The
Bedford
Introduction
to Drama

The Bedford Introduction to Drama

Lee A. Jacobus
University of Connecticut

A BEDFORD BOOK
ST. MARTIN'S PRESS • NEW YORK

For Bedford Books:
Publisher: Charles H. Christensen
Associate Publisher: Joan E. Feinberg
Managing Editor: Elizabeth M. Schaaf
Developmental Editor: Karen S. Henry
Production Editor: Chris Rutigliano
Text Design: Claire Seng-Niemoeller
Photo Researcher: Carole Frohlich, The Visual Connection
Cover Design: Hannus Design Associates
Cover Photo: Donald Cooper/Photostage, London

3   2   1   0   9

f   e   d   c   b   a

For information, write: St. Martin's Press, Inc.
175 Fifth Avenue, New York, NY 10010

Editorial Offices: Bedford Books of St. Martin's Press
29 Winchester Street, Boston, MA 02116

ISBN: 0–312–00363–3

Acknowledgments

Greek Drama

Figure 1. Theater at Epidaurus from *The Theatre of Dionysus in Athens* by Arthur Wallace Pickard-Cambridge. Reprinted by permission of Oxford University Press.

Acknowledgments and copyrights are continued at the back of the book on pages 1123–1126, which constitute an extension of the copyright page.

Preface for Instructors

The Bedford Introduction to Drama is, first and foremost, a collection of thirty-one important plays that have shaped dramatic literature from the time of the early Greek dramatists to the present. The book incorporates a number of features that distinguish it from other introductions to drama. Most notably, it presents five major playwrights in greater than usual depth. Sophocles, Shakespeare, Ibsen, Chekhov, and Beckett are each represented by two full-length plays. Commentaries — by the playwrights themselves and by other playwrights, directors, actors, and critics — about the playwrights and their works, together with the book's thorough biographical and critical introductions and photographs from recent important stage productions, offer beginning drama students a unique opportunity for studying (and writing about) these major figures in the development of drama.

Another distinctive feature of *The Bedford Introduction to Drama* is its strong representation of contemporary drama. Important plays by Sam Shepard, Athol Fugard, Martin Sherman, Caryl Churchill, Marsha Norman, and August Wilson, together with commentaries by and about these playwrights — including interviews and critical studies — give students an exposure to contemporary drama unavailable in any other introductory text. Moreover, the collection includes a broader range of plays by minority and women playwrights than most other introductory texts, including Caryl Churchill's *Top Girls*, Marsha Norman's *'night, Mother*, Lorraine Hansberry's *A Raisin in the Sun*, Lady Gregory's *The Rising of the Moon*, and August Wilson's *Fences*.

The Bedford Introduction to Drama is also a succinct but thorough history of Western drama. Even when it appears most timeless, all drama (like, of course, all literature) is a product of a language, an era, and a complex range of political, social, and ethnic influences. *The Bedford Introduction* highlights such influences. A general introduction gives an overview of the great ages of drama, the major genres and elements, and the cultural value of drama. Throughout the book, introductions to significant periods of drama, the playwrights, and the plays focus on the cultural contexts of the plays and on their stage history.

Finally, *The Bedford Introduction to Drama* is a complete resource book for the beginning student of drama. In the general introduction a discussion of the elements of drama defines important terms and concepts and demonstrates these concepts in action, drawing its examples from Lady Gregory's brief one-act play *The Rising of the Moon*.

Writing About Drama, a useful appendix, shows students possible approaches to commenting on dramatic literature and points the way to developing ideas that can result in probing essays. From prewriting to drafting and outlining, the process of writing about drama is illustrated by reference to Lady Gregory's play, and a sample essay on the play provides one example of drama criticism.

A second appendix, the Glossary of Dramatic Terms, defines concepts and terms clearly and concisely. When these terms are first introduced and defined in the text, they appear in small capital letters.

The Selected Bibliography, a third appendix, includes a list of reference works for the major periods of drama, the playwrights, and the plays by the five playwrights treated in depth. The cited general references, histories, biographies, critical studies, journal articles, reviews, and collections of plays will be especially useful for research in drama.

While the book emphasizes the plays as texts to be read, a fourth appendix, the Selected List of Films, Videos, and Recordings of the Plays, ensures that the element of performance is not ignored. This list, accompanied by a list of film, video, and record distributors, can help instructors and students find an illuminating treatment of the plays in performance.

Acknowledgments

First, I would like to thank those who offered their advice on what to include in this volume: Jeff Glauner, Park College; Susan Smith, University of Pittsburgh; and Jordan Miller, University of Rhode Island. Second, I am grateful to those who read the introductions and commentaries and who gave me the advantage of their knowledge and wisdom. G. Jennifer Wilson, University of California, Los Angeles; William Carroll, Boston University; Ronald Bryden, Graduate Centre for the Study of Drama, University of Toronto; Robert Dial, University of Akron; Jonnie Guerra, Mount Vernon College; and John Timpane, Lafayette College, were all unhesitating in offering suggestions and improvements. I am especially grateful to have had the guidance of Charles Christensen, publisher of Bedford Books of St. Martin's Press. Chris Rutigliano, Melissa Cook, and Jane Betz helped with extensive editing responsibilities; Virginia Creeden cleared the permissions for reprinting the plays and commentaries; and Carole Frohlich was instrumental in finding excellent photographs of key performances. But I owe most to the tireless creative efforts of my editor, Karen S. Henry. I also want to thank Jacqueline McCurry and Joseph Zwier, research assistants at the University of Connecticut, Storrs. John J. Manning, of the University of Connecticut, Storrs, who identified the Latin passage in *Top Girls*, deserves special mention for his collegial support.

Contents

Restoration and Eighteenth-Century Drama   319

Molière   329

Nineteenth-Century Drama to the Turn of the Century   355

Appendices

*The
Bedford
Introduction
to Drama*

Introduction: Thinking About Drama

What Is Drama?

Drama is the art of make-believe. It captivates children and adults from all societies and all walks of life. Make-believe consists in part of acting out events that happened or that we imagine happening. DRAMA consists of representing those actions for the pleasure of others. The primary ingredients of drama are characters, represented by players; action, described by gestures and movement; thought, implied by dialogue and action; spectacle, represented by scenery and costume; and, finally, audiences, who respond to this complex mixture.

Even when reading a play, we are encouraged to imagine actors speaking lines and to visualize a setting in which those lines are spoken. When we are in the theater, we see the actors, hear the lines, are aware of the setting, and sense the theatrical community of which we are a part. Drama is an experience in which we participate on many levels simultaneously. On one level, we may believe that what we see is really happening; on another level, we know it is only make-believe. On one level we may be amused, but on another level we realize that serious statements about our society are being made. Drama is like most other literature in that it both entertains and instructs.

When Aristotle wrote about drama in the *Poetics*, a work providing one of the earliest and most influential theories of drama, he began by explaining it as the IMITATION of an action. Those analyzing his work have interpreted this statement in several ways. One interpretation is that drama imitates life. On the surface, such an observation may seem simple, even obvious. But on reflection, we begin to find complex significance in his comment. The drama of the Greeks, for example, with its intense mythic structure, its formidable speeches, and its profound

1

actions, often seems larger than life or other than life. Yet we recognize characters saying words that we ourselves are capable of saying, doing things that we ourselves might do. The great Greek tragedies are certainly lifelike and certainly offer literary mirrors in which we can examine human nature. And the same is true of Greek comedies.

The relationship between drama and life has always been subtle and complex. In some plays, such as Luigi Pirandello's *Six Characters in Search of an Author*, it is one of the central issues. We begin our reading or viewing of most plays knowing that the dramatic experience is not absolutely real in the sense that, for example, the actor playing Hamlet does not truly die or truly see a ghost or truly frighten his mother. The play imitates those imagined actions, but when done properly it is realistic enough to make us fear, if only for a moment, that they could be real.

We are concerned for Hamlet as a person. We see significance in the actions he imitates; his actions help us live our own lives more deeply, more intensely, because they give us insight into the possibilities of life. We are all restricted to living this life as ourselves; drama is one art form that helps us realize the potentiality of life, for both the good and the bad. In an important sense, we can share the experience of a character such as Hamlet when he soliloquizes over the question of whether it is better to die than to live in a world filled with sin and crime. And we may find ourselves empathizing with a character like Faustus when he explains how unsatisfied he is with the worldly knowledge he has acquired and how much more meaningful the forbidden knowledge of the heavens would be to him were he only to have it at his bidding.

Drama and Ritual

Such imaginative participation is only a part of what we derive from drama. In its origins, drama probably evolved from ancient Egyptian and Greek rituals, ceremonies that were performed the same way again and again and were thought to have a propitious effect on the relationship between the people and their gods.

In ancient Egypt some religious rituals evolved into repeated passion plays, such as those celebrating Isis and Osiris at the festivals in Abydos some three thousand years ago. Greek drama was first performed during yearly religious celebrations to the god Dionysus. The early Greek playwrights, such as Sophocles in *Oedipus Rex* and *Antigone*, emphasized the will of the gods, pitting the truths of men and women against the truths of the gods. Such an emphasis suggests a high seriousness and perhaps a religious mission in the Greek tragedies.

The rebirth of drama in the Middle Ages — after the fall of Rome and the loss of classical artistic traditions — took place in the great cathedrals of Europe. It evolved from medieval religious ceremonies that fed the needs of the faithful to know more about their own moral predicament. *Everyman*, a late play in the medieval theater (it was written about 1500), concerns itself with the central issue of reward and punishment after this life because the soul is immortal.

Drama: The Illusion of Reality

From the beginning, drama has had the capacity to hold up an illusion of reality like the reflection in a mirror — we take the reality for granted while recognizing that it is nonetheless illusory. As we have seen, Aristotle described DRAMATIC ILLUSION as an imitation of an action. But unlike the reflection in a mirror, the action of most drama is not drawn from our actual experience of life, but from our potential or imagined experience. In the great Greek drama, the illusion includes the narratives of ancient myths that were thought to hold profound illumination for the populace. The interpretation of the myths by the Greek playwrights over a three-hundred-year period helped the Greek people participate in the myths, understand them, and integrate them into their daily lives.

Different ages have had different approaches toward representing reality onstage. The Greeks felt that their plays were exceptionally realistic, and yet their actors spoke in verse and wore masks. The staging consisted of very little setting and no special costumes. Medieval drama was often acted on pushwagons and carts, but the special machinery developed to suggest hellfire and the presence of devils was said to be so realistic as to be frightening. Elizabethan audiences were accustomed to actors occasionally conversing with the crowd at their feet near the apron of the stage. All Elizabethan plays were done in essentially contemporary clothing, with no more scenery than the suggestion of it in the spoken descriptions of the players. The actors recited their lines in verse, except when the author wanted to imply that the speaker was of low social station. Yet Elizabethans reported that their theater was very much like life itself.

Shakespeare's *A Midsummer Night's Dream* is not an illusion of waking reality, but an illusion of the reality of dreams — or the unreality of dreams. Fairies, enchantments, an ass's head on the shoulders of a man — all these are presented as illusions, and we accept them. They inform the audience — in Shakespeare's day and in modern times — not by showing us ourselves in a mirror but by proposing a reality that might be and then letting us delight in that reality, demonstrating that even fantastic realities have significance for us.

Certainly *A Midsummer Night's Dream* gives us insight into the profound range of human emotions. We learn about the pains of rejection when we see Helena longing for Demetrius, who in turn longs for Hermia. We learn about jealousy and possessiveness when we see Oberon cast a spell on his wife Titania over a dispute concerning a changeling. And we learn, too, about the worldly ambitions of the "rude mechanicals" who themselves put on a play whose reality they fear might frighten their audience. They solve the problem by reminding their audience that it is only a play and that they need not fear that reality will spoil their pleasure.

In modern drama the dramatic illusion of reality has grown to include not just the shape of an action, the events, and character but also the details of everyday life. In Bernard Shaw's *Major Barbara* we see Barbara in front of a Salvation Army band and we hear the music. When the action changes locale, the setting changes as well. Some contemporary playwrights make an effort to re-create a reality close to the one we live in. Some modern plays make a precise representation of reality a primary purpose, shaping the tone of the language to reflect the way modern people speak, re-creating contemporary reality in the setting, language, and other elements of the drama.

But describing a play as an illusion of reality in no way means that it represents the precise reality that we take for granted in our everyday experience. Rather, drama ranges widely and explores multiple realities, some of which may seem very close to our own and some of which may seem improbably removed from our everyday experience.

Seeing a Play on Stage

For an audience, drama is one of the most powerful artistic experiences. When we speak about participating in drama, we mean that as a member of the audience we become a part of the action that unfolds. This is a magical and a mysterious phenomenon.

When we see a play today we are usually seated in a darkened theater looking at a lighted stage. In ages past this contrast was not the norm. Greek plays took place outdoors during the morning and the afternoon; most Elizabethan plays were staged outdoors in the afternoon; in the Renaissance, some plays began to be staged indoors in darkened theaters with ingenious systems of lighting that involved candles and reflectors. In the early nineteenth century most theaters used gaslight onstage; electricity took over in the later part of the century, and its use has grown increasingly complex: in most large theaters today computerized lighting boards have replaced the Elizabethan candles.

Sitting in the darkness has made our experience of seeing Greek and Elizabethan plays much different for us than it was for the original audiences. We do not worry about being seen by the "right people" or about studying the quality of the audience, as people did during the Restoration. The darkness isolates us from all except those who sit adjacent to us. Yet we instantly respond when others in the audience laugh, when they gasp, when they shift restlessly. We recognize in those moments that we are part of a larger community drawn together by theater and that we are all involved in the dramatic experience.

Theaters and Their Effect

Different kinds of theaters make differing demands on actors and audiences. Despite their huge size, the open ARENA style theater of the early Greeks brought the audience into a special kind of intimacy with the actors. The players came very close to the first rows of seats and the acoustics permitted even a whisper onstage to be audible in the far seats. The Greek theater also imparted a sense of formality to the occasion of drama. For one thing, its regularity and circularity was accompanied by a relatively rigid seating plan. The officials of the competition and the judges sat with the nobility in special seats. Then each section of the theater was given over to specific families, with the edges of the seating area devoted to travelers and strangers to the town. One knew one's place in the Greek theater. Its regularity gave the community a sense of order.

The same may be said of the medieval theater, both when it used playing areas called mansions inside the churches and when it used portable wagons wheeled about outside the churches. That the medieval theater repeated the same cycles of plays again and again for about two hundred years, to the delight of many European communities, tells us something about the stability of those communities. Their drama was integrated with their religion, and both helped them express their sense of belonging to the church and the community.

In some medieval performances the actors came into the audience, breaking the sense of distance or the illusion of separation. It is difficult for us to know how much sense of participation and involvement of self the medieval audience would have felt. Modern audiences have responded very well to productions of medieval plays such as *The Second Shepherds' Play*, *Noah's Flood*, and *Everyman*, and we have every reason to think that medieval audiences enjoyed their dramas immensely. The guilds that performed them took pride in making their plays as exciting and involving as possible.

The Elizabethan playhouse was a wooden structure providing an enclosed space around a courtyard open to the sky. A covered stage thrust into the courtyard. As in the Greek theater, the audience was arranged somewhat by social station. Around the stage, which was about five feet off the ground, stood the groundlings, those who paid least for their entrance. Then in covered galleries in the building itself sat patrons who paid extra for a seat. The effect of the enclosed structure was of a small, contained world. Actors were in the habit of speaking directly to members of the audience, and the audience rarely kept a polite silence. It was a busy, humming theater that generated intimacy and involvement between actors and audience. It was also appropriate for the sometimes spectacular settings of plays like Christopher Marlowe's *Doctor Faustus* and Shakespeare's *Hamlet*.

The proscenium stage of the nineteenth century — and our century as well — distances the audience from the play, providing a clear frame (the proscenium) behind which the performers act out their scenes. This detachment is especially effective for plays that demand a high degree of realism because the effect of the proscenium is to make the audience feel it is witnessing the action as a silent observer, looking in as if through an imaginary fourth wall on a living room or other intimate space in which the action takes place. The proscenium arch gives the illusion that the actors are in a world of their own, unaware of the audience's presence.

In the twentieth century some of the virtues of theater in the round were rediscovered. Antonin Artaud in France developed a concept called the THEATER OF CRUELTY, which essentially closed the gap between actor and audience. One of its purposes was to confront the members of the audience individually to make them feel uncomfortable and force them to deal with the primary issues of the drama itself.

Twentieth-century theater is eclectic. It uses thrust, arena, proscenium, and every other kind of stage already described. Some contemporary theater also converts non-theatrical space, such as warehouses, or city streets, into space for performance.

Reading a Play

There is no question that reading a play is a different experience from seeing it enacted. For one thing, readers do not have the benefit of the interpretations made by a director, actors, and scene designers in presenting a performance. These interpretations are all critical judgments based both on their ideas of how the play should be presented and on their insights into the meaning of the play.

A reading of a play is largely an idealized version of the play. The interpretation remains in our heads and is not translated to the stage. The dramatic effect of the staging is lost to us unless we make a genuine effort to visualize the staging and to understand its contribution to the dramatic experience. For a fuller experience of the drama when reading plays, one should keep in mind the historical period and the conventions of staging that are appropriate to the period and that are specified by the playwright.

Some plays are meant to be read as well as staged, as evident in plays whose stage directions supply information that would be unavailable to an audience, such as the color of the characters' eyes, characters' secret motives, and other such details. Occasionally stage directions, such as those of Tennessee Williams, are written in a poetic prose that can be appreciated only by a reader.

It is not a certainty that seeing a play will produce an experience more "true" to the play's meaning than reading it. Every act of reading silently or speaking the lines aloud is an act of interpretation. No one can say which is the best interpretation. Each has its own merits, and the ideal is probably to do both for any play.

The Great Ages of Drama

Certain historical periods have produced great plays and great playwrights, although why some periods generate more dramatic activity than others is still a matter of conjecture for scholars examining the social, historical, and religious conditions of the times. Each of the great ages of drama has affected the way plays are written, acted, and staged in successive ages. Today, for example, drama borrows important elements from each earlier period.

Greek Drama

The Greeks of the fifth century B.C. are credited with the first dominating dramatic age, which lasted from the birth of Aeschylus (525 B.C.) to the death of Aristophanes (385 B.C.). Their theaters were supported by public funds, and the playwrights competed for prizes during the great feasts of Dionysus. Sometimes as many as ten to fifteen thousand people sat in the theaters and watched with a sense of delight and awe as the actors played out their tales.

Theater was extremely important to the Greeks as a way of interpreting their relationships with their gods and of reinforcing their sense of community. All classes enjoyed it; they came early in the morning and spent the entire day in the theater. Drama for the Greeks was not mere escapism or entertainment, not a frill or a luxury. Connected as it was with religious festivals, it was a cultural necessity.

Sophocles is perhaps the foremost of Greek playwrights, and his plays *Oedipus Rex* and *Antigone* are examples of the powerful tragedies that transfixed audiences for centuries. Euripides, who succeeded Sophocles, was also a prize-winning tragedian. His *Trojan Women*, *Alcestis*, *Medea*, and *Elektra* are still performed and still exert an influence on today's drama. The same is true of Aeschylus, who preceded both and whose *Agamemnon*, *The Libation Bearers*, *The Eumenides*, and *Prometheus Bound* have all been among the most lasting of plays.

In addition to such great tragedians, the Greeks also produced the important comedians Aristophanes and Menander, whose work has been plundered for plays as diverse as a Shakespeare comedy and a Broadway musical. Aristophanes was the master of the mix-up, mistaken identities, and preposterous situations. His *Lysistrata*, in which the Athenian and Spartan women agree to withhold sex from their husbands until the men promise to stop making war, is still played all over the world. Menander produced a more subtle comedy that made the culture laugh at itself. Both styles of comedy are the staple of popular entertainment even today. Menander's social comedies were the basis of the comedy of manners in which society's ways of behavior are criticized, exemplified in William Congreve's eighteenth-century *The Way of the World* and even in situation comedies on contemporary television.

Roman Drama

The Romans became aware of Greek drama in the third century B.C. and began to import Greek actors and playwrights. Because of many social and cultural differences between the societies, however, drama never took a central role in the life of the average Roman. Seneca, who is now viewed as Rome's most important tragedian, almost certainly wrote his plays to be read rather than to be seen on stage.

Roman comedy produced two great playwrights, Plautus and Terence, who helped develop the stock or type character, such as the skinflint or the prude, and used the device of mix-ups involving identical twins in their plays. Plautus was the great Roman comedian in the tradition of Menander's comedy of manners. Plautus's best-known plays are *The Braggart Warrior* and *The Twin Menaechmi*, and during the Renaissance, when all European schoolchildren read Latin, his works were favorites.

Terence's work was praised during the Renaissance as being smoother, more elegant, and more polished and refined than Plautus's. In his own age Terence was less admired by the general populace but more admired by connoisseurs of drama. His best-known plays are rarely performed today: *The Woman of Andros*, *The Phormio*, and *The Mother-in-Law*.

The Romans' concern for their gods seems to have been more abstract and more a matter of form than the Greeks' highly celebratory relationship with their gods. Consequently, drama never assumed the importance for Romans that it did for the Greeks. Roman entertainment took the form of sports events, spectacles, the slaughter of wild beasts, and mass sacrifices of Christians and others to animals. The Roman public, when it did attend plays, enjoyed farces and relatively coarse humor. The audiences for Plautus and Terence, aristocratic in taste, did not represent the cross section of the community that was typical of Greek audiences.

Medieval Drama

After the fall of Rome and the spread of the Goths and Visigoths across southern Europe in the fifth century, Europe experienced a total breakdown of the strong central government Rome had provided. When Rome fell, Greek and Roman culture virtually disappeared. Its great texts went unread until the end of the medieval period in the fourteenth and fifteenth centuries. Part of the medieval period, from about 476 to the tenth century, is known somewhat inaccurately as the Dark Ages. However, expressions of culture, including art forms such as drama, did not entirely disappear. During the medieval period the church's power and influence grew extensively and it tried to fill the gap left by the demise of the Roman Empire. The church became a focus of both religious and secular activity for people all over Europe.

After almost five centuries of relative inactivity, European drama was reborn in religious ceremonies in the great stone churches that dominate most European towns. It moved out of the churches by the twelfth century because its own demands outgrew its circumstances: It had become a competitor, not just an adjunct, of the religious ceremonies that had spawned it.

One reason that the medieval European communities regarded their drama so highly is that it was a direct expression of many of their concerns and values. The age was highly religious; in addition, the people who produced the plays were members of guilds whose personal pride was represented in their work. Their plays came to be called mystery plays because the trade that each guild represented was a special skill — a mystery to the average person.

Many of these plays told stories drawn from the Bible. The tales of Noah's Ark, Abraham and Isaac, and Samson and Delilah all had immense dramatic potential, and the mystery plays capitalized on that potential. Among them *The Second Shepherds' Play* and *The Play of Daniel* are still performed regularly.

Most mystery plays were gathered into groups of plays called cycles and were usually performed outdoors on movable wagons that doubled as stages. The audience either moved from wagon to wagon to see each play in a cycle, or the wagons moved among the audience. The interaction of the players and the audience was often taken for granted, and the distance between players and audience was often collapsed.

By the fifteenth and sixteenth centuries, another form of play developed that was not associated with cycles or with the guilds. These were the morality plays, and their purposes were to touch on larger contemporary issues that had a moral overtone. *Everyman* is certainly the best known of the morality plays and was performed in many nations in translation.

Renaissance Drama

The revival of learning in the Renaissance, beginning in the fourteenth century, had considerable effect on drama because classical Greek and Roman plays were discovered and studied. The late medieval traditions of the Italian theater's *commedia dell'arte,* a stylized improvisational slapstick comedy performed by actors' guilds, began to move outside Italy into other European nations. The *commedia's* stock characters, Harlequins and Pulcinellas, began to appear in many countries in Europe.

In the academies in Italy, some experiments in re-creating Greek and Roman plays introduced music into drama. New theaters were built in Italy to produce these plays, and while they did not have lasting effects on the modern stage, they allow us to see how the Renaissance reconceived the classical stage.

Elizabethan and Jacobean drama developed most fully during the fifty years from approximately 1590 to 1640. Audiences poured into the playhouses eager for plays about history and for the great tragedies of Christopher Marlowe, such as *Doctor Faustus,* and of Shakespeare, including *Macbeth, Hamlet, Othello, Julius Caesar,* and *King Lear.* But there were others as well: Cyril Tourneur's *Revenger's Tragedy* and John Webster's *The White Devil* and his touching but gory *The Duchess of Malfi.*

The great comedies of the age came mostly from the pen of William Shakespeare: *A Midsummer Night's Dream, The Comedy of Errors, Much Ado About Nothing, The Taming of the Shrew,* and *Twelfth Night.* Many of these comedies derived from Italian originals, usually novellas or popular poems and sometimes comedies. But Shakespeare, of course, elevated and vastly improved everything he borrowed.

Ben Jonson, a playwright who was significantly influenced by the classical writers, was also well represented on the Elizabethan stage, with *Volpone, The Alchemist, Everyman in His Humor, Bartholomew*

Fair, and other durable comedies. Jonson is also important for his contributions to the masque, an aristocratic entertainment that featured music, dance, and fantastic costuming.

The Elizabethan stage sometimes grew bloody, with playwrights and audiences showing a passion for tragedies that, like *Hamlet*, centered on revenge and often ended with most of the characters meeting a premature death. Elizabethan plays also show considerable variety, with many plays detailing the history of English kings and, therefore, the history of England. It was a theater of powerful effect, and contemporary diaries indicate that the audiences delighted in it.

Theaters in Shakespeare's day were built outside city limits in seamy neighborhoods near bear-baiting halls, where chained bears were set upon by large dogs for the crowd's amusement, and near brothels. Happily, their business was good; the plays were constructed of remarkable language that seems to have fascinated all social classes, since all flocked to the theater by the thousands.

Restoration and Eighteenth-Century Drama

After the Puritan reign in England from 1649 to 1660, during which dramatic productions were almost nonexistent, the theater was suddenly revived. In 1660 Prince Charles was invited back from France to be king, thus beginning what was known in England as the Restoration. It was a gay, exciting period in stark contrast with the gray Puritan era. During the period new indoor theaters modeled on those in France were built, and a new generation of actors and actresses (women took part in plays for the first time in England) came forth to participate in a revived drama.

Since the early 1600s, French writers had leaned toward development of a classical theater, which had long before been defined by Aristotle as following the "unities" of time, place, and action: A play had one plot and one setting and covered the action of one day. In 1637 Pierre Corneille wrote *Le Cid* using relatively modern Spanish history as his theme and carefully following classical techniques. Jean-Baptiste Racine was Corneille's successor, and his plays became even more classical by centering on classical topics. His work includes *Andromache*, *Britannicus*, and possibly his best play, *Phaedra*. Racine ended the century in retirement from the stage, but he left a powerful legacy of classicism that reached well into the eighteenth century.

Molière, an actor and producer whose work still holds center stage in contemporary productions, was the best comedian of seventeenth-century France. Among his plays, *The Misanthrope* and several others are still produced regularly in Western countries. Molière was classical in his way, borrowing Aristophanes' technique of using type, or stock, characters in his social satires.

Among the most important playwrights of the new generation were Aphra Behn, the first professional English female writer, whose play *The Rover* was one of the most popular plays of the late seventeenth century, and William Congreve, whose best-known play, *The Way of the World*, is often still produced. The latter play is a lively comedy of manners that aimed to chasten as well as entertain Congreve's audiences.

The eighteenth century saw the tradition of the comedy of manners continued in the work of Richard Brinsley Sheridan, whose *School for Scandal* continues to appeal even to modern audiences, and Oliver Goldsmith, whose *She Stoops to Conquer* is a much-produced play. The drama of this period focuses on an analysis of social manners, and much of it is satirical, that is, offering mild criticism of society and holding society up to comic ridicule. But underlying that ridicule is the relatively noble motive of reforming society. We can see some of that motive at work in the plays of Molière and Congreve.

During the eighteenth century, theater in France centered on the court and was in the control of a small coterie of snobbish people. The situation in England was not quite the same, although the audiences were snobbish and socially conscious. They went to the theater to be seen, and they often went in claques — groups of like-minded patrons who applauded or booed together to express their views. Theater was important, but attendance at it was like a material possession: something to be displayed for others to admire.

Nineteenth-Century Drama to the Turn of the Century

English playwrights alone produced more than thirty thousand plays during the nineteenth century. Most of the plays were sentimental, melodramatic, and dominated by a few very powerful actors, stars who often overwhelmed the works written for them. The audiences were quite different from those of the seventeenth and eighteenth centuries. The upwardly mobile urban middle classes and the moneyed factory and mill owners who had benefited economically from the industrial revolution demanded a drama that would entertain them.

The new audiences were not especially well educated, nor were they interested in plays that were intellectually demanding. Instead, they wanted escapist and sentimental entertainment that was easy to respond to and did not challenge their basic values. Revivals of old plays and adaptations of Shakespeare were common in the age, with great stars like Edward Forrest and William Macready using the plays as platforms for overwhelming, and sometimes overbearing, performances. Gothic thrillers were especially popular, as were historical plays and melodramatic plays featuring a helpless heroine.

As an antidote to such a diet, the new Realist movement in literature, marked by the achievements of French novelists Émile Zola and Gustave Flaubert, finally struck the stage in the 1870s in plays by August Strindberg and Henrik Ibsen. These Scandinavians revolutionized Western drama and forced their audiences, who were by then more sophisticated and better prepared, to pay attention to important issues and deeper psychological concerns than earlier audiences had done.

August Strindberg's *Miss Julie*, a psychological study, challenged social complacency based on class and social differences. Ibsen's *A Doll's House* was a blow struck for feminism, but it did not amuse all audiences. Some were horrified at the thought that Nora Helmer was to be taken as seriously as her husband. Such a view was heretical, but it was also thrilling for a newly awakened European conscience. Those intellectuals who responded positively to Ibsen acted as the new conscience and began a move that soon transformed drama. Feminism is also a theme, but perhaps less directly, of Ibsen's *Hedda Gabler*, the story of a woman whose frustration at being cast into an inferior role contributes toward a destructive — and ultimately self-destructive — impulse. Both plays are acted in a physical setting that seems to be as ordinary as a nineteenth-century sitting room, with characters as small — and yet as large — as the people who watched them.

The Russian Anton Chekhov's plays *Three Sisters* and *The Cherry Orchard*, both written at the turn of the twentieth century, are realistic as well, but they are also patient examinations of character rather than primarily problem plays, as were so many of Ibsen's successful dramas. Chekhov is aware of social change in Russia, especially the changes that revealed a hitherto repressed class of peasants evolving into landowners and merchants. Chekhov offers us a view of the Prozorov sisters who, unlike their brother's predatory wife, Natasha, are passive, helpless, and altogether too dependent. Their inability to act on their own behalf makes them prime targets for victimization.

The Cherry Orchard is suffused with an overpowering sense of inevitability through which Chekhov depicts the conflict between the necessity for change and a nostalgia for the past. Lyubov and Gaev, who live a false life of aristocratic privilege without the means to support it, choose to perish rather than to work or to change. Their estate is built on slave labor and while it is beautiful, it must perish with them. We watch them with fascination as they struggle to understand the new values that the landowner and former peasant Lopahin explains to them.

These plays introduce a modern realism of a kind that is quite rare in earlier drama. The melodrama of the earlier nineteenth century was especially satisfying to mass audiences because the good characters were very good, the bad characters were very bad, and justice was meted out at their end. But it is difficult in Chekhov to be sure who the heroes and villains are. Nothing is as white or as black in these plays as it is in popular melodramas. Instead, Chekhov's plays are as complicated as life itself. Such difficulties of distinction have become the norm of the most important drama of the twentieth century.

Drama in the Early and Mid-Twentieth Century

The drama of the early twentieth century nurtured the seeds of nineteenth-century realism into bloom, but sometimes with innovations such as experiments with the expectations of its audiences. John Millington Synge, for example, used the techniques of realism in *Riders to the Sea*, which might best be described as peasant tragedy. Synge contradicted the expectation of audiences that tragedy should focus on those who are elevated in social station. Maurya, the peasant mother who loses the last of her sons in the course of the play, is as tragic a figure as any in modern drama.

Eugene O'Neill's *Desire Under the Elms* is another tragedy that features the ordinary citizen rather than the noble. This play, while not a peasant tragedy, focuses on New England farmers as tragic characters. Arthur Miller's *Death of a Salesman* uses a Greek sense of fate and of inevitability within the world of the commercial salesman, the ordinary man. As in many other twentieth-century tragedies, the point is that the life of the ordinary man can be tragic just as Oedipus' life can be tragic.

Luigi Pirandello experiments with reality in *Six Characters in Search of an Author*, a play that has a distinctly absurd quality, since it expects us to accept the notion that the characters on the stage are waiting for an author to put them into a play. Pirandello plays with our sense of illusion and of expectation and realism to such an extent that he forces us to reexamine our concepts of reality.

Bertolt Brecht's *Mother Courage*, an example of what he called epic drama, explores the way modern people have acclimated to the constant warfare that marks the twentieth century. *Mother Courage* shows the defiance of peril, pain, and terror that are part of the modern condition. It is a social statement, like many of Brecht's plays and like many of the plays produced in the West in the first half of the century. Playwrights around the world responded to events such as World War I, the Communist revolution, and the Great Depression by writing plays that no longer permitted audiences to sit comfortably and securely in darkened theaters. Brecht and other playwrights came out to get their audiences, to make them feel, to make them realize their true condition.

The eternal dramatic questions concerning illusion and reality were certainly not ignored, any more than questions of a political and social nature affecting the playwright were ignored. Samuel Beckett's *Krapp's Last Tape* depicts the psychic withdrawal of a man who can hardly come to terms with his former selves in youth and young manhood. He cannot come to terms with life at all. Although he seems to be examining life in detail, in reality he is hiding from it. His obsessive tinkering with the tapes and tape recorder symbolizes the extent of his withdrawal. Tennessee Williams's study of withdrawal from life centers on a physically and psychically frail young woman in *The Glass Menagerie*. The play derives from personal experience: Williams's sister was such a woman.

Modern dramatists from the turn of the century to the Korean War explored in many different directions and developed new approaches to themes of dramatic illusion as well as to questions concerning the relationship of an audience to the stage and the players.

Contemporary Drama   Currently, the stage is vibrant. Although the commercial theaters in England and America are beset by high costs, they are producing remarkable plays. In Latin America, Germany, and France, the theater is very active and exciting. Poland produced some unusual experimental drama in the years before the present government clamped down on artistic expression. The Soviet Union, too, has produced a number of plays that have been given a worldwide currency.

The hallmark of most of these plays has been experimentalism. Caryl Churchill's *Top Girls* includes a scene in which great women of the past hold a discussion as if there were no historical distinctions between them. Top Girls is an employment agency and a pun useful for a treatment of the feminist issues that appear frequently in Churchill's plays.

Sam Shepard, probably the most productive major playwright in America today, gives us a glimpse of a family in *True West*. Part of Shepard's purpose is to shatter our cinematic illusions of the romantic West, and he does this by also shattering some of our illusions about the nature of families. The family in *True West* is, like many of Shepard's families, violent, murderous, and in an odd way indifferent. Shepard experiments in this play not only with violence but with unity of character, showing us ways in which one person can hope to usurp another's personality.

In *'night, Mother*, Marsha Norman portrays two women whose lives are constricted, limited, and painful. Thelma, the mother, is desperately trying to keep Jessie, her daughter, from committing suicide. But she fails. The structure of the play is traditional, but the material is experimental. The people in these modern plays would not be at ease in Ibsen's living rooms or Chekhov's cherry orchard. They are people who have been given a bad deal and who have given themselves a bad deal, and we must examine them because the playwrights insist that we will see into ourselves more deeply than we would if we — as most of us do in real life — turn away.

Not all modern theater is experimental, however. A substantial amount of good contemporary theater strives to respect conventional theatrical procedure. A play like Martin Sherman's *Bent* is in some ways quite conventional. It uses some of the Brechtian approach to rapid changes of scene, but the action is recognizably realistic and traditional. What is not traditional, however, is the subject matter — homosexual love and the horrors of Nazi concentration camps. Most middle-of-the-road theatergoers are aware of homosexuality, but few will have seen it portrayed as explicitly as it is in this play.

August Wilson's *Fences* shows us the pain of life at the lower end of the economic ladder and in a form that is recognizably realistic and plausible. The play is set in the 1950s and focuses on Troy Maxon, a black man, and his relationship with his son and his wife. Tenement life is one subject of the play, but the most important subject is the courage it takes to keep going after tasting defeat. The entire drama develops within the bounds of conventional nineteenth-century realism.

Contemporary Audiences. Audiences in the late twentieth century are an interesting study. Most theatergoers are middle or upper class and urban. The easy availability of dramatic entertainment on television has changed the nature of live drama. To some extent it is true that commercial theater in America depends on the wealthy to fill the house on Broadway. The "tired businessman" wants to be entertained. This is one reason why serious plays are often not performed on Broadway. But in light of such facts, it is striking to see that some plays of very high and lasting literary quality do reach Broadway.

Regional theaters, some of them extremely influential, have been springing up all over the world to provide a forum for new playwrights. Many of the new playwrights in this volume have had their work supported by regional theaters. Athol Fugard's plays now premiere at the Yale Repertory Company, as do August Wilson's plays. Marsha Norman's work was first produced by the Louisville Actor's Theatre. The Royal Court Theatre in London supported Harold Pinter and continues to support experimental writers such as Caryl Churchill today. All over the world, local theaters are producing adventurous theater.

Genres of Drama
Tragedy

Drama since the great age of the Greeks has taken several different forms. As we have seen, tragedies were one genre that pleased Greek audiences, and comedies pleased the Romans. In later ages, a blend of the comic and the tragic produced a hybrid genre: tragicomedy. In our time, unless a play is modeled on the Greek or Shakespearean tragedies, as is O'Neill's *Desire Under the Elms*, it is usually considered tragicomic rather than tragic. Our age still enjoys the kind of comedy that people laugh at, although most plays that are strictly comedy are frothy, temporarily entertaining, and not lasting.

TRAGEDY demands a specific worldview. Aristotle, in his *Poetics*, points out that the tragic hero or heroine should be noble of birth, perhaps a king like Oedipus or a princess like Antigone. The tragic hero or heroine should be more magnanimous, more daring, larger in spirit than the average person.

Modern tragedies have rediscovered tragic principles, and while Synge, O'Neill, and Miller rely on Aristotle's precepts, they have shown that in a modern society shorn of the distinctions between noble and peasant it is possible for audiences to see the greatness in all classes. This has given us a new way of orienting ourselves to the concept of fate; to HAMARTIA, the wrong act that leads people to a tragic end; and to the hero's or heroine's relationship to the social order.

Aristotle suggested that plot was the heart and soul of tragedy and that character came second. But most older tragedies take the name of the tragic hero or heroine as their title; such nomenclature signifies the importance that dramatists invested in their tragic characters. Yet they also heeded Aristotle's stipulation that tragic action should have one plot rather than the double or triple plots that often characterize comedies. (Shakespeare was soundly criticized in the eighteenth century for breaking this rule.) And they paid attention to the concept of PERIPETEIA, which specifies that the desires of the tragic characters sometimes lead them to a REVERSAL: They get what they want, but what they want turns out to be destructive. Aristotle especially valued a plot in which the reversal takes place simultaneously with the recognition of the truth, as it does in Sophocles' *Oedipus Rex.*

Playwrights in the seventeenth and eighteenth centuries in France were especially interested in following classical precepts. They were certain that Greek tragedy and Greek comedy were the epitome of excellence in drama. They were particular in following Aristotle's insistence on the integrity of the dramatic UNITIES when they demanded one plot, a single action that takes place in one day, a single setting, and characters who remained the same throughout the play. Their reinterpretations of the unities were probably much stricter than Aristotle intended them. Playwrights and critics in this period in France enjoyed following "rules," the proper way of doing things in drama, and one of their sacred rules was that of observing the unities.

Comedy

Two kinds of comedy developed among the ancient Greeks: OLD COMEDY, which resembles FARCE and often pokes fun at individuals who think of themselves as very important; and NEW COMEDY, which is a more suave, refined commentary on the condition of modern society.

Old Comedy survives in the masterful works of Aristophanes, such as *Lysistrata*, while New Comedy hearkens back to the lost plays of Menander and resurfaces in plays such as Molière's *The Misanthrope* and Bernard Shaw's *Major Barbara*. Both plays use humor but mix it with a serious level of social commentary. New Comedy has become the modern COMEDY OF MANNERS, studying and sometimes ridiculing modern society.

Comedy is usually thought to be funny. We laugh at *A Midsummer Night's Dream* as well as at most of Shakespeare's other comedies, but comedy is not a prisoner of laughter because laughter is not the only end of comedy. Chekhov thought *The Cherry Orchard* was a comedy, while his producer, the great Konstantin Stanislavsky, who trained actors to interpret his lines and who acted in other Chekhov plays, thought it was a tragedy. The argument may have centered on the ultimate effect of the play on its audiences, but it may also have centered on the question of laughter. There are laughs in *The Cherry Orchard*, but they usually come at the expense of a character or a social group. This is true, as well, of Samuel Beckett's *Krapp's Last Tape*. We laugh, but we also know that the play is at heart very serious.

This collection contains no sentimental comedies such as Neil Simon's *Biloxi Blues* — comedy that pulls a few heartstrings and provides many a belly laugh — although they are popular enough to be around us on television and on stage. The durability of sentimental comedies, such as Lindsay and Crouse's *Life with Father*, which was a perennial crowd-pleaser in the 1940s, is not great. To be put on modern stages, such works need to be emotionally as well as socially updated. Despite this fact, however, sentimental comedy will always be with us. Today we need only turn on any television situation comedy to see what sentimental comedy is like.

Tragicomedy

Since the early seventeenth century, serious plays have been called TRAGICOMEDIES when they do not adhere strictly to the structure of tragedy, which emphasizes the nobility of the hero or heroine, fate, the wrong action of the hero or heroine, and a resolution that includes death, exile, or a similar end. Many serious plays have these qualities, but they also have some of the qualities of comedy: a commentary on society, raucous behavior that draws laughs, and a relatively happy ending. Yet their darkness is such that we can hardly feel comfortable regarding them as comedies.

Plays such as Sam Shepard's *True West* and Lorraine Hansberry's *A Raisin in the Sun* can be considered tragicomedy. Indeed, the modern temperament has especially relied on the mixture of comic and tragic elements for its most serious plays. Eugene O'Neill, Tennessee Williams, Harold Pinter, and Caryl Churchill have all been masters of tragicomedy, and to some extent their worldview has helped us see the comic implications of tragic actions and the serious implications of comic actions.

In contemporary drama tragicomedy takes several forms. One is the play whose seriousness is relieved by comic moments; another is a play whose comic structure absorbs a tragic moment and continues to express affirmation. Yet another is the dark comedy whose sardonic humor leaves us wondering how we can laugh at something that is ultimately frightening. This is the case with some absurdist comedies, which insist that there is no meaning in events other than the meaning we invent for ourselves. Pinter's *The Dumb Waiter* and Beckett's *Happy Days* are such plays. They are funny yet sardonic, and when we laugh we do so very uneasily.

Other genres of drama exist, although they are generally versions of the three mentioned here. Improvisational theater, in which actors use no scripts and may switch roles at any moment, may defy generic description. Musical comedies and operas are dramatic entertainments that have established their own genres related in some ways to the standard genres of drama.

Genre distinctions are useful primarily because they establish expectations in the minds of audiences with theatrical experience. Tragedies and comedies make different demands on an audience. As Marsha Norman says in explaining her "rules" of drama: You have to know in a play just what is at stake. Understanding the principles that have developed over the centuries to create the genres of drama helps us know what is at stake.

The Cultural Value of Drama

In all ages drama has been an integral part of culture. For the Greeks, drama developed partly in reaction to the period of barbarism from which the society was emerging and reinforced and affirmed the moral values of civilization. The Greek experience of drama was centered in their religious festivals, which coincided with the agricultural cycle of the year. As the Greeks established themselves as communities, their drama became an important focus for their communal lives.

The Roman drama was entirely secular, and hence drama did not serve as a highly significant means of expression and as a community focus as it did for the Greeks. Drama received its impulses from religion once again in the medieval period, after several centuries of neglect. The populace was infused with a religious spirit and developed their drama as a way to interpret the Bible and the life of Christ and the saints.

One of the lasting cultural values in drama is its power to draw people together. We find ourselves in company of others like us when we sit watching a Shakespearean tragedy — just as Elizabethans did at the Globe Theatre in the early 1600s. When we laugh at a theatrical farce, we are sure to be laughing in the midst of others who echo our amusement and delight. The same is true when we see popular musicals such as *South Pacific* and *Les Misérables*.

We share with the nineteenth century a need for escapism when we find ourselves amused by a light situation comedy of Neil Simon or a mystery play by Anthony Shaffer. Drama is transporting, edifying, spiritually enriching, and blithely amusing — depending on the circumstances and the experience we choose.

The plays in this collection are not escapist pieces of writing. They reflect important achievements in theater, past and present. They are plays that have affected the history of drama and that reflect the ways in which audiences have been asked to adapt themselves to the changing needs of actor, playwright, and stage. They were designed to inform their audiences — and they continue to do so for modern audiences — about themselves, their limitations, and their capacities for triumphing. The plays show us how people react in the face of adversity, how they deal with the pressures in the world in which they — and we — live.

If the most modern plays in this collection are like mirrors, reflecting the society in which we live, then it is clear that our society is extraordinarily pluralistic — as plays ranging from *Bent*, *True West*, *"MASTER HAROLD" . . . and the boys* to *Top Girls*, *'night, Mother*, and *Fences* attest. They depict worlds within worlds, and they exhort their audiences to not be content with only a middle-class reflection of the world. Their success demonstrates that audiences are interested in seeing all the world, not just the little part in which they live.

Elements of Drama

All plays share some basic elements with which playwrights and producers work: plots, characters, settings, dialogue, movement, and themes. In addition, many modern plays pay close attention to lighting, costuming, and props. When we respond to a play, we observe the elements of drama in action together, and the total experience is rich, complex, and subtle. Occasionally, we respond primarily to an individual element — the theme or characterization, for instance — but that is rare. Our awareness of the elements of drama is most useful when we are thinking analytically about a play and the way it affects us.

For the sake of discussion, we will consider the way the basic elements of drama function in Lady Gregory's one-act play *The Rising of the Moon* (which follows this section). It has all the elements we expect from drama, and it is both a brief and very successful play.

Plot

PLOT is a term for the action of a drama. Plot implies that the ACTION has a shape and form that will ultimately prove satisfying to the audience. Generally, a carefully plotted play (sometimes called the WELL-MADE PLAY) begins with EXPOSITION, an explanation of what happened before the play began and of how the characters arrived at their present situation. The play then continues, using SUSPENSE to build tension in the audience and in the characters in developing further the pattern of RISING ACTION. The audience wonders what is going to happen, sees the characters set in motion, then watches as certain questions implied by the drama are answered one by one. The action achieves its greatest tension as it moves to a point of CLIMAX, when a revelation is experienced, usually by the chief characters. Once the climax has been reached, the plot continues, sometimes very briefly, in a pattern of FALLING ACTION as we reach the drama's conclusion and the characters understand their circumstances and themselves better than they did at the beginning of the play.

The function of plot is to give action a form that helps us understand elements of the drama in relation to one another. Often, plays can have several interrelated plots or only one. Lady Gregory's *The Rising of the Moon* has one very simple plot: a police sergeant is sent out with two policemen to make sure a political rebel does not escape from the area. The effect of the single plot is that the entire play focuses intensely on the interaction between the rebel, disguised as a ballad singer, and the sergeant. The sergeant meets the rebel, listens to him sing ballads, then recognizes in him certain qualities they both share. The audience wonders if a reward of one hundred pounds will cause the sergeant to arrest the ballad singer, or if instead, the ballad singer's sense that his cause is just will convince the sergeant to let him go. The climax of the action occurs when the sergeant's two policemen return, as the ballad singer hides behind a barrel, and ask if the sergeant has seen any signs of the rebel. Not until that moment does the audience know for sure what the sergeant will do. When he declares that he has not seen the rebel, the falling action begins. The rebel thanks the sergeant and takes his leave, and then the sergeant, left alone, appears to lament his loss of the reward, since he realizes he could have used it.

Plots depend on CONFLICT between characters, and in *The Rising of the Moon* the conflict is very deep. It is built into the characters themselves, but it is also part of the institution of law that the sergeant serves and the ongoing struggle for justice that the ballad-singer serves. This conflict, still evident today, was a very significant national issue in Ireland when the play was first produced in Dublin in 1907.

Lady Gregory works subtly with the conflict between the sergeant and the ballad-singer, showing that although they are on completely opposite sides of the law — and the important political issues — they are more alike than they are different. The ballad-singer begins to sing the "Granuaile," a revolutionary song about England's unlawful dominance over Ireland through seven centuries, and when he leaves out a line, the sergeant supplies it. In that action he reveals that, although he is paid by the English to keep law and order, his roots lie with the Irish people. By his knowledge of the revolutionary songs he reveals his sympathies, and we are prepared to accept his willingness to let the ballad-singer go free and to forfeit the substantial hundred-pound reward.

Characterization

Lady Gregory has effectively joined CHARACTER and conflict in *The Rising of the Moon*: As the conflict is revealed, the characters of the sergeant and the ballad-singer are also revealed. At first the sergeant seems eager to get the reward, and he acts bossy with Policeman X and Policeman B. And when he first meets the ballad-singer he seems demanding and policeman-like. It is only when he begins to sense who the ballad-singer really is that he changes and reveals a deep, sympathetic streak.

Lady Gregory, in a note to the play, said that in Ireland when the play was first produced, those who wanted Ireland to become part of England were incensed to see a policeman portrayed so as to show his sympathies with rebels. Those who wished Ireland to become a separate nation from England were equally shocked to see a policeman portrayed so sympathetically.

The sergeant and the ballad-singer are both major characters in the play, but it is not clear that either is the villain or the hero. When the play begins the sergeant seems to be the hero because he represents the law and the ballad-singer appears to be the villain because he has escaped from prison. But as the action develops, those characterizations change. What replaces them is an awareness of the complications that underlie the relationship between the law and the lawbreaker in some circumstances. This is part of the point of Lady Gregory's play.

Lady Gregory has given a very detailed portrait of both main characters, although in a one-act play she does not have enough space to be absolutely thorough in developing them. Yet we get an understanding of the personal ambitions of each character, and we understand both their relationship to Ireland and their particular allegiances as individuals. They speak with each other in enough detail to show that they understand each other, and when the ballad-singer hides behind the barrel at the approach of the other two policemen, he indicates that he trusts the sergeant not to reveal him.

Policeman X and Policeman B are only sketched in. Yet their presence is important. It is with them that the sergeant reveals his official personality, and it is their presence at the end that represents the most important threat to the security of the ballad-singer. However, we know little or nothing about them personally. They are characters who are functionaries, a little like Rosencrantz and Guildenstern in *Hamlet*, but without the differentiating characterizations that Shakespeare was able to give minor players in his full-length play.

The plays in this collection have some of the most remarkable characters ever created in literature. Tragedy usually demands highly complex characters, such as Oedipus, Antigone, Hamlet, and Willy Loman. We come to know them through their own words, through their interaction with other characters, through their expression of feelings, and through their presence on stage expressed in movement and gesture.

Characters in tragicomedies are individualized and complexly portrayed, such as Hedda Gabler, Miss Julie, Nora Helmer, and Maurya in *Riders to the Sea*. But just as effective in certain kinds of drama are characters drawn as types, such as Alceste, the misanthrope in Molière's play, Everyman in medieval drama, and the characters in the first act of Caryl Churchill's *Top Girls*. Type characters are especially effective in satires and comedies of manners.

In many plays we see that the entire shape of the action derives from the characters, from their strengths and weaknesses. In such plays we do not feel that the action lies outside the characters and that they must live through an arbitrary sequence of events. Instead we feel that they create their own opportunities and problems.

Setting   The SETTING of a play includes many things. First, it refers to the time and place in which the action occurs. Second, it refers to the scenery, the physical elements that appear on stage to vivify the author's stage directions. In Lady Gregory's play, we have a dock with barrels to suggest the locale, and darkness to suggest night. These are very important details that influence the emotional reaction of the audience.

Some plays make use of very elaborate settings, as does August Wilson's *Fences*, which is produced with a detailed tenement back yard onstage. Others make use of very simplified settings, such as the empty stage of Pirandello's *Six Characters in Search of an Author* or the strange mound that entraps Winnie in Samuel Beckett's *Happy Days*.

Lady Gregory's setting derives from her inspiration for the play. She visited the quays — places where boats dock and leave with goods — as a young girl and imagined how someone might escape from the nearby prison and make his getaway "under a load of kelp" in one of the ships. The quay represents the meeting of the land and water, and it represents the getaway, the possibility of freedom. The barrel is a symbol of trade, and the sergeant and the ballad-singer sit on its top and trade the words of a revolutionary song with each other.

The title of the play provides another element of the setting: the moonlight. The night protects the ballad-singer, and it permits the sergeant to bend his sworn principles a bit. The rising of the moon, as a rebel song suggests, signifies a change in society, the time when "the small shall rise up and the big shall fall down." Lady Gregory uses these elements in the play in a very effective way, interrelating them so that their significance becomes more and more apparent as the play progresses.

Dialogue

Plays depend for their unfolding on dialogue. The DIALOGUE is the speeches that the characters use to advance the action. Since there is no description or commentary on the action, as there is in most novels, the dialogue must tell the whole story. Fine playwrights have developed ways of revealing character, advancing action, and introducing themes by a highly efficient use of dialogue.

Ordinarily dialogue is spoken by one character to another, who then responds. But sometimes, as in Shakespeare's *Hamlet*, a character will deliver a SOLILOQUY, in which he or she will speak alone on stage, as if speaking to him or herself. Ordinarily, such speeches take on special importance because they are thought to be especially true. Characters, when they speak to each other, may well wish to deceive, but when they speak to themselves, they have no reason to say anything but the truth.

In *The Rising of the Moon* Lady Gregory has written an unusual form of dialogue that reveals a regional way of speech. Lady Gregory was Anglo-Irish, but she lived in the west of Ireland and was familiar with the speech patterns that the characters in this play would have used. She has been recognized for her ability to re-create the speech of the rural Irish, and passages such as the following are meant to reveal the peculiarities of the rhythms and syntax of English as it was spoken in Ireland at the turn of the century:

SERGEANT: Is he as bad as that?
MAN: He is then.
SERGEANT: Do you tell me so?

Lady Gregory makes a considerable effort to create dialogue that is rich in local color as well as rich in spirit. John Millington Synge, whose dialogue in *Riders to the Sea* is also an effort to re-create the sounds and rhythms of rural Irish speech, once said: "In a good play every speech should be as fully flavoured as a nut or apple, and such speeches cannot be written by anyone who works among people who have shut their lips on poetry." Lady Gregory, who produced the plays of Synge at the Abbey Theatre in Dublin, would certainly agree, as her dialogue in *The Rising of the Moon* amply shows.

Music

Lady Gregory introduces another, occasional dramatic element: music. In *The Rising of the Moon* the music is integral to the plot because it allows the ballad-singer, by omitting a line of a rebel song, gradually to expose the sergeant's sympathies with the rebel cause. The sergeant is at first mindful of his duty and insists that the balladeer stop, but eventually he is captivated by the music. As the ballad-singer continues, he sings a song containing the title of the play, and the audience or reader realizes that the title exposes the play's rebel sympathies right from the start.

Movement

When the Greeks performed their tragedies, the choruses danced in a ritualistic fashion from one side of the stage to the other. Their movement was keyed to the structure of their speeches. In plays such as *Hamlet*, specific movement is required, as in the ghost scene or in the final dueling scenes. We as readers or witnesses are energized by the movement of the characters in a play. As we read, stage directions inform us where the characters are, when they move, how they move, and perhaps even what the significance of their moving is. And in a live performance of a play, the playwright's directions enhance the actors' interpretations of their characters' actions.

Lady Gregory moves the ballad-singer and the sergeant in telling ways. They move physically closer to one another as they become closer in their thinking. Their movement seems to pivot around the barrel, and in one of the most charming moments of the play, they meet each other's eyes when the ballad-singer sits on the barrel and comments on the way the sergeant is pacing back and forth. They then both sit on the barrel, facing in opposite directions, and share a pipe between them, almost as a peace offering.

Theme

The theme of a play is its message, its central concerns — in short, what it is about. It is by no means a simple thing to decide what the theme of a play is, and many plays contain several rather than just a single theme. Often, the search for a theme tempts us to oversimplify and to reduce a complex play to a relatively simple catchphrase.

In Sophocles' *Antigone*, the play focuses on the conflict between human law and the law of the gods when following both sets of laws seems to be impossible. Antigone wishes to honor the gods by burying her brother, but the law of Kreon decrees that he shall have no burial, since her brother is technically a traitor to the state. Similar themes are present in other Greek plays. *Hamlet* has many themes. On a very elementary level, the main theme of *Hamlet* is revenge. This is played out in the obligation of a son to avenge the murder of a father, even when the murderer is a kinsman. Another theme centers on Hamlet's hesitation resulting from his need to have enough certainty to act in what he thinks is a just manner.

Lady Gregory's play has revolution as one theme. The rising of the moon is a sign for "the rising" or revolution of the people against their English oppressors. The sergeant is an especially English emblem of oppression, because the police were established by an Englishman, Robert

Peele. At one point the balladeer suggests a song, "The Peeler and the Goat," but rejects it because in Irish slang, a peeler is a policeman.

Another important theme in *The Rising of the Moon* is that of unity among the Irish people. The sergeant seems to be at an opposite pole from the ballad-singer when the play opens. He is posting signs announcing a reward that he could well use, since he is a family man. But as the play proceeds, the sergeant moves closer in thought to the Irish people, represented by the rebel, the ballad-singer.

Sometimes playwrights become anxious about readers and viewers missing their thematic intentions and reveal them in one or two speeches. Usually, a careful reader or viewer has already divined the theme, and the speeches are intrusive. But Lady Gregory is able to introduce thematic material in certain moments of dialogue, as in this comment by the sergeant, revealing that the police are necessary to prevent a revolution:

> SERGEANT: Well, we have to do our duty in the force. Haven't we the whole country depending on us to keep law and order? It's those that are down would be up and those that are up would be down, if it wasn't for us.

But the thematic material in *The Rising of the Moon* is spread evenly throughout, as is the case in most good plays.

In every play, the elements of drama will work differently, sometimes giving us the feeling that character is dominant over theme, or plot over character, or setting over both. Ordinarily, critics feel that character, plot, and theme are the most important elements of drama, while setting, dialogue, music, and movement come next. But in the best of dramas each has its importance and each balances the others. The interaction of the elements of drama, their balance and their harmony all imply excellence in the theater. The plays in this collection strive for that harmony and most achieve it memorably.

Lady Gregory

Isabella Augusta Persse (1852–1932) was born in the west of Ireland. Her family was known as "ascendancy stock," which is to say that it was educated, wealthy, and Protestant living in a land that was largely uneducated, poverty-ridden, and Roman Catholic. A huge gulf ordinarily existed between the rich ascendancy families, who lived in great houses with considerable style, partaking of lavish hunts and balls and parties, and the impoverished Irish, who lived in one-room straw-roofed homes and worked the soil with primitive tools.

Lady Gregory took a strong interest in the Irish language, stimulated in part by a nurse who often spoke the language to her when she was a child. Her nurse was an important source of Irish folklore and a contact with the people who lived in the modest cottages around her family estate. It was extraordinary for any wealthy Protestant to pay attention to the language or the life of the poor laborers of the west of Ireland. Yet these are the very people who figure most importantly in the plays that Lady Gregory wrote in later life.

Isabella Persse met Sir William Gregory when she was on a family trip to Nice and Rome. They were actually neighbors in Ireland, although they were only slightly acquainted. They were married the next year, when she was twenty-eight and he was sixty-three. He was also of Irish ascendancy stock and had been a governor of Ceylon for many years before they met. Their marriage was apparently quite successful. Their son, Robert Gregory, was born in 1881. They used the family home, Coole Park, as a retreat for short periods, but most of their time was spent traveling and living in London, where Sir Gregory was a trustee of the National Gallery of Art. W. B. Yeats, Bernard Shaw, and numerous other important literary figures spent time in Coole Park and its beautiful great house in the early part of the twentieth century.

Lady Gregory led a relatively conventional life until Sir Gregory died in 1892. According to the laws of that time, the estate passed to her son, so she looked forward to a life of relatively modest circumstances. She set herself to finishing Sir Gregory's memoirs and in the process found herself to be a gifted writer. She used some of her spare time to learn Irish well enough to talk with the old cottagers in the hills, where she went to gather folklore and old songs. W. B. Yeats and others had collected volumes of Irish stories and poems, but they did not know Irish well enough to authenticate what they heard. Lady Gregory published her Kiltartan tales (she had dubbed her neighborhood Kiltartan) as a way of preserving the rapidly disappearing myths and stories that were still told around the hearth as a matter of course in rural Ireland.

She was already an accomplished writer when she met W. B. Yeats in 1894. Their meeting was of immense importance for the history of drama, since they decided to forge their complementary talents and abilities in creating an Irish theater. Their discussions included certain Irish neighbors, among them Edward Martyn, a Catholic whose early plays were very successful. They also talked with Dr. Edward Hyde, a mythographer and linguist and the first president of modern Ireland. Another neighbor who took part, the flamboyant George Moore, was a well-established novelist and playwright.

Their first plays — Yeats's *The Countess Cathleen* and Martyn's *The Heather Field* — were performed on May 8 and 9, 1899, under the auspices of the Irish Literary Theatre in Dublin at the Ancient Concert Rooms. The Irish Literary Theatre was dedicated to producing plays by Irish playwrights on Irish themes, and when it became an immediate success the greatest problem the founders faced was finding more plays. Lady Gregory tried her own hand and discovered herself, at age fifty, to be a playwright.

Her ear for people's speech was unusually good — good enough that she was able to give the great poet Yeats lessons in dialogue and help him prepare his own plays for the stage. She collaborated with Yeats on *The Pot of Broth* in 1902, the year she wrote her first plays, *The Jackdaw* and *A Losing Game*. Her first produced play, *Twenty-Five*, was put on in 1903. By 1904, the group had rented the historic Abbey Theatre. Some of her plays were quite popular and were very successful even in later revivals: *Spreading the News* (1904); *Kincora* and *The White Cockade* (1905); and *Hyacinth Halvey*, *The Doctor in Spite of Himself*, *The Gaol Gate*, and *The Canavans*, all produced in 1906. In the next year, there were troubles at the Abbey over John Millington Synge's *Playboy of the Western World*. Lady Gregory faced down a rioting audience protesting what she felt was excellent drama.

In 1918 her son, a World War I pilot, was shot down over Italy. The years that followed were to some extent years of struggle. Lady Gregory managed the Abbey Theatre, directed its affairs, and developed new playwrights, among them Sean O'Casey. During the Irish Civil War (1920–1922), she was physically threatened and eventually her family home, Roxborough, was burned. When she found that she had cancer in 1926, she made arrangements to sell Coole Park to the government with the agreement that she could remain there for life. She died in 1932, the writer of a large number of satisfying plays and the prime mover in the development of one of the century's most important literary theaters.

THE RISING OF THE MOON

One of Lady Gregory's shortest but most popular plays, *The Rising of the Moon* is openly political in its themes. Lady Gregory had been writing plays only a short time, and she had been directing the Irish Literary Theatre when it became the Abbey Theatre Company and produced this play in 1907. Her interest in Irish politics developed, she said, when she was going through the papers of a distant relative of her husband. That man had been in the Castle, the offices of the English authorities given the task of ruling Ireland from Dublin. She said that the underhanded dealings that were revealed in those papers convinced her that Ireland should be a nation apart from England if justice were ever to be done.

In 1907 the question of union with England or separation and nationhood was on everyone's lips. Ireland was calm, and the people in Dublin were relatively prosperous and by no means readying for a fight or a revolution. Yet there had been a tradition of risings against the English dating back to 1698. In 1907 the average Irish person would have thought that revolution was a thing of the past. But the fact was that it was less than ten years in the future. Certain organizations had been developing, notably the widespread Gaelic League and the less known Sinn Féin (We Ourselves), to promote both Irish lore, Irish language, and Irish culture. English was the dominant language in Ireland, since it was the language of commerce, but it tended to obliterate the Irish culture. So Lady Gregory's work with the Abbey Theatre, which was making one of the age's most important contributions to Irish culture, coincided with growing interest in the rest of Ireland in rediscovering its literary past.

The title of *The Rising of the Moon* comes from a popular old rebel song that pointed to the rising of the moon as the signal for the rising of peoples against oppression. The main characters of the play represent the two opposing forces in Ireland: freedom and independence, personified by the ballad-singer ("a Ragged Man"), and law and order, represented by the sergeant. The ballad-singer is aligned with those who want to change the social structure of Ireland so that the people now on the bottom will be on top. The sergeant's job is to preserve the status quo and avoid such a turning of the tables.

In an important way, the sergeant and the ballad-singer represent the two alternatives that face the modern Irish — now as in the past. One alternative is to accept the power of the English and be in its pay, like the sergeant; one would then be well fed and capable of supporting a family. The other alternative is to follow the revolutionary path of the ballad-singer and risk prison, scorn, and impoverishment. The ballad-singer is a ragged man because he has been totally reduced in circumstances by his political choices.

For Lady Gregory, this play was a serious political statement. She and W. B. Yeats — both aristocratic Protestant Irish — were sympathetic to the Irish revolutionary causes. They each wrote plays that struck a revolutionary note during this period. Neither truly expected a revolution, and when the Easter Uprising of 1916 was put down with considerable loss of life and immense destruction of central Dublin, Yeats lamented that his plays may have sent some young men to their deaths.

It is possible that if either Yeats or Lady Gregory had thought there would be a revolution they would not have written such plays. They opposed violence, but it was clear to some that violence was the only means by which Ireland would be made into a separate nation.

The success of *The Rising of the Moon* lies in Lady Gregory's exceptional ear for dialogue. She captures the way people speak, and she also manages to draw the characters of the sergeant and ballad-singer so as to gain our sympathies for them both. In a remarkably economic fashion, she shapes the problem of politics in Ireland, characterizing the two polarities and revealing some of the complexities that face anyone who tries to understand them.

Lady Gregory (1852–1932)
THE RISING OF THE MOON

1907

Persons

SERGEANT	POLICEMAN B
POLICEMAN X	A RAGGED MAN

Scene: *Side of a quay in a seaport town. Some posts and chains. A large barrel. Enter three policemen. Moonlight.*

(Sergeant, who is older than the others, crosses the stage to right and looks down steps. The others put down a pastepot and unroll a bundle of placards.)

POLICEMAN B: I think this would be a good place to put up a notice. (*He points to barrel.*)

POLICEMAN X: Better ask him. (*Calls to Sergeant.*) Will this be a good place for a placard?

(No answer.)

POLICEMAN B: Will we put up a notice here on the barrel?

(No answer.)

SERGEANT: There's a flight of steps here that leads to the water. This is a place that should be minded well. If he got down here, his friends might have a boat to meet him; they might send it in here from outside.

POLICEMAN B: Would the barrel be a good place to put a notice up?

SERGEANT: It might; you can put it there.

(They paste the notice up.)

SERGEANT (*reading it*): Dark hair — dark eyes, smooth face, height five feet five — there's not much to take hold of in that — It's a pity I had no chance of seeing him before he broke out of jail. They say he's a wonder, that it's he makes all the plans for the whole organization. There isn't another man in Ireland would have broken jail the way he did. He must have some friends among the jailers.

POLICEMAN B: A hundred pounds is little enough for the Government to offer for him. You may be sure any man in the force that takes him will get promotion.

SERGEANT: I'll mind this place myself. I wouldn't wonder at all if he came this way. He might come slipping along there (*points to side of quay*), and his friends might be waiting for him there (*points down steps*), and once he got away it's little chance we'd have of finding him; it's maybe under a load of kelp he'd be in a fishing boat, and not one to help a married man that wants it to the reward.

POLICEMAN X: And if we get him itself, nothing but abuse on our heads for it from the people, and maybe from our own relations.

SERGEANT: Well, we have to do our duty in the force. Haven't we the whole country depending on us to keep law and order? It's those that are down would be up and those that are up would be down, if it wasn't for us. Well, hurry on, you have plenty of other places to placard yet, and come back here then to me. You can take the lantern. Don't be too long now. It's very lonesome here with nothing but the moon.

POLICEMAN B: It's a pity we can't stop with you. The Government should have brought more police into the town, with *him* in jail, and at assize° time too. Well, good luck to your watch.

(*They go out.*)

SERGEANT (*walks up and down once or twice and looks at placard*): A hundred pounds and promotion sure. There must be a great deal of spending in a hundred pounds. It's a pity some honest man not to be better of that.

(*A Ragged Man appears at left and tries to slip past. Sergeant suddenly turns.*)

SERGEANT: Where are you going?

MAN: I'm a poor ballad-singer, your honor. I thought to sell some of these (*holds out bundle of ballads*) to the sailors.

(*He goes on.*)

SERGEANT: Stop! Didn't I tell you to stop? You can't go on there.

MAN: Oh, very well. It's a hard thing to be poor. All the world's against the poor!

assize: Judicial inquest.

SERGEANT: Who are you?

MAN: You'd be as wise as myself if I told you, but I don't mind. I'm one Jimmy Walsh, a ballad-singer.

SERGEANT: Jimmy Walsh? I don't know that name.

MAN: Ah, sure, they know it well enough in Ennis. Were you ever in Ennis, sergeant?

SERGEANT: What brought you here?

MAN: Sure, it's to the assizes I came, thinking I might make a few shillings here or there. It's in the one train with the judges I came.

SERGEANT: Well, if you came so far, you may as well go farther, for you'll walk out of this.

MAN: I will, I will; I'll just go on where I was going.

(*Goes toward steps.*)

SERGEANT: Come back from those steps; no one has leave to pass down them tonight.

MAN: I'll just sit on the top of the steps till I see will some sailor buy a ballad off me that would give me my supper. They do be late going back to the ship. It's often I saw them in Cork carried down the quay in a handcart.

SERGEANT: Move on, I tell you. I won't have anyone lingering about the quay tonight.

MAN: Well, I'll go. It's the poor have the hard life! Maybe yourself might like one, sergeant. Here's a good sheet now. (*Turns one over.*) "Content and a pipe" — that's not much. "The Peeler and the goat" — you wouldn't like that. "Johnny Hart" — that's a lovely song.

SERGEANT: Move on.

MAN: Ah, wait till you hear it. (*Sings.*)
There was a rich farmer's daughter lived near the town of Ross;
She courted a Highland soldier, his name was Johnny Hart;
Says the mother to her daughter, "I'll go distracted mad
If you marry that Highland soldier dressed up in Highland plaid."

SERGEANT: Stop that noise.

(*Man wraps up his ballads and shuffles toward the steps.*)

SERGEANT: Where are you going?

MAN: Sure you told me to be going, and I am going.

SERGEANT: Don't be a fool. I didn't tell you to go that way; I told you to go back to the town.

MAN: Back to the town, is it?

SERGEANT (*taking him by the shoulder and shoving him before him*): Here, I'll show you the way. Be off with you. What are you stopping for?

MAN (*who has been keeping his eye on the notice, points to it*): I think I know what you're waiting for, sergeant.

SERGEANT: What's that to you?

MAN: And I know well the man you're waiting for — I know him well — I'll be going.

(*He shuffles on.*)

SERGEANT: You know him? Come back here. What sort is he?

MAN: Come back is it, sergeant? Do you want to have me killed?

SERGEANT: Why do you say that?

MAN: Never mind. I'm going. I wouldn't be in your shoes if the reward was ten times as much. (*Goes on off stage to left.*) Not if it was ten times as much.

SERGEANT (*rushing after him*): Come back here, come back. (*Drags him back.*) What sort is he? Where did you see him?

MAN: I saw him in my own place, in the County Clare. I tell you you wouldn't like to be looking at him. You'd be afraid to be in the one place with him. There isn't a weapon he doesn't know the use of, and as to strength, his muscles are as hard as that board (*slaps barrel*).

SERGEANT: Is he as bad as that?

MAN: He is then.

SERGEANT: Do you tell me so?

MAN: There was a poor man in our place, a sergeant from Ballyvaughan. — It was with a lump of stone he did it.

SERGEANT: I never heard of that.

MAN: And you wouldn't, sergeant. It's not everything that happens gets into the papers. And there was a policeman in plain clothes, too. . . . It is in Limerick he was. . . . It was after the time of the attack on the police barrack at Kilmallock. . . . Moonlight . . . just like this . . . waterside. . . . Nothing was known for certain.

SERGEANT: Do you say so? It's a terrible county to belong to.

MAN: That's so, indeed! You might be standing there, looking out that way, thinking you saw him coming up this side of the quay (*points*), and he might be coming up this other side (*points*), and he'd be on you before you knew where you were.

SERGEANT: It's a whole troop of police they ought to put here to stop a man like that.

MAN: But if you'd like me to stop with you, I could be looking down this side. I could be sitting up here on this barrel.

SERGEANT: And you know him well, too?

MAN: I'd know him a mile off, sergeant.

SERGEANT: But you wouldn't want to share the reward?

MAN: Is it a poor man like me, that has to be going the roads and singing in fairs, to have the name on him that he took a reward? But you don't want me. I'll be safer in the town.

SERGEANT: Well, you can stop.

MAN (*getting up on barrel*): All right, sergeant. I wonder, now, you're not tired out, sergeant, walking up and down the way you are.

SERGEANT: If I'm tired I'm used to it.

MAN: You might have hard work before you tonight yet. Take it easy while you can. There's plenty of room up here on the barrel, and you see farther when you're higher up.

SERGEANT: Maybe so. (*Gets up beside him on barrel, facing right. They sit back to back, looking different ways.*) You made me feel a bit queer with the way you talked.

MAN: Give me a match, sergeant (*he gives it and man lights pipe*); take a draw yourself? It'll quiet you. Wait now till I give you a light, but you needn't turn round. Don't take your eye off the quay for the life of you.

SERGEANT: Never fear, I won't. (*Lights pipe. They both smoke.*) Indeed it's a hard thing to be in the force, out at night and no thanks for it, for all the danger we're in. And it's little we get but abuse from the people, and no choice but to obey our orders, and never asked when a man is sent into danger, if you are a married man with a family.

MAN (*sings*): As through the hills I walked to view the hills and shamrock plain,
I stood awhile where nature smiles to view the rocks and streams,
On a matron fair I fixed my eyes beneath a fertile vale,
And she sang her song it was on the wrong of poor old Granuaile.

SERGEANT: Stop that; that's no song to be singing in these times.

MAN: Ah, sergeant, I was only singing to keep my heart up. It sinks when I think of him. To think of us two sitting here, and he creeping up the quay, maybe, to get to us.

SERGEANT: Are you keeping a good lookout?

MAN: I am; and for no reward too. Amn't I the foolish man? But when I saw a man in trouble, I never could help trying to get him out of it. What's that? Did something hit me?

(*Rubs his heart.*)

SERGEANT (*patting him on the shoulder*): You will get your reward in heaven.

MAN: I know that, I know that, sergeant, but life is precious.

SERGEANT: Well, you can sing if it gives you more courage.

MAN (*sings*): Her head was bare, her hands and feet with iron bands were bound,
Her pensive strain and plaintive wail mingles with the evening gale,

And the song she sang with mournful air, I am
    old Granuaile.
    Her lips so sweet that monarchs kissed . . .
SERGEANT: That's not it. . . . "Her gown she wore was
    stained with gore." . . . That's it — you missed
    that.
MAN: You're right, sergeant, so it is; I missed it. (*Repeats line.*) But to think of a man like you knowing
    a song like that.
SERGEANT: There's many a thing a man might know
    and might not have any wish for.
MAN: Now, I daresay, sergeant, in your youth, you
    used to be sitting up on a wall, the way you are
    sitting up on this barrel now, and the other lads
    beside you, and you singing "Granuaile"? . . .
SERGEANT: I did then.
MAN: And the "Shan Van Vocht"? . . .
SERGEANT: I did then.
MAN: And the "Green on the Cape?"
SERGEANT: That was one of them.
MAN: And maybe the man you are watching for tonight
    used to be sitting on the wall, when he was young,
    and singing those same songs. . . . It's a queer
    world. . . .
SERGEANT: Whisht! . . . I think I see something coming.
    . . . It's only a dog.
MAN: And isn't it a queer world? . . . Maybe it's one
    of the boys you used to be singing with that time
    you will be arresting today or tomorrow, and sending
    into the dock. . . .
SERGEANT: That's true indeed.
MAN: And maybe one night, after you had been singing,
    if the other boys had told you some plan they had,
    some plan to free the country, you might have
    joined with them . . . and maybe it is you might
    be in trouble now.
SERGEANT: Well, who knows but I might? I had a
    great spirit in those days.
MAN: It's a queer world, sergeant, and it's little any
    mother knows when she sees her child creeping on
    the floor what might happen to it before it has
    gone through its life, or who will be who in the
    end.
SERGEANT: That's a queer thought now, and a true
    thought. Wait now till I think it out. . . . If it wasn't
    for the sense I have, and for my wife and family,
    and for me joining the force the time I did, it might
    be myself now would be after breaking jail and
    hiding in the dark, and it might be him that's hiding
    in the dark and that got out of jail would be sitting
    up here where I am on this barrel. . . . And it might
    be myself would be creeping up trying to make my
    escape from himself, and it might be himself would
    be keeping the law, and myself would be breaking
    it, and myself would be trying to put a bullet in
    his head, or to take up a lump of stone the way

you said he did . . . no, that myself did. . . . Oh!
(*Gasps. After a pause.*) What's that? (*Grasps man's
arm.*)
MAN (*jumps off barrel and listens, looking out over
water*): It's nothing, sergeant.
SERGEANT: I thought it might be a boat. I had a notion
    there might be friends of his coming about the
    quays with a boat.
MAN: Sergeant, I am thinking it was with the people
    you were, and not with the law you were, when
    you were a young man.
SERGEANT: Well, if I was foolish then, that time's gone.
MAN: Maybe, sergeant, it comes into your head sometimes, in spite of your belt and your tunic, that it
    might have been as well for you to have followed
    Granuaile.
SERGEANT: It's no business of yours what I think.
MAN: Maybe, sergeant, you'll be on the side of the
    country yet.
SERGEANT (*gets off barrel*): Don't talk to me like that.
    I have my duties and I know them. (*Looks round.*)
    That was a boat; I hear the oars.

(*Goes to the steps and looks down.*)

MAN (*sings*): O, then, tell me, Shawn O'Farrell,
    Where the gathering is to be.
    In the old spot by the river
    Right well known to you and me!
SERGEANT: Stop that! Stop that, I tell you!
MAN (*sings louder*): One word more, for signal
    token,
    Whistle up the marching tune,
    With your pike upon your shoulder,
    At the Rising of the Moon.

SERGEANT: If you don't stop that, I'll arrest you.

(*A whistle from below answers, repeating the air.*)

SERGEANT: That's a signal. (*Stands between him and
    steps.*) You must not pass this way. . . . Step farther
    back. . . . Who are you? You are no ballad-singer.
MAN: You needn't ask who I am; that placard will
    tell you. (*Points to placard.*)
SERGEANT: You are the man I am looking for.
MAN (*Takes off hat and wig. Sergeant seizes them*):
    I am. There's a hundred pounds on my head. There
    is a friend of mine below in a boat. He knows a
    safe place to bring me to.
SERGEANT (*looking still at hat and wig*): It's a pity!
    It's a pity. You deceived me. You deceived me well.
MAN: I am a friend of Granuaile. There is a hundred
    pounds on my head.
SERGEANT: It's a pity, it's a pity!
MAN: Will you let me pass, or must I make you let
    me?
SERGEANT: I am in the force. I will not let you pass.

MAN: I thought to do it with my tongue. (*Puts hand in breast.*) What is that?

VOICE OF POLICEMAN X (*outside*): Here, this is where we left him.

SERGEANT: It's my comrades coming.

MAN: You won't betray me . . . the friend of Granuaile. (*Slips behind barrel.*)

VOICE OF POLICEMAN B: That was the last of the placards.

POLICEMAN X (*as they come in*): If he makes his escape it won't be unknown he'll make it.

(*Sergeant puts hat and wig behind his back.*)

POLICEMAN B: Did anyone come this way?

SERGEANT (*after a pause*): No one.

POLICEMAN B: No one at all?

SERGEANT: No one at all.

POLICEMAN B: We had no orders to go back to the station; we can stop along with you.

SERGEANT: I don't want you. There is nothing for you to do here.

POLICEMAN B: You bade us to come back here and keep watch with you.

SERGEANT: I'd sooner be alone. Would any man come this way and you making all that talk? It is better the place to be quiet.

POLICEMAN B: Well, we'll leave you the lantern anyhow.

(*Hands it to him.*)

SERGEANT: I don't want it. Bring it with you.

POLICEMAN B: You might want it. There are clouds coming up and you have the darkness of the night before you yet. I'll leave it over here on the barrel. (*Goes to barrel.*)

SERGEANT: Bring it with you, I tell you. No more talk.

POLICEMAN B: Well, I thought it might be a comfort to you. I often think when I have it in my hand and can be flashing it about into every dark corner (*doing so*) that it's the same as being beside the fire at home, and the bits of bogwood blazing up now and again.

(*Flashes it about, now on the barrel, now on Sergeant.*)

SERGEANT (*furious*): Be off the two of you, yourselves and your lantern!

(*They go out. Man comes from behind barrel. He and Sergeant stand looking at one another.*)

SERGEANT: What are you waiting for?

MAN: For my hat, of course, and my wig. You wouldn't wish me to get my death of cold?

(*Sergeant gives them.*)

MAN (*going toward steps*): Well, good night, comrade, and thank you. You did me a good turn tonight, and I'm obliged to you. Maybe I'll be able to do as much for you when the small rise up and the big fall down . . . when we all change places at the Rising (*waves his hand and disappears*) of the Moon.

SERGEANT (*turning his back to audience and reading placard*): A hundred pounds reward! A hundred pounds! (*Turns toward audience.*) I wonder, now, am I as great a fool as I think I am?

Greek Drama

Origins of Greek Drama

Because our historical knowledge of Greek drama is limited by the available contemporary commentaries and by partial archaeological remains — which are in the form of ruined theaters — we do not know when Greek theater began or what its original impulses were. Our best information points to the year 534 B.C. as the beginning of the formal competitions among playwrights for coveted prizes that continued to be awarded for several centuries. However, Greek drama could not have burst forth in full maturity in a given year, as Athena was said to have burst forth from the head of Zeus as a mature adult. Drama must have had a childhood and models to influence it, and it must have developed slowly.

One source that may well have influenced the Greeks was the Egyptian civilization of the first millennium B.C. Egyptian culture was fully formed, brilliant, and complex. And while Egyptologists do not credit it with having a formal theater, certain ceremonies, repeated annually at major festivals, seem to have counterparts in later Greek rituals and drama. The most important and most impressive Egyptian ritual was a passion play that told the dramatic story of Isis and Osiris and the treachery of Osiris's brother Set.

Nut, the sky goddess, married Isis and Osiris and declared Osiris to be the king of upper and lower Egypt, throwing Set into a jealous rage. Set plotted to kill Osiris and after careful planning fell upon him and threw him into the Nile, where he drowned. Isis searched for his body and found it in Byblos. But before she could give it a proper burial, Set found the body, tore it into fourteen pieces, and cast it about the kingdom. After great effort, Isis recovered the parts of her husband's body, reassembled it, and breathed life into it. Osiris's last resting place, reputed to be Abydos in Egypt, was for two thousand years the site of ritual dancing, music, and passion plays dramatizing the myths of death and rebirth that lay buried deep in the Egyptian imagination.

The closest Greek counterpart to Osiris was DIONYSUS, whose deeply buried mythical associations inspired orgiastic celebrations that found their way into early Greek drama. Dionysus was an agricultural deity, the Greek god of wine and the symbol of life-giving power. In several myths he, like Osiris, was ritually killed and dismembered and his parts scattered through the land. These myths paralleled the agricultural cycle of death and disintegration during the winter, followed by cultivation and rebirth in the spring, and reinforced the Greeks' understanding of the meaning of birth, life, and death. Death and rebirth, as embodied in the Egyptians' Osiris and in the Greeks' Dionysus, became a primary theme in Greek drama.

Drama developed in ancient Greece in close connection with the DIONYSIA, religious celebrations dedicated to Dionysus. Four Dionysiac celebrations were held each winter in Athens beginning at the time of the grape harvest and culminating at the time of the first wine tastings: the Rural Dionysia in December, the Lenaia in January, the Anthesteria in February, and the City Dionysia in March. Except for the Anthesteria, the festivals featured drama contests among playwrights, and some of the works performed in those competitions have endured through the centuries. Theories that connect the origins of drama with religion consider one function of the drama competitions within religious festivals to have been the ritual attempt to guarantee fertility and the growth of the crops, upon which the entire society depended.

The Greek Stage

At the center of the Greek theater was the round ORCHESTRA, where the chorus sang and danced (*orches* is Greek for dance). The audience, sometimes numbering fifteen thousand, sat in rising rows on three sides of the orchestra. Often the steep sides of a hill formed a natural amphitheater for Greek audiences. Eventually, on the rim of the orchestra, an obl ng building called the SKENE, or stage house, developed as a space for the actors and a background for the action. The term PROSKENION was sometimes used to refer to a raised stage in front of the *skene*, where the actors performed. The theater at Epidaurus (Figure 1) was a model for the basic Greek theater plan.

Greek theaters were widely dispersed from Greece to present-day Turkey, to Sicily, and even to southern France. Wherever the Greeks developed new colonies and city-states, they built theaters following the basic plan of Epidaurus. In many of the surviving theaters the acoustics are so fine that a human voice onstage can be heard at the level of a whisper from any seat in the theater.

Perhaps the most spectacular dramatic device used by the Greek playwrights, the DEUS EX MACHINA ("the god from the machine"), was implemented onstage by means of elaborate booms. Actors were lowered onto the stage to enact the roles of Olympian gods intervening in the affairs of humans. Some commentators, such as Aristotle (384–322 B.C.), felt that the *deus ex machina* should be used only if the intercession of

Figure 1. Theater at Epidaurus

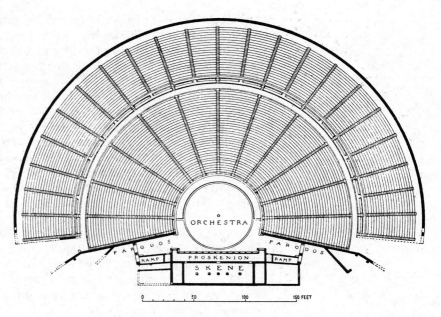

deities was in keeping with the character of the play. The last of the great Greek tragedians, Euripides (c. 480–c. 406 B.C.), used the device in almost half of his tragedies. Today the *deus ex machina* is usually frowned on by critics, who suggest that the device gives the playwright an easy way out of dramatic difficulties.

The evidence both in the drama itself and in writings contemporaneous with the plays suggests that attending the theater was usually a breathtaking experience. Besides the complex and sophisticated machinery, playwrights used inventive and colorful costumes. Costs of productions were underwritten by the state and by wealthy citizens, who were awarded the privilege of hiring the chorus.

That the state supported dramatic endeavors underscores the significance of drama in Greek life, as does the involvement of many wealthy citizens. Most playwrights came from well-to-do families and, like those who governed, must have felt that the role of drama and the practice of the festivals were of great value to the well-being of the state.

The Greek Chorus   The early Dionysiac festivals featured singing, music, and dancing. The choruses that sang DITHYRAMBS — emotional, almost uncontrollably intense songs — may have eventually developed into the CHORUSES of Greek plays. The first Greek tragedies apparently were not enacted by individual actors but were chanted by the choruses. At the height of its use, when Aeschylus (525?–456 B.C.) wrote and performed, the chorus numbered as many as fifty people, some of whom were prominent or talented citizens.

Some of the most important music of the drama accompanied the chorus. As the chorus sang one section of poetry, it moved from right to left on the stage (during the part of the choral ODE or song called the STROPHE), and then as it sang another section it moved to the right (during the ANTISTROPHE). A third section of its song was sung standing in front of the audience. The motion of the chorus implied that a dance, usually to the music of a flute, was part of the drama, but the nature of the dances is unknown.

The chorus assumed a very important part in most Greek tragedies. In some plays it represents the elders of the community, as in Aeschylus's *Agamemnon*. The chorus in Sophocles' *Oedipus Rex* is a group of serious and concerned citizens who eventually give Oedipus advice and make demands on him.

Thespis, the First Actor

According to legend, Thespis (sixth century B.C.) stepped out of a chorus to act in dialogue with it, thus creating the first AGON, or dramatic confrontation. He eventually won the first prize awarded for tragedy, in 534 B.C. As the only actor in the drama, Thespis took several roles, using MASKS to indicate the change from one character to another. Masks remained the norm in all Greek tragedies, even when the number of actors increased. Aeschylus, the first great Greek tragedian whose work survives, used two actors, while Sophocles (c. 496–c. 406 B.C.), one of the greatest of his successors, established the Greek pattern of using three actors in tragedy (only comedy used more: four actors). The actors' masks were large, sometimes decorated with golden hair, shorn hair, or other details to indicate the nature of the character: an old man, a woman, a youth, a ruler. The expressions on the masks were usually neutral.

Genres of Greek Drama
Tragedy

For the Greeks, the highest dramatic form was tragedy, which focused on a person who had risen to a great height and then fell precipitately. Tragedies showed humans at the mercy of MOIRA, their fate, which they only partly understood. One objective of Greek drama was that the audience experience a CATHARSIS, which Aristotle describes as a purging or purifying of the emotions of pity and fear. According to the Greeks, these are emotions that a person associates with the fall of someone higher in social station, such as a king or queen. A central character, or PROTAGONIST, of noble birth was therefore an essential element to the playwright striving to evoke catharsis in his audience. Twentieth-century experiments with tragic figures who are ordinary people, such as John Millington Synge's *Riders to the Sea* and Arthur Miller's *Death of a Salesman*, as masterful as they are, would not have been tolerated by the Greeks. For the Greeks, tragedy could befall only the great.

The modern critic Kenneth Burke identified a pattern for Greek tragedies. The tragic figure — who usually provides the name of the play

— experiences three stages of development: purpose, passion, and perception. The play begins with a purpose, such as finding the source of the plague in *Oedipus Rex*. Then as the path becomes tangled and events unfold, the tragic figure begins an extensive process of soul-searching and suffers an inner agony — the passion. The perception of the truth involves a fate that the tragic figure would rather not face. It might be death or, as in *Oedipus Rex*, exile. It always involves separation from the human community. For the Greeks, that was the greatest punishment.

According to Aristotle, the moment of perception of the truth is usually the most intense in the drama. He called it ANAGNORISIS, or recognition. When it comes at the same moment that the tragic figure's fortunes reverse — the *peripeteia* — Aristotle felt that the tragedy is most fulfilling and most intensely involving for the audience. This is the case in *Oedipus Rex*. Aristotle's comments in his *Poetics* on the structure and effect of *Oedipus Rex* remain the most penetrating, most significant critical observations made on Greek theater. (See the excerpt from the *Poetics* on page 86.)

Satyr Plays

The drama competitions held regularly from 534 B.C. consisted usually of the work of three playwrights who each produced three tragedies and one SATYR PLAY, a form of comic relief. In a satyr play, the chorus dressed as satyrs, comic half-beast, half-man figures who cavorted with a mock PHALLUS and engaged in riotous, almost slapstick antics. The characters were not fully developed, as they were in tragedy; the situations were not socially instructive, as they were in comedy. The satyr plays were rough-hewn and lighthearted and may have been a necessary antidote to the intensity of the tragedies.

One satyr play survives, perhaps an indication that the form was not as highly valued as tragedy. The surviving play is Euripides' *Cyclops*, based on Odysseus's confrontation with the vicious one-eyed giant who ate a number of his men. In the satyr play, Odysseus outwits the Cyclops with the aid of a well-filled wineskin. The powers of Bacchus (Dionysus) are often alluded to in the play, and drunkenness is a prime ingredient. The play is witty, entertaining, and brief. It might well have been the perfect way to end an otherwise serious drama festival.

Comedy

The works of Aristophanes (c. 448–c. 385 B.C.) represent the tradition of Old Comedy (which lasted from c. 486–c. 400 B.C.), in which individuals — sometimes well known to the audience — could be attacked in a very personal way. The nature of the humor was often ribald, coarse, and brassy, but, according to Aristotle, it was not vicious. Physical devices onstage, such as the erect phalluses beneath the togas in *Lysistrata*, accompanied ribald lines, and Athenian audiences were mightily entertained. Comedy appears to have provided an emotional release, but for entirely different emotions than those evoked by tragedy.

Aristotle comments briefly on comedy in the *Poetics*, but no coherent Greek theories on comedy have come down to us (Aristotle is said to have written a complete treatise on comedy, but it is lost). Aristotle points out that comedy shows people from a lower social order than the nobility, who are the main figures in tragedy. The Old Comedy of Aristophanes concentrated on the rollicking humor we associate with buffoonery and farce. The New Comedy of Menander and others whose work is now lost provided a more polished and refined humor that centered on the shortcomings of the middle classes.

Both forms of comedy are still evident in our theaters and on the screen. The Marx Brothers' movies are examples of Old Comedy, while the comedy of Neil Simon is an example of the New. We are still learning from the Greeks, and comparing our dramas with theirs demonstrates all the more how much we are their descendants in culture and art.

The Great Age of Greek Drama
Aeschylus

The fifth century B.C. was the great creative age in Athens. Theater survived until the Hellenistic period of the first century B.C., but the geniuses of Greek drama were clustered in the period dating from the birth of Aeschylus (525 B.C.) to the death of the philosopher Socrates (399 B.C.). Aeschylus was the first of the giants of Greek drama. He may have written as many as ninety plays, of which we have seven: *The Persians* (472); *Seven Against Thebes* (467); the *Oresteia* (458), a three-play cycle centering on Orestes and consisting of *Agamemnon*, *The Libation Bearers*, and *Eumenides*; *The Suppliants*; and *Prometheus Bound*, whose dates are uncertain.

Aeschylus's introduction of a second actor made it possible to intensify the dramatic value of each *agon*, the confrontation between ANTAGONISTS. He is also notable for giving minor characters, such as the watchman who opens *Agamemnon*, both dimension and depth.

The *Oresteia* has enjoyed successful modern production. In the three-play work, Orestes finds himself in a situation something like that of Shakespeare's Hamlet: His father, Agamemnon, returns from the Trojan War with his concubine, Cassandra, after having sacrificed his daughter Iphigenia. Agamemnon's wife, Clytemnestra, tricks him into defiling the gods and murders him in his bath, and Aegisthus, Clytemnestra's lover, accepts the kingship. Orestes flees, but when he returns in *The Libation Bearers* he resolves to kill his mother and Aegisthus to avenge Agamemnon's death. In *Eumenides*, Orestes is hounded by the Furies, female goddesses who avenge crimes against kinship. Finally, the Athenian judges render a split decision in the case against Orestes and Athena herself decides in favor of him. The power of this trilogy has established Aeschylus among the greatest of Greek dramatists.

Euripides

Euripides (c. 480–c. 406 B.C.) was the last of the great Greek dramatists. Sophocles (see page 40) expanded the number of actors to three, and Euripides followed that pattern. Some ninety-two plays have been ascribed to Euripides, and of the nineteen that survive the most important are the tragedies *Alcestis* (438), *Medea* (431), *Hippolytus* (428), *Elektra* (date uncertain), *The Trojan Women* (415), *Helen* (412), and *The Bacchae* (produced in 405) and the only surviving satyr play, *Cyclops*.

Euripides is noteworthy for his portrayal of powerful women, such as Medea and Elektra. He examines their suffering and their depth of character as few writers before or since have done with any of their creations. Euripides was interested in the psychology of his characters, so his portrayals are rounded, sometimes contradictory, and always intriguing. Late in his life his faith in the power of the gods grew dim and some of his later plays actually come close to being irreverent. Contemporaries enjoyed his work immensely, although his critical reputation was not as great as that of Sophocles or Aeschylus, whose plays were thought to be purer tragedy. Euripides was more of a romantic who appealed to the newer generation of theatergoer, those whose understanding of the great myths was not as deep as earlier theatergoers' had been.

Euripides was an experimentalist, but he was also sometimes careless of structure and craft. His use of the *deus ex machina* did not always win praise from critics, although it was always well received by audiences. The judges of the drama competitions awarded him only five first prizes, a small number for his fifty years in the theater.

Menander

The two greatest Greek comic writers were Aristophanes, whose *Lysistrata* appears in this collection, and Menander (c. 342–c. 291 B.C.). The first was a master of Old Comedy, which is similar to our modern slapstick. Menander was the master of New Comedy, a form of social commentary, sometimes satirical, sometimes biting.

Although Menander enjoyed a great reputation in his own time and was highly regarded by Roman playwrights much later, very little of his work has survived. He is said to have written a few more than one hundred plays, but only one, *The Grouch*, survives intact. Twenty-three of his plays existed in a manuscript in Constantinople in the sixteenth century, but nothing of that volume seems to have survived. We know a number of titles, such as *The Lady from Andros*, *The Flatterer*, and *The Suspicious Man*. And we know that the Romans pilfered liberally from his plays. Beyond that we know little.

Menander's New Comedy concentrated on social manners. Instead of attacking individuals, as Aristophanes frequently did, Menander was more likely to attack a vice, such as vanity, or to portray the foibles of a social class. He aimed at his own middle class and established the pattern of parents or guardians struggling, usually over the issue of marriage, against the wishes of their children. The children ordinarily foil their parents' wishes, frequently with the help of an acerbic slave who provides the comedy with most of its humor. This pattern has proved so durable that it is used virtually every day in modern situation comedies on television.

Sophocles

Sophocles (c. 496–c. 406 B.C.) is the best known of the fifth-century B.C. dramatists. His numerous first prizes in the Greek drama competitions outnumber those of any other playwright, and he never came in less than second in any of the competitions. His first victory was against the grand old master Aeschylus in 468 B.C. Sophocles' last plays, which he wrote in his eighties, were among his greatest. We have fragments of some ninety plays or poems and seven complete tragedies, while records suggest that his output numbered something over a hundred twenty plays.

Sophocles lived in interesting times. In 480 B.C. the Persian empire invaded Athens with an immense navy in one of its repeated attempts to conquer the Greek states. Through a guileful strategy, Themistocles left Athens with a handful of defenders and then, after the city was burned, lured the Persians out to sea for a battle at Salamis that turned out to be a total Greek victory that was astonishing and decisive. When it was over, Athens held superiority in the Aegean.

Sophocles was sixteen when the battle at Salamis was fought. In the ceremonies celebrating the victory, he led one of the most important choral performances. He was later to serve as a general with Pericles in the Samian War (440–439 B.C.), although tradition suggests that Pericles declared him a better poet than a general. We do not know if this ancient rumor is correct, but it is clear that Sophocles was a man of action who was able to serve his nation in more ways than one.

When Sophocles began writing, he broke with an old tradition. From the time of Thespis (mid-sixth century B.C.), the playwright acted in his own plays. Aeschylus, from what we know, probably acted in his own plays, but it is on record that Sophocles' voice was not strong enough to permit him to take a part in his plays. He played the lyre well enough to appear onstage, and he played a game of ball in one of his plays, but he did not appear as an actor. He also introduced innovations in the structure of his plays by reducing the size of the chorus from fifty to fifteen and by adding painted scenery, more props, and a third actor to the usual two that Aeschylus and other tragedians had used. In another twist that has affected virtually all subsequent ages of drama Sophocles wrote some of his plays with specific actors in mind. Shakespeare, Molière, and many other first-rank playwrights have done the same.

Sophocles was a deep reader of the epics of Homer. Many of his plays derive from the *Iliad* or the *Odyssey*, although Sophocles always adapted the material of others to his own distinct purposes. His nickname was the Attic Bee because he could investigate wonderful pieces of literature and always return with a useful idea. The approach he took to the structure of the play, measuring the effect of the rising action of complication and then ensuring that the moment of recognition occurred at the same time the falling action began, was thought, rightly, to demonstrate a skill of supreme elegance. Nowhere is this illustrated with more completeness than in *Oedipus Rex*.

The plays of Aeschylus, powerful though they are, do not have the same delicacy of construction as do Sophocles'. They are forceful but, in terms of structure, somewhat rude. The structure of the plays of Euripides, Sophocles' successor, was never as fully worked out, and when Aristotle came to discuss the nature of tragedy in his *Poetics*, it was to Sophocles he turned for a model, not to the other two master playwrights of the genre.

Besides the Oedipus trilogy, Sophocles' other surviving plays are *Philoctetes*, *Ajax*, *Trachiniae*, and *Elektra*.

OEDIPUS REX

Oedipus Rex is the first play in a group of three that are now linked because they treat the fate of Oedipus and his children. The plays were written over a period of thirty years: *Antigone* (first produced in 441 B.C.), *Oedipus Rex* (produced approximately fifteen years later, between 430 and 427 B.C.), and *Oedipus at Colonus* (produced in 401 B.C., after Sophocles' death). When these plays are produced together today, they are usually given in a different order — *Oedipus Rex*, *Oedipus at Colonus*, and *Antigone* — almost like the trilogy that Athenian audiences viewed at the drama competitions. In fact, they were never a unified trilogy, and one of Sophocles' distinctions is that he presented as trilogies plays that were not always thematically related, as poets before him had done.

The original narratives of the Oedipus plays were known to Sophocles' audience — with the possible exception of the story of Antigone — and one of the special pleasures for the audience watching the action of *Oedipus Rex* was that they knew the outcome. They watched for the steps, the choices, that led Oedipus to his fate.

Oedipus Rex is the story of a noble man who seeks knowledge that in the end destroys him. His greatness is measured in part by the fact that the gods have prophesied his fate: The gods do not take interest in insignificant men. Before the action of the play begins, Oedipus has set out to discover whether he was truly the son of Polybos and Merope, the people who have raised him. He learns from the oracle of Apollo at Delphi, the most powerful interpreter of the voice and the will of the gods, that he will kill his father and marry his mother. His response is overwhelmingly human: He has seen his *moira*, his fate, and he cannot accept it. His reaction is to do everything he can, including leaving his homeland as quickly as possible, to avoid the possibility of killing Polybos and marrying Merope.

Sophocles develops the drama in terms of IRONY — the disjunction between what seems to be true and what is true. Knowing the outcome of the action, the audience savors the ironic moments from the beginning of the play to the end. Oedipus flees his homeland to avoid fulfilling the prophecy, only to run headlong into the fate foretold by the oracle. He unwittingly returns to his original home, Thebes, and to his parents, murdering Laios, his true father, at a crossroads on the way and marrying Iokaste, his true mother, and becoming king of Thebes. The blind seer Teiresias warns Oedipus not to pursue the truth but, in human fashion, Oedipus refuses to heed Teiresias's warnings. When the complete truth becomes clear to Oedipus, he physically blinds himself in horror and expiation. Like the blind Teiresias, Oedipus must now look inward for the truth, without the distractions of surface experiences.

The belief that the moral health of the ruler reflected directly on the security of the *polis*, or city-state, was widespread in Athenian Greece. Indeed, the Athenians regarded their state as fragile — like a human being whose health, physical and moral, could change suddenly. Because of the concern of the Greeks for the well-being of their state, the *polis* often figures in the tragedies. The Sophoclean Oedipus trilogy is usually called the Theban Plays, a nomenclature that reminds us that the story of Oedipus can be read as the story of an individual or as the story of a state, depending on the political views of the reader.

Oedipus Rex examines the tension between and interdependence of the individual and the state. The agricultural and ritual basis of the Dionysian festivals — in which Greek drama developed — underscores the importance the Greeks attached to the individual's dependence on the state that feeds him and on the proper ways of doing things, whether planting and harvesting or worshiping the gods or living as part of a political entity.

The underlying conflict in the play is political. The political relationship of human beings to the gods, the arbiters of their fate, is dramatized in Oedipus's relationship with Teiresias. If he had his way, Oedipus might disregard Teiresias entirely. But Oedipus cannot command everything, even as ruler. His incomplete knowledge, despite his wisdom, is symptomatic of the limitations of every individual.

The contrast of Oedipus and Kreon, Iokaste's brother, is one of political style. Oedipus is a fully developed character who reveals himself as sympathetic but willful. He acts on his misunderstanding of the prophecy without reconsulting the oracle. He marries Iokaste and blinds himself without reconsulting the oracle. Kreon, who is much less complicated, never acts without consulting the oracle and thoughtfully reflecting on the oracle's message. Oedipus sometimes behaves tyrannically, and he appears eager for power. Kreon would take power only if forced to do so.

The depth of Sophocles' character development was unmatched, except by his contemporary Euripides, for almost fifteen hundred years. Before him, tragedy depended on action and difficult situations for its power; but Sophocles' drama is one of psychological development. His audiences saw Oedipus as a model for human greatness but also as a model for the human capacity to fall from a great height. This tragedy, in line with Aristotle's analysis, excites both terror — because it can happen to us — and pity — because we sympathize with the horrible suffering of Oedipus. In one important sense the play is about the limits of human knowledge. It is also about the limits and frailty of human happiness.

Sophocles (c. 496–c. 406 B.C.)

OEDIPUS REX

c. 430 B.C.

TRANSLATED BY DUDLEY FITTS AND ROBERT FITZGERALD

Characters

OEDIPUS, *King of Thebes, supposed son of Polybos and Merope, King and Queen of Corinth*
IOKASTE, *wife of Oedipus and widow of the late King Laios*
KREON, *brother of Iokaste, a prince of Thebes*
TEIRESIAS, *a blind seer who serves Apollo*
PRIEST
MESSENGER, *from Corinth*
SHEPHERD, *former servant of Laios*
SECOND MESSENGER, *from the palace*
CHORUS OF THEBAN ELDERS
CHORAGOS, *leader of the Chorus*
ANTIGONE *and* ISMENE, *young daughters of Oedipus and Iokaste. They appear in the Exodos but do not speak.*
SUPPLIANTS, GUARDS, SERVANTS

The Scene: *Before the palace of Oedipus, King of Thebes. A central door and two lateral doors open onto a platform which runs the length of the facade. On the platform, right and left, are altars; and three* steps *lead down into the orchestra, or chorus-ground. At the beginning of the action these steps are crowded by suppliants who have brought branches and chaplets of olive leaves and who sit in various attitudes of despair. Oedipus enters.*

PROLOGUE°

OEDIPUS: My children, generations of the living
  In the line of Kadmos,° nursed at his ancient hearth:
  Why have you strewn yourselves before these altars
  In supplication, with your boughs and garlands?
  The breath of incense rises from the city   5
  With a sound of prayer and lamentation.
                              Children,
  I would not have you speak through messengers,
  And therefore I have come myself to hear you —
  I, Oedipus, who bear the famous name.

Prologue: Portion of the play explaining the background and current action.   **2. Kadmos:** Founder of Thebes.

(*To a Priest.*) You, there, since you are eldest in
10   the company,
        Speak for them all, tell me what preys upon you,
        Whether you come in dread, or crave some
           blessing:
        Tell me, and never doubt that I will help you
        In every way I can; I should be heartless
15   Were I not moved to find you suppliant here.
        PRIEST: Great Oedipus, O powerful king of Thebes!
        You see how all the ages of our people
        Cling to your altar steps: here are boys
        Who can barely stand alone, and here are priests
20   By weight of age, as I am a priest of God,
        And young men chosen from those yet
           unmarried;
        As for the others, all that multitude,
        They wait with olive chaplets in the squares,
        At the two shrines of Pallas,° and where Apollo°
        Speaks in the glowing embers.
25   Your own eyes
        Must tell you: Thebes is tossed on a murdering
           sea
        And can not lift her head from the death surge.
        A rust consumes the buds and fruits of the
           earth;
        The herds are sick; children die unborn,
30   And labor is vain. The god of plague and pyre
        Raids like detestable lightning through the city,
        And all the house of Kadmos is laid waste,
        All emptied, and all darkened: Death alone
        Battens upon the misery of Thebes.

        You are not one of the immortal gods, we
35   know;
        Yet we have come to you to make our prayer
        As to the man surest in mortal ways
        And wisest in the ways of God. You saved us
        From the Sphinx,° that flinty singer, and the
           tribute
40   We paid to her so long; yet you were never
        Better informed than we, nor could we teach
           you:
        A god's touch, it seems, enabled you to help us.

        Therefore, O mighty power, we turn to you:
        Find us our safety, find us a remedy,
45   Whether by counsel of the gods or of men.

---

24. Pallas: Pallas Athene, daughter of Zeus and goddess of
wisdom;   **Apollo:** Son of Zeus and god of the sun, of light
and truth.   **39. Sphinx:** A winged monster with the body
of a lion and the face of a woman, the Sphinx had tormented
Thebes with her riddle, killing those who could not solve it.
When Oedipus solved the riddle, the Sphinx killed herself.

A king of wisdom tested in the past
Can act in a time of troubles, and act well.
Noblest of men, restore
Life to your city! Think how all men call you
Liberator for your boldness long ago;   50
Ah, when your years of kingship are
   remembered,
Let them not say *We rose, but later fell* —
Keep the State from going down in the storm!
Once, years ago, with happy augury,
You brought us fortune; be the same again!   55
No man questions your power to rule the land:
But rule over men, not over a dead city!
Ships are only hulls, high walls are nothing,
When no life moves in the empty passageways.
OEDIPUS: Poor children! You may be sure I know   60
All that you longed for in your coming here.
I know that you are deathly sick; and yet,
Sick as you are, not one is as sick as I.
Each of you suffers in himself alone
His anguish, not another's; but my spirit   65
Groans for the city, for myself, for you.

I was not sleeping, you are not waking me.
No, I have been in tears for a long while
And in my restless thought walked many ways.
In all my search I found one remedy,   70
And I have adopted it: I have sent Kreon,
Son of Menoikeus, brother of the queen,
To Delphi,° Apollo's place of revelation,
To learn there, if he can,
What act or pledge of mine may save the city.   75
I have counted the days, and now, this very day,
I am troubled, for he has overstayed his time.
What is he doing? He has been gone too long.
Yet whenever he comes back, I should do ill
Not to take any action the god orders.   80
PRIEST: It is a timely promise. At this instant
They tell me Kreon is here.
OEDIPUS: O Lord Apollo!
May his news be fair as his face is radiant!
PRIEST: Good news, I gather! he is crowned with
   bay,
The chaplet is thick with berries.
OEDIPUS: We shall soon know;   85
He is near enough to hear us now. (*Enter
   Kreon.*) O prince:
Brother: son of Menoikeus:
What answer do you bring us from the god?
KREON: A strong one. I can tell you, great
   afflictions
Will turn out well, if they are taken well.   90

---

73. Delphi: Site of the oracle, source of religious authority
and prophecy, under the protection of Apollo.

OEDIPUS: What was the oracle? These vague words
  Leave me still hanging between hope and fear.
KREON: Is it your pleasure to hear me with all
  these
  Gathered around us? I am prepared to speak,
  But should we not go in?
95 OEDIPUS: Speak to them all,
  It is for them I suffer, more than for myself.
KREON: Then I will tell you what I heard at Delphi.
  In plain words
  The god commands us to expel from the land of
  Thebes
100 An old defilement we are sheltering.
  It is a deathly thing, beyond cure;
  We must not let it feed upon us longer.
OEDIPUS: What defilement? How shall we rid
  ourselves of it?
KREON: By exile or death, blood for blood. It was
  Murder that brought the plague-wind on the
105 city.
OEDIPUS: Murder of whom? Surely the god has
  named him?
KREON: My Lord: Laios once ruled this land,
  Before you came to govern us.
OEDIPUS: I know;
  I learned of him from others; I never saw him.
KREON: He was murdered; and Apollo commands
110 us now
  To take revenge upon whoever killed him.
OEDIPUS: Upon whom? Where are they? Where
  shall we find a clue
  To solve that crime, after so many years?
KREON: Here in this land, he said. Search reveals
115 Things that escape an inattentive man.
OEDIPUS: Tell me: Was Laios murdered in his
  house,
  Or in the fields, or in some foreign country?
KREON: He said he planned to make a pilgrimage.
  He did not come home again.
OEDIPUS: And was there no one,
  No witness, no companion, to tell what
120 happened?
KREON: They were all killed but one, and he got
  away
  So frightened that he could remember one thing
  only.
OEDIPUS: What was that one thing? One may be
  the key
  To everything, if we resolve to use it.
KREON: He said that a band of highwaymen
125 attacked them,
  Outnumbered them, and overwhelmed the king.
OEDIPUS: Strange, that a highwayman should be so
  daring—
  Unless some faction here bribed him to do it.

KREON: We thought of that. But after Laios' death
  New troubles arose and we had no avenger. 130
OEDIPUS: What troubles could prevent your hunting
  down the killers?
KREON: The riddling Sphinx's song
  Made us deaf to all mysteries but her own.
OEDIPUS: Then once more I must bring what is
  dark to light.
  It is most fitting that Apollo shows, 135
  As you do, this compunction for the dead.
  You shall see how I stand by you, as I should,
  Avenging this country and the god as well,
  And not as though it were for some distant
  friend,
  But for my own sake, to be rid of evil. 140
  Whoever killed King Laios might — who
  knows? —
  Lay violent hands even on me — and soon.
  I act for the murdered king in my own interest.

  Come, then, my children: leave the altar steps,
  Lift up your olive boughs!
                              One of you go 145
  And summon the people of Kadmos to gather
  here.
  I will do all that I can; you may tell them that.
                                    (*Exit a Page.*)
  So, with the help of God,
  We shall be saved — or else indeed we are lost.
PRIEST: Let us rise, children. It was for this we
  came, 150
  And now the king has promised it.
  Phoibos° has sent us an oracle; may he descend
  Himself to save us and drive out the plague.

(*Exeunt*° *Oedipus and Kreon into the palace by the
central door. The Priest and the Suppliants disperse
right and left. After a short pause the Chorus enters
                                    the orchestra.*)

PARODOS° • Strophe° 1 _____

CHORUS: What is God singing in his profound
  Delphi of gold and shadow?
  What oracle for Thebes, the Sunwhipped city?
  Fear unjoints me, the roots of my heart tremble.
  Now I remember, O Healer, your power, and
  wonder:
  Will you send doom like a sudden cloud, or 5
  weave it

152. **Phoibos:** Apollo.   **Exeunt:** Latin for "they go out."
Parodos: The song or ode chanted by the Chorus on their
entry.   **Strophe:** Song sung by the Chorus as they danced
from stage right to stage left.

Like nightfall of the past?
Speak to me, tell me, O
Child of golden Hope, immortal Voice.

Antistrophe° 1

10 Let me pray to Athene, the immortal daughter of
     Zeus,
And to Artemis° her sister
Who keeps her famous throne in the market
     ring,
And to Apollo, archer from distant heaven —
15 O gods, descend! Like three streams leap against
The fires of our grief, the fires of darkness;
Be swift to bring us rest!
As in the old time from the brilliant house
Of air you stepped to save us, come again!

Strophe 2

Now our afflictions have no end,
20 Now all our stricken host lies down
And no man fights off death with his mind;
The noble plowland bears no grain,
And groaning mothers can not bear —
See, how our lives like birds take wing,
25 Like sparks that fly when a fire soars,
To the shore of the god of evening.

Antistrophe 2

The plague burns on, it is pitiless,
Though pallid children laden with death
Lie unwept in the stony ways,
30 And old gray women by every path
Flock to the strand about the altars
There to strike their breasts and cry
Worship of Phoibos in wailing prayers:
Be kind, God's golden child!

Strophe 3

35 There are no swords in this attack by fire,
No shields, but we are ringed with cries.
Send the besieger plunging from our homes
Into the vast sea-room of the Atlantic
Or into the waves that foam eastward of
     Thrace —
40 For the day ravages what the night spares —
Destroy our enemy, lord of the thunder!
Let him be riven by lightning from heaven!

Antistrophe: Song sung by the Chorus following the Strophe, as they danced back from stage left to stage right. **11. Artemis:** The huntress, daughter of Zeus, twin sister of Apollo.

Antistrophe 3

Phoibos Apollo, stretch the sun's bowstring,
That golden cord, until it sing for us,
Flashing arrows in heaven!
                              Artemis, Huntress,   45
Race with flaring lights upon our mountains!
O scarlet god,° O golden-banded brow,
O Theban Bacchos in a storm of Maenads,°

(*Enter Oedipus, center.*)

Whirl upon Death, that all the Undying hate!
Come with blinding torches, come in joy!   50

SCENE 1 _____

OEDIPUS: Is this your prayer? It may be answered.
     Come,
Listen to me, act as the crisis demands,
And you shall have relief from all these evils.

Until now I was a stranger to this tale,
As I had been a stranger to the crime.   5
Could I track down the murderer without a
     clue?
But now, friends,
As one who became a citizen after the murder,
I make this proclamation to all Thebans:
If any man knows by whose hand Laios, son of
     Labdakos,   10
Met his death, I direct that man to tell me
     everything,
No matter what he fears for having so long
     withheld it.
Let it stand as promised that no further trouble
Will come to him, but he may leave the land in
     safety.
Moreover: If anyone knows the murderer to be
     foreign,   15
Let him not keep silent: he shall have his reward
     from me.
However, if he does conceal it; if any man
Fearing for his friend or for himself disobeys this
     edict,
Hear what I propose to do:

I solemnly forbid the people of this country,   20
Where power and throne are mine, ever to
     receive that man
Or speak to him, no matter who he is, or let
     him
Join in sacrifice, lustration, or in prayer.

47. scarlet god: Bacchus, god of wine and revelry; also called Dionysus. **48. Maenads:** Female worshipers of Bacchus (Dionysus).

I decree that he be driven from every house,
Being, as he is, corruption itself to us: the
25   Delphic
Voice of Apollo has pronounced this revelation.
Thus I associate myself with the oracle
And take the side of the murdered king.

As for the criminal, I pray to God —
Whether it be a lurking thief, or one of a
30   number —
I pray that that man's life be consumed in evil
        and wretchedness.
And as for me, this curse applies no less
If it should turn out that the culprit is my guest
        here,
Sharing my hearth.
                        You have heard the penalty.
35   I lay it on you now to attend to this
For my sake, for Apollo's, for the sick
Sterile city that heaven has abandoned.
Suppose the oracle had given you no command:
Should this defilement go uncleansed for ever?
40   You should have found the murderer: your king,
A noble king, had been destroyed!
                                Now I,
Having the power that he held before me,
Having his bed, begetting children there
Upon his wife, as he would have, had he
        lived —
Their son would have been my children's
45   brother,
If Laios had had luck in fatherhood!
(And now his bad fortune has struck him
        down) —
I say I take the son's part, just as though
I were his son, to press the fight for him
50   And see it won! I'll find the hand that brought
Death to Labdakos' and Polydoros' child,
Heir of Kadmos' and Agenor's line.°
And as for those who fail me,
May the gods deny them the fruit of the earth,
55   Fruit of the womb, and may they rot utterly!
Let them be wretched as we are wretched, and
        worse!

For you, for loyal Thebans, and for all
Who find my actions right, I pray the favor
Of justice, and of all the immortal gods.
CHORAGOS: Since I am under oath, my lord, I
60   swear
I did not do the murder, I can not name

The murderer. Phoibos ordained the search;
Why did he not say who the culprit was?
OEDIPUS: An honest question. But no man in the
        world
Can make the gods do more than the gods will.   65
CHORAGOS: There is an alternative, I think —
OEDIPUS: Tell me.
Any or all, you must not fail to tell me.
CHORAGOS: A lord clairvoyant to the lord Apollo,
As we all know, is the skilled Teiresias.
One might learn much about this from him,
        Oedipus.   70
OEDIPUS: I am not wasting time:
Kreon spoke of this, and I have sent for him —
Twice, in fact; it is strange that he is not here.
CHORAGOS: The other matter — that old report —
        seems useless.
OEDIPUS: What was that? I am interested in all
        reports.   75
CHORAGOS: The king was said to have been killed
        by highwaymen.
OEDIPUS: I know. But we have no witnesses to that.
CHORAGOS: If the killer can feel a particle of dread,
Your curse will bring him out of hiding!
OEDIPUS: No.
The man who dared that act will fear no curse.   80

(*Enter the blind seer Teiresias, led by a Page.*)

CHORAGOS: But there is one man who may detect
        the criminal.
This is Teiresias, this is the holy prophet
In whom, alone of all men, truth was born.
OEDIPUS: Teiresias: seer: student of mysteries,
Of all that's taught and all that no man tells,   85
Secrets of Heaven and secrets of the earth:
Blind though you are, you know the city lies
Sick with plague; and from this plague, my lord,
We find that you alone can guard or save us.

Possibly you did not hear the messengers?   90
Apollo, when we sent to him,
Sent us back word that this great pestilence
Would lift, but only if we established clearly
The identity of those who murdered Laios.
They must be killed or exiled.
                                Can you use   95
Birdflight° or any art of divination
To purify yourself, and Thebes, and me
From this contagion? We are in your hands.
There is no fairer duty
Than that of helping others in distress.   100
TEIRESIAS: How dreadful knowledge of the truth
        can be

51–52. Labdakos, Polydoros, Kadmos, and Agenor: Father, grandfather, great-grandfather, and great-great-grandfather of Laios.

96. Birdflight: Prophets used the flight of birds to predict the future.

When there's no help in truth! I knew this well,
But did not act on it; else I should not have
come.
OEDIPUS: What is troubling you? Why are your eyes
so cold?
TEIRESIAS: Let me go home. Bear your own fate,
and I'll
Bear mine. It is better so: trust what I say.
OEDIPUS: What you say is ungracious and unhelpful
To your native country. Do not refuse to speak.
TEIRESIAS: When it comes to speech, your own is
neither temperate
Nor opportune. I wish to be more prudent.
OEDIPUS: In God's name, we all beg you —
TEIRESIAS: You are all ignorant.
No; I will never tell you what I know.
Now it is my misery; then, it would be yours.
OEDIPUS: What! You do know something, and will
not tell us?
You would betray us all and wreck the State?
TEIRESIAS: I do not intend to torture myself, or you.
Why persist in asking? You will not persuade
me.
OEDIPUS: What a wicked old man you are! You'd
try a stone's
Patience! Out with it! Have you no feeling at
all?
TEIRESIAS: You call me unfeeling. If you could only
see
The nature of your own feelings . . .
OEDIPUS: Why,
Who would not feel as I do? Who could endure
Your arrogance toward the city?
TEIRESIAS: What does it matter?
Whether I speak or not, it is bound to come.
OEDIPUS: Then, if "it" is bound to come, you are
bound to tell me.
TEIRESIAS: No, I will not go on. Rage as you please.
OEDIPUS: Rage? Why not!
                                    And I'll tell you what I think:
You planned it, you had it done, you all but
Killed him with your own hands: if you had
eyes,
I'd say the crime was yours, and yours alone.
TEIRESIAS: So? I charge you, then,
Abide by the proclamation you have made:
From this day forth
Never speak again to these men or to me;
You yourself are the pollution of this country.
OEDIPUS: You dare say that! Can you possibly think
you have
Some way of going free, after such insolence?
TEIRESIAS: I have gone free. It is the truth sustains
me.
OEDIPUS: Who taught you shamelessness? It was not
your craft.

TEIRESIAS: You did. You made me speak. I did not
want to.
OEDIPUS: Speak what? Let me hear it again more
clearly.
TEIRESIAS: Was it not clear before? Are you
tempting me?
OEDIPUS: I did not understand it. Say it again.
TEIRESIAS: I say that you are the murderer whom
you seek.
OEDIPUS: Now twice you have spat out infamy.
You'll pay for it!
TEIRESIAS: Would you care for more? Do you wish
to be really angry?
OEDIPUS: Say what you will. Whatever you say is
worthless.
TEIRESIAS: I say you live in hideous shame with
those
Most dear to you. You can not see the evil.
OEDIPUS: Can you go on babbling like this for ever?
TEIRESIAS: I can, if there is power in truth.
OEDIPUS: There is:
But not for you, not for you,
You sightless, witless, senseless, mad old man!
TEIRESIAS: You are the madman. There is no one
here
Who will not curse you soon, as you curse me.
OEDIPUS: You child of total night! I would not
touch you;
Neither would any man who sees the sun.
TEIRESIAS: True: it is not from you my fate will
come.
That lies within Apollo's competence,
As it is his concern.
OEDIPUS: Tell me, who made
These fine discoveries? Kreon? or someone else?
TEIRESIAS: Kreon is no threat. You weave your own
doom.
OEDIPUS: Wealth, power, craft of statemanship!
Kingly position, everywhere admired!
What savage envy is stored up against these,
If Kreon, whom I trusted, Kreon my friend,
For this great office which the city once
Put in my hands unsought — if for this power
Kreon desires in secret to destroy me!

He has bought this decrepit fortune-teller, this
Collector of dirty pennies, this prophet fraud —
Why, he is no more clairvoyant than I am!
                                              Tell us:
Has your mystic mummery ever approached the
truth?
When that hellcat the Sphinx was performing
here,
What help were you to these people?
Her magic was not for the first man who came
along:

It demanded a real exorcist. Your birds —
What good were they? or the gods, for the
   matter of that?
But I came by,
180   Oedipus, the simple man, who knows nothing —
I thought it out for myself, no birds helped me!
And this is the man you think you can destroy,
That you may be close to Kreon when he's king!
Well, you and your friend Kreon, it seems to
   me,
185   Will suffer most. If you were not an old man,
You would have paid already for your plot.
CHORAGOS: We can not see that his words or yours
Have been spoken except in anger, Oedipus,
And of anger we have no need. How to
   accomplish
The god's will best: that is what most concerns
190   us.
TEIRESIAS: You are a king. But where argument's
   concerned
I am your man, as much a king as you.
I am not your servant, but Apollo's.
I have no need of Kreon or Kreon's name.

195   Listen to me. You mock my blindness, do you?
But I say that you, with both your eyes, are
   blind:
You can not see the wretchedness of your life,
Nor in whose house you live, no, nor with
   whom.
Who are your father and mother? Can you tell
   me?
200   You do not even know the blind wrongs
That you have done them, on earth and in the
   world below.
But the double lash of your parents' curse will
   whip you
Out of this land some day, with only night
Upon your precious eyes.
205   Your cries then — where will they not be heard?
What fastness of Kithairon° will not echo them?
And that bridal-descant of yours — you'll know
   it then,
The song they sang when you came here to
   Thebes
And found your misguided berthing.
All this, and more, that you can not guess at
210   now,
Will bring you to yourself among your children.

Be angry, then. Curse Kreon. Curse my words.
I tell you, no man that walks upon the earth
Shall be rooted out more horribly than you.

206. Kithairon: The mountain where Oedipus was abandoned
as an infant.

OEDIPUS: Am I to bear this from him? —
   Damnation   215
Take you! Out of this place! Out of my sight!
TEIRESIAS: I would not have come at all if you had
   not asked me.
OEDIPUS: Could I have told that you'd talk
   nonsense, that
You'd come here to make a fool of yourself, and
   of me?
TEIRESIAS: A fool? Your parents thought me sane
   enough.   220
OEDIPUS: My parents again! — Wait: who were my
   parents?
TEIRESIAS: This day will give you a father, and
   break your heart.
OEDIPUS: Your infantile riddles! Your damned
   abracadabra!
TEIRESIAS: You were a great man once at solving
   riddles.
OEDIPUS: Mock me with that if you like; you will
   find it true.   225
TEIRESIAS: It was true enough. It brought about
   your ruin.
OEDIPUS: But if it saved this town?
TEIRESIAS (*to the Page*):   Boy, give me your hand.
OEDIPUS: Yes, boy; lead him away.
                         — While you are here
We can do nothing. Go; leave us in peace.
TEIRESIAS: I will go when I have said what I have
   to say.   230
How can you hurt me? And I tell you again:
The man you have been looking for all this time,
The damned man, the murderer of Laios,
That man is in Thebes. To your mind he is
   foreign-born,
But it will soon be shown that he is a Theban,   235
A revelation that will fail to please.
                             A blind man,
Who has his eyes now; a penniless man, who is
   rich now;
And he will go tapping the strange earth with
   his staff.
To the children with whom he lives now he will
   be
Brother and father — the very same; to her   240
Who bore him, son and husband — the very
   same
Who came to his father's bed, wet with his
   father's blood.
Enough. Go think that over.
If later you find error in what I have said,
You may say that I have no skill in prophecy.   245

(*Exit Teiresias, led by his Page. Oedipus goes into the
                                        palace.*)

ODE° 1 • Strophe 1 _____

CHORUS: The Delphic stone of prophecies
    Remembers ancient regicide
    And a still bloody hand.
    That killer's hour of flight has come.
5   He must be stronger than riderless
    Coursers of untiring wind,
    For the son of Zeus° armed with his father's
        thunder
    Leaps in lightning after him;
    And the Furies° hold his track, the sad Furies.

Antistrophe 1

10 Holy Parnassos'° peak of snow
    Flashes and blinds that secret man,
    That all shall hunt him down:
    Though he may roam the forest shade
    Like a bull gone wild from pasture
15 To rage through glooms of stone.
    Doom comes down on him; flight will not avail
        him;
    For the world's heart calls him desolate,
    And the immortal voices follow, for ever follow.

Strophe 2

    But now a wilder thing is heard
    From the old man skilled at hearing Fate in the
20   wing-beat of a bird.
    Bewildered as a blown bird, my soul hovers and
        can not find
    Foothold in this debate, or any reason or rest of
        mind.
    But no man ever brought — none can bring
    Proof of strife between Thebes' royal house,
25 Labdakos' line, and the son of Polybos;°
    And never until now has any man brought word
    Of Laios' dark death staining Oedipus the King.

Antistrophe 2

    Divine Zeus and Apollo hold
    Perfect intelligence alone of all tales ever told;
    And well though this diviner works, he works in
30   his own night;
    No man can judge that rough unknown or trust
        in second sight,
    For wisdom changes hands among the wise.

Ode: Song sung by the Chorus.   7. son of Zeus: Apollo.
9. Furies: Spirits called upon to avenge crimes, especially
against kin.   10. Parnassos: Mountain sacred to Apollo.
25. Polybos: King who adopted Oedipus.

Shall I believe my great lord criminal
At a raging word that a blind old man let fall?
I saw him, when the carrion woman° faced him
    of old,   35
Prove his heroic mind. These evil words are lies.

SCENE 2 _____

KREON: Men of Thebes:
    I am told that heavy accusations
    Have been brought against me by King Oedipus.

    I am not the kind of man to bear this tamely.

    If in these present difficulties   5
    He holds me accountable for any harm to him
    Through anything I have said or done — why,
        then,
    I do not value life in this dishonor.
    It is not as though this rumor touched upon
    Some private indiscretion. The matter is grave.   10
    The fact is that I am being called disloyal
    To the State, to my fellow citizens, to my
        friends.
CHORAGOS: He may have spoken in anger, not
        from his mind.
KREON: But did you not hear him say I was the
        one
    Who seduced the old prophet into lying?   15
CHORAGOS: The thing was said; I do not know
        how seriously.
KREON: But you were watching him! Were his eyes
        steady?
    Did he look like a man in his right mind?
CHORAGOS: I do not know.
    I can not judge the behavior of great men.
    But here is the king himself.

(Enter Oedipus.)

OEDIPUS: So you dared come back. 20
    Why? How brazen of you to come to my house,
    You murderer!
                    Do you think I do not know
    That you plotted to kill me, plotted to steal my
        throne?
    Tell me, in God's name: am I coward, a fool,
    That you should dream you could accomplish
        this?   25
    A fool who could not see your slippery game?
    A coward, not to fight back when I saw it?
    You are the fool, Kreon, are you not? hoping
    Without support or friends to get a throne?

35. woman: The Sphinx.

30   Thrones may be won or bought: you could do
     neither.
  KREON: Now listen to me. You have talked; let me
     talk, too.
    You can not judge unless you know the facts.
  OEDIPUS: You speak well: there is one fact; but I
     find it hard
    To learn from the deadliest enemy I have.
35   KREON: That above all I must dispute with you.
  OEDIPUS: That above all I will not hear you deny.
  KREON: If you think there is anything good in
     being stubborn
    Against all reason, then I say you are wrong.
  OEDIPUS: If you think a man can sin against his
     own kind
40   And not be punished for it, I say you are mad.
  KREON: I agree. But tell me: what have I done to
     you?
  OEDIPUS: You advised me to send for that wizard,
     did you not?
  KREON: I did. I should do it again.
  OEDIPUS: Very well. Now tell me:
    How long has it been since Laios —
  KREON: What of Laios?
  OEDIPUS: Since he vanished in that onset by the
45   road?
  KREON: It was long ago, a long time.
  OEDIPUS: And this prophet,
    Was he practicing here then?
  KREON: He was; and with honor, as now.
  OEDIPUS: Did he speak of me at that time?
  KREON: He never did,
    At least, not when I was present,
  OEDIPUS: But . . . the enquiry?
    I suppose you held one?
50   KREON: We did, but we learned nothing.
  OEDIPUS: Why did the prophet not speak against
     me then?
  KREON: I do not know; and I am the kind of man
    Who holds his tongue when he has no facts to
     go on.
  OEDIPUS: There's one fact that you know, and you
     could tell it.
  KREON: What fact is that? If I know it, you shall
55   have it.
  OEDIPUS: If he were not involved with you, he
     could not say
    That it was I who murdered Laios.
  KREON: If he says that, you are the one that knows
     it! —
    But now it is my turn to question you.
60   OEDIPUS: Put your questions. I am no murderer.
  KREON: First, then: You married my sister?
  OEDIPUS: I married your sister.
  KREON: And you rule the kingdom equally with her?

OEDIPUS: Everything that she wants she has from
    me.
KREON: And I am the third, equal to both of you?
OEDIPUS: That is why I call you a bad friend.   65
KREON: No. Reason it out, as I have done.
  Think of this first: would any sane man prefer
  Power, with all a king's anxieties,
  To that same power and the grace of sleep?
  Certainly not I.   70
  I have never longed for the king's power — only
    his rights.
  Would any wise man differ from me in this?
  As matters stand, I have my way in everything
  With your consent, and no responsibilities.
  If I were king, I should be a slave to policy.   75
  How could I desire a scepter more
  Than what is now mine — untroubled influence?
  No, I have not gone mad; I need no honors,
  Except those with the perquisites I have now.
  I am welcome everywhere; every man salutes me,   80
  And those who want your favor seek my ear,
  Since I know how to manage what they ask.
  Should I exchange this ease for that anxiety?
  Besides, no sober mind is treasonable.
  I hate anarchy   85
  And never would deal with any man who
    likes it.

  Test what I have said. Go to the priestess
  At Delphi, ask if I quoted her correctly.
  And as for this other thing: if I am found
  Guilty of treason with Teiresias,   90
  Then sentence me to death. You have my word
  It is a sentence I should cast my vote for —
  But not without evidence!
                You do wrong
  When you take good men for bad, bad men for
    good.
  A true friend thrown aside — why, life itself   95
  Is not more precious!
            In time you will know this well:
  For time, and time alone, will show the just
    man,
  Though scoundrels are discovered in a day.
CHORAGOS: This is well said, and a prudent man
    would ponder it.
  Judgments too quickly formed are dangerous.   100
OEDIPUS: But is he not quick in his duplicity?
  And shall I not be quick to parry him?
  Would you have me stand still, hold my peace,
    and let
  This man win everything, through my inaction?
KREON: And you want — what is it, then? To
    banish me?   105
OEDIPUS: No, not exile. It is your death I want,

So that all the world may see what treason
    means.
KREON: You will persist, then? You will not believe
    me?
OEDIPUS: How can I believe you?
KREON: Then you are a fool.
OEDIPUS: To save myself?
110 KREON: In justice, think of me.
OEDIPUS: You are evil incarnate.
KREON: But suppose that you are wrong?
OEDIPUS: Still I must rule.
KREON: But not if you rule badly.
OEDIPUS: O city, city!
KREON: It is my city, too!
CHORAGOS: Now, my lords, be still. I see the
    queen,
115 Iokaste, coming from her palace chambers;
    And it is time she came, for the sake of you
        both.
    This dreadful quarrel can be resolved through
        her.

(*Enter Iokaste.*)

IOKASTE: Poor foolish men, what wicked din is this?
    With Thebes sick to death, is it not shameful
120 That you should rake some private quarrel up?
    (*To Oedipus.*) Come into the house.
                    — And you, Kreon, go now:
    Let us have no more of this tumult over nothing.
KREON: Nothing? No, sister: what your husband
        plans for me
    Is one of two great evils: exile or death.
OEDIPUS: He is right.
125   Why, woman I have caught him squarely
    Plotting against my life.
KREON: No! Let me die
    Accurst if ever I have wished you harm!
IOKASTE: Ah, believe it, Oedipus!
    In the name of the gods, respect this oath of his
130 For my sake, for the sake of these people here!

Strophe 1

CHORAGOS: Open your mind to her, my lord. Be
        ruled by her, I beg you!
OEDIPUS: What would you have me do?
CHORAGOS: Respect Kreon's word. He has never
        spoken like a fool,
    And now he has sworn an oath.
OEDIPUS: You know what you ask?
CHORAGOS: I do.
OEDIPUS: Speak on, then.
CHORAGOS: A friend so sworn should not be baited
135 so,
    In blind malice, and without final proof.

OEDIPUS: You are aware, I hope, that what you say
    Means death for me, or exile at the least.

Strophe 2

CHORAGOS: No, I swear by Helios, first in heaven!
    May I die friendless and accurst,   140
    The worst of deaths, if ever I meant that!
    It is the withering fields
        That hurt my sick heart:
    Must we bear all these ills,
        And now your bad blood as well?   145
OEDIPUS: Then let him go. And let me die, if I
        must,
    Or be driven by him in shame from the land of
        Thebes.
    It is your unhappiness, and not his talk,
    That touches me.
                    As for him —
    Wherever he goes, hatred will follow him.   150
KREON: Ugly in yielding, as you were ugly in rage!
    Natures like yours chiefly torment themselves.
OEDIPUS: Can you not go? Can you not leave me?
KREON: I can.
    You do not know me; but the city knows me,
    And in its eyes I am just, if not in yours.   155
                    (*Exit Kreon.*)

Antistrophe 1

CHORAGOS: Lady Iokaste, did you not ask the King
        to go to his chambers?
IOKASTE: First tell me what has happened.
CHORAGOS: There was suspicion without evidence;
        yet it rankled
    As even false charges will.
IOKASTE: On both sides?
CHORAGOS: On both.
IOKASTE: But what was said?   160
CHORAGOS: Oh let it rest, let it be done with!
    Have we not suffered enough?
OEDIPUS: You see to what your decency has
        brought you:
    You have made difficulties where my heart saw
        none.

Antistrophe 2

CHORAGOS: Oedipus, it is not once only I have told
        you —   165
    You must know I should count myself unwise
    To the point of madness, should I now forsake
        you —
        You, under whose hand,

In the storm of another time,
170   Our dear land sailed out free.
But now stand fast at the helm!
IOKASTE: In God's name, Oedipus, inform your wife
as well:
Why are you so set in this hard anger?
OEDIPUS: I will tell you, for none of these men
deserves
175   My confidence as you do. It is Kreon's work,
His treachery, his plotting against me.
IOKASTE: Go on, if you can make this clear to me.
OEDIPUS: He charges me with the murder of Laios.
IOKASTE: Has he some knowledge? Or does he
speak from hearsay?
OEDIPUS: He would not commit himself to such a
180   charge,
But he has brought in that damnable soothsayer
To tell his story.
IOKASTE: Set your mind at rest.
If it is a question of soothsayers, I tell you
That you will find no man whose craft gives
knowledge
Of the unknowable.
185   Here is my proof:
An oracle was reported to Laios once
(I will not say from Phoibos himself, but from
His appointed ministers, at any rate)
That his doom would be death at the hands of
his own son —
190   His son, born of his flesh and of mine!

Now, you remember the story: Laios was killed
By marauding strangers where three highways
meet;
But his child had not been three days in this
world
Before the king had pierced the baby's ankles
195   And left him to die on a lonely mountainside.

Thus, Apollo never caused that child
To kill his father, and it was not Laios' fate
To die at the hands of his son, as he had feared.
This is what prophets and prophecies are worth!
Have no dread of them.
200   It is God himself
Who can show us what he wills, in his own
way.
OEDIPUS: How strange a shadowy memory crossed
my mind,
Just now while you were speaking; it chilled my
heart.
IOKASTE: What do you mean? What memory do
you speak of?
205 OEDIPUS: If I understand you, Laios was killed
At a place where three roads meet.

IOKASTE: So it was said;
We have no later story.
OEDIPUS: Where did it happen?
IOKASTE: Phokis, it is called: at a place where the
Theban Way
Divides into the roads toward Delphi and
Daulia.
OEDIPUS: When?
IOKASTE: We had the news not long before
you came   210
And proved the right to your succession here.
OEDIPUS: Ah, what net has God been weaving for
me?
IOKASTE: Oedipus! Why does this trouble you?
OEDIPUS: Do not ask me yet.
First, tell me how Laios looked, and tell me
How old he was.
IOKASTE: He was tall, his hair just touched   215
With white; his form was not unlike your own.
OEDIPUS: I think that I myself may be accurst
By my own ignorant edict.
IOKASTE: You speak strangely.
It makes me tremble to look at you, my king.
OEDIPUS: I am not sure that the blind man can not
see.   220
But I should know better if you were to tell
me —
IOKASTE: Anything — though I dread to hear you
ask it.
OEDIPUS: Was the king lightly escorted, or did he
ride
With a large company, as a ruler should?
IOKASTE: There were five men with him in all: one
was a herald;   225
And a single chariot, which he was driving.
OEDIPUS: Alas, that makes it plain enough!
                                                But who —
Who told you how it happened?
IOKASTE: A household servant,
The only one to escape.
OEDIPUS: And is he still
A servant of ours?
IOKASTE: No; for when he came back at last   230
And found you enthroned in the place of the
dead king,
He came to me, touched my hand with his, and
begged
That I would send him away to the frontier
district
Where only the shepherds go —
As far away from the city as I could send him.   235
I granted his prayer; for although the man was a
slave,
He had earned more than this favor at my
hands.

OEDIPUS: Can he be called back quickly?

IOKASTE: Easily.
　　But why?

OEDIPUS:　　I have taken too much upon myself
　　Without enquiry; therefore I wish to consult
　　him.

240 IOKASTE: Then he shall come.
　　　　　　　　　　　But am I not one also
　　To whom you might confide these fears of
　　yours?

OEDIPUS: That is your right; it will not be denied
　　you,
　　Now least of all; for I have reached a pitch
245 Of wild foreboding. Is there anyone
　　To whom I should sooner speak?

　　Polybos of Corinth is my father.
　　My mother is a Dorian: Merope.
　　I grew up chief among the men of Corinth
250 Until a strange thing happened —
　　Not worth my passion, it may be, but strange.
　　At a feast, a drunken man maundering in his
　　cups
　　Cries out that I am not my father's son!

　　I contained myself that night, though I felt anger
255 And a sinking heart. The next day I visited
　　My father and mother, and questioned them.
　　　They stormed,
　　Calling it all the slanderous rant of a fool;
　　And this relieved me. Yet the suspicion
　　Remained always aching in my mind;
260 I knew there was talk; I could not rest;
　　And finally, saying nothing to my parents,
　　I went to the shrine at Delphi.

　　The god dismissed my question without reply;
　　He spoke of other things.
　　　　　　　　　　Some were clear,
265 Full of wretchedness, dreadful, unbearable:
　　As, that I should lie with my own mother, breed
　　Children from whom all men would turn their
　　eyes;
　　And that I should be my father's murderer.

　　I heard all this, and fled. And from that day
270 Corinth to me was only in the stars
　　Descending in that quarter of the sky,
　　As I wandered farther and farther on my way
　　To a land where I should never see the evil
　　Sung by the oracle. And I came to this country
275 Where, so you say, King Laios was killed.

　　I will tell you all that happened there, my lady.

　　There were three highways
　　Coming together at a place I passed;
　　And there a herald came towards me, and a
　　chariot
　　Drawn by horses, with a man such as you
　　describe   280
　　Seated in it. The groom leading the horses
　　Forced me off the road at his lord's command;
　　But as this charioteer lurched over towards me
　　I struck him in my rage. The old man saw me
　　And brought his double goad down upon my
　　head   285
　　As I came abreast.
　　　　　　　　　　He was paid back, and more!
　　Swinging my club in this right hand I knocked
　　him
　　Out of his car, and he rolled on the ground.
　　　　　　　　　　　　　　I killed him.

　　I killed them all.
　　Now if that stranger and Laios were — kin,   290
　　Where is a man more miserable than I?
　　More hated by the gods? Citizen and alien alike
　　Must never shelter me or speak to me —
　　I must be shunned by all.
　　　　　　　　　　　　And I myself
　　Pronounced this malediction upon myself!   295

　　Think of it: I have touched you with these
　　hands,
　　These hands that killed your husband. What
　　defilement!

　　Am I all evil, then? It must be so,
　　Since I must flee from Thebes, yet never again
　　See my own countrymen, my own country,   300
　　For fear of joining my mother in marriage
　　And killing Polybos, my father.
　　　　　　　　　　　　　Ah,
　　If I was created so, born to this fate,
　　Who could deny the savagery of God?

　　O holy majesty of heavenly powers!   305
　　May I never see that day! Never!
　　Rather let me vanish from the race of men
　　Than know the abomination destined me!

CHORAGOS: We too, my lord, have felt dismay at
　　this.
　　But there is hope: you have yet to hear the
　　shepherd.   310

OEDIPUS: Indeed, I fear no other hope is left me.

IOKASTE: What do you hope from him when he
　　comes?

OEDIPUS:
　　　　　　　　　　　　　　This much:

If his account of the murder tallies with yours,
Then I am cleared.
IOKASTE: What was it that I said
Of such importance?
315 OEDIPUS: Why, "marauders," you said,
Killed the king, according to this man's story.
If he maintains that still, if there were several,
Clearly the guilt is not mine: I was alone.
But if he says one man, singlehanded, did it,
320 Then the evidence all points to me.
IOKASTE: You may be sure that he said there were
several;
And can he call back that story now? He can not.
The whole city heard it as plainly as I.
But suppose he alters some detail of it:
325 He can not ever show that Laios' death
Fulfilled the oracle: for Apollo said
My child was doomed to kill him; and my
child —
Poor baby! — it was my child that died first.

No. From now on, where oracles are concerned,
330 I would not waste a second thought on any.
OEDIPUS: You may be right.
                        But come: let someone go
For the shepherd at once. This matter must be
settled.
IOKASTE: I will send for him.
I would not wish to cross you in anything,
And surely not in this. — Let us go in.
                        (*Exeunt into the palace.*)

ODE 2 · Strophe 1 _____

CHORUS: Let me be reverent in the ways of right,
Lowly the paths I journey on;
Let all my words and actions keep
The laws of the pure universe
5   From highest Heaven handed down.
For Heaven is their bright nurse,
Those generations of the realms of light;
Ah, never of mortal kind were they begot,
Nor are they slaves of memory, lost in sleep:
10 Their Father is greater than Time, and ages not.

Antistrophe 1

The tyrant is a child of Pride
Who drinks from his great sickening cup
Recklessness and vanity,
Until from his high crest headlong
15 He plummets to the dust of hope.
That strong man is not strong.
But let no fair ambition be denied;

May God protect the wrestler for the State
In government, in comely policy,
Who will fear God, and on his ordinance wait.   20

Strophe 2

Haughtiness and the high hand of disdain
Tempt and outrage God's holy law;
And any mortal who dares hold
No immortal Power in awe
Will be caught up in a net of pain: 25
The price for which his levity is sold.
Let each man take due earnings, then,
And keep his hands from holy things,
And from blasphemy stand apart —
Else the crackling blast of heaven   30
Blows on his head, and on his desperate heart.
Though fools will honor impious men,
In their cities no tragic poet sings.

Antistrophe 2

Shall we lose faith in Delphi's obscurities,
We who have heard the world's core   35
Discredited, and the sacred wood
Of Zeus at Elis praised no more?
The deeds and the strange prophecies
Must make a pattern yet to be understood.
Zeus, if indeed you are lord of all,   40
Throned in light over night and day,
Mirror this in your endless mind:
Our masters call the oracle
Words on the wind, and the Delphic vision
blind!
Their hearts no longer know Apollo,   45
And reverence for the gods has died away.

SCENE 3 _____

(*Enter Iokaste.*)

IOKASTE: Princes of Thebes, it has occurred to me
To visit the altars of the gods, bearing
These branches as a suppliant, and this incense.
Our king is not himself: his noble soul
Is overwrought with fantasies of dread,   5
Else he would consider
The new prophecies in the light of the old.
He will listen to any voice that speaks disaster,
And my advice goes for nothing. (*She
approaches the altar, right.*)
                        To you, then, Apollo,
Lycean lord, since you are nearest, I turn in
prayer   10

Receive these offerings, and grant us deliverance
From defilement. Our hearts are heavy with fear
When we see our leader distracted, as helpless
        sailors
Are terrified by the confusion of their helmsman.

(*Enter Messenger.*)

15 MESSENGER: Friends, no doubt you can direct me:
Where shall I find the house of Oedipus,
Or, better still, where is the king himself?
CHORAGOS: It is this very place, stranger; he is
        inside.
This is his wife and mother of his children.
20 MESSENGER: I wish her happiness in a happy house,
Blest in all the fulfillment of her marriage.
IOKASTE: I wish as much for you: your courtesy
Deserves a like good fortune. But now, tell me:
Why have you come? What have you to say to
        us?
MESSENGER: Good news, my lady, for your house
25   and your husband.
IOKASTE: What news? Who sent you here?
MESSENGER: I am from Corinth.
The news I bring ought to mean joy for you,
Though it may be you will find some grief in it.
IOKASTE: What is it? How can it touch us in both
        ways?
MESSENGER: The word is that the people of the
30   Isthmus
Intend to call Oedipus to be their king.
IOKASTE: But old King Polybos — is he not reigning
        still?
MESSENGER: No. Death holds him in his sepulchre.
IOKASTE: What are you saying? Polybos is dead?
MESSENGER: If I am not telling the truth, may I die
35   myself.
IOKASTE (*to a Maidservant*): Go in, go quickly; tell
        this to your master.
O riddlers of God's will, where are you now!
This was the man whom Oedipus, long ago,
Feared so, fled so, in dread of destroying him —
40 But it was another fate by which he died.

(*Enter Oedipus, center.*)

OEDIPUS: Dearest Iokaste, why have you sent for
        me?
IOKASTE: Listen to what this man says, and then tell
        me
What has become of the solemn prophecies.
OEDIPUS: Who is this man? What is his news for
        me?
IOKASTE: He has come from Corinth to announce
45   your father's death!
OEDIPUS: Is it true, stranger? Tell me in your own
        words.

MESSENGER: I can not say it more clearly: the king
        is dead.
OEDIPUS: Was it by treason? Or by an attack of
        illness?
MESSENGER: A little thing brings old men to their
        rest.
OEDIPUS: It was sickness, then?
MESSENGER: Yes, and his many years. 50
OEDIPUS: Ah!
Why should a man respect the Pythian hearth,°
        or
Give heed to the birds that jangle above his
        head?
They prophesied that I should kill Polybos,
Kill my own father; but he is dead and buried, 55
And I am here — I never touched him, never,
Unless he died of grief for my departure,
And thus, in a sense, through me. No. Polybos
Has packed the oracles off with him
        underground.
They are empty words.
IOKASTE: Had I not told you so? 60
OEDIPUS: You had; it was my faint heart that
        betrayed me.
IOKASTE: From now on never think of those things
        again.
OEDIPUS: And yet — must I not fear my mother's
        bed?
IOKASTE: Why should anyone in this world be
        afraid,
Since Fate rules us and nothing can be foreseen? 65
A man should live only for the present day.

Have no more fear of sleeping with your
        mother:
How many men, in dreams, have lain with their
        mothers!
No reasonable man is troubled by such things.
OEDIPUS: That is true; only —   70
If only my mother were not still alive!
But she is alive. I can not help my dread.
IOKASTE: Yet this news of your father's death is
        wonderful.
OEDIPUS: Wonderful. But I fear the living woman.
MESSENGER: Tell me, who is this woman that you
        fear?   75
OEDIPUS: It is Merope, man; the wife of King
        Polybos.
MESSENGER: Merope? Why should you be afraid of
        her?
OEDIPUS: An oracle of the gods, a dreadful saying.
MESSENGER: Can you tell me about it or are you
        sworn to silence?

52. **Pythian hearth:** Delphi.

80 OEDIPUS: I can tell you, and I will.
　　Apollo said through his prophet that I was the
　　　　man
　　Who should marry his own mother, shed his
　　　　father's blood
　　With his own hands. And so, for all these years
　　I have kept clear of Corinth, and no harm has
　　　　come —
　　Though it would have been sweet to see my
85　　　parents again.
　MESSENGER: And is this the fear that drove you out
　　　of Corinth?
　OEDIPUS: Would you have me kill my father?
　MESSENGER:　　　　　　　　　　　　As for that
　　You must be reassured by the news I gave you.
　OEDIPUS: If you could reassure me, I would reward
　　you.
　MESSENGER: I had that in mind, I will confess: I
90　　thought
　　I could count on you when you returned to
　　　Corinth.
　OEDIPUS: No: I will never go near my parents
　　again.
　MESSENGER: Ah, son, you still do not know what
　　you are doing —
　OEDIPUS: What do you mean? In the name of God
　　tell me!
　MESSENGER: — If these are your reasons for not
95　　going home.
　OEDIPUS: I tell you, I fear the oracle may come
　　true.
　MESSENGER: And guilt may come upon you through
　　your parents?
　OEDIPUS: That is the dread that is always in my
　　heart.
　MESSENGER: Can you not see that all your fears are
　　groundless?
100 OEDIPUS: Groundless? Am I not my parents' son?
　MESSENGER: Polybos was not your father.
　OEDIPUS:　　　　　　　　　　　　Not my father?
　MESSENGER: No more your father than the man
　　speaking to you.
　OEDIPUS: But you are nothing to me!
　MESSENGER:　　　　　　　　　　　Neither was he.
　OEDIPUS: Then why did he call me son?
　MESSENGER:　　　　　　　　　　I will tell you:
105　Long ago he had you from my hands, as a gift.
　OEDIPUS: Then how could he love me so, if I was
　　not his?
　MESSENGER: He had no children, and his heart
　　turned to you.
　OEDIPUS: What of you? Did you buy me? Did you
　　find me by chance?
　MESSENGER: I came upon you in the woody vales
　　of Kithairon.

　OEDIPUS: And what were you doing there?
　MESSENGER:　　　　　　　　　Tending my flocks.   110
　OEDIPUS: A wandering shepherd?
　MESSENGER:　　　　　　But your savior, son, that day.
　OEDIPUS: From what did you save me?
　MESSENGER:　　　　Your ankles should tell you that.
　OEDIPUS: Ah, stranger, why do you speak of that
　　childhood pain?
　MESSENGER: I pulled the skewer that pinned your
　　feet together.
　OEDIPUS: I have had the mark as long as I can
　　remember.　　　　　　　　　　　　　　115
　MESSENGER: That was why you were given the
　　name you bear.
　OEDIPUS: God! Was it my father or my mother who
　　did it?
　　Tell me!
　MESSENGER:　　　　I do not know. The man who
　　gave you to me
　　Can tell you better than I.
　OEDIPUS: It was not you that found me, but
　　another?　　　　　　　　　　　　　　120
　MESSENGER: It was another shepherd gave you to
　　me.
　OEDIPUS: Who was he? Can you tell me who he
　　was?
　MESSENGER: I think he was said to be one of Laios'
　　people.
　OEDIPUS: You mean the Laios who was king here
　　years ago?
　MESSENGER: Yes; King Laios; and the man was one
　　of his herdsmen.　　　　　　　　　　125
　OEDIPUS: Is he still alive? Can I see him?
　MESSENGER:　　　　　　　　These men here
　　Know best about such things.
　OEDIPUS:　　　　　　　　　Does anyone here
　　Know this shepherd that he is talking about?
　　Have you seen him in the fields, or in the town?
　　If you have, tell me. It is time things were made
　　　plain.　　　　　　　　　　　　　　130
　CHORAGOS: I think the man he means is that same
　　shepherd
　　You have already asked to see. Iokaste perhaps
　　Could tell you something.
　OEDIPUS:　　　　　　　　Do you know anything
　　About him, Lady? Is he the man we have
　　summoned?
　　Is that the man this shepherd means?
　IOKASTE:　　　　　　　　　Why think of him?   135
　　Forget this herdsman. Forget it all.
　　This talk is a waste of time.
　OEDIPUS:　　　　　　　　　How can you say that,
　　When the clues to my true birth are in my hands?
　IOKASTE: For God's love, let us have no more
　　questioning!

140 Is your life nothing to you?
My own is pain enough for me to bear.
OEDIPUS: You need not worry. Suppose my mother
a slave,
And born of slaves: no baseness can touch you.
IOKASTE: Listen to me, I beg you: do not do this
thing!
OEDIPUS: I will not listen; the truth must be made
145 known.
IOKASTE: Everything that I say is for your own
good!
OEDIPUS: My own good
Snaps my patience, then; I want none of it.
IOKASTE: You are fatally wrong! May you never
learn who you are!
OEDIPUS: Go, one of you, and bring the shepherd
here.
Let us leave this woman to brag of her royal
150 name.
IOKASTE: Ah, miserable!
That is the only word I have for you now.
That is the only word I can ever have.
                              (*Exit into the palace.*)
CHORAGOS: Why has she left us, Oedipus? Why has
she gone
155 In such a passion of sorrow? I fear this silence:
Something dreadful may come of it.
OEDIPUS: Let it come!
However base my birth, I must know about it.
The Queen, like a woman, is perhaps ashamed
To think of my low origin. But I
160 Am a child of Luck; I can not be dishonored.
Luck is my mother; the passing months, my
brothers,
Have seen me rich and poor.
                              If this is so,
How could I wish that I were someone else?
How could I not be glad to know my birth?

ODE 3 • Strophe

CHORUS: If ever the coming time were known
To my heart's pondering,
Kithairon, now by Heaven I see the torches
At the festival of the next full moon,
5 And see the dance, and hear the choir sing
A grace to your gentle shade:
Mountain where Oedipus was found,
O mountain guard of a noble race!
May the god° who heals us lend his aid,
10 And let that glory come to pass
For our king's cradling-ground.

9. **god:** Apollo.

Antistrophe

Of the nymphs that flower beyond the years,
Who bore you,° royal child,
To Pan° of the hills or the timberline Apollo,
Cold in delight where the upland clears,   15
Or Hermes° for whom Kyllene's° heights are
piled?
Or flushed as evening cloud,
Great Dionysos,° roamer of mountains,
He — was it he who found you there,
And caught you up in his own proud   20
Arms from the sweet god-ravisher
Who laughed by the Muses'° fountains?

SCENE 4

OEDIPUS: Sirs: though I do not know the man,
I think I see him coming, this shepherd we want:
He is old, like our friend here, and the men
Bringing him seem to be servants of my house.
But you can tell, if you have ever seen him.   5

(*Enter Shepherd escorted by Servants.*)

CHORAGOS: I know him, he was Laios' man. You
can trust him.
OEDIPUS: Tell me first, you from Corinth: is this the
shepherd
We were discussing?
MESSENGER: This is the very man.
OEDIPUS (*to Shepherd*): Come here. No, look at me.
You must answer
Everything I ask. — You belonged to Laios?   10
SHEPHERD: Yes: born his slave, brought up in his
house.
OEDIPUS: Tell me: what kind of work did you do
for him?
SHEPHERD: I was a shepherd of his, most of my life.
OEDIPUS: Where mainly did you go for pasturage?
SHEPHERD: Sometimes Kithairon, sometimes the hills
near-by.   15
OEDIPUS: Do you remember ever seeing this man
out there?
SHEPHERD: What would he be doing there? This
man?

13. **Who bore you:** The Chorus is asking if Oedipus is the
son of an immortal nymph and a god: Pan, Apollo, Hermes,
or Dionysus.   14. **Pan:** God of nature, forests, flocks, and
shepherds, depicted as half-man and half-goat.   16. **Hermes:**
Son of Zeus, messenger of the gods.   **Kyllene:** Mountain
reputed to be the birthplace of Hermes; also the center of
a cult to Hermes.   18. **Dionysos:** (Dionysus) God of wine
around whom wild, orgiastic rituals developed; also called
Bacchus.   22. **Muses:** Nine sister goddesses who presided
over poetry and music, art and sciences.

OEDIPUS: This man standing here. Have you ever
    seen him before?
SHEPHERD: No. At least, not to my recollection.
MESSENGER: And that is not strange, my lord. But
    I'll refresh
    His memory: he must remember when we two
    Spent three whole seasons together, March to
        September,
    On Kithairon or thereabouts. He had two flocks;
    I had one. Each autumn I'd drive mine home
    And he would go back with his to Laios'
        sheepfold. —
    Is this not true, just as I have described it?
SHEPHERD: True, yes; but it was all so long ago.
MESSENGER: Well, then: do you remember, back in
        those days,
    That you gave me a baby boy to bring up as my
        own?
SHEPHERD: What if I did? What are you trying to
        say?
MESSENGER: King Oedipus was once that little
        child.
SHEPHERD: Damn you, hold your tongue!
OEDIPUS: No more of that!
    It is your tongue needs watching, not this man's.
SHEPHERD: My king, my master, what is it I have
        done wrong?
OEDIPUS: You have not answered his question about
        the boy.
SHEPHERD: He does not know . . . He is only
        making trouble . . .
OEDIPUS: Come, speak plainly, or it will go hard
        with you.
SHEPHERD: In God's name, do not torture an old
        man!
OEDIPUS: Come here, one of you; bind his arms
        behind him.
SHEPHERD: Unhappy king! What more do you wish
        to learn?
OEDIPUS: Did you give this man the child he speaks
        of?
SHEPHERD: I did.
    And I would to God I had died that very day.
OEDIPUS: You will die now unless you speak the
        truth.
SHEPHERD: Yet if I speak the truth, I am worse
        than dead.
OEDIPUS (to Attendant): He intends to draw it out,
        apparently —
SHEPHERD: No! I have told you already that I gave
        him the boy.
OEDIPUS: Where did you get him? From your
        house? From somewhere else?
SHEPHERD: Not from mine, no. A man gave him to
        me.

OEDIPUS: Is that man here? Whose house did he
        belong to?
SHEPHERD: For God's love, my king, do not ask me
        any more!
OEDIPUS: You are a dead man if I have to ask you
        again.
SHEPHERD: Then . . . Then the child was from the
        palace of Laios.
OEDIPUS: A slave child? or a child of his own line?
SHEPHERD: Ah, I am on the brink of dreadful
        speech!
OEDIPUS: And I of dreadful hearing. Yet I must
        hear.
SHEPHERD: If you must be told, then . . .
                            They said it was Laios' child;
    But it is your wife who can tell you about that.
OEDIPUS: My wife — Did she give it to you?
SHEPHERD: My lord, she did.
OEDIPUS: Do you know why?
SHEPHERD: I was told to get rid of it.
OEDIPUS: Oh heartless mother!
SHEPHERD: But in dread of prophecies . . .
OEDIPUS: Tell me.
SHEPHERD: It was said that the boy would
        kill his own father.
OEDIPUS: Then why did you give him over to this
        old man?
SHEPHERD: I pitied the baby, my king,
    And I thought that this man would take him far
        away
    To his own country.
                        He saved him — but for what a fate!
    For if you are what this man says you are,
    No man living is more wretched than Oedipus.
OEDIPUS: Ah God!
    It was true!
                    All the prophecies!
                                    — Now,
    O Light, may I look on you for the last time!
    I, Oedipus,
    Oedipus, damned in his birth, in his marriage
        damned,
    Damned in the blood he shed with his own
        hand!

(*He rushes into the palace.*)

ODE 4 • Strophe 1 _____

CHORUS: Alas for the seed of men.
    What measure shall I give these generations
    That breathe on the void and are void
    And exist and do not exist?
    Who bears more weight of joy
    Than mass of sunlight shifting in images,

The Shepherd (Oliver Cliff) tells Oedipus (Kenneth Welsh) the truth about his birth in the Guthrie Theater Company's 1973 production directed by Michael Langham.

Or who shall make his thought stay on
That down time drifts away?
Your splendor is all fallen.
10 O naked brow of wrath and tears,
O change of Oedipus!
I who saw your days call no man blest —
Your great days like ghosts gone.

Antistrophe 1

That mind was a strong bow.
15 Deep, how deep you drew it then, hard archer,
At a dim fearful range,
And brought dear glory down!
You overcame the stranger° —
The virgin with her hooking lion claws —
20 And though death sang, stood like a tower
To make pale Thebes take heart.
Fortress against our sorrow!
True king, giver of laws,
Majestic Oedipus!
25 No prince in Thebes had ever such renown,
No prince won such grace of power.

Strophe 2

And now of all men ever known
Most pitiful is this man's story:
His fortunes are most changed; his state
30 Fallen to a low slave's
Ground under bitter fate.
O Oedipus, most royal one!
The great door° that expelled you to the light
Gave at night — ah, gave night to your glory:
35 As to the father, to the fathering son.
All understood too late.
How could that queen whom Laios won,
The garden that he harrowed at his height,
Be silent when that act was done?

Antistrophe 2

40 But all eyes fail before time's eye,
All actions come to justice there.
Though never willed, though far down the deep
past,
Your bed, your dread sirings,
Are brought to book at last.
45 Child by Laios doomed to die,
Then doomed to lose that fortunate little death,
Would God you never took breath in this air
That with my wailing lips I take to cry:
For I weep the world's outcast.
50 I was blind, and now I can tell why:

18. **stranger:** The Sphinx. 33. **door:** Iokaste's womb.

Asleep, for you had given ease of breath
To Thebes, while the false years went by.

EXODOS°

(*Enter, from the palace, Second Messenger.*)

SECOND MESSENGER: Elders of Thebes, most
    honored in this land,
What horrors are yours to see and hear, what
    weight
Of sorrow to be endured, if, true to your birth,
You venerate the line of Labdakos!
I think neither Istros nor Phasis, those great
    rivers,   5
Could purify this place of all the evil
It shelters now, or soon must bring to light —
Evil not done unconsciously, but willed.

The greatest griefs are those we cause ourselves.
CHORAGOS: Surely, friend, we have grief enough
    already;   10
What new sorrow do you mean?
SECOND MESSENGER: The queen is dead.
CHORAGOS: O miserable queen! But at whose
    hand?
SECOND MESSENGER: Her own.
The full horror of what happened you can not
    know,
For you did not see it; but I, who did, will tell
    you
As clearly as I can how she met her death.   15

When she had left us,
In passionate silence, passing through the court,
She ran to her apartment in the house,
Her hair clutched by the fingers of both hands.
She closed the doors behind her; then, by that
    bed   20
Where long ago the fatal son was conceived —
That son who should bring about his father's
    death —
We heard her call upon Laios, dead so many
    years,
And heard her wail for the double fruit of her
    marriage,
A husband by her husband, children by her
    child.   25

Exactly how she died I do not know:
For Oedipus burst in moaning and would not let
    us
Keep vigil to the end: it was by him
As he stormed about the room that our eyes
    were caught.

Exodos: Final scene.

30 From one to another of us he went, begging a
       sword,
   Hunting the wife who was not his wife, the
       mother
   Whose womb had carried his own children and
       himself.
   I do not know: it was none of us aided him,
   But surely one of the gods was in control!
35 For with a dreadful cry
   He hurled his weight, as though wrenched out of
       himself,
   At the twin doors: the bolts gave, and he rushed
       in.
   And there we saw her hanging, her body
       swaying
   From the cruel cord she had noosed about her
       neck.
   A great sob broke from him, heartbreaking to
40   hear,
   As he loosed the rope and lowered her to the
       ground.

   I would blot out from my mind what happened
       next!
   For the king ripped from her gown the golden
       brooches
   That were her ornament, and raised them, and
       plunged them down
45 Straight into his own eyeballs, crying, "No more,
   No more shall you look on the misery about me,
   The horrors of my own doing! Too long you
       have known
   The faces of those whom I should never have
       seen,
   Too long been blind to those for whom I was
       searching!
   From this hour, go in darkness!" And as he
50   spoke,
   He struck at his eyes — not once, but many
       times;
   And the blood spattered his beard,
   Bursting from his ruined sockets like red hail.

   So from the unhappiness of two this evil has
       sprung,
55 A curse on the man and woman alike. The old
   Happiness of the house of Labdakos
   Was happiness enough: where is it today?
   It is all wailing and ruin, disgrace, death — all
   The misery of mankind that has a name —
60 And it is wholly and for ever theirs.
CHORAGOS: Is he in agony still? Is there no rest for
       him?
SECOND MESSENGER: He is calling for someone to
       open the doors wide

So that all the children of Kadmos may look
       upon
His father's murderer, his mother's — no,
I can not say it!
                           And then he will leave Thebes,   65
Self-exiled, in order that the curse
Which he himself pronounced may depart from
       the house.
He is weak, and there is none to lead him,
So terrible is his suffering.
                           But you will see:
Look, the doors are opening; in a moment   70
You will see a thing that would crush a heart of
       stone.

(The central door is opened; Oedipus, blinded, is led
in.)

CHORAGOS: Dreadful indeed for men to see.
   Never have my own eyes
   Looked on a sight so full of fear.

   Oedipus!   75
   What madness came upon you, what demon
   Leaped on your life with heavier
   Punishment than a mortal man can bear?
   No: I can not even
   Look at you, poor ruined one.   80
   And I would speak, question, ponder,
   If I were able. No.
   You make me shudder.
OEDIPUS: God. God.
   Is there a sorrow greater?   85
   Where shall I find harbor in this world?
   My voice is hurled far on a dark wind.
   What has God done to me?
CHORAGOS: Too terrible to think of, or to see.

Strophe 1

OEDIPUS: O cloud of night,   90
   Never to be turned away: night coming on,
   I can not tell how: night like a shroud!
   My fair winds brought me here.
                           O God. Again
   The pain of the spikes where I had sight,
   The flooding pain   95
   Of memory, never to be gouged out.
CHORAGOS: This is not strange.
   You suffer it all twice over, remorse in pain,
   Pain in remorse.

Antistrophe 1

OEDIPUS: Ah dear friend   100
   Are you faithful even yet, you alone?

Are you still standing near me, will you stay here,
　Patient, to care for the blind?
　　　　　　　　　　　　The blind man!
Yet even blind I know who it is attends me,
105　By the voice's tone —
　Though my new darkness hide the comforter.
CHORAGOS: Oh fearful act!
　What god was it drove you to rake black
　Night across your eyes?

Strophe 2

110　OEDIPUS: Apollo. Apollo. Dear
　Children, the god was Apollo.
　He brought my sick, sick fate upon me.
　But the blinding hand was my own!
　How could I bear to see
115　When all my sight was horror everywhere?
CHORAGOS: Everywhere; that is true.
OEDIPUS: And now what is left?
　Images? Love? A greeting even,
　Sweet to the senses? Is there anything?
120　Ah, no, friends: lead me away.
　Lead me away from Thebes.
　　　　　　　　　　Lead the great wreck
　And hell of Oedipus, whom the gods hate.
CHORAGOS: Your misery, you are not blind to that.
　Would God you had never found it out!

Antistrophe 2

125　OEDIPUS: Death take the man who unbound
　My feet on that hillside
　And delivered me from death to life! What life?
　If only I had died,
　This weight of monstrous doom
　Could not have dragged me and my darlings
130　down.
CHORAGOS: I would have wished the same.
OEDIPUS: Oh never to have come here
　With my father's blood upon me! Never
　To have been the man they call his mother's
　husband!
135　Oh accurst! Oh child of evil,
　To have entered that wretched bed —
　　　　　　　　　　the selfsame one!
　More primal than sin itself, this fell to me.
CHORAGOS: I do not know what words to offer
　you.
　You were better dead than alive and blind.
OEDIPUS: Do not counsel me any more. This
140　punishment
　That I have laid upon myself is just.
　If I had eyes,

I do not know how I could bear the sight
Of my father, when I came to the house of
　Death,
Or my mother: for I have sinned against them
　both　　　　　　　　　　　　　　　　　　　145
So vilely that I could not make my peace
By strangling my own life.
　　　　　　　Or do you think my children,
Born as they were born, would be sweet to my
　eyes?
Ah never, never! Nor this town with its high
　walls,
Nor the holy images of the gods.
　　　　　　　　　　　For I,　　　　　　　150
Thrice miserable! — Oedipus, noblest of all the
　line
Of Kadmos, have condemned myself to enjoy
These things no more, by my own malediction
Expelling that man whom the gods declared
To be a defilement in the house of Laios.　　155
After exposing the rankness of my own guilt,
How could I look men frankly in the eyes?
No, I swear it,
If I could have stifled my hearing at its source,
I would have done it and made all this body　160
A tight cell of misery, blank to light and sound:
So I should have been safe in my dark mind
Beyond external evil.
　　　　　Ah Kithairon!
Why did you shelter me? When I was cast upon
　you,
Why did I not die? Then I should never　　　165
Have shown the world my execrable birth.

Ah Polybos! Corinth, city that I believed
The ancient seat of my ancestors: how fair
I seemed, your child! And all the while this evil
Was cancerous within me!
　　　　　　　　For I am sick　　　170
In my own being, sick in my origin.

O three roads, dark ravine, woodland and way
Where three roads met; you, drinking my
　father's blood,
My own blood, spilled by my own hand: can
　you remember
The unspeakable things I did there, and the
　things　　　　　　　　　　　　　　　　　175
I went on from there to do?
　　　　　　　　　O marriage, marriage!
The act that engendered me, and again the act
Performed by the son in the same bed —
　　　　　　　　　　　　　Ah, the net
Of incest, mingling fathers, brothers, sons,
With brides, wives, mothers: the last evil　　180

That can be known by men: no tongue can say
How evil!
　　　No. For the love of God, conceal me
Somewhere far from Thebes; or kill me; or hurl
　　me
Into the sea, away from men's eyes for ever.

185 　Come, lead me. You need not fear to touch me.
Of all men, I alone can bear this guilt.

(*Enter Kreon.*)

CHORAGOS: Kreon is here now. As to what you
　　ask,
He may decide the course to take. He only
Is left to protect the city in your place.
OEDIPUS: Alas, how can I speak to him? What right
190 　have I
To beg his courtesy whom I have deeply
　　wronged?
KREON: I have not come to mock you, Oedipus,
Or to reproach you, either.
(*To Attendants.*)　　　— You, standing there:
If you have lost all respect for man's dignity,
195 　At least respect the flame of Lord Helios:
Do not allow this pollution to show itself
Openly here, an affront to the earth
And Heaven's rain and the light of day. No,
　　take him
Into the house as quickly as you can.
200 　For it is proper
That only the close kindred see his grief.
OEDIPUS: I pray you in God's name, since your
　　courtesy
Ignores my dark expectation, visiting
With mercy this man of all men most execrable:
Give me what I ask — for your good, not for
205 　mine.
KREON: And what is it that you turn to me begging
　　for?
OEDIPUS: Drive me out of this country as quickly as
　　may be
To a place where no human voice can ever greet
　　me.
KREON: I should have done that before now —
　　only,
210 　God's will had not been wholly revealed to me.
OEDIPUS: But his command is plain: the parricide
Must be destroyed. I am that evil man.
KREON: That is the sense of it, yes; but as things
　　are,
We had best discover clearly what is to be done.
OEDIPUS: You would learn more about a man like
215 　me?
KREON: You are ready now to listen to the god.

OEDIPUS: I will listen. But it is to you
That I must turn for help. I beg you, hear me.

The woman is there —
Give her whatever funeral you think proper:　220
She is your sister.
　　　— But let me go, Kreon!
Let me purge my father's Thebes of the pollution
Of my living here, and go out to the wild hills,
To Kithairon, that has won such fame with me,
The tomb my mother and father appointed for
　　me,　　　　　　　　　　　　　　　　　　225
And let me die there, as they willed I should.
And yet I know
Death will not ever come to me through sickness
Or in any natural way: I have been preserved
For some unthinkable fate. But let that be.　230

As for my sons, you need not care for them.
They are men, they will find some way to live.
But my poor daughters, who have shared my
　　table,
Who never before have been parted from their
　　father —
Take care of them, Kreon; do this for me.　235

And will you let me touch them with my hands
A last time, and let us weep together?
Be kind, my lord,
Great prince, be kind!
　　　　　Could I but touch them,
They would be mine again, as when I had my
　　eyes.　　　　　　　　　　　　　　　　　　240

(*Enter Antigone and Ismene, attended.*)

Ah, God!
Is it my dearest children I hear weeping?
Has Kreon pitied me and sent my daughters?
KREON: Yes, Oedipus: I knew that they were dear
　　to you
In the old days, and know you must love them
　　still.　　　　　　　　　　　　　　　　　　245
OEDIPUS: May God bless you for this — and be a
　　friendlier
Guardian to you than he has been to me!

Children, where are you?
Come quickly to my hands: they are your
　　brother's —
Hands that have brought your father's once clear
　　eyes　　　　　　　　　　　　　　　　　　250
To this way of seeing —
　　　　　Ah dearest ones,
I had neither sight nor knowledge then, your
　　father

By the woman who was the source of his own
    life!
And I weep for you — having no strength to see
    you — ,
255   I weep for you when I think of the bitterness
That men will visit upon you all your lives.
What homes, what festivals can you attend
Without being forced to depart again in tears?
And when you come to marriageable age,
Where is the man, my daughters, who would
260   dare
Risk the bane that lies on all my children?
Is there any evil wanting? Your father killed
His father; sowed the womb of her who bore
    him;
Engendered you at the fount of his own
    existence!
That is what they will say of you.

265   Then, whom
Can you ever marry? There are no bridegrooms
    for you,
And your lives must wither away in sterile
    dreaming.

O Kreon, son of Menoikeus!
You are the only father my daughters have,
Since we, their parents, are both of us gone for
270   ever.
They are your own blood: you will not let them
Fall into beggary and loneliness;
You will keep them from the miseries that are
    mine!
Take pity on them; see, they are only children,
275   Friendless except for you. Promise me this,
Great prince, and give me your hand in token
    of it.

(*Kreon clasps his right hand.*)

Children:
I could say much, if you could understand me,
But as it is, I have only this prayer for you:
Live where you can, be as happy as you can —   280
Happier, please God, than God has made your
    father.
KREON: Enough. You have wept enough. Now go
    within.
OEDIPUS: I must; but it is hard.
KREON: Time eases all things.
OEDIPUS: You know my mind, then?
KREON: Say what you desire.
OEDIPUS: Send me from Thebes!
KREON: God grant that I may! 285
OEDIPUS: But since God hates me . . .
KREON: No, he will grant your wish.
OEDIPUS: You promise?
KREON: I can not speak beyond my knowledge.
OEDIPUS: Then lead me in.
KREON: Come now, and leave your children.
OEDIPUS: No! Do not take them from me!
KREON: Think no longer
That you are in command here, but rather think 290
How, when you were, you served your own
    destruction.

(*Exeunt into the house all but the Chorus; the Choragos
chants directly to the audience.*)

CHORAGOS: Men of Thebes: look upon Oedipus.

This is the king who solved the famous riddle
And towered up, most powerful of men.
No mortal eyes but looked on him with envy,   295
Yet in the end ruin swept over him.

Let every man in mankind's frailty
Consider his last day; and let none
Presume on his good fortune until he find
Life, at his death, a memory without pain.   300

ANTIGONE

Antigone was probably the most popular of Sophocles' plays during his lifetime. It was his thirty-second play, and from its first production, probably in 441 B.C., it drew a powerful response from its audience. The reaction to the play was in part to the conflict between two profoundly willful people: Antigone, a daughter of Oedipus and Iokaste, and Kreon, Iokaste's brother and the king of Thebes, both of whom feel they are right and that they are following the law.

It has never been easy to see which character is correct. Yet the play is named for Antigone, not for Kreon. Kreon's portrayal as a tyrant content to take up the state as his private property tells us that he is not to be fully trusted. At the same time, Antigone knows that the social mores of Athens imply that a citizen must obey the ruler. Antigone's courage is great, and the audience feels intense sympathy and admiration for her. She is a martyr to her beliefs, an ancient Joan of Arc.

The main conflict in *Antigone* centers on a distinction between law and justice. In a sense, it is the conflict between a human law and a higher law. Kreon, the uncle of Antigone and Ismene, has made a decree: Polyneices, the brother of Antigone and Ismene, was guilty not only of killing his brother Eteocles but also of attacking the state and will therefore be denied a proper burial. When the action of the play begins, Antigone is determined to give her brother the burial that tradition and her religious beliefs demand.

The opening dialogue with Ismene clarifies the important distinction between human law and the higher law on which Antigone says she must act. Ismene declares simply that she cannot go against the law of the citizens. Kreon has been willful in establishing the law, but it is nonetheless the law. Antigone, knowing full well the consequences of defying Kreon, nonetheless acts on her principles.

The conflict between Antigone and Kreon is complex, occurring on the level of citizen and ruler and on a personal level in the relationship between Haimon, Kreon's son, and his intended bride, Antigone. The antagonism between Kreon and Haimon begins slowly, with Haimon appearing to yield to the will of his father, but culminates in Haimon's ultimate rejection of his father by choosing to join Antigone in death.

When Teiresias reveals a prophecy of death and punishment and begs Kreon, for the sake of the suffering Thebes, to rescind his decree and give Polyneices a proper burial, Kreon willfully continues to heed his own declarations rather than oracular wisdom or the pleas of others.

By the time Kreon accepts Teiresias's prophecy, it is too late: He has lost his son, and his wife has killed herself. Power not only has corrupted Kreon but has taken from him the people about whom he cared most.

He emerges as an unyielding tyrant, guilty of making some of the same mistakes that haunted Oedipus.

Antigone emerges as a heroine who presses forward in the full conviction that she is right. She must honor her dead brother, at all costs. Even if she must break the law of the state, she must answer to what she regards as a higher law. As she says early in the play, she has "dared the crime of piety." Yet she has within her the complexity of all humans: She is in one sense acting in the knowledge that she is right, but in another she is daring Kreon to punish her. She challenges Kreon so boldly that her every move, coupled with Kreon's pride, forces him to harden his position and set in motion the ultimate tragedy — the loss of all he holds dear. This is yet one more tragic irony in the Theban trilogy.

Sophocles (c. 496–c. 406 B.C.)

ANTIGONE   *441 B.C.*
TRANSLATED BY DUDLEY FITTS AND ROBERT FITZGERALD

Characters

ANTIGONE ⎱
ISMENE ⎰ *daughters of Oedipus*
EURYDICE, *wife of Kreon*
KREON, *King of Thebes*
HAIMON, *son of Kreon*
TEIRESIAS, *a blind seer*
A SENTRY
A MESSENGER
CHORUS

Scene: *Before the palace of Kreon, King of Thebes. A central double door, and two lateral doors. A platform extends the length of the facade, and from this platform three steps lead down into the orchestra, or chorus-ground.*

Time: *Dawn of the day after the repulse of the Argive army from the assault on Thebes.*

PROLOGUE° _____

(*Antigone and Ismene enter from the central door of the palace.*)

Prologue: Portion of the play explaining the background and current action.

ANTIGONE: Ismene, dear sister,
　　You would think that we had already suffered
　　　enough
　　For the curse on Oedipus.°
　　I cannot imagine any grief
　　That you and I have not gone through. And
　　　now —   5
　　Have they told you of the new decree of our
　　　King Kreon?
ISMENE: I have heard nothing: I know
　　That two sisters lost two brothers, a double
　　　death
　　In a single hour; and I know that the Argive
　　　army
　　Fled in the night; but beyond this, nothing.   10
ANTIGONE: I thought so. And that is why I wanted
　　you

3. curse on Oedipus: Oedipus, King of Thebes and the father of Antigone and Ismene, had been abandoned by his parents as an infant when the oracle foretold that he would one day kill his father and marry his mother. Rescued and raised by a shepherd, Oedipus returned years later to Thebes and unknowingly lived out the oracle's prophecy by killing Laios and marrying Iokaste. After his two sons, Eteocles and Polyneices, killed each other in combat, the throne went to Kreon, Iokaste's brother.

To come out here with me. There is something
  we must do.
ISMENE: Why do you speak so strangely?
ANTIGONE: Listen, Ismene:

15   Kreon buried our brother Eteocles
  With military honors, gave him a soldier's
    funeral,
  And it was right that he should; but Polyneices,
  Who fought as bravely and died as miserably, —
  They say that Kreon has sworn
20   No one shall bury him, no one mourn for him,
  But his body must lie in the fields, a sweet
    treasure
  For carrion birds to find as they search for food.
  That is what they say, and our good Kreon is
    coming here
  To announce it publicly; and the penalty —
  Stoning to death in the public square!
25   There it is,
  And now you can prove what you are:
  A true sister, or a traitor to your family.
ISMENE: Antigone, you are mad! What could I
    possibly do?
ANTIGONE: You must decide whether you will help
    me or not.
ISMENE: I do not understand you. Help you in
30   what?
ANTIGONE: Ismene, I am going to bury him. Will
    you come?
ISMENE: Bury him! You have just said the new law
    forbids it.
ANTIGONE: He is my brother. And he is your
    brother, too.
ISMENE: But think of the danger! Think what Kreon
    will do!
ANTIGONE: Kreon is not strong enough to stand in
35   my way.
ISMENE: Ah sister!
  Oedipus died, everyone hating him
  For what his own search brought to light, his
    eyes
  Ripped out by his own hand; and Iocaste died,
  His mother and wife at once: she twisted the
40   cords
  That strangled her life; and our two brothers
    died,
  Each killed by the other's sword. And we are
    left:
  But oh, Antigone,
  Think how much more terrible than these
  Our own death would be if we should go
45   against Kreon
  And do what he has forbidden! We are only
    women,
  We cannot fight with men, Antigone!

The law is strong, we must give in to the law
In this thing, and in worse. I beg the Dead
To forgive me, but I am helpless: I must yield   50
To those in authority. And I think it is
  dangerous business
To be always meddling.
ANTIGONE: If that is what you think,
  I should not want you, even if you asked to
    come.
  You have made your choice, you can be what
    you want to be.
  But I will bury him; and if I must die,   55
  I say that this crime is holy: I shall lie down
  With him in death, and I shall be as dear
  To him as he to me.
                   It is the dead,
  Not the living, who make the longest demands:
  We die for ever . . .
                   You may do as you like,   60
  Since apparently the laws of the gods mean
    nothing to you.
ISMENE: They mean a great deal to me; but I have
    no strength
  To break laws that were made for the public
    good.
ANTIGONE: That must be your excuse, I suppose.
    But as for me,
  I will bury the brother I love.
ISMENE: Antigone,   65
  I am so afraid for you!
ANTIGONE: You need not be:
  You have yourself to consider, after all.
ISMENE: But no one must hear of this, you must tell
    no one!
  I will keep it a secret, I promise!
ANTIGONE: O tell it! Tell everyone!
  Think how they'll hate you when it all comes
    out   70
  If they learn that you knew about it all the time!
ISMENE: So fiery! You should be cold with fear.
ANTIGONE: Perhaps. But I am doing only what I
    must.
ISMENE: But can you do it? I say that you cannot.
ANTIGONE: Very well: when my strength gives out, 75
  I shall do no more.
ISMENE: Impossible things should not be tried at all.
ANTIGONE: Go away, Ismene:
  I shall be hating you soon, and the dead will
    too,
  For your words are hateful. Leave me my foolish
    plan: 80
  I am not afraid of the danger; if it means death,
  It will not be the worst of deaths — death
    without honor.
ISMENE: Go then, if you feel that you must.

You are unwise,
85 But a loyal friend indeed to those who love you.

(Exit into the palace. Antigone goes off, left. Enter the Chorus.)

PARODOS° • Strophe° 1 _____

CHORUS: Now the long blade of the sun, lying
    Level east to west, touches with glory
    Thebes of the Seven Gates. Open, unlidded
    Eye of golden day! O marching light
5   Across the eddy and rush of Dirce's stream,°
    Striking the white shields of the enemy
    Thrown headlong backward from the blaze of
        morning!
CHORAGOS:° Polyneices their commander
    Roused them with windy phrases,
10   He the wild eagle screaming
    Insults above our land,
    His wings their shields of snow,
    His crest their marshalled helms.

Antistrophe° 1

CHORUS: Against our seven gates in a yawning ring
15   The famished spears came onward in the night;
    But before his jaws were sated with our blood,
    Or pinefire took the garland of our towers,
    He was thrown back, and as he turned, great
        Thebes —
    No tender victim for his noisy power —
20   Rose like a dragon behind him, shouting war.
CHORAGOS: For God hates utterly
    The bray of bragging tongues;
    And when he beheld their smiling,
    Their swagger of golden helms,
25   The frown of his thunder blasted
    Their first man from our walls.

Strophe 2

CHORUS: We heard his shout of triumph high in the
        air
    Turn to a scream; far out in a flaming arc
    He fell with his windy torch, and the earth
        struck him.
30   And others storming in fury no less than his
    Found shock of death in the dusty joy of battle.

Parodos: The song or ode chanted by the Chorus on their entry.   **Strophe:** Song sung by the Chorus as they danced from stage right to stage left.   **5. Dirce's stream:** River near Thebes.   **8. Choragos:** Leader of the Chorus.   **Antistrophe:** Song sung by the Chorus following the Strophe, as they danced back from stage left to stage right.

CHORAGOS: Seven captains at seven gates
    Yielded their clanging arms to the god
    That bends the battle-line and breaks it.
    These two only, brothers in blood,   35
    Face to face in matchless rage,
    Mirroring each the other's death,
    Clashed in long combat.

Antistrophe 2

CHORUS: But now in the beautiful morning of
        victory
    Let Thebes of the many chariots sing for joy!   40
    With hearts for dancing we'll take leave of war:
    Our temples shall be sweet with hymns of
        praise,
    And the long nights shall echo with our chorus.

SCENE 1 _____

CHORAGOS: But now at last our new King is
        coming:
    Kreon of Thebes, Menoikeus' son.
    In this auspicious dawn of his reign
    What are the new complexities
    That shifting Fate has woven for him?   5
    What is his counsel? Why has he summoned
    The old men to hear him?

(Enter Kreon from the palace, center. He addresses the Chorus from the top step.)

KREON: Gentlemen: I have the honor to inform you
that our Ship of State, which recent storms have
threatened to destroy, has come safely to harbor   10
at last, guided by the merciful wisdom of Heaven.
I have summoned you here this morning because
I know that I can depend upon you: your devotion
to King Laios was absolute; you never hesitated in
your duty to our late ruler Oedipus; and when   15
Oedipus died, your loyalty was transferred to his
children. Unfortunately, as you know, his two sons,
the princes Eteocles and Polyneices, have killed each
other in battle; and I, as the next in blood, have
succeeded to the full power of the throne.   20

    I am aware, of course, that no Ruler can expect
complete loyalty from his subjects until he has been
tested in office. Nevertheless, I say to you at the
very outset that I have nothing but contempt for
the kind of Governor who is afraid, for whatever   25
reason, to follow the course that he knows is best
for the State; and as for the man who sets private
friendship above the public welfare, — I have no
use for him, either. I call God to witness that if I
saw my country headed for ruin, I should not be   30
afraid to speak out plainly; and I need hardly remind

you that I would never have any dealings with an enemy of the people. No one values friendship more highly than I; but we must remember that friends
35 made at the risk of wrecking our Ship are not real friends at all.

These are my principles, at any rate, and that is why I have made the following decision concerning the sons of Oedipus: Eteocles, who died as a man
40 should die, fighting for his country, is to be buried with full military honors, with all the ceremony that is usual when the greatest heroes die; but his brother Polyneices, who broke his exile to come back with fire and sword against his native city
45 and the shrines of his fathers' gods, whose one idea was to spill the blood of his blood and sell his own people into slavery — Polyneices, I say, is to have no burial: no man is to touch him or say the least prayer for him; he shall lie on the plain, unburied;
50 and the birds and the scavenging dogs can do with him whatever they like.

This is my command, and you can see the wisdom behind it. As long as I am King, no traitor is going to be honored with the loyal man. But whoever
55 shows by word and deed that he is on the side of the State, — he shall have my respect while he is living and my reverence when he is dead.

CHORAGOS: If that is your will, Kreon son of Menoikeus,
You have the right to enforce it: we are yours.
KREON: That is my will. Take care that you do
60   your part.
CHORAGOS: We are old men: let the younger ones carry it out.
KREON: I do not mean that: the sentries have been appointed.
CHORAGOS: Then what is it that you would have us do?
KREON: You will give no support to whoever breaks this law.
CHORAGOS: Only a crazy man is in love with
65   death!
KREON: And death it is; yet money talks, and the wisest
Have sometimes been known to count a few coins too many.

(*Enter Sentry from left.*)

SENTRY: I'll not say that I'm out of breath from running, King, because every time I stopped to think about
70   what I have to tell you, I felt like going back. And all the time a voice kept saying, "You fool, don't you know you're walking straight into trouble?"; and then another voice: "Yes, but if you let somebody else get the news to Kreon first, it will be

even worse than that for you!" But good sense 75
won out, at least I hope it was good sense, and here I am with a story that makes no sense at all; but I'll tell it anyhow, because, as they say, what's going to happen's going to happen and —
KREON: Come to the point. What have you to say? 80
SENTRY: I did not do it. I did not see who did it. You must not punish me for what someone else has done.
KREON: A comprehensive defense! More effective, perhaps,
If I knew its purpose. Come: what is it? 85
SENTRY: A dreadful thing . . . I don't know how to put it —
KREON: Out with it!
SENTRY: Well, then;
The dead man —
                         Polyneices —

(*Pause. The Sentry is overcome, fumbles for words. Kreon waits impassively.*)

                                    out there —
                                    someone, —
The dead man — New dust on the slimy flesh!

(*Pause. No sign from Kreon.*)

Someone has given it burial that way, and 90
Gone . . .

(*Long pause. Kreon finally speaks with deadly control.*)

KREON: And the man who dared do this?
SENTRY: I swear I
Do not know! You must believe me!
                                    Listen:
The ground was dry, not a sign of digging, no,
Not a wheeltrack in the dust, no trace of anyone. 95
It was when they relieved us this morning: and one of them,
The corporal, pointed to it.
                              There it was,
The strangest —
              Look:
The body, just mounded over with light dust: you see?
Not buried really, but as if they'd covered it 100
Just enough for the ghost's peace. And no sign
Of dogs or any wild animal that had been there.

And then what a scene there was! Every man of us
Accusing the other: we all proved the other man did it,
We all had proof that we could not have done 105
it.

We were ready to take hot iron in our hands,
Walk through fire, swear by all the gods,
It was not I!
I do not know who it was, but it was not I!

(*Kreon's rage has been mounting steadily, but the Sentry is too intent upon his story to notice it.*)

And then, when this came to nothing, someone
110   said
A thing that silenced us and made us stare
Down at the ground: you had to be told the
    news,
And one of us had to do it! We threw the dice,
And the bad luck fell to me. So here I am,
115   No happier to be here than you are to have me:
Nobody likes the man who brings bad news.
CHORAGOS: I have been wondering, King: can it be
That the gods have done this?
KREON (*furiously*): Stop!
120   Must you doddering wrecks
Go out of your heads entirely? "The gods"!
Intolerable!
The gods favor this corpse? Why? How had he
    served them?
Tried to loot their temples, burn their images,
125   Yes, and the whole State, and its laws with it!
Is it your senile opinion that the gods love to
    honor bad men?
A pious thought! —
                  No, from the very beginning
There have been those who have whispered
    together,
Stiff-necked anarchists, putting their heads
    together,
Scheming against me in alleys. These are the
130   men,
And they have bribed my own guard to do this
    thing.
(*Sententiously.*) Money!
There's nothing in the world so demoralizing as
    money.
Down go your cities,
135   Homes gone, men gone, honest hearts corrupted,
Crookedness of all kinds, and all for money!
(*To Sentry.*)   But you —
I swear by God and by the throne of God,
The man who has done this thing shall pay for
    it!
Find that man, bring him here to me, or your
    death
Will be the least of your problems: I'll string
140   you up
Alive, and there will be certain ways to make
    you
Discover your employer before you die;

And the process may teach you a lesson you
    seem to have missed:
The dearest profit is sometimes all too dear:
That depends on the source. Do you understand
    me?   145
A fortune won is often misfortune.
SENTRY: King, may I speak?
KREON: Your very voice distresses me.
SENTRY: Are you sure that it is my voice, and not
    your conscience?
KREON: By God, he wants to analyze me now!
SENTRY: It is not what I say, but what has been
    done, that hurts you.   150
KREON: You talk too much.
SENTRY: Maybe; but I've done nothing.
KREON: Sold your soul for some silver: that's all
    you've done.
SENTRY: How dreadful it is when the right judge
    judges wrong!
KREON: Your figures of speech
May entertain you now; but unless you bring me
    the man,   155
You will get little profit from them in the end.
                    (*Exit Kreon into the palace.*)
SENTRY: "Bring me the man" — !
I'd like nothing better than bringing him the
    man!
But bring him or not, you have seen the last of
    me here.
At any rate, I am safe!   (*Exit Sentry.*)   160

ODE° 1 • Strophe 1 _____

CHORUS: Numberless are the world's wonders, but
    none
More wonderful than man; the stormgray sea
Yields to his prows, the huge crests bear him
    high;
Earth, holy and inexhaustible, is graven
With shining furrows where his plows have gone   5
Year after year, the timeless labor of stallions.

Antistrophe 1

The lightboned birds and beasts that cling to
    cover,
The lithe fish lighting their reaches of dim water,
All are taken, tamed in the net of his mind;
The lion on the hill, the wild horse windy-
    maned,   10
Resign to him; and his blunt yoke has broken
The sultry shoulders of the mountain bull.

Ode: Song sung by the Chorus.

Strophe 2

Words also, and thought as rapid as air,
He fashions to his good use; statecraft is his,
And his the skill that deflects the arrows of
15   snow,
The spears of winter rain: from every wind
He has made himself secure — from all but one:
In the late wind of death he cannot stand.

Antistrophe 2

O clear intelligence, force beyond all measure!
20 O fate of man, working both good and evil!
When the laws are kept, how proudly his city
    stands!
When the laws are broken, what of his city
    then?
Never may the anarchic man find rest at my
    hearth,
Never be it said that my thoughts are his
    thoughts.

SCENE 2

(Reenter Sentry leading Antigone.)

CHORAGOS: What does this mean? Surely this
    captive woman
Is the Princess, Antigone. Why should she be
    taken?
SENTRY: Here is the one who did it! We caught her
In the very act of burying him. — Where is
    Kreon?
CHORAGOS: Just coming from the house.

(Enter Kreon, center.)

5 KREON: What has happened?
Why have you come back so soon?
SENTRY (*expansively*):   O King,
A man should never be too sure of anything:
I would have sworn
That you'd not see me here again: your anger
Frightened me so, and the things you threatened
10   me with;
But how could I tell then
That I'd be able to solve the case so soon?
No dice-throwing this time: I was only too glad
    to come!
Here is this woman. She is the guilty one:
15 We found her trying to bury him.
Take her, then; question her; judge her as you
    will.
I am through with the whole thing now, and
    glad of it.

KREON: But this is Antigone! Why have you
    brought her here?
SENTRY: She was burying him, I tell you!
KREON (*severely*):   Is this the truth?
SENTRY: I saw her with my own eyes. Can I say
    more?   20
KREON: The details: come, tell me quickly!
SENTRY: It was like this:
After those terrible threats of yours, King,
We went back and brushed the dust away from
    the body.
The flesh was soft by now, and stinking,
So we sat on a hill to windward and kept guard. 25
No napping this time! We kept each other
    awake.
But nothing happened until the white round sun
Whirled in the center of the round sky over us:
Then, suddenly,
A storm of dust roared up from the earth, and
    the sky   30
Went out, the plain vanished with all its trees
In the stinging dark. We closed our eyes and
    endured it.
The whirlwind lasted a long time, but it passed;
And then we looked, and there was Antigone!
I have seen   35
A mother bird come back to a stripped nest,
    heard
Her crying bitterly a broken note or two
For the young ones stolen. Just so, when this girl
Found the bare corpse, and all her love's work
    wasted,
She wept, and cried on heaven to damn the
    hands   40
That had done this thing.
        And then she brought more dust
And sprinkled wine three times for her brother's
    ghost.

We ran and took her at once. She was not
    afraid,
Not even when we charged her with what she
    had done.
She denied nothing.
        And this was a comfort to me, 45
And some uneasiness: for it is a good thing
To escape from death, but it is no great pleasure
To bring death to a friend.
        Yet I always say
There is nothing so comfortable as your own
    safe skin!
KREON (*slowly, dangerously*): And you, Antigone, 50
You with your head hanging, — do you confess
    this thing?
ANTIGONE: I do. I deny nothing.

KREON (*to Sentry*): You may go.
(*Exit Sentry.*)
(*To Antigone.*) Tell me, tell me briefly:
Had you heard my proclamation touching this
matter?
55 ANTIGONE: It was public. Could I help hearing it?
KREON: And yet you dared defy the law.
ANTIGONE: I dared.
It was not God's proclamation. That final Justice
That rules the world below makes no such laws.

Your edict, King, was strong,
60 But all your strength is weakness itself against
The immortal unrecorded laws of God.
They are not merely now: they were, and shall
be,
Operative for ever, beyond man utterly.

I knew I must die, even without your decree:
65 I am only mortal. And if I must die
Now, before it is my time to die,
Surely this is no hardship: can anyone
Living, as I live, with evil all about me,
Think Death less than a friend? This death of
mine
70 Is of no importance; but if I had left my brother
Lying in death unburied, I should have suffered.
Now I do not.
You smile at me. Ah Kreon,
Think me a fool, if you like; but it may well be
That a fool convicts me of folly.
CHORAGOS: Like father, like daughter: both
75 headstrong, deaf to reason!
She has never learned to yield.
KREON: She has much to learn.
The inflexible heart breaks first, the toughest
iron
Cracks first, and the wildest horses bend their
necks
At the pull of the smallest curb.
Pride? In a slave?
80 This girl is guilty of a double insolence,
Breaking the given laws and boasting of it.
Who is the man here,
She or I, if this crime goes unpunished?
Sister's child, or more than sister's child,
85 Or closer yet in blood — she and her sister
Win bitter death for this!
(*To Servants.*) Go, some of you,
Arrest Ismene. I accuse her equally.
Bring her: you will find her sniffling in the house
there.

Her mind's a traitor: crimes kept in the dark
90 Cry for light, and the guardian brain shudders;

But how much worse than this
Is brazen boasting of barefaced anarchy!
ANTIGONE: Kreon, what more do you want than
my death?
KREON: Nothing.
That gives me everything.
ANTIGONE: Then I beg you: kill me.
This talking is a great weariness: your words 95
Are distasteful to me, and I am sure that mine
Seem so to you. And yet they should not seem
so:
I should have praise and honor for what I have
done.
All these men here would praise me
Were their lips not frozen shut with fear of you. 100
(*Bitterly.*) Ah the good fortune of kings,
Licensed to say and do whatever they please!
KREON: You are alone here in that opinion.
ANTIGONE: No, they are with me. But they keep
their tongues in leash.
KREON: Maybe. But you are guilty, and they are
not. 105
ANTIGONE: There is no guilt in reverence for the
dead.
KREON: But Eteocles — was he not your brother
too?
ANTIGONE: My brother too.
KREON: And you insult his memory?
ANTIGONE (*softly*): The dead man would not say
that I insult it.
KREON: He would: for you honor a traitor as much
as him. 110
ANTIGONE: His own brother, traitor or not, and
equal in blood.
KREON: He made war on his country. Eteocles
defended it.
ANTIGONE: Nevertheless, there are honors due all
the dead.
KREON: But not the same for the wicked as for the
just.
ANTIGONE: Ah Kreon, Kreon, 115
Which of us can say what the gods hold wicked?
KREON: An enemy is an enemy, even dead.
ANTIGONE: It is my nature to join in love, not hate.
KREON (*finally losing patience*): Go join them then;
if you must have your love,
Find it in hell! 120
CHORAGOS: But see, Ismene comes:

(*Enter Ismene, guarded.*)

Those tears are sisterly, the cloud
That shadows her eyes rains down gentle
sorrow.
KREON: You too, Ismene,
Snake in my ordered house, sucking my blood 125

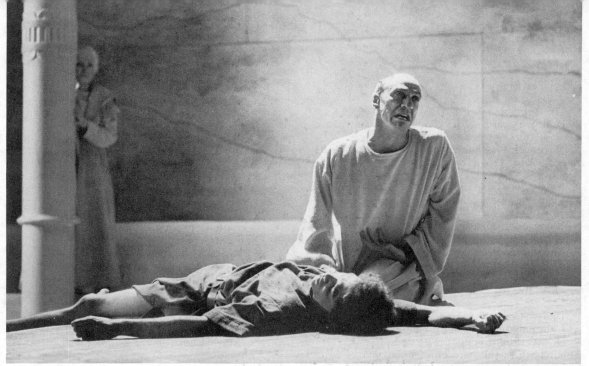

TOP LEFT: Kreon (F. Murray Abraham) in a scene from
the 1982 New York Shakespeare Festival production
directed by Joseph Chaikin. BOTTOM LEFT: Antigone (Lisa
Banes) steadfastly admitting her guilt. ABOVE: The Chorus
urges Kreon to change his decree before it is too late.

Stealthily — and all the time I never knew
That these two sisters were aiming at my throne!
                                            Ismene,
Do you confess your share in this crime, or deny
    it?
Answer me.
130 ISMENE: Yes, if she will let me say so. I am guilty.
    ANTIGONE (*coldly*): No, Ismene. You have no right
        to say so.
    You would not help me, and I will not have you
        help me.

ISMENE: But now I know what you meant; and I
    am here
    To join you, to take my share of punishment.
ANTIGONE: The dead man and the gods who rule
    the dead   135
    Know whose act this was. Words are not
    friends.
ISMENE: Do you refuse me, Antigone? I want to die
    with you:
    I too have a duty that I must discharge to the
    dead.
ANTIGONE: You shall not lessen my death by
    sharing it.
ISMENE: What do I care for life when you are dead?   140
ANTIGONE: Ask Kreon. You're always hanging on
    his opinions.
ISMENE: You are laughing at me. Why, Antigone?

ANTIGONE: It's a joyless laughter, Ismene.
ISMENE: But can I do nothing?
ANTIGONE: Yes. Save yourself. I shall not envy you.
There are those who will praise you; I shall have
145   honor, too.
ISMENE: But we are equally guilty!
ANTIGONE: No more, Ismene.
You are alive, but I belong to Death.
KREON (to the Chorus): Gentlemen, I beg you to
observe these girls:
One has just now lost her mind; the other,
150   It seems, has never had a mind at all.
ISMENE: Grief teaches the steadiest minds to waver,
King.
KREON: Yours certainly did, when you assumed
guilt with the guilty!
ISMENE: But how could I go on living without her?
KREON: You are.
She is already dead.
ISMENE: But your own son's bride!
KREON: There are places enough for him to push
155   his plow.
I want no wicked women for my sons!
ISMENE: O dearest Haimon, how your father
wrongs you!
KREON: I've had enough of your childish talk of
marriage!
CHORAGOS: Do you really intend to steal this girl
from your son?
KREON: No; Death will do that for me.
160 CHORAGOS: Then she must die?
KREON (ironically): You dazzle me.
— But enough of this talk!
(To Guards.) You, there, take them away and
guard them well:
For they are but women, and even brave men
run
When they see Death coming.
(Exeunt° Ismene, Antigone, and Guards.)

ODE 2 · Strophe 1 _____

CHORUS: Fortunate is the man who has never tasted
God's vengeance!
Where once the anger of heaven has struck, that
house is shaken
For ever: damnation rises behind each child
Like a wave cresting out of the black northeast,
5   When the long darkness under sea roars up
And bursts drumming death upon the
windwhipped sand.

Exeunt: Latin for "they go out."

Antistrophe 1

I have seen this gathering sorrow from time long
past
Loom upon Oedipus' children: generation from
generation
Takes the compulsive rage of the enemy god.
So lately this last flower of Oedipus' line   10
Drank the sunlight! but now a passionate word
And a handful of dust have closed up all its
beauty.

Strophe 2

What mortal arrogance
Transcends the wrath of Zeus?
Sleep cannot lull him nor the effortless long
months   15
Of the timeless gods: but he is young for ever,
And his house is the shining day of high
Olympos.
All that is and shall be,
And all the past, is his.
No pride on earth is free of the curse of heaven. 20

Antistrophe 2

The straying dreams of men
May bring them ghosts of joy:
But as they drowse, the waking embers burn
them;
Or they walk with fixed eyes, as blind men
walk.
But the ancient wisdom speaks for our own
time: 25
Fate works most for woe
With Folly's fairest show.
Man's little pleasure is the spring of sorrow.

SCENE 3 _____

CHORAGOS: But here is Haimon, King, the last of
all your sons.
Is it grief for Antigone that brings him here,
And bitterness at being robbed of his bride?

(Enter Haimon.)

KREON: We shall soon see, and no need of diviners.
— Son,
You have heard my final judgment on that girl: 5
Have you come here hating me, or have you
come
With deference and with love, whatever I do?
HAIMON: I am your son, father. You are my guide.

You make things clear for me, and I obey you.
No marriage means more to me than your
10   continuing wisdom.
KREON: Good. That is the way to behave:
        subordinate
Everything else, my son, to your father's will.
This is what a man prays for, that he may get
Sons attentive and dutiful in his house,
15   Each one hating his father's enemies,
Honoring his father's friends. But if his sons
Fail him, if they turn out unprofitably,
What has he fathered but trouble for himself
And amusement for the malicious?
                                    So you are right
20   Not to lose your head over this woman.
Your pleasure with her would soon grow cold,
        Haimon,
And then you'd have a hellcat in bed and
        elsewhere.
Let her find her husband in Hell!
Of all the people in this city, only she
25   Has had contempt for my law and broken it.

Do you want me to show myself weak before
        the people?
Or to break my sworn word? No, and I will
        not.
The woman dies.
I suppose she'll plead "family ties." Well, let her.
30   If I permit my own family to rebel,
How shall I earn the world's obedience?
Show me the man who keeps his house in hand,
He's fit for public authority.
                                    I'll have no dealings
With lawbreakers, critics of the government:
Whoever is chosen to govern should be
35   obeyed —
Must be obeyed, in all things, great and small,
Just and unjust! O Haimon,
The man who knows how to obey, and that
        man only,
Knows how to give commands when the time
        comes.
40   You can depend on him, no matter how fast
The spears come: he's a good soldier, he'll stick
        it out.
Anarchy, anarchy! Show me a greater evil!
This is why cities tumble and the great houses
        rain down,
This is what scatters armies!
45   No, no: good lives are made so by discipline.
We keep the laws then, and the lawmakers,
And no woman shall seduce us. If we must lose,
Let's lose to a man, at least! Is a woman
        stronger than we?

CHORAGOS: Unless time has rusted my wits,
What you say, King, is said with point and
        dignity.   50
HAIMON (*boyishly earnest*): Father:
Reason is God's crowning gift to man, and you
        are right
To warn me against losing mine. I cannot say —
I hope that I shall never want to say! — that
        you
Have reasoned badly. Yet there are other men   55
Who can reason, too; and their opinions might
        be helpful.
You are not in a position to know everything
That people say or do, or what they feel:
Your temper terrifies — everyone
Will tell you only what you like to hear.   60
But I, at any rate, can listen; and I have heard
        them
Muttering and whispering in the dark about this
        girl.
They say no woman has ever, so unreasonably,
Died so shameful a death for a generous act:
"She covered her brother's body. Is this
        indecent?   65
She kept him from dogs and vultures. Is this a
        crime?
Death? — She should have all the honor that we
        can give her!"

This is the way they talk out there in the city.

You must believe me:
Nothing is closer to me than your happiness.   70
What could be closer? Must not any son
Value his father's fortune as his father does his?
I beg you, do not be unchangeable:
Do not believe that you alone can be right.
The man who thinks that,   75
The man who maintains that only he has the
        power
To reason correctly, the gift to speak, the
        soul —
A man like that, when you know him, turns out
        empty.
It is not reason never to yield to reason!

In flood time you can see how some trees bend,   80
And because they bend, even their twigs are safe,
While stubborn trees are torn up, roots and all.
And the same thing happens in sailing:
Make your sheet fast, never slacken, — and over
        you go,
Head over heels and under: and there's your
        voyage.   85
Forget you are angry! Let yourself be moved!

I know I am young; but please let me say this:
The ideal condition
Would be, I admit, that men should be right by
instinct;
90 But since we are all too likely to go astray,
The reasonable thing is to learn from those who
can teach.
CHORAGOS: You will do well to listen to him, King,
If what he says is sensible. And you, Haimon,
Must listen to your father. — Both speak well.
KREON: You consider it right for a man of my
95   years and experience
To go to school to a boy?
HAIMON: It is not right
If I am wrong. But if I am young, and right,
What does my age matter?
KREON: You think it right to stand up for an
anarchist?
100 HAIMON: Not at all. I pay no respect to criminals.
KREON: Then she is not a criminal?
HAIMON: The City would deny it, to a man.
KREON: And the City proposes to teach me how to
rule?
HAIMON: Ah. Who is it that's talking like a boy
now?
KREON: My voice is the one voice giving orders in
105   this City!
HAIMON: It is no City if it takes orders from one
voice.
KREON: The State is the King!
HAIMON: Yes, if the State is a desert.

(Pause.)

KREON: This boy, it seems, has sold out to a
woman.
HAIMON: If you are a woman: my concern is only
for you.
KREON: So? Your "concern"! In a public brawl
110   with your father!
HAIMON: How about you, in a public brawl with
justice?
KREON: With justice, when all that I do is within
my rights?
HAIMON: You have no right to trample on God's
right.
KREON (completely out of control): Fool, adolescent
fool! Taken in by a woman!
HAIMON: You'll never see me taken in by anything
115   vile.
KREON: Every word you say is for her!
HAIMON (quietly, darkly):   And for you.
And for me. And for the gods under the earth.
KREON: You'll never marry her while she lives.
HAIMON: Then she must die. — But her death will
cause another.

KREON: Another?   120
Have you lost your senses? Is this an open
threat?
HAIMON: There is no threat in speaking to
emptiness.
KREON: I swear you'll regret this superior tone of
yours!
You are the empty one!
HAIMON: If you were not my father,
I'd say you were perverse.   125
KREON: You girl-struck fool, don't play at words
with me!
HAIMON: I am sorry. You prefer silence.
KREON: Now, by God —
I swear, by all the gods in heaven above us,
You'll watch it, I swear you shall!
(To the Servants.)   Bring her out!
Bring the woman out! Let her die before his
eyes!   130
Here, this instant, with her bridegroom beside
her!
HAIMON: Not here, no; she will not die here, King.
And you will never see my face again.
Go on raving as long as you've a friend to
endure you.   (Exit Haimon.)
CHORAGOS: Gone, gone.   135
Kreon, a young man in a rage is dangerous!
KREON: Let him do, or dream to do, more than a
man can.
He shall not save these girls from death.
CHORAGOS: These girls?
You have sentenced them both?
KREON: No, you are right.
I will not kill the one whose hands are clean.   140
CHORAGOS: But Antigone?
KREON (somberly):   I will carry her far away
Out there in the wilderness, and lock her
Living in a vault of stone. She shall have food,
As the custom is, to absolve the State of her
death.
And there let her pray to the gods of hell: 145
They are her only gods:
Perhaps they will show her an escape from
death,
Or she may learn,
                        though late,
That piety shown the dead is pity in vain.
(Exit Kreon.)

ODE 3 • Strophe

CHORUS: Love, unconquerable
Waster of rich men, keeper
Of warm lights and all-night vigil
In the soft face of a girl:

5   Sea-wanderer, forest-visitor!
Even the pure Immortals cannot escape you,
And mortal man, in his one day's dusk,
Trembles before your glory.

Antistrophe

10   Surely you swerve upon ruin
The just man's consenting heart,
As here you have made bright anger
Strike between father and son —
And none has conquered but Love!
15   A girl's glance working the will of heaven:
Pleasure to her alone who mocks us,
Merciless Aphrodite.°

SCENE 4 _____

CHORAGOS (*as Antigone enters guarded*): But I can
    no longer stand in awe of this,
Nor, seeing what I see, keep back my tears.
Here is Antigone, passing to that chamber
Where all find sleep at last.

Strophe 1

5 ANTIGONE: Look upon me, friends, and pity me
    Turning back at the night's edge to say
    Good-by to the sun that shines for me no
      longer;
    Now sleepy Death
    Summons me down to Acheron,° that cold
      shore:
10   There is no bridesong there, nor any music.
CHORUS: Yet not unpraised, not without a kind of
    honor,
    You walk at last into the underworld;
    Untouched by sickness, broken by no sword.
    What woman has ever found your way to death?

Antistrophe 1

15 ANTIGONE: How often I have heard the story of
    Niobe,°
    Tantalos' wretched daughter, how the stone
    Clung fast about her, ivy-close: and they say
    The rain falls endlessly

16. Aphrodite: Goddess of love and beauty.   **9. Acheron:**
River in Hades, domain of the dead.   **15. Niobe:** When
Niobe's many children (up to twenty in some accounts) were
slain in punishment for their mother's boastfulness, Niobe
was turned into a stone on Mount Sipylus. Her tears became
the mountain's streams.

And sifting soft snow; her tears are never done.
I feel the loneliness of her death in mine.   20
CHORUS: But she was born of heaven, and you
    Are woman, woman-born. If her death is yours,
    A mortal woman's, is this not for you
    Glory in our world and in the world beyond?

Strophe 2

ANTIGONE: You laugh at me. Ah, friends, friends, 25
    Can you not wait until I am dead? O Thebes,
    O men many-charioted, in love with Fortune,
    Dear springs of Dirce, sacred Theban grove,
    Be witnesses for me, denied all pity,
    Unjustly judged! and think a word of love   30
    For her whose path turns
    Under dark earth, where there are no more
      tears.
CHORUS: You have passed beyond human daring
    and come at last
    Into a place of stone where Justice sits.
    I cannot tell   35
    What shape of your father's guilt appears in this.

Antistrophe 2

ANTIGONE: You have touched it at last: that bridal
    bed
    Unspeakable, horror of son and mother
      mingling:
    Their crime, infection of all our family!
    O Oedipus, father and brother!   40
    Your marriage strikes from the grave to murder
      mine.
    I have been a stranger here in my own land:
    All my life
    The blasphemy of my birth has followed me.
CHORUS: Reverence is a virtue, but strength   45
    Lives in established law: that must prevail.
    You have made your choice,
    Your death is the doing of your conscious hand.

Epode°

ANTIGONE: Then let me go, since all your words
    are bitter,
    And the very light of the sun is cold to me.   50
    Lead me to my vigil, where I must have
    Neither love nor lamentation; no song, but
      silence.

(*Kreon interrupts impatiently.*)

Epode: Song sung by the chorus while standing still after
singing the strophe and antistrophe.

KREON: If dirges and planned lamentations could
    put off death,
    Men would be singing for ever.
    (*To the Servants.*)   ·Take her, go!
55   You know your orders: take her to the vault
    And leave her alone there. And if she lives or
    dies,
    That's her affair, not ours: our hands are clean.
ANTIGONE: O tomb, vaulted bride-bed in eternal
    rock,
    Soon I shall be with my own again
    Where Persephone° welcomes the thin ghosts
60   underground:
    And I shall see my father again, and you,
    mother,
    And dearest Polyneices —
                    dearest indeed
    To me, since it was my hand
    That washed him clean and poured the ritual
    wine:
65   And my reward is death before my time!

    And yet, as men's hearts know, I have done no
    wrong,
    I have not sinned before God. Or if I have,
    I shall know the truth in death. But if the guilt
    Lies upon Kreon who judged me, then, I pray,
    May his punishment equal my own.
70 CHORAGOS: O passionate heart,
    Unyielding, tormented still by the same winds!
KREON: Her guards shall have good cause to regret
    their delaying.
ANTIGONE: Ah! That voice is like the voice of
    death!
KREON: I can give you no reason to think you are
    mistaken.
75 ANTIGONE: Thebes, and you my fathers' gods,
    And rulers of Thebes, you see me now, the last
    Unhappy daughter of a line of kings,
    Your kings, led away to death. You will
    remember
    What things I suffer, and at what men's hands,
    Because I would not transgress the laws of
80   heaven.
    (*To the Guards, simply.*) Come: let us wait no
    longer.   (*Exit Antigone, left, guarded.*)

ODE 4 • Strophe 1 _____

CHORUS: All Danae's beauty was locked away
    In a brazen cell where the sunlight could not
    come:

60. **Persephone:** Abducted by Pluto, god of the underworld,
to be his queen.

A small room still as any grave, enclosed her.
Yet she was a princess too,
And Zeus in a rain of gold poured love upon
    her.°   5
O child, child,
No power in wealth or war
Or tough sea-blackened ships
Can prevail against untiring Destiny!

Antistrophe 1

And Dryas' son° also, that furious king,   10
Bore the god's prisoning anger for his pride:
Sealed up by Dionysos in deaf stone,
His madness died among echoes.
So at the last he learned what dreadful power
His tongue had mocked: 15
For he had profaned the revels,
And fired the wrath of the nine
Implacable Sisters° that love the sound of the
    flute.

Strophe 2

And old men tell a half-remembered tale
Of horror° where a dark ledge splits the sea   20
And a double surf beats on the gray shores:
How a king's new woman, sick
With hatred for the queen he had imprisoned,
Ripped out his two sons' eyes with her bloody
    hands
While grinning Ares° watched the shuttle plunge   25
Four times: four blind wounds crying for
    revenge,

Antistrophe 2

Crying, tears and blood mingled. — Piteously
    born,
Those sons whose mother was of heavenly birth!
Her father was the god of the North Wind

1–5. **All Danae's beauty . . . poured love upon her:** Locked
away to prevent the fulfillment of a prophecy that she would
bear a son who would kill her father, Danae was nonetheless
impregnated by Zeus, who came to her in a shower of gold.
The prophecy was fulfilled by the son that came of their
union.   **10. Dryas' son:** King Lycurgus of Thrace, whom
Dionysus, god of wine, caused to be stricken with madness.
18. Sisters: The Muses, nine sister goddesses who presided
over poetry and music, arts and sciences.   **19–20. half-
remembered tale of horror:** The second wife of King Phineas
blinded the sons of his first wife, Cleopatra, whom Phineas
had imprisoned in a cave.   **25. Ares:** God of war.

30 And she was cradled by gales,
    She raced with young colts on the glittering hills
    And walked untrammeled in the open light:
    But in her marriage deathless Fate found means
    To build a tomb like yours for all her joy.

SCENE 5 _____

*(Enter blind Teiresias, led by a boy. The opening
speeches of Teiresias should be in singsong contrast
to the realistic lines of Kreon.)*

TEIRESIAS: This is the way the blind man comes,
      Princes, Princes,
    Lockstep, two heads lit by the eyes of one.
KREON: What new thing have you to tell us, old
      Teiresias?
TEIRESIAS: I have much to tell you: listen to the
      prophet, Kreon.
KREON: I am not aware that I have ever failed to
5   listen.
TERESIAS: Then you have done wisely, King, and
      ruled well.
KREON: I admit my debt to you. But what have
      you to say?
TERESIAS: This, Kreon: you stand once more on the
      edge of fate.
KREON: What do you mean? Your words are a
      kind of dread.
10 TEIRESIAS: Listen, Kreon:
    I was sitting in my chair of augury, at the place
    Where the birds gather about me. They were all
      a-chatter,
    As is their habit, when suddenly I heard
    A strange note in their jangling, a scream, a
15   Whirring fury; I knew that they were fighting,
    Tearing each other, dying
    In a whirlwind of wings clashing. And I was
      afraid.
    I began the rites of burnt-offering at the altar,
    But Hephaistos° failed me: instead of bright
      flame,
    There was only the sputtering slime of the fat
20   thigh-flesh
    Melting: the entrails dissolved in gray smoke,
    The bare bone burst from the welter. And no
      blaze!

    This was a sign from heaven. My boy described
      it,
    Seeing for me as I see for others.

19. Hephaistos: God of fire.

I tell you, Kreon, you yourself have brought   25
This new calamity upon us. Our hearths and
      altars
Are stained with the corruption of dogs and
      carrion birds
That glut themselves on the corpse of Oedipus'
      son.
The gods are deaf when we pray to them, their
      fire
Recoils from our offering, their birds of omen   30
Have no cry of comfort, for they are gorged
With the thick blood of the dead.
                              O my son,
These are no trifles! Think: all men make
      mistakes,
But a good man yields when he knows his
      course is wrong,
And repairs the evil. The only crime is pride.   35

Give in to the dead man, then: do not fight with
      a corpse —
What glory is it to kill a man who is dead?
Think, I beg you:
It is for your own good that I speak as I do.
You should be able to yield for your own good.   40
KREON: It seems that prophets have made me their
      especial province.
All my life long
I have been a kind of butt for the dull arrows
Of doddering fortune-tellers!
                              No, Teiresias:
If your birds — if the great eagles of God
      himself   45
Should carry him stinking bit by bit to heaven,
I would not yield. I am not afraid of pollution:
No man can defile the gods.
                              Do what you will,
Go into business, make money, speculate
In India gold or that synthetic gold from Sardis, 50
Get rich otherwise than by my consent to bury
      him.
Teiresias, it is a sorry thing when a wise man
Sells his wisdom, lets out his words for hire!
TEIRESIAS: Ah Kreon! Is there no man left in the
      world —
KREON: To do what? — Come, let's have the
      aphorism!   55
TEIRESIAS: No man who knows that wisdom
      outweighs any wealth?
KREON: As surely as bribes are baser than any
      baseness.
TEIRESIAS: You are sick, Kreon! You are deathly
      sick!
KREON: As you say: it is not my place to challenge
      a prophet.

TEIRESIAS: Yet you have said my prophecy is for
60   sale.
KREON: The generation of prophets has always
    loved gold.
TEIRESIAS: The generation of kings has always loved
    brass.
KREON: You forget yourself! You are speaking to
    your King.
TEIRESIAS: I know it. You are a king because of me.
KREON: You have a certain skill; but you have sold
65   out.
TEIRESIAS: King, you will drive me to words that —
KREON: Say them, say them!
    Only remember: I will not pay you for them.
TEIRESIAS: No, you will find them too costly.
KREON: No doubt. Speak:
    Whatever you say, you will not change my will.
70 TEIRESIAS: Then take this, and take it to heart!
    The time is not far off when you shall pay back
    Corpse for corpse, flesh of your own flesh.
    You have thrust the child of this world into
        living night,
    You have kept from the gods below the child
        that is theirs:
75   The one in a grave before her death, the other,
    Dead, denied the grave. This is your crime:
    And the Furies° and the dark gods of Hell
    Are swift with terrible punishment for you.

    Do you want to buy me now, Kreon?

                               Not many days,
    And your house will be full of men and women
80   weeping,
    And curses will be hurled at you from far
    Cities grieving for sons unburied, left to rot
    Before the walls of Thebes.

    These are my arrows, Kreon: they are all for
        you.

85   (*To Boy.*) But come, child: lead me home.
    Let him waste his fine anger upon younger men.
    Maybe he will learn at last
    To control a wiser tongue in a better head.
                          (*Exit Teiresias.*)
CHORAGOS: The old man has gone, King, but his
    words
90   Remain to plague us. I am old, too,
    But I cannot remember that he was ever false.
KREON: That is true. . . . It troubles me.

---

77. Furies: Spirits called upon to avenge crimes, especially crimes committed against kin.

Oh it is hard to give in! but it is worse
To risk everything for stubborn pride.
CHORAGOS: Kreon: take my advice.
KREON: What shall I do?   95
CHORAGOS: Go quickly: free Antigone from her
    vault
    And build a tomb for the body of Polyneices.
KREON: You would have me do this!
CHORAGOS: Kreon, yes!
    And it must be done at once: God moves
    Swiftly to cancel the folly of stubborn men.   100
KREON: It is hard to deny the heart! But I
    Will do it: I will not fight with destiny.
CHORAGOS: You must go yourself, you cannot leave
    it to others.
KREON: I will go.
                  — Bring axes, servants:
    Come with me to the tomb. I buried her, I   105
    Will set her free.
                  Oh quickly!
    My mind misgives —
    The laws of the gods are mighty, and a man
        must serve them
    To the last day of his life!   (*Exit Kreon.*)

PAEAN° • Strophe 1 _____

CHORAGOS: God of many names
CHORUS: O Iacchos
                                son
    of Kadmeian Semele
                    O born of the Thunder!
    Guardian of the West
                    Regent
    of Eleusis' plain
                 O Prince of maenad Thebes
    and the Dragon Field by rippling Ismenos:°   5

Antistrophe 1

CHORAGOS: God of many names
CHORUS: the flame of torches
    flares on our hills
                 the nymphs of Iacchos
    dance at the spring of Castalia:°

Paean: A song of praise or prayer.   **1–5. God of many names . . . rippling Ismenos:** The following is a litany of names for Dionysus (Iacchos): He was son of Zeus ("Thunder") and Semele; he was honored in secret rites at Eleusis; and he was worshiped by the Maenads of Thebes. Kadmos, Semele's father, sowed dragon's teeth in a field beside the river Ismenos from which sprang warriors who became the first Thebans. **8. spring of Castalia:** A spring on Mount Parnassus used by Priestesses of Dionysus in rites of purification.

from the vine-close mountain
                      come ah come in ivy:
Evohe evohe!° sings through the streets of
10   Thebes

Strophe 2

CHORAGOS: God of many names
CHORUS: Iacchos of Thebes
  heavenly Child
             of Semele bride of the Thunderer!
  The shadow of plague is upon us:
                        come
with clement feet
           oh come from Parnasos
  down the long slopes
15   across the lamenting water

Antistrophe 2

CHORAGOS: Io° Fire! Chorister of the throbbing
  stars!
  O purest among the voices of the night!
  Thou son of God, blaze for us!
CHORUS: Come with choric rapture of circling
  Maenads
  Who cry *Io Iacche!*
20   *God of many names!*

EXODOS° _____

(Enter Messenger from left.)

MESSENGER: Men of the line of Kadmos, you who
  live
  Near Amphion's citadel,°
                I cannot say
Of any condition of human life "This is fixed,
This is clearly good, or bad." Fate raises up,
And Fate casts down the happy and unhappy
5   alike:
  No man can foretell his Fate.
               Take the case of Kreon:
Kreon was happy once, as I count happiness:
Victorious in battle, sole governor of the land,
Fortunate father of children nobly born.
10 And now it has all gone from him! Who can say
That a man is still alive when his life's joy fails?
He is a walking dead man. Grant him rich,
Let him live like a king in his great house:
If his pleasure is gone, I would not give

So much as the shadow of smoke for all he
  owns.   15
CHORAGOS: Your words hint at sorrow: what is
  your news for us?
MESSENGER: They are dead. The living are guilty of
  their death.
CHORAGOS: Who is guilty? Who is dead? Speak!
MESSENGER: Haimon.
  Haimon is dead; and the hand that killed him
  Is his own hand.
CHORAGOS: His father's? or his own?   20
MESSENGER: His own, driven mad by the murder
  his father had done.
CHORAGOS: Teiresias, Teiresias, how clearly you
  saw it all!
MESSENGER: This is my news: you must draw what
  conclusions you can from it.
CHORAGOS: But look: Eurydice, our Queen:
  Has she overheard us?   25

(Enter Eurydice from the palace, center.)

EURYDICE: I have heard something, friends:
  As I was unlocking the gate of Pallas'° shrine,
  For I needed her help today, I heard a voice
  Telling of some new sorrow. And I fainted
  There at the temple with all my maidens about
  me.   30
  But speak again: whatever it is, I can bear it:
  Grief and I are no strangers.
MESSENGER: Dearest Lady,
  I will tell you plainly all that I have seen.
  I shall not try to comfort you: what is the use,
  Since comfort could lie only in what is not true? 35
  The truth is always best.
                  I went with Kreon
  To the outer plain where Polyneices was lying,
  No friend to pity him, his body shredded by
  dogs.
  We made our prayers in that place to Hecate
  And Pluto,° that they would be merciful. And we
  bathed   40
  The corpse with holy water, and we brought
  Fresh-broken branches to burn what was left of
  it,
  And upon the urn we heaped up a towering
  barrow
  Of the earth of his own land.
                  When we were done, we ran
  To the vault where Antigone lay on her couch of
  stone.   45
  One of the servants had gone ahead,

---

10. *Evohe evohe!:* "Come forth, come forth!" Cry of the
Maenads to Dionysus. **16. Io:** "Hail!" **Exodos:** Final
scene. **2. Amphion's citadel:** A name for Thebes.

27. Pallas: Pallas Athene, goddess of wisdom.
39–40. Hecate and Pluto: Goddess of witchcraft and sorcery
and King of Hades, the underworld.

And while he was yet far off he heard a voice
Grieving within the chamber, and he came back
And told Kreon. And as the King went closer,
50   The air was full of wailing, the words lost,
And he begged us to make all haste. "Am I a
    prophet?"
He said, weeping, "And must I walk this road,
The saddest of all that I have gone before?
My son's voice calls me on. Oh quickly, quickly!
55   Look through the crevice there, and tell me
If it is Haimon, or some deception of the gods!"

We obeyed; and in the cavern's farthest corner
We saw her lying:
She had made a noose of her fine linen veil
60   And hanged herself. Haimon lay beside her,
His arms about her waist, lamenting her,
His love lost under ground, crying out
That his father had stolen her away from him.

When Kreon saw him the tears rushed to his
    eyes
And he called to him: "What have you done,
65   child? speak to me.
What are you thinking that makes your eyes so
        strange?
O my son, my son, I come to you on my
    knees!"
But Haimon spat in his face. He said not a
    word,
Staring —
            And suddenly drew his sword
And lunged. Kreon shrank back, the blade
70   missed; and the boy,
Desperate against himself, drove it half its length
Into his own side, and fell. And as he died
He gathered Antigone close in his arms again,
Choking, his blood bright red on her white
    cheek.
And now he lies dead with the dead, and she is
75   his
At last, his bride in the house of the dead.
                    (*Exit Eurydice into the palace.*)
CHORAGOS: She has left us without a word. What
    can this mean?
MESSENGER: It troubles me, too; yet she knows
    what is best,
Her grief is too great for public lamentation,
And doubtless she has gone to her chamber to
80   weep
For her dead son, leading her maidens in his
    dirge.

(*Pause.*)

CHORAGOS: It may be so: but I fear this deep
    silence.

MESSENGER: I will see what she is doing. I will go
    in.   (*Exit Messenger into the palace.*)

(*Enter Kreon with attendants, bearing Haimon's body.*)

CHORAGOS: But here is the king himself: oh look at
    him,
Bearing his own damnation in his arms.   85
KREON: Nothing you say can touch me any more.
My own blind heart has brought me
From darkness to final darkness. Here you see
The father murdering, the murdered son —
And all my civic wisdom!   90

Haimon my son, so young, so young to die,
I was the fool, not you; and you died for me.
CHORAGOS: That is the truth; but you were late in
    learning it.
KREON: This truth is hard to bear. Surely a god
Has crushed me beneath the hugest weight of
    heaven,   95
And driven me headlong a barbaric way
To trample out the thing I held most dear.

The pains that men will take to come to pain!

(*Enter Messenger from the palace.*)

MESSENGER: The burden you carry in your hands is
    heavy,
But it is not all: you will find more in your
    house.   100
KREON: What burden worse than this shall I find
    there?
MESSENGER: The Queen is dead.
KREON: O port of death, deaf world,
Is there no pity for me? And you, Angel of evil,
I was dead, and your words are death again.   105
Is it true, boy? Can it be true?
Is my wife dead? Has death bred death?
MESSENGER: You can see for yourself.

(*The doors are opened and the body of Eurydice is disclosed within.*)

KREON: Oh pity!
All true, all true, and more than I can bear!   110
O my wife, my son!
MESSENGER: She stood before the altar, and her
    heart
Welcomed the knife her own hand guided,
And a great cry burst from her lips for
    Megareus° dead,

---

114. Megareus: Son of Kreon and brother of Haimon, Megareus sacrificed himself in the unsuccessful attack upon Thebes, believing that his death was necessary to save Thebes.

115 And for Haimon dead, her sons; and her last
      breath
   Was a curse for their father, the murderer of her
      sons.
   And she fell, and the dark flowed in through her
      closing eyes.
   KREON: O God, I am sick with fear.
   Are there no swords here? Has no one a blow
      for me?
   MESSENGER: Her curse is upon you for the deaths
120   of both.
   KREON: It is right that it should be. I alone am
      guilty.
   I know it, and I say it. Lead me in,
   Quickly, friends.
   I have neither life nor substance. Lead me in.
   CHORAGOS: You are right, if there can be right in
125   so much wrong.
   The briefest way is best in a world of sorrow.
   KREON: Let it come,
   Let death come quickly, and be kind to me.
   I would not ever see the sun again.

CHORAGOS: All that will come when it will; but
      we, meanwhile,   130
   Have much to do. Leave the future to itself.
KREON: All my heart was in that prayer!
CHORAGOS: Then do not pray any more: the sky is
      deaf.
KREON: Lead me away. I have been rash and
      foolish.
   I have killed my son and my wife.   135
   I look for comfort; my comfort lies here dead.
   Whatever my hands have touched has come to
      nothing.
   Fate has brought all my pride to a thought of
      dust.

(*As Kreon is being led into the house, the Choragos
advances and speaks directly to the audience.*)

CHORAGOS: There is no happiness where there is no
      wisdom;
   No wisdom but in submission to the gods.   140
   Big words are always punished,
   And proud men in old age learn to be wise.

COMMENTARIES

Critical comment on the plays of Sophocles has been rich and various and has spanned the centuries. We are especially fortunate to have a commentary from the great age of Greek thought in which Sophocles himself flourished. In *Oedipus Rex* Sophocles gave the philosopher Aristotle a perfect drama on which to build a theory of tragedy, and Aristotle's observations have remained the most influential comments made on drama in the West. In some ways they have established the function, limits, and purposes of drama. In the twentieth century, for instance, when Bertolt Brecht tried to create a new theory of the drama, he specifically described his ideas as an alternative to the Aristotelian theory of the unities of time, place, character, and action.

Sigmund Freud, while not a critic, saw in the Oedipus myth as interpreted by Sophocles a basic psychological phenomenon experienced by all people in their infancy. His Oedipus complex is now well established in psychology and in the popular imagination.

The extraordinary range of commentary on the Oedipus story is demonstrated nowhere more amazingly than in Claude Lévi-Strauss's structural reading of the myth, both in Sophocles' version and in other versions. Lévi-Strauss shows that a pattern emerges when certain actions in the play are placed side by side. If he is correct, his theory offers us a way to interpret myths and to see why they were valued so highly by the Greeks in their drama.

Jean Anouilh, a major French playwright in the mid-twentieth century, wrote a version of *Antigone* while Nazi Germany occupied Paris and much of France. The political content of the play takes on interesting meaning in light of his experience. The excerpt that appears here offers us a modern interpretation of the struggle between Antigone and Kreon.

This sampling of commentaries on the drama and themes of Sophocles shows a range of thought and response to great and lasting works of art. These commentaries show that people from different ages, different political climates, and different cultures can all perceive value in plays that are primary not only in time but in importance to world drama. They also stimulate our own thoughts by revealing the many levels on which we can respond to the drama.

Aristotle (384–322 B.C.)
POETICS: COMEDY AND EPIC AND TRAGEDY
TRANSLATED BY GERALD F. ELSE

Aristotle was Plato's most brilliant student and the heir of his teaching mantle. He remained with Plato for twenty years, then began his own school, called the Lyceum. His extant work consists mainly of his lectures, which were written down by his students and carefully preserved. Called his treatises, they have greatly influenced later thought and deal with almost every branch of philosophy, science, and the arts. His Poetics *remains, more than two thousand years later, a document of immense importance for literary criticism. It provides insight into the theoretical basis of Greek tragedy and comedy, and it helps us see that the drama was significant enough in Greek intellectual life to warrant an examination by the most influential Greek minds.*

In the Poetics, *Aristotle establishes the theory of the unities: The action should be one action, taking place in one day, in one locale. He also establishes the nobility of the protagonist and the rhythms of action and emphasizes the peripeteia and recognition as the crucial moments of the drama. Further, he sets out a hierarchy of importance in the drama: plot, characters, verbal expression, thought, music, and visual adornment (or spectacle). His theories of MIMESIS, the way in which drama imitates life, are still subject to controversy. All drama criticism begins with Aristotle's* Poetics.

Comedy

Comedy is, as we said it was, an imitation of persons who are inferior; not, however, going all the way to full villainy, but imitating the ugly, of which the ludicrous is one part. The ludicrous, that is, is a failing or a piece of ugliness which causes no pain or destruction; thus, to go on farther, the comic mask[1] is something ugly and distorted but painless.

Now the stages of development of tragedy, and the men who were responsible for them, have not escaped notice but comedy did escape notice in the beginning because it was not taken seriously. (In fact it was late in its history that the presiding magistrate officially "granted a chorus" to the comic poets; until then they were volunteers.) Thus comedy already possessed certain defining characteristics when the first "comic poets," so-called, appear in the record. Who gave it masks, or prologues, or troupes of actors and all that sort of thing is not known. The composing of plots came originally from Sicily; of the Athenian poets, Crates[2] was the first to abandon the lampooning mode and compose arguments, that is, plots, of a general nature.

Epic and Tragedy

Well then, epic poetry followed in the wake of tragedy up to the point of being a (1) good-sized (2) imitation (3) in verse (4) of people who are to be taken seriously; but in its having its verse unmixed with any other and being narrative in character, there they differ. Further, so far as its length is concerned tragedy tries as hard as it can to exist during a single daylight period, or to vary but little, while the epic is not limited in its time and so differs in that respect. Yet originally they used to do this in tragedies just as much as they did in epic poems.

The constituent elements are partly identical and partly limited to tragedy. Hence anybody who knows about good and bad tragedy knows about epic also; for the elements that the epic possesses appertain to tragedy as well, but those of tragedy are not all found in the epic.

Tragedy and Its Six Constituent Elements

Our discussions of imitative poetry in hexameters,[3] and of comedy, will come later; at present let us deal with tragedy, recovering from what has been said so far the definition of its essential nature, as it was in development. Tragedy, then, is a process of imitating an action which has serious implications, is complete, and possesses magnitude; by means of language which has been made sensuously attractive, with each of its varieties found separately in the parts; enacted by the persons themselves and not presented through narrative; through a course of pity and fear completing the purification of tragic acts which have those emotional characteristics. By "language made sensuously attractive" I mean language that has rhythm and melody, and by "its varieties found separately" I mean the fact that certain parts of the play are carried on through spoken verses alone and others the other way around, through song.

Now first of all, since they perform the imitation through action (by acting it), the adornment of their visual appearance will perforce constitute some part

---

[1]**the comic mask**: Actors in Greek drama wore masks behind which they spoke their lines. The comic mask showed a smiling face; the tragic mask, a weeping face.

[2]**Crates (fl. 470 B.C.)**: Greek actor and playwright, credited by Aristotle with developing Greek comedy into a fully plotted, credible form. Aristophanes (450–c.388 B.C.), another Greek comic playwright, says that Crates was the first to portray a drunk onstage.

[3]**hexameters**: The first known metrical form for classical verse. Each line had six metrical feet, some of which were prescribed in advance. It is the meter used for epic poetry and for poetry designed to teach a lesson. The form has sometimes been used in comparatively modern poetry but rarely with success except in French.

of the making of tragedy; and song-composition and verbal expression also, for those are the media in which they perform the imitation. By "verbal expression" I mean the actual composition of the verses, and by "song-composition" something whose meaning is entirely clear.

Next, since it is an imitation of an action and is enacted by certain people who are performing the action, and since those people must necessarily have certain traits both of character and thought (for it is thanks to these two factors that we speak of people's actions also as having a defined character, and it is in accordance with their actions that all either succeed or fail); and since the imitation of the action is the plot, for by "plot" I mean here the structuring of the events, and by the "characters" that in accordance with which we say that the persons who are acting have a defined moral character, and by "thought" all the passages in which they attempt to prove some thesis or set forth an opinion — it follows of necessity, then, that tragedy as a whole has just six constituent elements, in relation to the essence that makes it a distinct species; and they are plot, characters, verbal expression, thought, visual adornment, and song-composition. For the elements by which they imitate are two (i.e., verbal expression and song-composition), the manner in which they imitate is one (visual adornment), the things they imitate are three (plot, characters, thought), and there is nothing more beyond these. These then are the constituent forms they use.

The Relative Importance of the Six Elements

The greatest of these elements is the structuring of the incidents. For tragedy is an imitation not of men but of a life, an action, and they have moral quality in accordance with their characters but are happy or unhappy in accordance with their actions; hence they are not active in order to imitate their characters, but they include the characters along with the actions for the sake of the latter. Thus the structure of events, the plot, is the goal of tragedy, and the goal is the greatest thing of all.

Again: a tragedy cannot exist without a plot, but it can without characters: thus the tragedies of most of our modern poets are devoid of character, and in general many poets are like that; so also with the relationship between Zeuxis and Polygnotus,[4] among the painters: Polygnotus is a good portrayer of character, while Zeuxis's painting has no dimension of character at all.

Again: if one strings end to end speeches that are expressive of character and carefully worked in thought and expression, he still will not achieve the result which we said was the aim of tragedy; the job will be done much better by a tragedy that is more deficient in these other respects but has a plot, a structure of events. It is much the same case as with painting: the most beautiful pigments smeared on at random will not give as much pleasure as a black-and-white outline picture. Besides, the most powerful means tragedy has for swaying our feelings, namely the peripeties and recognitions,[5] are elements of plot.

[4]**Zeuxis** (fl. 420–390 B.C.) **and Polygnotus** (c. 470–440 B.C.): Zeuxis developed a method of painting in which the figures were rounded and apparently three-dimensional. Thus, he was an illusionistic painter, imitating life in a realistic style. Polygnotus was famous as a painter, and his works were on the Akropolis as well as at Delphi. His draftsmanship was especially praised.

[5]**peripeties and recognitions**: The turning-about of fortune and the recognition on the part of the tragic hero of the truth. This is, for Aristotle, a critical moment in the drama, especially if both events happen simultaneously, as they do in *Oedipus Rex*. It is quite possible for these moments to happen apart from one another.

Again: an indicative sign is that those who are beginning a poetic career manage to hit the mark in verbal expression and character portrayal sooner than they do in plot construction; and the same is true of practically all the earliest poets.

So plot is the basic principle, the heart and soul, as it were, of tragedy, and the characters come second: . . . it is the imitation of an action and imitates the persons primarily for the sake of their action.

Third in rank is thought. This is the ability to state the issues and appropriate points pertaining to a given topic, an ability which springs from the arts of politics and rhetoric; in fact the earlier poets made their characters talk "politically," the present-day poets rhetorically. But "character" is that kind of utterance which clearly reveals the bent of a man's moral choice (hence there is no character in that class of utterances in which there is nothing at all that the speaker is choosing or rejecting), while "thought" is the passages in which they try to prove that something is so or not so, or state some general principle.

Fourth is the verbal expression of the speeches. I mean by this the same thing that was said earlier, that the "verbal expression" is the conveyance of thought through language: a statement which has the same meaning whether one says "verses" or "speeches."

The song-composition of the remaining parts is the greatest of the sensuous attractions, and the visual adornment of the dramatic persons can have a strong emotional effect but is the least artistic element, the least connected with the poetic art; in fact the force of tragedy can be felt even without benefit of public performance and actors, while for the production of the visual effect the property man's art is even more decisive than that of the poets.

General Principles
of the Tragic Plot

With these distinctions out of the way, let us next discuss what the structuring of the events should be like, since this is both the basic and the most important element in the tragic art. We have established, then, that tragedy is an imitation of an action which is complete and whole and has some magnitude (for there is also such a thing as a whole that has no magnitude). "Whole" is that which has beginning, middle, and end. "Beginning" is that which does not necessarily follow on something else, but after it something else naturally is or happens; "end," the other way around, is that which naturally follows on something else, either necessarily or for the most part, but nothing else after it; and "middle" that which naturally follows on something else and something else on it. So, then, well constructed plots should neither begin nor end at any chance point but follow the guidelines just laid down.

Furthermore, since the beautiful, whether a living creature or anything that is composed of parts, should not only have these in a fixed order to one another but also possess a definite size which does not depend on chance — for beauty depends on size and order; hence neither can a very tiny creature turn out to be beautiful (since our perception of it grows blurred as it approaches the period of imperceptibility) nor an excessively huge one (for then it cannot all be perceived at once and so its unity and wholeness are lost), if for example there were a creature a thousand miles long — so, just as in the case of living creatures they must have some size, but one that can be taken in a single view, so with plots: they should have length, but such that they are easy to remember. As to a limit of the length, the one is determined by the tragic competitions and the ordinary span of attention. (If they had to compete with a hundred tragedies they would compete by the water clock, as they say used to be done [?].) But the limit fixed by the very nature of the case is: the longer the plot, up to the point of still being perspicuous as a whole, the finer it is so far as size is concerned; or to put it in general terms, the length in which, with things happening in unbroken sequence, a shift takes place either probably or necessarily from bad to good fortune or from good to bad — that is an acceptable norm of length.

But a plot is not unified, as some people think, simply because it has to do with a single person. A large, indeed an indefinite number of things can happen to a given individual, some of which go to constitute no unified event; and in the same way there can be many acts of a given individual from which no single action emerges. Hence it seems clear that those poets are wrong who have composed *Heracleïds*, *Theseïds*, and the like. They think that since Heracles was a single person it follows that the plot will be single too. But Homer, superior as he is in all other respects, appears to have grasped this point well also, thanks either to art or nature, for in composing an *Odyssey* he did not incorporate into it everything that happened to the hero, for example how he was wounded on Mt. Parnassus[6] or how he feigned madness at the muster, neither of which events, by happening, made it at all necessary or probable that the other should happen. Instead, he composed the *Odyssey* — and the *Iliad* similarly — around a unified action of the kind we have been talking about.

A poetic imitation, then, ought to be unified in the same way as a single imitation in any other mimetic field, by having a single object: since the plot is an imitation of an action, the latter ought to be both unified and complete, and the component events ought to be so firmly compacted that if any one of them is shifted to another place, or removed, the whole is loosened up and dislocated; for an element whose addition or subtraction makes no perceptible extra difference is not really a part of the whole.

From what has been said it is also clear that the poet's job is not to report what has happened but what is likely to happen: that is, what is capable of happening according to the rule of probability or necessity. Thus the difference between the historian and the poet is not in their utterances being in verse or prose (it would be quite possible for Herodotus' work to be translated into verse, and it would not be any the less a history with verse than it is without it); the difference lies in the fact that the historian speaks of what has happened, the poet of the kind of thing that *can* happen. Hence also poetry is a more philosophical and serious business than history; for poetry speaks more of universals, history of particulars. "Universal" in this case is what kind of person is likely to do or say certain kinds of things, according to probability or necessity; that is what poetry aims at, although it gives its persons particular names afterward; while the "particular" is what Alcibiades did or what happened to him.

In the field of comedy this point has been grasped: our comic poets construct their plots on the basis of general probabilities and then assign names to the persons quite arbitrarily, instead of dealing with individuals as the old iambic poets[7] did. But in tragedy they still cling to the historically given names. The

[6]**Mt. Parnassus**: A mountain in central Greece traditionally sacred to Apollo. In legend, Odysseus was wounded there, but the point Aristotle is making is that the writer of epics need not include every detail of his hero's life in a given work. Homer, in writing the *Odyssey*, was working with a hero, Odysseus, whose story had been legendary long before he began writing.

[7]**old iambic poets**: Aristotle may be referring to Archilochus (fl. 650 B.C.) and the iambic style he developed. The iambic is a metrical foot of two syllables, a short and a

reason is that what is possible is persuasive; so what has not happened we are not yet ready to believe is possible, while what has happened is, we feel, obviously possible: for it would not have happened if it were impossible. Nevertheless, it is a fact that even in our tragedies, in some cases only one or two of the names are traditional, the rest being invented, and in some others none at all. It is so, for example, in Agathon's *Antheus* — the names in it are as fictional as the events — and it gives no less pleasure because of that. Hence the poets ought not to cling at all costs to the traditional plots, around which our tragedies are constructed. And in fact it is absurd to go searching for this kind of authentication, since even the familiar names are familiar to only a few in the audience and yet give the same kind of pleasure to all.

So from these considerations it is evident that the poet should be a maker of his plots more than of his verses, insofar as he is a poet by virtue of his imitations and what he imitates is actions. Hence even if it happens that he puts something that has actually taken place into poetry, he is none the less a poet; for there is nothing to prevent some of the things that have happened from being the kind of things that can happen, and that is the sense in which he is their maker.

Simple and Complex Plots

Among simple plots and actions the episodic are the worst. By "episodic" plot I mean one in which there is no probability or necessity for the order in which the episodes follow one another. Such structures are composed by the bad poets because they are bad poets, but by the good poets because of the actors: in composing contest pieces for them, and stretching out the plot beyond its capacity, they are forced frequently to dislocate the sequence.

Furthermore, since the tragic imitation is not only of a complete action but also of events that are fearful and pathetic,[8] and these come about best when they come about contrary to one's expectation yet logically, one following from the other; that way they will be more productive of wonder than if they happen merely at random, by chance — because even among chance occurrences the ones people consider most marvelous are those that seem to have come about as if on purpose: for example the way the statue of Mitys at Argos killed the man who had been the cause of Mitys' death, by falling on him while he was attending the festival; it stands to reason, people think, that such things don't happen by chance — so plots of that sort cannot fail to be artistically superior.

Some plots are simple, others are complex; indeed the actions of which the plots are imitations already fall into these two categories. By "simple" action I mean one the development of which being continuous and unified in the manner stated above, the reversal comes without peripety or recognition, and by "complex" action one in which the reversal is continuous but with recognition or peripety or both. And these developments must grow out of the very structure of the plot itself, in such a way that on the basis of what has happened previously

---

long syllable, and was the most popular metrical style before the time of Aristotle. "Dealing with individuals" implies using figures already known to the audience rather than figures whose names can be arbitrarily assigned because no one knows who they are.

[8]**fearful and pathetic**: Aristotle said that tragedy should evoke two emotions: terror and pity. The terror results from our realizing that what is happening to the hero might just as easily happen to us; the pity results from our human sympathy with a fellow sufferer. Therefore, the fearful and pathetic represent significant emotions appropriate to our witnessing drama.

this particular outcome follows either by necessity or in accordance with probability; for there is a great difference in whether these events happen because of those or merely after them.

"Peripety" is a shift of what is being undertaken to the opposite in the way previously stated, and that in accordance with probability or necessity as we have just been saying; as for example in the *Oedipus* the man who has come, thinking that he will reassure Oedipus, that is, relieve him of his fear with respect to his mother, by revealing who he once was, brings about the opposite; and in the *Lynceus*, as he (Lynceus) is being led away with every prospect of being executed, and Danaus pursuing him with every prospect of doing the executing, it comes about as a result of the other things that have happened in the play that *he* is executed and Lynceus is saved. And "recognition" is, as indeed the name indicates, a shift from ignorance to awareness, pointing in the direction either of close blood ties or of hostility, of people who have previously been in a clearly marked state of happiness or unhappiness.

The finest recognition is one that happens at the same time as a peripety, as is the case with the one in the *Oedipus*. Naturally, there are also other kinds of recognition: it is possible for one to take place in the prescribed manner in relation to inanimate objects and chance occurrences, and it is possible to recognize whether a person has acted or not acted. But the form that is most integrally a part of the plot, the action, is the one aforesaid; for that kind of recognition combined with peripety will excite either pity or fear (and these are the kinds of action of which tragedy is an imitation according to our definition), because both good and bad fortune will also be most likely to follow that kind of event. Since, further, the recognition is a recognition of persons, some are of one person by the other one only (when it is already known who the "other one" is), but sometimes it is necessary for both persons to go through a recognition, as for example Iphigenia is recognized by her brother through the sending of the letter, but of him by Iphigenia another recognition is required.

These then are two elements of plot: peripety and recognition; third is the *pathos*. Of these, peripety and recognition have been discussed; a *pathos* is a destructive or painful act, such as deaths on stage, paroxysms of pain, woundings, and all that sort of thing.

Edith Hamilton (1867–1963)
TRAGEDY

Edith Hamilton, a classics scholar, became famous for her works interpreting classical culture and mythology for a popular audience. The Greek Way, The Roman Way, *and* Mythology *have a rightful claim to being classics in their own right. In this brief excerpt from* The Greek Way, *she discusses the tragic view of life and the conditions that helped create two great ages of tragedy, one in Periclean Athens and one in Elizabethan England.*

Only twice in literary history has there been a great period of tragedy, in the Athens of Pericles and in Elizabethan England. What these two periods had in common, two thousand years and more apart in time, that they expressed themselves in the same fashion, may give us some hint of the nature of tragedy for, far from being periods of darkness and defeat, each was a time when life was seen exalted, a time of thrilling and unfathomable possibilities. They held their heads high, those men who conquered at Marathon and Salamis, and those who fought Spain and saw the Great Armada sink. The world was a place of wonder; mankind was beauteous; life was lived on the crest of the wave. More than all, the poignant joy of heroism had stirred men's hearts. Not stuff for tragedy, would you say? But on the crest of the wave one must feel either tragically or joyously; one cannot feel tamely. And the temper of mind that sees tragedy in life has not for its opposite the temper that sees joy. The opposite pole to the tragic view of life is the sordid view. When humanity is seen as devoid of dignity and significance, trivial, mean, and sunk in dreary hopelessness, then the spirit of tragedy departs.

Sigmund Freud (1856–1939)
THE OEDIPUS COMPLEX

Sigmund Freud is the most celebrated psychiatrist of the twentieth century and the father of psychoanalytic theory. His researches into the unconscious have changed the way we think about the human mind, and his explorations into the symbolic meaning of dreams have been widely regarded as a breakthrough in connecting the meaning of world myth to personal life.

In his Interpretation of Dreams *he turned to Sophocles' drama and developed his theories of the Oedipus complex, which explain that the desire to kill one parent and marry the other may be rooted in the deepest natural psychological development of the individual. The passage that follows provides insight not only into a psychological state that we may all share but also into the way in which a man of Freud's temperament read and interpreted a great piece of literature. Like Sophocles himself, Freud believed that the myth underlying* Oedipus Rex *has a meaning and importance for all human beings.*

In my experience, which is already extensive, the chief part in the mental lives of all children who later become psychoneurotics is played by their parents. Being in love with the one parent and hating the other are among the essential constituents of the stock of psychical impulses which is formed at that time and which is of such importance in determining the symptoms of the later neurosis. It is not my belief, however, that psychoneurotics differ sharply in this respect from other human beings who remain normal — that they are able, that is, to create something absolutely new and peculiar to themselves. It is far more probable — and this is confirmed by occasional observations on normal children — that they are only distinguished by exhibiting on a magnified scale feelings of love and hatred to their parents which occur less obviously and less intensely in the minds of most children.

This discovery is confirmed by a legend that has come down to us from classical antiquity: a legend whose profound and universal power to move can only be understood if the hypothesis I have put forward in regard to the psychology of children has an equally universal validity. What I have in mind is the legend of King Oedipus and Sophocles' drama which bears his name.

Oedipus, son of Laïus, King of Thebes, and of Jocasta, was exposed as an infant because an oracle had warned Laïus that the still unborn child would be his father's murderer. The child was rescued and grew up as a prince in an alien court, until, in doubts as to his origin, he too questioned the oracle and was warned to avoid his home since he was destined to murder his father and take his mother in marriage. On the road leading away from what he believed was his home, he met King Laïus and slew him in a sudden quarrel. He came next to Thebes and solved the riddle set him by the Sphinx who barred his way. Out of gratitude the Thebans made him their king and gave him Jocasta's hand in marriage. He reigned long in peace and honor, and she who, unknown to him, was his mother bore him two sons and two daughters. Then at last a plague broke out and the Thebans made inquiry once more of the oracle. It is at this point that Sophocles's tragedy opens. The messengers bring back the reply that the plague will cease when the murderer of Laïus has been driven from the land.

> But he, where is he? Where shall now be read
> The fading record of this ancient guilt?[1]

The action of the play consists in nothing other than the process of revealing, with cunning delays and ever-mounting excitement — a process that can be likened to the work of a psychoanalysis — that Oedipus himself is the murderer of Laïus, but further that he is the son of the murdered man and of Jocasta. Appalled at the abomination which he has unwittingly perpetrated, Oedipus blinds himself and forsakes his home. The oracle has been fulfilled.

Oedipus Rex is what is known as a tragedy of destiny. Its tragic effect is said to lie in the contrast between the supreme will of the gods and the vain attempts of mankind to escape the evil that threatens them. The lesson which, it is said, the deeply moved spectator should learn from the tragedy is submission to the divine will and realization of his own impotence. Modern dramatists have accordingly tried to achieve a similar tragic effect by weaving the same contrast into a plot invented by themselves. But the spectators have looked on unmoved while a curse or an oracle was fulfilled in spite of all the efforts of some innocent man: later tragedies of destiny have failed in their effect.

If *Oedipus Rex* moves a modern audience no less than it did the contemporary Greek one, the explanation can only be that its effect does not lie in the contrast between destiny and human will, but is to be looked for in the particular nature of the material on which that contrast is exemplified. There must be something which makes a voice within us ready to recognize the compelling force of destiny in the *Oedipus*, while we can dismiss as merely arbitrary such dispositions as are laid down in [Grillparzer's] *Die Ahnfrau* or other modern tragedies of destiny. And a factor of this kind is in fact involved in the story of King Oedipus. His destiny moves us only because it might have been ours — because the oracle laid the same curse upon us before our birth as upon him. It is the fate of all of us, perhaps, to direct our first sexual impulse toward our mother and our first hatred and our first murderous wish against our father. Our dreams convince

---

[1]Lewis Campbell's translation (1883), lines 108f.

us that that is so. King Oedipus, who slew his father Laïus and married his mother Jocasta, merely shows us the fulfillment of our own childhood wishes. But, more fortunate than he, we have meanwhile succeeded, in so far as we have not become psychoneurotics, in detaching our sexual impulses from our mothers and in forgetting our jealousy of our fathers. Here is one in whom these primeval wishes of our childhood have been fulfilled, and we shrink back from him with the whole force of the repression by which those wishes have since that time been held down within us. While the poet, as he unravels the past, brings to light the guilt of Oedipus, he is at the same time compelling us to recognize our own inner minds, in which those same impulses, though suppressed, are still to be found. The contrast with which the closing Chorus leaves us confronted —

> . . . Fix on Oedipus your eyes,
> Who resolved the dark enigma, noblest champion and most wise.
> Like a star his envied fortune mounted beaming far and wide:
> Now he sinks in seas of anguish, whelmed beneath a raging tide . . .[2]

— strikes as a warning at ourselves and our pride, at us who since our childhood have grown so wise and so mighty in our own eyes. Like Oedipus, we live in ignorance of these wishes, repugnant to morality, which have been forced upon us by Nature, and after their revelation we may all of us well seek to close our eyes to the scenes of our childhood.[3]

There is an unmistakable indication in the text of Sophocles' tragedy itself that the legend of Oedipus sprang from some primeval dream material which had as its content the distressing disturbance of a child's relation to his parents owing to the first stirrings of sexuality. At a point when Oedipus, though he is not yet enlightened, has begun to feel troubled by his recollection of the oracle, Jocasta consoles him by referring to a dream which many people dream, though, as she thinks, it has no meaning:

> Many a man ere now in dreams hath lain
> With her who bare him. He hath least annoy
> Who with such omens troubleth not his mind.[4]

Today, just as then, many men dream of having sexual relations with their mothers, and speak of the fact with indignation and astonishment. It is clearly the key to the tragedy and the complement to the dream of the dreamer's father being dead. The story of Oedipus is the reaction of the imagination to these two typical dreams. And just as these dreams, when dreamt by adults, are

[2]Lewis Campbell's translation, lines 1524ff.

[3][*Footnote added by Freud in 1914 Edition.*] None of the findings of psychoanalytic research has provoked such embittered denials, such fierce opposition — or such amusing contortions — on the part of critics as this indication of the childhood impulses toward incest which persist in the unconscious. An attempt has even been made recently to make out, in the face of all experience, that the incest should only be taken as "symbolic." — Ferenczi (1912) has proposed an ingenious "overinterpretation" of the Oedipus myth, based on a passage in one of Schopenhauer's letters. [*Added 1919.*] Later studies have shown that the "Oedipus complex," which was touched upon for the first time in the above paragraphs in the *Interpretation of Dreams*, throws a light of undreamt-of importance on the history of the human race and the evolution of religion and morality.

[4]Lewis Campbell's translation, lines 982ff.

accompanied by feelings of repulsion, so too the legend must include horror and self-punishment. Its further modification originates once again in a misconceived secondary revision of the material, which has sought to exploit it for theological purposes. . . . The attempt to harmonize divine omnipotence with human responsibility must naturally fail in connection with this subject matter just as with any other.

Claude Lévi-Strauss (b. 1908)
From "THE STRUCTURAL STUDY OF MYTH"

Claude Lévi-Strauss is one of a handful of modern anthropologists whose interests span the range of thought, culture, and understanding. His work has been of immense influence on French intellectual life and, by extension, on the intellectual life of our entire century. His works include Triste Tropiques *(translated as* A World on the Wane), *about his own experiences as an anthropologist;* Structural Anthropology, *about the ways in which the study of anthropology implies a study of the structure of thought; and* Mythologies, *a four-volume summation of his thought. The excerpt that follows is structuralist in scope in that it attempts to understand the myth of Oedipus by examining the patterns of repetition in the original narrative. By setting up a grid, Lévi-Strauss begins to sort out the implications of the myth and to seek a meaning that is not necessarily apparent in the chronological order of the narrative. He examines the myth diachronically — across the lines of time — and thereby sees a new range of implications, which he treats as the structural implications of the myth. His reading is complex, suggesting that the Oedipus myth is a vegetation myth explaining the origins of mankind. Lévi-Strauss gives us a new way to interpret the significance of literary myths.*

The time has come to give a concrete example of the method we propose. We will use the Oedipus myth which has the advantage of being well known to everybody and for which no preliminary explanation is therefore needed. By doing so, I am well aware that the Oedipus myth has only reached us under late forms and through literary transfigurations concerned more with esthetic and moral preoccupations than with religious or ritual ones, whatever these may have been. But as will be shown later, this apparently unsatisfactory situation will strengthen our demonstration rather than weaken it.

The myth will be treated as would be an orchestra score perversely presented as a unilinear series and where our task is to reestablish the correct disposition. As if, for instance, we were confronted with a sequence of the type: 1,2,4,7,8,2,3,4,6,8,1,4,5,7,8,1,2,5,7,3,4,5,6,8 . . . , the assignment being to put all the 1's together, all the 2's, the 3's, etc.; the result is a chart:

1	2		4			7	8
	2	3	4		6		8
1			4	5		7	8
1	2			5		7	
		3	4	5			
					6		8

We will attempt to perform the same kind of operation on the Oedipus myth, trying out several dispositions. . . . Let us suppose, for the sake of argument, that the best arrangement is the following (although it might certainly be improved by the help of a specialist in Greek mythology):

Kadmos seeks his sister Europa ravished by Zeus.		Kadmos kills the dragon.	
	The Spartoi kill each other.		Labdacos (Laios's father) = *lame* (?)
	Oedipus kills his father Laios.		Laios (Oedipus's father) = *left-sided* (?)
		Oedipus kills the Sphinx	
Oedipus marries his mother Jocasta	Eteocles kills his brother Polyneices		Oedipus = *swollen-foot* (?)
Antigone buries her brother Polyneices despite prohibition			

Thus, we find ourselves confronted with four vertical columns each of which includes several relations belonging to the same bundle. Were we to *tell* the myth, we would disregard the columns and read the rows from left to right and from top to bottom. But if we want to *understand* the myth, then we will have to disregard one half of the diachronic[1] dimension (top to bottom) and read from left to right, column after column, each one being considered as a unit.

All the relations belonging to the same column exhibit one common feature which it is our task to unravel. For instance, all the events grouped in the first column on the left have something to do with blood relations which are overemphasized, i.e. are subject to a more intimate treatment than they should be. Let us say, then, that the first column has as its common feature the *overrating of blood relations*. It is obvious that the second column expresses the same thing, but inverted: *underrating of blood relations*. The third column refers to monsters being slain. As to the fourth, a word of clarification is needed. The remarkable connotation of the surnames in Oedipus's father-line has often been

[1] **Diachronic:** Not ordered linearly in time, but across time in a structural fashion.

noticed. However, linguists usually disregard it, since to them the only way to define the meaning of a term is to investigate all the contexts in which it appears, and personal names, precisely because they are used as such, are not accompanied by any context. With the method we propose to follow the objection disappears since the myth itself provides its own context. The meaningful fact is no longer to be looked for in the eventual sense of each name, but in the fact that all the names have a common feature: i.e., that they may eventually mean something and that all these hypothetical meanings (which may well remain hypothetical) exhibit a common feature, namely they refer *to difficulties to walk and to behave straight.*

What is then the relationship between the two columns on the right? Column three refers to monsters. The dragon is a chthonian[2] being which has to be killed in order that mankind be born from the earth; the Sphinx is a monster unwilling to permit men to live. The last unit reproduces the first one which has to do with the *autochthonous*[3] *origin* of mankind. Since the monsters are overcome by men, we may thus say that the common feature of the third column is *the denial of the autochthonous origin of man.*

This immediately helps us to understand the meaning of the fourth column. In mythology it is a universal character of men born from the earth that at the moment they emerge from the depth, they either cannot walk or do it clumsily. This is the case of the chthonian beings in the mythology of the Pueblo: Masauwu, who leads the emergence, and the chthonian Shumaikoli are lame ("bleeding-foot," "sore-foot"). The same happens to the Koskimo of the Kwakiutl after they have been swallowed by the chthonian monster, Tsiakish: when they returned to the surface of the earth "they limped forward or tripped sideways." Then the common feature of the fourth column is: *the persistence of the autochthonous origin of man.* It follows that column four is to column three as column one is to column two. The inability to connect two kinds of relationships is overcome (or rather replaced) by the positive statement that contradictory relationships are identical inasmuch as they are both self-contradictory in a similar way. Although this is still a provisional formulation of the structure of mythical thought, it is sufficient at this stage.

Turning back to the Oedipus myth, we may now see what it means. The myth has to do with the inability, for a culture which holds the belief that mankind is autochthonous . . . to find a satisfactory transition between this theory and the knowledge that human beings are actually born from the union of man and woman. Although the problem obviously cannot be solved, the Oedipus myth provides a kind of logical tool which, to phrase it coarsely, replaces the original problem: born from one or born from two? born from different or born from same? By a correlation of this type, the overrating of blood relations is to the underrating of blood relations as the attempt to escape autochthony is to the impossibility to succeed in it. Although experience contradicts theory, social life verifies the cosmology by its similarity of structure. Hence cosmology is true.

Two remarks should be made at this stage.

In order to interpret the myth, we were able to leave aside a point which has until now worried the specialists, namely, that in the earlier (Homeric) versions of the Oedipus myth, some basic elements are lacking, such as Jocasta

[2]**Chthonian**: From the underworld.
[3]**Autochthonous**: Native, aboriginal; in this case, born of the earth.

killing herself and Oedipus piercing his own eyes. These events do not alter the substance of the myth although they can easily be integrated, the first one as a new case of autodestruction (column three) while the second is another case of crippledness (column four). At the same time there is something significant in these additions since the shift from foot to head is to be correlated with the shift from: autochthonous origin negated to: self-destruction.

Thus, our method eliminates a problem which has been so far one of the main obstacles to the progress of mythological studies, namely, the quest for the *true* version, or the *earlier* one. On the contrary, we define the myth as consisting of all its versions; to put it otherwise: a myth remains the same as long as it is felt as such. A striking example is offered by the fact that our interpretation may take into account, and is certainly applicable to, the Freudian use of the Oedipus myth. Although the Freudian problem has ceased to be that of autochthony *versus* bisexual reproduction, it is still the problem of understanding how *one* can be born from *two:* how is it that we do not have only one procreator, but a mother plus a father? Therefore, not only Sophocles, but Freud himself, should be included among the recorded versions of the Oedipus myth on a par with earlier or seemingly more "authentic" versions.

Jean Anouilh (b. 1910)
From ANTIGONE

TRANSLATED BY LEWIS GALANTIÈRE

Jean Anouilh began writing plays in 1931. Some of his best-known works, in addition to Antigone, *are* Eurydice *(1941),* Orestes *(1942),* Medea *(1946),* Ring Round the Moon *(1947),* The Waltz of the Toreadors *(1951), and* The Lark *(1952), which is about Joan of Arc. Anouilh wrote* Antigone *in 1942 in occupied Paris and produced it with his wife in the title role in February 1944, when the Nazis controlled most of Europe. The Parisian Resistance saw in* Antigone *a symbol of their cause. Kreon (spelled Creon in this excerpt) is more willing to compromise in Anouilh's version of the play, and for that reason some critics saw the play as pro-Nazi. But Anouilh's later plays seem to imply that his sympathies were with Antigone and that she represented the anti-Nazi view of the Parisian Resistance. Throughout its early run, the play was an inspiration to the patriotic French.*

Anouilh's interpretation is perhaps more understanding of Kreon and less sympathetic to Antigone than was Sophocles'. The problems of power, law, and the struggle to honor one's principles are central to the play. This excerpt begins when Ismene returns to accept some of the responsibility for Polyneices' burial and continues through the confrontation of Haimon (Haemon in this excerpt) and Kreon to the end of the play. The modern tone and quality of the text provide one of the best modern interpretations of this timeless masterpiece.

(Ismene enters through arch.)

ISMENE (*distraught*): Antigone!
ANTIGONE (*turns to Ismene*): You, too? What do you want?

ISMENE: Oh, forgive me, Antigone. I've come back. I'll be brave. I'll go with you now.

ANTIGONE: Where will you go with me?

ISMENE (*to Creon*): Creon! If you kill her, you'll have to kill me too.

ANTIGONE: Oh, no, Ismene. Not a bit of it. I die alone. You don't think I'm going to let you die with me after what I've been through? You don't deserve it.

ISMENE: If you die, I don't want to live. I don't want to be left behind, alone.

ANTIGONE: You chose life and I chose death. Now stop blubbering. You had your chance to come with me in the black night, creeping on your hands and knees. You had your chance to claw up the earth with your nails, as I did; to get yourself caught like a thief, as I did. And you refused it.

ISMENE: Not anymore. I'll do it alone tonight.

ANTIGONE (*turns round toward Creon*): You hear that, Creon? The thing is catching! Who knows but that lots of people will catch the disease from me! What are you waiting for? Call in your guards! Come on, Creon! Show a little courage! It only hurts for a minute! Come on, cook!

CREON (*turns toward arch and calls*): Guard!

(*Guards enter through arch.*)

ANTIGONE (*in a great cry of relief*): At last, Creon!

(*Chorus enters through left arch.*)

CREON (*to the Guards*): Take her away! (*Creon goes up on top step.*)

(*Guards grasp Antigone by her arms, turn and hustle her toward the arch, right, and exeunt.*[1] *Ismene mimes horror, backs away toward the arch, left, then turns and runs out through the arch. A long pause, as Creon moves slowly downstage.*)

CHORUS (*Behind Creon. Speaks in a deliberate voice.*): You are out of your mind, Creon. What have you done?

CREON (*his back to Chorus*): She had to die.

CHORUS: You must not let Antigone die. We shall carry the scar of her death for centuries.

CREON: She insisted. No man on earth was strong enough to dissuade her. Death was her purpose, whether she knew it or not. Polynices was a mere pretext. When she had to give up that pretext, she found another one — that life and happiness were tawdry things and not worth possessing. She was bent upon only one thing: to reject life and to die.

CHORUS: She is a mere child, Creon.

CREON: What do you want me to do for her? Condemn her to live?

HAEMON (*calls from offstage*): Father! (*Haemon enters through arch, right. Creon turns toward him.*)

CREON: Haemon, forget Antigone. Forget her, my dearest boy.

HAEMON: How can you talk like that?

CREON (*grasps Haemon by the hands*): I did everything I could to save her, Haemon. I used every argument. I swear I did. The girl doesn't love you. She could have gone on living for you; but she refused. She wanted it this way; she wanted to die.

HAEMON: Father! The guards are dragging Antigone away! You've got to stop them! (*He breaks away from Creon.*)

CREON (*looks away from Haemon*): I can't stop them. It's too late. Antigone has spoken. The story is all over Thebes. I cannot save her now.

---

[1]**exeunt:** Latin for "they go out."

CHORUS: Creon, you must find a way. Lock her up. Say that she has gone out of her mind.

CREON: Everybody will know it isn't so. The nation will say that I am making an exception of her because my son loves her. I cannot.

CHORUS: You can still gain time and get her out of Thebes.

CREON: The mob already knows the truth. It is howling for her blood. I can do nothing.

HAEMON: But, Father, you are master in Thebes!

CREON: I am master under the law. Not above the law.

HAEMON: You cannot let Antigone be taken from me. I am your son!

CREON: I cannot do anything else, my poor boy. She must die and you must live.

HAEMON: Live, you say! Live a life without Antigone? A life in which I am to go on admiring you as you busy yourself about your kingdom, make your persuasive speeches, strike your attitudes? Not without Antigone. I love Antigone. I will not live without Antigone!

CREON: Haemon — you will have to resign yourself to life without Antigone. (*He moves to left of Haemon*). Sooner or later there comes a day of sorrow in each man's life when he must cease to be a child and take up the burden of manhood. That day has come for you.

HAEMON (*backs away a step*): That giant strength, that courage. That massive god who used to pick me up in his arms and shelter me from shadows and monsters — was that you, Father? Was it of you I stood in awe? Was that man you?

CREON: For God's sake, Haemon, do not judge me! Not you, too!

HAEMON (*pleading now*): This is all a bad dream, Father. You are not yourself. It isn't true that we have been backed up against a wall, forced to surrender. We don't have to say *yes* to this terrible thing. You are still king. You are still the father I revered. You have no right to desert me, to shrink into nothingness. The world will be too bare, I shall be too alone in the world, if you force me to disown you.

CREON: The world *is* bare, Haemon, and you *are* alone. You must cease to think your father all-powerful. Look straight at me. See your father as he is. That is what it means to grow up and be a man.

HAEMON (*stares at Creon for a moment*): I tell you that I will not live without Antigone. (*Turns and goes quickly out through arch.*)

CHORUS: Creon, the boy will go mad.

CREON: Poor boy! He loves her.

CHORUS: Creon, the boy is wounded to death.

CREON: We are all wounded to death.

(*First Guard enters through arch, right, followed by Second and Third Guards pulling Antigone along with them.*)

FIRST GUARD: Sir, the people are crowding into the palace!

ANTIGONE: Creon, I don't want to see their faces. I don't want to hear them howl. You are going to kill me; let that be enough. I want to be alone until it is over.

CREON: Empty the palace! Guards at the gates!

(*Creon quickly crosses toward the arch; exit. Two Guards release Antigone; exeunt behind Creon. Chorus goes out through arch, left. The lighting dims so that only the area about the table is lighted. The cyclorama² is covered with a*

---

²**cyclorama:** Curved cloth or wall forming the back of many modern stage settings.

dark blue color. The scene is intended to suggest a prison cell, filled with shadows and dimly lit. Antigone moves to stool and sits. The First Guard stands upstage. He watches Antigone, and as she sits, he begins pacing slowly downstage, then upstage. A pause.)

ANTIGONE (*turns and looks at the Guard*): It's you, is it?

GUARD: What do you mean, me?

ANTIGONE: The last human face that I shall see. (*A pause as they look at each other, then Guard paces upstage, turns, and crosses behind table.*) Was it you that arrested me this morning?

GUARD: Yes, that was me.

ANTIGONE: You hurt me. There was no need for you to hurt me. Did I act as if I was trying to escape?

GUARD: Come on now, Miss. It was my business to bring you in. I did it. (*A pause. He paces to and fro upstage. Only the sound of his boots is heard.*)

ANTIGONE: How old are you?

GUARD: Thirty-nine.

ANTIGONE: Have you any children?

GUARD: Yes. Two.

ANTIGONE: Do you love your children?

GUARD: What's that got to with you? (*A pause. He paces upstage and downstage.*)

ANTIGONE: How long have you been in the Guard?

GUARD: Since the war. I was in the army. Sergeant. Then I joined the Guard.

ANTIGONE: Does one have to have been an army sergeant to get into the Guard?

GUARD: Supposed to be. Either that or on special detail. But when they make you a guard, you lose your stripes.

ANTIGONE (*murmurs*): I see.

GUARD: Yes. Of course, if you're a guard, everybody knows you're something special; they know you're an old N.C.O.[3] Take pay, for instance. When you're a guard you get your pay, and on top of that you get six months' extra pay, to make sure you don't lose anything by not being a sergeant anymore. And of course you do better than that. You get a house, coal, rations, extras for the wife and kids. If you've got two kids, like me, you draw better than a sergeant.

ANTIGONE (*barely audible*): I see.

GUARD: That's why sergeants, now, they don't like guards. Maybe you noticed they try to make out they're better than us? Promotion, that's what it is. In the army, anybody can get promoted. All you need is good conduct. Now in the Guard, it's slow, and you have to know your business — like how to make out a report and the like of that. But when you're an N.C.O. in the Guard, you've got something that even a sergeant major ain't got. For instance —

ANTIGONE (*breaking him off*): Listen.

GUARD: Yes, Miss.

ANTIGONE: I'm going to die soon.

(*The Guard looks at her for a moment, then turns and moves away.*)

GUARD: For instance, people have a lot of respect for guards, they have. A guard may be a soldier, but he's kind of in the civil service, too.

ANTIGONE: Do you think it hurts to die?

GUARD: How would I know? Of course, if somebody sticks a saber in your guts and turns it round, it hurts.

ANTIGONE: How are they going to put me to death?

---

[3]N.C.O.: Noncommissioned officer, usually of a subordinate rank such as sergeant.

GUARD: Well, I'll tell you. I heard the proclamation all right. Wait a minute. How did it go now? (*He stares into space and recites from memory.*) "In order that our fair city shall not be pol-luted with her sinful blood, she shall be im-mured — immured." That means, they shove you in a cave and wall up the cave.

ANTIGONE: Alive?

GUARD: Yes. . . . (*He moves away a few steps.*)

ANTIGONE (*murmurs*): O tomb! O bridal bed! Alone! (*Antigone sits there, a tiny figure in the middle of the stage. You would say she felt a little chilly. She wraps her arms round herself.*)

GUARD: Yes! Outside the southeast gate of the town. In the Cave of Hades. In broad daylight. Some detail, eh, for them that's on the job! First they thought maybe it was a job for the army. Now it looks like it's going to be the Guard. There's an outfit for you! Nothing the Guard can't do. No wonder the army's jealous.

ANTIGONE: A pair of animals.

GUARD: What do you mean, a pair of animals?

ANTIGONE: When the winds blow cold, all they need do is to press close against one another. I am all alone.

GUARD: Is there anything you want? I can send out for it, you know.

ANTIGONE: You are very kind. (*A pause. Antigone looks up at the Guard.*) Yes, there is something I want. I want you to give someone a letter from me, when I am dead.

GUARD: How's that again? A letter?

ANTIGONE: Yes, I want to write a letter; and I want you to give it to someone for me.

GUARD (*straightens up*): Now, wait a minute. Take it easy. It's as much as my job is worth to go handing out letters from prisoners.

ANTIGONE (*removes a ring from her finger and holds it out toward him*): I'll give you this ring if you will do it.

GUARD: Is it gold? (*He takes the ring from her.*)

ANTIGONE: Yes, it is gold.

GUARD (*shakes his head*): Uh-uh. No can do. Suppose they go through my pockets. I might get six months for a thing like that. (*He stares at the ring, then glances off right to make sure that he is not being watched.*) Listen, tell you what I'll do. You tell me what you want to say, and I'll write it down in my book. Then, afterwards, I'll tear out the pages and give them to the party, see? If it's in my handwriting, it's all right.

ANTIGONE (*winces*): In your handwriting? (*She shudders slightly.*) No. That would be awful. The poor darling! In your handwriting.

GUARD (*offers back the ring*): O.K. It's no skin off my nose.

ANTIGONE (*quickly*): Of course, of course. No, keep the ring. But hurry. Time is getting short. Where is your notebook? (*The Guard pockets the ring, takes his notebook and pencil from his pocket, puts his foot up on chair, and rests the notebook on his knee, licks his pencil.*) Ready? (*He nods.*) Write, now. "My darling . . ."

GUARD (*writes as he mutters*): The boyfriend, eh?

ANTIGONE: "My darling. I wanted to die, and perhaps you will not love me anymore . . ."

GUARD (*mutters as he writes*): ". . . will not love me anymore."

ANTIGONE: "Creon was right. It is terrible to die."

GUARD (*repeats as he writes*): ". . . terrible to die."

ANTIGONE: "And I don't even know what I am dying for. I am afraid . . ."

GUARD (*looks at her*): Wait a minute! How fast do you think I can write?

ANTIGONE (*takes hold of herself*): Where are you?

GUARD (*reads from his notebook*): "And I don't even know what I am dying for."

ANTIGONE: No. Scratch that out. Nobody must know that. They have no right to know. It's as if they saw me naked and touched me, after I was dead. Scratch it all out. Just write: "Forgive me."

GUARD (*looks at Antigone*): I cut out everything you said there at the end, and I put down, "Forgive me"?

ANTIGONE: Yes. "Forgive me, my darling. You would all have been so happy except for Antigone. I love you."

GUARD (*finishes the letter*): ". . . I love you." (*He looks at her.*) Is that all?

ANTIGONE: That's all.

GUARD (*straightens up, looks at notebook*): Damn funny letter.

ANTIGONE: I know.

GUARD (*looks at her*): Who is it to? (*A sudden roll of drums begins and continues until after Antigone's exit. The First Guard pockets the notebook and shouts at Antigone.*) O.K. That's enough out of you! Come on!

(*At the sound of the drum roll, Second and Third Guards enter through the arch. Antigone rises. Guards seize her and exeunt with her. The lighting moves up to suggest late afternoon. Chorus enters.*)

CHORUS: And now it is Creon's turn.

(*Messenger runs through the arch, right.*)

MESSENGER: The Queen . . . the Queen! Where is the Queen?

CHORUS: What do you want with the Queen? What have you to tell the Queen?

MESSENGER: News to break her heart. Antigone had just been thrust into the cave. They hadn't finished heaving the last block of stone into place when Creon and the rest heard a sudden moaning from the tomb. A hush fell over us all, for it was not the voice of Antigone. It was Haemon's voice that came forth from the tomb. Everybody looked at Creon; and he howled like a man demented: "Take away the stones! Take away the stones!" The slaves leaped at the wall of stones, and Creon worked with them, sweating and tearing at the blocks with his bleeding hands. Finally a narrow opening was forced, and into it slipped the smallest guard.

Antigone had hanged herself by the cord of her robe, by the red and golden twisted cord of her robe. The cord was round her neck like a child's collar. Haemon was on his knees, holding her in his arms and moaning, his face buried in her robe. More stones were removed, and Creon went into the tomb. He tried to raise Haemon to his feet. I could hear him begging Haemon to rise to his feet. Haemon was deaf to his father's voice, till suddenly he stood up of his own accord, his eyes dark and burning. Anguish was in his face, but it was the face of a little boy. He stared at his father. Then suddenly he struck him — hard; and he drew his sword. Creon leaped out of range. Haemon went on staring at him, his eyes full of contempt — a glance that was like a knife, and that Creon couldn't escape. The King stood trembling in the far corner of the tomb, and Haemon went on staring. Then, without a word, he stabbed himself and lay down beside Antigone, embracing her in a great pool of blood.

(*A pause as Creon and Page enter through arch on the Messenger's last words. Chorus and the Messenger both turn to look at Creon; then exit the Messenger through curtain.*)

CREON: I have had them laid out side by side. They are together at last, and at peace. Two lovers on the morrow of their bridal. Their work is done.

CHORUS: But not yours, Creon. You have still one thing to learn. Eurydice, the Queen, your wife —

CREON: A good woman. Always busy with her garden, her preserves, her sweaters — those sweaters she never stopped knitting for the poor. Strange, how the poor never stop needing sweaters. One would almost think that was all they needed.

CHORUS: The poor in Thebes are going to be cold this winter, Creon. When the Queen was told of her son's death, she waited carefully until she had finished her row, then put down her knitting calmly — as she did everything. She went up to her room, her lavender-scented room, with its embroidered doilies and its pictures framed in plush; and there, Creon, she cut her throat. She is laid out now in one of those two old-fashioned twin beds, exactly where you went to her one night when she was still a maiden. Her smile is still the same, scarcely a shade more melancholy. And if it were not for that great red blot on the bed linen by her neck, one might think she was asleep.

CREON (*in a dull voice*): She, too. They are all asleep. (*Pause.*) It must be good to sleep.

CHORUS: And now you are alone, Creon.

CREON: Yes, all alone. (*To Page.*) My lad.

PAGE: Sir?

CREON: Listen to me. They don't know it, but the truth is, the work is there to be done, and a man can't fold his arms and refuse to do it. They say it's dirty work. But if we didn't do it, who would?

PAGE: I don't know, sir.

CREON: Of course you don't. You'll be lucky if you never find out. In a hurry to grow up, aren't you?

PAGE: Oh, yes, sir.

CREON: I shouldn't be if I were you. Never grow up if you can help it. (*He is lost in thought as the hour chimes.*) What time is it?

PAGE: Five o'clock, sir.

CREON: What have we on at five o'clock?

PAGE: Cabinet meeting, sir.

CREON: Cabinet meeting. Then we had better go along to it.

(*Exeunt Creon and Page slowly through arch, left, and Chorus moves downstage.*)

CHORUS: And there we are. It is quite true that if it had not been for Antigone they would all have been at peace. But that is over now. And they are all at peace. All those who were meant to die have died: those who believed one thing, those who believed the contrary thing, and even those who believed nothing at all, yet were caught up in the web without knowing why. All dead: stiff, useless, rotting. And those who have survived will now begin quietly to forget the dead: they won't remember who was who or which was which. It is all over. Antigone is calm tonight, and we shall never know the name of the fever that consumed her. She has played her part.

(*Three Guards enter, resume their places on steps as at the rise of the curtain, and begin to play cards.*)

A great melancholy wave of peace now settles down upon Thebes, upon the empty palace, upon Creon, who can now begin to wait for his own death. Only the guards are left, and none of this matters to them. It's no skin off their noses. They go on playing cards.

(*Chorus walks toward the arch, left, as the curtain falls.*)

Aristophanes

The best known of the Greek comic playwrights, Aristophanes (c. 448–c. 385 B.C.) lived through some of the most difficult times in Athenian history. He watched Athenian democracy fade and decay as factionalism and war took their toll on the strength of the nation. By the time he died, Athens was caught up in a fierce struggle between supporters of democracy and supporters of oligarchy, government by a small group of leaders.

Aristophanes' plays are essentially democratic. He appealed not only to intellectuals, who immediately caught his sophisticated word plays, but also to the ordinary theatergoers who enjoyed his boisterous and rowdy comedy. He was a master of slapstick and sexual innuendo.

Aristophanes practiced Old Comedy, which was based on heaping insults on prominent people and important institutions. Nothing was sacred for the practitioner of Old Comedy. Aristophanes could taunt the leaders of Athens, its prominent citizens, its own sense of social order. But it was possible to do this only while Athenians felt secure enough as a people to tolerate criticism. It may be a sign of the health of a nation when its population can be amused at humor that is entirely at its own expense.

Of his more than thirty known plays, only eleven survive. They come from three main periods in his life, beginning, according to legend, when he was a young man, in 427 B.C. *The Acharnians*, from his first period, focuses on the theme of peace. Dicaeopolis (whose name means "honest" or "good citizen") decides to make peace after the Spartans have ravaged the Acharnian vineyards, for which the Acharnians vow revenge. Dicaeopolis explains that peace must begin as an individual decision. War, as Aristophanes saw it, was a corporate venture, and it was easier for an individual to make peace than for a group or a nation.

The Acharnians was followed by *The Peace* in 421 B.C., just before Sparta and Athens signed a treaty, and it seems clearly to have been written in support of the Athenian peace party, which had been growing powerful from the time of *The Acharnians* and whose cause had been aided by that play.

His second period is also dominated by the problems of war. Athens's ill-fated expedition to Sicily lies thematically beneath the surface of *The Birds* (414 B.C.), in which some citizens build Cloud-Cuckoo-Land to come between the world of humans and the world of the gods. *Lysistrata* (411 B.C.) is also from this period; its frank antiwar theme is related to the Sicilian wars and to the long-lasting and ultimately devastating Peloponnesian Wars. These wars were fought by Greek city-states in the areas south of Athens, the Peloponnesian Islands. The states had voluntarily contributed money to arm and support Athens against the Persians in 480 B.C. — resulting in the Athenian victory at Salamis. The states became angry when Pericles, the Athenian leader, demanded that they continue giving contributions, much of which he used in the rebuilding of the Akropolis and in other civic projects in Athens.

The other Greek city-states felt that Athens was becoming imperialistic and was overreaching itself. The struggles with the Peloponnesians and the difficulties of conducting a costly, long-distance war in Sicily combined eventually to exhaust the Athenian resources of men and funds. They were soundly defeated in 405 B.C. and surrendered to Sparta in 404. Unfortunately, Aristophanes lived to see the Spartan ships at rest in the harbors of Athens's chief port, the Piraeus. And he saw, too, the destruction of the walls of the city, leaving it essentially defenseless.

Aristophanes' third and final period, from 393 B.C. to his death, includes *The Ecclesiazusae* (translated as "The Women in Government"), in which women dress as men, find their way into parliament, and pass a new constitution. It is a highly topical play that points to the current situation in Athens and the people's general discontent and anxiety. The last part of *The Plutus*, written five years later, is an allegorical play about the god of wealth, who is eventually encouraged to make the just wealthy and the unjust poor.

Among the best known of Aristophanes' plays are several whose names refer to the disguises or costumes of the chorus, among them *The Knights*, *The Wasps*, and *The Frogs*. *The Frogs* (405 B.C.) is especially interesting for its focus on literary issues. It features a contest in the underworld between Aeschylus, who had been dead more than fifty years, and Euripides, who had just died at a relatively young age. In the course of the contest Aristophanes makes many interesting comments about Greek tragedy and the skills of the two authors.

Aristophanes is the only Greek comic playwright for whom we have more than one play. His legacy to the world of comedy is overwhelming, and his specific contribution — in the form of plays based on his work — from the Roman age to the present is incalculable.

LYSISTRATA

At the time *Lysistrata* was written (411 B.C.), Athens had had a steady diet of war for more than thirty years. Political groups were actively trying to convince Athenian leaders to discontinue the policies that had alienated Athens from the other city-states that were once its supporters in the Delian League, the group that had funded Athens' struggle against the Persian threat. The Athenian leaders were conducting distant wars and overextending their resources, and Aristophanes opposed the imperialist attitudes that seemed to contradict the democratic spirit of only a generation earlier.

Lysistrata makes it clear that war was the central business of the nation at this time. The men encountered by the heroine Lysistrata (whose name means "disband the army") on the Akropolis — men who guard the national security and the national treasury — are old and decrepit. The young men are in the field, and no sooner is one campaign ended than another begins. As Kalonike tells Lysistrata, her man has been away for five months. Such periods of separation were common, and these women are fed up. Lysistrata has gathered them together to propose a scheme to bring peace and negotiate a treaty.

The scheme is preposterous, but, typical of Old Comedy, its very outrageousness is its source of strength, and in time the idea begins to seem almost reasonable. Lysistrata asks the women to refuse to engage in sex with their husbands until the men stop making war. The women also seize the Akropolis and hold the treasury hostage. Without the national treasury there can be no war. And because they are confident of getting the support of the larger community of women in other nations — who suffer as they do — they do not fear the consequences of their acts.

The amusing scenes generated by this situation permit Aristophanes to poke fun at both sexes. We hear the gossipy conversation of the women, all of whom arrive late to Lysistrata's meeting. The men are dependent, helpless, and ineffectual and cannot resist the takeover. When the truth begins to settle in, the men solicit their wives' attention with enormous erections protruding beneath their gowns. The double meanings to the conversations are a great source of humor, but Aristophanes also counted on visual humor based on the ridiculous men roaming about with large, painful erections.

The wonderful scene (3) between Myrrhine (whose name means "fragrant and perfumed") and her husband Kinesias (whose name means "movement and agitation") is predicated on the audience's seeing the agony of the husband whose wife constantly promises, and then reneges, in order to build his sexual excitement to a fever pitch. It is no wonder that Lysistrata can eventually bring the men to sign any treaties she wants.

This heterosexual hilarity is also balanced by a number of homosexual allusions. Kleisthenes, possibly a bisexual Athenian, stands ready to relieve some of the men's sexual discomfort, while Lysistrata admits that if the men do not come around, the women will have to satisfy their own needs. Such frankness is typical of Athenian comedy. But the main source of humor is in the unrelieved sexual needs of the helpless and hapless men.

Women dominate the action of the play. They see the stupidity and waste of the war and devise the plan that will end it. They also observe that they pay their taxes in babies and that they are the ones who suffer most. The suffering of women had been a major theme in the tragedies of Euripides, and everyone in Aristophanes' audience would have understood Lysistrata's motivation. The idea that a woman should keep her place is expressed by several characters. And since Athenian audiences would have agreed that women should not meddle in war or government, Aristophanes offered them a play that challenged them on many levels.

Aristophanes praises Lysistrata's ingenuity and her perseverance. When the other women want to give up the plan because of their own sexual needs, she holds firm. She demands that they stand by their resolve. The picture of the strong, independent, intelligent, and capable woman obviously pleased the Athenians, since they permitted this play to be performed more than once (an unusual practice). Lysistrata became a recognizable and admirable character in Athenian life.

The following translation of *Lysistrata* has several interesting features. It is divided into scenes, a practice not done in the original Greek. The strophe and antistrophe are speeches given by the chorus moving first in one direction and then in the opposite direction. Instead of having a chorus of elders, as in *Antigone*, Aristophanes uses two choruses — one of men and one of women — that are truly representative of the people: They are as divided and antagonistic as Sophocles' chorus is united and wise. The KORYPHAIOS (leader) of the men's chorus speaks alone and often in opposition to the koryphaios of the women's chorus.

The rhyming patterns of some of the songs are approximated in English, and the sense of a country dialect is maintained in the speech of Lampito, who represents a kind of country bumpkin. She is also very muscular from the workouts that she and all other Spartans engaged in, and when she is taunted for her physique, Aristophanes reveals certain Athenian prejudices toward the Spartans.

Aristophanes is having fun with his audiences in this play. But as in so many comedies of all ages, the underlying themes are serious. As we laugh, we know we could almost as easily weep for the truth.

Aristophanes (c. 448–c. 385 B.C.)

LYSISTRATA   *411* B.C.
TRANSLATED BY DUDLEY FITTS

Persons Represented

LYSISTRATA ⎫
KALONIKE   ⎬ *Athenian women*
MYRRHINE   ⎭
LAMPITO, *a Spartan woman*
CHORUS
COMMISSIONER
KINESIAS, *husband of Myrrhine*
SPARTAN HERALD
SPARTAN AMBASSADOR
A SENTRY
[BABY SON OF KENESIAS
STRATYLLIS
SPARTANS
ATHENIANS]

Scene: *Athens. First, a public square; later, beneath the walls of the Akropolis;° later, a courtyard within the Akropolis.*

PROLOGUE° _____

(*Athens; a public square; early morning; Lysistrata alone.*)

LYSISTRATA: If someone had invited them to a
      festival —
   of Bacchos,° say; or to Pan's° shrine, or to
      Aphrodite's°
   over at Kolias — , you couldn't get through the
      streets,
   what with the drums and the dancing. But now,
   not a woman in sight!
5   Except — oh, yes!

(*Enter Kalonike.*)

Akropolis: Fortress of Athens, sacred to the goddess Athene.
Prologue: Portion of the play explaining the background and current action.   **2. Bacchos:** (Bacchus) God of wine and the object of wild, orgiastic ritual and celebration; also called Dionysos. **Pan:** God of nature, forests, flocks, and shepherds, depicted as half-man and half-goat. Pan was considered playful and lecherous.   **3. Aphrodite:** Goddess of love.

Here's one of my neighbors, at last. Good
      morning, Kalonike.
KALONIKE: Good morning, Lysistrata.
                                               Darling,
   don't frown so! You'll ruin your face!
LYSISTRATA: Never mind my face.
   Kalonike,
   the way we women behave! Really, I don't
      blame the men   10
   for what they say about us.
KALONIKE: No; I imagine they're right.
LYSISTRATA: For example: I call a meeting
   to think out a most important matter — and
      what happens?
   The women all stay in bed!
KALONIKE: Oh, they'll be along.
   It's hard to get away, you know: a husband, a
      cook,   15
   a child . . . Home life can be *so* demanding!
LYSISTRATA: What I have in mind is even more
   demanding.
KALONIKE: Tell me: what is it?
LYSISTRATA: It's big.
KALONIKE: Goodness! *How* big?
LYSISTRATA: Big enough for all of us.
KALONIKE: But we're not all here!
LYSISTRATA: We would be, if *that's* what was up!
                              No, Kalonike,   20
   this is something I've been turning over for
      nights,
   long sleepless nights.
KALONIKE: It must be getting worn down, then,
   if you've spent so much time on it.
LYSISTRATA: Worn down or not,
   it comes to this: Only we women can save
      Greece!
KALONIKE: Only we women? Poor Greece!
LYSISTRATA: Just the same,   25
   it's up to us. First, we must liquidate
   the Peloponnesians —
KALONIKE: Fun, fun!
LYSISTRATA: — and then the Boiotians.°

27. Boitians: Crude-mannered inhabitants of Boiotia, which was noted for its seafood.

KALONIKE: Oh! But not those heavenly eels!
LYSISTRATA: You needn't worry.
  I'm not talking about eels. — But here's the
    point:
30 If we can get the women from those places —
  all those Boiotians and Peloponnesians —
  to join us women here, why, we can save
  all Greece!
KALONIKE: But dearest Lysistrata!
  How can women do a thing so austere, so
35 political? We belong at home. Our only armor's
  our perfumes, our saffron dresses and
  our pretty little shoes!
LYSISTRATA: Exactly. Those
  transparent dresses, the saffron, the
    perfume, those pretty shoes —
KALONIKE: Oh?
LYSISTRATA: Not a single man would lift
  his spear —
KALONIKE: I'll send my dress to the dyer's
40 tomorrow!
LYSISTRATA: — or grab a shield —
KALONIKE: The sweetest little negligée —
LYSISTRATA: — or haul out his sword.
KALONIKE: I know where
  I can buy the dreamiest sandals!
LYSISTRATA: Well, so you see. Now, shouldn't
  the women have come?
KALONIKE: Come? They should have *flown!*
LYSISTRATA: Athenians are always late.
45 But imagine!
  There's no one here from the South Shore, or
    from Salamis.
KALONIKE: Things are hard over in Salamis, I
    swear.
  They have to get going at dawn.
LYSISTRATA: And nobody from Acharnai.
  I thought they'd be here hours ago.
KALONIKE: Well, you'll get
50 that awful Theagenes woman: she'll be
  a sheet or so in the wind.
    But look!
  Someone at last! Can you see who they are?

(Enter Myrrhine and other women.)

LYSISTRATA: They're from Anagyros.
KALONIKE: They certainly are.
  You'd know them anywhere, by the scent.
MYRRHINE: Sorry to be late, Lysistrata.
55 Oh come,
  don't scowl so. Say something!
LYSISTRATA: My dear Myrrhine,
  what is there to say? After all,
  you've been pretty casual about the whole thing.
MYRRHINE: Couldn't find

my girdle in the dark, that's all.
    But what *is*
  "the whole thing"?
KALONIKE: No, we've got to wait 60
  for those Boiotians and Peloponnesians.
LYSISTRATA: That's more like it. — But, look!
  Here's Lampito!

(Enter Lampito with women from Sparta.)

LYSISTRATA: Darling Lampito,
  how pretty you are today! What a nice color!
  Goodness, you look as though you could
    strangle a bull! 65
LAMPITO: Ah think Ah could! It's the work-out
  in the gym every day; and, of co'se that dance
    of ahs
  where y' kick yo' own tail.
KALONIKE: What an adorable figure!
LAMPITO: Lawdy, when y' touch me lahk that,
  Ah feel lahk a heifer at the altar!
LYSISTRATA: And this young lady? 70
  Where is she from?
LAMPITO: Boiotia. Social-Register type.
LYSISTRATA: Ah. "Boiotia of the fertile plain."
KALONIKE: And if you look,
  you'll find the fertile plain has just been mowed.
LYSISTRATA: And this lady?
LAMPITO: Hagh, wahd, handsome.
  She comes from Korinth.
KALONIKE: High and wide's the word for it.
LAMPITO: Which one of you 75
  called this heah meeting, and why?
LYSISTRATA: I did.
LAMPITO: Well, then, tell us:
  What's up?
MYRRHINE: Yes, darling, what *is* on your
  mind, after all?
LYSISTRATA: I'll tell you. — But first, one little
  question.
MYRRHINE: Well?
LYSISTRATA: It's your husbands. Fathers of your
  children. Doesn't it bother you
  that they're always off with the Army? I'll stake
    my life, 80
  not one of you has a man in the house this
    minute!
KALONIKE: Mine's been in Thrace the last five
  months, keeping an eye
  on that General.
MYRRHINE: Mine's been in Pylos for seven.
LAMPITO: And mahn,
  whenever he gets a *dis*charge, he goes raht back
  with that li'l ole shield of his, and enlists again! 85
LYSISTRATA: And not the ghost of a lover to be
  found!

From the very day the war began —

those Milesians!
I could skin them alive!

— I've not seen so much, even,
as one of those leather consolation prizes. —
But there! What's important is: If I've found a
90   way
to end the war, are you with me?
MYRRHINE: I should *say* so!
Even if I have to pawn my best dress and
drink up the proceeds.
KALONIKE: Me, too! Even if they split me
right up the middle, like a flounder.
LAMPITO: Ah'm shorely with you.
95   Ah'd crawl up Taygetos° on mah knees
if that'd bring peace.
LYSISTRATA: All right, then; here it is:
Women! Sisters!
If we really want our men to make peace,
we must be ready to give up —
MYRRHINE: Give up what?
Quick, tell us!
LYSISTRATA: But *will* you?
100 MYRRHINE: We will, even if it kills us.
LYSISTRATA: Then we must give up going to bed
with our men.

(*Long silence.*)

Oh? So now you're sorry? Won't look at me?
Doubtful? Pale? All teary-eyed?

But come: be frank with me.
Will you do it, or not? Well? Will you do it?
MYRRHINE: I couldn't. No.
Let the war go on.
105 KALONIKE: Nor I. Let the war go on.
LYSISTRATA: You, you little flounder,
ready to be split up the middle?
KALONIKE: Lysistrata, no!
I'd walk through fire for you — you *know* I
would! — but don't
ask us to give up *that!* Why, there's nothing like
it!
LYSISTRATA: And you?
BOIOTIAN: No. I must say *I'd* rather walk
110   through fire.
LYSISTRATA: What an utterly perverted sex we
women are!
No wonder poets write tragedies about us.
There's only one thing we can think of.

But you from Sparta:
if you stand by me, we may win yet! Will you?
It means so much!
115 LAMPITO: Ah sweah, it means *too* much!

95. Taygetos: A mountain range.

By the Two Goddesses,° it does! Asking a girl
to sleep — Heaven knows how long! — in a
great big bed
with nobody there but herself! But Ah'll stay
with you!
Peace comes first!
LYSISTRATA: Spoken like a true Spartan!
KALONIKE: But if —

oh dear!
— if we give up what you tell us to,   120
will there *be* any peace?
LYSISTRATA: Why, mercy, of course there will!
We'll just sit snug in our very thinnest gowns,
perfumed and powdered from top to bottom,
and those men
simply won't stand still! And when we say No,
they'll go out of their minds! And there's your
peace.   125
You can take my word for it.
LAMPITO: Ah seem to remember
that Colonel Menelaos threw his sword away
when he saw Helen's breast all bare.°
KALONIKE: But, goodness me!
What if they just get up and leave us?
LYSISTRATA: In that case
we'll have to fall back on ourselves, I suppose.   130
But they won't.
KALONIKE: I must say that's not much help. But
what if they drag us into the bedroom?
LYSISTRATA: Hang on to the door.
KALONIKE: What if they slap us?
LYSISTRATA: If they do, you'd better give in.
But be sulky about it. Do I have to teach you
how?
You know there's no fun for men when they
have to force you.   135
There are millions of ways of getting them to see
reason.
Don't you worry: a man
doesn't like it unless the girl cooperates.
KALONIKE: I suppose so. Oh, all right. We'll go
along.
LAMPITO: Ah imagine us Spahtans can arrange a
peace. But you   140
Athenians! Why, you're just war-mongerers!
LYSISTRATA: Leave that to me.
I know how to make them listen.
LAMPITO: Ah don't see how.
After all, they've got their boats; and there's lots
of money
piled up in the Akropolis.

116. Two Goddesses: A woman's oath referring to Demeter,
the earth goddess, and her daughter Persephone, who was
associated with seasonal cycles of fertility.

LYSISTRATA: The Akropolis? Darling,
145   we're taking over the Akropolis today!
        That's the older women's job. All the rest of us
        are going to the Citadel to sacrifice — you
        understand me?
        And once there, we're in for good!
LAMPITO: Whee! Up the rebels!
        Ah can see you're a good strat*ee*gist.
LYSISTRATA: Well, then, Lampito,
150   what we have to do now is take a solemn oath.
LAMPITO: Say it. We'll sweah.
LYSISTRATA: This is it.
        — But where's our Inner Guard?
                    — Look, Guard: you see this shield?
        Put it down here. Now bring me the victim's
        entrails.
KALONIKE: But the oath?
LYSISTRATA: You remember how in
        Aischylos' *Seven*°
        they killed a sheep and swore on a shield? Well,
155   then?
KALONIKE: But I don't see how you can swear for
        peace on a shield.
LYSISTRATA: What else do you suggest?
KALONIKE: Why not a white horse?
        We could swear by that.
LYSISTRATA: And where will you get
        a white horse?
KALONIKE: I never thought of that. *What* can we
        do?
LYSISTRATA: I have it!
160   Let's set this big black wine-bowl on the ground
        and pour in a gallon or so of Thasian,° and
        swear
        not to add one drop of water.
LAMPITO: Ah lahk *that* oath!
LYSISTRATA: Bring the bowl and the wine-jug.
KALONIKE: Oh, what a simply *huge* one!
LYSISTRATA: Set it down. Girls, place your hands on
        the gift-offering.
        O Goddess of Persuasion! And thou, O Loving-
165   cup:
        Look upon this our sacrifice, and
        be gracious!
KALONIKE: See the blood spill out. How red and
        pretty it is!
LAMPITO: And Ah must say it smells good.
MYRRHINE: Let me swear first!
170 KALONIKE: No, by Aphrodite, we'll match for it!

154. Seven: Aeschylus' *Seven Against Thebes*, which deals
with the war between the sons of Oedipus for the throne of
Thebes.   **161. Thasian:** Wine from Thasos.

LYSISTRATA: Lampito: all of you women: come,
        touch the bowl,
        and repeat after me — remember, this is an
        oath — :
        I WILL HAVE NOTHING TO DO WITH MY
        HUSBAND OR MY LOVER
KALONIKE: *I will have nothing to do with my
        husband or my lover*
LYSISTRATA: THOUGH HE COME TO ME IN
        PITIABLE CONDITION   175
KALONIKE: *Though he come to me in pitiable
        condition*
        (Oh Lysistrata! This is killing me!)
LYSISTRATA: IN MY HOUSE I WILL BE
        UNTOUCHABLE
KALONIKE: *In my house I will be untouchable*
LYSISTRATA: IN MY THINNEST SAFFRON SILK   180
KALONIKE: *In my thinnest saffron silk*
LYSISTRATA: AND MAKE HIM LONG FOR ME.
KALONIKE: *And make him long for me.*
LYSISTRATA: I WILL NOT GIVE MYSELF
KALONIKE: *I will not give myself*   185
LYSISTRATA: AND IF HE CONSTRAINS ME
KALONIKE: *And if he constrains me*
LYSISTRATA: I WILL BE COLD AS ICE AND
        NEVER MOVE
KALONIKE: *I will be cold as ice and never move*
LYSISTRATA: I WILL NOT LIFT MY SLIPPERS
        TOWARD THE CEILING   190
KALONIKE: *I will not lift my slippers toward the
        ceiling*
LYSISTRATA: OR CROUCH ON ALL FOURS LIKE
        THE LIONESS IN THE CARVING
KALONIKE: *Or crouch on all fours like the lioness
        in the carving*
LYSISTRATA: AND IF I KEEP THIS OATH LET ME
        DRINK FROM THIS BOWL
KALONIKE: *And if I keep this oath let me drink
        from this bowl*   195
LYSISTRATA: IF NOT, LET MY OWN BOWL BE
        FILLED WITH WATER.
KALONIKE: *If not, let my own bowl be filled with
        water.*
LYSISTRATA: You have all sworn?
MYRRHINE: We have.
LYSISTRATA: Then thus
        I sacrifice the victim.

(*Drinks largely.*)

KALONIKE: Save some for us!
        Here's to you, darling, and to you, and to you!   200

(*Loud cries off-stage.*)

LAMPITO: What's all *that* whoozy-goozy?
LYSISTRATA: Just what I told you.

The older women have taken the Akropolis.
Now you, Lampito,
rush back to Sparta. We'll take care of things
here. Leave
these girls here for hostages.
205   The rest of you,
up to the Citadel: and mind you push in the
bolts.
KALONIKE: But the men? Won't they be after us?
LYSISTRATA: Just you leave
the men to me. There's not fire enough in the
world,
or threats either, to make me open these doors
except on my own terms.
210 KALONIKE: I hope not, by Aphrodite!
After all,
we've got a reputation for bitchiness to live up
to.   (*Exeunt.°*)

PARODOS:°
CHORAL EPISODE _____

(*The hillside just under the Akropolis. Enter Chorus
of Old Men with burning torches and braziers; much
puffing and coughing.*)

KORYPHAIOS^(man)°: Forward march, Drakes, old
friend: never you mind
that damn big log banging hell down on your
back.

Strophe° 1

CHORUS^(men): There's this to be said for longevity:
You see things you thought that you'd never see.
Look, Strymodoros, who would have thought
5   it?
We've caught it —
the New Femininity!
The wives of our bosom, our board, our bed —
Now, by the gods, they've gone ahead
And taken the Citadel (Heaven knows why!),
10 Profanèd the sacred statuar-y,
And barred the doors,
The subversive whores!
KORYPHAIOS^(m): Shake a leg there, Philurgos, man:
the Akropolis or bust!

Put the kindling around here. We'll build one
almighty big
bonfire for the whole bunch of bitches, every last
one;   15
and the first we fry will be old Lykon's woman.

Antistrophe° 1

CHORUS^(m): They're not going to give me the old
horse-laugh!
No, by Demeter, they won't pull this off!
Think of Kleomenes: even he
Didn't go free
till he brought me his stuff.   20
A good man he was, all stinking and shaggy,
Bare as an eel except for the bag he
Covered his rear with. God, what a mess!
Never a bath in six years, I'd guess.
Pure Sparta, man!   25
He also ran.
KORYPHAIOS^(m): That was a siege, friends! Seventeen
ranks strong
we slept at the Gate. And shall we not do as
much
against these women, whom God and Euripides
hate?
If we don't, I'll turn in my medals from
Marathon.   30

Strophe 2

CHORUS^(m): Onward and upward! A little push,
And we're there.
Ouch, my shoulders! I could wish
For a pair
Of good strong oxen. Keep your eye   35
On the fire there, it mustn't die.
Akh! Akh!
The smoke would make a cadaver cough!

Antistrophe 2

Holy Herakles, a hot spark
Bit my eye!   40
Damn this hellfire, damn this work!
So say I.
Onward and upward just the same.
(Laches, remember the Goddess: for shame!)
Akh! Akh!   45
The smoke would make a cadaver cough!
KORYPHAIOS^(m): At last (and let us give suitable
thanks to God

Exeunt: Latin for "they go out." Parodos: The song or ode
chanted by the Chorus on their entry. Koryphaios: Leader
of the Chorus; also called Choragos. There are two Choruses
and two Koryphaioi, one male and one female. Strophe: Song
sung by the Chorus as they danced from stage right to stage
left.

Antistrophe: Song sung by the Chorus following the Strophe,
as they danced back from stage left to stage right.

for his infinite mercies) I have managed to bring
my personal flame to the common goal. It
    breathes, it lives.
50   Now, gentlemen, let us consider. Shall we insert
the torch, say, into the brazier, and thus extract
a kindling brand? And shall we then, do you
    think,
push on to the gate like valiant sheep? On the
    whole yes.
But I would have you consider this, too: if
    they —
55   I refer to the women — should refuse to open,
what then? Do we set the doors afire
and smoke them out? At ease, men. Meditate.
Akh, the smoke! Woof! What we really need
is the loan of a general or two from the Samos
    Command.°
60   At least we've got this lumber off our backs.
That's something. And now let's look to our fire.

O Pot, brave Brazier, touch my torch with
    flame!
Victory, Goddess, I invoke thy name!
Strike down these paradigms of female pride,
65   And we shall hang our trophies up inside.

(*Enter Chorus of Old Women on the walls of the
Akropolis, carrying jars of water.*)

KORYPHAIOS(woman): Smoke, girls, smoke! There's
    smoke all over the place!
Probably fire, too. Hurry, girls! Fire! Fire!

Strophe 1

CHORUS(women): Nikodike, run!
Or Kalyke's done
70   To a turn, and poor Kritylla's
Smoked like a ham.
            Damn
These old men! Are we too late?
I nearly died down at the place
Where we fill our jars:
75   Slaves pushing and jostling —
    Such a hustling
I never saw in all my days.

Antistrophe 1

But here's water at last.
Haste, sisters, haste!
80   Slosh it on them, slosh it down,
The silly old wrecks!

---

59. Samos Command: Headquarters of the Athenian military.

Sex
Almighty! What they want's
A hot bath? Good. Send one down.
Athena of Athens town,
    Trito-born!° Helm of Gold!   85
Cripple the old
Firemen! Help us help them drown!

(*The old men capture a woman, Stratyllis.*)

STRATYLLIS: Let me go! Let me go!
KORYPHAIOS(w):   You walking corpses,
have you no shame?
KORYPHAIOS(m):   I wouldn't have believed it!
An army of women in the Akropolis!   90
KORYPHAIOS(w): So we scare you, do we? Grandpa,
    you've seen
only our pickets yet!
KORYPHAIOS(m):   Hey, Phaidrias!
Help me with the necks of these jabbering hens!
KORYPHAIOS(w): Down with your pots, girls! We'll
    need both hands
if these antiques attack us!
KORYPHAIOS(m):   Want your face kicked in?   95
KORYPHAIOS(w): Want your balls chewed off?
KORYPHAIOS(m):   Look out! I've got a stick!
KORYPHAIOS(w): You lay a half-inch of your stick on
    Stratyllis,
and you'll never stick again!
KORYPHAIOS(m): Fall apart!
KORYPHAIOS(w):   I'll spit up your guts!
KORYPHAIOS(m):   Euripides! Master!
How well you knew women!
KORYPHAIOS(w):   Listen to him, Rhodippe,   100
up with the pots!
KORYPHAIOS(m):   Demolition of God,
what good are your pots?
KORYPHAIOS(w):   You refugee from the tomb,
what good is your fire?
KORYPHAIOS(m):   Good enough to make a pyre
to barbecue you!
KORYPHAIOS(w): We'll squizzle your kindling!
KORYPHAIOS(m): You think so?
KORYPHAIOS(w):   Yah! Just hang around a while!   105
KORYPHAIOS(m): Want a touch of my torch?
KORYPHAIOS(w):   It needs a good soaping.
KORYPHAIOS(m): How about you?
KORYPHAIOS(w):   Soap for a senile bridegroom!
KORYPHAIOS(m): Senile? Hold your trap
KORYPHAIOS(w):   Just *you* try to hold it!
KORYPHAIOS(m): The yammer of women!
KORYPHAIOS(w):   Oh is that so?
You're not in the jury room now, you know.   110

---

85. Trito-born: Athena, goddess of wisdom, was said to have
been born near Lake Tritonis, in Libya.

KORYPHAIOS[(m)]: Gentlemen, I beg you, burn off that
    woman's hair!
KORYPHAIOS[(w)]: Let it come down!

(*They empty their pots on the men.*)

KORYPHAIOS[(m)]: What a way to drown!
KORYPHAIOS[(w)]:   Hot, hey?
KORYPHAIOS[(m)]:   Say,
    enough!
KORYPHAIOS[(w)]: Dandruff
115   needs watering. I'll make you
    nice and fresh.
KORYPHAIOS[(m)]:   For God's sake, you,
    hold off!

SCENE 1

(*Enter a Commissioner accompanied by four
constables.*)

COMMISSIONER: These degenerate women! What a
    racket of little drums,
    what a yapping for Adonis° on every house-top!
    It's like the time in the Assembly when I was
      listening
    to a speech — out of order, as usual — by that
      fool
5   Demostratos,° all about troops for Sicily,°
    that kind of nonsense —
                and there was his wife
    trotting around in circles howling
    Alas for Adonis! —
               and Demostratos insisting
    we must draft every last Zakynthian that can
      walk —
10   and his wife up there on the roof,
    drunk as an owl, yowling
    Oh weep for Adonis! —
             and that damned ox Demostratos
    mooing away through the rumpus. That's what
      we get
    for putting up with this wretched woman-
      business!
KORYPHAIOS[(m)]: Sir, you haven't heard the half of it.
15   They laughed at us!
    Insulted us! They took pitchers of water
    and nearly drowned us! We're still wringing out
      our clothes,
    for all the world like unhousebroken brats.
COMMISSIONER: Serves you right, by Poseidon!

---

2. **Adonis:** Fertility god, loved by Aphrodite.   5. **Demostratos:**
Athenian orator and politician. **Sicily:** Reference to the Sicilian
Expedition (416 B.C.) in which Athens was decisively defeated.

Whose fault is it if these women-folk of ours   20
get out of hand? We coddle them,
we teach them to be wasteful and loose. You'll
    see a husband
go into a jeweler's. "Look," he'll say,
"jeweler," he'll say, "you remember that gold
    choker
you made for my wife? Well, she went to a
    dance last night   25
and broke the clasp. Now, I've got to go to
    Salamis,
and can't be bothered. Run over to my house
    tonight,
will you, and see if you can put it together for
    her."
Or another one
goes to a cobbler — a good strong workman,
    too,   30
with an awl that was never meant for child's
    play. "Here,"
he'll tell him, "one of my wife's shoes is
    pinching
her little toe. Could you come up about noon
and stretch it out for her?"
                   Well, what do you expect?
Look at me, for example, I'm a Public Officer,   35
and it's one of my duties to pay off the sailors.
And where's the money? Up there in the
    Akropolis!
And those blasted women slam the door in my
    face!
But what are we waiting for?
                 — Look here, constable,
stop sniffing around for a tavern, and get us   40
some crowbars. We'll force their gates! As a
    matter of fact,
I'll do a little forcing myself.

(*Enter Lysistrata, above, with Myrrhine, Kalonike,
and the Boiotian.*)

LYSISTRATA: No need of forcing.
Here I am, of my own accord. And all this talk
about locked doors — ! We don't need locked
    doors,
but just the least bit of common sense.   45
COMMISSIONER: Is that so, ma'am!
                — Where's my constable?
                    — Constable,
arrest that woman, and tie her hands behind her.
LYSISTRATA: If he touches me, I swear by Artemis
there'll be one scamp dropped from the public
    pay-roll tomorrow!
COMMISSIONER: Well, constable? You're not afraid,
    I suppose? Grab her,   50
two of you, around the middle!

KALONIKE: No, by Pandrosos!°
  Lay a hand on her, and I'll jump on you so hard
  your guts will come out the back door!
COMMISSIONER: That's what *you* think!
  Where's the sergeant? — Here, you: tie up that
    trollop first,
the one with the pretty talk!
55 MYRRHINE: By the Moon-Goddess,°
  just try! They'll have to scoop you up with a
    spoon!
COMMISSIONER: Another one!
                Officer, seize that woman!
                        I swear
  I'll put an end to this riot!
BOIOTIAN: By the Taurian,°
  one inch closer, you'll be one screaming bald-
    head!
COMMISSIONER: Lord, what a mess! And my
60   constables seem ineffective.
  But — women get the best of us? By God, no!
                    — Skythians!°
  Close ranks and forward march!
LYSISTRATA: "Forward," indeed!
  By the Two Goddesses, what's the sense in *that?*
  They're up against four companies of women
  armed from top to bottom.
65 COMMISSIONER: Forward, my Skythians!
LYSISTRATA: Forward, yourselves, dear comrades!
  You grainlettucebeanseedmarket girls!
  You garlicandonionbreadbakery girls!
  Give it to 'em! Knock 'em down! Scratch 'em!
  Tell 'em what you think of 'em!

(*General melee, the Skythians yield.*)

70   — Ah, that's enough!
  Sound a retreat: good soldiers don't rob the
    dead.
COMMISSIONER: A nice day *this* has been for the
    police!
LYSISTRATA: Well, there you are. — Did you really
    think we women
  would be driven like slaves? Maybe now you'll
    admit
  that a woman knows something about spirit.
75 COMMISSIONER: Spirit enough,
  especially spirits in bottles! Dear Lord Apollo!
KORYPHAIOS[(m)]: Your Honor, there's no use talking
    to them. Words

---

51. **Pandrosos:** A woman's oath referring to one of the
daughters of the founder of Athens.   55. **Moon-Goddess:**
Artemis, goddess of the hunt and of fertility, daughter of
Zeus.   58. **Taurian:** Reference to Artemis who was said to
have been worshiped in a cult at Taurica Chersonesos.   61.
Skythians: Athenian archers.

mean nothing whatever to wild animals like
  these.
Think of the sousing they gave us! and the water
  was not, I believe, of the purest.   80
KORYPHAIOS[(w)]: You shouldn't have come after us.
  And if you try it again,
  you'll be one eye short! — Although, as a matter
    .of fact,
what I like best is just to stay at home and read,
like a sweet little bride: never hurting a soul, no,
never going out. But if you *must* shake hornets'
    nests,   85
look out for the hornets.

Strophe 1

CHORUS[(m)]: Of all the beasts that God hath
    wrought
    What monster's worse than woman?
Who shall encompass with his thought
    Their guile unending? No man.   90

They've seized the Heights, the Rock, the
    Shrine —
    But to what end? I wot not.
Sure there's some clue to their design!
    Have you the key? I thought not.
KORYPHAIOS[(m)]: We might question them, I suppose.
  But I warn you, sir,   95
don't believe anything you hear! It would be un-
    Athenian
not to get to the bottom of this plot.
COMMISSIONER: Very well.
  My first question is this: Why, so help you God,
  did you bar the gates of the Akropolis?
LYSISTRATA: Why?
  To keep the money, of course. No money, no
    war.   100
COMMISSIONER: You think that money's the cause
    of war?
LYSISTRATA: I do.
  Money brought about that Peisandros° business
  and all the other attacks on the State. Well and
    good!
  They'll not get another cent here!
COMMISSIONER: And what will you do?
LYSISTRATA: What a question! From now on, we
    intend   105
  to control the Treasury.
COMMISSIONER: Control the Treasury!
LYSISTRATA: Why not? Does that seem strange?

---

102. **Peisandros:** A politician who plotted against the Athenian
democracy.

After all,
we control our household budgets.
COMMISSIONER: But that's different!
LYSISTRATA: "Different"? What do you mean?
COMMISSIONER: I mean simply this:
110   it's the Treasury that pays for National Defense.
LYSISTRATA: Unnecessary. We propose to abolish
  war.
COMMISSIONER: Good God. — And National
  Security?
LYSISTRATA: Leave that to us.
COMMISSIONER: You?
LYSISTRATA: Us.
COMMISSIONER: We're done for, then!
LYSISTRATA: Never mind.
  We women will save you in spite of yourselves.
COMMISSIONER: What nonsense!
LYSISTRATA: If you like. But you must accept it, like
115   it or not.
COMMISSIONER: Why, this is downright subversion!
LYSISTRATA: Maybe it is.
  But we're going to save you, Judge.
COMMISSIONER: I don't *want* to be saved.
LYSISTRATA: Tut. The death-wish. All the more
  reason.
COMMISSIONER: But the idea of women bothering
  themselves about peace and war!
LYSISTRATA: Will you listen to me?
120 COMMISSIONER: Yes. But be brief, or I'll —
LYSISTRATA: This is no time for stupid threats.
COMMISSIONER: By the gods,
  I can't stand any more!
AN OLD WOMAN: Can't stand? Well, well.
COMMISSIONER: That's enough out of you, you old
  buzzard!
  Now, Lysistrata: tell me what you're thinking.
LYSISTRATA: Glad to.
125   Ever since this war began
  We women have been watching you men,
    agreeing with you,
  keeping our thoughts to ourselves. That doesn't
    mean
  we were happy: we weren't, for we saw how
    things were going;
  but we'd listen to you at dinner
  arguing this way and that.
130   — Oh you, and your big
  Top Secrets! —
        And then we'd grin like little patriots
  (though goodness knows we didn't feel like
    grinning) and ask you:
  "Dear, did the Armistice come up in Assembly
    today?"
  And you'd say, "None of your business! Pipe
    down!," you'd say.
  And so we would.

AN OLD WOMAN: *I* wouldn't have, by God!   135
COMMISSIONER: You'd have taken a beating, then!
        — Go on.
LYSISTRATA: Well, we'd be quiet. But then, you
  know, all at once
  you men would think up something worse than
    ever.
  Even *I* could see it was fatal. And, "Darling,"
    I'd say,
  "have you gone completely mad?" And my
    husband would look at me   140
  and say, "Wife, you've got your weaving to
    attend to.
  Mind your tongue, if you don't want a slap.
    'War's
  a man's affair!' "°
COMMISSIONER: Good words, and well pronounced.
LYSISTRATA: You're a fool if you think so.
        It was hard enough
  to put up with all this banquet-hall strategy.   145
  But then we'd hear you out in the public square:
  "Nobody left for the draft-quota here in
    Athens?"
  you'd say; and, "No," someone else would say,
    "not a man!"
  And so we women decided to rescue Greece.
  You might as well listen to us now: you'll have
    to, later.   150
COMMISSIONER: *You* rescue Greece? Absurd.
LYSISTRATA: You're the absurd one.
COMMISSIONER: You expect me to take orders from
  a woman?
        I'd die first!
LYSISTRATA: Heavens, if that's what's bothering
  you, take my veil,
  here, and wrap it around your poor head.
KALONIKE: Yes,
  and you can have my market-basket, too.   155
  Go home, tighten your girdle, do the washing,
    mind
  your beans! "War's
  a woman's affair!"
KORYPHAIOS[w]: Ground pitchers! Close
  ranks!

Antistrophe

CHORUS[w]: This is a dance that I know well,
    My knees shall never yield.   160
  Wobble and creak I may, but still
    I'll keep the well-fought field.
  Valor and grace march on before,
    Love prods us from behind.

142–143. 'War's a man's affair!': Quoted from Homer's
Iliad, VI, 492, Hector's farewell to his wife, Andromache.

165 Our slogan is EXCELSIOR,
    Our watchword SAVE MANKIND.
KORYPHAIOS^(w): Women, remember your
    grandmothers! Remember
that little old mother of yours, what a stinger
    she was!
On, on, never slacken. There's a strong wind
    astern!
LYSISTRATA: O Eros of delight! O Aphrodite!
170   Kyprian!°
If ever desire has drenched our breasts or
    dreamed
in our thighs, let it work so now on the men of
    Hellas°
that they shall tail us through the land, slaves,
    slaves
to Woman, Breaker of Armies!
COMMISSIONER: And if we do?
LYSISTRATA: Well, for one thing, we shan't have to
175   watch you
going to market, a spear in one hand, and
    heaven knows
what in the other.
KALONIKE: Nicely said, by Aphrodite!
LYSISTRATA: As things stand now, you're neither
    men nor women.
Armor clanking with kitchen pans and pots —
180 You sound like a pack of Korybantes!°
COMMISSIONER: A man must do what a man must
    do.
LYSISTRATA: So I'm told.
But to see a General, complete with Gorgon-
    shield,
jingling along the dock to buy a couple of
    herrings!
KALONIKE: *I* saw a Captain the other day — lovely
    fellow he was,
nice curly hair — sitting on his horse; and —
185   can you believe it? —
he'd just bought some soup, and was pouring it
    into his helmet!
And there was a soldier from Thrace
swishing his lance like something out of
    Euripides,
and the poor fruit-store woman got so scared
190 that she ran away and let him have his figs free!
COMMISSIONER: All this is beside the point.
                Will you be so kind
as to tell me how you mean to save Greece?

170. **Kyprian:** Reference to Aphrodite's association with Cy-
prus (Kyprus), a place sacred to her and a center for her
worship.   172. **Hellas:** Greece.   180. **Korybantes:** Priestesses
of Cybele, a fertility goddess, who was celebrated in frenzied
rituals accompanied by the beating of cymbals.

LYSISTRATA: Of course.
Nothing could be simpler.
COMMISSIONER: I assure you, I'm all ears.
LYSISTRATA: Do you know anything about weaving?
Say the yarn gets tangled: we thread it   195
this way and that through the skein, up and
    down,
until it's free. And it's like that with war.
We'll send our envoys
up and down, this way and that, all over
    Greece,
until it's finished.
COMMISSIONER: Yarn? Thread? Skein?   200
Are you out of your mind? I tell you,
war is a serious business.
LYSISTRATA: So serious
that I'd like to go on talking about weaving.
COMMISSIONER: All right. Go ahead.
LYSISTRATA: The first thing we have to do
is to wash our yarn, get the dirt out of it.   205
You see? Isn't there too much dirt here in
    Athens?
You must wash those men away.
                Then our spoiled wool —
that's like your job-hunters, out for a life
of no work and big pay. Back to the basket,
citizens or not, allies or not,   210
or friendly immigrants.
               And your colonies?
Hanks of wool lost in various places. Pull them
together, weave them into one great whole,
and our voters are clothed for ever.
COMMISSIONER: It would take a woman
to reduce state questions to a matter of carding
    and weaving.   215
LYSISTRATA: You fool! Who were the mothers
    whose sons sailed off
to fight for Athens in Sicily?
COMMISSIONER: Enough!
I beg you, do not call back those memories.
LYSISTRATA: And then,
instead of the love that every woman needs,
we have only our single beds, where we can
    dream
of our husbands off with the Army.   220
               Bad enough for wives!
But what about our girls, getting older every
    day,
and older, and no kisses?
COMMISSIONER: Men get older, too.
LYSISTRATA: Not in the same sense.
          A soldier's discharged,
and he may be bald and toothless, yet he'll find   225
a pretty young thing to go to bed with.
             But a woman!
Her beauty is gone with the first gray hair.

She can spend her time
consulting the oracles and the fortune-tellers,
230   but they'll never send her a husband.
COMMISSIONER: Still, if a man can rise to the
    occasion —
LYSISTRATA: Rise? Rise, yourself!

(*Furiously.*)

Go invest in a coffin!
                        You've money enough.
                                    I'll bake you
a cake for the Underworld.
                        And here's your funeral
wreath!

(*She pours water upon him.*)

MYRRHINE: And here's another!

(*More water.*)

KALONIKE:
                                    And here's
my contribution!

(*More water.*)

LYSISTRATA: What are you waiting for?
All aboard Styx Ferry!
                        Charon's° calling for you!
It's sailing-time: don't disrupt the schedule!
COMMISSIONER: The insolence of women! And to
    me!
240   No, by God, I'll go back to town and show
    the rest of the Commission what might happen
    to them.   (*Exit Commissioner.*)
LYSISTRATA: Really, I suppose we should have laid
    out his corpse
on the doorstep, in the usual way.
                                    But never mind.
We'll give him the rites of the dead tomorrow
morning.
            (*Exit Lysistrata with Myrrhine and Kalonike.*)

PARABASIS:° CHORAL
EPISODE · Ode° 1 _____

KORYPHAIOS[(m)]: Sons of Liberty, awake! The day of
    glory is at hand.

---

237. **Charon:** The god who ferried the souls of the newly
dead across the river Styx to Hades. **Parabasis:** Section of
the play in which the author presented his own views through
the Koryphaios directly to the audience. The parabasis in
Lysistrata is shorter than those in Aristophanes' other works
and unusual in that the Koryphaios does not speak directly
for the author.   **Ode:** Song sung by the Chorus.

CHORUS[(m)]: I smell tyranny afoot, I smell it rising
    from the land.
I scent a trace of Hippias,° I sniff upon the
    breeze
A dismal Spartan hogo that suggests King
    Kleisthenes.°
Strip, strip for action, brothers!   5
Our wives, aunts, sisters, mothers
Have sold us out: the streets are full of godless
    female rages.
Shall we stand by and let our women confiscate
    our wages?

                                    [Epirrhema° 1]
KORYPHAIOS[(m)]: Gentlemen, it's a disgrace to
    Athens, a disgrace
to all that Athens stands for, if we allow these
    grandmas   10
to jabber about spears and shields and making
    friends
with the Spartans. What's a Spartan? Give me a
    wild wolf
any day. No. They want the Tyranny back, I
    suppose.
Are we going to take that? No. Let us look like
the innocent serpent, but be the flower under it,   15
as the poet sings. And just to begin with,
I propose to poke a number of teeth
down the gullet of that harridan over there.

Antode 1

KORYPHAIOS[(w)]: Oh, is that so? When you get
    home, your own mamma won't know you!
CHORUS[(w)]: Who do you think we are, you senile
    bravos? Well, I'll show you.   20
I bore the sacred vessels in my eighth year,° and
    at ten
I was pounding out the barley for Athena
    Goddess;° then
They made me Little Bear
At the Braunonian Fair;°

---

3. **Hippias:** An Athenian tyrant.   4. **Kleisthenes:** A bisexual
Athenian. **Epirrhema:** A part of the parabasis spoken by the
Koryphaios following an ode delivered by his or her half of
the Chorus.   21. **eighth year:** Young girls between the ages
of seven and eleven served in the temple of Athena in the
Akropolis.   22. **pounding out the barley for Athena goddess:**
At age ten a girl could be chosen to grind the sacred grain
of Athena.   24. **Braunonian Fair:** A ritual in the cult of
Artemis, who is associated with wild beasts, in which young
girls dressed up as bears and danced for the goddess.

25   I'd held the Holy Basket° by the time I was of
      age,
      The Blessed Dry Figs had adorned my plump
        decolletage.

[Antepirrhema° 1]

KORYPHAIOS⁽ʷ⁾: A "disgrace to Athens," and I, just
      at the moment
      I'm giving Athens the best advice she ever had?
      Don't I pay taxes to the State? Yes, I pay them
30   in baby boys. And what do you contribute,
      you impotent horrors? Nothing but waste: all
      our Treasury,° dating back to the Persian Wars,
      gone! rifled! And not a penny out of your
        pockets!
      Well, then? Can you cough up an answer to
        that?
35   Look out for your own gullet, or you'll get a
        crack
      from this old brogan that'll make your teeth see
        stars!

Ode 2

CHORUS⁽ᵐ⁾: Oh insolence!
      Am I unmanned?
      Incontinence!
40   Shall my scarred hand
      Strike never a blow
      To curb this flow-
      ing female curse?

      Leipsydrion!°
45   Shall I betray
      The laurels won
      On that great day?
      Come, shake a leg,
      Shed old age, beg
50   The years reverse!

[Epirrhema 2]

KORYPHAIOS⁽ᵐ⁾: Give them an inch, and we're done
      for! We'll have them
      launching boats next and planning naval
        strategy,
      sailing down on us like so many Artemisias.
      Or maybe they have ideas about the cavalry.
55   That's fair enough, women are certainly good

in the saddle. Just look at Mikon's paintings,
all those Amazons wrestling with all those men!
On the whole, a straitjacket's their best uniform.

Antode 2

CHORUS⁽ʷ⁾: Tangle with me,
      And you'll get cramps.   60
      Ferocity
      's no use now, Gramps!
      By the Two,
      I'll get through
      To you wrecks yet!   65

      I'll scramble your eggs,
      I'll burn your beans,
      With my two legs.
      You'll see such scenes
      As never yet   70
      Your two eyes met.
      A curse? You bet!

[Antepirrhema 2]

KORYPHAIOS⁽ʷ⁾: If Lampito stands by me, and that
      delicious Theban girl,
      Ismenia — what good are *you*? You and your
        seven
      Resolutions! Resolutions? Rationing Boiotian eels   75
      and making our girls go without them at
        Hekate's° Feast!
      That was statesmanship! And we'll have to put
        up with it
      and all the rest of your decrepit legislation
      until some patriot — God give him strength! —
      grabs you by the neck and kicks you off the
      Rock.   80

SCENE 2

(*Reenter Lysistrata and her lieutenants.*)

KORYPHAIOS⁽ʷ⁾ (*tragic tone*): Great Queen, fair
      Architect of our emprise,
      Why lookst thou on us with foreboding eyes?
LYSISTRATA: The behavior of these idiotic women!
      There's something about the female temperament
      that I can't bear!
KORYPHAIOS⁽ʷ⁾:   What in the world do you
      mean?   5
LYSISTRATA: Exactly what I say.
KORYPHAIOS⁽ʷ⁾: What dreadful thing has happened?
      Come, tell us: we're all your friends.

---

25. Holy Basket: In one ritual to Athena, young girls carried
baskets of objects sacred to the goddess. **Antepirrhema:** The
speech delivered by the second Koryphaios after the second
half of the Chorus had sung an ode.   **32. Treasury:** Athenian
politicians were raiding the funds that were collected by
Athens to finance a war against Persia.   **44. Leipsydrion:**
A place where Athenian patriots had heroically fought.

76. Hekate: Patron of successful wars, object of a Boiotian
cult (later associated with sorcery).

LYSISTRATA: It isn't easy
  to say it; yet, God knows, we can't hush it up.
KORYPHAIOS^(w): Well, then? Out with it!
LYSISTRATA: To put it bluntly,
  we're dying to get laid.
10 KORYPHAIOS^(w):   Almighty God!
LYSISTRATA: Why bring God into it? — No, it's just
    as I say.
  I can't manage them any longer: they've gone
    man-crazy,
  they're all trying to get out.
                  Why, look:
  one of them was sneaking out the back door
15 over there by Pan's cave; another
  was sliding down the walls with rope and tackle;
  another was climbing aboard a sparrow, ready
    to take off
  for the nearest brothel — I dragged *her* back by
    the hair!
  They're all finding some reason to leave.
                  Look there!
  There goes another one.
20   — Just a minute, you!
  Where are you off to so fast?
FIRST WOMAN: I've got to get home.
  I've a lot of Milesian wool, and the worms are
    spoiling it.
LYSISTRATA: Oh bother you and your worms! Get
    back inside!
FIRST WOMAN: I'll be back right away, I swear I
    will.
25 I just want to get it stretched out on my bed.
LYSISTRATA: You'll do no such thing. You'll stay
    right here.
FIRST WOMAN: And my wool?
  You want it ruined?
LYSISTRATA: Yes, for all I care.
SECOND WOMAN: Oh dear! My lovely new flax
    from Amorgos —
  I left it at home, all uncarded!
LYSISTRATA: Another one!
30 And all she wants is someone to card her flax.
  Get back in there!
SECOND WOMAN: But I swear by the Moon-
    Goddess,
  the minute I get it done, I'll be back!
LYSISTRATA: I say No.
  If you, why not all the other women as well?
THIRD WOMAN: O Lady Eileithyia!° Radiant
    goddess! Thou
  intercessor for women in childbirth! Stay, I pray
35   thee,

oh stay this parturition. Shall I pollute
  a sacred spot?°
LYSISTRATA: And what's the matter with *you?*
THIRD WOMAN: I'm having a baby — any minute
    now.
LYSISTRATA: But you weren't pregnant yesterday.
THIRD WOMAN: Well, I am today.
  Let me go home for a midwife, Lysistrata: 40
  there's not much time.
LYSISTRATA: I never heard such nonsense.
  What's that bulging under your cloak?
THIRD WOMAN: A little baby boy.
LYSISTRATA: It certainly isn't. But it's something
    hollow,
  like a basin or — Why, it's the helmet of
    Athena!
  And you said you were having a baby.
THIRD WOMAN: Well, I am! So there! 45
LYSISTRATA: Then why the helmet?
THIRD WOMAN: I was afraid that my pains
  might begin here in the Akropolis; and I wanted
  to drop my chick into it, just as the dear doves
    do.
LYSISTRATA: Lies! Evasions! — But at least one
    thing's clear:
  you can't leave the place before your
    purification.°   50
THIRD WOMAN: But I can't stay here in the
    Akropolis! Last night I dreamed
  of the Snake.
FIRST WOMAN: And those horrible owls, the
    noise they make!
  I can't get a bit of sleep; I'm just about dead.
LYSISTRATA: You useless girls, that's enough: Let's
  have no more lying.
  Of course you want your men. But don't you
    imagine   55
  that they want you just as much? I'll give you
    my word,
  their nights must be pretty hard.
               Just stick it out!
  A little patience, that's all, and our battle's won.
  I have heard an Oracle. Should you like to hear
    it?
FIRST WOMAN: An Oracle? Yes, tell us!
LYSISTRATA: Here is what it says: 60
  WHEN SWALLOWS SHALL THE HOOPOE
    SHUN
      AND SPURN HIS HOT DESIRE,
  ZEUS WILL PERFECT WHAT THEY'VE

---

34. Eileithyia: Goddess of childbirth.

36–37. pollute a sacred spot: Giving birth on the Akropolis was forbidden because it was sacred ground.   **50. purification:** A ritual cleansing of a woman after childbirth.

      BEGUN
      AND SET THE LOWER HIGHER.
65 FIRST WOMAN: Does that mean we'll be on top?
LYSISTRATA: BUT IF THE SWALLOWS SHALL
      FALL OUT
      AND TAKE THE HOOPOE'S BAIT,
    A CURSE MUST MARK THEIR HOUR OF
      DOUBT,
      INFAMY SEAL THEIR FATE.
THIRD WOMAN: I swear, *that* Oracle's all too clear.
70 FIRST WOMAN: Oh the dear gods!
LYSISTRATA: Let's not be downhearted, girls. Back
    to our places!
    The god has spoken. How can we possibly fail
    him?
        (*Exit Lysistrata with the dissident women.*)

CHORAL EPISODE · Strophe

CHORUS[(m)]: I know a little story that I learned way
    back in school
    Goes like this:
    Once upon a time there was a young man —
      and no fool —
    Named Melanion; and his
    One aversi-on was marriage. He loathed the very
5   thought.
    So he ran off to the hills, and in a special grot
    Raised a dog, and spent his days
    Hunting rabbits. And it says
    That he never never never did come home.
10 It might be called a refuge *from* the womb.
    All right,
        all right,
            all right!
    We're as bright as young Melanion, and we hate
    the very sight
    Of you women!
A MAN: How about a kiss, old lady?
15 A WOMAN: Here's an onion for your eye!
A MAN: A kick in the guts, then?
A WOMAN: Try, old bristle-tail, just try!
A MAN: Yet they say Myronides
    On hands and knees
20 Looked just as shaggy fore and aft as I!

Antistrophe

CHORUS[(w)]: Well, *I* know a little story, and it's just
    as good as yours.
    Goes like this:
    Once there was a man named Timon — a rough
      diamond, of course,
    And that whiskery face of his

Looked like murder in the shrubbery. By God, he
    was a son   25
Of the Furies, let me tell you! And what did he
    do but run
From the world and all its ways,
Cursing mankind! And it says
That his choicest execrations as of then
Were leveled almost wholly at *old* men.   30
All right,
      all right,
          all right!
But there's one thing about Timon: he could
    always stand the sight
of us women.
A WOMAN: How about a crack in the jaw, Pop?
A MAN: I can take it, Ma — no fear!   35
A WOMAN: How about a kick in the face?
A MAN: You'd reveal your old caboose?
A WOMAN: What I'd show,
    I'll have you know,
    Is an instrument you're too far gone to use.   40

SCENE 3

(*Reenter Lysistrata.*)

LYSISTRATA: Oh, quick, girls, quick! Come here!
A WOMAN: What is it?
LYSISTRATA: A man.
    A man simply bulging with love.
                    O Kyprian Queen,°
    O Paphian, O Kythereian! Hear us and aid us!
A WOMAN: Where is this enemy?
LYSISTRATA: Over there, by Demeter's shrine.
A WOMAN: Damned if he isn't. But who *is* he?
MYRRHINE: My husband.   5
    Kinesias.
LYSISTRATA: Oh then, get busy! Tease him!
    Undermine him!
    Wreck him! Give him everything — kissing,
    tickling, nudging,
    whatever you generally torture him with — :
    give him everything
    except what we swore on the wine we would
    not give.
MYRRHINE: Trust me.
LYSISTRATA: I do. But I'll help you get him started.   10
    The rest of you women, stay back.

(*Enter Kinesias.*)

KINESIAS: Oh God! Oh my God!
    I'm stiff from lack of exercise. All I can do to
    stand up.

2. **Kyprian Queen:** Aphrodite.

LYSISTRATA: Halt! Who are you, approaching our
  lines?
KINESIAS: Me? I.
LYSISTRATA: A man?
KINESIAS: You have eyes, haven't you?
LYSISTRATA: Go away.
KINESIAS: Who says so?
LYSISTRATA: Officer of the Day.
15 KINESIAS: Officer, I beg you,
  by all the gods at once, bring Myrrhine out.
LYSISTRATA: Myrrhine? And who, my good sir, are
  you?
KINESIAS: Kinesias. Last name's Pennison. Her
  husband.
LYSISTRATA: Oh, of course. I beg your pardon.
  We're glad to see you.
  We've heard so much about you. Dearest
20 Myrrhine
  is always talking about Kinesias — never nibbles
  an egg
  or an apple without saying
  "Here's to Kinesias!"
KINESIAS: Do you really mean it?
LYSISTRATA: I do.
  When we're discussing men, she always says
25 "Well, after all, there's nobody like Kinesias!"
KINESIAS: Good God. — Well, then, please send her
  down here.
LYSISTRATA: And what do *I* get out of it?
KINESIAS: A standing promise.
LYSISTRATA: I'll take it up with her.
                      (*Exit Lysistrata.*)
KINESIAS: But be quick about it!
  Lord, what's life without a wife? Can't eat.
  Can't sleep.
30 Every time I go home, the place is so empty, so
  insufferably sad. Love's killing me, Oh,
  hurry!

(*Enter Manes, a slave, with Kinesias' baby; the voice
of Myrrhine is heard off-stage.*)

MYRRHINE: But of course I love him! Adore
  him — But no,
  he hates love. No. I won't go down.

(*Enter Myrrhine, above.*)

KINESIAS: Myrrhine!
  Darlingest Myrrhinette! Come down quick!
MYRRHINE: Certainly not.
35 KINESIAS: Not? But why, Myrrhine?
MYRRHINE: Why? You don't need me.
KINESIAS: Need you? My God, *look* at me!
MYRRHINE: So long!

(*Turns to go.*)

KINESIAS: Myrrhine, Myrrhine, Myrrhine!
  If not for my sake, for our child!

(*Pinches Baby.*)

                      — All right, you: pipe up!
BABY: Mummie! Mummie! Mummie!
KINESIAS: You hear that?
  Pitiful, I call it. Six days now   40
  with never a bath; no food; enough to break
  your heart!
MYRRHINE: My darlingest child! What a father *you*
  acquired!
KINESIAS: At least come down for his sake.
MYRRHINE: I suppose I must.
  Oh, this mother business!   (*Exit.*)
KINESIAS: How pretty she is! And younger!
  The harder she treats me, the more bothered I
  get.

(*Myrrhine enters, below.*)

MYRRHINE: Dearest child,   45
  you're as sweet as your father's horrid. Give me
  a kiss.
KINESIAS: Now don't you see how wrong it was to
  get involved
  in this scheming League of women? It's bad
  for us both.
MYRRHINE: Keep your hands to yourself!
KINESIAS: But our house
  going to rack and ruin?
MYRRHINE: I don't care.
KINESIAS: And your knitting 50
  all torn to pieces by the chickens? Don't you
  care?
MYRRHINE: Not at all.
KINESIAS: And our debt to Aphrodite?
  Oh, *won't* you come back?
MYRRHINE: No. — At least, not until you
  men
  make a treaty and stop this war.
KINESIAS: Why, I suppose
  that might be arranged.
MYRRHINE: Oh? Well, I suppose   55
  I might come down then. But meanwhile,
  I've sworn not to.
KINESIAS: Don't worry. — Now let's have fun.
MYRRHINE: No! Stop it! I said no!
                      — Although, of course,
I *do* love you.
KINESIAS: I know you do. Darling Myrrhine:
  come, shall we?
MYRRHINE: Are you out of your mind? In front of
  the child?   60
KINESIAS: Take him home, Manes.
                      (*Exit Manes with Baby.*)

There. He's gone.
Come on!
There's nothing to stop us now.
MYRRHINE: You devil! But where?
KINESIAS: In Pan's cave. What could be snugger
    than that?
MYRRHINE: But my purification before I go back to
    the Citadel?
KINESIAS: Wash in the Klepsydra.°
MYRRHINE: And my oath?
65 KINESIAS: Leave the oath to me.
    After all, I'm the man.
MYRRHINE: Well . . . if you say so.
                      I'll go find a bed.
KINESIAS: Oh, bother a bed! The ground's good
    enough for me.
MYRRHINE: No. You're a bad man, but you deserve
    something better than dirt.   (Exit Myrrhine.)
KINESIAS: What a love she is! And how thoughtful!

(Reenter Myrrhine.)

MYRRHINE: Here's your bed.
    Now let me get my clothes off.
70   But, good horrors!
    We haven't a mattress.
KINESIAS: Oh, forget the mattress!
MYRRHINE: No.
    Just lying on blankets? Too sordid.
KINESIAS: Give me a kiss.
MYRRHINE: Just a second.   (Exit Myrrhine.)
KINESIAS: I swear, I'll explode!

(Reenter Myrrhine.)

MYRRHINE: Here's your mattress.
    I'll just take my dress off.
                        But look —
    where's our pillow?
KINESIAS: I don't need a pillow!
75 MYRRHINE: Well, I do.
                        (Exit Myrrhine.)
KINESIAS: I don't suppose even Herakles°
    would stand for this!

(Reenter Myrrhine.)

MYRRHINE: There we are. Ups-a-daisy!
KINESIAS: So we are. Well, come to bed.
MYRRHINE: But I wonder:
    is everything ready now?
KINESIAS: I can swear to that. Come, darling!

---

65. Klepsydra: A sacred spring beneath the walls of the
Akropolis. Kinesias' suggestion borders on blasphemy.   **76.
Herakles:** Greek hero known for his Twelve Labors.

MYRRHINE: Just getting out of my girdle.
                        But remember, now, 80
    what you promised about the treaty.
KINESIAS: Yes, yes, yes!
MYRRHINE: But no coverlet!
KINESIAS: Damn it, I'll be
    your coverlet!
MYRRHINE: Be right back.   (Exit Myrrhine.)
KINESIAS: This girl and her coverlets
    will be the death of me.

(Reenter Myrrhine.)

MYRRHINE: Here we are. Up you go!
KINESIAS: Up? I've been up for ages.
MYRRHINE: Some perfume? 85
KINESIAS: No, by Apollo!
MYRRHINE: Yes, by Aphrodite!
    I don't care whether you want it or not.
                        (Exit Myrrhine.)
KINESIAS: For love's sake, hurry!

(Reenter Myrrhine.)

MYRRHINE: Here, in your hand. Rub it right in.
KINESIAS: Never cared for perfume.
    And this is particularly strong. Still, here goes. 90
MYRRHINE: What a nitwit I am! I brought you the
    Rhodian bottle.
KINESIAS: Forget it.
MYRRHINE: No trouble at all. You just wait here.
                        (Exit Myrrhine.)
KINESIAS: God damn the man who invented
    perfume!

(Reenter Myrrhine.)

MYRRHINE: At last! The right bottle!
KINESIAS: I've got the rightest
    bottle of all, and it's right here waiting for you. 95
    Darling, forget everything else. Do come to bed.
MYRRHINE: Just let me get my shoes off.
                    — And, by the way,
    you'll vote for the treaty?
KINESIAS: I'll think about it.
                    (Myrrhine runs away.)
    There! That's done it! The damned woman,
    she gets me all bothered, she half kills me, 100
    and off she runs! What'll I do? Where
    can I get laid?
                — And you, little prodding pal,
    who's going to take care of you? No, you and I
    had better get down to old Foxdog's Nursing
    Clinic.
CHORUS[m]: Alas for the woes of man, alas 105
    Specifically for you.
    She's brought you to a pretty pass:
    What are you going to do?

Split, heart! Sag, flesh! Proud spirit, crack!
110   Myrrhine's got you on your back.
KINESIAS: The agony, the protraction!
KORYPHAIOS(m):   Friend,
      What woman's worth a damn?
      They bitch us all, world without end.
KINESIAS: Yet they're so damned sweet, man!
115 KORYPHAIOS(m): Calamitous, that's what I say.
      You should have learned that much today.
CHORUS(m): O blessed Zeus, roll womankind.
      Up into one great ball;
      Blast them aloft on a high wind,
120   And once there, let them fall.
      Down, down they'll come, the pretty dears,
      And split themselves on our thick spears.
                                              (Exit Kinesias.)

SCENE 4 _____

(Enter a Spartan Herald.)

HERALD: Gentlemen, Ah beg you will be so kind
      as to direct me to the Central Committee.
      Ah have a communication.

(Reenter Commissioner.)

COMMISSIONER: Are you a man,
      or a fertility symbol?
HERALD: Ah refuse to answer that question!
      Ah'm a certified herald from Spahta, and Ah've
5   come
      to talk about an ahmistice.
COMMISSIONER: Then why
      that spear under your cloak?
HERALD: Ah have no speah!
COMMISSIONER: You don't walk naturally, with
      your tunic
      poked out so. You have a tumor, maybe,
      or a hernia?
HERALD: You lost yo' mahnd, man?
10 COMMISSIONER: Well,
      something's up, I can see that. And I don't like
      it.
HERALD: Colonel, Ah resent this.
COMMISSIONER: So I see. But what is it?
HERALD: A staff
      with a message from Spahta.
COMMISSIONER: Oh, I know about those staffs.
      Well, then, man, speak out: How are things in
      Sparta?
HERALD: Hahd, Colonel, hahd! We're at a
15   standstill.
      Cain't seem to think of anything but women.
COMMISSIONER: How curious! Tell me, do you
      Spartans think
      that maybe Pan's to blame?

HERALD: Pan? No, Lampito and her little naked
      friends.
      They won't let a man come nigh them.   20
COMMISSIONER: How are you handling it?
HERALD: Losing our mahnds,
      if y' want to know, and walking around
      hunched over
      lahk men carrying candles in a gale.
      The women have swohn they'll have nothing to
      do with us
      until we get a treaty.
COMMISSIONER: Yes. I know.   25
      It's a general uprising, sir, in all parts of Greece.
      But as for the answer —
                        Sir: go back to Sparta
      and have them send us your Armistice
      Commission.
      I'll arrange things in Athens.
                              And I may say
      that my standing is good enough to make them
      listen.   30
HERALD: A man after mah own haht! Seh, Ah
      thank you.   (Exit Herald.)

CHORAL EPISODE · Strophe _____

CHORUS(m): Oh these women! Where will you find
      A slavering beast that's more unkind?
      Where's a hotter fire?
      Give me a panther, any day.
      He's not so merciless as they,   5
      And panthers don't conspire.

Antistrophe

CHORUS(w): We may be hard, you silly old ass,
      But who brought you to this stupid pass?
      You're the ones to blame.
      Fighting with us, your oldest friends,   10
      Simply to serve your selfish ends —
      Really, you have no shame!
KORYPHAIOS(m): No, I'm through with women for
      ever.
KORYPHAIOS(w):   If you say so.
      Still, you might put some clothes on. You look
      too absurd
      standing around naked. Come, get into this
      cloak.
KORYPHAIOS(m): Thank you; you're right. I merely
      took it off
      because I was in such a temper.
KORYPHAIOS(w):   That's much better.
      Now you resemble a man again.
                        Why have you been so horrid?
      And look: there's some sort of insect in your eye.

Shall I take it out?

20 KORYPHAIOS[m]:   An insect, is it? So that's
what's been bothering me. Lord, yes: take it out!
KORYPHAIOS[w]: You might be more polite.
                                        — But, heavens!
What an enormous mosquito!
KORYPHAIOS[m]:   You've saved my life.
That mosquito was drilling an artesian well
in my left eye.
25 KORYPHAIOS[w]:   Let me wipe
those tears away. — And now: one little kiss?
KORYPHAIOS[m]: No, no kisses.
KORYPHAIOS[w]: You're so difficult.
KORYPHAIOS[m]: You impossible women! How you
do get around us!
The poet was right: Can't live with you, or
without you.
30 But let's be friends. And to celebrate, you might join us in an Ode.

Strophe 1

CHORUS[m and w]: Let it never be said
That my tongue is malicious:
Both by word and by deed
I would set an example that's noble and
35   gracious.
We've had sorrow and care
Till we're sick of the tune.
Is there anyone here
Who would like a small loan?
40   My purse is crammed,
As you'll soon find;
And you needn't pay me back if the Peace gets
signed.

Strophe 2

I've invited to lunch
Some Karystian rips° —
45 An esurient bunch,
But I've ordered a menu to water their lips.
I can still make soup
And slaughter a pig.
You're all coming, I hope?
50 But a bath first, I beg!
Walk right up
As though you owned the place,
And you'll get the front door slammed to in
your face.

---

44. Karystian rips: The Karystians were allies of Athens but were scorned for their primitive ways and loose morals.

SCENE 5

(*Enter Spartan Ambassador, with entourage.*)

KORYPHAIOS[m]: The Commission has arrived from
Sparta.
                How oddly they're walking!
                        Gentlemen, welcome to Athens!
How is life in Lakonia?
AMBASSADOR: Need we discuss that?
Simply use your eyes.
CHORUS[m]:   The poor man's right:
                        What a sight!
AMBASSADOR: Words fail me.   5
But come, gentlemen, call in your
Commissioners,
and let's get down to a Peace.
CHORAGOS[m]:   The state we're in! Can't bear
a stitch below the waist. It's a kind of pelvic
paralysis.
COMMISSIONER: Won't somebody call
Lysistrata? — Gentlemen,
we're no better off than you.
AMBASSADOR: So I see.   10
A SPARTAN: Seh, do y'all feel a certain strain
early in the morning?
AN ATHENIAN: I do, sir. It's worse than a strain.
A few more days, and there's nothing for us but
Kleisthenes,
that broken blossom.
CHORAGOS[m]:   But you'd better get dressed again.
You know these people going around Athens
with chisels,   15
looking for statues of Hermes.°
ATHENIAN: Sir, you are right.
SPARTAN: He certainly is! Ah'll put mah own
clothes back on.

(*Enter Athenian Commissioners.*)

COMMISSIONER: Gentlemen from Sparta, welcome.
This is a sorry business.
SPARTAN (*To one of his own group*): Colonel, we
got dressed just in time. Ah sweah,
if they'd seen us the way we were, there'd have
been a new wah   20
between the states.
COMMISSIONER: Shall we call the meeting to order?
                        Now, Lakonians,
what's your proposal?
AMBASSADOR: We propose to consider peace.

---

16. statues of Hermes: The usual representation of Hermes was with an erect phallus. Statues of Hermes were scattered through Athens and were attacked by vandals just before the Sicilian Expedition.

COMMISSIONER: Good. That's on our minds, too.
                              — Summon Lysistrata.
  We'll never get anywhere without her.
25 AMBASSADOR: Lysistrata?
  Summon Lysis-*any*body! Only, summon!
  KORYPHAIOS[m]:   No need to summon:
  here she is, herself.

(*Enter Lysistrata.*)

COMMISSIONER: Lysistrata! Lion of women!
  This is your hour to be
  hard and yielding, outspoken and shy, austere
    and
30 gentle. You see here
  the best brains of Hellas (confused, I admit,
  by your devious charming) met as one man
  to turn the future over to you.
  LYSISTRATA: That's fair enough,
  unless you men take it into your heads
  to turn to each other instead of to us. But I'd
35 know
  soon enough if you did.
                    — Where is Reconciliation?
  Go, some of you: bring her here.
                    (*Exeunt two women.*)
                    And now, women,
  lead the Spartan delegates to me: not roughly
  or insultingly, as our men handle them, but
    gently,
  politely, as ladies should. Take them by the
40 hand,
  or by anything else if they won't give you their
    hands.

(*The Spartans are escorted over.*)

  There. — The Athenians next, by any convenient
    handle.

(*The Athenians are escorted.*)

  Stand there, please. — Now, all of you, listen to
    me.

(*During the following speech the two women reenter,
carrying an enormous statue of a naked girl; this is
Reconciliation.*)

  I'm only a woman, I know; but I've a mind,
  and, I think, not a bad one: I owe it to my
45   father
  and to listening to the local politicians.
  So much for that.
                    Now, gentlemen,
  since I have you here, I intend to give you a
    scolding.
  We are all Greeks.

Must I remind you of Thermopylai,° of Olympia, 50
  of Delphoi? names deep in all our hearts?
  Are they not a common heritage?
                              Yet you men
  go raiding through the country from both sides,
  Greek killing Greek, storming down Greek
    cities —
  and all the time the Barbarian across the sea   55
  is waiting for his chance!
                    — That's my first point.
AN ATHENIAN: Lord! I can hardly contain myself.
LYSISTRATA: As for you Spartans:
  Was it so long ago that Perikleides°
  came here to beg our help? I can see him still,
  his gray face, his sombre gown. And what did
    he want?   60
  An army from Athens. All Messene
  was hot at your heels, and the sea-god splitting
    your land.
  Well, Kimon and his men,
  four thousand strong, marched out and saved all
    Sparta.
  And what thanks do we get? You come back to
    murder us.   65
AN ATHENIAN: They're aggressors, Lysistrata!
A SPARTAN: Ah admit it.
  When Ah look at those laigs, Ah sweah Ah'll
    aggress mahself!
LYSISTRATA: And you, Athenians: do you think
    you're blameless?
  Remember that bad time when we were helpless, 70
  and an army came from Sparta,
    and that was the end of the Thessalian
    menace,
  the end of Hippias and his allies.
                    And that was Sparta,
  and only Sparta; but for Sparta, we'd be
  cringing slaves today, not free Athenians.

(*From this point, the male responses are less to Lysistrata than to the statue.*)

A SPARTAN: A well shaped speech.
AN ATHENIAN: Certainly it has its points. 75
LYSISTRATA: Why are we fighting each other? With
    all this history
  of favors given and taken, what stands in the
    way
  of making peace?

---

50. **Thermopylai:** A narrow pass where, in 480 B.C., an army
of three hundred Spartans held out for three days against a
superior Persian force. 58. **Perikleides:** Spartan ambassador
to Athens who successfully urged Athenians to aid Sparta in
quelling a rebellion.

AMBASSADOR: Spahta is ready, ma'am,
   so long as we get that place back.
LYSISTRATA: What place, man?
AMBASSADOR: Ah refer to Pylos.
80 COMMISSIONER: Not a chance, by God!
LYSISTRATA: Give it to them, friend.
COMMISSIONER: But — what shall we have to
   bargain with?
LYSISTRATA: Demand something in exchange.
COMMISSIONER: Good idea. — Well, then:
   Cockeville first, and the Happy Hills, and the
    country
   between the Legs of Megara.
AMBASSADOR: Mah government objects.
LYSISTRATA: Overruled. Why fuss about a pair of
85   legs?

(*General assent. The statue is removed.*)

AN ATHENIAN: I want to get out of these clothes
   and start my plowing.
A SPARTAN: Ah'll fertilize mahn first, by the
   Heavenly Twins!
LYSISTRATA: And so you shall,
   once you've made peace. If you are serious,
90   go, both of you, and talk with your allies.
COMMISSIONER: Too much talk already. No, we'll
   stand together.
   We've only one end in view. All that we want
   is our women; and I speak for our allies.
AMBASSADOR: Mah government concurs.
AN ATHENIAN: So does Karystos.
95 LYSISTRATA: Good. — But before you come inside
   to join your wives at supper, you must perform
   the usual lustration. Then we'll open
   our baskets for you, and all that we have is
   yours.
   But you must promise upright good behavior
   from this day on. Then each man home with his
100   woman!
AN ATHENIAN: Let's get it over with.
A SPARTAN: Lead on. Ah follow.
AN ATHENIAN: Quick as a cat can wink!
             (*Exeunt all but the Choruses.*)

Antistrophe 1

CHORUS[(w)]: Embroideries and
   Twinkling ornaments and
105   Pretty dresses — I hand
Them all over to you, and with never a qualm.
   They'll be nice for your daughters
   On festival days
   When the girls bring the Goddess
110   The ritual prize.

Come in, one and all:
Take what you will.
I've nothing here so tightly corked that you can't
   make it spill.

Antistrophe 2

You may search my house,
But you'll not find   115
The least thing of use,
Unless your two eyes are keener than mine.
   Your numberless brats
   Are half starved? and your slaves?
Courage, grandpa! I've lots   120
Of grain left, and big loaves.
   I'll fill your guts,
   I'll go the whole hog;
But if you come too close to me, remember:
   'ware the dog!   (*Exeunt Choruses.*)

EXODOS° _____

(*A Drunken Citizen enters, approaches the gate, and
is halted by a sentry.*)

CITIZEN: Open. The. Door.
SENTRY: Now, friend, just shove along!
   — So you want to sit down. If it weren't such
    an old joke,
   I'd tickle your tail with this torch. Just the sort
    of gag
   this audience appreciates.
CITIZEN: I. Stay. Right. Here.
SENTRY: Get away from there, or I'll scalp you!
   The gentlemen from Sparta   5
   are just coming back from dinner.

(*Exit Citizen; the general company reenters; the two
Choruses now represent Spartans and Athenians.*)

A SPARTAN: Ah must say,
   Ah never tasted better grub.
AN ATHENIAN: And those Lakonians!
   They're gentlemen, by the Lord! Just goes to
    show,
   a drink to the wise is sufficient.
COMMISSIONER: And why not?
   A sober man's an ass.   10
   Men of Athens, mark my words: the only
    efficient
   Ambassador's a drunk Ambassador. Is that
    clear?
   Look: we go to Sparta,

Exodos: Final scene.

and when we get there we're dead sober. The
   result?
Everyone cackling at everyone else. They make
15   speeches;
and even if we understand, we get it all wrong
when we file our reports in Athens. But
   today — !
Everybody's happy. Couldn't tell the difference
between *Drink to Me Only* and
The Star-Spangled Athens.
20   What's a few lies,
washed down in good strong drink?

(*Reenter the Drunken Citizen.*)

SENTRY: God almighty,
   he's back again!
CITIZEN: I. Resume. My. Place.
A SPARTAN (*to an Athenian*): Ah beg yo', seh,
take yo' instrument in yo' hand and play for us.
25   Ah'm told
yo' understand the in*tri*cacies of the floot?
Ah'd lahk to execute a song and dance
in honor of Athens,
                        and, of cohse, of Spahta.
CITIZEN: Toot. On. Your. Flute.

(*The following song is a solo — an aria — accompanied
by the flute. The Chorus of Spartans begins a slow
dance.*)

30 A SPARTAN: O Memory,
Let the Muse speak once more
In my young voice. Sing glory.
Sing Artemision's shore,
Where Athens fluttered the Persians. *Alalai,°*
35 Sing glory, that great
Victory! Sing also
Our Leonidas and his men,
Those wild boars, sweat and blood
Down in a red drench. Then, then
40 The barbarians broke, though they had stood
Numberless as the sands before!

O Artemis,
Virgin Goddess, whose darts
Flash in our forests: approve
45 This pact of peace and join our hearts,
From this day on, in love.
Huntress, descend!
LYSISTRATA: All that will come in time.
                        But now, Lakonians,
take home your wives. Athenians, take yours.
Each man be kind to his woman; and you,
50   women

34. **Alalai:** War cry.

be equally kind. Never again, pray God,
shall we lose our way in such madness.
KORYPHAIOS(Athenian):   And now
   let's dance our joy.

(*From this point the dance becomes general.*)

CHORUS(Athenian): Dance, you Graces
                              Artemis, dance
Dance, Phoibos,° Lord of dancing
                              Dance,   55
In a scurry of Maenads, Lord Dionysos°
                        Dance, Zeus Thunderer
                  Dance, Lady Hera°
Queen of the sky
                        Dance, dance, all you gods
Dance witness everlasting of our pact
Evohi Evohe°   60
Dance for the dearest
                        the Bringer of Peace
Deathless Aphrodite!
COMMISSIONER: Now let us have another song from
   Sparta.
CHORUS(Spartan): From Taygetos, from Taygetos,
Lakonian Muse, come down.   65
Sing to the Lord Apollo
   Who rules Amyklai Town.

Sing Athena of the House of Brass!°
Sing Leda's Twins,° that chivalry
Resplendent on the shore   70
Of our Eurotas; sing the girls
   That dance along before:

Sparkling in dust their gleaming feet,
   Their hair a Bacchant fire,
And Leda's daughter, thyrsos° raised,   75
   Leads their triumphant choir.

CHORUS(S and A): *Evohé!*
                        Evohaí!
                        Evohé!
                                    We pass
                  Dancing
                        dancing
                              to greet
Athena of the House of Brass.

55. **Phoibos:** Apollo, god of the sun.   56. **Maenads:** Female
worshipers of Bacchus (Dionysus).   57. **Hera:** Wife of Zeus.
60. **Evohi Evohe:** "Come forth! Come forth!" An orgiastic
cry associated with rituals of Bacchus.   68. **House of Brass:**
Temple to Athena on the Akropolis of Sparta.   69. **Leda's
Twins:** Leda, raped by Zeus, bore quadruplets, two daughters
(one of whom was Helen) and two sons.   75. **thyrsos:** A
staff twined with ivy and carried by Bacchus and his followers.

Roman Drama

Roman drama has several sources, not all of them well understood. The first and most literary is Greek drama, but among the more curious are the indigenous sources, which are especially difficult to trace. The Etruscans, members of an old and obscure civilization in northern Italy that reached its height in the sixth century B.C. and that the Romans eventually absorbed, had developed an improvised song and dance that was very entertaining. The town of Atella provided another indigenous comic tradition known as the ATELLAN FARCE, a very broad and sometimes coarse popular humor. Such entertainments may have been acted in open spaces or at fairs and at first probably did not demand a stage at all.

The Atellan farce is especially interesting for developments in later Roman drama and world drama. The characters in this farce seem to have been STOCK CHARACTERS, characters who are always recognizable and whose antics are predictable. The most common in the Stellan farce are Maccus the clown; Bucco the stupid, and probably fat, clown; Pappus the foolish or stubborn old man; and the hunchbacked, wily slave Dossennus. At first these pieces of drama were improvised to a repeatable pattern, often involving a master who tries to get his slave to do his bidding but who somehow ends up being made to look the fool by his cunning slave. When the farces began to develop in Rome, they were written down and played back in predictably comic form.

The concept of the stock character is associated with the masters of Roman comedy, Plautus and Terence, who often adapted Greek plays and made them their own. The braggart warrior (*miles gloriosus*) was a stock character on the Roman stage, and he reappears in modern plays such as George Bernard Shaw's *Arms and the Man* and Sean O'Casey's *Juno and the Paycock*. The miser has been a mainstay in literature since Roman times and probably is best known today as

131

Scrooge in Dickens' *A Christmas Carol* and in Molière's *The Miser*. The parasite was Roman in origin and can be seen today in numerous television situation comedies (Frank in M*A*S*H is an example). The use of identical twins for comic effect is a Roman invention, and because it permitted a wide range of comic misunderstandings, it has been used by many playwrights, including Shakespeare in *The Comedy of Errors*. The Roman use of masks made the device of identical twins much easier to perform than it is today.

The Greek Influence

According to legend, in 240 B.C., a former slave, Livius Andronicus, presented performances of his Latin translations of a Greek tragedy and a Greek comedy, giving the Romans their first real taste of Greek drama and literature. Livius soon earned his freedom, and his literary career became so firmly established that his translations from the Greek were standard in Rome for more than two hundred years. His translation of the *Odyssey* was the standard text through the time of Cicero (first century B.C.).

Roman comedy derived primarily from the New Comedy of Menander, although it could, like Aristophanes' work, sometimes be risqué. There is no question that comedy was the most well attended, the most performed, and the most beloved of Rome's drama. That is not to say that the Romans produced no tragedies. They did, and the effects of Roman tragedy have been as long-lasting as the effects of the comedy. However, the Roman people were much more pleased to laugh than to feel the pity and terror of tragic emotion.

Just as the Greek plays developed in connection with festivals, the Roman plays became associated with games held several times a year. During the games, performances were held on an average of five to eleven days. The Megalesian Games took place in early April, in honor of the Great Mother, the goddess Cybele, whose temple stood on the Palatine Hill. In late April the Floral Games were held in front of the temple of Flora on the Aventine Hill. The most important were the Roman Games in September and the Plebeian Games in November.

The Greek drama competitions had no counterpart among the Romans, for whom drama was not the primary entertainment. Roman playwrights were hired along with a group of actors to put on performances that were intended to entertain and divert the audiences watching gladiator fights, chariot races, animal baiting, and other spectacles. The producer had to get good results or else not have the chance to supply more entertainment. In a sense, this has a modern parallel in television ratings. The Roman audience was impatient as is the modern audience, and had many other diversions.

Roman comedies were sometimes revisions or amalgamations of Greek plays. The themes and characters of the tragedies also derived from Greek originals. The Trojan War figured largely in Roman plays, and the characters who fought the wars were reworked into new situations and their agonies reinterpreted.

For costumes, the actors wore the Greek tunic (called a CHITON) and a long white cloak or mantle called the PALLIUM. As did the Greeks, the Romans wore low shoes, called the SOCK, for comedy, and shoes with an elevated sole, the BUSKIN, for tragedy. For plays that had a totally Roman setting and narrative, the actors wore the Roman toga. Eventually, Roman actors used traditional Greek masks that immediately identified the characters for the audience. (The question of whether the earliest Roman actors wore masks as well has not been resolved.) The younger Roman characters wore black wigs, older characters wore white wigs, and characters representing slaves wore red wigs.

One of the most intriguing questions concerning Roman plays is the importance of music in the drama. In Greek plays, the chorus took most of the responsibility for the music, but since the chorus did not play as large a role in human drama (and was eliminated entirely from some works), the Roman plays may have resembled our musical comedies. The dialogue in some comedies turns the play over to an interlude of flute playing, indicating that there were times with no actor onstage, no spoken words, and no mimed action, but only a musician to entertain the audience.

The Roman Stage

In the third century B.C., the Romans began building wooden stages that could be taken down quickly and moved as necessary. Eventually, they built stone theaters following Greek plans; however, they varied from the Greek model in a number of important respects. They were built on flat ground, not carved into hillsides as the Greek theaters were. And the influence of their early wooden stage remained in the permanent buildings in several ways. The Roman stage was elevated, often three stories tall, and since there was little or no chorus, the orchestra, in which the chorus moved from place to place, was no longer needed. The SCAENA, or background, against which the action took place, apart from having three stories, was proportionally longer than the Greek *skene*. This lengthening of the place of action was helpful because so many Roman plays were set along a road on which the actors could set several houses, temples, or buildings.

The space in front of the *scaena* was known as the PROSCAENA, from which the PROSCENIUM ARCH, which frames the stage and separates the actors from the audience, developed in the seventeenth century. The action took place in the *proscaena*. The potentiality for the proscenium arch is evident in the plan of the Theater of Marcellus (Figure 2), where the sections to the left and the right of the stage already indicate a separation of the stage from the audience and already imply a frame.

As in the plan of the Theater of Marcellus, the SCAENA FRONS (the front wall) usually had three doors (some had only two), which were

Figure 2. Theater of Marcellus

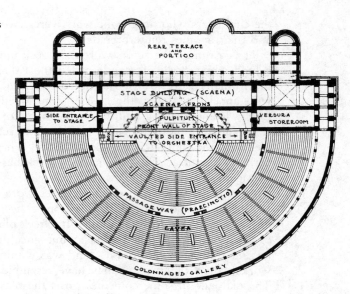

ordinarily established as doors to separate buildings, one a temple and the others the homes of chief characters. These doors were active "participants" in the drama; it has been said that the most common line heard in a Roman play is a statement that the door is opening and someone is coming in. The standard Roman play takes great care to justify the entrances and exits of its characters, which indicates that the Roman audience expected more realism in their comedies and tragedies than did their Greek counterparts.

The *scaena frons,* the front of the theater, not only was several stories high but also was much more architecturally developed than the *skene* of the Greek theater. The typical Roman architectural devices of multiple arches, columns, and pilasters decorated the *scaena,* giving it a stately appearance. Like the Greek theater, the Roman theater used machinery that permitted actors to be moved through the air and to make entrances from the heavens. Unlike the Greek theater, many Roman theaters had curtains.

Roman Dramatists
Plautus

All surviving Roman comedy shows the influence of Greek originals. Plautus (254–184 B.C.) is among Rome's most famous playwrights and he may have been a member of a troupe that performed Atellan comedy. His middle name is Maccius (a form of Maccus, the clown of the farces), which may allude to his history. Tradition has it that he was in the theater for a good while before he began writing comedies. His first plays date from 205 B.C., about thirty-five years after Livius introduced Greek drama to the Romans. No one knows how many plays he wrote, and it has been common to assign many titles to him that have not been authenticated. About twenty-one plays exist that are thought to be his, the most famous of which are *Amphitryon*, *The Pot of Gold*, *The Captives*, *Curculio*, *The Braggart Warrior*, *The Rope*, and *The Twin Menaechmi*.

The last play is probably the best-known Roman comedy. It features Menaechmus from Syracuse, who goes to Epidamnus searching for his lost twin. There he meets people who mistake him for his brother: a cook; a prostitute; Brush, a typical parasite; and even his brother's wife and father-in-law. The comedy uses all the confusions inherent in mistaken identity.

Terence

Terence (c. 195–159 B.C.) is said to have been a North African slave who was brought to Rome, where his master realized he was unusually intelligent and gifted. After he was freed, Terence took his place in Roman literary life and produced a body of six plays, all of which still exist: *The Woman of Andros*, *The Self-Tormentor*, *The Eunuch*, *The Phormio*, *The Mother-in-Law*, and *The Brothers*. Terence's plays are notable for including a subplot — carefully kept under control — and for avoiding the technique of addressing the audience directly.

The Romans preferred Plautus's broad farcical humor to Terence's more carefully plotted, elegantly styled plays, and it was not always easy for Terence to get his plays produced. A manager or producer worked with him on all his plays, and the musician who worked with him was a slave, Flaccus. Terence's productive life was relatively short. He died on a trip to Greece, apparently worrying over a piece of missing luggage said to have contained new plays.

Terence's situation was unusual: He had two wealthy Roman patrons who were interested in seeing the best Greek comedy brought to the Romans. Consequently, they paid for his productions and gave him more support than the average comic playwright could have expected. Terence was often accused of plagiarism, and he admitted that he adapted Greek plays so closely that they seemed to be little more than translations. However, his dramatic skills developed considerably from the beginning to the end of his work, contrasting sharply with the carelessness of Plautus. Terence was more than a translator, but he wrote at a time when Romans were interested in emulating the Greeks, and his fidelity to Greek originals was one of his strongest recommendations.

Seneca

The surviving Roman plays come from just three hands: Plautus, Terence, and Seneca (4 B.C.–65 A.D.). The comedies of Plautus are raucous, broad, and farcical; those of Terence are polished and carefully structured. Seneca wrote tragedies that were well known to Elizabethans such as Marlowe and Shakespeare, and it is clear that the Elizabethan Age found SENECAN TRAGEDY to be peculiarly suited to its own temperament.

Senecan tragedies were based on either Greek or Roman themes and included murder, bloodthirsty actions, horror of various kinds, ghosts, and long, bombastic speeches. Signs of Senecan influence can be seen in Elizabethan drama, with its taste for many of these devices; plays like *Hamlet* are notable for ending in a pool of blood, with most of the actors lying dead on stage. The theme of revenge was also prized by Seneca and, later, by the Elizabethans.

Seneca was not a professional theater person. He was wealthy and learned, a philosopher active in the government of Emperor Nero's Rome. His plays, most of which were adapted from Euripides, were probably written only to be read, as was common at his time; there is no record of their having been performed. It is instructive to realize that the Roman people thirsted for comedy and low-down farce but had much less taste for serious plays.

Ten plays attributed to Seneca exist, nine of which are surely his and one of which is only possibly his. His most famous are *Mad Hercules*, *The Phoenician Women*, *Medea*, *Phaedra*, *Agamemnon*, *Thyestes*, and *The Trojan Women*.

The surviving Roman plays offer enough variety to give us an idea of what the drama achieved. Like so much of Roman culture, Roman drama rested in the shadow of the Greek achievement. The Romans were responsible for maintaining the Greek texts, allowing us to see as much of their work as we have. If it is true that much of the Roman drama that was produced no longer exists, what survives shows variety and high quality.

Medieval Drama

The Role of the Church

The collapse of Rome in 476 A.D. was a calamity of such magnitude that the years between then and the beginning of the Crusades in 1095 have been traditionally called the Dark Ages. In fact, they were not dark, but they were a time in which no great central powers organized society or established patterns of behavior and standards in the arts.

Drama all but disappeared. The major institution to profit from the fall of the Roman Empire was the church, which in the ninth and tenth centuries enjoyed considerable power and considerable influence. The church considered drama, however, a godless activity, a distraction from the piety that it demanded of its members. During the great age of cathedral building and the great ages of religious painting and religious music — from the seventh century to the thirteenth — drama was not officially approved. Therefore, it is a striking irony that the rebirth of drama in the Western world should have taken place in the heart of the great cathedrals, developing slowly and inconspicuously until it outgrew its beginnings.

The church may well have intended nothing more than the simple dramatization of its message. Or it is possible that the people may have craved drama and the church's response could have been an attempt to answer their needs. In either event, the church could never have foreseen the outcome of adding a few moments of drama to the liturgy. Liturgical drama began in the ninth century with TROPES, or embellishments, which were sung during passages of the Mass that previously had been wordless. The earliest known example of a trope, called the *Quem Quaeritis* ("Whom seek ye?"), grew out of the Easter Mass and was sung in a monastic settlement in Switzerland called St. Gall:

ANGEL: Whom seek ye in the sepulchre, O ye Christians?
THREE MARYS: Jesus of Nazareth, who was crucified, O ye Angels.
ANGEL: He is not here; he is risen as he has foretold.
 Go, announce that he is risen from the sepulchre.

Some scholars think that in its earliest form this trope was sung by two monks in a dialogue pattern, one monk representing the three Marys at Christ's tomb and the other representing the angels. Tropes like the *Quem Quaeritis* trope evolved over the years to include a number of participants — monks, nuns, and choirboys — as the tropes spread from church to church throughout the Continent. These dramatic interpolations never became dramas separate from the Mass itself, although their success and popularity led to experiments with other dramatic sequences centering on moments in the Mass and in the life of Christ. The actors in these pieces did not think of themselves as specialists or professionals; they were simply monks who belonged to the church. The churchgoers obviously enjoyed the tropes, and more of them were created, despite the church's official position on drama.

In the twelfth century, for reasons that remain unclear, the church expelled the liturgical drama to the churchyard. It may be that the dramatic moments inside the church, which had begun to demand more elaborate equipment and settings, were too complex to remain in the spaces normally assigned them, or they may have begun to conflict with the liturgy of the Mass.

Mystery Plays

Once outside the church, the drama flourished and soon became independent, although its themes continued to be religious and its services were connected with religious festivals. In 1264, a new and important feast was added to the religious calendar by order of Pope Urban IV. Corpus Christi, as the feast was called, was celebrated beginning the first Thursday after Trinity Sunday — about two months after Easter. The purpose of the feast was to celebrate the new doctrine declaring that the body of Christ was real and present in the Host taken by the faithful in the sacrament of Communion.

At first the feast of Corpus Christi was localized in Liège, France. But in the fourteenth and fifteenth centuries it spread through papal decree and became one of the chief feasts of the church. Among other things, it featured a procession and pageant in which the Host was displayed publicly through the streets of a town. Because of the importance and excitement of this feast, entire communities took part in the celebration.

The craft guilds, professional organizations of workers involved in the same trade — carpenters, wool merchants, and so on — soon began competing with each other in producing plays that could be performed during the feast of Corpus Christi. Most of their plays derived from Bible stories and the life of Christ. Because the Bible is silent on many details of Christ's life, it was possible for plays to invent new material and illuminate dark areas, thereby satisfying the intense curiosity medieval Christians had about events the Bible omitted.

The church did not ignore drama after it cast it out of the church buildings. Since the subject matter of the plays was wholeheartedly religious and since the plays had an obvious use as a teaching device for the historical moments of the Bible as well as for modes of Christian behavior, they remained of considerable value to the church.

Because the plays were written, directed, and produced by members of craft guilds, they became known as CRAFT or MYSTERY PLAYS. The word *mystery* was used in the medieval period to describe a skill or trade that was known only to a few who apprenticed and mastered its special techniques.

By the fifteenth century mystery plays and the feast of Corpus Christi were popular almost everywhere in Europe, and in England certain towns produced exceptionally elaborate cycles with unusually complex and ambitious plays. The CYCLES were a group of plays numbering from twenty-four to forty-eight, depending on the cycle. Four cycles have been preserved: the Chester, York, Towneley (Wakefield), and N-Town cycles, named for their towns of origin. N-Town plays were a generic version of plays that any town could take and use as its own, although the plays were originally written near Lincoln, according to the best current information.

The plays were performed again and again during annual holidays and feasts and the texts were carefully preserved. Some of the plays are very short, such as *The Fall of Lucifer*. Others are more elaborate in length and complexity and resemble modern plays: *Noah*, from the Wakefield Cycle, which has been produced regularly in this century; *The Slaughter of Innocents*; and *The Second Shepherds' Play*, one of the most entertaining mystery plays.

The producers of the plays often had a sense of humor in their choice of subjects. For example, the Water-Drawers guild sponsored *Noah's Flood*, the Butchers (because they sold "flesh") *Temptation, The Woman Taken in Adultery*, and the Shipwrights *The Building of the Ark*.

Some of that sense of humor spilled over into the content of the plays as well. Among the best-known mystery plays is the somewhat farcical *The Second Shepherds' Play*, which is both funny and serious. It tells of a crafty shepherd named Mak who steals a lamb from his fellow shepherds and takes it home. His wife, Gill, then places it in a cradle and pretends it is her baby. Eventually the shepherds — who suspect Mak from the first — smoke out the fraud and give Mak a blanket-tossing for their trouble. But after they do so, they see a star in the heavens and turn their attention to the birth of baby Jesus, the Lamb of God. They join the Magi and come to pay homage to the Christ Child.

The easy way in which the profane elements of everyday life coexisted with the sacred in medieval times has long interested scholars. *The Second Shepherds' Play* virtually breaks into two parts, the first dedicated to the wickedness of Mak and Gill and the horseplay of the shepherds. But once Mak has had his due reward, the play alters in tone and the sense of devotion to Christian teachings becomes uppermost. The fact that the mystery plays moved away from Latin and to the vernacular (local) language made such a juxtaposition of sacred and profane much more possible.

Morality Plays

MORALITY PLAYS were never part of any cycle but developed independently in the late fourteenth or early fifteenth century on the Continent and in England as moral tales. They do not illustrate moments in the Bible, nor do they describe the life of Christ or the saints. Instead, they describe the circumstances of the lives of everyday people facing the temptations of the world. The plays are careful to present a warning to the unwary that their souls are always in peril, that the devil is on constant watch, and that people must behave properly if they are to be saved.

One feature of morality plays is the reliance on ALLEGORY, the use of which was a favorite medieval device. Allegory is the technique of giving abstract ideas or values a physical representation. In morality plays, abstractions such as goodness became characters in the drama. In modern times we use allegory in some sculpture, as when we represent justice as a blindfolded woman. Allegorically, justice acts impartially because she does not "see" any distinctions, such as of rank or privilege, that characterize most people standing before a judge.

The use of allegory permitted medieval dramatists to personify abstract values such as sloth, greed, daintiness, vanity, strength, and hope by making them characters and placing them onstage in action. The dramatist specified symbols, clothing, and gestures appropriate to these abstract figures, thus helping the audience recognize the ideas the characters represented. The use of allegory was an extremely durable technique that carried over into medieval painting, printed books, and books of emblems, in which, for example, sloth would be shown as a man reclining lazily on a bed or greed would be represented as overwhelmingly fat and vanity as a figure completely absorbed in a mirror.

The central problem in the morality play was the salvation of human beings, represented by an individual's struggle to avoid sin and damnation and achieve freedom in the otherworld. As in *Everyman,* the best known of the moralities, the subjects of these plays were usually abstract battles between certain vices and certain virtues for the possession of the human soul, a theme repeated in the Elizabethan age in Marlowe's *Doctor Faustus.*

In many ways, the morality play was a dramatized sermon, designed to teach a moral lesson. It was marked by high seriousness and, often, gloominess. The use of allegory to represent abstract qualities allowed the didactic playwrights to draw clearcut lines of moral force: Satan was always bad; angels were always good. The allegories were clear, direct, and observable by all who witnessed the plays.

We do not have much knowledge of the origins of morality plays, and many of them are lost, but some that remain are occasionally performed and have some power: *The Pride of Life*, the earliest extant morality play; *The Castle of Perseverance*; *Wisdom*; *Mankind*; and *Everyman* are the best known. They all enjoyed a remarkable popularity in the latter part of the medieval period, all the way up to the early Renaissance.

The Medieval Stage

Relatively little commentary survives about the conventions of medieval staging. What does exist sometimes contradicts the evidence that comes from other sources. We know that, in the earliest years, after the tropes developed into full-blown religious scenes acted inside the cathedrals, certain sections of the church were devoted to specific short plays. These areas of the church became known as MANSIONS, and each mansion represented a building or physical place known to the audience. The audience moved from one mansion to another, seeing play after play, accepting the dramatic reality of the events, characters, and locale associated with each mansion.

The tradition of moving from mansion to mansion inside the church carried over into the performances that took place later outside the church. Instead of mansions, movable wagons with raised stages provided the playing areas, called PAGEANTS. In some cases, the wagons moved to new audiences, and in others the wagons remained stationary and the audience moved from one to another. During the guild cycles, the pageants would move and the performers would give their plays at several locales so many people could see them.

According to contemporary descriptions, drawings, and reconstructions, the pageant was often a flat surface drawn on wheels that then had a wagon next to it. Their long sides touched and the pageant was used for exterior scenes and the wagon for interior scenes. In some cases a figure could descend from an upper area as if from the clouds, or actors could descend from the pageants onto the audience's level to effect a descent into an underworld. The stage was, then, a platform above the level of the audience so the action was visible (Figure 3).

A curtain concealed a space, usually inside or below the wagon, for changing costumes. The actors used costumes and props, sometimes very elaborate and expensive, in an effort to make the drama realistic. Indeed, between the thirteenth and the sixteenth centuries, a number of intense effects were developed to please a large audience. For instance, in the morality and mystery plays the devils were often portrayed as frightening, grotesque, and sometimes even comic figures. They became crowd pleasers. A sensational element was developed in some of the plays in the craft cycles, especially those that involved the lives of the saints and martyrs, in which there were plenty of chances to portray horrifying tortures.

The prop that seems to have pleased the most audiences was a complex

Figure 3. Pageant wagon

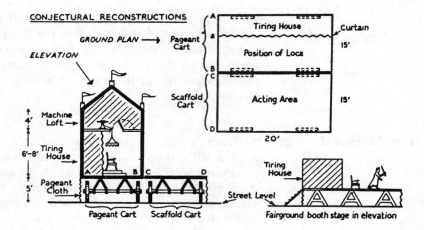

machine known as the MOUTH OF HELL, usually a large fish-shaped mouth from which smoke and explosions, fueled by gunpowder, belched constantly. The devils took great delight in stuffing their victims into these maws. According to a contemporary account, one of the machines required seventeen men to operate.

The level of realism achieved by medieval plays was at times startling. Numerous surviving illustrations show scenes that appear lifelike and authentic. In addition to visual realism, medieval plays involved a psychological level of participation on the part of both audience and actor. Sometimes they demanded that the actors suffer in accord with the characters they played. Some records attest to characters playing Christ on the cross having to be revived after their hearts stopped, and at least one Judas apparently was hanged just a little too long and had to be resuscitated.

The Actors

In the early days of liturgical drama, the actors in the tropes were monks and choirboys, and in the mystery plays they were drawn from the guilds. At first all the actors were male, but records show that eventually women took important roles.

The demands of more sophisticated plays encouraged the development of a kind of professionalism, although it seems unlikely that players in the cycles could have supported themselves on their earnings. Special skills became essential for the design and operation of complex stage machines and for the performance of acrobatics that were expected of certain characters, such as devils. As actors developed facility in delivering lines and writers found ways to incorporate more challenging elements in their plays, a professionalism no doubt arose even if actors and writers had few opportunities to earn a living on the stage.

By the second half of the sixteenth century, in the early Renaissance, groups of wandering actors were producing highly demanding and sophisticated plays, and writers such as Shakespeare were able to join them and make a living. When these professionals secured their own theaters, they had no problems filling them with good drama, with actors, and with an audience. The continuing growth and development of professionalism in the medieval theater account in large part for the power and appeal of much of the drama of the period.

EVERYMAN

This late medieval play may have origins in northern Europe. A Flemish play, *Elckerlijk* (Everyman), dates from c. 1495, and the question of whether the English *Everyman* was translated from it or whether it is a translation of *Everyman* has not been settled. Both plays may have had a common origin in an unknown play. The English *Everyman* was produced frequently in the early years of the sixteenth century. Its drama was largely theological and its purposes were aimed at reform of the audience. One indication that entertainment was not the primary goal of this morality play is its lack of the comic moments that other plays, such as *The Second Shepherds' Play*, contain.

The author of the play may have been a priest. This assumption has long been common because the play has so much theological content and offers a moral message of the kind one might expect to hear from the pulpit. The theme of the play is fundamental: the inevitability of death. And for that reason, in part, the play continues to have a universal appeal. Modern productions may not give the audience a suitable medieval chill, but the message of the play is still relevant for everyone.

The medieval reliance on allegory is apparent in the naming of the characters in *Everyman*: Death, Kindred, Cousin, Goods, Knowledge, Strength, Beauty, and Everyman himself. Each character not only stands for a specific quality; he or she is that quality. The allegorical way of thinking derived from the medieval faith that everything in the world had a moral meaning. Morality plays depended on this belief and always clarified setting, characters, and circumstances according to their moral value. This was in keeping with the medieval belief that the soul was always in jeopardy and that life was a test of one's moral condition. When Everyman meets a character, the most important information about his or her moral value is communicated instantly in the name of the character. Characters in allegorical plays also reveal themselves through their costumes and props. The character Good Deeds is simply good deeds — there is no need for psychological development because the medieval audience had a full understanding of what good deeds meant and how Good Deeds as a character would behave.

The structure of *Everyman* resembles a journey. Everyman undertakes to see who among all his acquaintances will accompany him on his most important trip: to the grave and the judgment of God Almighty. Seeing life as a journey — or as part of a journey — was especially natural for the medieval mind, which had as models the popular and costly religious pilgrimages to holy shrines and to the Holy Land itself. If life on earth is only part of the journey of the soul, then the morality play helps to put it into clear perspective. This life is not, the play tells us, the most important part of the soul's existence.

At its core, *Everyman* has a profound commercial metaphor: Everyman is called to square accounts with God. The metaphor of accounting appears early in the play, when Everyman talks about his accounts and reckonings as if they appeared in a book that should go with him to heaven. His life will be examined and if he is found wanting, he will go into the fires of hell. If he has lived profitably from a moral viewpoint, he will enjoy life everlasting. The language of the play is heavily loaded with accounting metaphors that indicate it is the product of a society quite unlike that of the Greeks or the Romans. Here the question is not centered on one's fate but rather on how well one has lived one's life.

Like many sermons, *Everyman* imparts a lesson that its auditors were expected to heed. Hence the key points of the play are repeated at the end by the Doctor. For moderns, didactic plays are sometimes tedious. For the medieval mind, they represented delightful ways of learning important messages.

Anonymous

EVERYMAN

c. 1495

EDITED BY A. C. CAWLEY

Characters

GOD	KNOWLEDGE
MESSENGER	CONFESSION
DEATH	BEAUTY
EVERYMAN	STRENGTH
FELLOWSHIP	DISCRETION
KINDRED	FIVE WITS
COUSIN	ANGEL
GOODS	DOCTOR
GOOD DEEDS	

Here beginneth a treatise how the high Father of Heaven sendeth Death to summon every creature to come and give account of their lives in this world, and is in manner of a moral play.

MESSENGER: I pray you all give your audience,
  And hear this matter with reverence,
By figure° a moral play:
The *Summoning of Everyman* called it is,
That of our lives and ending shows   5
How transitory we be all day.°
This matter is wondrous precious,
But the intent of it is more gracious,
And sweet to bear away.
The story saith: Man, in the beginning   10
Look well, and take good heed to the ending,
Be you never so gay!
Ye think sin in the beginning full sweet,
Which in the end causeth the soul to weep,
When the body lieth in clay.   15
Here shall you see how Fellowship and Jollity,
Both Strength, Pleasure, and Beauty,
Will fade from thee as flower in May;

3. By figure: In form. **6. all day:** Always.

For ye shall hear how our Heaven King
20 Calleth Everyman to a general reckoning:
Give audience, and hear what he doth say.
                                                (*Exit.*)

(*God speaketh.*)

GOD: I perceive, here in my majesty,
How that all creatures be to me unkind,°
Living without dread in worldly prosperity:
25 Of ghostly sight° the people be so blind,
Drowned in sin, they know me not for their
    God;
In worldly riches is all their mind,
They fear not my righteousness, the sharp rod.
My law that I showed, when I for them died,
They forget clean, and shedding of my blood
30   red;
I hanged between two, it cannot be denied;
To get them life I suffered to be dead;
I healed their feet, with thorns hurt was my
    head.
I could do no more than I did, truly;
35 And now I see the people do clean forsake me:
They use the seven deadly sins damnable,
As pride, covetise, wrath, and lechery
Now in the world be made commendable;
And thus they leave of angels the heavenly
    company.
40 Every man liveth so after his own pleasure,
And yet of their life they be nothing sure:
I see the more that I them forbear
The worse they be from year to year.
All that liveth appaireth° fast;
45 Therefore I will, in all the haste,
Have a reckoning of every man's person;
For, and° I leave the people thus alone
In their life and wicked tempests,
Verily they will become much worse than beasts;
50 For now one would by envy another up eat;
Charity they do all clean forget.
I hoped well that every man
In my glory should make his mansion,
And thereto I had them all elect;
55 But now I see, like traitors deject,°
They thank me not for the pleasure that I to
    them meant,
Nor yet for their being that I them have lent.
I proffered the people great multitude of mercy,
And few there be that asketh it heartily.
60 They be so cumbered with worldly riches
That needs on them I must do justice,

On every man living without fear.
Where art thou, Death, thou mighty messenger?

(*Enter Death.*)

DEATH: Almighty God, I am here at your will,
Your commandment to fulfill.   65
GOD: Go thou to Everyman,
And show him, in my name,
A pilgrimage he must on him take,
Which he in no wise may escape;
And that he bring with him a sure reckoning   70
Without delay or any tarrying.
                                    (*God withdraws.*)
DEATH: Lord, I will in the world go run overall,
And cruelly outsearch both great and small;
Every man will I beset that liveth beastly
Out of God's laws, and dreadeth not folly.   75
He that loveth riches I will strike with my dart,
His sight to blind, and from heaven to
    depart° —
Except that alms be his good friend —
In hell for to dwell, world without end.
Lo, yonder I see Everyman walking.   80
Full little he thinketh on my coming;
His mind is on fleshly lusts and his treasure,
And great pain it shall cause him to endure
Before the Lord, Heaven King.

(*Enter Everyman.*)

Everyman, stand still! Whither art thou going   85
Thus gaily? Hast thou thy Maker forget?
EVERYMAN: Why askest thou?
Wouldest thou wit?°
DEATH: Yea, sir; I will show you:
In great haste I am sent to thee   90
From God out of his majesty.
EVERYMAN: What, sent to me?
DEATH: Yea, certainly.
Though thou have forget him here,
He thinketh on thee in the heavenly sphere,   95
As, ere we depart, thou shalt know.
EVERYMAN: What desireth God of me?
DEATH: That shall I show thee:
A reckoning he will needs have
Without any longer respite.   100
EVERYMAN: To give a reckoning longer leisure I
    crave;
This blind matter troubleth my wit.
DEATH: On thee thou must take a long journey;
Therefore thy book of count° with thee thou
    bring,
For turn° again thou cannot by no way.   105

---

23. **unkind:** Ungrateful.   25. **ghostly sight:** Spiritual vision.
44. **appaireth:** Degenerates.   47. **and:** If.   55. **deject:** Abject.

77. **depart:** Separate.   88. **wit:** Know.   104. **count:** Account.
105. **turn:** Return.

And look thou be sure of thy reckoning,
For before God thou shalt answer, and show
Thy many bad deeds, and good but a few;
How thou hast spent thy life, and in what wise,
110 Before the chief Lord of paradise.
Have ado that we were in that way,°
For, wit thou well, thou shalt make none
attorney.°
EVERYMAN: Full unready I am such reckoning to
give.
I know thee not. What messenger art thou?
115 DEATH: I am Death, that no man dreadeth,°
For every man I rest,° and no man spareth;
For it is God's commandment
That all to me should be obedient.
EVERYMAN: O Death, thou comest when I had thee
least in mind!
120 In thy power it lieth me to save;
Yet of my good° will I give thee, if thou will be
kind:
Yea, a thousand pound shalt thou have,
And defer this matter till another day.
DEATH: Everyman, it may not be, by no way.
125 I set not by gold, silver, nor riches,
Ne by pope, emperor, king, duke, ne princes;
For, and I would receive gifts great,
All the world I might get;
But my custom is clean contrary.
I give thee no respite. Come hence, and not
130 tarry.
EVERYMAN: Alas, shall I have no longer respite?
I may say Death giveth no warning!
To think on thee, it maketh my heart sick,
For all unready is my book of reckoning.
135 But twelve year and I might have abiding,°
My counting-book I would make so clear
That my reckoning I should not need to fear.
Wherefore, Death, I pray thee, for God's mercy,
Spare me till I be provided of remedy.
140 DEATH: Thee availeth not to cry, weep, and pray;
But haste thee lightly that thou were gone that
journey,°
And prove thy friends if thou can;
For, wit thou well, the tide abideth no man,
And in the world each living creature
145 For Adam's sin must die of nature.°
EVERYMAN: Death, if I should this pilgrimage take,

And my reckoning surely make,
Show me, for saint charity,°
Should I not come again shortly?
DEATH: No, Everyman; and thou be once there,   150
Thou mayst never more come here,
Trust me verily.
EVERYMAN: O gracious God in the high seat
celestial,
Have mercy on me in this most need!
Shall I have no company from this vale
terrestrial   155
Of mine acquaintance, that way me to lead?
DEATH: Yea, if any be so hardy
That would go with thee and bear thee
company.
Hie thee that thou were gone to God's
magnificence,
Thy reckoning to give before his presence.   160
What, weenest° thou thy life is given thee,
And thy worldly goods also?
EVERYMAN: I had wend° so, verily.
DEATH: Nay, nay; it was but lent thee;
For as soon as thou art go,   165
Another a while shall have it, and then go
therefro,
Even as thou has done.
Everyman, thou art mad! Thou hast thy wits
five,
And here on earth will not amend thy life;
For suddenly I do come.   170
EVERYMAN: O wretched caitiff,° whither shall I flee,
That I might scape this endless sorrow?
Now, gentle Death, spare me till to-morrow,
That I may amend me
With good advisement.   175
DEATH: Nay, thereto I will not consent,
Nor no man will I respite;
But to the heart suddenly I shall smite
Without any advisement.
And now out of thy sight I will me hie;   180
See thou make thee ready shortly,
For thou mayst say this is the day
That no man living may scape away.
                                    (*Exit Death.*)
EVERYMAN: Alas, I may well weep with sighs deep!
Now have I no manner of company   185
To help me in my journey, and me to keep;
And also my writing is full unready,
How shall I do now for to excuse me?
I would to God I had never be get!°
To my soul a full great profit it had be;   190

---

111. **Have ado . . . that way:** Let us see about making that
journey.   112. **none attorney:** No one [your] advocate.   115.
no man dreadeth: Fears no man.   116. **rest:** Arrest.   121.
good: Goods.   135. **But twelve year . . . abiding:** If I could
stay for just twelve more years.   141. **But haste thee . . .
that journey:** But set off quickly on your journey.   145. **of
nature:** In the course of nature.

148. **for saint charity:** In the name of holy charity.   161.
weenest: Suppose.   163. **wend:** Supposed.   171. **caitiff:**
Captive.   189. **be get:** Been born.

For now I fear pains huge and great.
The time passeth. Lord, help, that all wrought!
For though I mourn it availeth nought.
The day passeth, and is almost ago;°
195 I wot not well what for to do.
To whom were I best my complaint to make?
What and I to Fellowship thereof spake,
And showed him of this sudden chance?
For in him is all mine affiance;°
200 We have in the world so many a day
Be good friends in sport and play.
I see him yonder, certainly.
I trust that he will bear me company;
Therefore to him will I speak to ease my sorrow.
205 Well met, good Fellowship, and good morrow!

(*Fellowship speaketh.*)

FELLOWSHIP: Everyman, good morrow, by this day!
Sir, why lookest thou so piteously?
If any thing be amiss, I pray thee me say,
That I may help to remedy.
210 EVERYMAN: Yea, good Fellowship, yea;
I am in great jeopardy.
FELLOWSHIP: My true friend, show to me your
mind;
I will not forsake thee to my life's end,
In the way of good company.
215 EVERYMAN: That was well spoken, and lovingly.
FELLOWSHIP: Sir, I must needs know your
heaviness;°
I have pity to see you in any distress.
If any have you wronged, ye shall revenged be,
Though I on the ground be slain for thee —
220 Though that I know before that I should die.
EVERYMAN: Verily, Fellowship, gramercy.°
FELLOWSHIP: Tush! by thy thanks I set not a straw.
Show me your grief, and say no more.
EVERYMAN: If I my heart should to you break,°
225 And then you to turn your mind from me,
And would not me comfort when ye hear me
speak,
Then should I ten times sorrier be.
FELLOWSHIP: Sir, I say as I will do indeed.
EVERYMAN: Then be you a good friend at need:
230 I have found you true herebefore.
FELLOWSHIP: And so ye shall evermore;
For, in faith, and thou go to hell,
I will not forsake thee by the way.
EVERYMAN: Ye speak like a good friend; I believe
you well.
235 I shall deserve° it, and I may.

FELLOWSHIP: I speak of no deserving, by this day!
For he that will say, and nothing do,
Is not worthy with good company to go;
Therefore show me the grief of your mind,
As to your friend most loving and kind.   240
EVERYMAN: I shall show you how it is:
Commanded I am to go a journey,
A long way, hard and dangerous,
And give a strait count, without delay,
Before the high Judge, Adonai.°   245
Wherefore, I pray you, bear me company,
As ye have promised, in this journey.
FELLOWSHIP: That is matter indeed.° Promise is
duty;
But, and I should take such a voyage on me,
I know it well, it should be to my pain;   250
Also it maketh me afeard, certain.
But let us take counsel here as well as we can,
For your words would fear a strong man.
EVERYMAN: Why, ye said if I had need
Ye would me never forsake, quick ne dead,   255
Though it were to hell, truly.
FELLOWSHIP: So I said, certainly,
But such pleasures be set aside, the sooth to say;
And also, if we took such a journey,
When should we come again?   260
EVERYMAN: Nay, never again, till the day of doom.
FELLOWSHIP: In faith, then will not I come there!
Who hath you these tidings brought?
EVERYMAN: Indeed, Death was with me here.
FELLOWSHIP: Now, by God that all hath bought,°   265
If Death were the messenger,
For no man that is living to-day
I will not go that loath journey —
Not for the father that begat me!
EVERYMAN: Ye promised otherwise, pardie.°   270
FELLOWSHIP: I wot well I said so, truly;
And yet if thou wilt eat, and drink, and make
good cheer,
Or haunt to women the lusty company,°
I would not forsake you while the day is clear,°
Trust me verily.   275
EVERYMAN: Yea, thereto ye would be ready!
To go to mirth, solace, and play,
Your mind will sooner apply,
Than to bear me company in my long journey.
FELLOWSHIP: Now, in good faith, I will not that
way.   280

---

194. **ago:** Gone.   199. **affiance:** Trust.   216. **heaviness:**
Sorrow.   221. **gramercy:** Thanks.   224. **break:** Open.   235.
deserve: Repay.

245. **Adonai:** Hebrew name for God.   248. **That is matter
indeed:** That is a good reason indeed [for asking me].   265.
bought: Redeemed.   270. **pardie.** By God.   273. **haunt to
women the lusty company:** Frequent the lively company of
women.   274. **while the day is clear:** Until daybreak.

But and thou will murder, or any man kill,
In that I will help thee with a good will.
EVERYMAN: O, that is a simple advice indeed.
Gentle fellow, help me in my necessity!
285 We have loved long, and now I need;
And now, gentle Fellowship, remember me.
FELLOWSHIP: Whether ye have loved me or no,
By Saint John, I will not with thee go.
EVERYMAN: Yet, I pray thee, take the labor, and do
so much for me
290 To bring me forward, for saint charity,
And comfort me till I come without the town.
FELLOWSHIP: Nay, and thou would give me a new
gown,
I will not a foot with thee go;
But, and thou had tarried, I would not have left
thee so.
295 And as now God speed thee in thy journey,
For from thee I will depart as fast as I may.
EVERYMAN: Whither away, Fellowship? Will thou
forsake me?
FELLOWSHIP: Yea, by my fay!° To God I betake°
thee.
EVERYMAN: Farewell, good Fellowship; for thee my
heart is sore.
300 Adieu for ever! I shall see thee no more.
FELLOWSHIP: In faith, Everyman, farewell now at
the ending;
For you I will remember that parting is
mourning. (*Exit Fellowship.*)
EVERYMAN: Alack! shall we thus depart° indeed —
Ah, Lady, help! — without any more comfort?
305 Lo, Fellowship forsaketh me in my most need.
For help in this world whither shall I resort?
Fellowship herebefore with me would merry
make,
And now little sorrow for me doth he take.
It is said, "In prosperity men friends may find,
310 Which in adversity be full unkind."
Now whither for succor shall I flee,
Sith° that Fellowship hath forsaken me?
To my kinsmen I will, truly,
Praying them to help me in my necessity;
315 I believe that they will do so,
For kind will creep where it may not go.°
I will go say,° for yonder I see them.
Where be ye now, my friends and kinsmen?

(*Enter Kindred and Cousin.*)

KINDRED: Here be we now at your commandment.
Cousin, I pray you show us your intent 320
In any wise, and do not spare.
COUSIN: Yea, Everyman, and to us declare
If ye be disposed to go anywhither;
For, wit you well, we will live and die together.
KINDRED: In wealth and woe we will with you
hold, 325
For over his kin a man may be bold.°
EVERYMAN: Gramercy, my friends and kinsmen
kind.
Now shall I show you the grief of my mind:
I was commanded by a messenger,
That is a high king's chief officer; 330
He bade me go a pilgrimage, to my pain,
And I know well I shall never come again;
Also I must give a reckoning strait,
For I have a great enemy° that hath me in wait,°
Which intendeth me for to hinder. 335
KINDRED: What account is that which ye must
render?
That would I know.
EVERYMAN: Of all my works I must show
How I have lived and my days spent;
Also of ill deeds that I have used 340
In my time, sith life was me lent;
And of all virtues that I have refused.
Therefore, I pray you, go thither with me
To help to make mine account, for saint charity.
COUSIN: What, to go thither? Is that the matter? 345
Nay, Everyman, I had liefer fast bread and
water°
All this five year and more.
EVERYMAN: Alas, that ever I was bore!
For now shall I never be merry,
If that you forsake me. 350
KINDRED: Ah, sir, what ye be a merry man!
Take good heart to you, and make no moan.
But one thing I warn you, by Saint Anne —
As for me, ye shall go alone.
EVERYMAN: My Cousin, will you not with me go? 355
COUSIN: No, by our Lady! I have the cramp in my
toe.
Trust not to me, for, so God me speed,
I will deceive you in your most need.
KINDRED: It availeth not us to tice.°
Ye shall have my maid with all my heart; 360
She loveth to go to feasts, there to be nice,°
And to dance, and abroad to start:

298. fay: Faith; betake: Commend. 303. depart: Part. 312.
Sith: Since. 316. for kind will creep where it may not go:
For kinship will creep where it cannot walk, i.e., blood is
thicker than water. 317. say: Essay, try.

326. For over his kin ... may be bold: For a man may be
sure of his kinsfolk. 334. enemy: Devil; hath me in wait:
Has me under observation. 346. liefer fast bread and water:
Rather fast on bread and water. 359. tice: Entice. 361.
nice: Wanton.

I will give her leave to help you in that journey,
If that you and she may agree.
EVERYMAN: Now show me the very effect° of your
365   mind:
Will you go with me, or abide behind?
KINDRED: Abide behind? Yea, that will I, and I
    may!
Therefore farewell till another day.
                      (*Exit Kindred.*)
EVERYMAN: How should I be merry or glad?
370   For fair promises men to me make,
But when I have most need they me forsake.
I am deceived; that maketh me sad.
COUSIN: Cousin Everyman, farewell now,
For verily I will not go with you.
375   Also of mine own an unready reckoning
I have to account; therefore I make tarrying.
Now God keep thee, for now I go.
                      (*Exit Cousin.*)
EVERYMAN: Ah, Jesus, is all come hereto?
Lo, fair words maketh fools fain;°
380   They promise, and nothing will do, certain.
My kinsmen promised me faithfully
For to abide with me steadfastly,
And now fast away do they flee:
Even so Fellowship promised me.
385   What friend were best me of to provide?°
I lose my time here longer to abide.
Yet in my mind a thing there is:
All my life I have loved riches;
If that my Good° now help me might,
390   He would make my heart full light.
I will speak to him in this distress —
Where art thou, my Goods and riches?

(*Goods speaks from a corner.*)

GOODS: Who calleth me? Everyman? What! hast
    thou haste?
I lie here in corners, trussed and piled so high,
395   And in chests I am locked so fast,
Also sacked in bags. Thou mayst see with thine
    eye
I cannot stir; in packs low I lie.
What would ye have? Lightly° me say.
EVERYMAN: Come hither, Good, in all the haste
    thou may,
400   For of counsel I must desire thee.
GOODS: Sir, and ye in the world have sorrow or
    adversity,
That can I help you to remedy shortly.
EVERYMAN: It is another disease that grieveth me;

In this world it is not, I tell thee so.
I am sent for, another way to go,   405
To give a strait count general
Before the highest Jupiter of all;
And all my life I have had joy and pleasure in
    thee,
Therefore, I pray thee, go with me;
For, peradventure, thou mayst before God
    Almighty   410
My reckoning help to clean and purify;
For it is said ever among
That money maketh all right that is wrong.
GOODS: Nay, Everyman, I sing another song.
I follow no man in such voyages;   415
For, and I went with thee,
Thou shouldst fare much the worse for me;
For because on me thou did set thy mind,
Thy reckoning I have made blotted and blind,
That thine account thou cannot make truly;   420
And that hast thou for the love of me.
EVERYMAN: That would grieve me full sore,
When I should come to that fearful answer.
Up, let us go thither together.
GOODS: Nay, not so! I am too brittle, I may not
    endure;   425
I will follow no man one foot, be ye sure.
EVERYMAN: Alas, I have thee loved, and had great
    pleasure
All my life-days on good and treasure.
GOODS: That is to thy damnation, without leasing,°
For my love is contrary to the love everlasting; 430
But if thou had me loved moderately during,
As to the poor to give part of me,
Then shouldst thou not in this dolor be,
Nor in this great sorrow and care.
EVERYMAN: Lo, now was I deceived ere I was ware, 435
And all I may wite° misspending of time.
GOODS: What, weenest thou that I am thine?
EVERYMAN: I had wend so.
GOODS: Nay, Everyman, I say no.
As for a while I was lent thee;   440
A season thou hast had me in prosperity.
My condition is man's soul to kill;
If I save one, a thousand I do spill.°
Weenest thou that I will follow thee?
Nay, not from this world, verily.   445
EVERYMAN: I had wend otherwise.
GOODS: Therefore to thy soul Good is a thief;
For when thou art dead, this is my guise —
Another to deceive in this same wise
As I have done thee, and all to his soul's
    reprief.°   450

---

365. **effect:** Tenor.   379. **fain:** Glad.   385. **me of to provide:**
To provide myself with.   389. **Good:** Goods.   398. **Lightly:**
Quickly.

429. **without leasing:** Without a lie, i.e., truly.   436. **wite:**
Blame.   443. **spill:** Ruin.   450. **reprief:** Shame.

EVERYMAN: O false Good, cursed may thou be,
   Thou traitor to God, that hast deceived me
   And caught me in thy snare!
GOODS: Marry, thou brought thyself in care,
455   Whereof I am glad;
   I must needs laugh, I cannot be sad.
EVERYMAN: Ah, Good, thou hast had long my
     heartly love;
   I gave thee that which should be the Lord's
     above.
   But wilt thou not go with me indeed?
460   I pray thee truth to say.
GOODS: No, so God me speed!
   Therefore farewell, and have good day.
                    (Exit Goods.)
EVERYMAN: O, to whom shall I make my moan
   For to go with me in that heavy journey?
465   First Fellowship said he would with me gone;
   His words were very pleasant and gay,
   But afterward he left me alone.
   Then spake I to my kinsmen, all in despair,
   And also they gave me words fair;
470   They lacked no fair speaking,
   But all forsook me in the ending.
   Then went I to my Goods, that I loved best,
   In hope to have comfort, but there had I least;
   For my Goods sharply did me tell
475   That he bringeth many into hell.
   Then of myself I was ashamed,
   And so I am worthy to be blamed;
   Thus may I well myself hate.
   Of whom shall I now counsel take?
480   I think that I shall never speed
   Till that I go to my Good Deed.
   But, alas, she is so weak
   That she can neither go nor speak;
   Yet will I venture on her now.
485   My Good Deeds, where be you?

(Good Deeds speaks from the ground.)

GOOD DEEDS: Here I lie, cold in the ground;
   Thy sins hath me sore bound,
   That I cannot stir.
EVERYMAN: O Good Deeds, I stand in fear!
490   I must you pray of counsel,
   For help now should come right well.°
GOOD DEEDS: Everyman, I have understanding
   That ye be summoned account to make
   Before Messias, of Jerusalem King;
   And you do by me,° that journey with you will I
495   take.

491. **should come right well:** Would be very welcome. **495.
by me:** As I advise.

EVERYMAN: Therefore I come to you, my moan to
     make;
   I pray you that ye will go with me.
GOOD DEEDS: I would full fain, but I cannot stand,
     verily.
EVERYMAN: Why, is there anything on you fall?
GOOD DEEDS: Yea, sir, I may thank you of° all;   500
   If ye had perfectly cheered me,
   Your book of count full ready had be.
   Look, the books of your works and deeds eke!°
   Behold how they lie under the feet,
   To your soul's heaviness.   505
EVERYMAN: Our Lord Jesus help me!
   For one letter here I cannot see.
GOOD DEEDS: There is a blind reckoning in time of
     distress.
EVERYMAN: Good Deeds, I pray you help me in this
     need,
   Or else I am for ever damned indeed;   510
   Therefore help me to make reckoning
   Before the Redeemer of all thing,
   That King is, and was, and ever shall.
GOOD DEEDS: Everyman, I am sorry of your fall,
   And fain would I help you, and I were able.   515
EVERYMAN: Good Deeds, your counsel I pray you
     give me.
GOOD DEEDS: That shall I do verily;
   Though that on my feet I may not go,
   I have a sister that shall with you also,
   Called Knowledge, which shall with you abide,   520
   To help you to make that dreadful reckoning.

(Enter Knowledge.)

KNOWLEDGE: Everyman, I will go with thee, and be
     thy guide,
   In thy most need to go by thy side.
EVERYMAN: In good condition I am now in every
     thing,
   And am wholly content with this good thing,   525
   Thanked be God my creator.
GOOD DEEDS: And when she hath brought you
     there
   Where thou shalt heal thee of thy smart,
   Then go you with your reckoning and your
     Good Deeds together,
   For to make you joyful at heart   530
   Before the blessed Trinity.
EVERYMAN: My Good Deeds, gramercy!
   I am well content, certainly,
   With your words sweet.
KNOWLEDGE: Now go we together lovingly   535
   To Confession, that cleansing river.

500. **of:** For.   503. **eke:** Also.

EVERYMAN: For joy I weep; I would we were there!
But, I pray you, give me cognition
Where dwelleth that holy man, Confession.
540 KNOWLEDGE: In the house of salvation:
We shall find him in that place,
That shall us comfort, by God's grace.

(*Knowledge takes Everyman to Confession.*)

Lo, this is Confession. Kneel down and ask
mercy,
For he is in good conceit° with God Almighty.
EVERYMAN: O glorious fountain, that all
545   uncleanness doth clarify,
Wash from me the spots of vice unclean,
That on me no sin may be seen.
I come with Knowledge for my redemption,
Redempt with heart° and full contrition;
550 For I am commanded a pilgrimage to take,
And great accounts before God to make.
Now I pray you, Shrift, mother of salvation,
Help my Good Deeds for my piteous
exclamation.
CONFESSION: I know your sorrow well, Everyman.
555 Because with Knowledge ye come to me,
I will you comfort as well as I can,
And a precious jewel I will give thee,
Called penance, voider of adversity;
Therewith shall your body chastised be,
With abstinence and perseverance in God's
560   service.
Here shall you receive that scourge of me,
Which is penance strong that ye must endure,
To remember thy Savior was scourged for thee
With sharp scourges, and suffered it patiently;
So must thou, ere thou scape that painful
565   pilgrimage.
Knowledge, keep him in this voyage,
And by that time Good Deeds will be with thee.
But in any wise be siker° of mercy,
For your time draweth fast; and° ye will saved
be,
570 Ask God mercy, and he will grant truly.
When with the scourge of penance man doth
him bind,
The oil of forgiveness then shall he find.
EVERYMAN: Thanked be God for his gracious work!
For now I will my penance begin;
575 This hath rejoiced and lighted my heart,
Though the knots be painful and hard within.
KNOWLEDGE: Everyman, look your penance that ye
fulfill,
What pain that ever it to you be;

544. conceit: Esteem.   549. heart: Heartfelt.   568. siker:
Sure.   569. and: If.

And Knowledge shall give you counsel at will
How your account ye shall make clearly.   580
EVERYMAN: O eternal God, O heavenly figure,
O way of righteousness, O goodly vision,
Which descended down in a virgin pure
Because he would every man redeem,
Which Adam forfeited by his disobedience: 585
O blessed Godhead, elect and high divine,
Forgive my grievous offense;
Here I cry thee mercy in this presence.°
O ghostly treasure, O ransomer and redeemer,
Of all the world hope and conductor,   590
Mirror of joy, and founder of mercy,
Which enlumineth heaven and earth thereby,
Hear my clamorous complaint, though it late be;
Receive my prayers, of thy benignity;
Though I be a sinner most abominable,   595
Yet let my name be written in Moses' table.°
O Mary, pray to the Maker of all thing,
Me for to help at my ending;
And save me from the power of my enemy,
For Death assaileth me strongly.   600
And, Lady, that I may by mean of thy prayer
Of your Son's glory to be partner,
By the means of his passion, I it crave;
I beseech you help my soul to save.
Knowledge, give me the scourge of penance;   605
My flesh therewith shall give acquittance:°
I will now begin, if God give me grace.
KNOWLEDGE: Everyman, God give you time and
space!
Thus I bequeath you in the hands of our
Saviour;
Now may you make your reckoning sure.   610
EVERYMAN: In the name of the Holy Trinity,
My body sore punished shall be:
Take this, body, for the sin of the flesh!

(*Scourges himself.*)

Also° thou delightest to go gay and fresh,
And in the way of damnation thou did me
bring,   615
Therefore suffer now strokes and punishing.
Now of penance I will wade the water clear,
To save me from purgatory, that sharp fire.

(*Good Deeds rises from the ground.*)

588. in this presence: In the presence of this company.   596.
Moses' table: Medieval theologians regarded the two tablets
given to Moses on Mount Sinai as symbols of baptism and
penance. Thus Everyman is asking to be numbered among
those who have escaped damnation by doing penance for
their sins.   606. acquittance: Satisfaction (as part of the
sacrament of penance).   614. Also: As.

GOOD DEEDS: I thank God, now I can walk and go,
620 And am delivered of my sickness and woe.
Therefore with Everyman I will go, and not
spare;
His good works I will help him to declare.
KNOWLEDGE: Now, Everyman, be merry and glad!
Your Good Deeds cometh now; ye may not be
sad.
625 Now is your Good Deeds whole and sound,
Going upright upon the ground.
EVERYMAN: My heart is light, and shall be
evermore;
Now will I smite° faster than I did before.
GOOD DEEDS: Everyman, pilgrim, my special friend,
630 Blessed be thou without end;
For thee is preparate the eternal glory.
Ye have me made whole and sound,
Therefore I will bide by thee in every stound.°
EVERYMAN: Welcome, my Good Deeds; now I hear
thy voice,
635 I weep for very sweetness of love.
KNOWLEDGE: Be no more sad, but ever rejoice;
God seeth thy living in his throne above.
Put on this garment to thy behoof,°
Which is wet with your tears,
640 Or else before God you may it miss,
When ye to your journey's end come shall.
EVERYMAN: Gentle Knowledge, what do ye it call?
KNOWLEDGE: It is a garment of sorrow:
From pain it will you borrow;°
645 Contrition it is,
That geteth forgiveness;
It pleaseth God passing well.
GOOD DEEDS: Everyman, will you wear it for your
heal?°
EVERYMAN: Now blessed be Jesu, Mary's Son,
650 For now have I on true contrition.
And let us go now without tarrying;
Good Deeds, have we clear our reckoning?
GOOD DEEDS: Yea, indeed, I have it here.
EVERYMAN: Then I trust we need not fear;
655 Now, friends, let us not part in twain.
KNOWLEDGE: Nay, Everyman, that will we not,
certain.
GOOD DEEDS: Yet must thou lead with thee
Three persons of great might.
EVERYMAN: Who should they be?
660 GOOD DEEDS: Discretion and Strength they hight,°
And thy Beauty may not abide behind.
KNOWLEDGE: Also ye must call to mind
Your Five Wits as for your counsellors.

GOOD DEEDS: You must have them ready at all
hours.
EVERYMAN: How shall I get them hither?   665
KNOWLEDGE: You must call them all together,
And they will hear you incontinent.°
EVERYMAN: My friends, come hither and be
present,
Discretion, Strength, my Five Wits, and Beauty.

(*Enter Beauty, Strength, Discretion, and Five Wits.*)

BEAUTY: Here at your will we be all ready.   670
What will ye that we should do?
GOOD DEEDS: That ye would with Everyman go,
And help him in his pilgrimage.
Advise you, will ye with him or not in that
voyage?
STRENGTH: We will bring him all thither,   675
To his help and comfort, ye may believe me.
DISCRETION: So will we go with him all together.
EVERYMAN: Almighty God, lofed° may thou be!
I give thee laud that I have hither brought
Strength, Discretion, Beauty, and Five Wits. Lack
I nought.   680
And my Good Deeds, with Knowledge clear,
All be in my company at my will here;
I desire no more to my business.
STRENGTH: And I, Strength, will by you stand in
distress,
Though thou would in battle fight on the
ground.   685
FIVE WITS: And though it were through the world
round,
We will not depart for sweet ne sour.
BEAUTY: No more will I unto death's hour,
Whatsoever thereof befall.
DISCRETION: Everyman, advise you first of all;   690
Go with a good advisement and deliberation.
We all give you virtuous monition°
That all shall be well.
EVERYMAN: My friends, harken what I will tell:
I pray God reward you in his heavenly sphere.   695
Now harken, all that be here,
For I will make my testament
Here before you all present:
In alms half my good I will give with my hands
twain
In the way of charity, with good intent,   700
And the other half still shall remain
In queth,° to be returned there it ought to be.°

---

628. **smite:** Strike.   633. **stound:** Trial.   638. **behoof:** Advantage.   644. **borrow:** Release.   648. **heal:** Salvation.   660. **hight:** Are called.

667. **incontinent:** Immediately.   678. **lofed:** Praised.   692. **monition:** Forewarning.   702. **queth:** Bequest; **returned there it ought to be:** This line probably refers to restitution, that is, the restoration to its proper owner of unlawfully acquired property.

This I do in despite of the fiend of hell,
To go quit out of his peril°
705 Ever after and this day.
KNOWLEDGE: Everyman, harken what I say:
Go to priesthood, I you advise,
And receive of him in any wise°
The holy sacrament and ointment together.
710 Then shortly see ye turn again hither;
We will all abide you here.
FIVE WITS: Yea, Everyman, hie you that ye ready
were.
There is no emperor, king, duke, ne baron,
That of God hath commission
715 As hath the least priest in the world being;
For of the blessed sacraments pure and benign
He beareth the keys, and thereof hath the cure°
For man's redemption — it is ever sure —
Which God for our soul's medicine
720 Gave us out of his heart with great pine.°
Here in this transitory life, for thee and me,
The blessed sacraments seven there be:
Baptism, confirmation, with priesthood good,
And the sacrament of God's precious flesh and
blood,
Marriage, the holy extreme unction, and
725 penance;
These seven be good to have in remembrance,
Gracious sacraments of high divinity.
EVERYMAN: Fain would I receive that holy body,
And meekly to my ghostly father I will go.
FIVE WITS: Everyman, that is the best that ye can
730 do.
God will you to salvation bring,
For priesthood exceedeth all other thing;
To us Holy Scripture they do teach,
And converteth man from sin heaven to reach;
735 God hath to them more power given
Than to any angel that is in heaven.
With five words° he may consecrate,
God's body in flesh and blood to make,
And handleth his Maker between his hands.
740 The priest bindeth and unbindeth all bands,
Both in earth and in heaven.
Thou ministers all the sacraments seven;
Though we kissed thy feet, thou were worthy;
Thou art surgeon that cureth sin deadly:
745 No remedy we find under God
But all only priesthood.°

Everyman, God gave priests that dignity,
And setteth them in his stead among us to be;
Thus be they above angels in degree.

(*Everyman goes to the priest to receive the last sacraments.*)

KNOWLEDGE: If priests be good, it is so, surely.   750
But when Jesus hanged on the cross with great
smart,
There he gave out of his blessed heart
The same sacrament in great torment:
He sold them not to us, that Lord omnipotent.
Therefore Saint Peter the apostle doth say   755
That Jesu's curse hath all they
Which God their Savior do buy or sell,
Or they for any money do take or tell.°
Sinful priests giveth the sinners example bad;
Their children sitteth by other men's fires, I have
heard;   760
And some haunteth women's company
With unclean life, as lusts of lechery:
These be with sin made blind.
FIVE WITS: I trust to God no such may we find;
Therefore let us priesthood honor,   765
And follow their doctrine for our souls' succor.
We be their sheep, and they shepherds be
By whom we all be kept in surety.
Peace, for yonder I see Everyman come,
Which hath made true satisfaction.   770
GOOD DEEDS: Methink it is he indeed.

(*Reenter Everyman.*)

EVERYMAN: Now Jesu be your alder speed!°
I have received the sacrament for my
redemption,
And then mine extreme unction:
Blessed be all they that counselled me to take it!   775
And now, friends, let us go without longer
respite;
I thank God that ye have tarried so long.
Now set each of you on this rood° your hand,
And shortly follow me:
I go before there I would be; God be our guide!   780
STRENGTH: Everyman, we will not from you go
Till ye have done this voyage long.
DISCRETION: I, Discretion, will bide by you also.
KNOWLEDGE: And though this pilgrimage be never
so strong,°
I will never part you fro.   785

704. quit out of his peril: Free out of his power.   708. in any wise: Without fail.   717. cure: Charge.   720. pine: Suffering.   737. five words: *Hoc est enim corpus meum* ("For this is My Body," the words of the consecration of the Body of Christ at Mass).   746. But all only priesthood: Except only from the priesthood.

755–758. Therefore Saint Peter . . . do take or tell: Reference to the sin of simony, the selling of Church offices or benefits.   758. tell: Count out, i.e., sell.   772. your alder speed: The helper of you all.   778. rood: Cross.   784. strong: Grievous.

STRENGTH: Everyman, I will be as sure by thee
    As ever I did by Judas Maccabee.°

(*Everyman comes to his grave.*)

EVERYMAN: Alas, I am so faint I may not stand;
    My limbs under me doth fold.
790   Friends, let us not turn again to this land,
    Not for all the world's gold;
    For into this cave must I creep
    And turn to earth, and there to sleep.
BEAUTY: What, into this grave? Alas!
EVERYMAN: Yea, there shall ye consume, more and
795   less.
BEAUTY: And what, should I smother here?
EVERYMAN: Yea, by my faith, and never more
    appear.
    In this world live no more we shall,
    But in heaven before the highest Lord of all.
800 BEAUTY: I cross out all this;° adieu, by Saint John!
    I take my cap in my lap,° and am gone.
EVERYMAN: What, Beauty, whither will ye?
BEAUTY: Peace, I am deaf; I look not behind me,
    Not and thou wouldest give me all the gold in
    thy chest.   (*Exit Beauty.*)
805 EVERYMAN: Alas, whereto may I trust?
    Beauty goeth fast away from me;
    She promised with me to live and die.
STRENGTH: Everyman, I will thee also forsake and
    deny;
    Thy game liketh° me not at all.
810 EVERYMAN: Why, then, ye will forsake me all?
    Sweet Strength, tarry a little space.
STRENGTH: Nay, sir, by the rood of grace!
    I will hie me from thee fast,
    Though thou weep till thy heart to-brast.°
815 EVERYMAN: Ye would ever bide by me, ye said.
STRENGTH: Yea, I have you far enough conveyed.
    Ye be old enough, I understand,
    Your pilgrimage to take on hand;
    I repent me that I hither came.
EVERYMAN: Strength, you to displease I am to
820   blame;
    Yet promise is debt, this ye well wot.
STRENGTH: In faith, I care not.
    Thou art but a fool to complain;
    You spend your speech and waste your brain.
825   Go thrust thee into the ground! (*Exit Strength.*)

---

787. Judas Maccabee: Judas Maccabeus, who overcame Syrian
domination and won religious freedom for the Jews in 165
B.C., believed that his strength came not from wordly might
but from heaven (1 Maccabees 3:19).   **800. I cross out all
this:** I cancel all this, i.e., my promise to stay with you.
801. take my cap in my lap: Doff my cap [so low that it
comes] into my lap.   **809. liketh:** Pleases.   **814. brast:** Break.

EVERYMAN: I had wend surer I should you have
    found.
    He that trusteth in his Strength
    She him deceiveth at the length.
    Both Strength and Beauty forsaketh me;
    Yet they promised me fair and lovingly.   830
DISCRETION: Everyman, I will after Strength be
    gone;
    As for me, I will leave you alone.
EVERYMAN: Why, Discretion, will ye forsake me?
DISCRETION: Yea, in faith, I will go from thee,
    For when Strength goeth before   835
    I follow after evermore.
EVERYMAN: Yet, I pray thee, for the love of the
    Trinity,
    Look in my grave once piteously.
DISCRETION: Nay, so nigh will I not come;
    Farewell, every one!   (*Exit Discretion.*) 840
EVERYMAN: O, all thing faileth, save God alone —
    Beauty, Strength, and Discretion;
    For when Death bloweth his blast,
    They all run from me full fast.
FIVE WITS: Everyman, my leave now of thee I take; 845
    I will follow the other, for here I thee forsake.
EVERYMAN: Alas, then may I wail and weep,
    For I took you for my best friend.
FIVE WITS: I will no longer thee keep;
    Now farewell, and there an end.   850
                         (*Exit Five Wits.*)
EVERYMAN: O Jesu, help! All hath forsaken me.
GOOD DEEDS: Nay, Everyman; I will bide with thee.
    I will not forsake thee indeed;
    Thou shalt find me a good friend at need.
EVERYMAN: Gramercy, Good Deeds! Now may I
    true friends see.   855
    They have forsaken me, every one;
    I loved them better than my Good Deeds alone.
    Knowledge, will ye forsake me also?
KNOWLEDGE: Yea, Everyman, when ye to Death
    shall go;
    But not yet, for no manner of danger.   860
EVERYMAN: Gramercy, Knowledge, with all my
    heart.
KNOWLEDGE: Nay, yet I will not from hence depart
    Till I see where ye shall become.
EVERYMAN: Methink, alas, that I must be gone
    To make my reckoning and my debts pay,   865
    For I see my time is nigh spent away.
    Take example, all ye that this do hear or see,
    How they that I loved best do forsake me,
    Except my Good Deeds that bideth truly.
GOOD DEEDS: All earthly things is but vanity: 870
    Beauty, Strength, and Discretion do man forsake,
    Foolish friends, and kinsmen, that fair spake —
    All fleeth save Good Deeds, and that am I.

EVERYMAN: Have mercy on me, God most mighty;
And stand by me, thou mother and maid, holy
875   Mary.
GOOD DEEDS: Fear not; I will speak for thee.
EVERYMAN: Here I cry God mercy.
GOOD DEEDS: Short our end, and minish our pain;
Let us go and never come again.
EVERYMAN: Into thy hands, Lord, my soul I
880   commend;
Receive it, Lord, that it be not lost.
As thou me boughtest, so me defend,
And save me from the fiend's boast,
That I may appear with that blessed host
885   That shall be saved at the day of doom.
In manus tuas, of mights most
For ever, *commendo spiritum meum.*°

(*He sinks into his grave.*)

KNOWLEDGE: Now hath he suffered that we all
shall endure;
The Good Deeds shall make all sure.
890   Now hath he made ending;
Methinketh that I hear angels sing,
And make great joy and melody
Where Everyman's soul received shall be.
ANGEL: Come, excellent elect spouse, to Jesu!
895   Hereabove thou shalt go
Because of thy singular virtue.
Now the soul is taken the body fro,
Thy reckoning is crystal-clear.
Now shalt thou into the heavenly sphere,

Unto the which all ye shall come   900
That liveth well before the day of doom.

(*Enter Doctor.*)

DOCTOR: This moral men may have in mind.
Ye hearers, take it of worth, old and young,
And forsake Pride, for he deceiveth you in the
end;
And remember Beauty, Five Wits, Strength, and
Discretion,   905
They all at the last do every man forsake,
Save his Good Deeds there doth he take.
But beware, for and they be small
Before God, he hath no help at all;
None excuse may be there for every man.   910
Alas, how shall he do then?
For after death amends may no man make,
For then mercy and pity doth him forsake.
If his reckoning be not clear when he doth
come,
God will say: *"Ite, maledicti, in ignem
eternum."*°   915
And he that hath his account whole and sound,
High in heaven he shall be crowned;
Unto which place God bring us all thither,
That we may live body and soul together.
Thereto help the Trinity!   920
Amen, say ye, for saint charity.

Thus endeth this moral play of Everyman.

886–887. *In manus tuas . . . commendo spiritum meum:* Into
your hands, most mighty One for ever, I commend my spirit.

915. *Ite, maledicti, in ignem eternum:* Depart, ye cursed, into
everlasting fire.

Renaissance Drama

Italian Drama

Renaissance means "rebirth." The spirit of the age (c. 1401–1600) centers on a profound rediscovery of the richness of Greek and Roman culture, including its arts, literature, and drama. When the Roman Empire fell, most ancient Greek and Roman literature was lost. But from the seventh to the fifteenth century, the Arabs had conquered immense territories in the Middle East and northern Africa and had preserved Greek and Roman texts in their academies. In the process of trading with the Arabs from 1200 to 1400, the Italians rediscovered the great classical texts and began to study them in academies of their own. Another source of the revival of classical learning was the material preserved by scholars who fled westward from the capital of Constantinople after the fall of the Byzantine empire.

Among the texts that were rediscovered were some of the works of Plato, Aristotle, Cicero, and the great Greek playwrights. These texts were immensely surprising to the Italians, whose medieval worldview had been shaped entirely by the church. The rediscovery of a pagan civilization that could produce such extraordinary texts, with such a deep understanding of human nature, had an overwhelming impact on the Italian worldview.

Vitruvius and the Rediscovery of Roman Design

Medieval Italian theater had depended on portable stages, but in the last decade of the fifteenth century and the first decade of the sixteenth it was clear that none of the rediscovered Roman comedies or other classical drama could be performed on those stages. Among the great rediscoveries of classical texts was the work of the Roman architect Vitruvius (written c. 16–13 B.C.), which included detailed plans for Roman theaters.

Using Vitruvius's designs, the Italians began building stages that were raised platforms with the FRONS SCAENA, the flat front wall used in the

Roman theater. The earliest Italian woodcuts show the stages to be relatively simple with pillars supporting a roof or cover. Curtains stretched between the pillars to permit the actors to enter and exit. Usually three "doors" with names over each indicated the houses of specific characters.

The study of Roman architecture eventually produced, in 1585, one of the wonders of the Renaissance, the Olympic Theater in Vicenza, designed by the great Renaissance architect, Andrea Palladio (1518–1580), whose interpretation of Roman architecture was so compelling that it influenced architecture all over the world. The Olympic Theater, which has been preserved and is still used for performances, has an orchestra, a semicircular seating area, and a multistory *frons scaena*. But it also has several entrances onstage constructed to give a view of characters entering from a great distance, an especially powerful setup for entrances with a large retinue.

The Olympic Theater was built with an essentially conservative design. It worked well for Roman plays, but not for Renaissance plays, and so did not inspire new theater designs. Italian plays had begun to use scenery and painted backdrops that could be changed to suggest a change in location of the action. Carefully painted backdrops were also effective in increasing the realism of the setting — one backdrop could immediately locate an action on a city street, while another could help shift the audience imaginatively to a pastoral woodland scene. These developments were not possible on a Roman stage.

The development of vanishing-point perspective by the architect Filippo Brunelleschi (1377–1446), published by Leon Battista Alberti in *On Painting* in 1435, helped revolutionize the design of theatrical backdrops. Earlier painters in the Renaissance had no way to establish a firm sense of perspective on a flat surface. Without that, all three-dimensional objects appeared flat; all space in a landscape or cityscape seemed shortened and unreal. The use of a single vanishing point — in which lines were lightly drawn from the edges of the canvas (or theatrical backdrop) so that they met in a single point in the center — made it possible to show buildings, trees, and figures in their proper proportion to one another. For the first time, Renaissance painters could achieve lifelike illusions on a flat surface.

The designer Sebastiano Serlio (1475–1554) used the vanishing-point technique, intensified by receding lines of tiles in the floor and on the painted backdrop. Serlio established all-purpose backdrops for comedy, tragedy, and satire. The rigidity of the backdrops for comedy and tragedy — both used a piazza, a small town square, ringed by stone buildings — restricted their use. But the setting for satire was rustic: trees, bushes, a couple of cottages. This style of backdrop was modified and used throughout Europe until the nineteenth century, not only for satires but for the proliferation of pastoral dramas in Italy and melodramas in the rest of Europe.

The most important and long-lasting development of Italian theater design in the mid-1500s was the *proscenium arch*, a "frame" that surrounds the stage, permitting the audience to look in on the scene, whether it be in a room or in a town square. The arch lent a finished touch to the theater, separating the action from the audience and distancing the actors. The proscenium arch is common in most theaters today.

Commedia dell'Arte

Renaissance Italy had two traditions of theater. *Commedia erudita* was learned, almost scholarly in its interests in Roman staging and Roman plays. COMMEDIA DELL'ARTE was less reverent, more slapstick, and generally more popular. It is difficult, however, to say which was more influential on literature over the years. Each had its power and each made its contribution.

In terms of acting and storytelling, the influence of the *commedia dell'arte* is almost unparalleled. The term means "comedy performed by professionals." They were usually actors who had grown up in performing families that made their living touring through the countryside, performing at fairs and on feast days. From the early Renaissance through the eighteenth century, the *commedia dell'arte* entertained all of Europe and influenced comic theater in every nation.

The essence of *commedia dell'arte* was improvised scripts — a general narrative outline served as a basis, but the speeches were improvised on the spot. Regional theaters today, such as Keith Johnstone's group in Calgary, Canada, and the many Theater Sports groups in New York City, use the same techniques of improvisation. "Improv" evenings are also common on television today, as in the work of Monteith and Rand. Their techniques naturally grew out of the *commedia dell'arte*. The lines that are delivered are created as the action occurs, but the underlying structure guides the actors.

The principal characters were types who soon became familiar all over Europe: Pantalone, the often magisterial but miserly old man; Arlecchino (Harlequin), the cunning clown; Pulcinella, the Punch of Punch and Judy; Columbina, the innocent; the *zanni*, shrewd and shifty servants who usually invented complications and got their way; and a host of other *stock characters* such as pedantic lawyers, a braggart captain, and a serving maid. Certain versions of general characters — such as Arlecchino, who began as a simple *zanni* — became famous and were copied in many countries.

The youthful lovers in the *commedia* did not require masks, but the old men, the *zanni*, and other characters all had masks that identified them and made them look, to modern eyes, rather grotesque. These masks survive today in the Venetian carnival and other celebrations. Stock characters thrive in popular comedies everywhere. Molière depended on them; later, Bernard Shaw and Sean O'Casey did as well. To a large extent, one of comedy's greatest sources of energy lies in the delight audiences have always taken in stock characters. Today hardly a situation comedy on television could survive without them.

The staging of *commedia dell'arte* was simple. It often took place in open air, but sometimes indoors in a more formal theatrical setting. Sometimes performers dispensed with the stage altogether and worked in marketplaces. The scenarios they wrote were broad, farcical, filled with buffoonery. Often they depended on elaborate practical jokes and tricks, and they seem to have uniformly pleased large audiences. The actors relied on two approaches to comedy: the LAZZI, which were instant comic moments, such as one character hitting another over the head with an inflated bladder, and the BURLE, slightly more elaborate routines such as the Abbott and Costello "Who's on first?" routine. From the second term, we get the modern word *burlesque*.

Elizabethan Drama

Today's English-speaking audience looks back at the English Renaissance with special interest because of the achievement of the Elizabethan playwrights, who produced an age of great theater unmatched except by the Greeks before them. The development of such a productive period may have resulted from the excitement generated by the discovery of the New World and its colossal riches or from the cultural upheaval caused by the Protestant Reformation, which began in the 1530s in England. Or it could have resulted from the more or less simultaneous arrival in London of several geniuses of theater: Christopher Marlowe (1564–1593), William Shakespeare (1564–1616), Ben Jonson (1572–1637), Inigo Jones (1573–1652), Thomas Kyd (1558–1594), John Fletcher (1597–1625), John Webster (1580–1638?), and John Ford (1586–1640?). Undoubtedly, the period's richness derived from a combination of all three elements, but there was one important additional ingredient: an audience that could appreciate and pay for high-quality theater. The Elizabethans were thrilled by histories, tragedies, and comedies. They appreciated the best.

That the Elizabethans enjoyed plays with a moral basis is plain from the fact that so much of the great drama of the late 1500s and early 1600s is moral in character. However, early Elizabethan plays were less obviously moralistic than the then popular morality plays. They did not aim specifically to teach a moral lesson, although it is true that there are many lessons to be learned from Shakespeare and his contemporaries.

During Shakespeare's youth wandering players put on a number of plays from REPERTORY, their stock of three or four current plays they could perform. How many players there were or what their source of plays was, we do not know. Much of what we know comes directly from *Hamlet* and the appearance of the players who perform Hamlet's *Mousetrap*. What we learn there tells us that dramatic styles had developed in the English countryside and that theater was thriving.

The First Professional Companies

Although professional players' groups had long been licensed to perform in France and Italy, until the 1570s professional actors — those who had no other trade — did not enjoy favor in England. Such people could be arrested for vagrancy. The law, however, changed, and when it did the history of theater changed too. In 1576, James Burbage (father of the famous star of Shakespeare's plays, Richard Burbage) built the first building made specially for plays in England. It was called The Theatre.

Soon there were other theaters: the Swan (Figure 4), the Globe, the Rose, the Fortune, the Hope. The Globe was large enough to accommodate two to three thousand people. All of these theaters were open-air, so they could not be used in winter, and all were extraordinarily successful. Shakespeare, who was part owner of the Globe and, later, the second indoor Blackfriars Theatre, received money from the tickets in the stalls, from his share as one of the actors in both companies, and from his role as chief playwright. He became rich enough to retire early in splendid style in Stratford, his hometown. Very few other Elizabethan actors and playwrights ever had as much of a financial stake in their work as Shakespeare did.

The Elizabethan Theater

The design of the Elizabethan theater is a matter of some speculation. Many of the plays popular before the theaters were built were performed in an inn yard, with a balcony above and a square yard on which actors performed. The audience looked out their windows or stood in the yard. As a result, Elizabethan theaters seem to have taken the inn yard structure as their basis. One location of the earliest English drama is the Inns at Court, essentially a college for law students in London. This audience would have been learned, bright, and imaginative. Indeed, the first English tragedy, *Gorboduc* by Thomas Sackville and Thomas Norton, was played at the Inner Temple, one of the Inns at Court, in 1562, before Marlowe and Shakespeare were born.

The shape of the early playhouses was often octagonal on the outside and circular on the inside, like the bearpits, the places in which bears, tied to stakes, were baited by dogs for the amusement of the audience. The stage was raised about five feet from the yard with levels of seating on both sides and in front. Approximately half the area over the stage was roofed and contained machinery to lower people from the "heavens," and it was painted blue with stars to simulate the sky. In most cases the stage was approximately twenty-five by forty feet. Doors or curtained areas at the back of the stage served for entrances and exits, and a special room to the back of the stage was for costume changes. There may have been a section of the stage that was normally curtained but that opened to reveal an interior, such as a bedroom. The existence of this feature is in considerable dispute, however.

The Elizabethan Audience

The entrance fee to the theaters was a penny, probably the equivalent of five to ten dollars in today's money. For another penny one could take a seat, probably on a bench, in one of the upper galleries. In some

Figure 4. The Swan Theater

theaters more private spaces were available as well. A great many playgoers were satisfied to stand around the stage and were thus nicknamed "groundlings." Hamlet calls them the "understanding gentlemen of the ground." But the more academic playwrights, Marlow and Jonson, used the term to mean those who would not perfectly understand the significance of the plays.

Shakespeare and other Elizabethan playwrights expected a widely diverse audience. Audiences could be coarse, or they could be extraordinarily polished. Shakespeare had the gift, as did Marlowe and even Jonson in his comedies, to play well to them all. Shakespeare's plays were given in public playhouses open to everyone. They were also given in university theaters, as in the case of *Macbeth*; Shakespeare's universality reveals itself in his appeal to many different kinds of people.

Women on the English Stage

Because women were not allowed to act on English stages, boys filled the parts of young characters such as Juliet, Desdemona, and Ophelia. Interestingly, no contemporary commentator makes any complaint about having to put up with a boy playing the part of Juliet or any of Shakespeare's other love interests, such as Katerina in *Taming of the Shrew*, Beatrice in *Much Ado About Nothing*, or even Queen Cleopatra. Helen of Troy in Marlowe's *Doctor Faustus* was played by a boy, a fact that seems remarkable in retrospect. Older women, such as the Nurse in *Romeo and Juliet*, were played by some of the gifted male character actors of the company.

The Masque

The Elizabethan MASQUE was a special entertainment of royalty. It was a celebration that included a rudimentary plot, a great deal of singing and dancing, and magnificent costumes and lighting. Masques were performed only once, often to celebrate a royal marriage. Masque audiences participated in the dances and were usually delighted by complex machinery that lifted or lowered characters from the skies. The masque was devised in Italy in the 1570s by Count Giovanni Bardi, founder of the Florentine Camerata, a Renaissance group of theatergoers sponsored by Lorenzo de'Medici.

The geniuses of the masque are generally admitted to have been Ben Jonson and Inigo Jones. Jones was the great architect whose Banquetting Rooms at Whitehall in London, which still stand, provided the setting for most of the great masques of the seventeenth century. Jonson and Jones worked together from 1605 to 1631 to produce a remarkable body of masques that today resemble the bones of a dinosaur: What we read on the page suggests in only the vaguest way what the presentation must have been like when the masques were mounted.

Because of the expenses of costuming and staging, masques were too costly to be produced more than once. The royal exchequer was frequently burdened in Queen Elizabeth's time, but more so in King James's time, after he took the throne in 1603. Masque costumes were impressive, the scenery astounding, and the effects amazing. In all of this, the words — which are, after all, at the center of Shakespeare's plays as well as other plays of the period — were of least account. As a result of the emphasis on the machinery and designs — the work of Inigo Jones — Jonson abandoned his partnership in something of a huff, complaining that he could not compete with the scene painters and carpenters.

The emphasis on spectacle in the Elizabethan and Jacobean masques (produced during the reign of King James) tells us something about the taste of the aristocrats, who enjoyed sumptuous foods, clothes, and amusements. Eventually, the more common audiences of the public theaters began demanding more and more spectacle, too, and huge storm machines were installed in the Globe. Some say that one reason Shakespeare wrote *The Tempest* was to take advantage of the new equipment. Foreign visitors described London theaters as gorgeous places of entertainment compared with their own. The quest for more intense spectacle led to disaster. The Globe actually burned down in 1613 because a piece of wadding from a stage cannon misfired, got caught in the roof, and brought the house down in real flames.

The royal demand for masques was unaffected, however. As Francis Bacon said in 1625 about masques, "These things are but toys to come amongst such serious observations. But yet, since princes will have such things, it is better they should be graced with elegancy than daubed with cost. Dancing to song is a thing of great state and pleasure."

Christopher Marlowe

Christopher Marlowe (1564–1593) was born two months before William Shakespeare and in somewhat similar social circumstances, to a shoemaker — Shakespeare's father was a glovemaker. But unlike Shakespeare, Marlowe won a scholarship to Cambridge, where he remained six years and began his career as a playwright. His first play, *Tamburlaine*, was finished before he left the university, and when it was performed in London it had the benefit of Edward Alleyn, the finest actor of his time, playing the title role.

Alleyn was the son-in-law of Philip Henslowe, who owned the Rose, the Fortune, and the Hope theaters in London. Alleyn was a rhetorical actor with a commanding voice and commanding gestures. His style was perfect for declaiming what Ben Jonson called Marlowe's "Mighty line": his IAMBIC PENTAMETER BLANK VERSE, which moves in stately rhythms and which dominated the Elizabethan stage. Marlowe's blank verse, especially in the emotional moments of Faustus's career — as in his invocation of the devils in act I, scene III — resonates and rolls from the tongue in mighty billows. It has a virtually incantatory effect on the listener, and in a London theater of the time, as spoken by Edward Alleyn, it must have been mesmerizing.

Marlowe had considerable success as a poet and as a translator of the classics. His version of Ovid's *Amores* is very lively, and his long poem *Hero and Leander* is a dynamic contribution to the poetry of Renaissance humanism. It shows his affection for the classics in a form that Shakespeare also employed: the longer narrative poem.

Marlowe had a university scholarship that was intended for those studying for the ministry. He began writing plays at college, and instead of entering the ministry, he went up to London in 1587. Some of his friends revealed that his beliefs were close to those of atheism, a charge that in his time could have resulted in death. Fortunately, when he applied for his master's degree and was on the verge of having it denied, Queen Elizabeth intervened on his behalf. Her comment was curiously veiled and has made subsequent generations think that he must have been a spy on her behalf for at least some of the time he was in Catholic sections of France.

Marlowe, partly as a result of his connection with Elizabeth, has often been portrayed as a romantic swashbuckler in the heart of complex intrigues. He was also well known to most of the literary people of London: Shakespeare, Sir Walter Raleigh, Francis Bacon, Thomas Kyd, and Thomas Harriot (an astronomer and writer) were all close associates. He knew the remarkable magician Dr. John Dee, who was known to some degree by all of those named. Most of them were members of a group, dubbed the School of Night by Frances Yates, who met privately to discuss ideas of the occult, Greek mystical philosophy, and skepticism that could not easily be talked about in the open.

Marlowe's first play was *Tamburlaine* (1587; in two parts), followed by *The Jew of Malta* (1589) and *Edward the Second* (1592). They are all powerful plays that feature a great tragic character. *The Massacre at Paris* (1593) is based on the St. Bartholomew Day's Massacre in 1573, when some thirty thousand Huguenots — French Protestants — were killed by Catholics in Paris. Marlowe's knowledge of the details of the events seems to have been considerable, although the play itself is not as powerful as his earlier tragedies. *Dido, Queen of Carthage* (1593; with Thomas Nashe) is a typical kind of collaboration of the period. None of these plays, good as they are, come to the level of *Doctor Faustus*, which stands as one of the greatest plays of the Elizabethan age.

Marlowe was apparently quick to anger and was involved in one murder before he himself was murdered over a bar bill at the inn of the Widow Bull in Deptford. His murder was avoidable. He was drinking with an acquaintance named Ingram Frizer, who worked for the great Walsingham family, a patron of Marlowe's. Over an argument, Marlowe grabbed Frizer from behind, but Frizer stabbed him while breaking free. Marlowe died instantly. When Marlowe died, Shakespeare was only beginning his career as a playwright.

DOCTOR FAUSTUS

Doctor Faustus was probably written between 1588 and 1593, shortly before Marlowe died. There is a record of its being readied for the press in 1601, but if that version was printed, no copies survive. The first printed version is from 1604, while a more amplified version was printed in 1616. Neither was supervised by Marlowe, and to make things more complicated, records indicate that Henslowe paid two writers a substantial sum to make additions to the original text. What the additions were, or what the original text was, we probably will never know.

Current scholarship has led us to believe that the 1616 text, which is printed here, is actually closer to the original acting version than the

1604 text. The breaking of the text into five acts and their scenes is a modern convention, as is the supplying of most of the stage directions. The five-act pattern was common in classical plays and it is natural to Elizabethan plays as well.

The influence of the medieval stage is readily apparent in *Doctor Faustus*. The emphasis on the devils, the seven deadly sins, and the terrifying vision of hell in act V is reminiscent of the devils of the mystery plays and their reliance on frightening hell's mouth props. The allusion to the tradition of the mansions of medieval theater in Mephistophilis's speech in act V also echoes the basic message of the morality plays:

> Aye, Faustus, now thou hast no hope of heaven;
> Therefore despair. Think only upon hell,
> For that must be thy mansion, there to dwell.

However, *Doctor Faustus* differs from the morality plays in one very important way. We are never led to think that Faustus would have lived a better or more interesting life if he had restrained his ambition. Faustus is a hero, especially of the romantic sort that strove to achieve great things and challenge the gods. The Elizabethans admired Faustus much more than they condemned him, no matter what moral tags Marlowe might have put in the play to satisfy the society's official view of itself.

Among the sources of the play are a medieval folklore tradition connected with the wizard who sold his soul to the devil for greater powers and a German book called *Historia von D. Johan Fausten*, published in 1587. Marlowe may have seen the book or, more likely, may have seen an English translation in 1592 called *The History of the damnable life, and deserved death of Doctor John Faustus*. In either event, the Faust legend goes back to the early medieval period and could have reached Marlowe in any number of ways.

Doctor Faustus is one of the earliest English tragedies. Its hero is in many ways larger than life, and while not a member of the nobility, he is at ease with royalty and clearly superior in intellectual abilities. The richness of the psychological portrayal of Faustus — as well as of Wagner and Mephistophilis — elevates the play from the best earlier efforts of English and European dramatists. Faustus represents an interesting tradition: the University of Wittenberg produced the most important Protestant of the sixteenth century, Martin Luther. His daring, comparable in some ways to Faustus's overreaching, led to the Reformation and one of the most cataclysmic changes in European thought in the Renaissance. Hamlet is also a student at Wittenberg, a fact that gives us insight into the Elizabethan imagination. Wittenberg to the Elizabethans meant fierce intellectual energy and daring.

As in the case of many of Shakespeare's tragedies, *Doctor Faustus* has interludes of comic relief, with the horse coursers who are bilked by Faustus and with other clowns and mechanicals who wonder openly about the terrifying skills of the magician. This linking of tragic and comic has annoyed some critics who have agreed with Aristotle that such a mixture is problematic and tends to diffuse the effect of the drama. Actually, in performance the comic scenes are in no way a dilution of effect. They tend to buoy the energy of the play and help us focus anew on the insatiable Faustus.

But *Doctor Faustus* has a modern twist that takes it out of the medieval mold. The Renaissance was a period of expansion, especially the expansion of knowledge. Astronomy was symbolic of the new age: Telescopes were beginning to give Europeans a sense of the vastness and complexity of the universe. When Faustus asks information of Mephistophilis, he begins with questions about the planets and the universe, knowledge of which had long been thought to be somehow secret. Mastering that knowledge was symbolic of mastering the knowledge of the innermost workings of science.

Faustus's quest for knowledge became for some people a Renaissance theme. The magicians who are referred to in the text, such as Roger Bacon and Cornelius Agrippa, were genuine. Their work was read throughout Europe, and the kinds of magic actions that Faustus aspires to were thought possible. The Elizabethans definitely believed in the presence of spirits, of ghosts, of intervention through witches of the otherworld. *Doctor Faustus* fed the contemporary interest in the occult. Faustus quests for forbidden knowledge; he must sell his soul to the devil to acquire it. His lust for knowledge — he says at the outset that he has dominated all the world of learning available to him — is without bounds.

Many of Marlowe's audience would have seen in Doctor Faustus an allusion to the magus John Dee, who cast the horoscope of Queen Elizabeth and who was known throughout Europe for his almost supernormal intellectual capacity. He was learned in many sciences, and his introduction to the first English edition of Euclid's *Geometry* made him not only respected in Europe but eventually known throughout the New World (that version of Euclid was used at Harvard until the late 1700s). Dee was a wizard, and his house at Mortlake was attacked and burned to the ground by frightened peasants while he was abroad. With his house went one of the most impressive personal libraries in Europe. Marlowe knew Dee, and his description of Faustus is quite like him.

Faustus was willing to seek forbidden knowledge — in the way Adam and Eve did — at all costs, in full awareness that he risked the loss of his soul. And while Marlowe condemns Faustus to hell and does not save him at the end, we have the feeling — as did Elizabethans — that there is something grand and heroic about Faustus's risk taking. He fails, yes, but he fails in a way that makes mediocre citizens who would never have had his imagination or daring seem pallid and weak. We find ourselves involved in Faustus's struggle.

Christopher Marlowe (1564–1593)

THE TRAGICAL HISTORY OF THE LIFE AND DEATH OF DOCTOR FAUSTUS

c. 1593

The Players

THE CHORUS
DOCTOR FAUSTUS
WAGNER, *his student and servant*
VALDES
CORNELIUS
THREE SCHOLARS
AN OLD MAN

POPE ADRIAN
RAYMOND, *King of Hungary*
BRUNO, *the rival Pope*
TWO CARDINALS
THE ARCHBISHOP OF RHEIMS
CHARLES V, *Emperor of Germany*
MARTINO ⎫
FREDERICK ⎬ *Gentlemen of the Emperor's court*
BENVOLIO ⎭
BEELZEBUB
DUKE OF SAXONY
DUKE OF ANHOLT
DUCHESS OF ANHOLT
ROBIN, *the clown, a hostler*
DICK
A VINTNER
A HORSE-COURSER
A CARTER
HOSTESS

GOOD ANGEL
BAD ANGEL
LUCIFER
MEPHISTOPHILIS
PRIDE ⎫
COVETOUSNESS ⎪
ENVY ⎪
WRATH ⎬ *The Seven Deadly Sins*
GLUTTONY ⎪
SLOTH ⎪
LECHERY ⎭
ALEXANDER, THE GREAT
HIS PARAMOUR
DARIUS, *King of Persia*

HELEN OF TROY
TWO CUPIDS
DEVILS, BISHOPS, MONKS, FRIARS, SOLDIERS

The Scene: *Wittenberg, Rome, the Emperor's court at Innsbruck, court of the Duke of Anholt, and the neighboring countryside.*

PROLOGUE

(*Enter Chorus.*)

CHORUS: Not marching in the fields of Trasimene
    Where Mars° did mate° the warlike Carthagens,°
    Nor sporting in the dalliance of love
    In courts of kings where state° is overturned,
    Nor in the pomp of proud audacious deeds   5
    Intends our muse to vaunt his heavenly verse.
    Only this, gentles: we must now perform
    The form of Faustus' fortunes, good or bad.
    And now to patient judgments we appeal,
    And speak for Faustus in his infancy.   10
    Now is he born, of parents base of stock,
    In Germany, within a town called Rhode.
    At riper years to Wittenberg he went,
    Whereas his kinsmen chiefly brought him up.
    So much he profits in divinity,   15
    The fruitful plot of scholarism graced,°
    That shortly he was graced with doctor's name,
    Excelling all whose sweet delight disputes°
    In th'heavenly matters of theology,
    Till swoll'n with cunning of a self-conceit,   20
    His waxen wings did mount above his reach,
    And melting,° heavens conspired his overthrow;

Note: Material in brackets has been added by the editor.
Prologue. 1–2. Trasimene . . . Carthagens: Perhaps an allusion to a lost play about the Carthaginian Hannibal, who achieved one of his greatest victories at Lake Trasimene in 217 B.C.
2. Mars: Roman god of war; **mate:** Rival, meet in battle.
4. state: Government. **16. fruitful plot . . . graced:** Adorned the university. **18. whose sweet delight disputes:** Who takes pleasure in disputing. **21–22. waxen wings . . . melting:** Metaphor referring to Icarus's attempt to fly with waxen wings, which melted when he ignored his father's warning and flew too near the sun.

For, falling to a devilish exercise
And glutted now with learning's golden gifts,
25 He surfeits upon cursèd necromancy.
Nothing so sweet as magic is to him,
Which he prefers before his chiefest bliss;
And this the man that in his study sits.

ACT I • Scene I

(*Faustus in his study.*)

FAUSTUS: Settle thy studies, Faustus, and begin
To sound the depth of that thou wilt profess.
Having commenced,° be a divine in show;
Yet level° at the end of every art,
5 And live and die in Aristotle's works.
Sweet Analytics, 'tis thou hast ravished me!
Bene disserere est finis logices.°
Is to dispute well logic's chiefest end?
Affords this art no greater miracle?
10 Then read no more; thou hast attained that end.
A greater subject fitteth Faustus' wit!
Bid *On cay mae on*° farewell; Galen° come.
Seeing *ubi desinit philosophus ibi incipit
medicus,*°
Be a physician, Faustus; heap up gold,
15 And be eternized for some wondrous cure.
Summum bonum medicinae sanitas.°
The end of physic is our body's health.
Why, Faustus, hast thou not attained that end?
Is not thy common talk sound aphorisms?
20 Are not thy bills° hung up as monuments,
Whereby whole cities have escaped the plague,
And divers desperate maladies been cured?
Yet art thou still but Faustus and a man.
Couldst thou make men to live eternally,
25 Or, being dead, raise them to life again,
Then this profession were to be esteemed.
Physic, farewell! Where is Justinian?°
Si una eademque res legatus duobus, [He reads.]

Alter rem, alter valorem rei, etc.°
A petty case of paltry legacies! 30
Exhaereditare filium non potest pater nisi° —
[*He reads.*]
Such is the subject of the Institute
And universal body of the law.
This study fits a mercenary drudge
Who aims at nothing but external trash, 35
Too servile and illiberal for me.
When all is done, divinity is best.
Jerome's Bible,° Faustus, view it well:
Stipendium peccati mors est.° Ha! *Stipendium,
etc.* [*He reads.*]
The reward of sin is death. That's hard. 40
Si pecasse negamus, fallimur [*He reads.*]
Et nulla est in nobis veritas.°
If we say that we have no sin,
We deceive ourselves, and there's no truth in us.
Why then belike we must sin, 45
And so consequently die.
Ay, we must die an everlasting death.
What doctrine call you this? *Che serà, serà:*
What will be, shall be! Divinity, adieu!
These metaphysics of magicians, 50
And necromantic books are heavenly.
Lines, circles, signs, letters, and characters —
Ay, these are those that Faustus most desires.
O, what a world of profit and delight,
Of power, of honor, of omnipotence 55
Is promised to the studious artisan!
All things that move between the quiet poles
Shall be at my command. Emperors and kings
Are but obeyed in their several provinces,
Nor can they raise the wind or rend the clouds, 60
But his dominion that exceeds in this
Stretcheth as far as doth the mind of man.
A sound magician is a demi-god.
Here try thy brains to get a deity!
Wagner!

(*Enter Wagner.*)

       Commend me to my dearest friends, 65
The German Valdes and Cornelius;
Request them earnestly to visit me.
WAGNER: I will sir.

(*Exit.*)

I, I. **3. commenced:** Taken a degree. **4. level:** Aim. **7.**
Bene disserere est finis logices: The end of logic is to dispute
well. A tenet of the anti-Aristotelian system introduced at
Cambridge when Marlowe was a student there. **12. On**
cay mae on: From Aristotle, being or not being; **Galen:** Greek
physician regarded throughout the Middle Ages as a medical
authority. **13. ubi desinit philosophus ibi incipit medicus:**
Where the philosopher stops, the doctor begins. **16. Summum
. . . sanitas:** Health is the highest good of the practice of
medicine. **20. bills:** Medical prescriptions. **27. Justinian:**
Roman emperor of Constantinople (527–565), responsible
for assembling the Roman law and renowned throughout
the Middle Ages as a jurist.

28–29. *Si . . . rei, etc.:* If the same object is willed to two
persons, let one have the thing itself and the other its value,
etc. This is an incorrect version of one of Justinian's rules.
31. Exhaereditare . . . nisi —: The father cannot disinherit
the son except —; another of Justinian's rules roughly para-
phrased. **38. Jerome's Bible:** St. Jerome's Vulgate [Latin]
translation of the Bible. **39. Stipendium . . . est:** Translated
in line 40 (Rom. 6:23). **41–42.** *Si . . . veritas:* Translated
in lines 43–44 (1 John 1:8).

FAUSTUS: Their conference will be a greater help to
     me
70   Than all my labors, plod I ne'er so fast.

(*Enter the Good Angel and the Evil Angel.*)

GOOD ANGEL: O, Faustus, lay that damnèd book
     aside,
     And gaze not on it, lest it tempt thy soul
     And heap God's heavy wrath upon thy head.
     Read, read the Scriptures. That is blasphemy.
BAD ANGEL: Go forward, Faustus, in that famous
75   art
     Wherein all nature's treasury is contained.
     Be thou on earth as Jove is in the sky,
     Lord and commander of these elements.
                              (*Exeunt° Angels.*)
FAUSTUS: How am I glutted with conceit° of this!
80   Shall I make spirits fetch me what I please,
     Resolve me of° all ambiguities,
     Perform what desperate enterprise I will?
     I'll have them fly to India for gold,
     Ransack the ocean for orient pearl,
85   And search all corners of the new-found world
     For pleasant fruits and princely delicates.
     I'll have them read me strange philosophy
     And tell the secrets of all foreign kings;
     I'll have them wall all Germany with brass
90   And make swift Rhine circle fair Wittenberg.°
     I'll have them fill the public schools with silk
     Wherewith the students shall be bravely clad.
     I'll levy soldiers with the coin they bring
     And chase the Prince of Parma from our land
95   And reign sole king of all the provinces.°
     Yea, stranger engines for the brunt of war
     Than was the fiery keel at Antwerp's bridge°
     I'll make my servile spirits to invent.
     Come, German Valdes and Cornelius,
                              [*He calls within.*]
100 And make me blessed with your sage conference!

(*Enter Valdes and Cornelius.*)

     Valdes, sweet Valdes, and Cornelius,
     Know that your words have won me at the last
     To practice magic and concealèd arts;
     Yet not your words only, but mine own fantasy
105 That will receive no object, for my head
     But ruminates on necromantic skill.

Philosophy is odious and obscure;
     Both law and physic are for petty wits;
     Divinity is basest of the three,
     Unpleasant, harsh, contemptible and vile.   110
     'Tis, magic, magic, that hath ravished me.
     Then, gentle friends, aid me in this attempt,
     And I, that have with subtle syllogisms
     Gravelled° the pastors of the German church,
     And made the flowering pride of Wittenberg   115
     Swarm to my problems° as th'infernal spirits
     On sweet Musaeus° when he came to hell,
     Will be as cunning as Agrippa was,
     Whose shadows° made all Europe honor him.
VALDES: Faustus, these books, thy wit, and our
     experience   120
     Shall make all nations to canonize us.
     As Indian Moors° obey their Spanish lords,
     So shall the spirits of every element
     Be always serviceable to us three.
     Like lions shall they guard us when we please, 125
     Like Almain rutters° with their horsemen's staves
     Or Lapland giants trotting by our sides,
     Sometimes like women or unwedded maids,
     Shadowing° more beauty in their airy brows
     Than in the white breasts of the queen of love. 130
     From Venice shall they drag huge argosies,
     And from America the golden fleece
     That yearly stuffs old Philip's treasury,
     If learnèd Faustus will be resolute.
FAUSTUS: Valdes, as resolute am I in this   135
     As thou to live; therefore object it not.
CORNELIUS: The miracles that magic will perform
     Will make thee vow to study nothing else.
     He that is grounded in astrology,
     Enriched with tongues,° well seen in minerals, 140
     Hath all the principles magic doth require.
     Then doubt not, Faustus, but to be renowned
     And more frequented for this mystery
     Than heretofore the Delphian oracle.°
     The spirits tell me they can dry the sea   145
     And fetch the treasure of all foreign wracks,
     Yea, all the wealth that our forefathers hid

---

78. [S.D.] *Exeunt:* Latin for "they go out."   79. **conceit:**
The conception of attaining.   81. **Resolve me of:** Explain
to me. 90. **Rhine . . . Wittenberg:** Wittenberg is actually on
the Elbe River, not the Rhine.   95. **provinces:** The Neth-
erlands.   97. **fiery . . . bridge:** In April 1584 the Dutch used
a fireship to destroy a bridge built across a river by the Prince
of Parma in an attempt to blockade Antwerp.

114. **Gravelled:** Puzzled and amazed.   116. **problems:** Public
disputations.   117. **Musaeus:** A semimythical Greek poet.
Following Virgil, Marlowe has him visit hell like the mythical
Orpheus.   118–119. **Agrippa . . . shadows:** Cornelius Agrippa
(1486?–1535), a German physician and student of the occult,
was said to have power to raise spirits (shadows) from the
dead.   122. **Indian Moors:** American Indians.   126. **Almain
rutters:** German cavalry.   129. **Shadowing:** Harboring, sheltering.   140. **Enriched with tongues:** Fluent in Latin, the
language used for communicating with spirits.   144. **Delphian
oracle:** The high priest of Apollo at Delphi who had power
to foretell the future.

Within the massy entrails of the earth.
Then tell me, Faustus, what shall we three want?
FAUSTUS: Nothing, Cornelius. O, this cheers my
150   soul!
Come, show me some demonstrations magical,
That I may conjure in some lusty grove
And have these joys in full possession.
VALDES: Then haste thee to some solitary grove,
155   And bear wise Bacon's and Abanus' works,°
The Hebrew Psalter, and New Testament;
And whatsoever else is requisite
We will inform thee ere our conference cease.
CORNELIUS: Valdes, first let him know the words of
art,
160   And then, all other ceremonies learned,
Faustus may try his cunning by himself.
VALDES: First I'll instruct thee in the rudiments,
And then wilt thou be perfecter than I.
FAUSTUS: Then come and dine with me, and after
meat
165   We'll canvass every quiddity° thereof,
For ere I sleep I'll try what I can do.
This night I'll conjure, though I die therefore.
                                        (*Exeunt.*)

Scene II

(*Enter two Scholars.*)

FIRST SCHOLAR: I wonder what's become of Faustus,
that was wont to make our schools ring with
sic probo.°

(*Enter Wagner.*)

SECOND SCHOLAR: That shall we presently know; here
5   comes his boy.
FIRST SCHOLAR: How now sirrah! Where's thy master?
WAGNER: God in heaven knows.
SECOND SCHOLAR: Why, dost not thou know then?
10   WAGNER: Yes, I know, but that follows not.
FIRST SCHOLAR: Go to, sirrah! Leave your jesting and
tell us where he is.
WAGNER: That follows not by force of argument, which
you, being licentiates,° should stand upon; therefore
15   acknowledge your error and be attentive.
SECOND SCHOLAR: Then you will not tell us?
WAGNER: You are deceived, for I will tell you. Yet if
you were not dunces, you would never ask me such

a question. For is he not *corpus naturale,* and is
not that *mobile?*° Then wherefore should you ask   20
such a question? But that I am by nature phlegmatic,
slow to wrath, and prone to lechery — to love, I
would say — it were not for you to come within
forty foot of the place of execution, although I do
not doubt but to see you both hanged the next   25
sessions. Thus having triumphed over you, I will
set my countenance like a precisian° and begin to
speak thus: Truly, my dear brethren, my master is
within at dinner with Valdes and Cornelius, as this
wine, if it could speak, would inform your worships.   30
And so, the Lord bless you, preserve you, and keep
you, my dear brethren.
                                        (*Exit.*)
FIRST SCHOLAR: O Faustus, then I fear that which I
have long suspected.
That thou art fall'n into that damnèd art
For which they two are infamous through the
world.   35
SECOND SCHOLAR: Were he a stranger, not allied to
me,
The danger of his soul would make me mourn.
But come, let us go and inform the rector.°
It may be his grave counsel may reclaim him.
FIRST SCHOLAR: I fear me nothing will reclaim him
now.   40
SECOND SCHOLAR: Yet let us see what we can do.
                                        (*Exeunt.*)

Scene III

(*Thunder. Enter [above] Lucifer and four Devils. Enter
Faustus to conjure.*)

FAUSTUS: Now that the gloomy shadow of the
night,
Longing to view Orion's drizzling look,
Leaps from th'Antarctic world unto the sky
And dims the welkin° with her pitchy breath,
Faustus begin thine incantations,   5
And try if devils will obey thy hest,
Seeing thou hast prayed and sacrificed to them.
Within this circle is Jehovah's name,
Forward and backward anagrammatized,
Th'abbreviated names of holy saints,   10
Figures of every adjunct to the heavens,
And characters of signs and erring° stars,
By which the spirits are enforced to rise.

---

155. Bacon's . . . works: Roger Bacon (1214?–1294) and
Pietro D'Abano (1250–1316) were famous in the Middle
Ages for their feats of magic.   **165. quiddity:** Essential element
(a term from scholastic logic). **I, II. 2. sic probo:** Thus I prove
(used in scholastic argument).   **14. licentiates:** Holders of
university degrees.

19–20. *corpus naturale . . . mobile:* The subject matter of
physics, in scholastic terms, was *corpus naturale seu mobile*
(natural body in motion).   **27. precisian:** Puritan.   **38. rector:**
Head of the university.   **I, III. 4. welkin:** Sky.   **12. erring:**
Wandering.

Then fear not, Faustus, to be resolute,
15   And try the utmost magic can peform.
                                          (*Thunder.*)
Sint mihi Dei Acherontis propitii! Valeat numen
triplex Jehovae. Ignei, aerii, aquatani spiritus, salvete!
Orientis princeps, Beelzebub, inferni ardentis mon-
archa, et Demogorgon, propitiamus vos, ut appareat
20   *et surgat Mephistophilis. Quid tu moraris? Per*
Jehovam Gehennam, et consecratam aquam quam
nunc spargo, signumque crucis quod nunc facio,
et per vota nostra, ipse nunc surgat nobis dicatus
Mephistophilis.°

(*Enter [Mephistophilis,] a Devil.*)

25   I charge thee to return and change thy shape;
Thou art too ugly to attend on me.
Go, and return an old Franciscan friar;
That holy shape becomes a devil best.
                                          (*Exit Devil.*)
I see there's virtue in my heavenly words.
30   Who would not be proficient in this art?
How pliant is this Mephistophilis,
Full of obedience and humility.
Such is the force of magic and my spells.
Now Faustus, thou art conjurer laureate,
35   That canst command great Mephistophilis.
Quin redis Mephistophilis fratris imagine.°

(*Enter Mephistophilis [dressed like a Franciscan friar].*)

MEPHISTOPHILIS: Now Faustus, what wouldst thou
      have me do?
FAUSTUS: I charge thee wait upon me whilst I live,
To do whatever Faustus shall command,
40   Be it to make the moon drop from her sphere
Or the ocean to overwhelm the world.
MEPHISTOPHILIS: I am a servant to great Lucifer
And may not follow thee without his leave.
No more than he commands must we perform.
45   FAUSTUS: Did not he charge thee to appear to me?
MEPHISTOPHILIS: No, I came hither of mine own
      accord.
FAUSTUS: Did not my conjuring speeches raise thee?
Speak.
MEPHISTOPHILIS: That was the cause, but yet *per*
      accidens,°

16–24. Sint . . . Mephistophilis: May the gods of Aceron be
propitious to me. Let the triple name of Jehova [the trinity]
be gone. Hail spirits of fire, air, and water. Prince of the
East, Beelzebub, monarch of burning hell, and Demogorgon,
we petition you that Mephistophilis may appear and rise.
Why do you linger? By Jehova, Gehenna and the holy water
which I now sprinkle and the sign of the cross which I now
make and by our vows, let Mephistophilis himself now rise
to serve us.   **36. Quin . . . imagine:** Return, Mephistophilis,
in the shape of a friar.   **48. cause . . . per accidens:** The
terms are from scholastic logic.

For when we hear one rack the name of God,
Abjure the Scriptures and his Savior Christ,   50
We fly in hope to get his glorious soul;
Nor will we come unless he use such means
Whereby he is in danger to be damned.
Therefore the shortest cut for conjuring
Is stoutly to abjure the Trinity   55
And pray devoutly to the prince of hell.
FAUSTUS: So Faustus hath
Already done, and holds this principle:
There is no chief but only Beelzebub,
To whom Faustus doth dedicate himself.   60
This word "damnation" terrifies not me,
For I confound hell in Elysium.
My ghost° be with the old philosophers!
But leaving these vain trifles of men's souls,
Tell me what is that Lucifer thy lord?   65
MEPHISTOPHILIS: Arch-regent and commander of all
      spirits.
FAUSTUS: Was not that Lucifer an angel once?
MEPHISTOPHILIS: Yes Faustus, and most dearly loved
      of God.
FAUSTUS: How comes it then that he is prince of
      devils?
MEPHISTOPHILIS: O, by aspiring pride and insolence, 70
For which God threw him from the face of
      heaven.
FAUSTUS: And what are you that live with Lucifer?
MEPHISTOPHILIS: Unhappy spirits that fell with
      Lucifer,
Conspired against our God with Lucifer,
And are for ever damned with Lucifer.   75
FAUSTUS: Where are you damned?
MEPHISTOPHILIS: In hell.
FAUSTUS: How comes it then that thou art out of
      hell?
MEPHISTOPHILIS: Why this is hell, nor am I out of
      it.
Think'st thou that I who saw the face of God
And tasted the eternal joys of heaven   80
Am not tormented with ten thousand hells
In being deprived of everlasting bliss?
O Faustus, leave these frivolous demands
Which strike a terror to my fainting soul.
FAUSTUS: What, is great Mephistophilis so   85
passionate
For being deprivèd of the joys of heaven?
Learn thou of Faustus' manly fortitude,
And scorn those joys thou never shalt possess.
Go bear these tidings to great Lucifer:
Seeing Faustus hath incurred eternal death   90
By desperate thoughts against Jove's deity,
Say he surrenders up to him his soul,

63. ghost: Spirit.

So he will spare him four and twenty years,
Letting him live in all voluptuousness,
95 Having thee ever to attend on me,
To give me whatsoever I shall ask,
To tell me whatsoever I demand,
To slay mine enemies, and aid my friends,
And always be obedient to my will.
100 Go, and return to mighty Lucifer,
And meet me in my study at midnight,
And then resolve me of thy master's mind.

MEPHISTOPHILIS: I will, Faustus.

(*Exit.*)

FAUSTUS: Had I as many souls as there be stars,
105 I'd give them all for Mephistophilis.
By him I'll be great emperor of the world,
And make a bridge thorough the moving air,
To pass the ocean with a band of men.
I'll join the hills that bind° the Afric shore,
110 And make that country continent to Spain,
And both contributory to my crown.
The Emperor shall not live but by my leave,
Nor any potentate of Germany.
Now that I have obtained what I desire,
115 I'll live in speculation of this art
Till Mephistophilis return again.

(*Exit.*)

Scene IV

(*Enter Wagner and* [*Robin,*] *the Clown.*)

WAGNER: Come hither, sirrah boy.

ROBIN: Boy! O disgrace to my person. Zounds, boy
in your face! You have seen many boys with such
pickedevants,° I am sure.

5 WAGNER: Sirrah, hast thou no comings in?°

ROBIN: Yes, and goings out too, you may see, sir.

WAGNER: Alas, poor slave! See how poverty jests in
his nakedness. I know the villain's out of service,
and so hungry that I know he would give his soul
10 to the devil for a shoulder of mutton, though it
were blood-raw.

ROBIN: Not so neither. I had need to have it well
roasted, and good sauce to it, if I pay so dear, I
can tell you.

15 WAGNER: Sirrah, wilt thou be my man and wait on
me, and I will make thee go like *Qui mihi
discipulus?*°

ROBIN: What, in verse?

WAGNER: No slave; in beaten° silk and staves-acre.°

ROBIN: Staves-acre? That's good to kill vermin. Then, 20
belike, if I serve you I shall be lousy.

WAGNER: Why, so thou shalt be, whether thou dost
it or no; for, sirrah, if thou dost not presently bind
thyself to me for seven years, I'll turn all the lice
about thee into familiars° and make them tear thee 25
in pieces.

ROBIN: Nay sir, you may save yourself a labor, for
they are as familiar with me as if they paid for
their meat and drink, I can tell you.

WAGNER: Well, sirrah, leave your jesting and take 30
these guilders.

ROBIN: Yes, marry sir, and I thank you too.

WAGNER: So, now thou art to be at an hour's warning,
whensoever and wheresoever the devil shall fetch
thee.   35

ROBIN: Here, take your guilders again. I'll none of
'em.

WAGNER: Not I. Thou art pressed.° Prepare thyself,
for I will presently raise up two devils to carry thee
away. Banio! Belcher!   40

ROBIN: Belcher? And Belcher come here, I'll belch him.
I am not afraid of a devil.

(*Enter two Devils.*)

WAGNER: How now, sir? Will you serve me now?

ROBIN: Ay, good Wagner; take away the devil then.

WAGNER: Spirits away! Now, sirrah, follow me.   45

[*Exeunt Devils.*]

ROBIN: I will sir. But hark you, master, will you teach
me this conjuring occupation?

WAGNER: Ay, sirrah. I'll teach thee to turn thyself to
a dog, or a cat, or a mouse, or a rat, or any thing.

ROBIN: A dog, or a cat, or a mouse, or a rat! O brave 50
Wagner!

WAGNER: Villain, call me Master Wagner, and see
that you walk attentively, and let your right eye
be always diametrally° fixed upon my left heel, that
thou may'st *quasi vestigias nostras insistere.*°   55

ROBIN: Well, sir, I warrant you.

(*Exeunt.*)

ACT II · Scene I _____

(*Enter Faustus in his Study.*)

FAUSTUS: Now Faustus must thou needs be damned,
And canst thou not be saved.
What boots° it then to think on God or heaven?

---

109. **bind:** Enclose. **I, IV. 4. pickedevants:** Pointed beards.
5. **comings in:** Earnings. **16–17.** *Qui mihi discipulus:* Who
is my disciple (the opening words of a Latin poem by William
Lyly, well known to Elizabethan schoolboys).

19. **beaten:** Embroidered with metal; **staves-acre:** A plant
used for killing vermin. **25. familiars:** Attendant evil spirits.
38. **pressed:** Enlisted into service in exchange for money.
54. **diametrally:** In a straight line. **55. quasi . . . insistere:**
As if to walk in our tracks. **II, I. 3. boots:** Avails.

Away with such vain fancies, and despair;
5 Despair in God, and trust in Beelzebub.
Now go not backward; Faustus, be resolute.
Why waver'st thou? O, something soundeth in
    mine ear:
"Abjure this magic; turn to God again."
Ay, and Faustus will turn to God again!
10 To God? He loves thee not.
The God thou serv'st is thine own appetite,
Wherein is fixed the love of Beelzebub.
To him I'll build an altar and a church,
And offer lukewarm blood of new-born babes.

(*Enter the two Angels.*)

BAD ANGEL: Go forward, Faustus, in that famous
15   art.
GOOD ANGEL: Sweet Faustus, leave that execrable
    art.
FAUSTUS: Contrition, prayer, repentance — what of
    these?
GOOD ANGEL: O, they are means to bring thee
    unto heaven.
BAD ANGEL: Rather illusions, fruits of lunacy,
20 That make men foolish that do use them most.
GOOD ANGEL: Sweet Faustus, think of heaven and
    heavenly things.
BAD ANGEL: No Faustus; think of honor and
    wealth.
                              (*Exeunt Angels.*)
FAUSTUS: Wealth? Why, the signory of Emden° shall
    be mine.
When Mephistophilis shall stand by me,
25 What power can hurt me? Faustus thou art safe.
Cast no more doubts. Mephistophilis, come
And bring glad tidings from great Lucifer.
Is't not midnight? Come, Mephistophilis.
Veni,° *veni, Mephistophile.*

(*Enter Mephistophilis.*)

30   Now tell me what saith Lucifer, thy lord?
MEPHISTOPHILIS: That I shall wait on Faustus whilst
    he lives,
So he will buy my service with his soul.
FAUSTUS: Already Faustus hath hazarded that for
    thee.
MEPHISTOPHILIS: But now thou must bequeath it
    solemnly
35 And write a deed of gift with thine own blood,
For that security craves great Lucifer.
If thou deny it, I must back to hell.

FAUSTUS: Stay, Mephistophilis! Tell me what good
    Will my soul do thy lord.
MEPHISTOPHILIS: Enlarge his kingdom.
FAUSTUS: Is that the reason why he tempts us thus?   40
MEPHISTOPHILIS: *Solamen miseris socios habuisse*
    doloris.°
FAUSTUS: Why, have you any pain that torture
    others?
MEPHISTOPHILIS: As great as have the human souls
    of men.
But tell me, Faustus, shall I have thy soul?
And I will be thy slave and wait on thee   45
And give thee more than thou hast wit to ask.
FAUSTUS: Ay, Mephistophilis, I'll give it him.
MEPHISTOPHILIS: Then Faustus, stab thy arm
    courageously,
And bind thy soul that at some certain day
Great Lucifer may claim it as his own,   50
And then be thou as great as Lucifer.
FAUSTUS: [*stabbing his arm*] Lo, Mephistophilis, for
    love of thee,
I cut mine arm, and with my proper° blood
Assure my soul to be great Lucifer's,
Chief lord and regent of perpetual night.   55
View here this blood that trickles from mine
    arm,
And let it be propitious for my wish.
MEPHISTOPHILIS: But Faustus,
Write it in manner of a deed of gift.
FAUSTUS: Ay, so I do. [*He writes.*] But
    Mephistophilis,   60
My blood congeals, and I can write no more.
MEPHISTOPHILIS: I'll fetch thee fire to dissolve it
    straight.
                              (*Exit.*)
FAUSTUS: What might the staying of my blood
    portend?
Is it unwilling I should write this bill?
Why streams it not that I may write afresh?   65
"Faustus gives to thee his soul." Ah, there it
    stayed.
Why shouldst thou not? Is not thy soul thine
    own?
Then write again: "Faustus gives to thee his
    soul."

(*Enter Mephistophilis with the chafer of fire.*)

MEPHISTOPHILIS: See Faustus, here is fire. Set it on.°
FAUSTUS: So. Now the blood begins to clear again.   70
Now will I make an end immediately.
                              [*He writes.*]

---

23. Emden: The chief city of East Friesland, near the mouth
of the river Ems, which had considerable trade relations with
Elizabethan England.

41. Solamen . . . doloris: It is a consolation in misery to have
a fellow sufferer. **53. proper:** Own. **69. Set it on:** Set the
dish of blood on the fire.

MEPHISTOPHILIS: [*Aside.*] What will not I do to
    obtain his soul?

FAUSTUS: *Consummatum est;°* this bill is ended,
    And Faustus hath bequeathed his soul to Lucifer.

75   But what is this inscription on mine arm?
    Homo fuge!° Whither should I fly?
    If unto God, he'll throw me down to hell.
    My senses are deceived; here's nothing writ.
    O yes, I see it plain. Even here is writ

80   *Homo fuge!* Yet shall not Faustus fly.

MEPHISTOPHILIS: [*Aside.*] I'll fetch him somewhat to
    delight his mind.

                        (*Exit.*)

(*Enter Devils, giving crowns and rich apparel to Faustus.
They dance and then depart. Enter Mephistophilis.*)

FAUSTUS: What means this show? Speak
    Mephistophilis.

MEPHISTOPHILIS: Nothing, Faustus, but to delight
    thy mind
    And let thee see what magic can perform.

85 FAUSTUS: But may I raise such spirits when I please?

MEPHISTOPHILIS: Ay Faustus, and do greater things
    than these.

FAUSTUS: Then, Mephistophilis, receive this scroll,
    A deed of gift of body and of soul,
    But yet conditionally that thou perform

90   All covenants and articles between us both.

MEPHISTOPHILIS: Faustus, I swear by hell and
    Lucifer
    To effect all promises between us made.

FAUSTUS: Then hear me read it Mephistophilis.
    On these conditions following:

95   *First, that Faustus may be a spirit in form and
    substance;*
    *Secondly, that Mephistophilis shall be his servant
    and be at his command;*
    Thirdly, that Mephistophilis shall do for him and

100   *bring him whatsoever;*
    *Fourthly, that he shall be in his chamber or house
    invisible;*
    *Lastly, that he shall appear to the said John Faustus
    at all times, in what form or shape soever he please:*

105   *I, John Faustus, of Wittenberg, doctor, by these
    presents, do give both body and soul to Lucifer,
    Prince of the East, and his minister, Mephistophilis;
    and furthermore grant unto them that four and
    twenty years being expired, the articles above writ-*

110   *ten inviolate, full power to fetch or carry the said
    John Faustus, body and soul, flesh, blood, or goods,
    into their habitation wheresoever.*
                By me, John Faustus.

MEPHISTOPHILIS: Speak Faustus. Do you deliver this
    as your deed?

FAUSTUS: Ay, take it, and the devil give thee good
    of it.   115

MEPHISTOPHILIS: So now, Faustus, ask me what
    thou wilt.

FAUSTUS: First will I question with thee about hell.
    Tell me, where is the place that men call hell?

MEPHISTOPHILIS: Under the heavens.

FAUSTUS: Ay, so are all things else. But
    whereabouts?   120

MEPHISTOPHILIS: Within the bowels of these
    elements,
    Where we are tortured and remain for ever.
    Hell hath no limits, nor is circumscribed
    In one self place, but where we are is hell,
    And where hell is, there must we ever be.   125
    And, to be short, when all the world dissolves
    And every creature shall be purified,
    All places shall be hell that is not heaven.

FAUSTUS: I think hell's a fable.

MEPHISTOPHILIS: Ay, think so still, till experience
    change thy mind.   130

FAUSTUS: Why, dost thou think that Faustus shall
    be damned?

MEPHISTOPHILIS: Ay, of necessity, for here's the
    scroll
    In which thou hast given thy soul to Lucifer.

FAUSTUS: Ay, and body too. But what of that?
    Think'st thou that Faustus is so fond° to imagine   135
    That after this life there is any pain?
    No, these are trifles and mere old wives' tales.

MEPHISTOPHILIS: But I am an instance to prove the
    contrary,
    For I tell thee I am damned and now in hell.

FAUSTUS: Nay, and this be hell, I'll willingly be
    damned.   140
    What? Sleeping, eating, walking and disputing?
    But, leaving off this, let me have a wife,
    The fairest maid in Germany,
    For I am wanton and lascivious,
    And cannot live without a wife.   145

MEPHISTOPHILIS: I prithee, Faustus, talk not of a
    wife.

FAUSTUS: Nay, sweet Mephistophilis, fetch me one,
    for I will have one.

MEPHISTOPHILIS: Well, Faustus, thou shalt have a
    wife.
    Sit there till I come.   [*Exit.*]

(*Enter [Mephistophilis] with a Devil dressed like a
woman, with fireworks.*)

---

73. Consummatum est: It is completed (the words of Jesus
at his Crucifixion; John 19:30).   **76. Homo fuge:** Fly, man.

135. fond: Foolish.

150 FAUSTUS: What sight is this?
MEPHISTOPHILIS: Now Faustus, how dost thou like
    thy wife?
FAUSTUS: Here's a hot whore indeed! No, I'll no
    wife.
MEPHISTOPHILIS: Marriage is but a ceremonial toy,
    And if thou lovest me, think no more of it.
155 I'll cull thee out the fairest courtesans
    And bring them every morning to thy bed.
    She whom thine eye shall like, thy heart shall
      have,
    Were she as chaste as was Penelope,°
    As wise as Saba,° or as beautiful
160 As was bright Lucifer before his fall.
    Hold; take this book; peruse it thoroughly.
    The iterating of these lines brings gold;
    The framing of this circle on the ground
    Brings thunder, whirlwinds, storm and lightning.
165 Pronounce this thrice devoutly to thyself,
    And men in harness° shall appear to thee,
    Ready to execute what thou command'st.
FAUSTUS: Thanks, Mephistophilis, for this sweet
    book.
    This will I keep as chary as my life.

                      (Exeunt.)

Scene II

(Enter Faustus in his study and Mephistophilis.)

FAUSTUS: When I behold the heavens, then I repent
    And curse thee, wicked Mephistophilis,
    Because thou hast deprived me of those joys.
MEPHISTOPHILIS: 'Twas thine own seeking, Faustus;
    thank thyself.
    But think'st thou heaven is such a glorious
5   thing?
    I tell thee, Faustus, 'tis not half so fair
    As thou, or any man that breathes on earth.
FAUSTUS: How prov'st thou that?
MEPHISTOPHILIS: 'Twas made for man; then he's
    more excellent.
FAUSTUS: If heaven was made for man, 'twas made
10   for me.
    I will renounce this magic and repent.

(Enter the two Angels.)

GOOD ANGEL: Faustus repent; yet God will pity
    thee.
BAD ANGEL: Thou art a spirit;° God cannot pity
    thee.

FAUSTUS: Who buzzeth in mine ears I am a spirit?
    Be I a devil, yet God may pity me;   15
    Yea, God will pity me if I repent.
BAD ANGEL: Ay, but Faustus never shall repent.
                      (Exeunt angels.)
FAUSTUS: My heart is hardened; I cannot repent.
    Scarce can I name salvation, faith, or heaven,
    But fearful echoes thunder in mine ears: 20
    "Faustus, thou art damned!" Then swords and
      knives,
    Poison, guns, halters, and envenomed steel
    Are laid before me to dispatch myself;
    And long ere this I should have done the deed,
    Had not sweet pleasure conquered deep despair. 25
    Have not I made blind Homer sing to me
    Of Alexander's love and Oenone's death?°
    And hath not he, that built the walls of Thebes
    With ravishing sound of his melodious harp,°
    Made music with my Mephistophilis?   30
    Why should I die then, or basely despair?
    I am resolved; Faustus shall not repent.
    Come, Mephistophilis, let us dispute again
    And reason of divine astrology.
    Speak; are there many spheres above the moon? 35
    Are all celestial bodies but one globe,
    As is the substance of this centric earth?
MEPHISTOPHILIS: As are the elements, such are the
    heavens,
    Even from the moon unto the empyreal orb,
    Mutually folded in each others' spheres,   40
    And jointly move upon one axle-tree.
    Whose terminè° is termed the world's wide pole;
    Nor are the names of Saturn, Mars, or Jupiter
    Feigned, but are erring stars.
FAUSTUS: But have they all
    One motion, both *situ et tempore?*°   45
MEPHISTOPHILIS: All move from east to west in four
    and twenty hours upon the poles of the world, but
    differ in their motions upon the poles of the zodiac.
FAUSTUS: These slender questions Wagner can
    decide.
    Hath Mephistophilis no greater skill?   50
    Who knows not the double motion of the
      planets?
    That the first is finished in a natural day?

---

27. Alexander's . . . death: Paris (also called Alexander) loved the nymph Oenone when he lived as a shepherd on Mt. Ida. Oenone died of a broken heart when he left her. **28–29. he . . . harp:** Amphion, son of Zeus and Antiope, caused stones to move and the walls of Thebes to be built simply by playing on the lyre given to him by Hermes. **42. terminè:** Limit. **44. erring stars:** Planets. **45. *situ et tempore:*** In position (direction of movement) and in the time they take to revolve about the earth.

158. Penelope: The faithful wife of Ulysses in Homer's *Odyssey.* **159. Saba:** The Queen of Sheba. **166. harness:** Armor. **II, II. 13. spirit:** Devil.

The second thus? Saturn in thirty years?
Jupiter in twelve; Mars in four; the sun, Venus and
55   Mercury in a year; the moon in twenty eight days
These are freshmen's suppositions. But tell me, hath
every sphere a dominion or *intelligentia?*°
MEPHISTOPHILIS: Ay.
FAUSTUS: How many heavens or spheres are there?
60   MEPHISTOPHILIS: Nine — the seven planets, the firmament, and the empyreal heaven.
FAUSTUS: But is there not *coelum igneum, et
crystallinum?*°
MEPHISTOPHILIS: No, Faustus, they be but fables.
65   FAUSTUS: Resolve me then in this one question: why
are not conjunctions, oppositions, aspects, eclipses°
all at one time, but in some years we have more,
in some less?
MEPHISTOPHILIS: *Per inaequalem motum respectu*
70   *totius.*°
FAUSTUS: Well, I am answered. Now tell me who made
the world.
MEPHISTOPHILIS: I will not.
FAUSTUS: Sweet Mephistophilis, tell me.
75   MEPHISTOPHILIS: Move me not, Faustus.
FAUSTUS: Villain, have not I bound thee to tell me any
thing?
MEPHISTOPHILIS: Ay, that is not against our
kingdom.
This is. Thou art damned. Think thou of hell.
FAUSTUS: Think, Faustus, upon God that made the
80   world.
MEPHISTOPHILIS: Remember this.
                                                  (*Exit.*)
FAUSTUS: Ay, go accursèd spirit to ugly hell.
'Tis thou hast damned distressèd Faustus' soul.
Is't not too late?

(*Enter the two Angels.*)

85   BAD ANGEL: Too late.
GOOD ANGEL: Never too late, if Faustus will
repent.
BAD ANGEL: If thou repent, devils will tear thee in
pieces.
GOOD ANGEL: Repent, and they shall never raze thy
skin.
                                     (*Exeunt Angels.*)

---

57. **dominion or** *intelligentia:* Governing angel.   **62–63.** *coelum . . . crystallinum:* The fiery heaven and crystalline sphere of Ptolemaic astronomy.   **66. conjunctions:** Seeming proximities of heavenly bodies; **oppositions:** Divergences of heavenly bodies; **aspects:** Any other relations of such bodies to one another; **eclipses:** The blottings out of one heavenly body by another.   **69–70.** *Per . . . totius:* By their unequal movements in respect to the whole (i.e., the different speeds of the various planets within the total cosmos).

FAUSTUS: O Christ, my Savior, my Savior,
Help to save distressèd Faustus' soul.   90

(*Enter Lucifer, Beelzebub, and Mephistophilis.*)

LUCIFER: Christ cannot save thy soul, for he is just.
There's none but I have interest in the same.
FAUSTUS: O, what art thou that look'st so terribly?
LUCIFER: I am Lucifer,
And this is my companion prince in hell.   95
FAUSTUS: O, Faustus, they are come to fetch thy
soul.
BEELZEBUB: We are come to tell thee thou dost
injure us.
LUCIFER: Thou call'st on Christ, contrary to thy
promise.
BEELZEBUB: Thou shouldst not think on God.
LUCIFER: Think on the devil.   100
BEELZEBUB: And his dam too.
FAUSTUS: Nor will I henceforth. Pardon me in this,
And Faustus vows never to look to heaven,
Never to name God, or to pray to him,
To burn his Scriptures, slay his ministers,   105
And make my spirits pull his churches down.
LUCIFER: So shalt thou show thyself an obedient
servant,
And we will highly gratify thee for it.
BEELZEBUB: Faustus, we are come from hell in person
to show thee some pastime. Sit down, and thou   110
shalt behold the Seven Deadly Sins appear to thee
in their own proper shapes and likeness.
FAUSTUS: That sight will be as pleasant to me as Paradise
was to Adam the first day of his creation.
LUCIFER: Talk not of Paradise or creation, but mark 115
the show. Go, Mephistophilis, fetch them in.
                              [*Exit Mephistophilis.*]

(*Enter the Seven Deadly Sins, [with Mephistophilis,
led by a Piper].*)

BEELZEBUB: Now Faustus, question them of their names
and dispositions.
FAUSTUS: That shall I soon. What art thou, the first?
PRIDE: I am Pride. I disdain to have any parents. I am 120
like to Ovid's flea:° I can creep into every corner
of a wench. Sometimes, like a periwig, I sit upon
her brow. Next, like a necklace, I hang about her
neck. Then, like a fan of feathers, I kiss her lips,
and then, turning myself to a wrought smock, do   125
what I list. But fie, what a smell is here! I'll not
speak another word unless the ground be perfumed
and covered with cloth of Arras.°

---

121. **Ovid's flea:** The medieval poem *Carmine de Pulice* (Poem of the Flea) was generally attributed to Ovid.   **128. cloth of Arras:** Flemish cloth used generally for tapestries.

FAUSTUS: Thou art a proud knave indeed. What art
130   thou, the second?
COVETOUSNESS: I am Covetousness, begotten of an
      old churl in a leather bag, and might I now obtain
      my wish, this house, you and all, should turn to
      gold, that I might lock you safe into my chest. O
135   my sweet gold!
FAUSTUS: And what art thou, the third?
ENVY: I am Envy, begotten of a chimney-sweeper and
      an oyster-wife. I cannot read and therefore wish
      all books burned. I am lean with seeing others eat.
140   O, that there would come a famine over all the
      world, that all might die, and I live alone; then
      thou shouldst see how fat I'd be. But must thou
      sit and I stand? Come down, with a vengeance.
FAUSTUS: Out envious wretch! But what are thou, the
145   fourth?
WRATH: I am Wrath. I had neither father nor mother.
      I leaped out of a lion's mouth when I was scarce
      an hour old, and ever since have run up and down
      the world with this case of rapiers, wounding myself
150   when I could get none to fight withal. I was born
      in hell, and look to it, for some of you shall be
      my father.
FAUSTUS: And what are you, the fifth?
GLUTTONY: I am Gluttony. My parents are all dead,
155   and the devil a penny they have left me but a small
      pension, and that buys me thirty meals a day and
      ten bevers° — a small trifle to suffice nature. I come
      of a royal pedigree. My father was a gammon of
      bacon, and my mother was a hogshead of claret
160   wine. My godfathers were these: Peter Pickled-her-
      ring and Martin Martlemas-beef.° But my god-
      mother, O, she was a jolly gentlewoman, and well
      beloved in every good town and city; her name
      was Mistress Margery March-beer.° Now Faustus,
165   thou hast heard all my progeny; wilt thou bid me
      to a supper.
FAUSTUS: Not I. Thou wilt eat up all my victuals.
GLUTTONY: Then the devil choke thee.
FAUSTUS: Choke thyself, glutton. What art thou, the
170   sixth?
SLOTH: Heigh ho! I am Sloth. I was begotten on a
      sunny bank, where I have lain ever since, and you
      have done me great injury to bring me from thence.
      Let me be carried thither again by Gluttony and
175   Lechery. Heigh ho! I'll not speak a word more for
      a king's ransom.

FAUSTUS: And what are you Mistress Minx, the seventh
      and last?
LECHERY: Who, I, sir? I am one that loves an inch of
      raw mutton° better than an ell of fried stockfish,°   180
      and the first letter of my name begins with lechery.
LUCIFER: Away to hell! Away! On piper!
            (*Exeunt the seven Sins [and the Piper].*)
FAUSTUS: O, how this sight doth delight my soul!
LUCIFER: But Faustus, in hell is all manner of delight.   185
FAUSTUS: O, might I see hell and return again safe,
      how happy were I then!
LUCIFER: Faustus, thou shalt. At midnight I will send
      for thee. Meanwhile peruse this book and view it
      thoroughly, and thou shalt turn thyself into what
      shape thou wilt.   190
FAUSTUS: Thanks, mighty Lucifer.
      This will I keep as chary as my life.
LUCIFER: Now Faustus, farewell.
FAUSTUS: Farewell, great Lucifer. Come, Mephistophilis.
            (*Exeunt, several ways.*)

Scene III

(*Enter the Clown, [Robin, holding a book].*)

ROBIN: What, Dick, look to the horses there till I
      come again. I have gotten one of Doctor Faustus'
      conjuring books, and now we'll have such knavery
      as't passes.

(*Enter Dick.*)

DICK: What, Robin, you must come away and walk   5
      the horses.
ROBIN: I walk the horses? I scorn't, 'faith. I have other
      matters in hand. Let the horses walk themselves
      and they will. [*He reads.*] *A per se a; t, h, e, the;*
      o per se o; deny orgon, gorgon. Keep further from   10
      me, O thou illiterate and unlearned hostler.
DICK: 'Snails,° what hast thou got there? A book?
      Why, thou canst not tell ne'er a word on't.
ROBIN: That thou shalt see presently. Keep out of the
      circle, I say, lest I send you into the hostry with a   15
      vengeance.
DICK: That's like, 'faith. You had best leave your
      foolery, for an my master come, he'll conjure you,
      'faith.
ROBIN: My master conjure me? I'll tell thee what: an   20
      my master come here, I'll clap as fair a pair of
      horns° on's head as e'er thou sawest in thy life.
DICK: Thou needst not do that, for my mistress hath
      done it.

---

157. **bevers:** Light snacks taken between regular meals.   **161.**
Martlemas-beef: Salted meat hung for the winter on Mar-
tinmas, November 11.   **164. March-beer:** A fine ale made
in the springtime and aged for two years before being drunk.

180. **raw mutton:** Common slang for "whore"; **stockfish:**
Dried codfish.   II, III. 12. **'Snails:** By God's nails.   **22. horns:**
The common sign of a cuckold.

25 ROBIN: Ay, there be of us here that have waded as
     deep into matters as other men, if they were disposed
     to talk.
    DICK: A plague take you! I thought you did not sneak
     up and down after her for nothing. But I prithee,
30   tell me in good sadness,° Robin, is that a conjuring
     book?
    ROBIN: Do but speak what thou'lt have me to do, and
     I'll do't. If thou'lt dance naked, put off thy clothes,
     and I'll conjure thee about presently. Or if thou'lt
35   go but to the tavern with me, I'll give thee white
     wine, red wine, claret wine, sack, muscadine, mal-
     mesey and whippincrust.° Hold belly, hold, and
     we'll not pay one penny for it.
    DICK: O brave! Prithee let's to it presently, for I am
     as dry as a dog.
    ROBIN: Come then, let's away.

                                                    (*Exeunt.*)

ACT III · Prologue _____

(*Enter the Chorus.*)

   CHORUS: Learnèd Faustus,
         To find the secrets of astronomy
         Graven in the book of Jove's high firmament,
         Did mount him up to scale Olympus' top,
5   Where, sitting in a chariot burning bright
         Drawn by the strength of yokèd dragons' necks,
         He views the clouds, the planets, and the stars,
         The tropics, zones, and quarters of the sky,
         From the bright circle of the hornèd moon
10   Even to the height of *Primum Mobile*.°
         And whirling round with this circumference,
         Within the concave compass of the pole,
         From east to west his dragons swiftly glide
         And in eight days did bring him home again.
15   Not long he stayed within his quiet house
         To rest his bones after his weary toil,
         But new exploits do hale him out again,
         And mounted then upon a dragon's back,
         That with his wings did part the subtle air,
20   He now is gone to prove cosmography,°
         That measures coasts and kingdoms of the earth,
         And, as I guess, will first arrive at Rome
         To see the Pope and manner of his court
         And take some part of holy Peter's feast,
25   The which this day is highly solemnized.

                                                    (*Exit.*)

Scene I

(*Enter Faustus and Mephistophilis.*)

FAUSTUS: Having now, my good Mephistophilis,
      Passed with delight the stately town of Trier,
      Environed round with airy mountain tops,
      With walls of flint, and deep entrenchèd lakes,°
      Not to be won by any conquering prince;   5
      From Paris next, coasting the realm of France,
      We saw the river Main fall into Rhine,
      Whose banks are set with groves of fruitful
          vines;
      Then up to Naples, rich Campania,
      Whose buildings fair and gorgeous to the eye,   10
      The streets straight forth and paved with finest
          brick,
      Quarters the town in four equivalents.
      There saw we learnèd Maro's° golden tomb,
      The way he cut, an English mile in length,
      Through a rock of stone in one night's space.°   15
      From thence to Venice, Padua, and the rest,
      In midst of which a sumptuous temple stands,
      That threats the stars with her aspiring top,
      Whose frame is paved with sundry colored
          stones,
      And roofed aloft with curious work in gold.°   20
      Thus hitherto hath Faustus spent his time.
      But tell me now, what resting-place is this?
      Hast thou, as erst I did command,
      Conducted me within the walls of Rome?
MEPHISTOPHILIS: I have, my Faustus, and for proof
          thereof   25
      This is the goodly palace of the Pope;
      And 'cause we are no common guests,
      I choose his privy chamber for our use.
FAUSTUS: I hope his holiness will bid us welcome.
MEPHISTOPHILIS: All's one, for we'll be bold with
          his venison.   30
      But now, my Faustus, that thou may'st perceive
      What Rome contains for to delight thine eyes,
      Know that this city stands upon seven hills
      That underprop the groundwork of the same.
      Just through the midst runs flowing Tiber's
          stream,   35
      With winding banks that cut it in two parts,
      Over the which four stately bridges lean,
      That make safe passage to each part of Rome.
      Upon the bridge called Ponte Angelo

---

30. **sadness:** Seriousness. 37. **whippincrust:** Possibly a corruption of "hippocras," a highly spiced and sugared wine.
III, Prologue. 10. *Primum Mobile:* In Ptolemaic astronomy
the outermost sphere of creation, which moves the other nine
spheres. 20. **prove cosmography:** Explore the universe.

III, I. 4. entrenchèd lakes: Castle moats. **13. Maro:** Virgil.
14–15. way . . . space: A tunnel between the bays of Naples
and Baiae, through Mt. Posilipo, was said to have been cut
by Virgil (regarded as a magician in the Middle Ages) by
supernatural art. **17–20. In midst . . . gold:** St. Mark's
cathedral in Venice.

40   Erected is a castle passing strong,
       Where thou shalt see such store of ordinance
       As that the double cannons, forged of brass,
       Do match the number of the days contained
       Within the compass of one complete year;
45   Beside the gates and high pyramidès
       That Julius Caesar brought from Africa.°
    FAUSTUS: Now, by the kingdoms of infernal rule,
       Of Styx, of Acheron, and the fiery lake
       Of ever-burning Phlegethon, I swear
50   That I do long to see the monuments
       And situation of bright-splendent Rome.
       Come, therefore, let's away.
    MEPHISTOPHILIS: Nay, stay my Faustus. I know
       you'd see the Pope
       And take some part of holy Peter's feast,
55   The which, in state and high solemnity,
       This day is held through Rome and Italy
       In honor of the Pope's triumphant victory.
    FAUSTUS: Sweet Mephistophilis, thou pleasest me.
       Whilst I am here on earth, let me be cloyed
60   With all things that delight the heart of man.
       My four and twenty years of liberty
       I'll spend in pleasure and in dalliance,
       That Faustus' name, whilst this bright frame
         doth stand,
       May be admirèd through the furthest land.
    MEPHISTOPHILIS: 'Tis well said, Faustus. Come then,
65   stand by me
       And thou shalt see them come immediately.
    FAUSTUS: Nay, stay, my gentle Mephistophilis,
       And grant me my request, and then I go.
       Thou know'st within the compass of eight days
70   We viewed the face of heaven, of earth, and hell.
       So high our dragons soared into the air,
       That looking down, the earth appeared to me
       No bigger than my hand in quantity.
       There did we view the kingdoms of the world,
75   And what might please mine eye I there beheld.
       Then in this show let me an actor be,
       That this proud Pope may Faustus' cunning see.
    MEPHISTOPHILIS: Let it be so, my Faustus. But, first
       stay
       And view their triumphs° as they pass this way,
80   And then devise what best contents thy mind
       By cunning in thine art to cross the Pope
       Or dash the pride of this solemnity,
       To make his monks and abbots stand like apes
       And point like antics at his triple crown,
85   To beat the beads about the friars' pates

       Or clap huge horns upon the cardinals' heads,
       Or any villainy thou canst devise,
       And I'll perform it, Faustus. Hark, they come.
       This day shall make thee be admired in Rome.

(Enter the Cardinals and Bishops, some bearing crosiers, some the pillars; Monks and Friars singing their procession. Then the Pope, and Raymond, King of Hungary, with Bruno, led in chains.)

POPE: Cast down our footstool.
RAYMOND: Saxon Bruno, stoop,   90
       Whilst on thy back his holiness ascends
       Saint Peter's chair and state pontifical.
BRUNO: Proud Lucifer, that state belongs to me,
       But thus I fall to Peter, not to thee.
POPE: To me and Peter shalt thou groveling lie   95
       And crouch before the papal dignity.
       Sound trumpets then, for thus Saint Peter's heir
       From Bruno's back ascends Saint Peter's chair.

(A flourish while he ascends.)

       Thus, as the gods creep on with feet of wool
       Long ere with iron hands they punish men,   100
       So shall our sleeping vengeance now arise
       And smite with death thy hated enterprise.
       Lord Cardinals of France and Padua,
       Go forthwith to our holy consistory,
       And read amongst the Statutes Decretal°   105
       What, by the holy council held at Trent,°
       The sacred synod hath decreed for him
       That doth assume the papal government
       Without election and a true consent.
       Away, and bring us word with speed.   110
FIRST CARDINAL: We go my Lord.
                (Exeunt Cardinals.)
POPE: Lord Raymond.   *[They talk apart.]*
FAUSTUS: Go, haste thee, gentle Mephistophilis,
       Follow the cardinals to the consistory,
       And as they turn their superstitious books,   115
       Strike them with sloth and drowsy idleness,
       And make them sleep so sound that in their
         shapes
       Thyself and I may parley with this Pope,
       This proud confronter of the Emperor,
       And in despite of all his holiness   120
       Restore this Bruno to his liberty
       And bear him to the states of Germany.
MEPHISTOPHILIS: Faustus, I go.
FAUSTUS: Dispatch it soon.

45–46. gates . . . Africa: Before the gates of St. Peter's there still stands the obelisk that was brought to Rome from Heliopolis by the Emperor Caligula in the first century A.D. **79. triumphs:** Spectacular displays.

105. Statutes Decretal: Papal decrees concerning religious doctrine or ecclesiastical law. **106. council . . . Trent:** The Council of Trent, held by the Church from 1545 to 1563.

The Pope shall curse that Faustus came to
125   Rome.
             (*Exeunt Faustus and Mephistophilis.*)
BRUNO: Pope Adrian,° let me have some right of
    law.
    I was elected by the Emperor.
POPE: We will depose the Emperor for that deed
    And curse the people that submit to him.
130   Both he and thou shalt stand excommunicate
    And interdict from church's privilege
    And all society of holy men.
    He grows too proud in his authority,
    Lifting his lofty head above the clouds,
135   And like a steeple overpeers the church.
    But we'll pull down his haughty insolence,
    And as Pope Alexander, our progenitor,
    Trod on the neck of German Frederick,°
    Adding this golden sentence to our praise,
140   "That Peter's heirs should tread on emperors
    And walk upon the dreadful adder's back,
    Treading the lion and the dragon down
    And fearless spurn the killing basilisk,"°
    So will we quell that haughty schismatic,
145   And by authority apostolical
    Depose him from his regal government.
BRUNO: Pope Julius swore to princely Sigismond,°
    For him and the succeeding popes of Rome,
    To hold the emperors their lawful lords.
150 POPE: Pope Julius did abuse the church's rites,
    And therefore none of his decrees can stand.
    Is not all power on earth bestowed on us?
    And therefore, though we would, we cannot err.
    Behold this silver belt, whereto is fixed
155   Seven golden keys fast sealed with seven seals
    In token of our sevenfold power from heaven,
    To bind or loose, lock fast, condemn or judge,
    Resign, or seal, or whatso pleaseth us.
    Then he and thou and all the world shall stoop,
160   Or be assurèd of our dreadful curse
    To light as heavy as the pains of hell.

---

126. **Pope Adrian:** Marlowe perhaps means Pope Hadrian
IV (1154–1159), who tried to assert his authority over Frederick Barbarossa, the Holy Roman Emperor. What historicity
there may be in these scenes at the papal court is badly
confused.   137–138. **Pope Alexander . . . Frederick:** Pope
Alexander III (1159–1181), successor to Hadrian IV, continued
the struggle against Barbarossa, forcing him to acknowledge
the papal supremacy at Canossa.   143. **basilisk:** A mythical
monster with power to kill by its looks.   147. **Pope Julius
. . . Sigismond:** None of the three popes named Julius was
contemporary with the Emperor Sigismund (1368–1437).
Sigismund did, however, in 1414 summon the Council of
Constance, which sought to end the Great Schism (1378–
1417), during which the papacy in Rome was challenged by
a line of popes in Avignon.

(*Enter Faustus and Mephistophilis, like the Cardinals.*)
MEPHISTOPHILIS: Now tell me, Faustus, are we not
    fitted well?
FAUSTUS: Yes, Mephistophilis, and two such
    cardinals
    Ne'er served a holy pope as we shall do.
    But whilst they sleep within the consistory,
    Let us salute his reverend fatherhood.   165
RAYMOND: Behold, my lord, the cardinals are
    returned.
POPE: Welcome, grave fathers. Answer presently:
    What have our holy council there decreed
    Concerning Bruno and the Emperor,   170
    In quittance of their late conspiracy
    Against our state and papal dignity?
FAUSTUS: Most sacred patron of the church of
    Rome,
    By full consent of all the synod
    Of priests and prelates it is thus decreed: 175
    That Bruno and the German Emperor
    Be held as Lollards° and bold schismatics
    And proud disturbers of the church's peace.
    And if that Bruno by his own assent,
    Without enforcement of the German peers,   180
    Did seek to wear the triple diadem
    And by your death to climb Saint Peter's chair,
    The Statutes Decretal have thus decreed:
    He shall be straight condemned of heresy
    And on a pile of fagots burned to death.   185
POPE: It is enough. Here, take him to your charge,
    And bear him straight to Ponte Angelo,
    And in the strongest tower enclose him fast.
    Tomorrow, sitting in our consistory
    With all our college of grave cardinals,   190
    We will determine of his life or death.
    Here, take his triple crown along with you,
    And leave it in the church's treasury.
    Make haste again, my good lord cardinals,
    And take our blessing apostolical.   195
MEPHISTOPHILIS: So, so. Was never devil thus
    blessed before.
FAUSTUS: Away, sweet Mephistophilis, be gone.
    The cardinals will be plagued for this anon.
        (*Exeunt Faustus and Mephistophilis [with
                        Bruno].*)
    POPE: Go presently and bring a banquet
    forth,
    That we may solemnize Saint Peter's feast,   200
    And with Lord Raymond, King of Hungary,
    Drink to our late and happy victory.   (*Exeunt.*)

---

177. **Lollards:** Followers of John Wyclif (1320?–1384), the
English reformer.

Scene II

(*A sennet [is sounded] while the banquet is brought in; and then enter Faustus and Mephistophilis in their own shapes.*)

MEPHISTOPHILIS: Now, Faustus, come, prepare
    thyself for mirth.
  The sleepy cardinals are hard at hand
  To censure Bruno, that is posted hence,
  And on a proud-paced steed, as swift as thought,
5 Flies o'er the Alps to fruitful Germany,
  There to salute the woeful Emperor.
FAUSTUS: The Pope will curse them for their sloth
    today,
  That slept both Bruno and his crown away.
  But now, that Faustus may delight his mind
10 And by their folly make some merriment,
  Sweet Mephistophilis, so charm me here
  That I may walk invisible to all
  And do whate'er I please unseen of any.
MEPHISTOPHILIS: Faustus, thou shalt. Then kneel
    down presently.
15 *Whilst on thy head I lay my hand*
  And charm thee with this magic wand.
  First wear this girdle; then appear
  Invisible to all are here.
  The planets seven, the gloomy air,
20 *Hell and the Furies'° forkèd hair,*
  Pluto's blue fire, and Hecate's tree,°
  With magic spells so compass thee
  That no eye may thy body see.
  So Faustus. Now, for all their holiness,
25 Do what thou wilt, thou shalt not be discerned.
FAUSTUS: Thanks, Mephistophilis. Now friars take
    heed
  Lest Faustus make your shaven crowns to bleed.
MEPHISTOPHILIS: Faustus, no more. See where the
    cardinals come.

(*Enter Pope and all the Lords. Enter the Cardinals with a book.*)

POPE: Welcome, lord cardinals. Come, sit down.
30 Lord Raymond, take your seat. Friars attend,
  And see that all things be in readiness,
  As best beseems this solemn festival.
FIRST CARDINAL: First, may it please your sacred
    holiness
  To view the sentence of the reverend synod
35 Concerning Bruno and the Emperor?
POPE: What needs this question? Did I not tell you
  Tomorrow we would sit i' th' consistory

And there determine of his punishment?
  You brought us word even now; it was decreed
  That Bruno and the cursèd Emperor   40
  Were by the holy council both condemned
  For loathèd Lollards and base schismatics.
  Then wherefore would you have me view that
    book?
FIRST CARDINAL: Your grace mistakes. You gave us
  no such charge.
RAYMOND: Deny it not. We all are witnesses   45
  That Bruno here was late delivered you,
  With his rich triple crown to be reserved
  And put into the church's treasury.
BOTH CARDINALS: By holy Paul, we saw them not.
POPE: By Peter, you shall die   50
  Unless you bring them forth immediately.
  Hale them to prison. Lade their limbs with
    gyves.°
  False prelates, for this hateful treachery
  Cursed be your souls to hellish misery.
    [*Exeunt the two Cardinals with Attendants.*]
FAUSTUS: So, they are safe. Now, Faustus, to the
    feast.   55
  The Pope had never such a frolic guest.
POPE: Lord Archbishop of Rheims, sit down with
    us.
ARCHBISHOP: I thank your holiness.
FAUSTUS: Fall to. The devil choke you an you
    spare.°
POPE: Who's that spoke? Friars look about.   60
FRIAR: Here's nobody, if it like your holiness.
POPE: Lord Raymond, pray fall to. I am beholding
  To the Bishop of Milan for this so rare a
    present.
FAUSTUS: I thank you, sir.   [*He snatches the dish.*]
POPE: How now? Who snatched the meat from me? 65
  Villains, why speak you not?
  My good Lord Archbishop, here's a most dainty
    dish
  Was sent me from a cardinal in France.
FAUSTUS: I'll have that too. [*He snatches the dish.*]
POPE: What Lollards do attend our holiness,   70
  That we receive such great indignity?
  Fetch me some wine.
FAUSTUS: Ay, pray do, for Faustus is a-dry.
POPE: Lord Raymond, I drink unto your grace.
FAUSTUS: I pledge your grace. [*He snatches the cup.*] 75
POPE: My wine gone too? Ye lubbers, look about
  And find the man that doth this villainy,
  Or by our sanctitude, you all shall die.
  I pray, my lords, have patience at this
  Troublesome banquet.   80

III, II. 20. *Furies:* Spirits called upon to avenge crimes, especially crimes against kin. 21. *Hecate's tree:* Hecate is the goddess of witchcraft.

52. Lade . . . gyves: Shackle their limbs. 59. an you spare: If you hold back.

ARCHBISHOP: Please it your holiness, I think it be some
    ghost crept out of purgatory, and now is come
    unto your holiness for his pardon.

POPE: It may be so.

85   Go then, command our priests to sing a dirge
    To lay the fury of this same troublesome ghost.
                            [*Exit an attendant.*]
    Once again, my lord, fall to.
                   (*The Pope crosseth himself.*)

FAUSTUS: How now?
    Must every bit be spicèd with a cross?

90   Nay then, take that.   [*He strikes the Pope.*]

POPE: O I am slain. Help me, my lords.
    O come and help to bear my body hence.
    Damned be this soul for ever for this deed.
               (*Exeunt the Pope and his train.*)

MEPHISTOPHILIS: Now, Faustus, what will you do now?

95   For I can tell you you'll be cursed with bell, book,
    and candle.°

FAUSTUS: Bell, book, and candle; candle, book, and
    bell,
    Forward and backward, to curse Faustus to hell.

(*Enter the Friars with bell, book, and candle for the
dirge.*)

FIRST FRIAR: Come, brethren, let's about our business

100   with good devotion.   [*They chant.*]
    Cursed be he that stole his holiness' meat
    from the table.
        Maledicat Dominus!°
    Cursed be he that struck his holiness a blow
    on the face.
        Maledicat Dominus!
    Cursed be he that struck Friar Sandelo a blow

105   *on the pate.*
        Maledicat Dominus!
    Cursed be he that disturbeth our holy dirge.
        Maledicat Dominus!
    Cursed be he that took away his holiness'
    wine.

110   *Maledicat Dominus! Et omnes sancti.°*
    Amen.

([*Faustus and Mephistophilis*] *beat the Friars, fling
fireworks among them, and exeunt.*)

Scene III

(*Enter* [*Robin,*] *the clown, and Dick, with a cup.*)

DICK: Sirrah Robin, we were best look that your devil

can answer the stealing of this same cup, for the
vintner's boy follows us at the hard heels.

ROBIN: 'Tis no matter. Let him come. An he follow
us, I'll so conjure him as he was never conjured in 5
his life, I warrant him. Let me see the cup.

(*Enter Vintner.*)

DICK: Here 'tis. Yonder he comes. Now, Robin, now
or never show thy cunning.

VINTNER: O, are you here? I am glad I have found
you. You are a couple of fine companions. Pray, 10
where's the cup you stole from the tavern?

ROBIN: How, how? We steal a cup? Take heed what
you say. We look not like cup stealers, I can tell
you.

VINTNER: Never deny't, for I know you have it, and 15
I'll search you.

ROBIN: Search me? Ay, and spare not. Hold the cup,
Dick. [*Aside to Dick.*] Come, come, search me,
search me.

[*The Vintner searches Robin.*]

VINTNER: [*to Dick*] Come on, sirrah, let me search 20
you now.

DICK: Ay, ay, do, do. Hold the cup, Robin. [*Aside to
Robin.*] I fear not your searching. We scorn to steal
your cups, I can tell you.

[*The Vintner searches Dick.*]

VINTNER: Never outface me for the matter, for sure 25
the cup is between you two.

ROBIN: Nay, there you lie. 'Tis beyond us both.

VINTNER: A plague take you! I thought 'twas your
knavery to take it away. Come, give it me again.

ROBIN: Ay, much. When? Can you tell? Dick, make 30
me a cirole, and stand close at my back, and stir
not for thy life. Vintner, you shall have your cup
anon. Say nothing, Dick, *O per se, O Demogorgon,
Belcher and Mephistophilis.*

(*Enter Mephistophilis.* [*Exit the Vintner, in fright.*])

MEPHISTOPHILIS: Monarch of hell, under whose
    black survey 35
Great potentates do kneel with awful fear,
Upon whose altars thousand souls do lie,
How am I vexèd by these villains' charms!
From Constantinople have they brought me now,
Only for pleasure of these damnèd slaves. 40

ROBIN: By Lady, sir, you have had a shrewd journey
of it. Will it please you to take a shoulder of mutton
to supper and a tester° in your purse, and go back
again?

95–96. **bell, book, and candle:** Used traditionally in the rite
of excommunication.   102. *Maledicat Dominus:* May the
Lord curse him.   110. *Et omnes sancti:* And all the saints.

III, III. 43. **tester:** Sixpence.

45 DICK: Ay, I pray you heartily, sir, for we called you
       but in jest, I promise you.
    MEPHISTOPHILIS: To purge the rashness of this
          cursèd deed,
       First be thou turnèd to this ugly shape,
       For apish deeds transformèd to an ape.
50 ROBIN: O brave, an ape! I pray sir, let me have the
       carrying of him about to show some tricks.
    MEPHISTOPHILIS: And so thou shalt. Be thou transformed
       to a dog, and carry him upon thy back. Away, be
       gone!
55 ROBIN: A dog? That's excellent. Let the maids look
       well to their porridge pots, for I'll into the
       kitchen presently. Come, Dick, come.
              (*Exeunt [Robin and Dick,] the two clowns.*)
    MEPHISTOPHILIS: Now with the flames of ever-
          burning fire,
       I'll wing myself and forthwith fly amain
60   Unto my Faustus, to the great Turk's court.
                                              (*Exit.*)

ACT IV · Prologue ────────────────

(*Enter Chorus.*)

CHORUS: When Faustus had with pleasure ta'en the
          view
       Of rarest things and royal courts of kings,
       He stayed his course and so returnèd home;
       Where such as bare his absence but with grief —
5   I mean his friends and nearest companions —
       Did gratulate his safety with kind words,
       And in their conference of what befell,
       Touching his journey through the world and air,
       They put forth questions of astrology,
10   Which Faustus answered with such learnèd skill
       As they admired and wondered at his wit.
       Now is his fame spread forth in every land.
       Amongst the rest, the Emperor is one —
       Carolus the fifth° — at whose palace now
15   Faustus is feasted 'mongst his noblemen.
       What there he did in trial of his art
       I leave untold, your eyes shall see performed.
                                              (*Exit.*)

Scene I

(*Enter Martino and Frederick, at several doors.*)

MARTINO: What ho, officers, gentlemen,
       Hie to the presence° to attend the Emperor.

Good Frederick, see the rooms be voided
          straight;
       His majesty is coming to the hall.
       Go back, and see the state° in readiness.   5
FREDERICK: But where is Bruno, our elected Pope,
       That on a fury's back came post from Rome?
       Will not his grace consort the Emperor?
MARTINO: O yes, and with him comes the German
          conjurer,
       The learnèd Faustus, fame of Wittenberg,   10
       The wonder of the world for magic art;
       And he intends to show great Carolus
       The race of all his stout progenitors,
       And bring in presence of his majesty
       The royal shapes and warlike semblances   15
       Of Alexander° and his beauteous paramour.
FREDERICK: Where is Benvolio?
MARTINO: Fast asleep, I warrant you.
       He took his rouse with stoups° of Rhenish wine
       So kindly yesternight to Bruno's health   20
       That all this day the sluggard keeps his bed.
FREDERICK: See, see, his window's ope. We'll call to
          him.
MARTINO: What ho, Benvolio!

(*Enter Benvolio above at a window, in his nightcap,
buttoning.*)

BENVOLIO: What a devil ail you two?
MARTINO: Speak softly, sir, lest the devil hear you,   25
       For Faustus at the court is late arrived,
       And at his heels a thousand furies wait
       To accomplish whatsoever the doctor please.
BENVOLIO: What of this?
MARTINO: Come, leave thy chamber first, and thou
          shalt see   30
       This conjurer perform such rare exploits
       Before the Pope° and royal Emperor
       As never yet was seen in Germany.
BENVOLIO: Has not the Pope enough of conjuring
          yet?
       He was upon the devil's back late enough,   35
       And if he be so far in love with him,
       I would he would post with him to Rome again.
FREDERICK: Speak, wilt thou come and see this
          sport?
BENVOLIO: Not I.
MARTINO: Wilt thou stand in thy window and see
       it then?
BENVOLIO: Ay, and I fall not asleep i' th' meantime.   40
MARTINO: The Emperor is at hand, who comes to
       see

IV, Prologue. 14. **Carolus the fifth:** Charles V, King of Spain
(as Charles I from 1516 to 1556) and Holy Roman Emperor
from 1519 to 1556.   **IV, I. 2. presence:** Emperor's chamber.

5. **state:** Throne.   16. **Alexander:** Alexander the Great.   19.
took . . . stoups: Had a drinking bout with brimming goblets.
32. **the Pope:** Bruno.

What wonders by black spells may compassed
    be.
BENVOLIO: Well, go you attend the Emperor. I am
    content for this once to thrust my head out at a
45   window, for they say if a man be drunk overnight
    the devil cannot hurt him in the morning. If that
    be true, I have a charm in my head shall control
    him as well as the conjurer, I warrant you.
    (*Exit [Frederick, with Martino. Benvolio remains*
               at the window above].)

Scene II

(*A* sennet [*is sounded. Enter] Charles, the German
Emperor, Bruno, [the Duke of] Saxony, Faustus, Mephistophilis, Frederick, Martino, and Attendants.*)

EMPEROR: Wonder of men, renowned magician,
    Thrice-learnèd Faustus, welcome to our court.
    This deed of thine, in setting Bruno free
    From his and our professèd enemy,
5   Shall add more excellence unto thine art
    Than if by powerful necromantic spells
    Thou couldst command the world's obedience.
    Forever be beloved of Carolus,
    And if this Bruno thou hast late redeemed°
10   In peace possess the triple diadem
    And sit in Peter's chair despite of chance,
    Thou shalt be famous through all Italy
    And honored of the German Emperor.
FAUSTUS: These gracious words, most royal Carolus,
15   Shall make poor Faustus to his utmost power
    Both love and serve the German Emperor
    And lay his life at holy Bruno's feet.
    For proof whereof, if so your grace be pleased,
    The doctor stands prepared by power of art
20   To cast his magic charms that shall pierce
        through
    The ebon gates of ever-burning hell,
    And hale the stubborn Furies from their caves
    To compass whatsoe'er your grace commands.
BENVOLIO: [*above*] Blood, he speaks terribly, but for
25   all that, I do not greatly believe him. He looks as
    like a conjurer as the Pope° to a costermonger.°
EMPEROR: Then, Faustus, as thou late did'st
        promise us,
    We would behold that famous conqueror,
    Great Alexander, and his paramour
30   In their true shapes and state majestical,
    That we may wonder at their excellence.
FAUSTUS: Your majesty shall see them presently.
    Mephistophilis, away,

And with a solemn noise of trumpets' sound
Present before this royal Emperor,   35
Great Alexander and his beauteous paramour.
MEPHISTOPHILIS: Faustus, I will.

                       [*Exit.*]

BENVOLIO: Well, master doctor, an your devils come
    not away quickly, you shall have me asleep presently.
    Zounds, I could eat myself for anger to think I 40
    have been such an ass all this while, to stand gaping
    after the devil's governor and can see nothing.
FAUSTUS: I'll make you feel something anon, if my
        art fail me not
    My lord, I must forewarn your majesty
    That when my spirits present the royal shapes 45
    Of Alexander and his paramour,
    Your grace demand no questions of the king,
    But in dumb silence let them come and go.
EMPEROR: Be it as Faustus please; we are content.
BENVOLIO: Ay, ay, and I am content too. And thou 50
    bring Alexander and his paramour before the Em-
    peror, I'll be Actaeon and turn myself to a stag.
FAUSTUS: And I'll play Diana and send you the
        horns presently.

(*[A]* sennet [*is sounded]. Enter at one [door] the Emperor Alexander, at the other Darius.° They meet [in
combat]. Darius is thrown down; Alexander kills him,
takes off his crown, and, offering to go out, his paramour meets him. He embraceth her and sets Darius'
crown upon her head; and coming back, both salute
the Emperor, who, leaving his state, offers to embrace
them, which Faustus seeing, suddenly stays him. Then
trumpets cease and music sounds.*)

My gracious lord, you do forget yourself.
These are but shadows, not substantial.   55
EMPEROR: O pardon me. My thoughts are so
        ravishèd
    With sight of this renownèd emperor,
    That in mine arms I would have compassed him.
    But, Faustus, since I may not speak to them,
    To satisfy my longing thoughts at full,   60
    Let me this tell thee: I have heard it said
    That this fair lady, whilst she lived on earth,
    Had on her neck a little wart or mole;
    How may I prove that saying to be true?
FAUSTUS: Your majesty may boldly go and see. 65
EMPEROR: Faustus, I see it plain,
    And in this sight thou better pleasest me
    Than if I gained another monarchy.
FAUSTUS: Away! Be gone!

                    (*Exit show.*)

---

52. [S.D.] *Darius:* King Darius III of Persia (336–330 B.C.),
defeated at Granicus in 334 B.C. by the Greeks under Alexander
the Great.

IV, II. **9. redeemed:** Rescued.   **26. the Pope:** Bruno; **coster-
monger:** Fruit vendor; a term of contempt.

70 See, see, my gracious lord, what strange beast is
yon, that thrusts his head out at window?
EMPEROR: O wondrous sight! See, Duke of Saxony,
Two spreading horns most strangely fastenèd
Upon the head of young Benvolio.
75 SAXONY: What? Is he asleep or dead?
FAUSTUS: He sleeps, my lord, but dreams not of his
horns.
EMPEROR: This sport is excellent. We'll call and
wake him.
What ho, Benvolio!
BENVOLIO: A plague upon you! Let me sleep a
while.
80 EMPEROR: I blame thee not to sleep much, having such
a head of thine own.
SAXONY: Look up, Benvolio; 'tis the Emperor calls.
BENVOLIO: The Emperor? Where? O zounds, my
head!
EMPEROR: Nay, and thy horns hold, 'tis no matter for
85 thy head, for that's armed sufficiently.
FAUSTUS: Why, how now, sir knight! What, hanged
by the horns? This is most horrible. Fie, fie, pull
in your head for shame. Let not all the world wonder
at you.
90 BENVOLIO: Zounds, doctor, is this your villainy?
FAUSTUS: O say not so, sir. The doctor has no skill,
No art, no cunning, to present these lords
Or bring before this royal Emperor
The mighty monarch, warlike Alexander.
95 If Faustus do it, you are straight resolved
In bold Actaeon's shape to turn a stag.
And therefore, my lord, so please your majesty,
I'll raise a kennel of hounds shall hunt him so
As all his footmanship shall scarce prevail
100 To keep his carcass from their bloody fangs
Ho, Belimote, Argiron, Asterote!
BENVOLIO: Hold, hold! Zounds, he'll raise up a kennel
of devils, I think, anon. Good, my lord, entreat for
me. 'Sblood, I am never able to endure these
105 torments.
EMPEROR: Then, good master doctor,
Let me entreat you to remove his horns.
He has done penance now sufficiently.
FAUSTUS: My gracious lord, not so much for injury
110 done to me, as to delight your majesty with some
mirth, hath Faustus justly requited this injurious°
knight; which being all I desire, I am content to
remove his horns. [*Mephistophilis removes the horns.*]
And hereafter, sir, look you speak well of scholars.
115 BENVOLIO: [*aside.*] Speak well of ye? 'Sblood, and
scholars be such cuckold makers to clap horns of

honest men's heads o' this order, I'll ne'er trust
smooth faces and small ruffs° more. But an I be
not revenged for this, would I might be turned to
a gaping oyster and drink nothing but salt   120
water.   [*Exit Benvolio above.*]
EMPEROR: Come, Faustus. While the Emperor lives,
In recompense of this thy high desert,
Thou shalt command the state of Germany
And live beloved of mighty Carolus.   125
(*Exeunt.*)

Scene III

(*Enter Benvolio, Martino, Frederick, and Soldiers.*)

MARTINO: Nay, sweet Benvolio, let us sway thy
thoughts
From this attempt against the conjurer.
BENVOLIO: Away! You love me not to urge me
thus.
Shall I let slip so great an injury,
When every servile groom jests at my wrongs   5
And in their rustic gambols proudly say,
"Benvolio's head was graced with horns today"?
O, may these eyelids never close again
Till with my sword I have that conjurer slain.
If you will aid me in this enterprise,   10
Then draw your weapons and be resolute.
If not, depart. Here will Benvolio die,
But Faustus' death shall quit° my infamy.
FREDERICK: Nay, we will stay with thee, betide
what may,
And kill that doctor if he come this way.   15
BENVOLIO: Then, gentle Frederick, hie thee to the
grove,
And place our servants and our followers
Close in an ambush there behind the trees.
By this, I know, the conjurer is near.
I saw him kneel and kiss the Emperor's hand   20
And take his leave, laden with rich rewards.
Then, soldiers, boldly fight. If Faustus die,
Take you the wealth; leave us the victory.
FREDERICK: Come, soldiers. Follow me unto the
grove.
Who kills him shall have gold and endless love.   25
(*Exit Frederick with the Soldiers.*)
BENVOLIO: My head is lighter than it was by
th'horns,
But yet my heart's more ponderous than my
head
And pants until I see that conjurer dead.
MARTINO: Where shall we place ourselves,
Benvolio?

---

111. injurious: Insulting.

118. small ruffs: Academic gowns.   **IV, III. 13. quit:** Pay
for.

BENVOLIO: Here will we stay to bide the first
30   assault.
        O, were that damnèd hell-hound but in place,
        Thou soon shouldst see me quit my foul
        disgrace.

(*Enter Frederick.*)

FREDERICK: Close, close, the conjurer is at hand
        And all alone comes walking in his gown.
35   Be ready then, and strike the peasant down.
BENVOLIO: Mine be that honor then. Now, sword,
        strike home.
        For horns he gave I'll have his head anon.

(*Enter Faustus with the false head.*)

MARTINO: See, see, he comes.
BENVOLIO: No words! This blow ends all.
        Hell take his soul; his body thus must fall.
                                    [*He stabs Faustus.*]
40 FAUSTUS: [*falling*] Oh!
FREDERICK: Groan you, master doctor?
BENVOLIO: Break may his heart with groans! Dear
        Frederick, see,
        Thus will I end his griefs immediately.
MARTINO: Strike with a willing hand. His head is
        off.

[*Benvolio strikes off Faustus' false head.*]

BENVOLIO: The devil's dead. The Furies now may
45   laugh.
FREDERICK: Was this that stern aspèct, that awful
        frown,
        Made the grim monarch of infernal spirits
        Tremble and quake at his commanding charms?
MARTINO: Was this that damnèd head whose heart
        conspired
50   Benvolio's shame before the Emperor?
BENVOLIO: Ay, that's the head, and here the body
        lies,
        Justly rewarded for his villainies.
FREDERICK: Come, let's devise how we may add
        more shame
        To the black scandal of his hated name.
BENVOLIO: First, on his head, in quittance of my
55   wrongs,
        I'll nail huge forkèd horns and let them hang
        Within the window where he yoked° me first,
        That all the world may see my just revenge.
MARTINO: What use shall we put his beard to?
60 BENVOLIO: We'll sell it to a chimney-sweeper. It will
        wear out ten birchen brooms, I warrant you.
FREDERICK: What shall eyes do?
BENVOLIO: We'll put out his eyes, and they shall serve

for buttons to his lips to keep his tongue from
catching cold.   65
MARTINO: An excellent policy! And now, sirs, having
        divided him, what shall the body do?

[*Faustus rises.*]

BENVOLIO: Zounds, the devil's alive again.
FREDERICK: Give him his head, for God's sake.
FAUSTUS: Nay, keep it. Faustus will have heads and
        hands,   70
        Ay, all your hearts, to recompense this deed.
        Knew you not, traitors, I was limited
        For four-and-twenty years to breathe on earth?
        And had you cut my body with your swords,
        Or hewed this flesh and bones as small as sand, 75
        Yet in a minute had my spirit returned,
        And I had breathed a man made free from
        harm.
        But wherefore do I dally my revenge?
        Asteroth, Belimoth, Mephistophilis!

(*Enter Mephistophilis and other Devils.*)

        Go, horse these traitors on your fiery backs,   80
        And mount aloft with them as high as heaven;
        Thence pitch them headlong to the lowest hell.
        Yet stay. The world shall see their misery,
        And hell shall after plague their treachery.
        Go, Belimoth, and take this caitiff° hence,   85
        And hurl him in some lake of mud and dirt.
        Take thou this other; drag him through the
        woods
        Amongst the pricking thorns and sharpest briars,
        Whilst with my gentle Mephistophilis
        This traitor flies unto some steepy rock   90
        That, rolling down, may break the villain's
        bones
        As he intended to dismember me.
        Fly hence. Dispatch my charge immediately.
FREDERICK: Pity us, gentle Faustus. Save our lives.
FAUSTUS: Away!
FREDERICK: He must needs go that the devil
        drives.   95
                        (*Exeunt Spirits with the Knights.*)

(*Enter the ambushed Soldiers.*)

FIRST SOLDIER: Come, sirs, prepare yourselves in
        readiness.
        Make haste to help these noble gentlemen;
        I heard them parley with the conjurer.
SECOND SOLDIER: See where he comes. Dispatch
        and kill the slave.
FAUSTUS: What's here? An ambush to betray my
        life?   100

---

57. yoked: Placed the horns on.

85. caitiff: Despicable wretch.

Then, Faustus, try thy skill. Base peasants, stand,
For lo, these trees remove at my command
And stand as bulwarks 'twixt yourselves and me,
To shield me from your hated treachery.
105   Yet to encounter this your weak attempt,
Behold an army comes incontinent.°

(*Faustus strikes the door, and enter a Devil playing on a drum, after him another bearing an ensign, and divers with weapons, Mephistophilis with fireworks. They set upon the Soldiers and drive them out. [Exit Faustus.]*)

Scene IV

(*Enter at several doors Benvolio, Frederick, and Martino, their heads and faces bloody and besmeared with mud and dirt, all having horns on their heads.*)

MARTINO: What ho, Benvolio!
BENVOLIO: Here! What, Frederick, ho!
FREDERICK: O help me, gentle friend. Where is
      Martino?
MARTINO: Dear Frederick, here,
5   Half smothered in a lake of mud and dirt,
      Through which the Furies dragged me by the
      heels.
FREDERICK: Martino, see! Benvolio's horns again.
MARTINO: O misery! How now, Benvolio?
BENVOLIO: Defend me, heaven. Shall I be haunted°
      still?
MARTINO: Nay, fear not man; we have not power
10   to kill.
BENVOLIO: My friends transformèd thus! O hellish
      spite!
      Your heads are all set with horns.
FREDERICK: You hit it right.
      It is your own you mean. Feel on your head.
BENVOLIO: Zounds, horns again!
15 MARTINO: Nay, chafe not man. We all are sped.°
BENVOLIO: What devil attends this damned
      magician,
      That, spite of spite, our wrongs are doublèd?
FREDERICK: What may we do, that we may hide
      our shames?
BENVOLIO: If we should follow him to work
      revenge,
20   He'd join long asses' ears to these huge horns,
      And make us laughing-stocks to all the world.
MARTINO: What shall we then do, dear Benvolio?
BENVOLIO: I have a castle joining near these woods,
      And thither we'll repair and live obscure

Till time shall alter these our brutish shapes.   25
Sith black disgrace hath thus eclipsed our fame,
We'll rather die with grief than live with shame.
                    (*Exeunt omnes.°*)

Scene V

(*Enter Faustus and Mephistophilis.*)

FAUSTUS: Now, Mephistophilis, the restless course
      That time doth run with calm and silent foot,
      Shortening my days and thread of vital life,
      Calls for the payment of my latest years.
      Therefore, sweet Mephistophilis, let us   5
      Make haste to Wittenberg.
MEPHISTOPHILIS: What, will you go on horseback,
      or on foot?
FAUSTUS: Nay, till I am past this fair and pleasant
      green,
      I'll walk on foot.
                    [*Exit Mephistophilis.*]
(*Enter a Horse-Courser.°*)

HORSE-COURSER: I have been all this day seeking one   10
      Master Fustian.° Mass, see where he is. God save
      you, master doctor.
FAUSTUS: What, horse-courser! You are well met.
HORSE-COURSER: I beseech your worship, accept of
      these forty dollars.   15
FAUSTUS: Friend, thou canst not buy so good a horse
      for so small a price. I have no great need to sell
      him, but if thou likest him for ten dollars more,
      take him, because I see thou hast a good mind to
      him.   20
HORSE-COURSER: I beseech you, sir, accept of this. I
      am a very poor man and have lost very much of
      late by horse-flesh, and this bargain will set me up
      again.
FAUSTUS: Well, I will not stand with thee.° Give me   25
      the money.

[*The Horse-Courser gives Faustus money.*]

      Now, sirrah, I must tell you that you may ride him
      o'er hedge and ditch, and spare him not. But, do
      you hear? In any case, ride him not into the water.
HORSE-COURSER: How sir? Not into the water? Why,   30
      will he not drink of all waters?°

---

106. **incontinent:** At once.   **IV, IV. 9. haunted:** (1) Bewitched; (2) hunted, pursued (since he is a stag).   **15. sped:** provided (with horns).

27. [S.D.] *Exeunt omnes:* Latin for "All go out."   **IV, V.** The first eleven lines of this scene do not appear in all versions of the play, but they provide a transition to the Horse-Courser episode and remind readers of Faustus's impending tragedy.   **11. Fustian:** The perversion of Faustus's name is a deliberate attempt at humor.   **9. [S.D.]** *Horse-Courser:* One who deals in horses.   **25. stand with thee:** Bargain.   **31. drink . . . waters:** Be ready for anything (a common proverb of the time).

FAUSTUS: Yes, he will drink of all waters, but ride him
not into the water — o'er hedge and ditch, or where
thou wilt, but not into the water. Go, bid the hostler
35   deliver him unto you, and remember what I say.
HORSE-COURSER: I warrant you, sir. O joyful day!
Now am I a man made forever.

(*Exit.*)

FAUSTUS: What art thou, Faustus, but a man
condemned to die?
Thy fatal time draws to a final end.
40   Despair doth drive distrust into my thoughts.
Confound these passions with a quiet sleep.
Tush! Christ did call the thief upon the cross;
Then rest thee, Faustus, quiet in conceit.°

(*He sits to sleep [in his chair].*)

(*Enter the Horse-Courser, wet.*)

HORSE-COURSER: O what a cozening doctor was this?
45   I riding my horse into the water, thinking some
hidden mystery° had been in the horse, I had nothing
under me but a little straw and had much ado to
escape drowning. Well, I'll go rouse him and make
him give me my forty dollars again. Ho, sirrah
50   doctor, you cozening scab!° Master doctor, awake
and rise, and give me my money again, for your
horse is turned to a bottle° of hay. Master doctor!

(*He [tries to wake Faustus, and in doing so] pulls off
his leg.*)

Alas, I am undone! What shall I do? I have pulled
off his leg.

[*Faustus awakes.*]

55   FAUSTUS: O, help, help! The villain hath murdered me.
HORSE-COURSER: Murder or not murder, now he has
but one leg, I'll outrun him and cast this leg into
some ditch or other.
FAUSTUS: Stop him, stop him, stop him! Ha, ha, ha,
60   Faustus hath his leg again, and the horse-courser
a bundle of hay for his forty dollars.

(*Enter Wagner.*)

How now, Wagner, what news with thee?
WAGNER: If it please you, the Duke of Anholt doth
earnestly entreat your company and hath sent some
65   of his men to attend you with provision fit for your
journey.
FAUSTUS: The Duke of Anholt's an honorable gentleman,
and one to whom I must be no niggard of my
cunning. Come away.

(*Exeunt.*)

Scene VI

(*Enter [Robin, the] Clown, Dick, [the] Horse-Courser,
and a Carter.°*)

CARTER: Come, my masters, I'll bring you to the best
beer in Europe. What ho, hostess! Where be these
whores?

(*Enter Hostess.*)

HOSTESS: How now, what lack you? What, my old
guests, welcome.   5
ROBIN: Sirrah, Dick, dost thou know why I stand so
mute?
DICK: No, Robin; why is't?
ROBIN: I am eighteen pence on the score.° But say
nothing; see if she have forgotten me.   10
HOSTESS: Who's this that stands so solemnly by himself?
What, my old guest?
ROBIN: O hostess, how do you? I hope my score stands
still.°
HOSTESS: Ay, there's no doubt of that, for methinks   15
you make no haste to wipe it out.
DICK: Why, hostess, I say, fetch us some beer.
HOSTESS: You shall presently. Look up into th'hall
there, ho!

(*Exit.*)

DICK: Come, sirs, what shall we do now till mine   20
hostess come?
CARTER: Marry, sir, I'll tell you the bravest tale how
a conjurer served me. You know Doctor Fauster?
HORSE-COURSER: Ay, a plague take him. Here's some
on's have cause to know him. Did he conjure thee   25
too?
CARTER: I'll tell you how he served me. As I was going
to Wittenberg t'other day with a load of hay, he
met me and asked me what he should give me for
as much hay as he could eat. Now, sir, I thinking   30
that a little would serve his turn, bade him take
as much as he would for three farthings. So he
presently gave me my money and fell to eating;
and as I am a cursen° man, he never left eating till
he had eat up all my load of hay.   35
ALL: O monstrous! Eat a whole load of hay!
ROBIN: Yes, yes, that may be, for I have heard of one
that has eat a load of logs.
HORSE-COURSER: Now, sirs, you shall hear how vil-
lainously he served me. I went to him yesterday to   40
buy a horse of him, and he would by no means
sell him under forty dollars. So, sir, because I knew
him to be such a horse as would run over hedge
and ditch and never tire, I gave him his money. So

---

43. **conceit:** Thoughts.   46. **mystery:** Quality.   50. **cozening
scab:** Deceitful, contemptible rascal.   52. **bottle:** Bundle.
IV, VI. [S.D.] *Carter:* A person who drives a cart.   9. **on
the score:** In debt.   13–14. **stands still:** Soes not go higher.
34. **cursen:** Christened.

45 when I had my horse, Doctor Fauster bade me ride
him night and day and spare him no time; but,
quoth he, in any case ride him not into the water.
Now sir, I thinking the horse had had some rare
quality that he would not have me know of, what
50 did I but rid him into a great river, and when I
came just in the midst, my horse vanished away,
and I sat straddling upon a bottle of hay.
ALL: O brave doctor!
HORSE-COURSER: But you shall hear how bravely I
55 served him for it. I went me home to his house,
and there I found him asleep. I kept a hallooing
and whooping in his ears, but all could not wake
him. I seeing that, took him by the leg and never
rested pulling till I had pulled me his leg quite off,
60 and now 'tis at home in mine hostry.
ROBIN: And has the doctor but one leg then? That's
excellent, for one of his devils turned me into the
likeness of an ape's face.
CARTER: Some more drink, hostess.
65 ROBIN: Hark you, we'll into another room and drink
a while, and then we'll go seek out the doctor.

                                                    (*Exeunt.*)

Scene VII

(*Enter the Duke of Anholt, his Duchess, Faustus, and
Mephistophilis, [Servants and Attendants].*)

DUKE: Thanks, master doctor, for these pleasant sights.
Nor know I how sufficiently to recompense your
great deserts° in erecting that enchanted castle in
the air, the sight whereof so delighted me, as nothing
5 in the world could please me more.
FAUSTUS: I do think myself, my good lord, highly re-
compensed in that it pleaseth your grace to think
but well of that which Faustus hath performed.
But, gracious lady, it may be that you have taken
10 no pleasure in those sights. Therefore, I pray you,
tell me what is the thing you most desire to have;
be it in the world, it shall be yours. I have heard
that great-bellied women do long for things are
rare and dainty.
15 DUCHESS: True, master doctor, and since I find you
so kind, I will make known unto you what my
heart desires to have. And were it now summer,
as it is January, a dead time of the winter, I would
request no better meat than a dish of ripe grapes.
20 FAUSTUS: This is but a small matter. Go, Mephistophilis,
away!

                              (*Exit Mephistophilis.*)
Madam I will do more than this for your content.

(*Enter Mephistophilis again with the grapes.*)

IV, VII. 3. deserts: Good deeds.

Here; now taste ye these. They should be good,
for they come from a far country, I can tell you.
DUKE: This makes me wonder more than all the rest, 25
that at this time of year, when every tree is barren
of his fruit, from whence you had these ripe grapes.
FAUSTUS: Please it, your grace, the year is divided into
two circles over the whole world, so that when it
is winter with us, in the contrary circle it is likewise 30
summer with them, as in India, Saba,° and such
countries that lie far east, where they have fruit
twice a year. From whence, by means of a swift
spirit that I have, I had these grapes brought, as
you see.   35
DUCHESS: And trust me, they are the sweetest grapes
that e'er I tasted.

(*The Clown[s, Robin, Dick, the Carter, and the Horse-
Courser,] bounce at the gate within.*)

DUKE: What rude disturbers have we at the gate?
Go, pacify their fury. Set it ope,
And then demand of them what they would
    have.   [*Exit a Servant.*] 40

(*They knock again and call out to talk with Faustus.*)

[*Enter Servant to them.*]

SERVANT: Why, how now, masters, what a coil° is
    there?
What is the reason you disturb the duke.
DICK: We have no reason for it; therefore a fig for
    him.
SERVANT: What, saucy varlets,° dare you be so
    bold?
HORSE-COURSER: I hope, sir, we have wit enough to 45
    be more bold than welcome.
SERVANT: It appears so. Pray be bold elsewhere,
    And trouble not the duke.
DUKE: What would they have?
SERVANT: They all cry out to speak with Doctor
    Faustus.
CARTER: Ay, and we will speak with him.   50
DUKE: Will you, sir? Commit the rascals.
DICK: Commit with us! He were as good commit with
    his father as commit with us.
FAUSTUS: I do beseech your grace, let them come in;
    They are good subject for a merriment.   55
DUKE: Do as thou wilt, Faustus. I give thee leave.
FAUSTUS: I thank your grace.

(*Enter Robin, Dick, Carter, and Horse-Courser.*)

            Why, how now, my good friends?

31. Saba: Sheba.   41. coil: Disturbance.   44. varlets: Knaves,
rascals.

'Faith you are too outrageous,° but come near;
I have procured your pardons. Welcome all!

60 ROBIN: Nay, sir, we will be welcome for our money,
and we will pay for what we take. What ho!
Give's half a dozen of beer here, and be
hanged.

FAUSTUS: Nay, hark you; can you tell me where
you are?

CARTER: Ay, marry can I: we are under heaven.

SERVANT: Ay, but sir sauce-box, know you in what
65 place?

HORSE-COURSER: Ay, ay, the house is good enough
to drink in. Zouns, fill us some beer, or we'll break
all the barrels in the house and dash out all your
brains with your bottles.

FAUSTUS: Be not so furious. Come, you shall have
70 beer.
My lord, beseech you give me leave a while:
I'll gage my credit, 'twill content your grace.

DUKE: With all my heart, kind doctor. Please
thyself;
Our servants and our court's at thy command.

FAUSTUS: I humbly thank your grace. Then fetch
75 some beer.

HORSE-COURSER: Ay, marry, there spake a doctor
indeed, and 'faith,
I'll drink a health to thy wooden leg for that
word.

FAUSTUS: My wooden leg? What dost thou mean by
that?

CARTER: Ha, ha, ha! Dost hear him, Dick? He has
forgot his leg.

HORSE-COURSER: Ay, ay, he does not stand much°
80 upon that.

FAUSTUS: No, faith; not much upon a wooden leg.

CARTER: Good lord, that flesh and blood should be
so frail with your worship! Do not you remember
a horse-courser you sold a horse to?

85 FAUSTUS: Yes, I remember I sold one a horse.

CARTER: And do you remember you bid he should
not ride into the water?

FAUSTUS: Yes, I do very well remember that.

CARTER: And do you remember nothing of your leg?

90 FAUSTUS: No, in good sooth.

CARTER: Then, I pray, remember your courtesy.°

FAUSTUS: I thank you, sir.

CARTER: 'Tis not so much worth. I pray you, tell me
one thing.

95 FAUSTUS: What's that?

CARTER: Be both your legs bedfellows every night
together?

FAUSTUS: Wouldst thou make a Colossus° of me, that
thou askest me such questions?

CARTER: No, truly, sir. I would make nothing of you, 100
but I would fain know that.

(*Enter Hostess with drink.*)

FAUSTUS: Then, I assure thee, certainly they are.

CARTER: I thank you; I am fully satisfied.

FAUSTUS: But wherefore dost thou ask?

CARTER: For nothing, sir. But methinks you should 105
have a wooden bedfellow of one of 'em.

HORSE-COURSER: Why, do you hear, sir; did not I pull
off one of your legs when you were asleep?

FAUSTUS: But I have it again, now I am awake. Look
you here, sir. 110

ALL: O horrible! Had the doctor three legs?

CARTER: Do you remember, sir, how you cozened me
and ate up my load of —

(*Faustus charms him dumb.*)

DICK: Do you remember how you made me wear an
ape's — 115

[*Faustus charms him dumb.*]

HORSE-COURSER: You whoreson conjuring scab, do
you remember how you cozened me with a ho —

[*Faustus charms him dumb.*]

ROBIN: Ha' you forgotten me? You think to carry it
away° with your *hey-pass* and *re-pass;* do you remember the dog's fa — 120

[*Faustus charms him dumb.*]   (*Exeunt Clowns.*)

HOSTESS: Who pays for the ale? Hear you, master
doctor, now you have sent away my guests, I pray
who shall pay me for my a —

[*Faustus charms her dumb.*]   (*Exit Hostess.*)

DUCHESS: My lord,
We are much beholding to this learnèd man. 125

DUKE: So are we, madam, which we will
recompense
With all the love and kindness that we may.
His artful sport drives all sad thoughts away.
                                        (*Exeunt.*)

ACT V • Scene I _____

(*Thunder and lightning. Enter Devils with covered
dishes. Mephistophilis leads them into Faustus' study.
Then enter Wagner.*)

---

58. outrageous: violent.   **80. stand much:** Make much of
(with a quibble).   **91. courtesy:** Curtsy, or leg.

98. Colossus: A giant statue said to have stood with its legs
astride at the entrance to the ancient harbor of Rhodes.
118–119. carry it away: Come off best.

WAGNER: I think my master means to die shortly.
    He has made his will and given me his wealth,
    His house, his goods, and store of golden plate,
    Besides two thousand ducats ready coined.
5   I wonder what he means. If death were nigh,
    He would not frolic thus. He's now at supper
    With the scholars, where there's such belly-cheer
    As Wagner in his life ne'er saw the like.
    And see where they come; belike the feast is
      done.

                                (*Exit.*)

(*Enter Faustus, Mephistophilis, and two or three Scholars.*)

10 FIRST SCHOLAR: Master Doctor Faustus, since our con-
    ference about fair ladies, which was the beautifulest
    in all the world, we have determined with ourselves
    that Helen of Greece was the admirablest lady that
    ever lived. Therefore, master doctor, if you will do
15   us so much favor as to let us see that peerless dame
    of Greece, whom all the world admires for majesty,
    we should think ourselves much beholding unto
    you.
FAUSTUS: Gentlemen,
20   For that I know your friendship is unfeigned,
    And Faustus' custom is not to deny
    The just requests of those that wish him well,
    You shall behold that peerless dame of Greece,
    No otherwise for pomp and majesty
25   Than when Sir Paris crossed the seas with her
    And brought the spoils to rich Dardania.°
    Be silent then, for danger is in words.

(*Music sounds. Mephistophilis brings in Helen; she passeth over the stage.*)

SECOND SCHOLAR: Was this fair Helen, whose
    admirèd worth
    Made Greece with ten years' war afflict poor
    Troy?
30   Too simple is my wit to tell her praise,
    Whom all the world admires for majesty.
THIRD SCHOLAR: No marvel though the angry
    Greeks pursued
    With ten years' war the rape of such a queen,
    Whose heavenly beauty passeth all compare.
FIRST SCHOLAR: Since we have seen the pride of
35   nature's works
    And only paragon of excellence,
    We'll take our leaves and for this blessèd sight
    Happy and blest be Faustus evermore.

FAUSTUS: Gentlemen, farewell; the same wish I to
    you.

                    (*Exeunt Scholars.*)

(*Enter an Old Man.*)

OLD MAN: O gentle Faustus, leave this damnèd art, 40
    This magic that will charm thy soul to hell
    And quite bereave thee of salvation.
    Though thou hast now offended like a man,
    Do not persevere in it like a devil.
    Yet, yet, thou hast an amiable° soul, 45
    If sin by custom grow not into nature.
    Then, Faustus, will repentance come too late;
    Then thou art banished from the sight of
      heaven.
    No mortal can express the pains of hell.
    It may be this my exhortation 50
    Seems harsh and all unpleasant; let it not,
    For, gentle son, I speak it not in wrath
    Or envy of° thee, but in tender love
    And pity of thy future misery.
    And so have hope that this my kind rebuke, 55
    Checking° thy body, may amend thy soul.
FAUSTUS: Where art thou, Faustus? Wretch, what
    hast thou done?
    Damned art thou, Faustus, damned; despair and
    die!
    Hell claims his right, and with a roaring voice
    Says, "Faustus, come; thine hour is almost
    come"; 60
    And Faustus now will come to do thee right.

(*Mephistophilis gives him a dagger.*)

OLD MAN: O stay, good Faustus, stay thy desperate
    steps.
    I see an angel hovers o'er thy head,
    And with a vial full of precious grace
    Offers to pour the same into thy soul. 65
    Then call for mercy and avoid despair.
FAUSTUS: Ah, my sweet friend, I feel thy words
    To comfort my distressèd soul.
    Leave me a while to ponder on my sins.
OLD MAN: Faustus, I leave thee, but with grief of
    heart, 70
    Fearing the enemy of thy hapless soul.

                    (*Exit.*)

FAUSTUS: Accursèd Faustus, where is mercy now?
    I do repent, and yet I do despair.
    Hell strives with grace for conquest in my
    breast.
    What shall I do to shun the snares of death? 75

V, I. 23–26. Peerless dame . . . Dardania: The Greek Helen
(the "peerless dame"), wife of Menelaus, was carried off to
Troy (Dardania) by Paris, sparking the Trojan War.

45. amiable: Worthy of divine love or grace. **53. envy of:**
Ill will toward. **56. Checking:** Admonishing.

MEPHISTOPHILIS: Thou traitor, Faustus, I arrest thy soul
  For disobedience to my sovereign lord.
  Revolt, or I'll in piecemeal tear thy flesh.
FAUSTUS: I do repent I e'er offended him.
80 Sweet Mephistophilis, entreat thy lord
  To pardon my unjust presumption,
  And with my blood again I will confirm
  The former vow I made to Lucifer.
MEPHISTOPHILIS: Do it then, Faustus, with unfeignèd° heart,
85 Lest greater dangers do attend thy drift.°

[*Faustus stabs his arm and writes on a paper with his blood.*]

FAUSTUS: Torment, sweet friend, that base and agèd man
  That durst dissuade me from thy Lucifer,
  With greatest torment that our hell affords.
MEPHISTOPHILIS: His faith is great; I cannot touch his soul,
90 But what I may afflict his body with
  I will attempt, which is but little worth.
FAUSTUS: One thing, good servant, let me crave of thee
  To glut the longing of my heart's desire —
  That I may have unto my paramour
95 That heavenly Helen which I saw of late,
  Whose sweet embracings may extinguish clear
  Those thoughts that do dissuade me from my vow,
  And keep mine oath I made to Lucifer.
MEPHISTOPHILIS: This, or what else my Faustus shall desire,
100 Shall be performed in twinkling of an eye.

(*Enter Helen again, passing over [the stage] between two Cupids.*)

FAUSTUS: Was this the face that launched a thousand ships
  And burnt the topless towers of Ilium?
  Sweet Helen, make me immortal with a kiss.

[*She kisses him.*]

  Her lips suck forth my soul. See where it flies!
105 Come, Helen, come, give me my soul again.
  Here will I dwell, for heaven is in these lips,
  And all is dross that is not Helena.

[*Enter the Old Man.*]

  I will be Paris, and for love of thee
  Instead of Troy shall Wittenberg be sacked;

And I will combat with weak Menelaus°   110
And wear thy colors on my plumèd crest.
Yea, I will wound Achilles° in the heel
And then return to Helen for a kiss.
O, thou art fairer than the evening's air,
Clad in the beauty of a thousand stars.   115
Brighter art thou than flaming Jupiter°
When he appeared to hapless Semele,°
More lovely than the monarch of the sky
In wanton Arethusa's azured arms,°
And none but thou shalt be my paramour.   120
        (*Exeunt [all but the Old Man].*)
OLD MAN: Accursèd Faustus, miserable man,
  That from thy soul exclud'st the grace of heaven
  And fliest the throne of his tribunal seat!

(*Enter the Devils.*)

  Satan begins to sift me with his pride.
  As in this furnace God shall try my faith,   125
  My faith, vile hell, shall triumph over thee.
  Ambitious fiends, see how the heavens smiles
  At your repulse and laughs your state° to scorn.
  Hence hell, for hence I fly unto my God.
        (*Exeunt.*)

Scene II

(*Thunder. Enter [above] Lucifer, Beelzebub, and Mephistophilis.*)

LUCIFER: Thus from infernal Dis° do we ascend
  To view the subjects of our monarchy,
  Those souls which sin seals the black sons of hell,
  'Mong which as chief, Faustus, we come to thee,
  Bringing with us lasting damnation   5
  To wait upon thy soul. The time is come
  Which makes it forfeit.
MEPHISTOPHILIS: And this gloomy night,
  Here in this room will wretched Faustus be.
BEELZEBUB: And here we'll stay
  To mark him how he doth demean himself.   10
MEPHISTOPHILIS: How should he, but in desperate lunacy?
  Fond worldling, now his heart-blood dries with grief;
  His conscience kills it, and his laboring brain

---

110. **Menelaus:** The husband of Helen of Troy.   112. **Achilles:** The Greek hero of the Trojan War, wounded in the heel by Paris.   116. **Jupiter:** Zeus.   117. **Semele:** The daughter of Cadmus and Harmonia who bore Zeus the child, Dionysus. 119–120. **monarch . . . arms:** Arethusa was a nymph, one of the Nereids, who governed a fountain on the isle of Ortygia near Syracuse.   128. **state:** Royal power.   V, II. 1. **Dis:** Hades, or hell.

84. **unfeignèd:** Honest.   85. **drift:** Purpose.

15 Begets a world of idle fantasies
To over-reach the devil. But all in vain;
His store of pleasures must be sauced° with pain.
He and his servant, Wagner, are at hand.
Both come from drawing Faustus' latest will.
See where they come.

(*Enter Faustus and Wagner.*)

20 FAUSTUS: Say, Wagner, thou has perused my will;
How dost thou like it?
WAGNER: Sir, so wondrous well
As in all humble duty I do yield
My life and lasting service for your love.

(*Enter the Scholars.*)

FAUSTUS: Gramercies,° Wagner. Welcome,
gentlemen.
                              [*Exit Wagner.*]
25 FIRST SCHOLAR: Now, worthy Faustus, methinks your
looks are changed.
FAUSTUS: Ah, gentlemen!
SECOND SCHOLAR: What ails Faustus?
FAUSTUS: Ah, my sweet chamber-fellow, had I lived
30 with thee, then had I lived still, but now must die
eternally. Look, sirs; comes he not? Comes he not?
FIRST SCHOLAR: O my dear Faustus, what imports this
fear?
SECOND SCHOLAR: Is all our pleasure turned to melan-
35 choly?
THIRD SCHOLAR: He is not well with being over-solitary.
SECOND SCHOLAR: If it be so, we'll have physicians,
and Faustus shall be cured.
THIRD SCHOLAR: 'Tis but a surfeit sir; fear nothing.
40 FAUSTUS: A surfeit of deadly sin that hath damned
both body and soul.
SECOND SCHOLAR: Yet Faustus, look up to heaven,
and remember mercy is infinite.
FAUSTUS: But Faustus' offence can ne'er be pardoned.
45 The serpent that tempted Eve may be saved, but
not Faustus. Ah gentlemen, hear me with patience
and tremble not at my speeches. Though my heart
pants and quivers to remember that I have been a
student here these thirty years, O, would I had
50 never seen Wittenberg, never read book. And what
wonders I have done, all Germany can witness —
yea, all the world — for which Faustus hath lost
both Germany and the world, yea heaven itself,
heaven the seat of God, the throne of the blessed,
55 the kingdom of joy, and must remain in hell for
ever. Hell, ah hell for ever! Sweet friends, what
shall become of Faustus, being in hell for ever?
SECOND SCHOLAR: Yet Faustus, call on God.

16. sauced: Paid for.   **24. Gramercies:** Thanks.

FAUSTUS: On God, whom Faustus hath abjured? On
God, whom Faustus hath blasphemed? Ah, my God, 60
I would weep, but the devil draws in my tears.
Gush forth blood instead of tears, yea life and soul.
O, he stays my tongue! I would lift up my hands,
but see, they hold 'em; they hold 'em.
ALL: Who, Faustus?   65
FAUSTUS: Why, Lucifer and Mephistophilis. Ah,
gentlemen, I gave them my soul for my cunning.
ALL: God forbid!
FAUSTUS: God forbade it indeed, but Faustus hath
done it. For the vain pleasure of four and twenty 70
years hath Faustus lost eternal joy and felicity. I
writ them a bill with mine own blood. The date
is expired. This is the time, and he will fetch me.
FIRST SCHOLAR: Why did not Faustus tell us of this
before, that divines might have prayed for thee? 75
FAUSTUS: Oft have I thought to have done so, but the
devil threatened to tear me in pieces if I named
God, to fetch me, body and soul, if I once gave
ear to divinity. And now 'tis too late. Gentlemen
away, lest you perish with me.   80
SECOND SCHOLAR: O, what may we do to save Faustus?
FAUSTUS: Talk not of me, but save yourselves and
depart.
THIRD SCHOLAR: God will strengthen me; I will stay
with Faustus.   85
FIRST SCHOLAR: Tempt not God, sweet friend, but let
us into the next room and there pray for him.
FAUSTUS: Ay, pray for me, pray for me; and what
noise soever you hear, come not unto me, for nothing
can rescue me.   90
SECOND SCHOLAR: Pray thou, and we will pray that
God may have mercy upon thee.
FAUSTUS: Gentlemen, farewell. If I live till morning,
I'll visit you; if not, Faustus is gone to hell.
ALL: Faustus, farewell.   95
                              (*Exeunt Scholars.*)
MEPHISTOPHILIS: [*above*] Ay, Faustus, now thou hast
no hope of heaven;
Therefore despair. Think only upon hell,
For that must be thy mansion, there to dwell.
FAUSTUS: O thou bewitching fiend, 'twas thy
temptation
Hath robbed me of eternal happiness.   100
MEPHISTOPHILIS: I do confess it, Faustus, and
rejoice.
'Twas I, that when thou wert i' the way to
heaven,
Damned up thy passage. When thou took'st the
book
To view the Scriptures, then I turned the leaves
And led thine eye.   105
What, weep'st thou? 'Tis too late. Despair!
Farewell!

Fools that will laugh on earth must weep in hell.

(*Exit.*)

(*Enter the Good Angel and the Bad Angel at several doors.*)

GOOD ANGEL: Ah, Faustus, if thou hadst given ear
    to me,
  Innumerable joys had followed thee;
  But thou didst love the world.

110 BAD ANGEL: Gave ear to me,
  And now must taste hell's pains perpetually.

GOOD ANGEL: O what will all thy riches, pleasures,
    pomps
  Avail thee now?

BAD ANGEL: Nothing but vex thee more,
  To want in hell, that had on earth such store.

(*Music while the throne descends.*)

115 GOOD ANGEL: O, thou hast lost celestial happiness,
  Pleasures unspeakable, bliss without end.
  Hadst thou affected sweet divinity,
  Hell or the devil had had no power on thee.
  Hadst thou kept on that way, Faustus, behold
120 In what resplendent glory thou hadst sat
  In yonder throne, like those bright shining saints,
  And triumphed over hell. That hast thou lost,
  And now, poor soul, must thy good angel leave
    thee.

[*The throne ascends.*]

  The jaws of hell are open to receive thee.

(*Exit.*)

(*Hell is discovered.*)

BAD ANGEL: Now, Faustus, let thine eyes with
125   horror stare
  Into that vast perpetual torture-house.
  There are the Furies tossing damnèd souls
  On burning forks; their bodies boil in lead.
  There are live quarters broiling on the coals,
130 That ne'er can die. This ever-burning chair
  Is for o'er-tortured souls to rest them in.
  These that are fed with sops of flaming fire
  Were gluttons and loved only delicates
  And laughed to see the poor starve at their
    gates.
135 But yet all these are nothing; thou shalt see
  Ten thousand tortures that more horrid be.

FAUSTUS: O, I have seen enough to torture me.

BAD ANGEL: Nay, thou must feel them, taste the
    smart of all.
  He that loves pleasure must for pleasure fall.
140 And so I leave thee, Faustus, till anon;
  Then wilt thou tumble in confusion.

(*Exit.*)

([*Hell disappears.*] *The clock strikes eleven.*)

FAUSTUS: Ah Faustus,
  Now hast thou but one bare hour to live,
  And then thou must be damned perpetually.
  Stand still, you ever-moving spheres of heaven,   145
  That time may cease and midnight never come.
  Fair nature's eye, rise, rise again, and make
  Perpetual day; or let this hour be but
  A year, a month, a week, a natural day,
  That Faustus may repent and save his soul.   150
  O lente, lente currite noctis equi!°
  The stars move still; time runs; the clock will
    strike;
  The devil will come, and Faustus must be
    damned.
  O, I'll leap up to my God! Who pulls me down?
  See, see, where Christ's blood streams in the
    firmament!   155
  One drop would save my soul, half a drop! Ah,
    my Christ!
  Rend not my heart for naming of my Christ!
  Yet will I call on him. O, spare me, Lucifer!
  Where is it now? 'Tis gone. And see where God
  Stretcheth out his arm and bends his ireful
    brows.   160
  Mountains and hills, come, come, and fall on
    me,
  And hide me from the heavy wrath of God.
  No, no!
  Then will I headlong run into the earth.
  Earth, gape! O no, it will not harbor me!   165
  You stars that reigned at my nativity,
  Whose influence hath allotted death and hell.
  Now draw up Faustus like a foggy mist
  Into the entrails of yon laboring cloud,
  That when you vomit forth into the air,   170
  My limbs may issue from your smoky mouths,
  So that my soul may but ascend to heaven.

(*The watch strikes.*)

  Ah, half the hour is past; 'twill all be past anon.
  O God,
  If thou wilt not have mercy on my soul,   175
  Yet for Christ's sake, whose blood hath
    ransomed me,
  Impose some end to my incessant pain.
  Let Faustus live in hell a thousand years,
  A hundred thousand, and at last be saved.
  O, no end is limited to damnèd souls.   180
  Why wert thou not a creature wanting soul?
  Or why is this immortal that thou hast?

151. *O . . . equi:* O slowly, slowly; run you horses of night
(adapted from Ovid's *Amores*).

Ah, Pythagoras' *metempsychosis,*° were that true,
This soul should fly from me and I be changed
185 Into some brutish beast. All beasts are happy,
For, when they die
Their souls are soon dissolved in elements,
But mine must live still to be plagued in hell.
Cursed be the parents that engendered me!
190 No, Faustus, curse thyself, curse Lucifer
That hath deprived thee of the joys of heaven.

(*The clock strikes twelve.*)

O, it strikes, it strikes! Now, body, turn to air,
Or Lucifer will bear thee quick° to hell.
O soul, be changed to little water-drops,
195 And fall into the ocean, ne'er be found!

(*Thunder, and enter the Devils.*)

My God, my God, look not so fierce on me!
Adders and serpents, let me breathe a while!
Ugly hell, gape not! Come not, Lucifer!
I'll burn my books! Ah, Mephistophilis!
                    (*Exeunt [Faustus and Devils].*)

Scene III

(*Enter the Scholars.*)

FIRST SCHOLAR: Come, gentlemen, let us go visit
          Faustus,
     For such a dreadful night was never seen
     Since first the world's creation did begin.
     Such fearful shrieks and cries were never heard.
5   Pray heaven the doctor have escaped the danger.
SECOND SCHOLAR: O help us, heaven! See, here are
          Faustus' limbs,
     All torn asunder by the hand of death.

---

183. metempsychosis: Belief in the transmigration of souls, associated with the Greek philosopher Pythagoras of Samos. **193. quick:** Alive.

THIRD SCHOLAR: The devils whom Faustus served
          have torn him thus;
     For 'twixt the hours of twelve and one,
          methought
     I heard him shriek and call aloud for help,   10
     At which self time the house seemed all on fire
     With dreadful horror of these damnèd fiends.
SECOND SCHOLAR: Well, gentlemen, though Faustus'
          end be such
     As every Christian heart laments to think on,
     Yet for he was a scholar, once admired   15
     For wondrous knowledge in our German
          schools,
     We'll give his mangled limbs due burial;
     And all the students clothed in mourning black,
     Shall wait upon° his heavy° funeral.
                    (*Exeunt.*)

EPILOGUE _____

(*Enter Chorus.*)

CHORUS: Cut is the branch that might have grown
          full straight,
     And burnèd is Apollo's laurel bough
     That sometime grew within this learnèd man.
     Faustus is gone. Regard his hellish fall,
     Whose fiendful fortune may exhort the wise   5
     Only to wonder at unlawful things,
     Whose deepness doth entice such forward wits
     To practice more than heavenly power permits.
                    [*Exit.*]
     Terminat hora diem; terminat author opus.°

V, III. 19. wait upon: By present at; **heavy:** Sorrowful.   Epilogue. **9. Terminat . . . opus:** The hour ends the day; the author ends his work.

William Shakespeare

Despite the fact that Shakespeare wrote some thirty-seven plays, owned part of his theatrical company, acted in plays, and retired a relatively wealthy man in the city of his birth, there is much we do not know about him. His father was a glovemaker with pretentions to being a gentleman, and Shakespeare himself had his coat of arms placed on his home, New Place, which he purchased in part because it was one of the grandest buildings in Stratford. Church records indicate that he was born in April 1564 and that he died in April 1616, after having been retired from the stage for two or three years. We know that he married Anne Hathaway in 1582, when he was eighteen and she twenty-six; that he had a daughter Susanna and twins, Judith and Hamnet; and that Hamnet, his only son, died at age eleven. He has no direct descendants today.

We know very little about his education. We assume he went to the local grammar school, since as the son of a burgess he was eligible to attend for free. If he did so, he would have received a very strong education based on rhetoric and logic and the reading of classical literature. He would have been exposed to the comedies of Plautus and the tragedies of Seneca as well as the poetry of Virgil, Ovid, and a host of other lesser writers.

A rumor has persisted that he spent some time as a Latin teacher, but that is uncertain. No evidence exists to suggest that Shakespeare went to a university, although his general learning and knowledge are so extraordinary and broad that generations of scholars have assumed that he was perhaps educated and then sent to the Inns at Court to study law. None of this has ever been proven. The lack of evidence to support any of these views has led some people to assume that his plays could not have been written by him but must have been written by someone with a considerable university education. However, no one in the Elizabethan theater had an education of the sort often proposed for Shakespeare. Marlowe and Ben Jonson were the most learned of Elizabethan playwrights, but they did not train as lawyers, and their work is quite different in character and feeling from that of Shakespeare.

One recent theory about Shakespeare's early years suggests that before he went up to London to work in theater Shakespeare had been a member of a wandering company of actors much like those who appear in *Hamlet*. It is an ingenious theory and has much to recommend it. For one thing, it would explain how Shakespeare could take the spotlight so quickly as to arouse the anger of more experienced London writers.

Shakespeare did not begin his career writing for the stage. He took a more conventional approach for the age and, because of his obvious skill as a poet, sought the support of an aristocratic patron, the Earl of Southampton. Southampton, like many wealthy and polished young courtiers, felt it a pleasant ornament to have a poet under his sponsorship whose works would be dedicated to him and would give him great credit. Shakespeare wrote sonnets apparently with Southampton in mind. And, hoping for preferment, he also wrote the long narrative poems *Venus and Adonis, The Rape of Lucrece,* and *The Phoenix and the Turtle.* However, Southampton eventually decided to become the patron of another poet, John Florio, an Italian who had translated Michel de Montaigne's *Essays.*

Shakespeare's response was to turn to the stage. His first plays were a considerable success: *King Henry VI* in three parts — three full-length plays. Satisfying London's taste for plays that told the history of England's tangled political past, Shakespeare wrote a lengthy series of plays ranging from *Richard II* through the two parts of *King Henry IV* to *Henry V* and won considerable renown. He was envied by competing playwrights. Audiences, however, were delighted. Francis Meres, in a famous book of the period called *Palladis Tamia: Wit's Treasury,* cites Shakespeare as the modern Plautus and Seneca, as the best in both comedy and tragedy. Meres says that by 1598 Shakespeare was known for a dozen plays. That his success was firm by this time is demonstrated by his having purchased his large house, New Place, in Stratford in 1597. He could not have done this without financial security.

In the next few years, Shakespeare made a number of interesting purchases of property in Stratford, and he also made deals with his own theater company to secure the rights to perform in London. These arrangements produced legal records that give us some of the clearest information we have concerning Shakespeare's activities during this period. His company was called the Lord Chamberlain's Men while Queen Elizabeth was alive, but King James, in the spring of 1603, less than two months after Elizabeth died, renamed the company the King's Men. As the King's Men, Shakespeare's company had considerable power and success. His company sometimes performed plays for an audience that included King James, as in the first performance of *Macbeth.*

Shakespeare was successful as a writer of histories, comedies, and tragedies. He also wrote in another genre, known as romance because the plays are certainly not comedies or tragedies and because they often depend on supernatural or improbable elements. *Cymbeline, The Winter's Tale,* and *The Tempest* are the best known of Shakespeare's romances. They are the work of his last years and have a fascinating complexity to them.

When Shakespeare died, on April 23, 1616, he was buried as a gentleman in the church in which he had been baptized in Stratford-upon-Avon. His will left most of his money and possessions to his two daughters, Judith and Susanna. His wife was left the second-best bed and its furniture — a bequest that has long baffled biographers. His wife was entitled to a third of the estate and the use of the house for life, so it may have been simply a special note that Shakespeare added to his will to ensure that she got the bed. Nonetheless, it has remained a curious mystery.

A MIDSUMMER NIGHT'S DREAM

A Midsummer Night's Dream, 1595–1596, is an early comedy of Shakespeare's and one of his most beloved works. It is also one of his most imaginative plays, introducing us to the world of fairies and the realm of dreams. Romantic painters, such as Fuseli, have long found in this play a rich store of images that stretch far beyond the limits of the real world of everyday experience.

For Shakespeare, the fun of the play is in the ways in which the world of the fairies intersects with the world of real people, and we can interpret the play as a hint of what would happen if the world of dreams were to intersect with the world of real experience. The fact that these worlds are more alike than they are different gives Shakespeare the comic basis on which to work. He finds some new and amusing ways to interpret the Aristophanic device of mistaken identities.

The play is set in Athens, with Duke Theseus about to wed Hippolyta, the queen of the Amazons. Helena and Hermia are young women in love with Demetrius and Lysander, respectively. However, Demetrius wants to marry Hermia, and he has the blessing of Hermia's father. Hermia's refusal to follow her father's wishes drives her into the woods, where she is followed by both young men and Helena, who does not want to lose Demetrius.

They find themselves in the world of the fairies, although the humans cannot see the fairies. Puck, an impish sprite, is ordered by Oberon, king of the fairies, to put a balm in Demetrius's eyes so he will fall in love with Helena, but Puck puts it in Lysander's eyes, and the plot backfires. Lysander is suddenly in love with Helena, and Hermia is confounded. Oberon, in the meantime, has had Puck place the same balm in the eyes of Titania, the queen of the fairies. She will fall in love with the first creature she sees when she awakes.

That creature is Bottom, the "rude mechanical" whose head has been transformed into an ass's head. Such a deception opens up possibilities for wonderful comic elements that go far beyond the simplistic comic devices used in the mix-ups with twins or other conventional mistaken identities. The richness of the illusions that operate onstage constantly draws us to the question of how we ever can know the truth of our own experiences, especially when some of them are dreams whose imaginative power is occasionally overwhelming.

Shakespeare plays here with some of the Aristotelian conventions of the drama, especially Aristotle's view that drama imitates life. One of the great comic devices in *A Midsummer Night's Dream* is the play within a play that Bottom, Quince, Snug, Flute, and Starveling are to put on before Theseus and Hippolyta. They tell the story of Pyramus and Thisby, lovers who lose each other because they misinterpret signs. It is "Merry and tragical! Tedious and brief!" But it is also a wonderful parody of what the playwright — including Shakespeare — often does when operating in the Aristotelian mode. The aim of the play is realism, and yet the players are naive and inexperienced in drama; they do their best constantly to remind the audience that it is only a play.

The comic ineptness of the rude mechanicals' play needs no disclaimers of this sort, and the immediate audience — Theseus, Hippolyta, Demetrius, Helena, Lysander, and Hermia — is the beneficiary of much laughter as a result of the ardor of the players. The audience in the theater is also mightily amused at the antics of the mechanicals, which, on the surface, are simply funny and a wonderful pastiche of artless playacting.

Beneath the surface, something more serious is going on. hakespeare is commenting on the entire function of drama in our lives. He constantly reminds us in this play that we are watching an illusion, even an illusion within an illusion, but he also convinces us that illusions teach us a great deal about reality. The setting of the real world in *A Midsummer Night's Dream* — Athens — is quite improbable. The mechanicals all have obviously English names and are out of place in an Athenian pastoral setting. The play on the level of Athens is pure fantasy, with even more fantastic goings-on at the level of the fairy world. But fantasy nourishes us. It helps us interpret our own experiences by permitting us to distance them and reflect on how they affect others. This is one of the deepest functions of drama.

As in all comedies, everything turns out exceptionally well — the way we would want it to. A multiple marriage, one of the delightful conventions of many comedies, ends the drama, and virtually everyone has gotten what she or he wanted. We are left with a sense of satisfaction because we, too, get our wish concerning how things should be in the play. And we also have a deep sense of consolation and of satisfaction in the human condition. Puck, one of the greatest of Shakespeare's characters, turns out to be sympathetic and human in his feelings about people. And Bottom, a clown whose origins are certainly Greek and

Roman, warms us with his sense of generosity and caring toward others. Shakespeare promotes a remarkably warm view of humanity in this play, leaving us with a sense of delight and a glow that is rare even in comedy. In this play Shakespeare somehow conveys to us a sense of goodness. It is as welcome today as it was in the sixteenth century.

William Shakespeare (1564–1616)
A MIDSUMMER NIGHT'S DREAM   *c. 1596*

[Dramatis Personae

THESEUS, *Duke of Athens*
EGEUS, *father to Hermia*
LYSANDER, ⎫
DEMETRIUS, ⎬ *in love with Hermia*
PHILOSTRATE, *Master of the Revels to Theseus*

QUINCE, *a carpenter*
SNUG, *a joiner*
BOTTOM, *a weaver*
FLUTE, *a bellows-mender*
SNOUT, *a tinker*
STARVELING, *a tailor*

HIPPOLYTA, *Queen of the Amazons, betrothed to Theseus*
HERMIA, *daughter to Egeus, in love with Lysander*
HELENA, *in love with Demetrius*

OBERON, *King of the Fairies*
TITANIA, *Queen of the Fairies*
PUCK, *or Robin Goodfellow*
PEASEBLOSSOM, ⎫
COBWEB,   ⎬ *fairies*
MOTH,   ⎪
MUSTARDSEED, ⎭
Other FAIRIES *attending their king and queen*
ATTENDANTS *on Theseus and Hippolyta*

Scene: *Athens, and a wood near it.*]

Note: The text of *A Midsummer Night's Dream* has come down to us in different versions — such as the first quarto, the second quarto, and the first Folio. The copy of the text used here is largely drawn from the first quarto. Passages enclosed in square brackets are taken from one of the other versions.

[ACT I • Scene I]° _____

(*Enter Theseus, Hippolyta, [Philostrate,] with others.*)

THESEUS: Now, fair Hippolyta, our nuptial hour
Draws on apace. Four happy days bring in
Another moon; but, O, methinks, how slow
This old moon wanes! She lingers° my desires,
Like to a step-dame° or a dowager°   5
Long withering out a young man's revenue.
HIPPOLYTA: Four days will quickly steep themselves in night,
Four nights will quickly dream away the time;
And then the moon, like to a silver bow
New-bent in heaven, shall behold the night   10
Of our solemnities.
THESEUS: Go, Philostrate,
Stir up the Athenian youth to merriments,
Awake the pert and nimble spirit of mirth,
Turn melancholy forth to funerals;
The pale companion° is not for our pomp.°   15
                                   [*Exit Philostrate.*]
Hippolyta, I woo'd thee with my sword,°
And won thy love doing thee injuries;
But I will wed thee in another key,
With pomp, with triumph,° and with reveling.

(*Enter Egeus and his daughter Hermia, and Lysander, and Demetrius.*)

EGEUS: Happy be Theseus, our renowned Duke!   20
THESEUS: Thanks, good Egeus. What's the news with thee?
EGEUS: Full of vexation come I, with complaint

I, I. Location: The palace of Theseus.   **4. lingers:** Lengthens, protects.   **5. step-dame:** Stepmother; **dowager:** Widow with a jointure or dower.   **15. companion:** Fellow; **pomp:** Ceremonial magnificence.   **16. with my sword:** In a military engagement against the Amazons, when Hippolyta was taken captive.   **19. triumph:** Public festivity.

Against my child, my daughter Hermia.
Stand forth, Demetrius. My noble lord,
25 This man hath my consent to marry her.
Stand forth, Lysander. And, my gracious Duke,
This man hath bewitch'd the bosom of my child.
Thou, thou, Lysander, thou hast given her
    rhymes
And interchang'd love tokens with my child.
30 Thou hast by moonlight at her window sung
With feigning voice verses of feigning love,°
And stol'n the impression of her fantasy,°
With bracelets of thy hair, rings, gauds,°
    conceits,°
Knacks,° trifles, nosegays, sweetmeats —
    messengers
35 Of strong prevailment in unhardened youth.
With cunning hast thou filch'd my daughter's
    heart,
Turn'd her obedience, which is due to me,
To stubborn harshness. And, my gracious Duke,
Be it so she will not here before your Grace
40 Consent to marry with Demetrius,
I beg the ancient privilege of Athens:
As she is mine, I may dispose of her,
Which shall be either to this gentleman
Or to her death, according to our law
45 Immediately° provided in that case.
THESEUS: What say you, Hermia? Be advis'd, fair
    maid.
To you your father should be as a god —
One that compos'd your beauties, yea, and one
To whom you are but as a form in wax
50 By him imprinted and within his power
To leave° the figure or disfigure° it.
Demetrius is a worthy gentleman.
HERMIA: So is Lysander.
THESEUS: In himself he is;
But in this kind,° wanting° your father's voice,°
55 The other must be held the worthier.
HERMIA: I would my father look'd but with my
    eyes.
THESEUS: Rather your eyes must with his judgment
    look.
HERMIA: I do entreat your Grace to pardon me.
I know not by what power I am made bold,
60 Nor how it may concern° my modesty,

In such a presence here to plead my thoughts;
But I beseech your Grace that I may know
The worst that may befall me in this case,
If I refuse to wed Demetrius.
THESEUS: Either to die the death, or to abjure   65
Forever the society of men.
Therefore, fair Hermia, question your desires,
Know of your youth, examine well your blood,°
Whether, if you yield not to your father's choice,
You can endure the livery° of a nun,   70
For aye° to be in shady cloister mew'd,°
To live a barren sister all your life,
Chanting faint hymns to the cold fruitless moon.
Thrice blessed they that master so their blood
To undergo such maiden pilgrimage,   75
But earthlier happy° is the rose distill'd,
Than that which withering on the virgin thorn
Grows, lives, and dies in single blessedness.
HERMIA: So will I grow, so live, so die, my lord,
Ere I will yield my virgin patent° up   80
Unto his lordship, whose unwished yoke
My soul consents not to give sovereignty.
THESEUS: Take time to pause; and, by the next new
    moon —
The sealing-day betwixt my love and me,
For everlasting bond of fellowship —   85
Upon that day either prepare to die
For disobedience to your father's will,
Or° else to wed Demetrius, as he would,
Or on Diana's altar° to protest°
For aye austerity and single life.   90
DEMETRIUS: Relent, sweet Hermia, and, Lysander,
    yield
Thy crazed° title to my certain right.
LYSANDER: You have her father's love, Demetrius;
Let me have Hermia's. Do you marry him.
EGEUS: Scornful Lysander! True, he hath my love,   95
And what is mine my love shall render him.
And she is mine, and all my right of her
I do estate unto° Demetrius.
LYSANDER: I am, my lord, as well deriv'd° as he,
As well possess'd;° my love is more than his;   100
My fortunes every way as fairly° rank'd,
If not with vantage,° as Demetrius';
And, which is more than all these boasts can be,
I am belov'd of beauteous Hermia.

---

31. feigning: (1) Counterfeiting, (2) Faining, desirous. **32. And . . . fantasy:** And made her fall in love with you (imprinting your image on her imagination) by stealthy and dishonest means. **33. gauds:** Playthings; **conceits:** Fanciful trifles. **34. Knacks:** Knickknacks. **45. Immediately:** Expressly. **51. leave:** Leave unaltered; **disfigure:** Obliterate. **54. kind:** Respect; **wanting:** Lacking; **voice:** Approval. **60. concern:** Befit.

68. blood: Passions. **70. livery:** Habit. **71. aye:** Ever; **mew'd:** Shut in. (Said of a hawk, poultry, etc.) **76. earthlier happy:** Happier as respects this world. **80. patent:** Privilege. **88. Or:** Either. **89. Diana's altar:** Diana was a virgin goddess; **protest:** Vow. **92. crazed:** Cracked, unsound. **98. estate unto:** Settle or bestow upon. **99. deriv'd:** Descended, i.e., "as well born." **100. possess'd:** Endowed with wealth. **101. fairly:** Handsomely. **102. vantage:** Superiority.

105 Why should not I then prosecute my right?
Demetrius, I'll avouch it to his head,°
Made love to Nedar's daughter, Helena,
And won her soul; and she, sweet lady, dotes,
Devoutly dotes, dotes in idolatry,
110 Upon this spotted° and inconstant man.
THESEUS: I must confess that I have heard so much,
And with Demetrius thought to have spoke
thereof;
But, being over-full of self-affairs,
My mind did lose it. But, Demetrius, come,
115 And come, Egeus, you shall go with me;
I have some private schooling for you both.
For you, fair Hermia, look you arm° yourself
To fit your fancies° to your father's will;
Or else the law of Athens yields you up —
120 Which by no means we may extenuate° —
To death, or to a vow of single life.
Come, my Hippolyta. What cheer, my love?
Demetrius and Egeus, go° along.
I must employ you in some business
125 Against° our nuptial, and confer with you
Of something nearly that° concerns yourselves.
EGEUS: With duty and desire we follow you.
    (*Exeunt*° [*all but Lysander and Hermia*].)
LYSANDER: How now, my love, why is your cheek
so pale?
How chance the roses there do fade so fast?
HERMIA: Belike° for want of rain, which I could
well
130 Beteem° them from the tempest of my eyes.
LYSANDER: Ay me! For aught that I could ever
read,
Could ever hear by tale or history,
The course of true love never did run smooth;
135 But either it was different in blood° —
HERMIA: O cross,° too high to be enthrall'd to low!
LYSANDER: Or else misgraffed° in respect of years —
HERMIA: O spite, too old to be engag'd to young!
LYSANDER: Or else it stood upon the choice of
friends° —
140 HERMIA: O hell, to choose love by another's eyes!
LYSANDER: Or, if there were a sympathy in choice,
War, death, or sickness did lay siege to it,
Making it momentany° as a sound,

Swift as a shadow, short as any dream,
Brief as the lightning in the collied° night,   145
That, in a spleen,° unfolds° both heaven and
earth,
And ere a man hath power to say "Behold!"
The jaws of darkness do devour it up.
So quick° bright things come to confusion.°
HERMIA: If then true lovers have been ever cross'd,°   150
It stands as an edict in destiny.
Then let us teach our trial patience,°
Because it is a customary cross,
As due to love as thoughts and dreams and
sighs,
Wishes and tears, poor fancy's° followers.   155
LYSANDER: A good persuasion. Therefore, hear me,
Hermia.
I have a widow aunt, a dowager
Of great revenue, and she hath no child.
From Athens is her house remote seven leagues;
And she respects° me as her only son.   160
There, gentle Hermia, may I marry thee,
And to that place the sharp Athenian law
Cannot pursue us. If thou lovest me, then,
Steal forth thy father's house tomorrow night;
And in the wood, a league without the town,   165
Where I did meet thee once with Helena
To do observance to a morn of May,°
There will I stay for thee.
HERMIA: My good Lysander!
I swear to thee, by Cupid's strongest bow,
By his best arrow° with the golden head,°   170
By the simplicity° of Venus' doves,°
By that which knitteth souls and prospers loves,
And by that fire which burn'd the Carthage
queen,
When the false Troyan° under sail was seen,
By all the vows that ever men have broke,   175
In number more than ever women spoke,
In that same place thou hast appointed me
Tomorrow truly will I meet with thee.
LYSANDER: Keep promise, love. Look, here comes
Helena.

145. collied: Blackened (as with coal dust), darkened.   146.
in a spleen: In a swift impulse, in a violent flash; unfolds:
Discloses.   149. quick: Quickly; or, perhaps, living, alive;
confusion: Ruin.   150. ever cross'd: Always thwarted.   152.
teach . . . patience: Teach ourselves patience in this trial.
155. fancy's: Amorous passion's.   160. respects: Regards.
167. do . . . May: Perform the ceremonies of May Day.
170. best arrow: Cupid's best gold-pointed arrows were sup-
poseed to induce love, his blunt leaden arrows aversion.
171. simplicity: Innocence; doves: Those that drew Venus'
chariot.   173, 174. Carthage queen, false Troyan: Dido,
Queen of Carthage, immolated herself on a funeral pyre after
having been deserted by the Trojan hero Aeneas.

106. head: Face.   110. spotted: Morally stained.   117. look
you arm: Take care you prepare.   118. fancies: Likings,
thoughts of love.   120. extenuate: Mitigate.   123. go: Come.
125. Against: In preparation for.   126. nearly that: That
closely.   127. [S.D.] Exeunt: Latin for "they go out."   130.
Belike: Very likely.   131. Beteem: Grant, afford.   135.
blood: Hereditary station.   136. cross: Vexation.   137.
misgraffed: Ill grafted, badly matched.   139. friends: Relatives.
143. momentany: Lasting but a moment.

(Enter Helena.)

180 HERMIA: God speed fair° Helena, whither away?
    HELENA: Call you me fair? That fair again unsay.
      Demetrius loves your fair.° O happy fair!°
      Your eyes are lodestars,° and your tongue's
        sweet air°
      More tuneable° than lark to shepherd's ear
      When wheat is green, when hawthorn buds
185   appear.
      Sickness is catching. O, were favor° so,
      Yours would I catch, fair Hermia, ere I go;
      My ear should catch your voice, my eye your
        eye,
      My tongue should catch your tongue's sweet
        melody.
190   Were the world mine, Demetrius being bated,°
      The rest I 'd give to be to you translated.°
      O, teach me how you look, and with what art
      You sway the motion° of Demetrius' heart.
    HERMIA: I frown upon him, yet he loves me still.
    HELENA: O that your frowns would teach my
195   smiles such skill!
    HERMIA: I give him curses, yet he gives me love.
    HELENA: O that my prayers could such affection°
     move!°
    HERMIA: The more I hate, the more he follows me.
    HELENA: The more I love, the more he hateth me.
200 HERMIA: His folly, Helena, is no fault of mine.
    HELENA: None, but your beauty. Would that fault
     were mine!
    HERMIA: Take comfort. He no more shall see my
     face.
      Lysander and myself will fly this place.
      Before the time I did Lysander see,
205   Seem'd Athens as a paradise to me.
      O, then, what graces in my love do dwell,
      That he hath turn'd a heaven unto a hell!
    LYSANDER: Helen, to you our minds we will unfold.
      Tomorrow night, when Phoebe° doth behold
210   Her silver visage in the wat'ry glass,°
      Decking with liquid pearl the bladed grass,
      A time that lovers' flights doth still° conceal,
      Through Athens' gates have we devis'd to steal.
    HERMIA: And in the wood, where often you and I

Upon faint° primrose beds were wont to lie,   215
Emptying our bosoms of their counsel° sweet,
There my Lysander and myself shall meet;
And thence from Athens turn away our eyes,
To seek new friends and stranger companies.
Farewell, sweet playfellow. Pray thou for us,   220
And good luck grant thee thy Demetrius!
Keep word, Lysander. We must starve our sight
From lovers' food till morrow deep midnight.
LYSANDER: I will, my Hermia.   *(Exit Hermia.)*
                 Helena, adieu.
As you on him, Demetrius dote on you!   225
               (Exit Lysander.)
HELENA: How happy some o'er other some can be!°
Through Athens I am thought as fair as she.
But what of that? Demetrius thinks not so;
He will not know what all but he do know.
And as he errs, doting on Hermia's eyes,   230
So I, admiring of° his qualities.
Things base and vile, holding no quantity,°
Love can transpose to form and dignity.
Love looks not with the eyes, but with the mind,
And therefore is wing'd Cupid painted blind.   235
Nor hath Love's mind of any judgment taste;°
Wings, and no eyes, figure° unheedy haste.
And therefore is Love said to be a child,
Because in choice he is so oft beguil'd.
As waggish boys in game° themselves forswear,   240
So the boy Love is perjur'd everywhere.
For ere Demetrius look'd on Hermia's eyne,°
He hail'd down oaths that he was only mine;
And when this hail some heat from Hermia felt,
So he dissolv'd, and show'rs of oaths did melt.   245
I will go tell him of fair Hermia's flight.
Then to the wood will he tomorrow night
Pursue her; and for this intelligence°
If I have thanks, it is a dear° expense.°
But herein mean I to enrich my pain,   250
To have his sight thither and back again. *(Exit.)*

[Scene II]°

*(Enter Quince the Carpenter, and Snug the Joiner,
and Bottom the Weaver, and Flute the Bellows-Mender,
and Snout the Tinker, and Starveling the Tailor.)*

---

180. fair: Fair-complexioned (generally regarded by the Elizabethans as more beautiful than dark complexioned). **182. your fair:** Your beauty (even though Hermia is dark-complexioned); **happy fair:** Lucky fair one. **183. lodestars:** Guiding stars; **air:** Music. **184. tuneable:** Tuneful, melodious. **186. favor:** Appearance, looks. **190. bated:** Excepted. **191. translated:** Transformed. **193. motion:** Impulse. **197. affection:** Passion; **move:** Arouse. **209. Phoebe:** Diana, the moon. **210. glass:** Mirror. **212. still:** Always. **215. faint:** Pale. **216. counsel:** Secret thought. **226. o'er . . . can be:** Can be in comparison to some others. **231. admiring of:** Wondering at. **232. holding no quantity:** I.e., unsubstantial, unshapely. **236. Nor . . . taste:** Nor has Love, which dwells in the fancy or imagination, any *taste* or least bit of judgment or reason. **237. figure:** Are a symbol of. **240. game:** Sport, jest. **242. eyne:** Eyes (old form of plural.) **248. intelligence:** Information. **249. dear:** Costly; **a dear expense:** A trouble worth taking. **I, II. Location:** Athens. Quince's house(?)

QUINCE: Is all our company here?

BOTTOM: You were best to call them generally,° man by man, according to the scrip.°

QUINCE: Here is the scroll of every man's name which
5   is thought fit, through all Athens, to play in our interlude before the Duke and the Duchess on his wedding-day at night.

BOTTOM: First, good Peter Quince, say what the play treats on, then read the names of the actors, and
10   so grow to° a point.

QUINCE: Marry,° our play is "The most lamentable comedy and most cruel death of Pyramus and Thisby."

BOTTOM: A very good piece of work, I assure you,
15   and a merry. Now, good Peter Quince, call forth your actors by the scroll. Masters, spread yourselves.

QUINCE: Answer as I call you. Nick Bottom, the weaver.

BOTTOM: Ready. Name what part I am for, and proceed.

QUINCE: You, Nick Bottom, are set down for Pyramus.

20 BOTTOM: What is Pyramus? A lover, or a tyrant?

QUINCE: A lover, that kills himself most gallant for love.

BOTTOM: That will ask some tears in the true performing of it. If I do it, let the audience look to their eyes.
25   I will move storms; I will condole° in some measure. To the rest — yet my chief humor° is for a tyrant. I could play Ercles° rarely, or a part to tear a cat° in, to make all split.°

    "The raging rocks
30   And shivering shocks
    Shall break the locks
      Of prison gates;
    And Phibbus' car°
    Shall shine from far
35   And make and mar
      The foolish Fates."

This was lofty! Now name the rest of the players. This is Ercles' vein, a tyrant's vein. A lover is more condoling.

40 QUINCE: Francis Flute, the bellows-mender.

FLUTE: Here, Peter Quince.

QUINCE: Flute, you must take Thisby on you.

FLUTE: What is Thisby? A wand'ring knight?

QUINCE: It is the lady that Pyramus must love.

45 FLUTE: Nay, faith, let not me play a woman. I have a beard coming.

QUINCE: That's all one.° You shall play it in a mask, and you may speak as small° as you will.

BOTTOM: An° I may hide my face, let me play Thisby
50   too. I'll speak in a monstrous little voice, "Thisne, Thisne!" "Ah Pyramus, my lover dear! Thy Thisby dear, and lady dear!"

QUINCE: No, no; you must play Pyramus; and, Flute, you Thisby.

55 BOTTOM: Well, proceed.

QUINCE: Robin Starveling, the tailor.

STARVELING: Here, Peter Quince.

QUINCE: Robin Starveling, you must play Thisby's mother. Tom Snout, the tinker.

60 SNOUT: Here, Peter Quince.

QUINCE: You, Pyramus' father; myself, Thisby's father; Snug, the joiner, you, the lion's part; and I hope here is a play fitted.

SNUG: Have you the lion's part written? Pray you, if
65   it be, give it me, for I am slow of study.

QUINCE: You may do it extempore, for it is nothing but roaring.

BOTTOM: Let me play the lion too. I will roar that I will do any man's heart good to hear me. I will
70   roar that I will make the Duke say, "Let him roar again, let him roar again."

QUINCE: An you should do it too terribly, you would fright the Duchess and the ladies, that they would shriek; and that were enough to hang us all.

75 ALL: That would hang us, every mother's son.

BOTTOM: I grant you, friends, if you should fright the ladies out of their wits, they would have no more discretion but to hang us; but I will aggravate° my voice so that I will roar you° as gently as any
80   sucking dove; I will roar you an 'twere any nightingale.

QUINCE: You can play no part but Pyramus; for Pyramus is a sweet-fac'd man, a proper° man as one shall see in a summer's day, a most lovely gentleman-
85   like man. Therefore you must needs play Pyramus.

BOTTOM: Well, I will undertake it. What beard were I best to play it in?

QUINCE: Why, what you will.

BOTTOM: I will discharge° it in either your° straw-
90   color beard, your orange-tawny beard, your purple-in-grain° beard, or your French-crown-color° beard, your perfect yellow.

---

2. **generally:** Bottom's blunder for *individually*.   3. **script:** Script, written list.   10. **grow to:** Come to.   11. **Marry:** A mild oath, originally the name of the Virgin Mary.   25. **condole:** Lament, arouse pity.   26. **humor:** Inclination, whim.   27. **Ercles:** Hercules (the tradition of ranting came from Seneca's *Hercules Furens*); **tear a cat:** Rant.   28. **make all split:** Cause a stir, bring the house down.   33. **Phibbus' car:** Phoebus', the sun-god's, chariot.

47. **That's all one:** It makes no difference.   48. **small:** High-pitched.   49. **An:** If.   78. **aggravate:** Bottom's blunder for *diminish*.   79. **roar you:** Roar for you.   83. **proper:** Handsome.   89. **discharge:** Perform; **your:** I.e., you know the kind I mean.   90–91. **purple-in-grain:** Dyed a very deep red (from *grain*, the name applied to the dried insect used to make the dye).   91. **French-crown-color:** Color of a French crown, a gold coin.

QUINCE: Some of your French crowns° have no hair
    at all, and then you will play barefac'd. But, masters,
95 here are your parts. [*He distributes parts.*] And I
    am to entreat you, request you, and desire you, to
    con° them by tomorrow night; and meet me in the
    palace wood, a mile without the town, by moonlight.
    There will we rehearse; for if we meet in the city,
100 we shall be dogg'd with company, and our devices°
    known. In the meantime I will draw a bill° of
    properties, such as our play wants. I pray you, fail
    me not.
BOTTOM: We will meet, and there we may rehearse
105 most obscenely° and courageously. Take pains, be
    perfect;° adieu.
QUINCE: At the Duke's oak we meet.
BOTTOM: Enough. Hold, or cut bow-strings.°

                               (*Exeunt.*)

[ACT II • Scene I]° _____

(*Enter a Fairy at one door, and Robin Goodfellow
[Puck] at another.*)

PUCK: How now, spirit! Whither wander you?
FAIRY: Over hill, over dale,
    Thorough° bush, thorough brier,
    Over park, over pale,°
5   Thorough flood, thorough fire,
    I do wander every where,
    Swifter than the moon's sphere;
    And I serve the Fairy Queen,
    To dew her orbs° upon the green.
10 The cowslips tall her pensioners° be.
    In their gold coats spots you see;
    Those be rubies, fairy favors,°
    In those freckles live their savors.°
    I must go seek some dewdrops here
15 And hang a pearl in every cowslip's ear.
    Farewell, thou lob° of spirits; I'll be gone.
    Our Queen and all her elves come here anon.°
PUCK: The King doth keep his revels here tonight.
    Take heed the Queen come not within his sight.
20 For Oberon is passing fell° and wrath,°

Because that she as her attendant hath
A lovely boy, stolen from an Indian king;
She never had so sweet a changeling.°
And jealous Oberon would have the child
Knight of his train, to trace° the forests wild.   25
But she perforce° withholds the loved boy,
Crowns him with flowers and makes him all her
    joy.
And now they never meet in grove or green,
By fountain° clear, or spangled starlight sheen,
But they do square,° that all their elves for fear   30
Creep into acorn-cups and hide them there.
FAIRY: Either I mistake your shape and making
    quite,
Or else you are that shrewd° and knavish sprite°
Call'd Robin Goodfellow. Are not you he
That frights the maidens of the villagery,   35
Skim milk, and sometimes labor in the quern,°
And bootless° make the breathless huswife
    churn,
And sometime make the drink to bear no barm,°
Mislead night-wanderers, laughing at their harm?
Those that Hobgoblin call you and sweet Puck,   40
You do their work, and they shall have good
    luck.
Are you not he?
PUCK: Thou speakest aright;
I am that merry wanderer of the night.
I jest to Oberon and make him smile
When I a fat and bean-fed horse beguile,   45
Neighing in likeness of a filly foal;
And sometime lurk I in a gossip's° bowl,
In very likeness of a roasted crab,°
And when she drinks, against her lips I bob
And on her withered dewlap° pour the ale.   50
The wisest aunt,° telling the saddest° tale,
Sometime for three-foot stool mistaketh me;
Then slip I from her bum, down topples she,
And "tailor"°cries, and falls into a cough;
And then the whole quire° hold their hips and
    laugh,   55
And waxen° in their mirth and neeze° and swear
A merrier hour was never wasted there.
But, room, fairy! Here comes Oberon.

---

93. crowns: Heads bald from syphilis, the "French disease".
97. con: Learn by heart.   **100. devices:** Plans.   **101. bill:**
List.   **105. obscenely:** An unintentionally funny blunder,
whatever Bottom meant to say.   **106. perfect:** Letter-perfect
in memorizing your parts.   **108. Hold . . . bow-strings:** An
archer's expression not definitely explained, but probably
meaning here "keep your promises, or give up the play."
II, I. Location: A wood near Athens.   **3. Thorough:** Through.
4. pale: Enclosure   **9. orbs:** Circles, i.e., fairy rings.   **10.**
pensioners: Retainers, members of the royal bodyguard.   **12.**
favors: Love tokens.   **13. savors:** Sweet smells.   **16. lob:**
Country bumpkin.   **17. anon:** At once.   **20. passing fell:**
Exceedingly angry; **wrath:** Wrathful.

23. changeling: Child exchanged for another by the fairies.
25. trace: Range through.   **26. perforce:** Forcibly.   **29.**
fountain: Spring.   **30. square:** Quarrel.   **33. shrewd:** Mischievous; **sprite:** Spirit.   **36. quern:** Handmill.   **37. bootless:**
In vain.   **38. barm:** Yeast, head on the ale.   **47. gossip's:**
Old woman's.   **48. crab:** Crab apple.   **50. dewlap:** Loose
skin on neck.   **51. aunt:** Old woman; **saddest:** Most serious.
54. tailor: Possibly because she ends up sitting cross-legged
on the floor, looking like a tailor.   **55. quire:** Company.
56. waxen: Increase; **neeze:** Sneeze.

FAIRY: And here my mistress. Would that he were gone!

(*Enter [Oberon] the King of Fairies at one door, with his train; and [Titania] the Queen at another, with hers.*)

60 OBERON: Ill met by moonlight, proud Titania.
TITANIA: What, jealous Oberon? Fairies, skip hence.
I have forsworn his bed and company.
OBERON: Tarry, rash wanton.° Am not I thy lord?
TITANIA: Then I must be thy lady; but I know
65 When thou hast stolen away from fairy land,
And in the shape of Corin° sat all day,
Playing on pipes of corn° and versing love
To amorous Phillida.° Why art thou here,
Come from the farthest steep° of India,
70 But that, forsooth, the bouncing Amazon,
Your buskin'd° mistress and your warrior love,
To Theseus must be wedded, and you come
To give their bed joy and prosperity.
OBERON: How canst thou thus for shame, Titania,
75 Glance at my credit with Hippolyta,°
Knowing I know thy love to Theseus?
Didst not thou lead him through the glimmering night
From Perigenia,° whom he ravished?
And make him with fair Aegles° break his faith,
80 With Ariadne and Antiopa?°
TITANIA: These are the forgeries of jealousy;
And never, since the middle summer's spring,°
Met we on hill, in dale, forest, or mead,
By paved° fountain or by rushy° brook,
85 Or in° the beached margent° of the sea,
To dance our ringlets° to the whistling wind,
But with thy brawls thou hast disturb'd our sport.
Therefore the winds, piping to us in vain,

As in revenge, have suck'd up from the sea
Contagious° fogs; which falling in the land   90
Hath every pelting° river made so proud
That they have overborne their continents.°
The ox hath therefore stretch'd his yoke in vain,
The ploughman lost his sweat, and the green corn°
Hath rotted ere his youth attain'd a beard;   95
The fold° stands empty in the drowned field,
And crows are fatted with the murrion° flock;
The nine men's morris° is fill'd up with mud,
And the quaint mazes° in the wanton° green
For lack of tread are undistinguishable.   100
The human mortals want° their winter° here;
No night is now with hymn or carol bless'd.
Therefore° the moon, the governess of floods,
Pale in her anger, washes all the air,
That rheumatic diseases° do abound.   105
And thorough this distemperature° we see
The seasons alter: hoary-headed frosts
Fall in the fresh lap of the crimson rose,
And on old Hiems'° thin and icy crown
An odorous chaplet of sweet summer buds   110
Is, as in mockery, set. The spring, the summer,
The childing° autumn, angry winter, change
Their wonted liveries,° and the mazed° world,
By their increase,° now knows not which is which.
And this same progeny of evils comes   115
From our debate,° from our dissension;
We are their parents and original.°
OBERON: Do you amend it then; it lies in you.
Why should Titania cross her Oberon?
I do but beg a little changeling boy,   120
To be my henchman.°
TITANIA: Set your heart at rest.
The fairy land buys not the child of me.

---

63. **wanton:** Headstrong creature.   **66, 68. Corin, Phillida:** Conventional names of pastoral lovers.   **67. corn:** Here, oat stalks.   **69. steep:** Mountain range.   **71. buskin'd:** Wearing half-boots called buskins.   **75. Glance . . . Hippolyta:** Make insinuations about my favored relationship with Hippolyta.   **78. Perigenia:** Perigouna, one of Theseus' conquests. (This and the following women are named in Thomas North's translation of Plutarch's *Life of Theseus*.).   **79. Aegles:** Aegle, for whom Theseus deserted Ariadne according to some accounts.   **80. Ariadne:** The daughter of Minos, King of Crete, who helped Theseus escape the labyrinth after killing the Minotaur; later she was abandoned by Theseus.   **Antiopa:** Queen of the Amazons and wife of Theseus; elsewhere identifed with Hippolyta, but here thought of as a separate woman.   **82. middle summer's spring:** Beginning of midsummer.   **84. paved:** With pebbled bottom; **rushy:** Bordered with rushes.   **85. in:** On; **margent:** edge, border.   **86. ringlets:** Dances in a ring. (See *orbs* in line 9.)

90. **Contagious:** Noxious.   **91. pelting:** Paltry; or striking, moving forcefully.   **92. continents:** Banks that contain them.   **94. corn:** Grain of any kind.   **96. fold:** Pen for sheep or cattle.   **97. murrion:** Having died of the murrain, plague.   **98. nine men's morris:** Portion of the village green marked out in a square for a game played with nine pebbles or pegs.   **99. quaint mazes:** Intricate paths marked out on the village green to be followed rapidly on foot as a kind of contest; **wanton:** Luxuriant.   **101. want:** Lack; **winter:** Regular winter season; or proper observances of winter, such as the *hymm or carol* in the next line(?).   **103. Therefore:** I.e., as a result of our quarrel.   **105. rheumatic diseases:** Colds, flu, and other respiratory infections.   **106. distemperature:** Disturbance in nature.   **109. Hiems:** The winter god.   **112. childing:** Fruitful, pregnant.   **113. wonted liveries:** Usual apparel; **mazed:** Bewildered.   **114. Their increase:** Their yield, what they produce.   **116. debate:** Quarrel.   **117. original:** Origin.   **121. henchman:** Attendant, page.

His mother was a vot'ress° of my order,
And, in the spiced Indian air, by night,
125 Full often hath she gossip'd by my side,
And sat with me on Neptune's yellow sands,
Marking th' embarked traders° on the flood,°
When we have laugh'd to see the sails conceive
And grow big-bellied with the wanton° wind;
130 Which she, with pretty and with swimming gait,
Following — her womb then rich with my
        young squire —
Would imitate, and sail upon the land
To fetch me trifles, and return again,
As from a voyage, rich with merchandise.
135 But she, being mortal, of that boy did die;
And for her sake do I rear up her boy,
And for her sake I will not part with him.
OBERON: How long within this wood intend you
        stay?
TITANIA: Perchance till after Theseus' wedding-day.
140 If you will patiently dance in our round°
And see our moonlight revels, go with us;
If not, shun me, and I will spare° your haunts.
OBERON: Give me that boy, and I will go with
        thee.
TITANIA: Not for thy fairy kingdom. Fairies, away!
145 We shall chide downright, if I longer stay.
              (*Exeunt* [*Titania with her train*].)
OBERON: Well, go thy way. Thou shalt not from°
        this grove
Till I torment thee for this injury.
My gentle Puck, come hither. Thou rememb'rest
Since° once I sat upon a promontory,
150 And heard a mermaid on a dolphin's back
Uttering such dulcet and harmonious breath°
That the rude sea grew civil at her song
And certain stars shot madly from their spheres,
To hear the sea-maid's music.
PUCK: I remember.
OBERON: That very time I saw, but thou couldst
155   not,
Flying between the cold moon and the earth,
Cupid all° arm'd. A certain aim he took
At a fair vestal° throned by the west,
And loos'd his love-shaft smartly from his bow,
160 As° it should pierce a hundred thousand hearts;
But I might° see young Cupid's fiery shaft

Quench'd in the chaste beams of the wat'ry
        moon,
And the imperial vot'ress passed on,
In maiden meditation, fancy-free.°
Yet mark'd I where the bolt of Cupid fell: 165
It fell upon a little western flower,
Before milk-white, now purple with love's
        wound,
And maidens call it love-in-idleness.°
Fetch me that flow'r; the herb I showed thee
        once.
The juice of it on sleeping eyelids laid   170
Will make or man or° woman madly dote
Upon the next live creature that it sees.
Fetch me this herb, and be thou here again
Ere the leviathan° can swim a league.
PUCK: I'll put a girdle round about the earth   175
In forty° minutes.   [*Exit.*]
OBERON: Having once this juice,
I'll watch Titania when she is asleep,
And drop the liquor of it in her eyes.
The next thing then she waking looks upon,
Be it on lion, bear, or wolf, or bull,   180
On meddling monkey, or on busy ape,
She shall pursue it with the soul of love.
And ere I take this charm from off her sight,
As I can take it with another herb,
I'll make her render up her page to me.   185
But who comes here? I am invisible,
And I will overhear their conference.

(*Enter Demetrius, Helena following him.*)

DEMETRIUS: I love thee not, therefore pursue me
        not.
Where is Lysander and fair Hermia?
The one I'll slay, the other slayeth me.   190
Thou told'st me they were stol'n unto this
        wood;
And here am I, and wode° within this wood,
Because I cannot meet my Hermia.
Hence, get thee gone, and follow me no more.
HELENA: You draw me, you hard-hearted
        adamant;°   195
But yet you draw not iron, for my heart
Is true as steel. Leave° you your power to draw,
And I shall have no power to follow you.

---

123. vot'ress: Female votary; devotee, worshiper.   **127. traders:** Trading vessels; **flood:** Flood tide.   **129. wanton:** Sportive.   **140. round:** Circular dance.   **142. spare:** Shun.   **146. from:** Go from.   **149. Since:** When.   **151. breath:** Voice, song.   **157. all:** Fully.   **158. vestal:** Vestal virgin (contains a complimentary allusion to Queen Elizabeth as a votaress of Diana and probably refers to an actual entertainment in her honor at Elvetham in 1591).   **160. As:** As if.   **161. might:** Could.

164. fancy-free: Free of love's spell.   **168. love-in-idleness:** Pansy, heartsease.   **171. or . . . or:** Either . . . or.   **174. leviathan:** Sea-monster, whale.   **176. forty:** Used indefinitely.   **192. wode:** Mad (pronounced *wood* and often spelled so).   **195. adamant:** Lodestone, magnet (with pun on *hard-hearted*, since adamant was also thought to be the hardest of all stones and was confused with the diamond).   **197. Leave:** Give up.

NEAR RIGHT: Oberon
instructing Puck in the power
of the "little western flower."
BELOW: The young lovers in
the American Repertory
Theater's 1986 production.
FAR LEFT: Oberon with
Titania upon his shoulder.
FAR RIGHT: The rude
mechanicals: Moonshine with
Lion.

210

DEMETRIUS: Do I entice you? Do I speak you fair?°
200   Or, rather, do I not in plainest truth
    Tell you I do not nor I cannot love you?
HELENA: And even for that do I love you the more.
    I am your spaniel; and, Demetrius,
    The more you beat me, I will fawn on you.
205   Use me but as your spaniel, spurn me, strike me,
    Neglect me, lose me; only give me leave,
    Unworthy as I am, to follow you.
    What worser place can I beg in your love —
    And yet a place of high respect with me —
210   Than to be used as you use your dog?
DEMETRIUS: Tempt not too much the hatred of my
    spirit,
    For I am sick when I do look on thee.
HELENA: And I am sick when I look not on you.

199. fair: Courteously.

DEMETRIUS: You do impeach° your modesty too
    much
    To leave the city and commit yourself   215
    Into the hands of one that loves you not,
    To trust the opportunity of night
    And the ill counsel of a desert° place
    With the rich worth of your virginity.
HELENA: Your virtue° is my privilege.° For that°   220
    It is not night when I do see your face,
    Therefore I think I am not in the night;
    Nor doth this wood lack worlds of company,
    For you in my respect° are all the world.
    Then how can it be said I am alone,   225
    When all the world is here to look on me?

214. impeach: Call into question.   **218. desert:** Deserted.
220. virtue: Goodness or power to attract; **privilege:** Safeguard,
warrant. **For that:** Because.   **224. in my respect:** As far as
I am concerned.

211

DEMETRIUS: I'll run from thee and hide me in the brakes,°
And leave thee to the mercy of wild beasts.
HELENA: The wildest hath not such a heart as you.
230 Run when you will, the story shall be chang'd:
Apollo flies and Daphne holds the chase,°
The dove pursues the griffin,° the mild hind°
Makes speed to catch the tiger — bootless° speed,
When cowardice pursues and valor flies.
DEMETRIUS: I will not stay° thy questions.° Let me
235 go!
Or if thou follow me, do not believe
But I shall do thee mischief in the wood.
HELENA: Ay, in the temple, in the town, the field,
You do me mischief. Fie, Demetrius!
240 Your wrongs do set a scandal on my sex.
We cannot fight for love, as men may do;
We should be woo'd and were not made to woo.

[*Exit Demetrius.*]

I'll follow thee and make a heaven of hell,
To die upon° the hand I love so well. [*Exit.*]
OBERON: Fare thee well, nymph. Ere he do leave
245 this grove,
Thou shalt fly him and he shall seek thy love.

(*Enter Puck.*)

Hast thou the flower there? Welcome, wanderer.
PUCK: Ay, there it is. [*Offers the flower.*]
OBERON: I pray thee, give it me.
I know a bank where the wild thyme blows,°
250 Where oxlips° and the nodding violet grows,
Quite over-canopied with luscious woodbine,°
With sweet musk-roses° and with eglantine.°
There sleeps Titania sometime of the night,
Lull'd in these flowers with dances and delight;
255 And there the snake throws° her enamel'd skin,
Weed° wide enough to wrap a fairy in.
And with the juice of this I'll streak° her eyes,
And make her full of hateful fantasies.

Take thou some of it, and seek through this grove.

[*Gives some love-juice.*]

A sweet Athenian lady is in love 260
With a disdainful youth. Anoint his eyes,
But do it when the next thing he espies
May be the lady. Thou shalt know the man
By the Athenian garments he hath on.
Effect it with some care, that he may prove 265
More fond on° her than she upon her love;
And look thou meet me ere the first cock crow.
PUCK: Fear not, my lord, your servant shall do so.

(*Exeunt.*)

[Scene II]°

(*Enter Titania, Queen of Fairies, with her train.*)

TITANIA: Come, now a roundel° and a fairy song;
Then, for the third part of a minute, hence —
Some to kill cankers° in the musk-rose buds,
Some war with rere-mice° for their leathern wings,
To make my small elves coats, and some keep back 5
The clamorous owl, that nightly hoots and wonders
At our quaint° spirits. Sing me now asleep.
Then to your offices and let me rest.

(*Fairies sing.*)

FIRST FAIRY: You spotted snakes with double° tongue,
Thorny hedgehogs, be not seen; 10
Newts° and blindworms, do no wrong,
Come not near our fairy queen.
[*Chorus.*] Philomel,° with melody
Sing in our sweet lullaby;
Lulla, lulla, lullaby, lulla, lulla, lullaby. 15
Never harm,
Nor spell nor charm,
Come our lovely lady nigh.
So, good night, with lullaby.
FIRST FAIRY: Weaving spiders, come not here; 20
Hence, you long-legg'd spinners, hence!
Beetles black, approach not near;

---

227. **brakes:** Thickets. 231. **Apollo . . . chase:** In the ancient myth, Daphne fled from Apollo and was saved from rape by being transformed into a laurel tree; here it is the female who *holds the chase,* or pursues, instead of the male. 232. **griffin:** A fabulous monster with the head of an eagle and the body of a lion; **hind:** Female deer. 233. **bootless:** Fruitless. 235. **stay:** Wait for; **questions:** Talk or argument. 244. **upon:** By. 249. **blows:** Blooms. 250. **oxlips:** Flowers resembling cowslip and primrose. 251. **woodbine:** Honeysuckle. 252. **musk-roses:** A kind of large, sweet-scented rose; **eglantine:** Sweetbriar, another kind of rose. 255. **throws:** Sloughs off, sheds. 256. **Weed:** Garment. 257. **streak:** Anoint, touch gently.

266. **fond on:** Doting on. **II, II. Location:** The wood. 1. **roundel:** Dance in a ring. 3. **cankers:** Cankerworms. 4. **rere-mice:** Bats. 7. **quaint:** Dainty. 9. **double:** Forked. 11. **Newts:** Water lizards (considered poisonous, as were *blindworms* — small snakes with tiny eyes — and spiders). 13. **Philomel:** The nightingale. (Philomela, daughter of King Pandion, was transformed into a nightingale, according to Ovid's *Metamorphoses,* after she had been raped by her sister Procne's husband, Tereus.)

Worm nor snail, do no offense.
[*Chorus.*] Philomel, with melody, etc.
25 SECOND FAIRY: Hence, away! Now all is well.
One aloof stand sentinel.
[*Exeunt Fairies. Titania sleeps.*]

(*Enter Oberon [and squeezes the flower on Titania's eyelids].*)

OBERON: What thou seest when thou dost wake,
Do it for thy true-love take;
Love and languish for his sake.
30 Be it ounce,° or cat, or bear,
Pard,° or boar with bristled hair,
In thy eye that shall appear
When thou wak'st, it is thy dear
Wake when some vile thing is near.   [*Exit.*]

(*Enter Lysander and Hermia.*)

LYSANDER: Fair love, you faint with wand'ring in
35   the wood;
And to speak troth,° I have forgot our way.
We'll rest us, Hermia, if you think it good,
And tarry for the comfort of the day.
HERMIA: Be 't so, Lysander. Find you out a bed,
40 For I upon this bank will rest my head.
LYSANDER: One turf shall serve as pillow for us
both,
One heart, one bed, two bosoms, and one troth.°
HERMIA: Nay, good Lysander; for my sake, my
dear,
Lie further off yet, do not lie so near.
LYSANDER: O, take the sense, sweet, of my
45   innocence!°
Love takes the meaning in love's conference.°
I mean, that my heart unto yours is knit
So that but one heart we can make of it;
Two bosoms interchained with an oath —
50 So then two bosoms and a single troth.
Then by your side no bed-room me deny,
For lying so, Hermia, I do not lie.°
HERMIA: Lysander riddles very prettily.
Now much beshrew° my manners and my pride
55 If Hermia meant to say Lysander lied.
But, gentle friend, for love and courtesy
Lie further off, in human° modesty;
Such separation as may well be said
Becomes a virtuous bachelor and a maid,

So far be distant; and, good night, sweet friend.   60
Thy love ne'er alter till thy sweet life end!
LYSANDER: Amen, amen, to that fair prayer, say I,
And then end life when I end loyalty!
Here is my bed. Sleep give thee all his rest!
HERMIA: With half that wish the wisher's eyes be
press'd!°   65
[*They sleep, separated by a short distance.*]

(*Enter Puck.*)

PUCK: Through the forest have I gone,
But Athenian found I none
On whose eyes I might approve°
This flower's force in stirring love.
Night and silence. — Who is here?   70
Weeds of Athens he doth wear.
This is he, my master said,
Despised the Athenian maid;
And here the maiden, sleeping sound,
On the dank and dirty ground.   75
Pretty soul! She durst not lie
Near this lack-love, this kill-courtesy.
Churl, upon thy eyes I throw
All the power this charm doth owe.°
[*Applies the love-juice.*]
When thou wak'st, let love forbid   80
Sleep his seat on thy eyelid.
So awake when I am gone,
For I must now to Oberon.   (*Exit.*)

(*Enter Demetrius and Helena, running.*)

HELENA: Stay, though thou kill me, sweet
Demetrius.
DEMETRIUS: I charge thee, hence, and do not haunt
me thus.   85
HELENA: O, wilt thou darkling° leave me? Do not
so.
DEMETRIUS: Stay, on thy peril!° I alone will go.
[*Exit.*]
HELENA: O, I am out of breath in this fond° chase!
The more my prayer, the lesser is my grace.°
Happy is Hermia, wheresoe'er she lies,°   90
For she hath blessed and attractive eyes.
How came her eyes so bright? Not with salt
tears;
If so, my eyes are oft'ner wash'd than hers.
No, no, I am as ugly as a bear;
For beasts that meet me run away for fear.   95

---

30. ounce: Lynx.   31. Pard: Leopard.   36. troth: Truth.
42. troth: Faith, troth-plight.   45. take . . . innocence: Interpret
my intention as innocent.   46. Love . . . conference: When
lovers confer, love teaches each lover to interpret the other's
meaning lovingly.   52. lie: Tell a falsehood (with a riddling
pun on *lie*, recline).   54. beshrew: Curse (but mildly meant).
57. human: Courteous.

65. With . . . press'd: May we share your wish, so that your
eyes too are *press'd*, closed, in sleep.   68. approve: Test.
79. owe: Own.   86. darkling: In the dark.   87. on thy
peril: On pain of danger to you if you don't obey me and
stay.   88. fond: Doting.   89. my grace: The favor I obtain.
90. lies: Dwells.

Therefore no marvel though Demetrius
Do, as a monster, fly my presence thus.
What wicked and dissembling glass of mine
Made me compare with Hermia's sphery eyne?°

100   But who is here? Lysander, on the ground?
Dead, or asleep? I see no blood, no wound.
Lysander, if you live, good sir, awake.
LYSANDER [*awaking*]: And run through fire I will
        for thy sweet sake.
Transparent° Helena! Nature shows art,
That through thy bosom makes me see thy

105   heart.
Where is Demetrius? O, how fit a word
Is that vile name to perish on my sword!
HELENA: Do not say so, Lysander, say not so.
What though he love your Hermia? Lord, what
        though?

110   Yet Hermia still loves you. Then be content.
LYSANDER: Content with Hermia? No! I do repent
The tedious minutes I with her have spent.
Not Hermia but Helena I love.
Who will not change a raven for a dove?

115   The will of man is by his reason sway'd,
And reason says you are the worthier maid.
Things growing are not ripe until their season;
So I, being young, till now ripe not° to reason.
And touching° now the point° of human skill,°

120   Reason becomes the marshal to my will
And leads me to your eyes, where I o'erlook°
Love's stories written in love's richest book.
HELENA: Wherefore was I to this keen mockery
        born?
When at your hands did I deserve this scorn?

125   Is 't not enough, is 't not enough, young man,
That I did never, no, nor never can,
Deserve a sweet look from Demetrius' eye,
But you must flout my insufficiency?
Good troth,° you do me wrong, good sooth,°
        you do,

130   In such disdainful manner me to woo.
But fare you well. Perforce I must confess
I thought you lord of° more true gentleness.°
O, that a lady, of° one man refus'd,
Should of another therefore be abus'd!°   (*Exit.*)
LYSANDER: She sees not Hermia. Hermia, sleep thou

135   there,
And never mayst thou come Lysander near!

For as a surfeit of the sweetest things
The deepest loathing to the stomach brings,
Or as the heresies that men do leave
Are hated most of those they did deceive,   140
So thou, my surfeit and my heresy,
Of all be hated, but the most of me!
And, all my powers, address your love and
        might
To honor Helen and to be her knight!   (*Exit.*)
HERMIA [*awaking*]: Help me, Lysander, help me!
        Do thy best   145
To pluck this crawling serpent from my breast!
Ay me, for pity! What a dream was here!
Lysander, look how I do quake with fear.
Methought a serpent eat° my heart away,
And you sat smiling at his cruel prey.°   150
Lysander! What, remov'd? Lysander! Lord!
What, out of hearing? Gone? No sound, no
        word?
Alack, where are you? Speak, an if you hear,
Speak, of all loves!° I swoon almost with fear.
No? Then I well perceive you are not nigh.   155
Either death, or you, I'll find immediately.
        (*Exit.* [*Manet Titania*° *lying asleep.*])

[ACT III • Scene I]°

(*Enter the Clowns* [*Quince, Snug, Bottom, Flute, Snout, and Starveling*].)

BOTTOM: Are we all met?
QUINCE: Pat, pat; and here's a marvailes° convenient
    place for our rehearsal. This green plot shall be
    our stage, this hawthorn brake° our tiring-house,°
    and we will do it in action as we will do it before   5
    the Duke.
BOTTOM: Peter Quince?
QUINCE: What sayest thou, bully° Bottom?
BOTTOM: There are things in this comedy of Pyramus
    and Thisby that will never please. First, Pyramus   10
    must draw a sword to kill himself, which the ladies
    cannot abide. How answer you that?
SNOUT: By 'r lakin,° a parlous° fear.
STARVELING: I believe we must leave the killing out,
    when all is done.°   15
BOTTOM: Not a whit. I have a device to make all well.

---

99. sphery eyne: Eyes as bright as stars in their spheres.
104. Transparent: (1) Radiant (2) able to be seen through.
118. ripe not: (Am) not ripened.   **119. touching:** Reaching;
point: Summit; **skill:** Judgment.   **121. o'erlook:** Read.   **129.
Good troth, good sooth:** Indeed, truly.   **132. lord of:** Possessor
of; **gentleness:** Courtesy.   **133. of:** By.   **134. abus'd:** Ill
treated.

149. eat: Ate (pronounced *et*).   **150. prey:** Act of preying.
154. of all loves: For all love's sake.   **156. [S.D.]** *Manet
Titania:* Titania remains.   **III, I. Location:** Scene continues.
2. marvailes: Marvelous.   **4. brake:** Thicket; **tiring-house:**
Attiring area, hence backstage.   **8. bully:** Worthy, jolly, fine
fellow.   **13. By'r lakin:** By our ladykin, the Virgin Mary;
parlous: Perilous.   **15. when all is done:** When all is said
and done.

Write me° a prologue; and let the prologue seem
to say, we will do no harm with our swords and
that Pyramus is not kill'd indeed; and, for the more
20 better assurance, tell them that I Pyramus am not
Pyramus, but Bottom the weaver. This will put
them out of fear.

QUINCE: Well, we will have such a prologue, and it
shall be written in eight and six.°

25 BOTTOM: No, make it two more; let it be written in
eight and eight.

SNOUT: Will not the ladies be afeard of the lion?

STARVELING: I fear it, I promise you.

BOTTOM: Masters, you ought to consider with your-
30 selves, to bring in — God shield us! — a lion among
ladies,° is a most dreadful thing. For there is not
a more fearful° wild-fowl than your lion living;
and we ought to look to 't.

SNOUT: Therefore another prologue must tell he is not
35 a lion.

BOTTOM: Nay, you must name his name, and half his
face must be seen through the lion's neck, and he
himself must speak through, saying thus, or to the
same defect:° "Ladies" — or "Fair ladies — I would
40 wish you" — or "I would request you" — or "I
would entreat you — not to fear, not to tremble;
my life for yours.° If you think I come hither as a
lion, it were pity of my life.° No, I am no such
thing; I am a man as other men are." And there
45 indeed let him name his name, and tell them plainly
he is Snug the joiner.

QUINCE: Well, it shall be so. But there is two hard
things: that is, to bring the moonlight into a chamber;
for, you know, Pyramus and Thisby meet by
50 moonlight.

SNOUT: Doth the moon shine that night we play our
play?

BOTTOM: A calendar, a calendar! Look in the almanac.
Find out moonshine, find out moonshine.

[*They consult an almanac.*]

55 QUINCE: Yes, it doth shine that night.

BOTTOM: Why then may you leave a casement of the
great chamber window, where we play, open, and
the moon may shine in at the casement.

QUINCE: Ay; or else one must come in with a bush
of thorns° and a lantern, and say he comes to   60
disfigure,° or to present,° the person of Moonshine.
Then there is another thing: we must have a wall
in the great chamber; for Pyramus and Thisby, says
the story, did talk through the chink of a wall.

SNOUT: You can never bring in a wall. What say you,   65
Bottom?

BOTTOM: Some man or other must present Wall. And
let him have some plaster, or some loam, or some
rough-cast° about him, to signify wall; and let him
hold his fingers thus, and through that cranny shall   70
Pyramus and Thisby whisper.

QUINCE: If that may be, then all is well. Come, sit
down, every mother's son, and rehearse your parts.
Pyramus, you begin. When you have spoken your
speech, enter into that brake, and so every one   75
according to his cue.

(*Enter Robin* [*Puck*].)

PUCK: What hempen° home-spuns have we
        swagg'ring here,
    So near the cradle of the Fairy Queen?
    What, a play toward?° I'll be an auditor;°
    An actor too perhaps, if I see cause.   80

QUINCE: Speak, Pyramus. Thisby, stand forth.

BOTTOM: "Thisby, the flowers of odious savors
        sweet," —

QUINCE: Odors, odors.

BOTTOM: — " Odors savors sweet;
    So hath thy breath, my dearest Thisby dear.   85
    But hark, a voice! Stay thou but here awhile,
    And by and by I will to thee appear."   (*Exit.*)

PUCK: A stranger Pyramus than e'er played here.°
                                              [*Exit.*]

FLUTE: Must I speak now?

QUINCE: Ay, marry, must you; for you must understand   90
he goes but to see a noise that he heard, and is to
come again.

FLUTE: "Most radiant Pyramus, most lily-white of
        hue,
    Of color like the red rose on triumphant brier,
    Most brisky juvenal° and eke° most lovely Jew,°   95

---

17. **Write me:** Write at my suggestion.   24. **eight and six:**
Alternate lines of eight and six syllables, a common ballad
measure.   30–31. **lion among ladies:** A contemporary pam-
phlet tells how at the christening in 1594 of Prince Henry,
eldest son of King James VI of Scotland, later James I of
England, a "blackmoor" instead of a lion drew the triumphal
chariot, since the lion's presence might have "brought some
fear to the nearest".   32. **fearful:** Fear-inspiring.   39. **defect:**
Bottom's blunder for *effect*.   42. **my life for yours:** I pledge
my life to make your lives safe.   43. **it were . . . life:** My
life would be endangered.

59–60. **bush of thorns:** Bundle of thornbush faggots (part
of the accoutrements of the man in the moon, according to
the popular notions of the time, along with his lantern and
his dog).   61. **disfigure:** Quince's blunder for *prefigure*; **present:** Represent.   69. **rough-cast:** A mixture of lime and gravel
used to plaster the outside of buildings.   77. **hempen:** Made
of hemp, a rough fiter.   79. **toward:** About to take place;
auditor: One who listens, i.e., part of the audience.   88.
here: In this theater(?)   95. **brisky juvenal:** Brisk youth; **eke:**
Also. **Jew:** Probably an absurd repetition of the first sysllable
of *juvenal*.

As true as truest horse that yet would never tire.
I'll meet thee, Pyramus, at Ninny's tomb."

QUINCE: "Ninus'° tomb," man. Why, you must not
speak that yet. That you answer to Pyramus. You
100   speak all your part at once, cues and all. Pyramus
enter. Your cue is past; it is, "never tire."

FLUTE: O — "As true as truest horse, that yet
would never tire."

*[Enter Puck, and Bottom as Pyramus with the ass
head.]°*

BOTTOM: "If I were fair,° Thisby, I were° only
thine."

QUINCE: O monstrous! O strange! We are haunted.
105   Pray, masters! Fly, masters! Help!
                    *[Exeunt Quince, Snug, Flute,
                    Snout, and Starveling.]*

PUCK: I'll follow you, I'll lead you about a round,°
Through bog, through bush, through brake,
through brier.
Sometime a horse I'll be, sometime a hound,
A hog, a headless bear, sometime a fire;°
And neigh, and bark, and grunt, and roar, and
110   burn,
Like horse, hound, hog, bear, fire, at every turn.
                                    (Exit.)

BOTTOM: Why do they run away? This is a knavery
of them to make me afeard.

(Enter Snout.)

SNOUT: O Bottom, thou art chang'd! What do I see
115   on thee?

BOTTOM: What do you see? You see an ass-head of
your own, do you?   *[Exit Snout.]*

(Enter Quince.)

QUINCE: Bless thee, Bottom, bless thee! Thou art
translated.°   *(Exit.)*
120   BOTTOM: I see their knavery. This is to make an ass
of me, to fright me, if they could. But I will not
stir from this place, do what they can. I will walk
up and down here, and I will sing, that they shall
hear I am not afraid.   *[Sings.]*
125   The woosel cock° so black of hue,
With orange-tawny bill,

The throstle° with his note so true,
The wren with little quill° —

TITANIA [*awaking*]: What angel wakes me from my
flow'ry bed?

BOTTOM [*sings*]: The finch, the sparrow, and the
lark,   130
The plain-song° cuckoo grey,
Whose note full many a man doth mark,
And dares not answer nay° —
For, indeed, who would set his wit to so foolish
a bird? Who would give a bird the lie,°   135
though he cry "cuckoo" never so?°

TITANIA: I pray thee, gentle mortal, sing again.
Mine ear is much enamored of thy note;
So is mine eye enthralled to thy shape;
And thy fair virtue's force° perforce doth move
me   140
On the first view to say, to swear, I love thee.

BOTTOM: Methinks, mistress, you should have little
reason for that. And yet, to say the truth, reason
and love keep little company together nowadays.
The more the pity that some honest neighbors will   145
not make them friends. Nay, I can gleek° upon
occasion.

TITANIA: Thou art as wise as thou art beautiful.

BOTTOM: Not so, neither. But if I had wit enough to
get out of this wood, I have enough to serve mine   150
own turn.°

TITANIA: Out of this wood do not desire to go.
Thou shalt remain here, whether thou wilt or
no.
I am a spirit of no common rate.°
The summer still° doth tend upon my state;°   155
And I do love thee. Therefore, go with me.
I'll give thee fairies to attend on thee,
And they shall fetch thee jewels from the deep,
And sing while thou on pressed flowers dost
sleep.
And I will purge thy mortal grossness so   160
That thou shalt like an airy spirit go.
Peaseblossom, Cobweb, Moth,° and
Mustardseed!

*(Enter four Fairies [Peaseblossom, Cobweb, Moth, and
Mustardseed].)*

---

98. **Ninus:** Mythical founder of Nineveh (whose wife, Semiramis, was supposed to have built the walls of Babylon where the story of Pyramis and Thisbe takes place).   102. **[S.D.] with the ass head:** This stage direction, taken from the Folio, presumably refers to a standard stage property. 103. **fair:** handsome; **were:** Would be.   106. **about a round:** Roundabout.   109. **fire:** Will-o'-the-wisp.   119. **translated:** Transformed.   125. **woosel cock:** Male ousel or ouzel, blackbird.

127. **throstle:** Song thrush.   128. **quill:** Literally, a reed pipe; hence, the bird's piping song.   131. **plain-song:** Singing a melody without variations.   133. **dares . . . nay:** Cannot deny that he is a cuckold.   135. **give . . . lie:** Call the bird a liar.   136. **never so:** Ever so much.   139. **thy . . . force:** The power of your beauty.   146. **gleek:** Scoff, jest.   150–151. **serve . . . turn:** Answer my purpose.   154. **rate:** Rank, value.   155. **still:** Ever always; **doth . . . state:** Waits upon me as part of my royal retinue.   162. **Moth:** Mote, speck. (The two words *moth* and *mote* were pronounced alike.)

PEASEBLOSSOM: Ready.
COBWEB: And I.
MOTH: And I.
MUSTARDSEED: And I.
ALL: Where shall we go?
165 TITANIA: Be kind and courteous to this gentleman.
      Hop in his walks and gambol in his eyes;
      Feed him with apricocks and dewberries,
      With purple grapes, green figs, and mulberries;
      The honey-bags steal from the humble-bees,
170   And for night-tapers crop their waxen thighs
      And light them at the fiery glow-worm's eyes,
      To have my love to bed and to arise;
      And pluck the wings from painted butterflies
      To fan the moonbeams from his sleeping eyes.
175   Nod to him, elves, and do him courtesies.
PEASEBLOSSOM: Hail, mortal!
COBWEB: Hail!
MOTH: Hail!
MUSTARDSEED: Hail!
180 BOTTOM: I cry your worship's mercy, heartily. I beseech
      your worship's name.
COBWEB: Cobweb.
BOTTOM: I shall desire you of more acquaintance,
      good Master Cobweb. If I cut my finger, I shall
185   make bold with you.° Your name, honest gentleman?
PEASEBLOSSOM: Peaseblossom.
BOTTOM: I pray you, commend me to Mistress Squash,°
      your mother, and to Master Peascod,° your father.
      Good Master Peaseblossom, I shall desire you of
190   more acquaintance too. Your name, I beseech you,
      sir?
MUSTARDSEED: Mustardseed.
BOTTOM: Good Master Mustardseed, I know your
      patience° well. That same cowardly, giant-like ox-
195   beef hath devour'd many a gentleman of your house.
      I promise you your kindred hath made my eyes
      water ere now. I desire you of more acquaintance,
      good Master Mustardseed.
TITANIA: Come wait upon him; lead him to my
      bower.
200   The moon methinks looks with a wat'ry eye;
      And when she weeps,° weeps every little flower,
      Lamenting some enforced° chastity.
      Tie up my lover's tongue, bring him silently.
                                      (*Exeunt*.)

[Scene II]°

(*Enter* [*Oberon*,] *King of Fairies*.)

OBERON: I wonder if Titania be awak'd;
      Then, what it was that next came in her eye,
      Which she must dote on in extremity.

([*Enter*] *Robin Goodfellow* [*Puck*].)

      Here comes my messenger. How now, mad
         spirit?
      What night-rule° now about this haunted° grove?   5
PUCK: My mistress with a monster is in love.
      Near to her close° and consecrated bower,
      While she was in her dull° and sleeping hour,
      A crew of patches,° rude mechanicals,°
      That work for bread upon Athenian stalls,   10
      Were met together to rehearse a play
      Intended for great Theseus' nuptial day.
      The shallowest thick-skin of that barren sort,°
      Who Pyramus presented,° in their sport
      Forsook his scene° and ent'red in a brake.   15
      When I did him at this advantage take,
      An ass's nole° I fixed on his head.
      Anon his Thisby must be answered,
      And forth my mimic° comes. When they him
         spy,
      As wild geese that the creeping fowler eye,   20
      Or russet-pated choughs,° many in sort,°
      Rising and cawing at the gun's report,
      Sever° themselves and madly sweep the sky,
      So, at his sight, away his fellows fly;
      And, at our stamp, here o'er and o'er one falls;   25
      He murder cries and help from Athens calls.
      Their sense thus weak, lost with their fears thus
         strong,
      Made senseless things begin to do them wrong,
      For briers and thorns at their apparel snatch;
      Some, sleeves — some, hats; from yielders all
         things catch.   30
      I led them on in this distracted fear
      And left sweet Pyramus translated there,
      When in that moment, so it came to pass,
      Titania wak'd and straightway lov'd an ass.
OBERON: This falls out better than I could devise.   35
      But hast thou yet latch'd° the Athenian's eyes
      With the love-juice, as I did bid thee do?

184–185. If . . . you: Cobwebs were used to stanch bleeding.
187. Squash: Unripe pea pod.   188. Peascod: Ripe pea pod.
193–194. your patience: What you have endured.   201. she
weeps: I.e., she causes dew.   202. enforced: Forced, violated;
or, possibly, constrained (since Titania at this moment is
hardly concerned about chastity).

III, II. Location: The wood.   5. night-rule: Diversion for the
night; haunted: Much frequented.   7. close: Secret, private.
8. dull: Drowsy.   9. patches: Clowns, fools; rude mechanicals:
Ignorant artisans.   13. barren sort: Stupid company or crew.
14. presented: Acted.   15. scene: Playing area.   17. nole:
Noddle, head.   19. mimic: Burlesque actor.   21. russet-
pated choughs: Gray-headed jackdaws; in sort: In a flock.
23. Sever: Scatter.   36. latch'd: Moistened, anointed.

PUCK: I took him sleeping — that is finish'd too —
And the Athenian woman by his side,
That, when he wak'd, of force° she must be
40   ey'd.

(*Enter Demetrius and Hermia.*)

OBERON: Stand close. This is the same Athenian.
PUCK: This is the woman, but not this the man.
                      [*They stand aside.*]
DEMETRIUS: O, why rebuke you him that loves you
    so?
Lay breath so bitter on your bitter foe.
HERMIA: Now I but chide; but I should use thee
45   worse,
For thou, I fear, hast given me cause to curse.
If thou hast slain Lysander in his sleep,
Being o'er shoes in blood, plunge in the deep,
And kill me too.
50 The sun was not so true unto the day
As he to me. Would he have stolen away
From sleeping Hermia? I'll believe as soon
This whole° earth may be bor'd and that the
    moon
May through the center creep and so displease
55 Her brother's° noontide with th' Antipodes.°
It cannot be but thou has murd'red him;
So should a murderer look, so dead,° so grim.
DEMETRIUS: So should the murdered look, and so
    should I,
Pierc'd through the heart with your stern cruelty.
60 Yet you, the murderer, look as bright, as clear,
As yonder Venus in her glimmering sphere.
HERMIA: What's this to my Lysander? Where is he?
Ah, good Demetrius, wilt thou give him me?
DEMETRIUS: I had rather give his carcass to my
    hounds.
HERMIA: Out dog! Out cur! Thou driv'st me past
65   the bounds
Of maiden's patience. Hast thou slain him, then?
Henceforth be never numb'red among men!
O, once tell true, tell true, even for my sake!
Durst thou have look'd upon him being awake,
And hast thou kill'd him sleeping? O brave
70   touch!°
Could not a worm,° an adder, do so much?
An adder did it; for with doubler tongue
Than thine, thou serpent, never adder stung.

DEMETRIUS: You spend your passion° on a mispris'd
    mood.°
I am not guilty of Lysander's blood,   75
Nor is he dead, for aught that I can tell.
HERMIA: I pray thee, tell me then that he is well.
DEMETRIUS: An if I could, what should I get
    therefore?
HERMIA: A privilege never to see me more.
And from thy hated presence part I so.   80
See me no more, whether he be dead or no.
                        (*Exit.*)
DEMETRIUS: There is no following her in this fierce
    vein.
Here therefore for a while I will remain.
So sorrow's heaviness doth heavier° grow
For debt that bankrupt° sleep doth sorrow owe;   85
Which now in some slight measure it will pay,
If for his tender here I make some stay.°
               (*Lie down [and sleep].*)
OBERON: What hast thou done? Thou hast
    mistaken quite
And laid the love-juice on some true-love's sight.
Of thy misprision° must perforce ensue   90
Some true love turn'd and not a false turn'd
    true.
PUCK: Then fate o'er-rules, that, one man holding
    troth,°
A million fail, confounding oath on oath.°
OBERON: About the wood go swifter than the wind,
And Helena of Athens look thou find.   95
All fancy-sick° she is and pale of cheer°
With sighs of love, that cost the fresh blood°
    dear.
By some illusion see thou bring her here.
I'll charm his eyes against she do appear.°
PUCK: I go, I go; look how I go   100
Swifter than arrow from the Tartar's bow.°
                        [*Exit.*]

---

74. passion: Violent feelings; **mispris'd mood:** Anger based on misconception.   **84. heavier:** (1) Harder to bear, (2) more drowsy.   **85. bankrupt:** Demetrius is saying that his sleepiness adds to the weariness caused by sorrow.   **86–87. Which . . . stay:** To a small extent I will be able to "pay back" and hence find some relief from sorrow, if I pause here a while (*make some stay*) while sleep "tenders" or offers itself by way of paying the debt owed to sorrow.   **90 misprision:** Mistake.   **92. troth:** Faith.   **93. confounding . . . oath:** Invalidating one oath with another.   **96. fancy-sick:** Lovesick; **cheer:** Face.   **97. sighs . . . blood:** An allusion to the physiological theory that each sigh costs the heart a drop of blood.   **99. against . . . appear:** in anticipation of her coming.   **101. Tartar's bow:** Tartars were famed for their skill with the bow.

---

40. of force: Perforce.   **53. whole:** Solid.   **55. Her brother's:** I.e., the sun's; **th' Antipodes:** The people on the opposite side of the earth.   **57. dead:** Deadly, or deathly pale.   **70. brave touch:** Noble exploit (said ironically).   **71. worm:** Serpent.

OBERON: Flower of this purple dye,
    Hit with Cupid's archery.
    Sink in apple of his eye.
        [*Applies love-juice to Demetrius' eyes.*]
105   When his love he doth espy,
    Let her shine as gloriously
    As the Venus of the sky.
    When thou wak'st, if she be by,
    Beg of her for remedy.

(*Enter Puck.*)

110 PUCK: Captain of our fairy band,
    Helena is here at hand,
    And the youth, mistook by me,
    Pleading for a lover's fee.°
    Shall we their fond pageant° see?
115   Lord, what fools these mortals be!
OBERON: Stand aside. The noise they make
    Will cause Demetrius to awake.
PUCK: Then will two at once woo one;
    That must needs be sport alone;°
120   And those things do best please me
    That befall prepost'rously.°
        [*They stand aside.*]

(*Enter Lysander and Helena.*)

LYSANDER: Why should you think that I should
        woo in scorn?
    Scorn and derision never come in tears.
    Look when° I vow, I weep; and vows so born,
125   In their nativity all truth appears.°
    How can these things in me seem scorn to you,
    Bearing the badge° of faith, to prove them true?
HELENA: You do advance° your cunning more and
        more.
    When truth kills truth,° O devilish-holy fray!
    These vows are Hermia's. Will you give her
130   o'er?
    Weigh oath with oath, and you will nothing
        weigh.
    Your vows to her and me, put in two scales,
    Will even weigh, and both as light as tales.°
LYSANDER: I had no judgment when to her I swore.

HELENA: Nor none, in my mind, now you give her
        o'er.   135
LYSANDER: Demetrius loves her, and he loves not
        you.
DEMETRIUS [*awaking*]: O Helen, goddess, nymph,
        perfect, divine!
    To what, my love, shall I compare thine eyne?
    Crystal is muddy. O, how ripe in show°
    Thy lips, those kissing cherries, tempting grow!   140
    That pure congealed white, high Taurus'° snow,
    Fann'd with the eastern wind, turns to a crow°
    When thou hold'st up thy hand. O, let me kiss
    This princess of pure white, this seal° of bliss!
HELENA: O spite! O hell! I see you all are bent   145
    To set against me for your merriment.
    If you were civil and knew courtesy,
    You would not do me thus much injury.
    Can you not hate me, as I know you do,
    But you must join in souls to mock me too?   150
    If you were men, as men you are in show,
    You would not use a gentle lady so —
    To vow, and swear, and superpraise° my parts,°
    When I am sure you hate me with your hearts.
    You both are rivals, and love Hermia;   155
    And now both rivals, to mock Helena.
    A trim° exploit, a manly enterprise,
    To conjure tears up in a poor maid's eyes
    With your derision! None of noble sort
    Would so offend a virgin and extort°   160
    A poor soul's patience, all to make you sport.
LYSANDER: You are unkind, Demetrius. Be not so;
    For you love Hermia; this you know I know.
    And here, with all good will, with all my heart,
    In Hermia's love I yield you up my part;   165
    And yours of Helena to me bequeath,
    Whom I do love and will do till my death.
HELENA: Never did mockers waste more idle
        breath.
DEMETRIUS: Lysander, keep thy Hermia; I will
        none.°
    If e'er I lov'd her, all that love is gone.   170
    My heart to her but as guest-wise sojourn'd,
    And now to Helen is it home return'd.
    There to remain.
LYSANDER: Helen, it is not so.
DEMETRIUS: Disparage not the faith thou dost not
        know,

---

113. **fee:** Privilege, reward.   114. **fond pageant:** Foolish
exhibition.   119. **alone:** Unequaled.   121. **prepost'rously:**
Out of the natural order.   124. **Look when:** Whenever.
124–125. **vows . . . appears:** Vows made by one who is
weeping give evidence thereby of their sincerity.   127. **badge:**
Identifying device such as that worn on servants' livery.   128.
advance: Carry forward, display.   129. **truth kills truth:**
One of Lysander's vows must invalidate the other.   133.
tales: Lies.

139. **show:** Appearance.   141. **Taurus:** A lofty mountain
range in Asia Minor.   142. **turns to a crow:** Seems black
by contrast.   144. **seal:** Pledge.   153. **superpraise:** Overpraise;
parts: Qualities.   157. **trim:** Pretty, fine (said ironically).
160. **extort:** Twist, torture.   169. **will none:** Wish none of
her.

175 Lest, to thy peril, thou aby° it dear.
    Look where thy love comes; yonder is thy dear.

(Enter Hermia.)

HERMIA: Dark night, that from the eye his°
        function takes,
    The ear more quick of apprehension makes;
    Wherein it doth impair the seeing sense,
180 It pays the hearing double recompense.
    Thou art not by mine eye, Lysander, found;
    Mine ear, I thank it, brought me to thy sound.
    But why unkindly didst thou leave me so?
LYSANDER: Why should he stay, whom love doth
        press to go?
HERMIA: What love could press Lysander from my
185   side?
LYSANDER: Lysander's love, that would not let him
        bide,
    Fair Helena, who more engilds the night
    Than all yon fiery oes° and eyes of light.
    Why seek'st thou me? Could not this make thee
        know,
190 The hate I bear thee made me leave thee so?
HERMIA: You speak not as you think. It cannot be.
HELENA: Lo, she is one of this confederacy!
    Now I perceive they have conjoin'd all three
    To fashion this false sport, in spite of me.°
195 Injurious Hermia, most ungrateful maid!
    Have you conspir'd, have you with these
        contriv'd°
    To bait° me with this foul derision?
    Is all the counsel° that we two have shar'd,
    The sisters' vows, the hours that we have spent,
200 When we have chid the hasty-footed time
    For parting us — O, is all forgot?
    All school-days friendship, childhood innocence?
    We, Hermia, like two artificial° gods,
    Have with our needles created both one flower,
205 Both on one sampler, sitting on one cushion,
    Both warbling of one song, both in one key,
    As if our hands, our sides, voices, and minds
    Had been incorporate. So we grew together,
    Like to a double cherry, seeming parted,
210 But yet an union in partition;
    Two lovely° berries molded on one stem;
    So, with two seeming bodies, but one heart;
    Two of the first, like coats in heraldry,

Due but to one and crowned with one crest.°
And will you rent° our ancient love asunder,   215
To join with men in scorning your poor friend?
It is not friendly, 'tis not maidenly.
Our sex, as well as I, may chide you for it,
Though I alone do feel the injury.
HERMIA: I am amazed at your passionate words.   220
    I scorn you not. It seems that you scorn me.
HELENA: Have you not set Lysander, as in scorn,
    To follow me and praise my eyes and face?
    And made your other love, Demetrius,
    Who even but now did spurn me with his foot,   225
    To call me goddess, nymph, divine and rare,
    Precious, celestial? Wherefore speaks he this
    To her he hates? And wherefore doth Lysander
    Deny your love, so rich within his soul,
    And tender° me, forsooth, affection,   230
    But by your setting on, by your consent?
    What though I be not so in grace° as you,
    So hung upon with love, so fortunate,
    But miserable most, to love unlov'd?
    This you should pity rather than despise.   235
HERMIA: I understand not what you mean by this.
HELENA: Ay, do! Persever, counterfeit sad° looks,
    Make mouths° upon° me when I turn my back,
    Wink each at other, hold the sweet jest up.
    This sport, well carried,° shall be chronicled.   240
    If you have any pity, grace, or manners,
    You would not make me such an argument.°
    But fare ye well. 'Tis partly my own fault,
    Which death, or absence, soon shall remedy.
LYSANDER: Stay, gentle Helena; hear my excuse,   245
    My love, my life, my soul, fair Helena!
HELENA: O excellent!
HERMIA: Sweet, do not scorn her so.
DEMETRIUS: If she cannot entreat,° I can compel.
LYSANDER: Thou canst compel no more than she
        entreat.
    Thy threats have no more strength than her
        weak prayers.   250
    Helen, I love thee, by my life, I do!
    I swear by that which I will lose for thee,
    To prove him false that says I love thee not.
DEMETRIUS: I say I love thee more than he can do.
LYSANDER: If thou say so, withdraw, and prove it
        too.   255

213–214. Two . . . crest: We have two separate bodies, just as a coat of arms in heraldry can be represented twice on a shield but surmounted by a single crest.   215. rent: Rend.   230. tender: Offer.   232. grace: Favor.   237. sad: Grave, serious.   238. mouths: Mows, faces, grimaces; upon: At.   240. carried: Managed.   242. argument: Subject for a jest.   248. entreat: Succeed by entreaty.

175. aby: Pay for.   177. his: Its.   188. oes: Circles, orbs, stars.   194. in spite of me: To vex me.   196. contriv'd: Plotted.   197. bait: Torment, as one sets on dogs to bait a bear.   198. counsel: Confidential talk.   203. artificial: Skilled in art or creation.   211. lovely: Loving.

DEMETRIUS: Quick, come!
HERMIA: Lysander, whereto tends all this?
LYSANDER: Away, you Ethiope!°
           [*He tries to break away from Hermia.*]
DEMETRIUS: No, no; he'll
  Seem to break loose; take on as you would
    follow,
  But yet come not. You are a tame man, go!
LYSANDER: Hang off,° thou cat, thou burr! Vile
260   thing, let loose,
  Or I will shake thee from me like a serpent!
HERMIA: Why are you grown so rude? What
    change is this,
  Sweet love?
LYSANDER: Thy love? Out, tawny Tartar, out!
  Out, loathed med'cine!° O hated potion, hence!
HERMIA: Do you not jest?
265 HELENA: Yes, sooth,° and so do you.
LYSANDER: Demetrius, I will keep my word with
  thee.
DEMETRIUS: I would I had your bond, for I perceive
  A weak bond° holds you. I'll not trust your
  word.
LYSANDER: What, should I hurt her, strike her, kill
  her dead?
270 Although I hate her, I'll not harm her so.
HERMIA: What, can you do me greater harm than
  hate?
  Hate me? Wherefore? O me, what news,° my
    love?
  Am not I Hermia? Are not you Lysander?
  I am as fair now as I was erewhile.°
275 Since night you lov'd me; yet since night you left
    me.
  Why, then you left me — O, the gods forbid! —
  In earnest, shall I say?
LYSANDER: Ay, by my life!
  And never did desire to see thee more.
  Therefore be out of hope, of question, of doubt;
280 Be certain, nothing truer. 'Tis no jest
  That I do hate thee and love Helena.
HERMIA: O me! You juggler! You cankerblossom!°
  You thief of love! What, have you come by
    night
  And stol'n my love's heart from him?
HELENA: Fine, i' faith!

Have you no modesty, no maiden shame,   285
No touch of bashfulness? What, will you tear
Impatient answers from my gentle tongue?
Fie, fie! You counterfeit, you puppet,° you!
HERMIA: Puppet? Why so? Ay, that way goes the
  game.
  Now I perceive that she hath made compare   290
  Between our statures; she hath urg'd her height,
  And with her personage, her tall personage,
  Her height, forsooth, she hath prevail'd with
    him.
  And are you grown so high in his esteem,
  Because I am so dwarfish and so low?   295
  How low am I, thou painted maypole? Speak!
  How low am I? I am not yet so low
  But that my nails can reach unto thine eyes.
     [*She flails at Helena, but is restrained.*]
HELENA: I pray you, though you mock me,
    gentlemen,
  Let her not hurt me. I was never curst;°   300
  I have no gift at all in shrewishness;
  I am a right° maid for my cowardice.
  Let her not strike me. You perhaps may think,
  Because she is something° lower than myself,
  That I can match her.
HERMIA: Lower! Hark, again!   305
HELENA: Good Hermia, do not be so bitter with
  me.
  I evermore did love you, Hermia,
  Did ever keep your counsels, never wrong'd you;
  Save that, in love unto Demetrius,
  I told him of your stealth° unto this wood.   310
  He followed you; for love I followed him.
  But he hath chid me hence and threat'ned me
  To strike me, spurn me, nay, to kill me too.
  And now, so° you will let me quiet go,
  To Athens will I bear my folly back   315
  And follow you no further. Let me go.
  You see how simple and how fond° I am.
HERMIA: Why, get you gone. Who is 't that hinders
  you?
HELENA: A foolish heart, that I leave here behind.
HERMIA: What, with Lysander?
HELENA: With Demetrius.   320
LYSANDER: Be not afraid; she shall not harm thee,
  Helena.
DEMETRIUS: No, sir, she shall not, though you take
  her part.

---

257. Ethiope: Referring to Hermia's relatively dark hair and complexion; see also *tawny Tartar* six lines later. **260. Hang off:** Let go. **264. sooth:** Poison. **265. sooth:** Truly. **268. weak bond:** Hermia's arm (with a pun on *bond*, oath, in the previous line). **272. what news:** What is the matter. **274. erewhile:** Just now. **282. cankerblossom:** Worm that destroys the flower bud(?).

288. puppet: (1) Counterfeit; (2) dwarfish woman (in reference to Hermia's smaller stature). **300. curst:** Shrewish. **302. right:** True. **304. something:** Somewhat. **310. stealth:** Stealing away. **314. so:** If only. **317. fond:** Foolish.

HELENA: O, when she is angry, she is keen and
 shrewd!°
 She was a vixen when she went to school;
325 And though she be but little, she is fierce.
HERMIA: "Little" again! Nothing but "low" and
 "little"!
 Why will you suffer her to flout me thus?
 Let me come to her.
LYSANDER: Get you gone, you dwarf!
 You minimus,° of hind'ring knot-grass° made!
 You bead, you acorn!
330 DEMETRIUS: You are too officious
 In her behalf that scorns your services.
 Let her alone. Speak not of Helena;
 Take not her part. For, if thou dost intend°
 Never so little show of love to her,
 Thou shalt aby° it.
335 LYSANDER: Now she holds me not;
 Now follow, if thou dar'st, to try whose right,
 Of thine or mine, is most in Helena. [Exit.]
DEMETRIUS: Follow? Nay, I'll go with thee, cheek
 by jowl.°
     [Exit, following Lysander.]
HERMIA: You, mistress, all this coil° is 'long of°
 you.
 Nay, go not back.°
340 HELENA: I will not trust you, I,
 Nor longer stay in your curst company.
 Your hands than mine are quicker for a fray;
 My legs are longer, though, to run away. [Exit.]
HERMIA: I am amaz'd, and know not what to say.
       (Exit.)
345 OBERON: This is thy negligence. Still thou mistak'st,
 Or else committ'st thy knaveries willfully.
PUCK: Believe me, king of shadows, I mistook.
 Did not you tell me I should know the man
 By the Athenian garments he had on?
350 And so far blameless proves my enterprise
 That I have 'nointed an Athenian's eyes;
 And so far am I glad it so did sort°
 As this their jangling I esteem a sport.
OBERON: Thou see'st these lovers seek a place to
 fight.
355 Hie therefore, Robin, overcast the night;
 The starry welkin° cover thou anon
 With drooping fog as black as Acheron,°

And lead these testy rivals so astray
As° one come not within another's way.
Like to Lysander sometime frame thy tongue, 360
Then stir Demetrius up with bitter wrong;°
And sometime rail thou like Demetrius.
And from each other look thou lead them thus,
Till o'er their brows death-counterfeiting sleep
With leaden legs and batty° wings doth creep. 365
Then crush this herb° into Lysander's eye,
      [Gives herb.]
Whose liquor hath this virtuous° property,
To take from thence all error with his° might
And make his eyeballs roll with wonted° sight.
When they next wake, all this derision° 370
Shall seem a dream and fruitless vision,
And back to Athens shall the lovers wend
With league whose date° till death shall never
 end.
Whiles I in this affair do thee employ,
I'll to my queen and beg her Indian boy; 375
And then I will her charmed eye release
From monster's view, and all things shall be
 peace.
PUCK: My fairy lord, this must be done with haste,
For night's swift dragons° cut the clouds full
 fast,
And yonder shines Aurora's harbinger,° 380
At whose approach, ghosts, wand'ring here and
 there,
Troop home to churchyards. Damned spirits all,
That in crossways and floods have burial,°
Already to their wormy beds are gone.
For fear lest day should look their shames upon, 385
They willfully themselves exile from light
And must for aye° consort with black-brow'd
 night.
OBERON: But we are spirits of another sort.
I with the Morning's love° have oft made sport,
And, like a forester,° the groves may tread 390
Even till the eastern gate, all fiery-red,

---

359. As: That. 361. wrong: Insults. 365. batty: Batlike.
366. this herb: The antidote (mentioned in III, I, line 184)
to love-in-idleness. 367. virtuous: Efficacious. 368. his:
Its. 369. wonted: Accustomed. 370. derision: Laughable
business. 373. date: Term of existence. 379. dragons:
Supposed by Shakespeare to be yoked to the car of the
goddess of night. 380. Aurora's harbinger: The morning
star, precursor of dawn. 383. crossways . . . burial: Those
who had committed suicide where buried at crossways, with
a stake driven through them; those drowned, i.e., buried in
floods or great waters, would be condemned to wander dis-
consolate for want of burial rites. 387. for aye: Forever.
389. Morning's love: Cephalus, a beautiful youth beloved
by Aurora; or perhaps the goddess of the dawn herself.
390. forester: Keeper of a royal forest.

---

323. shrewd: Shrewish. 329. minimus: Diminutive creature;
knot-grass: A weed, an infusion of which was thought to
stunt the growth. 333. intend: Give sign of. 335. aby:
Pay for. 338. cheek by jowl: Side by side. 339. coil:
Turmoil, dissension; 'long of: On account of. 340. go not
back: Don't retreat. (Hermia is again proposing a fight.)
352. sort: Turn out. 356. welkin: Sky. 357. Acheron:
River of Hades (here representing Hades itself).

Opening on Neptune with fair blessed beams,
Turns into yellow gold his salt green streams.
But, notwithstanding, haste; make no delay.
395 We may effect this business yet ere day.   [*Exit.*]
PUCK: Up and down, up and down,
I will lead them up and down.
I am fear'd in field and town.
Goblin, lead them up and down.
400 Here comes one.

(*Enter Lysander.*)

LYSANDER: Where art thou, proud Demetrius?
Speak thou now.
PUCK [*mimicking Demetrius*]: Here, villain, drawn°
and ready. Where art thou?
LYSANDER: I will be with thee straight.°
PUCK: Follow me, then,
To plainer° ground.
[*Lysander wanders about, following the voice.*]°

(*Enter Demetrius.*)

DEMETRIUS: Lysander! Speak again!
405 Thou runaway, thou coward, art thou fled?
Speak! In some bush? Where dost thou hide thy
head?
PUCK [*mimicking Lysander*]: Thou coward, art thou
bragging to the stars,
Telling the bushes that thou look'st for wars,
And wilt not come? Come, recreant;° come, thou
child,
410 I'll whip thee with a rod. He is defil'd
That draws a sword on thee.
DEMETRIUS: Yea, art thou there?
PUCK: Follow my voice. We'll try° no manhood
here.
(*Exeunt.*)

[*Lysander returns.*]

LYSANDER: He goes before me and still dares me
on.
When I come where he calls, then he is gone.
415 The villain is much lighter-heel'd than I.
I followed fast, but faster he did fly,
That fallen am I in dark uneven way,
And here will rest me. [*Lies down.*] Come, thou
gentle day!
For if but once thou show me thy gray light,
420 I'll find Demetrius and revenge this spite. [*Sleeps.*]

([*Enter*] *Robin* [*Puck*] *and Demetrius.*)

PUCK: Ho, ho, ho! Coward, why com'st thou not?
DEMETRIUS: Abide me, if thou dar'st; for well I
wot°
Thou runn'st before me, shifting every place,
And dar'st not stand nor look me in the face.
Where art thou now?
PUCK: Come hither. I am here.   425
DEMETRIUS: Nay, then, thou mock'st me. Thou
shalt buy° this dear,°
If ever I thy face by daylight see.
Now, go thy way. Faintness constraineth me
To measure out my length on this cold bed.
By day's approach look to be visited.   430
[*Lies down and sleeps.*]

(*Enter Helena.*)

HELENA: O weary night, O long and tedious night,
Abate° thy hours! Shine, comforts, from the east,
That I may back to Athens by daylight,
From these that my poor company detest;
And sleep, that sometimes shuts up sorrow's eye,   435
Steal me awhile from mine own company.
[*Lies down and*] *sleep*[*s*].
PUCK: Yet but three? Come one more;
Two of both kinds makes up four.
Here she comes, curst and sad.
Cupid is a knavish lad,   440
Thus to make poor females mad.

[*Enter Hermia.*]

HERMIA: Never so weary, never so in woe,
Bedabbled with the dew and torn with briers,
I can no further crawl, no further go;
My legs can keep no pace with my desires.   445
Here will I rest me till the break of day.
Heavens shield Lysander, if they mean a fray!
[*Lies down and sleeps.*]
PUCK: On the ground
Sleep sound.
I'll apply   450
To your eye,
Gentle lover, remedy.
[*Squeezing the juice on Lysander's eyes.*]
When thou wak'st,
Thou tak'st
True delight   455
In the sight
Of thy former lady's eye;
And the country proverb known,
That every man should take his own,

---

402. drawn: With drawn sword.   **403. straight:** Immediately.
404. plainer: Smoother.   **404.** [S.D.] *Lysander wanders about:*
It is not clearly necessary that Lysander exit at this point;
neither exit nor reentrance is indicated in the early texts.
409. recreant: Cowardly wretch.   **412. try:** Test.

422. wot: Know.   **426. buy:** Pay for; **dear:** Dearly.   **432.**
Abate: Lessen, shorten.

460   In your waking shall be shown:
     Jack shall have Jill;
     Nought shall go ill;
     The man shall have his mare again, and all shall
     be well.   *[Exit. Manent the four lovers.]*

[ACT IV · Scene I]°

(Enter [Titania,] Queen of Fairies, and [Bottom the] Clown, and Fairies; and [Oberon,] the King, behind them.)

TITANIA: Come, sit thee down upon this flow'ry
    bed,
   While I thy amiable° cheeks do coy,°
   And stick musk-roses in thy sleek smooth head,
   And kiss thy fair large ears, my gentle joy.
                      [They recline.]

5 BOTTOM: Where's Peaseblossom?
  PEASEBLOSSOM: Ready.
  BOTTOM: Scratch my head, Peaseblossom. Where's
    Mounsieur Cobweb?
  COBWEB: Ready.
10 BOTTOM: Mounsieur Cobweb, good mounsieur, get
    you your weapons in your hand, and kill me a red-
    hipp'd humble-bee on the top of a thistle; and,
    good mounsieur, bring me the honey-bag. Do not
    fret yourself too much in the action, mounsieur;
15   and, good mounsieur, have a care the honey-bag
    break not; I would be loath to have you overflown
    with a honey-bag, signior. Where's Mounsieur
    Mustardseed?
  MUSTARDSEED: Ready.
20 BOTTOM: Give me your neaf,° Mounsieur Mustardseed.
    Pray you, leave your curtsy,° good mounsieur.
  MUSTARDSEED: What's your will?
  BOTTOM: Nothing, good mounsieur, but to help Cav-
    alery° Cobweb° to scratch. I must to the barber's,
25   mounsieur; for methinks I am marvailes hairy about
    the face; and I am such a tender ass, if my hair
    do but tickle me, I must scratch.
  TITANIA: What, wilt thou hear some music, my
    sweet love?
  BOTTOM: I have a reasonable good ear in music. Let's
30   have the tongs and the bones.°

                  [Music: tongs, rural music.]°
TITANIA: Or say, sweet love, what thou desirest to
    eat.
BOTTOM: Truly, a peck of provender. I could munch
    your good dry oats. Methinks I have a great desire
    to a bottle° of hay. Good hay, sweet hay, hath no
    fellow.°   35
TITANIA: I have a venturous fairy that shall seek
    The squirrel's hoard, and fetch thee new nuts.
BOTTOM: I had rather have a handful or two of dried
    peas. But, I pray you, let none of your people stir
    me. I have an exposition° of sleep come upon me. 40
TITANIA: Sleep thou, and I will wind thee in my
    arms.
   Fairies, be gone, and be all ways° away.
                         [Exeunt fairies.]
   So doth the woodbine the sweet honeysuckle
   Gently entwist; the female ivy so
   Enrings the barky fingers of the elm.   45
   Oh, how I love thee! How I dote on thee!
                            [They sleep.]

(Enter Robin Goodfellow [Puck].)

OBERON [*advancing*]: Welcome, good Robin. See'st
    thou this sweet sight?
   Her dotage now I do begin to pity.
   For, meeting her of late behind the wood,
   Seeking sweet favors° for this hateful fool,   50
   I did upbraid her and fall out with her.
   For she his hairy temples then had rounded
   With coronet of fresh and fragrant flowers;
   And that same dew, which sometime° on the
    buds
   Was wont to swell like round and orient pearls,° 55
   Stood now within the pretty flouriets'° eyes
   Like tears that did their own disgrace bewail.
   When I had at my pleasure taunted her,
   And she in mild terms begg'd my patience,
   I then did ask of her her changeling child;   60
   Which straight she gave me, and her fairy sent
   To bear him to my bower in fairy land.
   And, now I have the boy, I will undo
   This hateful imperfection of her eyes.
   And, gentle Puck, take this transformed scalp 65
   From off the head of this Athenian swain,
   That, he awaking when the other° do,
   May all to Athens back again repair,

IV, I. **Location:** Scene continues. The four lovers are still asleep on stage. **2. amiable:** Lovely; **coy:** Caress. **20. neaf:** Fist. **21. leave your curtsy:** Put on your hat. **23–24. Cavalery:** Cavalier. Form of address for a gentleman. **24. Cobweb:** Seemingly an error, since Cobweb has been sent to bring honey while Peaseblossom has been asked to scratch. **30. tongs . . . bones:** Instruments for rustic music. (The tongs were played like a triangle, whereas the bones were held between the fingers and used as clappers.)

30. [S.D.] *Music . . . music:* This stage direction is added from the Folio. **34. bottle:** Bundle. **35. fellow:** Equal. **40. exposition:** Bottom's word for *disposition.* **42. all ways:** In all directions. **50. favors:** I.e., gifts of flowers. **54. sometime:** Formerly. **55. orient pearls:** The most beautiful of all pearls, those coming from the Orient. **56. flouriets':** Flowerets'. **67. other:** Others.

And think no more of this night's accidents
70 But as the fierce vexation of a dream.
But first I will release the Fairy Queen.
                              [*Squeezes juice in her eyes.*]
Be as thou wast wont to be;
See as thou wast wont to see.
Dian's bud° o'er Cupid's flower
75 Hath such force and blessed power.
Now, my Titania, wake you, my sweet queen.
TITANIA [*waking*]: My Oberon! What visions have I seen!
Methought I was enamor'd of an ass.
OBERON: There lies your love.
TITANIA: How came these things to pass?
80 O, how mine eyes do loathe his visage now!
OBERON: Silence awhile. Robin, take off this head.
Titania, music call, and strike more dead
Than common sleep of all these five° the sense.
TITANIA: Music, ho! Music, such as charmeth sleep!
                              [*Music.*]
PUCK [*removing the ass's head*]: Now, when thou
85 wak'st, with thine own fool's eyes peep.
OBERON: Sound, music! Come, my queen, take hands with me,
And rock the ground whereon these sleepers be.
                              [*Dance.*]
Now thou and I are new in amity,
And will tomorrow midnight solemnly°
90 Dance in Duke Theseus' house triumphantly
And bless it to all fair prosperity.
There shall the pairs of faithful lovers be
Wedded, with Theseus, all in jollity.
PUCK: Fairy King, attend, and mark:
95 I do hear the morning lark.
OBERON: Then, my queen, in silence sad,°
Trip we after night's shade.
We the globe can compass soon,
Swifter than the wand'ring moon.
100 TITANIA: Come, my lord, and in our flight
Tell me how it came this night
That I sleeping here was found
With these mortals on the ground.   (*Exeunt.*)
                              (*Wind horn* [*within*].)

(*Enter Theseus and all his train;* [*Hippolyta, Egeus*].)

THESEUS: Go, one of you, find out the forester,
105 For now our observation° is perform'd;

And since we have the vaward° of the day,
My love shall hear the music of my hounds.
Uncouple in the western valley; let them go.
Dispatch, I say, and find the forester.
                              [*Exit an Attendant.*]
We will, fair queen, up to the mountain's top   110
And mark the musical confusion
Of hounds and echo in conjunction.
HIPPOLYTA: I was with Hercules and Cadmus° once,
When in a wood of Crete they bay'd° the bear
With hounds of Sparta.° Never did I hear   115
Such gallant chiding; for, besides the groves,
The skies, the fountains, every region near
Seem'd all one mutual cry. I never heard
So musical a discord, such sweet thunder.
THESEUS: My hounds are bred out of the Spartan kind,   120
So flew'd,° so sanded;° and their heads are hung
With ears that sweep away the morning dew;
Crook-knee'd, and dewlapp'd° like Thessalian bulls;
Slow in pursuit, but match'd in mouth like bells,
Each under each.° A cry° more tuneable°   125
Was never holla'd to, nor cheer'd with horn,
In Crete, in Sparta, nor in Thessaly.
Judge when you hear. [*Sees the sleepers.*] But, soft! What nymphs are these?
EGEUS: My lord, this' my daughter here asleep;
And this, Lysander; this Demetrius is;   130
This Helena, old Nedar's Helena.
I wonder of their being here together.
THESEUS: No doubt they rose up early to observe
The rite of May, and, hearing our intent,
Came here in grace of our solemnity.°   135
But speak, Egeus. Is not this the day
That Hermia should give answer of her choice?
EGEUS: It is, my lord.
THESEUS: Go, bid the huntsmen wake them with their horns.
                              [*Exit an Attendant.*]

(*Shout within. Wind horns. They all start up.*)

---

74. **Dian's bud:** Perhaps the flower of the *agnus castus* or chaste-tree, supposed to preserve chastity; or perhaps referring simply to Oberon's herb by which he can undo the effects of "Cupid's flower," the love-in-idleness of II, I, lines 166–168.   83. **these five:** I.e., the four lovers and Bottom.   89. **solemnly:** Ceremoniously.   96. **sad:** Sober.   105. **observation:** Observance to a morn of May (I, I, line 167).

106. **vaward:** Vanguard, i.e., earliest part.   113. **Cadmus:** Mythical founder of Thebes. (This story about him is unknown.)   114. **bay'd:** Brought to bay.   115. **hounds of Sparta:** Breed famous in antiquity for their hunting skill.   121. **So flew'd:** Similarly having large hanging chaps or fleshy covering of the jaw; **sanded:** Of sandy color.   123. **dewlapp'd:** Having pendulous folds of skin under the neck.   124–125. **match'd ... each:** Harmoniously matched in their various cries like a set of bells, from treble down to bass.   125. **cry:** Pack of hounds; **tuneable:** Well tuned, melodious.   135. **solemnity:** Observance of these same rites of May.

140   Good morrow, friends. Saint Valentine° is past.
        Begin these wood-birds but to couple now?
LYSANDER: Pardon, my lord.   [*They kneel.*]
THESEUS: I pray you all, stand up.
        I know you two are rival enemies;
        How comes this gentle concord in the world,
145   That hatred is so far from jealousy
        To sleep by hate and fear no enmity?
LYSANDER: My lord, I shall reply amazedly,
        Half sleep, half waking; but as yet, I swear,
        I cannot truly say how I came here.
150   But, as I think — for truly would I speak,
        And now I do bethink me, so it is —
        I came with Hermia hither. Our intent
        Was to be gone from Athens, where° we might,
        Without° the peril of the Athenian law —
155 EGEUS: Enough, enough, my lord; you have enough.
        I beg the law, the law, upon his head.
        They would have stol'n away; they would,
            Demetrius,
        Thereby to have defeated you and me,
        You of your wife and me of my consent,
160   Of my consent that she should be your wife.
DEMETRIUS: My lord, fair Helen told me of their
            stealth,
        Of this their purpose hither to this wood,
        And I in fury hither followed them,
        Fair Helena in fancy following me.
165   But, my good lord, I wot not by what power —
        But by some power it is — my love to Hermia,
        Melted as the snow, seems to me now
        As the remembrance of an idle gaud.°
        Which in my childhood I did dote upon;
170   And all the faith, the virtue of my heart,
        The object and the pleasure of mine eye,
        Is only Helena. To her, my lord,
        Was I betroth'd ere I saw Hermia,
        But like a sickness did I loathe this food;
175   But, as in health, come to my natural taste,
        Now I do wish it, love it, long for it,
        And will for evermore be true to it.
THESEUS: Fair lovers, you are fortunately met.
        Of this discourse we more will hear anon.
180   Egeus, I will overbear your will;
        For in the temple, by and by, with us
        These couples shall eternally be knit.
        And, for° the morning now is something° worn,

        Our purpos'd hunting shall be set aside.
        Away with us to Athens. Three and three,   185
        We'll hold a feast in great solemnity.
        Come, Hippolyta.
            [*Exeunt Theseus, Hippolyta, Egeus, and train.*]
DEMETRIUS: These things seem small and
            undistinguishable,
        Like far-off mountains turned into clouds.
HERMIA: Methinks I see these things with parted°
            eye,   190
        When every thing seems double.
HELENA: So methinks;
        And I have found Demetrius like a jewel,
        Mine own, and not mine own.°
DEMETRIUS: Are you sure
        That we are awake? It seems to me
        That yet we sleep, we dream. Do not you think   195
        The Duke was here, and bid us follow him?
HERMIA: Yea, and my father.
HELENA: And Hippolyta.
LYSANDER: And he did bid us follow to the temple.
DEMETRIUS: Why, then, we are awake. Let's follow
            him,
        And by the way let us recount our dreams.   200
                                              [*Exeunt.*]
BOTTOM [*awaking*]: When my cue comes, call me,
        and I will answer. My next is, "Most fair Pyramus."
        Heigh-ho! Peter Quince! Flute, the bellows-mender!
        Snout, the tinker! Starveling! God's my life, stol'n
        hence, and left me asleep! I have had a most rare   205
        vision. I have had a dream, past the wit of man
        to say what dream it was. Man is but an ass, if
        he go about° to expound this dream. Methought
        I was — there is no man can tell what. Methought
        I was — and methought I had — but man is but   210
        a patch'd° fool, if he will offer° to say what me-
        thought I had. The eye of man hath not heard, the
        ear of man hath not seen, man's hand is not able
        to taste, his tongue to conceive, nor his heart to
        report, what my dream was. I will get Peter Quince 215
        to write a ballad of this dream. It shall be call'd
        "Bottom's Dream," because it hath no bottom; and
        I will sing it in the latter end of a play, before the
        Duke. Peradventure, to make it the more gracious,
        I shall sing it at her° death.   [*Exit.*]   220

---

140. Saint Valentine: Birds were supposed to choose their mates on St. Valentine's Day.   **153. where:** Wherever; or to where.   **154. Without:** Outside of, beyond.   **168. idle gaud:** Worthless trinket.   **183. for:** Since; **something:** Somewhat.

190. parted: Improperly focused.   **192–193. like . . . mine own:** Like a jewel that one finds by chance and therefore possesses but cannot certainly consider one's own property.   **208. go about:** Attempt.   **211. patch'd:** Wearing motley, i.e., a dress of various colors; **offer:** venture.   **220. her:** Thisby's(?)

[Scene II]°

(*Enter Quince, Flute, [Snout, and Starveling].*)

QUINCE: Have you sent to Bottom's house? Is he come
   home yet?

STARVELING: He cannot be heard of. Out of doubt he
   is transported.°

5 FLUTE: If he come not, then the play is marr'd. It goes
   not forward, doth it?

QUINCE: It is not possible. You have not a man in all
   Athens able to discharge° Pyramus but he.

FLUTE: No, he hath simply the best wit of any handicraft
10 man in Athens.

QUINCE: Yea, and the best person too; and he is a
   very paramour for a sweet voice.

FLUTE: You must say "paragon." A paramour is, God
   bless us, a thing of naught.

(*Enter Snug the Joiner.*)

15 SNUG: Masters, the Duke is coming from the temple,
   and there is two or three lords and ladies more
   married. If our sport had gone forward, we had
   all been made men.

FLUTE: O sweet bully Bottom! Thus hath he lost six-
20 pence a day° during his life; he could not have
   scap'd sixpence a day. An the Duke had not given
   him sixpence a day for playing Pyramus, I'll be
   hang'd. He would have deserv'd it. Sixpence a day
   in Pyramus, or nothing.

(*Enter Bottom.*)

25 BOTTOM: Where are these lads? Where are these hearts?°

QUINCE: Bottom! O most courageous day! O most
   happy hour!

BOTTOM: Masters, I am to discourse wonders.° But
   ask me not what; for if I tell you, I am no true
30 Athenian. I will tell you everything, right as it fell
   out.

QUINCE: Let us hear, sweet Bottom.

BOTTOM: Not a word of° me. All that I will tell you
   is, that the Duke hath din'd. Get your apparel
35 together, good strings° to your beards, new ribands°
   to your pumps; meet presently° at the palace; every
   man look o'er his part; for the short and the long
   is, our play is preferr'd.° In any case, let Thisby
   have clean linen; and let not him that plays the

lion pare his nails, for they shall hang out for the   40
lion's claws. And, most dear actors, eat no onions
nor garlic, for we are to utter sweet breath; and I
do not doubt but to hear them say, it is a sweet
comedy. No more words. Away! go, away!

                                [*Exeunt.*]

[ACT V • Scene I]°

(*Enter Theseus, Hippolyta, and Philostrate, [Lords,
and Attendants].*)

HIPPOLYTA: 'Tis strange, my Theseus, that° these
   lovers speak of.

THESEUS: More strange than true. I never may°
   believe
   These antic° fables, nor these fairy toys.°
   Lovers and madmen have such seething brains,
   Such shaping fantasies,° that apprehend   5
   More than cool reason ever comprehends.
   The lunatic, the lover, and the poet
   Are of imagination all compact.°
   One sees more devils than vast hell can hold;
   That is the madman. The lover, all as frantic,   10
   Sees Helen's° beauty in a brow of Egypt.°
   The poet's eye, in a fine frenzy rolling,
   Doth glance from heaven to earth, from earth to
      heaven;
   And as imagination bodies forth
   The forms of things unknown, the poet's pen   15
   Turns them to shapes and gives to airy nothing
   A local habitation and a name.
   Such tricks hath strong imagination
   That, if it would but apprehend some joy,
   It comprehends some bringer° of that joy;   20
   Or in the night, imagining some fear,°
   How easy is a bush suppos'd a bear!

HIPPOLYTA: But all the story of the night told over,
   And all their minds transfigur'd so together,
   More witnesseth than fancy's images°   25
   And grows to something of great constancy;°
   But, howsoever,° strange and admirable.°

(*Enter lovers: Lysander, Demetrius, Hermia, and
Helena.*)

V, I. **Location:** Athens. The palace of Theseus.   **1. that:**
That which.   **2. may:** Can.   **3. antic:** Strange, grotesque
(with additional punning sense of *antique*, ancient); **fairy
toys:** Trifling stories about fairies.   **5. fantasies:** Imaginations.
8. compact: Formed, composed.   **11. Helen's:** Of Helen of
Troy, pattern of beauty; **brow of Egypt:** Face of a gypsy.
20. bringer: Source.   **21. fear:** Object of fear.   **25. More
. . . images:** Testifies to something more substantial than mere
imaginings.   **26. constancy:** Certainty.   **27. howsoever:** In
any case; **admirable:** A source of wonder.

IV, II. **Location:** Athens. Quince's house(?).   **4. transported:**
Carried off by fairies; or, possibly, transformed.   **8. discharge:**
Perform.   **19–20. sixpence a day:** As a royal pension.   **25.**
hearts: Good fellows.   **28. am . . . wonders:** Have wonders
to relate.   **33. of:** Out of.   **35. strings:** To attach the beards;
ribands: ribbons.   **36. presently:** Immediately.   **38. preferr'd:**
Selected for consideration.

THESEUS: Here come the lovers, full of joy and
 mirth.
 Joy, gentle friends! Joy and fresh days of love
 Accompany your hearts!
30 LYSANDER: More than to us
 Wait in your royal walks, your board, your bed!
THESEUS: Come now, what masques, what dances
  shall we have,
 To wear away this long age of three hours
 Between our after-supper and bed-time?
35 Where is our usual manager of mirth?
 What revels are in hand? Is there no play,
 To ease the anguish of a torturing hour?
 Call Philostrate.
PHILOSTRATE: Here, mighty Theseus.
THESEUS: Say, what abridgement° have you for this
  evening?
 What masque? What music? How shall we
40 beguile
 The lazy time, if not with some delight?
PHILOSTRATE: There is a brief° how many sports are
  ripe.
 Make choice of which your Highness will see
 first.
          [Giving a paper.]
THESEUS [reads]: "The battle with the Centaurs,° to
  be sung
45 By an Athenian eunuch to the harp."
 We'll none of that. That have I told my love,
 In glory of my kinsman° Hercules.
 [Reads.] "The riot of the tipsy Bacchanals,
 Tearing the Thracian singer in their rage."°
50 That is an old device; and it was play'd
 When I from Thebes came last a conqueror.
 [Reads.] "The thrice three Muses mourning for
  the death
 Of Learning, late deceas'd in beggary."°
 That is some satire, keen and critical,
55 Not sorting° with a nuptial ceremony.
 [Reads.] "A tedious brief scene of young
  Pyramus

---

39. **abridgement:** Pastime (to abridge or shorten the evening).
42. **brief:** Short written statement, list.   **44. battle . . . Centaurs:** Probably refers to the battle of the Centaurs and the Lapithae, when the Centaurs attempted to carry off Hippodamia, bride of Theseus' friend Pirothous.   **47. kinsman:** Plutarch's *Life of Theseus* states that Hercules and Theseus were near-kinsmen. Theseus is referring to a version of the battle of the Centaurs in which Hercules was said to be present.   **48–49. The riot . . . rage:** This was the story of the death of Orpheus, as told in *Metamorphoses*.   **52–53. The thrice . . . beggary:** Possibly an allusion to Spenser's *Teares of the Muses* (1591), though "satires" deploring the neglect of learning and the creative arts were commonplace. **55. sorting with:** Befitting.

And his love Thisby; very tragical mirth."
 Merry and tragical? Tedious and brief?
 That is, hot ice and wondrous strange° snow.
 How shall we find the concord of this discord? 60
PHILOSTRATE: A play there is, my lord, some ten
  words long,
 Which is as brief as I have known a play;
 But by ten words, my lord, it is too long,
 Which makes it tedious. For in all the play
 There is not one word apt, one player fitted. 65
 And tragical, my noble lord, it is,
 For Pyramus therein doth kill himself.
 Which, when I saw rehears'd, I must confess,
 Made mine eyes water; but more merry tears
 The passion of loud laughter never shed. 70
THESEUS: What are they that do play it?
PHILOSTRATE: Hard-handed men that work in
  Athens here,
 Which never labor'd in their minds till now,
 And now have toil'd° their unbreathed°
  memories
 With this same play, against° your nuptial. 75
THESEUS: And we will hear it.
PHILOSTRATE: No, my noble lord,
 It is not for you. I have heard it over,
 And it is nothing, nothing in the world;
 Unless you can find sport in their intents,
 Extremely stretch'd° and conn'd° with cruel pain, 80
 To do you service.
THESEUS: I will hear that play;
 For never anything can be amiss'
 When simpleness and duty tender it.
 Go, bring them in; and take your places, ladies.
   [Philostrate goes to summon the players.]
HIPPOLYTA: I love not to see wretchedness
  o'ercharg'd° 85
 And duty in his service° perishing.
THESEUS: Why, gentle sweet, you shall see no such
  thing.
HIPPOLYTA: He says they can do nothing in this
  kind.°
THESEUS: The kinder we, to give them thanks for
  nothing.
 Our sport shall be to take what they mistake; 90
 And what poor duty cannot do, noble respect
 Takes it in might, not merit.°

---

59. **strange:** Seemingly an error for some adjective that would contrast with *snow,* just as *hot* contrasts with *ice.*   **74. toil'd:** Taxed; **unbreathed:** Unexercised.   **75. against:** In preparation for.   **80. stretch'd:** Strained; **conn'd:** Memorized.   **85. wretchedness o'ercharg'd:** Incompetence overburdened.   **86. his service:** Its attempt to serve.   **88. kind:** Kind of thing. **92. Takes . . . merit:** Values it for the effort made rather than for the excellence achieved.

Where I have come, great clerks° have purposed
To greet me with premeditated welcomes;
95 Where I have seen them shiver and look pale,
Make periods in the midst of sentences,
Throttle their practic'd accent° in their fears,
And in conclusion dumbly have broke off,
Not paying me a welcome. Trust me, sweet,
100 Out of this silence yet I pick'd a welcome;
And in the modesty of fearful duty
I read as much as from the rattling tongue
Of saucy and audacious eloquence.
Love, therefore, and tongue-tied simplicity
105 In least° speak most, to my capacity.°

[*Philostrate returns.*]

PHILOSTRATE: So please your Grace, the Prologue° is
 address'd.°
THESEUS: Let him approach. [*Flourish of trumpets.*]

(*Enter the Prologue* [*Quince*].)

PROLOGUE: If we offend, it is with our good will.
That you should think, we come not to offend,
110 But with good will. To show our simple skill,
That is the true beginning of our end.
Consider, then, we come but in despite.
We do not come, as minding° to content you,
Our true intent is. All for your delight
115 We are not here. That you should here repent
 you,
The actors are at hand; and, by their show,
You shall know all that you are like to know.
THESEUS: This fellow doth not stand upon points.°
LYSANDER: He hath rid his prologue like a rough°
120 colt; he knows not the stop.° A good moral, my
 lord: it is not enough to speak, but to speak true.
HIPPOLYTA: Indeed he hath play'd on his prologue like
 a child on a recorder;° a sound, but not in
 government.°
125 THESEUS: His speech was like a tangled chain, nothing°
 impair'd, but all disorder'd. Who is next?

(*Enter Pyramus and Thisby, and Wall, and Moonshine,
and Lion.*)

PROLOGUE: Gentles, perchance you wonder at this
 show;
But wonder on, till truth make all things plain.
This man is Pyramus, if you would know;
This beauteous lady Thisby is certain.   130
This man, with lime and rough-cast, doth
 present
Wall, that vile Wall which did these lovers
 sunder;
And through Wall's chink, poor souls, they are
 content
To whisper. At the which let no man wonder.
This man, with lantern, dog, and bush of thorn, 135
Presenteth Moonshine; for, if you will know,
By moonshine did these lovers think no scorn°
To meet at Ninus' tomb, there, there to woo.
This grisly beast, which Lion hight° by name,
The trusty Thisby, coming first by night, 140
Did scare away, or rather did affright;
And, as she fled, her mantle she did fall,°
Which Lion vile with bloody mouth did stain.
Anon comes Pyramus, sweet youth and tall,°
And finds his trusty Thisby's mantle slain; 145
Whereat, with blade, with bloody blameful
 blade,
He bravely broach'd° his boiling bloody breast.
And Thisby, tarrying in mulberry shade,
His dagger drew, and died. For all the rest,
Let Lion, Moonshine, Wall, and lovers twain 150
At large° discourse, while here they do remain.
   (*Exeunt Lion, Thisby, and Moonshine.*)
THESEUS: I wonder if the lion be to speak.
DEMETRIUS: No wonder, my lord. One lion may, when
 many asses do.
WALL: In this same interlude it doth befall 155
That I, one Snout by name, present a wall;
And such a wall, as I would have you think,
That had in it a crannied hole or chink,
Through which the lovers, Pyramus and Thisby,
Did whisper often very secretly. 160
This loam, this rough-cast, and this stone doth
 show
That I am that same wall; the truth is so.
And this the cranny is, right and sinister,°
Through which the fearful lovers are to whisper.
THESEUS: Would you desire lime and hair to speak 165
 better?

---

93. **clerks:** Learned men. 97. **practic'd accent:** Rehearsed
speech; or usual way of speaking. 105. **least:** Saying least;
to my capacity: In my judgment and understanding. 106.
Prologue: Speaker of the prologue; **address'd:** Ready. 113.
minding: Intending. 118. **stand upon points:** (1) Heed niceties
or small points, (2) pay attention to punctuation in his reading.
(The humor of Quince's speech is in the blunders of its
punctuation.) 119. **rough:** Unbroken. 120. **stop:** (1) The
stopping of a colt by reining it in, (2) punctuation mark.
123. **recorder:** A wind instrument like a flute. 124. **government:** Control. 125. **nothing:** Not at all.

137. **think no scorn:** Think it no disgraceful matter. 139.
hight: Is called. 142. **fall:** Let fall. 144. **tall:** Courageous.
147. **broach'd:** Stabbed. 151. **At large:** In full, at length.
163. **right and sinister:** The right side of it and the left
(sinister); or running from right to left, horizontally.

DEMETRIUS: It is the wittiest partition° that ever I
    heard discourse, my lord.

[*Pyramus comes forward.*]

THESEUS: Pyramus draws near the wall. Silence!

PYRAMUS: O grim-look'd° night! O night with hue
170   so black!
    O night, which ever art when day is not!
    O night, O night! Alack, alack, alack,
    I fear my Thisby's promise is forgot.
    And thou, O wall, O sweet, O lovely wall,
    That stand'st between her father's ground and
175   mine,
    Thou wall, O wall, O sweet and lovely wall,
    Show me thy chink, to blink through with mine
    eyne!   [*Wall holds up his fingers.*]
    Thanks, courteous wall. Jove shield thee well for
    this!
    But what see I? No Thisby do I see.
180   O wicked wall, through whom I see no bliss!
    Curs'd be thy stones for thus deceiving me!

THESEUS: The wall, methinks, being sensible,° should
    curse again.

PYRAMUS: No, in truth, sir, he should not. "Deceiving
185   me" is Thisby's cue: she is to enter now, and I am
    to spy her through the wall. You shall see, it will
    fall pat as I told you. Yonder she comes.

(*Enter Thisby.*)

THISBY: O wall, full often hast thou heard my
    moans,
    For parting my fair Pyramus and me.
190   My cherry lips have often kiss'd thy stones,
    Thy stones with lime and hair knit up in thee.

PYRAMUS: I see a voice. Now will I to the chink,
    To spy an° I can hear my Thisby's face.
    Thisby!

195 THISBY: My love! Thou art my love, I think.

PYRAMUS: Think what thou wilt, I am thy lover's
    grace;°
    And, like Limander,° am I trusty still.

THISBY: And I like Helen,° till the Fates me kill.

PYRAMUS: Not Shafalus to Procrus° was so true.

200 THISBY: As Shafalus to Procrus, I to you.

PYRAMUS: O, kiss me through the hole of this vile
    wall!

THISBY: I kiss the wall's hole, not your lips at all.

PYRAMUS: Wilt thou at Ninny's tomb meet me
    straightway?

THISBY: 'Tide° life, 'tide death, I come without
    delay.
               [*Exeunt Pyramus and Thisby.*]

WALL: Thus have I, Wall, my part discharged so; 205
    And, being done, thus Wall away doth go. [*Exit.*]

THESEUS: Now is the mural down between the two
    neighbors.

DEMETRIUS: No remedy, my lord, when walls are so
    willful to hear° without warning.°   210

HIPPOLYTA: This is the silliest stuff that ever I heard.

THESESUS: The best in this kind° are but shadows;°
    and the worst are no worse, if imagination amend
    them.

HIPPOLYTA: It must be your imagination then, and not 215
    theirs.

THESEUS: If we imagine no worse of them than they
    of themselves, they may pass for excellent men.
    Here come two noble beasts in, a man and a lion.

(*Enter Lion and Moonshine.*)

LION: You, ladies, you, whose gentle hearts do fear 220
    The smallest monstrous mouse that creeps on
    floor,
    May now perchance both quake and tremble
    here,
    When lion rough in wildest rage doth roar.
    Then know that I, as Snug the joiner, am
    A lion fell,° nor else no lion's dam;   225
    For, if I should as lion come in strife
    Into this place, 'twere pity on my life.

THESEUS: A very gentle beast, and of a good conscience.

DEMETRIUS: The very best at a beast, my lord, that
    e'er I saw.   230

LYSANDER: This lion is a very fox for his valor.°

THESEUS: True; and a goose for his discretion.°

DEMETRIUS: Not so, my lord; for his valor cannot
    carry his discretion; and the fox carries the goose.

THESEUS: His discretion, I am sure, cannot carry his 235
    valor; for the goose carries not the fox. It is well.
    Leave it to his discretion, and let us listen to the
    moon.

MOON: This lanthorn° doth the horned moon
    present —

---

167. **partition:** (1) Wall, (2) section of a learned treatise or
oration.   170. **grim-look'd:** Grim-looking.   182. **sensible:**
Capable of feeling.   193. **an:** If.   196. **lover's grace:** Gracious
lover.   197. **Limander:** Blunder for "Leander."   198. **Helen:**
Blunder for the "Hero."   199. **Shafalus, Procrus:** Blunders
for "Cephalus" and "Procris," also famous lovers.

204. **'Tide:** Betide, come.   210. **to hear:** As to hear; **without
warning:** Without warning the parents.   212. **in this kind:**
Of this sort; **shadows:** Likenesses, representations.   225.
lion fell: Fierce lion (with a play on the idea of *lion skin*).
231. **is . . . valor:** His valor consists of craftiness and discretion.
232. **goose . . . discretion:** As discreet as a goose, that is,
more foolish than discreet.   239. **lanthorn:** This original
spelling may suggest a play on the *horn* of which lanterns
were made and also on a cuckold's horns; but the spelling
lanthorn is not used consistently for comic effect in this play
or elsewhere. V, I, line 135, for example, the word is *lantern*
in the original.

240 DEMETRIUS: He should have worn the horns on his
head.°
THESEUS: He is no crescent, and his horns are invisible
within the circumference.
MOON: This lanthorn doth the horned moon
present;
245 Myself the man i' th' moon do seem to be.
THESEUS: This is the greatest error of all the rest. The
man should be put into the lanthorn. How is it
else the man i' th' moon?
DEMETRIUS: He dares not come there for the° candle;
250 for, you see, it is already in snuff.°
HIPPOLYTA: I am aweary of this moon. Would he
would change!
THESEUS: It appears, by his small light of discretion,
that he is in the wane; but yet, in courtesy, in all
255 reason, we must stay the time.
LYSANDER: Proceed, Moon.
MOON: All that I have to say is to tell you that the
lanthorn is the moon, I, the man in the moon, this
thorn-bush my thorn-bush, and this dog my dog.
260 DEMETRIUS: Why, all these should be in the lanthorn;
for all these are in the moon. But silence! Here
comes Thisby.

(*Enter Thisby.*)

THISBY: This is old Ninny's tomb. Where is my love?
LION [*roaring*]: Oh —   [*Thisby runs off.*]
265 DEMETRIUS: Well roar'd, Lion.
THESEUS: Well run, Thisby.
HIPPOLYTA: Well shone, Moon. Truly, the moon shines
with a good grace.
        [*The Lion shakes Thisby's mantle, and exit.*]'
THESEUS: Well mous'd,° Lion.
270 DEMETRIUS: And then came Pyramus.
LYSANDER: And so the lion vanish'd.

(*Enter Pyramus.*)

PYRAMUS: Sweet Moon, I thank thee for thy sunny
beams;
I thank thee, Moon, for shining now so bright;
For, by thy gracious, golden, glittering gleams,
275 I trust to take of truest Thisby sight.
    But stay, O spite!
    But mark, poor knight,
What dreadful dole° is here!
    Eyes, do you see?
280   How can it be?
O dainty duck! O dear!
    Thy mantle good,
    What, stain'd with blood!

Approach, ye Furies fell!°
    O Fates, come, come,   285
    Cut thread and thrum;°
Quail,° crush, conclude, and quell!°
THESEUS: This passion, and the death of a dear friend,
would go near to make a man look sad.°
HIPPOLYTA: Beshrew my heart, but I pity the man.   290
PYRAMUS: O wherefore, Nature, didst thou lions
frame?
Since lion vile hath here deflow'r'd my dear,
Which is — no, no — which was the fairest
dame
That liv'd, that lov'd, that lik'd, that look'd with
cheer.°
    Come, tears, confound,   295
    Out, sword, and wound
The pap of Pyramus;
    Ay, that left pap,
    Where heart doth hop.   [*Stabs himself.*]
Thus die I, thus, thus, thus.   300
    Now am I dead,
    Now am I fled;
My soul is in the sky.
    Tongue, lose thy light;
    Moon, take thy flight.   [*Exit Moonshine.*] 305
Now die, die, die, die, die.   [*Dies.*]
DEMETRIUS: No die, but an ace,° for him; for he is
but one.°
LYSANDER: Less than an ace, man; for he is dead, he
is nothing.   310
THESEUS: With the help of a surgeon he might yet
recover, and yet prove an ass.°
HIPPOLYTA: How chance Moonshine is gone before
Thisby comes back and finds her lover?
THESEUS: She will find him by starlight. Here she comes; 315
and her passion ends the play.

[*Enter Thisby.*]

HIPPOLYTA: Methinks she should not use a long one
for such a Pyramus. I hope she will be brief.
DEMETRIUS: A mote will turn the balance, which Pyramus, which° Thisby, is the better: he for a man,   320
God warr'nt us; she for a woman, God bless us.
LYSANDER: She hath spied him already with those
sweet eyes.

284. fell: Fierce.   **286. thread and thrum:** The warp in
weaving and the loose end of the warp.   **287. Quail:** Over-
power; **quell:** Kill, destroy.   **288–289. This . . . sad:** If one
had other reason to grieve, one might be sad, but not from
this absurd portrayal of passion.   **294. cheer:** Coutenance.
307. ace: The side of the die featuring the single pip, or spot.
(The pun is on *die* as a singular of *dice*; Bottom's performance
is not worth a whole *die* but rather one single face of it, one
small portion.)   **308. one:** (1) An individual person, (2)
unique.   **312. ass:** With a pun on *ace*.   **319–320. which
. . . which:** Whether . . . or.

240–241. on his head: As a sign of cuckoldry.   **249. for
the:** Because of the.   **250. in snuff:** (1) Offended, (2) in
need of snuffing.   **269. mous'd:** Shaken.   **278. dole:** Grievous
event.

DEMETRIUS: And thus she means,° videlicet:°
325 THISBY: Asleep, my love?
      What, dead, my dove?
      O Pyramus, arise!
      Speak, speak. Quite dumb?
      Dead, dead? A tomb
330 Must cover thy sweet eyes.
      These lily lips,
      This cherry nose,
      These yellow cowslip cheeks,
      Are gone, are gone!
335 Lovers, make moan.
      His eyes were green as leeks.
      O Sisters Three,°
      Come, come to me,
      With hands as pale as milk;
340 Lay them in gore,
      Since you have shore°
      With shears his thread of silk.
      Tongue, not a word.
      Come, trusty sword,
345 Come, blade, my breast imbrue!°   [Stabs herself.]
      And farewell, friends.
      Thus Thisby ends.
      Adieu, adieu, adieu.   [Dies.]
THESEUS: Moonshine and Lion are left to bury the
350 dead.
DEMETRIUS: Ay, and Wall too.
BOTTOM [starting up]: No, I assure you; the wall is
      down that parted their fathers. Will it please you
      to see the epilogue, or to hear a Bergomask dance°
355 between two of our company?
THESEUS: No epilogue, I pray you; for your play needs
      no excuse. Never excuse; for when the players are
      all dead, there need none to be blam'd. Marry, if
      he that writ it had play'd Pyramus and hang'd
360 himself in Thisby's garter, it would have been a
      fine tragedy; and so it is, truly, and very notably
      discharg'd. But, come, your Bergomask. Let your
      epilogue alone.   [A dance.]
      The iron tongue of midnight hath told° twelve.
365 Lovers, to bed; 'tis almost fairy time.
      I fear we shall outsleep the coming morn
      As much as we this night have overwatch'd.°
      This palpable-gross° play hath well beguil'd
      The heavy° gait of night. Sweet friends, to bed.
370 A fortnight hold we this solemnity,
      In nightly revels and new jollity.   (Exeunt.)

(Enter Puck)

PUCK: Now the hungry lion roars,
      And the wolf behowls the moon;
      Whilst the heavy ploughman snores,
      All with weary task fordone.°   375
      Now the wasted brands° do glow,
      Whilst the screech-owl, screeching loud,
      Puts the wretch that lies in woe
      In remembrance of a shroud.
      Now it is the time of night   380
      That the graves, all gaping wide,
      Every one lets forth his sprite,°
      In the churchway paths to glide.
      And we fairies, that do run
      By the triple Hecate's° team   385
      From the presence of the sun,
      Following darkness like a dream,
      Now are frolic.° Not a mouse
      Shall disturb this hallowed house.
      I am sent with broom before,   390
      To sweep the dust behind° the door.

(Enter [Oberon and Titania,] King and Queen of Fairies,
with all their train.)

OBERON: Through the house give glimmering light,
      By the dead and drowsy fire;
      Every elf and fairy sprite
      Hop as light as bird from brier;   395
      And this ditty, after me,
      Sing, and dance it trippingly.
TITANIA: First, rehearse your song by rote,
      To each word a warbling note.
      Hand in hand, with fairy grace,   400
      Will we sing, and bless this place.
                                        [Song and dance.]
OBERON: Now, until the break of day,
      Through this house each fairy stray.
      To the best bride-bed will we,
      Which by us shall blessed be;   405
      And the issue there create°
      Ever shall be fortunate.
      So shall all the couples three
      Ever true in loving be;
      And the blots of Nature's hand   410
      Shall not in their issue stand;
      Never mole, hare lip, nor scar,
      Nor mark prodigious,° such as are

---

324. **means:** Moans, laments; **videlicet:** To wit.   337. **Sisters Three:** The Fates.   341. **shore:** Shorn.   345. **imbrue:** Stain with blood.   354. **Bergomask dance:** A rustic dance named for Bergamo, a province in the state of Venice.   364. **told:** Counted, struck ("tolled").   367. **overwatch'd:** Stayed up too late.   368. **palpably-gross:** obviously crude.   369. **heavy:** Drowsy, dull.

375. **fordone:** Exhausted.   376. **wasted brands:** Burned-out logs.   382. **Every . . . sprite:** Every grave lets forth its ghost.   385. **triple Hecate's:** Hecate ruled in three capacities: as Luna or Cynthia in heaven, as Diana on earth, and as Proserpina in hell.   388. **frolic:** Merry.   391. **behind:** From behind. (Robin Goodfellow was a household spirit who helped good housemaids and punished lazy ones.)   406. **create:** Created.   413. **prodigious:** Monstrous, unnatural.

Despised in nativity,
415 Shall upon their children be.
With this field-dew consecrate,°
Every fairy take his gait,°
And each several° chamber bless,
Through this palace, with sweet peace;
420 And the owner of it blest
Ever shall in safety rest.
Trip away; make no stay;
Meet me all by break of day.
      (*Exeunt [Oberon, Titania, and train*].)
PUCK: If we shadows have offended,
425 Think but this, and all is mended,
That you have but slumb'red here°

While these visions did appear.
And this weak and idle theme,
No more yielding but° a dream,
Gentles, do not reprehend.   430
If you pardon, we will mend.
And, as I am an honest Puck,
If we have unearned luck
Now to scape the serpent's tongue,°
We will make amends ere long;   435
Else the Puck a liar call.
So, good night unto you all.
Give me your hands,° if we be friends,
And Robin shall restore amends.   [*Exit.*]

416. consecrate: Consecrated.   **417. take his gait:** Go his
way.   **418. several:** Separate.   **426. That . . . here:** That it
is a "midsummer night's dream".

429. No . . . but: Yielding no more than.   **434. serpent's
tongue:** Hissing.   **438. Give . . . hands:** Applaud.

HAMLET

Hamlet, 1600–1601, Shakespeare's boldest, most profound play, is
a landmark in the poet's work. It coincides with the new century and
the uncertainties of the last years of the old regime, brought to an end
by the death of Queen Elizabeth in 1603. Until the very moment of her
death, the succession was in doubt, but at her death she indicated that
her cousin James of Scotland would take the throne. The new age was
in many ways more complicated, more ambiguous, and more democratic
than the old. It was also more dangerous.

Almost like a voyager returning to England after the death of Elizabeth,
Hamlet returns to a Denmark and a court that he hardly recognizes,
to a mother newly wed to his uncle and in many ways not the woman
he remembers, and, finally, to a ghostly father who will not rest until
the crimes against him are avenged. Like Faustus, Hamlet was a scholar
at the University of Wittenberg, where he presumably had studied theology
and therefore had a special knowledge of the world of the spirits. Perhaps
he studied other sciences, medicine, and law as well. He gives evidence
of knowing literature and having a taste for theater, just as he gives
evidence of being physically ready with weapons when necessary.

Hamlet is also a melancholic. To the Elizabethan, *melancholic* does
not mean depressed, although Hamlet dresses in black and still mourns
for his father, even against the wishes of his uncle. The melancholic,
rather, is introspective, thoughtful, perhaps world-weary, and possibly

a touch sardonic. Above all things, he is an intellectual, a person of wide-ranging knowledge and intelligence, a reliable commentator with a probing mind.

Hamlet's broad intelligence and the penetrating introspection revealed in his soliloquies, such as his famous "To be, or not to be" meditation on suicide, make him a character with more psychological dimension, more "soul," than many people we know in life. In this sense the play is thoroughly modern; it satisfies our modern need to know the interior imaginations of characters who engage us on the stage. Hamlet's range of feeling, his range of felt and expressed emotion, is impressive to any audience.

Hamlet is a revenge tragedy, a type of play that was especially appealing to the Elizabethans. Thomas Kyd's *The Spanish Tragedy* and John Marston's *Antonio's Revenge* were very successful Elizabethan revenge tragedies. Shakespeare had written one earlier play that could be termed a revenge tragedy, *Titus Andronicus,* in 1594. Some characteristics of the revenge tragedy are the following:

The revenge of a father by a son or vice versa

The appearance of a ghost

The hesitation of the hero

The use of real or pretended insanity

Suicide

Political intrigue

An able, scheming villain

Philosophical soliloquies

Sensational use of horror (murder and gore onstage)

All these elements are present in *Hamlet.* But the play has other important qualities as well. The minor characters are developed in unexpected ways. Ophelia, the innocent, loving woman, becomes a touching heroine in her own right when, unable to understand the nature of evil in the Danish court and driven to insanity by Hamlet's rejection of her and by her father's murder, she permits herself to sink to a watery death in a stream. Her songs, her insane ramblings, and her devotion to her father as well as to Hamlet are all moving to audiences.

Characters such as Gertrude, Hamlet's mother, reveal a richness of psychology that sometimes startles us. Polonius, Ophelia's father, is virtually a stock character — the old, foolish philosopher — but he takes on special significance when he urges Ophelia to spy for him and when he ultimately dies at the hand of Hamlet. As Hamlet tells us, it was an unnecessary death for a "wretched, rash, intruding fool." But his son Laertes loved Polonius, and when Laertes returns with the people's support we see a character moved by grief, who, unlike Hamlet, will not hesitate a moment to get his revenge.

Hamlet's hesitation is linked with his reputation as a melancholic. Because he thinks things through so deeply, he does not act instantly, as does Laertes. Even when the ghost reveals himself as his father and tells him that he has been murdered and must be avenged, Hamlet fears it might be a dangerous fakery of the devil to lure him to murder.

Hamlet shows he can act swiftly — indeed, rashly. His killing of Polonius is a rash act. He thinks the man behind the tapestry is his uncle, since they are in his mother's bedroom and no other man but her husband has any right to be there. When Hamlet is sent to England with Rosencrantz and Guildenstern he quickly senses a plot, undoes it, leaps aboard a pirate ship, and negotiates his way home with relative alacrity. This is not the work of a man who cannot act. In the graveyard scene he acts just as impulsively as Laertes in leaping into Ophelia's grave.

His talents exhibited in his welcoming of the players in act II show him to be an experienced theatergoer, one with some skills onstage. He is also a skilled writer, since his additions to *The Murder of Gonzago* will convert that imaginary play into a "mousetrap" that will catch the murderer of his father. In early Renaissance paintings, the mousetrap is an allegory for Jesus Christ, who catches the devil. The allusion would not have been lost on the Elizabethan audience, who would have seen Hamlet's psychological approach as being quite reasonable.

Emotions are of great importance to Hamlet. He feels deeply and he watches others to see what their feelings are. He knows their demeanor may not reveal them as they are, so he must be a careful student of surfaces. As he tells his mother, "I know not 'seems.'" What seems is only what is apparent; his procedure is always to penetrate the surfaces of things to know their reality, which is why he uses drama as an instrument to penetrate psychological surfaces.

A connection between Seneca's tragedies and the Elizabethan revenge tragedy has prompted some Shakespeare scholars to declare that Elizabethan tragedy is all Senecan in nature. What they mean is that Seneca's preference for magic and ghosts as well as his penchant for onstage gore and murder translated well to the Elizabethan stage. Seneca has Iokaste kill herself onstage by ripping open her abdomen, for instance, and many such bloody scenes were enacted on the Elizabethan stage. Perhaps, however, the best remnant of Seneca in Elizabethan drama is the rhetorical, almost bombastic speeches of the player in act II, scene II. The lengthy nature of such speeches and their invitation to share a tragic emotion are much in the Senecan mold.

Hamlet has always deeply affected its audiences. Hamlet's situation has translated well into innumerable languages and cultures. Laura Bohannon, an anthropologist, tells of an African chieftain who lectured her on the logic of Hamlet's necessity to avenge himself. Such appreciation reminds us that Shakespeare's universality is one of his strongest qualities. It is nowhere in evidence more strongly than in this tragedy.

William Shakespeare (1564–1616)

HAMLET, PRINCE OF DENMARK   *c. 1600*

[Dramatis Personae

CLAUDIUS, *king of Denmark*
HAMLET, *son to the late King Hamlet, and nephew to the present king*
POLONIUS, *Lord Chamberlain*
HORATIO, *friend to Hamlet*
LAERTES, *son to Polonius*
VOLTIMAND,
CORNELIUS,
ROSENCRANTZ, } *courtiers*
GUILDENSTERN,
OSRIC,
GENTLEMAN,
PRIEST, OR DOCTOR OF DIVINITY
MARCELLUS, } *officers*
BERNARDO,
FRANCISCO, *a soldier*
REYNALDO, *servant to Polonius*
PLAYERS
TWO CLOWNS, *grave-diggers*
FORTINBRAS, *Prince of Norway*
CAPTAIN
ENGLISH AMBASSADORS

GERTRUDE, *Queen of Denmark, mother to Hamlet*
OPHELIA, *daughter to Polonius*

LORDS, LADIES, OFFICERS, SOLDIERS, SAILORS, MESSENGERS, AND OTHER ATTENDANTS
GHOST *of Hamlet's father*

Scene: *Denmark.*]

[ACT I • Scene I]° _____

(*Enter Bernardo and Francisco, two sentinels, [meeting].*)

BERNARDO: Who's there?

Note: The text of *Hamlet* has come down to us in different versions — such as the first quarto, the second quarto, and the first Folio. The copy of the text used here is largely drawn from the second quarto. Passages enclosed in square brackets are taken from one of the other versions, in most cases the first Folio. **I, I. Location:** Elsinore castle. A guard platform.

FRANCISCO: Nay, answer me.° Stand and unfold yourself.
BERNARDO: Long live the King!
FRANCISCO: Bernardo?
BERNARDO: He.   5
FRANCISCO: You come most carefully upon your hour.
BERNARDO: 'Tis now struck twelve. Get thee to bed, Francisco.
FRANCISCO: For this relief much thanks. 'Tis bitter cold,
   And I am sick at heart.
BERNARDO: Have you had quiet guard?
FRANCISCO: Not a mouse stirring.   10
BERNARDO: Well, good night.
   If you do meet Horatio and Marcellus,
   The rivals° of my watch, bid them make haste.

(*Enter Horatio and Marcellus.*)

FRANCISCO: I think I hear them. Stand, ho! Who is there?
HORATIO: Friends to this ground.
MARCELLUS: And liegemen to the Dane.°   15
FRANCISCO: Give you° good night.
MARCELLUS: O, farewell, honest soldier.
   Who hath relieved you?
FRANCISCO: Bernardo hath my place.
   Give you good night.   (*Exit Francisco.*)
MARCELLUS: Holla, Bernardo!
BERNARDO: Say,
   What, is Horatio there?
HORATIO: A piece of him.
BERNARDO: Welcome, Horatio. Welcome, good Marcellus.   20
HORATIO: What, has this thing appear'd again tonight?
BERNARDO: I have seen nothing.
MARCELLUS: Horatio says 'tis but our fantasy,
   And will not let belief take hold of him
   Touching this dreaded sight, twice seen of us.   25
   Therefore I have entreated him along
   With us to watch the minutes of this night,

---

2. me: Francisco emphasizes that *he* is the sentry currently on watch.   **13. rivals:** Partners.   **15. liegemen to the Dane:** Men sworn to serve the Danish king.   **16. Give you:** God give you.

That if again this apparition come
He may approve° our eyes and speak to it.
HORATIO: Tush, tush, 'twill not appear.

30 BERNARDO: Sit down awhile,
And let us once again assail your ears,
That are so fortified against our story,
What we have two nights seen.
HORATIO: Well, sit we down,
And let us hear Bernardo speak of this.

35 BERNARDO: Last night of all,
When yond same star that's westward from the
     pole°
Had made his° course t' illume that part of
     heaven
Where now it burns, Marcellus and myself,
The bell then beating one —

(Enter Ghost.)

MARCELLUS: Peace, break thee off! Look where it
40   comes again!
BERNARDO: In the same figure, like the King that's
     dead.
MARCELLUS: Thou art a scholar.° Speak to it,
     Horatio.
BERNARDO: Looks 'a° not like the King? Mark it,
     Horatio.
HORATIO: Most like. It harrows me with fear and
     wonder.
BERNARDO: It would be spoke to.
45 MARCELLUS: Speak to it,° Horatio.
HORATIO: What art thou that usurp'st this time of
     night,
Together with that fair and warlike form
In which the majesty of buried Denmark°
Did sometimes° march? By heaven I charge thee
     speak!
MARCELLUS: It is offended.
50 BERNARDO: See, it stalks away.
HORATIO: Stay! Speak, speak. I charge thee, speak.
                                   (Exit Ghost.)
MARCELLUS: 'Tis gone, and will not answer.
BERNARDO: How now, Horatio? You tremble and
     look pale.
Is not this something more than fantasy?
55 What think you on 't?
HORATIO: Before my God, I might not this believe
Without the sensible° and true avouch
Of mine own eyes.

MARCELLUS: Is it not like the King?
HORATIO: As thou art to thyself.
Such was the very armor he had on   60
When he the ambitious Norway° combated.
So frown'd he once when, in an angry parle,°
He smote the sledded° Polacks° on the ice.
'Tis strange.
MARCELLUS: Thus twice before, and jump° at this
     dead hour,   65
With martial stalk hath he gone by our watch.
HORATIO: In what particular thought to work I
     know not,
But, in the gross and scope° of mine opinion,
This bodes some strange eruption to our state.
MARCELLUS: Good now,° sit down, and tell me, he
     that knows,   70
Why this same strict and most observant watch
So nightly toils° the subject° of the land,
And why such daily cast° of brazen cannon,
And foreign mart° for implements of war,
Why such impress° of shipwrights, whose sore
     task   75
Does not divide the Sunday from the week.
What might be toward,° that this sweaty haste
Doth make the night joint-laborer with the day?
Who is 't that can inform me?
HORATIO: That can I,
At least, the whisper goes so. Our last king,   80
Whose image even but now appear'd to us,
Was, as you know, by Fortinbras of Norway,
Thereto prick'd on° by a most emulate° pride,
Dar'd to the combat; in which our valiant
     Hamlet —
For so this side of our known world esteem'd
     him —   85
Did slay this Fortinbras; who, by a seal'd
     compact,
Well ratified by law and heraldry,
Did forfeit, with his life, all those his lands
Which he stood seiz'd° of, to the conqueror;
Against the° which a moi'ty competent°   90
Was gaged° by our king, which had return'd
To the inheritance of Fortinbras

---

61. Norway: King of Norway. **62. parle:** Parley. **63. sledded:** Traveling on sleds; **Polacks:** Poles. **65. jump:** Exactly. **68. gross and scope:** General view. **70. Good now:** An expression denoting entreaty or expostulation. **72. toils:** Causes to toil; **subject:** Subjects. **73. cast:** Casting. **74. mart:** Buying and selling. **75. impress:** Impressment, conscription. **77. toward:** in preparation. **83. prick'd on:** incited; **emulate:** Ambitious. **89. seiz'd:** Possessed. **90. Against the:** In return for; **moi'ty competent:** Sufficient portion. **91. gaged:** Engaged, pledged.

29. approve: Corroborate. **36. pole:** Polestar. **37. his:** Its. **42. scholar:** One learned in Latin and able to address spirits. **43. 'a:** He. **45. It . . . to:** A ghost could not speak until spoken to. **48. buried Denmark:** The buried king of Denmark. **49. sometimes:** Formerly. **57. sensible:** Confirmed by the senses.

Had he been vanquisher, as, by the same comart°
And carriage° of the article design'd,
His fell to Hamlet. Now, sir, young Fortinbras, 95
Of unimproved° mettle hot and full,
Hath in the skirts° of Norway here and there
Shark'd up° a list of lawless resolutes°
For food and diet° to some enterprise
That hath a stomach° in 't, which is no other — 100
As it doth well appear unto our state —
But to recover of us, by strong hand
And terms compulsatory, those foresaid lands
So by his father lost. And this, I take it,
Is the main motive of our preparations, 105
The source of this our watch, and the chief head°
Of this post-haste and romage° in the land.
BERNARDO: I think it be no other but e'en so.
Well may it sort° that this portentous figure
Comes armed through our watch so like the King 110
That was and is the question of these wars.
HORATIO: A mote° it is to trouble the mind's eye.
In the most high and palmy° state of Rome,
A little ere the mightiest Julius fell,
The graves stood tenantless and the sheeted° dead 115
Did squeak and gibber in the Roman streets;
As° stars with trains of fire and dews of blood,
Disasters° in the sun; and the moist star°
Upon whose influence Neptune's° empire stands°
Was sick almost to doomsday° with eclipse. 120
And even the like precurse° of fear'd events,
As harbingers° preceding still° the fates
And prologue to the omen° coming on,
Have heaven and earth together demonstrated
Unto our climatures° and countrymen. 125

(*Enter Ghost.*)

93. comart: Joint bargain (?)   94. carriage: Import, bearing.
96. unimproved: Not turned to account (?) or untested (?)
97. skirts: Outlaying regions, outskirts.   98. Shark'd up:
Got together in haphazard fashion; resolutes: desperadoes.
99. food and diet: No pay but their keep.   100. stomach:
Relish of danger.   106. head: Source.   107. romage: Bustle,
commotion.   109. sort: Suit.   112. mote: Speck of dust.
113. palmy: Flourishing.   115. sheeted: Shrouded.   117.
As: This abrupt transition suggests that matter is possibly
omitted between lines 116 and 117.   118. Disasters: Un-
favorable signs of aspects; moist star: Moon, governing tides.
119. Neptune: God of the sea; stands: Depends.   120. sick
. . . doomsday: See Matt. 24:29 and Rev. 6:12.   121. precurse:
Heralding, foreshadowing.   122. harbingers: Forerunners;
still: Continually.   123. omen: Calamitous event.   125.
climatures: regions.

But soft, behold! Lo where it comes again!
I'll cross° it, though it blast me. Stay, illusion!
If thou hast any sound, or use of voice,
Speak to me!   (*It spreads his arms.*)
If there be any good thing to be done 130
That may to thee do ease and grace to me,
Speak to me!
If thou art privy to thy country's fate,
Which, happily,° foreknowing may avoid,
O, speak! 135
Or if thou hast uphoarded in thy life
Extorted treasure in the womb of earth,
For which, they say, you spirits oft walk in death,

(*The cock crows.*)

Speak of it. Stay, and speak! Stop it, Marcellus.
MARCELLUS: Shall I strike at it with my partisan?° 140
HORATIO: Do, if it will not stand. [*They strike at it.*]
BERNARDO: 'Tis here!
HORATIO: 'Tis here!
MARCELLUS: 'Tis gone.   [*Exit Ghost.*]
We do it wrong, being so majestical,
To offer it the show of violence;
For it is, as the air, invulnerable, 145
And our vain blows malicious mockery.
BERNARDO: It was about to speak when the cock crew.
HORATIO: And then it started like a guilty thing
Upon a fearful summons. I have heard,
The cock, that is the trumpet to the morn, 150
Doth with his lofty and shrill-sounding throat
Awake the god of day, and, at his warning,
Whether in sea or fire, in earth or air,
Th' extravagant and erring° spirit hies
To his confine; and of the truth herein 155
This present object made probation.°
MARCELLUS: It faded on the crowing of the cock.
Some say that ever 'gainst° that season comes
Wherein our Savior's birth is celebrated,
The bird of dawning singeth all night long, 160
And then, they say, no spirit dare stir abroad;
The nights are wholesome, then no planets strike,°
No fairy takes,° nor witch hath power to charm,
So hallowed and so gracious° is that time.
HORATIO: So have I heard and do in part believe it. 165
But, look, the morn, in russet mantle clad,

127. cross: Meet, face directly.   134. happily: Haply, perchance.   140. partisan: Long-handled spear.   154. extravagant and erring: Wandering. (The words have similar meaning.)   156. probation: Proof.   158. 'gainst: Just before.
162. strike: Exert evil influence.   163. takes: Bewitches.
164. gracious: Full of goodness.

Walks o'er the dew of yon high eastward hill.
Break we our watch up, and by my advice
Let us impart what we have seen tonight
170 Unto young Hamlet; for, upon my life,
This spirit, dumb to us, will speak to him.
Do you consent we shall acquaint him with it,
As needful in our loves, fitting our duty?
MARCELLUS: Let's do 't, I pray, and I this morning
    know
175 Where we shall find him most conveniently.
                                    (*Exeunt.*)°

[Scene II]°

(*Flourish. Enter Claudius, King of Denmark, Gertrude
the Queen, Councilors, Polonius and his son Laertes,
Hamlet, cum aliis*° [*including Voltimand and Cornelius*].)

KING: Though yet of Hamlet our dear brother's
    death
The memory be green, and that it us befitted
To bear our hearts in grief and our whole
    kingdom
To be contracted in one brow of woe,
5   Yet so far hath discretion fought with nature
That we with wisest sorrow think on him,
Together with remembrance of ourselves.
Therefore our sometime sister, now our queen,
Th' imperial jointress° to this warlike state,
10 Have we, as 'twere with a defeated joy —
With an auspicious and a dropping eye,
With mirth in funeral and with dirge in
    marriage,
In equal scale weighing delight and dole —
Taken to wife. Nor have we herein barr'd
15 Your better wisdoms, which have freely gone
With this affair along. For all, our thanks.
Now follows that you know° young Fortinbras,
Holding a weak supposal° of our worth,
Or thinking by our late dear brother's death
20 Our state to be disjoint and out of frame,
Colleagued with° this dream of his advantage,°
He hath not fail'd to pester us with message
Importing° the surrender of those lands
Lost by his father, with all bands° of law,
25 To our most valiant brother. So much for him.
Now for ourself and for this time of meeting.

Thus much the business is: we have here writ
To Norway, uncle of young Fortinbras —
Who, impotent and bed-rid, scarcely hears
Of this his nephew's purpose — to suppress   30
His° further gait° herein, in that the levies,
The lists, and full proportions are all made
Out of his subject;° and we here dispatch
You, good Cornelius, and you, Voltimand,
For bearers of this greeting to old Norway,   35
Giving to you no further personal power
To business with the King, more than the scope
Of these delated° articles allow. [*Gives a paper.*]
Farewell, and let your haste commend your duty.
CORNELIUS, VOLTIMAND: In that, and all things,
    will we show our duty.   40
KING: We doubt it nothing. Heartily farewell.
            [*Exit Voltimand and Cornelius.*]
And now, Laertes, what's the news with you?
You told us of some suit; what is 't, Laertes?
You cannot speak of reason to the Dane°
And lose your voice.° What wouldst thou beg,
    Laertes,   45
That shall not be my offer, not thy asking?
The head is not more native° to the heart,
The hand more instrumental° to the mouth,
Than is the throne of Denmark to thy father.
What wouldst thou have, Laertes?
LAERTES: My dread lord,   50
Your leave and favor to return to France,
From whence though willingly I came to
    Denmark
To show my duty in your coronation,
Yet now I must confess, that duty done,
My thoughts and wishes bend again toward
    France   55
And bow them to your gracious leave and
    pardon.°
KING: Have you your father's leave? What says
    Polonius?
POLONIUS: H'ath, my lord, wrung from me my slow
    leave
By laborsome petition, and at last
Upon his will I seal'd my hard° consent.   60
I do beseech you, give him leave to go.
KING: Take thy fair hour, Laertes. Time be thine,
And thy best graces spend it at thy will!

---

175. [S.D.] *Exeunt:* Latin for "they go out."   I, II. Location: The castle. **[S.D.] *cum aliis:* With others.   9. jointress:** Woman possessed of a joint tenancy of an estate.   **17. know:** Be informed (that).   **18. weak supposal:** Low estimate.   **21. Colleagued with:** Joined to, allied with; **dream . . . advantage:** Illusory hope of success.   **23. Importing:** Pertaining to.   **24. bands:** Contracts.

31. His: Fortinbras's; **gait:** Proceeding.   **31–33. in that . . . subject:** Since the levying of troops and supplies is drawn entirely from the King of Norway's own subjects.   **38. delated:** Detailed. (Variant of *dilated.*)   **44. the Dane:** The Danish king.   **45. lose your voice:** Waste your speech.   **47. native:** Closely connected, related.   **48. instrumental:** Serviceable.   **56. leave and pardon:** Permission to depart.   **60. hard:** Reluctant.

But now, my cousin° Hamlet, and my son —
HAMLET: A little more than kin, and less than
65   kind.°
KING: How is it that the clouds still hang on you?
HAMLET: Not so, my lord. I am too much in the
      sun.°
QUEEN: Good Hamlet, cast thy nighted color off,
      And let thine eye look like a friend on Denmark.
70   Do not forever with thy vailed° lids
      Seek for thy noble father in the dust.
      Thou know'st 'tis common,° all that lives must
        die,
      Passing through nature to eternity.
HAMLET: Ay, madam, it is common.
QUEEN: If it be,
75   Why seems it so particular with thee?
HAMLET: Seems, madam! Nay, it is. I know not
      "seems."
      'Tis not alone my inky cloak, good mother,
      Nor customary suits of solemn black,
      Nor windy suspiration of forc'd breath,
80   No, nor the fruitful° river in the eye,
      Nor the dejected havior of the visage,
      Together with all forms, moods, shapes of grief,
      That can denote me truly. These indeed seem,
      For they are actions that a man might play.
85   But I have that within which passes show;
      These but the trappings and the suits of woe.
KING: 'Tis sweet and commendable in your nature,
      Hamlet,
      To give these mourning duties to your father.
      But you must know your father lost a father,
90   That father lost, lost his, and the survivor bound
      In filial obligation for some term
      To do obsequious° sorrow. But to persever°
      In obstinate condolement° is a course
      Of impious stubbornness. 'Tis unmanly grief.
95   It shows a will most incorrect to heaven,
      A heart unfortified, a mind impatient,
      An understanding simple and unschool'd.
      For what we know must be and is as common
      As any the most vulgar thing to sense,°
100   Why should we in our peevish opposition
      Take it to heart? Fie, 'tis a fault to heaven,

A fault against the dead, a fault to nature,
To reason most absurd, whose common theme
Is death of fathers, and who still hath cried,
From the first corse° till he that died today,   105
"This must be so." We pray you, throw to earth
This unprevailing° woe, and think of us
As of a father; for let the world take note,
You are the most immediate° to our throne,
And with no less nobility of love   110
Than that which dearest father bears his son
Do I impart toward you. For your intent
In going back to school in Wittenberg,°
It is most retrograde° to our desire,
And we beseech you, bend you° to remain   115
Here in the cheer and comfort of our eye,
Our chiefest courtier, cousin, and our son.
QUEEN: Let not thy mother lose her prayers,
      Hamlet.
      I pray thee stay with us, go not to Wittenberg.
HAMLET: I shall in all my best obey you, madam.   120
KING: Why, 'tis a loving and a fair reply.
      Be as ourself in Denmark. Madam, come.
      This gentle and unforc'd accord of Hamlet
      Sits smiling to my heart, in grace whereof
      No jocund° health that Denmark drinks today   125
      But the great cannon to the clouds shall tell,
      And the King's rouse° the heaven shall bruit
      again,°
      Respeaking earthly thunder.° Come away.
            (*Flourish. Exeunt all but Hamlet.*)
HAMLET: O, that this too too sullied° flesh would
      melt,
      Thaw, and resolve itself into a dew!   130
      Or that the Everlasting had not fix'd
      His canon° 'gainst self-slaughter! O God, God,
      How weary, stale, flat, and unprofitable
      Seem to me all the uses of this world!
      Fie on 't, ah, fie! 'Tis an unweeded garden   135
      That grows to seed. Things rank and gross in
      nature
      Possess it merely.° That it should come to this!
      But two months dead — nay, not so much, not
      two.
      So excellent a king, that was to° this

---

64. cousin: Any kin not of the immediate family. **65. A little . . . kind:** Closer than an ordinary nephew (since I am stepson), and yet more separated in natural feeling (with pun on *kind*, meaning *affectionate* and *natural, lawful*. This line is often read as an aside, but it need not be.) **67. sun:** The sunshine of the King's royal favor (with pun on *son*). **70. vailed:** Downcast. **72. common:** Of universal occurrence. (But Hamlet plays on the sense of *vulgar* in line 74.) **80. fruitful:** Abundant. **92. obsequious:** Suited to obsequies or funerals; **persever:** persevere. **93. condolement:** Sorrowing. **99. As . . . sense:** As the most ordinary experience.

105. corse: Corpse. **107. unprevailing:** Unavailing. **109. most immediate:** Next in succession. **113. Wittenberg:** Famous German university founded in 1502. **114. retrograde:** Contrary. **115. bend you:** Incline yourself. **125. jocund:** Merry. **127. rouse:** Draft of liquor; **bruit again:** Loudly echo. **128. thunder:** Of trumpet and kettledrum, sounded when the King drinks; see I, IV, 8–12. **129. sullied:** Defiled. (The early quartos read *sallied,* the Folio *solid.*) **132. canon:** Law. **137. merely:** Completely. **139. to:** In comparison to.

140   Hyperion° to a satyr; so loving to my mother
       That he might not beteem° the winds of heaven
       Visit her face too roughly. Heaven and earth,
       Must I remember? Why, she would hang on him
       As if increase of appetite had grown
145   By what it fed on, and yet, within a month —
       Let me not think on 't. Frailty, thy name is
           woman! —
       A little month, or ere those shoes were old
       With which she followed my poor father's body,
       Like Niobe,° all tears, why she, even she —
150   O God, a beast, that wants discourse of reason,°
       Would have mourn'd longer — married with my
           uncle,
       My father's brother, but no more like my father
       Than I to Hercules. Within a month,
       Ere yet the salt of most unrighteous tears
155   Had left the flushing in her galled° eyes,
       She married. O, most wicked speed, to post
       With such dexterity to incestuous° sheets!
       It is not nor it cannot come to good.
       But break, my heart, for I must hold my tongue.

(*Enter Horatio, Marcellus, and Bernardo.*)

       HORATIO: Hail to your lordship!
160   HAMLET: I am glad to see you well.
           Horatio! — or I do forget myself.
       HORATIO: The same, my lord, and your poor
           servant ever.
       HAMLET: Sir, my good friend; I'll change° that
           name with you.
           And what make° you from Wittenberg, Horatio?
165   Marcellus?
       MARCELLUS: My good lord.
       HAMLET: I am very glad to see you. [*To Bernardo.*]
           Good even, sir. —
           But what, in faith, make you from Wittenberg?
       HORATIO: A truant disposition, good my lord.
170   HAMLET: I would not hear your enemy say so,
           Nor shall you do my ear that violence
           To make it truster of your own report
           Against yourself. I know you are no truant.

       But what is your affair in Elsinore?
       We'll teach you to drink deep ere you depart.   175
       HORATIO: My lord, I came to see your father's
           funeral.
       HAMLET: I prithee do not mock me, fellow student;
           I think it was to see my mother's wedding.
       HORATIO: Indeed, my lord, it followed hard° upon.
       HAMLET: Thrift, thrift, Horatio! The funeral bak'd
           meats   180
           Did coldly furnish forth the marriage tables.
           Would I had met my dearest° foe in heaven
           Or° ever I had seen that day, Horatio!
           My father! — Methinks I see my father.
       HORATIO: Where, my lord?
       HAMLET: In my mind's eye, Horatio.   185
       HORATIO: I saw him once. 'A° was a goodly king.
       HAMLET: 'A was a man, take him for all in all,
           I shall not look upon his like again.
       HORATIO: My lord, I think I saw him yesternight.
       HAMLET: Saw? Who?   190
       HORATIO: My lord, the King your father.
       HAMLET: The King my father?
       HORATIO: Season your admiration° for a while
           With an attent° ear, till I may deliver,
           Upon the witness of these gentlemen,
           This marvel to you.
       HAMLET: For God's love, let me hear!   195
       HORATIO: Two nights together had these gentlemen,
       HORATIO: Two nights together had these gentlemen,
           Marcellus and Bernardo, on their watch,
           In the dead waste and middle of the night,
           Been thus encount'red. A figure like your father,
           Armed at point° exactly, cap-a-pe,°   200
           Appears before them, and with solemn march
           Goes slow and stately by them. Thrice he walk'd
           By their oppress'd and fear-surprised eyes
           Within his truncheon's° length, whilst they,
              distill'd
           Almost to jelly with the act° of fear,   205
           Stand dumb and speak not to him. This to me
           In dreadful secrecy impart they did,
           And I with them the third night kept the watch,
           Where, as they had delivered, both in time,
           Form of the thing, each word made true and
              good,   210
           The apparition comes. I knew your father;
           These hands are not more like.
       HAMLET: But where was this?

---

140. Hyperion: Titan sun-god, father of Helios.   **141. beteem:**
Allow.   **149. Niobe:** Tantalus's daughter, Queen of Thebes,
who boasted that she had more sons and daughters than
Leto; for this, Apollo and Artemis, children of Leto, slew
her fourteen children. She was turned by Zeus into a stone
which continually dropped tears.   **150. wants . . . reason:**
Lacks the faculty of reason.   **155. galled:** Irritated, inflamed.
157. incestuous: In Shakespeare's day, the marriage of a man
like Claudius to his deceased brother's wife was considered
incestuous.   **163. change:** Exchange (i.e., the name of friend).
164. make: Do.

179. hard: Close.   **182. dearest:** Direst.   **183. or:** Ere, before.
186. 'A: he.   **192. Season your admiration:** Restrain your
astonishment.   **193. attent:** Attentive.   **200. at point:** Completely; **cap-a-pe:** From head to foot.   **204. truncheon:** Officer's staff.   **205. act:** Action, operation.

MARCELLUS: My lord, upon the platform where we
    watch.
HAMLET: Did you not speak to it?
HORATIO: My lord, I did,
215 But answer made it none. Yet once methought
It lifted up it° head and did address
Itself to motion, like as it would speak;
But even then the morning cock crew loud,
And at the sound it shrunk in haste away,
And vanish'd from our sight.
220 HAMLET: 'Tis very strange.
HORATIO: As I do live, my honor'd lord, 'tis true,
And we did think it writ down in our duty
To let you know of it.
HAMLET: Indeed, indeed, sirs. But this troubles me.
Hold you the watch tonight?
225 ALL: We do, my lord.
HAMLET: Arm'd, say you?
ALL: Arm'd, my lord.
HAMLET: From top to toe?
ALL: My lord, from head to foot.
HAMLET: Then saw you not his face?
230 HORATIO: O, yes, my lord. He wore his beaver° up.
HAMLET: What, looked he frowningly?
HORATIO: A countenance more
In sorrow than in anger.
HAMLET: Pale or red?
HORATIO: Nay, very pale.
HAMLET: And fix'd his eyes upon you?
HORATIO: Most constantly.
HAMLET: I would I had been there.
235 HORATIO: It would have much amaz'd you.
HAMLET: Very like, very like. Stay'd it long?
HORATIO: While one with moderate haste might
    tell° a hundred.
MARCELLUS, BERNARDO: Longer, longer.
HORATIO: Not when I saw 't.
HAMLET: His beard was grizzl'd, — no?
240 HORATIO: It was, as I have seen it in his life,
A sable silver'd.°
HAMLET: I will watch tonight.
Perchance 'twill walk again.
HORATIO: I warr'nt it will.
HAMLET: If it assume my noble father's person,
I'll speak to it, though hell itself should gape
245 And bid me hold my peace. I pray you all,
If you have hitherto conceal'd this sight,
Let it be tenable° in your silence still,
And whatsomever else shall hap tonight,
Give it an understanding, but no tongue.
250 I will requite your loves. So, fare you well.

216. it: Its.   230. beaver: Visor on the helmet.   237. tell:
Count.   241. sable silver'd: Black mixed with white.   247.
tenable: Held tightly.

Upon the platform, 'twixt eleven and twelve,
I'll visit you.
ALL: Our duty to your honor.
HAMLET: Your loves, as mine to you. Farewell.
             (*Exeunt [all but Hamlet]*.)
My father's spirit in arms! All is not well.
I doubt° some foul play. Would the night were
    come!   255
Till then sit still, my soul. Foul deeds will rise,
Though all the earth o'erwhelm them, to men's
    eyes.

                     (*Exit.*)

[Scene III]°

(*Enter Laertes and Ophelia, his sister.*)

LAERTES: My necessaries are embark'd. Farewell.
And, sister, as the winds give benefit
And convoy is assistant,° do not sleep
But let me hear from you.
OPHELIA: Do you doubt that?
LAERTES: For Hamlet, and the trifling of his favor,   5
Hold it a fashion and a toy in blood,°
A violet in the youth of primy° nature,
Forward,° not permanent, sweet, not lasting,
The perfume and suppliance° of a minute —
No more.
OPHELIA: No more but so?
LAERTES: Think it no more.   10
For nature crescent° does not grow alone
In thews° and bulk, but, as this temple° waxes,
The inward service of the mind and soul
Grows wide withal.° Perhaps he loves you now,
And now no soil° nor cautel° doth besmirch   15
The virtue of his will;° but you must fear,
His greatness weigh'd,° his will is not his own.
[For he himself is subject to his birth.]
He may not, as unvalued persons do,
Carve° for himself; for on his choice depends   20
The safety and health of this whole state,
And therefore must his choice be circumscrib'd
Unto the voice and yielding° of that body
Whereof he is the head. Then if he says he loves
    you,

255. doubt: Suspect.   I, III. Location: Polonius's chambers.
3. convoy is assistant: Means of conveyance are available.
6. toy in blood: Passing amorous fancy.   7. primy: In its
prime, springtime.   8. Forward: Precocious.   9. suppliance:
Supply, filler.   11. crescent: Growing, waxing.   12. thews:
Bodily strength; temple: Body.   14. Grows wide withal:
Grows along with it.   15. soil: Blemish; cautel: deceit.   16.
will: desire.   17. greatness weigh'd: High position considered.
20. Carve: Choose pleasure.   23. Voice and yielding: assent,
approval.

25 It fits your wisdom so far to believe it
    As he in his particular act and place
    May give his saying deed,° which is no further
    Than the main voice of Denmark goes withal.
    Then weigh what loss your honor may sustain
30 If with too credent° ear you list° his songs,
    Or lose your heart, or your chaste treasure open
    To his unmaster'd importunity.
    Fear it, Ophelia, fear it, my dear sister,
    And keep you in the rear of your affection,
35 Out of the shot° and danger of desire.
    The chariest° maid is prodigal enough
    If she unmask her beauty to the moon.
    Virtue itself scapes not calumnious strokes.
    The canker galls° the infants of the spring
40 Too oft before their buttons° be disclos'd,°
    And in the morn and liquid dew° of youth
    Contagious blastments° are most imminent.
    Be wary then; best safety lies in fear.
    Youth to itself rebels, though none else near.
45 OPHELIA: I shall the effect of this good lesson keep
    As watchman to my heart. But, good my
        brother,
    Do not, as some ungracious pastors do,
    Show me the steep and thorny way to heaven,
    Whiles, like a puff'd° and reckless libertine,
50 Himself the primrose path of dalliance treads,
    And recks° not his own rede.°

(Enter Polonius.)

LAERTES: O, fear me not.
    I stay too long. But here my father comes.
    A double blessing is a double° grace;
    Occasion° smiles upon a second leave.
POLONIUS: Yet here, Laertes? Aboard, aboard, for
55   shame!
    The wind sits in the shoulder of your sail,
    And you are stay'd for. There — my blessing
        with thee!
    And these few precepts in thy memory
    Look thou character.° Give thy thoughts no
        tongue,
60 Nor any unproportion'd thought his° act.
    Be thou familiar,° but by no means vulgar.°
    Those friends thou hast, and their adoption
        tried,°

Grapple them to thy soul with hoops of steel,
But do not dull thy palm with entertainment
Of each new-hatch'd, unfledg'd courage.° Beware 65
Of entrance to a quarrel, but, being in,
Bear't that° th' opposed may beware of thee.
Give every man thy ear, but few thy voice;
Take each man's censure,° but reserve thy
    judgment.
Costly thy habit as thy purse can buy,   70
But not express'd in fancy; rich, not gaudy,
For the apparel oft proclaims the man,
And they in France of the best rank and station
Are of a most select and generous chief° in that.
Neither a borrower nor a lender be,   75
For loan oft loses both itself and friend,
And borrowing dulleth edge of husbandry.°
This above all: to thine own self be true,
And it must follow, as the night the day,
Thou canst not then be false to any man.   80
Farewell. My blessing season° this in thee!
LAERTES: Most humbly do I take my leave, my
    lord.
POLONIUS: The time invests° you. Go, your servants
    tend.°
LAERTES: Farewell, Ophelia, and remember well
    What I have said to you.   85
OPHELIA: 'Tis in my memory lock'd,
    And you yourself shall keep the key of it.
LAERTES: Farewell.   *(Exit Laertes.)*
POLONIUS: What is 't, Ophelia, he hath said to you?
OPHELIA: So please you, something touching the
    Lord Hamlet.   90
POLONIUS: Marry,° well bethought.
    'Tis told me he hath very oft of late
    Given private time to you, and you yourself
    Have of your audience been most free and
        bounteous.
    If it be so — as so 'tis put on° me,   95
    And that in way of caution — I must tell you
    You do not understand yourself so clearly
    As it behooves my daughter and your honor.
    What is between you? Give me up the truth.
OPHELIA: He hath, my lord, of late made many
    tenders°   100
    Of his affection to me.
POLONIUS: Affection? Pooh! You speak like a green
    girl,

---

27. **deed:** Effect.   30. **credent:** Credulous; **list:** Listen to.
35. **shot:** Range.   36. **chariest:** Most scrupulously modest.
39. **canker galls:** Cankerworm destroys.   40. **buttons:** Buds;
disclos'd: Opened.   41. **liquid dew:** Time when dew is fresh.
42. **blastments:** Blights.   49. **puff'd:** Bloated.   51. **recks:**
Heeds; **rede:** Counsel.   53. **double:** I.e., Laertes has already
bidden his father good-by.   54. **Occasion:** Opportunity.
59. **character:** Inscribe.   60. **his:** Its.   61. **familiar:** Sociable;
vulgar: common.   62. **tried:** Tested.

65. **courage:** Young man of spirit.   67. **Bear't that:** Manage
it so that.   69. **censure:** Opinion, judgment.   74. **generous
chief:** Noble eminence (?)   77. **husbandry:** Thrift.   81. **season:** Mature.   83. **invests:** Besieges; **tend:** Attend, wait.   91.
Marry: By the Virgin Mary (a mild oath).   95. **put on:**
Impressed on, told to.   100. **tenders:** Offers.

Unsifted° in such perilous circumstance.
Do you believe his tenders, as you call them?
OPHELIA: I do not know, my lord, what I should
105 think.
POLONIUS: Marry, I will teach you. Think yourself
a baby
That you have ta'en these tenders° for true pay,
Which are not sterling.° Tender° yourself more
dearly,
Or — not to crack the wind° of the poor phrase,
110 Running it thus — you'll tender me a fool.°
OPHELIA: My lord, he hath importun'd me with
love
In honorable fashion.
POLONIUS: Ay, fashion° you may call it. Go to, go
to.
OPHELIA: And hath given countenance° to his
speech, my lord,
115 With almost all the holy vows of heaven.
POLONIUS: Ay, springes° to catch woodcocks.° I do
know,
When the blood burns, how prodigal the soul
Lends the tongue vows. These blazes, daughter,
Giving more light than heat, extinct in both
120 Even in their promise, as it is a-making,
You must not take for fire. From this time
Be something scanter of your maiden presence.
Set your entreatments° at a higher rate
Than a command to parle.° For Lord Hamlet,
125 Believe so much in him° that he is young,
And with a larger tether may he walk
Than may be given you. In few,° Ophelia,
Do not believe his vows, for they are brokers,°
Not of that dye° which their investments° show,
130 But mere implorators° of unholy suits,
Breathing° like sanctified and pious bawds,
The better to beguile. This is for all:

103. **Unsifted:** Untried. 107. **tenders:** With added meaning
here of *promises to pay.* 108. **sterling:** Legal currency;
Tender: Hold. 109. **crack the wind:** Run it until it is broken,
winded. 110. **tender me a fool:** (1) Show yourself to me
as a fool; (2) show me up as a fool; (3) present me with a
grandchild (*fool* was a term of endearment for a child).
113. **fashion:** Mere form, pretense. 114. **countenance:** Credit,
support. 116. **springes:** Snares; **woodcocks:** Birds easily
caught; here used to connote gullibility. 123. **entreatments:**
Negotiations for surrender (a military term). 124. **parle:**
Discuss terms with the enemy. (Polonius urges his daughter,
in the metaphor of military language, not to meet with Hamlet
and consider giving in to him merely because he requests an
interview.) 125. **so . . . him:** This much concerning him.
127. **In few:** Briefly. 128. **brokers:** Go-betweens, procurers.
129. **dye:** Color or sort; **investments:** Clothes (i.e., they are
not what they seem). 130. **mere implorators:** Out and out
solicitors. 131. **Breathing:** Speaking.

I would not, in plain terms, from this time forth
Have you so slander° any moment leisure
As to give words or talk with the Lord Hamlet. 135
Look to 't, I charge you. Come your ways.
OPHELIA: I shall obey, my lord. (*Exeunt.*)

[Scene IV]°

(*Enter Hamlet, Horatio, and Marcellus.*)

HAMLET: The air bites shrewdly; it is very cold.
HORATIO: It is a nipping and an eager air.
HAMLET: What hour now?
HORATIO: I think it lacks of twelve.
MARCELLUS: No, it is struck.
HORATIO: Indeed? I heard it not.
It then draws near the season 5
Wherein the spirit held his wont to walk.
(*A flourish of trumpets, and two pieces° go off
[within].*)
What does this mean, my lord?
HAMLET: The King doth wake° tonight and takes
his rouse,°
Keeps wassail,° and the swagg'ring up-spring°
reels;
And as he drains his draughts of Rhenish° down, 10
The kettle-drum and trumpet thus bray out
The triumph of his pledge.°
HORATIO: Is it a custom?
HAMLET: Ay, marry, is 't,
But to my mind, though I am native here
And to the manner° born, it is a custom 15
More honor'd in the breach than the
observance.°
This heavy-headed revel east and west°
Makes us traduc'd and tax'd of° other nations.
They clepe° us drunkards, and with swinish
phrase°
Soil our addition;° and indeed it takes 20
From our achievements, though perform'd at
height,°
The pith and marrow of our attribute.
So, oft it chances in particular men,

134. **slander:** Bring disgrace or reproach upon. **I, IV. Location:**
The guard platform. 6. **[S.D.]** *pieces:* I.e., of ordnance,
cannon. 8. **wake:** Stay awake and hold revel; **rouse:** Carouse,
drinking bout. 9. **wassail:** Carousal; **up-spring:** Wild German
dance. 10. **Rhenish:** Rhine wine. 12. **triumph . . . pledge:**
His feat in draining the wine in a single draught. 15. **manner:**
Custom (of drinking). 16. **More . . . observance:** Better
neglected than followed. 17. **east and west:** I.e., everywhere.
18. **tax'd of:** censured by. 19. **clepe:** Call; **with swinish
phrase:** By calling us swine. 20. **addition:** Reputation. 21.
at height: Outstandingly.

25 That for some vicious mole of nature° in them,
    As in their birth — wherein they are not guilty,
    Since nature cannot choose his° origin —
    By the o'ergrowth of some complexion,°
    Oft breaking down the pales° and forts of
        reason,
30 Or by some habit that too much o'er-leavens°
    The form of plausive° manners, that these men,
    Carrying, I say, the stamp of one defect,
    Being nature's livery,° or fortune's star,°
    Their virtues else, be they as pure as grace,
    As infinite as man may undergo,
35 Shall in the general censure take corruption
    From that particular fault. The dram of eale°
    Doth all the noble substance of a doubt°
    To his own scandal.°

(Enter Ghost.)

HORATIO: Look, my lord, it comes!
HAMLET: Angels and ministers of grace defend us!
40 Be thou a spirit of health° or goblin damn'd,
    Bring with thee airs from heaven or blasts from
        hell,
    Be thy intents wicked or charitable,
    Thou com'st in such a questionable° shape
    That I will speak to thee. I'll call thee Hamlet,
45 King, father, royal Dane. O, answer me!
    Let me not burst in ignorance; but tell
    Why thy canoniz'd° bones, hearsed° in death,
    Have burst their cerements;° why the sepulcher
    Wherein we saw thee quietly interr'd
50 Hath op'd his ponderous and marble jaws
    To cast thee up again. What may this mean,
    That thou, dead corse, again in complete steel
    Revisits thus the glimpses of the moon,°
    Making night hideous, and we fools of nature°
55 So horridly to shake our disposition
    With thoughts beyond the reaches of our souls?

Say, why is this? Wherefore? What should we
    do?
            ([Ghost] beckons [Hamlet].)
HORATIO: It beckons you to go away with it,
    As if it some impartment° did desire
    To you alone.
MARCELLUS: Look with what courteous action   60
    It waves you to a more removed ground.
    But do not go with it.
HORATIO: No, by no means.
HAMLET: It will not speak. Then I will follow it.
HORATIO: Do not, my lord.
HAMLET: Why, what should be the fear?
    I do not set my life at a pin's fee,°   65
    And for my soul, what can it do to that,
    Being a thing immortal as itself?
    It waves me forth again. I'll follow it.
HORATIO: What if it tempt you toward the flood,
        my lord,
    Or to the dreadful summit of the cliff   70
    That beetles o'er° his° base into the sea,
    And there assume some other horrible form
    Which might deprive your sovereignty of
        reason,°
    And draw you into madness? Think of it.
    The very place puts toys of desperation,°   75
    Without more motive, into every brain
    That looks so many fathoms to the sea
    And hears it roar beneath.
HAMLET: It waves me still.
    Go on, I'll follow thee.
MARCELLUS: You shall not go, my lord.
            [They try to stop him.]
HAMLET: Hold off your hands!   80
HORATIO: Be rul'd, you shall not go.
HAMLET: My fate cries out,
    And makes each petty artery° in this body
    As hardy as the Nemean lion's° nerve.°
    Still am I call'd. Unhand me, gentlemen.
    By heaven, I'll make a ghost of him that lets°
        me!   85
    I say, away! Go on. I'll follow thee.
            (Exeunt Ghost and Hamlet.)
HORATIO: He waxes desperate with imagination.
MARCELLUS: Let's follow. 'Tis not fit thus to obey
    him.
HORATIO: Have after. To what issue° will this
    come?

---

24. mole of nature: Natural blemish in one's constitution.
26. his: Its.   **27. complexion:** Humor (i.e., one of the four
humors or fluids thought to determine temperament).   **28.
pales:** Palings, fences (as of a fortification).   **29. o'er-leavens:**
Induces a change throughout (as yeast works in dough).   **30.
plausive:** Pleasing.   **32. nature's livery:** Endowment from
nature; **fortune's star:** Mark placed by fortune.   **36. dram
of eale:** Small amount of evil (?)   **37. of a doubt:** A famous
crux, sometimes emended to *oft about* or *often dout,* i.e.,
"often erase" or "do out," or to *antidote,* counteract.   **38.
To . . . scandal:** To the disgrace of the whole enterprise.
40. of health: Of spiritual good.   **43. questionable:** Inviting
question or conversation.   **47. canoniz'd:** Buried according
to the canons of the church; **hearsed:** coffined.   **48. cerements:**
Grave-clothes.   **53. glimpses of the moon:** Earth by night.
54. fools of nature: Mere men, limited to natural knowledge.

59. impartment: Communication.   **65. fee:** Value.   **71. beetles o'er:** Overhangs threateningly; **his:** Its.   **73. deprive . . .
reason:** Take away the rule of reason over your mind.   **75.
toys of desperation:** Fancies of desperate acts, i.e., suicide.
82. artery: Sinew.   **83. Nemean lion:** One of the monsters
slain by Hercules in his twelve labors; **nerve:** sinew.   **85.
lets:** Hinders.   **89. issue:** Outcome.

MARCELLUS: Something is rotten in the state of
90   Denmark.
HORATIO: Heaven will direct it.°
MARCELLUS: Nay, let's follow him. (*Exeunt.*)

[Scene v]°

(*Enter Ghost and Hamlet.*)

HAMLET: Whither wilt thou lead me? Speak. I'll go
      no further.
GHOST: Mark me.
HAMLET: I will.
GHOST: My hour is almost come,
      When I to sulph'rous and tormenting flames
      Must render up myself.
HAMLET: Alas, poor ghost!
5   GHOST: Pity me not, but lend thy serious hearing
      To what I shall unfold.
HAMLET: Speak. I am bound to hear.
GHOST: So art thou to revenge, when thou shalt
      hear.
HAMLET: What?
10 GHOST: I am thy father's spirit,
      Doom'd for a certain term to walk the night,
      And for the day confin'd to fast° in fires,
      Till the foul crimes° done in my days of nature
      Are burnt and purg'd away. But that° I am
      forbid
15   To tell the secrets of my prison-house,
      I could a tale unfold whose lightest word
      Would harrow up thy soul, freeze thy young
      blood,
      Make thy two eyes, like stars, start from their
      spheres,°
      Thy knotted and combined locks° to part,
20   And each particular hair to stand an end,°
      Like quills upon the fearful porpentine.°
      But this eternal blazon° must not be
      To ears of flesh and blood. List, list, O, list!
      If thou didst ever thy dear father love —
25 HAMLET: O God!
GHOST: Revenge his foul and most unnatural
      murder.
HAMLET: Murder?
GHOST: Murder most foul, as in the best it is,

But this most foul, strange, and unnatural.
HAMLET: Haste me to know 't, that I, with wings
      as swift   30
      As meditation or the thoughts of love,
      May sweep to my revenge.
GHOST: I find thee apt;
      And duller shouldst thou be than the fat weed
      That roots itself in ease on Lethe° wharf,°
      Wouldst thou not stir in this. Now, Hamlet,
      hear.   35
      'Tis given out that, sleeping in my orchard,
      A serpent stung me. So the whole ear of
      Denmark
      Is by a forged process° of my death
      Rankly abus'd.° But know, thou noble youth,
      The serpent that did sting thy father's life   40
      Now wears his crown.
HAMLET: O my prophetic soul!
      My uncle!
GHOST: Ay, that incestuous, that adulterate° beast,
      With witchcraft of his wits, with traitorous
      gifts —
      O wicked wit and gifts, that have the power   45
      So to seduce! — won to his shameful lust
      The will of my most seeming-virtuous queen.
      O Hamlet, what a falling-off was there!
      From me, whose love was of that dignity
      That it went hand in hand even with the vow   50
      I made to her in marriage, and to decline
      Upon a wretch whose natural gifts were poor
      To those of mine!
      But virtue, as it never will be moved,
      Though lewdness court it in a shape of heaven,°   55
      So lust, though to a radiant angel link'd,
      Will sate itself in a celestial bed,
      And prey on garbage.
      But, soft, methinks I scent the morning air.
      Brief let me be. Sleeping within my orchard,   60
      My custom always of the afternoon,
      Upon my secure° hour thy uncle stole,
      With juice of cursed hebona° in a vial,
      And in the porches of my ears did pour
      The leprous° distillment, whose effect   65
      Holds such an enmity with blood of man
      That swift as quicksilver it courses through
      The natural gates and alleys of the body,

---

91. **it:** The outcome.   **I, v. Location:** The battlements of
the castle.   **12. fast:** Do penance.   **13. crimes:** Sins.   **14.
But that:** Were it not that.   **18. spheres:** Eye sockets, here
compared to the orbits or transparent revolving spheres in
which, according to Ptolemaic astronomy, the heavenly bodies
were fixed.   **19. knotted . . . locks:** Hair neatly arranged
and confined.   **20. an end:** on end.   **21. fearful porpentine:**
Frightened porcupine.   **22. eternal blazon:** Revelation of the
secrets of eternity.

34. Lethe: The river of forgetfulness in Hades; **wharf:** Bank.
38. forged process: Falsified account.   **39. abus'd:** Deceived.
43. adulterate: Adulterous.   **55. shape of heaven:** Heavenly
form.   **62. secure:** Confident, unsuspicious.   **63. hebona:**
Poison. (The word seems to be a form of *ebony*, though it
is perhaps thought to be related to *henbane*, a poison, or to
ebenus, yew.)   **65. leprous:** Causing leprosy-like disfigurement.

And with a sudden vigor it doth posset°
70 And curd, like eager° droppings into milk,
The thin and wholesome blood. So did it mine,
And a most instant tetter° bark'd° about,
Most lazar-like,° with vile and loathsome crust,
All my smooth body.
75 Thus was I, sleeping, by a brother's hand
Of life, of crown, of queen, at once dispatch'd,°
Cut off even in the blossoms of my sin,
Unhous'led,° disappointed,° unanel'd,°
No reck'ning made, but sent to my account
80 With all my imperfections on my head.
O, horrible! O, horrible, most horrible!
If thou hast nature° in thee, bear it not.
Let not the royal bed of Denmark be
A couch for luxury° and damned incest.
85 But, howsomever thou pursues this act,
Taint not thy mind, nor let thy soul contrive
Against thy mother aught. Leave her to heaven
And to those thorns that in her bosom lodge,
To prick and sting her. Fare thee well at once.
90 The glow-worm shows the matin° to be near,
And 'gins to pale his uneffectual fire.°
Adieu, adieu, adieu! Remember me.   [*Exit.*]
HAMLET: O all you host of heaven! O earth! What
else?
And shall I couple° hell? O fie! Hold, hold, my
heart,
95 And you, my sinews, grow not instant old,
But bear me stiffly up. Remember thee!
Ay, thou poor ghost, whiles memory holds a
seat
In this distracted globe.° Remember thee!
Yea, from the table° of my memory
100 I'll wipe away all trivial fond° records,
All saws° of books, all forms,° all pressures° past
That youth and observation copied there,
And thy commandment all alone shall live
Within the book and volume of my brain,
105 Unmix'd with baser matter. Yes, by heaven!
O most pernicious woman!
O villain, villain, smiling, damned villain!

My tables — meet it is I set it down,
That one may smile, and smile, and be a villain.
At least I am sure it may be so in Denmark.   110
[*Writing.*]
So, uncle, there you are. Now to my word;
It is "Adieu, adieu! Remember me."
I have sworn 't.

(*Enter Horatio and Marcellus.*)

HORATIO: My lord, my lord!
MARCELLUS: Lord Hamlet!
HORATIO: Heavens secure him!
HAMLET: So be it!   115
MARCELLUS: Illo, ho, ho, my lord!
HAMLET: Hillo, ho, ho,° boy! Come, bird, come.
MARCELLUS: How is 't, my noble lord?
HORATIO: What news, my lord?
HAMLET: O, wonderful!
HORATIO: Good my lord, tell it.
HAMLET: No, you will reveal it.   120
HORATIO: Not I, my lord, by heaven.
MARCELLUS: Nor I, my lord.
HAMLET: How say you, then, would heart of man
once think it?
But you'll be secret?
HORATIO, MARCELLUS: Ay, by heaven, my
lord.
HAMLET: There's never a villain dwelling in all
Denmark
But he's an arrant° knave.   125
HORATIO: There needs no ghost, my lord, come
from the grave
To tell us this.
HAMLET: Why, right, you are in the right.
And so, without more circumstance° at all,
I hold it fit that we shake hands and part,
You, as your business and desire shall point
you —   130
For every man hath business and desire,
Such as it is — and for my own poor part,
Look you, I'll go pray.
HORATIO: These are but wild and whirling words,
my lord.
HAMLET: I am sorry they offend you, heartily;   135
Yes, faith, heartily.
HORATIO: There's no offense, my lord.
HAMLET: Yes, by Saint Patrick,° but there is,
Horatio,

---

69. **posset:** Coagulate, curdle.   70. **eager:** Sour, acid.   72.
tetter: Eruption of scabs; **bark'd:** covered with a rough covering, like bark on a tree.   73. **lazar-like:** Leper-like.   76.
dispatch'd: Suddenly deprived.   78. **Unhous'led:** Without
having received the sacrament [of Holy Communion]; **disappointed:** unready (spiritually) for the last journey; **unanel'd:**
Without having received extreme unction.   82. **nature:** The
promptings of a son.   84. **luxury:** Lechery.   90. **matin:**
Morning.   91. **uneffectual fire:** Cold light.   94. **couple:**
Add.   98. **globe:** Head.   99. **table:** Writing tablet.   100.
fond: Foolish.   101. **saws:** Wise sayings; **forms:** Images;
pressures: impressions stamped.

117. **Hillo, ho, ho:** A falconer's call to a hawk in air. Hamlet
is playing upon Marcellus's *Illo,* i.e., *halloo.*   125. **arrant:**
Thoroughgoing.   128. **circumstance:** Ceremony.   137. **Saint
Patrick:** The keeper of purgatory and patron saint of all
blunders and confusion.

And much offense too. Touching this vision here,
It is an honest° ghost, that let me tell you.
140 For your desire to know what is between us,
O'ermaster 't as you may. And now, good friends,
As you are friends, scholars, and soldiers,
Give me one poor request.
HORATIO: What is 't, my lord? We will.
HAMLET: Never make known what you have seen
145 tonight.
HORATIO, MARCELLUS: My lord, we will not.
HAMLET: Nay, but swear 't.
HORATIO: In faith,
My lord, not I.
MARCELLUS: Nor I, my lord, in faith.
HAMLET: Upon my sword.°   [Holds out his sword.]
MARCELLUS: We have sworn, my lord, already.
HAMLET: Indeed, upon my sword, indeed.
           (Ghost cries under the stage.)
150 GHOST: Swear.
HAMLET: Ha, ha, boy, say'st thou so? Art thou
there, truepenny?°
Come on, you hear this fellow in the cellarage.
Consent to swear.
HORATIO: Propose the oath, my lord.
HAMLET: Never to speak of this that you have seen,
155 Swear by my sword.
GHOST [beneath]: Swear.
HAMLET: Hic et ubique?° Then we'll shift our ground.
           [He moves to another spot.]
Come hither, gentlemen,
And lay your hands again upon my sword.
160 Swear by my sword
Never to speak of this that you have heard.
GHOST [beneath]: Swear by his sword.
HAMLET: Well said, old mole! Canst work i' th'
earth so fast?
A worthy pioner!° Once more remove, good friends.
           [Moves again.]
HORATIO: O day and night, but this is wondrous
165 strange!
HAMLET: And therefore as a stranger give it welcome.
There are more things in heaven and earth, Horatio,

Than are dreamt of in your philosophy.°
But come;
Here, as before, never, so help you mercy, 170
How strange or odd soe'er I bear myself —
As I perchance hereafter shall think meet
To put an antic° disposition on —
That you, at such times seeing me, never shall,
With arms encumb'red° thus, or this headshake, 175
Or by pronouncing of some doubtful phrase,
As "Well, well, we know," or "We could, an if°
we would,"
Or "If we list° to speak," or "There be, an if
they might,"
Or such ambiguous giving out,° to note°
That you know aught of me — this do swear, 180
So grace and mercy at your most need help you.
GHOST [beneath]: Swear.   [They swear.]
HAMLET: Rest, rest, perturbed spirit! So, gentlemen,
With all my love I do commend me to you;
And what so poor a man as Hamlet is 185
May do, t' express his love and friending to you,
God willing, shall not lack. Let us go in together,
And still° your fingers on your lips, I pray.
The time is out of joint. O cursed spite,
That ever I was born to set it right! 190
       [They wait for him to leave first.]
Nay, come, let's go together.   (Exeunt.)

[ACT II • Scene I]°

(Enter old Polonius, with his man [Reynaldo].)

POLONIUS: Give him this money and these notes,
Reynaldo.
REYNALDO: I will, my lord.
POLONIUS: You shall do marvel's° wisely, good
Reynaldo,
Before you visit him, to make inquire
Of his behavior.
REYNALDO: My lord, I did intend it. 5
POLONIUS: Marry, well said, very well said. Look
you, sir,
Inquire me first what Danskers° are in Paris,
And how, and who, what means,° and where
they keep,°

139. honest: I.e., a real ghost and not an evil spirit. 148. sword: The hilt in the form of a cross. 151. truepenny: Honest old fellow. 157. Hic et ubique: Here and everywhere (Latin). 164. pioner: Pioneer, digger, miner.

168. your philosophy: This subject called "natural philosophy" or "science" that people talk about. 173. antic: Fantastic. 175. encumb'red: Folded or entwined. 177. an if: If. 178. list: Were inclined. 179. giving out: Profession of knowledge; note: Give a sign, indicate. 188. still: Always. II, I. Location: Polonius's chambers. 3. marvel's: Marvelous(ly). 7. Danskers: Danes. 8. what means: What wealth (they have); keep: Dwell.

What company, at what expense; and finding
10   By this encompassment° and drift° of question
That they do know my son, come you more
     nearer
Than your particular demands will touch it.°
Take° you, as 'twere, some distant knowledge of
     him,
As thus, "I know his father and his friends,
15   And in part him." Do you mark this, Reynaldo?
REYNALDO: Ay, very well, my lord.
POLONIUS: "And in part him, but," you may say,
     "not well.
But, if 't be he I mean, he's very wild,
Addicted so and so," and there put on° him
What forgeries° you please — marry, none so
20   rank
As may dishonor, him take heed of that,
But, sir, such wanton,° wild, and usual slips,
As are companions noted and most known
To youth and liberty.
REYNALDO: As gaming, my lord.
25   POLONIUS: Ay, or drinking, fencing, swearing,
     Quarreling, drabbing° — you may go so far.
REYNALDO: My lord, that would dishonor him.
POLONIUS: Faith, no, as you may season° it in the
     charge.
You must not put another scandal on him
30   That he is open to incontinency;°
That's not my meaning. But breathe his faults so
     quaintly°
That they may seem the taints of liberty,°
The flash and outbreak of a fiery mind,
A savageness in unreclaimed° blood,
Of general assault.°
35   REYNALDO: But, my good lord —
POLONIUS: Wherefore should you do this?
REYNALDO: Ay, my lord,
I would know that.
POLONIUS: Marry, sir, here's my drift,
And, I believe, it is a fetch of wit.°
You laying these slight sullies on my son,
40   As 'twere a thing a little soil'd i' th' working,°

Mark you,
Your party in converse,° him you would sound,°
Having ever° seen in the prenominate crimes°
The youth you breathe° of guilty, be assur'd
He closes with you in this consequence:°   45
"Good sir," or so, or "friend," or "gentleman,"
According to the phrase or the addition°
Of man and country.
REYNALDO: Very good, my lord.
POLONIUS: And then, sir, does 'a this — 'a does —
     what was I about to say?
By the mass, I was about to say something.   50
Where did I leave?
REYNALDO: At "closes in the consequence."
POLONIUS: At "closes in the consequence," ay,
     marry.
He closes thus: "I know the gentleman;
I saw him yesterday, or th' other day,
Or then, or then, with such, or such, and, as
     you say,   55
There was 'a gaming, there o'ertook in 's rouse,°
There falling out° at tennis," or perchance,
"I saw him enter such a house of sale,"
Videlicet,° a brothel, or so forth. See you now,
Your bait of falsehood takes this carp° of truth; 60
And thus do we of wisdom and of reach,°
With windlasses° and with assays of bias,°
By indirections find directions° out.
So by my former lecture and advice
Shall you my son. You have me, have you not?   65
REYNALDO: My lord, I have.
POLONIUS: God buy ye; fare ye well.
REYNALDO: Good my lord.
POLONIUS: Observe his inclination in yourself.°
REYNALDO: I shall, my lord.
POLONIUS: And let him ply° his music.
REYNALDO: Well, my lord. 70
POLONIUS: Farewell.   (*Exit Reynaldo.*)

(*Enter Ophelia.*)

         How now, Ophelia, what's the matter?

10. **encompassment:** Roundabout talking; **drift:** Gradual approach or course.   **11–12. come . . . it:** You will find out more this way than by asking pointed questions (*particular demands*).   **13. Take:** Assume, pretend.   **19. put on:** Impute to.   **20. forgeries:** Invented tales.   **22. wanton:** Sportive, unrestrained.   **26. drabbing:** Whoring.   **28. season:** Temper, soften.   **30. incontinency:** Habitual loose behavior.   **31. quaintly:** Delicately, ingeniously.   **32. taints of liberty:** Faults resulting from freedom.   **34. unreclaimed:** Untamed.   **35. general assault:** Tendency that assails all unrestrained youth.   **38. fetch of wit:** Clever trick.   **40. soil'd i' th' working:** Shopworn.

42. **converse:** Conversation; **sound:** Sound out.   **43. Having ever:** If he has ever; **prenominate crimes:** Before-mentioned offenses.   **44. breathe:** Speak.   **45. closes . . . consequence:** Follows your lead in some fashion as follows.   **47. addition:** Title.   **56. o'ertook in 's rouse:** Overcome by drink.   **57. falling out:** Quarreling.   **59. Videlicet:** Namely.   **60. carp:** A fish.   **61. reach:** Capacity, ability.   **62. windlasses:** Circuitous paths (literally, circuits made to head off the game in hunting); **assays of bias:** Attempts through indirection (like the curving path of the bowling ball which is biased or weighted to one side).   **63. directions:** The way things really are.   **68. in yourself:** In your own person (as well as by asking questions).   **70. let him ply:** See that he continues to study.

OPHELIA: O, my lord, my lord, I have been so
    affrighted!

POLONIUS: With what, i' th' name of God?

OPHELIA: My lord, as I was sewing in my closet,°

75   Lord Hamlet, with his doublet° all unbrac'd,°
    No hat upon his head, his stockings fouled,
    Ungart'red, and down-gyved to his ankle,°
    Pale as his shirt, his knees knocking each other,
    And with a look so piteous in purport

80   As if he had been loosed out of hell
    To speak of horrors — he comes before me.

POLONIUS: Mad for thy love?

OPHELIA: My lord, I do not know,
    But truly I do fear it.

POLONIUS: What said he?

OPHELIA: He took me by the wrist and held me
    hard.

85   Then goes he to the length of all his arm,
    And, with his other hand thus o'er his brow,
    He falls to such perusal of my face
    As 'a would draw it. Long stay'd he so.
    At last, a little shaking of mine arm

90   And thrice his head thus waving up and down,
    He rais'd a sigh so piteous and profound
    As it did seem to shatter all his bulk°
    And end his being. That done, he lets me go,
    And, with his head over his shoulder turn'd,

95   He seem'd to find his way without his eyes,
    For out o' doors he went without their helps,
    And, to the last, bended their light on me.

POLONIUS: Come, go with me. I will go seek the
    King.
    This is the very ecstasy° of love,

100   Whose violent property° fordoes° itself
    And leads the will to desperate undertakings
    As oft as any passion under heaven
    That does afflict our natures. I am sorry.
    What, have you given him any hard words of
    late?

OPHELIA: No, my good lord, but, as you did
105   command,
    I did repel his letters and denied
    His access to me.

POLONIUS: That hath made him mad.
    I am sorry that with better heed and judgment
    I had not quoted° him. I fear'd he did but trifle

And meant to wrack thee; but, beshrew my
    jealousy!°   110

By heaven, it is as proper to our age°
To cast beyond° ourselves in our opinions
As it is common for the younger sort
To lack discretion. Come, go we to the King.
This must be known, which, being kept close,°
    might move   115

More grief to hide than hate to utter love.°
Come.   (*Exeunt.*)

[Scene II]°

(*Flourish. Enter King and Queen, Rosencrantz, and Guildenstern [with others].*)

KING: Welcome, dear Rosencrantz and
    Guildenstern.
    Moreover that° we much did long to see you,
    The need we have to use you did provoke
    Our hasty sending. Something have you heard
    Of Hamlet's transformation — so call it,   5
    Sith° nor th' exterior nor° the inward man
    Resembles that° it was. What it should be,
    More than his father's death, that thus hath put
    him
    So much from th' understanding of himself,
    I cannot dream of. I entreat you both   10
    That, being of so young days° brought up with
    him,
    And sith so neighbor'd to his youth and havior,
    That you vouchsafe your rest° here in our court
    Some little time, so by your companies
    To draw him on to pleasures, and to gather   15
    So much as from occasion you may glean,
    Whether aught to us unknown afflicts him thus,
    That, open'd,° lies within our remedy.

QUEEN: Good gentlemen, he hath much talk'd of
    you,
    And sure I am two men there is not living   20
    To whom he more adheres. If it will please you
    To show us so much gentry° and good will
    As to expend your time with us awhile
    For the supply and profit° of our hope,

---

74. **closet:** Private chamber.   75. **doublet:** Close-fitting jacket; **unbrac'd:** Unfastened.   77. **down-gyved to his ankle:** Fallen to the ankles (like gyves or fetters).   92. **bulk:** Body.   99. **ecstasy:** Madness.   100. **property:** Nature; **fordoes:** destroys. 109. **quoted:** Observed.

110. **beshrew my jealousy:** A plague upon my suspicious nature.   111. **proper . . . age:** Characteristic of us (old) men. 112. **cast beyond:** Overshoot, miscalculate.   115. **close:** Secret. **115–116 might . . . love:** Might cause more grief (to others) by hiding the knowledge of Hamlet's strange behavior to Ophelia than hatred by telling it.   **I, II. Location:** The castle. 2. **Moreover that:** Besides the fact that.   6. **Sith:** Since; **nor . . . nor:** Neither . . . nor.   7. **that:** What.   11. **of . . . days:** From such early youth.   13. **vouchsafe your rest:** Please to stay.   18. **open'd:** revealed.   22. **gentry:** Courtesy.   24. **supply and profit:** Aid and successful outcome.

25 Your visitation shall receive such thanks
    As fits a king's remembrance.
    ROSENCRANTZ: Both your Majesties
    Might, by the sovereign power you have of us,
    Put your dread pleasures more into command
    Than to entreaty.
    GUILDENSTERN: But we both obey,
30 And here give up ourselves in the full bent°
    To lay our service freely at your feet,
    To be commanded.
    KING: Thanks, Rosencrantz and gentle
        Guildenstern.
    QUEEN: Thanks, Guildenstern and gentle
        Rosencrantz.
35 And I beseech you instantly to visit
    My too much changed son. Go, some of you,
    And bring these gentlemen where Hamlet is.
    GUILDENSTERN: Heavens make our presence and
        our practices
    Pleasant and helpful to him!
    QUEEN: Ay, amen!
    (*Exeunt Rosencrantz and Guildenstern* [*with some
                              Attendants*].)

    (*Enter Polonius.*)

    POLONIUS: Th' ambassadors from Norway, my
40   good lord,
    Are joyfully return'd.
    KING: Thou still° hast been the father of good
        news.
    POLONIUS: Have I, my lord? I assure my good liege
    I hold my duty, as I hold my soul,
45 Both to my God and to my gracious king;
    And I do think, or else this brain of mine
    Hunts not the trail of policy so sure
    As it hath us'd to do, that I have found
    The very cause of Hamlet's lunacy.
50 KING: O, speak of that! That do I long to hear.
    POLONIUS: Give first admittance to th' ambassadors.
    My news shall be the fruit° to that great feast.
    KING: Thyself do grace to them, and bring them in.
                                (*Exit Polonius.*)
    He tells me, my dear Gertrude, he hath found
55 The head and source of all your son's distemper.
    QUEEN: I doubt° it is no other but the main,°
    His father's death, and our o'erhasty marriage.

    (*Enter Ambassadors* [*Voltimand and Cornelius, with
    Polonius*].)

    KING: Well, we shall sift him. — Welcome, my
        good friends!

    Say, Voltimand, what from our brother Norway?
    VOLTIMAND: Most fair return of greetings and
        desires.   60
    Upon our first,° he sent out to suppress
    His nephew's levies, which to him appear'd
    To be a preparation 'gainst the Polack,
    But, better look'd into, he truly found
    It was against your Highness. Whereat griev'd   65
    That so his sickness, age, and impotence
    Was falsely borne in hand,° sends out arrests
    On Fortinbras, which he, in brief, obeys,
    Receives rebuke from Norway, and in fine°
    Makes vow before his uncle never more   70
    To give th' assay° of arms against your Majesty.
    Whereon old Norway, overcome with joy,
    Gives him three score thousand crowns in
        annual fee,
    And his commission to employ those soldiers,
    So levied as before, against the Polack,   75
    With an entreaty, herein further shown,
                                  [*Giving a paper.*]
    That it might please you to give quiet pass
    Through your dominions for this enterprise,
    On such regards of safety and allowance°
    As therein are set down.
    KING: It likes° us well;   80
    And at our more consider'd° time we'll read,
    Answer, and think upon this business.
    Meantime we thank you for your well-took
        labor.
    Go to your rest; at night we'll feast together.
    Most welcome home!   (*Exeunt Ambassadors.*)
    POLONIUS: This business is well ended. 85
    My liege, and madam, to expostulate°
    What majesty should be, what duty is,
    Why day is day, night night, and time is time,
    Were nothing but to waste night, day, and time.
    Therefore, since brevity is the soul of wit,°   90
    And tediousness the limbs and outward
        flourishes,
    I will be brief. Your noble son is mad.
    Mad call I it, for, to define true madness,
    What is 't but to be nothing else but mad?
    But let that go.
    QUEEN: More matter, with less art.   95
    POLONIUS: Madam, I swear I use no art at all.
    That he is mad, 'tis true; 'tis true 'tis pity,

    ---

    30. **in . . . bent:** To the utmost degree of our capacity.   **42.
    still:** Always.   **52. fruit:** Dessert.   **56. doubt:** Fear, suspect;
    main: Chief point, principal concern.

    61. Upon our first: At our first words on the business.   **67.
    borne in hand:** Deluded, taken advantage of.   **69. in fine:**
    In the end.   **71. assay:** Trial.   **79. On . . . allowance:** With
    such pledges of safety and provisos.   **80. likes:** Pleases.   **81.
    consider'd:** Suitable for deliberation.   **86. expostulate:** ex-
    pound.   **90. wit:** Sound sense or judgment.

And pity 'tis 'tis true — a foolish figure,°
But farewell it, for I will use no art.
100 Mad let us grant him, then, and now remains
That we find out the cause of this effect,
Or rather say, the cause of this defect,
For this effect defective comes by cause.°
Thus it remains, and the remainder thus.
105 Perpend.°
I have a daughter — have while she is mine —
Who, in her duty and obedience, mark,
Hath given me this. Now gather, and surmise.
[*Reads the letter.*] "To the celestial and my
soul's idol,
110 the most beautified Ophelia" —
That's an ill phrase, a vile phrase; "beautified" is
a vile
phrase. But you shall hear. Thus: [*Reads.*]
"In her excellent white bosom, these, etc."
QUEEN: Came this from Hamlet to her?
POLONIUS: Good madam, stay awhile; I will be
115 faithful.
[*Reads.*]
"Doubt° thou the stars are fire,
Doubt that the sun doth move,
Doubt truth to be a liar,
But never doubt I love.
120 O dear Ophelia, I am ill at these numbers.° I have
not art to reckon° my groans. But that I love thee
best, O most best, believe it. Adieu.
Thine evermore, most dear lady, whilst this
machine° is to him, Hamlet."
125 This in obedience hath my daughter shown me,
And, more above,° hath his solicitings,
As they fell out° by time, by means, and place,
All given to mine ear.
KING: But how hath she
Receiv'd his love?
POLONIUS: What do you think of me?
130 KING: As of a man faithful and honorable.
POLONIUS: I would fain prove so. But what might
you think,
When I had seen this hot love on the wing —
As I perceiv'd it, I must tell you that,
Before my daughter told me — what might you,
135 Or my dear Majesty your Queen here, think,
If I had play'd the desk or table-book,°

Or given my heart a winking,° mute and dumb,
Or look'd upon this love with idle sight?°
What might you think? No, I went round° to
work,
And my young mistress thus I did bespeak:°   140
"Lord Hamlet is a prince, out of thy star;°
This must not be." And then I prescripts gave
her,
That she should lock herself from his resort,
Admit no messengers, receive no tokens.
Which done, she took the fruits of my advice;   145
And he, repelled — a short tale to make —
Fell into a sadness, then into a fast,
Thence to a watch,° thence into a weakness,
Thence to a lightness,° and, by this declension,°
Into the madness wherein now he raves,   150
And all we mourn for.
KING: Do you think this?
QUEEN: It may be, very like.
POLONIUS: Hath there been such a time — I would
fain know that —
That I have positively said " 'Tis so,"
When it prov'd otherwise?
KING: Not that I know.   155
POLONIUS [*pointing to his head and shoulder*]: Take
this from this, if this be otherwise.
If circumstances lead me, I will find
Where truth is hid, though it were hid indeed
Within the center.°
KING: How may we try it further?
POLONIUS: You know, sometimes he walks four
hours together   160
Here in the lobby.
QUEEN: So he does indeed.
POLONIUS: At such a time I'll loose my daughter to
him.
Be you and I behind an arras° then.
Mark the encounter. If he love her not
And be not from his reason fall'n thereon,°   165
Let me be no assistant for a state,
But keep a farm and carters.
KING: We will try it.

(*Enter Hamlet* [*reading on a book*].)

QUEEN: But look where sadly the poor wretch
comes reading.

98. figure: Figure of speech.   103. For . . . cause: I.e., for this defective behavior, this madness has a cause.   105. Perpend: Consider.   116. Doubt: Suspect, question.   120. ill . . . numbers: Unskilled at writing verses.   121. reckon: (1) Count, (2) Number metrically, scan.   124. machine: Body.   126. more above: Moreover.   127. fell out: Occurred. 136. play'd . . . table-book: Remained shut up, concealing the information.

137. winking: Closing of the eyes.   138. with idle sight: Complacently or incomprehendingly.   139. round: Roundly, plainly.   140. bespeak: Address.   141. out of thy star: Above your sphere, position.   148. watch: State of sleeplessness.   149. lightness: Lightheadedness; declension: Decline, deterioration.   159. center: Middle point of the earth (which is also the center of the Ptolemaic universe).   163. arras: Hanging, tapestry.   165. thereon: On that account.

POLONIUS: Away, I do beseech you both, away.
    I'll board° him presently.
        (*Exeunt King and Queen [with Attendants].*)
170   O, give me leave.
    How does my good Lord Hamlet?
HAMLET: Well, God-a-mercy.°
POLONIUS: Do you know me, my lord?
HAMLET: Excellent well. You are a fishmonger.°
175 POLONIUS: Not I, my lord.
HAMLET: Then I would you were so honest a man.
POLONIUS: Honest, my lord?
HAMLET: Ay, sir. To be honest, as this world goes, is
    to be one man pick'd out of ten thousand.
180 POLONIUS: That's very true, my lord.
HAMLET: For if the sun breed maggots in a dead dog,
    being a good kissing carrion° — Have you a
    daughter?
POLONIUS: I have, my lord.
185 HAMLET: Let her not walk i' th' sun.° Conception° is
    a blessing, but as your daughter may conceive,
    friend, look to 't.
POLONIUS [*aside*]: How say you by that? Still harping
    on my daughter. Yet he knew me not at first; 'a
190   said I was a fishmonger. 'A is far gone. And truly
    in my youth I suff'red much extremity for love,
    very near this. I'll speak to him again. — What do
    you read, my lord?
HAMLET: Words, words, words.
195 POLONIUS: What is the matter,° my lord?
HAMLET: Between who?
POLONIUS: I mean, the matter that you read, my lord.
HAMLET: Slanders, sir; for the satirical rogue says here
    that old men have gray beards, that their faces are
200   wrinkled, their eyes purging° thick amber and
    plum-tree gum, and that they have a plentiful lack
    of wit, together with most weak hams. All which,
    sir, though I most powerfully and potently believe,
    yet I hold it not honesty° to have it thus set down,
205   for you yourself, sir, shall grow old as I am, if like
    a crab you could go backward.
POLONIUS [*aside*]: Though this be madness, yet there
    is method in 't. — Will you walk out of the air,
    my lord?
210 HAMLET: Into my grave.
POLONIUS: Indeed, that's out of the air. [*Aside.*] How

pregnant° sometimes his replies are! A happiness°
that often madness hits on, which reason and sanity
could not so prosperously° be deliver'd of. I will
leave him, [and suddenly contrive the means of   215
meeting between him] and my daughter. — My
honorable lord, I will most humbly take my leave
of you.
HAMLET: You cannot, sir, take from me any thing
that I will more willingly part withal — except my   220
life, except my life, except my life.

(*Enter Guildenstern and Rosencrantz.*)

POLONIUS: Fare you well, my lord.
HAMLET: These tedious old fools!°
POLONIUS: You go to seek the Lord Hamlet; there he
    is.   225
ROSENCRANTZ [*to Polonius*]: God save you, sir!
              [*Exit Polonius.*]
GUILDENSTERN: My honor'd lord!
ROSENCRANTZ: My most dear lord!
HAMLET: My excellent good friends! How dost thou,
    Guildenstern? Ah, Rosencrantz! Good lads, how   230
    do you both?
ROSENCRANTZ: As the indifferent° children of the earth.
GUILDENSTERN: Happy in that we are not over-happy.
    On Fortune's cap we are not the very button.
HAMLET: Nor the soles of her shoe?   235
OSENCRANTZ: Neither, my lord.
HAMLET: Then you live about her waist, or in the
    middle of her favors?
GUILDENSTERN: Faith, her privates° we.
HAMLET: In the secret parts of Fortune? O, most true;   240
    she is a strumpet.° What news?
ROSENCRANTZ: None, my lord, but the world's grown
    honest.
HAMLET: Then is doomsday near. But your news is
    not true. [Let me question more in particular. What   245
    have you, my good friends, deserv'd at the hands
    of Fortune that she sends you to prison hither?
GUILDENSTERN: Prison, my lord?
HAMLET: Denmark's a prison.
ROSENCRANTZ: Then is the world one.   250
HAMLET: A goodly one, in which there are many con-
    fines,° wards,° and dungeons, Denmark being one
    o' th' worst.

---

170. board: Accost.   **172. God-a-mercy:** Thank you.   **174. fishmonger:** Fish merchant (with connotation of *bawd*, *procurer*?).   **182. good kissing carrion:** A good piece of flesh for kissing, or for the sun to kiss.   **185. i' th' sun:** With additional implication of the sunshine of princely favors; **Conception:** (1) Understanding, (2) pregnancy.   **195. matter:** Substance (but Hamlet plays on the sense of *basis for a dispute*).   **200. purging:** Discharging.   **204. honesty:** Decency.

212. pregnant: Full of meaning; **happiness:** Felicity of expression.   **214. prosperously:** Successfully.   **223. old fools:** I.e., old men like Polonius.   **232. indifferent:** Ordinary.   **239. privates:** Close acquaintances (with sexual pun on *private parts*).   **241. strumpet:** Prostitute (a common epithet for indiscriminate Fortune; see line 505, p. 257).   **251–252. confines:** Places of confinement.   **252. wards:** Cells.

ROSENCRANTZ: We think not so, my lord.

255 HAMLET: Why then 'tis none to you, for there is nothing
either good or bad but thinking makes it so. To
me it is a prison.

ROSENCRANTZ: Why then, your ambition makes it
one. 'Tis too narrow for your mind.

260 HAMLET: O God, I could be bounded in a nutshell
and count myself a king of infinite space, were it
not that I have bad dreams.

GUILDENSTERN: Which dreams indeed are ambition,
for the very substance of the ambitious° is merely
265 the shadow of a dream.

HAMLET: A dream itself is but a shadow.

ROSENCRANTZ: Truly, and I hold ambition of so airy
and light a quality that it is but a shadow's shadow.

HAMLET: Then are our beggars bodies,° and our mon-
270 archs and outstretch'd° heroes the beggars' shadows.
Shall we to th' court? For, by my fay,° I cannot
reason.

ROSENCRANTZ, GUILDENSTERN: We'll wait upon° you.

HAMLET: No such matter. I will not sort° you with
275 the rest of my servants, for, to speak to you like
an honest man, I am most dreadfully attended.°]
But, in the beaten way° of friendship, what make°
you at Elsinore?

ROSENCRANTZ: To visit you, my lord, no other occasion.

280 HAMLET: Beggar that I am, I am even poor in thanks;
but I thank you, and sure, dear friends, my thanks
are too dear a halfpenny.° Were you not sent for?
Is it your own inclining? Is it a free visitation?
Come, come, deal justly with me. Come, come;
285 nay, speak.

GUILDENSTERN: What should we say, my lord?

HAMLET: Why, anything, but to th' purpose. You were
sent for; and there is a kind of confession in your
looks which your modesties have not craft enough
290 to color. I know the good King and Queen have
sent for you.

ROSENCRANTZ: To what end, my lord?

HAMLET: That you must teach me. But let me conjure°
you, by the rights of our fellowship, by the con-
295 sonancy of our youth,° by the obligation of our

ever-preserv'd love, and by what more dear a better
proposer° could charge° you withal, be even° and
direct with me, whether you were sent for, or no?

ROSENCRANTZ [aside to Guildenstern]: What say you?

HAMLET [aside]: Nay then, I have an eye of° you. — 300
If you love me, hold not off.

GUILDENSTERN: My lord, we were sent for.

HAMLET: I will tell you why; so shall my anticipation
prevent your discovery,° and your secrecy to the
King and Queen molt no feather.° I have of late — 305
but wherefore I know not — lost all my mirth,
forgone all custom of exercises; and indeed it goes
so heavily with my disposition that this goodly
frame, the earth, seems to me a sterile promontory;
this most excellent canopy, the air, look you, this 310
brave° o'erhanging firmament, this majestical roof
fretted° with golden fire, why, it appeareth nothing
to me but a foul and pestilent congregation of
vapors. What a piece of work is a man! How noble
in reason, how infinite in faculties, in form and 315
moving how express° and admirable, in action how
like an angel, in apprehension how like a god! The
beauty of the world, the paragon of animals! And
yet, to me, what is this quintessence° of dust? Man
delights not me — no, nor woman neither, though 320
by your smiling you seem to say so.

ROSENCRANTZ: My lord, there was no such stuff in
my thoughts.

HAMLET: Why did you laugh then, when I said "man
delights not me"? 325

ROSENCRANTZ: To think, my lord, if you delight not
in man, what lenten entertainment° the players shall
receive from you. We coted° them on the way, and
hither are they coming, to offer you service.

HAMLET: He that plays the king shall be welcome; 330
his Majesty shall have tribute of me. The adventurous
knight shall use his foil and target,° the lover shall
not sigh gratis, the humorous man° shall end his
part in peace, [the clown shall make those laugh
whose lungs are tickle o' th' sere°], and the lady 335

---

264. the very . . . ambitious: That seemingly very substantial
thing which the ambitious pursue. **269. bodies:** Solid sub-
stances rather than shadows (since beggars are not ambitious).
270. outstretch'd: (1)Far-reaching in their ambition; (2) elon-
gated as shadows. **271. fay:** Faith. **273. wait upon:** Accompany, attend. **274. sort:** Class, associate: **276. dreadfully attended:** Waited upon in slovenly fashion. **277. beaten
way:** Familiar path; **make:** Do. **282. dear a halfpenny:**
Expensive at the price of a halfpenny, i.e., of little worth.
293. conjure: Adjure, entreat. **294–295. consonancy of our
youth:** The fact that we are of the same age.

296–297. better proposer: More skillful propounder. **297.
charge:** Urge; **even:** Straight, honest. **300. of:** On. **304.
prevent your discovery:** Forestall your disclosure. **305. molt
no feather:** Not diminish in the least. **311. brave:** Splendid.
312. fretted: Adorned (with fretwork, as in a vaulted ceiling).
316. express: Well-framed (?), exact (?). **319. quintessence:**
The fifth essence of ancient philosophy, beyond earth, water,
air, and fire, supposed to be the substance of the heavenly
bodies and to be latent in all things. **327. lenten entertainment:** Meager reception (appropriate to Lent). **328.
coted:** Overtook and passed beyond. **332. foil and target:**
Sword and shield. **333. humorous man:** Eccentric character,
dominated by one trait or "humor". **335. tickle o' th' sere:**
Easy on the trigger, ready to laugh easily. (*Sere* is part of a
gunlock.)

shall say her mind freely, or the blank verse shall
halt° for 't. What players are they?

ROSENCRANTZ: Even those you were wont to take
such delight in, the tragedians of the city.

340 HAMLET: How chances it they travel? Their residence,°
both in reputation and profit, was better both ways.

ROSENCRANTZ: I think their inhibition° comes by the
means of the innovation.°

HAMLET: Do they hold the same estimation they did
345 when I was in the city? Are they so follow'd?

ROSENCRANTZ: No, indeed, are they not.

[HAMLET: How comes it? Do they grow rusty?

ROSENCRANTZ: Nay, their endeavor keeps in the
wonted° pace. But there is, sir, an aery° of children,
350 little eyases,° that cry out on the top of question,°
and are most tyrannically° clapp'd for 't. These are
now the fashion, and so berattle° the common stages°
— so they call them — that many wearing rapiers°
are afraid of goose-quills° and dare scarce come
thither.

355 HAMLET: What, are they children? Who maintains
'em? How are they escoted?° Will they pursue the
quality° no longer than they can sing?° Will they
not say afterwards, if they should grow themselves
to common° players — as it is most like, if their
360 means are no better — their writers do them wrong,
to make them exclaim against their own succession?°

ROSENCRANTZ: Faith, there has been much to do° on
both sides; and the nation holds it no sin to tarre°
them to controversy. There was, for a while, no
365 money bid for argument° unless the poet and the
player went to cuffs in the question.°

HAMLET: Is 't possible?

GUILDENSTERN: O, there has been much throwing about
of brains.

370 HAMLET: Do the boys carry it away?°

ROSENCRANTZ: Ay, that they do, my lord — Hercules
and his load° too.°]

HAMLET: It is not very strange; for my uncle is King
of Denmark, and those that would make mouths°
at him while my father liv'd, give twenty, forty,   375
fifty, a hundred ducats° apiece for his picture in
little.° 'Sblood,° there is something in this more
than natural, if philosophy could find it out.

(*A flourish [of trumpets within].*)

GUILDENSTERN: There are the players.

HAMLET: Gentlemen, you are welcome to Elsinore.   380
Your hands, come then. Th' appurtenance of welcome is fashion and ceremony. Let me comply°
with you in this garb,° lest my extent° to the players,
which, I tell you, must show fairly outwards,° should
more appear like entertainment° than yours. You   385
are welcome. But my uncle-father and aunt-mother
are deceiv'd.

GUILDENSTERN: In what, my dear lord?

HAMLET: I am but mad north-north-west.° When the
wind is southerly I know a hawk from a handsaw.°   390

(*Enter Polonius.*)

POLONIUS: Well be with you, gentlemen!

HAMLET: Hark you, Guildenstern, and you too; at
each ear a hearer. That great baby you see there
is not yet out of his swaddling-clouts.°

ROSENCRANTZ: Happily° he is the second time come   395
to them; for they say an old man is twice a child.

HAMLET: I will prophesy he comes to tell me of the
players; mark it. — You say right, sir, o' Monday
morning, 'twas then indeed.

POLONIUS: My lord, I have news to tell you.   400

HAMLET: My lord, I have news to tell you. When
Roscius° was an actor in Rome —

POLONIUS: The actors are come hither, my lord.

---

337. halt: Limp.   **340. residence:** Remaining in one place,
i.e., in the city.   **342. inhibition:** Formal prohibition (from
acting plays in the city).   **343. innovation:** I.e., the new
fashion in satirical plays performed by boy actors in the
"private" theaters; or possibly a political uprising; or the
strict limitations set on the theater in London in 1600.   **349.
wonted:** Usual; **aery:** Nest.   **350. eyases:** Young hawks; **cry
. . . question:** Speak shrilly, dominating the controversy (in
decrying the public theaters).   **351. tyrannically:** Outrageous.
352. berattle: Berate; **common stages:** Public theaters.   **353.
many wearing rapiers:** Many men of fashion, who were afraid
to patronize the common players for fear of being satirized
by the poets who wrote for the children.   **354. goose-quills:**
pens of satirists.   **356. escoted:** maintained.   **357. quality:**
(acting) profession; **no longer . . . sing:** Only until their voices
change.   **359. common:** Regular, adult.   **361. succession:**
Future careers.   **362. to do:** Ado.   **363. tarre:** Set on (as
dogs).   **365. argument:** Plot for a play.   **366. went . . .
question:** Came to blows in the play itself.

370. carry it away: Win the day.   **371–372. Hercules . . .
load:** Thought to be an allusion to the sign of the Globe
Theatre, which was Hercules bearing the world on his shoulder.
347–372. How . . . load too: The passage omitted from the
early quartos, alludes to the so-called War of the Theatres,
1599–1602, the rivalry between the children companies and
the adult actors.   **374. mouths:** Faces.   **376. ducats:** Gold
coins.   **376–377. in little:** In miniature.   **377. 'Sblood:** by
His (God's, Christ's) blood.   **382. comply:** Observe the for-
malities of courtesy.   **383. garb:** Manner; **my extent:** The
extent of my showing courtesy.   **384. show fairly outwards:**
Look cordial to outward appearances.   **385. entertainment:**
A (warm) reception.   **389. north-north-west:** Only partly,
at times.   **390. hawk, handsaw:** Mattock (or *hack*) and a
carpenter's cutting tool respectively; also birds, with a play
on *hernshaw* or heron.   **394. swaddling-clouts:** Cloths in
which to wrap a newborn baby.   **395. Happily:** Haply,
perhaps.   **401. Roscius:** A famous Roman actor who died
in 62 B.C.

HAMLET: Buzz,° buzz!

405 POLONIUS: Upon my honor —

HAMLET: Then came each actor on his ass —

POLONIUS: The best actors in the world, either for tragedy, comedy, history, pastoral, pastoral-comical, historical-pastoral, tragical-historical, tragical-

410 comical-historical-pastoral, scene individable,° or poem unlimited.° Seneca° cannot be too heavy, nor Plautus° too light. For the law of writ and the liberty,° these are the only men.

HAMLET: O Jephthah, judge of Israel,° what a treasure

415 hadst thou!

POLONIUS: What a treasure had he, my lord?

HAMLET: Why,

"One fair daughter, and no more,
 The which he loved passing° well."

420 POLONIUS [aside]: Still on my daughter.

HAMLET: Am I not i' th' right, old Jephthah?

POLONIUS: If you call me Jephthah, my lord, I have a daughter that I love passing well.

HAMLET: Nay, that follows not.

425 POLONIUS: What follows, then, my lord?

HAMLET: Why,

"As by lot, God wot,"°
and then, you know,
"It came to pass, as most like° it was."

430 The first row° of the pious chanson° will show you more, for look where my abridgement° comes.

(Enter the Players.)

You are welcome, masters; welcome, all. I am glad to see thee well. Welcome, good friends. O, old

435 friend! Why, thy face is valanc'd° since I saw thee last. Com'st thou to beard° me in Denmark? What, my young lady° and mistress? By 'r lady, your ladyship is nearer to heaven than when I saw you last, by the altitude of a chopine.° Pray God your

440 voice, like a piece of uncurrent° gold, be not crack'd

within the ring.° Masters, you are all welcome. We'll e'en to 't like French falconers, fly at anything we see. We'll have a speech straight.° Come, give us a taste of your quality; come, a passionate speech.

FIRST PLAYER: What speech, my good lord?   445

HAMLET: I heard thee speak me a speech once, but it was never acted, or, if it was, not above once, for the play, I remember, pleas'd not the million; 'twas caviary to the general.° But it was — as I receiv'd it, and others, whose judgments in such matters cried   450 in the top of ° mine — an excellent play, well digested in the scenes, set down with as much modesty as cunning.° I remember one said there were no sallets° in the lines to make the matter savory, nor no matter in the phrase that might indict° the author   455 of affectation, but call'd it an honest method, as wholesome as sweet, and by very much more hand-some than fine.° One speech in 't I chiefly lov'd: 'twas Aeneas' tale to Dido, and thereabout of it especially when he speaks of Priam's slaughter.° If   460 it live in your memory, begin at this line: let me see, let me see —

"The rugged Pyrrhus,° like th' Hyrcanian beast"° —

'Tis not so. It begins with Pyrrhus:

"The rugged Pyrrhus, he whose sable° arms,   465
Black as his purpose, did the night resemble
When he lay couched in the ominous horse,°
Hath now this dread and black complexion
   smear'd
With heraldry more dismal.° Head to foot
Now is he total gules,° horridly trick'd°   470
With blood of fathers, mothers, daughters, sons,
Bak'd and impasted° with the parching streets,°

404. **Buzz:** An interjection used to denote stale news.   410. **scene individable:** A play observing the unity of place.   411. **poem unlimited:** A play disregarding the unities of time and place; **Seneca:** Writer of Latin tragedies.   412. **Plautus:** Writer of Latin comedy.   412–413. **law . . . liberty:** Dramatic composition both according to rules and without rules, i.e., "classical" and "romantic" dramas.   414. **Jephthah . . . Israel:** Jephthah had to sacrifice his daughter; see Judges 11. Hamlet goes on to quote from a ballad on the theme.   419. **passing:** Surpassingly.   427. **wot:** Knows.   429. **like:** Likely, probable.   430. **row:** Stanza; **chanson:** Ballad, song.   431. **my abridgement:** Something that cuts short my conversation; also, a diversion.   435. **valanc'd:** Fringed (with a beard).   436. **beard:** Confront (with obvious pun).   437. **young lady:** Boy playing women's parts.   439. **chopine:** Thick-soled shoe of Italian fashion.   440. **uncurrent:** Not passable as lawful coinage.

440–441. **crack'd . . . ring:** Changed from adolescent to male voice, no longer suitable for women's roles. (Coins featured rings enclosing the sovereign's head; if the coin was cracked within this ring, it was unfit for currency.)   443. **straight:** At once.   449. **caviary to the general:** Caviar to the multitude, i.e., a choice dish too elegant for coarse tastes.   450–451. **cried in the top of:** Spoke with greater authority than.   453. **cunning:** Skill; **sallets:** Salad, i.e., spicy improprieties.   455. **indict:** Convict.   458. **fine:** Elaborately ornamented, showy.   460. **Priam's slaughter:** The slaying of the rule of Troy, when the Greeks finally took the city.   463. **Pyrrhus:** a Greek hero in the Trojan War, also known as Neoptolemus, son of Achilles.   463–464. **Hyrcanian beast:** I.e., the tiger. (See Virgil, *Aeneid,* IV, 266; compare the whole speech with Marlowe's *Dido Queen of Carthage,* II, I 214 ff.)   465. **sable:** Black (for reasons of camouflage during the episode of the Trojan horse).   467. **ominous horse:** Trojan horse, by which the Greeks gained access to Troy.   469. **dismal:** Ill-omened.   470. **gules:** Red (a heraldic term); **trick'd:** Adorned, decorated.   472. **impasted:** Crusted, like a thick paste; **with . . . streets:** By the parching heat of the streets (because of the fires everywhere).

That lend a tyrannous and a damned light
To their lord's° murder. Roasted in wrath and
   fire,
475 And thus o'er-sized° with coagulate gore,
With eyes like carbuncles, the hellish Pyrrhus
Old grandsire Priam seeks."
So proceed you.
POLONIUS: 'Fore God, my lord, well spoken, with good
  accent and good discretion.
480 FIRST PLAYER: "Anon he finds him
Striking too short at Greeks. His antique sword,
Rebellious to his arm, lies where it falls,
Repugnant° to command. Unequal match'd,
Pyrrhus at Priam drives, in rage strikes wide,
485 But with the whiff and wind of his fell° sword
Th' unnerved father falls. [Then senseless Ilium,°]
Seeming to feel this blow, with flaming top
Stoops to his° base, and with a hideous crash
Takes prisoner Pyrrhus' ear. For, lo! His sword,
490 Which was declining on the milky head
Of reverend Priam, seem'd i' th' air to stick.
So as a painted° tyrant Pyrrhus stood,
And, like a neutral to his will and matter,°
Did nothing.
495 But, as we often see, against° some storm,
A silence in the heavens, the rack° stand still,
The bold winds speechless, and the orb below
As hush as death, anon the dreadful thunder
Doth rend the region,° so, after Pyrrhus' pause,
500 Aroused vengeance sets him new a-work,
And never did the Cyclops'° hammers fall
On Mars's armor forg'd for proof eterne°
With less remorse than Pyrrhus' bleeding sword
Now falls on Priam.
505 Out, out, thou strumpet Fortune! All you gods,
In general synod,° take away her power!
Break all the spokes and fellies° from her wheel,
And bowl the round nave° down the hill of
   heaven,
As low as to the fiends!"
510 POLONIUS: This is too long.
HAMLET: It shall to the barber's with your beard. —

Prithee say on. He's for a jig° or a tale of bawdry,
or he sleeps. Say on; come to Hecuba.°
FIRST PLAYER: "But who, ah woe! had seen the
  mobled° queen" —
HAMLET: "The mobled queen?"   515
POLONIUS: That's good. "Mobled queen" is good.
FIRST PLAYER: "Run barefoot up and down,
  threat'ning the flames
With bisson rheum,° a clout° upon that head
Where late the diadem stood, and for a robe,
About her lank and all o'er-teemed° loins,   520
A blanket, in the alarm of fear caught up —
Who this had seen, with tongue in venom
  steep'd,
'Gainst Fortune's state° would treason have
  pronounc'd.°
But if the gods themselves did see her then
When she saw Pyrrhus make malicious sport   525
In mincing with his sword her husband's limbs,
The instant burst of clamor that she made,
Unless things mortal move them not at all,
Would have made milch° the burning eyes of
  heaven,
And passion in the gods."   530
POLONIUS: Look whe'er° he has not turn'd his color
and has tears in 's eyes. Prithee, no more.
HAMLET: 'Tis well; I'll have thee speak out the rest
of this soon. Good my lord, will you see the players
well bestow'd?° Do you hear, let them be well us'd, 535
for they are the abstract° and brief chronicles of
the time. After your death you were better have a
bad epitaph than their ill report while you live.
POLONIUS: My lord, I will use them according to their
desert.   540
HAMLET: God's bodkin,° man, much better! Use every
man after his desert, and who shall scape whipping?
Use them after your own honor and dignity. The
less they deserve, the more merit is in your bounty.
Take them in.   545
POLONIUS: Come, sirs.
HAMLET: Follow him, friends. We'll hear a play tomorrow. [*As they start to leave, Hamlet detains
the First Player.*] Dost thou hear me, old friend?
Can you play the Murder of Gonzago?   550

---

474. their lord's: Priam's.   **475. o'er-sized:** Covered as with
size or glue.   **483. Repugnant:** Disobedient, resistant.   **485.
fell:** Cruel.   **486. senseless Ilium:** Insensate Troy.   **488. his:**
Its.   **492. painted:** Painted in a picture.   **493. like . . . matter:**
As though poised indecisively between his intention and its
fulfillment.   **495. against:** Just before.   **496. rack:** Mass of
clouds.   **499. region:** Sky.   **501. Cyclops:** Giant armor-
makers in the smithy of Vulcan.   **502. proof eterne:** Eternal
resistance to assault.   **506. synod:** Assembly: **507. fellies:**
Pieces of wood forming the rim of a wheel.   **508. nave:**
Hub.

512. jig: Comic song and dance often given at the end of a
play.   **513. Hecuba:** Wife of Priam.   **514. mobled:** Muffled.
518. bisson rheum: Blinding tears; **clout:** Cloth.   **520. o'er-
teemed:** Worn out with bearing children.   **523. state:** Rule,
managing; **pronounc'd:** Proclaimed.   **529. milch:** Milky, moist
with tears.   **531. whe'er:** Whether.   **535. bestow'd:** Lodged.
536. abstract: Summary account.   **541. God's bodkin:** By
God's (Christ's) little body, *bodykin* (not to be confused with
bodkin, dagger).

FIRST PLAYER: Ay, my lord.

HAMLET: We'll ha 't tomorrow night. You could, for
need, study a speech of some dozen or sixteen lines,
which I would set down and insert in 't, could you
555   not?

FIRST PLAYER: Ay, my lord.

HAMLET: Very well. Follow that lord, and look you
mock him not. — My good friends, I'll leave you
till night. You are welcome to Elsinore.
                          (*Exeunt Polonius and Players.*)

560   ROSENCRANTZ: Good my lord!
                          (*Exeunt [Rosencrantz and Guildenstern].*)

HAMLET: Ay, so, God buy you. — Now I am
alone.
O, what a rogue and peasant slave am I!
Is it not monstrous that this player here,
But in a fiction, in a dream of passion,
565   Could force his soul so to his own conceit°
That from her working all his visage wann'd,°
Tears in his eyes, distraction in his aspect,
A broken voice, and his whole function suiting
With forms to his conceit?° And all for nothing!
570   For Hecuba!
What's Hecuba to him, or he to Hecuba,
That he should weep for her? What would he
do,
Had he the motive and the cue for passion
That I have? He would drown the stage with
tears
575   And cleave the general ear with horrid speech,
Make mad the guilty and appall the free,°
Confound the ignorant, and amaze indeed
The very faculties of eyes and ears. Yet I,
A dull and muddy-mettled° rascal, peak,°
580   Like John-a-dreams,° unpregnant of° my cause,
And can say nothing — no, not for a king
Upon whose property° and most dear life
A damn'd defeat was made. Am I a coward?
Who calls me villain? Breaks my pate across?
585   Plucks off my beard, and blows it in my face?
Tweaks me by the nose? Gives me the lie° i' th'
throat,
As deep as to the lungs? Who does me this?
Ha, 'swounds, I should take it; for it cannot be
But I am pigeon-liver'd,° and lack gall

To make oppression bitter, or ere this   590
I should have fatted all the region kites°
With this slave's offal. Bloody, bawdy villain!
Remorseless, treacherous, lecherous, kindless°
villain!
[O, vengeance!]
Why, what an ass am I! This is most brave,   595
That I, the son of a dear father murder'd,
Prompted to my revenge by heaven and hell,
Must, like a whore, unpack my heart with
words,
And fall a-cursing, like a very drab,°
A stallion!° Fie upon 't, foh! About,° my brains!   600
Hum, I have heard
That guilty creatures sitting at a play
Have by the very cunning of the scene
Been struck so to the soul that presently°
They have proclaim'd their malefactions;   605
For murder, though it have no tongue, will
speak
With most miraculous organ. I'll have these
players
Play something like the murder of my father
Before mine uncle. I'll observe his looks;
I'll tent° him to the quick. If 'a do blench,°   610
I know my course. The spirit that I have seen
May be the devil, and the devil hath power
T' assume a pleasing shape; yea, and perhaps
Out of my weakness and my melancholy,
As he is very potent with such spirits,°   615
Abuses° me to damn me. I'll have grounds
More relative° than this. The play's the thing
Wherein I'll catch the conscience of the King.
                                                    (*Exit.*)

[ACT III • Scene I]°

(*Enter King, Queen, Polonius, Ophelia, Rosencrantz,
Guildenstern, Lords.*)

KING: And can you, by no drift of conference,°
Get from him why he puts on this confusion,
Grating so harshly all his days of quiet
With turbulent and dangerous lunacy?

ROSENCRANTZ: He does confess he feels himself
distracted,   5

---

565. conceit: Conception.   **566. wann'd:** Grew pale.   **569–570. his whole . . . conceit:** His whole being responded with actions to suit his thought.   **576. free:** Innocent.   **579. muddy-mettled:** Dull-spirited; **peak:** Mope, pine.   **580. John-a-dreams:** Sleepy dreaming idler; **unpregnant of:** Not quickened by.   **582. property:** The crown; perhaps also character, quality.   **586. Gives me the lie:** Calls me a liar.   **589. pigeon-liver'd:** The pigeon or dove was popularly supposed to be mild because it secreted no gall.

591. region kites: Kites (birds of prey) of the air, from the vicinity.   **593. kindless:** Unnatural.   **599. drab:** Prostitute.   **600. stallion:** Prostitute (male or female) (Many editors follow the Folio reading of *scullion.*); **About:** About it, to work.   **604. presently:** At once.   **610. tent:** Probe; **blench:** Quail, flinch.   **615. spirits:** Humors (of melancholy).   **616. Abuses:** Deludes.   **617. relative:** Closely related, pertinent.   **III, I. Location:** The castle.   **1. drift of conference:** Direction of conversation.

But from what cause 'a will by no means speak.
GUILDENSTERN: Nor do we find him forward° to be
    sounded,°
    But with a crafty madness keeps aloof
    When we would bring him on to some
       confession
    Of his true state.
10 QUEEN: Did he receive you well?
ROSENCRANTZ: Most like a gentleman.
GUILDENSTERN: But with much forcing of his
    disposition.°
ROSENCRANTZ: Niggard of question,° but of our
    demands
    Most free in his reply.
    QUEEN: Did you assay° him
15 To any pastime?
ROSENCRANTZ: Madam, it so fell out that certain
    players
    We o'er-raught° on the way. Of these we told
       him,
    And there did seem in him a kind of joy
    To hear of it. They are here about the court,
20 And, as I think, they have already order
    This night to play before him.
POLONIUS: 'Tis most true,
    And he beseech'd me to entreat your Majesties
    To hear and see the matter.
KING: With all my heart, and it doth much content
      me
25 To hear him so inclin'd.
    Good gentlemen, give him a further edge,°
    And drive his purpose into these delights.
ROSENCRANTZ: We shall, my lord.
          (*Exeunt Rosencrantz and Guildenstern.*)
KING: Sweet Gertrude, leave us too,
    For we have closely° sent for Hamlet hither,
30 That he, as 'twere by accident, may here
    Affront° Ophelia.
    Her father and myself, [lawful espials,°]
    Will so bestow ourselves that seeing, unseen,
    We may of their encounter frankly judge,
35 And gather by him, as he is behav'd,
    If 't be th' affliction of his love or no
    That thus he suffers for.
QUEEN: I shall obey you.
    And for your part, Ophelia, I do wish
    That your good beauties be the happy cause
    Of Hamlet's wildness. So shall I hope your
40   virtues

Will bring him to his wonted way again,
    To both your honors.
OPHELIA: Madam, I wish it may.
                    [*Exit Queen.*]
POLONIUS: Ophelia, walk you here. — Gracious,° so
    please you,
    We will bestow ourselves. [*To Ophelia.*] Read
      on this book,   [*Gives her a book.*]
    That show of such an exercise° may color°   45
    Your loneliness. We are oft to blame in this —
    'Tis too much prov'd° — that with devotion's
      visage
    And pious action we do sugar o'er
    The devil himself.
KING [*aside*]: O, 'tis too true!   50
    How smart a lash that speech doth give my
      conscience!
    The harlot's cheek, beautied with plast'ring art,
    Is not more ugly to° the thing° that helps it
    Than is my deed to my most painted word.
    O heavy burden!   55
POLONIUS: I hear him coming. Let's withdraw, my
    lord.   [*King and Polonius withdraw.*°]

(*Enter Hamlet. [Ophelia pretends to read a book.*])

HAMLET: To be, or not to be, that is the question:
    Whether 'tis nobler in the mind to suffer
    The slings and arrows of outrageous fortune,
    Or to take arms against a sea of troubles,   60
    And by opposing end them. To die, to sleep —
    No more — and by a sleep to say we end
    The heart-ache and the thousand natural shocks
    That flesh is heir to. 'Tis a consummation
    Devoutly to be wish'd. To die, to sleep;   65
    To sleep, perchance to dream. Ay, there's the
      rub,°
    For in that sleep of death what dreams may
      come
    When we have shuffled° off this mortal coil,°
    Must give us pause. There's the respect°
    That makes calamity of so long life.°   70
    For who would bear the whips and scorns of
      time,

---

43. Gracious: Your Grace (i.e., the King). **45. exercise:** Act of devotion (The book she reads is one of devotion.); **color:** Give a plausible appearance to. **47. too much prov'd:** Too often shown to be true, too often practiced. **53. to:** Compared to; **thing:** I.e., the cosmetic. **56. [S.D.]** *withdraw:* (The King and Polonius may retire behind an arras. The stage directions specify that they "enter" again near the end of the scene.) **66. rub:** Literally, an obstacle in the game of bowls. **68. shuffled:** Sloughed, cast; **coil:** Turmoil. **69. respect:** Consideration. **70. of . . . life:** So long-lived.

---

7. forward: Willing; **sounded:** Tested deeply. **12. disposition:** Inclination. **13. question:** Conversation. **14. assay:** Try to win. **17. o'er-raught:** Overtook and passed. **26. edge:** Incitement. **29. closely:** Privately. **31. Affront:** Confront, meet. **32. espials:** Spies.

Th' oppressor's wrong, the proud man's
   contumely,°
The pangs of despis'd° love, the law's delay,
The insolence of office,° and the spurns°
75 That patient merit of th' unworthy takes,
When he himself might his quietus° make
With a bare bodkin?° Who would fardels° bear,
To grunt and sweat under a weary life,
But that the dread of something after death,
80 The undiscover'd country from whose bourn°
No traveler returns, puzzles the will,
And makes us rather bear those ills we have
Than fly to others that we know not of?
Thus conscience does make cowards of us all
85 And thus the native hue° of resolution
Is sicklied o'er with the pale cast° of thought,
And enterprises of great pitch° and moment°
With this regard° their currents° turn awry,
And lose the name of action. — Soft you now,
90 The fair Ophelia. Nymph, in thy orisons°
Be all my sins rememb'red.
OPHELIA: Good my lord,
How does your honor for this many a day?
HAMLET: I humbly thank you; well, well, well.
OPHELIA: My lord, I have remembrances of yours,
95 That I have longed long to re-deliver.
I pray you, now receive them.   [Offers tokens.]
HAMLET: No, not I, I never gave you aught.
OPHELIA: My honor'd lord, you know right well
   you did,
And with them words of so sweet breath
   compos'd
As made these things more rich. Their perfume
100   lost,
Take these again, for to the noble mind
Rich gifts wax poor when givers prove unkind.
There, my lord.   [Gives tokens.]
HAMLET: Ha, ha! Are you honest?°
105 OPHELIA: My lord?
HAMLET: Are you fair?°
OPHELIA: What means your lordship?
HAMLET: That if you be honest and fair, your honesty°
   should admit no discourse° to your beauty.

OPHELIA: Could beauty, my lord, have better commerce° 110
   than with honesty?
HAMLET: Ay, truly; for the power of beauty will sooner
   transform honesty from what it is to a bawd than
   the force of honesty can translate beauty into his
   likeness. This was sometime° a paradox,° but now 115
   the time° gives it proof. I did love you once.
OPHELIA: Indeed, my lord, you made me believe so.
HAMLET: You should not have believ'd me, for virtue
   cannot so inoculate° our old stock but we shall
   relish of it.° I lov'd you not. 120
OPHELIA: I was the more deceiv'd.
HAMLET: Get thee to a nunn'ry.° Why wouldst thou
   be a breeder of sinners? I am myself indifferent
   honest;° but yet I could accuse me of such things
   that it were better my mother had not borne me: 125
   I am very proud, revengeful, ambitious, with more
   offenses at my beck° than I have thoughts to put
   them in, imagination to give them shape, or time
   to act them in. What should such fellows as I do
   crawling between earth and heaven? We are arrant 130
   knaves, all; believe none of us. Go thy ways to a
   nunn'ry. Where's your father?
OPHELIA: At home, my lord.
HAMLET: Let the doors be shut upon him, that he
   may play the fool nowhere but in 's own house. 135
   Farewell.
OPHELIA: O, help him, you sweet heavens!
HAMLET: If thou dost marry, I'll give thee this plague
   for thy dowry: be thou as chaste as ice, as pure as
   snow, thou shalt not escape calumny. Get thee to 140
   a nunn'ry, farewell. Or, if thou wilt needs marry,
   marry a fool, for wise men know well enough what
   monsters° you° make of them. To a nunn'ry, go,
   and quickly too. Farewell.
OPHELIA: Heavenly powers, restore him! 145
HAMLET: I have heard of your paintings too, well
   enough. God hath given you one face, and you
   make yourselves another. You jig,° and amble, and
   you lisp, you nickname God's creatures, and make
   your wantonness your ignorance.° Go to, I'll no 150
   more on 't; it hath made me mad. I say, we will
   have no moe marriage. Those that are married

---

72. **contumely:** Insolent abuse.   73. **despis'd:** Rejected.   74.
office: Officialdom; **spurns:** Insults.   76. **quietus:** Acquittance;
here, death.   77. **bodkin:** Dagger; **fardels:** Burdens.   80.
bourn: Boundary.   85. **native hue:** Natural color, complexion.
86. **cast:** Shade of color.   87. **pitch:** Height (as of a falcon's
flight); **moment:** Importance.   88. **regard:** Respect, consideration; **currents:** Courses.   90. **orisons:** Prayers.   104.
honest: (1) Truthful, (2) Chaste.   106. **fair:** (1) Beautiful,
(2) Just, honorable.   108. **your honesty:** Your chastity.   109.
discourse: Familiar dealings.

110. **commerce:** Dealings.   115. **sometime:** Formerly; **paradox:** A view opposite to commonly held opinion.   116.
the time: The present age.   119. **inoculate:** Graft, be engrafted
to.   119–120. **but . . . it:** That we do not still have about
us a taste of the old stock; i.e., retain our sinfulness.   122.
nunn'ry: (1) Convent, (2) Brothel.   122–123. **indifferent
honest:** Reasonably virtuous.   127. **beck:** Command.   143.
monsters: An allusion to the horns of a cuckold; **you:** You
women.   148. **jig:** Dance and sing affectedly and wantonly.
149–150. **make . . . ignorance:** Excuse your affection on the
grounds of your ignorance.

already — all but one — shall live. The rest shall
keep as they are. To a nunn'ry, go.   (*Exit.*)

155 OPHELIA: O, what a noble mind is here o'erthrown!
The courtier's, soldier's, scholar's, eye, tongue,
sword,
Th' expectancy and rose of the fair state,°
The glass of fashion and the mold of form,°
Th' observ'd of all observers,° quite, quite down!
160 And I, of ladies most deject and wretched,
That suck'd the honey of his music vows,
Now see that noble and most sovereign reason,
Like sweet bells jangled, out of time and harsh,
That unmatch'd form and feature of blown°
youth
165 Blasted with ecstasy.° O, woe is me,
T' have seen what I have seen, see what I see!

(*Enter King and Polonius.*)

KING: Love? His affections do not that way tend;
Nor what he spake, though it lack'd form a
little,
Was not like madness. There's something in his
soul,
170 O'er which his melancholy sits on brood,
And I do doubt° the hatch and the disclose°
Will be some danger; which for to prevent,
I have in quick determination
Thus set it down: he shall with speed to
England,
175 For the demand of° our neglected tribute.
Haply the seas and countries different
With variable° objects shall expel
This something-settled° matter in his heart,
Whereon his brains still beating puts him thus
180 From fashion of himself.° What think you on 't?
POLONIUS: It shall do well. But yet do I believe
The origin and commencement of his grief
Sprung from neglected love. — How now,
Ophelia?
You need not tell us what Lord Hamlet said;
185 We heard it all. — My lord, do as you please,
But, if you hold it fit, after the play
Let his queen mother all alone entreat him
To show his grief. Let her be round° with him;

And I'll be plac'd, so please you, in the ear
Of all their conference. If she find him not,   190
To England send him, or confine him where
Your wisdom best shall think.
KING: It shall be so.
Madness in great ones must not unwatch'd go.
(*Exeunt.*)

[Scene II]°

(*Enter Hamlet and three of the Players.*)

HAMLET: Speak the speech, I pray you, as I pronounc'd
it to you, trippingly on the tongue. But if you
mouth it, as many of our players° do, I had as lief
the town-crier spoke my lines. Nor do not saw the
air too much with your hand, thus, but use all   5
gently; for in the very torrent, tempest, and, as I
may say, whirlwind of your passion, you must acquire and beget a temperance that may give it
smoothness. O, it offends me to the soul to hear
a robustious° periwig-pated° fellow tear a passion   10
to tatters, to very rags, to split the ears of the
groundlings,° who for the most part are capable
of° nothing but inexplicable dumb-shows and noise.
I would have such a fellow whipp'd for o'er-doing
Termagant.° It out-herods Herod.° Pray you, avoid   15
it.
FIRST PLAYER: I warrant your honor.
HAMLET: Be not too tame neither, but let your own
discretion be your tutor. Suit the action to the
word, the word to the action, with this special   20
observance, that you o'erstep not the modesty of
nature. For anything so o'erdone is from° the purpose
of playing, whose end, both at the first and now,
was and is, to hold, as 't were, the mirror up to
nature, to show virtue her feature, scorn her own   25
image, and the very age and body of the time his°
form and pressure.° Now this overdone, or come
tardy off,° though it makes the unskillful laugh,
cannot but make the judicious grieve, the censure

---

157. Th' expectancy ... state: The hope and ornament of
the kingdom made fair (by him).   **158. The glass ... form:**
The mirror of fashion and the pattern of courtly behavior.
159. observ'd ... observers: The center of attention and
honor in the court.   **164. blown:** Booming.   **165. ecstasy:**
Madness.   **171. doubt:** Fear; **disclose:** Disclosure.   **175.
For ... of:** To demand.   **177. variable:** Various.   **178.
something-settled:** Somewhat settled.   **180. From ... himself:**
Out of his natural manner.   **188. round:** Blunt.

III, II. Location: The castle.   **3. our players:** Indefinite use;
i.e., *players nowadays.*   **10. robustious:** Violent, boisterous;
periwig-pated: Wearing a wig.   **12. groundlings:** Spectators
who paid least and stood in the yard of the theater.   **12–
13. capable of:** Susceptible of being influenced by.   **15.
Termagant:** A god of the Saracens; a character in the St.
Nicholas play, where one of his worshipers, leaving him in
charge of goods, returns to find them stolen; whereupon he
beats the god or idol, which howls vociferously; **Herod:**
Herod of Jewry (a character in *The Slaughter of the Innocents*
and other cycle plays. The part was played with great noise
and fury).   **22. from:** Contrary to.   **26. his:** Its.   **27. pressure:** Stamp, impressed character.   **27–28. come tardy off:**
Inadequately done.

FAR LEFT: Michael Pennington as Hamlet. NEAR LEFT: A scene from the ROYAL Shakespeare Company's 1980 production. BELOW LEFT: Gertrude watches Laertes and Hamlet dueling. The poisoned cup is in the foreground. RIGHT: The gravedigger holds up Yorick's skull as Hamlet and Horatio (Tom Wilkinson) look on. BELOW RIGHT: Carol Royale as Ophelia with Hamlet in the nunnery scene.

30 of which one° must in your allowance o'erweigh
a whole theater of others. O, there be players that
I have seen play, and heard others praise, and that
highly, not to speak it profanely, that, neither having
th' accent of Christians nor the gait of Christian,
35 pagan, nor man, have so strutted and bellow'd that
I have thought some of nature's journeymen° had
made men and not made them well, they imitated
humanity so abominably.
FIRST PLAYER: I hope we have reform'd that indiffer-
40 ently° with us, sir.
HAMLET: O, reform it altogether. And let those that
play your clowns speak no more than is set down
for them; for there be of them° that will themselves
laugh, to set on some quantity of barren° spectators
45 to laugh too, though in the mean time some necessary
question of the play be then to be consider'd. That's
villainous, and shows a most pitiful ambition in
the fool that uses it. Go, make you ready.
[*Exeunt Players.*]

(*Enter Polonius, Guildenstern, and Rosencrantz.*)

How now, my lord! Will the King hear this piece
50 of work?
POLONIUS: And the Queen too, and that presently.°
HAMLET: Bid the players make haste.
[*Exit Polonius.*]
Will you two help to hasten them?
ROSENCRANTZ: Ay, my lord.   (*Exeunt they two.*)
HAMLET: What ho, Horatio!

(*Enter Horatio.*)

55 HORATIO: Here, sweet lord, at your service.
HAMLET: Horatio, thou art e'en as just a man
As e'er my conversation cop'd withal.°
HORATIO: O, my dear lord —
                      Nay, do not think I flatter;
HAMLET: For what advancement may I hope from
thee
60 That no revenue hast but thy good spirits,
To feed and clothe thee? Why should the poor
be flatter'd?
No, let the candied° tongue lick absurd pomp,
And crook the pregnant° hinges of the knee
Where thrift° may follow fawning. Dost thou
hear?
65 Since my dear soul was mistress of her choice

And could of men distinguish her election,
Sh' hath seal'd thee for herself, for thou hast been
As one, in suff'ring all, that suffers nothing,
A man that Fortune's buffets and rewards
Hast ta'en with equal thanks; and blest are those 70
Whose blood° and judgment are so well
commeddled°
That they are not a pipe for Fortune's finger
To sound what stop° she please. Give me that
man
That is not passion's slave, and I will wear him
In my heart's core, ay, in my heart of heart, 75
As I do thee. — Something too much of this. —
There is a play tonight before the King.
One scene of it comes near the circumstance
Which I have told thee of my father's death.
I prithee, when thou seest that act afoot, 80
Even with the very comment of thy soul°
Observe my uncle. If his occulted° guilt
Do not itself unkennel in one speech,
It is a damned° ghost that we have seen,
And my imaginations are as foul 85
As Vulcan's stithy.° Give him heedful note,
For I mine eyes will rivet to his face,
And after we will both our judgments join
In censure of his seeming.°
HORATIO: Well, my lord.
If 'a steal aught the whilst this play is playing, 90
And scape detecting, I will pay the theft.

([*Flourish.*] *Enter trumpets and kettledrums, King,
Queen, Polonius, Ophelia, [Rosencrantz, Guildenstern,
and other Lords, with Guards carrying torches*].)

HAMLET: They are coming to the play. I must be idle.
Get you a place. [*The King, Queen, and courtiers
sit.*]
KING: How fares our cousin Hamlet?
HAMLET: Excellent, i' faith, of the chameleon's dish:° 95
I eat the air, promise-cramm'd. You cannot feed
capons so.
KING: I have nothing with° this answer, Hamlet. These
words are not mine.°

29–30. the censure . . . one: The judgment of even one of
whom. 36. journeymen: Laborers not yet masters in their
trade. 39–40 indifferently: Tolerably. 43. of them: Some
among them. 44. barren: I.e., of wit. 51. presently: At
once. 57. my . . . withal: My contact with people provided
opportunity for encounter with. 62. candied: Sugared, flattering. 63. pregnant: Compliant. 64. thrift: Profit.

71. blood: Passion; commeddled: Commingled. 73. stop:
Hole in a wind instrument for controlling the sound. 81.
very . . . soul: Inward and sagacious criticism. 82. occulted:
Hidden. 84. damned: In league with Satan. 86. stithy:
Smithy, place of stiths (anvils). 89. censure of his seeming:
Judgment of his appearance or behavior. 95. chameleon's
dish: Chameleons were supposed to feed on air. Hamlet
deliberately misinterprets the King's *fares* as *feeds*. By his
phrase *eat the air* he also plays on the idea of feeding himself
with the promise of succession, of being the *heir*. 98. have
. . . with: Make nothing of. 99. are not mine: Do not
respond to what I asked.

100 HAMLET: No, nor mine now. [*To Polonius.*] My lord,
you played once i' th' university, you say?
POLONIUS: That did I, my lord; and was accounted a
good actor.
HAMLET: What did you enact?
105 POLONIUS: I did enact Julius Caesar. I was killed i'
th' Capitol; Brutus kill'd me.
HAMLET: It was a brute part of him to kill so capital
a calf there. Be the players ready?
ROSENCRANTZ: Ay, my lord; they stay upon your
110 patience.
QUEEN: Come hither, my dear Hamlet, it by me.
HAMLET: No, good mother, here's metal more attractive.
POLONIUS [*to the King*]: O, ho, do you mark that?
HAMLET: Lady, shall I lie in your lap?
                           [*Lying down at Ophelia's feet.*]
115 OPHELIA: No, my lord.
[HAMLET: I mean, my head upon your lap?
OPHELIA: Ay, my lord.]
HAMLET: Do you think I meant country° matters?
OPHELIA: I think nothing, my lord.
120 HAMLET: That's a fair thought to lie between maids'
legs.
OPHELIA: What is, my lord?
HAMLET: Nothing.
OPHELIA: You are merry, my lord.
125 HAMLET: Who, I?
OPHELIA: Ay, my lord.
HAMLET: O God, your only jig-maker.° What should
a man do but be merry? For look you how cheerfully
my mother looks, and my father died within 's°
130 two hours.
OPHELIA: Nay, 'tis twice two months, my lord.
HAMLET: So long? Nay then, let the devil wear black,
for I'll have a suit of sables.° O heavens! Die two
months ago, and not forgotten yet? Then there's
135 hope a great man's memory may outlive his life
half a year. But, by 'r lady, 'a must build churches,
then, or else shall 'a suffer not thinking on,° with
the hobby-horse, whose epitaph is "For, O, for,
O, the hobby-horse is forgot."°

(*The trumpets sound. Dumb show follows.*)

(*Enter a King and a Queen [very lovingly]; the Queen
embracing him, and he her. [She kneels, and makes
show of protestation unto him.] He takes her up, and
declines his head upon her neck. He lies him down
upon a bank of flowers. She, seeing him asleep, leaves
him. Anon comes in another man, takes off his crown,
kisses it, pours poison in the sleeper's ears, and leaves
him. The Queen returns; finds the King dead, makes
passionate action. The Poisoner, with some three or
four, come in again, seem to condole with her. The
dead body is carried away. The Poisoner woos the
Queen with gifts; she seems harsh awhile, but in the
end accepts love.*)

                                        [*Exeunt.*]

OPHELIA: What means this, my lord?   140
HAMLET: Marry, this' miching mallecho;° it means
mischief.
OPHELIA: Belike° this show imports the argument° of
the play.

(*Enter Prologue.*)

HAMLET: We shall know by this fellow. The players   145
cannot keep counsel;° they'll tell all.
OPHELIA: Will 'a tell us what this show meant?
HAMLET: Ay, or any show that you will show him.
Be not you° asham'd to show, he'll not shame to
tell you what it means.   150
OPHELIA: You are naught, you are naught.° I'll mark
the play.
PROLOGUE: For us, and for our tragedy,
Here stooping° to your clemency,
We beg your hearing patiently.   [*Exit.*]   155
HAMLET: Is this a prologue, or the posy of a ring?°
OPHELIA: 'Tis brief, my lord.
HAMLET: As woman's love.

(*Enter [two Players as] King and Queen.*)

PLAYER KING: Full thirty times hath Phoebus' cart°
gone round
Neptune's salt wash° and Tellus'° orbed ground,   160
And thirty dozen moons with borrowed° sheen
About the world have times twelve thirties been,
Since love our hearts and Hymen° did our hands
Unite commutual° in most sacred bands.

---

118. country: With a bawdy pun.   **127. only jig-maker:**
Very best composer of jigs (song and dance).   **129. within
's:** Within this.   **133. suit of sables:** Garments trimmed with
the fur of the sable and hence suited for a wealthy person,
not a mourner (with a pun on *sable* black).   **137. suffer
. . . on:** Undergo oblivion.   **138–139.** "**For . . . forgot**":
Verse of a song occurring also in *Love's Labor's Lost*, III,
I, line 30. The hobby-horse was a character made up to
resemble a horse, appearing in the Morris Dance and such
May-game sports. This song laments the disappearance of
such customs under pressure from the Puritans.

141. this' miching mallecho: This is sneaking mischief.   **143.
Belike:** Probably; **argument:** Plot.   **146. counsel:** Secret.
149. Be not you: If you are not.   **151. naught:** Indecent.
154. stooping: Bowing.   **156. posy . . . ring:** Brief motto in
verse inscribed in a ring.   **159. Phoebus's cart:** The sun
god's chariot.   **160. salt wash:** The sea; **Tellus:** Goddess of
the earth, of the *orbed ground*.   **161. borrowed:** Reflected.
163. Hymen: God of matrimony.   **164. commutual:** Mutually.

PLAYER QUEEN: So many journeys may the sun and
165   moon
         Make us again count o'er ere love be done!
         But, woe is me, you are so sick of late,
         So far from cheer and from your former state,
         That I distrust you. Yet, though I distrust,°
170   Discomfort you, my lord, it nothing° must.
         For women's fear and love hold quantity;°
         In neither aught, or in extremity.
         Now, what my love is, proof° hath made you
             know,
         And as my love is siz'd, my fear is so.
175   Where love is great, the littlest doubts are fear;
         Where little fears grow great, great love grows
             there.
PLAYER KING: Faith, I must leave thee, love, and
             shortly too;
         My operant° powers their functions leave to do.°
         And thou shalt live in this fair world behind,
180   Honor'd, belov'd; and haply one as kind
         For husband shalt thou —
PLAYER QUEEN: O, confound the rest!
         Such love must needs be treason in my breast.
         In second husband let me be accurst!
         None wed the second but who kill'd the first.
185 HAMLET: Wormwood, wormwood.
PLAYER QUEEN: The instances° that second marriage
             move°
         Are base respects of thrift,° but none of love.
         A second time I kill my husband dead,
         When second husband kisses me in bed.
PLAYER KING: I do believe you think what now you
190   speak,
         But what we do determine oft we break.
         Purpose is but the slave to memory,°
         Of violent birth, but poor validity,°
         Which now, like fruit unripe, sticks on the tree,
195   But fall unshaken when they mellow be.
         Most necessary 'tis that we forget
         To pay ourselves what to ourselves is debt.°
         What to ourselves in passion we propose,
         The passion ending, doth the purpose lose.
200   The violence of either grief or joy
         Their own enactures° with themselves destroy.

Where joy most revels, grief doth most lament;
Grief joys, joy grieves, on slender accident.
This world is not for aye,° nor 'tis not strange
That even our loves should with our fortunes
    change;   205
For 'tis a question left us yet to prove,
Whether love lead fortune, or else fortune love.
The great man down, you mark his favorite flies;
The poor advanc'd makes friends of enemies.
And hitherto doth love on fortune tend;   210
For who not needs° shall never lack a friend,
And who in want° a hollow friend doth try,°
Directly seasons him° his enemy.
But, orderly to end where I begun,
Our wills and fates do so contrary run   215
That our devices still° are overthrown;
Our thoughts are ours, their ends° none of our
    own.
So think thou wilt no second husband wed,
But die thy thoughts when thy first lord is dead.
PLAYER QUEEN: Nor earth to me give food, nor
    heaven light,   220
Sport and repose lock from me day and night,
To desperation turn my trust and hope,
An anchor's cheer° in prison be my scope!°
Each opposite° that blanks° the face of joy
Meet what I would have well and it destroy!   225
Both here and hence° pursue me lasting strife,
If, once a widow, ever I be wife!
HAMLET: If she should break it now!
PLAYER KING: 'Tis deeply sworn. Sweet, leave me
    here awhile;
My spirits grow dull, and fain I would beguile   230
The tedious day with sleep.   [Sleeps.]
PLAYER QUEEN: Sleep rock thy brain,
And never come mischance between us twain!
                                          [Exit.]
HAMLET: Madam, how like you this play?
QUEEN: The lady doth protest too much, methinks.
HAMLET: O, but she'll keep her word.   235
KING: Have you heard the argument?° Is there no
    offense in 't?
HAMLET: No, no, they do but jest, poison in jest; no
    offense i' th' world.
KING: What do you call the play?   240

169. distrust: Am anxious about.   170. nothing: Not at all.
171. hold quantity: Keep proportion with one another.   173.
proof: Experience.   178. operant: Active; leave to do: Cease
to perform.   186. instances: Motives; move: Motivate.   187.
base . . . thrift: Ignoble considerations of material prosperity.
192. Purpose . . . memory: Our good intentions are subject
to forgetfulness.   193. validity: Strength, durability.   196–
197. Most . . . debt: It's inevitable that in time we forget
the obligations we have imposed on ourselves.   201. enactures:
Fulfillments.

203. aye: Ever.   211. who not needs: He who is not in need
(of wealth).   212. who in want: He who is in need; try:
Test (his generosity).   213. seasons him: Ripens him into.
216. devices still: Intentions continually.   217. ends: Results.
222. anchor's cheer: Anchorite's or hermit's fare; my scope:
The extent of my happiness.   224. opposite: Adverse thing;
blanks: Causes to blanch or grow pale.   226. hence: In the
life hereafter.   236. argument: Plot.

HAMLET: "The Mouse-trap." Marry, how? Tropically.°
  This play is the image of a murder done in Vienna.
  Gonzago is the Duke's name; his wife, Baptista.
  You shall see anon. 'Tis a knavish piece of work,
245 but what of that? Your Majesty, and we that have
  free° souls, it touches us not. Let the gall'd jade°
  winch,° our withers° are unwrung.°

(*Enter Lucianus.*)

  This is one Lucianus, nephew to the King.
OPHELIA: You are as good as a chorus,° my lord.
250 HAMLET: I could interpret between you and your love,
  if I could see the puppets dallying.°
OPHELIA: You are keen, my lord, you are keen.
HAMLET: It would cost you a groaning to take off
  mine edge.
255 OPHELIA: Still better, and worse.°
HAMLET: So° you mistake° your husbands. Begin, murderer; leave thy damnable faces, and begin. Come,
  the croaking raven doth bellow for revenge.
LUCIANUS: Thoughts black, hands apt, drugs fit, and
  time agreeing,
260   Confederate season,° else no creature seeing,
  Thou mixture rank, of midnight weeds collected,
  With Hecate's ban° thrice blasted, thrice infected,
  Thy natural magic and dire property
  On wholesome life usurp immediately.
        [*Pours the poison into the sleeper's ears.*]
265 HAMLET: 'A poisons him i' th' garden for his estate.
  His name's Gonzago. The story is extant, and written
  in very choice Italian. You shall see anon how the
  murderer gets the love of Gonzago's wife.
        [*Claudius rises.*]
OPHELIA: The King rises.
270 [HAMLET: What, frighted with false fire?°]
QUEEN: How fares my lord?
POLONIUS: Give o'er the play.

KING: Give me some light. Away!
POLONIUS: Lights, lights, lights!
        (*Exeunt all but Hamlet and Horatio.*)
HAMLET: "Why, let the strucken deer go weep,   275
  The hart ungalled° play.
  For some must watch,° while some must sleep;
  Thus runs the world away."°
  Would not this,° sir, and a forest of feathers° —
  if the rest of my fortunes turn Turk with° me —   280
  with two Provincial roses° on my raz'd° shoes, get
  me a fellowship in a cry of players?°
HORATIO: Half a share.
HAMLET: A whole one, I.
  "For thou dost know, O Damon dear,   285
  This realm dismantled° was
  Of Jove himself, and now reigns here
  A very, very — pajock."°
HORATIO: You might have rhym'd.
HAMLET: O good Horatio, I'll take the ghost's word   290
  for a thousand pound. Didst perceive?
HORATIO: Very well, my lord.
HAMLET: Upon the talk of pois'ning?
HORATIO: I did very well note him.
HAMLET: Ah, ha! Come, some music! Come, the   295
  recorders!°
  "For if the King like not the comedy,
  Why then, belike, he likes it not, perdy"°
  Come, some music!

(*Enter Rosencrantz and Guildenstern.*)

GUILDENSTERN: Good my lord, vouchsafe me a word   300
  with you.
HAMLET: Sir, a whole history.
GUILDENSTERN: The King, sir —
HAMLET: Ay, sir, what of him?
GUILDENSTERN: Is in his retirement marvelous   305
  distemp'red.
HAMLET: With drink, sir?
GUILDENSTERN: No, my lord, with choler.°

---

241. Tropically: Figuratively. (The first quarto reading, *trapically*, suggests a pun on *trap* in *Mouse-trap*.)   **246. free:** Guiltless; **gall'd jade:** Horse whose hide is rubbed by saddle or harness.   **246. Winch:** Wince; **withers:** The part between the horse's shoulder blades; **unwrung:** Not rubbed sore.   **249. chorus:** In many Elizabethan plays the forthcoming action was explained by an actor known as the "chorus"; at a puppet show the actor who spoke the dialogue was known as an "interpreter," as indicated by the lines following.   **251. dallying:** With sexual suggestion, continued in *keen*, i.e., sexually aroused, *groaning*, i.e., moaning in pregnancy, and *edge*, i.e., sexual desire or impetuosity.   **255. Still . . . worse:** More keen-witted and less decorous.   **256. So:** even thus (in marriage); **mistake:** Mis-take, take erringly, falseheartedly.   **260. Confederate season:** The time and occasion conspiring (to assist the murderer).   **262. Hecate's ban:** The curse of Hecate, the goddess of witchcraft.   **270. false fire:** The blank discharge of a gun loaded with powder but not shot.

276. ungalled: Unafflicted.   **277. watch:** Remain awake.   **275–278. Why . . . away:** Probably from an old ballad, with allusion to the popular belief that a wounded deer retires to weep and die; cf. *As You Like It*, II, I, line 66.   **279. this:** The play; **feathers:** Allusion to the plumes which Elizabethan actors were fond of wearing.   **280. turn Turk with:** Turn renegade against, go back on.   **281. provincial roses:** Rosettes of ribbon like the roses of a part of France; **raz'd:** With ornamental slashing.   **282. fellowship . . . players:** Partnership in a theatrical company.   **286. dismantled:** Stripped, divested.   **288. pajock:** Peacock, a bird with a bad reputation (here substituted for the obvious rhyme-word *ass*).   **296. recorders:** Wind instruments of the flute kind.   **298. perdy:** A corruption of the French *par dieu*, "by God."   **308. choler:** Anger. (But Hamlet takes the word in its more basic humors sense of *bilious disorder*.)

HAMLET: Your wisdom should show itself more richer
to signify this to the doctor, for for me to put him
to his purgation would perhaps plunge him into
more choler.

GUILDENSTERN: Good my lord, put your discourse into
some frame° and start not so wildly from my affair.

HAMLET: I am tame, sir. Pronounce.

GUILDENSTERN: The Queen, your mother, in most great
affliction of spirit, hath sent me to you.

HAMLET: You are welcome.

GUILDENSTERN: Nay, good my lord, this courtesy is
not of the right breed. If it shall please you to make
me a wholesome answer, I will do your mother's
commandment; if not, your pardon° and my return
shall be the end of my business.

HAMLET: Sir, I cannot.

ROSENCRANTZ: What, my lord?

HAMLET: Make you a wholesome answer; my wit's
diseas'd. But, sir, such answer as I can make, you
shall command, or rather, as you say, my mother.
Therefore no more, but to the matter. My mother,
you say —

ROSENCRANTZ: Then thus she says: your behavior hath
struck her into amazement and admiration.°

HAMLET: O wonderful son, that can so stonish a
mother! But is there no sequel at the heels of this
mother's admiration? Impart.

ROSENCRANTZ: She desires to speak with you in her
closet,° ere you go to bed.

HAMLET: We shall obey, were she ten times our mother.
Have you any further trade with us?

ROSENCRANTZ: My lord, you once did love me.

HAMLET: And do still, by these pickers and stealers.°

ROSENCRANTZ: Good my lord, what is your cause of
distemper? You do surely bar the door upon your
own liberty, if you deny your griefs to your friend.

HAMLET: Sir, I lack advancement.

ROSENCRANTZ: How can that be, when you have the
voice of the King himself for your succession in
Denmark?

HAMLET: Ay, sir, but "While the grass grows"° — the
proverb is something° musty.

(*Enter the Players with recorders.*)

O, the recorders! Let me see one. [*He takes a recorder.*] To withdraw° with you: why do you go

about to recover the wind° of me, as if you would
drive me into a toil?°

GUILDENSTERN: O, my lord, if my duty be too bold,
my love is too unmannerly.°

HAMLET: I do not well understand that. Will you play
upon this pipe?

GUILDENSTERN: My lord, I cannot.

HAMLET: I pray you.

GUILDENSTERN: Believe me, I cannot.

HAMLET: I do beseech you.

GUILDENSTERN: I know no touch of it, my lord.

HAMLET: It is as easy as lying. Govern these ventages°
with your fingers and thumb, give it breath with
your mouth, and it will discourse most eloquent
music. Look you, these are the stops.

GUILDENSTERN: But these cannot I command to any
utt'rance of harmony; I have not the skill.

HAMLET: Why, look you now, how unworthy a thing
you make of me! You would play upon me, you
would seem to know my stops, you would pluck
out the heart of my mystery, you would sound me
from my lowest note to the top of my compass,°
and there is much music, excellent voice, in this
little organ,° yet cannot you make it speak. 'Sblood,
do you think I am easier to be play'd on than a
pipe? Call me what instrument you will, though
you can fret° me, you cannot play upon me.

(*Enter Polonius.*)

God bless you, sir!

POLONIUS: My lord, the Queen would speak with you,
and presently.°

HAMLET: Do you see yonder cloud that's almost in
shape of a camel?

POLONIUS: By th' mass, and 'tis like a camel, indeed.

HAMLET: Methinks it is like a weasel.

POLONIUS: It is back'd like a weasel.

HAMLET: Or like a whale?

POLONIUS: Very like a whale.

HAMLET: Then I will come to my mother by and by.°
[*Aside.*] They fool me° to the top of my bent.° —
I will come by and by.

POLONIUS: I will say so.   [*Exit.*]

HAMLET: "By and by" is easily said. Leave me, friends.

---

314. frame: Order.   **322. pardon:** Permission to depart.
332. admiration: Wonder.   **337. closet:** Private chamber.
341. pickers and stealers: Hands (so called from the catechism,
"to keep my hands from picking and stealing").   **350. "While
. . . grows":** The rest of the proverb is "the silly horse starves";
Hamlet may not live long enough to succeed to the kingdom.
351. something: Somewhat.   **352. withdraw:** Speak privately.

353. recover the wind: Get the windward side.   **354. toil:**
Snare.   **355–356. if . . . unmannerly:** If I am using an unmannerly boldness, it is my love which occasions it.   **364.
ventages:** Stops of the recorder.   **374. compass:** Range (of
voice).   **376. organ:** Musical instrument.   **379. fret:** Irritate
(with a quibble on *fret* meaning the piece of wood, gut, or
metal which regulates the fingering on an instrument).   **382.
presently:** At once.   **390. by and by:** Immediately.   **391.
fool me:** Make me play the fool; **top of my bent:** Limit of
my ability or endurance (literally, the extent to which a bow
may be bent).

[*Exeunt all but Hamlet.*]

395 'Tis now the very witching time° of night,
When churchyards yawn and hell itself breathes
  out
Contagion to this world. Now could I drink hot
  blood,
And do such bitter business as the day
Would quake to look on. Soft, now to my
  mother.
400 O heart, lose not thy nature! Let not ever
The soul of Nero° enter this firm bosom.
Let me be cruel, not unnatural;
I will speak daggers to her, but use none.
My tongue and soul in this be hypocrites:
405 How in my words somever° she be shent,°
To give them seals° never, my soul, consent!

                                 (*Exit.*)

[Scene III]°

(*Enter King, Rosencrantz, and Guildenstern.*)

KING: I like him not, nor stands it safe with us
To let his madness range. Therefore prepare you.
I your commission will forthwith dispatch,°
And he to England shall along with you.
5 The terms° of our estate° may not endure
Hazard so near 's as doth hourly grow
Out of his brows.°
GUILDENSTERN: We will ourselves provide.
Most holy and religious fear it is
To keep those many many bodies safe
10 That live and feed upon your Majesty.
ROSENCRANTZ: The single and peculiar° life is
  bound
With all the strength and armor of the mind
To keep itself from noyance,° but much more
That spirit upon whose weal depends and rests
15 The lives of many. The cess° of majesty
Dies not alone, but like a gulf° doth draw
What's near it with it; or it is a massy wheel
Fix'd on the summit of the highest mount,
To whose huge spokes ten thousand lesser things
20 Are mortis'd and adjoin'd, which, when it falls,
Each small annexment, petty consequence,

Attends° the boist'rous ruin. Never alone
Did the King sigh, but with a general groan.
KING: Arm° you, I pray you, to this speedy voyage,
For we will fetters put about this fear,   25
Which now goes too free-footed.
ROSENCRANTZ: We will haste us.
(*Exeunt Gentlemen [Rosencrantz and Guildenstern].*)

(*Enter Polonius.*)

POLONIUS: My lord, he's going to his mother's
  closet.
Behind the arras° I'll convey myself
To hear the process.° I'll warrant she'll tax him
  home,°
And, as you said, and wisely was it said,   30
'Tis meet that some more audience than a
  mother,
Since nature makes them partial, should o'erhear
The speech, of vantage.° Fare you well, my liege.
I'll call upon you ere you go to bed,
And tell you what I know.
KING: Thanks, dear my lord.   35
                                 (*Exit [Polonius].*)
O, my offense is rank, it smells to heaven;
It hath the primal eldest curse° upon 't,
A brother's murder. Pray can I not,
Though inclination be as sharp as will.°
My stronger guilt defeats my strong intent,   40
And, like a man to double business bound,
I stand in pause where I shall first begin,
And both neglect. What if this cursed hand
Were thicker than itself with brother's blood,
Is there not rain enough in the sweet heavens   45
To wash it white as snow? Whereto serves
  mercy
But to confront the visage of offense?°
And what's in prayer but this twofold force,
To be forestalled° ere we come to fall,
Or pardon'd being down? Then I'll look up;   50
My fault is past. But, O, what form of prayer
Can serve my turn? "Forgive me my foul
  murder"?

---

395. witching time: Time when spells are cast and evil is abroad.   **401. Nero:** Murderer of his mother, Agrippina.   **405. How . . . somever:** However much by my words; **shent:** Rebuked.   **406. give them seals:** Confirm them with deeds.   **III, III. Location:** The castle.   **3. dispatch:** Prepare, cause to be drawn up.   **5. terms:** Condition, circumstances; **our estate:** My royal position.   **7. brows:** Effronteries, threatening frowns (?), brain (?).   **11. single and peculiar:** Individual and private.   **13. noyance:** Harm.   **15. cess:** Decease.   **16. gulf:** Whirlpool.

22. Attends: Participates in.   **24. Arm:** Prepare.   **28. arras:** Screen of tapestry placed around the walls of household apartments. (On the Elizabethan stage, the arras was presumably over a door or discovery space in the tiring house facade.)   **29. process:** Proceedings; **tax him home:** Reprove him severely.   **33. of vantage:** From an advantageous place.   **37. primal eldest curse:** The curse of Cain, the first murderer; he killed his brother Abel.   **39. Though . . . will:** Though my desire is as strong as my determination.   **46–47. Whereto . . . offense:** For what function does mercy serve other than to undo the effects of sin.   **49. forestalled:** Prevented (from sinning).

That cannot be, since I am still possess'd
Of those effects for which I did the murder,
55 My crown, mine own ambition, and my queen.
May one be pardon'd and retain th' offense?
In the corrupted currents° of this world
Offense's gilded hand° may shove by justice,
And oft 'tis seen the wicked prize° itself
60 Buys out the law. But 'tis not so above.
There is no shuffling,° there the action lies°
In his° true nature, and we ourselves compell'd,
Even to the teeth and forehead° of our faults,
To give in evidence. What then? What rests?°
65 Try what repentance can. What can it not?
Yet what can it, when one cannot repent?
O wretched state! O bosom black as death!
O limed° soul, that, struggling to be free,
Art more engag'd!° Help, angels! Make assay.°
Bow, stubborn knees, and heart with strings of
70   steel,
Be soft as sinews of the new-born babe!
All may be well.

                                              [*He kneels.*]

(*Enter Hamlet [with sword drawn].*)

HAMLET: Now might I do it pat,° now 'a is a-
        praying;
And now I'll do 't. And so 'a goes to heaven;
75 And so am I reveng'd. That would be scann'd:°
A villain kills my father, and for that,
I, his sole son, do this same villain send
To heaven.
Why, this is hire and salary, not revenge.
80 'A took my father grossly,° full of bread,°
With all his crimes broad blown,° as flush° as
        May;
And how his audit° stands who knows save
        heaven?
But in our circumstance and course° of thought,
'Tis heavy with him. And am I then reveng'd,
85 To take him in the purging of his soul,
When he is fit and season'd for his passage?

No!
Up, sword, and know thou a more horrid hent.°
                                    [*Puts up his sword.*]
When he is drunk asleep, or in his rage,
Or in th' incestuous pleasure of his bed,   90
At game a-swearing, or about some act
That has no relish of salvation in 't —
Then trip him, that his heels may kick at
        heaven,
And that his soul may be as damn'd and black
As hell, whereto it goes. My mother stays.   95
This physic° but prolongs thy sickly days. (*Exit.*)
KING: My words fly up, my thoughts remain below.
Words without thoughts never to heaven go.
                                              (*Exit.*)

[Scene IV]°

(*Enter [Queen] Gertrude and Polonius.*)

POLONIUS: 'A will come straight. Look you lay°
        home to him.
Tell him his pranks have been too broad° to
        bear with,
And that your Grace hath screen'd and stood
        between
Much heat° and him. I'll sconce° me even here.
Pray you, be round° [with him.   5
HAMLET (*within*): Mother, mother, mother!]
QUEEN: I'll warrant you, fear me not.
Withdraw, I hear him coming.
                    [*Polonius hides behind the arras.*]

(*Enter Hamlet.*)

HAMLET: Now, mother, what's the matter?
QUEEN: Hamlet, thou hast thy father° much
        offended.   10
HAMLET: Mother, you have my father much
        offended.
QUEEN: Come, come, you answer with an idle°
        tongue.
HAMLET: Go, go, you question with a wicked
        tongue.
QUEEN: Why, how now, Hamlet?
HAMLET: What's the matter now?
QUEEN: Have you forgot me?
HAMLET: No, by the rood,° not so: 15

---

57. **currents:** Courses.   58. **gilded hand:** Hand offering gold
as a bribe.   59. **wicked prize:** Prize won by wickedness.
61. **shuffling:** Escape by trickery; **the action lies:** The accusation
is made manifest, comes up for consideration (a legal metaphor).   62. **his:** Its.   63. **teeth and forehead:** Face to face,
concealing nothing.   64. **rests:** Remains.   68. **limed:** Caught
as with birdlime, a sticky substance used to ensnare birds.
69. **engag'd:** Embedded. **assay:** Trial.   73. **pat:** Opportunely.
75. **would be scann'd:** Needs to be looked into.   80. **grossly:**
Not spiritually prepared; **full of bread:** Enjoying his wordly
pleasures. (See Ezek. 16:49.)   81. **crimes broad blown:** Sins
in full bloom; **flush:** Lusty.   82. **audit:** Account.   83. **in
. . . course:** As we see it in our mortal situation.

88. **know . . . hent:** Await to be grasped by me on a more
horrid occasion.   96. **physic:** Purging (by prayer).   **III, IV.
Location:** The Queen's private chamber.   1. **lay:** Thrust (i.e.,
reprove him soundly).   2. **broad:** Unrestrained.   4. **Much
heat:** The King's anger; **sconce:** Ensconce, hide.   5. **round:**
Blunt.   10. **thy father:** Your stepfather, Claudius.   12. **idle:**
Foolish.   15. **rood:** Cross.

You are the Queen, your husband's brother's
    wife,
And — would it were not so! — you are my
    mother.
QUEEN: Nay, then, I'll set those to you that can
    speak.
HAMLET: Come, come, and sit you down; you shall
    not budge.
20 You go not till I set you up a glass
Where you may see the inmost part of you.
QUEEN: What wilt thou do? Thou wilt not murder
    me?
    Help, ho!
POLONIUS [behind]: What, ho! Help!
HAMLET [drawing]: How now? A rat? Dead, for a
25   ducat, dead!
                        [Makes a pass through the arras.]
POLONIUS [behind]: O, I am slain!   [Falls and dies.]
QUEEN: O me, what hast thou done?
HAMLET: Nay, I know not. Is it the King?
QUEEN: O, what a rash and bloody deed is this!
HAMLET: A bloody deed — almost as bad, good
    mother,
30 As kill a king, and marry with his brother.
QUEEN: As kill a king!
HAMLET: Ay, lady, it was my word.
            [Parts the arras and discovers Polonius.]
Thou wretched, rash, intruding fool, farewell!
I took thee for thy better. Take thy fortune.
Thou find'st to be too busy is some danger. —
Leave wringing of your hands. Peace, sit you
35   down,
And let me wring your heart, for so I shall,
If it be made of penetrable stuff,
If damned custom° have not braz'd° it so
That it be proof° and bulwark against sense.°
QUEEN: What have I done, that thou dar'st wag thy
40   tongue
In noise so rude against me?
HAMLET: Such an art
That blurs the grace and blush of modesty,
Calls virtue hypocrite, takes off the rose
From the fair forehead of an innocent love
45 And sets a blister° there, makes marriage-vows
As false as dicers' oaths. O, such a deed
As from the body of contraction° plucks
The very soul, and sweet religion° makes
A rhapsody° of words. Heaven's face does glow

O'er this solidity and compound mass   50
With heated visage, as against the doom,
Is thought-sick at the act.
QUEEN: Ay me, what act,°
That roars so loud and thunders in the index?°
HAMLET: Look here, upon this picture, and on this,
The counterfeit presentment° of two brothers.   55
                        [Shows her two likenesses.]
See, what a grace was seated on this brow:
Hyperion's° curls, the front° of Jove himself,
An eye like Mars, to threaten and command,
A station° like the herald Mercury
New-lighted on a heaven-kissing hill —   60
A combination and a form indeed,
Where every god did seem to set his seal,
To give the world assurance of a man.
This was your husband. Look you now, what
    follows:
Here is your husband, like a mildew'd ear,°   65
Blasting his wholesome brother. Have you eyes?
Could you on this fair mountain leave to feed,
And batten° on this moor?° Ha, have you eyes?
You cannot call it love, for at your age
The heyday° in the blood is tame, it's humble,   70
And waits upon the judgment, and what
    judgment
Would step from this to this? Sense,° sure, you
    have,
Else could you not have motion, but sure that
    sense
Is apoplex'd,° for madness would not err,
Nor sense to ecstasy was ne'er so thrall'd   75
But it reserv'd some quantity of choice
To serve in such a difference. What devil was 't
That thus hath cozen'd° you at hoodman-blind?°
Eyes without feeling, feeling without sight,
Ears without hands or eyes, smelling sans° all,   80
Or but a sickly part of one true sense

49–52. Heaven's . . . act: Heaven's face flushes with anger
to look down upon this solid world, this compound mass,
with hot face as though the day of doom were near, and is
thought-sick at the deed (i.e., Gertrude's marriage).   **53.
index:** Table of contents, prelude, or preface.   **55. counterfeit
presentment:** Portrayed representation.   **57. Hyperion:** The
sun god; **front:** Brow.   **59. station:** Manner of standing.
65. ear: I.e., of grain.   **68. batten:** Gorge; **moor:** Barren
upland.   **70. heyday:** State of excitement.   **72. Sense:** Perception through the five senses (the functions of the middle
or sensible soul).   **74. apoplex'd:** Paralyzed. (Hamlet goes
on to explain that without such a paralysis of will, mere
madness would not so err, nor would the five senses so
enthrall themselves to *ecstasy* or lunacy; even such deranged
states of mind would be able to make the obvious choice
between Hamlet Senior and Claudius.)   **78. cozen'd:** Cheated;
hoodman-blind: Blindman's buff.   **80. sans:** Without.

38. damned custom: Habitual wickedness; **braz'd:** Brazened,
hardened.   **39. proof:** Armor; **sense:** Feeling.   **45. sets a
blister:** Brands as a harlot;   **47. contraction:** The marriage
contract.   **48. religion:** Religious vows.   **49. rhapsody:**
Senseless string.

Could not so mope.°
O shame, where is thy blush? Rebellious hell,
If thou canst mutine° in a matron's bones,
85 To flaming youth let virtue be as wax,
And melt in her own fire. Proclaim no shame
When the compulsive ardor gives the charge,
Since frost itself as actively doth burn,
And reason panders will.°
90 QUEEN: O Hamlet, speak no more!
Thou turn'st mine eyes into my very soul,
And there I see such black and grained° spots
As will not leave their tint.°
HAMLET: Nay, but to live
In the rank sweat of an enseamed° bed,
95 Stew'd in corruption, honeying and making love
Over the nasty sty —
QUEEN: O, speak to me no more.
These words, like daggers, enter in my ears.
No more, sweet Hamlet!
HAMLET: A murderer and a villain,
100 A slave that is not twentieth part the tithe°
Of your precedent° lord, a vice° of kings,
A cutpurse of the empire and the rule,
That from a shelf the precious diadem stole,
And put it in his pocket!
105 QUEEN: No more!

(*Enter Ghost* [*in his nightgown*].)

HAMLET: A king of shreds and patches° —
Save me, and hover o'er me with your wings,
You heavenly guards! What would your gracious
  figure?
QUEEN: Alas, he's mad!
HAMLET: Do you not come your tardy son to
110 chide,
That, laps'd in time and passion,° lets go by
Th' important° acting of your dread command?
O, say!
GHOST: Do not forget. This visitation
115 Is but to whet thy almost blunted purpose.
But, look, amazement° on thy mother sits.

82. **mope:** Be dazed, act aimlessly.   84. **mutine:** Mutiny.
86–89. **Proclaim . . . will:** Call it no shameful business when
the compelling ardor of youth delivers the attack, i.e., commits
lechery, since the frost of advanced age burns with as active
a fire of lust and reason perverts itself by fomenting lust
rather than restraining it.   92. **grained:** Dyed in grain, in-
delible.   93. **tinct:** Color.   94. **enseamed:** Laden with grease.
100. **tithe:** Tenth part.   101. **precedent:** Former (i.e., the
elder Hamlet); **vice:** buffoon (a reference to the vice of the
morality plays).   106. **shreds and patches:** Motley, the traditional costume of the clown or fool.   111. **laps'd . . .
passion:** Having allowed time to lapse and passion to cool.
112. **important:** Importunate, urgent.   116. **amazement:**
Distraction.

O, step between her and her fighting soul!
Conceit° in weakest bodies strongest works.
Speak to her, Hamlet.
HAMLET: How is it with you, lady?
QUEEN: Alas, how is 't with you,   120
That you do bend your eye on vacancy,
And with th' incorporal° air do hold discourse?
Forth at your eyes your spirits wildly peep,
And, as the sleeping soldiers in th' alarm,
Your bedded° hair, like life in excrements,°   125
Start up and stand an° end. O gentle son,
Upon the heat and flame of thy distemper
Sprinkle cool patience. Whereon do you look?
HAMLET: On him, on him! Look you how pale he
  glares!
His form and cause conjoin'd,° preaching to
  stones,   130
Would make them capable.° — Do not look
  upon me,
Lest with this piteous action you convert
My stern effects.° Then what I have to do
Will want true color° — tears perchance for
  blood.
QUEEN: To whom do you speak this?   135
HAMLET: Do you see nothing there?
QUEEN: Nothing at all; yet all that is I see.
HAMLET: Nor did you nothing hear?
QUEEN: No, nothing but ourselves.
HAMLET: Why, look you there, look how it steals
  away!   140
My father, in his habit° as he lived!
Look, where he goes, even now, out at the
  portal!
                                        (*Exit Ghost.*)
QUEEN: This is the very coinage of your brain.
This bodiless creation ecstasy°
Is very cunning in.   145
HAMLET: Ecstasy?
My pulse, as yours, doth temperately keep time,
And makes as healthful music. It is not madness
That I have utter'd. Bring me to the test,
And I the matter will reword, which madness   150
Would gambol° from. Mother, for love of grace,
Lay not that flattering unction° to your soul
That not your trespass but my madness speaks.

118. **Conceit:** Imagination.   122. **incorporal:** Immaterial.
125. **bedded:** Laid in smooth layers; **excrements:** Outgrowths.
126. **an:** On.   130. **His . . . conjoin'd:** His appearance joined
to his cause for speaking.   131. **capable:** Receptive.   132–
133. **convert . . . effects:** Divert me from my stern duty.
134. **want true color:** Lack plausibility so that (with a play
on the normal sense of *color*) I shall shed tears instead of
blood.   141. **habit:** Dress.   144. **ecstasy:** Madness.   151.
gambol: Skip away.   152. **unction:** Ointment.

It will but skin and film the ulcerous place,
155 Whiles rank corruption, mining° all within,
Infects unseen. Confess yourself to heaven,
Repent what's past, avoid what is to come,
And do not spread the compost° on the weeds
To make them ranker. Forgive me this my
virtue;°
160 For in the fatness° of these pursy° times
Virtue itself of vice must pardon beg,
Yea, curb° and woo for leave° to do him good.
QUEEN: O Hamlet, thou hast cleft my heart in
twain.
HAMLET: O, throw away the worser part of it,
165 And live the purer with the other half.
Good night. But go not to my uncle's bed;
Assume a virtue, if you have it not.
That monster, custom, who all sense doth eat,°
Of habits devil,° is angel yet in this,
170 That to the use of actions fair and good
He likewise gives a frock or livery°
That aptly is put on. Refrain tonight,
And that shall lend a kind of easiness
To the next abstinence; the next more easy;
175 For use° almost can change the stamp of nature,
And either° . . . the devil, or throw him out
With wondrous potency. Once more, good night;
And when you are desirous to be bless'd,°
I'll blessing beg of you. For this same lord,
                      [*Pointing to Polonius.*]
180 I do repent; but heaven hath pleas'd it so
To punish me with this, and this with me,
That I must be their scourge and minister.°
I will bestow° him, and will answer well
The death I gave him. So, again, good night.
185 I must be cruel only to be kind.
Thus bad begins and worse remains behind.°
One word more, good lady.
QUEEN: What shall I do?
HAMLET: Not this, by no means, that I bid you do:

Let the bloat° king tempt you again to bed,
Pinch wanton on your cheek, call you his mouse, 190
And let him, for a pair of reechy° kisses,
Or paddling in your neck with his damn'd
fingers,
Make you to ravel all this matter out,
That I essentially am not in madness,
But mad in craft. 'Twere good° you let him
know,   195
For who that's but a queen, fair, sober, wise,
Would from a paddock,° from a bat, a gib,°
Such dear concernings° hide? Who would do so?
No, in despite of sense and secrecy,
Unpeg the basket° on the house's top,   200
Let the birds fly, and, like the famous ape,°
To try conclusions,° in the basket creep
And break your own neck down.
QUEEN: Be thou assur'd, if words be made of
breath,
And breath of life, I have no life to breathe   205
What thou hast said to me.
HAMLET: I must to England; you know that?
QUEEN: Alack,
I had forgot. 'Tis so concluded on.
HAMLET: There's letters seal'd, and my two school-
fellows,
Whom I will trust as I will adders fang'd,   210
They bear the mandate; they must sweep my
way,°
And marshal me to knavery. Let it work.
For 'tis the sport to have the enginer°
Hoist with° his own petar,° and 't shall go hard
But I will delve one yard below their mines,°   215
And blow them at the moon. O, 'tis most sweet,
When in one line two crafts° directly meet.
This man shall set me packing.°
I'll lug the guts into the neighbor room.
Mother, good night indeed. This counselor   220

---

155. **mining:** Working under the surface. 158. **compost:** Manure. 159. **this my virtue:** My virtuous talk in reproving you. 160. **fatness:** Grossness; **pursy:** Short-winded, corpulent. 162. **curb:** Bow, bend the knee; **leave:** Permission. 168. **who . . . eat:** Who consumes all proper or natural feeling. 169. **Of habits devil:** Devil-like in prompting evil habits. 171. **livery:** An outer appearance, a customary garb (and hence a predisposition easily assumed in time of stress). 175. **use:** Habit. 176. **And either:** A defective line usually emended by inserting the word *master* after *either,* following the fourth quarto and early editors. 178. **be bless'd:** Become blessed, i.e., repentant. 182. **their scourge and minister:** Agent of heavenly retribution. (By *scourge,* Hamlet also suggests that he himself will eventually suffer punishment in the process of fulfilling heaven's will.) 183. **bestow:** Stow, dispose of. 186. **behind:** To come.

189. **bloat:** Bloated. 191. **reechy:** Dirty, filthy. 195. **good:** Said ironically; also the following 8 lines. 197. **paddock:** Toad; **gib:** Tomcat. 198. **dear concernings:** Important affairs. 200. **Unpeg the basket:** Open the cage, i.e., let out the secret. 201. **famous ape:** In a story now lost. 202. **conclusions:** Experiments (in which the ape apparently enters a cage from which birds have been released and then tries to fly out of the cage as they have done, falling to his death). 211. **sweep my way:** Go before me. 213. **enginer:** Constructor of military contrivances. 214. **Hoist with:** Blown up by; **petar:** Petard, an explosive used to blow in a door or make a breach. 215. **mines:** Tunnels used in warfare to undermine the enemy's emplacements; Hamlet will countermine by going under their mines. 217. **crafts:** Acts of guile, plots. 218. **set me packing:** Set me to making schemes, and set me to lugging (him) and, also, send me off in a hurry.

Is now most still, most secret, and most grave,
Who was in life a foolish prating knave.
Come, sir, to draw toward an end° with you.
Good night, mother.
                    (*Exeunt* [*severally, Hamlet dragging in
                                            Polonius*].)

[ACT IV · Scene I]°

(*Enter King and Queen, with Rosencrantz and Guildenstern.*)

KING: There's matter in these sighs, these profound
        heaves
You must translate; 'tis fit we understand them.
Where is your son?
QUEEN: Bestow this place on us a little while.
            [*Exeunt Rosencrantz and Guildenstern.*]
5   Ah, mine own lord, what have I seen tonight!
KING: What, Gertrude? How does Hamlet?
QUEEN: Mad as the sea and wind when both
        contend
Which is the mightier. In his lawless fit,
Behind the arras hearing something stir,
10   Whips out his rapier, cries, "A rat, a rat!"
And, in this brainish apprehension,° kills
The unseen good old man.
KING: O heavy deed!
It had been so with us, had we been there.
His liberty is full of threats to all —
15   To you yourself, to us, to everyone.
Alas, how shall this bloody deed be answer'd?
It will be laid to us, whose providence°
Should have kept short,° restrain'd, and out of
        haunt°
This mad young man. But so much was our love
20   We would not understand what was most fit,
But, like the owner of a foul disease,
To keep it from divulging,° let it feed
Even on the pith of life. Where is he gone?
QUEEN: To draw apart the body he hath kill'd,
25   O'er whom his very madness, like some ore°
Among a mineral° of metals base,
Shows itself pure: 'a weeps for what is done.
KING: O Gertrude, come away!
The sun no sooner shall the mountains touch
30   But we will ship him hence; and this vile deed
We must, with all our majesty and skill,

Both countenance and excuse. Ho, Guildenstern!
(*Enter Rosencrantz and Guildenstern.*)
Friends both, go join you with some further aid.
Hamlet in madness hath Polonius slain,
And from his mother's closet hath he dragg'd
        him.   35
Go seek him out; speak fair, and bring the body
Into the chapel. I pray you, haste in this.
            [*Exeunt Rosencrantz and Guildenstern.*]
Come, Gertrude, we'll call up our wisest friends
And let them know both what we mean to do
And what's untimely done°   40
Whose whisper o'er the world's diameter,°
As level° as the cannon to his blank,°
Transports his pois'ned shot, may miss our
        name,
And hit the woundless° air. O, come away!
My soul is full of discord and dismay. (*Exeunt.*)   45

[Scene II]°

(*Enter Hamlet.*)

HAMLET: Safely stow'd.
[ROSENCRANTZ, GUILDENSTERN (*within*): Hamlet! Lord
        Hamlet!]
HAMLET: But soft, what noise? Who calls on Hamlet?
        O, here they come.   5

(*Enter Rosencrantz and Guildenstern.*)

ROSENCRANTZ: What have you done, my lord, with
        the dead body?
HAMLET: Compounded it with dust, whereto 'tis
        kin.
ROSENCRANTZ: Tell us where 'tis, that we may take
        it thence
And bear it to the chapel.
HAMLET: Do not believe it.   10
ROSENCRANTZ: Believe what?
HAMLET: That I can keep your counsel and not mine
        own. Besides, to be demanded of° a sponge, what
        replication° should be made by the son of a king?
ROSENCRANTZ: Take you me for a sponge, my lord?   15
HAMLET: Ay, sir, that soaks up the King's countenance,°
        his rewards, his authorities. But such officers do

---

223. **draw . . . end:** Finish up (with a pun on *draw*, pull).
IV, I. **Location:** The castle.   11. **brainish apprehension:**
Headstrong conception.   17. **providence:** Foresight.   18.
short: On a short tether; **out of haunt:** Secluded.   22. **divulging:** Becoming evident.   25. **ore:** Vein of gold.   26.
mineral: Mine.

40. **And . . . done:** A defective line; conjectures as to the
missing words include *so, haply, slander* (Capell and others);
for, haply, slander (Theobald and others).   41. **diameter:**
Extent from side to side.   42. **As level:** With as direct aim;
blank: White spot in the center of a target.   44. **woundless:**
Invulnerable.   IV, II. **Location:** The castle.   13. **demanded
of:** Questioned by.   14. **replication:** Reply.   16. **countenance:**
Favor.

the King best service in the end. He keeps them,
like an ape an apple, in the corner of his jaw, first
20 mouth'd, to be last swallow'd. When he needs what
you have glean'd, it is but squeezing you, and,
sponge, you shall be dry again.
ROSENCRANTZ: I understand you not, my lord.
HAMLET: I am glad of it. A knavish speech sleeps in°
25 a foolish ear.
ROSENCRANTZ: My lord, you must tell us where the
body is, and go with us to the King.
HAMLET: The body is with the King, but the King is
not with the body.° The King is a thing —
30 GUILDENSTERN: A thing, my lord?
HAMLET: Of nothing.° Bring me to him. [Hide fox,
and all after.°]   (*Exeunt.*)

[Scene III]°

(*Enter King, and two or three.*)

KING: I have sent to seek him, and to find the
      body.
   How dangerous is it that this man goes loose!
   Yet must not we put the strong law on him.
   He's lov'd of the distracted° multitude,
5   Who like not in their judgment, but their eyes,
   And where 'tis so, th' offender's scourge° is
      weigh'd,°
   But never the offense. To bear° all smooth and
      even,
   This sudden sending him away must seem
   Deliberate pause.° Diseases desperate grown
10 By desperate appliance are reliev'd,
   Or not at all.

(*Enter Rosencrantz, [Guildenstern,] and all the rest.*)

                     How now? What hath befall'n?
ROSENCRANTZ: Where the dead body is bestow'd,
      my lord,
   We cannot get from him.
KING: But where is he?
ROSENCRANTZ: Without, my lord; guarded, to
      know your pleasure.
KING: Bring him before us.

ROSENCRANTZ: Ho! Bring in the lord.   15

(*They enter [with Hamlet].*)

KING: Now, Hamlet, where's Polonius?
HAMLET: At supper.
KING: At supper? Where?
HAMLET: Not where he eats, but where 'a is eaten. A
   certain convocation of politic worms° are e'en at   20
   him. Your worm is your only emperor for diet.°
   We fat all creatures else to fat us, and we fat ourselves
   for maggots. Your fat king and your lean beggar
   is but variable service,° two dishes, but to one table
   — that's the end.
KING: Alas, alas!
HAMLET: A man may fish with the worm that hath
   eat° of a king, and eat of the fish that hath fed of
   that worm.
KING: What dost thou mean by this?   30
HAMLET: Nothing but to show you how a king may
   go a progress° through the guts of a beggar.
KING: Where is Polonius?
HAMLET: In heaven. Send thither to see. If your messenger
   find him not there, seek him i' th' other   35
   place yourself. But if indeed you find him not within
   this month, you shall nose him as you go up the
   stairs into the lobby.
KING [*to some Attendants*]: Go seek him there.
HAMLET: 'A will stay till you come.   40
                           [*Exit Attendants.*]
KING: Hamlet, this deed, for thine especial safety. —
   Which we do tender,° as we dearly° grieve
   For that which thou hast done — must send
      thee hence
   [With fiery quickness.] Therefore prepare thyself.
   The bark° is ready, and the wind at help,   45
   Th' associates tend,° and everything is bent°
   For England.
HAMLET: For England!
KING: Ay, Hamlet.
HAMLET: Good.   50
KING: So is it, if thou knew'st our purposes.
HAMLET: I see a cherub° that sees them. But, come,
   for England! Farewell, dear mother.
KING: Thy loving father, Hamlet.
HAMLET: My mother. Father and mother is man and   55

24. **sleeps in:** Has no meaning to.   28–29. **The . . . body:**
Perhaps alludes to the legal commonplace of "the king's two
bodies," which drew a distinction between the sacred office
of kingship and the particular mortal who possessed it at
any given time.   31. **Of nothing:** Of no account.   31–32.
Hide . . . after: An old signal cry in the game of hide-and-
seek, suggesting that Hamlet now runs away from them.
IV, III. Location: The castle.   4. **distracted:** Fickle, unstable.
6. **scourge:** Punishment; **weigh'd:** Taken into consideration.
7. **bear:** Manage.   9. **Deliberate pause:** Carefully considered
action.

20. **politic worms:** Crafty worms (suited to a master spy like
Polonius).   21. **diet:** Food, eating (with perhaps a punning
reference to the Diet of Worms, a famous *convocation* held
in 1521).   24. **variable service:** Different courses of a single
meal.   28. **eat:** Eaten (pronounced *et*).   32. **progress:** Royal
journey of state.   42. **tender:** Regard, hold dear; **dearly:**
Intensely.   45. **bark:** Sailing vessel.   46. **tend:** Wait; **bent:**
In readiness.   52. **cherub:** Cherubim are angels of knowledge.

wife, man and wife is one flesh, and so, my mother.
Come, for England!   (*Exit.*)
KING: Follow him at foot;° tempt him with speed
   aboard.
   Delay it not; I'll have him hence tonight.
60   Away! For everything is seal'd and done
   That else leans on° th' affair. Pray you, make
   haste.
               [*Exeunt all but the King.*]
   And, England,° if my love thou hold'st at aught —
   As my great power thereof may give thee sense,
   Since yet thy cicatrice° looks raw and red
65   After the Danish sword, and thy free awe°
   Pays homage to us — thou mayst not coldly set°
   Our sovereign process,° which imports at full,
   By letters congruing° to that effect,
   The present° death of Hamlet. Do it, England,
70   For like the hectic° in my blood he rages,
   And thou must cure me. Till I know 'tis done,
   Howe'er my haps,° my joys were ne'er begun.
                        (*Exit.*)

[Scene IV]°

(*Enter Fortinbras with his Army over the stage.*)

FORTINBRAS: Go, captain, from me greet the Danish
   king.
   Tell him that, by his license,° Fortinbras
   Craves the conveyance° of a promis'd march
   Over his kingdom. You know the rendezvous.
5   If that his Majesty would aught with us,
   We shall express our duty in his eye;°
   And let him know so.
CAPTAIN: I will do 't, my lord.
FORTINBRAS: Go softly° on.   [*Exeunt all but the
                               Captain.*]

(*Enter Hamlet, Rosencrantz, [Guildenstern,] etc.*)

HAMLET: Good sir, whose powers° are these?
10 CAPTAIN: They are of Norway, sir.
HAMLET: How purposed, sir, I pray you?
CAPTAIN: Against some part of Poland.
HAMLET: Who commands them, sir?
CAPTAIN: The nephew to old Norway, Fortinbras.
15 HAMLET: Goes it against the main° of Poland, sir,
   Or for some frontier?

CAPTAIN: Truly to speak, and with no addition,°
   We go to gain a little patch of ground
   That hath in it no profit but the name.
   To pay° five ducats, five, I would not farm it;°   20
   Nor will it yield to Norway or the Pole
   A ranker° rate, should it be sold in fee.°
HAMLET: Why, then the Polack never will defend it.
CAPTAIN: Yes, it is already garrison'd.
HAMLET: Two thousand souls and twenty thousand
   ducats   25
   Will not debate the question of this straw.°
   This is th' imposthume° of much wealth and
   peace,
   That inward breaks, and shows no cause
   without
   Why the man dies. I humbly thank you, sir.
CAPTAIN: God buy you, sir.   [*Exit.*]
ROSENCRANTZ: Will 't please you go, my lord? 30
HAMLET: I'll be with you straight. Go a little
   before.   [*Exit all except Hamlet.*]
   How all occasions do inform against° me,
   And spur my dull revenge! What is a man,
   If his chief good and market of° his time
   Be but to sleep and feed? A beast, no more. 35
   Sure he that made us with such large discourse,°
   Looking before and after, gave us not
   That capability and god-like reason
   To fust° in us unus'd. Now, whether it be
   Bestial oblivion,° or some craven scruple 40
   Of thinking too precisely on th' event° —
   A thought which, quarter'd, hath but one part
   wisdom
   And ever three parts coward — I do not know
   Why yet I live to say "This thing's to do,"
   Sith° I have cause and will and strength and
   means 45
   To do 't. Examples gross° as earth exhort me:
   Witness this army of such mass and charge°
   Led by a delicate and tender prince,
   Whose spirit, with divine ambition puff'd
   Makes mouths° at the invisible event, 50
   Exposing what is mortal and unsure
   To all that fortune, death, and danger dare,
   Even for an egg-shell. Rightly to be great

---

58. at foot: Close behind, at heel.   **61. leans on:** Bears upon, is related to.   **62. England:** King of England. **64. cicatrice:** Scar.   **65. free awe:** Voluntary show of respect.   **66. set:** Esteem.   **67. process:** Command.   **68. congruing:** Agreeing.   **69. present:** Immediate.   **70. hectic:** Persistent fever.   **72. haps:** Fortunes.   **IV, IV. Location:** The coast of Denmark.   **2. license:** Permission.   **3. conveyance:** Escort, convoy.   **6. eye:** Presence.   **8. softly:** Slowly.   **9. powers:** Forces.   **15. main:** Main part.

17. addition: Exaggeration.   **20. To pay:** I.e., for a yearly rental of; **farm it:** Take a lease of it.   **22. ranker:** Higher; **in fee:** Fee simple, outright.   **26. debate . . . straw:** Settle this trifling matter.   **27. imposthume:** Abscess.   **32. inform against:** Denounce, betray; take shape against.   **34. market of:** Profit of, compensation for.   **36. discourse:** Power of reasoning.   **39. fust:** Grow moldy.   **40. oblivion:** Forgetfulness.   **41. event:** Outcome.   **45. Sith:** Since.   **46. gross:** Obvious.   **47. charge:** Expense.   **50. Makes mouths:** Makes scornful faces.

Is not to stir without great argument,
55   But greatly to find quarrel in a straw
When honor's at the stake. How stand I then,
That have a father kill'd, a mother stain'd,
Excitements of° my reason and my blood,
And let all sleep, while, to my shame, I see
60   The imminent death of twenty thousand men,
That, for a fantasy° and trick° of fame,
Go to their graves like beds, fight for a plot°
Whereon the numbers cannot try the cause,°
Which is not tomb enough and continent°
65   To hide the slain? O, from this time forth,
My thoughts be bloody, or be nothing worth!

                                                      (*Exit.*)

[Scene V]°

(*Enter Horatio, [Queen] Gertrude, and a Gentleman.*)

QUEEN: I will not speak with her.
GENTLEMAN: She is importunate, indeed distract.
   Her mood will needs be pitied.
QUEEN: What would she have?
GENTLEMAN: She speaks much of her father, says
      she hears
   There's tricks° i' th' world, and hems, and beats
5   her heart,°
   Spurns enviously at straws,° speaks things in
         doubt°
   That carry but half sense. Her speech is nothing,
   Yet the unshaped use° of it doth move
   The hearers to collection;° they yawn° at it,
   And botch° the words up fit to their own
10   thoughts,
   Which, as her winks and nods and gestures
         yield° them,
   Indeed would make one think there might be
         thought,°
   Though nothing sure, yet much unhappily.
HORATIO: 'Twere good she were spoken with, for
      she may strew
15   Dangerous conjectures in ill-breeding° minds.

QUEEN: Let her come in.   [*Exit Gentlemen.*]
   [*Aside.*] To my sick soul, as sin's true nature is,
   Each toy° seems prologue to some great amiss.°
   So full of artless jealousy is guilt,
   It spills itself in fearing to be spilt.°   20

(*Enter Ophelia [distracted].*)

OPHELIA: Where is the beauteous majesty of
      Denmark?
QUEEN: How now, Ophelia?
OPHELIA (*she sings*): "How should I your true love
      know
   From another one?
   By his cockle hat° and staff,   25
   And his sandal shoon."°
QUEEN: Alas, sweet lady, what imports this song?
OPHELIA: Say you? Nay, pray you, mark.
   "He is dead and gone, lady,   (*Song.*)
   He is dead and gone;   30
   At his head a grass-green turf,
   At his heels a stone."
   O, ho!
QUEEN: Nay, but Ophelia —
OPHELIA: Pray you mark.   35
   [*Sings.*] "White his shroud as the mountain
      snow" —

(*Enter King.*)

QUEEN: Alas, look here, my lord.
OPHELIA: "Larded° all with flowers   (*Song.*)
   Which bewept to the ground did not go
   With true-love showers."   40
KING: How do you, pretty lady?
OPHELIA: Well, God 'ild° you! They say the owl° was
   a baker's daughter. Lord, we know what we are,
   but know not what we may be. God be at your
   table!   45
KING: Conceit° upon her father.
OPHELIA: Pray let's have no words of this; but when
   they ask you what it means, say you this:
   "Tomorrow is Saint Valentine's° day.   (*Song.*)
   All in the morning betime,   50

---

58. Excitements of: Promptings by.   **61. fantasy:** Fanciful
caprice; **trick:** Trifle.   **62. plot:** I.e., of ground.   **63. Whereon
. . . cause:** On which there is insufficient room for the soldiers
needed to engage in a military contest.   **64. continent:** Re-
ceptacle, container.   **IV, v. Location:** The castle.   **5. tricks:**
Deceptions; **heart:** Breast.   **6. Spurns . . . straws:** Kicks spite-
fully, takes offense at trifles; **in doubt:** Obscurely.   **8. unshaped
use:** Distracted manner.   **9. collection:** Inference, a guess at
some sort of meaning; **yawn:** Wonder, grasp.   **10. botch:**
Patch.   **11. yield:** Delivery, bring forth (her words).   **12.
thought:** Conjectured.   **15. ill-breeding:** Prone to suspect
the worst.

18. toy: Trifle; **amiss:** Calamity.   **19–20. So . . . spilt:** Guilt
is so full of suspicion that it unskillfully betrays itself in
fearing betrayal.   **25. cockle hat:** Hat with cockleshell stuck
in it as a sign that the wearer had been a pilgrim to the
shrine of St. James of Compostella in Spain.   **26. shoon:**
Shoes.   **38. Larded:** Decorated.   **42. God 'ild:** God yield
or reward; **owl:** Refers to a legend about a baker's daughter
who was turned into an owl for refusing Jesus bread.   **46.
Conceit:** Brooding.   **49. Valentine's:** This song alludes to
the belief that the first girl seen by a man on the morning
of this day was his valentine or true love.

And I a maid at your window,
  To be your Valentine.
Then up he rose, and donn'd his clo'es,
  And dupp'd° the chamber-door,
55 Let in the maid, that out a maid
  Never departed more."
KING: Pretty Ophelia!
OPHELIA: Indeed, la, without an oath, I'll make an
  end on 't:
60 [*Sings.*] "By Gis° and by Saint Charity,
  Alack, and fie for shame!
Young men will do 't, if they come to 't;
  By Cock,° they are to blame.
Quoth she, 'Before you tumbled me,
65   You promised me to wed.'"
He answers:
"'So would I ha' done, by yonder sun,
  An thou hadst not come to my bed.'"
KING: How long hath she been thus?
70 OPHELIA: I hope all will be well. We must be patient,
  but I cannot choose but weep, to think they would
  lay him i' th' cold ground. My brother shall know
  of it; and so I thank you for your good counsel.
  Come, my coach! Good night, ladies; good night,
75 sweet ladies; good night, good night.

                                                    [*Exit.*]

KING: Follow her close; give her good watch, I
  pray you.   [*Exit Horatio.*]
  O, this is the poison of deep grief; it springs
  All from her father's death — and now behold!
  O Gertrude, Gertrude,
80 When sorrows come, they come not single spies,°
  But in battalions. First, her father slain;
  Next, your son gone, and he most violent author
  Of his own just remove; the people muddied,°
  Thick and unwholesome in their thoughts and
  whispers,
  For good Polonius' death; and we have done but
85   greenly,°
  In hugger-mugger° to inter him; poor Ophelia
  Divided from herself and her fair judgment,
  Without the which we are pictures, or mere
  beasts;
  Last, and as much containing as all these,
90 Her brother is in secret come from France,
  Feeds on his wonder, keeps himself in clouds,°
  And wants° not buzzers° to infect his ear
  With pestilent speeches of his father's death,

Wherein necessity, of matter beggar'd,°
Will nothing stick our person to arraign   95
In ear and ear.° O my dear Gertrude, this,
Like to a murd'ring-piece,° in many places
Gives me superfluous death.   (*A noise within.*)
[QUEEN: Alack, what noise is this?]
KING: Attend!   100
Where are my Switzers?° Let them guard the
  door.

(*Enter a Messenger.*)

What is the matter?
MESSENGER: Save yourself, my lord!
The ocean, overpeering of his list,°
Eats not the flats° with more impiteous° haste
Than young Laertes, in a riotous head,°   105
O'erbears your officers. The rabble call him lord,
And, as° the world were now but to begin,
Antiquity forgot, custom not known,
The ratifiers and props° of every word,°
They cry, "Choose we! Laertes shall be king!"   110
Caps, hands, and tongues applaud it to the
  clouds,
"Laertes shall be king, Laertes king!"
                                (*A noise within.*)
QUEEN: How cheerfully on the false trail they cry!
  O, this is counter,° you false Danish dogs!

(*Enter Laertes with others.*)

KING: The doors are broke.   115
LAERTES: Where is this King? Sirs, stand you all
  without.
ALL: No, let's come in.
LAERTES: I pray you, give me leave.
ALL: We will, we will.
                    [*They retire without the door.*]
LAERTES: I thank you. Keep the door. O thou vile
  king,
  Give me my father!
QUEEN: Calmly, good Laertes.   120
                [*She tries to hold him back.*]
LAERTES: That drop of blood that's calm proclaims
  me bastard,
  Cries cuckold to my father, brands the harlot

---

54. **dupp'd:** Opened.   60. **Gis:** Jesus.   63. **Cock:** A perversion
of *God* in oaths.   80. **spies:** Scouts sent in advance of the
main force.   83. **muddied:** Stirred up, confused.   85. **greenly:**
Imprudently, foolishly.   86. **hugger-mugger:** Secret haste.
91. **in clouds:** I.e., of suspicion and rumor.   92. **wants:**
Lacks; **buzzers:** Gossipers, informers.

94. **of matter beggar'd:** Unprovided with facts.   **95–96. Will
. . . ear:** Will not hesitate to accuse my (royal) person in
everybody's ears.   97. **murd'ring-piece:** Cannon loaded so
as to scatter its shot.   101. **Switzers:** Swiss guards, mercenaries.
103. **overpeering of his list:** Overflowing its shore.   104.
flats: Flatlands near shore; **impiteous:** Pitiless.   105. **head:**
Armed force.   107. **as:** As if.   109. **ratifiers and props:**
Refer to *antiquity* and *custom*; **word:** Promise.   114. **counter:**
A hunting term meaning to follow the trail in a direction
opposite to that which the game has taken.

Even here, between the chaste unsmirched brow
Of my true mother.

KING: What is the cause, Laertes,
125   That thy rebellion looks so giant-like?
Let him go, Gertrude. Do not fear our° person.
There's such divinity doth hedge a king
That treason can but peep to what it would,°
Acts little of his will.° Tell me, Laertes,
Why thou art thus incens'd. Let him go,
130   Gertrude.
Speak, man.

LAERTES: Where is my father?

KING: Dead.

QUEEN: But not by him.

KING: Let him demand his fill.

LAERTES: How came he dead? I'll not be juggled
with.
To hell, allegiance! Vows, to the blackest devil!
135   Conscience and grace, to the profoundest pit!
I dare damnation. To this point I stand,
That both the worlds I give to negligence,°
Let come what comes, only I'll be reveng'd
Most throughly° for my father.

KING: Who shall stay you?

140 LAERTES: My will, not all the world's.°
And for my means, I'll husband them so well,
They shall go far with little.

KING: Good Laertes,
If you desire to know the certainty
Of your dear father, is 't writ in your revenge
That, swoopstake,° you will draw both friend
145   and foe,
Winner and loser?

LAERTES: None but his enemies.

KING: Will you know them then?

LAERTES: To his good friends thus wide I'll ope my
arms,
And, like the kind life-rend'ring pelican,°
Repast° them with my blood.

150 KING: Why, now you speak
Like a good child and a true gentleman.
That I am guiltless of your father's death,
And am most sensibly° in grief for it,

It shall as level° to your judgment 'pear
As day does to your eye.
                (*A noise within:*) "Let her come in."   155

LAERTES: How now? What noise is that?

(*Enter Ophelia.*)

O heat, dry up my brains! Tears seven times salt
Burn out the sense and virtue° of mine eye!
By heaven, thy madness shall be paid with
weight°
Till our scale turn the beam.° O rose of May!   160
Dear maid, kind sister, sweet Ophelia!
O heavens, is 't possible a young maid's wits
Should be as mortal as an old man's life?
[Nature is fine in° love, and where 'tis fine,
It sends some precious instance° of itself   165
After the thing it loves.°]

OPHELIA: "They bore him barefac'd on the bier;
                                        (*Song.*)
    [Hey non nonny, nonny, hey nonny,]
And in his grave rain'd many a tear" —
Fare you well, my dove!   170

LAERTES: Hadst thou thy wits, and didst persuade°
revenge,
It could not move thus.

OPHELIA: You must sing "A-down a-down,
And you call him a-down-a."
O, how the wheel° becomes it! It is the false steward°   175
that stole his master's daughter.

LAERTES: This nothing's more than matter.°

OPHELIA: There's rosemary,° that's for remembrance;
pray you, love, remember. And there is pansies,°
that's for thoughts.   180

LAERTES: A document° in madness, thoughts and remembrance fitted.

OPHELIA: There's fennel° for you, and columbines.°
There's rue° for you, and here's some for me; we
may call it herb of grace o' Sundays. You may   185

---

126. **fear our:** Fear for my.   128. **can . . . would:** Can only
glance; as from far off or through a barrier, at what it would
intend.   129. **Acts . . . will:** (But) performs little of what it
intends.   137. **both . . . negligence:** Both this world and the
next are of no consequence to me.   139. **throughly:** Thoroughly.   140. **My will . . . world's:** I'll stop (*stay*) when my
will is accomplished, not for anyone else's.   145. **swoopstake:**
Literally, taking all stakes on the gambling table at once,
i.e., indiscriminately; *draw* is also a gambling term.   149.
pelican: Refers to the belief that the female pelican fed its
young with its own blood.   150. **Repast:** Feed.   153. **sensibly:**
Feelingly.

154. **level:** Plain.   158. **virtue:** Faculty, power.   159. **paid
with weight:** Repaid, avenged equally or more.   160. **beam:**
Crossbar of a balance.   164. **fine in:** Refined by.   165.
instance: Token.   166. **After . . . loves:** Into the grave, along
with Polonius.   171. **persuade:** Argue cogently for.   175.
wheel: Spinning wheel as accompaniment to the song, or
refrain; **false steward:** The story is unknown.   177. **This
. . . matter:** This seeming nonsense is more meaningful than
sane utterance.   178. **rosemary:** Used as a symbol of remembrance both at weddings and at funerals.   179. **pansies:**
Emblems of love and courtship; perhaps from French *pensées,*
thoughts.   181. **document:** Instruction, lesson.   183. **fennel:**
Emblem of flattery; **columbines:** Emblems of unchastity (?)
or ingratitude (?).   184. **rue:** Emblem of repentance; when
mingled with holy water, it was known as *herb of grace.*

wear your rue with a difference.° There's a daisy.°
I would give you some violets,° but they wither'd
all when my father died. They say 'a made a good
end —

190 [*Sings.*] "For bonny sweet Robin is all my joy."
LAERTES: Thought° and affliction, passion, hell
    itself,
She turns to favor° and to prettiness.
OPHELIA: "And will 'a not come again?   (*Song.*)
And will 'a not come again?

195   No, no, he is dead,
    Go to thy death-bed,
He never will come again.

    "His beard was as white as snow,
    All flaxen was his poll.°

200   He is gone, he is gone,
    And we cast away moan.
God 'a' mercy on his soul!
And of all Christians' souls, I pray God. God buy
you.

                    [*Exit.*]

205 LAERTES: Do you see this, O God?
KING: Laertes, I must commune with your grief,
Or you deny me right. Go but apart,
Make choice of whom your wisest friends you
    will,
And they shall hear and judge 'twixt you and
    me.

210 If by direct or by collateral° hand
They find us touch'd,° we will our kingdom give,
Our crown, our life, and all that we call ours,
To you in satisfaction; but if not,
Be you content to lend your patience to us,

215 And we shall jointly labor with your soul
To give it due content.
LAERTES: Let this be so.
His means of death, his obscure funeral —
No trophy,° sword, nor hatchment° o'er his
    bones,
No noble rite nor formal ostentation° —

220 Cry to be heard, as 'twere from heaven to earth,
That I must call 't in question.
KING: So you shall;
And where th' offense is, let the great ax fall.
I pray you go with me.   (*Exeunt.*)

---

186. **with a difference:** Suggests that Ophelia and the Queen
have different causes of sorrow and repentance; perhaps with
a play on *rue* in the sense of ruth, pity; **daisy:** Emblem of
dissembling, faithlessness.   187. **violets:** Emblems of faithfulness.   191. **Thought:** Melancholy.   192. **favor:** Grace.
199. **poll:** Head.   210. **collateral:** Indirect.   211. **us touch'd:**
Me implicated.   218. **trophy:** Memorial; **hatchment:** Tablet
displaying the armorial bearings of a deceased person.   219.
ostentation: Ceremony.

[Scene VI]°

(*Enter Horatio and others.*)

HORATIO: What are they that would speak with me?
    GENTLEMAN: Seafaring men, sir. They say they have
letters for you.
HORATIO: Let them come in.   [*Exit Gentleman.*]
I do not know from what part of the world   5
I should be greeted, if not from lord Hamlet.

(*Enter Sailors.*)

FIRST SAILOR: God bless you sir.
HORATIO: Let him bless thee too.
FIRST SAILOR: 'A shall, sir, an 't please him. There's
a letter for you, sir — it came from th' ambassador   10
that was bound for England — if your name be
Horatio, as I am let to know it is. [*Gives letter.*]
HORATIO [*reads*]: "Horatio, when thou shalt have overlook'd this, give these fellows some means° to
the King; they have letters for him. Ere we were   15
two days old at sea, a pirate of very warlike ap-
pointment° gave us chase. Finding ourselves too
slow of sail, we put on a compell'd valor, and in
the grapple I boarded them. On the instant they
got clear of our ship, so I alone became their prisoner.   20
They have dealt with me like thieves of mercy,°
but they knew what they did: I am to do a good
turn for them. Let the King have the letters I have
sent, and repair thou to me with as much speed
as thou wouldest fly death. I have words to speak   25
in thine ear will make thee dumb; yet are they
much too light for the bore° of the matter. These
good fellows will bring thee where I am. Rosencrantz
and Guildenstern hold their course for England.
Of them I have much to tell thee. Farewell.   30
                    He that thou knowest thine, Hamlet."
Come, I will give you way for these your letters,
And do 't the speedier that you may direct me
To him from whom you brought them. (*Exeunt.*)

[Scene VII]°

(*Enter King and Laertes.*)

KING: Now must your conscience my acquittance
    seal,°
And you must put me in your heart for friend,
Sith you have heard, and with a knowing ear,

IV, VI. **Location:** The castle.   14. **means:** Means of access.
16–17. **appointment:** Equipage.   21. **thieves of mercy:** Merciful thieves.   27. **bore:** Caliber, i.e., importance.   IV, VII.
Location: The castle.   1. **my acquittance seal:** Confirm or
acknowledge my innocence.

That he which hath your noble father slain
Pursued my life.
5 LAERTES: It well appears. But tell me
Why you proceeded not against these feats°
So criminal and so capital° in nature,
As by your safety, greatness, wisdom, all things
     else,
You mainly° were stirr'd up.
KING: O, for two special reasons,
Which may to you, perhaps, seem much
10   unsinew'd,°
But yet to me th' are strong. The Queen his
     mother
Lives almost by his looks, and for myself —
My virtue or my plague, be it either which —
She's so conjunctive° to my life and soul
15 That, as the star moves not but in his sphere,°
I could not but by her. The other motive,
Why to a public count° I might not go,
Is the great love the general gender° bear him,
Who, dipping all his faults in their affection,
Would, like the spring° that turneth wood to
20   stone,
Convert his gyves° to graces, so that my arrows,
Too slightly timber'd° for so loud° a wind,
Would have reverted to my bow again
And not where I had aim'd them.
25 LAERTES: And so have I a noble father lost,
A sister driven into desp'rate terms,°
Whose worth, if praises may go back° again,
Stood challenger on mount° of all the age
For her perfections. But my revenge will come.
KING: Break not your sleeps for that. You must not
30   think
That we are made of stuff so flat and dull
That we can let our beard be shook with danger
And think it pastime. You shortly shall hear
     more.
I lov'd your father, and we love ourself;
35 And that, I hope, will teach you to imagine —

(*Enter a Messenger with letters.*)

[How now? What news?]

MESSENGER: [Letters, my lord, from Hamlet:]
These to your Majesty, this to the Queen.
                              [*Gives letters.*]
KING: From Hamlet? Who brought them?
MESSENGER: Sailors, my lord, they say; I saw them
     not.
They were given me by Claudio. He receiv'd
     them   40
Of him that brought them.
KING: Laertes, you shall hear them.
Leave us.   [*Exit Messenger.*]
[*Reads.*] "High and mighty, you shall know I am
set naked° on your kingdom. Tomorrow shall I beg
leave to see your kingly eyes, when I shall, first   45
asking your pardon° thereunto, recount the occasion
of my sudden and more strange return. Hamlet."
What should this mean? Are all the rest come back?
Or is it some abuse,° and no such thing?
LAERTES: Know you the hand?
KING: 'Tis Hamlet's character.° "Naked!"   50
And in a postscript here, he says "alone."
Can you devise° me?
LAERTES: I am lost in it, my lord. But let him come.
It warms the very sickness in my heart
That I shall live and tell him to his teeth,   55
"Thus didst thou."
KING: If it be so, Laertes —
As how should it be so? How otherwise?° —
Will you be ruled by me?
LAERTES: Ay, my lord,
So° you will not o'errule me to a peace.
KING: To thine own peace. If he be now returned,   60
As checking at° his voyage, and that he means
No more to undertake it, I will work him
To an exploit, now ripe in my device,
Under the which he shall not choose but fall;
And for his death no wind of blame shall
     breathe,   65
But even his mother shall uncharge the practice°
And call it accident.
LAERTES: My lord, I will be rul'd,
The rather if you could devise it so
That I might be the organ.°

---

6. **feats:** Acts.   7. **capital:** Punishable by death.   9. **mainly:**
Greatly.   10. **unsinew'd:** Weak.   14. **conjunctive:** Closely
united.   15. **sphere:** The hollow sphere in which, according
to Ptolemaic astronomy, the planets moved.   17. **count:**
Account, reckoning.   18. **general gender:** Common people.
20. **spring:** A spring with such a concentration of lime that
it coats a piece of wood with limestone, in effect gilding it.
21. **gyves:** Fetters (which, gilded by the people's praise, would
look like badges of honor).   22. **slightly timber'd:** Light;
loud: strong.   26. **terms:** State condition.   27. **go back:**
Recall Ophelia's former virtues.   28. **mount:** On high.

44. **naked:** Destitute, unarmed, without following.   46. **pardon:** Permission.   49. **abuse:** Deceit.   50. **character:** Handwriting.   52. **devise:** Explain to.   57. **As . . . otherwise:**
How can this (Hamlet's return) be true? Yet how otherwise
than true (since we have the evidence of his letter).   59. **So:**
Provided that.   61. **checking at:** Turning aside from (like a
falcon leaving the quarry to fly at a chance bird).   66.
uncharge the practice: Acquit the stratagem of being a plot.
69. **organ:** Agent, instrument.

KING: It falls right.
70   You have been talk'd of since your travel much,
     And that in Hamlet's hearing, for a quality
     Wherein, they say, you shine. Your sum of
          parts°
     Did not together pluck such envy from him
     As did that one, and that, in my regard,
75   Of the unworthiest siege.°
     LAERTES: What part is that, my lord?
     KING: A very riband in the cap of youth,
     Yet needful too, for youth no less becomes
     The light and careless livery that it wears
80   Than settled age his sables° and his weeds,°
     Importing health° and graveness. Two months
          since
     Here was a gentleman of Normandy.
     I have seen myself, and serv'd against, the
          French,
     And they can well° on horseback, but this
          gallant
85   Had witchcraft in 't; he grew unto his seat,
     And to such wondrous doing brought his horse
     As had he been incorps'd and demi-natured°
     With the brave beast. So far he topp'd° my
          thought
     That I, in forgery° of shapes and tricks,
     Come short of what he did.
90   LAERTES: A Norman was 't?
     KING: A Norman.
     LAERTES: Upon my life, Lamord.
     KING: The very same.
     LAERTES: I know him well. He is the brooch°
          indeed
     And gem of all the nation.
95   KING: He made confession° of you,
     And gave you such a masterly report
     For art and exercise in your defense,
     And for your rapier most especial,
     That he cried out, 'twould be a sight indeed,
     If one could match you. The scrimers° of their
100   nation,
     He swore, had neither motion, guard, nor eye,
     If you oppos'd them. Sir, this report of his
     Did Hamlet so envenom with his envy
     That he could nothing do but wish and beg

Your sudden coming o'er to play° with you.   105
Now, out of this —
LAERTES: What out of this, my lord?
KING: Laertes, was your father dear to you?
     Or are you like the painting of a sorrow,
     A face without a heart?
LAERTES: Why ask you this?
KING: Not that I think you did not love your
          father,   110
     But that I know love is begun by time,°
     And that I see, in passages of proof,°
     Time qualifies° the spark and fire of it.
     There lives within the very flame of love
     A kind of wick or snuff° that will abate it,   115
     And nothing is at a like goodness still,°
     For goodness, growing to a plurisy,°
     Dies in his own too much.° That° we would do,
     We should do when we would; for this "would"
          changes
     And hath abatements° and delays as many   120
     As there are tongues, are hands, are accidents,°
     And then this "should" is like a spendthrift's
          sigh,°
     That hurts by easing.° But, to the quick o' th'
          ulcer;
     Hamlet comes back. What would you undertake
     To show yourself your father's son in deed   125
     More than in words?
LAERTES: To cut his throat i' th' church!
KING: No place, indeed, should murder
          sanctuarize;°
     Revenge should have no bounds. But, good
          Laertes,
     Will you do this,° keep close within your
          chamber.
     Hamlet return'd shall know you are come home.   130
     We'll put on those° shall praise your excellence
     And set a double varnish on the fame
     The Frenchman gave you, bring you in fine°
          together,

72. **Your . . . parts:** All your other virtues.   75. **unworthiest siege:** Least important rank.   80. **sables:** Rich robes furred with sable; **weeds:** Garments.   81. **Importing health:** Indicating prosperity.   84. **can well:** Are skilled.   87. **incorps'd and demi-natur'd:** Of one body and nearly of one nature (like the centaur).   88. **topp'd:** Surpassed.   89. **forgery:** Invention.   93. **brooch:** Ornament.   95. **confession:** Admission of superiority.   100. **scrimers:** Fencers.

105. **play:** Fence.   111. **begun by time:** Subject to change.   112. **passages of proof:** Actual instances.   113. **qualifies:** Weakens.   115. **snuff:** The charred part of a candlewick.   116. **nothing . . . still:** Nothing remains at a constant level of perfection.   117. **plurisy:** Excess, plethora.   118. **in . . . much:** Of its own excess; **That:** That which.   120. **abatements:** Diminutions.   121. **accidents:** Occurrences, incidents.   122. **spendthrift's sigh:** An allusion to the belief that each sigh cost the heart a drop of blood.   123. **hurts by easing:** Costs the heart blood even while it affords emotional relief.   127. **sanctuarize:** Protect from punishment (alludes to the right of sanctuary with which certain religious places were invested).   129. **Will you do this:** If you wish to do this.   131. **put on those:** Instigate those who.   133. **in fine:** Finally.

And wager on your heads. He, being remiss,°
135   Most generous,° and free from all contriving,
Will not peruse the foils, so that, with ease,
Or with a little shuffling, you may choose
A sword unbated,° and in a pass of practice°
Requite him for your father.
LAERTES: I will do 't.
140   And for that purpose I'll anoint my sword.
I bought an unction° of a mountebank°
So mortal that, but dip a knife in it,
Where it draws blood no cataplasm° so rare,
Collected from all simples° that have virtue
145   Under the moon, can save the thing from death
That is but scratch'd withal. I'll touch my point
With this contagion, that, if I gall° him slightly,
It may be death.
KING: Let's further think of this,
Weigh what convenience both of time and means
150   May fit us to our shape.° If this should fail,
And that our drift look through our bad
      performance,°
'Twere better not assay'd. Therefore this project
Should have a back or second, that might hold
If this did blast in proof.° Soft, let me see.
155   We'll make a solemn wager on your cunnings —
I ha 't!
When in your motion you are hot and dry —
As° make your bouts more violent to that end —
And that he calls for drink, I'll have prepar'd
      him
160   A chalice for the nonce,° whereon but sipping,
If he by chance escape your venom'd stuck,°
Our purpose may hold there. [*A cry within.*] But
      stay, what noise?

(*Enter Queen.*)

QUEEN: One woe doth tread upon another's heel,
So fast they follow. Your sister's drowned,
      Laertes.
165   LAERTES: Drown'd! O, where?
QUEEN: There is a willow grows askant° the brook,
That shows his hoar° leaves in the glassy stream;
Therewith fantastic garlands did she make

Of crow-flowers, nettles, daisies, and long
      purples°
That liberal° shepherds give a grosser name,   170
But our cold° maids do dead men's fingers call
      them.
There on the pendent boughs her crownet°
      weeds
Clamb'ring to hang, an envious sliver° broke,
When down her weedy° trophies and herself
Fell in the weeping brook. Her clothes spread
      wide,   175
And mermaid-like awhile they bore her up,
Which time she chanted snatches of old lauds,°
As one incapable° of her own distress,
Or like a creature native and indued°
Unto that element. But long it could not be   180
Till that her garments, heavy with their drink,
Pull'd the poor wretch from her melodious lay
To muddy death.
LAERTES: Alas, then she is drown'd?
QUEEN: Drown'd, drown'd.
LAERTES: Too much of water hast thou, poor
      Ophelia,   185
And therefore I forbid my tears. But yet
It is our trick;° nature her custom holds,
Let shame say what it will. [*He weeps.*] When
      these are gone,
The woman will be out.° Adieu, my lord.
I have a speech of fire, that fain would blaze,   190
But that this folly drowns it.   (*Exit.*)
KING: Let's follow, Gertrude.
How much I had to do to calm his rage!
Now fear I this will give it start again;
Therefore let's follow.   (*Exeunt.*)

[ACT V · Scene I]° _____

(*Enter two Clowns.° [with spades, etc.])*)

FIRST CLOWN: Is she to be buried in Christian burial
when she willfully seeks her own salvation?
SECOND CLOWN: I tell thee she is; therefore make her
grave straight.° The crowner° hath sat on her, and
finds it Christian burial.   5

---

134. **remiss:** Negligently unsuspicious.   135. **generous:** Noble-
minded.   138. **unbated:** Not blunted, having no button;
pass of practice: Treacherous thrust.   141. **unction:** Ointment;
mountebank: Quack doctor.   143. **cataplasm:** Plaster or
poultice.   144. **simples:** Herbs.   147. **gall:** Graze, wound.
150. **shape:** Part that we propose to act.   151. **drift . . .
performance:** I.e., intention be disclosed by our bungling.
154. **blast in proof:** Burst in the test (like a cannon).   158.
As: And you should.   160. **nonce:** Occasion.   161. **stuck:**
Thrust (from *stoccado*, a fencing term).   166. **askant:** Aslant.
167. **hoar:** White or gray.

169. **long purples:** Early purple orchids.   170. **liberal:** Free-
spoken.   171. **cold:** Chaste.   172. **crownet:** Made into a
chaplet or coronet.   173. **envious sliver:** Malicious branch.
174. **weedy:** I.e., of plants.   177. **lauds:** Hymns.   178.
incapable: Lacking capacity to apprehend.   179. **indued:**
Adapted by nature.   187. **It is our trick:** Weeping is our
natural way (when sad).   188–189. **When . . . out:** When
my tears are all shed, the woman in me will be expended,
satisfied.   V, I. **Location:** A churchyard.   [S.D.] *Clowns:*
Rustics.   4. **straight:** Straightway, immediately; **crowner:**
Coroner.

FIRST CLOWN: How can that be, unless she drown'd herself in her own defense?

SECOND CLOWN: Why, 'tis found so.

FIRST CLOWN: It must be "se offendendo";° it cannot
10 be else. For here lies the point: if I drown myself wittingly, it argues an act, and an act hath three branches — it is to act, to do, and to perform. Argal,° she drown'd herself wittingly.

SECOND CLOWN: Nay, but hear you, goodman
15 delver —

FIRST CLOWN: Give me leave. Here lies the water; good. Here stands the man; good. If the man go to this water, and drown himself, it is, will he,° nill he, he goes, mark you that. But if the water
20 come to him and drown him, he drowns not himself. Argal, he that is not guilty of his own death shortens not his own life.

SECOND CLOWN: But is this law?

FIRST CLOWN: Ay, marry, is 't — crowner's quest°
25 law.

SECOND CLOWN: Will you ha' the truth on 't? If this had not been a gentlewoman, she should have been buried out o' Christian burial.

FIRST CLOWN: Why, there thou say'st.° And the more
30 pity that great folk should have count'nance° in this world to drown or hang themselves, more than their even-Christen.° Come, my spade. There is no ancient gentlemen but gard'ners, ditchers, and grave-makers. They hold up Adam's profession.

35 SECOND CLOWN: Was he a gentleman?

FIRST CLOWN: 'A was the first that ever bore arms.

[SECOND CLOWN: Why, he had none.

FIRST CLOWN: What, art a heathen? How dost thou understand the Scripture? The Scripture says "Adam
40 digg'd." Could he dig without arms?] I'll put another question to thee. If thou answerest me not to the purpose, confess thyself° —

SECOND CLOWN: Go to.

FIRST CLOWN: What is he that builds stronger than
45 either the mason, the shipwright, or the carpenter?

SECOND CLOWN: The gallows-maker, for that frame outlives a thousand tenants.

FIRST CLOWN: I like thy wit well, in good faith. The gallows does well; but how does it well? It does
50 well to those that do ill. Now thou dost ill to say the gallows is built stronger than the church. Argal, the gallows may do well to thee. To 't again, come.

SECOND CLOWN: "Who builds stronger than a mason, a shipwright, or a carpenter?"

FIRST CLOWN: Ay, tell me that, and unyoke.° 55

SECOND CLOWN: Marry, now I can tell.

FIRST CLOWN: To 't.

SECOND CLOWN: Mass,° I cannot tell.

(*Enter Hamlet and Horatio [at a distance].*)

FIRST CLOWN: Cudgel thy brains no more about it, for your dull ass will not mend his pace with beating; 60 and, when you are ask'd this question next, say "a grave-maker." The houses he makes lasts till doomsday. Go, get thee in, and fetch me a stoup° of liquor.

[*Exit Second Clown. First Clown digs.*]
(*Song.*)

"In youth, when I did love, did love,° 65
Methought it was very sweet,
To contract — O — the time for — a — my behove,°
O, methought there — a — was nothing — a — meet."°

HAMLET: Has this fellow no feeling of his business, that a sings at grave-making? 70

HORATIO: Custom hath made it in him a property of easiness.°

HAMLET: 'Tis e'en so. The hand of little employment hath the daintier sense.°

(*Song.*)

FIRST CLOWN: "But age, with his stealing steps, 75
Hath claw'd me in his clutch,
And hath shipped me into the land,°
As if I had never been such."

[*Throws up a skull.*]

HAMLET: That skull had a tongue in it, and could sing once. How the knave jowls° it to the ground, 80 as if 'twere Cain's jaw-bone, that did the first murder! This might be the pate of a politician,° which this ass now o'erreaches,° one that would circumvent God, might it not?

---

9. **se offendendo:** A comic mistake for *se defendendo*, term used in verdicts of justifiable homicide.   13. **Argal:** Corruption of *ergo*, therefore.   18. **will he:** Will he not.   24. **quest:** Inquest.   29. **there you say'st:** That's right.   30. **count'nance:** Privilege.   32. **even-Christen:** Fellow Christian.   42. **confess thyself:** The saying continues, "and be hanged."

55. **unyoke:** After this great effort you may unharness the team of your wits.   58. **Mass:** By the Mass.   63. **stoup:** Two-quart measure.   65. **In . . . love:** This and the two following stanzas, with nonsensical variations, are from a poem attributed to Lord Vaux and printed in *Tottel's Miscellany,* 1557. The O and a (for "ah") seemingly are the grunts of the digger.   67. **To contract . . . behove:** To make a betrothal agreement for my benefit (?)   68. **meet:** Suitable, i.e., more suitable: 71–72. **property of easiness:** Something he can do easily and without thinking.   74. **daintier sense:** More delicate sense of feeling.   77. **into the land:** Toward my grave (?) (but note the lack of rhyme in *steps, land*).   80. **jowls:** Dashes.   82. **politician:** Schemer, plotter.   83. **o'erreaches:** Circumvents, gets the better of (with a quibble on the literal sense).

85   HORATIO: It might, my lord.
      HAMLET: Or of a courtier, which could say "Good
        morrow, sweet lord! How dost thou, sweet lord?"
        This might be my Lord Such-a-one, that prais'd
        my Lord Such-a-one's horse when 'a meant to beg
90   it, might it not?
      HORATIO: Ay, my lord.
      HAMLET: Why, e'en so, and now my Lady Worm's,
        chapless,° and knock'd about the mazzard° with a
        sexton's spade. Here's fine revolution,° an° we had
95   the trick to see 't. Did these bones cost no more
        the breeding,° but to play at loggats° with them?
        Mine ache to think on 't.
                                                   (Song.)
      FIRST CLOWN: "A pick-axe, and a spade, a spade,
          For and° a shrouding sheet;
100   O, a pit of clay for to be made
          For such a guest is meet."
                                   [*Throws up another skull.*]
      HAMLET: There's another. Why may not that be the
        skull of a lawyer? Where be his quiddities° now,
        his quillities,° his cases, his tenures,° and his tricks?
105   Why does he suffer this mad knave now to knock
        him about the sconce° with a dirty shovel, and will
        not tell him of his action of battery? Hum! This
        fellow might be in 's time a great buyer of land,
        with his statutes, his recognizances,° his fines, his
110   double° vouchers,° his recoveries.° [Is this the fine
        of his fines, and the recovery of his recoveries,] to
        have his fine pate full of fine dirt?° Will his vouchers
        vouch him no more of his purchases, and double
        [ones too], than the length and breadth of a pair
115   of indentures?° The very conveyances° of his lands
        will scarcely lie in this box,° and must th' inheritor°
        himself have no more, ha?

93. chapless: Having no lower jaw; **mazzard:** Head (literally,
a drinking vessel). **94. revolution:** Change; **an:** If. **96.
the breeding:** In the breeding, raising; **loggats:** A game in
which pieces of hard wood are thrown to lie as near as
possible to a stake. **99. For and:** And moreover. **103.
quiddities:** Subtleties, quibbles (from Latin *quid,* a thing).
104. quillities: Verbal niceties, subtle distinctions (variation
of *quiddities*); **tenures:** The holding of a piece of property
or office, or the conditions or period of such holding. **106.
sconce:** Head. **109. statutes, recognizances:** Legal documents
guaranteeing a debt by attaching land and property. **109–
110. fines, recoveries:** Ways of converting entailed estates
into "fee simple" or freehold. **110. double:** Signed by two
signatories; **vouchers:** Guarantees of the legality of a title to
real estate. **110–112. fine of his fines . . . fine pate . . . fine
dirt:** End of his legal maneuvers . . . elegant head . . . minutely
sifted dirt. **114–115. pair of indentures:** Legal document
drawn up in duplicate on a single sheet and then cut apart
on a zigzag line so that each pair was uniquely matched.
(Hamlet may refer to two rows of teeth, or dentures.) **115.
conveyances:** Deeds. **116. this box:** The skull; **inheritor:**
Possessor, owner.

HORATIO: Not a jot more, my lord.
HAMLET: Is not parchment made of sheep-skins?
HORATIO: Ay, my lord, and of calf-skins too.   120
HAMLET: They are sheep and calves which seek out
  assurance in that.° I will speak to this fellow. —
  Whose grave's this, sirrah?°
FIRST CLOWN: Mine, sir.
  [*Sings.*] "O, a pit of clay for to be made   125
  [For such a guest is meet]."
HAMLET: I think it be thine, indeed, for thou liest
  in 't.
FIRST CLOWN: You lie out on 't, sir, and therefore 'tis
  not yours. For my part, I do not lie in 't, yet it is   130
  mine.
HAMLET: Thou dost lie in 't, to be in 't and say it is
  thine. 'Tis for the dead, not for the quick;° therefore
  thou liest.
FIRST CLOWN: 'Tis a quick lie, sir; 'twill away again   135
  from me to you.
HAMLET: What man dost thou dig it for?
FIRST CLOWN: For no man, sir.
HAMLET: What woman, then?
FIRST CLOWN: For none, neither.   140
HAMLET: Who is to be buried in 't?
FIRST CLOWN: One that was a woman, sir, but, rest
  her soul, she's dead.
HAMLET: How absolute° the knave is! We must speak
  by the card,° or equivocation° will undo us. By the   145
  Lord, Horatio, this three years I have taken note
  of it: the age is grown so pick'd° that the toe of
  the peasant comes so near the heel of the courtier,
  he galls his kibe.° How long hast thou been a grave-
  maker?   150
FIRST CLOWN: Of all the days i' th' year, I came to
  't that day that our last king Hamlet overcame
  Fortinbras.
HAMLET: How long is that since?
FIRST CLOWN: Cannot you tell that? Every fool can   155
  tell that. It was that very day that young Hamlet
  was born — he that is mad, and sent into England.
HAMLET: Ay, marry, why was he sent into England?
FIRST CLOWN: Why, because 'a was mad. 'A shall
  recover his wits there, or, if 'a do not, 'tis no great   160
  matter there.
HAMLET: Why?
FIRST CLOWN: 'Twill not be seen in him there. There
  the men are as mad as he.

122. assurance in that: Safety in legal parchments. **123.
sirrah:** Term of address to interiors. **133. quick:** Living.
144. absolute: Positive, decided. **145. by the card:** By the
mariner's card on which the points of the compass were
marked, i.e., with precision; **equivocation:** Ambiguity in the
use of terms. **147. pick'd:** Refined, fastidious. **149. galls
his kibe:** Chafes the courtier's chilblain.

165 HAMLET: How came he mad?
FIRST CLOWN: Very strangely, they say.
HAMLET: How strangely?
FIRST CLOWN: Faith, e'en with losing his wits.
HAMLET: Upon what ground?
170 FIRST CLOWN: Why, here in Denmark. I have been
sexton here, man and boy, thirty years.
HAMLET: How long will a man lie i' th' earth ere he
rot?
FIRST CLOWN: Faith, if 'a be not rotten before 'a die
175 — as we have many pocky° corses [now-a-days],
that will scarce hold the laying in — 'a will last
you some eight year or nine year. A tanner will
last you nine year.
HAMLET: Why he more than another?
180 FIRST CLOWN: Why, sir, his hide is so tann'd with his
trade that 'a will keep out water a great while, and
your water is a sore decayer of your whoreson dead
body. [Picks up a skull.] Here's a skull now hath
lain you° i' th' earth three and twenty years.
185 HAMLET: Whose was it?
FIRST CLOWN: A whoreson mad fellow's it was. Whose
do you think it was?
HAMLET: Nay, I know not.
FIRST CLOWN: A pestilence on him for a mad rogue!
190 'A pour'd a flagon of Rhenish° on my head once.
This same skull, sir, was Yorick's skull, the King's
jester.
HAMLET: This?
FIRST CLOWN: E'en that.
195 HAMLET: [Let me see.] [Takes the skull.] Alas, poor
Yorick! I knew him, Horatio, a fellow of infinite
jest, of most excellent fancy. He hath borne me on
his back a thousand times; and now, how abhorr'd
in my imagination it is! My gorge rises at it. Here
200 hung those lips that I have kiss'd I know not how
oft. Where be your gibes now? Your gambols, your
songs, your flashes of merriment that were wont
to set the table on a roar? Not one now, to mock
your own grinning? Quite chap-fall'n?° Now get
205 you to my lady's chamber, and tell her, let her
paint an inch thick, to this favor° she must come;
make her laugh at that. Prithee, Horatio, tell me
one thing.
HORATIO: What's that, my lord?
210 HAMLET: Dost thou think Alexander look'd o' this
fashion i' th' earth?
HORATIO: E'en so.
HAMLET: And smelt so? Pah! [Puts down the skull.]
HORATIO: E'en so, my lord.

HAMLET: To what base uses we may return, Horatio! 215
Why may not imagination trace the noble dust of
Alexander, till a' find it stopping a bung-hole?
HORATIO: 'Twere to consider too curiously,° to consider
so.
HAMLET: No, faith, not a jot, but to follow him thither 220
with modesty° enough, and likelihood to lead it.
[As thus]: Alexander died, Alexander was buried,
Alexander returneth to dust; the dust is earth; of
earth we make loam;° and why of that loam, whereto
he was converted, might they not stop a beer-barrel? 225
Imperious° Caesar, dead and turn'd to clay,
Might stop a hole to keep the wind away.
O, that that earth which kept the world in awe
Should patch a wall t' expel the winter's flaw!°
But soft, but soft awhile! Here comes the King. 230

(Enter King, Queen, Laertes, and the Corse [of Ophelia,
in procession, with Priest, Lords etc.].)

The Queen, the courtiers. Who is this they follow?
And with such maimed rites? This doth betoken
The corse they follow did with desp'rate hand
Fordo it° own life. 'Twas of some estate.°
Couch° we awhile, and mark. 235
        [He and Horatio conceal themselves.
        Ophelia's body is taken to the grave.]
LAERTES: What ceremony else?
HAMLET [to Horatio]: That is Laertes, a very noble
youth. Mark.
LAERTES: What ceremony else?
PRIEST: Her obsequies have been as far enlarg'd
As we have warranty. Her death was doubtful, 240
And, but that great command o'ersways the
order,
She should in ground unsanctified been lodg'd
Till the last trumpet. For° charitable prayers,
Shards,° flints, and pebbles should be thrown on
her.
Yet here she is allow'd her virgin crants,° 245
Her maiden strewments,° and the bringing home
Of bell and burial.°
LAERTES: Must there no more be done?
PRIEST: No more be done.
We should profane the service of the dead
To sing a requiem and such rest to her 250
As to peace-parted souls.

---

175. **pocky:** Rotten, diseased (literally, with the pox, or syphilis).   184. **lain you:** Lain.   190. **Rhenish:** Rhine wine.
204. **chap-fall'n:** (1) Lacking the lower jaw; (2) dejected.
206. **favor:** Aspect, appearance.

218. **curiously:** Minutely.   221. **modesty:** Moderation.   224.
loam: Clay mixture for brickmaking or other clay use.   226.
Imperious: Imperial.   229. **flaw:** Gust of wind.   234. **Fordo
it:** Destroy its; **estate:** Rank.   235. **Couch:** Hide, lurk.   243.
For: In place of.   244. **Shards:** Broken bits of pottery.   245.
crants: Garland.   246. **strewments:** Traditional stewing of
flowers.   246–247. **bringing ... burial:** Laying to rest of
the body in consecrated ground, to the sound of the bell.

LAERTES: Lay her i' th' earth,
And from her fair and unpolluted flesh
May violets° spring! I tell thee, churlish priest,
A minist'ring angel shall my sister be
When thou liest howling!

255 HAMLET [*To Horatio*]:   What, the fair Ophelia!
QUEEN [*Scattering flowers*]: Sweets to the sweet!
    Farewell.
I hoped thou shouldst have been my Hamlet's
    wife.
I thought thy bride-bed to have deck'd, sweet
    maid,
And not have strew'd thy grave.

LAERTES: O, treble woe
260 Fall ten times treble on that cursed head
Whose wicked deed thy most ingenious sense°
Depriv'd thee of! Hold off the earth awhile,
Till I have caught her once more in mine arms.
        [*Leaps into the grave and embraces Ophelia.*]
Now pile your dust upon the quick and dead,
265 Till of this flat a mountain you have made
T 'o'ertop old Pelion,° or the skyish head
Of blue Olympus.°

HAMLET [*coming forward*]: What is he whose grief
Bears such an emphasis, whose phrase of sorrow
Conjures the wand'ring stars,° and makes them
270   stand
Like wonder-wounded hearers? This is I,
Hamlet the Dane.°

LAERTES: The devil take thy soul!
                        [*Grappling with him.*]
HAMLET: Thou pray'st not well.
I prithee, take thy fingers from my throat;
275 For, though I am not splenitive° and rash,
Yet have I in me something dangerous,
Which let thy wisdom fear. Hold off thy hand.

KING: Pluck them asunder.
QUEEN: Hamlet, Hamlet!
ALL: Gentlemen!
HORATIO: Good my lord, be quiet.
                [*Hamlet and Horatio are parted.*]
HAMLET: Why, I will fight with him upon this
280   theme
Until my eyelids will no longer wag.
QUEEN: O my son, what theme?
HAMLET: I lov'd Ophelia. Forty thousand brothers
Could not with all their quantity of love
285 Make up my sum. What wilt thou do for her?
KING: O, he is mad, Laertes.

QUEEN: For love of God, forbear him.
HAMLET: 'Swounds,° show me what thou't do.
Woo 't° weep? Woo 't fight? Woo 't fast? Woo
    't tear thyself?
Woo 't drink up eisel?° Eat a crocodile?   290
I'll do 't. Dost thou come here to whine?
To outface me with leaping in her grave?
Be buried quick° with her, and so will I.
And, if thou prate of mountains, let them throw
Millions of acres on us, till our ground,   295
Singeing his pate° against the burning zone,°
Make Ossa° like a wart! Nay, an thou 'lt
    mouth,°
I'll rant as well as thou.

QUEEN: This is mere° madness,
And thus a while the fit will work on him;
Anon, as patient as the female dove
When that her golden couplets° are disclosed,°
His silence will sit drooping.

HAMLET: Hear you, sir.
What is the reason that you use me thus?
I lov'd you ever. But it is no matter.
Let Hercules himself do what he may,   305
The cat will mew, and dog will have his day.°

KING: I pray thee, good Horatio, wait upon him.
                (*Exit Hamlet and Horatio.*)
[*To Laertes.*] Strengthen your patience in° our
    last night's speech;
We'll put the matter to the present push.° —
Good Gertrude, set some watch over your
    son. —   310
This grave shall have a living° monument.
An hour of quiet shortly shall we see;
Till then, in patience our proceeding be.(*Exeunt.*)

[Scene II]°

(*Enter Hamlet and Horatio.*)

HAMLET: So much for this, sir; now shall you see
    the other.°
You do remember all the circumstance?

---

288. 'Swounds: By His (Christ's) wounds.   289. Woo 't:
Wilt thou.   290. eisel: Vinegar.   293. quick: Alive.   296.
his pate: Its head, i.e., top; **burning zone:** Sun's orbit.   297.
Ossa: Another mountain in Thessaly. (In their war against
the Olympian gods, the giants attempted to heap Ossa, Pelion,
and Olympus on one another to scale heaven.); **mouth:** Rant.
298. mere: Utter.   301. golden couplets: Two baby pigeons,
covered with yellow down; **disclos'd:** Hatched.   305–306.
Let . . . day: Despite any blustering attempts at interference
every person will sooner or later do what he must do.   308.
in: By recalling.   309. present push: Immediate test.   311.
living: Lasting; also refers (for Laertes's benefit) to the plot
against Hamlet. V, II. Location: The castle.   1. see the
other: Hear the other news.

---

253. violets: See IV, V, line 187 and note.   261. ingenious
sense: Mind endowed with finest qualities.   266, 267. Pelion,
Olympus: Mountains in the north of Thessaly; see also *Ossa*,
at line 297.   270. wand'ring stars: Planets.   272. the Dane:
This title normally signifies the King; see I, I, line 15 and
note.   275. splenitive: Quick-tempered.

HORATIO: Remember it, my lord!

HAMLET: Sir, in my heart there was a kind of
fighting

5   That would not let me sleep. Methought I lay
Worse than the mutines° in the bilboes.° Rashly,°
And prais'd be rashness for it — let us know,°
Our indiscretion sometime serves us well
When our deep plots do pall,° and that should
learn° us

10   There's a divinity that shapes our ends,
Rough-hew° them how we will —

HORATIO: That is most certain.

HAMLET: Up from my cabin,
My sea-gown scarf'd about me, in the dark
Grop'd I to find out them, had my desire,

15   Finger'd° their packet, and in fine° withdrew
To mine own room again, making so bold,
My fears forgetting manners, to unseal
Their grand commission; where I found,
Horatio —
Ah, royal knavery! — an exact command,

20   Larded° with many several sorts of reasons
Importing° Denmark's health and England's too,
With, ho, such bugs° and goblins in my life,°
That, on the supervise,° no leisure bated,°
No, not to stay the grinding of the axe,
My head should be struck off.

25   HORATIO: Is 't possible?

HAMLET: Here's the commission; read it at more
leisure.   [Gives document.]
But wilt thou hear now how I did proceed?

HORATIO: I beseech you.

HAMLET: Being thus benetted round with villainies,

30   Or I could make a prologue to my brains,
They had begun the play.° I sat me down,
Devis'd a new commission, wrote it fair.°
I once did hold it, as our statists° do,
A baseness° to write fair, and labor'd much

35   How to forget that learning, but, sir, now
It did me yeoman's° service. Wilt thou know
Th' effect° of what I wrote?

HORATIO: Ay, good my lord.

HAMLET: An earnest conjuration from the King,
As England was his faithful tributary,

As love between them like the palm might
flourish,   40
As peace should still her wheaten garland° wear
And stand a comma° 'tween their amities,
And many such-like as's° of great charge,°
That, on the view and knowing of these
contents,
Without debatement further, more or less,   45
He should those bearers put to sudden death,
Not shriving time° allow'd.

HORATIO: How was this seal'd?

HAMLET: Why, even in that was heaven ordinant.°
I had my father's signet° in my purse,
Which was the model of that Danish seal;   50
Folded the writ up in the form of th' other,
Subscrib'd° it, gave 't th' impression,° plac'd it
safely,
The changeling° never known. Now, the next
day
Was our sea-fight, and what to this was sequent
Thou knowest already.   55

HORATIO: So Guildenstern and Rosencrantz go
to 't.

HAMLET: [Why, man, they did make love to this
employment.]
They are not near my conscience. Their defeat
Does by their own insinuation° grow.
'Tis dangerous when the baser nature comes   60
Between the pass° and fell° incensed points
Of mighty opposites.

HORATIO: Why, what a king is this!

HAMLET: Does it not, think thee, stand° me now
upon —
He that hath killed my king and whor'd my
mother,
Popp'd in between th' election° and my hopes,   65
Thrown out his angle° for my proper° life,
And with such coz'nage° — is 't not perfect
conscience
[To quit° him with this arm? And is 't not to be
damn'd
To let this canker° of our nature come
In further evil?   70

---

6. **mutines:** Mutineers; **bilboes:** Shackles; **Rashly:** On impulse (this adverb goes with lines 12 ff.).   7. **know:** Acknowledge. 9. **pall:** Fail; **learn:** Teach.   11. **Rough-hew:** Shape roughly. 15. **Finger'd:** Pilfered, pinched; **in fine:** Finally, in conclusion. 20. **Larded:** Enriched.   21. **Importing:** Relating to.   22. **bugs:** Bugbears, hobgoblins; **in my life:** To be feared if I were allowed to live.   23. **supervise:** Reading; **leisure bated:** Delay allowed.   30–31. **Or . . . play:** Before I could consciously turn my brain to the matter, it had started working on a plan. (*Or* means *ere*.)   32. **fair:** In a clear hand.   33. **statists:** Statesmen.   34. **baseness:** Lower-class trait.   36. **yeoman's:** Substantial, workmanlike.   37. **effect:** Purport.

41. **wheaten garland:** Symbolic of fruitful agriculture, of peace. 42. **comma:** Indicating continuity, link.   43. **as's:** (1) The "whereases" of formal document, (2) asses; **charge:** (1) Import, (2) burden.   47. **shriving-time:** Time for confession and absolution.   48. **ordinant:** Directing.   49. **signet:** Small seal. 52. **Subscrib'd:** Signed; **impression:** With a wax seal.   53. **changeling:** The substituted letter (literally, a fairy child substituted for a human one).   59. **insinuation:** Interference. 61. **pass:** Thrust; **fell:** Fierce.   63. **stand:** Become incumbent. 65. **election:** The Danish monarch was "elected" by a small number of high-ranking electors.   66. **angle:** Fishing line; **proper:** Very.   67. **coz'nage:** Trickery.   68. **quit:** Repay. 69. **canker:** Ulcer.

HORATIO: It must be shortly known to him from
   England
   What is the issue of the business there.
HAMLET: It will be short. The interim is mine,
   And a man's life 's no more than to say "One."°
75 But I am very sorry, good Horatio,
   That to Laertes I forgot myself,
   For by the image of my cause I see
   The portraiture of his. I'll court his favors.
   But, sure, the bravery° of his grief did put me
   Into a tow'ring passion.
80 HORATIO: Peace, who comes here?]

(*Enter a Courtier* [*Osric*].)

OSRIC: Your lordship is right welcome back to
   Denmark.
HAMLET: I humbly thank you, sir. [*To Horatio.*] Dost
   know this water-fly?
85 HORATIO: No, my good lord.
HAMLET: Thy state is the more gracious, for 'tis a vice
   to know him. He hath much land, and fertile. Let
   a beast be lord of beasts, and his crib shall stand
   at the King's mess.° 'Tis a chough,° but, as I say,
90   spacious in the possession of dirt.
OSRIC: Sweet lord, if your lordship were at leisure, I
   should impart a thing to you from his Majesty.
HAMLET: I will receive it, sir, with all diligence of
   spirit. Put your bonnet to his right use; 'tis for the
95   head.
OSRIC: I thank your lordship, it is very hot.
HAMLET: No, believe me, 'tis very cold; the wind is
   northerly.
OSRIC: It is indifferent° cold, my lord, indeed.
100 HAMLET: But yet methinks it is very sultry and hot
   for my complexion.°
OSRIC: Exceedingly, my lord; it is very sultry, as 'twere
   — I cannot tell how. My lord, his Majesty bade
   me signify to you that 'a has laid a great wager
105   on your head. Sir, this is the matter —
HAMLET: I beseech you, remember —
          [*Hamlet moves him to put on his hat.*]
OSRIC: Nay, good my lord; for my ease,° in good
   faith. Sir, here is newly come to court Laertes —
   believe me, an absolute gentleman, full of most
110   excellent differences,° of very soft society° and great

showing.° Indeed, to speak feelingly° of him, he is
   the card° or calendar° of gentry,° for you shall find
   in him the continent of what part° a gentleman
   would see.
HAMLET: Sir, his definement° suffers no perdition° in 115
   you, though, I know, to divide him inventorially°
   would dozy° th' arithmetic of memory, and yet but
   yaw° neither° in respect of° his quick sail. But, in
   the verity of extolment,° I take him to be a soul
   of great article,° and his infusion° of such dearth 120
   and rareness,° as, to make true diction° of him, his
   semblable° is his mirror, and who else would trace°
   him, his umbrage,° nothing more.
OSRIC: Your lordship speaks most infallibly of him.
HAMLET: The concernancy,° sir? Why do we wrap the 125
   gentleman in our more rawer breath?°
OSRIC: Sir?
HORATIO: Is 't not possible to understand in another
   tongue?° You will do 't,° sir, really.
HAMLET: What imports the nomination° of this 130
   gentleman?
OSRIC: Of Laertes?
HORATIO [*to Hamlet*]: His purse is empty already; all
   's golden words are spent.
HAMLET: Of him, sir. 135
OSRIC: I know you are not ignorant —
HAMLET: I would you did, sir; yet, in faith, if you
   did, it would not much approve° me. Well, sir?
OSRIC: You are not ignorant of what excellence Laertes
   is — 140
HAMLET: I dare not confess that, lest I should compare°

---

74. a man's . . . "One": To take a man's life requires no
more than to count to one as one duels.   79. bravery:
Bravado.   87–89. Let . . . mess: If a man, no matter how
beastlike, is as rich in possessions as Osric, he may eat at
the King's table.   89. chough: Chattering jackdaw.   99.
indifferent: Somewhat.   100. complexion: Temperament.
107. for my ease: A conventional reply declining the invitation
to put his hat back on.   110. differences: Special qualities;
soft society: Agreeable manners.

110–111. great showing: Distinguished appearance.   111.
feelingly: With just perception.   112. card: Chart, map;
calendar: Guide; gentry: Good breeding.   113. the continent
. . . part: One who contains in him all the qualities (a *continent*
is that which contains).   115. definement: Definition. (Hamlet
proceeds to mock Osric by using his lofty diction back at
him.); perdition: Loss, diminution.   116. divide him inven-
torially: Enumerate his graces.   117. dozy: Dizzy.   118.
yaw: To move unsteadily (said of a ship); neither: For all
that; in respect of: In comparison with.   118–119. in . . .
extrolment: In true praise (of him).   120. article: Moment
or importance; infusion: Essence, character imparted by nature.
120–121. dearth and rareness: Rarity.   121. make true diction: Speak truly.   122. semblable: Only true likeness; who
. . . trace: Any other person who would wish to follow.
123. umbrage: Shadow.   125. concernancy: Import, relevance.
126. breath: Speech.   128–129. to understand . . . tongue:
For Osric to understand when someone else speaks in his
manner. (Horatio twits Osric for not being able to understand
the kind of flowery speech he himself uses when Hamlet
speaks in such a vein.)   129. You will do 't: You can if
you try.   130. nomination: Naming.   138. approve: Commend.   141. compare: Seem to compete.

with him in excellence; but to know a man well were to know himself.°

OSRIC: I mean, sir, for his weapon; but in the imputation
145   laid on him by them,° in his meed° he's unfellow'd.°

HAMLET: What's his weapon?

OSRIC: Rapier and dagger.

HAMLET: That's two of his weapons — but well.

OSRIC: The King, sir, hath wager'd with him six Barbary
150   horses, against the which he has impawn'd,° as I
take it, six French rapiers and poniards, with their
assigns,° as girdle, hangers,° and so. Three of the
carriages,° in faith, are very dear to fancy,° very
responsive° to the hilts, most delicate° carriages,
155   and of very liberal conceit.°

HAMLET: What call you the carriages?

HORATIO [to Hamlet]: I knew you must be edified by
the margent° ere you had done.

OSRIC: The carriages, sir, are the hangers.
160   HAMLET: The phrase would be more germane to the
matter if we could carry a cannon by our sides; I
would it might be hangers till then. But, on: six
Barb'ry horses against six French swords, their assigns, and three liberal-conceited carriages; that's
165   the French bet against the Danish. Why is this
impawn'd, as you call it?

OSRIC: The King, sir, hath laid,° sir, that in a dozen
passes° between yourself and him, he shall not exceed
you three hits. He hath laid on twelve for nine,
170   and it would come to immediate trial, if your lordship
would vouchsafe the answer.

HAMLET: How if I answer no?

OSRIC: I mean, my lord, the opposition of your person
in trial.
175   HAMLET: Sir, I will walk here in the hall. If it please
his Majesty, it is the breathing time° of day with
me. Let the foils be brought, the gentleman willing,
and the King hold his purpose, I will win for him
an I can; if not, I will gain nothing but my shame
180   and the odd hits.

142–143. but . . . himself: For, to recognize excellence in
another man, one must know oneself.   144–145. imputation
. . . them: Reputation given him by others.   145. meed:
Merit; unfellow'd: Unmatched.   150. impawn'd: Staked,
wagered.   152. assigns: Appurtenances; hangers: Straps on
the sword belt (girdle) from which the sword hung.   153.
carriages: An affected way of saying hangers; literally, gun-
carriages; dear to fancy: Fancifully designed, tasteful.   154.
responsive: Corresponding closely, matching; delicate: I.e.,
in workmanship.   155. liberal conceit: Elaborate design.
158. margent: Margin of a book, place for explanatory notes.
167. laid: Wagered.   168. passes: Bouts. (The odds of the
betting are hard to explain. Possibly the King bets that Hamlet
will win at least five out of twelve, at which point Laertes
raises the odds against himself by betting he will win nine.)
176. breathing time: Exercise period.

OSRIC: Shall I deliver you so?

HAMLET: To this effect, sir — after what flourish your
nature will.

OSRIC: I commend my duty to your lordship.

HAMLET: Yours, yours. [Exit Osric.] He does well to   185
commend it himself; there are no tongues else for
's turn.

HORATIO: This lapwing° runs away with the shell on
his head.

HAMLET: 'A did comply, sir, with his dug,° before 'a   190
suck'd it. Thus has he — and many more of the
same breed that I know the drossy° age dotes on
— only got the tune° of the time and, out of an
habit of encounter,° a kind of yesty° collection,°
which carries them through and through the most   195
fann'd and winnow'd° opinions; and do but blow
them to their trial, the bubbles are out.°

(Enter a Lord.)

LORD: My lord, his Majesty commended him to you
by young Osric, who brings back to him that you
attend him in the hall. He sends to know if your   200
pleasure hold to play with Laertes, or that you will
take longer time.

HAMLET: I am constant to my purposes; they follow
the King's pleasure. If his fitness speaks,° mine is
ready; now or whensoever, provided I be so able   205
as now.

LORD: The King and Queen and all are coming down.

HAMLET: In happy time.°

LORD: The Queen desires you to use some gentle en-
tertainment° to Laertes before you fall to play.   210

HAMLET: She well instructs me.   [Exit Lord.]

HORATIO: You will lose, my lord.

HAMLET: I do not think so. Since he went into France,
I have been in continual practice; I shall win at the
odds. But thou wouldst not think how ill all's here   215
about my heart; but it is no matter.

HORATIO: Nay, good my lord —

HAMLET: It is but foolery, but it is such a kind of
gain-giving,° as would perhaps trouble a woman.

HORATIO: If your mind dislike anything, obey it. I   220

---

188. lapwing: A bird that draws intruders away from its
nest and was thought to run about when newly hatched with
its head in the shell; a seeming reference to Osric's hat.   190.
comply . . . dug: Observe ceremonious formality toward his
mother's teat.   192. drossy: Frivolous.   193. tune: Temper,
mood, manner of speech.   194. habit of encounter: Demeanor
of social intercourse; yesty: Yeasty, frothy; collection: I.e.,
of current phrases.   196. fann'd and winnow'd: Select and
refined.   196–197. blow . . . out: Put them to the test, and
their ignorance is exposed.   204. if . . . speaks: If his readiness
answers to the time.   208. In happy time: A phrase of
courtesy indicating acceptance.   209–210. entertainment:
Greeting.   219. gain-giving: Misgiving.

will forestall their repair hither, and say you are
not fit.
HAMLET: Not a whit, we defy augury. There is special
providence in the fall of a sparrow. If it be now,
225 'tis not to come; if it be not to come, it will be
now; if it be not now; yet it will come. The readiness
is all. Since no man of aught he leaves knows what
is 't to leave betimes,° let be.

(*A table prepar'd.* [*Enter*] *trumpets, drums, and Officers
with cushions; King, Queen,* [*Osric,*] *and all the State;
foils, daggers,* [*and wine borne in;*] *and Laertes.*)

KING: Come, Hamlet, come, and take this hand
from me.
        [*The King puts Laertes' hand into Hamlet's.*]
HAMLET: Give me your pardon, sir. I have done
230   you wrong,
But pardon 't, as you are a gentleman.
This presence° knows,
And you must needs have heard, how I am
punish'd
With a sore distraction. What I have done
235 That might your nature, honor, and exception°
Roughly awake, I here proclaim was madness.
Was 't Hamlet wrong'd Laertes? Never Hamlet.
If Hamlet from himself be ta'en away,
And when he's not himself does wrong Laertes,
240 Then Hamlet does it not, Hamlet denies it.
Who does it, then? His madness. If 't be so,
Hamlet is of the faction that is wrong'd;
His madness is poor Hamlet's enemy.
[Sir, in this audience,]
245 Let my disclaiming from a purpos'd evil
Free me so far in your most generous thoughts
That I have shot my arrow o'er the house
And hurt my brother.
LAERTES: I am satisfied in nature,°
Whose motive in this case should stir me most
250 To my revenge. But in my terms of honor
I stand aloof, and will no reconcilement
Till by some elder masters of known honor
I have a voice° and precedent of peace
To keep my name ungor'd. But till that time,
255 I do receive your offer'd love like love,
And will not wrong it.
HAMLET: I embrace it freely,
And will this brothers' wager frankly play.
Give us the foils. Come on.
LAERTES: Come, one for me.

HAMLET: I'll be your foil,° Laertes. In mine
ignorance
Your skill shall, like a star i' th' darkest night,   260
Stick fiery off° indeed.
LAERTES: You mock me, sir.
HAMLET: No, by this hand.
KING: Give them the foils, young Osric. Cousin
Hamlet,
You know the wager?
HAMLET: Very well, my lord.
Your Grace has laid the odds o' th' weaker side.   265
KING: I do not fear it; I have seen you both.
But since he is better'd,° we have therefore odds.
LAERTES: This is too heavy, let me see another.
            [*Exchanges his foil for another.*]
HAMLET: This likes me well. These foils have all a
length?
            [*They prepare to play.*]
OSRIC: Ay, my good lord.   270
KING: Set me the stoups of wine upon that table.
If Hamlet give the first or second hit,
Or quit° in answer of the third exchange,
Let all the battlements their ordnance fire.
The King shall drink to Hamlet's better breath,   275
And in the cup an union° shall he throw,
Richer than that which four successive kings
In Denmark's crown have worn. Give me the
cups,
And let the kettle° to the trumpet speak,
The trumpet to the cannoneer without,   280
The cannons to the heavens, the heaven to earth,
"Now the King drinks to Hamlet." Come, begin.
            (*Trumpets the while.*)
And you, the judges, bear a wary eye.
HAMLET: Come on sir.
LAERTES: Come, my lord. [*They play. Hamlet scores* 285
                                        a hit.]
HAMLET: One.
LAERTES: No.
HAMLET: Judgment.
OSRIC: A hit, a very palpable hit.
            (*Drum, trumpets, and shot. Flourish.
                A piece goes off.*)
LAERTES: Well, again.
KING: Stay, give me drink. Hamlet, this pearl is
thine.   290
[*He throws a pearl in Hamlet's cup, and drinks.*]

227–228. what . . . betimes: What is the best time to leave
it.   **232. presence:** Royal assembly.   **235. exception:** Dis-
approval.   **248. in nature.** As to my personal feelings.   **253.
voice:** Authoritative pronouncement.

259. foil: Thin metal background which sets a jewel off (with
pun on the blunted rapier for fencing).   **261. Stick fiery off:**
Stand out brilliantly.   **267. is better'd:** Has improved; is the
odds-on-favorite.   **273. quit:** Repay (with a hit).   **276. union:**
Pearl (so called, according to Pliny's *Natural History,* IX,
because pearls are *unique,* never identical.   **279. kettle:**
Kettledrum.

Here's to thy health. Give him the cup.
HAMLET: I'll play this bout first; set it by awhile.
Come. [*They play.*] Another hit; what say you?
LAERTES: A touch, a touch, I do confess 't.
KING: Our son shall win.
295 QUEEN: He's fat,° and scant of breath.
Here, Hamlet, take my napkin,° rub thy brows.
The Queen carouses° to thy fortune, Hamlet.
HAMLET: Good madam!
KING: Gertrude, do not drink.
300 QUEEN: I will, my lord; I pray you pardon me.
[*Drinks.*]
KING [*aside*]: It is the pois'ned cup. It is too late.
HAMLET: I dare not drink yet, madam; by and by.
QUEEN: Come, let me wipe thy face.
LAERTES [*to King*]: My lord, I'll hit him now.
KING: I do not think 't.
LAERTES [*aside*]: And yet it is almost against my
305 conscience.
HAMLET: Come, for the third, Laertes. You do but
dally.
I pray you, pass with your best violence;
I am afeard you make a wanton of me.°
LAERTES: Say you so? Come on. [*They play.*]
310 OSRIC: Nothing, neither way.
LAERTES: Have at you now!
[*Laertes wounds Hamlet; then, in scuffling,
they change rapiers,° and Hamlet wounds Laertes.*]
KING: Part them! They are incens'd.
HAMLET: Nay, come, again. [*The Queen fails.*]
OSRIC: Look to the Queen there, ho!
HORATIO: They bleed on both sides. How is it, my
lord?
OSRIC: How is 't, Laertes?
LAERTES: Why, as a woodcock° to mine own
315 springe,° Osric;
I am justly kill'd with mine own treachery.
HAMLET: How does the Queen?
KING: She swoons to see them bleed.
QUEEN: No, no, the drink, the drink — O my dear
Hamlet —
The drink, the drink! I am pois'ned. [*Dies.*]
320 HAMLET: O villainy! Ho, let the door be lock'd!
Treachery! Seek it out. [*Laertes falls.*]
LAERTES: It is here, Hamlet. Hamlet, thou art slain.

No med'cine in the world can do thee good;
In thee there is not half an hour's life.
The treacherous instrument is in thy hand, 325
Unbated° and envenom'd. The foul practice
Hath turn'd itself on me. Lo, here I lie,
Never to rise again. Thy mother's pois'ned.
I can no more. The King, the King's to blame.
HAMLET: The point envenom'd too? Then, venom,
to thy work. [*Stabs the King.*] 330
ALL: Treason! Treason!
KING: O, yet defend me, friends; I am but hurt.
HAMLET: Here, thou incestuous, murd'rous, damned
Dane,
[*He forces the King to drink
the poisoned cup.*]
Drink off this potion. Is thy union° here?
Follow my mother. [*King dies.*]
LAERTES: He is justly serv'd. 335
It is a poison temper'd° by himself.
Exchange forgiveness with me, noble Hamlet.
Mine and my father's death come not upon thee,
Nor thine on me! [*Dies.*]
HAMLET: Heaven make thee free of it! I follow
thee. 340
I am dead, Horatio. Wretched Queen, adieu!
You that look pale and tremble at this chance,
That are but mutes° or audience to this act,
Had I but time — as this fell° sergeant,° Death,
Is strict in his arrest — O, I could tell you — 345
But let it be. Horatio, I am dead;
Thou livest. Report me and my cause aright
To the unsatisfied.
HORATIO: Never believe it.
I am more an antique Roman° than a Dane.
Here's yet some liquor left.
[*He attempts to drink from the poisoned cup.
Hamlet prevents him.*]
HAMLET: As th' art a man, 350
Give me the cup! Let go! By heaven, I'll ha 't.
O God, Horatio, what a wounded name,
Things standing thus unknown, shall I leave
behind me!
If thou didst ever hold me in thy heart,
Absent thee from felicity awhile, 355
And in this harsh world draw thy breath in pain
To tell my story.
(*A march afar off* [*and a volley within*].)
What warlike noise is this?

---

295. **fat:** Not physically fit, out of training.   296. **napkin:**
Handkerchief: 297. **carouses:** Drinks a toast.   308. **make
. . . me:** Treat me like a spoiled child, holding back to give
me an advantage.   311. [S.D.] *in scuffling, they change
rapiers:* This stage direction occurs in the Folio. According
to a widespread stage tradition, Hamlet receives a scratch,
realizes that Laertes's sword is unbated, and accordingly
forces an exchange.   315. **woodcock:** A bird, a type of
stupidity or as a decoy; **springe:** Trap, snare.

326. **Unbated:** Not blunted with a button.   334. **union:**
Pearl (see line 276; with grim puns on the word's other
meanings: marriage, shared death?).   336. **temper'd:** Mixed.
343. **mutes:** Silent observers.   344. **fell:** Cruel; **sergeant:**
Sheriff's officer.   349. **Roman:** It was the Roman custom
to follow masters in death.

OSRIC: Young Fortinbras, with conquest come from
    Poland,
  To the ambassadors of England gives
  This warlike volley.
360 HAMLET: O, I die, Horatio!
  The potent poison quite o'ercrows° my spirit.
  I cannot live to hear the news from England,
  But I do prophesy th' election lights
  On Fortinbras. He has my dying voice.°
365 So tell him, with th' occurrents° more and less
  Which have solicited° — the rest is silence.[*Dies.*]
  HORATIO: Now cracks a noble heart. Good night,
    sweet prince;
  And flights of angels sing thee to thy rest!
                        [*March within.*]
  Why does the drum come hither?

(*Enter Fortinbras, with the [English] Ambassadors [with
drum, colors, and attendants].*)

FORTINBRAS: Where is this sight?
370 HORATIO: What is it you would see?
  If aught of woe or wonder, cease your search.
  FORTINBRAS: This quarry° cries on havoc.° O proud
    Death,
  What feast is toward° in thine eternal cell,
  That thou so many princes at a shot
  So bloodily hast struck?
375 FIRST AMBASSADOR: The sight is dismal;
  And our affairs from England come too late.
  The ears are senseless that should give us
    hearing,
  To tell him his commandment is fulfill'd,
  That Rosencrantz and Guildenstern are dead.
  Where should we have our thanks?
380 HORATIO: Not from his° mouth,
  Had it th' ability of life to thank you.
  He never gave commandment for their death.
  But since, so jump° upon this bloody question,°

You from the Polack wars, and you from
  England,
Are here arriv'd, give order that these bodies   385
High on a stage° be placed to the view,
And let me speak to th' yet unknowing world
How these things came about. So shall you hear
Of carnal, bloody, and unnatural acts,
Of accidental judgments,° casual° slaughters,   390
Of deaths put on° by cunning and forc'd cause,
And, in this upshot, purposes mistook
Fall'n on th' inventors' heads. All this can I
Truly deliver.
FORTINBRAS: Let us haste to hear it,
And call the noblest to the audience.   395
For me, with sorrow I embrace my fortune.
I have some rights of memory° in this kingdom,
Which now to claim my vantage° doth invite me.
HORATIO: Of that I shall have also cause to speak,
And from his mouth whose voice will draw on
  more.°   400
But let this same be presently° perform'd,
Even while men's minds are wild, lest more
  mischance
On° plots and errors happen.
FORTINBRAS: Let four captains
Bear Hamlet, like a soldier, to the stage,
For he was likely, had he been put on,°   405
To have prov'd most royal; and, for his
  passage,°
The soldiers' music and the rite of war
Speak loudly for him.
Take up the bodies. Such a sight as this
Becomes the field,° but here shows much amiss.   410
Go, bid the soldiers shoot.
    (*Exeunt [marching, bearing off the dead bodies;
                  a peal of ordnance is shot off].*)

---

386. stage: Platform.   **390. judgments:** Retributions; **casual:**
Occurring by chance.   **391. put on:** Instigated.   **397. of
memory:** Traditional, remembered.   **398. vantage:** Presence
at this opportune moment.   **400. voice . . . more:** Vote will
influence still others.   **401. presently:** Immediately.   **403.
On:** On the basis of.   **405. put on:** Invested in royal office,
and so put to the test.   **406. passage:** Death.   **410. field:**
I.e., of battle.

---

361. o'ercrows: Triumphs over.   **364. voice:** Vote.   **365.
occurrents:** Events, incidents.   **366. solicited:** Moved, urged.
372. quarry: Heap of dead; **cries on havoc:** Proclaims a
general slaughter.   **373. toward:** In preparation.   **380. his:**
Claudius'   **383. jump:** Precisely; **question:** Dispute.

COMMENTARIES

Some of the finest critical commentary ever written has been devoted to the works of Shakespeare. From the seventeenth century to the present, critics have taken a considerable interest in the nuances of his work. His contemporaries knew that he was a force to be reckoned with, and some were jealous while others were proud to be his friends.

In the commentary on *A Midsummer Night's Dream* we find a wide range of interest. Enid Welsford's comments are in a special context, that of the court masque, the rich entertainments that were designed to please royalty. Since much of the entertainment of the play is designed to please Oberon or Theseus and Hippolyta, the play qualifies in many ways as a masque.

Ruth Nevo offers a careful assessment of the drama from the point of view of the critic of comedy. She gives some consideration to the ways in which the treatment of a character's gender contributes to the genre of comedy. In more specifically feminist observations, the critics Carol Thomas Neely and Linda Bamber show how assumptions regarding power in a male-female relationship affect our interpretation of the play. Their readings are fresh, exciting, and provocative. They show that Shakespeare is still the rich, remarkable playwright we've always known him to be.

Peter Brook, one of the most notable contemporary directors of Shakespeare, and the producer of the most striking recent production of *A Midsummer Night's Dream* (1970), gives us a director's view of the play. He centers the discussion on love, sensing that love, in many forms, is at the heart of the play.

The modern era of criticism on Shakespeare probably begins with Samuel Taylor Coleridge, whose lectures on Shakespeare were instrumental in helping a generation of early-nineteenth-century theatergoers take Shakespeare much more seriously than they might have done. Coleridge reached a wide and generally popular audience, and he stands as one of the most influential critics of the last century. His work on *Hamlet* centers on the character of Hamlet and his problems in the play. Coleridge shows how Hamlet reveals himself both to us and to himself.

Sigmund Freud's interests are naturally psychological. He sees in *Hamlet* the seeds of the Oedipus complex that he had already identified in Sophocles's *Oedipus Rex*. The question of how one psychoanalyzes a literary character is perhaps best raised in Freud's essay. Later, Ernest Jones, a follower of Freud, wrote an entire book on Hamlet, analyzing him much as a psychiatrist might.

A. C. Bradley's *Shakespearean Tragedy* (1904) was a landmark study of the tragedies. The excerpt included here from his essay on *Hamlet* focuses on Gertrude, Claudius, and the Ghost and on their relationships with the main character.

T. S. Eliot, speaking as a careful and noted student of Elizabethan and Jacobean drama, begins to point out some of the difficulties he sees with *Hamlet*. It is fascinating to see how great poets such as Coleridge and Eliot can approach the same play from such diverse points of view.

The commentaries on *Hamlet* show that it is possible to take even the minutest details in this play and examine them closely enough to have them yield a remarkable vision of the entire play. This demonstrates the extent to which Shakespeare wielded total control over all the elements of drama.

Enid Welsford
MASQUE ELEMENTS IN *A MIDSUMMER NIGHT'S DREAM*

One of the finest critics of the Elizabethan masque, Enid Welsford examines A Midsummer Night's Dream *from the point of view of its masque-like qualities. Shakespeare's* The Tempest *includes a masque and has certain scenic qualities that link it to that tradition, and so does* A Midsummer Night's Dream: *fantastic costumes, a remarkable fairy population that could be considered part of the antimasque (just as the rude mechanicals could), and music of the sort that characterizes many of the masques of Ben Jonson.*

The only character study in *A Midsummer Night's Dream* is to be found in the portrayal of Bottom, Theseus, and perhaps Hippolyta. Even in drawing these characters Shakespeare was evidently influenced by the memory of pageants, complimentary speeches, and entertainments addressed by townspeople and humble folk to the Queen or to the nobility. A glance through Nichols's *Public Progresses* shows what innumerable lengthy speeches, what innumerable disguisings and shows, Elizabeth was obliged to bear with gracious demeanor. Her experiences were similar to those of Theseus:

> Where I have come, great clerks have purposed
> To greet me with premeditated welcomes;
> Where I have seen them shiver and look pale,
> Make periods in the midst of sentences,
> Throttle their practic'd accent in their fears,
> And, in conclusion, dumbly have broke off,
> Not paying me a welcome.

One Sunday afternoon, at Kenilworth Castle, Elizabeth and her court whiled away the time by watching the countrypeople at a Brideale and Morris Dance. Their amused kindly tolerance is just that of Theseus and the lovers toward the Athenian workmen. So that even in the most solid and dramatic parts of his play Shakespeare is only giving an idealized version of courtly and country revels and of the people that played a part in them.

In *A Midsummer Night's Dream* Bottom and his companions serve the same purpose as the antimasque[1] in the courtly revels. It is true that Shakespeare's play was written before Ben Jonson had elaborated and defined the antimasque, but from the first grotesque dances were popular, and the principle of contrast was always latent in the masque. There is, however, a great difference between Jonson's and Shakespeare's management of foil and relief. In the antimasque the transition is sudden and the contrast complete, a method of composition effective enough in spectacle and ballet. But in a play, as Shakespeare well knew, the greatest beauty is gained through contrast when the difference is obvious and striking, but rises out of a deep though unobstrusive resemblance. This could not be better illustrated than by the picture of Titania winding the ass-headed Bottom in her arms. Why is it that this is a pleasing picture, why is it that the rude mechanicals do not, as a matter of fact, disturb or sully Titania's "close and consecrated bower"? Malvolio[2] in Bottom's place would be repellent, yet Malvolio, regarded superficially, is less violently contrasted to the Fairy Queen than is Nick Bottom. Bottom with his ass's head is grotesquely hideous, and in ordinary life he is crude, raw, and very stupid. We have no reason to suppose that Malvolio was anything but a well-set-up, proper-looking man, spruce, well dressed, the perfect family butler. His mentality too is of a distinctly higher order than Bottom's. He fills a responsible position with credit, he follows a reasoned line of conduct, he thinks nobly of the soul. Two things alone he lacks (and that is why no self-respecting fay could ever kiss him) — humor and imagination. Malvolio is, therefore, the only character who cannot be included in the final harmony of *Twelfth Night*. Bottom and his fellows did perhaps lack humor (though the interview with the fairies suggests that Bottom had a smack of it), but in its place they possessed unreason. Imagination they did have, of the most simple, primal, childlike kind. It is their artistic ambition that lifts them out of the humdrum world and turns them into Midsummer Dreamers, and we have seen how cunningly Shakespeare extracts from their very stupidity romance and moonshine. But, indeed, grotesqueness and stupidity (of a certain kind) have a kinship with beauty. For these qualities usually imply a measure of spiritual freedom, they lead to at least a temporary relief from the tyranny of reason and from the pressure of the external world. In *A Midsummer Night's Dream* the dominance of the Lord of Misrule is not marked by coarse parody, but by the partial repeal of the laws of cause and effect. By delicate beauty, gentle mockery, and simple romantic foolishness our freedom is gained.

[1]**antimasque:** Device introduced by Ben Jonson as a comic and grotesque foil to the main spectacle.
[2]**Malvolio:** A character in Shakespeare's *Twelfth Night*.

Ruth Nevo (b. 1924)
FANCY'S IMAGES

In her emphasis on the plays-within-plays in A Midsummer Night's Dream, *Ruth Nevo sheds light on a number of important relationships. She sees the play that the mechanicals put on,* Pyramus and Thisby, *to be an important study of the "sexual and individual roles" of the players, with this distinction helping to enlarge the meaning of the entire play. The question of who or what the players are is carefully, if briefly, treated in this excerpt.*

A Midsummer Night's Dream juggles conspicuously with multiple levels of representation, with plays-within-plays and visions within dreams. What is performed, what is meant, what is seen are often, as Theseus said of Peter Quince's prologue, "like a tangled chain; nothing impair'd, but all disorder'd" (V, I). The Athenian lovers, Lysander and Hermia, fall asleep and dream (in act II), fall asleep and wake (in act IV), and what happens to them is ambiguously dream/reality, just as Oberon, king of shadows, is ambiguously real/not real, visible to the audience but not to the lovers; and the "angel" that wakes Titania "from her flow'ry bed" (III, I) is visible to her but not to the audience, who perceive only Nick Bottom assified. Puck stage-manages these "transfigurations" for Oberon's delectation just as Peter Quince does for Theseus's and Shakespeare for ours. And the audience is more than once pointedly invited to conflate these frames. When Theseus says "The best in this kind are but shadows," his remark applies with equal validity to the artisans of Athens and the Lord Chamberlain's Men. By the same token Puck's "shadows" in the epilogue ("if we shadows have offended") refers, intentionally, both to the fairies and the actors — the visible and the invisible.

Act V dazzlingly catches up and refocuses the issues of the play, recapitulating its schooling of the imagination. When Theseus tempers Hippolyta's impatience with the mechanicals' efforts: "This is the silliest stuff that ever I heard" (V, I) with "The best in this kind are but shadows; and the worst are no worse, if imagination amend them" (V, I) he is retracting his previous repudiation of the imagination as the faculty which "sees more devils than vast hell can hold," or "Helen's beauty in a brow of Egypt," or some bringer of what is a merely "apprehended" joy, or a bear in a bush on a dark night. The rationalistic and empirically minded duke has been more than cautious about the seething tricks of that fertile and moonstruck faculty; and it is in reply to his dismissal of the lovers' story as so much irrational and illusory dream stuff that Hippolyta enters her caveat concerning the story of the night:

> But all the story of the night told over,
> And all their minds transfigur'd so together,
> More witnesseth than fancy's images,
> And grows to something of great constancy   (V, I)

The ducal pair . . . are a model of *concordia discors* ("How shall we find the concord of this discord?" Theseus asks of the "very tragical mirth" about to be presented by the artisans) and so it is fitting that they should conduct the dialectic of real and imaginary, meant and performed, visible and invisible toward a resolution for theatergoers and lovers alike. When Hippolyta reflects upon the story of the night, she is inviting not only Theseus but the theater audience as well to further reflection. She is inviting a retrospective reappraisal of all that has been enacted in the moonlit woods. Hippolyta's organic metaphor is interesting; cognition, it says, or re-cognition, grows in the mind in the process of recounting, retelling. What the play celebrates as remedial, beneficent, recuperative it will have discovered by working its way through the fantastic follies the initial deficiencies or infirmities generated. These follies, reduced (or expanded) to absurdity, will prove to have been homeopathically therapeutic, if imagination amend them by making them intelligible. "It must be your imagination then, not theirs," says wise Hippolyta, knowing that to stout bully Bottom nothing is invisible, not even a voice from behind a wall. So far as that parodic literalist of the imagination is concerned, moonlight cannot be better represented than by moonlight, shining in at the casement in all its factual actuality. And when a person is a wall, he must be well and truly plastered and roughcast. No fancy Brechtian placards will do for him, any more than he can conceive that anyone (of any size) called Mustardseed should not be instantly applied to roast beef.

Pyramus and Thisby presents a tragedy of lovers misprisions,[1] and neutralizes disaster with its ludicrous comicality. It is irresistibly amusing in itself and needs no amending, by imagination or any other means; and it is also the vehicle of Shakespeare's most ironic private joke to *his* audience over the heads, so to speak, of Peter Quince and his. The latter possess the capacity to distinguish between walls and witty partitions, between run-on and end-stopped pentameters, between a lion and a goose and between a man and a moon. But they haven't always been so good at distinguishing. Their own follies have been, in their own way, no less deconstructive; but also no less recreative.

"Your play needs no excuse," says Theseus, amused, ironic and kind. "Marry, if he that writ it had play'd Pyramus, and hang'd himself in Thisby's garter, it would have been a fine tragedy; and so it is truly, and very notably discharg'd" (V, I), A great deal, and of great constancy, has been "discharged" in this play. And not only Hippolyta, it has been suggested, has had an inkling that the fantasy of folly may grow into the wisdom of the imagination.

[1]**misprisions:** Misunderstanding.

Carol Thomas Neely (b. 1939)
BROKEN NUPTIALS

Carol Thomas Neely is interested in the problem of marriage in A Midsummer Night's Dream, *examining it not from the traditional point of view — which essentially accepted the status quo of the play and then ignored it — but from a modernist point of view that brings into question the institution of marriage and how it functions in the play. She is interested in the relationships of Titania and Oberon, who "make up" during the play, and of Theseus and Hippolyta, whose own nuptials have been postponed for the while it takes the action of the play to unfold. Neely reminds us how much "coupling" there is in the play.*

In *Midsummer Night's Dream* desire, symbolized by the operations of the fairy juice, is urgent, promiscuous, and threatening to women as well as to men. Its effects mock the protestations of constancy by Lysander and Demetrius and exaggerate the patriarchal possessiveness of Theseus and Oberon: "every man should take his own. . . . The man shall have his mare again, and all shall be well" (III, II). All is made well in part because the erratic or aggressive desires of the controlling men are "linger[ed]" (I, I) by the chaste constancy of Hermia and Helena and the poised detachment of Hippolyta, or tempered by the inconstancy of Titania with Bottom. Oberon, engineering this union, imagines it as an ugly, bestial coupling "with lion, bear, or wolf, or bull" (II, 1), an apt punishment for Titania's multiple desires and intimacies. But from Titania's perspective (and ours) it is a comically fulfilling alternate nuptial — and was staged as such by Peter Brook,[1] complete with streamers, the wedding march, a plumed bower of bliss, and a waving phallus. The union is a respite for Titania from the conflicts of her hierarchical marriage. She and Bottom experience not animal lust but a blissful, sensual, symbiotic union, characterized, like that of mother and child, by mutual affection and a shared sense of effortless omnipotence. Their eroticism, the opposite of Oberon's bestial fantasies or Theseus's phallic wooing, is tenderly gynocentric:[2] "So doth the woodbine the sweet honey-suckle/Gently entwist; the female ivy so/Enrings the barky fingers of the elm" (IV, 1). Although Titania disavows her "enamored" visions (IV, 1), and Oberon misconstrues them, the couple's "amity" (IV, 1) depends on that prior union: freed by it to relinquish her other love object, the Indian boy, to Oberon, Titania's submission generates in him the tenderness she craves.

While Theseus and Hippolyta await their nuptials, marital harmony is re-established by Titania and Oberon, and the chaotic desires of the young lovers are sorted out. During the last-act interval between the weddings and their consummations, the violent potentials in love, sex, and marriage are comically incorporated in the rejected and enacted entertainments. "The battle with the centaurs" interrupted the wedding of Theseus's friend Pirithous when the drunken centaurs attacked the Lapiths to capture the bride; during "the riot of the tipsy Bacchanals," the Bacchantes tore Orpheus to pieces, enraged by his devotion to Eurydice and his scorn of other women. The Pyramus and Thisby play dramatizes a lovers' union aborted by parental obstructions, and devouring lion, and the lovers' deaths. The play within the play's joining of parodic romance with bawdy innuendo brings into the festive conclusion the two dimensions of love — conventional romanticism and uncontrollable desire — which, converging, threatened but did not harm the couples in the forest and which facilitated the union of Titania and Bottom.

[1]**Peter Brook:** (b. 1925) innovative British film and theater director. His *Midsummer Night's Dream* was produced in 1970.
[2]**gynocentric:** Women-centered.

Linda Bamber (b. 1945)
ON A MIDSUMMER NIGHT'S DREAM

The question of masculine and feminine is central to A Midsummer Night's Dream. *Much of the action is precipitated by a power struggle between Titania and Oberon, and the young Athenians who rush off to the woods are there because a father has decided to oppose the will of his daughter regarding her marriage. Linda Bamber is a feminist critic interested in examining the centers of power in the play, particularly with an eye for what we accept as the natural order of relationships. She shows us that the action of the comedy is essentially tied into questions of gender, which begin to become questions of genre.*

The best example [in Shakespeare] of the relationship between male dominance and the status quo comes in *A Midsummer Night's Dream,* which begins with a rebellion of the feminine against the power of masculine authority. Hermia refuses the man both Aegeus and Theseus order her to marry; her refusal sends us off into the forest, beyond the power of the father and the masculine state. Once in the forest, of course, we find the social situation metaphorically repeated in this world of imagination and nature. The fairy king, Oberon, rules the forest. His rule, too, is troubled by the rebellion of the feminine. Titania has refused to give him her page, the child of a human friend who died in childbirth. But by the end of the story Titania is conquered, the child relinquished, and order restored. Even here the comic upheavals, whether we see them as May games or bad dreams, are associated with an uprising of women. David P. Young has pointed out how firmly this play connects order with masculine dominance and the disruption of order with the rebellion of the feminine:

> It is appropriate that Theseus, as representative of daylight and right reason, should have subdued his bride-to-be to the rule of his masculine will. That is the natural order of things. It is equally appropriate that Oberon, as king of darkness and fantasy, should have lost control of his wife, and that the corresponding natural disorder described by Titania should ensue.[1]

The natural order, the status quo, is for men to rule women. When they fail to do so, we have the exceptional situation, the festive, disruptive, disorderly moment of comedy.

A Midsummer Night's Dream is actually an anomaly among the festive comedies. It is unusual for the forces of the green world to be directed, as they are here, by a masculine figure. Because the green world here is a partial reproduction of the social world, the feminine is reduced to a kind of first cause of the action while a masculine power directs it. In the other festive comedies the feminine Other presides. She does not *command* the forces of the alternative world, as Oberon does, but since she acts in harmony with these forces her will and desire often prevail.

Where are we to bestow our sympathies? On the forces that make for the disruption of the status quo and therefore for the plot? Or on the force that asserts itself against the disruption and reestablishes a workable social order? Of course we cannot choose. We can only say that in comedy we owe our holiday to such forces as the tendency of the feminine to rebel, whereas to the successful reassertion of masculine power we owe our everyday order. Shakespearean comedy endorses both sides. Holiday is, of course, the subject and the analogue of each play; but the plays always end in a return to everyday life. The optimistic reading of Shakespearean comedy says that everyday life is clarified and enriched by our holiday from it; according to the pessimistic reading the temporary subversion of the social order has revealed how much that order excludes, how high a price we pay for it. But whether our return to everyday life is a comfortable one or not, the return itself is the inevitable conclusion to the journey out.

Does this make the comedies sexist? Is the association of women with the disruption of the social order an unconscious and insulting projection? It seems

---

[1]David P. Young, *Something of Great Constancy* (New Haven: CT, Yale UP, 1966), 183.

to begin as such; but as the form of Shakespearean comedy develops, the Otherness of the feminine develops into as powerful a force in the drama as the social authority of the masculine Self. For the feminine in Shakespearean comedy begins as a shrew but develops into a comic heroine. The shrew's rebellion directly challenges masculine authority, whereas the comic heroine merely presides over areas of experience to which masculine authority is irrelevant. But the shrew is essentially powerless against the social system, whereas the comic heroine is in alliance with forces that can never be finally overcome. The shrew is defeated by the superior strength, physical and social, of a man, or by women who support the status quo. She provokes a battle of the sexes, and the outcome of this battle, from Shakespeare's point of view, is inevitable. The comic heroine, on the other hand, does not fight the system but merely surfaces, again and again, when and where the social system is temporarily subverted. The comic heroine does not actively resist the social and political hegemony[2] of the men, but as an irresistible version of the Other she successfully competes for our favor with the (masculine) representatives of the social Self. The development of the feminine from the shrew to the comic heroine indicates a certain consciousness on the author's part of sexual politics; and it indicates a desire, at least, to create conditions of sexual equality within the drama even while reflecting the unequal conditions of men and women in the society at large.

[2]**hegemony:** Overriding authority.

Peter Brook (*b. 1925*)
THE PLAY IS THE MESSAGE . . .

When a distinguished director becomes a critic, we have the opportunity to understand a play from the point of view of one who has to make the play work in front of an audience. Brook's production of A Midsummer Night's Dream *was a sensation in England and America in 1970. It featured absolutely white lighting, white sets, and actors in swings. Brook had analyzed the play in such a fashion that he saw love as its constant concern, "constantly repeated." He concluded that to present the play, the players must embody the concept of love. They must bring to the play their own realization of the play's themes — even to the point of seeing theater anew, like the mechanicals "who are touching an extraordinary world with the tips of their fingers, a world which transcends their daily experience and which fills them with wonder" — the effect of the love they bring to their task.*

People have often asked me: "What is the theme of *A Midsummer Night's Dream?*" There is only one answer to that question, the same as one would give regarding a cup. The quality of a cup is its cupness. I say this by way of introduction, to show that if I lay so much stress on the dangers involved in trying to define the themes of the *Dream* it is because too many productions, too many attempts at visual interpretation are based on preconceived ideas, as if these had to be illustrated in some way. In my opinion we should first of all try to rediscover the play as a living thing; then we shall be able to analyze our discoveries. Once I have finished working on the play, I can begin to produce my theories. It was fortunate that I did not attempt to do so earlier because the play would not have yielded up its secrets.

At the center of the *Dream*, constantly repeated, we find the word "love." Everything comes back to this, even the structure of the play, even its music. The quality the play demands from its performers is to build up an atmosphere of love during the performance itself, so that this abstract idea — for the word "love" is in itself a complete abstraction — may become palpable. The play presents us with forms of love which become less and less blurred as it goes on. "Love" soon begins to resound like a musical scale and little by little we are introduced to its various modes and tones.

Love is, of course, a theme which touches all men. No one, not even the most hardened, the coldest, or the most despairing, is insensitive to it, even if he does not know what love is. Either his practical experience confirms its existence or he suffers from its absence, which is another way of recognizing that it exists. At every moment the play touches something which concerns everyone.

As this is theater, there must be conflicts, so this play about love is also a play about the opposite of love, love and its opposite force. We are brought to realize that love, liberty, and imagination are closely connected. Right at the beginning of the play, for example, the father in a long speech tries to obstruct his daughter's love and we are surprised that such a character, apparently a secondary role, should have so long a speech — until we discover the real importance of his words. What he says not only reflects a generation gap (a father opposing his daughter's love because he had intended her for someone else), it also explains the reasons for his feeling of suspicion toward the young man whom his daughter loves. He describes him as an individual prone to fantasy, led by his imagination — an unpardonable weakness in the father's eyes.

From this starting point we see, as in any of Shakespeare's plays, a confrontation. Here it is between love and its opposing qualities, between fantasy and solid common sense — caught in an endless series of mirrors. As usual, Shakespeare confuses the issue. If we asked someone's opinion on the father's point of view, he might say, for example, that "The father is in the wrong because he is against freedom of the imagination," a very widespread attitude today.

In this way, for most present-day audiences, the girl's father comes over as the classical father figure who misunderstands young people and their flights of fancy. But later on, we discover surprisingly that he is right, because the imaginative world in which this lover lives causes him to behave in a quite disgusting way toward the very same daughter: as soon as a drop of liquid falls into his eyes, acting as a drug which liberates natural tendencies, he not only jilts her but his love is transformed into violent hate. He uses words which might well be borrowed from *Measure for Measure,* denouncing the girl with the kind of vehemence that, in the Middle Ages, led people to burn one another at the stake. Yet at the end of the play we are once more in agreement with the Duke, who rejects the father in the name of love. The young man has now been transformed.

So we observe this game of love in a psychological and metaphysical context; we hear Titania's assertion that the opposition between herself and Oberon is fundamental, primordial. But Oberon's acts deny this, for he perceives that within their opposition a reconciliation is possible.

The play covers an extraordinarily broad range of universal forces and feelings in a mythical world, which suddenly changes, in the last part, into high society. We find ourselves back in the very real palace: and the same Shakespeare who, a few pages earlier, offered us a scene of pure fantasy between Titania and Oberon, where it would be absurd to ask prosaic questions like "Where does Oberon live?" or "When describing a queen like Titania did Shakespeare wish to express political ideas?," now takes us into a precise social environment. We are present at the meeting point of two worlds, that of the workmen and the court, the world of wealth and elegance, and alleged sensitivity, the world of people who have had the leisure to cultivate fine sentiments and are now shown as insensitive and even disgusting in their superior attitude toward the poor.

At the beginning of the court scene we see our former heroes, who have spent the entire play involved in the theme of love, and would no doubt be quite capable of giving academic lectures on the subject, suddenly finding themselves plunged into a context which has apparently nothing to do with love (with their own love, since all their problems have been solved). Now they are in the context of a relationship with each other and with another social class, and they are at a loss. They do not realize that here too scorn eliminates love.

We see how well Shakespeare has situated everything. Athens in the *Dream* resembles our Athens in the sixties: the workmen, as they state in the first scene, are very much afraid of the authorities; if they commit the slightest error they will be hanged, and there is nothing comical about that. Indeed, they risk hanging as soon as they shed their anonymity. At the same time they are irresistibly attracted by the carrot of "sixpence a day" which will enable them to escape poverty. Yet their real motive is neither glory nor adventure nor money (that is made very clear and should guide the actors who perform this scene). Those simple men who have only ever worked with their hands apply to the use of the imagination exactly the same quality of love which traditionally underlies the relationship between a craftsman and his tools. That is what gives these scenes both their strength and their comic quality. These craftsmen make efforts which are grotesque in one sense because they push awkwardness to its limit, but at another level they set themselves to their task with such love that the meaning of their clumsy efforts changes before our eyes.

The spectators can easily decide to adopt the same attitude as the courtiers: to find all this quite simply ridiculous; to laugh with the complacency of people who quite confidently mock the efforts of others. Yet the audience is invited to take a step back: to feel it cannot quite identify with the court, with people who are too grand and too unkind. Little by little, we come to see that the craftsmen, who behave with little understanding but who approach their new job with love, are discovering theater — an imaginary world for them, toward which they instinctively feel great respect. In fact, the "mechanicals" scene is often misinterpreted because the actors forget to look at theater through innocent eyes, they take a professional actor's views of good or bad acting, and in so doing they diminish the mystery and the sense of magic felt by these amateurs, who are touching an extraordinary world with the tips of their fingers, a world which transcends their daily experience and which fills them with wonder.

We see this quite clearly in the part of the boy who plays the girl, Thisby.

At first sight this tough lad is irresistibly absurd, but by degrees, through his love for what he is doing, we discover what more is involved. In our production, the actor playing the part is a professional plumber, who only took to acting a short while ago. He well understands what is involved, what it means to feel this nameless and shapeless kind of love. This boy, himself new to theater, acts the part of someone who is new to theater. Through his conviction and his identification we discover that these awkward craftsmen, without knowing it, are teaching us a lesson — or it might be preferable to say that a lesson is being taught us through them. These craftsmen are able to make the connection between love for their trade and for a completely different task, whereas the courtiers are not capable of linking the love about which they talk so well with their simple role as spectators.

Nonetheless, little by little the courtiers become involved, even touched by the play within the play, and if one follows very closely what is there in the text we see that for a moment the situation is completely transformed. One of the central images of the play is a wall, which, at a given moment, vanishes. Its disappearance, to which Bottom draws our attention, is caused by an act of love. Shakespeare is showing us how love can pervade a situation and act as a transforming force.

The *Dream* touches lightly on the fundamental question of the transformations which may occur if certain things are better understood. It requires us to reflect on the nature of love. All the landscapes of love are thrown into relief, and we are given a particular social context through which the other situations can be measured. Through the subtlety of its language the play removes all kinds of barriers. It is therefore not a play which provokes resistance, or creates disturbance in the usual sense. Rival politicians could sit side by side at a performance of *A Midsummer Night's Dream* and each leave with the impression that the play fits his point of view perfectly. But if they give it a fine, sensitive attention they cannot fail to perceive a world just like their own, more and more riddled with contradictions and, like their own, waiting for that mysterious force, love, without which harmony will never return.

Samuel Taylor Coleridge (1772–1834)
ON HAMLET

Samuel Taylor Coleridge was the first modern critic of Shakespeare to develop powerful, original readings of the great plays. He visited atheneums and lyceums (institutions promoting learning) on both sides of the Atlantic delivering his lectures on Shakespeare, and his interpretations stimulated a new age of thoughtful criticism. His lecture on Hamlet *includes a careful reading of difficult lines, but it also centers on questions of the relationship of Shakespeare to his creation. Further, the mental state of Hamlet becomes of central interest to Coleridge and a basis of much of his observation.*

The seeming inconsistencies in the conduct and character of Hamlet have long exercised the conjectural ingenuity of critics; and, as we are always loath to suppose that the cause of defective apprehension is in ourselves, the mystery has been too commonly explained by the very easy process of setting it down as in fact inexplicable, and by resolving the phenomenon into a misgrowth or *lusus* of the capricious and irregular genius of Shakespeare. The shallow and stupid arrogance of these vulgar and indolent decisions I would fain do my best to expose. I believe the character of Hamlet may be traced to Shakespeare's deep and accurate science in mental philosophy. Indeed, that this character must have some connection with the common fundamental laws of our nature may be assumed from the fact that Hamlet has been the darling of every country in which the literature of England has been fostered. In order to understand him, it is essential that we should reflect on the constitution of our own minds. Man is distinguished from the brute animals in proportion as thought prevails over sense: but in the healthy processes of the mind, a balance is constantly maintained between the impressions from outward objects and the inward operations of the intellect: — for if there be an overbalance in the contemplative faculty, man thereby becomes the creature of mere meditation, and loses his natural power of action. Now one of Shakespeare's modes of creating characters is to conceive any one intellectual or moral faculty in morbid excess, and then to place himself, Shakespeare, thus mutilated or diseased, under given circumstances. In Hamlet he seems to have wished to exemplify the moral necessity of a due balance between our attention to the objects of our senses, and our meditation on the workings of our minds, — an *equilibrium* between the real and the imaginary worlds. In Hamlet this balance is disturbed: his thoughts, and the images of his fancy, are far more vivid than his actual perceptions, and his very perceptions, instantly passing through the *medium* of his contemplations, acquire, as they pass, a form and a color not naturally their own. Hence we see a great, an almost enormous, intellectual activity, and a proportionate aversion to real action, consequent upon it, with all its symptoms and accompanying qualities. This character Shakespeare places in circumstances, under which it is obliged to act on the spur of the moment: — Hamlet is brave and careless of death; but he vacillates from sensibility, and procrastinates from thought, and loses the power of action in the energy of resolve. Thus it is that this tragedy presents a direct contrast to that of Macbeth; the one proceeds with the utmost slowness, the other with a crowded and breathless rapidity.

The effect of this overbalance of the imaginative power is beautifully illustrated in the everlasting broodings and superfluous activities of Hamlet's mind, which, unseated from its healthy relation, is constantly occupied with the world within, and abstracted from the world without, — giving substance to shadows, and throwing a mist over all commonplace actualities. It is the nature of thought to be indefinite; — definiteness belongs to external imagery alone. Hence it is that the sense of sublimity arises, not from the sight of an outward object, but from the beholder's reflection upon it; — not from the sensuous impression, but from the imaginative reflex. Few have seen a celebrated waterfall without feeling something akin to disappointment: it is only subsequently that the image comes back full into the mind, and brings with it a train of grand or beautiful associations. Hamlet feels this; his senses are in a state of trance, and he looks upon external things as hieroglyphics. His soliloquy —

Oh! that this too, too solid flesh would melt, &c.

springs from that craving after the indefinite — for that which is not — which most easily besets men of genius; and the self-delusion common to this temper of mind is finely exemplified in the character which Hamlet gives of himself: —

> — It can not be
> But I am pigeon-livered, and lack gall
> To make oppression bitter.

He mistakes the seeing his chains for the breaking of them, delays action till action is of no use, and dies the victim of mere circumstance and accident. . . .

Act I, scene IV. The unimportant conversation with which this scene opens is a proof of Shakespeare's minute knowledge of human nature. It is a well-established fact, that on the brink of any serious enterprise, or event of moment, men almost invariably endeavor to elude the pressure of their own thoughts by turning aside to trivial objects and familiar circumstances: thus this dialogue on the platform begins with remarks on the coldness of the air, and inquiries, obliquely connected, indeed, with the expected hour of the visitation, but thrown out in a seeming vacuity of topics, as to the striking of the clock and so forth. The same desire to escape from the impending thought is carried on in Hamlet's account of, and moralizing on, the Danish custom of wassailing: he runs off from the particular to the universal, and in his repugnance to personal and individual concerns, escapes, as it were, from himself in generalizations, and smothers the impatience and uneasy feelings of the moment in abstract reasoning. Besides this, another purpose is answered; — for by thus entangling the attention of the audience in the nice distinctions and parenthetical sentences of this speech of Hamlet's, Shakespeare takes them completely by surprise on the appearance of the Ghost, which comes upon them in all the suddenness of its visionary character. Indeed, no modern writer would have dared, like Shakespeare, to have preceded this last visitation by two distinct appearances, — or could have contrived that the third should rise upon the former two in impressiveness and solemnity of interest.

But in addition to all the other excellences of Hamlet's speech concerning the wassail-music — so finely revealing the predominant idealism, the ratiocinative[1] meditativeness, of his character — it has the advantage of giving nature and probability to the impassioned continuity of the speech instantly directed to the Ghost. The *momentum* had been given to his mental activity; the full current of the thoughts and words had set in, and the very forgetfulness, in the fervor of his augmentation, of the purpose for which he was there, aided in preventing the appearance from benumbing the mind. Consequently, it acted as a new impulse, — a sudden stroke which increased the velocity of the body already in motion, whilst it altered the direction. The copresence of Horatio, Marcellus, and Bernardo is most judiciously contrived; for it renders the courage of Hamlet and his impetuous eloquence perfectly intelligible. The knowledge, — the unthought of consciousness, — the sensation, — of human auditors — of flesh and blood sympathists — acts as a support and a stimulation of *a tergo*, while the front of the mind, the whole consciousness of the speaker, is filled, yea, absorbed, by the apparition. Add too, that the apparition itself has by its previous appearances been brought nearer to a thing of this world. This accrescence[2] of objectivity

---

[1]**ratiocinative:** Reasoned.
[2]**accrescence:** Accumulation or concentration.

in a Ghost that yet retains all its ghostly attributes and fearful subjectivity, is truly wonderful.

Act I, scene v. Hamlet's speech: —

> O all you host of heaven! O earth! What else?
> And shall I couple hell? —

I remember nothing equal to this burst unless it be the first speech of Prometheus in the Greek drama, after the exit of Vulcan and the two Afrites. But Shakespeare alone could have produced the vow of Hamlet to make his memory a blank of all maxims and generalized truths, that "observation had copied there," — followed immediately by the speaker noting down the generalized fact,

> That one may smile, and smile, and be a villain!

> MARCELLUS: Hillo, ho, ho, my lord!
> HAMLET: Hillo, ho, ho, boy! come bird, come, &c.

This part of the scene after Hamlet's interview with the Ghost has been charged with an improbable eccentricity. But the truth is that after the mind has been stretched beyond its usual pitch and tone, it must either sink into exhaustion and inanity, or seek relief by change. It is thus well known, that persons conversant in deeds of cruelty contrive to escape from conscience by connecting something of the ludicrous with them, and by inventing grotesque terms and a certain technical phraseology to disguise the horror of their practices. Indeed, paradoxical as it may appear, the terrible by a law of the human mind always touches on the verge of the ludicrous. Both arise from the perception of something out of the common order of things — something, in fact, out of its place; and if from this we can abstract danger, the uncommonness will alone remain, and the sense of the ridiculous be excited. The close alliance of these opposites — they are not contraries — appears from the circumstance, that laughter is equally the expression of extreme anguish and horror as of joy: as there are tears of sorrow and tears of joy, so is there a laugh of terror and a laugh of merriment. These complex causes will naturally have produced in Hamlet the disposition to escape from his own feelings of the overwhelming and supernatural by a wild transition to the ludicrous, — a sort of cunning bravado, bordering on the flights of delirium. For you may, perhaps, observe that Hamlet's wildness is but half false; he plays that subtle trick of pretending to act only when he is very near really being what he acts.

Sigmund Freud (1856–1939)
HAMLET'S SCRUPLES

Sigmund Freud is the most celebrated psychiatrist of the twentieth century. He was especially interested in Greek myth, as his comments on Oedipus Rex *suggest.* Hamlet *is another play that has taken on mythic proportions for him, in part because Freud sees in Hamlet the operation of his famous theory of the Oedipus complex. Freud examines not only the play but the circumstances of the play to see to what extent it fulfills his theory.*

Another of the great creations of tragic poetry, Shakespeare's *Hamlet*, has its roots in the same soil as *Oedipus Rex*. But the changed treatment of the same material reveals the whole difference in the mental life of these two widely separated epochs of civilization: the secular advance of repression in the emotional life of mankind. In the *Oedipus* the child's wishful fantasy that underlies it is brought into the open and realized as it would be in a dream. In *Hamlet* it remains repressed; and — just as in the case of a neurosis — we only learn of its existence from its inhibiting consequences. Strangely enough, the overwhelming effect produced by the more modern tragedy has turned out to be compatible with the fact that people have remained completely in the dark as to the hero's character. The play is built up on Hamlet's hesitations over fulfilling the task of revenge that is assigned to him; but its text offers no reasons or motives for these hesitations and an immense variety of attempts at interpreting them have failed to produce a result. According to the view which was originated by Goethe and is still the prevailing one today, Hamlet represents the type of man whose power of direct action is paralyzed by an excessive development of his intellect. (He is "sicklied o'er with the pale cast of thought.") According to another view, the dramatist has tried to portray a pathologically irresolute character which might be classed as neurasthenic. The plot of the drama shows us, however, that Hamlet is far from being represented as a person incapable of taking any action. We see him doing so on two occasions: first in a sudden outburst of temper, when he runs his sword through the eavesdropper behind the arras, and secondly in a premeditated and even crafty fashion, when, with all the callousness of a Renaissance prince, he sends the two courtiers to the death that had been planned for himself. What is it, then, that inhibits him in fulfilling the task set him by his father's ghost? The answer, once again, is that it is the peculiar nature of the task. Hamlet is able to do anything — except take vengeance on the man who did away with his father and took that father's place with his mother, the man who shows him the repressed wishes of his own childhood realized. Thus the loathing which should drive him on to revenge is replaced in him by self-reproaches, by scruples of conscience, which remind him that he himself is literally no better than the sinner whom he is to punish. Here I have translated into conscious terms what was bound to remain unconscious in Hamlet's mind; and if anyone is inclined to call him a hysteric, I can only accept the fact as one that is implied by my interpretation. The distaste for sexuality expressed by Hamlet in his conversation with Ophelia fits in very well with this: the same distaste which was destined to take possession of the poet's mind more and more during the years that followed, and which reached its extreme expression in *Timon of Athens*. For it can of course only be the poet's own mind which confronts us in Hamlet. I observe in a book on Shakespeare by Georg Brandes (1896) a statement that *Hamlet* was written immediately after the death of Shakespeare's father (in 1601), that is, under the immediate impact of his bereavement and, as we may well assume, while his childhood feelings about his father had been freshly revived. It is known, too, that Shakespeare's own son who died at an early age bore the name of "Hamnet," which is identical with "Hamlet." Just as *Hamlet* deals with the relation of a son to his parents, so *Macbeth* (written at approximately the same period) is concerned with the subject of childlessness. But just as all neurotic symptoms, and, for that matter, dreams, are capable of being "overinterpreted" and indeed need to be, if they are to be fully understood, so all genuinely creative writings are the product of more than a single motive and more than a single impulse in the poet's mind, and are open to more than a single interpretation. In what I have written I have only attempted to interpret the deepest layer of impulses in the mind of the creative writer.

A. C. Bradley (1851–1935)
On Hamlet

Andrew Cecil Bradley was among the most distinguished English critics of literature at Oxford University before World War I. His lectures, gathered as Shakespearean Tragedy (1904), discuss Hamlet, Othello, King Lear, and Macbeth with a depth and range that have earned the book a reputation as the single most important work of criticism on the tragedies in the twentieth century. The following selection is from the end of his lectures on Hamlet, when he turns his thoughts to the Queen, the King, and the Ghost. He reminds us how powerful these minor characters are in our imagination.

The answers to two questions asked about the Queen are, it seems to me, practically certain. (1) She did not merely marry a second time with indecent haste; she was false to her husband while he lived. This is surely the most natural interpretation of the words of the Ghost (I, v), coming, as they do, before his account of the murder. And against this testimony what force has the objection that the queen in the "Murder of Gonzago" is not represented as an adulteress? Hamlet's mark in arranging the play scene was not his mother, whom besides he had been expressly ordered to spare (I, v).

(2) On the other hand, she was *not* privy to the murder of her husband, either before the deed or after it. There is no sign of her being so, and there are clear signs that she was not. The representation of the murder in the play scene does not move her; and when her husband starts from his throne, she innocently asks him, "How fares my lord?" In the interview with Hamlet, when her son says of his slaughter of Polonius,

"A bloody deed!" Almost as bad, good mother,
As kill a king and marry with his brother,

the astonishment of her repetition "As kill a king!" is evidently genuine; and, if it had not been so, she would never have had the hardihood to exclaim:

What have I done, that thou darest wag thy tongue
In noise so rude against me?

Further, it is most significant that when she and the King speak together alone, nothing that is said by her or to her implies her knowledge of the secret.

The Queen was not a badhearted woman, not at all the woman to think little of murder. But she had a soft animal nature, and was very dull and very shallow. She loved to be happy, like a sheep in the sun; and, to do her justice, it pleased her to see others happy, like more sheep in the sun. She never saw that drunkenness is disgusting till Hamlet told her so; and, though she knew that he considered her marriage "o'er-hasty" (II, II), she was untroubled by any shame at the feelings which had led to it. It was pleasant to sit upon her throne and see smiling faces round her, and foolish and unkind in Hamlet to persist in grieving for his father instead of marrying Ophelia and making everything comfortable. She was fond of Ophelia and genuinely attached to her son (though willing to see her lover exclude him from the throne); and, no doubt, she considered equality of rank a mere trifle compared with the claims of love. The belief at the bottom of her heart was that the world is a place constructed simply that people may be happy in it in a good-humored sensual fashion.

Her only chance was to be made unhappy. When affliction comes to her, the good in her nature struggles to the surface through the heavy mass of sloth. Like other faulty characters in Shakespeare's tragedies, she dies a better woman than she had lived. When Hamlet shows her what she has done she feels genuine remorse. It is true, Hamlet fears it will not last, and so at the end of the interview (III, IV) he adds a warning that, if she betrays him, she will ruin herself as well.[1] It is true too that there is no sign of her obeying Hamlet in breaking off her most intimate connection with the King. Still she does feel remorse; and she loves her son, and does not betray him. She gives her husband a false account of Polonius's death, and is silent about the appearance of the Ghost. She becomes miserable:

> To her sick soul, as sin's true nature is,
> Each toy seems prologue to some great amiss.

She shows spirit when Laertes raises the mob, and one respects her for standing up for her husband when she can do nothing to help her son. If she had sense to realize Hamlet's purpose, or the probability of the King's taking some desperate step to foil it, she must have suffered torture in those days. But perhaps she was too dull.

The last we see of her, at the fencing match, is most characteristic. She is perfectly serene. Things have slipped back into their groove, and she has no apprehensions. She is, however, disturbed and full of sympathy for her son, who is out of condition and pants and perspires. These are afflictions she can thoroughly feel for, though they are even more common than the death of a father. But then she meets her death because she cannot resist the wish to please her son by drinking to his success. And more: when she falls dying, and the King tries to make out that she is merely swooning at the sight of blood, she collects her energies to deny it and to warn Hamlet:

> No, no, the drink, the drink, — O my dear Hamlet, —
> The drink, the drink! I am poison'd.   (*Dies.*)

Was ever any other writer at once so pitiless and so just as Shakespeare? Did ever any other mingle the grotesque and the pathetic with a realism so daring and yet so true to "the modesty of nature"?

King Claudius rarely gets from the reader the attention he deserves. But he is very interesting, both psychologically and dramatically. On the one hand, he is not without respectable qualities. As a king he is courteous and never undignified; he performs his ceremonial duties efficiently; and he takes good care of the

---

[1] I.e., the King will kill *her* to make all sure.

national interests. He nowhere shows cowardice, and when Laertes and the mob force their way into the palace, he confronts a dangerous situation with coolness and address. His love for his ill-gotten wife seems to be quite genuine, and there is no ground for suspecting him of having used her as a mere means to the crown.[2] His conscience, though ineffective, is far from being dead. In spite of its reproaches he plots new crimes to ensure the prize of the old one; but still it makes him unhappy (III, I, III, III). Nor is he cruel or malevolent.

On the other hand, he is no tragic character. He had a small nature. If Hamlet may be trusted, he was a man of mean appearance — a mildewed ear, a toad, a bat; and he was also bloated by excess in drinking. People made mouths at him in contempt while his brother lived; and though, when he came to the throne, they spent large sums in buying his portrait, he evidently put little reliance on their loyalty. He was no villain of force, who thought of winning his brother's crown by a bold and open stroke, but a cut-purse who stole the diadem from a shelf and put it in his pocket. He had the inclination of natures physically weak and morally small toward intrigue and crooked dealing. His instinctive predilection was for poison: this was the means he used in his first murder, and he at once recurred to it when he had failed to get Hamlet executed by deputy. Though in danger he showed no cowardice, his first thought was always for himself.

> I like him not, nor stands it safe with *us*
> To let his madness range,

— these are the first words we hear him speak after the play scene. His first comment on the death of Polonius is

> It had been so with *us* had we been there

and his second is

> Alas, how shall this bloody deed be answered?
> It will be laid to *us*.

He was not, however, stupid, but rather quick-witted and adroit. He won the Queen partly indeed by presents (how pitifully characteristic of her!), but also by "witch-craft of his wit" or intellect. He seems to have been soft-spoken, ingratiating in manner, and given to smiling on the person he addressed ("that one may smile, and smile, and be a villain"). We see this in his speech to Laertes about the young man's desire to return to Paris (I, II). Hamlet scarcely ever speaks to him without an insult, but he never shows resentment, hardly even annoyance. He makes use of Laertes with great dexterity. He had evidently found that a clear head, a general complaisance, a willingness to bend and oblige where he could not overawe, would lead him to his objects — that he could trick men and manage them. Unfortunately he imagined he could trick something more than men.

This error, together with a decided trait of temperament, leads him to his ruin. He has a sanguine disposition. When first we see him, all has fallen out to his wishes, and he confidently looks forward to a happy life. He believes his

---

[2]I do not rely so much on his own statement to Laertes (IV, VII) as on the absence of contrary indications, on his tone in speaking to her, and on such signs as his mention of her in soliloquy (III, III).

secret to be absolutely safe, and he is quite ready to be kind to Hamlet, in whose melancholy he sees only excess of grief. He has no desire to see him leave the Court; he promises him his voice for the succession (I, II; III, II); he will be a father to him. Before long, indeed, he becomes very uneasy, and then more and more alarmed; but when, much later, he has contrived Hamlet's death in England, he has still no suspicion that he need not hope for happiness:

> till I know 'tis done,
> Howe'er my haps, my *joys* were ne'er begun.

Nay, his very last words show that he goes to death unchanged:

> Oh yet defend me, friends, I am but hurt [= wounded],

he cries, although in half a minute he is dead. That his crime has failed, and that it could do nothing else, never once comes home to him. He thinks he can overreach Heaven. When he is praying for pardon, he is all the while perfectly determined to keep his crown; and he knows it. More — it is one of the grimmest things in Shakespeare, but he puts such things so quietly that we are apt to miss them — when the King is praying for pardon for his first murder he has just made his final arrangements for a second, the murder of Hamlet. But he does not allude to that fact in his prayer. If Hamlet had really wished to kill him at a moment that had no relish of salvation in it, he had no need to wait.[3] So we are inclined to say; and yet it was not so. For this was the crisis for Claudius as well as Hamlet. He had better have died at once, before he had added to his guilt a share in the responsibility for all the woe and death that followed. And so, we may allow ourselves to say, here also Hamlet's indiscretion served him well. The power that shaped his end shaped the King's no less.

For — to return in conclusion to the action of the play — in all that happens or is done we seem to apprehend some vaster power. We do not define it, or even name it, or perhaps even say to ourselves that it is there; but our imagination is haunted by the sense of it, as it works its way through the deeds or the delays of men to its inevitable end. And most of all do we feel this in regard to Hamlet and the King. For these two, the one by his shrinking from his appointed task, and the other by efforts growing ever more feverish to rid himself of his enemy, seem to be bent on avoiding each other. But they cannot. Through devious paths, the very paths they take in order to escape, something is pushing them silently step by step toward one another, until they meet and it puts the sword into Hamlet's hand. He himself must die, for he needed this compulsion before he could fulfill the demand of destiny; but he *must* fulfill it. And the King too, turn and twist as he may, must reach the appointed goal, and is only hastening to it by the windings which seem to lead elsewhere. Concentration on the character of the hero is apt to withdraw our attention from this aspect of the drama; but in no other tragedy of Shakespeare's, not even in *Macbeth,* is this aspect so impressive.

I mention *Macbeth* for a further reason. In *Macbeth* and *Hamlet* not only is the feeling of a supreme power or destiny peculiarly marked, but it has also

---

[3]This also is quietly indicated. Hamlet spares the King, he says, because if the King is killed praying he will *go to heaven.* On Hamlet's departure, the King rises from his knees, and mutters:

> My words fly up, my thoughts remain below:
> Words without thoughts *never to heaven go.*

at times a peculiar tone, which may be called, in a sense, religious. I cannot make my meaning clear without using language too definite to describe truly the imaginative impression produced; but it is roughly true that, while we do not imagine the supreme power as a divine being who avenges crime, or as a providence which supernaturally interferes, our sense of it is influenced by the fact that Shakespeare uses current religious ideas here much more decidedly than in *Othello* or *King Lear*. The horror in Macbeth's soul is more than once represented as desperation at the thought that he is eternally "lost"; the same idea appears in the attempt of Claudius at repentance; and as *Hamlet* nears its close the "religious" tone of the tragedy is deepened in two ways. In the first place, "accident" is introduced into the plot in its barest and least dramatic form, when Hamlet is brought back to Denmark by the chance of the meeting with the pirate ship. This incident has been therefore severely criticized as a lame expedient,[4] but it appears probable that the "accident" is meant to impress the imagination as the very reverse of accidental, and with many readers it certainly does so. And that this was the intention is made the more likely by a second fact, the fact that in connection with the events of the voyage Shakespeare introduces that feeling, on Hamlet's part, of his being in the hands of Providence. The repeated expressions of this feeling are not, I have maintained, a sign that Hamlet has now formed a fixed resolution to do his duty forthwith; but their effect is to strengthen in the spectator the feeling that, whatever may become of Hamlet, and whether he wills it or not, his task will surely be accomplished, because it is the purpose of a power against which both he and his enemy are impotent, and which makes of them the instruments of its own will.

Observing this, we may remember another significant point of resemblance between *Hamlet* and *Macbeth*, the appearance in each play of a Ghost — a figure which seems quite in place in either, whereas it would seem utterly out of place in *Othello* or *King Lear*. Much might be said of the Ghost in *Hamlet*, but I confine myself to the matter which we are now considering. What is the effect of the appearance of the Ghost? And, in particular, why does Shakespeare make this Ghost so *majestical* a phantom, giving it that measured and solemn utterance, and that air of impersonal abstraction which forbids, for example, all expression of affection for Hamlet and checks in Hamlet the outburst of pity for his father? Whatever the intention may have been, the result is that the Ghost affects imagination not simply as the apparition of a dead king who desires the accomplishment of *his* purposes, but also as the representative of that hidden ultimate power, the messenger of divine justice set upon the expiation of offenses which it appeared impossible for man to discover and avenge, a reminder or a symbol of the connection of the limited world of ordinary experience with the vaster life of which it is but a partial appearance. And as, at the beginning of the play, we have this intimation, conveyed through the medium of the received religious idea of a soul come from purgatory, so at the end, conveyed through the similar idea of a soul carried by angels to its rest, we have an intimation of the same character, and a reminder that the apparent failure of Hamlet's life is not the ultimate truth concerning him.

If these various peculiarities of the tragedy are considered, it will be agreed that, while *Hamlet* certainly cannot be called in the specific sense a "religious

[4]The attempt to explain this meeting as prearranged by Hamlet is scarcely worth mention.

drama," there is in it nevertheless both a freer use of popular religious ideas, and a more decided, though always imaginative, intimation of a supreme power concerned in human evil and good, than can be found in any other of Shakespeare's tragedies. And this is probably one of the causes of the special popularity of this play, just as *Macbeth,* the tragedy which in these respects most nearly approaches it, has also the place next to it in general esteem.

T. S. Eliot (1888–1965)
HAMLET AND HIS PROBLEMS

T. S. Eliot not only was one of the most important poets of the modernist period in the twentieth century, but he was also an extremely interesting critic of Elizabethan literature. His several collections of essays have in some cases defined important critical terms that later readers have used to gain insight into great writers. One of those terms is developed here: the objective correlative, which Eliot feels is missing in Hamlet. *His argument is provocative and revealing.*

Few critics have ever admitted that *Hamlet* the play is the primary problem, and Hamlet the character only secondary. And Hamlet the character has had an especial temptation for that most dangerous type of critic: the critic with a mind which is naturally of the creative order, but which through some weakness in creative power exercises itself in criticism instead. These minds often find in Hamlet a vicarious existence for their own artistic realization. Such a mind had Goethe, who made of Hamlet a Werther; and such had Coleridge who made of Hamlet a Coleridge; and probably neither of these men in writing about Hamlet remembered that his first business was to study a work of art. The kind of criticism that Goethe and Coleridge produced, in writing of Hamlet, is the most misleading kind possible. For they both possessed unquestionable critical insight, and both make their critical aberrations the more plausible by the substitution — of their own Hamlet for Shakespeare's — which their creative gift effects. We should be thankful that Walter Pater[1] did not fix his attention on this play.

Two writers of our time, Mr. J. M. Robertson and Professor Stoll of the University of Minnesota, have issued small books which can be praised for moving in the other direction. Mr. Stoll performs a service in recalling to our attention the labors of the critics of the seventeenth and eighteenth centuries, observing that

> they knew less about psychology than more recent Hamlet critics, but they were nearer in spirit to Shakespeare's art; and as they insisted on the importance of the effect of the whole rather than on the importance of the leading character, they were nearer, in their old-fashioned way, to the secret of dramatic art in general.

Qua work of art, the work of art cannot be interpreted; there is nothing to interpret; we can only criticize it according to standards, in comparison to other

---

[1]**Walter Pater:** (1839–1894) English writer and critic. His writings were often morbidly violent.

works of art; and for "interpretation" the chief task is the presentation of relevant historical facts which the reader is not assumed to know. Mr. Robertson points out, very pertinently, how critics have failed in their "interpretation" of *Hamlet* by ignoring what ought to be very obvious: that *Hamlet* is a stratification, that it represents the efforts of a series of men, each making what he could out of the work of his predecessors. The *Hamlet* of Shakespeare will appear to us very differently if, instead of treating the whole action of the play as due to Shakespeare's design, we perceive his *Hamlet* to be superposed upon much cruder material which persists even in the final form.

We know that there was an older play by Thomas Kyd, that extraordinary dramatic (if not poetic) genius who was in all probability the author of two plays so dissimilar as the *Spanish Tragedy* and *Arden of Feversham;* and what this play was like we can guess from three clues: from the *Spanish Tragedy* itself, from the tale of Belleforest upon which Kyd's *Hamlet* must have been based, and from a version acted in Germany in Shakespeare's lifetime which bears strong evidence of having been adapted from the earlier, not from the later, play. From these three sources it is clear that in the earlier play the motive was a revenge motive simply; that the action or delay is caused, as in the *Spanish Tragedy,* solely by the difficulty of assassinating a monarch surrounded by guards; and that the "madness" of Hamlet was feigned in order to escape suspicion, and successfully. In the final play of Shakespeare, on the other hand, there is a motive which is more important than that of revenge, and which explicitly "blunts" the latter; the delay in revenge is unexplained on grounds of necessity or expediency; and the effect of the "madness" is not to lull but to arouse the king's suspicion. The alteration is not complete enough, however, to be convincing. Furthermore, there are verbal parallels so close to the *Spanish Tragedy* as to leave no doubt that in places Shakespeare was merely *revising* the text of Kyd. And finally there are unexplained scenes — the Polonius-Laertes and the Polonius-Reynaldo scenes — for which there is little excuse; these scenes are not in the verse style of Kyd, and not beyond doubt in the style of Shakespeare. These Mr. Robertson believes to be scenes in the original play of Kyd reworked by a third hand, perhaps Chapman,[2] before Shakespeare touched the play. And he concludes, with very strong show of reason, that the original play of Kyd was, like certain other revenge plays, in two parts of five acts each. The upshot of Mr. Robertson's examination is, we believe, irrefragable: that Shakespeare's *Hamlet,* so far as it is Shakespeare's, is a play dealing with the effect of a mother's guilt upon her son, and that Shakespeare was unable to impose this motive successfully upon the "intractable" material of the old play.

Of the intractability there can be no doubt. So far from being Shakespeare's masterpiece, the play is most certainly an artistic failure. In several ways the play is puzzling, and disquieting as is none of the others. Of all the plays it is the longest and is possibly the one on which Shakespeare spent most pains; and yet he has left in it superfluous and inconsistent scenes which even hasty revision should have noticed. The versification is variable. Lines like

> Look, the morn, in russet mantle clad,
> Walks o'er the dew of yon high eastern hill,

are of the Shakespeare of *Romeo and Juliet.* The lines in act V, scene II,

---

[2]**Chapman:** (?1559–1634) Elizabethan poet and playwright.

> Sir, in my heart there was a kind of fighting
> That would not let me sleep . . .
> Up from my cabin,
> My sea-grown scarf'd about me, in the dark
> Grop'd I to find out them: had my desire;
> Finger'd their packet;

are of his quite mature. Both workmanship and thought are in an unstable position. We are surely justified in attributing the play, with that other profoundly interesting play of "intractable" material and astonishing versification, *Measure for Measure,* to a period of crisis, after which follow the tragic successes which culminate in *Coriolanus. Coriolanus* may be not as "interesting" as *Hamlet,* but it is, with *Antony and Cleopatra,* Shakespeare's most assured artistic success. And probably more people have thought *Hamlet* a work of art because they found it interesting, than have found it interesting because it is a work of art. It is the *Mona Lisa* of literature.

The grounds of *Hamlet*'s failure are not immediately obvious. Mr. Robertson is undoubtedly correct in concluding that the essential emotion of the play is the feeling of a son toward a guilty mother:

> [Hamlet's] tone is that of one who has suffered tortures on the score of his mother's degradation. . . . The guilt of a mother is an almost intolerable motive for drama, but it had to be maintained and emphasized to supply a psychological solution, or rather a hint of one.

This, however, is by no means the whole story. It is not merely the "guilt of a mother" that cannot be handled as Shakespeare handled the suspicion of Othello, the infatuation of Antony, or the pride of Coriolanus. The subject might conceivably have expanded into a tragedy like these, intelligible, self-complete, in the sunlight. *Hamlet,* like the sonnets, is full of some stuff that the writer could not drag to light, contemplate, or manipulate into art. And when we search for this feeling, we find it, as in the sonnets, very difficult to localize. You cannot point to it in the speeches; indeed, if you examine the two famous soliloquies you see the versification of Shakespeare, but a content which might be claimed by another, perhaps by the author of the *Revenge of Bussy d'Ambois,*[3] act V, scene I. We find Shakespeare's Hamlet not in the action, not in any quotations that we might select, so much as in an unmistakable tone which is unmistakably not in the earlier play.

The only way of expressing emotion in the form of art is by finding an "objective correlative"; in other words, a set of objects, a situation, a chain of events which shall be the formula of that *particular* emotion; such that when the external facts, which must terminate in sensory experience, are given, the emotion is immediately evoked. If you examine any of Shakespeare's more successful tragedies, you will find this exact equivalence; you will find that the state of mind of Lady Macbeth walking in her sleep has been communicated to you by a skillful accumulation of imagined sensory impressions; the words of Macbeth on hearing of his wife's death strike us as if, given the sequence of events, these words were automatically released by the last event in the series. The artistic "inevitability" lies in this complete adequacy of the external to the emotion; and this is precisely what is deficient in *Hamlet.* Hamlet (the man) is

---

[3] *Revenge of Bussy d'Ambois:* Tragedy (1610–1611) by George Chapman, dealing with the reluctance of Clement d'Ambois to avenge his brother's death.

dominated by an emotion which is inexpressible, because it is in *excess* of the facts as they appear. And the supposed identity of Hamlet with his author is genuine to this point: that Hamlet's bafflement at the absence of objective equivalent to his feelings is a prolongation of the bafflement of his creator in the face of his artistic problem. Hamlet is up against the difficulty that his disgust is occasioned by his mother, but that his mother is not an adequte equivalent for it; his disgust envelops and exceeds her. It is thus a feeling which he cannot understand; he cannot objectify it, and it therefore remains to poison life and obstruct action. None of the possible actions can satisfy it; and nothing that Shakespeare can do with the plot can express Hamlet for him. And it must be noticed that the very nature of the *données* of the problem precludes objective equivalence. To have heightened the criminality of Gertrude would have been to provide the formula for a totally different emotion in Hamlet; it is just *because* her character is so negative and insignificant that she arouses in Hamlet the feeling which she is incapable of representing.

The "madness" of Hamlet lay to Shakespeare's hand; in the earlier play a simple ruse, and to the end, we may presume, understood as a ruse by the audience. For Shakespeare it is less than madness and more than feigned. The levity of Hamlet, his repetition of phrase, his puns, are not part of a deliberate plan of dissimulation, but a form of emotional relief. In the character Hamlet it is the buffoonery of an emotion which can find no outlet in action; in the dramatist it is the buffoonery of an emotion which he cannot express in art. The intense feeling, ecstatic or terrible, without an object or exceeding its object, is something which every person of sensibility has known; it is doubtless a subject of study for pathologists. It often occurs in adolescence: the ordinary person puts these feelings to sleep, or trims down his feelings to fit the business world; the artist keeps them alive by his ability to intensify the world to his emotions. The Hamlet of Laforgue[4] is an adolescent; the Hamlet of Shakespeare is not, he has not that explanation and excuse. We must simply admit that here Shakespeare tackled a problem which proved too much for him. Why he attempted it at all is an insoluble puzzle; under compulsion of what experience he attempted to express the inexpressibly horrible, we cannot ever know. We need a great many facts in his biography; and we should like to know whether, and when, and after or at the same time as what personal experience, he read Montaigne's *Apologie de Raimond Sebond*. We should have, finally, to know something which is by hypothesis unknowable, for we assume it to be an experience which, in the manner indicated, exceeded the facts. We should have to understand things which Shakespeare did not understand himself.

[4]**Laforgue:** (1860–1887) French poet who was an important influence on Eliot.

C. Walter Hodges
HAMLET'S GHOST

The drawing by C. Walter Hodges gives us an interesting possible reconstruction for the manner in which Hamlet's ghost could have entered and exited. We get a good idea of the resources of the Elizabethan stage from the illustration on page 318.

Restoration and Eighteenth-Century Drama

The Restoration: Rebirth of Drama

Theater in England continued to thrive after Shakespeare's death, with a host of successful playwrights, including John Webster (1580?–1638?), who emerged with two important plays: *The White Devil* (1609) and the much performed *Duchess of Malfi* (1613). But in 1642 long-standing religious and political conflicts between King Charles I and Parliament finally erupted into civil war, with the Parliament, under the influence of Puritanism, eventually winning.

The Puritans were religious extremists with narrow, specific values. They were essentially an emerging merchant class of well-to-do citizens who viewed the aristocracy as immoral wastrels. Theater for them was associated with both the aristocracy and the low life. Theatergoing was synonymous with wasting time and with immoral behavior, since by then the theaters were often a focus for immoral activity and the neighborhoods around the theaters were as unsavory as any in England. Under the Puritan government, the theaters were totally closed in England for almost twenty years. They became disused and when the new king, Charles II, was crowned in 1660, those that had not been converted to other uses had become completely outmoded.

As fate would have it, Charles II was sent with his mother and brother to the Continent in the early stages of the civil war. When Charles I was beheaded, the future king and his family were in France, where they were in a position to see the remarkable achievements of French comedy and French classical tragedy. Charles II developed a taste for theater that was to accompany him back to England. And when he returned in triumph to usher in the gay, exciting, and swashbuckling period known as the Restoration, he had new theaters built and plays written to fill them.

Theater on the Continent: Neoclassicism

Interaction between the leading European countries — England, Spain, and France — was sporadic at best in the seventeenth century because of intermittent wars among the nations, yet the development of theater in all three countries took similar turns throughout the early 1600s.

The Spanish developed, independently, a corral resembling the Elizabethan inn yard, in which they produced plays. This development may have been an accident of architecture — because of the widespread need for inns and for places to store horses — that permitted the symmetry of growth of the English Elizabethan and the Spanish Golden Age theaters.

The most important playwright of the Spanish theater was Lope de Vega (1562–1635), who is said to have written twelve hundred plays (seven hundred fifty survive). Many of them are relatively brief, and some are like the scenarios for the *commedia dell'arte*. But a good number are full-length and impressive works, such as *The King, The Greatest Alcalde*, and *The Gardener's Dog*.

The French became aware of Spanish achievements in the theater in the 1630s, and Pierre Corneille (1606–1684), who emerged as France's leading playwright of the time, adapted a play by de Vega that became one of his most important plays, *Le Cid*.

By the time Charles II took up residence in France in the 1640s, the French had developed a suave, polished, and intellectually demanding approach to drama. Corneille and the neoclassicists were part of a large movement in European culture and the arts that tried to codify the achievement of the ancients and emulate them. Qualities such as harmony, symmetry, balance in everything structural, and clear moral themes were most in evidence. NEOCLASSICISM privileged thought over feeling, so the thematic material in neoclassical drama was very important. The thematic material was sometimes political in nature, reflecting the political values of Augustan Rome — 27 BC to 17 AD — when Virgil lived, and when it was appropriate to think in terms of subordinating the self to the interests of the state. Dramatists focused on honor, moral integrity, self-sacrifice, and heroic political subjects, and the tragic stage took on the greatest apparent importance for the time.

In addition, the Aristotelian concepts of the unities of time, place, character, and action became central to the art of playwriting. A school of critics arose, who criticized by the rules. These "rules critics" demanded a perfect observance of the unities. In most cases the plays that satisfied them are now often thought of as static, cold, limited, and dull. Their perfection is seen today as rigid and emotionally icy.

Corneille eventually gave way to a much younger competitor, Jean Baptiste Racine (1639–1699), who brought the tradition of French tragedy to its fullest. Most of his plays are on classical subjects, beginning in 1667 with *Andromache*, continuing with *Britannicus* (1669), *Iphigenia* (1674), and *Mithridate* (1673), and ending in 1677 with his most famous and possibly best play, *Phaedra*.

Phaedra is a deeply passionate, deeply moral play centering on the love of Phaedra for her stepson, Hippolytus. Venus is responsible for her incestuous love — which is the playwright's way of saying that Phaedra is impelled by destiny, almost against her will.

The French stage, unlike the English, never substituted boys for female roles, and so plays such as *Phaedra* were opportunities for brilliant actresses. Phaedra, in particular, dominates the stage — she is a commanding and infinitely complex figure. It is no wonder that this play was a favorite of Sarah Bernhardt (1844–1923), one of France's greatest actresses.

French Comedy: Molière

At the same time as Racine commanded the tragic stage, Jean Baptiste Poquelin (1622–1673), known as Molière, was beginning his dominance of the comic stage. He was aware of Racine's achievements and applauded them strongly. His career began in a family-run theater company that spent most of its time touring the countryside beyond Paris. The plays the company developed were obviously influenced by some of the stock characters and situations of the *commedia dell'arte* style, but they also began to reflect Molière's own genius for composition.

King Louis XIV saw the company in 1658 and found it so much to his liking that he installed it in a theater and demanded to see more of its work. From that time until his death, Molière wrote, produced, and acted in one comedy after another, most of which have become part of the permanent repertoire of the French stage. Plays such as *The Misanthrope, The Miser, The Imaginary Invalid, The Bourgeois Gentleman,* and his satire on the theme of Puritanism, *Tartuffe,* are also staged all over the world.

Theater in England: Restoration Comedy of Manners

When the theaters reopened in England in the 1660s with the return of Charles II, it was clear that they could not survive merely by reviving older plays. Times had changed, England had suffered enormous upheaval, and the Puritan-dominated, theater-darkened past was quickly undone. The new age wanted glitter, excitement, sensuality, and dramatic dazzle. Tastes had changed so much that the audiences demanded new endings for old plays, such as Shakespeare's tragedies. They wanted upbeat comedies that would poke fun at the stuffed shirts of society and at old-fashioned institutions and fashions.

Several important physical changes took effect immediately. The new stages were in indoor theaters using artificial light. They could be operated year-round and they segregated people according to social class. The middle class sat in the orchestra before the proscenium-arched stage (Figure 5). The first level boxes against the walls were occupied by the upper classes, while the lower classes took the upper ranges of the balconies.

Figure 5. Proscenium arch

At the side of the APRON of the stage (a forward space not usually used by the actors) were several doors used as entrances and exits for some of the actors. These doors extended the stage somewhat forward, providing at times the convenience of the front space of the Roman stage. Because the stage was essentially broken into two parts, forward and rear, a character could come in through a door and then be whisked into the action and hidden within in a closet or beneath a bed (as was often the case).

Once women were permitted to take part in theater, actresses appeared who commanded the stage immediately. The actresses of the period were bright, witty, and charming and were often the most important "draw" for seventeenth-century audiences. Nell Gwynne (1650–1687), the most famous actress of her day, became one of the legends of the English stage.

Among England's most notable playwrights from 1660 to the early years of the eighteenth century were Aphra Behn (1640–1689), the first professional woman playwright on the English stage and author of *The Rover,* one of the most frequently performed plays of the period; William Wycherley (1640–1716), whose *The Plain Dealer,* adapted from Molière, is regarded as his best work; William Congreve (1670–1729), whose *The Way of the World* is usually said to epitomize the period; and Richard Brinsley Sheridan (1751–1816), whose *School for Scandal* is still bright, lively, and engaging for modern audiences.

The English playwrights produced a wide range of comedy, drawing on their understanding of their audience and their desire to entertain them with bright, gay, and witty work. The comedies of the period came to be known as comedies of manners because they reveal the foibles of the society that watched them. Society enjoyed laughing at itself. Although some of the English drama of the eighteenth century developed a moralistic tone and was often heavily classical, the earlier Restoration comedies of manners were less interested in reforming the society than in capitalizing on its faults.

Eighteenth-Century Drama

Eighteenth-century Europe absorbed much of the spirit of France and the French neoclassicists. England, like other European countries, began to see the effects of neoclassicism in the arts and literature. Emulation of classical art and classical values was common throughout Europe, and critics established standards of excellence in the arts to guarantee quality.

The most famous name in eighteenth-century English drama is David Garrick, the legendary actor and manager of the Drury Lane Theatre. The theaters, including his own, often reworked French drama and earlier English and Italian drama, but they began to develop a new SENTIMENTAL COMEDY to balance the neoclassical heroic tragedies of the period. It was a comedy in which the emotions of the audience were played on, manipulated, and exploited to arouse sympathy for the characters in the play.

Colley Cibber (1671–1757) is sometimes credited with beginning the sentimental comedy with his *Love's Last Shift* (1696). The play centers on Loveless, who wanders from his marriage only to find that his wife has disguised herself as a prostitute in order to win him back. As in all sentimental comedies, what the audience most wants is what it gets: a certain amount of tears, a contrasting amount of laughter, and a happy ending. Cibber was especially well known as an actor for his portrayal of fops, his way of poking satiric fun at his own society and its pretentions.

Sir Richard Steele (1672–1729) wrote one of the best known sentimental comedies in his *The Conscious Lovers* (1722). His play is among the few that are still occasionally performed. Steele's coauthor of *The Spectator*, Joseph Addison (1672–1719), also distinguished himself with his contribution to the heroic tragedy of the age, the long neoclassical *Cato*. The most often played tragedy of its day, it was considered to be the finest example of the moral, heroic style. Today it is not a playable drama because the action is too slow, the speeches too long, and the theme too obscure, although it is a perfect model of what the age preferred.

The audiences at the time seem to have preferred bright, amusing comedies of manners that often taunted wayward youth, overprotective parents, dishonest financial dealings, and social expectations. Their taste in tragedies veered toward a moralizing heroism that extolled the ideals of dedication to the values of the community, self-sacrifice on the part of the hero, and steadfastness in all moral activities.

William Congreve (1670–1729)
THE WAY OF THE WORLD   *1700*

Congreve had a brief career. His first play was produced when he was twenty-three and his last when he was thirty. His concern for satisfying his audiences before satisfying himself was not as strong as it apparently was in some other popular playwrights of the age. When at the beginning of the eighteenth century the public's taste began to shift from preferring sharply intellectual and witty comedy to a more sentimental and emotional comedy, his work did not shift with it. For that reason, his best play, *The Way of the World* (1700), was not well received. His reaction was to give up drama altogether.

Congreve was especially skilled at examining and analyzing conventional theater devices and putting them to good use. His interest in plot led him to conceive myriad complications. Indeed, in *The Way of the World* the complexities of plot and the interrelations of Fainall, Mirabell, Witwoud, Petulant, and Mrs. Millamant dazzled many audiences. From their very names we see that the characters are types cast into typical situations. Type characters have always been popular in all ages of comic drama, especially in the Restoration.

The genius of Congreve shows up in his witty REPARTEE, or quick replies. He is a master of the one-liner and the RIPOSTE, a sharp return in speech. In this sense, he reflects the interest of his audiences in brilliant exchanges. Wit was a rapier, to be used for the amusement of those intelligent enough to follow the exchanges. Seventeenth-century audiences respected intelligence in language, and the very young especially reveled in one-upping each other — and their seniors as well — by force of their wit. In the hands of Congreve, the use of wit served to critique the society.

The plot of *The Way of the World* centers on a sum of money that was the equivalent of a fortune in Congreve's time. Mirabell loves Millamant, who inherits six thousand pounds but who will receive another six thousand if she marries according to her aunt's wishes. Her aunt, Lady Wishfort (an older woman in the "full vigor of fifty-five"), feels betrayed by Mirabell, who pretended to be in love with her to get close to Millamant.

The plot to get Lady Wishfort to relent in her determination to marry Millamant to Sir Wilfull Witwoud is carried forth on a wave of disguise, deception, and comic mix-ups. The play proceeds breathlessly from beginning to end.

Mirabell and Millamant are the center of the comedy. They engage in classic jousts of wit in the tradition of Shakespeare's comic lovers, and Millamant demonstrates a great poise and a sense of appropriate modern behavior. She is not a shrinking violet or a mere innocent. She is every bit a match for Mirabell, and as a result their comic scenes are intense, involving, and revealing of the beliefs of Congreve's society.

The "contract" scene excerpted here is one of the funniest and most memorable in the play. Millamant and Mirabell discuss the terms of their marriage. He asks what conditions she intends to lay down for their marriage, and she responds that she wants to receive and send letters without his interference, to wear what she wants, "and choose conversation with regard only to my own taste; to have no obligation upon me to converse with wits that I don't like, because they are your acquaintance, or to be intimate with fools, because they may be your relations." Her other conditions ("to be sole empress of my tea-table") are amusing, especially to an audience who understands her social circumstances. She establishes herself as an independent woman.

Mirabell's counterdemands are couched in legalese: "I thank you. *Imprimis* then, I covenant that your acquaintance be general; that you admit no sworn confidante, or intimate of your own sex . . . No decoy-duck to wheedle you a fop." Millamant's response to his conditions is to ridicule and reject them. She has the upper hand.

Eventually, of course, everything comes out as any audience would wish: All deceptions are revealed; the proper lovers are joined; and the improbable complications are smoothed out. Based on the relationship between the sexes and on the impediments a sophisticated society can throw between them, it is virtually a timeless comedy. It has played to delighted audiences for almost three hundred years.

EXCERPT FROM ACT IV

MRS. MILLAMANT: If it is of no great importance, Sir Wilfull, you will oblige me to leave me; I have just now a little business —

SIR WILFULL: Enough, enough, cousin, yes, yes, all a case;[1] when you're disposed, when you're disposed. Now's as well as another time; and another time as well as now. All's one for that. Yes, yes, if your concerns call you, there's no haste; it will keep cold, as they say. Cousin, your servant. I think this door's locked.

MRS. MILLAMANT: You may go this way, sir.

SIR WILFULL: Your servant; then with your leave I'll return to my company.

MRS. MILLAMANT: Aye, aye; ha! ha! ha!
"Like Phoebus sung the no less am'rous boy."[2]

(*Enter* MIRABELL.)

MIRABELL: "Like Daphne she, as lovely and as coy."[3]
Do you lock yourself up from me, to make my search more curious?[4] Or is

---

[1] **all a case:** Idiomatic for "It's all the same."

[2] **"Like . . . boy":** The third line of Waller's *Story of Phoebus and Daphne, Applied,* referring to Apollo (Phoebus) and his pursuit of the nymph Daphne.

[3] **"Like . . . coy":** Line 4 from Waller's play. Mirabell completes the couplet begun by Millamant.

[4] **curious:** Difficult.

this pretty artifice contrived, to signify that here the chase must end and my pursuit be crowned, for you can fly no further?

MRS. MILLMANT: Vanity! No. I'll fly and be followed to the last moment. Though I am upon the very verge of matrimony, I expect you should solicit me as much as if I were wavering at the grate of a monastery, with one foot over the threshold. I'll be solicited to the very last, nay, and afterwards.

MIRABELL: What, after the last?

MRS. MILLAMANT: Oh, I should think I was poor and had nothing to bestow, if I were reduced to an inglorious ease and freed from the agreeable fatigues of solicitation.

MIRABELL: But do not you know that when favors are conferred upon instant and tedious solicitation, that they diminish in their value, and that both the giver loses the grace, and the receiver lessens his pleasure?

MRS. MILLAMANT: It may be in things of common application; but never sure in love. Oh, I hate a lover that can dare to think he draws a moment's air independent on the bounty of his mistress. There is not so impudent a thing in nature as the saucy look of an assured man, confident of success. The pedantic arrogance of a very husband has not so pragmatical[5] an air. Ah! I'll never marry, unless I am first made sure of my will and pleasure.

MIRABELL: Would you have 'em both before marriage? Or will you be contented with the first now, and stay for the other till after grace?

MRS. MILLAMANT: Ah! don't be impertinent. My dear liberty, shall I leave thee? My faithful solitude, my darling contemplation, must I bid you then adieu? Ay-h adieu, my morning thoughts, agreeable wakings, indolent slumbers, all ye *douceurs*,[6] ye *sommeils du matin*,[7] adieu. I can't do't, 'tis more than impossible. Positively, Mirabell, I'll lie abed in a morning as long as I please.

MIRABELL: Then I'll get up in a morning as early as I please.

MRS. MILLAMANT: Ah! idle creature, get up when you will. And d'ye hear, I won't be called names after I'm married; positively I won't be called names.

MIRABELL: Names!

MRS. MILLAMANT: Aye, as wife, spouse, my dear, joy, jewel, love, sweetheart, and the rest of that nauseous cant, in which men and their wives are so fulsomely familiar; I shall never bear that. Good Mirabell, don't let us be familiar or fond, nor kiss before folks, like my Lady Fadler and Sir Francis; nor go to Hyde Park together the first Sunday in a new chariot, to provoke eyes and whispers, and then never be seen there together again, as if we were proud of one another the first week, and ashamed of one another ever after. Let us never visit together, nor go to a play together. But let us be very strange and well bred; let us be as strange as if we had been married a great while, and as well bred as if we were not married at all.

MIRABELL: Have you any more conditions to offer? Hitherto your demands are pretty reasonable.

MRS. MILLAMANT: Trifles! As liberty to pay and receive visits to and from whom I please; to write and receive letters, without interrogatories or wry faces on your part; to wear what I please, and choose conversation with regard only to my own taste; to have no obligation upon me to converse with wits that I don't like, because they are your acquaintance, or to be intimate with fools, because they may be your relations. Come to dinner when I please; dine in my dressing-room when I'm out of humor, without giving a reason. To have my closet inviolate; to be sole empress of my tea-table, which you must never

---

[5]**pragmatical:** Officious.
[6]*douceurs:* Sweet pleasures.
[7]*sommeils du matin:* Morning sleeps.

presume to approach without first asking leave. And lastly, wherever I am, you shall always knock at the door before you come in. These articles subscribed, if I continue to endure you a little longer, I may by degrees dwindle into a wife.

MIRABELL: Your bill of fare is something advanced in this latter account. Well, have I liberty to offer conditions, that when you are dwindled into a wife, I may not be beyond measure enlarged into a husband?

MRS. MILLAMANT: You have free leave. Propose your utmost; speak and spare not.

MIRABELL: I thank you. *Imprimis*[8] then, I covenant[9] that your acquaintance be general; that you admit no sworn confidante, or intimate of your own sex; no she-friend to screen her affairs under your countenance, and tempt you to make trial of a mutual secrecy. No decoy-duck to wheedle[10] you a fop, scrambling[11] to the play in a mask; then bring you home in a pretended fright, when you think you shall be found out, and rail at me for missing the play, and disappointing the frolic which you had to pick me up and prove my constancy.

MRS. MILLAMANT: Detestable *imprimis!* I go to the play in a mask!

MIRABELL: *Item*,[12] I article that you continue to like your own face, as long as I shall; and while it passes current with me, that you endeavor not to new-coin it. To which end, together with all vizards[13] for the day, I prohibit all masks for the night, made of oiled skins and I know not what: hog's bones, hare's gall, pig-water, and the marrow of a roasted cat.[14] In short, I forbid all commerce with the gentlewoman in What-d'ye-call-it Court. *Item,* I shut my doors against all bawds with baskets, and pennyworths of muslin, china, fans, atlases,[15] etc. *Item,* when you shall be breeding —

MRS. MILLAMANT: Ah! name it not.

MIRABELL: Which may be presumed, with a blessing on our endeavors —

MRS. MILLAMANT: Odious endeavors!

MIRABELL: I denounce against all straitlacing, squeezing for a shape, till you mold my boy's head like a sugar-loaf, and instead of a man child, make me father to a crooked billet.[16] Lastly, to the dominion of the tea-table I submit, but with *proviso* that you exceed not in your province, but restrain yourself to native and simple tea-table drinks, as tea, chocolate, and coffee, as likewise to genuine and authorized tea-table talk, such as mending of fashions, spoiling reputations, railing at absent friends, and so forth; but that on no account you encroach upon the men's prerogative, and presume to drink healths, or toast fellows; for prevention of which, I banish all foreign forces, all auxiliaries to the tea-table, as orange-brandy, all aniseed, cinnamon, citron, and Barbadoes waters, together with ratafia and the most noble spirt of clary.[17] But for cowslip-wine, poppy-water, and all dormitives,[18] those I allow. These *provisos* admitted, in other things I may prove a tractable and complying husband.

[8]*Imprimis:* First.
[9]**covenant:** Decree.
[10]**wheedle:** Procure.
[11]**scrambling:** Going without suitable dignity.
[12]*Item:* Also
[13]**vizards:** Masks.
[14]**hog's bones . . . roasted cat:** All were ingredients in cosmetics.
[15]**atlases:** A kind of satin.
[16]**billet:** Stick.
[17]**orange-brandy . . . clary:** All these "auxiliaries" were cordials made of brandy, variously flavored.
[18]**dormitives:** Sedatives.

MRS. MILLAMANT: O horrid *provisos!* filthy strong-waters! I toast fellows, odious men! I hate your odious *provisos*.

MIRABELL: Then we're agreed. Shall I kiss your hand upon the contract? And here comes one to be a witness to the sealing of the deed.

(*Reenter Mrs. Fainall.*)

MRS. MILLAMANT: Fainall, what shall I do? Shall I have him? I think I must have him.

MRS. FAINALL: Aye, aye, take him, take him; what should you do?

MRS. MILLAMANT: Well then — I'll take my death I'm in a horrid fright. Fainall, I shall never say it. Well — I think — I'll endure you.

MRS. FAINALL: Fie! fie! have him, have him, and tell him so in plain terms; for I am sure you have a mind to him.

MRS. MILLAMANT: Are you? I think I have; and the horrid man looks as if he thought so too. Well, you ridiculous thing you, I'll have you; I won't be kissed, nor I won't be thanked. Here, kiss my hand, though. So, hold your tongue now; don't say a word.

MRS. FAINALL: Mirabell, there's a necessity for your obedience; you have neither time to talk nor stay. My mother is coming; and in my conscience, if she should see you, would fall into fits and maybe not recover, time enough to return to Sir Rowland, who, as Foible tells me, is in a fair way to succeed. Therefore spare your ecstasies for another occasion, and slip down the back stairs, where Foible waits to consult you.

MRS. MILLAMANT: Aye, go, go. In the meantime I suppose you have said something to please me.

MIRABELL: I am all obedience. (*Exit.*)

MRS. FAINALL: Yonder Sir Wilfull's drunk, and so noisy that my mother has been forced to leave Sir Rowland to appease him; but he answers her only with singing and drinking. What they may have done by this time I know not; but Petulant and he were upon quarreling as I came by.

MRS. MILLAMANT: Well, if Mirabell should not make a good husband, I am a lost thing; for I find I love him violently.

MRS. FAINALL: So it seems; for you mind not what's said to you. If you doubt him, you had best take up with Sir Wilfull.

MRS. MILLAMANT: How can you name that superannuated lubber? foh!

Molière

Molière (1622–1673, born Jean Baptiste Poquelin) came from a distinguished family attached to the glittering court of King Louis XIV, the Sun King. His father had purchased an appointment to the king and as a result both Molière and his family were familiar with the exciting court life of Paris. That is not to say that they were on intimate terms with the courtiers that surrounded the king. Molière's father was a furnisher and upholsterer to the king, so the family, while well-to-do and in a position of some power, was still apart from royalty and the privileged aristocracy.

Molière's education was exceptional. He went to Jesuit schools and spent more than five years at Collège de Clermont, which he left in 1641 having studied both the humanities and philosophy. His knowledge of philosophy was unusually deep and his background in the classics, including the classical philosophers, was exceptionally strong. He also took a degree in the law in 1641 at Orleans, but never practiced. His father's dream was that his son should inherit his appoinment as furnisher to the king, thereby guaranteeing himself a comfortable future.

That, however, was not to be. Instead of following the law, Molière decided at the last minute to abandon his secure future, change his name so as not to scandalize his family, and take up a career in the theater. He began by joining a company of actors run by the Béjart family. They established a theater based in Paris called the Illustre Théâtre. It was run by Madeleine Béjart, with whom Molière had a professional relationship until she died in 1672. Eventually Molière began writing plays but only after he had worked extensively as an actor.

The famed *commedia dell'arte* actor Tiberio Fiorillo, known as Scaramouche, was a close friend of Molière and may be responsible for his having chosen a career in theater. Scaramouche may have been part of the Illustre Théâtre, or he may have acted in it. Unfortunately, the Illustre Théâtre lasted only a year. It was one of several Parisian theatrical groups, and none of them prospered.

Eventually the company went bankrupt in 1644, and Molière, forced to leave Paris for about thirteen years, played in the provinces and remote towns. Before he left he had to be bailed out of debtors prison. What was left of the Béjart group merged with another company on tour, and Molière became director of that company. During this time he suffered most of the indignities typical of the traveling life, including impoverishment.

In October of 1658 Louis XIV saw Molière's troupe acting in one of his comedies at the Louvre. The royal court was so impressed with what it saw that Molière was installed in residence. His work remained, until his death in 1673, immensely popular and controversial. He acted in his own plays, produced his own plays, and wrote a succession of major works that are still favorites.

Because other companies envied his success and favor with the king, a number of "scandals" arose around some of his plays. The first play to invite controversy was *The School for Wives*, in which Arnolphe reacts in horror to the infidelities he sees in the wives all around him. He decides that his wife-to-be must be raised far from the world, where she will be ignorant of the wayward lives of the Parisians. A man who intends to seduce her tells Arnolphe (not knowing who he is) how he will get her out of Arnolphe's grasp. The play is highly comic, but groups of theatergoers protested that it was immoral and scandalous. In response Molière wrote *Criticism of the School for Wives*, in which the debate over the play is enacted. The result of the controversy was to lend an air of importance to comedy, since it was clear that the ensuing debate took on important social issues that comedy had tried to clarify.

One of Molière's most popular plays, *Tartuffe* (written in 1664; first performed in 1669), concerns a religious hypocrite who weasels his way into a noble household and then goes about trying to seduce its mistress. Molière envisioned the religious con man as his target in this play, and the name *Tartuffe* became shorthand for a religious hypocrite. The name still implies hypocrisy in France.

A French church group, the Society of the Holy Sacrament, thought it saw itself being portrayed in the title role and protested that the play was totally immoral and offensive. Its condemnation of the play effectively prevented it from being performed. Molière tried rewriting it; but the Society would not approve its production.

The Society was dissolved in a restructuring of the French church in 1669, and *Tartuffe* was finally permitted to be played to large audiences. Theatergoers loved the play and found great amusement in the sly, lecherous rogue who completely beguiles Orgon, the man who thinks Tartuffe is a great saint and who introduces him into his household. In most modern productions, Tartuffe is played broadly, almost as a caricature or a clown. Audiences find him amusing, scabrous, and irresistible. They usually find the play irresistible as well, since it involves crafty maneuvering on stage and complicated deceptions.

Among Molière's other successes are *The Miser* (1668), *The Bourgeois Gentleman* (1670), and his final play, *The Imaginary Invalid* (1673). He had a bad cough for most of the last decade of his life, and he often made it seem onstage like a stage cough. But it was genuine, and he died playing the title role of *The Imaginary Invalid* after its fourth performance.

THE MISANTHROPE

The Misanthrope (1666) in its own age was not the most successful of Molière's plays, but it has certainly been one of the most produced of all the plays in his canon. It is typical of his work in that it derives from a close and careful observation of French life and French manners. Recently English language audiences have been able to savor this play in Richard Wilbur's superb translation, which catches the sharpness of the French wit and the elegance of the verse — both hallmarks of French seventeenth-century drama.

In one sense the play is based on the type of improbability that marks Greek New Comedy: the romance of two very different people, Alceste, the misanthrope who speaks his mind and brashly tells people what he thinks of them, and Célimène, the coquette who rarely says what she thinks but who enjoys the attention of many suitors. She enjoys society and her capacity to dominate it. Alceste cannot abide society and its superficialities. At the end of the play he resolves to leave it.

One of the revelations of the play is that while Alceste and Célimène are different on the surface, beneath the surface they are similar. They are extreme types who behave extremely. Célimène carries coquetry to great lengths, leading on as many men as possible. Alceste is the epitome of a misanthrope, refusing to flatter people just to make them feel good. He says that he must tell the truth, and he does — even when it hurts, perhaps especially when it hurts. For him to fall in love with a coquette who must deceive those around her to keep herself at the center of attention is a wonderful comic irony. But beneath that irony lies the thought that Alceste himself may have flaws that are the opposites of Célimène's.

The ending of *The Misanthrope*, which is not typical of comedies, may have contributed to the disappointment of its initial audiences. Another comic playwright would have brought the two lovers together at the end. But Molière chose a more complex and, for some, a less satisfying ending. While two secondary characters marry, the main characters — Alceste and Célimène — agree to disagree and decide not to marry after all. Molière leaves his audience simply hoping that the two will change their minds. But as the play ends, the audience has no real reason to expect that they will come together.

This is a very French drama. The society is elegant, formal, and mannered. Molière knows every character and reveals each one totally. The surface elegance of the verse is such that the manners of the society seem polished, artificial, and ritualistic without being especially deceptive. The deception in this play is not at the center of things; the play does not depend on mix-ups and misapprehensions for its success. This in itself gives us a rather intriguing hint about Molière's intentions. The theme of honesty is at the play's center, but it is no simple thing to decide, in a social situation such as these characters enjoy, exactly how honest honesty should be or when honesty is the best policy. Alceste has one view and Célimène has another.

Molière enjoys pitting the values of Célimène and Alceste against one another, but it is clear that he does not want to offer sweeping or simple solutions to their conflict. Instead, he is content to leave his audience thinking and wondering.

Molière [*Jean Baptiste Poquelin*] (1622–1673)

THE MISANTHROPE   *1666*
TRANSLATED BY RICHARD WILBUR

Characters

ALCESTE, *in love with Célimène*
PHILINTE, *Alceste's friend*
ORONTE, *in love with Célimène*
CÉLIMÈNE, *Alceste's beloved*
ÉLIANTE, *Célimène's cousin*
ARSINOÉ, *a friend of Célimène's*
ACASTE }
CLITANDRE } *Marquesses*
BASQUE, *Célimène's servant*
A GUARD *of the Marshalsea*
DUBOIS, *Alceste's valet*

The scene throughout is in Célimène's house at Paris.

ACT I · Scene I [*Philinte, Alceste.*] _____

PHILINTE: Now, what's got into you?
ALCESTE (*seated*):   Kindly leave me alone.
PHILINTE: Come, come, what is it? This lugubrious
     tone . . .
ALCESTE: Leave me, I said; you spoil my solitude.
PHILINTE: Oh, listen to me, now, and don't be
     rude.
ALCESTE: I choose to be rude, Sir, and to be hard
5   of hearing.
PHILINTE: These ugly moods of yours are not
     endearing;
     Friends though we are, I really must insist . . .
ALCESTE (*abruptly rising*): Friends? Friends, you
     say? Well, cross me off your list.

I've been your friend till now, as you well know;
But after what I saw a moment ago   10
I tell you flatly that our ways must part.
I wish no place in a dishonest heart.
PHILINTE: Why, what have I done, Alceste? Is this
     quite just?
ALCESTE: My God, you ought to die of self-disgust.
I call your conduct inexcusable, Sir,   15
And every man of honor will concur.
I see you almost hug a man to death,
Exclaim for joy until you're out of breath,
And supplement these loving demonstrations
With endless offers, vows, and protestations;   20
Then when I ask you "Who was that?" I find
That you can barely bring his name to mind!
Once the man's back is turned, you cease to love
     him,
And speak with absolute indifference of him!
By God, I say it's base and scandalous   25
To falsify the heart's affections thus;
If I caught myself behaving in such a way,
I'd hang myself for shame, without delay.
PHILINTE: It hardly seems a hanging matter to me;
I hope that you will take it graciously   30
If I extend myself a slight reprieve,
And live a little longer, by your leave.
ALCESTE: How dare you joke about a crime so
     grave?
PHILINTE: What crime? How else are people to
     behave?
ALCESTE: I'd have them be sincere, and never part   35
With any word that isn't from the heart.

PHILINTE: When someone greets us with a show of
    pleasure,
    It's but polite to give him equal measure,
    Return his love the best that we know how,
40   And trade him offer for offer, vow for vow.
ALCESTE: No, no, this formula you'd have me
    follow,
    However fashionable, is false and hollow,
    And I despise the frenzied operations
    Of all these barterers of protestations,
45   These lavishers of meaningless embraces,
    These utterers of obliging commonplaces,
    Who court and flatter everyone on earth
    And praise the fool no less than the man of
    worth.
    Should you rejoice that someone fondles you,
50   Offers his love and service, swears to be true,
    And fills your ears with praises of your name,
    When to the first damned fop he'll say the same?
    No, no: no self-respecting heart would dream
    Of prizing so promiscuous an esteem;
55   However high the praise, there's nothing worse
    Than sharing honors with the universe.
    Esteem is founded on comparison:
    To honor all men is to honor none.
    Since you embrace this indiscriminate vice,
60   Your friendship comes at far too cheap a price;
    I spurn the easy tribute of a heart
    Which will not set the worthy man apart:
    I choose, Sir, to be chosen; and in fine,
    The friend of mankind is no friend of mine.
65 PHILINTE: But in polite society, custom decrees
    That we show certain outward courtesies. . . .
ALCESTE: Ah, no! we should condemn with all our
    force
    Such false and artificial intercourse.
    Let men behave like men; let them display
70   Their inmost hearts in everything they say;
    Let the heart speak, and let our sentiments
    Not mask themselves in silly compliments.
PHILINTE: In certain cases it would be uncouth
    And most absurd to speak the naked truth;
75   With all respect for your exalted notions,
    It's often best to veil one's true emotions.
    Wouldn't the social fabric come undone
    If we were wholly frank with everyone?
    Suppose you met with someone you couldn't
    bear;
80   Would you inform him of it then and there?
ALCESTE: Yes.
PHILINTE: Then you'd tell old Emilie it's
    pathetic
    The way she daubs her features with cosmetic
    And plays the gay coquette at sixty-four?
ALCESTE: I would.
PHILINTE: And you'd call Dorilas a bore,

And tell him every ear at court is lame   85
From hearing him brag about his noble name?
ALCESTE: Precisely.
PHILINTE: Ah, you're joking.
ALCESTE: *Au contraire:*°
    In this regard there's none I'd choose to spare.
    All are corrupt; there's nothing to be seen
    In court or town but aggravates my spleen.°   90
    I fall into deep gloom and melancholy
    When I survey the scene of human folly,
    Finding on every hand base flattery,
    Injustice, fraud, self-interest, treachery. . . .
    Ah, it's too much; mankind has grown so base,   95
    I mean to break with the whole human race.
PHILINTE: This philosophic rage is a bit extreme;
    You've no idea how comical you seem;
    Indeed, we're like those brothers in the play
    Called *School for Husbands,*° one of whom was
    prey . . .   100
ALCESTE: Enough, now! None of your stupid
    similes.
PHILINTE: Then let's have no more tirades, if you
    please.
    The world won't change, whatever you say or
    do;
    And since plain speaking means so much to you,
    I'll tell you plainly that by being frank   105
    You've earned the reputation of a crank,
    And that you're thought ridiculous when you
    rage
    And rant against the manners of the age.
ALCESTE: So much the better; just what I wish to
    hear.
    No news could be more grateful to my ear.   110
    All men are so detestable in my eyes,
    I should be sorry if they thought me wise.
PHILINTE: Your hatred's very sweeping, is it not?
ALCESTE: Quite right: I hate the whole degraded
    lot.
PHILINTE: Must all poor human creatures be
    embraced,   115
    Without distinction, by your vast distaste?
    Even in these bad times, there are surely a
    few . . .
ALCESTE: No, I include all men in one dim view:
    Some men I hate for being rogues: the others

---

87. *Au contraire:* On the contrary.   **90. spleen:** A body
organ thought to be the seat of melancholy, one of the four
humors of medieval physiology.   **100. *School for Husbands:***
A play by Molière (1661) in which two brothers, Sganarelle
and Ariste, are guardians of two orphan girls. Sganarelle
hopes to marry one of the girls, Isabelle, but she frees herself
by trickery from his domineering ways and marries someone
else.

I hate because they treat the rogues like
120   brothers,
And, lacking a virtuous scorn for what is vile,
Receive the villain with a complaisant smile.
Notice how tolerant people choose to be
Toward that bold rascal who's at law with me.
125 His social polish can't conceal his nature;
One sees at once that he's a treacherous
      creature;
No one could possibly be taken in
By those soft speeches and that sugary grin.
The whole world knows the shady means by
      which
130 The low-brow's grown so powerful and rich,
And risen to a rank so bright and high
That virtue can but blush, and merit sigh.
Whenever his name comes up in conversation,
None will defend his wretched reputation;
135 Call him knave, liar, scoundrel, and all the rest,
Each head will nod, and no one will protest.
And yet his smirk is seen in every house,
He's greeted everywhere with smiles and bows,
And when there's any honor that can be got
140 By pulling strings, he'll get it, like as not.
My God! It chills my heart to see the ways
Men come to terms with evil nowadays;
Sometimes, I swear, I'm moved to flee and find
Some desert land unfouled by humankind.
145 PHILINTE: Come, let's forget the follies of the times
And pardon mankind for its petty crimes;
Let's have an end of rantings and of railings,
And show some leniency toward human failings.
This world requires a pliant rectitude;
150 Too stern a virtue makes one stiff and rude;
Good sense views all extremes with detestation,
And bids us to be noble in moderation.
The rigid virtues of the ancient days
Are not for us; they jar with all our ways
155 And ask of us too lofty a perfection.
Wise men accept their times without objection,
And there's no greater folly, if you ask me,
Than trying to reform society.
Like you, I see each day a hundred and one
160 Unhandsome deeds that might be better done,
But still, for all the faults that meet my view,
I'm never known to storm and rave like you.
I take men as they are, or let them be,
And teach my soul to bear their frailty;
And whether in court or town, whatever the
165   scene,
My phlegm's° as philosophic as your spleen.

166. phlegm: In medieval physiology, the humor thought to
be cold and moist and to cause sluggishness.

ALCESTE: This phlegm which you so eloquently
      commend,
Does nothing ever rile it up, my friend?
Suppose some man you trust should
      treacherously
Conspire to rob you of your property,   170
And do his best to wreck your reputation?
Wouldn't you feel a certain indignation?
PHILINTE: Why, no. These faults of which you so
      complain
Are part of human nature, I maintain,
And it's no more a matter for disgust   175
That men are knavish, selfish and unjust,
Than that the vulture dines upon the dead,
And wolves are furious, and apes ill-bred.
ALCESTE: Shall I see myself betrayed, robbed, torn
      to bits,
And not . . . Oh, let's be still and rest our wits.   180
Enough of reasoning, now. I've had my fill.
PHILINTE: Indeed, you would do well, Sir, to be
      still.
Rage less at your opponent, and give some
      thought
To how you'll win this lawsuit that he's
      brought.
ALCESTE: I assure you I'll do nothing of the sort.   185
PHILINTE: Then who will plead your case before the
      court?
ALCESTE: Reason and right and justice will plead
      for me.
PHILINTE: Oh, Lord. What judges do you plan to
      see?
ALCESTE: Why, none. The justice of my cause is
      clear.
PHILINTE: Of course, man; but there's politics to
      fear. . . .   190
ALCESTE: No, I refuse to lift a hand. That's flat.
I'm either right, or wrong.
PHILINTE: Don't count on that.
ALCESTE: No, I'll do nothing.
PHILINTE: Your enemy's influence
Is great, you know . . .
ALCESTE: That makes no difference.
PHILINTE: It will; you'll see.
ALCESTE: Must honor bow to guile?   195
If so, I shall be proud to lose the trial.
PHILINTE: Oh, really . . .
ALCESTE: I'll discover by this case
Whether or not men are sufficiently base
And impudent and villainous and perverse
To do me wrong before the universe.   200
PHILINTE: What a man!
ALCESTE: Oh, I could wish, whatever the cost,
Just for the beauty of it, that my trial were lost.
PHILINTE: If people heard you talking so, Alceste,

They'd split their sides. Your name would be a
    jest.
ALCESTE: So much the worse for jesters.
205 PHILINTE: May I enquire
    Whether this rectitude you so admire,
    And these hard virtues you're enamored of
    Are qualities of the lady whom you love?
    It much surprises me that you, who seem
210   To view mankind with furious disesteem,
    Have yet found something to enchant your eyes
    Amidst a species which you so despise.
    And what is more amazing, I'm afraid,
    Is the most curious choice your heart has made.
215   The honest Éliante is fond of you,
    Arsinoé, the prude, admires you too;
    And yet your spirit's been perversely led
    To choose the flighty Célimène instead,
    Whose brittle malice and coquettish ways
220   So typify the manners of our days.
    How is it that the traits you most abhor
    Are bearable in this lady you adore?
    Are you so blind with love that you can't find
        them?
    Or do you contrive, in her case, not to mind
        them?
ALCESTE: My love for that young widow's not the
225   kind
    That can't perceive defects; no, I'm not blind.
    I see her faults, despite my ardent love,
    And all I see I fervently reprove.
    And yet I'm weak; for all her falsity,
230   That woman knows the art of pleasing me,
    And though I never cease complaining of her,
    I swear I cannot manage not to love her.
    Her charm outweighs her faults; I can but aim
    To cleanse her spirit in my love's pure flame.
PHILINTE: That's no small task; I wish you all
235   success.
    You think then that she loves you?
ALCESTE: Heavens, yes!
    I wouldn't love her did she not love me.
PHILINTE: Well, if her taste for you is plain to see,
    Why do these rivals cause you such despair?
ALCESTE: True love, Sir, is possessive, and cannot
240   bear
    To share with all the world. I'm here today
    To tell her she must send that mob away.
PHILINTE: If I were you, and had your choice to
    make,
    Éliante, her cousin, would be the one I'd take;
245   That honest heart, which cares for you alone,
    Would harmonize far better with your own.
ALCESTE: True, true: each day my reason tells me
    so;
    But reason doesn't rule in love, you know.

PHILINTE: I fear some bitter sorrow is in store;
    This love . . .

Scene II [*Oronte, Alceste, Philinte.*]

ORONTE (*to Alceste*): The servants told me at the
    door
    That Éliante and Célimène were out,
    But when I heard, dear Sir, that you were about,
    I came to say, without exaggeration,
    That I hold you in the vastest admiration,   5
    And that it's always been my dearest desire
    To be the friend of one I so admire.
    I hope to see my love of merit requited,
    And you and I in friendship's bond united.
    I'm sure you won't refuse — if I may be
        frank —   10
    A friend of my devotedness — and rank.

(*During this speech of Oronte's Alceste is abstracted
and seems unaware that he is being spoken to. He
only breaks off his reverie when Oronte says:*)

    It was for you, if you please, that my words
        were intended.
ALCESTE: For me, Sir?
ORONTE: Yes, for you. You're not offended?
ALCESTE: By no means. But this much surprises
    me. . . .
    The honor comes most unexpectedly. . . .   15
ORONTE: My high regard should not astonish you;
    The whole world feels the same. It is your due.
ALCESTE: Sir . . .
ORONTE: Why, in all the State there isn't one
    Can match your merits; they shine, Sir, like the
        sun.
ALCESTE: Sir . . .
ORONTE: You are higher in my estimation   20
    Than all that's most illustrious in the nation.
ALCESTE: Sir . . .
ORONTE: If I lie, may heaven strike me dead!
    To show you that I mean what I have said,
    Permit me, Sir, to embrace you most sincerely,
    And swear that I will prize our friendship dearly.   25
    Give me your hand. And now, Sir, if you
        choose,
    We'll make our vows.
ALCESTE: Sir . . .
ORONTE: What! You refuse?
ALCESTE: Sir, it's a very great honor you extend:
    But friendship is a sacred thing, my friend;
    It would be profanation to bestow   30
    The name of friend on one you hardly know.
    All parts are better played when well-rehearsed;
    Let's put off friendship, and get acquainted first.

We may discover it would be unwise
35 To try to make our natures harmonize.
ORONTE: By heaven! You're sagacious to the core;
This speech has made me admire you even more.
Let time, then, bring us closer day by day;
Meanwhile, I shall be yours in every way.
40 If, for example, there should be anything
You wish at court, I'll mention it to the King.
I have his ear, of course; it's quite well known
That I am much in favor with the throne.
In short, I am your servant. And now, dear
    friend,
45 Since you have such fine judgment, I intend
To please you, if I can, with a small sonnet
I wrote not long ago. Please comment on it,
And tell me whether I ought to publish it.
ALCESTE: You must excuse me, Sir; I'm hardly fit
To judge such matters.
ORONTE: Why not?
50 ALCESTE: I am, I fear,
Inclined to be unfashionably sincere.
ORONTE: Just what I ask; I'd take no satisfaction
In anything but your sincere reaction.
I beg you not to dream of being kind.
ALCESTE: Since you desire it, Sir, I'll speak my
55   mind.
ORONTE: *Sonnet*. It's a sonnet. . . . *Hope* . . . The
    poem's addressed
To a lady who wakened hopes within my breast.
Hope . . . this is not the pompous sort of thing,
Just modest little verses, with a tender ring.
ALCESTE: Well, we shall see.
60 ORONTE: *Hope* . . . I'm anxious to hear
Whether the style seems properly smooth and
    clear,
And whether the choice of words is good or
    bad.
ALCESTE: We'll see, we'll see.
ORONTE: Perhaps I ought to add
That it took me only a quarter-hour to write it.
65 ALCESTE: The time's irrelevant, Sir: kindly recite it.
ORONTE (*reading*): Hope comforts us awhile, 'tis
    true,
    Lulling our cares with careless laughter,
    And yet such joy is full of rue,
    My Phyllis, if nothing follows after.
PHILINTE: I'm charmed by this already; the style's
70   delightful.
ALCESTE (*sotto voce,*° *to Philinte*): How can you
    say that? Why, the thing is frightful.
ORONTE: Your fair face smiled on me awhile,
    But was it kindness so to enchant me?

71. [S.D.] *sotto voce:* In a soft voice or stage whisper.

    'Twould have been fairer not to smile,
    If hope was all you meant to grant me. 75
PHILINTE: What a clever thought! How handsomely
    you phrase it!
ALCESTE (*sotto voce, to Philinte*): You know the
    thing is trash. How dare you praise it?
ORONTE: If it's to be my passion's fate
    Thus everlastingly to wait,
    Then death will come to set me free: 80

    For death is fairer than the fair;
    Phyllis, to hope is to despair
    When one must hope eternally.
PHILINTE: The close is exquisite — full of feeling
    and grace.
ALCESTE (*sotto voce, aside*): Oh, blast the close;
    you'd better close your face 85
Before you send your lying soul to hell.
PHILINTE: I can't remember a poem I've liked so
    well.
ALCESTE (*sotto voce, aside*): Good Lord!
ORONTE (*to Philinte*):   I fear you're flattering
    me a bit.
PHILINTE: Oh, no!
ALCESTE (*sotto voce, aside*):   What else d'you
    call it, you hypocrite?
ORONTE (*to Alceste*): But you, Sir, keep your
    promise now: don't shrink 90
From telling me sincerely what you think.
ALCESTE: Sir, these are delicate matters; we all
    desire
To be told that we've the true poetic fire.
But once, to one whose name I shall not
    mention,
I said, regarding some verse of his invention, 95
That gentlemen should rigorously control
That itch to write which often afflicts the soul;
That one should curb the heady inclination
To publicize one's little avocation;
And that in showing off one's works of art 100
One often plays a very clownish part.
ORONTE: Are you suggesting in a devious way
That I ought not . . .
ALCESTE: Oh, that I do not say.
Further, I told him that no fault is worse
That that of writing frigid, lifeless verse, 105
And that the merest whisper of such a shame
Suffices to destroy a man's good name.
ORONTE: D'you mean to say my sonnet's dull and
    trite?
ALCESTE: I don't say that. But I went on to cite
Numerous cases of once-respected men 110
Who came to grief by taking up the pen.
ORONTE: And am I like them? Do I write so
    poorly?

ALCESTE: I don't say that. But I told this person, "Surely
　　You're under no necessity to compose;
115　Why you should wish to publish, heaven knows.
　　There's no excuse for printing tedious rot
　　Unless one writes for bread, as you do not.
　　Resist temptation, then, I beg of you;
　　Conceal your pastimes from the public view;
120　And don't give up, on any provocation,
　　Your present high and courtly reputation,
　　To purchase at a greedy printer's shop
　　The name of silly author and scribbling fop."
　　These were the points I tried to make him see.
125 ORONTE: I sense that they are also aimed at me;
　　But now — about my sonnet — I'd like to be told . . .
ALCESTE: Frankly, that sonnet should be pigeonholed.
　　You've chosen the worst models to imitate.
　　The style's unnatural. Let me illustrate:
　　For example, Your fair face smiled on me
130　awhile,
　　Followed by, 'Twould have been fairer not to smile!
　　Or this: such joy is full of rue;
　　Or this: For death is fairer than the fair;
　　Or, Phyllis, to hope is to despair
135　When one must hope eternally!
　　This artificial style, that's all the fashion,
　　Has neither taste, nor honesty, nor passion;
　　It's nothing but a sort of wordy play,
　　And nature never spoke in such a way.
140　What, in this shallow age, is not debased?
　　Our fathers, though less refined, had better taste;
　　I'd barter all that men admire today
　　For one old love song I shall try to say:
　　If the King had given me for my own
145　Paris, his citadel,
　　And I for that must leave alone
　　Her whom I love so well,
　　I'd say then to the Crown,
　　Take back your glittering town;
150　My darling is more fair, I swear,
　　My darling is more fair.
　　The rhyme's not rich, the style is rough and old,
　　But don't you see that it's the purest gold
　　Beside the tinsel nonsense now preferred,
155　And that there's passion in its every word?
　　If the King had given me for my own
　　Paris, his citadel,
　　And I for that must leave alone
　　Her whom I love so well,

160　I'd say then to the Crown,
　　Take back your glittering town;

My darling is more fair, I swear,
My darling is more fair.
There speaks a loving heart. (*To Philinte.*)
　　You're laughing, eh?
Laugh on, my precious wit. Whatever you say,   165
I hold that song's worth all the bibelots°
That people hail today with ah's and oh's.
ORONTE: And I maintain my sonnet's very good.
ALCESTE: It's not at all surprising that you should.
　　You have your reasons; permit me to have mine   170
　　For thinking that you cannot write a line.
ORONTE: Others have praised my sonnet to the skies.
ALCESTE: I lack their art of telling pleasant lies.
ORONTE: You seem to think you've got no end of wit.
ALCESTE: To praise your verse, I'd need still more of it.   175
ORONTE: I'm not in need of your approval, Sir.
ALCESTE: That's good; you couldn't have it if you were.
ORONTE: Come now, I'll lend you the subject of my sonnet;
　　I'd like to see you try to improve upon it.
ALCESTE: I might, by chance, write something just as shoddy;   180
　　But then I wouldn't show it to everybody.
ORONTE: You're most opinionated and conceited.
ALCESTE: Go find your flatterers, and be better treated.
ORONTE: Look here, my little fellow, pray watch your tone.
ALCESTE: My great big fellow, you'd better watch your own.   185
PHILINTE (*stepping between them*): Oh, please, please, gentlemen! This will never do.
ORONTE: The fault is mine, and I leave the field to you.
　　I am your servant, Sir, in every way.
ALCESTE: And I, Sir, am your most abject valet.

Scene III [*Philinte, Alceste.*]

PHILINTE: Well, as you see, sincerity in excess
　　Can get you into a very pretty mess;
　　Oronte was hungry for appreciation. . . .
ALCESTE: Don't speak to me.
PHILINTE:　　　　　　　　　What?
ALCESTE:　　　　　　　　　　　　No more conversation.
PHILINTE: Really, now . . .
ALCESTE:　　　　　　　Leave me alone.
PHILINTE:　　　　　　　　　　　If I . . .

166. **bibelots:** Trinkets.

5 ALCESTE: Out of my sight!
PHILINTE: But what . . .
ALCESTE: I won't listen.
PHILINTE: But . . .
ALCESTE: Silence!
PHILINTE: Now, is it polite . . .
ALCESTE: By heaven, I've had enough. Don't follow
    me.
PHILINTE: Ah, you're just joking. I'll keep you
    company.

ACT II • Scene I [*Alceste, Célimène.*] ————

ALCESTE: Shall I speak plainly, Madam? I confess
    Your conduct gives me infinite distress,
    And my resentment's grown too hot to smother.
    Soon, I foresee, we'll break with one another.
5   If I said otherwise, I should deceive you;
    Sooner or later, I shall be forced to leave you,
    And if I swore that we shall never part,
    I should misread the omens of my heart.
CÉLIMÈNE: You kindly saw me home, it would
    appear,
10 So as to pour invectives in my ear.
ALCESTE: I've no desire to quarrel. But I deplore
    Your inability to shut the door
    On all these suitors who beset you so.
    There's what annoys me, if you care to know.
CÉLIMÈNE: Is it my fault that all these men pursue
15   me?
    Am I to blame if they're attracted to me?
    And when they gently beg an audience,
    Ought I to take a stick and drive them hence?
ALCESTE: Madam, there's no necessity for a stick;
20 A less responsive heart would do the trick.
    Of your attractiveness I don't complain;
    But those your charms attract, you then detain
    By a most melting and receptive manner,
    And so enlist their hearts beneath your banner.
25 It's the agreeable hopes which you excite
    That keep these lovers round you day and night;
    Were they less liberally smiled upon,
    That sighing troop would very soon be gone.
    But tell me, Madam, why it is that lately
30 This man Clitandre interests you so greatly?
    Because of what high merits do you deem
    Him worthy of the honor of your esteem?
    Is it that your admiring glances linger
    On the splendidly long nail of his little finger?
35 Or do you share the general deep respect
    For the blond wig he chooses to affect?
    Are you in love with his embroidered hose?
    Do you adore his ribbons and his bows?
    Or is it that this paragon bewitches
40 Your tasteful eye with his vast German breeches?

Perhaps his giggle, or his falsetto voice,
    Makes him the latest gallant of your choice?
CÉLIMÈNE: You're much mistaken to resent him so.
    Why I put up with him you surely know:
    My lawsuit's very shortly to be tried,   45
    And I must have his influence on my side.
ALCESTE: Then lose your lawsuit, Madam, or let it
    drop;
    Don't torture me by humoring such a fop.
CÉLIMÈNE: You're jealous of the whole world, Sir.
ALCESTE: That's true,
    Since the whole world is well-received by you.   50
CÉLIMÈNE: That my good nature is so unconfined
    Should serve to pacify your jealous mind;
    Were I to smile on one, and scorn the rest,
    Then you might have some cause to be
        distressed.
ALCESTE: Well, if I mustn't be jealous, tell me, then, 55
    Just how I'm better treated than other men.
CÉLIMÈNE: You know you have my love. Will that
    not do?
ALCESTE: What proof have I that what you say is
    true?
CÉLIMÈNE: I would expect, Sir, that my having said
    it
    Might give the statement a sufficient credit.   60
ALCESTE: But how can I be sure that you don't tell
    The selfsame thing to other men as well?
CÉLIMÈNE: What a gallant speech! How flattering to
    me!
    What a sweet creature you make me out to be!
    Well then, to save you from the pangs of doubt,   65
    All that I've said I hereby cancel out;
    Now, none but yourself shall make a monkey of
        you:
    Are you content?
ALCESTE: Why, why am I doomed to love you?
    I swear that I shall bless the blissful hour
    When this poor heart's no longer in your power!   70
    I make no secret of it: I've done my best
    To exorcise this passion from my breast;
    But thus far all in vain; it will not go;
    It's for my sins that I must love you so.
CÉLIMÈNE: Your love for me is matchless, Sir; that's
    clear.   75
ALCESTE: Indeed, in all the world it has no peer;
    Words can't describe the nature of my passion,
    And no man ever loved in such a fashion.
CÉLIMÈNE: Yes, it's a brand-new fashion, I agree:
    You show your love by castigating me,   80
    And all your speeches are enraged and rude.
    I've never been so furiously wooed.
ALCESTE: Yet you could calm that fury, if you
    chose.
    Come, shall we bring our quarrels to a close?

85   Let's speak with open hearts, then, and
        begin . . .

Scene II [*Célimène, Alceste, Basque.*]

CÉLIMÈNE: What is it?
BASQUE: Acaste is here.
CÉLIMÈNE: Well, send him in.

Scene III [*Célimène, Alceste.*]

ALCESTE: What! Shall we never be alone at all?
    You're always ready to receive a call,
    And you can't bear, for ten ticks of the clock,
    Not to keep open house for all who knock.
CÉLIMÈNE: I couldn't refuse him: he'd be most put
5   out.
ALCESTE: Surely that's not worth worrying about.
CÉLIMÈNE: Acaste would never forgive me if he
        guessed
    That I consider him a dreadful pest.
ALCESTE: If he's a pest, why bother with him then?
CÉLIMÈNE: Heavens! One can't antagonize such
10   men;
    Why, they're the chartered gossips of the court,
    And have a say in things of every sort.
    One must receive them, and be full of charm;
    They're no great help, but they can do you
        harm,
15 And though your influence be ever so great,
    They're hardly the best people to alienate.
ALCESTE: I see, dear lady, that you could make a
        case
    For putting up with the whole human race;
    These friendships that you calculate so nicely . . .

Scene IV [*Alceste, Célimène, Basque.*]

BASQUE: Madam, Clitandre is here as well.
ALCESTE: Precisely.
CÉLIMÈNE: Where are you going?
ALCESTE: Elsewhere.
CÉLIMÈNE: Stay.
ALCESTE: No, no.
CÉLIMÈNE: Stay, Sir.
ALCESTE: I can't
CÉLIMÈNE: I wish it.
ALCESTE: No, I must go.
    I beg you, Madam, not to press the matter;
5   You know I have no taste for idle chatter.
CÉLIMÈNE: Stay. I command you.
ALCESTE: No, I cannot stay.
CÉLIMÈNE: Very well; you have my leave to go
        away.

Scene V [*Éliante, Philinte, Acaste, Clitandre, Alceste, Célimène, Basque.*]

ÉLIANTE (*to Célimène*): The Marquesses have kindly
        come to call.
    Were they announced?
CÉLIMÈNE: Yes. Basque, bring chairs for all.

(*Basque provides the chairs and exits.*)

    (*To Alceste.*) You haven't gone?
ALCESTE: No; and I shan't depart
    Till you decide who's foremost in your heart.
CÉLIMÈNE: Oh, hush.
ALCESTE: It's time to choose; take them, or me. 5
CÉLIMÈNE: You're mad.
ALCESTE: I'm not, as you shall shortly see.
CÉLIMÈNE: Oh?
ALCESTE: You'll decide.
CÉLIMÈNE: You're joking now, dear friend.
ALCESTE: No, no; you'll choose; my patience is at
        an end.
CLITANDRE: Madam, I come from court, where
        poor Cléonte
    Behaved like a perfect fool, as is his wont.   10
    Has he no friend to counsel him, I wonder,
    And teach him less unerringly to blunder?
CÉLIMÈNE: It's true, the man's a most accomplished
        dunce;
    His gauche behavior charms the eye at once;
    And every time one sees him, on my word,   15
    His manner's grown a trifle more absurd.
ACASTE: Speaking of dunces, I've just now
        conversed
    With old Damon, who's one of the very worst;
    I stood a lifetime in the broiling sun
    Before his dreary monologue was done.   20
CÉLIMÈNE: Oh, he's a wondrous talker, and has the
        power
    To tell you nothing hour after hour:
    If, by mistake, he ever came to the point,
    The shock would put his jawbone out of joint.
ÉLIANTE (*to Philinte*): The conversation takes its
        usual turn,   25
    And all our dear friends' ears will shortly burn.
CLITANDRE: Timante's a character, Madam.
CÉLIMÈNE: Isn't he, though?
    A man of mystery from top to toe,
    Who moves about in a romantic mist
    On secret missions which do not exist.   30
    His talk is full of eyebrows and grimaces;
    How tired one gets of his momentous faces;
    He's always whispering something confidential
    Which turns out to be quite inconsequential;
    Nothing's too slight for him to mystify;   35
    He even whispers when he says "good-by."

ACASTE: Tell us about Géralde.

CÉLIMÈNE: That tiresome ass.
   He mixes only with the titled class,
   And fawns on dukes and princes, and is bored
40   With anyone who's not at least a lord.
   The man's obsessed with rank, and his
      discourses
   Are all of hounds and carriages and horses;
   He uses Christian names with all the great,
   And the word Milord, with him, is out of date.

45 CLITANDRE: He's very taken with Bélisc, I hear.

CÉLIMÈNE: She is the dreariest company, poor dear.
   Whenever she comes to call, I grope about
   To find some topic which will draw her out,
   But, owing to her dry and faint replies,
50   The conversation wilts, and droops, and dies.
   In vain one hopes to animate her face
   By mentioning the ultimate commonplace;
   But sun or shower, even hail or frost
   Are matters she can instantly exhaust.
55   Meanwhile her visit, painful though it is,
   Drags on and on through mute eternities,
   And though you ask the time, and yawn, and
      yawn,
   She sits there like a stone and won't be gone.

ACASTE: Now for Adraste.

CÉLIMÈNE: Oh, that conceited elf
60   Has a gigantic passion for himself;
   He rails against the court, and cannot bear it
   That none will recognize his hidden merit;
   All honors given to others give offense
   To his imaginary excellence.

CLITANDRE: What about young Cléon? His house,
65   they say,
   Is full of the best society, night and day.

CÉLIMÈNE: His cook has made him popular, not he:
   It's Cléon's table that people come to see.

ÉLIANTE: He gives a splendid dinner, you must
   admit.

70 CÉLIMÈNE: But must he serve himself along with it?
   For my taste, he's a most insipid dish
   Whose presence sours the wine and spoils the
      fish.

PHILINTE: Damis, his uncle is admired no end.
   What's your opinion, Madam?

CÉLIMÈNE: Why, he's my friend.

PHILINTE: He seems a decent fellow, and rather
75   clever.

CÉLIMÈNE: He works too hard at cleverness,
   however.
   I hate to see him sweat and struggle so
   To fill his conversation with *bons mots*.°
   Since he's decided to become a wit

His taste's so pure that nothing pleases it;   80
He scolds at all the latest books and plays,
Thinking that wit must never stoop to praise,
That finding fault's a sign of intellect,
That all appreciation is abject,
And that by damning everything in sight   85
One shows oneself in a distinguished light.
He's scornful even of our conversations:
Their trivial nature sorely tries his patience;
He folds his arms, and stands above the battle,
And listens sadly to our childish prattle.   90

ACASTE: Wonderful, Madam! You've hit him off
   precisely.

CLITANDRE: No one can sketch a character so
   nicely.

ALCESTE: How bravely, Sirs, you cut and thrust at
   all
   These absent fools, till one by one they fall:
   But let one come in sight, and you'll at once   95
   Embrace the man you lately called a dunce,
   Telling him in a tone sincere and fervent
   How proud you are to be his humble servant.

CLITANDRE: Why pick on us? *Madame's* been
   speaking, Sir.
   And you should quarrel, if you must, with her.   100

ALCESTE: No, no, by God, the fault is yours,
   because
   You lead her on with laughter and applause,
   And make her think that she's the more
      delightful
   The more her talk is scandalous and spiteful.
   Oh, she would stoop to malice far, far less   105
   If no such claque approved her cleverness.
   It's flatterers like you whose foolish praise
   Nourishes all the vices of these days.

PHILINTE: But why protest when someone ridicules
   Those you'd condemn, yourself, as knaves or
      fools?   110

CÉLIMÈNE: Why, Sir? Because he loves to make a
   fuss.
   You don't expect him to agree with us,
   When there's an opportunity to express
   His heaven-sent spirit of contrariness?
   What other people think, he can't abide;   115
   Whatever they say, he's on the other side;
   He lives in deadly terror of agreeing;
   'Twould make him seem an ordinary being.
   Indeed, he's so in love with contradiction,
   He'll turn against his most profound conviction   120
   And with a furious eloquence deplore it,
   If only someone else is speaking for it.

ALCESTE: Go on, dear lady, mock me as you please;
   You have your audience in ecstasies.

PHILINTE: But what she says is true: you have a
   way   125

----

78. ***bons mots:*** Clever remarks, witticisms.

Of bridling at whatever people say;
Whether they praise or blame, your angry spirit
Is equally unsatisfied to hear it.
ALCESTE: Men, Sir, are always wrong, and that's
    the reason
130 That righteous anger's never out of season;
All that I hear in all their conversation
Is flattering praise or reckless condemnation.
CÉLIMÈNE: But . . .
ALCESTE: No, no, Madam, I am forced to state
That you have pleasures which I deprecate,
135 And that these others, here, are much to blame
For nourishing the faults which are your shame.
CLITANDRE: I shan't defend myself, Sir; but I vow
I'd thought this lady faultless until now.
ACASTE: I see her charms and graces, which are
    many;
140 But as for faults, I've never noticed any.
ALCESTE: I see them, Sir; and rather than ignore
    them,
I strenuously criticize her for them.
The more one loves, the more one should object
To every blemish, every least defect.
145 Were I this lady, I would soon get rid
Of lovers who approved of all I did,
And by their slack indulgence and applause
Endorsed my follies and excused my flaws.
CÉLIMÈNE: If all hearts beat according to your
    measure,
150 The dawn of love would be the end of pleasure;
And love would find its perfect consummation
In ecstasies of rage and reprobation.
ÉLIANTE: Love, as a rule, affects men otherwise,
And lovers rarely love to criticize.
155 They see their lady as a charming blur,
And find all things commendable in her.
If she has any blemish, fault, or shame,
They will redeem it by a pleasing name.
The pale-faced lady's lily-white, perforce;
160 The swarthy one's a sweet brunette, of course;
The spindly lady has a slender grace;
The fat one has a most majestic pace;
The plain one, with her dress in disarray,
They classify as *beauté négligée;°*
165 The hulking one's a goddess in their eyes,
The dwarf, a concentrate of Paradise;
The haughty lady has a noble mind;
The mean one's witty, and the dull one's kind;
The chatterbox has liveliness and verve,
170 The mute one has a virtuous reserve.
So lovers manage, in their passion's cause,
To love their ladies even for their flaws.
ALCESTE: But I still say . . .

164. *beauté négligée:* Slovenly beauty.

CÉLIMÈNE: I think it would be nice
To stroll around the gallery once or twice.
What! You're not going, Sirs?
CLITANDRE AND ACASTE: No, Madam, no.   175
ALCESTE: You seem to be in terror lest they go.
Do what you will, Sirs; leave, or linger on,
But I shan't go till after you are gone.
ACASTE: I'm free to linger, unless I should perceive
Madame is tired, and wishes me to leave.   180
CLITANDRE: And as for me, I needn't go today
Until the hour of the King's *coucher.°*
CÉLIMÈNE (*to Alceste*): You're joking, surely?
ALCESTE: Not in the least; we'll see
Whether you'd rather part with them, or me.

Scene VI [*Alceste, Célimène, Éliante, Acaste, Philinte, Clitandre, Basque.*]

BASQUE (*to Alceste*): Sir, there's a fellow here who
    bids me state
That he must see you, and that it can't wait.
ALCESTE: Tell him that I have no such pressing
    affairs.
BASQUE: It's a long tailcoat that this fellow wears,
With gold all over.
CÉLIMÈNE (*to Alceste*):   You'd best go down
    and see.   5
Or — have him enter.

Scene VII [*Alceste, Célimène, Éliante, Acaste, Philinte, Clitandre, Guard.*]

ALCESTE (*confronting the Guard*):   Well, what
    do you want with me?
Come in, Sir.
GUARD: I've a word, Sir, for your ear.
ALCESTE: Speak it aloud, Sir; I shall strive to hear.
GUARD: The Marshals have instructed me to say
You must report to them without delay.   5
ALCESTE: Who? Me, Sir?
GUARD: Yes, Sir; you.
ALCESTE: But what do they want?
PHILINTE (*to Alceste*): To scotch your silly quarrel
    with Oronte.
CÉLIMÈNE (*to Philinte*): What quarrel?
PHILINTE: Oronte and he have fallen out
Over some verse he spoke his mind about;
The Marshals wish to arbitrate the matter.   10
ALCESTE: Never shall I equivocate or flatter!
PHILINTE: You'd best obey their summons; come,
    let's go.

182. the King's *coucher:* The King's bedtime, a ceremonial
occasion.

ALCESTE: How can they mend our quarrel, I'd like
to know?
Am I to make a cowardly retraction,
15   And praise those jingles to his satisfaction?
I'll not recant; I've judged that sonnet rightly.
It's bad.
PHILINTE: But you might say so more
politely. . . .
ALCESTE: I'll not back down; his verses make me
sick.
PHILINTE: If only you could be more politic!
But come, let's go.
20   ALCESTE: I'll go, but I won't unsay
A single word.
PHILINTE: Well, let's be on our way.
ALCESTE: Till I am ordered by my lord the King
To praise that poem, I shall say the thing
Is scandalous, by God, and that the poet
Ought to be hanged for having the nerve to
25   show it.

(*To Clitandre and Acaste, who are laughing.*)

By heaven, Sirs, I really didn't know
That I was being humorous.
CÉLIMÈNE: Go, Sir, go;
Settle your business.
ALCESTE: I shall, and when I'm through,
I shall return to settle things with you.

ACT III · Scene I [*Clitandre, Acaste.*] ————

CLITANDRE: Dear Marquess, how contented you
appear;
All things delight you, nothing mars your cheer.
Can you, in perfect honesty, declare
That you've a right to be so debonair?
5   ACASTE: By Jove, when I survey myself, I find
No cause whatever for distress of mind.
I'm young and rich; I can in modesty
Lay claim to an exalted pedigree;
And owing to my name and my condition
10   I shall not want for honors and position.
Then as to courage, that most precious trait,
I seem to have it, as was proved of late
Upon the field of honor, where my bearing,
They say, was very cool and rather daring.
15   I've wit, of course; and taste in such perfection
That I can judge without the least reflection,
And at the theater, which is my delight,
Can make or break a play on opening night,
And lead the crowd in hisses or bravos,
20   And generally be known as one who knows.
I'm clever, handsome, gracefully polite;
My waist is small, my teeth are strong and
white;

As for my dress, the world's astonished eyes
Assure me that I bear away the prize.
I find myself in favor everywhere,   25
Honored by men, and worshiped by the fair;
And since these things are so, it seems to me
I'm justified in my complacency.
CLITANDRE: Well, if so many ladies hold you dear,
Why do you press a hopeless courtship here?   30
ACASTE: Hopeless, you say? I'm not the sort of fool
That likes his ladies difficult and cool.
Men who are awkward, shy, and peasantish
May pine for heartless beauties, if they wish,
Grovel before them, bear their cruelties,   35
Woo them with tears and sighs and bended
knees,
And hope by dogged faithfulness to gain
What their poor merits never could obtain.
For men like me, however, it makes no sense
To love on trust, and foot the whole expense.   40
Whatever any lady's merits be,
I think, thank God, that I'm as choice as she;
That if my heart is kind enough to burn
For her, she owes me something in return;
And that in any proper love affair   45
The partners must invest an equal share.
CLITANDRE: You think, then, that our hostess
favors you?
ACASTE: I've reason to believe that that is true.
CLITANDRE: How did you come to such a mad
conclusion?
You're blind, dear fellow. This is sheer delusion. 50
ACASTE: All right, then: I'm deluded and I'm blind.
CLITANDRE: Whatever put the notion in your mind?
ACASTE: Delusion.
CLITANDRE: What persuades you that you're
right?
ACASTE: I'm blind.
CLITANDRE: But have you any proofs to cite?
ACASTE: I tell you I'm deluded.
CLITANDRE: Have you, then,   55
Received some secret pledge from Célimène?
ACASTE: Oh, no: she scorns me.
CLITANDRE: Tell me the truth, I beg.
ACASTE: She just can't bear me.
CLITANDRE: Ah, don't pull my leg.
Tell me what hope she's given you, I pray.
ACASTE: I'm hopeless, and it's you who win the
day.   60
She hates me thoroughly, and I'm so vexed
I mean to hang myself on Tuesday next.
CLITANDRE: Dear Marquess, let us have an
armistice
And make a treaty. What do you say to this?
If ever one of us can plainly prove   65
That Célimène encourages his love,

The other must abandon hope, and yield,
And leave him in possession of the field.
ACASTE: Now, there's a bargain that appeals to me;
70   With all my heart, dear Marquess, I agree.
But hush.

Scene II [*Célimène, Acaste, Clitandre.*]

CÉLIMÈNE: Still here?
CLITANDRE: 'Twas love that stayed our feet.
CÉLIMÈNE: I think I heard a carriage in the street.
Whose is it? D'you know?

Scene III [*Célimène, Acaste, Clitandre, Basque.*]

BASQUE: Arsinoé is here,
Madame.
CÉLIMÈNE: Arsinoé, you say? Oh, dear.
BASQUE: Éliante is entertaining her below.
CÉLIMÈNE: What brings the creature here, I'd like
to know?
ACASTE: They say she's dreadfully prudish, but in
5   fact
I think her piety . . .
CÉLIMÈNE: It's all an act.
At heart she's worldly, and her poor success
In snaring men explains her prudishness.
It breaks her heart to see the beaux and gallants
10   Engrossed by other women's charms and talents,
And so she's always in a jealous rage
Against the faulty standards of the age.
She lets the world believe that she's a prude
To justify her loveless solitude,
15   And strives to put a brand of moral shame
On all the graces that she cannot claim.
But still she'd love a lover; and Alceste
Appears to be the one she'd love the best.
His visits here are poison to her pride;
20   She seems to think I've lured him from her side;
And everywhere, at court or in the town,
The spiteful, envious woman runs me down.
In short, she's just as stupid as can be,
Vicious and arrogant in the last degree,
25   And . . .

Scene IV [*Arsinoé, Célimène, Clitandre, Acaste.*]

CÉLIMÈNE: Ah! What happy chance has
brought you here?
I've thought about you ever so much, my dear.
ARSINOÉ: I've come to tell you something you
should know.
CÉLIMÈNE: How good of you to think of doing so!

(*Clitandre and Acaste go out, laughing.*)

Scene V [*Arsinoé, Célimène.*]

ARSINOÉ: It's just as well those gentlemen didn't
tarry.
CÉLIMÈNE: Shall we sit down?
ARSINOÉ: That won't be necessary.
Madam, the flame of friendship ought to burn
Brightest in matters of the most concern,
And as there's nothing which concerns us more   5
Than honor, I have hastened to your door
To bring you, as your friend, some information
About the status of your reputation.
I visited, last night, some virtuous folk,
And, quite by chance, it was of you they spoke;   10
There was, I fear, no tendency to praise
Your light behavior and your dashing ways.
The quantity of gentlemen you see
And your by now notorious coquetry
Were both so vehemently criticized   15
By everyone, that I was much surprised.
Of course, I needn't tell you where I stood;
I came to your defense as best I could,
Assured them you were harmless, and declared
Your soul was absolutely unimpaired.   20
But there are some things, you must realize,
One can't excuse, however hard one tries,
And I was forced at last into conceding
That your behavior, Madam, is misleading,
That it makes a bad impression, giving rise   25
To ugly gossip and obscene surmise,
And that if you were more *overtly* good,
You wouldn't be so much misunderstood.
Not that I think you've been unchaste — no!
no!
The saints preserve me from a thought so low!   30
But mere good conscience never did suffice:
One must avoid the outward show of vice.
Madam, you're too intelligent, I'm sure,
To think my motives anything but pure
In offering you this counsel — which I do   35
Out of a zealous interest in you.
CÉLIMÈNE: Madam, I haven't taken you amiss;
I'm very much obliged to you for this;
And I'll at once discharge the obligation
By telling you about *your* reputation.   40
You've been so friendly as to let me know
What certain people say of me, and so
I mean to follow your benign example
By offering you a somewhat similar sample.
The other day, I went to an affair   45
And found some most distinguished people there
Discussing piety, both false and true.
The conversation soon came round to you.
Alas! Your prudery and bustling zeal
Appeared to have a very slight appeal.   50

Your affectation of a grave demeanor,
Your endless talk of virtue and of honor,
The aptitude of your suspicious mind
For finding sin where there is none to find,
55   Your towering self-esteem, that pitying face
With which you contemplate the human race,
Your sermonizings and your sharp aspersions
On people's pure and innocent diversions —
All these were mentioned, Madam, and, in fact,
60   Were roundly and concertedly attacked.
"What good," they said, "are all these outward
     shows,
When everything belies her pious pose?
She prays incessantly; but then, they say,
She beats her maids and cheats them of their
     pay;
65   She shows her zeal in every holy place,
But still she's vain enough to paint her face;
She holds that naked statues are immoral,
But with a naked *man* she'd have no quarrel."
Of course, I said to everybody there
70   That they were being viciously unfair;
But still they were disposed to criticize you,
And all agreed that someone should advise you
To leave the morals of the world alone,
And worry rather more about your own.
They felt that one's self-knowledge should be
75   great
Before one thinks of setting others straight;
That one should learn the art of living well
Before one threatens other men with hell,
And that the Church is best equipped, no doubt,
80   To guide our souls and root our vices out.
Madam, you're too intelligent, I'm sure,
To think my motives anything but pure
In offering you this counsel — which I do
Out of a zealous interest in you.
85   ARSINOÉ: I dared not hope for gratitude, but I
Did not expect so acid a reply;
I judge, since you've been so extremely tart,
That my good counsel pierced you to the heart.
CÉLIMÈNE: Far from it, Madam. Indeed, it seems to
     me
90   We ought to trade advice more frequently.
One's vision of oneself is so defective
That it would be an excellent corrective.
If you are willing, Madam, let's arrange
Shortly to have another frank exchange
95   In which we'll tell each other, *entre nous,*°
What you've heard tell of me, and I of you.
ARSINOÉ: Oh, people never censure you, my dear;
It's me they criticize. Or so I hear.
CÉLIMÈNE: Madam, I think we either blame or
     praise

According to our taste and length of days.   100
There is a time of life for coquetry,
And there's a season, too, for prudery.
When all one's charms are gone, it is, I'm sure,
Good strategy to be devout and pure:
It makes one seem a little less forsaken.   105
Some day, perhaps, I'll take the road you've
     taken:
Time brings all things. But I have time aplenty,
And see no cause to be a prude at twenty.
ARSINOÉ: You give your age in such a gloating tone
That one would think I was an ancient crone;   110
We're not so far apart, in sober truth,
That you can mock me with a boast of youth!
Madam, you baffle me. I wish I knew
What moves you to provoke me as you do.
CÉLIMÈNE: For my part, Madam, I should like to
     know   115
Why you abuse me everywhere you go.
Is it my fault, dear lady, that your hand
Is not, alas, in very great demand?
If men admire me, if they pay me court
And daily make me offers of the sort   120
You'd dearly love to have them make to you,
How can I help it? What would you have me
     do?
If what you want is lovers, please feel free
To take as many as you can from me.
ARSINOÉ: Oh, come. D'you think the world is
     losing sleep   125
Over the flock of lovers which you keep,
Or that we find it difficult to guess
What price you pay for their devotedness?
Surely you don't expect us to suppose
Mere merit could attract so many beaux?   130
It's not your virtue that they're dazzled by;
Nor is it virtuous love for which they sigh.
You're fooling no one, Madam; the world's not
     blind;
There's many a lady heaven has designed
To call men's noblest, tenderest feelings out,   135
Who has no lovers dogging her about;
From which it's plain that lovers nowadays
Must be acquired in bold and shameless ways,
And only pay one court for such reward
As modesty and virtue can't afford.   140
Then don't be quite so puffed up, if you please,
About your tawdry little victories;
Try, if you can, to be a shade less vain,
And treat the world with somewhat less disdain.
If one were envious of your amours,   145
One soon could have a following like yours;
Lovers are no great trouble to collect
If one prefers them to one's self-respect.
CÉLIMÈNE: Collect them then, my dear; I'd love to
     see

---

95. entre nous: Between ourselves.

150 You demonstrate that charming theory;
     Who knows, you might . . .
     ARSINOÉ: Now, Madam, that will do;
     It's time to end this trying interview.
     My coach is late in coming to your door,
     Or I'd have taken leave of you before.
     CÉLIMÈNE: Oh, please don't feel that you must rush
155   away;
     I'd be delighted, Madam, if you'd stay.
     However, lest my conversation bore you,
     Let me provide some better company for you;
     This gentleman, who comes most apropos,
160 Will please you more than I could do, I know.

Scene VI [*Alceste, Célimène, Arsinoé.*]

CÉLIMÈNE: Alceste, I have a little note to write
     Which simply must go out before tonight;
     Please entertain *Madame;* I'm sure that she
     Will overlook my incivility.

Scene VII [*Alceste, Arsinoé.*]

ARSINOÉ: Well, Sir, our hostess graciously contrives
     For us to chat until my coach arrives;
     And I shall be forever in her debt
     For granting me this little *tête-à-tête.*°
  5 We women very rightly give our hearts
     To men of noble character and parts,
     And your especial merits, dear Alceste,
     Have roused the deepest sympathy in my breast.
     Oh, how I wish they had sufficient sense
 10 At court, to recognize your excellence!
     They wrong you greatly, Sir. How it must hurt
         you
     Never to be rewarded for your virtue!
     ALCESTE: Why, Madam, what cause have I to feel
         aggrieved?
     What great and brilliant thing have I achieved?
 15 What service have I rendered to the King
     That I should look to him for anything?
     ARSINOÉ: Not everyone who's honored by the State
     Has done great services. A man must wait
     Till time and fortune offer him the chance.
 20 Your merit, Sir, is obvious at a glance,
     And . . .
     ALCESTE: Ah, forget my merit; I am not
         neglected.
     The court, I think, can hardly be expected
     To mine men's souls for merit, and unearth
     Our hidden virtues and our secret worth.
     ARSINOÉ: *Some* virtues, though, are far too bright
         to hide;
 25

4. *tête-à-tête:* French for "head-to-head," in private
conversation.

     Yours are acknowledged, Sir, on every side.
     Indeed, I've heard you warmly praised of late
     By persons of considerable weight.
     ALCESTE: This fawning age has praise for everyone,
     And all distinctions, Madam, are undone.   30
     All things have equal honor nowadays,
     And no one should be gratified by praise.
     To be admired, one only need exist,
     And every lackey's on the honors list.
     ARSINOÉ: I only wish, Sir, that you had your eye   35
     On some position at court, however high;
     You'd only have to hint at such a notion
     For me to set the proper wheels in motion;
     I've certain friendships I'd be glad to use
     To get you any office you might choose.   40
     ALCESTE: Madam, I fear that any such ambition
     Is wholly foreign to my disposition.
     The soul God gave me isn't of the sort
     That prospers in the weather of a court.
     It's all too obvious that I don't possess   45
     The virtues necessary for success.
     My one great talent is for speaking plain;
     I've never learned to flatter or to feign;
     And anyone so stupidly sincere
     Had best not seek a courtier's career.   50
     Outside the court, I know, one must dispense
     With honors, privilege, and influence;
     But still one gains the right, foregoing these,
     Not to be tortured by the wish to please.
     One needn't live in dread of snubs and slights,   55
     Nor praise the verse that every idiot writes,
     Nor humor silly Marquesses, nor bestow
     Politic sighs on Madam So-and-So.
     ARSINOÉ: Forget the court, then; let the matter rest.
     But I've another cause to be distressed   60
     About your present situation, Sir.
     It's to your love affair that I refer.
     She whom you love, and who pretends to love
         you,
     Is, I regret to say, unworthy of you.
     ALCESTE: Why, Madam? Can you seriously intend   65
     To make so grave a charge against your friend?
     ARSINOÉ: Alas, I must. I've stood aside too long
     And let that lady do you grievous wrong;
     But now my debt to conscience shall be paid:
     I tell you that your love has been betrayed.   70
     ALCESTE: I thank you, Madam; you're extremely
         kind.
     Such words are soothing to a lover's mind.
     ARSINOÉ: Yes, though she *is* my friend, I say again
     You're very much too good for Célimène.
     She's wantonly misled you from the start.   75
     ALCESTE: You may be right; who knows another's
         heart?
     But ask yourself if it's the part of charity
     To shake my soul with doubts of her sincerity.

ARSINOÉ: Well, if you'd rather be a dupe than
    doubt her,
80   That's your affair. I'll say no more about her.
ALCESTE: Madam, you know that doubt and vague
    suspicion
    Are painful to a man in my position;
    It's most unkind to worry me this way
    Unless you've some real proof of what you say.
ARSINOÉ: Sir, say no more: all doubts shall be
85   removed,
    And all that I've been saying shall be proved.
    You've only to escort me home, and there
    We'll look into the heart of this affair.
    I've ocular evidence which will persuade you
90   Beyond a doubt, that Célimène's betrayed you.
    Then, if you're saddened by that revelation,
    Perhaps I can provide some consolation.

ACT IV · Scene I [*Éliante, Philinte.*] ───────

PHILINTE: Madam, he acted like a stubborn child;
    I thought they never would be reconciled;
    In vain we reasoned, threatened, and appealed;
    He stood his ground and simply would not
    yield.
5   The Marshals, I feel sure, have never heard
    An argument so splendidly absurd.
    "No, gentlemen," said he, "I'll not retract.
    His verse is bad: extremely bad, in fact.
    Surely it does the man no harm to know it.
10   Does it disgrace him, not to be a poet?
    A gentleman may be respected still,
    Whether he writes a sonnet well or ill.
    That I dislike his verse should not offend him;
    In all that touches honor, I commend him;
15   He's noble, brave, and virtuous — but I fear
    He can't in truth be called a sonneteer.
    I'll gladly praise his wardrobe; I'll endorse
    His dancing, or the way he sits a horse;
    But, gentlemen, I cannot praise his rhyme.
20   In fact, it ought to be a capital crime
    For anyone so sadly unendowed
    To write a sonnet, and read the thing aloud."
    At length he fell into a gentler mood
    And, striking a concessive attitude,
25   He paid Oronte the following courtesies:
    "Sir, I regret that I'm so hard to please,
    And I'm profoundly sorry that your lyric
    Failed to provoke me to a panegyric."°
    After these curious words, the two embraced,
30   And then the hearing was adjourned — in haste.
ÉLIANTE: His conduct has been very singular lately;
    Still, I confess that I respect him greatly.

28. **panegyric:** Elaborate praise.

The honesty in which he takes such pride
Has — to my mind — its noble, heroic side.
In this false age, such candor seems outrageous; 35
But I could wish that it were more contagious.
PHILINTE: What most intrigues me in our friend
    Alceste
    Is the grand passion that rages in his breast.
    The sullen humors he's compounded of
    Should not, I think, dispose his heart to love; 40
    But since they do, it puzzles me still more
    That he should choose your cousin to adore.
ÉLIANTE: It does, indeed, belie the theory
    That love is born of gentle sympathy,
    And that the tender passion must be based 45
    On sweet accords of temper and of taste.
PHILINTE: Does she return his love, do you
    suppose?
ÉLIANTE: Ah, that's a difficult question, Sir. Who
    knows?
    How can we judge the truth of her devotion?
    Her heart's a stranger to its own emotion. 50
    Sometimes it thinks it loves, when no love's
    there;
    At other times it loves quite unaware.
PHILINTE: I rather think Alceste is in for more
    Distress and sorrow than he's bargained for;
    Were he of my mind, Madam, his affection 55
    Would turn in quite a different direction,
    And we would see him more responsive to
    The kind regard which he receives from you.
ELIANTE: Sir, I believe in frankness, and I'm
    inclined,
    In matters of the heart, to speak my mind. 60
    I don't oppose his love for her; indeed,
    I hope with all my heart that he'll succeed,
    And were it in my power, I'd rejoice
    In giving him the lady of his choice.
    But if, as happens frequently enough 65
    In love affairs, he meets with a rebuff —
    If Célimène should grant some rival's suit —
    I'd gladly play the role of substitute;
    Nor would his tender speeches please me less
    Because they'd once been made without success. 70
PHILINTE: Well, Madam, as for me, I don't oppose
    Your hopes in this affair; and heaven knows
    That in my conversations with the man
    I plead your cause as often as I can.
    But if those two should marry, and so remove 75
    All chance that he will offer you his love,
    Then I'll declare my own, and hope to see
    Your gracious favor pass from him to me.
    In short, should you be cheated of Alceste,
    I'd be most happy to be second best. 80
ÉLIANTE: Philinte, you're teasing.
PHILINTE: Ah, Madam, never fear;

No words of mine were ever so sincere,
And I shall live in fretful expectation
Till I can make a fuller declaration.

Scene II [*Alceste, Éliante, Philinte.*]

ALCESTE: Avenge me, Madam! I must have
          satisfaction,
    Or this great wrong will drive me to distraction!
ÉLIANTE: Why, what's the matter? What's upset you
          so?
ALCESTE: Madam, I've had a mortal, mortal blow.
5   If Chaos repossessed the universe,
    I swear I'd not be shaken any worse.
    I'm ruined. . . . I can say no more. . . . My
          soul . . .
ÉLIANTE: Do try, Sir, to regain your self-control.
ALCESTE: Just heaven! Why were so much beauty
          and grace
10   Bestowed on one so vicious and so base?
ÉLIANTE: Once more, Sir, tell us. . . .
ALCESTE: My world has gone to wrack;
    I'm — I'm betrayed; she's stabbed me in the
          back:
    Yes, Célimène (who would have thought it of
          her?)
    Is false to me, and has another lover.
ÉLIANTE: Are you quite certain? Can you prove
15   these things?
PHILINTE: Lovers are prey to wild imaginings
    And jealous fancies. No doubt there's some
          mistake. . . .
ALCESTE: Mind your own business, Sir, for heaven's
          sake.
    (*To Éliante.*) Madam, I have the proof that you
          demand
20   Here in my pocket, penned by her own hand.
    Yes, all the shameful evidence one could want
    Lies in this letter written to Oronte —
    Oronte! whom I felt sure she couldn't love,
    And hardly bothered to be jealous of.
25 PHILINTE: Still, in a letter, appearances may deceive;
    This may not be so bad as you believe.
ALCESTE: Once more I beg you, Sir, to let me be;
    Tend to your own affairs; leave mine to me.
ÉLIANTE: Compose yourself; this anguish that you
          feel . . .
30 ALCESTE: Is something, Madam, you alone can heal.
    My outraged heart, beside itself with grief,
    Appeals to you for comfort and relief.
    Avenge me on your cousin, whose unjust
    And faithless nature has deceived my trust;
35   Avenge a crime your pure soul must detest.
ÉLIANTE: But how, Sir?
ALCESTE: Madam, this heart within my breast

Is yours; pray take it; redeem my heart from
          her,
    And so avenge me on my torturer.
    Let her be punished by the fond emotion,
    The ardent love, the bottomless devotion,   40
    The faithful worship which this heart of mine
    Will offer up to yours as to a shrine.
ÉLIANTE: You have my sympathy, Sir, in all you
          suffer;
    Nor do I scorn the noble heart you offer;
    But I suspect you'll soon be mollified,   45
    And this desire for vengeance will subside.
    When some belovèd hand has done us wrong
    We thirst for retribution — but not for long;
    However dark the deed that she's committed,
    A lovely culprit's very soon acquitted.   50
    Nothing's so stormy as an injured lover,
    And yet no storm so quickly passes over.
ALCESTE: No, Madam, no — this is no lovers' spat;
    I'll not forgive her; it's gone too far for that;
    My mind's made up; I'll kill myself before   55
    I waste my hopes upon her any more.
    Ah, here she is. My wrath intensifies.
    I shall confront her with her tricks and lies,
    And crush her utterly, and bring you then
    A heart no longer slave to Célimène.   60

Scene III [*Célimène, Alceste.*]

ALCESTE (*aside*): Sweet heaven, help me to control
          my passion.
CÉLIMÈNE (*aside*): Oh, Lord. (*To Alceste.*) Why
          stand there staring in that fashion?
    And what d'you mean by those dramatic sighs,
    And that malignant glitter in your eyes?
ALCESTE: I mean that sins which cause the blood to
          freeze   5
    Look innocent beside your treacheries;
    That nothing Hell's or Heaven's wrath could do
    Ever produced so bad a thing as you.
CÉLIMÈNE: Your compliments were always sweet
          and pretty.
ALCESTE: Madam, it's not the moment to be witty.   10
    No, blush and hang your head; you've ample
          reason,
    Since I've the fullest evidence of your treason.
    Ah, this is what my sad heart prophesied;
    Now all my anxious fears are verified;
    My dark suspicion and my gloomy doubt   15
    Divined the truth, and now the truth is out.
    For all your trickery, I was not deceived;
    It was my bitter stars that I believed.
    But don't imagine that you'll go scot-free;
    You shan't misuse me with impunity.   20
    I know that love's irrational and blind;

I know the heart's not subject to the mind,
And can't be reasoned into beating faster;
I know each soul is free to choose its master;
25   Therefore had you but spoken from the heart,
Rejecting my attention from the start,
I'd have no grievance, or at any rate
I could complain of nothing but my fate.
Ah, but so falsely to encourage me —
30   That was a treason and a treachery
For which you cannot suffer too severely,
And you shall pay for that behavior dearly.
Yes, now I have no pity, not a shred;
My temper's out of hand; I've lost my head;
Shocked by the knowledge of your double-
35   dealings,
My reason can't restrain my savage feelings;
A righteous wrath deprives me of my senses,
And I won't answer for the consequences.
CÉLIMÈNE: What does this outburst mean? Will you
    please explain?
40   Have you, by any chance, gone quite insane?
ALCESTE: Yes, yes, I went insane the day I fell
A victim to your black and fatal spell,
Thinking to meet with some sincerity
Among the treacherous charms that beckoned
    me.
CÉLIMÈNE: Pooh. Of what treachery can you
45   complain?
ALCESTE: How sly you are, how cleverly you feign!
But you'll not victimize me any more.
Look: here's a document you've seen before.
This evidence, which I acquired today,
50   Leaves you, I think, without a thing to say.
CÉLIMÈNE: Is this what sent you into such a fit?
ALCESTE: You should be blushing at the sight of it.
CÉLIMÈNE: Ought I to blush? I truly don't see why.
ALCESTE: Ah, now you're being bold as well as sly;
Since there's no signature, perhaps you'll
55   claim . . .
CÉLIMÈNE: I wrote it, whether or not it bears my
    name.
ALCESTE: And you can view with equanimity
This proof of your disloyalty to me!
CÉLIMÈNE: Oh, don't be so outrageous and
    extreme.
ALCESTE: You take this matter lightly, it would
60   seem.
Was it no wrong to me, no shame to you,
That you should send Oronte this *billet-doux?*°
CÉLIMÈNE: Oronte! Who said it was for him?

62. *billet-doux:* Love letter.

ALCESTE: Why, those
Who brought me this example of your prose.
But what's the difference? If you wrote the letter 65
To someone else, it pleases me no better.
My grievance and your guilt remain the same.
CÉLIMÈNE: But need you rage, and need I blush for
    shame,
If this was written to a *woman* friend?
ALCESTE: Ah! Most ingenious. I'm impressed no
    end; 70
And after that incredible evasion
Your guilt is clear. I need no more persuasion.
How dare you try so clumsy a deception?
D'you think I'm wholly wanting in perception?
Come, come, let's see how brazenly you'll try 75
To bolster up so palpable a lie:
Kindly construe this ardent closing section
As nothing more than sisterly affection!
Here, let me read it. Tell me, if you dare to,
That this is for a woman . . .
CÉLIMÈNE: I don't care to. 80
What right have you to badger and berate me,
And so high-handedly interrogate me?
ALCESTE: Now, don't be angry; all I ask of you
Is that you justify a phrase or two . . .
CÉLIMÈNE: No, I shall not. I utterly refuse, 85
And you may take those phrases as you choose.
ALCESTE: Just show me how this letter could be
    meant
For a woman's eyes, and I shall be content.
CÉLIMÈNE: No, no, it's for Oronte; you're perfectly
    right.
I welcome his attentions with delight, 90
I prize his character and his intellect,
And everything is just as you suspect.
Come, do your worst now; give your rage free
    rein;
But kindly cease to bicker and complain.
ALCESTE (*aside*): Good God! Could anything be
    more inhuman? 95
Was ever a heart so mangled by a woman?
When I complain of how she has betrayed me,
She bridles, and commences to upbraid me!
She tries my tortured patience to the limit;
She won't deny her guilt; she glories in it! 100
And yet my heart's too faint and cowardly
To break these chains of passion, and be free,
To scorn her as it should, and rise above
This unrewarded, mad, and bitter love.
(*To Célimène.*) Ah, traitress, in how confident a
    fashion 105
You take advantage of my helpless passion,
And use my weakness for your faithless charms
To make me once again throw down my arms!

But do at least deny this black transgression;
110 Take back that mocking and perverse confession;
Defend this letter and your innocence,
And I, poor fool, will aid in your defense.
Pretend, pretend, that you are just and true,
And I shall make myself believe in you.
CÉLIMÈNE: Oh, stop it. Don't be such a jealous
115   dunce,
Or I shall leave off loving you at once.
Just why should I *pretend?* What could impel me
To stoop so low as that? And kindly tell me
Why, if I loved another, I shouldn't merely
120 Inform you of it, simply and sincerely!
I've told you where you stand, and that
      admission
Should altogether clear me of suspicion;
After so generous a guarantee,
What right have you to harbor doubts of me?
125 Since women are (from natural reticence)
Reluctant to declare their sentiments,
And since the honor of our sex requires
That we conceal our amorous desires,
Ought any man for whom such laws are broken
130 To question what the oracle has spoken?
Should he not rather feel an obligation
To trust that most obliging declaration?
Enough, now. Your suspicions quite disgust me;
Why should I love a man who doesn't trust me?
135 I cannot understand why I continue,
Fool that I am, to take an interest in you.
I ought to choose a man less prone to doubt,
And give you something to be vexed about.
ALCESTE: Ah, what a poor enchanted fool I am,
140 These gentle words, no doubt, were all a sham,
But destiny requires me to entrust
My happiness to you, and so I must.
I'll love you to the bitter end, and see
How false and treacherous you dare to be.
CÉLIMÈNE: No, you don't really love me as you
145   ought.
ALCESTE: I love you more than can be said or
      thought;
Indeed, I wish you were in such distress
That I might show my deep devotedness.
Yes, I could wish that you were wretchedly
      poor,
150 Unloved, uncherished, utterly obscure;
That fate had set you down upon the earth
Without possessions, rank, or gentle birth;
Then, by the offer of my heart, I might
Repair the great injustice of your plight;
155 I'd raise you from the dust, and proudly prove
The purity and vastness of my love.
CÉLIMÈNE: This is a strange benevolence indeed!

God grant that I may never be in need. . . .
Ah, here's Monsieur Dubois in quaint disguise.

Scene IV [*Célimène, Alceste, Dubois.*]

ALCESTE: Well, why this costume? Why those
      frightened eyes?
   What ails you?
DUBOIS: Well, Sir, things are most mysterious.
ALCESTE: What do you mean?
DUBOIS: I fear they're very serious.
ALCESTE: What?
DUBOIS: Shall I speak more loudly?
ALCESTE: Yes; speak out.
DUBOIS: Isn't there someone here, Sir?
ALCESTE: Speak, you lout! 5
   Stop wasting time.
DUBOIS: Sir, we must slip away.
ALCESTE: How's that?
DUBOIS: We must decamp without delay.
ALCESTE: Explain yourself.
DUBOIS: I tell you we must fly.
ALCESTE: What for?
DUBOIS: We mustn't pause to say good-by.
ALCESTE: Now what d'you mean by all of this,
      you clown?   10
DUBOIS: I mean, Sir, that we've got to leave this
      town.
ALCESTE: I'll tear you limb from limb and joint
      from joint
   If you don't come more quickly to the point.
DUBOIS: Well, Sir, today a man in a black suit,
   Who wore a black and ugly scowl to boot,   15
   Left us a document scrawled in such a hand
   As even Satan couldn't understand.
   It bears upon your lawsuit, I don't doubt;
   But all hell's devils couldn't make it out.
ALCESTE: Well, well, go on. What then? I fail to see 20
   How this event obliges us to flee.
DUBOIS: Well, Sir, an hour later, hardly more,
   A gentleman who's often called before
   Came looking for you in an anxious way.
   Not finding you, he asked me to convey   25
   (Knowing I could be trusted with the same)
   The following message. . . . Now, what *was* his
      name?
ALCESTE: Forget his name, you idiot. What did he
      say?
DUBOIS: Well, it was one of your friends, Sir,
      anyway.
   He warned you to begone, and he suggested   30
   That if you stay, you may well be arrested.
ALCESTE: What? Nothing more specific? Think,
      man, think!

DUBOIS: No, Sir. He had me bring him pen and
  ink,
  And dashed you off a letter which, I'm sure,
35 Will render things distinctly less obscure.
ALCESTE: Well — let me have it!
CÉLIMÈNE: What *is* this all about?
ALCESTE: God knows; but I have hopes of finding
  out.
  How long am I to wait, you blitherer?
DUBOIS (*after a protracted search for the letter*): I
  must have left it on your table, Sir.
ALCESTE: I ought to . . .
40 CÉLIMÈNE: No, no, keep your self-control;
  Go find out what's behind his rigmarole.
ALCESTE: It seems that fate, no matter what I do,
  Has sworn that I may not converse with you;
  But, Madam, pray permit your faithful lover
45 To try once more before the day is over.

ACT V · Scene I [*Alceste, Philinte.*] ——————

ALCESTE: No, it's too much. My mind's made up, I
  tell you.
PHILINTE: Why should this blow, however hard,
  compel you . . .
ALCESTE: No, no, don't waste your breath in
  argument;
  Nothing you say will alter my intent;
5 This age is vile, and I've made up my mind
  To have no further commerce with mankind.
  Did not truth, honor, decency, and the laws
  Oppose my enemy and approve my cause?
  My claims were justified in all men's sight;
10 I put my trust in equity and right;
  Yet, to my horror and the world's disgrace,
  Justice is mocked, and I have lost my case!
  A scoundrel whose dishonesty is notorious
  Emerges from another lie victorious!
15 Honor and right condone his brazen fraud,
  While rectitude and decency applaud!
  Before his smirking face, the truth stands
  charmed,
  And virtue conquered, and the law disarmed!
  His crime is sanctioned by a court decree!
20 And not content with what he's done to me,
  The dog now seeks to ruin me by stating
  That I composed a book now circulating,
  A book so wholly criminal and vicious
  That even to speak its title is seditious!
25 Meanwhile Oronte, my rival, lends his credit
  To the same libelous tale, and helps to spread it!
  Oronte! a man of honor and of rank,
  With whom I've been entirely fair and frank;
  Who sought me out and forced me, willy-nilly,

To judge some verse I found extremely silly;   30
And who, because I properly refused
To flatter him, or see the truth abused,
35 Abets my enemy in a rotten slander!
There's the reward of honesty and candor!
The man will hate me to the end of time   35
For failing to commend his wretched rhyme!
And not this man alone, but all humanity
Do what they do from interest and vanity;
They prate of honor, truth, and righteousness,
But lie, betray, and swindle nonetheless.   40
Come then: man's villainy is too much to bear;
Let's leave this jungle and this jackal's lair.
Yes! treacherous and savage race of men,
You shall not look upon my face again.
PHILINTE: Oh, don't rush into exile prematurely;   45
  Things aren't as dreadful as you make them,
  surely.
  It's rather obvious, since you're still at large,
  That people don't believe your enemy's charge.
  Indeed, his tale's so patently untrue
  That it may do more harm to him than you.   50
ALCESTE: Nothing could do that scoundrel any
  harm:
  His frank corruption is his greatest charm,
  And, far from hurting him, a further shame
  Would only serve to magnify his name.
PHILINTE: In any case, his bald prevarication   55
  Has done no injury to your reputation,
  And you may feel secure in that regard.
  As for your lawsuit, it should not be hard
  To have the case reopened, and contest
  This judgment . . .
ALCESTE: No, no, let the verdict rest.   60
  Whatever cruel penalty it may bring,
  I wouldn't have it changed for anything.
  It shows the times' injustice with such clarity
  That I shall pass it down to our posterity
  As a great proof and signal demonstration   65
  Of the black wickedness of this generation.
  It may cost twenty thousand francs; but I
  Shall pay their twenty thousand, and gain
  thereby
  The right to storm and rage at human evil,
  And send the race of mankind to the devil.   70
PHILINTE: Listen to me . . .
ALCESTE: Why? What can you possibly say?
  Don't argue, Sir; your labor's thrown away.
  Do you propose to offer lame excuses
  For men's behavior and the times' abuses?
PHILINTE: No, all you say I'll readily concede: 75
  This is a low, conniving age, indeed;
  Nothing but trickery prospers nowadays,
  And people ought to mend their shabby ways.

Yes, man's a beastly creature; but must we then
80   Abandon the society of men?
Here in the world, each human frailty
Provides occasion for philosophy,
And that is virtue's noblest exercise;
If honesty shone forth from all men's eyes,
85   If every heart were frank and kind and just.
What could our virtues do but gather dust
(Since their employment is to help us bear
The villainies of men without despair)?
A heart well-armed with virtue can endure. . . .
ALCESTE: Sir, you're a matchless reasoner, to be
90   sure;
Your words are fine and full of cogency;
But don't waste time and eloquence on me.
My reason bids me go, for my own good.
My tongue won't lie and flatter as it should;
God knows what frankness it might next
95   commit,
And what I'd suffer on account of it.
Pray let me wait for Célimène's return
In peace and quiet. I shall shortly learn,
By her response to what I have in view,
100   Whether her love for me is feigned or true.
PHILINTE: Till then, let's visit Éliante upstairs.
ALCESTE: No, I am too weighed down with somber
    cares.
Go to her, do; and leave me with my gloom
Here in the darkened corner of this room.
PHILINTE: Why, that's no sort of company, my
105   friend;
I'll see if Éliante will not descend.

Scene II [*Célimène, Oronte, Alceste.*]

ORONTE: Yes, Madam, if you wish me to remain
Your true and ardent lover, you must deign
To give me some more positive assurance.
All this suspense is quite beyond endurance.
5   If your heart shares the sweet desires of mine,
Show me as much by some convincing sign;
And here's the sign I urgently suggest:
That you no longer tolerate Alceste,
But sacrifice him to my love, and sever
10   All your relations with the man forever.
CÉLIMÈNE: Why do you suddenly dislike him so?
You praised him to the skies not long ago.
ORONTE: Madam, that's not the point. I'm here to
    find
Which way your tender feelings are inclined.
15   Choose, if you please, between Alceste and me,
And I shall stay or go accordingly.
ALCESTE (*emerging from the corner*): Yes, Madam,
    choose; this gentleman's demand

Is wholly just, and I support his stand.
I too am true and ardent; I too am here
To ask you that you make your feelings clear.   20
No more delays, now; no equivocation;
The time has come to make your declaration.
ORONTE: Sir, I've no wish in any way to be
An obstacle to your felicity.
ALCESTE: Sir, I've no wish to share her heart with
    you;   25
That may sound jealous, but at least it's true.
ORONTE: If, weighing us, she leans in your
    direction . . .
ALCESTE: If she regards you with the least
    affection . . .
ORONTE: I swear I'll yield her to you there and
    then.
ALCESTE: I swear I'll never see her face again.   30
ORONTE: Now, Madam, tell us what we've come to
    hear.
ALCESTE: Madam, speak openly and have no fear.
ORONTE: Just say which one is to remain your
    lover.
ALCESTE: Just name one name, and it will all be
    over.
ORONTE: What! Is it possible that you're
    undecided?   35
ALCESTE: What! Can your feelings possibly be
    divided?
CÉLIMÈNE: Enough: this inquisition's gone too far:
How utterly unreasonable you are!
Not that I couldn't make the choice with ease;
My heart has no conflicting sympathies;   40
I know full well which one of you I favor,
And you'd not see me hesitate or waver.
But how can you expect me to reveal
So cruelly and bluntly what I feel?
I think it altogether too unpleasant   45
To choose between two men when both are
    present;
One's heart has means more subtle and more
    kind
Of letting its affections be divined,
Nor need one be uncharitably plain
To let a lover know he loves in vain.   50
ORONTE: No, no, speak plainly; I for one can stand
    it.
I beg you to be frank.
ALCESTE: And I demand it.
The simple truth is what I wish to know,
And there's no need for softening the blow.
You've made an art of pleasing everyone,   55
But now your days of coquetry are done:
You have no choice now, Madam, but to
    choose,

For I'll know what to think if you refuse;
I'll take your silence for a clear admission
60 That I'm entitled to my worst suspicion.
ORONTE: I thank you for this ultimatum, Sir.
And I may say I heartily concur.
CÉLIMÈNE: Really, this foolishness is very wearing:
Must you be so unjust and overbearing?
65 Haven't I told you why I must demur?
Ah, here's Éliante; I'll put the case to her.

Scene III [*Éliante, Philinte, Célimène, Oronte, Alceste.*]

CÉLIMÈNE: Cousin, I'm being persecuted here
By these two persons, who, it would appear,
Will not be satisfied till I confess
Which one I love the more, and which the less,
5 And tell the latter to his face that he
Is henceforth banished from my company.
Tell me, has ever such a thing been done?
ÉLIANTE: You'd best not turn to me; I'm not the one
To back you in a matter of this kind:
10 I'm all for those who frankly speak their mind.
ORONTE: Madam, you'll search in vain for a defender.
ALCESTE: You're beaten, Madam, and may as well surrender.
ORONTE: Speak, speak, you must; and end this awful strain.
ALCESTE: Or don't, and your position will be plain.
ORONTE: A single word will close this painful
15 scene.
ALCESTE: But if you're silent, I'll know what you mean.

Scene IV [*Arsinoé, Célimène, Éliante, Alceste, Philinte, Acaste, Clitandre, Oronte.*]

ACASTE (*to Célimène*): Madam, with all due deference, we two
Have come to pick a little bone with you.
CLITANDRE (*to Oronte and Alceste*): I'm glad you're present, Sirs, as you'll soon learn,
Our business here is also your concern.
ARSINOÉ (*to Célimène*): Madam, I visit you so soon
5 again
Only because of these two gentlemen,
Who came to me indignant and aggrieved
About a crime too base to be believed.
Knowing your virtue, having such confidence in it,
10 I couldn't think you guilty for a minute,
In spite of all their telling evidence;
And, rising above our little difference,

I've hastened here in friendship's name to see
You clear yourself of this great calumny.
ACASTE: Yes, Madam, let us see with what composure 15
You'll manage to respond to this disclosure.
You lately sent Clitandre this tender note.
CLITANDRE: And this one, for Acaste, you also wrote.
ACASTE (*to Oronte and Alceste*): You'll recognize this writing, Sirs, I think;
The lady is so free with pen and ink 20
That you must know it all too well, I fear.
But listen: this is something you should hear.

"How absurd you are to condemn my light-heartedness in society, and to accuse me of being happiest in the company of others. Nothing could 25 be more unjust; and if you do not come to me instantly and beg pardon for saying such a thing, I shall never forgive you as long as I live. Our big bumbling friend the Viscount . . ."

What a shame that he's not here. 30

"Our big bumbling friend the Viscount, whose name stands first in your complaint, is hardly a man to my taste; and ever since the day I watched him spend three-quarters of an hour spitting into a well, so as to make circles in the water, I have 35 been unable to think highly of him. As for the little Marquess . . ."

In all modesty, gentlemen, that is I.

"As for the little Marquess, who sat squeezing my hand for such a long while yesterday, I find 40 him in all respects the most trifling creature alive; and the only things of value about him are his cape and his sword. As for the man with the green ribbons . . ."

(*To Alceste.*) It's your turn now, Sir. 45

"As for the man with the green ribbons, he amuses me now and then with his bluntness and his bearish ill-humor; but there are many times indeed when I think him the greatest bore in the world. And as for the sonneteer . . ." 50

(*To Oronte.*) Here's your helping.

"And as for the sonneteer, who has taken it into his head to be witty, and insists on being an author in the teeth of opinion, I simply cannot be bothered to listen to him, and his prose wearies me quite as 55

much as his poetry. Be assured that I am not always
so well-entertained as you suppose; that I long for
your company, more than I dare to say, at all these
entertainments to which people drag me; and that
60 the presence of those one loves is the true and
perfect seasoning to all one's pleasures."

CLITANDRE: And now for me.

"Clitandre, whom you mention, and who so
pesters me with his saccharine speeches, is the last
65 man on earth for whom I could feel any affection.
He is quite mad to suppose that I love him, and
so are you, to doubt that you are loved. Do come
to your senses; exchange your suppositions for his;
and visit me as often as possible, to help me bear
70 the annoyance of his unwelcome attentions."

It's sweet character that these letters show,
And what to call it, Madam, you well know.
Enough. We're off to make the world acquainted
With this sublime self-portrait that you've
painted.
75 ACASTE: Madam, I'll make you no farewell oration;
No, you're not worthy of my indignation.
Far choicer hearts than yours, as you'll discover,
Would like this little Marquess for a lover.

Scene V [*Célimène, Éliante, Arsinoé, Alceste, Oronte, Philinte.*]

ORONTE: So! After all those loving letters you
wrote,
You turn on me like this, and cut my throat!
And your dissembling, faithless heart, I find,
Has pledged itself by turns to all mankind!
5   How blind I've been! But now I clearly see;
I thank you, Madam, for enlightening me.
My heart is mine once more, and I'm content;
The loss of it shall be your punishment.
(*To Alceste.*) Sir, she is yours; I'll seek no more
to stand
10 Between your wishes and this lady's hand.

Scene VI [*Célimène, Éliante, Arsinoé, Alceste, Philinte.*]

ARSINOÉ: (*to Célimène*): Madam, I'm forced to
speak. I'm far too stirred
To keep my counsel, after what I've heard.
I'm shocked and staggered by your want of
morals.
It's not my way to mix in others' quarrels;
5   But really, when this fine and noble spirit,
This man of honor and surpassing merit,

Laid down the offering of his heart before you,
How *could* you . . .
ALCESTE: Madam, permit me, I implore you,
To represent myself in this debate.
Don't bother, please, to be my advocate.   10
My heart, in any case, could not afford
To give your services their due reward;
And if I chose, for consolation's sake,
Some other lady, 'twould not be you I'd take.
ARSINOÉ: What makes you think you could, Sir?
And how dare you   15
Imply that I've been trying to ensnare you?
If you can for a moment entertain
Such flattering fancies, you're extremely vain.
I'm not so interested as you suppose
In Célimène's discarded gigolos.   20
Get rid of that absurd illusion, do.
Women like me are not for such as you.
Stay with this creature, to whom you're so
attached;
I've never seen two people better matched.

Scene VII [*Célimène, Éliante, Alceste, Philinte.*]

ALCESTE (*to Célimène*): Well, I've been still
throughout this exposé,
Till everyone but me has said his say.
Come, have I shown sufficient self-restraint?
And may I now . . .
CÉLIMÈNE: Yes, make your just complaint.
Reproach me freely, call me what you will;   5
You've every right to say I've used you ill.
I've wronged you, I confess it; and in my shame
I'll make no effort to escape the blame.
The anger of those others I could despise;
My guilt toward you I sadly recognize.   10
Your wrath is wholly justified, I fear;
I know how culpable I must appear,
I know all things bespeak my treachery,
And that, in short, you've grounds for hating
me.
Do so; I give you leave.
ALCESTE: Ah, traitress — how,   15
How should I cease to love you, even now?
Though mind and will were passionately bent
On hating you, my heart would not consent.
(*To Éliante and Philinte.*) Be witness to my
madness, both of you;
See what infatuation drives one to;   20
But wait; my folly's only just begun,
And I shall prove to you before I'm done
How strange the human heart is, and how far
From rational we sorry creatures are.
(*To Célimène.*) Woman, I'm willing to forget
your shame,   25

And clothe your treacheries in a sweeter name;
I'll call them youthful errors, instead of crimes,
And lay the blame on these corrupting times.
My one condition is that you agree
30   To share my chosen fate, and fly with me
To that wild, trackless, solitary place
In which I shall forget the human race.
Only by such a course can you atone
For those atrocious letters; by that alone
35   Can you remove my present horror of you,
And make it possible for me to love you.
CÉLIMÈNE: What! *I* renounce the world at my
         young age,
And die of boredom in some hermitage?
ALCESTE: Ah, if you really loved me as you ought,
You wouldn't give the world a moment's
40   thought;
Must you have me, and all the world beside?
CÉLIMÈNE: Alas, at twenty one is terrified
Of solitude. I fear I lack the force
And depth of soul to take so stern a course.
45   But if my hand in marriage will content you,
Why, there's a plan which I might well consent
         to,
And . . .
ALCESTE: No, I detest you now. I could excuse
Everything else, but since you thus refuse
Everything else, but since you thus refuse
To love me wholly, as a wife should do,
50   And see the world in me, as I in you,
Go! I reject your hand, and disenthrall
My heart from your enchantments, once for all.

Scene VIII [*Éliante, Alceste, Philinte.*]

ALCESTE (*to Éliante*): Madam, your virtuous beauty
         has no peer;
Of all this world you only are sincere;
I've long esteemed you highly, as you know;
Permit me ever to esteem you so,
And if I do not now request your hand,   5
Forgive me, Madam, and try to understand.
I feel unworthy of it; I sense that fate
Does not intend me for the married state,
That I should do you wrong by offering you
My shattered heart's unhappy residue,   10
And that in short . . .
ÉLIANTE: Your argument's well taken:
Nor need you fear that I shall feel forsaken.
Were I to offer him this hand of mine,
Your friend Philinte, I think, would not decline.
PHILINTE: Ah, Madam, that's my heart's most
         cherished goal,   15
For which I'd gladly give my life and soul.
ALCESTE (*to Éliante and Philinte*): May you be true
         to all you now profess,
And so deserve unending happiness.
Meanwhile, betrayed and wronged in everything,
I'll flee this bitter world where vice is king,   20
And seek some spot unpeopled and apart
Where I'll be free to have an honest heart.
PHILINTE: Come, Madam, let's do everything we
         can
To change the mind of this unhappy man.

Nineteenth-Century Drama to the Turn of the Century

Romantic Drama

The early nineteenth century was the age of Romanticism, an artistic movement that countered in large measure the neoclassical emphasis on community, nation, rules, and narrow interpretations of moral behavior. The romanticists, Coleridge, Wordsworth, Byron, Keats, and Shelley, were individualists and sometimes aesthetic renegades. Most of the best work in literature in the age was done in poetry and the novel, and relatively little was done in drama. One of the most interesting plays of the period is an example of CLOSET DRAMA, drama that is meant to be read rather than performed — Lord Byron's remarkable but unproducible *Manfred* (1817). And some of the most remarkable dramatic material was written originally as fiction; Mary Shelley's novel, *Frankenstein* (1817), for instance, was made into a play in the late 1880s. Sir Walter Scott's novels were also transformed into plays. Popular classic novels were a favorite in the period, with plays developed from *A Tale of Two Cities*, *Sherlock Holmes*, and *The Count of Monte Cristo* reaching enormous audiences for decades. Eugene O'Neill's father was the star of *The Count of Monte Cristo* for years when Eugene was a child, and his early experiences with theater colored the rest of his life and provided him with material for his own plays. This pattern of adapting novels for the stage continued through the end of the nineteenth and into the twentieth century and is sustained now in motion pictures.

Johann Wolfgang von Goethe's play *Faust*, Part 1 (1808), is a depiction of the self-analytic and individualistic Romantic hero who has fascinated the German mind ever since. It is based on Marlowe's *Doctor Faustus* as well as the original German material from which Marlowe drew his play. However, like closet drama, its effect has been much greater on the reader than on any theater audience. Victor Hugo's *Hernani* (1830) was a popular favorite, as was his *Ruy Blas*, a play with a Spanish —

and therefore to its French audiences somewhat exotic — theme. The Romantics often used exotic locales, especially the Near East, Greece, and sometimes northern Africa.

Alexander Dumas *fils* (meaning son; his father had the same name) became celebrated in 1848 for a novel, *La Dame aux camélias* (*The Lady of the Camillias*), which became a theatrical hit in 1852. It has remained a popular favorite, inspiring an opera, *La Traviata* (1853), as well as popular revivals as recently as 1987 in a version by the British feminist playwright Pam Gems. It is the story of a wealthy young man who falls in love with a courtesan, Marguerite Gauthier. She has lived by love and has manipulated many men, but she truly loves the young nobleman. The young man's father is opposed to the match, of course, but even he is moved by the majesty of their love. Marguerite eventually dies of tuberculosis, and her death is taken as a sign that her life had been sullied, that she had sinned and must pay. It is a sentimental triumph that still works on the stage.

The works of Shakespeare, Molière, and other important earlier writers enjoyed many revivals. What the early nineteenth century did not produce, however, was a group of great playwrights. Until the 1870s and the arrival of Strindberg and Ibsen, the nineteenth-century stage was dominated not by writers and plays but by a succession of brilliant actors.

The Star System

The early nineteenth century produced a star system in which a small number of especially appealing actors dominated the stage for a considerable period of time. We see the beginnings of this trend in Restoration theater, in the career of the actress Nell Gwynne, and then later in the eighteenth century in the dominance of David Garrick. But in the nineteenth century, the stars were of such magnitude that modern actors still refer to them; Edmund Kean, Charles Kean, Henry Irving, Marie Dorval, J. P. Kemble, Mrs. Sarah Siddons, Edwin Booth, Mme. Lucia Elizabeth Vestris, William Macready and Edwin Forrest were among the most memorable English, American, and French actors of the period. They dominated the stage and obviously wanted to play only in established classics that would showcase their talents.

The passions of audiences for the stars often ran high, sometimes even erupting in riots. Probably the best known fracas is the Astor Place Riots in 1849 in New York, when the great English actor William Macready brought his troupe to perform. Edwin Forrest, an American actor, had claimed that his own tour of England had been scuttled by Macready, and their personal feud became exacerbated by the antagonism of the crowd. The result was two nights of disturbance in which the crowd prevented Macready from performing his plays. The second night produced more than twenty deaths. Such disturbances happened elsewhere, although not on such a destructive scale.

The New Audiences

The star system definitely altered the way drama developed in the Romantic period, but so did the audiences. For all its horrors — well documented in the period by Charles Dickens and others — the industrial revolution brought with it changes that included newly moneyed classes of people. Modern society was becoming less agricultural, more urban, more independent. These changes produced a new group of theatergoers whose demands and needs were quite different from those of the seventeenth- and eighteenth-century audiences.

Legitimate theater was only one of the many diversions available to the nineteenth-century spectator. The circus, which developed in this period, attracted huge audiences. P. T. Barnum (1810–1891) sold almost 40 million tickets to his shows in New York alone. And there were traveling variety shows, burlesque and minstrel shows, as well as opera companies in many major cities. The tastes of the middle classes created by the new industrial age were not defined by unusual learning, a knowledge of the classics, or tutored intellects. On the contrary, theatergoers seem to have been interested primarily in sentimental escapist drama that came to be called, for convenience, melodrama.

Melodrama

Despite the competition from other sources, theater in the first eighty years of the nineteenth century was probably more popular and better attended than in any other era before or since. Thirty thousand plays were produced in England during the century, and more people had the financial ability to attend theater than at any other time. A huge audience naturally made its demands known at the box office, and as a result the dramatists of the period were quick to produce what the audience wanted: melodramas, plays that were usually superficial but always effective.

The term MELODRAMA comes from the combination of music (*melos*) and drama. Many of the earliest melodramas played to background music that altered according to the mood of the scene. This tradition continues today in films and on television, and the conventions of melodrama, reshaped to fit the growing sophistication of audiences that no longer adhere to strict moralistic standards, remain firmly in place in popular entertainment.

Nineteenth-century melodramas featured familiar crises: the virtuous maiden who has fallen into the hands of an unscrupulous landlord, for instance. Such plays produced very well-defined heroes, heroines, and villains. There were no subtleties or shadings: the good were well rewarded for their virtue, and the bad were soundly trounced. The moralistic tone of nineteenth-century melodrama reflected the relatively simple moral standards of the emerging middle class audience.

Probably the most famous and most successful playwright of the period was the Irish-born melodramatist Dion Boucicault (1820–1890), who had great success on the New York stage. His best-known plays *The Octoroon* (1859), *The Colleen Bawn* (1860), *Arrah-na-Pogue* (1864), and *The Shaughraun* (1874) are only a portion of his output. Some of his works are still played, but they do seem — despite their occasional strength — to have been designed as commercial vehicles to appeal to the masses.

The most notable success of the period was George L. Aiken's adaptation of Harriet Beecher Stowe's novel *Uncle Tom's Cabin* (1852), which portrays the black slave Uncle Tom as a pious fellow willing to sacrifice his life for Little Eva. By modern standards the play is difficult to accept, particularly in its characterizations of Uncle Tom, the devoted black slave who ultimately supports his white master, and of the white slave master whose evil ways are almost unbelievable and whose name is still a synonym for viciousness: Simon Legree. The stereotypes of white evil and black goodness are virtually unrelieved, with the exception of Little Eva, the white girl whose goodness lives after her in a lock of hair, which in turn converts a few temporarily difficult and renegade black characters, such as Topsy.

Today we find such drama almost comic, but it is important to remind ourselves that our forebears took it very seriously. The play had well over a quarter of a million performances, and it is the first American play to be produced without the customary ballet or comedy interludes between the acts. Such interludes were normal in all plays. To an extent the music and dance segments that center on Topsy and the black community substitute for the normal interludes that maintained audience interest.

Uncle Tom's Cabin contributed, both in novel and play form, to the ferment concerning emancipating the slaves and keeping the states together in the Union. Lincoln once said, on meeting Harriet Beecher Stowe, that she was the little woman who started such a big war.

The Comedy of Oscar Wilde

The drawing room comedies of Oscar Wilde offered an alternative to melodrama and realistic drama in the late nineteenth century. Wilde, an Irish writer who had a brilliant career as a classicist at Trinity College, and then again at Oxford, had spent much of his literary life promoting the philosophy of art for art's sake. He asserted that the pleasure of poetry was in its sounds, images, and thoughts. Poetry did not serve religious, political, social, or even personal goals. Art served itself.

Wilde was a remarkable conversationalist. The Irish poet W. B. Yeats remarked that Wilde was the only person he ever heard who spoke complete, rounded sentences that sounded as if he had written and polished them the night before. His witticisms, notorious in London, were often barbed and vicious but always appropriate and thoughtful.

His life was marked, as he said himself, by an overindulgence in sensuality. "What paradox was to me in the sphere of thought, perversity became to me in the sphere of passion." His personal life was marked by an unhappy marriage followed by the discovery that he was more fulfilled by a homosexual than a heterosexual relationship. He soon pursued a young man, Lord Alfred Douglas, whose father, the Marquess of Queensberry, accused Wilde publicly of being a homosexual. Wilde foolishly and self-destructively sued for libel and lost. Consequently he was put on trial for homosexuality and was convicted. He spent two years in jail, and suffered bankruptcy, total ruin, and death in exile three years after he left England.

His most well-known novel is *The Picture of Dorian Gray* (1891), about a young man whose sensual life eats away at him and eventually destroys him. His best known poem is *The Ballad of Reading Gaol* (1898), published after he had served two years hard labor. Today he is still regarded as a late-Victorian writer of great importance, and his plays are often produced.

His plays were written and produced in a remarkably short time, from 1892 to 1895, when he was convicted and jailed. *Lady Windermere's Fan* (1892), *A Woman of No Importance* (1893), *An Ideal Husband* (1895), and *The Importance of Being Earnest* (1895) are all bright, witty, comic portraits of the society that Wilde knew best. They owe a great deal to the witty comedies of the English Restoration, such as William Congreve's *The Way of the World*. They rely on the clever use of language for their effect. The dialogue in Wilde's plays is as scintillating as one could find in any comedy of manners. His analysis of the behavior of the upper classes is incisive, merciless, and comic. We still laugh today even though the class which is being satirized has largely disappeared.

The Importance of Being Earnest was a remarkable success when it was first produced in 1895, but it closed after fewer than one hundred performances when the scandal of Wilde's conviction became public. The play was revived in 1898, which gratified Wilde even though he was in exile by that time.

Oscar Wilde (1854–1900)
THE IMPORTANCE OF BEING EARNEST

The excerpt that follows is from Act I. The primary characters are Algernon Moncrieff and Jack Worthing, young gentlemen of marriageable age. The women in this excerpt are Algernon's cousin Gwendolen Fairfax, who adores the name Ernest and is in love with Jack, and Lady Bracknell, her mother. Algernon's butler is Lane, trained well enough to cover for his employer's minor indiscretions, such as his earlier consumption of the cucumber sandwiches that were originally ordered for his aunt, Lady Bracknell.

Bunbury seems to be a character in the play, but he is not. He is a convenience for Algernon, who invented him to avoid going to social events he disliked, such as Lady Bracknell's dinner. When Algernon does not want to appear, he simply tells everyone that Bunbury is ill in the country and that he must visit his sick friend. Jack, who lives in the country, has created a similar figure to help him escape to town — an imaginary brother, Ernest. In town, Jack pretends to be Ernest; and all his town acquaintances, including Algernon and Gwendolen, know Jack by that name.

The excerpt that appears here is in the same comic vein as the excerpt from *The Way of the World*; both are proposal scenes. The contractual aspect of marriage in this social class is the only aspect that interests Lady Bracknell, who needs to know everything of importance about Jack Worthing before she can approve of his engagement to her daughter. What she discovers is one of the key comic situations of the play: Jack is a foundling who had been left in a handbag in Victoria Station, the Brighton Line. He does not know his true identity — a situation that is much used in melodrama, which Wilde here satirizes.

The spirited young women in Wilde's play are reminiscent of Congreve's female characters. Gwendolen is an independent young woman who makes up her own mind and waits for her man to see the light and propose. She is determined to have Jack Worthing, and when he is sluggish about proposing, she urges him on with promises of acceptance.

Ultimately, it turns out that Jack is not Jack, but the son and namesake of Ernest John Moncrieff, and is none other than Algernon's older brother. The discovery takes place at the last minute of the last act, and it pleases everyone, especially Gwendolen, who all along had had her heart set on marrying a man named Ernest.

The wit of this delightful farce is verbal, rapid, and acerbic. Very little actually happens, and nothing significant is at stake in the play, but its trivialities are charming and amusing. Its characters, while lacking in psychological depth, are fascinating and sympathetic. Brilliant actors and actresses, such as John Giulgud and Margaret Rutherfod, have played this comedy in memorable fashion. Wilde's language is what makes the play such a success.

EXCERPT FROM ACT I

(*Enter Lane.*)

LANE: Lady Bracknell and Miss Fairfax.

(*Algernon goes forward to meet them. Enter Lady Bracknell and Gwendolen.*)

LADY BRACKNELL: Good afternoon, dear Algernon, I hope you are behaving very well.

ALGERNON: I'm feeling very well, Aunt Augusta.

LADY BRACKNELL: That's not quite the same thing. In fact the two things rarely go together. (*Sees Jack and bows to him with icy coldness.*)

ALGERNON (*to Gwendolen*): Dear me, you are smart!

GWENDOLEN: I am always smart! Am I not, Mr. Worthing?

JACK: You're quite perfect, Miss Fairfax.

GWENDOLEN: Oh! I hope I am not that. It would leave no room for developments, and I intend to develop in many directions. (*Gwendolen and Jack sit down together in the corner.*)

LADY BRACKNELL: I'm sorry if we are a little late, Algernon, but I was obliged to call on dear Lady Harbury. I hadn't been there since her poor husband's death. I never saw a woman so altered; she looks quite twenty years younger. And now I'll have a cup of tea and one of those nice cucumber sandwiches you promised me.

ALGERNON: Certainly, Aunt Augusta. (*Goes over to teatable.*)

LADY BRACKNELL: Won't you come and sit here, Gwendolen?

GWENDOLEN: Thanks, mamma, I'm quite comfortable where I am.

ALGERNON (*picking up empty plate in horror*): Good heavens! Lane! Why are there no cucumber sandwiches? I ordered them specially.

LANE (*gravely*): There were no cucumbers in the market this morning, sir. I went down twice.

ALGERNON: No cucumbers!

LANE: No, sir. Not even for ready money.

ALGERNON: That will do, Lane, thank you.

LANE: Thank you, sir. (*Goes out.*)

ALGERNON: I am greatly distressed, Aunt Augusta, about there being no cucumbers, not even for ready money.

LADY BRACKNELL: It really makes no matter, Algernon. I had some crumpets with Lady Harbury, who seems to me to be living entirely for pleasure now.

ALGERNON: I hear her hair has turned quite gold from grief.

LADY BRACKNELL: It certainly has changed its color. From what cause I, of course, cannot say. (*Algernon crosses and hands tea.*) Thank you. I've quite a treat for you tonight, Algernon. I am going to send you down with Mary Farquhar. She is such a nice woman, and so attentive to her husband. It's delightful to watch them.

ALGERNON: I am afraid, Aunt Augusta, I shall have to give up the pleasure of dining with you tonight after all.

LADY BRACKNELL (*frowning*): I hope not, Algernon. It would put my table completely out. Your uncle would have to dine upstairs. Fortunately he is accustomed to that.

ALGERNON: It is a great bore, and, I need hardly say, a terrible disappointment to me, but the fact is I have just had a telegram to say that my poor friend Bunbury is very ill again. (*Exchanges glances with Jack.*) They seem to think I should be with him.

LADY BRACKNELL: It is very strange. This Mr. Bunbury seems to suffer from curiously bad health.

ALGERNON: Yes; poor Bunbury is a dreadful invalid.

LADY BRACKNELL: Well, I must say, Algernon, that I think it is high time that Mr. Bunbury made up his mind whether he was going to live or to die. This shilly-shallying with the question is absurd. Nor do I in any way approve of the modern sympathy with invalids. I consider it morbid. Illness of any kind is hardly a thing to be encouraged in others. Health is the primary duty of life. I am always telling that to your poor uncle, but he never seems to take much notice . . . as far as any improvement in his ailments goes. I should be much obliged if you would ask Mr. Bunbury, from me, to be kind enough not to have a relapse on Saturday, for I rely on you to arrange my music for me. It is my last reception, and one wants something that will encourage conversation, particularly at the end of the season when every one has practically said whatever they had to say, which, in most cases, was probably not much.

ALGERNON: I'll speak to Bunbury, Aunt Augusta, if he is still conscious, and I

think I can promise you he'll be all right by Saturday. Of course the music
is a great difficulty. You see, if one plays good music, people don't listen,
and if one plays bad music, people don't talk. But I'll run over the program
I've drawn out, if you will kindly come into the next room for a moment.

LADY BRACKNELL: Thank you, Algernon. It is very thoughtful of you. (*Rising,
and following Algernon.*) I'm sure the program will be delightful, after a few
expurgations. French songs I cannot possibly allow. People always seem to
think that they are improper, and either look shocked, which is vulgar, or
laugh, which is worse. But German sounds a thoroughly respectable language,
and, indeed I believe is so. Gwendolen, you will accompany me.

GWENDOLEN: Certainly, mamma.

(*Lady Bracknell and Algernon go into the music room; Gwendolen remains
behind.*)

JACK: Charming day it has been, Miss Fairfax.

GWENDOLEN: Pray don't talk to me about the weather, Mr. Worthing. Whenever
people talk to me about the weather, I always feel quite certain that they
mean something else. And that makes me so nervous.

JACK: I do mean something else.

GWENDOLEN: I thought so. In fact, I am never wrong.

JACK: And I would like to be allowed to take advantage of Lady Bracknell's
temporary absence. . . .

GWENDOLEN: I would certainly advise you to do so. Mamma has a way of
coming back suddenly into a room that I have often had to speak to her
about.

JACK (*nervously*): Miss Fairfax, ever since I met you I have admired you more
than any girl . . . I have ever met since . . . I met you.

GWENDOLEN: Yes, I am quite aware of the fact. And I often wish that in public,
at any rate, you had been more demonstrative. For me you have always had
an irresistible fascination. Even before I met you I was far from indifferent
to you. (*Jack looks at her in amazement.*) We live, as I hope you know, Mr.
Worthing, in an age of ideals. The fact is constantly mentioned in the more
expensive monthly magazines, and has reached the provincial pulpits, I am
told; and my ideal has always been to love someone of the name of Ernest.
There is something in that name that inspires absolute confidence. The moment
Algernon first mentioned to me that he had a friend called Ernest, I knew
I was destined to love you.

JACK: You really love me, Gwendolen?

GWENDOLEN: Passionately!

JACK: Darling! You don't know how happy you've made me.

GWENDOLEN: My own Ernest!

JACK: But you don't really mean to say that you couldn't love me if my name
wasn't Ernest?

GWENDOLEN: But your name is Ernest.

JACK: Yes, I know it is. But supposing it was something else? Do you mean to
say you couldn't love me then?

GWENDOLEN (*glibly*): Ah! that is clearly a metaphysical speculation, and like
most metaphysical speculations has very little reference at all to the actual
facts of real life, as we know them.

JACK: Personally, darling, to speak quite candidly, I don't much care about the
name of Ernest. . . . I don't think the name suits me at all.

GWENDOLEN: It suits you perfectly. It is a divine name. It has a music of its
own. It produces vibrations.

JACK: Well, really, Gwendolen, I must say that I think there are lots of other
much nicer names. I think Jack, for instance, a charming name.

GWENDOLEN: Jack? . . . No, there is very little music in the name Jack, if any at all, indeed. It does not thrill. It produces absolutely no vibrations. . . . I have known several Jacks, and they all, without exception, were more than usually plain. Besides, Jack is a notorious domesticity for John! And I pity any woman who is married to a man called John. She would probably never be allowed to know the entrancing pleasure of a single moment's solitude. The only really safe name is Ernest.

JACK: Gwendolen, I must get christened at once — I mean we must get married at once. There is no time to be lost.

GWENDOLEN: Married, Mr. Worthing?

JACK (*astounded*): Well . . . surely. You know that I love you, and you led me to believe, Miss Fairfax, that you were not absolutely indifferent to me.

GWENDOLEN: I adore you. But you haven't proposed to me yet. Nothing has been said at all about marriage. The subject has not even been touched on.

JACK: Well . . . may I propose to you now?

GWENDOLEN: I think it would be an admirable opportunity. And to spare you any possible disappointment, Mr. Worthing, I think it only fair to tell you quite frankly beforehand that I am fully determined to accept you.

JACK: Gwendolen!

GWENDOLEN: Yes, Mr. Worthing, what have you got to say to me?

JACK: You know what I have got to say to you.

GWENDOLEN: Yes, but you don't say it.

JACK: Gwendolen, will you marry me? (*Goes on his knees.*)

GWENDOLEN: Of course I will, darling. How long you have been about it! I am afraid you have had very little experience in how to propose.

JACK: My own one, I have never loved anyone in the world but you.

GWENDOLEN: Yes, but men often propose for practice. I know my brother Gerald does. All my girlfriends tell me so. What wonderfully blue eyes you have, Ernest! They are quite, quite blue. I hope you will always look at me just like that, especially when there are other people present.

(*Enter Lady Bracknell.*)

LADY BRACKNELL: Mr. Worthing! Rise sir, from this semirecumbent posture. It is most indecorous.

GWENDOLEN: Mamma! (*He tries to rise; she restrains him.*) I must beg you to retire. This is no place for you. Besides, Mr. Worthing has not quite finished yet.

LADY BRACKNELL: Finished what, may I ask?

GWENDOLEN: I am engaged to Mr. Worthing, mamma. (*They rise together.*)

LADY BRACKNELL: Pardon me, you are not engaged to anyone. When you do become engaged to some one, I, or your father, should his health permit him, will inform you of the fact. An engagement should come on a young girl as a surprise, pleasant or unpleasant, as the case may be. It is hardly a matter that she could be allowed to arrange for herself. . . . And now I have a few questions to put to you, Mr. Worthing. While I am making these inquiries, you, Gwendolen, will wait for me below in the carriage.

GWENDOLEN (*reproachfully*): Mamma!

LADY BRACKNELL: In the carriage, Gwendolen! (*Gwendolen goes to the door. She and Jack blow kisses to each other behind Lady Bracknell's back. Lady Bracknell looks vaguely about as if she could not understand what the noise was. Finally turns round.*) Gwendolen, the carriage!

GWENDOLEN: Yes, mamma. (*Goes out, looking back at Jack.*)

LADY BRACKNELL (*sitting down*): You can take a seat, Mr. Worthing.

(*Looks in her pocket for notebook and pencil.*)

JACK: Thank you, Lady Bracknell, I prefer standing.

LADY BRACKNELL (*pencil and notebook in hand*): I feel bound to tell you that you are not down on my list of eligible young men, although I have the same list as the dear Duchess of Bolton has. We work together, in fact. However, I am quite ready to enter your name, should your answers be what a really affectionate mother requires. Do you smoke?

JACK: Well, yes, I must admit I smoke.

LADY BRACKNELL: I am glad to hear it. A man should always have an occupation of some kind. There are far too many idle men in London as it is. How old are you?

JACK: Twenty-nine.

LADY BRACKNELL: A very good age to be married at. I have always been of opinion that a man who desires to get married should know either everything or nothing. Which do you know?

JACK (*after some hesitation*): I know nothing, Lady Bracknell.

LADY BRACKNELL: I am pleased to hear it. I do not approve of anything that tampers with natural ignorance. Ignorance is like a delicate exotic fruit; touch it and the bloom is gone. The whole theory of modern education is radically unsound. Fortunately in England, at any rate, education produces no effect whatsoever. If it did, it would prove a serious danger to the upper classes, and probably lead to acts of violence in Grosvenor Square. What is your income?

JACK: Between seven and eight thousand a year.

LADY BRACKNELL (*makes a note in her book*): In land, or in investments?

JACK: In investments, chiefly.

LADY BRACKNELL: That is satisfactory. What between the duties expected of one during one's lifetime, and the duties exacted from one after one's death, land has ceased to be either a profit or a pleasure. It gives one position, and prevents one from keeping it up. That's all that can be said about land.

JACK: I have a country house with some land, of course, attached to it, about fifteen hundred acres, I believe; but I don't depend on that for my real income. In fact, as far as I can make out, the poachers are the only people who make anything out of it.

LADY BRACKNELL: A country house! How many bedrooms? Well, that point can be cleared up afterwards. You have a town house, I hope? A girl with a simple, unspoiled nature, like Gwendolen, could hardly be expected to reside in the country.

JACK: Well, I own a house in Belgrave Square, but it is let by the year to Lady Bloxham. Of course, I can get it back whenever I like, at six months' notice.

LADY BRACKNELL: Lady Bloxham? I don't know her.

JACK: Oh, she goes about very little. She is a lady considerably advanced in years.

LADY BRACKNELL: Ah, nowadays that is no guarantee of respectability of character. What number in Belgrave Square?

JACK: 149.

LADY BRACKNELL (*shaking her head*): The unfashionable side. I thought there was something. However, that could easily be altered.

JACK: Do you mean the fashion, or the side?

LADY BRACKNELL (*sternly*): Both, if necessary, I presume. What are your politics?

JACK: Well, I am afraid I really have none. I am a Liberal Unionist.

LADY BRACKNELL: Oh, they count as Tories. They dine with us. Or come in the evening, at any rate. Now to minor matters. Are your parents living?

JACK: I have lost both my parents.

LADY BRACKNELL: To lose one parent, Mr. Worthing, may be regarded as a misfortune; to lose both looks like carelessness. Who was your father? He was evidently a man of some wealth. Was he born in what the Radical papers call the purple of commerce, or did he rise from the ranks of the aristocracy?

JACK: I am afraid I really don't know. The fact is, Lady Bracknell, I said I had lost my parents. It would be nearer the truth to say that my parents seem to have lost me. . . . I don't actually know who I am by birth. I was . . . well, I was found.

LADY BRACKNELL: Found!

JACK: The late Mr. Thomas Cardew, an old gentleman of a very charitable and kindly disposition, found me, and gave me the name of Worthing, because he happened to have a first-class ticket for Worthing in his pocket at the time. Worthing is a place in Sussex. It is a seaside resort.

LADY BRACKNELL: Where did the charitable gentleman who had a first-class ticket for this seaside resort find you?

JACK (*gravely*): In a handbag.

LADY BRACKNELL: A handbag?

JACK (*very seriously*): Yes, Lady Bracknell. I was in a handbag — a somewhat large, black leather handbag, with handles to it — an ordinary handbag in fact.

LADY BRACKNELL: In what locality did this Mr. James, or Thomas, Cardew come across this ordinary handbag?

JACK: In the cloak room at Victoria Station. It was given to him in mistake for his own.

LADY BRACKNELL: The cloak room at Victoria Station?

JACK: Yes. The Brighton line.

LADY BRACKNELL: The line is immaterial. Mr. Worthing, I confess I feel somewhat bewildered by what you have just told me. To be born, or at any rate bred, in a handbag, whether it had handles or not, seems to me to display a contempt for the ordinary decencies of family life that reminds one of the worst excesses of the French Revolution. And I presume you know what that unfortunate movement led to? As for the particular locality in which the handbag was found, a cloak room at a railway station might serve to conceal a social indiscretion — has probably, indeed, been used for that purpose before now — but it could hardly be regarded as an assured basis for a recognized position in good society.

JACK: May I ask you then what you would advise me to do? I need hardly say I would do anything in the world to ensure Gwendolen's happiness.

LADY BRACKNELL: I would strongly advise you, Mr. Worthing, to try and acquire some relations as soon as possible, and to make a definite effort to produce at any rate one parent, of either sex, before the season is quite over.

JACK: Well, I don't see how I could possibly manage to do that. I can produce the handbag at any moment. It is in my dressing room at home. I really think that should satisfy you, Lady Bracknell.

LADY BRACKNELL: Me, sir! What has it to do with me? You can hardly imagine that I and Lord Bracknell would dream of allowing our only daughter — a girl brought up with the utmost care — to marry into a cloak room, and form an alliance with a parcel. Good morning, Mr. Worthing!

(*Lady Bracknell sweeps out in majestic indignation.*)

Realism

Melodrama held the stage for years, even long after the Civil War. But eventually a movement in the arts and literature found its way slowly onto the stage, first in the 1870s in Scandinavia and ultimately in the early 1920s in the United States. The movement was REALISM, and the drama told a modern story in modern ways with modern frankness. Drama, such as Ibsen's *Ghosts* and Strindberg's *Miss Julie*, was likely to shock the sensibilities of proper audiences both by its frank language and its treatment of themes that had never been seen on the stage before.

Realism occasionally included fantasy as a way of expanding the psychological dimension of a play. However, a development from realism called NATURALISM avoided anything that departed from life as it occurs in all its minute details. The goals of naturalism were to present life without the shaping influences of plot and a sense of completion. The ideal was to produce a slice of life. Such dramas would by necessity include trivial conversation and random moments of dialogue. But most of all, because of the somewhat pessimistic philosophy of the naturalists — Stendhal, Émile Zola, Gerhart Hauptmann (whose *Weavers* is one of the best naturalistic plays) — the life that was portrayed was often gloomy. Naturalism is sometimes said to have derived from a reaction to Darwin's *On the Origin of Species* (1859), a work setting forth his doctrine of the survival of the fittest.

The introduction of gas lights to the theater, which began early in the century at the Chestnut Street Theater in Philadelphia, helped spur realistic drama. Even though gas light could be relatively soft, and even sometimes dreamy, when it was bright the audience could easily see that the three-dimensional details of the setting were illusions created by painting. Thereafter, and especially when electric lighting was introduced, settings had to be constructed with three-dimensional details that more closely simulated real locations. Such realistic settings complemented the emerging realistic drama.

Costuming became an advanced theatrical art, and although the first history of theatrical costume was written late in the eighteenth century, it was the nineteenth century that began to demand accurate period costumes in historical dramas. The first such drama was Shakespeare's *King John*, produced at Covent Garden in London in 1823. Later historical productions soon followed that pattern.

It was a long way from the realism of 1823 to the realism of 1879, when Strindberg and Ibsen were writing, but in a sense the path was straight. The stage itself began in the century with a proscenium arch that acted as the imaginary fourth wall of a room for the action. As the century drew to a close, the audience felt itself to be eavesdropping on actors who were less and less aware of the presence of onlookers.

Eventually this type of staging became the norm in theaters in the latter part of the century (Figure 6). But the dramas of Strindberg and Ibsen were not always absolutely realistic in detail, but rather in effect. Theatergoers had the feeling that they searched into the psychological lives of the characters onstage. Certain remarkable, almost fantastical things happened in the plays, but the playwrights always expected the audience to concern itself with the underlying realism of theme and substance. It was rarely easy for audiences to watch drama about such

Figure 6. Realistic setting in
Anton Chekhov's *Three
Sisters*

issues as feminism, madness, venereal disease, and municipal corruption
— all subjects that were hardly the norm on the popular stage.

It is little wonder, then, that realist playwrights were sometimes under
fire. Ibsen's *Ghosts* was thought to be reprehensible by many theatergoers.
Plays such as Strindberg's *Miss Julie*, Ibsen's *A Doll's House*, and Chekhov's
The Cherry Orchard were so frank that for a short time they alienated
their audiences. Other artists, however, were excited by the new drama.
As a college student, James Joyce, the great Irish novelist, learned Dano-
Norwegian so he could correspond with Ibsen in his native language
to express his delight in Ibsen's achievement of realism. Joyce felt that
realism was the direction that modern literature had, by necessity, to
take. Joyce was right and Ibsen's detractors were wrong.

The nineteenth century began with a powerful move in the direction
of new technical achievement and ended with an entirely new kind of
drama, a drama that showed people as they were, blemishes and all. It
was not a theater of wit, light comedy, or cunning satire that entranced
the audience at the end of the century. Rather, it was a drama of high
intensity, high seriousness, and sometimes gloomy outlook. But it was
also a theater of ideas, as Shaw's *Major Barbara* demonstrates.

Henrik Ibsen

Henrik Ibsen (1828–1906) wrote the most powerful and influential plays in the new style of realism. Subjects that had been ignored on the stage became the center of his work. But the price he paid for his honesty was enormous. He was an isolated and lonely man throughout his life; and after his first drama to hint at the new style of realism, *Pillars of Society*, was produced in 1877, he also became one of the most attacked playwrights of his time.

He wrote many kinds of plays, from his early idealized romances to late symbolist dramas, but those that most affected future playwrights such as Eugene O'Neill, Arthur Miller, and others were the great realist works such as *A Doll's House*, *Ghosts*, *The Wild Duck*, and *Hedda Gabler*. All these plays examine powerful characters who are to some extent overwhelmed by forces in their society.

Ibsen was born into a middle-class family, but his father, a merchant, went bankrupt early. When he was fifteen, Ibsen worked in a drug store in a small Norwegian town called Grimstad, where, in complete poverty, he stayed for six years. Although his life at this time was difficult, in 1849 he wrote his first play, on a classical subject: *Catiline*. Eventually he left Grimstad for Bergen and worked in a theatrical company writing, directing, and designing. He wrote numerous verse plays, most on romantic themes, and he received very little notice and little success.

By 1860 he was married with a child and still in deep poverty. His first success was *Brand* (1866), but it was a verse play that was intended to be read, not acted. It is a powerful portrait of a priest who takes the strictures of religion so seriously that he rejects the New Testament doctrine of love and accepts the Old Testament doctrine of the will of God. He destroys himself in the process and ends the play on a mountaintop in the Ice Church, facing an avalanche about to kill him. Out of the clouds comes the answer to his question of whether love or will achieves salvation: "He is the God of Love."

Ibsen followed *Brand* with *Peer Gynt* in 1867, a play about a character, quite unlike Brand, who avoids the rigors of morality and ends up unable to know if he has been saved or condemned. In 1877 Ibsen finished *The Pillars of Society*, which is about a merchant, Bernick, who prospers by all manner of double dealing and betraying his relatives. Eventually, he confesses his crimes and is accepted back into society. The work was a complete success and gave Ibsen an international reputation. Two years later, *A Doll's House* was a sensation in Copenhagen; this first play in his new style of realism slowly established Ibsen as a world-famous playwright. The next play, *Ghosts* (1881), was denounced violently because it dared to treat a subject that had been taboo on the stage: syphilis. *Ghosts* introduced a respectable family, the Alvings, who harbor the secret that the late father was accustomed to sexual dalliance, contracted the disease, and passed it on to Oswald, his son. In addition, the theme of incest is suggested in the presence of Alving's illegitimate daughter, Regina, who falls in love with Oswald. This kind of material was so foreign to the late nineteenth-century stage that Ibsen was vilified and isolated by the literary community in Norway. He became an exile for most of the remainder of his life in Rome, Amalfi, and Munich.

Ibsen's last years were filled with activity. He wrote some of his best-known plays in rapid succession: *An Enemy of the People* (1882), *The Wild Duck* (1884), *Hedda Gabler* (1890), *The Master Builder* (1892), and *John Gabriel Borkman* (1896). In 1891 he returned to live in Norway, where he died fifteen years later.

Ibsen was the most influential European dramatist in the late nineteenth century. He inspired emerging writers in the United States, Ireland, and many other nations. But his full influence was not felt until the early decades of the twentieth century, when other writers were able to spread the revolutionary doctrine that was implied in realism as practiced by Ibsen and Strindberg. Being direct, honest, and unsparing in treating character and theme became the normal mode of serious drama after Ibsen.

A DOLL'S HOUSE

Once Henrik Ibsen found his voice as a realist playwright, he began to develop plays centering on social problems and the problems of the individual in society. In *A Doll's House* (1879) he found a ready-made problem, the repression of women by society. It was a subject that deeply offended conservatives and was very much on the minds of progressive and liberal Scandinavians. It was therefore a rather daring theme. The play opens with the dutiful, eager wife Nora Helmer twittering like a lark and nattering like a squirrel pleasing her husband, Torvald. Helmer is himself so fatuous as to leave a modern audience almost breathless with alarm and amusement. As far as he is concerned, Nora is only a woman, an empty-headed ornament in a house designed to keep his life functioning smoothly.

Nora is portrayed as a macaroon-eating, sweet-toothed creature looking for ways to please her husband. When she reveals that she borrowed the money that took them to Italy for a year to save her husband's life, she shows us that she is made of much stronger stuff than anyone has given her credit for. Yet the manner in which she borrowed the money is potentially criminal because she forged her father's signature, and she finds herself at the mercy of the lender, Nils Krogstad.

From a modern perspective, Nora's action seems daring and imaginative rather than merely illegal and surreptitious. Torvald Helmer's moralistic position is to us essentially stifling. He condemns Nora's father for a similar failure to secure proper signatures, just as he condemns Nils Krogstad for doing the same. He condemns people for their crimes without considering their circumstances or motives. He is moralistic rather than moral.

The atmosphere of the Helmer household is oppressive. Everything is set up to amuse Torvald, and he lacks any awareness that other people might be his equal. Early in the play Ibsen establishes Nora's longings: she explains that to pay back her loan she has had to take in copying work, and rather than resent her labor she observes that it made her feel wonderful, the way a man must feel. Ibsen said that his intention in the play was not primarily to promote the emancipation of women; it was to establish, as Ibsen's biographer Michael Meyer says, "that the primary duty of anyone was to find out who he or she really was and to become that person."

However, the play from the first was seen as addressing the problems of women, especially married women who were treated as their husbands' property. When the play was first performed, the slam of the door at Nora's leaving was much louder than it is today. It was shocking to late-nineteenth-century society, which took Torvald Helmer's attitudes for granted. The first audiences would have been split in their opinions about Nora's actions. As Meyer reminds us, "No play had ever before contributed so momentously to the social debate, or been so widely and furiously discussed among people who were not normally interested in theatrical or even artistic matters." Although the critics in Copenhagen and England were very negative, the audiences were filled with curiosity and flocked to the theaters to see the play.

What the audiences saw was that once Nora is awakened, the kind of life Torvald imagines for her is death to Nora. Torvald cannot see how his self-absorbed concern and fear for his own social standing reveal his limitations and selfishness. Nora sees immediately the limits of his concern, and her only choice is to leave him so that she can grow morally and spiritually.

What she does and where she goes have been a matter of speculation since the play was first performed. Ibsen refused to encourage any specific conjecture. It is enough that she has the courage to leave. But the ending of the play bothered audiences as well as critics, and it was performed in Germany in 1880 with a happy ending that Ibsen himself wrote to forestall anyone else from doing so. The first German actress to play the part demanded the ending. She insisted that she would never leave her children and would not do the play as written. In the revised version, instead of leaving, Nora is led to the door of her children's room and falls weeping as the curtain goes down. No one was satisfied with this ending, and eventually the play reverted to its original form.

Through the proscenium arch of the theater in Ibsen's day audiences were permitted to eavesdrop on themselves, since Ibsen clearly was analyzing their own mores. In a way the audience was looking at a doll's house, a room with one wall removed; but instead of containing miniature furniture and miniature people, it contained replicas of those watching. That very sense of intimacy, made possible by the late-nineteenth-century theater, heightened the intensity of the play.

Henrik Ibsen (1828–1906)

A Doll's House

1879

TRANSLATED BY MICHAEL MEYER

Characters

TORVALD HELMER, *a lawyer*
NORA, *his wife*
DR. RANK
MRS. LINDE
NILS KROGSTAD, *also a lawyer*
THE HELMERS' *three small children*
ANNE-MARIE, *their nurse*
HELEN, *the maid*
A PORTER

Scene: *The action takes place in the Helmers' apartment.*

ACT I

(*A comfortably and tastefully, but not expensively, furnished room. Backstage right a door leads out to the hall; backstage left, another door to Helmer's study. Between these two doors stands a piano. In the middle of the left-hand wall is a door, with a window downstage of it. Near the window, a round table with armchairs and a small sofa. In the right-hand wall, slightly upstage, is a door; downstage of this, against the same wall, a stove lined with porcelain tiles, with a couple of armchairs and a rocking-chair in front of it. Between the stove and the side door is a small table. Engravings on the wall. A what-not with china* and other bric-a-brac; a small bookcase with leather-bound books. A carpet on the floor; a fire in the stove. A winter day.*)

(*A bell rings in the hall outside. After a moment, we hear the front door being opened. Nora enters the room, humming contentedly to herself. She is wearing outdoor clothes and carrying a lot of parcels, which she puts down on the table right. She leaves the door to the hall open; through it, we can see a Porter carrying a Christmas tree and a basket. He gives these to the Maid, who has opened the door for them.*)

NORA: Hide that Christmas tree away, Helen. The children mustn't see it before I've decorated it this evening. (*To the Porter, taking out her purse.*) How much —?
PORTER: A shilling.
NORA: Here's half a crown. No, keep it.

(*The Porter touches his cap and goes. Nora closes the door. She continues to laugh happily to herself as she removes her coat, etc. She takes from her pocket a bag containing macaroons and eats a couple. Then she tiptoes across and listens at her husband's door.*)

NORA: Yes, he's here. (*Starts humming again as she goes over to the table, right.*)
HELMER (*from his room*): Is that my skylark twittering out there?
NORA (*opening some of the parcels*): It is!

HELMER: Is that my squirrel rustling?

NORA: Yes!

HELMER: When did my squirrel come home?

NORA: Just now. (*Pops the bag of macaroons in her pocket and wipes her mouth.*) Come out here, Torvald, and see what I've bought.

HELMER: You mustn't disturb me! (*Short pause; then he opens the door and looks in, his pen in his hand.*) Bought, did you say? All that? Has my little squanderbird been overspending again?

NORA: Oh, Torvald, surely we can let ourselves go a little this year! It's the first Christmas we don't have to scrape.

HELMER: Well, you know, we can't afford to be extravagant.

NORA: Oh yes, Torvald, we can be a little extravagant now. Can't we? Just a tiny bit? You've got a big salary now, and you're going to make lots and lots of money.

HELMER: Next year, yes. But my new salary doesn't start till April.

NORA: Pooh; we can borrow till then.

HELMER: Nora! (*Goes over to her and takes her playfully by the ear.*) What a little spendthrift you are! Suppose I were to borrow fifty pounds today, and you spent it all over Christmas, and then on New Year's Eve a tile fell off a roof on to my head —

NORA (*puts her hand over his mouth*): Oh, Torvald! Don't say such dreadful things!

HELMER: Yes, but suppose something like that did happen? What then?

NORA: If anything as frightful as that happened, it wouldn't make much difference whether I was in debt or not.

HELMER: But what about the people I'd borrowed from?

NORA: Them? Who cares about them? They're strangers.

HELMER: Oh, Nora, Nora, how like a woman! No, but seriously, Nora, you know how I feel about this. No debts! Never borrow! A home that is founded on debts can never be a place of freedom and beauty. We two have stuck it out bravely up to now; and we shall continue to do so for the short time we still have to.

NORA (*goes over toward the stove*): Very well, Torvald. As you say.

HELMER (*follows her*): Now, now! My little songbird mustn't droop her wings. What's this? Is little squirrel sulking? (*Takes out his purse.*) Nora; guess what I've got here!

NORA (*turns quickly*): Money!

HELMER: Look. (*Hands her some banknotes.*) I know how these small expenses crop up at Christmas.

NORA (*counts them*): One — two — three — four.

Oh, thank you, Torvald, thank you! I should be able to manage with this.

HELMER: You'll have to.

NORA: Yes, yes, of course I will. But come over here, I want to show you everything I've bought. And so cheaply! Look, here are new clothes for Ivar — and a sword. And a horse and a trumpet for Bob. And a doll and a cradle for Emmy — they're nothing much, but she'll pull them apart in a few days. And some bits of material and handkerchiefs for the maids. Old Anne-Marie ought to have had something better, really.

HELMER: And what's in that parcel?

NORA (*cries*): No. Torvald, you mustn't see that before this evening!

HELMER: Very well. But now, tell me, you little spendthrift, what do you want for Christmas?

NORA: Me? Oh, pooh, I don't want anything.

HELMER: Oh, yes, you do. Now tell me, what, within reason, would you most like?

NORA: No, I really don't know. Oh, yes — Torvald —!

HELMER: Well?

NORA (*plays with his coat buttons; not looking at him*): If you really want to give me something, you could — you could —

HELMER: Come on, out with it.

NORA (*quickly*): You could give me money, Torvald. Only as much as you feel you can afford; then later I'll buy something with it.

HELMER: But, Nora —

NORA: Oh yes, Torvald dear, please! Please! Then I'll wrap up the notes in pretty gold paper and hang them on the Christmas tree. Wouldn't that be fun?

HELMER: What's the name of that little bird that can never keep any money?

NORA: Yes, yes, squanderbird; I know. But let's do as I say, Torvald; then I'll have time to think about what I need most. Isn't that the best way? Mm?

HELMER (*smiles*): To be sure it would be, if you could keep what I give you and really buy yourself something with it. But you'll spend it on all sorts of useless things for the house, and then I'll have to put my hand in my pocket again.

NORA: Oh, but Torvald —

HELMER: You can't deny it, Nora dear. (*Puts his arm round her waist.*) The squanderbird's a pretty little creature, but she gets through an awful lot of money. It's incredible what an expensive pet she is for a man to keep.

NORA: For shame! How can you say such a thing? I save every penny I can.

HELMER (*laughs*): That's quite true. Every penny you can. But you can't.

NORA (*hums and smiles, quietly gleeful*): Hm. If you

only knew how many expenses we larks and squirrels have, Torvald.

HELMER: You're a funny little creature. Just like your father used to be. Always on the look-out for some way to get money, but as soon as you have any it just runs through your fingers, and you never know where it's gone. Well, I suppose I must take you as you are. It's in your blood. Yes, yes, yes, these things are hereditary, Nora.

NORA: Oh, I wish I'd inherited more of Papa's qualities.

HELMER: And I wouldn't wish my darling little songbird to be any different from what she is. By the way, that reminds me. You look awfully — how shall I put it? — awfully guilty today.

NORA: Do I?

HELMER: Yes, you do. Look me in the eyes.

NORA (*looks at him*): Well?

HELMER (*wags his finger*): Has my little sweet-tooth been indulging herself in town today, by any chance?

NORA: No, how can you think such a thing?

HELMER: Not a tiny little digression into a pastry shop?

NORA: No, Torvald, I promise —

HELMER: Not just a wee jam tart?

NORA: Certainly not.

HELMER: Not a little nibble at a macaroon?

NORA: No, Torvald — I promise you, honestly —

HELMER: There, there. I was only joking.

NORA (*goes over to the table, right*): You know I could never act against your wishes.

HELMER: Of course not. And you've given me your word — (*Goes over to her.*) Well, my beloved Nora, you keep your little Christmas secrets to yourself. They'll be revealed this evening, I've no doubt, once the Christmas tree has been lit.

NORA: Have you remembered to invite Dr. Rank?

HELMER: No. But there's no need; he knows he'll be dining with us. Anyway, I'll ask him when he comes this morning. I've ordered some good wine. Oh, Nora, you can't imagine how I'm looking forward to this evening.

NORA: So am I. And, Torvald, how the children will love it!

HELMER: Yes, it's a wonderful thing to know that one's position is assured and that one has an ample income. Don't you agree? It's good to know that, isn't it?

NORA: Yes, it's almost like a miracle.

HELMER: Do you remember last Christmas? For three whole weeks you shut yourself away every evening to make flowers for the Christmas tree, and all those other things you were going to surprise us with. Ugh, it was the most boring time I've ever had in my life.

NORA: I didn't find it boring.

HELMER (*smiles*): But it all came to nothing in the end, didn't it?

NORA: Oh, are you going to bring that up again? How could I help the cat getting in and tearing everything to bits?

HELMER: No, my poor little Nora, of course you couldn't. You simply wanted to make us happy, and that's all that matters. But it's good that those hard times are past.

NORA: Yes, it's wonderful.

HELMER: I don't have to sit by myself and be bored. And you don't have to tire your pretty eyes and your delicate little hands —

NORA (*claps her hands*): No, Torvald, that's true, isn't it — I don't have to any longer? Oh, it's really all just like a miracle. (*Takes his arm.*) Now, I'm going to tell you what I thought we might do, Torvald. As soon as Christmas is over — (*A bell rings in the hall.*) Oh, there's the doorbell. (*Tidies up one or two things in the room*). Someone's coming. What a bore.

HELMER: I'm not at home to any visitors. Remember!

MAID (*in the doorway*): A lady's called, madam. A stranger.

NORA: Well, ask her to come in.

MAID: And the doctor's here too, sir.

HELMER: Has he gone to my room?

MAID: Yes, sir.

(*Helmer goes into his room. The Maid shows in Mrs. Linde, who is dressed in traveling clothes, and closes the door.*)

MRS. LINDE (*shyly and a little hesitantly*): Good evening, Nora.

NORA (*uncertainly*): Good evening —

MRS. LINDE: I don't suppose you recognize me.

NORA: No, I'm afraid I — Yes, wait a minute — surely — (*Exclaims.*) Why, Christine! Is it really you?

MRS. LINDE: Yes, it's me.

NORA: Christine! And I didn't recognize you! But how could I —? (*More quietly.*) How you've changed, Christine!

MRS. LINDE: Yes, I know. It's been nine years — nearly ten —

NORA: Is it so long? Yes, it must be. Oh, these last eight years have been such a happy time for me! So you've come to town? All that way in winter! How brave of you!

MRS. LINDE: I arrived by the steamer this morning.

NORA: Yes, of course — to enjoy yourself over Christmas. Oh, how splendid! We'll have to celebrate! But take off your coat. You're not cold, are you? (*Helps her off with it.*) There! Now let's sit down here by the stove and be comfortable. No, you take the armchair. I'll sit here in the rocking-chair. (*Clasps Mrs. Linde's hands.*) Yes, now you look like your old self. It was just at first that — you've got a little paler, though, Christine. And perhaps a bit thinner.

MRS. LINDE: And older, Nora. Much, much older.

NORA: Yes, perhaps a little older. Just a tiny bit. Not much. (*Checks herself suddenly and says earnestly.*) Oh, but how thoughtless of me to sit here and chatter away like this! Dear, sweet Christine, can you forgive me?

MRS. LINDE: What do you mean, Nora?

NORA (*quietly*): Poor Christine, you've become a widow.

MRS. LINDE: Yes. Three years ago.

NORA: I know, I know — I read it in the papers. Oh, Christine, I meant to write to you so often, honestly. But I always put it off, and something else always cropped up.

MRS. LINDE: I understand, Nora dear.

NORA: No, Christine, it was beastly of me. Oh, my poor darling, what you've gone through! And he didn't leave you anything?

MRS. LINDE: No.

NORA: No children, either?

MRS. LINDE: No.

NORA: Nothing at all, then?

MRS. LINDE: Not even a feeling of loss or sorrow.

NORA (*looks incredulously at her*): But, Christine, how is that possible?

MRS. LINDE (*smiles sadly and strokes Nora's hair*): Oh, these things happen, Nora.

NORA: All alone. How dreadful that must be for you. I've three lovely children. I'm afraid you can't see them now, because they're out with nanny. But you must tell me everything —

MRS. LINDE: No, no, no. I want to hear about you.

NORA: No, you start. I'm not going to be selfish today, I'm just going to think about you. Oh, but there's one thing I *must* tell you. Have you heard of the wonderful luck we've just had?

MRS. LINDE: No. What?

NORA: Would you believe it — my husband's just been made manager of the bank!

MRS. LINDE: Your husband? Oh, how lucky —!

NORA: Yes, isn't it? Being a lawyer is so uncertain, you know, especially if one isn't prepared to touch any case that isn't — well — quite nice. And of course Torvald's been very firm about that — and I'm absolutely with him. Oh, you can imagine how happy we are! He's joining the bank in the New Year; and he'll be getting a big salary, and lots of percentages too. From now on we'll be able to live quite differently — we'll be able to do whatever

we want. Oh Christine, it's such a relief! I feel so happy! Well, I mean, it's lovely to have heaps of money and not to have to worry about anything. Don't you think?

MRS. LINDE: It must be lovely to have enough to cover one's needs, anyway.

NORA: Not just our needs! We're going to have heaps and heaps of money!

MRS. LINDE (*smiles*): Nora, Nora, haven't you grown up yet? When we were at school you were a terrible little spendthrift.

NORA (*laughs quietly*): Yes, Torvald still says that. (*Wags her finger.*) But "Nora, Nora" isn't as silly as you think. Oh, we've been in no position for me to waste money. We've both had to work.

MRS. LINDE: You too?

NORA: Yes, little things — fancy work, crocheting, embroidery and so forth. (*Casually.*) And other things too. I suppose you know Torvald left the Ministry when we got married? There were no prospects of promotion in his department, and of course he needed more money. But the first year he overworked himself quite dreadfully. He had to take on all sorts of extra jobs, and worked day and night. But it was too much for him, and he became frightfully ill. The doctors said he'd have to go to a warmer climate.

MRS. LINDE: Yes, you spent a whole year in Italy, didn't you?

NORA: Yes. It wasn't easy for me to get away, you know. I'd just had Ivar. But of course we had to do it. Oh, it was a marvelous trip! And it saved Torvald's life. But it cost an awful lot of money, Christine.

MRS. LINDE: I can imagine.

NORA: Two hundred and fifty pounds. That's a lot of money, you know.

MRS. LINDE: How lucky you had it.

NORA: Well, actually, we got it from my father.

MRS. LINDE: Oh, I see. Didn't he die just about that time?

NORA: Yes, Christine, just about then. Wasn't it dreadful, I couldn't go and look after him. I was expecting little Ivar any day. And then I had my poor Torvald to care for — we really didn't think he'd live. Dear, kind Papa! I never saw him again, Christine. Oh, it's the saddest thing that's happened to me since I got married.

MRS. LINDE: I know you were very fond of him. But you went to Italy —

NORA: Yes. Well, we had the money, you see, and the doctors said we mustn't delay. So we went the month after Papa died.

MRS. LINDE: And your husband came back completely cured?

NORA: Fit as a fiddle!

MRS. LINDE: But — the doctor?

NORA: How do you mean?

MRS. LINDE: I thought the maid said that the gentleman who arrived with me was the doctor.

NORA: Oh yes, that's Doctor Rank, but he doesn't come because anyone's ill. He's our best friend, and he looks us up at least once every day. No, Torvald hasn't had a moment's illness since we went away. And the children are fit and healthy and so am I. (*Jumps up and claps her hands.*) Oh God, oh God, Christine, isn't it a wonderful thing to be alive and happy! Oh, but how beastly of me! I'm only talking about myself. (*Sits on a footstool and rests her arms on Mrs. Linde's knee.*) Oh, please don't be angry with me! Tell me, is it really true you didn't love your husband? Why did you marry him, then?

MRS. LINDE: Well, my mother was still alive; and she was helpless and bedridden. And I had my two little brothers to take care of. I didn't feel I could say no.

NORA: Yes, well, perhaps you're right. He was rich then, was he?

MRS. LINDE: Quite comfortably off, I believe. But his business was unsound, you see, Nora. When he died it went bankrupt, and there was nothing left.

NORA: What did you do?

MRS. LINDE: Well, I had to try to make ends meet somehow, so I started a little shop, and a little school, and anything else I could turn my hand to. These last three years have been just one endless slog for me, without a moment's rest. But now it's over, Nora. My poor dear mother doesn't need me anymore; she's passed away. And the boys don't need me either; they've got jobs now and can look after themselves.

NORA: How relieved you must feel —

MRS. LINDE: No, Nora. Just unspeakably empty. No one to live for anymore. (*Gets up restlessly.*) That's why I couldn't bear to stay out there any longer, cut off from the world. I thought it'd be easier to find some work here that will exercise and occupy my mind. If only I could get a regular job — office work of some kind —

NORA: Oh but, Christine, that's dreadfully exhausting; and you look practically finished already. It'd be much better for you if you could go away somewhere.

MRS. LINDE (*goes over to the window*): I have no Papa to pay for my holidays, Nora.

NORA (*gets up*): Oh, please don't be angry with me.

MRS. LINDE: My dear Nora, it's I who should ask you not to be angry. That's the worst thing about this kind of situation — it makes one so bitter. One has no one to work for; and yet one has to be continually sponging for jobs. One has to live; and so one becomes completely egocentric. When you told me about this luck you've just had with Torvald's new job — can you imagine? — I was happy not so much on your account, as on my own.

NORA: How do you mean? Oh, I understand. You mean Torvald might be able to do something for you?

MRS. LINDE: Yes, I was thinking that.

NORA: He will too, Christine. Just you leave it to me. I'll lead up to it so delicately, so delicately; I'll get him in the right mood. Oh, Christine, I do so want to help you.

MRS. LINDE: It's sweet of you to bother so much about me, Nora. Especially since you know so little of the worries and hardships of life.

NORA: I? You say *I* know little of —?

MRS. LINDE (*smiles*): Well, good heavens — those bits of fancy work of yours — well, really —! You're a child, Nora.

NORA (*tosses her head and walks across the room*): You shouldn't say that so patronizingly.

MRS. LINDE: Oh?

NORA: You're like the rest. You all think I'm incapable of getting down to anything serious —

MRS. LINDE: My dear —

NORA: You think I've never had any worries like the rest of you.

MRS. LINDE: Nora dear, you've just told me about all your difficulties —

NORA: Pooh — that! (*Quietly.*) I haven't told you about the big thing.

MRS. LINDE: What big thing? What do you mean?

NORA: You patronize me, Christine; but you shouldn't. You're proud that you've worked so long and so hard for your mother.

MRS. LINDE: I don't patronize anyone, Nora. But you're right — I am both proud and happy that I was able to make my mother's last months on earth comparatively easy.

NORA: And you're also proud of what you've done for your brothers.

MRS. LINDE: I think I have a right to be.

NORA: I think so too. But let me tell you something, Christine. I too have done something to be proud and happy about.

MRS. LINDE: I don't doubt it. But — how do you mean?

NORA: Speak quietly! Suppose Torvald should hear! He mustn't, at any price — no one must know, Christine — no one but you.

MRS. LINDE: But what is this?

NORA: Come over here. (*Pulls her down on to the sofa beside her.*) Yes, Christine — I too have done something to be happy and proud about. It was I who saved Torvald's life.

MRS. LINDE: Saved his —? How did you save it?

NORA: I told you about our trip to Italy. Torvald couldn't have lived if he hadn't managed to get down there —

MRS. LINDE: Yes, well — your father provided the money —

NORA (*smiles*): So Torvald and everyone else thinks. But —

MRS. LINDE: Yes?

NORA: Papa didn't give us a penny. It was I who found the money.

MRS. LINDE: You? All of it?

NORA: Two hundred and fifty pounds. What do you say to that?

MRS. LINDE: But Nora, how could you? Did you win a lottery or something?

NORA (*scornfully*): Lottery? (*Sniffs.*) What would there be to be proud of in that?

MRS. LINDE: But where did you get it from, then?

NORA (*hums and smiles secretively*): Hm; tra-la-la-la!

MRS. LINDE: You couldn't have borrowed it.

NORA: Oh? Why not?

MRS. LINDE: Well, a wife can't borrow money without her husband's consent.

NORA (*tosses her head*): Ah, but when a wife has a little business sense, and knows how to be clever —

MRS. LINDE: But Nora, I simply don't understand —

NORA: You don't have to. No one has said I borrowed the money. I could have got it in some other way. (*Throws herself back on the sofa.*) I could have got it from an admirer. When a girl's as pretty as I am —

MRS. LINDE: Nora, you're crazy!

NORA: You're dying of curiosity now, aren't you, Christine?

MRS. LINDE: Nora dear, you haven't done anything foolish?

NORA (*sits up again*): Is it foolish to save one's husband's life?

MRS. LINDE: I think it's foolish if without his knowledge you —

NORA: But the whole point was that he mustn't know! Great heavens, don't you see? He hadn't to know how dangerously ill he was. I was the one they told that his life was in danger and that only going to a warm climate could save him. Do you suppose I didn't try to think of other ways of getting him down there? I told him how wonderful it would be for me to go abroad like other young wives; I cried and prayed; I asked him to remember my condition, and said he ought to be nice and tender to me; and then I suggested he might quite easily borrow the money. But then he got almost angry with me, Christine. He said I was frivolous, and that it was his duty as a husband not to pander to my moods and caprices — I think that's what he called them. Well, well, I thought, you've got to be saved somehow. And then I thought of a way —

MRS. LINDE: But didn't your husband find out from your father that the money hadn't come from him?

NORA: No, never. Papa died just then. I'd thought of letting him into the plot and asking him not to tell. But since he was so ill —! And as things turned out, it didn't become necessary.

MRS. LINDE: And you've never told your husband about this?

NORA: For heaven's sake, no! What an idea! He's frightfully strict about such matters. And besides — he's so proud of being a *man* — it'd be so painful and humiliating for him to know that he owed anything to me. It'd completely wreck our relationship. This life we have built together would no longer exist.

MRS. LINDE: Will you never tell him?

NORA (*thoughtfully, half-smiling*): Yes — some time, perhaps. Years from now, when I'm no longer pretty. You mustn't laugh! I mean of course, when Torvald no longer loves me as he does now; when it no longer amuses him to see me dance and dress up and play the fool for him. Then it might be useful to have something up my sleeve. (*Breaks off.*) Stupid, stupid, stupid! That time will never come. Well, what do you think of my big secret, Christine? I'm not completely useless, am I? Mind you, all this has caused me a frightful lot of worry. It hasn't been easy for me to meet my obligations punctually. In case you don't know, in the world of business there are things called quarterly installments and interest, and they're a terrible problem to cope with. So I've had to scrape a little here and save a little there as best I can. I haven't been able to save much on the housekeeping money, because Torvald likes to live well; and I couldn't let the children go short of clothes — I couldn't take anything out of what he gives me for them. The poor little angels!

MRS. LINDE: So you've had to stint yourself, my poor Nora?

NORA: Of course. Well, after all, it was my problem. Whenever Torvald gave me money to buy myself new clothes, I never used more than half of it; and I always bought what was cheapest and plainest. Thank heaven anything suits me, so that Torvald's never noticed. But it made me a bit sad sometimes, because it's lovely to wear pretty clothes. Don't you think?

MRS. LINDE: Indeed it is.

NORA: And then I've found one or two other sources of income. Last winter I managed to get a lot of copying to do. So I shut myself away and wrote every evening, late into the night. Oh, I often got so tired. But it was great fun, though, sitting there working and earning money. It was almost like being a man.

MRS. LINDE: But how much have you managed to pay off like this?

NORA: Well, I can't say exactly. It's awfully difficult to keep an exact check on these kind of transactions. I only know I've paid everything I've managed to scrape together. Sometimes I really didn't know where to turn. (*Smiles.*) Then I'd sit here and imagine some rich old gentleman had fallen in love with me —

MRS. LINDE: What! What gentleman?

NORA: Silly! And that now he'd died and when they opened his will it said in big letters: "Everything I possess is to be paid forthwith to my beloved Mrs. Nora Helmer in cash."

MRS. LINDE: But, Nora dear, who was this gentleman?

NORA: Great heavens, don't you understand? There wasn't any old gentleman; he was just something I used to dream up as I sat here evening after evening wondering how on earth I could raise some money. But what does it matter? The old bore can stay imaginary as far as I'm concerned, because now I don't have to worry any longer! (*Jumps up.*) Oh, Christine, isn't it wonderful? I don't have to worry any more! No more troubles! I can play all day with the children, I can fill the house with pretty things, just the way Torvald likes. And, Christine, it'll soon be spring, and the air'll be fresh and the skies blue, — and then perhaps we'll be able to take a little trip somewhere. I shall be able to see the sea again. Oh, yes, yes, it's a wonderful thing to be alive and happy!

(*The bell rings in the hall.*)

MRS. LINDE (*gets up*): You've a visitor. Perhaps I'd better go.

NORA: No, stay. It won't be for me. It's someone for Torvald —

MAID (*in the doorway*): Excuse me, madam, a gentleman's called who says he wants to speak to the master. But I didn't know — seeing as the doctor's with him —

NORA: Who is this gentleman?

KROGSTAD (*in the doorway*): It's me, Mrs. Helmer.

(*Mrs. Linde starts, composes herself, and turns away to the window.*)

NORA (*takes a step toward him and whispers tensely*):

You? What is it? What do you want to talk to my husband about?

KROGSTAD: Business — you might call it. I hold a minor post in the bank, and I hear your husband is to become our new chief —

NORA: Oh — then it isn't —?

KROGSTAD: Pure business, Mrs. Helmer. Nothing more.

NORA: Well, you'll find him in his study.

(*Nods indifferently as she closes the hall door behind him. Then she walks across the room and sees to the stove.*)

MRS. LINDE: Nora, who was that man?

NORA: A lawyer called Krogstad.

MRS. LINDE: It was him, then.

NORA: Do you know that man?

MRS. LINDE: I used to know him — some years ago. He was a solicitor's clerk in our town, for a while.

NORA: Yes, of course, so he was.

MRS. LINDE: How he's changed!

NORA: He was very unhappily married, I believe.

MRS. LINDE: Is he a widower now?

NORA: Yes, with a lot of children. Ah, now it's alight.

(*She closes the door of the stove and moves the rocking-chair a little to one side.*)

MRS. LINDE: He does — various things now, I hear?

NORA: Does he? It's quite possible — I really don't know. But don't let's talk about business. It's so boring.

(*Dr. Rank enters from Helmer's study.*)

RANK (*still in the doorway*): No, no, my dear chap, don't see me out. I'll go and have a word with your wife. (*Closes the door and notices Mrs. Linde.*) Oh, I beg your pardon. I seem to be *de trop°* here too.

NORA: Not in the least. (*Introduces them.*) Dr. Rank. Mrs. Linde.

RANK: Ah! A name I have often heard in this house. I believe I passed you on the stairs as I came up.

MRS. LINDE: Yes. Stairs tire me; I have to take them slowly.

RANK: Oh, have you hurt yourself?

MRS. LINDE: No, I'm just a little run down.

RANK: Ah, is that all? Then I take it you've come to town to cure yourself by a round of parties?

MRS. LINDE: I have come here to find work.

RANK: Is that an approved remedy for being run down?

MRS. LINDE: One has to live, Doctor.

RANK: Yes, people do seem to regard it as a necessity.

NORA: Oh, really, Dr. Rank. I bet you want to stay alive.

---

de trop: Too much, superfluous.

RANK: You bet I do. However miserable I sometimes feel, I still want to go on being tortured for as long as possible. It's the same with all my patients; and with people who are morally sick, too. There's a moral cripple in with Helmer at this very moment —

MRS. LINDE (*softly*): Oh!

NORA: Whom do you mean?

RANK: Oh, a lawyer fellow called Krogstad — you wouldn't know him. He's crippled all right; morally twisted. But even he started off by announcing, as though it were a matter of enormous importance, that he had to live.

NORA: Oh? What did he want to talk to Torvald about?

RANK: I haven't the faintest idea. All I heard was something about the bank.

NORA: I didn't know that Krog — that this man Krogstad had any connection with the bank.

RANK: Yes, he's got some kind of job down there. (*To Mrs. Linde.*) I wonder if in your part of the world you too have a species of human being that spends its time fussing around trying to smell out moral corruption? And when they find a case they give him some nice, comfortable position so that they can keep a good watch on him. The healthy ones just have to lump it.

MRS. LINDE: But surely it's the sick who need care most?

RANK (*shrugs his shoulders*): Well, there we have it. It's that attitude that's turning human society into a hospital.

(*Nora, lost in her own thoughts, laughs half to herself and claps her hands.*)

RANK: Why are you laughing? Do you really know what society is?

NORA: What do I care about society? I think it's a bore. I was laughing at something else — something frightfully funny. Tell me, Dr. Rank — will everyone who works at the bank come under Torvald now?

RANK: Do you find that particularly funny?

NORA (*smiles and hums*): Never you mind! Never you mind! (*Walks around the room.*) Yes, I find it very amusing to think that we — I mean, Torvald — has obtained so much influence over so many people. (*Takes the paper bag from her pocket.*) Dr. Rank, would you like a small macaroon?

RANK: Macaroons! I say! I thought they were forbidden here.

NORA: Yes, well, these are some Christine gave me.

MRS. LINDE: What? I —?

NORA: All right, all right, don't get frightened. You weren't to know Torvald had forbidden them. He's afraid they'll ruin my teeth. But, dash it — for once

—! Don't you agree, Dr. Rank? Here! (*Pops a macaroon into his mouth.*) You too, Christine. And I'll have one too. Just a little one. Two at the most. (*Begins to walk round again.*) Yes, now I feel really, really happy. Now there's just one thing in the world I'd really love to do.

RANK: Oh? And what is that?

NORA: Just something I'd love to say to Torvald.

RANK: Well, why don't you say it?

NORA: No, I daren't. It's too dreadful.

MRS. LINDE: Dreadful?

RANK: Well, then, you'd better not. But you can say it to us. What is it you'd so love to say to Torvald?

NORA: I've the most extraordinary longing to say: "Bloody hell!"

RANK: Are you mad?

MRS. LINDE: My dear Nora —!

RANK: Say it. Here he is.

NORA (*hiding the bag of macaroons*): Ssh! Ssh!

(*Helmer, with his overcoat on his arm and his hat in his hand, enters from his study.*)

NORA (*goes to meet him*): Well, Torvald dear, did you get rid of him?

HELMER: Yes, he's just gone.

NORA: May I introduce you —? This is Christine. She's just arrived in town.

HELMER: Christine —? Forgive me, but I don't think —

NORA: Mrs. Linde, Torvald dear. Christine Linde.

HELMER: Ah. A childhood friend of my wife's, I presume?

MRS. LINDE: Yes, we knew each other in earlier days.

NORA: And imagine, now she's traveled all this way to talk to you.

HELMER: Oh?

MRS. LINDE: Well, I didn't really —

NORA: You see, Christine's frightfully good at office work, and she's mad to come under some really clever man who can teach her even more than she knows already —

HELMER: Very sensible, madam.

NORA: So when she heard you'd become head of the bank — it was in her local paper — she came here as quickly as she could and — Torvald, you will, won't you? Do a little something to help Christine? For my sake?

HELMER: Well, that shouldn't be impossible. You are a widow, I take it, Mrs. Linde?

MRS. LINDE: Yes.

HELMER: And you have experience of office work?

MRS. LINDE: Yes, quite a bit.

HELMER: Well then, it's quite likely I may be able to find some job for you —

NORA (*claps her hands*): You see, you see!

HELMER: You've come at a lucky moment, Mrs. Linde.

MRS. LINDE: Oh, how can I ever thank you —?

HELMER: There's absolutely no need. (*Puts on his overcoat.*) But now I'm afraid I must ask you to excuse me —

RANK: Wait. I'll come with you.

(*He gets his fur coat from the hall and warms it at the stove.*)

NORA: Don't be long, Torvald dear.

HELMER: I'll only be an hour.

NORA: Are you going too, Christine?

MRS. LINDE (*puts on her outdoor clothes*): Yes, I must start to look round for a room.

HELMER: Then perhaps we can walk part of the way together.

NORA (*helps her*): It's such a nuisance we're so cramped here — I'm afraid we can't offer to —

MRS. LINDE: Oh, I wouldn't dream of it. Goodbye, Nora dear, and thanks for everything.

NORA: *Au revoir.* You'll be coming back this evening, of course. And you too, Dr. Rank. What? If you're well enough? Of course you'll be well enough. Wrap up warmly, though.

(*They go out, talking, into the hall. Children's voices are heard from the stairs.*)

NORA: Here they are! Here they are!

(*She runs out and opens the door. Anne-Marie, the nurse, enters with the children.*)

NORA: Come in, come in! (*Stoops down and kisses them.*) Oh, my sweet darlings —! Look at them, Christine! Aren't they beautiful?

RANK: Don't stand here chattering in this draught!

HELMER: Come, Mrs. Linde. This is for mothers only.

(*Dr. Rank, Helmer, and Mrs. Linde go down the stairs. The nurse brings the children into the room. Nora follows, and closes the door to the hall.*)

NORA: How well you look! What red cheeks you've got! Like apples and roses! (*The children answer her inaudibly as she talks to them.*) Have you had fun? That's splendid. You gave Emmy and Bob a ride on the sledge? What, both together? I say! What a clever boy you are, Ivar! Oh, let me hold her for a moment, Anne-Marie! My sweet little baby doll! (*Takes the smallest child from the nurse and dances with her.*) Yes, yes, Mummy will dance with Bob too. What? Have you been throwing snowballs? Oh, I wish I'd been there! No, don't — I'll undress them myself, Anne-Marie. No, please let me; it's such fun. Go inside and warm yourself; you look frozen. There's some hot coffee on the stove. (*The nurse goes into the room on the left.*

Nora takes off the children's outdoor clothes and throws them anywhere while they all chatter simultaneously.) What? A big dog ran after you? But he didn't bite you? No, dogs don't bite lovely little baby dolls. Leave those parcels alone, Ivar. What's in them? Ah, wouldn't you like to know! No, no; it's nothing nice. Come on, let's play a game. What shall we play? Hide and seek. Yes, let's play hide and seek. Bob shall hide first. You want me to? All right, let me hide first.

(*Nora and the children play around the room, and in the adjacent room to the left, laughing and shouting. At length Nora hides under the table. The children rush in, look, but cannot find her. Then they hear her half-stifled laughter, run to the table, lift up the cloth, and see her. Great excitement. She crawls out as though to frighten them. Further excitement. Meanwhile, there has been a knock on the door leading from the hall, but no one has noticed it. Now the door is half-opened and Krogstad enters. He waits for a moment; the game continues.*)

KROGSTAD: Excuse me, Mrs. Helmer —

NORA (*turns with a stifled cry and half jumps up*): Oh! What do you want?

KROGSTAD: I beg your pardon; the front door was ajar. Someone must have forgotten to close it.

NORA (*gets up*): My husband is not at home, Mr. Krogstad.

KROGSTAD: I know.

NORA: Well, what do want here, then?

KROGSTAD: A word with you.

NORA: With —? (*To the children, quietly.*) Go inside to Anne-Marie. What? No, the strange gentleman won't do anything to hurt Mummy. When he's gone we'll start playing again.

(*She takes the children into the room on the left and closes the door behind them.*)

NORA (*uneasy, tense*): You want to speak to me?

KROGSTAD: Yes.

NORA: Today? But it's not the first of the month yet.

KROGSTAD: No, it is Christmas Eve. Whether or not you have a merry Christmas depends on you.

NORA: What do you want? I can't give you anything today —

KROGSTAD: We won't talk about that for the present. There's something else. You have a moment to spare?

NORA: Oh, yes. Yes, I suppose so; though —

KROGSTAD: Good. I was sitting in the café down below and I saw your husband cross the street —

NORA: Yes.

KROGSTAD: With a lady.

NORA: Well?

KROGSTAD: Might I be so bold as to ask: was not that lady a Mrs. Linde?

NORA: Yes.

KROGSTAD: Recently arrived in town?

NORA: Yes, today.

KROGSTAD: She is a good friend of yours, is she not?

NORA: Yes, she is. But I don't see —

KROGSTAD: I used to know her too once.

NORA: I know.

KROGSTAD: Oh? You've discovered that. Yes, I thought you would. Well then, may I ask you a straight question: is Mrs. Linde to be employed at the bank?

NORA: How dare you presume to cross-examine me, Mr. Krogstad? You, one of my husband's employees? But since you ask, you shall have an answer. Yes, Mrs. Linde is to be employed by the bank. And I arranged it, Mr. Krogstad. Now you know.

KROGSTAD: I guessed right, then.

NORA (*walks up and down the room*): Oh, one has a little influence, you know. Just because one's a woman it doesn't necessarily mean that — When one is in a humble position, Mr. Krogstad, one should think twice before offending someone who — hm —

KROGSTAD: — who has influence?

ABOVE: Nora (Claire Bloom) is troubled as Helmer (Donald Madden) kisses her in Patrick Garland's 1971 production. BELOW: Helmer, Nora, and Mrs. Linde (Patricia Elliott) discuss the possibility of finding a suitable job for Mrs. Linde in the bank. FAR RIGHT: Krogstad (Robert Gerringer) explains the seriousness of her actions to Nora.

NORA: Precisely.

KROGSTAD (*changes his tone*): Mrs. Helmer, will you have the kindness to use your influence on my behalf?

NORA: What? What do you mean?

KROGSTAD: Will you be so good as to see that I keep my humble position at the bank?

NORA: What do you mean? Who is thinking of removing you from your position?

KROGSTAD: Oh, you don't need to play innocent with me. I realize it can't be very pleasant for your friend to risk bumping into me; and now I also realize whom I have to thank for being hounded out like this.

NORA: But I assure you —

KROGSTAD: Look, let's not beat about the bush. There's still time, and I'd advise you to use your influence to stop it.

NORA: But, Mr. Krogstad, I have no influence!

KROGSTAD: Oh? I thought you just said —

NORA: But I didn't mean it like that! I? How on earth could you imagine that I would have any influence over my husband?

KROGSTAD: Oh, I've known your husband since we were students together. I imagine he has his weaknesses like other married men.

NORA: If you speak impertinently of my husband, I shall show you the door.

KROGSTAD: You're a bold woman, Mrs. Helmer.

NORA: I'm not afraid of you any longer. Once the New Year is in, I'll soon be rid of you.

KROGSTAD (*more controlled*): Now listen to me, Mrs. Helmer. If I'm forced to, I shall fight for my little job at the bank as I would fight for my life.

NORA: So it sounds.

KROGSTAD: It isn't just the money; that's the last thing I care about. There's something else — well, you might as well know. It's like this, you see. You know of course, as everyone else does, that some years ago I committed an indiscretion.

NORA: I think I did hear something —

KROGSTAD: It never came into court; but from that day, every opening was barred to me. So I turned my hand to the kind of business you know about. I had to do something; and I don't think I was one of the worst. But now I want to give up all that. My sons are growing up; for their sake, I must try to regain what respectability I can. This job in the bank was the first step on the ladder. And now your husband wants to kick me off that ladder back into the dirt.

NORA: But my dear Mr. Krogstad, it simply isn't in my power to help you.

KROGSTAD: You say that because you don't want to help me. But I have the means to make you.

NORA: You don't mean you'd tell my husband that I owe you money?

KROGSTAD: And if I did?

NORA: That'd be a filthy trick! (*Almost in tears.*) This secret that is my pride and my joy — that he should hear about it in such a filthy, beastly way — hear about it from you! It'd involve me in the most dreadful unpleasantness —

KROGSTAD: Only — unpleasantness?

NORA (*vehemently*): All right, do it! You'll be the one who'll suffer. It'll show my husband the kind of man you are, and then you'll never keep your job.

KROGSTAD: I asked you whether it was merely domestic unpleasantness you were afraid of.

NORA: If my husband hears about it, he will of course immediately pay you whatever is owing. And then we shall have nothing more to do with you.

KROGSTAD (*takes a step closer*): Listen, Mrs. Helmer.

Either you've a bad memory or else you know very little about financial transactions. I had better enlighten you.

NORA: What do you mean?

KROGSTAD: When your husband was ill, you came to me to borrow two hundred and fifty pounds.

NORA: I didn't know anyone else.

KROGSTAD: I promised to find that sum for you —

NORA: And you did find it.

KROGSTAD: I promised to find that sum for you on certain conditions. You were so worried about your husband's illness and so keen to get the money to take him abroad that I don't think you bothered much about the details. So it won't be out of place if I refresh your memory. Well — I promised to get you the money in exchange for an I.O.U., which I drew up.

NORA: Yes, and which I signed.

KROGSTAD: Exactly. But then I added a few lines naming your father as security for the debt. This paragraph was to be signed by your father.

NORA: Was to be? He did sign it.

KROGSTAD: I left the date blank for your father to fill in when he signed this paper. You remember, Mrs. Helmer?

NORA: Yes, I think so —

KROGSTAD: Then I gave you back this I.O.U. for you to post to your father. Is that not correct?

NORA: Yes.

KROGSTAD: And of course you posted it at once; for within five or six days you brought it along to me with your father's signature on it. Whereupon I handed you the money.

NORA: Yes, well. Haven't I repaid the installments as agreed?

KROGSTAD: Mm — yes, more or less. But to return to what we were speaking about — that was a difficult time for you just then, wasn't it, Mrs. Helmer?

NORA: Yes, it was.

KROGSTAD: And your father was very ill, if I am not mistaken.

NORA: He was dying.

KROGSTAD: He did in fact die shortly afterwards?

NORA: Yes.

KROGSTAD: Tell me, Mrs. Helmer, do you by any chance remember the date of your father's death? The day of the month, I mean.

NORA: Papa died on the twenty-ninth of September.

KROGSTAD: Quite correct; I took the trouble to confirm it. And that leaves me with a curious little problem — (Takes out a paper.) — which I simply cannot solve.

NORA: Problem? I don't see —

KROGSTAD: The problem, Mrs. Helmer, is that your father signed this paper three days after his death.

NORA: What? I don't understand —

KROGSTAD: Your father died on the twenty-ninth of September. But look at this. Here your father has dated his signature the second of October. Isn't that a curious little problem, Mrs. Helmer? (Nora is silent.) Can you suggest any explanation? (She remains silent.) And there's another curious thing. The words "second of October" and the year are written in a hand which is not your father's, but which I seem to know. Well, there's a simple explanation to that. Your father could have forgotten to write in the date when he signed and someone else could have added it before news came of his death. There's nothing criminal about that. It's the signature itself I'm wondering about. It is genuine, I suppose, Mrs. Helmer? It was your father who wrote his name here?

NORA (after a short silence, throws back her head and looks defiantly at him): No, it was not. It was I who wrote Papa's name there.

KROGSTAD: Look, Mrs. Helmer, do you realize this is a dangerous admission?

NORA: Why? You'll get your money.

KROGSTAD: May I ask you a question? Why didn't you send this paper to your father?

NORA: I couldn't. Papa was very ill. If I'd asked him to sign this, I'd have had to tell him what the money was for. But I couldn't have told him in his condition that my husband's life was in danger. I couldn't have done that!

KROGSTAD: Then you would have been wiser to have given up your idea of a holiday.

NORA: But I couldn't! It was to save my husband's life. I couldn't put it off.

KROGSTAD: But didn't it occur to you that you were being dishonest towards me?

NORA: I couldn't bother about that. I didn't care about you. I hated you because of all the beastly difficulties you'd put in my way when you knew how dangerously ill my husband was.

KROGSTAD: Mrs. Helmer, you evidently don't appreciate exactly what you have done. But I can assure you that it is no bigger nor worse a crime than the one I once committed, and thereby ruined my whole social position.

NORA: You? Do you expect me to believe that you would have taken a risk like that to save your wife's life?

KROGSTAD: The law does not concern itself with motives.

NORA: Then the law must be very stupid.

KROGSTAD: Stupid or not, if I show this paper to the police, you will be judged according to it.

NORA: I don't believe that. Hasn't a daughter the right to shield her father from worry and anxiety when he's old and dying? Hasn't a wife the right to save her husband's life? I don't know much about the law, but there must be something somewhere that says that such things are allowed. You ought to know about that, you're meant to be a lawyer, aren't you? You can't be a very good lawyer, Mr. Krogstad.

KROGSTAD: Possibly not. But business, the kind of business we two have been transacting — I think you'll admit I understand something about that? Good. Do as you please. But I tell you this. If I get thrown into the gutter for a second time, I shall take you with me.

(*He bows and goes out through the hall.*)

NORA (*stands for a moment in thought, then tosses her head*): What nonsense! He's trying to frighten me! I'm not that stupid. (*Busies herself gathering together the children's clothes; then she suddenly stops.*) But —? No, it's impossible. I did it for love, didn't I?

CHILDREN (*in the doorway, left*): Mummy, the strange gentleman's gone out into the street.

NORA: Yes, yes, I know. But don't talk to anyone about the strange gentleman. You hear? Not even to Daddy.

CHILDREN: No, Mummy. Will you play with us again now?

NORA: No, no. Not now.

CHILDREN: Oh but, Mummy, you promised!

NORA: I know, but I can't just now. Go back to the nursery. I've a lot to do. Go away, my darlings, go away. (*She pushes them gently into the other room, and closes the door behind them. She sits on the sofa, takes up her embroidery, stitches for a few moments, but soon stops.*) No! (*Throws the embroidery aside, gets up, goes to the door leading to the hall, and calls.*) Helen! Bring in the Christmas tree! (*She goes to the table on the left and opens the drawer in it; then pauses again.*) No, but it's utterly impossible!

MAID (*enters with the tree*): Where shall I put it, madam?

NORA: There, in the middle of the room.

MAID: Will you be wanting anything else?

NORA: No, thank you, I have everything I need.

(*The maid puts down the tree and goes out.*)

NORA (*busy decorating the tree*): Now — candles here — and flowers here. That loathsome man! Nonsense, nonsense, there's nothing to be frightened about. The Christmas tree must be beautiful. I'll do everything that you like, Torvald. I'll sing for you, dance for you —

(*Helmer, with a bundle of papers under his arm, enters.*)

NORA: Oh — are you back already?

HELMER: Yes. Has anyone been here?

NORA: Here? No.

HELMER: That's strange. I saw Krogstad come out of the front door.

NORA: Did you? Oh yes, that's quite right — Krogstad was here for a few minutes.

HELMER: Nora, I can tell from your face, he's been here and asked you to put in a good word for him.

NORA: Yes.

HELMER: And you were to pretend you were doing it of your own accord? You weren't going to tell me he'd been here? He asked you to do that too, didn't he?

NORA: Yes, Torvald. But —

HELMER: Nora, Nora! And you were ready to enter into such a conspiracy? Talking to a man like that, and making him promises — and then, on top of it all, to tell me an untruth!

NORA: An untruth?

HELMER: Didn't you say no one had been here? (*Wags his finger.*) My little songbird must never do that again. A songbird must have a clean beak to sing with; otherwise she'll start twittering out of tune. (*Puts his arm round her waist.*) Isn't that the way we want things? Yes, of course it is. (*Lets go of her.*) So let's hear no more about that. (*Sits down in front of the stove.*) Ah, how cozy and peaceful it is here. (*Glances for a few moments at his papers.*)

NORA (*busy with the tree; after a short silence*): Torvald.

HELMER: Yes.

NORA: I'm terribly looking forward to that fancy dress ball at the Stenborgs on Boxing Day.°

HELMER: And I'm terribly curious to see what you're going to surprise me with.

NORA: Oh, it's so maddening.

HELMER: What is?

NORA: I can't think of anything to wear. It all seems so stupid and meaningless.

HELMER: So my little Nora's come to that conclusion, has she?

NORA (*behind his chair, resting her arms on its back*): Are you very busy, Torvald?

HELMER: Oh —

NORA: What are those papers?

HELMER: Just something to do with the bank.

NORA: Already?

HELMER: I persuaded the trustees to give me authority to make certain immediate changes in the staff and organization. I want to have everything straight by the New Year.

NORA: Then that's why this poor man Krogstad —

HELMER: Hm.

NORA (*still leaning over his chair, slowly strokes the*

Boxing Day: The first weekday after Christmas.

back of his head): If you hadn't been so busy, I was going to ask you an enormous favor, Torvald.

HELMER: Well, tell me. What was it to be?

NORA: You know I trust your taste more than anyone's. I'm so anxious to look really beautiful at the fancy dress ball. Torvald, couldn't you help me to decide what I shall go as, and what kind of costume I ought to wear?

HELMER: Aha! So little Miss Independent's in trouble and needs a man to rescue her, does she?

NORA: Yes, Torvald. I can't get anywhere without your help.

HELMER: Well, well, I'll give the matter thought. We'll find something.

NORA: Oh, how kind of you! (*Goes back to the tree. Pause.*) How pretty these red flowers look! But, tell me, is it so dreadful, this thing that Krogstad's done?

HELMER: He forged someone else's name. Have you any idea what that means?

NORA: Mightn't he have been forced to do it by some emergency?

HELMER: He probably just didn't think — that's what usually happens. I'm not so heartless as to condemn a man for an isolated action.

NORA: No, Torvald, of course not!

HELMER: Men often succeed in re-establishing themselves if they admit their crime and take their punishment.

NORA: Punishment?

HELMER: But Krogstad didn't do that. He chose to try and trick his way out of it; and that's what has morally destroyed him.

NORA: You think that would —?

HELMER: Just think how a man with that load on his conscience must always be lying and cheating and dissembling; how he must wear a mask even in the presence of those who are dearest to him, even his own wife and children! Yes, the children. That's the worst danger, Nora.

NORA: Why?

HELMER: Because an atmosphere of lies contaminates and poisons every corner of the home. Every breath that the children draw in such a house contains the germs of evil.

NORA (*comes closer behind him*): Do you really believe that?

HELMER: Oh, my dear, I've come across it so often in my work at the bar. Nearly all young criminals are the children of mothers who are constitutional liars.

NORA: Why do you say mothers?

HELMER: It's usually the mother; though of course the father can have the same influence. Every lawyer knows that only too well. And yet this fellow Krogstad has been sitting at home all these years poisoning his children with his lies and pretenses. That's why I say that, morally speaking, he is dead. (*Stretches out his hands toward her.*) So my pretty little Nora must promise me not to plead his case. Your hand on it. Come, come, what's this? Give me your hand. There. That's settled, now. I assure you it'd be quite impossible for me to work in the same building as him. I literally feel physically ill in the presence of a man like that.

NORA (*draws her hand from his and goes over to the other side of the Christmas tree*): How hot it is in here! And I've so much to do.

HELMER (*gets up and gathers his papers*): Yes, and I must try to get some of this read before dinner. I'll think about your costume too. And I may even have something up my sleeve to hang in gold paper on the Christmas tree. (*Lays his hand on her head.*) My precious little songbird!

(*He goes into his study and closes the door.*)

NORA (*softly, after a pause*): It's nonsense. It must be. It's impossible. It *must* be impossible!

NURSE (*in the doorway, left*): The children are asking if they can come in to Mummy.

NORA: No, no, no; don't let them in! You stay with them, Anne-Marie.

NURSE: Very good, madam. (*Closes the door.*)

NORA (*pale with fear*): Corrupt my little children —! Poison my home! (*Short pause. She throws back her head.*) It isn't true! It *couldn't* be true!

ACT II

(*The same room. In the corner by the piano the Christmas tree stands, stripped and disheveled, its candles burned to their sockets. Nora's outdoor clothes lie on the sofa. She is alone in the room, walking restlessly to and fro. At length she stops by the sofa and picks up her coat.*)

NORA (*drops the coat again*): There's someone coming! (*Goes to the door and listens.*) No, it's no one. Of course — no one'll come today, it's Christmas Day. Nor tomorrow. But perhaps —! (*Opens the door and looks out.*) No. Nothing in the letter-box. Quite empty. (*Walks across the room.*) Silly, silly. Of course he won't do anything. It couldn't happen. It isn't possible. Why, I've three small children.

(*The Nurse, carrying a large cardboard box, enters from the room on the left.*)

NURSE: I found those fancy dress clothes at last, madam.

NORA: Thank you. Put them on the table.

NURSE (*does so*): They're all rumpled up.

NORA: Oh, I wish I could tear them into a million pieces!

NURSE: Why, madam! They'll be all right. Just a little patience.

NORA: Yes, of course. I'll go and get Mrs. Linde to help me.

NURSE: What, out again? In this dreadful weather? You'll catch a chill, madam.

NORA: Well, that wouldn't be the worst. How are the children?

NURSE: Playing with their Christmas presents, poor little dears. But —

NORA: Are they still asking to see me?

NURSE: They're so used to having their Mummy with them.

NORA: Yes, but, Anne-Marie, from now on I shan't be able to spend so much time with them.

NURSE: Well, children get used to anything in time.

NORA: Do you think so? Do you think they'd forget their mother if she went away from them — for ever?

NURSE: Mercy's sake, madam! — For ever?

NORA: Tell me, Anne-Marie — I've so often wondered. How could you bear to give your child away — to strangers?

NURSE: But I had to when I came to nurse my little Miss Nora.

NORA: Do you mean you wanted to?

NURSE: When I had the chance of such a good job? A poor girl what's got into trouble can't afford to pick and choose. That good-for-nothing didn't lift a finger.

NORA: But your daughter must have completely forgotten you.

NURSE: Oh no, indeed she hasn't. She's written to me twice, once when she got confirmed and then again when she got married.

NORA (hugs her): Dear old Anne-Marie, you were a good mother to me.

NURSE: Poor little Miss Nora, you never had any mother but me.

NORA: And if my little ones had no one else, I know you would — no, silly, silly, silly! (Opens the cardboard box.) Go back to them, Anne-Marie. Now I must — Tomorrow you'll see how pretty I shall look.

NURSE: Why, there'll be no one at the ball as beautiful as my Miss Nora.

(She goes into the room, left.)

NORA (begins to unpack the clothes from the box, but soon throws them down again): Oh, if only I dared to go out! If I could be sure no one would come, and nothing would happen while I was away! Stupid, stupid! No one will come. I just mustn't think about it. Brush this muff. Pretty gloves, pretty gloves! Don't think about it, don't think about it! One, two, three, four, five, six — (Cries.) Ah — they're coming —!

(She begins to run toward the door, but stops uncertainly. Mrs. Linde enters from the hall, where she has been taking off her outdoor clothes.)

NORA: Oh, it's you, Christine. There's no one else out there, is there? Oh, I'm so glad you've come.

MRS. LINDE: I hear you were at my room asking for me.

NORA: Yes, I just happened to be passing. I want to ask you to help me with something. Let's sit down here on the sofa. Look at this. There's going to be a fancy dress ball tomorrow night upstairs at Consul Stenborg's, and Torvald wants me to go as a Neapolitan fisher-girl and dance the tarantella. I learned it on Capri.

MRS. LINDE: I say, are you going to give a performance?

NORA: Yes, Torvald says I should. Look, here's the dress. Torvald had it made for me in Italy; but now it's all so torn. I don't know —

MRS. LINDE: Oh, we'll soon put that right; the stitching's just come away. Needle and thread? Ah, here we are.

NORA: You're being awfully sweet.

MRS. LINDE (sews): So you're going to dress up tomorrow, Nora? I must pop over for a moment to see how you look. Oh, but I've completely forgotten to thank you for that nice evening yesterday.

NORA (gets up and walks across the room): Oh, I didn't think it was as nice as usual. You ought to have come to town a little earlier, Christine. . . . Yes, Torvald understands how to make a home look attractive.

MRS. LINDE: I'm sure you do, too. You're not your father's daughter for nothing. But, tell me. Is Dr. Rank always in such low spirits as he was yesterday?

NORA: No, last night it was very noticeable. But he's got a terrible disease; he's got spinal tuberculosis, poor man. His father was a frightful creature who kept mistresses and so on. As a result Dr. Rank has been sickly ever since he was a child — you understand —

MRS. LINDE (puts down her sewing): But, my dear Nora, how on earth did you get to know about such things?

NORA (walks about the room): Oh, don't be silly, Christine — when one has three children, one comes into contact with women who — well, who know about medical matters, and they tell one a thing or two.

MRS. LINDE (sews again; a short silence): Does Dr. Rank visit you every day?

NORA: Yes, every day. He's Torvald's oldest friend, and a good friend to me too. Dr. Rank's almost one of the family.

MRS. LINDE: But, tell me — is he quite sincere? I mean, doesn't he rather say the sort of thing he thinks people want to hear?

NORA: No, quite the contrary. What gave you that idea?

MRS. LINDE: When you introduced me to him yesterday, he said he'd often heard my name mentioned here. But later I noticed your husband had no idea who I was. So how could Dr. Rank —?

NORA: Yes, that's quite right, Christine. You see, Torvald's so hopelessly in love with me that he wants to have me all to himself — those were his very words. When we were first married, he got quite jealous if I as much as mentioned any of my old friends back home. So naturally, I stopped talking about them. But I often chat with Dr. Rank about that kind of thing. He enjoys it, you see.

MRS. LINDE: Now listen, Nora. In many ways you're still a child; I'm a bit older than you and have a little more experience of the world. There's something I want to say to you. You ought to give up this business with Dr. Rank.

NORA: What business?

MRS. LINDE: Well, everything. Last night you were speaking about this rich admirer of yours who was going to give you money —

NORA: Yes, and who doesn't exist — unfortunately. But what's that got to do with —?

MRS. LINDE: Is Dr. Rank rich?

NORA: Yes.

MRS. LINDE: And he has no dependents?

NORA: No, no one. But —

MRS. LINDE: And he comes here to see you every day?

NORA: Yes, I've told you.

MRS. LINDE: But how dare a man of his education be so forward?

NORA: What on earth are you talking about?

MRS. LINDE: Oh, stop pretending, Nora. Do you think I haven't guessed who it was who lent you that two hundred pounds?

NORA: Are you out of your mind? How could you imagine such a thing? A friend, someone who comes here every day! Why, that'd be an impossible situation!

MRS. LINDE: Then it really wasn't him?

NORA: No, of course not. I've never for a moment dreamed of — anyway, he hadn't any money to lend then. He didn't come into that till later.

MRS. LINDE: Well, I think that was a lucky thing for you, Nora dear.

NORA: No, I could never have dreamed of asking Dr. Rank — Though I'm sure that if I ever did ask him —

MRS. LINDE: But of course you won't.

NORA: Of course not. I can't imagine that it should ever become necessary. But I'm perfectly sure that if I did speak to Dr. Rank —

MRS. LINDE: Behind your husband's back?

NORA: I've got to get out of this other business; and *that's* been going on behind his back. I've *got* to get out of it.

MRS. LINDE: Yes, well, that's what I told you yesterday. But —

NORA (*walking up and down*): It's much easier for a man to arrange these things than a woman —

MRS. LINDE: One's own husband, yes.

NORA: Oh, bosh. (*Stops walking.*) When you've completely repaid a debt, you get your I.O.U. back, don't you?

MRS. LINDE: Yes, of course.

NORA: And you can tear it into a thousand pieces and burn the filthy, beastly thing!

MRS. LINDE (*looks hard at her, puts down her sewing, and gets up slowly*): Nora, you're hiding something from me.

NORA: Can you see that?

MRS. LINDE: Something has happened since yesterday morning. Nora, what is it?

NORA (*goes toward her*): Christine! (*Listens.*) Ssh! There's Torvald. Would you mind going into the nursery for a few minutes? Torvald can't bear to see sewing around. Anne-Marie'll help you.

MRS. LINDE (*gathers some of her things together*): Very well. But I shan't leave this house until we've talked this matter out.

(*She goes into the nursery, left. As she does so, Helmer enters from the hall.*)

NORA (*runs to meet him*): Oh, Torvald dear, I've been so longing for you to come back!

HELMER: Was that the dressmaker?

NORA: No, it was Christine. She's helping me mend my costume. I'm going to look rather splendid in that.

HELMER: Yes, that was quite a bright idea of mine, wasn't it?

NORA: Wonderful! But wasn't it nice of me to give in to you?

HELMER (*takes her chin in his hand*): Nice — to give in to your husband? All right, little silly, I know you didn't mean it like that. But I won't disturb you. I expect you'll be wanting to try it on.

NORA: Are you going to work now?

HELMER: Yes. (*Shows her a bundle of papers.*) Look

at these. I've been down to the bank — (*Turns to go into his study.*)

NORA: Torvald.

HELMER (*stops*): Yes.

NORA: If little squirrel asked you really prettily to grant her a wish —

HELMER: Well?

NORA: Would you grant it to her?

HELMER: First I should naturally have to know what it was.

NORA: Squirrel would do lots of pretty tricks for you if you granted her wish.

HELMER: Out with it, then.

NORA: Your little skylark would sing in every room —

HELMER: My little skylark does that already.

NORA: I'd turn myself into a little fairy and dance for you in the moonlight, Torvald.

HELMER: Nora, it isn't that business you were talking about this morning?

NORA (*comes closer*): Yes, Torvald — oh, please! I beg of you!

HELMER: Have you really the nerve to bring that up again?

NORA: Yes, Torvald, yes, you must do as I ask! You must let Krogstad keep his place at the bank!

HELMER: My dear Nora, his is the job I'm giving to Mrs. Linde.

NORA: Yes, that's terribly sweet of you. But you can get rid of one of the other clerks instead of Krogstad.

HELMER: Really, you're being incredibly obstinate. Just because you thoughtlessly promised to put in a word for him, you expect me to —

NORA: No, it isn't that, Helmer. It's for your own sake. That man writes for the most beastly newspapers — you said so yourself. He could do you tremendous harm. I'm so dreadfully frightened of him —

HELMER: Oh, I understand. Memories of the past. That's what's frightening you.

NORA: What do you mean?

HELMER: You're thinking of your father, aren't you?

NORA: Yes, yes. Of course. Just think what those dreadful men wrote in the papers about Papa! The most frightful slanders. I really believe it would have lost him his job if the Ministry hadn't sent you down to investigate, and you hadn't been so kind and helpful to him.

HELMER: But my dear little Nora, there's a considerable difference between your father and me. Your father was not a man of unassailable reputation. But I am; and I hope to remain so all my life.

NORA: But no one knows what spiteful people may not dig up. We could be so peaceful and happy now, Torvald — we could be free from every worry — you and I and the children. Oh, please, Torvald, please —!

HELMER: The very fact of your pleading his cause makes it impossible for me to keep him. Everyone at the bank already knows that I intend to dismiss Krogstad. If the rumor got about that the new manager had allowed his wife to persuade him to change his mind —

NORA: Well, what then?

HELMER: Oh, nothing, nothing. As long as my little Miss Obstinate gets her way — Do you expect me to make a laughing-stock of myself before my entire staff — give people the idea that I am open to outside influence? Believe me, I'd soon feel the consequences! Besides — there's something else that makes it impossible for Krogstad to remain in the bank while I am its manager.

NORA: What is that?

HELMER: I might conceivably have allowed myself to ignore his moral obloquies° —

NORA: Yes, Torvald, surely?

HELMER: And I hear he's quite efficient at his job. But we — well, we were schoolfriends. It was one of those friendships that one enters into over-hastily and so often comes to regret later in life. I might as well confess the truth. We — well, we're on Christian name terms. And the tactless idiot makes no attempt to conceal it when other people are present. On the contrary, he thinks it gives him the right to be familiar with me. He shows off the whole time, with "Torvald this," and "Torvald that." I can tell you, I find it damned annoying. If he stayed, he'd make my position intolerable.

NORA: Torvald, you can't mean this seriously.

HELMER: Oh? And why not?

NORA: But it's so petty.

HELMER: What did you say? Petty? You think *I* am petty?

NORA: No, Torvald dear, of course you're not. That's just why —

HELMER: Don't quibble! You call my motives petty. Then I must be petty too. Petty! I see. Well, I've had enough of this. (*Goes to the door and calls into the hall.*) Helen!

NORA: What are you going to do?

HELMER (*searching among his papers*): I'm going to settle this matter once and for all. (*The Maid enters.*) Take this letter downstairs at once. Find a messenger and see that he delivers it. Immediately! The address is on the envelope. Here's the money.

MAID: Very good, sir. (*Goes out with the letter.*)

obloquies: Disreputableness.

HELMER (*putting his papers in order*): There now, little Miss Obstinate.

NORA (*tensely*): Torvald — what was in that letter?

HELMER: Krogstad's dismissal.

NORA: Call her back, Torvald! There's still time. Oh, Torvald, call her back! Do it for my sake — for your own sake — for the children! Do you hear me, Torvald? Please do it! You don't realize what this may do to us all!

HELMER: Too late.

NORA: Yes. Too late.

HELMER: My dear Nora, I forgive you this anxiety. Though it is a bit of an insult to me. Oh, but it is! Isn't it an insult to imply that I should be frightened by the vindictiveness of a depraved hack journalist? But I forgive you, because it so charmingly testifies to the love you bear me. (*Takes her in his arms.*) Which is as it should be, my own dearest Nora. Let what will happen, happen. When the real crisis comes, you will not find me lacking in strength or courage. I am man enough to bear the burden for us both.

NORA (*fearfully*): What do you mean?

HELMER: The whole burden, I say —

NORA (*calmly*): I shall never let you do that.

HELMER: Very well. We shall share it, Nora — as man and wife. And that is as it should be. (*Caresses her.*) Are you happy now? There, there, there; don't look at me with those frightened little eyes. You're simply imagining things. You go ahead now and do your tarantella, and get some practice on that tambourine. I'll sit in my study and close the door. Then I won't hear anything, and you can make all the noise you want. (*Turns in the doorway.*) When Dr. Rank comes, tell him where to find me. (*He nods to her, goes into his room with his papers, and closes the door.*)

NORA (*desperate with anxiety, stands as though transfixed, and whispers*): He said he'd do it. He will do it. He will do it, and nothing'll stop him. No, never that. I'd rather anything. There must be some escape — Some way out —! (*The bell rings in the hall.*) Dr. Rank —! Anything but that! Anything, I don't care —!

(*She passes her hand across her face, composes herself, walks across, and opens the door to the hall. Dr. Rank is standing there, hanging up his fur coat. During the following scene, it begins to grow dark.*)

NORA: Good evening, Dr. Rank. I recognized your ring. But you mustn't go to Torvald yet. I think he's busy.

RANK: And — you?

NORA (*as he enters the room and she closes the door behind him*): Oh, you know very well I've always time to talk to you.

RANK: Thank you. I shall avail myself of that privilege as long as I can.

NORA: What do you mean by that? As long as you *can*?

RANK: Yes. Does that frighten you?

NORA: Well, it's rather a curious expression. Is something going to happen?

RANK: Something I've been expecting to happen for a long time. But I didn't think it would happen quite so soon.

NORA (*seizes his arm*): What is it? Dr. Rank, you must tell me!

RANK (*sits down by the stove*): I'm on the way out. And there's nothing to be done about it.

NORA (*sighs with relief*): Oh, it's you —?

RANK: Who else? No, it's no good lying to oneself. I am the most wretched of all my patients, Mrs. Helmer. These last few days I've been going through the books of this poor body of mine, and I find I am bankrupt. Within a month I may be rotting up there in the churchyard.

NORA: Ugh, what a nasty way to talk!

RANK: The facts aren't exactly nice. But the worst is that there's so much else that's nasty to come first. I've only one more test to make. When that's done I'll have a pretty accurate idea of when the final disintegration is likely to begin. I want to ask you a favor. Helmer's a sensitive chap, and I know how he hates anything ugly. I don't want him to visit me when I'm in hospital —

NORA: Oh but, Dr. Rank —

RANK: I don't want him there. On any pretext. I shan't have him allowed in. As soon as I know the worst, I'll send you my visiting card with a black cross on it, and then you'll know that the final filthy process has begun.

NORA: Really, you're being quite impossible this evening. And I did hope you'd be in a good mood.

RANK: With death on my hands? And all this to atone for someone else's sin? Is there justice in that? And in every single family, in one way or another, the same merciless law of retribution is at work —

NORA (*holds her hands to her ears*): Nonsense! Cheer up! Laugh!

RANK: Yes, you're right. Laughter's all the damned thing's fit for. My poor innocent spine must pay for the fun my father had as a gay young lieutenant.

NORA (*at the table, left*): You mean he was too fond of asparagus and *foie gras*?

RANK: Yes, and truffles too.

NORA: Yes, of course, truffles, yes. And oysters too, I suppose?

RANK: Yes, oysters, oysters. Of course.

NORA: And all that port and champagne to wash them down. It's too sad that all those lovely things should affect one's spine.

RANK: Especially a poor spine that never got any pleasure out of them.

NORA: Oh yes, that's the saddest thing of all.

RANK (*looks searchingly at her*): Hm —

NORA (*after a moment*): Why did you smile?

RANK: No, it was you who laughed.

NORA: No, it was you who smiled, Dr. Rank!

RANK (*gets up*): You're a worse little rogue than I thought.

NORA: Oh, I'm full of stupid tricks today.

RANK: So it seems.

NORA (*puts both her hands on his shoulders*): Dear, dear Dr. Rank, you mustn't die and leave Torvald and me.

RANK: Oh, you'll soon get over it. Once one is gone, one is soon forgotten.

NORA (*looks at him anxiously*): Do you believe that?

RANK: One finds replacements, and then —

NORA: Who will find a replacement?

RANK: You and Helmer both will, when I am gone. You seem to have made a start already, haven't you? What was this Mrs. Linde doing here yesterday evening?

NORA: Aha! But surely you can't be jealous of poor Christine?

RANK: Indeed I am. She will be my successor in this house. When I have moved on, this lady will —

NORA: Ssh! — don't speak so loud! She's in there!

RANK: Today again? You see!

NORA: She's only come to mend my dress. Good heavens, how unreasonable you are! (*Sits on the sofa.*) Be nice now, Dr. Rank. Tomorrow you'll see how beautifully I shall dance; and you must imagine that I'm doing it just for you. And for Torvald of course; obviously. (*Takes some things out of the box.*) Dr. Rank, sit down here and I'll show you something.

RANK (*sits*): What's this?

NORA: Look here! Look!

RANK: Silk stockings!

NORA: Flesh-colored. Aren't they beautiful? It's very dark in here now, of course, but tomorrow — No, no, no; only the soles. Oh well, I suppose you can look a bit higher if you want to.

RANK: Hm —

NORA: Why are you looking so critical? Don't you think they'll fit me?

RANK: I can't really give you a qualified opinion on that.

NORA (*looks at him for a moment*): Shame on you! (*Flicks him on the ear with the stockings.*) Take that. (*Puts them back in the box.*)

RANK: What other wonders are to be revealed to me?

NORA: I shan't show you anything else. You're being naughty.

(*She hums a little and looks among the things in the box.*)

RANK (*after a short silence*): When I sit here like this being so intimate with you, I can't think — I cannot imagine what would have become of me if I had never entered this house.

NORA (*smiles*): Yes, I think you enjoy being with us, don't you?

RANK (*more quietly, looking into the middle distance*): And now to have to leave it all —

NORA: Nonsense. You're not leaving us.

RANK (*as before*): And not to be able to leave even the most wretched token of gratitude behind; hardly even a passing sense of loss; only an empty place, to be filled by the next comer.

NORA: Suppose I were to ask you to —? No —

RANK: To do what?

NORA: To give me proof of your friendship —

RANK: Yes, yes?

NORA: No, I mean — to do me a very great service —

RANK: Would you really for once grant me that happiness?

NORA: But you've no idea what it is.

RANK: Very well, tell me, then.

NORA: No, but, Dr. Rank, I can't. It's far too much — I want your help and advice, and I want you to do something for me.

RANK: The more the better. I've no idea what it can be. But tell me. You do trust me, don't you?

NORA: Oh, yes, more than anyone. You're my best and truest friend. Otherwise I couldn't tell you. Well then, Dr. Rank — there's something you must help me to prevent. You know how much Torvald loves me — he'd never hesitate for an instant to lay down his life for me —

RANK (*leans over toward her*): Nora — do you think he is the only one —?

NORA (*with a slight start*): What do you mean?

RANK: Who would gladly lay down his life for you?

NORA (*sadly*): Oh, I see.

RANK: I swore to myself I would let you know that before I go. I shall never have a better opportunity. . . . Well, Nora, now you know that. And now you also know that you can trust me as you can trust nobody else.

NORA (*rises; calmly and quietly*): Let me pass, please.

RANK (*makes room for her but remains seated*): Nora —

NORA (*in the doorway to the hall*): Helen, bring the lamp. (*Goes over to the stove.*) Oh, dear Dr. Rank, this was really horrid of you.

RANK (*gets up*): That I have loved you as deeply as anyone else has? Was that horrid of me?

NORA: No — but that you should go and tell me. That was quite unnecessary —

RANK: What do you mean? Did you know, then —?

(*The Maid enters with the lamp, puts it on the table, and goes out.*)

RANK: Nora — Mrs. Helmer — I am asking you, did you know this?

NORA: Oh, what do I know, what did I know, what didn't I know — I really can't say. How could you be so stupid, Dr. Rank? Everything was so nice.

RANK: Well, at any rate now you know that I am ready to serve you, body and soul. So — please continue.

NORA (*looks at him*): After this?

RANK: Please tell me what it is.

NORA: I can't possibly tell you now.

RANK: Yes, yes! You mustn't punish me like this. Let me be allowed to do what I can for you.

NORA: You can't do anything for me now. Anyway, I don't need any help. It was only my imagination — you'll see. Yes, really. Honestly. (*Sits in the rocking-chair, looks at him, and smiles.*) Well, upon my word you *are* a fine gentleman, Dr. Rank. Aren't you ashamed of yourself, now that the lamp's been lit?

RANK: Frankly, no. But perhaps I ought to say — *adieu*?

NORA: Of course not. You will naturally continue to visit us as before. You know quite well how Torvald depends on your company.

RANK: Yes, but you?

NORA: Oh, I always think it's enormous fun having you here.

RANK: That was what misled me. You're a riddle to me, you know. I'd often felt you'd just as soon be with me as with Helmer.

NORA: Well, you see, there are some people whom one loves, and others whom it's almost more fun to be with.

RANK: Oh yes, there's some truth in that.

NORA: When I was at home, of course I loved Papa best. But I always used to think it was terribly amusing to go down and talk to the servants; because they never told me what I ought to do; and they were such fun to listen to.

RANK: I see. So I've taken their place?

NORA (*jumps up and runs over to him*): Oh, dear, sweet Dr. Rank, I didn't mean that at all. But I'm sure you understand — I feel the same about Torvald as I did about Papa.

MAID (*enters from the hall*): Excuse me, madam. (*Whispers to her and hands her a visiting card.*)

NORA (*glances at the card*): Oh! (*Puts it quickly in her pocket.*)

RANK: Anything wrong?

NORA: No, no, nothing at all. It's just something that — it's my new dress.

RANK: What? But your costume is lying over there.

NORA: Oh — that, yes — but there's another — I ordered it specially — Torvald mustn't know —

RANK: Ah, so that's your big secret?

NORA: Yes, yes. Go in and talk to him — he's in his study — keep him talking for a bit —

RANK: Don't worry. He won't get away from me. (*Goes into Helmer's study.*)

NORA (*to the Maid*): Is he waiting in the kitchen?

MAID: Yes, madam, he came up the back way —

NORA: But didn't you tell him I had a visitor?

MAID: Yes, but he wouldn't go.

NORA: Wouldn't go?

MAID: No, madam, not until he'd spoken with you.

NORA: Very well, show him in; but quietly. Helen, you mustn't tell anyone about this. It's a surprise for my husband.

MAID: Very good, madam. I understand. (*Goes.*)

NORA: It's happening. It's happening after all. No, no, no, it can't happen, it mustn't happen.

(*She walks across and bolts the door of Helmer's study. The Maid opens the door from the hall to admit Krogstad, and closes it behind him. He is wearing an overcoat, heavy boots, and a fur cap.*)

NORA (*goes toward him*): Speak quietly. My husband's at home.

KROGSTAD: Let him hear.

NORA: What do you want from me?

KROGSTAD: Information.

NORA: Hurry up, then. What is it?

KROGSTAD: I suppose you know I've been given the sack.

NORA: I couldn't stop it, Mr. Krogstad. I did my best for you, but it didn't help.

KROGSTAD: Does your husband love you so little? He knows what I can do to you, and yet he dares to —

NORA: Surely you don't imagine I told him?

KROGSTAD: No. I didn't really think you had. It wouldn't have been like my old friend Torvald Helmer to show that much courage —

NORA: Mr. Krogstad, I'll trouble you to speak respectfully of my husband.

KROGSTAD: Don't worry, I'll show him all the respect

he deserves. But since you're so anxious to keep this matter hushed up, I presume you're better informed than you were yesterday of the gravity of what you've done?

NORA: I've learned more than you could ever teach me.

KROGSTAD: Yes, a bad lawyer like me —

NORA: What do you want from me?

KROGSTAD: I just wanted to see how things were with you, Mrs. Helmer. I've been thinking about you all day. Even duns° and hack journalists have hearts, you know.

NORA: Show some heart, then. Think of my little children.

KROGSTAD: Have you and your husband thought of mine? Well, let's forget that. I just wanted to tell you, you don't need to take this business too seriously. I'm not going to take any action, for the present.

NORA: Oh, no — you won't, will you? I knew it.

KROGSTAD: It can all be settled quite amicably. There's no need for it to become public. We'll keep it among the three of us.

NORA: My husband must never know about this.

KROGSTAD: How can you stop him? Can you pay the balance of what you owe me?

NORA: Not immediately.

KROGSTAD: Have you any means of raising the money during the next few days?

NORA: None that I would care to use.

KROGSTAD: Well, it wouldn't have helped anyway. However much money you offered me now I wouldn't give you back that paper.

NORA: What are you going to do with it?

KROGSTAD: Just keep it. No one else need ever hear about it. So in case you were thinking of doing anything desperate —

NORA: I am.

KROGSTAD: Such as running away —

NORA: I am.

KROGSTAD: Or anything more desperate —

NORA: How did you know?

KROGSTAD: — just give up the idea.

NORA: How did you know?

KROGSTAD: Most of us think of that at first. I did. But I hadn't the courage —

NORA (*dully*): Neither have I.

KROGSTAD (*relieved*): It's true, isn't it? You haven't the courage either?

NORA: No. I haven't. I haven't.

KROGSTAD: It'd be a stupid thing to do anyway. Once the first little domestic explosion is over. . . . I've

got a letter in my pocket here addressed to your husband —

NORA: Telling him everything?

KROGSTAD: As delicately as possible.

NORA (*quickly*): He must never see that letter. Tear it up. I'll find the money somehow —

KROGSTAD: I'm sorry, Mrs. Helmer, I thought I'd explained —

NORA: Oh, I don't mean the money I owe you. Let me know how much you want from my husband, and I'll find it for you.

KROGSTAD: I'm not asking your husband for money.

NORA: What do you want, then?

KROGSTAD: I'll tell you. I want to get on my feet again, Mrs. Helmer. I want to get to the top. And your husband's going to help me. For eighteen months now my record's been clean. I've been in hard straits all that time; I was content to fight my way back inch by inch. Now I've been chucked back into the mud, and I'm not going to be satisfied with just getting back my job. I'm going to get to the top, I tell you. I'm going to get back into the bank, and it's going to be higher up. Your husband's going to create a new job for me —

NORA: He'll never do that!

KROGSTAD: Oh, yes he will. I know him. He won't dare to risk a scandal. And once I'm in there with him, you'll see! Within a year I'll be his right-hand man. It'll be Nils Krogstad who'll be running that bank, not Torvald Helmer!

NORA: That will never happen.

KROGSTAD: Are you thinking of —?

NORA: Now I *have* the courage.

KROGSTAD: Oh, you can't frighten me. A pampered little pretty like you —

NORA: You'll see! You'll see!

KROGSTAD: Under the ice? Down in the cold, black water? And then, in the spring, to float up again, ugly, unrecognizable, hairless —?

NORA: You can't frighten me.

KROGSTAD: And you can't frighten me. People don't do such things, Mrs. Helmer. And anyway, what'd be the use? I've got him in my pocket.

NORA: But afterwards? When I'm no longer —?

KROGSTAD: Have you forgotten that then your reputation will be in my hands? (*She looks at him speechlessly.*) Well, I've warned you. Don't do anything silly. When Helmer's read my letter, he'll get in touch with me. And remember, it's your husband who's forced me to act like this. And for that I'll never forgive him. Goodbye, Mrs. Helmer. (*He goes out through the hall.*)

NORA (*runs to the hall door, opens it a few inches, and listens*): He's going. He's not going to give him the letter. Oh, no, no, it couldn't possibly happen.

---

duns: Bill collectors.

(*Opens the door a little wider.*) What's he doing? Standing outside the front door. He's not going downstairs. Is he changing his mind? Yes, he —!

(*A letter falls into the letter-box. Krogstad's footsteps die away down the stairs.*)

NORA (*with a stifled cry, runs across the room toward the table by the sofa. A pause*): In the letter-box. (*Steals timidly over toward the hall door.*) There it is! Oh, Torvald, Torvald! Now we're lost!

MRS. LINDE (*enters from the nursery with Nora's costume*): Well, I've done the best I can. Shall we see how it looks —?

NORA (*whispers hoarsely*): Christine, come here.

MRS. LINDE (*throws the dress on the sofa*): What's wrong with you? You look as though you'd seen a ghost!

NORA: Come here. Do you see that letter? There — look — through the glass of the letter-box.

MRS. LINDE: Yes, yes, I see it.

NORA: That letter's from Krogstad —

MRS. LINDE: Nora! It was Krogstad who lent you the money!

NORA: Yes. And now Torvald's going to discover everything.

MRS. LINDE: Oh, believe me, Nora, it'll be best for you both.

NORA: You don't know what's happened. I've committed a forgery —

MRS. LINDE: But, for heaven's sake —!

NORA: Christine, all I want is for you to be my witness.

MRS. LINDE: What do you mean? Witness what?

NORA: If I should go out of my mind — and it might easily happen —

MRS. LINDE: Nora!

NORA: Or if anything else should happen to me — so that I wasn't here any longer —

MRS. LINDE: Nora, Nora, you don't know what you're saying!

NORA: If anyone should try to take the blame, and say it was all his fault — you understand —?

MRS. LINDE: Yes, yes — but how can you think —?

NORA: Then you must testify that it isn't true, Christine. I'm not mad — I know exactly what I'm saying — and I'm telling you, no one else knows anything about this. I did it entirely on my own. Remember that.

MRS. LINDE: All right. But I simply don't understand —

NORA: Oh, how could you understand? A — miracle — is about to happen.

MRS. LINDE: Miracle?

NORA: Yes. A miracle. But it's so frightening, Christine. It *mustn't* happen, not for anything in the world.

MRS. LINDE: I'll go over and talk to Krogstad.

NORA: Don't go near him. He'll only do something to hurt you.

MRS. LINDE: Once upon a time he'd have done anything for my sake.

NORA: He?

MRS. LINDE: Where does he live?

NORA: Oh, how should I know —? Oh, yes, wait a moment —! (*Feels in her pocket.*) Here's his card. But the letter, the letter —!

HELMER (*from his study, knocks on the door*): Nora!

NORA (*cries in alarm*): What is it?

HELMER: Now, now, don't get alarmed. We're not coming in; you've closed the door. Are you trying on your costume?

NORA: Yes, yes — I'm trying on my costume. I'm going to look so pretty for you, Torvald.

MRS. LINDE (*who has been reading the card*): Why, he lives just around the corner.

NORA: Yes, but it's no use. There's nothing to be done now. The letter's lying there in the box.

MRS. LINDE: And your husband has the key?

NORA: Yes, he always keeps it.

MRS. LINDE: Krogstad must ask him to send the letter back unread. He must find some excuse —

NORA: But Torvald always opens the box at just about this time —

MRS. LINDE: You must stop him. Go in and keep him talking. I'll be back as quickly as I can.

(*She hurries out through the hall.*)

NORA (*goes over to Helmer's door, opens it and peeps in*): Torvald!

HELMER (*offstage*): Well, may a man enter his own drawing-room again? Come on, Rank, now we'll see what — (*In the doorway.*) But what's this?

NORA: What, Torvald dear?

HELMER: Rank's been preparing me for some great transformation scene.

RANK (*in the doorway*): So I understood. But I seem to have been mistaken.

NORA: Yes, no one's to be allowed to see me before tomorrow night.

HELMER: But, my dear Nora, you look quite worn out. Have you been practicing too hard?

NORA: No, I haven't practiced at all yet.

HELMER: Well, you must.

NORA: Yes, Torvald, I must, I know. But I can't get anywhere without your help. I've completely forgotten everything.

HELMER: Oh, we'll soon put that to rights.

NORA: Yes, help me, Torvald. Promise me you will? Oh, I'm so nervous. All those people —! You must forget everything except me this evening. You mustn't think of business — I won't even let you touch a pen. Promise me, Torvald?

HELMER: I promise. This evening I shall think of nothing but you — my poor, helpless little darling. Oh, there's just one thing I must see to — (*Goes toward the hall door.*)

NORA: What do you want out there?

HELMER: I'm only going to see if any letters have come.

NORA: No, Torvald, no!

HELMER: Why, what's the matter?

NORA: Torvald, I beg you. There's nothing there.

HELMER: Well, I'll just make sure.

(*He moves towards the door. Nora runs to the piano and plays the first bars of the tarantella.*)

HELMER (*at the door, turns*): Aha!

NORA: I can't dance tomorrow if I don't practice with you now.

HELMER (*goes over to her*): Are you really so frightened, Nora dear?

NORA: Yes, terribly frightened. Let me start practicing now, at once — we've still time before dinner. Oh, do sit down and play for me, Torvald dear. Correct me, lead me, the way you always do.

HELMER: Very well, my dear, if you wish it.

(*He sits down at the piano. Nora seizes the tambourine and a long multicolored shawl from the cardboard box, wraps the latter hastily around her, then takes a quick leap into the center of the room.*)

NORA: Play for me! I want to dance!

(*Helmer plays and Nora dances. Dr. Rank stands behind Helmer at the piano and watches her.*)

HELMER (*as he plays*): Slower, slower!

NORA: I can't!

HELMER: Not so violently, Nora.

NORA: I must!

HELMER: (*stops playing*): No, no, this won't do at all.

NORA (*laughs and swings her tambourine*): Isn't that what I told you?

RANK: Let me play for her.

HELMER (*gets up*): Yes, would you? Then it'll be easier for me to show her.

(*Rank sits down at the piano and plays. Nora dances more and more wildly. Helmer has stationed himself by the stove and tries repeatedly to correct her, but she seems not to hear him. Her hair works loose and falls over her shoulders; she ignores it and continues to dance. Mrs. Linde enters.*)

MRS. LINDE (*stands in the doorway as though tongue-tied*): Ah —!

NORA (*as she dances*): Oh, Christine, we're having such fun!

HELMER: But, Nora darling, you're dancing as if your life depended on it.

NORA: It does.

HELMER: Rank, stop it! This is sheer lunacy. Stop it, I say!

(*Rank ceases playing. Nora suddenly stops dancing.*)

HELMER (*goes over to her*): I'd never have believed it. You've forgotten everything I taught you.

NORA (*throws away the tambourine*): You see!

HELMER: I'll have to show you every step.

NORA: You see how much I need you! You must show me every step of the way. Right to the end of the dance. Promise me you will, Torvald?

HELMER: Never fear. I will.

NORA: You mustn't think about anything but me — today or tomorrow. Don't open any letters — don't even open the letter-box —

HELMER: Aha, you're still worried about that fellow —

NORA: Oh, yes, yes, him too.

HELMER: Nora, I can tell from the way you're behaving, there's a letter from him already lying there.

NORA: I don't know. I think so. But you mustn't read it now. I don't want anything ugly to come between us till it's all over.

RANK (*quietly, to Helmer*): Better give her her way.

HELMER (*puts his arm round her*): My child shall have her way. But tomorrow night, when your dance is over —

NORA: Then you will be free.

MAID (*appears in the doorway, right*): Dinner is served, madam.

NORA: Put out some champagne, Helen.

MAID: Very good, madam. (*Goes.*)

HELMER: I say! What's this, a banquet?

NORA: We'll drink champagne until dawn! (*Calls.*) And, Helen! Put out some macaroons! Lots of macaroons — for once!

HELMER (*takes her hands in his*): Now, now, now. Don't get so excited. Where's my little songbird, the one I know?

NORA: All right. Go and sit down — and you too, Dr. Rank. I'll be with you in a minute. Christine, you must help me put my hair up.

RANK (*quietly, as they go*): There's nothing wrong, is there? I mean, she isn't — er — expecting —?

HELMER: Good heavens no, my dear chap. She just gets scared like a child sometimes — I told you before —

(*They go out right.*)

NORA: Well?

MRS. LINDE: He's left town.

NORA: I saw it from your face.

MRS. LINDE: He'll be back tomorrow evening. I left a note for him.

NORA: You needn't have bothered. You can't stop anything now. Anyway, it's wonderful really, in a way — sitting here and waiting for the miracle to happen.

MRS. LINDE: Waiting for what?

NORA: Oh, you wouldn't understand. Go in and join them. I'll be with you in a moment.

(*Mrs. Linde goes into the dining room.*)

NORA (*stands for a moment as though collecting herself. Then she looks at her watch*): Five o'clock. Seven hours till midnight. Then another twenty-four hours till midnight tomorrow. And then the tarantella will be finished. Twenty-four and seven? Thirty-one hours to live.

HELMER (*appears in the doorway, right*): What's happened to my little songbird?

NORA (*runs to him with her arms wide*): Your songbird is here!

ACT III

(*The same room. The table which was formerly by the sofa has been moved into the center of the room; the chairs surround it as before. The door to the hall stands open. Dance music can be heard from the floor above. Mrs. Linde is seated at the table, absent-mindedly glancing through a book. She is trying to read, but seems unable to keep her mind on it. More than once she turns and listens anxiously toward the front door.*)

MRS. LINDE (*looks at her watch*): Not here yet. There's not much time left. Please God he hasn't —! (*Listens again.*) Ah, here he is. (*Goes out into the hall and cautiously opens the front door. Footsteps can be heard softly ascending the stairs. She whispers.*) Come in. There's no one here.

KROGSTAD (*in the doorway*): I found a note from you at my lodgings. What does this mean?

MRS. LINDE: I must speak with you.

KROGSTAD: Oh? And must our conversation take place in this house?

MRS. LINDE: We couldn't meet at my place; my room has no separate entrance. Come in. We're quite alone. The maid's asleep, and the Helmers are at the dance upstairs.

KROGSTAD (*comes into the room*): Well, well! So the Helmers are dancing this evening? Are they indeed?

MRS. LINDE: Yes. Why not?

KROGSTAD: True enough. Why not?

MRS. LINDE: Well, Krogstad. You and I must have a talk together.

KROGSTAD: Have we two anything further to discuss?

MRS. LINDE: We have a great deal to discuss.

KROGSTAD: I wasn't aware of it.

MRS. LINDE: That's because you've never really understood me.

KROGSTAD: Was there anything to understand? It's the old story, isn't it — a woman chucking a man because something better turns up?

MRS. LINDE: Do you really think I'm so utterly heartless? You think it was easy for me to give you up?

KROGSTAD: Wasn't it?

MRS. LINDE: Oh, Nils, did you really believe that?

KROGSTAD: Then why did you write to me the way you did?

MRS. LINDE: I had to. Since I had to break with you, I thought it my duty to destroy all the feelings you had for me.

KROGSTAD (*clenches his fists*): So that was it. And you did this for money!

MRS. LINDE: You mustn't forget I had a helpless mother to take care of, and two little brothers. We couldn't wait for you, Nils. It would have been so long before you'd had enough to support us.

KROGSTAD: Maybe. But you had no right to cast me off for someone else.

MRS. LINDE: Perhaps not. I've often asked myself that.

KROGSTAD (*more quietly*): When I lost you, it was just as though all solid ground had been swept from under my feet. Look at me. Now I am a shipwrecked man, clinging to a spar.

MRS. LINDE: Help may be near at hand.

KROGSTAD: It was near. But then you came, and stood between it and me.

MRS. LINDE: I didn't know, Nils. No one told me till today that this job I'd found was yours.

KROGSTAD: I believe you, since you say so. But now you know, won't you give it up?

MRS. LINDE: No — because it wouldn't help you even if I did.

KROGSTAD: Wouldn't it? I'd do it all the same.

MRS. LINDE: I've learned to look at things practically. Life and poverty have taught me that.

KROGSTAD: And life has taught me to distrust fine words.

MRS. LINDE: Then it's taught you a useful lesson. But surely you still believe in actions?

KROGSTAD: What do you mean?

MRS. LINDE: You said you were like a shipwrecked man clinging to a spar.

KROGSTAD: I have good reason to say it.

MRS. LINDE: I'm in the same position as you. No one to care about, no one to care for.

KROGSTAD: You made your own choice.

MRS. LINDE: I had no choice — then.

KROGSTAD: Well?

MRS. LINDE: Nils, suppose we two shipwrecked souls could join hands?

KROGSTAD: What are you saying?

MRS. LINDE: Castaways have a better chance of survival together than on their own.

KROGSTAD: Christine!

MRS. LINDE: Why do you suppose I came to this town?

KROGSTAD: You mean — you came because of me?

MRS. LINDE: I must work if I'm to find life worth living. I've always worked, for as long as I can remember; it's been the greatest joy of my life — my only joy. But now I'm alone in the world, and I feel so dreadfully lost and empty. There's no joy in working just for oneself. Oh, Nils, give me something — someone — to work for.

KROGSTAD: I don't believe all that. You're just being hysterical and romantic. You want to find an excuse for self-sacrifice.

MRS. LINDE: Have you ever known me to be hysterical?

KROGSTAD: You mean you really —? Is it possible? Tell me — you know all about my past?

MRS. LINDE: Yes.

KROGSTAD: And you know what people think of me here?

MRS. LINDE: You said just now that with me you might have become a different person.

KROGSTAD: I know I could have.

MRS. LINDE: Couldn't it still happen?

KROGSTAD: Christine — do you really mean this? Yes — you do — I see it in your face. Have you really the courage —?

MRS. LINDE: I need someone to be a mother to; and your children need a mother. And you and I need each other. I believe in you, Nils. I am afraid of nothing — with you.

KROGSTAD (*clasps her hands*): Thank you, Christine — thank you! Now I shall make the world believe in me as you do! Oh — but I'd forgotten —

MRS. LINDE (*listens*): Ssh! The tarantella! Go quickly, go!

KROGSTAD: Why? What is it?

MRS. LINDE: You hear that dance? As soon as it's finished, they'll be coming down.

KROGSTAD: All right, I'll go. It's no good, Christine. I'd forgotten — you don't know what I've just done to the Helmers.

MRS. LINDE: Yes, Nils. I know.

KROGSTAD: And yet you'd still have the courage to —?

MRS. LINDE: I know what despair can drive a man like you to.

KROGSTAD: Oh, if only I could undo this!

MRS. LINDE: You can. Your letter is still lying in the box.

KROGSTAD: Are you sure?

MRS. LINDE: Quite sure. But —

KROGSTAD (*looks searchingly at her*): Is that why you're doing this? You want to save your friend at any price? Tell me the truth. Is that the reason?

MRS. LINDE: Nils, a woman who has sold herself once for the sake of others doesn't make the same mistake again.

KROGSTAD: I shall demand my letter back.

MRS. LINDE: No, no.

KROGSTAD: Of course I shall. I shall stay here till Helmer comes down. I'll tell him he must give me back my letter — I'll say it was only to do with my dismissal, and that I don't want him to read it —

MRS. LINDE: No, Nils, you mustn't ask for that letter back.

KROGSTAD: But — tell me — wasn't that the real reason you asked me to come here?

MRS. LINDE: Yes — at first, when I was frightened. But a day has passed since then, and in that time I've seen incredible things happen in this house. Helmer must know the truth. This unhappy secret of Nora's must be revealed. They must come to a full understanding; there must be an end of all these shiftings and evasions.

KROGSTAD: Very well. If you're prepared to risk it. But one thing I can do — and at once —

MRS. LINDE (*listens*): Hurry! Go, go! The dance is over. We aren't safe here another moment.

KROGSTAD: I'll wait for you downstairs.

MRS. LINDE: Yes, do. You can see me home.

KROGSTAD: I've never been so happy in my life before!

(*He goes out through the front door. The door leading from the room into the hall remains open.*)

MRS. LINDE (*tidies the room a little and gets her hat and coat*): What a change! Oh, what a change! Someone to work for — to live for! A home to bring joy into! I won't let this chance of happiness slip through my fingers. Oh, why don't they come? (*Listens.*) Ah, here they are. I must get my coat on.

(*She takes her hat and coat. Helmer's and Nora's voices become audible outside. A key is turned in the lock and Helmer leads Nora almost forcibly into the hall. She is dressed in an Italian costume with a large black shawl. He is in evening dress, with a black cloak.*)

NORA (*still in the doorway, resisting him*): No, no, no — not in here! I want to go back upstairs. I don't want to leave so early.

HELMER: But my dearest Nora —

NORA: Oh, please, Torvald, please! Just another hour!

HELMER: Not another minute, Nora, my sweet. You

know what we agreed. Come along, now. Into the drawing room. You'll catch cold if you stay out here.

(*He leads her, despite her efforts to resist him, gently into the room.*)

MRS. LINDE: Good evening.

NORA: Christine!

HELMER: Oh, hullo, Mrs. Linde. You still here?

MRS. LINDE: Please forgive me. I did so want to see Nora in her costume.

NORA: Have you been sitting here waiting for me?

MRS. LINDE: Yes. I got here too late, I'm afraid. You'd already gone up. And I felt I really couldn't go back home without seeing you.

HELMER (*takes off Nora's shawl*): Well, take a good look at her. She's worth looking at, don't you think? Isn't she beautiful, Mrs. Linde?

MRS. LINDE: Oh, yes, indeed —

HELMER: Isn't she unbelievably beautiful? Everyone at the party said so. But dreadfully stubborn she is, bless her pretty little heart. What's to be done about that? Would you believe it, I practically had to use force to get her away!

NORA: Oh, Torvald, you're going to regret not letting me stay — just half an hour longer.

HELMER: Hear that, Mrs. Linde? She dances her tarantella — makes a roaring success — and very well deserved — though possibly a trifle too realistic — more so than was aesthetically necessary, strictly speaking. But never mind that. Main thing is — she had a success — roaring success. Was I going to let her stay on after that and spoil the impression? No, thank you. I took my beautiful little Capri signorina — my capricious little Capricienne, what? — under my arm — a swift round of the ballroom, a curtsey to the company, and, as they say in novels, the beautiful apparition disappeared! An exit should always be dramatic, Mrs. Linde. But unfortunately that's just what I can't get Nora to realize. I say, it's hot in here. (*Throws his cloak on a chair and opens the door to his study.*) What's this? It's dark in here. Ah, yes, of course — excuse me. (*Goes in and lights a couple of candles.*)

NORA (*whispers swiftly, breathlessly*): Well?

MRS. LINDE (*quietly*): I've spoken to him.

NORA: Yes?

MRS. LINDE: Nora — you must tell your husband everything.

NORA (*dully*): I knew it.

MRS. LINDE: You've nothing to fear from Krogstad. But you must tell him.

NORA: I shan't tell him anything.

MRS. LINDE: Then the letter will.

NORA: Thank you, Christine. Now I know what I must do. Ssh!

HELMER (*returns*): Well, Mrs. Linde, finished admiring her?

MRS. LINDE: Yes. Now I must say good night.

HELMER: Oh, already? Does this knitting belong to you?

MRS. LINDE (*takes it*): Thank you, yes. I nearly forgot it.

HELMER: You knit, then?

MRS. LINDE: Why, yes.

HELMER: Know what? You ought to take up embroidery.

MRS. LINDE: Oh? Why?

HELMER: It's much prettier. Watch me, now. You hold the embroidery in your left hand, like this, and then you take the needle in your right hand and go in and out in a slow, easy movement — like this. I am right, aren't I?

MRS. LINDE: Yes, I'm sure —

HELMER: But knitting, now — that's an ugly business — can't help it. Look — arms all huddled up — great clumsy needles going up and down — makes you look like a damned Chinaman. I say, that really was a magnificent champagne they served us.

MRS. LINDE: Well, good night, Nora. And stop being stubborn. Remember!

HELMER: Quite right, Mrs. Linde!

MRS. LINDE: Good night, Mr. Helmer.

HELMER (*accompanies her to the door*): Good night, good night! I hope you'll manage to get home all right? I'd gladly — but you haven't far to go, have you? Good night, good night. (*She goes. He closes the door behind her and returns.*) Well, we've got rid of her at last. Dreadful bore that woman is!

NORA: Aren't you very tired, Torvald?

HELMER: No, not in the least.

NORA: Aren't you sleepy?

HELMER: Not a bit. On the contrary, I feel extraordinarily exhilarated. But what about you? Yes, you look very sleepy and tired.

NORA: Yes, I am very tired. Soon I shall sleep.

HELMER: You see, you see! How right I was not to let you stay longer!

NORA: Oh, you're always right, whatever you do.

HELMER (*kisses her on the forehead*): Now my little songbird's talking just like a real big human being. I say, did you notice how cheerful Rank was this evening?

NORA: Oh? Was he? I didn't have a chance to speak with him.

HELMER: I hardly did. But I haven't seen him in such a jolly mood for ages. (*Looks at her for a moment, then comes closer.*) I say, it's nice to get back to one's home again, and be all alone with you. Upon my word, you're a distractingly beautiful young woman.

NORA: Don't look at me like that, Torvald!

HELMER: What, not look at my most treasured possession? At all this wonderful beauty that's mine, mine alone, all mine.

NORA (*goes round to the other side of the table*): You mustn't talk to me like that tonight.

HELMER (*follows her*): You've still the tarantella in your blood, I see. And that makes you even more desirable. Listen! Now the other guests are beginning to go. (*More quietly.*) Nora — soon the whole house will be absolutely quiet.

NORA: Yes, I hope so.

HELMER: Yes, my beloved Nora, of course you do! Do you know — when I'm out with you among other people like we were tonight, do you know why I say so little to you, why I keep so aloof from you, and just throw you an occasional glance? Do you know why I do that? It's because I pretend to myself that you're my secret mistress, my clandestine little sweetheart, and that nobody knows there's anything at all between us.

NORA: Oh, yes, yes, yes — I know you never think of anything but me.

HELMER: And then when we're about to go, and I wrap the shawl round your lovely young shoulders, over this wonderful curve of your neck — then I pretend to myself that you are my young bride, that we've just come from the wedding, that I'm taking you to my house for the first time — that, for the first time, I am alone with you — quite alone with you, as you stand there young and trembling and beautiful. All evening I've had no eyes for anyone but you. When I saw you dance the tarantella, like a huntress, a temptress, my blood grew hot, I couldn't stand it any longer! That was why I seized you and dragged you down here with me —

NORA: Leave me, Torvald! Get away from me! I don't want all this.

HELMER: What? Now, Nora, you're joking with me. Don't want, don't want —? Aren't I your husband —?

(*There is a knock on the front door.*)

NORA (*starts*): What was that?

HELMER (*goes toward the hall*): Who is it?

RANK (*outside*): It's me. May I come in for a moment?

HELMER (*quietly, annoyed*): Oh, what does he want now? (*Calls.*) Wait a moment. (*Walks over and opens the door.*) Well! Nice of you not to go by without looking in.

RANK: I thought I heard your voice, so I felt I had to say goodbye. (*His eyes travel swiftly around the room.*) Ah, yes — these dear rooms, how well I know them. What a happy, peaceful home you two have.

HELMER: You seemed to be having a pretty happy time yourself upstairs.

RANK: Indeed I did. Why not? Why shouldn't one make the most of this world? As much as one can, and for as long as one can. The wine was excellent —

HELMER: Especially the champagne.

RANK: You noticed that too? It's almost incredible how much I managed to get down.

NORA: Torvald drank a lot of champagne too, this evening.

RANK: Oh?

NORA: Yes. It always makes him merry afterwards.

RANK: Well, why shouldn't a man have a merry evening after a well-spent day?

HELMER: Well-spent? Oh, I don't know that I can claim that.

RANK (*slaps him across the back*): I can, though, my dear fellow!

NORA: Yes, of course, Dr. Rank — you've been carrying out a scientific experiment today, haven't you?

RANK: Exactly.

HELMER: Scientific experiment! Those are big words for my little Nora to use!

NORA: And may I congratulate you on the finding?

RANK: You may indeed.

NORA: It was good, then?

RANK: The best possible finding — both for the doctor and the patient. Certainty.

NORA (*quickly*): Certainty?

RANK: Absolute certainty. So aren't I entitled to have a merry evening after that?

NORA: Yes, Dr. Rank. You were quite right to.

HELMER: I agree. Provided you don't have to regret it tomorrow.

RANK: Well, you never get anything in this life without paying for it.

NORA: Dr. Rank — you like masquerades, don't you?

RANK: Yes, if the disguises are sufficiently amusing.

NORA: Tell me. What shall we two wear at the next masquerade?

HELMER: You little gadabout! Are you thinking about the next one already?

RANK: We two? Yes, I'll tell you. You must go as the Spirit of Happiness —

HELMER: You try to think of a costume that'll convey that.

RANK: Your wife need only appear as her normal, everyday self —

HELMER: Quite right! Well said! But what are you going to be? Have you decided that?

RANK: Yes, my dear friend. I have decided that.

HELMER: Well?

RANK: At the next masquerade, I shall be invisible.

HELMER: Well, that's a funny idea.

RANK: There's a big, black hat — haven't you heard of the invisible hat? Once it's over your head, no one can see you anymore.

HELMER (*represses a smile*): Ah yes, of course.

RANK: But I'm forgetting what I came for. Helmer, give me a cigar. One of your black Havanas.

HELMER: With the greatest pleasure. (*Offers him the box.*)

RANK (*takes one and cuts off the tip*): Thank you.

NORA (*strikes a match*): Let me give you a light.

RANK: Thank you. (*She holds out the match for him. He lights his cigar.*) And now — goodbye.

HELMER: Goodbye, my dear chap, goodbye.

NORA: Sleep well, Dr. Rank.

RANK: Thank you for that kind wish.

NORA: Wish me the same.

RANK: You? Very well — since you ask. Sleep well. And thank you for the light. (*He nods to them both and goes.*)

HELMER (*quietly*): He's been drinking too much.

NORA (*abstractedly*): Perhaps.

(*Helmer takes his bunch of keys from his pocket and goes out into the hall.*)

NORA: Torvald, what do you want out there?

HELMER: I must empty the letter-box. It's absolutely full. There'll be no room for the newspapers in the morning.

NORA: Are you going to work tonight?

HELMER: You know very well I'm not. Hullo, what's this? Someone's been at the lock.

NORA: At the lock —?

HELMER: Yes, I'm sure of it. Who on earth —? Surely not one of the maids? Here's a broken hairpin. Nora, it's yours —

NORA (*quickly*): Then it must have been the children.

HELMER: Well, you'll have to break them of that habit. Hm, hm. Ah, that's done it. (*Takes out the contents of the box and calls into the kitchen.*) Helen! Put out the light on the staircase. (*Comes back into the drawing room with the letters in his hand and closes the door to the hall.*) Look at this! You see how they've piled up? (*Glances through them.*) What on earth's this?

NORA (*at the window*): The letter! Oh, no, Torvald, no!

HELMER: Two visiting cards — from Rank.

NORA: From Dr. Rank?

HELMER (*looks at them*): Peter Rank, M.D. They were on top. He must have dropped them in as he left.

NORA: Has he written anything on them?

HELMER: There's a black cross above his name. Look. Rather gruesome, isn't it? It looks just as though he was announcing his death.

NORA: He is.

HELMER: What? Do you know something? Has he told you anything?

NORA: Yes. When these cards come, it means he's said goodbye to us. He wants to shut himself up in his house and die.

HELMER: Ah, poor fellow. I knew I wouldn't be seeing him for much longer. But so soon —! And now he's going to slink away and hide like a wounded beast.

NORA: When the time comes, it's best to go silently. Don't you think so, Torvald?

HELMER (*walks up and down*): He was so much a part of our life. I can't realize that he's gone. His suffering and loneliness seemed to provide a kind of dark background to the happy sunlight of our marriage. Well, perhaps it's best this way. For him, anyway. (*Stops walking.*) And perhaps for us too, Nora. Now we have only each other. (*Embraces her.*) Oh, my beloved wife — I feel as though I could never hold you close enough. Do you know, Nora, often I wish some terrible danger might threaten you, so that I could offer my life and my blood, everything, for your sake.

NORA (*tears herself loose and says in a clear, firm voice*): Read your letters now, Torvald.

HELMER: No, no. Not tonight. Tonight I want to be with you, my darling wife —

NORA: When your friend is about to die —?

HELMER: You're right. This news has upset us both. An ugliness has come between us; thoughts of death and dissolution. We must try to forget them. Until then — you go to your room; I shall go to mine.

NORA (*throws her arms round his neck*): Good night, Torvald! Good night!

HELMER (*kisses her on the forehead*): Good night, my darling little songbird. Sleep well, Nora. I'll go and read my letters.

(*He goes into the study with the letters in his hand, and closes the door.*)

NORA (*wild-eyed, fumbles around, seizes Helmer's cloak, throws it round herself and whispers quickly, hoarsely*): Never see him again. Never. Never. Never. (*Throws the shawl over her head.*) Never see the children again. Them too. Never. Never. Oh — the icy black water! Oh — that bottomless — that —! Oh, if only it were all over! Now he's got it

— he's reading it. Oh, no, no! Not yet! Goodbye, Torvald! Goodbye, my darlings!

(*She turns to run into the hall. As she does so, Helmer throws open his door and stands there with an open letter in his hand.*)

HELMER: Nora!

NORA (*shrieks*): Ah —!

HELMER: What is this? Do you know what is in this letter?

NORA: Yes, I know. Let me go! Let me go!

HELMER (*holds her back*): Go? Where?

NORA (*tries to tear herself loose*): You mustn't try to save me, Torvald!

HELMER (*staggers back*): Is it true? Is it true, what he writes? Oh, my God! No, no — it's impossible, it can't be true!

NORA: It *is* true. I've loved you more than anything else in the world.

HELMER: Oh, don't try to make silly excuses.

NORA (*takes a step toward him*): Torvald —

HELMER: Wretched woman! What have you done?

NORA: Let me go! You're not going to suffer for my sake. I won't let you!

HELMER: Stop being theatrical. (*Locks the front door.*) You're going to stay here and explain yourself. Do you understand what you've done? Answer me! Do you understand?

NORA (*looks unflinchingly at him and, her expression growing colder, says*): Yes. Now I am beginning to understand.

HELMER (*walking around the room*): Oh, what a dreadful awakening! For eight whole years — she who was my joy and my pride — a hypocrite, a liar — worse, worse — a criminal! Oh, the hideousness of it! Shame on you, shame!

(*Nora is silent and stares unblinkingly at him.*)

HELMER (*stops in front of her*): I ought to have guessed that something of this sort would happen. I should have foreseen it. All your father's recklessness and instability — be quiet! — I repeat, all your father's recklessness and instability he has handed on to you. No religion, no morals, no sense of duty! Oh, how I have been punished for closing my eyes to his faults! I did it for your sake. And now you reward me like this.

NORA: Yes. Like this.

HELMER: Now you have destroyed all my happiness. You have ruined my whole future. Oh, it's too dreadful to contemplate! I am in the power of a man who is completely without scruples. He can do what he likes with me, demand what he pleases, order me to do anything — I dare not disobey him.

I am condemned to humiliation and ruin simply for the weakness of a woman.

NORA: When I am gone from this world, you will be free.

HELMER: Oh, don't be melodramatic. Your father was always ready with that kind of remark. How would it help me if you were "gone from this world," as you put it? It wouldn't assist me in the slightest. He can still make all the facts public; and if he does, I may quite easily be suspected of having been an accomplice in your crime. People may think that I was behind it — that it was I who encouraged you! And for all this I have to thank you, you whom I have carried on my hands through all the years of our marriage! Now do you realize what you've done to me?

NORA (*coldly calm*): Yes.

HELMER: It's so unbelievable I can hardly credit it. But we must try to find some way out. Take off that shawl. Take it off, I say! I must try to buy him off somehow. This thing must be hushed up at any price. As regards our relationship — we must appear to be living together just as before. Only *appear*, of course. You will therefore continue to reside here. That is understood. But the children shall be taken out of your hands. I dare no longer entrust them to you. Oh, to have to say this to the woman I once loved so dearly — and whom I still —! Well, all that must be finished. Henceforth there can be no question of happiness; we must merely strive to save what shreds and tatters — (*The front door bell rings. Helmer starts.*) What can that be? At this hour? Surely not —? He wouldn't —? Hide yourself, Nora. Say you're ill.

(*Nora does not move. Helmer goes to the door of the room and opens it. The Maid is standing half-dressed in the hall.*)

MAID: A letter for madam.

HELMER: Give it to me. (*Seizes the letter and shuts the door.*) Yes, it's from him. You're not having it. I'll read this myself.

NORA: Read it.

HELMER (*by the lamp*): I hardly dare to. This may mean the end for us both. No, I must know. (*Tears open the letter hastily; reads a few lines; looks at a piece of paper which is enclosed with it; utters a cry of joy.*) Nora! (*She looks at him questioningly.*) Nora! No — I must read it once more. Yes, yes, it's true! I am saved! Nora, I am saved!

NORA: What about me?

HELMER: You too, of course. We're both saved, you and I. Look! He's returning your I.O.U. He writes that he is sorry for what has happened — a happy accident has changed his life — oh, what does it matter what he writes? We are saved, Nora! No one can harm you now. Oh, Nora, Nora — no, first let me destroy this filthy thing. Let me see —! (*Glances at the I.O.U.*) No, I don't want to look at it. I shall merely regard the whole business as a dream. (*He tears the I.O.U. and both letters into pieces, throws them into the stove, and watches them burn.*) There. Now they're destroyed. He wrote that ever since Christmas Eve you've been — oh, these must have been three dreadful days for you, Nora.

NORA: Yes. It's been a hard fight.

HELMER: It must have been terrible — seeing no way out except — no, we'll forget the whole sordid business. We'll just be happy and go on telling ourselves over and over again: "It's over! It's over!" Listen to me, Nora. You don't seem to realize. It's over! Why are you looking so pale? Ah, my poor little Nora, I understand. You can't believe that I have forgiven you. But I have, Nora. I swear it to you. I have forgiven you everything. I know that what you did you did for your love of me.

NORA: That is true.

HELMER: You have loved me as a wife should love her husband. It was simply that in your inexperience you chose the wrong means. But do you think I love you any less because you don't know how to act on your own initiative? No, no. Just lean on me. I shall counsel you. I shall guide you. I would not be a true man if your feminine helplessness did not make you doubly attractive in my eyes. You mustn't mind the hard words I said to you in those first dreadful moments when my whole world seemed to be tumbling about my ears. I have forgiven you, Nora. I swear it to you; I have forgiven you.

NORA: Thank you for your forgiveness.

(*She goes out through the door, right.*)

HELMER: No, don't go — (*Looks in.*) What are you doing there?

NORA (*offstage*): Taking off my fancy dress.

HELMER (*by the open door*): Yes, do that. Try to calm yourself and get your balance again, my frightened little songbird. Don't be afraid. I have broad wings to shield you. (*Begins to walk around near the door.*) How lovely and peaceful this little home of ours is, Nora. You are safe here; I shall watch over you like a hunted dove which I have snatched unharmed from the claws of the falcon. Your wildly beating little heart shall find peace with me. It will happen, Nora; it will take time, but it will happen, believe me. Tomorrow all this will seem quite different. Soon everything will be as it was before. I shall no longer need to remind you that I have forgiven you; your own heart will tell you that it

is true. Do you really think I could ever bring myself to disown you, or even to reproach you? Ah, Nora, you don't understand what goes on in a husband's heart. There is something indescribably wonderful and satisfying for a husband in knowing that he has forgiven his wife — forgiven her unreservedly, from the bottom of his heart. It means that she has become his property in a double sense; he has, as it were, brought her into the world anew; she is now not only his wife but also his child. From now on that is what you shall be to me, my poor, helpless, bewildered little creature. Never be frightened of anything again, Nora. Just open your heart to me. I shall be both your will and your conscience. What's this? Not in bed? Have you changed?

NORA (*in her everyday dress*): Yes, Torvald. I've changed.

HELMER: But why now — so late —?

NORA: I shall not sleep tonight.

HELMER: But, my dear Nora —

NORA (*looks at her watch*): It isn't that late. Sit down here, Torvald. You and I have a lot to talk about.

(*She sits down on one side of the table.*)

HELMER: Nora, what does this mean? You look quite drawn —

NORA: Sit down. It's going to take a long time. I've a lot to say to you.

HELMER (*sits down on the other side of the table*): You alarm me, Nora. I don't understand you.

NORA: No, that's just it. You don't understand me. And I've never understood you — until this evening. No, don't interrupt me. Just listen to what I have to say. You and I have got to face facts, Torvald.

HELMER: What do you mean by that?

NORA (*after a short silence*): Doesn't anything strike you about the way we're sitting here?

HELMER: What?

NORA: We've been married for eight years. Does it occur to you that this is the first time that we two, you and I, man and wife, have ever had a serious talk together?

HELMER: Serious? What do you mean, serious?

NORA: In eight whole years — no, longer — ever since we first met — we have never exchanged a serious word on a serious subject.

HELMER: Did you expect me to drag you into all my worries — worries you couldn't possibly have helped me with?

NORA: I'm not talking about worries. I'm simply saying that we have never sat down seriously to try to get to the bottom of anything.

HELMER: But, my dear Nora, what on earth has that got to do with you?

NORA: That's just the point. You have never understood

me. A great wrong has been done to me, Torvald. First by Papa, and then by you.

HELMER: What? But we two have loved you more than anyone in the world!

NORA (*shakes her head*): You have never loved me. You just thought it was fun to be in love with me.

HELMER: Nora, what kind of a way is this to talk?

NORA: It's the truth, Torvald. When I lived with Papa, he used to tell me what he thought about everything, so that I never had any opinions but his. And if I did have any of my own, I kept them quiet, because he wouldn't have liked them. He called me his little doll, and he played with me just the way I played with my dolls. Then I came here to live in your house —

HELMER: What kind of a way is that to describe our marriage?

NORA (*undisturbed*): I mean, then I passed from Papa's hands into yours. You arranged everything the way you wanted it, so that I simply took over your taste in everything — or pretended I did — I don't really know — I think it was a little of both — first one and then the other. Now I look back on it, it's as if I've been living here like a pauper, from hand to mouth. I performed tricks for you, and you gave me food and drink. But that was how you wanted it. You and Papa have done me a great wrong. It's your fault that I have done nothing with my life.

HELMER: Nora, how can you be so unreasonable and ungrateful? Haven't you been happy here?

NORA: No, never. I used to think I was; but I haven't ever been happy.

HELMER: Not — not happy?

NORA: No. I've just had fun. You've always been very kind to me. But our home has never been anything but a playroom. I've been your doll-wife, just as I used to be Papa's doll-child. And the children have been my dolls. I used to think it was fun when you came in and played with me, just as they think it's fun when I go in and play games with them. That's all our marriage has been, Torvald.

HELMER: There may be a little truth in what you say, though you exaggerate and romanticize. But from now on it'll be different. Playtime is over. Now the time has come for education.

NORA: Whose education? Mine or the children's?

HELMER: Both yours and the children's, my dearest Nora.

NORA: Oh, Torvald, you're not the man to educate me into being the right wife for you.

HELMER: How can you say that?

NORA: And what about me? Am I fit to educate the children?

HELMER: Nora!

NORA: Didn't you say yourself a few minutes ago that you dare not leave them in my charge?

HELMER: In a moment of excitement. Surely you don't think I meant it seriously?

NORA: Yes. You were perfectly right. I'm not fitted to educate them. There's something else I must do first. I must educate myself. And you can't help me with that. It's something I must do by myself. That's why I'm leaving you.

HELMER (*jumps up*): What did you say?

NORA: I must stand on my own feet if I am to find out the truth about myself and about life. So I can't go on living here with you any longer.

HELMER: Nora, Nora!

NORA: I'm leaving you now, at once. Christine will put me up for tonight —

HELMER: You're out of your mind! You can't do this! I forbid you!

NORA: It's no use your trying to forbid me anymore. I shall take with me nothing but what is mine. I don't want anything from you, now or ever.

HELMER: What kind of madness is this?

NORA: Tomorrow I shall go home — I mean, to where I was born. It'll be easiest for me to find some kind of a job there.

HELMER: But you're blind! You've no experience of the world —

NORA: I must try to get some, Torvald.

HELMER: But to leave your home, your husband, your children! Have you thought what people will say?

NORA: I can't help that. I only know that I must do this.

HELMER: But this is monstrous! Can you neglect your most sacred duties?

NORA: What do you call my most sacred duties?

HELMER: Do I have to tell you? Your duties towards your husband, and your children.

NORA: I have another duty which is equally sacred.

HELMER: You have not. What on earth could that be?

NORA: My duty towards myself.

HELMER: First and foremost you are a wife and a mother.

NORA: I don't believe that any longer. I believe that I am first and foremost a human being, like you — or anyway, that I must try to become one. I know most people think as you do, Torvald, and I know there's something of the sort to be found in books. But I'm no longer prepared to accept what people say and what's written in books. I must think things out for myself, and try to find my own answer.

HELMER: Do you need to ask where your duty lies in your own home? Haven't you an infallible guide in such matters — your religion?

NORA: Oh, Torvald, I don't really know what religion means.

HELMER: What are you saying?

NORA: I only know what Pastor Hensen told me when

I went to confirmation. He explained that religion meant this and that. When I get away from all this and can think things out on my own, that's one of the questions I want to look into. I want to find out whether what Pastor Hensen said was right — or anyway, whether it is right for me.

HELMER: But it's unheard of for so young a woman to behave like this! If religion cannot guide you, let me at least appeal to your conscience. I presume you have some moral feelings left? Or — perhaps you haven't? Well, answer me.

NORA: Oh, Torvald, that isn't an easy question to answer. I simply don't know. I don't know where I am in these matters. I only know that these things mean something quite different to me from what they do to you. I've learned now that certain laws are different from what I'd imagined them to be; but I can't accept that such laws can be right. Has a woman really not the right to spare her dying father pain, or save her husband's life? I can't believe that.

HELMER: You're talking like a child. You don't understand how society works.

NORA: No, I don't. But now I intend to learn. I must try to satisfy myself which is right, society or I.

HELMER: Nora, you're ill; you're feverish. I almost believe you're out of your mind.

NORA: I've never felt so sane and sure in my life.

HELMER: You feel sure that it is right to leave your husband and your children?

NORA: Yes, I do.

HELMER: Then there is only one possible explanation.

NORA: What?

HELMER: That you don't love me any longer.

NORA: No, that's exactly it.

HELMER: Nora! How can you say this to me?

NORA: Oh, Torvald, it hurts me terribly to have to say it, because you've always been so kind to me. But I can't help it. I don't love you any longer.

HELMER (controlling his emotions with difficulty): And you feel quite sure about this too?

NORA: Yes, absolutely sure. That's why I can't go on living here any longer.

HELMER: Can you also explain why I have lost your love?

NORA: Yes, I can. It happened this evening, when the miracle failed to happen. It was then that I realized you weren't the man I'd thought you to be.

HELMER: Explain more clearly. I don't understand you.

NORA: I've waited so patiently, for eight whole years — well, good heavens, I'm not such a fool as to suppose that miracles occur every day. Then this dreadful thing happened to me, and then I *knew:* "Now the miracle will take place!" When Krogstad's letter was lying out there, it never occurred to me

for a moment that you would let that man trample over you. I *knew* that you would say to him: "Publish the facts to the world." And when he had done this —

HELMER: Yes, what then? When I'd exposed my wife's name to shame and scandal —

NORA: I was certain that you would step forward and take all the blame on yourself, and say: "I am the one who is guilty!"

HELMER: Nora!

NORA: You're thinking I wouldn't have accepted such a sacrifice from you? No, of course I wouldn't! But what would my word have counted for against yours? That was the miracle I was hoping for, and dreading. And it was to prevent it happening that I wanted to end my life.

HELMER: Nora, I would gladly work for you night and day, and endure sorrow and hardship for your sake. But no man can be expected to sacrifice his honor, even for the person he loves.

NORA: Millions of women have done it.

HELMER: Oh, you think and talk like a stupid child.

NORA: That may be. But you neither think nor talk like the man I could share my life with. Once you'd got over your fright — and you weren't frightened of what might threaten me, but only of what threatened you — once the danger was past, then as far as you were concerned it was exactly as though nothing had happened. I was your little songbird just as before — your doll whom henceforth you would take particular care to protect from the world because she was so weak and fragile. (*Gets up.*) Torvald, in that moment I realized that for eight years I had been living here with a complete stranger, and had borne him three children —! Oh, I can't bear to think of it! I could tear myself to pieces!

HELMER (*sadly*): I see it, I see it. A gulf has indeed opened between us. Oh, but Nora — couldn't it be bridged?

NORA: As I am now, I am no wife for you.

HELMER: I have the strength to change.

NORA: Perhaps — if your doll is taken from you.

HELMER: But to be parted — to be parted from you! No, no, Nora, I can't conceive of it happening!

NORA (*goes into the room, right*): All the more necessary that it should happen.

(*She comes back with her outdoor things and a small traveling bag, which she puts down on a chair by the table.*)

HELMER: Nora, Nora, not now! Wait till tomorrow!

NORA (*puts on her coat*): I can't spend the night in a strange man's house.

HELMER: But can't we live here as brother and sister, then —?

NORA (*fastens her hat*): You know quite well it wouldn't last. (*Puts on her shawl.*) Goodbye, Torvald. I don't want to see the children. I know they're in better hands than mine. As I am now, I can be nothing to them.

HELMER: But some time, Nora — some time —?

NORA: How can I tell? I've no idea what will happen to me.

HELMER: But you are my wife, both as you are and as you will be.

NORA: Listen, Torvald. When a wife leaves her husband's house, as I'm doing now, I'm told that according to the law he is freed of any obligations towards her. In any case, I release you from any such obligations. You mustn't feel bound to me in any way, however small, just as I shall not feel bound to you. We must both be quite free. Here is your ring back. Give me mine.

HELMER: That too?

NORA: That too.

HELMER: Here it is.

NORA: Good. Well, now it's over. I'll leave the keys here. The servants know about everything to do with the house — much better than I do. Tomorrow, when I have left town, Christine will come to pack the things I brought here from home. I'll have them sent on after me.

HELMER: This is the end then! Nora, will you never think of me anymore?

NORA: Yes, of course. I shall often think of you and the children and this house.

HELMER: May I write to you, Nora?

NORA: No, never. You mustn't do that.

HELMER: But at least you must let me send you —

NORA: Nothing. Nothing.

HELMER: But if you should need help —?

NORA: I tell you, no. I don't accept things from strangers.

HELMER: Nora — can I never be anything but a stranger to you?

NORA (*picks up her bag*): Oh, Torvald! Then the miracle of miracles would have to happen.

HELMER: The miracle of miracles?

NORA: You and I would both have to change so much that — oh, Torvald, I don't believe in miracles any longer.

HELMER: But I want to believe in them. Tell me. We should have to change so much that —?

NORA: That life together between us two could become a marriage. Goodbye.

(*She goes out through the hall.*)

HELMER (*sinks down on a chair by the door and buries his face in his hands*): Nora! Nora! (*Looks round and gets up.*) Empty! She's gone! (*A hope strikes him.*) The miracle of miracles —?

(*The street door is slammed shut downstairs.*)

HEDDA GABLER

Hedda Gabler (1890) is today Ibsen's most produced and perhaps his most respected play. But when it was first performed, it provoked a more uniformly negative response than any of his other plays. Critics were alarmed at the depressing environment that Ibsen created, and some Scandinavian critics were especially annoyed by the sense that Ibsen was condemning their entire society. The critics denounced the play "as a base escape of moral sewage gas" and Hedda herself as "a-crawl with the foulest passions of humanity."

Hedda Gabler is an intense, powerful woman living in a world totally dominated by men. She is herself dominated by her memory of her father, the General, a man of action whose pistols she now uses to amuse herself. What she enjoys is something of the General's prerogative:

the shaping of the destiny of men, especially the manner of their death. But her rejection of anything she deems bourgeois, including sex, which seems to repulse her, drives her to reject the baby she is about to have and to lure Eilert Loevborg to her only to destroy him.

She wants to be an independent woman just as her father was independent and free. She chooses marriage not because she wants to give herself to George Tesman but because she anticipates, on the strength of his expectations of a professorship, a life of comfort and influence. The play opens on Hedda's return from her wedding trip abroad, and the question on the characters' minds is whether or not she is pregnant. Hedda is not interested in children and constantly denies that she is or wants to be pregnant. We realize that Hedda and Tesman's marriage is bound for failure, but Tesman cannot see the truth about her.

Eilert Loevborg, Hedda's suitor before she married, is also Tesman's professional rival. Loevborg has the fire and genius needed to be truly distinguished — unlike Tesman, who is most comfortable gathering material for other people's books. But Loevborg is intemperate. He does everything to excess, including drinking. Hedda drives Loevborg to drink after he has been "renovated" by her friend Mrs. Elvsted. This is only one way in which Hedda's cruelty is revealed. She abuses the innocent Aunt Julia and actually burns Loevborg's book because it was created in part by Mrs. Elvsted and is therefore their "baby."

Hedda is a frustrated woman who cannot satisfy herself in the stifling society she hoped to dominate. To ensure that Loevborg commits suicide in an elegant, romantic way, she gives him one of the General's pistols, but her dreams for a romantic shot in the temple are shattered when Judge Brack reveals that Loevborg actually died miserably in a brothel from a shot in the bowels.

Hedda watches on as Mrs. Elvsted and Tesman team up to somehow rewrite Loevborg's lost book, and when she turns from them she discovers that she has lost all her independence. Judge Brack knows about the pistol, and his price of silence must be paid, he explains, by her becoming his mistress.

Hedda's tragic fate has been variously interpreted. Is she a worthwhile character? Is her behavior excusable because she is a woman in a society that will value her not for what she can do but only for who she is? Is her fate determined by the fact that as a woman she cannot live the life she knows she should? Hedda does some frightful things in the play, but how are we to take her? She is clearly larger than anyone else in the play, and certainly more interesting. The men are all weak: Tesman is tied to his aunt's apron strings; Loevborg cannot control himself; and Brack is corrupt. Mrs. Elvsted is a sympathetic character, but her ambition is to be nothing more than a helpmate. None of these fates would satisfy Hedda, and so she takes the action she does at the end of the play.

The sense in which this is a realistic play is qualified by Ibsen's adherence to most of the standards of classical theater. The characters, plot, and setting are established according to the principles of earlier drama, and the effort to maintain a sense that the play is a "slice of life" seems minimal. The play is structured in four acts, and its rhythms resemble those of a tragedy. There is no attempt to raise issues that are especially shocking to the society or the audiences, as Ibsen had done, for instance, in dealing with syphilis in his play *Ghosts*.

The way we are to interpret Hedda is complicated by some facts that we know about the composition of the play. When Ibsen was writing it, he was himself an unfulfilled husband, with a profoundly repressed sex life. But he was also famous and as a result attracted a great many young women who were interested in him sexually. One of these, Emilie Bardach, age eighteen, fell in love with him, and he with her. They agreed to go off together, but soon Ibsen had second thoughts. He was afraid to take the chance of happiness when it was finally offered.

Ibsen's biographer, Michael Meyer, in a commentary on the play refers to Hedda Gabler as "a merciless self-portrait of Ibsen in skirts." The psychologist Arne Duve has argued that Hedda is a portrait of Ibsen's "repressed and crippled emotional life." Such an interpretation makes the situation in the play less straightforward, less simple to interpret. Whether this biographical interpretation is fully warranted is difficult to say, but if it is true, then the character of Hedda and our interpretation of the play are intensely complicated.

Henrik Ibsen (1828–1906)

HEDDA GABLER
TRANSLATED BY MICHAEL MEYER

1890

Characters

GEORGE TESMAN, *research graduate in cultural history*
HEDDA, *his wife*
MISS JULIANA TESMAN, *his aunt*
MRS. ELVSTED
JUDGE BRACK
EILERT LOEVBORG
BERTHA, *a maid*

The action takes place in Tesman's villa in the fashionable quarter of town.

ACT I _____

(A large drawing room, handsomely and tastefully furnished; decorated in dark colors. In the rear wall is a broad open doorway, with curtains drawn back to either side. It leads to a smaller room, decorated in the same style as the drawing room. In the right-hand wall of the drawing room a folding door leads out to the hall. The opposite wall, on the left, contains French windows, also with curtains drawn back on either side. Through the glass we can see part of a veranda, and trees in autumn colors. Downstage stands an oval table, covered by a cloth and surrounded by chairs. Downstage right, against the wall, is a broad stove tiled with dark porcelain; in front of it stand a high-backed armchair, a cushioned footrest, and two footstools. Upstage right, in an alcove, is a corner sofa, with a small, round table. Downstage left, a little away from the wall, is another sofa. Upstage of the French windows, a piano. On either side of the open doorway in the rear wall stand what-nots holding

ornaments of terra-cotta and majolica. Against the rear wall of the smaller room can be seen a sofa, a table, and a couple of chairs. Above this sofa hangs the portrait of a handsome old man in general's uniform. Above the table a lamp hangs from the ceiling, with a shade of opalescent, milky glass. All round the drawing room bunches of flowers stand in vases and glasses. More bunches lie on the tables. The floors of both rooms are covered with thick carpets. Morning light. The sun shines in through the French windows.)

(Miss Juliana Tesman, wearing a hat and carrying a parasol, enters from the hall, followed by Bertha, who is carrying a bunch of flowers wrapped in paper. Miss Tesman is about sixty-five, of pleasant and kindly appearance. She is neatly but simply dressed in gray outdoor clothes. Bertha, the maid, is rather simple and rustic-looking. She is getting on in years.)

MISS TESMAN (*stops just inside the door, listens, and says in a hushed voice*): Well, fancy that! They're not up yet!

BERTHA (*also in hushed tones*): What did I tell you, miss? The boat didn't get in till midnight. And when they did turn up — Jesus, miss, you should have seen all the things madam made me unpack before she'd go to bed!

MISS TESMAN: Ah, well. Let them have a good lie in. But let's have some nice fresh air waiting for them when they do come down. (*Goes to the French windows and throws them wide open.*)

BERTHA (*bewildered at the table, the bunch of flowers in her hand*): I'm blessed if there's a square inch left to put anything. I'll have to let it lie here, miss. (*Puts it on the piano.*)

MISS TESMAN: Well, Bertha dear, so now you have a new mistress. Heaven knows it nearly broke my heart to have to part with you.

BERTHA (*snivels*): What about me, Miss Juju? How do you suppose I felt? After all the happy years I've spent with you and Miss Rena?

MISS TESMAN: We must accept it bravely, Bertha. It was the only way. George needs you to take care of him. He could never manage without you. You've looked after him ever since he was a tiny boy.

BERTHA: Oh, but, Miss Juju, I can't help thinking about Miss Rena, lying there all helpless, poor dear. And that new girl! She'll never learn the proper way to handle an invalid.

MISS TESMAN: Oh, I'll manage to train her. I'll do most of the work myself, you know. You needn't worry about my poor sister, Bertha dear.

BERTHA: But, Miss Juju, there's another thing. I'm frightened madam may not find me suitable.

MISS TESMAN: Oh, nonsense, Bertha. There may be one or two little things to begin with —

BERTHA: She's a real lady. Wants everything just so.

MISS TESMAN: But of course she does! General Gabler's daughter! Think of what she was accustomed to when the general was alive. You remember how we used to see her out riding with her father? In that long black skirt? With the feather in her hat?

BERTHA: Oh, yes, miss. As if I could forget! But, Lord! I never dreamed I'd live to see a match between her and Master Georgie.

MISS TESMAN: Neither did I. By the way, Bertha, from now on you must stop calling him Master Georgie. You must say Dr. Tesman.

BERTHA: Yes, madam said something about that too. Last night — the moment they'd set foot inside the door. Is it true, then, miss?

MISS TESMAN: Indeed it is. Just fancy, Bertha, some foreigners have made him a doctor. It happened while they were away. I had no idea till he told me when they got off the boat.

BERTHA: Well, I suppose there's no limit to what he won't become. He's that clever. I never thought he'd go in for hospital work, though.

MISS TESMAN: No, he's not that kind of doctor. (*Nods impressively.*) In any case, you may soon have to address him by an even grander title.

BERTHA: You don't say! What might that be, miss?

MISS TESMAN (*smiles*): Ah! If you only knew! (*Moved.*) Dear God, if only poor Joachim could rise out of his grave and see what his little son has grown into! (*Looks round.*) But, Bertha, why have you done this? Taken the chintz covers off all the furniture!

BERTHA: Madam said I was to. Can't stand chintz covers on chairs, she said.

MISS TESMAN: But surely they're not going to use this room as a parlor?

BERTHA: So I gathered, miss. From what madam said. He didn't say anything. The Doctor.

(George Tesman comes into the rear room from the right, humming, with an open, empty traveling bag in his hand. He is about thirty-three, of medium height and youthful appearance, rather plump, with an open, round, contented face, and fair hair and beard. He wears spectacles, and is dressed in comfortable indoor clothes.)

MISS TESMAN: Good morning! Good morning, George!

TESMAN (*in open doorway*): Auntie Juju! Dear Auntie Juju! (*Comes forward and shakes her hand.*) You've come all the way out here! And so early! What?

MISS TESMAN: Well, I had to make sure you'd settled in comfortably.

TESMAN: But you can't have had a proper night's sleep.

MISS TESMAN: Oh, never mind that.

TESMAN: But you got home safely?

MISS TESMAN: Oh, yes. Judge Brack kindly saw me home.

TESMAN: We were so sorry we couldn't give you a lift. But you saw how it was — Hedda had so much luggage — and she insisted on having it all with her.

MISS TESMAN: Yes, I've never seen so much luggage.

BERTHA (*to Tesman*): Shall I go and ask madam if there's anything I can lend her a hand with?

TESMAN: Er — thank you, Bertha, no, you needn't bother. She says if she wants you for anything she'll ring.

BERTHA (*over to right*): Oh. Very good.

TESMAN: Oh, Bertha — take this bag, will you?

BERTHA (*takes it*): I'll put it in the attic.

(*She goes out into the hall.*)

TESMAN: Just fancy, Auntie Juju, I filled that whole bag with notes for my book. You know, it's really incredible what I've managed to find rooting through those archives. By Jove! Wonderful old things no one even knew existed —

MISS TESMAN: I'm sure you didn't waste a single moment of your honeymoon, George dear.

TESMAN: No, I think I can truthfully claim that. But, Auntie Juju, do take your hat off. Here. Let me untie it for you. What?

MISS TESMAN (*as he does so*): Oh dear, oh dear! It's just as if you were still living at home with us.

TESMAN (*turns the hat in his hand and looks at it*): I say! What a splendid new hat!

MISS TESMAN: I bought it for Hedda's sake.

TESMAN: For Hedda's sake? What?

MISS TESMAN: So that Hedda needn't be ashamed of me, in case we ever go for a walk together.

TESMAN (*pats her cheek*): You still think of everything, don't you, Auntie Juju? (*Puts the hat down on a chair by the table.*) Come on, let's sit down here on the sofa. And have a little chat while we wait for Hedda.

(*They sit. She puts her parasol in the corner of the sofa.*)

MISS TESMAN (*clasps both his hands and looks at him*): Oh, George, it's so wonderful to have you back, and be able to see you with my own eyes again! Poor dear Joachim's own son!

TESMAN: What about me? It's wonderful for me to see you again, Auntie Juju. You've been a mother to me. And a father, too.

MISS TESMAN: You'll always keep a soft spot in your heart for your old aunties, won't you, George dear?

TESMAN: I suppose Auntie Rena's no better? What?

MISS TESMAN: Alas, no. I'm afraid she'll never get better, poor dear. She's lying there just as she has for all these years. Please God I may be allowed to keep her for a little longer. If I lost her I don't know what I'd do. Especially now I haven't you to look after.

TESMAN (*pats her on the back*): There, there, there!

MISS TESMAN (*with a sudden change of mood*): Oh, but, George, fancy you being a married man! And to think it's you who've won Hedda Gabler! The beautiful Hedda Gabler! Fancy! She was always so surrounded by admirers.

TESMAN (*hums a little and smiles contentedly*): Yes, I suppose there are quite a few people in this town who wouldn't mind being in my shoes. What?

MISS TESMAN: And what a honeymoon! Five months! Nearly six.

TESMAN: Well, I've done a lot of work, you know. All those archives to go through. And I've had to read lots of books.

MISS TESMAN: Yes, dear, of course. (*Lowers her voice confidentially.*) But tell me, George — haven't you any — any extra little piece of news to give me?

TESMAN: You mean, arising out of the honeymoon?

MISS TESMAN: Yes.

TESMAN: No, I don't think there's anything I didn't tell you in my letters. My doctorate, of course — but I told you about that last night, didn't I?

MISS TESMAN: Yes, yes, I didn't mean that kind of thing. I was just wondering — are you — are you expecting —?

TESMAN: Expecting what?

MISS TESMAN: Oh, come on, George, I'm your old aunt!

TESMAN: Well, actually — yes, I am expecting something.

MISS TESMAN: I knew it!

TESMAN: You'll be happy to learn that before very long I expect to become a — professor.

MISS TESMAN: Professor?

TESMAN: I think I may say that the matter has been decided. But, Auntie Juju, you know about this.

MISS TESMAN (*gives a little laugh*): Yes, of course. I'd forgotten. (*Changes her tone.*) But we were talking about your honeymoon. It must have cost a dreadful amount of money, George?

TESMAN: Oh well, you know, that big research grant I got helped a good deal.

MISS TESMAN: But how on earth did you manage to make it do for two?

TESMAN: Well, to tell the truth it was a bit tricky. What?

MISS TESMAN: Especially when one's traveling with a lady. A little bird tells me that makes things very much more expensive.

TESMAN: Well, yes, of course it does make things a little more expensive. But Hedda has to do things in style, Auntie Juju. I mean, she has to. Anything less grand wouldn't have suited her.

MISS TESMAN: No, no, I suppose not. A honeymoon abroad seems to be the vogue nowadays. But tell me, have you had time to look round the house?

TESMAN: You bet. I've been up since the crack of dawn.

MISS TESMAN: Well, what do you think of it?

TESMAN: Splendid. Absolutely splendid. I'm only wondering what we're going to do with those two empty rooms between that little one and Hedda's bedroom.

MISS TESMAN (*laughs slyly*): Ah, George dear, I'm sure you'll manage to find some use for them — in time.

TESMAN: Yes, of course, Auntie Juju, how stupid of me. You're thinking of my books? What?

MISS TESMAN: Yes, yes, dear boy. I was thinking of your books.

TESMAN: You know, I'm so happy for Hedda's sake that we've managed to get this house. Before we became engaged she often used to say this was the only house in town she felt she could really bear to live in. It used to belong to Mrs. Falk — you know, the Prime Minister's widow.

MISS TESMAN: Fancy that! And what a stroke of luck it happened to come into the market. Just as you'd left on your honeymoon.

TESMAN: Yes, Auntie Juju, we've certainly had all the luck with us. What?

MISS TESMAN: But, George dear, the expense! It's going to make a dreadful hole in your pocket, all this.

TESMAN (*a little downcast*): Yes, I — I suppose it will, won't it?

MISS TESMAN: Oh, George, really!

TESMAN: How much do you think it'll cost? Roughly, I mean? What?

MISS TESMAN: I can't possibly say till I see the bills.

TESMAN: Well, luckily Judge Brack's managed to get it on very favorable terms. He wrote and told Hedda so.

MISS TESMAN: Don't you worry, George dear. Anyway, I've stood security for all the furniture and carpets.

TESMAN: Security? But dear, sweet Auntie Juju, how could you possibly stand security?

MISS TESMAN: I've arranged a mortgage on our annuity.

TESMAN (*jumps up*): What? On your annuity? And — Auntie Rena's?

MISS TESMAN: Yes. Well, I couldn't think of any other way.

TESMAN (*stands in front of her*): Auntie Juju, have you gone completely out of your mind? That annuity's all you and Auntie Rena have.

MISS TESMAN: All right, there's no need to get so excited about it. It's a pure formality, you know. Judge Brack told me so. He was so kind as to arrange it all for me. A pure formality; those were his very words.

TESMAN: I dare say. All the same —

MISS TESMAN: Anyway, you'll have a salary of your own now. And, good heavens, even if we did have to fork out a little — tighten our belts for a week or two — why, we'd be happy to do so for your sake.

TESMAN: Oh, Auntie Juju! Will you never stop sacrificing yourself for me?

MISS TESMAN (*gets up and puts her hands on his shoulders*): What else have I to live for but to smooth your road a little, my dear boy? You've never had any mother or father to turn to. And now at last we've achieved our goal. I won't deny we've had our little difficulties now and then. But now, thank the good Lord, George dear, all your worries are past.

TESMAN: Yes, it's wonderful really how everything's gone just right for me.

MISS TESMAN: Yes! And the enemies who tried to bar your way have been struck down. They have been made to bite the dust. The man who was your most dangerous rival has had the mightiest fall. And now he's lying there in the pit he dug for himself, poor misguided creature.

TESMAN: Have you heard any news of Eilert? Since I went away?

MISS TESMAN: Only that he's said to have published a new book.

TESMAN: What! Eilert Loevborg? You mean — just recently? What?

MISS TESMAN: So they say. I don't imagine it can be of any value, do you? When your new book comes out, that'll be another story. What's it going to be about?

TESMAN: The domestic industries of Brabant in the Middle Ages.

MISS TESMAN: Oh, George! The things you know about!

TESMAN: Mind you, it may be some time before I actually get down to writing it. I've made these very extensive notes, and I've got to file and index them first.

MISS TESMAN: Ah, yes! Making notes; filing and indexing; you've always been wonderful at that. Poor dear Joachim was just the same.

TESMAN: I'm looking forward so much to getting down to that. Especially now I've a home of my own to work in.

MISS TESMAN: And above all, now that you have the girl you set your heart on, George dear.

TESMAN (*embraces her*): Oh, yes, Auntie Juju, yes!

Hedda's the loveliest thing of all! (*Looks toward the doorway.*) I think I hear her coming. What?

(*Hedda enters the rear room from the left, and comes into the drawing room. She is a woman of twenty-nine. Distinguished, aristocratic face and figure. Her complexion is pale and opalescent. Her eyes are steel-gray, with an expression of cold, calm serenity. Her hair is of a handsome auburn color, but is not especially abundant. She is dressed in an elegant, somewhat loose-fitting morning gown.*)

MISS TESMAN (*goes to greet her*): Good morning, Hedda dear! Good morning!

HEDDA (*holds out her hand*): Good morning, dear Miss Tesman. What an early hour to call. So kind of you.

MISS TESMAN (*seems somewhat embarrassed*): And has the young bride slept well in her new home?

HEDDA: Oh — thank you, yes. Passably well.

TESMAN (*laughs*): Passably? I say. Hedda, that's good! When I jumped out of bed, you were sleeping like a top.

HEDDA: Yes. Fortunately. One has to accustom oneself to anything new, Miss Tesman. It takes time. (*Looks left.*) Oh, that maid's left the French windows open. This room's flooded with sun.

MISS TESMAN (*goes toward the windows*): Oh — let me close them.

HEDDA: No, no, don't do that. Tesman dear, draw the curtains. This light's blinding me.

TESMAN (*at the windows*): Yes, yes, dear. There, Hedda, now you've got shade and fresh air.

HEDDA: This room needs fresh air. All these flowers —! But my dear Miss Tesman, won't you take a seat?

MISS TESMAN: No, really not, thank you. I just wanted to make sure you have everything you need. I must see about getting back home. My poor dear sister will be waiting for me.

TESMAN: Be sure to give her my love, won't you? Tell her I'll run over and see her later today.

MISS TESMAN: Oh yes, I'll tell her that. Oh, George — (*Fumbles in the pocket of her skirt.*) I almost forgot. I've brought something for you.

TESMAN: What's that, Auntie Juju? What?

MISS TESMAN (*pulls out a flat package wrapped in newspaper and gives it to him*): Open and see, dear boy.

TESMAN (*opens the package*): Good heavens! Auntie Juju, you've kept them! Hedda, this is really very touching. What?

HEDDA (*by the what-nots, on the right*): What is it, Tesman?

TESMAN: My old shoes! My slippers, Hedda!

HEDDA: Oh, them. I remember you kept talking about them on our honeymoon.

TESMAN: Yes, I missed them dreadfully. (*Goes over to her.*) Here, Hedda, take a look.

HEDDA (*goes away toward the stove*): Thanks, I won't bother.

TESMAN (*follows her*): Fancy, Hedda, Auntie Rena's embroidered them for me. Despite her being so ill. Oh, you can't imagine what memories they have for me.

HEDDA (*by the table*): Not for me.

MISS TESMAN: No, Hedda's right there, George.

TESMAN: Yes, but I thought since she's one of the family now —

HEDDA (*interrupts*): Tesman, we really can't go on keeping this maid.

MISS TESMAN: Not keep Bertha?

TESMAN: What makes you say that, dear? What?

HEDDA (*points*): Look at that! She's left her old hat lying on the chair.

TESMAN (*appalled, drops his slippers on the floor*): But, Hedda —!

HEDDA: Suppose someone came in and saw it?

TESMAN: But, Hedda — that's Auntie Juju's hat.

HEDDA: Oh?

MISS TESMAN (*picks up the hat*): Indeed it's mine. And it doesn't happen to be old, Hedda dear.

HEDDA: I didn't look at it very closely, Miss Tesman.

MISS TESMAN (*tying on the hat*): As a matter of fact, it's the first time I've worn it. As the good Lord is my witness.

TESMAN: It's very pretty, too. Really smart.

MISS TESMAN: Oh, I'm afraid it's nothing much really. (*Looks around.*) My parasol. Ah, there it is. (*Takes it.*) This is mine, too. (*Murmurs.*) Not Bertha's.

TESMAN: A new hat and a new parasol! I say, Hedda, fancy that!

HEDDA: Very pretty and charming.

TESMAN: Yes, isn't it? What? But, Auntie Juju, take a good look at Hedda before you go. Isn't she pretty and charming?

MISS TESMAN: Dear boy, there's nothing new in that. Hedda's been a beauty ever since the day she was born. (*Nods and goes right.*)

TESMAN (*follows her*): Yes, but have you noticed how strong and healthy she's looking? And how she's filled out since we went away?

MISS TESMAN (*stops and turns*): Filled out?

HEDDA (*walks across the room*): Oh, can't we forget it?

TESMAN: Yes, Auntie Juju — you can't see it so clearly with that dress on. But I've good reason to know —

HEDDA (*by the French windows, impatiently*): You haven't good reason to know anything.

TESMAN: It must have been the mountain air up there in the Tyrol —

HEDDA (*curtly, interrupts him*): I'm exactly the same as when I went away.

TESMAN: You keep on saying so. But you're not. I'm right, aren't I, Auntie Juju?

MISS TESMAN (*has folded her hands and is gazing at her*): She's beautiful — beautiful. Hedda is beautiful. (*Goes over to Hedda, takes her head between her hands, draws it down, and kisses her hair.*) God bless and keep you, Hedda Tesman. For George's sake.

HEDDA (*frees herself politely*): Oh — let me go, please.

MISS TESMAN (*quietly, emotionally*): I shall come and see you both every day.

TESMAN: Yes, Auntie Juju, please do. What?

MISS TESMAN: Good-bye! Good-bye!

(*She goes out into the hall. Tesman follows her. The door remains open. Tesman is heard sending his love to Aunt Rena and thanking Miss Tesman for his slippers. Meanwhile Hedda walks up and down the room, raising her arms and clenching her fists as though in desperation. Then she throws aside the curtains from the French windows and stands there, looking out. A few moments later Tesman returns and closes the door behind him.*)

TESMAN (*picks up his slippers from the floor*): What are you looking at, Hedda?

HEDDA (*calm and controlled again*): Only the leaves. They're so golden and withered.

TESMAN (*wraps up the slippers and lays them on the table*): Well, we're in September now.

HEDDA (*restless again*): Yes. We're already into September.

TESMAN: Auntie Juju was behaving rather oddly, I thought, didn't you? Almost as though she was in church or something. I wonder what came over her. Any idea?

HEDDA: I hardly know her. Does she often act like that?

TESMAN: Not to the extent she did today.

HEDDA (*goes away from the French windows*): Do you think she was hurt by what I said about the hat?

TESMAN: Oh, I don't think so. A little at first, perhaps —

HEDDA: But what a thing to do, throw her hat down in someone's drawing room. People don't do such things.

TESMAN: I'm sure Auntie Juju doesn't do it very often.

HEDDA: Oh well, I'll make it up with her.

TESMAN: Oh Hedda, would you?

HEDDA: When you see them this afternoon invite her to come out here this evening.

TESMAN: You bet I will! I say, there's another thing which would please her enormously.

HEDDA: Oh?

TESMAN: If you could bring yourself to call her Auntie Juju. For my sake, Hedda? What?

HEDDA: Oh no, really, Tesman, you mustn't ask me to do that. I've told you so once before. I'll try to call her Aunt Juliana. That's as far as I'll go.

TESMAN (*after a moment*): I say, Hedda, is anything wrong?

HEDDA: I'm just looking at my old piano. It doesn't really go with all this.

TESMAN: As soon as I start getting my salary we'll see about changing it.

HEDDA: No, no, don't let's change it. I don't want to part with it. We can move it into that little room and get another one to put in here.

TESMAN (*a little downcast*): Yes, we — might do that.

HEDDA (*picks up the bunch of flowers from the piano*): These flowers weren't here when we arrived last night.

TESMAN: I expect Auntie Juju brought them.

HEDDA: Here's a card. (*Takes it out and reads.*) "Will come back later today." Guess who it's from?

TESMAN: No idea. Who? What?

HEDDA: It says: "Mrs. Elvsted."

TESMAN: No, really? Mrs. Elvsted! She used to be Miss Rysing, didn't she?

HEDDA: Yes. She was the one with that irritating hair she was always showing off. I hear she used to be an old flame of yours.

TESMAN (*laughs*): That didn't last long. Anyway, that was before I got to know you, Hedda. By Jove, fancy her being in town!

HEDDA: Strange she should call. I only knew her at school.

TESMAN: Yes, I haven't seen her for — oh, heaven knows how long. I don't know how she manages to stick it out up there in the north. What?

HEDDA (*thinks for a moment, then says suddenly*): Tell me, Tesman, doesn't he live somewhere up in those parts? You know — Eilert Loevborg?

TESMAN: Yes, that's right. So he does.

(*Bertha enters from the hall.*)

BERTHA: She's here again, madam. The lady who came and left the flowers. (*Points.*) The ones you're holding.

HEDDA: Oh, is she? Well, show her in.

(*Bertha opens the door for Mrs. Elvsted and goes out. Mrs. Elvsted is a delicately built woman with gentle, attractive features. Her eyes are light blue, large, and somewhat prominent, with a frightened, questioning expression. Her hair is extremely fair, almost flaxen, and is exceptionally wavy and abundant. She is two or three years younger than Hedda. She is wearing a dark visiting dress, in good taste but not quite in the latest fashion.*)

HEDDA (*goes cordially to greet her*): Dear Mrs. Elvsted, good morning! How delightful to see you again after all this time!

MRS. ELVSTED (*nervously, trying to control herself*): Yes, it's many years since we met.

TESMAN: And since *we* met. What?

HEDDA: Thank you for your lovely flowers.

MRS. ELVSTED: I wanted to come yesterday afternoon. But they told me you were away —

TESMAN: You've only just arrived in town, then? What?

MRS. ELVSTED: I got here yesterday, around midday. Oh, I became almost desperate when I heard you weren't here.

HEDDA: Desperate? Why?

TESMAN: My dear Mrs. Rysing — Elvsted —

HEDDA: There's nothing wrong, I hope?

MRS. ELVSTED: Yes, there is. And I don't know anyone else here whom I can turn to.

HEDDA (*puts the flowers down on the table*): Come and sit with me on the sofa —

MRS. ELVSTED: Oh, I feel too restless to sit down.

HEDDA: You must. Come along, now.

(*She pulls Mrs. Elvsted down on to the sofa and sits beside her.*)

TESMAN: Well? Tell us, Mrs. — er —

HEDDA: Has something happened at home?

MRS. ELVSTED: Yes — that is, yes and no. Oh, I do hope you won't misunderstand me —

HEDDA: Then you'd better tell us the whole story, Mrs. Elvsted.

TESMAN: That's why you've come. What?

MRS. ELVSTED: Yes — yes, it is. Well, then — in case you don't already know — Eilert Loevborg is in town.

HEDDA: Loevborg here?

TESMAN: Eilert back in town? Fancy, Hedda, did you hear that?

HEDDA: Yes, of course I heard.

MRS. ELVSTED: He's been here a week. A whole week! In this city. Alone. With all those dreadful people —

HEDDA: But, my dear Mrs. Elvsted, what concern is he of yours?

MRS. ELVSTED (*gives her a frightened look and says quickly*): He's been tutoring the children.

HEDDA: Your children?

MRS. ELVSTED: My husband's. I have none.

HEDDA: Oh, you mean your stepchildren.

MRS. ELVSTED: Yes.

TESMAN (*gropingly*): But was he sufficiently — I don't know how to put it — sufficiently regular in his habits to be suited to such a post? What?

MRS. ELVSTED: For the past two to three years he has been living irreproachably.

TESMAN: You don't say! Hedda, do you hear that?

HEDDA: I hear.

MRS. ELVSTED: Quite irreproachably, I assure you. In every respect. All the same — in this big city — with money in his pockets — I'm so dreadfully frightened something may happen to him.

TESMAN: But why didn't he stay up there with you and your husband?

MRS. ELVSTED: Once his book had come out, he became restless.

TESMAN: Oh, yes — Auntie Juju said he's brought out a new book.

MRS. ELVSTED: Yes, a big new book about the history of civilization. A kind of general survey. It came out a fortnight ago. Everyone's been buying it and reading it — it's created a tremendous stir —

TESMAN: Has it really? It must be something he's dug up, then.

MRS. ELVSTED: You mean from the old days?

TESMAN: Yes.

MRS. ELVSTED: No, he's written it all since he came to live with us.

TESMAN: Well, that's splendid news, Hedda. Fancy that!

MRS. ELVSTED: Oh, yes! If only he can go on like this!

HEDDA: Have you met him since you came here?

MRS. ELVSTED: No, not yet. I had such dreadful difficulty finding his address. But this morning I managed to track him down at last.

HEDDA (*looks searchingly at her*): I must say I find it a little strange that your husband — hm —

MRS. ELVSTED (*starts nervously*): My husband! What do you mean?

HEDDA: That he should send you all the way here on an errand of this kind. I'm surprised he didn't come himself to keep an eye on his friend.

MRS. ELVSTED: Oh, no, no — my husband hasn't the time. Besides, I — er — wanted to do some shopping here.

HEDDA (*with a slight smile*): Ah. Well, that's different.

MRS. ELVSTED (*gets up quickly, restlessly*): Please, Mr. Tesman, I beg you — be kind to Eilert Loevborg if he comes here. I'm sure he will. I mean, you used to be such good friends in the old days. And you're both studying the same subject, as far as I can understand. You're in the same field, aren't you?

TESMAN: Well, we used to be, anyway.

MRS. ELVSTED: Yes — so I beg you earnestly, do please, please, keep an eye on him. Oh, Mr. Tesman, do promise me you will.

TESMAN: I shall be only too happy to do so, Mrs. Rysing.

HEDDA: Elvsted.

TESMAN: I'll do everything for Eilert that lies in my power. You can rely on that.

MRS. ELVSTED: Oh, how good and kind you are! (*Presses his hands.*) Thank you, thank you, thank you. (*Frightened.*) My husband's so fond of him, you see.

HEDDA (*gets up*): You'd better send him a note, Tesman. He may not come to you of his own accord.

TESMAN: Yes, that'd probably be the best plan, Hedda. What?

HEDDA: The sooner the better. Why not do it now?

MRS. ELVSTED (*pleadingly*): Oh yes, if only you would!

TESMAN: I'll do it this very moment. Do you have his address, Mrs. — er — Elvsted?

MRS. ELVSTED: Yes. (*Takes a small piece of paper from her pocket and gives it to him.*)

TESMAN: Good, good. Right, well, I'll go inside and — (*Looks around.*) Where are my slippers? Oh yes, here. (*Picks up the package and is about to go.*)

HEDDA: Try to sound friendly. Make it a nice long letter.

TESMAN: Right, I will.

MRS. ELVSTED: Please don't say anything about my having seen you.

TESMAN: Good heavens, no, of course not. What?

(*He goes out through the rear room to the right.*)

HEDDA (*goes over to Mrs. Elvsted, smiles, and says softly*): Well! Now we've killed two birds with one stone.

MRS. ELVSTED: What do you mean?

HEDDA: Didn't you realize I wanted to get him out of the room?

MRS. ELVSTED: So that he could write the letter?

HEDDA: And so that I could talk to you alone.

MRS. ELVSTED (*confused*): About this?

HEDDA: Yes, about this.

MRS. ELVSTED (*in alarm*): But there's nothing more to tell, Mrs. Tesman. Really there isn't.

HEDDA: Oh, yes, there is. There's a lot more. I can see that. Come along, let's sit down and have a little chat.

(*She pushes Mrs. Elvsted down into the armchair by the stove and seats herself on one of the footstools.*)

MRS. ELVSTED (*looks anxiously at her watch*): Really, Mrs. Tesman, I think I ought to be going now.

HEDDA: There's no hurry. Well? How are things at home?

MRS. ELVSTED: I'd rather not speak about that.

HEDDA: But, my dear, you can tell me. Good heavens, we were at school together.

MRS. ELVSTED: Yes, but you were a year senior to me. Oh, I used to be terribly frightened of you in those days.

HEDDA: Frightened of me?

MRS. ELVSTED: Yes, terribly frightened. Whenever you met me on the staircase you used to pull my hair.

HEDDA: No, did I?

MRS. ELVSTED: Yes. And once you said you'd burn it all off.

HEDDA: Oh, that was only in fun.

MRS. ELVSTED: Yes, but I was so silly in those days. And then afterwards — I mean, we've drifted so far apart. Our backgrounds were so different.

HEDDA: Well, now we must try to drift together again. Now listen. When we were at school we used to call each other by our Christian names —

MRS. ELVSTED: No, I'm sure you're mistaken.

HEDDA: I'm sure I'm not. I remember it quite clearly. Let's tell each other our secrets, as we used to in the old days. (*Moves closer on her footstool.*) There, now. (*Kisses her on the cheek.*) You must call me Hedda.

MRS. ELVSTED (*squeezes her hands and pats them*): Oh, you're so kind. I'm not used to people being so nice to me.

HEDDA: Now, now, now. And I shall call you Tora, the way I used to.

MRS. ELVSTED: My name is Thea.

HEDDA: Yes, of course. Of course. I meant Thea. (*Looks at her sympathetically.*) So you're not used to kindness, Thea? In your own home?

MRS. ELVSTED: Oh, if only I had a home! But I haven't. I've never had one.

HEDDA (*looks at her for a moment*): I thought that was it.

MRS. ELVSTED (*stares blankly and helplessly*): Yes — yes — yes.

HEDDA: I can't remember exactly, but didn't you first go to Mr. Elvsted as a housekeeper?

MRS. ELVSTED: Governess, actually. But his wife — at the time, I mean — she was an invalid, and had to spend most of her time in bed. So I had to look after the house, too.

HEDDA: But in the end, you became mistress of the house.

MRS. ELVSTED (*sadly*): Yes, I did.

HEDDA: Let me see. Roughly how long ago was that?

MRS. ELVSTED: When I got married, you mean?

HEDDA: Yes.

MRS. ELVSTED: About five years.

HEDDA: Yes; it must be about that.

MRS. ELVSTED: Oh, those five years! Especially the last two or three. Oh, Mrs. Tesman, if you only knew —!

HEDDA (*slaps her hand gently*): Mrs. Tesman? Oh, Thea!

MRS. ELVSTED: I'm sorry, I'll try to remember. Yes — if you had any idea —

HEDDA (*casually*): Eilert Loevborg's been up there, too, for about three years, hasn't he?

MRS. ELVSTED (*looks at her uncertainly*): Eilert Loevborg? Yes, he has.

HEDDA: Did you know him before? When you were here?

MRS. ELVSTED: No, not really. That is — I knew him by name, of course.

HEDDA: But up there, he used to visit you?

MRS. ELVSTED: Yes, he used to come and see us every day. To give the children lessons. I found I couldn't do that as well as manage the house.

HEDDA: I'm sure you couldn't. And your husband — ? I suppose being a magistrate he has to be away from home a good deal?

MRS. ELVSTED: Yes. You see, Mrs. — you see, Hedda, he has to cover the whole district.

HEDDA (*leans against the arm of Mrs. Elvsted's chair*): Poor, pretty little Thea! Now you must tell me the whole story. From beginning to end.

MRS. ELVSTED: Well — what do you want to know?

HEDDA: What kind of a man is your husband, Thea? I mean, as a person. Is he kind to you?

MRS. ELVSTED (*evasively*): I'm sure he does his best to be.

HEDDA: I only wonder if he isn't too old for you. There's more than twenty years between you, isn't there?

MRS. ELVSTED (*irritably*): Yes, there's that, too. Oh, there are so many things. We're different in every way. We've nothing in common. Nothing whatever.

HEDDA: But he loves you, surely? In his own way?

MRS. ELVSTED: Oh, I don't know. I think he just finds me useful. And then I don't cost much to keep. I'm cheap.

HEDDA: Now you're being stupid.

MRS. ELVSTED (*shakes her head*): It can't be any different. With him. He doesn't love anyone except himself. And perhaps the children — a little.

HEDDA: He must be fond of Eilert Loevborg, Thea.

MRS. ELVSTED (*looks at her*): Eilert Loevborg? What makes you think that?

HEDDA: Well, if he sends you all the way down here to look for him — (*Smiles almost imperceptibly.*) Besides, you said so yourself to Tesman.

MRS. ELVSTED (*with a nervous twitch*): Did I? Oh yes, I suppose I did. (*Impulsively, but keeping her voice low.*) Well, I might as well tell you the whole story. It's bound to come out sooner or later.

HEDDA: But, my dear Thea —?

MRS. ELVSTED: My husband had no idea I was coming here.

HEDDA: What? Your husband didn't know?

MRS. ELVSTED: No, of course not. As a matter of fact, he wasn't even there. He was away at the assizes.° Oh, I couldn't stand it any longer, Hedda! I just couldn't. I'd be so dreadfully lonely up there now.

HEDDA: Go on.

MRS. ELVSTED: So I packed a few things. Secretly. And went.

HEDDA: Without telling anyone?

MRS. ELVSTED: Yes. I caught the train and came straight here.

HEDDA: But, my dear Thea! How brave of you!

MRS. ELVSTED (*gets up and walks across the room*): Well, what else could I do?

HEDDA: But what do you suppose your husband will say when you get back?

MRS. ELVSTED (*by the table, looks at her*): Back there? To him?

HEDDA: Yes. Surely —?

MRS. ELVSTED: I shall never go back to him.

HEDDA (*gets up and goes closer*): You mean you've left your home for good?

MRS. ELVSTED: Yes. I didn't see what else I could do.

HEDDA: But to do it so openly!

MRS. ELVSTED: Oh, it's no use trying to keep a thing like that secret.

HEDDA: But what do you suppose people will say?

MRS. ELVSTED: They can say what they like. (*Sits sadly, wearily on the sofa.*) I had to do it.

HEDDA (*after a short silence*): What do you intend to do now? How are you going to live?

MRS. ELVSTED: I don't know. I only know that I must live wherever Eilert Loevborg is. If I am to go on living.

HEDDA (*moves a chair from the table, sits on it near Mrs. Elvsted and strokes her hands*): Tell me, Thea, how did this — friendship between you and Eilert Loevborg begin?

MRS. ELVSTED: Oh, it came about gradually. I developed a kind of — power over him.

HEDDA: Oh?

MRS. ELVSTED: He gave up his old habits. Not because I asked him to. I'd never have dared to do that. I suppose he just noticed I didn't like that kind of thing. So he gave it up.

assizes: Sessions of court.

HEDDA (*hides a smile*): So you've made a new man of him! Clever little Thea!

MRS. ELVSTED: Yes — anyway, he says I have. And he's made a — sort of — real person of me. Taught me to think — and to understand all kinds of things.

HEDDA: Did he give you lessons, too?

MRS. ELVSTED: Not exactly lessons. But he talked to me. About — oh, you've no idea — so many things! And then he let me work with him. Oh, it was wonderful. I was so happy to be allowed to help him.

HEDDA: Did he allow you to help him?

MRS. ELVSTED: Yes. Whenever he wrote anything we always — did it together.

HEDDA: Like good friends?

MRS. ELVSTED (*eagerly*): Friends! Yes — why, Hedda, that's exactly the word he used! Oh, I ought to feel so happy. But I can't. I don't know if it will last.

HEDDA: You don't seem very sure of him.

MRS. ELVSTED (*sadly*): Something stands between Eilert Loevborg and me. The shadow of another woman.

HEDDA: Who can that be?

MRS. ELVSTED: I don't know. Someone he used to be friendly with in — in the old days. Someone he's never been able to forget.

HEDDA: What has he told you about her?

MRS. ELVSTED: Oh, he only mentioned her once, casually.

HEDDA: Well! What did he say?

MRS. ELVSTED: He said when he left her she tried to shoot him with a pistol.

HEDDA (*cold, controlled*): What nonsense. People don't do such things. The kind of people we know.

MRS. ELVSTED: No. I think it must have been that red-haired singer he used to —

HEDDA: Ah yes, very probably.

MRS. ELVSTED: I remember they used to say she always carried a loaded pistol.

HEDDA: Well then, it must be her.

MRS. ELVSTED: But, Hedda, I hear she's come back, and is living here. Oh, I'm so desperate —!

HEDDA (*glances toward the rear room*): Ssh! Tesman's coming. (*Gets up and whispers.*) Thea, we mustn't breathe a word about this to anyone.

MRS. ELVSTED (*jumps up*): Oh, no, no! Please don't!

(*George Tesman appears from the right in the rear room with a letter in his hand, and comes into the drawing room.*)

TESMAN: Well, here's my little epistle all signed and sealed.

HEDDA: Good. I think Mrs. Elvsted wants to go now. Wait a moment — I'll see you as far as the garden gate.

TESMAN: Er — Hedda, do you think Bertha could deal with this?

HEDDA (*takes the letter*): I'll give her instructions.

(*Bertha enters from the hall.*)

BERTHA: Judge Brack is here and asks if he may pay his respects to madam and the Doctor.

HEDDA: Yes, ask him to be so good as to come in. And — wait a moment — drop this letter in the post box.

BERTHA (*takes the letter*): Very good, madam.

(*She opens the door for Judge Brack, and goes out. Judge Brack is forty-five; rather short, but well built, and elastic in his movements. He has a roundish face with an aristocratic profile. His hair, cut short, is still almost black, and is carefully barbered. Eyes lively and humorous. Thick eyebrows. His mustache is also thick, and is trimmed square at the ends. He is wearing outdoor clothes which are elegant but a little too youthful for him. He has a monocle in one eye; now and then he lets it drop.*)

BRACK (*hat in hand, bows*): May one presume to call so early?

HEDDA: One may presume.

TESMAN (*shakes his hand*): You're welcome here any time. Judge Brack — Mrs. Rysing.

(*Hedda sighs.*)

BRACK (*bows*): Ah — charmed —

HEDDA (*looks at him and laughs*): What fun to be able to see you by daylight for once, Judge.

BRACK: Do I look — different?

HEDDA: Yes. A little younger, I think.

BRACK: Too kind.

TESMAN: Well, what do you think of Hedda? What? Doesn't she look well? Hasn't she filled out —?

HEDDA: Oh, do stop it. You ought to be thanking Judge Brack for all the inconvenience he's put himself to —

BRACK: Nonsense, it was a pleasure —

HEDDA: You're a loyal friend. But my other friend is pining to get away. Au revoir, Judge. I won't be a minute.

(*Mutual salutations. Mrs. Elvsted and Hedda go out through the hall.*)

BRACK: Well, is your wife satisfied with everything?

TESMAN: Yes, we can't thank you enough. That is — we may have to shift one or two things around, she tells me. And we're short of one or two little items we'll have to purchase.

BRACK: Oh? Really?

TESMAN: But you mustn't worry your head about that. Hedda says she'll get what's needed. I say, why don't we sit down? What?

BRACK: Thanks, just for a moment. (*Sits at the table.*) There's something I'd like to talk to you about, my dear Tesman.

TESMAN: Oh? Ah yes, of course. (*Sits.*) After the feast comes the reckoning. What?

BRACK: Oh, never mind about the financial side — there's no hurry about that. Though I could wish we'd arranged things a little less palatially.

TESMAN: Good heavens, that'd never have done. Think of Hedda, my dear chap. You know her. I couldn't possibly ask her to live like a petty bourgeois.

BRACK: No, no — that's just the problem.

TESMAN: Anyway, it can't be long now before my nomination comes through.

BRACK: Well, you know, these things often take time.

TESMAN: Have you heard any more news? What?

BRACK: Nothing definite. (*Changing the subject.*) Oh, by the way, I have one piece of news for you.

TESMAN: What?

BRACK: Your old friend Eilert Loevborg is back in town.

TESMAN: I know that already.

BRACK: Oh? How did you hear that?

TESMAN: She told me. That lady who went out with Hedda.

BRACK: I see. What was her name? I didn't catch it.

TESMAN: Mrs. Elvsted.

BRACK: Oh, the magistrate's wife. Yes, Loevborg's been living up near them, hasn't he?

TESMAN: I'm delighted to hear he's become a decent human being again.

BRACK: Yes, so they say.

TESMAN: I gather he's published a new book, too. What?

BRACK: Indeed he has.

TESMAN: I hear it's created rather a stir.

BRACK: Quite an unusual stir.

TESMAN: I say, isn't that splendid news! He's such a gifted chap — and I was afraid he'd gone to the dogs for good.

BRACK: Most people thought he had.

TESMAN: But I can't think what he'll do now. How on earth will he manage to make ends meet? What?

(*As he speaks his last words Hedda enters from the hall.*)

HEDDA (*to Brack, laughs slightly scornfully*): Tesman is always worrying about making ends meet.

TESMAN: We were talking about poor Eilert Loevborg, Hedda dear.

HEDDA (*gives him a quick look*): Oh, were you? (*Sits in the armchair by the stove and asks casually*) Is he in trouble?

TESMAN: Well, he must have run through his inheritance long ago by now. And he can't write a new book every year. What? So I'm wondering what's going to become of him.

BRACK: I may be able to enlighten you there.

TESMAN: Oh?

BRACK: You mustn't forget he has relatives who wield a good deal of influence.

TESMAN: Relatives? Oh, they've quite washed their hands of him, I'm afraid.

BRACK: They used to regard him as the hope of the family.

TESMAN: Used to, yes. But he's put an end to that.

HEDDA: Who knows? (*With a little smile.*) I hear the Elvsteds have made a new man of him.

BRACK: And then this book he's just published —

TESMAN: Well, let's hope they find something for him. I've just written him a note. Oh, by the way, Hedda, I asked him to come over and see us this evening.

BRACK: But, my dear chap, you're coming to me this evening. My bachelor party. You promised me last night when I met you at the boat.

HEDDA: Had you forgotten, Tesman?

TESMAN: Good heavens, yes, I'd quite forgotten.

BRACK: Anyway, you can be quite sure he won't turn up here.

TESMAN: Why do you think that? What?

BRACK (*a little unwillingly, gets up and rests his hands on the back of his chair*): My dear Tesman — and you, too, Mrs. Tesman — there's something I feel you ought to know.

TESMAN: Concerning Eilert?

BRACK: Concerning him and you.

TESMAN: Well, my dear Judge, tell us, please!

BRACK: You must be prepared for your nomination not to come through quite as quickly as you hope and expect.

TESMAN (*jumps up uneasily*): Is anything wrong? What?

BRACK: There's a possibility that the appointment may be decided by competition —

TESMAN: Competition! Hedda, fancy that!

HEDDA (*leans further back in her chair*): Ah! How interesting!

TESMAN: But who else —? I say, you don't mean — ?

BRACK: Exactly. By competition with Eilert Loevborg.

TESMAN (*clasps his hands in alarm*): No, no, but this is inconceivable! It's absolutely impossible! What?

BRACK: Hm. We may find it'll happen, all the same.

TESMAN: No, but — Judge Brack, they couldn't be so inconsiderate towards me! (*Waves his arms.*) I mean, by Jove, I — I'm a married man! It was on the strength of this that Hedda and I *got* married! We've run up some pretty hefty debts. And borrowed money from Auntie Juju! I mean, good heavens, they practically promised me the appointment. What?

BRACK: Well, well, I'm sure you'll get it. But you'll have to go through a competition.

HEDDA (*motionless in her armchair*): How exciting, Tesman. It'll be a kind of duel, by Jove.

TESMAN: My dear Hedda, how can you take it so lightly?

HEDDA (*as before*): I'm not. I can't wait to see who's going to win.

BRACK: In any case, Mrs. Tesman, it's best you should know how things stand. I mean before you commit yourself to these little items I hear you're threatening to purchase.

HEDDA: I can't allow this to alter my plans.

BRACK: Indeed? Well, that's your business. Good-bye. (*To Tesman.*) I'll come and collect you on the way home from my afternoon walk.

TESMAN: Oh, yes, yes. I'm sorry, I'm all upside down just now.

HEDDA (*lying in her chair, holds out her hand*): Good-bye, Judge. See you this afternoon.

BRACK: Thank you. Good-bye, good-bye.

TESMAN (*sees him to the door*): Good-bye, my dear Judge. You will excuse me, won't you?

(*Judge Brack goes out through the hall.*)

TESMAN (*pacing up and down*): Oh, Hedda! One oughtn't to go plunging off on wild adventures. What?

HEDDA (*looks at him and smiles*): Like you're doing?

TESMAN: Yes. I mean, there's no denying it, it was a pretty big adventure to go off and get married and set up house merely on expectation.

HEDDA: Perhaps you're right.

TESMAN: Well, anyway, we have our home, Hedda. My word, yes! The home we dreamed of. And set our hearts on. What?

HEDDA (*gets up slowly, wearily*): You agreed that we should enter society. And keep open house. That was the bargain.

TESMAN: Yes. Good heavens, I was looking forward to it all so much. To seeing you play hostess to a select circle! By Jove! What? Ah, well, for the time being we shall have to make do with each other's company, Hedda. Perhaps have Auntie Juju in now and then. Oh dear, this wasn't at all what you had in mind —

HEDDA: I won't be able to have a liveried footman. For a start.

TESMAN: Oh no, we couldn't possibly afford a footman.

HEDDA: And the bay mare you promised me —

TESMAN (*fearfully*): Bay mare!

HEDDA: I mustn't even think of that now.

TESMAN: Heaven forbid!

HEDDA (*walks across the room*): Ah, well. I still have one thing left to amuse myself with.

TESMAN (*joyfully*): Thank goodness for that. What's that, Hedda? What?

HEDDA (*in the open doorway, looks at him with concealed scorn*): My pistols, George darling.

TESMAN (*alarmed*): Pistols!

HEDDA (*her eyes cold*): General Gabler's pistols.

(*She goes into the rear room and disappears.*)

TESMAN (*runs to the doorway and calls after her*): For heaven's sake, Hedda dear, don't touch those things. They're dangerous. Hedda — please — for my sake! What?

ACT II

(*The same as in Act 1, except that the piano has been removed and an elegant little writing table, with a bookcase, stands in its place. By the sofa on the left a smaller table has been placed. Most of the flowers have been removed. Mrs. Elvsted's bouquet stands on the larger table, downstage. It is afternoon.*)

(*Hedda, dressed to receive callers, is alone in the room. She is standing by the open French windows, loading a revolver. The pair to it is lying in an open pistol case on the writing table.*)

HEDDA (*looks down into the garden and calls*): Good afternoon, Judge.

BRACK (*in the distance, below*): Afternoon, Mrs. Tesman.

HEDDA (*raises the pistol and takes aim*): I'm going to shoot you, Judge Brack.

BRACK (*shouts from below*): No, no, no! Don't aim that thing at me!

HEDDA: This'll teach you to enter houses by the back door.

(*She fires.*)

BRACK (*below*): Have you gone completely out of your mind?

HEDDA: Oh dear! Did I hit you?

BRACK (*still outside*): Stop playing these silly tricks.

HEDDA: All right, Judge. Come along in.

(*Judge Brack, dressed for a bachelor party, enters through the French windows. He has a light overcoat on his arm.*)

BRACK: For God's sake, haven't you stopped fooling

around with those things yet? What are you trying to hit?

HEDDA: Oh, I was just shooting at the sky.

BRACK (*takes the pistol gently from her hand*): By your leave, ma'am. (*Looks at it.*) Ah, yes — I know this old friend well. (*Looks around.*) Where's the case? Oh, yes. (*Puts the pistol in the case and closes it.*) That's enough of that little game for today.

HEDDA: Well, what on earth *am* I to do?

BRACK: You haven't had any visitors?

HEDDA (*closes the French windows*): Not one. I suppose the best people are all still in the country.

BRACK: Your husband isn't home yet?

HEDDA (*locks the pistol case away in a drawer of the writing table*): No. The moment he'd finished eating he ran off to his aunties. He wasn't expecting you so early.

BRACK: Ah, why didn't I think of that? How stupid of me.

HEDDA (*turns her head and looks at him*): Why stupid?

BRACK: I'd have come a little sooner.

HEDDA (*walks across the room*): There'd have been no one to receive you. I've been in my room since lunch, dressing.

BRACK: You haven't a tiny crack in the door through which we might have negotiated?

HEDDA: You forgot to arrange one.

BRACK: Another stupidity.

HEDDA: Well, we'll have to sit down here. And wait. Tesman won't be back for some time.

BRACK: Sad. Well, I'll be patient.

(*Hedda sits on the corner of the sofa. Brack puts his coat over the back of the nearest chair and seats himself, keeping his hat in his hand. Short pause. They look at each other.*)

HEDDA: Well?

BRACK (*in the same tone of voice*): Well?

HEDDA: I asked first.

BRACK (*leans forward slightly*): Yes, well, now we can enjoy a nice, cozy little chat — Mrs. Hedda.

HEDDA (*leans further back in her chair*): It seems ages since we had a talk. I don't count last night or this morning.

BRACK: You mean: *à deux*?°

HEDDA: Mm — yes. That's roughly what I meant.

BRACK: I've been longing so much for you to come home.

HEDDA: So have I.

BRACK: You? Really, Mrs. Hedda? And I thought you were having such a wonderful honeymoon.

HEDDA: Oh, yes. Wonderful!

à deux: Between the two of us.

BRACK: But your husband wrote such ecstatic letters.

HEDDA: He! Oh, yes! He thinks life has nothing better to offer than rooting around in libraries and copying old pieces of parchment, or whatever it is he does.

BRACK (*a little maliciously*): Well, that *is* his life. Most of it, anyway.

HEDDA: Yes, I know. Well, it's all right for him. But for me! Oh no, my dear Judge. I've been bored to death.

BRACK (*sympathetically*): Do you mean that? Seriously?

HEDDA: Yes. Can you imagine? Six whole months without ever meeting a single person who was one of us, and to whom I could talk about the kind of things we talk about.

BRACK: Yes, I can understand. I'd miss that, too.

HEDDA: That wasn't the worst, though.

BRACK: What was?

HEDDA: Having to spend every minute of one's life with — with the same person.

BRACK (*nods*): Yes. What a thought! Morning; noon; *and* —

HEDDA (*coldly*): As I said: every minute of one's life.

BRACK: I stand corrected. But dear Tesman is such a clever fellow, I should have thought one ought to be able —

HEDDA: Tesman is only interested in one thing, my dear Judge. His special subject.

BRACK: True.

HEDDA: And people who are only interested in one thing don't make the most amusing company. Not for long, anyway.

BRACK: Not even when they happen to be the person one loves?

HEDDA: Oh, don't use that sickly, stupid word.

BRACK (*starts*): But, Mrs. Hedda —!

HEDDA (*half laughing, half annoyed*): You just try it, Judge. Listening to the history of civilization morning, noon and —

BRACK (*corrects her*): Every minute of one's life.

HEDDA: All right. Oh, and those domestic industries of Brabant in the Middle Ages! That really is beyond the limit.

BRACK (*looks at her searchingly*): But, tell me — if you feel like this why on earth did you —? Hm —

HEDDA: Why on earth did I marry George Tesman?

BRACK: If you like to put it that way.

HEDDA: Do you think it so very strange?

BRACK: Yes — and no, Mrs. Hedda.

HEDDA: I'd danced myself tired, Judge. I felt my time was up — (*Gives a slight shudder.*) No, I mustn't say that. Or even think it.

BRACK: You've no rational cause to think it.

HEDDA: Oh — cause, cause — (*Looks searchingly at*

him.) After all, George Tesman — well, I mean, he's a very respectable man.

BRACK: Very respectable, sound as a rock. No denying that.

HEDDA: And there's nothing exactly ridiculous about him. Is there?

BRACK: Ridiculous? N-no, I wouldn't say that.

HEDDA: Mm. He's very clever at collecting material and all that, isn't he? I mean, he may go quite far in time.

BRACK (*looks at her a little uncertainly*): I thought you believed, like everyone else, that he would become a very prominent man.

HEDDA (*looks tired*): Yes, I did. And when he came and begged me on his bended knees to be allowed to love and to cherish me, I didn't see why I shouldn't let him.

BRACK: No, well — if one looks at it like that —

HEDDA: It was more than my other admirers were prepared to do, Judge dear.

BRACK (*laughs*): Well, I can't answer for the others. As far as I myself am concerned, you know I've always had a considerable respect for the institution of marriage. As an institution.

HEDDA (*lightly*): Oh, I've never entertained any hopes of you.

BRACK: All I want is to have a circle of friends whom I can trust, whom I can help with advice or — or by any other means, and into whose houses I may come and go as a — trusted friend.

HEDDA: Of the husband?

BRACK (*bows*): Preferably, to be frank, of the wife. And of the husband too, of course. Yes, you know, this kind of triangle is a delightful arrangement for all parties concerned.

HEDDA: Yes, I often longed for a third person while

FAR LEFT: Hedda silhouetted near a portrait of her father, the General, in the Hartford Stage Company's 1988 production. NEAR LEFT: Tesman (Scott Wentworth), Loevborg (Richard Bekins), and Hedda (Mary Layne) discuss Loevborg's manuscript. RIGHT: Tesman and Mrs. Elvsted (Elisabeth Berridge) plan to rewrite Loevborg's lost manuscript. BELOW RIGHT: Judge Brack (William Duff-Griffin) examines Hedda's father's pistol.

I was away. Oh, those hours we spent alone in railway compartments —

BRACK: Fortunately your honeymoon is now over.

HEDDA (*shakes her head*): There's a long, long way still to go. I've only reached a stop on the line.

BRACK: Why not jump out and stretch your legs a little, Mrs. Hedda?

HEDDA: I'm not the jumping sort.

BRACK: Aren't you?

HEDDA: No. There's always someone around who —

BRACK (*laughs*): Who looks at one's legs?

HEDDA: Yes. Exactly.

BRACK: Well, but surely —

HEDDA (*with a gesture of rejection*): I don't like it. I'd rather stay where I am. Sitting in the compartment. *À deux.*

BRACK: But suppose a third person were to step into the compartment?

HEDDA: That would be different.

BRACK: A trusted friend — someone who understood —

HEDDA: And was lively and amusing —

BRACK: And interested in — more subjects than one —

HEDDA (*sighs audibly*): Yes, that'd be a relief.

BRACK (*hears the front door open and shut*): The triangle is completed.

HEDDA (*half under her breath*): And the train goes on.

(*George Tesman, in gray walking dress with a soft felt hat, enters from the hall. He has a number of paper-covered books under his arm and in his pockets.*)

TESMAN (*goes over to the table by the corner sofa*): Phew! It's too hot to be lugging all this around. (*Puts the books down.*) I'm positively sweating, Hedda. Why, hullo, hullo! You here already, Judge? What? Bertha didn't tell me.

BRACK (*gets up*): I came in through the garden.

HEDDA: What are all those books you've got there?

TESMAN (*stands glancing through them*): Oh, some new publications dealing with my special subject. I had to buy them.

HEDDA: Your special subject?

BRACK: His special subject, Mrs. Tesman.

(*Brack and Hedda exchange a smile.*)

HEDDA: Haven't you collected enough material on your special subject?

TESMAN: My dear Hedda, one can never have too much. One must keep abreast of what other people are writing.

HEDDA: Yes. Of course.

TESMAN (*rooting among the books*): Look — I bought a copy of Eilert Loevborg's new book, too. (*Holds it out to her.*) Perhaps you'd like to have a look at it, Hedda? What?

HEDDA: No, thank you. Er — yes, perhaps I will, later.

TESMAN: I glanced through it on my way home.

BRACK: What's your opinion — as a specialist on the subject?

TESMAN: I'm amazed how sound and balanced it is. He never used to write like that. (*Gathers his books together.*) Well, I must get down to these at once. I can hardly wait to cut the pages.° Oh, I've got to change, too. (*To Brack*) We don't have to be off just yet, do we? What?

BRACK: Heavens, no. We've plenty of time yet.

TESMAN: Good, I needn't hurry, then. (*Goes with his books, but stops and turns in the doorway.*) Oh, by the way, Hedda, Auntie Juju won't be coming to see you this evening.

HEDDA: Won't she? Oh — the hat, I suppose.

TESMAN: Good heavens, no. How could you think such a thing of Auntie Juju? Fancy —! No, Auntie Rena's very ill.

HEDDA: She always is.

TESMAN: Yes, but today she's been taken really bad.

HEDDA: Oh, then it's quite understandable that the other one should want to stay with her. Well, I shall have to swallow my disappointment.

TESMAN: You can't imagine how happy Auntie Juju was in spite of everything. At your looking so well after the honeymoon!

HEDDA (*half beneath her breath, as she rises*): Oh, these everlasting aunts!

TESMAN: What?

HEDDA (*goes over to the French windows*): Nothing.

TESMAN: Oh. All right. (*Goes into the rear room and out of sight.*)

BRACK: What was that about the hat?

HEDDA: Oh, something that happened with Miss Tesman this morning. She'd put her hat down on a chair. (*Looks at him and smiles.*) And I pretended to think it was the servant's.

BRACK (*shakes his head*): But, my dear Mrs. Hedda, how could you do such a thing? To that poor old lady?

HEDDA (*nervously, walking across the room*): Sometimes a mood like that hits me. And I can't stop myself. (*Throws herself down in the armchair by the stove.*) Oh, I don't know how to explain it.

BRACK (*behind her chair*): You're not really happy. That's the answer.

---

cut the pages: At the time of this play, books were constructed with their pages folded and bound in groups of four; the pages were cut apart at the outside edges not by the book manufacturer but by the user of the book.

HEDDA (*stares ahead of her*): Why on earth should I be happy? Can you give me a reason?

BRACK: Yes. For one thing you've got the home you always wanted.

HEDDA (*looks at him*): You really believe that story?

BRACK: You mean it isn't true?

HEDDA: Oh, yes, it's partly true.

BRACK: Well?

HEDDA: It's true I got Tesman to see me home from parties last summer —

BRACK: It was a pity my home lay in another direction.

HEDDA: Yes. Your interests lay in another direction, too.

BRACK (*laughs*): That's naughty of you, Mrs. Hedda. But to return to you and George —

HEDDA: Well, we walked past this house one evening. And poor Tesman was fidgeting in his boots trying to find something to talk about. I felt sorry for the great scholar —

BRACK (*smiles incredulously*): Did you? Hm.

HEDDA: Yes, honestly I did. Well, to help him out of his misery, I happened to say quite frivolously how much I'd love to live in this house.

BRACK: Was that all?

HEDDA: That evening, yes.

BRACK: But — afterwards?

HEDDA: Yes. My little frivolity had its consequences, my dear Judge.

BRACK: Our little frivolities do. Much too often, unfortunately.

HEDDA: Thank you. Well, it was our mutual admiration for the late Prime Minister's house that brought George Tesman and me together on common ground. So we got engaged, and we got married, and we went on our honeymoon, and — Ah well, Judge, I've — made my bed and I must lie in it, I was about to say.

BRACK: How utterly fantastic! And you didn't really care in the least about the house?

HEDDA: God knows I didn't.

BRACK: Yes, but now that we've furnished it so beautifully for you?

HEDDA: Ugh — all the rooms smell of lavender and dried roses. But perhaps Auntie Juju brought that in.

BRACK (*laughs*): More likely the Prime Minister's widow, rest her soul.

HEDDA: Yes, it's got the odor of death about it. It reminds me of the flowers one has worn at a ball — the morning after. (*Clasps her hands behind her neck, leans back in the chair and looks up at him.*) Oh, my dear Judge, you've no idea how hideously bored I'm going to be out here.

BRACK: Couldn't you find some — occupation, Mrs. Hedda? Like your husband?

HEDDA: Occupation? That'd interest me?

BRACK: Well — preferably.

HEDDA: God knows what. I've often thought — (*Breaks off.*) No, that wouldn't work either.

BRACK: Who knows? Tell me about it.

HEDDA: I was thinking — if I could persuade Tesman to go into politics, for example.

BRACK (*laughs*): Tesman! No, honestly, I don't think he's quite cut out to be a politician.

HEDDA: Perhaps not. But if I could persuade him to have a go at it?

BRACK: What satisfaction would that give you? If he turned out to be no good? Why do you want to make him do that?

HEDDA: Because I'm bored. (*After a moment.*) You feel there's absolutely no possibility of Tesman becoming Prime Minister, then?

BRACK: Well, you know, Mrs. Hedda, for one thing he'd have to be pretty well off before he could become that.

HEDDA (*gets up impatiently*): There you are! (*Walks across the room.*) It's this wretched poverty that makes life so hateful. And ludicrous. Well, it is!

BRACK: I don't think that's the real cause.

HEDDA: What is, then?

BRACK: Nothing really exciting has ever happened to you.

HEDDA: Nothing serious, you mean?

BRACK: Call it that if you like. But now perhaps it may.

HEDDA (*tosses her head*): Oh, you're thinking of this competition for that wretched professorship? That's Tesman's affair. I'm not going to waste my time worrying about that.

BRACK: Very well, let's forget about that, then. But suppose you were to find yourself faced with what people call — to use the conventional phrase — the most solemn of human responsibilities? (*Smiles.*) A new responsibility, little Mrs. Hedda.

HEDDA (*angrily*): Be quiet! Nothing like that's going to happen.

BRACK (*warily*): We'll talk about it again in a year's time. If not earlier.

HEDDA (*curtly*): I've no leanings in that direction, Judge. I don't want any — responsibilities.

BRACK: But surely you must feel some inclination to make use of that — natural talent which every woman —

HEDDA (*over by the French windows*): Oh, be quiet, I say! I often think there's only one thing for which I have any natural talent.

BRACK (*goes closer*): And what is that, if I may be so bold as to ask?

HEDDA (*stands looking out*): For boring myself to death. Now you know. (*Turns, looks toward the rear room and laughs.*) Talking of boring, here comes the professor.

BRACK (*quietly, warningly*): Now, now, now, Mrs. Hedda!

(*George Tesman, in evening dress, with gloves and hat in his hand, enters through the rear room from the right.*)

TESMAN: Hedda, hasn't any message come from Eilert? What?

HEDDA: No.

TESMAN: Ah, then we'll have him here presently. You wait and see.

BRACK: You really think he'll come?

TESMAN: Yes, I'm almost sure he will. What you were saying about him this morning is just gossip.

BRACK: Oh?

TESMAN: Yes. Auntie Juju said she didn't believe he'd ever dare to stand in my way again. Fancy that!

BRACK: Then everything in the garden's lovely.

TESMAN (*puts his hat, with his gloves in it, on a chair, right*): Yes, but you really must let me wait for him as long as possible.

BRACK: We've plenty of time. No one'll be turning up at my place before seven or half past.

TESMAN: Ah, then we can keep Hedda company a little longer. And see if he turns up. What?

HEDDA (*picks up Brack's coat and hat and carries them over to the corner sofa*): And if the worst comes to the worst, Mr. Loevborg can sit here and talk to me.

BRACK (*offering to take his things from her*): No, please. What do you mean by "if the worst comes to the worst"?

HEDDA: If he doesn't want to go with you and Tesman.

TESMAN (*looks doubtfully at her*): I say, Hedda, do you think it'll be all right for him to stay here with you? What? Remember Auntie Juju isn't coming.

HEDDA: Yes, but Mrs. Elvsted is. The three of us can have a cup of tea together.

TESMAN: Ah, that'll be all right.

BRACK (*smiles*): It's probably the safest solution as far as he's concerned.

HEDDA: Why?

BRACK: My dear Mrs. Tesman, you always say of my little bachelor parties that they should only be attended by men of the strongest principles.

HEDDA: But Mr. Loevborg is a man of principle now. You know what they say about a reformed sinner —

(*Bertha enters from the hall.*)

BERTHA: Madam, there's a gentleman here who wants to see you —

HEDDA: Ask him to come in.

TESMAN (*quietly*): I'm sure it's him. By Jove. Fancy that!

(*Eilert Loevborg enters from the hall. He is slim and lean, of the same age as Tesman, but looks older and somewhat haggard. His hair and beard are of a blackish-brown; his face is long and pale, but with a couple of reddish patches on his cheekbones. He is dressed in an elegant and fairly new black suit, and carries black gloves and a top hat in his hand. He stops just inside the door and bows abruptly. He seems somewhat embarrassed.*)

TESMAN (*goes over and shakes his hand*): My dear Eilert! How grand to see you again after all these years!

EILERT LOEVBORG (*speaks softly*): It was good of you to write, George. (*Goes near to Hedda.*) May I shake hands with you, too, Mrs. Tesman?

HEDDA (*accepts his hand*): Delighted to see you, Mr. Loevborg. (*With a gesture.*) I don't know if you two gentlemen —

LOEVBORG (*bows slightly*): Judge Brack, I believe.

BRACK (*also with a slight bow*): Correct. We — met some years ago —

TESMAN (*puts his hands on Loevborg's shoulders*): Now, you're to treat this house just as though it were your own home, Eilert. Isn't that right, Hedda? I hear you've decided to settle here again. What?

LOEVBORG: Yes, I have.

TESMAN: Quite understandable. Oh, by the by — I've just bought your new book. Though to tell the truth I haven't found time to read it yet.

LOEVBORG: You needn't bother.

TESMAN: Oh? Why?

LOEVBORG: There's nothing much in it.

TESMAN: By Jove, fancy hearing that from you!

BRACK: But everyone's praising it.

LOEVBORG: That was exactly what I wanted to happen. So I only wrote what I knew everyone would agree with.

BRACK: Very sensible.

TESMAN: Yes, but my dear Eilert —

LOEVBORG: I want to try to re-establish myself. To begin again — from the beginning.

TESMAN (*a little embarrassed*): Yes, I — er — suppose you do. What?

LOEVBORG (*smiles, puts down his hat and takes a package wrapped in paper from his coat pocket*): But when this gets published — George Tesman — read it. This is my real book. The one in which I have spoken with my own voice.

TESMAN: Oh, really? What's it about?

LOEVBORG: It's the sequel.

TESMAN: Sequel? To what?

LOEVBORG: To the other book.

TESMAN: The one that's just come out?

LOEVBORG: Yes.

TESMAN: But my dear Eilert, that covers the subject right up to the present day.

LOEVBORG: It does. But this is about the future.

TESMAN: The future! But, I say, we don't know anything about that.

LOEVBORG: No. But there are one or two things that need to be said about it. (*Opens the package.*) Here, have a look.

TESMAN: Surely that's not your handwriting?

LOEVBORG: I dictated it. (*Turns the pages.*) It's in two parts. The first deals with the forces that will shape our civilization. (*Turns further on toward the end.*) And the second indicates the direction in which that civilization may develop.

TESMAN: Amazing! I'd never think of writing about anything like that.

HEDDA (*by the French windows, drumming on the pane*): No. You wouldn't.

LOEVBORG (*puts the pages back into their cover and lays the package on the table*): I brought it because I thought I might possibly read you a few pages this evening.

TESMAN: I say, what a kind idea! Oh, but this evening —? (*Glances at Brack.*) I'm not quite sure whether —

LOEVBORG: Well, some other time, then. There's no hurry.

BRACK: The truth is, Mr. Loevborg, I'm giving a little dinner this evening. In Tesman's honor, you know.

LOEVBORG (*looks round for his hat*): Oh — then I mustn't —

BRACK: No, wait a minute. Won't you do me the honor of joining us?

LOEVBORG (*curtly, with decision*): No. I can't. Thank you so much.

BRACK: Oh, nonsense. Do — please. There'll only be a few of us. And I can promise you we shall have some good sport, as Hed — as Mrs. Tesman puts it.

LOEVBORG: I've no doubt. Nevertheless —

BRACK: You could bring your manuscript along and read it to Tesman at my place. I could lend you a room.

TESMAN: Well, yes, that's an idea. What?

HEDDA (*interposes*): But, Tesman, Mr. Loevborg doesn't want to go. I'm sure Mr. Loevborg would much rather sit here and have supper with me.

LOEVBORG (*looks at her*): With you, Mrs. Tesman?

HEDDA: And Mrs. Elvsted.

LOEVBORG: Oh. (*Casually.*) I ran into her this afternoon.

HEDDA: Did you? Well, she's coming here this evening. So you really must stay, Mr. Loevborg. Otherwise she'll have no one to see her home.

LOEVBORG: That's true. Well — thank you, Mrs. Tesman, I'll stay then.

HEDDA: I'll just tell the servant.

(*She goes to the door which leads into the hall, and rings. Bertha enters. Hedda talks softly to her and points toward the rear room. Bertha nods and goes out.*)

TESMAN (*to Loevborg, as Hedda does this*): I say, Eilert. This new subject of yours — the — er — future — is that the one you're going to lecture about?

LOEVBORG: Yes.

TESMAN: They told me down at the bookshop that you're going to hold a series of lectures here during the autumn.

LOEVBORG: Yes, I am. I — hope you don't mind, Tesman.

TESMAN: Good heavens, no! But —?

LOEVBORG: I can quite understand it might queer your pitch a little.

TESMAN (*dejectedly*): Oh well, I can't expect you to put them off for my sake.

LOEVBORG: I'll wait till your appointment's been announced.

TESMAN: You'll wait! But — but — aren't you going to compete with me for the post? What?

LOEVBORG: No. I only want to defeat you in the eyes of the world.

TESMAN: Good heavens! Then Auntie Juju was right after all! Oh, I knew it, I knew it! Hear that, Hedda? Fancy! Eilert *doesn't* want to stand in our way.

HEDDA (*curtly*): Our? Leave me out of it, please.

(*She goes toward the rear room, where Bertha is setting a tray with decanters and glasses on the table. Hedda nods approval, and comes back into the drawing room. Bertha goes out.*)

TESMAN (*while this is happening*): Judge Brack, what do you think about all this? What?

BRACK: Oh, I think honor and victory can be very splendid things —

TESMAN: Of course they can. Still —

HEDDA (*looks at Tesman, with a cold smile*): You look as if you'd been hit by a thunderbolt.

TESMAN: Yes, I feel rather like it.

BRACK: There was a black cloud looming up, Mrs. Tesman. But it seems to have passed over.

HEDDA (*points toward the rear room*): Well, gentlemen, won't you go in and take a glass of cold punch?

BRACK (*glances at his watch*): One for the road? Yes, why not?

TESMAN: An admirable suggestion, Hedda. Admirable! Oh, I feel so relieved!

HEDDA: Won't you have one, too, Mr. Loevborg?

LOEVBORG: No, thank you. I'd rather not.

BRACK: Great heavens, man, cold punch isn't poison. Take my word for it.

LOEVBORG: Not for everyone, perhaps.

HEDDA: I'll keep Mr. Loevborg company while you drink.

TESMAN: Yes, Hedda dear, would you?

(*He and Brack go into the rear room, sit down, drink punch, smoke cigarettes, and talk cheerfully during the following scene. Eilert Loevborg remains standing by the stove. Hedda goes to the writing table.*)

HEDDA (*raising her voice slightly*): I've some photographs I'd like to show you, if you'd care to see them. Tesman and I visited the Tyrol on our way home.

(*She comes back with an album, places it on the table by the sofa and sits in the upstage corner of the sofa. Eilert Loevborg comes toward her, stops, and looks at her. Then he takes a chair and sits down on her left, with his back toward the rear room.*)

HEDDA (*opens the album*): You see these mountains, Mr. Loevborg? That's the Ortler group. Tesman has written the name underneath. You see: "The Ortler Group near Meran."

LOEVBORG (*has not taken his eyes from her; says softly, slowly*): Hedda — Gabler!

HEDDA (*gives him a quick glance*): Ssh!

LOEVBORG (*repeats softly*): Hedda Gabler!

HEDDA (*looks at the album*): Yes, that used to be my name. When we first knew each other.

LOEVBORG: And from now on — for the rest of my life — I must teach myself never to say: Hedda Gabler.

HEDDA (*still turning the pages*): Yes, you must. You'd better start getting into practice. The sooner the better.

LOEVBORG (*bitterly*): Hedda Gabler married? And to George Tesman!

HEDDA: Yes. Well — that's life.

LOEVBORG: Oh, Hedda, Hedda! How could you throw yourself away like that?

HEDDA (*looks sharply at him*): Stop it.

LOEVBORG: What do you mean?

(*Tesman comes in and goes toward the sofa.*)

HEDDA (*hears him coming and says casually*): And this, Mr. Loevborg, is the view from the Ampezzo valley. Look at those mountains. (*Glances affectionately up at Tesman.*) What did you say those curious mountains were called, dear?

TESMAN: Let me have a look. Oh, those are the Dolomites.

HEDDA: Of course. Those are the Dolomites, Mr. Loevborg.

TESMAN: Hedda, I just wanted to ask you, can't we bring some punch in here? A glass for you, anyway. What?

HEDDA: Thank you, yes. And a biscuit or two, perhaps.

TESMAN: You wouldn't like a cigarette?

HEDDA: No.

TESMAN: Right.

(*He goes into the rear room and over to the right. Brack is seated there, glancing occasionally at Hedda and Loevborg.*)

LOEVBORG (*softly, as before*): Answer me, Hedda. How could you do it?

HEDDA (*apparently absorbed in the album*): If you go on calling me Hedda I won't talk to you anymore.

LOEVBORG: Mayn't I even when we're alone?

HEDDA: No. You can think it. But you mustn't say it.

LOEVBORG: Oh, I see. Because you love George Tesman.

HEDDA (*glances at him and smiles*): Love? Don't be funny.

LOEVBORG: You don't love him?

HEDDA: I don't intend to be unfaithful to him. That's not what I want.

LOEVBORG: Hedda — just tell me one thing —

HEDDA: Ssh!

(*Tesman enters from the rear room, carrying a tray.*)

TESMAN: Here we are! Here come the refreshments.

(*He puts the tray down on the table.*)

HEDDA: Why didn't you ask the servant to bring it in?

TESMAN (*fills the glasses*): I like waiting on you, Hedda.

HEDDA: But you've filled both glasses. Mr. Loevborg doesn't want to drink.

TESMAN: Yes, but Mrs. Elvsted'll be here soon.

HEDDA: Oh yes, that's true. Mrs. Elvsted —

TESMAN: Had you forgotten her? What?

HEDDA: We're so absorbed with these photographs. (*Shows him one.*) You remember this little village?

TESMAN: Oh, that one down by the Brenner Pass. We spent a night there —

HEDDA: Yes, and met all those amusing people.

TESMAN: Oh yes, it was there, wasn't it? By Jove, if only we could have had you with us, Eilert! Ah, well.

(*He goes back into the other room and sits down with Brack.*)

LOEVBORG: Tell me one thing, Hedda.

HEDDA: Yes?

LOEVBORG: Didn't you love me either? Not — just a little?

HEDDA: Well now, I wonder? No, I think we were just good friends. (*Smiles.*) You certainly poured your heart out to me.

LOEVBORG: You begged me to.

HEDDA: Looking back on it, there was something beautiful and fascinating — and brave — about the way we told each other everything. That secret friendship no one else knew about.

LOEVBORG: Yes, Hedda, yes! Do you remember? How I used to come up to your father's house in the afternoon — and the General sat by the window and read his newspapers — with his back towards us —

HEDDA: And we sat on the sofa in the corner —

LOEVBORG: Always reading the same illustrated magazine —

HEDDA: We hadn't any photograph album.

LOEVBORG: Yes, Hedda. I regarded you as a kind of confessor. Told you things about myself which no one else knew about — then. Those days and nights of drinking and — oh, Hedda, what power did you have to make me confess such things?

HEDDA: Power? You think I had some power over you?

LOEVBORG: Yes — I don't know how else to explain it. And all those — oblique questions you asked me —

HEDDA: You knew what they meant.

LOEVBORG: But that you could sit there and ask me such questions! So unashamedly —

HEDDA: I thought you said they were oblique.

LOEVBORG: Yes, but you asked them so unashamedly. That you could question me about — about that kind of thing!

HEDDA: You answered willingly enough.

LOEVBORG: Yes — that's what I can't understand — looking back on it. But tell me, Hedda — what you felt for me — wasn't that — love? When you asked me those questions and made me confess my sins to you, wasn't it because you wanted to wash me clean?

HEDDA: No, not exactly.

LOEVBORG: Why did you do it, then?

HEDDA: Do you find it so incredible that a young girl, given the chance in secret, should want to be allowed a glimpse into a forbidden world of whose existence she is supposed to be ignorant?

LOEVBORG: So that was it?

HEDDA: One reason. One reason — I think.

LOEVBORG: You didn't love me, then. You just wanted — knowledge. But if that was so, why did you break it off?

HEDDA: That was your fault.

LOEVBORG: It was you who put an end to it.

HEDDA: Yes, when I realized that our friendship was threatening to develop into something — something else. Shame on you, Eilert Loevborg! How could you abuse the trust of your dearest friend?

LOEVBORG (*clenches his fist*): Oh, why didn't you do it? Why didn't you shoot me dead? As you threatened to!

HEDDA: I was afraid. Of the scandal.

LOEVBORG: Yes, Hedda. You're a coward at heart.

HEDDA: A dreadful coward. (*Changes her tone.*) Luckily for you. Well, now you've found consolation with the Elvsteds.

LOEVBORG: I know what Thea's been telling you.

HEDDA: I dare say you told her about us.

LOEVBORG: Not a word. She's too silly to understand that kind of thing.

HEDDA: Silly?

LOEVBORG: She's silly about that kind of thing.

HEDDA: And I'm a coward. (*Leans closer to him, without looking him in the eyes, and says quietly*) But let me tell you something. Something you don't know.

LOEVBORG (*tensely*): Yes?

HEDDA: My failure to shoot you wasn't my worst act of cowardice that evening.

LOEVBORG (*looks at her for a moment, realizes her meaning, and whispers passionately*): Oh, Hedda! Hedda Gabler! Now I see what was behind those questions. Yes! It wasn't knowledge you wanted! It was life!

HEDDA (*flashes a look at him and says quietly*): Take care! Don't you delude yourself!

(*It has begun to grow dark. Bertha, from outside, opens the door leading into the hall.*)

HEDDA (*closes the album with a snap and cries, smiling*): Ah, at last! Come in, Thea dear!

(*Mrs. Elvsted enters from the hall, in evening dress. The door is closed behind her.*)

HEDDA (*on the sofa, stretches out her arms toward her*): Thea darling, I thought you were never coming!

(*Mrs. Elvsted makes a slight bow to the gentlemen in the rear room as she passes the open doorway, and they to her. Then she goes to the table and holds out her hand to Hedda. Eilert Loevborg has risen from his chair. He and Mrs. Elvsted nod silently to each other.*)

MRS. ELVSTED: Perhaps I ought to go in and say a few words to your husband?

HEDDA: Oh, there's no need. They're happy by themselves. They'll be going soon.

MRS. ELVSTED: Going?

HEDDA: Yes, they're off on a spree this evening.

MRS. ELVSTED (*quickly, to Loevborg*): You're not going with them?

LOEVBORG: No.

HEDDA: Mr. Loevborg is staying here with us.

MRS. ELVSTED (*takes a chair and is about to sit down beside him*): Oh, how nice it is to be here!

HEDDA: No, Thea darling, not there. Come over here and sit beside me. I want to be in the middle.

MRS. ELVSTED: Yes, just as you wish.

(*She goes round the table and sits on the sofa, on Hedda's right. Loevborg sits down again in his chair.*)

LOEVBORG (*after a short pause, to Hedda*): Isn't she lovely to look at?

HEDDA (*strokes her hair gently*): Only to look at?

LOEVBORG: Yes. We're just good friends. We trust each other implicitly. We can talk to each other quite unashamedly.

HEDDA: No need to be oblique?

MRS. ELVSTED (*nestles close to Hedda and says quietly*): Oh, Hedda, I'm so happy. Imagine — he says I've inspired him!

HEDDA (*looks at her with a smile*): Dear Thea! Does he really?

LOEVBORG: She has the courage of her convictions, Mrs. Tesman.

MRS. ELVSTED: I? Courage?

LOEVBORG: Absolute courage. Where friendship is concerned.

HEDDA: Yes. Courage. Yes. If only one had that —

LOEVBORG: Yes?

HEDDA: One might be able to live. In spite of everything. (*Changes her tone suddenly.*) Well, Thea darling, now you're going to drink a nice glass of cold punch.

MRS. ELVSTED: No thank you. I never drink anything like that.

HEDDA: Oh. You, Mr. Loevborg?

LOEVBORG: Thank you, I don't either.

MRS. ELVSTED: No, he doesn't, either.

HEDDA (*looks into his eyes*): But if I want you to.

LOEVBORG: That doesn't make any difference.

HEDDA (*laughs*): Have I no power over you at all? Poor me!

LOEVBORG: Not where this is concerned.

HEDDA: Seriously, I think you should. For your own sake.

MRS. ELVSTED: Hedda!

LOEVBORG: Why?

HEDDA: Or perhaps I should say for other people's sake.

LOEVBORG: What do you mean?

HEDDA: People might think you didn't feel absolutely and unashamedly sure of yourself. In your heart of hearts.

MRS. ELVSTED (*quietly*): Oh, Hedda, no!

LOEVBORG: People can think what they like. For the present.

MRS. ELVSTED (*happily*): Yes, that's true.

HEDDA: I saw it so clearly in Judge Brack a few minutes ago.

LOEVBORG: Oh. What did you see?

HEDDA: He smiled so scornfully when he saw you were afraid to go in there and drink with them.

LOEVBORG: Afraid! I wanted to stay here and talk to you.

MRS. ELVSTED: That was only natural, Hedda.

HEDDA: But the Judge wasn't to know that. I saw him wink at Tesman when you showed you didn't dare to join their wretched little party.

LOEVBORG: Didn't dare! Are you saying I didn't dare?

HEDDA: I'm not saying so. But that was what Judge Brack thought.

LOEVBORG: Well, let him.

HEDDA: You're not going, then?

LOEVBORG: I'm staying here with you and Thea.

MRS. ELVSTED: Yes, Hedda, of course he is.

HEDDA (*smiles, and nods approvingly to Loevborg*): Firm as a rock! A man of principle! That's how a man should be! (*Turns to Mrs. Elvsted and strokes her cheek.*) Didn't I tell you so this morning when you came here in such a panic —?

LOEVBORG (*starts*): Panic?

MRS. ELVSTED (*frightened*): Hedda! But — Hedda!

HEDDA: Well, now you can see for yourself. There's no earthly need for you to get scared to death just because — (*Stops.*) Well! Let's all three cheer up and enjoy ourselves.

LOEVBORG: Mrs. Tesman, would you mind explaining to me what this is all about?

MRS. ELVSTED: Oh, my God, my God, Hedda, what are you saying? What are you doing?

HEDDA: Keep calm. That horrid Judge has his eye on you.

LOEVBORG: Scared to death, were you? For my sake?

MRS. ELVSTED (*quietly, trembling*): Oh, Hedda! You've made me so unhappy!

LOEVBORG (*looks coldly at her for a moment. His face is distorted*): So that was how much you trusted me.

MRS. ELVSTED: Eilert dear, please listen to me —

LOEVBORG (*takes one of the glasses of punch, raises it, and says quietly, hoarsely*): Skoal, Thea!

(*He empties the glass, puts it down, and picks up one of the others.*)

MRS. ELVSTED (*quietly*): Hedda, Hedda! Why did you want this to happen?

HEDDA: *I* — want it? Are you mad?

LOEVBORG: Skoal to you, too, Mrs. Tesman. Thanks for telling me the truth. Here's to the truth!

(*He empties his glass and refills it.*)

HEDDA (*puts her hand on his arm*): Steady. That's enough for now. Don't forget the party.

MRS. ELVSTED: No, no, no!

HEDDA: Ssh! They're looking at you.

LOEVBORG (*puts down his glass*): Thea, tell me the truth —

MRS. ELVSTED: Yes!

LOEVBORG: Did your husband know you were following me?

MRS. ELVSTED: Oh, Hedda!

LOEVBORG: Did you and he have an agreement that you should come here and keep an eye on me? Perhaps he gave you the idea? After all, he's a magistrate. I suppose he needed me back in his office. Or did he miss my companionship at the card table?

MRS. ELVSTED (*quietly, sobbing*): Eilert, Eilert!

LOEVBORG (*seizes a glass and is about to fill it*): Let's drink to him, too.

HEDDA: No more now. Remember you're going to read your book to Tesman.

LOEVBORG (*calm again, puts down his glass*): That was silly of me, Thea. To take it like that, I mean. Don't be angry with me, my dear. You'll see — yes, and they'll see, too — that though I fell, I — I have raised myself up again. With your help, Thea.

MRS. ELVSTED (*happily*): Oh, thank God!

(*Brack has meanwhile glanced at his watch. He and Tesman get up and come into the drawing room.*)

BRACK (*takes his hat and overcoat*): Well, Mrs. Tesman, it's time for us to go.

HEDDA: Yes, I suppose it must be.

LOEVBORG (*gets up*): Time for me, too, Judge.

MRS. ELVSTED (*quietly, pleadingly*): Eilert, please don't!

HEDDA (*pinches her arm*): They can hear you.

MRS. ELVSTED (*gives a little cry*): Oh!

LOEVBORG (*to Brack*): You were kind enough to ask me to join you.

BRACK: Are you coming?

LOEVBORG: If I may.

BRACK: Delighted.

LOEVBORG (*puts the paper package in his pocket and says to Tesman*): I'd like to show you one or two things before I send it off to the printer.

TESMAN: I say, that'll be fun. Fancy —! Oh, but, Hedda, how'll Mrs. Elvsted get home? What?

HEDDA: Oh, we'll manage somehow.

LOEVBORG (*glances over toward the ladies*): Mrs. Elvsted? I shall come back and collect her, naturally. (*Goes closer.*) About ten o'clock, Mrs. Tesman? Will that suit you?

HEDDA: Yes. That'll suit me admirably.

TESMAN: Good, that's settled. But you mustn't expect me back so early, Hedda.

HEDDA: Stay as long as you c — as long as you like, dear.

MRS. ELVSTED (*trying to hide her anxiety*): Well then, Mr. Loevborg, I'll wait here till you come.

LOEVBORG (*his hat in his hand*): Pray do, Mrs. Elvsted.

BRACK: Well, gentlemen, now the party begins. I trust that, in the words of a certain fair lady, we shall enjoy good sport.

HEDDA: What a pity the fair lady can't be there, invisible.

BRACK: Why invisible?

HEDDA: So as to be able to hear some of your uncensored witticisms, your honor.

BRACK (*laughs*): Oh, I shouldn't advise the fair lady to do that.

TESMAN (*laughs, too*): I say, Hedda, that's good. What!

BRACK: Well, good night, ladies, good night!

LOEVBORG (*bows farewell*): About ten o'clock then.

(*Brack, Loevborg, and Tesman go out through the hall. As they do so, Bertha enters from the rear room with a lighted lamp. She puts it on the drawing room table, then goes out the way she came.*)

MRS. ELVSTED (*has got up and is walking uneasily to and fro*): Oh, Hedda, Hedda! How is all this going to end?

HEDDA: At ten o'clock, then. He'll be here. I can see him. With a crown of vine leaves in his hair. Burning and unashamed!

MRS. ELVSTED: Oh, I do hope so!

HEDDA: Can't you see? Then he'll be himself again! He'll be a free man for the rest of his days!

MRS. ELVSTED: Please God you're right.

HEDDA: That's how he'll come! (*Gets up and goes closer.*) You can doubt him as much as you like. I believe in him! Now we'll see which of us —

MRS. ELVSTED: You're after something, Hedda.

HEDDA: Yes, I am. For once in my life I want to have the power to shape a man's destiny.

MRS. ELVSTED: Haven't you that power already?

HEDDA: No, I haven't. I've never had it.

MRS. ELVSTED: What about your husband?

HEDDA: Him! Oh, if you could only understand how poor I am. And you're allowed to be so rich, so rich! (*Clasps her passionately.*) I think I'll burn your hair off after all!

MRS. ELVSTED: Let me go! Let me go! You frighten me, Hedda!

BERTHA (*in the open doorway*): I've laid tea in the dining room, madam.

HEDDA: Good, we're coming.

MRS. ELVSTED: No, no, no! I'd rather go home alone! Now — at once!

HEDDA: Rubbish! First you're going to have some tea, you little idiot. And then — at ten o'clock — Eilert Loevborg will come. With a crown of vine leaves in his hair!

(*She drags Mrs. Elvsted almost forcibly toward the open doorway.*)

ACT III

(*The same. The curtains are drawn across the open doorway, and also across the French windows. The lamp, half turned down, with a shade over it, is burning on the table. In the stove, the door of which is open, a fire has been burning, but it is now almost out. Mrs. Elvsted, wrapped in a large shawl and with her feet resting on a footstool, is sitting near the stove, huddled in the armchair. Hedda is lying asleep on the sofa, fully dressed, with a blanket over her.*)

MRS. ELVSTED (*After a pause, suddenly sits up in her chair and listens tensely. Then she sinks wearily back again and sighs.*): Not back yet! Oh, God! Oh, God! Not back yet!

(*Bertha tiptoes cautiously in from the hall. She has a letter in her hand.*)

MRS. ELVSTED (*turns and whispers*): What is it? Has someone come?

BERTHA (*quietly*): Yes, a servant's just called with this letter.

MRS. ELVSTED (*quickly, holding out her hand*): A letter! Give it to me!

BERTHA: But it's for the Doctor, madam.

MRS. ELVSTED: Oh, I see.

BERTHA: Miss Tesman's maid brought it. I'll leave it here on the table.

MRS. ELVSTED: Yes, do.

BERTHA (*puts down the letter*): I'd better put the lamp out. It's starting to smoke.

MRS. ELVSTED: Yes, put it out. It'll soon be daylight.

BERTHA (*puts out the lamp*): It's daylight already, madam.

MRS. ELVSTED: Yes. Broad day. And not home yet!

BERTHA: Oh dear, I was afraid this would happen.

MRS. ELVSTED: Were you?

BERTHA: Yes. When I heard that a certain gentleman had returned to town, and saw him go off with them. I've heard all about him.

MRS. ELVSTED: Don't talk so loud. You'll wake your mistress.

BERTHA (*looks at the sofa and sighs*): Yes. Let her go on sleeping, poor dear. Shall I put some more wood on the fire?

MRS. ELVSTED: Thank you, don't bother on my account.

BERTHA: Very good.

(*She goes quietly out through the hall.*)

HEDDA (*wakes as the door closes and looks up*): What's that?

MRS. ELVSTED: It was only the maid.

HEDDA (*looks round*): What am I doing here? Oh, now I remember. (*Sits up on the sofa, stretches herself, and rubs her eyes.*) What time is it, Thea?

MRS. ELVSTED: It's gone seven.

HEDDA: When did Tesman get back?

MRS. ELVSTED: He's not back yet.

HEDDA: Not home yet?

MRS. ELVSTED (*gets up*): No one's come.

HEDDA: And we sat up waiting for them till four o'clock.

MRS. ELVSTED: God! How I waited for him!

HEDDA (*yawns and says with her hand in front of her mouth*): Oh, dear. We might have saved ourselves the trouble.

MRS. ELVSTED: Did you manage to sleep?

HEDDA: Oh, yes. Quite well, I think. Didn't you get any?

MRS. ELVSTED: Not a wink. I couldn't, Hedda. I just couldn't.

HEDDA (*gets up and comes over to her*): Now, now, now. There's nothing to worry about. I know what's happened.

MRS. ELVSTED: What? Please tell me.

HEDDA: Well, obviously the party went on very late —

MRS. ELVSTED: Oh dear, I suppose it must have. But —

HEDDA: And Tesman didn't want to come home and wake us all up in the middle of the night. (*Laughs.*) Probably wasn't too keen to show his face either, after a spree like that.

MRS. ELVSTED: But where could he have gone?

HEDDA: I should think he's probably slept at his aunts'. They keep his old room for him.

MRS. ELVSTED: No, he can't be with them. A letter came for him just now from Miss Tesman. It's over there.

HEDDA: Oh? (*Looks at the envelope.*) Yes, it's Auntie Juju's handwriting. Well, he must still be at Judge Brack's, then. And Eilert Loevborg is sitting there, reading to him. With a crown of vine leaves in his hair.

MRS. ELVSTED: Hedda, you're only saying that. You don't believe it.

HEDDA: Thea, you really are a little fool.

MRS. ELVSTED: Perhaps I am.

HEDDA: You look tired to death.

MRS. ELVSTED: Yes. I am tired to death.

HEDDA: Go to my room and lie down for a little. Do as I say, now; don't argue.

MRS. ELVSTED: No, no. I couldn't possibly sleep.

HEDDA: Of course you can.

MRS. ELVSTED: But your husband'll be home soon. And I must know at once —

HEDDA: I'll tell you when he comes.

MRS. ELVSTED: Promise me, Hedda?

HEDDA: Yes, don't worry. Go and get some sleep.

MRS. ELVSTED: Thank you. All right, I'll try.

(*She goes out through the rear room. Hedda goes to the French windows and draws the curtains. Broad daylight floods into the room. She goes to the writing table, takes a small hand mirror from it, and arranges her hair. Then she goes to the door leading into the hall and presses the bell. After a few moments, Bertha enters.*)

BERTHA: Did you want anything, madam?

HEDDA: Yes, put some more wood on the fire. I'm freezing.

BERTHA: Bless you, I'll soon have this room warmed up. (*She rakes the embers together and puts a fresh piece of wood on them. Suddenly she stops and listens.*) There's someone at the front door, madam.

HEDDA: Well, go and open it. I'll see to the fire.

BERTHA: It'll burn up in a moment.

(*She goes out through the hall. Hedda kneels on the footstool and puts more wood in the stove. After a few seconds, George Tesman enters from the hall. He looks tired, and rather worried. He tiptoes toward the open doorway and is about to slip through the curtains.*)

HEDDA (*at the stove, without looking up*): Good morning.

TESMAN (*turns*): Hedda! (*Comes nearer.*) Good heavens, are you up already? What?

HEDDA: Yes, I got up very early this morning.

TESMAN: I was sure you'd still be sleeping. Fancy that!

HEDDA: Don't talk so loud. Mrs. Elvsted's asleep in my room.

TESMAN: Mrs. Elvsted? Has she stayed the night here?

HEDDA: Yes. No one came to escort her home.

TESMAN: Oh. No, I suppose not.

HEDDA (*closes the door of the stove and gets up*): Well. Was it fun?

TESMAN: Have you been anxious about me? What?

HEDDA: Not in the least. I asked if you'd had fun.

TESMAN: Oh yes, rather! Well, I thought, for once in a while —! The first part was the best; when Eilert read his book to me. We arrived over an hour too early — what about that, eh? Fancy —! Brack had a lot of things to see to, so Eilert read to me.

HEDDA (*sits at the right-hand side of the table*): Well? Tell me about it.

TESMAN (*sits on a footstool by the stove*): Honestly, Hedda, you've no idea what a book that's going to be. It's really one of the most remarkable things that's ever been written. By Jove!

HEDDA: Oh, never mind about the book —

TESMAN: I'm going to make a confession to you, Hedda. When he'd finished reading a sort of beastly feeling came over me.

HEDDA: Beastly feeling?

TESMAN: I found myself envying Eilert for being able to write like that. Imagine that, Hedda!

HEDDA: Yes. I can imagine.

TESMAN: What a tragedy that with all those gifts he should be so incorrigible.

HEDDA: You mean he's less afraid of life than most men?

TESMAN: Good heavens, no. He just doesn't know the meaning of the word moderation.

HEDDA: What happened afterwards?

TESMAN: Well, looking back on it, I suppose you might almost call it an orgy, Hedda.

HEDDA: Had he vine leaves in his hair?

TESMAN: Vine leaves? No, I didn't see any of them. He made a long, rambling oration in honor of the woman who'd inspired him to write this book. Yes, those were the words he used.

HEDDA: Did he name her?

TESMAN: No. But I suppose it must be Mrs. Elvsted. You wait and see!

HEDDA: Where did you leave him?

TESMAN: On the way home. We left in a bunch — the last of us, that is — and Brack came with us to get a little fresh air. Well, then, you see, we agreed we ought to see Eilert home. He'd had a drop too much.

HEDDA: You don't say?

TESMAN: But now comes the funny part, Hedda. Or I should really say the tragic part. Oh, I'm almost ashamed to tell you. For Eilert's sake, I mean —

HEDDA: Why, what happened?

TESMAN: Well, you see, as we were walking towards town I happened to drop behind for a minute. Only for a minute — er — you understand —

HEDDA: Yes, yes —?

TESMAN: Well then, when I ran on to catch them up, what do you think I found by the roadside. What?

HEDDA: How on earth should I know?

TESMAN: You mustn't tell anyone, Hedda. What? Promise me that — for Eilert's sake. (*Takes a package wrapped in paper from his coat pocket.*) Just fancy! I found this.

HEDDA: Isn't this the one he brought here yesterday?

TESMAN: Yes! The whole of that precious, irreplaceable manuscript! And he went and lost it! Didn't even notice! What about that? Tragic.

HEDDA: But why didn't you give it back to him?

TESMAN: I didn't dare to, in the state he was in.

HEDDA: Didn't you tell any of the others?

TESMAN: Good heavens, no. I didn't want to do that. For Eilert's sake, you understand.

HEDDA: Then no one else knows you have his manuscript?

TESMAN: No. And no one must be allowed to know.

HEDDA: Didn't it come up in the conversation later?

TESMAN: I didn't get a chance to talk to him anymore. As soon as we got into the outskirts of town, he and one or two of the others gave us the slip. Disappeared, by Jove!

HEDDA: Oh? I suppose they took him home.

TESMAN: Yes, I imagine that was the idea. Brack left us, too.

HEDDA: And what have you been up to since then?

TESMAN: Well, I and one or two of the others — awfully jolly chaps, they were — went back to where one of them lived and had a cup of morning coffee. Morning-after coffee — what? Ah, well. I'll just lie down for a bit and give Eilert time to sleep it off, poor chap, then I'll run over and give this back to him.

HEDDA (*holds out her hand for the package*): No, don't do that. Not just yet. Let me read it first.

TESMAN: Oh no, really, Hedda dear, honestly, I daren't do that.

HEDDA: Daren't?

TESMAN: No — imagine how desperate he'll be when he wakes up and finds his manuscript's missing. He hasn't any copy, you see. He told me so himself.

HEDDA: Can't a thing like that be rewritten?

TESMAN: Oh no, not possibly, I shouldn't think. I mean, the inspiration, you know —

HEDDA: Oh, yes, I'd forgotten that. (*Casually.*) By the way, there's a letter for you.

TESMAN: Is there? Fancy that!

HEDDA (*holds it out to him*): It came early this morning.

TESMAN: I say, it's from Auntie Juju! What on earth can it be? (*Puts the package on the other footstool, opens the letter, reads it, and jumps up.*) Oh, Hedda! She says poor Auntie Rena's dying.

HEDDA: Well, we've been expecting that.

TESMAN: She says if I want to see her I must go quickly. I'll run over at once.

HEDDA (*hides a smile*): Run?

TESMAN: Hedda dear, I suppose you wouldn't like to come with me? What about that, eh?

HEDDA (*gets up and says wearily and with repulsion*): No, no, don't ask me to do anything like that. I can't bear illness or death. I loathe anything ugly.

TESMAN: Yes, yes. Of course. (*In a dither.*) My hat? My overcoat? Oh yes, in the hall. I do hope I won't get there too late, Hedda! What?

HEDDA: You'll be all right if you run.

(*Bertha enters from the hall.*)

BERTHA: Judge Brack's outside and wants to know if he can come in.

TESMAN: At this hour? No, I can't possibly receive him now.

HEDDA: I can. (*To Bertha.*) Ask his honor to come in.

(*Bertha goes.*)

HEDDA (*whispers quickly*): The manuscript, Tesman.

(*She snatches it from the footstool.*)

TESMAN: Yes, give it to me.

HEDDA: No, I'll look after it for now.

(*She goes over to the writing table and puts it in the bookcase. Tesman stands dithering, unable to get his gloves on. Judge Brack enters from the hall.*)

HEDDA (*nods to him*): Well, you're an early bird.

BRACK: Yes, aren't I? (*To Tesman.*) Are you up and about, too?

TESMAN: Yes, I've got to go and see my aunts. Poor Auntie Rena's dying.

BRACK: Oh dear, is she? Then you mustn't let me detain you. At so tragic a —

TESMAN: Yes, I really must run. Good-bye! Good-bye!

(*He runs out through the hall.*)

HEDDA (*goes nearer*): You seem to have had excellent sport last night — Judge.

BRACK: Indeed yes, Mrs. Hedda. I haven't even had time to take my clothes off.

HEDDA: *You* haven't either?

BRACK: As you see. What's Tesman told you about last night's escapades?

HEDDA: Oh, only some boring story about having gone and drunk coffee somewhere.

BRACK: Yes, I've heard about that coffee-party. Eilert Loevborg wasn't with them, I gather?

HEDDA: No, they took him home first.

BRACK: Did Tesman go with him?

HEDDA: No, one or two of the others, he said.

BRACK (*smiles*): George Tesman is a credulous man, Mrs. Hedda.

HEDDA: God knows. But — has something happened?

BRACK: Well, yes, I'm afraid it has.

HEDDA: I see. Sit down and tell me.

(*She sits on the left of the table, Brack at the long side of it, near her.*)

HEDDA: Well?

BRACK: I had a special reason for keeping track of my guests last night. Or perhaps I should say some of my guests.

HEDDA: Including Eilert Loevborg?

BRACK: I must confess — yes.

HEDDA: You're beginning to make me curious.

BRACK: Do you know where he and some of my other guests spent the latter half of last night, Mrs. Hedda?

HEDDA: Tell me. If it won't shock me.

BRACK: Oh, I don't think it'll shock you. They found themselves participating in an exceedingly animated *soirée*.

HEDDA: Of a sporting character?

BRACK: Of a highly sporting character.

HEDDA: Tell me more.

BRACK: Loevborg had received an invitation in advance — as had the others. I knew all about that. But he had refused. As you know, he's become a new man.

HEDDA: Up at the Elvsteds', yes. But he went?

BRACK: Well, you see, Mrs. Hedda, last night at my house, unhappily, the spirit moved him.

HEDDA: Yes, I hear he became inspired.

BRACK: Somewhat violently inspired. And as a result, I suppose, his thoughts strayed. We men, alas, don't always stick to our principles as firmly as we should.

HEDDA: I'm sure you're an exception, Judge Brack. But go on about Loevborg.

BRACK: Well, to cut a long story short, he ended up in the establishment of a certain Mademoiselle Danielle.

HEDDA: Mademoiselle Danielle?

BRACK: She was holding the *soirée*. For a selected circle of friends and admirers.

HEDDA: Has she got red hair?

BRACK: She has.

HEDDA: A singer of some kind?

BRACK: Yes — among other accomplishments. She's also a celebrated huntress — of men, Mrs. Hedda. I'm sure you've heard about her. Eilert Loevborg used to be one of her most ardent patrons. In his salad days.

HEDDA: And how did all this end?

BRACK: Not entirely amicably, from all accounts. Mademoiselle Danielle began by receiving him with the utmost tenderness and ended by resorting to her fists.

HEDDA: Against Loevborg?

BRACK: Yes. He accused her, or her friends, of having robbed him. He claimed his pocketbook had been stolen. Among other things. In short, he seems to have made a bloodthirsty scene.

HEDDA: And what did this lead to?

BRACK: It led to a general free-for-all, in which both sexes participated. Fortunately, in the end the police arrived.

HEDDA: The police, too?

BRACK: Yes. I'm afraid it may turn out to be rather an expensive joke for Master Eilert. Crazy fool!

HEDDA: Oh?

BRACK: Apparently he put up a very violent resistance. Hit one of the constables on the ear and tore his uniform. He had to accompany them to the police station.

HEDDA: Where did you learn all this?

BRACK: From the police.

HEDDA (*to herself*): So that's what happened. He didn't have a crown of vine leaves in his hair.

BRACK: Vine leaves, Mrs. Hedda?

HEDDA (*in her normal voice again*): But, tell me, Judge, why do you take such a close interest in Eilert Loevborg?

BRACK: For one thing it'll hardly be a matter of complete indifference to me if it's revealed in court that he came there straight from my house.

HEDDA: Will it come to court?

BRACK: Of course. Well, I don't regard that as particularly serious. Still, I thought it my duty, as a friend of the family, to give you and your husband a full account of his nocturnal adventures.

HEDDA: Why?

BRACK: Because I've a shrewd suspicion that he's hoping to use you as a kind of screen.

HEDDA: What makes you think that?

BRACK: Oh, for heaven's sake, Mrs. Hedda, we're not blind. You wait and see. This Mrs. Elvsted won't be going back to her husband just yet.

HEDDA: Well, if there were anything between those two there are plenty of other places where they could meet.

BRACK: Not in anyone's home. From now on every respectable house will once again be closed to Eilert Loevborg.

HEDDA: And mine should be, too, you mean?

BRACK: Yes. I confess I should find it more than irksome if this gentleman were to be granted unrestricted access to this house. If he were superfluously to intrude into —

HEDDA: The triangle?

BRACK: Precisely. For me it would be like losing a home.

HEDDA (*looks at him and smiles*): I see. You want to be the cock of the walk.

BRACK (*nods slowly and lowers his voice*): Yes, that is my aim. And I shall fight for it with — every weapon at my disposal.

HEDDA (*as her smile fades*): You're a dangerous man, aren't you? When you really want something.

BRACK: You think so?

HEDDA: Yes, I'm beginning to think so. I'm deeply thankful you haven't any kind of hold over me.

BRACK (*laughs equivocally*): Well, well, Mrs. Hedda — perhaps you're right. If I had, who knows what I might not think up?

HEDDA: Come, Judge Brack. That sounds almost like a threat.

BRACK (*gets up*): Heaven forbid! In the creation of a triangle — and its continuance — the question of compulsion should never arise.

HEDDA: Exactly what I was thinking.

BRACK: Well, I've said what I came to say. I must be getting back. Good-bye, Mrs. Hedda. (*Goes toward the French windows.*)

HEDDA (*gets up*): Are you going out through the garden?

BRACK: Yes, it's shorter.

HEDDA: Yes. And it's the back door, isn't it?

BRACK: I've nothing against back doors. They can be quite intriguing — sometimes.

HEDDA: When people fire pistols out of them, for example?

BRACK (*in the doorway, laughs*): Oh, people don't shoot tame cocks.

HEDDA (*laughs, too*): I suppose not. When they've only got one.

(*They nod good-bye, laughing. He goes. She closes the French windows behind him, and stands for a moment, looking out pensively. Then she walks across the room and glances through the curtains in the open doorway. Goes to the writing table, takes Loevborg's package from the bookcase, and is about to turn through the pages when Bertha is heard remonstrating loudly in the hall. Hedda turns and listens. She hastily puts the package back in the drawer, locks it, and puts the key on the inkstand. Eilert Loevborg, with his overcoat on and his hat in his hand, throws the door open. He looks somewhat confused and excited.*)

LOEVBORG (*shouts as he enters*): I must come in, I tell you! Let me pass!

(*He closes the door, turns, sees Hedda, controls himself immediately, and bows.*)

HEDDA (*at the writing table*): Well, Mr. Loevborg, this is rather a late hour to be collecting Thea.

LOEVBORG: And an early hour to call on you. Please forgive me.

HEDDA: How do you know she's still here?

LOEVBORG: They told me at her lodgings that she has been out all night.

HEDDA (*goes to the table*): Did you notice anything about their behavior when they told you?

LOEVBORG (*looks at her, puzzled*): Notice anything?

HEDDA: Did they sound as if they thought it — strange?

LOEVBORG (*suddenly understands*): Oh, I see what you mean. I'm dragging her down with me. No, as a matter of fact I didn't notice anything. I suppose Tesman isn't up yet?

HEDDA: No, I don't think so.

LOEVBORG: When did he get home?

HEDDA: Very late.

LOEVBORG: Did he tell you anything?

HEDDA: Yes. I gather you had a merry party at Judge Brack's last night.

LOEVBORG: He didn't tell you anything else?

HEDDA: I don't think so. I was so terribly sleepy —

(*Mrs. Elvsted comes through the curtains in the open doorway.*)

MRS. ELVSTED (*runs toward him*): Oh, Eilert! At last!

LOEVBORG: Yes — at last. And too late.

MRS. ELVSTED: What is too late?

LOEVBORG: Everything — now. I'm finished, Thea.

MRS. ELVSTED: Oh, no, no! Don't say that!

LOEVBORG: You'll say it yourself, when you've heard what I —

MRS. ELVSTED: I don't want to hear anything!

HEDDA: Perhaps you'd rather speak to her alone? I'd better go.

LOEVBORG: No, stay.

MRS. ELVSTED: But I don't want to hear anything, I tell you!

LOEVBORG: It's not about last night.

MRS. ELVSTED: Then what —?

LOEVBORG: I want to tell you that from now on we must stop seeing each other.

MRS. ELVSTED: Stop seeing each other!

HEDDA (*involuntarily*): I knew it!

LOEVBORG: I have no further use for you, Thea.

MRS. ELVSTED: You can stand there and say that! No further use for me! Surely I can go on helping you? We'll go on working together, won't we?

LOEVBORG: I don't intend to do any more work from now on.

MRS. ELVSTED (*desperately*): Then what use have I for my life?

LOEVBORG: You must try to live as if you had never known me.

MRS. ELVSTED: But I can't!

LOEVBORG: Try to, Thea. Go back home —

MRS. ELVSTED: Never! I want to be wherever you are! I won't let myself be driven away like this! I want to stay here — and be with you when the book comes out.

HEDDA (*whispers*): Ah, yes! The book!

LOEVBORG (*looks at her*): Our book; Thea's and mine. It belongs to both of us.

MRS. ELVSTED: Oh, yes! I feel that, too! And I've a right to be with you when it comes into the world.

I want to see people respect and honor you again. And the joy! The joy! I want to share it with you!

LOEVBORG: Thea — our book will never come into the world.

HEDDA: Ah!

MRS. ELVSTED: Not —?

LOEVBORG: It cannot. Ever.

MRS. ELVSTED: Eilert — what have you done with the manuscript?

HEDDA: Yes — the manuscript?

MRS. ELVSTED: Where is it?

LOEVBORG: Oh, Thea, please don't ask me that!

MRS. ELVSTED: Yes, yes — I must know. I've a right to know. Now!

LOEVBORG: The manuscript. Yes. I've torn it up.

MRS. ELVSTED (*screams*): No, no!

HEDDA (*involuntarily*): But that's not —!

LOEVBORG (*looks at her*): Not true, you think.

HEDDA (*controls herself*): Why — yes, of course it is, if you say so. It sounded so incredible —

LOEVBORG: It's true, nevertheless.

MRS. ELVSTED: Oh, my God, my God, Hedda — he's destroyed his own book!

LOEVBORG: I have destroyed my life. Why not my life's work, too?

MRS. ELVSTED: And you — did this last night?

LOEVBORG: Yes, Thea. I tore it into a thousand pieces. And scattered them out across the fjord. It's good, clean, salt water. Let it carry them away; let them drift in the current and the wind. And in a little while, they will sink. Deeper and deeper. As I shall, Thea.

MRS. ELVSTED: Do you know, Eilert — this book — all my life I shall feel as though you'd killed a little child.

LOEVBORG: You're right. It is like killing a child.

MRS. ELVSTED: But how could you? It was my child, too!

HEDDA (*almost inaudibly*): Oh — the child —!

MRS. ELVSTED (*breathes heavily*): It's all over, then. Well — I'll go now, Hedda.

HEDDA: You're not leaving town?

MRS. ELVSTED: I don't know what I'm going to do. I can't see anything except — darkness.

(*She goes out through the hall.*)

HEDDA (*waits a moment*): Aren't you going to escort her home, Mr. Loevborg?

LOEVBORG: I? Through the streets? Do you want me to let people see her with me?

HEDDA: Of course, I don't know what else may have happened last night. But is it so utterly beyond redress?

LOEVBORG: It isn't just last night. It'll go on happening. I know it. But the curse of it is, I don't want to live that kind of life. I don't want to start all that again. She's broken my courage. I can't spit in the eyes of the world any longer.

HEDDA (*as though to herself*): That pretty little fool's been trying to shape a man's destiny. (*Looks at him.*) But how could you be so heartless towards her?

LOEVBORG: Don't call me heartless!

HEDDA: To go and destroy the one thing that's made her life worth living? You don't call that heartless?

LOEVBORG: Do you want to know the truth, Hedda?

HEDDA: The truth?

LOEVBORG: Promise me first — give me your word — that you'll never let Thea know about this.

HEDDA: I give you my word.

LOEVBORG: Good. Well; what I told her just now was a lie.

HEDDA: About the manuscript?

LOEVBORG: Yes. I didn't tear it up. Or throw it in the fjord.

HEDDA: You didn't? But where is it, then?

LOEVBORG: I destroyed it, all the same. I destroyed it, Hedda!

HEDDA: I don't understand.

LOEVBORG: Thea said that what I had done was like killing a child.

HEDDA: Yes. That's what she said.

LOEVBORG: But to kill a child isn't the worst thing a father can do to it.

HEDDA: What could be worse than that?

LOEVBORG: Hedda — suppose a man came home one morning, after a night of debauchery, and said to the mother of his child: "Look here. I've been wandering round all night. I've been to — such-and-such a place and such-and-such a place. And I had our child with me. I took him to — these places. And I've lost him. Just — lost him. God knows where he is or whose hands he's fallen into."

HEDDA: I see. But when all's said and done, this was only a book —

LOEVBORG: Thea's heart and soul were in that book. It was her whole life.

HEDDA: Yes, I understand.

LOEVBORG: Well, then you must also understand that she and I cannot possibly ever see each other again.

HEDDA: Where will you go?

LOEVBORG: Nowhere. I just want to put an end to it all. As soon as possible.

HEDDA (*takes a step toward him*): Eilert Loevborg, listen to me. Do it — beautifully!

LOEVBORG: Beautifully? (*Smiles.*) With a crown of vine leaves in my hair? The way you used to dream of me — in the old days?

HEDDA: No. I don't believe in that crown any longer. But — do it beautifully, all the same. Just this once.

Good-bye. You must go now. And don't come back.

LOEVBORG: Adieu, madame. Give my love to George Tesman. (*Turns to go.*)

HEDDA: Wait. I want to give you a souvenir to take with you.

(*She goes over to the writing table, opens the drawer and the pistol case, and comes back to Loevborg with one of the pistols.*)

LOEVBORG (*looks at her*): This? Is this the souvenir?

HEDDA (*nods slowly*): You recognize it? You looked down its barrel once.

LOEVBORG: You should have used it then.

HEDDA: Here! Use it now!

LOEVBORG (*puts the pistol in his breast pocket*): Thank you.

HEDDA: Do it beautifully, Eilert Loevborg. Only promise me that!

LOEVBORG: Good-bye, Hedda Gabler.

(*He goes out through the hall. Hedda stands by the door for a moment, listening. Then she goes over to the writing table, takes out the package containing the manuscript, glances inside it, pulls some of the pages half out and looks at them. Then she takes it to the armchair by the stove and sits down with the package in her lap. After a moment, she opens the door of the stove; then she opens the packet.*)

HEDDA (*throws one of the pages into the stove and whispers to herself*): I'm burning your child, Thea! You with your beautiful, wavy hair! (*She throws a few more pages into the stove.*) The child Eilert Loevborg gave you. (*Throws the rest of the manuscript in.*) I'm burning it! I'm burning your child!

ACT IV

(*The same. It is evening. The drawing room is in darkness. The small room is illuminated by the hanging lamp over the table. The curtains are drawn across the French windows. Hedda, dressed in black, is walking up and down in the darkened room. Then she goes into the small room and crosses to the left. A few chords are heard from the piano. She comes back into the drawing room.*)

(*Bertha comes through the small room from the right with a lighted lamp, which she places on the table in front of the corner sofa in the drawing room. Her eyes are red with crying, and she has black ribbons on her cap. She goes quietly out, right. Hedda goes over to the French windows, draws the curtains slightly to one side, and looks out into the darkness.*)

(*A few moments later, Miss Tesman enters from the hall. She is dressed in mourning, with a black hat and veil. Hedda goes to meet her and holds out her hand.*)

MISS TESMAN: Well, Hedda, here I am in the weeds of sorrow. My poor sister has ended her struggles at last.

HEDDA: I've already heard. Tesman sent me a card.

MISS TESMAN: Yes, he promised me he would. But I thought, no, I must go and break the news of death to Hedda myself — here, in the house of life.

HEDDA: It's very kind of you.

MISS TESMAN: Ah, Rena shouldn't have chosen a time like this to pass away. This is no moment for Hedda's house to be a place of mourning.

HEDDA (*changing the subject*): She died peacefully, Miss Tesman?

MISS TESMAN: Oh, it was quite beautiful! The end came so calmly. And she was so happy at being able to see George once again. And say good-bye to him. Hasn't he come home yet?

HEDDA: No. He wrote that I mustn't expect him too soon. But please sit down.

MISS TESMAN: No, thank you, Hedda dear — bless you. I'd like to. But I've so little time. I must dress her and lay her out as well as I can. She shall go to her grave looking really beautiful.

HEDDA: Can't I help with anything?

MISS TESMAN: Why, you mustn't think of such a thing! Hedda Tesman mustn't let her hands be soiled by contact with death. Or her thoughts. Not at this time.

HEDDA: One can't always control one's thoughts.

MISS TESMAN (*continues*): Ah, well, that's life. Now we must start to sew poor Rena's shroud. There'll be sewing to be done in this house, too, before long, I shouldn't wonder. But not for a shroud, praise God.

(*George Tesman enters from the hall.*)

HEDDA: You've come at last! Thank heavens!

TESMAN: Are you here, Auntie Juju? With Hedda? Fancy that!

MISS TESMAN: I was just on the point of leaving, dear boy. Well, have you done everything you promised me?

TESMAN: No, I'm afraid I forgot half of it. I'll have to run over again tomorrow. My head's in a complete whirl today. I can't collect my thoughts.

MISS TESMAN: But, George dear, you mustn't take it like this.

TESMAN: Oh? Well — er — how should I?

MISS TESMAN: You must be happy in your grief. Happy for what's happened. As I am.

TESMAN: Oh, yes, yes. You're thinking of Aunt Rena.

HEDDA: It'll be lonely for you now, Miss Tesman.

MISS TESMAN: For the first few days, yes. But it won't last long, I hope. Poor dear Rena's little room isn't going to stay empty.

TESMAN: Oh? Whom are you going to move in there? What?

MISS TESMAN: Oh, there's always some poor invalid who needs care and attention.

HEDDA: Do you really want another cross like that to bear?

MISS TESMAN: Cross! God forgive you, child. It's been no cross for me.

HEDDA: But now — if a complete stranger comes to live with you —?

MISS TESMAN: Oh, one soon makes friends with invalids. And I need so much to have someone to live for. Like you, my dear. Well, I expect there'll soon be work in this house too for an old aunt, praise God!

HEDDA: Oh — please!

TESMAN: My word, yes! What a splendid time the three of us could have together if —

HEDDA: If?

TESMAN (*uneasily*): Oh, never mind. It'll all work out. Let's hope so — what?

MISS TESMAN: Yes, yes. Well, I'm sure you two would like to be alone. (*Smiles.*) Perhaps Hedda may have something to tell you, George. Good-bye. I must go home to Rena. (*Turns to the door.*) Dear God, how strange! Now Rena is with me and with poor dear Joachim.

TESMAN: Why, yes, Auntie Juju! What?

(*Miss Tesman goes out through the hall.*)

HEDDA (*follows Tesman coldly and searchingly with her eyes*): I really believe this death distresses you more than it does her.

TESMAN: Oh, it isn't just Auntie Rena. It's Eilert I'm so worried about.

HEDDA (*quickly*): Is there any news of him?

TESMAN: I ran over to see him this afternoon. I wanted to tell him his manuscript was in safe hands.

HEDDA: Oh? You didn't find him?

TESMAN: No. He wasn't at home. But later I met Mrs. Elvsted and she told me he'd been here early this morning.

HEDDA: Yes, just after you'd left.

TESMAN: It seems he said he'd torn the manuscript up. What?

HEDDA: Yes, he claimed to have done so.

TESMAN: You told him we had it, of course?

HEDDA: No. (*Quickly.*) Did you tell Mrs. Elvsted?

TESMAN: No, I didn't like to. But you ought to have told him. Think if he should go home and do something desperate! Give me the manuscript, Hedda. I'll run over to him with it right away. Where did you put it?

HEDDA (*cold and motionless, leaning against the armchair*): I haven't got it any longer.

TESMAN: Haven't got it? What on earth do you mean?

HEDDA: I've burned it.

TESMAN (*starts, terrified*): Burned it! Burned Eilert's manuscript!

HEDDA: Don't shout. The servant will hear you.

TESMAN: Burned it! But in heaven's name —! Oh, no, no, no! This is impossible!

HEDDA: Well, it's true.

TESMAN: But, Hedda, do you realize what you've done? That's appropriating lost property! It's against the law! By God! You ask Judge Brack and see if I'm not right.

HEDDA: You'd be well advised not to talk about it to Judge Brack or anyone else.

TESMAN: But how could you go and do such a dreadful thing? What on earth put the idea into your head? What came over you? Answer me! What?

HEDDA (*represses an almost imperceptible smile*): I did it for your sake, George.

TESMAN: For my sake?

HEDDA: When you came home this morning and described how he'd read his book to you —

TESMAN: Yes, yes?

HEDDA: You admitted you were jealous of him.

TESMAN: But, good heavens, I didn't mean it literally!

HEDDA: No matter. I couldn't bear the thought that anyone else should push you into the background.

TESMAN (*torn between doubt and joy*): Hedda — is this true? But — but — but I never realized you loved me like that! Fancy that!

HEDDA: Well, I suppose you'd better know. I'm going to have — (*Breaks off and says violently*) No, no — you'd better ask your Auntie Juju. She'll tell you.

TESMAN: Hedda! I think I understand what you mean. (*Clasps his hands.*) Good heavens, can it really be true? What?

HEDDA: Don't shout. The servant will hear you.

TESMAN (*laughing with joy*): The servant! I say, that's good! The servant! Why, that's Bertha! I'll run out and tell her at once!

HEDDA (*clenches her hands in despair*): Oh, it's destroying me, all this — it's destroying me!

TESMAN: I say, Hedda, what's up? What?

HEDDA (*cold, controlled*): Oh, it's all so — absurd — George.

TESMAN: Absurd? That I'm so happy? But surely —? Ah, well — perhaps I won't say anything to Bertha.

HEDDA: No, do. She might as well know, too.

TESMAN: No, no, I won't tell her yet. But Auntie Juju — I must let her know! And you — you called me George! For the first time! Fancy that! Oh, it'll make Auntie Juju so happy, all this! So very happy!

HEDDA: Will she be happy when she hears I've burned Eilert Loevborg's manuscript — for your sake?

TESMAN: No, I'd forgotten about that. Of course, no one must be allowed to know about the manuscript. But that you're burning with love for me, Hedda, I must certainly let Auntie Juju know that. I say, I wonder if young wives often feel like that towards their husbands? What?

HEDDA: You might ask Auntie Juju about that, too.

TESMAN: I will, as soon as I get the chance. (*Looks uneasy and thoughtful again.*) But I say, you know, that manuscript. Dreadful business. Poor Eilert!

(*Mrs. Elvsted, dressed as on her first visit, with hat and overcoat, enters from the hall.*)

MRS. ELVSTED (*greets them hastily and tremulously*): Oh, Hedda dear, do please forgive me for coming here again.

HEDDA: Why, Thea, what's happened?

TESMAN: Is it anything to do with Eilert Loevborg? What?

MRS. ELVSTED: Yes — I'm so dreadfully afraid he may have met with an accident.

HEDDA (*grips her arm*): You think so?

TESMAN: But, good heavens, Mrs. Elvsted, what makes you think that?

MRS. ELVSTED: I heard them talking about him at the boarding house, as I went in. Oh, there are the most terrible rumors being spread about him in town today.

TESMAN: Er — yes, I heard about them, too. But I can testify that he went straight home to bed. Fancy —!

HEDDA: Well — what did they say in the boarding-house?

MRS. ELVSTED: Oh, I couldn't find out anything. Either they didn't know, or else — They stopped talking when they saw me. And I didn't dare to ask.

TESMAN (*fidgets uneasily*): We must hope — we must hope you misheard them, Mrs. Elvsted.

MRS. ELVSTED: No, no, I'm sure it was him they were talking about. I heard them say something about a hospital —

TESMAN: Hospital!

HEDDA: Oh no, surely that's impossible!

MRS. ELVSTED: Oh, I became so afraid. So I went up to his rooms and asked to see him.

HEDDA: Do you think that was wise, Thea?

MRS. ELVSTED: Well, what else could I do? I couldn't bear the uncertainty any longer.

TESMAN: But *you* didn't manage to find him either? What?

MRS. ELVSTED: No. And they had no idea where he was. They said he hadn't been home since yesterday afternoon.

TESMAN: Since yesterday? Fancy that!

MRS. ELVSTED: I'm sure he must have met with an accident.

TESMAN: Hedda, I wonder if I ought to go into town and make one or two enquiries?

HEDDA: No, no, don't you get mixed up in this.

(*Judge Brack enters from the hall, hat in hand. Bertha, who has opened the door for him, closes it. He looks serious and greets them silently.*)

TESMAN: Hullo, my dear Judge. Fancy seeing you!

BRACK: I had to come and talk to you.

TESMAN: I can see Auntie Juju's told you the news.

BRACK: Yes, I've heard about that, too.

TESMAN: Tragic, isn't it?

BRACK: Well, my dear chap, that depends how you look at it.

TESMAN (*looks uncertainly at him*): Has something else happened?

BRACK: Yes.

HEDDA: Another tragedy?

BRACK: That also depends on how you look at it, Mrs. Tesman.

MRS. ELVSTED: Oh, it's something to do with Eilert Loevborg!

BRACK (*looks at her for a moment*): How did you guess? Perhaps you've heard already —?

MRS. ELVSTED (*confused*): No, no, not at all — I —

TESMAN: For heaven's sake, tell us!

BRACK (*shrugs his shoulders*): Well, I'm afraid they've taken him to the hospital. He's dying.

MRS. ELVSTED (*screams*): Oh God, God!

TESMAN: The hospital! Dying!

HEDDA (*involuntarily*): So quickly!

MRS. ELVSTED (*weeping*): Oh, Hedda! And we parted enemies!

HEDDA (*whispers*): Thea — Thea!

MRS. ELVSTED (*ignoring her*): I must see him! I must see him before he dies!

BRACK: It's no use, Mrs. Elvsted. No one's allowed to see him now.

MRS. ELVSTED: But what's happened to him? You must tell me!

TESMAN: He hasn't tried to do anything to himself? What?

HEDDA: Yes, he has. I'm sure of it.

TESMAN: Hedda, how can you —?

BRACK (*who has not taken his eyes from her*): I'm afraid you've guessed correctly, Mrs. Tesman.

MRS. ELVSTED: How dreadful!

TESMAN: Attempted suicide! Fancy that!

HEDDA: Shot himself!

BRACK: Right again, Mrs. Tesman.

MRS. ELVSTED (*tries to compose herself*): When did this happen, Judge Brack?

BRACK: This afternoon. Between three and four.

TESMAN: But, good heavens — where? What?

BRACK (*a little hesitantly*): Where? Why, my dear chap, in his rooms, of course.

MRS. ELVSTED: No, that's impossible. I was there soon after six.

BRACK: Well, it must have been somewhere else, then. I don't know exactly. I only know that they found him. He's shot himself — through the breast.

MRS. ELVSTED: Oh, how horrible! That he should end like that!

HEDDA (*to Brack*): Through the breast, you said?

BRACK: That is what I said.

HEDDA: Not through the head?

BRACK: Through the breast, Mrs. Tesman.

HEDDA: The breast. Yes; yes. That's good, too.

BRACK: Why, Mrs. Tesman?

HEDDA: Oh — no, I didn't mean anything.

TESMAN: And the wound's dangerous, you say? What?

BRACK: Mortal. He's probably already dead.

MRS. ELVSTED: Yes, yes — I feel it! It's all over. All over. Oh Hedda —!

TESMAN: But, tell me, how did you manage to learn all this?

BRACK (*curtly*): From the police. I spoke to one of them.

HEDDA (*loudly, clearly*): Thank God! At last!

TESMAN (*appalled*): For God's sake, Hedda, what are you saying?

HEDDA: I am saying there's beauty in what he has done.

BRACK: Hm — Mrs. Tesman —

TESMAN: Beauty! Oh, but I say!

MRS. ELVSTED: Hedda, how can you talk of beauty in connection with a thing like this?

HEDDA: Eilert Loevborg has settled his account with life. He's had the courage to do what — what he had to do.

MRS. ELVSTED: No, that's not why it happened. He did it because he was mad.

TESMAN: He did it because he was desperate.

HEDDA: You're wrong! I know!

MRS. ELVSTED: He must have been mad. The same as when he tore up the manuscript.

BRACK (*starts*): Manuscript? Did he tear it up?

MRS. ELVSTED: Yes. Last night.

TESMAN (*whispers*): Oh, Hedda, we shall never be able to escape from this.

BRACK: Hm. Strange.

TESMAN (*wanders round the room*): To think of Eilert dying like that. And not leaving behind him the thing that would have made his name endure.

MRS. ELVSTED: If only it could be pieced together again!

TESMAN: Yes, yes, yes! If only it could! I'd give anything —

MRS. ELVSTED: Perhaps it can, Mr. Tesman.

TESMAN: What do you mean?

MRS. ELVSTED (*searches in the pocket of her dress*): Look. I kept the notes he dictated it from.

HEDDA (*takes a step nearer*): Ah!

TESMAN: You kept them, Mrs. Elvsted! What?

MRS. ELVSTED: Yes, here they are. I brought them with me when I left home. They've been in my pocket ever since.

TESMAN: Let me have a look.

MRS. ELVSTED (*hands him a wad of small sheets of paper*): They're in a terrible muddle. All mixed up.

TESMAN: I say, just fancy if we could sort them out! Perhaps if we work on them together —?

MRS. ELVSTED: Oh, yes! Let's try, anyway!

TESMAN: We'll manage it. We must! I shall dedicate my life to this. ·

HEDDA: *You*, George? Your life?

TESMAN: Yes — well, all the time I can spare. My book'll have to wait. Hedda, you do understand? What? I owe it to Eilert's memory.

HEDDA: Perhaps.

TESMAN: Well, my dear Mrs. Elvsted, you and I'll have to pool our brains. No use crying over spilt milk, what? We must try to approach this matter calmly.

MRS. ELVSTED: Yes, yes, Mr. Tesman. I'll do my best.

TESMAN: Well, come over here and let's start looking at these notes right away. Where shall we sit? Here? No, the other room. You'll excuse us, won't you, Judge? Come along with me, Mrs. Elvsted.

MRS. ELVSTED: Oh, God! If only we can manage to do it!

(*Tesman and Mrs. Elvsted go into the rear room. He takes off his hat and overcoat. They sit at the table beneath the hanging lamp and absorb themselves in the notes. Hedda walks across to the stove and sits in the armchair. After a moment, Brack goes over to her.*)

HEDDA (*half aloud*): Oh, Judge! This act of Eilert Loevborg's — doesn't it give one a sense of release!

BRACK: Release, Mrs. Hedda? Well, it's a release for him, of course —

HEDDA: Oh, I don't mean him — I mean me! The release of knowing that someone can do something really brave! Something beautiful!

BRACK (*smiles*): Hm — my dear Mrs. Hedda —

HEDDA: Oh, I know what you're going to say. You're a *bourgeois* at heart, too, just like — ah, well!

BRACK (*looks at her*): Eilert Loevborg has meant more to you than you're willing to admit to yourself. Or am I wrong?

HEDDA: I'm not answering questions like that from you. I only know that Eilert Loevborg has had the courage to live according to his own principles.

And now, at last, he's done something big! Something beautiful! To have the courage and the will to rise from the feast of life so early!

BRACK: It distresses me deeply, Mrs. Hedda, but I'm afraid I must rob you of that charming illusion.

HEDDA: Illusion?

BRACK: You wouldn't have been allowed to keep it for long, anyway.

HEDDA: What do you mean?

BRACK: He didn't shoot himself on purpose.

HEDDA: Not on purpose?

BRACK: No. It didn't happen quite the way I told you.

HEDDA: Have you been hiding something? What is it?

BRACK: In order to spare poor Mrs. Elvsted's feelings, I permitted myself one or two small — equivocations.

HEDDA: What?

BRACK: To begin with, he is already dead.

HEDDA: He died at the hospital?

BRACK: Yes. Without regaining consciousness.

HEDDA: What else haven't you told us?

BRACK: The incident didn't take place at his lodgings.

HEDDA: Well, that's utterly unimportant.

BRACK: Not utterly. The fact is, you see, that Eilert Loevborg was found shot in Mademoiselle Danielle's boudoir.

HEDDA (*almost jumps up, but instead sinks back in her chair*): That's impossible. He can't have been there today.

BRACK: He was there this afternoon. He went to ask for something he claimed they'd taken from him. Talked some crazy nonsense about a child which had got lost —

HEDDA: Oh! So that was the reason!

BRACK: I thought at first he might have been referring to his manuscript. But I hear he destroyed that himself. So he must have meant his pocketbook — I suppose.

HEDDA: Yes, I suppose so. So they found him there?

BRACK: Yes; there. With a discharged pistol in his breast pocket. The shot had wounded him mortally.

HEDDA: Yes. In the breast.

BRACK: No. In the — stomach. The — lower part —

HEDDA (*looks at him with an expression of repulsion*): That, too! Oh, why does everything I touch become mean and ludicrous? It's like a curse!

BRACK: There's something else, Mrs. Hedda. It's rather disagreeable, too.

HEDDA: What?

BRACK: The pistol he had on him —

HEDDA: Yes? What about it?

BRACK: He must have stolen it.

HEDDA (*jumps up*): Stolen it! That isn't true! He didn't!

BRACK: It's the only explanation. He must have stolen it. Ssh!

(*Tesman and Mrs. Elvsted have got up from the table in the rear room and come into the drawing room.*)

TESMAN (*his hands full of papers*): Hedda, I can't see properly under that lamp. Do you think —?

HEDDA: I am thinking.

TESMAN: Do you think we could possibly use your writing table for a little? What?

HEDDA: Yes, of course. (*Quickly.*) No, wait! Let me tidy it up first.

TESMAN: Oh, don't you trouble about that. There's plenty of room.

HEDDA: No, no, let me tidy it up first, I say. I'll take these in and put them on the piano. Here.

(*She pulls an object, covered with sheets of music, out from under the bookcase, puts some more sheets on top, and carries it all into the rear room and away to the left. Tesman puts his papers on the writing table and moves the lamp over from the corner table. He and Mrs. Elvsted sit down and begin working again. Hedda comes back.*)

HEDDA (*behind Mrs. Elvsted's chair, ruffles her hair gently*): Well, my pretty Thea. And how is work progressing on Eilert Loevborg's memorial?

MRS. ELVSTED (*looks up at her, dejectedly*): Oh, it's going to be terribly difficult to get these into any order.

TESMAN: We've got to do it. We must! After all, putting other people's papers into order is rather my speciality, what?

(*Hedda goes over to the stove and sits on one of the footstools. Brack stands over her, leaning against the armchair.*)

HEDDA (*whispers*): What was that you were saying about the pistol?

BRACK (*softly*): I said he must have stolen it.

HEDDA: Why do you think that?

BRACK: Because any other explanation is unthinkable, Mrs. Hedda. Or ought to be.

HEDDA: I see.

BRACK (*looks at her for a moment*): Eilert Loevborg was here this morning. Wasn't he?

HEDDA: Yes.

BRACK: Were you alone with him?

HEDDA: For a few moments.

BRACK: You didn't leave the room while he was here?

HEDDA: No.

BRACK: Think again. Are you sure you didn't go out for a moment?

HEDDA: Oh — yes, I might have gone into the hall. Just for a few seconds.

BRACK: And where was your pistol case during this time?

HEDDA: I'd locked it in that —

BRACK: Er — Mrs. Hedda?

HEDDA: It was lying over there on my writing table.

BRACK: Have you looked to see if both the pistols are still there?

HEDDA: No.

BRACK: You needn't bother. I saw the pistol Loevborg had when they found him. I recognized it at once. From yesterday. And other occasions.

HEDDA: Have you got it?

BRACK: No. The police have it.

HEDDA: What will the police do with this pistol?

BRACK: Try to trace the owner.

HEDDA: Do you think they'll succeed?

BRACK (*leans down and whispers*): No, Hedda Gabler. Not as long as I hold my tongue.

HEDDA (*looks nervously at him*): And if you don't?

BRACK (*shrugs his shoulders*): You could always say he'd stolen it.

HEDDA: I'd rather die!

BRACK (*smiles*): People say that. They never do it.

HEDDA (*not replying*): And suppose the pistol wasn't stolen? And they trace the owner? What then?

BRACK: There'll be a scandal, Hedda.

HEDDA: A scandal!

BRACK: Yes, a scandal. The thing you're so frightened of. You'll have to appear in court together with Mademoiselle Danielle. She'll have to explain how it all happened. Was it an accident, or was it — homicide? Was he about to take the pistol from his pocket to threaten her? And did it go off? Or did she snatch the pistol from his hand, shoot him, and then put it back in his pocket? She might quite easily have done it. She's a resourceful lady, is Mademoiselle Danielle.

HEDDA: But I have nothing to do with this repulsive business.

BRACK: No. But you'll have to answer one question. Why did you give Eilert Loevborg this pistol? And what conclusions will people draw when it is proved you did give it to him?

HEDDA (*bows her head*): That's true. I hadn't thought of that.

BRACK: Well, luckily there's no danger as long as I hold my tongue.

HEDDA (*looks up at him*): In other words, I'm in your power, Judge. From now on, you've got your hold over me.

BRACK (*whispers, more slowly*): Hedda, my dearest — believe me — I will not abuse my position.

HEDDA: Nevertheless, I'm in your power. Dependent on your will, and your demands. Not free. Still not free! (*Rises passionately.*) No. I couldn't bear that. No.

BRACK (*looks half-derisively at her*): Most people resign themselves to the inevitable, sooner or later.

HEDDA (*returns his gaze*): Possibly they do.

(*She goes across to the writing table.*)

HEDDA (*represses an involuntary smile and says in Tesman's voice*): Well, George. Think you'll be able to manage? What?

TESMAN: Heaven knows, dear. This is going to take months and months.

HEDDA (*in the same tone as before*): Fancy that, by Jove! (*Runs her hands gently through Mrs. Elvsted's hair.*) Doesn't it feel strange, Thea? Here you are working away with Tesman just the way you used to work with Eilert Loevborg.

MRS. ELVSTED: Oh — if only I can inspire your husband, too!

HEDDA: Oh, it'll come. In time.

TESMAN: Yes — do you know, Hedda, I really think I'm beginning to feel a bit — well — that way. But you go back and talk to Judge Brack.

HEDDA: Can't I be of use to you two in any way?

TESMAN: No, none at all. (*Turns his head.*) You'll have to keep Hedda company from now on, Judge, and see she doesn't get bored. If you don't mind.

BRACK (*glances at Hedda*): It'll be a pleasure.

HEDDA: Thank you. But I'm tired this evening. I think I'll lie down on the sofa in there for a little while.

TESMAN: Yes, dear — do. What?

(*Hedda goes into the rear room and draws the curtains behind her. Short pause. Suddenly she begins to play a frenzied dance melody on the piano.*)

MRS. ELVSTED (*starts up from her chair*): Oh, what's that?

TESMAN (*runs to the doorway*): Hedda dear, please! Don't play dance music tonight! Think of Auntie Rena. And Eilert.

HEDDA (*puts her head through the curtains*): And Auntie Juju. And all the rest of them. From now on I'll be quiet.

(*She closes the curtains behind her.*)

TESMAN (*at the writing table*): It distresses her to watch us doing this. I say, Mrs. Elvsted, I've an idea. Why don't you move in with Auntie Juju? I'll run over each evening, and we can sit and work there. What?

MRS. ELVSTED: Yes, that might be the best plan.

HEDDA (*from the rear room*): I can hear what you're saying, Tesman. But how shall I spend the evenings out here?

TESMAN (*looking through his papers*): Oh, I'm sure Judge Brack'll be kind enough to come over and keep you company. You won't mind my not being here, Judge?

BRACK (*in the armchair, calls gaily*): I'll be delighted,

Mrs. Tesman. I'll be here every evening. We'll have great fun together, you and I.

HEDDA (*loud and clear*): Yes, that'll suit you, won't it, Judge? The only cock on the dunghill —

(*A shot is heard from the rear room. Tesman, Mrs. Elvsted, and Judge Brack start from their chairs.*)

TESMAN: Oh, she's playing with those pistols again.

(*He pulls the curtains aside and runs in. Mrs. Elvsted follows him. Hedda is lying dead on the sofa. Confusion and shouting. Bertha enters in alarm from the right.*)

TESMAN (*screams to Brack*): She's shot herself! Shot herself in the head! Fancy that!

BRACK (*half paralyzed in the armchair*): But, good God! People don't do such things!

COMMENTARIES

Ibsen wrote about his own work, both in his letters to producers and actors and in his notes describing the development of his plays. Such notes reveal his concern, his insights as he wrote the plays, and his motives. Sometimes he says things about the plays that do not completely square with modern interpretations of the plays. On the other hand, he explains in his notes that the circumstances of women in modern society were much on his mind when he was working on *A Doll's House*.

Ibsen's "Notes for the Modern Tragedy" is remarkable for establishing a separate sensibility (spiritual law) for men and for women. His observations about the society in which women live — and in which Nora is confounded — sound as if they could have been written a century later than they were. When Bernard Shaw wrote his comments on *A Doll's House* the play was a popular shocker and Shaw's observations were designed to help audiences interpret the play's actions more carefully. He is one of the earliest critics of the play and one must remember while reading Shaw that some productions of the play had changed the ending to make it happy. Muriel Bradbrook's discussion of *A Doll's House* focuses on the moral bankruptcy of Nora's situation, which is to say the situation of all wives of the period.

Ibsen's notes to *Hedda Gabler* show us what a complex process he went through to conceive the character and to put her in action. One sees his method of sketching out the action of the play, then commenting to himself on what the action implies. We also gain insight by listening to those who produce Ibsen, such as the distinguished American actress Eva Le Gallienne. Her understanding of the play, and especially the relationship between Hedda and her husband, is informed by her experience acting in the title role. Caroline Mayerson's extensive commentary gives us insight into the symbolic levels of meaning in the play. Since the play has been considered a masterpiece of realism, some critics have assumed that it has no symbolic texture. Mayerson counters that view with a detailed analysis. Jan Kott's interpretation of Hedda's pistols, which he sees as explicit sexual symbols, helps to expand Mayerson's claim that the drama, while realistic, does not ignore the deeper significance of its own imagery.

Both of Ibsen's plays focus on the role of women in the kind of society with which he was familiar in Europe and especially in Norway and Denmark at the end of the nineteenth century. These plays shocked the conservative members of their society enough that Ibsen was denounced. Such a reaction reveals the limits of social tolerance in the late nineteenth century. It also shows us that drama can help produce social change. Our own society reflects changes that Ibsen would have approved.

Henrik Ibsen (1828–1906)
NOTES FOR THE MODERN TRAGEDY

Ibsen's first notes for A Doll's House *were jotted down on October 19, 1878. They show that his thinking on the relations between men and women was considerably sophisticated at this time and that the material for the play had been gestating. His comments indicate that the essentially male society he knew was one of his central concerns in the play.*

There are two kinds of spiritual law, two kinds of conscience, one in man and another, altogether different, in woman. They do not understand each other; but in practical life the woman is judged by man's law, as though she were not a woman but a man.

The wife in the play ends by having no idea of what is right or wrong; natural feeling on the one hand and belief in authority on the other have altogether bewildered her.

A woman cannot be herself in the society of the present day, which is an exclusively masculine society, with laws framed by men and with a judicial system that judges feminine conduct from a masculine point of view.

She has committed forgery, and she is proud of it; for she did it out of love for her husband, to save his life. But this husband with his commonplace principles of honor is on the side of the law and looks at the question from the masculine point of view.

Spiritual conflicts. Oppressed and bewildered by the belief in authority, she loses faith in her moral right and ability to bring up her children. Bitterness. A mother in modern society, like certain insects who go away and die when she has done her duty in the propagation of the race. Love of life, of home, of husband and children and family. Now and then a womanly shaking off of her thoughts. Sudden return of anxiety and terror. She must bear it all alone. The catastrophe approaches, inexorably, inevitably. Despair, conflict, and destruction.

(Krogstad has acted dishonorably and thereby become well-to-do; now his prosperity does not help him, he cannot recover his honor.)

Bernard Shaw (1856–1950)
A DOLL'S HOUSE

One of the first English men of letters to pay close attention to Ibsen's work was Bernard Shaw. Shaw was beginning to write his own plays, but he also spent time in the theater as a critic. His landmark book The Quintessence of Ibsenism, *in which this comment on* A Doll's House *appears, is a thorough discussion not only of the individual plays that Ibsen had produced but of their implication for future literature. Shaw saw the significance of the new realism and its implications for the audiences of the later nineteenth century. He saw, too, that Ibsen's brand of realism would have an effect on the beliefs of his audiences, that Ibsen's drama was a drama of important ideas. In the following excerpt Shaw is especially sensitive to the feminist issues that are at the heart of the play and pays close attention to Nora's character development.*

Unfortunately, *Pillars of Society,* as a propagandist play, is disabled by the circumstance that the hero, being a fraudulent hypocrite in the ordinary police-court sense of the phrase, would hardly be accepted as a typical pillar of society by the class he represents. Accordingly, Ibsen took care next time to make his idealist irreproachable from the standpoint of the ordinary idealist morality. In the famous *Doll's House,* the pillar of society who owns the doll is a model husband, father, and citizen. In his little household, with the three darling children and the affectionate little wife, all on the most loving terms with one another, we have the sweet home, the womanly woman, the happy family life of the idealist's dream. Mrs. Nora Helmer is happy in the belief that she has attained a valid realization of all these illusions; that she is an ideal wife and mother; and that Helmer is an ideal husband who would, if the necessity arose, give his life to save her reputation. A few simply contrived incidents disabuse her effectually on all these points. One of her earliest acts of devotion to her husband has been the secret raising of a sum of money to enable him to make a tour which was necessary to restore his health. As he would have broken down sooner than go into debt, she has had to persuade him that the money was a gift from her father. It was really obtained from a moneylender, who refused to make her the loan unless she induced her father to endorse the promissory note. This being impossible, as her father was dying at the time, she took the shortest way out of the difficulty by writing the name herself, to the entire satisfaction of the moneylender, who, though not at all duped, knew that forged bills are often the surest to be paid. Since then she has slaved in secret at scrivener's work until she has nearly paid off the debt.

At this point Helmer is made manager of the bank in which he is employed; and the moneylender, wishing to obtain a post there, uses the forged bill to force Nora to exert her influence with Helmer on his behalf. But she, having a hearty contempt for the man, cannot be persuaded by him that there was any harm in putting her father's name on the bill, and ridicules the suggestion that the law would not recognize that she was right under the circumstances. It is her husband's own contemptuous denunciation of a forgery formerly committed by the moneylender himself that destroys her self-satisfaction and opens her eyes to her ignorance of the serious business of the world to which her husband belongs: the world outside the home he shares with her. When he goes on to tell her that commercial dishonesty is generally to be traced to the influence of bad mothers, she begins to perceive that the happy way in which she plays with the children, and the care she takes to dress them nicely, are not sufficient to constitute her a fit person to train them. To redeem the forged bill, she resolves to borrow the balance due upon it from an intimate friend of the family. She has learnt to coax her husband into giving her what she asks by appealing to his affection for her: that is, by playing all sorts of pretty tricks until he is wheedled into an amorous humor. This plan she has adopted without thinking about it, instinctively taking the line of least resistance with him. And now she naturally takes the same line with her husband's friend. An unexpected declaration of love from him is the result; and it at once explains to her the real nature of the domestic influence she has been so proud of.

All her illusions about herself are now shattered. She sees herself as an ignorant and silly woman, a dangerous mother, and a wife kept for her husband's pleasure merely; but she clings all the harder to her illusion about him: he is still the ideal husband who would make any sacrifice to rescue her from ruin. She resolves to kill herself rather than allow him to destroy his own career by taking the forgery on himself to save her reputation. The final disillusion comes when he, instead of at once proposing to pursue this ideal line of conduct when he hears of the forgery, naturally enough flies into a vulgar rage and heaps invective on her for disgracing him. Then she sees that their whole family life has been a fiction: their home a mere doll's house in which they have been playing at ideal husband and father, wife and mother. So she leaves him then and there and goes out into the real world to find out its reality for herself, and to gain some position not fundamentally false, refusing to see her children again until she is fit to be in charge of them, or to live with him until she and he become capable of a more honorable relation to one another. He at first cannot understand what has happened, and flourishes the shattered ideals over her as if they were as potent as ever. He presents the course most agreeable to him — that of her staying at home and avoiding a scandal — as her duty to her husband, to her children, and to her religion; but the magic of these disguises is gone; and at last even he understands what has really happened, and sits down alone to wonder whether that more honorable relation can ever come to pass between them.

Muriel C. Bradbrook
A DOLL'S HOUSE: IBSEN THE MORALIST

In her important study of Ibsen, Ibsen: The Norwegian, *Muriel Bradbrook discusses all the important plays, but she reserves a special place for* A Doll's House. *In her analysis she suggests that Nora slowly discovers the fundamental bankruptcy of her marriage. Bradbrook calls it "eight years' prostitution." She also shows the true extent to which Torvald is both possessive and immature. As Bradbrook says, the true moment of recognition — in the Greek tragic sense — occurs when Nora sees both herself and Torvald in their true nature. Bradbrook also helps us see the full implication of Nora's leaving her home. She can never hope again for the comforts she has enjoyed as Torvald's wife.*

Poor Nora, living by playing her tricks like a little pet animal, sensing how to manage Torvald by those pettinesses in his character she does not know she knows of, is too vulnerably sympathetic to find her life-work in reading John Stuart Mill. At the end she still does not understand the strange world in which she has done wrong by forging a signature. She does understand that she has lived by what Virginia Woolf called "the slow waterlogged sinking of her will into his." And this picture is built up for her and for us by the power of structural implication, a form of writing particularly suited to drama, where the latent possibilities of a long stretch of past time can be thrown into relief by a crisis. In *A Doll's House*, the past is not only lighted up by the present, as a transparency might be lit up with a lamp; the past is changed by the present so that it becomes a different thing. Nora's marriage becomes eight years' prostitution, as she gradually learns the true nature of her relations with Torvald and the true nature of Torvald's feelings for her.

In Act I, no less than six different episodes bring out the war that is secretly waged between his masculine dictatorship and her feminine wiles:

Her wheedling him for money with a simple transference: "Let us do as *you* suggest. . . ."

Her promise to Christine: "Just leave it to me: I will broach the matter very cleverly." She is evidently habituated to and aware of her own technique.

Her description of how she tried to coax Torvald into taking the holiday and how she was saving up the story of the bond "for when I am no longer as good-looking as I am now." She knows the precarious nature of her hold.

Her method of asking work for Christine by putting Christine also into a (completely bogus) position of worshipping subservience to Torvald.

Her boast to Krogstad about her influence. Whilst this may be a justifiable triumph over her tormentor, it is an unconscious betrayal of Torvald (witness his fury in Act II at the idea of being thought uxorious).

After this faceted exposition, the treatment grows much broader. Nora admits Torvald's jealousy: yet she flirts with Rank, aware but not acknowledging the grounds of her control. The pressure of implication remains constant throughout: it is comparable with the effect of a dialect, coloring all that is said. To take a few lines at random from the dialogue of Nora and Rank in Act II:

> NORA (*putting her hand on his shoulder*): Dear, dear Dr. Rank! Death mustn't take you away from Torvald and me. [Nora is getting demonstrative as she senses Rank's responsiveness, and her hopes of obtaining a loan from him rise. Hence her warmth of feeling, purely seductive.]
>
> RANK: It is a loss you will easily recover from. Those who are gone away are soon forgotten. [Poor Rank is reminded by that "Torvald and me" how little he really counts to Nora.]
>
> NORA (*anxiously*): Do you believe that? [Rank has awakened her thoughts of what may happen if *she* has to go away.]

Her methods grow more desperate — the open appeal to Torvald to keep Krogstad and the frantic expedient of the tarantella. In the last act her fate is upon her; yet in spite of all her terror and Torvald's tipsy amorousness, she still believes in his chivalry and devotion. This extraordinary self-deception is perhaps the subtlest and most telling implication of all. Practice had left her theory unshaken: so when the crash comes, she cries, "I have been living with a strange man," yet it was but the kind of man her actions had always implied him to be. Her vanity had completely prevented her from recognizing what she was doing, even though she had become such an expert at doing it.

Torvald is more gradually revealed. In the first act he appears indulgent, perhaps a trifle inclined to nag about the macaroons and to preach, but virtually a more efficient David Copperfield curbing a rather better-trained Dora. In the second act, his resentment and his pleasure alike uncover the deeper bases of his dominance. His anger at the prospect of being thought under his wife's influence and his fury at the imputation of narrow-mindedness show that it is really based on his own cowardice, the need for something weaker to bully: this is confirmed when he gloats over Nora's panic as evidence of her love for him, and over her agitation in the tarantella ("you little helpless thing!"). His love of order and his fastidiousness, when joined to such qualities, betray a set personality; and the last act shows that he has neither control nor sympathy on the physical level. But he is no fool, and his integrity is not all cowardice. Doubtless, debt or forgery really was abhorrent to him.

The climax of the play comes when Nora sees Torvald and sees herself: it is an *anagnorisis,* a recognition. Her life is cored like an apple. For she has had no life apart from this. Behind the irrelevant program for self-education there stands a woman, pitifully inexperienced, numbed by emotional shock, but with a newfound will to face what has happened, to accept her bankruptcy, as, in a very different way, Peer Gynt had at last accepted his.

"Yes, I am beginning to understand. . . ." she says. "What you did," observes the now magnanimous Torvald, "you did out of love for me." "That is true," says Nora: and she calls him to a "settling of accounts," not in any spirit of hostility but in an attempt to organize vacancy. "I have made nothing of my life. . . . I must stand quite alone . . . it is necessary to me . . ." That is really the program. *Ainsi tout leur a craqué dans les mains.*[1]

The spare and laminated speech gains its effect by inference and riddle. But these are the characteristic virtues of Norse. Irony is its natural weapon. Ibsen was working with the grain of the language. It was no accident that it fell to a Norwegian to take that most finely tooled art, the drama, and bring it to a point and precision so nice that literally not a phrase is without its direct contribution to the structure. The unrelenting cohesion of *A Doll's House* is perhaps, like that of the *Oedipus the King,* too hard on the playgoer; he is allowed no relief. Nora cannot coo to her baby without saying: "My sweet little *baby doll!*" or play with her children without choosing, significantly, *Hide and Seek.* Ibsen will not allow the smallest action to escape from the psychopathology of everyday life. However, a play cannot be acted so that every moment is tense with significance, and, in practice, an actor, for the sake of light and shade, will probably slur some of Ibsen's points, deliberately or unconsciously. The tension between the characters is such that the slightest movement of one sets all the others quivering. But this is partly because they are seen with such detachment, like a clear-cut intaglio. The play is, above all, articulated.

That is not to say that it is the mere dissection of a problem. Perhaps Rank and Mrs. Linde would have been more subtly wrought into the action at a later date; but the tight control kept over Nora and Torvald does not mean that

---

[1]*Ainsi . . . mains:* Thus everything has shattered in their hands.

they can be exhausted by analysis or staled by custom. They are so far in advance of the characters of *Pillars of Society* that they are capable of the surprising yet inevitable development that marks the character conceived "in the round," the character that is, in Ibsen's phrase, fully "seen."

Consider, for example, Torvald's soliloquy whilst Nora is taking off her masquerade dress. It recalls at one moment Dickens's most unctuous hypocrites — "Here I will protect you like a hunted dove that I have saved from the claws of the hawk!" — at another Meredith's Willoughby Patterne[2] — "Only be frank and open with me and I will be both will and conscience to you" — yet from broadest caricature to sharpest analysis, it remains the self-glorified strut of the one character, the bank clerk in his pride, cousin to Peer Gynt, that typical Norwegian, and to Hjalmer Ekdal, the toiling breadwinner of the studio.

Whilst the Ibsenites might have conceded that Torvald is Art, they would probably have contended that Nora is Truth. Nora, however, is much more than a Revolting Wife. She is not a sour misanthropist or a fighting suffragette, but a lovely young woman who knows that she still holds her husband firmly infatuated after eight years of marriage. . . .

In leaving her husband Nora is seeking a fuller life as a human being. She is emancipating herself. Yet the seeking itself is also a renunciation, a kind of death — "I must stand alone." No less than Falk, or the hero of *On the Vidda*, she gives up something that has been her whole life. She is as broken as Torvald in the end: but she is a strong character and he is a weak one. In the "happy ending" which Ibsen reluctantly allowed to be used, it was the sight of the children that persuaded her to stay, and unless it is remembered that leaving Torvald means leaving the children, the full measure of Nora's decision cannot be taken. An actress gets her chance to make this point in the reply to Torvald's plea that Nora should stay for the children's sake.

It should be remembered, too, that the seriousness of the step she takes is lost on the present generation. She was putting herself outside society, inviting insult, destitution and loneliness. She went out into a very dark night.

Henrik Ibsen (1828–1906)
NOTES FOR *HEDDA GABLER*

Like most playwrights, Ibsen kept a notebook into which he jotted ideas as he was writing his plays. The notes that follow are some of those he gathered as he was writing Hedda Gabler. *They show how his mind worked on the material, how he considered alternatives to what he was doing, and how he permitted his material to grow and develop.*

. . . ¶ One talks about building railways and highways for the cause of progress. But no, no, that is not what is needed. Space must be cleared so that the spirit of man can make its great turnabout. For it has gone astray. The spirit of man has gone astray. . . .

[2]The protagonist in George Meredith's novel *The Egoist* (1879), an arrogant aristocrat who lacks awareness of the needs and desires of the women in his life.

¶ *Notes:* One evening as Hedda and Tesman, together with some others, were on their way home from a party, Hedda remarked as they walked by a charming house that was where she would like to live. She meant it, but she said it only to keep the conversation with Tesman going. "He simply cannot carry on a conversation."

The house was actually for rent or sale. Tesman had been pointed out as the coming young man. And later when he proposed, and let slip that he too had dreamed of living there, she accepted.

He too had liked the house very much.

They get married. And they rent the house.[1]

But when Hedda returns as a young wife, with a vague sense of responsibility, the whole thing seems distasteful to her. She conceives a kind of hatred for the house just because it has become her home. She confides this to Brack. She evades the question with Tesman.

¶ The play shall deal with "the impossible," that is, to aspire to and strive for something which is against all the conventions, against that which is acceptable to conscious minds — Hedda's included.

¶ The episode of the hat makes Aunt Rising[2] lose her composure. She leaves — That it could be taken for the maid's hat — no, that's going too far!

That my hat, which I've had for over nine years, could be taken for the maid's — no, that's really too much! . . .

¶ Very few true parents are to be found in the world. Most people grow up under the influence of aunts or uncles — either neglected and misunderstood or else spoiled. . . .

¶ Hedda feels herself demoniacally attracted by the tendencies of the times. But she lacks courage. Her thoughts remain theories, ineffective dreams.

¶ The feminine imagination is not active and independently creative like the masculine. It needs a bit of reality as a help.

¶ Loevborg has had inclinations toward "the bohemian life." Hedda is attracted in the same direction, but she does not dare to take the leap.

¶ Buried deep within Hedda there is a level of poetry. But the environment frightens her. Suppose she were to make herself ridiculous!

¶ Hedda realizes that she, much more than Thea, has abandoned her husband.

¶ The newly wedded couple return home in September — as the summer is dying. In the second act they sit in the garden — but with their coats on.

¶ Being frightened by one's own voice. Something strange, foreign.

¶ NEWEST PLAN: The festivities in Tesman's garden — and Loevborg's defeat — already prepared for in the 1st act. Second act: the party —

¶ Hedda energetically refuses to serve as hostess. She will not celebrate their marriage because (in her opinion, it isn't a marriage) . . .

---

[1] Both of them, each in his and her own way, have seen in their common love for this house a sign of their mutual understanding. As if they sought and were drawn to a common home.

Then he rents the house. They get married and go abroad. He orders the house bought and his aunt furnishes it at his expense. Now it is their home. It is theirs and yet it is not, because it is not paid for. Everything depends on his getting the professorship. (Ibsen's note.)

[2] Aunt Rising (or Rysing) becomes Aunt Juliana Tesman in the final version of the play.

¶ Hedda is the type of woman in her position and with her character. She marries Tesman but she devotes her imagination to Eilert Loevborg. She leans back in her chair, closes her eyes, and dreams of his adventures. . . . This is the enormous difference: Mrs. Elvsted "works for his moral improvement." But for Hedda he is the object of cowardly, tempting daydreams. In reality she does not have the courage to be a part of anything like that. Then she realizes her condition. Caught! Can't comprehend it. Ridiculous! Ridiculous!

¶ The traditional delusion that one man and one woman are made for each other. Hedda has her roots in the conventional. She marries Tesman but she dreams of Eilert Loevborg. . . . She is disgusted by the latter's flight from life. He believes that this has raised him in her estimation. . . . Thea Elvsted is the conventional, sentimental, hysterical Philistine.

¶ Those Philistines, Mrs. E. and Tesman, explain my behavior by saying first I drink myself drunk and that the rest is done in insanity. It's a flight from reality which is an absolute necessity to me.

¶ *E. L.*: Give me something — a flower — at our parting. Hedda hands him the revolver.

Then Tesman arrives: Has he gone? "Yes." Do you think he will still compete against me? No, I don't think so. You can set your mind at rest.

¶ Tesman relates that when they were in Gratz she did not want to visit her relatives —

He misunderstands her real motives.

¶ In the last act as Tesman, Mrs. Elvsted, and Miss Rysing are consulting, Hedda plays in the small room at the back. She stops. The conversation continues. She appears in the doorway — Good night — I'm going now. Do you need me for anything? Tesman: No, nothing at all. Good night, my dear! . . . The shot is fired —

¶ CONCLUSION: All rush into the back room. Brack sinks as if paralyzed into a chair near the stove: But God have mercy — people don't *do* such things!

¶ When Hedda hints at her ideas to Brack, he says: Yes, yes, that's extraordinarily amusing — Ha ha ha! He does not understand that she is quite serious.

¶ Hedda is right in this: There is no love on Tesman's part. Nor on the aunt's part. However full of love she may be.

Eilert Loevborg has a double nature. It is a fiction that one loves only *one* person. He loves two — or many — alternately (to put it frivolously). But how can he explain his position? Mrs. Elvsted, who forces him to behave correctly, runs away from her husband. Hedda, who drives him beyond all limits, draws back at the thought of a scandal.

¶ Neither he nor Mrs. Elvsted understands the point. Tesman reads in the manuscript that was left behind about "the two ideals." Mrs. Elvsted can't explain to him what E. L. meant. Then comes the burlesque note: both T. and Mrs. E. are going to devote their future lives to interpreting the mystery.

¶ Tesman thinks that Hedda hates E. L.

Mrs. Elvsted thinks so too.

Hedda sees their delusion but dares not disabuse them of it. There is something beautiful about having an aim in life. Even if it is a delusion —

She cannot do it. Take part in someone else's.

That is when she shoots herself.

The destroyed manuscript is entitled "The ~~Philosophy~~ Ethics of Future Society."

¶ Tesman is on the verge of losing his head. All this work meaningless. New thoughts! New visions! A whole new world! Then the two of them sit there, trying to find the meaning in it. Can't make any sense of it. . . .

¶ The greatest misery in this world is that so many have nothing to do but pursue happiness without being able to find it. . . .

¶ The simile: The journey of life = the journey on a train.

H.: One doesn't usually jump out of the compartment.

No, not when the train is moving.

Nor stand still when it is stationary. There's always someone on the platform, staring in.

¶ *Hedda*: Dream of a scandal — yes, I understand that well enough. But commit one — no, no, no.

¶ *Loevborg*: Now I understand. My ideal was an illusion. You aren't a bit better than I. Now I have nothing left to live for. Except pleasure — dissipation — as you call it . . . Wait, here's a present (The pistol)

¶ Tesman is nearsighted. Wears glasses. My, what a beautiful rose! Then he stuck his nose in the cactus. Ever since then —!

¶ NB: The mutual hatred of women. Women have no influence on external matters of government. Therefore they want to have an influence on souls. And then so many of them have no aim in life (the lack thereof is inherited) — . . .

¶ Men and women don't belong to the same century. . . . What a great prejudice that one should love only *one*! . . .

¶ The demoniacal element in Hedda is this: She wants to exert her influence on someone — But once she has done so, she despises him. . . . The manuscript?

¶ In the third act Hedda questions Mrs. Elvsted. But if he's like that, why is he worth holding on to. . . . Yes, yes, I know — . . .

¶ NB!! The reversal in the play occurs during the big scene between Hedda and E. L. *He*: What a wretched business it is to conform to the existing morals. It would be ideal if a man of the present could live the life of the future. What a miserable business it is to fight over a professorship!

Hedda — that lovely girl! *H.*: No! *E. L.*: Yes, I'm going to say it. That lovely, cold girl — cold as marble.

I'm not dissipated fundamentally. But the life of reality isn't livable — . . .

¶ Life becomes for Hedda a ridiculous affair that isn't "worth seeing through to the end."

¶ The happiest mission in life is to place the people of today in the conditions of the future.

L.: Never put a child in this world, H.!

¶ When Brack speaks of a "triangular affair," Hedda thinks about what is going to happen and refers ambiguously to it. Brack doesn't understand.

¶ Brack cannot bear to be in a house where there are small children. "Children shouldn't be allowed to exist until they are fourteen or fifteen. That is, girls. What about boys? Shouldn't be allowed to exist at all — or else they should be raised outside the house."

¶ H. admits that children have always been a horror to her too.

¶ Hedda is strongly but imprecisely opposed to the idea that one should love "the family." The aunts mean nothing to her.

¶ It liberated Hedda's spirit to serve as a confessor to E. L. Her sympathy has secretly been on his side — But it became ugly when the public found out everything. Then she backed out.

¶ MAIN POINTS: (1) They are not all made to be mothers. (2) They are passionate but they are afraid of scandal. (3) They perceive that the times are full of missions worth devoting one's life to, but they cannot discover them.

¶ And besides Tesman is not exactly a professional, but he is a specialist. The Middle Ages are dead —

¶ *T.:* Now there you see also the great advantages to my studies. I can lose manuscripts and rewrite them — no inspiration needed —

¶ Hedda is completely taken up by the child that is to come, but when it is born she dreads what is to follow —

¶ Hedda must say somewhere in the play that she did not like to get out of her compartment while on the trip. Why not? I don't like to show my legs. . . . Ah, Mrs. H., but they do indeed show themselves. Nevertheless, I don't.

¶ Shot herself! Shot herself!

Brack (collapsing in the easy chair): But great God — people don't *do* such things!

¶NB!! Eilert Loevborg believes that a comradeship must be formed between man and woman out of which the truly spiritual human being can arise. Whatever else the two of them do is of no concern. This is what the people around him do not understand. To them he is dissolute. Inwardly he is not.

¶ If a man can have several male friends, why can't he have several lady friends?

¶ It is precisely the sensual feelings that are aroused while in the company of his female "friends" or "comrades" that seek release in his excesses.

¶ Now I'm going. Don't you have some little remembrance to give me —? You have flowers — and so many other things — (The story of the pistol from before) — But you won't use it anyhow —

¶ In the fourth act when Hedda finds out that he has shot himself, she is jubilant. . . . He had courage.

Here is the rest of the manuscript.

¶ CONCLUSION: Life isn't tragic. . . . Life is ridiculous. . . . And that's what I can't bear.

¶ Do you know what happens in novels? All those who kill themselves — through the head — not in the stomach. . . . How ridiculous — how baroque — . . .

Eva Le Gallienne
From PREFACE TO IBSEN'S HEDDA GABLER

Eva Le Gallienne is one of the most durable American actresses. She was especially popular in the 1930s and continued to act into the 1960s. One of her roles was Hamlet, when she was thirty-six. She was able to command the stage in important female roles as well. Her comments on how one ought to produce Hedda Gabler *give us the insights not of playwright or critic but of the actress who would play the title role.*

Some actresses have played the part completely disregarding Ibsen's wishes; have dressed Hedda in an exaggerated *femme fatale* style; have made her appearance so extremely neurotic and peculiar that Tesman would never have dreamed of marrying her, even had he wished to, which would be doubtful, for his tastes would surely lean toward the conventional, and outwardly it is important that Hedda should seem conventional and in every way impress one as a highly bred woman of distinction and poise.

Ibsen describes her clothes as "tasteful." They should be becoming and should have a certain individuality, no matter what period is chosen for the play; they should never look like exaggerated fashion-plates, for a European woman of taste is not nearly as regimented in her dress as her American equivalent. Hedda would choose her clothes carefully and with a subtle art. They would be quite definitely "her own," for she is in everything an individualist while never going beyond the bounds of good taste and refinement. She is enormously aware of the impression she creates, very self-conscious always, and exquisite. She thinks of herself, one can be sure, as someone rare and romantic, a kind of *princesse lointaine*.[1] It is probable that one of the most irritating things she found on the "wedding journey" was Tesman's good-natured willingness to conform to all the petty rules and regulations, his exactness about trains and timetables, his careful economy and budgeting, all so "vulgar" and bourgeois; never the slightest inclination toward the unscheduled or the unexpected. And then for nearly six months to be cooped up in small hotel rooms or tiny railroad carriages; under such conditions to find oneself "everlastingly with one and the same person" — yes, indeed — poor Hedda must have been "bored to distraction."

So, on this morning, when we first meet her, she is probably in a good mood. When she woke up, Tesman had already disappeared and she was able to get up in a leisurely fashion, to prepare herself gradually to face the day, without the irritation of Tesman's noisy, bustling vitality.

. . . When Thea is first announced, Hedda has no idea of the reason of her visit. She only knows that Loevborg has, for the past few years, been living near the Elvsteds and she is avid for news of him. Her feeling for Loevborg is not love — is Hedda capable of that? What is it then? Certainly there was between them a strong physical attraction. Hedda had a great, a consuming desire for Loevborg. But she is not like Thea. Passion with her could never be simple, pure, and inevitable. It must always be perverse and complicated. . . .

Hedda is now acutely aware that Thea is in love with Loevborg and is determined to find out the whole truth of the matter.

All during Thea's scene with Tesman she watches her, taking note of every expression, every nuance of tone and emphasis. She realizes that she must get Thea alone if she is to win her confidence.

During this scene she hears for the first time about Loevborg's rehabilitation, about the success of his published book, and the fact that Thea was closely associated with it. With a woman's eye for detail she observes her plain, almost shabby dress, the poorness of her accessories; her gloves, her bag; all meticulously neat, but indicative of the strictest economy. Thea later says: "It doesn't cost much to keep me — I'm not expensive." This has been obvious to Hedda from the beginning.

She now sends Tesman into his study to write a "long friendly letter" to Loevborg, asking him to call. In this way she manages to get Thea to herself.

[1]***princesse lointaine:*** Remote or detached princess.

Also, knowing Loevborg as she does, she is probably right in thinking that "he may not care to come of his own accord" and she is consumed with curiosity to see him again and judge for herself the extent of his "reformation." Tesman bustles happily off to write the letter and the two women are alone. The scene that follows must be played by Hedda with the utmost finesse.

In order to achieve a successful performance in an Ibsen play, it is necessary that the actor be capable of such concentrated thinking that his thoughts actually take shape; the audience must see the thought, must be made a part of it. And this must be achieved without any external commotion whatever; not even a flick of the eyelash should be needed. The actor must, through the truth and power of his thinking, transfer his thought to the audience, compel them into awareness of the hidden inner life of the character portrayed. This is not a simple business. All great actors make use of this power to some extent, no matter what the play. But Ibsen makes the use of it imperative.

In the scene under discussion we have a perfect example.

Thea must be genuinely convinced of Hedda's good will, of her friendly sympathy and understanding. In everything she does and says Hedda must inspire confidence, must charm Thea and disarm her; the external pattern of the actress's performance must take care of that. Yet the audience must be acutely aware of the true thread of Hedda's thinking; to them her motives must be unmistakable. And this must be achieved by power of thought; there must be no dark looks behind Thea's back, no baleful glances toward the auditorium. It must all be very quiet, very relaxed, very sure. If the actress playing Hedda handles the scene clumsily, Thea will seem a fool. And that would be wrong.

It is true that when she finds herself alone with Hedda, Thea's first impulse is to escape. She mistrusts her; her clear, uncluttered instinct warns her against this woman. Hedda is quite aware of this. She is insistent that Thea "can't be in such a hurry," that they must have "a nice friendly chat"; she conjures up a purely fictitious childhood friendship — makes much of "after all, we were at school together" — refuses to notice Thea's weak denials of former intimacy, and finally overwhelms her into staying. Thea is shy and unwilling to give offense, she gives in.

And then her loneliness, confronted by this charming woman, who seems all warmth and strength and understanding, betrays her into revealing her secret.

Hedda starts by asking her questions about her "life at home." She is now in full control of the situation and plays with Thea as a cat plays with a mouse. There is always in her attitude a slightly superior tone — the snob in her comes out in almost imperceptible ways as in her question "You were engaged as housekeeper, weren't you?" — the color of the word "housekeeper" is unmistakable, though veiled with the good manners of the high-born talking to an inferior. Thea just senses it, for she comes back quite strongly with "I was supposed to go as governess," etc., and then in a few minutes Hedda brings out the frustration of her married life. She prompts her skillfully. "But isn't he a bit old for you, dear? There must be about twenty years between you." All this with the greatest concern and sympathy.

Gradually Thea forgets her shyness, and all the pent-up grievances and misery of the past few years come tumbling out. She has been so alone, and it is a relief to talk about herself.

When it transpires that Thea has left her home for good, has run away, in fact, to be where Loevborg is, Hedda is definitely taken by surprise. To begin with, she hadn't suspected the importance of the Thea-Loevborg relationship; she now realizes that she is face to face with a woman who loves so deeply and so purely that she will dare anything for the sake of that love. Here is no little "ninny," no weak little female without character or courage; on the contrary, Hedda understands only too well the power and integrity of Thea's love. She is filled with envy as well as amazement. She would be entirely incapable of such an act. To face the condemnation of society, to dare to stand alone against all criticism, to be that true to oneself and to God — these are things that Hedda in the innermost recesses of her being would long to do — but would always refuse. She understands that Thea is far stronger than she.

I think there is a grudging admiration in her feeling; but her envy and resentment, yes, her jealousy, overcome it and her every thought, from now on, will be to poison and destroy Thea's love.

She herself dared not take Loevborg, but she can't endure the fact of anyone else having him.

Though Thea is unaware of it, Hedda has now become her bitter enemy. And the more she gives herself away, the truer this becomes. She feeds, through her guileless trust in Hedda, the resentment and jealousy that smolder there.

When she speaks of sharing Loevborg's work, and particularly when she admits Loevborg's use of the term "comrade," she has unwittingly delivered herself and her love into Hedda's ruthless and destructive power. Loevborg had called Hedda, too, in the "old days," his "comrade" (men have an unfortunate way of repeating their patterns where women are concerned), and it is unbearable for Hedda to realize that he found "ample consolation" (as she puts it) elsewhere.

Her egotistical nature would have had him forever crushed and lost, since he could not have her. In fact, it is she who has been frustrated and lost through not having dared accept his love, through not having had the courage to really live.

But, at the very end of the scene, Thea lets fall a remark that provides Hedda with a very dangerous weapon. She reveals the fact that she feels "there is a shadow between Loevborg and me; a woman's shadow"; Hedda instinctively guesses who this woman is, and when Thea admits that "when they parted she threatened to shoot him" there is no room for doubt. This knowledge makes it clear to Hedda that she still has the "power" to disturb Loevborg, that the poison of their unresolved passion still works in him as it does in her. It is now only a question of how she can make circumstances serve her purpose. She is resolved.

This is a masterly scene. It is so clearly and brilliantly conceived from a psychological point of view, so closely knit, so economical in writing, so unerringly accurate, that the actresses concerned need do nothing but be honest. But they must be that. There is considerable comedy in the scene, for it is handled with a light touch, and the double values, of which the audience is aware, provide a number of reasons for ironic laughter.

In general, it is true that Ibsen's mordant humor is too often neglected. Actors are prone to handle his plays too heavily. They are afraid of "getting laughs." This is a mistake. Ibsen's sense of humor may not be gay or pleasant, but it is very potent all the same, and to discount it is to rob his plays of one of their most powerful assets.

Caroline W. Mayerson
THEMATIC SYMBOLS IN *HEDDA GABLER*

Sometimes the designation of realism has been applied to Ibsen in such a way as to suggest that all we get in his plays is a slice of life, with details that are meaningless except that they are there. The fact is that, like Gustave Flaubert, James Joyce, August Strindberg, and other realistic writers of his time, Ibsen was a craftsman who tried to make every detail in his plays add up to something. Caroline Mayerson shows us how loaded with significance certain otherwise innocent-looking objects are in Hedda Gabler. *She begins with Thea's hair, the manuscript that Loevborg loses, and General Gabler's pistols. By examining them, she shows us just how rich the surfaces of Ibsen's plays can be.*

During the course of the play, Ibsen places considerable emphasis upon Thea's hair, upon the manuscript as her "child," and upon General Gabler's pistols, and his treatment of these items suggests that he intended them to have symbolic significance. We shall be concerned in this essay with determining this significance and its effect upon the total meaning of the play. My analysis of the three symbols in their relationship to the theme, the characters, and the action will be based upon several broad assumptions which reflect views of Ibsen's concepts and methods implied or expressed by a number of previous commentators: (1) In *Hedda Gabler*, Ibsen examines the possibility of attaining freedom and fulfillment in modern society. (2) Hedda is a woman, not a monster; neurotic, but not psychotic. Thus, she may be held accountable for her behavior. But she is spiritually sterile. Her yearning for self-realization through exercise of her natural endowments is in conflict with her enslavement to a narrow standard of conduct. This conflict is complicated by her incomplete understanding of what freedom and fulfillment mean and how they may be achieved. She fails to realize that one must earn his inheritance in order to possess it, and she romanticizes the destructive and sensational aspects of Dionysiac ecstasy without perceiving that its true end is regeneration through sublimation of the ego in a larger unity. (3) Ibsen, as an experienced artist, was aware of the impact of minutiae and the need for integrating these with the general impression to be projected; therefore we may regard his descriptions, his stage directions, and his properties, no less than his dialogue, as means whereby intention and significance are conveyed.

While all the other characters in *Hedda Gabler* are implicitly compared to Hedda and serve, in one way or another, to throw light upon her personality, Thea Elvsted is the one with whom she is most obviously contrasted. Furthermore, their contest for the control of Loevborg is the most prominent external conflict in the play. The sterility-fertility antithesis from which central action proceeds is chiefly realized through the opposition of these two. Hedda is pregnant, and Thea is physically barren. But in emotionally repudiating her unborn child, Hedda rejects what Ibsen considered woman's opportunity to advance the march of progress.[1] The many other symptoms of her psychic sterility need little en-

[1] Cf. Ibsen's speech to the Norwegian Women's Rights League (1898): "It is women who are to solve the social problems. As mothers they are to do it. And only as such can they do it. Here lies a great task for woman" (*Speeches and New Letters of Henrik Ibsen*, trans. by Arne Kildal [Boston, 1901], p. 66).

largement. Unwilling to give or even share herself, she maintains her independence at the price of complete frustration. Ibsen uses Thea, on the other hand, to indicate a way to freedom which Hedda never apprehends. Through her ability to extend herself in comradeship with Loevborg, Thea not only brings about the rebirth of his creative powers, but merges her own best self with his to produce a prophecy of the future, conceivably of the "Third Kingdom," in which Ibsen believed that the ideals of the past would coalesce in a new and more perfect unity. Having lost herself to find herself, she almost instinctively breaks with the mores of her culture in order to ensure continuance of function. Despite her palpitating femininity, she is the most truly emancipated person in the play. And it is she who wins at least a limited victory in the end. Although Loevborg has failed her, her fecundity is indefatigable; as Hedda kills herself, Thea is busily preparing to recreate her "child" with Tesman, thereby at once enabling him to realize his own little talents and weakening even further the tenuous bond which ties him to Hedda.

The contrast outlined above is reinforced by the procreative imagery of the play. The manuscript is Loevborg's and Thea's "child," the idea of progress born of a union between individuals who have freed themselves from the pre-conceptions of their environment.[2] This manuscript the sterile Hedda throws into the fire at the climax of her vindictive passion. Her impulse to annihilate by burning is directed both toward Thea's "child" and toward Thea's hair and calls attention to the relationship between them. Even without other indications that Ibsen was using hair as a symbol of fertility, such an inference might be made from the words which accompany the destruction of the manuscript:

> Now I am burning your child, Thea! Burning it, curly-locks! Your child and Eilert Loevborg's. I am burning — I am burning your child.

There is, however, considerable evidence, both before and after this scene, that Thea's hair is a sign of that potency which Hedda envies even while she ridicules and bullies its possessor. Ibsen, of course, had ample precedent for employing hair as a symbol of fertility. Perhaps the best support for the argument that he made a literary adaptation of this well-known, ancient idea in *Hedda Gabler* is a summary of the instances in which the hair is mentioned.

Although Ibsen's unobtrusive description of the hair of each of these women at her initial entrance may seem at the time only a casual stroke in the sketch, it assumes importance in retrospect. Hedda's hair is "not particularly abundant," whereas Thea's is "unusually abundant and wavy." Hedda's strongest impression of Thea is of that abundance: she recalls her as "the girl with the irritating hair, that she was always showing off." Moreover, Thea fearfully recollects Hedda's schoolgirl reaction to it: ". . . when we met on the stairs you used always to pull my hair. . . . Yes, and once you said you would burn it off my head." When Thea and Loevborg first meet in the play, Hedda seats herself, significantly, between them; the brief exchange of questions and answers which ensues is notable for its overtones: "Is not she [Thea] lovely to look at?" Loevborg asks. Hedda, lightly stroking Thea's hair, answers, "Only to look at?" Loevborg understands the innuendo, for he replies, "Yes. For we two — she and I — we two are real comrades." Later, when the women are alone, Hedda,

---

[2] Cf. Ibsen's statement: "I firmly believe in the capacity for procreation and development of ideals" (*Speeches and New Letters*, p. 57).

now fully informed of the extent to which Thea has realized her generative powers, laments her own meager endowment and renews her threat in its adolescent terms:

> Oh, if you could only understand how poor I am, and fate has made you so rich! (*Clasps her passionately in her arms.*) I think I must burn your hair off after all.

Hedda's violent gesture and Thea's almost hysterical reaction ("Let me go! Let me go! I am afraid of you, Hedda!") indicate the dangerous seriousness of words which otherwise might be mistaken for a joke; the threat prepares us for the burning of the manuscript, which follows in Act III. In the last tense scene of the play Hedda twice handles Thea's hair. The reader's imagination readily constructs the expressions and gestures whereby an actress could show Hedda's true attitude toward the hair which Ibsen directs her to ruffle "gently" and to pass her hands "softly through." The first gesture follows immediately upon an important action — Hedda has just removed the pistol to the inner room. The second accompanies dialogue which for the last time emphasizes Hedda's association of the hair with Thea's fertility and which brings home to Hedda her own predicament:

> HEDDA (*passes her hands softly through Mrs. Elvsted's hair*): Doesn't it seem strange to you, Thea? Here you are sitting with Tesman — just as you used to sit with Eilert Loevborg?
> MRS. ELVSTED: Ah, if I could only inspire your husband in the same way!
> HEDDA: Oh, that will come too — in time.
> TESMAN: Yes, do you know, Hedda — I really think I begin to feel something of the sort. But won't you go to sit with Brack again?
> HEDDA: Is there nothing I can do to help you two?
> TESMAN: No, nothing in the world.

These scenes in which the hair plays a part not only call attention to Hedda's limitations but show her reaction to her partial apprehension of them. In adapting a primitive symbol, Ibsen slightly altered its conventional meaning, substituting psychic for physical potency. Its primitivistic associations nevertheless pervade the fundamental relationships between the two women. The weapons Hedda uses against Thea are her hands and fire. The shock of the climactic scene results chiefly from seeing the savage emerge from behind her veneer of sophistication — the Hedda who feeds the manuscript to the flames is a naked woman engaged in a barbaric act. In contrast, the Hedda who handles her father's pistols is self-consciously cloaked in illusions of her hereditary participation in a chivalric tradition.

The pistols, like many other symbols used by Ibsen, quite obviously are not merely symbols, but have important plot function as well. Moreover, their symbolic significance cannot be reduced to a simple formula, but must be thought of in the light of the complex of associations which they carry as Hedda's legacy from General Gabler. Through Hedda's attitude toward and uses of the pistols, Ibsen constantly reminds us that Hedda "is to be regarded rather as her father's daughter than as her husband's wife."[3] Clearly the pistols are linked with certain values in her background which Hedda cherishes. Complete definition of these values is difficult without a more thorough knowledge of Ibsen's conception of

---

[3]*The Correspondence of Henrik Ibsen*, trans. & ed. by Mary Morison (London, 1905), p. 435.

a Norwegian general than the play or contemporary comment on it allows. Perhaps, as Brandes said, nineteenth-century audiences recognized that Hedda's pretensions to dignity and grandeur as a general's daughter were falsely based, "that a Norwegian general is a cavalry officer, who as a rule, has never smelt powder, and whose pistols are innocent of bloodshed."[4] Such a realization, however, by no means nullifies the *theoretical* attributes and privileges of generalship to which Hedda aspires. Possibly Ibsen intended us to understand that Hedda is a member of a second generation of "ham actors" who betray their proud tradition by their melodramatic posturings. But it is this tradition, however ignoble its carrier, to which the pistols and Hedda (in her own mind) belong, and it is, after all, the general only as glimpsed through his daughter's ambitions and conceptions of worth that is of real importance in the play. These conceptions, as embodied in Hedda's romantic ideal of manhood, may be synthesized from the action and dialogue. The aristocrat possesses, above all, courage and self-control. He expresses himself through direct and independent action, living to capacity and scorning security and public opinion. Danger only piques his appetite, and death with honor is the victory to be plucked from defeat. But the recklessness of this Hotspur is tempered by a disciplined will, by means of which he "beautifully" orders both his own actions and those of others on whom his power is imposed. Such a one uses his pistols with deliberation, with calculated aim. He shoots straight — to defend his life or his honor, and to maintain his authority. Pistols, however, have an intrinsic glamor. Of the several possible accoutrements of a general, his pistols are those least likely to evoke thoughts of chivalric principles and most likely to recall the menace of the power vested in him. And such power, as *Hedda Gabler* shows us, delivered into the hands of a confused and irresponsible egotist, brings only meaningless destruction to all who come within its range.

The manipulation of the pistols throughout the play is a mockery of their traditional role. Except at target practice, Hedda does not even shoot straight until her suicide. Her potential danger is recognized by both men whom she threatens, but both understand (Brack, immediately; Loevborg, in Act II) that her threat is a theatrical gesture and that she has no real intention of acting directly, in defiance of the conventions which bid her "go roundabout." Her crass dishonesty in her sexual encounters is highlighted by this gun play. She uses the pistols, to be sure, to ward off or warn off encroachments upon her "honor." This honor, however, is rooted in social expedience rather than in a moral code. Having indirectly encouraged Loevborg by a succession of intimate *tête-à-têtes,* she poses as an outraged maiden when he makes amorous advances, thereby, as she later hints, thwarting her own emotional needs. Subsequently she sells her body to Tesman as cynically as (and far less honestly than) Madame Diana[5] sells hers, then deliberately participates in the form, if not the substance, of marital infidelity with Brack in order to relieve her boredom. Both Hedda and Brack become aware of the cold ruthlessness of the other and the consequent danger to the loser if the delicate equilibrium of their relationship should be disturbed. But until the end Brack is so complacently convinced that Hedda is his female counterpart that he has no fear she will do more than shoot over

---

[4]Georg Brandes, *Henrik Ibsen. Björnstjerne Björnson: Critical Studies* (New York, 1899), p. 94.

[5]Madame Danielle in Meyer's translation.

his head; even as she lies dead, he can hardly believe that she has resorted to direct action — "People don't do such things."

The part the pistols play in Loevborg's death makes a central contribution to our understanding of the degree to which the ideals they represent are distorted by the clouded perspective from which Hedda views them. She has no real comprehension of, nor interest in, the vital creative powers Thea helps Loevborg to realize. Instead, she glorifies his weaknesses, mistaking bravado for courage, the indulgence of physical appetites for godlike participation in "the banquet of life," a flight from reality for a heroic quest for totality of experience. Even more important is the fact that as she inhibits her own instinctive urge for fulfillment, she romanticizes its converse. Thus, having instigated his ruin, she incites Loevborg to commit suicide with her pistol. This radical denial of the will to live she arbitrarily invests with the heroism and beauty one associates with a sacrificial death; Hedda is incapable of making the distinction between an exhibitionistic gesture which inflates the ego and the tragic death, in which the ego is sublimated in order that the values of life may be extended and reborn.

Her inability to perceive the difference between melodrama and tragedy accounts for the disparity between Hedda's presumptive view of her own suicide and our evaluation of its significance. Ibsen with diabolical irony arranged a situation which bears close superficial resemblance to the traditional tragic end. Symbolically withdrawing herself from the bourgeois environment into the inner chamber which contains the relics of her earlier life, Hedda plays a "wild dance" upon her piano and, beneath her father's portrait, shoots herself "beautifully" through the temple with her father's pistol. She dies to vindicate her heritage of independence; with disciplined and direct aim she at last defeats the Boyg, which hitherto she has unsuccessfully attempted to circumvent. So Hedda would see her death, we are led to believe, could she be both principal and spectator; and no doubt she would find high-sounding phrases with which to memorialize it. But of course it is Brack and Tesman who have the curtain lines, and these lines show how little of her intent Hedda has conveyed to her world. And we, having the opportunity to judge the act with relation to its full context, may properly interpret it as the final self-dramatization of the consistently sterile protagonist. Hedda gains no insight; her death affirms nothing of importance. She never understands why, at her touch, everything becomes "ludicrous and mean." She dies to escape a sordid situation that is largely of her own making; she will not face reality nor assume responsibility for the consequences of her acts. The pistols, having descended to a coward and a cheat, bring only death without honor.

It would appear, then, that the symbols, while they do not carry the whole thematic burden of *Hedda Gabler*, illuminate the meaning of the characters and the action with which they are associated. As Eric Bentley has suggested, the characters, like those in the other plays of Ibsen's last period, are the living dead who dwell in a waste-land that resembles T. S. Eliot's. And, like Eliot later, Ibsen emphasized the aridity of the present by contrasting it with the heroic past. Indeed, *Hedda Gabler* may be thought of as a mock-tragedy, a sardonically contrived travesty of tragic action, which Ibsen shows us is no longer possible in the world of the play. This world is sick with a disease less curable than that of Oedipus's Thebes or Hamlet's Denmark. For its hereditary leaders are shrunken in stature, maimed and paralyzed by their enslavement to the ideals of the dominant middle class. With the other hollow men, they despise but nonetheless worship the false gods of respectability and security, paying only lip service to their ancestral principles. Such geniuses as this society produces are, when left to themselves, too weak to do more than batter their own heads against constricting barriers. They dissipate their talents and so fail in their mission as prophets and disseminators of Western culture; its interpretation is left to the unimaginative pedant, picking over the dry bones of the past. Women, the natural seminal vesicles of that culture, the mothers of the future, are those most cruelly inhibited by the sterilizing atmosphere of their environment. At one extreme is Aunt Julia, the genteel spinster, overcompensating for her starved emotions with obsessive self-dedication. At the other is Diana, the harlot. Even Thea, the progenitive spirit, the girl with the abundant hair, is a frail and colorless repository for the seeds of generation. Her break with convention when it threatens her maternity is shown to be the one mode of escape from the fate that overtakes the others. But Ibsen gives her triumph, too, a ludicrous twist. Hardly having begun the mourning song for her Adonis, she brings forth her embryonic offspring from her pocket and proceeds to mold it into shape with the aid of a Tesman — an echo of the classic death and rebirth, to be sure, but one not likely to produce the glorious Third Kingdom of which Ibsen dreamed. And appropriately holding the center of the stage throughout is Hedda, in whom the shadows of the past still struggle in a losing battle with the sterile specter of the present. Her pistols are engraved with insignia which the others understand not at all and which she only dimly comprehends. Her colossal egotism, her lack of self-knowledge, her cowardice, render her search for fulfillment but a succession of futile blunders which culminate in the supreme futility of death. Like Peer Gynt, she is fit only for the ladle of the button-molder;[6] she fails to realize a capacity either for great good or for great evil. Her mirror-image wears the mask of tragedy, but Ibsen makes certain that we see the horns and pointed ears of the satyr protruding from behind it.

Jan Kott (b. 1914)
ON HEDDA GABLER

Jan Kott is one of the most interesting modern commentators on drama. His book Shakespeare Our Contemporary *(1964) established him as having original insights into Shakespeare's plays. But his comments on most major playwrights show him to be equally original in interpreting Ibsen, as he does here. His sexual analysis of Hedda's pistols introduces important levels of metaphor into a play that is already laden with sexual imagery.*

Chekhov wrote: "If in the first act a gun hangs on the wall, in the last act it must go off." In laying down this dramatic precept, he must surely have had *Hedda Gabler* in mind. Hedda inherits two pistols from her father. She fires the first one over Judge Brack's head when he approaches the house from the

[6]At the end of Ibsen's play *Peer Gynt*, the Button Molder tries to melt Peer in his ladle, an action that symbolizes loss of identity.

garden; and again at the end, when she shoots herself. The other pistol is fired offstage. It kills Eilert Loevborg. But the two pistols in *Hedda Gabler* are not only props exploited by Ibsen with iron-clad dramatic logic and preordained consequences; they also have sexual undertones. A Scandinavian Madame Bovary, well read in romantic novels, gives Loevborg a pistol: "use it now . . . and beautifully." But the fatal shot wounds him "in the stomach — more or less," and is fired in the parlor of the red-haired Mademoiselle Diana.[1]

Ibsen's setting for *Hedda Gabler* is striking. The action takes place in a spacious salon with French windows which open out on a veranda and a garden in the "fashionable part of town," not a fjord. The windows are curtained; the theater had already learned the advantages of gaslight.

In the first scene, Hedda orders the curtains drawn. She can't stand sunlight. This is our first glimpse of her character. The salon is spacious and the furniture arrangement makes it possible for two separate conversations to be carried on at the same time. The old-fashioned *a parte*[2] is no longer necessary. Chekhov borrowed this "contrapuntal" dialogue from Ibsen and masterfully refined it.

The crucial part of the stage design is the room in the background, with a huge portrait of "a handsome, elderly man in a general's uniform" hanging on the wall behind the sofa. In the last scene Hedda will enter this room, draw the curtains, and shoot herself in front of her father's portrait. Hedda Tesman, two months pregnant, kills Hedda Gabler. The inner room, whose only exit leads to the salon in the foreground, is at once the concrete and the symbolic setting of the conflict between the Father/superego and the id. By shooting herself, Hedda kills the shadow of her Father and the child she never wanted. The "shadow" of the father kills the daughter. In contrast to the earlier dramas [by Ibsen], *Lady from the Sea* and *Rosmersholm*, where the prehistory of the conflicts, traumas, and sexual complexes festers beneath the surface, and though continuing to grow they are never seen, in *Hedda Gabler* nothing remains unspoken.

In this case study of a neurosis, the mother's place is left empty. Hedda was raised by her father, who would have preferred a son. She rode horses and learned to shoot guns. In school, like a tomboy, she pulled her girlfriends' hair. She can barely resist pulling Thea's blond locks in Act II. In the last *Hedda Gabler* I saw, in Bochum in 1977, Peter Zadek directed the scene of Hedda's and Thea's drinking bout with distinct lesbian undertones. It is an extreme though not arbitrary reading of the text. In this record of sexual neurosis, the inversion and displacement of libido are intended. Thirty-year-old Hedda Gabler is frigid.

General Gabler's daughter not only wants to rule in a man's world. Unable to assume her female sexual role, she escapes by playing out the male one in her imagination. She demands that Loevborg initiate her into masculine rites and describe his visits to the red-haired Diana. Imaginary sex is vicarious. Hedda, rejecting the traditional roles of wife and mother, is condemned to live vicariously, full of the frustration and sense of emptiness which she calls deadly boredom. Madame Bovary's love affairs with shallow men were substitutions for the romantic ecstasies she read about in contemporary novels. For General Gabler's

[1]Madame Danielle in Meyer's translation.
[2]*a parte*: Keeping different conversations separate from one another as if in different spaces.

daughter these flights and escapes are ruled out. She has only her inner room "with its heavy curtains and her father's portrait."

It is not only sexual fulfillment that Hedda strives for through imagination. Until the very last scene, all her passions and hatreds are realized only by acts of substitution. The manuscript of Loevborg's new book is twice called his and Thea's "child"; Hedda commits a substitute "infanticide" by burning it in the fireplace. The pistol shot above Judge Brack's head was a substitute murder and a substitute sexual act. Fear paralyzed her twice before: once when she was afraid to shoot Loevborg for his aggressive advances, and then a second time when she was afraid to sleep with him. Handing the pistol to Loevborg is murder by intent: the shot that kills him, in keeping with the logic of the dramaturgy, symbolically castrates him as well.

In coded messages, myths, dreams, and unconscious acts, opposite terms are interchangeable: they assume the guise of their antitheses. As in Racine and Chekhov (although in Chekhov it is deeply hidden), the appeal of death in Ibsen disguises itself as the pulse of life, the instinct toward self-destruction is masked as libido. *Hedda Gabler* appears to return to the realistic technique of the earlier dramas, but along with *Rosmersholm*, it marks the beginning of Ibsen's last cycle of plays, from *Little Eyolf* to *When We Dead Awaken*, each of which repeats the theme of sexual frustration leading to self-destruction. With the exception of his final masterpiece, *John Gabriel Borkman*, in all these plays the balance between the realistic world and its symbolic projection is broken.

In his biography of Ibsen (1957), Michael Meyer entitled his chapter on *Hedda Gabler* "Portrait of the Dramatist as a Young Woman." "*Madame Bovary — c'est moi,*" Flaubert once wrote, and Hedda Gabler is in some sense Ibsen's alter ego. The psychoanalysis of Hedda would no doubt become the merciless psychoanalysis of her author. But in psychoanalytic interpretations of the author or of his work Ibsen's invention and artistic discoveries are usually neglected, and what is even more important, the historical context, the customs and atmospheric realism of the *fin de siècle*,[3] are altogether lost.

Ibsen never read a page of Freud. Neither did Strindberg. In the early 1890s Freud began his first methodical studies of hysteria; in 1895 he announced his first analysis of dreams; and he used the term "psychoanalysis" for the first time in 1896. The Scandinavian Miss Julies and Heddas were finding their dramatists in Strindberg and Ibsen while the Viennese Julies and Heddas were finding their analyst in Freud.

[3]*fin de siècle:* Turn of the century.

August Strindberg

August Strindberg (1849–1912) was one of the pioneers of literary naturalism in Scandinavia. He was born to parents whose social situation was a bit unusual for the age. His father's family did not have a great deal of wealth, but it was considered very respectable nonetheless. His mother had been a servant. This disjunction between the status of mother and father was the source of a great deal of unhappiness in the family, and Strindberg himself was so distraught as a young person that he was sure that his parents did not love him. In mid-nineteenth-century Stockholm, distinctions in social status were much more attended to than they are today.

The society Strindberg grew up in was essentially quite comfortable. It was bourgeois — which is to say self-satisfied and well-to-do — and in most things it was very conservative. He decided early to work in a naturalistic mode, to portray life as he saw it and not to avoid calling his audiences' attention to unpleasant realities. Naturalism was dedicated to representing life with as much simple fidelity to facts as possible, to the point of presenting dramatic moments as if they were "slices of life." His decision to work within naturalism was extremely painful to Strindberg because, to a great extent, it cost him a large audience.

In Strindberg's time naturalism was thought to be synonymous with vulgarity, an explicit insult to polite society. His major plays, *The Father* (1887) and *Creditors* (1889), were denounced at one time in Sweden and elsewhere. His first play, *Master Olof* (1872), was denied production at the Royal Dramatic Theater because it was much too realistic in its portrayal of Swedish heroes. It made an effort to tell the truth, and the theater rejected it. It has since been recognized as the first great drama written by a Swede. Later, in 1879, Strindberg wrote a realistic novel based on his experiences in Stockholm; while it was denounced on all sides, *The Red Room* made him almost instantly famous.

During his early years he made a living as a translator and journalist, among other professions. He married three times, but none of his marriages lasted very long. One of his collections of short stories is called *Married* (1886), and it shocked Stockholm because it was much more frank about sexual matters than any Swedish fiction had ever been. Paradoxically, Strindberg was very conservative about the role of women in society, preferring that they stay home and tend to their husbands. In the later nineteenth century, this conservative view made him unwelcome in the circles of liberal intellectuals in Sweden despite the success of *Miss Julie* (1888).

At one point he went into voluntary exile and his enemies charged him with blasphemy in the courts forcing him to return to Sweden to defend himself. He was acquitted, but he always felt thereafter that he was being persecuted in Sweden. After a period of mental crisis in which he went almost completely mad, Strindberg became convinced that the occult held all the secrets that would restore him to prominence and ease his financial stress.

His period of instability was recorded in a book called *Inferno* (1897), and after he returned to sanity he wrote another twenty-nine plays and many other works. Plays such as *There Are Crimes and Crimes* (1899), *Easter, The Dance of Death* (both 1901), and *A Dream Play* (1902) all date from this period.

Throughout his career, Strindberg was a misogynist. His distrust of women and his sense that they were best occupied in supporting a man were central to his thinking. Such attitudes contributed to the breakup of his three marriages.

Some of Strindberg's final works move away from realism and toward a powerful expressionism. EXPRESSIONISM disregarded the strict demands of realism and used materials that resembled dreams — or nightmares. Strindberg's work has had profound influence on a number of modern playwrights. In some ways, he is the first of the modern dramatists.

MISS JULIE

Like Strindberg's parents, Miss Julie, daughter of a count, and Jean, the count's valet, come from different social strata. Though *Miss Julie* (1888) may owe something to Strindberg's family background, it is certainly not clear that the play was in any way autobiographical or that it described his parents' relationship.

The play is intense, produced, as it would have occurred in life, without an intermission. Miss Julie had a fiancé, but he has been disposed of before the play begins because he refuses to debase himself slavishly to her will. She is a free spirit, but her breeding is suspect because her mother, like her, took a lover and defied the Count. Miss Julie's mother raised her to think like a man, to have the same independent spirit as a man. To get back at her husband, Miss Julie's mother burned the house down after the insurance expired. Moreover, she arranged to have her lover loan the Count the money to rebuild it.

Miss Julie was raised to manipulate men, but she cannot accept them totally. She also seems to feel a mixture of contempt for herself as a woman along with her contempt for men. In his foreward to the play, Strindberg says that Julie is a modern "half-woman" "man-hater" who sells herself for honors of various kinds. His comments reveal his misogyny — the reverse of modern feminism.

The play has a mysterious quality. It takes place on Midsummer Eve, when lovers are sometimes revealed to one another and when almost anything can happen. In primitive fertility rites it was a time associated with sexual awakening. Kristine mentions that it is the feast of St. John and alludes to his beheading for spurning Salome's advances. Jean, French for John, in one violent moment of the play beheads Julie's pet bird as a sign of the violence that lies pent up in him.

The fairy-tale quality that creeps into the play — as in *A Midsummer Night's Dream,* set on the same day — may seem out of place in a realistic drama, but it is profoundly compelling. It is also typical of Strindberg, who often uses a form of expressionism to explore a dream quality and deepen the significance of the action. Dreams are a part of reality that modern playwrights have taken great pains to explore.

The Count himself is nightmarish. He never appears in the play, but his presence is always ominous and intense, very much as in folktale or fairy tale. Jean tells Miss Julie that he would willingly kill himself if the Count were to order it. The cook, Kristine, is like a witch, demanding retribution because she was spurned by Jean, who once was her lover. Near the end of the play she prevents Julie and Jean from running away from the Count by impounding the horses in the stable. She has her revenge on both of them.

Although Julie may be seen as the princess, Jean has very little claim to being Prince Charming of the play, especially since he has little strength of character. He feels superior to his station as a valet, and Strindberg in his foreword refers to him as a nobleman. However, like Kristine, he is slavish. His highest ambition is to be the proprietor of a first-class hotel, a prospect he wants to share with Julie.

One of the most striking passages in the play is the dream that Jean reveals to Julie. He portrays himself as having found his way into an "enchanted" garden. He exits through the outhouse only to come upon a vision of Julie dressed in pink and white. The dream is fairy-tale-like, including elements of sexual mystery and desire, of an awareness of inferiority, and of a longing for innocence. By contrast, Miss Julie dreams of desperately trying to descend from a pillar.

The fairy tale has a special value in Scandinavia, which produced Hans Christian Andersen and the Brothers Grimm. In an otherwise naturalistic play, the invocation of the power of myth expands the psychological dimension of the individual characters and intensifies the impact of the play on the audience.

Miss Julie depends on intensity. It moves swiftly to its conclusion. The contrast between the willfulness of Julie and the caution of Jean makes their situation especially desperate. When Julie leaves at the end of the play to seal her fate, we sense the terrible weight of their society's values. Those values are symbolized by the return of the Count and the expectations he had of Julie's behavior while he was gone.

August Strindberg (1849–1912)

MISS JULIE   *1888*
TRANSLATED BY HARRY G. CARLSON

Characters

MISS JULIE, *25 years old*
JEAN, *her father's valet, 30 years old*
KRISTINE, *her father's cook, 35 years old*

(*The action takes place in the count's kitchen on midsummer eve.*)

Setting: (*A large kitchen, the ceiling and side walls of which are hidden by draperies. The rear wall runs diagonally from down left to up right. On the wall down left are two shelves with copper, iron, and pewter utensils; the shelves are lined with scalloped paper. Visible to the right is most of a set of large, arched glass doors, through which can be seen a fountain with a statue of Cupid, lilac bushes in bloom, and the tops of some Lombardy poplars. At down left is the corner of a large tiled stove; a portion of its hood is showing. At right, one end of the servants' white pine dining table juts out; several chairs stand around it. The stove is decorated with birch branches; juniper twigs are strewn on the floor. On the end of the table stands a large Japanese spice jar, filled with lilac blossoms. An ice box, a sink, and a washstand. Above the door is an old-fashioned bell on a spring; to the left of the door, the mouthpiece of a speaking tube is visible.*)

(*Kristine is frying something on the stove. She is wearing a light-colored cotton dress and an apron. Jean enters. He is wearing livery and carries a pair of high riding boots with spurs, which he puts down on the floor where they can be seen by the audience.*)

JEAN: Miss Julie's crazy again tonight; absolutely crazy!
KRISTINE: So you finally came back?
JEAN: I took the Count to the station and when I returned past the barn I stopped in for a dance. Who do I see but Miss Julie leading off the dance with the gamekeeper! But as soon as she saw me she rushed over to ask me for the next waltz. And she's been waltzing ever since — I've never seen anything like it. She's crazy!
KRISTINE: She always has been, but never as bad as the last two weeks since her engagement was broken off.
JEAN: Yes, I wonder what the real story was there. He was a gentleman, even if he wasn't rich. Ah! These people have such romantic ideas. (*Sits at the end of the table.*) Still, it's strange, isn't it? I mean that she'd rather stay home with the servants on midsummer eve instead of going with her father to visit relatives?
KRISTINE: She's probably embarrassed after that row with her fiancé.
JEAN: Probably! He gave a good account of himself, though. Do you know how it happened, Kristine? I saw it, you know, though I didn't let on I had.
KRISTINE: No! You saw it?
JEAN: Yes, I did. —— That evening they were out near the stable, and she was "training" him — as she called it. Do you know what she did? She made him jump over her riding crop, the way you'd teach a dog to jump. He jumped twice and she hit him each time. But the third time he grabbed the crop out of her hand, hit her with it across the cheek, and broke it in pieces. Then he left.
KRISTINE: So, that's what happened! I can't believe it!
JEAN: Yes, that's the way it went! —— What have you got for me that's tasty, Kristine?
KRISTINE (*serving him from the pan*): Oh, it's only a piece of kidney I cut from the veal roast.
JEAN (*smelling the food*): Beautiful! That's my favorite *délice.*° (*Feeling the plate.*) But you could have warmed the plate!

---

délice: Delight.

KRISTINE: You're fussier than the Count himself, once you start! (*She pulls his hair affectionately.*)

JEAN (*angry*): Stop it, leave my hair alone! You know I'm touchy about that.

KRISTINE: Now, now, it's only love, you know that. (*Jean eats. Kristine opens a bottle of beer.*)

JEAN: Beer? On midsummer eve? No thank you! I can do better than that. (*Opens a drawer in the table and takes out a bottle of red wine with yellow sealing wax.*) See that? Yellow seal! Give me a glass! A wine glass! I'm drinking this *pur*.°

KRISTINE (*returns to the stove and puts on a small saucepan*): God help the woman who gets you for a husband! What a fussbudget.

JEAN: Nonsense! You'd be damned lucky to get a man like me. It certainly hasn't done you any harm to have people call me your sweetheart. (*Tastes the wine.*) Good! Very good! Just needs a little warming. (*Warms the glass between his hands.*) We bought this in Dijon. Four francs a liter, not counting the cost of the bottle, or the customs duty. ——— What are you cooking now? It stinks like hell!

KRISTINE: Oh, some slop Miss Julie wants to give Diana.

JEAN: Watch your language, Kristine. But why should you have to cook for that damn mutt on midsummer eve? Is she sick?

KRISTINE: Yes, she's sick! She sneaked out with the gatekeeper's dog — and now there's hell to pay. Miss Julie won't have it!

JEAN: Miss Julie has too much pride about some things and not enough about others, just like her mother was. The Countess was most at home in the kitchen and the cowsheds, but a *one*-horse carriage wasn't elegant enough for her. The cuffs of her blouse were dirty, but she had to have her coat of arms on her cufflinks. ——— And Miss Julie won't take proper care of herself either. If you ask me, she just isn't refined. Just now, when she was dancing in the barn, she pulled the gamekeeper away from Anna and made him dance with her. *We* wouldn't behave like that, but that's what happens when aristocrats pretend they're common people — they get *common!* ——— But she is quite a woman! Magnificent! What shoulders, and what — et cetera!

KRISTINE: Oh, don't overdo it! I've heard what Clara says, and she dresses her.

JEAN: Ha, Clara! You're all jealous of each other! I've been out riding with her. . . . And the way she dances!

KRISTINE: Listen, Jean! You've going to dance with me, when I'm finished here, aren't you?

JEAN: Of course I will.

KRISTINE: Promise?

JEAN: Promise? When I say I'll do something, I do it! By the way, the kidney was very good. (*Corks the bottle.*)

JULIE (*in the doorway to someone outside*): I'll be right back! You go ahead for now! (*Jean sneaks the bottle back into the table drawer and gets up respectfully. Miss Julie enters and crosses to Kristine by the stove.*) Well? Is it ready? (*Kristine indicates that Jean is present.*)

JEAN (*gallantly*): Are you ladies up to something secret?

JULIE (*flicking her handkerchief in his face*): None of your business!

JEAN: Hmm! I like the smell of violets!

JULIE (*coquettishly*): Shame on you! So you know about perfumes, too? You certainly know how to dance. Ah, ah! No peeking! Go away.

JEAN (*boldly but respectfully*): Are you brewing up a magic potion for midsummer eve? Something to prophesy by under a lucky star, so you'll catch a glimpse of your future husband!

JULIE (*caustically*): You'd need sharp eyes to see him! (*To Kristine.*) Pour out half a bottle and cork it well. ——— Come and dance a schottische° with me, Jean . . .

JEAN (*hesitating*): I don't want to be impolite to anyone, and I've already promised this dance to Kristine . . .

JULIE: Oh, she can have another one — can't you, Kristine? Won't you lend me Jean?

KRISTINE: It's not up to me, ma'am. (*To Jean.*) If the mistress is so generous, it wouldn't do for you to say no. Go on, Jean, and thank her for the honor.

JEAN: To be honest, and no offense intended, I wonder whether it's wise for you to dance twice running with the same partner, especially since these people are quick to jump to conclusions . . .

JULIE (*flaring up*): What's that? What sort of conclusions? What do you mean?

JEAN (*submissively*): If you don't understand, ma'am, I must speak more plainly. It doesn't look good to play favorites with your servants. . . .

JULIE: Play favorites! What an idea! I'm astonished! As mistress of the house, I honor your dance with my presence. And when I dance, I want to dance with someone who can lead, so I won't look ridiculous.

JEAN: As you order, ma'am! I'm at your service!

JULIE (*gently*): Don't take it as an order! On a night like this we're all just ordinary people having fun, so we'll forget about rank. Now, take my arm! ——— Don't worry, Kristine! I won't steal your

---

pur: Pure; the first drink from the bottle.

schottische: A Scottish round dance resembling a polka.

sweetheart! (*Jean offers his arm and leads Miss Julie out.*)

Mime

(*The following should be played as if the actress playing Kristine were really alone. When she has to, she turns her back to the audience. She does not look toward them, nor does she hurry as if she were afraid they would grow impatient. Schottische music played on a fiddle sounds in the distance. Kristine hums along with the music. She clears the table, washes the dishes, dries them, and puts them away. She takes off her apron. From a table drawer she removes a small mirror and leans it against the bowl of lilacs on the table. She lights a candle, heats a hairpin over the flame, and uses it to set a curl on her forehead. She crosses to the door and listens, then returns to the table. She finds the handkerchief Miss Julie left behind, picks it up, and smells it. Then, preoccupied, she spreads it out, stretches it, smoothes out the wrinkles, and folds it into quarters, and so forth.*)

JEAN (*enters alone*): God, she really *is* crazy! What a way to dance! Everybody's laughing at her behind her back. What do you make of it, Kristine?

KRISTINE: Ah! It's that time of the month for her, and she always gets peculiar like that. Are you going to dance with me now?

JEAN: You're not mad at me, are you, for leaving . . . ?

KRISTINE: Of course not! ——— Why should I be, for a little thing like that? Besides, I know my place . . .

JEAN (*puts his arm around her waist*): You're a sensible girl, Kristine, and you'd make a good wife . . .

JULIE (*entering; uncomfortably surprised; with forced good humor*): What a charming escort — running away from his partner.

JEAN: On the contrary, Miss Julie. Don't you see how I rushed back to the partner I abandoned!

JULIE (*changing her tone*): You know, you're a superb dancer! ——— But why are you wearing livery on a holiday? Take it off at once!

JEAN: Then I must ask you to go outside for a moment. You see, my black coat is hanging over here . . . (*Gestures and crosses right.*)

JULIE: Are you embarrassed about changing your coat in front of me? Well, go in your room then. Either that or stay and I'll turn my back.

JEAN: With your permission, ma'am! (*He crosses right. His arm is visible as he changes his jacket.*)

JULIE (*to Kristine*): Tell me, Kristine — you two are so close —. Is Jean your fiancé?

KRISTINE: Fiancé? Yes, if you wish. We can call him that.

JULIE: What do you mean?

KRISTINE: You had a fiancé yourself, didn't you? So . . .

JULIE: Well, we were properly engaged . . .

KRISTINE: But nothing came of it, did it? (*Jean returns dressed in a frock coat and bowler hat.*)

JULIE: *Très gentil, monsieur Jean! Très gentil!*

JEAN: *Vous voulez plaisanter, madame!*

JULIE: *Et vous voulez parler français!°* Where did you learn that?

JEAN: In Switzerland, when I was wine steward in one of the biggest hotels in Lucerne!

JULIE: You look like a real gentleman in that coat! *Charmant!°* (*Sits at the table.*)

JEAN: Oh, you're flattering me!

JULIE (*offended*): Flattering you?

JEAN: My natural modesty forbids me to believe that you would really compliment someone like me, and so I took the liberty of assuming that you were exaggerating, which polite people call flattering.

JULIE: Where did you learn to talk like that? You must have been to the theater often.

JEAN: Of course. And I've done a lot of traveling.

JULIE: But you come from here, don't you?

JEAN: My father was a farmhand on the district attorney's estate nearby. I used to see you when you were little, but you never noticed me.

JULIE: No! Really?

JEAN: Sure. I remember one time especially . . . but I can't talk about that.

JULIE: Oh, come now! Why not? Just this once!

JEAN: No, I really couldn't, not now. Some other time, perhaps.

JULIE: Why some other time? What's so dangerous about now?

JEAN: It's not dangerous, but there are obstacles. ——— Her, for example. (*Indicating Kristine, who has fallen asleep in a chair by the stove.*)

JULIE: What a pleasant wife she'll make! She probably snores, too.

JEAN: No, she doesn't, but she talks in her sleep.

JULIE (*cynically*): How do *you* know?

JEAN (*audaciously*): I've heard her! (*Pause, during which they stare at each other.*)

JULIE: Why don't you sit down?

JEAN: I couldn't do that in your presence.

JULIE: But if I order you to?

JEAN: Then I'd obey.

Très gentil . . . français!:
    Very pleasing, Mr. Jean! Very pleasing.
    You would trifle with me, madam!
    And you want to speak French!
Charmant: Charming.

JULIE: Sit down, then. ——— No, wait. Can you get me something to drink first?

JEAN: I don't know what we have in the ice box. I think there's only beer.

JULIE: Why do you say "only"? My tastes are so simple I prefer beer to wine. (*Jean takes a bottle of beer from the ice box and opens it. He looks for a glass and a plate in the cupboard and serves her.*)

JEAN: Here you are, ma'am.

JULIE: Thank you. Won't you have something yourself?

JEAN: I'm not partial to beer, but if it's an order . . .

JULIE: An order? ——— Surely a gentleman can keep his lady company.

JEAN: You're right, of course. (*Opens a bottle and gets a glass.*)

JULIE: Now, drink to my health! (*He hesitates.*) What? A man of the world — and shy?

JEAN (*in mock romantic fashion, he kneels and raises his glass*): Skål to my mistress!

JULIE: Bravo! ——— Now kiss my shoe, to finish it properly. (*Jean hesitates, then boldly seizes her foot and kisses it lightly.*) Perfect! You should have been an actor.

JEAN (*rising*): That's enough now, Miss Julie! Someone might come in and see us.

JULIE: What of it?

JEAN: People talk, that's what! If you knew how their tongues were wagging just now at the dance, you'd . . .

JULIE: What were they saying? Tell me! ——— Sit down!

JEAN (*sits*): I don't want to hurt you, but they were sayings things ——— suggestive things, that, that . . . well, you can figure it out for yourself! You're not a child. If a woman is seen drinking alone with a man — let alone a servant — at night — then . . .

JULIE: Then what? Besides, we're not alone. Kristine is here.

JEAN: Asleep!

JULIE: Then I'll wake her up. (*Rising.*) Kristine! Are you asleep? (*Kristine mumbles in her sleep.*)

JULIE: Kristine! ——— She certainly can sleep!

KRISTINE (*in her sleep*): The Count's boots are brushed — put the coffee on — right away, right away — uh, huh — oh!

JULIE (*grabbing Kristine's nose*): Will you wake up!

JEAN (*severely*): Leave her alone — let her sleep!

JULIE (*sharply*): What?

JEAN: Someone who's been standing over a stove all day has a right to be tired by now. Sleep should be respected . . .

JULIE (*changing her tone*): What a considerate thought — it does you credit — thank you! (*Offering her hand.*) Come outside and pick some lilacs for me!

(*During the following, Kristine awakens and shambles sleepily off right to bed.*)

JEAN: Go with you?

JULIE: With me!

JEAN: We couldn't do that! Absolutely not!

JULIE: I don't understand. Surely you don't imagine . . .

JEAN: No, I don't, but the others might.

JULIE: What? That I've fallen in love with a servant?

JEAN: I'm not a conceited man, but such things happen — and for these people, nothing is sacred.

JULIE: I do believe you're an aristocrat!

JEAN: Yes, I am.

JULIE: And I'm stepping down . . .

JEAN: Don't step down, Miss Julie, take my advice. No one'll believe you stepped down voluntarily. People will always say you fell.

JULIE: I have a higher opinion of people than you. Come and see! ——— Come! (*She stares at him broodingly.*)

JEAN: You're very strange, do you know that?

JULIE: Perhaps! But so are you! ——— For that matter, everything is strange. Life, people, everything. Like floating scum, drifting on and on across the water, until it sinks down and down! That reminds me of a dream I have now and then. I've climbed up on top of a pillar. I sit there and see no way of getting down. I get dizzy when I look down, and I must get down, but I don't have the courage to jump. I can't hold on firmly, and I long to be able to fall, but I don't fall. And yet I'll have no peace until I get down, no rest unless I get down, down on the ground! And if I did get down to the ground, I'd want to be under the earth . . . Have you ever felt anything like that?

JEAN: No. I dream that I'm lying under a high tree in a dark forest. I want to get up, up on top, and look out over the bright landscape, where the sun is shining, and plunder the bird's nest up there, where the golden eggs lie. And I climb and climb, but the trunk's so thick and smooth, and it's so far to the first branch. But I know if I just reached that first branch, I'd go right to the top, like up a ladder. I haven't reached it yet, but I will, even if it's only in a dream!

JULIE: Here I am chattering with you about dreams. Come, let's go out! Just into the park! (*She offers him her arm, and they start to leave.*)

JEAN: We'll have to sleep on nine midsummer flowers, Miss Julie, to make our dreams come true! (*They turn at the door. Jean puts his hand to his eye.*)

JULIE: Did you get something in your eye?

JEAN: It's nothing — just a speck — it'll be gone in a minute.

JULIE: My sleeve must have brushed against you. Sit

down and let me help you. (*She takes him by the arm and seats him. She tilts his head back and with the tip of a handkerchief tries to remove the speck.*) Sit still, absolutely still! (*She slaps his hand.*) Didn't you hear me? —— Why, you're trembling; the big, strong man is trembling! (*Feels his biceps.*) What muscles you have!

JEAN (*warning*): Miss Julie!

JULIE: Yes, *monsieur* Jean.

JEAN: *Attention! Je ne suis qu'un homme!*°

JULIE: Will you sit still! —— There! Now it's gone! Kiss my hand and thank me.

JEAN (*rising*): Miss Julie, listen to me! —— Kristine has gone to bed! —— Will you listen to me!

JULIE: Kiss my hand first!

JEAN: Listen to me!

JULIE: Kiss my hand first!

JEAN: All right, but you've only yourself to blame!

JULIE: For what?

JEAN: For what? Are you still a child at twenty-five? Don't you know that it's dangerous to play with fire?

JULIE: Not for me. I'm insured.

JEAN (*boldly*): No, you're not! But even if you were, there's combustible material close by.

JULIE: Meaning you?

JEAN: Yes! Not because it's me, but because I'm young ——

JULIE: And handsome — what incredible conceit! A Don Juan perhaps! Or a Joseph!° Yes, that's it, I do believe you're a Joseph!

JEAN: Do you?

JULIE: I'm almost afraid so. (*Jean boldly tries to put his arm around her waist and kiss her. She slaps his face.*) How dare you?

JEAN: Are you serious or joking?

JULIE: Serious.

JEAN: Then so was what just happened. You play games too seriously, and that's dangerous. Well, I'm tired of games. You'll excuse me if I get back to work. I haven't done the Count's boots yet and it's long past midnight.

JULIE: Put the boots down!

JEAN: No! It's the work I have to do. I never agreed to be your playmate, and never will. It's beneath me.

JULIE: You're proud.

JEAN: In certain ways, but not in others.

JULIE: Have you ever been in love?

Attention! Je ne suis qu'un homme!: Watch out! I am only a man!

Don Juan . . . Joseph: Don Juan in Spanish legend is a seducer of women; in Genesis, Joseph resists the advances of Potiphar's wife.

JEAN: We don't use that word, but I've been fond of many girls, and once I was sick because I couldn't have the one I wanted. That's right, sick, like those princes in the Arabian Nights — who couldn't eat or drink because of love.

JULIE: Who was she? (*Jean is silent.*) Who was she?

JEAN: You can't force me to tell you that.

JULIE: But if I ask you as an equal, as a — friend! Who was she?

JEAN: You!

JULIE (*sits*): How amusing . . .

JEAN: Yes, if you like! It was ridiculous! —— You see, that was the story I didn't want to tell you earlier. Maybe I will now. Do you know how the world looks from down below? —— Of course you don't. Neither do hawks and falcons, whose backs we can't see because they're usually soaring up there above us. I grew up in a shack with seven brothers and sisters and a pig, in the middle of a wasteland, where there wasn't a single tree. But from our window I could see the tops of apple trees above the wall of your father's garden. That was the Garden of Eden, guarded by angry angels with flaming swords. All the same, the other boys and I managed to find our way to the Tree of Life. —— Now you think I'm contemptible, I suppose.

JULIE: Oh, all boys steal apples.

JEAN: You say that, but you think I'm contemptible anyway. Oh well! One day I went into the Garden of Eden with my mother, to weed the onion beds. Near the vegetable garden was a small Turkish pavilion in the shadow of jasmine bushes and overgrown with honeysuckle. I had no idea what it was used for, but I'd never seen such a beautiful building. People went in and came out again, and one day the door was left open. I sneaked close and saw walls covered with pictures of kings and emperors, and red curtains with fringes at the windows — now you know the place I mean. I —— (*Breaks off a sprig of lilac and holds it in front of Miss Julie's nose.*) —— I'd never been inside the manor house, never seen anything except the church — but this was more beautiful. From then on, no matter where my thoughts wandered, they returned — there. And gradually I got a longing to experience, just once, the full pleasure of — *enfin,*° I sneaked in, saw, and marveled! But then I heard someone coming! There was only one exit for ladies and gentlemen, but for me there was another, and I had no choice but to take it! (*Miss Julie, who has taken the lilac sprig, lets it fall on the table.*) Afterwards, I started running. I crashed through a raspberry bush, flew over a strawberry patch, and

---

enfin: Finally.

came up onto the rose terrace. There I caught sight of a pink dress and a pair of white stockings — it was you. I crawled under a pile of weeds, and I mean under — under thistles that pricked me and wet dirt that stank. And I looked at you as you walked among the roses, and I thought: if it's true that a thief can enter heaven and be with the angels, then why can't a farmhand's son here on God's earth enter the manor house garden and play with the Count's daughter?

JULIE (*romantically*): Do you think all poor children would have thought the way you did?

JEAN (*at first hesitant, then with conviction*): If *all* poor — yes — of course. Of course!

JULIE: It must be terrible to be poor!

JEAN (*with exaggerated suffering*): Oh, Miss Julie! Oh! ——— A dog can lie on the Countess's sofa, a horse can have his nose patted by a young lady's hand, but a servant ——— (*Changing his tone.*) ——— oh, I know — now and then you find one with enough stuff in him to get ahead in the world, but how often? ——— Anyhow, do you know what I did then? ——— I jumped in the millstream with my clothes on, was pulled out, and got a beating. But the following Sunday, when my father and all the others went to my grandmother's, I arranged to stay home. I scrubbed myself with soap and water, put on my best clothes, and went to church so that I could see you! I saw you and returned home, determined to die. But I wanted to die beautifully and pleasantly, without pain. And then I remembered that it was dangerous to sleep under an elder bush. We had a big one, and it was in full flower. I plundered its treasures and bedded down under them in the oat bin. Have you ever noticed how smooth oats are? — and soft to the touch, like human skin . . . ! Well, I shut the lid and closed my eyes. I fell asleep and woke up feeling very sick. But I didn't die, as you can see. What was I after? ——— I don't know. There was no hope of winning you, of course. ——— You were a symbol of the hopelessness of ever rising out of the class in which I was born.

JULIE: You're a charming storyteller. Did you ever go to school?

JEAN: A bit, but I've read lots of novels and been to the theater often. And then I've listened to people like you talk — that's where I learned most.

JULIE: Do you listen to what we say?

JEAN: Naturally! And I've heard plenty, too, driving the carriage or rowing the boat. Once I heard you and a friend . . .

JULIE: Oh? ——— What did you hear?

JEAN: I'd better not say. But I was surprised a little.

I couldn't imagine where you learned such words. Maybe at bottom there isn't such a great difference between people as we think.

JULIE: Shame on you! We don't act like you when we're engaged.

JEAN (*staring at her*): Is that true? ——— You don't have to play innocent with me, Miss . . .

JULIE: The man I gave my love to was a swine.

JEAN: That's what you all say — afterwards.

JULIE: All?

JEAN: I think so. I know I've heard that phrase before, on similar occasions.

JULIE: What occasions?

JEAN: Like the one I'm talking about. The last time . . .

JULIE (*rising*): Quiet! I don't want to hear any more!

JEAN: That's interesting — that's what *she* said, too. Well, if you'll excuse me, I'm going to bed.

JULIE (*gently*): To bed? On midsummer eve?

JEAN: Yes! Dancing with the rabble out there doesn't amuse me much.

JULIE: Get the key to the boat and row me out on the lake. I want to see the sun come up.

JEAN: Is that wise?

JULIE: Are you worried about your reputation?

JEAN: Why not? Why should I risk looking ridiculous and getting fired without a reference, just when I'm trying to establish myself. Besides, I think I owe something to Kristine.

JULIE: So, now it's Kristine . . .

JEAN: Yes, but you, too. ——— Take my advice, go up and go to bed!

JULIE: Am I to obey you?

JEAN: Just this once — for your own good! Please! It's very late. Drowsiness makes people giddy and liable to lose their heads! Go to bed! Besides — unless I'm mistaken — I hear the others coming to look for me. And if they find us together, you'll be lost!

(*The Chorus approaches, singing.*)

The swineherd found his true love
a pretty girl so fair,
The swineherd found his true love
but let the girl beware.

For then he saw the princess
the princess on the golden hill,
but then saw the princess,
so much fairer still.

So the swineherd and the princess
they danced the whole night through,
and he forgot his first love,
to her he was untrue.

And when the long night ended,
and in the light of day, of day,
the dancing too was ended,
and the princess could not stay.

Then the swineherd lost his true love,
and the princess grieves him still,
and never more she'll wander
from atop the golden hill.

JULIE: I know all these people and I love them, just as they love me. Let them come in and you'll see.

JEAN: No, Miss Julie, they don't love you. They take your food, but they spit on it! Believe me! Listen to them, listen to what they're singing! —— No, don't listen to them!

JULIE (*listening*): What are they singing?

JEAN: It's a dirty song! About you and me!

JULIE: Disgusting! Oh! How deceitful! ——

JEAN: The rabble is always cowardly! And in a battle like this, you don't fight; you can only run away!

JULIE: Run away? But where? We can't go out — or into Kristine's room.

JEAN: True. But there's my room. Necessity knows no rules. Besides, you can trust me. I'm your friend and I respect you.

JULIE: But suppose — suppose they look for you in there?

JEAN: I'll bolt the door, and if anyone tries to break in, I'll shoot! —— Come! (*On his knees.*) Come!

JULIE (*urgently*): Promise me . . . ?

JEAN: I swear! (*Miss Julie runs off right. Jean hastens after her.*)

Ballet

(*Led by a fiddler, the servants and farm people enter, dressed festively, with flowers in their hats. On the table they place a small barrel of beer and a keg of schnapps, both garlanded. Glasses are brought out, and the drinking starts. A dance circle is formed and "The Swineherd and the Princess" is sung. When the dance is finished, everyone leaves, singing.*)

(*Miss Julie enters alone. She notices the mess in the kitchen, wrings her hands, then takes out her powder puff and powders her nose.*)

JEAN (*enters, agitated*): There, you see? And you heard them. We can't possibly stay here now, you know that.

JULIE: Yes, I know. But what can we do?

JEAN: Leave, travel, far away from here.

JULIE: Travel? Yes, but where?

JEAN: To Switzerland, to the Italian lakes. Have you ever been there?

JULIE: No. Is it beautiful?

JEAN: Oh, an eternal summer — oranges growing everywhere, laurel trees, always green . . .

JULIE: But what'll we do there?

JEAN: I'll open a hotel — with first-class service for first-class people.

JULIE: Hotel?

JEAN: That's the life, you know. Always new faces, new languages. No time to worry or be nervous. No hunting for something to do — there's always work to be done: bells ringing night and day, train whistles blowing, carriages coming and going, and all the while gold rolling into the till! That's the life!

JULIE: Yes, it sounds wonderful. But what'll I do?

JEAN: You'll be mistress of the house: the jewel in our crown! With your looks . . . and your manner — oh — success is guaranteed! It'll be wonderful! You'll sit in your office like a queen and push an electric button to set your slaves in motion. The guests will file past your throne and timidly lay their treasures before you. —— You have no idea how people tremble when they get their bill. —— I'll salt the bills° and you'll sweeten them with your prettiest smile. —— Let's get away from here —— (*Takes a timetable out of his pocket.*) —— Right away, on the next train! —— We'll be in Malmö six-thirty tomorrow morning, Hamburg at eight-forty; from Frankfort to Basel will take a day, then on to Como by way of the St. Gotthard Tunnel, in, let's see, three days. Three days!

JULIE: That's all very well! But Jean — you must give me courage! —— Tell me you love me! Put your arms around me!

JEAN (*hesitating*): I want to — but I don't dare. Not in this house, not again. I love you — never doubt that — you don't doubt it, do you, Miss Julie?

JULIE (*shy; very feminine*): "Miss!" —— Call me Julie! There are no barriers between us anymore. Call me Julie!

JEAN (*tormented*): I can't! There'll always be barriers between us as long as we stay in this house. —— There's the past and there's the Count. I've never met anyone I had such respect for. —— When I see his gloves lying on a chair, I feel small. —— When I hear that bell up there ring, I jump like a skittish horse. —— And when I look at his boots standing there so stiff and proud, I feel like bowing! (*Kicking the boots.*) Superstitions and prejudices we learned as children — but they can easily be forgotten. If I can just get to another country, a republic, people will bow and scrape when they

---

salt the bills: Inflate or pad the bills.

see my livery — *they'll* bow and scrape, you hear, not me! I wasn't born to cringe. I've got stuff in me, I've got character, and if I can only grab onto that first branch, you watch me climb! I'm a servant today, but next year I'll own my own hotel. In ten years I'll have enough to retire. Then I'll go to Rumania and be decorated. I could — mind you I said *could* — end up a count!

JULIE: Wonderful, wonderful!

JEAN: Ah, in Rumania you just buy your title, and so you'll be a countess after all. My countess!

JULIE: But I don't care about that — that's what I'm putting behind me! Show me you love me, otherwise — otherwise, what am I?

JEAN: I'll show you a thousand times — afterwards! Not here! And whatever you do, no emotional outbursts, or we'll both be lost! We must think this through coolly, like sensible people. (*He takes out a cigar, snips the end, and lights it.*) You sit there, and I'll sit here. We'll talk as if nothing happened.

JULIE (*desperately*): Oh, my God! Have you no feelings?

JEAN: Me? No one has more feelings than I do, but I know how to control them.

JULIE: A little while ago you could kiss my shoe — and now!

JEAN (*harshly*): Yes, but that was before. Now we have other things to think about.

JULIE: Don't speak harshly to me!

JEAN: I'm not — just sensibly! We've already done one foolish thing, let's not have any more. The Count could return any minute, and by then we've got to decide what to do with our lives. What do you think of my plans for the future? Do you approve?

JULIE: They sound reasonable enough. I have only one question: for such a big undertaking you need capital — do you have it?

JEAN (*chewing on the cigar*): Me? Certainly! I have my professional expertise, my wide experience, and my knowledge of languages. That's capital enough, I should think!

JULIE: But all that won't even buy a train ticket.

JEAN: That's true. That's why I'm looking for a partner to advance me the money.

JULIE: Where will you find one quickly enough?

JEAN: That's up to you, if you want to come with me.

JULIE: But I can't; I have no money of my own. (*Pause.*)

JEAN: Then it's all off . . .

JULIE: And . . .

JEAN: Things stay as they are.

JULIE: Do you think I'm going to stay in this house as your lover? With all the servants pointing their fingers at me? Do you imagine I can face my father

after this? No! Take me away from here, away from shame and dishonor —— Oh, what have I done! My God, my God! (*She cries.*)

JEAN: Now, don't start that old song! —— What have you done? The same as many others before you.

JULIE (*screaming convulsively*): And now you think I'm contemptible! —— I'm falling, I'm falling!

JEAN: Fall down to my level and I'll lift you up again.

JULIE: What terrible power drew me to you? The attraction of the weak to the strong? The falling to the rising? Or was it love? Was this love? Do you know what love is?

JEAN: Me? What do you take me for? You don't think this was my first time, do you?

JULIE: The things you say, the thoughts you think!

JEAN: That's the way I was taught, and that's the way I am! Now don't get excited and don't play the grand lady, because we're in the same boat now! —— Come on, Julie, I'll pour you a glass of something special! (*He opens a drawer in the table, takes out a wine bottle, and fills two glasses already used.*)

JULIE: Where did you get that wine?

JEAN: From the cellar.

JULIE: My father's burgundy!

JEAN: That'll do for his son-in-law, won't it?

JULIE: And I drink beer! Beer!

JEAN: That only shows I have better taste.

JULIE: Thief!

JEAN: Planning to tell?

JULIE: Oh, oh! Accomplice of a common thief! Was I drunk? Have I been walking in a dream the whole evening? Midsummer eve! A time of innocent fun!

JEAN: Innocent, eh?

JULIE (*pacing back and forth*): Is there anyone on earth more miserable than I am at this moment?

JEAN: Why should you be? After such a conquest? Think of Kristine in there. Don't you think she has feelings, too?

JULIE: I thought so awhile ago, but not any more. No, a servant is a servant . . .

JEAN: And a whore is a whore!

JULIE (*on her knees, her hands clasped*): Oh, God in heaven, end my wretched life! Take me away from the filth I'm sinking into! Save me! Save me!

JEAN: I can't deny I feel sorry for you. When I lay in that onion bed and saw you in the rose garden, well . . . I'll be frank . . . I had the same dirty thoughts all boys have.

JULIE: And you wanted to die for me!

JEAN: In the oat bin? That was just talk.

JULIE: A lie, in other words!

JEAN (*beginning to feel sleepy*): More or less! I got

the idea from a newspaper story about a chimney sweep who curled up in a firewood bin full of lilacs because he got a summons for not supporting his illegitimate child . . .

JULIE: So, that's what you're like . . .

JEAN: I had to think of something. And that's the kind of story women always go for.

JULIE: Swine!

JEAN: *Merde!*

JULIE: And now you've seen the hawk's back . . .

JEAN: Not exactly its *back* . . .

JULIE: And I was to be the first branch . . .

JEAN: But the branch was rotten . . .

JULIE: I was to be the sign on the hotel . . .

JEAN: And I the hotel . . .

JULIE: Sit at your desk, entice your customers, pad their bills . . .

JEAN: That I'd do myself . . .

JULIE: How can anyone be so thoroughly filthy?

JEAN: Better clean up then!

JULIE: You lackey, you menial, stand up, when I speak to you!

JEAN: Menial's strumpet, lackey's whore, shut up and get out of here! Who are you to lecture me on coarseness? None of my kind is ever as coarse as you were tonight. Do you think one of your maids would throw herself at a man the way you did? Have you ever seen any girl of my class offer herself like that? I've only seen it among animals and streetwalkers.

JULIE (*crushed*): You're right. Hit me, trample on me. I don't deserve any better. I'm worthless. But help me! If you see any way out of this, help me, Jean, please!

JEAN (*more gently*): I'd be lying if I didn't admit to a sense of triumph in all this, but do you think that a person like me would have dared even to look at someone like you if you hadn't invited it? I'm still amazed . . .

JULIE: And proud . . .

JEAN: Why not? Though I must say it was too easy to be really exciting.

JULIE: Go on, hit me, hit me harder!

JEAN (*rising*): No! Forgive me for what I've said! I don't hit a man when he's down, let alone a woman. I can't deny though, that I'm pleased to find out that what looked so dazzling to us from below was only tinsel, that the hawk's back was only gray, after all, that the lovely complexion was only powder, that those polished fingernails had black edges, and that a dirty handkerchief is still dirty, even if it smells of perfume . . . ! On the other hand, it hurts me to find out that what I was striving for wasn't finer, more substantial. It hurts me to see

you sunk so low that you're inferior to your own cook. It hurts like watching flowers beaten down by autumn rains and turned into mud.

JULIE: You talk as if you were already above me.

JEAN: I am. You see, I could make you a countess, but you could never make me a count.

JULIE: But I'm the child of a count — something you could never be!

JEAN: That's true. But I could be the father of counts — if . . .

JULIE: But you're a thief. I'm not.

JEAN: There are worse things than being a thief! Besides, when I'm working in a house, I consider myself sort of a member of the family, like one of the children. And you don't call it stealing when a child snatches a berry off a full bush. (*His passion is aroused again.*) Miss Julie, you're a glorious woman, much too good for someone like me! You were drinking and you lost your head. Now you want to cover up your mistake by telling yourself that you love me! You don't. Maybe there was a physical attraction — but then your love is no better than mine. ——— I could never be satisfied to be no more than an animal to you, and I could never arouse real love in you.

JULIE: Are you sure of that?

JEAN: You're suggesting it's possible ——— Oh, I could fall in love with you, no doubt about it. You're beautiful, you're refined——— (*Approaching and taking her hand.*) ——— cultured, lovable when you want to be, and once you start a fire in a man, it never goes out. (*Putting his arm around her waist.*) You're like hot, spicy wine, and one kiss from you . . . (*He tries to lead her out, but she slowly frees herself.*)

JULIE: Let me go!? ——— You'll never win me like that.

JEAN: *How* then? ——— Not like that? Not with caresses and pretty speeches. Not with plans about the future or rescue from disgrace! *How* then?

JULIE: How? How? I don't know! ——— I have no idea! ——— I detest you as I detest rats, but I can't escape from you.

JEAN: Escape with me!

JULIE (*pulling herself together*): Escape? Yes, we must escape! ——— But I'm so tired. Give me a glass of wine? (*Jean pours the wine. She looks at her watch.*) But we must talk first. We still have a little time. (*She drains the glass, then holds it out for more.*)

JEAN: Don't drink so fast. It'll go to your head.

JULIE: What does it matter?

JEAN: What does it matter? It's vulgar to get drunk! What did you want to tell me?

JULIE: We must escape! But first we must talk, I mean I must talk. You've done all the talking up to now. You told about your life, now I want to tell about mine, so we'll know all about each other before we go off together.

JEAN: Just a minute! Forgive me! If you don't want to regret it afterwards, you'd better think twice before revealing any secrets about yourself.

JULIE: Aren't you my friend?

JEAN: Yes, sometimes! But don't rely on me.

JULIE: You're only saying that. —— Besides, everyone already knows my secrets. —— You see, my mother was a commoner — very humble background. She was brought up believing in social equality, women's rights, and all that. The idea of marriage repelled her. So, when my father proposed, she replied that she would never become his wife, but he could be her lover. He insisted that he didn't want the woman he loved to be less respected than he. But his passion ruled him, and when she explained that the world's respect meant nothing to her, he accepted her conditions.

But now his friends avoided him and his life was restricted to taking care of the estate, which couldn't satisfy him. I came into the world — against my mother's wishes, as far as I can understand. She wanted to bring me up as a child of nature, and, what's more, to learn everything a boy had to learn, so that I might be an example of how a woman can be as good as a man. I had to wear boy's clothes and learn to take care of horses, but I was never allowed in the cowshed. I had to groom and harness the horses and go hunting — and even had to watch them slaughter animals — that was disgusting! On the estate men were put on women's jobs and women on men's jobs — with the result that the property became run down and we became the laughingstock of the district. Finally, my father must have awakened from his trance because he rebelled and changed everything his way. My parents were then married quietly. Mother became ill — I don't know what illness it was — but she often had convulsions, hid in the attic and in the garden, and sometimes stayed out all night. Then came the great fire, which you've heard about. The house, the stables, and the cowshed all burned down, under very curious circumstances, suggesting arson, because the accident happened the day after the insurance had expired. The quarterly premium my father sent in was delayed because of a messenger's carelessness and didn't arrive in time. (*She fills her glass and drinks.*)

JEAN: Don't drink any more!

JULIE: Oh, what does it matter. —— We were left penniless and had to sleep in the carriages. My father had no idea where to find money to rebuild the house because he had so slighted his old friends that they had forgotten him. Then my mother suggested that he borrow from a childhood friend of hers, a brick manufacturer who lived nearby. Father got the loan without having to pay interest, which surprised him. And that's how the estate was rebuilt. —— (*Drinks again.*) Do you know who started the fire?

JEAN: The Countess, your mother.

JULIE: Do you know who the brick manufacturer was?

JEAN: Your mother's lover?

JULIE: Do you know whose money it was?

JEAN: Wait a moment — no, I don't.

JULIE: It was my mother's.

JEAN: You mean the Count's, unless they didn't sign an agreement when they were married.

JULIE: They didn't. —— My mother had a small inheritance which she didn't want under my father's control, so she entrusted it to her — friend.

JEAN: Who stole it!

JULIE: Exactly! He kept it. —— All this my father found out, but he couldn't bring it to court, couldn't repay his wife's lover, couldn't prove it was his wife's money! It was my mother's revenge for being forced into marriage against her will. It nearly drove him to suicide — there was a rumor that he tried with a pistol, but failed. So, he managed to live through it and my mother had to suffer for what she'd done. You can imagine that those were a terrible five years for me. I loved my father, but I sided with my mother because I didn't know the circumstances. I learned from her to hate men — you've heard how she hated the whole male sex — and I swore to her I'd never be a slave to any man.

JEAN: But you got engaged to that lawyer.

JULIE: In order to make him my slave.

JEAN: And he wasn't willing?

JULIE: He was willing, all right, but I wouldn't let him. I got tired of him.

JEAN: I saw it — out near the stable.

JULIE: What did you see?

JEAN: I saw — how he broke off the engagement.

JULIE: That's a lie! I was the one who broke it off. Has he said that he did? That swine . . .

JEAN: He was no swine, I'm sure. So, you hate men, Miss Julie?

JULIE: Yes! —— Most of the time! But sometimes — when the weakness comes, when passion burns! Oh, God, will the fire never die out?

JEAN: Do you hate me, too?

JULIE: Immeasurably! I'd like to have you put to death, like an animal . . .

JEAN: I see — the penalty for bestiality — the woman

gets two years at hard labor and the animal is put to death. Right?

JULIE: Exactly!

JEAN: But there's no prosecutor here — and no animal. So, what'll we do?

JULIE: Go away!

JEAN: To torment each other to death?

JULIE: No! To be happy for — two days, a week, as long as we can be happy, and then — die . . .

JEAN: Die? That's stupid! It's better to open a hotel!

JULIE (*without listening*): ——— on the shore of Lake Como, where the sun always shines, where the laurels are green at Christmas and the oranges glow.

JEAN: Lake Como is a rainy hole, and I never saw any oranges outside the stores. But tourists are attracted there because there are plenty of villas to be rented out to lovers, and that's a profitable business. ——— Do you know why? Because they sign a lease for six months — and then leave after three weeks!

JULIE (*naively*): Why after three weeks?

JEAN: They quarrel, of course! But they still have to pay the rent in full! And so you rent the villas out again. And that's the way it goes, time after time. There's never a shortage of love — even if it doesn't last long!

JULIE: You don't want to die with me?

JEAN: I don't want to die at all! For one thing, I like living, and for another, I think suicide is a crime against the Providence which gave us life.

JULIE: You believe in God? *You?*

JEAN: Of course I do. And I go to church every other Sunday. ——— To be honest, I'm tired of all this, and I'm going to bed.

JULIE: Are you? And do you think I can let it go at that? A man owes something to the woman he's shamed.

JEAN (*taking out his purse and throwing a silver coin on the table*): Here! I don't like owing anything to anybody.

JULIE (*pretending not to notice the insult*): Do you know what the law states . . .

JEAN: Unfortunately the law doesn't state any punishment for the woman who seduces a man!

JULIE (*as before*): Do you see any way out but to leave, get married, and then separate?

JEAN: Suppose I refuse such a *mésalliance?*°

JULIE: *Mésalliance* . . .

JEAN: Yes, for me! You see, I come from better stock than you. There's no arsonist in my family.

JULIE: How do you know?

JEAN: You can't prove otherwise. We don't keep charts

on our ancestors — there's just the police records! But I've read about your family. Do you know who the founder was? He was a miller who let the king sleep with his wife one night during the Danish War. I don't have any noble ancestors like that. I don't have any noble ancestors at all, but I could become one myself.

JULIE: This is what I get for opening my heart to someone unworthy, for giving my family's honor . . .

JEAN: Dishonor! ——— Well, I told you so: when people drink, they talk, and talk is dangerous!

JULIE: Oh, how I regret it! ——— How I regret it! ——— If you at least loved me.

JEAN: For the last time — what do you want? Shall I cry; shall I jump over your riding crop? Shall I kiss you and lure you off to Lake Como for three weeks, and then God knows what . . . ? What shall I do? What do you want? This is getting painfully embarrassing! But that's what happens when you stick your nose in women's business. Miss Julie! I see that you're unhappy. I know you're suffering, but I can't understand you. We don't have such romantic ideas; there's not this kind of hate between us. Love is a game we play when we get time off from work, but we don't have all day and night, like you. I think you're sick, really sick. Your mother was crazy, and her ideas have poisoned your life.

JULIE: Be kind to me. At least now you're talking like a human being.

JEAN: Be human yourself, then. You spit on me, and you won't let me wipe myself off ———

JULIE: Help me! Help me! Just tell me what to do, where to go!

JEAN: In God's name, if I only knew myself!

JULIE: I've been crazy, out of my mind, but isn't there any way out?

JEAN: Stay here and keep calm! No one knows anything!

JULIE: Impossible! The others know and Kristine knows.

JEAN: No they don't, and they'd never believe a thing like that!

JULIE (*hesitantly*): But — it could happen again!

JEAN: That's true!

JULIE: And then?

JEAN (*frightened*): Then? ——— Why didn't I think about that? Yes, there is only one thing to do — get away from here! Right away! I can't come with you, then we'd be finished, so you'll have to go alone — away — anywhere!

JULIE: Alone? ——— Where? ——— I can't do that!

JEAN: You must! And before the Count gets back! If you stay, you know what'll happen. Once you make a mistake like this, you want to continue because the damage has already been done. . . . Then you get bolder and bolder — until finally you're caught! So leave! Later you can write to the Count and

mésalliance: Misalliance or mismatch, especially regarding relative social status.

confess everything — except that it was me! He'll never guess who it was, and he's not going to be eager to find out, anyway.

JULIE: I'll go if you come with me.

JEAN: Are you out of your head? Miss Julie runs away with her servant! In two days it would be in the newspapers, and that's something your father would never live through.

JULIE: I can't go and I can't stay! Help me! I'm so tired, so terribly tired. ——— Order me! Set me in motion — I can't think or act on my own . . .

JEAN: What miserable creatures you people are! You strut around with your noses in the air as if you were the lords of creation! All right, I'll order you. Go upstairs and get dressed! Get some money for the trip, and then come back down!

JULIE (in a half-whisper): Come up with me!

JEAN: To your room? ——— Now you're crazy again! (Hesitates for a moment.) No! Go, at once! (Takes her hand to lead her out.)

JULIE (as she leaves): Speak kindly to me, Jean!

JEAN: An order always sounds unkind — now you know how it feels. (Jean, alone, sighs with relief. He sits at the table, takes out a notebook and pencil, and begins adding up figures, counting aloud as he works. He continues in dumb show until Kristine enters, dressed for church. She is carrying a white tie and shirt front.)

KRISTINE: Lord Jesus, what a mess! What have you been up to?

JEAN: Oh, Miss Julie dragged everybody in here. You mean you didn't hear anything? You must have been sleeping soundly.

KRISTINE: Like a log.

JEAN: And dressed for church already?

KRISTINE: Of course! You remember you promised to come with me to communion today!

JEAN: Oh, yes, that's right. ——— And you brought my things. Come on, then! (He sits down. Kristine starts to put on his shirt front and tie. Pause. Jean begins sleepily.) What's the gospel text for today?

KRISTINE: On St. John's Day? — the beheading of John the Baptist, I should think!

JEAN: Ah, that'll be a long one, for sure. ——— Hey, you're choking me! ——— Oh, I'm sleepy, so sleepy!

KRISTINE: Yes, what have you been doing, up all night? Your face is absolutely green.

JEAN: I've been sitting here gabbing with Miss Julie.

KRISTINE: She has no idea what's proper, that one! (Pause.)

JEAN: You know, Kristine . . .

KRISTINE: What?

JEAN: It's really strange when you think about it. ——— Her!

KRISTINE: What's so strange?

JEAN: Everything! (Pause.)

KRISTINE (looking at the half-empty glasses standing on the table): Have you been drinking together, too?

JEAN: Yes.

KRISTINE: Shame on you! ——— Look me in the eye!

JEAN: Well?

KRISTINE: Is it possible? Is it possible?

JEAN (thinking it over for a moment): Yes, it is.

KRISTINE: Ugh! I never would have believed it! No, shame on you, shame!

JEAN: You're not jealous of her, are you?

KRISTINE: No, not of her! If it had been Clara or Sofie I'd have scratched your eyes out! ——— I don't know why, but that's the way I feel. ——— Oh, it's disgusting!

JEAN: Are you angry at her, then?

KRISTINE: No, at you! That was an awful thing to do, awful! Poor girl! ——— No, I don't care who knows it — I won't stay in a house where we can't respect the people we work for.

JEAN: Why should we respect them?

KRISTINE: You're so clever, you tell me! Do you want to wait on people who can't behave decently? Do you? You disgrace yourself that way, if you ask me.

JEAN: But it's a comfort to know they aren't any better than us.

KRISTINE: Not for me. If they're no better, what do we have to strive for to better ourselves. ——— And think of the Count! Think of him! As if he hasn't had enough misery in his life! Lord Jesus! No, I won't stay in this house any longer! ——— And it had to be with someone like you! If it had been that lawyer, if it had been a real gentleman . . .

JEAN: What do you mean?

KRISTINE: Oh, you're all right for what you are, but there are men and gentlemen, after all! ——— No, this business with Miss Julie I can never forget. She was so proud, so arrogant with men, you wouldn't have believed she could just go and give herself — and to someone like you! And she was going to have poor Diana shot for running after the gatekeepers' mutt! ——— Yes, I'm giving my notice, I mean it — I won't stay here any longer. On the twenty-fourth of October, I leave!

JEAN: And then?

KRISTINE: Well, since the subject has come up, it's about time you looked around for something since we're going to get married, in any case.

JEAN: Where am I going to look? I couldn't find a job like this if I was married.

KRISTINE: No, that's true. But you can find work as a porter or as a caretaker in some government office. The state doesn't pay much, I know, but it's secure, and there's a pension for the wife and children . . .

JEAN (*grimacing*): That's all very well, but it's a bit early for me to think about dying for a wife and children. My ambitions are a little higher than that.

KRISTINE: Your ambitions, yes! Well, you have obligations, too! Think about them!

JEAN: Don't start nagging me about obligations. I know what I have to do! (*Listening for something outside.*) Besides, this is something we have plenty of time to think over. Go and get ready for church.

KRISTINE: Who's that walking around up there?

JEAN: I don't know, unless it's Clara.

KRISTINE (*going*): You don't suppose it's the Count, who came home without us hearing him?

JEAN (*frightened*): The Count? No, I don't think so. He'd have rung.

KRISTINE (*going*): Well, God help us! I've never seen anything like this before. (*The sun has risen and shines through the treetops in the park. The light shifts gradually until it slants in through the windows. Jean goes to the door and signals. Miss Julie enters, dressed in travel clothes and carrying a small bird cage, covered with a cloth, which she places on a chair.*)

JULIE: I'm ready now.

JEAN: Shh! Kristine is awake.

JULIE (*very nervous during the following*): Does she suspect something?

JEAN: She doesn't know anything. But my God, you look awful!

JULIE: Why? How do I look?

JEAN: You're pale as a ghost and — excuse me, but your face is dirty.

JULIE: Let me wash up then. ——— (*She goes to the basin and washes her hands and face.*) Give me a towel! ——— Oh — the sun's coming up.

JEAN: Then the goblins will disappear.

JULIE: Yes, there must have been goblins out last night! ——— Jean, listen, come with me! I have some money now.

JEAN (*hesitantly*): Enough?

JULIE: Enough to start with. Come with me! I just can't travel alone on a day like this — midsummer day on a stuffy train — jammed in among crowds of people staring at me. Eternal delays at every station, while I'd wish I had wings. No, I can't, I can't! And then there'll be memories, memories of midsummer days when I was little. The church — decorated with birch leaves and lilacs; dinner at the big table with relatives and friends; the afternoons

in the park, dancing, music, flowers, and games. Oh, no matter how far we travel, the memories will follow in the baggage car, with remorse and guilt!

JEAN: I'll go with you — but right away, before it's too late. Right this minute!

JULIE: Get dressed, then! (*Picking up the bird cage.*)

JEAN: But no baggage! It would give us away!

JULIE: No, nothing! Only what we can have in the compartment with us.

JEAN (*has taken his hat*): What've you got there? What is it?

JULIE: It's only my greenfinch. I couldn't leave her behind.

JEAN: What? Bring a bird cage with us? You're out of your head! Put it down!

JULIE: It's the only thing I'm taking from my home — the only living being that loves me, since Diana was unfaithful. Don't be cruel! Let me take her!

JEAN: Put the cage down, I said! ——— And don't talk so loudly — Kristine will hear us!

JULIE: No, I won't leave her in the hands of strangers! I'd rather you killed her.

JEAN: Bring the thing here, then, I'll cut its head off!

JULIE: Oh! But don't hurt her! Don't . . . no, I can't.

JEAN: Bring it here! I can!

JULIE (*taking the bird out of the cage and kissing it*): Oh, my little Serena, must you die and leave your mistress?

JEAN: Please don't make a scene! Your whole future is at stake! Hurry up! (*He snatches the bird from her, carries it over to the chopping block, and picks up a meat cleaver. Miss Julie turns away.*) You should have learned how to slaughter chickens instead of how to fire pistols. (*He chops off the bird's head.*) Then you wouldn't feel faint at the sight of blood.

JULIE (*screaming*): Kill me, too! Kill me! You, who can slaughter an innocent animal without blinking an eye! Oh, how I hate, how I detest you! There's blood between us now! I curse the moment I set eyes on you! I curse the moment I was conceived in my mother's womb!

JEAN: What good does cursing do? Let's go!

JULIE (*approaching the chopping block, as if drawn against her will*): No, I don't want to go yet. I can't . . . until I see . . . Shh! I hear a carriage ——— (*She listens, but her eyes never leave the cleaver and the chopping block.*) Do you think I can't stand the sight of blood? You think I'm so weak . . . Oh — I'd like to see your blood and your brains on a chopping block! ——— I'd like to see your whole sex swimming in a sea of blood, like my little bird . . . I think I could drink from your skull! I'd like to bathe my feet in your open chest and eat your heart roasted whole! —— You think I'm weak. You think I love you because my womb craved your seed. You think I want to carry your spawn under my heart and nourish it with my blood — bear your child and take your name! By the way, what is your family name? I've never heard it. —— Do you have one? I was to be Mrs. Bootblack — or Madame Pigsty. —— You dog, who wears my collar, you lackey, who bears my coat of arms on your buttons — do I have to share you with my cook, compete with my own servant? Oh! Oh! Oh! —— You think I'm a coward who wants to run away! No, now I'm staying — and let the storm break! My father will come home . . . to find his desk broken open . . . and his money gone! Then he'll ring — that bell . . . twice for his valet — and then he'll send for the police . . . and then I'll tell everything! Everything! Oh, what a relief it'll be to have it all end — if only it will end! —— And then he'll have a stroke and die . . . That'll be the end of all of us — and there'll be peace . . . quiet . . . eternal rest! —— And then our coat of arms will be broken against his coffin — the family title extinct — but the valet's line will go on in an orphanage . . . win laurels in the gutter, and end in jail!

JEAN: There's the blue blood talking! Very good, Miss Julie! Just don't let that miller out of the closet! (*Kristine enters, dressed for church, with a psalm-book in her hand.*)

JULIE (*rushing to Kristine and falling into her arms, as if seeking protection*): Help, me Kristine! Help me against this man!

KRISTINE (*unmoved and cold*): What a fine way to behave on a Sunday morning! (*Sees the chopping block.*) And look at this mess! —— What does all this mean? Why all this screaming and carrying on?

JULIE: Kristine! You're a woman and my friend! Beware of this swine!

JEAN (*uncomfortable*): While you ladies discuss this, I'll go in and shave. (*Slips off right.*)

JULIE: You must listen to me so you'll understand!

KRISTINE: No, I could never understand such disgusting behavior! Where are you off to in your traveling clothes? —— And he had his hat on. —— Well? —— Well? ——

JULIE: Listen to me, Kristine! Listen, and I'll tell you everything ——

KRISTINE: I don't want to hear it . . .

JULIE: But you must listen to me . . .

KRISTINE: What about? If it's about this silliness with Jean, I'm not interested, because it's none of my business. But if you're thinking of tricking him into running out, we'll soon put a stop to that!

JULIE (*extremely nervous*): Try to be calm now, Kristine, and listen to me! I can't stay here, and neither can Jean — so we must go away . . .

KRISTINE: Hm, hm!

JULIE (*brightening*): You see, I just had an idea —— What if all three of us go — abroad — to Switzerland and start a hotel together? —— I have money, you see — and Jean and I could run it — and I thought you, you could take care of the kitchen . . . Wouldn't that be wonderful? —— Say yes! And come with us, and then everything will be settled! —— Oh, do say yes! (*Embracing Kristine and patting her warmly.*)

KRISTINE (*coolly, thoughtfully*): Hm, hm!

JULIE (*presto tempo*):° You've never traveled, Kristine. —— You must get out and see the world. You can't imagine how much fun it is to travel by train — always new faces — new countries. —— And when we get to Hamburg, we'll stop off at the zoo — you'll like that. —— and then we'll go to the theater and the opera — and when we get to Munich, dear, there we have museums, with Rubens and Raphael, the great painters, as you know. —— You've heard of Munich, where King Ludwig lived — the king who went mad. —— And then we'll see his castles — they're still there and they're like castles in fairy tales. —— And from there it isn't far to Switzerland — and the Alps. —— Imagine — the Alps have snow on them even in the middle of summer! —— And oranges grow there and laurel trees that are green all year round —— (*Jean can be seen in the wings right, sharpening his razor on a strop which he holds with his teeth and his left hand. He listens to the conversation with satisfaction, nodding now and then in approval. Miss Julie continues tempo prestissimo.*)° And then we'll start a hotel — and I'll be at the desk, while Jean greets the guests . . . does the shopping . . . writes letters. —— You have no idea what a life it'll be — the train whistles blowing and the carriages arriving and the bells ringing in the rooms and down in the restaurant. —— And I'll make out the bills — and I know how to salt them! . . . You'll never believe how timid travelers are when they have to pay their bills! —— And you — you'll be in charge of the kitchen. —— Naturally, you won't have to stand over the stove yourself. —— And since you're going to be seen by people, you'll have to wear beautiful clothes. —— And you,

---

presto tempo: At a rapid pace.
tempo prestissimo: At a very rapid pace.

with your looks — no, I'm not flattering you —
one fine day you'll grab yourself a husband! ———
You'll see! ——— A rich Englishman — they're so
easy to ——— (*Slowing down.*) ——— catch —
and then we'll get rich — and build ourselves a
villa on Lake Como. ——— It's true it rains there
a little now and then, but ——— (*Dully.*) ———
the sun has to shine sometimes — although it looks
dark — and then . . . of course we could always
come back home again ——— (*Pause.*) ——— here
— or somewhere else ———

KRISTINE: Listen, Miss Julie, do you believe all this?

JULIE (*crushed*): Do I believe it?

KRISTINE: Yes!

JULIE (*wearily*): I don't know. I don't believe in anything
anymore. (*She sinks down on the bench and cradles
her head in her arms on the table.*) Nothing! Nothing
at all!

KRISTINE (*turning right to where Jean is standing*):
So, you thought you'd run out!

JEAN (*embarrassed; puts the razor on the table*): Run
out? That's no way to put it. You hear Miss Julie's
plan, and even if she is tired after being up all
night, it's still a practical plan.

KRISTINE: Now you listen to me! Did you think I'd
work as a cook for that . . .

JEAN (*sharply*): You watch what you say in front of
your mistress! Do you understand?

KRISTINE: Mistress!

JEAN: Yes!

KRISTINE: Listen to him! Listen to him!

JEAN: Yes, you listen! It'd do you good to listen more
and talk less! Miss Julie is your mistress. If you
despise her, you have to despise yourself for the
same reason!

KRISTINE: I've always had enough self-respect ———

JEAN: ——— to be able to despise other people!

KRISTINE: ——— to stop me from doing anything
that's beneath me. You can't say that the Count's
cook has been up to something with the groom or
the swineherd! Can you?

JEAN: No, you were lucky enough to get hold of a
gentleman!

KRISTINE: Yes, a gentleman who sells the Count's oats
from the stable.

JEAN: You should talk — taking a commission from
the grocer and bribes from the butcher.

KRISTINE: What?

JEAN: And you say you can't respect your employers
any longer. You, you, you!

KRISTINE: Are you coming to church with me, now?
You could use a good sermon after your fine deed!

JEAN: No, I'm not going to church today. You'll have
to go alone and confess what you've been up to.

KRISTINE: Yes, I'll do that, and I'll bring back enough
forgiveness for you, too. The Savior suffered and
died on the Cross for all our sins, and if we go to
Him with faith and a penitent heart, He takes all
our sins on Himself.

JEAN: Even grocery sins?

JULIE: And do you believe that, Kristine?

KRISTINE: It's my living faith, as sure as I stand here.
It's the faith I learned as a child, Miss Julie, and
kept ever since. "Where sin abounded, grace did
much more abound!"

JULIE: Oh, if I only had your faith. If only . . .

KRISTINE: Well, you see, we can't have it without
God's special grace, and that isn't given to everyone ———

JULIE: Who is it given to then?

KRISTINE: That's the great secret of the workings of
grace, Miss Julie, and God is no respecter of persons,
for the last shall be the first . . .

JULIE: Then He does respect the last.

KRISTINE (*continuing*): . . . and it is easier for a camel
to go through the eye of a needle, than for a rich
man to enter the Kingdom of God. That's how it
is, Miss Julie! Anyhow, I'm going now — alone,
and on the way I'm going to tell the groom not to
let any horses out, in case anyone wants to leave
before the Count gets back! ——— Goodbye!
(*Leaves.*)

JEAN: What a witch! ——— And all this because of
a greenfinch! ———

JULIE (*dully*): Never mind the greenfinch! ——— Can
you see any way out of this? Any end to it?

JEAN (*thinking*): No!

JULIE: What would you do in my place?

JEAN: In your place? Let's see — as a person of position,
as a woman who had — fallen. I don't know —
wait, now I know.

JULIE (*taking the razor and making a gesture*): You
mean like this?

JEAN: Yes! But — understand — *I* wouldn't do it!
That's the difference between us!

JULIE: Because you're a man and I'm a woman? What
sort of difference is that?

JEAN: The usual difference — between a man and a
woman.

JULIE (*with the razor in her hand*): I want to, but I
can't! ——— My father couldn't either, the time
he should have done it.

JEAN: No, he shouldn't have! He had to revenge himself
first.

JULIE: And now my mother is revenged again, through
me.

JEAN: Didn't you ever love your father, Miss Julie?

JULIE: Oh yes, deeply, but I've hated him, too. I must

have done so without realizing it! It was he who brought me up to despise my own sex, making me half woman, half man. Whose fault is what's happened? My father's, my mother's, my own? My own? I don't have anything that's my own. I don't have a single thought that I didn't get from my father, not an emotion that I didn't get from my mother, and this last idea — that all people are equal — I got that from my fiancé. ———— That's why I called him a swine! How can it be my fault? Shall I let Jesus take on the blame, the way Kristine does? ———— No, I'm too proud to do that and too sensible — thanks to my father's teachings. ———— And as for someone rich not going to heaven, that's a lie. But Kristine won't get in — how will she explain the money she has in the savings bank? Whose fault is it? ———— What does it matter whose fault it is? I'm still the one who has to bear the blame, face the consequences . . .

JEAN: Yes, but . . . (*The bell rings sharply twice. Miss Julie jumps up. Jean changes his coat.*) The Count is back! Do you suppose Kristine — (*He goes to the speaking tube, taps the lid, and listens.*)

JULIE: He's been to his desk!

JEAN: It's Jean, sir! (*Listening; the audience cannot hear the Count's voice.*) Yes, sir! (*Listening.*) Yes, sir! Right away! (*Listening.*) At once, sir! (*Listening.*) I see, in half an hour!

JULIE (*desperately frightened*): What did he say? Dear Lord, what did he say?

JEAN: He wants his boots and his coffee in half an hour.

JULIE: So, in half an hour! Oh, I'm so tired. I'm not able to do anything. I can't repent, can't run away, can't stay, can't live — can't die! Help me now! Order me, and I'll obey like a dog! Do me this last service, save my honor, save his name! You know what I *should* do, but don't have the will to . . . You will it, you order me to do it!

JEAN: I don't know why ———— but now I can't either ———— I don't understand. ———— It's as if this coat made it impossible for me to order you to do anything. ———— And now, since the Count spoke to me — I — I can't really explain it — but — ah, it's the damn lackey in me! ———— I think if the Count came down here now — and ordered me to cut my throat, I'd do it on the spot.

JULIE: Then pretend you're he, and I'm you! ————

You gave such a good performance before when you knelt at my feet. ———— You were a real nobleman. ———— Or — have you ever seen a hypnotist in the theater? (*Jean nods.*) He says to his subject: "Take the broom," and he takes it. He says: "Sweep," and he sweeps ————

JEAN: But the subject has to be asleep.

JULIE (*ecstatically*): I'm already asleep. ———— The whole room is like smoke around me . . . and you look like an iron stove . . . shaped like a man in black, with a tall hat — and your eyes glow like coals when the fire is dying — and your face is a white patch, like ashes — (*The sunlight has reached the floor and now shines on Jean.*) ———— it's so warm and good ———— (*She rubs her hands as if warming them before a fire.*) ———— and bright — and so peaceful!

JEAN (*taking the razor and putting it in her hand*): Here's the broom! Go now while it's bright — out to the barn — and . . . (*Whispers in her ear.*)

JULIE (*awake*): Thank you. I'm going now to rest! But just tell me — that those who are first can also receive the gift of grace. Say it, even if you don't believe it.

JEAN: The first? No, I can't ———— But wait — Miss Julie — now I know! You're no longer among the first — you're now among — the last!

JULIE: That's true. ———— I'm among the very last. I'm the last one of all! Oh! ———— But now I can't go! ———— Tell me once more to go!

JEAN: No, now I can't either! I can't!

JULIE: And the first shall be the last!

JEAN: Don't think, don't think! You're taking all my strength from me, making me a coward. ———— What was that? I thought the bell moved! No! Shall we stuff paper in it? ———— To be so afraid of a bell! ———— But it isn't just a bell. ———— There's someone behind it — a hand sets it in motion — and something else sets the hand in motion. ———— Maybe if you cover your ears — cover your ears! But then it rings even louder! rings until someone answers. ———— And then it's too late! And then the police come — and — then ———— (*The bell rings twice loudly. Jean flinches, then straightens up.*) It's horrible! But there's no other way! ———— Go! (*Miss Julie walks firmly out through the door.*)

Anton Chekhov

Anton Chekhov (1860–1904) spent most of his childhood in relative poverty. His family managed to set up its household in Moscow after years spent in remote Taganrog, six hundred miles south of the capital. He studied medicine in Moscow and eventually took his degree. However, he did not practice medicine with any zeal and instead began writing. His earliest efforts were done for the essential purpose of relieving his family's poverty.

His first theatrical works, apart from his farces, were not successful. *Ivanov* (1887–1889) was rushed to production and was a failure. *The Wood Demon* (1889) was also a failure, but it helped Chekhov eventually produce one of his great plays, *Uncle Vanya* (1897). His most important plays are *The Seagull* (1896); *Three Sisters* (1901); and his last, *The Cherry Orchard* (1903). These plays essentially reshaped modern drama and created a realist style that has endured into the latter part of the twentieth century.

One of the first plays that Chekhov saw was *Uncle Tom's Cabin* in a Moscow performance in 1877. Afterward, he wrote a number of plays that are now lost. By 1879 he was in medical school for a five-year course and divided his literary attention between drama and short stories. The number of stories in his collected works far outnumbers his plays, and his reputation, had he never written a single play, would still be in the first ranks of literature.

Unfortunately, Chekhov showed the first signs of tuberculosis when he finished his medical training in 1884. He suffered from the disease until it killed him twenty years later. His brother died of it in 1889.

He worked continually writing stories and plays. By the time he had written *The Seagull* in 1896 he had published more than three hundred stories. *The Seagull* attracted the attention of the Moscow Art Theatre, which planned a production of it in 1898. Stanislavsky, the great Russian director and actor, played Trigorin, the lead character, in that production, but Chekhov felt he was overacting. They often had disagreements about his work, but the Moscow Art Theatre supported Chekhov fully.

The surfaces of Chekhov's plays are so lifelike that at times one feels his dramatic purposes are submerged, and to an extent that is true. Chekhov is the master of the SUBTEXT, a modern technique in which the surface of the dialogue seems innocuous or meandering, but in which deeper meanings are implied. In *Three Sisters* a great deal of time is spent discussing the wonders of the Moscow neighborhood that the

Prozorovs left behind, and certain characters are valued simply for their connection with that neighborhood. Beneath the surface of the text is another message: The past represents a form of security for the Prozorov sisters and their taking refuge in the past implies an unwillingness to live in the future. Natasha, in contrast, is filled with ambition and constantly talks about what she plans to do, showing us that her vision is forward-looking. The question of which vision is superior is left to us to decide.

Because Chekhov's subtexts are always present, it is not a simple matter to read his work. One must constantly probe, analyze, ask what is implied by what is being said. Chekhov resists "explaining" his plays by having key characters give key thematic speeches. Instead, the meaning accretes slowly. Our understanding of what a situation or circumstance finally means will change as we read and as we gather more understanding of the subtleties veiled by surfaces.

Chekhov's style is remarkable for its modernity. His approach to writing was direct, simple, and effective. Even his short stories have a clear dramatic center, and the characters he chose to observe are exceptionally modern in one important way: they are not heroes and not villains. The dramatic concept of a hero who, like Oedipus, is larger than life, or a villain, like Mephistophilis, who is essentially a devil, is nowhere to be seen in his work. Chekhov's characters are like the people we know. They are limited, recognizable, and in many ways completely ordinary.

Chekhov's genius was in taking such characters and showing their ambitions, their pain, and their successes. He was quite aware of important social changes taking place in Russia, especially changes that saw the old aristocratic classes, who once owned serfs, being reduced to a genteel impoverishment while the children of former slaves were beginning to succeed in business and real estate ventures. Chekhov's grandfather had been a serf who bought his freedom in 1841, so it is likely that Chekhov was especially supportive of such social change. His best plays provide ample evidence of his concern for the changes taking place in modern Russia.

THREE SISTERS

Three Sisters (1901) seems to be derived from Chekhov's observation of families in Moscow during a period in which social values were rapidly changing. To a large extent, the play is in the same vein as his other dramas, with very little action but a large cumulative effect. *Three Sisters* seems to meander rather than press on with urgency to a fated conclusion. Chekhov is careful to avoid giving us the sense that the action is plotted, that each gesture, each speech is moving toward an inevitable conclusion. Life, as he observed it, was not like that, and he wanted his plays to be lifelike.

In an age that took melodrama and overacting as a norm, such a lifelike portrayal of experience was sometimes baffling and unappreciated. But Chekhov persisted in his efforts to make his work understood. In all his plays the action is played down rather than being inflated or overdone. His theater is a theater of nuance, of subtle mood, of shifting emotions. Things happen slowly, but in retrospect they move toward a conclusion that is usually a change like that in *Three Sisters,* in which the sisters must leave to begin again elsewhere.

One of the constant complaints in *Three Sisters* is that the sisters must keep on living in a provincial wasteland where nothing happens and there is no excitement. They long for Moscow, where they grew up. Their interest in Vershinin is based in part on the fact that he lived on their old street, the street to which they want to return. They constantly imply that being in Moscow would solve their problems, yet the audience is not convinced. Their problems lie within themselves, not within the environment of a city. The sisters have been too dependent on their father, the General, and they repeat their mistake by becoming too dependent on their brother Andrey.

Andrey's wife, Natasha, is a grasping, materialistic, and manipulative woman. She comes from a social class that the Prozorovs look down upon. She is the only person in the play with a clear sense of an objective: to have the house all to herself and to dominate her family. Andrey is unable to see her for what she is, even though he admits at the end of the play that he realizes she is evil and cruel. He loves her nonetheless. Her machinations eventually secure the house for herself through mortgages, and soon she is able to oust all the Prozorovs and essentially evict them from their own home. Natasha's cruelty is most clearly revealed when she wants to send the old maid Anfisa back to her village because there is no room for her in the household.

Protopopov never appears onstage, yet he is an ominous presence. He is Andrey's employer, but he is also Natasha's lover, and Natasha has plans to move him into the house, pushing the baby's carriage. She will ultimately have everything her own way.

Natasha can have her own way because the Prozorovs are unable to look after their best interests. They are not grasping, not ambitious, not predatory. Consequently they are used. The sisters are generally unhappy. Olga does not like teaching, yet she ends up as a headmistress. Masha is stuck with Kuligin, the pedantic, Latin-spouting teacher, and Irina, the youngest, finally accepts her loveless marriage to Tusenbach only to lose him in a senseless duel.

Most of the Prozorovs can say, as Masha does, that they have made a mess of their lives. Andrey never realized his ambition to become a professor any more than the sisters realized their ambitions. They work, and they have a vague faith that their work is somehow important, but it is as unsatisfying to them as living in their provincial town is.

The characters frequently say that times will be better in Russia, that the sacrifices people make today will pay off in the achievements of the next generation. But this sounds like wishful thinking. The future is in the hands of Natasha, and that is — to an extent — the result of the Prozorovs' failure to understand her or to emulate her.

Three Sisters is not a nostalgic look at the old ways. Rather it is a study of people whose fecklessness makes them easy for Natasha to manipulate. The play is about people who pay a dear price simply for being the people they are.

Anton Chekhov (1860–1904)

THREE SISTERS   *1901*
TRANSLATED BY CONSTANCE GARNETT

Characters

ANDREY SERGEYEVITCH PROZOROV

NATALYA IVANOVNA (*also called* NATASHA), *his fiancée, afterward his wife*

OLGA ⎫
MASHA ⎬ *his sisters*
IRINA ⎭

FYODOR ILYITCH KULIGIN, *a high school teacher, husband of Masha*

LIEUTENANT COLONEL ALEXANDER IGNATYEVITCH VERSHININ, *Battery Commander*

BARON NIKOLAY LVOVITCH TUSENBACH, *Lieutenant*

VASSILY VASSILYEVITCH SOLYONY, *Captain*

IVAN ROMANITCH TCHEBUTYKIN, *army doctor*

ALEXEY PETROVITCH FEDOTIK, *Second Lieutenant*

VLADIMIR KARLOVITCH RODDEY, *Second Lieutenant*

FERAPONT, *an old porter from the Rural Board*°

ANFISA, *the nurse, an old woman of eighty*

Scene: *The action takes place in a provincial town.*

ACT I _____

(*In the house of the Prozorovs. A drawing room with columns beyond which a large room is visible. Midday;*

Rural Board: A local form of government.

it is bright and sunny. The table in the farther room is being laid for lunch.)

(*Olga, in the dark-blue uniform of a high school teacher, is correcting exercise books, at times standing still and then walking up and down; Masha, in a black dress, with her hat on her knee, is reading a book; Irina, in a white dress, is standing plunged in thought.*)

OLGA: Father died just a year ago, on this very day — the fifth of May, your name day,° Irina. It was very cold, snow was falling. I felt as though I should not live through it; you lay fainting as though you were dead. But now a year has passed and we can think of it calmly; you are already in a white dress, your face radiant. (*The clock strikes twelve.*) The clock was striking then too. (*A pause.*) I remember the band playing and the firing at the cemetery as they carried the coffin. Though he was a general in command of a brigade, yet there weren't many people. It was raining, though. Heavy rain and snow.

IRINA: Why recall it!

(*Baron Tusenbach, Tchebutykin, and Solyony appear near the table in the dining room, beyond the columns.*)

name day: The feast day of the saint after whom Irina was named. Many Russians celebrate a feast day as if it were a birthday.

OLGA: It is warm today, we can have the windows open, but the birches are not in leaf yet. Father was given his brigade and came here with us from Moscow eleven years ago and I remember distinctly that in Moscow at this time, at the beginning of May, everything was already in flower; it was warm, and everything was bathed in sunshine. It's eleven years ago, and yet I remember it all as though we had left it yesterday. Oh, dear! I woke up this morning, I saw a blaze of sunshine. I saw the spring, and joy stirred in my heart. I had a passionate longing to be back at home again!

TCHEBUTYKIN: The devil it is!

TUSENBACH: Of course, it's nonsense.

(*Masha, brooding over a book, softly whistles a song.*)

OLGA: Don't whistle, Masha. How can you! (*A pause.*) Being all day in school and then at my lessons till the evening gives me a perpetual headache and thoughts as gloomy as though I' were old. And really these four years that I have been at the high school I have felt my strength and my youth oozing away from me every day. And only one yearning grows stronger and stronger. . . .

IRINA: To go back to Moscow. To sell the house, to make an end of everything here, and off to Moscow. . . .

OLGA: Yes! To Moscow, and quickly.

(*Tchebutykin and Tusenbach laugh.*)

IRINA: Andrey will probably be a professor; he will not live here anyhow. The only difficulty is poor Masha.

OLGA: Masha will come and spend the whole summer in Moscow every year.

(*Masha softly whistles a tune.*)

IRINA: Please God it will all be managed. (*Looking out of window.*) How fine it is today. I don't know why I feel so lighthearted! I remembered this morning that it was my name day and at once I felt joyful and thought of my childhood when Mother was living. And I was thrilled by such wonderful thoughts, such thoughts!

OLGA: You are radiant today and looking lovelier than usual. And Masha is lovely too. Andrey would be nice-looking, but he has grown too fat and that does not suit him. And I have grown older and ever so much thinner. I suppose it's because I get so cross with the girls at school. Today now I am free, I am at home, and my head doesn't ache, and I feel younger than yesterday. I am only twenty-eight . . . It's all quite right, it's all from God, but it seems to me that if I were married and sitting at home all day, it would be better. (*A pause.*) I should be fond of my husband.

TUSENBACH (*to Solyony*): You talk such nonsense, I am tired of listening to you. (*Coming into the drawing room.*) I forgot to tell you, you will receive a visit today from Vershinin, the new commander of our battery. (*Sits down to the piano.*)

OLGA: Well, I shall be delighted.

IRINA: Is he old?

TUSENBACH: No, nothing to speak of. Forty or forty-five at the most. (*Softly plays the piano.*) He seems to be a nice fellow. He is not stupid, that's certain. Only he talks a lot.

IRINA: Is he interesting?

TUSENBACH: Yes, he is all right, only he has a wife, a mother-in-law, and two little girls. And it's his second wife too. He is paying calls and telling everyone that he has a wife and two little girls. He'll tell you so too. His wife seems a bit crazy, with her hair in a long plait like a girl's, always talks in a high-flown style, makes philosophical reflections and frequently attempts to commit suicide, evidently to annoy her husband. I should have left a woman like that years ago, but he puts up with her and merely complains.

SOLYONY (*coming into the drawing room with Tchebutykin*): With one hand I can only lift up half a hundredweight, but with both hands I can lift up a hundredweight and a half or even a hundredweight and three-quarters.° From that I conclude that two men are not only twice but three times as strong as one man, or even more. . . .

TCHEBUTYKIN (*reading the newspaper as he comes in*): For hair falling out . . . two ounces of naphthalene in half a bottle of spirit . . . to be dissolved and used daily. . . . (*Puts it down in his notebook.*) Let's make a note of it! No, I don't want it. . . . (*Scratches it out.*) It doesn't matter.

IRINA: Ivan Romanitch, dear Ivan Romanitch!

TCHEBUTYKIN: What is it, my child, my joy?

IRINA: Tell me, why is it I am so happy today? As though I were sailing with the great blue sky above me and big white birds flying over it. Why is it? Why?

TCHEBUTYKIN (*kissing both her hands, tenderly*): My white bird. . . .

IRINA: When I woke up this morning, got up and washed, it suddenly seemed to me as though everything in the world was clear to me and that I knew how one ought to live. Dear Ivan Romanitch, I know all about it. A man ought to work, to toil in the sweat of his brow, whoever he may be, and all the purpose and meaning of his life, his happiness, his ecstasies lie in that alone. How delightful to be a workman who gets up before dawn and breaks stones on the road, or a shepherd, or a schoolmaster

hundredweight . . . and three-quarters: 150 to 175 pounds.

teaching children, or an engine driver. . . . Oh, dear! to say nothing of human beings, it would be better to be an ox, better to be a humble horse and work, than a young woman who wakes at twelve o'clock, then has coffee in bed, then spends two hours dressing. . . . Oh, how awful that is! Just as one has a craving for water in hot weather I have a craving for work. And if I don't get up early and work, give me up as a friend, Ivan Romanitch.

TCHEBUTYKIN (*tenderly*): I'll give you up, I'll give you up. . . .

OLGA: Father trained us to get up at seven o'clock. Now Irina wakes at seven and lies in bed at least till nine thinking. And she looks so serious! (*Laughs.*)

IRINA: You are used to thinking of me as a child and are surprised when I look serious. I am twenty!

TUSENBACH: The yearning for work, oh dear, how well I understand it! I have never worked in my life. I was born in cold, idle Petersburg, in a family that had known nothing of work or cares of any kind. I remember, when I came home from the school of cadets, a footman used to pull off my boots. I used to be troublesome, but my mother looked at me with reverential awe, and was surprised when other people did not do the same. I was guarded from work. But I doubt if they have succeeded in guarding me completely, I doubt it! The time is at hand, an avalanche is moving down upon us, a mighty clearing storm which is coming, is already near and will soon blow the laziness, the indifference, the distaste for work, the rotten boredom out of our society. I shall work, and in another twenty-five or thirty years everyone will have to work. Everyone!

TCHEBUTYKIN: I am not going to work.

TUSENBACH: You don't count.

SOLYONY: In another twenty-five years you won't be here, thank God. In two or three years you will kick the bucket, or I shall lose my temper and put a bullet through your head, my angel.

(*Pulls a scent bottle out of his pocket and sprinkles his chest and hands.*)

TCHEBUTYKIN (*laughs*): And I really have never done anything at all. I haven't done a stroke of work since I left the university, I have never read a book, I read nothing but newspapers. . . . (*Takes another newspaper out of his pocket.*) Here . . . I know, for instance, from the newspapers that there was such a person as Dobrolyubov,° but what he wrote, I can't say. . . . Goodness only knows. . . . (*A knock*

Dobrolyubov: Nicholas A. Dobrolyubov (1836–1861), a literary and social critic.

is heard on the floor from the story below.) There . . . they are calling me downstairs, someone has come for me. I'll be back directly. . . . Wait a minute. . . . (*Goes out hurriedly, combing his beard.*)

IRINA: He's got something up his sleeve.

TUSENBACH: Yes, he went out with a solemn face; evidently he is just going to bring you a present.

IRINA: What a nuisance!

OLGA: Yes, it's awful. He is always doing something silly.

MASHA: By the sea strand an oak tree green . . . upon that oak a chain of gold . . . upon that oak a chain of gold. (*Gets up, humming softly.*)

OLGA: You are not very cheerful today, Masha.

(*Masha, humming, puts on her hat.*)

OLGA: Where are you going?

MASHA: Home.

IRINA: How queer! . . .

TUSENBACH: To go away from a name day party!

MASHA: Never mind. . . . I'll come in the evening. Goodbye, my darling. . . . (*Kisses Irina.*) Once again I wish you, be well and happy. In old days, when Father was alive, we always had thirty or forty officers here on name days; it was noisy, but today there is only a man and a half, and it is as still as the desert. . . . I'll go. . . . I am in the blues today, I am feeling glum, so don't you mind what I say. (*Laughing through her tears.*) We'll talk some other time, and so for now good-bye, darling, I am going. . . .

IRINA (*discontentedly*) Oh, how tiresome you are. . . .

OLGA (*with tears*): I understand you, Masha.

SOLYONY: If a man philosophizes, there will be philosophy or sophistry, anyway, but if a woman philosophizes, or two do it, then you may just snap your fingers!

MASHA: What do you mean to say by that, you terrible person?

SOLYONY: Nothing. He had not time to say "alack," before the bear was on his back. (*A pause.*)

MASHA (*to Olga, angrily*): Don't blubber!

(*Enter Anfisa and Ferapont carrying a cake.*)

ANFISA: This way, my good man. Come in, your boots are clean. (*To Irina.*) From the Rural Board, from Mihail Ivanitch Protopopov. . . . A cake.

IRINA: Thanks. Thank him. (*Takes the cake.*)

FERAPONT: What?

IRINA (*more loudly*): Thank him from me!

OLGA: Nurse dear, give him some pie. Ferapont, go along, they will give you some pie.

FERAPONT: Eh?

ANFISA: Come along, Ferapont Spiridonitch, my good soul, come along. . . .

(*Goes out with Ferapont.*)

MASHA: I don't like that Protopopov, that Mihail Potapitch or Ivanitch. He ought not to be invited.

IRINA: I did not invite him.

MASHA: That's a good thing.

(*Enter Tchebutykin, followed by an orderly with a silver samovar; a hum of surprise and displeasure.*)

OLGA (*putting her hands over her face*): A samovar! How awful! (*Goes out to the table in the dining room.*)

IRINA: My dear Ivan Romanitch, what are you thinking about!

TUSENBACH (*laughs*): I warned you!

MASHA: Ivan Romanitch, you really have no conscience!

TCHEBUTYKIN: My dear girls, my darlings, you are all that I have, you are the most precious treasures I have on earth. I shall soon be sixty, I am an old man, alone in the world, a useless old man. . . . There is nothing good in me, except my love for you, and if it were not for you, I should have been dead long ago. . . . (*To Irina.*) My dear, my little girl, I've known you from a baby. . . . I've carried you in my arms. . . . I loved your dear mother. . . .

IRINA: But why such expensive presents?

TCHEBUTYKIN (*angry and tearful*): Expensive presents. . . . Get along with you! (*To the orderly.*) Take the samovar in there. . . .(*Mimicking.*) Expensive presents. . . .

(*The orderly carries the samovar into the dining room.*)

ANFISA (*crossing the room*): My dears, a colonel is here, a stranger. . . . He has taken off his greatcoat, children, he is coming in here. Irinushka, you must be nice and polite, dear. . . . (*As she goes out.*) And it's time for lunch already . . . mercy on us. . . .

TUSENBACH: Vershinin, I suppose.

(*Enter Vershinin.*)

TUSENBACH: Colonel Vershinin.

VERSHININ (*to Masha and Irina*): I have the honor to introduce myself, my name is Vershinin. I am very, very glad to be in your house at last. How you have grown up! Aie-Aie!

IRINA: Please sit down. We are delighted to see you.

VERSHININ (*with animation*): How glad I am, how glad I am! But there are three of you sisters. I remember — three little girls. I don't remember your faces, but that your father, Colonel Prozorov, had three little girls I remember perfectly, and saw them with my own eyes. How time passes! Hey-ho, how it passes!

TUSENBACH: Alexandr Ignatyevitch has come from Moscow.

IRINA: From Moscow? You have come from Moscow?

VERSHININ: Yes. Your father was in command of a battery there, and I was an officer in the same brigade. (*To Masha.*) Your face, now, I seem to remember.

MASHA: I don't remember you.

IRINA: Olya! Olya! (*Calls into the dining room.*) Olya, come!

(*Olga comes out of the dining room into the drawing room.*)

IRINA: Colonel Vershinin is from Moscow, it appears.

VERSHININ: So you are Olga Sergeyevna, the eldest. . . . And you are Marya. . . . And you are Irina, the youngest. . . .

OLGA: You come from Moscow?

VERSHININ: Yes. I studied in Moscow. I began my service there, I served there for years, and at last I have been given a battery here — I have come here as you see. I don't remember you exactly, I only remember you were three sisters. I remember your father. If I shut my eyes, I can see him as though he were living. I used to visit you in Moscow. . . .

OLGA: I thought I remembered everyone, and now all at once . . .

VERSHININ: My name is Alexandr Ignatyevitch.

IRINA: Alexandr Ignatyevitch, you have come from Moscow. . . . What a surprise!

OLGA: We are going to move there, you know.

IRINA: We are hoping to be there by the autumn. It's our native town, we were born there. . . . In Old Basmanny Street. . . . (*Both laugh with delight.*)

MASHA: To see someone from our own town unexpectedly! (*Eagerly.*) Now I remember! Do you remember, Olya, they used to talk of the "love-sick major"? You were a lieutenant at that time and were in love, and for some reason everyone called you "major" to tease you. . . .

VERSHININ (*laughs*): Yes, yes. . . . The love-sick major, that was it.

MASHA: You only had a mustache then. . . . Oh, how much older you look! (*Through tears.*) How much older!

VERSHININ: Yes, when I was called the love-sick major I was young, I was in love. Now it's very different.

OLGA: But you haven't a single gray hair. You have grown older but you are not old.

VERSHININ: I am in my forty-third year, though. Is it long since you left Moscow?

IRINA: Eleven years. But why are you crying, Masha, you queer girl? . . . (*Through her tears.*) I shall cry too. . . .

MASHA: I am all right. And in which street did you live?

VERSHININ: In Old Basmanny.

OLGA: And that's where we lived too. . . .

VERSHININ: At one time I lived in Nyemetsky Street. I used to go from there to the Red Barracks. There is a gloomy-looking bridge on the way, where the water makes a noise. It makes a lonely man feel melancholy. (*A pause.*) And here what a broad, splendid river! A marvelous river!

OLGA: Yes, but it is cold. It's cold here and there are gnats. . . .

VERSHININ: How can you! You've such a splendid healthy Russian climate here. Forest, river . . . and birches here too. Charming, modest birches, I love them better than any other trees. It's nice to live here. The only strange thing is that the railway station is fifteen miles away. . . . And no one knows why it is so.

SOLYONY: I know why it is. (*They all look at him.*) Because if the station had been near it would not have been so far, and if it is far, it's because it is not near.

(*An awkward silence.*)

TUSENBACH: He is fond of his joke, Vassily Vassilyevitch.

OLGA: Now I recall you, too. I remember.

VERSHININ: I knew your mother.

TCHEBUTYKIN: She was a fine woman, the Kingdom of Heaven be hers.

IRINA: Mother is buried in Moscow.

OLGA: In the Novo-Dyevitchy.° . . .

MASHA: Would you believe it, I am already beginning to forget her face. So people will not remember us either . . . they will forget us.

VERSHININ: Yes. They will forget us. Such is our fate, there is no help for it. What seems to us serious, significant, very important, will one day be forgotten or will seem unimportant. (*A pause.*) And it's curious that we can't possibly tell what exactly will be considered great and important, and what will seem paltry and ridiculous. Did not the discoveries of Copernicus or Columbus, let us say, seem useless and ridiculous at first, while the nonsensical writings of some wiseacre seemed true? And it may be that our present life, which we accept so readily, will in time seem queer, uncomfortable, not sensible, not clean enough, perhaps even sinful. . . .

TUSENBACH: Who knows? Perhaps our age will be called a great one and remembered with respect. Now we have no torture-chamber, no executions, no invasions, but at the same time how much unhappiness there is!

SOLYONY (*in a high-pitched voice*): Chook, chook, chook. . . . It's bread and meat to the baron to talk about ideas.

Novo-Dyevitchy: A famous cemetery in Moscow.

TUSENBACH: Vassily Vassilyevitch, I ask you to let me alone. . . . (*Moves to another seat.*) It gets boring, at last.

SOLYONY (*in a high-pitched voice*): Chook, chook, chook. . . .

TUSENBACH (*to Vershinin*): The unhappiness which one observes now — there is so much of it — does indicate, however, that society has reached a certain moral level.

VERSHININ: Yes, yes, of course.

TCHEBUTYKIN: You said just now, baron, that our age will be called great; but people are small all the same. . . . (*Gets up.*) Look how small I am.

(*A violin is played behind the scenes.*)

MASHA: That's Andrey playing, our brother.

IRINA: He is the learned one of the family We expect him to become a professor. Father was a military man, but his son has gone in for a learned career.

MASHA: It was father's wish.

OLGA: We have been teasing him today. We think he is a little in love.

IRINA: With a young lady living here. She will come in today most likely.

MASHA: Oh, how she dresses! It's not that her clothes are merely ugly or out of fashion, they are simply pitiful. A queer gaudy yellowish skirt with some sort of vulgar fringe and a red blouse. And her cheeks scrubbed till they shine! Andrey is not in love with her — I won't admit that, he has some taste anyway — it's simply for fun, he is teasing us, playing the fool. I heard yesterday that she is going to be married to Protopopov, the chairman of our Rural Board. And a very good thing too. . . . (*At the side door.*) Andrey, come here, dear, for a minute!

(*Enter Andrey.*)

OLGA: This is my brother, Andrey Sergeyevitch.

VERSHININ: My name is Vershinin.

ANDREY: And mine is Prozorov. (*Mops his perspiring face.*) You are our new battery commander?

OLGA: Only fancy, Alexandr Ignatyevitch comes from Moscow.

ANDREY: Really? Well, then, I congratulate you. My sisters will let you have no peace.

VERSHININ: I have had time to bore your sisters already.

IRINA: See what a pretty picture-frame Andrey has given me today! (*Shows the frame.*) He made it himself.

VERSHININ (*looking at the frame and not knowing what to say*): Yes . . . it is a thing. . . .

IRINA: And that frame above the piano, he made that too!

(*Andrey waves his hand in despair and moves away.*)

OLGA: He is learned, and he plays the violin, and he makes all sorts of things with the fretsaw. In fact he is good all round. Andrey, don't go! That's a way he has — he always tries to make off! Come here!

(*Masha and Irina take him by the arms and, laughing, lead him back.*)

MASHA: Come, come!

ANDREY: Leave me alone, please!

MASHA: How absurd he is! Alexandr Ignatyevitch used to be called the love-sick major at one time, and he was not a bit offended.

VERSHININ: Not in the least!

MASHA: And I should like to call you the love-sick violinist!

IRINA: Or the love-sick professor!

OLGA: He is in love! Andryusha is in love!

IRINA (*claps her hands*): Bravo, bravo! Encore! Andryusha is in love!

TCHEBUTYKIN (*comes up behind Andrey and puts both arms round his waist*): Nature our hearts for love created! (*Laughs, then sits down and reads the newspaper which he takes out of his pocket.*)

ANDREY: Come, that's enough, that's enough. . . . (*Mops his face.*) I haven't slept all night and this morning I don't feel quite myself, as they say. I read till four o'clock and then went to bed, but it was no use. I thought of one thing and another, and then it gets light so early; the sun simply pours into my bedroom. I want while I am here during the summer to translate a book from the English. . . .

VERSHININ: You read English then?

ANDREY: Yes. Our father, the Kingdom of Heaven be his, oppressed us with education. It's absurd and silly, but it must be confessed I began to get fatter after his death, and I have grown too fat in one year, as though a weight had been taken off my body. Thanks to our father we all know English, French, and German, and Irina knows Italian too. But what it cost us!

MASHA: In this town to know three languages is an unnecessary luxury! Not even a luxury, but an unnecessary encumbrance, like a sixth finger. We know a great deal that is unnecessary.

VERSHININ: What next! (*Laughs.*) You know a great deal that is unnecessary! I don't think there can be a town so dull and dismal that intelligent and educated people are unnecessary in it. Let us suppose that of the hundred thousand people living in this town, which is, of course, uncultured and behind the times, there are only three of your sort. It goes without saying that you cannot conquer the mass of darkness round you; little by little, as you go on living, you will be lost in the crowd. You will have to give in to it. Life will get the better of you, but still you will not disappear without a trace. After you there may appear perhaps six like you, then twelve and so on until such as you form a majority. In two or three hundred years life on earth will be unimaginably beautiful, marvelous. Man needs such a life and, though he hasn't it yet, he must have a presentiment of it, expect it, dream of it, prepare for it; for that he must see and know more than his father and grandfather. (*Laughs.*) And you complain of knowing a great deal that's unnecessary.

MASHA (*takes off her hat*): I'll stay to lunch.

IRINA (*with a sigh*): All that really ought to be written down. . . .

(*Andrey has slipped away unobserved.*)

TUSENBACH: You say that after many years life on earth will be beautiful and marvelous. That's true. But in order to have any share, however far off, in it now one must be preparing for it, one must be working. . . .

VERSHININ (*gets up*): Yes. What a lot of flowers you have! (*Looking round.*) And delightful rooms. I envy you! I've been knocking about all my life from one wretched lodging to another, always with two chairs and a sofa and stoves which smoke. What I have been lacking all my life is just such flowers. . . . (*Rubs his hands.*) But there, it's no use thinking about it!

TUSENBACH: Yes, we must work. I'll be bound you think the German° is getting sentimental. But on my honor I am Russian and I can't even speak German. My father belongd to the Orthodox Church. . . . (*A pause.*)

VERSHININ (*walks about the stage*): I often think, what if one were to begin life over again, knowing what one is about! If one life, which has been already lived, were only a rough sketch so to say, and the second were the fair copy! Then, I fancy, every one of us would try before everything not to repeat himself, anyway he would create a different setting for his life; would have a house like this with plenty of light and masses of flowers. . . . I have a wife and two little girls, my wife is in delicate health and so on and so on, but if I were to begin life over again I would not marry. . . . No, no!

(*Enter Kuligin in the uniform of a schoolmaster.*)

KULIGIN (*goes up to Irina*): Dear sister, allow me to congratulate you on your name day and with all my heart to wish you good health and everything else that one can desire for a girl of your age. And to offer you as a gift this little book. (*Gives her a book.*) The history of our high school for fifty

---

German: A term once used in Russia to refer to all foreigners.

years, written by myself. An insignificant little book, written because I had nothing better to do, but still you can read it. Good morning, friends. (*To Vershinin.*) My name is Kuligin, teacher in the high school here. (*To Irina.*) In that book you will find a list of all who have finished their studies in our high school during the last fifty years. *Feci quod potui, faciant meliora potentes.*° (*Kisses Masha.*)

IRINA: Why, but you gave me a copy of this book at Easter.

KULIGIN (*laughs*): Impossible! If that's so, give it back, or better still, give it to the Colonel. Please accept it, Colonel. Some day when you are bored you can read it.

VERSHININ: Thank you. (*Is about to take leave.*) I am extremely glad to have made your acquaintance. . . .

OLGA: You are going? No, no!

IRINA: You must stay to lunch with us. Please do.

OLGA: Pray do!

VERSHININ (*bows*): I believe I have chanced on a name day. Forgive me, I did not know and have not congratulated you. . . . (*Walks away with Olga into the dining room.*)

KULIGIN: Today, gentlemen, is Sunday, a day of rest. Let us all rest and enjoy ourselves each in accordance with our age and our position. The carpets should be taken up for the summer and put away till the winter . . . Persian powder or naphthalene. . . . The Romans were healthy because they knew how to work and they knew how to rest, they had *mens sana in corpore sano.*° Their life was molded into a certain framework. Our headmaster says that the most important thing in every life is its framework. . . . What loses its framework, comes to an end — and it's the same in our everyday life. (*Puts his arm round Masha's waist, laughing.*) Masha loves me. My wife loves me. And the window curtains, too, ought to be put away together with the carpets. . . . Today I feel cheerful and in the best of spirits. Masha, at four o'clock this afternoon we have to be at the headmaster's. An excursion has been arranged for the teachers and their families.

MASHA: I am not going.

KULIGIN (*grieved*): Dear Masha, why not?

MASHA: We'll talk about it afterward. . . . (*Angrily.*) Very well, I will go, only let me alone, please. . . . (*Walks away.*)

KULIGIN: And then we shall spend the evening at the headmaster's. In spite of the delicate state of his health, that man tries before all things to be sociable. He is an excellent, noble personality. A splendid

Feci . . . potentes: Latin for "I have done what I can; let those who are more able do better."
mens . . . sano: Latin for "a sound mind in a sound body."

man. Yesterday, after the meeting, he said to me, "I am tired, Fyodor Ilyitch, I am tired." (*Looks at the clock, then at his watch.*) Your clock is seven minutes fast. "Yes," he said, "I am tired."

(*Sounds of a violin behind the scenes.*)

OLGA: Come to lunch, please. There's a pie!

KULIGIN: Ah, Olga, my dear Olga! Yesterday I was working from early morning till eleven o'clock at night and was tired out, and today I feel happy. (*Goes up to the table in the dining room.*) My dear. . . .

TCHEBUTYKIN (*puts the newspaper in his pocket and combs his beard*): Pie? Splendid!

MASHA (*to Tchebutykin, sternly*): Only mind you don't drink today! Do you hear? It's bad for you to drink.

TCHEBUTYKIN: Oh, come, that's a thing of the past. It's two years since I got drunk. (*Impatiently.*) But there, my good girl, what does it matter!

MASHA: Anyway, don't you dare to drink. Don't dare. (*Angrily, but so as not to be heard by her husband.*) Again, damnation take it, I am to be bored a whole evening at the headmaster's!

TUSENBACH: I wouldn't go if I were you. . . . It's very simple.

TCHEBUTYKIN: Don't go, my love.

MASHA: Oh, yes, don't go! . . . It's a damnable life, insufferable. . . . (*Goes to the dining room.*)

TCHEBUTYKIN (*following her*): Come, come. . . .

SOLYONY (*going to the dining room*): Chook, chook, chook. . . .

TUSENBACH: Enough, Vassily Vassilyevitch! Leave off!

SOLYONY: Chook, chook, chook. . . .

KULIGIN (*gaily*): Your health, Colonel! I am a schoolmaster and one of the family here, Masha's husband. . . . She is very kind, really, very kind. . . .

VERSHININ: I'll have some of this dark-colored vodka. . . . (*Drinks.*) To your health! (*To Olga.*) I feel so happy with all of you!

(*No one is left in the drawing room but Irina and Tusenbach.*)

IRINA: Masha is in low spirits today. She was married at eighteen, when she thought him the cleverest of men. But now it's not the same. He is the kindest of men, but he is not the cleverest.

OLGA (*impatiently*): Andrey, do come!

ANDREY (*behind the scenes*): I am coming. (*Comes in and goes to the table.*)

TUSENBACH: What are you thinking about?

IRINA: Nothing. I don't like that Solyony of yours, I am afraid of him. He keeps on saying such stupid things. . . .

TUSENBACH: He is a queer man. I am sorry for him and annoyed by him, but more sorry. I think he is shy. . . . When one is alone with him he is very intelligent and friendly, but in company he is rude, a bully. Dont go yet, let them sit down to the table. Let me be by you. What are you thinking of? (*A pause.*) You are twenty, I am not yet thirty. How many years have we got before us, a long, long chain of days full of my love for you. . . .

IRINA: Nikolay Lvovitch, don't talk to me about love.

TUSENBACH (*not listening*): I have a passionate craving for life, for struggle, for work, and that craving is mingled in my soul with my love for you, Irina, and just because you are beautiful it seems to me that life too is beautiful! What are you thinking of?

IRINA: You say life is beautiful. . . . Yes, but what if it only seems so! Life for us three sisters has not been beautiful yet, we have been stifled by it as plants are choked by weeds. . . . I am shedding tears. . . . I mustn't do that. (*Hurriedly wipes her eyes and smiles.*) I must work, I must work. The reason we are depressed and take such a gloomy view of life is that we know nothing of work. We come of people who despised work. . . .

(*Enter Natalya Ivanovna; she is wearing a pink dress with a green sash.*)

NATASHA: They are sitting down to lunch already . . . I am late . . . (*Steals a glance at herself in the glass and sets herself to rights.*) I think my hair is all right. (*Seeing Irina.*) Dear Irina Sergeyevna, I congratulate you! (*Gives her a vigorous and prolonged kiss.*) You have a lot of visitors, I really feel shy. . . . Good day, Baron!

OLGA (*coming into the drawing room*): Well, here is Natalya Ivanovna! How are you, my dear? (*Kisses her.*)

NATASHA: Congratulations on the name day. You have such a big party and I feel awfully shy. . . .

OLGA: Nonsense, we have only our own people. (*In an undertone, in alarm.*) You've got on a green sash! My dear, that's not nice!

NATASHA: Why, is that a bad omen?

OLGA: No, it's only that it doesn't go with your dress . . . and it looks queer. . . .

NATASHA (*in a tearful voice*): Really? But you know it's not green exactly, it's more a neutral color. (*Follows Olga into the dining room.*)

(*In the dining room they are all sitting down to lunch; there is no one in the drawing room.*)

KULIGIN: I wish you a good husband, Irina. It's time for you to think of getting married.

TCHEBUTYKIN: Natalya Ivanovna, I hope we may hear of your engagement, too.

KULIGIN: Natalya Ivanovna has got a suitor already.

MASHA (*strikes her plate with her fork*): Ladies and gentlemen, I want to make a speech!

KULIGIN: You deserve three bad marks for conduct.

VERSHININ: How nice this cordial is! What is it made of?

SOLYONY: Beetles.

IRINA (*in a tearful voice*): Ugh ugh! How disgusting.

OLGA: We are going to have roast turkey and apple pie for supper. Thank God I am at home all day and shall be at home in the evening. . . . Friends, won't you come this evening?

VERSHININ: Allow me to come too.

IRINA: Please do.

NATASHA: They don't stand on ceremony.

TCHEBUTYKIN: Nature our hearts for love created! (*Laughs.*)

ANDREY (*angrily*): Do leave off, I wonder you are not tired of it!

(*Fedotik and Roddey come in with a big basket of flowers.*)

FEDOTIK: I say, they are at lunch already.

RODDEY (*speaking loudly, with a lisp*): At lunch? Yes, they are at lunch already. . . .

FEDOTIK: Wait a minute. (*Takes a snapshot.*) One! Wait another minute. . . . (*Takes another snapshot.*) Two! Now it's ready.

(*They take the basket and walk into the dining room, where they are greeted noisily.*)

RODDEY (*loudly*): My congratulations! I wish you everything, everything! The weather is delightful, perfectly magnificent. I've been out all the morning for a walk with the high school boys. I teach them gymnastics.

FEDOTIK: You may move, Irina Sergeyevna, you may move. (*Taking a photograph.*) You look charming today. (*Taking a top out of his pocket.*) Here is a top, by the way. . . . It has a wonderful note. . . .

IRINA: How lovely!

MASHA: By the seashore an oak tree green. . . . Upon that oak a chain of gold. . . . (*Complainingly.*) Why do I keep saying that? That phrase has been haunting me all day. . . .

KULIGIN: Thirteen at table!

RODDEY (*loudly*): Surely you do not attach importance to such superstitions? (*Laughter.*)

KULIGIN: If there are thirteen at table, it means that someone present is in love. It's not you, Ivan Romanitch, by any chance? (*Laughter.*)

TCHEBUTYKIN: I am an old sinner, but why Natalya Ivanovna is overcome, I can't imagine . . .

(*Loud laughter; Natasha runs out from the dining room into the drawing room followed by Andrey.*)

ABOVE: The Prozorovs and their guests are sitting down for lunch in Liviu Ciulei's 1984 production at the Guthrie Theater. RIGHT: Masha (Joan MacIntosh) talking with Tchebutykin (Michael Egan) with Andrey (Jay Patterson) wheeling the sleeping baby in a perambulator in the background.

ANDREY: Come, don't take any notice! Wait a minute
. . . stop, I entreat you. . . .

NATASHA: I am ashamed. . . . I don't know what's the
matter with me and they make fun of me. I know
it's improper for me to leave the table like this,
but I can't help it. . . . I can't . . . (*Covers her face
with her hands.*)

ANDREY: My dear girl, I entreat you, I implore you,
don't be upset. I assure you they are only joking,
they do it in all kindness. My dear, my sweet, they
are all kind, warmhearted people and they are fond
of me and of you. Come here to the window, here
they can't see us. . . . (*Looks round.*)

NATASHA: I am so unaccustomed to society! . . .

ANDREY: Oh youth, lovely, marvelous youth! My dear,
my sweet, don't be so distressed! Believe me, believe
me. . . . I feel so happy, my soul is full of love and
rapture. . . . Oh, they can't see us, they can't see
us! Why, why, I love you, when I first loved you
— oh, I don't know. My dear, my sweet, pure one,
be my wife! I love you, I love you . . . as I have
never loved anyone . . . (*A kiss.*)

(*Two officers come in and, seeing the pair kissing,
stop in amazement.*)

ACT II _____

(*The same scene as in Act I. Eight o'clock in the
evening. Behind the scenes in the street there is the
faintly audible sound of a concertina. There is no light.
Natalya Ivanovna enters in a dressing gown, carrying
a candle; she comes in and stops at the door leading
to Andrey's room.*)

NATASHA: What are you doing, Andryusha? Reading?
Never mind, I only just asked. . . . (*Goes and opens
another door and, peeping into it, shuts it again.*)
Is there a light?

ANDREY (*enters with a book in his hand*): What is it,
Natasha?

NATASHA: I was looking to see whether there was a
light. . . . It's Carnival, the servants are not themselves; one has always to be on the lookout for
fear something goes wrong. Last night at twelve
o'clock I passed through the dining room, and there
was a candle left burning. I couldn't find out who
had lighted it. (*Puts down the candle.*) What's the
time?

ANDREY (*looking at his watch*): A quarter past eight.

NATASHA: And Olga and Irina aren't in yet. They
haven't come in. Still at work, poor dears! Olga is
at the teachers' council and Irina at the telegraph
office. . . . (*Sighs.*) I was saying to your sister this
morning, "Take care of yourself, Irina darling,"

said I. But she won't listen. A quarter past eight,
you say? I am afraid our Бobik is not at all well.
Why is he so cold? Yesterday he was feverish and
today he is cold all over. . . . I am so anxious!

ANDREY: It's all right, Natasha. The boy is quite well.

NATASHA: We had better be careful about his food,
anyway. I am anxious. And I am told that the
mummers are going to be here for the Carnival at
nine o'clock this evening. It would be better for
them not to come, Andryusha.

ANDREY: I really don't know. They've been invited,
you know.

NATASHA: Baby woke up this morning, looked at me,
and all at once he gave a smile; so he knew me.
"Good morning, Bobik!" said I. "Good morning,
darling!" And he laughed. Children understand;
they understand very well. So I shall tell them,
Andryusha, not to let the Carnival party come in.

ANDREY (*irresolutely*): That's for my sisters to say. It's
for them to give orders.

NATASHA: Yes, for them too; I will speak to them.
They are so kind. . . . (*Is going.*) I've ordered junket
for supper. The doctor says you must eat nothing
but junket, or you will never get thinner. (*Stops.*)
Bobik is cold. I am afraid his room is chilly, perhaps.
We ought to put him in a different room till the
warm weather comes, anyway. Irina's room, for
instance, is just right for a nursery: it's dry and the
sun shines there all day. I must tell her; she might
share Olga's room for the time. . . . She is never at
home, anyway, except for the night. . . . (*A pause.*)
Andryushantchik, why don't you speak?

ANDREY: Nothing. I was thinking. . . . Besides, I have
nothing to say.

NATASHA: Yes . . . what was it I meant to tell
you? . . . Oh, yes; Ferapont has come from the Rural
Board, and is asking for you.

ANDREY (*yawns*): Send him in.

(*Natasha goes out; Andrey, bending down to the candle
which she has left behind, reads. Enter Ferapont; he
wears an old shabby overcoat, with the collar turned
up, and has a scarf over his ears.*)

ANDREY: Good evening, my good man. What is it?

FERAPONT: The chairman has sent a book and a paper
of some sort here. . . . (*Gives the book and an
envelope.*)

ANDREY: Thanks. Very good. But why have you come
so late? It is past eight.

FERAPONT: Eh?

ANDREY (*louder*): I say, you have come late. It is eight
o'clock.

FERAPONT: Just so. I came before it was dark, but
they wouldn't let me see you. The master is busy,
they told me. Well, of course, if you are busy, I

am in no hurry. (*Thinking that Andrey has asked him a question.*) Eh?

ANDREY: Nothing. (*Examines the book.*) Tomorrow is Friday. We haven't a sitting, but I'll come all the same . . . and do my work. It's dull at home. . . . (*A pause.*) Dear old man, how strangely life changes and deceives one! Today I was so bored and had nothing to do, so I picked up this book — old university lectures — and I laughed. . . . Good heavens! I am the secretary of the Rural Board of which Protopopov is the chairman. I am the secretary, and the most I can hope for is to become a member of the Board! Me, a member of the local Rural Board, while I dream every night I am professor of the University of Moscow — a distinguished man, of whom all Russia is proud!

FERAPONT: I can't say, sir. . . . I don't hear well. . . .

ANDREY: If you did hear well, perhaps I should not talk to you. I must talk to somebody, and my wife does not understand me. My sisters I am somehow afraid of — I'm afraid they will laugh at me and make me ashamed. . . . I don't drink, I am not fond of restaurants, but how I should enjoy sitting at Tyestov's in Moscow at this moment, dear old chap!

FERAPONT: A contractor was saying at the Board the other day that there were some merchants in Moscow eating pancakes; one who ate forty, it seems, died. It was either forty or fifty, I don't remember.

ANDREY: In Moscow you sit in a huge room at a restaurant; you know no one and no one knows you, and at the same time you don't feel a stranger. . . . But here you know everyone and everyone knows you, and yet you are a stranger — a stranger. . . . A stranger, and lonely. . . .

FERAPONT: Eh? (*A pause.*) And the same contractor says — maybe it's not true — that there's a rope stretched right across Moscow.

ANDREY: What for?

FERAPONT: I can't say, sir. The contractor said so.

ANDREY: Nonsense. (*Reads.*) Have you ever been in Moscow?

FERAPONT (*after a pause*): No, never. It was not God's will I should. (*A pause.*) Am I to go?

ANDREY: You can go. Good-bye. (*Ferapont goes out.*) Good-bye. (*Reading.*) Come tomorrow morning and take some papers here. . . . Go. . . . (*A pause.*) He has gone. (*A ring.*) Yes, it is a business. . . . (*Stretches and goes slowly into his own room.*)

(*Behind the scenes a nurse is singing, rocking a baby to sleep. Enter Masha and Vershinin. While they are talking a maidservant is lighting a lamp and candles in the dining room.*)

MASHA: I don't know. (*A pause.*) I don't know. Of course habit does a great deal. After Father's death, for instance, it was a long time before we could get used to having no orderlies in the house. But apart from habit, I think it's a feeling of justice makes me say so. Perhaps it is not so in other places, but in our town the most decent, honorable, and well-bred people are all in the army.

VERSHININ: I am thirsty. I should like some tea.

MASHA (*glancing at the clock*): They will soon be bringing it. I was married when I was eighteen, and I was afraid of my husband because he was a teacher, and I had only just left school. In those days I thought him an awfully learned, clever, and important person. And now it is not the same, unfortunately. . . .

VERSHININ: Yes. . . . I see. . . .

MASHA: I am not speaking of my husband — I am used to him; but among civilians generally there are so many rude, ill-mannered, badly brought-up people. Rudeness upsets and distresses me: I am unhappy when I see that a man is not refined, not gentle, not polite enough. When I have to be among the teachers, my husband's colleagues, it makes me quite miserable.

VERSHININ: Yes. . . . But, to my mind, it makes no difference whether they are civilians or military men — they are equally uninteresting, in this town anyway. It's all the same! If one listens to a man of the educated class here, civilian or military, he is worried to death by his wife, worried to death by his house, worried to death by his estate, worried to death by his horses. . . . A Russian is peculiarly given to exalted ideas, but why is it he always falls so short in life? Why?

MASHA: Why?

VERSHININ: Why is he worried to death by his children and by his wife? And why are his wife and children worried to death by him?

MASHA: You are rather depressed this evening.

VERSHININ: Perhaps. . . . I've had no dinner today, and had nothing to eat since the morning. My daughter is not quite well, and when my little girls are ill I am consumed by anxiety; my conscience reproaches me for having given them such a mother. Oh, if you had seen her today! She is a wretched creature! We began quarreling at seven o'clock in the morning, and at nine I slammed the door and went away. (*A pause.*) I never talk about it. Strange, it's only to you I complain. (*Kisses her hand.*) Don't be angry with me. . . . Except for you I have no one — no one. . . .

(*A pause.*)

MASHA: What a noise in the stove! Before Father died there was howling in the chimney. There, just like that.

VERSHININ: Are you superstitious?

MASHA: Yes.

VERSHININ: That's strange. (*Kisses her hand.*) You are a splendid, wonderful woman. Splendid! Wonderful! It's dark, but I see the light in your eyes.

MASHA: (*moves to another chair*) It's lighter here.

VERSHININ: I love you — love, love. . . . I love your eyes, your movements, I see them in my dreams. . . . Splendid, wonderful woman!

MASHA: (*laughing softly*): When you talk to me like that, for some reason I laugh, though I am frightened. . . . Please don't do it again. . . . (*In an undertone.*) You may say it, though; I don't mind. . . . (*Covers her face with her hands.*) I don't mind. . . . Someone is coming. Talk of something else.

(*Irina and Tusenbach come in through the dining room.*)

TUSENBACH: I've got a three-barreled name. My name is Baron Tusenbach-Krone-Altschauer, but I belong to the Orthodox Church and am just as Russian as you. There is very little of the German left in me — nothing, perhaps, but the patience and perseverance with which I bore you. I see you home every evening.

IRINA: How tired I am!

TUSENBACH: And every day I will come to the telegraph office and see you home. I'll do it for ten years, for twenty years, till you drive me away. . . . (*Seeing Masha and Vershinin, delightedly.*) Oh, it's you! How are you?

IRINA: Well, I am home at last. (*To Masha.*) A lady came just now to telegraph to her brother in Saratov that her son died today, and she could not think of the address. So she sent it without an address — simply to Saratov. She was crying. And I was rude to her for no sort of reason. Told her I had no time to waste. It was so stupid. Are the Carnival people coming tonight?

MASHA: Yes.

IRINA (*sits down in an armchair*): I must rest. I am tired.

TUSENBACH (*with a smile*): When you come from the office you seem so young, so forlorn. . . . (*A pause.*)

IRINA: I am tired. No, I don't like telegraph work. I don't like it.

MASHA: You've grown thinner. . . . (*Whistles.*) And you look younger, rather like a boy in the face.

TUSENBACH: That's the way she does her hair.

IRINA: I must find some other job, this does not suit me. What I so longed for, what I dream of, is the very thing that it's lacking in. . . . It is work without poetry, without meaning. . . . (*A knock on the floor.*) There's the doctor knocking. . . . (*To Tusenbach.*) Do knock, dear. . . . I can't. . . . I am tired.

(*Tusenbach knocks on the floor.*)

IRINA: He will come directly. We ought to do something about it. The doctor and our Andrey were at the Club yesterday and they lost again. I am told Andrey lost two hundred rubles.

MASHA (*indifferently*): Well, it can't be helped now.

IRINA: A fortnight ago he lost money, in December he lost money. I wish he'd make haste and lose everything, then perhaps we should go away from this town. By God, every night I dream of Moscow, it's perfect madness. (*Laughs.*) We'll move there in June and there is still left February, March, April, May . . . almost half a year.

MASHA: The only thing is Natasha must not hear of his losses.

IRINA: I don't suppose she cares.

(*Tchebutykin, who has only just got off his bed — he has been resting after dinner — comes into the dining room combing his beard, then sits down to the table, and takes a newspaper out of his pocket.*)

MASHA: Here he is . . . has he paid his rent?

IRINA (*laughs*): No. Not a kopek° for eight months. Evidently he has forgotten.

MASHA (*laughs*): How gravely he sits. (*They all laugh; a pause.*)

IRINA: Why are you so quiet, Alexandr Ignatyevitch?

VERSHININ: I don't know. I am longing for tea. I'd give half my life for a glass of tea. I have had nothing to eat since the morning.

TCHEBUTYKIN: Irina Sergeyevna!

IRINA: What is it?

TCHEBUTYKIN: Come here. *Venez ici.*° (*Irina goes and sits down at the table.*) I can't do without you. (*Irina lays out the cards for patience.*)

VERSHININ: Well, if they won't bring tea, let us discuss something.

TUSENBACH: By all means. What?

VERSHININ: What? Let us dream . . . for instance of the life that will come after us, in two or three hundred years.

TUSENBACH: Well? When we are dead, men will fly in balloons, change the fashion of their coats, will discover a sixth sense, perhaps, and develop it, but life will remain just the same; difficult, full of mysteries and happiness. In a thousand years man will sigh just the same, "Ah, how hard life is," and yet just as now he will be afraid of death and not want it.

VERSHININ (*after a moment's thought*): Well, I don't know. . . . It seems to me that everything on earth is bound to change by degrees and is already changing before our eyes. In two or three hundred, perhaps in a thousand years — the time does not matter

kopek: One hundred kopeks make one ruble.
Venez ici: French for "come here."

— a new, happy life will come. We shall have no share in that life, of course, but we are living for it, we are working, well, yes, and suffering for it, we are creating it — and that alone is the purpose of our existence, and is our happiness, if you like.

(*Masha laughs softly.*)

TUSENBACH: What is it?

MASHA: I don't know. I've been laughing all day.

VERSHININ: I was at the same school as you were, I did not go to the Military Academy; I read a great deal, but I do not know how to choose my books, and very likely I read quite the wrong things, and yet the longer I live the more I want to know. My hair is turning gray, I am almost an old man, but I know so little, oh so little! But all the same I fancy that I do know and thoroughly grasp what is essential and matters most. And how I should like to make you see that there is no happiness for us, that there ought not to be and will not be. . . . We must work and work, and happiness is the portion of our remote descendants. (*A pause.*) If it is not for me, at least it is for the descendants of my descendants. . . . (*Fedotik and Roddey appear in the dining room; they sit down and sing softly, playing the guitar.*)

TUSENBACH: You think it's no use even dreaming of happiness! But what if I am happy?

VERSHININ: No.

TUSENBACH (*flinging up his hands and laughing*): It is clear we don't understand each other. Well, how am I to convince you? (*Masha laughs softly. Tusenbach holds up a finger to her.*) Laugh! (*To Vershinin.*) Not only in two or three hundred years but in a million years life will be just the same; it does not change, it remains stationary, following its own laws which we have nothing to do with or which, anyway, we shall never find out. Migratory birds, cranes for instance, fly backward and forward, and whatever ideas, great or small, stray through their minds, they will still go on flying just the same without knowing where or why. They fly and will continue to fly, however philosophic they may become; and it doesn't matter how philosophical they are so long as they go on flying. . . .

MASHA: But still there is a meaning?

TUSENBACH: Meaning. . . . Here it is snowing. What meaning is there in that? (*A pause.*)

MASHA: I think man ought to have faith or ought to seek a faith, or else his life is empty, empty. . . . To live and not to understand why cranes fly; why children are born; why there are stars in the sky. . . . One must know what one is living for or else it is all nonsense and waste. (*A pause.*)

VERSHININ: And yet one is sorry that youth is over. . . .

MASHA: Gogol says: it's dull living in this world, friends!

TUSENBACH: And I say: it is difficult to argue with you, my friends, God bless you. . . .

TCHEBUTYKIN (*reading the newspaper*): Balzac° was married at Berditchev. (*Irina hums softly.*) I really must put that down in my book. (*Writes.*) Balzac was married at Berditchev. (*Reads the paper.*)

IRINA (*lays out the cards for patience, dreamily*): Balzac was married at Berditchev.

TUSENBACH: The die is cast. You know, Marya Sergeyevna, I've resigned my commission.

MASHA: So I hear. And I see nothing good in that. I don't like civilians.

TUSENBACH: Never mind. . . . (*Gets up.*) I am not good-looking enough for a soldier. But that does not matter, though. . . . I am going to work. If only for one day in my life, to work so that I come home at night tired out and fall asleep as soon as I get into bed. . . . (*Going into the dining room.*) Workmen must sleep soundly!

FEDOTIK (*to Irina*): I bought these chalks for you just now as I passed the shop. . . . And this penknife. . . .

IRINA: You've got into the way of treating me as though I were little, but I am grown up, you know. . . . (*Takes the chalks and the penknife, joyfully.*) How lovely!

FEDOTIK: And I bought a knife for myself . . . look . . . one blade, and another blade, a third, and this is for the ears, and here are scissors, and that's for cleaning the nails. . . .

RODDEY (*loudly*): Doctor, how old are you?

TCHEBUTYKIN: I? Thirty-two. (*Laughter.*)

FEDOTIK: I'll show you another patience. . . . (*Lays out the cards.*)

(*The samovar is brought in; Anfisa is at the samovar; a little later Natasha comes in and is also busy at the table; Solyony comes in and, after greeting the others, sits down at the table.*)

VERSHININ: What a wind there is!

MASHA: Yes. I am sick of the winter. I've forgotten what summer is like.

IRINA: It's coming out right, I see. We shall go to Moscow.

FEDOTIK: No, it's not coming out. You see, the eight is over the two of spades. (*Laughs.*) So that means you won't go to Moscow.

TCHEBUTYKIN (*reads from the newspaper*): Tsi-tsi-kar.° Smallpox is raging there.

ANFISA (*going up to Masha*): Masha, come to tea, my dear. (*To Vershinin.*) Come, your honor . . . excuse me, sir, I have forgotten your name. . . .

Balzac: Honoré de Balzac (1799–1850), French novelist.
Tsi-tsi-kar: A resort city in northeast China.

MASHA: Bring it here, nurse, I am not going there.

IRINA: Nurse!

ANFISA: I am coming!

NATASHA (*to Solyony*): Little babies understand very well. "Good morning, Bobik, good morning, darling," I said. He looked at me in quite a special way. You think I say that because I am a mother, but no, I assure you! He is an extraordinary child.

SOLYONY: If that child were mine, I'd fry him in a frying-pan and eat him.

(*Takes his glass, comes into the drawing room, and sits down in a corner.*)

NATASHA (*covers her face with her hands*): Rude, ill-bred man!

MASHA: Happy people don't notice whether it is winter or summer. I fancy if I lived in Moscow I should not mind what the weather was like. . . .

VERSHININ: The other day I was reading the diary of a French minister written in prison. The minister was condemned for the Panama affair.° With what enthusiasm and delight he describes the birds he sees from the prison window, which he never noticed before when he was a minister. Now that he is released, of course, he notices birds no more than he did before. In the same way, you won't notice Moscow when you live in it. We have no happiness and never do have, we only long for it.

TUSENBACH (*takes a box from the table*): What has become of the sweets?

IRINA: Solyony has eaten them.

TUSENBACH: All?

ANFISA (*handing tea*): There's a letter for you, sir.

VERSHININ: For me? (*Takes the letter.*) From my daughter. (*Reads.*) Yes, of course. . . . Excuse me, Marya Sergeyevna, I'll slip away. I won't have tea. (*Gets up in agitation.*) Always these upsets. . . .

MASHA: What is it? Not a secret?

VERSHININ (*in a low voice*): My wife has taken poison again. I must go. I'll slip off unnoticed. Horribly unpleasant it all is. (*Kisses Masha's hand.*) My fine, dear, splendid woman. . . . I'll go this way without being seen. . . . (*Goes out.*)

ANFISA: Where is he off to? I've just given him his tea. . . . What a man.

MASHA (*getting angry*): Leave off! Don't pester, you give one no peace. . . . (*Goes with her cup to the table.*) You bother me, old lady.

ANFISA: Why are you so huffy? Darling!

ANDREY'S VOICE: "Anfisa!"

ANFISA (*mimicking*): Anfisa! He sits there. . . . (*Goes out.*)

Panama affair: French officials were convicted of fraud and bribery during the construction of the Panama Canal.

MASHA (*by the table in the dining room, angrily*): Let me sit down! (*Mixes the cards on the table.*) You take up all the table with your cards. Drink your tea!

IRINA: How cross you are, Masha!

MASHA: If I'm cross, don't talk to me. Don't interfere with me.

TCHEBUTYKIN (*laughing*): Don't touch her, don't touch her!

MASHA: You are sixty, but you talk rot like a schoolboy.

NATASHA (*sighs*): Dear Masha, why make use of such expressions in conversations? With your attractive appearance, I tell you straight out, you would be simply fascinating in a well-bred social circle if it were not for the things you say. *Je vous prie, pardonnez-moi, Marie, mais vous avez des manières un peu grossières.*°

TUSENBACH (*suppressing a laugh*): Give me . . . give me . . . I think there is some brandy there.

NATASHA: *Il paraît que mon Bobik déjà ne dort pas,*° he is awake. He is not well today. I must go to him, excuse me. . . . (*Goes out.*)

IRINA: Where has Alexandr Ignatyevitch gone?

MASHA: Home. Something queer with his wife again.

TUSENBACH (*goes up to Solyony with a decanter of brandy in his hand*): You always sit alone, thinking, and there's no making out what you think about. Come, let us make it up. Let us have a drink of brandy. (*They drink.*) I shall have to play the piano all night, I suppose, play all sorts of trash. . . . Here goes!

SOLYONY: Why make it up? I haven't quarreled with you.

TUSENBACH: You always make me feel as though something had gone wrong between us. You are a queer character, there's no denying that.

SOLYONY (*declaims*): I am strange, who is not strange! Be not wroth, Aleko!°

TUSENBACH: I don't see what Aleko has got to do with it. . . .

SOLYONY: When I am *tête-à-tête*° with somebody, I am all right, just like anyone else, but in company I am depressed, ill at ease and . . . say all sorts of idiotic things, but at the same time I am more conscientious and straightforward than many. And I can prove it. . . .

Je . . . grossières: French for "I beg your pardon, Marie, but your manners are a bit gross."

Il . . . pas: French for "It seems that my Bobik is already no longer asleep." Chekhov intentionally makes Natasha's French awkward.

Aleko: A character in Alexander Pushkin's (1799–1837) poem "The Gypsies" who kills his lover when she rejects him for another.

tête-à-tête: French for "head-to-head," in private conversation.

TUSENBACH: I often feel angry with you, you are always attacking me when we are in company, and yet I somehow like you. Here goes, I am going to drink a lot today. Let's drink!

SOLYONY: Let us. (*Drinks.*) I have never had anything against you, Baron. But I have the temperament of Lermontov.° (*In a low voice.*) In fact I am rather like Lermontov to look at . . . so I am told. (*Takes out scent bottle and sprinkles scent on his hands.*)

TUSENBACH: I have sent in my papers. I've had enough of it! I have been thinking of it for five years and at last I have come up to the scratch. I am going to work.

SOLYONY (*declaims*): Be not wroth, Aleko. . . . Forget, forget thy dreams. . . .

(*While they are talking Andrey comes in quietly with a book and sits down by a candle.*)

TUSENBACH: I am going to work.

TCHEBUTYKIN (*coming into the drawing room with Irina*): And the food too was real Caucasian stuff: onion soup and for the meat course *tchehartma.* . . .

SOLYONY: *Tcheremsha* is not meat at all, it's a plant rather like our onion.

TCHEBUTYKIN: No, my dear soul, it's not onion, but mutton roasted in a special way.

SOLYONY: But I tell you that *tcheremsha* is an onion.

TCHEBUTYKIN: And I tell you that *tchehartma* is mutton.

SOLYONY: And I tell you that *tcheremsha* is an onion.

TCHEBUTYKIN: What's the use of my arguing with you? You have never been to the Caucasus or eaten *tchehartma.*

SOLYONY: I haven't eaten it because I can't bear it. *Tcheremsha* smells like garlic.

ANDREY (*imploringly*): That's enough! Please!

TUSENBACH: When are the Carnival party coming?

IRINA: They promised to come at nine, so they will be here directly.

TUSENBACH (*embraces Andrey and sings*): "Oh my porch, oh my new porch . . ."

ANDREY (*dances and sings*): "With posts of maple wood. . . ."

TCHEBUTYKIN (*dances*): "And lattice work complete. . . ."° (*Laughter.*)

TUSENBACH (*kisses Andrey*): Hang it all, let us have a drink. Andryusha, let us drink to our everlasting friendship. I'll go to the university when you do, Andryusha.

SOLYONY: Which? There are two universities in Moscow.

ANDREY: There is only one university in Moscow.

SOLYONY: I tell you there are two.

ANDREY: There may be three for aught I care. So much the better.

SOLYONY: There are two universities in Moscow! (*A murmur and hisses.*) There are two universities in Moscow: the old one and the new one. And if you don't care to hear, if what I say irritates you, I can keep quiet. I can even go into another room. (*Goes out at one of the doors.*)

TUSENBACH: Bravo, bravo! (*Laughs.*) Friends, begin, I'll sit down and play! Funny fellow that Solyony. . . . (*Sits down to the piano and plays a waltz.*)

MASHA (*dances a waltz alone*): The baron is drunk, the baron is drunk, the baron is drunk.

(*Enter Natasha.*)

NATASHA (*to Tchebutykin*): Ivan Romanitch!

(*Says something to Tchebutykin, then goes out softly. Tchebutykin touches Tusenbach on the shoulder and whispers something to him.*)

IRINA: What is it?

TCHEBUTYKIN: It's time we were going. Good night.

TUSENBACH: Good night. It's time to be going.

IRINA: But I say . . . what about the Carnival party?

ANDREY (*with embarrassment*): They won't be coming. You see, dear, Natasha says Bobik is not well, and so . . . In fact I know nothing about it, and don't care either.

IRINA (*shrugs her shoulders*): Bobik is not well!

MASHA: Well, it's not the first time we've had to lump it! If we are turned out, we must go. (*To Irina.*) It's not Bobik that is ill, but she is a bit . . . (*Taps her forehead with her finger.*) Petty, vulgar creature!

(*Andrey goes by door on right to his own room, Tchebutykin following him; they are saying good-bye in the dining room.*)

FEDOTIK: What a pity! I was meaning to spend the evening, but of course if the child is ill . . . I'll bring him a toy tomorrow.

RODDEY (*loudly*): I had a nap today after dinner on purpose, I thought I would be dancing all night. . . . Why it's only nine o'clock.

MASHA: Let us go into the street; there we can talk. We'll decide what to do.

(*Sounds of "Good-bye! Good night!" The good-humored laugh of Tusenbach is heard. All go out. Anfisa and the maidservant clear the table and put out the light. There is the sound of the nurse singing. Andrey, in his hat and coat, and Tchebutykin come in quietly.*)

TCHEBUTYKIN: I never had time to get married, because life has flashed by like lightning and because I was

---

Lermontov: Mikhail Yurievitch Lermontov (1814–1841), a Russian poet famous for his romantic, introspective verse. **"Oh my porch . . . complete":** A traditional Russian song.

passionately in love with your mother, who was married.

ANDREY: One shouldn't get married. One shouldn't, because it's boring.

TCHEBUTYKIN: That's all very well, but what about loneliness? Say what you like, it's a dreadful thing to be lonely, my dear boy. . . . But no matter, though!

ANDREY: Let's make haste and go.

TCHEBUTYKIN: What's the hurry? We have plenty of time.

ANDREY: I am afraid my wife may stop me.

TCHEBUTYKIN: Oh!

ANDREY: I am not going to play today, I shall just sit and look on. I don't feel well. . . . What am I to do, Ivan Romanitch, I am so short of breath?

TCHEBUTYKIN: It's no use asking me! I don't remember, dear boy. . . . I don't know. . .

ANDREY: Let us go through the kitchen. (*They go out.*)

(*A ring, then another ring; there is a sound of voices and laughter.*)

IRINA (*enters*): What is it?

ANFISA (*in a whisper*): The mummers, all dressed up. (*A ring.*)

IRINA: Nurse, dear, say there is no one at home. They must excuse us.

(*Anfisa goes out. Irina walks about the room in hesitation; she is excited. Enter Solyony.*)

SOLYONY (*in perplexity*): No one here. . . . Where are they all?

IRINA: They have gone home.

SOLYONY: How queer. Are you alone here?

IRINA: Yes. (*A pause.*) Good night.

SOLYONY: I behaved tactlessly, without sufficient restraint just now. But you are not like other people, you are pure and lofty, you see the truth. You alone can understand me. I love you, I love you deeply, infinitely.

IRINA: Good night! You must go.

SOLYONY: I can't live without you. (*Following her.*) Oh, my bliss! (*Through his tears.*) Oh, happiness! Those glorious, exquisite, marvelous eyes such as I have never seen in any other woman.

IRINA (*coldly*): Don't, Vassily Vassilyevitch!

SOLYONY: For the first time I am speaking of love to you, and I feel as though I were not on earth but on another planet. (*Rubs his forehead.*) But there, it does not matter. There is no forcing kindness, of course. . . . But there must be no happy rivals. . . . There must not. . . . I swear by all that is sacred I will kill any rival. . . . O exquisite being!

(*Natasha passes with a candle.*)

NATASHA (*peeps in at one door, then at another and passes by the door that leads to her husband's room*): Andrey is there. Let him read. Excuse me, Vassily Vassilyevitch, I did not know you were here, and I am in my dressing gown. . . .

SOLYONY: I don't care. Good-bye! (*Goes out.*)

NATASHA: You are tired, my poor, dear little girl! (*Kisses Irina.*) You ought to go to bed earlier. . . .

IRINA: Is Bobik asleep?

NATASHA: He is asleep, but not sleeping quietly. By the way, dear, I keep meaning to speak to you, but either you are out or else I haven't the time. . . . I think Bobik's nursery is cold and damp. And your room is so nice for a baby. My sweet, my dear, you might move for a time into Olya's room!

IRINA (*not understanding*): Where?

(*The sound of a three-horse sledge with bells driving up to the door.*)

NATASHA: You would be in the same room with Olya, and Bobik in your room. He is such a poppet. I said to him today, "Bobik, you are mine, you are mine!" and he looked at me with his funny little eyes. (*A ring.*) That must be Olya. How late she is!

(*The maid comes up to Natasha and whispers in her ear.*)

NATASHA: Protopopov? What a queer fellow he is! Protopopov has come, and asks me to go out with him in his sledge. (*Laughs*) How strange men are! . . . (*A ring.*) Somebody has come. I might go for a quarter of an hour. . . . (*To the maid.*) Tell him I'll come directly. (*A ring.*) You hear . . . it must be Olya. (*Goes out.*)

(*The maid runs out; Irina sits lost in thought; Kuligin, Olga, and Vershinin come in.*)

KULIGIN: Well, this is a surprise! They said they were going to have an evening party.

VERSHININ: Strange! And when I went away half an hour ago they were expecting the Carnival people. . . .

IRINA: They have all gone.

KULIGIN: Has Masha gone too? Where has she gone? And why is Protopopov waiting below with his sledge? Whom is he waiting for?

IRINA: Don't ask questions. . . . I am tired.

KULIGIN: Oh, you little cross-patch. . . .

OLGA: The meeting is only just over. I am tired out. Our headmistress is ill and I have to take her place. Oh, my head, my head does ache; oh, my head! (*Sits down.*) Andrey lost two hundred rubles yesterday at cards. . . . The whole town is talking about it. . . .

KULIGIN: Yes, I am tired out by the meeting too. (*Sits down.*)

VERSHININ: My wife took it into her head to give me a fright, she nearly poisoned herself. It's all right now, and I'm glad, it's a relief. . . . So we are to go away? Very well, then, I will say good night. Fyodor Ilyitch, let us go somewhere together! I can't stay at home, I absolutely can't. . . . Come along!

KULIGIN: I am tired. I am not coming. (*Gets up.*) I am tired. Has my wife gone home?

IRINA: I expect so.

KULIGIN (*kisses Irina's hand*): Good-bye! I have all day tomorrow and next day to rest. Good night! (*Going.*) I do want some tea. I was reckoning on spending the evening in pleasant company. . . . *O fallacem hominum spem!°* . . . Accusative of exclamation.

VERSHININ: Well, then, I must go alone. (*Goes out with Kuligin, whistling.*)

OLGA: My head aches, oh, how my head aches. . . . Andrey has lost at cards. . . . The whole town is talking about it. . . . I'll go and lie down. (*Is going.*) Tomorrow I shall be free. . . . Oh, goodness, how nice that is! Tomorrow I am free, and the day after I am free. . . . My head does ache, oh, my head. . . . (*Goes out.*)

IRINA (*alone*): They have all gone away. There is no one left.

(*A concertina plays in the street, the nurse sings.*)

NATASHA (*in a fur cap and coat crosses the dining room, followed by the maid*): I shall be back in half an hour. I shall only go a little way. (*Goes out.*)

IRINA (*left alone, in dejection*): Oh, to go to Moscow, to Moscow!

ACT III

(*The bedroom of Olga and Irina. On left and right beds with screens round them. Past two o'clock in the night. Behind the scenes a bell is ringing on account of a fire in the town, which has been going on for some time. It can be seen that no one in the house has gone to bed yet. On the sofa Masha is lying, dressed as usual in black. Enter Olga and Anfisa.*)

ANFISA: They are sitting below, under the stairs. . . . I said to them, "Come upstairs; why, you mustn't stay there" — they only cried. "We don't know where father is," they said. "What if he is burned!" What an idea! And the poor souls in the yard. . . . They are all undressed too.

OLGA (*taking clothes out of the cupboard*): Take this gray dress . . . and this one . . . and the blouse too . . . and that skirt, nurse. . . . Oh, dear, what a dreadful thing! Kirsanov Street is burned to the ground, it seems. . . . Take this . . . take this. . . . (*Throws clothes into her arms.*) The Vershinins have had a fright, poor things. . . . Their house was very nearly burned. Let them stay the night here . . . we can't let them go home. . . . Poor Fedotik has had everything burned, he has not a thing left. . . .

ANFISA: You had better call Ferapont, Olya darling, I can't carry it all.

OLGA (*rings*): No one will answer the bell. (*At the door.*) Come here, whoever is there! (*Through the open door can be seen a window red with fire; the fire brigade is heard passing the house.*) How awful it is! And how sickening!

(*Enter Ferapont.*)

OLGA: Here take these, carry them downstairs. . . . The Kolotilin young ladies are downstairs . . . give it to them . . . and give this too.

FERAPONT: Yes, miss. In 1812 Moscow was burned too. . . . Mercy on us! The French marveled.°

OLGA: You can go now.

FERAPONT: Yes, miss. (*Goes out.*)

OLGA: Nurse darling, give them everything. We don't want anything, give it all to them. . . . I am tired, I can hardly stand on my feet. . . . We mustn't let the Vershinins go home. . . . The little girls can sleep in the drawing room, and Alexandr Ignatyevitch down below at the baron's. . . . Fedotik can go to the baron's, too, or sleep in our dining room. . . . As ill-luck will have it, the doctor is drunk, frightfully drunk, and no one can be put in his room. And Vershinin's wife can be in the drawing room too.

ANFISA (*wearily*): Olya darling, don't send me away; don't send me away!

OLGA: That's nonsense, nurse. No one is sending you away.

ANFISA (*lays her head on Olga's shoulder*): My own, my treasure, I work, I do my best. . . . I'm getting weak, everyone will say "Be off!" And where am I to go? Where? I am eighty. Eighty-one.

OLGA: Sit down, nurse darling. . . . You are tired, poor thing. . . . (*Makes her sit down.*) Rest, dear good nurse. . . . How pale you are!

(*Enter Natasha.*)

NATASHA: They are saying we must form a committee

O . . . spem: Latin for "O the futility of human hope."

marveled: Russians burned their own cities as they retreated from Napoleon's invading army.

at once for the assistance of those whose houses have been burned. Well, that's a good idea. Indeed, one ought always to be ready to help the poor, it's the duty of the rich. Bobik and baby Sophie are both asleep, sleeping as though nothing were happening. There are such a lot of people everywhere, wherever one goes, the house is full. There is influenza in the town now; I am so afraid the children may get it.

OLGA (*not listening*): In this room one does not see the fire, it's quiet here.

NATASHA: Yes . . . my hair must be untidy. (*In front of the looking glass.*) They say I have grown fatter . . . but it's not true! Not a bit! Masha is asleep, she is tired out, poor dear. . . . (*To Anfisa coldly.*) Don't dare to sit down in my presence! Get up! Go out of the room! (*Anfisa goes out; a pause.*) Why you keep that old woman, I can't understand!

OLGA (*taken aback*): Excuse me, I don't understand either. . . .

NATASHA: She is no use here. She is a peasant; she ought to be in the country. . . . You spoil people! I like order in the house! There ought to be no useless servants in the house. (*Strokes her cheek.*) You are tired, poor darling. Our headmistress is tired! When baby Sophie is a big girl and goes to the high school, I shall be afraid of you.

OLGA: I shan't be headmistress.

NATASHA: You will be elected, Olya. That's a settled thing.

OLGA: I shall refuse. I can't. . . . It's too much for me. . . . (*Drinks water.*) You were so rude to nurse just now. . . . Excuse me, I can't endure it. . . . It makes me feel faint.

NATASHA (*perturbed*): Forgive me, Olya; forgive me. . . . I did not mean to hurt your feelings.

(*Masha gets up, takes her pillow, and goes out in a rage.*)

OLGA: You must understand, my dear, it may be that we have been strangely brought up, but I can't endure it. . . . Such an attitude oppresses me, it makes me ill. . . . I feel simply unnerved by it. . . .

NATASHA: Forgive me; forgive me. . . . (*Kisses her.*)

OLGA: The very slightest rudeness, a tactless word, upsets me. . . .

NATASHA: I often say too much, that's true, but you must admit, dear, that she might just as well be in the country.

OLGA: She has been thirty years with us.

NATASHA: But now she can't work! Either I don't understand, or you won't understand me. She is not fit for work. She does nothing but sleep or sit still.

OLGA: Well, let her sit still.

NATASHA (*surprised*): How, sit still? Why, she is a servant. (*Through tears.*) I don't understand you, Olya. I have a nurse to look after the children as well as a wet nurse for baby, and we have a housemaid and a cook, what do we want that old woman for? What's the use of her?

(*The alarm bell rings behind the scenes.*)

OLGA: This night has made me ten years older.

NATASHA: We must come to an understanding, Olya. You are at the high school, I am at home; you are teaching while I look after the house, and if I say anything about the servants, I know what I'm talking about; I do know what I'm talking about. . . . And that old thief, that old hag . . . (*Stamps.*) that old witch shall clear out of the house tomorrow! . . . I won't have people annoy me! I won't have it! (*Feeling that she has gone too far.*) Really, if you don't move downstairs, we shall always be quarreling. It's awful.

(*Enter Kuligin.*)

KULIGIN: Where is Masha? It's time to be going home. The fire is dying down, so they say. (*Stretches.*) Only one part of the town has been burned, and yet there was a wind; it seemed at first as though the whole town would be destroyed. (*Sits down.*) I am exhausted. Olya, my dear . . . I often think if it had not been for Masha I should have married you. You are so good. . . . I am tired out. (*Listens.*)

OLGA: What is it?

KULIGIN: It is unfortunate the doctor should have a drinking bout just now; he is helplessly drunk. Most unfortunate. (*Gets up.*) Here he comes, I do believe. . . . Do you hear? Yes, he is coming this way. . . . (*Laughs.*) What a man he is really. . . . I shall hide. (*Goes to the cupboard and stands in the corner.*) Isn't he a ruffian!

OLGA: He has not drunk for two years and now he has gone and done it. . . . (*Walks away with Natasha to the back of the room.*)

(*Tchebutykin comes in; walking as though sober without staggering, he walks across the room, stops, looks round; then goes up to the washing stand and begins to wash his hands.*)

TCHEBUTYKIN (*morosely*): The devil take them all . . . damn them all. They think I am a doctor, that I can treat all sorts of complaints, and I really know nothing about it, I have forgotten all I did know, I remember nothing, absolutely nothing. (*Olga and Natasha go out unnoticed by him.*) The devil take them. Last Wednesday I treated a woman at Zasyp — she died, and it's my fault that she died. Yes . . . I did know something twenty-five years ago, but now I remember nothing, nothing. Perhaps I am not a man at all but only pretend to have arms and legs and head; perhaps I don't exist at all and only fancy that I walk about, eat, and sleep. (*Weeps.*) Oh, if only I did not exist! (*Leaves off weeping, morosely.*) I don't care! I don't care a scrap! (*A pause.*) Goodness knows. . . . The day before yesterday there was a conversation at the club: they talked about Shakespeare, Voltaire. . . . I have read nothing, nothing at all, but I looked as though I had read them. And the others did the same as I did. The vulgarity! The meanness! And that woman I killed on Wednesday came back to my mind . . . and it all came back to my mind and everything seemed nasty, disgusting, and all awry in my soul. . . . I went and got drunk. . . .

(*Enter Irina, Vershinin, and Tusenbach; Tusenbach is wearing a fashionable new civilian suit.*)

IRINA: Let us sit here. No one will come here.

VERSHININ: If it had not been for the soldiers, the whole town would have been burned down. Splendid fellows! (*Rubs his hands with pleasure.*) They are first-rate men! Splendid fellows!

KULIGIN (*going up to them*): What time is it?

TUSENBACH: It's past three. It's getting light already.

IRINA: They are all sitting in the dining room. No one seems to think of going. And that Solyony of yours is sitting there too. . . . (*To Tchebutykin.*) You had better go to bed, doctor.

TCHEBUTYKIN: It's all right. . . . Thank you! (*Combs his beard.*)

KULIGIN (*laughs*): You are a bit fuddled, Ivan Romanitch! (*Slaps him on the shoulder.*) Bravo! *In vino veritas,*° the ancients used to say.

TUSENBACH: Everyone is asking me to get up a concert for the benefit of the families whose houses have been burned down.

IRINA: Why, who is there? . . .

TUSENBACH: We could get it up, if we wanted to. Marya Sergeyevna plays the piano splendidly, to my thinking.

KULIGIN: Yes, she plays splendidly.

IRINA: She has forgotten. She has not played for three . . . or four years.

TUSENBACH: There is absolutely no one who understands music in this town, not one soul, but I do understand and on my honor I assure you that Marya Sergeyevna plays magnificently, almost with genius.

KULIGIN: You are right, Baron. I am very fond of her; Masha, I mean. She is a good sort.

TUSENBACH: To be able to play so gloriously and to know that no one understands you!

KULIGIN (*sighs*): Yes . . . But would it be suitable for her to take part in a concert? (*A pause.*) I know nothing about it, my friends. Perhaps it would be all right. There is no denying that our director is a fine man, indeed a very fine man, very intelligent, but he has such views. . . . Of course it is not his business, still if you like I'll speak to him about it.

(*Tchebutykin takes up a china clock and examines it.*)

VERSHININ: I got dirty all over at the fire. I am a sight. (*A pause.*) I heard a word dropped yesterday about our brigade being transferred ever so far away. Some say to Poland, and others to Tchita.°

TUSENBACH: I've heard something about it too. Well! The town will be a wilderness then.

IRINA: We shall go away too.

TCHEBUTYKIN (*drops the clock, which smashes*): To smithereens!

KULIGIN (*picking up the pieces*): To smash such a valuable thing — oh, Ivan Romanitch, Ivan Romanitch! I should give you minus zero for conduct!

IRINA: That was Mother's clock.

TCHEBUTYKIN: Perhaps. . . . Well, if it was hers, it was. Perhaps I did not smash it, but it only seems as though I had. Perhaps it only seems to us that we exist, but really we are not here at all. I don't know anything — nobody knows anything. (*By the door.*) What are you staring at? Natasha has got a little affair with Protopopov, and you don't see it. . . . You sit here and see nothing, while Natasha has a little affair with Protopopov. . . . (*Sings.*) May I offer you this date?° . . . (*Goes out.*)

VERSHININ: Yes. . . . (*Laughs.*) How very queer it all is, really! (*A pause.*) When the fire began I ran home as fast as I could. I went up and saw our house was safe and sound and out of danger, but my little girls were standing in the doorway in their nightgowns; their mother was nowhere to be seen, people were bustling about, horses and dogs were running about, and my children's faces were full of alarm, horror, entreaty, and I don't know what; it wrung my heart to see their faces. My God, I thought, what more have these children to go through in the long years to come! I took their hands and ran along with them, and could think of nothing else but what more they would have to go through in this world! (*A pause.*) When I came to your house I found their mother here, screaming, angry. (*Masha comes in with the pillow and sits*

Tchita: A town in Siberia.
May . . . date: Chekhov explained that he had forgotten the name of the operetta from which this line comes.

In vino veritas: Latin for "In wine there is truth."

down on the sofa.) And while my little girls were standing in the doorway in their nightgowns and the street was red with the fire, and there was a fearful noise, I thought that something like it used to happen years ago when the enemy would suddenly make a raid and begin plundering and burning. . . . And yet, in reality, what a difference there is between what is now and has been in the past! And when a little more time has passed — another two or three hundred years — people will look at our present manner of life with horror and derision, and everything of today will seem awkward and heavy, and very strange and uncomfortable. Oh, what a wonderful life that will be — what a wonderful life! (*Laughs.*) Forgive me, here I am airing my theories again! Allow me to go on. I have such a desire to talk about the future. I am in the mood. (*A pause.*) It's as though everyone were asleep. And so, I say, what a wonderful life it will be! Can you only imagine? . . . There are only three of your sort in the town now, but in generations to come there will be more and more and more; and the time will come when everything will be changed and be as you would have it; they will live in your way, and later on you too will be out of date — people will be born who will be better than you. . . . (*Laughs.*) I am in such a strange state of mind today. I have a fiendish longing for life. . . . (*Sings.*) Young and old are bound by love, and precious are its pangs.° . . . (*Laughs.*)

MASHA: Tram-tam-tam!

VERSHININ: Tam-tam!

MASHA: Tra-ra-ra?

VERSHININ: Tra-ta-ta! (*Laughs.*)

(*Enter Fedotik.*)

FEDOTIK (*dances*): Burned to ashes! Burned to ashes! Everything I had in the world. (*Laughter.*)

IRINA: A queer thing to joke about. Is everything burned?

FEDOTIK (*laughs*): Everything I had in the world. Nothing is left. My guitar is burned, and the camera and all my letters. . . . And the notebook I meant to give you — that's burned too.

(*Enter Solyony.*)

IRINA: No; please go, Vassily Vassilyevitch. You can't stay here.

SOLYONY: How is it the baron can be here and I can't?

VERSHININ: We must be going, really. How is the fire?

SOLYONY: They say it is dying down. No, I really can't understand why the baron may be here and

not I. (*Takes out a bottle of scent and sprinkles himself.*)

VERSHININ: Tram-tam-tam!

MASHA: Tram-tam!

VERSHININ (*laughs, to Solyony*): Let us go into the dining room.

SOLYONY: Very well; we'll make a note of it. I might explain my meaning further, but fear I may provoke the geese.° . . . (*Looking at Tusenbach.*) Chook, chook, chook! . . . (*Goes out with Vershinin and Fedotik.*)

IRINA: How that horrid Solyony has made the room smell of tobacco! . . . (*In surprise.*) The baron is asleep! Baron, Baron!

TUSENBACH (*waking up*): I am tired, though. . . . The brickyard. I am not talking in my sleep. I really am going to the brickyard directly, to begin work. . . . It's nearly settled. (*To Irina, tenderly.*) You are so pale and lovely and fascinating. . . . It seems to me as though your paleness sheds a light through the dark air. . . . You are melancholy; you are dissatisfied with life. . . . Ah, come with me; let us go and work together!

MASHA: Nikolay Lvovitch, do go!

TUSENBACH (*laughing*): Are you here? I didn't see you. . . . (*Kisses Irina's hand.*) Good-bye, I am going. . . . I look at you now, and I remember as though it were long ago how on your name day you talked of the joy of work, and were so gay and confident. . . . And what a happy life I was dreaming of then! What has become of it? (*Kisses her hand.*) There are tears in your eyes. Go to bed, it's getting light . . . it is nearly morning. . . . If it were granted to me to give my life for you!

MASHA: Nikolay Lvovitch, do go! Come, really. . . .

TUSENBACH: I am going. (*Goes out.*)

MASHA (*lying down*): Are you asleep, Fyodor?

KULIGIN: Eh?

MASHA: You had better go home.

KULIGIN: My darling Masha, my precious girl! . . .

IRINA: She is tired out. Let her rest, Fedya.

KULIGIN: I'll go at once. . . . My dear, charming wife! . . . I love you, my only one! . . .

MASHA (*angrily*): Amo, amas, amat; amamus, amatis, amant.°

KULIGIN (*laughs*): Yes, really she is wonderful. You have been my wife for seven years, and it seems to me as though we were only married yesterday. Honor bright! Yes, really you are a wonderful woman! I am content, I am content, I am content!

MASHA: I am bored, I am bored, I am bored! . . . (*Gets up and speaks, sitting down.*) And there's something

---

Young . . . pangs: From Tchaikovsky's opera *Eugene Onegin*.

Amo . . . amant: Latin for "I love, you love, he loves," etc.

I can't get out of my head. . . . It's simply revolting. It sticks in my head like a nail; I must speak of it. I mean about Andrey. . . . He has mortgaged this house in the bank and his wife has grabbed all the money, and you know the house does not belong to him alone, but to us four! He ought to know that, if he is a decent man.

KULIGIN: Why do you want to bother about it, Masha? What is it to you? Andryusha is in debt all round, so there it is.

MASHA: It's revolting, anyway. (*Lies down.*)

KULIGIN: We are not poor. I work — I go to the high school, and then I give private lessons. . . . I do my duty. . . . There's no nonsense about me. *Omnia mea mecum porto,°* as the saying is.

MASHA: I want nothing, but it's the injustice that revolts me. (*A pause.*) Go, Fyodor.

KULIGIN (*kisses her*): You are tired, rest for half an hour, and I'll sit and wait for you. . . . Sleep. . . . (*Goes.*) I am content, I am content, I am content. (*Goes out.*)

IRINA: Yes, how petty our Andrey has grown, how dull and old he has become beside that woman! At one time he was working to get a professorship and yesterday he was boasting of having succeeded at last in becoming a member of the Rural Board. He is a member, and Protopopov is chairman. . . . The whole town is laughing and talking of it and he is the only one who sees and knows nothing. . . . And here everyone has been running to the fire while he sits still in his room and takes no notice. He does nothing but play his violin. . . . (*Nervously.*) Oh, it's awful, awful, awful! (*Weeps.*) I can't bear it anymore, I can't! I can't, I can't! (*Olga comes in and begins tidying up her table. Irina sobs loudly.*) Turn me out, turn me out, I can't bear it anymore!

OLGA (*alarmed*): What is it? What is it, darling?

IRINA (*sobbing*): Where? Where has it all gone? Where is it? Oh, my God, my God! I have forgotten everything, everything . . . everything is in a tangle in my mind. . . . I don't remember the Italian for window or ceiling . . . I am forgetting everything; every day I forget something more and life is slipping away and will never come back, we shall never, never go to Moscow. . . . I see that we shan't go. . . .

OLGA: Darling, darling. . . .

IRINA (*restraining herself*): Oh, I am wretched. . . . I can't work, I am not going to work. I have had enough of it, enough of it! I have been a telegraph clerk and now I have a job in the town council and I hate and despise every bit of the work they give me. . . . I am nearly twenty-four, I have been working for years, my brains are drying up, I am getting thin and old and ugly and there is nothing, nothing, not the slightest satisfaction, and time is passing and one feels that one is moving away from a real, fine life, moving farther and farther away and being drawn into the depths. I am in despair and I don't know how it is I am alive and have not killed myself yet. . . .

OLGA: Don't cry, my child, don't cry. It makes me miserable.

IRINA: I am not crying, I am not crying. . . . It's over. . . . There, I am not crying now. I won't . . . I won't.

OLGA: Darling, I am speaking to you as a sister, as a friend, if you care for my advice, marry the baron! (*Irina weeps. Olga speaks softly.*) You know you respect him, you think highly of him. . . . It's true he is ugly, but he is such a thoroughly nice man, so good. . . . One doesn't marry for love, but to do one's duty. . . . That's what I think, anyway, and I would marry without love. Whoever proposed to me I would marry him, if only he were a good man. . . . I would even marry an old man. . . .

IRINA: I kept expecting we should move to Moscow and there I should meet my real one. I've been dreaming of him, loving him. . . . But it seems that was all nonsense, nonsense. . . .

OLGA (*puts her arms round her sister*): My darling, lovely sister, I understand it all; when the baron left the army and came to us in a plain coat, I thought he looked so ugly that it positively made me cry. . . . He asked me, "Why are you crying?" How could I tell him! But if God brought you together I should be happy. That's a different thing, you know, quite different.

(*Natasha with a candle in her hand walks across the stage from door on right to door on left without speaking.*)

MASHA (*sits up*): She walks about as though it were she had set fire to the town.

OLGA: Masha, you are silly. The very silliest of the family, that's you. Please forgive me. (*A pause.*)

MASHA: I want to confess my sins, dear sisters. My soul is yearning. I am going to confess to you and never again to anyone. . . . I'll tell you this minute. (*Softly.*) It's my secret, but you must know everything. . . . I can't be silent. . . . (*A pause.*) I am in love, I am in love. . . . I love that man. . . . You have just seen him. . . . Well, I may as well say it straight out. I love Vershinin.

OLGA (*going behind her screen*): Leave off. I don't hear anyway.

MASHA: But what am I to do? (*Clutches her head.*)

Omnia . . . porto: Latin for "Everything I have I carry with me."

At first I thought him queer . . . then I was sorry for him . . . then I came to love him . . . to love him with his voice, his words, his misfortunes, his two little girls. . . .

OLGA (*behind the screen*): I don't hear you anyway. Whatever silly things you say I shan't hear them.

MASHA: Oh, Olya, you are silly. I love him — so that's my fate. It means that that's my lot. . . . And he loves me. . . . It's all dreadful. Yes? Is it wrong? (*Takes Irina by the hand and draws her to herself.*) Oh, my darling. . . . How are we going to live our lives, what will become of us? . . . When one reads a novel it all seems stale and easy to understand, but when you are in love yourself you see that no one knows anything and we all have to settle things for ourselves. . . . My darling, my sister. . . . I have confessed it to you, now I'll hold my tongue. . . . I'll be like Gogol's madman° . . . silence . . . silence. . . .

(*Enter Andrey and after him Ferapont.*)

ANDREY (*angrily*): What do you want? I can't make it out.

FERAPONT (*in the doorway, impatiently*): I've told you ten times already, Andrey Sergeyevitch.

ANDREY: In the first place I am not Andrey Sergeyevitch, but Your Honor, to you!

FERAPONT: The firemen ask leave, Your Honor, to go through the garden on their way to the river. Or else they have to go round and round, an awful nuisance for them.

ANDREY: Very good. Tell them, very good. (*Ferapont goes out.*) I am sick of them. Where is Olga? (*Olga comes from behind the screen.*) I've come to ask you for the key of the cupboard, I have lost mine. You've got one, it's a little key.

(*Olga gives him the key in silence; Irina goes behind her screen; a pause.*)

ANDREY: What a tremendous fire! Now it's begun to die down. Hang it all, that Ferapont made me so cross I said something silly to him. Your Honor. . . . (*A pause.*) Why don't you speak, Olya? (*A pause.*) It's time to drop this foolishness and sulking all about nothing. . . . You are here, Masha, and you too, Irina — very well, then, let us have things out thoroughly, once for all. What have you against me? What is it?

OLGA: Leave off, Andryusha. Let us talk tomorrow. (*Nervously.*) What an agonizing night!

ANDREY (*greatly confused*): Don't excite yourself. I ask you quite coolly, what have you against me? Tell me straight out.

VERSHININ'S VOICE: Tram-tam-tam!

MASHA (*standing up, loudly*): Tra-ta-ta! (*To Olga.*) Good night, Olya, God bless you. . . .(*Goes behind the screen and kisses Irina.*) Sleep well. . . . Good night, Andrey. You'd better leave them now, they are tired out . . . you can go into things tomorrow. (*Goes out.*)

OLGA: Yes, really, Andryusha, let us put it off until tomorrow. . . . (*Goes behind her screen.*) It's time we were in bed.

ANDREY: I'll say what I have to say and then go. Directly. . . . First, you have something against Natasha, my wife, and I've noticed that from the very day of my marriage. Natasha is a splendid woman, conscientious, straightforward, and honorable — that's my opinion! I love and respect my wife, do you understand? I respect her, and I insist on other people respecting her too. I repeat, she is a conscientious, honorable woman, and all your disagreements are simply caprice, or rather the whims of old maids. Old maids never like and never have liked their sisters-in-law — that's the rule. (*A pause.*) Secondly, you seem to be cross with me for not being a professor, not working at something learned. But I am in the service of the Zemstvo,° I am a member of the Rural Board, and I consider this service just as sacred and elevated as the service of learning. I am a member of the Rural Board and I am proud of it, if you care to know. . . . (*A pause.*) Thirdly . . . there's something else I have to say. . . . I have mortgaged the house without asking your permission. . . . For that I am to blame, yes, and I ask your pardon for it. I was driven to it by my debts . . . thirty-five thousand. . . . I am not gambling now — I gave up cards long ago; but the chief thing I can say in self-defense is that you are, so to say, of the privileged sex — you get a pension . . . while I had not . . . my wages, so to speak. . . . (*A pause.*)

KULIGIN (*at the door*): Isn't Masha here? (*Perturbed.*) Where is she? It's strange. . . . (*Goes out.*)

ANDREY: They won't listen. Natasha is an excellent, conscientious woman. (*Paces up and down the stage in silence, then stops.*) When I married her, I thought we should be happy . . . happy, all of us. . . . But, my God! (*Weeps.*) Dear sisters, darling sisters, you must not believe what I say, you mustn't believe it. . . . (*Goes out.*)

KULIGIN (*at the door, uneasily*): Where is Masha? Isn't Masha here? How strange! (*Goes out.*)

(*The fire bell rings in the street. The stage is empty.*)

---

madman: An allusion to "The Memoirs of a Madman" by Nikolay Gogol (1809–1852).

Zemstvo: A local governing board.

IRINA (*behind the screen*): Olya! Who is that knocking on the floor?

OLGA: It's the doctor, Ivan Romanitch. He is drunk.

IRINA: What a troubled night! (*A pause.*) Olya! (*Peeps out from behind the screen.*) Have you heard? The brigade is going to be taken away; they are being transferred to some place very far off.

OLGA: That's only a rumor.

IRINA: Then we shall be alone. . . . Olya!

OLGA: Well?

IRINA: My dear, my darling, I respect the baron, I think highly of him, he is a fine man — I will marry him, I consent, only let us go to Moscow! I entreat you, do let us go! There's nothing in the world better than Moscow! Let us go, Olya! Let us go!

ACT IV

(*Old garden of the Prozorovs' house. A long avenue of fir trees, at the end of which is a view of the river. On the farther side of the river there is a wood. On the right the veranda of the house; on the table in it are bottles and glasses; evidently they have just been drinking champagne. It is twelve o'clock noon. People pass occasionally from the street across the garden to the river; five soldiers pass rapidly. Tchebutykin, in an affable mood, which persists throughout the act, is sitting in an easy chair in the garden, waiting to be summoned; he is wearing a military cap and has a stick. Irina, Kuligin with a decoration on his breast and with no mustache, and Tusenbach, standing on the veranda, are saying good-bye to Fedotik and Roddey, who are going down the steps; both officers are in marching uniform.*)

TUSENBACH (*kissing Fedotik*): You are a good fellow; we've got on so happily together. (*Kisses Roddey.*) Once more. . . . Good-bye, my dear boy. . . .

IRINA: Till we meet again!

FEDOTIK: No, it's good-bye for good; we shall never meet again.

KULIGIN: Who knows! (*Wipes his eyes, smiles.*) Here I am crying too.

IRINA: We shall meet some day.

FEDOTIK: In ten years, or fifteen perhaps? But then we shall scarcely recognize each other — we shall greet each other coldly. . . . (*Takes a snapshot.*) Stand still. . . . Once more, for the last time.

RODDEY (*embraces Tusenbach*): We shall not see each other again. . . . (*Kisses Irina's hand.*) Thank you for everything, everything. . . .

FEDOTIK (*with vexation*): Oh, do wait!

TUSENBACH: Please God we shall meet again. Write to us. Be sure to write to us.

RODDEY (*taking a long look at the garden*): Good-bye, trees! (*Shouts.*) Halloo! (*A pause.*) Good-bye, echo!

KULIGIN: I shouldn't wonder if you get married in Poland. . . . Your Polish wife will clasp you in her arms and call you *kochany!*° (*Laughs.*)

FEDOTIK (*looking at his watch*): We have less than an hour. Of our battery only Solyony is going on the barge; we are going with the rank and file. Three divisions of the battery are going today and three more tomorrow — and peace and quiet will descend upon the town.

TUSENBACH: And dreadful boredom too.

RODDEY: And where is Marya Sergeyevna?

KULIGIN: Masha is in the garden.

FEDOTIK: We must say good-bye to her.

RODDEY: Good-bye. We must go, or I shall begin to cry. . . .(*Hurriedly embraces Tusenbach and Kuligin and kisses Irina's hand.*) We've had a splendid time here.

FEDOTIK (*to Kuligin*): This is a little souvenir for you . . . a notebook with a pencil. . . . We'll go down here to the river. . . . (*As they go away both look back.*)

RODDEY (*shouts*): Halloo-oo!

KULIGIN (*shouts*): Good-bye!

(*Roddey and Fedotik meet Masha in the background and say good-bye to her; she walks away with them.*)

IRINA: They've gone. . . . (*She sits down on the bottom step of the veranda.*)

TCHEBUTYKIN: They have forgotten to say good-bye to me.

IRINA: And what were you thinking about?

TCHEBUTYKIN: Why, I somehow forget, too. But I shall see them again soon, I am setting off tomorrow. Yes . . . I have one day more. In a year I shall be on the retired list. Then I shall come here again and shall spend the rest of my life near you. . . . There is only one year now before I get my pension. (*Puts a newspaper into his pocket and takes out another.*) I shall come here to you and arrange my life quite differently. . . . I shall become such a quiet . . . God-fearing . . . well-behaved person.

IRINA: Well, you do need to arrange your life differently, dear Ivan Romanitch. You certainly ought to somehow.

TCHEBUTYKIN: Yes, I feel it. (*Softly hums.*) "Tarara-boom-dee-ay — Tarara-boom-dee-ay."°

KULIGIN: Ivan Romanitch is incorrigible! Incorrigible!

---

kochany: A Polish term indicating affection.
Tarara-boom-dee-ay: From a popular American song of the 1890s.

TCHEBUTYKIN: You ought to take me in hand. Then I should reform.

IRINA: Fyodor has shaved off his mustache. I can't bear to look at him!

KULIGIN: Why, what's wrong?

TCHEBUTYKIN: I might tell you what your countenance looks like now, but I really can't.

KULIGIN: Well! It's the thing now, *modus vivendi.*° Our headmaster is clean-shaven and now I am second to him I have taken to shaving too. Nobody likes it, but I don't care. I am content. With mustache or without mustache I am equally content. (*Sits down.*)

(*In the background Andrey is wheeling a baby asleep in a perambulator.*)

IRINA: Ivan Romanitch, darling, I am dreadfully uneasy. You were on the boulevard yesterday, tell me what was it that happened?

TCHEBUTYKIN: What happened? Nothing. Nothing much. (*Reads the newspaper.*) It doesn't matter!

KULIGIN: The story is that Solyony and the baron met yesterday on the boulevard near the theater. . . .

TUSENBACH: Oh, stop it! Really. . . . (*With a wave of his hand walks away into the house.*)

KULIGIN: Near the theater. . . . Solyony began pestering the baron and he couldn't keep his temper and said something offensive. . . .

TCHEBUTYKIN: I don't know. It's all nonsense.

KULIGIN: A teacher at a divinity school wrote "nonsense" at the bottom of an essay and the pupil puzzled over it thinking it was a Latin word. . . . (*Laughs.*) It was fearfully funny. . . . They say Solyony is in love with Irina and hates the baron. . . . That's natural. Irina is a very nice girl.

(*From the background behind the scenes, "Aa-oo! Halloo!"*)

IRINA (*starts*): Everything frightens me somehow today. (*A pause.*) All my things are ready, after dinner I shall send off my luggage. The baron and I are to be married tomorrow, tomorrow we go to the brickyard and the day after that I shall be in the school. A new life is beginning. God will help me! How will it fare with me? When I passed my exam as a teacher I felt so happy, so blissful, that I cried. . . . (*A pause.*) The cart will soon be coming for my things. . . .

KULIGIN: That's all very well, but it does not seem serious. It's all nothing but ideas and very little that is serious. However, I wish you success with all my heart.

TCHEBUTYKIN (*moved to tenderness*): My good, delightful darling. . . . My heart of gold. . . .

KULIGIN: Well, today the officers will be gone and everything will go on in the old way. Whatever people may say, Masha is a true, good woman. I love her dearly and am thankful for my lot! . . . People have different lots in life. . . . There is a man called Kozyrev serving in the Excise° here. He was at school with me, but he was expelled from the fifth form because he could never understand *ut consecutivum.*° Now he is frightfully poor and ill, and when I meet him I say, "How are you, *ut consecutivum?*" "Yes," he says, "just so — *consecutivum*" . . . and then he coughs. . . . Now I have always been successful, I am fortunate, I have even got the order of the Stanislav of the second degree° and I am teaching others that *ut consecutivum.* Of course I am clever, cleverer than very many people, but happiness does not lie in that. . . . (*A pause.*)

(*In the house the "Maiden's Prayer" is played on the piano.*)

IRINA: Tomorrow evening I shall not be hearing that "Maiden's Prayer," I shan't be meeting Protopopov. . . . (*A pause.*) Protopopov is sitting there in the drawing room; he has come again today. . . .

KULIGIN: The headmistress has not come yet?

IRINA: No. They have sent for her. If only you knew how hard it is for me to live here alone, without Olya. . . . Now that she is headmistress and lives at the high school and is busy all day long. I am alone, I am bored, I have nothing to do, and I hate the room I live in. . . . I have made up my mind, since I am not fated to be in Moscow, that so it must be. It must be destiny. There is no help for it. . . . It's all in God's hands, that's the truth. When Nikolay Lvovitch made me an offer again . . . I thought it over and made up my mind. . . . He is a good man, it's wonderful really how good he is. . . . And I suddenly felt as though my soul had grown wings, my heart felt so light and again I longed for work, work. . . . Only something happened yesterday, there is some mystery hanging over me.

TCHEBUTYKIN: Nonsense.

NATASHA (*at the window*): Our headmistress!

KULIGIN: The headmistress has come. Let us go in. (*Goes into the house with Irina.*)

Excise: Tax office.
ut consecutivum: Latin for "and so it follows." Kozyrev was not good at Latin grammar.
Stanislav of the second degree: An award for civil service.

modus vivendi: Latin for "manner of living."

TCHEBUTYKIN (*reads the newspaper, humming softly*): "Tarara-boom-dee-ay."

(*Masha approaches; in the background Andrey is pushing the perambulator.*)

MASHA: Here he sits, snug and settled.

TCHEBUTYKIN: Well, what then?

MASHA (*sits down*): Nothing. . . . (*A pause.*) Did you love my mother?

TCHEBUTYKIN: Very much.

MASHA: And did she love you?

TCHEBUTYKIN (*after a pause*): That I don't remember.

MASHA: Is my man here? It's just like our cook Marfa used to say about her policeman: is my man here?

TCHEBUTYKIN: Not yet.

MASHA: When you get happiness by snatches, by little bits, and then lose it, as I am losing it, by degrees one grows coarse and spiteful. . . . (*Points to her bosom.*) I'm boiling here inside. . . . (*Looking at Andrey, who is pushing the perambulator.*) Here is our Andrey. . . . All our hopes are shattered. Thousands of people raised the bell, a lot of money and of labor was spent on it, and it suddenly fell and smashed. All at once, for no reason whatever. That's just how it is with Andrey. . . .

ANDREY: When will they be quiet in the house? There is such a noise.

TCHEBUTYKIN: Soon. (*Looks at his watch.*) My watch is an old-fashioned one with a repeater. . . . (*Winds his watch, it strikes.*) The first, the second, and the fifth batteries are going at one o'clock. (*A pause.*) And I am going tomorrow.

ANDREY: For good?

TCHEBUTYKIN: I don't know. Perhaps I shall come back in a year. Though goodness knows. . . . It doesn't matter one way or another.

(*There is the sound of a harp and violin being played far away in the street.*)

ANDREY: The town will be empty. It's as though one put an extinguisher over it. (*A pause.*) Something happened yesterday near the theater; everyone is talking of it, and I know nothing about it.

TCHEBUTYKIN: It was nothing. Foolishness. Solyony began annoying the baron and he lost his temper and insulted him, and it came in the end to Solyony's having to challenge him. (*Looks at his watch.*) It's time, I fancy. . . . It was to be at half-past twelve in the Crown forest that we can see from here beyond the river. . . . Piff-paff! (*Laughs.*) Solyony imagines he is a Lermontov and even writes verses. Joking apart, this is his third duel.

MASHA: Whose?

TCHEBUTYKIN: Solyony's.

MASHA: And the baron's?

TCHEBUTYKIN: What about the baron? (*A pause.*)

MASHA: My thoughts are in a muddle. . . . Anyway, I tell you, you ought not to let them do it. He may wound the baron or even kill him.

TCHEBUTYKIN: The baron is a very good fellow, but one baron more or less in the world, what does it matter? Let them! It doesn't matter. (*Beyond the garden a shout of "Aa-oo! Halloo!"*) You can wait. That is Skvortsov, the second, shouting. He is in a boat. (*A pause.*)

ANDREY: In my opinion to take part in a duel, or to be present at it even in the capacity of a doctor, is simply immoral.

TCHEBUTYKIN: That only seems so. . . . We are not real, nothing in the world is real, we don't exist, but only seem to exist. . . . Nothing matters!

MASHA: How they keep on talking, talking all day long. (*Goes.*) To live in such a climate, it may snow any minute, and then all this talk on the top of it. (*Stops.*) I am not going indoors, I can't go in there. . . . When Vershinin comes, tell me. . . . (*Goes down the avenue.*) And the birds are already flying south. . . . (*Looks up.*) Swans or geese. . . . Darlings, happy things. . . . (*Goes out.*)

ANDREY: Our house will be empty. The officers are going, you are going, Irina is getting married, and I shall be left in the house alone.

TCHEBUTYKIN: What about your wife?

(*Enter Ferapont with papers.*)

ANDREY: A wife is a wife. She is a straightforward, upright woman, good-natured, perhaps, but for all that there is something in her which makes her no better than some petty, blind, hairy animal. Anyway she is not a human being. I speak to you as a friend, the one man to whom I can open my soul. I love Natasha, that is so, but sometimes she seems to me wonderfully vulgar, and then I don't know what to think, I can't account for my loving her or, anyway, having loved her.

TCHEBUTYKIN (*gets up*): I am going away tomorrow, my boy, perhaps we shall never meet again, so this is my advice to you. Put on your cap, you know, take your stick, and walk off . . . walk off and just go, go without looking back. And the farther you go, the better. (*A pause.*) But do as you like! It doesn't matter. . . .

(*Solyony crosses the stage in the background with two officers; seeing Tchebutykin he turns toward him; the officers walk on.*)

SOLYONY: Doctor, it's time! It's half-past twelve. (*Greets Andrey.*)

TCHEBUTYKIN: Directly. I am sick of you all. (*To Andrey.*) If anyone asks for me, Andryusha, say I'll be back directly. . . . (*Sighs.*) Oho-ho-ho!

SOLYONY: He had not time to say alack before the bear was on his back. (*Walks away with the doctor.*) Why are you croaking, old chap?

TCHEBUTYKIN: Come!

SOLYONY: How do you feel?

TCHEBUTYKIN (*angrily*): Like a pig in clover.°

SOLYONY: The old chap need not excite himself. I won't do anything much, I'll only shoot him like a snipe. (*Takes out scent and sprinkles his hands.*) I've used a whole bottle today, and still they smell. My hands smell like a corpse. (*A pause.*) Yes. . . . Do you remember the poem? "And, restless, seeks the stormy ocean, as though in tempest there were peace."°

TCHEBUTYKIN: Yes. He had not time to say alack before the bear was on his back.

(*Goes out with Solyony. Shouts are heard: "Halloo!-Oo-oo!" Andrey and Ferapont come in.*)

FERAPONT: Papers for you to sign. . . .

ANDREY (*nervously*): Let me alone! Let me alone! I entreat you! (*Walks away with the perambulator.*)

FERAPONT: That's what the papers are for — to be signed. (*Retires into the background.*)

(*Enter Irina and Tusenbach wearing a straw hat; Kuligin crosses the stage shouting "Aa-oo, Masha, aa-oo!"*)

TUSENBACH: I believe that's the only man in the town who is glad that the officers are going away.

IRINA: That's very natural. (*A pause.*) Our town will be empty now.

TUSENBACH: Dear, I'll be back directly.

IRINA: Where are you going?

TUSENBACH: I must go into the town, and then . . . to see my comrades off.

IRINA: That's not true. . . . Nikolay, why are you so absentminded today? (*A pause.*) What happened yesterday near the theater?

TUSENBACH (*with a gesture of impatience*): My beautiful one . . . (*Looks into her face.*) For five years now I have loved you and still I can't get used to it, and you seem to me more and more lovely. What wonderful, exquisite hair! What eyes! I shall carry you off tomorrow, we will work, we will be rich, my dreams will come true. You shall be happy. There is only one thing, one thing: you don't love me!

IRINA: That's not in my power! I'll be your wife and

be faithful and obedient, but there is no love. I can't help it. (*Weeps.*) I've never been in love in my life! Oh, I have so dreamed of love, I've been dreaming of it for years, day and night, but my soul is like a wonderful piano of which the key has been lost. (*A pause.*) You look uneasy.

TUSENBACH: I have not slept all night. There has never been anything in my life so dreadful that it could frighten me, and only that lost key frets at my heart and won't let me sleep. . . . Say something to me. . . . (*A pause.*) Say something to me. . . .

IRINA: What? What am I to say to you? What?

TUSENBACH: Anything.

IRINA: There, there! (*A pause.*)

TUSENBACH: What trifles, what little things suddenly *à propos* of nothing acquire importance in life! One laughs at them as before, thinks them nonsense, but still one goes on and feels that one has not the power to stop. Don't let us talk about it! I am happy. I feel as though I were seeing these pines, these maples, these birch trees for the first time in my life, and they all seem to be looking at me with curiosity and waiting. What beautiful trees, and, really, how beautiful life ought to be under them! (*A shout of "Halloo! Aa-oo!"*) I must be off; it's time. . . . See, that tree is dead, but it waves in the wind with the others. And so it seems to me that if I die I shall still have part in life, one way or another. Good-bye, my darling. . . . (*Kisses her hands.*) Those papers of yours you gave me are lying under the calendar on my table.

IRINA: I am coming with you.

TUSENBACH (*in alarm*): No, no! (*Goes off quickly, stops in the avenue.*) Irina!

IRINA: What is it?

TUSENBACH (*not knowing what to say*): I didn't have any coffee this morning. Ask them to make me some. (*Goes out quickly.*)

(*Irina stands lost in thought, then walks away into the background of the scene and sits down on the swing. Enter Andrey with the perambulator, and Ferapont comes into sight.*)

FERAPONT: Andrey Sergeyevitch, the papers aren't mine; they are government papers. I didn't invent them.

ANDREY: Oh, where is it all gone? What has become of my past, when I was young, gay, and clever, when my dreams and thoughts were exquisite, when my present and my past were lighted up by hope? Why on the very threshold of life do we become dull, gray, uninteresting, lazy, indifferent, useless, unhappy? . . . Our town has been going on for two hundred years — there are a hundred thousand people living in it; and there is not one who is not

---

Like a pig in clover: Distracted.
"And . . . peace": From Lermontov's poem "The Sail."

like the rest, not one saint in the past, or the present, not one man of learning, not one artist, not one man in the least remarkable who could inspire envy or a passionate desire to imitate him. . . . They only eat, drink, sleep, and not to be bored to stupefaction they vary their lives by nasty gossip, vodka, cards, litigation; and the wives deceive their husbands, and the husbands tell lies and pretend that they see and hear nothing, and an overwhelmingly vulgar influence weighs upon the children, and the divine spark is quenched in them, and they become the same sort of pitiful, dead creatures, all exactly alike, as their fathers and mothers. . . . (*To Ferapont, angrily.*) What do you want?

FERAPONT: Eh? There are papers to sign.

ANDREY: You bother me!

FERAPONT (*handing him the papers*): The porter from the local treasury was saying just now that there was as much as two hundred degrees of frost in Petersburg this winter.

ANDREY: The present is hateful, but when I think of the future, it is so nice! I feel so lighthearted, so free. A light dawns in the distance, I see freedom. I see how I and my children will become free from sloth, from kvass, from goose and cabbage, from sleeping after dinner, from mean, parasitic living. . . .

FERAPONT: He says that two thousand people were frozen to death. The people were terrified. It was either in Petersburg or Moscow, I don't remember.

ANDREY (*in a rush of tender feeling*): My dear sisters, my wonderful sisters! (*Through tears.*) Masha, my sister!

NATASHA (*in the window*): Who is talking so loud out there? Is that you, Andryusha? You will wake baby Sophie. *Il ne faut pas faire de bruit, la Sophie est dormée déja: Vous êtes un ours.°* (*Getting angry.*) If you want to talk, give the perambulator with the baby to somebody else. Ferapont, take the perambulator from the master!

FERAPONT: Yes, ma'am. (*Takes the pram.*)

ANDREY (*in confusion*): I am talking quietly.

NATASHA (*petting her child, inside the room*): Bobik! Naughty Bobik! Little rascal!

ANDREY (*looking through the papers*): Very well, I'll look through them and sign what wants signing, and then you can take them back to the Board. . . .

(*Goes into the house reading the papers; Ferapont pushes the pram farther into the garden.*)

NATASHA (*speaking indoors*): Bobik, what is mamma's name? Darling, darling! And who is this? This is Auntie Olya. Say to Auntie, "Good morning, Olya!"

Il . . . ours: French for "Don't make any noise; Sophie is already asleep. You are a bear."

(*Two wandering musicians, a man and a girl, enter and play a violin and a harp; from the house enter Vershinin with Olga and Anfisa, and stand for a minute listening in silence; Irina comes up.*)

OLGA: Our garden is like a public passage; they walk and ride through. Nurse, give those people something.

ANFISA (*gives money to the musicians*): Go away, and God bless you, my dear souls! (*The musicians bow and go away.*) Poor things. People don't play if they have plenty to eat. (*To Irina.*) Good morning, Irisha! (*Kisses her.*) Aye, aye, my little girl, I am having a time of it! Living in the high school, in a government flat, with dear Olya — that's what the Lord has vouchsafed me in my old age! I have never lived so well in my life, sinful woman that I am. . . . It's a big flat, and I have a room to myself and a bedstead. All at the government expense. I wake up in the night and, O Lord, Mother of God, there is no one in the world happier than I!

VERSHININ (*looks at his watch*): We are just going, Olga Sergeyevna. It's time to be off. (*A pause.*) I wish you everything, everything. . . . Where is Marya Sergeyevna?

IRINA: She is somewhere in the garden. . . . I'll go and look for her.

VERSHININ: Please be so good. I am in a hurry.

ANFISA: I'll go and look for her too. (*Shouts.*) Mashenka, aa-oo! (*Goes with Irina into the farther part of the garden.*) Aa-oo! Aa-oo!

VERSHININ: Everything comes to an end. Here we are parting. (*Looks at his watch.*) The town has given us something like a lunch; we have been drinking champagne, the mayor made a speech. I ate and listened, but my heart was here, with you all. . . . (*Looks round the garden.*) I've grown used to you. . . .

OLGA: Shall we ever see each other again?

VERSHININ: Most likely not. (*A pause.*) My wife and two little girls will stay here for another two months; please, if anything happens, if they need anything . . .

OLGA: Yes, yes, of course. Set your mind at rest. (*A pause.*) By tomorrow there won't be a soldier in the town — it will all turn into a memory, and of course for us it will be like beginning a new life. . . . (*A pause.*) Nothing turns out as we would have it. I did not want to be a headmistress, and yet I am. It seems we are not to live in Moscow. . . .

VERSHININ: Well. . . . Thank you for everything. . . . Forgive me if anything was amiss. . . . I have talked a great deal: forgive me for that too — don't remember evil against me.

OLGA (*wipes her eyes*): Why doesn't Masha come?

VERSHININ: What else am I to say to you at parting?

What am I to theorize about? . . . (*Laughs.*) Life is hard. It seems to many of us blank and hopeless; but yet we must admit that it goes on getting clearer and easier, and it looks as though the time were not far off when it will be full of happiness. (*Looks at his watch.*) It's time for me to go! In old days men were absorbed in wars, filling all their existence with marches, raids, victories, but now all that is a thing of the past, leaving behind it a great void which there is so far nothing to fill: humanity is searching for it passionately, and of course will find it. Ah, if only it could be quickly! (*A pause.*) If, don't you know, industry were united with culture and culture with industry. . . . (*Looks at his watch.*) But, I say, it's time for me to go. . . .

OLGA: Here she comes.

(*Masha comes in*)

VERSHININ: I have come to say good-bye. . . .

(*Olga moves a little away to leave them free to say good-bye.*)

MASHA (*looking into his face*): Good-bye. . . . (*A prolonged kiss.*)

OLGA: Come, come. . . .

(*Masha sobs violently.*)

VERSHININ: Write to me. . . . Don't forget me! Let me go! . . . Time is up! . . . Olga Sergeyevna, take her, I must . . . go . . . I am late. . . . (*Much moved, kisses Olga's hands; then again embraces Masha and quickly goes off.*)

OLGA: Come, Masha! Leave off, darling.

(*Enter Kuligin.*)

KULIGIN (*embarrassed*): Never mind, let her cry — let her. . . . My good Masha, my dear Masha! . . . You are my wife, and I am happy, anyway. . . . I don't complain; I don't say a word of blame. . . . Here Olya is my witness. . . . We'll begin the old life again, and I won't say one word, not a hint. . . .

MASHA (*restraining her sobs*): By the seastrand an oak tree green. . . . Upon that oak a chain of gold. . . . Upon that oak a chain of gold. . . . I am going mad. . . . By the seastrand . . . an oak tree green. . . .

OLGA: Calm yourself, Masha. . . . Calm yourself. . . . Give her some water.

MASHA: I am not crying now. . . .

KULIGIN: She is not crying now . . . she is good. . . .

(*The dim sound of a faraway shot.*)

MASHA: By the seastrand an oak tree green, upon that oak a chain of gold. . . . The cat is green . . . the oak is green. . . . I am mixing it up. . . . (*Drinks water.*) My life is a failure. . . . I want nothing now. . . . I shall be calm directly. . . . It doesn't matter. . . . What does "strand" mean? Why do these words haunt me? My thoughts are in a tangle.

(*Enter Irina.*)

OLGA: Calm yourself, Masha. Come, that's a good girl. Let us go indoors.

MASHA (*angrily*): I am not going in. Let me alone! (*Sobs, but at once checks herself.*) I don't go into that house now and I won't.

IRINA: Let us sit together, even if we don't say anything. I am going away tomorrow, you know. . . . (*A pause.*)

KULIGIN: I took a false beard and mustache from a boy in the third grade yesterday, just look. . . . (*Puts on the beard and mustache.*) I look like the German teacher. . . . (*Laughs.*) Don't I? Funny creatures, those boys.

MASHA: You really do look like the German teacher.

OLGA (*laughs*): Yes.

(*Masha weeps.*)

IRINA: There, Masha!

KULIGIN: Awfully like. . . .

(*Enter Natasha.*)

NATASHA (*to the maid*): What? Mr. Protopopov will sit with Sophie, and let Andrey Sergeyevitch wheel Bobik up and down. What a lot there is to do with children. . . . (*To Irina.*) Irina, you are going away tomorrow, what a pity. Do stay just another week. (*Seeing Kuligin utters a shriek; the latter laughs and takes off the beard and mustache.*) Well, what next, you gave me such a fright! (*To Irina.*) I am used to you and do you suppose that I don't feel parting with you? I shall put Andrey with his violin into your room — let him saw away there! — and we will put baby Sophie in his room. Adorable, delightful baby! Isn't she a child! Today she looked at me with such eyes and said "Mamma"!

KULIGIN: A fine child, that's true.

NATASHA: So tomorrow I shall be all alone here. (*Sighs.*) First of all I shall have this avenue of fir trees cut down, and then that maple. . . . It looks so ugly in the evening. . . . (*To Irina.*) My dear, that sash does not suit you at all. . . . It's in bad taste. You want something light. And then I shall have flowers, flowers planted everywhere, and there will be such a scent. . . . (*Severely.*) Why is there a fork lying about on that seat? (*Going into the house, to the maid.*) Why is there a fork lying about on this seat, I ask you? (*Shouts.*) Hold your tongue!

KULIGIN: She is at it!

(*Behind the scenes the band plays a march; they all listen.*)

OLGA: They are going.

(*Enter Tchebutykin.*)

MASHA: Our people are going. Well . . . a happy journey to them! (*To her husband.*) We must go home. . . . Where are my hat and cape?

KULIGIN: I took them into the house. . . . I'll get them directly. . . .

OLGA: Yes, now we can go home, it's time.

TCHEBUTYKIN: Olga Sergeyevna!

OLGA: What is it? (*A pause.*) What?

TCHEBUTYKIN: Nothing. . . . I don't know how to tell you. (*Whispers in her ear.*)

OLGA (*in alarm*): It can't be!

TCHEBUTYKIN: Yes . . . such a business. . . . I am so worried and worn out, I don't want to say another word. . . . (*With vexation.*) But there, it doesn't matter!

MASHA: What has happened?

OLGA (*puts her arms round Irina*): This is a terrible day. . . . I don't know how to tell you, my precious. . . .

IRINA: What is it? Tell me quickly, what is it? For God's sake! (*Cries.*)

TCHEBUTYKIN: The baron has just been killed in a duel.

IRINA (*weeping quietly*): I knew, I knew. . . .

TCHEBUTYKIN (*in the background of the scene sits down on a garden seat*): I am worn out. . . . (*Takes a newspaper out of his pocket.*) Let them cry. . . . (*Sings softly.*) "Tarara-boom-dee-ay." . . . It doesn't matter.

(*The three sisters stand with their arms round one another.*)

MASHA: Oh, listen to that band! They are going away from us; one has gone altogether, gone forever. We are left alone to begin our life over again. . . . We've got to live . . . we've got to live. . . .

IRINA (*lays her head on Olga's bosom*): A time will come when everyone will know what all this is for, why there is this misery; there will be no mysteries and, meanwhile, we have got to live . . . we have got to work, only to work! Tomorrow I shall go alone; I shall teach in the school, and I will give all my life to those to whom it may be of use. Now it's autumn; soon winter will come and cover us with snow, and I will work, I will work.

OLGA (*embraces both her sisters*): The music is so gay, so confident, and one longs for life! O my God! Time will pass, and we shall go away forever, and we shall be forgotten, our faces will be forgotten, our voices, and how many there were of us; but our sufferings will pass into joy for those who will live after us, happiness and peace will be established upon earth, and they will remember kindly and bless those who have lived before. Oh, dear sisters, our life is not ended yet. We shall live! The music is so gay, so joyful, and it seems as though a little more and we shall know what we are living for, why we are suffering. . . . If we only knew — if we only knew!

(*The music grows more and more subdued; Kuligin, cheerful and smiling, brings the hat and cape; Andrey pushes the perambulator in which Bobik is sitting.*)

TCHEBUTYKIN (*humming softly*): "Tarara-boom-dee-ay!" (*Reads his paper.*) It doesn't matter, it doesn't matter.

OLGA: If we only knew, if we only knew!

THE CHERRY ORCHARD

Chekhov's most popular play is his last, *The Cherry Orchard* (1903), which premiered on his birthday, January 17, in 1904. The Moscow Art Theatre performance was directed by Konstantin Stanislavsky, an actor-director who pioneered a new method of realistic acting. (Stanislavsky is still read and admired the world over. His techniques were modified in the United States and form the basis of METHOD ACTING.) However, when Chekhov saw him acting in his plays, he was alarmed. He found Stanislavsky too stagey, too flamboyant and melodramatic, for the effects he wanted. He and Stanislavsky argued hotly over what should happen in his plays, and all too often Stanislavsky prevailed.

They argued over whether *The Cherry Orchard* was a tragedy. Chekhov steadfastly called it a comedy, but Stanislavsky saw the ruin of Lyuba and the destruction of the cherry orchard as tragic. The old beauty was giving way to modern necessity and materialism. The cherry orchard, which was a notable ornament of that part of Russia, was to become tract housing for summer residents. Stanislavsky saw this as a tragic loss. Chekhov perhaps saw it the same way, but he also considered its potential as the beginning of a new, more realistic life for Lyuba and Gayev. Their impracticality was an important cause of their having lost their wealth and estate.

How audiences interpret Lopahin depends on how they view the ambition of the new class of businessmen whose zeal, work, and cleverness earn them the estates that previously they could only have hoped to work on. Social change is fueled by money, which replaces an inherited aristocracy with ambitious moneymakers who earn the power to force changes on the old, less flexible aristocrats. In Russia massive social change was eventually effected by revolution and the institution of communism. But *The Cherry Orchard* shows that change would have come to Russia in any event.

Perhaps Chekhov's peasant blood helped him see the play as more of a comedy than a tragedy even though he portrays the characters with greater complexity than we might expect in comedy. Lopahin is not a simple unsympathetic character; Trofimov is not a simple dreamer. These characters are complicated by history. We need to look closely at what they do and why they do it. For example, when thinking about preserving the beauties of the cherry orchard, Trofimov reminds people that all of Russia is an orchard, that the world is filled with beautiful places. Such a view makes it difficult for him to feel nostalgia for aristocratic privilege.

Trofimov sounds a striking note about the practice of slavery in Russia. He tells Lyuba and Gayev that they are living on credit, that they have debts that must be paid back to the Russian people. The cherry orchard is beautiful because each tree represents the soul of a serf. The beautiful class of people to which the impractical Lyuba belongs owes its beauty and grace to the institution of slavery, and soon the note will be presented for payment. The sound of the breaking string in Act I, repeated at the end of the play, is Chekhov's graphic way of dramatizing the changes represented in the play.

Lyuba, however, cannot change. Her habits of mind are fully formed before the play begins and nothing that Lopahin can say will help change her. Even though she knows she is dangerously in debt, she gives a gold coin to a beggar. *Noblesse oblige* — the duty of the upper class to help the poor — is still part of her ethos, even if it also involves her own ruin.

A sense of tragedy is apparent in Lyuba's feelings and her helplessness. She seems incapable of renovating herself, no matter how much she may wish to change. We see her as a victim of fate, a fate that is formed by her expectations and training. But the play also contains comic and nonsensical moments. In his letters, Chekhov mentions that the play is happy and frivolous, "in places even a farce."

The Cherry Orchard has a more direct, less diffuse quality than *Three Sisters* if only because the conclusion, the loss of the cherry orchard — in every sense of its loss — seems a more complete action than the eviction of the Prozorovs. We anticipate it more clearly and sense that we have been prepared for it more thoroughly. Yet Chekhov has by no means provided a neatly plotted vehicle of melodrama. He has remained faithful to his own vision of reality as a series of unfolding moments that constantly reveal character and qualify behavior.

Anton Chekhov (1860–1904)

THE CHERRY ORCHARD   *1903*
TRANSLATED BY CONSTANCE GARNETT

Characters

MADAME RANEVSKY (LYUBOV ANDREYEVNA), *the owner of the Cherry Orchard*
ANYA, *her daughter, aged 17*
VARYA, *her adopted daughter, aged 24*
GAEV (LEONID ANDREYEVITCH), *brother of Madame Ranevsky*
LOPAHIN (YERMOLAY ALEXEYEVITCH), *a merchant*
TROFIMOV (PYOTR SERGEYEVITCH), *a student*
SEMYONOV-PISHTCHIK, *a landowner*
CHARLOTTA IVANOVNA, *a governess*
EPIHODOV (SEMYON PANTALEYEVITCH), *a clerk*
DUNYASHA, *a maid*
FIRS, *an old valet, aged 87*
YASHA, *a young valet*
A WAYFARER
THE STATION MASTER
A POST OFFICE CLERK
VISITORS, SERVANTS

(*The action takes place on the estate of Madame Ranevsky.*)

ACT I

(*A room, which has always been called the nursery. One of the doors leads into Anya's room. Dawn, sun rises during the scene. May, the cherry trees in flower, but it is cold in the garden with the frost of early morning. Windows closed.*)

(*Enter Dunyasha with a candle and Lopahin with a book in his hand.*)

LOPAHIN: The train's in, thank God. What time is it?

DUNYASHA: Nearly two o'clock. (*Puts out the candle.*) It's daylight already.

LOPAHIN: The train's late! Two hours, at least. (*Yawns and stretches.*) I'm a pretty one; what a fool I've been. Came here on purpose to meet them at the station and dropped asleep. . . . Dozed off as I sat in the chair. It's annoying. . . . You might have waked me.

DUNYASHA: I thought you had gone. (*Listens.*) There, I do believe they're coming!

LOPAHIN (*listens*): No, what with the luggage and one thing and another. (*A pause.*) Lyubov Andreyevna has been abroad five years; I don't know what she is like now. . . . She's a splendid woman. A good-natured, kind-hearted woman. I remember when I was a lad of fifteen, my poor father — he used to keep a little shop here in the village in those days — gave me a punch in the face with his fist and made my nose bleed. We were in the yard here, I forget what we'd come about — he had had a drop. Lyubov Andreyevna — I can see her now — she was a slim young girl then — took me to wash my face, and then brought me into this very room, into the nursery. "Don't cry, little peasant," says she, "it will be well in time for your wedding day." . . . (*A pause.*) Little peasant. . . . My father was a peasant, it's true, but here am I in a white waistcoat and brown shoes, like a pig in a bun shop. Yes, I'm a rich man, but for all my money, come to think, a peasant I was, and a peasant I am. (*Turns over the pages of the book.*) I've been reading this book and I can't make head or tail of it. I fell asleep over it. (*A pause.*)

DUNYASHA: The dogs have been awake all night, they feel that the mistress is coming.

LOPAHIN: Why, what's the matter with you, Dunyasha?

DUNYASHA: My hands are all of a tremble. I feel as though I should faint.

LOPAHIN: You're a spoilt soft creature, Dunyasha. And dressed like a lady too, and your hair done up. That's not the thing. One must know one's place.

(*Enter Epihodov with a nosegay; he wears a pea jacket and highly polished creaking top boots; he drops the nosegay as he comes in.*)

EPIHODOV (*picking up the nosegay*): Here! the gardener's sent this, says you're to put it in the dining room. (*Gives Dunyasha the nosegay.*)

LOPAHIN: And bring me some kvass.

DUNYASHA: I will. (*Goes out.*)

EPIHODOV: It's chilly this morning, three degrees of frost, though the cherries are all in flower. I can't say much for our climate. (*Sighs.*) I can't. Our climate is not often propitious to the occasion. Yermolay Alexeyevitch, permit me to call your attention to the fact that I purchased myself a pair of boots the day before yesterday, and they creak, I venture to assure you, so that there's no tolerating them. What ought I to grease them with?

LOPAHIN: Oh, shut up! Don't bother me.

EPIHODOV: Every day some misfortune befalls me. I don't complain, I'm used to it, and I wear a smiling face.

(*Dunyasha comes in, hands Lopahin the kvass.*)

EPIHODOV: I am going. (*Stumbles against a chair, which falls over.*) There! (*As though triumphant.*) There

you see now, excuse the expression, an accident like that among others. . . . It's positively remarkable. (*Goes out.*)

DUNYASHA: Do you know, Yermolay Alexeyevitch, I must confess, Epihodov has made me a proposal.

LOPAHIN: Ah!

DUNYASHA: I'm sure I don't know. . . . He's a harmless fellow, but sometimes when he begins talking, there's no making anything of it. It's all very fine and expressive, only there's no understanding it. I've a sort of liking for him too. He loves me to distraction. He's an unfortunate man; every day there's something. They tease him about it — two and twenty misfortunes they call him.

LOPAHIN (*listening*): There! I do believe they're coming.

DUNYASHA: They are coming! What's the matter with me? . . . I'm cold all over.

LOPAHIN: They really are coming. Let's go and meet them. Will she know me? It's five years since I saw her.

DUNYASHA (*in a flutter*): I shall drop this very minute. . . . Ah, I shall drop.

(*There is a sound of two carriages driving up to the house. Lopahin and Dunyasha go out quickly. The stage is left empty. A noise is heard in the adjoining rooms. Firs, who has driven to meet Madame Ranevsky, crosses the stage hurriedly leaning on a stick. He is wearing old-fashioned livery and a high hat. He says something to himself, but not a word can be distinguished. The noise behind the scenes goes on increasing. A voice: "Come, let's go in here." Enter Lyubov Andreyevna, Anya, and Charlotta Ivanovna with a pet dog on a chain, all in traveling dresses. Varya in an outdoor coat with a kerchief over her head, Gaev, Semyonov-Pishtchik, Lopahin, Dunyasha with bag and parasol, servants with other articles. All walk across the room.*)

ANYA: Let's come in here. Do you remember what room this is, mamma?

LYUBOV (*joyfully, through her tears*): The nursery!

VARYA: How cold it is, my hands are numb. (*To Lyubov Andreyevna.*) Your rooms, the white room and the lavender one, are just the same as ever, mamma.

LYUBOV: My nursery, dear delightful room. . . . I used to sleep here when I was little. . . . (*Cries.*) And here I am, like a little child. . . . (*Kisses her brother and Varya, and then her brother again.*) Varya's just the same as ever, like a nun. And I knew Dunyasha. (*Kisses Dunyasha.*)

GAEV: The train was two hours late. What do you think of that? Is that the way to do things?

CHARLOTTA (*to Pishtchik*): My dog eats nuts, too.

PISHTCHIK (*wonderingly*): Fancy that!

(They all go out except Anya and Dunyasha.)

DUNYASHA: We've been expecting you so long. *(Takes Anya's hat and coat.)*

ANYA: I haven't slept for four nights on the journey. I feel dreadfully cold.

DUNYASHA: You set out in Lent, there was snow and frost, and now? My darling! *(Laughs and kisses her.)* I *have* missed you, my precious, my joy. I must tell you . . . I can't put it off a minute. . . .

ANYA *(wearily)*: What now?

DUNYASHA: Epihodov, the clerk, made me a proposal just after Easter.

ANYA: It's always the same thing with you. . . . *(Straightening her hair.)* I've lost all my hairpins. *(She is staggering from exhaustion.)*

DUNYASHA: I don't know what to think, really. He does love me, he does love me so!

ANYA *(looking toward her door, tenderly)*: My own room, my windows just as though I had never gone away. I'm home! Tomorrow morning I shall get up and run into the garden. . . . Oh, if I could get to sleep! I haven't slept all the journey, I was so anxious and worried.

DUNYASHA: Pyotr Sergeyevitch came the day before yesterday.

ANYA *(joyfully)*: Petya!

DUNYASHA: He's asleep in the bath house, he has settled in there. I'm afraid of being in their way, says he. *(Glancing at her watch.)* I was to have waked him, but Varvara Mihalovna told me not to. Don't you wake him, says she.

(Enter Varya with a bunch of keys at her waist.)

VARYA: Dunyasha, coffee and make haste. . . . Mamma's asking for coffee.

DUNYASHA: This very minute. *(Goes out.)*

VARYA: Well, thank God, you've come. You're home again. *(Petting her.)* My little darling has come back! My precious beauty has come back again!

ANYA: I have had a time of it!

VARYA: I can fancy.

ANYA: We set off in Holy Week — it was so cold then, and all the way Charlotta would talk and show off her tricks. What did you want to burden me with Charlotta for?

VARYA: You couldn't have traveled all alone, darling. At seventeen!

ANYA: We got to Paris at last, it was cold there — snow. I speak French shockingly. Mamma lives on the fifth floor, I went up to her and there were a lot of French people, ladies, an old priest with a book. The place smelt of tobacco and so comfortless. I felt sorry, oh! so sorry for mamma all at once. I put my arms round her neck, and hugged her and wouldn't let her go. Mamma was as kind as she could be, and she cried. . . .

VARYA *(through her tears)*: Don't speak of it, don't speak of it!

ANYA: She had sold her villa at Mentone, she had nothing left, nothing. I hadn't a farthing left either, we only just had enough to get here. And mamma doesn't understand! When we had dinner at the stations, she always ordered the most expensive things and gave the waiters a whole ruble. Charlotta's just the same. Yasha too must have the same as we do; it's simply awful. You know Yasha is mamma's valet now, we brought him here with us.

VARYA: Yes, I've seen the young rascal.

ANYA: Well, tell me — have you paid the arrears on the mortgage?

VARYA: How could we get the money?

ANYA: Oh, dear! Oh, dear!

VARYA: In August the place will be sold.

ANYA: My goodness!

LOPAHIN *(peeps in at the door and moos like a cow)*: Moo! *(Disappears.)*

VARYA *(weeping)*: There, that's what I could do to him. *(Shakes her fist.)*

ANYA *(embracing Varya, softly)*: Varya, has he made you an offer? *(Varya shakes her head.)* Why, but he loves you. Why is it you don't come to an understanding? What are you waiting for?

VARYA: I believe that there never will be anything between us. He has a lot to do, he has not time for me . . . and takes no notice of me. Bless the man, it makes me miserable to see him. . . . Everyone's talking of our being married, everyone's congratulating me, and all the while there's really nothing in it; it's all like a dream. *(In another tone.)* You have a new brooch like a bee.

ANYA *(mournfully)*: Mamma bought it. *(Goes into her own room and in a lighthearted childish tone.)* And you know, in Paris I went up in a balloon!

VARYA: My darling's home again! My pretty is home again!

(Dunyasha returns with the coffee pot and is making the coffee.)

VARYA *(standing at the door)*: All day long, darling, as I go about looking after the house, I keep dreaming all the time. If only we could marry you to a rich man, then I should feel more at rest. Then I would go off by myself on a pilgrimage to Kiev, to Moscow . . . and so I would spend my life going from one holy place to another. . . . I would go on and on. . . . What bliss!

ANYA: The birds are singing in the garden. What time is it?

VARYA: It must be nearly three. It's time you were

asleep, darling. (*Going into Anya's room.*) What bliss!

(*Yasha enters with a rug and a traveling bag.*)

YASHA (*crosses the stage, mincingly*): May one come in here, pray?

DUNYASHA: I shouldn't have known you, Yasha. How you have changed abroad.

YASHA: H'm! . . . And who are you?

DUNYASHA: When you went away, I was that high. (*Shows distance from floor.*) Dunyasha, Fyodor's daughter. . . . You don't remember me!

YASHA: H'm! . . . You're a peach! (*Looks round and embraces her: she shrieks and drops a saucer. Yasha goes out hastily.*)

VARYA (*in the doorway, in a tone of vexation*): What now?

DUNYASHA (*through her tears*): I have broken a saucer.

VARYA: Well, that brings good luck.

ANYA (*coming out of her room*): We ought to prepare mamma: Petya is here.

VARYA: I told them not to wake him.

ANYA (*dreamily*): It's six years since father died. Then only a month later little brother Grisha was drowned in the river, such a pretty boy he was, only seven. It was more than mamma could bear, so she went away, went away without looking back. (*Shuddering.*) . . . How well I understand her, if only she knew! (*A pause.*) And Petya Trofimov was Grisha's tutor, he may remind her.

(*Enter Firs: he is wearing a pea jacket and a white waistcoat.*)

FIRS (*Goes up to the coffee pot, anxiously*): The mistress will be served here. (*Puts on white gloves.*) Is the coffee ready? (*Sternly to Dunyasha.*) Girl! Where's the cream?

DUNYASHA: Ah, mercy on us! (*Goes out quickly.*)

FIRS (*fussing round the coffee pot*): Ech! you good-for-nothing! (*Muttering to himself.*) Come back from Paris. And the old master used to go to Paris too . . . horses all the way. (*Laughs.*)

VARYA: What is it, Firs?

FIRS: What is your pleasure? (*Gleefully.*) My lady has come home! I have lived to see her again! Now I can die. (*Weeps with joy.*)

(*Enter Lyubov Andreyevna, Gaev, and Semyonov-Pishtchik; the latter is in a short-waisted full coat of fine cloth, and full trousers. Gaev, as he comes in, makes a gesture with his arms and his whole body, as though he were playing billiards.*)

LYUBOV: How does it go? Let me remember. Cannon off the red!

GAEV: That's it — in off the white! Why, once, sister,

we used to sleep together in this very room, and now I'm fifty-one, strange as it seems.

LOPAHIN: Yes, time flies.

GAEV: What do you say?

LOPAHIN: Time, I say, flies.

GAEV: What a smell of patchouli!

ANYA: I'm going to bed. Good night, mamma. (*Kisses her mother.*)

LYUBOV: My precious darling. (*Kisses her hands.*) Are you glad to be home? I can't believe it.

ANYA: Good night, uncle.

GAEV (*kissing her face and hands*): God bless you! How like you are to your mother! (*To his sister.*) At her age you were just the same, Lyuba.

(*Anya shakes hands with Lopahin and Pishtchik, then goes out, shutting the door after her.*)

LYUBOV: She's quite worn out.

PISHTCHIK: Aye, it's a long journey, to be sure.

VARYA (*to Lopahin and Pishtchik*): Well, gentlemen? It's three o'clock and time to say good-bye.

LYUBOV (*laughs*): You're just the same as ever, Varya. (*Draws her to her and kisses her.*) I'll just drink my coffee and then we will all go and rest. (*Firs puts a cushion under her feet.*) Thanks, friend. I am so fond of coffee, I drink it day and night. Thanks, dear old man. (*Kisses Firs.*)

VARYA: I'll just see whether all the things have been brought in. (*Goes out.*)

LYUBOV: Can it really be me sitting here? (*Laughs.*) I want to dance about and clap my hands. (*Covers her face with her hands.*) And I could drop asleep in a moment! God knows I love my country, I love it tenderly; I couldn't look out of the window in the train, I kept crying so. (*Through her tears.*) But I must drink my coffee, though. Thank you, Firs, thanks, dear old man. I'm so glad to find you still alive.

FIRS: The day before yesterday.

GAEV: He's rather deaf.

LOPAHIN: I have to set off for Harkov directly, at five o'clock. . . . It is annoying! I wanted to have a look at you, and a little talk. . . . You are just as splendid as ever.

PISHTCHIK (*breathing heavily*): Handsomer, indeed. . . . Dressed in Parisian style . . . completely bowled me over.

LOPAHIN: Your brother, Leonid Andreyevitch here, is always saying that I'm a low-born knave, that I'm a money grubber, but I don't care one straw for that. Let him talk. Only I do want you to believe in me as you used to. I do want your wonderful tender eyes to look at me as they used to in the old days. Merciful God! My father was a serf of your father and of your grandfather, but you —

you — did so much for me once, that I've forgotten all that; I love you as though you were my kin . . . more than my kin.

LYUBOV: I can't sit still, I simply can't. . . . (*Jumps up and walks about in violent agitation.*) This happiness is too much for me. . . . You may laugh at me, I know I'm silly. . . . My own bookcase. (*Kisses the bookcase.*) My little table.

GAEV: Nurse died while you were away.

LYUBOV (*sits down and drinks coffee*): Yes, the Kingdom of Heaven be hers! You wrote me of her death.

GAEV: And Anastasy is dead. Squinting Petruchka has left me and is in service now with the police captain in the town. (*Takes a box of caramels out of his pocket and sucks one.*)

PISHTCHIK: My daughter, Dashenka, wishes to be remembered to you.

LOPAHIN: I want to tell you something very pleasant and cheering. (*Glancing at his watch.*) I'm going directly . . . there's no time to say much . . . well, I can say it in a couple of words. I needn't tell you your cherry orchard is to be sold to pay your debts; the twenty-second of August is the date fixed for the sale; but don't you worry, dearest lady, you may sleep in peace, there is a way of saving it. . . . This is what I propose. I beg your attention! Your estate is not twenty miles from the town, the railway runs close by it, and if the cherry orchard and the land along the river bank were cut up into building plots and then let on lease for summer villas, you would make an income of at least twenty-five thousand rubles a year out of it.

GAEV: That's all rot, if you'll excuse me.

LYUBOV: I don't quite understand you, Yermolay Alexeyevitch.

LOPAHIN: You will get a rent of at least twenty-five rubles a year for a three-acre plot from summer visitors, and if you say the word now, I'll bet you what you like there won't be one square foot of ground vacant by the autumn, all the plots will be taken up. I congratulate you; in fact, you are saved. It's a perfect situation with that deep river. Only, of course, it must be cleared — all the old buildings, for example, must be removed, this house too, which is really good for nothing and the old cherry orchard must be cut down.

LYUBOV: Cut down? My dear fellow, forgive me, but you don't know what you are talking about. If there is one thing interesting — remarkable indeed — in the whole province, it's just our cherry orchard.

LOPAHIN: The only thing remarkable about the orchard is that it's a very large one. There's a crop of cherries every alternate year, and then there's nothing to be done with them, no one buys them.

GAEV: This orchard is mentioned in the *Encyclopedia*.

LOPAHIN (*glancing at his watch*): If we don't decide on something and don't take some steps, on the twenty-second of August the cherry orchard and the whole estate too will be sold by auction. Make up your minds! There is no other way of saving it, I'll take my oath on that. No, No!

FIRS: In old days, forty or fifty years ago, they used to dry the cherries, soak them, pickle them, make jam too, and they used —

GAEV: Be quiet, Firs.

FIRS: And they used to send the preserved cherries to Moscow and to Harkov by the wagon load. That brought the money in! And the preserved cherries in those days were soft and juicy, sweet and fragrant. . . . They knew the way to do them then. . . .

LYUBOV: And where is the recipe now?

FIRS: It's forgotten. Nobody remembers it.

PISHTCHIK (*to Lyubov Andreyevna*): What's it like in Paris? Did you eat frogs there?

LYUBOV: Oh, I ate crocodiles.

PISHTCHIK: Fancy that now!

LOPAHIN: There used to be only the gentlefolks and the peasants in the country, but now there are these summer visitors. All the towns, even the small ones, are surrounded nowadays by these summer villas. And one may say for sure that in another twenty years there'll be many more of these people and that they'll be everywhere. At present the summer visitor only drinks tea in his veranda, but maybe he'll take to working his bit of land too, and then your cherry orchard would become happy, rich, and prosperous. . . .

GAEV (*indignant*): What rot!

(*Enter Varya and Yasha.*)

VARYA: There are two telegrams for you, mamma. (*Takes out keys and opens an old-fashioned bookcase with a loud crack.*) Here they are.

LYUBOV: From Paris. (*Tears the telegrams, without reading them.*) I have done with Paris.

GAEV: Do you know, Lyuba, how old that bookcase is? Last week I pulled out the bottom drawer and there I found the date branded on it. The bookcase was made just a hundred years ago. What do you say to that? We might have celebrated its jubilee. Though it's an inanimate object, still it is a *book*case.

PISHTCHIK (*amazed*): A hundred years! Fancy that now.

GAEV: Yes. . . . It is a thing. . . . (*Feeling the bookcase.*) Dear, honored, bookcase! Hail to thee who for more than a hundred years hast served the pure ideals of good and justice; thy silent call to fruitful labor has never flagged in those hundred years, maintaining (*In tears.*) in the generations of man, courage and faith in a brighter future and fostering in us ideals of good and social consciousness. (*A pause.*)

LOPAHIN: Yes. . . .

LYUBOV: You are just the same as ever, Leonid.

GAEV (*a little embarrassed*): Cannon off the right into the pocket!

LOPAHIN (*looking at his watch*): Well, it's time I was off.

YASHA (*handing Lyubov Andreyevna medicine*): Perhaps you will take your pills now.

PISHTCHIK: You shouldn't take medicines, my dear madam . . . they do no harm and no good. Give them here . . . honored lady. (*Takes the pillbox, pours the pills into the hollow of his hand, blows on them, puts them in his mouth and drinks off some kvass.*) There!

LYUBOV (*in alarm*): Why, you must be out of your mind!

PISHTCHIK: I have taken all the pills.

LOPAHIN: What a glutton! (*All laugh.*)

FIRS: His honor stayed with us in Easter week, ate a gallon and a half of cucumbers. . . . (*Mutters.*)

LYUBOV: What is he saying?

VARYA: He has taken to muttering like that for the last three years. We are used to it.

YASHA: His declining years!

(*Charlotta Ivanovna, a very thin, lanky figure in a white dress with a lorgnette in her belt, walks across the stage.*)

LOPAHIN: I beg your pardon, Charlotta Ivanovna, I have not had time to greet you. (*Tries to kiss her hand.*)

CHARLOTTA (*pulling away her hand*): If I let you kiss my hand, you'll be wanting to kiss my elbow, and then my shoulder.

LOPAHIN: I've no luck today! (*All laugh.*) Charlotta Ivanovna, show us some tricks!

LYUBOV: Charlotta, do show us some tricks!

CHARLOTTA: I don't want to. I'm sleepy. (*Goes out.*)

LOPAHIN: In three weeks' time we shall meet again. (*Kisses Lyubov Andreyevna's hand.*) Good-bye till then — I must go. (*To Gaev.*) Good-bye. (*Kisses Pishtchik.*) Good-bye. (*Gives his hand to Varya, then to Firs and Yasha.*) I don't want to go. (*To Lyubov Andreyevna.*) If you think over my plan for the villas and make up your mind, then let me know; I will lend you fifty thousand rubles. Think of it seriously.

VARYA (*angrily*): Well, do go, for goodness sake.

LOPAHIN: I'm going, I'm going. (*Goes out.*)

GAEV: Low-born knave! I beg pardon, though . . . Varya is going to marry him, he's Varya's fiancé.

VARYA: Don't talk nonsense, uncle.

LYUBOV: Well, Varya, I shall be delighted. He's a good man.

PISHTCHIK: He is, one must acknowledge, a most worthy man. And my Dashenka . . . says too that . . . she

says . . . various things. (*Snores, but at once wakes up.*) But all the same, honored lady, could you oblige me . . . with a loan of two hundred forty rubles . . . to pay the interest on my mortgage tomorrow?

VARYA (*dismayed*): No, no.

LYUBOV: I really haven't any money.

PISHTCHIK: It will turn up. (*Laughs.*) I never lose hope. I thought everything was over, I was a ruined man, and lo and behold — the railway passed through my land and . . . they paid me for it. And something else will turn up again, if not today, then tomorrow . . . Dashenka'll win two hundred thousand . . . she's got a lottery ticket.

LYUBOV: Well, we've finished our coffee, we can go to bed.

FIRS (*brushes Gaev, reprovingly*): You have got on the wrong trousers again! What am I to do with you?

VARYA (*softly*): Anya's asleep. (*Softly opens the window.*) Now the sun's risen, it's not a bit cold. Look, mamma, what exquisite trees! My goodness! And the air! The starlings are singing!

GAEV (*opens another window*): The orchard is all white. You've not forgotten it, Lyuba? That long avenue that runs straight, straight as an arrow, how it shines on a moonlight night. You remember? You've not forgotten?

LYUBOV (*looking out of the window into the garden*): Oh, my childhood, my innocence! It was in this nursery I used to sleep, from here I looked out into the orchard, happiness waked with me every morning and in those days the orchard was just the same, nothing has changed. (*Laughs with delight.*) All, all white! Oh, my orchard! After the dark gloomy autumn, and the cold winter; you are young again, and full of happiness, the heavenly angels have never left you. . . . If I could cast off the burden that weighs on my heart, if I could forget the past!

GAEV: Hm! and the orchard will be sold to pay our debts; it seems strange. . . .

LYUBOV: See, our mother walking . . . all in white, down the avenue! (*Laughs with delight.*) It is she!

GAEV: Where?

VARYA: Oh, don't, mamma!

LYUBOV: There is no one. It was my fancy. On the right there, by the path to the arbor, there is a white tree bending like a woman. . . .

(*Enter Trofimov wearing a shabby student's uniform and spectacles.*)

LYUBOV: What a ravishing orchard! White masses of blossom, blue sky. . . .

TROFIMOV: Lyubov Andreyevna! (*She looks round at him.*) I will just pay my respects to you and then leave you at once. (*Kisses her hand warmly.*) I was told to wait until morning, but I hadn't the patience to wait any longer. . . .

(*Lyubov Andreyevna looks at him in perplexity.*)

VARYA (*through her tears*): This is Petya Trofimov.

TROFIMOV: Petya Trofimov, who was your Grisha's tutor. . . . Can I have changed so much?

(*Lyubov Andreyevna embraces him and weeps quietly.*)

GAEV (*in confusion*): There, there, Lyuba.

VARYA (*crying*): I told you, Petya, to wait till tomorrow.

LYUBOV: My Grisha . . . my boy . . . Grisha . . . my son!

VARYA: We can't help it, mamma, it is God's will.

TROFIMOV (*softly through his tears*): There . . . there.

LYUBOV (*weeping quietly*): My boy was lost . . . drowned. Why? Oh, why, dear Petya? (*More quietly.*) Anya is asleep in there, and I'm talking loudly . . . making this noise. . . . But, Petya? Why have you grown so ugly? Why do you look so old?

TROFIMOV: A peasant woman in the train called me a mangy-looking gentleman.

LYUBOV: You were quite a boy then, a pretty little student, and now your hair's thin — and spectacles. Are you really a student still? (*Goes toward the door.*)

TROFIMOV: I seem likely to be a perpetual student.

LYUBOV (*kisses her brother, then Varya*): Well, go to bed. . . . You are older too, Leonid.

PISHTCHIK (*follows her*): I suppose it's time we were asleep. . . . Ugh! my gout. I'm staying the night! Lyubov Andreyevna, my dear soul, if you could . . . tomorrow morning . . . two hundred forty rubles.

GAEV: That's always his story.

PISHTCHIK: Two hundred forty rubles . . . to pay the interest on my mortgage.

LYUBOV: My dear man, I have no money.

PISHTCHIK: I'll pay it back, my dear . . . a trifling sum.

LYUBOV: Oh, well, Leonid will give it you. . . . You give him the money, Leonid.

GAEV: Me give it him! Let him wait till he gets it!

LYUBOV: It can't be helped, give it him. He needs it. He'll pay it back.

(*Lyubov Andreyevna, Trofimov, Pishtchik, and Firs go out. Gaev, Varya, and Yasha remain.*)

GAEV: Sister hasn't got out of the habit of flinging away her money. (*To Yasha.*) Get away, my good fellow, you smell of the henhouse.

YASHA (*with a grin*): And you, Leonid Andreyevitch, are just the same as ever.

GAEV: What's that? (*To Varya.*) What did he say?

VARYA (*to Yasha*): Your mother has come from the village; she has been sitting in the servants' room since yesterday, waiting to see you.

YASHA: Oh, bother her!

VARYA: For shame!

YASHA: What's the hurry? She might just as well have come tomorrow. (*Goes out.*)

VARYA: Mamma's just the same as ever, she hasn't changed a bit. If she had her own way, she'd give away everything.

GAEV: Yes. (*A pause.*) If a great many remedies are suggested for some disease, it means that the disease is incurable. I keep thinking and racking my brains; I have many schemes, a great many, and that really means none. If we could only come in for a legacy from somebody, or marry our Anya to a very rich man, or we might go to Yaroslavl and try our luck with our old aunt, the Countess. She's very, very rich, you know.

VARYA (*weeps*): If God would help us.

GAEV: Don't blubber. Aunt's very rich, but she doesn't like us. First, sister married a lawyer instead of a nobleman. . . .

(*Anya appears in the doorway.*)

GAEV: And then her conduct, one can't call it virtuous. She is good, and kind, and nice, and I love her, but, however one allows for extenuating circumstances, there's no denying that she's an immoral woman. One feels it in her slightest gesture.

VARYA (*in a whisper*): Anya's in the doorway.

GAEV: What do you say? (*A pause.*) It's queer, there seems to be something wrong with my right eye. I don't see as well as I did. And on Thursday when I was in the district court . . .

(*Enter Anya.*)

VARYA: Why aren't you asleep, Anya?

ANYA: I can't get to sleep.

GAEV: My pet. (*Kisses Anya's face and hands.*) My child. (*Weeps.*) You are not my niece, you are my angel, you are everything to me. Believe me, believe. . . .

ANYA: I believe you, uncle. Everyone loves you and respects you . . . but, uncle dear, you must be silent . . . simply be silent. What were you saying just now about my mother, about your own sister? What made you say that?

GAEV: Yes, yes. . . . (*Puts his hand over his face.*) Really, that was awful! My God, save me! And today I made a speech to the bookcase . . . so stupid! And only when I had finished, I saw how stupid it was.

VARYA: It's true, uncle, you ought to keep quiet. Don't talk, that's all.

ANYA: If you could keep from talking, it would make things easier for you, too.

GAEV: I won't speak. (*Kisses Anya's and Varya's hands.*)

I'll be silent. Only this is about business. On Thursday I was in the district court; well, there was a large party of us there and we began talking of one thing and another, and this and that, and do you know, I believe that it will be possible to raise a loan on an I.O.U. to pay the arrears on the mortgage.

VARYA: If the Lord would help us!

GAEV: I'm going on Tuesday; I'll talk of it again. (*To Varya.*) Don't blubber. (*To Anya.*) Your mamma will talk to Lopahin; of course, he won't refuse her. And as soon as you're rested you shall go to Yaroslavl to the Countess, your great-aunt. So we shall all set to work in three directions at once, and the business is done. We shall pay off arrears, I'm convinced of it. (*Puts a caramel in his mouth.*) I swear on my honor, I swear by anything you like, the estate shan't be sold. (*Excitedly.*) By my own happiness, I swear it! Here's my hand on it, call me the basest, vilest of men, if I let it come to an auction! Upon my soul I swear it!

ANYA (*her equanimity has returned, she is quite happy*): How good you are, uncle, and how clever! (*Embraces her uncle.*) I'm at peace now! Quite at peace! I'm happy!

(*Enter Firs.*)

FIRS (*reproachfully*): Leonid Andreyevitch, have you no fear of God? When are you going to bed?

GAEV: Directly, directly. You can go, Firs. I'll . . . yes, I will undress myself. Come, children, bye-bye. We'll go into details tomorrow, but now go to bed. (*Kisses Anya and Varya.*) I'm a man of the eighties. They run down that period, but still I can say I have had to suffer not a little for my convictions in my life, it's not for nothing that the peasant loves me. One must know the peasant! One must know how. . . .

ANYA: At it again, uncle!

VARYA: Uncle dear, you'd better be quiet!

FIRS (*angrily*): Leonid Andreyevitch!

GAEV: I'm coming. I'm coming. Go to bed. Potted the shot — there's a shot for you! A beauty! (*Goes out, Firs hobbling after him.*)

ANYA: My mind's at rest now. I don't want to go to Yaroslavl, I don't like my great-aunt, but still my mind's at rest. Thanks to uncle. (*Sits down.*)

VARYA: We must go to bed. I'm going. Something unpleasant happened while you were away. In the old servants' quarters there are only the old servants, as you know — Efimyushka, Polya, and Yevstigney — and Karp too. They began letting stray people in to spend the night — I said nothing. But all at once I heard they had been spreading a report that I gave them nothing but pease pudding to eat. Out

of stinginess, you know. . . . And it was all Yevstigney's doing. . . . Very well, I said to myself. . . . If that's how it is, I thought, wait a bit. I sent for Yevstigney. . . . (*Yawns.*) He comes. . . . "How's this, Yevstigney," I said, "you could be such a fool as to? . . ." (*Looking at Anya.*) Anitchka! (*A pause.*) She's asleep. (*Puts her arm around Anya.*) Come to bed . . . come along! (*Leads her.*) My darling has fallen asleep! Come . . . (*They go.*)

(*Far away beyond the orchard a shepherd plays on a pipe. Trofimov crosses the stage and, seeing Varya and Anya, stands still.*)

VARYA: Sh! asleep, asleep. Come, my own.

ANYA (*softly, half-asleep*): I'm so tired. Still those bells. Uncle . . . dear . . . mamma and uncle. . . .

VARYA: Come, my own, come along.

(*They go into Anya's room.*)

TROFIMOV (*tenderly*): My sunshine! My spring.

ACT II

(*The open country. An old shrine, long abandoned and fallen out of the perpendicular; near it a well, large stones that have apparently once been tombstones, and an old garden seat. The road to Gaev's house is seen. On one side rise dark poplars; and there the cherry orchard begins. In the distance a row of telegraph poles and far, far away on the horizon there is faintly outlined a great town, only visible in very fine clear weather. It is near sunset. Charlotta, Yasha, and Dunyasha are sitting on the seat. Epihodov is standing near, playing something mournful on a guitar. All sit plunged in thought. Charlotta wears an old forage cap; she has taken a gun from her shoulder and is tightening the buckle on the strap.*)

CHARLOTTA (*musingly*): I haven't a real passport of my own, and I don't know how old I am, and I always feel that I'm a young thing. When I was a little girl, my father and mother used to travel about to fairs and give performances — very good ones. And I used to dance *salto-mortale*° and all sorts of things. And when papa and mamma died, a German lady took me and had me educated. And so I grew up and became a governess. But where I came from, and who I am, I don't know. . . . Who my parents were, very likely they weren't married. . . . I don't know. (*Takes a cucumber out of her pocket and eats.*) I know nothing at all. (*A pause.*) One wants to talk and has no one to talk to. . . . I have nobody.

salto-mortale: Somersault.

EPIHODOV (*plays on the guitar and sings*): "What care I for the noisy world! What care I for friends or foes?" How agreeable it is to play on the mandolin!

DUNYASHA: That's a guitar, not a mandolin. (*Looks in a hand mirror and powders herself.*)

EPIHODOV: To a man mad with love, it's a mandolin. (*Sings.*) "Were her heart but aglow with love's mutual flame."

(*Yasha joins in.*)

CHARLOTTA: How shockingly these people sing! Foo! Like jackals!

DUNYASHA (*to Yasha*): What happiness, though, to visit foreign lands.

YASHA: Ah, yes! I rather agree with you there. (*Yawns, then lights a cigar.*)

EPIHODOV: That's comprehensible. In foreign lands everything has long since reached full complexion.

YASHA: That's so, of course.

EPIHODOV: I'm a cultivated man, I read remarkable books of all sorts, but I can never make out the tendency I am myself precisely inclined for, whether to live or to shoot myself, speaking precisely, but nevertheless I always carry a revolver. Here it is. . . . (*Shows revolver.*)

CHARLOTTA: I've had enough, and now I'm going. (*Puts on the gun.*) Epihodov, you're a very clever fellow, and a very terrible one too, all the women must be wild about you. Br-r-r! (*Goes.*) These clever fellows are all so stupid; there's not a creature for me to speak to. . . . Always alone, alone, nobody belonging to me . . . and who I am, and why I'm on earth, I don't know. (*Walks away slowly.*)

EPIHODOV: Speaking precisely, not touching upon other subjects, I'm bound to admit about myself, that destiny behaves mercilessly to me, as a storm to a little boat. If, let us suppose, I am mistaken, then why did I wake up this morning, to quote an example, and look round, and there on my chest was a spider of fearful magnitude . . . like this. (*Shows with both hands.*) And then I take up a jug of kvass, to quench my thirst, and in it there is something in the highest degree unseemly of the nature of a cockroach. (*A pause.*) Have you read Buckle?° (*A pause.*) I am desirous of troubling you, Dunyasha, with a couple of words.

DUNYASHA: Well, speak.

EPIHODOV: I should be desirous to speak with you alone. (*Sighs.*)

DUNYASHA (*embarrassed*): Well — only bring me my

Buckle: Henry Thomas Buckle (1821–1862) was a radical historian who formulated a scientific basis for history emphasizing the interrelationship of climate, food production, population, and wealth.

mantle first. It's by the cupboard. It's rather damp here.

EPIHODOV: Certainly. I will fetch it. Now I know what I must do with my revolver. (*Takes guitar and goes off playing on it.*)

YASHA: Two and twenty misfortunes! Between ourselves, he's a fool. (*Yawns.*)

DUNYASHA: God grant he doesn't shoot himself! (*A pause.*) I am so nervous, I'm always in a flutter. I was a little girl when I was taken into our lady's house, and now I have quite grown out of peasant ways, and my hands are white, as white as a lady's. I'm such a delicate, sensitive creature, I'm afraid of everything. I'm so frightened. And if you deceive me, Yasha, I don't know what will become of my nerves.

YASHA (*kisses her*): You're a peach! Of course a girl must never forget herself; what I dislike more than anything is a girl being flighty in her behavior.

DUNYASHA: I'm passionately in love with you, Yasha; you are a man of culture — you can give your opinion about anything. (*A pause.*)

YASHA (*yawns*): Yes, that's so. My opinion is this: if a girl loves anyone, that means that she has no principles. (*A pause.*) It's pleasant smoking a cigar in the open air. (*Listens.*) Someone's coming this way . . . it's the gentlefolk. (*Dunyasha embraces him impulsively.*) Go home, as though you had been to the river to bathe; go by that path, or else they'll meet you and suppose I have made an appointment with you here. That I can't endure.

DUNYASHA (*coughing softly*): The cigar has made my head ache. . . . (*Goes off.*)

(*Yasha remains sitting near the shrine. Enter Lyubov Andreyevna, Gaev, and Lopahin.*)

LOPAHIN: You must make up your mind once for all — there's no time to lose. It's quite a simple question, you know. Will you consent to letting the land for building or not? One word in answer: Yes or no? Only one word!

LYUBOV: Who is smoking such horrible cigars here? (*Sits down.*)

GAEV: Now the railway line has been brought near, it's made things very convenient. (*Sits down.*) Here we have been over and lunched in town. Cannon off the white! I should like to go home and have a game.

LYUBOV: You have plenty of time.

LOPAHIN: Only one word! (*Beseechingly.*) Give me an answer!

GAEV (*yawning*): What do you say?

LYUBOV (*looks in her purse*): I had quite a lot of money here yesterday, and there's scarcely any left today. My poor Varya feeds us all on milk soup for the sake of economy; the old folks in the kitchen get nothing but pease pudding, while I waste my money in a senseless way. (*Drops purse, scattering gold pieces.*) There, they have all fallen out! (*Annoyed.*)

YASHA: Allow me, I'll soon pick them up. (*Collects the coins.*)

LYUBOV: Pray do, Yasha. And what did I go off to the town to lunch for? Your restaurant's a wretched place with its music and the tablecloth smelling of soap. . . . Why drink so much, Leonid? And eat so much? And talk so much? Today you talked a great deal again in the restaurant, and all so inappropriately. About the era of the seventies, about the decadents. And to whom? Talking to waiters about decadents!

LOPAHIN: Yes.

GAEV (*waving his hand*): I'm incorrigible; that's evident. (*Irritably to Yasha.*) Why is it you keep fidgeting about in front of us!

YASHA (*laughs*): I can't help laughing when I hear your voice.

GAEV (*to his sister*): Either I or he. . . .

LYUBOV: Get along! Go away, Yasha.

YASHA (*gives Lyubov Andreyevna her purse*): Directly. (*Hardly able to suppress his laughter.*) This minute. . . . (*Goes off.*)

LOPAHIN: Deriganov, the millionaire, means to buy your estate. They say he is coming to the sale himself.

LYUBOV: Where did you hear that?

LOPAHIN: That's what they say in town.

GAEV: Our aunt in Yaroslavl has promised to send help; but when, and how much she will send, we don't know.

LOPAHIN: How much will she send? A hundred thousand? Two hundred?

LYUBOV: Oh, well! . . . Ten or fifteen thousand, and we must be thankful to get that.

LOPAHIN: Forgive me, but such reckless people as you are — such queer, unbusinesslike people — I never met in my life. One tells you in plain Russian your estate is going to be sold, and you seem not to understand it.

LYUBOV: What are we to do? Tell us what to do.

LOPAHIN: I do tell you every day. Every day I say the same thing. You absolutely must let the cherry orchard and the land on building leases; and do it at once, as quick as may be — the auction's close upon us! Do understand! Once make up your mind to build villas, and you can raise as much money as you like, and then you are saved.

LYUBOV: Villas and summer visitors — forgive me saying so — it's so vulgar.

GAEV: There I perfectly agree with you.

LOPAHIN: I shall sob, or scream, or fall into a fit. I can't stand it! You drive me mad! (*To Gaev.*) You're an old woman!

GAEV: What do you say?

LOPAHIN: An old woman! (*Gets up to go.*)

LYUBOV (*in dismay*): No, don't go! Do stay, my dear friend! Perhaps we shall think of something.

LOPAHIN: What is there to think of?

LYUBOV: Don't go, I entreat you! With you here it's more cheerful, anyway. (*A pause.*) I keep expecting something, as though the house were going to fall about our ears.

GAEV (*in profound dejection*): Potted the white! It fails — a kiss.

LYUBOV: We have been great sinners. . . .

LOPAHIN: You have no sins to repent of.

GAEV (*puts a caramel in his mouth*): They say I've eaten up my property in caramels. (*Laughs.*)

LYUBOV: Oh, my sins! I've always thrown my money away recklessly like a lunatic. I married a man who made nothing but debts. My husband died of champagne — he drank dreadfully. To my misery I loved another man, and immediately — it was my first punishment — the blow fell upon me, here, in the river . . . my boy was drowned and I went abroad — went away forever, never to return, not to see that river again . . . I shut my eyes, and fled, distracted, and *he* after me . . . pitilessly, brutally. I bought a villa at Mentone, for *he* fell ill there, and for three years I had no rest day or night. His illness wore me out, my soul was dried up. And last year, when my villa was sold to pay my debts, I went to Paris and there he robbed me of everything and abandoned me for another woman; and I tried to poison myself. . . . So stupid, so shameful! . . . And suddenly I felt a yearning for Russia, for my country, for my little girl. . . . (*Dries her tears.*) Lord, Lord, be merciful! Forgive my sins! Do not chastise me more! (*Takes a telegram out of her pocket.*) I got this today from Paris. He implores forgiveness, entreats me to return. (*Tears up the telegram.*) I fancy there is music somewhere. (*Listens.*)

GAEV: That's our famous Jewish orchestra. You remember, four violins, a flute, and a double bass.

LYUBOV: That still in existence? We ought to send for them one evening and give a dance.

LOPAHIN (*listens*): I can't hear. . . . (*Hums softly.*) "For money the Germans will turn a Russian into a Frenchman." (*Laughs.*) I did see such a piece at the theater yesterday! It was funny!

LYUBOV: And most likely there was nothing funny in it. You shouldn't look at plays, you should look at yourselves a little oftener. How gray your lives are! How much nonsense you talk.

LOPAHIN: That's true. One may say honestly, we live

NEAR RIGHT: Madame Ranevsky (Natasha Perry) and Gaev (Erland Josephson) return from the auction in Peter Brook's 1988 production at the Brooklyn Academy of Music. BELOW: Lopahin (Brian Dennehy), Gaev, and Madame Ranevsky reminisce. TOP FAR RIGHT: Varya (Stephanie Roth) and Anya (Rebecca Miller) face the fact that the Cherry Orchard could be sold. BOTTOM FAR RIGHT: Anya, Madame Ranevsky, and Varya prepare to leave their home.

a fool's life. (*Pause.*) My father was a peasant, an idiot; he knew nothing and taught me nothing, only beat me when he was drunk, and always with his stick. In reality I am just such another blockhead and idiot. I've learnt nothing properly. I write a wretched hand. I write so that I feel ashamed before folks, like a pig.

LYUBOV: You ought to get married, my dear fellow.

LOPAHIN: Yes . . . that's true.

LYUBOV: You should marry our Varya, she's a good girl.

LOPAHIN: Yes.

LYUBOV: She's a good-natured girl, she's busy all day long, and what's more, she loves you. And you have liked her for ever so long.

LOPAHIN: Well? I'm not against it. . . . She's a good girl. (*Pause.*)

GAEV: I've been offered a place in the bank: six thousand rubles a year. Did you know?

LYUBOV: You would never do for that! You must stay as you are.

(*Enter Firs with overcoat.*)

FIRS: Put it on, sir, it's damp.

GAEV (*putting it on*): You bother me, old fellow.

FIRS: You can't go on like this. You went away in the morning without leaving word. (*Looks him over.*)

LYUBOV: You look older, Firs!

FIRS: What is your pleasure?

LOPAHIN: You look older, she said.

FIRS: I've had a long life. They were arranging my wedding before your papa was born. . . . (*Laughs.*) I was the head footman before the emancipation came. I wouldn't consent to be set free then; I stayed on with the old master. . . . (*A pause.*) I remember what rejoicings they made and didn't know themselves what they were rejoicing over.

LOPAHIN: Those were fine old times. There was flogging anyway.

FIRS (*not hearing*): To be sure! The peasants knew their place, and the masters knew theirs; but now they're all at sixes and sevens,° there's no making it out.

GAEV: Hold your tongue, Firs. I must go to town tomorrow. I have been promised an introduction to a general, who might let us have a loan.

LOPAHIN: You won't bring that off. And you won't pay your arrears, you may rest assured of that.

LYUBOV: That's all his nonsense. There is no such general.

(*Enter Trofimov, Anya, and Varya.*)

GAEV: Here come our girls.

at sixes and sevens: In disorder.

ANYA: There's mamma on the seat.

LYUBOV (*tenderly*): Come here, come along. My darlings! (*Embraces Anya and Varya.*) If you only knew how I love you both. Sit beside me, there, like that. (*All sit down.*)

LOPAHIN: Our perpetual student is always with the young ladies.

TROFIMOV: That's not your business.

LOPAHIN: He'll soon be fifty, and he's still a student.

TROFIMOV: Drop your idiotic jokes.

LOPAHIN: Why are you so cross, you queer fish?

TROFIMOV: Oh, don't persist!

LOPAHIN (*laughs*): Allow me to ask you what's your idea of me?

TROFIMOV: I'll tell you my idea of you, Yermolay Alexeyevitch: you are a rich man, you'll soon be a millionaire. Well, just as in the economy of nature a wild beast is of use, who devours everything that comes in his way, so you too have your use.

(*All laugh.*)

VARYA: Better tell us something about the planets, Petya.

LYUBOV: No, let us go on with the conversation we had yesterday.

TROFIMOV: What was it about?

GAEV: About pride.

TROFIMOV: We had a long conversation yesterday, but we came to no conclusion. In pride, in your sense of it, there is something mystical. Perhaps you are right from your point of view; but if one looks at it simply, without subtlety, what sort of pride can there be, what sense is there in it, if man in his physiological formation is very imperfect, if in the immense majority of cases he is coarse, dull-witted, profoundly unhappy? One must give up glorification of self. One should work, and nothing else.

GAEV: One must die in any case.

TROFIMOV: Who knows? And what does it mean — dying? Perhaps man has a hundred senses, and only the five we know are lost at death, while the other ninety-five remain alive.

LYUBOV: How clever you are, Petya!

LOPAHIN (*ironically*): Fearfully clever!

TROFIMOV: Humanity progresses, perfecting its powers. Everything that is beyond its ken now will one day become familiar and comprehensible; only we must work, we must with all our powers aid the seeker after truth. Here among us in Russia the workers are few in number as yet. The vast majority of the intellectual people I know seek nothing, do nothing, are not fit as yet for work of any kind. They call themselves intellectual, but they treat their servants as inferiors, behave to the peasants as though they were animals, learn little, read nothing seriously, do practically nothing, only talk about science, and know very little about art. They are all serious people, they all have severe faces, they all talk of weighty matters and air their theories, and yet the vast majority of us — ninety-nine percent — live like savages, at the least thing fly to blows and abuse, eat piggishly, sleep in filth and stuffiness, bugs everywhere, stench and damp and moral impurity. And it's clear all our fine talk is only to divert our attention and other people's. Show me where to find the *crèches*° there's so much talk about, and the reading rooms? They only exist in novels: in real life there are none of them. There is nothing but filth and vulgarity and Asiatic apathy. I fear and dislike very serious faces. I'm afraid of serious conversation. We should do better to be silent.

LOPAHIN: You know, I get up at five o'clock in the morning, and I work from morning to night; and I've money, my own and other people's, always passing through my hands, and I see what people are made of all round me. One has only to begin to do anything to see how few honest decent people there are. Sometimes when I lie awake at night, I think: "Oh! Lord, thou hast given us immense forests, boundless plains, the widest horizons, and living here we ourselves ought really to be giants."

LYUBOV: You ask for giants! They are no good except in storybooks; in real life they frighten us.

(*Epihodov advances in the background, playing on the guitar.*)

LYUBOV (*dreamily*): There goes Epihodov.
ANYA (*dreamily*): There goes Epihodov.
GAEV: The sun has set, my friends.
TROFIMOV: Yes.
GAEV (*not loudly but, as it were, declaiming*): O nature, divine nature, thou art bright with eternal luster, beautiful and indifferent! Thou, whom we call mother, thou dost unite within thee life and death! Thou dost give life and dost destroy!
VARYA (*in a tone of supplication*): Uncle!
ANYA: Uncle, you are at it again!
TROFIMOV: You'd much better be cannoning off the red!
GAEV: I'll hold my tongue, I will.

(*All sit plunged in thought. Perfect stillness. The only thing audible is the muttering of Firs. Suddenly there is a sound in the distance, as it were from the sky — the sound of a breaking harp string, mournfully dying away.*)

LYUBOV: What is that?
LOPAHIN: I don't know. Somewhere far away a bucket

fallen and broken in the pits. But somewhere very far away.
GAEV: It might be a bird of some sort — such as a heron.
TROFIMOV: Or an owl.
LYUBOV (*shudders*): I don't know why, but it's horrid. (*A pause.*)
FIRS: It was the same before the calamity — the owl hooted and the samovar hissed all the time.
GAEV: Before what calamity?
FIRS: Before the emancipation. (*A pause.*)
LYUBOV: Come, my friends, let us be going; evening is falling. (*To Anya.*) There are tears in your eyes. What is it, darling? (*Embraces her.*)
ANYA: Nothing, mamma; it's nothing.
TROFIMOV: There is somebody coming.

(*The Wayfarer appears in a shabby white forage cap and an overcoat; he is slightly drunk.*)

WAYFARER: Allow me to inquire, can I get to the station this way?
GAEV: Yes. Go along that road.
WAYFARER: I thank you most feelingly. (*Coughing.*) The weather is superb. (*Declaims.*) My brother, my suffering brother! . . . Come out to the Volga! Whose groan do you hear? . . . (*To Varya.*) Mademoiselle, vouchsafe a hungry Russian thirty kopeks.

(*Varya utters a shriek of alarm.*)

LOPAHIN (*angrily*): There's a right and a wrong way of doing everything!
LYUBOV (*hurriedly*): Here, take this. (*Looks in her purse.*) I've no silver. No matter — here's gold for you.
WAYFARER: I thank you most feelingly! (*Goes off.*)

(*Laughter.*)

VARYA (*frightened*): I'm going home — I'm going. . . . Oh, mamma, the servants have nothing to eat, and you gave him gold!
LYUBOV: There's no doing anything with me. I'm so silly! When we get home, I'll give you all I possess. Yermolay Alexeyevitch, you will lend me some more! . . .
LOPAHIN: I will.
LYUBOV: Come, friends, it's time to be going. And Varya, we have made a match of it for you. I congratulate you.
VARYA (*through her tears*): Mamma, that's not a joking matter.
LOPAHIN: "Ophelia, get thee to a nunnery!"°

---

crèches: Day nurseries, day-care centers.

"Ophelia . . . nunnery!": In Shakespeare's *Hamlet*, Hamlet's famous line rejecting Ophelia.

GAEV: My hands are trembling; it's a long while since I had a game of billiards.

LOPAHIN: "Ophelia! Nymph, in thy orisons be all my sins remember'd."

LYUBOV: Come, it will soon be suppertime.

VARYA: How he frightened me! My heart's simply throbbing.

LOPAHIN: Let me remind you, ladies and gentlemen: on the twenty-second of August the cherry orchard will be sold. Think about that! Think about it!

(*All go off, except Trofimov and Anya.*)

ANYA (*laughing*): I'm grateful to the wayfarer! He frightened Varya and we are left alone.

TROFIMOV: Varya's afraid we shall fall in love with each other, and for days together she won't leave us. With her narrow brain she can't grasp that we are above love. To eliminate the petty and transitory which hinder us from being free and happy — that is the aim and meaning of our life. Forward! We go forward irresistibly toward the bright star that shines yonder in the distance. Forward! Do not lag behind, friends.

ANYA (*claps her hands*): How well you speak! (*A pause.*) It is divine here today.

TROFIMOV: Yes, it's glorious weather.

ANYA: Somehow, Petya, you've made me so that I don't love the cherry orchard as I used to. I used to love it so dearly. I used to think that there was no spot on earth like our garden.

TROFIMOV: All Russia is our garden. The earth is great and beautiful — there are many beautiful places in it. (*A pause.*) Think only, Anya, your grandfather, and great-grandfather, and all your ancestors were slave owners — the owners of living souls — and from every cherry in the orchard, from every leaf, from every trunk there are human creatures looking at you. Cannot you hear their voices? Oh, it is awful! Your orchard is a fearful thing, and when in the evening or at night one walks about the orchard, the old bark on the trees glimmers dimly in the dusk, and the old cherry trees seem to be dreaming of centuries gone by and tortured by fearful visions. Yes! We are at least two hundred years behind, we have really gained nothing yet, we have no definite attitude to the past, we do nothing but theorize or complain of depression or drink vodka. It is clear that to begin to live in the present, we must first expiate our past; we must break with it; and we can expiate it only by suffering, by extraordinary unceasing labor. Understand that, Anya.

ANYA: The house we live in has long ceased to be our own, and I shall leave it, I give you my word.

TROFIMOV: If you have the house keys, fling them into the well and go away. Be free as the wind.

ANYA (*in ecstasy*): How beautifully you said that!

TROFIMOV: Believe me, Anya, believe me! I am not thirty yet, I am young, I am still a student, but I have gone through so much already! As soon as winter comes I am hungry, sick, careworn, poor as a beggar, and what ups and downs of fortune have I not known! And my soul was always, every minute, day and night, full of inexplicable forebodings. I have a foreboding of happiness, Anya. I see glimpses of it already.

ANYA (*pensively*): The moon is rising.

(*Epihodov is heard playing still the same mournful song on the guitar. The moon rises. Somewhere near the poplars Varya is looking for Anya and calling "Anya! where are you?"*)

TROFIMOV: Yes, the moon is rising. (*A pause.*) Here is happiness — here it comes! It is coming nearer and nearer; already I can hear its footsteps. And if we never see it — if we may never know it — what does it matter? Others will see it after us.

VARYA'S VOICE: Anya! Where are you?

TROFIMOV: That Varya again! (*Angrily.*) It's revolting!

ANYA: Well, let's go down to the river. It's lovely there.

TROFIMOV: Yes, let's go. (*They go.*)

VARYA'S VOICE: Anya! Anya!

ACT III

(*A drawing room divided by an arch from a larger drawing room. A chandelier burning. The Jewish orchestra, the same that was mentioned in Act II, is heard playing in the anteroom. It is evening. In the larger drawing room they are dancing the grand chain. The voice of Semyonov-Pishtchik: "Promenade à une paire!"° Then enter the drawing room in couples first Pishtchik and Charlotta Ivanova, then Trofimov and Lyubov Andreyevna, thirdly Anya with the Post Office Clerk, fourthly Varya with the Station Master, and other guests. Varya is quietly weeping and wiping away her tears as she dances. In the last couple is Dunyasha. They move across the drawing room. Pishtchik shouts: "Grand rond, balancez!" and "Les Cavaliers à genou et remerciez vos dames."°*)

(*Firs in a swallowtail coat brings in seltzer water on a tray. Pishtchik and Trofimov enter the drawing room.*)

PISHTCHIK: I am a full-blooded man; I have already had two strokes. Dancing's hard work for me, but as they say, if you're in the pack, you must bark

---

"Promenade à une paire!": French for "Walk in pairs."
"Grand rond . . . dames": Instructions in the dance: "Large circle, . . . Men, kneel down and thank your ladies."

with the rest. I'm as strong, I may say, as a horse. My parent, who would have his joke — may the Kingdom of Heaven be his! — used to say about our origin that the ancient stock of the Semyonov-Pishtchiks was derived from the very horse that Caligula made a member of the senate.° (*Sits down.*) But I've no money, that's where the mischief is. A hungry dog believes in nothing but meat. (*Snores, but at once wakes up.*) That's like me ... I can think of nothing but money.

TROFIMOV: There really is something horsy about your appearance.

PISHTCHIK: Well ... a horse is a fine beast ... a horse can be sold.

(*There is the sound of billiards being played in an adjoining room. Varya appears in the arch leading to the larger drawing room.*)

TROFIMOV (*teasing*): Madame Lopahin! Madame Lopahin!

VARYA (*angrily*): Mangy-looking gentleman!

TROFIMOV: Yes, I am a mangy-looking gentleman, and I'm proud of it!

VARYA (*pondering bitterly*): Here we have hired musicians and nothing to pay them! (*Goes out.*)

TROFIMOV (*to Pishtchik*): If the energy you have wasted during your lifetime in trying to find the money to pay your interest had gone to something else, you might in the end have turned the world upside down.

PISHTCHIK: Nietzsche, the philosopher, a very great and celebrated man ... of enormous intellect ... says in his works that one can make forged bank notes.

TROFIMOV: Why, have you read Nietzsche?

PISHTCHIK: What next ... Dashenka told me. ... And now I am in such a position, I might just as well forge bank notes. The day after tomorrow I must pay three hundred ten rubles — one hundred thirty I have procured. (*Feels in his pockets, in alarm.*) The money's gone! I have lost my money! (*Through his tears.*) Where's the money? (*Gleefully.*) Why, here it is behind the lining. ... It has made me hot all over.

(*Enter Lyubov Andreyevna and Charlotta Ivanova.*)

LYUBOV (*hums the Lezginka°*): Why is Leonid so long? What can he be doing in town? (*To Dunyasha.*) Offer the musicians some tea.

TROFIMOV: The sale hasn't taken place, most likely.

LYUBOV: It's the wrong time to have the orchestra, and the wrong time to give a dance. Well, never mind. (*Sits down and hums softly.*)

CHARLOTTA (*gives Pishtchik a pack of cards*): Here's a pack of cards. Think of any card you like.

PISHTCHIK: I've thought of one.

CHARLOTTA: Shuffle the pack now. That's right. Give it here, my dear Mr. Pishtchik. *Ein, zwei, drei°* — now look, it's in your breast pocket.

PISHTCHIK (*taking a card out of his breast pocket*): The eight of spades! Perfectly right! (*Wonderingly.*) Fancy that now!

CHARLOTTA (*holding pack of cards in her hands, to Trofimov*): Tell me quickly which is the top card.

TROFIMOV: Well, the queen of spades.

CHARLOTTA: It is! (*To Pishtchik.*) Well, which card is uppermost?

PISHTCHIK: The ace of hearts.

CHARLOTTA: It is! (*Claps her hands, pack of cards disappears.*) Ah! what lovely weather it is today!

(*A mysterious feminine voice which seems coming out of the floor answers her, "Oh, yes, it's magnificent weather, madam."*)

CHARLOTTA: You are my perfect ideal.

VOICE: And I greatly admire you too, madam.

STATION MASTER (*applauding*): The lady ventriloquist — bravo!

PISHTCHIK (*wonderingly*): Fancy that now! Most enchanting, Charlotta Ivanovna. I'm simply in love with you.

CHARLOTTA: In love? (*Shrugging shoulders.*) What do you know of love, *guter Mensch, aber schlechter Musikant.°*

TROFIMOV (*pats Pishtchik on the shoulder*): You dear old horse. ...

CHARLOTTA: Attention, please! Another trick! (*Takes a traveling rug from a chair.*) Here's a very good rug; I want to sell it. (*Shaking it out.*) Doesn't anyone want to buy it?

PISHTCHIK (*wonderingly*): Fancy that!

CHARLOTTA: *Ein, zwei, drei!* (*Quickly picks up rug she has dropped; behind the rug stands Anya; she makes a curtsy, runs to her mother, embraces her, and runs back into the larger drawing room amidst general enthusiasm.*)

LYUBOV (*applauds*): Bravo! Bravo!

CHARLOTTA: Now again! *Ein, zwei, drei!* (*Lifts up the rug; behind the rug stands Varya, bowing.*)

PISHTCHIK (*wonderingly*): Fancy that now!

CHARLOTTA: That's the end. (*Throws the rug at Pishtchik, makes a curtsy, runs into the larger drawing room.*)

Caligula ... senate: Caligula (A.D. 12–41), a cavalry soldier, was Roman emperor (37–41).
Lezginka: A popular, lively Russian dance.

Ein, zwei, drei: German for "One, two, three."
guter Mensch, aber schlechter Musikant: German for "Good man, but poor musician."

PISHTCHIK (*hurries after her*): Mischievous creature! Fancy! (*Goes out.*)

LYUBOV: And still Leonid doesn't come. I can't understand what he's doing in the town so long! Why, everything must be over by now. The estate is sold, or the sale has not taken place. Why keep us so long in suspense?

VARYA (*trying to console her*): Uncle's bought it. I feel sure of that.

TROFIMOV (*ironically*): Oh, yes!

VARYA: Great-aunt sent him an authorization to buy it in her name and transfer the debt. She's doing it for Anya's sake, and I'm sure God will be merciful. Uncle will buy it.

LYUBOV: My aunt in Yaroslavl sent fifteen thousand to buy the estate in her name, she doesn't trust us — but that's not enough even to pay the arrears. (*Hides her face in her hands.*) My fate is being sealed today, my fate. . . .

TROFIMOV (*teasing Varya*): Madame Lopahin.

VARYA (*angrily*): Perpetual student! Twice already you've been sent down from the university.

LYUBOV: Why are you angry, Varya? He's teasing you about Lopahin. Well, what of that? Marry Lopahin if you like, he's a good man, and interesting; if you don't want to, don't! Nobody compels you, darling.

VARYA: I must tell you plainly, mamma, I look at the matter seriously; he's a good man, I like him.

LYUBOV: Well, marry him. I can't see what you're waiting for.

VARYA: Mamma. I can't make him an offer myself. For the last two years, everyone's been talking to me about him. Everyone talks; but he says nothing or else makes a joke. I see what it means. He's growing rich, he's absorbed in business, he has no thoughts for me. If I had money, were it ever so little, if I had only a hundred rubles, I'd throw everything up and go far away. I would go into a nunnery.

TROFIMOV: What bliss!

VARYA (*to Trofimov*): A student ought to have sense! (*In a soft tone with tears.*) How ugly you've grown, Petya! How old you look! (*To Lyubov Andreyevna, no longer crying.*) But I can't do without work, mamma; I must have something to do every minute.

(*Enter Yasha.*)

YASHA (*hardly restraining his laughter*): Epihodov has broken a billiard cue! (*Goes out.*)

VARYA: What is Epihodov doing here? Who gave him leave to play billiards? I can't make these people out. (*Goes out.*)

LYUBOV: Don't tease her, Petya. You see she has grief enough without that.

TROFIMOV: She is so very officious, meddling in what's not her business. All the summer she's given Anya and me no peace. She's afraid of a love affair between us. What's it to do with her? Besides, I have given no grounds for it. Such triviality is not in my line. We are above love!

LYUBOV: And I suppose I am beneath love. (*Very uneasily.*) Why is it Leonid's not here? If only I could know whether the estate is sold or not! It seems such an incredible calamity that I really don't know what to think. I am distracted . . . I shall scream in a minute . . . I shall do something stupid. Save me, Petya, tell me something, talk to me!

TROFIMOV: What does it matter whether the estate is sold today or not? That's all done with long ago. There's no turning back, the path is overgrown. Don't worry yourself, dear Lyubov Andreyevna. You mustn't deceive yourself; for once in your life you must face the truth!

LYUBOV: What truth? You see where the truth lies, but I seem to have lost my sight, I see nothing. You settle every great problem so boldly, but tell me, my dear boy, isn't it because you're young — because you haven't yet understood one of your problems through suffering? You look forward boldly, and isn't it that you don't see and don't expect anything dreadful because life is still hidden from your young eyes? You're bolder, more honest, deeper than we are, but think, be just a little magnanimous, have pity on me. I was born here, you know, my father and mother lived here, my grandfather lived here, I love this house. I can't conceive of life without the cherry orchard, and if it really must be sold, then sell me with the orchard. (*Embraces Trofimov, kisses him on the forehead.*) My boy was drowned here. (*Weeps.*) Pity me, my dear kind fellow.

TROFIMOV: You know I feel for you with all my heart.

LYUBOV: But that should have been said differently, so differently. (*Takes out her handkerchief, telegram falls on the floor.*) My heart is so heavy today. It's so noisy here, my soul is quivering at every sound, I'm shuddering all over, but I can't go away; I'm afraid to be quiet and alone. Don't be hard on me, Petya . . . I love you as though you were one of ourselves. I would gladly let you marry Anya — I swear I would — only, my dear boy, you must take your degree, you do nothing — you're simply tossed by fate from place to place. That's so strange. It is, isn't it? And you must do something with your beard to make it grow somehow. (*Laughs.*) You look so funny!

TROFIMOV (*picks up the telegram*): I've no wish to be a beauty.

LYUBOV: That's a telegram from Paris. I get one every day. One yesterday and one today. That savage creature is ill again, he's in trouble again. He begs forgiveness, beseeches me to go, and really I ought to go to Paris to see him. You look shocked, Petya. What am I to do, my dear boy, what am I to do? He is ill, he is alone and unhappy, and who'll look after him, who'll keep him from doing the wrong thing, who'll give him his medicine at the right time? And why hide it or be silent? I love him, that's clear. I love him! I love him! He's a millstone about my neck, I'm going to the bottom with him, but I love that stone and can't live without it. (*Presses Trofimov's hand.*) Don't think ill of me, Petya, don't tell me anything, don't tell me. . . .

TROFIMOV (*through his tears*): For God's sake forgive my frankness: why, he robbed you!

LYUBOV: No! No! No! You mustn't speak like that. (*Covers her ears.*)

TROFIMOV: He is a wretch! You're the only person that doesn't know it! He's a worthless creature! A despicable wretch!

LYUBOV (*getting angry, but speaking with restraint*): You're twenty-six or twenty-seven years old, but you're still a schoolboy.

TROFIMOV: Possibly.

LYUBOV: You should be a man at your age! You should understand what love means! And you ought to be in love yourself! You ought to fall in love! (*Angrily.*) Yes, yes, and it's not purity in you, you're simply a prude, a comic fool, a freak.

TROFIMOV (*in horror*): The things she's saying!

LYUBOV: I am above love! You're not above love, but simply as our Firs here says, "You are a good-for-nothing." At your age not to have a mistress!

TROFIMOV (*in horror*): This is awful! The things she is saying! (*Goes rapidly into the larger drawing room clutching his head.*) This is awful! I can't stand it! I'm going. (*Goes off, but at once returns.*) All is over between us! (*Goes off into the anteroom.*)

LYUBOV (*shouts after him*): Petya! Wait a minute! You funny creature! I was joking! Petya! (*There is a sound of somebody running quickly downstairs and suddenly falling with a crash. Anya and Varya scream, but there is a sound of laughter at once.*)

LYUBOV: What has happened?

(*Anya runs in.*)

ANYA (*laughing*): Petya's fallen downstairs! (*Runs out.*)

LYUBOV: What a queer fellow that Petya is!

(*The Station Master stands in the middle of the larger room and reads* The Magdalene, *by Alexey Tolstoy.°*)

Alexey Tolstoy: Alexey Konstantinovich Tolstoy (1817–1875), Russian novelist (*Prince Serebryany*, 1863), dramatist (*The Death of Ivan the Terrible*, 1866), and poet.

They listen to him, but before he has recited many lines strains of a waltz are heard from the anteroom and the reading is broken off. All dance. Trofimov, Anya, Varya, and Lyubov Andreyevna come in from the anteroom.)

LYUBOV: Come, Petya — come, pure heart! I beg your pardon. Let's have a dance! (*Dances with Petya.*)

(*Anya and Varya dance. Firs comes in, puts his stick down near the side door. Yasha also comes into the drawing room and looks on at the dancing.*)

YASHA: What is it, old man?

FIRS: I don't feel well. In old days we used to have generals, barons, and admirals dancing at our balls, and now we send for the post office clerk and the station master and even they're not overanxious to come. I am getting feeble. The old master, the grandfather, used to give sealing wax for all complaints. I have been taking sealing wax for twenty years or more. Perhaps that's what's kept me alive.

YASHA: You bore me, old man! (*Yawns.*) It's time you were done with.

FIRS: Ach, you're a good-for-nothing! (*Mutters.*)

(*Trofimov and Lyubov Andreyevna dance in larger room and then on to the stage.*)

LYUBOV: *Merci.* I'll sit down a little. (*Sits down.*) I'm tired.

(*Enter Anya.*)

ANYA (*excitedly*): There's a man in the kitchen has been saying that the cherry orchard's been sold today.

LYUBOV: Sold to whom?

ANYA: He didn't say to whom. He's gone away.

(*She dances with Trofimov, and they go off into the larger room.*)

YASHA: There was an old man gossiping there, a stranger.

FIRS: Leonid Andreyevitch isn't here yet, he hasn't come back. He has his light overcoat on, *demi-saison,°* he'll catch cold for sure. *Ach!* Foolish young things!

LYUBOV: I feel as though I should die. Go, Yasha, find out to whom it has been sold.

YASHA: But he went away long ago, the old chap. (*Laughs.*)

LYUBOV (*with slight vexation*): What are you laughing at? What are you pleased at?

YASHA: Epihodov is so funny. He's a silly fellow, two and twenty misfortunes.

demi-saison: Between-season.

LYUBOV: Firs, if the estate is sold, where will you go?

FIRS: Where you bid me, there I'll go.

LYUBOV: Why do you look like that? Are you ill? You ought to be in bed.

FIRS: Yes. (*Ironically.*) Me go to bed and who's to wait here? Who's to see to things without me? I'm the only one in all the house.

YASHA (*to Lyubov Andreyevna*): Lyubov Andreyevna, permit me to make a request of you; if you go back to Paris again, be so kind as to take me with you. It's positively impossible for me to stay here. (*Looking about him; in an undertone.*) There's no need to say it, you see for yourself — an uncivilized country, the people have no morals, and then the dullness! The food in the kitchen's abominable, and then Firs runs after one muttering all sorts of unsuitable words. Take me with you, please do!

(*Enter Pishtchik.*)

PISHTCHIK: Allow me to ask you for a waltz, my dear lady. (*Lyubov Andreyevna goes with him.*) Enchanting lady, I really must borrow of you just one hundred eighty rubles, (*dances*) only one hundred eighty rubles. (*They pass into the larger room.*)

(*In the larger drawing room, a figure in a gray top hat and in checked trousers is gesticulating and jumping about. Shouts of "Bravo, Charlotta Ivanovna."*)

DUNYASHA (*she has stopped to powder herself*): My young lady tells me to dance. There are plenty of gentlemen and too few ladies, but dancing makes me giddy and makes my heart beat. Firs, the post office clerk said something to me just now that quite took my breath away.

(*Music becomes more subdued.*)

FIRS: What did he say to you?

DUNYASHA: He said I was like a flower.

YASHA (*yawns*): What ignorance! (*Goes out.*)

DUNYASHA: Like a flower. I am a girl of such delicate feelings, I am awfully fond of soft speeches.

FIRS: Your head's being turned.

(*Enter Epihodov.*)

EPIHODOV: You have no desire to see me, Dunyasha. I might be an insect. (*Sighs.*) Ah! life!

DUNYASHA: What is it you want?

EPIHODOV: Undoubtedly you may be right. (*Sighs.*) But, of course, if one looks at it from that point of view, if I may so express myself, you have, excuse my plain speaking, reduced me to a complete state of mind. I know my destiny. Every day some misfortune befalls me and I have long ago grown accustomed to it, so that I look upon my fate with a smile. You gave me your word, and though I —

DUNYASHA: Let us have a talk later, I entreat you, but now leave me in peace, for I am lost in reverie. (*Plays with her fan.*)

EPIHODOV: I have a misfortune every day, and if I may venture to express myself, I merely smile at it, I even laugh.

(*Varya enters from the larger drawing room.*)

VARYA: You still have not gone, Epihodov. What a disrespectful creature you are, really! (*To Dunyasha.*) Go along, Dunyasha! (*To Epihodov.*) First you play billiards and break the cue, then you go wandering about the drawing room like a visitor!

EPIHODOV: You really cannot, if I may so express myself, call me to account like this.

VARYA: I'm not calling you to account, I'm speaking to you. You do nothing but wander from place to place and don't do your work. We keep you as a counting house clerk, but what use you are I can't say.

EPIHODOV (*offended*): Whether I work or whether I walk, whether I eat or whether I play billiards, is a matter to be judged by persons of understanding and my elders.

VARYA: You dare to tell me that! (*Firing up.*) You dare! You mean to say I've no understanding. Begone from here! This minute!

EPIHODOV (*intimidated*): I beg you to express yourself with delicacy.

VARYA (*beside herself with anger*): This moment! get out! away! (*He goes toward the door, she following him.*) Two and twenty misfortunes! Take yourself off! Don't let me set eyes on you! (*Epihodov has gone out, behind the door his voice, "I shall lodge a complaint against you."*) What! You're coming back? (*Snatches up the stick Firs has put down near the door.*) Come! Come! Come! I'll show you! What! you're coming? Then take that! (*She swings the stick, at the very moment that Lopahin comes in.*)

LOPAHIN: Very much obliged to you!

VARYA (*angrily and ironically*): I beg your pardon!

LOPAHIN: Not at all! I humbly thank you for your kind reception!

VARYA: No need of thanks for it. (*Moves away, then looks round and asks softly.*) I haven't hurt you?

LOPAHIN: Oh, no! Not at all! There's an immense bump coming up, though!

VOICES FROM LARGER ROOM: Lopahin has come! Yermolay Alexeyevitch!

PISHTCHIK: What do I see and hear? (*Kisses Lopahin.*) There's a whiff of cognac about you, my dear soul, and we're making merry here too!

(*Enter Lyubov Andreyevna.*)

LYUBOV: Is it you, Yermolay Alexeyevitch? Why have you been so long? Where's Leonid?

LOPAHIN: Leonid Andreyevitch arrived with me. He is coming.

LYUBOV (*in agitation*): Well! Well! Was there a sale? Speak!

LOPAHIN (*embarrassed, afraid of betraying his joy*): The sale was over at four o'clock. We missed our train — had to wait till half-past nine. (*Sighing heavily.*) Ugh! I feel a little giddy.

(*Enter Gaev. In his right hand he has purchases, with his left hand he is wiping away his tears.*)

LYUBOV: Well, Leonid? What news? (*Impatiently, with tears.*) Make haste, for God's sake!

GAEV (*makes her no answer, simply waves his hand; to Firs, weeping*): Here, take them; there's anchovies, Kertch herrings. I have eaten nothing all day. What I have been through! (*Door into the billiard room is open. There is heard a knocking of balls and the voice of Yasha saying "Eighty-seven." Gaev's expression changes, he leaves off weeping.*) I am fearfully tired. Firs, come and help me change my things. (*Goes to his own room across the larger drawing room.*)

PISHTCHIK: How about the sale? Tell us, do!

LYUBOV: Is the cherry orchard sold?

LOPAHIN: It is sold.

LYUBOV: Who has bought it?

LOPAHIN: I have bought it. (*A pause. Lyubov is crushed; she would fall down if she were not standing near a chair and table.*)

(*Varya takes keys from her waistband, flings them on the floor in middle of drawing room and goes out.*)

LOPAHIN: I have bought it! Wait a bit, ladies and gentlemen, pray. My head's a bit muddled, I can't speak. (*Laughs.*) We came to the auction. Deriganov was there already. Leonid Andreyevitch only had fifteen thousand and Deriganov bid thirty thousand, besides the arrears, straight off. I saw how the land lay. I bid against him. I bid forty thousand, he bid forty-five thousand, I said fifty-five, and so he went on, adding five thousands and I adding ten. Well . . . So it ended. I bid ninety, and it was knocked down to me. Now the cherry orchard's mine! Mine! (*Chuckles.*) My God, the cherry orchard's mine! Tell me that I'm drunk, that I'm out of my mind, that it's all a dream. (*Stamps with his feet.*) Don't laugh at me! If my father and my grandfather could rise from their graves and see all that has happened! How their Yermolay, ignorant, beaten Yermolay, who used to run about barefoot in winter, how that very Yermolay has bought the finest estate in the world! I have bought the estate where my father

and grandfather were slaves, where they weren't even admitted into the kitchen. I am asleep, I am dreaming! It is all fancy, it is the work of your imagination plunged in the darkness of ignorance. (*Picks up keys, smiling fondly.*) She threw away the keys; she means to show she's not the housewife now. (*Jingles the keys.*) Well, no matter. (*The orchestra is heard tuning up.*) Hey, musicians! Play! I want to hear you. Come, all of you, and look how Yermolay Lopahin will take the ax to the cherry orchard, how the trees will fall to the ground! We will build houses on it and our grandsons and great-grandsons will see a new life springing up there. Music! Play up!

(*Music begins to play. Lyubov Andreyevna has sunk into a chair and is weeping bitterly.*)

LOPAHIN (*reproachfully*): Why, why didn't you listen to me? My poor friend! Dear lady, there's no turning back now. (*With tears.*) Oh, if all this could be over, oh, if our miserable disjointed life could somehow soon be changed!

PISHTCHIK (*takes him by the arm, in an undertone*): She's weeping, let us go and leave her alone. Come. (*Takes him by the arm and leads him into the larger drawing room.*)

LOPAHIN: What's that? Musicians, play up! All must be as I wish it. (*With irony.*) Here comes the new master, the owner of the cherry orchard! (*Accidentally tips over a little table, almost upsetting the candelabra.*) I can pay for everything! (*Goes out with Pishtchik. No one remains on the stage or in the larger drawing room except Lyubov, who sits huddled up, weeping bitterly. The music plays softly. Anya and Trofimov come in quickly. Anya goes up to her mother and falls on her knees before her. Trofimov stands at the entrance to the larger drawing room.*)

ANYA: Mamma! Mamma, you're crying, dear, kind, good mamma! My precious! I love you! I bless you! The cherry orchard is sold, it is gone, that's true, that's true! But don't weep, mamma! Life is still before you, you have still your good, pure heart! Let us go, let us go, darling, away from here! We will make a new garden, more splendid than this one; you will see it, you will understand. And joy, quiet, deep joy, will sink into your soul like the sun at evening! And you will smile, mamma! Come, darling, let us go!

ACT IV

(*Same as in first act. There are neither curtains on the windows nor pictures on the walls: only a little furniture remains piled up in a corner as if for sale. There is a sense of desolation; near the outer door and in the background of the scene are packed trunks, traveling bags, etc. On the left the door is open, and from here the voices of Varya and Anya are audible. Lopahin is standing waiting. Yasha is holding a tray with glasses full of champagne. In front of the stage Epihodov is tying up a box. In the background behind the scene a hum of talk from the peasants who have come to say good-bye. The voice of Gaev: "Thanks, brothers, thanks!")*

YASHA: The peasants have come to say good-bye. In my opinion, Yermolay Alexeyevitch, the peasants are good-natured, but they don't know much about things.

(The hum of talk dies away. Enter across front of stage Lyubov Andreyevna and Gaev. She is not weeping, but is pale; her face is quivering — she cannot speak.)

GAEV: You gave them your purse, Lyuba. That won't do — that won't do!

LYUBOV: I couldn't help it! I couldn't help it!
(Both go out.)

LOPAHIN *(in the doorway, calls after them)*: You will take a glass at parting? Please do. I didn't think to bring any from the town, and at the station I could only get one bottle. Please take a glass. (*A pause.*) What? You don't care for any? (*Comes away from the door.*) If I'd known, I wouldn't have bought it. Well, and I'm not going to drink it. (*Yasha carefully sets the tray down on a chair.*) You have a glass, Yasha, anyway.

YASHA: Good luck to the travelers, and luck to those that stay behind! (*Drinks.*) This champagne isn't the real thing, I can assure you.

LOPAHIN: It cost eight rubles the bottle. (*A pause.*) It's devilish cold here.

YASHA: They haven't heated the stove today — it's all the same since we're going. (*Laughs.*)

LOPAHIN: What are you laughing for?

YASHA: For pleasure.

LOPAHIN: Though it's October, it's as still and sunny as though it were summer. It's just right for building! (*Looks at his watch; says in doorway.*) Take note, ladies and gentlemen, the train goes in forty-seven minutes; so you ought to start for the station in twenty minutes. You must hurry up!

(Trofimov comes in from out of doors wearing a greatcoat.)

TROFIMOV: I think it must be time to start, the horses are ready. The devil only knows what's become of my galoshes; they're lost. (*In the doorway.*) Anya! My galoshes aren't here. I can't find them.

LOPAHIN: And I'm getting off to Harkov. I am going in the same train with you. I'm spending all the winter at Harkov. I've been wasting all my time gossiping with you and fretting with no work to do. I can't get on without work. I don't know what to do with my hands, they flap about so queerly, as if they didn't belong to me.

TROFIMOV: Well, we're just going away, and you will take up your profitable labors again.

LOPAHIN: Do take a glass.

TROFIMOV: No, thanks.

LOPAHIN: Then you're going to Moscow now?

TROFIMOV: Yes. I shall see them as far as the town, and tomorrow I shall go on to Moscow.

LOPAHIN: Yes, I daresay, the professors aren't giving any lectures, they're waiting for your arrival.

TROFIMOV: That's not your business.

LOPAHIN: How many years have you been at the university?

TROFIMOV: Do think of something newer than that — that's stale and flat. (*Hunts for galoshes.*) You know we shall most likely never see each other again, so let me give you one piece of advice at parting: don't wave your arms about — get out of the habit. And another thing, building villas, reckoning up that the summer visitors will in time become independent farmers — reckoning like that, that's not the thing to do either. After all, I am fond of you: you have fine delicate fingers like an artist, you've a fine delicate soul.

LOPAHIN *(embraces him)*: Good-bye, my dear fellow. Thanks for everything. Let me give you money for the journey, if you need it.

TROFIMOV: What for? I don't need it.

LOPAHIN: Why, you haven't got a half-penny.

TROFIMOV: Yes, I have, thank you. I got some money for a translation. Here it is in my pocket, (*Anxiously.*) but where can my galoshes be!

VARYA *(from the next room)*: Take the nasty things! (*Flings a pair of galoshes onto the stage.*)

TROFIMOV: Why are you so cross, Varya? hm! . . . but those aren't my galoshes.

LOPAHIN: I sowed three thousand acres with poppies in the spring, and now I have cleared forty thousand profit. And when my poppies were in flower, wasn't it a picture! So here, as I say, I made forty thousand, and I'm offering you a loan because I can afford to. Why turn up your nose? I am a peasant — I speak bluntly.

TROFIMOV: Your father was a peasant, mine was a chemist — and that proves absolutely nothing whatever. (*Lopahin takes out his pocketbook.*) Stop that — stop that. If you were to offer me two hundred thousand I wouldn't take it. I am an independent man, and everything that all of you, rich and poor alike, prize so highly and hold so dear hasn't the slightest power over me — it's like so much fluff fluttering in the air. I can get on without you. I can pass by you. I am strong and proud. Humanity is advancing towards the highest truth, the highest happiness, which is possible on earth, and I am in the front ranks.

LOPAHIN: Will you get there?

TROFIMOV: I shall get there. (*A pause.*) I shall get there, or I shall show others the way to get there.

(*In the distance is heard the stroke of an ax on a tree.*)

LOPAHIN: Good-bye, my dear fellow; it's time to be off. We turn up our noses at one another, but life is passing all the while. When I am working hard without resting, then my mind is more at ease, and it seems to me as though I too know what I exist for; but how many people are in Russia, my dear boy, who exist, one doesn't know what for. Well, it doesn't matter. That's not what keeps things spinning. They tell me Leonid Andreyevitch has taken a situation. He is going to be a clerk at the bank — six thousand rubles a year. Only, of course, he won't stick to it — he's too lazy.

ANYA (*in the doorway*): Mamma begs you not to let them chop down the orchard until she's gone.

TROFIMOV: Yes, really, you might have the tact. (*Walks out across the front of the stage.*)

LOPAHIN: I'll see to it! I'll see to it! Stupid fellows! (*Goes out after him.*)

ANYA: Has Firs been taken to the hospital?

YASHA: I told them this morning. No doubt they have taken him.

ANYA (*to Epihodov, who passes across the drawing room*): Semyon Pantaleyevitch, inquire, please, if Firs has been taken to the hospital.

YASHA (*in a tone of offense*): I told Yegor this morning — why ask a dozen times?

EPIHODOV: Firs is advanced in years. It's my conclusive opinion no treatment would do him good; it's time he was gathered to his fathers. And I can only envy him. (*Puts a trunk down on a cardboard hatbox and crushes it.*) There, now, of course — I knew it would be so.

YASHA (*jeeringly*): Two and twenty misfortunes!

VARYA (*through the door*): Has Firs been taken to the hospital?

ANYA: Yes.

VARYA: Why wasn't the note for the doctor taken too?

ANYA: Oh, then, we must send it after them. (*Goes out.*)

VARYA (*from the adjoining room*): Where's Yasha? Tell him his mother's come to say good-bye to him.

YASHA (*waves his hand*): They put me out of all pa-

tience! (*Dunyasha has all this time been busy about the luggage. Now, when Yasha is left alone, she goes up to him.*)

DUNYASHA: You might just give me one look, Yasha. You're going away. You're leaving me. (*Weeps and throws herself on his neck.*)

YASHA: What are you crying for? (*Drinks the champagne.*) In six days I shall be in Paris again. Tomorrow we shall get into the express train and roll away in a flash. I can scarcely believe it! *Vive la France!* It doesn't suit me here — it's not the life for me; there's no doing anything. I have seen enough of the ignorance here. I have had enough of it. (*Drinks champagne.*) What are you crying for? Behave yourself properly, and then you won't cry.

DUNYASHA (*powders her face, looking in a pocket mirror*): Do send me a letter from Paris. You know how I loved you, Yasha — how I loved you! I am a tender creature, Yasha.

YASHA: Here they are coming!

(*Busies himself about the trunks, humming softly. Enter Lyubov Andreyevna, Gaev, Anya, and Charlotta Ivanovna.*)

GAEV: We ought to be off. There's not much time now. (*Looking at Yasha.*) What a smell of herrings!

LYUBOV: In ten minutes we must get into the carriage. (*Casts a look about the room.*) Farewell, dear house, dear old home of our fathers! Winter will pass and spring will come, and then you will be no more; they will tear you down! How much those walls have seen! (*Kisses her daughter passionately.*) My treasure, how bright you look! Your eyes are sparkling like diamonds! Are you glad? Very glad?

ANYA: Very glad! A new life is beginning, mamma.

GAEV: Yes, really, everything is all right now. Before the cherry orchard was sold, we were all worried and wretched, but afterwards, when once the question was settled conclusively, irrevocably, we all felt calm and even cheerful. I am a bank clerk now — I am a financier — cannon off the red. And you, Lyuba, after all, you are looking better; there's no question of that.

LYUBOV: Yes. My nerves are better, that's true. (*Her hat and coat are handed to her.*) I'm sleeping well. Carry out my things, Yasha. It's time. (*To Anya.*) My darling, we shall soon see each other again. I am going to Paris. I can live there on the money your Yaroslavl auntie sent us to buy the estate with — hurrah for auntie! — but that money won't last long.

ANYA: You'll come back soon, mamma, won't you? I'll be working up for my examination in the high school, and when I have passed that, I shall set to work and be a help to you. We will read all sorts of things together, mamma, won't we? (*Kisses her mother's hands.*) We will read in the autumn evenings. We'll read lots of books, and a new wonderful world will open out before us. (*Dreamily.*) Mamma, come soon.

LYUBOV: I shall come, my precious treasure. (*Embraces her.*)

(*Enter Lopahin. Charlotta softly hums a song.*)

GAEV: Charlotta's happy; she's singing!

CHARLOTTA (*picks up a bundle like a swaddled baby*): Bye, bye, my baby. (*A baby is heard crying: "Ooah! ooah!"*) Hush, hush, my pretty boy! ("*Ooah! ooah!*") Poor little thing! (*Throws the bundle back.*) You must please find me a situation. I can't go on like this.

LOPAHIN: We'll find you one, Charlotta Ivanovna. Don't you worry yourself.

GAEV: Everyone's leaving us. Varya's going away. We have become of no use all at once.

CHARLOTTA: There's nowhere for me to be in the town. I must go away. (*Hums.*) What care I . . .

(*Enter Pishtchik.*)

LOPAHIN: The freak of nature.

PISHTCHIK (*gasping*): Oh . . . let me get my breath. . . . I'm worn out . . . my most honored . . . Give me some water.

GAEV: Want some money, I suppose? Your humble servant! I'll go out of the way of temptation. (*Goes out.*)

PISHTCHIK: It's a long while since I have been to see you . . . dearest lady. (*To Lopahin.*) You are here . . . glad to see you . . . a man of immense intellect . . . take . . . here (*Gives Lopahin.*) four hundred rubles. That leaves me owing eight hundred forty.

LOPAHIN (*shrugging his shoulders in amazement*): It's like a dream. Where did you get it?

PISHTCHIK: Wait a bit . . . I'm hot . . . a most extraordinary occurrence! Some Englishmen came along and found in my land some sort of white clay. (*To Lyubov Andreyevna.*) And four hundred for you . . . most lovely . . . wonderful. (*Gives money.*) The rest later. (*Sips water.*) A young man in the train was telling me just now that a great philosopher advises jumping off a housetop. "Jump!" says he; "the whole gist of the problem lies in that." (*Wonderingly.*) Fancy that, now! Water, please!

LOPAHIN: What Englishmen?

PISHTCHIK: I have made over to them the rights to dig the clay for twenty-four years . . . and now, excuse me . . . I can't stay . . . I must be trotting on. I'm going to Znoikovo . . . to Kardamanovo. . . . I'm in debt all round. (*Sips.*) . . . To your very good health! . . . I'll come in on Thursday.

LYUBOV: We are just off to the town, and tomorrow I start for abroad.

PISHTCHIK: What! (*In agitation.*) Why to the town? Oh, I see the furniture . . . the boxes. No matter . . . (*Through his tears.*) . . . no matter . . . men of enormous intellect . . . these Englishmen. . . . Never mind . . . be happy. God will succor you . . . no matter . . . everything in this world must have an end. (*Kisses Lyubov Andreyevna's hand.*) If the rumor reaches you that my end has come, think of this . . . old horse, and say: "There once was such a man in the world . . . Semyonov-Pishtchik . . . the Kingdom of Heaven be his!" . . . most extraordinary weather . . . yes. (*Goes out in violent agitation, but at once returns and says in the doorway.*) Dashenka wishes to be remembered to you. (*Goes out.*)

LYUBOV: Now we can start. I leave with two cares in my heart. The first is leaving Firs ill. (*Looking at her watch.*) We have still five minutes.

ANYA: Mamma, Firs has been taken to the hospital. Yasha sent him off this morning.

LYUBOV: My other anxiety is Varya. She is used to getting up early and working; and now, without work, she's like a fish out of water. She is thin and pale, and she's crying, poor dear! (*A pause.*) You are well aware, Yermolay Alexeyevitch, I dreamed of marrying her to you, and everything seemed to show that you would get married. (*Whispers to Anya and motions to Charlotta and both go out.*) She loves you — she suits you. And I don't know — I don't know why it is you seem, as it were, to avoid each other. I can't understand it!

LOPAHIN: I don't understand it myself, I confess. It's queer somehow, altogether. If there's still time, I'm ready now at once. Let's settle it straight off, and go ahead; but without you, I feel I shan't make her an offer.

LYUBOV: That's excellent. Why, a single moment's all that's necessary. I'll call her at once.

LOPAHIN: And there's champagne all ready too. (*Looking into the glasses.*) Empty! Someone's emptied them already. (*Yasha coughs.*) I call that greedy.

LYUBOV (*eagerly*): Capital! We will go out. Yasha, *allez!*° I'll call her in. (*At the door.*) Varya, leave all that; come here. Come along! (*Goes out with Yasha.*)

LOPAHIN (*looking at his watch*): Yes.

(*A pause. Behind the door, smothered laughter and whispering, and, at last, enter Varya.*)

VARYA (*looking a long while over the things*): It is strange, I can't find it anywhere.

allez: French for "Go."

LOPAHIN: What are you looking for?

VARYA: I packed it myself, and I can't remember. (*A pause.*)

LOPAHIN: Where are you going now, Varvara Mihailova?

VARYA: I? To the Ragulins. I have arranged to go to them to look after the house — as a housekeeper.

LOPAHIN: That's in Yashnovo? It'll be seventy miles away. (*A pause.*) So this is the end of life in this house!

VARYA (*looking among the things*): Where is it? Perhaps I put it in the trunk. Yes, life in this house is over — there will be no more of it.

LOPAHIN: And I'm just off to Harkov — by this next train. I've a lot of business there. I'm leaving Epihodov here, and I've taken him on.

VARYA: Really!

LOPAHIN: This time last year we had snow already, if you remember; but now it's so fine and sunny. Though it's cold, to be sure — three degrees of frost.

VARYA: I haven't looked. (*A pause.*) And besides, our thermometer's broken. (*A pause.*)

(*Voice at the door from the yard: "Yermolay Alexeyevitch!"*)

LOPAHIN (*as though he had long been expecting this summons*): This minute!

(*Lopahin goes out quickly. Varya sitting on the floor and laying her head on a bag full of clothes, sobs quietly. The door opens. Lyubov Andreyevna comes in cautiously.*)

LYUBOV: Well? (*A pause.*) We must be going.

VARYA (*has wiped her eyes and is no longer crying*): Yes, mamma, it's time to start. I shall have time to get to the Ragulins today, if only you're not late for the train.

LYUBOV (*in the doorway*): Anya, put your things on.

(*Enter Anya, then Gaev and Charlotta Ivanovna. Gaev has on a warm coat with a hood. Servants and cabmen come in. Epihodov bustles about the luggage.*)

LYUBOV: Now we can start on our travels.

ANYA (*joyfully*): On our travels!

GAEV: My friends — my dear, my precious friends! Leaving this house forever, can I be silent? Can I refrain from giving utterance at leave-taking to those emotions which now flood all my being?

ANYA (*supplicatingly*): Uncle!

VARYA: Uncle, you mustn't!

GAEV (*dejectedly*): Cannon and into the pocket . . . I'll be quiet. . . .

(*Enter Trofimov and afterward Lopahin.*)

TROFIMOV: Well, ladies and gentlemen, we must start.

LOPAHIN: Epihodov, my coat!

LYUBOV: I'll stay just one minute. It seems as though I have never seen before what the walls, what the ceilings in this house were like, and now I look at them with greediness, with such tender love.

GAEV: I remember when I was six years old sitting in that window on Trinity Day watching my father going to church.

LYUBOV: Have all the things been taken?

LOPAHIN: I think all. (*Putting on overcoat, to Epihodov.*) You, Epihodov, mind you see everything is right.

EPIHODOV (*in a husky voice*): Don't you trouble, Yermolay Alexeyevitch!

LOPAHIN: Why, what's wrong with your voice?

EPIHODOV: I've just had a drink of water, and I choked over something.

YASHA (*contemptuously*): The ignorance!

LYUBOV: We are going — and not a soul will be left here.

LOPAHIN: Not till the spring.

VARYA (*pulls a parasol out of a bundle, as though about to hit someone with it; Lopahin makes a gesture as though alarmed*): What is it? I didn't mean anything.

TROFIMOV: Ladies and gentlemen, let us get into the carriage. It's time. The train will be in directly.

VARYA: Petya, here they are, your galoshes, by that box. (*With tears.*) And what dirty old things they are!

TROFIMOV (*putting on his galoshes*): Let us go, friends!

GAEV (*greatly agitated, afraid of weeping*): The train — the station! Double balk,° ah!

LYUBOV: Let us go!

LOPAHIN: Are we all here? (*Locks the side door on left.*) The things are all here. We must lock up. Let us go!

ANYA: Good-bye, home! Good-bye to the old life!

TROFIMOV: Welcome to the new life!

(*Trofimov goes out with Anya. Varya looks round the room and goes out slowly. Yasha and Charlotta Ivanovna, with her dog, go out.*)

LOPAHIN: Till the spring, then! Come, friends, till we meet! (*Goes out.*)

(*Lyubov Andreyevna and Gaev remain alone. As though they had been waiting for this, they throw themselves on each other's necks, and break into subdued smothered sobbing, afraid of being overheard.*)

GAEV (*in despair*): Sister, my sister!

LYUBOV: Oh, my orchard! — my sweet, beautiful orchard! My life, my youth, my happiness, good-bye! Good-bye!

balk: A term in billiards.

VOICE OF ANYA (*calling gaily*): Mamma!

VOICE OF TROFIMOV (*gaily, excitedly*): Aa — oo!

LYUBOV: One last look at the walls, at the windows. My dear mother loved to walk about this room.

GAEV: Sister, sister!

VOICE OF ANYA: Mamma!

VOICE OF TROFIMOV: Aa — oo!

LYUBOV: We are coming. (*They go out.*)

(*The stage is empty. There is the sound of the doors being locked up, then of the carriages driving away. There is silence. In the stillness there is the dull stroke of an ax in a tree, clanging with a mournful, lonely sound. Footsteps are heard. Firs appears in the doorway on the right. He is dressed as always — in a pea jacket and white waistcoat, with slippers on his feet. He is ill.*)

FIRS (*goes up to the doors, and tries the handles*): Locked! They have gone . . . (*Sits down on sofa.*) They have forgotten me. . . . Never mind . . . I'll sit here a bit. . . . I'll be bound Leonid Andreyevitch hasn't put his fur coat on and has gone off in his thin overcoat. (*Sighs anxiously.*) I didn't see after him. . . . These young people . . . (*Mutters something that can't be distinguished.*) Life has slipped by as though I hadn't lived. (*Lies down.*) I'll lie down a bit. . . . There's no strength in you, nothing left you — all gone! Ech! I'm good for nothing. (*Lies motionless.*)

(*A sound is heard that seems to come from the sky, like a breaking harp string, dying away mournfully. All is still again, and there is heard nothing but the strokes of the ax far away in the orchard.*)

COMMENTARIES

Chekhov often commented on his stories and plays in his letters. In the selections from his letters included here, he talks about the difficulties he faced in writing *Three Sisters*. The characters themselves gave him problems, and he feared the play would be dull. But his letters about *The Cherry Orchard* show him in a state of excitement. He is able to plan the play carefully and to consider the nature of the characters carefully.

Konstantin Stanislavsky, director of the Moscow Art Theatre, describes the first moments of hearing a staged reading of *Three Sisters* with Chekhov present. Most interesting is Stanislavsky's observation that he and the actors thought the play was a comedy, while Chekhov thought it a tragedy. Maxim Gorky, himself a famous playwright and a poet of the people, incisively analyzes several of Chekhov's chief characters, reminding us that they refuse to live in the present, although they anticipate a glorious future. Beverly Hahn's comments on *Three Sisters* focuses on the role of each woman in the play, especially as they illustrate Chekhov's views on dependence and ambition. Hahn looks beyond questions of social class to questions of gender.

Virginia Woolf's comments on *The Cherry Orchard* center on language and music. As a distinguished writer, Woolf naturally responds to the Chekhovian language and its effect upon his audiences. Peter Brook, whose recent (1987) production of the play was well received by critics, gives us a director's point of view. He shows us the kind of preparation that must go into a professional performer's interpretation before the play can be realized. Brook's comments are especially interesting in light of Stanislavsky's experiences working with Chekhov, since both Brook and Stanislavsky explore the ways in which Chekhov's characters respond to life's challenges.

All the commentaries on Chekhov show us the richness of interpretation possible in these plays. From the examination of individual characters and the social significance of the action, to the appreciation of the language — these comments help us see how different points of view open up various avenues of concern in each play. We cannot help but be impressed at the complexity of Chekhov's work, especially in light of the apparent simplicity of its surfaces.

Anton Chekhov (1860–1904)
FROM CHEKHOV'S LETTERS

Chekhov, like Ibsen, was an inveterate letter writer. In letters to family members and colleagues, he spoke quite frankly about his hopes, expectations, and difficulties regarding his work. Chekhov's letters concerning Three Sisters *and* The Cherry Orchard *give us some insight into the anxieties and hopes that Chekhov had for his work. His awareness of the difficulties he faced in his writing helps us understand how his plays developed into complex and demanding works.*

October 4, 1888

The people I fear are those who look for tendentiousness between the lines and are determined to see me as either liberal or conservative. I am neither liberal, nor conservative, nor gradualist, nor monk, nor indifferentist. I should like to be a free artist and nothing else. That is why I cultivate no particular predilection for policemen, butchers, scientists, writers, or the younger generation. I look upon tags and labels as prejudices. My holy of holies is the human body, health, intelligence, talent, inspiration, love and the most absolute freedom imaginable, freedom from violence and lies.

November 25, 1892

Keep in mind that the writers we call eternal or simply good, the writers who intoxicate us, have one highly important trait in common: they are moving towards something definite and beckon you to follow, and you feel with your entire being, not only with your mind, that they have a certain goal, like the ghost of Hamlet's father, which had a motive for coming and stirring Hamlet's imagination. Depending on their caliber, some have immediate goals — the abolition of serfdom, the liberation of one's country, politics, beauty, or simply vodka . . . — while the goals of others are more remote — God, life after death, the happiness of mankind, etc. The best of them are realistic and describe life as it is, but because each line is saturated with the consciousness of its goal, you feel life as it should be in addition to life as it is, and you are captivated by it. But what about us? Us! We describe life as it is and stop dead right there. We wouldn't lift a hoof if you lit into us with a whip. We have neither immediate nor remote goals, and there is an emptiness in our souls. We have no politics, we don't believe in revolution, there is no God, we're not afraid of ghosts, and I personally am not even afraid of death or blindness. If you want nothing, hope for nothing, and fear nothing, you cannot be an artist.

Three Sisters

To His Sister
Yalta. Sept. 9, 1900

"The Three Sisters" is very difficult to write, more difficult than my other plays. Oh well, it doesn't matter; perhaps something will come of it, next season if not this. It's very hard to write in Yalta, by the way: I am interrupted, and I feel as though I had no object in writing; what I wrote yesterday I don't like today. . . .

To Maxim Gorky
Yalta. Oct. 16, 1900

. . . On the 21st of this month I am going to Moscow, and from there abroad. Can you imagine — I have written a play; but as it will be produced not now, but next season, I have not made a fair copy of it yet. It can lie as it is. It was very difficult to write "The Three Sisters." Three heroines, you see, each a separate type and all the daughters of a general. The action is laid in a provincial town, — it might be Perm, — in the background military, artillery.

To V. F. Kommissarzhevskaya[1]
Moscow. Nov. 13, 1900

"The Three Sisters" is completed, but its future, at least its immediate future, is obscure to me. The play turned out dull, verbose, and awkward. I say awkward because it has only four female roles, and its mood is duller than dull. Your artists would not take to it if I sent it to them at the Alexandra Theatre. Nevertheless, I shall send it to you. Read it and let me know if it would be a good idea to take it on tour for the summer.

To G. M. Chekhov
Yalta. March 8, 1901

"The Three Sisters" met with great success. Ah, if only there were three good, young actresses, and actors who know how to wear military uniforms. The play is not intended for the provinces.

The Cherry Orchard

To V. F. Kommissarzhevskaya
Yalta. Jan. 27, 1903

This much about the play:
(1) The play is already in my mind, it is true, and the title chosen ("The Cherry Orchard," — but this is a secret), and I shall start on it not later than the end of February, providing, of course, I am well.

[1]Vera F. Kommissarzhevskaya, an actress of whom Chekhov said, she "acts amazingly."

(2) In this play the central person is a woman along in years, to the great regret of the author.

(3) Should I turn it over to the Art Theatre, then according to existing rules and regulations of the theater the play is given over to the sole disposal of the Art Theatre in Moscow and Petersburg, — and I can in no way help this. If the Art Theatre does not travel to Petersburg in 1904 (which is altogether possible), I shall assign the play to you without further ado, providing it is suitable for your theater. Or, here is something else: why not a play for you? Not for this or the other theater, but for you. This has been a long-cherished desire of mine. . . .

You write: "I have in me such faith that, should it break, it would kill me. . . ." etc. Right, you are right, but, for Heaven's sake, do not place all this faith on the new theater. You are an artist, and that is like being a good sailor: no matter on what ship he sails, be it a government vessel or a merchant ship, he remains under all circumstances a good sailor.

To K. S. Stanislavsky
Yalta. July 28, 1903

My play "The Cherry Orchard" is not yet finished; it makes slow progress, which I put down to laziness, fine weather, and the difficulty of the subject. . . . .

I think your part is all right, though I can't undertake to decide, as I can judge very little of a play by reading it. . . .

To Vl. I. Nemirovich-Danchenko[2]
Yalta. August 22, 1903

Now as to my play, "The Cherry Orchard," — so far I am making good progress. I work on it each day, but not too hard, and if I am a bit late in completing it, it would make little difference. I reduced the stage set to a minimum; no special decorations will be required.

In the second act I substituted for the river an old chapel and a well. This is better. But in the second act you will make provision for a real green field, and a path, and a horizon wider than is usual on the stage.

To Vl. I. Nemirovich-Danchenko
Yalta. Sept. 2, 1903

My play (if I continue to make as much headway as up to the present) will be completed very soon; don't worry. The second act presented many difficulties, but I seem to have overcome them. I shall call the play a comedy.

To Madame Stanislavsky
Yalta. Sept. 15, 1903

. . . Don't believe anybody — no living soul has read my play yet; I have written for you not the part of a "canting hypocrite," but of a very nice girl, with which you will, I hope, be satisfied. I have almost finished the play, but eight or ten days ago I was taken ill with coughing and weakness — in fact, last year's business over again. Now — that is today — it is warmer and I feel better, but still I cannot write, as my head is aching. Olga [Mme. Knipper-

[2]Vladimir Ivanovich Nemirovich-Danchenko was a novelist and co-director of the Moscow Art Theatre.

Chekhova, Chekhov's wife] will not bring the play; I will send the four acts together as soon as it is possible for me to set to work for a whole day. It has turned out not a drama, but a comedy, in parts a farce, indeed, and I am afraid I shall catch it from Vladimir Ivanich [Nemirovich-Danchenko]. . . .

I can't come for the opening of your season, I must stay in Yalta till November. Olga, who has grown fatter and stronger in the summer, will probably come to Moscow on Sunday. I shall remain alone, and of course shall take advantage of that. As a writer it is essential for me to observe women, to study them, and so, I regret to say, I cannot be a faithful husband. As I observe women chiefly for the sake of my plays, in my opinion the Art Theatre ought to increase my wife's salary or give her a pension! . . .

> To K. S. Stanislavsky
> Yalta. Oct. 30, 1903

When I was writing Lopahin, I thought of it as a part for you. If for any reason you don't care for it, take the part of Gaev. Lopahin is a merchant, of course, but he is a very decent person in every sense. He must behave with perfect decorum, like an educated man, with no petty ways or tricks of any sort, and it seemed to me this part, the central one of the play, would come out brilliantly in your hands. . . . In choosing an actor for the part you must remember that Varya, a serious and religious girl, is in love with Lopahin; she wouldn't be in love with a mere money-grubber. . . .

> To Vl. I. Nemirovich-Danchenko
> Yalta. Nov. 2, 1903

And now about the play.

(1) Anya can be played by anybody convenient, even by an altogether unknown actress, — only she must be young and look young, and her voice must be youthful and ringing. This is not one of the important roles.

(2) Varya is a more serious part, if Marya Petrovna [Mme. Stanislavsky] takes it. Without Marya Petrovna it will be a little insipid and crude, and will have to be changed, softened. M. P. cannot repeat herself, first, because she is talented, and second, because Varya does not resemble Sonya and Natasha; she is a figure in a black dress, a bit nunlike, a bit stupid, somewhat tearful, etc., etc.

(3) Gaev and Lopahin — let these roles be left to Konst. Serg [Stanislavsky] to try to make his choice. If he were to take Lopahin and the role pleased him, then the play would be successful. But if Lopahin is poorly played by a second-rate actor, both the role and the play will fail.

(4) Pishtchik — Gribunin. God keep N. from this role.

(5) Charlotta — a question mark . . . of course, you must not give it away; Muratova will perhaps be good, but not comical. For this role Mme. Knipper.

(6) Epihodov — if Moskvin wants it, let him have it. He will be an excellent Epihodov. I supposed that Luzhsky was to play it.

(7) Firs — Artyom.

(8) Dunyasha — Khalutina.

(9) Yasha. If Alexandrov, of whom you write, is the one who is your assistant manager, let him have Yasha. Moskvin would make a wonderful Yasha. And I should not object to Leonidov for the part.

(10) The Tramp — Gromov.

(11) The station-master, the one who reads "The Transgressor" in the third act, — an actor who has a bass voice.

Charlotta does not speak in a hybrid way, but uses the pure Russian tongue; but, on rare occasions, she pronounces the soft ending of a word, hard, and she confuses the masculine and feminine genders of adjectives. Pishtchik is a Russian, an old man, worn out by the gout, age, and satiety; stout, dressed in a sleeveless undercoat (à la Simov [an actor in the Moscow Art Theatre], boots without heels. Lopahin — a white waistcoat, yellow shoes; when walking, swings his arms, a broad stride, thinks deeply while walking, walks as if on a straight line. Hair not short, and therefore often throws back his head; while in thought he passes his hand through his beard, combing it from the back forward, i.e., from the neck toward the mouth. Trofimov, I think, is clear. Varya — black dress, wide belt.

Three years I spent writing "The Cherry Orchard," and for three years I have been telling you that it is necessary to invite an actress for the role of Lyubov Andreyevna. And now you see you are trying to solve a puzzle that won't work out.

> To K. S. Alekseyev (Stanislavsky)
> Yalta. Nov. 5, 1903

The house in the play is two-storied, a large one. But in the third act does it not speak of a stairway leading down? Nevertheless, this third act worries me.... N. has it that the third act takes place in "some kind of hotel"; ... evidently I made an error in the play. The action does not pass in "some kind of hotel," but in a *drawing-room*. If I mention a hotel in the play, which I cannot now doubt, after Vl. Iv.'s [Nemirovich-Danchenko] letter, please telegraph me. We must correct it; we cannot issue it thus, with grave errors distorting its meaning.

The house must be large, solid; wooden (like Aksakov's, which, I think, S. T. Morozov has seen) or stone, it is all the same. It is very old and imposing; country residents do not take such houses; such houses are usually wrecked and the material employed for the construction of a country house. The furniture is ancient, stylish, solid; ruin and debt have not affected the surroundings.

When they buy such a house, they reason thus: it is cheaper and easier to build a new and smaller one than to repair this old one.

Your shepherd played well. That was most essential.

> To K. S. Stanislavsky
> Yalta. Nov. 10, 1903

Of course the scenery for III and IV can be the same, the hall and the staircase. Please do just as you like about the scenery, I leave it entirely to you; I am amazed and generally sit with my mouth wide open at your theater. There can be no question about it, whatever you do will be excellent, a hundred times better than anything I could invent. . . .

> To K. S. Alekseyev (Stanislavsky)
> Yalta. Nov. 23, 1903

Hay-mowing time is usually from the 20–22 of June; by that time the rail-birds have become still, and the frogs, too. It is not a graveyard now; long ago there was a cemetery on the spot. Two or three scattered slabs of sandstone are all that remains. The bridge is very good. If one can present the train without noise, without the least sound, then go ahead. I do not oppose the plan of the single setting for Acts III and IV; only, in Act IV the exits and entrances must be natural.

To V. F. Kommissarzhevskaya
Moscow. Jan. 6, 1904

I write you this with a light heart, because of my deep conviction that "The Cherry Orchard" is not for you. The central figure in the play is a woman, an old woman, wholly of the past, with nothing in her of the present; the other roles, at least the women, are trivial and uninteresting, not in the least suited for you.

To F. D. Batiushkov[3]
Moscow. Jan. 19, 1904

. . . At the first performance of "The Cherry Orchard" on the 17th of January, they gave me an ovation, so lavish, warm, and really so unexpected, that I can't get over it even now. . . .

Konstantin Stanislavsky (1863–1938)
ON THE FIRST PRODUCTION OF *THREE SISTERS*

Konstantin Stanislavsky is the actor and director whose methods produced an entire school of acting. He urged actors to relive deeply emotional moments from their own past in order to portray their characters with more depth and realism. In addition, he had actors learn entire scripts so they could fully understand their role in relation to other roles. The deep analysis of the characters' motivation was among his most significant innovations. He is still studied in depth by the Russians and other European theater people. He was an actor in Chekhov's plays and a director with the Moscow Art Theatre, which produced most of Chekhov's great dramas. Stanislavsky is known not only for his theories of production and his theories of acting, but for his lucid commentaries on the work done by his theater.

Now, after the success of both Chekhov's plays [*Ivanov* and *The Seagull*], our Theatre could not get along without a new play from his pen. We began to attack Anton Pavlovich [Chekhov] to have him fulfill the promise he gave us in the Crimea to write us a new play. We were forced to tire him with our continual questions and hints. It was hard for him to have us continually beating at the gates of his soul, it was hard for us to force ourselves to violate his will. But there was nothing else for us to do. The fate of the Theatre from that time on was in his hands; if he gave us a play we would have another season, if he didn't the Theatre would lose all of its prestige. Unhappily the health of Chekhov

[3]Fiodor Dmitriyevich Batiushkov was a critic and professor in Moscow.

seemed to be on the wane. The freshest news from his quarters came from Olga Knipper [Chekhov's wife] from the Crimea. — Strange! — We began to suspect her. — She knew altogether too much about everything that was going on in Yalta — of the state of health of Chekhov, of the weather in the Crimea, of the progress of work on the play, of the coming or not coming of Chekhov to Moscow.

"Aha," said we, Petr Ivanovich and I.

At last, to the pleasure of all, Anton Pavlovich sent the first act of the new play, still unnamed. Then there arrived the second act and the third. Only the last act was missing. Finally Chekhov came himself with the fourth act, and a reading of the play was arranged, with the author present. As was our custom, a large table was placed in the foyer of the theater and covered with cloth, and we all sat down around it, the author and the stage directors in the center. The atmosphere was triumphant and uplifted. All the members of the company, the ushers, some of the stagehands and even a tailor or two were present. The author was apparently excited and felt out of place in the chairman's seat. Now and then he would leap from his chair and walk about, especially at those moments when the conversation, in his opinion, took a false or unpleasant direction. After the reading of the play, some of us, in talking of our impressions of the play, called it a drama, and others, even a tragedy, without noticing that these definitions amazed Chekhov. One of the speakers, who had a self-evident Eastern accent and tried to display his eloquence, began to speak of his impressions with pathos and the common vocabulary of a tried orator:

"Although I do not agree with the author in principle, still —"

Anton Pavlovich could not survive this "in principle." Confused, hurt, and even insulted, he left the meeting, trying to go out without being noticed. He succeeded, for we had not understood what had happened, and least of all could explain the cause that had made him leave us. Afraid that it was his state of health that had forced him to leave the Theatre, I went at once to his home and found him not only out of spirits and insulted, but angry. I do not remember ever seeing him so angry again.

"It is impossible. Listen — 'in principle'!"

At first I thought that the flatness and the out-of-place use of the commonplace phrase and the vulgarity of pronunciation had made Anton Pavlovich lose his patience. But the real reason was that he had written a happy comedy and all of us had considered the play a tragedy and even wept over it. Evidently Chekhov thought that the play had been misunderstood and that it was already a failure.

The work of stage direction began. As was the custom I wrote a detailed *mise en scène* [description of the arrangement of actors and scenery], who must cross to where and why, what he must feel, what he must do, how he must look — things that are considered strange, superfluous, and harmful at the present time, but which were unavoidable and necessary at that time because of the immaturity of the actors and the swiftness of production.

We worked with spirit. We rehearsed the play, everything was clear, comprehensive, true, but the play did not live; it was hollow, it seemed tiresome and long. There was something missing. How torturing it is to seek this something without knowing what it is. All was ready, it was necessary to advertise the production, but if it were to be allowed on the stage in the form in which it had congealed, we were faced with certain failure. And then what would happen to Anton Pavlovich? And what would happen to the Theatre? Yet, nevertheless, we felt that there were elements that augured great success, that everything with the exception of that little something was present. But we could not guess what that something was. We met daily, we rehearsed to a point of despair, we parted company, and next day we would meet again and reach despair once more.

"Friends, this all happens because we are trying to be smart," someone suddenly pronounced judgment. "We are dragging the thing out, we are playing bores on the stage. We must lift the tone and play in quick tempo, as in vaudeville, without any foolishness."

We began to play quickly, that is, we tried to speak and move swiftly, and this forced us to crumple up the action, to lose the text of our speeches and to pronounce our sentences meaninglessly. The result was that the play became worse, more tiresome, from the general disorder, hurry, and flying about of actors on the stage. It was hard to understand what was taking place on the stage and of what the actors were talking. The prevalent mistake of beginning stage directors and actors is that they think that the heightening of tone is the quickening of tempo; that playing in full tone is loud and quick talking and strained action. But the expressions the "heightening of tone," "full tone," "quickening of tempo" have nothing to do with the actor and all with the spectator. To heighten tone means to heighten the mood of the audience, to strengthen the interest of the spectator in the performance; to quicken tempo means to live more strongly and intensively and to live over all that one says and does on the stage. And in talking and acting so that the spectator does not understand either the words or the problems of the actors, all that the actor really accomplishes is the letting down and lowering of the interest of the spectator in the performance and the general tone of his spiritual state of being.

At one of our torturing rehearsals the actors stopped in the middle of the play, ceased to act, seeing no sense in their work and feeling that we were standing in one place and not moving forward. At such times the distrust of the actors in the stage director and in each other reaches its greatest height and threatens to cause demoralization and the disappearance of energy. This took place late at night. Two or three electric lights burned dimly. We sat in the corners, hardly able to restrain our tears, silent, in the semigloom. Our hearts beat with anxiety and the helplessness of our position. Someone was nervously scratching the bench on which he sat with his fingernails. The sound was like that of a mouse. Now again there happened to me something incomprehensible, something that had remained a secret to me ever since an analogous happening during the rehearsals of "The Snow Maiden." Apparently the sound of a scratching mouse, which must have had some meaning for me at an early period of my life, in conjunction with the darkness and the condition and the mood of the entire night, together with the helplessness and depression, reminded me of something important, deep and bright that I had experienced somewhere and at some time. A spiritual spring was touched and I at last understood the nature of the something that was missing. I had known it before also, but I had known it with my mind and not my emotions.

The men of Chekhov do not bathe, as we did at that time, in their own sorrow. Just the opposite; they, like Chekhov himself, seek life, joy, laughter, courage. The men and women of Chekhov want to live and not to die. They are active and surge to overcome the hard and unbearable impasses into which life has plunged them. It is not their fault that Russian life kills initiative and the best of beginnings and interferes with the free action and life of men and women.

I came to life and knew what it was I had to show the actors. I had to show them what was to be done on the stage and how. And they also came to life. We began to work; it was clear to everybody that the dress rehearsal was not far away at last. Olga Knipper still had some trouble with her part, but Nemirovich-Danchenko worked privately with her. At one of the rehearsals something seemed to open in her soul and her role began to progress excellently.

Poor Anton Pavlovich did not wait, not only for the first night, but even for the dress rehearsal. He left Russia, giving his failing health as an excuse for going. I think there was another reason also — his anxiety over the play. This suspicion of mine was borne out by the fact that Chekhov did not leave an address where we could telegraph him of the reception of the play. Even Olga Knipper did not know where he had gone. And it seemed —

But Chekhov had left a viceroy in the person of a lovable colonel who was to see that there should be no mistakes made in the customs of military life, in the manner and method of the officers' bearing in the play, in the details of their uniforms, and so on. Anton Pavlovich paid a great deal of attention to this detail of his play because there had been rumors that he had written a play against the army, and these had aroused confusion, expectation, and bad feelings on the part of military men. In truth, Anton Pavlovich always had the best of opinion about military men, especially those in active service, for they, in his own words, were to a certain extent the bearers of a cultural mission, since, coming into the farthest corners of the provinces, they brought with them new demands on life, knowledge, art, happiness, and joy. Chekhov least of all desired to hurt the self-esteem of the military men.

During the dress rehearsals we received a letter from Chekhov abroad, but again there was no mention of his address. His letter stated, "Cross out the whole speech of Andrey and use instead of it the words 'A wife is a wife.'" This was typical, for it gives a good picture of the laconism of Chekhov. In the original manuscript Andrey delivered a fine speech which defined wonderfully and censured strongly the prosiness and smallness of many Russian women. Till marriage they kept alive in themselves a bit of poetry and femininity. But once married, they wore dressing gowns and slippers at home, and rich but tasteless clothes outside. The same dressing gown and the same tasteless clothes were apparent in their spiritual life and relationships. Is not this whole thought of Chekhov expressed without the use of unnecessary words in the secret meaning and the undercurrent of his short sentence, so full of helplessness and sadness: "A wife is a wife"?

Maxim Gorky (1868–1936)
FROM *RECOLLECTIONS*

Alexei Maximovitch Pyeshkov changed his name to Maxim Gorky, which in Russian means Maxim the Bitter. His childhood and early years gave him great reason for bitterness, because he was raised by a brutal grandfather who regularly beat Maxim and his mother. Once, when he was eight, he attacked his grandfather with a bread knife for beating his frail and sick mother. Gorky spent many years tramping through Russia and became a writer of the common people. He was introduced to the Moscow Art Theatre by Chekhov, and his first play, The Lower Depths *(1902), starred Chekhov's wife, Olga Knipper. It was a mercilessly realistic portrait of the homeless, impoverished, castaways of Russian life. It established Gorky as a major writer, and after the Russian revolution he became the most revered of Soviet writers.*

Reading Anton Chekhov's stories, one feels oneself in a melancholy day of late autumn, when the air is transparent and the outline of naked trees, narrow houses, grayish people, is sharp. Everything is strange, lonely, motionless, helpless. The horizon, blue and empty, melts into the pale sky, and its breath is terribly cold upon the earth, which is covered with frozen mud. The author's mind, like the autumn sun, shows up in hard outline the monotonous roads, the crooked streets, the little squalid houses in which tiny, miserable people are stifled by boredom and laziness and fill the houses with an unintelligible, drowsy bustle. Here, anxiously, like a gray mouse, scurries *The Darling*, the dear, meek woman who loves so slavishly and who can love so much. You can slap her cheek and she won't even dare to utter a sigh aloud, the meek slave. . . . And by her side is Olga of *The Three Sisters*: she too loves much, and submits with resignation to the caprices of the dissolute, banal wife of her good-for-nothing brother; the life of her sisters crumbles before her eyes, she weeps and cannot help anyone in anything, and she has not within her a single live, strong word of protest against banality.

And here is the lachrymose Ranevskaya and the other owners of *The Cherry Orchard*, egotistical like children, with the flabbiness of senility. They missed the right moment for dying; they whine, seeing nothing of what is going on around them, understanding nothing, parasites without the power of again taking root in life. The wretched little student, Trofimov, speaks eloquently of the necessity of working — and does nothing but amuse himself, out of sheer boredom, with stupid mockery of Varya, who works ceaselessly for the good of idlers.

Vershinin dreams of how pleasant life will be in three hundred years, and lives without perceiving that everything around him is falling into ruin before his eyes; Solyony, from boredom and stupidity, is ready to kill the pitiable Baron Tusenbach.

There passes before one a long file of men and women, slaves of their love, of their stupidity and idleness, of their greed for the good things of life; there walk the slaves of the dark fear of life; they straggle anxiously along, filling life with incoherent words about the future, feeling that in the present there is no place for them.

At moments out of the gray mass of them one hears the sound of a shot: Ivanov [in *Ivanov*] or Treplev [in *The Seagull*] has guessed what he ought to do and has died.

Many of them have nice dreams of how pleasant life will be in three hundred years, but it occurs to none of them to ask themselves who will make life pleasant if we only dream.

In front of that dreary, gray crowd of helpless people there passed a great, wise, and observant man; he looked at all these dreary inhabitants of his country, and, with a sad smile, with a tone of gentle but deep reproach, with anguish in his face and in his heart, in a beautiful and sincere voice, he said to them: "You live badly, my friends. It is shameful to live like that."

Beverly Hahn
THE WOMEN IN *THREE SISTERS*

Beverly Hahn analyzes Chekhov's treatment of women in Three Sisters. *The relationships among the sisters are complex and subtle, if only because they demonstrate a variety of forms of dependence and ambition. The Prozorov sisters stand in sharp contrast with Natasha, but it is not absolutely clear that either they or Natasha should be condemned for being as they are. Hahn demonstrates that the play is about more than social change or even social class. She suggests that Chekhov's concern is, at a deep level, for gender issues — the ways in which women have been exploited by men. All the women have qualities that are both admirable and self-destructive. In this sense, our reaction to any of them is determined in part by our sympathies, and Chekhov works on our sympathies in such a way as to prevent us from viewing the play simplistically.*

Natasha and her way of life are set against the sisters and theirs. Irina is sensitive and well bred, and her way of expressing herself has a smooth and attractive lyricism. Natasha, obviously, is vulgar, affected, and incorrigibly vain. Her staccato phrases and jerky movements, along with her pink dress and green sash, reveal by contrast with Irina a complete lack of taste. Yet, as most audiences realize, Natasha's gaudiness and clumsy energy also signify a rough vitality in her which contrasts with the lack of energy of the sisters. Irina is educated and refined but also exceptionally vulnerable, and behind her tears there is a dangerous passivity to life. Her lyricism gives her predicament real pathos: ". . . we have been stifled by [life] as plants are choked by weeds . . ."; but it is a lyricism which comes from an unusual quality of submission. Irina lacks real will, perhaps from the very nature of her upper-class education and what is hidden in it — what W. H. Bruford, in his "sociological study" of Chekhov's Russia, calls "a concealed fear of life."[1] As Natasha enters, Irina makes the very important observation, "We come of people who despised work"; and that is just where Natasha is different. Natasha feigns — she may actually feel — a sense of her social inferiority when she proclaims that she is shy; but in fact she has all the self-assertive energy of one who feels herself rising in the world. She does not seem actually to calculate her effects: she does not need to. With the steely, self-enclosed will of a person who, all her life, has had to "know [something] of work," she is bound to triumph over the superior delicacy of the sisters.

Yet it is important that *Three Sisters* not be seen simply as a drama of class conflict, with Natasha the representative of the bourgeoisie. It appeals to us in terms quite different from those of *The Cherry Orchard,* with its more directly social emphases. For one thing, there is no simple choice to be made between one class and another, since Andrey, in actually marrying Natasha, creates something in between. Also, . . . Natasha herself too often borders on caricature to occupy such an important role. Though she is frighteningly destructive as she gradually takes over the sisters' house, she remains an individual figure rather than a representative one, and she is less subtly and less interestingly developed than any other major character in the play. Her purpose in the drama

---

[1]*Chekhov and His Russia: A Sociological Study* (London, 1948), p. 36.

is as the agent of the sisters' defeat; but the way she defeats them — personal as it is — simply focuses more intently the vulnerability of the sisters' fineness and refined aspiration to the coarser and more primitively energetic elements of life.

Three Sisters, then, is less concerned with the outside threat to civilized standards represented by Natasha than with the paradoxical — and tragic — vulnerability of civilization to weaknesses within itself. The sisters, it is true, are caught in an environment peculiar to late-nineteenth-century Russia; but the social and psychological aspects of their predicament, as Chekhov portrays them, have the utmost relevance to other cultures as well. As civilized people surrounded by, and in some ways embodying, an almost defunct culture, the sisters make us aware of the dilemma which later preoccupied Yeats in "Ancestral Houses," that of cultural refinement working unconsciously towards its own defeat. So although Natasha is necessary to the bolder dramatic outlines of the play, Chekhov I think puts proportionately much more stress on the *internal* nature of the sisters' world and its inbuilt momentum towards destruction. He is intensely sympathetic to the sisters, whose fineness and sensitivity is contrasted with Natasha's coarseness and bluntness; but he is likewise aware of their lack of energy and purpose (again by contrast with Natasha), which signals the decline of a previous phase of Russian civilization.

All three sisters are very attractive, I think, and from moment to moment they behave with a spontaneous — if rather brittle — gaiety:

> MASHA (*strikes her plate with her fork*): Ladies
> and gentlemen, I want to make a speech!
> KULIGIN: You deserve three bad marks for
> conduct.

But beneath the liveliness and humor of these momentary outbursts there is in the sisters a deep-rooted and tragic inability to act. Beyond their openness — even spiritedness — in daily conversation there is an element of defeatism in their psychological make-up which makes them unusally vulnerable to the frustrating conditions of their lives. Masha exemplifies it least: in her manner — her whistling, her recitations from Pushkin and her occasional bluntness of speech — there is a sensuousness of a distinctly sexual kind. She does find fulfillment, with Vershinin, and her tragedy is that she has to forfeit it. But in Olga particularly, despite her dignity and gentleness, there is finally a damaging lack of flexibility — a deep inability to adapt and to make something positive of life. Olga is the most responsible of the sisters, the one with the most developed sense of duty. At times she acts towards Irina and Masha with the strength and stabilizing force which compensate for the loss of their mother. Yet her strength and stability at some points are matched by complete exhaustion at others, as we see in Act III on the night of the fire. Being the eldest, she has the longest memory, and the sheer strength of her memory of Moscow seems to leave her oddly disabled and unfitted for the present. She feels old, although she is only twenty-eight; and at twenty-eight her life does seem already in the past. Of her personal life she speaks with resignation, and in an implied past tense:

> It's all quite right, it's all from God, but it seems to me that if I were married and sitting at home all day, it would be better (*a pause*). I should be fond of my husband.

Olga's gentleness and reserve give her an air of assurance, but she is in an intangible way prematurely aged. She cannot really conceive of a different future:

her opportunities all seem to have been missed. She seems, on the surface, the very opposite of Irina; but while Irina, as the youngest, does have innocence and hope — her whole personality suspended towards that mythical future in Moscow — she too shares Olga's passivity. She waits for the happier future to happen to her, rather than taking initiatives of her own. In Act III, in fact, her passivity becomes almost a kind of living death:

> You are so pale and lovely and fascinating. . . . It seems to me as though your paleness sheds a light through the dark air. . . . You are melancholy; you are dissatisfied with life.

So, attractive as Irina certainly is, her very refinement seems to shut out those more vigorous energies on which personal happiness often depends. Throughout *Three Sisters* her vitality remains conspicuously chaste, and her adolescence seems rather painfully extended. The fulfillment she awaits does not come. Like her sisters, she has not the psychological resources to seek it out. The sisters, as a group, have much to offer, but they are caught in circumstances that have very little to offer them. Worse, in this situation, where Olga and Irina find no real opportunity for fulfillment and Masha's is only fleeting, the sisters' very differentness from the provincial life around them seems to turn back on them to disable them. Their psychological disabilities, as they emerge to us, stem directly from their embodiment of certain standards of civilization in a world upon which such civilization has no hold. It is on this that the tragedy turns.

Virginia Woolf (1882–1941)
ON *THE CHERRY ORCHARD*

Virginia Woolf was one of the most important experimental writers of fiction in the first half of the twentieth century. Her best-known works include Mrs. Dalloway *(1925),* To the Lighthouse *(1927),* Orlando, *(1928),* A Room of One's Own *(1930), and* The Waves *(1931). But in addition to these landmark works, she wrote a huge number of essays and commentaries, not to mention letters that have now been gathered into five large volumes. Her insight into literature is always keen and original. Her approach, for instance, to a 1920 production of* The Cherry Orchard *is through language. She is naturally sensitive to careful use of language, and it is therefore important for her to observe that out of the apparently disjointed use of sentences comes extraordinary drama. She ends her commentary with an interesting comparison that delves into the realm of music — or, more properly, into an imaginative realm in which the theatergoers themselves are musical instruments.*

It is, as a rule, when a critic does not wish to commit himself or to trouble himself, that he refers to atmosphere. And, given time, something might be said in greater detail of the causes which produced this atmosphere — the strange dislocated sentences, each so erratic and yet cutting out the shape so firmly, of the realism, of the humor, of the artistic unity. But let the word atmosphere be taken literally to mean that Chekhov has contrived to shed over us a luminous vapor in which life appears as it is, without veils, transparent and visible to the depths. Long before the play was over, we seemed to have sunk below the surface of things and to be feeling our way among submerged but recognizable emotions. "I have no proper passport. I don't know how old I am; I always feel I am still young" — how the words go sounding on in one's mind — how the whole play resounds with such sentences, which reverberate, melt into each other, and pass far away out beyond everything! In short, if it is permissible to use such vague language, I do not know how better to describe the sensation at the end of *The Cherry Orchard*, than by saying that it sends one into the street feeling like a piano played upon at last, not in the middle only but all over the keyboard and with the lid left open so that the sound goes on.

Peter Brook (b. 1925)
ON CHEKHOV

Peter Brook has established himself as one of the most distinguished modern directors. He was educated at Oxford University and has been a director of the Royal Shakespeare Company in England. In 1987 he directed The Cherry Orchard *at the Brooklyn Academy of Music. Some of his thoughts as he prepared to direct the play are presented here, showing his awareness of Chekhov's "film sense" in a play that was written just as film was emerging as a popular form. He is also aware of Chekhov's personal vision of death and sees it expressed in the circumstances of the play.*

Chekhov always looked for what's natural; he wanted performances and productions to be as limpid as life itself. Chekhov's writing is extremely concentrated, employing a minimum of words; in a way, it is similar to Pinter or Beckett. As with them, it is construction that counts, rhythm, the purely theatrical poetry that comes not from beautiful words but from the right word at the right moment. In the theater, someone can say "yes" in such a way that the "yes" is no longer ordinary — it can become a beautiful word, because it is the perfect expression of what cannot be expressed in any other way. With Chekhov, periods, commas, points of suspension are all of a fundamental importance, as fundamental as the "pauses" precisely indicated by Beckett. If one fails to observe them, one loses the rhythm and tensions of the play. In Chekhov's work, the punctuation represents a series of coded messages which record characters' relationships and emotions, the moments at which ideas come together or follow their own course. The punctuation enables us to grasp what the words conceal.

Chekhov is like a perfect filmmaker. Instead of cutting from one image to another — perhaps from one place to another — he switches from one emotion to another just before it gets too heavy. At the precise moment when the spectator risks becoming too involved in a character, an unexpected situation cuts across: nothing is stable. Chekhov portrays individuals and a society in a state of perpetual change, he is the dramatist of life's movement, simultaneously smiling and serious, amusing and bitter — completely free from the "music," the Slav "nostalgia" that Paris nightclubs still preserve. He often stated that his plays were comedies — this was the central issue of his conflict with Stanislavsky.

But it's wrong to conclude that *The Cherry Orchard* should be performed as a vaudeville. Chekhov is an infinitely detailed observer of the human comedy. As a doctor, he knew the meaning of certain kinds of behavior, how to discern what was essential, to expose what he diagnosed. Although he shows tenderness and an attentive sympathy, he never sentimentalizes. One doesn't imagine a doctor shedding tears over the illnesses of his patients. He learns how to balance compassion with distance.

In Chekhov's work, death is omnipresent — he knew it well — but there is nothing negative or unsavory in its presence. The awareness of death is balanced with a desire to live. His characters possess a sense of the present moment, and the need to taste it fully. As in great tragedies, one finds a harmony between life and death.

Chekhov died young, having traveled, written, and loved enormously, having taken part in the events of his day, in great schemes of social reform. He died shortly after asking for some champagne, and his coffin was transported in a wagon bearing the inscription "Fresh Oysters." His awareness of death, and of the precious moments that could be lived, endow his work with a sense of the relative: in other words, a viewpoint from which the tragic is always a bit absurd.

In Chekhov's work, each character has its own existence: not one of them resembles another, particularly in *The Cherry Orchard*, which presents a microcosm of the political tendencies of the time. There are those who believe in social transformations, others attached to a disappearing past. None of them can achieve satisfaction or plenitude, and seen from outside, their existences might well appear empty, senseless. But they all burn with intense desires. They are not disillusioned, quite the contrary: in their own ways, they are all searching for a better quality of life, emotionally and socially. Their drama is that society — the outside world — blocks their energy. The complexity of their behavior is not indicated in the words, it emerges from the mosaic construction of an infinite number of details. What is essential is to see that these are not plays about lethargic people. They are hypervital people in a lethargic world, forced to dramatize the minutest happening out of a passionate desire to live. They have not given up.

Bernard Shaw

The Irish playwright Bernard Shaw (1856–1950) was astonishing not only for the range of his writing but for the length and vigor of his life. He was a public figure for most of his days, with an especially keen ability to catch public attention and make his presence felt. His early work was devoted to criticism in newspapers, then to a series of fairly successful novels. He began writing plays in his late thirties; once he began, he realized that he had discovered his vocation, and he continued to write more than fifty. Some of them, such as *Arms and the Man* (1894); *Candida* (1897); *Mrs. Warren's Profession* (1898); *Man and Superman* (1901–1903); *John Bull's Other Island* (1904); *Heartbreak House* (1919); *Back to Methuselah* (1921); and *St. Joan* (1923) are among the most performed plays by any English language writer of his time.

Shaw's gift of analysis and philosophical reflection created in his works a new kind of drama that has sometimes been named for him — Shavian. The term implies a deep interest in ideas rather than character and a propensity for elaborate discourse between characters who represent different points of view. Shaw assumed that drama should amuse and entertain, but of much greater importance was his didactic motive. Drama should teach a lesson about something of great moral importance.

This is not to say that Shaw was unable to be entertaining. Some of his comedies, still played today, are light, bright, and witty. *You Never Can Tell* (1898), a comedy about a dentist, and *Pygmalion* (1913), a comedy about a man who teaches a cockney girl how to speak with an upper-class accent and then falls in love with her, are both funny plays. *Pygmalion* was redone as a musical, *My Fair Lady*, and has been Shaw's most financially successful play.

However, Shaw was a basically philosophical writer. His plays can usually be seen as having a specific theme on which the characters constantly discourse. Whether it is on the question of the relation of England to Ireland, on the state of the medical profession, on genetics and propagation, or on poverty, Shaw always focused on an issue. His concern for issues was so important that he once commented that Shakespeare's shortcoming was that his plays have no message.

He frequently wrote elaborate and lengthy prefaces to his published plays. The Preface to *Major Barbara* is included as a commentary and it is a representative exploration of the issues of morality and poverty in the play. In his other prefaces, Shaw takes time to explain — and fully explore — the messages of his plays. He discusses the questions of genetic planning and the improvement of the race in his Preface to *Man and Superman*; in The Preface to *Candida* he discusses the relationship of pity to love. In other prefaces he raises questions about the English medical profession, the exploitation of Ireland by the English, and matters of love and religion.

Shaw's lifelong socialism affected his work and his thinking. The Fabian Society, a political group to which he belonged, was the socialist conscience of British politics, and he himself was a socialist politician for a short period. Consequently, it is not uncommon to see political concerns expressed and debated in his plays.

His political ideas were essentially shaped by his involvement with economics as a discipline of study in 1882. The Fabian Society, which he joined in 1884, disseminated information about socialist ideals, and among the works that affected him at this time was Marx's *Das Kapital*. Shaw never became a Marxist or a Communist, but he did visit Russia in 1931 and felt that its communes, cooperatives, and socialist politics were essentially Fabian in character. He wrote many essays for the Fabian Society and published a collection called *Fabian Essays* in 1889. His activity in the group continued until 1911.

While he studied economics he grew to believe that all social values were built on an economic base. He developed this idea in his Fabian essays and maintained it throughout his plays. He also maintained a presence as a critic of theater and accepted Ibsen as a major playwright when most London critics found his work unacceptable. Shaw's *Quintessence of Ibsenism* (1891; revised after Ibsen's death in 1913) is still one of the most important books on that playwright's work.

MAJOR BARBARA

Major Barbara (1905) centers on the question of poverty, which, as Shaw says in his preface to the play, is a modern kind of crime. The play is not realistic in the way that Ibsen's or Strindberg's plays are, and yet it maintains a sense of naturalness, a suitably convincing surface of realism that works well enough within the limits of the drama.

It soon becomes clear that the extreme positions of Major Barbara of the Salvation Army and her father, Andrew Undershaft, the millionaire owner of the largest munitions factories in England, represent two sides of a debate. Andrew Undershaft wins easily, perhaps too easily. The Salvation Army cannot save souls without the cash needed to feed them. The cash comes from two sources: Bodger, the distiller who has provided liquor to most of the impoverished of the area, and Undershaft himself, who in effect buys the Salvation Army by giving it the wherewithal to continue operating.

The conflict is expressed through a series of oppositions. The most effective is the conflict between Major Barbara the idealist who thinks that the munitions maker is evil and Undershaft who takes life as it is, seeing the munitions maker as neither good nor evil, but simply as an instrument. The creed of the munitions maker is simple: Sell weapons to anyone who can afford them. The outcome of that creed was illustrated the year before the play was produced, in the Russo-Japanese War, when better-equipped Japanese troops defeated a much larger Russian army.

If we can talk about realists in the play, then we must point to Andrew Undershaft and his constant reminders about what really counts in Europe. He attacks the idealists and reminds people of the harsh economic realities that rule their lives. The man who falls in love with Barbara, the professor of Greek Adolphus Cusins, turns out to be the perfect successor to Andrew Undershaft, who, according to tradition, must retire and pass his succession on to a foundling. Adolphus qualifies on a technicality and, after some hard dealing, accepts the offer of the business with a clear understanding of what the power of the office means.

At the same time, he proposes to Major Barbara, who has left the Salvation Army with some of her ideals bruised. But she, too, is much more realistic about life than any mere idealist could be, and when Adolphus chooses to accept the job, Barbara is completely behind him. She can see that more good can be done from a position of power than from a position of weakness.

Major Barbara is more a drama of ideas than it is of character, so the characters are sometimes two-dimensional. But they are always interesting enough to carry the drama forward. Barbara may be enigmatic at the end, but Andrew is clear-thinking, warning Adolphus that he will be driven by the business, not just drive it. This is an important bit of wisdom.

Some of the questions the play raises center on issues of morality. The play opens with the Salvation Army attempting to do good and to maintain a high moral level among the people. But the fact that the Army's money comes from enterprises that, at root, contribute to immoral behavior — the sale of liquor and munitions manufacturing — points to a serious question about Major Barbara's behavior. Shaw asks whether she is realistic and knowledgeable about what she is doing. Is she aware of the contradictions that are already built into the pattern of behavior she has chosen?

Major Barbara learns a great many things in the course of the play, not the least of which is that Andrew Undershaft's money can buy not only things, but people. Somehow she thought that her work went beyond such banal facts. Her leaving the Salvation Army is her acknowledgment that in an indirect way even she had been bought by Undershaft's money.

From Shaw's position, the most important question of the play concerns poverty. It is unforgivable, a crime. Andrew Undershaft does his best to expose the myths of idealism and relate them to the horrors of poverty. In this sense the play has an extremely modern tone. We cannot help but reflect on the extent to which modern prosperity is built on the ideals of Andrew Undershaft more than on the ideals of Major Barbara. Shaw, in his preface to the play, tells his readers that most of them refuse to look at the truth, that "the greatest of our crimes is poverty, and that our first duty, to which every other consideration should be sacrificed, is not to be poor." Those are very difficult words for an idealist like Major Barbara, who could never have conceived of poverty growing up as she did in Andrew Undershaft's house.

Bernard Shaw (1856–1950)

MAJOR BARBARA   *1905*

Characters

ANDREW UNDERSHAFT	RUMMY MITCHENS
LADY BRITOMART	SNOBBY PRICE
STEPHEN UNDERSHAFT	PETER SHIRLEY
BARBARA UNDERSHAFT	BILL WALKER
SARAH UNDERSHAFT	JENNY HILL
ADOLPHUS CUSINS	MRS. BAINES
CHARLES LOMAX	BILTON
MORRISON	

ACT I _____

(It is after dinner in January 1906, in the library in Lady Britomart Undershaft's house in Wilton Crescent. A large and comfortable settee is in the middle of the room, upholstered in dark leather. A person sitting on it (it is vacant at present) would have, on his right, Lady Britomart's writing table, with the lady herself busy at it; a smaller writing table behind him on his left; the door behind him on Lady Britomart's side; and a window with a window seat directly on his left. Near the window is an armchair.)

(Lady Britomart is a woman of fifty or thereabouts, well dressed and yet careless of her dress, well bred and quite reckless of her breeding, well mannered and yet appallingly outspoken and indifferent to the opinion of her interlocutors, amiable and yet peremptory, arbitrary, and high-tempered to the last bearable degree, and withal a very typical managing matron of the upper class, treated as a naughty child until she grew into a scolding mother, and finally settling down with plenty of practical ability and worldly experience, limited in the oddest way with domestic and class limitations, conceiving the universe exactly as if it were a large house in Wilton Crescent, though handling her corner of it very effectively on that assumption, and being quite enlightened and liberal as to the books in the library, the pictures on the walls, the music in the portfolios, and the articles in the papers.)

(Her son, Stephen, comes in. He is a gravely correct young man under 25, taking himself very seriously, but still in some awe of his mother, from childish habit and bachelor shyness rather than from any weakness of character.)

STEPHEN: Whats the matter?

LADY BRITOMART: Presently, Stephen.

(*Stephen submissively walks to the settee and sits down. He takes up a Liberal weekly called* The Speaker.)

LADY BRITOMART: Dont begin to read, Stephen. I shall require all your attention.

STEPHEN: It was only while I was waiting —

LADY BRITOMART: Dont make excuses, Stephen. (*He puts down* The Speaker.) Now! (*She finishes her writing; rises; and comes to the settee.*) I have not kept you waiting very long, I think.

STEPHEN: Not at all, mother.

LADY BRITOMART: Bring me my cushion. (*He takes the cushion from the chair at the desk and arranges it for her as she sits down on the settee.*) Sit down. (*He sits down and fingers his tie nervously.*) Dont fiddle with your tie, Stephen: there is nothing the matter with it.

STEPHEN: I beg your pardon. (*He fiddles with his watch chain instead.*)

LADY BRITOMART: Now are you attending to me, Stephen?

STEPHEN: Of course, mother.

LADY BRITOMART: No: it's not of course. I want something much more than your everyday matter-of-course attention. I am going to speak to you very seriously, Stephen. I wish you would let that chain alone.

STEPHEN (*hastily relinquishing the chain*): Have I done anything to annoy you, mother? If so, it was quite unintentional.

LADY BRITOMART (*astonished*): Nonsense! (*With some remorse.*) My poor boy, did you think I was angry with you?

STEPHEN: What is it, then, mother? You are making me very uneasy.

LADY BRITOMART (*squaring herself at him rather aggressively*): Stephen: may I ask how soon you intend to realize that you are a grown-up man, and that I am only a woman?

STEPHEN (*amazed*): Only a —

LADY BRITOMART: Dont repeat my words, please: it is a most aggravating habit. You must learn to face life seriously, Stephen. I really cannot bear the whole burden of our family affairs any longer. You must advise me: you must assume the responsibility.

STEPHEN: I!

LADY BRITOMART: Yes, you, of course. You were 24 last June. Youve been at Harrow and Cambridge. Youve been to India and Japan. You must know a lot of things, now; unless you have wasted your time most scandalously. Well, advise me.

STEPHEN (*much perplexed*): You know I have never interfered in the household —

LADY BRITOMART: No: I should think not. I dont want you to order the dinner.

STEPHEN: I mean in our family affairs.

LADY BRITOMART: Well, you must interfere now for they are getting quite beyond me.

STEPHEN (*troubled*): I have thought sometimes that perhaps I ought; but really, mother, I know so little about them; and what I do know is so painful! it is so impossible to mention some things to you — (*He stops, ashamed.*)

LADY BRITOMART: I suppose you mean your father.

STEPHEN (*almost inaudibly*): Yes.

LADY BRITOMART: My dear: we cant go on all our lives not mentioning him. Of course you were quite right not to open the subject until I asked you to; but you are old enough now to be taken into my confidence, and to help me to deal with him about the girls.

STEPHEN: But the girls are all right. They are engaged.

LADY BRITOMART (*complacently*): Yes: I have made a very good match for Sarah. Charles Lomax will be a millionaire at 35. But that is ten years ahead; and in the meantime his trustees cannot under the terms of his father's will allow him more than £800 a year.

STEPHEN: But the will says also that if he increases his income by his own exertions, they may double the increase.

LADY BRITOMART: Charles Lomax's exertions are much more likely to decrease his income than to increase it. Sarah will have to find at least another £800 a year for the next ten years; and even then they will be as poor as church mice. And what about Barbara? I thought Barbara was going to make the most brilliant career of all of you. And what does she do? Joins the Salvation Army; discharges her maid; lives on a pound a week and walks in one evening with a professor of Greek whom she has picked up in the street, and who pretends to be a Salvationist, and actually plays the big drum for her in public because he has fallen head over ears in love with her.

STEPHEN: I was certainly rather taken aback when I heard they were engaged. Cusins is a very nice fellow, certainly: nobody would ever guess that he was born in Australia; but —

LADY BRITOMART: Oh, Adolphus Cusins will make a very good husband. After all, nobody can say a word against Greek: it stamps a man at once as an educated gentleman. And my family, thank Heaven, is not a pig-headed Tory one. We are Whigs, and believe in liberty. Let snobbish people say what they please: Barbara shall marry, not the man they like, but the man *I* like.

STEPHEN: Of course I was thinking only of his income. However, he is not likely to be extravagant.

LADY BRITOMART: Dont be too sure of that, Stephen. I know your quiet, simple, refined, poetic people like Adolphus: quite content with the best of everything! They cost more than your extravagant people, who are always as mean as they are second rate. No: Barbara will need at least £2000 a year. You see it means two additional households. Besides, my dear, you must marry soon. I dont approve of the present fashion of philandering bachelors and late marriages; and I am trying to arrange something for you.

STEPHEN: It's very good of you, mother; but perhaps I had better arrange that for myself.

LADY BRITOMART: Nonsense! you are much too young to begin matchmaking: you would be taken in by some pretty little nobody. Of course I dont mean that you are not to be consulted: you know that as well as I do. (*Stephen closes his lips and is silent.*) Now dont sulk, Stephen.

STEPHEN: I am not sulking, mother. What has all this got to do with — with — with my father?

LADY BRITOMART: My dear Stephen: where is the money to come from? It is easy enough for you and the other children to live on my income as long as we are in the same house; but I cant keep four families in four separate houses. You know how poor my father is: he has barely seven thousand a year now; and really, if he were not the Earl of Stevenage, he would have to give up society. He can do nothing for us. He says, naturally enough, that it is absurd that he should be asked to provide for the children of a man who is rolling in money. You see, Stephen, your father must be fabulously wealthy, because there is always a war going on somewhere.

STEPHEN: You need not remind me of that, mother. I have hardly ever opened a newspaper in my life without seeing our name in it. The Undershaft torpedo! The Undershaft quick firers! The Undershaft ten inch! the Undershaft disappearing rampart gun! the Undershaft submarine! and now the Undershaft aerial battleship! At Harrow they called me the Woolwich Infant.° At Cambridge it was the same. A little brute at King's who was always trying to get up revivals, spoilt my Bible — your first birthday present to me — by writing under my name, "Son and heir to Undershaft and Lazarus, Death and Destruction Dealers: address Christendom and Judea." But that was not so bad as the way I was kowtowed to everywhere because my father was making millions by selling cannons.

LADY BRITOMART: It is not only the cannons, but the war loans that Lazarus arranges under cover of giving credit for the cannons. You know, Stephen, it's perfectly scandalous. Those two men, Andrew Undershaft and Lazarus, positively have Europe under their thumbs. That is why your father is able to behave as he does. He is above the law. Do you think Bismarck or Gladstone or Disraeli° could have openly defied every social and moral obligation all their lives as your father has? They simply wouldnt have dared. I asked Gladstone to take it up. I asked *The Times* to take it up. I asked the Lord Chamberlain to take it up. But it was just like asking them to declare war on the Sultan. They wouldnt. They said they couldnt touch him. I believe they were afraid.

STEPHEN: What could they do? He does not actually break the law.

LADY BRITOMART: Not break the law! He is always breaking the law. He broke the law when he was born: his parents were not married.

STEPHEN: Mother! Is that true?

LADY BRITOMART: Of course it's true: that was why we separated.

STEPHEN: He married without letting you know that!

LADY BRITOMART (*rather taken aback by this inference*): Oh no. To do Andrew justice, that was not the sort of thing he did. Besides, you know the Undershaft motto: Unashamed. Everybody knew.

STEPHEN: But you said that was why you separated.

LADY BRITOMART: Yes, because he was not content with being a foundling himself: he wanted to disinherit you for another foundling. That was what I couldnt stand.

STEPHEN (*ashamed*): Do you mean for — for — for —

LADY BRITOMART: Dont stammer, Stephen. Speak distinctly.

STEPHEN: But this is so frightful to me, mother. To have to speak to you about such things!

LADY BRITOMART: It's not pleasant for me, either, especially if you are still so childish that you must make it worse by a display of embarrassment. It is only in the middle classes, Stephen, that people get into a state of dumb helpless horror when they find that there are wicked people in the world. In our class, we have to decide what is to be done

---

Woolwich Infant: A term used for a class of heavy guns.

Bismarck or Gladstone or Disraeli: Otto von Bismark (1815–1898) was a powerful and influential German statesman; William Gladstone (1809–1898) was four-time British prime minister; Benjamin Disraeli (1804–1881) was also a British statesman and two-time prime minister. All were noted for their social reforms.

with wicked people; and nothing should disturb our self-possession. Now ask your question properly.

STEPHEN: Mother: have you no consideration for me? For Heaven's sake either treat me as a child, as you always do, and tell me nothing at all or tell me everything and let me take it as best I can.

LADY BRITOMART: Treat you as a child! What do you mean? It is most unkind and ungrateful of you to say such a thing. You know I have never treated any of you as children. I have always made you my companions and friends, and allowed you perfect freedom to do and say whatever you like, so long as you liked what I could approve of.

STEPHEN (*desperately*): I daresay we have been the very imperfect children of a very perfect mother; but I do beg you to let me alone for once, and tell me about this horrible business of my father wanting to set me aside for another son.

LADY BRITOMART (*amazed*): Another son! I never said anything of the kind. I never dreamt of such a thing. This is what comes of interrupting me.

STEPHEN: But you said —

LADY BRITOMART (*cutting him short*): Now be a good boy, Stephen, and listen to me patiently. The Undershafts are descended from a foundling in the parish of St. Andrew Undershaft in the city. That was long ago, in the reign of James the First. Well, this foundling was adopted by an armorer and gun-maker. In the course of time the foundling succeeded to the business; and from some notion of gratitude, or some vow or something, he adopted another foundling, and left the business to him. And that foundling did the same. Ever since that, the cannon business has always been left to an adopted foundling named Andrew Undershaft.

STEPHEN: But did they never marry? Were there no legitimate sons?

LADY BRITOMART: Oh yes: they married just as your father did; and they were rich enough to buy land for their own children and leave them well provided for. But they always adopted and trained some foundling to succeed them in the business; and of course they always quarreled with their wives furiously over it. Your father was adopted in that way and he pretends to consider himself bound to keep up the tradition and adopt somebody to leave the business to. Of course I was not going to stand that. There may have been some reason for it when the Undershafts could only marry women in their own class, whose sons were not fit to govern great estates. But there could be no excuse for passing over my son.

STEPHEN (*dubiously*): I am afraid I should make a poor hand of managing a cannon foundry.

LADY BRITOMART: Nonsense! you could easily get a manager and pay him a salary.

STEPHEN: My father evidently had no great opinion of my capacity.

LADY BRITOMART: Stuff, child! you were only a baby: it had nothing to do with your capacity. Andrew did it on principle, just as he did every perverse and wicked thing on principle. When my father remonstrated, Andrew actually told him to his face that history tells us of only two successful institutions: one the Undershaft firm and the other the Roman Empire under the Antonines. That was because the Antonine emperors all adopted their successors. Such rubbish! The Stevenages are as good as the Antonines, I hope: and you are a Stevenage. But that was Andrew all over. There you have the man! Always clever and unanswerable when he was defending nonsense and wickedness: always awkward and sullen when he had to behave sensibly and decently!

STEPHEN: Then it was on my account that your home life was broken up, mother. I am sorry.

LADY BRITOMART: Well, dear, there were other differences. I really cannot bear an immoral man. I am not a Pharisee, I hope; and I should not have minded his merely doing wrong things: we are none of us perfect. But your father didnt exactly do wrong things: he said them and thought them: that was what was so dreadful. He really had a sort of religion of wrongness. Just as one doesnt mind men practicing immorality so long as they own that they are in the wrong by preaching morality; so I couldnt forgive Andrew for preaching immorality while he practiced morality. You would all have grown up without principles, without any knowledge of right and wrong, if he had been in the house. You know, my dear, your father was a very attractive man in some ways. Children did not dislike him; and he took advantage of it to put the wickedest ideas into their heads, and make them quite unmanageable. I did not dislike him myself: very far from it; but nothing can bridge over moral disagreement.

STEPHEN: All this simply bewilders me, mother. People may differ about matters of opinion, or even about religion; but how can they differ about right and wrong? Right is right; and wrong is wrong; and if a man cannot distinguish them properly, he is either a fool or a rascal: thats all.

LADY BRITOMART (*touched*): Thats my own boy (*she pats his cheek*)! Your father never could answer that: he used to laugh and get out of it under cover of some affectionate nonsense. And now that you understand the situation, what do you advise me to do?

STEPHEN: Well, what can you do?

LADY BRITOMART: I must get the money somehow.

STEPHEN: We cannot take money from him. I had rather go and live in some cheap place like Bedford

Square or even Hampstead than take a farthing of his money.

LADY BRITOMART: But after all, Stephen, our present income comes from Andrew.

STEPHEN (*shocked*): I never knew that.

LADY BRITOMART: Well, you surely didnt suppose your grandfather had anything to give me. The Stevenages could not do everything for you. We gave you social position. Andrew had to contribute something. He had a very good bargain, I think.

STEPHEN (*bitterly*): We are utterly dependent on him and his cannons, then?

LADY BRITOMART: Certainly not: the money is settled. But he provided it. So you see it is not a question of taking money from him or not: it is simply a question of how much. I dont want any more for myself.

STEPHEN: Nor do I.

LADY BRITOMART: But Sarah does; and Barbara does. That is, Charles Lomax and Adolphus Cusins will cost them more. So I must put my pride in my pocket and ask for it, I suppose. That is your advice, Stephen, is it not?

STEPHEN: No.

LADY BRITOMART (*sharply*): Stephen!

STEPHEN: Of course if you are determined —

LADY BRITOMART: I am not determined: I ask your advice; and I am waiting for it. I will not have all the responsibility thrown on my shoulders.

STEPHEN (*obstinately*): I would die sooner than ask him for another penny.

LADY BRITOMART (*resignedly*): You mean that I must ask him. Very well, Stephen: it shall be as you wish. You will be glad to know that your grandfather concurs. But he thinks I ought to ask Andrew to come here and see the girls. After all, he must have some natural affection for them.

STEPHEN: Ask him here!!!

LADY BRITOMART: Do not repeat my words, Stephen. Where else can I ask him?

STEPHEN: I never expected you to ask him at all.

LADY BRITOMART: Now dont tease, Stephen. Come! you see that it is necessary that he should pay us a visit, dont you?

STEPHEN (*reluctantly*): I suppose so, if the girls cannot do without his money.

LADY BRITOMART: Thank you, Stephen: I knew you would give me the right advice when it was properly explained to you. I have asked your father to come this evening. (*Stephen bounds from his seat.*) Dont jump, Stephen: it fidgets me.

STEPHEN (*in utter consternation*): Do you mean to say that my father is coming here tonight — that he may be here at any moment?

LADY BRITOMART (*looking at her watch*): I said nine. (*He gasps. She rises.*) Ring the bell, please. (*Stephen*

goes to the smaller writing table; presses a button on it; and sits at it with his elbows on the table and his head in his hands, outwitted and overwhelmed.) It is ten minutes to nine yet; and I have to prepare the girls. I asked Charles Lomax and Adolphus to dinner on purpose that they might be here. Andrew had better see them in case he should cherish any delusion as to their being capable of supporting their wives. (*The butler enters: Lady Britomart goes behind the settee to speak to him.*) Morrison: go up to the drawing room and tell everybody to come down here at once. (*Morrison withdraws. Lady Britomart turns to Stephen.*) Now remember, Stephen: I shall need all your countenance and authority. (*He rises and tries to recover some vestige of these attributes.*) Give me a chair, dear. (*He pushes a chair forward from the wall to where she stands, near the smaller writing table. She sits down; and he goes to the armchair, into which he throws himself.*) I dont know how Barbara will take it. Ever since they made her a major in the Salvation Army she has developed a propensity to have her own way and order people about which quite cows me sometimes. It's not ladylike: I'm sure I dont know where she picked it up. Anyhow, Barbara shant bully me but still it's just as well that your father should be here before she has time to refuse to meet him or make a fuss. Dont look nervous, Stephen: it will only encourage Barbara to make difficulties. *I* am nervous enough, goodness knows; but I dont show it.

(*Sarah and Barbara come in with their respective young men, Charles Lomax and Adolphus Cusins. Sarah is slender, bored, and mundane. Barbara is robuster, jollier, much more energetic. Sarah is fashionably dressed: Barbara is in Salvation Army uniform. Lomax, a young man about town, is like many other young men about town. He is afflicted with a frivolous sense of humor which plunges him at the most inopportune moments into paroxysms of imperfectly suppressed laughter. Cusins is a spectacled student, slight, thin-haired, and sweet-voiced, with a more complex form of Lomax's complaint. His sense of humor is intellectual and subtle and is complicated by an appalling temper. The lifelong struggle of a benevolent temperament and a high conscience against impulses of inhuman ridicule and fierce impatience has visibly wrecked his constitution. He is a most implacable, determined, tenacious, intolerant person who by mere force of character presents himself as — and indeed actually is — considerate, gentle, explanatory, even mild and apologetic, capable possibly of murder, but not of cruelty or coarseness. By the operation of some instinct which is not merciful enough to blind him with the illusions of love, he is obstinately bent on marrying Barbara. Lomax likes Sarah and thinks it will be rather a lark to marry her. Consequently he has not attempted to resist Lady Britomart's arrangements to that end.)*

(All four look as if they had been having a good deal of fun in the drawing room. The girls enter first, leaving the swains outside. Sarah comes to the settee. Barbara comes in after her and stops at the door.)

BARBARA: Are Cholly and Dolly to come in?

LADY BRITOMART (*forcibly*): Barbara: I will not have Charles called Cholly: the vulgarity of it positively makes me ill.

BARBARA: It's all right, mother: Cholly is quite correct nowadays. Are they to come in?

LADY BRITOMART: Yes, if they will behave themselves.

BARBARA (*through the door*): Come in, Dolly; and behave yourself.

(Barbara comes to her mother's writing table. Cusins enters smiling, and wanders towards Lady Britomart.)

SARAH (*calling*): Come in, Cholly. (*Lomax enters, controlling his features very imperfectly, and places himself vaguely between Sarah and Barbara.*)

LADY BRITOMART (*peremptorily*): Sit down, all of you. (*They sit. Cusins crosses to the window and seats himself there. Lomax takes a chair. Barbara sits at the writing table and Sarah on the settee.*) I dont in the least know what you are laughing at, Adolphus. I am surprised at you, though I expected nothing better from Charles Lomax.

CUSINS (*in a remarkably gentle voice*): Barbara has been trying to teach me the West Ham Salvation March.

LADY BRITOMART: I see nothing to laugh at in that; nor should you if you are really converted.

CUSINS (*sweetly*): You were not present. It was really funny, I believe.

LOMAX: Ripping.

LADY BRITOMART: Be quiet, Charles. Now listen to me, children. Your father is coming here this evening.

(General stupefaction. Lomax, Sarah, and Barbara rise: Sarah scared, and Barbara amused and expectant.)

LOMAX (*remonstrating*): Oh I say!

LADY BRITOMART: You are not called on to say anything, Charles.

SARAH: Are you serious, mother?

LADY BRITOMART: Of course I am serious. It is on your account, Sarah, and also on Charles's. (*Silence. Sarah sits, with a shrug. Charles looks painfully unworthy.*) I hope you are not going to object, Barbara.

BARBARA: I! why should I? My father has a soul to be saved like everybody else. He's quite welcome as far as I am concerned. (*She sits on the table, and softly whistles "Onward, Christian Soldiers."*)

LOMAX (*still remonstrant*): But really, dont you know! Oh I say!

LADY BRITOMART (*frigidly*): What do you wish to convey, Charles?

LOMAX: Well, you must admit that this is a bit thick.

LADY BRITOMART (*turning with ominous suavity to Cusins*): Adolphus: you are a professor of Greek. Can you translate Charles Lomax's remarks into reputable English for us?

CUSINS (*cautiously*): If I may say so, Lady Brit, I think Charles has rather happily expressed what we feel. Homer, speaking of Autolycus, uses the same phrase. πυκινὸν δόμον ἐλθεῖν means a bit thick.

LOMAX (*handsomely*): Not that I mind, you know, if Sarah dont. (*He sits.*)

LADY BRITOMART (*crushingly*): Thank you. Have I your permission, Adolphus, to invite my own husband to my own house?

CUSINS (*gallantly*): You have my unhesitating support in everything you do.

LADY BRITOMART: Tush! Sarah: have you nothing to say?

SARAH: Do you mean that he is coming regularly to live here?

LADY BRITOMART: Certainly not. The spare room is ready for him if he likes to stay for a day or two and see a little more of you; but there are limits.

SARAH: Well, he cant eat us, I suppose. *I* dont mind.

LOMAX (*chuckling*): I wonder how the old man will take it.

LADY BRITOMART: Much as the old woman will, no doubt, Charles.

LOMAX (*abashed*): I didnt mean — at least —

LADY BRITOMART: You didnt think, Charles. You never do; and the result is, you never mean anything. And now please attend to me, children. Your father will be quite a stranger to us.

LOMAX: I suppose he hasnt seen Sarah since she was a little kid.

LADY BRITOMART: Not since she was a little kid, Charles, as you express it with that elegance of diction and refinement of thought that seem never to desert you. Accordingly — er — (*Impatiently.*) Now I have forgotten what I was going to say. That comes of your provoking me to be sarcastic, Charles. Adolphus: will you kindly tell me where I was.

CUSINS (*sweetly*): You were saying that as Mr. Undershaft has not seen his children since they were babies, he will form his opinion of the way you have brought them up from their behavior tonight, and that therefore you wish us all to be particularly careful to conduct ourselves well, especially Charles.

LADY BRITOMART (*with emphatic approval*): Precisely.

LOMAX: Look here, Dolly: Lady Brit didnt say that.

LADY BRITOMART (*vehemently*): I did, Charles. Adolphus's recollection is perfectly correct. It is most important that you should be good; and I do beg you for once not to pair off into opposite corners and giggle and whisper while I am speaking to your father.

BARBARA: All right, mother. We'll do you credit. (*She comes off the table and sits in her chair with ladylike elegance.*)

LADY BRITOMART: Remember, Charles, that Sarah will want to feel proud of you instead of ashamed of you.

LOMAX: Oh I say! theres nothing to be exactly proud of, dont you know.

LADY BRITOMART: Well, try and look as if there was.

(*Morrison, pale and dismayed, breaks into the room in unconcealed disorder.*)

MORRISON: Might I speak a word to you, my lady?

LADY BRITOMART: Nonsense! Show him up.

MORRISON: Yes, my lady. (*He goes.*)

LOMAX: Does Morrison know who it is?

LADY BRITOMART: Of course. Morrison has always been with us.

LOMAX: It must be a regular corker for him, dont you know.

LADY BRITOMART: Is this a moment to get on my nerves, Charles, with your outrageous expressions?

LOMAX: But this is something out of the ordinary, really —

MORRISON (*at the door*): The — er — Mr. Undershaft. (*He retreats in confusion.*)

(*Andrew Undershaft comes in. All rise. Lady Britomart meets him in the middle of the room behind the settee.*)

(*Andrew is, on the surface, a stoutish, easygoing elderly man, with kindly patient manners and an engaging simplicity of character. But he has a watchful, deliberate, waiting, listening face and formidable reserves of power, both bodily and mental, in his capacious chest and long head. His gentleness is partly that of a strong man who has learnt by experience that his natural grip hurts ordinary people unless he handles them very carefully, and partly the mellowness of age and success. He is also a little shy in his present very delicate situation.*)

LADY BRITOMART: Good evening, Andrew.

UNDERSHAFT: How d'ye do, my dear.

LADY BRITOMART: You look a good deal older.

UNDERSHAFT (*apologetically*): I am somewhat older. (*Taking her hand with a touch of courtship.*) Time has stood still with you.

LADY BRITOMART (*throwing away his hand*): Rubbish! This is your family.

UNDERSHAFT (*surprised*): Is it so large? I am sorry to say my memory is failing very badly in some things. (*He offers his hand with paternal kindness to Lomax.*)

LOMAX (*jerkily shaking his hand*): Ahdedoo.

UNDERSHAFT: I can see you are my eldest. I am very glad to meet you again, my boy.

LOMAX (*remonstrating*): No, but look here dont you know — (*Overcome.*) Oh I say!

LADY BRITOMART (*recovering from momentary speechlessness*): Andrew: do you mean to say that you dont remember how many children you have?

UNDERSHAFT: Well, I am afraid I —. They have grown so much — er. Am I making any ridiculous mistake? I may as well confess: I recollect only one son. But so many things have happened since, of course — er —

LADY BRITOMART (*decisively*): Andrew: you are talking nonsense. Of course you have only one son.

UNDERSHAFT: Perhaps you will be good enough to introduce me, my dear.

LADY BRITOMART: That is Charles Lomax, who is engaged to Sarah.

UNDERSHAFT: My dear sir, I beg your pardon.

LOMAX: Notatall. Delighted, I assure you.

LADY BRITOMART: This is Stephen.

UNDERSHAFT (*bowing*): Happy to make your acquaintance, Mr. Stephen. Then (*going to Cusins*) you must be my son. (*Taking Cusins' hands in his.*) How are you, my young friend? (*To Lady Britomart.*) He is very like you, my love.

CUSINS: You flatter me, Mr. Undershaft. My name is Cusins: engaged to Barbara. (*Very explicitly.*) That is Major Barbara Undershaft, of the Salvation Army. This is Sarah, your second daughter. This is Stephen Undershaft, your son.

UNDERSHAFT: My dear Stephen, I beg your pardon.

STEPHEN: Not at all.

UNDERSHAFT: Mr. Cusins: I am much indebted to you for explaining so precisely. (*Turning to Sarah.*) Barbara, my dear —

SARAH (*prompting him*): Sarah.

UNDERSHAFT: Sarah, of course. (*They shake hands. He goes over to Barbara.*) Barbara — I am right this time, I hope?

BARBARA: Quite right. (*They shake hands.*)

LADY BRITOMART (*resuming command*): Sit down, all of you. Sit down, Andrew. (*She comes forward and sits on the settee. Cusins also brings his chair forward on her left. Barbara and Stephen resume their seats. Lomax gives his chair to Sarah and goes for another.*)

UNDERSHAFT: Thank you, my love.

LOMAX (*conversationally, as he brings a chair forward*

between the writing table and the settee, and offers it to Undershaft): Takes you some time to find out exactly where you are, dont it?

UNDERSHAFT (*accepting the chair, but remaining standing*): That is not what embarrasses me, Mr. Lomax. My difficulty is that if I play the part of a father, I shall produce the effect of an intrusive stranger; and if I play the part of a discreet stranger, I may appear a callous father.

LADY BRITOMART: There is no need for you to play any part at all, Andrew. You had much better be sincere and natural.

UNDERSHAFT (*submissively*): Yes, my dear: I daresay that will be best. (*He sits down comfortably.*) Well, here I am. Now what can I do for you all?

LADY BRITOMART: You need not do anything, Andrew. You are one of the family. You can sit with us and enjoy yourself.

(*A painfully conscious pause. Barbara makes a face at Lomax, whose too long suppressed mirth immediately explodes in agonized neighings.*)

LADY BRITOMART (*outraged*): Charles Lomax: if you can behave yourself, behave yourself. If not, leave the room.

LOMAX: I'm awfully sorry, Lady Brit; but really you know, upon my soul! (*He sits on the settee between Lady Britomart and Undershaft, quite overcome.*)

BARBARA: Why dont you laugh if you want to, Cholly? It's good for your inside.

LADY BRITOMART: Barbara: you have had the education of a lady. Please let your father see that; and dont talk like a street girl.

UNDERSHAFT: Never mind me, my dear. As you know, I am not a gentleman; and I was never educated.

LOMAX (*encouragingly*): Nobody'd know it, I assure you. You look all right, you know.

CUSINS: Let me advise you to study Greek, Mr. Undershaft. Greek scholars are privileged men. Few of them know Greek; and none of them know anything else; but their position is unchallengeable. Other languages are the qualifications of waiters and commercial travelers: Greek is to a man of position what the hallmark is to silver.

BARBARA: Dolly: dont be insincere. Cholly: fetch your concertina and play something for us.

LOMAX (*jumps up eagerly, but checks himself to remark doubtfully to Undershaft*): Perhaps that sort of thing isnt in your line, eh?

UNDERSHAFT: I am particularly fond of music.

LOMAX (*delighted*): Are you? Then I'll get it. (*He goes upstairs for the instrument.*)

UNDERSHAFT: Do you play, Barbara?

BARBARA: Only the tambourine. But Cholly's teaching me the concertina.

UNDERSHAFT: Is Cholly also a member of the Salvation Army?

BARBARA: No: he says it's bad form to be a dissenter. But I dont despair of Cholly. I made him come yesterday to a meeting at the dock gates, and take the collection in his hat.

UNDERSHAFT (*looks whimsically at his wife*): !!

LADY BRITOMART: It is not my doing, Andrew. Barbara is old enough to take her own way. She has no father to advise her.

BARBARA: Oh yes she has. There are no orphans in the Salvation Army.

UNDERSHAFT: Your father there has a great many children and plenty of experience, eh?

BARBARA (*looking at him with quick interest and nodding*): Just so. How did you come to understand that? (*Lomax is heard at the door trying the concertina.*)

LADY BRITOMART: Come in, Charles. Play us something at once.

LOMAX: Righto! (*He sits down in his former place, and preludes.*)

UNDERSHAFT: One moment, Mr. Lomax. I am rather interested in the Salvation Army. Its motto might be my own: Blood and Fire.

LOMAX (*shocked*): But not your sort of blood and fire, you know.

UNDERSHAFT: My sort of blood cleanses: my sort of fire purifies.

BARBARA: So do ours. Come down tomorrow to my shelter — the West Ham shelter — and see what we're doing. We're going to march to a great meeting in the Assembly Hall at Mile End. Come and see the shelter and then march with us: it will do you a lot of good. Can you play anything?

UNDERSHAFT: In my youth I earned pennies, and even shillings occasionally, in the streets and in public house parlors by my natural talent for stepdancing. Later on, I became a member of the Undershaft orchestral society, and performed passably on the tenor trombone.

LOMAX (*scandalized — putting down the concertina*): Oh I say!

BARBARA: Many a sinner has played himself into heaven on the trombone, thanks to the Army.

LOMAX (*to Barbara, still rather shocked*): Yes, but what about the cannon business, dont you know? (*To Undershaft.*) Getting into heaven is not exactly in your line, is it?

LADY BRITOMART: Charles!!!

LOMAX: Well; but it stands to reason, dont it? The cannon business may be necessary and all that: we cant get on without cannons; but it isnt right, you know. On the other hand, there may be a certain amount of tosh about the Salvation Army — I belong to the Established Church myself — but still you cant deny that it's religion; and you cant go against religion, can you? At least unless youre downright immoral, dont you know.

UNDERSHAFT: You hardly appreciate my position, Mr. Lomax —

LOMAX (*hastily*): I'm not saying anything against you personally —

UNDERSHAFT: Quite so, quite so. But consider for a moment. Here I am, a profiteer in mutilation and murder. I find myself in a specially amiable humor just now because, this morning, down at the foundry, we blew twenty-seven dummy soldiers into fragments with a gun which formerly destroyed only thirteen.

LOMAX (*leniently*): Well, the more destructive war becomes, the sooner it will be abolished, eh?

UNDERSHAFT: Not at all. The more destructive war becomes the more fascinating we find it. No, Mr. Lomax: I am obliged to you for making the usual excuse for my trade; but I am not ashamed of it. I am not one of those men who keep their morals and their business in watertight compartments. All the spare money my trade rivals spend on hospitals, cathedrals, and other receptacles for conscience money, I devote to experiments and researches in improved methods of destroying life and property. I have always done so; and I always shall. Therefore your Christmas card moralities of peace on earth and goodwill among men are of no use to me. Your Christianity, which enjoins you to resist not evil, and to turn the other cheek, would make me a bankrupt. My morality — my religion — must have a place for cannons and torpedoes in it.

STEPHEN (*coldly — almost sullenly*): You speak as if there were half a dozen moralities and religions to choose from, instead of one true morality and one true religion.

UNDERSHAFT: For me there is only one true morality; but it might not fit you, as you do not manufacture aerial battleships. There is only one true morality for every man; but every man has not the same true morality.

LOMAX (*overtaxed*): Would you mind saying that again? I didnt quite follow it.

CUSINS: It's quite simple. As Euripides says, one man's meat is another man's poison morally as well as physically.

UNDERSHAFT: Precisely.

LOMAX: Oh, that! Yes, yes, yes. True. True.

STEPHEN: In other words, some men are honest and some are scoundrels.

BARBARA: Bosh! There are no scoundrels.

UNDERSHAFT: Indeed? Are there any good men?

BARBARA: No. Not one. There are neither good men nor scoundrels: there are just children of one Father;

and the sooner they stop calling one another names the better. You neednt talk to me: I know them. Ive had scores of them through my hands: scoundrels, criminals, infidels, philanthropists, missionaries, county councillors, all sorts. Theyre all just the same sort of sinner; and theres the same salvation ready for them all.

UNDERSHAFT: May I ask have you ever saved a maker of cannons?

BARBARA: No. Will you let me try?

UNDERSHAFT: Well, I will make a bargain with you. If I go to see you tomorrow in your Salvation Shelter, will you come the day after to see me in my cannon works?

BARBARA: Take care. It may end in your giving up the cannons for the sake of the Salvation Army.

UNDERSHAFT: Are you sure it will not end in your giving up the Salvation Army for the sake of the cannons?

BARBARA: I will take my chance of that.

UNDERSHAFT: And I will take my chance of the other. (*They shake hands on it.*) Where is your shelter?

BARBARA: In West Ham. At the sign of the cross. Ask anybody in Canning Town. Where are your works?

UNDERSHAFT: In Perivale St. Andrews. At the sign of the sword. Ask anybody in Europe.

LOMAX: Hadnt I better play something?

BARBARA: Yes. Give us Onward, Christian Soldiers.

LOMAX: Well, thats rather a strong order to begin with, dont you know. Suppose I sing Thourt passing hence, my brother. It's much the same tune.

BARBARA: It's too melancholy. You get saved, Cholly; and youll pass hence, my brother, without making such a fuss about it.

LADY BRITOMART: Really, Barbara, you go on as if religion were a pleasant subject. Do have some sense of propriety.

UNDERSHAFT: I do not find it an unpleasant subject, my dear. It is the only one that capable people really care for.

LADY BRITOMART (*looking at her watch*): Well, if you are determined to have it, I insist on having it in a proper and respectable way. Charles: ring for prayers.

(*General amazement. Stephen rises in dismay.*)

LOMAX (*rising*): Oh I say!

UNDERSHAFT (*rising*): I am afraid I must be going.

LADY BRITOMART: You cannot go now, Andrew: it would be most improper. Sit down. What will the servants think?

UNDERSHAFT: My dear: I have conscientious scruples. May I suggest a compromise? If Barbara will conduct a little service in the drawing room, with Mr. Lomax as organist, I will attend it willingly. I will even take part, if a trombone can be procured.

LADY BRITOMART: Dont mock, Andrew.

UNDERSHAFT (*shocked — to Barbara*): You dont think I am mocking, my love, I hope.

BARBARA: No, of course not; and it wouldnt matter if you were: half the Army came to their first meeting for a lark. (*Rising.*) Come along. (*She throws her arm round her father and sweeps him out, calling to the others from the threshold.*) Come, Dolly. Come, Cholly.

LADY BRITOMART: I will not be disobeyed by everybody. Adolphus: sit down. (*He does not.*) Charles: you may go. You are not fit for prayers: you cannot keep your countenance.

LOMAX: Oh I say! (*He goes out.*)

LADY BRITOMART (*continuing*): But you, Adolphus, can behave yourself if you choose to. I insist on your staying.

CUSINS: My dear Lady Brit: there are things in the family prayer book that I couldnt bear to hear you say.

LADY BRITOMART: What things, pray?

CUSINS: Well, you would have to say before all the servants that we have done things we ought not to have done, and left undone things we ought to have done, and that there is no health in us. I cannot bear to hear you doing yourself such an injustice, and Barbara such an injustice. As for myself, I flatly deny it: I have done my best. I shouldnt dare to marry Barbara — I couldnt look you in the face — if it were true. So I must go to the drawing room.

LADY BRITOMART (*offended*): Well, go. (*He starts for the door.*) And remember this, Adolphus (*he turns to listen*): I have a very strong suspicion that you went to the Salvation Army to worship Barbara and nothing else. And I quite appreciate the very clever way in which you systematically humbug me. I have found you out. Take care Barbara doesnt. Thats all.

CUSINS (*with unruffled sweetness*): Dont tell on me. (*He steals out.*)

LADY BRITOMART: Sarah: if you want to go, go. Anything's better than to sit there as if you wished you were a thousand miles away.

SARAH (*languidly*): Very well, mamma. (*She goes.*)

(*Lady Britomart, with a sudden flounce, gives way to a little gust of tears.*)

STEPHEN (*going to her*): Mother: whats the matter?

LADY BRITOMART (*swishing away her tears with her handkerchief*): Nothing. Foolishness. You can go with him, too, if you like, and leave me with the servants.

STEPHEN: Oh, you mustnt think that, mother. I — I dont like him.

LADY BRITOMART: The others do. That is the injustice of a woman's lot. A woman has to bring up her children; and that means to restrain them, to deny them things they want, to set them tasks, to punish them when they do wrong, to do all the unpleasant things. And then the father, who has nothing to do but pet them and spoil them, comes in when all her work is done and steals their affection from her.

STEPHEN: He has not stolen our affection from you. It is only curiosity.

LADY BRITOMART (*violently*): I wont be consoled, Stephen. There is nothing the matter with me. (*She rises and goes towards the door.*)

STEPHEN: Where are you going, mother?

LADY BRITOMART: To the drawing room, of course. (*She goes out. Onward, Christian Soldiers, on the concertina, with tambourine accompaniment, is heard when the door opens.*) Are you coming, Stephen?

STEPHEN: No. Certainly not. (*She goes. He sits down on the settee, with compressed lips and an expression of strong dislike.*)

ACT II

(*The yard of the West Ham shelter of the Salvation Army is a cold place on a January morning. The building itself, an old warehouse, is newly whitewashed. Its gabled end projects into the yard in the middle, with a door on the ground floor, and another in the loft above it without any balcony or ladder, but with a pulley rigged over it for hoisting sacks. Those who come from this central gable end into the yard have the gateway leading to the street on their left, with a stone horse-trough just beyond it, and, on the right, a penthouse shielding a table from the weather. There are forms at the table; and on them are seated a man and a woman, both much down on their luck, finishing a meal of bread (one thick slice each, with margarine and golden syrup) and diluted milk.*)

(*The man, a workman out of employment, is young, agile, a talker, a poser, sharp enough to be capable of anything in reason except honesty or altruistic considerations of any kind. The woman is a commonplace old bundle of poverty and hard-worn humanity. She looks sixty and probably is forty-five. If they were rich people, gloved and muffed and well wrapped up in furs and overcoats, they would be numbed and miserable; for it is a grindingly cold raw January day; and a glance at the background of grimy warehouses and leaden sky visible over the whitewashed walls of the yard would drive any idle rich person straight to*) *the Mediterranean. But these two, being no more trou-bled with visions of the Mediterranean than of the moon, and being compelled to keep more of their clothes in the pawnshop, and less on their persons, in winter than in summer, are not depressed by the cold: rather are they stung into vivacity, to which their meal has just now given an almost jolly turn. The man takes a pull at his mug, and then gets up and moves about the yard with his hands deep in his pockets, occasionally breaking into a stepdance.)*

THE WOMAN: Feel better arter your meal, sir?

THE MAN: No. Call that a meal! Good enough for you, praps, but wot is it to me, an intelligent workin man.

THE WOMAN: Workin man! Wot are you?

THE MAN: Painter.

THE WOMAN (*skeptically*): Yus, I dessay.

THE MAN: Yus, you dessay! I know. Every loafer that cant do nothink calls isself a painter. Well, I'm a real painter: grainer, finisher, thirty-eight bob a week when I can get it.

THE WOMAN: Then why dont you go and get it?

THE MAN: I'll tell you why. Fust: I'm intelligent — fffff! it's rotten cold here (*He dances a step or two.*) — yes: intelligent beyond the station o life into which it has pleased the capitalists to call me: and they dont like a man that sees through em. Second, an intelligent bein needs a doo share of appiness; so I drink somethink cruel when I get the chawnce. Third, I stand by my class and do as little as I can so's to leave arf the job for me fellow workers. Fourth, I'm fly enough to know wots inside the law and wots outside it; and inside it I do as the capitalists do: pinch wot I can lay me ands on. In a proper state of society I am sober, industrious and honest: in Rome, so to speak, I do as the Romans do. Wots the consequence? When trade is bad — and it's rotten bad just now — and the employers az to sack arf their men, they generally start on me.

THE WOMAN: Whats your name?

THE MAN: Price. Bronterre O'Brien Price. Usually called Snobby Price, for short.

THE WOMAN: Snobby's a carpenter, aint it? You said you was a painter.

PRICE: Not that kind of snob, but the genteel sort. I'm too uppish, owing to my intelligence, and my father being a Chartist° and a reading, thinking man: a stationer, too. I'm none of your common hewers of wood and drawers of water; and dont you forget it. (*He returns to his seat at the table and takes up his mug.*) Wots your name?

Chartist: Member of the British working-class reform move-ment known as chartism (1838–1848).

THE WOMAN: Rummy Mitchens, sir.

PRICE (*quaffing the remains of his milk to her*): Your elth, Miss Mitchens.

RUMMY (*correcting him*): Missis Mitchens.

PRICE: Wot! Oh Rummy, Rummy! Respectable married woman, Rummy, gittin rescued by the Salvation Army by pretendin to be a bad un. Same old game!

RUMMY: What am I to do? I cant starve. Them Salvation lasses is dear good girls; but the better you are, the worse they likes to think you were before they rescued you. Why shouldnt they av a bit o credit, poor loves? theyre worn to rags by their work. And where would they get the money to rescue us if we was to let on we're no worse than other people? You know what ladies and gentlemen are.

PRICE: Thievin swine! Wish I ad their job, Rummy, all the same. Wot does Rummy stand for? Pet name praps?

RUMMY: Short for Romola.

PRICE: For wot!?

RUMMY: Romola. It was out of a new book. Somebody me mother wanted me to grow up like.

PRICE: We're companions in misfortune, Rummy. Both on us got names that nobody cawnt pronounce. Consequently I'm Snobby and youre Rummy because Bill and Sally wasnt good enough for our parents. Such is life!

RUMMY: Who saved you, Mr. Price? Was it Major Barbara?

PRICE: No: I come here on my own. I'm going to be Bronterre O'Brien Price, the converted painter. I know wot they like. I'll tell em how I blasphemed and gambled and wopped my poor old mother —

RUMMY (*shocked*): Used you to beat your mother?

PRICE: Not likely. She used to beat me. No matter: you come and listen to the converted painter, and youll hear how she was a pious woman that taught me me prayers at er knee, an how I used to come home drunk and drag her out o bed be er snow white airs, an lam into er with the poker.

RUMMY: Thats whats so unfair to us women. Your confessions is just as big lies as ours: you dont tell what you really done no more than us; but you men can tell your lies right out at the meetins and be made much of for it, while the sort o confessions we az to make az to be whispered to one lady at a time. It aint right, spite of all their piety.

PRICE: Right! Do you spose the Army'd be allowed if it went and did right? Not much. It combs our air and makes us good little blokes to be robbed and put upon. But I'll play the game as good as any of em. I'll see somebody struck by lightnin, or hear a voice sayin "Snobby Price: where will you spend eternity?" I'll av a time of it, I tell you.

RUMMY: You wont be let drink, though.

PRICE: I'll take it out in gorspellin, then. I dont want to drink if I can get fun enough any other way.

(*Jenny Hill, a pale, overwrought, pretty Salvation lass of 18, comes in through the yard gate, leading Peter Shirley, a half hardened, half worn-out elderly man, weak with hunger.*)

JENNY (*supporting him*): Come! pluck up. I'll get you something to eat. Youll be all right then.

PRICE (*rising and hurrying officiously to take the old man off Jenny's hands*): Poor old man! Cheer up, brother: youll find rest and peace and appiness ere. Hurry up with the food, miss: e's fair done. (*Jenny hurries into the shelter.*) Ere, buck up, daddy! she's fetchin y'a thick slice of breadn treacle, an a mug o skyblue. (*He seats him at the corner of the table.*)

RUMMY (*gaily*): Keep up your old art! Never say die!

SHIRLEY: I'm not an old man. I'm only forty-six. I'm as good as ever I was. The grey patch come in my hair before I was 30. All it wants is three pennorth o hair dye: am I to be turned on the streets to starve for it? Holy God! I've worked ten to twelve hours a day since I was thirteen, and paid my way all through; and now am I to be thrown into the gutter and my job given to a young man that can do it no better than me because Ive black hair that goes white at the first change?

PRICE (*cheerfully*): No good jawrin about it. Youre ony a jumped-up, jerked-off, orspittle-turned-out incurable of an ole workin man: who cares about you? Eh? Make the thievin swine give you a meal: theyve stole many a one from you. Get a bit o your own back. (*Jenny returns with the usual meal.*) There you are, brother. Awsk a blessin an tuck that into you.

SHIRLEY (*looking at it ravenously but not touching it, and crying like a child*): I never took anything before.

JENNY (*petting him*): Come, come! the Lord sends it to you: he wasn't above taking bread from his friends; and why should you be? Besides, when we find you a job you can pay us for it if you like.

SHIRLEY (*eagerly*): Yes, yes: thats true. I can pay you back: it's only a loan. (*Shivering.*) Oh Lord! oh Lord! (*He turns to the table and attacks the meal ravenously.*)

JENNY: Well, Rummy, are you more comfortable now?

RUMMY: God bless you, lovey! youve fed my body and saved my soul, havent you? (*Jenny, touched, kisses her.*) Sit down and rest a bit: you must be ready to drop.

JENNY: Ive been going hard since morning. But theres more work than we can do. I mustnt stop.

RUMMY: Try a prayer for just two minutes. Youll work all the better after.

JENNY (*her eyes lighting up*): Oh isnt it wonderful how a few minutes prayer revives you! I was quite lightheaded at twelve o'clock, I was so tired; but Major Barbara just sent me to pray for five minutes; and I was able to go on as if I had only just begun. (*To Price.*) Did you have a piece of bread?

PRICE (*with unction*): Yes, miss; but Ive got the piece that I value more; and thats the peace that passeth hall hannerstennin.

RUMMY (*fervently*): Glory Hallelujah!

(*Bill Walker, a rough customer of about 25, appears at the yard gate and looks malevolently at Jenny.*)

JENNY: That makes me so happy. When you say that, I feel wicked for loitering here. I must get to work again.

(*She is hurrying to the shelter, when the newcomer moves quickly up to the door and intercepts her. His manner is so threatening that she retreats as he comes at her truculently, driving her down the yard.*)

BILL: Aw knaow you. Youre the one that took awy maw girl. Youre the one that set er agen me. Well, I'm gowin to ev er aht. Not that Aw care a carse for er or you: see? Bat Aw'll let er knaow; and Aw'll let you knaow. Aw'm gowing to give her a doin thatll teach er to cat awy from me. Nah in wiv you and tell er to cam aht afore Aw cam in and kick er aht. Tell er Bill Walker wants er. She'll knaow wot thet means; and if she keeps me witin itll be worse. You stop to jawr beck at me: and Aw'll stawt on you: d'ye eah? Theres your wy. In you gow. (*He takes her by the arm and slings her towards the door of the shelter. She falls on her hand and knee. Rummy helps her up again.*)

PRICE (*rising, and venturing irresolutely towards Bill*): Easy there, mate. She aint doin you no arm.

BILL: Oo are you callin mite? (*Standing over him threateningly.*) Youre gowin to stend ap for er, aw yer? Put ap your ends.

RUMMY (*running indignantly to him to scold him*): Oh, you great brute — (*He instantly swings his left hand back against her face. She screams and reels back to the trough, where she sits down, covering her bruised face with her hands and rocking herself and moaning with pain.*)

JENNY (*going to her*): Oh, God forgive you! How could you strike an old woman like that?

BILL (*seizing her by the hair so violently that she also screams, and tearing her away from the old woman*): You Gawd forgimme again an Aw'll Gawd forgive you one on the jawr thetll stop you pryin for a week. (*Holding her and turning fiercely on Price.*) Ev you ennything to sy agen it?

PRICE (*intimidated*): No, matey: she aint anything to do with me.

BILL: Good job for you! Aw'd pat two meals into you and fawt you with one finger arter, you stawved cur. (*To Jenny.*) Nah are you gowin to fetch aht Mog Ebbijem; or em Aw to knock your fice off you and fetch her meself?

JENNY (*writhing in his grasp*): Oh please someone go in and tell Major Barbara — (*She screams again as he wrenches her head down; and Price and Rummy flee into the shelter.*)

BILL: You want to gow in and tell your Mijor of me, do you?

JENNY: Oh please dont drag my hair. Let me go.

BILL: Do you or downt you? (*She stifles a scream.*) Yus or nao?

JENNY: God give me strength —

BILL (*striking her with his fist in the face*): Gow an shaow her thet, and tell her if she wants one lawk it to cam and interfere with me. (*Jenny, crying with pain, goes into the shed. He goes to the form and addresses the old man.*) Eah: finish your mess; an git aht o mah wy.

SHIRLEY (*springing up and facing him fiercely, with the mug in his hand*): You take a liberty with me, and I'll smash you over the face with the mug and cut your eye out. Aint you satisfied — young whelps like you — with takin the bread out o the mouths of your elders that have brought you up and slaved for you, but you must come shovin and cheekin and bullyin in here, where the bread o charity is sickenin in our stummicks?

BILL (*contemptuously, but backing a little*): Wot good are you, you aold palsy mag? Wot good are you?

SHIRLEY: As good as you and better. I'll do a day's work agen you or any fat young soaker of your age. Go and take my job at Horrockses, where I worked for ten year. They want young men there: they cant afford to keep men over forty-five. Theyre very sorry — give you a character and happy to help you to get anything suited to your years — sure a steady man wont be long out of a job. Well, let em try you. Theyll find the differ. What do you know? Not as much as how to beeyave yourself — layin your dirty fist across the mouth of a respectable woman!

BILL: Downt provowk me to ly it acrost yours: d'ye eah?

SHIRLEY (*with blighting contempt*): Yes: you like an old man to hit, dont you, when youve finished with the women. I ain't seen you hit a young one yet.

BILL (*stung*): You loy, you aold soupkitchener, you. There was a yang menn eah. Did Aw offer to itt him or did Aw not?

SHIRLEY: Was he starvin or was he not? Was he a man or only a crossed-eyed thief an a loafer? Would you hit my son-in-law's brother?

BILL: Oo's ee?

SHIRLEY: Todger Fairmile o Balls Pond. Him that won £20 off the Japanese wrastler at the music hall by standin out 17 minutes 4 seconds agen him.

BILL (*sullenly*): Aw'm nao music awl wrastler. Ken he box?

SHIRLEY: Yes: an you cant.

BILL: Wot! Aw cawnt, cawnt Aw? Wots thet you sy (*threatening him*)?

SHIRLEY (*not budging an inch*): Will you box Todger Fairmile if I put him on to you? Say the word.

BILL (*subsiding with a slouch*): Aw'll stend ap to enny menn alawv, if he was ten Todger Fairmawls. But Aw dont set ap to be a perfeshnal.

SHIRLEY (*looking down on him with unfathomable disdain*): You box! Slap an old woman with the back o your hand! You hadnt even the sense to hit her where the magistrate couldnt see the mark of it, you silly young lump of conceit and ignorance. Hit a girl in the jaw and ony make her cry! If Todger Fairmile's done it, she wouldnt a got up inside o ten minutes, no more than you would if he got on to you. Yah! I'd set about you myself if I had a week's feedin in me instead o two months' starvation. (*He turns his back on him and sits down moodily at the table.*)

BILL (*following him and stooping over him to drive the taunt in*): You loy! youve the bread and treacle in you that you cam eah to beg.

SHIRLEY (*bursting into tears*): Oh God! it's true: I'm only an old pauper on the scrap heap. (*Furiously.*) But youll come to it yourself; and then youll know. Youll come to it sooner than a teetotaller like me, fillin yourself with gin at this hour o the mornin!

BILL: Aw'm nao gin drinker, you oald lawr; but wen Aw want to give my girl a bloomin good awdin Aw lawk to ev a bit o devil in me: see? An eah Aw emm, talkin to a rotten aold blawter like you sted o givin her wot for. (*Working himself into a rage.*) Aw'm gowin in there to fetch her aht. (*He makes vengefully for the shelter door.*)

SHIRLEY: Youre goin to the station on a stretcher, more likely; and theyll take the gin and the devil out of you there when they get you inside. You mind what youre about: the major here is the Earl o Stevenage's granddaughter.

BILL (*checked*): Garn!

SHIRLEY: Youll see.

BILL (*his resolution oozing*): Well, Aw aint dan nathin to er.

SHIRLEY: Spose she said you did! who'd believe you?

BILL (*very uneasy, skulking back to the corner of the penthouse*): Gawd! theres no jastice in this cantry.

To think wot them people can do! Aw'm as good as er.

SHIRLEY: Tell her so. It's just what a fool like you would do.

(*Barbara, brisk and businesslike, comes from the shelter with a notebook, and addresses herself to Shirley. Bill, cowed, sits down in the corner on a form, and turns his back on them.*)

BARBARA: Good morning.

SHIRLEY (*standing up and taking off his hat*): Good morning, miss.

BARBARA: Sit down: make yourself at home. (*He hesitates; but she puts a friendly hand on his shoulder and makes him obey.*) Now then! since youve made friends with us, we want to know all about you. Names and addresses and trades.

SHIRLEY: Peter Shirley. Fitter. Chucked out two months ago because I was too old.

BARBARA (*not at all surprised*): Youd pass still. Why didnt you dye your hair?

SHIRLEY: I did. Me age come out at a coroner's inquest on me daughter.

BARBARA: Steady?

SHIRLEY: Teetotaler. Never out of a job before. Good worker. And sent to the knackers like an old horse!

BARBARA: No matter: if you did your part God will do his.

SHIRLEY (*suddenly stubborn*): My religion's no concern of anybody but myself.

BARBARA (*guessing*): I know. Secularist?

SHIRLEY (*hotly*): Did I offer to deny it?

BARBARA: Why should you? My own father's a Secularist, I think. Our Father — yours and mine — fulfills himself in many ways; and I daresay he knew what he was about when he made a Secularist of you. So buck up, Peter! we can always find a job for a steady man like you. (*Shirley, disarmed and a little bewildered, touches his hat. She turns from him to Bill.*) Whats your name?

BILL (*insolently*): Wots thet to you?

BARBARA (*calmly making a note*): Afraid to give his name. Any trade?

BILL: Oo's afride to give is nime? (*Doggedly, with a sense of heroically defying the House of Lords in the person of Lord Stevenage.*) If you want to bring a chawge agen me, bring it. (*She waits, unruffled.*) Moy nime's Bill Walker.

BARBARA (*as if the name were familiar: trying to remember how*): Bill Walker? (*Recollecting.*) Oh, I know: youre the man that Jenny Hill was praying for inside just now. (*She enters his name in her notebook.*)

BILL: Oo's Jenny Ill? And wot call as she to pry for me?

BARBARA: I dont know. Perhaps it was you that cut her lip.

BILL (*defiantly*): Yus, it was me that cat her lip. Aw aint afride o you.

BARBARA: How could you be, since youre not afraid of God? Youre a brave man, Mr. Walker. It takes some pluck to do our work here; but none of us dare lift our hand against a girl like that, for fear of her father in heaven.

BILL (*sullenly*): I want nan o your kentin jawr. I spowse you think Aw cam eah to beg from you, like this demmiged lot eah. Not me. Aw downt want your bread and scripe and ketlep. Aw dont belive in your Gawd, no more than you do yourself.

BARBARA (*sunnily apologetic and ladylike, as on a new footing with him*): Oh, I beg your pardon for putting your name down, Mr. Walker. I didn't understand. I'll strike it out.

BILL (*taking this as a slight, and deeply wounded by it*): Eah! you let maw nime alown. Aint it good enaff to be in your book?

BARBARA (*considering*): Well, you see, theres no use putting down your name unless I can do something for you, is there? Whats your trade?

BILL (*still smarting*): Thets nao concern o yours.

BARBARA: Just so. (*Very businesslike.*) I'll put you down as (*writing*) the man who — struck — poor little Jenny Hill — in the mouth.

BILL (*rising threateningly*): See eah. Awve ed enaff o this.

BARBARA (*quite sunny and fearless*): What did you come to us for?

BILL: Aw cam for maw gel, see? Aw cam to tike her aht o this and to brike er jawr for er.

BARBARA (*complacently*): You see I was right about your trade. (*Bill, on the point of retorting furiously, finds himself, to his great shame and terror, in danger of crying instead. He sits down again suddenly.*) Whats her name?

BILL (*dogged*): Er nime's Mog Ebbijem: thets wot her nime is.

BARBARA: Mog Habbijam! Oh, she's gone to Canning Town, to our barracks there.

BILL (*fortified by his resentment of Mog's perfidy*): Is she? (*Vindictively.*) Then Aw'm gowin to Kennintahn arter her. (*He crosses to the gate; hesitates; finally comes back at Barbara.*) Are you loyin to me to git shat o me?

BARBARA: I dont want to get shut of you. I want to keep you here and save your soul. Youd better stay: youre going to have a bad time today, Bill.

BILL: Oo's gowin to give it to me? You, preps?

BARBARA: Someone you dont believe in. But youll be glad afterwards.

BILL (*slinking off*): Aw'll gow to Kennintahn to be

aht o reach o your tangue. (*Suddenly turning on her with intense malice.*) And if Aw downt fawnd Mog there, Aw'll cam beck and do two years for you, selp me Gawd if Aw downt!

BARBARA (*a shade kindlier, if possible*): It's no use, Bill. She's got another bloke.

BILL: Wot!

BARBARA: One of her own converts. He fell in love with her when he saw her with her soul saved, and her face clean, and her hair washed.

BILL (*surprised*): Wottud she wash it for, the carroty slat? It's red.

BARBARA: It's quite lovely now, because she wears a new look in her eyes with it. It's a pity youre too late. The new bloke has put your nose out of joint, Bill.

BILL: Aw'll put his nowse aht o joint for him. Not that Aw care a carse for er, mawnd thet. But Aw'll teach him to drop me as if Aw was dirt. And Aw'll teach him to meddle with maw Judy. Wots iz bleedin nime?

BARBARA: Sergeant Todger Fairmile.

SHIRLEY (*rising with grim joy*): I'll go with him, miss. I want to see them two meet. I'll take him to the infirmary when it's over.

BILL (*to Shirley, with undissembled misgiving*): Is thet im you was speakin on?

SHIRLEY: Thats him.

BILL: Im that wrastled in the music awl?

SHIRLEY: The competitions at the National Sportin Club was worth nigh a hundred a year to him. He's gev em up now for religion; so he's a bit fresh for want of the exercise he was accustomed to. He'll be glad to see you. Come along.

BILL: Wots is wight?

SHIRLEY: Thirteen four.° (*Bill's last hope expires.*)

BARBARA: Go and talk to him, Bill. He'll convert you.

SHIRLEY: He'll convert your head into a mashed potato.

BILL (*sullenly*): Aw aint afride of im. Aw aint afride of ennybody. Bat e can lick me. She's dan me. (*He sits down moodily on the edge of the horse trough.*)

SHIRLEY: You aint going. I thought not. (*He resumes his seat.*)

BARBARA (*calling*): Jenny!

JENNY (*appearing at the shelter door with a plaster on the corner of her mouth*): Yes, Major.

BARBARA: Send Rummy Mitchens out to clear away here.

JENNY: I think she's afraid.

BARBARA (*her resemblance to her mother flashing out for a moment*): Nonsense! she must do as she's told.

Thirteen four: Thirteen stone, four pounds. (A stone is a British weight equal to fourteen pounds.)

JENNY (*calling into the shelter*): Rummy: the Major says you must come.

(*Jenny comes to Barbara, purposely keeping on the side next Bill, lest he should suppose that she shrank from him or bore malice.*)

BARBARA: Poor little Jenny! Are you tired? (*Looking at the wounded cheek.*) Does it hurt?

JENNY: No: it's all right now. It was nothing.

BARBARA (*critically*): It was as hard as he could hit, I expect. Poor Bill! You dont feel angry with him, do you?

JENNY: Oh no, no, no: indeed I dont, Major, bless his poor heart! (*Barbara kisses her; and she runs away merrily into the shelter. Bill writhes with an agonizing return of his new and alarming symptoms, but says nothing. Rummy Mitchens comes from the shelter.*)

BARBARA (*going to meet Rummy*): Now Rummy, bustle. Take in those mugs and plates to be washed; and throw the crumbs about for the birds.

(*Rummy takes the three plates and mugs; but Shirley takes back his mug from her, as there is still some milk left in it.*)

RUMMY: There aint any crumbs. This aint a time to waste good bread on birds.

PRICE (*appearing at the shelter door*): Gentleman come to see the shelter, Major. Says he's your father.

BARBARA: All right. Coming. (*Snobby goes back into the shelter, followed by Barbara.*)

RUMMY (*stealing across to Bill and addressing him in a subdued voice, but with intense conviction*): I'd av the lor of you, you flat eared pignosed potwalloper, if she'd let me. Youre no gentleman, to hit a lady in the face. (*Bill, with greater things moving in him, takes no notice.*)

SHIRLEY (*following her*): Here! in with you and dont get yourself into more trouble by talking.

RUMMY (*with hauteur*): I aint ad the pleasure o being hintroduced to you, as I can remember. (*She goes into the shelter with the plates.*)

SHIRLEY: Thats the —

BILL (*savagely*): Downt you talk to me, d'ye eah? You lea me alown, or Aw'll do you a mischief. Aw'm not dirt under your feet, ennywy.

SHIRLEY (*calmly*): Dont you be afeerd. You aint such prime company that you need expect to be sought after. (*He is about to go into the shelter when Barbara comes out, with Undershaft on her right.*)

BARBARA: Oh, there you are, Mr. Shirley! (*Between them.*) This is my father: I told you he was a Secularist, didn't I? Perhaps youll be able to comfort one another.

UNDERSHAFT (*startled*): A Secularist! Not the least in the world: on the contrary, a confirmed mystic.

BARBARA: Sorry, I'm sure. By the way, papa, what is your religion? in case I have to introduce you again.

UNDERSHAFT: My religion? Well, my dear, I am a Millionaire. That is my religion.

BARBARA: Then I'm afraid you and Mr. Shirley wont be able to comfort one another after all. Youre not a Millionaire, are you, Peter?

SHIRLEY: No; and proud of it.

UNDERSHAFT (*gravely*): Poverty, my friend, is not a thing to be proud of.

SHIRLEY (*angrily*): Who made your millions for you? Me and my like. Whats kep us poor? Keepin you rich. I wouldnt have your conscience, not for all your income.

UNDERSHAFT: I wouldnt have your income, not for all your conscience, Mr. Shirley. (*He goes to the penthouse and sits down on a form.*)

BARBARA (*stopping Shirley adroitly as he is about to retort*): You wouldnt think he was my father, would you, Peter? Will you go into the shelter and lend the lasses a hand for a while: we're worked off our feet.

SHIRLEY (*bitterly*): Yes: I'm in their debt for a meal, aint I?

BARBARA: Oh, not because youre in their debt, but for love of them, Peter, for love of them. (*He cannot understand, and is rather scandalized.*) There! dont stare at me. In with you; and give that conscience of yours a holiday. (*Bustling him into the shelter.*)

SHIRLEY (*as he goes in*): Ah! it's a pity you never was trained to use your reason, miss. Youd have been a very taking lecturer on Secularism.

(*Barbara turns to her father.*)

UNDERSHAFT: Never mind me, my dear. Go about your work; and let me watch it for a while.

BARBARA: All right.

UNDERSHAFT: For instance, whats the matter with that outpatient over there?

BARBARA (*looking at Bill, whose attitude has never changed, and whose expression of brooding wrath has deepened*): Oh, we shall cure him in no time. Just watch. (*She goes over to Bill and waits. He glances up at her and casts his eyes down again, uneasy, but grimmer than ever.*) It would be nice to just stamp on Mog Habbijam's face, wouldnt it, Bill?

BILL (*starting up from the trough in consternation*): It's a loy: Aw never said so. (*She shakes her head.*) Oo taold you wot was in moy mawnd?

BARBARA: Only your new friend.

BILL: Wot new friend?

BARBARA: The devil, Bill. When he gets round people they get miserable, just like you.

BILL (*with a heartbreaking attempt at devil-may-care cheerfulness*): Aw aint miserable. (*He sits down again and stretches his legs in an attempt to seem indifferent.*)

BARBARA: Well, if youre happy, why dont you look happy, as we do?

BILL (*his legs curling back in spite of him*): Aw'm eppy enaff, Aw tell you. Woy cawnt you lea me alown? Wot ev I dan to you? Aw aint smashed your fice, ev Aw?

BARBARA (*softly: wooing his soul*): It's not me thats getting at you, Bill.

BILL: Oo else is it?

BARBARA: Somebody that doesnt intend you to smash women's faces, I suppose. Somebody or something that wants to make a man of you.

BILL (*blustering*): Mike a menn o me! Aint Aw a menn? eh? Oo sez Aw'm not a menn?

BARBARA: Theres a man in you somewhere, I suppose. But why did he let you hit poor little Jenny Hill? That wasn't very manly of him, was it?

BILL (*tormented*): Ev dan wiv it, Aw tell you. Chack it. Aw'm sick o your Jenny Ill and er silly little fice.

BARBARA: Then why do you keep thinking about it? Why does it keep coming up against you in your mind? Youre not getting converted, are you?

BILL (*with conviction*): Not ME. Not lawkly.

BARBARA: Thats right, Bill. Hold out against it. Put out your strength. Dont lets get you cheap. Todger Fairmile said he wrestled for three nights against his salvation harder than he ever wrestled with the Jap at the music hall. He gave in to the Jap when his arm was going to break. But he didnt give in to his salvation until his heart was going to break. Perhaps youll escape that. You havnt any heart, have you?

BILL: Wot d'ye mean? Woy aint Aw got a awt the sime as ennybody else?

BARBARA: A man with a heart wouldnt have bashed poor little Jenny's face, would he?

BILL (*almost crying*): Ow, will you lea me alown? Ev Aw ever offered to meddle with you, that you cam neggin and provowkin me lawk this? (*He writhes convulsively from his eyes to his toes.*)

BARBARA (*with a steady soothing hand on his arm and a gentle voice that never lets him go*): It's your soul thats hurting you, Bill, and not me. Weve been through it all ourselves. Come with us, Bill. (*He looks wildly round.*) To brave manhood on earth and eternal glory in heaven. (*He is on the point of breaking down.*) Come. (*A drum is heard in the shelter; and Bill, with a gasp, escapes from the spell as Barbara turns quickly. Adolphus enters from the shelter with a big drum.*) Oh! there you are, Dolly. Let me introduce a new friend of mine, Mr. Bill Walker. This is my bloke, Bill: Mr. Cusins. (*Cusins salutes with his drumstick.*)

BILL: Gowin to merry im?

BARBARA: Yes.

BILL (*fervently*): Gawd elp im! Gaw-aw-aw-awd elp him!

BARBARA: Why? Do you think he wont be happy with me?

BILL: Awve aony ed to stend it for a mawnin: e'll ev to stend it for a lawftawm.

CUSINS: That is a frightful reflection, Mr. Walker. But I cant tear myself away from her.

BILL: Well, Aw ken. (*To Barbara.*) Eah do you knaow where Aw'm gowin to, and wot Aw'm gowin to do?

BARBARA: Yes: youre going to heaven; and youre coming back here before the week's out to tell me so.

BILL: You loy. Aw'm gowin to Kennintahn, to spit in Todger Fairmawl's eye. Aw beshed Jenny Ill's fice; an nar Aw'll git me aown fice beshed and cam bec and shaow it to er. Ee'll itt me ardern Aw itt her. Thatll mike us square. (*To Adolphus.*) Is thet fair or is it not? Youre a genlmn: you oughter knaow.

BARBARA: Two black eyes wont make one white one, Bill.

BILL: Aw didnt awst you. Cawnt you never keep your mahth shat? Oy awst the genlmn.

CUSINS (*reflectively*): Yes: I think youre right, Mr. Walker. Yes: I should do it. It's curious: it's exactly what an ancient Greek would have done.

BARBARA: But what good will it do?

CUSINS: Well, it will give Mr. Fairmile some exercise; and it will satisfy Mr. Walker's soul.

BILL: Rot! there aint nao such a thing as a saoul. Ah kin you tell wevver Awve a saoul or not? You never seen it.

BARBARA: Ive seen it hurting you when you went against it.

BILL (*with compressed aggravation*): If you was maw gel and took the word awt o me mahth lawk thet, Aw'd give you sathink youd feel urtin, Aw would. (*To Adolphus.*) You tike maw tip, mite. Stop er jawr or youll doy afoah your tawm (*With intense expression.*) Wore aht: thets wot youll be: wore aht. (*He goes away through the gate.*)

CUSINS (*looking after him*): I wonder!

BARBARA: Dolly! (*Indignant, in her mother's manner.*)

CUSINS: Yes, my dear, it's very wearing to be in love with you. If it lasts, I quite think I shall die young.

BARBARA: Should you mind?

CUSINS: Not at all. (*He is suddenly softened, and kisses her over the drum, evidently not for the first time, as people cannot kiss over a big drum without practice. Undershaft coughs.*)

BARBARA: It's all right, papa, weve not forgotten you. Dolly: explain the place to papa: I havnt time. (*She goes busily into the shelter.*)

(*Undershaft and Adolphus now have the yard to themselves. Undershaft, seated on a form, and still keenly attentive, looks hard at Adolphus. Adolphus looks hard at him.*)

UNDERSHAFT: I fancy you guess something of what is in my mind, Mr. Cusins. (*Cusins flourishes his drumsticks as if in the act of beating a lively rataplan, but makes no sound.*) Exactly so. But suppose Barbara finds you out!

CUSINS: You know, I do not admit that I am imposing on Barbara. I am quite genuinely interested in the views of the Salvation Army. The fact is, I am a sort of collector of religions; and the curious thing is that I find I can believe them all. By the way, have you any religion?

UNDERSHAFT: Yes.

CUSINS: Anything out of the common?

UNDERSHAFT: Only that there are two things necessary to Salvation.

CUSINS (*disappointed, but polite*): Ah, the Church Catechism. Charles Lomax also belongs to the Established Church.

UNDERSHAFT: The two things are —

CUSINS: Baptism and —

UNDERSHAFT: No. Money and gunpowder.

CUSINS (*surprised, but interested*): That is the general opinion of our governing classes. The novelty is in hearing any man confess it.

UNDERSHAFT: Just so.

CUSINS: Excuse me: is there any place in your religion for honor, justice, truth, love, mercy, and so forth?

UNDERSHAFT: Yes: they are the graces and luxuries of a rich, strong, and safe life.

CUSINS: Suppose one is forced to choose between them and money or gunpowder?

UNDERSHAFT: Choose money and gunpowder; for without enough of both you cannot afford the others.

CUSINS: That is your religion?

UNDERSHAFT: Yes.

(*The cadence of this reply makes a full close in the conversation. Cusins twists his face dubiously and contemplates Undershaft. Undershaft contemplates him.*)

CUSINS: Barbara wont stand that. You will have to choose between your religion and Barbara.

UNDERSHAFT: So will you, my friend. She will find out that that drum of yours is hollow.

CUSINS: Father Undershaft: you are mistaken: I am a sincere Salvationist. You do not understand the Salvation Army. It is the army of joy, of love, of courage: it has banished the fear and remorse and despair of the old hell-ridden evangelical sects: it marches to fight the devil with trumpet and drum, with music and dancing, with banner and palm, as becomes a sally from heaven by its happy garrison. It picks the waster out of the public house and makes a man of him: it finds a worm wriggling in a back kitchen, and lo! a woman! Men and women of rank too, sons and daughters of the Highest. It takes the poor professor of Greek, the most artificial and self-suppressed of human creatures, from his meal of roots, and lets loose the rhapsodist in him; reveals the true worship of Dionysos to him; sends him down the public street drumming dithyrambs. (*He plays a thundering flourish on the drum.*)

UNDERSHAFT: You will alarm the shelter.

CUSINS: Oh, they are accustomed to these sudden ecstasies. However, if the drum worries you — (*He pockets the drumsticks, unhooks the drum, and stands it on the ground opposite the gateway.*)

UNDERSHAFT: Thank you.

CUSINS: You remember what Euripides says about your money and gunpowder?°

UNDERSHAFT: No.

CUSINS (*declaiming*): One and another
  In money and guns may outpass his brother;
  And men in their millions float and flow
  And seethe with a million hopes as leaven;
  And they win their will; or they miss their will;
  And their hopes are dead or are pined for still;
    But who'er can know
    As the long days go
  That to live is happy, has found his heaven.

My translation: what do you think of it?

UNDERSHAFT: I think, my friend, that if you wish to know, as the long days go, that to live is happy, you must first acquire money enough for a decent life, and power enough to be your own master.

CUSINS: You are damnably discouraging. (*He resumes his declamation.*)
  Is it so hard a thing to see
  That the spirit of God — whate'er it be —

N.B.: The Euripidean verses in the second act of *Major Barbara* are not by me, nor even directly by Euripides. They are by Professor Gilbert Murray, whose English version of *The Bacchae* came into our dramatic literature with all the impulsive power of an original work shortly before *Major Barbara* was begun. The play, indeed, stands indebted to him in more ways than one. B.S.

  The law that abides and changes not, ages long,
  The Eternal and Nature-born: these things be
    strong?
  What else is Wisdom? What of Man's endeavor,
  Of God's high grace so lovely and so great?
  To stand from fear set free? to breathe and
    wait?
  To hold a hand uplifted over Fate?
  And shall not Barbara be loved for ever?

UNDERSHAFT: Euripides mentions Barbara, does he?

CUSINS: It is a fair translation. The word means Loveliness.

UNDERSHAFT: May I ask — as Barbara's father — how much a year she is to be loved for ever on?

CUSINS: As for Barbara's father, that is more your affair than mine. I can feed her by teaching Greek: that is about all.

UNDERSHAFT: Do you consider it a good match for her?

CUSINS (*with polite obstinacy*): Mr. Undershaft: I am in many ways a weak, timid, ineffectual person; and my health is far from satisfactory. But whenever I feel that I must have anything, I get it, sooner or later. I feel that way about Barbara. I dont like marriage: I feel intensely afraid of it; and I dont know what I shall do with Barbara or what she will do with me. But I feel that I and nobody else must marry her. Please regard that as settled. — Not that I wish to be arbitrary; but why should I waste your time in discussing what is inevitable?

UNDERSHAFT: You mean that you will stick at nothing: not even the conversion of the Salvation Army to the worship of Dionysos.

CUSINS: The business of the Salvation Army is to save, not to wrangle about the name of the pathfinder. Dionysos or another: what does it matter?

UNDERSHAFT (*rising and approaching him*): Professor Cusins: you are a young man after my own heart.

CUSINS: Mr. Undershaft: you are, as far as I am able to gather, a most infernal old rascal; but you appeal very strongly to my sense of ironic humor.

(*Undershaft mutely offers his hand. They shake.*)

UNDERSHAFT (*suddenly concentrating himself*): And now to business.

CUSINS: Pardon me. We are discussing religion. Why go back to such an uninteresting and unimportant subject as business?

UNDERSHAFT: Religion is our business at present, because it is through religion alone that we can win Barbara.

CUSINS: Have you, too, fallen in love with Barbara?

UNDERSHAFT: Yes, with a father's love.

CUSINS: A father's love for a grown-up daughter is

the most dangerous of all infatuations. I apologize for mentioning my own pale, coy, mistrustful fancy in the same breath with it.

UNDERSHAFT: Keep to the point. We have to win her; and we are neither of us Methodists.

CUSINS: That doesnt matter. The power Barbara wields here — the power that wields Barbara herself — is not Calvinism, not Presbyterianism, not Methodism —

UNDERSHAFT: Not Greek Paganism either, eh?

CUSINS: I admit that. Barbara is quite original in her religion.

UNDERSHAFT (*triumphantly*): Aha! Barbara Undershaft would be. Her inspiration comes from within herself.

CUSINS: How do you suppose it got there?

UNDERSHAFT (*in towering excitement*): It is the Undershaft inheritance. I shall hand on my torch to my daughter. She shall make my converts and preach my gospel —

CUSINS: What! Money and gunpowder!

UNDERSHAFT: Yes, money and gunpowder. Freedom and power. Command of life and command of death.

CUSINS (*urbanely: trying to bring him down to earth*): This is extremely interesting, Mr. Undershaft. Of course you know that you are mad.

UNDERSHAFT (*with redoubled force*): And you?

CUSINS: Oh, mad as a hatter. You are welcome to my secret since I have discovered yours. But I am astonished. Can a madman make cannons?

UNDERSHAFT: Would anyone else than a madman make them? And now (*with surging energy*) question for question. Can a sane man translate Euripides?

CUSINS: No.

UNDERSHAFT (*seizing him by the shoulder*): Can a sane woman make a man of a waster or a woman of a worm?

CUSINS (*reeling before the storm*): Father Colossus — Mammoth Millionaire —

UNDERSHAFT (*pressing him*): Are there two mad people or three in this Salvation shelter today?

CUSINS: You mean Barbara is as mad as we are?

UNDERSHAFT (*pushing him lightly off and resuming his equanimity suddenly and completely*): Pooh, Professor! let us call things by their proper names. I am a millionaire; you are a poet: Barbara is a savior of souls. What have we three to do with the common mob of slaves and idolators? (*He sits down again with a shrug of contempt for the mob.*)

CUSINS: Take care! Barbara is in love with the common people. So am I. Have you never felt the romance of that love?

UNDERSHAFT (*cold and sardonic*): Have you ever been in love with Poverty, like St. Francis? Have you ever been in love with Dirt, like St. Simeon! Have

you ever been in love with disease and suffering, like our nurses and philanthropists? Such passions are not virtues, but the most unnatural of all the vices. This love of the common people may please an earl's granddaughter and a university professor; but I have been a common man and a poor man; and it has no romance for me. Leave it to the poor to pretend that poverty is a blessing: leave it to the coward to make a religion of his cowardice by preaching humility: we know better than that. We three must stand together above the common people: how else can we help their children to climb up beside us? Barbara must belong to us, not to the Salvation Army.

CUSINS: Well, I can only say that if you think you will get her away from the Salvation Army by talking to her as you have been talking to me, you dont know Barbara.

UNDERSHAFT: My friend: I never ask for what I can buy.

CUSINS (*in a white fury*): Do I understand you to imply that you can buy Barbara?

UNDERSHAFT: No; but I can buy the Salvation Army.

CUSINS: Quite impossible.

UNDERSHAFT: You shall see. All religious organizations exist by selling themselves to the rich.

CUSINS: Not the Army. That is the Church of the poor.

UNDERSHAFT: All the more reason for buying it.

CUSINS: I dont think you quite know what the Army does for the poor.

UNDERSHAFT: Oh yes I do. It draws their teeth: that is enough for me as a man of business.

CUSINS: Nonsense! It makes them sober —

UNDERSHAFT: I prefer sober workmen. The profits are larger.

CUSINS: — honest —

UNDERSHAFT: Honest workmen are the most economical.

CUSINS: — attached to their homes —

UNDERSHAFT: So much the better: they will put up with anything sooner than change their shop.

CUSINS: — happy —

UNDERSHAFT: An invaluable safeguard against revolution.

CUSINS: — unselfish —

UNDERSHAFT: Indifferent to their own interests, which suits me exactly.

CUSINS: — with their thoughts on heavenly things —

UNDERSHAFT (*rising*): And not on Trade Unionism nor Socialism. Excellent.

CUSINS (*revolted*): You really are an infernal old rascal.

UNDERSHAFT (*indicating Peter Shirley, who has just come from the shelter and strolled dejectedly down the yard between them*): And this is an honest man!

SHIRLEY: Yes; and what av I got by it? (*He passes on

bitterly and sits on the form, in the corner of the penthouse.)

(*Snobby Price, beaming sanctimoniously, and Jenny Hill, with a tambourine full of coppers, come from the shelter and go to the drum, on which Jenny begins to count the money.*)

UNDERSHAFT (*replying to Shirley*): Oh, your employers must have got a good deal by it from first to last. (*He sits on the table, with one foot on the side form, Cusins, overwhelmed, sits down on the same form nearer the shelter. Barbara comes from the shelter to the middle of the yard. She is excited and a little overwrought.*)

BARBARA: Weve just had a splendid experience meeting at the other gate in Cripps's lane. Ive hardly ever seen them so much moved as they were by your confession, Mr. Price.

PRICE: I could almost be glad of my past wickedness if I could believe that it would elp to keep hathers stright.

BARBARA: So it will, Snobby. How much, Jenny?

JENNY: Four and tenpence, Major.

BARBARA: Oh Snobby, if you had given your poor mother just one more kick, we should have got the whole five shillings!

PRICE: If she heard you say that, miss, she'd be sorry I didnt. But I'm glad. Oh what a joy it will be to her when she hears I'm saved!

UNDERSHAFT: Shall I contribute the odd twopence, Barbara? The millionaire's mite, eh? (*He takes a couple of pennies from his pocket.*)

BARBARA: How did you make that twopence?

UNDERSHAFT: As usual. By selling cannons, torpedoes, submarines, and my new patent Grand Duke hand grenade.

BARBARA: Put it back in your pocket. You cant buy your salvation here for twopence: you must work it out.

UNDERSHAFT: Is twopence not enough? I can afford a little more, if you press me.

BARBARA: Two million millions would not be enough. There is bad blood on your hands; and nothing but good blood can cleanse them. Money is no use. Take it away. (*She turns to Cusins.*) Dolly: you must write another letter for me to the papers. (*He makes a wry face.*) Yes: I know you dont like it; but it must be done. The starvation this winter is beating us: everybody is unemployed. The General says we must close this shelter if we cant get more money. I force the collections at the meetings until I am ashamed: dont I, Snobby?

PRICE: It's a fair treat to see you work it, miss. The way you got them up from three-and-six to four-and-ten with that hymn, penny by penny and verse by verse, was a caution. Not a Cheap Jack on Mile End Waste could touch you at it.

BARBARA: Yes: but I wish we could do without it. I am getting at last to think more of the collection than of the people's souls. And what are those hatfuls of pence and halfpence? We want thousands! tens of thousands! hundreds of thousands! I want to convert people, not to be always begging for the Army in a way I'd die sooner than beg for myself.

UNDERSHAFT (*in profound irony*): Genuine unselfishness is capable of anything, my dear.

BARBARA (*unsuspectingly, as she turns away to take the money from the drum and put it in a cash bag she carries*): Yes, isnt it? (*Undershaft looks sardonically at Cusins.*)

CUSINS (*aside to Undershaft*): Mephistopheles! Machiavelli!°

BARBARA (*tears coming into her eyes as she ties the bag and pockets it*): How are we to feed them? I cant talk religion to a man with bodily hunger in his eyes. (*Almost breaking down.*) It's frightful.

JENNY (*running to her*): Major, dear —

BARBARA (*rebounding*): No: dont comfort me. It will be all right. We shall get the money.

UNDERSHAFT: How?

JENNY: By praying for it, of course. Mrs. Baines says she prayed for it last night; and she has never prayed for it in vain: never once. (*She goes to the gate and looks out into the street.*)

BARBARA (*who has dried her eyes and regained her composure*): By the way, dad, Mrs. Baines has come to march with us to our big meeting this afternoon and she is very anxious to meet you, for some reason or other. Perhaps she'll convert you.

UNDERSHAFT: I shall be delighted, my dear.

JENNY (*at the gate: excitedly*): Major! Major! here's that man back again.

BARBARA: What man?

JENNY: The man that hit me. Oh, I hope he's coming back to join us.

(*Bill Walker, with frost on his jacket, comes through the gate, his hands deep in his pockets and his chin sunk between his shoulders, like a cleaned-out gambler. He halts between Barbara and the drum.*)

BARBARA: Hullo, Bill! Back already!

BILL (*nagging at her*): Bin talkin ever sence, ev you?

Mephistopheles! Machiavelli!: In the Faust legend Mephistopheles tempts Faust with worldly promises and strikes a bargain for Faust's soul. Niccolò Machiavelli (1469–1527) was an Italian political philosopher whose name became synonymous with political cynicism and treachery.

BARBARA: Pretty nearly. Well, has Todger paid you out for poor Jenny's jaw?

BILL: Nao e aint.

BARBARA: I thought your jacket looked a bit snowy.

BILL: Sao it is snaowy. You want to knaow where the snaow cam from, downt you?

BARBARA: Yes.

BILL: Well, it cam from orf the grahnd in Pawkinses Corner in Kennintahn. It got rabbed orf be maw shaoulders: see?

BARBARA: Pity you didnt rub some off with your knees, Bill! That would have done you a lot of good.

BILL (*with sour mirthless humor*): Aw was sivin anather menn's knees at the tawm. E was kneelin on moy ed, e was.

JENNY: Who was kneeling on your head?

BILL: Todger was. E was pryin for me: pryin camfortable wiv me as a cawpet. Sow was Mog. Sao was the aol bloomin meeting. Mog she sez "Ow Lawd brike is stabborn sperrit; bat downt urt is dear art." Thet was wot she said. "Downt urt is dear art"! An er blowk — thirteen stun four! — kneelin wiv all is wight on me. Fanny, aint it?

JENNY: Oh no. We're so sorry, Mr. Walker.

BARBARA (*enjoying it frankly*): Nonsense! of course it's funny. Served you right, Bill! You must have done something to him first.

BILL (*doggedly*): Aw did wot Aw said Aw'd do. Aw spit in is eye. E looks ap at the skoy and sez, "Ow that Aw should be fahnd worthy to be spit upon for the gospel's sike!" e sez; an Mog sez "Glaory Allelloolier!"; and then e called me Braddher an dahned me as if Aw was a kid and he was me mather worshin me a Setterda nawt. Aw ednt jast nao shaow wiv im at all. Arf the street pryed; an the tather arf larfed fit to split theirselves. (*To Barbara.*) There are you settisfawd nah?

BARBARA (*her eyes dancing*): Wish I'd been there, Bill.

BILL: Yus: youd a got in a hextra bit o talk on me, wouldnt you?

JENNY: I'm so sorry, Mr. Walker.

BILL (*fiercely*): Downt you gow being sorry for me: youve no call. Listen eah. Aw browk your jawr.

JENNY: No, it didnt hurt me: indeed it didnt, except for a moment. It was only that I was frightened.

BILL: Aw downt want to be forgive be you, or be ennybody. Wot Aw did Aw'll py for. Aw trawd to gat me aown jawr browk to settisfaw you —

JENNY (*distressed*): Oh no —

BILL (*impatiently*): Tell y' Aw did: cawnt you listen to wots being taold you? All Aw got be it was being mide a sawt of in the pablic street for me pines. Well, if Aw cawnt settisfaw you one wy, Aw ken anather. Listen eah! Aw ed two quid sived

agen the frost; an Awve a pahnd of it left. A mite o mawn last week ed words with the judy e's gowing to merry. E give er wot-for; an e's bin fawned fifteen bob. E ed a rawt to itt er cause they was gowin to be merrid; but Aw ednt nao rawt to itt you; sao put anather fawv bob on an call it a pahnd's worth. (*He produces a sovereign.*) Eahs the manney. Tike it, and lets ev no more o your forgivin an prying and your Mijor jawrin me. Let wot Aw dan be dan an pide for; and let there be a end of it.

JENNY: Oh, I couldn't take it, Mr. Walker. But if you would give a shilling or two to poor Rummy Mitchens! you really did hurt her; and she's old.

BILL (*contemptuously*): Not lawkly. Aw'd give her anather as soon as look at er. Let her ev the lawr o me as she threatened! She aint forgiven me: not mach. Wot Aw dan to er is not on me mawnd — wot she (*indicating Barbara*) mawt call on me conscience — no more than stickin a pig. It's this Christian gime o yours that Aw wownt ev plyed agen me: this bloomin forgivin an neggin an jawrin that mikes a menn thet sore that iz lawf's a burdn to im. Aw wownt ev it, Aw tell you; sao tike your manney and stop thraowin your silly beshed fice hap agen me.

JENNY: Major: may I take a little of it for the Army?

BARBARA: No: the Army is not to be bought. We want your soul, Bill; and we'll take nothing less.

BILL (*bitterly*): Aw knaow. Me an maw few shillins is not good enaff for you. Youre a earl's grendorter, you are. Nathink less than a andered pahnd for you.

UNDERSHAFT: Come, Barbara! you could do a great deal of good with a hundred pounds. If you will set this gentleman's mind at ease by taking his pound, I will give the other ninety-nine.

(*Bill, dazed by such opulence, instinctively touches his cap.*)

BARBARA: Oh, youre too extravagant, papa. Bill offers twenty pieces of silver. All you need offer is the other ten. That will make the standard price to buy anybody who's for sale. I'm not; and the Army's not. (*To Bill.*) Youll never have another quiet moment, Bill, until you come around to us. You cant stand out against your salvation.

BILL (*sullenly*): Aw cawnt stend aht agen music awl wrastlers and awtful tangued women. Awve offered to py. Aw can do no more. Tike it or leave it. There it is. (*He throws the sovereign on the drum and sits down on the horse trough. The coin fascinates Snobby Price, who takes an early opportunity of dropping his cap on it.*)

(*Mrs. Baines comes from the shelter. She is dressed as a Salvation Army Commissioner. She is an earnest looking woman of about 40, with a caressing, urgent voice, and an appealing manner.*)

BARBARA: This is my father, Mrs. Baines. (*Undershaft comes from the table, taking his hat off with marked civility.*) Try what you can do with him. He wont listen to me, because he remembers what a fool I was when I was a baby. (*She leaves them together and chats with Jenny.*)

MRS. BAINES: Have you been shown over the shelter, Mr. Undershaft? You know the work we're doing, of course.

UNDERSHAFT (*very civilly*): The whole nation knows it, Mrs. Baines.

MRS. BAINES: No, sir: the whole nation does not know it, or we should not be crippled as we are for want of money to carry our work through the length and breadth of the land. Let me tell you that there would have been rioting this winter in London but for us.

UNDERSHAFT: You really think so?

MRS. BAINES: I know it. I remember 1886, when you rich gentlemen hardened your hearts against the cry of the poor. They broke the windows of your clubs in Pall Mall.

UNDERSHAFT (*gleaming with approval of their method*): And the Mansion House Fund went up next day from thirty thousand pounds to seventy-nine thousand! I remember quite well.

MRS. BAINES: Well, wont you help me to get at the people? They wont break windows then. Come here, Price. Let me show you to this gentleman (*Price comes to be inspected*). Do you remember the window breaking?

PRICE: My ole father thought it was the revolution, maam.

MRS. BAINES: Would you break windows now?

PRICE: Oh no, maam. The windows of eaven av bin opened to me. I know now that the rich man is a sinner like myself.

RUMMY (*appearing above at the loft door*): Snobby Price!

SNOBBY: Wot is it?

RUMMY: Your mother's askin for you at the other gate in Cripps's Lane. She's heard about your confession (*Price turns pale.*)

MRS. BAINES: Go, Mr. Price; and pray with her.

JENNY: You can go through the shelter, Snobby.

PRICE (*to Mrs. Baines*): I couldnt face her now, maam, with all the weight of my sins fresh on me. Tell her she'll find her son at ome, waitin for her in prayer. (*He skulks off through the gate, incidentally stealing the sovereign on his way out by picking up his cap from the drum.*)

MRS. BAINES (*with swimming eyes*): You see how we take the anger and the bitterness against you out of their hearts, Mr. Undershaft.

UNDERSHAFT: It is certainly most convenient and gratifying to all large employers of labor, Mrs. Baines.

MRS. BAINES: Barbara: Jenny: I have good news: most wonderful news. (*Jenny runs to her.*) My prayers have been answered. I told you they would, Jenny, didnt I?

JENNY: Yes, yes.

BARBARA (*moving nearer to the drum*): Have we got money enough to keep the shelter open?

MRS. BAINES: I hope we shall have enough to keep all the shelters open. Lord Saxmundham has promised us five thousand pounds —

BARBARA: Hooray!

JENNY: Glory!

MRS. BAINES: — if —

BARBARA: "If!" If what?

MRS. BAINES: — if five other gentlemen will give a thousand each to make it up to ten thousand.

BARBARA: Who is Lord Saxmundham? I never heard of him.

UNDERSHAFT (*who has pricked up his ears at the peer's name, and is now watching Barbara curiously*): A new creation, my dear. You have heard of Sir Horace Bodger?

BARBARA: Bodger! Do you mean the distiller? Bodger's whisky!

UNDERSHAFT: That is the man. He is one of the greatest of our public benefactors. He restored the cathedral at Hakington. They made him a baronet for that. He gave half a million to the funds of his party: they made him a baron for that.

SHIRLEY: What will they give him for the five thousand?

UNDERSHAFT: There is nothing left to give him. So the five thousand, I should think, is to save his soul.

MRS. BAINES: Heaven grant it may! Oh Mr. Undershaft, you have some very rich friends. Cant you help us towards the other five thousand? We are going to hold a great meeting this afternoon at the Assembly Hall in the Mile End Road. If I could only announce that one gentleman had come forward to support Lord Saxmundham, others would follow. Dont you know somebody? couldnt you? wouldnt you? (*Her eyes fill with tears.*) Oh, think of those poor people, Mr. Undershaft: think of how much it means to them, and how little to a great man like you.

UNDERSHAFT (*sardonically gallant*): Mrs. Baines: you are irresistible. I cant disappoint you; and I cant deny myself the satisfaction of making Bodger pay up. You shall have your five thousand pounds.

MRS. BAINES: Thank God!

UNDERSHAFT: You dont thank me?

MRS. BAINES: Oh sir, dont try to be cynical: dont be ashamed of being a good man. The Lord will bless you abundantly; and our prayers will be like a strong fortification round you all the days of your life. (*With a touch of caution.*) You will let me have the check to show at the meeting, wont you? Jenny: go in and fetch a pen and ink. (*Jenny runs to the shelter door.*)

UNDERSHAFT: Do not disturb Miss Hill: I have a fountain pen. (*Jenny halts. He sits at the table and writes the check. Cusins rises to make room for him. They all watch him silently.*)

BILL (*cynically, aside to Barbara, his voice and accent horribly debased*): Wot prawce selvytion nah?

BARBARA: Stop. (*Undershaft stops writing: they all turn to her in surprise.*) Mrs. Baines: are you really going to take this money?

MRS. BAINES (*astonished*): Why not, dear?

BARBARA: Why not! Do you know what my father is? Have you forgotten that Lord Saxmundham is Bodger the whisky man? Do you remember how we implored the County Council to stop him from writing Bodger's Whisky in letters of fire against the sky; so that the poor drink-ruined creatures on the Embankment could not wake up from their snatches of sleep without being reminded of their deadly thirst by that wicked sky sign? Do you know that the worst thing I have had to fight here is not the devil, but Bodger, Bodger, Bodger, with his whisky, his distilleries, and his tied houses? Are you going to make our shelter another tied house for him, and ask me to keep it?

BILL: Rotten dranken whisky it is too.

MRS. BAINES: Dear Barbara: Lord Saxmundham has a soul to be saved like any of us. If heaven had found the way to make a good use of his money, are we to set ourselves up against the answer to our prayers?

BARBARA: I know he has a soul to be saved. Let him come down here; and I'll do my best to help him to his salvation. But he wants to send his check down to buy us, and go on being as wicked as ever.

UNDERSHAFT (*with a reasonableness which Cusins alone perceives to be ironical*): My dear Barbara: alcohol is a very necessary article. It heals the sick —

BARBARA: It does nothing of the sort.

UNDERSHAFT: Well, it assists the doctor: that is perhaps a less questionable way of putting it. It makes life bearable to millions of people who could not endure their existence if they were quite sober. It enables Parliament to do things at eleven at night that no sane person would do at eleven in the morning. Is it Bodger's fault that this inestimable gift is deplorably abused by less than one per cent of the poor? (*He turns again to the table; signs the check; and crosses it.*)

MRS. BAINES: Barbara: will there be less drinking or more if all those poor souls we are saving come tomorrow and find the doors of our shelters shut in their faces? Lord Saxmundham gives us the money to stop drinking — to take his own business from him.

CUSINS (*impishly*): Pure self-sacrifice on Bodger's part, clearly! Bless dear Bodger! (*Barbara almost breaks down as Adolphus, too, fails her.*)

UNDERSHAFT (*tearing out the check and pocketing the book as he rises and goes past Cusins to Mrs. Baines*): I also, Mrs. Baines, may claim a little disinterestedness. Think of my business! think of the widows and orphans! the men and lads torn to pieces with shrapnel and poisoned with lyddite! (*Mrs. Baines shrinks; but he goes on remorselessly.*) the oceans of blood, not one drop of which is shed in a really just cause! the ravaged crops! the peaceful peasants forced, women and men, to till their fields under the fire of opposing armies on pain of starvation! the bad blood of the fierce little cowards at home who egg on others to fight for the gratification of their national vanity! All this makes money for me: I am never richer, never busier than when the papers are full of it. Well, it is your work to preach peace on earth and good will to men. (*Mrs. Baines's face lights up again.*) Every convert you make is a vote against war. (*Her lips move in prayer.*) Yet I give you this money to help you to hasten my own commercial ruin. (*He gives her the check.*)

CUSINS (*mounting the form in an ecstasy of mischief*): The millennium will be inaugurated by the unselfishness of Undershaft and Bodger. Oh be joyful! (*He takes the drumsticks from his pocket and flourishes them.*)

MRS. BAINES (*taking the check*): The longer I live the more proof I see that there is an Infinite Goodness that turns everything to the work of salvation sooner or later. Who would have thought that any good could have come out of war and drink? And yet their profits are brought today to the feet of salvation to do its blessed work. (*She is affected to tears.*)

JENNY (*running to Mrs. Baines and throwing her arms round her*): Oh dear! how blessed, how glorious it all is!

CUSINS (*in a convulsion of irony*): Let us seize this unspeakable moment. Let us march to the great meeting at once. Excuse me just an instant. (*He rushes into the shelter. Jenny takes her tambourine from the drum head.*)

MRS. BAINES: Mr. Undershaft: have you ever seen a thousand people fall on their knees with one impulse and pray? Come with us to the meeting. Barbara shall tell them that the Army is saved, and saved through you.

CUSINS (*returning impetuously from the shelter with a flag and a trombone, and coming between Mrs. Baines and Undershaft*): You shall carry the flag down the first street, Mrs. Baines. (*He gives her the flag.*) Mr. Undershaft is a gifted trombonist: he shall intone an Olympian diapason° to the West Ham Salvation March. (*Aside to Undershaft, as he forces the trombone on him.*) Blow, Machiavelli, blow.

UNDERSHAFT (*aside to him, as he takes the trombone*): The Trumpet in Zion! (*Cusins rushes to the drum, which he takes up and puts on. Undershaft continues, aloud.*) I will do my best. I could vamp a bass if I knew the tune.

CUSINS: It is a wedding chorus from one of Donizetti's operas; but we have converted it. We convert everything to good here, including Bodger. You remember the chorus. "For thee immense rejoicing — immenso giubilo — immenso giubilo." (*With drum obbligato.*) Rum tum ti tum tum, tum tum ti ta —

BARBARA: Dolly: you are breaking my heart.

CUSINS: What is a broken heart more or less here? Dionysos° Undershaft has descended. I am possessed.

MRS. BAINES: Come, Barbara: I must have my dear Major to carry the flag with me.

JENNY: Yes, yes, Major darling.

CUSINS (*Snatches the tambourine out of Jenny's hand and mutely offers it to Barbara.*)

BARBARA (*coming forward a little as she puts the offer behind her with a shudder, while Cusins recklessly tosses the tambourine back to Jenny and goes to the gate*): I cant come.

JENNY: Not come!

MRS. BAINES (*with tears in her eyes*): Barbara: do you think I am wrong to take the money?

BARBARA (*impulsively going to her and kissing her*): No, no: God help you, dear, you must: you are saving the Army. Go; and may you have a great meeting!

JENNY: But arnt you coming?

BARBARA: No. (*She begins taking off the silver S brooch from her collar.*)

MRS. BAINES: Barbara: what are you doing?

diapason: An outburst of harmonious sound.
Dionysos: The Greek god of wine and the symbol of life-giving power.

JENNY: Why are you taking your badge off? You cant be going to leave us, Major.

BARBARA (*quietly*): Father: come here.

UNDERSHAFT (*coming to her*): My dear! (*Seeing that she is going to pin the badge on his collar, he retreats to the penthouse in some alarm.*)

BARBARA (*following him*): Don't be frightened. (*She pins the badge on and steps back towards the table, showing him to the others.*) There! It's not much for £5000, is it?

MRS. BAINES: Barbara: if you wont come and pray with us, promise me you will pray for us.

BARBARA: I cant pray now. Perhaps I shall never pray again.

MRS. BAINES: Barbara!

JENNY: Major!

BARBARA (*almost delirious*): I cant bear any more. Quick march!

CUSINS (*calling to the procession in the street outside*): Off we go. Play up, there! Immenso giubilo. (*He gives the time with his drum; and the band strikes up the march, which rapidly becomes more distant as the procession moves briskly away.*)

MRS. BAINES: I must go, dear. Youre overworked: you will be all right tomorrow. We'll never lose you. Now Jenny: step out with the old flag. Blood and Fire! (*She marches out through the gate with her flag.*)

JENNY: Glory Hallelujah! (*Flourishing her tambourine and marching.*)

UNDERSHAFT (*to Cusins, as he marches out past him easing the slide of his trombone*): "My ducats and my daughter"!°

CUSINS (*following him out*): Money and gunpowder!

BARBARA: Drunkenness and Murder! My God: why hast thou forsaken me?

(*She sinks on the form with her face buried in her hands. The march passes away into silence. Bill Walker steals across to her.*)

BILL (*taunting*): Wot prawce selvytion nah?

SHIRLEY: Don't you hit her when she's down.

BILL: She it me wen aw wiz dahn. Waw shouldnt Aw git a bit o me aown beck?

BARBARA (*raising her head*): I didnt take your money, Bill. (*She crosses the yard to the gate and turns her back on the two men to hide her face from them.*)

BILL (*sneering after her*): Naow, it warnt enaff for you. (*Turning to the drum, he misses the money.*)

"**My . . . daughter**"! Shylock's line in Shakespeare's *Merchant of Venice*. When Shylock's daughter elopes, taking some of her father's money with her, Shylock is more concerned with the loss of his money (ducats) than with the loss of his daughter.

Ellow! If you aint took it sammun else ez. Weres it gorn? Bly me if Jenny Ill didnt tike it arter all!

RUMMY (*screaming at him from the loft*): You lie, you dirty blackguard! Snobby Price pinched it off the drum when he took up his cap. I was up here all the time an see im do it.

BILL: Wot! Stowl may manney! Waw didnt you call thief on him, you silly aold macker you?

RUMMY: To serve you aht for ittin me across the fice. It's cost y'pahnd, that az. (*Raising a paeon of squalid triumph.*) I done you. I'm even with you. Uve ad it aht o y — (*Bill snatches up Shirley's mug and hurls it at her. She slams the loft door and vanishes. The mug smashes against the door and falls in fragments.*)

BILL (*beginning to chuckle*): Tell us, aol menn, wot o'clock this mawnin was it wen im as they call Snobby Prawce was sived?

BARBARA (*turning to him more composedly, and with unspoiled sweetness*): About half past twelve, Bill. And he pinched your pound at a quarter to two. I know. Well, you cant afford to lose it. I'll send it to you.

BILL (*his voice and accent suddenly improving*): Not if Aw wiz to stawve for it. Aw aint to be bought.

SHIRLEY: Aint you? Youd sell yourself to the devil for a pint o beer; only there aint no devil to make the offer.

BILL (*unashamed*): Sao Aw would, mite, and often ev, cheerful. But she cawnt baw me. (*Approaching Barbara.*) You wanted maw soul, did you? Well, you aint got it.

BARBARA: I nearly got it, Bill. But weve sold it back to you for ten thousand pounds.

SHIRLEY: And dear at the money!

BARBARA: No, Peter: it was worth more than money.

BILL (*salvationproof*): It's nao good: you cawnt get rahnd me nah. Aw downt blieve in it; and Awve seen tody that Aw was rawt. (*Going.*) Sao long, aol soupkitchener! Ta, ta, Mijor Earl's Grendorter! (*Turning at the gate.*) Wot prawce selvytion nah? Snobby Prawce! Ha! ha!

BARBARA (*offering her hand*): Goodbye, Bill.

BILL (*taken aback, half plucks his cap off; then shoves it on again defiantly*): Get aht. (*Barbara drops her hand, discouraged. He has a twinge of remorse.*) But thets aw rawt, you knaow. Nathink pasnl. Naow mellice. Sao long, Judy. (*He goes.*)

BARBARA: No malice. So long, Bill.

SHIRLEY (*shaking his head*): You make too much of him, miss, in your innocence.

BARBARA (*going to him*): Peter: I'm like you now. Cleaned out, and lost my job.

SHIRLEY: Youve youth an hope. Thats two better than me.

BARBARA: I'll get you a job, Peter. Thats hope for you: the youth will have to be enough for me. (*She counts her money.*) I have just enough left for two teas at Lockharts, a Rowton doss for you, and my tram and bus home. (*He frowns and rises with offended pride. She takes his arm.*) Dont be proud, Peter: it's sharing between friends. And promise me youll talk to me and not let me cry. (*She draws him towards the gate.*)

SHIRLEY: Well, I'm not accustomed to talk to the like of you —

BARBARA (*gently*): Yes, yes: you must talk to me. Tell me about Tom Paine's books and Bradlaugh's lectures.° Come along.

SHIRLEY: Ah, if you would only read Tom Paine in the proper spirit, miss! (*They go out through the gate together.*)

ACT III

(*Next day after lunch Lady Britomart is writing in the library in Wilton Crescent. Sarah is reading in the armchair near the window. Barbara, in ordinary fashionable dress, pale and brooding, is on the settee. Charles Lomax enters. He starts on seeing Barbara fashionably attired and in low spirits.*)

LOMAX: Youve left off your uniform!

(*Barbara says nothing; but an expression of pain passes over her face.*)

LADY BRITOMART (*warning him in low tones to be careful*): Charles!

LOMAX (*much concerned, coming behind the settee and bending sympathetically over Barbara*): I'm awfully sorry, Barbara. You know I helped you all I could with the concertina and so forth. (*Momentously.*) Still, I have never shut my eyes to the fact that there is a certain amount of tosh about the Salvation Army. Now the claims of the Church of England —

LADY BRITOMART: Thats enough, Charles. Speak of something suited to your mental capacity.

LOMAX: But surely the Church of England is suited to all our capacities.

BARBARA (*pressing his hand*): Thank you for your sympathy, Cholly. Now go and spoon with Sarah.

LOMAX (*dragging a chair from the writing table and seating himself affectionately by Sarah's side*): How is my ownest today?

Tom Paine's . . . Bradlaugh's lectures: Thomas Paine (1737–1809) was a political radical whose works urged revolution, particularly in France and the United States. Charles Bradlaugh (1833–1891) was a social reformer and political free thinker who gave lectures under the pseudonym Iconoclast.

SARAH: I wish you wouldnt tell Cholly to do things, Barbara. He always comes straight and does them. Cholly: we're going to the works this afternoon.

LOMAX: What works?

SARAH: The cannon works.

LOMAX: What? your governor's shop!

SARAH: Yes.

LOMAX: Oh I say!

(*Cusins enters in poor condition. He also starts visibly when he sees Barbara without her uniform.*)

BARBARA: I expected you this morning, Dolly. Didnt you guess that?

CUSINS (*sitting down beside her*): I'm sorry. I have only just breakfasted.

SARAH: But weve just finished lunch.

BARBARA: Have you had one of your bad nights?

CUSINS: No: I had rather a good night: in fact, one of the most remarkable nights I have ever passed.

BARBARA: The meeting?

CUSINS: No: after the meeting.

LADY BRITOMART: You should have gone to bed after the meeting. What were you doing?

CUSINS: Drinking.

LADY BRITOMART:⎤ Adolphus!
SARAH: ⎟ Dolly!
BARBARA: ⎟ Dolly!
LOMAX: ⎦ Oh I say!

LADY BRITOMART: What were you drinking, may I ask?

CUSINS: A most devilish kind of Spanish burgundy, warranted free from added alcohol: a Temperance burgundy in fact. Its richness in natural alcohol made any addition superfluous.

BARBARA: Are you joking, Dolly?

CUSINS (*patiently*): No. I have been making a night of it with the nominal head of this household: that is all.

LADY BRITOMART: Andrew made you drunk!

CUSINS: No: he only provided the wine. I think it was Dionysos who made me drunk. (*To Barbara.*) I told you I was possessed.

LADY BRITOMART: Youre not sober yet. Go home to bed at once.

CUSINS: I have never before ventured to reproach you, Lady Brit; but how could you marry the Prince of Darkness?

LADY BRITOMART: It was much more excusable to marry him than to get drunk with him. That is a new accomplishment of Andrew's, by the way. He usent to drink.

CUSINS: He doesnt now. He only sat there and completed the wreck of my moral basis, the rout of my convictions, the purchase of my soul. He cares for you, Barbara. That is what makes him so dangerous to me.

BARBARA: That has nothing to do with it, Dolly. There are larger loves and diviner dreams than the fireside ones. You know that, dont you?

CUSINS: Yes: that is our understanding. I know it. I hold to it. Unless he can win me on that holier ground he may amuse me for a while; but he can get no deeper hold, strong as he is.

BARBARA: Keep to that; and the end will be right. Now tell me what happened at the meeting?

CUSINS: It was an amazing meeting. Mrs. Baines almost died of emotion. Jenny Hill simply gibbered with hysteria. The Prince of Darkness played his trombone like a madman: its brazen roarings were like the laughter of the damned. 117 conversions took place then and there. They prayed with the most touching sincerity and gratitude for Bodger, and for the anonymous donor of the £5000. Your father would not let his name be given.

LOMAX: That was rather fine of the old man, you know. Most chaps would have wanted the advertisement.

CUSINS: He said all the charitable institutions would be down on him like kites on a battlefield if he gave his name.

LADY BRITOMART: Thats Andrew all over. He never does a proper thing without giving an improper reason for it.

CUSINS: He convinced me that I have all my life been doing improper things for proper reasons.

LADY BRITOMART: Adolphus: now that Barbara has left the Salvation Army, you had better leave it too. I will not have you playing that drum in the streets.

CUSINS: Your orders are already obeyed, Lady Brit.

BARBARA: Dolly: were you ever really in earnest about it? Would you have joined if you had never seen me?

CUSINS (*disingenuously*): Well — er — well, possibly, as a collector of religions —

LOMAX (*cunningly*): Not as a drummer, though, you know. You are a very clearheaded brainy chap, Dolly; and it must have been apparent to you that there is a certain amount of tosh about —

LADY BRITOMART: Charles: if you must drivel, drivel like a grown-up man and not like a schoolboy.

LOMAX (*out of countenance*): Well, drivel is drivel, dont you know, whatever a man's age.

LADY BRITOMART: In good society in England, Charles, men drivel at all ages by repeating silly formulas with an air of wisdom. Schoolboys make their own formulas out of slang, like you. When they reach your age, and get political private secretaryships and things of that sort, they drop slang and get their formulas out of the *Spectator* or *The Times*. You had better confine yourself to *The Times*. You will find that there is a certain amount of tosh about *The Times*; but at least its language is reputable.

LOMAX (*overwhelmed*): You are so awfully strong-minded, Lady Brit —

LADY BRITOMART: Rubbish! (*Morrison comes in.*) What is it?

MORRISON: If you please, my lady, Mr. Undershaft has just drove up to the door.

LADY BRITOMART: Well, let him in. (*Morrison hesitates.*) Whats the matter with you?

MORRISON: Shall I announce him, my lady; or is he at home here, so to speak, my lady?

LADY BRITOMART: Announce him.

MORRISON: Thank you, my lady. You wont mind my asking, I hope. The occasion is in a manner of speaking new to me.

LADY BRITOMART: Quite right. Go and let him in.

MORRISON: Thank you, my lady. (*He withdraws.*)

LADY BRITOMART: Children: go and get ready. (*Sarah and Barbara go upstairs for their out-of-door wraps.*) Charles: go and tell Stephen to come down here in five minutes: you will find him in the drawing room. (*Charles goes.*) Adolphus: tell them to send round the carriage in about fifteen minutes. (*Adolphus goes.*)

MORRISON (*at the door*): Mr. Undershaft.

(*Undershaft comes in. Morrison goes out.*)

UNDERSHAFT: Alone! How fortunate!

LADY BRITOMART (*rising*): Dont be sentimental, Andrew. Sit down. (*She sits on the settee: he sits beside her, on her left. She comes to the point before he has time to breathe.*) Sarah must have £800 a year until Charles Lomax comes into his property. Barbara will need more, and need it permanently, because Adolphus hasnt any property.

UNDERSHAFT (*resignedly*): Yes, my dear: I will see to it. Anything else? for yourself, for instance?

LADY BRITOMART: I want to talk to you about Stephen.

UNDERSHAFT (*rather wearily*): Dont, my dear. Stephen doesnt interest me.

LADY BRITOMART: He does interest me. He is our son.

UNDERSHAFT: Do you really think so? He has induced us to bring him into the world; but he chose his parents very incongruously, I think. I see nothing of myself in him, and less of you.

LADY BRITOMART: Andrew: Stephen is an excellent son, and a most steady, capable, highminded young man. You are simply trying to find an excuse for disinheriting him.

UNDERSHAFT: My dear Biddy: the Undershaft tradition disinherits him. It would be dishonest of me to leave the cannon foundry to my son.

LADY BRITOMART: It would be most unnatural and improper of you to leave it to anyone else, Andrew. Do you suppose this wicked and immoral tradition can be kept up for ever? Do you pretend that Stephen could not carry on the foundry just as well as all the other sons of the big business houses?

UNDERSHAFT: Yes: he could learn the office routine without understanding the business, like all the other sons; and the firm would go by its own momentum until the real Undershaft — probably an Italian or a German — would invent a new method and cut him out.

LADY BRITOMART: There is nothing that any Italian or German could do that Stephen could not do. And Stephen at least has breeding.

UNDERSHAFT: The son of a foundling! Nonsense!

LADY BRITOMART: My son, Andrew! And even you may have good blood in your veins for all you know.

UNDERSHAFT: True. Probably I have. That is another argument in favor of a foundling.

LADY BRITOMART: Andrew: dont be aggravating. And dont be wicked. At present you are both.

UNDERSHAFT: This conversation is part of the Undershaft tradition, Biddy. Every Undershaft's wife has treated him to it ever since the house was founded. It is mere waste of breath. If the tradition be ever broken it will be for an abler man than Stephen.

LADY BRITOMART (*pouting*): Then go away.

UNDERSHAFT (*deprecatory*): Go away!

LADY BRITOMART: Yes: go away. If you will do nothing for Stephen, you are not wanted here. Go to your foundling, whoever he is; and look after him.

UNDERSHAFT: The fact is, Biddy —

LADY BRITOMART: Dont call me Biddy. I dont call you Andy.

UNDERSHAFT: I will not call my wife Britomart: it is not good sense. Seriously, my love, the Undershaft tradition has landed me in a difficulty. I am getting on in years; and my partner Lazarus has at last made a stand and insisted that the succession must be settled one way or the other; and of course he is quite right. You see, I havent found a fit successor yet.

LADY BRITOMART (*obstinately*): There is Stephen.

UNDERSHAFT: Thats just it: all the foundlings I can find are exactly like Stephen.

LADY BRITOMART: Andrew!

UNDERSHAFT: I want a man with no relations and no schooling: that is, a man who would be out of the running altogether if he were not a strong man. And I cant find him. Every blessed foundling nowadays is snapped up in his infancy by Barnardo homes, or School Board officers, or Boards of Guardians; and if he shows the least ability he is fastened on by schoolmasters; trained to win scholarships like a racehorse; crammed with secondhand ideas; drilled and disciplined in docility and what they call good taste; and lamed for life so that he is fit for nothing but teaching. If you want to keep the foundry in the family, you had better find an eligible foundling and marry him to Barbara.

LADY BRITOMART: Ah! Barbara! Your Pet! You would sacrifice Stephen to Barbara.

UNDERSHAFT: Cheerfully. And you, my dear, would boil Barbara to make soup for Stephen.

LADY BRITOMART: Andrew: this is not a question of our likings and dislikings: it is a question of duty. It is your duty to make Stephen your successor.

UNDERSHAFT: Just as much as it is your duty to submit to your husband. Come, Biddy! these tricks of the governing class are of no use with me. I am one of the governing class myself; and it is waste of time giving tracts to a missionary. I have the power in this matter; and I am not to be humbugged into using it for your purposes.

LADY BRITOMART: Andrew: you can talk my head off; but you cant change wrong into right. And your tie is all on one side. Put it straight.

UNDERSHAFT (disconcerted): It won't stay unless it's pinned (he fumbles at it with childish grimaces) —

(Stephen comes in.)

STEPHEN (at the door): I beg your pardon. (About to retire.)

LADY BRITOMART: No: come in, Stephen. (Stephen comes forward to his mother's writing table.)

UNDERSHAFT (not very cordially): Good afternoon.

STEPHEN (coldly): Good afternoon.

UNDERSHAFT (to Lady Britomart): He knows all about the tradition, I suppose?

LADY BRITOMART: Yes. (To Stephen.) It is what I told you last night, Stephen.

UNDERSHAFT (sulkily): I understand you want to come into the cannon business.

STEPHEN: I go into trade! Certainly not.

UNDERSHAFT (opening his eyes, greatly eased in mind and manner): Oh! in that case —

LADY BRITOMART: Cannons are not trade, Stephen. They are enterprise.

STEPHEN: I have no intention of becoming a man of business in any sense. I have no capacity for business and no taste for it. I intend to devote myself to politics.

UNDERSHAFT (rising): My dear boy: this is an immense relief to me. And I trust it may prove an equally good thing for the country. I was afraid you would consider yourself disparaged and slighted. (He moves towards Stephen as if to shake hands with him.)

LADY BRITOMART (rising and interposing): Stephen: I cannot allow you to throw away an enormous property like this.

STEPHEN (stiffly): Mother: there must be an end of treating me as a child, if you please. (Lady Britomart recoils, deeply wounded by his tone.) Until last night I did not take your attitude seriously, because I did not think you meant it seriously. But I find now that you left me in the dark as to matters which you should have explained to me years ago. I am extremely hurt and offended. Any further discussion of my intentions had better take place with my father, as between one man and another.

LADY BRITOMART: Stephen! (She sits down again, her eyes filling with tears.)

UNDERSHAFT (with grave compassion): You see, my dear, it is only the big men who can be treated as children.

STEPHEN: I am sorry, mother, that you have forced me —

UNDERSHAFT (stopping him): Yes, yes, yes, yes: thats all right, Stephen. She wont interfere with you any more: your independence is achieved: you have won your latchkey. Dont rub it in; and above all, dont apologize. (He resumes his seat.) Now what about your future, as between one man and another — I beg your pardon, Biddy: as between two men and a woman.

LADY BRITOMART (who has pulled herself together strongly): I quite understand, Stephen. By all means go your own way if you feel strong enough. (Stephen sits down magisterially in the chair at the writing table with an air of affirming his majority.)

UNDERSHAFT: It is settled that you do not ask for the succession to the cannon business.

STEPHEN: I hope it is settled that I repudiate the cannon business.

UNDERSHAFT: Come, come! dont be so devilishly sulky: it's boyish. Freedom should be generous. Besides, I owe you a fair start in life in exchange for disinheriting you. You cant become prime minister all at once. Havent you a turn for something? What about literature, art, and so forth?

STEPHEN: I have nothing of the artist about me, either in faculty or character, thank Heaven!

UNDERSHAFT: A philosopher, perhaps? Eh?

STEPHEN: I make no such ridiculous pretension.

UNDERSHAFT: Just so. Well, there is the army, the navy, the Church, the Bar. The Bar requires some ability. What about the Bar?

STEPHEN: I have not studied law. And I am afraid I

have not the necessary push — I believe that is the name barristers give to their vulgarity — for success in pleading.

UNDERSHAFT: Rather a difficult case, Stephen. Hardly anything left but the stage, is there? (*Stephen makes an impatient movement.*) Well, come! is there anything you know or care for?

STEPHEN (*rising and looking at him steadily*): I know the difference between right and wrong.

UNDERSHAFT (*hugely tickled*): You dont say so! What! no capacity for business, no knowledge of law, no sympathy with art, no pretension to philosophy; only a simple knowledge of the secret that has puzzled all the philosophers, baffled all the lawyers, muddled all the men of business, and ruined most of the artists: the secret of right and wrong. Why, man, youre a genius, a master of masters, a god! At twenty-four, too!

STEPHEN (*keeping his temper with difficulty*): You are pleased to be facetious. I pretend to nothing more than any honorable English gentleman claims as his birthright. (*He sits down angrily.*)

UNDERSHAFT: Oh, thats everybody's birthright. Look at poor little Jenny Hill, the Salvation lassie! she would think you were laughing at her if you asked her to stand up in the street and teach grammar or geography or mathematics or even drawing room dancing; but it never occurs to her to doubt that she can teach morals and religion. You are all alike, you respectable people. You cant tell me the bursting strain of a ten-inch gun, which is a very simple matter; but you all think you can tell me the bursting strain of a man under temptation. You darent handle high explosives; but youre all ready to handle honesty and truth and justice and the whole duty of man, and kill one another at that game. What a country! What a world!

LADY BRITOMART (*uneasily*): What do you think he had better do, Andrew?

UNDERSHAFT: Oh, just what he wants to do. He knows nothing and he thinks he knows everything. That points clearly to a political career. Get him a private secretaryship to someone who can get him an Under Secretaryship; and then leave him alone. He will find his natural and proper place in the end on the Treasury Bench.

STEPHEN (*springing up again*): I am sorry, sir, that you force me to forget the respect due to you as my father. I am an Englishman and I will not hear the Government of my country insulted. (*He thrusts his hands in his pockets and walks angrily across to the window.*)

UNDERSHAFT (*with a touch of brutality*): The government of your country! I am the government of your country: I, and Lazarus. Do you suppose that you and half a dozen amateurs like you, sitting in a row in that foolish gabble shop, can govern Undershaft and Lazarus? No, my friend: you will do what pays us. You will make war when it suits us, and keep peace when it doesnt. You will find out that trade requires certain measures when we have decided on those measures. When I want anything to keep my dividends up, you will discover that my want is a national need. When other people want something to keep my dividends down, you will call out the police and military. And in return you shall have the support and applause of my newspapers, and the delight of imagining that you are a great statesman. Government of your country! Be off with you, my boy, and play with your caucuses and leading articles and historic parties and great leaders and burning questions and the rest of your toys. *I* am going back to my counting-house to pay the piper and call the tune.

STEPHEN (*actually smiling, and putting his hand on his father's shoulder with indulgent patronage*): Really, my dear father, it is impossible to be angry with you. You dont know how absurd all this sounds to me. You are very properly proud of having been industrious enough to make money; and it is greatly to your credit that you have made so much of it. But it has kept you in circles where you are valued for your money and deferred to for it, instead of in the doubtless very old-fashioned and behind-the-times public school and university where I formed my habits of mind. It is natural for you to think that money governs England; but you must allow me to think I know better.

UNDERSHAFT: And what does govern England, pray?

STEPHEN: Character, father, character.

UNDERSHAFT: Whose character? Yours or mine?

STEPHEN: Neither yours nor mine, father, but the best elements in the English national character.

UNDERSHAFT: Stephen: Ive found your profession for you. Youre a born journalist. I'll start you with a high-toned weekly review. There!

(*Before Stephen can reply Sarah, Barbara, Lomax, and Cusins come in ready for walking. Barbara crosses the room to the window and looks out. Cusins drifts amiably to the armchair. Lomax remains near the door, while Sarah comes to her mother.*)

(*Stephen goes to the smaller writing table and busies himself with his letters.*)

SARAH: Go and get ready, mamma: the carriage is waiting. (*Lady Britomart leaves the room.*)

UNDERSHAFT (*to Sarah*): Good day, my dear. Good afternoon, Mr. Lomax.

LOMAX (*vaguely*): Ahdedoo.

UNDERSHAFT (*to Cusins*): Quite well after last night, Euripides, eh?

CUSINS: As well as can be expected.

UNDERSHAFT: Thats right. (*To Barbara.*) So you are coming to see my death and devastation factory, Barbara?

BARBARA (*at the window*): You came yesterday to see my salvation factory. I promised you a return visit.

LOMAX (*coming forward between Sarah and Undershaft*): Youll find it awfully interesting. Ive been through the Woolwich Arsenal and it gives you a ripping feeling of security, you know, to think of the lot of beggars we could kill if it came to fighting. (*To Undershaft, with sudden solemnity.*) Still, it must be rather an awful reflection for you, from the religious point of view as it were. Youre getting on, you know, and all that.

SARAH: You dont mind Cholly's imbecility, papa, do you?

LOMAX (*much taken aback*): Oh I say!

UNDERSHAFT: Mr. Lomax looks at the matter in a very proper spirit, my dear.

LOMAX: Just so. Thats all I meant, I assure you.

SARAH: Are you coming, Stephen?

STEPHEN: Well, I am rather busy — er — (*Magnanimously.*) Oh well, yes: I'll come. That is, if there is room for me.

UNDERSHAFT: I can take two with me in a little motor I am experimenting with for field use. You wont mind its being rather unfashionable. It's not painted yet; but it's bulletproof.

LOMAX (*appalled at the prospect of confronting Wilton Crescent in an unpainted motor*): Oh I say!

SARAH: The carriage for me, thank you. Barbara doesnt mind what she's seen in.

LOMAX: I say, Dolly, old chap: do you really mind the car being a guy?° Because of course if you do I'll go in it. Still —

CUSINS: I prefer it.

LOMAX: Thanks awfully, old man. Come, my ownest. (*He hurries out to secure his seat in the carriage. Sarah follows him.*)

CUSINS (*moodily walking across to Lady Britomart's writing table*): Why are we two coming to this Works Department of Hell? that is what I ask myself.

BARBARA: I have always thought of it as a sort of pit where lost creatures with blackened faces stirred up smoky fires and were driven and tormented by my father. Is it like that, dad?

guy: A person (or thing) of grotesque appearance.

UNDERSHAFT (*scandalized*): My dear! It is a spotlessly clean and beautiful hillside town.

CUSINS: With a Methodist chapel? Oh do say theres a Methodist chapel.

UNDERSHAFT: There are two: a Primitive one and a sophisticated one. There is even an Ethical Society; but it is not much patronized, as my men are all strongly religious. In the High Explosives Sheds they object to the presence of Agnostics as unsafe.

CUSINS: And yet they dont object to you!

BARBARA: Do they obey all your orders?

UNDERSHAFT: I never give them any orders. When I speak to one of them it is "Well, Jones, is the baby doing well? and has Mrs. Jones made a good recovery?" "Nicely, thank you, sir." And thats all.

CUSINS: But Jones has to be kept in order. How do you maintain discipline among your men?

UNDERSHAFT: I dont. They do. You see, the one thing Jones wont stand is any rebellion from the man under him, or any assertion of social equality between the wife of the man with 4 shillings a week less than himself, and Mrs. Jones! Of course they all rebel against me, theoretically. Practically, every man of them keeps the man just below him in his place. I never meddle with them. I never bully them. I dont even bully Lazarus. I say that certain things are to be done; but I dont order anybody to do them. I dont say, mind you, that there is no ordering about and snubbing and even bullying. The men snub the boys and order them about; the carmen snub the sweepers; the artisans snub the unskilled laborers; the foremen drive and bully both the laborers and artisans; the assistant engineers find fault with the foremen; the chief engineers drop on the assistants; the departmental managers worry the chiefs; and the clerks have tall hats and hymnbooks and keep up the social tone by refusing to associate on equal terms with anybody. The result is a colossal profit, which comes to me.

CUSINS (*revolted*): You really are a — well, what I was saying yesterday.

BARBARA: What was he saying yesterday?

UNDERSHAFT: Never mind, my dear. He thinks I have made you unhappy. Have I?

BARBARA: Do you think I can be happy in this vulgar silly dress? I! who have worn the uniform. Do you understand what you have done to me? Yesterday I had a man's soul in my hand. I set him in the way of life with his face to salvation. But when we took your money he turned back to drunkenness and derision. (*With intense conviction.*) I will never forgive you that. If I had a child, and you destroyed its body with your explosives — if you murdered Dolly with your horrible guns — I could forgive you if my forgiveness would open the gates of heaven to you. But to take a human soul from me, and turn it into the soul of a wolf! that is worse than any murder.

UNDERSHAFT: Does my daughter despair so easily? Can you strike a man to the heart and leave no mark on him?

BARBARA (*her face lighting up*): Oh, you are right: he can never be lost now: where was my faith?

CUSINS: Oh, clever clever devil!

BARBARA: You may be a devil; but God speaks through you sometimes. (*She takes her father's hands and kisses them.*) You have given me back my happiness: I feel it deep down now, though my spirit is troubled.

UNDERSHAFT: You have learnt something. That always feels at first as if you had lost something.

BARBARA: Well, take me to the factory of death; and let me learn something more. There must be some truth or other behind all this frightful irony. Come, Dolly. (*She goes out.*)

CUSINS: My guardian angel! (*To Undershaft.*) Avaunt! (*He follows Barbara.*)

STEPHEN (*quietly, at the writing table*): You must not mind Cusins, father. He is a very amiable good fellow; but he is a Greek scholar and naturally a little eccentric.

UNDERSHAFT: Ah, quite so. Thank you, Stephen. Thank you. (*He goes out.*)

(*Stephen smiles patronizingly; buttons his coat responsibly; and crosses the room to the door. Lady Britomart, dressed for out of doors, opens it before he reaches it. She looks round for the others; looks at Stephen and turns to go without a word.*)

STEPHEN (*embarrassed*): Mother —

LADY BRITOMART: Dont be apologetic, Stephen. And dont forget that you have outgrown your mother. (*She goes out.*)

(*Perivale St. Andrews lies between two Middlesex hills, half climbing the northern one. It is an almost smokeless town of white walls, roofs of narrow green slates or red tiles, tall trees, domes, campaniles, and slender chimney shafts, beautifully situated and beautiful in itself. The best view of it is obtained from the crest of a slope about half a mile to the east, where the high explosives are dealt with. The foundry lies hidden in the depths between, the tops of its chimneys sprouting like huge skittles into the middle distance. Across the crest runs an emplacement of concrete, with a firestep, and a parapet which suggests a fortification, because there is a huge cannon of the obsolete Woolwich Infant pattern peering across it at the town. The cannon is mounted on an experimental gun carriage: possibly*

the original model of the Undershaft disappearing rampart gun alluded to by Stephen. The firestep, being a convenient place to sit, is furnished here and there with straw disc cushions; and at one place there is the additional luxury of a fur rug.)

(*Barbara is standing on the firestep, looking over the parapet towards the town. On her right is the cannon; on her left the end of a shed raised on piles, with a ladder of three or four steps up to the door, which opens outwards and has a little wooden landing at the threshold, with a fire bucket in the corner of the landing. Several dummy soldiers more or less mutilated, with straw protruding from their gashes, have been shoved out of the way under the landing. A few others are nearly upright against the shed; and one has fallen forward and lies, like a grotesque corpse, on the emplacement. The parapet stops short of the shed, leaving a gap which is the beginning of the path down the hill through the foundry to the town. The rug is on the firestep near this gap. Down on the emplacement behind the cannon is a trolley carrying a huge conical bombshell with a red band painted on it. Further to the right is the door of an office, which, like the sheds, is of the lightest possible construction.*)

(*Cusins arrives by the path from the town.*)

BARBARA: Well?

CUSINS: Not a ray of hope. Everything perfect! wonderful! real! It only needs a cathedral to be a heavenly city instead of a hellish one.

BARBARA: Have you found out whether they have done anything for old Peter Shirley?

CUSINS: They have found him a job as gatekeeper and timekeeper. He's frightfully miserable. He calls the timekeeping brainwork, and says he isnt used to it; and his gate lodge is so splendid that he's ashamed to use the rooms, and skulks in the scullery.

BARBARA: Poor Peter!

(*Stephen arrives from the town. He carries a fieldglass.*)

STEPHEN (*enthusiastically*): Have you two seen the place? Why did you leave us?

CUSINS: I wanted to see everything I was not intended to see; and Barbara wanted to make the men talk.

STEPHEN: Have you found anything discreditable?

CUSINS: No. They call him Dandy Andy and are proud of his being a cunning old rascal; but it's all horribly, frightfully, immorally, unanswerably perfect.

(*Sarah arrives.*)

SARAH: Heavens! what a place! (*She crosses to the trolley.*) Did you see the nursing home? (*She sits down on the shell.*)

STEPHEN: Did you see the libraries and schools?

SARAH: Did you see the ballroom and the banqueting chamber in the Town Hall!?

STEPHEN: Have you gone into the insurance fund, the pension fund, the building society, the various applications of cooperation!?

(*Undershaft comes from the office, with a sheaf of telegrams in his hand.*)

UNDERSHAFT: Well, have you seen everything? I'm sorry I was called away. (*Indicating the telegrams.*) Good news from Manchuria.

STEPHEN: Another Japanese victory?

UNDERSHAFT: Oh, I dont know. Which side wins does not concern us here. No: the good news is that the aerial battleship is a tremendous success. At the first trial it has wiped out a fort with three hundred soldiers in it.

CUSINS (*from the platform*): Dummy soldiers?

UNDERSHAFT (*striding across to Stephen and kicking the prostrate dummy brutally out of his way*): No: the real thing.

(*Cusins and Barbara exchange glances. Then Cusins sits on the step and buries his face in his hands. Barbara gravely lays her hand on his shoulder. He looks up at her in whimsical desperation.*)

UNDERSHAFT: Well, Stephen, what do you think of the place?

STEPHEN: Oh, magnificent. A perfect triumph of modern industry. Frankly, my dear father, I have been a fool: I had no idea of what it all meant: of the wonderful forethought, the power of organization, the administrative capacity, the financial genius, the colossal capital it represents. I have been repeating to myself as I came through your streets "Peace hath her victories no less renowned than War." I have only one misgiving about it all.

UNDERSHAFT: Out with it.

STEPHEN: Well, I cannot help thinking that all this provision for every want of your workmen may sap their independence and weaken their sense of responsibility. And greatly as we enjoyed our tea at that splendid restaurant — how they gave us all that luxury and cake and jam and cream for three-pence I really cannot imagine! — still you must remember that restaurants break up home life. Look at the continent, for instance! Are you sure so much pampering is really good for the men's characters?

UNDERSHAFT: Well you see, my dear boy, when you are organizing civilization you have to make up your mind whether trouble and anxiety are good things or not. If you decide that they are, then, I take it, you simply dont organize civilization; and there you are, with trouble and anxiety enough to make us all angels! But if you decide the other way, you may as well go through with it. However, Stephen, our characters are safe here. A sufficient dose of anxiety is always provided by the fact that we may be blown to smithereens at any moment.

SARAH: By the way, papa, where do you make the explosives?

UNDERSHAFT: In separate little sheds like that one. When one of them blows up, it costs very little, and only the people quite close to it are killed.

(*Stephen, who is quite close to it, looks at it rather scaredly, and moves away quickly to the cannon. At the same moment the door of the shed is thrown abruptly open; and a foreman in overalls and list slippers comes out on the little landing and holds the door for Lomax, who appears in the doorway.*)

LOMAX (*with studied coolness*): My good fellow: you neednt get into a state of nerves. Nothing's going to happen to you; and I suppose it wouldnt be the end of the world if anything did. A little bit of British pluck is what you want, old chap. (*He descends and strolls across to Sarah.*)

UNDERSHAFT (*to the foreman*): Anything wrong, Bilton?

BILTON (*with ironic calm*): Gentleman walked into the high explosives shed and lit a cigarette, sir: thats all.

UNDERSHAFT: Ah, quite so. (*Going over to Lomax.*) Do you happen to remember what you did with the match?

LOMAX: Oh come! I'm not a fool. I took jolly good care to blow it out before I chucked it away.

BILTON: The top of it was red hot inside, sir.

LOMAX: Well, suppose it was! I didnt chuck it into any of your messes.

UNDERSHAFT: Think no more of it, Mr. Lomax. By the way, would you mind lending me your matches.

LOMAX (*offering his box*): Certainly.

UNDERSHAFT: Thanks. (*He pockets the matches.*)

LOMAX (*lecturing to the company generally*): You know, these high explosives dont go off like gunpowder, except when theyre in a gun. When theyre spread loose, you can put a match to them without the least risk: they just burn quietly like a bit of paper. (*Warming to the scientific interest of the subject.*) Did you know that, Undershaft? Have you ever tried?

UNDERSHAFT: Not on a large scale, Mr. Lomax. Bilton will give you a sample of guncotton when you are leaving if you ask him. You can experiment with it at home. (*Bilton looks puzzled.*)

SARAH: Bilton will do nothing of the sort, papa. I suppose it's your business to blow up the Russians and Japs; but you might really stop short of blowing up poor Cholly. (*Bilton gives it up and retires into the shed.*)

LOMAX: My ownest, there is no danger. (*He sits beside her on the shell.*)

(*Lady Britomart arrives from the town with a bouquet.*)

LADY BRITOMART (*impetuously*): Andrew: you shouldnt have let me see this place.

UNDERSHAFT: Why, my dear?

LADY BRITOMART: Never mind why: you shouldnt have: thats all. To think of all that (*indicating the town*) being yours! and that you have kept it to yourself all these years!

UNDERSHAFT: It does not belong to me. I belong to it. It is the Undershaft inheritance.

LADY BRITOMART: It is not. Your ridiculous cannons and that noisy banking foundry may be the Undershaft inheritance; but all that plate and linen, all that furniture and those houses and orchards and gardens belong to us. They belong to me: they are not a man's business. I wont give them up. You must be out of your senses to throw them all away; and if you persist in such folly, I will call in a doctor.

UNDERSHAFT (*stooping to smell the bouquet*): Where did you get the flowers, my dear?

LADY BRITOMART: Your men presented them to me in your William Morris Labor Church.

CUSINS: Oh! It needed only that. A Labor Church! (*He mounts the firestep distractedly and leans with his elbows on the parapet, turning his back to them.*)

LADY BRITOMART: Yes, with Morris's words in mosaic letters ten feet high around the dome. NO MAN IS GOOD ENOUGH TO BE ANOTHER MAN'S MASTER. The cynicism of it!

UNDERSHAFT: It shocked the men at first, I am afraid. But now they take no more notice of it than of the ten commandments in church.

LADY BRITOMART: Andrew: you are trying to put me off the subject of the inheritance by profane jokes. Well, you shant. I dont ask it any longer for Stephen: he has inherited far too much of your perversity to be fit for it. But Barbara has rights as well as Stephen. Why should not Adolphus succeed to the inheritance? I could manage the town for him and he can look after the cannons, if they are really necessary.

UNDERSHAFT: I should ask nothing better if Adolphus were a foundling. He is exactly the sort of new blood that is wanted in English business. But he's not a foundling; and theres an end of it. (*He makes for the office door.*)

CUSINS (*turning to them*): Not quite. (*They all turn and stare at him.*) I think — Mind! I am not committing myself in any way as to my future course — but I think the foundling difficulty can be got over. (*He jumps down to the emplacement.*)

UNDERSHAFT (*coming back to him*): What do you mean?

CUSINS: Well, I have something to say which is in the nature of a confession.

SARAH:
LADY BRITOMART: } Confession!
BARBARA:
STEPHEN:

LOMAX: Oh I say!

CUSINS: Yes, a confession. Listen, all. Until I met Barbara I thought myself in the main an honorable, truthful man, because I wanted the approval of my conscience more than I wanted anything else. But the moment I saw Barbara, I wanted her far more than the approval of my conscience.

LADY BRITOMART: Adolphus!

CUSINS: It is true. You accused me yourself, Lady Brit, of joining the Army to worship Barbara; and so I did. She bought my soul like a flower at a street corner; but she bought it for herself.

UNDERSHAFT: What! Not for Dionysos or another?

CUSINS: Dionysos and all the others are in herself. I adored what was divine in her, and was therefore a true worshipper. But I was romantic about her too. I thought she was a woman of the people, and that a marriage with a professor of Greek would be far beyond the wildest social ambitions of her rank.

LADY BRITOMART: Adolphus!!

LOMAX: Oh I say!!!

CUSINS: When I learnt the horrible truth —

LADY BRITOMART: What do you mean by the horrible truth, pray?

CUSINS: That she was enormously rich; that her grandfather was an earl; that her father was the Prince of Darkness —

UNDERSHAFT: Chut!

CUSINS: — and that I was only an adventurer trying to catch a rich wife, then I stooped to deceive her about my birth.

BARBARA (*rising*): Dolly!

LADY BRITOMART: Your birth! Now Adolphus, dont dare to make up a wicked story for the sake of these wretched cannons. Remember: I have seen photographs of your parents; and the Agent General for South Western Australia knows them personally and has assured me that they are most respectable married people.

CUSINS: So they are in Australia; but here they are outcasts. Their marriage is legal in Australia, but not in England. My mother is my father's deceased wife's sister; and in this island I am consequently a foundling. (*Sensation.*)

BARBARA: Silly! (*She climbs to the cannon, and leans, listening, in the angle it makes with the parapet.*)

CUSINS: Is the subterfuge good enough, Machiavelli?

UNDERSHAFT (*thoughtfully*): Biddy: this may be a way out of the difficulty.

LADY BRITOMART: Stuff! A man cant make cannons any the better for being his own cousin instead of his proper self. (*She sits down on the rug with a bounce that expresses her downright contempt for their casuistry.*)

UNDERSHAFT (*to Cusins*): You are an educated man. That is against the tradition.

CUSINS: Once in ten thousand times it happens that the schoolboy is a born master of what they try to teach him. Greek has not destroyed my mind: it has nourished it. Besides, I did not learn it at an English public school.

UNDERSHAFT: Hm! Well, I cannot afford to be too particular: you have cornered the foundling market. Let it pass. You are eligible, Euripides: you are eligible.

BARBARA: Dolly: yesterday morning, when Stephen told us all about the tradition, you became very silent, and you have been strange and excited ever since. Were you thinking of your birth then?

CUSINS: When the finger of Destiny suddenly points at a man in the middle of his breakfast, it makes him thoughtful.

UNDERSHAFT: Aha! You have had your eye on the business, my young friend, have you?

CUSINS: Take care! There is an abyss of moral horror between me and your accursed aerial battleships.

UNDERSHAFT: Never mind the abyss for the present. Let us settle the practical details and leave your final decision open. You know that you will have to change your name. Do you object to that?

CUSINS: Would any man named Adolphus — any man called Dolly! — object to be called something else?

UNDERSHAFT: Good. Now, as to money! I propose to treat you handsomely from the beginning. You shall start at a thousand a year.

CUSINS (*with sudden heat, his spectacles twinkling with mischief*): A thousand! You dare offer a miserable thousand to the son-in-law of a millionaire! No, by Heavens, Machiavelli! you shall not cheat me. You cannot do without me; and I can do without you. I must have two thousand five hundred a year for two years. At the end of that time, if I am a failure, I go. But if I am a success, and stay on, you must give me the other five thousand.

UNDERSHAFT: What other five thousand?

CUSINS: To make the two years up to five thousand a year. The two thousand five hundred is only half pay in case I should turn out a failure. The third year I must have ten percent on the profits.

UNDERSHAFT (*taken aback*): Ten percent! Why, man, do you know what my profits are?

CUSINS: Enormous, I hope: otherwise I shall require twenty-five percent.

UNDERSHAFT: But, Mr. Cusins, this is a serious matter of business. You are not bringing any capital into the concern.

CUSINS: What! no capital! Is my mastery of Greek no capital? Is my access to the subtlest thought, the loftiest poetry yet attained by humanity, no capital? My character! my intellect! my life! my career! what Barbara calls my soul! are these no capital? Say another word; and I double my salary.

UNDERSHAFT: Be reasonable —

CUSINS (*peremptorily*): Mr. Undershaft: you have my terms. Take them or leave them.

UNDERSHAFT (*recovering himself*): Very well, I note your terms; and I offer you half.

CUSINS (*disgusted*): Half!

UNDERSHAFT (*firmly*): Half.

CUSINS: You call yourself a gentleman; and you offer me half!!

UNDERSHAFT: I do not call myself a gentleman; but I offer you half.

CUSINS: This to your future partner! your successor! your son-in-law!

BARBARA: You are selling your own soul, Dolly, not mine. Leave me out of the bargain, please.

UNDERSHAFT: Come! I will go a step further for Barbara's sake. I will give you three-fifths; but that is my last word.

CUSINS: Done!

LOMAX: Done in the eye! Why, *I* get only eight hundred, you know.

CUSINS: By the way, Mac, I am a classical scholar not an arithmetical one. Is three-fifths more than half or less?

UNDERSHAFT: More, of course.

CUSINS: I would have taken two hundred and fifty. How you can succeed in business when you are willing to pay all that money to a University don who is obviously not worth a junior clerk's wages! — well! What will Lazarus say?

UNDERSHAFT: Lazarus is a gentle romantic Jew who cares for nothing but string quartets and stalls at fashionable theaters. He will be blamed for your rapacity in money matters, poor fellow! as he has hitherto been blamed for mine. You are a shark of the first order, Euripides. So much the better for the firm!

BARBARA: Is the bargain closed, Dolly? Does your soul belong to him now?

CUSINS: No: the price is settled: that is all. The real tug of war is still to come. What about the moral question?

LADY BRITOMART: There is no moral question in the matter at all, Adolphus. You must simply sell cannons and weapons to people whose cause is right and just, and refuse them to foreigners and criminals.

UNDERSHAFT (*determinedly*): No: none of that. You must keep the true faith of an Armorer, or you dont come in here.

CUSINS: What on earth is the true faith of an Armorer?

UNDERSHAFT: To give arms to all men who offer an honest price for them, without respect of persons or principles: to aristocrat and republican, to Nihilist and Tsar, to Capitalist and Socialist, to Protestant and Catholic, to burglar and policeman, to black man, white man, and yellow man, to all sorts and conditions, all nationalities, all faiths, all follies, all causes, and all crimes. The first Undershaft wrote up in his shop IF GOD GAVE THE HAND, LET NOT MAN WITHHOLD THE SWORD. The second wrote up ALL HAVE THE RIGHT TO FIGHT: NONE HAVE THE RIGHT TO JUDGE. The third wrote up TO MAN THE WEAPON: TO HEAVEN THE VICTORY. The fourth had no literary turn; so he did not write up anything; but he sold cannons to Napoleon under the nose of George the Third. The fifth wrote up PEACE SHALL NOT PREVAIL SAVE WITH A SWORD IN HER HAND. The sixth, my master, was the best of all. He wrote up NOTHING IS EVER DONE IN THIS WORLD UNTIL MEN ARE PREPARED TO KILL ONE ANOTHER IF IT IS NOT DONE. After that, there was nothing left for the seventh to say. So he wrote up, simply, UNASHAMED.

CUSINS: My good Machiavelli. I shall certainly write something up on the wall; only, as I shall write it in Greek, you wont be able to read it. But as to your Armorer's faith, if I take my neck out of the noose of my own morality I am not going to put it into the noose of yours. I shall sell cannons to whom I please and refuse them to whom I please. So there!

UNDERSHAFT: From the moment when you become Andrew Undershaft, you will never do as you please again. Dont come here lusting for power, young man.

CUSINS: If power were my aim I should not come here for it. You have no power.

UNDERSHAFT: None of my own, certainly.

CUSINS: I have more power than you, more will. You do not drive this place: it drives you. And what drives the place?

UNDERSHAFT (*enigmatically*): A will of which I am a part.

BARBARA (*startled*): Father! Do you know what you are saying; or are you laying a snare for my soul?

CUSINS: Dont listen to his metaphysics, Barbara. The place is driven by the most rascally part of society, the money hunters, the pleasure hunters, the military promotion hunters; and he is their slave.

UNDERSHAFT: Not necessarily. Remember the Armorer's Faith. I will take an order from a good man as cheerfully as from a bad one. If you good people prefer preaching and shirking to buying my weapons and fighting the rascals, dont blame me. I can make cannons: I cannot make courage and conviction. Bah! you tire me, Euripides, with your morality mongering. Ask Barbara: she understands. (*He suddenly reaches up and takes Barbara's hands, looking powerfully into her eyes.*) Tell him, my love, what power really means.

BARBARA (*hypnotized*): Before I joined the Salvation Army, I was in my own power and the consequence was that I never knew what to do with myself. When I joined it, I had not time enough for all the things I had to do.

UNDERSHAFT (*approvingly*): Just so. And why was that, do you suppose?

BARBARA: Yesterday I should have said, because I was in the power of God. (*She resumes her self-possession, withdrawing her hands from his with a power equal to his own.*) But you came and showed me that I was in the power of Bodger and Undershaft. Today I feel — oh! how can I put it into words? Sarah: do you remember the earthquake at Cannes, when we were little children? — how little the surprise of the first shock mattered compared to the dread and horror of waiting for the second? That is how I feel in this place today. I stood on the rock I thought eternal; and without a word of warning it reeled and crumbled under me. I was safe with an infinite wisdom watching me, an army marching to Salvation with me; and in a moment, at a stroke of your pen in a check book, I stood alone; and the heavens were empty. That was the first shock of the earthquake: I am waiting for the second.

UNDERSHAFT: Come, come, my daughter! dont make too much of your little tinpot tragedy. What do we do here when we spend years of work and thought and thousands of pounds of solid cash on a new gun or an aerial battleship that turns out just a hairsbreadth wrong after all? Scrap it. Scrap it without wasting another hour or another pound on it. Well, you have made for yourself something that you call a morality or a religion or what not. It doesnt fit the facts. Well, scrap it. Scrap it and get one that does fit. That is what is wrong with the world at present. It scraps its obsolete steam engines and dynamos; but it wont scrap its old prejudices and its old moralities and its old religions and its old political constitutions. Whats the result? In machinery it does very well; but in morals and religion and politics it is working at a loss that brings it nearer bankruptcy every year. Dont persist in that folly. If your old religion broke down yesterday, get a newer and a better one for tomorrow.

BARBARA: Oh how gladly I would take a better one to my soul! But you offer me a worse one. (*Turning on him with sudden vehemence.*) Justify yourself: show me some light through the darkness of this dreadful place, with its beautifully clean workshops, and respectable workmen, and model homes.

UNDERSHAFT: Cleanliness and respectability do not need justification, Barbara: they justify themselves. I see no darkness here, no dreadfulness. In your Salvation shelter I saw poverty, misery, cold, and hunger. You gave them bread and treacle and dreams of heaven. I give from thirty shillings a week to twelve thousand a year. They find their own dreams but I look after the drainage.

BARBARA: And their souls?

UNDERSHAFT: I save their souls just as I saved yours.

BARBARA (*revolted*): You saved my soul! What do you mean?

UNDERSHAFT: I fed you and clothed you and housed you. I took care that you should have money enough to live handsomely — more than enough; so that you could be wasteful, careless, generous. That saved your soul from the seven deadly sins.

BARBARA (*bewildered*): The seven deadly sins!

UNDERSHAFT: Yes, the deadly seven. (*Counting on his fingers.*) Food, clothing, firing, rent, taxes, respectability, and children. Nothing can lift those seven millstones from Man's neck but money and the spirit cannot soar until the millstones are lifted. I lifted them from your spirit. I enabled Barbara to become Major Barbara; and I saved her from the crime of poverty.

CUSINS: Do you call poverty a crime?

UNDERSHAFT: The worst of crimes. All the other crimes are virtues beside it: all the other dishonors are chivalry itself by comparison. Poverty blights whole cities; spreads horrible pestilences; strikes dead the very souls of all who come within sight, sound, or smell of it. What you call crime is nothing: a murder here and a theft there, a blow now and a curse then: what do they matter? they are only the accidents and illnesses of life: there are not fifty genuine professional criminals in London. But there are millions of poor people, abject people, dirty people, ill fed, ill clothed people. They poison us morally and physically: they kill the happiness of society: they force us to do away with our own liberties and to organize unnatural cruelties for fear they

should rise against us and drag us down into their abyss. Only fools fear crime: we all fear poverty. Pah! (*Turning on Barbara.*) you talk of your half-saved ruffian in West Ham: you accuse me of dragging his soul back to perdition. Well, bring him to me here; and I will drag his soul back again to salvation for you. Not by words and dreams; but by thirty-eight shillings a week, a sound house in a handsome street, and a permanent job. In three weeks he will have a fancy waistcoat; in three months a tall hat and a chapel sitting; before the end of the year he will shake hands with a duchess at a Primrose League meeting, and join the Conservative Party.

BARBARA: And will he be the better for that?

UNDERSHAFT: You know he will. Dont be a hypocrite, Barbara. He will be better fed, better housed, better clothed, better behaved; and his children will be pounds heavier and bigger. That will be better than an American cloth mattress in a shelter, chopping firewood, eating bread and treacle, and being forced to kneel down from time to time to thank heaven for it: knee drill, I think you call it. It is cheap work converting starving men with a Bible in one hand and a slice of bread in the other. I will undertake to convert West Ham to Mahometanism° on the same terms. Try your hand on my men: their souls are hungry because their bodies are full.

BARBARA: And leave the east end to starve?

UNDERSHAFT (*his energetic tone dropping into one of bitter and brooding remembrance*): I was an east ender. I moralized and starved until one day I swore that I would be a full-fed free man at all costs; that nothing should stop me except a bullet, neither reason nor morals nor the lives of other men. I said "Thou shalt starve ere I starve"; and with that word I became free and great. I was a dangerous man until I had my will: now I am a useful, beneficent, kindly person. That is the history of most self-made millionaires, I fancy. When it is the history of every Englishman we shall have an England worth living in.

LADY BRITOMART: Stop making speeches, Andrew. This is not the place for them.

UNDERSHAFT (*punctured*): My dear: I have no other means of conveying my ideas.

LADY BRITOMART: Your ideas are nonsense. You got on because you were selfish and unscrupulous.

UNDERSHAFT: Not at all. I had the strongest scruples about poverty and starvation. Your moralists are quite unscrupulous about both: they make virtues

Mahometanism: Islam.

of them. I had rather be a thief than a pauper. I had rather be a murderer than a slave. I dont want to be either; but if you force the alternative on me, then, by Heaven, I'll choose the braver and more moral one. I hate poverty and slavery worse than any other crimes whatsoever. And let me tell you this. Poverty and slavery have stood up for centuries to your sermons and leading articles: they will not stand up to my machine guns. Dont preach at them: dont reason with them. Kill them.

BARBARA: Killing. Is that your remedy for everything?

UNDERSHAFT: It is the final test of conviction, the only lever strong enough to overturn a social system, the only way of saying Must. Let six hundred and seventy fools loose in the streets; and three policemen can scatter them. But huddle them together in a certain house in Westminster; and let them go through certain ceremonies and call themselves certain names until at last they get the courage to kill; and your six hundred and seventy fools become a government. Your pious mob fills up ballot papers and imagines it is governing its masters; but the ballot paper that really governs is the paper that has a bullet wrapped up in it.

CUSINS: That is perhaps why, like most intelligent people, I never vote.

UNDERSHAFT: Vote! Bah! When you vote, you only change the names of the cabinet. When you shoot, you pull down governments, inaugurate new epochs, abolish old orders, and set up new. Is that historically true, Mr. Learned Man, or is it not?

CUSINS: It is historically true. I loathe having to admit it. I repudiate your sentiments. I abhor your nature. I defy you in every possible way. Still, it is true. But it ought not to be true.

UNDERSHAFT: Ought! ought! ought! ought! ought! Are you going to spend your life saying ought, like the rest of our moralists? Turn your oughts into shalls, man. Come and make explosives with me. Whatever can blow men up can blow society up. The history of the world is the history of those who had courage enough to embrace this truth. Have you the courage to embrace it, Barbara?

LADY BRITOMART: Barbara: I positively forbid you to listen to your father's abominable wickedness. And you, Adolphus, ought to know better than to go about saying that wrong things are true. What does it matter whether they are true if they are wrong?

UNDERSHAFT: What does it matter whether they are wrong if they are true?

LADY BRITOMART (rising): Children: come home instantly. Andrew: I am exceedingly sorry I allowed you to call on us. You are wickeder than ever. Come at once.

BARBARA (shaking her head): It's no use running away from wicked people, mamma.

LADY BRITOMART: It is every use. It shows your disapprobation of them.

BARBARA: It does not save them.

LADY BRITOMART: I can see that you are going to disobey me. Sarah: are you coming home or are you not?

SARAH: I daresay it's very wicked of papa to make cannons; but I dont think I shall cut him on that account.

LOMAX (pouring oil on the troubled waters): The fact is, you know, there is a certain amount of tosh about this notion of wickedness. It doesnt work. You must look at facts. Not that I would say a word in favor of anything wrong; but then, you see, all sorts of chaps are always doing all sorts of things; and we have to fit them in somehow, dont you know. What I mean is that you cant go cutting everybody; and thats about what it comes to. (Their rapt attention to his eloquence makes him nervous.) Perhaps I dont make myself clear.

LADY BRITOMART: You are lucidity itself, Charles. Because Andrew is successful and has plenty of money to give to Sarah, you will flatter him and encourage him in his wickedness.

LOMAX (unruffled): Well, where the carcase is, there will the eagles be gathered, dont you know. (To Undershaft.) Eh? What?

UNDERSHAFT: Precisely. By the way, may I call you Charles?

LOMAX: Delighted. Cholly is the usual ticket.

UNDERSHAFT (to Lady Britomart): Biddy —

LADY BRITOMART (violently): Dont dare call me Biddy. Charles Lomax: you are a fool. Adolphus Cusins: you are a Jesuit. Stephen: you are a prig. Barbara: you are a lunatic. Andrew: you are a vulgar tradesman. Now you all know my opinion; and my conscience is clear, at all events. (She sits down with a vehemence that the rug fortunately softens.)

UNDERSHAFT: My dear: you are the incarnation of morality. (She snorts.) Your conscience is clear and your duty done when you have called everybody names. Come, Euripides! it is getting late; and we all want to get home. Make up your mind.

CUSINS: Understand this, you old demon —

LADY BRITOMART: Adolphus!

UNDERSHAFT: Let him alone, Biddy. Proceed, Euripides.

CUSINS: You have me in a horrible dilemma. I want Barbara.

UNDERSHAFT: Like all young men, you greatly exaggerate the difference between one young woman and another.

BARBARA: Quite true, Dolly.

CUSINS: I also want to avoid being a rascal.

UNDERSHAFT (*with biting contempt*): You lust for personal righteousness, for self-approval, for what you call a good conscience, for what Barbara calls salvation, for what I call patronizing people who are not so lucky as yourself.

CUSINS: I do not: all the poet in me recoils from being a good man. But there are things in me that I must reckon with. Pity —

UNDERSHAFT: Pity! The scavenger of misery.

CUSINS: Well, love.

UNDERSHAFT: I know. You love the needy and the outcast: you love the oppressed races, the negro, the Indian ryot, the underdog everywhere. Do you love the Japanese? Do you love the French? Do you love the English?

CUSINS: No. Every true Englishman detests the English. We are the wickedest nation on earth; and our success is a moral horror.

UNDERSHAFT: That is what comes of your gospel of love, is it?

CUSINS: May I not love even my father-in-law?

UNDERSHAFT: Who wants your love, man? By what right do you take the liberty of offering it to me? I will have your due heed and respect, or I will kill you. But your love! Damn your impertinence!

CUSINS (*grinning*): I may not be able to control my affections, Mac.

UNDERSHAFT: You are fencing, Euripides. You are weakening: your grip is slipping. Come! try your last weapon. Pity and love have broken in your hand: forgiveness is still left.

CUSINS: No: forgiveness is a beggar's refuge. I am with you there: we must pay our debts.

UNDERSHAFT: Well said. Come! you will suit me. Remember the words of Plato.

CUSINS (*starting*): Plato! You dare quote Plato to me!

UNDERSHAFT: Plato says, my friend, that society cannot be saved until either the Professors of Greek take to making gunpowder, or else the makers of gunpowder become Professors of Greek.

CUSINS: Oh, tempter, cunning tempter!

UNDERSHAFT: Come! choose, man, choose.

CUSINS: But perhaps Barbara will not marry me if I make the wrong choice.

BARBARA: Perhaps not.

CUSINS (*desperately perplexed*): You hear!

BARBARA: Father: do you love nobody?

UNDERSHAFT: I love my best friend.

LADY BRITOMART: And who is that, pray?

UNDERSHAFT: My bravest enemy. That is the man who keeps me up to the mark.

CUSINS: You know, the creature is really a sort of poet in his way. Suppose he is a great man, after all!

UNDERSHAFT: Suppose you stop talking and make up your mind, my young friend.

CUSINS: But you are driving me against my nature. I hate war.

UNDERSHAFT: Hatred is the coward's revenge for being intimidated. Dare you make war on war? Here are the means: my friend Mr. Lomax is sitting on them.

LOMAX (*springing up*): Oh I say! You dont mean that this thing is loaded, do you? My ownest: come off it.

SARAH (*sitting placidly on the shell*): If I am to be blown up, the more thoroughly it is done the better. Dont fuss, Cholly.

LOMAX (*to Undershaft, strongly remonstrant*): Your own daughter, you know!

UNDERSHAFT: So I see. (*To Cusins.*) Well, my friend, may we expect you here at six tomorrow morning?

CUSINS (*firmly*): Not on any account. I will see the whole establishment blown up with its own dynamite before I will get up at five. My hours are healthy, rational hours: eleven to five.

UNDERSHAFT: Come when you please: before a week you will come at six and stay until I turn you out for the sake of your health. (*Calling.*) Bilton! (*He turns to Lady Britomart, who rises.*) My dear: let us leave these two young people to themselves for a moment. (*Bilton comes from the shed.*) I am going to take you through the guncotton shed.

BILTON (*barring the way*): You cant take anything explosive in here, sir.

LADY BRITOMART: What do you mean? Are you alluding to me?

BILTON (*unmoved*): No, maam. Mr. Undershaft has the other gentleman's matches in his pocket.

LADY BRITOMART (*abruptly*): Oh! I beg your pardon! (*She goes into the shed.*)

UNDERSHAFT: Quite right, Bilton, quite right: here you are. (*He gives Bilton the box of matches.*) Come, Stephen. Come, Charles. Bring Sarah. (*He passes into the shed.*)

(*Bilton opens the box and deliberately drops the matches into the fire bucket.*)

LOMAX: Oh! I say. (*Bilton stolidly hands him the empty box.*) Infernal nonsense! Pure scientific ignorance! (*He goes in.*)

SARAH: Am I all right, Bilton?

BILTON: Youll have to put on list slippers, miss: thats all. Weve got em inside. (*She goes in.*)

STEPHEN (*very seriously to Cusins*): Dolly, old fellow, think. Think before you decide. Do you feel that you are a sufficiently practical man? It is a huge undertaking, an enormous responsibility. All this mass of business will be Greek to you.

CUSINS: Oh, I think it will be much less difficult than Greek.

STEPHEN: Well, I just want to say this before I leave you to yourselves. Dont let anything I have said about right and wrong prejudice you against this great chance in life. I have satisfied myself that the business is one of the highest character and a credit to our country. (*Emotionally.*) I am very proud of my father. I — (*Unable to proceed, he presses Cusins' hand and goes hastily into the shed, followed by Bilton.*)

(*Barbara and Cusins, left alone together, look at one another silently.*)

CUSINS: Barbara: I am going to accept this offer.

BARBARA: I thought you would.

CUSINS: You understand, dont you, that I had to decide without consulting you. If I had thrown the burden of the choice on you, you would sooner or later have despised me for it.

BARBARA: Yes: I did not want you to sell your soul for me any more than for this inheritance.

CUSINS: It is not the sale of my soul that troubles me: I have sold it too often to care about that. I have sold it for a professorship. I have sold it for an income. I have sold it to escape being imprisoned for refusing to pay taxes for hangmen's ropes and unjust wars and things that I abhor. What is all human conduct but the daily and hourly sale of our souls for trifles? What I am now selling it for is neither money nor position nor comfort, but for reality and for power.

BARBARA: You know that you will have no power, and that he has none.

CUSINS: I know. It is not for myself alone. I want to make power for the world.

BARBARA: I want to make power for the world too; but it must be spiritual power.

CUSINS: I think all power is spiritual: these cannons will not go off by themselves. I have tried to make spiritual power by teaching Greek. But the world can never be really touched by a dead language and a dead civilization. The people must have power; and the people cannot have Greek. Now the power that is made here can be wielded by all men.

BARBARA: Power to burn women's houses down and kill their sons and tear their husbands to pieces.

CUSINS: You cannot have power for good without having power for evil too. Even mother's milk nourishes murderers as well as heroes. This power which only tears men's bodies to pieces has never been so horribly abused as the intellectual power, the imaginative power, the poetic, religious power that can enslave men's souls. As a teacher of Greek I gave the intellectual man weapons against the common man. I now want to give the common man weapons against the intellectual man. I love the common people. I want to arm them against the lawyers, the doctors, the priests, the literary men, the professors, the artists, and the politicians, who, once in authority, are more disastrous and tyrannical than all the fools, rascals, and impostors. I want a power simple enough for common men to use, yet strong enough to force the intellectual oligarchy to use its genius for the general good.

BARBARA: Is there no higher power than that (*pointing to the shell*)?

CUSINS: Yes; but that power can destroy the higher powers just as a tiger can destroy a man: therefore Man must master that power first. I admitted this when the Turks and Greeks were last at war. My best pupil went out to fight for Hellas. My parting gift to him was not a copy of Plato's *Republic*, but a revolver and a hundred Undershaft cartridges. The blood of every Turk he shot — if he shot any — is on my head as well as on Undershaft's. That act committed me to this place for ever. Your father's challenge has beaten me. Dare I make war on war? I must. I will. And now, is it all over between us?

BARBARA (*touched by his evident dread of her answer*): Silly baby Dolly! How could it be!

CUSINS (*overjoyed*): Then you — you — you — Oh for my drum! (*He flourishes imaginary drumsticks.*)

BARBARA (*angered by his levity*): Take care, Dolly, take care. Oh, if only I could get away from you and from father and from it all! if I could have the wings of a dove and fly away to heaven!

CUSINS: And leave me!

BARBARA: Yes, you, and all the other naughty mischievous children of men. But I cant. I was happy in the Salvation Army for a moment. I escaped from the world into a paradise of enthusiasm and prayer and soul saving; but the moment our money ran short, it all came back to Bodger: it was he who saved our people: he, and the Prince of Darkness, my papa. Undershaft and Bodger: their hands stretch everywhere: when we feed a starving fellow creature, it is with their bread, because there is no other bread; when we tend the sick, it is in the hospitals they endow; if we turn from the churches they build, we must kneel on the stones of the streets they pave. As long as that lasts, there is no getting away from them. Turning our backs on Bodger and Undershaft is turning our backs on life.

CUSINS: I thought you were determined to turn your back on the wicked side of life.

BARBARA: There is no wicked side: life is all one. And

I never wanted to shirk my share in whatever evil must be endured, whether it be sin or suffering. I wish I could cure you of middle-class ideas, Dolly.

CUSINS (*gasping*): Middle cl —! A snub! A social snub to me from the daughter of a foundling!

BARBARA: That is why I have no class, Dolly: I come straight out of the heart of the whole people. If I were middle class I should turn my back on my father's business; and we should both live in an artistic drawing room, with you reading the reviews in one corner, and I in the other at the piano, playing Schumann: both very superior persons, and neither of us a bit of use. Sooner than that, I would sweep out the guncotton shed, or be one of Bodger's barmaids. Do you know what would have happened if you had refused papa's offer?

CUSINS: I wonder!

BARBARA: I should have given you up and married the man who accepted it. After all, my dear old mother has more sense than any of you. I felt like her when I saw this place — felt that I must have it — that never, never, never could I let it go; only she thought it was the houses and the kitchen ranges and the linen and china, when it was really all the human souls to be saved: not weak souls in starved bodies, sobbing with gratitude for a scrap of bread and treacle, but fullfed, quarrelsome, snobbish, uppish creatures, all standing on their little rights and dignities, and thinking that my father ought to be greatly obliged to them for making so much money for him — and so he ought. That is where salvation is really wanted. My father shall never throw it in my teeth again that my converts were bribed with bread. (*She is transfigured.*) I have got rid of the bribe of bread. I have got rid of the bribe of heaven. Let God's work be done for its own sake: the work he had to create us to do because it cannot be done except by living men and women. When I die, let him be in my debt, not I in his; and let me forgive him as becomes a woman of my rank.

CUSINS: Then the way of life lies through the factory of death?

BARBARA: Yes, through the raising of hell to heaven and of man to God, through the unveiling of an eternal light in the Valley of The Shadow. (*Seizing him with both hands.*) Oh, did you think my courage would never come back? did you believe that I was a deserter? that I, who have stood in the streets, and taken my people to my heart, and talked of the holiest and greatest things with them, could ever turn back and chatter foolishly to fashionable people about nothing in a drawing room? Never, never, never, never: Major Barbara will die with the colors. Oh! and I have my dear little Dolly boy still; and he has found me my place and my work. Glory Hallelujah! (*She kisses him.*)

CUSINS: My dearest: consider my delicate health. I cannot stand as much happiness as you can.

BARBARA: Yes: it is not easy work being in love with me, is it? But it's good for you. (*She runs to the shed, and calls, childlike.*) Mamma! Mamma! (*Bilton comes out of the shed, followed by Undershaft.*) I want Mamma.

UNDERSHAFT: She is taking off her list slippers, dear. (*He passes on to Cusins.*) Well? What does she say?

CUSINS: She has gone right up into the skies.

LADY BRITOMART (*coming from the shed and stopping on the steps, obstructing Sarah, who follows with Lomax. Barbara clutches like a baby at her mother's skirt*): Barbara: when will you learn to be independent and to act and think for yourself? I know, as well as possible what that cry of "Mamma, Mamma," means. Always running to me!

SARAH (*touching Lady Britomart's ribs with her fingertips and imitating a bicycle horn*): Pip! pip!

LADY BRITOMART (*highly indignant*): How dare you say Pip! pip! to me, Sarah? You are both very naughty children. What do you want, Barbara?

BARBARA: I want a house in the village to live in with Dolly. (*Dragging at the skirt.*) Come and tell me which one to take.

UNDERSHAFT (*to Cusins*): Six o'clock tomorrow morning, Euripides.

COMMENTARY

Bernard Shaw (1856–1950)
FROM THE PREFACE TO MAJOR BARBARA

Shaw's plays were always about something important, and at times he indicated that the critics missed the point. In his preface to Major Barbara, *Shaw gives the critics something to say by going through the play himself, talking about its situations and its characters as well as about its ideas and deepest concerns. His comments generally focus on the economic issues underlying the play. Shaw's socialist views come to the fore in his preface as he condemns poverty as a crime and urges society to give every citizen a stipend on which to live. The moral issues of the play — concerning the ethics of making munitions — shift their ground in the preface, since it is shown that moral issues involved in avoiding poverty far outweigh the question of how a person earns money.*

The Gospel of St Andrew Undershaft

In the millionaire Undershaft I have represented a man who has become intellectually and spiritually as well as practically conscious of the irrestible natural truth which we all abhor and repudiate; to wit, that the greatest of our evils, and the worst of our crimes is poverty, and that our first duty, to which every other consideration should be sacrificed, is not to be poor. "Poor but honest," "the respectable poor," and such phrases are as intolerable and as immoral as "drunken but amiable," "fraudulent but a good after-dinner speaker," "splendidly criminal," or the like. Security, the chief pretense of civilization, cannot exist where the worst of dangers, the danger of poverty, hangs over everyone's head, and where the alleged protection of our persons from violence is only an accidental result of the existence of a police force whose real business is to force the poor man to see his children starve whilst idle people overfeed pet dogs with the money that might feed and clothe them.

It is exceedingly difficult to make people realize that an evil is an evil. For instance, we seize a man and deliberately do him a malicious injury: say, imprison him for years. One would not suppose that it needed any exceptional clearness of wit to recognize in this an act of diabolical cruelty. But in England such a recognition provokes a stare of surprise, followed by an explanation that the outrage is punishment or justice or something else that is all right, or perhaps by a heated attempt to argue that we should all be robbed and murdered in our beds if such stupid villainies as sentences of imprisonment were not committed daily. It is useless to argue that even if this were true, which it is not, the alternative to adding crimes of our own to the crimes from which we suffer is not helpless submission. Chickenpox is an evil; but if I were to declare that we must either submit to it or else repress it sternly by seizing everyone who suffers from it and punishing them by inoculation with smallpox, I should be laughed at; for though nobody could deny that the result would be to prevent chickenpox to some extent by making people avoid it much more carefully, and to effect a further apparent prevention by making them conceal it very anxiously, yet people would have sense enough to see that the deliberate propagation of smallpox was a creation of evil, and must therefore be ruled out in favor of purely humane and hygienic measures. Yet in the precisely parallel case of a man breaking into my house and stealing my wife's diamonds I am expected as a matter of course to steal ten years of his life, torturing him all the time. If he tries to defeat that monstrous retaliation by shooting me, my survivors hang him. The net result suggested by the police statistics is that we inflict atrocious injuries on the burglars we catch in order to make the rest take effectual precautions against detection; so that instead of saving our wives' diamonds from burglary we only greatly decrease our chances of ever getting them back, and increase our chances of being shot by the robber if we are unlucky enough to disturb him at his work.

But the thoughtless wickedness with which we scatter sentences of imprisonment, torture in the solitary cell and on the plank bed, and flogging, on moral invalids and energetic rebels, is as nothing compared to the silly levity with which we tolerate poverty as if it were either a wholesome tonic for lazy people or else a virtue to be embraced as St Francis embraced it. If a man is indolent, let him be poor. If he is drunken, let him be poor. If he is not a gentleman, let him be poor. If he is addicted to the fine arts or to pure science instead of to trade and finance, let him be poor. If he chooses to spend his urban eighteen shillings a week or his agricultural thirteen shillings a week on his beer and his family instead of saving it up for his old age, let him be poor. Let nothing be done for "the undeserving": let him be poor. Serve him right! Also — somewhat inconsistently — blessed are the poor!

Now what does this Let Him Be Poor mean? It means let him be weak. Let him be ignorant. Let him become a nucleus of disease. Let him be a standing exhibition and example of ugliness and dirt. Let him have rickety children. Let him be cheap, and drag his fellows down to his own price by selling himself to do their work. Let his habitations turn our cities into poisonous congeries of slums. Let his daughters infect our young men with the diseases of the streets, and his sons revenge him by turning the nation's manhood into scrofula, cowardice, cruelty, hypocrisy, political imbecility, and all the other fruits of oppression and malnutrition. Let the undeserving become still less deserving; and let the deserving lay up for himself, not treasures in heaven, but horrors in hell upon earth. This being so, is it really wise to let him be poor? Would he not do ten times less harm as a prosperous burglar, incendiary, ravisher or murderer, to the utmost limits of humanity's comparatively negligible impulses in these directions? Suppose we were to abolish all penalties for such activities, and decide that poverty is the one thing we will not tolerate — that every adult with less than, say, £365 a year, shall be painlessly but inexorably killed, and every hungry half naked child forcibly fattened and clothed, would not that be an enormous improvement on our existing system, which has already destroyed so many civilizations, and is visibly destroying ours in the same way?

Is there any radicle of such legislation in our parliamentary system? Well, there are two measures just sprouting in the political soil, which may conceivably grow to something valuable. One is the institution of a Legal Minimum Wage. The other, Old Age Pensions. But there is a better plan than either of these.

Some time ago I mentioned the subject of Universal Old Age Pensions to my fellow Socialist Cobden-Sanderson, famous as an artist-craftsman in bookbinding and printing. "Why not Universal Pensions for Life?" said Cobden-Sanderson. In saying this, he solved the industrial problem at a stroke. At present we say callously to each citizen "If you want money, earn it" as if his having or not having it were a matter that concerned himself alone. We do not even secure for him the opportunity of earning it: on the contrary, we allow our industry to be organized in open dependence on the maintenance of "a reserve army of unemployed" for the sake of "elasticity." The sensible course would be Cobden-Sanderson's: that is, to give every man enough to live well on, so as to guarantee the community against the possibility of a case of the malignant disease of poverty, and then (necessarily) to see that he earned it.

Undershaft, the hero of Major Barbara, is simply a man who, having grasped the fact that poverty is a crime, knows that when society offered him the alternative of poverty or a lucrative trade in death and destruction, it offered him, not a choice between opulent villainy and humble virtue, but between energetic enterprise and cowardly infamy. His conduct stands the Kantian test, which Peter Shirley's does not.[1] Peter Shirley is what we call the honest poor man. Undershaft is what we call the wicked rich one: Shirley is Lazarus, Undershaft Dives.[2] Well, the misery of the world is due to the fact that the great mass of men act and believe as Peter Shirley acts and believes. If they acted and believed as Undershaft acts and believes, the immediate result would be a revolution of incalculable beneficence. To be wealthy, says Undershaft, is with me a point of honor for which I am prepared to kill at the risk of my own life. This preparedness is, as he says, the final test of sincerity. Like Froissart's medieval hero, who saw that "to rob and pill was a good life," he is not the dupe of that public sentiment against killing which is propagated and endowed by people who would otherwise be killed themselves, or of the mouth-honor paid to poverty and obedience by rich and insubordinate do-nothings who want to rob the poor without courage and command them without superiority. Froissart's knight, in placing the achievement of a good life before all the other duties — which indeed are not duties at all when they conflict with it, but plain wickedness — behaved bravely, admirably, and, in the final analysis, public-spiritedly. Medieval society, on the other hand, behaved very badly indeed in organizing itself so stupidly that a good life could be achieved by robbing and pilling. If the knight's contemporaries had been all as resolute as he, robbing and pilling would have been the shortest way to the gallows, just as, if we were all as resolute and clearsighted as Undershaft, an attempt to live by means of what is called "an independent income" would be the shortest way to the lethal chamber. But as, thanks to our political imbecility and personal cowardice (fruits of poverty, both), the best imitation of a good life now procurable is life on an independent income, all sensible people aim at securing such an income, and are, of course, careful to legalize and moralize both it and all the actions and sentiments which

---

[1]Immanuel Kant (1724–1804) in the *Kritik* of practical reason urges that the moral imperative is possible when the worlds of sense and reason are balanced and when self-determination is achieved.

[2]In Luke 16:19–31 Jesus tells a parable about a poor man, Lazarus, who begs crumbs from a rich man, Dives. Lazarus is turned away. After they die, however, Lazarus receives a place in Abraham's bosom and Dives suffers in anguish.

lead to it and support it as an institution. What else can they do? They know, of course, that they are rich because others are poor. But they cannot help that: it is for the poor to repudiate poverty when they have had enough of it. The thing can be done easily enough: the demonstrations to the contrary made by the economists, jurists, moralists and sentimentalists hired by the rich to defend them, or even doing the work gratuitously out of sheer folly and abjectness, impose only on those who want to be imposed on.

The reason why the independent income-tax payers are not solid in defense of their position is that since we are not medieval rovers through a sparsely populated country, the poverty of those we rob prevents our having the good life for which we sacrifice them. Rich men or aristocrats with a developed sense of life — men like Ruskin and William Morris and Kropotkin — have enormous social appetites and very fastidious personal ones. They are not content with handsome houses: they want handsome cities. They are not content with be-diamonded wives and blooming daughters: they complain because the charwoman is badly dressed, because the laundress smells of gin, because the sempstress is anemic, because every man they meet is not a friend and every woman not a romance. They turn up their noses at their neighbor's drains, and are made ill by the architecture of their neighbor's houses. Trade patterns made to suit vulgar people do not please them (and they can get nothing else): they cannot sleep nor sit at ease upon "slaughtered" cabinet makers' furniture. The very air is not good enough for them: there is too much factory smoke in it. They even demand abstract conditions: justice, honor, a noble moral atmosphere, a mystic nexus to replace the cash nexus. Finally they declare that though to rob and pill with your own hand on horseback and in steel coat may have been a good life, to rob and pill by the hands of the policeman, the bailiff, and the soldier, and to underpay them meanly for doing it, is not a good life, but rather fatal to all possibility of even a tolerable one. They call on the poor to revolt, and, finding the poor shocked at their ungentlemanliness, despairingly revile the proletariat for its "damned wantlessness" (*verdammte Bedürfnislosigkeit*).

So far, however, their attack on society has lacked simplicity. The poor do not share their tastes nor understand their art-criticisms. They do not want the simple life, nor the esthetic life; on the contrary, they want very much to wallow in all the costly vulgarities from which the elect souls among the rich turn away with loathing. It is by surfeit and not by abstinence that they will be cured of their hankering after unwholesome sweets. What they do dislike and despise and are ashamed of is poverty. To ask them to fight for the difference between the Christmas number of the Illustrated London News and the Kelmscott Chaucer is silly: they prefer the News. The difference between a stock-broker's cheap and dirty starched white shirt and collar and the comparatively costly and carefully dyed blue shirt of William Morris is a difference so disgraceful to Morris in their eyes that if they fought on the subject at all, they would fight in defense of the starch. "Cease to be slaves, in order that you may become cranks" is not a very inspiring call to arms; nor is it really improved by substituting saints for cranks. Both terms denote men of genius; and the common man does not want to live the life of a man of genius: he would much rather live the life of a pet collie if that were the only alternative. But he does want more money. Whatever else he may be vague about, he is clear about that. He may or may not prefer Major Barbara to the Drury Lane pantomime; but he always prefers five hundred pounds to five hundred shillings.

Now to deplore this preference as sordid, and teach children that it is sinful to desire money, is to strain towards the extreme possible limit of impudence in lying and corruption in hypocrisy. The universal regard for money is the one hopeful fact in our civilization, the one sound spot in our social conscience. Money is the most important thing in the world. It represents health, strength, honor, generosity and beauty as conspicuously and undeniably as the want of it represents illness, weakness, disgrace, meanness and ugliness. Not the least of its virtues is that it destroys base people as certainly as it fortifies and dignifies noble people. It is only when it is cheapened to worthlessness for some and made impossibly dear to others, that it becomes a curse. In short, it is a curse only in such foolish social conditions that life itself is a curse. For the two things are inseparable: money is the counter that enables life to be distributed socially: it *is* life as truly as sovereigns and bank notes are money. The first duty of every citizen is to insist on having money on reasonable terms; and this demand is not complied with by giving four men three shillings each for ten or twelve hours' drudgery and one man a thousand pounds for nothing. The crying need of the nation is not for better morals, cheaper bread, temperance, liberty, culture, redemption of fallen sisters and erring brothers, nor the grace, love and fellowship of the Trinity, but simply for enough money. And the evil to be attacked is not sin, suffering, greed, priestcraft, kingcraft, demagogy, monopoly, ignorance, drink, war, pestilence, nor any other of the scapegoats which reformers sacrifice, but simply poverty.

Once take your eyes from the ends of the earth and fix them on this truth just under your nose; and Andrew Undershaft's views will not perplex you in the least. Unless indeed his constant sense that he is only the instrument of a Will or Life Force which uses him for purposes wider than his own, may puzzle you. If so, that is because you are walking either in artificial Darwinian darkness, or in mere stupidity. All genuinely religious people have that consciousness. To them Undershaft the Mystic will be quite intelligible, and his perfect comprehension of his daughter the Salvationist and her lover the Euripidean republican natural and inevitable. That, however, is not new, even on the stage. What is new, as far as I know, is that article in Undershaft's religion which recognizes in Money the first need and in poverty the vilest sin of man and society.

This dramatic conception has not, of course, been attained *per saltum.*[3] Nor has it been borrowed from Nietzsche or from any man born beyond the Channel. The late Samuel Butler, in his own department the greatest English writer of the latter half of the XIX century, steadily inculcated the necessity and morality of a conscientious Laodiceanism in religion and of an earnest and constant sense of the importance of money. It drives one almost to despair of English literature when one sees so extraordinary a study of English life as Butler's posthumous *Way of All Flesh* making so little impression that when, some years later, I produce plays in which Butler's extraordinarily fresh, free and future-piercing suggestions have an obvious share, I am met with nothing but vague cacklings about Ibsen and Nietzsche, and am only too thankful that they are not about Alfred de Musset and Georges Sand. Really, the English do not deserve to have great men. They allowed Butler to die practically unknown, whilst I, a comparatively insignificant Irish journalist, was leading them by the nose into an advertisement of me which has made my own life a burden. In Sicily there is a Via Samuele

---

[3]*per saltum:* With gestures.

Butler. When an English tourist sees it, he either asks "Who the devil was Samuele Butler?" or wonders why the Sicilians should perpetuate the memory of the author of *Hudibras*.

Well, it cannot be denied that the English are only too anxious to recognize a man of genius if somebody will kindly point him out to them. Having pointed myself out in this manner with some success, I now point out Samuel Butler, and trust that in consequence I shall hear a little less in future of the novelty and foreign origin of the ideas which are now making their way into the English theater through plays written by Socialists. There are living men whose originality and power are as obvious as Butler's and when they die that fact will be discovered. Meanwhile I recommend them to insist on their own merits as an important part of their own business.

The Salvation Army

When *Major Barbara* was produced in London, the second act was reported in an important northern newspaper as a withering attack on the Salvation Army, and the despairing ejaculation of Barbara deplored by a London daily as a tasteless blasphemy. And they were set right, not by the professed critics of the theater, but by religious and philosophical publicists like Sir Oliver Lodge and Dr. Stanton Coit, and strenuous Nonconformist journalists like William Stead, who not only understood the act as well as the Salvationists themselves, but also saw it in its relation to the religious life of the nation, a life which seems to lie not only outside the sympathy of many of our theater critics, but actually outside their knowledge of society. Indeed nothing could be more ironically curious than the confrontation Major Barbara effected of the theater enthusiasts with the religious enthusiasts. On the one hand was the playgoer, always seeking pleasure, paying exorbitantly for it, suffering unbearable discomforts for it, and hardly ever getting it. On the other hand was the Salvationist, repudiating gaiety and courting effort and sacrifice, yet always in the wildest spirits, laughing, joking, singing, rejoicing, drumming, and tambourining: his life flying by in a flash of excitement, and his death arriving as a climax of triumph. And, if you please, the playgoer despising the Salvationist as a joyless person, shut out from the heaven of the theater, self-condemned to a life of hideous gloom; and the Salvationist mourning over the playgoer as over a prodigal with vine leaves in his hair, careering outrageously to hell amid the popping of champagne corks and the ribald laughter of sirens! Could misunderstanding be more complete, or sympathy worse misplaced?

Fortunately, the Salvationists are more accessible to the religious character of the drama than the playgoers to the gay energy and artistic fertility of religion. They can see, when it is pointed out to them, that a theater, as a place where two or three are gathered together, takes from that divine presence an inalienable sanctity of which the grossest and profanest farce can no more deprive it than a hypocritical sermon by a snobbish bishop can desecrate Westminster Abbey. But in our professional playgoers this indispensable preliminary conception of sanctity seems wanting. They talk of actors as mimes and mummers, and I fear, think of dramatic authors as liars and pandars, whose main business is the voluptuous soothing of the tired city speculator when what he calls the serious business of the day is over. Passion, the life of drama, means nothing to them but primitive sexual excitement: such phrases as "impassioned poetry" or "passionate love of truth" have fallen quite out of their vocabulary and been replaced by "passional crime" and the like. They assume, as far as I can gather, that people in whom passion has a larger scope are passionless and therefore uninteresting. Consequently they come to think of religious people as people who are not interesting and not amusing. And so, when Barbara cuts the regular Salvation Army jokes, and snatches a kiss from her lover across his drum, the devotees of the theater think they ought to appear shocked, and conclude that the whole play is an elaborate mockery of the Army. And then either hypocritically rebuke me for mocking, or foolishly take part in the supposed mockery!

Even the handful of mentally competent critics got into difficulties over my demonstration of the economic deadlock in which the Salvation Army finds itself. Some of them thought that the Army would not have taken money from a distiller and a cannon founder: others thought it should not have taken it: all assumed more or less definitely that it reduced itself to absurdity or hypocrisy by taking it. On the first point the reply of the Army itself was prompt and conclusive. As one of its officers said, they would take money from the devil himself and be only too glad to get it out of his hands and into God's. They gratefully acknowledged that publicans not only give them money but allow them to collect it in the bar — sometimes even when there is a Salvation meeting outside preaching teetotalism. In fact, they questioned the verisimilitude of the play, not because Mrs Baines took the money, but because Barbara refused it.

On the point that the Army ought not to take such money, its justification is obvious. It must take the money because it cannot exist without money, and there is no other money to be had. Practically all the spare money in the country consists of a mass of rent, interest, and profit, every penny of which is bound up with crime, drink, prostitution, disease, and all the evil fruits of poverty, as inextricably as with enterprise, wealth, commercial probity, and national prosperity. The notion that you can earmark certain coins as tainted is an unpractical individualist superstition. Nonetheless the fact that all our money is tainted gives a very severe shock to earnest young souls when some dramatic instance of the taint first makes them conscious of it. When an enthusiastic young clergyman of the Established Church first realizes that the Ecclesiastical Commissioners receive the rents of sporting public houses, brothels, and sweating dens; or that the most generous contributor at his last charity sermon was an employer trading in female labor cheapened by prostitution as unscrupulously as a hotel keeper trades in waiters' labor cheapened by tips, or commissionaires' labor cheapened by pensions; or that the only patron who can afford to rebuild his church or his schools or give his boys' brigade a gymnasium or a library is the son-in-law of a Chicago meat King, that young clergyman has, like Barbara, a very bad quarter hour. But he cannot help himself by refusing to accept money from anybody except sweet old ladies with independent incomes and gentle and lovely ways of life. He has only to follow up the income of the sweet ladies to its industrial source, and there he will find Mrs Warren's profession[4] and the poisonous canned meat and all the rest of it. His own stipend has the same root. He must either share the world's guilt or go to another planet. He must save the world's honor if he is to save his own. This is what all the Churches find just as the Salvation Army and Barbara find it in the play. Her discovery that she is her father's accomplice; that the Salvation Army is the accomplice of the distiller and the dynamite maker; that they can no more escape one

---

[4]Prostitution, as in his play *Mrs Warren's Profession.*

another than they can escape the air they breathe; that there is no salvation for them through personal righteousness, but only through the redemption of the whole nation from its vicious, lazy, competitive anarchy: this discovery has been made by everyone except the Pharisees and (apparently) the professional playgoers, who still wear their Tom Hood shirts and underpay their washerwoman without the slightest misgiving as to the elevation of their private characters, the purity of their private atmospheres, and their right to repudiate as foreign to themselves the coarse depravity of the garret and the slum. Not that they mean any harm: they only desire to be, in their little private way, what they call gentlemen. They do not understand Barbara's lesson because they have not, like her, learnt it by taking their part in the larger life of the nation.

Barbara's Return to the Colors

Barbara's return to the colors may yet provide a subject for the dramatic historian of the future. To get back to the Salvation Army with the knowledge that even the Salvationists themselves are not saved yet; that poverty is not blessed, but a most damnable sin; and that when General Booth chose Blood and Fire for the emblem of Salvation instead of the Cross, he was perhaps better inspired than he knew: such knowledge, for the daughter of Andrew Undershaft, will clearly lead to something hopefuller than distributing bread and treacle at the expense of Bodger.

It is a very significant thing, this instinctive choice of the military form of organization, this substitution of the drum for the organ, by the Salvation Army. Does it not suggest that the Salvationists divine that they must actually fight the devil instead of merely praying at him? At present, it is true, they have not quite ascertained his correct address. When they do, they may give a very rude shock to that sense of security which he has gained from his experience of the fact that hard words, even when uttered by eloquent essayists and lecturers, or carried unanimously at enthusiastic public meetings on the motion of eminent reformers, break no bones. It has been said that the French Revolution was the work of Voltaire, Rousseau, and the Encyclopedists. It seems to me to have been the work of men who had observed that virtuous indignation, caustic criticism, conclusive argument, and instructive pamphleteering, even when done by the most earnest and witty literary geniuses, were as useless as praying, things going steadily from bad to worse whilst the Social Contract and the pamphlets of Voltaire were at the height of their vogue. Eventually, as we know, perfectly respectable citizens and earnest philanthropists connived at the September massacres because hard experience had convinced them that if they contented themselves with appeals to humanity and patriotism, the aristocracy, though it would read their appeals with the greatest enjoyment and appreciation, flattering and admiring the writers, would nonetheless continue to conspire with foreign monarchists to undo the revolution and restore the old system with every circumstance of savage vengeance and ruthless repression of popular liberties.

The nineteenth century saw the same lesson repeated in England. It had its Utilitarians, its Christian Socialists, its Fabians (still extant): it had Bentham, Mill, Dickens, Ruskin, Carlyle, Butler, Henry George, and Morris. And the end of all their efforts is in the Chicago described by Mr Upton Sinclair, and the London in which the people who pay to be amused by my dramatic representation of Peter Shirley turned out to starve at forty because there are younger slaves to be had for his wages, do not take, and have not the slightest intention of taking, any effective step to organize society in such a way as to make that everyday infamy impossible. I, who have preached and pamphleteered like any Encyclopedist, have to confess that my methods are no use, and would be no use if I were Voltaire, Rousseau, Bentham, Marx, Mill, Dickens, Carlyle, Ruskin, Butler, and Morris all rolled into one, with Euripides, More, Montaigne, Molière, Beaumarchais, Swift, Goethe, Ibsen, Tolstoy, Jesus, and the prophets all thrown in (as indeed in some sort I actually am, standing as I do on all their shoulders). The problem being to make heroes out of cowards, we paper apostles and artist-magicians have succeeded only in giving cowards all the sensations of heroes whilst they tolerate every abomination, accept every plunder, and submit to every oppression. Christianity, in making a merit of such submission, has marked only that depth in the abyss at which the very sense of shame is lost. The Christian has been like Dickens's doctor in the debtor's prison, who tells the newcomer of its ineffable peace and security: no duns; no tyrannical collectors of rates, taxes, and rent; no importunate hopes nor exacting duties; nothing but the rest and safety of having no farther to fall.

Yet in the poorest corner of this soul-destroying Christendom vitality suddenly begins to germinate again. Joyousness, a sacred gift long dethroned by the hellish laughter of derision and obscenity, rises like a flood miraculously out of the fetid dust and mud of the slums; rousing marches and impetuous dithyrambs rise to the heavens from people among whom the depressing noise called "sacred music" is a standing joke; a flag with Blood and Fire on it is unfurled, not in murderous rancor, but because fire is beautiful and blood a vital and splendid red; Fear, which we flatter by calling Self, vanishes; and transfigured men and women carry their gospel through a transfigured world, calling their leader General, themselves captains and brigadiers, and their whole body an Army: praying, but praying only for refreshment, for strength to fight, and for needful MONEY (a notable sign, that); preaching, but not preaching submission; daring ill-usage and abuse, but not putting up with more of it than is inevitable; and practicing what the world will let them practice, including soap and water, color and music. There is danger in such activity; and where there is danger there is hope. Our present security is nothing, and can be nothing, but evil made irresistible.

Weaknesses of the Salvation Army

For the present, however, it is not my business to flatter the Salvation Army. Rather must I point out to it that it has almost as many weaknesses as the Church of England itself. It is building up a business organization which will compel it eventually to see that its present staff of enthusiast-commanders shall be succeeded by a bureaucracy of men of business who will be no better than bishops, and perhaps a good deal more unscrupulous. That has always happened sooner or later to great orders founded by saints; and the order founded by St William Booth is not exempt from the same danger. It is even more dependent than the Church on rich people who would cut off supplies at once if it began to preach that indispensable revolt against poverty which must also be a revolt against riches. It is hampered by a heavy contingent of pious elders who are not really Salvationists at all, but Evangelicals of the old school. It still, as Commissioner Howard affirms, "sticks to Moses," which is flat nonsense at this time of day if the Commissioner means, as I am afraid he does, that the Book of Genesis contains a trustworthy scientific account of the origin of species, and that the god to whom Jephthah sacrificed his daughter is any less obviously a tribal idol than Dagon or Chemosh.

Further, there is still too much other-worldliness about the Army. Like Frederick's grenadier, the Salvationist wants to live forever (the most monstrous way of crying for the moon); and though it is evident to anyone who has ever heard General Booth and his best officers that they would work as hard for human salvation as they do at present if they believed that death would be the end of them individually, they and their followers have a bad habit of talking as if the Salvationists were heroically enduring a very bad time on earth as an investment which will bring them in dividends later on in the form, not of a better life to come for the whole world, but of an eternity spent by themselves personally in a sort of bliss which would bore any active person to a second death. Surely the truth is that the Salvationists are unusually happy people. And is it not the very diagnostic of true salvation that it shall overcome the fear of death? Now the man who has come to believe that there is no such thing as death, the change so called being merely the transition to an exquisitely happy and utterly careless life, has not overcome the fear of death at all: on the contrary, it has overcome him so completely that he refuses to die on any terms whatever. I do not call a Salvationist really saved until he is ready to lie down cheerfully on the scrap heap, having paid scot and lot and something over, and let his eternal life pass on to renew its youth in the battalions of the future.

Then there is the nasty lying habit called confession, which the Army encourages because it lends itself to dramatic oratory, with plenty of thrilling incident. For my part, when I hear a convert relating the violences and oaths and blasphemies he was guilty of before he was saved, making out that he was a very terrible fellow then and is the most contrite and chastened of Christians now, I believe him no more than I believe the millionaire who says he came up to London or Chicago as a boy with only three halfpence in his pocket. Salvationists have said to me that Barbara in my play would never have been taken in by so transparent a humbug as Snobby Price; and certainly I do not think Snobby could have taken in any experienced Salvationist on a point on which the Salvationist did not wish to be taken in. But on the point of conversion all Salvationists wish to be taken in; for the more obvious the sinner the more obvious the miracle of his conversion. When you advertise a converted burglar or reclaimed drunkard as one of the attractions at an experience meeting, your burglar can hardly have been too burglarious or your drunkard too drunken. As long as such attractions are relied on, you will have your Snobbies claiming to have beaten their mothers when they were as a matter of prosaic fact habitually beaten by them, and your Rummies of the tamest respectability pretending to a past of reckless and dazzling vice. Even when confessions are sincerely autobiographic we should beware of assuming that the impulse to make them was pious or that the interest of the hearers is wholesome. As well might we assume that the poor people who insist on showing disgusting ulcers to district visitors are convinced hygienists, or that the curiosity which sometimes welcomes such exhibitions is a pleasant and creditable one. One is often tempted to suggest that those who pester our police superintendents with confessions of murder might very wisely be taken at their word and executed, except in the few cases in which a real murderer is seeking to be relieved of his guilt by confession and expiation. For though I am not, I hope, an unmerciful person, I do not think that the inexorability of the deed once done should be disguised by any ritual, whether in the confessional or on the scaffold.

And here my disagreement with the Salvation Army, and with all propagandists of the Cross (which I loathe as I loathe all gibbets) becomes deep indeed. Forgiveness, absolution, atonement, are figments: punishment is only a pretense of canceling one crime by another; and you can no more have forgiveness without vindictiveness than you can have a cure without a disease. You will never get a high morality from people who conceive that their misdeeds are revocable and pardonable, or in a society where absolution and expiation are officially provided for us all. The demand may be very real; but the supply is spurious. Thus Bill Walker, in my play, having assaulted the Salvation Lass, presently finds himself overwhelmed with an intolerable conviction of sin under the skilled treatment of Barbara. Straightway he begins to try to unassault the lass and deruffianize his deed, first by getting punished for it in kind, and, when that relief is denied him, by fining himself a pound to compensate the girl. He is foiled both ways. He finds the Salvation Army is inexorable as fact itself. It will not punish him: it will not take his money. It will not tolerate a redeemed ruffian: it leaves him no means of salvation except ceasing to be a ruffian. In doing this, the Salvation Army instinctively grasps the central truth of Christianity, and discards its central superstition: that central truth being the vanity of revenge and punishment, and that central superstition the salvation of the world by the gibbet.

For, be it noted, Bill has assaulted an old and starving woman also; and for this worse offense he feels no remorse whatever, because she makes it clear that her malice is as great as his own. "Let her have the law of me, as she said she would," says Bill: "what I done to her is no more on what you might call my conscience than sticking a pig." This shows a perfectly natural and wholesome state of mind on his part. The old woman, like the law she threatens him with, is perfectly ready to play the game of retaliation with him: to rob him if he steals, to flog him if he strikes, to murder him if he kills. By example and precept the law and public opinion teach him to impose his will on others by anger, violence, and cruelty, and to wipe off the moral score by punishment. That is sound Crosstianity. But his Crosstianity has got entangled with something which Barbara calls Christianity, and which unexpectedly causes her to refuse to play the hangman's game of Satan casting out Satan. She refuses to prosecute a drunken ruffian; she converses on equal terms with a blackguard to whom no lady should be seen speaking in the public street: in short, she imitates Christ. Bill's conscience reacts to this just as naturally as it does to the old woman's threats. He is placed in a position of unbearable moral inferiority, and strives by every means in his power to escape from it, whilst he is still quite ready to meet the abuse of the old woman by attempting to smash a mug on her face. And that is the triumphant justification of Barbara's Christianity as against our system of judicial punishment and the vindictive villain-thrashings and "poetic justice" of the romantic stage.

For the credit of literature it must be pointed out that the situation is only partly novel. Victor Hugo long ago gave us the epic of the convict and the bishop's candlesticks, of the Crosstian policeman annihilated by his encounter with the Christian Valjean. But Bill Walker is not, like Valjean, romantically changed from a demon into an angel. There are millions of Bill Walkers in all classes of society today; and the point which I, as a professor of natural psychology, desire to demonstrate, is that Bill, without any change in his character or circumstances whatsoever, will react one way to one sort of treatment and another way to another.

In proof I might point to the sensational object lesson provided by our commercial millionaires today. They begin as brigands: merciless, unscrupulous, dealing out ruin and death and slavery to their competitors and employees, and facing desperately the worst that their competitors can do to them. The history of the English factories, the American Trusts, the exploitation of African gold, diamonds, ivory and rubber, outdoes in villainy the worst that has ever been imagined of the buccaneers of the Spanish Main. Captain Kidd would have marooned a modern Trust magnate for conduct unworthy of a gentleman of fortune. The law every day seizes on unsuccessful scoundrels of this type and punishes them with a cruelty worse than their own, with the result that they come out of the torture house more dangerous than they went in, and renew their evil doing (nobody will employ them at anything else) until they are again seized, again tormented, and again let loose, with the same result.

But the successful scoundrel is dealt with very differently, and very Christianly. He is not only forgiven: he is idolized, respected, made much of, all but worshiped. Society returns him good for evil in the most extravagant overmeasure. And with what result? He begins to idolize himself, to respect himself, to live up to the treatment he receives. He preaches sermons; he writes books of the most edifying advice to young men, and actually persuades himself that he got on by taking his own advice; he endows educational institutions; he supports charities; he dies finally in the odor of sanctity, leaving a will which is a monument of public spirit and bounty. And all this without any change in his character. The spots of the leopard and the stripes of the tiger are as brilliant as ever; but the conduct of the world towards him has changed; and his conduct has changed accordingly. You have only to reverse your attitude towards him — to lay hands on his property, revile him, assault him, and he will be a brigand again in a moment, as ready to crush you as you are to crush him, and quite as full of pretentious moral reasons for doing it.

In short, when Major Barbara says that there are no scoundrels, she is right: there are no absolute scoundrels, though there are impracticable people of whom I shall treat presently. Every reasonable man (and woman) is a potential scoundrel and a potential good citizen. What a man is depends on his character; but what he does, and what we think of what he does, depends on his circumstances. The characteristics that ruin a man in one class make him eminent in another. The characters that behave differently in different circumstances behave alike in similar circumstances. Take a common English character like that of Bill Walker. We meet Bill everywhere: on the judicial bench, on the episcopal bench, in the Privy Council, at the War Office and Admiralty, as well as in the Old Bailey dock or in the ranks of casual unskilled labor. And the morality of Bill's characteristics varies with these various circumstances. The faults of the burglar are the qualities of the financier: the manners and habits of a duke would cost a city clerk his situation. In short, though character is independent of circumstances, conduct is not; and our moral judgments of character are not: both are circumstantial. Take any condition of life in which the circumstances are for a mass of men practically alike: felony, the House of Lords, the factory, the stables, the gipsy encampment or where you please! In spite of diversity of character and temperament, the conduct and morals of the individuals in each group are as predicable and as alike in the main as if they were a flock of sheep, morals being mostly only social habits and circumstantial necessities. Strong people know this and count upon it. In nothing have the master-minds of the world been distinguished from the ordinary suburban season-ticket holder more than in their straightforward perception of the fact that mankind is practically a single species, and not a menagerie of gentlemen and bounders, villains and heroes, cowards and daredevils, peers and peasants, grocers and aristocrats, artisans and laborers, washerwomen and duchesses, in which all the grades of income and caste represent distinct animals who must not be introduced to one another or intermarry. Napoleon constructing a galaxy of generals and courtiers, and even of monarchs, out of his collection of social nobodies; Julius Caesar appointing as governor of Egypt the son of a freedman — one who but a short time before would have been legally disqualified for the post even of a private soldier in the Roman army; Louis XI making his barber his privy councillor: all these had in their different ways a firm hold of the scientific fact of human equality, expressed by Barbara in the Christian formula that all men are children of one father. A man who believes that men are naturally divided into upper and lower and middle classes morally is making exactly the same mistake as the man who believes that they are naturally divided in the same way socially. And just as our persistent attempts to found political institutions on a basis of social inequality have always produced long periods of destructive friction relieved from time to time by violent explosions of revolution; so the attempt — will Americans please note — to found moral institutions on a basis of moral inequality can lead to nothing but unnatural Reigns of the Saints relieved by licentious Restorations; to Americans who have made divorce a public institution turning the face of Europe into one huge sardonic smile by refusing to stay in the same hotel with a Russian man of genius who has changed wives without the sanction of South Dakota; to grotesque hypocrisy, cruel persecution, and final utter confusion of conventions and compliances with benevolence and respectability. It is quite useless to declare that all men are born free if you deny that they are born good. Guarantee a man's goodness and his liberty will take care of itself. To guarantee his freedom on condition that you approve of his moral character is formally to abolish all freedom whatsoever, as every man's liberty is at the mercy of a moral indictment which any fool can trump up against everyone who violates custom, whether as a prophet or as a rascal. This is the lesson Democracy has to learn before it can become anything but the most oppressive of all the priesthoods.

Let us now return to Bill Walker and his case of conscience against the Salvation Army. Major Barbara, not being a modern Tetzel, or the treasurer of a hospital, refuses to sell absolution to Bill for a sovereign. Unfortunately, what the Army can afford to refuse in the case of Bill Walker, it cannot refuse in the case of Bodger. Bodger is master of the situation because he holds the purse strings. "Strive as you will," says Bodger, in effect: "me you cannot do without. You cannot save Bill Walker without my money." And the Army answers, quite rightly under the circumstances, "We will take money from the devil himself sooner than abandon the work of Salvation." So Bodger pays his conscience-money and gets the absolution that is refused to Bill. In real life Bill would perhaps never know this. But I, the dramatist whose business it is to show the connection between things that seem apart and unrelated in the haphazard order of events in real life, have contrived to make it known to Bill, with the result that the Salvation Army loses its hold of him at once.

But Bill may not be lost, for all that. He is still in the grip of the facts and of his own conscience, and may find his taste for blackguardism permanently spoiled. Still, I cannot guarantee that happy ending. Walk through the poorer quarters of our cities on Sunday when the men are not working, but resting and chewing the cud of their reflections. You will find one expression common to every mature face: the expression of cynicism. The discovery made by Bill Walker about the Salvation Army has been made by everyone there. They have found that every man has his price; and they have been foolishly or corruptly taught to mistrust and despise him for that necessary and salutary condition of social existence. When they learn that General Booth, too, has his price, they do not admire him because it is a high one, and admit the need of organizing society so that he shall get it in an honorable way: they conclude that his character is unsound and that all religious men are hypocrites and allies of their sweaters and oppressors. They know that the large subscriptions which help to support the Army are endowments, not of religion, but of the wicked doctrine of docility in poverty and humility under oppression; and they are rent by the most agonizing of all the doubts of the soul, the doubt whether their true salvation must not come from their most abhorrent passions, from murder, envy, greed, stubbornness, rage, and terrorism, rather than from public spirit, reasonableness, humanity, generosity, tenderness, delicacy, pity, and kindness. The confirmation of that doubt, at which our newspapers have been working so hard for years past, is the morality of militarism; and the justification of militarism is that circumstances may at any time make it the true morality of the moment. It is by producing such moments that we produce violent and sanguinary revolutions, such as the one now in progress in Russia and the one which Capitalism in England and America is daily and diligently provoking.

At such moments it becomes the duty of the Churches to evoke all the powers of destruction against the existing order. But if they do this, the existing order must forcibly suppress them. Churches are suffered to exist only on condition that they preach submission to the State as at present capitalistically organized. The Church of England itself is compelled to add to the thirty-six articles in which it formulates its religious tenets, three more in which it apologetically protests that the moment any of these articles comes in conflict with the State it is to be entirely renounced, abjured, violated, abrogated and abhorred, the policeman being a much more important person than any of the Persons of the Trinity. And this is why no tolerated Church nor Salvation Army can ever win the entire confidence of the poor. It must be on the side of the police and the military, no matter what it believes or disbelieves; and as the police and the military are the instruments by which the rich rob and oppress the poor (on legal and moral principles made for the purpose), it is not possible to be on the side of the poor and of the police at the same time. Indeed the religious bodies, as the almoners of the rich, become a sort of auxiliary police, taking off the insurrectionary edge of poverty with coals and blankets, bread and treacle, and soothing and cheering the victims with hopes of immense and inexpensive happiness in another world when the process of working them to premature death in the service of the rich is complete in this.

Christianity and Anarchism

Such is the false position from which neither the Salvation Army nor the Church of England nor any other religious organization whatever can escape except through a reconstition of society. Nor can they merely endure the State passively, washing their hands of its sins. The State is constantly forcing the consciences of men by violence and cruelty. Not content with exacting money from us for the maintenance of its soldiers and policemen, its jailers and executioners, it forces us to take an active personal part in its proceedings on pain of becoming ourselves the victims of its violence. As I write these lines, a sensational example is given to the world. A royal marriage has been celebrated, first by sacrament in a cathedral, and then by a bullfight having for its main amusement the spectacle of horses gored and disemboweled by the bull, after which, when the bull is so exhausted as to be no longer dangerous, he is killed by a cautious matador. But the ironic contrast between the bullfight and the sacrament of marriage does not move anyone. Another contrast — that between the splendor, the happiness, the atmosphere of kindly admiration surrounding the young couple, and the price paid for it under our abominable social arrangements in the misery, squalor and degradation of millions of other young couples — is drawn at the same moment by a novelist, Mr Upton Sinclair, who chips a corner of the veneering from the huge meat packing industries of Chicago, and shows it to us as a sample of what is going on all over the world underneath the top layer of prosperous plutocracy. One man is sufficiently moved by that contrast to pay his own life as the price of one terrible blow at the responsible parties. His poverty has left him ignorant enough to be duped by the pretense that the innocent young bride and bridegroom, put forth and crowned by plutocracy as the heads of a State in which they have less personal power than any policeman, and less influence than any Chairman of a Trust, are responsible. At them accordingly he launches his sixpennorth of fulminate, missing his mark, but scattering the bowels of as many horses as any bull in the arena, and slaying twenty-three persons, besides wounding ninety-nine. And of all these, the horses alone are innocent of the guilt he is avenging: had he blown all Madrid to atoms with every adult person in it, not one could have escaped the charge of being an accessory, before, at, and after the fact, to poverty and prostitution, to such wholesale massacre of infants as Herod never dreamt of, to plague, pestilence and famine, battle, murder and lingering death — perhaps not one who had not helped, through example, precept, connivance, and even clamor, to teach the dynamiter his well-learnt gospel of hatred and vengeance, by approving every day of sentences of years of imprisonment so infernal in their unnatural stupidity and panic-stricken cruelty, that their advocates can disavow neither the dagger nor the bomb without stripping the mask of justice and humanity from themselves also.

Be it noted that at this very moment there appears the biography of one of our dukes, who, being a Scot, could argue about politics, and therefore stood out as a great brain among our aristocrats. And what, if you please, was his grace's favorite historical episode, which he declared he never read without intense satisfaction? Why, the young General Bonaparte's pounding of the Paris mob to pieces in 1795, called in playful approval by our respectable classes "the whiff of grapeshot," though Napoleon, to do him justice, took a deeper view of it, and would fain have had it forgotten. And since the Duke of Argyll was not a demon, but a man of like passions with ourselves, by no means rancorous or cruel as men go, who can doubt that all over the world proletarians of the ducal kidney are now reveling in "the whiff of dynamite" (the flavor of the joke seems to evaporate a little, does it not?) because it was aimed at the class they hate even as our argute duke hated what he called the mob.

In such an atmosphere there can be only one sequel to the Madrid explosion. All Europe burns to emulate it. Vengeance! More blood! Tear "the Anarchist beast" to shreds. Drag him to the scaffold. Imprison him for life. Let all civilized States band together to drive his like off the face of the earth; and if any State refuses to join, make war on it. This time the leading London newspaper, anti-Liberal and therefore anti-Russian in politics, does not say "Serve you right" to the victims, as it did, in effect, when Bobrikoff, and De Plehve, and Grand Duke Sergius, were in the same manner unofficially fulminated into fragments. No: fulminate our rivals in Asia by all means, ye brave Russian revolutionaries; but to aim at an English princess! monstrous! hideous! hound down the wretch to his doom; and observe, please, that we are a civilized and merciful people, and, however much we may regret it, must not treat him as Ravaillac and Damiens were treated. And meanwhile, since we have not yet caught him, let us soothe our quivering nerves with the bullfight, and comment in a courtly way on the unfailing tact and good taste of the ladies of our royal houses, who, though presumably of full normal natural tenderness, have been so effectually broken in to fashionable routine that they can be taken to see the horses slaughtered as helplessly as they could no doubt be taken to a gladiator show, if that happened to be the mode just now.

Strangely enough, in the midst of this raging fire of malice, the one man who still has faith in the kindness and intelligence of human nature is the fulminator, now a hunted wretch, with nothing, apparently, to secure his triumph over all the prisons and scaffolds of infuriate Europe except the revolver in his pocket and his readiness to discharge it at a moment's notice into his own or any other head. Think of him setting out to find a gentleman and a Christian in the multitude of human wolves howling for his blood. Think also of this: that at the very first essay he finds what he seeks, a veritable grandee of Spain, a noble, high-thinking, unterrified, malice-void soul, in the guise — of all masquerades in the world! — of a modern editor. The Anarchist wolf, flying from the wolves of plutocracy, throws himself on the honor of the man. The man, not being a wolf (nor a London editor), and therefore not having enough sympathy with his exploit to be made bloodthirsty by it, does not throw him back to the pursuing wolves — gives him, instead, what help he can to escape, and sends him off acquainted at last with a force that goes deeper than dynamite, though you cannot buy so much of it for sixpence. That righteous and honorable high human deed is not wasted on Europe, let us hope, though it benefits the fugitive wolf only for a moment. The plutocratic wolves presently smell him out. The fugitive shoots the unlucky wolf whose nose is nearest; shoots himself; and then convinces the world, by his photograph, that he was no monstrous freak of reversion to the tiger, but a good looking young man with nothing abnormal about him except his appalling courage and resolution (that is why the terrified shriek Coward at him): one to whom murdering a happy young couple on their wedding morning would have been an unthinkably unnatural abomination under rational and kindly human circumstances.

Then comes the climax of irony and blind stupidity. The wolves, balked of their meal of fellow-wolf, turn on the man, and proceed to torture him, after their manner, by imprisonment, for refusing to fasten his teeth in the throat of the dynamiter and hold him down until they came to finish him.

Thus, you see, a man may not be a gentleman nowadays even if he wishes to. As to being a Christian, he is allowed some latitude in that matter, because, I repeat, Christianity has two faces. Popular Christianity has for its emblem a gibbet, for its chief sensation a sanguinary execution after torture, for its central mystery an insane vengeance bought off by a trumpery expiation. But there is a nobler and profounder Christianity which affirms the sacred mystery of Equality, and forbids the glaring futility and folly of vengeance, often politely called punishment or justice. The gibbet part of Christianity is tolerated. The other is criminal felony. Connoisseurs in irony are well aware of the fact that the only editor in England who denounces punishment as radically wrong, also repudiates Christianity; calls his paper The Freethinker; and has been imprisoned for "bad taste" under the law against blasphemy.

Sane Conclusions

And now I must ask the excited reader not to lose his head on one side or the other, but to draw a sane moral from these grim absurdities. It is not good sense to propose that laws against crime should apply to principals only and not to accessories whose consent, counsel, or silence may secure impunity to the principal. If you institute punishment as part of the law, you must punish people for refusing to punish. If you have a police, part of its duty must be to compel everybody to assist the police. No doubt if your laws are unjust, and your policemen agents of oppression, the result will be an unbearable violation of the private consciences of citizens. But that cannot be helped: the remedy is, not to license everybody to thwart the law if they please, but to make laws that will command the public assent, and not to deal cruelly and stupidly with law-breakers. Everybody disapproves of burglars; but the modern burglar, when caught and overpowered by a householder, usually appeals, and often, let us hope, with success, to his captor not to deliver him over to the useless horrors of penal servitude. In other cases the law-breaker escapes because those who could give him up do not consider his breach of the law a guilty action. Sometimes, even, private tribunals are formed in opposition to the official tribunals; and these private tribunals employ assassins as executioners, as was done, for example, by Mahomet before he had established his power officially, and by the Ribbon lodges of Ireland in their long struggle with the landlords. Under such circumstances, the assassin goes free although everybody in the district knows who he is and what he has done. They do not betray him, partly because they justify him exactly as the regular Government justifies its official executioner, and partly because they would themselves be assassinated if they betrayed him: another method learnt from the official government. Given a tribunal employing a slayer who has no personal quarrel with the slain; and there is clearly no moral difference between official and unofficial killing.

In short, all men are anarchists with regard to laws which are against their consciences, either in the preamble or in the penalty. In London our worst anarchists are the magistrates, because many of them are so old and ignorant that when they are called upon to administer any law that is based on ideas or knowledge less than half a century old, they disagree with it, and being mere ordinary homebred private Englishmen without any respect for law in the abstract, naively set the example of violating it. In this instance the man lags behind the law; but when the law lags behind the man, he becomes equally an anarchist. When some huge change in social conditions, such as the industrial revolution of the eighteenth and nineteenth centuries, throws our legal and industrial institutions out of date, Anarchism becomes almost a religion. The whole force of the most energetic geniuses of the time in philosophy, economics, and art, concentrates itself on demonstrations and reminders that morality and law are only conventions, fallible and continually obsolescing. Tragedies in which the heroes are bandits, and comedies in which law-abiding and conventionally moral folk are compelled to satirize themselves by outraging the conscience of the spectators every time they do their duty, appear simultaneously with economic treatises entitled "What Is Property? Theft!" and with histories of "The Conflict Between Religion and Science."

Now this is not a healthy state of things. The advantages of living in society are proportionate, not to the freedom of the individual from a code, but to the complexity and subtlety of the code he is prepared not only to accept but to uphold as a matter of such vital importance that a law-breaker at large is hardly to be tolerated on any plea. Such an attitude becomes impossible when the only men who can make themselves heard and remembered throughout the world spend all their energy in raising our gorge against current law, current morality, current respectability, and legal property. The ordinary man, uneducated in social theory even when he is schooled in Latin verse, cannot be set against all the laws of his country and yet persuaded to regard law in the abstract as vitally necessary to society. Once he is brought to repudiate the laws and institutions he knows, he will repudiate the very conception of law and the very groundwork of institutions, ridiculing human rights, extolling brainless methods as "historical," and tolerating nothing except pure empiricism in conduct, with dynamite as the basis of politics and vivisection as the basis of science. That is hideous; but what is to be done? Here am I, for instance, by class a respectable man, by common sense a hater of waste and disorder, by intellectual constitution legally minded to the verge of pedantry, and by temperament apprehensive and economically disposed to the limit of old-maidishness; yet I am, and have always been, and shall now always be, a revolutionary writer, because our laws make law impossible; our liberties destroy all freedom; our property is organized robbery; our morality is an impudent hypocrisy; our wisdom is administered by inexperienced or malexperienced dupes, our power wielded by cowards and weaklings, and our honor false in all its points. I am an enemy of the existing order for good reasons; but that does not make my attacks any less encouraging or helpful to people who are its enemies for bad reasons. The existing order may shriek that if I tell the truth about it, some foolish person may drive it to become still worse by trying to assassinate it. I cannot help that, even if I could see what worse it could do than it is already doing. And the disadvantage of that worst even from its own point of view is that society, with all its prisons and bayonets and whips and ostracisms and starvations, is powerless in the face of the Anarchist who is prepared to sacrifice his own life in the battle with it. Our natural safety from the cheap and devastating explosives which every Russian student can make, and every Russian grenadier has learnt to handle in Manchuria, lies in the fact that brave and resolute men, when they are rascals, will not risk their skins for the good of humanity, and, when they are not, are sympathetic enough to care for humanity, abhorring murder, and never committing it until their consciences are outraged beyond endurance. The remedy is, then, simply not to outrage their consciences.

Do not be afraid that they will not make allowances. All men make very large allowances indeed before they stake their own lives in a war to the death with society. Nobody demands or expects the millennium. But there are two things that must be set right, or we shall perish, like Rome, of soul atrophy disguised as empire.

The first is, that the daily ceremony of dividing the wealth of the country among its inhabitants shall be so conducted that no crumb shall, save as a criminal's ration, go to any able-bodied adults who are not producing by their personal exertions not only a full equivalent for what they take, but a surplus sufficient to provide for their superannuation and pay back the debt due for their nurture.

The second is that the deliberate infliction of malicious injuries which now goes on under the name of punishment be abandoned; so that the thief, the ruffian, the gambler, and the beggar, may without inhumanity be handed over to the law, and made to understand that a State which is too humane to punish will also be too thrifty to waste the life of honest men in watching or restraining dishonest ones. That is why we do not imprison dogs. We even take our chance of their first bite. But if a dog delights to bark and bite, it goes to the lethal chamber. That seems to me sensible. To allow the dog to expiate his bite by a period of torment, and then let him loose in a much more savage condition (for the chain makes a dog savage) to bite again and expiate again, having meanwhile spent a great deal of human life and happiness in the task of chaining and feeding and tormenting him, seems to me idiotic and superstitious. Yet that is what we do to men who bark and bite and steal. It would be far more sensible to put up with their vices, as we put up with their illnesses, until they give more trouble than they are worth, at which point we should, with many apologies and expressions of sympathy, and some generosity in complying with their last wishes, place them in the lethal chamber and get rid of them. Under no circumstances should they be allowed to expiate their misdeeds by a man-ufactured penalty, to subscribe to a charity, or to compensate the victims. If there is to be no punishment there can be no forgiveness. We shall never have real moral responsibility until everyone knows that his deeds are irrevocable, and that his life depends on his usefulness. Hitherto, alas! humanity has never dared face these hard facts. We frantically scatter conscience money and invent systems of conscience banking, with expiatory penalties, atonements, redemptions, salvations, hospital subscription lists and what not, to enable us to contract-out of the moral code. Not content with the old scapegoat and sacrificial lamb, we deify human saviors, and pray to miraculous virgin intercessors. We attribute mercy to the inexorable; soothe our consciences after commiting murder by throwing ourselves on the bosom of divine love; and shrink even from our own gallows because we are forced to admit that it, at least, is irrevocable — as if one hour of imprisonment were not as irrevocable as any execution!

If a man cannot look evil in the face without illusion, he will never know what it really is, or combat it effectually. The few men who have been able (relatively) to do this have been called cynics, and have sometimes had an abnormal share of evil in themselves, corresponding to the abnormal strength of their minds; but they have never done mischief unless they intended to do it. That is why great scoundrels have been beneficent rulers whilst amiable and privately harmless monarchs have ruined their countries by trusting to the hocus-pocus of innocence and guilt, reward and punishment, virtuous indignation and pardon, instead of standing up to the facts without either malice or mercy. Major Barbara stands up to Bill Walker in that way, with the result that the ruffian who cannot get hated, has to hate himself. To relieve this agony he tries to get punished; but the Salvationist whom he tries to provoke is as merciless as Barbara, and only prays for him. Then he tries to pay, but can get nobody to take his money. His doom is the doom of Cain, who, failing to find either a savior, a policeman, or an almoner to help him to pretend that his brother's blood no longer cried from the ground, had to live and die a murderer. Cain took care not to commit another murder, unlike our railway shareholders (I am one) who kill and maim shunters by hundreds to save the cost of automatic couplings, and make atonement by annual subscriptions to deserving charities. Had Cain been allowed to pay off his score, he might possibly have killed Adam and Eve for the mere sake of a second luxurious reconciliation with God afterwards. Bodger, who may depend on it, will go on to the end of his life poisoning people with bad whisky, because he can always depend on the Salvation Army or the Church of England to negotiate a redemption for him in consideration of a trifling percentage of his profits.

There is a third condition too, which must be fulfilled before the great teachers of the world will cease to scoff at its religions. Creeds must become intellectually honest. At present there is not a single credible established religion in the world. That is perhaps the most stupendous fact in the whole world-situation. This play of mine, *Major Barbara*, is, I hope, both true and inspired; but whoever says that it all happened, and that faith in it and understanding of it consist in believing that it is a record of an actual occurrence, is, to speak according to Scripture, a fool and a liar, and is hereby solemnly denounced and cursed as such by me, the author, to all posterity.

Drama in the Early and Mid-Twentieth Century

The realist tradition in drama had certain EXPRESSIONIST qualities, evident in the dream passages in Strindberg's *Miss Julie* and the romantic fantasies of Hedda in *Hedda Gabler*. But the surfaces of the plays appear naturalistic, consisting of a sequence of events that we might imagine happening in real life. The subject matter of these plays is also in the tradition of naturalism because it is drawn from life and not beautified or toned down for the middle-class audience.

But in the early to mid-twentieth century realistic drama took a new turn, incorporating distortions of reality that border on the unreal or *surreal*. From the time of John Millington Synge in 1905 to Harold Pinter in the 1960s, drama exploited the possibilities of realism, anti-realism, and the poetic expansion of expressionism.

The Heritage of Realism

In the late nineteenth century realism was often perceived as too severe on an audience that had applauded melodrama with great approval. Realistic plays forced comfortable audiences to observe psychological and physical problems that their status as members of the middle class usually allowed them to avoid. It was a painful experience for these audiences, and they often protested loudly.

However, the technique of realism could be adapted for many different purposes, and eventually realism was reshaped to satisfy the middle-class sensibilities of the audiences. The techniques of realistic theater were quickly mastered by commercial playwrights, who produced popular, pleasant plays. It took a few decades for this to happen, but by the 1920s in Europe and the 1930s in America, realism was the norm of expectation of theatergoing audiences. Even the light comedies dominating the commercial stage — or, as the revolutionary French playwright/actor Antonin Artaud put it, the theater of the boulevard — were in a more or less realistic mode. Anything that disturbed the illusion of realism was thought to be a flaw.

Reactions to the comfortable use of realistic techniques were numerous, especially after the First World War. One extreme reaction was that of the Dadaists. Through the group's chief propagandist, Tristan Tzara (1896–1963), they promoted an art that was essentially enigmatic and incoherent to the average person. That was its point. The Dadaists blamed World War I on sensible, middle-class people who were logical and well intentioned. The brief plays that were performed in many Dadaist clubs in Europe often featured actors speaking simultaneously so that nothing they said could be understood. The purpose was to confound the normal expectations of theatergoers.

Other developments also were making it possible for playwrights to experiment and move away from a strict reliance on "comfortable" realism. By World War I motion pictures began to make melodramatic entertainment available to most people in the world. Even when films were silent, they relied on techniques that had been common on the nineteenth-century stage. Their growing domination of popular dramatic entertainment provided an outlet for the expectations of middle-class audiences and freed more imaginative playwrights to experiment and develop in different directions.

Realism and Myth

The incorporation of myth in drama offered new opportunities to expand the limits of realism. Sigmund Freud's theories of psychoanalysis at the turn of the century stimulated a new interest in myth and dreams as a psychological link between people. Freud studied Greek myths for clues to the psychic state of his patients, and he published a number of commentaries on Greek plays and on *Hamlet*. The psychologist Carl Jung, a follower of Freud who eventually split with him, helped give a powerful impetus to the interest in dreams and the symbolism of myth by suggesting that all members of a culture share an inborn knowledge of the basic myths of the culture. Jung postulated a collective unconscious, a repository of mythic material in the mind that all humans inherit as part of their birthright. This theory gave credence to the power of myth in everyday life, and it is, along with Freud's theories, one of the most important ideas empowering drama and other art forms in this century. Playwrights who used elements of myth in their plays produced a poetic form of realism that deals with a level of truth — common to a given culture.

Poetic Realism

The Abbey Theatre in Dublin, which functioned with distinction from the turn of the century to 1930, produced major works by John Millington Synge, W. B. Yeats, Sean O'Casey, and Lady Augusta Gregory. Lady Gregory's peasant plays concentrated on the charming, the amusing, and occasionally the grotesque. She tried to represent the dialect she heard in the west of Ireland, a dialect that was distinctive, poetic, and colorful. She also took advantage of local Irish myths and used some of them for her most powerful plays, such as *Dervorgilla* and *Grania*, both portraits of passionate women whose stories were told in Irish legend and ancient Irish myth.

John Millington Synge, like Lady Gregory, was interested in the twin forces of myth and the peasant dialects. He wrote plays that are very difficult to fit into a realist mold, although their surfaces are sometimes naturalistic. Some audiences reacted violently to his realistic portrayals of peasant life because it was unflattering.

Synge's plays were sometimes directly connected with ancient Irish myth, as in *Deirdre of the Sorrows* (1910), which is about a willful Irish princess who runs off with a young warrior and his brothers on the eve of her wedding to an old king. The story ends sadly for Deirdre, and she is regarded as a fated heroine, almost a Greek figure. The influence of Irish anecdote is present in *The Playboy of the Western World* (1907), which is said to have been suggested by a story told to Yeats and Synge when they first arrived on the Aran Islands — the far western Irish islands where Synge spent much time observing the peasant culture and language. Synge's great short tragedy *Riders to the Sea* may also have derived from an anecdote or legend; it is an expressionist play in its use of unreal moments, such as Maurya's encounter with the ghost of her son Michael and her vision of her dead son Bartley.

In the United States, Eugene O'Neill experimented with realism, first by presenting stark, powerful, realistic plays that disturbed his audiences. *The Hairy Ape* (1922) portrayed a primitive coal stoker on a passenger liner who awakened base emotions in the more refined passengers. But O'Neill also experimented with more poetic forms of realism. In *Desire Under the Elms* (1924), he explores the myth of Phaedra — centering on her incestuous love for her husband's son — but sets it in rural New England on a rock-hard farm. It is as close as O'Neill can get to a peasant reality drawing on myth in America.

In the tradition of realism, the play treats unpleasant themes: sons' distrust of their father and their dishonoring him; lust between a son and his stepmother; and the murder of a baby to "prove" love. There is neither melodrama in the play nor comic relief. But it is not simply realistic. Without its underpinning of myth, the play would be sordid. The myth helps us see things much more clearly: Fate operates even today, but not in terms of messages from the gods. Rather, it works in terms of messages from our hearts and bodies. Lust is a force in nature. It drives and it destroys.

Social Realism

Ten years after *Desire Under the Elms* enjoyed popularity, a new kind of play based on social realism developed. This was realism with a political conscience. Since the world was in the throes of a depression that reduced otherwise secure people to absolute poverty and homelessness, drama began to aim at awakening governments to the consequences of unbridled capitalism and the depressions that freewheeling economies produced.

Plays like Jack Kirkland's *Tobacco Road* (1933), adapted from Erskine Caldwell's novel, presented a grim portrait of rural poverty in America. Sidney Kingsley's *Dead End* (1935) portrayed the life of virtually homeless boys on the Lower East Side of Manhattan. In the same year Maxwell Anderson produced a verse comedy, *Winterset*, with gangsters and gangsterism at its core. Also in 1935 Clifford Odets produced *Waiting for Lefty*, an openly leftist labor drama. These plays were mainly naturalistic in style, but their realist credentials lay primarily in their effort to show audiences portraits of real life that might shock their middle-class sensibilities.

Meanwhile, in Fascist Spain, Federico García Lorca was pointing to dark emotional centers of the psyche in his *House of Bernarda Alba* (1936), which explores erotic forces repressed and then set loose. Lorca was opposed to fascism and was murdered by a Fascist agent. His plays reveal a darkness of spirit that makes us take note of the darkness — moral and psychological — that enveloped Europe in the 1940s.

Realism and Expressionism

After Eugene O'Neill's experiments in combining myth and realism, later American dramatists looked for new ways to expand the resources of realism while retaining its power. The use of expressionism — often poetic in language and effect — was one solution that appealed to both Tennessee Williams and Arthur Miller.

Tennessee Williams's *The Glass Menagerie* (1944) and Arthur Miller's *Death of a Salesman* (1949) both use expressionist techniques. Williams's poetic stage directions make clear that he is drawing upon nonrealistic dramatic devices. He describes the scene as "memory and . . . therefore nonrealistic." He calls for an interior "rather dim and poetic," and he uses a character who also steps outside the staged action to serve as a narrator — one who "takes whatever license with dramatic convention as is convenient to his purposes." As the narrator tells his story, the walls of the building seem to melt away, revealing the inside of a house and the lives and fantasies of his mother and sister, both caught in their own distorted visions of life.

Arthur Miller's original idea for *Death of a Salesman* was to build a set that would represent the inside of Willie Loman's mind; but the final, expressionist set represented a cross section of his house instead. As the action in one room concluded, lights went up to begin action in another (Figure 7). This evocative staging affected the production of numerous plays by later writers. *Death of a Salesman* examines the values that led Willie and his family to their state of desperation. They

Figure 7. Expressionistic setting in Arthur Miller's *Death of a Salesman*

are the values that many American businesspeople hold: If you are well liked you will get ahead; petty crimes such as stealing and adultery are evidence of high spirits; being an athlete confers glory and privileges; being studious leads nowhere.

Miller used expressionist techniques to create the hallucinative sequences in which Willie talks with Ben, the man who walked into the jungle poor and walked out a millionaire, and Biff recalls seeing Willie with the woman in Boston.

Lorraine Hansberry's *A Raisin in the Sun* (1959) uses basically realistic staging and dialogue to portray the difficulties of a family that struggles to take advantage of its opportunity to overcome poverty. For Williams and Miller, expressionism offered a way to bring other worlds to bear on the staged action — the worlds of dream and fantasy. Hansberry does not use the expressionist techniques of Miller. She chooses another path to a similar end when she introduces an exotic touch in the visit of the African young man, Asagai, and offers a moment of cultural counterpoint that is as effective in bringing in another world as a dream or hallucinative sequence. Hansberry's realism is essentially conservative.

Antirealism

SURREALISM (literally, "beyond realism") in the early twentieth century was based originally on an interpretation of experience not through the lucid mind of the waking person but through the mind of the dreamer, the unconscious mind that Freud described. Surrealism augmented or, for some playwrights, supplanted realism and became a means of distorting reality for emotional purposes.

When Pirandello's six characters come onstage looking for their author in *Six Characters in Search of an Author* (1921), no one can believe that they are characters rather than actors. Least of all does the audience believe that. Pirandello's play is an examination of the realities we take for granted in drama. He turns the world of expectation in drama upside down. He reminds us that what we assume to be real is always questionable — we cannot be sure of anything; we must presume things are true, and in some cases we must take them on faith.

Pirandello's philosophy dominated his stories, plays, and novels. His questioning of the certainty of human knowledge was designed to undermine his audience's faith in an absolute reality. Modern physicists have concurred with philosophers, ancient and modern, who question everyday reality. Pirandello was influenced by the modern theories of relativity that physicists were developing, and he found in them validation of his own attack on certainty.

Epic Theater

Bertolt Brecht (1898–1956) began writing plays before World War II. He was a political dramatist who rejected the theater of his day, which valued the realistic "well-made play," in which all the parts fit perfectly together and function like a machine. His feeling was that such plays were too mechanical, like a "clockwork mouse."

Brecht conceived a new style that he called EPIC THEATER. The term implies a sequence of actions or episodes of the kind found in Homer's *Iliad*. In epic theater the sense of dramatic illusion is constantly voided by reminders from the stage that one is watching a play. Stark, harsh lighting, blank stages, placards announcing changes of scenes, bands playing music onstage, and long, discomfiting pauses make it impossible for an audience to become totally immersed in a realistic illusion. Brecht wanted the audience to analyze the play's thematic content rather than sit back and be entertained. Brecht offered a genuine alternative to realistic drama. His complaints about realistic drama were focused on the power of such drama to convince audiences that their realism described not just things as they are, but things as they must be. He thought such drama helped maintain the social problems that they portrayed by reinforcing, rather than challenging, their realities.

Brecht's *Mother Courage* (1941) is an antiwar drama written on the eve of World War II. The use of song, an unreal setting, and an unusual historical perspective (the Thirty Years War in the seventeenth century) help to achieve the "strangeness" that Brecht thought drama ought to have for its audiences. The techniques of epic theater as developed in *Mother Courage* and also *The Good Woman of Setzuan* (1943), a study of the immoralities that prosper under capitalism, were imitated by playwrights in the 1950s. Hardly a major play in that period is free of Brecht's influence.

Absurdist Drama

The critic Martin Esslin coined the term THEATER OF THE ABSURD when describing the work of Samuel Beckett (b. 1906), the Irish playwright whose dramas often dispense with almost everything that makes the well-made play well made. Some of his plays have no actors onstage — amplified breathing is the only hint of human presence in one case. Some have little or no plot; others have no words. His theater is minimalist, offering a stage reality that seems cut to the bone, without the usual realistic devices of plot, character development, and intricate setting.

Waiting for Godot (1952) captured the modern imagination and established a landmark in absurdist drama. The theater of the absurd assumes that the world is meaningless, that meaning is a human concept, and that individuals must create significance and not rely on institutions or traditions to provide it. The absurdist movement grew out of existentialism, a postwar French philosophy that demanded that the individual face the emptiness of the universe and create meaning in a life that has no essential meaning within itself.

In *Waiting for Godot* two tramps, Vladimir and Estragon, meet near a tree where they expect Godot to arrive to talk with them. The play has two acts that end with a small boy explaining that Godot cannot come today but will come tomorrow. Godot is not coming, and the tramps who wait for Godot will wait forever. While they wait they entertain themselves with vaudeville routines and eventually are met by a rich man, Pozzo, and his slave, Lucky. Lucky, on the command "Think, pig," speaks in a highly technical language that runs through themes of western philosophy and religion but that remains meaningless. Pozzo and Lucky have no interest in joining Vladimir and Estragon in waiting for Godot. They leave the two alone, waiting — afraid to leave for fear of missing Godot, but uncertain that Godot will ever arrive.

The situation bears a resemblance to the situation of all those who faithfully wait for God's enlightenment. Beckett seems to be saying that in an absurd world, such gestures are necessary to create the sense of significance that people need to live. His stark lighting, his characters' awareness of an audience, and his refusal to create a drama in which an audience can "lose" itself in a comfortable surface of realistic illusion are all, in their own way, indebted to Brecht.

Beckett's *Krapp's Last Tape* (1958) and *Happy Days* (1961) place some extraordinary limitations on performance. For example, Winnie in *Happy Days* appears onstage buried in a mound almost up to her shoulders. She never leaves it. Krapp is the only person onstage throughout *Krapp's Last Tape*, and his dialogues are with tapes of himself made many years before. The situation is absurd, but as Beckett reveals to us, the absurd has its own complexities, and situations such as Krapp's can sustain complex interpretations. Like Brecht, Beckett expects his audience to analyze the drama, not sit back and merely be entertained.

Harold Pinter's *The Dumb Waiter* (1957) features an absurdist situation, with Gus and Ben waiting for a message much as Vladimir and Estragon do, but their message is to be delivered by a dumbwaiter. Their circumstances seem all too ordinary, and their conversation, like that between Vladimir and Estragon, seems pointless, meandering chatter. Unlike Vladimir and Estragon, they actually receive their message, but it comes as a dreadful surprise.

The great plays of this period reflect the values of the cultures from which they spring. They make comments on life in the modern world and question the values that the culture takes for granted. The drama of this part of the twentieth century is a drama of examination.

John Millington Synge

John Millington Synge (1871–1909) was one of the brilliant discoveries of the Irish Literary Renaissance, which was largely the product of Lady Isabella Augusta Gregory and William Butler Yeats, the codirectors of the Abbey Theatre in Dublin. The Abbey ranks as one of the most influential and successful national theaters in European history. From 1904 to the present, it has been devoted to producing plays by Irish writers, some of whom have gone on to be ranked among the greatest of their age. Besides Synge, Bernard Shaw, Lady Gregory, Yeats, Sean O'Casey, and Brian Friel are among the many whose names still loom impressively as having contributed to building the reputation of the Abbey.

Synge was gifted in languages, with a degree in German from Trinity College, Dublin. But he was also a violinist and went to Paris to study music and live the bohemian life of the artist. It was there in 1896 that Yeats and Lady Gregory met him and convinced him to return to Ireland and write plays for what was to become the Abbey. They convinced him to spend time in the Aran Islands, the westernmost — and the wildest — part of Ireland. It is there that *Riders to the Sea* is set. Yeats felt the Arans were an important source of the literary energy of the nation because the Islanders' colorful language sounded like English filtered through Irish Gaelic.

Synge wrote a number of important plays, all within less than ten years. Most of them remain in the repertory of modern drama: *In the Shadow of the Glen* (1903); *Riders to the Sea* (1904); *The Well of the Saints* (1905); *The Tinker's Wedding* (1907); *The Playboy of the Western World* (1907); and *Deirdre of the Sorrows* (1910). With the exception of *The Tinker's Wedding*, which is so anticlerical that it has never been given a production at the Abbey, they are all still regularly produced there.

Synge was not always a popular playwright in Ireland. He felt he faithfully represented peasant ways, but his Dublin audiences often protested that he insulted the Irish. Synge's kind of realism, while not especially harsh or critical, was an unvarnished view of the west of Ireland. The Abbey audiences wanted an idealized portrait of their countrymen and countrywomen, not straightforward and sometimes embarrassing portraits such as the one Synge offered them in *The Playboy of the Western World*. That play caused riots in the Abbey Theatre when it was first performed. The "Playboy Riots" demonstrated the extent to which Irish audiences would go to express their dislike of the new realism, which had begun in Scandinavia with Strindberg and Ibsen and seemed to have finally reached Ireland in the work of Synge. That impression, however, was ironic, since Synge had no special intention of creating a realistic drama in Ireland.

The Playboy of the Western World is about a young man who, thinking he has killed his father, arrives at a shebeen — a kind of tavern — in Mayo where the townfolk make a kind of hero of him rather than turning him in to the police. He joins in their games and wins all the prizes and woos and almost wins Pegeen Mike, the local beauty. The subject matter — Irish people lionizing a presumed murderer — and the frank language were departures from previous Irish drama, but neither the playwright nor his producers at the Abbey Theatre were prepared for the audience's reaction. At its first performance when Christy, the Playboy, actually hits his father (who was not really dead) onstage late in the play, the audience could sit still no longer. Such an act was perceived as an offense against all the Irish.

But vocal protest finally erupted at a line that describes women standing in their slips in front of the hero. At that point the crowd was so noisy that no one could hear what was said onstage. For subsequent performances, Lady Gregory advised the actors to move their lips when the crowd roared, but not to waste their voices unless the crowd noise died down. Eventually, the police were called in to throw out troublemakers and to keep the audience noise down. When the Abbey company toured the United States in 1909 and performed the play in Boston, riots ensued again, with the local chapter of the nationalist Irish organization Sinn Fein enlisted to make a deafening racket during the performances.

Synge was shocked at the uproar; he had never expected his play to stimulate such a response. The question of realism was probably not on Synge's mind at all — he did not think of himself as an heir of Ibsen. *Playboy* is less a realistic play than *Riders to the Sea*, and both are rooted not in any effort to force the audience to look at life as it is really lived but rather in the mythic and symbolic forces that underlie everyone's experiences of heroism, life, and death. The deep roots of both plays are in Irish myth and the Christian religion. Synge was amazed to think that audiences ignored those important aspects and focused on other, less significant issues.

Synge's early death robbed world drama of a figure who certainly would have been among the greatest writers of the century. As it is, his work is remarkable; but in his last play, which he never finished, we can see the promise of a body of work that would have taken its place with the best plays of our time.

RIDERS TO THE SEA

Riders to the Sea (1904) was the first success that Synge produced for the Abbey Theatre. In some ways it is still one of the most impressive plays to come out of the Irish Literary Renaissance. It is a one-act play, which the Abbey found congenial for its early programs, but its length in no way mitigates its power.

The play is set in the westernmost part of Ireland, the part least touched by English influence. Aran Islanders speak both Gaelic and English, but their English is marked with a very expressive and idiosyncratic flavor, which Synge tries to replicate in this play. The syntax of Synge's peasants benefits from his excellent ear — acquired in his training as a musician — as well as from his having lived in an inn in Wicklow where he eavesdropped on the local Irish kitchen girls speaking naturally and unaffectedly.

Riders to the Sea owes much of its power to the local speech and the local way of life portrayed faithfully in the play. In his preface to *The Playboy of the Western World*, Synge credits Irish writers with the advantage of listening "for a few years more" to a language that is "rich as a nut."

The richness of the dialogue in *Riders to the Sea* is striking. Maurya's long speeches at the end of the play are filled with the rhythms of the sea and the agony of someone who has suffered as much as the world can demand. Even the speeches of the lesser characters have an extraordinarily expressive flavor.

The drama has tragic overtones, although it does not fulfill the Aristotelian demands for tragedy in that it does not portray the agony of a person of noble birth. Instead, it depicts the sufferings of a superstitious peasant woman. Yet the drama contains the same kinds of intensity of dramatic action found in Greek tragedies. It maintains a unity of time, place, character, and action, as well as an intense sense of fate and impending doom. Synge may well have begun developing a new genre of folk tragedy, just as Arthur Miller later began developing a genre of bourgeois tragedy in *Death of A Salesman*. *Riders to the Sea* is permeated by a sense of fate, and Maurya, whose name is remarkably close in sound to *moira*, the Greek word for fate, senses the inevitability of the premature death of her last son on the sea. The feeling of inevitability is heightened by the discussion between the daughters about the son Michael, who has been feared lost at sea, by their identification of his sock that was recovered from the sea, and by the willful insistence of the last son, Bartley, to ride the mares across the sea to the mainland, knowingly risking his life. (In fact, men did swim their animals from the islands to the mainland, and they often went out to meet the large boats that came near. Even today those waters are difficult, and Aran Islanders still use the same black curraghs their ancestors used to ferry themselves, their goods, and their livestock between the mainland and their homes.)

As in so many Irish plays, the women remain to suffer after the men have perished. The play ends with the sound of women keening for the dead, knowing that there are no men left to help them survive in a harsh environment. A question that begs to be asked is why Bartley dares the sea, knowing the risks he is taking. What drives him on, as it drove his father and brothers? Nothing Maurya can say will make him swerve from his progress. Maurya's horrifying vision of Michael and Bartley on the mares confirms even more painfully her premonitions and fears. It also provides an element of supernatural intensity.

Perhaps because of its tragic Greek pattern, *Riders to the Sea* has a mythic force. The sense of destiny that Maurya feels is built into her life. Her sense of resignation and deep faith help her grow in our imagination and give her a heroic dimension. Synge's approach to realism is much different from Ibsen's or Chekhov's. It is more elemental, based on the spiritual life of the folk as expressed in the eloquence of their language.

John Millington Synge (1871–1909)
RIDERS TO THE SEA

1904

Persons in the Play

MAURYA (*an old woman*)
BARTLEY (*her son*)
CATHLEEN (*her daughter*)
NORA (*a younger daughter*)
MEN *and* WOMEN

Scene: *An Island off the West of Ireland.*

(*Cottage kitchen, with nets, oilskins, spinning wheel, some new boards standing by the wall, etc. Cathleen, a girl of about twenty, finishes kneading cake, and puts it down in the pot-oven by the fire; then wipes her hands, and begins to spin at the wheel. Nora, a young girl, puts her head in at the door.*)

NORA (*in a low voice*): Where is she?
CATHLEEN: She's lying down, God help her, and may be sleeping, if she's able.

(*Nora comes in softly and takes a bundle from under her shawl.*)

CATHLEEN (*spinning the wheel rapidly*): What is it you have?
NORA: The young priest is after bringing them. It's a shirt and a plain stocking were got off a drowned man in Donegal.

(*Cathleen stops her wheel with a sudden movement, and leans out to listen.*)

NORA: We're to find out if it's Michael's they are, some time herself will be down looking by the sea.
CATHLEEN: How would they be Michael's, Nora. How would he go the length of that way to the far north?
NORA: The young priest says he's known the like of it. "If it's Michael's they are," says he, "you can tell herself he's got a clean burial by the grace of God, and if they're not his, let no one say a word

about them, for she'll be getting her death," says he, "with crying and lamenting."

(*The door which Nora half closed is blown open by a gust of wind.*)

CATHLEEN (*looking out anxiously*): Did you ask him would he stop Bartley going this day with the horses to the Galway fair?

NORA: "I won't stop him," says he, "but let you not be afraid. Herself does be saying prayers half through the night, and the Almighty God won't leave her destitute," says he, "with no son living."

CATHLEEN: Is the sea bad by the white rocks, Nora?

NORA: Middling bad, God help us. There's a great roaring in the west, and it's worse it'll be getting when the tide's turned to the wind. (*She goes over to the table with the bundle.*) Shall I open it now?

CATHLEEN: Maybe she'd wake up on us, and come in before we'd done. (*Coming to the table.*) It's a long time we'll be, and the two of us crying.

NORA (*goes to the inner door and listens*): She's moving about on the bed. She'll be coming in a minute.

CATHLEEN: Give me the ladder, and I'll put them up in the turf-loft, the way she won't know of them at all, and maybe when the tide turns she'll be going down to see would he be floating from the east.

(*They put the ladder against the gable of the chimney; Cathleen goes up a few steps and hides the bundle in the turf-loft. Maurya comes from the inner room.*)

MAURYA (*looking up at Cathleen and speaking querulously*): Isn't it turf enough you have for this day and evening?

CATHLEEN: There's a cake baking at the fire for a short space (*throwing down the turf*) and Bartley will want it when the tide turns if he goes to Connemara.

(*Nora picks up the turf and puts it round the pot-oven.*)

MAURYA (*sitting down on a stool at the fire*): He won't go this day with the wind rising from the south and west. He won't go this day, for the young priest will stop him surely.

NORA: He'll not stop him, mother, and I heard Eamon Simon and Stephen Pheety and Colum Shawn saying he would go.

MAURYA: Where is he itself?

NORA: He went down to see would there be another boat sailing in the week, and I'm thinking it won't be long till he's here now, for the tide's turning at the green head, and the hooker's tacking from the east.

CATHLEEN: I hear some one passing the big stones.

NORA (*looking out*): He's coming now, and he in a hurry.

BARTLEY (*Comes in and looks round the room. Speaking sadly and quietly*): Where is the bit of new rope, Cathleen, was bought in Connemara?

CATHLEEN (*coming down*): Give it to him, Nora; it's on a nail by the white boards. I hung it up this morning, for the pig with the black feet was eating it.

NORA (*giving him a rope*): Is that it, Bartley?

MAURYA: You'd do right to leave that rope, Bartley, hanging by the boards. (*Bartley takes the rope.*) It will be wanting in this place, I'm telling you, if Michael is washed up tomorrow morning, or the next morning, or any morning in the week, for it's a deep grave we'll make him by the grace of God.

BARTLEY (*beginning to work with the rope*): I've no halter the way I can ride down on the mare, and I must go now quickly. This is the one boat going for two weeks or beyond it, and the fair will be a good fair for horses I heard them saying below.

MAURYA: It's a hard thing they'll be saying below if the body is washed up and there's no man in it to make the coffin, and I after giving a big price for the finest white boards you'd find in Connemara.

(*She looks round at the boards.*)

BARTLEY: How would it be washed up, and we after looking each day for nine days, and a strong wind blowing a while back from the west and south?

MAURYA: If it wasn't found itself, that wind is raising the sea, and there was a star up against the moon, and it rising in the night. If it was a hundred horses, or a thousand horses you had itself, what is the price of a thousand horses against a son where there is one son only?

BARTLEY (*working at the halter, to Cathleen*): Let you go down each day, and see the sheep aren't jumping in on the rye, and if the jobber comes you can sell the pig with the black feet if there is a good price going.

MAURYA: How would the like of her get a good price for a pig?

BARTLEY (*to Cathleen*): If the west wind holds with the last bit of the moon let you and Nora get up weed enough for another cock for the kelp. It's hard set we'll be from this day with no one in it but one man to work.

MAURYA: It's hard set we'll be surely the day you're drown'd with the rest. What way will I live and the girls with me, and I an old woman looking for the grave?

(*Bartley lays down the halter, takes off his old coat, and puts on a newer one of the same flannel.*)

BARTLEY (*to Nora*): Is she coming to the pier?

NORA (*looking out*): She's passing the green head and letting fall her sails.

BARTLEY (*getting his purse and tobacco*): I'll have half an hour to go down, and you'll see me coming again in two days, or in three days, or maybe in four days if the wind is bad.

MAURYA (*turning round to the fire, and putting her shawl over her head*): Isn't it a hard and cruel man won't hear a word from an old woman, and she holding him from the sea?

CATHLEEN: It's the life of a young man to be going on the sea, and who would listen to an old woman with one thing and she saying it over?

BARTLEY (*taking the halter*): I must go now quickly. I'll ride down on the red mare, and the gray pony 'll run behind me. . . . The blessing of God on you.

(*He goes out.*)

MAURYA (*crying out as he is in the door*): He's gone now, God spare us, and we'll not see him again. He's gone now, and when the black night is falling I'll have no son left me in the world.

CATHLEEN: Why wouldn't you give him your blessing and he looking round in the door? Isn't it sorrow enough is on every one in this house without your sending him out with an unlucky word behind him, and a hard word in his ear?

(*Maurya takes up the tongs and begins raking the fire aimlessly without looking round.*)

NORA (*turning toward her*): You're taking away the turf from the cake.

CATHLEEN (*crying out*): The Son of God forgive us, Nora, we're after forgetting his bit of bread.

(*She comes over to the fire.*)

NORA: And it's destroyed he'll be going till dark night, and he after eating nothing since the sun went up.

CATHLEEN (*turning the cake out of the oven*): It's destroyed he'll be, surely. There's no sense left on any person in a house where an old woman will be talking forever.

(*Maurya sways herself on her stool.*)

CATHLEEN (*cutting off some of the bread and rolling it in a cloth; to Maurya*): Let you go down now to the spring well and give him this and he passing. You'll see him then and the dark word will be broken, and you can say "God speed you," the way he'll be easy in his mind.

MAURYA (*taking the bread*): Will I be in it as soon as himself?

CATHLEEN: If you go now quickly.

MAURYA (*standing up unsteadily*): It's hard set I am to walk.

CATHLEEN (*looking at her anxiously*): Give her the stick, Nora, or maybe she'll slip on the big stones.

NORA: What stick?

CATHLEEN: The stick Michael brought from Connemara.

MAURYA (*taking a stick Nora gives her*): In the big world the old people do be leaving things after them for their sons and children, but in this place it is the young men do be leaving things behind for them that do be old.

(*She goes out slowly. Nora goes over to the ladder.*)

CATHLEEN: Wait, Nora, maybe she'd turn back quickly. She's that sorry, God help her, you wouldn't know the thing she'd do.

NORA: Is she gone round by the bush?

CATHLEEN (*looking out*): She's gone now. Throw it down quickly, for the Lord knows when she'll be out of it again.

NORA (*getting the bundle from the loft*): The young priest said he'd be passing tomorrow, and we might go down and speak to him below if it's Michael's they are surely.

CATHLEEN (*taking the bundle*): Did he say what way they were found?

NORA (*coming down*): "There were two men," says he, "and they rowing round with poteen before the cocks crowed, and the oar of one of them caught the body, and they passing the black cliffs of the north."

CATHLEEN (*trying to open the bundle*): Give me a knife, Nora, the string's perished with the salt water, and there's a black knot on it you wouldn't loosen in a week.

NORA (*giving her a knife*): I've heard tell it was a long way to Donegal.

CATHLEEN (*cutting the string*): It is surely. There was a man in here a while ago — the man sold us that knife — and he said if you set off walking from the rocks beyond, it would be seven days you'd be in Donegal.

NORA: And what time would a man take, and he floating?

(*Cathleen opens the bundle and takes out a bit of a stocking. They look at them eagerly.*)

CATHLEEN (*in a low voice*): The Lord spare us, Nora! isn't it a queer hard thing to say if it's his they are surely?

NORA: I'll get his shirt off the hook the way we can put the one flannel on the other. (*She looks through some clothes hanging in the corner.*) It's not with them, Cathleen, and where will it be?

CATHLEEN: I'm thinking Bartley put it on him in the morning, for his own shirt was heavy with the salt in it (*pointing to the corner*). There's a bit of a sleeve was of the same stuff. Give me that and it will do.

(*Nora brings it to her and they compare the flannel.*)

CATHLEEN: It's the same stuff, Nora; but if it is itself aren't there great rolls of it in the shops of Galway, and isn't it many another man may have a shirt of it as well as Michael himself?

NORA (*who has taken up the stocking and counted the stitches, crying out*): It's Michael, Cathleen, it's Michael; God spare his soul, and what will herself say when she hears this story, and Bartley on the sea?

CATHLEEN (*taking the stocking*): It's a plain stocking.

NORA: It's the second one of the third pair I knitted, and I put up three score stitches, and I dropped four of them.

CATHLEEN (*counts the stitches*): It's that number is in it. (*Crying out.*) Ah, Nora, isn't it a bitter thing to think of him floating that way to the far north, and no one to keen him but the black hags that do be flying on the sea?

NORA (*swinging herself round, and throwing out her arms on the clothes*): And isn't it a pitiful thing when there is nothing left of a man who was a great rower and fisher, but a bit of an old shirt and a plain stocking?

CATHLEEN (*after an instant*): Tell me is herself coming, Nora? I hear a little sound on the path.

NORA (*looking out*): She is, Cathleen. She's coming up to the door.

CATHLEEN: Put these things away before she'll come in. Maybe it's easier she'll be after giving her blessing to Bartley, and we won't let on we've heard anything the time he's on the sea.

NORA (*helping Cathleen to close the bundle*): We'll put them here in the corner.

(*They put them into a hole in the chimney corner. Cathleen goes back to the spinning wheel.*)

NORA: Will she see it was crying I was?

CATHLEEN: Keep your back to the door the way the light'll not be on you.

(*Nora sits down at the chimney corner, with her back to the door. Maurya comes in very slowly, without looking at the girls, and goes over to her stool at the other side of the fire. The cloth with the bread is still in her hand. The girls look at each other, and Nora points to the bundle of bread.*)

CATHLEEN (*after spinning for a moment*): You didn't give him his bit of bread?

(*Maurya begins to keen softly, without turning round.*)

CATHLEEN: Did you see him riding down?

(*Maurya goes on keening.*)

CATHLEEN (*a little impatiently*): God forgive you; isn't it a better thing to raise your voice and tell what you seen, than to be making lamentation for a thing that's done? Did you see Bartley, I'm saying to you.

MAURYA (*with a weak voice*): My heart's broken from this day.

CATHLEEN (*as before*): Did you see Bartley?

MAURYA: I seen the fearfulest thing.

CATHLEEN (*leaves her wheel and looks out*): God forgive you; he's riding the mare now over the green head, and the gray pony behind him.

MAURYA (*Starts, so that her shawl falls back from her head and shows her white tossed hair. With a frightened voice.*): The gray pony behind him.

CATHLEEN (*coming to the fire*): What is it ails you, at all?

MAURYA (*speaking very slowly*): I've seen the fearfulest thing any person has seen, since the day Bride Dara seen the dead man with the child in his arms.

CATHLEEN AND NORA: Uah.

(*They crouch down in front of the old woman at the fire.*)

NORA: Tell us what it is you seen.

MAURYA: I went down to the spring well, and I stood there saying a prayer to myself. Then Bartley came along, and he riding on the red mare with the gray pony behind him. (*She puts up her hands, as if to hide something from her eyes.*) The Son of God spare us, Nora!

CATHLEEN: What is it you seen.

MAURYA: I seen Michael himself.

CATHLEEN (*speaking softly*): You did not, mother; It wasn't Michael you seen, for his body is after being found in the far north, and he's got a clean burial by the grace of God.

MAURYA (*a little defiantly*): I'm after seeing him this day, and he riding and galloping. Bartley came first on the red mare; and I tried to say "God speed you," but something choked the words in my throat. He went by quickly; and "the blessing of God on you," says he, and I could say nothing. I looked up then, and I crying, at the gray pony, and there was Michael upon it — with fine clothes on him, and new shoes on his feet.

CATHLEEN (*begins to keen*): It's destroyed we are from this day. It's destroyed, surely.

NORA: Didn't the young priest say the Almighty God wouldn't leave her destitute with no son living?

MAURYA (*in a low voice, but clearly*): It's little the like of him knows of the sea. . . . Bartley will be lost now, and let you call in Eamon and make me a good coffin out of the white boards, for I won't live after them. I've had a husband, and a husband's father, and six sons in this house — six fine men, though it was a hard birth I had with every one of them and they coming to the world — and some of them were found and some of them were not found, but they're gone now the lot of them. ... There were Stephen, and Shawn, were lost in the great wind, and found after in the Bay of Gregory of the Golden Mouth, and carried up the two of them on the one plank, and in by that door.

(*She pauses for a moment, the girls start as if they heard something through the door that is half open behind them.*)

NORA (*in a whisper*): Did you hear that, Cathleen? Did you hear a noise in the northeast?

CATHLEEN (*in a whisper*): There's some one after crying out by the seashore.

MAURYA (*continues without hearing anything*): There was Sheamus and his father, and his own father again, were lost in a dark night, and not a stick or sign was seen of them when the sun went up. There was Patch after was drowned out of a curagh° that turned over. I was sitting here with Bartley, and he a baby, lying on my two knees, and I seen two women, and three women, and four women coming in, and they crossing themselves, and not saying a word. I looked out then, and there were men coming after them, and they holding a thing in the half of a red sail, and water dripping out of it — it was a dry day, Nora — and leaving a track to the door.

(*She pauses again with her hand stretched out toward the door. It opens softly and old women begin to come in, crossing themselves on the threshold, and kneeling down in front of the stage with red petticoats over their heads.*)

MAURYA (*half in a dream, to Cathleen*): Is it Patch, or Michael, or what is it at all?

CATHLEEN: Michael is after being found in the far north, and when he is found there how could he be here in this place?

MAURYA: There does be a power of young men floating round in the sea, and what way would they know if it was Michael they had, or another man like him, for when a man is nine days in the sea, and the wind blowing, it's hard set his own mother would be to say what man was it.

CATHLEEN: It's Michael, God spare him, for they're after sending us a bit of his clothes from the far north.

(*She reaches out and hands Maurya the clothes that belonged to Michael. Maurya stands up slowly and takes them in her hands. Nora looks out.*)

curagh: A small boat with a hide- or tarpaulin-covered frame.

NORA: They're carrying a thing among them and there's water dripping out of it and leaving a track by the big stones.

CATHLEEN (*in a whisper to the women who have come in*): Is it Bartley it is?

ONE OF THE WOMEN: It is surely, God rest his soul.

(*Two younger women come in and pull out the table. Then men carry in the body of Bartley, laid on a plank, with a bit of a sail over it, and lay it on the table.*)

CATHLEEN (*to the women, as they are doing so*): What way was he drowned?

ONE OF THE WOMEN: The gray pony knocked him into the sea, and he was washed out where there is a great surf on the white rocks.

(*Maurya has gone over and knelt down at the head of the table. The women are keening softly and swaying themselves with a slow movement. Cathleen and Nora kneel at the other end of the table. The men kneel near the door.*)

MAURYA (*raising her head and speaking as if she did not see the people around her*): They're all gone now, and there isn't anything more the sea can do to me. ... I'll have no call now to be up crying and praying when the wind breaks from the south, and you can hear the surf is in the east, and the surf is in the west, making a great stir with the two noises, and they hitting one on the other. I'll have no call now to be going down and getting Holy Water in the dark nights after Samhain,° and I won't care what way the sea is when the other women will be keening. (*To Nora.*) Give me the Holy Water, Nora, there's a small sup still on the dresser.

(*Nora gives it to her.*)

MAURYA (*drops Michael's clothes across Bartley's feet, and sprinkles the Holy Water over him*): It isn't that I haven't prayed for you, Bartley, to the Almighty God. It isn't that I haven't said prayers in the dark night till you wouldn't know what I'd be saying; but it's a great rest I'll have now, and it's time surely. It's a great rest I'll have now, and great sleeping in the long nights after Samhain, if it's only a bit of wet flour we do have to eat, and maybe a fish that would be stinking.

(*She kneels down again, crossing herself, and saying prayers under her breath.*)

CATHLEEN (*to an old man*): Maybe yourself and Eamon would make a coffin when the sun rises. We have

Samhain: Feast of All Saints, November 1.

fine white boards herself bought, God help her, thinking Michael would be found, and I have a new cake you can eat while you'll be working.

THE OLD MAN (*looking at the boards*): Are there nails with them?

CATHLEEN: There are not, Colum; we didn't think of the nails.

ANOTHER MAN: It's a great wonder she wouldn't think of the nails, and all the coffins she's seen made already.

CATHLEEN: It's getting old she is, and broken.

(*Maurya stands up again very slowly and spreads out the pieces of Michael's clothes beside the body, sprinkling them with the last of the Holy Water.*)

NORA (*in a whisper to Cathleen*): She's quiet now and easy; but the day Michael was drowned you could hear her crying out from this to the spring well. It's fonder she was of Michael, and would any one have thought that?

CATHLEEN (*slowly and clearly*): An old woman will be soon tired with anything she will do, and isn't it nine days herself is after crying and keening, and making great sorrow in the house?

MAURYA (*puts the empty cup mouth downward on the table, and lays her hands together on Bartley's feet*): They're all together this time, and the end is come. May the Almighty God have mercy on Bartley's soul, and on Michael's soul, and on the souls of Sheamus and Patch, and Stephen and Shawn (*bending her head*); and may He have mercy on my soul, Nora, and on the soul of every one is left living in the world.

(*She pauses, and the keen rises a little more loudly from the women, then sinks away.*)

MAURYA (*continuing*): Michael has a clean burial in the far north, by the grace of the Almighty God. Bartley will have a fine coffin out of the white boards, and a deep grave surely. What more can we want than that? No man at all can be living forever, and we must be satisfied.

(*She kneels down again and the curtain falls slowly.*)

Luigi Pirandello

Luigi Pirandello (1867–1936) was a short-story writer and novelist, a secondary school teacher, and finally a playwright. His life was complicated by business failures that wiped out his personal income and threw his wife into a psychological depression that Pirandello quite bluntly described as madness. Out of his acquaintance with madness — he remained with his wife for fourteen years after she lost touch with reality — Pirandello claimed to have developed much of his attitude toward the shifting surfaces of appearances.

Pirandello's short stories and novels show the consistent pattern of his plays: a deep examination of what we know to be real and a questioning of our confidence in our beliefs. His novels such as *Shoot* (1915) question the surfaces of cinema reality, a reality to which contemporary Italy had yielded with great enthusiasm. His relentless examination of the paradoxes of experience has given him a reputation for pessimism. Virtually all of his work is unified in outlook. He himself said, "I think of life as a very sad piece of buffoonery," and he insisted that people bear within them a deep need to deceive themselves "by creating a reality . . . which . . . is discovered to be vain and illusory."

Pirandello was not a popular writer in Italy, and much of his dramatic work was first performed abroad. But he did win the Nobel Prize for literature in 1934, an indication that his particular brand of modernism was indeed influential. At that time Pirandello was a member of the Fascist party in Italy, although his participation was limited primarily to his work in the state-supported Art Theater of Rome, which he founded.

Pirandello's influence in modern theater resulted from his experimentation with the concept of realism that dominated the stage from the time of Strindberg and Ibsen. The concept of the imaginary "fourth wall" of the stage through which the audience observed the action of characters in their living rooms had become the norm in theater. Pirandello, however, questioned all thought of norms by returning to the stage itself and bringing the very idea of reality under philosophical scrutiny. His relentless questioning helped playwrights around the world open themselves up to new approaches to theater in the early part of the twentieth century. Pirandello was one of the first, and one of the best, experimentalists.

SIX CHARACTERS IN SEARCH OF AN AUTHOR

Pirandello's play is part of a trilogy: *Six Characters in Search of an Author* (1921); *Each in His Own Way* (1924); and *Tonight We Improvise* (1930). These plays all examine the impossibility of knowing reality. There is no objective truth to know, Pirandello tells us, and what we think of as reality is totally subjective, something that each of us maintains independently of other people and that none of us can communicate. We are, in other words, apart, permanently sealed into our own limited world.

These ideas were hardly novel. Playwrights had dealt with them before, even during the Elizabethan age, at a time when — because of the Reformation — the absolute systems of reality promoted by the church had crumbled. Pirandello's plays were also produced in a time — the 1920s — when his culture was uncertain, frightened, and still reeling in shock from the destruction of World War I. It was a depressed time, and in Pirandello's work his audience saw a reflection of their own dispirited, fearful selves. While the films of the period were slapstick escapist pieces of entertainment, the legitimate stage reflected the more thought-provoking issues of the day.

In a sense, *Six Characters in Search of an Author* is about the relationship of art and life, and especially about the relationship of drama and life. The premise of the play is absurd. In the middle of a rehearsal of a Pirandello play, several characters appear and request that an author be present to cobble them into a play. The stage manager assumes they mean they are actors come to be in a play, but they explain that they are not actors. They are real characters. This implies a very complex paradox, since there are such things as characters and such things as actors. However, we are used to the characters being only on paper. When they demand actors to represent them we know that one limit of impossibility has been reached.

The characters who appear are, in a sense, types: a father, a mother, a stepdaughter, a son, two silent figures, — the boy and the child — and, finally, a milliner, Madame Pace. Besides these characters are the actors of the company who are rehearsing the Pirandello play *Mixing It Up*. The six characters have been abandoned by their creator, the author who has absconded, leaving them in search of a substitute. The stepdaughter, late in the play, surmises that their author abandoned them "in a fit of depression, of disgust for the ordinary theater as the public knows it and likes it."

Pirandello uses his characters and their situation to comment on the life of the theater as the public knew it in the 1920s, and he also uses them to begin a series of speculations on the relationship of a public to the actors they see in plays, the characters the actors play, and the authors who create them. To an extent, the relationship between an author and his or her characters will always imply a metaphor for the relationship between a creator and all creation, and it is tempting to think of Samuel Beckett years later in his *Waiting for Godot* imagining an "author" having abandoned his creations because they failed to satisfy him. The six characters — or creations — who invade the stage in this play have a very firm sense of themselves and their actions. They bring with them a story — as all characters in plays do — and they invite the manager to participate in their stories, just as characters invite audiences to become one with their narratives.

One of the more amusing scenes depicts the characters' reactions to seeing actors play their parts. Since they are "real" characters, they have the utmost authority in knowing how their parts should be played, and they end up laughing at the inept efforts of the actors in Act II. When the manager disputes with them, wondering why they protest so vigorously, they explain that they want to make sure the truth is told. The truth. The concept seems so simple on the surface, but in the situation that Pirandello has conceived, it is loaded with complexities that the stage manager cannot fathom.

By the time the question of the truth has been raised, the manager has begun to get a sense of the poignancy of the story that these characters have to tell. He has also begun to see that he must let them continue to tell their story — except that they are not telling it; they are living it. When the climax of their story is reached in the last moments of the play, the line between what is acted and what is lived onstage has become almost completely blurred. When the play ends, there is no telling what has truly occurred and what has truly been acted out.

Six Characters in Search of an Author has endured because it still rings true in its examination of the relationship of art to life, illusion to reality. The very word "illusion" is rejected by the characters — since as characters they are part of the illusion of reality. They reject the thought that they are literature, asserting, "This is Life, this is passion!"

Luigi Pirandello (1867–1936)

SIX CHARACTERS IN SEARCH OF AN AUTHOR   1921
A COMEDY IN THE MAKING

TRANSLATED BY EDWARD STORER

Characters of the Comedy in the Making

THE FATHER	THE BOY
THE MOTHER	THE CHILD
THE STEPDAUGHTER	MADAME PACE
THE SON	

} *do not speak*

Actors of the Company

THE MANAGER	OTHER ACTORS AND ACTRESSES
LEADING LADY	PROPERTY MAN
LEADING MAN	PROMPTER
SECOND LADY LEAD	MACHINIST
L'INGÉNUE	MANAGER'S SECRETARY
JUVENILE LEAD	DOOR-KEEPER
	SCENE-SHIFTERS

Scene: *Daytime. The stage of a theater.*

(**N.B.:** *The Comedy is without acts or scenes. The performance is interrupted once, without the curtain being lowered, when the Manager and the chief characters withdraw to arrange a scenario. A second interruption of the action takes place when, by mistake, the stage hands let the curtain down.*)

ACT I

(*The spectators will find the curtain raised and the stage as it usually is during the daytime. It will be half dark, and empty, so that from the beginning the public may have the impression of an impromptu performance.*)

(*Prompter's box and a small table and chair for the Manager.*)

(*Two other small tables and several chairs scattered about as during rehearsals.*)

(*The Actors and Actresses of the company enter from the back of the stage: first one, then another, then two together; nine or ten in all. They are about to rehearse a Pirandello play: Mixing It Up. Some of the company move off toward their dressing rooms. The Prompter, who has the "book" under his arm,* is waiting for the Manager in order to begin the rehearsal.*)

(*The Actors and Actresses, some standing, some sitting, chat and smoke. One perhaps reads a paper; another cons his part.*)

(*Finally, the Manager enters and goes to the table prepared for him. His Secretary brings him his mail, through which he glances. The Prompter takes his seat, turns on a light, and opens the "book."*)

THE MANAGER (*throwing a letter down on the table*): I can't see. (*To Property Man.*) Let's have a little light, please!

PROPERTY MAN: Yes, sir, yes, at once. (*A light comes down on to the stage.*)

THE MANAGER (*clapping his hands*): Come along! Come along! Second act of "Mixing It Up." (*Sits down.*)

(*The Actors and Actresses go from the front of the stage to the wings, all except the three who are to begin the rehearsal.*)

THE PROMPTER (*reading the "book"*): "Leo Gala's house. A curious room serving as dining-room and study."

THE MANAGER (*to Property Man*): Fix up the old red room.

PROPERTY MAN (*noting it down*): Red set. All right!

THE PROMPTER (*continuing to read from the "book"*): "Table already laid and writing desk with books and papers. Bookshelves. Exit rear to Leo's bedroom. Exit left to kitchen. Principal exit to right."

THE MANAGER (*energetically*): Well, you understand: The principal exit over there; here, the kitchen. (*Turning to actor who is to play the part of Socrates.*) You make your entrances and exits here. (*To Property Man.*) The baize doors at the rear, and curtains.

PROPERTY MAN (*noting it down*): Right!

PROMPTER (*reading as before*): "When the curtain rises, Leo Gala, dressed in cook's cap and apron, is busy beating an egg in a cup. Philip, also dressed as a cook, is beating another egg. Guidi Venanzi is seated and listening."

LEADING MAN (*to Manager*): Excuse me, but must I absolutely wear a cook's cap?

THE MANAGER (*annoyed*): I imagine so. It says so there anyway. (*Pointing to the "book."*)

LEADING MAN: But it's ridiculous!

THE MANAGER (*jumping up in a rage*): Ridiculous? Ridiculous? Is it my fault if France won't send us any more good comedies, and we are reduced to putting on Pirandello's works, where nobody understands anything, and where the author plays the fool with us all? (*The Actors grin. The Manager goes to Leading Man and shouts.*) Yes sir, you put on the cook's cap and beat eggs. Do you suppose that with all this egg-beating business you are on an ordinary stage? Get that out of your head. You represent the shell of the eggs you are beating! (*Laughter and comments among the Actors.*) Silence! and listen to my explanations, please! (*To Leading Man.*) "The empty form of reason without the fullness of instinct, which is blind." — You stand for reason, your wife is instinct. It's a mixing up of the parts, according to which you who act your own part become the puppet of yourself. Do you understand?

LEADING MAN: I'm hanged if I do.

THE MANAGER: Neither do I. But let's get on with it. It's sure to be a glorious failure anyway. (*Confidentially.*) But I say, please face three-quarters. Otherwise, what with the abstruseness of the dialogue, and the public that won't be able to hear you, the whole thing will go to hell. Come on! come on!

PROMPTER: Pardon sir, may I get into my box? There's a bit of a draft.

THE MANAGER: Yes, yes, of course!

(*At this point, the Door-Keeper has entered from the stage door and advances toward the Manager's table, taking off his braided cap. During this maneuver, the Six Characters enter, and stop by the door at back of stage, so that when the Door-Keeper is about to announce their coming to the Manager, they are already on the stage. A tenuous light surrounds them, almost as if irradiated by them — the faint breath of their fantastic reality.*)

(*This light will disappear when they come forward toward the actors. They preserve, however, something of the dream lightness in which they seem almost suspended; but this does not detract from the essential reality of their forms and expressions.*)

(*He who is known as The Father is a man of about 50: hair, reddish in color, thin at the temples; he is not bald, however; thick mustaches, falling over his still fresh mouth, which often opens in an empty and uncertain smile. He is fattish, pale; with an especially wide forehead. He has blue, oval-shaped eyes, very clear and piercing. Wears light trousers and a dark jacket. He is alternatively mellifluous and violent in his manner.*)

(*The Mother seems crushed and terrified as if by an intolerable weight of shame and abasement. She is dressed in modest black and wears a thick widow's veil of crepe. When she lifts this, she reveals a waxlike face. She always keeps her eyes downcast.*)

(*The Stepdaughter is dashing, almost impudent, beautiful. She wears mourning too, but with great elegance. She shows contempt for the timid half-frightened manner of the wretched Boy (14 years old, and also dressed in black); on the other hand, she displays a lively tenderness for her little sister, The Child (about four), who is dressed in white, with a black silk sash at the waist.*)

(*The Son (22) is tall, severe in his attitude of contempt for The Father, supercilious and indifferent to The Mother. He looks as if he had come on the stage against his will.*)

DOOR-KEEPER (*cap in hand*): Excuse me, sir . . .

THE MANAGER (*rudely*): Eh? What is it?

DOOR-KEEPER (*timidly*): These people are asking for you, sir.

THE MANAGER (*furious*): I am rehearsing, and you know perfectly well no one's allowed to come in during rehearsals! (*Turning to the Characters.*) Who are you, please? What do you want?

THE FATHER (*coming forward a little, followed by the others who seem embarrassed*): As a matter of fact . . . we have come here in search of an author . . .

THE MANAGER (*half angry, half amazed*): An author? What author?

THE FATHER: Any author, sir.

THE MANAGER: But there's no author here. We are not rehearsing a new piece.

THE STEPDAUGHTER (*vivaciously*): So much the better, so much the better! We can be your new piece.

AN ACTOR (*coming forward from the others*): Oh, do you hear that?

THE FATHER (*to Stepdaughter*): Yes, but if the author isn't here . . . (*To Manager.*) unless you would be willing . . .

THE MANAGER: You are trying to be funny.

THE FATHER: No, for Heaven's sake, what are you saying? We bring you a drama, sir.

THE STEPDAUGHTER: We may be your fortune.

THE MANAGER: Will you oblige me by going away? We haven't time to waste with mad people.

THE FATHER (*mellifluously*): Oh sir, you know well that life is full of infinite absurdities, which, strangely enough, do not even need to appear plausible, since they are true.

THE MANAGER: What the devil is he talking about?

THE FATHER: I say that to reverse the ordinary process

may well be considered a madness: that is, to create credible situations, in order that they may appear true. But permit me to observe that if this be madness, it is the sole *raison d'être*° of your profession, gentlemen. (*The Actors look hurt and perplexed.*)

THE MANAGER (*getting up and looking at him*): So our profession seems to you one worthy of madmen then?

THE FATHER: Well, to make seem true that which isn't true . . . without any need . . . for a joke as it were . . . Isn't that your mission, gentlemen: to give life to fantastic characters on the stage?

THE MANAGER (*interpreting the rising anger of the Company*): But I would beg you to believe, my dear sir, that the profession of the comedian is a noble one. If today, as things go, the playwrights give us stupid comedies to play and puppets to represent instead of men, remember we are proud to have given life to immortal works here on these very boards! (*The Actors, satisfied, applaud their Manager.*)

THE FATHER (*interrupting furiously*): Exactly, perfectly, to living beings more alive than those who breathe and wear clothes: beings less real perhaps, but truer! I agree with you entirely. (*The Actors look at one another in amazement.*)

THE MANAGER: But what do you mean? Before, you said . . .

THE FATHER: No, excuse me, I meant it for you, sir, who were crying out that you had no time to lose with madmen, while no one better than yourself knows that nature uses the instrument of human fantasy in order to pursue her high creative purpose.

THE MANAGER: Very well, — but where does all this take us?

THE FATHER: Nowhere! It is merely to show you that one is born to life in many forms, in many shapes, as tree, or as stone, as water, as butterfly, or as woman. So one may also be born a character in a play.

THE MANAGER (*with feigned comic dismay*): So you and these other friends of yours have been born characters?

THE FATHER: Exactly, and alive as you see! (*Manager and Actors burst out laughing.*)

THE FATHER (*hurt*): I am sorry you laugh, because we carry in us a drama, as you can guess from this woman here veiled in black.

THE MANAGER (*losing patience at last and almost indignant*): Oh, chuck it! Get away please! Clear out of here! (*To Property Man.*) For Heaven's sake, turn them out!

THE FATHER (*resisting*): No, no, look here, we . . .

THE MANAGER (*roaring*): We come here to work, you know.

LEADING ACTOR: One cannot let oneself be made such a fool of.

THE FATHER (*determined, coming forward*): I marvel at your incredulity, gentlemen. Are you not accustomed to see the characters created by an author spring to life in yourselves and face each other? Just because there is no "book" (*pointing to the Prompter's box*) which contains us, you refuse to believe . . .

THE STEPDAUGHTER (*advances toward Manager, smiling and coquettish*): Believe me, we are really six most interesting characters, sir; sidetracked however.

THE FATHER: Yes, that is the word! (*To Manager all at once.*) In the sense, that is, that the author who created us alive no longer wished, or was no longer able, materially to put us into a work of art. And this was a real crime, sir; because he who has had the luck to be born a character can laugh even at death. He cannot die. The man, the writer, the instrument of the creation will die, but his creation does not die. And to live for ever, it does not need to have extraordinary gifts or to be able to work wonders. Who was Sancho Panza? Who was Don Abbondio?° Yet they live eternally because — live germs as they were — they had the fortune to find a fecundating matrix, a fantasy which could raise and nourish them: make them live for ever!

THE MANAGER: That is quite all right. But what do you want here, all of you?

THE FATHER: We want to live.

THE MANAGER (*ironically*): For Eternity?

THE FATHER: No, sir, only for a moment . . . in you.

AN ACTOR: Just listen to him!

LEADING LADY: They want to live, in us . . . !

JUVENILE LEAD (*pointing to the Stepdaughter*): I've no objection, as far as that one is concerned!

THE FATHER: Look here! look here! The comedy has to be made. (*To the Manager.*) But if you and your actors are willing, we can soon concert it among ourselves.

THE MANAGER (*annoyed*): But what do you want to concert? We don't go in for concerts here. Here we play dramas and comedies!

THE FATHER: Exactly! That is just why we have come to you.

THE MANAGER: And where is the "book"?

THE FATHER: It is in us! (*The Actors laugh.*) The drama is in us, and we are the drama. We are

---

raison d'être: French for "reason to exist."

Sancho Panza . . . Don Abbondio: Memorable characters in novels: the squire in Cervantes's *Don Quixote* and the priest in Manzoni's *I Promessi Sposi* (*The Betrothed*), respectively.

impatient to play it. Our inner passion drives us on to this.

THE STEPDAUGHTER (*disdainful, alluring, treacherous, full of impudence*): My passion, sir! Ah, if you only knew! My passion for him! (*Points to the Father and makes a pretense of embracing him. Then she breaks out into a loud laugh.*)

THE FATHER (*angrily*): Behave yourself! And please don't laugh in that fashion.

THE STEPDAUGHTER: With your permission, gentlemen, I, who am a two months orphan, will show you how I can dance and sing. (*Sings and then dances Prenez garde à Tchou-Tchin-Tchou.*)

Les chinois sont un peuple malin,
De Shangaî à Pékin,
Ils ont mis des écriteaux partout:
Prenez garde à Tchou-Tchin-Tchou.°

ACTORS AND ACTRESSES: Bravo! Well done! Tip-top!

THE MANAGER: Silence! This isn't a café concert, you know! (*Turning to the Father in consternation.*) Is she mad?

THE FATHER: Mad? No, she's worse than mad.

THE STEPDAUGHTER (*to Manager*): Worse? Worse? Listen! Stage this drama for us at once! Then you will see that at a certain moment I . . . when this little darling here. . . . (*Takes the Child by the hand and leads her to the Manager.*) Isn't she a dear? (*Takes her up and kisses her.*) Darling! Darling! (*Puts her down again and adds feelingly.*) Well, when God suddenly takes this dear little child away from that poor mother there; and this imbecile here (*seizing hold of the Boy roughly and pushing him forward*) does the stupidest things, like the fool he is, you will see me run away. Yes, gentlemen, I shall be off. But the moment hasn't arrived yet. After what has taken place between him and me (*indicates the Father with a horrible wink*) I can't remain any longer in this society, to have to witness the anguish of this mother here for that fool. . . . (*Indicates the Son.*) Look at him! Look at him! See how indifferent, how frigid he is, because he is the legitimate son. He despises me, despises him (*pointing to the Boy*), despises this baby here; because . . . we are bastards. (*Goes to the Mother and embraces her.*) And he doesn't want to recognize her as his mother — she who is the common mother of us all. He looks down upon her as if she were only the mother of us three bastards. Wretch! (*She

Prenez . . . Tchou:** This French popular song is an adaptation of "Chu-Chin-Chow," and old Broadway show tune. "The Chinese are a sly people; / From Shanghai to Peking, / They've stuck up warning signs: / Beware of Tchou-Tchin-Tchou." (The words are funnier in French because *chou* means "cabbage.")

says all this very rapidly, excitedly. At the word "bastards" she raises her voice, and almost spits out the final "Wretch!"*)

THE MOTHER (*to the Manager, in anguish*): In the name of these two little children, I beg you. . . . (*She grows faint and is about to fall.*) Oh God!

THE FATHER (*coming forward to support her as do some of the Actors*): Quick, a chair, a chair for this poor widow!

THE ACTORS: Is it true? Has she really fainted?

THE MANAGER: Quick, a chair! Here!

(*One of the Actors brings a chair, the others proffer assistance. The Mother tries to prevent the Father from lifting the veil which covers her face.*)

THE FATHER: Look at her! Look at her!

THE MOTHER: No, no; stop it please!

THE FATHER (*raising her veil*): Let them see you!

THE MOTHER (*rising and covering her face with her hands, in desperation*): I beg you, sir, to prevent this man from carrying out his plan which is loathsome to me.

THE MANAGER (*dumbfounded*): I don't understand at all. What is the situation? (*To the Father.*) Is this lady your wife?

THE FATHER: Yes, gentlemen: my wife!

THE MANAGER: But how can she be a widow if you are alive? (*The Actors find relief for their astonishment in a loud laugh.*)

THE FATHER: Don't laugh! Don't laugh like that, for Heaven's sake. Her drama lies just here in this: she has had a lover, a man who ought to be here.

THE MOTHER (*with a cry*): No! No!

THE STEPDAUGHTER: Fortunately for her, he is dead. Two months ago as I said. We are in mourning, as you see.

THE FATHER: He isn't here, you see, not because he is dead. He isn't here — look at her a moment and you will understand — because her drama isn't a drama of the love of two men for whom she was incapable of feeling anything except possibly a little gratitude — gratitude not for me but for the other. She isn't a woman, she is a mother, and her drama — powerful, sir, I assure you — lies, as a matter of fact, all in these four children she has had by two men.

THE MOTHER: I had them? Have you got the courage to say that I wanted them? (*To the Company.*) It was his doing. It was he who gave me that other man, who forced me to go away with him.

THE STEPDAUGHTER: It isn't true.

THE MOTHER (*startled*): Not true, isn't it?

THE STEPDAUGHTER: No, it isn't true, it just isn't true.

THE MOTHER: And what can you know about it?

THE STEPDAUGHTER: It isn't true. Don't believe it. (*To

Manager.) Do you know why she says so? For that fellow there. (*Indicates the Son.*) She tortures herself, destroys herself on account of the neglect of that son there; and she wants him to believe that if she abandoned him when he was only two years old, it was because he (*indicates the Father*) made her do so.

THE MOTHER (*vigorously*): He forced me to it, and I call God to witness it. (*To the Manager.*) Ask him (*indicates Husband*) if it isn't true. Let him speak. You (*to Daughter*) are not in a position to know anything about it.

THE STEPDAUGHTER: I know you lived in peace and happiness with my father while he lived. Can you deny it?

THE MOTHER: No, I don't deny it. . . .

THE STEPDAUGHTER: He was always full of affection and kindness for you. (*To the Boy, angrily.*) It's true, isn't it? Tell them! Why don't you speak, you little fool?

THE MOTHER: Leave the poor boy alone. Why do you want to make me appear ungrateful, daughter? I don't want to offend your father. I have answered him that I didn't abandon my house and my son through any fault of mine, nor from any wilful passion.

THE FATHER: It is true. It was my doing.

LEADING MAN (*to the Company*): What a spectacle!

LEADING LADY: We are the audience this time.

JUVENILE LEAD: For once, in a way.

THE MANAGER (*beginning to get really interested*): Let's hear them out. Listen!

THE SON: Oh yes, you're going to hear a fine bit now. He will talk to you of the Demon of Experiment.

THE FATHER: You are a cynical imbecile. I've told you so already a hundred times. (*To the Manager.*) He tries to make fun of me on account of this expression which I have found to excuse myself with.

THE SON (*with disgust*): Yes, phrases! phrases!

THE FATHER: Phrases! Isn't everyone consoled when faced with a trouble or fact he doesn't understand, by a word, some simple word, which tells us nothing and yet calms us?

THE STEPDAUGHTER: Even in the case of remorse. In fact, especially then.

THE FATHER: Remorse? No, that isn't true. I've done more than use words to quiet the remorse in me.

THE STEPDAUGHTER: Yes, there was a bit of money too. Yes, yes, a bit of money. There were the hundred lire he was about to offer me in payment, gentlemen. . . . (*Sensation of horror among the Actors.*)

THE SON (*to the Stepdaughter*): This is vile.

THE STEPDAUGHTER: Vile? There they were in a pale blue envelope on a little mahogany table in the back of Madame Pace's shop. You know Madame Pace — one of those ladies who attract poor girls of good family into their ateliers, under the pretext of their selling *robes et manteaux.*°

THE SON: And he thinks he has bought the right to tyrannize over us all with those hundred lire he was going to pay; but which, fortunately — note this, gentlemen — he had no chance of paying.

THE STEPDAUGHTER: It was a near thing, though, you know! (*Laughs ironically.*)

THE MOTHER (*protesting*): Shame, my daughter, shame!

THE STEPDAUGHTER: Shame indeed! This is my revenge! I am dying to live that scene . . . The room . . . I see it . . . Here is the window with the mantles exposed, there the divan, the looking-glass, a screen, there in front of the window the little mahogany table with the blue envelope containing one hundred lire. I see it. I see it. I could take hold of it. . . . But you, gentlemen, you ought to turn your backs now: I am almost nude, you know. But I don't blush: I leave that to him. (*Indicating Father.*)

THE MANAGER: I don't understand this at all.

THE FATHER: Naturally enough. I would ask you, sir, to exercise your authority a little here, and let me speak before you believe all she is trying to blame me with. Let me explain.

THE STEPDAUGHTER: Ah yes, explain it in your own way.

THE FATHER: But don't you see that the whole trouble lies here? In words, words. Each one of us has within him a whole world of things, each man of us his own special world. And how can we ever come to an understanding if I put in the words I utter the sense and value of things as I see them; while you who listen to me must inevitably translate them according to the conception of things each one of you has within himself. We think we understand each other, but we never really do. Look here! This woman (*indicating the Mother*) takes all my pity for her as a specially ferocious form of cruelty.

THE MOTHER: But you drove me away.

THE FATHER: Do you hear her? I drove her away! She believes I really sent her away.

THE MOTHER: You know how to talk, and I don't; but, believe me, sir (*To Manager.*), after he had married me . . . who knows why? . . . I was a poor insignificant woman. . . .

THE FATHER: But, good Heavens! it was just for your humility that I married you. I loved this simplicity in you. (*He stops when he sees she makes signs to contradict him, opens his arms wide in sign of desperation, seeing how hopeless it is to make himself understood.*) You see she denies it. Her mental

robes et manteaux: French for "dresses and capes."

deafness, believe me, is phenomenal, the limit: (*touches his forehead*) deaf, deaf, mentally deaf! She has plenty of feeling. Oh yes, a good heart for the children; but the brain — deaf, to the point of desperation —!

THE STEPDAUGHTER: Yes, but ask him how his intelligence has helped us.

THE FATHER: If we could see all the evil that may spring from good, what should we do? (*At this point the Leading Lady, who is biting her lips with rage at seeing the Leading Man flirting with the Stepdaughter, comes forward and speaks to the Manager.*)

LEADING LADY: Excuse me, but are we going to rehearse today?

MANAGER: Of course, of course; but let's hear them out.

JUVENILE LEAD: This is something quite new.

L'INGÉNUE: Most interesting!

LEADING LADY: Yes, for the people who like that kind of thing. (*Casts a glance at Leading Man.*)

THE MANAGER (*to Father*): You must please explain yourself quite clearly. (*Sits down.*)

THE FATHER: Very well then: listen! I had in my service a poor man, a clerk, a secretary of mine, full of devotion, who became friends with her. (*Indicating the Mother.*) They understood one another, were kindred souls in fact, without, however, the least suspicion of any evil existing. They were incapable even of thinking of it.

THE STEPDAUGHTER: So he thought of it — for them!

THE FATHER: That's not true. I meant to do good to them — and to myself, I confess, at the same time. Things had come to the point that I could not say a word to either of them without their making a mute appeal, one to the other, with their eyes. I could see them silently asking each other how I was to be kept in countenance, how I was to be kept quiet. And this, believe me, was just about enough of itself to keep me in a constant rage, to exasperate me beyond measure.

THE MANAGER: And why didn't you send him away then — this secretary of yours?

THE FATHER: Precisely what I did, sir. And then I had to watch this poor woman drifting forlornly about the house like an animal without a master, like an animal one has taken in out of pity.

THE MOTHER: Ah yes . . . !

THE FATHER (*suddenly turning to the Mother*): It's true about the son anyway, isn't it?

THE MOTHER: He took my son away from me first of all.

THE FATHER: But not from cruelty. I did it so that he should grow up healthy and strong by living in the country.

THE STEPDAUGHTER (*pointing to him ironically*): As one can see.

THE FATHER (*quickly*): Is it my fault if he has grown up like this? I sent him to a wet nurse in the country, a peasant, as *she* did not seem to me strong enough, though she is of humble origin. That was, anyway, the reason I married her. Unpleasant all this may be, but how can it be helped? My mistake possibly, but there we are! All my life I have had these confounded aspirations towards a certain moral sanity. (*At this point the Stepdaughter bursts into a noisy laugh.*) Oh, stop it! Stop it! I can't stand it.

THE MANAGER: Yes, please stop it, for Heaven's sake.

THE STEPDAUGHTER: But imagine moral sanity from him, if you please — the client of certain ateliers like that of Madame Pace!

THE FATHER: Fool! That is the proof that I am a man! This seeming contradiction, gentlemen, is the strongest proof that I stand here a live man before you. Why, it is just for this very incongruity in my nature that I have had to suffer what I have. I could not live by the side of that woman (*indicating the Mother*) any longer; but not so much for the boredom she inspired me with as for the pity I felt for her.

THE MOTHER: And so he turned me out —.

THE FATHER: — well provided for! Yes, I sent her to that man, gentlemen . . . to let her go free of me.

THE MOTHER: And to free himself.

THE FATHER: Yes, I admit it. It was also a liberation for me. But great evil has come of it. I meant well when I did it; and I did it more for her sake than mine. I swear it. (*Crosses his arms on his chest; then turns suddenly to the Mother.*) Did I ever lose sight of you until that other man carried you off to another town, like the angry fool he was? And on account of my pure interest in you . . . my pure interest, I repeat, that had no base motive in it . . . I watched with the tenderest concern the new family that grew up around her. She can bear witness to this. (*Points to the Stepdaughter.*)

THE STEPDAUGHTER: Oh yes, that's true enough. When I was a kiddie, so so high, you know, with plaits over my shoulders and knickers longer than my skirts, I used to see him waiting outside the school for me to come out. He came to see how I was growing up.

THE FATHER: This is infamous, shameful!

THE STEPDAUGHTER: No. Why?

THE FATHER: Infamous! infamous! (*Then excitedly to Manager, explaining.*) After she (*indicating the Mother*) went away, my house seemed suddenly empty. She was my incubus, but she filled my house. I was like a dazed fly alone in the empty rooms.

This boy here (*indicating the Son*) was educated away from home, and when he came back, he seemed to me to be no more mine. With no mother to stand between him and me, he grew up entirely for himself, on his own, apart, with no tie of intellect or affection binding him to me. And then — strange but true — I was driven, by curiosity at first and then by some tender sentiment, towards her family, which had come into being through my will. The thought of her began gradually to fill up the emptiness I felt all around me. I wanted to know if she were happy in living out the simple daily duties of life. I wanted to think of her as fortunate and happy because far away from the complicated torments of my spirit. And so, to have proof of this, I used to watch that child coming out of school.

THE STEPDAUGHTER: Yes, yes. True. He used to follow me in the street and smiled at me, waved his hand, like this. I would look at him with interest, wondering who he might be. I told my mother, who guessed at once. (*The Mother agrees with a nod.*) Then she didn't want to send me to school for some days; and when I finally went back, there he was again — looking so ridiculous — with a paper parcel in his hands. He came close to me, caressed me, and drew out a fine straw hat from the parcel, with a bouquet of flowers — all for me!

THE MANAGER: A bit discursive this, you know!

THE SON (*contemptuously*): Literature! Literature!

THE FATHER: Literature indeed! This is life, this is passion!

THE MANAGER: It may be, but it won't act.

THE FATHER: I agree. This is only the part leading up. I don't suggest this should be staged. She (*pointing to the Stepdaughter*), as you see, is no longer the flapper with plaits down her back —

THE STEPDAUGHTER: — and knickers showing below the skirt!

THE FATHER: The drama is coming now, sir; something new, complex, most interesting.

THE STEPDAUGHTER: As soon as my father died . . .

THE FATHER: — there was absolute misery for them. They came back here, unknown to me. Through her stupidity! (*Pointing to the Mother.*) It is true she can barely write her own name; but she could anyhow have got her daughter to write to me that they were in need . . .

THE MOTHER: And how was I to divine all this sentiment in him?

THE FATHER: That is exactly your mistake, never to have guessed any of my sentiments.

THE MOTHER: After so many years apart, and all that had happened . . .

THE FATHER: Was it my fault if that fellow carried you away? It happened quite suddenly; for after he had obtained some job or other, I could find no trace of them; and so, not unnaturally, my interest in them dwindled. But the drama culminated unforeseen and violent on their return, when I was impelled by my miserable flesh that still lives. . . . Ah! what misery, what wretchedness is that of the man who is alone and disdains debasing *liaisons*! Not old enough to do without women, and not young enough to go and look for one without shame. Misery? It's worse than misery; it's a horror; for no woman can any longer give him love; and when a man feels this. . . . One ought to do without, you say? Yes, yes, I know. Each of us when he appears before his fellows is clothed in a certain dignity. But every man knows what unconfessable things pass within the secrecy of his own heart. One gives way to the temptation, only to rise from it again, afterwards, with a great eagerness to re-establish one's dignity, as if it were a tombstone to place on the grave of one's shame, and a monument to hide and sign the memory of our weaknesses. Everybody's in the same case. Some folks haven't the courage to say certain things, that's all!

THE STEPDAUGHTER: All appear to have the courage to do them though.

THE FATHER: Yes, but in secret. Therefore, you want more courage to say these things. Let a man but speak these things out, and folks at once label him a cynic. But it isn't true. He is like all the others, better indeed, because he isn't afraid to reveal with the light of the intelligence the red shame of human bestiality on which most men close their eyes so as not to see it.

Woman — for example, look at her case! She turns tantalizing inviting glances on you. You seize her. No sooner does she feel herself in your grasp than she closes her eyes. It is the sign of her mission, the sign by which she says to man: "Blind yourself, for I am blind."

THE STEPDAUGHTER: Sometimes she can close them no more: when she no longer feels the need of hiding her shame to herself, but dry-eyed and dispassionately, sees only that of the man who has blinded himself without love. Oh, all these intellectual complications make me sick, disgust me — all this philosophy that uncovers the beast in man, and then seeks to save him, excuse him . . . I can't stand it, sir. When a man seeks to "simplify" life bestially, throwing aside every relic of humanity, every chaste aspiration, every pure feeling, all sense of ideality, duty, modesty, shame . . . then nothing is more revolting and nauseous than a certain kind of remorse — crocodiles' tears, that's what it is.

THE MANAGER: Let's come to the point. This is only discussion.

THE FATHER: Very good, sir! But a fact is like a sack which won't stand up when it's empty. In order that it may stand up, one has to put into it the reason and sentiment which have caused it to exist. I couldn't possibly know that after the death of that man, they had decided to return here, that they were in misery, and that she (*pointing to the Mother*) had gone to work as a modiste,° and at a shop of the type of that of Madame Pace.

THE STEPDAUGHTER: A real high-class modiste, you must know, gentlemen. In appearance, she works for the leaders of the best society; but she arranges matters so that these elegant ladies serve her purpose . . . without prejudice to other ladies who are . . . well . . . only so so.

THE MOTHER: You will believe me, gentlemen, that it never entered my mind that the old hag offered me work because she had her eye on my daughter.

THE STEPDAUGHTER: Poor mamma! Do you know, sir, what that woman did when I brought her back the work my mother had finished? She would point out to me that I had torn one of my frocks, and she would give it back to my mother to mend. It was I who paid for it, always I; while this poor creature here believed she was sacrificing herself for me and these two children here, sitting up at night sewing Madame Pace's robes.

THE MANAGER: And one day you met there . . .

THE STEPDAUGHTER: Him, him. Yes sir, an old client. There's a scene for you to play! Superb!

THE FATHER: She, the Mother arrived just then . . .

THE STEPDAUGHTER (*treacherously*): Almost in time!

THE FATHER (*crying out*): No, in time! in time! Fortunately I recognized her . . . in time. And I took them back home with me to my house. You can imagine now her position and mine; she, as you see her; and I who cannot look her in the face.

THE STEPDAUGHTER: Absurd! How can I possibly be expected — after that — to be a modest young miss, a fit person to go with his confounded aspirations for "a solid moral sanity"?

THE FATHER: For the drama lies all in this — in the conscience that I have, that each one of us has. We believe this conscience to be a single thing, but it is many-sided. There is one for this person, and another for that. Diverse consciences. So we have this illusion of being one person for all, of having a personality that is unique in all our acts. But it isn't true. We perceive this when, tragically perhaps, in something we do, we are as it were, suspended, caught up in the air on a kind of hook. Then we perceive that all of us was not in that act, and that

modiste: A person who makes fashionable clothing for women.

it would be an atrocious injustice to judge us by that action alone, as if all our existence were summed up in that one deed. Now do you understand the perfidy of this girl? She surprised me in a place, where she ought not to have known me, just as I could not exist for her; and she now seeks to attach to me a reality such as I could never suppose I should have to assume for her in a shameful and fleeting moment of my life. I feel this above all else. And the drama, you will see, acquires a tremendous value from this point. Then there is the position of the others . . . his. . . . (*Indicating the Son.*)

THE SON (*shrugging his shoulders scornfully*): Leave me alone! I don't come into this.

THE FATHER: What? You don't come into this?

THE SON: I've got nothing to do with it, and don't want to have; because you know well enough I wasn't made to be mixed up in all this with the rest of you.

THE STEPDAUGHTER: We are only vulgar folk! He is the fine gentleman. You may have noticed, Mr. Manager, that I fix him now and again with a look of scorn while he lowers his eyes — for he knows the evil he has done me.

THE SON (*scarcely looking at her*): I?

THE STEPDAUGHTER: You! you! I owe my life on the streets to you. Did you or did you not deny us, with your behavior, I won't say the intimacy of home, but even that mere hospitality which makes guests feel at their ease? We were intruders who had come to disturb the kingdom of your legitimacy. I should like to have you witness, Mr. Manager, certain scenes between him and me. He says I have tyrannized over everyone. But it was just his behavior which made me insist on the reason for which I had come into the house, — this reason he calls "vile" — into his house, with my mother who is his mother too. And I came as mistress of the house.

THE SON: It's easy for them to put me always in the wrong. But imagine, gentlemen, the position of a son, whose fate it is to see arrive one day at his home a young woman of impudent bearing, a young woman who inquires for his father, with whom who knows what business she has. This young man has then to witness her return bolder than ever, accompanied by that child there. He is obliged to watch her treat his father in an equivocal and confidential manner. She asks for money of him in a way that lets one suppose he must give it to her, *must,* do you understand, because he has every obligation to do so.

THE FATHER: But I have, as a matter of fact, this obligation. I owe it to your mother.

THE SON: How should I know? When had I ever seen

or heard of her? One day there arrive with her (*indicating Stepdaughter*) that lad and this baby here. I am told: "This is *your* mother too, you know." I divine from her manner (*indicating Stepdaughter again*) why it is they have come home. I had rather not say what I feel and think about it. I shouldn't even care to confess to myself. No action can therefore be hoped for from me in this affair. Believe me, Mr. Manager, I am an "unrealized" character, dramatically speaking; and I find myself not at all at ease in their company. Leave me out of it, I beg you.

THE FATHER: What? It is just because you are so that . . .

THE SON: How do you know what I am like? When did you ever bother your head about me?

THE FATHER: I admit it. I admit it. But isn't that a situation in itself? This aloofness of yours which is so cruel to me and to your mother, who returns home and sees you almost for·the first time grown up, who doesn't recognize you but knows you are her son. . . . (*Pointing out the Mother to the Manager.*) See, she's crying!

THE STEPDAUGHTER (*angrily, stamping her foot*): Like a fool!

THE FATHER (*indicating Stepdaughter*): She can't stand him, you know. (*Then referring again to the Son.*) He says he doesn't come into the affair, whereas he is really the hinge of the whole action. Look at that lad who is always clinging to his mother, frightened and humiliated. It is on account of this fellow here. Possibly his situation is the most painful of all. He feels himself a stranger more than the others. The poor little chap feels mortified, humiliated at being brought into a home out of charity as it were. (*In confidence.*) He is the image of his father. Hardly talks at all. Humble and quiet.

THE MANAGER: Oh, we'll cut him out. You've no notion what a nuisance boys are on the stage. . . .

THE FATHER: He disappears soon, you know. And the baby too. She is the first to vanish from the scene. The drama consists finally in this: when that mother reenters my house, her family born outside of it, and shall we say superimposed on the original, ends with the death of the little girl, the tragedy of the boy and the flight of the elder daughter. It cannot go on, because it is foreign to its surroundings. So after much torment, we three remain: I, the mother, that son. Then, owing to the disappearance of that extraneous family, we too find ourselves strange to one another. We find we are living in an atmosphere of mortal desolation which is the revenge, as he (*indicating Son*) scornfully said of the Demon of Experiment, that unfortunately hides in me. Thus, sir, you see when faith is lacking, it becomes impossible to create certain states of happiness, for we lack the necessary humility. Vaingloriously, we try to substitute ourselves for this faith, creating thus for the rest of the world a reality which we believe after their fashion, while, actually, it doesn't exist. For each one of us has his own reality to be respected before God, even when it is harmful to one's very self.

THE MANAGER: There is something in what you say. I assure you all this interests me very much. I begin to think there's the stuff for a drama in all this, and not a bad drama either.

THE STEPDAUGHTER (*coming forward*): When you've got a character like me.

THE FATHER (*shutting her up, all excited to learn the decision of the Manager*): You be quiet!

THE MANAGER (*reflecting, heedless of interruption*): It's new . . . hem . . . yes. . . .

THE FATHER: Absolutely new!

THE MANAGER: You've got a nerve though, I must say, to come here and fling it at me like this . . .

THE FATHER: You will understand, sir, born as we are for the stage . . .

THE MANAGER: Are you amateur actors then?

THE FATHER: No, I say born for the stage, because . . .

THE MANAGER: Oh, nonsense. You're an old hand, you know.

THE FATHER: No sir, no. We act that role for which we have been cast, that role which we are given in life. And in my own case, passion itself, as usually happens, becomes a trifle theatrical when it is exalted.

THE MANAGER: Well, well, that will do. But you see, without an author. . . . I could give you the address of an author if you like . . .

THE FATHER: No, no. Look here! You must be the author.

THE MANAGER: I? What are you talking about?

THE FATHER: Yes, you, you! Why not?

THE MANAGER: Because I have never been an author: that's why.

THE FATHER: Then why not turn author now? Everybody does it. You don't want any special qualities. Your task is made much easier by the fact that we are all here alive before you. . . .

THE MANAGER: It won't do.

THE FATHER: What? When you see us live our drama. . . .

THE MANAGER: Yes, that's all right. But you want someone to write it.

THE FATHER: No, no. Someone to take it down, possibly, while we play it, scene by scene! It will be enough to sketch it out at first, and then try it over.

THE MANAGER: Well . . . I am almost tempted. It's a bit of an idea. One might have a shot at it.

THE FATHER: Of course. You'll see what scenes will come out of it. I can give you one, at once . . .

THE MANAGER: By Jove, it tempts me. I'd like to have a go at it. Let's try it out. Come with me to my office. (*Turning to the Actors.*) You are at liberty for a bit, but don't step out of the theater for long. In a quarter of an hour, twenty minutes, all back here again! (*To the Father.*) We'll see what can be done. Who knows if we don't get something really extraordinary out of it?

THE FATHER: There's no doubt about it. They (*indicating the Characters*) had better come with us too, hadn't they?

THE MANAGER: Yes, yes. Come on! come on! (*Moves away and then turning to the Actors.*) Be punctual, please! (*Manager and the Six Characters cross the stage and go off. The other Actors remain, looking at one another in astonishment.*)

LEADING MAN: Is he serious? What the devil does he want to do?

JUVENILE LEAD: This is rank madness.

THIRD ACTOR: Does he expect to knock up a drama in five minutes?

JUVENILE LEAD: Like the improvisers!

LEADING LADY: If he thinks I'm going to take part in a joke like this. . . .

JUVENILE LEAD: I'm out of it anyway.

FOURTH ACTOR: I should like to know who they are. (*Alludes to Characters.*)

THIRD ACTOR: What do you suppose? Madmen or rascals!

JUVENILE LEAD: And he takes them seriously!

L'INGÉNUE: Vanity! He fancies himself as an author now.

LEADING MAN: It's absolutely unheard of. If the stage has come to this . . . well I'm . . .

FIFTH ACTOR: It's rather a joke.

THIRD ACTOR: Well, we'll see what's going to happen next.

(*Thus talking, the Actors leave the stage, some going out by the little door at the back, others retiring to their dressing rooms.*)

(*The curtain remains up.*)

(*The action of the play is suspended for twenty minutes.*)

ACT II _____

(*The stage call-bells ring to warn the company that the play is about to begin again.*)

(*The Stepdaughter comes out of the Manager's office along with the Child and the Boy. As she comes out of the office, she cries: —*)

Nonsense! nonsense! Do it yourselves! I'm not going to mix myself up in this mess. (*Turning to the Child and coming quickly with her on to the stage.*) Come on, Rosetta, let's run!

(*The Boy follows them slowly, remaining a little behind and seeming perplexed.*)

THE STEPDAUGHTER (*stops, bends over the Child and takes the latter's face between her hands*): My little darling! You're frightened, aren't you? You don't know where we are, do you? (*Pretending to reply to a question of the Child.*) What is the stage? It's a place, baby, you know, where people play at being serious, a place where they act comedies. We've got to act a comedy now, dead serious, you know; and you're in it also, little one. (*Embraces her, pressing the little head to her breast, and rocking the Child for a moment.*) Oh darling, darling, what a horrid comedy you've got to play! What a wretched part they've found for you! A garden . . . a fountain . . . look . . . just suppose, kiddie, it's here. Where, you say? Why, right here in the middle. It's all pretense you know. That's the trouble, my pet: it's all make-believe here. It's better to imagine it though, because if they fix it up for you, it'll only be painted cardboard, painted cardboard for the rockery, the water, the plants. . . . Ah, but I think a baby like this one would sooner have a make-believe fountain than a real one, so she could play with it. What a joke it'll be for the others! But for you, alas! not quite such a joke: you who are real, baby dear, and really play by a real fountain that is big and green and beautiful, with ever so many bamboos around it that are reflected in the water, and a whole lot of little ducks swimming about. . . . No, Rosetta, no, your mother doesn't bother about you on account of that wretch of a son there. I'm in the devil of a temper, and as for that lad. . . . (*Seizes Boy by the arm to force him to take one of his hands out of his pockets.*) What have you got there? What are you hiding? (*Pulls his hand out of his pocket, looks into it, and catches the glint of a revolver.*) Ah! where did you get this? (*The Boy, very pale in the face, looks at her, but does not answer.*) Idiot! If I'd been in your place, instead of killing myself, I'd have shot one of those two, or both of them: father and son.

(*The Father enters from the office, all excited from his work. The Manager follows him.*)

THE FATHER: Come on, come on dear! Come here for a minute! We've arranged everything. It's all fixed up.

THE MANAGER (*also excited*): If you please, young lady, there are one or two points to settle still. Will you come along?

THE STEPDAUGHTER (*following him toward the office*): Ouff! what's the good, if you've arranged everything.

(*The Father, Manager, and Stepdaughter go back into the office again [off] for a moment. At the same time, the Son, followed by the Mother, comes out.*)

THE SON (*looking at the three entering office*): Oh this is fine, fine! And to think I can't even get away!

(*The Mother attempts to look at him, but lowers her eyes immediately when he turns away from her. She then sits down. The Boy and the Child approach her. She casts a glance again at the Son, and speaks with humble tones, trying to draw him into conversation.*)

THE MOTHER: And isn't my punishment the worst of all? (*Then seeing from the Son's manner that he will not bother himself about her.*) My God! Why are you so cruel? Isn't it enough for one person to support all this torment? Must you then insist on others seeing it also?

THE SON (*half to himself, meaning the Mother to hear, however*): And they want to put it on the stage! If there was at least a reason for it! He thinks he has got at the meaning of it all. Just as if each one of us in every circumstance of life couldn't find his own explanation of it! (*Pauses.*) He complains he was discovered in a place where he ought not to have been seen, in a moment of his life which ought to have remained hidden and kept out of the reach of that convention which he has to maintain for other people. And what about my case? Haven't I had to reveal what no son ought ever to reveal: how father and mother live and are man and wife for themselves quite apart from that idea of father and mother which we give them? When this idea is revealed, our life is then linked at one point only to that man and that woman; and as such it should shame them, shouldn't it?

(*The Mother hides her face in her hands. From the dressing rooms and the little door at the back of the stage the Actors and Stage Manager return, followed by the Property Man and the Prompter. At the same moment, the Manager comes out of his office, accompanied by the Father and the Stepdaughter.*)

THE MANAGER: Come on, come on, ladies and gentlemen! Heh! you there, machinist!

MACHINIST: Yes sir?

THE MANAGER: Fix up the parlor with the floral decorations. Two wings and a drop with a door will do. Hurry up!

(*The Machinist runs off at once to prepare the scene and arranges it while the Manager talks with the Stage Manager, the Property Man, and the Prompter on matters of detail.*)

THE MANAGER (*to Property Man*): Just have a look, and see if there isn't a sofa or a divan in the wardrobe . . .

PROPERTY MAN: There's the green one.

THE STEPDAUGHTER: No no! Green won't do. It was yellow, ornamented with flowers — very large! and most comfortable!

PROPERTY MAN: There isn't one like that.

THE MANAGER: It doesn't matter. Use the one we've got.

THE STEPDAUGHTER: Doesn't matter? It's most important!

THE MANAGER: We're only trying it now. Please don't interfere. (*To Property Man.*) See if we've got a shop window — long and narrowish.

THE STEPDAUGHTER: And the little table! The little mahogany table for the pale blue envelope!

PROPERTY MAN (*to Manager*): There's that little gilt one.

THE MANAGER: That'll do fine.

THE FATHER: A mirror.

THE STEPDAUGHTER: And the screen! We must have a screen. Otherwise how can I manage?

PROPERTY MAN: That's all right, Miss. We've got any amount of them.

THE MANAGER (*to the Stepdaughter*): We want some clothes pegs too, don't we?

THE STEPDAUGHTER: Yes, several, several!

THE MANAGER: See how many we've got and bring them all.

PROPERTY MAN: All right!

(*The Property Man hurries off to obey his orders. While he is putting the things in their places, the Manager talks to the Prompter and then with the Characters and the Actors.*)

THE MANAGER (*to Prompter*): Take your seat. Look here: this is the outline of the scenes, act by act. (*Hands him some sheets of paper.*) And now I'm going to ask you to do something out of the ordinary.

PROMPTER: Take it down in shorthand?

THE MANAGER (*pleasantly surprised*): Exactly! Can you do shorthand?

PROMPTER: Yes, a little.

THE MANAGER: Good! (*Turning to a Stage Hand.*) Go and get some paper from my office, plenty, as much as you can find.

(*The Stage Hand goes off and soon returns with a handful of paper which he gives to the Prompter.*)

THE MANAGER (*to Prompter*): You follow the scenes as we play them, and try and get the points down, at any rate the most important ones. (*Then addressing the Actors.*) Clear the stage, ladies and gentlemen! Come over here (*pointing to the left*) and listen attentively.

LEADING LADY: But, excuse me, we . . .

THE MANAGER (*guessing her thought*): Don't worry! You won't have to improvise.

LEADING MAN: What have we to do then?

THE MANAGER: Nothing. For the moment you just watch and listen. Everybody will get his part written out afterwards. At present we're going to try the thing as best we can. They're going to act now.

THE FATHER (*as if fallen from the clouds into the confusion of the stage*): We? What do you mean, if you please, by a rehearsal?

THE MANAGER: A rehearsal for them. (*Points to the Actors.*)

THE FATHER: But since we are the characters . . .

THE MANAGER: All right: "characters" then, if you insist on calling yourselves such. But here, my dear sir, the characters don't act. Here the actors do the acting. The characters are there, in the "book" (*pointing toward Prompter's box*) — when there is a "book"!

THE FATHER: I won't contradict you; but excuse me, the actors aren't the characters. They want to be, they pretend to be, don't they? Now if these gentlemen here are fortunate enough to have us alive before them . . .

THE MANAGER: Oh, this is grand! You want to come before the public yourselves then?

THE FATHER: As we are. . . .

THE MANAGER: I can assure you it would be a magnificent spectacle!

LEADING MAN: What's the use of us here anyway then?

THE MANAGER: You're not going to pretend that you can act? It makes me laugh! (*The Actors laugh.*) There, you see, they are laughing at the notion. But, by the way, I must cast the parts. That won't be difficult. They cast themselves. (*To the Second Lady Lead.*) You play the Mother. (*To the Father.*) We must find her a name.

THE FATHER: Amalia, sir.

THE MANAGER: But that is the real name of your wife. We don't want to call her by her real name.

THE FATHER: Why ever not, if it is her name? . . . Still, perhaps, if that lady must . . . (*Makes a slight motion of the hand to indicate the Second Lady Lead.*) I see this woman here (*means the Mother*) as Amalia. But do as you like. (*Gets more and more confused.*) I don't know what to say to you. Already, I begin to hear my own words ring false, as if they had another sound . . .

THE MANAGER: Don't you worry about it. It'll be our job to find the right tones. And as for her name, if you want her Amalia, Amalia it shall be; and if you don't like it, we'll find another! For the moment though, we'll call the characters in this way: (*To Juvenile Lead.*) You are the Son. (*To the Leading Lady.*) You naturally are the Stepdaughter. . . .

THE STEPDAUGHTER (*excitedly*): What? what? I, that woman there? (*Bursts out laughing.*)

THE MANAGER (*angry*): What is there to laugh at?

LEADING LADY (*indignant*): Nobody has ever dared to laugh at me. I insist on being treated with respect; otherwise I go away.

THE STEPDAUGHTER: No, no, excuse me . . . I am not laughing at you. . . .

THE MANAGER (*to Stepdaughter*): You ought to feel honored to be played by . . .

LEADING LADY (*at once, contemptuously*): "That woman there" . . .

THE STEPDAUGHTER: But I wasn't speaking of you, you know. I was speaking of myself — whom I can't see at all in you! That is all. I don't know . . . but . . . you . . . aren't in the least like me. . . .

THE FATHER: True, Here's the point. Look here, sir, our temperaments, our souls. . . .

THE MANAGER: Temperament, soul, be hanged! Do you suppose the spirit of the piece is in you? Nothing of the kind!

THE FATHER: What, haven't we our own temperaments, our own souls?

THE MANAGER: Not at all. Your soul or whatever you like to call it takes shape here. The actors give body and form to it, voice and gesture. And my actors — I may tell you — have given expression to much more lofty material than this little drama of yours, which may or may not hold up on the stage. But if it does, the merit of it, believe me, will be due to my actors.

THE FATHER: I don't dare contradict you, sir; but, believe me, it is a terrible suffering for us who are as we are, with these bodies of ours, these features to see. . . .

THE MANAGER (*cutting him short and out of patience*): Good heavens! The make-up will remedy all that, man, the make-up. . . .

THE FATHER: Maybe. But the voice, the gestures . . .

THE MANAGER: Now, look here! On the stage, you as yourself, cannot exist. The actor here acts you, and that's an end to it!

THE FATHER: I understand. And now I think I see why our author who conceived us as we are, all alive, didn't want to put us on the stage after all. I haven't the least desire to offend your actors. Far from it! But when I think that I am to be acted by . . . I don't know by whom. . . .

LEADING MAN (*on his dignity*): By me, if you've no objection!

THE FATHER (*humbly, mellifluously*): Honored, I assure you, sir. (*Bows.*) Still, I must say that try as this gentleman may, with all his good will and wonderful art, to absorb me into himself. . . .

LEADING MAN: Oh chuck it! "Wonderful art!" Withdraw that, please!

THE FATHER: The performance he will give, even doing his best with make-up to look like me. . . .

LEADING MAN: It will certainly be a bit difficult! (*The Actors laugh.*)

THE FATHER: Exactly! It will be difficult to act me as I really am. The effect will be rather — apart from the make-up — according as to how he supposes I am, as he senses me — if he does sense me — and not as I inside of myself feel myself to be. It seems to me then that account should be taken of this by everyone whose duty it may become to criticize us. . . .

THE MANAGER: Heavens! The man's starting to think about the critics now! Let them say what they like. It's up to us to put on the play if we can. (*Looking around.*) Come on! come on! Is the stage set? (*To the Actors and Characters.*) Stand back — stand back! Let me see, and don't let's lose any more time! (*To the Stepdaughter.*) Is it all right as it is now?

THE STEPDAUGHTER: Well, to tell the truth, I don't recognize the scene.

THE MANAGER: My dear lady, you can't possibly suppose that we can construct that shop of Madame Pace piece by piece here? (*To the Father.*) You said a white room with flowered wallpaper, didn't you?

THE FATHER: Yes.

THE MANAGER: Well then. We've got the furniture right more or less. Bring that little table a bit further forward. (*The Stage Hands obey the order. To Property Man.*) You go and find an envelope, if possible, a pale blue one; and give it to that gentleman. (*Indicates Father.*)

PROPERTY MAN: An ordinary envelope?

MANAGER AND FATHER: Yes, yes, an ordinary envelope.

PROPERTY MAN: At once, sir. (*Exit.*)

THE MANAGER: Ready, everyone! First scene — the Young Lady. (*The Leading Lady comes forward.*) No, no, you must wait. I meant her. (*Indicating the Stepdaughter.*) You just watch —

THE STEPDAUGHTER (*adding at once*): How I shall play it, how I shall live it! . . .

LEADING LADY (*offended*): I shall live it also, you may be sure, as soon as I begin!

THE MANAGER (*with his hands to his head*): Ladies and gentlemen, if you please! No more useless discussions! Scene I: the Young Lady with Madame Pace: Oh! (*Looks around as if lost.*) And this Madame Pace, where is she?

THE FATHER: She isn't with us, sir.

THE MANAGER: Then what the devil's to be done?

THE FATHER: But she is alive too.

THE MANAGER: Yes, but where is she?

THE FATHER: One minute. Let me speak! (*Turning to the Actresses.*) If these ladies would be so good as to give me their hats for a moment. . . .

THE ACTRESSES (*half surprised, half laughing, in chorus*): What? Why? Our hats? What does he say?

THE MANAGER: What are you going to do with the ladies' hats? (*The Actors laugh.*)

THE FATHER: Oh nothing. I just want to put them on these pegs for a moment. And one of the ladies will be so kind as to take off her mantle. . . .

THE ACTORS: Oh, what d'you think of that? Only the mantle? He must be mad.

SOME ACTRESSES: But why? Mantles as well?

THE FATHER: To hang them up here for a moment. Please be so kind, will you?

THE ACTRESSES (*taking off their hats, one or two also their cloaks, and going to hang them on the racks*): After all, why not? There you are! This is really funny. We've got to put them on show.

THE FATHER: Exactly; just like that, on show.

THE MANAGER: May we know why?

THE FATHER: I'll tell you. Who knows if, by arranging the stage for her, she does not come here herself, attracted by the very articles of her trade? (*Inviting the Actors to look toward the exit at back of stage.*) Look! Look!

(*The door at the back of stage opens and Madame Pace enters and takes a few steps forward. She is a fat, oldish woman with puffy oxygenated hair. She is rouged and powdered, dressed with a comical elegance in black silk. Round her waist is a long silver chain from which hangs a pair of scissors. The Stepdaughter runs over to her at once amid the stupor of the Actors.*)

THE STEPDAUGHTER (*turning toward her*): There she is! There she is!

THE FATHER (*radiant*): It's she! I said so, didn't I! There she is!

THE MANAGER (*conquering his surprise, and then becoming indignant*): What sort of a trick is this?

LEADING MAN (*almost at the same time*): What's going to happen next?

JUVENILE LEAD: Where does *she* come from?

L'INGÉNUE: They've been holding her in reserve, I guess.

LEADING LADY: A vulgar trick!

THE FATHER (*dominating the protests*): Excuse me, all of you! Why are you so anxious to destroy in the name of a vulgar, commonplace sense of truth, this reality which comes to birth attracted and formed by the magic of the stage itself, which has indeed more right to live here than you, since it is much truer than you — if you don't mind my saying so? Which is the actress among you who is to play Madame Pace? Well, here is Madame Pace herself. And you will allow, I fancy, that the actress who acts her will be less true than this woman here, who is herself in person. You see my daughter recognized her and went over to her at once. Now you're going to witness the scene!

(*But the scene between the Stepdaughter and Madame Pace has already begun despite the protest of the Actors and the reply of the Father. It has begun quietly, naturally, in a manner impossible for the stage. So when the Actors, called to attention by the Father, turn round and see Madame Pace, who has placed one hand under the Stepdaughter's chin to raise her head, they observe her at first with great attention, but hearing her speak in an unintelligible manner their interest begins to wane.*)

THE MANAGER: Well? well?

LEADING MAN: What does she say?

LEADING LADY: One can't hear a word.

JUVENILE LEAD: Louder! Louder please!

THE STEPDAUGHTER (*leaving Madame Pace, who smiles a Sphinx-like smile, and advancing toward the Actors*): Louder? Louder? What are you talking about? These aren't matters which can be shouted at the top of one's voice. If I have spoken them out loud, it was to shame him and have my revenge. (*Indicates Father.*) But for Madame it's quite a different matter.

THE MANAGER: Indeed? indeed? But here, you know, people have got to make themselves heard, my dear. Even we who are on the stage can't hear you. What will it be when the public's in the theater? And anyway, you can very well speak up now among yourselves, since we shan't be present to listen to you as we are now. You've got to pretend to be alone in a room at the back of a shop where no one can hear you.

(*The Stepdaughter coquettishly and with a touch of malice makes a sign of disagreement two or three times with her finger.*)

THE MANAGER: What do you mean by no?

THE STEPDAUGHTER (*sotto voce,° mysteriously*): There's someone who will hear us if she (*indicating Madame Pace*) speaks out loud.

THE MANAGER (*in consternation*): What? Have you got someone else to spring on us now? (*The Actors burst out laughing.*)

THE FATHER: No, no sir. She is alluding to me. I've got to be here — there behind that door, in waiting; and Madame Pace knows it. In fact, if you will allow me, I'll go there at once, so I can be quite ready. (*Moves away.*)

THE MANAGER (*stopping him*): No! wait! wait! We must observe the conventions of the theater. Before you are ready ...

THE STEPDAUGHTER (*interrupting him*): No, get on with it at once! I'm just dying, I tell you, to act this scene. If he's ready, I'm more than ready.

THE MANAGER (*shouting*): But, my dear young lady, first of all, we must have the scene between you and this lady. ... (*Indicates Madame Pace.*) Do you understand?

THE STEPDAUGHTER: Good Heavens! She's been telling me what you know already: that mama's work is badly done again, that the material's ruined; and that if I want her to continue to help us in our misery I must be patient. ...

MADAME PACE (*coming forward with an air of great importance*): Yes indeed, sir, I no wanta take advantage of her, I no wanta be hard. ...

(*Note: Madame Pace is supposed to talk in a jargon half Italian, half English.*)

THE MANAGER (*alarmed*): What? What? She talks like that? (*The Actors burst out laughing again.*)

THE STEPDAUGHTER (*also laughing*): Yes yes, that's the way she talks, half English, half Italian! Most comical it is!

MADAME PACE: Itta seem not verra polite gentlemen laugha atta me eeff I trya best speaka English.

THE MANAGER: *Diamine!°* Of course! Of course! Let her talk like that! Just what we want. Talk just like that, Madame, if you please! The effect will be certain. Exactly what was wanted to put a little comic relief into the crudity of the situation. Of course she talks like that! Magnificent!

THE STEPDAUGHTER: Magnificent? Certainly! When certain suggestions are made to one in language of that kind, the effect is certain, since it seems almost a joke. One feels inclined to laugh when one hears her talk about an "old signore" "who wanta talka nicely with you." Nice old signore, eh, Madame?

MADAME PACE: Not so old my dear, not so old! And even if you no lika him, he won't make any scandal!

THE MOTHER (*jumping up amid the amazement and consternation of the Actors, who had not been noticing her. They move to restrain her*): You old devil! You murderess!

THE STEPDAUGHTER (*running over to calm her Mother*): Calm yourself, Mother, calm yourself! Please don't. ...

THE FATHER (*going to her also at the same time*): Calm yourself! Don't get excited! Sit down now!

THE MOTHER: Well then, take that woman away out of my sight!

THE STEPDAUGHTER (*to Manager*): It is impossible for my mother to remain here.

THE FATHER (*to Manager*): They can't be here together. And for this reason, you see: that woman there was not with us when we came. ... If they are on

---

sotto voce: In a soft voice or stage whisper.   *Diamine!:* Italian for "Well, I'll be damned!"

together, the whole thing is given away inevitably, as you see.

THE MANAGER: It doesn't matter. This is only a first rough sketch — just to get an idea of the various points of the scene, even confusedly. . . . (*Turning to the Mother and leading her to her chair.*) Come along, my dear lady, sit down now, and let's get on with the scene. . . .

(*Meanwhile, the Stepdaughter, coming forward again, turns to Madame Pace.*)

THE STEPDAUGHTER: Come on, Madame, come on!

MADAME PACE (*offended*): No, no, *grazie*. I do not do anything witha your mother present.

THE STEPDAUGHTER: Nonsense! Introduce this "old signore" who wants to talk nicely to me. (*Addressing the Company imperiously.*) We've got to do this scene one way or another, haven't we? Come on! (*To Madame Pace.*) You can go!

MADAME PACE: Ah yes! I go'way! I go'way! Certainly! (*Exits furious.*)

THE STEPDAUGHTER (*to the Father*): Now you make your entry. No, you needn't go over there. Come here. Let's suppose you've already come in. Like that, yes! I'm here with bowed head, modest like. Come on! Out with your voice! Say "Good morning, Miss" in that peculiar tone, that special tone. . . .

THE MANAGER: Excuse me, but are you the Manager, or am I? (*To the Father, who looks undecided and perplexed.*) Get on with it, man! Go down there to the back of the stage. You needn't go off. Then come right forward here.

(*The Father does as he is told, looking troubled and perplexed at first. But as soon as he begins to move, the reality of the action affects him, and he begins to smile and to be more natural. The Actors watch intently.*)

THE MANAGER (*sotto voce, quickly to the Prompter in his box*): Ready! ready! Get ready to write now.

THE FATHER (*coming forward and speaking in a different tone*): Good afternoon, Miss!

THE STEPDAUGHTER (*head bowed down slightly, with restrained disgust*): Good afternoon!

THE FATHER (*looks under her hat which partly covers her face. Perceiving she is very young, he makes an exclamation, partly of surprise, partly of fear lest he compromise himself in a risky adventure*): Ah . . . but . . . ah . . . I say . . . this is not the first time that you have come here, is it?

THE STEPDAUGHTER (*modestly*): No sir.

THE FATHER: You've been here before, eh? (*Then seeing her nod agreement.*) More than once? (*Waits for her to answer, looks under her hat, smiles, and then says:*) Well then, there's no need to be so shy, is there? May I take off your hat?

THE STEPDAUGHTER (*anticipating him and with veiled disgust*): No sir . . . I'll do it myself. (*Takes it off quickly.*)

(*The Mother, who watches the progress of the scene with the Son and the other two children who cling to her, is on thorns; and follows with varying expressions of sorrow, indignation, anxiety, and horror the words and actions of the other two. From time to time she hides her face in her hands and sobs.*)

THE MOTHER: Oh, my God, my God!

THE FATHER (*playing his part with a touch of gallantry*): Give it to me! I'll put it down. (*Takes hat from her hands.*) But a dear little head like yours ought to have a smarter hat. Come and help me choose one from the stock, won't you?

L'INGÉNUE (*interrupting*): I say . . . those are our hats you know.

THE MANAGER (*furious*): Silence! silence! Don't try and be funny, if you please. . . . We're playing the scene now, I'd have you notice. (*To the Stepdaughter.*) Begin again, please!

THE STEPDAUGHTER (*continuing*): No thank you, sir.

THE FATHER: Oh, come now. Don't talk like that. You must take it. I shall be upset if you don't. There are some lovely little hats here; and then — Madame will be pleased. She expects it, anyway, you know.

THE STEPDAUGHTER: No, no! I couldn't wear it!

THE FATHER: Oh, you're thinking about what they'd say at home if they saw you come in with a new hat? My dear girl, there's always a way round these little matters, you know.

THE STEPDAUGHTER (*all keyed up*): No, it's not that. I couldn't wear it because I am . . . as you see . . . you might have noticed . . .

(*Showing her black dress.*)

THE FATHER: . . . in mourning! Of course: I beg your pardon: I'm frightfully sorry. . . .

THE STEPDAUGHTER (*forcing herself to conquer her indignation and nausea*): Stop! Stop! It's I who must thank you. There's no need for you to feel mortified or specially sorry. Don't think any more of what I've said. (*Tries to smile.*) I must forget that I am dressed so. . . .

THE MANAGER (*interrupting and turning to the Prompter*): Stop a minute! Stop! Don't write that down. Cut out that last bit. (*Then to the Father and Stepdaughter.*) Fine! it's going fine! (*To the Father only.*) And now you can go on as we arranged. (*To the Actors.*) Pretty good that scene, where he offers her the hat, eh?

THE STEPDAUGHTER: The best's coming now. Why can't we go on?

THE MANAGER: Have a little patience! (*To the Actors.*) Of course, it must be treated rather lightly.

LEADING MAN: Still, with a bit of go in it!

LEADING LADY: Of course! It's easy enough! (*To Leading Man.*) Shall you and I try it now?

LEADING MAN: Why, yes! I'll prepare my entrance. (*Exit in order to make his entrance.*)

THE MANAGER (*to Leading Lady*): See here! The scene between you and Madame Pace is finished. I'll have it written out properly after. You remain here . . . oh, where are you going?

LEADING LADY: One minute. I want to put my hat on again. (*Goes over to hatrack and puts her hat on her head.*)

THE MANAGER: Good! You stay here with your head bowed down a bit.

THE STEPDAUGHTER: But she isn't dressed in black.

LEADING LADY: But I shall be, and much more effectively than you.

THE MANAGER (*to Stepdaughter*): Be quiet please, and watch! You'll be able to learn something. (*Clapping his hands.*) Come on! come on! Entrance, please!

(*The door at rear of stage opens, and the Leading Man enters with the lively manner of an old gallant. The rendering of the scene by the Actors from the very first words is seen to be quite a different thing, though it has not in any way the air of a parody. Naturally, the Stepdaughter and the Father, not being able to recognize themselves in the Leading Lady and the Leading Man, who deliver their words in different tones and with a different psychology, express, sometimes with smiles, sometimes with gestures, the impression they receive.*)

LEADING MAN: Good afternoon, Miss . . .

THE FATHER (*at once unable to contain himself*): No! no!

(*The Stepdaughter, noticing the way the Leading Man enters, bursts out laughing.*)

THE MANAGER (*furious*): Silence! And you, please, just stop that laughing. If we go on like this, we shall never finish.

THE STEPDAUGHTER: Forgive me, sir, but it's natural enough. This lady (*indicating Leading Lady*) stands there still; but if she is supposed to be me, I can assure you that if I heard anyone say "Good afternoon" in that manner and in that tone, I should burst out laughing as I did.

THE FATHER: Yes, yes, the manner, the tone . . .

THE MANAGER: Nonsense! Rubbish! Stand aside and let me see the action.

LEADING MAN: If I've got to represent an old fellow who's coming into a house of an equivocal character . . .

THE MANAGER: Don't listen to them, for Heaven's sake! Do it again! It goes fine. (*Waiting for the Actors to begin again.*) Well?

LEADING MAN: Good afternoon, Miss.

LEADING LADY: Good afternoon.

LEADING MAN (*imitating the gesture of the Father when he looked under the hat, and then expressing quite clearly first satisfaction and then fear*): Ah, but . . . I say . . . this is not the first time that you have come here, is it?

THE MANAGER: Good, but not quite so heavily. Like this. (*Acts himself.*) "This isn't the first time that you have come here" . . . (*To Leading Lady.*) And you say: "No, sir."

LEADING LADY: No, sir.

LEADING MAN: You've been here before, more than once.

THE MANAGER: No, no, stop! Let her nod "yes" first. "You've been here before, eh?" (*The Leading Lady lifts up her head slightly and closes her eyes as though in disgust. Then she inclines her head twice.*)

THE STEPDAUGHTER (*unable to contain herself*): Oh my God! (*Puts a hand to her mouth to prevent herself from laughing.*)

THE MANAGER (*turning round*): What's the matter?

THE STEPDAUGHTER: Nothing, nothing!

THE MANAGER (*to Leading Man*): Go on!

LEADING MAN: You've been here before, eh? Well then, there's no need to be so shy, is there? May I take off your hat?

(*The Leading Man says this last speech in such a tone and with such gestures that the Stepdaughter, though she has her hand to her mouth, cannot keep from laughing.*)

LEADING LADY (*indignant*): I'm not going to stop here to be made a fool of by that woman there.

LEADING MAN: Neither am I! I'm through with it!

THE MANAGER (*shouting to Stepdaughter*): Silence! for once and all, I tell you!

THE STEPDAUGHTER: Forgive me! forgive me!

THE MANAGER: You haven't any manners: that's what it is! You go too far.

THE FATHER (*endeavoring to intervene*): Yes, it's true, but excuse her . . .

THE MANAGER: Excuse what? It's absolutely disgusting.

THE FATHER: Yes, sir, but believe me, it has such a strange effect when . . .

THE MANAGER: Strange? Why strange? Where is it strange?

THE FATHER: No, sir; I admire your actors — this gentleman here, this lady; but they are certainly not us!

THE MANAGER: I should hope not. Evidently they cannot be you, if they are actors.

THE FATHER: Just so: actors! Both of them act our parts exceedingly well. But, believe me, it produces quite a different effect on us. They want to be us, but they aren't, all the same.

THE MANAGER: What is it then anyway?

THE FATHER: Something that is . . . that is theirs — and no longer ours . . .

THE MANAGER: But naturally, inevitably, I've told you so already.

THE FATHER: Yes, I understand . . . I understand . . .

THE MANAGER: Well then, let's have no more of it! (*Turning to the Actors.*) We'll have the rehearsals by ourselves, afterwards, in the ordinary way. I never could stand rehearsing with the author present. He's never satisfied! (*Turning to Father and Stepdaughter.*) Come on! Let's get on with it again; and try and see if you can't keep from laughing.

THE STEPDAUGHTER: Oh, I shan't laugh any more. There's a nice little bit coming from me now: you'll see.

THE MANAGER: Well then: when she says "Don't think any more of what I've said, I must forget, etc.," you (*addressing the Father*) come in sharp with "I understand"; and then you ask her . . .

THE STEPDAUGHTER (*interrupting*): What?

THE MANAGER: Why she is in mourning.

THE STEPDAUGHTER: Not at all! See here: when I told him that it was useless for me to be thinking about my wearing mourning, do you know how he answered me? "Ah well," he said, "then let's take off this little frock."

THE MANAGER: Great! Just what we want, to make a riot in the theater!

THE STEPDAUGHTER: But it's the truth!

THE MANAGER: What does that matter? Acting is our business here. Truth up to a certain point, but no further.

THE STEPDAUGHTER: What do you want to do then?

THE MANAGER: You'll see, you'll see! Leave it to me.

THE STEPDAUGHTER: No sir! What you want to do is to piece together a little romantic sentimental scene out of my disgust, out of all the reasons, each more cruel and viler than the other, why I am what I am. He is to ask me why I'm in mourning; and I'm to answer with tears in my eyes, that it is just two months since papa died. No sir, no! He's got to say to me, as he did say. "Well, let's take off this little dress at once." And I, with my two months' mourning in my heart, went there behind that screen, and with these fingers tingling with shame . . .

THE MANAGER (*running his hands through his hair*): For Heaven's sake! What are you saying?

THE STEPDAUGHTER (*crying out excitedly*): The truth! The truth!

THE MANAGER: It may be. I don't deny it, and I can understand all your horror; but you must surely see that you can't have this kind of thing on the stage. It won't go.

THE STEPDAUGHTER: Not possible, eh? Very well! I'm much obliged to you — but I'm off.

THE MANAGER: Now be reasonable! Don't lose your temper!

THE STEPDAUGHTER: I won't stop here! I won't! I can see you fixed it all up with him in your office. All this talk about what is possible for the stage . . . I understand! He wants to get at his complicated "cerebral drama," to have his famous remorses and torments acted; but I want to act my part, *my part!*

THE MANAGER (*annoyed, shaking his shoulders*): Ah! Just *your* part! But, if you will pardon me, there are other parts than yours: His (*indicating the Father*) and hers (*indicating the Mother*)! On the stage you can't have a character becoming too prominent and overshadowing all the others. The thing is to pack them all into a neat little framework and then act what is actable. I am aware of the fact that everyone has his own interior life which he wants very much to put forward. But the difficulty lies in this fact: to set out just so much as is necessary for the stage, taking the other characters into consideration, and at the same time hint at the unrevealed interior life of each. I am willing to admit, my dear young lady, that from your point of view it would be a fine idea if each character could tell the public all his troubles in a nice monologue or a regular one hour lecture. (*Good humoredly.*) You must restrain yourself, my dear, and in your own interest, too; because this fury of yours, this exaggerated disgust you show, may make a bad impression, you know. After you have confessed to me that there were others before him at Madame Pace's and more than once . . .

THE STEPDAUGHTER (*bowing her head, impressed*): It's true. But remember those others mean him for me all the same.

THE MANAGER (*not understanding*): What? The others? What do you mean?

THE STEPDAUGHTER: For one who has gone wrong, sir, he who was responsible for the first fault is responsible for all that follow. He is responsible for my faults, was, even before I was born. Look at him, and see if it isn't true!

THE MANAGER: Well, well! And does the weight of so much responsibility seem nothing to you? Give him a chance to act it, to get it over!

THE STEPDAUGHTER: How? How can he act all his "noble remorses," all his "moral torments," if you want to spare him the horror of being discovered one day — after he had asked her what he did ask her — in the arms of her, that already fallen woman, that child, sir, that child he used to watch come out of school? (*She is moved.*)

(*The Mother at this point is overcome with emotion and breaks out into a fit of crying. All are touched. A long pause.*)

THE STEPDAUGHTER (*as soon as the Mother becomes a little quieter, adds resolutely and gravely*): At present, we are unknown to the public. Tomorrow, you will act us as you wish, treating us in your own manner. But do you really want to see drama, do you want to see it flash out as it really did?

THE MANAGER: Of course! That's just what I do want, so I can use as much of it as is possible.

THE STEPDAUGHTER: Well then, ask that Mother there to leave us.

THE MOTHER (*changing her low plaint into a sharp cry*): No! No! Don't permit, it, sir, don't permit it!

THE MANAGER: But it's only to try it.

THE MOTHER: I can't bear it. I can't.

THE MANAGER: But since it has happened already . . . I don't understand!

THE MOTHER: It's taking place now. It happens all the time. My torment isn't a pretended one. I live and feel every minute of my torture. Those two children there — have you heard them speak? They can't speak anymore. They cling to me to keep my torment actual and vivid for me. But for themselves, they do not exist, they aren't anymore. And she (*indicating the Stepdaughter*) has run away, she has left me, and is lost. If I now see her here before me, it is only to renew for me the tortures I have suffered for her too.

THE FATHER: The eternal moment! She (*indicating the Stepdaughter*) is here to catch me, fix me, and hold me eternally in the stocks for that one fleeting and shameful moment of my life. She can't give it up! And you, sir, cannot either fairly spare me it.

THE MANAGER: I never said I didn't want to act it. It will form, as a matter of fact, the nucleus of the whole first act right up to her surprise. (*Indicates the Mother.*)

THE FATHER: Just so! This is my punishment: the passion in all of us that must culminate in her final cry.

THE STEPDAUGHTER: I can hear it still in my ears. It's driven me mad, that cry! — You can put me on as you like; it doesn't matter. Fully dressed, if you like — provided I have at least the arm bare; because, standing like this (*she goes close to the Father and leans her head on his breast*) with my head so, and my arms round his neck, I saw a vein pulsing in my arm here; and then, as if that live vein had awakened disgust in me, I closed my eyes like this, and let my head sink on his breast. (*Turning to the Mother.*) Cry out, mother! Cry out! (*Buries head in Father's breast, and with her shoulders raised as if to prevent her hearing the cry, adds in tones of intense emotion.*) Cry out as you did then!

THE MOTHER (*coming forward to separate them*): No! My daughter, my daughter! (*And after having pulled her away from him.*) You brute! you brute! She is my daughter! Don't you see she's my daughter?

THE MANAGER (*walking backward toward footlights*): Fine! fine! Damned good! And then, of course — curtain!

THE FATHER (*going toward him excitedly*): Yes, of course, because that's the way it really happened.

THE MANAGER (*convinced and pleased*): Oh, yes, no doubt about it. Curtain here, curtain!

(*At the reiterated cry of the Manager, the Machinist lets the curtain down, leaving the Manager and the Father in front of it before the footlights.*)

THE MANAGER: The darned idiot! I said "curtain" to show the act should end there, and he goes and lets it down in earnest. (*To the Father, while he pulls the curtain back to go on to the stage again.*) Yes, yes, it's all right. Effect certain! That's the right ending. I'll guarantee the first act at any rate.

ACT III

(*When the curtain goes up again, it is seen that the stage hands have shifted the bit of scenery used in the last part and have rigged up instead at the back of the stage a drop, with some trees, and one or two wings. A portion of a fountain basin is visible. The Mother is sitting on the right with the two children by her side. The Son is on the same side, but away from the others. He seems bored, angry, and full of shame. The Father and the Stepdaughter are also seated toward the right front. On the other side (left) are the Actors, much in the positions they occupied before the curtain was lowered. Only the Manager is standing up in the middle of the stage, with his hand closed over his mouth, in the act of meditating.*)

THE MANAGER (*shaking his shoulders after a brief pause*): Ah yes: the second act! Leave it to me, leave it all to me as we arranged, and you'll see! It'll go fine!

THE STEPDAUGHTER: Our entry into his house (*indicates Father*) in spite of him . . . (*Indicates the Son.*)

THE MANAGER (*out of patience*): Leave it to me, I tell you!

THE STEPDAUGHTER: Do let it be clear, at any rate, that it is in spite of my wishes.

THE MOTHER (*from her corner, shaking her head*): For all the good that's come of it . . .

THE STEPDAUGHTER (*turning toward her quickly*): It

doesn't matter. The more harm done us, the more remorse for him.

THE MANAGER (*impatiently*): I understand! Good Heavens! I understand! I'm taking it into account.

THE MOTHER (*supplicatingly*): I beg you, sir, to let it appear quite plain that for conscience' sake I did try in every way . . .

THE STEPDAUGHTER (*interrupting indignantly and continuing for the Mother*): . . . to pacify me, to dissuade me from spiting him. (*To Manager*.) Do as she wants: satisfy her, because it is true! I enjoy it immensely. Anyhow, as you can see, the meeker she is, the more she tries to get at his heart, the more distant and aloof does he become.

THE MANAGER: Are we going to begin this second act or not?

THE STEPDAUGHTER: I'm not going to talk any more now. But I must tell you this: you can't have the whole action take place in the garden, as you suggest. It isn't possible!

THE MANAGER: Why not?

THE STEPDAUGHTER: Because he (*indicates the Son again*) is always shut up alone in his room. And then there's all the part of that poor dazed-looking boy there which takes place indoors.

THE MANAGER: Maybe! On the other hand, you will understand — we can't change scenes three or four times in one act.

LEADING MAN: They used to once.

THE MANAGER: Yes, when the public was up to the level of that child there.

LEADING LADY: It makes the illusion easier.

THE FATHER (*irritated*): The illusion! For Heaven's sake, don't say illusion. Please don't use that word, which is particularly painful for us.

THE MANAGER (*astounded*): And why, if you please?

THE FATHER: It's painful, cruel, really cruel; and you ought to understand that.

THE MANAGER: But why? What ought we to say then? The illusion, I tell you, sir, which we've got to create for the audience. . . .

THE LEADING MAN: With our acting.

THE MANAGER: The illusion of a reality.

THE FATHER: I understand; but you, perhaps, do not understand us. Forgive me! You see . . . here for you and your actors, the thing is only — and rightly so . . . a kind of game.

THE LEADING LADY (*interrupting indignantly*): A game! We're not children here, if you please! We are serious actors.

THE FATHER: I don't deny it. What I mean is the game, or play, of your art, which has to give, as the gentleman says, a perfect illusion of reality.

THE MANAGER: Precisely —!

THE FATHER: Now, if you consider the fact that we (*indicates himself and the other five Characters*),

as we are, have no other reality outside of this illusion. . . .

THE MANAGER (*astonished, looking at his Actors, who are also amazed*): And what does that mean?

THE FATHER (*after watching them for a moment with a wan smile*): As I say, sir, that which is a game of art for you is our sole reality. (*Brief pause. He goes a step or two nearer the Manager and adds.*) But not only for us, you know, by the way. Just you think it over well. (*Looks him in the eyes.*) Can you tell me who you are?

THE MANAGER (*perplexed, half smiling*): What? Who am I? I am myself.

THE FATHER: And if I were to tell you that that isn't true, because you and I . . . ?

THE MANAGER: I should say you were mad —! (*The Actors laugh.*)

THE FATHER: You're quite right to laugh: because we are all making believe here. (*To Manager.*) And you can therefore object that it's only for a joke that that gentleman there (*indicates the Leading Man*), who naturally is himself, has to be me, who am on the contrary myself — this thing you see here. You see I've caught you in a trap! (*The Actors laugh.*)

THE MANAGER (*annoyed*): But we've had all this over once before. Do you want to begin again?

THE FATHER: No, no! That wasn't my meaning! In fact, I should like to request you to abandon this game of art (*looking at the Leading Lady as if anticipating her*) which you are accustomed to play here with your actors, and to ask you seriously once again: who are you?

THE MANAGER (*astonished and irritated, turning to his Actors*): If this fellow here hasn't got a nerve! A man who calls himself a character comes and asks me who I am!

THE FATHER (*with dignity, but not offended*): A character, sir, may always ask a man who he is. Because a character has really a life of his own, marked with his especial characteristics; for which reason he is always "somebody." But a man — I'm not speaking of you now — may very well be "nobody."

THE MANAGER: Yes, but you are asking these questions of me, the boss, the manager! Do you understand?

THE FATHER: But only in order to know if you, as you really are now, see yourself as you once were with all the illusions that were yours then, with all the things both inside and outside of you as they seemed to you — as they were then indeed for you. Well, sir, if you think of all those illusions that mean nothing to you now, of all those things which don't even *seem* to you to exist anymore, while once they *were* for you, don't you feel that — I won't say these boards — but the very earth under your feet is sinking away from you when you reflect that in the same way this *you* as you feel it today — all this present reality of yours — is fated to seem a mere illusion to you tomorrow?

THE MANAGER (*without having understood much, but astonished by the specious argument*): Well, well! And where does all this take us anyway?

THE FATHER: Oh, nowhere! It's only to show you that if we (*indicating the Characters*) have no other reality beyond the illusion, you too must not count overmuch on your reality as you feel it today, since, like that of yesterday, it may prove an illusion for you tomorrow.

THE MANAGER (*determining to make fun of him*): Ah, excellent! Then you'll be saying next that you, with this comedy of yours that you brought here to act, are truer and more real than I am.

THE FATHER (*with the greatest seriousness*): But of course; without doubt!

THE MANAGER: Ah, really?

THE FATHER: Why, I thought you'd understand that from the beginning.

THE MANAGER: More real than I?

THE FATHER: If your reality can change from one day to another. . . .

THE MANAGER: But everyone knows it can change. It is always changing, the same as anyone else's.

THE FATHER (*with a cry*): No, sir, not ours! Look here! That is the very difference! Our reality doesn't change: it can't change! It can't be other than what it is, because it is already fixed for ever. It's terrible. Ours is an immutable reality which should make you shudder when you approach us if you are really conscious of the fact that your reality is a mere transitory and fleeting illusion, taking this form today and that tomorrow, according to the conditions, according to your will, your sentiments, which in turn are controlled by an intellect that shows them to you today in one manner and tomorrow . . . who knows how? . . . Illusions of reality represented in this fatuous comedy of life that never ends, nor can ever end! Because if tomorrow it were to end . . . then why, all would be finished.

THE MANAGER: Oh for God's sake, will you *at least* finish with this philosophizing and let us try and shape this comedy which you yourself have brought me here? You argue and philosophize a bit too much, my dear sir. You know you seem to me almost, almost . . . (*Stops and looks him over from head to foot.*) Ah, by the way, I think you introduced yourself to me as a — what shall . . . we say — a "character," created by an author who did not afterward care to make a drama of his own creations.

THE FATHER: It is the simple truth, sir.

THE MANAGER: Nonsense! Cut that out, please! None of us believes it, because it isn't a thing, as you must recognize yourself, which one can believe seriously. If you want to know, it seems to me you are trying to imitate the manner of a certain author whom I heartily detest — I warn you — although I have unfortunately bound myself to put on one of his works. As a matter of fact, I was just starting to rehearse it, when you arrived. (*Turning to the Actors.*) And this is what we've gained — out of the frying-pan into the fire!

THE FATHER: I don't know to what author you may be alluding, but believe me I feel what I think; and I seem to be philosophizing only for those who do not think what they feel, because they blind themselves with their own sentiment. I know that for many people this self-blinding seems much more "human"; but the contrary is really true. For man never reasons so much and becomes so introspective as when he suffers; since he is anxious to get at the cause of his sufferings, to learn who has produced them, and whether it is just or unjust that he should have to bear them. On the other hand, when he is happy, he takes his happiness as it comes and doesn't analyze it, just as if happiness were his right. The animals suffer without reasoning about their sufferings. But take the case of a man who suffers and begins to reason about it. Oh no! it can't be allowed! Let him suffer like an animal, and then — ah yes, he is "human"!

THE MANAGER: Look here! Look here! You're off again, philosophizing worse than ever.

THE FATHER: Because I suffer, sir! I'm not philosophizing: I'm crying aloud the reason of my sufferings.

THE MANAGER (*makes brusque movement as he is taken with a new idea*): I should like to know if anyone has ever heard of a character who gets right out of his part and perorates and speechifies as you do. Have you ever heard of a case? I haven't.

THE FATHER: You have never met such a case, sir, because authors, as a rule, hide the labor of their creations. When the characters are really alive before their author, the latter does nothing but follow them in their action, in other words, in the situations which they suggest to him; and he has to will them the way they will themselves — for there's trouble if he doesn't. When a character is born, he acquires at once such an independence, even of his own author, that he can be imagined by everybody even in many other situations where the author never dreamed of placing him; and so he acquires for himself a meaning which the author never thought of giving him.

THE MANAGER: Yes, yes, I know this.

THE FATHER: What is there then to marvel at in us? Imagine such a misfortune for characters as I have described to you: to be born of an author's fantasy, and be denied life by him; and then answer me if these characters left alive, and yet without life, weren't right in doing what they did do and are doing now, after they have attempted everything in their power to persuade him to give them their stage life. We've all tried him in turn, I, she (*indicating the Stepdaughter*) and she (*indicating the Mother*).

THE STEPDAUGHTER: It's true. I too have sought to tempt him, many, many times, when he has been sitting at his writing table, feeling a bit melancholy, at the twilight hour. He would sit in his armchair too lazy to switch on the light, and all the shadows that crept into his room were full of our presence coming to tempt him. (*As if she saw herself still there by the writing table, and was annoyed by the presence of the Actors.*) Oh, if you would only go away, go away and leave us alone — mother here with that son of hers — I with that child — that boy there always alone — and then I with him (*just hints at the Father*) — and then I alone, alone . . . in those shadows! (*Makes a sudden movement as if in the vision she has of herself illuminating those shadows she wanted to seize hold of herself.*) Ah! my life! my life! Oh, what scenes we proposed to him — and I tempted him more than any of the others!

THE FATHER: Maybe. But perhaps it was your fault that he refused to give us life: because you were too insistent, too troublesome.

THE STEPDAUGHTER: Nonsense! Didn't he make me so himself? (*Goes close to the Manager to tell him as if in confidence.*) In my opinion he abandoned us in a fit of depression, of disgust for the ordinary theater as the public knows it and likes it.

THE SON: Exactly what it was, sir; exactly that!

THE FATHER: Not at all! Don't believe it for a minute. Listen to me! You'll be doing quite right to modify, as you suggest, the excesses both of this girl here, who wants to do too much, and of this young man, who won't do anything at all.

THE SON: No, nothing!

THE MANAGER: You too get over the mark occasionally, my dear sir, if I may say so.

THE FATHER: I? When? Where?

THE MANAGER: Always! Continuously! Then there's this insistence of yours in trying to make us believe you are a character. And then too, you must really argue and philosophize less, you know, much less.

THE FATHER: Well, if you want to take away from me the possibility of representing the torment of my spirit which never gives me peace, you will be suppressing me: that's all. Every true man, sir, who is a little above the level of the beasts and plants does not live for the sake of living, without knowing how to live; but he lives so as to give a meaning and a value of his own to life. For me this is *everything*. I cannot give up this, just to represent a mere fact as she (*indicating the Stepdaughter*) wants. It's all very well for her, since her "vendetta" lies in the "fact." I'm not going to do it. It destroys my *raison d'être*.

THE MANAGER: Your *raison d'être*! Oh, we're going ahead fine! First she starts off, and then you jump in. At this rate, we'll never finish.

THE FATHER: Now, don't be offended! Have it your own way — provided, however, that within the limits of the parts you assign us each one's sacrifice isn't too great.

THE MANAGER: You've got to understand that you can't go on arguing at your own pleasure. Drama is action, sir, action and not confounded philosophy.

THE FATHER: All right. I'll do just as much arguing and philosophizing as everybody does when he is considering his own torments.

THE MANAGER: If the drama permits! But for Heaven's sake, man, let's get along and come to the scene.

THE STEPDAUGHTER: It seems to me we've got too much action with our coming into his house. (*Indicating Father.*) You said, before, you couldn't change the scene every five minutes.

THE MANAGER: Of course not. What we've got to do is to combine and group up all the facts in one simultaneous, close-knit action. We can't have it as you want, with your little brother wandering like a ghost from room to room, hiding behind doors and meditating a project which — what did you say it did to him?

THE STEPDAUGHTER: Consumes him, sir, wastes him away!

THE MANAGER: Well, it may be. And then at the same time, you want the little girl there to be playing in the garden . . . one in the house, and the other in the garden; isn't that it?

THE STEPDAUGHTER: Yes, in the sun, in the sun! That is my only pleasure: to see her happy and careless in the garden after the misery and squalor of the horrible room where we all four slept together. And I had to sleep with her — I, do you understand? — with my vile contaminated body next to hers; with her folding me fast in her loving little arms. In the garden, whenever she spied me, she would run to take me by the hand. She didn't care for the big flowers, only the little ones; and she loved to show me them and pet me.

THE MANAGER: Well then, we'll have it in the garden. Everything shall happen in the garden; and we'll group the other scenes there. (*Calls a Stage Hand.*) Here, a backcloth with trees and something to do as a fountain basin. (*Turning round to look at the back of the stage.*) Ah, you've fixed it up. Good! (*To Stepdaughter.*) This is just to give an idea, of course. The Boy, instead of hiding behind the doors, will wander about here in the garden, hiding behind the trees. But it's going to be rather difficult to find a child to do that scene with you where she shows you the flowers. (*Turning to the Boy.*) Come forward a little, will you please? Let's try it now! Come along! come along! (*Then seeing him come shyly forward, full of fear and looking lost.*) It's a nice business, this lad here. What's the matter with him? We'll have to give him a word or two to say. (*Goes close to him, puts a hand on his shoulders, and leads him behind one of the trees.*) Come on! come on! Let me see you a little! Hide here . . . yes, like that. Try and show your head just a little as if you were looking for someone. . . . (*Goes back to observe the effect, when the Boy at once goes through the action.*) Excellent! fine! (*Turning to Stepdaughter.*) Suppose the little girl there were to surprise him as he looks round, and run over to him, so we could give him a word or two to say?

THE STEPDAUGHTER: It's useless to hope he will speak, as long as that fellow there is here. . . . (*Indicates the Son.*) You must send him away first.

THE SON (*jumping up*): Delighted! Delighted! I don't ask for anything better. (*Begins to move away.*)

THE MANAGER (*at once stopping him*): No! No! Where are you going? Wait a bit!

(*The Mother gets up alarmed and terrified at the thought that he is really about to go away. Instinctively she lifts her arms to prevent him, without, however, leaving her seat.*)

THE SON (*to Manager, who stops him*): I've got nothing to do with this affair. Let me go, please! Let me go!

THE MANAGER: What do you mean by saying you've got nothing to do with this?

THE STEPDAUGHTER (*calmly, with irony*): Don't bother to stop him: he won't go away.

THE FATHER: He has to act the terrible scene in the garden with his mother.

THE SON (*suddenly resolute and with dignity*): I shall act nothing at all. I've said so from the very beginning. (*To the Manager.*) Let me go!

THE STEPDAUGHTER (*going over to the Manager*): Allow me? (*Puts down the Manager's arm which is restraining the Son.*) Well, go away then, if you want to! (*The Son looks at her with contempt and hatred. She laughs and says.*) You see, he can't, he can't go away! He is obliged to stay here, indissolubly bound to the chain. If I, who fly off when that happens which has to happen because I can't bear him — if I am still here and support that face and expression of his, you can well imagine that he is unable to move. He has to remain here, has to stop with that nice father of his, and that mother whose only son he is. (*Turning to the Mother.*) Come on, mother, come along! (*Turning to Manager to indicate her.*) You see, she was getting up to keep him back. (*To the Mother, beckoning her with her hand.*) Come on, come on! (*Then to Manager.*) You can imagine how little she wants to show these actors of yours what she really feels; but so eager is she to get near him that. . . . There, you see? She is willing to act her part. (*And in fact, the Mother approaches him; and as soon as the Stepdaughter has finished speaking, opens her arms to signify that she consents.*)

THE SON (*suddenly*): No! no! If I can't go away, then I'll stop here; but I repeat: I act nothing!

THE FATHER (*to Manager excitedly*): You can force him, sir.

THE SON: Nobody can force me.

THE FATHER: I can.

THE STEPDAUGHTER: Wait a minute, wait . . . First of all, the baby has to go to the fountain. . . . (*Runs to take the Child and leads her to the fountain.*)

THE MANAGER: Yes, yes of course; that's it. Both at the same time.

(*The Second Lady Lead and the Juvenile Lead at this point separate themselves from the group of Actors. One watches the Mother attentively; the other moves about studying the movements and manner of the Son whom he will have to act.*)

THE SON (*to Manager*): What do you mean by both at the same time? It isn't right. There was no scene between me and her. (*Indicates the Mother.*) Ask her how it was!

THE MOTHER: Yes, it's true. I had come into his room. . . .

THE SON: Into my room, do you understand? Nothing to do with the garden.

THE MANAGER: It doesn't matter. Haven't I told you we've got to group the action?

THE SON (*observing the Juvenile Lead studying him*): What do you want?

THE JUVENILE LEAD: Nothing! I was just looking at you.

THE SON (*turning toward the Second Lady Lead*): Ah! she's at it too: to re-act her part! (*Indicating the Mother.*)

THE MANAGER: Exactly! And it seems to me that you ought to be grateful to them for their interest.

THE SON: Yes, but haven't you yet perceived that it

isn't possible to live in front of a mirror which not only freezes us with the image of ourselves, but throws our likeness back at us with a horrible grimace?

THE FATHER: That is true, absolutely true. You must see that.

THE MANAGER (*to Second Lady Lead and Juvenile Lead*): He's right! Move away from them!

THE SON: Do as you like. I'm out of this!

THE MANAGER: Be quiet, you, will you? And let me hear your mother! (*To Mother.*) You were saying you had entered. . . .

THE MOTHER: Yes, into his room, because I couldn't stand it any longer. I went to empty my heart to him of all the anguish that tortures me. . . . But as soon as he saw me come in. . . .

THE SON: Nothing happened! There was no scene. I went away, that's all! I don't care for scenes!

THE MOTHER: It's true, true. That's how it was.

THE MANAGER: Well now, we've got to do this bit between you and him. It's indispensable.

THE MOTHER: I'm ready . . . when you are ready. If you could only find a chance for me to tell him what I feel here in my heart.

THE FATHER (*going to Son in a great rage*): You'll do this for your mother, for your mother, do you understand?

THE SON (*quite determined*): I do nothing!

THE FATHER (*taking hold of him and shaking him*): For God's sake, do as I tell you! Don't you hear your mother asking you for a favor? Haven't you even got the guts to be a son?

THE SON (*taking hold of the Father*): No! No! And for God's sake stop it, or else. . . . (*General agitation. The Mother, frightened, tries to separate them.*)

THE MOTHER (*pleading*): Please! please!

THE FATHER (*not leaving hold of the Son*): You've got to obey, do you hear?

THE SON (*almost crying from rage*): What does it mean, this madness you've got? (*They separate.*) Have you no decency, that you insist on showing everyone our shame? I won't do it! I won't! And I stand for the will of our author in this. He didn't want to put us on the stage, after all!

THE MANAGER: Man alive! You came here . . .

THE SON (*indicating Father*): *He* did! I didn't!

THE MANAGER: Aren't you here now?

THE SON: It was his wish, and he dragged us along with him. He's told you not only the things that did happen, but also things that have never happened at all.

THE MANAGER: Well, tell me then what did happen. You went out of your room without saying a word?

THE SON: Without a word, so as to avoid a scene!

THE MANAGER: And then what did you do?

THE SON: Nothing . . . walking in the garden. . . . (*Hesitates for a moment with expression of gloom.*)

THE MANAGER (*coming closer to him, interested by his extraordinary reserve*): Well, well . . . walking in the garden. . . .

THE SON (*exasperated*): Why on earth do you insist? It's horrible!

(*The Mother trembles, sobs, and looks toward the fountain.*)

THE MANAGER (*slowly observing the glance and turning toward the Son with increasing apprehension*): The baby?

THE SON: There in the fountain. . . .

THE FATHER (*pointing with tender pity to the Mother*): She was following him at the moment. . . .

THE MANAGER (*to the Son anxiously*): And then you. . . .

THE SON: I ran over to her; I was jumping in to drag her out when I saw something that froze my blood . . . the boy standing stock still, with eyes like a madman's, watching his little drowned sister, in the fountain! (*The Stepdaughter bends over the fountain to hide the Child. She sobs.*) Then. . . . (*A revolver shot rings out behind the trees where the Boy is hidden.*)

THE MOTHER (*with a cry of terror runs over in that direction together with several of the Actors amid general confusion*): My son! My son! (*Then amid the cries and exclamations one hears her voice.*) Help! Help!

THE MANAGER (*pushing the Actors aside while they lift up the Boy and carry him off*): Is he really wounded?

SOME ACTORS: He's dead! dead!

OTHER ACTORS: No, no, it's only make-believe, it's only pretense!

THE FATHER (*with a terrible cry*): Pretense? Reality, sir, reality!

THE MANAGER: Pretense? Reality? To hell with it all! Never in my life has such a thing happened to me. I've lost a whole day over these people, a whole day!

Eugene O'Neill

Eugene O'Neill (1888–1953) is today a major figure in American drama. His enormous output is in the tradition of realism established by Strindberg and Ibsen, and his early plays, such as *Anna Christie* (1921), introduced Americans to the techniques of the great European realists. Realism for Americans was a move away from the sentimental comedies, the pathetic dramas, and melodrama that dominated the American stage since before the Civil War until World War I. O'Neill rejected the theater in which his father had thrived. James O'Neill had been a star in the American theater, traveling across the country in his production of *The Count of Monte Cristo*, which had made him rich but also had made him a prisoner of a single part.

Eugene O'Neill won the Pulitzer Prize for drama three times in the 1920s and the Nobel Prize for literature in 1936, but he was rarely a popular success in his own day. His plays have been mainstays of the American theater since his death, partly because some of his important work was published posthumously and partly because some of America's finest actors have taken a strong interest in his work and have produced it and acted in it both on the stage and on television. From the late 1950s to the present, Colleen Dewhurst and Jason Robards, Jr., in particular, have given some magnificent performances and interpretations of O'Neill's work.

The young O'Neill was a romantic in the popular sense of the word. After a year at Princeton University, he began to travel on the sea. His jaunts took him to South America as a young man, and he once wound up virtually broke and without resources in Buenos Aires. When he returned to America he worked with George Pierce Baker, the most famous drama teacher of his day. Eventually he took up residence in Provincetown, Massachusetts, where a group of people dedicated to theater — including the playwright Susan Glaspell — began to put on plays in their living rooms. When their audiences spilled over, they created the Provincetown Playhouse, the theater in which many of O'Neill's earliest pieces were first performed.

The subjects of many of O'Neill's plays were not especially appealing to general theater audiences. Those who hoped for light comedy and a good laugh or light comedy and a good cry found the intensity of his dark vision of the world to be overwhelming. They came for mere entertainment, and he was providing them with frightening visions of the soul's interior. The glum and painful surroundings of *Anna Christie*

(1921) and the brutality of the lower-class coal stoker in *The Hairy Ape* (1922) were completely foreign to the comfortable middle-class audiences who supported commercial theater in America. Despite his remarkable abilities and the power of his drama, audiences often did not know what to make of him. To a large extent, his acceptance came on waves of shock, as the acceptance of the Scandinavian realists had come.

O'Neill's early work is marked by a variety of experiments with theatrical effects and moods. He tried to use the primary influences of Greek drama in such plays as *Desire Under the Elms* (1924), which has been described by critics as Greek tragedy, and *Mourning Becomes Electra* (1931), which in its original version took three days to perform. But many of his early plays now seem dated and strange. His most impressive plays are his later work, such as *Ah, Wilderness!* (1933), *The Iceman Cometh* (1939), *Long Day's Journey into Night* (1939–1941), *A Moon for the Misbegotten* (1943), and *A Touch of the Poet* (1935–1942), which was performed posthumously in 1957.

Now, more than a hundred years after his birth, O'Neill's work continues to provide a special vision of the world. In his plays the characters are haunted by family agonies, affections never given, ambitions never realized, pains never assuaged. O'Neill looked deep into himself for his subject matter, especially in his later plays. He remains the major figure in American drama of the twentieth century.

DESIRE UNDER THE ELMS

Desire Under the Elms (1924) is Eugene O'Neill's first effort at writing in the style of Greek tragedy. He did not follow the Greek tradition and choose a great figure of noble birth about whom the fates would unravel their mystery. Rather, he was deliberately democratic and American, choosing a New England farmer and his family as the protagonists of his drama. The powers of fate are expressed in the emotional forces of jealousy, resentment, lust, and incestuous love. The mix is immediately recognizable to a student of Greek tragedy.

O'Neill chose to place his play on a typically rocky New England soil, which in many ways bears a striking resemblance to the rocky soil of Athens and the Greek coastline. The unyielding toughness of life on that land contrasts with the easy life to be made from gold mining in California. Ephraim Cabot, the seventy-five-year-old father, has been made hard and physically powerful by his work. He has just taken a young and scheming wife, Abbie. Eben Cabot has decided to stay on the farm while his two brothers go to California and try to put New England behind them.

The sense of having been dispossessed of his farm drives Eben to hate his new mother, who married the elder Cabot merely to inherit his farm when he died. Abbie knows that Cabot is not a satisfying sexual partner, but she sees Eben as a reasonable substitute. At first the sparring between Abbie and Eben is based on calculating self-interest, but eventually their feelings for each other become overpowering. Lust turns to love, and the desires and emotions they thought they could control are quite out of control. The son they produce is passed off as old Cabot's, although the townspeople have no illusion about whose child it is.

The farm itself is a powerful presence in the play. Whenever old Cabot thinks he should give up and follow the promise of easy money in California, he gets vibrations from God telling him to stay. God operates for Ephraim as the oracle in *Oedipus Rex* does, giving him a message that is painful but that he is compelled to obey. The rocks on the farm are unforgiving, and so is the fate that Abbie and Eben face. Theirs is an impossible love; everything they do to prove their love condemns them even more. The forces of fate center on the farm. When the play opens, Eben says of it, "God! Purty!" When the play ends, the sheriff praises the farm and says he surely would like to own it, striking a clear note of irony: The agony of the play is rooted in lust — lust for the farm that parallels the lust between Abbie and Eben.

The play is haunted by the ghost of Eben's mother, whom Ephraim married primarily for her farm. When the ghost of Eben's mother is exorcised it is only because the cycle of retribution has begun. Old Cabot has committed a crime against her, and now he must become the victim.

The language of the dialogue is that of New England in the mid-nineteenth century. O'Neill lived in New England and understood the ways and the language of its people. He seems to have imagined the "down-east" flavor of Maine in the language, and he has been careful to build the proper pronunciation into the dialogue. This folksy way of speaking helps emphasize the peasantlike qualities in these New England farmers. O'Neill's careful use of language is reminiscent of Synge's masterful representation of the Irish-English speech of the Aran Islanders in *Riders to the Sea*, a play that is also a kind of folk tragedy.

The language of O'Neill's characters has a rocky toughness at times. Characters are laconic — they often answer in a single word: "Ay-eh." Faithful to his vision of the simple speech of country folk, O'Neill avoids giving them elaborate poetic soliloquies, no matter how tempting such poetry might be. Instead, he shows how, despite their limited language, rural people feel profound emotions and act on them.

O'Neill carefully links Abbie with Queen Phaedra, who in Euripides's play *Hippolytus* and in Racine's seventeenth-century play *Phèdre* finds herself uncontrollably desiring her husband's son as a lover. Racine and Racine's audience could easily imagine such intense emotions overwhelming a noblewoman because they thought that nobility felt everything more intensely and lived more intensely than ordinary people. But O'Neill is trying to make his audience see that even unlettered farm people can feel as deeply as tragic heroes of any age. The Cabots are victims of passion. They share their fate with the great families of the Greek tragedies.

Eugene O'Neill (1888–1953)
DESIRE UNDER THE ELMS   *1924*

Characters

EPHRAIM CABOT
SIMEON ⎫
PETER ⎬ *his sons*
EBEN   ⎭

ABBIE PUTNAM
YOUNG GIRL, TWO FARMERS, *the* FIDDLER, *a* SHERIFF, *and other folk from the neighboring farms.*

The action of the entire play takes place in, and immediately outside of, the Cabot farmhouse in New England, in the year 1850. The south end of the house faces front to a stone wall with a wooden gate at center opening on a country road. The house is in good condition but in need of paint. Its walls are a sickly grayish, the green of the shutters faded. Two enormous elms are on each side of the house. They bend their trailing branches down over the roof. They appear to protect and at the same time subdue. There is a sinister maternity in their aspect, a crushing, jealous absorption. They have developed from their intimate contact with the life of man in the house an appalling humaneness. They brood oppressively over the house. They are like exhausted women resting their sagging breasts and hands and hair on its roof, and when it rains their tears trickle down monotonously and rot on the shingles.

There is a path running from the gate around the right corner of the house to the front door. A narrow porch is on this side. The end wall facing us has two windows in its upper story, two larger ones on the floor below. The two upper are those of the father's

bedroom and that of the brothers. On the left, ground floor, is the kitchen — on the right, the parlor, the shades of which are always drawn down.

PART I • Scene I

(Exterior of the farmhouse. It is sunset of a day at the beginning of summer in the year 1850. There is no wind and everything is still. The sky above the roof is suffused with deep colors, the green of the elms glows, but the house is in shadow, seeming pale and washed out by contrast.)

(A door opens and Eben Cabot comes to the end of the porch and stands looking down the road to the right. He has a large bell in his hand and this he swings mechanically, awakening a deafening clangor. Then he puts his hands on his hips and stares up at the sky. He sighs with a puzzled awe and blurts out with halting appreciation.)

EBEN: God! Purty! *(His eyes fall and he stares about him frowningly. He is twenty-five, tall and sinewy. His face is well formed, good-looking, but its expression is resentful and defensive. His defiant, dark eyes remind one of a wild animal's in captivity. Each day is a cage in which he finds himself trapped but inwardly unsubdued. There is a fierce repressed vitality about him. He has black hair, mustache, a thin curly trace of beard. He is dressed in rough farm clothes.)*

(He spits on the ground with intense disgust, turns, and goes back into the house.)

(*Simeon and Peter come in from their work in the fields. They are tall men, much older than their half-brother [Simeon is thirty-nine and Peter thirty-seven], built on a squarer, simpler model, fleshier in body, more bovine and homelier in face, shrewder and more practical. Their shoulders stoop a bit from years of farm work. They clump heavily along in their clumsy thick-soled boots caked with earth. Their clothes, their faces, hands, bare arms, and throats are earth-stained. They smell of earth. They stand together for a moment in front of the house and, as if with the one impulse, stare dumbly up at the sky, leaning on their hoes. Their faces have a compressed, unresigned expression. As they look upward, this softens.*)

SIMEON (*grudgingly*): Purty.

PETER: Ay-eh.

SIMEON (*suddenly*): Eighteen year ago.

PETER: What?

SIMEON: Jenn. My woman. She died.

PETER: I'd fergot.

SIMEON: I rec'lect — now an' agin. Makes it lonesome. She'd hair long's a hoss' tail — an' yaller like gold!

PETER: Waal — she's gone. (*This with indifferent finality — then after a pause.*) They's gold in the West, Sim.

SIMEON (*still under the influence of sunset — vaguely*): In the sky?

PETER: Waal — in a manner o' speakin' — that's the promise. (*Growing excited.*) Gold in the sky — in the West — Golden Gate — Californi-a! — Goldest West! — fields o' gold!

SIMEON (*excited in his turn*): Fortunes layin' just atop o' the ground waitin' t' be picked! Solomon's mines, they says! (*For a moment they continue looking up at the sky — then their eyes drop.*)

PETER (*with sardonic bitterness*): Here — it's stones atop o' the ground — stones atop o' stones — makin' stone walls — year atop o' year — him 'n' yew 'n' me 'n' then Eben — makin' stone walls fur him to fence us in!

SIMEON: We've wuked. Give our strength. Give our years. Plowed 'em under in the ground — (*He stamps rebelliously.*) — rottin' — makin' soil for his crops! (*A pause.*) Waal — the farm pays good for hereabouts.

PETER: If we plowed in Californi-a, they'd be lumps o' gold in the furrow!

SIMEON: Californi-a's t'other side o' earth, a'most. We got t' calc'late —

PETER (*after a pause*): 'Twould be hard fur me, too, to give up what we've 'arned here by our sweat. (*A pause. Eben sticks his head out of the dining room window, listening.*)

SIMEON: Ay-eh. (*A pause.*) Mebbe — he'll die soon.

PETER (*doubtfully*): Mebbe.

SIMEON: Mebbe — fur all we knows — he's dead now.

PETER: Ye'd need proof.

SIMEON: He's been gone two months — with no word.

PETER: Left us in the fields an evenin' like this. Hitched up an' druv off into the West. That's plum onnateral. He hain't never been off this farm 'ceptin' t' the village in thirty year or more, not since he married Eben's maw. (*A pause. Shrewdly.*) I calc'late we might git him declared crazy by the court.

SIMEON: He skinned 'em too slick. He got the best o' all on 'em. They'd never b'lieve him crazy. (*A pause.*) We got t' wait — till he's underground.

EBEN (*with a sardonic chuckle*): Honor thy father! (*They turn startled, and stare at him. He grins, then scowls.*) I pray he's died. (*They stare at him. He continues matter-of-factly.*) Supper's ready.

SIMEON AND PETER (*together*): Ayeh.

EBEN (*gazing up at the sky*): Sun's downin' purty.

SIMEON AND PETER (*together*): Ay-eh. They's gold in the West.

EBEN: Ay-eh. (*Pointing.*) Yonder atop o' the hill pasture, ye mean?

SIMEON AND PETER (*together*): In Californi-a!

EBEN: Hunh? (*Stares at them indifferently for a second, then drawls.*) Waal — supper's gittin' cold. (*He turns back into kitchen.*)

SIMEON (*startled — smacks his lips*): I air hungry!

PETER (*sniffing*): I smells bacon!

SIMEON (*with hungry appreciation*): Bacon's good!

PETER (*in same tone*): Bacon's bacon! (*They turn, shouldering each other, their bodies bumping and rubbing together as they hurry clumsily to their food, like two friendly oxen toward their evening meal. They disappear around the right corner of house and can be heard entering the door.*)

Scene II

(*The color fades from the sky. Twilight begins. The interior of the kitchen is now visible. A pine table is at center, a cook-stove in the right rear corner, four rough wooden chairs, a tallow candle on the table. In the middle of the rear wall is fastened a big advertising poster with a ship in full sail and the word "California" in big letters. Kitchen utensils hang from nails. Everything is neat and in order but the atmosphere is of a men's camp kitchen rather than that of a home.*)

(*Places for three are laid. Eben takes boiled potatoes and bacon from the stove and puts them on the table, also a loaf of bread and a crock of water. Simeon and Peter shoulder in, slump down in their chairs without a word. Eben joins them. The three eat in silence for a moment, the two elder as naturally unrestrained as beasts of the field, Eben picking at his food without appetite, glancing at them with a tolerant dislike.)*

SIMEON (*suddenly turns to Eben*): Looky here! Ye'd oughtn't t' said that, Eben.
PETER: 'Twa'n't righteous.
EBEN: What?
SIMEON: Ye prayed he'd died.
EBEN: Waal — don't yew pray it? (*A pause.*)
PETER: He's our Paw.
EBEN (*violently*): Not mine!
SIMEON (*dryly*): Ye'd not let no one else say that about yer Maw! Ha! (*He gives one abrupt sardonic guffaw. Peter grins.*)
EBEN (*very pale*): I meant — I hain't his'n — I hain't like him — he hain't me!
PETER (*dryly*): Wait till ye've growed his age!
EBEN (*intensely*): I'm Maw — every drop o' blood! (*A pause. They stare at him with indifferent curiosity.*)
PETER (*reminiscently*): She was good t' Sim 'n' me. A good Stepmaw's scurse.
SIMEON: She was good t' everyone.
EBEN (*greatly moved, gets to his feet and makes an awkward bow to each of them — stammering*): I be thankful t' ye. I'm her — her heir. (*He sits down in confusion.*)
PETER (*after a pause — judicially*): She was good even t' him.
EBEN (*fiercely*): An' fur thanks he killed her!
SIMEON (*after a pause*): No one never kills nobody. It's allus somethin'. That's the murderer.
EBEN: Didn't he slave Maw t' death?
PETER: He's slaved himself t' death. He's slaved Sim 'n' me 'n' yew t' death — on'y none o' us hain't died — yit.
SIMEON: It's somethin' — drivin' him — t' drive us!
EBEN (*vengefully*): Waal — I hold him t' jedgment! (*Then scornfully.*) Somethin'! What's somethin'?
SIMEON: Dunno.
EBEN (*sardonically*): What's drivin' yew to California, mebbe? (*They look at him in surprise.*) Oh, I've heerd ye! (*Then, after a pause.*) But ye'll never go t' the gold fields!
PETER (*assertively*): Mebbe!
EBEN: Whar'll ye git the money?
PETER: We kin walk. It's an a'mighty ways — California — but if yew was t' put all the steps we've walked on this farm end t' end we'd be in the moon!
EBEN: The Injuns'll skulp ye on the plains.
SIMEON (*with grim humor*): We'll mebbe make 'em pay a hair fur a hair!
EBEN (*decisively*): But t'aint that. Ye won't never go

because ye'll wait here fur yer share o' the farm, thinkin' allus he'll die soon.
SIMEON (*after a pause*): We've a right.
PETER: Two-thirds belongs t'us.
EBEN (*jumping to his feet*): Ye've no right! She wa'n't yewr Maw! It was her farm! Didn't he steal it from her? She's dead. It's my farm.
SIMEON (*sardonically*): Tell that t' Paw — when he comes! I'll bet ye a dollar he'll laugh — fur once in his life. Ha! (*He laughs himself in one single mirthless bark.*)
PETER (*amused in turn, echoes his brother*): Ha!
SIMEON (*after a pause*): What've ye got held agin us, Eben? Year arter year it's skulked in yer eye — somethin'.
PETER: Ay-eh.
EBEN: Ay-eh. They's somethin'. (*Suddenly exploding.*) Why didn't ye never stand between him 'n' my Maw when he was slavin' her to her grave — t' pay her back fur the kindness she done t' yew? (*There is a long pause. They stare at him in surprise.*)
SIMEON: Waal — the stock'd got t' be watered.
PETER: 'R they was woodin' t' do.
SIMEON: 'R plowin'.
PETER: 'R hayin'.
SIMEON: 'R spreadin' manure.
PETER: 'R weedin'.
SIMEON: 'R prunin'.
PETER: 'R milkin'.
EBEN (*breaking in harshly*): An' makin' walls — stone atop o' stone — makin' walls till yer heart's a stone ye heft up out o' the way o' growth onto a stone wall t' wall in yer heart!
SIMEON (*matter-of-factly*): We never had no time t' meddle.
PETER (*to Eben*): Yew was fifteen afore yer Maw died — an' big fur yer age. Why didn't ye never do nothin'?
EBEN (*harshly*): They was chores t' do, wa'n't they? (*A pause — then slowly.*) It was on'y arter she died I come to think o' it. Me cookin' — doin' her work — that made me know her, suffer her sufferin' — she'd come back t' help — come back t' bile potatoes — come back t' fry bacon — come back t' bake biscuits — come back all cramped up t' shake the fire, an' carry ashes, her eyes weepin' an' bloody with smoke an' cinders same's they used t' be. She still comes back — stands by the stove thar in the evenin' — she can't find it nateral sleepin' an' restin' in peace. She can't git used t' bein' free — even in her grave.
SIMEON: She never complained none.
EBEN: She'd got too tired. She'd got too used t' bein' too tired. That was what he done. (*With vengeful passion.*) An' sooner'r later, I'll meddle. I'll say the

thin's I didn't say then t' him! I'll yell 'em at the top o' my lungs. I'll see t' it my Maw gits some rest an' sleep in her grave! (*He sits down again, relapsing into a brooding silence. They look at him with a queer indifferent curiosity.*)

PETER (*after a pause*): Whar in tarnation d'ye s'pose he went, Sim?

SIMEON: Dunno. He druv off in the buggy, all spick an' span, with the mare all breshed an' shiny, druv off clackin' his tongue an' wavin' his whip. I remember it right well. I was finishin' plowin', it was spring an' May an' sunset, an' gold in the West, an' he druv off into it. I yells "Whar ye goin', Paw?" an' he hauls up by the stone wall a jiffy. His old snake's eyes was glitterin' in the sun like he'd been drinkin' a jugful an' he says with a mule's grin: "Don't ye run away till I come back!"

PETER: Wonder if he knowed we was wantin' fur Californi-a?

SIMEON: Mebbe. I didn't say nothin' and he says, lookin' kinder queer an' sick: "I been hearin' the hens cluckin' an' the roosters crowin' all the durn day. I been listenin' t' the cows lowin' an' everythin' else kickin' up till I can't stand it no more. It's spring an' I'm feelin' damned," he says. "Damned like an old bare hickory tree fit on'y fur burnin','" he says. An' then I calc'late I must've looked a mite hopeful, fur he adds real spry and vicious: "But don't git no fool idee I'm dead. I've sworn t' live a hundred an' I'll do it, if on'y t' spite yer sinful greed! An' now I'm ridin' out t' learn God's message t' me in the spring, like the prophets done. An' yew git back t' yer plowin','" he says. An' he druv off singin' a hymn. I thought he was drunk — 'r I'd stopped him goin'.

EBEN (*scornfully*): No, ye wouldn't! Ye're scared o' him. He's stronger — inside — than both o' ye put together!

PETER (*sardonically*): An' yew — be yew Samson?°

EBEN: I'm gittin' stronger. I kin feel it growin' in me — growin' an' growin' — till it'll bust out —! (*He gets up and puts on his coat and a hat. They watch him, gradually breaking into grins. Eben avoids their eyes sheepishly.*) I'm goin' out fur a spell — up the road.

PETER: T' the village.

SIMEON: T' see Minnie?

EBEN (*defiantly*): Ay-eh!

PETER (*jeeringly*): The Scarlet Woman!

SIMEON: Lust — that's what's growin' in ye!

EBEN: Waal — she's purty!

PETER: She's been purty fur twenty year.

Samson: A biblical hero known for his great physical strength.

SIMEON: A new coat o' paint'll make a heifer out of forty.

EBEN: She hain't forty!

PETER: If she hain't, she's teeterin' on the edge.

EBEN (*desperately*): What d'yew know —

PETER: All they is . . . Sim knew her — an' then me arter —

SIMEON: An' Paw kin tell yew somethin' too! He was fust!

EBEN: D'ye mean t' say he . . . ?

SIMEON (*with a grin*): Ay-eh! We air his heirs in everythin'!

EBEN (*intensely*): That's more to it! That grows on it! It'll bust soon! (*Then violently.*) I'll go smash my fist in her face! (*He pulls open the door in rear violently.*)

SIMEON (*with a wink at Peter — drawlingly*): Mebbe — but the night's wa'm — purty — by the time ye git thar mebbe ye'll kiss her instead!

PETER: Sart'n he will! (*They both roar with coarse laughter. Eben rushes out and slams the door — then the outside front door — comes around the corner of the house and stands still by the gate, staring up at the sky.*)

SIMEON (*looking after him*): Like his Paw.

PETER: Dead spit an' image!

SIMEON: Dog'll eat dog!

PETER: Ay-eh. (*Pause. With yearning.*) Mebbe a year from now we'll be in Californi-a.

SIMEON: Ay-eh. (*A pause. Both yawn.*) Let's git t'bed. (*He blows out the candle. They go out door in rear. Eben stretches his arms up to the sky — rebelliously.*)

EBEN: Waal — thar's a star, an' somewhar's they's him, an' here's me, an' thar's Min up the road — in the same night. What if I does kiss her? She's like t'night, she's soft 'n' wa'm, her eyes kin wink like a star, her mouth's wa'm, her arms're wa'm, she smells like a wa'm plowed field, she's purty . . . Ay-eh! By God A'mighty she's purty, an' I don't give a damn how many sins she's sinned afore mine or who she's sinned 'em with, my sin's as purty as any one on 'em! (*He strides off down the road to the left.*)

Scene III

(*It is the pitch darkness just before dawn. Eben comes in from the left and goes around to the porch, feeling his way, chuckling bitterly and cursing half-aloud to himself.*)

EBEN: The cussed old miser! (*He can be heard going in the front door. There is a pause as he goes*

upstairs, then a loud knock on the bedroom door
of the brothers.) Wake up!

SIMEON (*startledly*): Who's thar?

EBEN (*Pushing open the door and coming in, a lighted
candle in his hand. The bedroom of the brothers
is revealed. Its ceiling is the sloping roof. They can
stand upright only close to the center dividing wall
of the upstairs. Simeon and Peter are in a double
bed, front. Eben's cot is to the rear. Eben has a
mixture of silly grin and vicious scowl on his face.*):
I be!

PETER (*angrily*): What in hell's-fire . . . ?

EBEN: I got news fur ye! Ha! (*He gives one abrupt
sardonic guffaw.*)

SIMEON (*angrily*): Couldn't ye hold it 'til we'd got our
sleep?

EBEN: It's nigh sunup. (*Then explosively.*) He's gone
an' married agen!

SIMEON AND PETER (*explosively*): Paw?

EBEN: Got himself hitched to a female 'bout thirty-
five — an' purty, they says . . .

SIMEON (*aghast*): It's a durn lie!

PETER: Who says?

SIMEON: They been stringin' ye!

EBEN: Think I'm a dunce, do ye? The hull village says.
The preacher from New Dover, he brung the news
— told it t'our preacher — New Dover, that's whar
the old loon got himself hitched — that's whar the
woman lived —

PETER (*no longer doubting — stunned*): Waal . . . !

SIMEON (*the same*): Waal . . . !

EBEN (*sitting down on a bed — with vicious hatred*):
Ain't he a devil out o' hell? It's jest t' spite us —
the damned old mule!

PETER (*after a pause*): Everythin'll go t'her now.

SIMEON: Ay-eh. (*A pause — dully.*) Waal — if it's
done —

PETER: It's done us. (*Pause — then persuasively.*) They's
gold in the fields o' Californi-a, Sim. No good a-
stayin' here now.

SIMEON: Jest what I was a-thinkin'. (*Then with decision.*) S'well fust's last! Let's light out and git this
mornin'.

PETER: Suits me.

EBEN: Ye must like walkin'.

SIMEON (*sardonically*): If ye'd grow wings on us we'd
fly thar!

EBEN: Ye'd like ridin' better — on a boat, wouldn't
ye? (*Fumbles in his pocket and takes out a crumpled
sheet of foolscap.*) Waal, if ye sign this ye kin ride
on a boat. I've had it writ out an' ready in case
ye'd ever go. It says fur three hundred dollars t'
each ye agree yewr shares o' the farm is sold t'
me. (*They look suspiciously at the paper. A pause.*)

SIMEON (*wonderingly*): But if he's hitched agen —

PETER: An' whar'd yew git that sum o' money, anyways?

EBEN (*cunningly*): I know whar it's hid. I been waitin'
— Maw told me. She knew whar it lay fur years,
but she was waitin' . . . It's her'n — the money he
hoarded from her farm an' hid from Maw. It's my
money by rights now.

PETER: Whar's it hid?

EBEN (*cunningly*): Whar yew won't never find it without
me. Maw spied on him — 'r she'd never knowed.
(*A pause. They look at him suspiciously, and he
at them.*) Waal, is it fa'r trade?

SIMEON: Dunno.

PETER: Dunno.

SIMEON (*looking at window*): Sky's grayin'.

PETER: Ye better start the fire, Eben.

SIMEON: An' fix some vittles.

EBEN: Ay-eh. (*Then with a forced jocular heartiness.*)
I'll git ye a good one. If ye're startin' t' hoof it t'
Californi-a ye'll need somethin' that'll stick t' yer
ribs. (*He turns to the door, adding meaningly.*) But
ye kin ride on a boat if ye'll swap. (*He stops at
the door and pauses. They stare at him.*)

SIMEON (*suspiciously*): Whar was ye all night?

EBEN (*defiantly*): Up t' Min's. (*Then slowly.*) Walkin'
thar, fust I felt 's if I'd kiss her; then I got a-thinkin'
o' what ye'd said o' him an' her an' I says, I'll bust
her nose fur that! Then I got t' the village an' heerd
the news an' I got madder'n hell an' run all the
way t' Min's not knowin' what I'd do — (*He pauses
— then sheepishly but more defiantly.*) Waal —
when I seen her, I didn't hit her — nor I didn't
kiss her nuther — I begun t' beller like a calf an'
cuss at the same time, I was so durn mad — an'
she got scared — an' I jest grabbed holt an' tuk
her! (*Proudly.*) Yes, sirree! I tuk her. She may've
been his'n — an' your'n, too — but she's mine
now!

SIMEON (*dryly*): In love, air yew?

EBEN (*with lofty scorn*): Love! I don't take no stock
in sech slop!

PETER (*winking at Simeon*): Mebbe Eben's aimin' t'
marry, too.

SIMEON: Min'd make a true faithful he'pmeet! (*They
snicker.*)

EBEN: What do I care fur her — 'ceptin' she's round
an' wa'm? The p'int is she was his'n — an' now
she b'longs t' me! (*He goes to the door — then
turns — rebelliously.*) An' Min hain't sech a bad
un. They's worse'n Min in the world, I'll bet ye!
Wait'll we see this cow the Old Man's hitched t'!
She'll beat Min, I got a notion! (*He starts to go
out.*)

SIMEON (*suddenly*): Mebbe ye'll try t' make her your'n,
too?

PETER: Ha! (*He gives a sardonic laugh of relish at this idea.*)

EBEN (*spitting with disgust*): Her — here — sleepin' with him — stealin' my Maw's farm! I'd as soon pet a skunk 'r kiss a snake! (*He goes out. The two stare after him suspiciously. A pause. They listen to his steps receding.*)

PETER: He's startin' the fire.

SIMEON: I'd like t' ride t' Californi-a — but —

PETER: Min might o' put some scheme in his head.

SIMEON: Mebbe it's all a lie 'bout Paw marryin'. We'd best wait an' see the bride.

PETER: An' don't sign nothin' till we does!

SIMEON: Nor till we've tested it's good money! (*Then with a grin.*) But if Paw's hitched we'd be sellin' Eben somethin' we'd never git nohow!

PETER: We'll wait an' see. (*Then with sudden vindictive anger.*) An' till he comes, let's yew 'n' me not wuk a lick, let Eben tend to thin's if he's a mind t', let's us jest sleep an' eat an' drink likker, an' let the hull damned farm go t' blazes!

SIMEON (*excitedly*): By God, we've 'arned a rest! We'll play rich fur a change. I hain't a-going to stir outa bed till breakfast's ready.

PETER: An' on the table!

SIMEON (*after a pause — thoughtfully*): What d'ye calc'late she'll be like — our new Maw? Like Eben thinks?

PETER: More'n' likely.

SIMEON (*vindictively*): Waal — I hope she's a she-devil that'll make him wish he was dead an' livin' in the pit o' hell fur comfort!

PETER (*fervently*): Amen!

SIMEON (*imitating his father's voice*): "I'm ridin' out t' learn God's message t' me in the spring like the prophets done," he says. I'll bet right then an' thar he knew plumb well he was goin' whorin', the stinkin' old hypocrite!

Scene IV

(*Same as Scene II — shows the interior of the kitchen with a lighted candle on table. It is gray dawn outside. Simeon and Peter are just finishing their breakfast. Eben sits before his plate of untouched food, brooding frowningly.*)

PETER (*glancing at him rather irritably*): Lookin' glum don't help none.

SIMEON (*sarcastically*): Sorrowin' over his lust o' the flesh!

PETER (*with a grin*): Was she yer fust?

EBEN (*angrily*): None o' yer business. (*A pause.*) I was thinkin' o' him. I got a notion he's gittin' near — I kin feel him comin' on like yew kin feel malaria chill afore it takes ye.

PETER: It's too early yet.

SIMEON: Dunno. He'd like t' catch us nappin' — jest t' have somethin' t' hoss us 'round over.

PETER (*Mechanically gets to his feet. Simeon does the same.*): Waal — let's git t'wuk. (*They both plod mechanically toward the door before they realize. Then they stop short.*)

SIMEON (*grinning*): Ye're a cussed fool, Pete — and I be wuss! Let him see we hain't wukin'! We don't give a durn!

PETER (*as they go back to the table*): Not a damned durn! It'll serve t' show him we're done with him. (*They sit down again. Eben stares from one to the other with surprise.*)

SIMEON (*grins at him*): We're aimin' t' start bein' lilies o' the field.

PETER: Nary a toil 'r spin 'r lick o' wuk do we put in!

SIMEON: Ye're sole owner — till he comes — that's what ye wanted. Waal, ye got t' be sole hand, too.

PETER: The cows air bellerin'. Ye better hustle at the milkin'.

EBEN (*with excited joy*): Ye mean ye'll sign the paper?

SIMEON (*dryly*): Mebbe.

PETER: Mebbe.

SIMEON: We're considerin'. (*Peremptorily.*) Ye better git t' wuk.

EBEN (*with queer excitement*): It's Maw's farm agen! It's my farm! Them's my cows! I'll milk my durn fingers off fur cows o' mine! (*He goes out door in rear, they stare after him indifferently.*)

SIMEON: Like his Paw.

PETER: Dead spit 'n' image!

SIMEON: Waal — let dog eat dog! (*Eben comes out of front door and around the corner of the house. The sky is beginning to grow flushed with sunrise. Eben stops by the gate and stares around him with glowing, possessive eyes. He takes in the whole farm with his embracing glance of desire.*)

EBEN: It's purty! It's damned purty! It's mine! (*He suddenly throws his head back boldly and glares with hard, defiant eyes at the sky.*) Mine, d'ye hear? Mine! (*He turns and walks quickly off left, rear, toward the barn. The two brothers light their pipes.*)

SIMEON (*putting his muddy boots up on the table, tilting back his chair, and puffing defiantly*): Waal — this air solid comfort — fur once.

PETER: Ay-eh. (*He follows suit. A pause. Unconsciously they both sigh.*)

SIMEON (*suddenly*): He never was much o' a hand at milkin', Eben wa'n't.

PETER (*with a snort*): His hands air like hoofs! (*A pause.*)

SIMEON: Reach down the jug thar! Let's take a swaller. I'm feelin' kind o' low.

PETER: Good idee! (*He does so — gets two glasses —*

they pour out drinks of whisky.) Here's t' the gold in Californi-a!

SIMEON: An' luck t' find it! (*They drink — puff resolutely — sigh — take their feet down from the table.*)

PETER: Likker don't pear t' sot right.

SIMEON: We hain't used t' it this early. (*A pause. They become very restless.*)

PETER: Gittin' close in this kitchen.

SIMEON (*with immense relief*): Let's git a breath o' air. (*They arise briskly and go out rear — appear around house and stop by the gate. They stare up at the sky with a numbed appreciation.*)

PETER: Purty!

SIMEON: Ay-eh. Gold's t' the East now.

PETER: Sun's startin' with us fur the Golden West.

SIMEON (*staring around the farm, his compressed face tightened, unable to conceal his emotion*): Waal — it's our last mornin' — mebbe.

PETER (*the same*): Ay-eh.

SIMEON (*stamps his foot on the earth and addresses it desperately*): Waal — ye've thirty year o' me buried in ye — spread out over ye — blood an' bone an' sweat — rotted away — fertilizin' ye — richin' yer soul — prime manure, by God, that's what I been t' ye!

PETER: Ay-eh! An' me.

SIMEON: An' yew, Peter. (*He sighs — then spits.*) Waal — no use'n cryin' over spilt milk.

PETER: They's gold in the West — an' freedom, mebbe. We been slaves t' stone walls here.

SIMEON (*defiantly*): We hain't nobody's slaves from this out — nor nothin's slaves nuther. (*A pause — restlessly.*) Speaking o' milk, wonder how Eben's managin'?

PETER: I s'pose he's managin'.

SIMEON: Mebbe we'd ought t' help — this once.

PETER: Mebbe. The cows knows us.

SIMEON: An' likes us. They don't know him much.

PETER: An' the hosses, an' pigs, an' chickens. They don't know him much.

SIMEON: They knows us like brothers — an' likes us! (*Proudly.*) Hain't we raised 'em t' be fust-rate, number one prize stock?

PETER: We hain't — not no more.

SIMEON (*dully*): I was fergittin'. (*Then resignedly.*) Waal, let's go help Eben a spell an' git waked up.

PETER: Suits me. (*They are starting off down left, rear, for the barn when Eben appears from there hurrying toward them, his face excited.*)

EBEN (*breathlessly*): Waal — har they be! The old mule an' the bride! I seen 'em from the barn down below at the turnin'.

PETER: How could ye tell that far?

EBEN: Hain't I as far-sight as he's near-sight? Don't I know the mare 'n' buggy, an' two people settin'

in it? Who else . . . ? An' I tell ye I kin feel 'em a-comin', too! (*He squirms as if he had the itch.*)

PETER (*beginning to be angry*): Waal — let him do his own unhitchin'!

SIMEON (*angry in his turn*): Let's hustle in an' git our bundles an' be a-goin' as he's a-comin'. I don't want never t' step inside the door agen arter he's back. (*They both start back around the corner of the house. Eben follows them.*)

EBEN (*anxiously*): Will ye sign it afore ye go?

PETER: Let's see the color o' the old skinflint's money an' we'll sign. (*They disappear left. The two brothers clump upstairs to get their bundles. Eben appears in the kitchen, runs to window, peers out, comes back and pulls up a strip of flooring in under stove, takes out a canvas bag and puts it on table, then sets the floorboard back in place. The two brothers appear a moment after. They carry old carpetbags.*)

EBEN (*puts his hand on bag guardingly*): Have ye signed?

SIMEON (*shows paper in his hand*): Ay-eh. (*Greedily.*) Be that the money?

EBEN (*opens bag and pours out pile of twenty-dollar gold pieces*): Twenty-dollar pieces — thirty on 'em. Count 'em. (*Peter does so, arranging them in stacks of five, biting one or two to test them.*)

PETER: Six hundred. (*He puts them in bag and puts it inside his shirt carefully.*)

SIMEON (*handing paper to Eben*): Har ye be.

EBEN (*after a glance, folds it carefully and hides it under his shirt — gratefully*): Thank yew.

PETER: Thank yew fur the ride.

SIMEON: We'll send ye a lump o' gold fur Christmas. (*A pause. Eben stares at them and they at him.*)

PETER (*awkwardly*): Waal — we're a-goin'.

SIMEON: Comin' out t' the yard?

EBEN: No. I'm waitin' in here a spell. (*Another silence. The brothers edge awkwardly to door in rear — then turn and stand.*)

SIMEON: Waal — good-by.

PETER: Good-by.

EBEN: Good-by. (*They go out. He sits down at the table, faces the stove and pulls out the paper. He looks from it to the stove. His face, lighted up by the shaft of sunlight from the window, has an expression of trance. His lips move. The two brothers come out to the gate.*)

PETER (*looking off toward barn*): Thar he be — unhitchin'.

SIMEON (*with a chuckle*): I'll bet ye he's riled!

PETER: An' thar she be.

SIMEON: Let's wait 'n' see what our new Maw looks like.

PETER (*with a grin*): An' give him our partin' cuss!

SIMEON (*grinning*): I feel like raisin' fun. I feel light in my head an' feet.

PETER: Me, too. I feel like laffin' till I'd split up the middle.

SIMEON: Reckon it's the likker?

PETER: No. My feet feel itchin' t' walk an' walk — an' jump high over thin's — an'. . . .

SIMEON: Dance? (*A pause.*)

PETER (*puzzled*): It's plumb onnateral.

SIMEON (*a light coming over his face*): I calc'late it's 'cause school's out. It's holiday. Fur once we're free!

PETER (*dazedly*): Free?

SIMEON: The halter's broke — the harness is busted — the fence bars is down — the stone walls air crumblin' an' tumblin'! We'll be kickin' up an' tearin' away down the road!

PETER (*drawing a deep breath — oratorically*): Anybody that wants this stinkin' old rock-pile of a farm kin hev it. T'ain't our'n, no sirree!

SIMEON (*takes the gate off its hinges and puts it under his arm*): We harby 'bolishes shet gates, an' open gates, an' all gates, by thunder!

PETER: We'll take it with us fur luck an' let 'er sail free down some river.

SIMEON (*as a sound of voices comes from left, rear*): Har they comes! (*The two brothers congeal into two stiff, grim-visaged statues. Ephraim Cabot and Abbie Putnam come in. Cabot is seventy-five, tall and gaunt, with great, wiry, concentrated power, but stoop-shouldered from toil. His face is as hard as if it were hewn out of a boulder, yet there is a weakness in it, a petty pride in its own narrow strength. His eyes are small, close together, and extremely near-sighted, blinking continually in the effort to focus on objects, their stare having a straining, ingrowing quality. He is dressed in his dismal black Sunday suit. Abbie is thirty-five, buxom, full of vitality. Her round face is pretty but marred by its rather gross sensuality. There is strength and obstinacy in her jaw, a hard determination in her eyes, and about her whole personality the same unsettled, untamed, desperate quality which is so apparent in Eben.*)

CABOT (*as they enter — a queer strangled emotion in his dry cracking voice*): Har we be t' hum, Abbie.

ABBIE (*with lust for the word*): Hum! (*Her eyes gloating on the house without seeming to see the two stiff figures at the gate.*) It's purty — purty! I can't b'lieve it's r'ally mine.

CABOT (*sharply*): Yewr'n? Mine! (*He stares at her penetratingly. She stares back. He adds relentingly.*) Our'n — mebbe! It was lonesome too long. I was growin' old in the spring. A hum's got t' hev a woman.

ABBIE (*her voice taking possession*): A woman's got t' hev a hum!

CABOT (*nodding uncertainly*): Ay-eh. (*Then irritably.*) Whar be they? Ain't thar nobody about — 'r wukin' — 'r nothin'?

ABBIE (*Sees the brothers. She returns their stare of cold appraising contempt with interest — slowly.*): Thar's two men loafin' at the gate an' starin' at me like a couple o' strayed hogs.

CABOT (*straining his eyes*): I kin see 'em — but I can't make out. . . .

SIMEON: It's Simeon.

PETER: It's Peter.

CABOT (*exploding*): Why hain't ye wukin'?

SIMEON (*dryly*): We're waitin' t' welcome ye hum — yew an' the bride!

CABOT (*confusedly*): Huh? Waal — this be yer new Maw, boys. (*She stares at them and they at her.*)

SIMEON (*turns away and spits contemptuously*): I see her!

PETER (*spits also*): An' I see her!

ABBIE (*with the conqueror's conscious superiority*): I'll go in an' look at *my* house. (*She goes slowly around to porch.*)

SIMEON (*with a snort*): *Her* house!

PETER (*calls after her*): Ye'll find Eben inside. Ye better not tell him it's *yewr* house.

ABBIE (*mouthing the name*): Eben. (*Then quietly.*) I'll tell Eben.

CABOT (*with a contemptuous sneer*): Ye needn't heed Eben. Eben's a dumb fool — like his Maw — soft an' simple!

SIMEON (*with his sardonic burst of laughter*): Ha! Eben's a chip o' yew — spit 'n' image — hard 'n' bitter's a hickory tree! Dog'll eat dog. He'll eat ye yet, old man!

CABOT (*commandingly*): Ye git t' wuk.

SIMEON (*as Abbie disappears in house — winks at Peter and says tauntingly*): So that thar's our new Maw, be it? Whar in hell did ye dig her up? (*He and Peter laugh.*)

PETER: Ha! Ye'd better turn her in the pen with the other sows. (*They laugh uproariously, slapping their thighs.*)

CABOT (*so amazed at their effrontery that he stutters in confusion*): Simeon! Peter! What's come over ye? Air ye drunk?

SIMEON: We're free, old man — free o' yew an' the hull damned farm! (*They grow more and more hilarious and excited.*)

PETER: An' we're startin' out fur the gold fields o' Californi-a!

SIMEON: Ye kin take this place an' burn it!

PETER: An' bury it — fur all we cares!

SIMEON: We're free, old man! (*He cuts a caper.*)

PETER: Free! (*He gives a kick in the air.*)

SIMEON (*in a frenzy*): Whoop!

PETER: Whoop! (*They do an absurd Indian war dance about the old man who is petrified between rage and the fear that they are insane.*)

SIMEON: We're free as Injuns! Lucky we don't skulp ye!

PETER: An' burn yer barn an' kill the stock!

SIMEON: An' rape yer new woman! Whoop! (*He and Peter stop their dance, holding their sides, rocking with wild laughter.*)

CABOT (*edging away*): Lust fur gold — fur the sinful, easy gold o' Californi-a! It's made ye mad!

SIMEON (*tauntingly*): Wouldn't ye like us to send ye back some sinful gold, ye old sinner?

PETER: They's gold besides what's in Californi-a! (*He retreats back beyond the vision of the old man and takes the bag of money and flaunts it in the air above his head, laughing.*)

SIMEON: And sinfuller, too!

PETER: We'll be voyagin' on the sea! Whoop! (*He leaps up and down.*)

SIMEON: Livin' free! Whoop! (*He leaps in turn.*)

CABOT (*suddenly roaring with rage*): My cuss on ye!

SIMEON: Take our'n in trade fur it! Whoop!

CABOT: I'll hev ye both chained up in the asylum!

PETER: Ye old skinflint! Good-by!

SIMEON: Ye old blood sucker! Good-by!

CABOT: Go afore I . . . !

PETER: Whoop! (*He picks a stone from the road. Simeon does the same.*)

SIMEON: Maw'll be in the parlor.

PETER: Ay-eh! One! Two!

CABOT (*frightened*): What air ye . . . ?

PETER: Three! (*They both throw, the stones hitting the parlor window with a crash of glass, tearing the shade.*)

SIMEON: Whoop!

PETER: Whoop!

CABOT (*in a fury now, rushing toward them*): If I kin lay hands on ye — I'll break yer bones fur ye! (*But they beat a capering retreat before him, Simeon with the gate still under his arm. Cabot comes back, panting with impotent rage. Their voices as they go off take up the song of the gold-seekers to the old tune of "Oh, Susannah!"*)

"I jumped aboard the Liza ship,
And traveled on the sea,
And every time I thought of home
I wished it wasn't me!
Oh! Californi-a,
That's the land fur me!
I'm off to Californi-a!
With my wash bowl on my knee."

(*In the meantime, the window of the upper bedroom on right is raised and Abbie sticks her head out. She looks down at Cabot — with a sigh of relief.*)

ABBIE: Waal — that's the last o' them two, hain't it? (*He doesn't answer. Then in possessive tones.*) This here's a nice bedroom, Ephraim. It's a r'al nice bed. Is it my room, Ephraim?

CABOT (*grimly — without looking up*): Our'n! (*She cannot control a grimace of aversion and pulls back her head slowly and shuts the window. A sudden horrible thought seems to enter Cabot's head.*) They been up to somethin'! Mebbe — mebbe they've pizened the stock — 'r somethin'! (*He almost runs off down toward the barn. A moment later the kitchen door is slowly pushed open and Abbie enters. For a moment she stands looking at Eben. He does not notice her at first. Her eyes take him in penetratingly with a calculating appraisal of his strength as against hers. But under this her desire is dimly awakened by his youth and good looks. Suddenly he becomes conscious of her presence and looks up. Their eyes meet. He leaps to his feet, glowering at her speechlessly.*)

ABBIE (*in her most seductive tones which she uses all through this scene*): Be you — Eben? I'm Abbie — (*She laughs.*) I mean, I'm yer new Maw.

EBEN (*viciously*): No, damn ye!

ABBIE (*as if she hadn't heard — with a queer smile*): Yer Paw's spoke a lot o' yew. . . .

EBEN: Ha!

ABBIE: Ye mustn't mind him. He's an old man. (*A long pause. They stare at each other.*) I don't want t' pretend playin' Maw t' ye, Eben. (*Admiringly.*) Ye're too big an' too strong fur that. I want t' be frens with ye. Mebbe with me fur a fren ye'd find ye'd like livin' here better. I kin make it easy fur ye with him, mebbe. (*With a scornful sense of power.*) I calc'late I kin git him t' do most anythin' fur me.

EBEN (*with bitter scorn*): Ha! (*They stare again, Eben obscurely moved, physically attracted to her — in forced stilted tones.*) Yew kin go t' the devil!

ABBIE (*calmly*): If cussin' me does ye good, cuss all ye've a mind t'. I'm all prepared t' have ye agin me — at fust. I don't blame ye nuther. I'd feel the same at any stranger comin' t' take my Maw's place. (*He shudders. She is watching him carefully.*) Yew must've cared a lot fur yewr Maw, didn't ye? My Maw died afore I'd growed. I don't remember her none. (*A pause.*) But yew won't hate me long, Eben. I'm not the wust in the world — an' yew an' me've got a lot in common. I kin tell that by lookin' at ye. Waal — I've had a hard life, too — oceans o' trouble an' nuthin' but wuk fur reward. I was a orphan early an' had t' wuk fur others in other folks' hums. Then I married an' he turned out a drunken spreer an' so he had to wuk fur others an' me too agen in other folks' hums, an' the baby died, an' my husband got sick an' died too, an' I was glad sayin' now I'm free fur once, on'y I diskivered right away all I was free fur was t' wuk agen in other folks' hums, doin' other folks' wuk till I'd most give up hope o' ever doin' my own wuk in my own hum, an' then your Paw come. . . . (*Cabot appears returning from the barn. He comes to the gate and looks down the road the brothers have gone. A faint strain of their retreating voices is heard: "Oh, Californi-a! That's the place for me." He stands glowering, his fist clenched, his face grim with rage.*)

EBEN (*fighting against his growing attraction and sympathy — harshly*): An' bought yew — like a harlot! (*She is stung and flushes angrily. She has been sincerely moved by the recital of her troubles. He adds furiously.*) An' the price he's payin' ye — this farm — was my Maw's, damn ye! — an' mine now!

ABBIE (*with a cool laugh of confidence*): Yewr'n? We'll see 'bout that! (*Then strongly.*) Waal — what if I did need a hum? What else'd I marry an old man like him fur?

EBEN (*maliciously*): I'll tell him ye said that!

ABBIE (*smiling*): I'll say ye're lyin' a-purpose — an' he'll drive ye off the place!

EBEN: Ye devil!

ABBIE (*defying him*): This be my farm — this be my hum — this be my kitchen —!

EBEN (*furiously, as if he were going to attack her*): Shut up, damn ye!

ABBIE (*walks up to him — a queer coarse expression of desire in her face and body — slowly*): An' upstairs — that be my bedroom — an' my bed! (*He stares into her eyes, terribly confused and torn. She adds softly.*) I hain't bad nor mean — 'ceptin' fur an enemy — but I got t' fight fur what's due me out o' life, if I ever 'spect t' git it. (*Then putting her hand on his arm — seductively.*) Let's yew 'n' me be frens, Eben.

EBEN (*stupidly — as if hypnotized*): Ay-eh. (*Then furiously flinging off her arm.*) No, ye durned old witch! I hate ye! (*He rushes out the door.*)

ABBIE (*looks after him smiling satisfiedly — then half to herself, mouthing the word*): Eben's nice. (*She looks at the table, proudly.*) I'll wash up *my* dishes now. (*Eben appears outside, slamming the door behind him. He comes around corner, stops on seeing his father, and stands staring at him with hate.*)

CABOT (*raising his arms to heaven in the fury he can no longer control*): Lord God o' Hosts, smite the undutiful sons with Thy wust cuss!

EBEN (*breaking in violently*): Yew 'n' yewr God! Allus cussin' folks — allus naggin' 'em!

CABOT (*oblivious to him — summoningly*): God o' the old! God o' the lonesome!

EBEN (*mockingly*): Naggin' His sheep t' sin! T' hell with yewr God! (*Cabot turns. He and Eben glower at each other.*)

CABOT (*harshly*): So it's yew. I might've knowed it. (*Shaking his finger threateningly at him.*) Blasphemin' fool! (*Then quickly.*) Why hain't ye t' wuk?

EBEN: Why hain't yew? They've went. I can't wuk it all alone.

CABOT (*contemptuously*): Nor noways! I'm wuth ten o' ye yit, old's I be! Ye'll never be more'n half a man! (*Then, matter-of-factly.*) Waal — let's git t' the barn. (*They go. A last faint note of the "Californi-a" song is heard from the distance. Abbie is washing her dishes.*)

PART II • Scene I

(*The exterior of the farmhouse, as in Part I — a hot Sunday afternoon two months later. Abbie, dressed in her best, is discovered sitting in a rocker at the end of the porch. She rocks listlessly, enervated by the heat, staring in front of her with bored, half-closed eyes.*)

(*Eben sticks his head out of his bedroom window. He looks around furtively and tries to see — or hear — if anyone is on the porch, but although he has been careful to make no noise, Abbie has sensed his movement. She stops rocking, her face grows animated and eager, she waits attentively. Eben seems to feel her presence, he scowls back his thoughts of her and spits with exaggerated disdain — then withdraws back into the room. Abbie waits, holding her breath as she listens with passionate eagerness for every sound within the house.*)

(*Eben comes out. Their eyes meet; his falter. He is confused, he turns away and slams the door resentfully. At this gesture, Abbie laughs tantalizingly, amused but at the same time piqued and irritated. He scowls, strides off the porch to the path and starts to walk past her to the road with a grand swagger of ignoring her existence. He is dressed in his store suit, spruced up, his face shines from soap and water. Abbie leans forward on her chair, her eyes hard and angry now, and, as he passes her, gives a sneering, taunting chuckle.*)

EBEN (*stung — turns on her furiously*): What air yew cacklin' 'bout?

ABBIE (*triumphant*): Yew!

EBEN: What about me?

ABBIE: Ye look all slicked up like a prize bull.

EBEN (*with a sneer*): Waal — ye hain't so durned purty yerself, be ye? (*They stare into each other's eyes, his held by hers in spite of himself, hers glowingly possessive. Their physical attraction becomes a palpable force quivering in the hot air.*)

ABBIE (*softly*): Ye don't mean that, Eben. Ye may think ye mean it, mebbe, but ye don't. Ye can't. It's agin nature, Eben. Ye been fightin' yer nature ever since the day I come — tryin' t' tell yerself I hain't purty t'ye. (*She laughs a low humid laugh without taking her eyes from his. A pause — her body squirms desirously — she murmurs languorously.*) Hain't the sun strong an' hot? Ye kin feel it burnin' into the earth — Nature — makin' thin's grow — bigger 'n' bigger — burnin' inside ye — makin' ye want t' grow — into somethin' else — till ye're jined with it — an' it's your'n — but it owns ye, too — an' makes ye grow bigger — like a tree — like them elums — (*She laughs again softly, holding his eyes. He takes a step toward her, compelled against his will.*) Nature'll beat ye, Eben. Ye might's well own up t' it fust 's last.

EBEN (*trying to break from her spell — confusedly*): If Paw'd hear us goin' on. . . . (*Resentfully.*) But ye've made such a damned idjit out o' the old devil . . .! (*Abbie laughs.*)

ABBIE: Waal — hain't it easier fur yew with him changed softer?

EBEN (*defiantly*): No. I'm fightin' him — fightin' yew — fightin' fur Maw's rights t' her hum! (*This breaks her spell for him. He glowers at her.*) An' I'm onto ye. Ye hain't foolin' me a mite. Ye're aimin' t' swaller up everythin' an' make it your'n. Waal, you'll find I'm a heap sight bigger hunk nor yew kin chew! (*He turns from her with a sneer.*)

ABBIE (*trying to regain her ascendancy — seductively*): Eben!

EBEN: Leave me be! (*He starts to walk away.*)

ABBIE (*more commandingly*): Eben!

EBEN (*stops — resentfully*): What d'ye want?

ABBIE (*trying to conceal a growing excitement*): Whar air ye goin'?

EBEN (*with malicious nonchalance*): Oh — up the road a spell.

ABBIE: T' the village?

EBEN (*airily*): Mebbe.

ABBIE (*excitedly*): T' see that Min, I s'pose?

EBEN: Mebbe.

ABBIE (*weakly*): What d'ye want t' waste time on her fur?

EBEN (*revenging himself now — grinning at her*): Ye can't beat Nature, didn't ye say? (*He laughs and again starts to walk away.*)

ABBIE (*bursting out*): An ugly old hake!

EBEN (*with a tantalizing sneer*): She's purtier'n yew be!

ABBIE: That every wuthless drunk in the country has. . . .

EBEN (*tauntingly*): Mebbe — but she's better'n yew. She owns up fa'r 'n' squar' t' her doin's.

ABBIE (*furiously*): Don't ye dare compare. . . .

EBEN: She don't go sneakin' an' stealin' — what's mine.

ABBIE (*savagely seizing on his weak point*): Your'n? Yew mean — my farm?

EBEN: I mean the farm yew sold yerself fur like any other old whore — my farm!

ABBIE (*stung — fiercely*): Ye'll never live t' see the day when even a stinkin' weed on it'll belong t' ye! (*Then in a scream.*) Git out o' my sight! Go on t' yer slut — disgracin' yer Paw 'n' me! I'll git yer Paw t' horsewhip ye off the place if I want t'! Ye're only livin' here 'cause I tolerate ye! Git along! I hate the sight o' ye! (*She stops, panting and glaring at him.*)

EBEN (*returning her glance in kind*): An' I hate the sight o' yew! (*He turns and strides off up the road. She follows his retreating figure with concentrated hate. Old Cabot appears coming up from the barn. The hard, grim expression of his face has changed. He seems in some queer way softened, mellowed. His eyes have taken on a strange, incongruous dreamy quality. Yet there is no hint of physical weakness about him — rather he looks more robust and younger. Abbie sees him and turns away quickly with unconcealed aversion. He comes slowly up to her.*)

CABOT (*mildly*): War yew an' Eben quarrelin' agen?

ABBIE (*shortly*): No.

CABOT: Ye was talkin' a'mighty loud. (*He sits down on the edge of porch.*)

ABBIE (*snappishly*): If ye heerd us they hain't no need askin' questions.

CABOT: I didn't hear what ye said.

ABBIE (*relieved*): Waal — it wa'n't nothin' t' speak on.

CABOT (*after a pause*): Eben's queer.

ABBIE (*bitterly*): He's the dead spit 'n' image o' yew!

CABOT (*queerly interested*): D'ye think so, Abbie? (*After a pause, ruminatingly.*) Me 'n' Eben's allus fit 'n' fit. I never could b'ar him noways. He's so thunderin' soft — like his Maw.

ABBIE (*scornfully*): Ay-eh! 'Bout as soft as yew be!

CABOT (*as if he hadn't heard*): Mebbe I been too hard on him.

ABBIE (*jeeringly*): Waal — ye're gittin' soft now — soft as slop! That's what Eben was sayin'.

CABOT (*his face instantly grim and ominous*): Eben was sayin'? Waal, he'd best not do nothin' t' try me 'r he'll soon diskiver. . . . (*A pause. She keeps her face turned away. His gradually softens. He stares up at the sky.*) Purty, hain't it?

ABBIE (*crossly*): I don't see nothin' purty.

CABOT: The sky. Feels like a wa'm field up thar.

ABBIE (*sarcastically*): Air yew aimin' t' buy up over the farm too? (*She snickers contemptuously.*)

CABOT (*strangely*): I'd like t' own my place up thar. (*A pause.*) I'm gittin' old, Abbie. I'm gittin' ripe on the bough. (*A pause. She stares at him mystified. He goes on.*) It's allus lonesome cold in the house — even when it's bilin' hot outside. Hain't yew noticed?

ABBIE: No.

CABOT: It's wa'm down t' the barn — nice smellin' an' warm — with the cows. (*A pause.*) Cows is queer.

ABBIE: Like yew?

CABOT: Like Eben. (*A pause.*) I'm gittin' t' feel resigned t' Eben — jest as I got t' feel 'bout his Maw. I'm gittin' t' learn to b'ar his softness — jest like her'n. I calc'late I c'd a'most take t' him — if he wa'n't sech a dumb fool! (*A pause.*) I s'pose it's old age a-creepin' in my bones.

ABBIE (*indifferently*): Waal — ye hain't dead yet.

CABOT (*roused*): No, I hain't, yew bet — not by a hell of a sight — I'm sound 'n' tough as hickory! (*Then moodily.*) But arter three score and ten the Lord warns ye t' prepare. (*A pause.*) That's why Eben's come in my head. Now that his cussed sinful brothers is gone their path t' hell, they's no one left but Eben.

ABBIE (*resentfully*): They's me, hain't they? (*Agitatedly.*) What's all this sudden likin' ye've tuk to Eben? Why don't ye say nothin' 'bout me? Hain't I yer lawful wife?

CABOT (*simply*): Ay-eh. Ye be. (*A pause — he stares at her desirously — his eyes grow avid — then with a sudden movement he seizes her hands and squeezes them, declaiming in a queer camp meeting preacher's tempo.*) Yew air my Rose o' Sharon! Behold, yew air fair; yer eyes air doves; yer lips air like scarlet; yer two breasts air like two fawns; yer navel be like a round goblet; yer belly be like a heap o' wheat. . . . (*He covers her hand with kisses. She does not seem to notice. She stares before her with hard angry eyes.*)

ABBIE (*jerking her hands away — harshly*): So ye're plannin' t' leave the farm t' Eben, air ye?

CABOT (*dazedly*): Leave . . . ? (*Then with resentful obstinacy.*) I hain't a-givin' it t' no one!

ABBIE (*remorselessly*): Ye can't take it with ye.

CABOT (*thinks a moment — then reluctantly*): No, I calc'late not. (*After a pause — with a strange passion.*) But if I could, I would, by the Eternal! 'R if I could, in my dyin' hour, I'd set it afire an' watch it burn — this house an' every ear o' corn an' every tree down t' the last blade o' hay! I'd sit an' know it was all a-dying with me an' no one else'd ever own what was mine, what I'd made out o' nothin' with my own sweat 'n' blood! (*A pause — then he adds with a queer affection.*) 'Ceptin' the cows. Them I'd turn free.

ABBIE (*harshly*): An' me?

CABOT (*with a queer smile*): Ye'd be turned free, too.

ABBIE (*furiously*): So that's the thanks I git fur marryin' ye — t' have ye change kind to Eben who hates ye, an' talk o' turnin' me out in the road.

CABOT (*hastily*): Abbie! Ye know I wa'n't. . . .

ABBIE (*vengefully*): Just let me tell ye a thing or two 'bout Eben! Whar's he gone? T' see that harlot, Min! I tried fur t' stop him. Disgracin' yew an' me — on the Sabbath, too!

CABOT (*rather guiltily*): He's a sinner — nateral-born. It's lust eatin' his heart.

ABBIE (*enraged beyond endurance — wildly vindictive*): An' his lust fur me! Kin ye find excuses fur that?

CABOT (*stares at her — after a dead pause*): Lust — fur yew?

ABBIE (*defiantly*): He was tryin' t' make love t' me — when ye heerd us quarrelin'.

CABOT (*stares at her — then a terrible expression of rage comes over his face — he springs to his feet shaking all over*): By the A'mighty God — I'll end him!

ABBIE (*frightened now for Eben*): No! Don't ye!

CABOT (*violently*): I'll git the shotgun an' blow his soft brains t' the top o' them elums!

ABBIE (*throwing her arms around him*): No, Ephraim!

CABOT (*pushing her away violently*): I will, by God!

ABBIE (*in a quieting tone*): Listen, Ephraim. 'Twa'n't nothin' bad — on'y a boy's foolin' — 'twa'n't meant serious — jest jokin' an' teasin'. . . .

CABOT: Then why did ye say — lust?

ABBIE: It must hev sounded wusser'n I meant. An' I was mad at thinkin' — ye'd leave him the farm.

CABOT (*quieter but still grim and cruel*): Waal then, I'll horsewhip him off the place if that much'll content ye.

ABBIE (*reaching out and taking his hand*): No. Don't think o' me! Ye mustn't drive him off. 'Tain't sensible. Who'll ye get to help ye on the farm? They's no one hereabouts.

CABOT (*considers this — then nodding his appreciation*): Ye got a head on ye. (*Then irritably.*) Waal, let him stay. (*He sits down on the edge of the porch. She sits beside him. He murmurs contemptuously.*) I oughtn't t' git riled so — at that 'ere fool calf. (*A pause.*) But har's the p'int. What son o' mine'll keep on here t' the farm — when the Lord does call me? Simeon an' Peter air gone t' hell — an' Eben's follerin' 'em.

ABBIE: They's me.

CABOT: Ye're on'y a woman.

ABBIE: I'm yewr wife.

CABOT: That hain't me. A son is me — my blood — mine. Mine ought t' git mine. An' then it's still mine — even though I be six foot under. D'ye see?

ABBIE (*giving him a look of hatred*): Ay-eh. I see. (*She becomes very thoughtful, her face growing shrewd, her eyes studying Cabot craftily.*)

CABOT: I'm gittin' old — ripe on the bough. (*Then with a sudden forced reassurance.*) Not but what I hain't a hard nut t' crack even yet — an' fur many a year t' come! By the Etarnal, I kin break most o' the young fellers' backs at any kind o' work any day o' the year!

ABBIE (*suddenly*): Mebbe the Lord'll give *us* a son.

CABOT (*turns and stares at her eagerly*): Ye mean — a son — t' me 'n' yew?

ABBIE (*with a cajoling smile*): Ye're a strong man yet, hain't ye? 'Tain't noways impossible, be it? We know that. Why d'ye stare so? Hain't ye never thought o' that afore? I been thinkin' o' it all along. Ay-eh — an' I been prayin' it'd happen, too.

CABOT (*his face growing full of joyous pride and a sort of religious ecstasy*): Ye been prayin', Abbie? — fur a son? — t' us?

ABBIE: Ay-eh. (*With a grim resolution.*) I want a son now.

CABOT (*excitedly clutching both of her hands in his*): It'd be the blessin' o' God, Abbie — the blessin' o' God A'mighty on me — in my old age — in my lonesomeness! They hain't nothin' I wouldn't do fur ye then, Abbie. Ye'd hev on'y t' ask it — anythin' ye'd a mind t'!

ABBIE (*interrupting*): Would ye will the farm t' me then — t' me an' it . . . ?

CABOT (*vehemently*): I'd do anythin' ye axed, I tell ye! I swar it! May I be everlastin' damned t' hell if I wouldn't! (*He sinks to his knees pulling her down with him. He trembles all over with the fervor of his hopes.*) Pray t' the Lord agen, Abbie. It's the Sabbath! I'll jine ye! Two prayers air better nor one. "An' God hearkened unto Rachel"! An' God hearkened unto Abbie! Pray, Abbie! Pray fur him to hearken! (*He bows his head, mumbling. She pretends to do likewise but gives him a side glance of scorn and triumph.*)

Scene II

(*About eight in the evening. The interior of the two bedrooms on the top floor is shown. Eben is sitting on the side of his bed in the room on the left. On account of the heat he has taken off everything but his undershirt and pants. His feet are bare. He faces front, brooding moodily, his chin propped on his hands, a desperate expression on his face.*)

(*In the other room Cabot and Abbie are sitting side by side on the edge of their bed, an old four-poster with feather mattress. He is in his nightshirt, she in her nightdress. He is still in the queer, excited mood into which the notion of a son has thrown him. Both rooms are lighted dimly and flickeringly by tallow candles.*)

CABOT: The farm needs a son.

ABBIE: I need a son.

CABOT: Ay-eh. Sometimes ye air the farm an' sometimes the farm be yew. That's why I clove t' ye in my lonesomeness. (*A pause. He pounds his knee with his fist.*) Me an' the farm has got t' beget a son!

ABBIE: Ye'd best go t' sleep. Ye're gittin' thin's all mixed.

CABOT (*with an impatient gesture*): No, I hain't. My mind's clear's a well. Ye don't know me, that's it. (*He stares hopelessly at the floor.*)

ABBIE (*indifferently*): Mebbe. (*In the next room Eben gets up and paces up and down distractedly. Abbie hears him. Her eyes fasten on the intervening wall with concentrated attention. Eben stops and stares. Their hot glances seem to meet through the wall. Unconsciously he stretches out his arms for her and she half rises. Then aware, he mutters a curse at himself and flings himself face downward on the bed, his clenched fists above his head, his face buried in the pillow. Abbie relaxes with a faint sigh but her eyes remain fixed on the wall; she listens with all her attention for some movement from Eben.*)

CABOT (*suddenly raises his head and looks at her — scornfully*): Will ye ever know me — 'r will any man 'r woman? (*Shaking his head.*) No. I calc'late wa'n't t' be. (*He turns away. Abbie looks at the wall. Then, evidently unable to keep silent about his thoughts, without looking at his wife, he puts out his hand and clutches her knee. She starts violently, looks at him, sees he is not watching her, concentrates again on the wall, and pays no attention to what he says.*) Listen, Abbie. When I come here fifty odd year ago — I was jest twenty an' the strongest an' hardest ye ever seen — ten times as strong an' fifty times as hard as Eben. Waal — this place was nothin' but fields o' stones. Folks laughed when I tuk it. They couldn't know what I knowed. When ye kin make corn sprout out o' stones, God's livin' in yew! They wa'n't strong enuf fur that! They reckoned God was easy. They laughed. They don't laugh no more. Some died hereabouts. Some went West an' died. They're all underground — fur follerin' arter an easy God. God hain't easy. (*He shakes his head slowly.*) An' I growed hard. Folks kept allus sayin' he's a hard man like 'twas sinful t' be hard, so's at last I said back at 'em:

Waal then, by thunder, ye'll git me hard an' see how ye like it! (*Then suddenly.*) But I give in t' weakness once. 'Twas arter I'd been here two year. I got weak — despairful — they was so many stones. They was a party leavin', givin' up, goin' West. I jined 'em. We tracked on 'n' on. We come t' broad medders, plains, whar the soil was black an' rich as gold. Nary a stone. Easy. Ye'd on'y to plow an' sow an' then set an' smoke yer pipe an' watch thin's grow. I could o' been a rich man — but somethin' in me fit me an' fit me — the voice o' God sayin': "This hain't wuth nothin' t' Me. Git ye back t' hum!" I got afeerd o' that voice an' I lit out back t' hum here, leavin' my claim an' crops t' whoever'd a mind t' take 'em. Ay-eh. I actoolly give up what was rightful mine! God's hard, not easy! God's in the stones! Build my church on a rock — out o' stones an' I'll be in them! That's what He meant t' Peter! (*He sighs heavily — a pause.*) Stones. I picked 'em up an' piled 'em into walls. Ye kin read the years of my life in them walls, every day a hefted stone, climbin' over the hills up and down, fencin' in the fields that was mine, whar I'd made thin's grow out o' nothin' — like the will o' God, like the servant o' His hand. It wa'n't easy. It was hard an' He made me hard fur it. (*He pauses.*) All the time I kept gittin' lonesomer. I tuk a wife. She bore Simeon an' Peter. She was a good woman. She wuked hard. We was married twenty year. She never knowed me. She helped but she never knowed what she was helpin'. I was allus lonesome. She died. After that it wa'n't so lonesome fur a spell. (*A pause.*) I lost count o' the years. I had no time t' fool away countin' 'em. Sim an' Peter helped. The farm growed. It was all mine! When I thought o' that I didn't feel lonesome. (*A pause.*) But ye can't hitch yer mind t' one thin' day an' night. I tuk another wife — Eben's Maw. Her folks was contestin' me at law over my deeds t' the farm — my farm! That's why Eben keeps a-talkin' his fool talk o' this bein' his Maw's farm. She bore Eben. She was purty — but soft. She tried t' be hard. She couldn't. She never knowed me nor nothin'. It was lonesomer 'n hell with her. After a matter o' sixteen odd years, she died. (*A pause.*) I lived with the boys. They hated me 'cause I was hard. I hated them 'cause they was soft. They coveted the farm without knowin' what it meant. It made me bitter 'n wormwood. It aged me — them coveting what I'd made fur mine. Then this spring the call come — the voice o' God cryin' in my wilderness, in my lonesomeness — t' go out an' seek an' find! (*Turning to her with strange passion.*) I sought ye an' I found ye! Yew air my Rose o' Sharon! Yer eyes air like. . . . (*She has turned a blank face,*

resentful eyes to his. He stares at her for a moment — then harshly.*) Air ye any the wiser fur all I've told ye?

ABBIE (*confusedly*): Mebbe.

CABOT (*pushing her away from him — angrily*): Ye don't know nothin' — nor never will. If ye don't hev a son t' redeem ye. . . . (*This in a tone of cold threat.*)

ABBIE (*resentfully*): I've prayed, hain't I?

CABOT (*bitterly*): Pray agen — fur understandin'!

ABBIE (*a veiled threat in her tone*): Ye'll have a son out o' me, I promise ye.

CABOT: How kin ye promise?

ABBIE: I got second-sight mebbe. I kin foretell. (*She gives a queer smile.*)

CABOT: I believe ye have. Ye give me the chills sometimes. (*He shivers.*) It's cold in this house. It's oneasy. They's thin's pokin' about in the dark — in the corners. (*He pulls on his trousers, tucking in his nightshirt, and pulls on his boots.*)

ABBIE (*surprised*): Whar air ye goin'?

CABOT (*queerly*): Down whar it's restful — whar it's warm — down t' the barn. (*Bitterly.*) I kin talk t' the cows. They know. They know the farm an' me. They'll give me peace. (*He turns to go out the door.*)

ABBIE (*a bit frightenedly*): Air ye ailin' tonight, Ephraim?

CABOT: Growin'. Growin' ripe on the bough. (*He turns and goes, his boots clumping down the stairs. Eben sits up with a start, listening. Abbie is conscious of his movement and stares at the wall. Cabot comes out of the house around the corner and stands by the gate, blinking at the sky. He stretches up his hands in a tortured gesture.*) God A'mighty, call from the dark! (*He listens as if expecting an answer. Then his arms drop, he shakes his head and plods off toward the barn. Eben and Abbie stare at each other through the wall. Eben sighs heavily and Abbie echoes it. Both become terribly nervous, uneasy. Finally Abbie gets up and listens, her ear to the wall. He acts as if he saw every move she was making, he becomes resolutely still. She seems driven into a decision — goes out the door in rear determinedly. His eyes follow her. Then as the door of his room is opened softly, he turns away, waits in an attitude of strained fixity. Abbie stands for a second staring at him, her eyes burning with desire. Then with a little cry she runs over and throws her arms about his neck, she pulls his head back and covers his mouth with kisses. At first, he submits dumbly; then he puts his arms about her neck and returns her kisses, but finally, suddenly aware of his hatred, he hurls her away from him, springing to his feet. They stand speechless and breathless, panting like two animals.*)

ABBIE (*at last — painfully*): Ye shouldn't, Eben — ye shouldn't — I'd make ye happy!

EBEN (*harshly*): I don't want t' be happy — from yew!

ABBIE (*helplessly*): Ye do, Eben! Ye do! Why d'ye lie?

EBEN (*viciously*): I don't take t'ye, I tell ye! I hate the sight o' ye!

ABBIE (*with an uncertain troubled laugh*): Waal, I kissed ye anyways — an' ye kissed back — yer lips was burnin' — ye can't lie 'bout that! (*Intensely.*) If ye don't care, why did ye kiss me back — why was yer lips burnin'?

EBEN (*wiping his mouth*): It was like pizen on 'em. (*Then tauntingly.*) When I kissed ye back, mebbe I thought 'twas someone else.

ABBIE (*wildly*): Min?

EBEN: Mebbe.

ABBIE (*torturedly*): Did ye go t' see her? Did ye r'ally go? I thought ye mightn't. Is that why ye throwed me off jest now?

EBEN (*sneeringly*): What if it be?

ABBIE (*raging*): Then ye're a dog, Eben Cabot!

EBEN (*threateningly*): Ye can't talk that way t' me!

ABBIE (*with a shrill laugh*): Can't I? Did ye think I was in love with ye — a weak thin' like yew? Not much! I on'y wanted ye fur a purpose o' my own — an' I'll hev ye fur it yet 'cause I'm stronger'n yew be!

EBEN (*resentfully*): I knowed well it was on'y part o' yer plan t' swaller everythin'!

ABBIE (*tauntingly*): Mebbe!

EBEN (*furious*): Git out o' my room!

ABBIE: This air my room an' ye're on'y hired help!

EBEN (*threateningly*): Git out afore I murder ye!

ABBIE (*quite confident now*): I hain't a mite afeerd. Ye want me, don't ye? Yes, ye do! An' yer Paw's son'll never kill what he wants! Look at yer eyes! They's lust fur me in 'em, burnin' 'em up! Look at yer lips now! They're tremblin' an' longin' t' kiss me, an' yer teeth t' bite! (*He is watching her now with a horrible fascination. She laughs a crazy triumphant laugh.*) I'm a-goin' t' make all o' this hum my hum! They's one room hain't mine yet, but it's a-goin' t' be tonight. I'm a-goin' down now an' light up! (*She makes him a mocking bow.*) Won't ye come courtin' me in the best parlor, Mister Cabot?

EBEN (*staring at her — horribly confused — dully*): Don't ye dare! It hain't been opened since Maw died an' was laid out thar! Don't ye . . . ! (*But her eyes are fixed on his so burningly that his will seems to wither before hers. He stands swaying toward her helplessly.*)

ABBIE (*holding his eyes and putting all her will into her words as she backs out the door*): I'll expect ye afore long, Eben.

EBEN (*Stares after her for a while, walking toward the door. A light appears in the parlor window. He murmurs.*): In the parlor? (*This seems to arouse connotations, for he comes back and puts on his white shirt, collar, half ties the tie mechanically, puts on coat, takes his hat, stands barefooted looking about him in bewilderment, mutters wonderingly.*) Maw! Whar air yew? (*Then goes slowly toward the door in rear.*)

Scene III

(*A few minutes later. The interior of the parlor is shown. A grim, repressed room like a tomb in which the family has been interred alive. Abbie sits on the edge of the horsehair sofa. She has lighted all the candles and the room is revealed in all its preserved ugliness. A change has come over the woman. She looks awed and frightened now, ready to run away.*)

(*The door is opened and Eben appears. His face wears an expression of obsessed confusion. He stands staring at her, his arms hanging disjointedly from his shoulders, his feet bare, his hat in his hand.*)

ABBIE (*after a pause — with a nervous, formal politeness*): Won't ye set?

EBEN (*dully*): Ay-eh. (*Mechanically he places his hat carefully on the floor near the door and sits stiffly beside her on the edge of the sofa. A pause. They both remain rigid, looking straight ahead with eyes full of fear.*)

ABBIE: When I fust come in — in the dark — they seemed somethin' here.

EBEN (*simply*): Maw.

ABBIE: I kin still feel — somethin'. . . .

EBEN: It's Maw.

ABBIE: At fust I was feered o' it. I wanted t' yell an' run. Now — since yew come — seems like it's growin' soft an' kind t' me. (*Addressing the air — queerly.*) Thank yew.

EBEN: Maw allus loved me.

ABBIE: Mebbe it knows I love yew, too. Mebbe that makes it kind t' me.

EBEN (*dully*): I dunno. I should think she'd hate ye.

ABBIE (*with certainty*): No. I kin feel it don't — not no more.

EBEN: Hate ye fur stealin' her place — here in her hum — settin' in her parlor whar she was laid — (*He suddenly stops, staring stupidly before him.*)

ABBIE: What is it, Eben?

EBEN (*in a whisper*): Seems like Maw didn't want me t' remind ye.

ABBIE (*excitedly*): I knowed, Eben! It's kind t' me! It don't b'ar me no grudges fur what I never knowed an' couldn't help!

EBEN: Maw b'ars him a grudge.

ABBIE: Waal, so does all o' us.

EBEN: Ay-eh. (*With passion.*) I does, by God!

ABBIE (*taking one of his hands in hers and patting it*): Thar! Don't git riled thinkin' o' him. Think o' yer Maw who's kind t' us. Tell me about yer Maw, Eben.

EBEN: They hain't nothin' much. She was kind. She was good.

ABBIE (*Putting one arm over his shoulder. He does not seem to notice — passionately.*): I'll be kind an' good t' ye!

EBEN: Sometimes she used t' sing fur me.

ABBIE: I'll sing fur ye!

EBEN: This was her hum. This was her farm.

ABBIE: This is my hum! This is my farm!

EBEN: He married her t' steal 'em. She was soft an' easy. He couldn't 'preciate her.

ABBIE: He can't 'preciate me!

EBEN: He murdered her with his hardness.

ABBIE: He's murderin' me!

EBEN: She died. (*A pause.*) Sometimes she used to sing fur me. (*He bursts into a fit of sobbing.*)

ABBIE (*both her arms around him — with wild passion*): I'll sing fur ye! I'll die fur ye! (*In spite of her overwhelming desire for him, there is a sincere maternal love in her manner and voice — a horribly frank mixture of lust and mother love.*) Don't cry, Eben! I'll take yer Maw's place! I'll be everythin' she was t' ye! Let me kiss ye, Eben! (*She pulls his head around. He makes a bewildered pretense of resistance. She is tender.*) Don't be afeered! I'll kiss ye pure, Eben — same 's if I was a Maw t' ye — an' ye kin kiss me back 's if yew was my son — my boy — sayin' good-night t' me! Kiss me, Eben. (*They kiss in restrained fashion. Then suddenly wild passion overcomes her. She kisses him lustfully again and again and he flings his arms about her and returns her kisses. Suddenly, as in the bedroom, he frees himself from her violently and springs to his feet. He is trembling all over, in a strange state of terror. Abbie strains her arms toward him with fierce pleading.*) Don't ye leave me, Eben! Can't ye see it hain't enuf — lovin' ye like a Maw — can't ye see it's got t' be that an' more — much more — a hundred times more — fur me t' be happy — fur yew t' be happy?

EBEN (*to the presence he feels in the room*): Maw! Maw! What d'ye want? What air ye tellin' me?

ABBIE: She's tellin' ye t' love me. She knows I love ye an' I'll be good t' ye. Can't ye feel it? Don't ye know? She's tellin' ye t' love me, Eben!

EBEN: Ay-eh. I feel — mebbe she — but — I can't figger out — why — when ye've stole her place — here in her hum — in the parlor whar she was —

ABBIE (*fiercely*): She knows I love ye!

EBEN (*his face suddenly lighting up with a fierce, triumphant grin*): I see it! I sees why. It's her vengeance on him — so's she kin rest quiet in her grave!

ABBIE (*wildly*): Vengeance o' God on the hull o' us! What d'we give a durn? I love ye, Eben! God knows I love ye! (*She stretches out her arms for him.*)

EBEN (*throws himself on his knees beside the sofa and grabs her in his arms — releasing all his pent-up passion*): An' I love ye, Abbie! — now I kin say it! I been dyin' fur want o' ye — every hour since ye come! I love ye! (*Their lips meet in a fierce, bruising kiss.*)

Scene IV

(*Exterior of the farmhouse. It is just dawn. The front door at right is opened and Eben comes out and walks around to the gate. He is dressed in his working clothes. He seems changed. His face wears a bold and confident expression, he is grinning to himself with evident satisfaction. As he gets near the gate, the window of the parlor is heard opening and the shutters are flung back and Abbie sticks her head out. Her hair tumbles over her shoulders in disarray, her face is flushed, she looks at Eben with tender, languorous eyes and calls softly.*)

ABBIE: Eben. (*As he turns — playfully.*) Jest one more kiss afore ye go. I'm goin' to miss ye fearful all day.

EBEN: An' me yew, ye kin bet! (*He goes to her. They kiss several times. He draws away, laughingly.*) Thar. That's enuf, hain't it? Ye won't hev none left fur next time.

ABBIE: I got a million o' 'em left fur yew! (*Then a bit anxiously.*) D'ye r'ally love me, Eben?

EBEN (*emphatically*): I like ye better'n any gal I ever knowed! That's gospel!

ABBIE: Likin' hain't lovin'.

EBEN: Waal then — I love ye. Now air yew satisfied?

ABBIE: Ay-eh, I be. (*She smiles at him adoringly.*)

EBEN: I better git t' the barn. The old critter's liable t' suspicion an' come sneakin' up.

ABBIE (*with a confident laugh*): Let him! I kin allus pull the wool over his eyes. I'm goin' t' leave the shutters open and let in the sun 'n' air. This room's been dead long enuf. Now it's goin' t' be my room!

EBEN (*frowning*): Ay-eh.

ABBIE (*hastily*): I meant — our room.

EBEN: Ay-eh.

ABBIE: We made it our'n last night, didn't we? We give it life — our lovin' did. (*A pause.*)

EBEN (*with a strange look*): Maw's gone back t' her grave. She kin sleep now.

ABBIE: May she rest in peace! (*Then tenderly rebuking.*) Ye oughtn't t' talk o' sad thin's — this mornin'.

EBEN: It jest come up in my mind o' itself.

ABBIE: Don't let it. (*He doesn't answer. She yawns.*) Waal, I'm a-goin' t' steal a wink o' sleep. I'll tell the Old Man I hain't feelin' pert. Let him git his own vittles.

EBEN: I see him comin' from the barn. Ye better look smart an' git upstairs.

ABBIE: Ay-eh. Good-by. Don't ferget me. (*She throws him a kiss. He grins — then squares his shoulders and awaits his father confidently. Cabot walks slowly up from the left, staring up at the sky with a vague face.*)

EBEN (*jovially*): Mornin', Paw. Star-gazin' in daylight?

CABOT: Purty, hain't it?

EBEN (*looking around him possessively*): It's a durned purty farm.

CABOT: I mean the sky.

EBEN (*grinning*): How d'ye know? Them eyes o' your'n can't see that fur. (*This tickles his humor and he slaps his thigh and laughs.*) Ho-ho! That's a good un!

CABOT (*grimly sarcastic*): Ye're feelin' right chipper, hain't ye? Whar'd ye steal the likker?

EBEN (*good-naturedly*): 'Tain't likker. Jest life. (*Suddenly holding out his hand — soberly.*) Yew 'n' me is quits. Let's shake hands.

CABOT (*suspiciously*): What's come over ye?

EBEN: Then don't. Mebbe it's jest as well. (*A moment's pause.*) What's come over me? (*Queerly.*) Didn't ye feel her passin' — goin' back t' her grave?

CABOT (*dully*): Who?

EBEN: Maw. She kin rest now an' sleep content. She's quit with ye.

CABOT (*confusedly*): I rested. I slept good — down with the cows. They know how t' sleep. They're teachin' me.

EBEN (*suddenly jovial again*): Good fur the cows! Waal — ye better git t' work.

CABOT (*grimly amused*): Air yew bossin' me, ye calf?

EBEN (*beginning to laugh*): Ay-eh! I'm bossin' yew! Ha-ha-ha! See how ye like it! Ha-ha-ha! I'm the prize rooster o' this roost. Ha-ha-ha! (*He goes off toward the barn laughing.*)

CABOT (*looks after him with scornful pity*): Soft-headed. Like his Maw. Dead spit 'n' image. No hope in him! (*He spits with contemptuous disgust.*) A born fool! (*Then matter-of-factly.*) Waal — I'm gittin' peckish. (*He goes toward door.*)

PART III · Scene I

(*A night in late spring the following year. The kitchen and the two bedrooms upstairs are shown. The two*

bedrooms are dimly lighted by a tallow candle in each. Eben is sitting on the side of the bed in his room, his chin propped on his fists, his face a study of the struggle he is making to understand his conflicting emotions. The noisy laughter and music from below where a kitchen dance is in progress annoy and distract him. He scowls at the floor.)

(*In the next room a cradle stands beside the double bed.*)

(*In the kitchen all is festivity. The stove has been taken down to give more room to the dancers. The chairs, with wooden benches added, have been pushed back against the walls. On these are seated, squeezed in tight against one another, farmers and their wives and their young folks of both sexes from the neighboring farms. They are all chattering and laughing loudly. They evidently have some secret joke in common. There is no end of winking, of nudging, of meaning nods of the head toward Cabot who, in a state of extreme hilarious excitement increased by the amount he has drunk, is standing near the rear door where there is a small keg of whisky and serving drinks to all the men. In the left corner, front, dividing the attention with her husband, Abbie is sitting in a rocking chair, a shawl wrapped about her shoulders. She is very pale, her face is thin and drawn, her eyes are fixed anxiously on the open door in rear as if waiting for someone.*)

(*The musician is tuning up his fiddle, seated in the far right corner. He is a lanky young fellow with a long, weak face. His pale eyes blink incessantly and he grins about him slyly with a greedy malice.*)

ABBIE (*suddenly turning to a young girl on her right*): Whar's Eben?

YOUNG GIRL (*eyeing her scornfully*): I dunno, Mrs. Cabot. I hain't seen Eben in ages. (*Meaningly.*) Seems like he's spent most o' his time t' hum since yew come.

ABBIE (*vaguely*): I tuk his Maw's place.

YOUNG GIRL: Ay-eh. So I've heerd. (*She turns away to retail this bit of gossip to her mother sitting next to her. Abbie turns to her left to a big stoutish middle-aged man whose flushed face and starting eyes show the amount of "likker" he has consumed.*)

ABBIE: Ye hain't seen Eben, hev ye?

MAN: No, I hain't. (*Then he adds with a wink.*) If yew hain't, who would?

ABBIE: He's the best dancer in the county. He'd ought t' come an' dance.

MAN (*with a wink*): Mebbe he's doin' the dutiful an' walkin' the kid t' sleep. It's a boy, hain't it?

ABBIE (*nodding vaguely*): Ay-eh — born two weeks back — purty's a picter.

MAN: They all is — t' their Maws. (*Then in a whisper,*

with a nudge and a leer.) Listen, Abbie — if ye ever git tired o' Eben, remember me! Don't fergit now! (*He looks at her uncomprehending face for a second — then grunts disgustedly.*) Waal — guess I'll likker agin. (*He goes over and joins Cabot who is arguing noisily with an old farmer over cows. They all drink.*)

ABBIE (*this time appealing to nobody in particular*): Wonder what Eben's a-doin'? (*Her remark is repeated down the line with many a guffaw and titter until it reaches the fiddler. He fastens his blinking eyes on Abbie.*)

FIDDLER (*raising his voice*): Bet I kin tell ye, Abbie, what Eben's doin'! He's down t' the church offerin' up prayers o' thanksgivin'. (*They all titter expectantly.*)

A MAN: What fur? (*Another titter.*)

FIDDLER: 'Cause unto him a — (*He hesitates just long enough.*) brother is born! (*A roar of laughter. They all look from Abbie to Cabot. She is oblivious, staring at the door. Cabot, although he hasn't heard the words, is irritated by the laughter and steps forward, glaring about him. There is an immediate silence.*)

CABOT: What're ye all bleatin' about — like a flock o' goats? Why don't ye dance, damn ye? I axed ye here t' dance — t' eat, drink an' be merry — an' thar ye set cacklin' like a lot o' wet hens with the pip! Ye've swilled my likker an' guzzled my vittles like hogs, hain't ye? Then dance fur me, can't ye? That's fa'r an' squar', hain't it? (*A grumble of resentment goes around but they are all evidently in too much awe of him to express it openly.*)

FIDDLER (*slyly*): We're waitin' fur Eben. (*A suppressed laugh.*)

CABOT (*with a fierce exultation*): T'hell with Eben! Eben's done fur now! I got a new son! (*His mood switching with drunken suddenness.*) But ye needn't t' laugh at Eben, none o' ye! He's my blood, if he be a dumb fool. He's better nor any o' yew! He kin do a day's work a'most up t' what I kin — an' that'd put any o' yew pore critters t' shame!

FIDDLER: An' he kin do a good night's work, too! (*A roar of laughter.*)

CABOT: Laugh, ye damn fools! Ye're right jist the same, Fiddler. He kin work day an' night too, like I kin, if need be!

OLD FARMER (*from behind the keg where he is weaving drunkenly back and forth — with great simplicity*): They hain't many t' touch ye, Ephraim — a son at seventy-six. That's a hard man fur ye! I be on'y sixty-eight an' I couldn't do it. (*A roar of laughter in which Cabot joins uproariously.*)

CABOT (*slapping him on the back*): I'm sorry fur ye, Hi. I'd never suspicion sech weakness from a boy like yew!

OLD FARMER: An' I never reckoned yew had it in ye nuther, Ephraim. (*There is another laugh.*)

CABOT (*suddenly grim*): I got a lot in me — a hell of a lot — folks don't know on. (*Turning to the fiddler.*) Fiddle 'er up, durn ye! Give 'em somethin' t' dance t'! What air ye, an ornament? Hain't this a celebration? Then grease yer elbow an' go it!

FIDDLER (*seizes a drink which the Old Farmer holds out to him and downs it*): Here goes! (*He starts to fiddle "Lady of the Lake." Four young fellows and four girls form in two lines and dance a square dance. The Fiddler shouts directions for the different movements, keeping his words in the rhythm of the music and interspersing them with jocular personal remarks to the dancers themselves. The people seated along the walls stamp their feet and clap their hands in unison. Cabot is especially active in this respect. Only Abbie remains apathetic, staring at the door as if she were alone in a silent room.*)

FIDDLER: Swing your partner t' the right! That's it, Jim! Give her a b'ar hug! Her Maw hain't lookin'. (*Laughter.*) Change partners! That suits ye, don't it, Essie, now ye got Reub afore ye? Look at her redden up, will ye? Waal, life is short an' so's love, as the feller says. (*Laughter.*)

CABOT (*excitedly, stamping his foot*): Go it, boys! Go it, gals!

FIDDLER (*with a wink at the others*): Ye're the spryest seventy-six ever I sees, Ephraim! Now if ye'd on'y good eyesight . . . ! (*Suppressed laughter. He gives Cabot no chance to retort but roars.*) Promenade! Ye're walkin' like a bride down the aisle, Sarah! Waal, while they's life they's allus hope, I've heerd tell. Swing your partner to the left! Gosh A'mighty, look at Johnny Cook high-steppin'! They hain't goin' t' be much strength left fur howin' in the corn lot t'morrow. (*Laughter.*)

CABOT: Go it! Go it! (*Then suddenly, unable to restrain himself any longer, he prances into the midst of the dancers, scattering them, waving his arms about wildly.*) Ye're all hoofs! Git out o' my road! Give me room! I'll show ye dancin'. Ye're all too soft! (*He pushes them roughly away. They crowd back toward the walls, muttering, looking at him resentfully.*)

FIDDLER (*jeeringly*): Go it, Ephraim! Go it! (*He starts "Pop, Goes the Weasel," increasing the tempo with every verse until at the end he is fiddling crazily as fast as he can go.*)

CABOT (*Starts to dance, which he does very well and with tremendous vigor. Then he begins to improvise, cuts incredibly grotesque capers, leaping up and *cracking his heels together, prancing around in a circle with body bent in an Indian war dance, then suddenly straightening up and kicking as high as he can with both legs. He is like a monkey on a string. And all the while he intersperses his antics with shouts and derisive comments.*): Whoop! Here's dancin' fur ye! Whoop! See that! Seventy-six, if I'm a day! Hard as iron yet! Beatin' the young 'uns like I allus done! Look at me! I'd invite ye t' dance on my hundredth birthday on'y ye'll all be dead by then. Ye're a sickly generation! Yer hearts air pink, not red! Yer veins is full o' mud an' water! I be the on'y man in the county! Whoop! See that! I'm a Injun! I've killed Injuns in the West afore ye was born — an' skulped 'em too! They's a arrer wound on my backside I c'd show ye! The hull tribe chased me. I outrun 'em all — with the arrer stuck in me! An' I tuk vengeance on 'em. Ten eyes fur an eye, that was my motter! Whoop! Look at me! I kin kick the ceilin' off the room! Whoop!

FIDDLER (*stops playing — exhaustedly*): God A'mighty, I got enuf. Ye got the devil's strength in ye.

CABOT (*delightedly*): Did I beat yew, too? Waal, ye played smart. Hev a swig. (*He pours whisky for himself and Fiddler. They drink. The others watch Cabot silently with cold, hostile eyes. There is a dead pause. The Fiddler rests. Cabot leans against the keg, panting, glaring around him confusedly. In the room above, Eben gets to his feet and tiptoes out the door in rear, appearing a moment later in the other bedroom. He moves silently, even frightenedly, toward the cradle and stands there looking down at the baby. His face is as vague as his reactions are confused, but there is a trace of tenderness, of interested discovery. At the same moment that he reaches the cradle, Abbie seems to sense something. She gets up weakly and goes to Cabot.*)

ABBIE: I'm goin' up t' the baby.

CABOT (*with real solicitation*): Air ye able fur the stairs? D'ye want me t' help ye, Abbie?

ABBIE: No. I'm able. I'll be down agen soon.

CABOT: Don't ye git wore out! He needs ye, remember — our son does! (*He grins affectionately, patting her on the back. She shrinks from his touch.*)

ABBIE (*dully*): Don't — tech me. I'm goin' — up. (*She goes. Cabot looks after her. A whisper goes around the room. Cabot turns. It ceases. He wipes his forehead streaming with sweat. He is breathing pantingly.*)

CABOT: I'm a-goin' out t' git fresh air. I'm feelin' a mite dizzy. Fiddle up thar! Dance, all o' ye! Here's likker fur them as wants it. Enjoy yerselves. I'll be back. (*He goes, closing the door behind him.*)

FIDDLER (*sarcastically*): Don't hurry none on our account! (*A suppressed laugh. He imitates Abbie.*) Whar's Eben? (*More laughter.*)

A WOMAN (*loudly*): What's happened in this house is plain as the nose on yer face! (*Abbie appears in the doorway upstairs and stands looking in surprise and adoration at Eben who does not see her.*)

A MAN: Ssshh! He's li'ble t' be listenin' at the door. That'd be like him. (*Their voices die to an intensive whispering. Their faces are concentrated on this gossip. A noise as of dead leaves in the wind comes from the room. Cabot has come out from the porch and stands by the gate, leaning on it, staring at the sky blinkingly. Abbie comes across the room silently. Eben does not notice her until quite near.*)

EBEN (*starting*): Abbie!

ABBIE: Ssshh! (*She throws her arms around him. They kiss — then bend over the cradle together.*) Ain't he purty? — dead spit 'n' image o' yew!

EBEN (*pleased*): Air he? I can't tell none.

ABBIE: E-zactly like!

EBEN (*frowningly*): I don't like this. I don't like lettin' on what's mine's his'n. I been doin' that all my life. I'm gittin' t' the end o' b'arin' it!

ABBIE (*putting her finger on his lips*): We're doin' the best we kin. We got t' wait. Somethin's bound t' happen. (*She puts her arms around him.*) I got t' go back.

EBEN: I'm goin' out. I can't b'ar it with the fiddle playin' an' the laughin'.

ABBIE: Don't git feelin' low. I love ye, Eben. Kiss me. (*He kisses her. They remain in each other's arms.*)

CABOT (*at the gate, confusedly*): Even the music can't drive it out — somethin'. Ye kin feel it droppin' off the elums, climbin' up the roof, sneakin' down the chimney, pokin' in the corners! They's no peace in houses, they's no rest livin' with folks. Somethin's always livin' with ye. (*With a deep sigh.*) I'll go t' the barn an' rest a spell. (*He goes wearily toward the barn.*)

FIDDLER (*tuning up*): Let's celebrate the old skunk gittin' fooled! We kin have some fun now he's went. (*He starts to fiddle "Turkey in the Straw." There is real merriment now. The young folks get up to dance.*)

Scene II

(*A half hour later — exterior — Eben is standing by the gate looking up at the sky, an expression of dumb pain bewildered by itself on his face. Cabot appears, returning from the barn, walking wearily, his eyes on the ground. He sees Eben and his whole mood immediately changes. He becomes excited, a cruel, triumphant grin comes to his lips, he strides up and slaps*

Eben on the back. From within comes the whining of the fiddle and the noise of stamping feet and laughing voices.)

CABOT: So har ye be!

EBEN (*startled, stares at him with hatred for a moment — then dully*): Ay-eh.

CABOT (*surveying him jeeringly*): Why hain't ye been in t' dance? They was all axin' fur ye.

EBEN: Let 'em ax!

CABOT: They's a hull passel o' purty gals.

EBEN: T' hell with 'em!

CABOT: Ye'd ought t' be marryin' one o' 'em soon.

EBEN: I hain't marryin' no one.

CABOT: Ye might 'arn a share o' a farm that way.

EBEN (*with a sneer*): Like yew did, ye mean? I hain't that kind.

CABOT (*stung*): Ye lie! 'Twas yer Maw's folks aimed t' steal my farm from me.

EBEN: Other folks don't say so. (*After a pause — defiantly.*) An' I got a farm, anyways!

CABOT (*derisively*): Whar?

EBEN (*stamps a foot on the ground*): Har!

CABOT (*throws his head back and laughs coarsely*): Ho-ho! Ye hev, hev ye? Waal, that's a good un!

EBEN (*controlling himself — grimly*): Ye'll see!

CABOT (*stares at him suspiciously, trying to make him out — a pause — then with scornful confidence*): Ay-eh. I'll see. So'll ye. It's ye that's blind — blind as a mole underground. (*Eben suddenly laughs, one short sardonic bark: "Ha." A pause. Cabot peers at him with renewed suspicion.*) What air ye hawin' 'bout? (*Eben turns away without answering. Cabot grows angry.*) God A'mighty, yew air a dumb dunce! They's nothin' in that thick skull o' your'n but noise — like an empty keg it be! (*Eben doesn't seem to hear. Cabot's rage grows.*) Yewr farm! God A'mighty! If ye wa'n't a born donkey ye'd know ye'll never own stick nor stone on it, specially now arter him bein' born. It's his'n, I tell ye — his'n arter I die — but I'll live a hundred jest t' fool ye all — an' he'll be growed then — yewr age a'most! (*Eben laughs again his sardonic "Ha." This drives Cabot into a fury.*) Ha? Ye think ye kin git 'round that someways, do ye? Waal, it'll be her'n, too — Abbie's — ye won't git 'round her — she knows yer tricks — she'll be too much fur ye — she wants the farm her'n — she was afeerd o' ye — she told me ye was sneakin' 'round tryin' t' make love t' her t' git her on yer side . . . ye . . . ye mad fool, ye! (*He raises his clenched fists threateningly.*)

EBEN (*is confronting him, choking with rage*): Ye lie, ye old skunk! Abbie never said no sech thing!

CABOT (*suddenly triumphant when he sees how shaken Eben is*): She did. An' I says, I'll blow his brains

t' the top o' them elums — an' she says no, that hain't sense, who'll ye git t'help ye on the farm in his place — an' then she says yew'n me ought t' have a son — I know we kin, she says — an' I says, if we do, ye kin have anythin' I've got ye've a mind t'. An' she says, I wants Eben cut off so's this farm'll be mine when ye die! (*With terrible gloating.*) An' that's what's happened, hain't it? An' the farm's her'n! An' the dust o' the road — that's you'rn! Ha! Now who's hawin'?

EBEN (*has been listening, petrified with grief and rage — suddenly laughs wildly and brokenly*): Ha-ha-ha! So that's her sneakin' game — all along! — like I suspicioned at fust — t' swaller it all — an' me, too . . . ! (*Madly.*) I'll murder her! (*He springs toward the porch but Cabot is quicker and gets in between.*)

CABOT: No, ye don't!

EBEN: Git out o' my road! (*He tries to throw Cabot aside. They grapple in what becomes immediately a murderous struggle. The old man's concentrated strength is too much for Eben. Cabot gets one hand on his throat and presses him back across the stone wall. At the same moment, Abbie comes out on the porch. With a stifled cry she runs toward them.*)

ABBIE: Eben! Ephraim! (*She tugs at the hand on Eben's throat.*) Let go, Ephraim! Ye're chokin' him!

CABOT (*Removes his hand and flings Eben sideways full length on the grass, gasping and choking. With a cry, Abbie kneels beside him, trying to take his head on her lap, but he pushes her away. Cabot stands looking down with fierce triumph.*): Ye needn't t've fret, Abbie, I wa'n't aimin' t' kill him. He hain't wuth hangin' fur — not by a hell of a sight! (*More and more triumphantly.*) Seventy-six an' him not thirty yit — an' look whar he be fur thinkin' his Paw was easy! No, by God, I hain't easy! An' him upstairs, I'll raise him t' be like me! (*He turns to leave them.*) I'm goin' in an' dance! — sing an' celebrate! (*He walks to the porch — then turns with a great grin.*) I don't calc'late it's left in him, but if he gits pesky, Abbie, ye jest sing out. I'll come a-runnin' an' by the Etarnal, I'll put him across my knee an' birch him! Ha-ha-ha! (*He goes into the house laughing. A moment later his loud "whoop" is heard.*)

ABBIE (*tenderly*): Eben. Air ye hurt? (*She tries to kiss him but he pushes her violently away and struggles to a sitting position.*)

EBEN (*gaspingly*): T'hell — with ye!

ABBIE (*not believing her ears*): It's me, Eben — Abbie — don't ye know me?

EBEN (*glowering at her with hatred*): Ay-eh — I know ye — now! (*He suddenly breaks down, sobbing weakly.*)

ABBIE (*fearfully*): Eben — what's happened t' ye — why did ye look at me 's if ye hated me?

EBEN (*violently, between sobs and gasps*): I do hate ye! Ye're a whore — a damn trickin' whore!

ABBIE (*shrinking back horrified*): Eben! Ye don't know what ye're sayin'!

EBEN (*scrambling to his feet and following her — accusingly*): Ye're nothin' but a stinkin' passel o' lies! Ye've been lyin' t' me every word ye spoke, day an' night, since we fust — done it. Ye've kept sayin' ye loved me....

ABBIE (*frantically*): I do love ye! (*She takes his hand but he flings hers away.*)

EBEN (*unheeding*): Ye've made a fool o' me — a sick, dumb fool — a-purpose! Ye've been on'y playin' yer sneakin', stealin' game all along — gittin' me t' lie with ye so's ye'd hev a son he'd think was his'n, an' makin' him promise he'd give ye the farm and let me eat dust, if ye did git him a son! (*Staring at her with anguished, bewildered eyes.*) They must be a devil livin' in ye! T'ain't human t' be as bad as that be!

ABBIE (*stunned — dully*): He told yew ...?

EBEN: Hain't it true? It hain't no good in yew lyin'.

ABBIE (*pleadingly*): Eben, listen — ye must listen — it was long ago — afore we done nothin' — yew was scornin' me — goin' t' see Min — when I was lovin' ye — an' I said it t' him t' git vengeance on ye!

EBEN (*Unheedingly. With tortured passion.*): I wish ye was dead! I wish I was dead along with ye afore this come! (*Ragingly.*) But I'll git my vengeance too! I'll pray Maw t' come back t' help me — t' put her cuss on yew an' him!

ABBIE (*brokenly*): Don't ye, Eben! Don't ye! (*She throws herself on her knees before him, weeping.*) I didn't mean t' do bad t'ye! Fergive me, won't ye?

EBEN (*not seeming to hear her — fiercely*): I'll git squar' with the old skunk — an' yew! I'll tell him the truth 'bout the son he's so proud o'! Then I'll leave ye here t' pizen each other — with Maw comin' out o' her grave at nights — an' I'll go t' the gold fields o' Californi-a whar Sim an' Peter be!

ABBIE (*terrified*): Ye won't — leave me? Ye can't!

EBEN (*with fierce determination*): I'm a-goin', I tell ye! I'll git rich thar an' come back an' fight him fur the farm he stole — an' I'll kick ye both out in the road — t' beg an' sleep in the woods — an' yer son along with ye — t' starve an' die! (*He is hysterical at the end.*)

ABBIE (*with a shudder — humbly*): He's yewr son, too, Eben.

EBEN (*torturedly*): I wish he never was born! I wish he'd die this minit! I wish I'd never sot eyes on him! It's him — yew havin' him — a-purpose t' steal — that's changed everythin'!

ABBIE (*gently*): Did ye believe I loved ye — afore he come?

EBEN: Aye-eh — like a dumb ox!

ABBIE: An' ye don't believe no more?

EBEN: B'lieve a lyin' thief! Ha!

ABBIE (*shudders — then humbly*): An' did ye r'ally love me afore?

EBEN (*brokenly*): Ay-eh — an' ye was trickin' me!

ABBIE: An' ye don't love me now!

EBEN (*violently*): I hate ye, I tell ye!

ABBIE: An' ye're truly goin' West — goin' t' leave me — all account o' him being born?

EBEN: I'm a-goin' in the mornin' — or may God strike me t' hell!

ABBIE (*after a pause — with a dreadful cold intensity — slowly*): If that's what his comin's done t' me — killin' yewr love — takin' yew away — my on'y joy — the on'y joy I ever knowed — like heaven t' me — purtier'n heaven — then I hate him, too, even if I be his Maw!

EBEN (*bitterly*): Lies! Ye love him! He'll steal the farm fur ye! (*Brokenly.*) But t'ain't the farm so much — not no more — it's yew foolin' me — gittin' me t' love ye — lyin' yew loved me — jest t' git a son t' steal!

ABBIE (*distractedly*): He won't steal! I'd kill him fust! I do love ye! I'll prove t' ye ...!

EBEN (*harshly*): T'ain't no use lyin' no more. I'm deaf t' ye! (*He turns away.*) I hain't seein' ye agen. Good-by!

ABBIE (*pale with anguish*): Hain't ye even goin' t' kiss me — not once — arter all we loved?

EBEN (*in a hard voice*): I hain't wantin' t' kiss ye never agen! I'm wantin' t' forgit I ever sot eyes on ye!

ABBIE: Eben! — ye mustn't — wait a spell — I want t' tell ye....

EBEN: I'm a-goin' in t' git drunk. I'm a-goin' t' dance.

ABBIE (*clinging to his arm — with passionate earnestness*): If I could make it — 's if he'd never come up between us — if I could prove t' ye I wa'n't schemin' t' steal from ye — so's everythin' could be jest the same with us, lovin' each other jest the same, kissin' an' happy the same's we've been happy afore he come — if I could do it — ye'd love me agen, wouldn't ye? Ye'd kiss me agen? Ye wouldn't never leave me, would ye?

EBEN (*moved*): I calc'late not. (*Then shaking her hand off his arm — with a bitter smile.*) But ye hain't God, be ye?

ABBIE (*exultantly*): Remember ye've promised! (*Then with strange intensity.*) Mebbe I kin take back one thin' God does!

EBEN (*peering at her*): Ye're gittin' cracked, hain't ye? (*Then going toward door.*) I'm a-goin' t' dance.

ABBIE (*calls after him intensely*): I'll prove t' ye! I'll prove I love ye better'n. . . . (*He goes in the door, not seeming to hear. She remains standing where she is, looking after him — then she finishes desperately.*) Better'n everythin' else in the world!

Scene III

(*Just before dawn in the morning — shows the kitchen and Cabot's bedroom. In the kitchen, by the light of a tallow candle on the table, Eben is sitting, his chin propped on his hands, his drawn face blank and expressionless. His carpetbag is on the floor beside him. In the bedroom, dimly lighted by a small whale-oil lamp, Cabot lies asleep. Abbie is bending over the cradle, listening, her face full of terror yet with an undercurrent of desperate triumph. Suddenly, she breaks down and sobs, appears about to throw herself on her knees beside the cradle; but the old man turns restlessly, groaning in his sleep, and she controls herself, and, shrinking away from the cradle with a gesture of horror, backs swiftly toward the door in rear and goes out. A moment later she comes into the kitchen and, running to Eben, flings her arms about his neck and kisses him wildly. He hardens himself, he remains unmoved and cold, he keeps his eyes straight ahead.*)

ABBIE (*hysterically*): I done it, Eben! I told ye I'd do it! I've proved I love ye — better'n everythin' — so's ye can't never doubt me no more!

EBEN (*dully*): Whatever ye done, it hain't no good now.

ABBIE (*wildly*): Don't ye say that! Kiss me, Eben, won't ye? I need ye t' kiss me arter what I done! I need ye t' say ye love me!

EBEN (*kisses her without emotion — dully*): That's fur good-by. I'm a-goin' soon.

ABBIE: No! No! Ye won't go — not now!

EBEN (*going on with his own thoughts*): I been a-thinkin' — an' I hain't goin' t' tell Paw nothin'. I'll leave Maw t' take vengeance on ye. If I told him, the old skunk'd jest be stinkin' mean enuf to take it out on that baby. (*His voice showing emotion in spite of him.*) An' I don't want nothin' bad t' happen t' him. He hain't t' blame fur yew. (*He adds with a certain queer pride.*) An' he looks like me! An' by God, he's mine! An' some day I'll be a-comin' back an' . . . !

ABBIE (*too absorbed in her own thoughts to listen to him — pleadingly*): They's no cause fur ye t' go now — they's no sense — it's all the same's it was — they's nothin' come b'tween us now — arter what I done!

EBEN (*Something in her voice arouses him. He stares at her a bit frightenedly.*): Ye look mad, Abbie. What did ye do?

ABBIE: I — I killed him, Eben.

EBEN (*amazed*): Ye killed him?

ABBIE (*dully*): Ay-eh.

EBEN (*recovering from his astonishment — savagely*): An' serves him right! But we got t' do somethin' quick t' make it look s'if the old skunk'd killed himself when he was drunk. We kin prove by 'em all how drunk he got.

ABBIE (*wildly*): No! No! Not him! (*Laughing distractedly.*) But that's what I ought t' done, hain't it? I oughter killed him instead! Why didn't ye tell me?

EBEN (*appalled*): Instead? What d'ye mean?

ABBIE: Not him.

EBEN (*his face grown ghastly*): Not — not that baby!

ABBIE (*dully*): Ay-eh!

EBEN (*falls to his knees as if he'd been struck — his voice trembling with horror*): Oh, God A'mighty! A'mighty God! Maw, whar was ye, why didn't ye stop her?

ABBIE (*simply*): She went back t' her grave that night we fust done it, remember? I hain't felt her about since. (*A pause. Eben hides his head in his hands, trembling all over as if he had the ague. She goes on dully.*) I left the piller over his little face. Then he killed himself. He stopped breathin'. (*She begins to weep softly.*)

EBEN (*rage beginning to mingle with grief*): He looked like me. He was mine, damn ye!

ABBIE (*slowly and brokenly*): I didn't want t' do it. I hated myself fur doin' it. I loved him. He was so purty — dead spit 'n' image o' yew. But I loved yew more — an' yew was goin' away — far off whar I'd never see ye agen, never kiss ye, never feel ye pressed agin me agen — an' ye said ye hated me fur havin' him — ye said ye hated him an' wished he was dead — ye said if it hadn't been fur him comin' it'd be the same's afore between us.

EBEN (*unable to endure this, springs to his feet in a fury, threatening her, his twitching fingers seeming to reach out for her throat*): Ye lie! I never said — I never dreamed ye'd — I'd cut off my head afore I'd hurt his finger!

ABBIE (*piteously, sinking on her knees*): Eben, don't ye look at me like that — hatin' me — not after what I done fur ye — fur us — so's we could be happy agen —

EBEN (*furiously now*): Shut up, or I'll kill ye! I see yer game now — the same old sneakin' trick — ye're aimin' t' blame me fur the murder ye done!

ABBIE (*moaning — putting her hands over her ears*): Don't ye, Eben! Don't ye! (*She grasps his legs.*)

EBEN (*his mood suddenly changing to horror, shrinks away from her*): Don't ye tech me! Ye're pizen! How could ye — t' murder a pore little critter — Ye must've swapped yer soul t' hell! (*Suddenly raging.*) Ha! I kin see why ye done it! Not the lies ye jest told — but 'cause ye wanted t' steal agen — steal the last thin' ye'd left me — my part o' him — no, the hull o' him — ye saw he looked like me — ye knowed he was all mine — an' ye couldn't b'ar it — I know ye! Ye killed him fur bein' mine! (*All this has driven him almost insane. He makes a rush past her for the door — then turns — shaking both fists at her, violently.*) But I'll take vengeance now! I'll git the Sheriff! I'll tell him everythin'! Then I'll sing "I'm off to California-a!" an' go — gold — Golden Gate — gold sun — fields o' gold in the West! (*This last he half shouts, half croons incoherently, suddenly breaking off passionately.*) I'm a-goin' fur the Sheriff t' come an' git ye! I want ye tuk away, locked up from me! I want ye tuk away out o' my sight! Murderer an' thief 'r not, ye still tempt me! I'll give ye up t' the Sheriff! (*He turns and runs out, around the corner of house, panting and sobbing, and breaks into a swerving sprint down the road.*)

ABBIE (*struggling to her feet, runs to the door, calling after him*): I love ye, Eben! I love ye! (*She stops at the door weakly, swaying, about to fall.*) I don't care what ye do — if ye'll on'y love me agen — (*She falls limply to the floor in a faint.*)

Scene IV

(*About an hour later. Same as Scene III. Shows the kitchen and Cabot's bedroom. It is after dawn. The sky is brilliant with the sunrise. In the kitchen, Abbie sits at the table, her body limp and exhausted, her head bowed down over her arms, her face hidden. Upstairs, Cabot is still asleep but awakens with a start. He looks toward the window and gives a snort of surprise and irritation — throws back the covers and begins hurriedly pulling on his clothes. Without looking behind him, he begins talking to Abbie whom he supposes beside him.*)

CABOT: Thunder 'n' lightin', Abbie! I hain't slept this late in fifty year! Looks 's if the sun was full riz a'most. Must've been the dancin' an' likker. Must be gittin' old. I hope Eben's t' wuk. Ye might've tuk the trouble t' rouse me, Abbie. (*He turns — sees no one there — surprised.*) Waal — whar air she? Gittin' vittles, I calc'late. (*He tiptoes to the cradle and peers down — proudly.*) Mornin', sonny. Purty's a picter! Sleepin' sound. He don't beller all night like most o' 'em. (*He goes quietly out the door in rear — a few moments later enters kitchen — sees Abbie — with satisfaction.*) So thar ye be. Ye got any vittles cooked?

ABBIE (*without moving*): No.

CABOT (*coming to her, almost sympathetically*): Ye feelin' sick?

ABBIE: No.

CABOT (*Pats her on shoulder. She shudders.*): Ye'd best lie down a spell. (*Half jocularly.*) Yer son'll be needin' ye soon. He'd ought t' wake up with a gnashin' appetite, the sound way he's sleepin'.

ABBIE (*shudders — then in a dead voice*): He hain't never goin' t' wake up.

CABOT (*jokingly*): Takes after me this mornin'. I hain't slept so late in . . .

ABBIE: He's dead.

CABOT (*stares at her — bewilderedly*): What. . . .

ABBIE: I killed him.

CABOT (*stepping back from her — aghast*): Air ye drunk — 'r crazy — 'r . . . ?

ABBIE (*suddenly lifts her head and turns on him — wildly*): I killed him, I tell ye! I smothered him. Go up an' see if ye don't b'lieve me!

(*Cabot stares at her a second, then bolts out the rear door, can be heard bounding up the stairs, and rushes into the bedroom and over to the cradle. Abbie has sunk back lifelessly into her former position. Cabot puts his hand down on the body in the crib. An expression of fear and horror comes over his face.*)

CABOT (*shrinking away — tremblingly*): God A'mighty! God A'mighty. (*He stumbles out the door — in a short while returns to the kitchen — comes to Abbie, the stunned expression still on his face — hoarsely.*) Why did ye do it? Why? (*As she doesn't answer, he grabs her violently by the shoulder and shakes her.*) I ax ye why ye done it! Ye'd better tell me 'r . . . !

ABBIE (*gives him a furious push which sends him staggering back and springs to her feet — with wild rage and hatred*): Don't ye dare tech me! What right hev ye t' question me 'bout him? He wa'n't yewr son! Think I'd have a son by yew? I'd die fust! I hate the sight o' ye an' allus did! It's yew I should've murdered, if I'd had good sense! I hate ye! I love Eben. I did from the fust. An' he was Eben's son — mine an' Eben's — not your'n!

CABOT (*stands looking at her dazedly — a pause — finding his words with an effort — dully*): That was it — what I felt — pokin' round the corners — while ye lied — holdin' yerself from me — sayin' ye'd a'ready conceived — (*He lapses into crushed silence — then with a strange emotion.*) He's dead, sart'n. I felt his heart. Pore little critter! (*He blinks back one tear, wiping his sleeve across his nose.*)

ABBIE (*hysterically*): Don't ye! Don't ye! (*She sobs unrestrainedly.*)

CABOT (*with a concentrated effort that stiffens his body into a rigid line and hardens his face into a stony mask — through his teeth to himself*): I got t' be — like a stone — a rock o' jedgment! (*A pause. He gets complete control over himself — harshly.*) If he was Eben's, I be glad he air gone! An' mebbe I suspicioned it all along. I felt thar was somethin' onnateral — somewhars — the house got so lonesome — an' cold — drivin' me down t' the barn — t' the beasts o' the field. . . . Ay-eh. I must've suspicioned — somethin'. Ye didn't fool me — not altogether, leastways — I'm too old a bird — growin' ripe on the bough. . . . (*He becomes aware he is wandering, straightens again, looks at Abbie with a cruel grin.*) So ye'd liked t' hev murdered me 'stead o' him, would ye? Waal, I'll live to a hundred! I'll live t' see ye hung! I'll deliver ye up t' the jedgment o' God an' the law! I'll git the Sheriff now. (*Starts for the door.*)

ABBIE (*dully*): Ye needn't. Eben's gone fur him.

CABOT (*amazed*): Eben — gone fur the Sheriff?

ABBIE: Ay-eh.

CABOT: T' inform agen ye?

ABBIE: Ay-eh.

CABOT (*considers this — a pause — then in a hard voice*): Waal, I'm thankful fur him savin' me the trouble. I'll git t' wuk. (*He goes to the door — then turns — in a voice full of strange emotion.*) He'd ought t' been my son, Abbie. Ye'd ought t' loved me. I'm a man. If ye'd loved me, I'd never told no Sheriff on ye no matter what ye did, if they was t' brile me alive!

ABBIE (*defensively*): They's more to it nor yew know, makes him tell.

CABOT (*dryly*): Fur yewr sake, I hope they be. (*He goes out — comes around to the gate — stares up at the sky. His control relaxes. For a moment he is old and weary. He murmurs despairingly.*) God A'mighty, I be lonesomer'n ever! (*He hears running footsteps from the left, immediately is himself again. Eben runs in, panting exhaustedly, wild-eyed and mad looking. He lurches through the gate. Cabot grabs him by the shoulder. Eben stares at him dumbly.*) Did ye tell the Sheriff?

EBEN (*nodding stupidly*): Ay-eh.

CABOT (*gives him a push away that sends him sprawling — laughing with withering contempt*): Good fur ye! A prime chip o' yer Maw ye be! (*He goes toward the barn, laughing harshly. Eben scrambles to his feet. Suddenly Cabot turns — grimly threatening.*) Git off this farm when the Sheriff takes her — or, by God, he'll have t' come back an' git me fur murder, too! (*He stalks off. Eben does not appear to have heard him. He runs to the door and comes into the kitchen. Abbie looks up with a cry of anguished joy. Eben stumbles over and throws himself on his knees beside her sobbing brokenly.*)

EBEN: Fergive me!

ABBIE (*happily*): Eben! (*She kisses him and pulls his head over against her breast.*)

EBEN: I love ye! Fergive me!

ABBIE (*ecstatically*): I'd fergive ye all the sins in hell fur sayin' that! (*She kisses his head, pressing it to her with a fierce passion of possession.*)

EBEN (*brokenly*): But I told the Sheriff. He's comin' fur ye!

ABBIE: I kin b'ar what happens t' me — now!

EBEN: I woke him up. I told him. He says, wait 'til I git dressed. I was waiting. I got to thinkin' o' yew. I got to thinkin' how I'd loved ye. It hurt like somethin' was bustin' in my chest an' head. I got t' cryin'. I knowed sudden I loved ye yet, an' allus would love ye!

ABBIE (*caressing his hair — tenderly*): My boy, hain't ye?

EBEN: I begun t' run back. I cut across the fields an' through the woods. I thought ye might have time t' run away — with me — an' . . .

ABBIE (*shaking her head*): I got t' take my punishment — t' pay fur my sin.

EBEN: Then I want t' share it with ye.

ABBIE: Ye didn't do nothin'.

EBEN: I put it in yer head. I wisht he was dead! I as much as urged ye t' do it!

ABBIE: No. It was me alone!

EBEN: I'm as guilty as yew be! He was the child o' our sin.

ABBIE (*lifting her head as if defying God*): I don't repent that sin! I hain't askin' God t' fergive that!

EBEN: Nor me — but it led up t' the other — an' the murder ye did, ye did 'count o' me — an' it's my murder, too, I'll tell the Sheriff — an' if ye deny it, I'll say we planned it t'gether — an' they'll all b'lieve me, fur they suspicion everythin' we've done, an' it'll seem likely an' true to 'em. An' it is true — way down. I did help ye — somehow.

ABBIE (*laying her head on his — sobbing*): No! I don't want yew t' suffer!

EBEN: I got t' pay fur my part o' the sin! An' I'd suffer wuss leavin' ye, goin' West, thinkin' o' ye day an' night, bein' out when yew was in — (*Lowering his voice.*) 'r bein' alive when yew was dead. (*A pause.*) I want t' share with ye, Abbie — prison 'r death 'r hell 'r anythin'! (*He looks into her eyes and forces a trembling smile.*) If I'm sharin' with ye, I won't feel lonesome, leastways.

ABBIE (*weakly*): Eben! I won't let ye! I can't let ye!

EBEN (*kissing her — tenderly*): Ye can't he'p yerself. I got ye beat fur once!

ABBIE (*forcing a smile — adoringly*): I hain't beat — s'long's I got ye!

EBEN (*hears the sound of feet outside*): Ssshh! Listen! They've come t' take us!

ABBIE: No, it's him. Don't give him no chance to fight ye, Eben. Don't say nothin' — no matter what he says. An' I won't neither. (*It is Cabot. He comes up from the barn in a great state of excitement and strides into the house and then into the kitchen. Eben is kneeling beside Abbie, his arm around her, hers around him. They stare straight ahead.*)

CABOT (*Stares at them, his face hard. A long pause — vindictively.*): Ye make a slick pair o' murderin' turtle doves! Ye'd ought t' be both hung on the same limb an' left thar t' swing in the breeze an' rot — a warnin' t' old fools like me t' b'ar their lonesomeness alone — an' fur young fools like ye t' hobble their lust. (*A pause. The excitement returns to his face, his eyes snap, he looks a bit crazy.*) I couldn't work today. I couldn't take no interest. T' hell with the farm! I'm leavin' it! I've turned the cows an' other stock loose! I've druv 'em into the woods whar they kin be free! By freein' 'em, I'm freein' myself! I'm quittin' here today! I'll set fire t' house an' barn an' watch 'em burn, an' I'll leave yer Maw t' haunt the ashes, an' I'll will the fields back t' God, so that nothin' human kin never touch 'em! I'll be a-goin' to Californi-a — t' jine Simeon an' Peter — true sons o' mine if they be dumb fools — an' the Cabots'll find Solomon's Mines t'gether! (*He suddenly cuts a mad caper.*) Whoop! What was the song they sung? "Oh, Californi-a! That's the land fur me." (*He sings this — then gets on his knees by the floorboard under which the money was hid.*) An' I'll sail thar on one o' the finest clippers I kin find! I've got the money! Pity ye didn't know whar this was hidden so's ye could steal. . . . (*He has pulled up the board. He stares — feels — stares again. A pause of dead silence. He slowly turns, slumping into a sitting position on the floor, his eyes like those of a dead fish, his face the sickly green of an attack of nausea. He swallows painfully several times — forces a weak smile at last.*) So — ye did steal it!

EBEN (*emotionlessly*): I swapped it t' Sim an' Peter fur their share o' the farm — t' pay their passage t' Californi-a.

CABOT (*with one sardonic*): Ha! (*He begins to recover. Gets slowly to his feet — strangely.*) I calc'late God give it to 'em — not yew! God's hard, not easy! Mebbe they's easy gold in the West but it hain't God's gold. It hain't fur me. I kin hear His voice warnin' me agen t' be hard an' stay on my farm. I kin see his hand usin' Eben t' steal t' keep me from weakness. I kin feel I be in the palm o' His hand, His fingers guidin' me. (*A pause — then he mutters sadly.*) It's a-goin' t' be lonesomer now than ever it war afore — an' I'm gittin' old, Lord — ripe on the bough. . . . (*Then stiffening.*) Waal — what d'ye want? God's lonesome, hain't He? God's hard an' lonesome! (*A pause. The Sheriff with two men comes up the road from the left. They move cautiously to the door. The Sheriff knocks on it with the butt of his pistol.*)

SHERIFF: Open in the name o' the law! (*They start.*)

CABOT: They've come fur ye. (*He goes to the rear door.*) Come in, Jim! (*The three men enter. Cabot meets them in doorway.*) Jest a minit, Jim. I got 'em safe here. (*The Sheriff nods. He and his companions remain in the doorway.*)

EBEN (*suddenly calls*): I lied this mornin', Jim. I helped her to do it. Ye kin take me, too.

ABBIE (*brokenly*): No!

CABOT: Take 'em both. (*He comes forward — stares at Eben with a trace of grudging admiration.*) Purty good — fur yew! Waal, I got t' round up the stock. Good-by.

EBEN: Good-by.

ABBIE: Good-by. (*Cabot turns and strides past the men — comes out and around the corner of the house, his shoulders squared, his face stony, and stalks grimly toward the barn. In the meantime the Sheriff and men have come into the room.*)

SHERIFF (*embarrassedly*): Waal — we'd best start.

ABBIE: Wait. (*Turns to Eben.*) I love ye, Eben.

EBEN: I love ye, Abbie. (*They kiss. The three men grin and shuffle embarrassedly. Eben takes Abbie's hand. They go out the door in rear, the men following, and come from the house, walking hand in hand to the gate. Eben stops there and points to the sunrise sky.*) Sun's a-rizin'. Purty, hain't it?

ABBIE: Ay-eh. (*They both stand for a moment looking up raptly in attitudes strangely aloof and devout.*)

SHERIFF (*looking around at the farm enviously — to his companions*): It's a jim-dandy farm, no denyin'. Wished I owned it!

Bertolt Brecht

Among the most inventive and influential of modern playwrights, Bertolt Brecht (1898–1956) has left a legacy of important plays and theories about how those plays should be produced. His work is inextricably connected with politics, and throughout most of his career he felt that drama should inform and awaken sensibilities, not just entertain or anesthetize an audience. Most of his plays concern philosophical and political issues, and some of them so threatened the Nazi regime that his works were burned publicly in Germany during the Third Reich.

When he was nineteen, Brecht was an orderly in a hospital during the last months of World War I. He saw so much carnage and misery in the medical wards that he became a lifelong pacifist. After the war he began writing plays while he was a student in Munich. His first successes in the Munich theater took the form of commentary on returned war veterans, on the questions of duty and heroism — which he treated negatively — and on issues related to spiritual values. His materialistic attitude (his rejection of spiritual concepts of an after life) was influenced by his readings of Hegel and the doctrines of Marx's dialectical materialism. Marx's theories predicted class struggles and based most social values in economic realities. Brecht eventually moved to Berlin, the theatrical center of Germany, and by 1926 was on his way to becoming a Communist.

Brecht found the political pressures in early Nazi Germany too frightening and dangerous for his writing, and he went into exile in 1933. He lived for a time in Scandinavia and later in the United States. After World War II Brecht and his wife returned to Berlin where, in 1949, he founded the Berliner Ensemble, which produced most of his later work. Brecht chose East Berlin as his home, in part because he felt his work could best be understood in a Communist setting. One irony is that his work has been even more widely appreciated and accepted in the West than in the Communist bloc.

Brecht wrote his most popular play in 1928, a musical in collaboration with the German composer Kurt Weill: *The Threepenny Opera*. The model for this play, the English writer John Gay's 1728 opera-drama *The Beggar's Opera*, provided Brecht with a perfect platform on which to comment satirically on the political and economic circumstances in Germany two hundred years after Gay wrote. The success of the Brecht-Weill collaboration — the work is still performed regularly — is due in part to Brecht's capacity to create appealing underworld characters such as Polly Peachum and Macheath, known as Mackie the Knife.

Brecht's wife, Helene Weigel, played Peachum, the madam of the brothel in which the action takes place. Kurt Weill's second wife, Lotte Lenya, was an overnight sensation in the part of Jenny, and she had a reprise in New York almost twenty-five years later when she was as highly acclaimed as she was in the original Berlin production. Songs like "Mack the Knife" are still popular. The Brecht-Weill style has been imitated widely in popular musicals worldwide.

Brecht's use of other plays as sources for his work came to be a virtual trademark. Brecht borrowed not only from Gay but from Sophocles, Molière, Gorky, Shakespeare, and John Webster, among others. His most successful plays are *The Private Lives of the Master Race* (1945); *Mother Courage* (1941); *The Life of Galileo* (1938–1939); *The Good Woman of Setzuan* (1943); and *The Caucasian Chalk Circle* (1948). But these represent only a tiny fraction of a mass of work, including plays, poetry, criticism, and fiction. His output is extraordinary in volume and quality.

Brecht developed a number of theories regarding drama. He defined the concept of epic theater as an alternative to the traditional Aristotelian theory, in which the audience remained apart from the drama. Brecht wanted his audience to be in a dialectical and sometimes alienating relationship with the drama. He expected his audience to observe, but to observe critically, to draw conclusions and participate in an intellectual argument with the work at hand. The confrontational relationship he intended would engage the audience in analyzing what they saw rather than simply being bathed in a wash of sentimentality or emotion.

One of the ways in which Brecht hoped to achieve his ends was by making the production's props, lights, sets, and equipment visible, thereby reminding the audience that they were seeing a play. He also liked his plays to be staged with intense light so that the audience's attention would not drift away allowing them to imagine they were watching a realistic spectacle. In a sense, he was hoping to alienate his audience from the drama, to separate them so that they could seriously consider what was taking place onstage. He used the term ALIENATION to establish his principles and position his audience so that they would have the attitude toward his work that he intended. The alienation effect in his plays resulted from his ability to keep the audience emotionally detached from the characters' situations. His best audiences were alert and critical.

Brecht's theories produced interesting results and helped stimulate audiences that had sunk rapidly into the expectation of being entertained by realistic and often sentimental plays. His style spread rapidly throughout the world of theater, and it is still being used and developed by contemporary playwrights.

MOTHER COURAGE

Since *Mother Courage* was first produced in 1941 in Zurich, it has become a true classic of modern theater. It has been performed successfully in the United States, most Western theaters, and East Germany. Brecht conceived of the drama as a powerful antiwar play. He set it in Germany during the Thirty Years War, in which the German Protestants, supported by countries such as France, Denmark, and England, fought against the Hapsburg empire, which was allied with the Holy Roman Empire and the German Catholic princes. Actually a combination of many wars fought during the period of thirty years, the "War" was bloody and seemingly interminable, devastating Germany's towns and citizenry as well as its agriculture and commerce. Though the armies fought to control territory and economic markets, the religious differences between the German Lutherans and the Roman Catholics provided further reason for conflict.

Brecht was not interested in the immediate causes underlying the Thirty Years War, any more than he was interested in the causes of the war that raged while he wrote. He was interested in making a statement against war entirely, regardless of its cause. To do this he deliberately avoided making his play realistic. The stage setting is essentially barren; the play is structured in scenes that are very intense but that avoid any sense of continuity of action — and therefore prohibit audiences from losing all sense of themselves by becoming involved in unfolding action. Moreover, the lighting is high intensity, almost cruel at times, spotlighting the action in a way that is completely unnatural. In the early productions, Brecht included slide projections of the headings that accompany each of the twelve scenes so that the audience was always reminded of the presence of the playwright and the fact that they were seeing a play. These headings provided yet another break in the continuity of the action.

Although the printed text does not convey it, the play in production employs long silences, some of which can be unsettling to the audience. When Swiss Cheese, Mother Courage's "honest" son, has a moment of rest in Scene 3, he is in an intense ring of stage light as he comments on sitting in the sun in his shirtsleeves. He is relaxing for the last time, and the intensity of the light becomes an ironic device: He is dragged off to his death as a result of having stolen the cash box from the regiment. Swiss Cheese has been corrupted by the war, just as virtually everyone is corrupted.

Mother Courage herself lives off the war by selling goods to the soldiers. She and her children haul their wagon across the battlefields with no concern for who is winning, who is losing, or even where they are. Her only ambition is to stock her wagon, sell her goods, and make sure she does not get stuck with any useless inventory. At one point, the Chaplain tells her that peace has broken out, and she laments their condition because without war they have no livelihood.

As Mother Courage continues to pull her wagon across field after field, she learns how to survive. But she also loses her children, one by one, to the war. Eilif is seduced into joining the army by a recruitment officer, and is led into battle thinking that war is a heroic adventure. Swiss Cheese thinks he found a good deal in a paymaster's uniform, but both of them are wrong: There is no security in war and they eventually perish.

Kattrin, the daughter, is likewise a victim of the violence of war. Having been violated by a Swedish soldier, she becomes mute. Near the end of the play she is treated violently again, and the terrible scar on her face leaves her unmarriageable. At the end of the play, Kattrin dies while sounding an alarm to give the sleeping town warning of an imminent attack.

Finally, Mother Courage is left alone. She picks up her wagon and finds that she can maneuver it herself. The play ends as she circles the stage, with everything around her consumed by war.

Brecht's stated intentions were somewhat thwarted by the reactions of the play's first audiences. They were struck by the power of Brecht's characterization of Mother Courage and treated her with immense sympathy. They saw her as an indomitable woman whose strength in the face of adversity was so great that she could not be overwhelmed. But Brecht intended the audience to further analyze Mother Courage and to see in her a reflection of society's wrong values. She conducts business on the field of battle, paying no attention to the moral question of war itself. She makes her living from the war but cannot see that it is the war that causes her anguish.

In response to the audiences' sympathetic reactions, Brecht tried to revise the play, adding new lines to help audiences see the venality of Mother Courage's motives. But subsequent audiences have continued to treat her as a survivor — almost a biblical figure. Brecht's East German critics still see her as a model for one who endures all the terrors of war, and yet remains a testament for the resilience of humankind. No matter how one decides to interpret her, Mother Courage remains one of the most unusual and haunting characters in modern drama.

Bertolt Brecht *(1898–1956)*

MOTHER COURAGE AND HER CHILDREN   *1941*
A CHRONICLE OF THE THIRTY YEARS' WAR

TRANSLATED BY RALPH MANHEIM

Characters

MOTHER COURAGE	THE OTHER SERGEANT
KATTRIN, *her mute*	THE OLD COLONEL
daughter	A CLERK
EILIF, *her elder son*	A YOUNG SOLDIER
SWISS CHEESE, *her younger*	AN OLDER SOLDIER
son	A PEASANT
THE RECRUITER	THE PEASANT'S WIFE
THE SERGEANT	THE YOUNG MAN
THE COOK	THE OLD WOMAN
THE GENERAL	ANOTHER PEASANT
THE CHAPLAIN	THE PEASANT WOMAN
THE ORDNANCE OFFICER	A YOUNG PEASANT
YVETTE POTTIER	THE LIEUTENANT
THE MAN WITH THE PATCH	SOLDIERS
OVER HIS EYE	A VOICE

SCENE 1 _____

(*Spring, 1624. General Oxenstjerna recruits troops in Dalarna for the Polish campaign. The canteen woman, Anna Fierling, known as Mother Courage, loses a son.*)

(*Highway near a city.*)

(*A sergeant and a recruiter stand shivering.*)

THE RECRUITER: How can anybody get a company together in a place like this? Sergeant, sometimes I feel like committing suicide. The general wants me to recruit four platoons by the twelfth, and the people around here are so depraved I can't sleep at night. I finally get hold of a man, I close my eyes and pretend not to see that he's chicken-breasted and he's got varicose veins, I get him good and drunk and he signs up. While I'm paying for the drinks, he steps out, I follow him to the door because I smell a rat: Sure enough, he's gone, like a fart out of a goose. A man's word doesn't mean a thing, there's no honor, no loyalty. This place has undermined my faith in humanity, sergeant.

THE SERGEANT: It's easy to see these people have gone too long without a war. How can you have morality without a war, I ask you? Peace is a mess, it takes a war to put things in order. In peacetime the human race goes to the dogs. Man and beast are treated like so much dirt. Everybody eats what they like, a big piece of cheese on white bread, with a slice of meat on top of the cheese. Nobody knows how many young men or good horses there are in that town up ahead, they've never been counted. I've been in places where they hadn't had a war in as much as seventy years, the people had no names, they didn't even know who they were. It takes a war before you get decent lists and records; then your boots are done up in bales and your grain in sacks, man and beast are properly counted and marched away, because people realize that without order they can't have a war.

THE RECRUITER: How right you are!

THE SERGEANT: Like all good things, a war is hard to get started. But once it takes root, it's vigorous; then people are as scared of peace as dice players are of laying off, because they'll have to reckon up their losses. But at first they're scared of war. It's the novelty.

THE RECRUITER: Say, there comes a wagon. Two women and two young fellows. Keep the old woman busy, sergeant. If this is another flop, you won't catch me standing out in this April wind any more.

(*A Jew's harp is heard. Drawn by two young men, a covered wagon approaches. In the wagon sit Mother Courage and her mute daughter Kattrin.*)

MOTHER COURAGE: Good morning, sergeant.

SERGEANT (*barring the way*): Good morning, friends. Who are you?

MOTHER COURAGE: Business people. (*Sings.*)

Hey, Captains, make the drum stop drumming
And let your soldiers take a seat.
Here's Mother Courage, with boots she's coming
To help along their aching feet.
How can they march off to the slaughter
With baggage, cannon, lice and fleas
Across the rocks and through the water
Unless their boots are in one piece?

The spring is come. Christian, revive!
The snowdrifts melt. The dead lie dead.
And if by chance you're still alive
It's time to rise and shake a leg.
O Captains, don't expect to send them
To death with nothing in their crops.
First you must let Mother Courage mend them
In mind and body with her schnapps.
On empty bellies it's distressing
To stand up under shot and shell.
But once they're full, you have my blessing
To lead them to the jaws of hell.
  The spring is come. Christian, revive!
  The snowdrifts melt, the dead lie dead.
  And if by chance you're still alive
  It's time to rise and shake a leg.

THE SERGEANT: Halt, you scum. Where do you belong?

THE ELDER SON: Second Finnish Regiment.

THE SERGEANT: Where are your papers?

MOTHER COURAGE: Papers?

THE YOUNGER SON: But she's Mother Courage!

THE SERGEANT: Never heard of her. Why Courage?

MOTHER COURAGE: They call me Courage, sergeant, because when I saw ruin staring me in the face I drove out of Riga through cannon fire with fifty loaves of bread in my wagon. They were getting moldy, it was high time, I had no choice.

THE SERGEANT: No wisecracks. Where are your papers?

MOTHER COURAGE (*fishing a pile of papers out of a tin box and climbing down*): Here are my papers, sergeant. There's a whole missal, picked it up in Alt-Ötting to wrap cucumbers in, and a map of Moravia, God knows if I'll ever get there, if I don't it's a total loss. And this here certifies that my horse hasn't got foot-and-mouth disease, too bad, he croaked on us, he cost fifteen guilders, but not out of my pocket, glory be. Is that enough paper?

THE SERGEANT: Are you trying to pull my leg? I'll teach you to get smart. You know you need a license.

MOTHER COURAGE: You mind your manners and don't go telling my innocent children that I'd go anywhere near your leg, it's indecent. I want no truck with you. My license in the Second Regiment is my honest face, and if you can't read it, that's not my fault. I'm not letting anybody put his seal on it.

THE RECRUITER: Sergeant, I detect a spirit of insubordination in this woman. In our camp we need respect for authority.

MOTHER COURAGE: Wouldn't sausage be better?

THE SERGEANT: Name.

MOTHER COURAGE: Anna Fierling.

THE SERGEANT: Then you're all Fierlings?

MOTHER COURAGE: What do you mean? Fierling is my name. Not theirs.

THE SERGEANT: Aren't they all your children?

MOTHER COURAGE: That they are, but why should they all have the same name? (*Pointing at the elder son.*) This one, for instance. His name is Eilif Nojocki. How come? Because his father always claimed to be called Kojocki or Mojocki. The boy remembers him well, except the one he remembers was somebody else, a Frenchman with a goatee. But aside from that, he inherited his father's intelligence; that man could strip the pants off a peasant's ass without his knowing it. So, you see, we've each got our own name.

THE SERGEANT: Each different, you mean?

MOTHER COURAGE: Don't act so innocent.

THE SERGEANT: I suppose that one's a Chinaman? (*Indicating the younger son.*)

MOTHER COURAGE: Wrong. He's Swiss.

THE SERGEANT: After the Frenchman?

MOTHER COURAGE: What Frenchman? I never heard of any Frenchman. Don't get everything balled up or we'll be here all day. He's Swiss, but his name is Fejos, the name has nothing to do with his father. He had an entirely different name, he was an engineer, built fortifications, but he drank.

(*Swiss Cheese nods, beaming; the mute Kattrin is also tickled.*)

THE SERGEANT: Then how can his name be Fejos?

MOTHER COURAGE: I wouldn't want to offend you, but you haven't got much imagination. Naturally his name is Fejos because when he came I was with a Hungarian, it was all the same to him, he was dying of kidney trouble though he never touched a drop, a very decent man. The boy takes after him.

THE SERGEANT: But you said he wasn't his father?

MOTHER COURAGE: He takes after him all the same. I call him Swiss Cheese, how come, because he's good at pulling the wagon. (*Pointing at her daughter.*) Her name is Kattrin Haupt, she's half German.

THE SERGEANT: A fine family, I must say.

MOTHER COURAGE: Yes, I've been all over the world with my wagon.

THE SERGEANT: It's all being taken down. (*He takes it down.*) You're from Bamberg, Bavaria. What brings you here?

MOTHER COURAGE: I couldn't wait for the war to kindly come to Bamberg.

THE RECRUITER: You wagon pullers ought to be called Jacob Ox and Esau Ox. Do you ever get out of harness?

EILIF: Mother, can I clout him one on the kisser? I'd like to.

MOTHER COURAGE: And I forbid you. You stay put. And now, gentlemen, wouldn't you need a nice pistol, or a belt buckle, yours is all worn out, sergeant.

THE SERGEANT: I need something else. I'm not blind. Those young fellows are built like tree trunks, big broad chests, sturdy legs. Why aren't they in the army? That's what I'd like to know.

MOTHER COURAGE (*quickly*): Nothing doing, sergeant. My children aren't cut out for soldiers.

THE RECRUITER: Why not? There's profit in it, and glory. Peddling shoes is woman's work. (*To Eilif.*) Step up; let's feel if you've got muscles or if you're a sissy.

MOTHER COURAGE: He's a sissy. Give him a mean look and he'll fall flat on his face.

THE RECRUITER: And kill a calf if it happens to be standing in the way. (*Tries to lead him away.*)

MOTHER COURAGE: Leave him alone. He's not for you.

THE RECRUITER: He insulted me. He referred to my face as a kisser. Him and me will now step out in the field and discuss this thing as man to man.

EILIF: Don't worry, mother. I'll take care of him.

MOTHER COURAGE: You stay put. You no-good! I know you, always fighting. He's got a knife in his boot, he's a knifer.

THE RECRUITER: I'll pull it out of him like a milk tooth. Come on, boy.

MOTHER COURAGE: Sergeant, I'll report you to the colonel. He'll throw you in the lock-up. The lieutenant is courting my daughter.

THE SERGEANT: No rough stuff, brother. (*To Mother Courage.*) What have you got against the army? Wasn't his father a soldier? Didn't he die fair and square? You said so yourself.

MOTHER COURAGE: He's only a child. You want to lead him off to slaughter, I know you. You'll get five guilders for him.

THE RECRUITER: He'll get a beautiful cap and top boots.

EILIF: Not from you.

MOTHER COURAGE: Oh, won't you come fishing with me? said the fisherman to the worm. (*To Swiss Cheese.*) Run and yell that they're trying to steal your brother. (*She pulls a knife.*) Just try and steal him. I'll cut you down, you dogs. I'll teach you to put him in your war! We do an honest business in ham and shirts, we're peaceful folk.

THE SERGEANT: I can see by the knife how peaceful you are. You ought to be ashamed of yourself, put that knife away, you bitch. A minute ago you admitted you lived off war, how else would you live, on what? How can you have a war without soldiers?

MOTHER COURAGE: It doesn't have to be my children.

THE SERGEANT: I see. You'd like the war to eat the core and spit out the apple. You want your brood

to batten on war, tax-free. The war can look out for itself, is that it? You call yourself Courage, eh? And you're afraid of the war that feeds you. Your sons aren't afraid of it, I can see that.

EILIF: I'm not afraid of any war.

THE SERGEANT: Why should you be? Look at me: Has the soldier's life disagreed with me? I was seventeen when I joined up.

MOTHER COURAGE: You're not seventy yet.

THE SERGEANT: I can wait.

MOTHER COURAGE: Sure. Under ground.

THE SERGEANT: Are you trying to insult me? Telling me I'm going to die?

MOTHER COURAGE: But suppose it's the truth? I can see the mark on you. You look like a corpse on leave.

SWISS CHEESE: She's got second sight. Everybody says so. She can tell the future.

THE RECRUITER: Then tell the sergeant his future. It might amuse him.

THE SERGEANT: I don't believe in that stuff.

MOTHER COURAGE: Give me your helmet. (*He gives it to her.*)

THE SERGEANT: It doesn't mean any more than taking a shit in the grass. But go ahead for the laugh.

MOTHER COURAGE (*takes a sheet of parchment and tears it in two*): Eilif, Swiss Cheese, Kattrin: That's how we'd all be torn apart if we got mixed up too deep in the war. (*To the sergeant.*) Seeing it's you, I'll do it for nothing. I make a black cross on this piece. Black is death.

SWISS CHEESE: She leaves the other one blank. Get it?

MOTHER COURAGE: Now I fold them, and now I shake them up together. Same as we're all mixed up together from the cradle to the grave. And now you draw, and you'll know the answer. (*The sergeant hesitates.*)

THE RECRUITER (*to Eilif*): I don't take everybody, I'm known to be picky and choosy, but you've got spirit, I like that.

THE SERGEANT (*fishing in the helmet*): Damn foolishness! Hocus-pocus!

SWISS CHEESE: He's pulled a black cross. He's through.

THE RECRUITER: Don't let them scare you, there's not enough bullets for everybody.

THE SERGEANT (*hoarsely*): You've fouled me up.

MOTHER COURAGE: You fouled yourself up the day you joined the army. And now we'll be going, there isn't a war every day, I've got to take advantage.

THE SERGEANT: Hell and damnation! Don't try to hornswoggle me. We're taking your bastard to be a soldier.

EILIF: I'd like to be a soldier, mother.

MOTHER COURAGE: You shut your trap, you Finnish devil.

EILIF: Swiss Cheese wants to be a soldier too.

MOTHER COURAGE: That's news to me. I'd better let you draw too, all three of you. (*She goes to the rear to mark crosses on slips of parchment.*)

THE RECRUITER (*to Eilif*): It's been said to our discredit that a lot of religion goes on in the Swedish camp, but that's slander to blacken our reputation. Hymn singing only on Sunday, one verse! And only if you've got a voice.

MOTHER COURAGE (*comes back with the slips in the sergeant's helmet*): Want to sneak away from their mother, the devils, and run off to war like calves to a salt lick. But we'll draw lots on it, then they'll see that the world is no vale of smiles with a "Come along, son, we're short on generals." Sergeant, I'm very much afraid they won't come through the war. They've got terrible characters, all three of them. (*She holds out the helmet to Eilif.*) There. Pick a slip. (*He picks one and unfolds it. She snatches it away from him.*) There you have it. A cross! Oh, unhappy mother that I am, oh, mother of sorrows. Has he got to die? Doomed to perish in the springtime of his life? If he joins the army, he'll bite the dust, that's sure. He's too brave, just like his father. If he's not smart, he'll go the way of all flesh, the slip proves it. (*She roars at him.*) Are you going to be smart?

EILIF: Why not?

MOTHER COURAGE: The smart thing to do is to stay with your mother, and if they make fun of you and call you a sissy, just laugh.

THE RECRUITER: If you're shitting in your pants, we'll take your brother.

MOTHER COURAGE: I told you to laugh. Laugh! And now you pick, Swiss Cheese. I'm not so worried about you, you're honest. (*He picks a slip.*) Oh! Why, have you got that strange look? It's got to be blank. There can't be a cross on it. No, I can't lose you. (*She takes the slip.*) A cross? Him too? Maybe it's because he's so stupid. Oh, Swiss Cheese, you'll die too, unless you're very honest the whole time, the way I've taught you since you were a baby, always bringing back the change when I sent you to buy bread. That's the only way you can save yourself. Look, sergeant, isn't that a black cross?

THE SERGEANT: It's a cross all right. I don't see how I could have pulled one. I always stay in the rear. (*To the recruiter.*) It's on the up and up. Her own get it too.

SWISS CHEESE: I get it too. But I can take a hint.

MOTHER COURAGE (*to Kattrin*): Now you're the only one I'm sure of, you're a cross yourself because you've got a good heart. (*She holds up the helmet to Kattrin in the wagon, but she herself takes out the slip.*) It's driving me to despair. It can't be right, maybe I mixed them wrong. Don't be too good-natured, Kattrin, don't, there's a cross on your path too. Always keep very quiet, that ought to be easy seeing you're dumb. Well, now you know. Be careful, all of you, you'll need to be. And now we'll climb up and drive on. (*She returns the sergeant's helmet and climbs up into the wagon.*)

THE RECRUITER (*to the sergeant*): Do something!

THE SERGEANT: I'm not feeling so good.

THE RECRUITER: Maybe you caught cold when you took your helmet off in the wind. Tell her you want to buy something. Keep her busy. (*Aloud.*) You could at least take a look at that buckle, sergeant. After all, selling things is these good people's living. Hey, you, the sergeant wants to buy that belt buckle.

MOTHER COURAGE: Half a guilder. A buckle like that is worth two guilders. (*She climbs down.*)

THE SERGEANT: It's not new. This wind! I can't examine it here. Let's go where it's quiet. (*He goes behind the wagon with the buckle.*)

MOTHER COURAGE: I haven't noticed any wind.

THE SERGEANT: Maybe it is worth half a guilder. It's silver.

MOTHER COURAGE (*joins him behind the wagon*): Six solid ounces.

THE RECRUITER (*to Eilif*): And then we'll have a drink, just you and me. I've got your enlistment bonus right here. Come on. (*Eilif stands undecided.*)

MOTHER COURAGE: All right. Half a guilder.

THE SERGEANT: I don't get it. I always stay in the rear. There's no safer place for a sergeant. You can send the men up forward to win glory. You've spoiled my dinner. It won't go down, I know it, not a bite.

MOTHER COURAGE: Don't take it to heart. Don't let it spoil your appetite. Just keep behind the lines. Here, take a drink of schnapps, man. (*She hands him the bottle.*)

THE RECRUITER (*has taken Eilif's arm and is pulling him away toward the rear*): A bonus of ten guilders, and you'll be a brave man and you'll fight for the king, and the women will tear each other's hair out over you. And you can clout me one on the kisser for insulting you. (*Both go out.*)

(*Mute Kattrin jumps down from the wagon and emits raucous sounds.*)

MOTHER COURAGE: Just a minute, Kattrin, just a minute. The sergeant's paying up. (*Bites the half guilder.*) I'm always suspicious of money. I'm a burnt child, sergeant. But your coin is good. And now we'll be going. Where's Eilif?

SWISS CHEESE: He's gone with the recruiter.

MOTHER COURAGE (*stands motionless, then*): You simple soul. (*To Kattrin.*) I know. You can't talk, you couldn't help it.

THE SERGEANT: You could do with a drink yourself, mother. That's the way it goes. Soldiering isn't the worst thing in the world. You want to live off the war, but you want to keep you and yours out of it. Is that it?

MOTHER COURAGE: Now you'll have to pull with your brother, Kattrin.

(*Brother and sister harness themselves to the wagon and start pulling. Mother Courage walks beside them. The wagon rolls off.*)

THE SERGEANT (*looking after them*): If you want the war to work for you
You've got to give the war its due.

SCENE 2 _____

(*In 1625 and 1626 Mother Courage crosses Poland in the train of the Swedish armies. Outside the fortress of Wallhof she meets her son again. — A capon is successfully sold, the brave son's fortunes are at their zenith.*)

(*The general's tent.*)

(*Beside it the kitchen. The thunder of cannon. The cook is arguing with Mother Courage, who is trying to sell him a capon.*)

THE COOK: Sixty hellers for that pathetic bird?

MOTHER COURAGE: Pathetic bird? You mean this plump beauty? Are you trying to tell me that a general who's the biggest eater for miles around — God help you if you haven't got anything for his dinner — can't afford a measly sixty hellers?

THE COOK: I can get a dozen like it for ten hellers right around the corner.

MOTHER COURAGE: What, you'll find a capon like this right around the corner? With a siege on and everybody so starved you can see right through them. Maybe you'll scare up a rat, maybe, I say, 'cause they've all been eaten, I've seen five men chasing a starved rat for hours. Fifty hellers for a giant capon in the middle of a siege.

THE COOK: We're not besieged; they are. We're the besiegers, can't you get that through your head?

MOTHER COURAGE: But we haven't got anything to eat either, in fact we've got less than the people in the city. They've hauled it all inside. I hear their life is one big orgy. And look at us. I've been around to the peasants, they haven't got a thing.

THE COOK: They've got plenty. They hide it.

MOTHER COURAGE (*triumphantly*): Oh, no! They're ruined, that's what they are. They're starving. I've seen them. They're so hungry they're digging up roots. They lick their fingers when they've eaten a boiled strap. That's the situation. And here I've got a capon and I'm supposed to let it go for forty hellers.

THE COOK: Thirty, not forty. Thirty, I said.

MOTHER COURAGE: It's no common capon. They tell me this bird was so talented that he wouldn't eat unless they played music, he had his own favorite march. He could add and subtract, that's how intelligent he was. And you're trying to tell me forty hellers is too much. The general will bite your head off if there's nothing to eat.

THE COOK: You know what I'm going to do? (*He takes a piece of beef and sets his knife to it.*) Here I've got a piece of beef. I'll roast it. Think it over. This is your last chance.

MOTHER COURAGE: Roast and be damned. It's a year old.

THE COOK: A day old. That ox was running around only yesterday afternoon, I saw him with my own eyes.

MOTHER COURAGE: Then he must have stunk on the hoof.

THE COOK: I'll cook it five hours if I have to. We'll see if it's still tough. (*He cuts into it.*)

MOTHER COURAGE: Use plenty of pepper, maybe the general won't notice the stink.

(*The general, a chaplain, and Eilif enter the tent.*)

THE GENERAL (*slapping Eilif on the back*): All right, son, into your general's tent you go, you'll sit at my right hand. You've done a heroic deed and you're a pious trooper, because this is a war of religion and what you did was done for God, that's what counts with me. I'll reward you with a gold bracelet when I take the city. We come here to save their souls and what do those filthy, shameless peasants do? They drive their cattle away. And they stuff their priests with meat, front and back. But you taught them a lesson. Here's a tankard of red wine for you. (*He pours.*) We'll down it in one gulp. (*They do so.*) None for the chaplain, he's got his religion. What would you like for dinner, sweetheart?

EILIF: A scrap of meat. Why not?

THE GENERAL: Cook! Meat!

THE COOK: And now he brings company when there's nothing to eat.

(*Wanting to listen, Mother Courage makes him stop talking.*)

EILIF: Cutting down peasants whets the appetite.

MOTHER COURAGE: God, it's my Eilif.

THE COOK: Who?

MOTHER COURAGE: My eldest. I haven't seen hide nor hair of him in two years, he was stolen from me on the highway. He must be in good if the general invites him to dinner, and what have you got to offer? Nothing. Did you hear what the general's guest wants for dinner? Meat! Take my advice, snap up this capon. The price is one guilder.

THE GENERAL (*Has sat down with Eilif. Bellows.*): Food, Lamb, you lousy, no-good cook, or I'll kill you.

THE COOK: All right, hand it over. This is extortion.

MOTHER COURAGE: I thought it was a pathetic bird.

THE COOK: Pathetic is the word. Hand it over. Fifty hellers! It's highway robbery.

MOTHER COURAGE: One guilder, I say. For my eldest son, the general's honored guest, I spare no expense.

THE COOK (*gives her the money*): Then pluck it at least while I make the fire.

MOTHER COURAGE (*sits down to pluck the capon*): Won't he be glad to see me! He's my brave, intelligent son. I've got a stupid one too, but he's honest. The girl's a total loss. But at least she doesn't talk, that's something.

THE GENERAL: Take another drink, son, it's my best Falerno, I've only got another barrel or two at the most, but it's worth it to see that there's still some true faith in my army. The good shepherd here just looks on, all he knows how to do is preach. Can he do anything? No. And now, Eilif my son, tell us all about it, how cleverly you hoodwinked those peasants and captured those twenty head of cattle. I hope they'll be here soon.

EILIF: Tomorrow. Maybe the day after.

MOTHER COURAGE: Isn't my Eilif considerate, not bringing those oxen in until tomorrow, or you wouldn't have even said hello to my capon.

EILIF: Well, it was like this: I heard the peasants were secretly — mostly at night — rounding up the oxen they'd hidden in a certain forest. The city people had arranged to come and get them. I let them round the oxen up, I figured they'd find them easier than I would. I made my men ravenous for meat, put them on short rations for two days until their mouths watered if they even heard a word beginning with *me* . . . like measles.

THE GENERAL: That was clever of you.

EILIF: Maybe. The rest was a pushover. Except the peasants had clubs and there were three times more of them and they fell on us like bloody murder. Four of them drove me into a clump of bushes, they knocked my sword out of my hand and yelled: Surrender! Now what'll I do, I says to myself, they'll make hash out of me.

THE GENERAL: What did you do?

EILIF: I laughed.

THE GENERAL: You laughed?

EILIF: I laughed. Which led to a conversation. The first thing you know, I'm bargaining. Twenty guilders is too much for that ox, I say, how about fifteen? Like I'm meaning to pay. They're flummoxed, they scratch their heads. Quick, I reach for my sword and mow them down. Necessity knows no law. See what I mean?

THE GENERAL: What do you say to that, shepherd?

CHAPLAIN: Strictly speaking, that maxim is not in the Bible. But our Lord was able to turn five loaves into five hundred. So there was no question of poverty; he could tell people to love their neighbors because their bellies were full. Nowadays it's different.

THE GENERAL (*laughs*): Very different. All right, you Pharisee,° take a swig. (*To Eilif.*) You mowed them down, splendid, so my fine troops could have a decent bite to eat. Doesn't the Good Book say: "Whatsoever thou doest for the least of my brethren, thou doest for me"? And what have you done for them? You've got them a good chunk of beef for their dinner. They're not used to moldy crusts; in the old days they had a helmetful of white bread and wine before they went out to fight for God.

EILIF: Yes, I reached for my sword and I mowed them down.

THE GENERAL: You're a young Caesar. You deserve to see the king.

EILIF: I have, in the distance. He shines like a light. He's my ideal.

THE GENERAL: You're something like him already, Eilif. I know the worth of a brave soldier like you. When I find one, I treat him like my own son. (*He leads him to the map.*) Take a look at the situation, Eilif; we've still got a long way to go.

MOTHER COURAGE (*who has been listening starts plucking her capon furiously*): He must be a rotten general.

THE COOK: Eats like a pig, but why rotten?

MOTHER COURAGE: Because he needs brave soldiers, that's why. If he planned his campaigns right, what would he need brave soldiers for? The run-of-the-mill would do. Take it from me, whenever you find a lot of virtues, it shows that something's wrong.

THE COOK: I'd say it proves that something is all right.

MOTHER COURAGE: No, that something's wrong. See, when a general or a king is real stupid and leads his men up shit creek, his troops need courage, that's a virtue. If he's stingy and doesn't hire enough soldiers, they've all got to be Herculeses. And if

---

Pharisee: A member of a Jewish sect current in biblical days; the term is now commonly used to refer to a hypocritical, self-righteous person.

he's a slob and lets everything go to pot, they've
got to be as sly as serpents or they're done for.
And if he's always expecting too much of them,
they need an extra dose of loyalty. A country that's
run right, or a good king or a good general, doesn't
need any of these virtues. You don't need virtues
in a decent country, the people can all be perfectly
ordinary, medium-bright, and cowards too for my
money.

THE GENERAL: I bet your father was a soldier.

EILIF: A great soldier, I'm told. My mother warned
me about it. Makes me think of a song.

THE GENERAL: Sing it! (*Bellowing.*) Where's that food!

EILIF: It's called: The Song of the Old Wife and the
Soldier. (*He sings, doing a war dance with his
saber.*)

A gun or a pike, they can kill who they like
And the torrent will swallow a wader
You had better think twice before battling with
   ice
Said the old wife to the soldier.
Cocking his rifle he leapt to his feet
Laughing for joy as he heard the drum beat
The wars cannot hurt me, he told her.
He shouldered his gun and he picked up his
   knife
To see the wide world. That's the soldier's life.
Those were the words of the soldier.

Ah, deep will they lie who wise counsel defy
Learn wisdom from those that are older
Oh, don't venture too high or you'll fall from
   the sky
Said the old wife to the soldier.
But the young soldier with knife and with gun
Only laughed a cold laugh and stepped into the
   run.
The water can't hurt me, he told her.
And when the moon on the rooftop shines white
We'll be coming back. You can pray for that
   night.
Those were the words of the soldier.

MOTHER COURAGE (*in the kitchen, continues the song,
beating a pot with a spoon*):
Like the smoke you'll be gone and no warmth
   linger on
And your deeds only leave me the colder!
Oh, see the smoke race. Oh, dear God keep him
   safe!
That's what she said of the soldier.

EILIF: What's that?

MOTHER COURAGE (*goes on singing*): And the
   young soldier with knife and with gun
Was swept from his feet till he sank in the run
And the torrent swallowed the waders.

Cold shone the moon on the rooftop white
But the soldier was carried away with the ice
And what was it she heard from the soldiers?

Like the smoke he was gone and no warmth
   lingered on
And his deeds only left her the colder.
Ah, deep will they lie who wise counsel defy!
That's what she said to the soldiers.

THE GENERAL: What do they think they're doing in
my kitchen?

EILIF (*Has gone into the kitchen. He embraces his
mother.*): Mother! It's you! Where are the others?

MOTHER COURAGE (*in his arms*): Snug as a bug in a
rug. Swiss Cheese is paymaster of the Second Regiment; at least he won't be fighting, I couldn't keep
him out altogether.

ELLIE: And how about your feet?

MOTHER COURAGE: Well, it's hard getting my shoes
on in the morning.

THE GENERAL (*has joined them*): Ah, so you're his
mother. I hope you've got more sons for me like
this fellow here.

EILIF: Am I lucky! There you're sitting in the kitchen
hearing your son being praised.

MOTHER COURAGE: I heard it all right! (*She gives him
a slap in the face.*)

EILIF (*holding his cheek*): For capturing the oxen?

MOTHER COURAGE: No. For not surrendering when
the four of them were threatening to make hash
out of you! Didn't I teach you to take care of
yourself? You Finnish devil!

(*The general and the chaplain laugh.*)

SCENE 3

(*Three years later Mother Courage and parts of a
Finnish regiment are taken prisoner. She is able to
save her daughter and her wagon, but her honest son
dies.*)

(*Army camp.*)

(*Afternoon. On a pole the regimental flag. Mother
Courage has stretched a clothesline between her wagon,
on which all sorts of merchandise is hung in display,
and a large cannon. She and Kattrin are folding washing
and piling it on the cannon. At the same time she is
negotiating with an ordnance officer over a sack of
bullets. Swiss Cheese, now in the uniform of a paymaster, is looking on. A pretty woman, Yvette Pottier,
is sitting with a glass of brandy in front of her, sewing
a gaudy-colored hat. She is in her stocking feet, her
red high-heeled shoes are on the ground beside her.*)

THE ORDNANCE OFFICER: I'll let you have these bullets
for two guilders. It's cheap, I need the money,

because the colonel's been drinking with the officers for two days and we're out of liquor.

MOTHER COURAGE: That's ammunition for the troops. If it's found here, I'll be court-martialed. You punks sell their bullets and the men have nothing to shoot at the enemy.

THE ORDNANCE OFFICER: Don't be hard-hearted, you scratch my back, I'll scratch yours.

MOTHER COURAGE: I'm not taking any army property. Not at that price.

THE ORDNANCE OFFICER: You can sell it for five guilders, maybe eight, to the ordnance officer of the Fourth before the day is out, if you're quiet about it and give him a receipt for twelve. He hasn't an ounce of ammunition left.

MOTHER COURAGE: Why don't you do it yourself?

THE ORDNANCE OFFICER: Because I don't trust him, he's a friend of mine.

MOTHER COURAGE (*takes the sack*): Hand it over. (*To Kattrin.*) Take it back there and pay him one and a half guilders. (*In response to the ordnance officer's protest.*) One and a half guilders, I say. (*Kattrin drags the sack behind the wagon, the ordnance officer follows her. Mother Courage to Swiss Cheese.*) Here's your underdrawers, take good care of them, this is October, might be coming on fall, I don't say it will be, because I've learned that nothing is sure to happen the way we think, not even the seasons. But whatever happens, your regimental funds have to be in order. Are your funds in order?

SWISS CHEESE: Yes, mother.

MOTHER COURAGE: Never forget that they made you paymaster because you're honest and not brave like your brother, and especially because you're too simple-minded to get the idea of making off with the money. That's a comfort to me. And don't go mislaying your drawers.

SWISS CHEESE: No, mother. I'll put them under my mattress. (*Starts to go.*)

ORDNANCE OFFICER: I'll go with you, paymaster.

MOTHER COURAGE: Just don't teach him any of your tricks. (*Without saying good-bye the ordnance officer goes out with Swiss Cheese.*)

YVETTE (*waves her hand after the ordnance officer*): You might say good-bye, officer.

MOTHER COURAGE (*to Yvette*): I don't like to see those two together. He's not the right kind of company for my Swiss Cheese. But the war's getting along pretty well. More countries are joining in all the time, it can go on for another four, five years, easy. With a little planning ahead, I can do good business if I'm careful. Don't you know you shouldn't drink in the morning with your sickness?

YVETTE: Who says I'm sick, it's slander.

MOTHER COURAGE: Everybody says so.

YVETTE: Because they're all liars. Mother Courage, I'm desperate. They all keep out of my way like I'm a rotten fish on account of those lies. What's the good of fixing my hat? (*She throws it down.*) That's why I drink in the morning, I never used to, I'm getting crow's-feet, but it doesn't matter now. In the Second Finnish Regiment they all know me. I should have stayed home when my first love walked out on me. Pride isn't for the likes of us. If we can't put up with shit, we're through.

MOTHER COURAGE: Just don't start in on your Pieter and how it all happened in front of my innocent daughter.

YVETTE: She's just the one to hear it, it'll harden her against love.

MOTHER COURAGE: Nothing can harden them.

YVETTE: Then I'll talk about it because it makes me feel better. It begins with my growing up in fair Flanders, because if I hadn't I'd never have laid eyes on him and I wouldn't be here in Poland now, because he was an army cook, blond, a Dutchman, but skinny. Kattrin, watch out for the skinny ones, but I didn't know that then, and another thing I didn't know is that he had another girl even then, and they all called him Pete the Pipe, because he didn't even take his pipe out of his mouth when he was doing it, that's all it meant to him. (*She sings the Song of Fraternization.*)

When I was only sixteen
The foe came into our land.
He laid aside his sabre
And with a smile he took my hand.
   After the May parade
   The May light starts to fade.
   The regiment dressed by the right
   Then drums were beaten, that's the drill.
   The foe took us behind the hill
   And fraternized all night.

There were so many foes came
And mine worked in the mess.
I loathed him in the daytime.
At night I loved him none the less.
   After the May parade
   The May light starts to fade.
   The regiment dressed by the right
   Then drums were beaten, that's the drill.
   The foe took us behind the hill
   And fraternized all night.

The love which came upon me
Was wished on me by fate.
My friends could never grasp why
I found it hard to share their hate.
   The fields were wet with dew
   When sorrow first I knew.

The regiment dressed by the right
Then drums were beaten, that's the drill
And then the foe, my lover still
Went marching from our sight.

Well, I followed him, but I never found him. That was five years ago. (*She goes behind the wagon with an unsteady gait.*)

MOTHER COURAGE: You've left your hat.

YVETTE: Anybody that wants it can have it.

MOTHER COURAGE: Let that be a lesson to you, Kattrin. Have no truck with soldiers. It's love that makes the world go round, so you'd better watch out. Even with a civilian it's no picnic. He says he'd kiss the ground you put your little feet on, talking of feet, did you wash yours yesterday, and then you're his slave. Be glad you're dumb, that way you'll never contradict yourself or want to bite your tongue off because you've told the truth, it's a gift of God to be dumb. Here comes the general's cook, I wonder what he wants.

(*The cook and the chaplain enter.*)

THE CHAPLAIN: I've got a message for you from your son Eilif. The cook here thought he'd come along, he's taken a shine to you.

THE COOK: I only came to get a breath of air.

MOTHER COURAGE: You can always do that here if you behave, and if you don't, I can handle you. Well, what does he want? I've got no money to spare.

THE CHAPLAIN: Actually he wanted me to see his brother, the paymaster.

MOTHER COURAGE: He's not here any more, or anywhere else either. He's not his brother's paymaster. I don't want him leading him into temptation and being smart at his expense. (*Gives him money from the bag slung around her waist.*) Give him this, it's a sin, he's speculating on mother love and he ought to be ashamed.

THE COOK: He won't do it much longer, then he'll be marching off with his regiment, maybe to his death, you never can tell. Better make it a little more, you'll be sorry later. You women are hardhearted, but afterwards you're sorry. A drop of brandy wouldn't have cost much when it was wanted, but it wasn't given, and later, for all you know, he'll be lying in the cold ground and you can't dig him up again.

THE CHAPLAIN: Don't be sentimental, cook. There's nothing wrong with dying in battle, it's a blessing, and I'll tell you why. This is a war of religion. Not a common war, but a war for the faith, and therefore pleasing to God.

THE COOK: That's a fact. In a way you could call it a war, because of the extortion and killing and looting, not to mention a bit of rape, but it's a war of religion, which makes it different from all other wars, that's obvious. But it makes a man thirsty all the same, you've got to admit that.

THE CHAPLAIN (*to Mother Courage, pointing at the cook*): I tried to discourage him, but he says you've turned his head, he sees you in his dreams.

THE COOK (*lights a short-stemmed pipe*): All I want is a glass of brandy from your fair hand, nothing more sinful. I'm already so shocked by the jokes the chaplain's been telling me, I bet I'm still red in the face.

MOTHER COURAGE: And him a clergyman! I'd better give you fellows something to drink or you'll be making me immoral propositions just to pass the time.

THE CHAPLAIN: This is temptation, said the deacon, and succumbed to it. (*Turning toward Kattrin as he leaves.*) And who is this delightful young lady?

MOTHER COURAGE: She's not delightful, she's a respectable young lady.

(*The chaplain and the cook go behind the wagon with Mother Courage. Kattrin looks after them, then she walks away from the washing and approaches the hat. She picks it up, sits down, and puts on the red shoes. From the rear Mother Courage is heard talking politics with the chaplain and the cook.*)

MOTHER COURAGE: The Poles here in Poland shouldn't have butted in. All right, our king marched his army into their country. But instead of keeping the peace, the Poles start butting into their own affairs and attack the king while he's marching quietly through the landscape. That was a breach of the peace and the blood is on their head.

THE CHAPLAIN: Our king had only one thing in mind: freedom. The emperor had everybody under his yoke, the Poles as much as the Germans; the king had to set them free.

THE COOK: I see it this way, your brandy's first-rate, I can see why I liked your face, but we were talking about the king. This freedom he was trying to introduce into Germany cost him a fortune, he had to levy a salt tax in Sweden, which, as I said, cost the poor people a fortune. Then he had to put the Germans in jail and break them on the rack because they liked being the emperor's slaves. Oh yes, the king made short shrift of anybody that didn't want to be free. In the beginning he only wanted to protect Poland against wicked people, especially the emperor, but the more he ate the more he wanted, and pretty soon he was protecting all of Germany. But the Germans didn't take it lying down and the king got nothing but trouble for all his kindness and expense, which he naturally had to defray from taxes, which made for bad blood, but that didn't discourage him. He had one thing in his favor, the word of God, which was lucky, because otherwise people would have said he was doing it all for himself and what he hoped to get out of it. As it was, he always had a clear conscience and that was all he really cared about.

MOTHER COURAGE: It's easy to see you're not a Swede, or you wouldn't talk like that about the Hero-King.

THE CHAPLAIN: You're eating his bread, aren't you?

THE COOK: I don't eat his bread, I bake it.

MOTHER COURAGE: He can't be defeated because his men believe in him. (*Earnestly.*) When you listen to the big wheels talk, they're making war for reasons of piety, in the name of everything that's fine and noble. But when you take another look, you see that they're not so dumb; they're making war for profit. If they weren't, the small fry like me wouldn't have anything to do with it.

THE COOK: That's a fact.

THE CHAPLAIN: And it wouldn't hurt you as a Dutchman to take a look at that flag up there before you express opinions in Poland.

MOTHER COURAGE: We're all good Protestants here! Prosit!°

(*Kattrin has started strutting about with Yvette's hat on, imitating Yvette's gait.*)

(*Suddenly cannon fire and shots are heard. Drums. Mother Courage, the cook, and the chaplain run out from behind the wagon, the two men still with glasses in hand. The ordnance officer and a soldier rush up to the cannon and try to push it away.*)

MOTHER COURAGE: What's going on? Let me get my washing first, you lugs. (*She tries to rescue her washing.*)

THE ORDNANCE OFFICER: The Catholics. They're attacking. I don't know as we'll get away. (*To the soldier.*) Get rid of the gun! (*Runs off.*)

THE COOK: Christ, I've got to find the general. Courage, I'll be back for a little chat in a day or two. (*Rushes out.*)

MOTHER COURAGE: Stop, you've forgotten your pipe.

THE COOK (*from the distance*): Keep it for me! I'll need it.

MOTHER COURAGE: Just when we were making a little money!

THE CHAPLAIN: Well, I guess I'll be going too. It might be dangerous though, with the enemy so close. Blessed are the peaceful is the best motto in wartime. If only I had a cloak to cover up with.

Prosit: A toast to good health.

MOTHER COURAGE: I'm not lending any cloaks, not on your life. I've had bitter experience in that line.

THE CHAPLAIN: But my religion puts me in special danger.

MOTHER COURAGE (*bringing him a cloak*): It's against my better conscience. And now run along.

THE CHAPLAIN: Thank you kindly, you've got a good heart. But maybe I'd better sit here a while. The enemy might get suspicious if they see me running.

MOTHER COURAGE (*to the soldier*): Leave it lay, you fool, you won't get paid extra. I'll take care of it for you, you'd only get killed.

THE SOLDIER (*running away*): I tried. You're my witness.

MOTHER COURAGE: I'll swear it on the Bible. (*Sees her daughter with the hat.*) What are you doing with that floozy hat? Take it off, have you gone out of your mind? Now of all times, with the enemy on top of us? (*She tears the hat off Kattrin's head.*) You want them to find you and make a whore out of you? And those shoes! Take them off, you woman of Babylon! (*She tries to pull them off.*) Jesus Christ, chaplain, make her take those shoes off! I'll be right back. (*She runs to the wagon.*)

YVETTE (*enters, powdering her face*): What's this I hear? The Catholics are coming? Where's my hat? Who's been stamping on it? I can't be seen like this if the Catholics are coming. What'll they think of me? I haven't even got a mirror. (*To the chaplain.*) How do I look? Too much powder?

THE CHAPLAIN: Just right.

YVETTE: And where are my red shoes? (*She doesn't see them because Kattrin hides her feet under her skirt.*) I left them here. I've got to get back to my tent. In my bare feet. It's disgraceful! (*Goes out.*)

(*Swiss Cheese runs in carrying a small box.*)

MOTHER COURAGE (*Comes out with her hands full of ashes. To Kattrin.*): Ashes. (*To Swiss Cheese.*) What you got there?

SWISS CHEESE: The regimental funds.

MOTHER COURAGE: Throw it away! No more paymastering for you.

SWISS CHEESE: I'm responsible for it. (*He goes rear.*)

MOTHER COURAGE (*to the chaplain*): Take your clergyman's coat off, chaplain, or they'll recognize you, cloak or no cloak. (*She rubs Kattrin's face with ashes.*) Hold still! There. With a little dirt you'll be safe. What a mess! The sentries were drunk. Hide your light under a bushel, as the Good Book says. When a soldier, especially a Catholic, sees a clean face, she's a whore before she knows it. Nobody feeds them for weeks. When they finally loot some provisions, the next thing they want is women. That'll do it. Let me look at you. Not bad. Like you'd been wallowing in a pigsty. Stop shaking.

You're safe now. (*To Swiss Cheese.*) What did you do with the cashbox?

SWISS CHEESE: I thought I'd put it in the wagon.

MOTHER COURAGE (*horrified*): What! In my wagon? Of all the sinful stupidity! If my back is turned for half a second! They'll hang us all!

SWISS CHEESE: Then I'll put it somewhere else, or I'll run away with it.

MOTHER COURAGE: You'll stay right here. It's too late.

THE CHAPLAIN (*still changing, comes forward*): Heavens, the flag!

MOTHER COURAGE (*takes down the regimental flag*): Bozhe moi! I'm so used to it I don't see it. Twenty-five years I've had it.

(*The cannon fire grows louder.*)

(*Morning, three days later. The cannon is gone. Mother Courage, Kattrin, the chaplain, and Swiss Cheese are sitting dejectedly over a meal.*)

SWISS CHEESE: This is the third day I've been sitting here doing nothing; the sergeant has always been easy on me, but now he must be starting to wonder: where can Swiss Cheese be with the cashbox?

MOTHER COURAGE: Be glad they haven't tracked you down.

THE CHAPLAIN: What about me? I can't hold a service here either. The Good Book says: "Whosoever hath a full heart, his tongue runneth over." Heaven help me if mine runneth over.

MOTHER COURAGE: That's the way it is. Look what I've got on my hands: one with a religion and one with a cashbox. I don't know which is worse.

THE CHAPLAIN: Tell yourself that we're in the hands of God.

MOTHER COURAGE: I don't think we're that bad off, but all the same I can't sleep at night. If it weren't for you, Swiss Cheese, it'd be easier. I think I've put myself in the clear. I told them I was against the antichrist; he's a Swede with horns, I told them, and I'd noticed the left horn was kind of worn down. I interrupted the questioning to ask where I could buy holy candles cheap. I knew what to say because Swiss Cheese's father was a Catholic and he used to make jokes about it. They didn't really believe me, but their regiment had no provisioner, so they looked the other way. Maybe we stand to gain. We're prisoners, but so are lice on a dog.

THE CHAPLAIN: This milk is good. Though there's not very much of it or of anything else. Maybe we'll have to cut down on our Swedish appetites. But such is the lot of the vanquished.

MOTHER COURAGE: Who's vanquished? Victory and defeat don't always mean the same thing to the big wheels up top and the small fry underneath. Not by a long shot. In some cases defeat is a blessing to the small fry. Honor's lost, but nothing else. One time in Livonia our general got such a shellacking from the enemy that in the confusion I laid hands on a beautiful white horse from the baggage train. That horse pulled my wagon for seven months, until we had a victory and they checked up. On the whole, you can say that victory and defeat cost us plain people plenty. The best thing for us is when politics gets bogged down. (*To Swiss Cheese.*) Eat!

SWISS CHEESE: I've lost my appetite. How's the sergeant going to pay the men?

MOTHER COURAGE: Troops never get paid when they're running away.

SWISS CHEESE: But they've got it coming to them. If they're not paid, they don't need to run. Not a step.

MOTHER COURAGE: Swiss Cheese, you're too conscientious, it almost frightens me. I brought you up to be honest, because you're not bright, but somewhere it's got to stop. And now me and the chaplain are going to buy a Catholic flag and some meat. Nobody can buy meat like the chaplain, he goes into a trance and heads straight for the best piece, I guess it makes his mouth water and that shows him the way. At least they let me carry on my business. Nobody cares about a shopkeeper's religion, all they want to know is the price. Protestant pants are as warm as any other kind.

THE CHAPLAIN: Like the friar said when somebody told him the Lutherans were going to stand the whole country on its head. They'll always need beggars, he says. (*Mother Courage disappears into the wagon.*) But she's worried about that cashbox. They've taken no notice of us so far, they think we're all part of the wagon, but how long can that go on?

SWISS CHEESE: I can take it away.

THE CHAPLAIN: That would be almost more dangerous. What if somebody sees you? They've got spies. Yesterday morning, just as I'm relieving myself, one of them jumps out of the ditch. I was so scared I almost let out a prayer. That would have given me away. I suppose they think they can tell a Protestant by the smell of his shit. He was a little runt with a patch over one eye.

MOTHER COURAGE (*climbing down from the wagon with a basket*): Look what I've found. You shameless slut! (*She holds up the red shoes triumphantly.*) Yvette's red shoes! She's swiped them in cold blood. It's your fault. Who told her she was a delightful young lady? (*She puts them into the basket.*) I'm giving them back. Stealing Yvette's shoes! She ruins herself for money, that I can understand. But you'd like to do it free of charge, for pleasure. I've told you, you'll have to wait for peace. No soldiers! Just wait for peace with your worldly ways.

THE CHAPLAIN: She doesn't seem very worldly to me.

MOTHER COURAGE: Too worldly for me. In Dalarna she was like a stone, which is all they've got around there. The people used to say: We don't see the cripple. That's the way I like it. That way she's safe. (*To Swiss Cheese.*) You leave that box where it is, hear? And keep an eye on your sister, she needs it. The two of you will be the death of me. I'd sooner take care of a bag of fleas. (*She goes off with the chaplain. Kattrin starts clearing away the dishes.*)

SWISS CHEESE: Won't be many more days when I can sit in the sun in my shirtsleeves. (*Kattrin points to a tree.*) Yes, the leaves are all yellow. (*Kattrin asks him, by means of gestures, whether he wants a drink.*) Not now. I'm thinking. (*Pause.*) She says she can't sleep. I'd better get the cashbox out of here, I've found a hiding place. All right, get me a drink. (*Kattrin goes behind the wagon.*) I'll hide it in the rabbit hole down by the river until I can take it away. Maybe late tonight. I'll go get it and take it to the regiment. I wonder how far they've run in three days? Won't the sergeant be surprised! Well, Swiss Cheese, this is a pleasant disappointment, that's what he'll say. I trust you with the regimental cashbox and you bring it back.

(*As Kattrin comes out from behind the wagon with a glass of brandy, she comes face to face with two men. One is a sergeant. The other removes his hat and swings it through the air in a ceremonious greeting. He has a patch over one eye.*)

THE MAN WITH THE PATCH: Good morning, my dear. Have you by any chance seen a man from the headquarters of the Second Finnish Regiment?

(*Scared out of her wits, Kattrin runs front, spilling the brandy. The two exchange looks and withdraw after seeing Swiss Cheese sitting there.*)

SWISS CHEESE (*starting up from his thoughts*): You've spilled half of it. What's the fuss about? Poke yourself in the eye? I don't understand you. I'm getting out of here, I've made up my mind, it's best. (*He stands up. She does everything she can think of to call his attention to the danger. He only evades her.*) I wish I could understand you. Poor thing, I know you're trying to tell me something, you just can't say it. Don't worry about spilling the brandy, I'll be drinking plenty more. What's one glass? (*He takes the cashbox out of the wagon and hides it under his jacket.*) I'll be right back. Let me go,

you're making me angry. I know you mean well. If only you could talk.

(*When she tries to hold him back, he kisses her and tears himself away. He goes out. She is desperate, she races back and forth, uttering short inarticulate sounds. The chaplain and Mother Courage come back. Kattrin gesticulates wildly at her mother.*)

MOTHER COURAGE: What's the matter? You're all upset. Has somebody hurt you? Where's Swiss Cheese? Tell it to me in order, Kattrin. Your mother understands you. What, the no-good's taken the cashbox? I'll hit him over the head with it, the sneak. Take your time, don't talk nonsense, use your hands, I don't like it when you howl like a dog, what will the chaplain think? It gives him the creeps. A one-eyed man?

THE CHAPLAIN: The one-eyed man is a spy. Did they arrest Swiss Cheese? (*Kattrin shakes her head and shrugs her shoulders.*) We're done for.

MOTHER COURAGE (*Takes a Catholic flag out of her basket. The chaplain fastens it to the flagpole.*): Hoist the new flag!

THE CHAPLAIN (*bitterly*): All good Catholics here.

(*Voices are heard from the rear. The two men bring in Swiss Cheese.*)

SWISS CHEESE: Let me go, I haven't got anything. Stop twisting my shoulder, I'm innocent.

THE SERGEANT: He belongs here. You know each other.

MOTHER COURAGE: What makes you think that?

SWISS CHEESE: I don't know them. I don't even know who they are. I had a meal here, it cost me ten hellers. Maybe you saw me sitting here, it was too salty.

THE SERGEANT: Who are you anyway?

MOTHER COURAGE: We're respectable people. And it's true. He had a meal here. He said it was too salty.

THE SERGEANT: Are you trying to tell me you don't know each other?

MOTHER COURAGE: Why should I know him? I don't know everybody. I don't ask people what their name is or if they're heathens; if they pay, they're not heathens. Are you a heathen?

SWISS CHEESE: Of course not.

THE CHAPLAIN: He ate his meal and he behaved himself. He didn't open his mouth except when he was eating. Then you have to.

THE SERGEANT: And who are you?

MOTHER COURAGE: He's only my bartender. You gentlemen must be thirsty, I'll get you a drink of brandy, you must be hot and tired.

THE SERGEANT: We don't drink on duty. (*To Swiss Cheese.*) You were carrying something. You must have hidden it by the river. You had something under your jacket when you left here.

MOTHER COURAGE: Was it really him?

SWISS CHEESE: I think you must have seen somebody else. I saw a man running with something under his jacket. You've got the wrong man.

MOTHER COURAGE: That's what I think too, it's a misunderstanding. These things happen. I'm a good judge of people, I'm Mother Courage, you've heard of me, everybody knows me. Take it from me, this man has an honest face.

THE SERGEANT: We're looking for the cashbox of the Second Finnish Regiment. We know what the man in charge of it looks like. We've been after him for two days. You're him.

SWISS CHEESE: I'm not.

THE SERGEANT: Hand it over. If you don't you're a goner, you know that. Where is it?

MOTHER COURAGE (with urgency): He'd hand it over, wouldn't he, knowing he was a goner if he didn't? I've got it, he'd say, take it, you're stronger. He's not that stupid. Speak up, you stupid idiot, the sergeant's giving you a chance.

SWISS CHEESE: But I haven't got it.

THE SERGEANT: In that case come along. We'll get it out of you. (They lead him away.)

MOTHER COURAGE (shouts after them): He'd tell you. He's not that stupid. And don't twist his shoulder off! (Runs after them.)

(The same evening. The chaplain and mute Kattrin are washing dishes and scouring knives.)

THE CHAPLAIN: That boy's in trouble. There are cases like that in the Bible. Take the Passion of our Lord and Savior. There's an old song about it. (He sings the Song of the Hours.)

In the first hour Jesus mild
Who had prayed since even
Was betrayed and led before
Pontius the heathen.

Pilate found him innocent
Free from fault and error.
Therefore, having washed his hands
Sent him to King Herod.

In the third hour he was scourged
Stripped and clad in scarlet
And a plaited crown of thorns
Set upon his forehead.

On the Son of Man they spat
Mocked him and made merry.
Then the cross of death was brought
Given him to carry.

At the sixth hour with two thieves
To the cross they nailed him
And the people and the thieves
Mocked him and reviled him.

This is Jesus King of Jews
Cried they in derision
Till the sun withdrew its light
From that awful vision.

At the ninth hour Jesus wailed
Why hast thou me forsaken?
Soldiers brought him vinegar
Which he left untaken.

Then he yielded up the ghost
And the earth was shaken.
Rended was the temple's veil
And the saints were wakened.

Soldiers broke the two thieves' legs
As the night descended
Thrust a spear in Jesus' side
When his life had ended.

Still they mocked, as from his wound
Flowed the blood and water
Thus blasphemed the Son of Man
With their cruel laughter.

MOTHER COURAGE (enters in a state of agitation): His life's at stake. But they say the sergeant will listen to reason. Only it mustn't come out that he's our Swiss Cheese, or they'll say we've been giving him aid and comfort. All they want is money. But where will we get the money? Hasn't Yvette been here? I met her just now, she's latched onto a colonel, he's thinking of buying her a provisioner's business.

THE CHAPLAIN: Are you really thinking of selling?

MOTHER COURAGE: How else can I get the money for the sergeant?

THE CHAPLAIN: But what will you live on?

MOTHER COURAGE: That's the hitch.

(Yvette Pottier comes in with a doddering colonel.)

YVETTE (embracing Mother Courage): My dear Mother Courage. Here we are again! (Whispering.) He's willing. (Aloud.) This is my dear friend who advises me on business matters. I just chanced to hear that you wish to sell your wagon, due to circumstances. I might be interested.

MOTHER COURAGE: Mortgage it, not sell it, let's not be hasty. It's not so easy to buy a wagon like this in wartime.

YVETTE (disappointed): Only mortgage it? I thought you wanted to sell it. In that case, I don't know if I'm interested. (To the colonel.) What do you think?

THE COLONEL: Just as you say, my dear.

MOTHER COURAGE: It's only being mortgaged.

YVETTE: I thought you needed money.

MOTHER COURAGE (*firmly*): I need the money, but I'd rather run myself ragged looking for an offer than sell now. The wagon is our livelihood. It's an opportunity for you, Yvette, God knows when you'll find another like it and have such a good friend to advise you. See what I mean?

YVETTE: My friend thinks I should snap it up, but I don't know. If it's only being mortgaged . . . Don't you agree that we ought to buy?

THE COLONEL: Yes, my dear.

MOTHER COURAGE: Then you'll have to look for something that's for sale, maybe you'll find something if you take your time and your friend goes around with you. Maybe in a week or two you'll find the right thing.

YVETTE: Then we'll go looking, I love to go looking for things, and I love to go around with you, Poldi, it's a real pleasure. Even if it takes two weeks. When would you pay the money back if you get it?

MOTHER COURAGE: I can pay it back in two weeks, maybe one.

YVETTE: I can't make up my mind, Poldi, chéri, tell me what to do. (*She takes the colonel aside.*) I know she's got to sell, that's definite. The lieutenant, you know who I mean, the blond one, he'd be glad to lend me the money. He's mad about me, he says I remind him of somebody. What do you think?

THE COLONEL: Keep away from that lieutenant. He's no good. He'll take advantage. Haven't I told you I'd buy you something, pussykins?

YVETTE: I can't accept it from you. But then if you think the lieutenant might take advantage . . . Poldi, I'll accept it from you.

THE COLONEL: I hope so.

YVETTE: Your advice is to take it?

THE COLONEL: That's my advice.

YVETTE (*goes back to Mother Courage*): My friend advises me to do it. Write me out a receipt, say the wagon belongs to me complete with stock and furnishings when the two weeks are up. We'll take inventory right now, then I'll bring you the two hundred guilders. (*To the colonel.*) You go back to camp, I'll join you in a little while, I've got to take inventory, I don't want anything missing from my wagon. (*She kisses him. He leaves. She climbs up in the wagon.*) I don't see very many boots.

MOTHER COURAGE: Yvette. This is no time to inspect your wagon if it is yours. You promised to see the sergeant about my Swiss Cheese, you've got to hurry. They say he's to be court-martialed in an hour.

YVETTE: Just let me count the shirts.

MOTHER COURAGE (*pulls her down by the skirt*): You hyena, it's Swiss Cheese, his life's at stake. And don't tell anybody where the offer comes from, in heaven's name say it's your gentleman friend, or we'll all get it, they'll say we helped him.

YVETTE: I've arranged to meet One-Eye in the woods, he must be there already.

THE CHAPLAIN: And there's no need to start out with the whole two hundred, offer a hundred and fifty, that's plenty.

MOTHER COURAGE: Is it your money? You just keep out of this. Don't worry, you'll get your bread and soup. Go on now and don't haggle. It's his life. (*She gives Yvette a push to start her on her way.*)

THE CHAPLAIN: I didn't mean to butt in, but what are we going to live on? You've got an unemployable daughter on your hands.

MOTHER COURAGE: You muddlehead, I'm counting on the regimental cashbox. They'll allow for his expenses, won't they?

THE CHAPLAIN: But will she handle it right?

MOTHER COURAGE: It's in her own interest. If I spend her two hundred, she gets the wagon. She's mighty keen on it, how long can she expect to hold on to her colonel? Kattrin, you scour the knives, use pumice. And you, don't stand around like Jesus on the Mount of Olives,° bestir yourself, wash those glasses, we're expecting at least fifty for dinner, and then it'll be the same old story: "Oh my feet, I'm not used to running around, I don't run around in the pulpit." I think they'll set him free. Thank God they're open to bribery. They're not wolves, they're human and out for money. Bribe-taking in humans is the same as mercy in God. It's our only hope. As long as people take bribes, you'll have mild sentences and even the innocent will get off once in a while.

YVETTE (*comes in panting*): They want two hundred. And we've got to be quick. Or it'll be out of their hands. I'd better take One-Eye to see my colonel right away. He confessed that he'd had the cashbox, they put the thumb screws on him. But he threw it in the river when he saw they were after him. The box is gone. Should I run and get the money from my colonel?

MOTHER COURAGE: The box is gone. How will I get my two hundred back?

YVETTE: Ah, so you thought you could take it out of the cashbox? You thought you'd put one over on

---

Jesus on the Mount of Olives: Two biblical scenes depict Jesus on the Mount of Olives: when he delivers the Sermon on the Mount and when he meditates just before his betrayal and death.

me. Forget it. If you want to save Swiss Cheese, you'll just have to pay, or maybe you'd like me to drop the whole thing and let you keep your wagon?

MOTHER COURAGE: This is something I hadn't reckoned with. But don't rush me, you'll get the wagon, I know it's down the drain, I've had it for seventeen years. Just let me think a second, it's all so sudden. What'll I do, I can't give them two hundred, I guess you should have bargained. If I haven't got a few guilders to fall back on, I'll be at the mercy of the first Tom, Dick, or Harry. Say I'll give them a hundred and twenty, I'll lose my wagon anyway.

YVETTE: They won't go along. One-Eye's in a hurry, he's so keyed-up he keeps looking behind him. Hadn't I better give them the whole two hundred?

MOTHER COURAGE (*in despair*): I can't do it. Thirty years I've worked. She's twenty-five and no husband. I've got her to keep too. Don't needle me, I know what I'm doing. Say a hundred and twenty or nothing doing.

YVETTE: It's up to you. (*Goes out quickly.*)

(*Mother Courage looks neither at the chaplain nor at her daughter. She sits down to help Kattrin scour the knives.*)

MOTHER COURAGE: Don't break the glasses. They're not ours anymore. Watch what you're doing, you'll cut yourself. Swiss Cheese will be back, I'll pay two hundred if I have to. You'll have your brother. With eighty guilders we can buy a peddler's pack and start all over. Worse things have happened.

THE CHAPLAIN: The Lord will provide.

MOTHER COURAGE: Rub them dry. (*They scour the knives in silence. Suddenly Kattrin runs sobbing behind the wagon.*)

YVETTE (*comes running*): They won't go along. I warned you. One-Eye wanted to run out on me, he said it was no use. He said we'd hear the drums any minute, meaning he'd been sentenced. I offered a hundred and fifty. He didn't even bother to shrug his shoulders. When I begged and pleaded, he promised to wait till I'd spoken to you again.

MOTHER COURAGE: Say I'll give him the two hundred. Run. (*Yvette runs off. They sit in silence. The chaplain has stopped washing the glasses.*) Maybe I bargained too long. (*Drums are heard in the distance. The chaplain stands up and goes to the rear. Mother Courage remains seated. It grows dark. The drums stop. It grows light again. Mother Courage has not moved.*)

YVETTE (*enters, very pale*): Now you've done it with your haggling and wanting to keep your wagon. Eleven bullets he got, that's all. I don't know why I bother with you any more, you don't deserve it.

But I've picked up a little information. They don't believe the cashbox is really in the river. They suspect it's here and they think you were connected with him. They're going to bring him here, they think maybe you'll give yourself away when you see him. I'm warning you: You don't know him, or you're all dead ducks. I may as well tell you, they're right behind me. Should I keep Kattrin out of the way? (*Mother Courage shakes her head.*) Does she know? Maybe she didn't hear the drums or maybe she didn't understand.

MOTHER COURAGE: She knows. Get her.

(*Yvette brings Kattrin, who goes to her mother and stands beside her. Mother Courage takes her by the hand. Two soldiers come in with a stretcher on which something is lying under a sheet. The sergeant walks beside them. They set the stretcher down.*)

THE SERGEANT: We've got a man here and we don't know his name. We need it for the records. He had a meal with you. Take a look, see if you know him. (*He removes the sheet.*) Do you know him? (*Mother Courage shakes her head.*) What? You'd never seen him before he came here for a meal? (*Mother Courage shakes her head.*) Pick him up. Throw him on the dump. Nobody knows him. (*They carry him away.*)

SCENE 4

(*Mother Courage sings the Song of the Great Capitulation.*)

(*Outside an officer's tent.*)

(*Mother Courage is waiting. A clerk looks out of the tent.*)

THE CLERK: I know you. You had a Protestant paymaster at your place, he was hiding. I wouldn't put in any complaints if I were you.

MOTHER COURAGE: I'm putting in a complaint. I'm innocent. If I take this lying down, it'll look as if I had a guilty conscience. First they ripped up my whole wagon with their sabers, then they wanted me to pay a fine of five thalers for no reason at all.

THE CLERK: I'm advising you for your own good: Keep your trap shut. We haven't got many provisioners and we'll let you keep on with your business, especially if you've got a guilty conscience and pay a fine now and then.

MOTHER COURAGE: I'm putting in a complaint.

THE CLERK: Have it your way. But you'll have to wait till the captain can see you. (*Disappears into the tent.*)

A YOUNG SOLDIER (*enters in a rage*): Bouque la Ma-

donne!° Where's that stinking captain? He embezzled
my reward and now he's drinking it up with his
whores. I'm going to get him!

AN OLDER SOLDIER (*comes running after him*): Shut
up. They'll put you in the stocks!

THE YOUNG SOLDIER: Come on out, you crook! I'll
make chops out of you. Embezzling my reward!
Who jumps in the river? Not another man in the
whole squad, only me. And I can't even buy myself
a beer. I won't stand for it. Come on out and let
me cut you to pieces!

THE OLDER SOLDIER: Holy Mary! He'll ruin himself.

MOTHER COURAGE: They didn't give him a reward?

THE YOUNG SOLDIER: Let me go. I'll run you through
too, the more the merrier.

THE OLDER SOLDIER: He saved the colonel's horse
and they didn't give him a reward. He's young, he
hasn't been around long.

MOTHER COURAGE: Let him go, he's not a dog, you
don't have to tie him up. Wanting a reward is
perfectly reasonable. Why else would he distinguish
himself?

THE YOUNG SOLDIER: And him drinking in there! You're
all a lot of yellowbellies. I distinguished myself and
I want my reward.

MOTHER COURAGE: Young man, don't shout at me.
I've got my own worries and besides, go easy on
your voice, you may need it. You'll be hoarse when
the captain comes out, you won't be able to say
boo and he won't be able to put you in the stocks
till you're blue in the face. People that yell like that
don't last long, maybe half an hour, then they're
so exhausted you have to sing them to sleep.

THE YOUNG SOLDIER: I'm not exhausted and who
wants to sleep? I'm hungry. They make our bread
out of acorns and hemp seed, and they skimp on
that. He's whoring away my reward and I'm hungry.
I'll murder him.

MOTHER COURAGE: I see. You're hungry. Last year
your general made you cut across the fields to trample down the grain. I could have sold a pair of
boots for ten guilders if anybody'd had ten guilders
and if I'd had any boots. He thought he'd be someplace else this year, but now he's still here and
everybody's starving. I can see that you might be
good and mad.

THE YOUNG SOLDIER: He can't do this to me, save
your breath, I won't put up with injustice.

MOTHER COURAGE: You're right, but for how long?
How long won't you put up with injustice? An
hour? Two hours? You see, you never thought of
that, though it's very important, because it's mi-

Bouque la Madonne: Vulgar expression.

serable in the stocks when it suddenly dawns on
you that you *can* put up with injustice.

THE YOUNG SOLDIER: I don't know why I listen to
you. Bouque la Madonne! Where's the captain?

MOTHER COURAGE: You listen to me because I'm not
telling you anything new. You know your temper
has gone up in smoke, it was a short temper and
you need a long one, but that's a hard thing to
come by.

THE YOUNG SOLDIER: Are you trying to say I've no
right to claim my reward?

MOTHER COURAGE: Not at all. I'm only saying your
temper isn't long enough, it won't get you anywhere.
Too bad. If you had a long temper, I'd even egg
you on. Chop the bastard up, that's what I'd say,
but suppose you don't chop him up, because your
tail's drooping and you know it. I'm left standing
there like a fool and the captain takes it out on
me.

THE OLDER SOLDIER: You're right. He's only blowing
off steam.

THE YOUNG SOLDIER: We'll see about that. I'll cut
him to pieces. (*He draws his sword.*) When he
comes out, I'll cut him to pieces.

THE CLERK (*looks out*): The captain will be here in
a moment. Sit down.

(*The young soldier sits down.*)

MOTHER COURAGE: There he sits. What did I tell you?
Sitting, aren't you? Oh, they know us like a book,
they know how to handle us. Sit down! And down
we sit. You can't start a riot sitting down. Better
not stand up again, you won't be able to stand the
way you were standing before. Don't be embarrassed
on my account, I'm no better, not a bit of it. We
were full of piss and vinegar, but they've bought
it off. Look at me. No back talk, it's bad for business.
Let me tell you about the great capitulation. (*She
sings the Song of the Great Capitulation.*)

When I was young, no more than a spring
    chicken
I too thought that I was really quite the cheese
(No common peddler's daughter, not I with my
    looks and my talent and striving for higher
    things!)
One little hair in the soup would make me
    sicken
And at me no man would dare to sneeze.
(It's all or nothing, no second best for me. I've
    got what it takes, the rules are for somebody
    else!)

But a chickadee
Sang wait and see!

And you go marching with the show
In step, however fast or slow
And rattle off your little song:
It won't be long.
And then the whole thing slides.
You think God provides —
But you've got it wrong.

And before one single year had wasted
I had learned to swallow down the bitter brew
(Two kids on my hands and the price of bread
    and who do they take me for anyway!)
Man, the double-edged shellacking that I tasted
On my ass and knees I was when they were
    through.
(You've got to get along with people, one good
    turn deserves another, no use trying to ram
    your head through the wall!)
And the chickadee
Sang wait and see!
    And she goes marching with the show
    In step, however fast or slow
    And rattles off her little song:
    It won't be long.
    And then the whole thing slides
    You think God provides —
    But you've got it wrong.

I've seen many fired by high ambition
No star's big or high enough to reach out for.
(It's ability that counts, where there's a will
    there's a way, one way or another we'll swing
    it!)
Then while moving mountains they get a
    suspicion
That to wear a straw hat is too big a chore.
(No use being too big for your britches!)
And the chickadee
Sings wait and see!
    And they go marching with the show
    In step, however fast or slow
    And rattle off their little song:
    It won't be long.
    And then the whole thing slides!
    You think God provides —
    But you've got it wrong!

MOTHER COURAGE (*to the young soldier*): So here's
what I think: Stay here with your sword if your
anger's big enough, I know you have good reason,
but if it's a short quick anger, better make tracks!
THE YOUNG SOLDIER: Kiss my ass! (*He staggers off,
the older soldier after him.*)
THE CLERK (*sticking his head out*): The captain is
here. You can put in your complaint now.
MOTHER COURAGE: I've changed my mind. No complaint. (*She goes out.*)

SCENE 5

(*Two years have passed. The war has spread far and
wide. With scarcely a pause Mother Courage's little
wagon rolls through Poland, Moravia, Bavaria, Italy,
and back again to Bavaria. 1631. Tilly's victory at
Magdeburg costs Mother Courage four officers' shirts.*)

(*Mother Courage's wagon has stopped in a dev-
astated village.*)

(*Thin military music is heard from the distance.
Two soldiers at the bar are being waited on by Kattrin
and Mother Courage. One of them is wearing a lady's
fur coat over his shoulders.*)

MOTHER COURAGE: What's that? You can't pay? No
money, no schnapps. Plenty of victory marches for
the Lord but no pay for the men.
THE SOLDIER: I want my schnapps. I came too late
for the looting. The general skunked us: permission
to loot the city for exactly one hour. Says he's not
a monster; the mayor must have paid him.
THE CHAPLAIN (*staggers in*): There's still some wounded
in the house. The peasant and his family. Help me,
somebody, I need linen.

(*The second soldier goes out with him. Kattrin gets
very excited and tries to persuade her mother to hand
out linen.*)

MOTHER COURAGE: I haven't got any. The regiment's
bought up all my bandages. You think I'm going
to rip up my officers' shirts for the likes of them?
THE CHAPLAIN (*calling back*): I need linen, I tell you.
MOTHER COURAGE (*sitting down on the wagon steps
to keep Kattrin out*): Nothing doing. They don't
pay, they got nothing to pay with.
THE CHAPLAIN (*bending over a woman whom he has
carried out*): Why did you stay here in all that
gunfire?
THE PEASANT WOMAN (*feebly*): Farm.
MOTHER COURAGE: You won't catch them leaving
their property. And I'm expected to foot the bill.
I won't do it.
THE FIRST SOLDIER: They're Protestants. Why do they
have to be Protestants?
MOTHER COURAGE: Religion is the least of their worries.
They've lost their farm.
THE SECOND SOLDIER: They're no Protestants. They're
Catholics like us.
THE FIRST SOLDIER: How do we know who we're
shooting at?
A PEASANT (*whom the Chaplain brings in*): They got
my arm.
THE CHAPLAIN: Where's the linen?

(*All look at Mother Courage, who does not move.*)

MOTHER COURAGE: I can't give you a thing. What

with all my taxes, duties, fees and bribes! (*Making guttural sounds, Kattrin picks up a board and threatens her mother with it.*) Are you crazy? Put that board down, you slut, or I'll smack you. I'm not giving anything, you can't make me, I've got to think of myself. (*The chaplain picks her up from the step and puts her down on the ground. Then he fishes out some shirts and tears them into strips.*) My shirts! Half a guilder apiece! I'm ruined!

(*The anguished cry of a baby is heard from the house.*)

THE PEASANT: The baby's still in there!

(*Kattrin runs in.*)

THE CHAPLAIN (*to the woman*): Don't move. They're bringing him out.

MOTHER COURAGE: Get her out of there. The roof'll cave in.

THE CHAPLAIN: I'm not going in there again.

MOTHER COURAGE (*torn*): Don't run hog-wild with my expensive linen.

(*Kattrin emerges from the ruins carrying an infant.*)

MOTHER COURAGE: Oh, so you've found another baby to carry around with you? Give that baby back to its mother this minute, or it'll take me all day to get it away from you. Do you hear me? (*To the second soldier.*) Don't stand there gaping, go back and tell them to stop that music, I can see right here that they've won a victory. Your victory's costing me a pretty penny.

(*Kattrin rocks the baby in her arms, humming a lullaby.*)

MOTHER COURAGE: There she sits, happy in all this misery; give it back this minute, the mother's coming to. (*She pounces on the first soldier who has been helping himself to the drinks and is now making off with the bottle.*) Pshagreff! Beast! Haven't you had enough victories for today? Pay up.

FIRST SOLDIER: I'm broke.

MOTHER COURAGE (*tears the fur coat off him*): Then leave the coat here, it's stolen anyway.

THE CHAPLAIN: There's still somebody in there.

SCENE 6

(*Outside Ingolstadt in Bavaria Mother Courage attends the funeral of Tilly, the imperial field marshal. Conversations about heroes and the longevity of the war. The chaplain deplores the waste of his talents. Mute Kattrin gets the red shoes. 1632.*)

(*Inside Mother Courage's tent.*)

(*A bar open to the rear. Rain. In the distance drum rolls and funeral music. The chaplain and the regimental clerk are playing a board game. Mother Courage and her daughter are taking inventory.*)

THE CHAPLAIN: The procession's starting.

MOTHER COURAGE: It's a shame about the general — socks: twenty-two pairs — I hear he was killed by accident. On account of the fog in the fields. He's up front encouraging the troops. "Fight to the death, boys," he sings out. Then he rides back, but he gets lost in the fog and rides back forward. Before you know it he's in the middle of the battle and stops a bullet — lanterns: we're down to four. (*A whistle from the rear. She goes to the bar.*) You men ought to be ashamed, running out on your late general's funeral! (*She pours drinks.*)

THE CLERK: They shouldn't have been paid before the funeral. Now they're getting drunk instead.

THE CHAPLAIN (*to the clerk*): Shouldn't you be at the funeral?

THE CLERK: In this rain?

MOTHER COURAGE: With you it's different, the rain might spoil your uniform. It seems they wanted to ring the bells, naturally, but it turned out the churches had all been shot to pieces by his orders, so the poor general won't hear any bells when they lower him into his grave. They're going to fire a three-gun salute instead, so it won't be too dull — seventeen sword belts.

CRIES (*from the bar*): Hey! Brandy!

MOTHER COURAGE: Money first! No, you can't come into my tent with your muddy boots! You can drink outside, rain or no rain. (*To the clerk.*) I'm only letting officers in. It seems the general had been having his troubles. Mutiny in the Second Regiment because he hadn't paid them. It's a war of religion, he says, should they profit by their faith?

(*Funeral march. All look to the rear.*)

THE CHAPLAIN: Now they're marching past the body.

MOTHER COURAGE: I feel sorry when a general or an emperor passes away like this, maybe he thought he'd do something big, that posterity would still be talking about and maybe put up a statue in his honor, conquer the world, for instance, that's a nice ambition for a general, he doesn't know any better. So he knocks himself out, and then the common people come and spoil it all, because what do they care about greatness, all they care about is a mug of beer and maybe a little company. The most beautiful plans have been wrecked by the smallness of the people that are supposed to carry them out. Even an emperor can't do anything by himself, he needs the support of his soldiers and his people. Am I right?

THE CHAPLAIN (*laughing*): Courage, you're right, except about the soldiers. They do their best. With those fellows out there, for instance, drinking their brandy in the rain, I'll undertake to carry on one war after another for a hundred years, two at once if I have to, and I'm not a general by trade.

MOTHER COURAGE: Then you don't think the war might stop?

THE CHAPLAIN: Because the general's dead? Don't be childish. They grow by the dozen, there'll always be plenty of heroes.

MOTHER COURAGE: Look here, I'm not asking you for the hell of it. I've been wondering whether to lay in supplies while they're cheap, but if the war stops, I can throw them out the window.

THE CHAPLAIN: I understand. You want a serious answer. There have always been people who say: "The war will be over some day." I say there's no guarantee the war will ever be over. Naturally a brief intermission is conceivable. Maybe the war needs a breather, a war can even break its neck, so to speak. There's always a chance of that, nothing is perfect here below. Maybe there never will be a perfect war, one that lives up to all our expectations. Suddenly, for some unforeseen reason, a war can bog down, you can't think of everything. Some little oversight and your war's in trouble. And then you've got to pull it out of the mud. But the kings and emperors, not to mention the pope, will always come to its help in adversity. On the whole, I'd say this war has very little to worry about, it'll live to a ripe old age.

A SOLDIER (*sings at the bar*): A drink, and don't be slow!
A soldier's got to go
And fight for his religion.

Make it double, this is a holiday.

MOTHER COURAGE: If I could only be sure . . .

THE CHAPLAIN: Figure it out for yourself. What's to stop the war?

THE SOLDIER (*sings*): Your breasts, girl, don't be slow!
A soldier's got to go
And ride away to Pilsen.

THE CLERK (*suddenly*): But why can't we have peace? I'm from Bohemia, I'd like to go home when the time comes.

THE CHAPLAIN: Oh, you'd like to go home? Ah, peace! What becomes of the hole when the cheese has been eaten?

THE SOLDIER (*sings*): Play cards, friends, don't be slow!
A soldier's got to go
No matter if it's Sunday.

A prayer, priest, don't be slow!
A soldier's got to go
And die for king and country.

THE CLERK: In the long run nobody can live without peace.

THE CHAPLAIN: The way I see it, war gives you plenty of peace. It has its peaceful moments. War meets every need, including the peaceful ones, everything's taken care of, or your war couldn't hold its own. In a war you can shit the same as in the dead of peace, you can stop for a beer between battles, and even on the march you can always lie down on your elbows and take a little nap by the roadside. You can't play cards when you're fighting; but then you can't when you're plowing in the dead of peace either, but after a victory the sky's the limit. Maybe you've had a leg shot off, at first you raise a howl, you make a big thing of it. But then you calm down or they give you schnapps, and in the end you're hopping around again and the war's no worse off than before. And what's to prevent you from multiplying in the thick of the slaughter, behind a barn or someplace, in the long run how can they stop you, and then the war has your progeny to help it along. Take it from me, the war will always find an answer. Why would it have to stop?

(*Kattrin has stopped working and is staring at the chaplain.*)

MOTHER COURAGE: Then I'll buy the merchandise. You've convinced me. (*Kattrin suddenly throws down a basket full of bottles and runs out.*) Kattrin! (*Laughs.*) My goodness, the poor thing's been hoping for peace. I promised her she'd get a husband when peace comes. (*She runs after her.*)

THE CLERK (*getting up*): I win, you've been too busy talking. Pay up.

MOTHER COURAGE (*comes back with Kattrin*): Be reasonable, the war'll go on a little longer and we'll make a little more money, then peace will be even better. Run along to town now, it won't take you ten minutes, and get the stuff from the Golden Lion, only the expensive things, we'll pick up the rest in the wagon later, it's all arranged, the regimental clerk here will go with you. They've almost all gone to the general's funeral, nothing can happen to you. Look sharp, don't let them take anything away from you, think of your dowry.

(*Kattrin puts a kerchief over her head and goes with the clerk.*)

THE CHAPLAIN: Is it all right letting her go with the clerk?

MOTHER COURAGE: Who'd want to ruin her? She's not pretty enough.

THE CHAPLAIN: I've come to admire the way you handle your business and pull through every time. I can see why they call you Mother Courage.

MOTHER COURAGE: Poor people need courage. Why? Because they're sunk. In their situation it takes gumption just to get up in the morning. Or to plow a field in the middle of a war. They even show courage by bringing children into the world, because look at the prospects. The way they butcher and execute each other, think of the courage they need to look each other in the face. And putting up with an emperor and a pope takes a whale of a lot of courage, because those two are the death of the poor. (*She sits down, takes a small pipe from her pocket and smokes.*) You could be making some kindling.

THE CHAPLAIN (*reluctantly takes his jacket off and prepares to chop*): Chopping wood isn't really my trade, you know, I'm a shepherd of souls.

MOTHER COURAGE: Sure. But I have no soul and I need firewood.

THE CHAPLAIN: What's that pipe?

MOTHER COURAGE: Just a pipe.

THE CHAPLAIN: No, it's not "just a pipe," it's a very particular pipe.

MOTHER COURAGE: Really?

THE CHAPLAIN: It's the cook's pipe from the Oxen-stjerna regiment.

MOTHER COURAGE: If you know it all, why the mealy-mouthed questions?

THE CHAPLAIN: I didn't know if *you* knew. You could have been rummaging through your belongings and laid hands on some pipe and picked it up without thinking.

MOTHER COURAGE: Yes. Maybe that's how it was.

THE CHAPLAIN: Except it wasn't. You knew who that pipe belongs to.

MOTHER COURAGE: What of it?

THE CHAPLAIN: Courage, I'm warning you. It's my duty. I doubt if you ever lay eyes on the man again, but that's no calamity, in fact you're lucky. If you ask me, he wasn't steady. Not at all.

MOTHER COURAGE: What makes you say that? He was a nice man.

THE CHAPLAIN: Oh, you think he was nice? I differ. Far be it from me to wish him any harm, but I can't say he was nice. I'd say he was a scheming Don Juan. If you don't believe me, take a look at his pipe. You'll have to admit that it shows up his character.

MOTHER COURAGE: I don't see anything. It's beat up.

THE CHAPLAIN: It's half bitten through. A violent man. That is the pipe of a ruthless, violent man, you must see that if you've still got an ounce of good sense.

MOTHER COURAGE: Don't wreck my chopping block.

THE CHAPLAIN: I've told you I wasn't trained to chop wood. I studied theology. My gifts and abilities are being wasted on muscular effort. The talents that God gave me are lying fallow. That's a sin. You've never heard me preach. With one sermon I can whip a regiment into such a state that they take the enemy for a flock of sheep. Then men care no more about their lives than they would about a smelly old sock that they're ready to throw away in hopes of final victory. God has made me eloquent. You'll swoon when you hear me preach.

MOTHER COURAGE: I don't want to swoon. What good would that do me?

THE CHAPLAIN: Courage, I've often wondered if maybe you didn't conceal a warm heart under that hard-bitten talk of yours. You too are human, you need warmth.

MOTHER COURAGE: The best way to keep this tent warm is with plenty of firewood.

THE CHAPLAIN: Don't try to put me off. Seriously, Courage, I sometimes wonder if we couldn't make our relationship a little closer. I mean, seeing that the whirlwind of war has whirled us so strangely together.

MOTHER COURAGE: Seems to me it's close enough. I cook your meals and you do chores, such as chopping wood, for instance.

THE CHAPLAIN (*goes toward her*): You know what I mean by "closer"; it has nothing to do with meals and chopping wood and such mundane needs. Don't harden your heart, let it speak.

MOTHER COURAGE: Don't come at me with that ax. That's too close a relationship.

THE CHAPLAIN: Don't turn it to ridicule. I'm serious, I've given it careful thought.

MOTHER COURAGE: Chaplain, don't be silly. I like you, I don't want to have to scold you. My aim in life is to get through, me and my children and my wagon. I don't think of it as mine and besides I'm not in the mood for private affairs. Right now I'm taking a big risk, buying up merchandise with the general dead and everybody talking peace. What'll you do if I'm ruined? See? You don't know. Chop that wood, then we'll be warm in the evening, which is a good thing in times like these. Now what? (*She stands up.*)

(*Enter Kattrin out of breath, with a wound across her forehead and over one eye. She is carrying all sorts of things, packages, leather goods, a drum, etc.*)

MOTHER COURAGE: What's that? Assaulted? On the way back? She was assaulted on the way back. Must have been that soldier that got drunk here!

I shouldn't have let you go! Throw the stuff down! It's not bad, only a flesh wound. I'll bandage it, it'll heal in a week. They're worse than wild beasts. (*She bandages the wound.*)

THE CHAPLAIN: I can't find fault with them. At home they never raped anybody. I blame the people that start wars, they're the ones that dredge up man's lowest instincts.

MOTHER COURAGE: Didn't the clerk bring you back? That's because you're respectable, they don't give a damn. It's not a deep wound, it won't leave a mark. There, all bandaged. Don't fret, I've got something for you. I've been keeping it for you on the sly, it'll be a surprise. (*She fishes Yvette's red shoes out of a sack.*) See? You've always wanted them. Now you've got them. Put them on quick before I regret it. It won't leave a mark, though I wouldn't mind if it did. The girls that attract them get the worst of it. They drag them around till there's nothing left of them. If you don't appeal to them, they won't harm you. I've seen girls with pretty faces, a few years later they'd have given a wolf the creeps. They can't step behind a bush without fearing the worst. It's like trees. The straight tall ones get chopped down for ridgepoles, the crooked ones enjoy life. In other words, it's a lucky break. The shoes are still in good condition, I've keep them nicely polished.

(*Kattrin leaves the shoes where they are and crawls into the wagon.*)

THE CHAPLAIN: I hope she won't be disfigured.

MOTHER COURAGE: There'll be a scar. She can stop waiting for peace.

THE CHAPLAIN: She didn't let them take anything.

MOTHER COURAGE: Maybe I shouldn't have drummed it into her. If I only knew what went on in her head. One night she stayed out, the only time in all these years. Afterwards she traipsed around as usual, except she worked harder. I never could find out what happened. I racked my brains for quite some time. (*She picks up the articles brought by Kattrin and sorts them angrily.*) That's war for you! A fine way to make a living! (*Cannon salutes are heard.*)

THE CHAPLAIN: Now they're burying the general. This is a historic moment.

MOTHER COURAGE: To me it's a historic moment when they hit my daughter over the eye. She's a wreck, she'll never get a husband now, and she's so crazy about children. It's the war that made her dumb too, a soldier stuffed something in her mouth when she was little. I'll never see Swiss Cheese again and where Eilif is, God knows. God damn the war.

SCENE 7

(*Mother Courage at the height of her business career.*)
(*Highway.*)
(*The chaplain, Mother Courage, and her daughter Kattrin are pulling the wagon. New wares are banging on it. Mother Courage is wearing a necklace of silver talers.*)

MOTHER COURAGE: Stop running down the war. I won't have it. I know it destroys the weak, but the weak haven't a chance in peacetime either. And war is a better provider. (*Sings.*)
If you're not strong enough to take it
The victory will find you dead.
A war is only what you make it.
It's business, not with cheese but lead.
And what good is it staying in one place? The stay-at-homes are the first to get it. (*Sings.*)
Some people think they'd like to ride out
The war, leave danger to the brave
And dig themselves a cozy hideout —
They'll dig themselves an early grave.
I've seen them running from the thunder
To find a refuge from the war
But once they're resting six feet under
They wonder what they hurried for.

(*They plod on.*)

SCENE 8

(*In the same year Gustavus Adolphus, King of Sweden, is killed at the battle of Lützen. Peace threatens to ruin Mother Courage's business. Her brave son performs one heroic deed too many and dies an ignominious death.*)
(*A camp.*)
(*A summer morning. An old woman and her son are standing by the wagon. The son is carrying a large sack of bedding.*)

MOTHER COURAGE'S VOICE (*from the wagon*): Does it have to be at this unearthly hour?

THE YOUNG MAN: We've walked all night, twenty miles, and we've got to go back today.

MOTHER COURAGE'S VOICE: What can I do with bedding? The people haven't any houses.

THE YOUNG MAN: Wait till you've seen it.

THE OLD WOMAN: She won't take it either. Come on.

THE YOUNG MAN: They'll sell the roof from over our heads for taxes. Maybe she'll give us three guilders if you throw in the cross. (*Bells start ringing.*) Listen, mother!

VOICES (*from the rear*): Peace! The king of Sweden is dead!

MOTHER COURAGE (*Sticks her head out of the wagon.*

She has not yet done her hair.): Why are the bells ringing in the middle of the week?

THE CHAPLAIN (*crawls out from under the wagon*): What are they shouting?

MOTHER COURAGE: Don't tell me peace has broken out when I've just taken in more supplies.

THE CHAPLAIN (*shouting toward the rear*): Is it true? Peace?

VOICE: Three weeks ago, they say. But we just found out.

THE CHAPLAIN (*to Mother Courage*): What else would they ring the bells for?

VOICE: There's a whole crowd of Lutherans, they've driven their carts into town. They brought the news.

THE YOUNG MAN: Mother, it's peace. What's the matter?

(*The old woman has collapsed.*)

MOTHER COURAGE (*going back into the wagon*): Heavenly saints! Kattrin, peace! Put your black dress on! We're going to church. We owe it to Swiss Cheese. Can it be true?

THE YOUNG MAN: The people here say the same thing. They've made peace. Can you get up? (*The old woman stands up, still stunned.*) I'll get the saddle shop started again. I promise. Everything will be all right. Father will get his bed back. Can you walk? (*To the chaplain.*) She fainted. It was the news. She thought peace would never come again. Father said it would. We'll go straight home. (*Both go out.*)

MOTHER COURAGE'S VOICE: Give her some brandy.

THE CHAPLAIN: They're gone.

MOTHER COURAGE'S VOICE: What's going on in camp?

THE CHAPLAIN: A big crowd. I'll go see. Shouldn't I put on my clericals?

MOTHER COURAGE'S VOICE: Better make sure before you step out in your antichrist costume. I'm glad to see peace, even if I'm ruined. At least I've brought two of my children through the war. Now I'll see my Eilif again.

THE CHAPLAIN: Look who's coming down the road. If it isn't the general's cook!

THE COOK (*rather bedraggled, carrying a bundle*): Can I believe my eyes? The chaplain!

THE CHAPLAIN: Courage! A visitor!

(*Mother Courage climbs down.*)

THE COOK: Didn't I promise to come over for a little chat as soon as I had time? I've never forgotten your brandy, Mrs. Fierling.

MOTHER COURAGE: Mercy, the general's cook! After all these years! Where's Eilif, my eldest?

THE COOK: Isn't he here yet? He left ahead of me, he was coming to see you too.

THE CHAPLAIN: I'll put on my clericals, wait for me. (*Goes out behind the wagon.*)

MOTHER COURAGE: Then he'll be here any minute. (*Calls into wagon.*) Kattrin, Eilif's coming! Bring the cook a glass of brandy! (*Kattrin does not appear.*) Put a lock of hair over it, and forget it! Mr. Lamb is no stranger. (*Gets the brandy herself.*) She won't come out. Peace doesn't mean a thing to her, it's come too late. They hit her over the eye, there's hardly any mark, but she thinks people are staring at her.

THE COOK: Ech, war! (*He and Mother Courage sit down.*)

MOTHER COURAGE: Cook, you find me in trouble. I'm ruined.

THE COOK: What? Say, that's a shame.

MOTHER COURAGE: Peace has done me in. Only the other day I stocked up. The chaplain's advice. And now they'll all demobilize and leave me sitting on my merchandise.

THE COOK: How could you listen to the chaplain? If I'd had time, I'd have warned you against him, but the Catholics came too soon. He's a fly-by-night. So now he's the boss here?

MOTHER COURAGE: He washed my dishes and helped me pull the wagon.

THE COOK: Him? Pulling? I guess he's told you a few of his jokes too, I wouldn't put it past him, he has an unsavory attitude toward women, I tried to reform him, it was hopeless. He's not steady.

MOTHER COURAGE: Are you steady?

THE COOK: If nothing else, I'm steady. Prosit!

MOTHER COURAGE: Steady is no good. I've only lived with one steady man, thank the Lord. I never had to work so hard, he sold the children's blankets when spring came, and he thought my harmonica was unchristian. In my opinion you're not doing yourself any good by admitting you're steady.

THE COOK: You've still got your old bite, but I respect you for it.

MOTHER COURAGE: Don't tell me you've been dreaming about my old bite.

THE COOK: Well, here we sit, with the bells of peace and your world-famous brandy, that hasn't its equal.

MOTHER COURAGE: The bells of peace don't strike my fancy right now. I don't see them paying the men, they're behind-hand already. Where does that leave me with my famous brandy? Have you been paid?

THE COOK (*hesitantly*): Not really. That's why we demobilized ourselves. Under the circumstances, I says to myself, why should I stay on? I'll go see my friends in the meantime. So here we are.

MOTHER COURAGE: You mean you're out of funds?

THE COOK: If only they'd stop those damn bells! I'd

be glad to go into some kind of business. I'm sick of being a cook. They give me roots and shoe leather to work with, and then they throw the hot soup in my face. A cook's got a dog's life these days. I'd rather be in combat, but now we've got peace. (*The chaplain appears in his original dress.*) We'll discuss it later.

THE CHAPLAIN: It's still in good condition. There were only a few moths in it.

THE COOK: I don't see why you bother. They won't take you back. Who are you going to inspire now to be an honest soldier and earn his pay at the risk of his life? Besides, I've got a bone to pick with you. Advising this lady to buy useless merchandise on the ground that the war would last forever.

THE CHAPLAIN (*heatedly*): And why, I'd like to know, is it any of your business?

THE COOK: Because it's unscrupulous. How can you meddle in other people's business and give unsolicited advice?

THE CHAPLAIN: Who's meddling? (*To Mother Courage.*) I didn't know you were accountable to this gentleman, I didn't know you were so intimate with him.

MOTHER COURAGE: Don't get excited, the cook is only giving his private opinion. And you can't deny that your war was a dud.

THE CHAPLAIN: Courage, don't blaspheme against peace. You're a battlefield hyena.

MOTHER COURAGE: What am I?

THE COOK: If you insult this lady, you'll hear from me.

THE CHAPLAIN: I'm not talking to you. Your intentions are too obvious. (*To Mother Courage.*) But when I see you picking up peace with thumb and forefinger like a snotty handkerchief, it revolts my humanity; you don't want peace, you want war, because you profit by it, but don't forget the old saying: "He hath need of a long spoon that eateth with the devil."

MOTHER COURAGE: I've no use for war and war hasn't much use for me. Anyway, I'm not letting anybody call me a hyena, you and me are through.

THE CHAPLAIN: How can you complain about peace when it's such a relief to everybody else? On account of the old rags in your wagon?

MOTHER COURAGE: My merchandise isn't old rags, it's what I live off, and so did you.

THE CHAPLAIN: Off war, you mean. Aha!

THE COOK (*to the chaplain*): You're a grown man, you ought to know there's no sense in giving advice. (*To Mother Courage.*) The best thing you can do now is to sell off certain articles quick, before the prices hit the floor. Dress yourself and get started, there's no time to lose.

MOTHER COURAGE: That's very sensible advice. I think I'll do it.

THE CHAPLAIN: Because the cook says so!

MOTHER COURAGE: Why didn't *you* say so? He's right, I'd better run over to the market. (*She goes into the wagon.*)

THE COOK: My round, chaplain. No presence of mind. Here's what you should have said: me give you advice? All I ever did was talk politics! Don't try to take me on. Cockfighting is undignified in a clergyman.

THE CHAPLAIN: If you don't shut up, I'll murder you, undignified or not.

THE COOK (*taking off his shoe and unwinding the wrappings from his feet*): If the war hadn't made a godless bum out of you, you could easily come by a parsonage now that peace is here. They won't need cooks, there's nothing to cook, but people still do a lot of believing, that hasn't changed.

THE CHAPLAIN: See here, Mr. Lamb. Don't try to squeeze me out. Being a bum has made me a better man. I couldn't preach to them any more.

(*Yvette Pottier enters, elaborately dressed in black, with a cane. She is much older and fatter and heavily powdered. Behind her a servant.*)

YVETTE: Hello there! Is this the residence of Mother Courage?

CHAPLAIN: Right you are. With whom have we the pleasure?

YVETTE: The Countess Starhemberg, my good people. Where is Mother Courage?

THE CHAPLAIN (*calls into the wagon*): Countess Starhemberg wishes to speak to you!

MOTHER COURAGE: I'm coming.

YVETTE: It's Yvette!

MOTHER COURAGE'S VOICE: My goodness! It's Yvette!

YVETTE: Just dropped in to see how you're doing. (*The cook has turned around in horror.*) Pieter!

THE COOK: Yvette!

YVETTE: Blow me down! How did you get here?

THE COOK: In a cart.

THE CHAPLAIN: Oh, you know each other? Intimately?

YVETTE: I should think so. (*She looks the cook over.*) Fat!

THE COOK: You're not exactly willowy yourself.

YVETTE: All the same I'm glad I ran into you, you bum. Now I can tell you what I think of you.

THE CHAPLAIN: Go right ahead, spare no details, but wait until Courage comes out.

MOTHER COURAGE (*comes out with all sorts of merchandise*): Yvette! (*They embrace.*) But what are you in mourning for?

YVETTE: Isn't it becoming? My husband the colonel died a few years ago.

MOTHER COURAGE: The old geezer that almost bought my wagon?

YVETTE: His elder brother.

MOTHER COURAGE: You must be pretty well fixed. It's nice to find somebody that's made a good thing out of the war.

YVETTE: Oh well, it's been up and down and back up again.

MOTHER COURAGE: Let's not say anything bad about colonels. They make money by the bushel.

THE CHAPLAIN: If I were you, I'd put my shoes back on again. (*To Yvette.*) Countess Starhemberg, you promised to tell us what you think of this gentleman.

THE COOK: Don't make a scene here.

MOTHER COURAGE: He's a friend of mine, Yvette.

YVETTE: He's Pete the Pipe, that's who he is.

THE COOK: Forget the nicknames, my name is Lamb.

MOTHER COURAGE (*laughs*): Pete the Pipe! That drove the women crazy! Say, I've saved your pipe.

THE CHAPLAIN: And smoked it.

YVETTE: It's lucky I'm here to warn you. He's the worst rotter that ever infested the coast of Flanders. He ruined more girls than he's got fingers.

THE COOK: That was a long time ago. I've changed.

YVETTE: Stand up when a lady draws you into a conversation! How I loved this man! And all the while he was seeing a little bandylegged brunette, ruined her too, naturally.

THE COOK: Seems to me I started you off on a prosperous career.

YVETTE: Shut up, you depressing wreck! Watch your step with him, his kind are dangerous even when they've gone to seed.

MOTHER COURAGE (*to Yvette*): Come along, I've got to sell my stuff before the prices drop. Maybe you can help me, with your army connections. (*Calls into the wagon.*) Kattrin, forget about church, I'm running over to the market. When Eilif comes, give him a drink. (*Goes out with Yvette.*)

YVETTE (*in leaving*): To think that such a man could lead me astray! I can thank my lucky stars that I was able to rise in the world after that. I've put a spoke in your wheel, Pete the Pipe, and they'll give me credit for it in heaven when my time comes.

THE CHAPLAIN: Our conversation seems to illustrate the old adage: The mills of God grind slowly. What do you think of my jokes now?

THE COOK: I'm just unlucky. I'll come clean: I was hoping for a hot meal. I'm starving. And now they're talking about me, and she'll get the wrong idea. I think I'll beat it before she comes back.

THE CHAPLAIN: I think so too.

THE COOK: Chaplain, I'm fed up on peace already. Men are sinners from the cradle, fire and sword are their natural lot. I wish I were cooking for the general again, God knows where he is, I'd roast a fine fat capon, with mustard sauce and a few carrots.

THE CHAPLAIN: Red cabbage. Red cabbage with capon.

THE COOK: That's right, but he wanted carrots.

THE CHAPLAIN: He was ignorant.

THE COOK: That didn't prevent you from gorging yourself.

THE CHAPLAIN: With repugnance.

THE COOK: Anyway you'll have to admit those were good times.

THE CHAPLAIN: I might admit that.

THE COOK: Now you've called her a hyena, your good times here are over. What are you staring at?

THE CHAPLAIN: Eilif! (*Eilif enters, followed by soldiers with pikes. His hands are fettered. He is deathly pale.*) What's wrong?

EILIF: Where's mother?

THE CHAPLAIN: Gone to town.

EILIF: I heard she was here. They let me come and see her.

THE COOK (*to the soldiers*): Where are you taking him?

A SOLDIER: No good place.

THE CHAPLAIN: What has he done?

THE SOLDIER: Broke into a farm. The peasant's wife is dead.

THE CHAPLAIN: How could you do such a thing?

EILIF: It's what I've been doing all along.

THE COOK: But in peacetime!

EILIF: Shut your trap. Can I sit down till she comes?

THE SOLDIER: We haven't time.

THE CHAPLAIN: During the war they honored him for it, he sat at the general's right hand. Then it was bravery. Couldn't we speak to the officer?

THE SOLDIER: No use. What's brave about taking a peasant's cattle?

THE COOK: It was stupid.

EILIF: If I'd been stupid, I'd have starved, wise guy.

THE COOK: And for being smart your head comes off.

THE CHAPLAIN: Let's get Kattrin at least.

EILIF: Leave her be. Get me a drink of schnapps.

THE SOLDIER: No time. Let's go!

THE CHAPLAIN: And what should we tell your mother?

EILIF: Tell her it wasn't any different, tell her it was the same. Or don't tell her anything.

(*The soldiers drive him away.*)

THE CHAPLAIN: I'll go with you on your hard journey.

EILIF: I don't need any sky pilot.

THE CHAPLAIN: You don't know yet. (*He follows him.*)

THE COOK (*calls after them*): I'll have to tell her, she'll want to see him.

THE CHAPLAIN: Better not tell her anything. Or say he was here and he'll come again, maybe tomorrow. I'll break it to her when I get back. (*Hurries out.*)

(*The cook looks after them, shaking his head, then he walks anxiously about. Finally he approaches the wagon.*)

THE COOK: Hey! Come on out! I can see why you'd

hide from peace. I wish I could do it myself. I'm the general's cook, remember? Wouldn't you have a bite to eat, to do me till your mother gets back? A slice of ham or just a piece of bread while I'm waiting. (*He looks in.*) She's buried her head in a blanket. (*The sound of gunfire in the rear.*)

MOTHER COURAGE (*Runs in. She is out of breath and still has her merchandise.*): Cook, the peace is over, the war started up again three days ago. I hadn't sold my stuff yet when I found out. Heaven be praised! They're shooting each other up in town, the Catholics and Lutherans. We've got to get out of here. Kattrin, start packing. What have *you* got such a long face about? What's wrong?

THE COOK: Nothing.

MOTHER COURAGE: Something's wrong, I can tell by your expression.

THE COOK: Maybe it's the war starting up again. Now I probably won't get anything hot to eat before tomorrow night.

MOTHER COURAGE: That's a lie, cook.

THE COOK: Eilif was here. He couldn't stay.

MOTHER COURAGE: He was here? Then we'll see him on the march. I'm going with our troops this time. How does he look?

THE COOK: The same.

MOTHER COURAGE: He'll never change. The war couldn't take him away from me. He's smart. Could you help me pack? (*She starts packing.*) Did he tell you anything? Is he in good with the general? Did he say anything about his heroic deeds?

THE COOK (*gloomily*): They say he's been at one of them again.

MOTHER COURAGE: Tell me later, we've got to be going. (*Kattrin emerges.*) Kattrin, peace is over. We're moving. (*To the cook.*) What's the matter with you?

THE COOK: I'm going to enlist.

MOTHER COURAGE: I've got a suggestion. Why don't . . . ? Where's the chaplain?

THE COOK: Gone to town with Eilif.

MOTHER COURAGE: Then come a little way with me, Lamb. I need help.

THE COOK: That incident with Yvette . . .

MOTHER COURAGE: It hasn't lowered you in my estimation. Far from it. Where there's smoke there's fire. Coming?

THE COOK: I won't say no.

MOTHER COURAGE: The Twelfth Regiment has shoved off. Take the shaft. Here's a chunk of bread. We'll have to circle around to meet the Lutherans. Maybe I'll see Eilif tonight. He's my favorite. It's been a short peace. And we're on the move again. (*She sings, while the cook and Kattrin harness themselves to the wagon.*)

From Ulm to Metz, from Metz to Pilsen
Courage is right there in the van.
The war both in and out of season
With shot and shell will feed its man.
But lead alone is not sufficient
The war needs soldiers to subsist!
Its diet elseways is deficient.
The war is hungry! So enlist!

SCENE 9

(*The great war of religion has been going on for sixteen years. Germany has lost more than half its population. Those whom the slaughter has spared have been laid low by epidemics. Once-flourishing countrysides are ravaged by famine. Wolves prowl through the charred ruins of the cities. In the fall of 1634 we find Mother Courage in Germany, in the Fichtelgebirge, at some distance from the road followed by the Swedish armies. Winter comes early and is exceptionally severe. Business is bad, begging is the only resort. The cook receives a letter from Utrecht and is dismissed.*)

(*Outside a half-demolished presbytery.*)

(*Gray morning in early winter. Gusts of wind. Mother Courage and the cook in shabby sheepskins by the wagon.*)

THE COOK: No light. Nobody's up yet.

MOTHER COURAGE: But it's a priest. He'll have to crawl out of bed to ring the bells. Then he'll get himself a nice bowl of hot soup.

THE COOK: Go on, you saw the village, everything's been burned to a crisp.

MOTHER COURAGE: But somebody's here, I heard a dog bark.

THE COOK: If the priest's got anything, he won't give it away.

MOTHER COURAGE: Maybe if we sing . . .

THE COOK: I've had it up to here. (*Suddenly.*) I got a letter from Utrecht. My mother's died of cholera and the tavern belongs to me. Here's the letter if you don't believe me. It's no business of yours what my aunt says about my evil ways, but never mind, read it.

MOTHER COURAGE (*reads the letter*): Lamb, I'm sick of roaming around, myself. I feel like a butcher's dog that pulls the meat cart but doesn't get any for himself. I've nothing left to sell and the people have no money to pay for it. In Saxony a man in rags tried to foist a cord of books on me for two eggs, and in Württemberg they'd have let their plow go for a little bag of salt. What's the good of plowing? Nothing grows but brambles. In Pomerania they say the villagers have eaten up all the babies, and that nuns have been caught at highway robbery.

THE COOK: It's the end of the world.

MOTHER COURAGE: Sometimes I have visions of myself driving through hell, selling sulphur and brimstone, or through heaven peddling refreshments to the roaming souls. If me and the children I've got left could find a place where there's no shooting, I wouldn't mind a few years of peace and quiet.

THE COOK: We could open up the tavern again. Think it over, Anna. I made up my mind last night; with or without you, I'm going back to Utrecht. In fact I'm leaving today.

MOTHER COURAGE: I'll have to talk to Kattrin. It's kind of sudden, and I don't like to make decisions in the cold with nothing in my stomach. Kattrin! (*Kattrin climbs out of the wagon.*) Kattrin, I've got something to tell you. The cook and me are thinking of going to Utrecht. They've left him a tavern there. You'd be living in one place, you'd meet people. A lot of men would be glad to get a nice, well-behaved girl, looks aren't everything. I'm all for it. I get along fine with the cook. I've got to hand it to him: He's got a head for business. We'd eat regular meals, wouldn't that be nice? And you'd have your own bed, wouldn't you like that? It's no life on the road, year in year out. You'll go to rack and ruin. You're crawling with lice already. We've got to decide, you see, we could go north with the Swedes, they must be over there. (*She points to the left.*) I think we'll do it, Kattrin.

THE COOK: Anna, could I have a word with you alone?

MOTHER COURAGE: Get back in the wagon, Kattrin.

(*Kattrin climbs back in.*)

THE COOK: I interrupted you because I see there's been a misunderstanding. I thought it was too obvious to need saying. But if it isn't, I'll just have to say it. You can't take her, it's out of the question. Is that plain enough for you?

(*Kattrin sticks her head out of the wagon and listens.*)

MOTHER COURAGE: You want me to leave Kattrin?

THE COOK: Look at it this way. There's no room in the tavern. It's not one of those places with three taprooms. If the two of us put our shoulder to the wheel, we can make a living, but not three, it can't be done. Kattrin can keep the wagon.

MOTHER COURAGE: I'd been thinking she could find a husband in Utrecht.

THE COOK: Don't make me laugh! How's she going to find a husband? At her age? And dumb! And with that scar!

MOTHER COURAGE: Not so loud.

THE COOK: Shout or whisper, the truth's the truth. And that's another reason why I can't have her in the tavern. The customers won't want a sight like that staring them in the face. Can you blame them?

MOTHER COURAGE: Shut up. Not so loud, I say.

THE COOK: There's a light in the presbytery. Let's sing.

MOTHER COURAGE: How could she pull the wagon by herself? She's afraid of the war. She couldn't stand it. The dreams she must have! I hear her groaning at night. Especially after battles. What she sees in her dreams, God knows. It's pity that makes her suffer so. The other day the wagon hit a hedgehog, I found it hidden in her blanket.

THE COOK: The tavern's too small. (*He calls.*) Worthy gentleman and members of the household! We shall now sing the Song of Solomon, Julius Caesar, and other great men, whose greatness didn't help them any. Just to show you that we're God-fearing people ourselves, which makes it hard for us, especially in the winter. (*They sing.*)

You saw the wise King Solomon
You know what came of him.
To him all hidden things were plain.
He cursed the hour gave birth to him
And saw that everything was vain.
How great and wise was Solomon!
Now think about his case. Alas
A useful lesson can be won
It's wisdom that had brought him to that pass!
How happy is the man with none!

Our beautiful song proves that virtues are dangerous things, better steer clear of them, enjoy life, eat a good breakfast, a bowl of hot soup, for instance. Take me, I haven't got any soup and wish I had, I'm a soldier, but what has my bravery in all those battles got me, nothing, I'm starving, I'd be better off if I'd stayed home like a yellowbelly. And I'll tell you why.

You saw the daring Caesar next
You know what he became.
They deified him in his life
But then they killed him just the same.
And as they raised the fatal knife
How loud he cried: "You too, my son!"
Now think about his case. Alas
A useful lesson can be won.
It's daring that had brought him to that pass!
How happy is the man with none!
(*In an undertone.*) They're not even looking out.
Worthy gentleman and members of the household! Maybe you'll say, all right, if bravery won't keep body and soul together, try honesty. That may fill your belly or at least get you a drop to drink. Let's look into it.

You've heard of honest Socrates
Who never told a lie.

They weren't so grateful as you'd think
Instead they sentenced him to die
And handed him the poisoned drink.
How honest was the people's noble son!
Now think about his case. Alas
A useful lesson can be won.
His honesty had brought him to that pass.
How happy is the man with none!
Yes, they tell us to be charitable and to share what
we have, but what if we haven't got anything?
Maybe philanthropists have a rough time of it too,
it stands to reason, they need a little something for
themselves. Yes, charity is a rare virtue, because it
doesn't pay.
St. Martin couldn't bear to see
His fellows in distress.
He saw a poor man in the snow.
"Take half my cloak!" He did, and lo!
They both of them froze none the less.
He thought his heavenly reward was won.
Now think about his case. Alas
A useful lesson can be won.
Unselfishness had brought him to that pass.
How happy is the man with none!
That's our situation. We're God-fearing folk, we
stick together, we don't steal, we don't murder, we
don't set fire to anything! You could say that we
set an example which bears out the song, we sink
lower and lower, we seldom see any soup, but if
we were different, if we were thieves and murderers,
maybe our bellies would be full. Because virtue isn't
rewarded, only wickedness, the world needn't be
like this, but it is.
And here you see God-fearing folk
Observing God's ten laws.
So far He hasn't taken heed.
You people sitting warm indoors
Help to relieve our bitter need!
Our virtue can be counted on.
Now think about our case. Alas
A useful lesson can be won.
The fear of God has brought us to this pass.
How happy is the man with none!

VOICE (*from above*): Hey, down there! Come on up!
We've got some good thick soup.
MOTHER COURAGE: Lamb, I couldn't get anything
down. I know what you say makes sense, but is it
your last word? We've always been good friends.
THE COOK: My last word. Think it over.
MOTHER COURAGE: I don't need to think it over. I
won't leave her.
THE COOK: It wouldn't be wise, but there's nothing
I can do. I'm not inhuman, but it's a small tavern.
We'd better go in now, or there won't be anything
left, we'll have been singing in the cold for nothing.

MOTHER COURAGE: I'll get Kattrin.
THE COOK: Better bring it down for her. They'll get
a fright if the three of us barge in. (*They go out.*)

(*Kattrin climbs out of the wagon. She is carrying a
bundle. She looks around to make sure the others are
gone. Then she spreads out an old pair of the cook's
trousers and a skirt belonging to her mother side by
side on a wheel of the wagon so they can easily be
seen. She is about to leave with her bundle when
Mother Courage comes out of the house.*)

MOTHER COURAGE (*with a dish of soup*): Kattrin!
Stop! Kattrin! Where do you think you're going
with that bundle? Have you taken leave of your
wits? (*She examines the bundle.*) She's packed her
things. Were you listening? I've told him it's no go
with Utrecht and his lousy tavern, what would we
do there? A tavern's no place for you and me. The
war still has a thing or two up its sleeve for us.
(*She sees the trousers and skirt.*) You're stupid.
Suppose I'd seen that and you'd been gone? (*Kattrin
tries to leave, Mother Courage holds her back.*)
And don't go thinking I've given him the gate on
your account. It's the wagon. I won't part with the
wagon, I'm used to it, it's not you, it's the wagon.
We'll go in the other direction, we'll put the cook's
stuff out here where he'll find it, the fool. (*She
climbs up and throws down a few odds and ends
to join the trousers.*) There. Now we're shut of
him, you won't see me taking anyone else into the
business. From now on it's you and me. This winter
will go by like all the rest. Harness up, it looks
like snow.

(*They harness themselves to the wagon, turn it around,
and pull it away. When the cook comes out he sees
his things and stands dumbfounded.*)

SCENE 10

(*Throughout 1635 Mother Courage and her daughter
Kattrin pull the wagon over the roads of central Ger-
many in the wake of the increasingly bedraggled armies.*)
(*Highway.*)
(*Mother Courage and Kattrin are pulling the wagon.
They come to a peasant's house. A voice is heard
singing from within.*)

THE VOICE: The rose bush in our garden
Rejoiced our hearts in spring
It bore such lovely flowers.
We planted it last season
Before the April showers.
A garden is a blessèd thing
It bore such lovely flowers.

When winter comes a-stalking
And gales great snow storms bring
They trouble us but little.
We've lately finished caulking
The roof with moss and wattle.
A sheltering roof's a blessèd thing
When winter comes a-stalking.

(*Mother Courage and Kattrin have stopped to listen. Then they move on.*)

SCENE 11 _____

(*January 1636. The imperial troops threaten the Protestant city of Halle. The stone speaks. Mother Courage loses her daughter and goes on alone. The end of the war is not in sight.*)

(*The wagon, much the worse for wear, is standing beside a peasant house with an enormous thatch roof. The house is built against the side of a stony hill. Night.*)

(*A lieutenant and three soldiers in heavy armor step out of the woods.*)

THE LIEUTENANT: I don't want any noise. If anybody yells, run him through with your pikes.
FIRST SOLDIER: But we need a guide. We'll have to knock if we want them to come out.
THE LIEUTENANT: Knocking sounds natural. It could be a cow bumping against the barn wall.

(*The soldiers knock on the door. A peasant woman opens. They hold their hands over her mouth. Two soldiers go in.*)

A MAN'S VOICE (*inside*): Who's there?

(*The soldiers bring out a peasant and his son.*)

THE LIEUTENANT (*points to the wagon, in which Kattrin has appeared*): There's another one. (*A soldier pulls her out.*) Anybody else live here?
THE PEASANT COUPLE: This is our son. — That's a dumb girl. — Her mother's gone into the town on business. — Buying up people's belongings, they're selling cheap because they're getting out. — They're provisioners.
THE LIEUTENANT: I'm warning you to keep quiet, one squawk and you'll get a pike over the head. All right. I need somebody who can show us the path into the city. (*Points to the young peasant.*) You. Come here!
THE YOUNG PEASANT: I don't know no path.
THE SECOND SOLDIER (*grinning*): He don't know no path.
THE YOUNG PEASANT: I'm not helping the Catholics.
THE LIEUTENANT (*to the second soldier*): Give him a feel of your pike!

THE YOUNG PEASANT (*forced down on his knees and threatened with the pike*): You can kill me. I won't do it.
THE FIRST SOLDIER: I know what'll make him think twice. (*He goes over to the barn.*) Two cows and an ox. Get this: If you don't help us, I'll cut them down.
THE YOUNG PEASANT: Not the animals!
THE PEASANT WOMAN (*in tears*): Captain, spare our animals or we'll starve.
THE LIEUTENANT: If he insists on being stubborn, they're done for.
THE FIRST SOLDIER: I'll start with the ox.
THE YOUNG PEASANT (*to the old man*): Do I have to? (*The old woman nods.*) I'll do it.
THE PEASANT WOMAN: And thank you kindly for your forbearance, Captain, for ever and ever, amen.

(*The peasant stops her from giving further thanks.*)

THE FIRST SOLDIER: Didn't I tell you? With them it's the animals that come first.

(*Led by the young peasant, the lieutenant and the soldiers continue on their way.*)

THE PEASANT: I wish I knew what they're up to. Nothing good.
THE PEASANT WOMAN: Maybe they're only scouts. — What are you doing?
THE PEASANT (*putting a ladder against the roof and climbing up*): See if they're alone. (*On the roof.*) Men moving in the woods. All the way to the quarry. Armor in the clearing. And a cannon. It's more than a regiment. God have mercy on the city and everybody in it.
THE PEASANT WOMAN: See any light in the city?
THE PEASANT: No. They're all asleep. (*He climbs down.*) If they get in, they'll kill everybody.
THE PEASANT WOMAN: The sentry will see them in time.
THE PEASANT: They must have killed the sentry in the tower on the hill, or he'd have blown his horn.
THE PEASANT WOMAN: If there were more of us ...
THE PEASANT: All by ourselves up here with a cripple ...
THE PEASANT WOMAN: We can't do a thing. Do you think ...
THE PEASANT: Not a thing.
THE PEASANT WOMAN: We couldn't get down there in the dark.
THE PEASANT: The whole hillside is full of them. We can't even give a signal.
THE PEASANT WOMAN: They'd kill us.
THE PEASANT: No, we can't do a thing.
THE PEASANT WOMAN (*to Kattrin*): Pray, poor thing, pray! We can't stop the bloodshed. If you can't

talk, at least you can pray. He'll hear you if nobody else does. I'll help you. (*All kneel, Kattrin behind the peasants.*) Our Father which art in heaven, hear our prayer. Don't let the town perish with everybody in it, all asleep and unsuspecting. Wake them, make them get up and climb the walls and see the enemy coming through the night with cannon and pikes, through the fields and down the hillside. (*Back to Kattrin.*) Protect our mother and don't let the watchman sleep, wake him before it's too late. And succor our brother-in-law, he's in there with his four children, let them not perish, they're innocent and don't know a thing. (*To Kattrin, who groans.*) The littlest is less than two, the oldest is seven. (*Horrified, Kattrin stands up.*) Our Father, hear us, for Thou alone canst help, we'll all be killed, we're weak, we haven't any pikes or anything, we are powerless and in Thine hands, we and our animals and the whole farm, and the city too, it's in Thine hands, and the enemy is under the walls with great might.

(*Kattrin has crept unnoticed to the wagon, taken something out of it, put it under her apron, and climbed up the ladder to the roof of the barn.*)

THE PEASANT WOMAN: Think upon the children in peril, especially the babes in arms and the old people that can't help themselves and all God's creatures.

THE PEASANT: And forgive us our trespasses as we forgive them that trespass against us. Amen.

(*Kattrin, sitting on the roof, starts beating the drum that she has taken out from under her apron.*)

THE PEASANT WOMAN: Jesus! What's she doing?
THE PEASANT: She's gone crazy.
THE PEASANT WOMAN: Get her down, quick!

(*The peasant runs toward the ladder, but Kattrin pulls it up on the roof.*)

THE PEASANT WOMAN: She'll be the death of us all.
THE PEASANT: Stop that, you cripple!
THE PEASANT WOMAN: She'll have the Catholics down on us.
THE PEASANT (*looking around for stones*): I'll throw rocks at you.
THE PEASANT WOMAN: Have you no pity? Have you no heart? We're dead if they find out it's us! They'll run us through!

(*Kattrin stares in the direction of the city and goes on drumming.*)

THE PEASANT WOMAN (*to the peasant*): I told you not to let those tramps stop here. What do they care if the soldiers drive our last animals away?

THE LIEUTENANT (*rushes in with his soldiers and the young peasant*): I'll cut you to pieces!
THE PEASANT WOMAN: We're innocent, captain. We couldn't help it. She sneaked up there. We don't know her.
THE LIEUTENANT: Where's the ladder?
THE PEASANT: Up top.
THE LIEUTENANT (*to Kattrin*): Throw down that drum. It's an order!

(*Kattrin goes on drumming.*)

THE LIEUTENANT: You're all in this together! This'll be the end of you!
THE PEASANT: They've felled some pine trees in the woods over there. We could get one and knock her down . . .
THE FIRST SOLDIER (*to the lieutenant*): Request permission to make a suggestion. (*He whispers something in the lieutenant's ear. He nods.*) Listen. We've got a friendly proposition. Come down, we'll take you into town with us. Show us your mother and we won't touch a hair of her head.

(*Kattrin goes on drumming.*)

THE LIEUTENANT (*pushes him roughly aside*): She doesn't trust you. No wonder with your mug. (*He calls up.*) If I give you my word? I'm an officer, you can trust my word of honor.

(*She drums still louder.*)

THE LIEUTENANT: Nothing is sacred to her.
THE YOUNG PEASANT: It's not just her mother, lieutenant!
THE FIRST SOLDIER: We can't let this go on. They'll hear it in the city.
THE LIEUTENANT: We'll have to make some kind of noise that's louder than the drums. What could we make noise with?
THE FIRST SOLDIER: But we're not supposed to make noise.
THE LIEUTENANT: An innocent noise, stupid. A peaceable noise.
THE PEASANT: I could chop wood.
THE LIEUTENANT: That's it, chop! (*The peasant gets an ax and chops at a log.*) Harder! Harder! You're chopping for your life.

(*Listening, Kattrin has been drumming more softly. Now she looks anxiously around and goes on drumming as before.*)

THE LIEUTENANT (*to the peasant*): Not loud enough. (*To the first soldier.*) You chop too.
THE PEASANT: There's only one ax. (*Stops chopping.*)
THE LIEUTENANT: We'll have to set the house on fire. Smoke her out.

THE PEASANT: That won't do any good, captain. If the city people see fire up here, they'll know what's afoot.

(*Still drumming, Kattrin has been listening again. Now she laughs.*)

THE LIEUTENANT: Look, she's laughing at us. I'll shoot her down, regardless. Get the musket!

(*Two soldiers run out. Kattrin goes on drumming.*)

THE PEASANT WOMAN: I've got it, captain. That's their wagon over there. If we start smashing it up, she'll stop. The wagon's all they've got.

THE LIEUTENANT (*to the young peasant*): Smash away. (*To Kattrin.*) We'll smash your wagon if you don't stop.

(*The young peasant strikes a few feeble blows at the wagon.*)

THE PEASANT WOMAN: Stop it, you beast!

(*Kattrin stares despairingly at the wagon and emits pitiful sounds. But she goes on drumming.*)

THE LIEUTENANT: Where are those stinkers with the musket?

THE FIRST SOLDIER: They haven't heard anything in the city yet, or we'd hear their guns.

THE LIEUTENANT (*to Kattrin*): They don't hear you. And now we're going to shoot you down. For the last time: Drop that drum!

THE YOUNG PEASANT (*suddenly throws the plank away*): Keep on drumming! Or they'll all be killed! Keep on drumming, keep on drumming . . .

(*The soldier throws him down and hits him with his pike. Kattrin starts crying but goes on drumming.*)

THE PEASANT WOMAN: Don't hit him in the back! My God, you're killing him.

(*The soldiers run in with the musket.*)

THE SECOND SOLDIER: The colonel's foaming at the mouth. We'll be court-martialed.

THE LIEUTENANT: Set it up! Set it up! (*To Kattrin, while the musket is being set up on its stand.*) For the last time: Stop that drumming! (*Kattrin in tears drums as loud as she can.*) Fire!

(*The soldiers fire. Kattrin is hit. She beats the drum a few times more and then slowly collapses.*)

THE LIEUTENANT: Now we'll have some quiet.

(*But Kattrin's last drumbeats are answered by the city's cannon. A confused hubbub of alarm bells and cannon is heard in the distance.*)

FIRST SOLDIER: She's done it.

SCENE 12

(*Night, toward morning. The fifes and drums of troops marching away.*)

(*Outside the wagon Mother Courage sits huddled over her daughter. The peasant couple are standing beside them.*)

THE PEASANT (*hostile*): You'll have to be going, woman. There's only one more regiment to come. You can't go alone.

MOTHER COURAGE: Maybe I can get her to sleep. (*She sings.*)
Lullaby baby
What stirs in the hay?
The neighbor brats whimper
Mine are happy and gay.
They go in tatters
And you in silk down
Cut from an angel's
Best party gown.

They've nothing to munch on
And you will have pie
Just tell your mother
In case it's too dry.
Lullaby baby
What stirs in the hay?
The one lies in Poland
The other — who can say?

Now she's asleep. You shouldn't have told her about your brother-in-law's children.

THE PEASANT: Maybe it wouldn't have happened if you hadn't gone to town to swindle people.

MOTHER COURAGE: I'm glad she's sleeping now.

THE PEASANT WOMAN: She's not sleeping, you'll have to face it, she's dead.

THE PEASANT: And it's time you got started. There are wolves around here, and what's worse, marauders.

MOTHER COURAGE: Yes. (*She goes to the wagon and takes out a sheet of canvas to cover the body with.*)

THE PEASANT WOMAN: Haven't you anybody else? Somebody you can go to?

MOTHER COURAGE: Yes, there's one of them left. Eilif.

THE PEASANT (*while Mother Courage covers the body*): Go find him. We'll attend to this one, give her a decent burial. Set your mind at rest.

MOTHER COURAGE: Here's money for your expenses. (*She gives the peasant money.*)

(*The peasant and his son shake hands with her and carry Kattrin away.*)

THE PEASANT WOMAN (*on the way out*): Hurry up!

MOTHER COURAGE (*harnesses herself to the wagon*):

I hope I can pull the wagon alone. I'll manage, there isn't much in it. I've got to get back in business.

(*Another regiment marches by with fifes and drums in the rear.*)

MOTHER COURAGE: Hey, take me with you! (*She starts to pull.*)

(*Singing is heard in the rear.*)
    With all the killing and recruiting
    The war will worry on a while
In ninety years they'll still be shooting.
It's hardest on the rank-and-file.
Our food is swill, our pants all patches
The higher-ups steal half our pay
And still we dream of God-sent riches.
Tomorrow is another day!
    The spring is come! Christian, revive!
    The snowdrifts melt, the dead lie dead!
    And if by chance you're still alive
    It's time to rise and shake a leg.

Tennessee Williams

Tennessee Williams (1911–1983) was one of a handful of post-World War II American playwrights to achieve an international reputation. He was born Thomas Lanier Williams in Columbus, Mississippi, the son of a traveling shoe salesman who eventually moved the family to a dark and dreary tenement in St. Louis. Because he was a precocious child, Williams's mother gave him a typewriter when he was eleven years old. The instrument helped him create fantasy worlds that seemed more real, more important to him than the dark and sometimes threatening world in which he lived. His parents, when they were expecting a third child, bought a house whose gloominess depressed virtually everyone in it. His mother and father found themselves arguing, and his sister, Rose, took refuge from the real world by closeting herself with a collection of glass animals.

Both Rose and Tennessee responded badly to their environment, and both had breakdowns. Tennessee was so ill that he suffered a partial paralysis of his legs, a disorder that made him a victim of bullies at school and a disappointment to his father at home. He could never participate in sports and was always somewhat frail, but he published his first story when he was sixteen.

His education was sporadic. He attended the University of Missouri, but failed ROTC because of his physical limitations and soon dropped out of school to work in a shoe company. Then he went to Washington University in St. Louis and dropped out again. Finally, he took a bachelor's degree in playwrighting from the State University of Iowa when he was twenty-four. During this time he was writing plays, some of which were produced at Washington University. Two years after he was graduated, the Theatre Guild produced his first commercial play, *Battle of Angels* (1940), in Boston. It was such a distinct failure that he feared his career was stunted from the beginning. But he kept writing and managed to live for a few years on foundation grants. It was not until the production of *The Glass Menagerie* (1944 in Chicago, 1945 in New York) that he achieved the kind of notice he knew he deserved. His first real success, the play was given the New York Drama Critics' Circle Award, the sign of his having achieved a measure of professional recognition and financial independence.

Although he had tried his hand at many activities — including an unsuccessful attempt at screenwriting — to make a living, he had no more worries about work after *The Glass Menagerie* ran on Broadway for 561 performances. In 1947 his second success, *A Streetcar Named Desire*, starring the then unknown Marlon Brando, was an even bigger box-office smash. It ran for 855 performances and won the Pulitzer Prize. By the time Tennessee Williams was thirty-six, he was thought of as one of the most important playwrights in America.

Williams followed these successes with a number of plays that were not all as well received as his first works. *Summer and Smoke* (1948), *The Rose Tattoo*, (1951), and *Camino Real* (1953), were met with measured enthusiasm from the public, although the critics thought highly of Williams's work. These plays were followed by the saga of a southern family, *Cat on a Hot Tin Roof*, which won all the major drama prizes in 1955, including the Pulitzer.

Williams's energy was unfailing in the next several years. He authored a screenplay, *Baby Doll*, with the legendary producer Elia Kazan, in 1956. In 1958 he wrote a one-act play, *Suddenly Last Summer*, and in 1959 *Sweet Bird of Youth*. Some of his later plays are *The Night of the Iguana* (1961), *The Milk Train Doesn't Stop Here Anymore* (1963), and *Small Craft Warnings* (1972). He also wrote a novel and several volumes of short stories, establishing himself as an important writer in every sense of the word. His accidental death in 1983 was a total shock to the theater world.

THE GLASS MENAGERIE

Tennessee Williams has often been accused of exorcising his family demons in his plays and of therefore sometimes cloaking events in a personal symbolism that is impossible for an audience to penetrate totally. *The Glass Menagerie* (1944) certainly derives from his personal experience growing up in St. Louis in a tenement, the setting for the play. The characters in the play are drawn from his own family, particularly the character Laura, who is based on his sister. But the symbolism in the play is not so obscure as to give an audience special difficulty.

In a way, Williams thought of the play as a tribute to his sister, Rose. Rose's depressions were so severe that eventually she received a lobotomy, which rendered her more passive and, to a certain extent, more hopeless than she had been before. The operation did not achieve anything positive, and Williams felt somewhat responsible because he had not urged the family to refuse the treatment.

In the play, Amanda Wingfield is obsessed with finding gentleman callers and a suitable career for her daughter, Laura, who is partially lame and exceedingly shy. Amanda lives in a world of imagination, inventing stories about a glorious past she never lived and about all the suitors she could have had before she married. Amanda bullies Laura, whose only defense is to bury herself in her own fantasy world of spun-glass animals. Tom, the son and narrator of the play, is also a victim of Amanda's bullying, but he is more independent and better able to withstand her assaults.

Both children are great disappointments to Amanda. Tom is aloof, indolent, something like his father, whose presence is felt only by his picture on the wall. Laura calls herself a cripple and has no self-esteem or hope for a future such as the one her mother conceives for her. Laura's shyness is almost uncontrollable. It has ruined any hope of a business career, to Amanda's intense distress. When Tom brings home Jim, the one boy Laura remembers from high school, Laura is nearly too shy to come to the dinner table. And when it becomes clear that Jim is not the gentleman caller of Amanda's dreams, Amanda and Laura are left to face reality or to continue living in their fantasy worlds.

Amanda confronts Tom at the end of the play and asserts that he "live[s] in a dream" and "manufactures[s] illusions." She could be speaking about any character in the play, including Jim, who lives according to popular illusions about self-fulfillment. But the Wingfields in particular pay dearly for their illusions, perhaps Laura more than anyone because of her mother's inability to relinquish her intense but unrealistic hopes for her.

Williams's written presentation of the play provides more insights than usual for a reading audience. His stage directions are elaborate, poetic, and exceptionally evocative. Through Tom, as narrator, he says that the play is not realistic but rather is a memory play, an enactment of moments in Tom's memory.

Williams specifies a setting that is almost dreamlike, using Brechtian devices such as the visual images and screen legends flashed at appropriate moments. Like Brecht in certain plays, Williams also uses music to establish a mood or stimulate an association. These devices may be thought of as expressionistic, although they fall short of the fullness of expressionism, which usually involves a distortion of reality to express the feelings of the author.

Modern productions rarely follow Williams's directions, however, so the dreamlike quality is sometimes lost. In fact, ironically, modern productions of this play are often realistic rather than symbolic, although they usually maintain the sentimental effect that Williams hoped to achieve.

Tennessee Williams (1911–1983)
THE GLASS MENAGERIE   *1944*

Nobody, not even the rain, has such small hands.   — E. E. CUMMINGS

Production Notes by Tennessee Williams

Being a "memory play," *The Glass Menagerie* can be presented with unusual freedom of convention. Because of its considerably delicate or tenuous material, atmospheric touches and subtleties of direction play a particularly important part. Expressionism and all other unconventional techniques in drama have only one valid aim, and this is a closer approach to truth. When a play employs unconventional techniques, it is not, or certainly shouldn't be, trying to escape its responsibility of dealing with reality, or interpreting experience, but is actually or should be attempting to find a closer approach, or more penetrating and vivid expression of things as they are. The straight realistic play with its genuine frigidaire and authentic ice cubes, its characters that speak exactly as its audience speaks, corresponds to the academic landscape and has the same virtue of a photographic likeness. Everyone should know nowadays the unimportance of the photographic in art: that truth, life, or reality is an organic thing which the poetic imagination can represent or suggest, in essence, only through transformation, through changing into other forms than those which were merely present in appearance.

These remarks are not meant as a preface only to this particular play. They have to do with a conception of a new, plastic theatre which must take the place of the exhausted theatre of realistic conventions if the theatre is to resume vitality as a part of our culture.

The Screen Device. There is *only one important difference between the original and acting version of the play* and that is the *omission* in the latter of the device which I tentatively included in my *original* script. This device was the use of a screen on which were projected magic-lantern slides bearing images or titles. I do not regret the omission of this device from the present Broadway production. The extraordinary power of Miss Taylor's performance made it suitable to have the utmost simplicity in the physical production. But I think it may be interesting to some readers to see how this device was conceived. So I am putting it into the published manuscript. These images and legends, projected from behind, were cast on a section of wall between the front-room and dining-room areas, which should be indistinguishable from the rest when not in use.

The purpose of this will probably be apparent. It is to give accent to certain values in each scene. Each scene contains a particular point (or several) which is structurally the most important. In an episodic play, such as this, the basic structure or narrative line may be obscured from the audience; the effect may seem fragmentary rather than architectural. This may not be the fault of the play so much as a lack of attention in the audience. The legend or image upon the screen will strengthen the effect of what is merely allusion in the writing and allow the primary point to be made more simply and lightly than if the entire responsibility were on the spoken lines. Aside from this structural value, I think the screen will have a definite emotional appeal, less definable but just as important. An imaginative producer or director may invent many other uses for this device than those indicated in the present script. In fact the possibilities of the device seem much larger to me than the instance of this play can possibly utilize.

The Music. Another extra-literary accent in this play is provided by the use of music. A single recurring tune, "The Glass Menagerie," is used to give emotional emphasis to suitable passages. This tune is like circus music, not when you are on the grounds or in the immediate vicinity of the parade, but when you are at some distance and very likely thinking of something else. It seems under those circumstances to continue almost interminably and it weaves in and out of your preoccupied consciousness; then it is the lightest, most delicate music in the world and perhaps the saddest. It expresses the surface vivacity of life with the underlying strain of immutable and inexpressible sorrow. When you look at a piece of delicately spun glass you think of two things: how beautiful it is and how easily it can be broken. Both of those ideas should be woven into the recurring tune, which dips in and out of the play as if it were carried on a wind that changes. It serves as a thread of connection and allusion between the narrator with his separate point in time and space and the subject of his story. Between each episode it returns as reference to the emotion, nostalgia, which is the first condition of the play. It is primarily Laura's music and therefore comes out most clearly when the play focuses upon her and the lovely fragility of glass which is her image.

The Lighting. The lighting in the play is not realistic. In keeping with the atmosphere of memory, the stage is dim. Shafts of light are focused on selected areas or actors, sometimes in contradistinction to what is the apparent center. For instance, in the quarrel scene between Tom and Amanda, in which Laura has no active part, the clearest pool of light is on her figure. This is also true of the supper scene, when her silent figure on the sofa should remain the visual center. The light upon Laura should be distinct from the others, having a peculiar pristine clarity such as light used in early religious portraits of female saints or madonnas. A certain correspondence to light in religious paintings, such as El Greco's, where the figures are radiant in atmosphere that is relatively dusky, could be effectively used throughout the play. (It will also permit a more effective use of the screen.) A free, imaginative use of light can be of enormous value in giving a mobile, plastic quality to plays of a more or less static nature.

Characters

AMANDA WINGFIELD, *the mother. A little woman of great but confused vitality clinging frantically to another time and place. Her characterization must be carefully created, not copied from type. She is not paranoiac, but her life is paranoia. There is much to admire in Amanda, and as much to love and pity as there is to laugh at. Certainly she has endurance and a kind of heroism, and though her foolishness makes her unwittingly cruel at times, there is tenderness in her slight person.*

LAURA WINGFIELD, *her daughter. Amanda, having failed to establish contact with reality, continues to live vitally in her illusions, but Laura's situation is even graver. A childhood illness has left her crippled, one leg slightly shorter than the other, and held in a brace. This defect need not be more than suggested on the stage. Stemming from this, Laura's separation increases till she is like a piece of her own glass collection, too exquisitely fragile to move from the shelf.*

TOM WINGFIELD, *her son. And the narrator of the play. A poet with a job in a warehouse. His nature is not remorseless, but to escape from a trap he has to act without pity.*

JIM O'CONNOR, *the gentleman caller. A nice, ordinary, young man.*

Scene: *An alley in St. Louis.*
Part I: *Preparation for a Gentleman Caller.*
Part II: *The Gentleman Calls.*
Time: *Now and the Past.*

SCENE 1

(*The Wingfield apartment is in the rear of the building, one of those vast hive-like conglomerations of cellular living-units that flower as warty growths in overcrowded urban centers of lower middle-class population and are symptomatic of the impulse of this largest and fundamentally enslaved section of American society to avoid fluidity and differentiation and to exist and function as one interfused mass of automatism.*)

(*The apartment faces an alley and is entered by a fire escape, a structure whose name is a touch of accidental poetic truth, for all of these huge buildings are always burning with the slow and implacable fires of human desperation. The fire escape is included in the set — that is, the landing of it and steps descending from it.*)

(*The scene is memory and is therefore nonrealistic. Memory takes a lot of poetic license. It omits some details; others are exaggerated, according to the emotional value of the articles it touches, for memory is seated predominantly in the heart. The interior is therefore rather dim and poetic.*)

(*At the rise of the curtain, the audience is faced with the dark, grim rear wall of the Wingfield tenement. This building, which runs parallel to the footlights, is flanked on both sides by dark, narrow alleys which run into murky canyons of tangled clotheslines, garbage cans, and the sinister latticework of neighboring fire escapes. It is up and down these side alleys that exterior entrances and exits are made, during the play. At the end of Tom's opening commentary, the dark tenement wall slowly reveals (by means of a transparency) the interior of the ground floor Wingfield apartment.*)

(*Downstage is the living room, which also serves as a sleeping room for Laura, the sofa unfolding to make her bed. Upstage, center, and divided by a wide arch or second proscenium with transparent faded portieres (or second curtain), is the dining room. In an old-fashioned what-not in the living room are seen scores of transparent glass animals. A blown-up photograph of the father hangs on the wall of the living room, facing the audience, to the left of the archway. It is the face of a very handsome young man in a doughboy's First World War cap. He is gallantly smiling, ineluctably smiling, as if to say, "I will be smiling forever."*)

(*The audience hears and sees the opening scene in the dining room through both the transparent fourth wall of the building and the transparent gauze portieres of the dining-room arch. It is during this revealing scene that the fourth wall slowly ascends, out of sight. This transparent exterior wall is not brought down again until the very end of the play, during Tom's final speech.)*

(The narrator is an undisguised convention of the play. He takes whatever license with dramatic convention as is convenient to his purposes.)

(Tom enters dressed as a merchant sailor from alley, stage left, and strolls across the front of the stage to the fire escape. There he stops and lights a cigarette. He addresses the audience.)

TOM: Yes, I have tricks in my pocket, I have things up my sleeve. But I am the opposite of a stage magician. He gives you illusion that has the appearance of truth. I give you truth in the pleasant disguise of illusion. To begin with, I turn back time. I reverse it to that quaint period, the thirties, when the huge middle class of America was matriculating in a school for the blind. Their eyes had failed them, or they had failed their eyes, and so they were having their fingers pressed forcibly down on the fiery Braille alphabet of a dissolving economy. In Spain there was revolution. Here there was only shouting and confusion. In Spain there was Guernica. Here there were disturbances of labor, sometimes pretty violent, in otherwise peaceful cities such as Chicago, Cleveland, Saint Louis. . . . This is the social background of the play.

(Music.)

The play is memory. Being a memory play, it is dimly lighted, it is sentimental, it is not realistic. In memory everything seems to happen to music. That explains the fiddle in the wings. I am the narrator of the play, and also a character in it. The other characters are my mother, Amanda, my sister, Laura, and a gentleman caller who appears in the final scenes. He is the most realistic character in the play, being an emissary from a world of reality that we were somehow set apart from. But since I have a poet's weakness for symbols, I am using this character also as a symbol; he is the long delayed but always expected something that we live for. There is a fifth character in the play who doesn't appear except in this larger-than-life photograph over the mantel. This is our father who left us a long time ago. He was a telephone man who fell in love with long distances; he gave up his job with the telephone company and skipped the light fantastic out of town . . . The last we heard of him was a picture postcard from Mazatlan, on the Pacific coast of Mexico, containing a message of two words

— "Hello — Goodbye!" and no address. I think the rest of the play will explain itself. . . .

(Amanda's voice becomes audible through the portieres.)
(Legend on Screen: "Où Sont les Neiges.")°
(He divides the portieres and enters the upstage area.)
(Amanda and Laura are seated at a drop-leaf table. Eating is indicated by gestures without food or utensils. Amanda faces the audience. Tom and Laura are seated in profile.)
(The interior has lit up softly and through the scrim we see Amanda and Laura seated at the table in the upstage area.)

AMANDA *(calling)*: Tom?
TOM: Yes, Mother.
AMANDA: We can't say grace until you come to the table!
TOM: Coming, Mother. *(He bows slightly and withdraws, reappearing a few moments later in his place at the table.)*
AMANDA *(to her son)*: Honey, don't *push* with your fingers. If you have to push with something, the thing to push with is a crust of bread. And chew — chew! Animals have sections in their stomachs which enable them to digest food without mastication, but human beings are supposed to chew their food before they swallow it down. Eat food leisurely, son, and really enjoy it. A well-cooked meal has lots of delicate flavors that have to be held in the mouth for appreciation. So chew your food and give your salivary glands a chance to function!

(Tom deliberately lays his imaginary fork down and pushes his chair back from the table.)

TOM: I haven't enjoyed one bite of this dinner because of your constant directions on how to eat it. It's you that makes me rush through meals with your hawk-like attention to every bite I take. Sickening — spoils my appetite — all this discussion of animals' secretion — salivary glands — mastication!
AMANDA *(lightly)*: Temperament like a Metropolitan° star! *(He rises and crosses downstage.)* You're not excused from the table.
TOM: I'm getting a cigarette.
AMANDA: You smoke too much.

(Laura rises.)

LAURA: I'll bring in the blanc mange.

(He remains standing with his cigarette by the portieres during the following.)

Où Sont les Neiges: Where are the snows [of yesteryear].
Metropolitan: The Metropolitan Opera in New York City.

AMANDA (*rising*): No, sister, no, sister — you be the lady this time and I'll be the darky.

LAURA: I'm already up.

AMANDA: Resume your seat, little sister — I want you to stay fresh and pretty — for gentlemen callers!

LAURA: I'm not expecting any gentlemen callers.

AMANDA (*Crossing out to kitchenette. Airily.*): Sometimes they come when they are least expected! Why, I remember one Sunday afternoon in Blue Mountain — (*Enters kitchenette.*)

TOM: I know what's coming!

LAURA: Yes. But let her tell it.

TOM: Again?

LAURA: She loves to tell it.

(*Amanda returns with bowl of dessert.*)

AMANDA: One Sunday afternoon in Blue Mountain — your mother received — *seventeen!* — gentlemen callers! Why, sometimes there weren't chairs enough to accommodate them all. We had to send the nigger over to bring in folding chairs from the parish house.

TOM (*remaining at portieres*): How did you entertain those gentlemen callers?

AMANDA: I understood the art of conversation!

TOM: I bet you could talk.

AMANDA: Girls in those days *knew* how to talk, I can tell you.

TOM: Yes?

(*Image: Amanda as a girl on a porch greeting callers.*)

AMANDA: They knew how to entertain their gentlemen callers. It wasn't enough for a girl to be possessed of a pretty face and a graceful figure — although I wasn't slighted in either respect. She also needed to have a nimble wit and a tongue to meet all occasions.

TOM: What did you talk about?

AMANDA: Things of importance going on in the world! Never anything coarse or common or vulgar. (*She addresses Tom as though he were seated in the vacant chair at the table though he remains by portieres. He plays this scene as though he held the book.*) My callers were gentlemen — all! Among my callers were some of the most prominent young planters of the Mississippi Delta — planters and sons of planters!

(*Tom motions for music and a spot of light on Amanda.*)
(*Her eyes lift, her face glows, her voice becomes rich and elegiac.*)
(*Screen legend: "Où Sont les Neiges."*)

There was young Champ Laughlin who later became vice-president of the Delta Planters Bank. Hadley Stevenson who was drowned in Moon Lake and left his widow one hundred and fifty thousand in Government bonds. There were the Cutrere brothers, Wesley and Bates. Bates was one of my bright particular beaux! He got in a quarrel with that wild Wainright boy. They shot it out on the floor of Moon Lake Casino. Bates was shot through the stomach. Died in the ambulance on his way to Memphis. His widow was also well-provided for, came into eight or ten thousand acres, that's all. She married him on the rebound — never loved her — carried my picture on him the night he died! And there was that boy that every girl in the Delta had set her cap for! That beautiful, brilliant young Fitzhugh boy from Greene County!

TOM: What did he leave his widow?

AMANDA: He never married! Gracious, you talk as though all of my old admirers had turned up their toes to the daisies!

TOM: Isn't this the first you mentioned that still survives?

AMANDA: That Fitzhugh boy went North and made a fortune — came to be known as the Wolf of Wall Street! He had the Midas touch, whatever he touched turned to gold! And I could have been Mrs. Duncan J. Fitzhugh, mind you! But — I picked your *father!*

LAURA (*rising*): Mother, let me clear the table.

AMANDA: No, dear, you go in front and study your typewriter chart. Or practice your shorthand a little. Stay fresh and pretty! — It's almost time for our gentlemen callers to start arriving. (*She flounces girlishly toward the kitchenette.*) How many do you suppose we're going to entertain this afternoon?

(*Tom throws down the paper and jumps up with a groan.*)

LAURA (*alone in the dining room*): I don't believe we're going to receive any, Mother.

AMANDA (*reappearing, airily*): What? No one — not one? You must be joking! (*Laura nervously echoes her laugh. She slips in a fugitive manner through the half-open portieres and draws them gently behind her. A shaft of very clear light is thrown on her face against the faded tapestry of the curtains. Music: "The Glass Menagerie" under faintly. Lightly.*) Not one gentleman caller? It can't be true! There must be a flood, there must have been a tornado!

LAURA: It isn't a flood, it's not a tornado, Mother. I'm just not popular like you were in Blue Mountain. . . . (*Tom utters another groan. Laura glances at him with a faint, apologetic smile. Her voice catching a little.*) Mother's afraid I'm going to be an old maid.

(*The scene dims out with "Glass Menagerie" music.*)

SCENE 2

("*Laura, Haven't You Ever Liked Some Boy?*")

(*On the dark stage the screen is lighted with the image of blue roses.*)

(*Gradually Laura's figure becomes apparent and the screen goes out.*)

(*The music subsides.*)

(*Laura is seated in the delicate ivory chair at the small clawfoot table.*)

(*She wears a dress of soft violet material for a kimono — her hair tied back from her forehead with a ribbon.*)

(*She is washing and polishing her collection of glass.*)

(*Amanda appears on the fire escape steps. At the sound of her ascent, Laura catches her breath, thrusts the bowl of ornaments away and seats herself stiffly before the diagram of the typewriter keyboard as though it held her spellbound. Something has happened to Amanda. It is written in her face as she climbs to the landing: a look that is grim and hopeless and a little absurd.*)

(*She has on one of those cheap or imitation velvety-looking cloth coats with imitation fur collar. Her hat is five or six years old, one of those dreadful cloche hats that were worn in the late twenties, and she is clasping an enormous black patent-leather pocketbook with nickel clasp and initials. This is her full-dress outfit, the one she usually wears to the D.A.R.°*)

(*Before entering she looks through the door.*)

(*She purses her lips, opens her eyes wide, rolls them upward and shakes her head.*)

(*Then she slowly lets herself in the door. Seeing her mother's expression Laura touches her lips with a nervous gesture.*)

LAURA: Hello, Mother, I was — (*She makes a nervous gesture toward the chart on the wall. Amanda leans against the shut door and stares at Laura with a martyred look.*)

AMANDA: Deception? Deception? (*She slowly removes her hat and gloves, continuing the swift suffering stare. She lets the hat and gloves fall on the floor — a bit of acting.*)

LAURA (*shakily*): How was the D.A.R. meeting? (*Amanda slowly opens her purse and removes a dainty white handkerchief which she shakes out delicately and delicately touches to her lips and nostrils.*) Didn't you go to the D.A.R. meeting, Mother?

AMANDA (*faintly, almost inaudibly*): — No. — No. (*Then more forcibly*). I did not have the strength

D.A.R.: Daughters of the American Revolution, a conservative, patriotic organization for women whose ancestors were involved in the American Revolutionary War.

— to go to the D.A.R. In fact, I did not have the courage! I wanted to find a hole in the ground and hide myself in it forever! (*She crosses slowly to the wall and removes the diagram of the typewriter keyboard. She holds it in front of her for a second, staring at it sweetly and sorrowfully — then bites her lips and tears it in two pieces.*)

LAURA (*faintly*): Why did you do that, Mother? (*Amanda repeats the same procedure with the chart of the Gregg Alphabet.*) Why are you —

AMANDA: Why? Why? How old are you, Laura?

LAURA: Mother, you know my age.

AMANDA: I thought that you were an adult; it seems that I was mistaken. (*She crosses slowly to the sofa and sinks down and stares at Laura.*)

LAURA: Please don't stare at me, Mother.

(*Amanda closes her eyes and lowers her head. Count ten.*)

AMANDA: What are we going to do, what is going to become of us, what is the future?

(*Count ten.*)

LAURA: Has something happened, Mother? (*Amanda draws a long breath and takes out the handkerchief again. Dabbing process.*) Mother, has — something happened?

AMANDA: I'll be all right in a minute. I'm just bewildered — (*Count five.*) — by life. . . .

LAURA: Mother, I wish that you would tell me what's happened.

AMANDA: As you know, I was supposed to be inducted into my office at the D.A.R. this afternoon. (*Image: a swarm of typewriters.*) But I stopped off at Rubicam's Business College to speak to your teachers about your having a cold and ask them what progress they thought you were making down there.

LAURA: Oh. . . .

AMANDA: I went to the typing instructor and introduced myself as your mother. She didn't know who you were. Wingfield, she said. We don't have any such student enrolled at the school! I assured her she did, that you had been going to classes since early in January. "I wonder," she said, "if you could be talking about that terribly shy little girl who dropped out of school after only a few days' attendance?" "No," I said, "Laura, my daughter, has been going to school every day for the past six weeks!" "Excuse me," she said. She took the attendance book out and there was your name, unmistakably printed, and all the dates you were absent until they decided that you had dropped out of school. I still said, "No, there must have been some mistake! There must have been some mix-up in the records!" And she said, "No — I remember her perfectly now.

Her hands shook so that she couldn't hit the right keys! The first time we gave a speed test, she broke down completely — was sick at the stomach and almost had to be carried into the wash-room! After that morning she never showed up any more. We phoned the house but never got any answer" — while I was working at Famous and Barr, I suppose, demonstrating those — Oh! I felt so weak I could barely keep on my feet. I had to sit down while they got me a glass of water! Fifty dollars' tuition, all of our plans — my hopes and ambitions for you — just gone up the spout, just gone up the spout like that. (*Laura draws a long breath and gets awkwardly to her feet. She crosses to the victrola and winds it up.*) What are you doing?

LAURA: Oh! (*She releases the handle and returns to her seat.*)

AMANDA: Laura, where have you been going when you've gone out pretending that you were going to business college?

LAURA: I've just been going out walking.

AMANDA: That's not true.

LAURA: It is. I just went walking.

AMANDA: Walking? Walking? In winter? Deliberately courting pneumonia in that light coat? Where did you walk to, Laura?

LAURA: All sorts of places — mostly in the park.

AMANDA: Even after you'd started catching that cold?

LAURA: It was the lesser of two evils, Mother. (*Image: winter scene in park.*) I couldn't go back up. I — threw up — on the floor!

AMANDA: From half past seven till after five every day you mean to tell me you walked around in the park, because you wanted to make me think that you were still going to Rubicam's Business College?

LAURA: It wasn't as bad as it sounds. I went inside places to get warmed up.

AMANDA: Inside where?

LAURA: I went in the art museum and the bird houses at the Zoo. I visited the penguins every day! Sometimes I did without lunch and went to the movies. Lately I've been spending most of my afternoons in the Jewel-box, that big glass house where they raise the tropical flowers.

AMANDA: You did all this to deceive me, just for the deception? (*Laura looks down.*) Why?

LAURA: Mother, when you're disappointed, you get that awful suffering look on your face, like the picture of Jesus' mother in the museum!

AMANDA: Hush!

LAURA: I couldn't face it.

(*Pause. A whisper of strings.*)
(*Legend: "The Crust of Humility."*)

AMANDA (*hopelessly fingering the huge pocketbook*):

So what are we going to do the rest of our lives? Stay home and watch the parades go by? Amuse ourselves with the glass menagerie, darling? Eternally play those worn-out phonograph records your father left as a painful reminder of him? We won't have a business career — we've given that up because it gave us nervous indigestion! (*Laughs wearily.*) What is there left but dependency all our lives? I know so well what becomes of unmarried women who aren't prepared to occupy a position. I've seen such pitiful cases in the South — barely tolerated spinsters living upon the grudging patronage of sister's husband or brother's wife! — stuck away in some little mousetrap of a room — encouraged by one in-law to visit another — little birdlike women without any nest — eating the crust of humility all their life! Is that the future that we've mapped out for ourselves? I swear it's the only alternative I can think of! It isn't a very pleasant alternative, is it? Of course — some girls do *marry*. (*Laura twists her hands nervously.*) Haven't you ever liked some boy?

LAURA: Yes. I liked one once. (*Rises.*) I came across his picture a while ago.

AMANDA (*with some interest*): He gave you his picture?

LAURA: No, it's in the yearbook.

AMANDA (*disappointed*): Oh — a high-school boy.

(*Screen image: Jim as high school hero bearing a silver cup.*)

LAURA: Yes. His name was Jim. (*Laura lifts the heavy annual from the clawfoot table.*) Here he is in *The Pirates of Penzance.*

AMANDA (*absently*): The what?

LAURA: The operetta the senior class put on. He had a wonderful voice and we sat across the aisle from each other Mondays, Wednesdays, and Fridays in the Aud. Here he is with the silver cup for debating! See his grin?

AMANDA (*absently*): He must have had a jolly disposition.

LAURA: He used to call me — Blue Roses.

(*Image: blue roses.*)

AMANDA: Why did he call you such a name as that?

LAURA: When I had that attack of pleurosis — he asked me what was the matter when I came back. I said pleurosis — he thought that I said Blue Roses! So that's what he always called me after that. Whenever he saw me, he'd holler, "Hello, Blue Roses!" I didn't care for the girl that he went out with. Emily Meisenbach. Emily was the best-dressed girl at Soldan. She never struck me, though, as being sincere . . . It says in the Personal Section —

they're engaged. That's — six years ago! They must be married by now.

AMANDA: Girls that aren't cut out for business careers usually wind up married to some nice man. (*Gets up with a spark of revival.*) Sister, that's what you'll do!

(*Laura utters a startled, doubtful laugh. She reaches quickly for a piece of glass.*)

LAURA: But, Mother —
AMANDA: Yes? (*Crossing to photograph.*)
LAURA (*in a tone of frightened apology*): I'm — crippled!

(*Image: screen.*)

AMANDA: Nonsense! Laura, I've told you never, never to use that word. Why, you're not crippled, you just have a little defect — hardly noticeable, even! When people have some slight disadvantage like that, they cultivate other things to make up for it — develop charm — and vivacity — and — *charm!* That's all you have to do! (*She turns again to the photograph.*) One thing your father had *plenty of* — was *charm!*

(*Tom motions to the fiddle in the wings.*)
(*The scene fades out with music.*)

SCENE 3

(*Legend on screen: "After the Fiasco — "*)
(*Tom speaks from the fire escape landing.*)

TOM: After the fiasco at Rubicam's Business College, the idea of getting a gentleman caller for Laura began to play a more important part in Mother's calculations. It became an obsession. Like some archetype of the universal unconscious, the image of the gentleman caller haunted our small apartment. . . . (*Image: young man at door with flowers.*) An evening at home rarely passed without some allusion to this image, this specter, this hope. . . . Even when he wasn't mentioned, his presence hung in Mother's preoccupied look and in my sister's frightened, apologetic manner — hung like a sentence passed upon the Wingfields! Mother was a woman of action as well as words. She began to take logical steps in the planned direction. Late that winter and in the early spring — realizing that extra money would be needed to properly feather the nest and plume the bird — she conducted a vigorous campaign on the telephone, roping in subscribers to one of those magazines for matrons called *The Home-maker's Companion*, the type of journal that features the serialized sublimations of ladies of letters who think in terms of delicate cuplike breasts, slim, tapering waists, rich, creamy thighs, eyes like wood smoke in autumn, fingers that soothe and caress like strains of music, bodies as powerful as Etruscan sculpture.

(*Screen image: glamor magazine cover.*)
(*Amanda enters with phone on long extension cord. She is spotted in the dim stage.*)

AMANDA: Ida Scott? This is Amanda Wingfield! We *missed* you at the D.A.R. last Monday! I said to myself: She's probably suffering with that sinus condition! How is that sinus condition? Horrors! Heaven have mercy! — You're a Christian martyr, yes, that's what you are, a Christian martyr! Well, I just now happened to notice that your subscription to the *Companion's* about to expire! Yes, it expires with the next issue, honey! — just when that wonderful new serial by Bessie Mae Hopper is getting off to such an exciting start. Oh, honey, it's something that you can't miss! You remember how *Gone With the Wind* took everybody by storm? You simply couldn't go out if you hadn't read it. All everybody *talked* was Scarlett O'Hara. Well, this is a book that critics already compare to *Gone With the Wind*. It's the *Gone With the Wind* of the post-World War generation! — What? — Burning? — Oh, honey, don't let them burn, go take a look in the oven and I'll hold the wire! Heavens — I think she's hung up!

(*Dim out.*)
(*Legend on screen: "You Think I'm in Love with Continental Shoemakers?"*)
(*Before the stage is lighted, the violent voices of Tom and Amanda are heard.*)
(*They are quarreling behind the portieres. In front of them stands Laura with clenched hands and panicky expression.*)
(*A clear pool of light on her figure throughout this scene.*)

TOM: What in Christ's name am I —
AMANDA (*shrilly*): Don't you use that —
TOM: Supposed to do!
AMANDA: Expression! Not in my —
TOM: Ohhh!
AMANDA: Presence! Have you gone out of your senses?
TOM: I have, that's true, *driven* out!
AMANDA: What is the matter with you, you — big — big — IDIOT!
TOM: Look — I've got *no thing*, no single thing —
AMANDA: Lower your voice!
TOM: In my life here that I can call my OWN! Everything is —
AMANDA: Stop that shouting!
TOM: Yesterday you confiscated my books! You had the nerve to —

AMANDA: I took that horrible novel back to the library — yes! That hideous book by that insane Mr. Lawrence. (*Tom laughs wildly.*) I cannot control the output of diseased minds or people who cater to them — (*Tom laughs still more wildly.*) BUT I WON'T ALLOW SUCH FILTH BROUGHT INTO MY HOUSE! No, no, no, no, no!

TOM: House, house! Who pays rent on it, who makes a slave of himself to —

AMANDA (*fairly screeching*): Don't you DARE to —

TOM: No, no, I musn't say things! *I've* got to just —

AMANDA: Let me tell you —

TOM: I don't want to hear any more! (*He tears the portieres open. The upstage area is lit with a turgid smoky red glow.*)

(*Amanda's hair is in metal curlers and she wears a very old bathrobe, much too large for her slight figure, a relic of the faithless Mr. Wingfield.*)

(*An upright typewriter and a wild disarray of manuscripts are on the dropleaf table. The quarrel was probably precipitated by Amanda's interruption of his creative labor. A chair lying overthrown on the floor.*)

(*Their gesticulating shadows are cast on the ceiling by the fiery glow.*)

AMANDA: You *will* hear more, you —

TOM: No, I won't hear more, I'm going out!

AMANDA: You come right back in —

TOM: Out, out out! Because I'm —

AMANDA: Come back here, Tom Wingfield! I'm not through talking to you!

TOM: Oh, go —

LAURA (*desperately*): Tom!

AMANDA: You're going to listen, and no more insolence from you! I'm at the end of my patience! (*He comes back toward her.*)

TOM: What do you think I'm at? Aren't I supposed to have any patience to reach the end of, Mother? I know, I know. It seems unimportant to you, what I'm *doing* — what I *want* to do — having a little *difference* between them! You don't think that —

AMANDA: I think you've been doing things that you're ashamed of. That's why you act like this. I don't believe that you go every night to the movies. Nobody goes to the movies night after night. Nobody in their right minds goes to the movies as often as you pretend to. People don't go to the movies at nearly midnight, and movies don't let out at two A.M. Come in stumbling. Muttering to yourself like a maniac! You get three hours' sleep and then go to work. Oh, I can picture the way you're doing down there. Moping, doping, because you're in no condition.

TOM (*wildly*): No, I'm in no condition!

AMANDA: What right have you got to jeopardize your job? Jeopardize the security of us all? How do you think we'd manage if you were —

TOM: Listen! You think I'm crazy *about* the *warehouse*? (*He bends fiercely toward her slight figure.*) You think I'm in love with the Continental Shoemakers? You think I want to spend fifty-five *years* down there in that — *celotex interior!* with — *fluorescent* — *tubes!* Look! I'd rather somebody picked up a crowbar and battered out my brains — than go back mornings! I *go!* Every time you come in yelling that God damn "*Rise and Shine!*" "*Rise and Shine!*" I say to myself, "How *lucky dead* people are!" But I get up. I *go!* For sixty-five dollars a month I give up all that I dream of doing and being *ever!* And you say self — *self*'s all I ever think of. Why, listen, if self is what I thought of, Mother, I'd be where he is — GONE! (*Pointing to father's picture.*) As far as the system of transportation reaches! (*He starts past her. She grabs his arm.*) Don't grab at me, Mother!

AMANDA: Where are you going?

TOM: I'm going to the *movies!*

AMANDA: I don't believe that lie!

TOM (*Crouching toward her, overtowering her tiny figure. She backs away, gasping.*): I'm going to opium dens! Yes, opium dens, dens of vice and criminals' hangouts, Mother. I've joined the Hogan gang, I'm a hired assassin, I carry a tommy-gun in a violin case! I run a string of cathouses in the Valley! They call me Killer, Killer Wingfield, I'm leading a double life, a simple, honest warehouse worker by day, by night, a dynamic *czar* of the *underworld, Mother.* I go to gambling casinos, I spin away fortunes on the roulette table! I wear a patch over one eye and a false mustache, sometimes I put on green whiskers. On those occasions they call me — *El Diablo!* Oh, I could tell you things to make you sleepless! My enemies plan to dynamite this place. They're going to blow us all sky-high some night! I'll be glad, very happy, and so will you! You'll go up, up on a broomstick, over Blue Mountain with seventeen gentlemen callers! You ugly — babbling old — *witch....* (*He goes through a series of violent, clumsy movements, seizing his overcoat, lunging to the door, pulling it fiercely open. The women watch him, aghast. His arm catches in the sleeve of the coat as he struggles to pull it on. For a moment he is pinioned by the bulky garment. With an outraged groan he tears the coat off again, splitting the shoulders of it, and hurls it across the room. It strikes against the shelf of Laura's glass collection, there is a tinkle of shattering glass. Laura cries out as if wounded.*)

(*Music legend: "The Glass Menagerie."*)

LAURA (*shrilly*): *My glass!* — menagerie. . . . (*She covers her face and turns away.*)

(*But Amanda is still stunned and stupefied by the "ugly witch" so that she barely notices this occurrence. Now she recovers her speech.*)

AMANDA (*in an awful voice*): I won't speak to you — until you apologize! (*She crosses through portieres and draws them together behind her. Tom is left with Laura. Laura clings weakly to the mantel with her face averted. Tom stares at her stupidly for a moment. Then he crosses to shelf. Drops awkwardly to his knees to collect the fallen glass, glancing at Laura as if he would speak but couldn't.*)

(*"The Glass Menagerie" steals in as the scene dims out.*)

SCENE 4

(*The interior is dark. Faint light in the alley.*)

(*A deep-voiced bell in a church is tolling the hour of five as the scene commences.*)

(*Tom appears at the top of the alley. After each solemn boom of the bell in the tower, he shakes a little noisemaker or rattle as if to express the tiny spasm of man in contrast to the sustained power and dignity of the Almighty. This and the unsteadiness of his advance make it evident that he has been drinking.*)

(*As he climbs the few steps to the fire escape landing light steals up inside. Laura appears in nightdress, observing Tom's empty bed in the front room.*)

(*Tom fishes in his pockets for the door key, removing a motley assortment of articles in the search, including a perfect shower of movie ticket stubs and an empty bottle. At last he finds the key, but just as he is about to insert it, it slips from his fingers. He strikes a match and crouches below the door.*)

TOM (*bitterly*): One crack — and it falls through!

(*Laura opens the door.*)

LAURA: Tom! Tom, what are you doing?
TOM: Looking for a door key.
LAURA: Where have you been all this time?
TOM: I have been to the movies.
LAURA: All this time at the movies?
TOM: There was a very long program. There was a Garbo picture and a Mickey Mouse and a travelogue and a newsreel and a preview of coming attractions. And there was an organ solo and a collection for the milk fund — simultaneously — which ended up in a terrible fight between a fat lady and an usher!

LAURA (*innocently*): Did you have to stay through everything?
TOM: Of course! And, oh, I forgot! There was a big stage show! The headliner on this stage show was Malvolio the Magician. He performed wonderful tricks, many of them, such as pouring water back and forth between pitchers. First it turned to wine and then it turned to beer and then it turned to whiskey. I know it was whiskey it finally turned into because he needed somebody to come up out of the audience to help him, and I came up — both shows! It was Kentucky Straight Bourbon. A very generous fellow, he gave souvenirs. (*He pulls from his back pocket a shimmering rainbow-colored scarf.*) He gave me this. This is his magic scarf. You can have it, Laura. You wave it over a canary cage and you get a bowl of goldfish. You wave it over the goldfish bowl and they fly away canaries. . . . But the wonderfullest trick of all was the coffin trick. We nailed him into a coffin and he got out of the coffin without removing one nail. (*He has come inside.*) There is a trick that would come in handy for me — get me out of this 2 by 4 situation! (*Flops onto bed and starts removing shoes.*)
LAURA: Tom — Shhh!
TOM: What you shushing me for?
LAURA: You'll wake up Mother.
TOM: Goody, goody! Pay 'er back for all those "Rise an' Shines." (*Lies down, groaning.*) You know it don't take much intelligence to get yourself into a nailed-up coffin, Laura. But who in hell ever got himself out of one without removing one nail?

(*As if in answer, the father's grinning photograph lights up.*)

(*Scene dims out.*)

(*Immediately following: The church bell is heard striking six. At the sixth stroke the alarm clock goes off in Amanda's room, and after a few moments we hear her calling: "Rise and Shine! Rise and Shine! Laura, go tell your brother to rise and shine!"*)

TOM (*sitting up slowly*): I'll rise — but I won't shine.

(*The light increases.*)

AMANDA: Laura, tell your brother his coffee is ready.

(*Laura slips into front room.*)

LAURA: Tom! it's nearly seven. Don't make Mother nervous. (*He stares at her stupidly. Beseechingly.*) Tom, speak to Mother this morning. Make up with her, apologize, speak to her!
TOM: She won't to me. It's her that started not speaking.
LAURA: If you just say you're sorry she'll start speaking.
TOM: Her not speaking — is that such a tragedy?

LAURA: Please — please!

AMANDA (*calling from kitchenette*): Laura, are you going to do what I asked you to do, or do I have to get dressed and go out myself?

LAURA: Going, going — soon as I get on my coat! (*She pulls on a shapeless felt hat with nervous, jerky movement, pleadingly glancing at Tom. Rushes awkwardly for coat. The coat is one of Amanda's, inaccurately made over, the sleeves too short for Laura.*) Butter and what else?

AMANDA (*entering upstage*): Just butter. Tell them to charge it.

LAURA: Mother, they make such faces when I do that.

AMANDA: Sticks and stones may break my bones, but the expression on Mr. Garfinkel's face won't harm us! Tell your brother his coffee is getting cold.

LAURA (*at door*): Do what I asked you, will you, will you, Tom?

(*He looks sullenly away.*)

AMANDA: Laura, go now or just don't go at all!

LAURA (*rushing out*): Going — going! (*A second later she cries out. Tom springs up and crosses to the door. Amanda rushes anxiously in. Tom opens the door.*)

TOM: Laura?

LAURA: I'm all right. I slipped, but I'm all right.

AMANDA (*peering anxiously after her*): If anyone breaks a leg on those fire escape steps, the landlord ought to be sued for every cent he possesses! (*She shuts door. Remembers she isn't speaking and returns to other room.*)

(*As Tom enters listlessly for his coffee, she turns her back to him and stands rigidly facing the window on the gloomy gray vault of the areaway. Its light on her face with its aged but childish features is cruelly sharp, satirical as a Daumier print.*)

(*Music under: "Ave Maria."*)

(*Tom glances sheepishly but sullenly at her averted figure and slumps at the table. The coffee is scalding hot; he sips it and gasps and spits it back in the cup. At his gasp, Amanda catches her breath and half turns. Then catches herself and turns back to window.*)

(*Tom blows on his coffee, glancing sidewise at his mother. She clears her throat. Tom clears his. He starts to rise. Sinks back down again, scratches his head, clears his throat again. Amanda coughs. Tom raises his cup in both hands to blow on it, his eyes staring over the rim of it at his mother for several moments. Then he slowly sets the cup down and awkwardly and hesitantly rises from the chair.*)

TOM (*hoarsely*): Mother. I — I apologize. Mother. (*Amanda draws a quick, shuddering breath. Her face works grotesquely. She breaks into childlike tears.*) I'm sorry for what I said, for everything that I said, I didn't mean it.

AMANDA (*sobbingly*): My devotion has made me a witch and so I make myself hateful to my children!

TOM: No, you *don't*.

AMANDA: I worry so much, don't sleep, it makes me nervous!

TOM (*gently*): I understand that.

AMANDA: I've had to put up a solitary battle all these years. But you're my right-hand bower! Don't fall down, don't fail!

TOM (*gently*): I try, Mother.

AMANDA (*with great enthusiasm*): Try and you will SUCCEED! (*The notion makes her breathless.*) Why, you — you're just *full* of natural endowments! Both of my children — they're *unusual* children! Don't you think I know it? I'm so — *proud*! Happy and — feel I've — so much to be thankful for but — Promise me one thing, son!

TOM: What, Mother?

AMANDA: Promise, son, you'll — never be a drunkard!

TOM (*turns to her grinning*): I will never be a drunkard, Mother.

AMANDA: That's what frightened me so, that you'd be drinking! Eat a bowl of Purina!

TOM: Just coffee, Mother.

AMANDA: Shredded wheat biscuit?

TOM: No, no, Mother, just coffee.

AMANDA: You can't put in a day's work on an empty stomach. You've got ten minutes — don't gulp! Drinking too-hot liquids makes cancer of the stomach. . . . Put cream in.

TOM: No, thank you.

AMANDA: To cool it.

TOM: No! No, thank you, I want it black.

AMANDA: I know, but it's not good for you. We have to do all that we can to build ourselves up. In these trying times we live in, all that we have to cling to is — each other. . . . That's why it's so important to — Tom, I — I sent out your sister so I could discuss something with you. If you hadn't spoken I would have spoken to you. (*Sits down.*)

TOM (*gently*): What is it, Mother, that you want to discuss?

AMANDA: *Laura!*

(*Tom puts his cup down slowly.*)
(*Legend on screen: "Laura."*)
(*Music: "The Glass Menagerie."*)

TOM: — Oh. — Laura . . .

AMANDA (*touching his sleeve*): You know how Laura is. So quiet but — still water runs deep! She notices things and I think she — broods about them. (*Tom looks up.*) A few days ago I came in and she was crying.

TOM: What about?

AMANDA: You.

TOM: Me?

AMANDA: She has an idea that you're not happy here.

TOM: What gave her that idea?

AMANDA: What gives her any idea? However, you do act strangely. I — I'm not criticizing, understand *that!* I know your ambitions do not lie in the warehouse, that like everybody in the whole wide world — you've had to — make sacrifices, but — Tom — Tom — life's not easy, it calls for — Spartan endurance! There's so many things in my heart that I cannot describe to you! I've never told you but I — *loved your father.* . . .

TOM (*gently*): I know that, Mother.

AMANDA: And you — when I see you taking after his ways! Staying out late — and — well, you *had* been drinking the night you were in that — terrifying condition! Laura says that you hate the apartment and that you go out nights to get away from it! Is that true, Tom?

TOM: No. You say there's so much in your heart that you can't describe to me. That's true of me, too. There's so much in my heart that I can't describe to *you!* So let's respect each other's —

AMANDA: But, why — *why*, Tom — are you always so *restless?* Where do you go to, nights?

TOM: I — go to the movies.

AMANDA: Why do you go to the movies so much, Tom?

TOM: I go to the movies because — I like adventure. Adventure is something I don't have much of at work, so I go to the movies.

AMANDA: But, Tom, you go to the movies *entirely* too *much!*

TOM: I like a lot of adventure.

(*Amanda looks baffled, then hurt. As the familiar inquisition resumes he becomes hard and impatient again. Amanda slips back into her querulous attitude toward him.*)

(*Image on screen: sailing vessel with Jolly Roger.°*)

AMANDA: Most young men find adventure in their careers.

TOM: Then most young men are not employed in a warehouse.

AMANDA: The world is full of young men employed in warehouses and offices and factories.

TOM: Do all of them find adventure in their careers?

Jolly Roger: The black flag with white skull and crossbones used by pirates.

AMANDA: They do or they do without it! Not everybody has a craze for adventure.

TOM: Man is by instinct a lover, a hunter, a fighter, and none of those instincts are given much play at the warehouse!

AMANDA: Man is by instinct! Don't quote instinct to me! Instinct is something that people have got away from! It belongs to animals! Christian adults don't want it!

TOM: What do Christian adults want, then, Mother?

AMANDA: Superior things! Things of the mind and the spirit! Only animals have to satisfy instincts! Surely your aims are somewhat higher than theirs! Than monkeys — pigs —

TOM: I reckon they're not.

AMANDA: You're joking. However, that isn't what I wanted to discuss.

TOM (*rising*): I haven't much time.

AMANDA (*pushing his shoulders*): Sit down.

TOM: You want me to punch in red at the warehouse, Mother?

AMANDA: You have five minutes. I want to talk about Laura.

(*Legend: "Plans and Provisions."*)

TOM: All right! What about Laura?

AMANDA: We have to be making plans and provisions for her. She's older than you, two years, and nothing has happened. She just drifts along doing nothing. It frightens me terribly how she just drifts along.

TOM: I guess she's the type that people call home girls.

AMANDA: There's no such type, and if there is, it's a pity! That is unless the home is hers, with a husband!

TOM: What?

AMANDA: Oh, I can see the handwriting on the wall as plain as I see the nose in front of my face! It's terrifying! More and more you remind me of your father! He was out all hours without explanation — Then *left! Goodbye!* And me with a bag to hold. I saw that letter you got from the Merchant Marine. I know what you're dreaming of. I'm not standing here blindfolded. Very well, then. Then *do* it! But not till there's somebody to take your place.

TOM: What do you mean?

AMANDA: I mean that as soon as Laura has got somebody to take care of her, married, a home of her own, independent — why, then you'll be free to go wherever you please, on land, on sea, whichever way the wind blows you! But until that time you've got to look out for your sister. I don't say me because I'm old and don't matter! I say for your sister because she's young and dependent. I put her in business college — a dismal failure! Frightened her so it made her sick to her stomach. I took her over to the Young People's League at the church. Another fiasco. She spoke to nobody, nobody spoke to her. Now all she does is fool with those pieces of glass and play those worn-out records. What kind of a life is that for a girl to lead!

TOM: What can I do about it?

AMANDA: Overcome selfishness! Self, self, self is all that you ever think of! (*Tom springs up and crosses to get his coat. It is ugly and bulky. He pulls on a cap with earmuffs.*) Where is your muffler? Put your wool muffler on! (*He snatches it angrily from the closet and tosses it around his neck and pulls both ends tight.*) Tom! I haven't said what I had in mind to ask you.

TOM: I'm too late to —

AMANDA (*Catching his arms — very importunately. Then shyly*): Down at the warehouse, aren't there some — nice young men?

TOM: No!

AMANDA: There *must* be — *some* . . .

TOM: Mother —

(*Gesture.*)

AMANDA: Find out one that's clean-living — doesn't drink and — ask him out for sister!

TOM: What?

AMANDA: For *sister!* To *meet!* Get *acquainted!*

TOM (*stamping to door*): Oh, my go-osh!

AMANDA: Will you? (*He opens door. Imploringly.*) Will you? (*He starts down.*) Will you? *Will* you, dear?

TOM (*calling back*): YES!

(*Amanda closes the door hesitantly and with a troubled but faintly hopeful expression.*)
(*Screen image: glamor magazine cover.*)
(*Spot° Amanda at phone.*)

AMANDA: Ella Cartwright? This is Amanda Wingfield! How are you, honey? How is that kidney condition? (*Count five.*) Horrors! (*Count five.*) You're a Christian martyr, yes, honey, that's what you are, a Christian martyr! Well, I just happened to notice in my little red book that your subscription to the *Companion* has just run out! I knew that you wouldn't want to miss out on the wonderful serial starting in this new issue. It's by Bessie Mae Hopper, the first thing she's written since *Honeymoon for Three.* Wasn't that a strange and interesting story? Well, this one is even lovelier, I believe. It has a sophisticated society background. It's all about the horsey set on Long Island!

(*Fade out.*)

Spot: Spotlight.

SCENE 5 _____

(*Legend on screen: "Annunciation." Fade with music.*)
(*It is early dusk of a spring evening. Supper has just been finished in the Wingfield apartment. Amanda and Laura in light colored dresses are removing dishes from the table, in the upstage area, which is shadowy, their movements formalized almost as a dance or ritual, their moving forms as pale and silent as moths.*)
(*Tom, in white shirt and trousers, rises from the table and crosses toward the fire escape.*)

AMANDA (*as he passes her*): Son, will you do me a favor?

TOM: What?

AMANDA: Comb your hair! You look so pretty when your hair is combed! (*Tom slouches on sofa with evening paper. Enormous caption "Franco Triumphs."*) There is only one respect in which I would like you to emulate your father.

TOM: What respect is that?

AMANDA: The care he always took of his appearance. He never allowed himself to look untidy. (*He throws down the paper and crosses to fire escape.*) Where are you going?

TOM: I'm going out to smoke.

AMANDA: You smoke too much. A pack a day at fifteen cents a pack. How much would that amount to in a month? Thirty times fifteen is how much, Tom? Figure it out and you will be astounded at what you could save. Enough to give you a night school course in accounting at Washington U! Just think what a wonderful thing that would be for you, son!

(*Tom is unmoved by the thought.*)

TOM: I'd rather smoke. (*He steps out on landing, letting the screen door slam.*)

AMANDA (*sharply*): I know! That's the tragedy of it. . . . (*Alone, she turns to look at her husband's picture.*)

(*Dance music: "All the World is Waiting for the Sunrise!"*)

TOM (*to the audience*): Across the alley from us was the Paradise Dance Hall. On evenings in spring the windows and doors were open and the music came outdoors. Sometimes the lights were turned out except for a large glass sphere that hung from the ceiling. It would turn slowly about and filter the dusk with delicate rainbow colors. Then the orchestra played a waltz or a tango, something that had a slow and sensuous rhythm. Couples would come outside, to the relative privacy of the alley. You could see them kissing behind ash-pits and telephone poles. This was the compensation for lives that passed like mine, without any change or adventure. Adventure and change were imminent in this year. They were waiting around the corner for all these kids. Suspended in the mist over Berchtesgaden, caught in the folds of Chamberlain's umbrella — In Spain there was Guernica!° But here there was only hot swing music and liquor, dance halls, bars, and movies, and sex that hung in the gloom like a chandelier and flooded the world with brief, deceptive rainbows. . . . All the world was waiting for bombardments!

(*Amanda turns from the picture and comes outside.*)

AMANDA (*sighing*): A fire escape landing's a poor excuse for a porch. (*She spreads a newspaper on a step and sits down, gracefully and demurely as if she were settling into a swing on a Mississippi veranda.*) What are you looking at?

TOM: The moon.

AMANDA: Is there a moon this evening?

TOM: It's rising over Garfinkel's Delicatessen.

AMANDA: So it is! A little silver slipper of a moon. Have you made a wish on it yet?

TOM: Um-hum.

AMANDA: What did you wish for?

TOM: That's a secret.

AMANDA: A secret, huh? Well, I won't tell mine either. I will be just as mysterious as you.

TOM: I bet I can guess what yours is.

AMANDA: Is my head so transparent?

TOM: You're not a sphinx.

AMANDA: No, I don't have secrets. I'll tell you what I wished for on the moon. Success and happiness for my precious children! I wish for that whenever there's a moon, and when there isn't a moon, I wish for it, too.

TOM: I thought perhaps you wished for a gentleman caller.

AMANDA: Why do you say that?

TOM: Don't you remember asking me to fetch one?

AMANDA: I remember suggesting that it would be nice for your sister if you brought home some nice young man from the warehouse. I think I've made that suggestion more than once.

TOM: Yes, you have made it repeatedly.

AMANDA: Well?

TOM: We are going to have one.

AMANDA: *What?*

TOM: A gentleman caller!

Berchtesgaden . . . Chamberlain . . . Guernica: All references to the approach of World War II in Europe. Berchtesgaden was Hitler's summer home; Neville Chamberlain was the prime minister of England who signed the Munich Pact, which was regarded as a capitulation to Hitler; and the Spanish town Guernica was destroyed by German bombs during the Spanish Civil War in the late 1930s.

(*The annunciation is celebrated with music.*)
(*Amanda rises.*)
(*Image on screen: caller with bouquet.*)

AMANDA: You mean you have asked some nice young man to come over?

TOM: Yep. I've asked him to dinner.

AMANDA: You really did?

TOM: I did!

AMANDA: You did, and did he — *accept?*

TOM: He did!

AMANDA: Well, well — well, well! That's — lovely!

TOM: I thought that you would be pleased.

AMANDA: It's definite, then?

TOM: Very definite.

AMANDA: Soon?

TOM: Very soon.

AMANDA: For heaven's sake, stop putting on and tell me some things, will you?

TOM: What things do you want me to tell you?

AMANDA: *Naturally* I would like to know when he's *coming!*

TOM: He's coming tomorrow.

AMANDA: *Tomorrow?*

TOM: Yep. Tomorrow.

AMANDA: But, Tom!

TOM: Yes, Mother?

AMANDA: Tomorrow gives me no time!

TOM: Time for what?

AMANDA: Preparations! Why didn't you phone me at once, as soon as you asked him, the minute that he accepted? Then, don't you see, I could have been getting ready!

TOM: You don't have to make any fuss.

AMANDA: Oh, Tom, Tom, Tom, of course I have to make a fuss! I want things nice, not sloppy! Not thrown together. I'll certainly have to do some fast thinking, won't I?

TOM: I don't see why you have to think at all.

AMANDA: You just don't know. We can't have a gentleman caller in a pigsty! All my wedding silver has to be polished, the monogrammed table linen ought to be laundered! The windows have to be washed and fresh curtains put up. And how about clothes? We have to *wear* something, don't we?

TOM: Mother, this boy is no one to make a fuss over!

AMANDA: Do you realize he's the first young man we've introduced to your sister? It's terrible, dreadful, disgraceful that poor little sister has never received a single gentleman caller! Tom, come inside! (*She opens the screen door.*)

TOM: What for?

AMANDA: I want to ask you some things.

TOM: If you're going to make such a fuss, I'll call it off, I'll tell him not to come.

AMANDA: You certainly won't do anything of the kind. Nothing offends people worse than broken engagements. It simply means I'll have to work like a Turk! We won't be brilliant, but we'll pass inspection. Come on inside. (*Tom follows, groaning.*) Sit down.

TOM: Any particular place you would like me to sit?

AMANDA: Thank heavens I've got that new sofa! I'm also making payments on a floor lamp I'll have sent out! And put the chintz covers on, they'll brighten things up! Of course I'd hoped to have these walls repapered. . . . What is the young man's name?

TOM: His name is O'Connor.

AMANDA: That, of course, means fish — tomorrow is Friday!° I'll have that salmon loaf — with Durkee's dressing! What does he do? He works at the warehouse?

TOM: Of course! How else would I —

AMANDA: Tom, he — doesn't drink?

TOM: Why do you ask me that?

AMANDA: Your father *did*!

TOM: Don't get started on that!

AMANDA: He *does* drink, then?

TOM: Not that I know of!

AMANDA: Make sure, be certain! The last thing I want for my daughter's a boy who drinks!

TOM: Aren't you being a little premature? Mr. O'Connor has not yet appeared on the scene!

AMANDA: But will tomorrow. To meet your sister, and what do I know about his character? Nothing! Old maids are better off than wives of drunkards!

TOM: Oh, my God!

AMANDA: Be still!

TOM (*leaning forward to whisper*): Lots of fellows meet girls whom they don't marry!

AMANDA: Oh, talk sensibly, Tom — and don't be sarcastic! (*She has gotten a hairbrush.*)

TOM: What are you doing?

AMANDA: I'm brushing that cowlick down! What is this young man's position at the warehouse?

TOM (*submitting grimly to the brush and the interrogation*): This young man's position is that of a shipping clerk, Mother.

AMANDA: Sounds to me like a fairly responsible job, the sort of a job *you* would be in if you just had more *get-up*. What is his salary? Have you got any idea?

TOM: I would judge it to be approximately eighty-five dollars a month.

AMANDA: Well — not princely, but —

TOM: Twenty more than I make.

fish . . . Friday: Until recent decades, Catholics were prohibited from eating meat on Fridays.

AMANDA: Yes, how well I know! But for a family man, eighty-five dollars a month is not much more than you can just get by on. . . .

TOM: Yes, but Mr. O'Connor is not a family man.

AMANDA: He might be, mightn't he? Some time in the future?

TOM: I see. Plans and provisions.

AMANDA: You are the only young man that I know of who ignores the fact that the future becomes the present, the present the past, and the past turns into everlasting regret if you don't plan for it!

TOM: I will think that over and see what I can make of it.

AMANDA: Don't be supercilious with your mother! Tell me some more about this — what do you call him?

TOM: James D. O'Connor. The D. is for Delaney.

AMANDA: Irish on *both* sides! *Gracious!* And doesn't drink?

TOM: Shall I call him up and ask him right this minute?

AMANDA: The only way to find out about those things is to make discreet inquiries at the proper moment. When I was a girl in Blue Mountain and it was suspected that a young man drank, the girl whose attentions he had been receiving, if any girl *was*, would sometimes speak to the minister of his church, or rather her father would if her father was living, and sort of feel him out on the young man's character. That is the way such things are discreetly handled to keep a young woman from making a tragic mistake!

TOM: Then how did you happen to make a tragic mistake?

AMANDA: That innocent look of your father's had everyone fooled! He *smiled* — the world was *enchanted*! No girl can do worse than put herself at the mercy of a handsome appearance! I hope that Mr. O'Connor is not too good-looking.

TOM: No, he's not too good-looking. He's covered with freckles and hasn't too much of a nose.

AMANDA: He's not right-down homely, though?

TOM: Not right-down homely. Just medium homely, I'd say.

AMANDA: Character's what to look for in a man.

TOM: That's what I've always said, Mother.

AMANDA: You've never said anything of the kind and I suspect you would never give it a thought.

TOM: Don't be suspicious of me.

AMANDA: At least I hope he's the type that's up and coming.

TOM: I think he really goes in for self-improvement.

AMANDA: What reason have you to think so?

TOM: He goes to night school.

AMANDA (*beaming*): Splendid! What does he do, I mean study?

TOM: Radio engineering and public speaking!

AMANDA: Then he has visions of being advanced in the world! Any young man who studies public speaking is aiming to have an executive job some day! And radio engineering? A thing for the future! Both of these facts are very illuminating. Those are the sort of things that a mother should know concerning any young man who comes to call on her daughter. Seriously or — not.

TOM: One little warning. He doesn't know about Laura. I didn't let on that we had dark ulterior motives. I just said, why don't you come have dinner with us? He said okay and that was the whole conversation.

AMANDA: I bet it was! You're eloquent as an oyster. However, he'll know about Laura when he gets here. When he sees how lovely and sweet and pretty she is, he'll thank his lucky stars he was asked to dinner.

TOM: Mother, you mustn't expect too much of Laura.

AMANDA: What do you mean?

TOM: Laura seems all those things to you and me because she's ours and we love her. We don't even notice she's crippled anymore.

AMANDA: Don't say crippled! You know that I never allow that word to be used!

TOM: But face facts, Mother. She is and — that's not all —

AMANDA: What do you mean "not all"?

TOM: Laura is very different from other girls.

AMANDA: I think the difference is all to her advantage.

TOM: Not quite all — in the eyes of others — strangers — she's terribly shy and lives in a world of her own and those things make her seem a little peculiar to people outside the house.

AMANDA: Don't say peculiar.

TOM: Face the facts. She is.

(*The dance-hall music changes to a tango that has a minor and somewhat ominous tone.*)

AMANDA: In what way is she peculiar — may I ask?

TOM (*gently*): She lives in a world of her own — a world of — little glass ornaments, Mother. . . . (*Gets up. Amanda remains holding brush, looking at him, troubled.*) She plays old phonograph records and — that's about all — (*He glances at himself in the mirror and crosses to door.*)

AMANDA (*sharply*): Where are you going?

TOM: I'm going to the movies. (*Out screen door.*)

AMANDA: Not to the movies, every night to the movies! (*Follows quickly to screen door.*) I don't believe you always go to the movies! (*He is gone. Amanda looks worriedly after him for a moment. Then vitality and optimism return and she turns from the door. Crossing to portieres.*) Laura! Laura! (*Laura answers from kitchenette.*)

LAURA: Yes, Mother.

AMANDA: Let those dishes go and come in front! (*Laura appears with dish towel. Gaily.*) Laura, come here and make a wish on the moon!

LAURA (*entering*): Moon — moon?

AMANDA: A little silver slipper of a moon. Look over your left shoulder, Laura, and make a wish! (*Laura looks faintly puzzled as if called out of sleep. Amanda seizes her shoulders and turns her at an angle by the door.*) Now! Now, darling, *wish!*

LAURA: What shall I wish for, Mother?

AMANDA (*her voice trembling and her eyes suddenly filling with tears*): Happiness! Good Fortune!

(*The violin rises and the stage dims out.*)

SCENE 6

(*Image: high school hero.*)

TOM: And so the following evening I brought Jim home to dinner. I had known Jim slightly in high school. In high school Jim was a hero. He had tremendous Irish good nature and vitality with the scrubbed and polished look of white chinaware. He seemed to move in a continual spotlight. He was a star in basketball, captain of the debating club, president of the senior class and the glee club and he sang the male lead in the annual light operas. He was always running or bounding, never just walking. He seemed always at the point of defeating the law of gravity. He was shooting with such velocity through his adolescence that you would logically expect him to arrive at nothing short of the White House by the time he was thirty. But Jim apparently ran into more interference after his graduation from Soldan. His speed had definitely slowed. Six years after he left high school he was holding a job that wasn't much better than mine.

(*Image: clerk.*)

He was the only one at the warehouse with whom I was on friendly terms. I was valuable to him as someone who could remember his former glory, who had seen him win basketball games and the silver cup in debating. He knew of my secret practice of retiring to a cabinet of the washroom to work on poems when business was slack in the warehouse. He called me Shakespeare. And while the other boys in the warehouse regarded me with suspicious hostility, Jim took a humorous attitude toward me. Gradually his attitude affected the others, their hostility wore off and they also began to smile at me as people smile at an oddly fashioned dog who trots across their path at some distance.

I knew that Jim and Laura had known each other at Soldan, and I had heard Laura speak admiringly of his voice. I didn't know if Jim remembered her or not. In high school Laura had been as unobtrusive as Jim had been astonishing. If he did remember Laura, it was not as my sister, for when I asked him to dinner, he grinned and said, "You know, Shakespeare, I never thought of you as having folks!"

He was about to discover that I did. . . .

(*Light up stage.*)

(*Legend on screen: "The Accent of a Coming Foot."*)

(*Friday evening. It is about five o'clock of a late spring evening which comes "scattering poems in the sky."*)

(*A delicate lemony light is in the Wingfield apartment.*)

(*Amanda has worked like a Turk in preparation for the gentleman caller. The results are astonishing. The new floor lamp with its rose-silk shade is in place, a colored paper lantern conceals the broken light fixture in the ceiling, new billowing white curtains are at the windows, chintz covers are on chairs and sofa, a pair of new sofa pillows make their initial appearance.*)

(*Open boxes and tissue paper are scattered on the floor.*)

(*Laura stands in the middle with lifted arms while Amanda crouches before her, adjusting the hem of the new dress, devout and ritualistic. The dress is colored and designed by memory. The arrangement of Laura's hair is changed; it is softer and more becoming. A fragile, unearthly prettiness has come out in Laura: she is like a piece of translucent glass touched by light, given a momentary radiance, not actual, not lasting.*)

AMANDA (*impatiently*): Why are you trembling?

LAURA: Mother, you've made me so nervous!

AMANDA: How have I made you nervous?

LAURA: By all this fuss! You make it seem so important!

AMANDA: I don't understand you, Laura. You couldn't be satisfied with just sitting home, and yet whenever I try to arrange something for you, you seem to resist it. (*She gets up.*) Now take a look at yourself. No, wait! Wait just a moment — I have an idea!

LAURA: What is it now?

(*Amanda produces two powder puffs which she wraps in handkerchiefs and stuffs in Laura's bosom.*)

LAURA: Mother, what are you doing?

AMANDA: They call them "Gay Deceivers"!

LAURA: I won't wear them!

AMANDA: You will!

LAURA: Why should I?

AMANDA: Because, to be painfully honest, your chest is flat.

LAURA: You make it seem like we were setting a trap.

AMANDA: All pretty girls are a trap, a pretty trap, and men expect them to be. (*Legend: "A Pretty Trap."*) Now look at yourself, young lady. This is the prettiest you will ever be! I've got to fix myself now! You're going to be surprised by your mother's appearance! (*She crosses through portieres, humming gaily.*)

(*Laura moves slowly to the long mirror and stares solemnly at herself.*)

(*A wind blows the white curtains inward in a slow, graceful motion and with a faint, sorrowful sighing.*)

AMANDA (*offstage*): It isn't dark enough yet. (*She turns slowly before the mirror with a troubled look.*)

(*Legend on screen: "This Is My Sister: Celebrate Her with Strings!" Music.*)

AMANDA (*laughing, off*): I'm going to show you something. I'm going to make a spectacular appearance!

LAURA: What is it, Mother?

AMANDA: Possess your soul in patience — you will see! Something I've resurrected from that old trunk! Styles haven't changed so terribly much after all. . . . (*She parts the portieres.*) Now just look at your mother! (*She wears a girlish frock of yellowed voile with a blue silk sash. She carries a bunch of jonquils — the legend of her youth is nearly revived. Feverishly.*) This is the dress in which I led the cotillion. Won the cakewalk twice at Sunset Hill, wore one spring to the Governor's ball in Jackson! See how I sashayed around the ballroom, Laura? (*She raises her skirt and does a mincing step around the room.*) I wore it on Sundays for my gentlemen callers! I had it on the day I met your father — I had malaria fever all that spring. The change of climate from East Tennessee to the Delta — weakened resistance — I had a little temperature all the time — not enough to be serious — just enough to make me restless and giddy! Invitations poured in — parties all over the Delta! — "Stay in bed," said Mother, "you have fever!" — but I just wouldn't. — I took quinine but kept on going, going! — Evenings, dances! — Afternoons, long, long rides! Picnics — lovely! — So lovely, that country in May. — All lacy with dogwood, literally flooded with jonquils! — That was the spring I had the craze for jonquils. Jonquils became an absolute obsession. Mother said, "Honey, there's no more room for jonquils." And still I kept on bringing in more jonquils. Whenever, wherever I saw them, I'd say, "Stop! Stop! I see jonquils!" I made the young men help me gather the jonquils! It was a joke, Amanda and her jonquils! Finally there were no more vases to hold them, every available space was filled with jonquils. No vases to hold them? All right, I'll hold them myself! And then I — (*She stops in front of the picture. Music.*) met your father! Malaria fever and jonquils and then — this — boy.... (*She switches on the rose-colored lamp.*) I hope they get here before it starts to rain. (*She crosses upstage and places the jonquils in bowl on table.*) I gave your brother a little extra change so he and Mr. O'Connor could take the service car home.

LAURA (*with altered look*): What did you say his name was?

AMANDA: O'Connor.

LAURA: What is his first name?

AMANDA: I don't remember. Oh, yes, I do. It was — Jim!

(*Laura sways slightly and catches hold of a chair.*)
(*Legend on screen: "Not Jim!"*)

LAURA (*faintly*): Not — Jim!

AMANDA: Yes, that was it, it was Jim! I've never known a Jim that wasn't nice!

(*Music: ominous.*)

LAURA: Are you sure his name is Jim O'Connor?

AMANDA: Yes. Why?

LAURA: Is he the one that Tom used to know in high school?

AMANDA: He didn't say so. I think he just got to know him at the warehouse.

LAURA: There was a Jim O'Connor we both knew in high school — (*Then, with effort.*) If that is the one that Tom is bringing to dinner — you'll have to excuse me, I won't come to the table.

AMANDA: What sort of nonsense is this?

LAURA: You asked me once if I'd ever liked a boy. Don't you remember I showed you this boy's picture?

AMANDA: You mean the boy you showed me in the yearbook?

LAURA: Yes, that boy.

AMANDA: Laura, Laura, were you in love with that boy?

LAURA: I don't know, Mother. All I know is I couldn't sit at the table if it was him!

AMANDA: It won't be him! It isn't the least bit likely. But whether it is or not, you will come to the table. You will not be excused.

LAURA: I'll have to be, Mother.

AMANDA: I don't intend to humor your silliness, Laura. I've had too much from you and your brother, both! So just sit down and compose yourself till

they come. Tom has forgotten his key so you'll have to let them in, when they arrive.

LAURA (*panicky*): Oh, Mother — *you* answer the door!

AMANDA (*lightly*): I'll be in the kitchen — busy!

LAURA: Oh, Mother, please answer the door, don't make me do it!

AMANDA (*crossing into kitchenette*): I've got to fix the dressing for the salmon. Fuss, fuss — silliness! — over a gentleman caller!

(*Door swings shut. Laura is left alone.*)
(*Legend: "Terror!"*)
(*She utters a low moan and turns off the lamp — sits stiffly on the edge of the sofa, knotting her fingers together.*)
(*Legend on screen: "The Opening of a Door!"*)
(*Tom and Jim appear on the fire escape steps and climb to landing. Hearing their approach, Laura rises with a panicky gesture. She retreats to the portieres.*)
(*The doorbell. Laura catches her breath and touches her throat. Low drums.*)

AMANDA (*calling*): Laura, sweetheart! The door!

(*Laura stares at it without moving.*)

JIM: I think we just beat the rain.

TOM: Uh-huh. (*He rings again, nervously. Jim whistles and fishes for a cigarette.*)

AMANDA (*very, very gaily*): Laura, that is your brother and Mr. O'Connor! Will you let them in, darling?

(*Laura crosses toward kitchenette door.*)

LAURA (*breathlessly*): Mother — you go to the door!

(*Amanda steps out of kitchenette and stares furiously at Laura. She points imperiously at the door.*)

LAURA: Please, please!

AMANDA (*in a fierce whisper*): What is the matter with you, you silly thing?

LAURA (*desperately*): Please, you answer it, *please!*

AMANDA: I told you I wasn't going to humor you, Laura. Why have you chosen this moment to lose your mind?

LAURA: Please, please, please, you go!

AMANDA: You'll have to go to the door because I can't!

LAURA (*despairingly*): I can't either!

AMANDA: *Why?*

LAURA: I'm *sick!*

AMANDA: I'm sick, too — of your nonsense! Why can't you and your brother be normal people? Fantastic whims and behavior! (*Tom gives a long ring.*) Preposterous goings on! Can you give me one reason — (*Calls out lyrically.*) COMING! JUST ONE SECOND! — why should you be afraid to open a door? Now you answer it, Laura!

LAURA: Oh, oh, oh . . . (*She returns through the portieres. Darts to the victrola and winds it frantically and turns it on.*)

AMANDA: Laura Wingfield, you march right to that door!

LAURA: Yes — yes, Mother!

(*A faraway, scratchy rendition of "Dardanella" softens the air and gives her strength to move through it. She slips to the door and draws it cautiously open.*)
(*Tom enters with the caller, Jim O'Connor.*)

TOM: Laura, this is Jim. Jim, this is my sister, Laura.

JIM (*stepping inside*): I didn't know that Shakespeare had a sister!

LAURA (*retreating stiff and trembling from the door*): How — how do you do?

JIM (*heartily extending his hand*): Okay!

(*Laura touches it hesitantly with hers.*)

JIM: Your hand's *cold*, Laura!

LAURA: Yes, well — I've been playing the victrola. . . .

JIM: Must have been playing classical music on it! You ought to play a little hot swing music to warm you up!

LAURA: Excuse me — I haven't finished playing the victrola. . . .

(*She turns awkwardly and hurries into the front room. She pauses a second by the victrola. Then catches her breath and darts through the portieres like a frightened deer.*)

JIM (*grinning*): What was the matter?

TOM: Oh — with Laura? Laura is — terribly shy.

JIM: Shy, huh? It's unusual to meet a shy girl nowadays. I don't believe you ever mentioned you had a sister.

TOM: Well, now you know. I have one. Here is the *Post Dispatch.* You want a piece of it?

JIM: Uh-huh.

TOM: What piece? The comics?

JIM: Sports! (*Glances at it.*) Ole Dizzy Dean is on his bad behavior.

TOM (*disinterest*): Yeah? (*Lights cigarette and crosses back to fire escape door.*)

JIM: Where are *you* going?

TOM: I'm going out on the terrace.

JIM (*goes after him*): You know, Shakespeare — I'm going to sell you a bill of goods!

TOM: What goods?

JIM: A course I'm taking.

TOM: Huh?

JIM: In public speaking! You and me, we're not the warehouse type.

TOM: Thanks — that's good news. But what has public speaking got to do with it?

JIM: It fits you for — executive positions!

TOM: Awww.

JIM: I tell you it's done a helluva lot for me.

(*Image: executive at desk.*)

TOM: In what respect?

JIM: In every! Ask yourself what is the difference between you an' me and men in the office down front? Brains? — No! — Ability? — No! Then what? Just one little thing —

TOM: What is that one little thing?

JIM: Primarily it amounts to — social poise! Being able to square up to people and hold your own on any social level!

AMANDA (*offstage*): Tom?

TOM: Yes, Mother?

AMANDA: Is that you and Mr. O'Connor?

TOM: Yes, Mother.

AMANDA: Well, you just make yourselves comfortable in there.

TOM: Yes, Mother.

AMANDA: Ask Mr. O'Connor if he would like to wash his hands.

JIM: Aw, — no — no — thank you — I took care of that at the warehouse. Tom —

TOM: Yes?

JIM: Mr. Mendoza was speaking to me about you.

TOM: Favorably?

JIM: What do you think?

TOM: Well —

JIM: You're going to be out of a job if you don't wake up.

TOM: I am waking up —

JIM: You show no signs.

TOM: The signs are interior.

(*Image on screen: the sailing vessel with Jolly Roger again.*)

TOM: I'm planning to change. (*He leans over the rail speaking with quiet exhilaration. The incandescent marquees and signs of the first-run movie houses light his face from across the alley. He looks like a voyager.*) I'm right at the point of committing myself to a future that doesn't include the warehouse and Mr. Mendoza or even a night school course in public speaking.

JIM: What are you gassing about?

TOM: I'm tired of the movies.

JIM: Movies!

TOM: Yes, movies! Look at them — (*A wave toward the marvels of Grand Avenue.*) All of those glamorous people — having adventures — hogging it all, gobbling the whole thing up! You know what happens? People go to the *movies* instead of *moving!*

Hollywood characters are supposed to have all the adventures for everybody in America, while everybody in America sits in a dark room and watches them have them! Yes, until there's a war. That's when adventure becomes available to the masses! *Everyone's* dish, not only Gable's! Then the people in the dark room come out of the dark room to have some adventures themselves — Goody, goody! — It's our turn now, to go to the South Sea Island — to make a safari — to be exotic, far-off! — But I'm not patient. I don't want to wait till then. I'm tired of the *movies* and I am *about* to *move!*

JIM (*incredulously*): Move?

TOM: Yes.

JIM: When?

TOM: Soon!

JIM: Where? Where?

(*Theme three music seems to answer the question, while Tom thinks it over. He searches among his pockets.*)

TOM: I'm starting to boil inside. I know I seem dreamy, but inside — well, I'm boiling! Whenever I pick up a shoe, I shudder a little thinking how short life is and what I am doing! — Whatever that means. I know it doesn't mean shoes — except as something to wear on a traveler's feet! (*Finds paper.*) Look —

JIM: What?

TOM: I'm a member.

JIM (*reading*): The Union of Merchant Seamen.

TOM: I paid my dues this month, instead of the light bill.

JIM: You will regret it when they turn the lights off.

TOM: I won't be here.

JIM: How about your mother?

TOM: I'm like my father. The bastard son of a bastard! See how he grins? And he's been absent going on sixteen years!

JIM: You're just talking, you drip. How does your mother feel about it?

TOM: Shhh! — Here comes Mother! Mother is not acquainted with my plans!

AMANDA (*enters portieres*): Where are you all?

TOM: On the terrace, Mother.

(*They start inside. She advances to them. Tom is distinctly shocked at her appearance. Even Jim blinks a little. He is making his first contact with girlish Southern vivacity and in spite of the night school course in public speaking is somewhat thrown off the beam by the unexpected outlay of social charm.*)

(*Certain responses are attempted by Jim but are swept aside by Amanda's gay laughter and chatter. Tom is embarrassed but after the first shock Jim reacts very warmly. Grins and chuckles, is altogether won over.*)

(*Image: Amanda as a girl.*)

AMANDA (*coyly smiling, shaking her girlish ringlets*): Well, well, well, so this is Mr. O'Connor. Introductions entirely unnecessary. I've heard so much about you from my boy. I finally said to him, Tom — good gracious! — why don't you bring this paragon to supper? I'd like to meet this nice young man at the warehouse! — Instead of just hearing him sing your praises so much! I don't know why my son is so standoffish — that's not Southern behavior! Let's sit down and — I think we could stand a little more air in here! Tom, leave the door open. I felt a nice fresh breeze a moment ago. Where has it gone to? Mmm, so warm already! And not quite summer, even. We're going to burn up when summer really gets started. However, we're having — we're having a very light supper. I think light things are better fo' this time of year. The same as light clothes are. Light clothes an' light food are what warm weather calls fo'. You know our blood gets so thick during th' winter — it takes a while fo' us to *adjust* ou'selves! — when the season changes . . . It's come so quick this year. I wasn't prepared. All of a sudden — heavens! Already summer! — I ran to the trunk an' pulled out this light dress — Terribly old! Historical almost! But feels so good — so good an' co-ol, y'know. . . .

TOM: Mother —

AMANDA: Yes, honey?

TOM: How about — supper?

AMANDA: Honey, you go ask Sister if supper is ready! You know that Sister is in full charge of supper! Tell her you hungry boys are waiting for it. (*To Jim.*) Have you met Laura?

JIM: She —

AMANDA: Let you in? Oh, good, you've met already! It's rare for a girl as sweet an' pretty as Laura to be domestic! But Laura is, thank heavens, not only pretty but also very domestic. I'm not at all. I never was a bit. I never could make a thing but angel food cake. Well, in the South we had so many servants. Gone, gone, gone. All vestiges of gracious living! Gone completely! I wasn't prepared for what the future brought me. All of my gentlemen callers were sons of planters and so of course I assumed that I would be married to one and raise my family on a large piece of land with plenty of servants. But man proposes — and woman accepts the proposal! — To vary that old, old saying a little bit — I married no planter! I married a man who worked for the telephone company! — That gallantly smiling gentleman over there! (*Points to the picture.*)

A telephone man who — fell in love with long distance! — Now he travels and I don't even know where! — But what am I going on for about my — tribulations! Tell me yours — I hope you don't have any! Tom?

TOM (*returning*): Yes, Mother?

AMANDA: Is supper nearly ready?

TOM: It looks to me like supper is on the table.

AMANDA: Let me look — (*She rises prettily and looks through portieres.*) Oh, lovely! — But where is Sister?

TOM: Laura is not feeling well and she says that she thinks she'd better not come to the table.

AMANDA: What? — Nonsense! — Laura? Oh, Laura!

LAURA (*off stage, faintly*): Yes, Mother.

AMANDA: You really must come to the table. We won't be seated until you come to the table! Come in, Mr. O'Connor. You sit over there, and I'll — Laura? Laura Wingfield! You're keeping us waiting, honey! We can't say grace until you come to the table!

(*The back door is pushed weakly open and Laura comes in. She is obviously quite faint, her lips trembling, her eyes wide and staring. She moves unsteadily toward the table.*)

(*Legend: "Terror!"*)

(*Outside a summer storm is coming abruptly. The white curtains billow inward at the windows and there is a sorrowful murmur and deep blue dusk.*)

(*Laura suddenly stumbles — she catches at a chair with a faint moan.*)

TOM: Laura!

AMANDA: Laura! (*There is a clap of thunder.*) (*Legend: "Ah!"*) (*Despairingly.*) Why, Laura, you *are* sick, darling! Tom, help your sister into the living room, dear! Sit in the living room, Laura — rest on the sofa. Well! (*To the gentleman caller.*) Standing over the hot stove made her ill! — I told her that it was just too warm this evening, but — (*Tom comes back in. Laura is on the sofa.*) Is Laura all right now?

TOM: Yes.

AMANDA: What *is* that? Rain? A nice cool rain has come up! (*She gives the gentleman caller a frightened look.*) I think we may — have grace — now ... (*Tom looks at her stupidly.*) Tom, honey — you say grace!

TOM: Oh ... "For these and all thy mercies — " (*They bow their heads, Amanda stealing a nervous glance at Jim. In the living room Laura, stretched on the sofa, clenches her hand to her lips, to hold back a shuddering sob.*) God's Holy Name be praised —

(*The scene dims out.*)

SCENE 7

(*A Souvenir*)

(*Half an hour later. Dinner is just being finished in the upstage area which is concealed by the drawn portieres.*)

(*As the curtain rises Laura is still huddled upon the sofa, her feet drawn under her, her head resting on a pale blue pillow, her eyes wide and mysteriously watchful. The new floor lamp with its shade of rose-colored silk gives a soft, becoming light to her face, bringing out the fragile, unearthly prettiness which usually escapes attention. There is a steady murmur of rain, but it is slackening and stops soon after the scene begins; the air outside becomes pale and luminous as the moon breaks out.*)

(*A moment after the curtain rises, the lights in both rooms flicker and go out.*)

JIM: Hey, there, Mr. Light Bulb!

(*Amanda laughs nervously.*)

(*Legend: "Suspension of a Public Service."*)

AMANDA: Where was Moses when the lights went out? Ha-ha. Do you know the answer to that one, Mr. O'Connor?

JIM: No, Ma'am, what's the answer?

AMANDA: In the dark! (*Jim laughs appreciably.*) Everybody sit still. I'll light the candles. Isn't it lucky we have them on the table? Where's a match? Which of you gentlemen can provide a match?

JIM: Here.

AMANDA: Thank you, sir.

JIM: Not at all, Ma'am!

AMANDA: I guess the fuse has burnt out. Mr. O'Connor, can you tell a burnt-out fuse? I know I can't and Tom is a total loss when it comes to mechanics. (*Sound: getting up: voices recede a little to kitchenette.*) Oh, be careful you don't bump into something. We don't want our gentleman caller to break his neck. Now wouldn't that be a fine howdy-do?

JIM: Ha-ha! Where is the fuse box?

AMANDA: Right here next to the stove. Can you see anything?

JIM: Just a minute.

AMANDA: Isn't electricity a mysterious thing? Wasn't it Benjamin Franklin who tied a key to a kite? We live in such a mysterious universe, don't we? Some people say that science clears up all the mysteries for us. In my opinion it only creates more! Have you found it yet?

JIM: No, Ma'am. All these fuses look okay to me.

AMANDA: Tom!

TOM: Yes, Mother?

AMANDA: That light bill I gave you several days ago. The one I told you we got the notices about?

TOM: Oh. — Yeah.

(*Legend: "Ha!"*)

AMANDA: You didn't neglect to pay it by any chance?

TOM: Why, I —

AMANDA: Didn't! I might have known it!

JIM: Shakespeare probably wrote a poem on that light bill, Mrs. Wingfield.

AMANDA: I might have known better than to trust him with it! There's such a high price for negligence in this world!

JIM: Maybe the poem will win a ten-dollar prize.

AMANDA: We'll just have to spend the remainder of the evening in the nineteenth century, before Mr. Edison made the Mazda lamp!

JIM: Candlelight is my favorite kind of light.

AMANDA: That shows you're romantic! But that's no excuse for Tom. Well, we got through dinner. Very considerate of them to let us get through dinner before they plunged us into everlasting darkness, wasn't it, Mr. O'Connor?

JIM: Ha-ha!

AMANDA: Tom, as a penalty for your carelessness you can help me with the dishes.

JIM: Let me give you a hand.

AMANDA: Indeed you will not!

JIM: I ought to be good for something.

AMANDA: Good for something? (*Her tone is rhapsodic.*) You? Why, Mr. O'Connor, nobody, *nobody's* given me this much entertainment in years — as you have!

JIM: Aw, now, Mrs. Wingfield!

AMANDA: I'm not exaggerating, not one bit! But Sister is all by her lonesome. You go keep her company in the parlor! I'll give you this lovely old candelabrum that used to be on the altar at the church of the Heavenly Rest. It was melted a little out of shape when the church burnt down. Lightning struck it one spring. Gypsy Jones was holding a revival at the time and he intimated that the church was destroyed because the Episcopalians gave card parties.

JIM: Ha-ha.

AMANDA: And how about coaxing Sister to drink a little wine? I think it would be good for her! Can you carry both at once?

JIM: Sure. I'm Superman!

AMANDA: Now, Thomas, get into this apron!

(*The door of kitchenette swings closed on Amanda's gay laughter; the flickering light approaches the portieres.*)

(*Laura sits up nervously as he enters. Her speech at first is low and breathless from the almost intolerable strain of being alone with a stranger.*)

(*The legend: "I Don't Suppose You Remember Me at All!"*)

(*In her first speeches in this scene, before Jim's warmth overcomes her paralyzing shyness, Laura's voice is thin and breathless as though she has just run up a steep flight of stairs.*)

(*Jim's attitude is gently humorous. In playing this scene it should be stressed that while the incident is apparently unimportant, it is to Laura the climax of her secret life.*)

JIM: Hello, there, Laura.

LAURA (*faintly*): Hello. (*She clears her throat.*)

JIM: How are you feeling now? Better?

LAURA: Yes. Yes, thank you.

JIM: This is for you. A little dandelion wine. (*He extends it toward her with extravagant gallantry.*)

LAURA: Thank you.

JIM: Drink it — but don't get drunk! (*He laughs heartily. Laura takes the glass uncertainly; laughs shyly.*) Where shall I set the candles?

LAURA: Oh — oh, anywhere . . .

JIM: How about here on the floor? Any objections?

LAURA: No.

JIM: I'll spread a newspaper under to catch the drippings. I like to sit on the floor. Mind if I do?

LAURA: Oh, no.

JIM: Give me a pillow?

LAURA: What?

JIM: A pillow!

LAURA: Oh . . . (*Hands him one quickly.*)

JIM: How about you? Don't you like to sit on the floor?

LAURA: Oh — yes.

JIM: Why don't you, then?

LAURA: I — will.

JIM: Take a pillow! (*Laura does. Sits on the other side of the candelabrum. Jim crosses his legs and smiles engagingly at her.*) I can't hardly see you sitting way over there.

LAURA: I can — see you.

JIM: I know, but that's not fair, I'm in the limelight. (*Laura moves her pillow closer.*) Good! Now I can see you! Comfortable?

LAURA: Yes.

JIM: So am I. Comfortable as a cow. Will you have some gum?

LAURA: No, thank you.

JIM: I think that I will indulge, with your permission. (*Musingly unwraps it and holds it up.*) Think of the fortune made by the guy that invented the first piece of chewing gum. Amazing, huh? The Wrigley Building is one of the sights of Chicago. — I saw it summer before last when I went up to the Century of Progress. Did you take in the Century of Progress?

LAURA: No, I didn't.

JIM: Well, it was quite a wonderful exposition. What impressed me most was the Hall of Science. Gives you an idea of what the future will be in America, even more wonderful than the present time is! (*Pause. Smiling at her.*) Your brother tells me you're shy. Is that right, Laura?

LAURA: I — don't know.

JIM: I judge you to be an old-fashioned type of girl. Well, I think that's a pretty good type to be. Hope you don't think I'm being too personal — do you?

LAURA (*hastily, out of embarrassment*): I believe I *will* take a piece of gum, if you — don't mind. (*Clearing her throat.*) Mr. O'Connor, have you — kept up with your singing?

JIM: Singing? Me?

LAURA: Yes. I remember what a beautiful voice you had.

JIM: When did you hear me sing?

(*Voice offstage in the pause.*)

VOICE (*offstage*): O blow, ye winds, heigh-ho,
    A-roving I will go!
        I'm off to my love
        With a boxing glove —
    Ten thousand miles away!

JIM: You say you've heard me sing?

LAURA: Oh, yes! Yes, very often . . . I — don't suppose you remember me — at all?

JIM (*smiling doubtfully*): You know I have an idea I've seen you before. I had that idea soon as you opened the door. It seemed almost like I was about to remember your name. But the name that I started to call you — wasn't a name! And so I stopped myself before I said it.

LAURA: Wasn't it — Blue Roses?

JIM (*Springs up. Grinning.*): Blue Roses! My gosh, yes — Blue Roses! That's what I had on my tongue when you opened the door! Isn't it funny what tricks your memory plays? I didn't connect you with the high school somehow or other. But that's where it was; it was high school. I didn't even know you were Shakespeare's sister! Gosh, I'm sorry.

LAURA: I didn't expect you to. You — barely knew me!

JIM: But we did have a speaking acquaintance, huh?

LAURA: Yes, we — spoke to each other.

JIM: When did you recognize me?

LAURA: Oh, right away!

JIM: Soon as I came in the door?

LAURA: When I heard your name I thought it was probably you. I knew that Tom used to know you a little in high school. So when you came in the door — Well, then I was — sure.

JIM: Why didn't you *say* something, then?

LAURA (*breathlessly*): I didn't know what to say, I was — too surprised!

JIM: For goodness' sakes! You know, this sure is funny!

LAURA: Yes! Yes, isn't it, though . . .

JIM: Didn't we have a class in something together?

LAURA: Yes, we did.

JIM: What class was that?

LAURA: It was — singing — Chorus!

JIM: Aw!

LAURA: I sat across the aisle from you in the Aud.

JIM: Aw.

LAURA: Mondays, Wednesdays, and Fridays.

JIM: Now I remember — you always came in late.

LAURA: Yes, it was so hard for me, getting upstairs. I had that brace on my leg — it clumped so loud!

JIM: I never heard any clumping.

LAURA (*wincing at the recollection*): To me it sounded like — thunder!

JIM: Well, well, well, I never even noticed.

LAURA: And everybody was seated before I came in. I had to walk in front of all those people. My seat was in the back row. I had to go clumping all the way up the aisle with everyone watching!

JIM: You shouldn't have been self-conscious.

LAURA: I know, but I was. It was always such a relief when the singing started.

JIM: Aw, yes, I've placed you now! I used to call you Blue Roses. How was it that I got started calling you that?

LAURA: I was out of school a little while with pleurosis. When I came back you asked me what was the matter. I said I had pleurosis — you thought I said Blue Roses. That's what you always called me after that!

JIM: I hope you didn't mind.

LAURA: Oh, no — I liked it. You see, I wasn't acquainted with many — people. . . .

JIM: As I remember you sort of stuck by yourself.

LAURA: I — I — never had much luck at — making friends.

JIM: I don't see why you wouldn't.

LAURA: Well, I — started out badly.

JIM: You mean being —

LAURA: Yes, it sort of — stood between me —

JIM: You shouldn't have let it!

LAURA: I know, but it did, and —

JIM: You were shy with people!

LAURA: I tried not to be but never could —

JIM: Overcome it?

LAURA: No, I — I never could!

JIM: I guess being shy is something you have to work out of kind of gradually.

LAURA (*sorrowfully*): Yes — I guess it —

JIM: Takes time!

LAURA: Yes —

JIM: People are not so dreadful when you know them. That's what you have to remember! And everybody has problems, not just you, but practically everybody has got some problems. You think of yourself as having the only problems, as being the only one who is disappointed. But just look around you and you will see lots of people as disappointed as you are. For instance, I hoped when I was going to high school that I would be further along at this time, six years later, than I am now — You remember that wonderful write-up I had in *The Torch?*

LAURA: Yes! (*She rises and crosses to table.*)

JIM: It said I was bound to succeed in anything I went into! (*Laura returns with the annual.*) Holy Jeez! *The Torch!* (*He accepts it reverently. They smile across it with mutual wonder. Laura crouches beside him and they begin to turn through it. Laura's shyness is dissolving in his warmth.*)

LAURA: Here you are in *Pirates of Penzance!*

JIM (*wistfully*): I sang the baritone lead in that operetta.

LAURA (*rapidly*): So — *beautifully!*

JIM (*protesting*): Aw —

LAURA: Yes, yes — beautifully — beautifully!

JIM: You heard me?

LAURA: All three times!

JIM: No!

LAURA: Yes!

JIM: All three performances?

LAURA (*looking down*): Yes.

JIM: Why?

LAURA: I — wanted to ask you to — autograph my program.

JIM: Why didn't you ask me to?

LAURA: You were always surrounded by your own friends so much that I never had a chance to.

JIM: You should have just —

LAURA: Well, I — thought you might think I was —

JIM: Thought I might think you was — what?

LAURA: Oh —

JIM (*with reflective relish*): I was beleaguered by females in those days.

LAURA: You were terribly popular!

JIM: Yeah —

LAURA: You had such a — friendly way —

JIM: I was spoiled in high school.

LAURA: Everybody — liked you!

JIM: Including you?

LAURA: I — yes, I — I did, too — (*She gently closes the book in her lap.*)

JIM: Well, well, well! — Give me that program, Laura. (*She hands it to him. He signs it with a flourish.*) There you are — better late than never!

LAURA: Oh, I — what a — surprise!

JIM: My signature isn't worth very much right now. But some day — maybe — it will increase in value!

Being disappointed is one thing and being discouraged is something else. I am disappointed but I am not discouraged. I'm twenty-three years old. How old are you?

LAURA: I'll be twenty-four in June.

JIM: That's not old age!

LAURA: No, but —

JIM: You finished high school?

LAURA (*with difficulty*): I didn't go back.

JIM: You mean you dropped out?

LAURA: I made bad grades in my final examinations. (*She rises and replaces the book and the program. Her voice strained.*) How is — Emily Meisenbach getting along?

JIM: Oh, that kraut-head!

LAURA: Why do you call her that?

JIM: That's what she was.

LAURA: You're not still — going with her?

JIM: I never see her.

LAURA: It said in the Personal Section that you were — engaged!

JIM: I know, but I wasn't impressed by that — propaganda!

LAURA: It wasn't — the truth?

JIM: Only in Emily's optimistic opinion!

LAURA: Oh —

(*Legend: "What Have You Done since High School?"*)
(*Jim lights a cigarette and leans indolently back on his elbows smiling at Laura with a warmth and charm which lights her inwardly with altar candles. She remains by the table and turns in her hands a piece of glass to cover her tumult.*)

JIM (*after several reflective puffs on a cigarette*): What have you done since high school? (*She seems not to hear him.*) Huh? (*Laura looks up.*) I said what have you done since high school, Laura?

LAURA: Nothing much.

JIM: You must have been doing something these six long years.

LAURA: Yes.

JIM: Well, then, such as what?

LAURA: I took a business course at business college —

JIM: How did that work out?

LAURA: Well, not very — well — I had to drop out, it gave me — indigestion —

(*Jim laughs gently.*)

JIM: What are you doing now?

LAURA: I don't do anything — much. Oh, please don't think I sit around doing nothing! My glass collection takes up a good deal of my time. Glass is something you have to take good care of.

JIM: What did you say — about glass?

LAURA: Collection I said — I have one — (*She clears her throat and turns away again, acutely shy.*)

JIM (*abruptly*): You know what I judge to be the trouble with you? Inferiority complex! Know what that is? That's what they call it when someone low-rates himself! I understand it because I had it, too. Although my case was not so aggravated as yours seems to be. I had it until I took up public speaking, developed my voice, and learned that I had an aptitude for science. Before that time I never thought of myself as being outstanding in any way whatsoever! Now I've never made a regular study of it, but I have a friend who says I can analyze people better than doctors that make a profession of it. I don't claim that to be necessarily true, but I can sure guess a person's psychology, Laura! (*Takes out his gum.*) Excuse me, Laura. I always take it out when the flavor is gone. I'll use this scrap of paper to wrap it in. I know how it is to get it stuck on a shoe. Yep — that's what I judge to be your principal trouble. A lack of confidence in yourself as a person. You don't have the proper amount of faith in yourself. I'm basing that fact on a number of your remarks and also on certain observations I've made. For instance that clumping you thought was so awful in high school. You say that you even dreaded to walk into class. You see what you did? You dropped out of school, you gave up an education because of a clump, which as far as I know was practically nonexistent! A little physical defect is what you have. Hardly noticeable even! Magnified thousands of times by imagination! You know what my strong advice to you is? Think of yourself as *superior* in some way!

LAURA: In what way would I think?

JIM: Why, man alive, Laura! Just look about you a little. What do you see? A world full of common people! All of 'em born and all of 'em going to die! Which of them has one-tenth of your good points! Or mine! Or anyone else's, as far as that goes — Gosh! Everybody excels in some one thing. Some in many! (*Unconsciously glances at himself in the mirror.*) All you've got to do is discover in *what!* Take me, for instance. (*He adjusts his tie at the mirror.*) My interest happens to lie in electro-dynamics. I'm taking a course in radio engineering at night school, Laura, on top of a fairly responsible job at the warehouse. I'm taking that course and studying public speaking.

LAURA: Ohhhh.

JIM: Because I believe in the future of television! (*Turning back to her.*) I wish to be ready to go up right along with it. Therefore I'm planning to get in on the ground floor. In fact, I've already made the right connections and all that remains is for the industry itself to get under way! Full steam — (*His eyes are starry.*) Knowledge — Zzzzzp! Money — Zzzzzzp! — Power! That's the cycle democracy is built on! (*His attitude is convincingly dynamic. Laura stares at him, even her shyness eclipsed in her absolute wonder. He suddenly grins.*) I guess you think I think a lot of myself!

LAURA: No — o-o-o, I —

JIM: Now how about you? Isn't there something you take more interest in than anything else?

LAURA: Well, I do — as I said — have my — glass collection —

(*A peal of girlish laughter from the kitchen.*)

JIM: I'm not right sure I know what you're talking about. What kind of glass is it?

LAURA: Little articles of it, they're ornaments mostly! Most of them are little animals made out of glass, the tiniest little animals in the world. Mother calls them a glass menagerie! Here's an example of one, if you'd like to see it! This one is one of the oldest. It's nearly thirteen. (*He stretches out his hand.*) (*Music: "The Glass Menagerie."*) Oh, be careful — if you breathe, it breaks!

JIM: I'd better not take it. I'm pretty clumsy with things.

LAURA: Go on, I trust you with him! (*Places it in his palm.*) There now — you're holding him gently! Hold him over the light, he loves the light! You see how the light shines through him?

JIM: It sure does shine!

LAURA: I shouldn't be partial, but he is my favorite one.

JIM: What kind of a thing is this one supposed to be?

LAURA: Haven't you noticed the single horn on his forehead?

JIM: A unicorn, huh?

LAURA: Mmm-hmmm!

JIM: Unicorns, aren't they extinct in the modern world?

LAURA: I know!

JIM: Poor little fellow, he must feel sort of lonesome.

LAURA (*smiling*): Well, if he does he doesn't complain about it. He stays on a shelf with some horses that don't have horns and all of them seem to get along nicely together.

JIM: How do you know?

LAURA (*lightly*): I haven't heard any arguments among them!

JIM (*grinning*): No arguments, huh? Well, that's a pretty good sign! Where shall I set him?

LAURA: Put him on the table. They all like a change of scenery once in a while!

JIM (*stretching*): Well, well, well, well — Look how big my shadow is when I stretch!

LAURA: Oh, oh, yes — it stretches across the ceiling!

JIM (*crossing to door*): I think it's stopped raining. (*Opens fire escape door.*) Where does the music come from?

LAURA: From the Paradise Dance Hall across the alley.

JIM: How about cutting the rug a little, Miss Wingfield?

LAURA: Oh, I —

JIM: Or is your program filled up? Let me have a look at it. (*Grasps imaginary card.*) Why, every dance is taken! I'll just have to scratch some out. (*Waltz music: "La Golondrina."*) Ahhh, a waltz! (*He executes some sweeping turns by himself then holds his arms toward Laura.*)

LAURA (*breathlessly*): I — can't dance!

JIM: There you go, that inferiority stuff!

LAURA: I've never danced in my life!

JIM: Come on, try!

LAURA: Oh, but I'd step on you!

JIM: I'm not made out of glass.

LAURA: How — how — how do we start?

JIM: Just leave it to me. You hold your arms out a little.

LAURA: Like this?

JIM: A little bit higher. Right. Now don't tighten up, that's the main thing about it — relax.

LAURA (*laughing breathlessly*): It's hard not to.

JIM: Okay.

LAURA: I'm afraid you can't budge me.

JIM: What do you bet I can't? (*He swings her into motion.*)

LAURA: Goodness, yes, you can!

JIM: Let yourself go, now, Laura, just let yourself go.

LAURA: I'm —

JIM: Come on!

LAURA: Trying!

JIM: Not so stiff — Easy does it!

LAURA: I know but I'm —

JIM: Loosen th' backbone! There now, that's a lot better.

LAURA: Am I?

JIM: Lots, lots better! (*He moves her about the room in a clumsy waltz.*)

LAURA: Oh, my!

JIM: Ha-ha!

LAURA: Oh, my goodness!

JIM: Ha-ha-ha! (*They suddenly bump into the table. Jim stops.*) What did we hit on?

LAURA: Table.

JIM: Did something fall off it? I think —

LAURA: Yes.

JIM: I hope that it wasn't the little glass horse with the horn!

LAURA: Yes.

JIM: Aw, aw, aw. Is it broken?

LAURA: Now it is just like all the other horses.

JIM: It's lost its —

LAURA: Horn! It doesn't matter. Maybe it's a blessing in disguise.

JIM: You'll never forgive me. I bet that that was your favorite piece of glass.

LAURA: I don't have favorites much. It's no tragedy, Freckles. Glass breaks so easily. No matter how careful you are. The traffic jars the shelves and things fall off them.

JIM: Still I'm awfully sorry that I was the cause.

LAURA (*smiling*): I'll just imagine he had an operation. The horn was removed to make him feel less — freakish! (*They both laugh.*) Now he will feel more at home with the other horses, the ones that don't have horns . . .

JIM: Ha-ha, that's very funny! (*Suddenly serious.*) I'm glad to see that you have a sense of humor. You know — you're — well — very different! Surprisingly different from anyone else I know! (*His voice becomes soft and hesitant with a genuine feeling.*) Do you mind me telling you that? (*Laura is abashed beyond speech.*) I mean it in a nice way . . . (*Laura nods shyly, looking away.*) You make me feel sort of — I don't know how to put it! I'm usually pretty good at expressing things, but — This is something that I don't know how to say! (*Laura touches her throat and clears it — turns the broken unicorn in her hands.*) (*Even softer.*) Has anyone ever told you that you were pretty? (*Pause: Music.*) (*Laura looks up slowly, with wonder, and shakes her head.*) Well, you are! In a very different way from anyone else. And all the nicer because of the difference, too. (*His voice becomes low and husky. Laura turns away, nearly faint with the novelty of her emotions.*) I wish that you were my sister. I'd teach you to have some confidence in yourself. The different people are not like other people, but being different is nothing to be ashamed of. Because other people are not such wonderful people. They're one hundred times one thousand. You're one times one! They walk all over the earth. You just stay here. They're common as — weeds, but — you — well, you're — *Blue Roses!*

(*Image on screen: blue roses.*)
(*Music changes.*)

LAURA: But blue is wrong for — roses . . .

JIM: It's right for you — You're — pretty!

LAURA: In what respect am I pretty?

JIM: In all respects — believe me! Your eyes — your hair — are pretty! Your hands are pretty! (*He catches hold of her hand.*) You think I'm making this up because I'm invited to dinner and have to be nice. Oh, I could do that! I could put on an act for you, Laura, and say lots of things without being very sincere. But this time I am. I'm talking to you sincerely. I happened to notice you had this inferiority complex that keeps you from feeling comfortable with people. Somebody needs to build your confidence up and make you proud instead of shy and turning away and — blushing — Somebody ought to — Ought to — *kiss you, Laura!* (*His hand slips slowly up her arm to her shoulder.*) (*Music swells tumultuously.*) (*He suddenly turns her about and kisses her on the lips. When he releases her Laura sinks on the sofa with a bright, dazed look. Jim backs away and fishes in his pocket for a cigarette.*) (*Legend on screen: "Souvenir."*) Stumble-john! (*He lights the cigarette, avoiding her look. There is a peal of girlish laughter from Amanda in the kitchen. Laura slowly raises and opens her hand. It still contains the little broken glass animal. She looks at it with a tender, bewildered expression.*) Stumble-john! I shouldn't have done that — That was way off the beam. You don't smoke, do you? (*She looks up, smiling, not hearing the question. He sits beside her a little gingerly. She looks at him speechlessly — waiting. He coughs decorously and moves a little farther aside as he considers the situation and senses her feelings, dimly, with perturbation. Gently.*) Would you — care for a — mint? (*She doesn't seem to hear him but her look grows brighter even.*) Peppermint — Life Saver? My pocket's a regular drugstore — wherever I go . . . (*He pops a mint in his mouth. Then gulps and decides to make a clean breast of it. He speaks slowly and gingerly.*) Laura, you know, if I had a sister like you, I'd do the same thing as Tom. I'd bring out fellows and — introduce her to them. The right type of boys of a type to — appreciate her. Only — well — he made a mistake about me. Maybe I've got no call to be saying this. That may not have been the idea in having me over. But what if it was? There's nothing wrong about that. The only trouble is that in my case — I'm not in a situation to — do the right thing. I can't take down your number and say I'll phone. I can't call up next week and — ask for a date. I thought I had better explain the situation in case you misunderstood it and — hurt your feelings. . . . (*Pause. Slowly, very slowly, Laura's look changes, her eyes returning slowly from his to the ornament in her palm.*)

(*Amanda utters another gay laugh in the kitchen.*)

LAURA (*faintly*): You — won't — call again?
JIM: No, Laura, I can't. (*He rises from the sofa.*) As I was just explaining, I've — got strings on me, Laura, I've — been going steady! I go out all the time with a girl named Betty. She's a home-girl like you, and Catholic, and Irish, and in a great many ways we — get along fine. I met her last

summer on a moonlight boat trip up the river to Alton, on the *Majestic*. Well — right away from the start it was — love! (*Legend: Love!*) (*Laura sways slightly forward and grips the arm of the sofa. He fails to notice, now enrapt in his own comfortable being.*) Being in love has made a new man of me! (*Leaning stiffly forward, clutching the arm of the sofa, Laura struggles visibly with her storm. But Jim is oblivious, she is a long way off.*) The power of love is really pretty tremendous! Love is something that — changes the whole world, Laura! (*The storm abates a little and Laura leans back. He notices her again.*) It happened that Betty's aunt took sick, she got a wire and had to go to Centralia. So Tom — when he asked me to dinner — I naturally just accepted the invitation, not knowing that you — that he — that I — (*He stops awkwardly.*) Huh — I'm a stumble-john! (*He flops back on the sofa. The holy candles in the altar of Laura's face have been snuffed out! There is a look of almost infinite desolation. Jim glances at her uneasily.*) I wish that you would — say something. (*She bites her lip which was trembling and then bravely smiles. She opens her hand again on the broken glass ornament. Then she gently takes his hand and raises it level with her own. She carefully places the unicorn in the palm of his hand, then pushes his fingers closed upon it.*) What are you — doing that for? You want me to have him? — Laura? (*She nods.*) What for?

LAURA: A — souvenir . . .

(*She rises unsteadily and crouches beside the victrola to wind it up.*)

(*Legend on screen: "Things Have a Way of Turning out so Badly."*)

(*Or Image: "Gentleman Caller Waving Good-bye! — Gaily."*)

(*At this moment Amanda rushes brightly back in the front room. She bears a pitcher of fruit punch in an old-fashioned cut-glass pitcher and a plate of macaroons. The plate has a gold border and poppies painted on it.*)

AMANDA: Well, well, well! Isn't the air delightful after the shower? I've made you children a little liquid refreshment. (*Turns gaily to the gentleman caller.*) Jim, do you know that song about lemonade?
"Lemonade, lemonade
   Made in the shade and stirred with a spade —
Good enough for any old maid!"
JIM (*uneasily*): Ha-ha! No — I never heard it.
AMANDA: Why, Laura! You look so serious!
JIM: We were having a serious conversation.
AMANDA: Good! Now you're better acquainted!
JIM (*uncertainly*): Ha-ha! Yes.

AMANDA: You modern young people are much more serious-minded than my generation. I was so gay as a girl!

JIM: You haven't changed, Mrs. Wingfield.

AMANDA: Tonight I'm rejuvenated! The gaiety of the occasion, Mr. O'Connor! (*She tosses her head with a peal of laughter. Spills lemonade.*) Oooo! I'm baptizing myself!

JIM: Here — let me —

AMANDA (*setting the pitcher down*): There now. I discovered we had some maraschino cherries. I dumped them in, juice and all!

JIM: You shouldn't have gone to that trouble, Mrs. Wingfield.

AMANDA: Trouble, trouble? Why it was loads of fun! Didn't you hear me cutting up in the kitchen? I bet your ears were burning! I told Tom how outdone with him I was for keeping you to himself so long a time! He should have brought you over much, much sooner! Well, now that you've found your way, I want you to be a very frequent caller! Not just occasional but all the time. Oh, we're going to have a lot of gay times together! I see them coming! Mmm, just breathe that air! So fresh, and the moon's so pretty! I'll skip back out — I know where my place is when young folks are having a — serious conversation!

JIM: Oh, don't go out, Mrs. Wingfield. The fact of the matter is I've got to be going.

AMANDA: Going, now? You're joking! Why, it's only the shank of the evening, Mr. O'Connor!

JIM: Well, you know how it is.

AMANDA: You mean you're a young workingman and have to keep workingmen's hours. We'll let you off early tonight. But only on the condition that next time you stay later. What's the best night for you? Isn't Saturday night the best night for you workingmen?

JIM: I have a couple of time clocks to punch, Mrs. Wingfield. One at morning, another one at night!

AMANDA: My, but you *are* ambitious! You work at night, too?

JIM: No, Ma'am, not work but — Betty! (*He crosses deliberately to pick up his hat. The band at the Paradise Dance Hall goes into a tender waltz.*)

AMANDA: Betty? Betty? Who's — Betty! (*There is an ominous cracking sound in the sky.*)

JIM: Oh, just a girl. The girl I go steady with! (*He smiles charmingly. The sky falls.*)

(*Legend: "The Sky Falls."*)

AMANDA (*a long-drawn exhalation*): Ohhhh . . . Is it a serious romance, Mr. O'Connor?

JIM: We're going to be married the second Sunday in June.

AMANDA: Ohhhh — how nice! Tom didn't mention that you were engaged to be married.

JIM: The cat's not out of the bag at the warehouse yet. You know how they are. They call you Romeo and stuff like that. (*He stops at the oval mirror to put on his hat. He carefully shapes the brim and the crown to give a discreetly dashing effect.*) It's been a wonderful evening, Mrs. Wingfield. I guess this is what they mean by Southern hospitality.

AMANDA: It really wasn't anything at all.

JIM: I hope it don't seem like I'm rushing off. But I promised Betty I'd pick her up at the Wabash depot, an' by the time I get my jalopy down there her train'll be in. Some women are pretty upset if you keep 'em waiting.

AMANDA: Yes, I know — The tyranny of women! (*Extends her hand.*) Good-bye, Mr. O'Connor. I wish you luck — and happiness — and success! All three of them, and so does Laura! — Don't you, Laura?

LAURA: Yes!

JIM (*taking her hand*): Good-bye, Laura. I'm certainly going to treasure that souvenir. And don't you forget the good advice I gave you. (*Raises his voice to a cheery shout.*) So long, Shakespeare! Thanks again, ladies — Good night!

(*He grins and ducks jauntily out.*)

(*Still bravely grimacing, Amanda closes the door on the gentleman caller. Then she turns back to the room with a puzzled expression. She and Laura don't dare to face each other. Laura crouches beside the victrola to wind it.*)

AMANDA (*faintly*): Things have a way of turning out so badly. I don't believe that I would play the victrola. Well, well — well — Our gentleman caller was engaged to be married! Tom!

TOM (*from back*): Yes, Mother?

AMANDA: Come in here a minute. I want to tell you something awfully funny.

TOM (*enters with macaroon and a glass of the lemonade*): Has the gentleman caller gotten away already?

AMANDA: The gentleman caller has made an early departure. What a wonderful joke you played on us!

TOM: How do you mean?

AMANDA: You didn't mention that he was engaged to be married.

TOM: Jim? Engaged?

AMANDA: That's what he just informed us.

TOM: I'll be jiggered! I didn't know about that.

AMANDA: That seems very peculiar.

TOM: What's peculiar about it?

AMANDA: Didn't you call him your best friend down at the warehouse?

TOM: He is, but how did I know?

AMANDA: It seems extremely peculiar that you wouldn't know your best friend was going to be married!

TOM: The warehouse is where I work, not where I know things about people!

AMANDA: You don't know things anywhere! You live in a dream; you manufacture illusions! (*He crosses to door.*) Where are you going?

TOM: I'm going to the movies.

AMANDA: That's right, now that you've had us make such fools of ourselves. The effort, the preparations, all the expense! The new floor lamp, the rug, the clothes for Laura! All for what? To entertain some other girl's fiancé! Go to the movies, go! Don't think about us, a mother deserted, an unmarried sister who's crippled and has no job! Don't let anything interfere with your selfish pleasure! Just go, go, go — to the movies!

TOM: All right, I will! The more you shout about my selfishness to me the quicker I'll go, and I *won't* go to the movies!

AMANDA: Go, then! Then go to the moon — you selfish dreamer!

(*Tom smashes his glass on the floor. He plunges out on the fire escape, slamming the door. Laura screams — cut by door.*)

(*Dance hall music up. Tom goes to the rail and grips it desperately, lifting his face in the chill white moonlight penetrating the narrow abyss of the alley.*)

(*Legend on screen: "And so Good-bye . . ."*)

(*Tom's closing speech is timed with the interior pantomime. The interior scene is played as though viewed through soundproof glass. Amanda appears to be making a comforting speech to Laura who is huddled upon the sofa. Now that we cannot hear the mother's speech, her silliness is gone and she has dignity and tragic beauty. Laura's dark hair hides her face until* at the end of the speech she lifts it to smile at her mother. Amanda's gestures are slow and graceful, almost dancelike, as she comforts the daughter. At the end of her speech she glances a moment at the father's picture — then withdraws through the portieres. At close of Tom's speech, Laura blows out the candles, ending the play.*)

TOM: I didn't go to the moon, I went much further — for time is the longest distance between two places — Not long after that I was fired for writing a poem on the lid of a shoebox. I left Saint Louis. I descended the steps of this fire escape for a last time and followed, from then on, in my father's footsteps, attempting to find in motion what was lost in space — I traveled around a great deal. The cities swept about me like dead leaves, leaves that were brightly colored but torn away from the branches. I would have stopped, but I was pursued by something. It always came upon me unawares, taking me altogether by surprise. Perhaps it was a familiar bit of music. Perhaps it was only a piece of transparent glass — Perhaps I am walking along a street at night, in some strange city, before I have found companions. I pass the lighted window of a shop where perfume is sold. The window is filled with pieces of colored glass, tiny transparent bottles in delicate colors, like bits of a shattered rainbow. Then all at once my sister touches my shoulder. I turn around and look into her eyes . . . Oh, Laura, Laura, I tried to leave you behind me, but I am more faithful than I intended to be! I reach for a cigarette, I cross the street, I run into the movies or a bar, I buy a drink, I speak to the nearest stranger — anything that can blow your candles out! (*Laura bends over the candles.*) — for nowadays the world is lit by lightning! Blow out your candles, Laura — and so good-bye. . . .

(*She blows the candles out.*)
(*The scene dissolves.*)

Arthur Miller

Arthur Miller (b. 1915) has been the dean of American playwrights since the opening of *Death of a Salesman* in 1949. His steady output as a writer and a playwright began with his first publications after college in 1939, when he worked in the New York Federal Theatre Project, a branch of the Work Projects Administration (WPA), Franklin D. Roosevelt's huge Depression effort to put Americans back to work.

Miller, the son of a Jewish immigrant, was born and raised during his early years in the Harlem section of Manhattan and later in Brooklyn after his father's business failed. In high school, Miller thought of himself more as an athlete than a student, and he had trouble getting teachers' recommendations for college. After considerable struggle and waiting, he entered the University of Michigan, where his talent as a playwright emerged under the tutelage of Kenneth Rowe, his playwriting professor. His undergraduate plays won important university awards and he became noticed by the Theatre Guild, a highly respected theater founded to present excellent plays (not necessarily commercial successes). His career was under way.

Miller wrote radio plays, screenplays, articles, stories, and a novel in the eight years it took him to write a successful Broadway play. His work covered a wide range of material, much of it growing out of his childhood memories of a tightly knit and somewhat eccentric family that provided him with a large gallery of characters. But he also dealt with political issues and problems of anti-Semitism, which was widespread in the 1930s and 1940s. Miller's political concerns have been a constant presence in his work since his earliest writings.

All My Sons (1947) was his first successful play. It ran on Broadway for 300 performances, a remarkable record for a serious drama. The story centers on a man who knowingly produces defective parts for airplanes and then blames the subsequent crashes on his business partner, who is ruined and imprisoned. When the man's son finds out the truth, he confronts his father and rebukes him. Ultimately, the man realizes not only that he has lost his son because of his deceit, but that the dead pilots were also "all my sons." The play won the New York Critics Circle Award.

Miller's next play, *Death of a Salesman* (1949), was written in six weeks. Its concerns were rooted in the American ideal of business success, and its conclusions were a challenge to standard American business values. Willy Loman, first performed by Lee J. Cobb, became a symbol for Americans in the postwar period of growing wealth and affluence. The play won the New York Critics Circle Award and the Pulitzer Prize and ran for an incredible 742 performances on Broadway. It was revived on Broadway in 1984 and was performed on television with Dustin Hoffman as Willy Loman. It was an immense success thirty-five years after its first performance.

Miller's next play was *The Crucible* (1953), which portrayed witch hunts of seventeenth-century New England. However, it was clear to most people that the play had a subtext: It was about contemporary witch hunts orchestrated by Senator Joseph McCarthy (1909–1957) in the early 1950s. McCarthy conducted Senate hearings that were supposed to flush out suspected communists from government and other areas of American life, including the arts. In the anti-communist hysteria that possessed the nation, many writers, artists, and performers came under close, often unfair, scrutiny for their political views and allegiances. Some were blacklisted — prevented from working in commercial theaters and movie companies — some were imprisoned for not testifying at others' trials, and some had reputations and careers destroyed.

Arthur Miller was fearless in facing down McCarthy's committee. He was convicted of contempt of court for not testifying against his friends. For a time he too was blacklisted, but the conviction was soon reversed, and he was not imprisoned for his resistance to the committee. Given his personal political stance during this dangerous time, it is not a surprise to find that his themes usually center on matters of social concern.

DEATH OF A SALESMAN

Death of a Salesman (1949) was a hit from its first performances and has remained at the center of modern American drama ever since. It was staged on Broadway for 742 performances, an achievement that very few plays can claim. Moreover, it was produced on television in the mid-1960s for an audience of seventeen million and again in the late 1980s for an audience of twenty-five million. It has been successful in China, where there are no salesmen, and in Europe, where many salesmen dominate certain industries. Everywhere it has been seen it has touched the hearts and minds of its audiences. Its success is a phenomenon of American drama.

The play was first performed in an environment that must be called experimental. Miller had originally conceived of a model of a man's head as the stage setting. He has said: "The first image that occurred to me which was to result in *Death of a Salesman* was of an enormous face the height of the proscenium arch which would appear and then open up, and we would see the inside of a man's head. In fact, *The Inside of His Head* was the first title." This technique was not used, but when Miller worked with the director and producer of the first production, he helped develop a setting that became a model for the "American style" in drama. The multilevel set permitted the play to shift from Willy Loman and his wife, Linda, having a conversation in their kitchen to their son's bedroom on the second level of the house. It permitted portions of the stage to be reserved for Willy's visions of his brother, Ben, and for scenes outside the house such as Willy's interlude with the woman in Boston.

In a way, the setup of the stage respected Miller's original plan, but instead of portraying a cross section of Willy's head, it presented a metaphor for a cross section of his life. The audience felt that they were looking in on more than a living room — as in the nineteenth-century Ibsenist approach — they were looking in on an entire house and an entire life.

Using a cross section of a house as a metaphor was an especially important device in this play because of the play's obvious allusions to Greek tragedy. The great Greek tragedies usually portray the destruction of a house — such as the house of Atreus — as a way of making a metaphor for a whole family, not just an individual. When Hamlet dies, for example, his entire line dies with him. His family is gone at the end of Act V. The death in *Death of a Salesman* implies the destruction of a family that has held certain beliefs, which have been wrong from the start.

The life of the salesman has given Willy a sense of dignity and worth, and he imagines that the modern world has corrupted that sense by robbing salesmen of the value of their personality. He thinks the modern world has failed him, but he is wrong. His original belief that what counts is not *what* you know but *whom* you know and how well you are liked lies at the heart of his failure. When the play opens, he has failed. He cannot do the traveling salesman's job because he can no longer drive to the territory. He cannot sell what he needs to sell.

Willy has inculcated his beliefs in his sons, Happy and Biff, and both are as ineffectual as their father. Willy doted on Biff and encouraged him to become a high school football star at the expense of his studies. But when Biff cannot pass an important course, his dreams of a college football career are gone. He cannot change, cannot recover from this defeat, because to do so he would have to ignore his father's philosophy and the foundation of his beliefs. Happy, like his father, builds castles in the air and assumes somehow that he will be successful when he has nothing to back himself up with. He wants the glory — and he spends time in fanciful imaginings, as Willy does — but he cannot do the basic work that makes it possible to achieve glory. Ironically, it is the "anemic" Bernard — who studies hard, stresses personal honesty and diligence, and never brags — who is successful.

Linda supports Willy's illusions, allowing him to be a fraud by believing — or pretending to believe — in his dream with him. Willy has permitted himself to feel that integrity, honesty, and fidelity are not so important as being well liked.

The play ends with Willy still unable to face the deceptions he has perpetuated. He commits suicide in the firm belief that his sons will be able to follow in his footsteps and succeed where he did not. He thinks that his insurance money will be just what they need to save the house and the family. What he does not realize is that they are no more capable than he is. They have been corrupted by his thinking, his values, his beliefs. And they cannot solve the problems that overwhelmed him.

Death of a Salesman has been given a privileged position in American drama because it is a modern tragedy. Aristotle felt that only characters of noble birth could be tragic heroes, but Miller confounds this theory, as John Millington Synge did, by showing the human integrity in even the lowliest characters. Miller's Willy Loman is not a peasant, nor is he noble in the savage way that Maurya is in *Riders to the Sea*. In fact, Miller took a frightening risk in producing a figure that we find hard to like. Willy wants to be well liked, but as an audience we find it difficult to like a person who whines, complains, and accepts petty immorality as a normal way of life. It is despite his character that we are awed by his fate.

One Chinese commentator said after the Chinese production that China is filled with such dreamers as Willy. Certainly America has been filled with them. Willy stands as an aspect of our culture, commercial and otherwise, that is at the center of our reflection of ourselves. Perhaps we react so strongly to Willy because we are afraid that we might easily become a Willy Loman if we are not vigilant about our moral views, our psychological well-being, and the limits of our commitment to success. Willy Loman has mesmerized audiences in America in many different economic circumstances: during prosperity, recession, rapid growth, and cautious development. No matter what those circumstances, we have looked at the play as if looking in a mirror. What we have seen has always involved us, although it may not always make us pleased with ourselves.

Arthur Miller (*b. 1915*)
DEATH OF A SALESMAN   1949

Characters

WILLY LOMAN   UNCLE BEN
LINDA   HOWARD WAGNER
BIFF   JENNY
HAPPY   STANLEY
BERNARD   MISS FORSYTHE
THE WOMAN   LETTA
CHARLEY

The action takes place in Willy Loman's house and yard and in various places he visits in the New York and Boston of today.

(Throughout the play, in the stage directions, left and right mean stage left and stage right.)

ACT I _____

(A melody is heard, played upon a flute. It is small and fine, telling of grass and trees and the horizon. The curtain rises.)

(Before us is the Salesman's house. We are aware of towering, angular shapes behind it, surrounding it on all sides. Only the blue light of the sky falls upon the house and forestage; the surrounding area shows an angry glow of orange. As more light appears, we see a solid vault of apartment houses around the small, fragile-seeming home. An air of the dream clings to the place, a dream rising out of reality. The kitchen at center seems actual enough, for there is a kitchen table with three chairs, and a refrigerator. But no other fixtures are seen. At the back of the kitchen there is a draped entrance, which leads to the living room. To the right of the kitchen, on a level raised two feet, is a bedroom furnished only with a brass bedstead and a straight chair. On a shelf over the bed a silver athletic trophy stands. A window opens onto the apartment house at the side.)

(Behind the kitchen, on a level raised six and a half feet, is the boys' bedroom, at present barely visible. Two beds are dimly seen, and at the back of the room a dormer window. [This bedroom is above the unseen living room.] At the left a stairway curves up to it from the kitchen.)

(The entire setting is wholly or, in some places, partially transparent. The roofline of the house is one-dimensional; under and over it we see the apartment buildings. Before the house lies an apron, curving beyond the forestage into the orchestra. This forward area serves as the back yard as well as the locale of all Willy's imaginings and of his city scenes. Whenever the action is in the present the actors observe the imaginary wall-lines, entering the house only through its door at the left. But in the scenes of the past these boundaries are broken, and characters enter or leave a room by stepping "through" a wall onto the forestage.)

(From the right, Willy Loman, the Salesman, enters, carrying two large sample cases. The flute plays on. He hears but is not aware of it. He is past sixty years of age, dressed quietly. Even as he crosses the stage to the doorway of the house, his exhaustion is apparent. He unlocks the door, comes into the kitchen, and thankfully lets his burden down, feeling the soreness of his palms. A word-sigh escapes his lips — it might be "Oh, boy, oh, boy." He closes the door, then carries his cases out into the living room, through the draped kitchen doorway.)

(Linda, his wife, has stirred in her bed at the right. She gets out and puts on a robe, listening. Most often jovial, she has developed an iron repression of her exceptions to Willy's behavior — she more than loves him, she admires him, as though his mercurial nature, his temper, his massive dreams and little cruelties, served her only as sharp reminders of the turbulent longings within him, longings which she shares but lacks the temperament to utter and follow to their end.)

LINDA (*hearing Willy outside the bedroom, calls with some trepidation*): Willy!

WILLY: It's all right. I came back.

LINDA: Why? What happened? (*Slight pause.*) Did something happen, Willy?

WILLY: No, nothing happened.

LINDA: You didn't smash the car, did you?

WILLY (*with casual irritation*): I said nothing happened. Didn't you hear me?

LINDA: Don't you feel well?

WILLY: I'm tired to the death. (*The flute has faded away. He sits on the bed beside her, a little numb.*) I couldn't make it. I just couldn't make it, Linda.

LINDA (*very carefully, delicately*): Where were you all day? You look terrible.

WILLY: I got as far as a little above Yonkers. I stopped for a cup of coffee. Maybe it was the coffee.

LINDA: What?

WILLY (*after a pause*): I suddenly couldn't drive anymore. The car kept going off onto the shoulder, y'know?

LINDA (*helpfully*): Oh. Maybe it was the steering again. I don't think Angelo knows the Studebaker.

WILLY: No, it's me, it's me. Suddenly I realize I'm goin' sixty miles an hour and I don't remember the last five minutes. I'm — I can't seem to — keep my mind to it.

LINDA: Maybe it's your glasses. You never went for your new glasses.

WILLY: No, I see everything. I came back ten miles an hour. It took me nearly four hours from Yonkers.

LINDA (*resigned*): Well, you'll just have to take a rest, Willy, you can't continue this way.

WILLY: I just got back from Florida.

LINDA: But you didn't rest your mind. Your mind is overactive, and the mind is what counts, dear.

WILLY: I'll start out in the morning. Maybe I'll feel better in the morning. (*She is taking off his shoes.*) These goddam arch supports are killing me.

LINDA: Take an aspirin. Should I get you an aspirin? It'll soothe you.

WILLY (*with wonder*): I was driving along, you understand? And I was fine. I was even observing the scenery. You can imagine, me looking at scenery, on the road every week of my life. But it's so beautiful up there, Linda, the trees are so thick, and the sun is warm. I opened the windshield and just let the warm air bathe over me. And then all of a sudden I'm goin' off the road! I'm tellin' ya, I absolutely forgot I was driving. If I'd've gone the other way over the white line I might've killed somebody. So I went on again — and five minutes later I'm dreamin' again, and I nearly — (*He presses two fingers against his eyes.*) I have such thoughts, I have such strange thoughts.

LINDA: Willy, dear. Talk to them again. There's no reason why you can't work in New York.

WILLY: They don't need me in New York. I'm the New England man. I'm vital in New England.

LINDA: But you're sixty years old. They can't expect you to keep traveling every week.

WILLY: I'll have to send a wire to Portland. I'm supposed to see Brown and Morrison tomorrow morning at ten o'clock to show the line. Goddammit, I could sell them! (*He starts putting on his jacket.*)

LINDA (*taking the jacket from him*): Why don't you go down to the place tomorrow and tell Howard you've simply got to work in New York? You're too accommodating, dear.

WILLY: If old man Wagner was alive I'd a been in charge of New York now! That man was a prince, he was a masterful man. But that boy of his, that Howard, he don't appreciate. When I went north the first time, the Wagner Company didn't know where New England was!

LINDA: Why don't you tell those things to Howard, dear?

WILLY (*encouraged*): I will, I definitely will. Is there any cheese?

LINDA: I'll make you a sandwich.

WILLY: No, go to sleep. I'll take some milk. I'll be up right away. The boys in?

LINDA: They're sleeping. Happy took Biff on a date tonight.

WILLY (*interested*): That so?

LINDA: It was so nice to see them shaving together, one behind the other, in the bathroom. And going out together. You notice? The whole house smells of shaving lotion.

WILLY: Figure it out. Work a lifetime to pay off a house. You finally own it, and there's nobody to live in it.

LINDA: Well, dear, life is a casting off. It's always that way.

WILLY: No, no, some people — some people accomplish something. Did Biff say anything after I went this morning?

LINDA: You shouldn't have criticized him, Willy, especially after he just got off the train. You mustn't lose your temper with him.

WILLY: When the hell did I lose my temper? I simply asked him if he was making any money. Is that a criticism?

LINDA: But, dear, how could he make any money?

WILLY (*worried and angered*): There's such an undercurrent in him. He became a moody man. Did he apologize when I left this morning?

LINDA: He was crestfallen, Willy. You know how he admires you. I think if he finds himself, then you'll both be happier and not fight any more.

WILLY: How can he find himself on a farm? Is that a life? A farmhand? In the beginning, when he was young, I thought, well, a young man, it's good for him to tramp around, take a lot of different jobs. But it's more than ten years now and he has yet to make thirty-five dollars a week!

LINDA: He's finding himself, Willy.

WILLY: Not finding yourself at the age of thirty-four is a disgrace!

LINDA: Shh!

WILLY: The trouble is he's lazy, goddammit!

LINDA: Willy, please!

WILLY: Biff is a lazy bum!

LINDA: They're sleeping. Get something to eat. Go on down.

WILLY: Why did he come home? I would like to know what brought him home.

LINDA: I don't know. I think he's still lost, Willy. I think he's very lost.

WILLY: Biff Loman is lost. In the greatest country in the world a young man with such — personal attractiveness, gets lost. And such a hard worker. There's one thing about Biff — he's not lazy.

LINDA: Never.

WILLY (*with pity and resolve*): I'll see him in the morning; I'll have a nice talk with him. I'll get him a job selling. He could be big in no time. My God! Remember how they used to follow him around in high school? When he smiled at one of them their faces lit up. When he walked down the street ... (*He loses himself in reminiscences.*)

LINDA (*trying to bring him out of it*): Willy, dear, I got a new kind of American-type cheese today. It's whipped.

WILLY: Why do you get American when I like Swiss?

LINDA: I just thought you'd like a change —

WILLY: I don't want a change! I want Swiss cheese. Why am I always being contradicted?

LINDA (*with a covering laugh*): I thought it would be a surprise.

WILLY: Why don't you open a window in here, for God's sake?

LINDA (*with infinite patience*): They're all open, dear.

WILLY: The way they boxed us in here. Bricks and windows, windows and bricks.

LINDA: We should've bought the land next door.

WILLY: The street is lined with cars. There's not a breath of fresh air in the neighborhood. The grass don't grow anymore, you can't raise a carrot in the back yard. They should've had a law against apartment houses. Remember those two beautiful elm trees out there? When I and Biff hung the swing between them?

LINDA: Yeah, like being a million miles from the city.

WILLY: They should've arrested the builder for cutting those down. They massacred the neighborhood. (*Lost.*) More and more I think of those days, Linda. This time of year it was lilac and wisteria. And then the peonies would come out, and the daffodils. What fragrance in this room!

LINDA: Well, after all, people had to move somewhere.

WILLY: No, there's more people now.

LINDA: I don't think there's more people. I think —

WILLY: There's more people! That's what's ruining this country! Population is getting out of control. The competition is maddening! Smell the stink from that apartment house! And another one on the other side ... How can they whip cheese?

(*On Willy's last line, Biff and Happy raise themselves up in their beds, listening.*)

LINDA: Go down, try it. And be quiet.

WILLY (*turning to Linda, guiltily*): You're not worried about me, are you, sweetheart?

BIFF: What's the matter?

HAPPY: Listen!

LINDA: You've got too much on the ball to worry about.

WILLY: You're my foundation and my support, Linda.

LINDA: Just try to relax, dear. You make mountains out of molehills.

WILLY: I won't fight with him any more. If he wants to go back to Texas, let him go.

LINDA: He'll find his way.

WILLY: Sure. Certain men just don't get started till later in life. Like Thomas Edison, I think. Or B. F. Goodrich. One of them was deaf. (*He starts for the bedroom doorway.*) I'll put my money on Biff.

LINDA: And Willy — if it's warm Sunday we'll drive in the country. And we'll open the windshield, and take lunch.

WILLY: No, the windshields don't open on the new cars.

LINDA: But you opened it today.

WILLY: Me? I didn't. (*He stops.*) Now isn't that peculiar! Isn't that a remarkable — (*He breaks off in amazement and fright as the flute is heard distantly.*)

LINDA: What, darling?

WILLY: That is the most remarkable thing.

LINDA: What, dear?

WILLY: I was thinking of the Chevvy. (*Slight pause.*) Nineteen twenty-eight ... when I had that red Chevvy — (*Breaks off.*) That funny? I coulda sworn I was driving that Chevvy today.

LINDA: Well, that's nothing. Something must've reminded you.

WILLY: Remarkable. Ts. Remember those days? The way Biff used to simonize that car? The dealer refused to believe there was eighty thousand miles on it. (*He shakes his head.*) Heh! (*To Linda.*) Close your eyes, I'll be right up. (*He walks out of the bedroom.*)

HAPPY (*to Biff*): Jesus, maybe he smashed up the car again!

LINDA (*calling after Willy*): Be careful on the stairs, dear! The cheese is on the middle shelf! (*She turns, goes over to the bed, takes his jacket, and goes out of the bedroom.*)

(*Light has risen on the boys' room. Unseen, Willy is heard talking to himself, "Eighty thousand miles," and a little laugh. Biff gets out of bed, comes downstage a bit, and stands attentively. Biff is two years older than his brother Happy, well built, but in these days bears a worn air and seems less self-assured. He has succeeded less, and his dreams are stronger and less*) *acceptable than Happy's. Happy is tall, powerfully made. Sexuality is like a visible color on him, or a scent that many women have discovered. He, like his brother, is lost, but in a different way, for he has never allowed himself to turn his face toward defeat and is thus more confused and hard-skinned, although seemingly more content.*)

HAPPY (*getting out of bed*): He's going to get his license taken away if he keeps that up. I'm getting nervous about him, y'know, Biff?

BIFF: His eyes are going.

HAPPY: No, I've driven with him. He sees all right. He just doesn't keep his mind on it. I drove into the city with him last week. He stops at a green light and then it turns red and he goes. (*He laughs.*)

BIFF: Maybe he's color-blind.

HAPPY: Pop? Why he's got the finest eye for color in the business. You know that.

BIFF (*sitting down on his bed*): I'm going to sleep.

HAPPY: You're not still sour on Dad, are you, Biff?

BIFF: He's all right, I guess.

WILLY (*underneath them, in the living room*): Yes, sir, eighty thousand miles — eighty-two thousand!

BIFF: You smoking?

HAPPY (*holding out a pack of cigarettes*): Want one?

BIFF (*taking a cigarette*): I can never sleep when I smell it.

WILLY: What a simonizing job, heh!

HAPPY (*with deep sentiment*): Funny, Biff, y'know? Us sleeping in here again? The old beds. (*He pats his bed affectionately.*) All the talk that went across those two beds, huh? Our whole lives.

BIFF: Yeah. Lotta dreams and plans.

HAPPY (*with a deep and masculine laugh*): About five hundred women would like to know what was said in this room.

(*They share a soft laugh.*)

BIFF: Remember that big Betsy something — what the hell was her name — over on Bushwick Avenue?

HAPPY (*combing his hair*): With the collie dog!

BIFF: That's the one. I got you in there, remember?

HAPPY: Yeah, that was my first time — I think. Boy, there was a pig. (*They laugh, almost crudely.*) You taught me everything I know about women. Don't forget that.

BIFF: I bet you forgot how bashful you used to be. Especially with girls.

HAPPY: Oh, I still am, Biff.

BIFF: Oh, go on.

HAPPY: I just control it, that's all. I think I got less bashful and you got more so. What happened, Biff? Where's the old humor, the old confidence? (*He shakes Biff's knee. Biff gets up and moves restlessly about the room.*) What's the matter?

BIFF: Why does Dad mock me all the time?

HAPPY: He's not mocking you, he —

BIFF: Everything I say there's a twist of mockery on his face. I can't get near him.

HAPPY: He just wants you to make good, that's all. I wanted to talk to you about Dad for a long time, Biff. Something's — happening to him. He — talks to himself.

BIFF: I noticed that this morning. But he always mumbled.

HAPPY: But not so noticeable. It got so embarrassing I sent him to Florida. And you know something? Most of the time he's talking to you.

BIFF: What's he say about me?

HAPPY: I can't make it out.

BIFF: What's he say about me?

HAPPY: I think the fact that you're not settled, that you're still kind of up in the air . . .

BIFF: There's one or two other things depressing him, Happy.

HAPPY: What do you mean?

BIFF: Never mind. Just don't lay it all to me.

HAPPY: But I think if you just got started — I mean — is there any future for you out there?

BIFF: I tell ya, Hap, I don't know what the future is. I don't know — what I'm supposed to want.

HAPPY: What do you mean?

BIFF: Well, I spent six or seven years after high school trying to work myself up. Shipping clerk, salesman, business of one kind or another. And it's a measly manner of existence. To get on that subway on the hot mornings in summer. To devote your whole life to keeping stock, or making phone calls, or selling or buying. To suffer fifty weeks of the year for the sake of a two-week vacation, when all you really desire is to be outdoors, with your shirt off. And always to have to get ahead of the next fella. And still — that's how you build a future.

HAPPY: Well, you really enjoy it on a farm? Are you content out there?

BIFF (*with rising agitation*): Hap, I've had twenty or thirty different kinds of jobs since I left home before the war, and it always turns out the same. I just realized it lately. In Nebraska when I herded cattle, and the Dakotas, and Arizona, and now in Texas. It's why I came home now, I guess, because I realized it. This farm I work on, it's spring there now, see? And they've got about fifteen new colts. There's nothing more inspiring or — beautiful than the sight of a mare and a new colt. And it's cool there now, see? Texas is cool now, and it's spring. And whenever spring comes to where I am, I suddenly get the feeling, my God, I'm not gettin' anywhere! What the hell am I doing, playing around with horses, twenty-eight dollars a week! I'm thirty-four years old, I oughta be makin' my future. That's when I come running home. And now, I get here, and I don't know what to do with myself. (*After a pause.*) I've always made a point of not wasting my life, and every time I come back here I know that all I've done is to waste my life.

HAPPY: You're a poet, you know that, Biff? You're a — you're an idealist!

BIFF: No, I'm mixed up very bad. Maybe I oughta get married. Maybe I oughta get stuck into something. Maybe that's my trouble. I'm like a boy. I'm not married, I'm not in business, I just — I'm like a boy. Are you content, Hap? You're a success, aren't you? Are you content?

HAPPY: Hell, no!

BIFF: Why? You're making money, aren't you?

HAPPY (*moving about with energy, expressiveness*): All I can do now is wait for the merchandise manager to die. And suppose I get to be merchandise manager? He's a good friend of mine, and he just built a terrific estate on Long Island. And he lived there about two months and sold it, and now he's building another one. He can't enjoy it once it's finished. And I know that's just what I would do. I don't know what the hell I'm workin' for. Sometimes I sit in my apartment — all alone. And I think of the rent I'm paying. And it's crazy. But then, it's what I always wanted. My own apartment, a car, and plenty of women. And still, goddammit, I'm lonely.

BIFF (*with enthusiasm*): Listen, why don't you come out West with me?

HAPPY: You and I, heh?

BIFF: Sure, maybe we could buy a ranch. Raise cattle, use our muscles. Men built like we are should be working out in the open.

HAPPY (*avidly*): The Loman Brothers, heh?

BIFF (*with vast affection*): Sure, we'd be known all over the counties!

HAPPY (*enthralled*): That's what I dream about, Biff. Sometimes I want to just rip my clothes off in the middle of the store and outbox that goddam merchandise manager. I mean I can outbox, outrun, and outlift anybody in that store, and I have to take orders from those common, petty sons-of-bitches till I can't stand it anymore.

BIFF: I'm tellin' you, kid, if you were with me I'd be happy out there.

HAPPY (*enthused*): See, Biff, everybody around me is so false that I'm constantly lowering my ideals . . .

BIFF: Baby, together we'd stand up for one another, we'd have someone to trust.

HAPPY: If I were around you —

BIFF: Hap, the trouble is we weren't brought up to grub for money. I don't know how to do it.

HAPPY: Neither can I!

BIFF: Then let's go!

HAPPY: The only thing is — what can you make out there?

BIFF: But look at your friend. Builds an estate and then hasn't the peace of mind to live in it.

HAPPY: Yeah, but when he walks into the store the waves part in front of him. That's fifty-two thousand dollars a year coming through the revolving door, and I got more in my pinky finger than he's got in his head.

BIFF: Yeah, but you just said —

HAPPY: I gotta show some of those pompous, self-important executives over there that Hap Loman can make the grade. I want to walk into the store the way he walks in. Then I'll go with you, Biff. We'll be together yet, I swear. But take those two we had tonight. Now weren't they gorgeous creatures?

BIFF: Yeah, yeah, most gorgeous I've had in years.

HAPPY: I get that any time I want, Biff. Whenever I feel disgusted. The only trouble is, it gets like bowling or something. I just keep knockin' them over and it doesn't mean anything. You still run around a lot?

BIFF: Naa. I'd like to find a girl — steady, somebody with substance.

HAPPY: That's what I long for.

BIFF: Go on! You'd never come home.

HAPPY: I would! Somebody with character, with re-sistance! Like Mom, y'know? You're gonna call me a bastard when I tell you this. That girl Charlotte I was with tonight is engaged to be married in five weeks. (*He tries on his new hat.*)

BIFF: No kiddin'!

HAPPY: Sure, the guy's in line for the vice-presidency of the store. I don't know what gets into me, maybe I just have an overdeveloped sense of competition or something, but I went and ruined her, and fur-thermore I can't get rid of her. And he's the third executive I've done that to. Isn't that a crummy characteristic? And to top it all, I go to their wed-dings! (*Indignantly, but laughing.*) Like I'm not supposed to take bribes. Manufacturers offer me a hundred-dollar bill now and then to throw an order their way. You know how honest I am, but it's like this girl, see. I hate myself for it. Because I don't want the girl, and, still, I take it and — I love it!

BIFF: Let's go to sleep.

HAPPY: I guess we didn't settle anything, heh?

BIFF: I just got one idea that I think I'm going to try.

HAPPY: What's that?

BIFF: Remember Bill Oliver?

HAPPY: Sure, Oliver is very big now. You want to work for him again?

BIFF: No, but when I quit he said something to me. He put his arm on my shoulder, and he said, "Biff, if you ever need anything, come to me."

HAPPY: I remember that. That sounds good.

BIFF: I think I'll go to see him. If I could get ten thousand or even seven or eight thousand dollars I could buy a beautiful ranch.

HAPPY: I bet he'd back you. 'Cause he thought highly of you, Biff. I mean, they all do. You're well liked, Biff. That's why I say to come back here, and we both have the apartment. And I'm tellin' you, Biff, any babe you want . . .

BIFF: No, with a ranch I could do the work I like and still be something. I just wonder though. I wonder if Oliver still thinks I stole that carton of basketballs.

HAPPY: Oh, he probably forgot that long ago. It's almost ten years. You're too sensitive. Anyway, he didn't really fire you.

BIFF: Well, I think he was going to. I think that's why I quit. I was never sure whether he knew or not. I know he thought the world of me, though. I was the only one he'd let lock up the place.

WILLY (*below*): You gonna wash the engine, Biff?

HAPPY: Shh!

(*Biff looks at Happy, who is gazing down, listening. Willy is mumbling in the parlor.*)

HAPPY: You hear that?

(*They listen. Willy laughs warmly.*)

BIFF (*growing angry*): Doesn't he know Mom can hear that?

WILLY: Don't get your sweater dirty, Biff!

(*A look of pain crosses Biff's face.*)

HAPPY: Isn't that terrible? Don't leave again, will you? You'll find a job here. You gotta stick around. I don't know what to do about him, it's getting embarrassing.

WILLY: What a simonizing job!

BIFF: Mom's hearing that!

WILLY: No kiddin', Biff, you got a date? Wonderful!

HAPPY: Go on to sleep. But talk to him in the morning, will you?

BIFF (*reluctantly getting into bed*): With her in the house. Brother!

HAPPY (*getting into bed*): I wish you'd have a good talk with him.

(*The light on their room begins to fade.*)

BIFF (*to himself in bed*): That selfish, stupid . . .

HAPPY: Sh . . . Sleep, Biff.

(*Their light is out. Well before they have finished speaking, Willy's form is dimly seen below in the darkened kitchen. He opens the refrigerator, searches in there, and takes out a bottle of milk. The apartment houses are fading out, and the entire house and surroundings become covered with leaves. Music insinuates itself as the leaves appear.*)

WILLY: Just wanna be careful with those girls, Biff, that's all. Don't make any promises. No promises of any kind. Because a girl, y'know, they always believe what you tell 'em, and you're very young, Biff, you're too young to be talking seriously to girls.

(*Light rises on the kitchen. Willy, talking, shuts the refrigerator door and comes downstage to the kitchen table. He pours milk into a glass. He is totally immersed in himself, smiling faintly.*)

WILLY: Too young entirely, Biff. You want to watch your schooling first. Then when you're all set, there'll be plenty of girls for a boy like you. (*He smiles broadly at a kitchen chair.*) That so? The girls pay for you? (*He laughs.*) Boy, you must really be makin' a hit.

(*Willy is gradually addressing — physically — a point offstage, speaking through the wall of the kitchen, and his voice has been rising in volume to that of a normal conversation.*)

WILLY: I been wondering why you polish the car so careful. Ha! Don't leave the hubcaps, boys. Get the chamois to the hubcaps. Happy, use newspaper on the windows, it's the easiest thing. Show him how to do it, Biff! You see, Happy? Pad it up, use it like a pad. That's it, that's it, good work. You're doin' all right, Hap. (*He pauses, then nods in approbation for a few seconds, then looks upward.*) Biff, first thing we gotta do when we get time is clip that big branch over the house. Afraid it's gonna fall in a storm and hit the roof. Tell you what. We get a rope and sling her around, and then we climb up there with a couple of saws and take her down. Soon as you finish the car, boys, I wanna see ya. I got a surprise for you, boys.

BIFF (*offstage*): Whatta ya got, Dad?

WILLY: No, you finish first. Never leave a job till you're finished — remember that. (*Looking toward the "big trees."*) Biff, up in Albany I saw a beautiful hammock. I think I'll buy it next trip, and we'll hang it right between those two elms. Wouldn't that be something? Just swingin' there under those branches. Boy, that would be . . .

(*Young Biff and Young Happy appear from the direction Willy was addressing. Happy carries rags and a pail of water. Biff, wearing a sweater with a block "S," carries a football.*)

BIFF (*pointing in the direction of the car offstage*): How's that, Pop, professional?

WILLY: Terrific. Terrific job, boys. Good work, Biff.

HAPPY: Where's the surprise, Pop?

WILLY: In the back seat of the car.

HAPPY: Boy! (*He runs off.*)

BIFF: What is it, Dad? Tell me, what'd you buy?

WILLY (*laughing, cuffs him*): Never mind, something I want you to have.

BIFF (*turns and starts off*): What is it, Hap?

HAPPY (*offstage*): It's a punching bag!

BIFF: Oh, Pop!

WILLY: It's got Gene Tunney's signature on it!

(*Happy runs onstage with a punching bag.*)

BIFF: Gee, how'd you know we wanted a punching bag?

WILLY: Well, it's the finest thing for the timing.

HAPPY (*lies down on his back and pedals with his feet*): I'm losing weight, you notice, Pop?

WILLY (*to Happy*): Jumping rope is good too.

BIFF: Did you see the new football I got?

WILLY (*examining the ball*): Where'd you get a new ball?

BIFF: The coach told me to practice my passing.

WILLY: That so? And he gave you the ball, heh?

BIFF: Well, I borrowed it from the locker room. (*He laughs confidentially.*)

WILLY (*laughing with him at the theft*): I want you to return that.

HAPPY: I told you he wouldn't like it!

BIFF (*angrily*): Well, I'm bringing it back!

WILLY (*stopping the incipient argument, to Happy*): Sure, he's gotta practice with a regulation ball, doesn't he? (*To Biff.*) Coach'll probably congratulate you on your initiative!

BIFF: Oh, he keeps congratulating my initiative all the time, Pop.

WILLY: That's because he likes you. If somebody else took that ball there'd be an uproar. So what's the report, boys, what's the report?

BIFF: Where'd you go this time, Dad? Gee we were lonesome for you.

WILLY (*pleased, puts an arm around each boy and they come down to the apron*): Lonesome, heh?

BIFF: Missed you every minute.

WILLY: Don't say? Tell you a secret, boys. Don't breathe it to a soul. Someday I'll have my own business, and I'll never have to leave home anymore.

HAPPY: Like Uncle Charley, heh?

WILLY: Bigger than Uncle Charley! Because Charley is not — liked. He's liked, but he's not — well liked.

BIFF: Where'd you go this time, Dad?

WILLY: Well, I got on the road, and I went north to Providence. Met the Mayor.

BIFF: The Mayor of Providence!

WILLY: He was sitting in the hotel lobby.

BIFF: What'd he say?

WILLY: He said, "Morning!" And I said, "You got a fine city here, Mayor." And then he had coffee with me. And then I went to Waterbury. Waterbury is a fine city. Big clock city, the famous Waterbury clock. Sold a nice bill there. And then Boston — Boston is the cradle of the Revolution. A fine city. And a couple of other towns in Mass., and on to Portland and Bangor and straight home!

BIFF: Gee, I'd love to go with you sometime, Dad.

WILLY: Soon as summer comes.

HAPPY: Promise?

WILLY: You and Hap and I, and I'll show you all the towns. America is full of beautiful towns and fine, upstanding people. And they know me, boys, they know me up and down New England. The finest people. And when I bring you fellas up, there'll be open sesame for all of us, 'cause one thing, boys: I have friends. I can park my car in any street in New England, and the cops protect it like their own. This summer, heh?

BIFF AND HAPPY (*together*): Yeah! You bet!

WILLY: We'll take our bathing suits.

HAPPY: We'll carry your bags, Pop!

WILLY: Oh, won't that be something! Me comin' into the Boston stores with you boys carryin' my bags. What a sensation!

(*Biff is prancing around, practicing passing the ball.*)

WILLY: You nervous, Biff, about the game?

BIFF: Not if you're gonna be there.

WILLY: What do they say about you in school, now that they made you captain?

HAPPY: There's a crowd of girls behind him every time the classes change.

BIFF (*taking Willy's hand*): This Saturday, Pop, this Saturday — just for you, I'm going to break through for a touchdown.

HAPPY: You're supposed to pass.

BIFF: I'm takin' one play for Pop. You watch me, Pop, and when I take off my helmet, that means I'm breakin' out. Then you watch me crash through that line!

WILLY (*kisses Biff*): Oh, wait'll I tell this in Boston!

(*Bernard enters in knickers. He is younger than Biff, earnest and loyal, a worried boy.*)

BERNARD: Biff, where are you? You're supposed to study with me today.

WILLY: Hey, looka Bernard. What're you lookin' so anemic about, Bernard?

BERNARD: He's gotta study, Uncle Willy. He's got Regents next week.

HAPPY (*tauntingly, spinning Bernard around*): Let's box, Bernard!

BERNARD: Biff! (*He gets away from Happy.*) Listen, Biff, I heard Mr. Birnbaum say that if you don't start studyin' math he's gonna flunk you, and you won't graduate. I heard him!

WILLY: You better study with him, Biff. Go ahead now.

BERNARD: I heard him!

BIFF: Oh, Pop, you didn't see my sneakers! (*He holds up a foot for Willy to look at.*)

WILLY: Hey, that's a beautiful job of printing!

BERNARD (*wiping his glasses*): Just because he printed University of Virginia on his sneakers doesn't mean they've got to graduate him, Uncle Willy!

WILLY (*angrily*): What're you talking about? With scholarships to three universities they're gonna flunk him?

BERNARD: But I heard Mr. Birnbaum say —

WILLY: Don't be a pest, Bernard! (*To his boys.*) What an anemic!

BERNARD: Okay, I'm waiting for you in my house, Biff.

(*Bernard goes off. The Lomans laugh.*)

WILLY: Bernard is not well liked, is he?

BIFF: He's liked, but he's not well liked.

HAPPY: That's right, Pop.

WILLY: That's just what I mean. Bernard can get the best marks in school, y'understand, but when he gets out in the business world, y'understand, you are going to be five times ahead of him. That's why I thank Almighty God you're both built like Adonises. Because the man who makes an appearance in the business world, the man who creates personal interest, is the man who gets ahead. Be liked and you will never want. You take me, for instance. I never have to wait in line to see a buyer. "Willy Loman is here!" That's all they have to know, and I go right through.

BIFF: Did you knock them dead, Pop?

WILLY: Knocked 'em cold in Providence, slaughtered 'em in Boston.

HAPPY (*on his back, pedaling again*): I'm losing weight, you notice, Pop?

(*Linda enters as of old, a ribbon in her hair, carrying a basket of washing.*)

LINDA (*with youthful energy*): Hello, dear!

WILLY: Sweetheart!

LINDA: How'd the Chevvy run?

WILLY: Chevrolet, Linda, is the greatest car ever built. (*To the boys.*) Since when do you let your mother carry wash up the stairs?

BIFF: Grab hold there, boy!

HAPPY: Where to, Mom?

LINDA: Hang them up on the line. And you better go down to your friends, Biff. The cellar is full of boys. They don't know what to do with themselves.

BIFF: Ah, when Pop comes home they can wait!

WILLY (*laughs appreciatively*): You better go down and tell them what to do, Biff.

BIFF: I think I'll have them sweep out the furnace room.

WILLY: Good work, Biff.

BIFF (*goes through wall-line of kitchen to doorway at back and calls down*): Fellas! Everybody sweep out the furnace room! I'll be right down!

VOICES: All right! Okay, Biff.

BIFF: George and Sam and Frank, come out back! We're hangin' up the wash! Come on, Hap, on the double! (*He and Happy carry out the basket.*)

LINDA: The way they obey him!

WILLY: Well, that's training, the training. I'm tellin' you, I was sellin' thousands and thousands, but I had to come home.

LINDA: Oh, the whole block'll be at that game. Did you sell anything?

WILLY: I did five hundred gross in Providence and seven hundred gross in Boston.

LINDA: No! Wait a minute, I've got a pencil. (*She pulls pencil and paper out of her apron pocket.*) That makes your commission . . . Two hundred — my God! Two hundred and twelve dollars!

WILLY: Well, I didn't figure it yet, but . . .

LINDA: How much did you do?

WILLY: Well, I — I did — about a hundred and eighty gross in Providence. Well, no — it came to — roughly two hundred gross on the whole trip.

LINDA (*without hesitation*): Two hundred gross. That's . . . (*She figures.*)

WILLY: The trouble was that three of the stores were half-closed for inventory in Boston. Otherwise I woulda broke records.

LINDA: Well, it makes seventy dollars and some pennies. That's very good.

WILLY: What do we owe?

LINDA: Well, on the first there's sixteen dollars on the refrigerator —

WILLY: Why sixteen?

LINDA: Well, the fan belt broke, so it was a dollar eighty.

WILLY: But it's brand new.

LINDA: Well, the man said that's the way it is. Till they work themselves in, y'know.

(*They move through the wall-line into the kitchen.*)

WILLY: I hope we didn't get stuck on that machine.

LINDA: They got the biggest ads of any of them!

WILLY: I know, it's a fine machine. What else?

LINDA: Well, there's nine-sixty for the washing machine. And for the vacuum cleaner there's three and a half due on the fifteenth. Then the roof, you got twenty-one dollars remaining.

WILLY: It don't leak, does it?

LINDA: No, they did a wonderful job. Then you owe Frank for the carburetor.

WILLY: I'm not going to pay that man! That goddam Chevrolet, they ought to prohibit the manufacture of that car!

LINDA: Well, you owe him three and a half. And odds and ends, comes to around a hundred and twenty dollars by the fifteenth.

WILLY: A hundred and twenty dollars! My God, if business don't pick up I don't know what I'm gonna do!

LINDA: Well, next week you'll do better.

WILLY: Oh, I'll knock 'em dead next week. I'll go to Hartford. I'm very well liked in Hartford. You know, the trouble is, Linda, people don't seem to take to me.

(*They move onto the forestage.*)

LINDA: Oh, don't be foolish.

WILLY: I know it when I walk in. They seem to laugh at me.

LINDA: Why? Why would they laugh at you? Don't talk that way, Willy.

(*Willy moves to the edge of the stage. Linda goes into the kitchen and starts to darn stockings.*)

WILLY: I don't know the reason for it, but they just pass me by. I'm not noticed.

LINDA: But you're doing wonderful, dear. You're making seventy to a hundred dollars a week.

WILLY: But I gotta be at it ten, twelve hours a day. Other men — I don't know — they do it easier. I don't know why — I can't stop myself — I talk too much. A man oughta come in with a few words. One thing about Charley. He's a man of few words, and they respect him.

LINDA: You don't talk too much, you're just lively.

WILLY (*smiling*): Well, I figure, what the hell, life is short, a couple of jokes. (*To himself.*) I joke too much! (*The smile goes.*)

LINDA: Why? You're —

WILLY: I'm fat. I'm very — foolish to look at, Linda.

I didn't tell you, but Christmas time I happened to be calling on F. H. Stewarts, and a salesman I know, as I was going in to see the buyer I heard him say something about — walrus. And I — I cracked him right across the face. I won't take that. I simply will not take that. But they do laugh at me. I know that.

LINDA: Darling . . .

WILLY: I gotta overcome it. I know I gotta overcome it. I'm not dressing to advantage, maybe.

LINDA: Willy, darling, you're the handsomest man in the world —

WILLY: Oh, no, Linda.

LINDA: To me you are. (*Slight pause.*) The handsomest.

(*From the darkness is heard the laughter of a woman. Willy doesn't turn to it, but it continues through Linda's lines.*)

LINDA: And the boys, Willy. Few men are idolized by their children the way you are.

(*Music is heard as behind a scrim, to the left of the house, The Woman, dimly seen, is dressing.*)

WILLY (*with great feeling*): You're the best there is, Linda, you're a pal, you know that? On the road — on the road I want to grab you sometimes and just kiss the life outa you.

(*The laughter is loud now, and he moves into a brightening area at the left, where The Woman has come from behind the scrim and is standing, putting on her hat, looking into a "mirror" and laughing.*)

WILLY: 'Cause I get so lonely — especially when business is bad and there's nobody to talk to. I get the feeling that I'll never sell anything again, that I won't make a living for you, or a business, a business for the boys. (*He talks through The Woman's subsiding laughter; The Woman primps at the "mirror."*) There's so much I want to make for —

THE WOMAN: Me? You didn't make me, Willy. I picked you.

WILLY (*pleased*): You picked me?

THE WOMAN (*who is quite proper-looking, Willy's age*): I did. I've been sitting at that desk watching all the salesmen go by, day in, day out. But you've got such a sense of humor, and we do have such a good time together, don't we?

WILLY: Sure, sure. (*He takes her in his arms.*) Why do you have to go now?

THE WOMAN: It's two o'clock . . .

WILLY: No, come on in! (*He pulls her.*)

THE WOMAN: . . . my sisters'll be scandalized. When'll you be back?

WILLY: Oh, two weeks about. Will you come up again?

THE WOMAN: Sure thing. You do make me laugh. It's good for me. (*She squeezes his arm, kisses him.*) And I think you're a wonderful man.

WILLY: You picked me, heh?

THE WOMAN: Sure. Because you're so sweet. And such a kidder.

WILLY: Well, I'll see you next time I'm in Boston.

THE WOMAN: I'll put you right through to the buyers.

WILLY (*slapping her bottom*): Right. Well, bottoms up!

THE WOMAN (*slaps him gently and laughs*): You just kill me, Willy. (*He suddenly grabs her and kisses her roughly.*) You kill me. And thanks for the stockings. I love a lot of stockings. Well, good night.

WILLY: Good night. And keep your pores open!

THE WOMAN: Oh, Willy!

(*The Woman bursts out laughing, and Linda's laughter blends in. The Woman disappears into the dark. Now the area at the kitchen table brightens. Linda is sitting where she was at the kitchen table, but now is mending a pair of her silk stockings.*)

LINDA: You are, Willy. The handsomest man. You've got no reason to feel that —

WILLY (*coming out of The Woman's dimming area and going over to Linda*): I'll make it all up to you, Linda, I'll —

LINDA: There's nothing to make up, dear. You're doing fine, better than —

WILLY (*noticing her mending*): What's that?

LINDA: Just mending my stockings. They're so expensive —

WILLY (*angrily, taking them from her*): I won't have you mending stockings in this house! Now throw them out!

(*Linda puts the stockings in her pocket.*)

BERNARD (*entering on the run*): Where is he? If he doesn't study!

WILLY (*moving to the forestage, with great agitation*): You'll give him the answers!

BERNARD: I do, but I can't on a Regents! That's a state exam! They're liable to arrest me!

WILLY: Where is he? I'll whip him, I'll whip him!

LINDA: And he'd better give back that football, Willy, it's not nice.

WILLY: Biff! Where is he? Why is he taking everything?

LINDA: He's too rough with the girls, Willy. All the mothers are afraid of him!

WILLY: I'll whip him!

BERNARD: He's driving the car without a license!

(*The Woman's laugh is heard.*)

WILLY: Shut up!

LINDA: All the mothers —

WILLY: Shut up!

BERNARD (*backing quietly away and out*): Mr. Birnbaum says he's stuck up.

WILLY: Get outa here!

BERNARD: If he doesn't buckle down he'll flunk math! (*He goes off.*)

LINDA: He's right, Willy, you've gotta —

WILLY (*exploding at her*): There's nothing the matter with him! You want him to be a worm like Bernard? He's got spirit, personality . . .

(*As he speaks, Linda, almost in tears, exits into the living room. Willy is alone in the kitchen, wilting and staring. The leaves are gone. It is night again, and the apartment houses look down from behind.*)

WILLY: Loaded with it. Loaded! What is he stealing? He's giving it back, isn't he? Why is he stealing? What did I tell him? I never in my life told him anything but decent things.

(*Happy in pajamas has come down the stairs; Willy suddenly becomes aware of Happy's presence.*)

HAPPY: Let's go now, come on.

WILLY (*sitting down at the kitchen table*): Huh! Why did she have to wax the floors herself? Everytime she waxes the floors she keels over. She knows that!

HAPPY: Shh! Take it easy. What brought you back tonight?

WILLY: I got an awful scare. Nearly hit a kid in Yonkers. God! Why didn't I go to Alaska with my brother Ben that time! Ben! That man was a genius, that man was success incarnate! What a mistake! He begged me to go.

HAPPY: Well, there's no use in —

WILLY: You guys! There was a man started with the clothes on his back and ended up with diamond mines!

HAPPY: Boy, someday I'd like to know how he did it.

WILLY: What's the mystery? The man knew what he wanted and went out and got it! Walked into a jungle, and comes out, the age of twenty-one, and he's rich! The world is an oyster, but you don't crack it open on a mattress!

HAPPY: Pop, I told you I'm gonna retire you for life.

WILLY: You'll retire me for life on seventy goddam dollars a week? And your women and your car and your apartment, and you'll retire me for life! Christ's sake, I couldn't get past Yonkers today! Where are you guys, where are you? The woods are burning! I can't drive a car!

(*Charley has appeared in the doorway. He is a large man, slow of speech, laconic, immovable. In all he says, despite what he says, there is pity, and, now, trepidation. He has a robe over pajamas, slippers on his feet. He enters the kitchen.*)

CHARLEY: Everything all right?
HAPPY: Yeah, Charley, everything's . . .
WILLY: What's the matter?
CHARLEY: I heard some noise. I thought something happened. Can't we do something about the walls? You sneeze in here, and in my house hats blow off.
HAPPY: Let's go to bed, Dad. Come on.

(*Charley signals to Happy to go.*)

WILLY: You go ahead, I'm not tired at the moment.
HAPPY (*to Willy*): Take it easy, huh? (*He exits.*)
WILLY: What're you doin' up?
CHARLEY (*sitting down at the kitchen table opposite Willy*): Couldn't sleep good. I had a heartburn.
WILLY: Well, you don't know how to eat.
CHARLEY: I eat with my mouth.
WILLY: No, you're ignorant. You gotta know about vitamins and things like that.
CHARLEY: Come on, let's shoot. Tire you out a little.
WILLY (*hesitantly*): All right. You got cards?
CHARLEY (*taking a deck from his pocket*): Yeah, I got them. Someplace. What is it with those vitamins?
WILLY (*dealing*): They build up your bones. Chemistry.
CHARLEY: Yeah, but there's no bones in a heartburn.
WILLY: What are you talkin' about? Do you know the first thing about it?
CHARLEY: Don't get insulted.
WILLY: Don't talk about something you don't know anything about.

(*They are playing. Pause.*)

CHARLEY: What're you doin' home?
WILLY: A little trouble with the car.
CHARLEY: Oh. (*Pause.*) I'd like to take a trip to California.
WILLY: Don't say.
CHARLEY: You want a job?
WILLY: I got a job, I told you that. (*After a slight pause.*) What the hell are you offering me a job for?
CHARLEY: Don't get insulted.
WILLY: Don't insult me.
CHARLEY: I don't see no sense in it. You don't have to go on this way.
WILLY: I got a good job. (*Slight pause.*) What do you keep comin' in here for?
CHARLEY: You want me to go?
WILLY (*after a pause, withering*): I can't understand it. He's going back to Texas again. What the hell is that?
CHARLEY: Let him go.
WILLY: I got nothin' to give him, Charley, I'm clean, I'm clean.
CHARLEY: He won't starve. None a them starve. Forget about him.
WILLY: Then what have I got to remember?
CHARLEY: You take it too hard. To hell with it. When a deposit bottle is broken you don't get your nickel back.
WILLY: That's easy enough for you to say.
CHARLEY: That ain't easy for me to say.
WILLY: Did you see the ceiling I put up in the living room?
CHARLEY: Yeah, that's a piece of work. To put up a ceiling is a mystery to me. How do you do it?
WILLY: What's the difference?
CHARLEY: Well, talk about it.
WILLY: You gonna put up a ceiling?
CHARLEY: How could I put up a ceiling?
WILLY: Then what the hell are you bothering me for?
CHARLEY: You're insulted again.
WILLY: A man who can't handle tools is not a man. You're disgusting.
CHARLEY: Don't call me disgusting, Willy.

(*Uncle Ben, carrying a valise and an umbrella, enters the forestage from around the right corner of the house. He is a stolid man, in his sixties, with a mustache and an authoritative air. He is utterly certain of his destiny, and there is an aura of far places about him. He enters exactly as Willy speaks.*)

WILLY: I'm getting awfully tired, Ben.

(*Ben's music is heard. Ben looks around at everything.*)

CHARLEY: Good, keep playing; you'll sleep better. Did you call me Ben?

(*Ben looks at his watch.*)

WILLY: That's funny. For a second there you reminded me of my brother Ben.
BEN: I only have a few minutes. (*He strolls, inspecting the place. Willy and Charley continue playing.*)
CHARLEY: You never heard from him again, heh? Since that time?
WILLY: Didn't Linda tell you? Couple of weeks ago we got a letter from his wife in Africa. He died.
CHARLEY: That so.
BEN (*chuckling*): So this is Brooklyn, eh?
CHARLEY: Maybe you're in for some of his money.
WILLY: Naa, he had seven sons. There's just one opportunity I had with that man . . .
BEN: I must make a train, William. There are several properties I'm looking at in Alaska.

WILLY: Sure, sure! If I'd gone with him to Alaska that time, everything would've been totally different.

CHARLEY: Go on, you'd froze to death up there.

WILLY: What're you talking about?

BEN: Opportunity is tremendous in Alaska, William. Surprised you're not up there.

WILLY: Sure, tremendous.

CHARLEY: Heh?

WILLY: There was the only man I ever met who knew the answers.

CHARLEY: Who?

BEN: How are you all?

WILLY (*taking a pot, smiling*): Fine, fine.

CHARLEY: Pretty sharp tonight.

BEN: Is Mother living with you?

WILLY: No, she died a long time ago.

CHARLEY: Who?

BEN: That's too bad. Fine specimen of a lady, Mother.

WILLY (*to Charley*): Heh?

BEN: I'd hoped to see the old girl.

CHARLEY: Who died?

BEN: Heard anything from Father, have you?

WILLY (*unnerved*): What do you mean, who died?

CHARLEY (*taking a pot*): What're you talkin' about?

BEN (*looking at his watch*): William, it's half-past eight!

WILLY (*as though to dispel his confusion he angrily stops Charley's hand*): That's my build!

CHARLEY: I put the ace —

WILLY: If you don't know how to play the game I'm not gonna throw my money away on you!

CHARLEY (*rising*): It was my ace, for God's sake!

WILLY: I'm through, I'm through!

BEN: When did Mother die?

WILLY: Long ago. Since the beginning you never knew how to play cards.

CHARLEY (*picks up the cards and goes to the door*): All right! Next time I'll bring a deck with five aces.

WILLY: I don't play that kind of game!

CHARLEY (*turning to him*): You ought to be ashamed of yourself!

WILLY: Yeah?

CHARLEY: Yeah! (*He goes out.*)

WILLY (*slamming the door after him*): Ignoramus!

BEN (*as Willy comes toward him through the wall-line of the kitchen*): So you're William.

WILLY (*shaking Ben's hand*): Ben! I've been waiting for you so long! What's the answer? How did you do it?

BEN: Oh, there's a story in that.

(*Linda enters the forestage, as of old, carrying the wash basket.*)

LINDA: Is this Ben?

BEN (*gallantly*): How do you do, my dear.

LINDA: Where've you been all these years? Willy's always wondered why you —

WILLY (*pulling Ben away from her impatiently*): Where is Dad? Didn't you follow him? How did you get started?

BEN: Well, I don't know how much you remember.

WILLY: Well, I was just a baby, of course, only three or four years old —

BEN: Three years and eleven months.

WILLY: What a memory, Ben!

BEN: I have many enterprises, William, and I have never kept books.

WILLY: I remember I was sitting under the wagon in — was it Nebraska?

BEN: It was South Dakota, and I gave you a bunch of wild flowers.

WILLY: I remember you walking away down some open road.

BEN (*laughing*): I was going to find Father in Alaska.

WILLY: Where is he?

BEN: At that age I had a very faulty view of geography, William. I discovered after a few days that I was heading due south, so instead of Alaska, I ended up in Africa.

LINDA: Africa!

WILLY: The Gold Coast!

BEN: Principally diamond mines.

LINDA: Diamond mines!

BEN: Yes, my dear. But I've only a few minutes —

WILLY: No! Boys! Boys! (*Young Biff and Happy appear.*) Listen to this. This is your Uncle Ben, a great man! Tell my boys, Ben!

BEN: Why, boys, when I was seventeen I walked into the jungle, and when I was twenty-one I walked out. (*He laughs.*) And by God I was rich.

WILLY (*to the boys*): You see what I been talking about? The greatest things can happen!

BEN (*glancing at his watch*): I have an appointment in Ketchikan Tuesday week.

WILLY: No, Ben! Please tell about Dad. I want my boys to hear. I want them to know the kind of stock they spring from. All I remember is a man with a big beard, and I was in Mamma's lap, sitting around a fire, and some kind of high music.

BEN: His flute. He played the flute.

WILLY: Sure, the flute, that's right!

(*New music is heard, a high, rollicking tune.*)

BEN: Father was a very great and a very wild-hearted man. We would start in Boston, and he'd toss the whole family into the wagon, and then he'd drive the team right across the country; through Ohio, and Indiana, Michigan, Illinois, and all the Western states. And we'd stop in the towns and sell the flutes that he'd made on the way. Great inventor,

Father. With one gadget he made more in a week than a man like you could make in a lifetime.

WILLY: That's just the way I'm bringing them up, Ben — rugged, well liked, all-around.

BEN: Yeah? (*To Biff.*) Hit that, boy — hard as you can. (*He pounds his stomach.*)

BIFF: Oh, no, sir!

BEN (*taking boxing stance*): Come on, get to me! (*He laughs.*)

WILLY: Go to it, Biff! Go ahead, show him!

BIFF: Okay! (*He cocks his fists and starts in.*)

LINDA (*to Willy*): Why must he fight, dear?

BEN (*sparring with Biff*): Good boy! Good boy!

WILLY: How's that, Ben, heh?

HAPPY: Give him the left, Biff!

LINDA: Why are you fighting?

BEN: Good boy! (*Suddenly comes in, trips Biff, and stands over him, the point of his umbrella poised over Biff's eye.*)

LINDA: Look out, Biff!

BIFF: Gee!

BEN (*patting Biff's knee*): Never fight fair with a stranger, boy. You'll never get out of the jungle that way. (*Taking Linda's hand and bowing.*) It was an honor and a pleasure to meet you, Linda.

LINDA (*withdrawing her hand coldly, frightened*): Have a nice — trip.

BEN (*to Willy*): And good luck with your — what do you do?

WILLY: Selling.

BEN: Yes. Well . . . (*He raises his hand in farewell to all.*)

WILLY: No, Ben, I don't want you to think . . . (*He takes Ben's arm to show him.*) It's Brooklyn, I know, but we hunt too.

BEN: Really, now.

WILLY: Oh, sure, there's snakes and rabbits and — that's why I moved out here. Why, Biff can fell any one of these trees in no time! Boys! Go right over to where they're building the apartment house and get some sand. We're gonna rebuild the entire front stoop right now! Watch this, Ben!

BIFF: Yes, sir! On the double, Hap!

HAPPY (*as he and Biff run off*): I lost weight, Pop, you notice?

(*Charley enters in knickers, even before the boys are gone.*)

CHARLEY: Listen, if they steal any more from that building the watchman'll put the cops on them!

LINDA (*to Willy*): Don't let Biff . . .

(*Ben laughs lustily.*)

WILLY: You shoulda seen the lumber they brought home last week. At least a dozen six-by-tens worth all kinds a money.

CHARLEY: Listen, if that watchman —

WILLY: I gave them hell, understand. But I got a couple of fearless characters there.

CHARLEY: Willy, the jails are full of fearless characters.

BEN (*clapping Willy on the back, with a laugh at Charley*): And the stock exchange, friend!

WILLY (*joining in Ben's laughter*): Where are the rest of your pants?

CHARLEY: My wife bought them.

WILLY: Now all you need is a golf club and you can go upstairs and go to sleep. (*To Ben.*) Great athlete! Between him and his son Bernard they can't hammer a nail!

BERNARD (*rushing in*): The watchman's chasing Biff!

WILLY (*angrily*): Shut up! He's not stealing anything!

LINDA (*alarmed, hurrying off left*): Where is he? Biff, dear! (*She exits.*)

WILLY (*moving toward the left, away from Ben*): There's nothing wrong. What's the matter with you?

BEN: Nervy boy. Good!

WILLY (*laughing*): Oh, nerves of iron, that Biff!

CHARLEY: Don't know what it is. My New England man comes back and he's bleedin', they murdered him up there.

WILLY: It's contacts, Charley, I got important contacts!

CHARLEY (*sarcastically*): Glad to hear it, Willy. Come in later, we'll shoot a little casino. I'll take some of your Portland money. (*He laughs at Willy and exits.*)

WILLY (*turning to Ben*): Business is bad, it's murderous. But not for me, of course.

BEN: I'll stop by on my way back to Africa.

WILLY (*longingly*): Can't you stay a few days? You're just what I need, Ben, because I — I have a fine position here, but I — well, Dad left when I was such a baby and I never had a chance to talk to him and I still feel — kind of temporary about myself.

BEN: I'll be late for my train.

(*They are at opposite ends of the stage.*)

WILLY: Ben, my boys — can't we talk? They'd go into the jaws of hell for me, see, but I —

BEN: William, you're being first-rate with your boys. Outstanding, manly chaps!

WILLY (*hanging on to his words*): Oh, Ben, that's good to hear! Because sometimes I'm afraid that I'm not teaching them the right kind of — Ben, how should I teach them?

BEN (*giving great weight to each word, and with a certain vicious audacity*): William, when I walked into the jungle, I was seventeen. When I walked out I was twenty-one. And, by God, I was rich! (*He goes off into darkness around the right corner of the house.*)

WILLY: . . . was rich! That's just the spirit I want to imbue them with! To walk into a jungle! I was right! I was right! I was right!

(*Ben is gone, but Willy is still speaking to him as Linda, in nightgown and robe, enters the kitchen, glances around for Willy, then goes to the door of the house, looks out and sees him. Comes down to his left. He looks at her.*)

LINDA: Willy, dear? Willy?

WILLY: I was right!

LINDA: Did you have some cheese? (*He can't answer.*) It's very late, darling. Come to bed, heh?

WILLY (*looking straight up*): Gotta break your neck to see a star in this yard.

LINDA: You coming in?

WILLY: Whatever happened to that diamond watch fob? Remember? When Ben came from Africa that time? Didn't he give me a watch fob with a diamond in it?

LINDA: You pawned it, dear. Twelve, thirteen years ago. For Biff's radio correspondence course.

WILLY: Gee, that was a beautiful thing. I'll take a walk.

LINDA: But you're in your slippers.

WILLY (*starting to go around the house at the left*): I was right! I was! (*Half to Linda, as he goes, shaking his head.*) What a man! There was a man worth talking to. I was right!

LINDA (*calling after Willy*): But in your slippers, Willy!

(*Willy is almost gone when Biff, in his pajamas, comes down the stairs and enters the kitchen.*)

BIFF: What is he doing out there?

LINDA: Sh!

BIFF: God Almighty, Mom, how long has he been doing this?

LINDA: Don't, he'll hear you.

BIFF: What the hell is the matter with him?

LINDA: It'll pass by morning.

BIFF: Shouldn't we do anything?

LINDA: Oh, my dear, you should do a lot of things, but there's nothing to do, so go to sleep.

(*Happy comes down the stair and sits on the steps.*)

HAPPY: I never heard him so loud, Mom.

LINDA: Well, come around more often; you'll hear him. (*She sits down at the table and mends the lining of Willy's jacket.*)

BIFF: Why didn't you ever write me about this, Mom?

LINDA: How would I write to you? For over three months you had no address.

BIFF: I was on the move. But you know I thought of you all the time. You know that, don't you, pal?

LINDA: I know, dear, I know. But he likes to have a letter. Just to know that there's still a possibility for better things.

BIFF: He's not like this all the time, is he?

LINDA: It's when you come home he's always the worst.

BIFF: When I come home?

LINDA: When you write you're coming, he's all smiles, and talks about the future, and — he's just wonderful. And then the closer you seem to come, the more shaky he gets, and then, by the time you get here, he's arguing, and he seems angry at you. I think it's just that maybe he can't bring himself to — to open up to you. Why are you so hateful to each other? Why is that?

BIFF (*evasively*): I'm not hateful, Mom.

LINDA: But you no sooner come in the door than you're fighting!

BIFF: I don't know why. I mean to change. I'm tryin', Mom, you understand?

LINDA: Are you home to stay now?

BIFF: I don't know. I want to look around, see what's doin'.

LINDA: Biff, you can't look around all your life, can you?

BIFF: I just can't take hold, Mom. I can't take hold of some kind of a life.

LINDA: Biff, a man is not a bird, to come and go with the springtime.

BIFF: Your hair . . . (*He touches her hair.*) Your hair got so gray.

LINDA: Oh, it's been gray since you were in high school. I just stopped dyeing it, that's all.

BIFF: Dye it again, will ya? I don't want my pal looking old. (*He smiles.*)

LINDA: You're such a boy! You think you can go away for a year and . . . You've got to get it into your head now that one day you'll knock on this door and there'll be strange people here —

BIFF: What are you talking about? You're not even sixty, Mom.

LINDA: But what about your father?

BIFF (*lamely*): Well, I meant him too.

HAPPY: He admires Pop.

LINDA: Biff, dear, if you don't have any feeling for him, then you can't have any feeling for me.

BIFF: Sure I can, Mom.

LINDA: No. You can't just come to see me, because I love him. (*With a threat, but only a threat, of tears.*) He's the dearest man in the world to me, and I won't have anyone making him feel unwanted and low and blue. You've got to make up your mind now, darling, there's no leeway any more. Either he's your father and you pay him that respect, or else you're not to come here. I know he's not easy to get along with — nobody knows that better than me — but . . .

WILLY (*from the left, with a laugh*): Hey, hey, Biffo!

BIFF (*starting to go out after Willy*): What the hell is the matter with him? (*Happy stops him.*)

LINDA: Don't — don't go near him!

BIFF: Stop making excuses for him! He always, always wiped the floor with you. Never had an ounce of respect for you.

HAPPY: He's always had respect for —

BIFF: What the hell do you know about it?

HAPPY (*surlily*): Just don't call him crazy!

BIFF: He's got no character — Charley wouldn't do this. Not in his own house — spewing out that vomit from his mind.

HAPPY: Charley never had to cope with what he's got to.

BIFF: People are worse off than Willy Loman. Believe me, I've seen them!

LINDA: Then make Charley your father, Biff. You can't do that, can you? I don't say he's a great man. Willy Loman never made a lot of money. His name was never in the paper. He's not the finest character that ever lived. But he's a human being, and a terrible thing is happening to him. So attention must be paid. He's not to be allowed to fall into his grave like an old dog. Attention, attention must be finally paid to such a person. You called him crazy —

BIFF: I didn't mean —

LINDA: No, a lot of people think he's lost his — balance. But you don't have to be very smart to know what his trouble is. The man is exhausted.

HAPPY: Sure!

LINDA: A small man can be just as exhausted as a great man. He works for a company thirty-six years this March, opens up unheard-of territories to their trademark, and now in his old age they take his salary away.

HAPPY (*indignantly*): I didn't know that, Mom.

LINDA: You never asked, my dear! Now that you get your spending money someplace else you don't trouble your mind with him.

HAPPY: But I gave you money last —

LINDA: Christmas time, fifty dollars! To fix the hot water it cost ninety-seven fifty! For five weeks he's been on straight commission, like a beginner, an unknown!

BIFF: Those ungrateful bastards!

LINDA: Are they any worse than his sons? When he brought them business, when he was young, they were glad to see him. But now his old friends, the old buyers that loved him so and always found some order to hand him in a pinch — they're all dead, retired. He used to be able to make six, seven calls a day in Boston. Now he takes his valises out of the car and puts them back and takes them out again and he's exhausted. Instead of walking he talks now. He drives seven hundred miles, and when he gets there no one knows him anymore, no one welcomes him. And what goes through a man's mind, driving seven hundred miles home without having earned a cent? Why shouldn't he talk to himself? Why? When he has to go to Charley and borrow fifty dollars a week and pretend to me that it's his pay? How long can that go on? How long? You see what I'm sitting here and waiting for? And you tell me he has no character? The man who never worked a day but for your benefit? When does he get the medal for that? Is this his reward — to turn around at the age of sixty-three and find his sons, who he loved better than his life, one a philandering bum —

HAPPY: Mom!

LINDA: That's all you are, my baby! (*To Biff.*) And you! What happened to the love you had for him? You were such pals! How you used to talk to him on the phone every night! How lonely he was till he could come home to you!

BIFF: All right, Mom. I'll live here in my room, and I'll get a job. I'll keep away from him, that's all.

LINDA: No, Biff. You can't stay here and fight all the time.

BIFF: He threw me out of this house, remember that.

LINDA: Why did he do that? I never knew why.

BIFF: Because I know he's a fake and he doesn't like anybody around who knows!

LINDA: Why a fake? In what way? What do you mean?

BIFF: Just don't lay it all at my feet. It's between me and him — that's all I have to say. I'll chip in from now on. He'll settle for half my pay check. He'll be all right. I'm going to bed. (*He starts for the stairs.*)

LINDA: He won't be all right.

BIFF (*turning on the stairs, furiously*): I hate this city and I'll stay here. Now what do you want?

LINDA: He's dying, Biff.

(*Happy turns quickly to her, shocked.*)

BIFF (*after a pause*): Why is he dying?

LINDA: He's been trying to kill himself.

BIFF (*with great horror*): How?

LINDA: I live from day to day.

BIFF: What're you talking about?

LINDA: Remember I wrote you that he smashed up the car again? In February?

BIFF: Well?

LINDA: The insurance inspector came. He said that they have evidence. That all these accidents in the last year — weren't — weren't — accidents.

HAPPY: How can they tell that? That's a lie.

LINDA: It seems there's a woman . . . (*She takes a breath as*)

BIFF (*sharply but contained*): ⎱What woman?
LINDA (*simultaneously*):   ⎰ . . . and this woman . . .

LINDA: What?

BIFF: Nothing. Go ahead.

LINDA: What did you say?

BIFF: Nothing. I just said what woman?

HAPPY: What about her?

LINDA: Well, it seems she was walking down the road and saw his car. She says that he wasn't driving fast at all, and that he didn't skid. She says he came to that little bridge, and then deliberately smashed into the railing, and it was only the shallowness of the water that saved him.

BIFF: Oh, no, he probably just fell asleep again.

LINDA: I don't think he fell asleep.

BIFF: Why not?

LINDA: Last month . . . (*With great difficulty.*) Oh, boys, it's so hard to say a thing like this! He's just a big stupid man to you, but I tell you there's more good in him than in many other people. (*She chokes, wipes her eyes.*) I was looking for a fuse. The lights blew out, and I went down the cellar. And behind the fuse box — it happened to fall out — was a length of rubber pipe — just short.

HAPPY: No kidding!

LINDA: There's a little attachment on the end of it. I knew right away. And sure enough, on the bottom of the water heater there's a new little nipple on the gas pipe.

HAPPY (*angrily*): That — jerk.

BIFF: Did you have it taken off?

LINDA: I'm — I'm ashamed to. How can I mention it to him? Every day I go down and take away that little rubber pipe. But, when he comes home, I put it back where it was. How can I insult him that way? I don't know what to do. I live from day to day, boys. I tell you, I know every thought in his mind. It sounds so old-fashioned and silly, but I tell you he put his whole life into you and you've turned your backs on him. (*She is bent over in the chair, weeping, her face in her hands.*) Biff, I swear to God! Biff, his life is in your hands!

HAPPY (*to Biff*): How do you like that damned fool!

BIFF (*kissing her*): All right, pal, all right. It's all settled

now. I've been remiss. I know that, Mom. But now I'll stay, and I swear to you, I'll apply myself. (*Kneeling in front of her, in a fever of self-reproach.*) It's just — you see, Mom, I don't fit in business. Not that I won't try. I'll try, and I'll make good.

HAPPY: Sure you will. The trouble with you in business was you never tried to please people.

BIFF: I know, I —

HAPPY: Like when you worked for Harrison's. Bob Harrison said you were tops, and then you go and do some damn fool thing like whistling whole songs in the elevator like a comedian.

BIFF (*against Happy*): So what? I like to whistle sometimes.

HAPPY: You don't raise a guy to a responsible job who whistles in the elevator!

LINDA: Well, don't argue about it now.

HAPPY: Like when you'd go off and swim in the middle of the day instead of taking the line around.

BIFF (*his resentment rising*): Well, don't you run off? You take off sometimes, don't you? On a nice summer day?

HAPPY: Yeah, but I cover myself!

LINDA: Boys!

HAPPY: If I'm going to take a fade the boss can call any number where I'm supposed to be and they'll swear to him that I just left. I'll tell you something that I hate to say, Biff, but in the business world some of them think you're crazy.

BIFF (*angered*): Screw the business world!

HAPPY: All right, screw it! Great, but cover yourself!

LINDA: Hap, Hap!

BIFF: I don't care what they think! They've laughed at Dad for years, and you know why? Because we don't belong in this nuthouse of a city! We should be mixing cement on some open plain, or — or carpenters. A carpenter is allowed to whistle!

(*Willy walks in from the entrance of the house, at left.*)

WILLY: Even your grandfather was better than a carpenter. (*Pause. They watch him.*) You never grew up. Bernard does not whistle in the elevator, I assure you.

BIFF (*as though to laugh Willy out of it*): Yeah, but you do, Pop.

WILLY: I never in my life whistled in an elevator! And who in the business world thinks I'm crazy?

BIFF: I didn't mean it like that, Pop. Now don't make a whole thing out of it, will ya?

WILLY: Go back to the West! Be a carpenter, a cowboy, enjoy yourself!

LINDA: Willy, he was just saying —

WILLY: I heard what he said!

HAPPY (*trying to quiet Willy*): Hey, Pop, come on now . . .

WILLY (*continuing over Happy's line*): They laugh at me, heh? Go to Filene's, go to the Hub, go to Slattery's, Boston. Call out the name Willy Loman and see what happens! Big shot!

BIFF: All right, Pop.

WILLY: Big!

BIFF: All right!

WILLY: Why do you always insult me?

BIFF: I didn't say a word. (*To Linda.*) Did I say a word?

LINDA: He didn't say anything, Willy.

WILLY (*going to the doorway of the living room*): All right, good night, good night.

LINDA: Willy, dear, he just decided . . .

WILLY (*to Biff*): If you get tired hanging around tomorrow, paint the ceiling I put up in the living room.

BIFF: I'm leaving early tomorrow.

HAPPY: He's going to see Bill Oliver, Pop.

WILLY (*interestedly*): Oliver? For what?

BIFF (*with reserve, but trying, trying*): He always said he'd stake me. I'd like to go into business, so maybe I can take him up on it.

LINDA: Isn't that wonderful?

WILLY: Don't interrupt. What's wonderful about it? There's fifty men in the City of New York who'd stake him. (*To Biff.*) Sporting goods?

BIFF: I guess so. I know something about it and —

WILLY: He knows something about it! You know sporting goods better than Spalding, for God's sake! How much is he giving you?

BIFF: I don't know, I didn't even see him yet, but —

WILLY: Then what're you talkin' about?

BIFF (*getting angry*): Well, all I said was I'm gonna see him, that's all!

WILLY (*turning away*): Ah, you're counting your chickens again.

BIFF (*starting left for the stairs*): Oh, Jesus, I'm going to sleep!

WILLY (*calling after him*): Don't curse in this house!

BIFF (*turning*): Since when did you get so clean?

HAPPY (*trying to stop them*): Wait a . . .

WILLY: Don't use that language to me! I won't have it!

HAPPY (*grabbing Biff, shouts*): Wait a minute! I got an idea. I got a feasible idea. Come here, Biff, let's talk this over now, let's talk some sense here. When I was down in Florida last time, I thought of a great idea to sell sporting goods. It just came back to me. You and I, Biff — we have a line, the Loman Line. We train a couple of weeks, and put on a couple of exhibitions, see?

WILLY: That's an idea!

HAPPY: Wait! We form two basketball teams, see? Two water polo teams. We play each other. It's a million dollars' worth of publicity. Two brothers, see? The Loman Brothers. Displays in the Royal Palms — all the hotels. And banners over the ring and the basketball court: "Loman Brothers." Baby, we could sell sporting goods!

WILLY: That is a one-million-dollar idea!

LINDA: Marvelous!

BIFF: I'm in great shape as far as that's concerned.

HAPPY: And the beauty of it is, Biff, it wouldn't be like a business. We'd be out playin' ball again . . .

BIFF (*enthused*): Yeah, that's . . .

WILLY: Million-dollar . . .

HAPPY: And you wouldn't get fed up with it, Biff. It'd be the family again. There'd be the old honor, and comradeship, and if you wanted to go off for a swim or somethin' — well, you'd do it! Without some smart cooky gettin' up ahead of you!

WILLY: Lick the world! You guys together could absolutely lick the civilized world.

BIFF: I'll see Oliver tomorrow. Hap, if we could work that out . . .

LINDA: Maybe things are beginning to —

WILLY (*wildly enthused, to Linda*): Stop interrupting! (*To Biff.*) But don't wear sport jacket and slacks when you see Oliver.

BIFF: No, I'll —

WILLY: A business suit, and talk as little as possible, and don't crack any jokes.

BIFF: He did like me. Always liked me.

LINDA: He loved you!

WILLY (*to Linda*): Will you stop! (*To Biff.*) Walk in very serious. You are not applying for a boy's job. Money is to pass. Be quiet, fine, and serious. Everybody likes a kidder, but nobody lends him money.

HAPPY: I'll try to get some myself, Biff. I'm sure I can.

WILLY: I see great things for you kids, I think your troubles are over. But remember, start big and you'll end big. Ask for fifteen. How much you gonna ask for?

BIFF: Gee, I don't know —

WILLY: And don't say "Gee." "Gee" is a boy's word. A man walking in for fifteen thousand dollars does not say "Gee!"

BIFF: Ten, I think, would be top though.

WILLY: Don't be so modest. You always started too low. Walk in with a big laugh. Don't look worried. Start off with a couple of your good stories to lighten things up. It's not what you say, it's how you say it — because personality always wins the day.

LINDA: Oliver always thought the highest of him —

WILLY: Will you let me talk?

BIFF: Don't yell at her, Pop, will ya?

WILLY (*angrily*): I was talking, wasn't I?

BIFF: I don't like you yelling at her all the time, and I'm tellin' you, that's all.

WILLY: What're you, takin' over this house?

LINDA: Willy —

WILLY (*turning to her*): Don't take his side all the time, goddammit!

BIFF (*furiously*): Stop yelling at her!

WILLY (*suddenly pulling on his cheek, beaten down, guilt ridden*): Give my best to Bill Oliver — he may remember me. (*He exits through the living room doorway.*)

LINDA (*her voice subdued*): What'd you have to start that for? (*Biff turns away.*) You see how sweet he was as soon as you talked hopefully? (*She goes over to Biff.*) Come up and say good night to him. Don't let him go to bed that way.

HAPPY: Come on, Biff, let's buck him up.

LINDA: Please, dear. Just say good night. It takes so little to make him happy. Come. (*She goes through the living room doorway, calling upstairs from within the living room.*) Your pajamas are hanging in the bathroom, Willy!

HAPPY (*looking toward where Linda went out*): What a woman! They broke the mold when they made her. You know that, Biff?

BIFF: He's off salary. My God, working on commission!

HAPPY: Well, let's face it: he's no hot-shot selling man. Except that sometimes, you have to admit, he's a sweet personality.

BIFF (*deciding*): Lend me ten bucks, will ya? I want to buy some new ties.

HAPPY: I'll take you to a place I know. Beautiful stuff. Wear one of my striped shirts tomorrow.

BIFF: She got gray. Mom got awful old. Gee, I'm gonna go in to Oliver tomorrow and knock him for a —

HAPPY: Come on up. Tell that to Dad. Let's give him a whirl. Come on.

BIFF (*steamed up*): You know, with ten thousand bucks, boy!

HAPPY (*as they go into the living room*): That's the talk, Biff, that's the first time I've heard the old confidence out of you! (*From within the living room, fading off.*) You're gonna live with me, kid, and any babe you want just say the word . . . (*The last lines are hardly heard. They are mounting the stairs to their parents' bedroom.*)

LINDA (*entering her bedroom and addressing Willy, who is in the bathroom. She is straightening the bed for him.*): Can you do anything about the shower? It drips.

WILLY (*from the bathroom*): All of a sudden everything falls to pieces. Goddam plumbing, oughta be sued, those people. I hardly finished putting it in and the thing . . . (*His words rumble off.*)

LINDA: I'm just wondering if Oliver will remember him. You think he might?

WILLY (*coming out of the bathroom in his pajamas*): Remember him? What's the matter with you, you crazy? If he'd've stayed with Oliver he'd be on top by now! Wait'll Oliver gets a look at him. You don't know the average caliber any more. The average young man today — (*he is getting into bed*) — is got a caliber of zero. Greatest thing in the world for him was to bum around.

(*Biff and Happy enter the bedroom. Slight pause.*)

WILLY (*stops short, looking at Biff*): Glad to hear it, boy.

HAPPY: He wanted to say good night to you, sport.

WILLY (*to Biff*): Yeah. Knock him dead, boy. What'd you want to tell me?

BIFF: Just take it easy, Pop. Good night. (*He turns to go.*)

WILLY (*unable to resist*): And if anything falls off the desk while you're talking to him — like a package or something — don't you pick it up. They have office boys for that.

LINDA: I'll make a big breakfast —

WILLY: Will you let me finish? (*To Biff.*) Tell him you were in the business in the West. Not farm work.

BIFF: All right, Dad.

LINDA: I think everything —

WILLY (*going right through her speech*): And don't undersell yourself. No less than fifteen thousand dollars.

BIFF (*unable to bear him*): Okay. Good night, Mom. (*He starts moving.*)

WILLY: Because you got a greatness in you, Biff, remember that. You got all kinds of greatness . . . (*He lies back, exhausted. Biff walks out.*)

LINDA (*calling after Biff*): Sleep well, darling!

HAPPY: I'm gonna get married, Mom. I wanted to tell you.

LINDA: Go to sleep, dear.

HAPPY (*going*): I just wanted to tell you.

WILLY: Keep up the good work. (*Happy exits.*) God . . . remember that Ebbets Field game? The championship of the city?

LINDA: Just rest. Should I sing to you?

WILLY: Yeah. Sing to me. (*Linda hums a soft lullaby.*) When that team came out — he was the tallest, remember?

LINDA: Oh, yes. And in gold.

(*Biff enters the darkened kitchen, takes a cigarette, and leaves the house. He comes downstage into a golden pool of light. He smokes, staring at the night.*)

WILLY: Like a young god. Hercules — something like that. And the sun, the sun all around him. Remember how he waved to me? Right up from the field, with the representatives of three colleges standing by? And the buyers I brought, and the cheers when he came out — Loman, Loman, Loman! God Almighty, he'll be great yet. A star like that, magnificent, can never really fade away!

(*The light on Willy is fading. The gas heater begins to glow through the kitchen wall, near the stairs, a blue flame beneath red coils.*)

LINDA (*timidly*): Willy dear, what has he got against you?

WILLY: I'm so tired. Don't talk anymore.

(*Biff slowly returns to the kitchen. He stops, stares toward the heater.*)

LINDA: Will you ask Howard to let you work in New York?

WILLY: First thing in the morning. Everything'll be all right.

(*Biff reaches behind the heater and draws out a length of rubber tubing. He is horrified and turns his head toward Willy's room, still dimly lit, from which the strains of Linda's desperate but monotonous humming rise.*)

WILLY (*staring through the window into the moonlight*): Gee, look at the moon moving between the buildings!

(*Biff wraps the tubing around his hand and quickly goes up the stairs.*)

ACT II

(*Music is heard, gay and bright. The curtain rises as the music fades away. Willy, in shirt sleeves, is sitting at the kitchen table, sipping coffee, his hat in his lap. Linda is filling his cup when she can.*)

WILLY: Wonderful coffee. Meal in itself.

LINDA: Can I make you some eggs?

WILLY: No. Take a breath.

LINDA: You look so rested, dear.

WILLY: I slept like a dead one. First time in months. Imagine, sleeping till ten on a Tuesday morning. Boys left nice and early, heh?

LINDA: They were out of here by eight o'clock.

WILLY: Good work!

LINDA: It was so thrilling to see them leaving together. I can't get over the shaving lotion in this house!

WILLY (*smiling*): Mmm —

LINDA: Biff was very changed this morning. His whole attitude seemed to be hopeful. He couldn't wait to get downtown to see Oliver.

WILLY: He's heading for a change. There's no question, there simply are certain men that take longer to get — solidified. How did he dress?

LINDA: His blue suit. He's so handsome in that suit. He could be a — anything in that suit!

(*Willy gets up from the table. Linda holds his jacket for him.*)

WILLY: There's no question, no question at all. Gee, on the way home tonight I'd like to buy some seeds.

LINDA (*laughing*): That'd be wonderful. But not enough sun gets back there. Nothing'll grow any more.

WILLY: You wait, kid, before it's all over we're gonna get a little place out in the country, and I'll raise some vegetables, a couple of chickens . . .

LINDA: You'll do it yet, dear.

(*Willy walks out of his jacket. Linda follows him.*)

WILLY: And they'll get married, and come for a week-end. I'd build a little guest house. 'Cause I got so many fine tools, all I'd need would be a little lumber and some peace of mind.

LINDA (*joyfully*): I sewed the lining . . .

WILLY: I could build two guest houses, so they'd both come. Did he decide how much he's going to ask Oliver for?

LINDA (*getting him into the jacket*): He didn't mention it, but I imagine ten or fifteen thousand. You going to talk to Howard today?

WILLY: Yeah. I'll put it to him straight and simple. He'll just have to take me off the road.

LINDA: And Willy, don't forget to ask for a little advance, because we've got the insurance premium. It's the grace period now.

WILLY: That's a hundred . . . ?

LINDA: A hundred and eight, sixty-eight. Because we're a little short again.

WILLY: Why are we short?

LINDA: Well, you had the motor job on the car . . .

WILLY: That goddam Studebaker!

LINDA: And you got one more payment on the refrigerator . . .

WILLY: But it just broke again!

LINDA: Well, it's old, dear.

WILLY: I told you we should've bought a well-advertised machine. Charley bought a General Electric and it's twenty years old and it's still good, that son-of-a-bitch.

LINDA: But, Willy —

WILLY: Whoever heard of a Hastings refrigerator? Once in my life I would like to own something outright before it's broken! I'm always in a race with the junkyard! I just finished paying for the car and it's on its last legs. The refrigerator consumes belts like a goddamn maniac. They time those things. They time them so when you finally paid for them, they're used up.

LINDA (*buttoning up his jacket as he unbuttons it*): All told, about two hundred dollars would carry us, dear. But that includes the last payment on the mortgage. After this payment, Willy, the house belongs to us.

WILLY: It's twenty-five years!

LINDA: Biff was nine years old when we bought it.

WILLY: Well, that's a great thing. To weather a twenty-five year mortgage is —

LINDA: It's an accomplishment.

WILLY: All the cement, the lumber, the reconstruction I put in this house! There ain't a crack to be found in it anymore.

LINDA: Well, it served its purpose.

WILLY: What purpose? Some stranger'll come along, move in, and that's that. If only Biff would take this house, and raise a family . . . (*He starts to go.*) Good-by, I'm late.

LINDA (*suddenly remembering*): Oh, I forgot! You're supposed to meet them for dinner.

WILLY: Me?

LINDA: At Frank's Chop House on Forty-eighth near Sixth Avenue.

WILLY: Is that so! How about you?

LINDA: No, just the three of you. They're gonna blow you to a big meal!

WILLY: Don't say! Who thought of that?

LINDA: Biff came to me this morning, Willy, and he said, "Tell Dad, we want to blow him to a big meal." Be there six o'clock. You and your two boys are going to have dinner.

WILLY: Gee whiz! That's really somethin'. I'm gonna knock Howard for a loop, kid. I'll get an advance, and I'll come home with a New York job. Goddammit, now I'm gonna do it!

LINDA: Oh, that's the spirit, Willy!

WILLY: I will never get behind a wheel the rest of my life!

LINDA: It's changing, Willy, I can feel it changing!

WILLY: Beyond a question. G'by, I'm late. (*He starts to go again.*)

LINDA (*calling after him as she runs to the kitchen table for a handkerchief*): You got your glasses?

WILLY (*feels for them, then comes back in*): Yeah, yeah, got my glasses.

LINDA (*giving him the handkerchief*): And a handkerchief.

WILLY: Yeah, handkerchief.

LINDA: And your saccharine?

WILLY: Yeah, my saccharine.

LINDA: Be careful on the subway stairs.

(*She kisses him, and a silk stocking is seen hanging from her hand. Willy notices it.*)

WILLY: Will you stop mending stockings? At least while I'm in the house. It gets me nervous. I can't tell you. Please.

(*Linda hides the stocking in her hand as she follows Willy across the forestage in front of the house.*)

LINDA: Remember, Frank's Chop House.

WILLY (*passing the apron*): Maybe beets would grow out there.

LINDA (*laughing*): But you tried so many times.

WILLY: Yeah. Well, don't work hard today. (*He disappears around the right corner of the house.*)

LINDA: Be careful!

(*As Willy vanishes, Linda waves to him. Suddenly the phone rings. She runs across the stage and into the kitchen and lifts it.*)

LINDA: Hello? Oh, Biff! I'm so glad you called, I just . . . Yes, sure, I just told him. Yes, he'll be there for dinner at six o'clock, I didn't forget. Listen, I was just dying to tell you. You know that little rubber pipe I told you about? That he connected to the gas heater? I finally decided to go down the cellar this morning and take it away and destroy it. But it's gone! Imagine? He took it away himself, it isn't there! (*She listens.*) When? Oh, then you took it. Oh — nothing, it's just that I'd hoped he'd taken it away himself. Oh, I'm not worried, darling, because this morning he left in such high spirits, it was like the old days! I'm not afraid any more. Did Mr. Oliver see you? . . . Well, you wait there then. And make a nice impression on him, darling. Just don't perspire too much before you see him. And have a nice time with Dad. He may have big news too! . . . That's right, a New York job. And be sweet to him tonight, dear. Be loving to him. Because he's only a little boat looking for a harbor. (*She is trembling with sorrow and joy.*) Oh, that's wonderful, Biff, you'll save his life. Thanks, darling. Just put your arm around him when he comes into the restaurant. Give him a smile. That's the boy . . . Good-by, dear. . . . You got your comb? . . . That's fine. Good-by, Biff dear.

(*In the middle of her speech, Howard Wagner, thirty-six, wheels in a small typewriter table on which is a wire-recording machine and proceeds to plug it in. This is on the left forestage. Light slowly fades on Linda as it rises on Howard. Howard is intent on threading the machine and only glances over his shoulder as Willy appears.*)

WILLY: Pst! Pst!

HOWARD: Hello, Willy, come in.

WILLY: Like to have a little talk with you, Howard.

HOWARD: Sorry to keep you waiting. I'll be with you in a minute.

WILLY: What's that, Howard?

HOWARD: Didn't you ever see one of these? Wire recorder.

WILLY: Oh. Can we talk a minute?

HOWARD: Records things. Just got delivery yesterday. Been driving me crazy, the most terrific machine I ever saw in my life. I was up all night with it.

WILLY: What do you do with it?

HOWARD: I bought it for dictation, but you can do anything with it. Listen to this. I had it home last night. Listen to what I picked up. The first one is my daughter. Get this. (*He flicks the switch and "Roll out the Barrel" is heard being whistled.*) Listen to that kid whistle.

WILLY: That is lifelike, isn't it?

HOWARD: Seven years old. Get that tone.

WILLY: Ts, ts. Like to ask a little favor if you . . .

(*The whistling breaks off, and the voice of Howard's daughter is heard.*)

HIS DAUGHTER: "Now you, Daddy."

HOWARD: She's crazy for me! (*Again the same song is whistled.*) That's me! Ha! (*He winks.*)

WILLY: You're very good!

(*The whistling breaks off again. The machine runs silent for a moment.*)

HOWARD: Sh! Get this now, this is my son.

HIS SON: "The capital of Alabama is Montgomery; the capital of Arizona is Phoenix; the capital of Arkansas is Little Rock; the capital of California is Sacramento . . ." (*and on, and on.*)

HOWARD (*holding up five fingers*): Five years old, Willy!

WILLY: He'll make an announcer some day!

HIS SON (*continuing*): "The capital . . ."

HOWARD: Get that — alphabetical order! (*The machine breaks off suddenly.*) Wait a minute. The maid kicked the plug out.

WILLY: It certainly is a —

HOWARD: Sh, for God's sake!

HIS SON: "It's nine o'clock, Bulova watch time. So I have to go to sleep."

WILLY: That really is —

HOWARD: Wait a minute! The next is my wife.

(*They wait.*)

HOWARD'S VOICE: "Go on, say something." (*Pause.*) "Well, you gonna talk?"

HIS WIFE: "I can't think of anything."

HOWARD'S VOICE: "Well, talk — it's turning."

HIS WIFE (*shyly, beaten*): "Hello." (*Silence.*) "Oh, Howard, I can't talk into this . . ."

HOWARD (*snapping the machine off*): That was my wife.

WILLY: That is a wonderful machine. Can we —

HOWARD: I tell you, Willy, I'm gonna take my camera, and my bandsaw, and all my hobbies, and out they go. This is the most fascinating relaxation I ever found.

WILLY: I think I'll get one myself.

HOWARD: Sure, they're only a hundred and a half. You can't do without it. Supposing you wanna hear Jack Benny, see? But you can't be at home at that hour. So you tell the maid to turn the radio on when Jack Benny comes on, and this automatically goes on with the radio . . .

WILLY: And when you come home you . . .

HOWARD: You can come home twelve o'clock, one o'clock, any time you like, and you get yourself a Coke and sit yourself down, throw the switch, and there's Jack Benny's program in the middle of the night!

WILLY: I'm definitely going to get one. Because lots of times I'm on the road, and I think to myself, what I must be missing on the radio!

HOWARD: Don't you have a radio in the car?

WILLY: Well, yeah, but who ever thinks of turning it on?

HOWARD: Say, aren't you supposed to be in Boston?

WILLY: That's what I want to talk to you about, Howard. You got a minute? (*He draws a chair in from the wing.*)

HOWARD: What happened? What're you doing here?

WILLY: Well . . .

HOWARD: You didn't crack up again, did you?

WILLY: Oh, no. No . . .

HOWARD: Geez, you had me worried there for a minute. What's the trouble?

WILLY: Well, tell you the truth, Howard. I've come to the decision that I'd rather not travel anymore.

HOWARD: Not travel! Well, what'll you do?

WILLY: Remember, Christmas time, when you had the party here? You said you'd try to think of some spot for me here in town.

HOWARD: With us?

WILLY: Well, sure.

HOWARD: Oh, yeah, yeah. I remember. Well, I couldn't think of anything for you, Willy.

WILLY: I tell ya, Howard. The kids are all grown up, y'know. I don't need much anymore. If I could take home — well, sixty-five dollars a week, I could swing it.

HOWARD: Yeah, but Willy, see I —

WILLY: I tell ya why, Howard. Speaking frankly and between the two of us, y'know — I'm just a little tired.

HOWARD: Oh, I could understand that, Willy. But you're a road man, Willy, and we do a road business. We've only got a half-dozen salesmen on the floor here.

WILLY: God knows, Howard, I never asked a favor of any man. But I was with the firm when your father used to carry you in here in his arms.

HOWARD: I know that, Willy, but —

WILLY: Your father came to me the day you were born and asked me what I thought of the name Howard, may he rest in peace.

HOWARD: I appreciate that, Willy, but there just is no spot here for you. If I had a spot I'd slam you right in, but I just don't have a single solitary spot.

(*He looks for his lighter. Willy has picked it up and gives it to him. Pause.*)

WILLY (*with increasing anger*): Howard, all I need to set my table is fifty dollars a week.

HOWARD: But where am I going to put you, kid?

WILLY: Look, it isn't a question of whether I can sell merchandise, is it?

HOWARD: No, but it's business, kid, and everybody's gotta pull his own weight.

WILLY (*desperately*): Just let me tell you a story, Howard —

HOWARD: 'Cause you gotta admit, business is business.

WILLY (*angrily*): Business is definitely business, but just listen for a minute. You don't understand this. When I was a boy — eighteen, nineteen — I was already on the road. And there was a question in my mind as to whether selling had a future for me. Because in those days I had a yearning to go to Alaska. See, there were three gold strikes in one month in Alaska, and I felt like going out. Just for the ride, you might say.

HOWARD (*barely interested*): Don't say.

WILLY: Oh, yeah, my father lived many years in Alaska. He was an adventurous man. We've got quite a little streak of self-reliance in our family. I thought I'd go out with my older brother and try to locate him, and maybe settle in the North with the old man. And I was almost decided to go, when I met a salesman in the Parker House. His name was Dave Singleman. And he was eighty-four years old, and he'd drummed merchandise in thirty-one states. And old Dave, he'd go up to his room, y'understand, put on his green velvet slippers — I'll never forget — and pick up his phone and call the buyers, and without ever leaving his room, at the age of eighty-four, he made his living. And when I saw that, I realized that selling was the greatest career a man could want. 'Cause what could be more satisfying than to be able to go, at the age of eighty-four, into twenty or thirty different cities, and pick up a phone, and be remembered and loved and helped by so many different people? Do you know? When he died — and by the way he died the death of a salesman, in his green velvet slippers in the smoker of the New York, New Haven and Hartford, going into Boston — when he died, hundreds of salesmen and buyers were at his funeral. Things were sad on a lotta trains for months after that. (*He stands up. Howard has not looked at him.*) In those days there was personality in it, Howard. There was respect, and comradeship, and gratitude in it. Today, it's all cut and dried, and there's no chance for bringing friendship to bear — or personality. You see what I mean? They don't know me any more.

HOWARD (*moving away, to the right*): That's just the thing, Willy.

WILLY: If I had forty dollars a week — that's all I'd need. Forty dollars, Howard.

HOWARD: Kid, I can't take blood from a stone, I —

WILLY (*desperation is on him now*): Howard, the year Al Smith was nominated, your father came to me and —

HOWARD (*starting to go off*): I've got to see some people, kid.

WILLY (*stopping him*): I'm talking about your father! There were promises made across this desk! You mustn't tell me you've got people to see — I put thirty-four years into this firm, Howard, and now I can't pay my insurance! You can't eat the orange and throw the peel away — a man is not a piece of fruit! (*After a pause.*) Now pay attention. Your father — in 1928 I had a big year. I averaged a hundred and seventy dollars a week in commissions.

HOWARD (*impatiently*): Now, Willy, you never averaged —

WILLY (*banging his hand on the desk*): I averaged a hundred and seventy dollars a week in the year of 1928! And your father came to me — or rather, I was in the office here — it was right over this desk — and he put his hand on my shoulder —

HOWARD (*getting up*): You'll have to excuse me, Willy, I gotta see some people. Pull yourself together. (*Going out.*) I'll be back in a little while.

(*On Howard's exit, the light on his chair grows very bright and strange.*)

WILLY: Pull myself together! What the hell did I say to him? My God, I was yelling at him! How could I? (*Willy breaks off, staring at the light, which occupies the chair, animating it. He approaches this chair, standing across the desk from it.*) Frank, Frank, don't you remember what you told me that time? How you put your hand on my shoulder, and Frank . . . (*He leans on the desk and as he speaks the dead man's name he accidentally switches on the recorder, and instantly*)

HOWARD'S SON: ". . . of New York is Albany. The capital of Ohio is Cincinnati, the capital of Rhode Island is . . ." (*The recitation continues.*)

WILLY (*leaping away with fright, shouting*): Ha! Howard! Howard! Howard!

HOWARD (*rushing in*): What happened?

WILLY (*pointing at the machine, which continues nasally, childishly, with the capital cities*): Shut it off! Shut it off!

HOWARD (*pulling the plug out*): Look, Willy . . .

WILLY (*pressing his hands to his eyes*): I gotta get myself some coffee. I'll get some coffee . . .

(*Willy starts to walk out. Howard stops him.*)

HOWARD (*rolling up the cord*): Willy, look . . .

WILLY: I'll go to Boston.

HOWARD: Willy, you can't go to Boston for us.

WILLY: Why can't I go?

HOWARD: I don't want you to represent us. I've been meaning to tell you for a long time now.

WILLY: Howard, are you firing me?

HOWARD: I think you need a good long rest, Willy.

WILLY: Howard —

HOWARD: And when you feel better, come back, and we'll see if we can work something out.

WILLY: But I gotta earn money, Howard. I'm in no position to —

HOWARD: Where are your sons? Why don't your sons give you a hand?

WILLY: They're working on a very big deal.

HOWARD: This is no time for false pride, Willy. You go to your sons and you tell them that you're tired. You've got two great boys, haven't you?

WILLY: Oh, no question, no question, but in the meantime . . .

HOWARD: Then that's that, heh?

WILLY: All right, I'll go to Boston tomorrow.

HOWARD: No, no.

WILLY: I can't throw myself on my sons. I'm not a cripple!

HOWARD: Look, kid, I'm busy this morning.

WILLY (*grasping Howard's arm*): Howard, you've got to let me go to Boston!

HOWARD (*hard, keeping himself under control*): I've got a line of people to see this morning. Sit down, take five minutes, and pull yourself together, and then go home, will ya? I need the office, Willy. (*He starts to go, turns, remembering the recorder, starts to push off the table holding the recorder.*) Oh, yeah. Whenever you can this week, stop by and drop off the samples. You'll feel better, Willy, and then come back and we'll talk. Pull yourself together, kid, there's people outside.

(*Howard exits, pushing the table off left. Willy stares into space, exhausted. Now the music is heard — Ben's music — first distantly, then closer, closer. As Willy speaks, Ben enters from the right. He carries valise and umbrella.*)

WILLY: Oh, Ben, how did you do it? What is the answer? Did you wind up the Alaska deal already?

BEN: Doesn't take much time if you know what you're doing. Just a short business trip. Boarding ship in an hour. Wanted to say good-by.

WILLY: Ben, I've got to talk to you.

BEN (*glancing at his watch*): Haven't the time, William.

WILLY (*crossing the apron to Ben*): Ben, nothing's working out. I don't know what to do.

BEN: Now, look here, William. I've bought timberland in Alaska and I need a man to look after things for me.

WILLY: God, timberland! Me and my boys in those grand outdoors!

BEN: You've a new continent at your doorstep, William. Get out of these cities, they're full of talk and time payments and courts of law. Screw on your fists and you can fight for a fortune up there.

WILLY: Yes, yes! Linda, Linda!

(*Linda enters as of old, with the wash.*)

LINDA: Oh, you're back?

BEN: I haven't much time.

WILLY: No, wait! Linda, he's got a proposition for me in Alaska.

LINDA: But you've got — (*To Ben.*) He's got a beautiful job here.

WILLY: But in Alaska, kid, I could —

LINDA: You're doing well enough, Willy!

BEN (*to Linda*): Enough for what, my dear?

LINDA (*frightened of Ben and angry at him*): Don't say those things to him! Enough to be happy right here, right now. (*To Willy, while Ben laughs.*) Why must everybody conquer the world? You're well liked, and the boys love you, and someday — (*To Ben*) — why, old man Wagner told him just the other day that if he keeps it up he'll be a member of the firm, didn't he, Willy?

WILLY: Sure, sure. I am building something with this firm, Ben, and if a man is building something he must be on the right track, mustn't he?

BEN: What are you building? Lay your hand on it. Where is it?

WILLY (*hesitantly*): That's true, Linda, there's nothing.

LINDA: Why? (*To Ben.*) There's a man eighty-four years old —

WILLY: That's right, Ben, that's right. When I look at that man I say, what is there to worry about?

BEN: Bah!

WILLY: It's true, Ben. All he has to do is go into any city, pick up the phone, and he's making his living and you know why?

BEN (*picking up his valise*): I've got to go.

WILLY (*holding Ben back*): Look at this boy!

(*Biff, in his high school sweater, enters carrying suitcase. Happy carries Biff's shoulder guards, gold helmet, and football pants.*)

WILLY: Without a penny to his name, three great universities are begging for him, and from there the sky's the limit, because it's not what you do, Ben. It's who you know and the smile on your face! It's contacts, Ben, contacts! The whole wealth of Alaska passes over the lunch table at the Commodore Hotel, and that's the wonder, the wonder of this country, that a man can end with diamonds here on the basis of being liked! (*He turns to Biff.*) And that's why when you get out on that field today it's important. Because thousands of people will be rooting for you and loving you. (*To Ben, who has again begun to leave.*) And Ben! when he walks into a business office his name will sound out like a bell and all the doors will open to him! I've seen it, Ben, I've seen it a thousand times! You can't feel it with your hand like timber, but it's there!

BEN: Good-by, William.

WILLY: Ben, am I right? Don't you think I'm right? I value your advice.

BEN: There's a new continent at your doorstep, William. You could walk out rich. Rich! (*He is gone.*)

WILLY: We'll do it here, Ben! You hear me? We're gonna do it here!

(*Young Bernard rushes in. The gay music of the Boys is heard.*)

BERNARD: Oh, gee, I was afraid you left already!

WILLY: Why? What time is it?

BERNARD: It's half-past one!

WILLY: Well, come on, everybody! Ebbets Field next stop! Where's the pennants? (*He rushes through the wall-line of the kitchen and out into the living room.*)

LINDA (*to Biff*): Did you pack fresh underwear?

BIFF (*who has been limbering up*): I want to go!

BERNARD: Biff, I'm carrying your helmet, ain't I?

HAPPY: No, I'm carrying the helmet.

BERNARD: Oh, Biff, you promised me.

HAPPY: I'm carrying the helmet.

BERNARD: How am I going to get in the locker room?

LINDA: Let him carry the shoulder guards. (*She puts her coat and hat on in the kitchen.*)

BERNARD: Can I, Biff? 'Cause I told everybody I'm going to be in the locker room.

HAPPY: In Ebbets Field it's the clubhouse.

BERNARD: I meant the clubhouse. Biff!

HAPPY: Biff!

BIFF (*grandly, after a slight pause*): Let him carry the shoulder guards.

HAPPY (*as he gives Bernard the shoulder guards*): Stay close to us now.

(*Willy rushes in with the pennants.*)

WILLY (*handing them out*): Everybody wave when Biff comes out on the field. (*Happy and Bernard run off.*) You set now, boy?

(*The music has died away.*)

BIFF: Ready to go, Pop. Every muscle is ready.

WILLY (*at the edge of the apron*): You realize what this means?

BIFF: That's right, Pop.

WILLY (*feeling Biff's muscles*): You're comin' home this afternoon captain of the All-Scholastic Championship Team of the City of New York.

BIFF: I got it, Pop. And remember, pal, when I take off my helmet, that touchdown is for you.

WILLY: Let's go! (*He is starting out, with his arm around Biff, when Charley enters, as of old, in knickers.*) I got no room for you, Charley.

CHARLEY: Room? For what?

WILLY: In the car.

CHARLEY: You goin' for a ride? I wanted to shoot some casino.

WILLY (*furiously*): Casino! (*Incredulously.*) Don't you realize what today is?

LINDA: Oh, he knows, Willy. He's just kidding you.

WILLY: That's nothing to kid about!

CHARLEY: No, Linda, what's goin' on?

LINDA: He's playing in Ebbets Field.

CHARLEY: Baseball in this weather?

WILLY: Don't talk to him. Come on, come on! (*He is pushing them out.*)

CHARLEY: Wait a minute, didn't you hear the news?

WILLY: What?

CHARLEY: Don't you listen to the radio? Ebbets Field just blew up.

WILLY: You go to hell! (*Charley laughs. Pushing them out.*) Come on, come on! We're late.

CHARLEY (*as they go*): Knock a homer, Biff, knock a homer!

WILLY (*the last to leave, turning to Charley*): I don't

think that was funny, Charley. This is the greatest day of his life.

CHARLEY: Willy, when are you going to grow up?

WILLY: Yeah, heh? When this game is over, Charley, you'll be laughing out of the other side of your face. They'll be calling him another Red Grange. Twenty-five thousand a year.

CHARLEY (*kidding*): Is that so?

WILLY: Yeah, that's so.

CHARLEY: Well, then, I'm sorry, Willy. But tell me something.

WILLY: What?

CHARLEY: Who is Red Grange?

WILLY: Put up your hands. Goddam you, put up your hands!

(*Charley, chuckling, shakes his head and walks away, around the left corner of the stage. Willy follows him. The music rises to a mocking frenzy.*)

WILLY: Who the hell do you think you are, better than everybody else? You don't know everything, you big, ignorant, stupid . . . Put up your hands!

(*Light rises, on the right side of the forestage, on a small table in the reception room of Charley's office. Traffic sounds are heard. Bernard, now mature, sits whistling to himself. A pair of tennis rackets and an overnight bag are on the floor beside him.*)

WILLY (*offstage*): What are you walking away for? Don't walk away! If you're going to say something say it to my face! I know you laugh at me behind my back. You'll laugh out of the other side of your goddam face after this game. Touchdown! Touchdown! Eighty thousand people! Touchdown! Right between the goal posts.

(*Bernard is a quiet, earnest, but self-assured young man. Willy's voice is coming from right upstage now. Bernard lowers his feet off the table and listens. Jenny, his father's secretary, enters.*)

JENNY (*distressed*): Say, Bernard, will you go out in the hall?

BERNARD: What is that noise? Who is it?

JENNY: Mr. Loman. He just got off the elevator.

BERNARD (*getting up*): Who's he arguing with?

JENNY: Nobody. There's nobody with him. I can't deal with him anymore, and your father gets all upset everytime he comes. I've got a lot of typing to do, and your father's waiting to sign it. Will you see him?

WILLY (*entering*): Touchdown! Touch — (*He sees Jenny.*) Jenny, Jenny, good to see you. How're ya? Workin'? Or still honest?

JENNY: Fine. How've you been feeling?

WILLY: Not much any more, Jenny. Ha, ha! (*He is surprised to see the rackets.*)

BERNARD: Hello, Uncle Willy.

WILLY (*almost shocked*): Bernard! Well, look who's here! (*He comes quickly, guiltily, to Bernard and warmly shakes his hand.*)

BERNARD: How are you? Good to see you.

WILLY: What are you doing here?

BERNARD: Oh, just stopped by to see Pop. Get off my feet till my train leaves. I'm going to Washington in a few minutes.

WILLY: Is he in?

BERNARD: Yes, he's in his office with the accountant. Sit down.

WILLY (*sitting down*): What're you going to do in Washington?

BERNARD: Oh, just a case I've got there, Willy.

WILLY: That so? (*Indicating the rackets.*) You going to play tennis there?

BERNARD: I'm staying with a friend who's got a court.

WILLY: Don't say. His own tennis court. Must be fine people, I bet.

BERNARD: They are, very nice. Dad tells me Biff's in town.

WILLY (*with a big smile*): Yeah, Biff's in. Working on a very big deal, Bernard.

BERNARD: What's Biff doing?

WILLY: Well, he's been doing very big things in the West. But he decided to establish himself here. Very big. We're having dinner. Did I hear your wife had a boy?

BERNARD: That's right. Our second.

WILLY: Two boys! What do you know!

BERNARD: What kind of a deal has Biff got?

WILLY: Well, Bill Oliver — very big sporting-goods man — he wants Biff very badly. Called him in from the West. Long distance, carte blanche, special deliveries. Your friends have their own private tennis court?

BERNARD: You still with the old firm, Willy?

WILLY (*after a pause*): I'm — I'm overjoyed to see how you made the grade, Bernard, overjoyed. It's an encouraging thing to see a young man really — really — Looks very good for Biff — very — (*He breaks off, then.*) Bernard — (*He is so full of emotion, he breaks off again.*)

BERNARD: What is it, Willy?

WILLY (*small and alone*): What — what's the secret?

BERNARD: What secret?

WILLY: How — how did you? Why didn't he ever catch on?

BERNARD: I wouldn't know that, Willy.

WILLY (*confidentially, desperately*): You were his friend, his boyhood friend. There's something I don't understand about it. His life ended after that Ebbets Field game. From the age of seventeen nothing good ever happened to him.

BERNARD: He never trained himself for anything.

WILLY: But he did, he did. After high school he took so many correspondence courses. Radio mechanics; television; God knows what, and never made the slightest mark.

BERNARD (*taking off his glasses*): Willy, do you want to talk candidly?

WILLY (*rising, faces Bernard*): I regard you as a very brilliant man, Bernard. I value your advice.

BERNARD: Oh, the hell with the advice, Willy. I couldn't advise you. There's just one thing I've always wanted to ask you. When he was supposed to graduate, and the math teacher flunked him —

WILLY: Oh, that son-of-a-bitch ruined his life.

BERNARD: Yeah, but, Willy, all he had to do was go to summer school and make up that subject.

WILLY: That's right, that's right.

BERNARD: Did you tell him not to go to summer school?

WILLY: Me? I begged him to go. I ordered him to go!

BERNARD: Then why wouldn't he go?

WILLY: Why? Why! Bernard, that question has been trailing me like a ghost for the last fifteen years. He flunked the subject, and laid down and died like a hammer hit him!

BERNARD: Take it easy, kid.

WILLY: Let me talk to you — I got nobody to talk to. Bernard, Bernard, was it my fault? Y'see? It keeps going around in my mind, maybe I did something to him. I got nothing to give him.

BERNARD: Don't take it so hard.

WILLY: Why did he lay down? What is the story there? You were his friend!

BERNARD: Willy, I remember, it was June, and our grades came out. And he'd flunked math.

WILLY: That son-of-a-bitch!

BERNARD: No, it wasn't right then. Biff just got very angry, I remember, and he was ready to enroll in summer school.

WILLY (*surprised*): He was?

BERNARD: He wasn't beaten by it at all. But then, Willy, he disappeared from the block for almost a month. And I got the idea that he'd gone up to New England to see you. Did he have a talk with you then?

(*Willy stares in silence.*)

BERNARD: Willy?

WILLY (*with a strong edge of resentment in his voice*): Yeah, he came to Boston. What about it?

BERNARD: Well, just that when he came back — I'll never forget this, it always mystifies me. Because I'd thought so well of Biff, even though he'd always taken advantage of me. I loved him, Willy, y'know? And he came back after that month and took his sneakers — remember those sneakers with "University of Virginia" printed on them? He was so proud of those, wore them every day. And he took them down in the cellar, and burned them up in the furnace. We had a fist fight. It lasted at least half an hour. Just the two of us, punching each other down the cellar, and crying right through it. I've often thought of how strange it was that I knew he'd given up his life. What happened in Boston, Willy?

(*Willy looks at him as at an intruder.*)

BERNARD: I just bring it up because you asked me.

WILLY (*angrily*): Nothing. What do you mean, "What happened?" What's that got to do with anything?

BERNARD: Well, don't get sore.

WILLY: What are you trying to do, blame it on me? If a boy lays down is that my fault?

BERNARD: Now, Willy, don't get —

WILLY: Well, don't — don't talk to me that way! What does that mean, "What happened?"

(*Charley enters. He is in his vest, and he carries a bottle of bourbon.*)

CHARLEY: Hey, you're going to miss that train. (*He waves the bottle.*)

BERNARD: Yeah, I'm going. (*He takes the bottle.*) Thanks, Pop. (*He picks up his rackets and bag.*) Good-by, Willy, and don't worry about it. You know, "If at first you don't succeed . . ."

WILLY: Yes, I believe in that.

BERNARD: But sometimes, Willy, it's better for a man just to walk away.

WILLY: Walk away?

BERNARD: That's right.

WILLY: But if you can't walk away?

BERNARD (*after a slight pause*): I guess that's when it's tough. (*Extending his hand.*) Good-by, Willy.

WILLY (*shaking Bernard's hand*): Good-by, boy.

CHARLEY (*an arm on Bernard's shoulder*): How do you like this kid? Gonna argue a case in front of the Supreme Court.

BERNARD (*protesting*): Pop!

WILLY (*genuinely shocked, pained, and happy*): No! The Supreme Court!

BERNARD: I gotta run. 'By, Dad!

CHARLEY: Knock 'em dead, Bernard!

(*Bernard goes off.*)

WILLY (*as Charley takes out his wallet*): The Supreme Court! And he didn't even mention it!

CHARLEY (*counting out money on the desk*): He don't have to — he's gonna do it.

WILLY: And you never told him what to do, did you? You never took any interest in him.

CHARLEY: My salvation is that I never took any interest in anything. There's some money — fifty dollars. I got an accountant inside.

WILLY: Charley, look . . . (*With difficulty.*) I got my insurance to pay. If you can manage it — I need a hundred and ten dollars.

(*Charley doesn't reply for a moment; merely stops moving.*)

WILLY: I'd draw it from my bank but Linda would know, and I . . .

CHARLEY: Sit down, Willy.

WILLY (*moving toward the chair*): I'm keeping an account of everything, remember. I'll pay every penny back. (*He sits.*)

CHARLEY: Now listen to me, Willy.

WILLY: I want you to know I appreciate . . .

CHARLEY (*sitting down on the table*): Willy, what're you doin'? What the hell is goin' on in your head?

WILLY: Why? I'm simply . . .

CHARLEY: I offered you a job. You make fifty dollars a week. And I won't send you on the road.

WILLY: I've got a job.

CHARLEY: Without pay? What kind of a job is a job without pay? (*He rises.*) Now, look, kid, enough is enough. I'm no genius but I know when I'm being insulted.

WILLY: Insulted!

CHARLEY: Why don't you want to work for me?

WILLY: What's the matter with you? I've got a job.

CHARLEY: Then what're you walkin' in here every week for?

WILLY (*getting up*): Well, if you don't want me to walk in here —

CHARLEY: I'm offering you a job.

WILLY: I don't want your goddam job!

CHARLEY: When the hell are you going to grow up?

WILLY (*furiously*): You big ignoramus, if you say that to me again I'll rap you one! I don't care how big you are! (*He's ready to fight.*)

(*Pause.*)

CHARLEY (*kindly, going to him*): How much do you need, Willy?

WILLY: Charley, I'm strapped. I'm strapped. I don't know what to do. I was just fired.

CHARLEY: Howard fired you?

WILLY: That snotnose. Imagine that? I named him. I named him Howard.

CHARLEY: Willy, when're you gonna realize that them things don't mean anything? You named him How-

ard, but you can't sell that. The only thing you got in this world is what you can sell. And the funny thing is that you're a salesman, and you don't know that.

WILLY: I've always tried to think otherwise, I guess. I always felt that if a man was impressive, and well liked, that nothing —

CHARLEY: Why must everybody like you? Who liked J. P. Morgan?° Was he impressive? In a Turkish bath he'd look like a butcher. But with his pockets on he was very well liked. Now listen, Willy, I know you don't like me, and nobody can say I'm in love with you, but I'll give you a job because — just for the hell of it, put it that way. Now what do you say?

WILLY: I — I just can't work for you, Charley.

CHARLEY: What're you, jealous of me?

WILLY: I can't work for you, that's all, don't ask me why.

CHARLEY (*angered, takes out more bills*): You been jealous of me all your life, you dammed fool! Here, pay your insurance. (*He puts the money in Willy's hand.*)

WILLY: I'm keeping strict accounts.

CHARLEY: I've got some work to do. Take care of yourself. And pay your insurance.

WILLY (*moving to the right*): Funny, y'know? After all the highways, and the trains, and the appointments, and the years, you end up worth more dead than alive.

CHARLEY: Willy, nobody's worth nothin' dead. (*After a slight pause.*) Did you hear what I said?

(*Willy stands still, dreaming.*)

CHARLEY: Willy!

WILLY: Apologize to Bernard for me when you see him. I didn't mean to argue with him. He's a fine boy. They're all fine boys, and they'll end up big — all of them. Someday they'll all play tennis together. Wish me luck, Charley. He saw Bill Oliver today.

CHARLEY: Good luck.

WILLY (*on the verge of tears*): Charley, you're the only friend I got. Isn't that a remarkable thing? (*He goes out.*)

CHARLEY: Jesus!

(*Charley stares after him a moment and follows. All light blacks out. Suddenly raucous music is heard, and a red glow rises behind the screen at right. Stanley, a young waiter, appears, carrying a table, followed by Happy, who is carrying two chairs.*)

J. P. Morgan: (1837–1913), wealthy financier and art collector whose money was made chiefly in banking, railroads, and steel.

STANLEY (*putting the table down*): That's all right, Mr. Loman, I can handle it myself. (*He turns and takes the chairs from Happy and places them at the table.*)

HAPPY (*glancing around*): Oh, this is better.

STANLEY: Sure, in the front there you're in the middle of all kinds of noise. Whenever you got a party, Mr. Loman, you just tell me and I'll put you back here. Y'know, there's a lotta people they don't like it private, because when they go out they like to see a lotta action around them because they're sick and tired to stay in the house by theirself. But I know you, you ain't from Hackensack. You know what I mean?

HAPPY (*sitting down*): So how's it coming, Stanley?

STANLEY: Ah, it's a dog life. I only wish during the war they'd a took me in the Army. I coulda been dead by now.

HAPPY: My brother's back, Stanley.

STANLEY: Oh, he come back, heh? From the Far West.

HAPPY: Yeah, big cattle man, my brother, so treat him right. And my father's coming too.

STANLEY: Oh, your father too!

HAPPY: You got a couple of nice lobsters?

STANLEY: Hundred percent, big.

HAPPY: I want them with the claws.

STANLEY: Don't worry, I don't give you no mice. (*Happy laughs.*) How about some wine? It'll put a head on the meal.

HAPPY: No. You remember, Stanley, that recipe I brought you from overseas? With the champagne in it?

STANLEY: Oh, yeah, sure. I still got it tacked up yet in the kitchen. But that'll have to cost a buck apiece anyways.

HAPPY: That's all right.

STANLEY: What'd you, hit a number or somethin'?

HAPPY: No, it's a little celebration. My brother is — I think he pulled off a big deal today. I think we're going into business together.

STANLEY: Great! That's the best for you. Because a family business, you know what I mean? — that's the best.

HAPPY: That's what I think.

STANLEY: 'Cause what's the difference? Somebody steals? It's in the family. Know what I mean? (*Sotto voce.°*) Like this bartender here. The boss is goin' crazy what kinda leak he's got in the cash register. You put it in but it don't come out.

HAPPY (*raising his head*): Sh!

STANLEY: What?

HAPPY: You notice I wasn't lookin' right or left, was I?

Sotto voce: In a soft voice or stage whisper.

STANLEY: No.

HAPPY: And my eyes are closed.

STANLEY: So what's the — ?

HAPPY: Strudel's comin'.

STANLEY (*catching on, looks around*): Ah, no, there's no —

(*He breaks off as a furred, lavishly dressed girl enters and sits at the next table. Both follow her with their eyes.*)

STANLEY: Geez, how'd ya know?

HAPPY: I got radar or something. (*Staring directly at her profile.*) Oooooooo . . . Stanley.

STANLEY: I think that's for you, Mr. Loman.

HAPPY: Look at that mouth. Oh, God. And the binoculars.

STANLEY: Geez, you got a life, Mr. Loman.

HAPPY: Wait on her.

STANLEY (*going to the girl's table*): Would you like a menu, ma'am?

GIRL: I'm expecting someone, but I'd like a —

HAPPY: Why don't you bring her — excuse me, miss, do you mind? I sell champagne, and I'd like you to try my brand. Bring her a champagne, Stanley.

GIRL: That's awfully nice of you.

HAPPY: Don't mention it. It's all company money. (*He laughs.*)

GIRL: That's a charming product to be selling, isn't it?

HAPPY: Oh, gets to be like everything else. Selling is selling, y'know.

GIRL: I suppose.

HAPPY: You don't happen to sell, do you?

GIRL: No, I don't sell.

HAPPY: Would you object to a compliment from a stranger? You ought to be on a magazine cover.

GIRL (*looking at him a little archly*): I have been.

(*Stanley comes in with a glass of champagne.*)

HAPPY: What'd I say before, Stanley? You see? She's a cover girl.

STANLEY: Oh, I could see, I could see.

HAPPY (*to the Girl*): What magazine?

GIRL: Oh, a lot of them. (*She takes the drink.*) Thank you.

HAPPY: You know what they say in France, don't you? "Champagne is the drink of the complexion" — Hya, Biff!

(*Biff has entered and sits with Happy.*)

BIFF: Hello, kid. Sorry I'm late.

HAPPY: I just got here. Uh, Miss — ?

GIRL: Forsythe.

HAPPY: Miss Forsythe, this is my brother.

BIFF: Is Dad here?

HAPPY: His name is Biff. You might've heard of him. Great football player.

GIRL: Really? What team?

HAPPY: Are you familiar with football?

GIRL: No, I'm afraid I'm not.

HAPPY: Biff is quarterback with the New York Giants.

GIRL: Well, that is nice, isn't it? (*She drinks.*)

HAPPY: Good health.

GIRL: I'm happy to meet you.

HAPPY: That's my name. Hap. It's really Harold, but at West Point they called me Happy.

GIRL (*now really impressed*): Oh, I see. How do you do? (*She turns her profile.*)

BIFF: Isn't Dad coming?

HAPPY: You want her?

BIFF: Oh, I could never make that.

HAPPY: I remember the time that idea would never come into your head. Where's the old confidence, Biff?

BIFF: I just saw Oliver —

HAPPY: Wait a minute. I've got to see that old confidence again. Do you want her? She's on call.

BIFF: Oh, no. (*He turns to look at the Girl.*)

HAPPY: I'm telling you. Watch this. (*Turning to the Girl*): Honey? (*She turns to him.*) Are you busy?

GIRL: Well, I am . . . but I could make a phone call.

HAPPY: Do that, will you, honey? And see if you can get a friend. We'll be here for a while. Biff is one of the greatest football players in the country.

GIRL (*standing up*): Well, I'm certainly happy to meet you.

HAPPY: Come back soon.

GIRL: I'll try.

HAPPY: Don't try, honey, try hard.

(*The Girl exits. Stanley follows, shaking his head in bewildered admiration.*)

HAPPY: Isn't that a shame now? A beautiful girl like that? That's why I can't get married. There's not a good woman in a thousand. New York is loaded with them, kid!

BIFF: Hap, look —

HAPPY: I told you she was on call!

BIFF (*strangely unnerved*): Cut it out, will ya? I want to say something to you.

HAPPY: Did you see Oliver?

BIFF: I saw him all right. Now look, I want to tell Dad a couple of things and I want you to help me.

HAPPY: What? Is he going to back you?

BIFF: Are you crazy? You're out of your goddam head, you know that?

HAPPY: Why? What happened?

BIFF (*breathlessly*): I did a terrible thing today, Hap. It's been the strangest day I ever went through. I'm all numb, I swear.

HAPPY: You mean he wouldn't see you?

BIFF: Well, I waited six hours for him, see? All day. Kept sending my name in. Even tried to date his secretary so she'd get me to him, but no soap.

HAPPY: Because you're not showin' the old confidence, Biff. He remembered you, didn't he?

BIFF (*stopping Happy with a gesture*): Finally, about five o'clock, he comes out. Didn't remember who I was or anything. I felt like such an idiot, Hap.

HAPPY: Did you tell him my Florida idea?

BIFF: He walked away. I saw him for one minute. I got so mad I could've torn the walls down! How the hell did I ever get the idea I was a salesman there? I even believed myself that I'd been a salesman for him! And then he gave me one look and — I realized what a ridiculous lie my whole life has been! We've been talking in a dream for fifteen years. I was a shipping clerk.

HAPPY: What'd you do?

BIFF (*with great tension and wonder*): Well, he left, see. And the secretary went out. I was all alone in the waiting room. I don't know what came over me, Hap. The next thing I know I'm in his office — paneled walls, everything. I can't explain it. I — Hap, I took his fountain pen.

HAPPY: Geez, did he catch you?

BIFF: I ran out. I ran down all eleven flights. I ran and ran and ran.

HAPPY: That was an awful dumb — what'd you do that for?

BIFF (*agonized*): I don't know, I just — wanted to take something, I don't know. You gotta help me, Hap. I'm gonna tell Pop.

HAPPY: You crazy? What for?

BIFF: Hap, he's got to understand that I'm not the man somebody lends that kind of money to. He thinks I've been spiting him all these years and it's eating him up.

HAPPY: That's just it. You tell him something nice.

BIFF: I can't.

HAPPY: Say you got a lunch date with Oliver tomorrow.

BIFF: So what do I do tomorrow?

HAPPY: You leave the house tomorrow and come back at night and say Oliver is thinking it over. And he thinks it over for a couple of weeks, and gradually it fades away and nobody's the worse.

BIFF: But it'll go on forever!

HAPPY: Dad is never so happy as when he's looking forward to something!

(*Willy enters.*)

HAPPY: Hello, scout!

WILLY: Gee, I haven't been here in years!

(*Stanley has followed Willy in and sets a chair for him. Stanley starts off but Happy stops him.*)

HAPPY: Stanley!

(*Stanley stands by, waiting for an order.*)

BIFF (*going to Willy with guilt, as to an invalid*): Sit down, Pop. You want a drink?

WILLY: Sure, I don't mind.

BIFF: Let's get a load on.

WILLY: You look worried.

BIFF: N-no. (*To Stanley.*) Scotch all around. Make it doubles.

STANLEY: Doubles, right. (*He goes.*)

WILLY: You had a couple already, didn't you?

BIFF: Just a couple, yeah.

WILLY: Well, what happened, boy? (*Nodding affirmatively, with a smile.*) Everything go all right?

BIFF (*takes a breath, then reaches out and grasps Willy's hand*): Pal . . . (*He is smiling bravely, and Willy is smiling too.*) I had an experience today.

HAPPY: Terrific, Pop.

WILLY: That so? What happened?

BIFF (*high, slightly alcoholic, above the earth*): I'm going to tell you everything from first to last. It's been a strange day. (*Silence. He looks around, composes himself as best he can, but his breath keeps breaking the rhythm of his voice.*) I had to wait quite a while for him, and —

WILLY: Oliver?

BIFF: Yeah, Oliver. All day, as a matter of cold fact. And a lot of — instances — facts, Pop, facts about my life came back to me. Who was it, Pop? Who ever said I was a salesman with Oliver?

WILLY: Well, you were.

BIFF: No, Dad, I was a shipping clerk.

WILLY: But you were practically —

BIFF (*with determination*): Dad, I don't know who said it first, but I was never a salesman for Bill Oliver.

WILLY: What're you talking about?

BIFF: Let's hold on to the facts tonight, Pop. We're not going to get anywhere bullin' around. I was a shipping clerk.

WILLY (*angrily*): All right, now listen to me —

BIFF: Why don't you let me finish?

WILLY: I'm not interested in stories about the past or any crap of that kind because the woods are burning, boys, you understand? There's a big blaze going on all around. I was fired today.

BIFF (*shocked*): How could you be?

WILLY: I was fired, and I'm looking for a little good news to tell your mother, because the woman has waited and the woman has suffered. The gist of it is that I haven't got a story left in my head, Biff. So don't give me a lecture about facts and aspects. I am not interested. Now what've you got to say to me?

(*Stanley enters with three drinks. They wait until he leaves.*)

WILLY: Did you see Oliver?

BIFF: Jesus, Dad!

WILLY: You mean you didn't go up there?

HAPPY: Sure he went up there.

BIFF: I did. I — saw him. How could they fire you?

WILLY (*on the edge of his chair*): What kind of a welcome did he give you?

BIFF: He won't even let you work on commission?

WILLY: I'm out! (*Driving.*) So tell me, he gave you a warm welcome?

HAPPY: Sure, Pop, sure!

BIFF (*driven*): Well, it was kind of —

WILLY: I was wondering if he'd remember you. (*To Happy.*) Imagine, man doesn't see him for ten, twelve years and gives him that kind of a welcome!

HAPPY: Damn right!

BIFF (*trying to return to the offensive*): Pop, look —

WILLY: You know why he remembered you, don't you? Because you impressed him in those days.

BIFF: Let's talk quietly and get this down to the facts, huh?

WILLY (*as though Biff had been interrupting*): Well, what happened? It's great news, Biff. Did he take you into his office or'd you talk in the waiting room?

BIFF: Well, he came in, see, and —

WILLY (*with a big smile*): What'd he say? Betcha he threw his arm around you.

BIFF: Well, he kinda —

WILLY: He's a fine man. (*To Happy.*) Very hard man to see, y'know.

HAPPY (*agreeing*): Oh, I know.

WILLY (*to Biff*): Is that where you had the drinks?

BIFF: Yeah, he gave me a couple of — no, no!

HAPPY (*cutting in*): He told him my Florida idea.

WILLY: Don't interrupt. (*To Biff.*) How'd he react to the Florida idea?

BIFF: Dad, will you give me a minute to explain?

WILLY: I've been waiting for you to explain since I sat down here! What happened? He took you into his office and what?

BIFF: Well — I talked. And — and he listened, see.

WILLY: Famous for the way he listens, y'know. What was his answer?

BIFF: His answer was — (*He breaks off, suddenly angry.*) Dad, you're not letting me tell you what I want to tell you!

WILLY (*accusing, angered*): You didn't see him, did you?

BIFF: I did see him!

WILLY: What'd you insult him or something? You insulted him, didn't you?

BIFF: Listen, will you let me out of it, will you just let me out of it!

HAPPY: What the hell!

WILLY: Tell me what happened!

BIFF (*to Happy*): I can't talk to him!

(*A single trumpet note jars the ear. The light of green leaves stains the house, which holds the air of night and a dream. Young Bernard enters and knocks on the door of the house.*)

YOUNG BERNARD (*frantically*): Mrs. Loman, Mrs. Loman!

HAPPY: Tell him what happened!

BIFF (*to Happy*): Shut up and leave me alone!

WILLY: No, no! You had to go and flunk math!

BIFF: What math? What're you talking about?

YOUNG BERNARD: Mrs. Loman, Mrs. Loman!

(*Linda appears in the house, as of old.*)

WILLY (*wildly*): Math, math, math!

BIFF: Take it easy, Pop!

YOUNG BERNARD: Mrs. Loman!

WILLY (*furiously*): If you hadn't flunked you'd've been set by now!

BIFF: Now, look, I'm gonna tell you what happened, and you're going to listen to me.

YOUNG BERNARD: Mrs. Loman!

BIFF: I waited six hours —

HAPPY: What the hell are you saying?

BIFF: I kept sending in my name but he wouldn't see me. So finally he . . . (*He continues unheard as light fades low on the restaurant.*)

YOUNG BERNARD: Biff flunked math!

LINDA: No!

YOUNG BERNARD: Birnbaum flunked him! They won't graduate him!

LINDA: But they have to. He's gotta go to the university. Where is he? Biff! Biff!

YOUNG BERNARD: No, he left. He went to Grand Central.

LINDA: Grand — You mean he went to Boston!

YOUNG BERNARD: Is Uncle Willy in Boston?

LINDA: Oh, maybe Willy can talk to the teacher. Oh, the poor, poor boy!

(*Light on house area snaps out.*)

BIFF (*at the table, now audible, holding up a gold fountain pen*): . . . so I'm washed up with Oliver, you understand? Are you listening to me?

WILLY (*at a loss*): Yeah, sure. If you hadn't flunked —

BIFF: Flunked what? What're you talking about?

WILLY: Don't blame everything on me! I didn't flunk math — you did! What pen?

HAPPY: That was awful dumb, Biff, a pen like that is worth —

WILLY (*seeing the pen for the first time*): You took Oliver's pen?

BIFF (*weakening*): Dad, I just explained it to you.

WILLY: You stole Bill Oliver's fountain pen!

BIFF: I didn't exactly steal it! That's just what I've been explaining to you!

HAPPY: He had it in his hand and just then Oliver walked in, so he got nervous and stuck it in his pocket!

WILLY: My God, Biff!

BIFF: I never intended to do it, Dad!

OPERATOR'S VOICE: Standish Arms, good evening!

WILLY (*shouting*): I'm not in my room!

BIFF (*frightened*): Dad, what's the matter? (*He and Happy stand up.*)

OPERATOR: Ringing Mr. Loman for you!

WILLY: I'm not there, stop it!

BIFF (*horrified, gets down on one knee before Willy*): Dad, I'll make good, I'll make good. (*Willy tries to get to his feet. Biff holds him down.*) Sit down now.

WILLY: No, you're no good, you're no good for anything.

BIFF: I am, Dad, I'll find something else, you understand? Now don't worry about anything. (*He holds up Willy's face.*) Talk to me, Dad.

OPERATOR: Mr. Loman does not answer. Shall I page him?

WILLY (*attempting to stand, as though to rush and silence the Operator*): No, no, no!

HAPPY: He'll strike something, Pop.

WILLY: No, no . . .

BIFF (*desperately, standing over Willy*): Pop, listen! Listen to me! I'm telling you something good. Oliver talked to his partner about the Florida idea. You listening? He — he talked to his partner, and he came to me . . . I'm going to be all right, you hear? Dad, listen to me, he said it was just a question of the amount!

WILLY: Then you . . . got it?

HAPPY: He's gonna be terrific, Pop!

WILLY (*trying to stand*): Then you got it, haven't you? You got it! You got it!

BIFF (*agonized, holds Willy down*): No, no. Look, Pop. I'm supposed to have lunch with them tomorrow. I'm just telling you this so you'll know that I can still make an impression, Pop. And I'll make good somewhere, but I can't go tomorrow, see?

WILLY: Why not? You simply —

BIFF: But the pen, Pop!

WILLY: You give it to him and tell him it was an oversight!

HAPPY: Sure, have lunch tomorrow!

BIFF: I can't say that —

WILLY: You were doing a crossword puzzle and accidentally used his pen!

BIFF: Listen, kid, I took those balls years ago, now I walk in with his fountain pen? That clinches it, don't you see? I can't face him like that! I'll try elsewhere.

PAGE'S VOICE: Paging Mr. Loman!

WILLY: Don't you want to be anything?

BIFF: Pop, how can I go back?

WILLY: You don't want to be anything, is that what's behind it?

BIFF (*now angry at Willy for not crediting his sympathy*): Don't take it that way! You think it was easy walking into that office after what I'd done to him? A team of horses couldn't have dragged me back to Bill Oliver!

WILLY: Then why'd you go?

BIFF: Why did I go? Why did I go! Look at you! Look at what's become of you!

(*Off left, The Woman laughs.*)

WILLY: Biff, you're going to go to that lunch tomorrow, or —

BIFF: I can't go. I've got no appointment!

HAPPY: Biff, for . . . !

WILLY: Are you spiting me?

BIFF: Don't take it that way! Goddammit!

WILLY (*strikes Biff and falters away from the table*): You rotten little louse! Are you spiting me?

THE WOMAN: Someone's at the door, Willy!

BIFF: I'm no good, can't you see what I am?

HAPPY (*separating them*): Hey, you're in a restaurant! Now cut it out, both of you! (*The girls enter.*) Hello, girls, sit down.

(*The Woman laughs, off left.*)

MISS FORSYTHE: I guess we might as well. This is Letta.

THE WOMAN: Willy, are you going to wake up?

BIFF (*ignoring Willy*): How're ya, miss, sit down. What do you drink?

MISS FORSYTHE: Letta might not be able to stay long.

LETTA: I gotta get up very early tomorrow. I got jury duty. I'm so excited! Were you fellows ever on a jury?

BIFF: No, but I been in front of them! (*The girls laugh.*) This is my father.

LETTA: Isn't he cute? Sit down with us, Pop.

HAPPY: Sit him down, Biff!

BIFF (*going to him*): Come on, slugger, drink us under the table. To hell with it! Come on, sit down, pal.

(*On Biff's last insistence, Willy is about to sit.*)

THE WOMAN (*now urgently*): Willy, are you going to answer the door!

(*The Woman's call pulls Willy back. He starts right, befuddled.*)

BIFF: Hey, where are you going?

WILLY: Open the door.

BIFF: The door?

WILLY: The washroom . . . the door . . . where's the door?

BIFF (*leading Willy to the left*): Just go straight down.

(*Willy moves left.*)

THE WOMAN: Willy, Willy, are you going to get up, get up, get up, get up?

(*Willy exits left.*)

LETTA: I think it's sweet you bring your daddy along.

MISS FORSYTHE: Oh, he isn't really your father!

BIFF (*at left, turning to her resentfully*): Miss Forsythe, you've just seen a prince walk by. A fine, troubled prince. A hard-working, unappreciated prince. A pal, you understand? A good companion. Always for his boys.

LETTA: That's so sweet.

HAPPY: Well, girls, what's the program? We're wasting time. Come on, Biff. Gather round. Where would you like to go?

BIFF: Why don't you do something for him?

HAPPY: Me!

BIFF: Don't you give a damn for him, Hap?

HAPPY: What're you talking about? I'm the one who —

BIFF: I sense it, you don't give a good goddam about him. (*He takes the rolled-up hose from his pocket and puts it on the table in front of Happy.*) Look what I found in the cellar, for Christ's sake. How can you bear to let it go on?

HAPPY: Me? Who goes away? Who runs off and —

BIFF: Yeah, but he doesn't mean anything to you. You could help him — I can't! Don't you understand what I'm talking about? He's going to kill himself, don't you know that?

HAPPY: Don't I know it! Me!

BIFF: Hap, help him! Jesus . . . help him . . . Help me, help me, I can't bear to look at his face! (*Ready to weep, he hurries out, up right.*)

HAPPY (*starting after him*): Where are you going?

MISS FORSYTHE: What's he so mad about?

HAPPY: Come on, girls, we'll catch up with him.

MISS FORSYTHE (*as Happy pushes her out*): Say, I don't like that temper of his!

HAPPY: He's just a little overstrung, he'll be all right!

WILLY (*off left, as The Woman laughs*): Don't answer! Don't answer!

LETTA: Don't you want to tell your father —

HAPPY: No, that's not my father. He's just a guy. Come on, we'll catch Biff, and, honey, we're going to paint this town! Stanley, where's the check! Hey, Stanley!

(*They exit. Stanley looks toward left.*)

STANLEY (*calling to Happy indignantly*): Mr. Loman! Mr. Loman!

(*Stanley picks up a chair and follows them off. Knocking is heard off left. The Woman enters, laughing. Willy follows her. She is in a black slip; he is buttoning his shirt. Raw, sensuous music accompanies their speech.*)

WILLY: Will you stop laughing? Will you stop?

THE WOMAN: Aren't you going to answer the door? He'll wake the whole hotel.

WILLY: I'm not expecting anybody.

THE WOMAN: Whyn't you have another drink, honey, and stop being so damn self-centered?

WILLY: I'm so lonely.

THE WOMAN: You know you ruined me, Willy? From now on, whenever you come to the office, I'll see that you go right through to the buyers. No waiting at my desk anymore, Willy. You ruined me.

WILLY: That's nice of you to say that.

THE WOMAN: Gee, you are self-centered! Why so sad? You are the saddest, self-centeredest soul I ever did see-saw. (*She laughs. He kisses her.*) Come on inside, drummer boy. It's silly to be dressing in the middle of the night. (*As knocking is heard.*) Aren't you going to answer the door?

WILLY: They're knocking on the wrong door.

THE WOMAN: But I felt the knocking. And he heard us talking in here. Maybe the hotel's on fire!

WILLY (*his terror rising*): It's a mistake.

THE WOMAN: Then tell him to go away!

WILLY: There's nobody there.

THE WOMAN: It's getting on my nerves, Willy. There's somebody standing out there and it's getting on my nerves!

WILLY (*pushing her away from him*): All right, stay in the bathroom here, and don't come out. I think there's a law in Massachusetts about it, so don't come out. It may be that new room clerk. He looked very mean. So don't come out. It's a mistake, there's no fire.

(*The knocking is heard again. He takes a few steps away from her, and she vanishes into the wing. The light follows him, and now he is facing Young Biff, who carries a suitcase. Biff steps toward him. The music is gone.*)

BIFF: Why didn't you answer?

WILLY: Biff! What are you doing in Boston?

BIFF: Why didn't you answer? I've been knocking for five minutes, I called you on the phone —

WILLY: I just heard you. I was in the bathroom and had the door shut. Did anything happen home?

BIFF: Dad — I let you down.

WILLY: What do you mean?

BIFF: Dad . . .

WILLY: Biffo, what's this about? (*Putting his arm around Biff.*) Come on, let's go downstairs and get you a malted.

BIFF: Dad, I flunked math.

WILLY: Not for the term?

BIFF: The term. I haven't got enough credits to graduate.

WILLY: You mean to say Bernard wouldn't give you the answers?

BIFF: He did, he tried, but I only got a sixty-one.

WILLY: And they wouldn't give you four points?

BIFF: Birnbaum refused absolutely. I begged him, Pop, but he won't give me those points. You gotta talk to him before they close the school. Because if he saw the kind of man you are, and you just talked to him in your way, I'm sure he'd come through for me. The class came right before practice, see, and I didn't go enough. Would you talk to him? He'd like you, Pop. You know the way you could talk.

WILLY: You're on. We'll drive right back.

BIFF: Oh, Dad, good work! I'm sure he'll change it for you!

WILLY: Go downstairs and tell the clerk I'm checkin' out. Go right down.

BIFF: Yes, sir! See, the reason he hates me, Pop — one day he was late for class so I got up at the blackboard and imitated him. I crossed my eyes and talked with a lithp.

WILLY (*laughing*): You did? The kids like it?

BIFF: They nearly died laughing!

WILLY: Yeah? What'd you do?

BIFF: The thquare root of thixthy twee is . . . (*Willy bursts out laughing; Biff joins.*) And in the middle of it he walked in!

(*Willy laughs and The Woman joins in offstage.*)

WILLY (*without hesitation*): Hurry downstairs and —

BIFF: Somebody in there?

WILLY: No, that was next door.

(*The Woman laughs offstage.*)

BIFF: Somebody got in your bathroom!

WILLY: No, it's the next room, there's a party —

THE WOMAN (*enters, laughing. She lisps this.*): Can I come in? There's something in the bathtub, Willy, and it's moving!

(*Willy looks at Biff, who is staring open-mouthed and horrified at The Woman.*)

WILLY: Ah — you better go back to your room. They must be finished painting by now. They're painting her room so I let her take a shower here. Go back, go back . . . (*He pushes her.*)

THE WOMAN (*resisting*): But I've got to get dressed, Willy, I can't —

WILLY: Get out of here! Go back, go back . . . (*Suddenly striving for the ordinary.*) This is Miss Francis, Biff, she's a buyer. They're painting her room. Go back, Miss Francis, go back . . .

THE WOMAN: But my clothes, I can't go out naked in the hall!

WILLY (*pushing her offstage*): Get outa here! Go back, go back!

(*Biff slowly sits down on his suitcase as the argument continues offstage.*)

THE WOMAN: Where's my stockings? You promised me stockings, Willy!

WILLY: I have no stockings here!

THE WOMAN: You had two boxes of size nine sheers for me, and I want them!

WILLY: Here, for God's sake, will you get outa here!

THE WOMAN (*enters holding a box of stockings*): I just hope there's nobody in the hall. That's all I hope. (*To Biff.*) Are you football or baseball?

BIFF: Football.

THE WOMAN (*angry, humiliated*): That's me too. G'night. (*She snatches her clothes from Willy, and walks out.*)

WILLY (*after a pause*): Well, better get going. I want to get to the school first thing in the morning. Get my suits out of the closet. I'll get my valise. (*Biff doesn't move.*) What's the matter! (*Biff remains motionless, tears falling.*) She's a buyer. Buys for J. H. Simmons. She lives down the hall — they're painting. You don't imagine — (*He breaks off. After a pause.*) Now listen, pal, she's just a buyer. She sees merchandise in her room and they have to keep it looking just so . . . (*Pause. Assuming command.*) All right, get my suits. (*Biff doesn't move.*) Now stop crying and do as I say. I gave you an order. Biff, I gave you an order! Is that what you do when I give you an order? How dare you cry! (*Putting his arm around Biff.*) Now look, Biff, when you grow up you'll understand about these things. You mustn't — you mustn't over-emphasize a thing like this. I'll see Birnbaum first thing in the morning.

BIFF: Never mind.

WILLY (*getting down beside Biff*): Never mind! He's going to give you those points. I'll see to it.

BIFF: He wouldn't listen to you.

WILLY: He certainly will listen to me. You need those points for the U. of Virginia.

BIFF: I'm not going there.

WILLY: Heh? If I can't get him to change that mark you'll make it up in summer school. You've got all summer to —

BIFF (*his weeping breaking from him*): Dad . . .

WILLY (*infected by it*): Oh, my boy . . .

BIFF: Dad . . .

WILLY: She's nothing to me, Biff. I was lonely, I was terribly lonely.

BIFF: You — you gave her Mama's stockings! (*His tears break through and he rises to go.*)

WILLY (*grabbing for Biff*): I gave you an order!

BIFF: Don't touch me, you — liar!

WILLY: Apologize for that!

BIFF: You fake! You phony little fake! You fake! (*Overcome, he turns quickly and weeping fully goes out with his suitcase. Willy is left on the floor on his knees.*)

WILLY: I gave you an order! Biff, come back here or I'll beat you! Come back here! I'll whip you!

(*Stanley comes quickly in from the right and stands in front of Willy.*)

WILLY (*shouts at Stanley*): I gave you an order . . .

STANLEY: Hey, let's pick it up, pick it up, Mr. Loman. (*He helps Willy to his feet.*) Your boys left with the chippies. They said they'll see you home.

(*A second waiter watches some distance away.*)

WILLY: But we were supposed to have dinner together.

(*Music is heard, Willy's theme.*)

STANLEY: Can you make it?

WILLY: I'll — sure, I can make it. (*Suddenly concerned about his clothes.*) Do I — I look all right?

STANLEY: Sure, you look all right. (*He flicks a speck off Willy's lapel.*)

WILLY: Here — here's a dollar.

STANLEY: Oh, your son paid me. It's all right.

WILLY (*putting it in Stanley's hand*): No, take it. You're a good boy.

STANLEY: Oh, no, you don't have to . . .

WILLY: Here — here's some more, I don't need it anymore. (*After a slight pause.*) Tell me — is there a seed store in the neighborhood?

STANLEY: Seeds? You mean like to plant?

(*As Willy turns, Stanley slips the money back into his jacket pocket.*)

WILLY: Yes. Carrots, peas . . .

STANLEY: Well, there's hardware stores on Sixth Avenue, but it may be too late now.

WILLY (*anxiously*): Oh, I'd better hurry. I've got to get some seeds. (*He starts off to the right.*) I've got to get some seeds, right away. Nothing's planted. I don't have a thing in the ground.

(*Willy hurries out as the light goes down. Stanley moves over to the right after him, watches him off. The other waiter has been staring at Willy.*)

STANLEY (*to the waiter*): Well, whatta you looking at?

(*The waiter picks up the chairs and moves off right. Stanley takes the table and follows him. The light fades on this area. There is a long pause, the sound of the flute coming over. The light gradually rises on the kitchen, which is empty. Happy appears at the door of the house, followed by Biff. Happy is carrying a large bunch of long-stemmed roses. He enters the kitchen, looks around for Linda. Not seeing her, he turns to Biff, who is just outside the house door, and makes a gesture with his hands, indicating "Not here, I guess." He looks into the living room and freezes. Inside, Linda, unseen, is seated, Willy's coat on her lap. She rises ominously and quietly and moves toward Happy, who backs up into the kitchen, afraid.*)

HAPPY: Hey, what're you doing up? (*Linda says nothing but moves toward him implacably.*) Where's Pop? (*He keeps backing to the right, and now Linda is in full view in the doorway to the living room.*) Is he sleeping?

LINDA: Where were you?

HAPPY (*trying to laugh it off*): We met two girls, Mom, very fine types. Here, we brought you some flowers. (*Offering them to her.*) Put them in your room, Ma.

(*She knocks them to the floor at Biff's feet. He has now come inside and closed the door behind him. She stares at Biff, silent.*)

HAPPY: Now what'd you do that for? Mom, I want you to have some flowers —

LINDA (*cutting Happy off, violently to Biff*): Don't you care whether he lives or dies?

HAPPY (*going to the stairs*): Come upstairs, Biff.

BIFF (*with a flare of disgust, to Happy*): Go away from me! (*To Linda.*) What do you mean, lives or dies? Nobody's dying around here, pal.

LINDA: Get out of my sight! Get out of here!

BIFF: I wanna see the boss.

LINDA: You're not going near him!

BIFF: Where is he? (*He moves into the living room and Linda follows.*)

LINDA (*shouting after Biff*): You invite him for dinner. He looks forward to it all day — (*Biff appears in his parents' bedroom, looks around, and exits*) — and then you desert him there. There's no stranger you'd do that to!

HAPPY: Why? He had a swell time with us. Listen, when I — (*Linda comes back into the kitchen*) — desert him I hope I don't outlive the day!

LINDA: Get out of here!

HAPPY: Now look, Mom . . .

LINDA: Did you have to go to women tonight? You and your lousy rotten whores!

(*Biff reenters the kitchen.*)

HAPPY: Mom, all we did was follow Biff around trying to cheer him up! (*To Biff.*) Boy, what a night you gave me!

LINDA: Get out of here, both of you, and don't come back! I don't want you tormenting him any more. Go on now, get your things together! (*To Biff.*) You can sleep in his apartment. (*She starts to pick up the flowers and stops herself.*) Pick up this stuff, I'm not your maid anymore. Pick it up, you bum, you!

(*Happy turns his back to her in refusal. Biff slowly moves over and gets down on his knees, picking up the flowers.*)

LINDA: You're a pair of animals! Not one, not another living soul would have had the cruelty to walk out on that man in a restaurant!

BIFF (*not looking at her*): Is that what he said?

LINDA: He didn't have to say anything. He was so humiliated he nearly limped when he came in.

HAPPY: But, Mom, he had a great time with us —

BIFF (*cutting him off violently*): Shut up!

(*Without another word, Happy goes upstairs.*)

LINDA: You! You didn't even go in to see if he was all right!

BIFF (*still on the floor in front of Linda, the flowers in his hand; with self-loathing*): No. Didn't. Didn't do a damned thing. How do you like that, heh? Left him babbling in a toilet.

LINDA: You louse. You . . .

BIFF: Now you hit it on the nose! (*He gets up, throws the flowers in the wastebasket.*) The scum of the earth, and you're looking at him!

LINDA: Get out of here!

BIFF: I gotta talk to the boss, Mom. Where is he?

LINDA: You're not going near him. Get out of this house!

BIFF (*with absolute assurance, determination*): No. We're gonna have an abrupt conversation, him and me.

LINDA: You're not talking to him.

(*Hammering is heard from outside the house, off right. Biff turns toward the noise.*)

LINDA (*suddenly pleading*): Will you please leave him alone?

BIFF: What's he doing out there?

LINDA: He's planting the garden!

BIFF (*quietly*): Now? Oh, my God!

(*Biff moves outside, Linda following. The light dies down on them and comes up on the center of the apron as Willy walks into it. He is carrying a flashlight, a hoe, and a handful of seed packets. He raps the top of the hoe sharply to fix it firmly, and then moves to the left, measuring off the distance with his foot. He holds the flashlight to look at the seed packets, reading off the instructions. He is in the blue of night.*)

WILLY: Carrots . . . quarter-inch apart. Rows . . . one-foot rows. (*He measures it off.*) One foot. (*He puts down a package and measures off.*) Beets. (*He puts down another package and measures again.*) Lettuce. (*He reads the package, puts it down.*) One foot — (*He breaks off as Ben appears at the right and moves slowly down to him.*) What a proposition, ts, ts. Terrific, terrific. 'Cause she's suffered, Ben, the woman has suffered. You understand me? A man can't go out the way he came in, Ben, a man has got to add up to something. You can't, you can't — (*Ben moves toward him as though to interrupt.*) You gotta consider, now. Don't answer so quick. Remember, it's a guaranteed twenty-thousand-dollar proposition. Now look, Ben, I want you to go through the ins and outs of this thing with me. I've got nobody to talk to, Ben, and the woman has suffered, you hear me?

BEN (*standing still, considering*): What's the proposition?

WILLY: It's twenty thousand dollars on the barrelhead. Guaranteed, gilt-edged, you understand?

BEN: You don't want to make a fool of yourself. They might not honor the policy.

WILLY: How can they dare refuse? Didn't I work like a coolie to meet every premium on the nose? And now they don't pay off? Impossible!

BEN: It's called a cowardly thing, William.

WILLY: Why? Does it take more guts to stand here the rest of my life ringing up a zero?

BEN (*yielding*): That's a point, William. (*He moves, thinking, turns.*) And twenty thousand — that *is* something one can feel with the hand, it is there.

WILLY (*now assured, with rising power*): Oh, Ben, that's the whole beauty of it! I see it like a diamond, shining in the dark, hard and rough, that I can pick up and touch in my hand. Not like — like an appointment! This would not be another damned-fool appointment, Ben, and it changes all the aspects. Because he thinks I'm nothing, see, and so he spites me. But the funeral — (*Straightening up.*) Ben, that funeral will be massive! They'll come from Maine, Massachusetts, Vermont, New Hampshire! All the old-timers with the strange license plates — that boy will be thunderstruck, Ben, because he never

realized — I am known! Rhode Island, New York, New Jersey — I am known, Ben, and he'll see it with his eyes once and for all. He'll see what I am, Ben! He's in for a shock, that boy!

BEN (*coming down to the edge of the garden*): He'll call you a coward.

WILLY (*suddenly fearful*): No, that would be terrible.

BEN: Yes. And a damned fool.

WILLY: No, no, he mustn't, I won't have that! (*He is broken and desperate.*)

BEN: He'll hate you, William.

(*The gay music of the Boys is heard.*)

WILLY: Oh, Ben, how do we get back to all the great times? Used to be so full of light, and comradeship, the sleigh-riding in winter, and the ruddiness on his cheeks. And always some kind of good news coming up, always something nice coming up ahead. And never even let me carry the valises in the house, and simonizing, simonizing that little red car! Why, why can't I give him something and not have him hate me?

BEN: Let me think about it. (*He glances at his watch.*) I still have a little time. Remarkable proposition, but you've got to be sure you're not making a fool of yourself.

(*Ben drifts off upstage and goes out of sight. Biff comes down from the left.*)

WILLY (*suddenly conscious of Biff, turns and looks up at him, then begins picking up the packages of seeds in confusion*): Where the hell is that seed? (*Indignantly.*) You can't see nothing out here! They boxed in the whole goddam neighborhood!

BIFF: There are people all around here. Don't you realize that?

WILLY: I'm busy. Don't bother me.

BIFF (*taking the hoe from Willy*): I'm saying good-by to you, Pop. (*Willy looks at him, silent, unable to move.*) I'm not coming back any more.

WILLY: You're not going to see Oliver tomorrow?

BIFF: I've got no appointment, Dad.

WILLY: He put his arm around you, and you've got no appointment?

BIFF: Pop, get this now, will you? Everytime I've left it's been a fight that sent me out of here. Today I realized something about myself and I tried to explain it to you and I — I think I'm just not smart enough to make any sense out of it for you. To hell with whose fault it is or anything like that. (*He takes Willy's arm.*) Let's just wrap it up, heh? Come on in, we'll tell Mom. (*He gently tries to pull Willy to left.*)

WILLY (*frozen, immobile, with guilt in his voice*): No, I don't want to see her.

BIFF: Come on! (*He pulls again, and Willy tries to pull away.*)

WILLY (*highly nervous*): No, no, I don't want to see her.

BIFF (*tries to look into Willy's face, as if to find the answer there*): Why don't you want to see her?

WILLY (*more harshly now*): Don't bother me, will you?

BIFF: What do you mean, you don't want to see her? You don't want them calling you yellow, do you? This isn't your fault; it's me, I'm a bum. Now come inside! (*Willy strains to get away.*) Did you hear what I said to you?

(*Willy pulls away and quickly goes by himself into the house. Biff follows.*)

LINDA (*to Willy*): Did you plant, dear?

BIFF (*at the door, to Linda*): All right, we had it out. I'm going and I'm not writing any more.

LINDA (*going to Willy in the kitchen*): I think that's the best way, dear. 'Cause there's no use drawing it out, you'll just never get along.

(*Willy doesn't respond.*)

BIFF: People ask where I am and what I'm doing, you don't know, and you don't care. That way it'll be off your mind and you can start brightening up again. All right? That clears it, doesn't it? (*Willy is silent, and Biff goes to him.*) You gonna wish me luck, scout? (*He extends his hand.*) What do you say?

LINDA: Shake his hand, Willy.

WILLY (*turning to her, seething with hurt*): There's no necessity to mention the pen at all, y'know.

BIFF (*gently*): I've got no appointment, Dad.

WILLY (*erupting fiercely*): He put his arm around . . . ?

BIFF: Dad, you're never going to see what I am, so what's the use of arguing? If I strike oil I'll send you a check. Meantime forget I'm alive.

WILLY (*to Linda*): Spite, see?

BIFF: Shake hands, Dad.

WILLY: Not my hand.

BIFF: I was hoping not to go this way.

WILLY: Well, this is the way you're going. Good-by.

(*Biff looks at him a moment, then turns sharply and goes to the stairs.*)

WILLY (*stops him with*): May you rot in hell if you leave this house!

BIFF (*turning*): Exactly what is it that you want from me?

WILLY: I want you to know, on the train, in the mountains, in the valleys, wherever you go, that you cut down your life for spite!

BIFF: No, no.

WILLY: Spite, spite, is the word of your undoing! And when you're down and out, remember what did it. When you're rotting somewhere beside the railroad tracks, remember, and don't you dare blame it on me!

BIFF: I'm not blaming it on you!

WILLY: I won't take the rap for this, you hear?

(*Happy comes down the stairs and stands on the bottom step, watching.*)

BIFF: That's just what I'm telling you!

WILLY (*sinking into a chair at a table, with full accusation*): You're trying to put a knife in me — don't think I don't know what you're doing!

BIFF: All right, phony! Then let's lay it on the line. (*He whips the rubber tube out of his pocket and puts it on the table.*)

HAPPY: You crazy . . .

LINDA: Biff! (*She moves to grab the hose, but Biff holds it down with his hand.*)

BIFF: Leave it there! Don't move it!

WILLY (*not looking at it*): What is that?

BIFF: You know goddam well what that is.

WILLY (*caged, wanting to escape*): I never saw that.

BIFF: You saw it. The mice didn't bring it into the cellar! What is this supposed to do, make a hero out of you? This supposed to make me sorry for you?

WILLY: Never heard of it.

BIFF: There'll be no pity for you, you hear it? No pity!

WILLY (*to Linda*): You hear the spite!

BIFF: No, you're going to hear the truth — what you are and what I am!

LINDA: Stop it!

WILLY: Spite!

HAPPY (*coming down toward Biff*): You cut it now!

BIFF (*to Happy*): The man don't know who we are! The man is gonna know! (*To Willy.*) We never told the truth for ten minutes in this house!

HAPPY: We always told the truth!

BIFF (*turning on him*): You big blow, are you the assistant buyer? You're one of the two assistants to the assistant, aren't you?

HAPPY: Well, I'm practically . . .

BIFF: You're practically full of it! We all are! and I'm through with it. (*To Willy.*) Now hear this, Willy, this is me.

WILLY: I know you!

BIFF: You know why I had no address for three months? I stole a suit in Kansas City and I was in jail. (*To*

Linda, who is sobbing.) Stop crying. I'm through with it.

(*Linda turns away from them, her hands covering her face.*)

WILLY: I suppose that's my fault!

BIFF: I stole myself out of every good job since high school!

WILLY: And whose fault is that?

BIFF: And I never got anywhere because you blew me so full of hot air I could never stand taking orders from anybody! That's whose fault it is!

WILLY: I hear that!

LINDA: Don't, Biff!

BIFF: It's goddam time you heard that! I had to be boss big shot in two weeks, and I'm through with it!

WILLY: Then hang yourself! For spite, hang yourself!

BIFF: No! Nobody's hanging himself, Willy! I ran down eleven flights with a pen in my hand today. And suddenly I stopped, you hear me? And in the middle of that office building, do you hear this? I stopped in the middle of that building and I saw — the sky. I saw the things that I love in this world. The work and the food and time to sit and smoke. And I looked at the pen and said to myself, what the hell am I grabbing this for? Why am I trying to become what I don't want to be? What am I doing in an office, making a contemptuous, begging fool of myself, when all I want is out there, waiting for me the minute I say I know who I am! Why can't I say that, Willy? (*He tries to make Willy face him, but Willy pulls away and moves to the left.*)

WILLY (*with hatred, threateningly*): The door of your life is wide open!

BIFF: Pop! I'm a dime a dozen, and so are you!

WILLY (*turning on him now in an uncontrolled outburst*): I am not a dime a dozen! I am Willy Loman, and you are Biff Loman!

(*Biff starts for Willy, but is blocked by Happy. In his fury, Biff seems on the verge of attacking his father.*)

BIFF: I am not a leader of men, Willy, and neither are you. You were never anything but a hard-working drummer who landed in the ash can like all the rest of them! I'm one dollar an hour, Willy! I tried seven states and couldn't raise it. A buck an hour! Do you gather my meaning? I'm not bringing home any prizes any more, and you're going to stop waiting for me to bring them home!

WILLY (*directly to Biff*): You vengeful, spiteful mutt!

(*Biff breaks from Happy. Willy, in fright, starts up the stairs. Biff grabs him:*)

BIFF (*at the peak of his fury*): Pop, I'm nothing! I'm nothing, Pop. Can't you understand that? There's no spite in it any more. I'm just what I am, that's all.

(*Biff's fury has spent itself and he breaks down, sobbing, holding on to Willy, who dumbly fumbles for Biff's face.*)

WILLY (*astonished*): What're you doing? What're you doing? (*To Linda.*) Why is he crying?

BIFF (*crying, broken*): Will you let me go, for Christ's sake? Will you take that phony dream and burn it before something happens? (*Struggling to contain himself he pulls away and moves to the stairs.*) I'll go in the morning. Put him — put him to bed. (*Exhausted, Biff moves up the stairs to his room.*)

WILLY (*after a long pause, astonished, elevated*): Isn't that — isn't that remarkable? Biff — he likes me!

LINDA: He loves you, Willy!

HAPPY (*deeply moved*): Always did, Pop.

WILLY: Oh, Biff! (*Staring wildly.*) He cried! Cried to me. (*He is choking with his love, and now cries out his promise.*) That boy — that boy is going to be magnificent!

(*Ben appears in the light just outside the kitchen.*)

BEN: Yes, outstanding, with twenty thousand behind him.

LINDA (*sensing the racing of his mind, fearfully, carefully*): Now come to bed, Willy. It's all settled now.

WILLY (*finding it difficult not to rush out of the house*): Yes, we'll sleep. Come on. Go to sleep, Hap.

BEN: And it does take a great kind of a man to crack the jungle.

(*In accents of dread, Ben's idyllic music starts up.*)

HAPPY (*his arm around Linda*): I'm getting married, Pop, don't forget it. I'm changing everything. I'm gonna run that department before the year is up. You'll see, Mom. (*He kisses her.*)

BEN: The jungle is dark but full of diamonds, Willy.

(*Willy turns, moves, listening to Ben.*)

LINDA: Be good. You're both good boys, just act that way, that's all.

HAPPY: 'Night, Pop. (*He goes upstairs.*)

LINDA (*to Willy*): Come, dear.

BEN (*with greater force*): One must go in to fetch a diamond out.

WILLY (*to Linda, as he moves slowly along the edge of kitchen, toward the door*): I just want to get settled down, Linda. Let me sit alone for a little.

LINDA (*almost uttering her fear*): I want you upstairs.

WILLY (*taking her in his arms*): In a few minutes,

Linda. I couldn't sleep right now. Go on, you look awful tired. (*He kisses her.*)

BEN: Not like an appointment at all. A diamond is rough and hard to the touch.

WILLY: Go on now. I'll be right up.

LINDA: I think this is the only way, Willy.

WILLY: Sure, it's the best thing.

BEN: Best thing!

WILLY: The only way. Everything is gonna be — go on, kid, get to bed. You look so tired.

LINDA: Come right up.

WILLY: Two minutes.

(*Linda goes into the living room, then reappears in her bedroom. Willy moves just outside the kitchen door.*)

WILLY: Loves me. (*Wonderingly.*) Always loved me. Isn't that a remarkable thing? Ben, he'll worship me for it!

BEN (*with promise*): It's dark there, but full of diamonds.

WILLY: Can you imagine that magnificence with twenty thousand dollars in his pocket?

LINDA (*calling from her room*): Willy! Come up!

WILLY (*calling into the kitchen*): Yes! yes. Coming! It's very smart, you realize that, don't you, sweetheart? Even Ben sees it. I gotta go, baby. 'By! 'By! (*Going over to Ben, almost dancing.*) Imagine? When the mail comes he'll be ahead of Bernard again!

BEN: A perfect proposition all around.

WILLY: Did you see how he cried to me? Oh, if I could kiss him, Ben!

BEN: Time, William, time!

WILLY: Oh, Ben, I always knew one way or another we were gonna make it, Biff and I!

BEN (*looking at his watch*): The boat. We'll be late. (*He moves slowly off into the darkness.*)

WILLY (*elegiacally, turning to the house*): Now when you kick off, boy, I want a seventy-yard boot, and get right down the field under the ball, and when you hit, hit low and hit hard, because it's important, boy. (*He swings around and faces the audience.*) There's all kinds of important people in the stands, and the first thing you know . . . (*Suddenly realizing he is alone.*) Ben! Ben, where do I . . . ? (*He makes a sudden movement of search.*) Ben, how do I . . . ?

LINDA (*calling*): Willy, you coming up?

WILLY (*uttering a gasp of fear, whirling about as if to quiet her*): Sh! (*He turns around as if to find his way; sounds, faces, voices, seem to be swarming in upon him and he flicks at them, crying, Sh! Sh! Suddenly music, faint and high, stops him. It rises in intensity, almost to an unbearable scream. He goes up and down on his toes, and rushes off around the house.*) Shhh!

LINDA: Willy?

(*There is no answer. Linda waits. Biff gets up off his bed. He is still in his clothes. Happy sits up. Biff stands listening.*)

LINDA (*with real fear*): Willy, answer me! Willy!

(*There is the sound of a car starting and moving away at full speed.*)

LINDA: No!

BIFF (*rushing down the stairs*): Pop!

(*As the car speeds off, the music crashes down in a frenzy of sound, which becomes the soft pulsation of a single cello string. Biff slowly returns to his bedroom. He and Happy gravely don their jackets. Linda slowly walks out of her room. The music has developed into a dead march. The leaves of day are appearing over everything. Charley and Bernard, somberly dressed, appear and knock on the kitchen door. Biff and Happy slowly descend the stairs to the kitchen as Charley and Bernard enter. All stop a moment when Linda, in clothes of mourning, bearing a little bunch of roses, comes through the draped doorway into the kitchen. She goes to Charley and takes his arm. Now all move toward the audience, through the wall-line of the kitchen. At the limit of the apron, Linda lays down the flowers, kneels, and sits back on her heels. All stare down at the grave.*)

REQUIEM

CHARLEY: It's getting dark, Linda.

(*Linda doesn't react. She stares at the grave.*)

BIFF: How about it, Mom? Better get some rest, heh? They'll be closing the gate soon.

(*Linda makes no move. Pause.*)

HAPPY (*deeply angered*): He had no right to do that. There was no necessity for it. We would've helped him.

CHARLEY (*grunting*): Hmmm.

BIFF: Come along, Mom.

LINDA: Why didn't anybody come?

CHARLEY: It was a very nice funeral.

LINDA: But where are all the people he knew? Maybe they blame him.

CHARLEY: Naa. It's a rough world, Linda. They wouldn't blame him.

LINDA: I can't understand it. At this time especially. First time in thirty-five years we were just about free and clear. He only needed a little salary. He was even finished with the dentist.

CHARLEY: No man only needs a little salary.

LINDA: I can't understand it.

BIFF: There were a lot of nice days. When he'd come

home from a trip; or on Sundays, making the stoop; finishing the cellar; putting on the new porch; when he built the extra bathroom; and put up the garage. You know something, Charley, there's more of him in that front stoop than in all the sales he ever made.

CHARLEY: Yeah. He was a happy man with a batch of cement.

LINDA: He was so wonderful with his hands.

BIFF: He had the wrong dreams. All, all, wrong.

HAPPY (*almost ready to fight Biff*): Don't say that!

BIFF: He never knew who he was.

CHARLEY (*Stopping Happy's movement and reply. To Biff.*): Nobody dast blame this man. You don't understand: Willy was a salesman. And for a salesman, there is no rock bottom to the life. He don't put a bolt to a nut, he don't tell you the law or give you medicine. He's a man way out there in the blue, riding on a smile and a shoeshine. And when they start not smiling back — that's an earthquake. And then you get yourself a couple of spots on your hat, and you're finished. Nobody dast blame this man. A salesman is got to dream, boy. It comes with the territory.

BIFF: Charley, the man didn't know who he was.

HAPPY (*infuriated*): Don't say that!

BIFF: Why don't you come with me, Happy?

HAPPY: I'm not licked that easily. I'm staying right in this city, and I'm gonna beat this racket! (*He looks at Biff, his chin set.*) The Loman Brothers!

BIFF: I know who I am, kid.

HAPPY: All right, boy. I'm gonna show you and everybody else that Willy Loman did not die in vain.

He had a good dream. It's the only dream you can have — to come out number-one man. He fought it out here, and this is where I'm gonna win it for him.

BIFF (*with a hopeless glance at Happy, bends toward his mother*): Let's go, Mom.

LINDA: I'll be with you in a minute. Go on, Charley. (*He hesitates.*) I want to, just for a minute. I never had a chance to say good-by.

(*Charley moves away, followed by Happy. Biff remains a slight distance up and left of Linda. She sits there, summoning herself. The flute begins, not far away, playing behind her speech.*)

LINDA: Forgive me, dear. I can't cry. I don't know what it is, but I can't cry. I don't understand it. Why did you ever do that? Help me, Willy, I can't cry. It seems to me that you're just on another trip. I keep expecting you. Willy, dear, I can't cry. Why did you do it? I search and search and I search, and I can't understand it, Willy. I made the last payment on the house today. Today, dear. And there'll be nobody home. (*A sob rises in her throat.*) We're free and clear. (*Sobbing more fully, released.*) We're free. (*Biff comes slowly toward her.*) We're free . . . We're free . . .

(*Biff lifts her to her feet and moves out up right with her in his arms. Linda sobs quietly. Bernard and Charley come together and follow them, followed by Happy. Only the music of the flute is left on the darkening stage as over the house the hard towers of the apartment buildings rise into sharp focus, and the curtain falls.*)

Samuel Beckett

Samuel Beckett (b. 1906) was born into an upper-middle-class family in Dublin. His people were Protestants and he received a privileged education at the Portora Royal School and then went to Trinity College, Dublin, where he studied French and Italian. He was an unusually good student and, in 1928 after graduation, went to Paris to teach English at the École Normale Supérieure, an unusual reward for good scholarship.

Beckett early on straddled two literary cultures: Irish and Anglo-Irish. Most of the literary energy in Ireland in the 1920s and 1930s was split between the essentially conservative Anglo-Irish Protestants, such as William Butler Yeats and Lady Isabella Augusta Gregory, and the more avant-garde Catholics, such as James Joyce, with whom Beckett formed an enduring personal and literary friendship in Paris. Although much younger than Joyce, Beckett developed a close artistic sympathy with him. Beckett's first published work (1929) was an essay on Joyce, and he wrote one of the earliest critical essays on Joyce's most radical literary composition, *Finnegans Wake*.

When he was first in France, Beckett began reading French philosophers, especially Descartes, and this reading exerted a strong influence on his work. Beckett's earliest writings appeared in Eugene Jolas's avant-garde literary journal *transition*, which put him in the center of Parisian literary activity in the late 1920s. After 1930, his series of short stories published under the title *More Pricks than Kicks* (1934) established him as an important writer. After settling in Paris in 1937, Beckett wrote the novel *Murphy* (1938), on a recognizably Irish theme of economic impoverishment, alienation, and of inward meditation and spiritual complexity.

When the war began in 1939 Beckett took up the cause of the French Resistance. His activity caught the eye of the Gestapo, and for two years he lay low in unoccupied France by working as a farmhand and also writing another novel, *Watt* (written in 1944 but published in 1953). After the war he took up residence again in Paris and began writing most of his work in French. His greatest novels were written in the five years after the war, and they are often referred to as his trilogy: *Molloy*, *Malone Dies*, and *The Unnamable*. All these novels are about men who have become disaffected with society and who have strange and compelling urgencies to be alone and to follow exacting and repetitive patterns of behavior. In a sense, they are archetypes of the kinds of heroes — if that word can be used for them — that Beckett created in most of his work.

Beckett's first published play, *Waiting for Godot* (1952), was produced in Paris in 1953, in London in 1955, and in Miami in 1956. From the first, its repetitive, whimsical, and sometimes nonsensical style established the play as a major post-war statement. In a barren setting, Vladimir and Estragon, two tramps who echo the comic vision of Charlie Chaplin, wait for Godot to come. They amuse themselves by doing vaudeville routines, but their loneliness and isolation are painfully apparent to the audience. Godot has promised to come, and as they wait, Vladimir and Estragon speculate on whether or not Godot will come.

The comic moments in the play, along with the enigma of Vladimir and Estragon's fruitless waiting, combined to capture the imagination of audiences and the press. They saw the play as a modern statement about the condition of humankind, although there was never any agreement on just what the statement was. Godot sends a boy to say that he will, indeed, come, but when the play ends, he has not arrived. The implication seems to be that he will never arrive. Most audiences saw Godot as a metaphor for God. Despite the critics' constant inquiries, Beckett was careful never to confirm the view that Godot was God and to keep Godot's identity open-ended.

The play itself was open-ended, as Beckett had hoped, and therefore could be interpreted many ways. One was to see the play as a commentary on the futility of religion; another was to suggest that it underscored the loneliness of humankind in an empty universe; yet a third implied that it was up to individuals, represented by the hapless Vladimir and Estragon, to shape the significance of their own lives, and their waiting represented that effort.

Many of the themes in *Waiting for Godot* are apparent in Beckett's later plays. The radio play *All That Fall* (1957) was followed by the very successful *Krapp's Last Tape* (1958). Also in 1958, *Endgame*, a play on the themes of the end of the world, was produced, followed in 1961 by *Happy Days*. Beckett experimented with minimalist approaches to drama, exemplified in *Act Without Words I* and *Act Without Words II*, which are both mime plays. Other plays experiment with the least necessary in setting, props, and — in the mime plays — even words.

Beckett's plays reveal the deep influence of French post-war philosophers, such as Albert Camus and Jean-Paul Sartre, both existentialists. Their philosophy declares that people are not essentially good, bad, kind, or anything else, but what they make of themselves. Beckett's adaptation of existentialism sometimes borders on pessimism because his vision seems to negate many of the consolations of religious and secular philosophy. His style is antirealist, but the question of realism — the search for beliefs that are reasonable and plausible in a fundamentally absurd world and the plight of individuals who must make their own meanings — is central to most of his work.

Beckett's view of the world is not cheerful. We are not cheered by Krapp or Winnie and Willie. But his vision is consistent, honest, and sympathetic to the persistence of his characters, who endure even in the face of apparent defeat. The significance of Beckett's achievements was recognized in 1969 when he was awarded the Nobel Prize for literature.

KRAPP'S LAST TAPE

Krapp's Last Tape was first performed in 1958 at the Royal Court Theatre in London, a theater that developed an impressive reputation for producing avant-garde drama. By the time this play was produced, Samuel Beckett had achieved a worldwide reputation as an avant-garde playwright. His absurdist drama *Waiting for Godot* had been staged in 1953 and had caused a sensation as one of the first major works of the literature of the absurd that caught the attention of a large, popular audience.

The absurdist writers inherited the philosopher Nietzsche's view that god, as an idea that could explain the meaning of life, was dead. Therefore, the universe was meaningless, or absurd, and people must search out their own meanings and shape their own lives.

Krapp is in many ways a typical Beckett protagonist. He is totally alone, with no friends that he can count on, no connections with the lives of others except through memory. Yet he is in constant contact with his past self, through the medium of tape recordings he made on previous birthdays. The tapes attempt a kind of summary of events in the life of a lonely and withdrawn man. Krapp of the present time (which the stage directions tell us is actually a future time) looks back on the younger man who represents a version of himself that embarrasses him. He constantly says he is glad that the year on this particular tape — his thirty-ninth year — is over.

Krapp has deliberately chosen the way he lives now, and in listening to himself on tape he maintains a continual contact with his earlier personae and congratulates himself on no longer being the man he was. He fears that his best years may be gone but is convinced that he is better now.

Krapp borrows a page from the philosophy of Socrates, who said, "The unexamined life is not worth living." In his way, Krapp examines his life as intensely as anyone could. He listens to the young man he was, watches himself grow older, if not wiser, and cavorts onstage like a magpie. He keeps a ledger filled with his thoughts — as if they might add up to something meaningful. He examines himself in detail: His opinions, the strength of his voice, the thoughts he is able to form at any given moment. He thinks about his mother, who turns out to be the only woman with whom he had any genuine relationship.

He scrutinizes himself but seems to come to no definitive conclusions, other than satisfaction that he is not the man he was. To some extent his feelings reflect one critical point: His past, which absorbs all his energy, organizational skill, and technical know-how, was not devoted to a life that was lived. It was devoted to a life that was left unlived; Krapp has avoided the world. Krapp's is a life of denial.

The use of the tape recorder was very effective in the play's first performances, when the technology of recording was still a novelty. In one production given by London's Young Vic company in the mid-1970s, the sound tapes were replaced by television tapes, with several monitors onstage. Television works as well as sound tapes and in some ways is even more striking to an audience. The lighting in early productions was harsh, brilliant, and totally revealing.

Audiences are impressed by Krapp's antiquity, his grizzledness, his sense that his youth is gone and good riddance. The audience may or may not give him much sympathy, but it will always see him as a strange, compelling figure, someone who is almost pitiable for the way in which he "lost" his life while all the time imagining he was preserving it.

Samuel Beckett (b. 1906)

KRAPP'S LAST TAPE

1958

(*A late evening in the future.*)

(*Krapp's den.*)

(*Front center a small table, the two drawers of which open toward audience.*)

(*Sitting at the table, facing front, i.e., across from the drawers, a wearish° old man: Krapp.*)

(*Rusty black narrow trousers too short for him. Rusty black sleeveless waistcoat, four capacious pockets. Heavy silver watch and chain. Grimy white shirt open at neck, no collar. Surprising pair of dirty white boots, size ten at least, very narrow and pointed.*)

(*White face. Purple nose. Disordered gray hair. Unshaven.*)

(*Very near-sighted [but unspectacled]. Hard of hearing.*)

(*Cracked voice. Distinctive intonation.*)

wearish: Sickly, withered.

(*Laborious walk.*)

(*On the table a tape recorder with microphone and a number of cardboard boxes containing reels of recorded tapes.*)

(*Table and immediately adjacent area in strong white light. Rest of stage in darkness.*)

(*Krapp remains a moment motionless, heaves a great sigh, looks at his watch, fumbles in his pockets, takes out an envelope, puts it back, fumbles, takes out a small bunch of keys, raises it to his eyes, chooses a key, gets up and moves to front of table. He stoops, unlocks first drawer, peers into it, feels about inside it, takes out a reel of tape, peers at it, puts it back, locks drawer, unlocks second drawer, peers into it, feels about inside it, takes out a large banana, peers at it, locks drawer, puts keys back in his pocket. He turns, advances to edge of stage, halts, strokes banana, peels it, drops skin at his feet, puts end of banana in*) *his mouth, and remains motionless, staring vacuously before him. Finally he bites off the end, turns aside, and begins pacing to and fro at edge of stage, in the light, i.e., not more than four or five paces either way, meditatively eating banana. He treads on skin, slips, nearly falls, recovers himself, stoops and peers at skin and finally pushes it, still stooping, with his foot over the edge of stage into pit. He resumes his pacing, finishes banana, returns to table, sits down, remains a moment motionless, heaves a great sigh, takes keys from his pockets, raises them to his eyes, chooses key, gets up and moves to front of table, unlocks second drawer, takes out a second large banana, peers at it, locks drawer, puts back keys in his pocket, turns, advances to edge of stage, halts, strokes banana, peels it, tosses skin into pit, puts end of banana in his mouth, and remains motionless, staring vacuously before him. Finally he has an idea, puts banana in his waistcoat pocket, the end emerging, and goes with all the speed he can muster backstage into darkness. Ten seconds. Loud pop of cork. Fifteen seconds. He comes back into light carrying an old ledger and sits down at table. He lays ledger on table, wipes his mouth, wipes his hands on the front of his waistcoat, brings them smartly together and rubs them.)*

LEFT: Krapp (Rich Cluchy) prepares to eat his banana in Samuel Beckett's 1986 production of *Krapp's Last Tape*. BELOW LEFT: Krapp listens to his voice on tape. RIGHT: The tape recorder speaks to Krapp.

KRAPP (*briskly*): Ah! (*He bends over ledger, turns the pages, finds the entry he wants, reads.*) Box . . . thrree . . . spool . . . five. (*He raises his head and stares front. With relish.*) Spool! (*Pause.*) Spooool! (*Happy smile. Pause. He bends over table, starts peering and poking at the boxes.*) Box . . . thrree . . . thrree . . . four . . . two . . . (*with surprise*) nine! good God! . . . seven . . . ah! the little rascal! (*He takes up box, peers at it.*) Box thrree. (*He lays it on table, opens it and peers at spools inside.*) Spool . . . (*he peers at ledger*) . . . five . . . (*he peers at spools*) . . . five . . . five . . . ah! the little scoundrel! (*He takes out a spool, peers at it.*) Spool five. (*He lays it on table, closes box three, puts it back with the others, takes up the spool.*) Box thrree, spool five. (*He bends over the machine, looks up. With relish.*) Spooool! (*Happy smile. He bends, loads spool on machine, rubs his hands.*) Ah! (*He peers at ledger, reads entry at foot of page.*) Mother at rest at last . . . Hm . . . The black ball . . . (*He raises his head, stares blankly front. Puzzled.*) Black ball? . . . (*He peers again at ledger, reads.*) The dark nurse . . . (*He raises his head, broods, peers again at ledger, reads.*) Slight improvement in bowel condition . . . Hm . . . Memorable . . . what? (*He peers closer.*) Equinox, memorable equinox. (*He raises his head, stares blankly front. Puzzled.*) Memorable equinox? . . . (*Pause. He shrugs his shoulders, peers again at ledger, reads.*) Farewell to — (*he turns the page*) — love.

(*He raises his head, broods, bends over machine, switches on and assumes listening posture, i.e., leaning forward, elbows on table, hand cupping ear toward machine, face front.*)

TAPE (*strong voice, rather pompous, clearly Krapp's at a much earlier time*): Thirty-nine today, sound as a — (*Settling himself more comfortably he knocks one of the boxes off the table, curses, switches off, sweeps boxes and ledger violently to the ground, winds tape back to beginning, switches on, resumes posture.*) Thirty-nine today, sound as a bell, apart from my old weakness, and intellectually I have now every reason to suspect at the . . . (*hesitates*) . . . crest of the wave — or thereabouts. Celebrated the awful occasion, as in recent years, quietly at the Winehouse. Not a soul. Sat before the fire with closed eyes, separating the grain from the husks. Jotted down a few notes, on the back of an envelope. Good to be back in my den, in my old rags. Have just eaten I regret to say three bananas and only with difficulty refrained from a fourth. Fatal things for a man with my condition. (*Vehemently.*) Cut 'em out! (*Pause.*) The new light above my table is a great improvement. With all this darkness round me I feel less alone. (*Pause.*) In a way. (*Pause.*) I love to get up and move about in it, then back here to . . . (*hesitates*) . . . me. (*Pause.*) Krapp.

(*Pause.*)

The grain, now what I wonder do I mean by that, I mean . . . (*hesitates*) . . . I suppose I mean those things worth having when all the dust has — when all *my* dust has settled. I close my eyes and try and imagine them.

(*Pause. Krapp closes his eyes briefly.*)

Extraordinary silence this evening, I strain my ears and do not hear a sound. Old Miss McGlome always sings at this hour. But not tonight. Songs of her girlhood, she says. Hard to think of her as a girl. Wonderful woman though. Connaught, I fancy. (*Pause.*) Shall I sing when I am her age, if I ever am? No. (*Pause.*) Did I sing as a boy? No. (*Pause.*) Did I ever sing? No.

(*Pause.*)

Just been listening to an old year, passages at random. I did not check in the book, but it must be at least ten or twelve years ago. At that time I think I was still living on and off with Bianca in Kedar Street. Well out of that, Jesus yes! Hopeless business. (*Pause.*) Not much about her, apart from a tribute to her eyes. Very warm. I suddenly saw them again. (*Pause.*) Incomparable! (*Pause.*) Ah well . . . (*Pause.*) These old P.M.s are gruesome, but I often find them — (*Krapp switches off, broods, switches on*) — a help before embarking on a new . . . (*hesitates*) . . . retrospect. Hard to believe I was ever that young whelp. The voice! Jesus! And the aspirations! (*Brief laugh in which Krapp joins.*) And the resolutions! (*Brief laugh in which Krapp joins.*) To drink less, in particular. (*Brief laugh of Krapp alone.*) Statistics. Seventeen hundred hours, out of the preceding eight thousand odd, consumed on licensed premises alone. More than 20%, say 40% of his waking life. (*Pause.*) Plans for a less . . . (*hesitates*) . . . engrossing sexual life. Last illness of his father. Flagging pursuit of happiness. Unattainable laxation. Sneers at what he calls his youth and thanks to God that it's over.

(*Pause.*) False ring there. (*Pause.*) Shadows of the opus . . . magnum. Closing with a — (*brief laugh*) — yelp to Providence. (*Prolonged laugh in which Krapp joins.*) What remains of all that misery? A girl in a shabby green coat, on a railway-station platform? No?

(*Pause.*)

When I look —

(*Krapp switches off, broods, looks at his watch, gets up, goes backstage into darkness. Ten seconds. Pop of cork. Ten seconds. Second cork. Ten seconds. Third cork. Ten seconds. Brief burst of quavering song.*)

KRAPP (*sings*): Now the day is over,
Night is drawing nigh-igh,
Shadows —

(*Fit of coughing. He comes back into light, sits down, wipes his mouth, switches on, resumes his listening posture.*)

TAPE: — back on the year that is gone, with what I hope is perhaps a glint of the old eye to come, there is of course the house on the canal where mother lay a-dying, in the late autumn, after her long viduity (*Krapp gives a start*), and the — (*Krapp switches off, winds back tape a little, bends his ear closer to machine, switches on*) — a-dying, after her long viduity, and the —

(*Krapp switches off, raises his head, stares blankly before him. His lips move in the syllables of "viduity." No sound. He gets up, goes backstage into darkness, comes back with an enormous dictionary, lays it on table, sits down and looks up the word.*)

KRAPP (*reading from dictionary*): State — or condition of being — or remaining — a widow — or widower. (*Looks up. Puzzled.*) Being — or remaining? . . . (*Pause. He peers again at dictionary. Reading.*) "Deep weeds of viduity" . . . Also of an animal, especially a bird . . . the vidua or weaver-bird . . . Black plumage of male . . . (*He looks up. With relish.*) The vidua-bird!

(*Pause. He closes dictionary, switches on, resumes listening posture.*)

TAPE: — bench by the weir from where I could see her window. There I sat, in the biting wind, wishing she were gone. (*Pause.*) Hardly a soul, just a few regulars, nursemaids, infants, old men, dogs. I got to know them quite well — oh by appearance of course I mean! One dark young beauty I recollect particularly, all white and starch, incomparable bosom, with a big black hooded perambulator, most funereal thing. Whenever I looked in her direction she had her eyes on me. And yet when I was bold enough to speak to her — not having been introduced — she threatened to call a policeman. As if I had designs on her virtue! (*Laugh. Pause.*) The face she had! The eyes! Like . . . (*hesitates*) . . . chrysolite! (*Pause.*) Ah well . . . (*Pause.*) I was there when — (*Krapp switches off, broods, switches on again*) — the blind went down, one of those dirty brown roller affairs, throwing a ball for a little white dog, as chance would have it. I happened to look up and there it was. All over and done with, at last. I sat on for a few moments with the ball in my hand and the dog yelping and pawing at me. (*Pause.*) Moments. Her moments, my moments. (*Pause.*) The dog's moments. (*Pause.*) In the end I held it out to him and he took it in his mouth, gently, gently. A small, old, black, hard, solid rubber ball. (*Pause.*) I shall feel it, in my hand, until my dying day. (*Pause.*) I might have kept it. (*Pause.*) But I gave it to the dog.

(*Pause.*)

Ah well . . .

(*Pause.*)

Spiritually a year of profound gloom and indigence until that memorable night in March, at the end of the jetty, in the howling wind, never to be forgotten, when suddenly I saw the whole thing. The vision, at last. This I fancy is what I have chiefly to record this evening, against the day when my work will be done and perhaps no place left in my memory, warm or cold, for the miracle that . . . (*hesitates*) . . . for the fire that set it alight. What I suddenly saw then was this, that the belief I had been going on all my life, namely — (*Krapp switches off impatiently, winds tape forward, switches on again*) — great granite rocks the foam flying up in the light of the lighthouse and the wind-gauge spinning like a propellor, clear to me at last that the dark I have always struggled to keep under is in reality my most — (*Krapp curses, switches off, winds tape forward, switches on again*) — unshatterable association until my dissolution of storm and night with the light of the understanding and the fire — (*Krapp curses louder, switches off, winds tape forward, switches on again*) — my face in her breasts and my hand on her. We lay there without moving. But under us all moved, and moved us, gently, up and down, and from side to side.

(*Pause.*)

Past midnight. Never knew such silence. The earth might be uninhabited.

(*Pause.*)

Here I end —

(*Krapp switches off, winds tape back, switches on again.*)

— upper lake, with the punt, bathed off the bank, then pushed out into the stream and drifted. She lay stretched out on the floorboards with her hands under her head and her eyes closed. Sun blazing down, bit of a breeze, water nice and lively. I noticed a scratch on her thigh and asked her how she came by it. Picking gooseberries, she said. I said again I thought it was hopeless and no good going on, and she agreed, without opening her eyes. (*Pause.*) I asked her to look at me and after a few moments — (*pause*) — after a few moments she did, but the eyes just slits, because of the glare. I bent over her to get them in the shadow and they opened. (*Pause. Low.*) Let me in. (*Pause.*) We drifted in among the flags and stuck. The way they went down, sighing, before the stem! (*Pause.*) I lay down across her with my face in her breasts and my hand on her. We lay there without moving. But under us all moved, and moved us, gently, up and down, and from side to side.

(*Pause.*)

Past midnight. Never knew —

(*Krapp switches off, broods. Finally he fumbles in his pockets, encounters the banana, takes it out, peers at it, puts it back, fumbles, brings out the envelope, fumbles, puts back envelope, looks at his watch, gets up and goes backstage into darkness. Ten seconds. Sound of bottle against glass, then brief siphon. Ten seconds. Bottle against glass alone. Ten seconds. He comes back a little unsteadily into light, goes to front of table, takes out keys, raises them to his eyes, chooses key, unlocks first drawer, peers into it, feels about inside, takes out reel, peers at it, locks drawer, puts keys back in his pocket, goes and sits down, takes reel off machine, lays it on dictionary, loads virgin reel on machine, takes envelope from his pocket, consults back of it, lays it on table, switches on, clears his throat, and begins to record.*)

KRAPP: Just been listening to that stupid bastard I took myself for thirty years ago, hard to believe I was ever as bad as that. Thank God that's all done with anyway. (*Pause.*) The eyes she had! (*Broods, realizes he is recording silence, switches off, broods. Finally.*) Everything there, everything all the — (*Realizes this is not being recorded, switches on.*) Everything there, everything on this old muckball, all the light and dark and famine and feasting of . . . (*hesitates*)

... the ages! (*In a shout.*) Yes! (*Pause.*) Let that go! Jesus! Take his mind off his homework! Jesus! (*Pause. Weary.*) Ah well, maybe he was right. (*Pause.*) Maybe he was right. (*Broods. Realizes. Switches off. Consults envelope.*) Pah! (*Crumples it and throws it away. Broods. Switches on.*) Nothing to say, not a squeak. What's a year now? The sour cud and the iron stool. (*Pause.*) Reveled in the word spool. (*With relish.*) Spooool! Happiest moment of the past half million. (*Pause.*) Seventeen copies sold, of which eleven at trade price to free circulating libraries beyond the seas. Getting known. (*Pause.*) One pound six and something, eight I have little doubt. (*Pause.*) Crawled out once or twice, before the summer was cold. Sat shivering in the park, drowned in dreams and burning to be gone. Not a soul. (*Pause.*) Last fancies. (*Vehemently.*) Keep 'em under! (*Pause.*) Scalded the eyes out of me reading *Effie* again, a page a day, with tears again. Effie ... (*Pause.*) Could have been happy with her, up there on the Baltic, and the pines, and the dunes. (*Pause.*) Could I? (*Pause.*) And she? (*Pause.*) Pah! (*Pause.*) Fanny came in a couple of times. Bony old ghost of a whore. Couldn't do much, but I suppose better than a kick in the crutch. The last time wasn't so bad. How do you manage it, she said, at your age? I told her I'd been saving up for her all my life. (*Pause.*) Went to Vespers once, like when I was in short trousers. (*Pause. Sings.*)
Now the day is over,
Night is drawing nigh-igh,
Shadows — (*coughing, then almost
   inaudible*) — of the evening
Steal across the sky.
(*Gasping.*) Went to sleep and fell off the pew. (*Pause.*) Sometimes wondered in the night if a last effort mightn't — (*Pause.*) Ah finish your booze now and get to your bed. Go on with this drivel in the morning. Or leave it at that. (*Pause.*) Leave it at that. (*Pause.*) Lie propped up in the dark —

and wander. Be again in the dingle on a Christmas Eve, gathering holly, the red-berried. (*Pause.*) Be again on Croghan on a Sunday morning, in the haze, with the bitch, stop and listen to the bells. (*Pause.*) And so on. (*Pause.*) Be again, be again. (*Pause.*) All that old misery. (*Pause.*) Once wasn't enough for you. (*Pause.*) Lie down across her.

(*Long pause. He suddenly bends over machine, switches off, wrenches off tape, throws it away, puts on the other, winds it forward to the passage he wants, switches on, listens staring front.*)

TAPE: — gooseberries, she said. I said again I thought it was hopeless and no good going on, and she agreed, without opening her eyes. (*Pause.*) I asked her to look at me and after a few moments — (*pause*) — after a few moments she did, but the eyes just slits, because of the glare. I bent over her to get them in the shadow and they opened. (*Pause. Low.*) Let me in. (*Pause.*) We drifted in among the flags and stuck. The way they went down, sighing, before the stem! (*Pause.*) I lay down across her with my face in her breasts and my hand on her. We lay there without moving. But under us all moved, and moved us, gently, up and down, and from side to side.

(*Pause. Krapp's lips move. No sound.*)

Past midnight. Never knew such silence. The earth might be uninhabited.

(*Pause.*)

Here I end this reel. Box — (*pause*) — three, spool — (*pause*) — five. (*Pause.*) Perhaps my best years are gone. When there was a chance of happiness. But I wouldn't want them back. Not with the fire in me now. No, I wouldn't want them back.

(*Krapp motionless staring before him. The tape runs on in silence.*)

HAPPY DAYS

British writer and critic Nigel Dennis praised *Happy Days* (1961) for introducing a woman "spokesperson" into Beckett's cast of characters. Winnie, buried in a mound of earth first up to her waist, then up to her neck, is a nonstop talker who ruminates about every trivial thing around her. She looks at the contents of her bag and examines every item in detail to get some concrete information that she thinks is required for living sensibly. No matter what happens or does not happen, Winnie believes firmly that this day has been a happy day.

Winnie, a true believer, needs to know the truth, although her truths tend to be details that are essentially useless for a meaningful life. She does not seem to demand that her life be meaningful; she simply trusts that it is. As if the opposite side of the coin represented by Krapp, she lives a life that is essentially unexamined except for the trivial details.

Time and again she calls out to Willie, a portrait of an absent, newspaper-reading husband. His mere presence throughout the play provides one of the details that so please Winnie. At the end he himself appears in a full dress outfit and makes an effort to climb Winnie's mound apparently to reach her revolver. What his purposes are, we do not know. Winnie puts a good face on it and thinks his actions must be a sign of affection. The audience may think that he could simply be tired of her talking. He is, after all, as laconic as she is loquacious.

Winnie's situation is hopeless. She is rooted in the earth and cannot move. In this sense, she is a reflection of Oedipus — if Claude Lévi-Strauss is right about Oedipus' origins as a man plucked from the earth. Winnie is embedded in the earth. In Act 2 she is drawn down even more deeply than in Act 1, yet she never gives much notice of her confinement. She ignores this important detail of reality and insists on maintaining a number of broad illusions. One of them is her pious faith in religion, which opens the play. Another is her faith in Willie as a devoted husband and helpmate. Finally, she seems completely unaware that the earth that holds her so firmly is a metaphor for the grave.

Beckett may be graphically illustrating the fact that everyone alive is slowly slipping back into the earth from which we came. Beckett's philosophy of absurdism is especially bleak about facing the facts of life. Life is short; it is grim. It is — regardless of what we may do to endow it with meaning — meaningless. But these are facts that Winnie reveals no awareness of.

Beckett, like the Irish satirist Jonathan Swift, is rather savage in his treatment of those who willfully ignore the painful realities of life. The Miltonic allusion in the opening of Act 2 ("Hail, holy light") reminds us that the characters in this play are their own Adam and Eve, but their paradise leaves much wanting. God walked in Eden with Adam and Eve, but Winnie's mound lacks the presence of God. In a way, it is paradise in reverse, although if it is a Mephistophelean hell, Winnie is quite unaware of it.

Samuel Beckett (b. 1906)

HAPPY DAYS

1961

Characters

WINNIE, *a woman about fifty*
WILLIE, *a man about sixty*

ACT I

(*Expanse of scorched grass rising center to low mound. Gentle slopes down to front and either side of stage. Back an abrupter fall to stage level. Maximum of simplicity and symmetry.*)

(*Blazing light.*)

(*Very pompier trompe-l'oeil° backcloth to represent unbroken plain and sky receding to meet in far distance.*)

(*Imbedded up to above her waist in exact centre of mound, Winnie. About fifty, well preserved, blond for preference, plump, arms and shoulders bare, low bodice, big bosom, pearl necklet. She is discovered sleeping, her arms on the ground before her, her head on her arms. Beside her on ground to her left a capacious black bag, shopping variety, and to her right a collapsible collapsed parasol, beak of handle emerging from sheath.*)

(*To her right and rear, lying asleep on ground, hidden by mound, Willie.*)

(*Long pause. A bell rings piercingly, say ten seconds, stops. She does not move. Pause. Bell more piercingly, say five seconds. She wakes. Bell stops. She raises her head, gazes front. Long pause. She straightens up, lays her hands flat on ground, throws back her head and gazes at zenith. Long pause.*)

WINNIE (*gazing at zenith*): Another heavenly day. (*Pause. Head back level, eyes front, pause. She clasps hands to breast, closes eyes. Lips move in inaudible prayer, say ten seconds. Lips still. Hands remain clasped. Low.*) For Jesus Christ sake Amen. (*Eyes open, hands unclasp, return to mound. Pause. She clasps hands to breast again, closes eyes, lips move again in inaudible addendum, say five seconds. Low.*) World without end Amen. (*Eyes open, hands unclasp, return to mound. Pause.*) Begin, Winnie. (*Pause.*) Begin your day, Winnie. (*Pause. She turns to bag, rummages in it without moving it from its place, brings out toothbrush, rummages again, brings*

---

pompier trompe-l'oeil: Ordinary illusionistic.

out flat tube of toothpaste, turns back front, unscrews cap of tube, lays cap on ground, squeezes with difficulty small blob of paste on brush, holds tube in one hand and brushes teeth with other. She turns modestly aside and back to her right to spit out behind mound. In this position her eyes rest on Willie. She spits out. She cranes a little further back and down. Loud.*) Hoo-oo! (*Pause. Louder.*) Hoo-oo! (*Pause. Tender smile as she turns back front, lays down brush.*) Poor Willie — (*examines tube, smile off*) — running out — (*looks for cap*) — ah well — (*finds cap*) — can't be helped — (*screws on cap*) — just one of those old things — (*lays down tube*) — another of those old things — (*turns toward bag*) — just can't be cured — (*rummages in bag*) — cannot be cured — (*brings out small mirror, turns back front*) — ah yes — (*inspects teeth in mirror*) — poor dear Willie — (*testing upper front teeth with thumb, indistinctly*) — good Lord! — (*pulling back upper lip to inspect gums, do.*) — good God! — (*pulling back corner of mouth, mouth open, do.*) — ah well — (*other corner, do.*) — no worse — (*abandons inspection, normal speech*) — no better, no worse — (*lays down miror*) — no change — (*wipes fingers on grass*) — no pain — (*looks for toothbrush*) — hardly any — (*takes up toothbrush*) — great thing that — (*examines handle of brush*) — nothing like it — (*examines handle, reads*) — pure . . . what? — (*pause*) — what? — (*lays down brush*) — ah yes — (*turns toward bag*) — poor Willie — (*rummages in bag*) — no zest — (*rummages*) — for anything — (*brings out spectacles in case*) — no interest — (*turns back front*) — in life — (*takes spectacles from case*) — poor dear Willie — (*lays down case*) — sleep forever — (*opens spectacles*) — marvelous gift — (*puts on spectacles*) — nothing to touch it — (*looks for toothbrush*) — in my opinion — (*takes up toothbrush*) — always said so — (*examines handle of brush*) — wish I had it — (*examines handle, reads*) — genuine . . . pure . . . what? — (*lays down brush*) — blind next — (*takes off spectacles*) — ah well — (*lays down spectacles*) — seen enough — (*feels in bodice for handkerchief*) — I suppose — (*takes out folded handkerchief*) — by now — (*shakes out handkerchief*) — what are those wonderful lines — (*wipes* *one eye*) — woe woe is me — (*wipes the other*) — to see what I see — (*looks for spectacles*) — ah yes — (*takes up spectacles*) — wouldn't miss it — (*starts polishing spectacles, breathing on lenses*) — or would I? — (*polishes*) — holy light — (*polishes*) — bob up out of dark — (*polishes*) — blaze of hellish light. (*Stops polishing, raises face to sky, pause, head back level, resumes polishing, stops polishing, cranes back to her right and down.*) Hoo-oo! (*Pause. Tender smile as she turns back front and resumes polishing. Smile off.*) Marvelous gift — (*stops polishing, lays down spectacles*) — wish I had it — (*folds handkerchief*) — ah well — (*puts handkerchief back in bodice*) — can't complain — (*looks for spectacles*) — no no — (*takes up spectacles*) — mustn't complain — (*holds up spectacles, looks through lens*) — so much to be thankful for — (*looks through other lens*) — no pain — (*puts on spectacles*) — hardly any — (*looks for toothbrush*) — wonderful thing that — (*takes up toothbrush*) — nothing like it — (*examines handle of brush*) — slight headache sometimes — (*examines handle, reads*) — guaranteed . . . genuine . . . pure . . . what? — (*looks closer*) — genuine pure . . . — (*takes handkerchief from bodice*) — ah yes — (*shakes out handkerchief*) — occasional mild migraine — (*starts wiping handle of brush*) — it comes — (*wipes*) — then goes — (*wiping mechanically*) — ah yes — (*wiping*) — many mercies — (*wiping*) — great mercies — (*stops wiping, fixed lost gaze, brokenly*) — prayers perhaps not for naught — (*pause, do.*) — first thing — (*pause, do.*) — last thing — (*head down, resumes wiping, stops wiping, head up, calmed, wipes eyes, folds handkerchief, puts it back in bodice, examines handle of brush, reads*) — fully guaranteed . . . genuine pure . . . — (*looks closer*) — genuine pure . . . (*Takes off spectacles, lays them and brush down, gazes before her.*) Old things. (*Pause.*) Old eyes. (*Long pause.*) On, Winnie. (*She casts about her, sees parasol, considers it at length, takes it up, and develops from sheath a handle of surprising length. Holding butt of parasol in right hand she cranes back and down to her right to hang over Willie.*) Hoo-oo! (*Pause.*) Willie! (*Pause.*) Wonderful gift. (*She strikes down at him with beak of parasol.*) Wish I had it. (*She strikes again. The parasol slips from her grasp and falls behind mound. It is immediately restored to her by Willie's invisible hand.*) Thank you, dear. (*She transfers parasol to left hand, turns back front and examines right palm.*) Damp. (*Returns parasol to right hand, examines left palm.*) Ah well, no worse. (*Head up, cheerfully.*) No better, no worse, no change. (*Pause. Do.*) No pain. (*Cranes back to look down at Willie, holding parasol by butt as before.*) Don't go off on me

again now dear will you please, I may need you. (*Pause.*) No hurry, no hurry, just don't curl up on me again. (*Turns back front, lays down parasol, examines palms together, wipes them on grass.*) Perhaps a shade off color just the same. (*Turns to bag, rummages in it, brings out revolver, holds it up, kisses it rapidly, puts it back, rummages, brings out almost empty bottle of red medicine, turns back front, looks for spectacles, puts them on, reads label.*) Loss of spirits . . . lack of keenness . . . want of appetite . . . infants . . . children . . . adults . . . six level . . . tablespoonfuls daily — (*head up, smile*) — the old style! — (*smile off, head down, reads*) — daily . . . before and after . . . meals . . . instantaneous . . . (*looks closer*) . . . improvement. (*Takes off spectacles, lays them down, holds up bottle at arm's length to see level, unscrews cap, swigs it off head well back, tosses cap and bottle away in Willie's direction. Sound of breaking glass.*) Ah that's better! (*Turns to bag, rummages in it, brings out lipstick, turns back front, examines lipstick.*) Running out. (*Looks for spectacles.*) Ah well. (*Puts on spectacles, looks for mirror.*) Musn't complain. (*Takes up mirror, starts doing lips.*) What is that wonderful line? (*Lips.*) Oh fleeting joys — (*lips*) — oh something lasting woe. (*Lips. She is interrupted by disturbance from Willie. He is sitting up. She lowers lipstick and mirror and cranes back and down to look at him. Pause. Top back of Willie's bald head, trickling blood, rises to view above slope, comes to rest. Winnie pushes up her spectacles. Pause. His hand appears with handkerchief, spreads it on skull, disappears. Pause. The hand appears with boater, club ribbon, settles it on head, rakish angle, disappears. Pause. Winnie cranes a little further back and down.*) Slip on your drawers, dear, before you get singed. (*Pause.*) No? (*Pause.*) Oh I see, you still have some of that stuff left. (*Pause.*) Work it well in, dear. (*Pause.*) Now the other. (*Pause. She turns back front, gazes before her. Happy expression.*) Oh this is going to be another happy day! (*Pause. Happy expression off. She pulls down spectacles and resumes lips. Willie opens newspaper, hands invisible. Tops of yellow sheets appear on either side of his head. Winnie finishes lips, inspects them in mirror held a little further away.*) Ensign crimson. (*Willie turns page. Winnie lays down lipstick and mirror, turns toward bag.*) Pale flag.

(*Willie turns page. Winnie rummages in bag, brings out small ornate brimless hat with crumpled feather, turns back front, straightens hat, smooths feather, raises it toward head, arrests gesture as Willie reads.*)

WILLIE: His Grace and Most Reverend Father in God Dr. Carolus Hunter dead in tub.

Top Left: Willie (George Voskovec) reads the newspaper while Winnie (Irene Worth) talks in Andrei Serban's 1979 New York Shakespeare Festival production of *Happy Days*. Bottom Left: Winnie searches through her things, ransacking memory. Above: Willie finally comes, dressed to kill.

(*Pause.*)

Winnie (*gazing front, hat in hand, tone of fervent reminiscence*): Charlie Hunter! (*Pause.*) I close my eyes — (*she takes off spectacles and does so, hat in one hand, spectacles in other, Willie turns page*) — and am sitting on his knees again, in the back garden at Borough Green, under the horse-beech. (*Pause. She opens eyes, puts on spectacles, fiddles with hat.*) Oh the happy memories!

(*Pause. She raises hat toward head, arrests gesture as Willie reads.*)

Willie: Opening for smart youth.

(*Pause. She raises hat toward head, arrests gesture, takes off spectacles, gazes front, hat in one hand, spectacles in other.*)

Winnie: My first ball! (*Long pause.*) My second ball! (*Long pause. Closes eyes.*) My first kiss! (*Pause. Willie turns page. Winnie opens eyes.*) A Mr. Johnson, or Johnston, or perhaps I should say Johnstone. Very bushy mustache, very tawny. (*Reverently.*)

Almost ginger! (*Pause.*) Within a toolshed, though whose I cannot conceive. We had no toolshed and he most certainly had no toolshed. (*Closes eyes.*) I see the piles of pots. (*Pause.*) The tangles of bast. (*Pause.*) The shadows deepening among the rafters.

(*Pause. She opens eyes, puts on spectacles, raises hat toward head, arrests gesture as Willie reads.*)

Willie: Wanted bright boy.

(*Pause. Winnie puts on hat hurriedly, looks for mirror. Willie turns page. Winnie takes up mirror, inspects hat, lays down mirror, turns toward bag. Paper disappears. Winnie rummages in bag, brings out magnifying-glass, turns back front, looks for toothbrush. Paper reappears, folded, and begins to fan Willie's face, hand invisible. Winnie takes up toothbrush and examines handle through glass.*)

Winnie: Fully guaranteed . . . (*Willie stops fanning*) . . . genuine pure . . . (*Pause. Willie resumes fanning. Winnie looks closer, reads.*) Fully guaranteed . . . (*Willie stops fanning*) . . . genuine pure . . . (*Pause.*

Willie resumes fanning. Winnie lays down glass and brush, takes handkerchief from bodice, takes off and polishes spectacles, puts on spectacles, looks for glass, takes up and polishes glass, lays down glass, looks for brush, takes up brush and wipes handle, lays down brush, puts handkerchief back in bodice, looks for glass, takes up glass, looks for brush, takes up brush and examines handle through glass.) Fully guaranteed . . . (*Willie stops fanning*) . . . genuine pure . . . (*pause, Willie resumes fanning*) . . . hog's (*Willie stops fanning, pause*) . . . setae.° (*Pause. Winnie lays down glass and brush, paper disappears, Winnie takes of spectacles, lays them down, gazes front.*) Hog's setae. (*Pause.*) That is what I find so wonderful, that not a day goes by — (*smile*) — to speak in the old style — (*smile off*) — hardly a day, without some addition to one's knowledge however trifling, the addition I mean, provided one takes the pains. (*Willie's hand reappears with a postcard which he examines close to eyes.*) And if for some strange reason no further pains are possible, why then just close the eyes — (*she does so*) — and wait for the day to come — (*opens eyes*) — the happy day to come when flesh melts at so many degrees and the night of the moon has so many hundred hours. (*Pause.*) That is what I find so comforting when I lose heart and envy the brute beast. (*Turning toward Willie.*) I hope you are taking in — (*She sees postcard, bends lower.*) What is that you have there, Willie, may I see? (*She reaches down with hand and Willie hands her card. The hairy forearm appears above slope, raised in gesture of giving, the hand open to take back, and remains in this position till card is returned. Winnie turns back front and examines card.*) Heavens what are they up to! (*She looks for spectacles, puts them on and examines card.*) No but this is just genuine pure filth! (*Examines card.*) Make any nice-minded person want to vomit! (*Impatience of Willie's fingers. She looks for glass, takes it up and examines card through glass. Long pause.*) What does that creature in the background think he's doing? (*Looks closer.*) Oh no really! (*Impatience of fingers. Last long look. She lays down glass, takes edge of card between right forefinger and thumb, averts head, takes nose between left forefinger and thumb.*) Pah! (*Drops card.*) Take it away! (*Willie's arm disappears. His hand reappears immediately, holding card. Winnie takes off spectacles, lays them down, gazes before her. During what follows Willie continues to relish card, varying angles and distance from his eyes.*) Hog's setae. (*Puzzled expression.*) What exactly is a hog? (*Pause. Do.*)

setae: Body organs.

A sow of course I know, but a hog . . . (*Puzzled expression off.*) Oh well what does it matter, that is what I always say, it will come back, that is what I find so wonderful, all comes back. (*Pause.*) All? (*Pause.*) No, not all. (*Smile.*) No no. (*Smile off.*) Not quite. (*Pause.*) A part. (*Pause.*) Floats up, one fine day, out of the blue. (*Pause.*) That is what I find so wonderful. (*Pause. She turns toward bag. Hand and card disappear. She makes to rummage in bag, arrests gesture.*) No. (*She turns back front. Smile.*) No no. (*Smile off.*) Gently Winnie. (*She gazes front. Willie's hand reappears, takes off hat, disappears with hat.*) What then? (*Hand reappears, takes handkerchief from skull, disappears with handkerchief. Sharply, as to one not paying attention.*) Winnie! (*Willie bows head out of sight.*) What is the alternative? (*Pause.*) What is the al — (*Willie blows nose loud and long, head and hands invisible. She turns to look at him. Pause. Head reappears. Pause. Hand reappears with handkerchief, spreads it on skull, disappears. Pause. Hand reappears with boater, settles it on head, rakish angle, disappears. Pause.*) Would I had let you sleep on. (*She turns back front. Intermittent plucking at grass, head up and down, to animate following.*) Ah yes, if only I could bear to be alone, I mean prattle away with not a soul to hear. (*Pause.*) Not that I flatter myself you hear much, no Willie, God forbid. (*Pause.*) Days perhaps when you hear nothing. (*Pause.*) But days too when you answer. (*Pause.*) So that I may say at all times, even when you do not answer and perhaps hear nothing, something of this is being heard, I am not merely talking to myself, that is in the wilderness, a thing I could never bear to do — for any length of time. (*Pause.*) That is what enables me to go on, go on talking that is. (*Pause.*) Whereas if you were to die — (*smile*) — to speak in the old style — (*smile off*) — or go away and leave me, then what would I do, what *could* I do, all day long, I mean between the bell for waking and the bell for sleep? (*Pause.*) Simply gaze before me with compressed lips. (*Long pause while she does so. No more plucking.*) Not another word as long as I drew breath, nothing to break the silence of this place. (*Pause.*) Save possibly, now and then, every now and then, a sigh into my looking-glass. (*Pause.*) Or a brief . . . gale of laughter, should I happen to see the old joke again. (*Pause. Smile appears, broadens and seems about to culminate in laugh when suddenly replaced by expression of anxiety.*) My hair! (*Pause.*) Did I brush and comb my hair? (*Pause.*) I may have done. (*Pause.*) Normally I do. (*Pause.*) There is so little one *can* do. (*Pause.*) One does it all. (*Pause.*) All one can. (*Pause.*) Tis only human. (*Pause.*) Human nature. (*She begins to inspect mound, looks up.*) Human weakness. (*She resumes inspection of mound, looks up.*) Natural weakness. (*She resumes inspection of mound.*) I see no comb. (*Inspects.*) Nor any hairbrush. (*Looks up. Puzzled expression. She turns to bag, rummages in it.*) The comb is here. (*Back front. Puzzled expression. Back to bag. Rummages.*) The brush is here. (*Back front. Puzzled expression.*) Perhaps I put them back, after use. (*Pause. Do.*) But normally I do not put things back, after use, no, I leave them lying about and put them back all together, at the end of the day. (*Smile.*) To speak in the old style. (*Pause.*) The sweet old style. (*Smile off.*) And yet . . . I seem . . . to remember . . . (*Suddenly careless.*) Oh well, what does it matter, that is what I always say, I shall simply brush and comb them later on, purely and simply, I have the whole — (*Pause. Puzzled.*) Them? (*Pause.*) Or it? (*Pause.*) Brush and comb it? (*Pause.*) Sounds improper somehow. (*Pause. Turning a little toward Willie.*) What would you say, Willie? (*Pause. Turning a little further.*) What would you say, Willie, speaking of your hair, them or it? (*Pause.*) The hair on your head, I mean. (*Pause. Turning a little further.*) The hair on your head, Willie, what would you say speaking of the hair on your head, them or it?

(*Long pause.*)

WILLIE: It.

WINNIE (*turning back front, joyful*): Oh you are going to talk to me today, this is going to be a happy day! (*Pause. Joy off.*) Another happy day. (*Pause.*) Ah well, where was I, my hair, yes, later on, I shall be thankful for it later on. (*Pause.*) I have my — (*raises hands to hat*) — yes, on, my hat on — (*lowers hands*) — I cannot take it off now. (*Pause.*) To think there are times one cannot take off one's hat, not if one's life were at stake. Times one cannot put it on, times one cannot take it off. (*Pause.*) How often I have said, Put on your hat now, Winnie, there is nothing else for it, take off your hat now, Winnie, like a good girl, it will do you good, and did not. (*Pause.*) Could not. (*Pause. She raises hand, frees a strand of hair from under hat, draws it toward eye, squints at it, lets it go, hand down.*) Golden you called it, that day, when the last guest was gone — (*hand up in gesture of raising a glass*) — to your golden . . . may it never (*voice breaks*) . . . may it never . . . (*Hand down. Head down. Pause. Low.*) That day. (*Pause. Do.*) What day? (*Pause. Head up. Normal voice.*) What now? (*Pause.*) Words fail, there are times when even they fail. (*Turning a little toward Willie.*) Is that not so, Willie? (*Pause. Turning a little further.*) Is not that so, Willie, that even words fail, at times? (*Pause.*

Back front.) What is one to do then, until they come again? Brush and comb the hair, if it has not been done, or if there is some doubt, trim the nails if they are in need of trimming, these things tide one over. (*Pause.*) That is what I mean. (*Pause.*) That is all I mean. (*Pause.*) That is what I find so wonderful, that not a day goes by — (*smile*) — to speak in the old style — (*smile off*) — without some blessing — (*Willie collapses behind slope, his head disappears, Winnie turns toward event*) — in disguise. (*She cranes back and down.*) Go back into your hole now, Willie, you've exposed yourself enough. (*Pause.*) Do as I say, Willie, don't lie sprawling there in this hellish sun, go back into your hole. (*Pause.*) Go on now, Willie. (*Willie invisible starts crawling left toward hole.*) That's the man. (*She follows his progress with her eyes.*) Not head first, stupid, how are you going to turn? (*Pause.*) That's it . . . right round . . . now . . . back in. (*Pause.*) Oh I know it is not easy, dear, crawling backwards, but it is rewarding in the end. (*Pause.*) You have left your vaseline behind. (*She watches as he crawls back for vaseline.*) The lid! (*She watches as he crawls back toward hole. Irritated.*) Not head first, I tell you! (*Pause.*) More to the right. (*Pause.*) The *right,* I said. (*Pause. Irritated.*) Keep your tail down, can't you! (*Pause.*) Now. (*Pause.*) There! (*All these directions loud. Now in her normal voice, still turned toward him.*) Can you hear me? (*Pause.*) I beseech you, Willie, just yes or no, can you hear me, just yes or nothing.

(*Pause.*)

WILLIE: Yes.

WINNIE (*turning front, same voice*): And now?

WILLIE (*irritated*): Yes.

WINNIE (*less loud*): And now?

WILLIE (*more irritated*): Yes.

WINNIE (*still less loud*): And now? (*A little louder.*) And now?

WILLIE (*violently*): Yes!

WINNIE (*same voice*): Fear no more the heat o' the sun. (*Pause.*) Did you hear that?

WILLIE (*irritated*): Yes.

WINNIE (*same voice*): What? (*Pause.*) What?

WILLIE (*more irritated*): Fear no more.

(*Pause.*)

WINNIE (*same voice*): No more what? (*Pause.*) Fear no more what?

WILLIE (*violently*): Fear no more!

WINNIE (*normal voice, gabbled*): Bless you Willie I do appreciate your goodness I know what an effort it costs you, now you may relax I shall not trouble you again unless I am obliged to, by that I mean unless I come to the end of my own resources which is most unlikely, just to know that in theory you can hear me even though in fact you don't is all I need, just to feel you there within earshot and conceivably on the qui vive° is all I ask, not to say anything I would not wish you to hear or liable to cause you pain, not to be just babbling away on trust as it is were not knowing and something gnawing at me. (*Pause for breath.*) Doubt. (*Places index and second finger on heart area, moves them about, brings them to rest.*) Here. (*Moves them slightly.*) Abouts. (*Hand away.*) Oh no doubt the time will come when before I can utter a word I must make sure you heard the one that went before and then no doubt another come another time when I must learn to talk to myself a thing I could never bear to do such wilderness. (*Pause.*) Or gaze before me with compressed lips. (*She does so.*) All day long. (*Gaze and lips again.*) No. (*Smile.*) No no. (*Smile off.*) There is of course the bag. (*Turns toward it.*) There will always be the bag. (*Back front.*) Yes, I suppose so. (*Pause.*) Even when you are gone, Willie. (*She turns a little toward him.*) You *are* going, Willie, aren't you? (*Pause. Louder.*) You *will* be going soon, Willie, won't you? (*Pause. Louder.*) Willie! (*Pause. She cranes back and down to look at him.*) So you have taken off your straw, that is wise. (*Pause.*) You do look snug, I must say, with your chin on your hands and the old blue eyes like saucers in the shadows. (*Pause.*) Can you see me from there I wonder, I still wonder. (*Pause.*) No? (*Back front.*) Oh I know it does not follow when two are gathered together — (*faltering*) — in this way — (*normal*) — that because one sees the other the other sees the one, life has taught me that . . . too. (*Pause.*) Yes, life I suppose, there is no other word. (*She turns a little toward him.*) Could you see me, Willie, do you think, from where you are, if you were to raise your eyes in my direction? (*Turns a little further.*) Lift up your eyes to me, Willie, and tell me can you see me, do that for me, I'll lean back as far as I can. (*Does so. Pause.*) No? (*Pause.*) Well never mind. (*Turns back painfully front.*) The earth is very tight today, can it be I have put on flesh, I trust not. (*Pause. Absently, eyes lowered.*) The great heat possibly. (*Starts to pat and stroke ground.*) All things expanding, some more than others. (*Pause. Patting and stroking.*) Some less. (*Pause. Do.*) Oh I can well imagine what is passing through your mind, it is not enough to have to listen to the woman, now I must look at her as well. (*Pause. Do.*) Well it is very understandable. (*Pause. Do.*) Most understandable.

(*Pause. Do.*) One does not appear to be asking a great deal, indeed at times it would seem hardly possible — (*voice breaks, falls to a murmur*) — to ask less — of a fellow creature — to put it mildly — whereas actually — when you think about it — look into your heart — see the other — what he needs — peace — to be left in peace — then perhaps the moon — all this time — asking for the moon. (*Pause. Stroking hand suddenly still. Lively.*) Oh I say, what have we here? (*Bending head to ground, incredulous.*) Looks like life of some kind! (*Looks for spectacles, puts them on, bends closer. Pause.*) An emmet! (*Recoils. Shrill.*) Willie, an emmet, a live emmet! (*Seizes magnifying glass, bends to ground again, inspects through glass.*) Where's it gone? (*Inspects.*) Ah! (*Follows its progress through grass.*) Has like a little white ball in its arms. (*Follows progress. Hand still. Pause.*) It's gone in. (*Continues a moment to gaze at spot through glass, then slowly straightens up, lays down glass, takes off spectacles and gazes before her, spectacles in hand. Finally.*) Like a little white ball.

(*Long pause. Gesture to lay down spectacles.*)

WILLIE: Eggs.
WINNIE (*arresting gesture*): What?

(*Pause.*)

WILLIE: Eggs. (*Pause. Gesture to lay down glasses.*) Formication.
WINNIE (*arresting gesture*): What?

(*Pause.*)

WILLIE: Formication.

(*Pause. She lays down spectacles, gazes before her. Finally.*)

WINNIE (*murmur*): God. (*Pause. Willie laughs quietly. After a moment she joins in. They laugh quietly together. Willie stops. She laughs on a moment alone. Willie joins in. They laugh together. She stops. Willie laughs on a moment alone. He stops. Pause. Normal voice.*) Ah well what a joy in any case to hear you laugh again, Willie, I was convinced I never would, you never would. (*Pause.*) I suppose some people might think us a trifle irreverent, but I doubt it. (*Pause.*) How can one better magnify the Almighty than by sniggering with him at his little jokes, particularly the poorer ones? (*Pause.*) I think you would back me up there, Willie. (*Pause.*) Or were we perhaps diverted by two quite different things? (*Pause.*) Oh well, what does it matter, that is what I always say, so long as one . . . you know . . . what is that wonderful line . . . laughing wild . . . something something laughing wild amid severest

on the qui vive: On the alert, on the lookout.

woe. (*Pause.*) And now? (*Long pause.*) Was I lovable once, Willie? (*Pause.*) Was I ever lovable? (*Pause.*) Do not misunderstand my question, I am not asking you if you loved me, we know all about that, I am asking you if you found me lovable — at one stage. (*Pause.*) No? (*Pause.*) You can't? (*Pause.*) Well I admit it is a teaser. And you have done more than your bit already, for the time being, just lie back now and relax, I shall not trouble you again unless I am compelled to, just to know you are there within hearing and conceivably on the semi-alert is … er … paradise enow. (*Pause.*) The day is now well advanced. (*Smile.*) To speak in the old style. (*Smile off.*) And yet it is perhaps a little soon for my song. (*Pause.*) To sing too soon is a great mistake, I find. (*Turning toward bag.*) There is of course the bag. (*Looking at bag.*) The bag. (*Back front.*) Could I enumerate its contents? (*Pause.*) No. (*Pause.*) Could I, if some kind person were to come along and ask, What all have you got in that big black bag, Winnie? give an exhaustive answer? (*Pause.*) No. (*Pause.*) The depths in particular, who knows what treasures. (*Pause.*) What comforts. (*Turns to look at bag.*) Yes, there is the bag. (*Back front.*) But something tells me. Do not overdo the bag, Winnie, make use of it of course, let it help you … along, when stuck, by all means, but cast your mind forward, something tells me, cast your mind forward, Winnie, to the time when words must fail — (*she closes eyes, pause, opens eyes*) — and do not overdo the bag. (*Pause. She turns to look at bag.*) Perhaps just one quick dip. (*She turns back front, closes eyes, throws out left arm, plunges hand in bag and brings out revolver. Disgusted.*) You again! (*She opens eyes, brings revolver front and contemplates it. She weighs it in her palm.*) You'd think the weight of this thing would bring it down among the … last rounds. But no. It doesn't. Ever uppermost, like Browning. (*Pause.*) Brownie … (*Turning a little toward Willie.*) Remember Brownie, Willie? (*Pause.*) Remember how you used to keep on at me to take it away from you? Take it away, Winnie, take it away, before I put myself out of my misery. (*Back front. Derisive.*) *Your* misery! (*To revolver.*) Oh I suppose it's a comfort to know you're there, but I'm tired of you. (*Pause.*) I'll leave you out, that's what I'll do. (*She lays revolver on ground to her right.*) There, that's your home from this day out. (*Smile.*) The old style! (*Smile off.*) And now? (*Long pause.*) Is gravity what it was, Willie, I fancy not. (*Pause.*) Yes, the feeling more and more that if I were not held — (*gesture*) — in this way, I would simply float up into the blue. (*Pause.*) And that perhaps some day the earth will yield and let me go, the pull is so great, yes,

crack all round me and let me out. (*Pause.*) Don't you ever have that feeling, Willie, of being sucked up? (*Pause.*) Don't you have to cling on sometimes, Willie? (*Pause. She turns a little toward him.*) Willie.

(*Pause.*)

WILLIE: *Sucked* up?

WINNIE: Yes love, up into the blue, like gossamer. (*Pause.*) No? (*Pause.*) You don't? (*Pause.*) Ah well, natural laws, natural laws, I suppose it's like everything else, it all depends on the creature you happen to be. All I can say is for my part is that for me they are not what they were when I was young and … foolish and … (*faltering, head down*) … beautiful … possibly … lovely … in a way … to look at. (*Pause. Head up.*) Forgive me, Willie, sorrow keeps breaking in. (*Normal voice.*) Ah well what a joy in any case to know you are there, as usual, and perhaps awake, and perhaps taking all this in, some of all this, what a happy day for me … it will have been. (*Pause.*) So far. (*Pause.*) What a blessing nothing grows, imagine if all this stuff were to start growing. (*Pause.*) Imagine. (*Pause.*) Ah yes, great mercies. (*Long pause.*) I can say no more. (*Pause.*) For the moment. (*Pause. Turns to look at bag. Back front. Smile.*) No no. (*Smile off. Looks at parasol.*) I suppose I might — (*takes up parasol*) — yes, I suppose I might … hoist this thing now. (*Begins to unfurl it. Following punctuated by mechanical difficulties overcome.*) One keeps putting off — putting up — for fear of putting up — too soon — and the day goes by — quite by — without one's having put up — at all. (*Parasol now fully open. Turned to her right she twirls it idly this way and that.*) Ah yes, so little to say, so little to do, and the fear so great, certain days, of finding oneself … left, with hours still to run, before the bell for sleep, and nothing more to say, nothing more to do, that the days go by, certain days go by, quite by, the bell goes, and little or nothing said, little or nothing done. (*Raising parasol.*) That is the danger. (*Turning front.*) To be guarded against. (*She gazes front, holding up parasol with right hand. Maximum pause.*) I used to perspire freely. (*Pause.*) Now hardly at all. (*Pause.*) The heat is much greater. (*Pause.*) The perspiration much less. (*Pause.*) That is what I find so wonderful. (*Pause.*) The way man adapts himself. (*Pause.*) To changing conditions. (*She transfers parasol to left hand. Long pause.*) Holding up wearies the arm. (*Pause.*) Not if one is going along. (*Pause.*) Only if one is at rest. (*Pause.*) That is a curious observation. (*Pause.*) I hope you heard that, Willie, I should be grieved to think you had not heard that. (*She takes parasol in both hands. Long pause.*) I am weary,

holding it up, and I cannot put it down. (*Pause.*)
I am worse off with it up than with it down, and
I cannot put it down. (*Pause.*) Reason says, Put it
down, Winnie, it is not helping you, put the thing
down and get on with something else. (*Pause.*) I
cannot. (*Pause.*) I cannot move. (*Pause.*) No, something must happen, in the world, take place, some
change, I cannot, if I am to move again. (*Pause.*)
Willie. (*Mildly.*) Help. (*Pause.*) No? (*Pause.*) Bid
me put this thing down, Willie, I would obey you
instantly, as I have always done, honored and
obeyed. (*Pause.*) Please, Willie. (*Mildly.*) For pity's
sake. (*Pause.*) No? (*Pause.*) You can't? (*Pause.*)
Well I don't blame you, no, it would ill become
me, who cannot move, to blame my Willie because
he cannot speak. (*Pause.*) Fortunately I am in tongue
again. (*Pause.*) That is what I find so wonderful,
my two lamps, when one goes out the other burns
brighter. (*Pause.*) Oh yes, great mercies. (*Maximum
pause. The parasol goes on fire. Smoke, flames if
feasible. She sniffs, looks up, throws parasol to her
right behind mound, cranes back to watch it burning.
Pause.*) Ah earth you old extinguisher. (*Back front.*)
I presume this has occurred before, though I cannot
recall it. (*Pause.*) Can you, Willie? (*Turns a little
toward him.*) Can you recall this having occurred
before? (*Pause. Cranes back to look at him.*) Do
you know what has occurred, Willie? (*Pause.*) Have
you gone off on me again? (*Pause.*) I do not ask
if you are alive to all that is going on, I merely ask
if you have not gone off on me again. (*Pause.*)
Your eyes appear to be closed, but that has no
particular significance we know. (*Pause.*) Raise a
finger, dear, will you please, if you are not quite
senseless. (*Pause.*) Do that for me, Willie please,
just the little finger, if you are still conscious. (*Pause.
Joyful.*) Oh all five, you are a darling today, now
I may continue with an easy mind. (*Back front.*)
Yes, what ever occurred that did not occur before
and yet . . . I wonder, yes, I confess I wonder.
(*Pause.*) With the sun blazing so much fiercer down,
and hourly fiercer, is it not natural things should
go on fire never known to do so, in this way I
mean, spontaneous like. (*Pause.*) Shall I myself not
melt perhaps in the end, or burn, oh I do not mean
necessarily burst into flames, no, just little by little
be charred to a black cinder, all this — (*ample
gesture of arms*) — visible flesh. (*Pause.*) On the
other hand, did I ever know a temperate time?
(*Pause.*) No. (*Pause.*) I speak of temperate times
and torrid times, they are empty words. (*Pause.*) I
speak of when I was not yet caught — in this way
— and had my legs and had the use of my legs,
and could seek out a shady place, like you, when
I was tired of the sun, or a sunny place when I

was tired of the shade, like you, and they are all
empty words. (*Pause.*) It is no hotter today than
yesterday, it will be no hotter tomorrow than today,
how could it, and so on back into the far past,
forward into the far future. (*Pause.*) And should
one day the earth cover my breasts, then I shall
never have seen my breasts, no one ever seen my
breasts. (*Pause.*) I hope you caught something of
that, Willie, I should be sorry to think you had
caught nothing of all that, it is not every day I rise
to such heights. (*Pause.*) Yes, something seems to
have occurred, something has seemed to occur, and
nothing has occurred, nothing at all, you are quite
right, Willie. (*Pause.*) The sunshade will be there
again tomorrow, beside me on this mound, to help
me through the day. (*Pause. She takes up mirror.*)
I take up this little glass, I shiver it on a stone —
(*does so*) — I throw it away — (*does so far behind
her*) — it will be in the bag again tomorrow, without
a scratch, to help me through the day. (*Pause.*) No,
one can do nothing. (*Pause.*) That is what I find
so wonderful, the way things . . . (*voice breaks,
head down*) . . . things . . . so wonderful. (*Long
pause, head down. Finally turns, still bowed, to
bag, brings out unidentifiable odds and ends, stuffs
them back, fumbles deeper, brings out finally musical-box, winds it up, turns it on, listens for a
moment holding it in both hands, huddled over it,
turns back front, straightens up and listens to tune,
holding box to breast with both hands. It plays
the Waltz Duet "I love you so" from* The Merry
Widow. *Gradually happy expression. She sways to
the rhythm. Music stops. Pause. Brief burst of hoarse
song without words — musical-box tune — from
Willie. Increase of happy expression. She lays down
box.*) Oh this will have been a happy day! (*She
claps hands.*) Again, Willie, again! (*Claps.*) Encore,
Willie, please! (*Pause. Happy expression off.*) No?
You won't do that for me? (*Pause.*) Well it is very
understandable, very understandable. One cannot
sing just to please someone, however much one
loves them, no, song must come from the heart,
that is what I always say, pour out from the inmost,
like a thrush. (*Pause.*) How often I have said, in
evil hours, Sing now, Winnie, sing your song, there
is nothing else for it, and did not. (*Pause.*) Could
not. (*Pause.*) No, like the thrush, or the bird of
dawning, with no thought of benefit, to oneself or
anyone else. (*Pause.*) And now? (*Long pause. Low.*)
Strange feeling. (*Pause. Do.*) Strange feeling that
someone is looking at me. I am clear, then dim,
then gone, then dim again, then clear again, and
so on, back and forth, in and out of someone's
eye. (*Pause. Do.*) Strange? (*Pause. Do.*) No, here
all is strange. (*Pause. Normal voice.*) Something

says, Stop talking now, Winnie, for a minute, don't squander all your words for the day, stop talking and do something for a change, will you? (*She raises hands and holds them open before her eyes. Apostrophic.*) Do something! (*She closes hands.*) What claws! (*She turns to bag, rummages in it, brings out finally a nailfile, turns back front and begins to file nails. Files for a time in silence, then the following punctuated by filing.*) There floats up — into my thoughts — a Mr. Shower — a Mr. and perhaps a Mrs. Shower — no — they are holding hands — his fiancée then more likely — or just some — loved one. (*Looks closer at nails.*) Very brittle today. (*Resumes filing.*) Shower — Shower — does the name mean anything — to you, Willie — evoke any reality, I mean — for you, Willie — don't answer if you don't — feel up to it — you have done more — than your bit — already — Shower — Shower. (*Inspects filed nails.*) Bit more like it. (*Raises head, gazes front.*) Keep yourself nice, Winnie, that's what I always say, come what may, keep yourself nice. (*Pause. Resumes filing.*) Yes — Shower — Shower — (*stops filing, raises head, gazes front, pause*) — or Cooker, perhaps I should say Cooker. (*Turning a little toward Willie.*) Cooker, Willie, does Cooker strike a chord? (*Pause. Turns a little further. Louder.*) Cooker, Willie, does Cooker ring a bell, the name Cooker? (*Pause. She cranes back to look at him. Pause.*) Oh really! (*Pause.*) Have you no handkerchief, darling? (*Pause.*) Have you no delicacy? (*Pause.*) Oh, Willie, you're not eating it! Spit it out, dear, spit it out! (*Pause. Back front.*) Ah well, I suppose it's only natural. (*Break in voice.*) Human. (*Pause. Do.*) What *is* one to do? (*Head down. Do.*) All day long. (*Pause. Do.*) Day after day. (*Pause. Head up. Smile. Calm.*) The old style! (*Smile off. Resumes nails.*) No, done him. (*Passes on to next.*) Should have put on my glasses. (*Pause.*) Too late now. (*Finishes left hand, inspects it.*) Bit more human. (*Starts right hand. Following punctuated as before.*) Well anyway — this man Shower — or Cooker — no matter — and the woman — hand in hand — in the other hands bags — kind of big brown grips — standing there gaping at me — and at last this man Shower — or Cooker — ends in er anyway — stake my life on that — What's she doing? he says — What's the idea? he says — stuck up to her diddies in the bleeding ground — coarse fellow — What does it mean? he says — What's it meant to mean? — and so on — lot more stuff like that — usual drivel — Do you hear me? he says — I do, she says, God help me — What do you mean, he says, God help you? (*Stops filing, raises head, gazes front.*) And you, she says, what's the idea of you, she says,

what are you meant to mean? It is because you're still on your two flat feet, with your old ditty full of tinned muck and changes of underwear, dragging me up and down this fornicating wilderness, coarse creature, fit mate — (*with sudden violence*) — let go of my hand and drop for God's sake, she says, drop! (*Pause. Resumes filing.*) Why doesn't he dig her out? he says — referring to you, my dear — What good is she to him like that? — What good is he to her like that? — and so on — usual tosh — Good! she says, have a heart for God's sake — Dig her out, he says, dig her out, no sense in her like that — Dig her out with what? she says — I'd dig her out with my bare hands, he says — must have been man and — wife. (*Files in silence.*) Next thing they're away — hand in hand — and the bags — dim — then gone — last human kind — to stray this way. (*Finishes right hand, inspects it, lays down file, gazes front.*) Strange thing, time like this, drift up into the mind. (*Pause.*) Strange? (*Pause.*) No, here all is strange. (*Pause.*) Thankful for it in any case. (*Voice breaks.*) Most thankful. (*Head down. Pause. Head up. Calm.*) Bow and raise the head, bow and raise, always that. (*Pause.*) And now? (*Long pause. Starts putting things back in bag, toothbrush last. This operation, interrupted by pauses as indicated, punctuates following.*) It is perhaps a little soon — to make ready — for the night — (*stops tidying, head up, smile*) — the old style! — (*smile off, resumes tidying*) — and yet I do — make ready for the night — feeling it at hand — the bell for sleep — saying to myself — Winnie — it will not be long now, Winnie — until the bell for sleep. (*Stops tidying, head up.*) Sometimes I am wrong. (*Smile.*) But not often. (*Smile off.*) Sometimes all is over, for the day, all done, all said, all ready for the night, and the day not over, far from over, the night not ready, far, far from ready. (*Smile.*) But not often. (*Smile off.*) Yes, the bell for sleep, when I feel it at hand, and so make ready for the night — (*gesture*) — in this way, sometimes I am wrong — (*smile*) — but not often. (*Smile off. Resumes tidying.*) I used to think — I say I used to think — that all these things — put back into the bag — if too soon — put back too soon — could be taken out again — if necessary — if needed — and so on — indefinitely — back into the bag — back out of the bag — until the bell — went. (*Stops tidying, head up, smile.*) But no. (*Smile broader.*) No no. (*Smile off. Resumes tidying.*) I suppose this — might seem strange — this — what shall I say — this what I have said — yes — (*she takes up revolver*) — strange — (*she turns to put revolver in bag*) — were it not — (*about to put revolver in bag she arrests gesture and turns back front*) —

were it not — (*she lays down revolver to her right, stops tidying, head up*) — that all seems strange. (*Pause.*) Most strange. (*Pause.*) Never any change. (*Pause.*) And more and more strange. (*Pause. She bends to mound again, takes up last object, i.e., toothbrush, and turns to put it in bag when her attention is drawn to disturbance from Willie. She cranes back and to her right to see. Pause.*) Weary of your hole, dear? (*Pause.*) Well I can understand that. (*Pause.*) Don't forget your straw. (*Pause.*) Not the crawler you were, poor darling. (*Pause.*) No, not the crawler I gave my heart to. (*Pause.*) The hands and knees, love, try the hands and knees. (*Pause.*) The knees! The knees! (*Pause.*) What a curse, mobility! (*She follows with eyes his progress toward her behind mound, i.e., toward place he occupied at beginning of act.*) Another foot, Willie, and you're home. (*Pause as she observes last foot.*) Ah! (*Turns back front laboriously, rubs neck.*) Crick in my neck admiring you. (*Rubs neck.*) But it's worth it, well worth it. (*Turning slightly toward him.*) Do you know what I dream sometimes? (*Pause.*) What I dream sometimes, Willie. (*Pause.*) That you'll come round and live this side where I could see you. (*Pause. Back front.*) I'd be a different woman. (*Pause.*) Unrecognizable. (*Turning slightly toward him.*) Or just now and then, come round this side just every now and then and let me feast on you. (*Back front.*) But you can't, I know. (*Head down.*) I know. (*Pause. Head up.*) Well anyway — (*looks at toothbrush in her hand*) — can't be long now — (*looks at brush*) — until the bell. (*Top back of Willie's head appears above slope. Winnie looks closer at brush.*) Fully guaranteed . . . (*head up*) . . . what's this it was? (*Willie's hand appears with handkerchief, spreads it on skull, disappears.*) Genuine pure . . . fully guaranteed . . . (*Willie's hand appears with boater, settles it on head, rakish angle, disappears*) . . . genuine pure . . . ah! hog's setae. (*Pause.*) What is a hog exactly? (*Pause. Turns slightly toward Willie.*) What exactly is a hog, Willie, do you know, I can't remember. (*Pause. Turning a little further, pleading.*) What *is* a hog, Willie, please!

(*Pause.*)

WILLIE: Castrated male swine. (*Happy expression appears on Winnie's face.*) Reared for slaughter.

(*Happy expression increases. Willie opens newspaper, hands invisible. Tops of yellow sheets appear on either side of his head. Winnie gazes before her with happy expression.*)

WINNIE: Oh this *is* a happy day! This will have been another happy day! (*Pause.*) After all. (*Pause.*) So far.

(*Pause. Happy expression off. Willie turns page. Pause. He turns another page. Pause.*)

WILLIE: Opening for smart youth.

(*Pause. Winnie takes off hat, turns to put it in bag, arrests gesture, turns back front. Smile.*)

WINNIE: No. (*Smile broader.*) No no. (*Smile off. Puts on hat again, gazes front, pause.*) And now? (*Pause.*) Sing. (*Pause.*) Sing your song, Winnie. (*Pause.*) No? (*Pause.*) Then pray. (*Pause.*) Pray your prayer, Winnie.

(*Pause. Willie turns page. Pause.*)

WILLIE: Wanted bright boy.

(*Pause. Winnie gazes before her. Willie turns page. Pause. Newspaper disappears. Long pause.*)

WINNIE: Pray your old prayer, Winnie.

(*Long pause.*)

ACT II

(*Scene as before.*)

(*Winnie imbedded up to neck, hat on head, eyes closed. Her head, which she can no longer turn, nor bow, nor raise, faces front motionless throughout act. Movements of eyes as indicated.*)

(*Bag and parasol as before. Revolver conspicuous to her right on mound.*)

(*Long pause.*)

(*Bell rings loudly. She opens eyes at once. Bell stops. She gazes front. Long pause.*)

WINNIE: Hail, holy light. (*Long pause. She closes her eyes. Bell rings loudly. She opens eyes at once. Bell stops. She gazes front. Long smile. Smile off. Long pause.*) Someone is looking at me still. (*Pause.*) Caring for me still. (*Pause.*) That is what I find so wonderful. (*Pause.*) Eyes on my eyes. (*Pause.*) What is that unforgettable line? (*Pause. Eyes right.*) Willie. (*Pause. Louder.*) Willie. (*Pause. Eyes front.*) May one still speak of time? (*Pause.*) Say it is a long time now, Willie, since I saw you. (*Pause.*) Since I heard you. (*Pause.*) May one? (*Pause.*) One does. (*Smile.*) The old style! (*Smile off.*) There is so little one can speak of. (*Pause.*) One speaks of it all. (*Pause.*) All one can. (*Pause.*) I used to think . . . (*pause*) . . . I say I used to think that I would learn to talk alone. (*Pause.*) By that I mean to myself, the wilderness. (*Smile.*) But no. (*Smile broader.*) No no. (*Smile off.*) Ergo° you are there. (*Pause.*) Oh no doubt you are dead, like the others, no

Ergo: Latin for "therefore."

doubt you have died, or gone away and left me, like the others, it doesn't matter, you are there. (*Pause. Eyes left.*) The bag too is there, the same as ever, I can see it. (*Pause. Eyes right. Louder.*) The bag is there, Willie, as good as ever, the one you gave me that day . . . to go to market. (*Pause. Eyes front.*) That day. (*Pause.*) What day? (*Pause.*) I used to pray. (*Pause.*) I say I used to pray. (*Pause.*) Yes, I must confess I did. (*Smile.*) Not now. (*Smile broader.*) No no. (*Smile off. Pause.*) Then . . . now . . . what difficulties here, for the mind. (*Pause.*) To have been always what I am — and so changed from what I was. (*Pause.*) I am the one, I say the one, then the other. (*Pause.*) Now the one, then the other. (*Pause.*) There is so little one can say, one says it all. (*Pause.*) All one can. (*Pause.*) And no truth in it anywhere. (*Pause.*) My arms. (*Pause.*) My breasts. (*Pause.*) What arms? (*Pause.*) What breasts? (*Pause.*) Willie. (*Pause.*) What Willie? (*Sudden vehement affirmation.*) My Willie! (*Eyes right, calling.*) Willie! (*Pause. Louder.*) Willie! (*Pause. Eyes front.*) Ah well, not to know, not to know for sure, great mercy, all I ask. (*Pause.*) Ah yes . . . then . . . now . . . beechen green . . . this . . . Charlie . . . kisses . . . this . . . all that . . . deep trouble for the mind. (*Pause.*) But it does not trouble mine. (*Smile.*) Not now. (*Smile broader.*) No no. (*Smile off. Long pause. She closes eyes. Bell rings loudly. She opens eyes. Pause.*) Eyes float up that seem to close in peace . . . to see . . . in peace. (*Pause.*) Not mine. (*Smile.*) Not now. (*Smile broader.*) No no. (*Smile off. Long pause.*) Willie. (*Pause.*) Do you think the earth has lost its atmosphere, Willie? (*Pause.*) Do you, Willie? (*Pause.*) You have no opinion? (*Pause.*) Well that is like you, you never had any opinion about anything. (*Pause.*) It's understandable. (*Pause.*) Most. (*Pause.*) The earthball. (*Pause.*) I sometimes wonder. (*Pause.*) Perhaps not quite all. (*Pause.*) There always remains something. (*Pause.*) Of everything. (*Pause.*) Some remains. (*Pause.*) If the mind were to go. (*Pause.*) It won't of course. (*Pause.*) Not quite. (*Pause.*) Not mine. (*Smile.*) Not now. (*Smile broader.*) No no. (*Smile off. Long pause.*) It might be the eternal cold. (*Pause.*) Everlasting perishing cold. (*Pause.*) Just chance, I take it, happy chance. (*Pause.*) Oh yes, great mercies, great mercies. (*Pause.*) And now? (*Long pause.*) The face. (*Pause.*) The nose. (*She squints down.*) I can see it . . . (*squinting down*) . . . the tip . . . the nostrils . . . breath of life . . . that curve you so admired . . . (*pouts*) . . . a hint of lip . . . (*pouts again*) . . . if I pout them out . . . (*sticks out tongue*) . . . the tongue of course . . . you so admired . . . if I stick it out . . . (*sticks it out again*) . . . the tip . . . (*eyes up*) . . . suspicion of brow . . . eyebrow

. . . imagination possibly . . . (*eyes left*) . . . cheek . . . no . . . (*eyes right*) . . . no . . . (*distends cheeks*) . . . even if I puff them out . . . (*eyes left, distends cheeks again*) . . . no . . . no damask. (*Eyes front.*) That is all. (*Pause.*) The bag of course . . . (*eyes left*) . . . a little blurred perhaps . . . but the bag. (*Eyes front. Offhand.*) The earth of course and sky. (*Eyes right.*) The sunshade you gave me . . . that day . . . (*pause*) . . . that day . . . the lake . . . the reeds. (*Eyes front. Pause.*) What day? (*Pause.*) What reeds? (*Long pause. Eyes close. Bell rings loudly. Eyes open. Pause. Eyes right.*) Brownie of course. (*Pause.*) You remember Brownie, Willie, I can see him. (*Pause.*) Brownie is there, Willie, beside me. (*Pause. Loud.*) Brownie is there, Willie. (*Pause. Eyes front.*) That is all. (*Pause.*) What would I do without them? (*Pause.*) What would I do without them, when words fail? (*Pause.*) Gaze before me, with compressed lips. (*Long pause while she does so.*) I cannot. (*Pause.*) Ah yes, great mercies, great mercies. (*Long pause. Low.*) Sometimes I hear sounds. (*Listening expression. Normal voice.*) But not often. (*Pause.*) They are a boon, sounds are a boon, they help me . . . through the day. (*Smile.*) The old style! (*Smile off.*) Yes, those are happy days, when there are sounds. (*Pause.*) When I hear sounds. (*Pause.*) I used to think . . . (*pause*) . . . I say I used to think they were in my head. (*Smile.*) But no. (*Smile broader.*) No no. (*Smile off.*) That was just logic. (*Pause.*) Reason. (*Pause.*) I have not lost my reason. (*Pause.*) Not yet. (*Pause.*) Not all. (*Pause.*) Some remains. (*Pause.*) Sounds. (*Pause.*) Like little . . . sunderings, little falls . . . apart. (*Pause. Low.*) It's things, Willie. (*Pause. Normal voice.*) In the bag, outside the bag. (*Pause.*) Ah yes, things have their life, that is what I always say, *things* have a life. (*Pause.*) Take my looking-glass, it doesn't need me. (*Pause.*) The bell. (*Pause.*) It hurts like a knife. (*Pause.*) A gouge. (*Pause.*) One cannot ignore it. (*Pause.*) How often . . . (*pause*) . . . I say how often I have said, Ignore it, Winnie, ignore the bell, pay no heed, just sleep and wake, sleep and wake, as you please, open and close the eyes, as you please, or in the way you find most helpful. (*Pause.*) Open and close the eyes, Winnie, open and close, always that. (*Pause.*) But no. (*Smile.*) Not now. (*Smile broader.*) No no. (*Smile off. Pause.*) What now? (*Pause.*) What now, Willie? (*Long pause.*) There is my story of course, when all else fails. (*Pause.*) A life. (*Smile.*) A long life. (*Smile off.*) Beginning in the womb, where life used to begin, Mildred has memories, she will have memories, of the womb, before she dies, the mother's womb. (*Pause.*) She is now four or five already and has recently been given a big waxen dolly. (*Pause.*)

Fully clothed, complete outfit. (*Pause.*) Shoes, socks, undies, complete set, frilly frock, gloves. (*Pause.*) White mesh. (*Pause.*) A little white straw hat with a chin elastic. (*Pause.*) Pearly necklet. (*Pause.*) A little picture-book with legends in real print to go under her arm when she takes her walk. (*Pause.*) China blue eyes that open and shut. (*Pause. Narrative.*) The sun was not well up when Milly rose, descended the steep . . . (*pause*) . . . slipped on her nightgown, descended all alone the steep wooden stairs, backwards on all fours, though she had been forbidden to do so, entered the . . . (*pause*) . . . tiptoed down the silent passage, entered the nursery and began to undress Dolly. (*Pause.*) Crept under the table and began to undress Dolly. (*Pause.*) Scolding her . . . the while. (*Pause.*) Suddenly a mouse — (*Long pause.*) Gently, Winnie. (*Long pause. Calling.*) Willie! (*Pause. Louder.*) Willie! (*Pause. Mild reproach.*) I sometimes find your attitude a little strange, Willie, all this time, it is not like you to be wantonly cruel. (*Pause.*) Strange? (*Pause.*) No. (*Smile.*) Not here. (*Smile broader.*) Not now. (*Smile off.*) And yet . . . (*Suddenly anxious.*) I do hope nothing is amiss. (*Eyes right, loud.*) Is all well, dear? (*Pause. Eyes front. To herself.*) God grant he did not go in head foremost! (*Eyes right, loud.*) You're not stuck, Willie? (*Pause. Do.*) You're not jammed, Willie? (*Eyes front, distressed.*) Perhaps he is crying out for help all this time and I do not hear him! (*Pause.*) I do of course hear cries. (*Pause.*) But they are in my head surely. (*Pause.*) Is it possible that . . . (*Pause. With finality.*) No no, my head was always full of cries. (*Pause.*) Faint confused cries. (*Pause.*) They come. (*Pause.*) Then go. (*Pause.*) As on a wind. (*Pause.*) That is what I find so wonderful. (*Pause.*) They cease. (*Pause.*) Ah yes, great mercies, great mercies. (*Pause.*) The day is now well advanced. (*Smile. Smile off.*) And yet it is perhaps a little soon for my song. (*Pause.*) To sing too soon is fatal, I always find. (*Pause.*) On the other hand it is possible to leave it too late. (*Pause.*) The bell goes for sleep and one has not sung. (*Pause.*) The whole day has flown — (*smile, smile off*) — flown by, quite by, and no song of any class, kind or description. (*Pause.*) There is a problem here. (*Pause.*) One cannot sing . . . just like that, no. (*Pause.*) It bubbles up, for some unknown reason, the time is ill chosen, one chokes it back. (*Pause.*) One says, Now is the time, it is now or never, and one cannot. (*Pause.*) Simply cannot sing. (*Pause.*) Not a note. (*Pause.*) Another thing, Willie, while we are on this subject. (*Pause.*) The sadness after song. (*Pause.*) Have you run across that, Willie? (*Pause.*) In the course of your experience. (*Pause.*) No? (*Pause.*) Sadness after intimate

sexual intercourse one is familiar with of course. (*Pause.*) You would concur with Aristotle there, Willie, I fancy. (*Pause.*) Yes, that one knows and is prepared to face. (*Pause.*) But after song . . . (*Pause.*) It does not last of course. (*Pause.*) That is what I find so wonderful. (*Pause.*) It wears away. (*Pause.*) What are those exquisite lines? (*Pause.*) Go forget me why should something o'er that something shadow fling . . . go forget me . . . why should sorrow . . . brightly smile . . . go forget me . . . never hear me . . . sweetly smile . . . brightly sing . . . (*Pause. With a sigh.*) One loses one's classics. (*Pause.*) Oh not all. (*Pause.*) A part. (*Pause.*) A part remains. (*Pause.*) That is what I find so wonderful, a part remains, of one's classics, to help one through the day. (*Pause.*) Oh yes, many mercies, many mercies. (*Pause.*) And now? (*Pause.*) And now, Willie? (*Long pause.*) I call to the eye of the mind . . . Mr. Shower — or Cooker. (*She closes her eyes. Bell rings loudly. She opens her eyes. Pause.*) Hand in hand, in the other hands bags. (*Pause.*) Getting on . . . in life. (*Pause.*) No longer young, not yet old. (*Pause.*) Standing there gaping at me. (*Pause.*) Can't have been a bad bosom, he says, in its day. (*Pause.*) Seen worse shoulders, he says, in my time. (*Pause.*) Does she feel her legs? he says. (*Pause.*) Is there any life in her legs? he says. (*Pause.*) Has she anything on underneath? he says. (*Pause.*) Ask her, he says, I'm shy. (*Pause.*) Ask her what? she says. (*Pause.*) Is there any life in her legs. (*Pause.*) Has she anything on underneath. (*Pause.*) Ask her, she says. (*Pause. With sudden violence.*) Let go of me for Christ sake and drop! (*Pause. Do.*) Drop dead! (*Smile.*) But no. (*Smile broader.*) No no. (*Smile off.*) I watch them recede. (*Pause.*) Hand in hand — and the bags. (*Pause.*) Dim. (*Pause.*) Then gone. (*Pause.*) Last human kind — to stray this way. (*Pause.*) Up to date. (*Pause.*) And now? (*Pause. Low.*) Help. (*Pause. Do.*) Help, Willie. (*Pause. Do.*) No? (*Long pause. Narrative.*) Suddenly a mouse . . . (*Pause.*) Suddenly a mouse ran up her little thigh and Mildred, dropping Dolly in her fright, began to scream — (*Winnie gives a sudden piercing scream*) — and screamed and screamed — (*Winnie screams twice*) — screamed and screamed and screamed and screamed till all came running, in their night attire, papa, mamma, Bibby and . . . old Annie, to see what was the matter . . . (*pause*) . . . what on earth could possibly be the matter. (*Pause.*) Too late. (*Pause.*) Too late. (*Long pause. Just audible.*) Willie. (*Pause. Normal voice.*) Ah well, not long now, Winnie, can't be long now, until the bell for sleep. (*Pause.*) Then you may close your eyes, then you *must* close your eyes — and keep them closed. (*Pause.*) Why say

that again? (*Pause.*) I used to think . . . (*pause*) . . .
I say I used to think there was no difference between
one fraction of a second and the next. (*Pause.*) I
used to say . . . (*pause*) . . . I say I used to say,
Winnie, you are changeless, there is never any difference between one fraction of a second and the
next. (*Pause.*) Why bring that up again? (*Pause.*)
There is so little one can bring up, one brings up
all. (*Pause.*) All one can. (*Pause.*) My neck is hurting
me. (*Pause. With sudden violence.*) My neck is
hurting me! (*Pause.*) Ah that's better. (*With mild
irritation.*) Everything within reason. (*Long pause.*)
I can do no more. (*Pause.*) Say no more. (*Pause.*)
But I must say more. (*Pause.*) Problem here. (*Pause.*)
No, something must move, in the world, I can't
any more. (*Pause.*) A zephyr. (*Pause.*) A breath.
(*Pause.*) What are those immortal lines? (*Pause.*)
It might be the eternal dark. (*Pause.*) Black night
without end. (*Pause.*) Just chance, I take it, happy
chance. (*Pause.*) Oh yes, abounding mercies. (*Long
pause.*) And now? (*Pause.*) And now, Willie? (*Long
pause.*) That day. (*Pause.*) The pink fizz. (*Pause.*)
The flute glasses. (*Pause.*) The last guest gone.
(*Pause.*) The last bumper with the bodies nearly
touching. (*Pause.*) The look. (*Long pause.*) What
day? (*Long pause.*) What look? (*Long pause.*) I
hear cries. (*Pause.*) Sing. (*Pause.*) Sing your old
song, Winnie.

(*Long pause. Suddenly alert expression. Eyes switch
right. Willie's head appears to her right round corner
of mound. He is on all fours, dressed to kill — top
hat, morning coat, striped trousers, etc., white gloves
in hand. Very long bushy white Battle of Britain mustache. He halts, gazes front, smooths mustache. He
emerges completely from behind mound, turns to his
left, halts, looks up at Winnie. He advances on all
fours toward center, halts, turns head front, gazes
front, strokes mustache, straightens tie, adjusts hat,
advances a little further, halts, takes off hat and looks
up at Winnie. He is now not far from center and
within her field of vision. Unable to sustain effort of
looking up he sinks head to ground.*)

WINNIE (*mondaine*):° Well this is an unexpected pleasure! (*Pause.*) Reminds me of the day you came
whining for my hand. (*Pause.*) I worship you, Winnie, be mine. (*He looks up.*) Life a mockery without
Win. (*She goes off into a giggle.*) What a get up,
you do look a sight! (*Giggles.*) Where are the flowers?
(*Pause.*) That smile today. (*Willie sinks head.*) What's
that on your neck, an anthrax? (*Pause.*) Want to
watch that, Willie, before it gets a hold on you.

mondaine: Worldly.

(*Pause.*) Where were you all this time? (*Pause.*)
What were you doing all this time? (*Pause.*) Changing? (*Pause.*) Did you not hear me screaming for
you? (*Pause.*) Did you get stuck in your hole? (*Pause.
He looks up.*) That's right, Willie, look at me.
(*Pause.*) Feast your old eyes, Willie. (*Pause.*) Does
anything remain? (*Pause.*) Any remains? (*Pause.*)
No? (*Pause.*) I haven't been able to look after it,
you know. (*He sinks his head.*) You are still recognizable, in a way. (*Pause.*) Are you thinking of
coming to live this side now . . . for a bit maybe?
(*Pause.*) No? (*Pause.*) Just a brief call? (*Pause.*)
Have you gone deaf, Willie? (*Pause.*) Dumb? (*Pause.*)
Oh I know you were never one to talk, I worship
you Winnie be mine and then nothing from that
day forth only titbits from Reynolds' News. (*Eyes
front. Pause.*) Ah well, what matter, that's what I
always say, it will have been a happy day, after
all, another happy day. (*Pause.*) Not long now,
Winnie. (*Pause.*) I hear cries. (*Pause.*) Do you ever
hear cries, Willie? (*Pause.*) No? (*Eyes back on Willie.*)
Willie. (*Pause.*) Look at me again, Willie. (*Pause.*)
Once more, Willie. (*He looks up. Happily.*) Ah!
(*Pause. Shocked.*) What ails you, Willie, I never
saw such an expression! (*Pause.*) Put on your hat,
dear, it's the sun, don't stand on ceremony, I won't
mind. (*He drops hat and gloves and starts to crawl
up mound toward her. Gleeful.*) Oh I say, this is
terrific! (*He halts, clinging to mound with one hand,
reaching up with the other.*) Come on, dear, put
a bit of jizz into it, I'll cheer you on. (*Pause.*) Is it
me you're after, Willie . . . or is it something else?
(*Pause.*) Do you want to touch my face . . . again?
(*Pause.*) Is it a kiss you're after, Willie . . . or is it
something else? (*Pause.*) There was a time when I
could have given you a hand. (*Pause.*) And then a
time before that again when I did give you a hand.
(*Pause.*) You were always in dire need of a hand,
Willie. (*He slithers back to foot of mound and lies
with face to ground.*) Brrum! (*Pause. He rises to
hands and knees, raises his face toward her.*) Have
another go, Willie, I'll cheer you on. (*Pause.*) Don't
look at me like that! (*Pause. Vehement.*) Don't look
at me like that! (*Pause. Low.*) Have you gone off
your head, Willie? (*Pause. Do.*) Out of your poor
old wits, Willie?

(*Pause.*)

WILLIE (*just audible*): Win.

(*Pause. Winnie's eyes front. Happy expression appears,
grows.*)

WINNIE: Win! (*Pause.*) Oh this *is* a happy day, this
will have been another happy day! (*Pause.*) After
all. (*Pause.*) So far.

(*Pause. She hums tentatively beginning of song, then sings softly, musical-box tune.*)

> Though I say not
> What I may not
> Let you hear,
> Yet the swaying
> Dance is saying,
> Love me dear!
> Every touch of fingers

> Tells me what I know,
> Says for you,
> It's true, it's true,
> You love me so!

(*Pause. Happy expression off. She closes her eyes. Bell rings loudly. She opens her eyes. She smiles, gazing front. She turns her eyes, smiling, to Willie, still on his hands and knees looking up at her. Smile off. They look at each other. Long pause.*)

COMMENTARIES

Samuel Beckett's plays are considered difficult, obscure, experimental, and, since Martin Esslin defined the term, absurd. Absurd literature might seem to require no commentary because absurdity ought to have no significant content, but quite the opposite is true. One of the anomalies of absurdist literature is that it may require more commentary than other kinds of literature.

Martin Esslin's essay defined the term by which we describe work by Beckett and a few other playwrights influenced by him. The essay tries to establish the character of absurd drama, its limits and its importance. Audiences were certainly baffled by Beckett's work, starting with his very successful *Waiting for Godot* and including *Krapp's Last Tape* and *Happy Days*. All these plays are restricted by space and in action. Their very essence is restriction. Esslin shows the possible range of significance in Beckett's plays and explains that if we see them properly, we can understand how they interpret experience.

Ruby Cohn is interested in performance problems and discusses Beckett's own experiences in staging and directing *Krapp's Last Tape*. Her observations provide insight into Beckett's hopes for the play and into his understanding of the way the play works onstage. Professional critics Bernard Dukore, Sidney Homan, and Eugene Webb describe some of the range of possible interpretation when aspects of the play are focused on with intensity. Absurdist drama is not without meaning; rather, it seems capable of absorbing a wide range of meanings and of reflecting the interpreter's attitudes and observations in remarkably subtle ways.

Martin Esslin (b. 1918)
The Theater of the Absurd

Martin Esslin is a drama critic whose work has had wide currency. He was the first to write extensively about the theater of the absurd, a term that has come to describe the plays of Samuel Beckett and a number of other post-World War II playwrights such as Eugène Ionesco and Harold Pinter. The question of what use playwrights make of the absurd and why it is an appropriate term to reflect the achievement of Beckett is explored briefly in this excerpt.

The Theater of the Absurd shows the world as an incomprehensible place. The spectators see the happenings on the stage entirely from the outside, without ever understanding the full meaning of these strange patterns of events, as newly arrived visitors might watch life in a country of which they have not yet mastered the language. The confrontation of the audience with characters and happenings which they are not quite able to comprehend makes it impossible for them to share the aspirations and emotions depicted in the play. Brecht's famous "Verfremdungseffekt" (alienation effect), the inhibition of any identification between spectator and actor, which Brecht could never successfully achieve in his own highly rational theater, really comes into its own in the Theater of the Absurd. It is impossible to identify oneself with characters one does not understand or whose motives remain a closed book, and so the distance between the public and the happenings on the stage can be maintained. Emotional identification with the characters is replaced by a puzzled, critical attention. For while the happenings on the stage are absurd, they yet remain recognizable as somehow related to real life with *its* absurdity, so that eventually the spectators are brought face to face with the irrational side of their existence. Thus, the absurd and fantastic goings-on of the Theater of the Absurd will, in the end, be found to reveal the irrationality of the human condition and the illusion of what we thought was its apparent logical structure.

If the dialogue in these plays consists of meaningless clichés and the mechanical, circular repetition of stereotyped phrases — how many meaningless clichés and stereotyped phrases do we use in our day-to-day conversation? If the characters change their personality halfway through the action, how consistent and truly integrated are the people we meet in our real life? And if people in these plays appear as mere marionettes, helpless puppets without any will of their own, passively at the mercy of blind fate and meaningless circumstance, do we, in fact, in our overorganized world, still possess any genuine initiative or power to decide our own destiny? The spectators of the Theater of the Absurd are thus confronted with a grotesquely heightened picture of their own world: a world without faith, meaning, and genuine freedom of will. In this sense, the Theater of the Absurd is the true theater of our time.

The theater of most previous epochs reflected an accepted moral order, a world whose aims and objectives were clearly present to the minds of all its public, whether it was the audience of the medieval mystery plays with their solidly accepted faith in the Christian world order or the audience of the drama of Ibsen, Shaw, or Hauptmann with their unquestioned belief in evolution and progress. To such audiences, right and wrong were never in doubt, nor did they question the then accepted goals of human endeavor. Our own time, at least in the Western world, wholly lacks such a generally accepted and completely integrated world picture. The decline of religious faith, the destruction of the belief in automatic social and biological progress, the discovery of vast areas of irrational and unconscious forces within the human psyche, the loss of a sense of control over rational human development in an age of totalitarianism and weapons of mass destruction, have all contributed to the erosion of the basis for a dramatic convention in which the action proceeds within a fixed and self-evident framework of generally accepted values. Faced with the vacuum left by the destruction of a universally accepted and unified set of beliefs, most serious playwrights have felt the need to fit their work into the frame of values and objectives expressed in one of the contemporary ideologies: Marxism, psychoanalysis, aestheticism, or nature worship. But these, in the eyes of a writer like Adamov, are nothing but superficial rationalizations which try to hide the depth of man's predicament, his loneliness and his anxiety. Or, as Ionesco puts it:

> As far as I am concerned, I believe sincerely in the poverty of the poor, I deplore it; it is real; it can become a subject for the theatre; I also believe in the anxieties and serious troubles the rich may suffer from; but it is neither in the misery of the former nor in the melancholia of the latter, that I, for one, find my dramatic subject matter. Theatre is for me the outward projection onto the stage of an inner world; it is in my dreams, in my anxieties, in my obscure desires, in my internal contradictions that I, for one, reserve for myself the right of finding my dramatic subject matter. As I am not alone in the world, as each of us, in the depth of his being, is at the same time part and parcel of all others, my dreams, my desires, my anxieties, my obsessions do not belong to me alone. They form part of an ancestral heritage, a very ancient storehouse which is a portion of the common property of all mankind. It is this, which, transcending their outward diversity, reunites all human beings and constitutes our profound common patrimony, the universal language.[1]

In other words, the commonly acceptable framework of beliefs and values of former epochs which has now been shattered is to be replaced by the community of dreams and desires of a collective unconscious. And, to quote Ionesco again:

> ... the new dramatist is one ... who tries to link up with what is most ancient: new language and subject matter in a dramatic structure which aims at being clearer, more stripped of inessentials and more purely theatrical; the rejection of traditionalism to rediscover tradition; a synthesis of knowledge and invention, of the real and imaginary, of the particular and the universal, or as they say now, of the individual and the collective. ... By expressing my deepest obsessions, I express my deepest humanity. I become one with all others, spontaneously, over and above all the barriers of caste and different psychologies. I express my solitude and become one with all other solitudes.[2]

What is the tradition with which the Theater of the Absurd — at first sight the most revolutionary and radically new movement — is trying to link itself? It is in fact a very ancient and a very rich tradition, nourished from many and varied sources: the verbal exuberance and extravagant inventions of Rabelais, the age-old clowning of the Roman mimes and the Italian *Commedia dell'Arte*,

---

[1] Eugène Ionesco, "L'Impromptu de l'Alma," *Théâtre II*, Paris, 1958.
[2] Ionesco, "The Avant-Garde Theatre," *World Theatre*, VIII, No. 3 (Autumn 1959).

the knock-about humor of circus clowns like Grock; the wild, archetypal symbolism of English nonsense verse, the baroque horror of Jacobean dramatists like Webster or Tourneur, the harsh, incisive and often brutal tones of the German drama of Grabbe, Büchner, Kleist, and Wedekind with its delirious language and grotesque inventiveness; and the Nordic paranoia of the dreams and persecution fantasies of Strindberg.

Ruby Cohn (b. 1922)
BECKETT DIRECTING

Ruby Cohn has written books and articles about Beckett and has become one of the most important Beckett scholars. This discussion focuses on the way in which Beckett works with actors, directors, and other people in the theater. Cohn's description of the directions Beckett gave to the actors in Krapp's Last Tape *reveals his imaginative attitude toward the play. The thought that he once felt Krapp should wear clown white and behave farcically could certainly affect the way we interpret the play. Cohn is careful to give us information about the way Beckett responded to performances and actors, thus emphasizing the play as a performed work of art, not just something to read.*

After the intricate cross-relationships and complex repetitive texture of *Endgame*, directing *Krapp's Last Tape* might seem like child's play. It will be recalled that Beckett wrote the one-character piece in English for actor Pat Magee, who was first directed by Donald McWhinnie. In 1958 in London Beckett worked closely with actor and director. The three of them played hard and then pub-crawled, but there was no pub crawling in 1969 in Berlin, where Krapp's role went to ponderous Martin Held.

James Knowlson has discussed the complex symbolism of *Krapp's Last Tape*, succinctly summarized in Beckett's Director's Notebook:

Krapp decrees physical (ethical) incompatibility of light (Spiritual) and dark (Sensual) only when he intuits possibility of their reconciliation as rational-irrational. He turns from fact of anti-mind alien to mind to thought of anti-mind constituent of mind.[1]

Despite this esoteric and symbolic background, the surface of *Krapp's Last Tape* is realistic, but Beckett's Director's Notebook dwells on realistic and nonrealistic detail.

Unlike the *Endgame* notebook, that for *Krapp* does not divide the play into rehearsal scenes. Instead, Beckett lists twenty-seven matters needing directorial attention, from the metaphysical "1. *Choix-hasard*" (choice-guess) to the very physical "27. *Endgültig Werkstatt*" (final . . . Werkstatt [version]). Beckett calculates that Krapp has been recording for forty-five years, since there are nine boxes, each containing five spools of tape. The notebook designates the tape recorder as a masturbatory agent, and Beckett instructed Held to hold the box erotically. His separation of speech from motion, introduced into *Come and Go* and

---

[1]Qtd. in Pierre Chabert, "Beckett as Director," *Gambit* (28): 62.

Endgame, becomes the fulcrum of performance: "Play therefore composed of two approximately equal parts, listening-immobility and nonlistening-motion." For the *écoute* (listening) Beckett began rehearsals with a provisional tape of thirty-nine-year-old Krapp, but this was replaced.

Beckett wished abrupt and vivid disjunction between still listening and agitated nonlistening. Toward this end, he amplified his stage directions and simplified his stage picture. He eliminated Krapp's clown makeup and endowed him with worn-out rather than farcical clothes. Krapp's table was clean at the start, and Beckett excised the comic business with keys and envelope, but he introduced fumbling rheumatic fingers. He suggested to Held a moving "rest" gesture; Krapp hugs himself shivering. Realistically, an old man seeks warmth; symbolically, Krapp loves himself.

Because of Beckett's stage simplification, we more easily grasp similarities between the young and the old Krapp. Action begins when Krapp peers short-sightedly at his large silver watch, and it proves to be time for his banana. After two bananas are eaten onstage, Krapp on tape mentions three. The man who has stepped from his spotlighted circle into darkness and back listens to a tape announcing that he loves to return from darkness to himself, Krapp. And yet, Krapp-Held looks in astonishment at the tape recorder when he hears the voice say: "Me. (*pause*) Krapp." For Krapp as for Rimbaud, "*Je est un autre*" ("I is another").

Separating speech from motion, Beckett moved Krapp toward pathos, although the effect in *Endgame* was lugubriously comic. In the opening mime Krapp makes clumsy comic gestures, but it is a rheumatic old man who makes them, and it is a lonely old man who personifies tapes as "little rascal" and "little scoundrel." Whenever Krapp-Held rises from the table, he leans heavily on both hands. Whenever Krapp walks away from the table, he crosses in front and to the right; he fears the darkness at his left. His love-hate relation with objects is comic, for pathos is a greater danger to *Krapp's Last Tape* than to *Endgame*. Beckett dissolved pathos by beating time for Krapp-Held's nonverbal and comic noises — wheezing, walking, turning pages, drinking, and even slamming objects on his table.

When taped speech fills the theater, Krapp listens motionless, comic gestures spent. His head is bent at an angle of 45 degrees, his left hand caresses the tape recorder, and the fingers of his right hand sometimes drum impatiently. Unrecorded in Beckett's notebook is the frequent ternary rhythm evident in performance. Krapp listens to three main events; there are three breaks in the equinox account and three in the "Farewell to Love." At the play's beginning Krapp walks three times out of his spotlight into darkness and back. He disappears through his backstage curtain three times — for his ledger, pile of tapes, and tape recorder, the increased weight of the objects revealed by increased fatigue. In the later action Beckett changed the three backstage exits to offstage drinking, search for a dictionary, offstage drinking and search for a microphone. Krapp consults his watch three times; he moves the tape ahead three times and back three times. After he records, he looks at the machine three times before he wrenches off his last tape.

Within this ternary pattern Krapp shows emotional variety — his lubricity on peeling a banana, his impatience with a younger self, his contained grief at his mother's death, his boast to a whore, his extrapolation of a novel, his fear of dark at his left, his inability to sustain love, which he perhaps regrets when he plays and replays the "Farewell to Love." Krapp-Held squinted when he tremulously spoke of eyes — in the words of the notebook, "*ein Traumgefressener Mensch*" ("A man consumed by dreams").

With improved vision of his own (after operations to remove cataracts), Beckett returned to *Krapp* in 1975 — in his French translation, to accompany the French premiere of *Not I* at the Petit d'Orsay. Ten years after *L'Hypothèse* Beckett and Chabert again worked together on a one-character play. In Paris as in Berlin, the central image remained a Krapp who was "one body with the machine." As in *L'Hypothèse* Beckett divided the small stage into areas: the central table (place of reverie) and the backstage alcove (place of practicality).

Because of [the young actor Pierre] Chabert's relative youth, Beckett dressed him in a frayed dressing gown to hide his tall frame, a toque to hide his abundant hair, and black half gloves that evoke premonitions of death. Pale and thin, Krapp-Chabert shivered with an old man's cold, and his myopic eyes seemed intent on piercing the dark. He stretched to listen so as to compensate for his deafness, one hand curled round the recorder handle. Immobile, he sucked at his cheeks, leaving his mouth open. Tall, he bumped the overhead light when he rose from the table, and the light continued to move while he listened, still, to the "moves" of the "Farewell to Love."

Musically trained, Chabert readily responded to Beckett's sonata breakdown of the dialogue into b-A(b)-A-B-a, A being the taped voice, B the live voice, and small letters standing for short duration. Much of the brief (three-week) rehearsal period was devoted to the B-voice, sharp and staccato in b and (b), but rhythmically varied in B; the high-pitched quaver of the conventional stage old man was especially to be avoided. In both A and B, Beckett wished counterpoint between objectivity and self-disgust or between objectivity and fascination with a woman or a word.

In Paris Beckett revised key scenes of both nonlistening and listening. When Krapp goes backstage to drink, he leaves a curtain open, so that his guzzling shadow is seen in a long light rectangle, projected from a Chinese lantern on a screen. This space is sharply different from the dream-memory space of Krapp's table. Thus, Krapp versus his past is theatricalized audibly as Krapp versus his taped voice; visually as a shrunken actual Krapp versus his enlarged shadow. In the three playbacks of the love scene, Krapp listens first with bowed head, then with his face on the table, and finally, after a long look over his left shoulder into darkness, with stony erectness. Krapp-Chabert's last playback of "Farewell to Love" is clarified as his stoic farewell to life as well. After the stage lights go out, the tape-recorder light continues to glow — a small *memento mori*.

A little over two years later, in 1977, Beckett found himself directing an English *Krapp* in Berlin's Akademie der Künste, as a favor to his friend Rick Cluchey. Despite two previous productions, he made extensive director's notes, which have been published in the San Quentin Drama Workshop Program and in Bethanien Center Publications. His headings summarize the areas of his concern: "Tape Montage, Costume, Props [a long list], Lighting, Opening, *Hain* ["friend Death" in a poem by Matthias Claudius], Drinks, Song, Microphone, End." Visual details were carried over from the Paris production — a dressing gown, modified banana business, enlarged shadow of drinking, erect posture at the end as at the beginning.

This time Beckett divided the play into four rehearsal scenes: (1) Beginning to ledger note: "Farewell to — love"; (2) "Thirty-nine today . . ." to "A girl in a shabby green coat. . . . No?" (with "Connaught" replaced by "Kerry" and the hymn cut); (3) "When I look back —" to preparations for recording. (Watch business is cut. Looking up "viduity" in the dictionary, near-sighted Krapp first reads "vicar" and "vicious"); (4) From the newly introduced "Fanny" before "Just been listening . . ." to the end. ("One pound . . . doubt" disappears. "Finger and thumb" replaces "a kick in the crutch," and "dozed away" replaces "went to sleep.")

In contrast to Held's erotic recorder, Cluchey's is both friend and enemy, alternately caressed and cursed. Even more sharply than earlier, the Akademie *Krapp* points up opposites: stillness-movement, silence-noise, dark-light, black-white. As a corollary to such polarity, Beckett had Cluchey emphasize the "or"s in the "viduity" definition.

Beckett never spoke to the Workshop members of the symbolic genesis of the play, but they worried together in the inadequately equipped Akademie about nuances of light and sound. To the ternary rhythms of the earlier productions Beckett added long still "brood"s after the words "Incomparable," "crystolite," and "side by side." He sought tonal interest for the often-repeated phrase "Ah well," which had nearly become the play's title. Live Krapp's "Be again, be again" was to sound like the churchbells of his youth. Clinging to rhythm in the face of death, Krapp-Cluchey was sometimes rehearsed with Beckett beating time — for the little rushes of seven steps to and from the table, for the longer series of thirteen steps to and from the alcove, for the offstage drinking sounds (clink of bottle against glass, bottle down, drink, glass down, cough-sigh), and for the long *Hain* (sudden stiffening, slow head turn to left, hold, slow return to right, resume tape). Although the American group knew little German, they prattled glibly of the *Hain*, unaware that it derived from the Matthias Claudius poem. Seeking the precise shuffle sound he wanted from Krapp's run-walk, Beckett gave Cluchey his own worn slippers. In the last week (of nearly four) of rehearsals Beckett changed Krapp-Cluchey's listening position, right hand embracing the recorder, left hand behind it, head angled about 60 degrees to the table. Under a conical dunce-cap light, the metallic rotating tape was reflected on Cluchey's left cheek — a kind of shadow pulse. San Quentin technical men Hauptle and Thorpe conferred on how to eliminate it, but Beckett told them softly, "I love it."

Bernard F. Dukore (b. 1931)
KRAPP'S LAST TAPE AS TRAGICOMEDY

Bernard Dukore is a distinguished scholar of modern drama. His comments on Krapp's Last Tape *center on a careful description of the play in an effort to divine its genre. In the process of his discussion, Dukore sheds some light on interesting qualities of the play, especially the relationship of the Krapp we see onstage with the Krapp that he hears speaking from the tape recorder.*

First things first: the title, followed by the subtitle. Virtually every word of both is a pun: *Krapp's Last Tape: A Play in One Act.* As numerous critics have observed, *Krapp* is both the man's name and excrement; man is therefore symbolized by and reduced to excrement. As Ruby Cohn points out,[1] *Tape* may refer both to the recording device and to an alcoholic beverage. *A Play*, a work for the stage, also describes how one records and how one listens to a recording device; and such meanings of the word as amusement, game, or diversionary activity (as distinguished from meaningful employment) are apposite. Perhaps more important in the context of tragicomedy are the remaining words. *Last* may mean final or it may mean the most recent. Descriptive of the theater piece, *One Act* at the same time suggests that all of Krapp's tape recording sessions are ultimately the same, are essentially one act. Thus, Krapp's final and/or his most recent tape is essentially the same as the others.

Similarly, old Krapp is himself essentially the same as middle-aged Krapp (whose tape voice he hears), who is essentially the same as young Krapp (unheard by the audience but discussed by middle-aged Krapp). Paradoxically, *Krapp's Last Tape* is a *mono*drama for *two* voices: in alternating strips of monologue, Beckett presents the voice and presence of Old Krapp and the taped voice of middle-aged Krapp, the latter very much (to use the television phrase) "live on tape," both in the sense of vividness of impression and in the sense that he lives still in the old clown he has become. The assertion of Vladimir in *Waiting for Godot* holds equally for *Krapp's Last Tape*: "The essential doesn't change." Using similar phrases, old Krapp and the voice of Krapp thirty years earlier speak of similar pleasures, similar hopes, similar disappointments. When old Krapp calls middle-aged Krapp a "stupid bastard," one recalls the latter's reference to younger Krapp as a foolish "young whelp." As if to underscore their resemblances, old Krapp joins middle-aged Krapp in laughing at young Krapp. As Leonard C. Pronko remarks, "The tragedy of Krapp, and of all men in Beckett's view, is not that we become what we were not, but that we are now and evermore the same."[2] But, as Pronko recognizes, such a tragedy, and this play in particular, is comic as well. Indeed, this sort of sameness is also a pattern of comedy.

The essential may not change, but as in *Waiting for Godot* other changes take place. Krapp's memory is failing: he can no longer recall either the black ball or what he once called a "memorable equinox," and he has to look up the meaning of words he used to use. His sexual abilities and his sexual pleasures, moreover, are also diminishing. From Bianca and an "engrossing sexual life" he has dwindled to Fanny, a "Bony old ghost of a whore" with whom old Krapp "Couldn't do much." From the "incomparable" Bianca, whose name suggests virginal purity (it means *white* in Italian), he has degenerated to Fanny, whose name (slang for *behind*) reinforces his description of her as a mere piece of ass. All of this is both tragic and comic, for though he has achieved what he said he wanted (middle-aged Krapp, who expressed relief that his affair with Bianca was over, hoped his sexual life would be less absorbing), the result (ignobility and a thwarting of basic desire) is far from what he had hoped.

Similarly tragicomic — and similarly simultaneously so — is the coupling of bodily functionings and the intellect. With Krapp, neither crap nor thought moves freely, though mere words do; in both cases, only gas flows. Constipated

[1]Ruby Cohn, *Samuel Beckett: The Comic Gamut* (New Brunswick, N.J.: Rutgers University Press, 1962), p. 249.

[2]Leonard C. Pronko, *Avant-Garde: The Experimental Theatre in France* (Berkeley: University of California Press, 1962), p. 51.

physically, Krapp is constipated intellectually, for the results of his thought — books — do not circulate. In the past year only seventeen copies of his books have been sold, that is, have been dropped into their intended receptacles. When man's noblest function, or what is generally held to be his noblest function, is related in this manner to constipation, the result is grotesque tragicomedy.

Combining the two traditional dramatic genres, tragedy and comedy, *Krapp's Last Tape* employs comic, even farcical techniques, which are visual as well as verbal. Krapp looks like a decrepit old man but in addition, with his "White face" and "Purple nose," he resembles a clown, and he has clown business: slipping on a banana skin, for instance, he nearly falls, but he recovers himself and after a comic take kicks the skin into the orchestra pit. Nevertheless, the play follows a traditional tragic pattern: the protagonist achieves a goal but loses what makes that goal meaningful. Beneath the activity of recording tapes is an underlying objective: to be alone with himself. "I love to get up and move about in [the darkness]," says the voice on the tape, "then back here to . . . me. (*Pause.*) Krapp." Figuratively as well as literally, he has moved about in the darkness, but in achieving his self-centered, solipsistic objective, he has failed utterly in achieving an understanding of himself. Because Krapp does not understand himself, which is necessary (though insufficient) for tragedy, the tragic pattern is followed only to an extent. If he were to comprehend what we do, the play might become less comic, more tragic. But Beckett provides no indication that Krapp has achieved any self-understanding, no indication of anything but that he thinks he has advanced beyond the "stupid bastard" of a middle-aged Krapp who himself thought he had advanced beyond the "young whelp" he used to be. Were Krapp to realize the absurdity of his position and abandon his solipsism, leave his dank, dark "den" and join the rest of the world in an integration of man and society, which is a comic ending, *Krapp's Last Tape* might be less tragic, more comic. As it is, the play is tragicomic. Krapp repeats his futile gestures, does pretty much what he has been doing, and achieves no self-understanding.

The traditional order of tragedy is from good fortune to bad, from happiness to unhappiness, from order to chaos; that of comedy the reverse: from bad fortune to good, from unhappiness to happiness, from chaos to order. The order of *Krapp's Last Tape*, returning us to Vladimir's perception, suggests an absence of essential change: the opening action is comic, underlined by pathos; the play's final moment is bleak (Krapp stares motionlessly as the tape runs silently) but it is given a comic edge by the ironically comic words (the last on the tape) immediately preceding this silent finale: "Perhaps my best years are gone. When there was a chance of happiness. But I wouldn't want them back. Not with the fire in me now. No, I wouldn't want them back." Not only is there a basic absence of change but, more important, for this may be a characteristic of modern tragicomedy in general, there is a denial of either type of change associated with tragedy or comedy. Unlike the protagonist of tragedy, the protagonist of tragicomedy is unaware of or deliberately blind to the worsening of fortune, for he lacks self-understanding. Unlike comedy, there is no "happy ending"; in fact, the ending of *Krapp's Last Tape* is grimmer than that of a tragedy that ends in the death of the protagonist. And unlike either tragedy or comedy, *Krapp's Last Tape* reveals no moral order.

In this play, Beckett usually mingles the tragic and the comic simultaneously rather than alternately. As I mentioned earlier, the scene in which old Krapp and middle-aged Krapp laugh together at young Krapp is tragicomic. Old Krapp's reference to having had sex with a superannuated whore is both comic and tragic: comic in its parody of sex; tragic in the sense of great loss which inheres in that same parody, for youthful desire persists in the aged bodies, now unable to do more than "manage it," and feebly to perform only the motions, as it were, of pleasure.

Let us further explore Beckett's tragicomic synthesis in terms of the sexual motif. Though glad his love affair with Bianca is over, middle-aged Krapp recalls with great pleasure — in a truly beautiful and affecting scene — some moments of love in a rowboat. Not at all comic, the scene touches the tragic in a sense just alluded to, that of great loss. Shortly thereafter, old Krapp describes a more recent sexual encounter, this time with Fanny, with whom he could not do much, says he, but it's better than a kick in the crutch. A comic description — particularly when, answering her question as to how he manages to make love at his age, he replies that he has been saving up for her all his life — the scene is for several reasons tragicomic. That this old wreck of a man needs sex and barely manages to satisfy that need is comic, though pathetically so. When Krapp observes that the last time with Fanny "wasn't so bad," the effect is enormously funny, but the laugh freezes when one realizes that "not so bad" is a ghastly description of maximal pleasure. The chiefly comic description of the encounter with Fanny also serves as a grotesque commentary on the beautiful, perhaps tragic love scene just heard on the tape. Following the account of Fanny, old Krapp *re*plays the description of the rowboat episode, with its now intensified sense of tragic loss, and the replay thereby serves to comment on the scene which had commented on it. That is, the repetition of the rowboat scene casts a reflection on the bony old whore scene which had cast a reflection on the rowboat scene. The tragic aspect is intensified through the recollection of the comic.

In conclusion, then, to alter Ruby Cohn's observation about the modern blend of tragicomedy,[3] Beckett in *Krapp's Last Tape* joins the tragic and the comic in a way that makes us aware of *both* their opposition and their union. In its essence, as in its title, the play embraces different referents and different perceptions.

[3]Ruby Cohn, *Currents in Contemporary Drama* (Bloomington: Indiana University Press, 1969), p. 197.

Steven J. Rosen (b. 1944)
From SAMUEL BECKETT AND THE PESSIMISTIC TRADITION

Steven Rosen comments on Beckett's use of philosophy and allusion in Krapp's Last Tape. *Beckett is well read in philosophy and it is natural to think that he would derive much of his thinking from the philosophers he has studied. Early in this essay, Rosen says, "One of Beckett's greatest achievements is his distinctive treatment of thought as it is weighed down by time." In a way, philosophy is the thought that Beckett weighs down by time, and in* Krapp's Last Tape, *time is graphically presented. Rosen helps us see what its shape and significance can be.*

In *Krapp's Last Tape*, Beckett has no need of philosophical allusions, for the tapes provide the same effects his allusions normally supply. Krapp is a failed sage; his tapes form his own sage tradition and the repetition of his concerns both discredits and amplifies them. Similarly, but on a larger plane, Beckett's allusions to philosophers comment on the failure of philosophical tradition, the futile repetition of philosophical activity. This commentary authorizes his own pessimism; but at the same time, the evocation of the sage tradition lends dignity and weight to the preoccupations of Beckett's heroes — thoughts usually fleeting and trivial in themselves. All of his writing can be regarded as successive versions of Lucky's speech in *Waiting for Godot*, a testament to the futility of philosophical labors; but while this testament is pathetic and nearly incoherent, it does not lower Lucky in the audience's estimation. There is something awesome in the persistence of his consciousness.

At least since Aristotle, man has been defined as a creature of consciousness, as opposed to instinct, instinctive behavior consisting of purposive action without consciousness of purpose.[1] It has always been recognized that man could suffer from excessive consciousness, and be "sicklied o'er with the pale cast of thought," but Beckett's critique of consciousness goes much further than this and questions whether awareness of purpose ever has any value. Moran studies his bees' dance, wondering what its purpose is and whether bees "are capable of such notions" as conscious intention. But the implication here is that their dance would be in no way enhanced by such awareness. Lichtenberg, the German aphorist, once remarked that

> Perhaps a dog, shortly before it falls asleep, or a drunken elephant has ideas which would not be unworthy of a master of philosophy. But these are of no use to them.[2]

According to Beckett, they are of no use to the master of philosophy either. Consequently, his speakers all disclaim having any good reason for expressing themselves, and Beckett's writing exhausts the standard poses of excuse: ignorance, insanity, and "obligation."

Such an approach can be termed neither tragic or comic; it is tragicomic. The narrative structures of Beckett's works, rather than leaving the reader with a definitive sense of completion, suggest a situation infinitely perpetuated. If comedies end well and tragedies unhappily (though with a consoling sense of order reaffirmed), the characteristic conclusion of tragicomedy is endlessness. Beckett calls *Waiting for Godot* a "tragicomedy in two acts" because the second act substantially repeats the first, leaving the audience with no anticipation other than that of the tramps "going on."

[1] Eduoard von Hartman cited by Mitchell Ginsberg, "Nietzschean Psychiatry," in Robert Solomon, ed., *Nietzsche: A Collection of Critical Essays* (Garden City: Anchor Press, 1973), p. 304.

[2] George von Lichtenberg, The Lichtenberg Reader, tr. F. Mautner and H. Hartfield (Boston: Beacon Press, 1959), p. 50.

Sidney Homan (b. 1938)
Happy Days: Creation in Spite of Habit

Sidney Homan's focus in his discussion of Happy Days *is on the question of sexuality, especially as it relates to Winnie. He sees the props and settings on stage as symbolic of sexual organs. He also sees interesting connections with the sexual imagination as expressed in other plays, such as* A Midsummer Night's Dream. *Homan is especially sensitive to the double-meanings implied in some of the play's language, and it is through a cautious but close interpretation of gestures and language that he builds his case for his approach to the play.*

Sexuality, in the broadest sense of the word, is inseparable from Winnie's creation. Even if they are immobile, or undesirable, Beckett's women all breathe a sexuality, wholesome or otherwise, that is either at one with their own sense of creativity or with that creativity they inspire in others. One thinks, first of all, of Mrs. Rooney in *All That Fall*, still eager, albeit somewhat incapacitated because of age and weight, to do the "trick," a creature lusting after something more than friendly taps on the shoulder. From her fertile mind spews a torrent of suggestive, symbolic, playful words. In *Embers*, Ada, however browbeaten by Henry, at length serves as stimulus for her husband, inspiring him with her description of his own Belacqua-like father. We might also think of the woman in the boat with Krapp, or the woman who berates Joe in Beckett's first television play, or the woman in the photograph examined by O in *Film*, even Sucky Moll in *Malone Dies*, serving the dying narrator, at the very least, as the subject for a fiction as he tries to escape his own death room.

As in Shakespeare's own *A Midsummer Night's Dream*, sex and the imagination are one: the poet is also a lover, giving birth to the creatures of his fictive venture. To love is to have empathy for that creation, for the ability to "go on." However inferior the shallow Athenians or the rustic Bottom are to the rationalist Theseus, the five lovers are still given the chance to experience Shakespeare's expansive, imaginative world, that forest expanding from finite Athens to the infinite dimensions of Oberon's kingdom. And this power, this chance is denied rationalists like Theseus. Similarly, in *The Taming of the Shrew* Petruchio's imaginative re-creation of Kate from shrew to model wife, or the imaginative capacity they both share in fashioning a world that denies the surface facts, is at one with their status as lovers. It is therefore no surprise that Winnie's sexuality, however faded, is stressed from the opening. We learn early that she is *"well preserved,"* with *"bare"* arms and shoulders, a *"low bodice, big bosom."* Though no shapely young girl, she is still miles beyond that dried virgin Miss Fitt.

If anything, the sexual problem in the play belongs to Willie, the husband, and this point is emphasized by the double entendres. Winnie's juxtaposition of commentary on the toothpaste and addresses to her husband suggests that, like the toothpaste, he is "running out," that the situation cannot be helped, and that both he and his sexual organ are "just one of those old things [which] . . . can't be cured." There is even a coda for this hymn joining fading toiletry and sexuality: "ah yes . . . poor dear Willie . . . good Lord."

Holding the butt of the parasol in her hand, a handle of "*surprising length,*" Winnie brings Willie into the comparison as she stretches back and to her right, hanging over him with "Willie" and then "wonderful gift." As she strikes her impotent husband with the handle, she cries, "Wish I had it," whereupon the parasol slips from her grasp and falls beneath the mound. After such sexual taunting she finds that her palm is "damp," perhaps as if from passion.

It is true that at times Winnie seems to be part of a large, symbolic travesty of sexuality: the various phallic instruments at her command (the parasol, the toothbrush, the revolver) arrayed against the vaginal hole into which Willie retreats, and the lubricant that she counsels him to "work it well in." The fact remains that it is Willie who seems to have lost his zest, his "jizz." Almost dead in his use of language, confined to a few monosyllabic utterances, some wordless play, and drawing comments not from his imagination but from the newspaper, he is, until the end of the play, almost extinct as a creative force. For Willie takes only a vicarious verbal pleasure from obscene postcards, from wordplay on "suck," or allusions to an old lover of Winnie. Winnie thus tries to lead him, to bring him out, both sexually and imaginatively. Again, sexuality and the imagination are inseparable: one feeds on the other. She reminds him that he once found her lovable, that in the past he had complimented her hair. Now the relationship is failing, despite Winnie's purposeful distortions of the situation: her attempts to dredge up a more romantic past and the fact that her standards for social intercourse have become so minimal that a mere grunt or monosyllable from Willie can move her to conclude that it will be a happy day.

Eugene Webb (*b. 1938*)
ON *HAPPY DAYS*

Eugene Webb begins his discussion of the play with a description of what happens, emphasizing the setting and the visual circumstances of the action. He also focuses on the limitations that dominate the play: limitations of action, movement, and the design of the set. The symbolic value of Winnie's being buried in the earth suggests to Webb that her situation is one not only of necessity but of choice. He examines her uses of language and shows that "she talks so that she will not have to think." Talk has become a form of defense. The value of Willie as an audience for her talk becomes apparent by the end of the play.

The basic situation is . . . that of a person thrown into a condition with frustrating limitations and with the choice of either facing this directly and clearly or evading it. The central character in this case is Winnie, a rather full-blown, blond woman of about fifty, who is buried to above her waist in the center of a mound. Since Willie, her husband, rarely speaks or shows himself, he is largely peripheral to the play and is present primarily as an object of relationship for Winnie. All one sees of the earth is covered by scorched grass. On the backcloth an unbroken plain and sky recede to meet in the distance.

The design of the set, with its *"maximum of simplicity and symmetry,"* carries our eyes to the center of attention, Winnie. The fact that she is buried in the earth is a symbol both of the way the absurd is closing in on her as death approaches, making it harder and harder for her to find distractions from herself, and also of the way she has given up her freedom to objects outside her by burying herself in that which is not herself. That the mound has not only been imposed on her by life but is also something she has chosen for herself is made clear by the reference to her feeling of having "to cling on" so as not to float up out of it.

The action begins when a piercing bell rings to awaken her. . . . It has to ring twice, first for ten seconds, then for five, before it finally gets through to her. Evidently she would prefer to remain asleep — in fact she says a little later that Willie's faculty for sleeping most of the time is a "marvelous gift" and that she wishes she had it — but nevertheless when she finally wakes, her first effort is to muster up her courage and look at life cheerfully: "Another heavenly day." Her next act is to pray in the traditional way — "For Jesus Christ sake Amen" — before commanding herself to "begin" her "day."

The fact that Winnie wants to make her experience a "day" is significant. Man cannot live without order, and in a world without a time scheme he will impose a pattern of his own making. There are no more days now, and when she is not busy making them up she knows this. "The old style," she says at one point when she sees the label on her medicine bottle telling her to take six level tablespoons "daily." "All day long" in the world she lives in now means only "between the bell for waking and the bell for sleep," but she likes the "old style" the way Hamm [in *Endgame*] liked the "old questions" and the "old answers" and does her best to retain what she can of it in her "daily" life.

In structuring her day she tries to give it, like an Aristotelian plot, a beginning, middle, and end. There has to be a time for brushing her teeth, which comes at the beginning, for rummaging among her things, for singing her song, which should come sometime near the end, and finally for going back to sleep when the bell rings. The trouble, of course, is that never knowing when the bell will ring to signal the end, she can never be certain the middle is being adequately arranged: "To sing too soon is fatal, I always find. . . . On the other hand it is possible to leave it too late. . . . The bell goes for sleep and one has not sung." Anxieties of this kind are something of a blessing for her, however; they distract her from the situation as it really is: a formless chaos on which patterns can be fitted only by self-deception.

Another important distraction, as well as a deep compulsion, is the need she has to know. The object of knowledge is not important; it need not be anything particularly significant. All that is required is that the search for it keep her mind occupied. There is her toothbrush, for example. When she finishes brushing her teeth, she looks at the handle of the brush and tries to make out the writing on it: ". . . genuine . . . pure . . . what?" She polishes her spectacles and tries again, then gets a magnifying glass out of her bag and finally manages to decipher it: "Fully guaranteed . . . genuine pure . . . hog's . . . setae." Every now and then, as in this instance, such a quest for knowledge brings her up against a reminder of the emptiness and sterility of this world in which "nothing grows." In this case, inquiring from Willie the difference between a hog and a swine, she finds that a hog is a "castrated male swine. . . . Reared for slaughter." She manages, however, to avoid thinking about the associations that go with this, the parallel to her own situation and to Willie's, by shifting her attention to her joy in the fact that Willie has finally spoken to her: "Oh this *is* a happy day!" Another object of curiosity, with similarly unpleasant associations for her, is a pornographic picture Willie shows her when she asks if she can see it. "No but this is just genuine pure filth," she exclaims as she examines it intently. "Make any nice-minded person want to vomit." Then she gets her magnifying glass to give it a better look: "What does that creature in the background think he's doing? (*Looks closer.*) Oh no really!" Finally she gives it a "last long look" before returning it with a "Pah! . . . Take it away!" No source of curiosity is too trivial or too repulsive to defeat her. She is always grateful for something — whether the hairs of the head are called "it" or "them," how the comb and brush got back into her bag if she did not put them there — that can keep her mind occupied and diverted from the real unpleasantness of her life.

And when these distractions fail her, when she loses heart and envies the brute beast, as she says, she turns to thoughts of death, either the death that will come, she hopes, with the end of the world — "the happy day to come when flesh melts at so many degrees and the night of the moon has so many hundred hours" — or suicide. Of course, as might be expected, her feelings about death are as equivocal as those of any of Beckett's other characters. This is made clear by her reaction to her revolver when she runs across it while rummaging in her bag: she brings it out, holds it up, "kisses it rapidly," then puts it back. She calls it by a pet name, "Brownie," and likes to know that it is there, but the sight of it makes her uncomfortable. Death is a pleasant fantasy as long as it remains at some remove, but when it comes too close it is as disturbing as reality itself.

The most important of her defenses is talk. Like Vladimir and Estragon [in *Waiting for Godot*], she talks so that she will not have to think, and what she is most afraid of is the possibility that there may come a time when she will no longer be able to talk, either because words will fail her — "Words fail, there are times when even they fail" — or because there will be nobody left to talk to. If it were simply words that failed she would still be able to occupy herself with her possessions, and consequently she is careful not to "overdo the bag" lest she exhaust its interest before the time when she will really need it. But if she were to lose Willie so that she were left entirely alone, she would have to face the emptiness that would be left in her by the absence of the other whose perception of her she had relied on to constitute her personality. The thought of no longer having an interlocutor to direct herself toward is especially abhorrent to her: "Oh no doubt the time will come when before I can utter a word I must make sure you heard the one that went before and then no doubt another come another time when I must learn to talk to myself a thing I could never bear to do such wilderness." Since what Winnie knows of her being is largely confined to that which is reflected in the eyes of others, to be deprived of those eyes, or ears, would be something more frightening to her than death itself. . . .

Does this steadfast refusal on Winnie's part to face reality mean . . . that her story is purely static, that she does not go through any kind of growth during the play? Not at all. Her life brings her closer to the vision she seeks to avoid even if it does so against her will. Reality presses upon her, both from the outside and from within. Even if it does not break through to her during the course of the play, we can see the direction in which things are moving. . . .

Act 2 carries this process of growth still further, even if not to completion. Whereas Winnie opened and closed the first act with conventional prayers and tried to persuade herself that they would be effective in bringing her relief from her misfortunes — "prayers perhaps not for naught," she says at one point on thinking of how sometimes her headaches go away — the second act opens without petitionary prayer, but only with "Hail, holy light" and an attempt to believe that "someone is looking at me still." Of course the "someone" is still the God of "the sweet old style," and the greeting to the "holy light" is a quotation from Milton's invocation to the uncreated light of God, but the fact that she is not explicitly praying for something to be given her would seem to indicate some growth in self-reliance. "I used to pray," she says, "I say I used to pray. . . . Yes, I must confess I did. (*Smile.*) Not now."

The reason she smiles as she says this is probably that she feels some degree of liberation in being able to get along without prayer. Her smile does not last, however; freedom may have its pleasant side, but it is also rather frightening. She stops to reflect that if this indicates a change in her, it is not clear what kind of change is involved and that perhaps it may be leading toward more change than she wants: "Then . . . now . . . what difficulties here, for the mind. (*Pause.*) To have been always what I am — and so changed from what I was." She goes on both to introduce and avoid the idea that something might be happening inside her that could eventually lead to a radical break with her past: "Eyes float up that seem to close in peace . . . to see . . . in peace. (*Pause.*) Not mine. (*Smile.*) Not now." The eyes she feels floating up inside her would seem to be the eyes of a new vision that would enable her to look on the reality of her world without anxiety over its lack of meaning. She does not want them yet, though: the "old style" is still too precious to her. She turns aside from these thoughts to return to the old question and answer game, to concern with her appearance, and to the last of her possessions, the gun. Even this flight from what is happening, however, leads her inescapably back to the heart of the problem. Thinking about her things she is forced to face for a moment the fact that like all the rest of reality they are not hers: they are only what they are. Possession is an artificial meaning imposed on an indifferent reality by man's imagination: "It's things, Willie. . . . In the bag, outside the bag. . . . Ah yes, things have their life, that is what I always say, *things* have a life. . . . Take my looking-glass, it doesn't need me." Things have a life of their own; they do not need her or any other person. Of course this is not what she "always" says — quite the contrary — but this thought, like so many others, feels more comfortable to her when she can take the edge off its newness by persuading herself that it is not unfamiliar.

These thoughts in turn lead to reflections on the role of the bell in her life, raising the question of the possibility of autonomy:

> The bell. . . . It hurts like a knife. . . . A gouge. . . . One cannot ignore it. . . . How often . . . I say how often I have said, Ignore it, Winnie, ignore the bell, pay no heed, just sleep and wake, sleep and wake, as you please, open and close the eyes as you please. . . . But no. (*Smile.*) Not now. (*Smile broader.*) No no.

Perhaps the new life that would emerge from the new vision that seems to be growing inside her would involve both freedom from the need to impose artificial patterns on a reality they do not fit and freedom to direct her own acts with her own will, no longer submitting to the authority of the bell any more than to that of the God she imagines or to that of the possessions which in fact possess her. This is not something she can accept, however. Freedom is no more endurable to her than meaninglessness.

She retreats into a story. Still, this turns out to be no more satisfactory an escape than any other. All roads lead to the same end: defeat. In this case the story is a thinly veiled projection of her own life into fiction. It is about a little girl named Mildred or Millie who has a doll with "china blue eyes that open and shut," like Winnie's, and a "pearly necklet," like that Winnie wears. Millie decides "to undress Dolly," rather the way the new self in Winnie represented by the eyes floating up from her depths is undressing Winnie by stripping from her all the conventional ideas that shield her from naked contact with the hard light of reality. Then suddenly a mouse appears in the story, disturbing Winnie sufficiently to make her discontinue it for a while. Evidently the mouse is a symbol to her of the destructive element she feels threatened by in the process of change she is undergoing. When she returns to the story later, she describes the mouse running up Millie's "little thigh." And as the little girl begins to scream in the story, Winnie gives a "*sudden piercing scream*" of her own, an indication of how closely she identifies with her protagonist. When the parents come, she says, it is "too late." Evidently Winnie feels the same of her own case: that the undressing that is taking place in her will lead to the destruction not only of her superficial identity, the self that lives in conventional ideas and in the eyes of others, but also of the deeper self within. She cannot believe that the loss of all her normal patterns of thought and behaviour would not destroy her very being as well.

At the end she retreats as usual to what she believes is the safer ground of her fortress of illusions, to the old dream of her "happy day." It does not seem likely, however, that this fortress will be able to stand indefinitely. The signs of change are too great. It is hard to tell just what it means when Willie appears, for the first time, dressed up in morning clothes, complete with top hat and white gloves, and tries without success to crawl up the mound to reach her. The attire suggests that the occasion is one of some solemnity, perhaps a death, though just what kind of death is not clear. Winnie makes of it what she must, a sign that this "will have been a happy day, after all, another happy day," and when Willie gasps her name, she rejoices and makes of it another occasion for flight into song. We already know of the sadness that comes after song, however, and we know how fragile the illusion of the "happy day" is. All we can be certain of about this ending is that Winnie will not find in it the meaning she expects. It would seem more likely that the process of change we have seen working itself out in her will lead her to an end she cannot imagine and into which we cannot follow her.

Harold Pinter

Harold Pinter (b. 1930) has successfully written plays for the commercial stage, radio, and television as well as film scripts produced by some of the best directors of his time. Pinter was born into relatively humble circumstances in East London, but his early schooling distinguished him and he eventually enrolled in London's prestigious Royal Academy of Dramatic Arts, where he studied acting. When he finished his studies, he joined a company and toured for several years, married an actress, and began to write for the stage. His previous writing efforts were in prose: He wrote short stories and a long novel, *The Dwarfs* (1956), purportedly autobiographical, but never finished and never published as a novel. Produced as a radio play in 1960, it expresses some of the themes of his best work: the disintegration of a mind and the cruelty of people to their fellow beings.

In 1957, Pinter turned to playwriting and wrote three important plays, the one-act *The Room* and *The Dumb Waiter* and the full-length *The Birthday Party* (finished in 1958). All these plays were well received, and they established his method in dialogue and to a large extent the style that has dominated his work. The critic Martin Esslin, who coined the term "theater of the absurd," saw in Pinter's work an absurdist strain, especially in the nihilism — the belief in nothing — that sometimes shows up in his work. Pinter's characters usually reveal no spiritual awareness and no longing for spiritual values.

Pinter's dialogue sometimes has qualities of aimlessness, at least on the surface. But always the dialogue penetrates the unconsciousness of the audience and reveals the nature of the characters and their situation. Even the repetitious dialogue makes the audience more aware of the limitations and the pain of the circumstances in which Pinter's people find themselves.

Early reaction to the plays sometimes saw the aimless dialogue and the absurdist qualities as shortcomings rather than as indictments of the social order from which the plays arose. Yet the brutality of his characters to one another, their lack of sympathy for one another, and their demands for dominance have all become hallmarks of late-twentieth-century life, especially in the cities of the West.

The first of Pinter's plays to catch the attention of the general theater public was the commercially produced *The Caretaker* (1960), a play about two brothers, one of whom, Aston, invites a bewildered and all but mentally destroyed tramp, Davies, to become a caretaker in his room. Davies hardly knows who he is. His identity is essentially reduced to nothing by his aimless, soul-destroying life, and he speaks in shards of language, especially when he is trying to explain that he left his identity papers in his beloved Sidcup — some fifteen years before — and that if they could find those papers, he would know where he was born and who he was. At the end of the play the younger brother, Mick, torments Davies, demanding that he leave, twisting his arm, verbally abusing him, but then relenting. The play ends with the shards of a life, as Davies says: "Listen . . . if I . . . go down . . . if I was to . . . get my papers . . . would you . . . would you let . . . would you . . . if I got down . . . and got my . . . (*Long silence.*)"

Pinter's other well-known play is *The Homecoming* (1965), which has a brutal, shocking quality. A professor returns to England from America with his wife, and it becomes clear that he plans to return to America but that his wife will stay on as a mistress to his father and his brothers. The matter-of-factness with which the situation is treated and the relationships are portrayed provides part of the play's shock value.

Beginning in the late 1960s and continuing to the present, Pinter has been writing screenplays, some of which are adaptations of his own plays. His other screenwriting credits include *The Servant, The Quiller Memorandum, Accident, The Go-Between,* and *The French Lieutenant's Woman.*

THE DUMB WAITER

The claustrophobic qualities of *The Dumb Waiter* (1957), with all its action taking place in a confined basement room, are typical of Pinter's plays, which are often constrained by limits of space. To an extent, such constraint is a metaphor for the constraints that life itself places on people and that people place upon themselves.

The title of the play refers to the machine that ferries clothing and messages from Gus and Ben's room to someone whose identity is unknown. It also refers to Gus and Ben themselves, who are waiting dumbly for a job. They do what they are told and follow orders.

There is an ironic hominess to the domestic scene at the beginning of the play. Ben reads the newspaper and retells the important bits with some relish. Gus's reaction is what we might expect of a wife — if one of them had a wife. The stories they read and analyze give a glimpse of sensationalism that is an appropriate preamble to their own story. Gus and Ben have a sense of propriety and order that is as banal as we would expect from thugs. They like things to be orderly and neat. They want the toilet to work, and they can't help but wonder who cleans up after their jobs.

Ben and Gus are masters of small talk. The language of the play has a meandering, aimless quality that characterizes much of Pinter's style. Ben says one thing, and Gus repeats it. Ben begins a sentence, and Gus finishes. After a point has been made, one hears silence, then the point is made again:

> BEN: We do the same.
> GUS: Exactly the same?
> BEN: Exactly.
> (*Pause.*)
> GUS: We don't do anything different?
> BEN: We do exactly the same.
> GUS: Oh.

This technique results in the buildup of tension and anticipation. The technique also contributes to creating a sense of enigma — the audience strains to make meaning out of what appear to be banal observations, and in the process those observations begin to take on more importance. And, indeed, from the accretion of banalities a deeper meaning grows until trivial matters become matters of life and death.

The play seems almost to amble. There is no detectable direction, no detectable climax toward which it is building, and virtually no conflict. The only conflict that develops is limited to the trivial disagreements the two old hands have about things that are of no abiding importance. Certainly, this is not the kind of dramatic conflict that engages Ibsen's characters or characters of a more traditional stripe. The petty disagreements seem very natural, and the play itself seems naturalistic. But the improbable intrusion of the dumb waiter changes our sense of what is and is not realistic. The dumb waiter sends down messages virtually in the manner of the oracle at Delphi, and it is up to those who receive them to act accordingly.

When the play ends, with the next victim walking into the room out of the lavatory, we can only assume that Ben will act on the oracle. And if he does, the message that has come down from on high is terrifying indeed.

Harold Pinter (b. 1930)
THE DUMB WAITER

1957

Scene: *A basement room. Two beds, flat against the back wall. A serving hatch, closed, between the beds. A door to the kitchen and lavatory, left. A door to a passage, right. Ben is lying on a bed, left, reading a paper. Gus is sitting on a bed, right, tying his shoelaces, with difficulty. Both are dressed in shirts, trousers, and braces.*

Silence.

Gus ties his laces, rises, yawns, and begins to walk slowly to the door, left. He stops, looks down, and shakes his foot.

Ben lowers his paper and watches him. Gus kneels and unties his shoelace and slowly takes off the shoe. He looks inside it and brings out a flattened matchbox. He shakes it and examines it. Their eyes meet. Ben rattles his paper and reads. Gus puts the matchbox in his pocket and bends down to put on his shoe. He ties his lace, with difficulty. Ben lowers his paper and watches him. Gus walks to the door, left, stops, and shakes the other foot. He kneels, unties his shoelace, and slowly takes off the shoe. He looks inside it and brings out a flattened cigarette packet. He shakes it and examines it. Their eyes meet. Ben rattles his paper and reads. Gus puts the packet in his pocket, bends down, puts on his shoe, and ties the lace.

He wanders off, left.

Ben slams the paper down on the bed and glares after him. He picks up the paper and lies on his back, reading.

Silence.

A lavatory chain is pulled twice, off left, but the lavatory does not flush.

Silence.

Gus reenters, left, and halts at the door, scratching his head.

Ben slams down the paper.

BEN: Kaw!

(*He picks up the paper.*)

What about this? Listen to this!

(*He refers to the paper.*)

A man of eighty-seven wanted to cross the road. But there was a lot of traffic, see? He couldn't see how he was going to squeeze through. So he crawled under a lorry.°

GUS: He what?

BEN: He crawled under a lorry. A stationary lorry.

GUS: No?

BEN: The lorry started and ran over him.

GUS: Go on!

BEN: That's what it says here.

GUS: Get away.

BEN: It's enough to make you want to puke, isn't it?

GUS: Who advised him to do a thing like that?

BEN: A man of eighty-seven crawling under a lorry!

GUS: It's unbelievable.

BEN: It's down here in black and white.

GUS: Incredible.

(*Silence.*)

(*Gus shakes his head and exits. Ben lies back and reads.*)

(*The lavatory chain is pulled once off left, but the lavatory does not flush.*)

(*Ben whistles at an item in the paper.*)

(*Gus reenters.*)

I want to ask you something.

BEN: What are you doing out there?

GUS: Well, I was just —

BEN: What about the tea?

GUS: I'm just going to make it.

BEN: Well, go on, make it.

GUS: Yes, I will. (*He sits in a chair. Ruminatively.*) He's laid on some very nice crockery this time, I'll say that. It's sort of striped. There's a white stripe.

(*Ben reads.*)

It's very nice. I'll say that.

(*Ben turns the page.*)

You know, sort of round the cup. Round the rim. All the rest of it's black, you see. Then the saucer's black, except for right in the middle, where the cup goes, where it's white.

(*Ben reads.*)

lorry: Truck.

Then the plates are the same, you see. Only they've got a black stripe — the plates — right across the middle. Yes, I'm quite taken with the crockery.

BEN (*still reading*): What do you want plates for? You're not going to eat.

GUS: I've brought a few biscuits.

BEN: Well, you'd better eat them quick.

GUS: I always bring a few biscuits. Or a pie. You know I can't drink tea without anything to eat.

BEN: Well, make the tea then, will you? Time's getting on.

(*Gus brings out the flattened cigarette packet and examines it.*)

GUS: You got any cigarettes? I think I've run out.

(*He throws the packet high up and leans forward to catch it.*)

I hope it won't be a long job, this one.

(*Aiming carefully, he flips the packet under his bed.*)

Oh, I wanted to ask you something.

BEN (*slamming his paper down*): Kaw!

GUS: What's that?

BEN: A child of eight killed a cat!

GUS: Get away.

BEN: It's a fact. What about that, eh? A child of eight killing a cat!

GUS: How did he do it?

BEN: It was a girl.

GUS: How did she do it?

BEN: She —

(*He picks up the paper and studies it.*)

It doesn't say.

GUS: Why not?

BEN: Wait a minute. It just says — Her brother, aged eleven, viewed the incident from the toolshed.

GUS: Go on!

BEN: That's bloody ridiculous.

(*Pause.*)

GUS: I bet he did it.

BEN: Who?

GUS: The brother.

BEN: I think you're right.

(*Pause.*)

(*Slamming down the paper.*) What about that, eh? A kid of eleven killing a cat and blaming it on his little sister of eight! It's enough to —

(*He breaks off in disgust and seizes the paper. Gus rises.*)

GUS: What time is he getting in touch?

(*Ben reads.*)

What time is he getting in touch?

BEN: What's the matter with you? It could be any time. Any time.

GUS (*moves to the foot of Ben's bed*): Well, I was going to ask you something.

BEN: What?

GUS: Have you noticed the time that tank takes to fill?

BEN: What tank?

GUS: In the lavatory.

BEN: No. Does it?

GUS: Terrible.

BEN: Well, what about it?

GUS: What do you think's the matter with it?

BEN: Nothing.

GUS: Nothing?

BEN: It's got a deficient ballcock, that's all.

GUS: A deficient what?

BEN: Ballcock.

GUS: No? Really?

BEN: That's what I should say.

GUS: Go on! That didn't occur to me.

(*Gus wanders to his bed and presses the mattress.*)

I didn't have a very restful sleep today, did you? It's not much of a bed. I could have done with another blanket too. (*He catches sight of a picture on the wall.*) Hello, what's this? (*Peering at it.*) "The First Eleven."° Cricketers. You seen this, Ben?

BEN (*reading*): What?

GUS: The first eleven.

BEN: What?

GUS: There's a photo here of the first eleven.

BEN: What first eleven?

GUS (*studying the photo*): It doesn't say.

BEN: What about that tea?

GUS: They all look a bit old to me.

(*Gus wanders downstage, looks out front, then all about the room.*)

I wouldn't like to live in this dump. I wouldn't mind if you had a window, you could see what it looked like outside.

BEN: What do you want a window for?

GUS: Well, I like to have a bit of a view, Ben. It wiles away the time.

(*He walks about the room.*)

The First Eleven: A cricket team.

I mean, you come into a place when it's still dark, you come into a room you've never seen before, you sleep all day, you do your job, and then you go away in the night again.

(*Pause.*)

I like to get a look at the scenery. You never get the chance in this job.

BEN: You get your holidays, don't you?

GUS: Only a fortnight.

BEN (*lowering the paper*): You kill me. Anyone would think you're working every day. How often do we do a job? Once a week? What are you complaining about?

GUS: Yes, but we've got to be on tap though, haven't we? You can't move out of the house in case a call comes.

BEN: You know what your trouble is?

GUS: What?

BEN: You haven't got any interests.

GUS: I've got interests.

BEN: What? Tell me one of your interests.

(*Pause.*)

GUS: I've got interests.

BEN: Look at me. What have I got?

GUS: I don't know. What?

BEN: I've got my woodwork. I've got my model boats. Have you ever seen me idle? I'm never idle. I know how to occupy my time, to its best advantage. Then when a call comes, I'm ready.

GUS: Don't you ever get a bit fed up?

BEN: Fed up? What with?

(*Silence.*)

(*Ben reads. Gus feels in the pocket of his jacket, which hangs on the bed.*)

GUS: You got any cigarettes? I've run out.

(*The lavatory flushes off left.*)

There she goes.

(*Gus sits on his bed.*)

No, I mean, I say the crockery's good. It is. It's very nice. But that's about all I can say for this place. It's worse than the last one. Remember that last place we were in? Last time, where was it? At least there was a wireless there. No, honest. He doesn't seem to bother much about our comfort these days.

BEN: When are you going to stop jabbering?

GUS: You'd get rheumatism in a place like this, if you stay long.

BEN: We're not staying long. Make the tea, will you? We'll be on the job in a minute.

(*Gus picks up a small bag by his bed and brings out a packet of tea. He examines it and looks up.*)

GUS: Eh, I've been meaning to ask you.

BEN: What the hell is it now?

GUS: Why did you stop the car this morning, in the middle of that road?

BEN (*lowering the paper*): I thought you were asleep.

GUS: I was, but I woke up when you stopped. You did stop, didn't you?

(*Pause.*)

In the middle of that road. It was still dark, don't you remember? I looked out. It was all misty. I thought perhaps you wanted to kip,° but you were sitting up dead straight, like you were waiting for something.

BEN: I wasn't waiting for anything.

GUS: I must have fallen asleep again. What was all that about then? Why did you stop?

BEN (*picking up the paper*): We were too early.

GUS: Early? (*He rises.*) What do you mean? We got the call, didn't we, saying we were to start right away. We did. We shoved out on the dot. So how could we be too early?

BEN (*quietly*): Who took the call, me or you?

GUS: You.

BEN: We were too early.

GUS: Too early for what?

(*Pause.*)

You mean someone had to get out before we got in?

(*He examines the bedclothes.*)

I thought these sheets didn't look too bright. I thought they ponged° a bit. I was too tired to notice when I got in this morning. Eh, that's taking a bit of a liberty, isn't it? I don't want to share my bed sheets. I told you things were going down the drain. I mean, we've always had clean sheets laid on up till now. I've noticed it.

BEN: How do you know those sheets weren't clean?

GUS: What do you mean?

BEN: How do you know they weren't clean? You've spent the whole day in them, haven't you?

GUS: What, you mean it might be my pong? (*He sniffs sheets.*) Yes. (*He sits slowly on bed.*) It could be my pong, I suppose. It's difficult to tell. I don't really know what I pong like, that's the trouble.

BEN (*referring to the paper*): Kaw!

GUS: Eh, Ben.

kip: Nap.
ponged: Smelled.

BEN: Kaw!

GUS: Ben.

BEN: What?

GUS: What town are we in? I've forgotten.

BEN: I've told you. Birmingham.

GUS: Go on!

(*He looks with interest about the room.*)

That's in the Midlands. The second biggest city in Great Britain. I'd never have guessed.

(*He snaps his fingers.*)

Eh, it's Friday today, isn't it? It'll be Saturday tomorrow.

BEN: What about it?

GUS (*excited*): We could go and watch the Villa.°

BEN: They're playing away.

GUS: No, are they? Caarr! What a pity.

BEN: Anyway, there's no time. We've got to get straight back.

GUS: Well, we have done in the past, haven't we? Stayed over and watched a game, haven't we? For a bit of relaxation.

BEN: Things have tightened up, mate. They've tightened up.

(*Gus chuckles to himself.*)

GUS: I saw the Villa get beat in a cup tie once. Who was it against now? White shirts. It was one-all at halftime. I'll never forget it. Their opponents won by a penalty. Talk about drama. Yes, it was a disputed penalty. Disputed. They got beat two-one, anyway, because of it. You were there yourself.

BEN: Not me.

GUS: Yes, you were there. Don't you remember that disputed penalty?

BEN: No.

GUS: He went down just inside the area. Then they said he was just acting. I didn't think the other bloke touched him myself. But the referee had the ball on the spot.

BEN: Didn't touch him! What are you talking about? He laid him out flat!

GUS: Not the Villa. The Villa don't play that sort of game.

BEN: Get out of it.

(*Pause.*)

GUS: Eh, that must have been here, in Birmingham.

BEN: What must?

GUS: The Villa. That must have been here.

BEN: They were playing away.

Villa: A soccer team.

GUS: Because you know who the other team was? It was the Spurs. It was Tottenham Hotspur.

BEN: Well, what about it?

GUS: We've never done a job in Tottenham.

BEN: How do you know?

GUS: I'd remember Tottenham.

(*Ben turns on his bed to look at him.*)

BEN: Don't make me laugh, will you?

(*Ben turns back and reads. Gus yawns and speaks through his yawn.*)

GUS: When's he going to get in touch?

(*Pause.*)

Yes, I'd like to see another football° match. I've always been an ardent football fan. Here, what about coming to see the Spurs tomorrow?

BEN (*tonelessly*): They're playing away.

GUS: Who are?

BEN: The Spurs.

GUS: Then they might be playing here.

BEN: Don't be silly.

GUS: If they're playing away they might be playing here. They might be playing the Villa.

BEN (*tonelessly*): But the Villa are playing away.

(*Pause. An envelope slides under the door, right. Gus sees it. He stands, looking at it.*)

GUS: Ben.

BEN: Away. They're all playing away.

GUS: Ben, look here.

BEN: What?

GUS: Look.

(*Ben turns his head and sees the envelope. He stands.*)

BEN: What's that?

GUS: I don't know.

BEN: Where did it come from?

GUS: Under the door.

BEN: Well, what is it?

GUS: I don't know.

(*They stare at it.*)

BEN: Pick it up.

GUS: What do you mean?

BEN: Pick it up!

(*Gus slowly moves toward it, bends, and picks it up.*)

What is it?

GUS: An envelope.

BEN: Is there anything on it?

GUS: No.

football: Soccer.

BEN: Is it sealed?
GUS: Yes.
BEN: Open it.
GUS: What?
BEN: Open it!

(*Gus opens it and looks inside.*)

What's in it?

(*Gus empties twelve matches into his hand.*)

GUS: Matches.
BEN: Matches?
GUS: Yes.
BEN: Show it to me.

(*Gus passes the envelope. Ben examines it.*)

Nothing on it. Not a word.
GUS: That's funny, isn't it?
BEN: It came under the door?
GUS: Must have done.
BEN: Well, go on.
GUS: Go on where?
BEN: Open the door and see if you can catch anyone outside.
GUS: Who, me?
BEN: Go on!

(*Gus stares at him; puts the matches in his pocket, goes to his bed, and brings a revolver from under the pillow. He goes to the door, opens it, looks out, and shuts it.*)

GUS: No one.

(*He replaces the revolver.*)

BEN: What did you see?
GUS: Nothing.
BEN: They must have been pretty quick.

(*Gus takes the matches from pocket and looks at them.*)

GUS: Well, they'll come in handy.
BEN: Yes.
GUS: Won't they?
BEN: Yes, you're always running out, aren't you?
GUS: All the time.
BEN: Well, they'll come in handy then.
GUS: Yes.
BEN: Won't they?
GUS: Yes, I could do with them. I could do with them too.
BEN: You could, eh?
GUS: Yes.
BEN: Why?
GUS: We haven't got any.
BEN: Well, you've got some now, haven't you?

GUS: I can light the kettle now.
BEN: Yes, you're always cadging° matches. How many have you got there?
GUS: About a dozen.
BEN: Well, don't lose them. Red too. You don't even need a box.

(*Gus probes his ear with a match.*)

(*Slapping his hand.*) Don't waste them! Go on, go and light it.
GUS: Eh?
BEN: Go and light it.
GUS: Light what?
BEN: The kettle.
GUS: You mean the gas.
BEN: Who does?
GUS: You do.
BEN (*his eyes narrowing*): What do you mean, I mean the gas?
GUS: Well, that's what you mean, don't you? The gas.
BEN (*powerfully*): If I say go and light the kettle I mean go and light the kettle.
GUS: How can you light a kettle?
BEN: It's a figure of speech! Light the kettle. It's a figure of speech!
GUS: I've never heard it.
BEN: Light the kettle! It's common usage!
GUS: I think you've got it wrong.
BEN (*menacing*): What do you mean?
GUS: They say put on the kettle.
BEN (*taut*): Who says?

(*They stare at each other, breathing hard.*)

(*Deliberately.*) I have never in all my life heard anyone say put on the kettle.
GUS: I bet my mother used to say it.
BEN: Your mother? When did you last see your mother?
GUS: I don't know, about —
BEN: Well, what are you talking about your mother for?

(*They stare.*)

Gus, I'm not trying to be unreasonable. I'm just trying to point out something to you.
GUS: Yes, but —
BEN: Who's the senior partner here, me or you?
GUS: You.
BEN: I'm only looking after your interests, Gus. You've got to learn, mate.
GUS: Yes, but I've never heard —
BEN (*vehemently*): Nobody says light the gas! What does the gas light?
GUS: What does the gas —?

cadging: Begging.

BEN (*grabbing him with two hands by the throat, at arm's length*): THE KETTLE, YOU FOOL!

(*Gus takes the hands from his throat.*)

GUS: All right, all right.

(*Pause.*)

BEN: Well, what are you waiting for?
GUS: I want to see if they light.
BEN: What?
GUS: The matches.

(*He takes out the flattened box and tries to strike.*)

No.

(*He throws the box under the bed.*)
(*Ben stares at him.*)
(*Gus raises his foot.*)

Shall I try it on here?

(*Ben stares. Gus strikes a match on his shoe. It lights.*)

Here we are.
BEN (*wearily*): Put on the bloody kettle, for Christ's sake.

(*Ben goes to his bed, but, realizing what he has said, stops and half turns. They look at each other. Gus slowly exits, left. Ben slams his paper down on the bed and sits on it, head in hands.*)

GUS (*entering*): It's going.
BEN: What?
GUS: The stove.

(*Gus goes to his bed and sits.*)

I wonder who it'll be tonight.

(*Silence.*)

Eh, I've been wanting to ask you something.
BEN (*putting his legs on the bed*): Oh, for Christ's sake.
GUS: No. I was going to ask you something.

(*He rises and sits on Ben's bed.*)

BEN: What are you sitting on my bed for?

(*Gus sits.*)

What's the matter with you? You're always asking me questions. What's the matter with you?
GUS: Nothing.
BEN: You never used to ask me so many damn questions. What's come over you?
GUS: No, I was just wondering.
BEN: Stop wondering. You've got a job to do. Why don't you just do it and shut up?
GUS: That's what I was wondering about.

BEN: What?
GUS: The job.
BEN: What job?
GUS (*tentatively*): I thought perhaps you might know something.

(*Ben looks at him.*)

I thought perhaps you — I mean — have you got any idea — who it's going to be tonight?
BEN: Who what's going to be?

(*They look at each other.*)

GUS (*at length*): Who it's going to be.

(*Silence.*)

BEN: Are you feeling all right?
GUS: Sure.
BEN: Go and make the tea.
GUS: Yes, sure.

(*Gus exits, left, Ben looks after him. He then takes his revolver from under the pillow and checks it for ammunition. Gus reenters.*)

The gas has gone out.
BEN: Well, what about it?
GUS: There's a meter.
BEN: I haven't got any money.
GUS: Nor have I.
BEN: You'll have to wait.
GUS: What for?
BEN: For Wilson.
GUS: He might not come. He might just send a message. He doesn't always come.
BEN: Well, you'll have to do without it, won't you?
GUS: Blimey.
BEN: You'll have a cup of tea afterwards. What's the matter with you?
GUS: I like to have one before.

(*Ben holds the revolver up to the light and polishes it.*)

BEN: You'd better get ready anyway.
GUS: Well, I don't know, that's a bit much, you know, for my money.

(*He picks up a packet of tea from the bed and throws it into the bag.*)

I hope he's got a shilling, anyway, if he comes. He's entitled to have. After all, it's his place, he could have seen there was enough gas for a cup of tea.
BEN: What do you mean, it's his place?
GUS: Well, isn't it?
BEN: He's probably only rented it. It doesn't have to be his place.

GUS: I know it's his place. I bet the whole house is. He's not even laying on any gas now either.

(*Gus sits on his bed.*)

It's his place all right. Look at all the other places. You go to this address, there's a key there, there's a teapot, there's never a soul in sight — (*He pauses.*) Eh, nobody ever hears a thing, have you ever thought of that? We never get any complaints, do we, too much noise or anything like that? You never see a soul, do you? — except the bloke who comes. You ever noticed that? I wonder if the walls are soundproof. (*He touches the wall above his bed.*) Can't tell. All you do is wait, eh? Half the time he doesn't even bother to put in an appearance, Wilson.

BEN: Why should he? He's a busy man.

GUS (*thoughtfully*): I find him hard to talk to, Wilson. Do you know that, Ben?

BEN: Scrub round it, will you?

(*Pause.*)

GUS: There are a number of things I want to ask him. But I can never get round to it, when I see him.

(*Pause.*)

I've been thinking about the last one.

BEN: What last one?

GUS: That girl.

(*Ben grabs the paper, which he reads.*)

(*Rising, looking down at Ben.*) How many times have you read that paper?

(*Ben slams the paper down and rises.*)

BEN (*angrily*): What do you mean?

GUS: I was just wondering how many times you'd —

BEN: What are you doing, criticizing me?

GUS: No, I was just —

BEN: You'll get a swipe round your earhole if you don't watch your step.

GUS: Now look here, Ben —

BEN: I'm not looking anywhere! (*He addresses the room.*) How many times have I —! A bloody liberty!

GUS: I didn't mean that.

BEN: You just get on with it, mate. Get on with it, that's all.

(*Ben gets back on the bed.*)

GUS: I was just thinking about that girl, that's all.

(*Gus sits on his bed.*)

She wasn't much to look at, I know, but still. It was a mess though, wasn't it? What a mess. Honest, I can't remember a mess like that one. They don't seem to hold together like men, women. A looser texture, like. Didn't she spread, eh? She didn't half spread. Kaw! But I've been meaning to ask you.

(*Ben sits up and clenches his eyes.*)

Who clears up after we've gone? I'm curious about that. Who does the clearing up? Maybe they don't clear up. Maybe they just leave them there, eh? What do you think? How many jobs have we done? Blimey, I can't count them. What if they never clear anything up after we've gone.

BEN (*pityingly*): You mutt. Do you think we're the only branch of this organization? Have a bit of common. They got departments for everything.

GUS: What cleaners and all?

BEN: You birk!°

GUS: No, it was that girl made me start to think —

(*There is a loud clatter and racket in the bulge of wall between the beds, of something descending. They grab their revolvers, jump up, and face the wall. The noise comes to a stop. Silence. They look at each other. Ben gestures sharply toward the wall. Gus approaches the wall slowly. He bangs it with his revolver. It is hollow. Ben moves to the head of his bed, his revolver cocked. Gus puts his revolver on his bed and pats along the bottom of the center panel. He finds a rim. He lifts the panel. Disclosed is a serving hatch, a "dumb waiter." A wide box is held by pulleys. Gus peers into the box. He brings out a piece of paper.*)

BEN: What is it?

GUS: You have a look at it.

BEN: Read it.

GUS (*reading*): Two braised steak and chips. Two sago puddings. Two teas without sugar.

BEN: Let me see that. (*He takes the paper.*)

GUS (*to himself*): Two teas without sugar.

BEN: Mmnn.

GUS: What do you think of that?

BEN: Well —

(*The box goes up. Ben levels his revolver.*)

GUS: Give us a chance? They're in a hurry, aren't they?

(*Ben rereads the note. Gus looks over his shoulder.*)

That's a bit — that's a bit funny, isn't it?

BEN (*quickly*): No. It's not funny. It probably used to be a café here, that's all. Upstairs. These places change hands very quickly.

GUS: A café?

---

birk: Fool.

BEN: Yes.

GUS: What, you mean this was the kitchen, down here?

BEN: Yes, they change hands overnight, these places. Go into liquidation. The people who run it, you know, they don't find it a going concern, they move out.

GUS: You mean the people who ran this place didn't find it a going concern and moved out?

BEN: Sure.

GUS: WELL, WHO'S GOT IT NOW?

(*Silence.*)

BEN: What do you mean, who's got it now?

GUS: Who's got it now? If they moved out, who moved in?

BEN: Well, that all depends —

(*The box descends with a clatter and bang. Ben levels his revolver. Gus goes to the box and brings out a piece of paper.*)

GUS (*reading*): Soup of the day. Liver and onions. Jam tart.

(*A pause. Gus looks at Ben. Ben takes the note and reads it. He walks slowly to the hatch. Gus follows. Ben looks into the hatch but not up it. Gus puts his hand on Ben's shoulder. Ben throws it off. Gus puts his finger to his mouth. He leans on the hatch and swiftly looks up it. Ben flings him away in alarm. Ben looks at the note. He throws his revolver on the bed and speaks with decision.*)

BEN: We'd better send something up.

GUS: Eh?

BEN: We'd better send something up.

GUS: Oh! Yes. Yes. Maybe you're right.

(*They are both relieved at the decision.*)

BEN (*purposefully*): Quick! What have you got in that bag?

GUS: Not much.

(*Gus goes to the hatch and shouts up it.*)

   Wait a minute!

BEN: Don't do that!

(*Gus examines the contents of the bag and brings them out, one by one.*)

GUS: Biscuits. A bar of chocolate. Half a pint of milk.

BEN: That all?

GUS: Packet of tea.

BEN: Good.

GUS: We can't send the tea. That's all the tea we've got.

BEN: Well, there's no gas. You can't do anything with it, can you?

GUS: Maybe they can send us down a bob.°

BEN: What else is there?

GUS (*reaching into bag*): One Eccles cake.°

BEN: One Eccles cake?

GUS: Yes.

BEN: You never told me you had an Eccles cake.

GUS: Didn't I?

BEN: Why only one? Didn't you bring one for me?

GUS: I didn't think you'd be keen.

BEN: Well, you can't send up one Eccles cake, anyway.

GUS: Why not?

BEN: Fetch one of those plates.

GUS: All right.

(*Gus goes toward the door, left, and stops.*)

   Do you mean I can keep the Eccles cake then?

BEN: Keep it?

GUS: Well, they don't know we've got it, do they?

BEN: That's not the point.

GUS: Can't I keep it?

BEN: No, you can't. Get the plate.

(*Gus exits, left. Ben looks in the bag. He brings out a packet of crisps.° Enter Gus with a plate.*)

   (*Accusingly, holding up the crisps.*) Where did these come from?

GUS: What?

BEN: Where did these crisps come from?

GUS: Where did you find them?

BEN (*hitting him on the shoulder*): You're playing a dirty game, my lad!

GUS: I only eat those with beer!

BEN: Well, where were you going to get the beer?

GUS: I was saving them till I did.

BEN: I'll remember this. Put everything on the plate.

(*They pile everything on to the plate. The box goes up without the plate.*)

   Wait a minute!

(*They stand.*)

GUS: It's gone up.

BEN: It's all your stupid fault, playing about!

GUS: What do we do now?

BEN: We'll have to wait till it comes down.

(*Ben puts the plate on the bed, puts on his shoulder holster, and starts to put on his tie.*)

bob: A shilling for the gas meter.
Eccles cake: A sugared pastry.
crisps: Potato chips.

You'd better get ready.

(*Gus goes to his bed, puts on his tie, and starts to fix his holster.*)

GUS: Hey, Ben.
BEN: What?
GUS: What's going on here?

(*Pause.*)

BEN: What do you mean?
GUS: How can this be a café?
BEN: It used to be a café.
GUS: Have you seen the gas stove?
BEN: What about it?
GUS: It's only got three rings.
BEN: So what?
GUS: Well, you couldn't cook much on three rings, not for a busy place like this.
BEN (*irritably*): That's why the service is slow!

(*Ben puts on his waistcoat.*)

GUS: Yes, but what happens when we're not here? What do they do then? All these menus coming down and nothing going up. It might have been going on like this for years.

(*Ben brushes his jacket.*)

What happens when we go?

(*Ben puts on his jacket.*)

They can't do much business.

(*The box descends. They turn about. Gus goes to the hatch and brings out a note.*)

GUS (*reading*): Macaroni Pastitsio. Ormitha Macarounada.
BEN: What was that?
GUS: Macaroni Pastitsio. Ormitha Macarounada.
BEN: Greek dishes.
GUS: No.
BEN: That's right.
GUS: That's pretty high class.
BEN: Quick before it goes up.

(*Gus puts the plate in the box.*)

GUS (*calling up the hatch*): Three McVitie and Price! One Lyons Red Label! One Smith's Crisps! One Eccles cake! One Fruit and Nut!
BEN: Cadbury's.
GUS (*up the hatch*): Cadbury's!
BEN (*handing the milk*): One bottle of milk.
GUS (*up the hatch*): One bottle of milk! Half a pint! (*He looks at the label.*) Express Dairy! (*He puts the bottle in the box.*)

(*The box goes up.*)

Just did it.
BEN: You shouldn't shout like that.
GUS: Why not?
BEN: It isn't done.

(*Ben goes to his bed.*)

Well, that should be all right, anyway, for the time being.
GUS: You think so, eh?
BEN: Get dressed, will you? It'll be any minute now.

(*Gus puts on his waistcoat. Ben lies down and looks up at the ceiling.*)

GUS: This is some place. No tea and no biscuits.
BEN: Eating makes you lazy, mate. You're getting lazy, you know that? You don't want to get slack on your job.
GUS: Who me?
BEN: Slack, mate, slack.
GUS: Who me? Slack?
BEN: Have you checked your gun? You haven't even checked your gun. It looks disgraceful, anyway. Why don't you ever polish it?

(*Gus rubs his revolver on the sheet. Ben takes out a pocket mirror and straightens his tie.*)

GUS: I wonder where the cook is. They must have had a few, to cope with that. Maybe they had a few more gas stoves. Eh! Maybe there's another kitchen along the passage.
BEN: Of course there is! Do you know what it takes to make an Ormitha Macarounada?
GUS: No, what?
BEN: An Ormitha —! Buck your ideas up,° will you?
GUS: Takes a few cooks, eh?

(*Gus puts his revolver in its holster.*)

The sooner we're out of this place the better.

(*He puts on his jacket.*)

Why doesn't he get in touch? I feel like I've been here years. (*He takes his revolver out of its holster to check the ammunition.*) We've never let him down though, have we? We've never let him down. I was thinking only the other day, Ben. We're reliable, aren't we?

(*He puts his revolver back in its holster.*)

Still, I'll be glad when it's over tonight.

(*He brushes his jacket.*)

Buck . . . up: Be quiet.

I hope the bloke's not going to get excited tonight, or anything. I'm feeling a bit off. I've got a splitting headache.

(*Silence.*)

(*The box descends. Ben jumps up.*)
(*Gus collects the note.*)

(*Reading.*) One Bamboo Shoots, Water Chestnuts and Chicken. One Char Siu and Beansprouts.
BEN: Beansprouts?
GUS: Yes.
BEN: Blimey.
GUS: I wouldn't know where to begin.

(*He looks back at the box. The packet of tea is inside it. He picks it up.*)

They've sent back the tea.
BEN (*anxious*): What'd they do that for?
GUS: Maybe it isn't tea-time.

(*The box goes up. Silence.*)

BEN (*throwing the tea on the bed, and speaking urgently*): Look here. We'd better tell them.
GUS: Tell them what?
BEN: That we can't do it, we haven't got it.
GUS: All right then.
BEN: Lend us your pencil. We'll write a note.

(*Gus, turning for a pencil, suddenly discovers the speaking tube, which hangs on the right wall of the hatch facing his bed.*)

GUS: What's this?
BEN: What?
GUS: This.
BEN (*examining it*): This? It's a speaking tube.
GUS: How long has that been there?
BEN: Just the job. We should have used it before, instead of shouting up there.
GUS: Funny I never noticed it before.
BEN: Well, come on.
GUS: What do you do?
BEN: See that? That's a whistle.
GUS: What, this?
BEN: Yes, take it out. Pull it out.

(*Gus does so.*)

That's it.
GUS: What do we do now?
BEN: Blow into it.
GUS: Blow?
BEN: It whistles up there if you blow. Then they know you want to speak. Blow.

(*Gus blows. Silence.*)

GUS (*tube at mouth*): I can't hear a thing.
BEN: Now you speak! Speak into it!

(*Gus looks at Ben, then speaks into the tube.*)

GUS: The larder's bare!
BEN: Give me that!

(*He grabs the tube and puts it to his mouth.*)

(*Speaking with great deference.*) Good evening. I'm sorry to — bother you, but we just thought we'd better let you know that we haven't got anything left. We sent up all we had. There's no more food down here.

(*He brings the tube slowly to his ear.*)

What?

(*To mouth.*)

What?

(*To ear. He listens. To mouth.*)

No, all we had we sent up.

(*To ear. He listens. To mouth.*)

Oh, I'm very sorry to hear that.

(*To ear. He listens. To Gus.*)

The Eccles cake was stale.

(*He listens. To Gus.*)

The chocolate was melted.

(*He listens. To Gus.*)

The milk was sour.
GUS: What about the crisps?
BEN (*listening*): The biscuits were moldy.

(*He glares at Gus. Tube to mouth.*)

Well, we're very sorry about that.

(*Tube to ear.*)

What?

(*To mouth.*)

What?

(*To ear.*)

Yes. Yes.

(*To mouth.*)

Yes certainly. Certainly. Right away.

(*To ear. The voice has ceased. He hangs up the tube.*)

(*Excitedly.*) Did you hear that?

GUS: What?

BEN: You know what he said? Light the kettle! Not put on the kettle! Not light the gas! But light the kettle!

GUS: How can we light the kettle?

BEN: What do you mean?

GUS: There's no gas.

BEN (*clapping hand to head*): Now what do we do?

GUS: What did he want us to light the kettle for?

BEN: For tea. He wanted a cup of tea.

GUS: *He* wanted a cup of tea! What about me? I've been wanting a cup of tea all night!

BEN (*despairingly*): What do we do now?

GUS: What are we supposed to drink?

(*Ben sits on his bed, staring.*)

What about us?

(*Ben sits.*)

I'm thirsty too. I'm starving. And he wants a cup of tea. That beats the band, that does.

(*Ben lets his head sink on to his chest.*)

I could do with a bit of sustenance myself. What about you? You look as if you could do with something too.

(*Gus sits on his bed.*)

We send him up all we've got and he's not satisfied. No, honest, it's enough to make the cat laugh. Why did you send him up all that stuff? (*Thoughtfully.*) Why did I send it up?

(*Pause.*)

Who knows what he's got upstairs? He's probably got a salad bowl. They must have something up there. They won't get much from down here. You notice they didn't ask for any salads? They've probably got a salad bowl up there. Cold meat, radishes, cucumbers. Watercress. Roll mops.°

(*Pause.*)

Hardboiled eggs.

(*Pause.*)

The lot. They've probably got a crate of beer too. Probably eating my crisps with a pint of beer now. Didn't have anything to say about those crisps, did he? They do all right, don't worry about that. You don't think they're just going to sit there and wait for stuff to come up from down here, do you? That'll get them nowhere.

Roll mops: Skewered herring with pickles.

(*Pause.*)

They do all right.

(*Pause.*)

And he wants a cup of tea.

(*Pause.*)

That's past a joke, in my opinion.

(*He looks over at Ben, rises, and goes to him.*)

What's the matter with you? You don't look too bright. I feel like an Alka-Seltzer myself.

(*Ben sits up.*)

BEN (*in a low voice*): Time's getting on.

GUS: I know. I don't like doing a job on an empty stomach.

BEN (*wearily*): Be quiet a minute. Let me give you your instructions.

GUS: What for? We always do it the same way, don't we?

BEN: Let me give you your instructions.

(*Gus sighs and sits next to Ben on the bed. The instructions are stated and repeated automatically.*)

When we get the call, you go over and stand behind the door.

GUS: Stand behind the door.

BEN: If there's a knock on the door you don't answer it.

GUS: If there's a knock on the door I don't answer it.

BEN: But there won't be a knock on the door.

GUS: So I won't answer it.

BEN: When the bloke comes in —

GUS: When the bloke comes in —

BEN: Shut the door behind him.

GUS: Shut the door behind him.

BEN: Without divulging your presence.

GUS: Without divulging my presence.

BEN: He'll see me and come towards me.

GUS: He'll see you and come towards you.

BEN: He won't see you.

GUS (*absently*): Eh?

BEN: He won't see you.

GUS: He won't see me.

BEN: But he'll see me.

GUS: He'll see you.

BEN: He won't know you're there.

GUS: He won't know you're there.

BEN: He won't know *you're* there.

GUS: He won't know I'm there.

BEN: I take out my gun.

GUS: You take out your gun.

BEN: He stops in his tracks.
GUS: He stops in his tracks.
BEN: If he turns round —
GUS: If he turns round —
BEN: You're there.
GUS: I'm here.

(*Ben frowns and presses his forehead.*)

You've missed something out.
BEN: I know. What?
GUS: I haven't taken my gun out, according to you.
BEN: You take your gun out —
GUS: After I've closed the door.
BEN: After you've closed the door.
GUS: You've never missed that out before, you know that?
BEN: When he sees you behind him —
GUS: Me behind him —
BEN: And me in front of him —
GUS: And you in front of him —
BEN: He'll feel uncertain —
GUS: Uneasy.
BEN: He won't know what to do.
GUS: So what will he do?
BEN: He'll look at me and he'll look at you.
GUS: We won't say a word.
BEN: We'll look at him.
GUS: He won't say a word.
BEN: He'll look at us.
GUS: And we'll look at him.
BEN: Nobody says a word.

(*Pause.*)

GUS: What do we do if it's a girl?
BEN: We do the same.
GUS: Exactly the same?
BEN: Exactly.

(*Pause.*)

GUS: We don't do anything different?
BEN: We do exactly the same.
GUS: Oh.

(*Gus rises and shivers.*)

Excuse me.

(*He exits through the door on the left. Ben remains sitting on the bed, still.*)
    (*The lavatory chain is pulled once off left, but the lavatory does not flush.*)
    (*Silence.*)
    (*Gus reenters and stops inside the door, deep in thought. He looks at Ben, then walks slowly across to his own bed. He is troubled. He stands, thinking.*

He turns and looks at Ben. He moves a few paces toward him.)

    (*Slowly in a low, tense voice.*) Why did he send us matches if he knew there was no gas?

(*Silence.*)
    (*Ben stares in front of him. Gus crosses to the left side of Ben, to the foot of his bed, to get to his other ear.*)

    Ben. Why did he send us matches if he knew there was no gas?

(*Ben looks up.*)

    Why did he do that?
BEN: Who?
GUS: Who sent us those matches?
BEN: What are you talking about?

(*Gus stares down at him.*)

GUS (*thickly*): Who is it upstairs?
BEN (*nervously*): What's one thing to do with another?
GUS: Who is it, though?
BEN: What's one thing to do with another?

(*Ben fumbles for his paper on the bed.*)

GUS: I asked you a question.
BEN: Enough!
GUS (*with growing agitation*): I asked you before. Who moved in? I asked you. You said the people who had it before moved out. Well, who moved in?
BEN (*hunched*): Shut up.
GUS: I told you, didn't I?
BEN (*standing*): Shut up!
GUS (*feverishly*): I told you before who owned this place, didn't I? I told you.

(*Ben hits him viciously on the shoulder.*)

    I told you who ran this place, didn't I?

(*Ben hits him viciously on the shoulder.*)

    (*Violently.*) Well, what's he playing all these games for? That's what I want to know. What's he doing it for?
BEN: What games?
GUS (*passionately, advancing*): What's he doing it for? We've been through our tests, haven't we? We got right through our tests, years ago, didn't we? We took them together, don't you remember, didn't we? We've proved ourselves before now, haven't we? We've always done our job. What's he doing all this for? What's the idea? What's he playing these games for?

(The box in the shaft comes down behind them. The noise is this time accompanied by a shrill whistle, as it falls. Gus rushes to the hatch and seizes the note.)

(*Reading.*) Scampi!

(He crumples the note, picks up the tube, takes out the whistle, blows, and speaks.)

WE'VE GOT NOTHING LEFT! NOTHING! DO YOU UNDERSTAND?

(Ben seizes the tube and flings Gus away. He follows Gus and slaps him hard, back-handed, across the chest.)

BEN: Stop it! You maniac!
GUS: But you heard!
BEN (*savagely*): That's enough! I'm warning you!

(Silence.)

(Ben hangs the tube. He goes to his bed and lies down. He picks up his paper and reads.)
(Silence.)
(The box goes up.)
(They turn quickly, their eyes meet. Ben turns to his paper.)
(Slowly Gus goes back to his bed, and sits.)
(Silence.)
(The hatch falls back into place.)
(They turn quickly, their eyes meet. Ben turns back to his paper.)
(Silence.)
(Ben throws his paper down.)

BEN: Kaw!

(He picks up the paper and looks at it.)

Listen to this!

(Pause.)

What about that, eh?

(Pause.)

Kaw!

(Pause.)

Have you ever heard such a thing?
GUS (*dully*): Go on!
BEN: It's true.
GUS: Get away.
BEN: It's down here in black and white.
GUS (*very low*): Is that a fact?
BEN: Can you imagine it.
GUS: It's unbelievable.

BEN: It's enough to make you want to puke, isn't it?
GUS (*almost inaudible*): Incredible.

(Ben shakes his head. He puts the paper down and rises. He fixes the revolver in his holster.)
(Gus stands up. He goes toward the door on the left.)

BEN: Where are you going?
GUS: I'm going to have a glass of water.

(He exits. Ben brushes dust off his clothes and shoes. The whistle in the speaking tube blows. He goes to it, takes the whistle out, and puts the tube to his ear. He listens. He puts it to his mouth.)

BEN: Yes.

(To ear. He listens. To mouth.)

Straight away. Right.

(To ear. He listens. To mouth.)

Sure we're ready.

(To ear. He listens. To mouth.)

Understood. Repeat. He has arrived and will be coming in straight away. The normal method to be employed. Understood.

(To ear. He listens. To mouth.)

Sure we're ready.

(To ear. He listens. To mouth.)

Right.

(He hangs the tube up.)

Gus!

(He takes out a comb and combs his hair, adjusts his jacket to diminish the bulge of the revolver. The lavatory flushes off left. Ben goes quickly to the door, left.)

Gus!

(The door right opens sharply. Ben turns, his revolver leveled at the door.)
(Gus stumbles in.)
(He is stripped of his jacket, waistcoat, tie, holster, and revolver.)
(He stops, body stooping, his arms at his sides.)
(He raises his head and looks at Ben.)
(A long silence.)
(They stare at each other.)

Lorraine Hansberry

Lorraine Hansberry (1930–1965), like John Millington Synge, died tragically young. Her loss to the American stage is incalculable; her successes were only beginning, and at her death she seemed on the verge of a remarkable career.

Hansberry grew up in a middle-class black family in Chicago. Her father, a successful real estate man, founded one of the first banks for blacks in Chicago. However, he spent much of his life trying to find a way to make a decent life for himself and his family in America. He eventually gave up on the United States and, when he died in 1945, he was scouting for a place in Mexico where he could move his family to live in decency.

Lorraine Hansberry went to college after her father died, and her first ambition was to become a visual artist. She attended the Art Institute of Chicago and numerous other schools before moving to New York. Once there, she became interested in some drama groups and soon married the playwright Howard Nemiroff. She began writing, sharing parts of her first play with friends in her own living room. They helped raise money to stage the play and, with black director Lloyd Richards and little-known Sidney Poitier as Walter Lee Younger, *A Raisin in the Sun* (1959) thrust her into the drama spotlight.

In 1959, when she was twenty-nine years old, she was the most promising woman writing for the American stage. She was also the first black American to win the New York Drama Critics' Circle Award for the best play of the year. She died the day her second produced play, *The Sign in Sidney Brustein's Window*, closed. She had finished a third play, *Les Blancs*, which was brought to Broadway by Nemiroff in 1970. Neither of her other plays was as popular as *Raisin*, but the two later plays demonstrate a deepening concern for and understanding of some of the key issues of racial and sexual politics that interested her throughout her career.

The Sign in Sidney Brustein's Window is about a Jewish intellectual in the 1950s in Greenwich Village who feels that all the radical struggle of the 1930s has been lost. He agitates for personal involvement, for emotional and intellectual action. It is an especially idealistic play, considering that it anticipates the political agitation in the United States during the era of the middle 1960s and early 1970s. *Les Blancs* takes as its central character a black African intellectual, Tshembe, and explores his relationship to both Europe and Africa. In his uneasiness with both cultures he discovers that he cannot live outside his own history. In this play, Hansberry reveals some of her deep interest in Pan-Africanism and the search for a personal heritage.

A last, posthumous work was put together by Howard Nemiroff from Hansberry's notes, letters, and early writings. Titled *To Be Young, Gifted, and Black* (1971), it has helped solidify her achievements. It is certainly impossible to know just how Hansberry's career would have developed had she lived, but her gifts were so remarkable that we can only lament that she is not writing for the stage today.

A Raisin in the Sun

When it was produced on Broadway in 1959, *A Raisin in the Sun* was somewhat prophetic. Lorraine Hansberry's themes of blacks pressing forward with legitimate demands and expressing interest in their African heritage were to become primary themes of black culture in the 1960s, 1970s, and, indeed, to this day. The title of her play is from a poem by Langston Hughes, one of the poets of the Harlem Renaissance. It warns of the social explosions that might occur if society permits blacks to remain unequal and unfree.

The play appeared at the beginning of renewed political activity on the part of blacks, and it reveals its historical position in the use of the word *Negro*, which black activists rejected in the 1960s as an enslaving euphemism. In a way, the term was used at the time out of the same politeness that asked blacks to understand the feelings of whites who did not want to share their neighborhoods with them.

This play illustrates the American dream as it is felt not just by blacks but by all Americans: If you work hard and save your money, if you hold to the proper values and hope, then you can one day buy your own home and have the kind of space and privacy that permit people to live with dignity. Yet this very theme has plagued the play from the beginning: its apparent emphasis on middle-class, bourgeois values. On the surface, it seems to celebrate a mild form of consumerism — the desire for the little house in the suburbs with the TV set inside to anesthetize its occupants. Hansberry was shocked when such criticisms, from black critics as well as white, were leveled against the play. She had written it very carefully to explore just those issues, but in a context that demonstrated that black families' needs paralleled white families' while also having a different dimension that most white families could not understand.

Hansberry was quick to admit that Walter Lee Younger was affected by the same craziness that affected all Americans who lusted after possessions and the power they might confer. Walter wants to take his father's insurance money and buy a liquor store, which he plans to do in partnership with a con man. Lena Younger argues against her son's plan as a profanation of her husband's memory as well as an abuse of the American dream: She believes that the product of a liquor store will further poison the community. What she wants is not a consumer product. She wants the emblem of identity and security that she feels her family deserves.

Being able to live where she wishes, how she wishes, and with other members of her society as equals is a reasonable desire. As head of the family she brings a measure of wisdom and of human ambition to the family and strives to make each member aim toward worthwhile values. She is fighting segregation, neighborhood associations that jealously guard property values, and the fear of making reasonable demands on society.

Hansberry is painfully honest in this play. Walter Lee's weaknesses are recognizable. His black male chauvinistic behavior undoes him. He is caught up in the old, failing pattern of male dominance over women. But none of the women in his life will tolerate his behavior. Hansberry also admits of the social distinctions between blacks. George Murchison is a young man from a wealthy black family, and when Beneatha tells Lena that she will not marry George, she says, "The only people in the world who are more snobbish than rich white people are rich colored people." Beneatha's desire to be a doctor is obviously not rooted in consumerism any more than in the middle-class need to be comfortable and rich.

The confusion in the family when the African Asagai enters is realistically portrayed. In the early days of the Pan-African movement in the 1960s, blacks were often bemused by the way Africans presented themselves. Interest in Africa on the part of the American blacks was distorted by Tarzan movies and National Geographic ethnographic studies, none of which presented black Africans as role models. Therefore, the adjustment to black African pride — while made swiftly — was not made without difficulties. The Youngers are presented as no more sophisticated about black Africans than the rest of black society.

The pride of the Younger family finally triumphs. When Walter Lee stands up for himself, he is not asserting his macho domination. He is asserting black manhood — a manhood that needs no domination over women. He is not expressing a desire for a big house — as he had done when he reflected on the possessions of his rich employer — but a desire to demonstrate to the Clybourne Park Improvement Association that the Youngers are not socially inferior and that they have a right to live wherever they choose.

Lorraine Hansberry (1930–1965)

A RAISIN IN THE SUN

1959

Characters

RUTH YOUNGER
TRAVIS YOUNGER
WALTER LEE YOUNGER (*brother*)
BENEATHA YOUNGER
LENA YOUNGER (*Mama*)
JOSEPH ASAGAI
GEORGE MURCHISON
MRS. JOHNSON
KARL LINDNER
BOBO
MOVING MEN

The action of the play is set in Chicago's Southside, sometime between World War II and the present.

Act I
Scene I: *Friday morning.*
Scene II: *The following morning.*

Act II
Scene I: *Later, the same day.*
Scene II: *Friday night, a few weeks later.*
Scene III: *Moving day, one week later.*

Act III
An hour later.

ACT I • Scene I

(*The Younger living room would be a comfortable and well-ordered room if it were not for a number of indestructible contradictions to this state of being. Its furnishings are typical and undistinguished and their primary feature now is that they have clearly had to accommodate the living of too many people for too many years — and they are tired. Still, we can see that at some time, a time probably no longer remembered by the family [except perhaps for Mama], the furnishings of this room were actually selected with care and love and even hope — and brought to this apartment and arranged with taste and pride.*)

(*That was a long time ago. Now the once loved pattern of the couch upholstery has to fight to show itself from under acres of crocheted doilies and couch covers which have themselves finally come to be more important than the upholstery. And here a table or a chair has been moved to disguise the worn places in the carpet; but the carpet has fought back by showing its weariness, with depressing uniformity, elsewhere on its surface.*)

(*Weariness has, in fact, won in this room. Everything has been polished, washed, sat on, used, scrubbed too often. All pretenses but living itself have long since vanished from the very atmosphere of this room.*)

(*Moreover, a section of this room, for it is not really a room unto itself, though the landlord's lease would make it seem so, slopes backward to provide a small kitchen area, where the family prepares the meals that are eaten in the living room proper, which must also serve as dining room. The single window that has been provided for these "two" rooms is located in this kitchen area. The sole natural light the family may enjoy in the course of a day is only that which fights its way through this little window.*)

(*At left, a door leads to a bedroom which is shared by Mama and her daughter, Beneatha. At right, opposite, is a second room [which in the beginning of the life of this apartment was probably a breakfast room] which serves as a bedroom for Walter and his wife, Ruth.*)

(*Time: Sometime between World War II and the present.*)

(*Place: Chicago's Southside.*)

(*At rise: It is morning dark in the living room. Travis is asleep on the make-down bed at center. An alarm clock sounds from within the bedroom at right, and presently Ruth enters from that room and closes the door behind her. She crosses sleepily toward the window. As she passes her sleeping son she reaches down and shakes him a little. At the window she raises the shade and a dusky Southside morning light comes in feebly. She fills a pot with water and puts it on to boil. She calls to the boy, between yawns, in a slightly muffled voice.*)

(*Ruth is about thirty. We can see that she was a pretty girl, even exceptionally so, but now it is apparent that life has been little that she expected, and disappointment has already begun to hang in her face. In a few years, before thirty-five even, she will be known among her people as a "settled woman."*)

(*She crosses to her son and gives him a good, final, rousing shake.*)

RUTH: Come on now, boy, it's seven thirty! (*Her son sits up at last, in a stupor of sleepiness.*) I say hurry up, Travis! You ain't the only person in the world got to use a bathroom! (*The child, a sturdy, handsome little boy of ten or eleven, drags himself out of the bed and almost blindly takes his towels and "today's clothes" from drawers and a closet and goes out to the bathroom, which is in an outside hall and which is shared by another family or families on the same floor. Ruth crosses to the bedroom door at right and opens it and calls in to her husband.*) Walter Lee! . . . It's after seven thirty! Lemme see you do some waking up in there now! (*She waits.*) You better get up from there, man! It's after seven thirty I tell you. (*She waits again.*) All right, you just go ahead and lay there and next thing you know Travis be finished and Mr. Johnson'll be in there and you'll be fussing and cussing round here like a madman! And be late too! (*She waits, at the end of patience.*) Walter Lee — it's time for you to GET UP!

(*She waits another second and then starts to go into the bedroom, but is apparently satisfied that her husband has begun to get up. She stops, pulls the door to, and returns to the kitchen area. She wipes her face with a moist cloth and runs her fingers through her sleep-disheveled hair in a vain effort and ties an apron around her housecoat. The bedroom door at right opens and her husband stands in the doorway in his pajamas, which are rumpled and mismated. He is a lean, intense young man in his middle thirties, inclined to quick nervous movements and erratic speech habits — and always in his voice there is a quality of indictment.*)

WALTER: Is he out yet?

RUTH: What you mean *out*? He ain't hardly got in there good yet.

WALTER (*wandering in, still more oriented to sleep than to a new day*): Well, what was you doing all that yelling for if I can't even get in there yet? (*Stopping and thinking.*) Check coming today?

RUTH: They *said* Saturday and this is just Friday and I hopes to God you ain't going to get up here first thing this morning and start talking to me 'bout no money — 'cause I 'bout don't want to hear it.

WALTER: Something the matter with you this morning?

RUTH: No — I'm just sleepy as the devil. What kind of eggs you want?

WALTER: Not scrambled. (*Ruth starts to scramble eggs.*) Paper come? (*Ruth points impatiently to the rolled up Tribune on the table, and he gets it and spreads it out and vaguely reads the front page.*) Set off another bomb yesterday.

RUTH (*maximum indifference*): Did they?

WALTER (*looking up*): What's the matter with you?

RUTH: Ain't nothing the matter with me. And don't keep asking me that this morning.

WALTER: Ain't nobody bothering you. (*Reading the news of the day absently again.*) Say Colonel McCormick is sick.

RUTH (*affecting tea-party interest*): Is he now? Poor thing.

WALTER (*sighing and looking at his watch*): Oh, me. (*He waits.*) Now what is that boy doing in that bathroom all this time? He just going to have to start getting up earlier. I can't be being late to work on account of him fooling around in there.

RUTH (*turning on him*): Oh, no he ain't going to be getting up no earlier no such thing! It ain't his fault that he can't get to bed no earlier nights 'cause he got a bunch of crazy good-for-nothing clowns sitting up running their mouths in what is supposed to be his bedroom after ten o'clock at night . . .

WALTER: That's what you mad about, ain't it? The things I want to talk about with my friends just couldn't be important in your mind, could they?

(*He rises and finds a cigarette in her handbag on the table and crosses to the little window and looks out, smoking and deeply enjoying this first one.*)

RUTH (*almost matter of factly, a complaint too automatic to deserve emphasis*): Why you always got to smoke before you eat in the morning?

WALTER (*at the window*): Just look at 'em down there . . . Running and racing to work . . . (*He turns and faces his wife and watches her a moment at the stove, and then, suddenly.*) You look young this morning, baby.

RUTH (*indifferently*): Yeah?

WALTER: Just for a second — stirring them eggs. Just for a second it was — you looked real young again. (*He reaches for her; she crosses away. Then, drily.*) It's gone now — you look like yourself again!

RUTH: Man, if you don't shut up and leave me alone.

WALTER (*looking out to the street again*): First thing a man ought to learn in life is not to make love to no colored woman first thing in the morning. You all some eeeevil people at eight o'clock in the morning.

(*Travis appears in the hall doorway, almost fully dressed and quite wide awake now, his towels and pajamas across his shoulders. He opens the door and signals for his father to make the bathroom in a hurry.*)

TRAVIS (*watching the bathroom*): Daddy, come on!

(*Walter gets his bathroom utensils and flies out to the bathroom.*)

RUTH: Sit down and have your breakfast, Travis.

TRAVIS: Mama, this is Friday. (*Gleefully.*) Check coming tomorrow, huh?

RUTH: You get your mind off money and eat your breakfast.

TRAVIS (*eating*): This is the morning we supposed to bring the fifty cents to school.

RUTH: Well, I ain't got no fifty cents this morning.

TRAVIS: Teacher say we have to.

RUTH: I don't care what teacher say. I ain't got it. Eat your breakfast, Travis.

TRAVIS: I *am* eating.

RUTH: Hush up now and just eat!

(*The boy gives her an exasperated look for her lack of understanding and eats grudgingly.*)

TRAVIS: You think Grandmama would have it?

RUTH: No! And I want you to stop asking your grandmother for money, you hear me?

TRAVIS (*outraged*): Gaaaleee! I don't ask her, she just gimme it sometimes!

RUTH: Travis Willard Younger — I got too much on me this morning to be —

TRAVIS: Maybe Daddy —

RUTH: *Travis!*

(*The boy hushes abruptly. They are both quiet and tense for several seconds.*)

TRAVIS (*presently*): Could I maybe go carry some groceries in front of the supermarket for a little while after school then?

RUTH: Just hush, I said. (*Travis jabs his spoon into his cereal bowl viciously and rests his head in anger upon his fists.*) If you through eating, you can get over there and make up your bed.

(*The boy obeys stiffly and crosses the room, almost mechanically, to the bed and more or less folds the bedding into a heap, then angrily gets his books and cap.*)

TRAVIS (*sulking and standing apart from her unnaturally*): I'm gone.

RUTH (*looking up from the stove to inspect him automatically*): Come here. (*He crosses to her and she studies his head.*) If you don't take this comb and fix this here head, you better! (*Travis puts down his books with a great sigh of oppression and crosses to the mirror. His mother mutters under her breath about his "slubbornness."*) 'Bout to march out of here with that head looking just like chickens slept in it! I just don't know where you get your slubborn ways . . . And get your jacket, too. Looks chilly out this morning.

TRAVIS (*with conspicuously brushed hair and jacket*): I'm gone.

RUTH: Get carfare and milk money — (*waving one finger*) — and not a single penny for no caps, you hear me?

TRAVIS (*with sullen politeness*): Yes'm.

(*He turns in outrage to leave. His mother watches after him as in his frustration he approaches the door almost comically. When she speaks to him, her voice has become a very gentle tease.*)

RUTH (*mocking; as she thinks he would say it*): Oh, Mama makes me so mad sometimes, I don't know what to do! (*She waits and continues to his back as he stands stock-still in front of the door.*) I wouldn't kiss that woman good-bye for nothing in this world this morning! (*The boy finally turns around and rolls his eyes at her, knowing the mood has changed and he is vindicated; he does not, however, move toward her yet.*) Not for nothing in this world! (*She finally laughs aloud at him and holds out her arms to him and we see that it is a way between them, very old and practiced. He crosses to her and allows her to embrace him warmly but keeps his face fixed with masculine rigidity. She holds him back from her presently and looks at him and runs her fingers over the features of his face. With utter gentleness —*) Now — whose little old angry man are you?

TRAVIS (*the masculinity and gruffness start to fade at last*): Aw gaalee — Mama . . .

RUTH (*mimicking*): Aw — gaaaaalleeeee, Mama! (*She pushes him, with rough playfulness and finality, toward the door.*) Get on out of here or you going to be late.

TRAVIS (*in the face of love, new aggressiveness*): Mama, could I *please* go carry groceries?

RUTH: Honey, it's starting to get so cold evenings.

WALTER (*coming in from the bathroom and drawing a make-believe gun from a make-believe holster and shooting at his son*): What is it he wants to do?

RUTH: Go carry groceries after school at the supermarket.

WALTER: Well, let him go . . .

TRAVIS (*quickly, to the ally*): I have to — she won't gimme the fifty cents . . .

WALTER (*to his wife only*): Why not?

RUTH (*simply, and with flavor*): 'Cause we don't have it.

WALTER (*to Ruth only*): What you tell the boy things like that for? (*Reaching down into his pants with a rather important gesture.*) Here, son —

(*He hands the boy the coin, but his eyes are directed to his wife's. Travis takes the money happily.*)

TRAVIS: Thanks, Daddy.

(*He starts out. Ruth watches both of them with murder in her eyes. Walter stands and stares back at her with defiance and suddenly reaches into his pocket again on an afterthought.*)

WALTER (*without even looking at his son, still staring hard at his wife*): In fact, here's another fifty cents . . . Buy yourself some fruit today — or take a taxicab to school or something!

TRAVIS: Whoopee —

(*He leaps up and clasps his father around the middle with his legs, and they face each other in mutual appreciation; slowly Walter Lee peeks around the boy to catch the violent rays from his wife's eyes and draws his head back as if shot.*)

WALTER: You better get down now — and get to school, man.

TRAVIS (*at the door*): O.K. Good-bye.

(*He exits.*)

WALTER (*after him, pointing with pride*): That's *my* boy. (*She looks at him in disgust and turns back to her work.*) You know what I was thinking 'bout in the bathroom this morning?

RUTH: No.

WALTER: How come you always try to be so pleasant!

RUTH: What is there to be pleasant 'bout!

WALTER: You want to know what I was thinking 'bout in the bathroom or not!

RUTH: I know what you thinking 'bout.

WALTER (*ignoring her*): 'Bout what me and Willy Harris was talking about last night.

RUTH (*immediately — a refrain*): Willy Harris is a good-for-nothing loudmouth.

WALTER: Anybody who talks to me has got to be a good-for-nothing loudmouth, ain't he? And what you know about who is just a good-for-nothing loudmouth? Charlie Atkins was just a "good-for-nothing loudmouth" too, wasn't he! When he wanted me to go in the dry-cleaning business with him. And now — he's grossing a hundred thousand a year. A hundred thousand dollars a year! You still call *him* a loudmouth!

RUTH (*bitterly*): Oh, Walter Lee . . .

(*She folds her head on her arms over the table.*)

WALTER (*rising and coming to her and standing over her*): You tired, ain't you? Tired of everything. Me, the boy, the way we live — this beat-up hole — everything. Ain't you? (*She doesn't look up, doesn't answer.*) So tired — moaning and groaning all the time, but you wouldn't do nothing to help, would you? You couldn't be on my side that long for nothing, could you?

RUTH: Walter, please leave me alone.

WALTER: A man needs for a woman to back him up . . .

RUTH: Walter —

WALTER: Mama would listen to you. You know she listen to you more than she do me and Bennie. She think more of you. All you have to do is just sit down with her when you drinking your coffee one morning and talking 'bout things like you do and — (*He sits down beside her and demonstrates graphically what he thinks her methods and tone shoud be.*) — you just sip your coffee, see, and say easy like that you been thinking 'bout that deal Walter Lee is so interested in, 'bout the store and all, and sip some more coffee, like what you saying ain't really that important to you — And the next thing you know, she be listening good and asking you questions and when I come home — I can tell her the details. This ain't no fly-by-night proposition, baby. I mean we figured it out, me and Willy and Bobo.

RUTH (*with a frown*): Bobo?

WALTER: Yeah. You see, this little liquor store we got in mind cost seventy-five thousand and we figured the initial investment on the place be 'bout thirty thousand, see. That be ten thousand each. Course, there's a couple of hundred you got to pay so's you don't spend your life just waiting for them clowns to let your license get approved —

RUTH: You mean graft?

WALTER (*frowning impatiently*): Don't call it that. See there, that just goes to show you what women understand about the world. Baby, don't *nothing* happen for you in this world 'less you pay *somebody* off!

RUTH: Walter, leave me alone! (*She raises her head and stares at him vigorously — then says, more quietly.*) Eat your eggs, they gonna be cold.

WALTER (*straightening up from her and looking off*): That's it. There you are. Man say to his woman: I got me a dream. His woman say: Eat your eggs. (*Sadly, but gaining in power.*) Man say: I got to take hold of this here world, baby! And a woman will say: Eat your eggs and go to work. (*Passionately now.*) Man say: I got to change my life, I'm choking to death, baby! And his woman say — (*in utter anguish as he brings his fists down on his thighs*) — Your eggs is getting cold!

RUTH (*softly*): Walter, that ain't none of our money.

WALTER (*not listening at all or even looking at her*): This morning, I was lookin' in the mirror and thinking about it . . . I'm thirty-five years old; I been married eleven years and I got a boy who sleeps in the living room — (*very, very quietly*) — and all I got to give him is stories about how rich white people live . . .

RUTH: Eat your eggs, Walter.

WALTER (*slams the table and jumps up*): — DAMN MY EGGS — DAMN ALL THE EGGS THAT EVER WAS!

RUTH: Then go to work.

WALTER (*looking up at her*): See — I'm trying to talk to you 'bout myself — (*Shaking his head with the repetition*) — and all you can say is eat them eggs and go to work.

RUTH (*wearily*): Honey, you never say nothing new. I listen to you every day, every night and every morning, and you never say nothing new. (*Shrugging.*) So you would rather *be* Mr. Arnold than be his chauffeur. So — I would *rather* be living in Buckingham Palace.

WALTER: That is just what is wrong with the colored woman in this world . . . Don't understand about building their men up and making 'em feel like they somebody. Like they can do something.

RUTH (*drily, but to hurt*): There *are* colored men who do things.

WALTER: No thanks to the colored woman.

RUTH: Well, being a colored woman, I guess I can't help myself none.

(*She rises and gets the ironing board and sets it up and attacks a huge pile of rough-dried clothes, sprinkling them in preparation for the ironing and then rolling them into tight fat balls.*)

WALTER (*mumbling*): We one group of men tied to a race of women with small minds!

(*His sister Beneatha enters. She is about twenty, as slim and intense as her brother. She is not as pretty as her sister-in-law, but her lean, almost intellectual face has a handsomeness of its own. She wears a bright red flannel nightie, and her thick hair stands wildly about her head. Her speech is a mixture of many things; it is different from the rest of the family's insofar as education has permeated her sense of English — and perhaps the Midwest rather than the South has finally — at last — won out in her inflection; but not altogether, because over all of it is a soft slurring and transformed use of vowels which is the decided influence of the Southside. She passes through the room without looking at either Ruth or Walter and goes to the outside door and looks, a little blindly, out to the bathroom. She sees that it has been lost to the Johnsons. She closes the door with a sleepy vengeance and crosses to the table and sits down a little defeated.*)

BENEATHA: I am going to start timing those people.

WALTER: You should get up earlier.

BENEATHA (*Her face in her hands. She is still fighting the urge to go back to bed.*): Really — would you suggest dawn? Where's the paper?

WALTER (*pushing the paper across the table to her as he studies her almost clinically, as though he has never seen her before*): You a horrible-looking chick at this hour.

BENEATHA (*drily*): Good morning, everybody.

WALTER (*senselessly*): How is school coming?

BENEATHA (*in the same spirit*): Lovely. Lovely. And you know, biology is the greatest. (*Looking up at him.*) I dissected something that looked just like you yesterday.

WALTER: I just wondered if you've made up your mind and everything.

BENEATHA (*gaining in sharpness and impatience*): And what did I answer yesterday morning — and the day before that?

RUTH (*from the ironing board, like someone disinterested and old*): Don't be so nasty, Bennie.

BENEATHA (*still to her brother*): And the day before that and the day before that!

WALTER (*defensively*): I'm interested in you. Something wrong with that? Ain't many girls who decide —

WALTER AND BENEATHA (*in unison*): — "to be a doctor."

(*Silence.*)

WALTER: Have we figured out yet just exactly how much medical school is going to cost?

RUTH: Walter Lee, why don't you leave that girl alone and get out of here to work?

BENEATHA (*exits to the bathroom and bangs on the door*): Come on out of there, please!

(*She comes back into the room.*)

WALTER (*looking at his sister intently*): You know the check is coming tomorrow.

BENEATHA (*turning on him with a sharpness all her own*): That money belongs to Mama, Walter, and it's for her to decide how she wants to use it. I don't care if she wants to buy a house or a rocketship or just nail it up somewhere and look at it. It's hers. Not ours — *hers*.

WALTER (*bitterly*): Now ain't that fine! You just got your mother's interest at heart, ain't you, girl? You such a nice girl — but if Mama got that money she can always take a few thousand and help you through school too — can't she?

BENEATHA: I have never asked anyone around here to do anything for me!

WALTER: No! And the line between asking and just accepting when the time comes is big and wide — ain't it!

BENEATHA (*with fury*): What do you want from me, Brother — that I quit school or just drop dead, which!

WALTER: I don't want nothing but for you to stop

acting holy 'round here. Me and Ruth done made some sacrifices for you — why can't you do something for the family?

RUTH: Walter, don't be dragging me in it.

WALTER: You are in it — Don't you get up and go work in somebody's kitchen for the last three years to help put clothes on her back?

RUTH: Oh, Walter — that's not fair . . .

WALTER: It ain't that nobody expects you to get on your knees and say thank you, Brother; thank you, Ruth; thank you, Mama — and thank you, Travis, for wearing the same pair of shoes for two semesters —

BENEATHA (*dropping to her knees*): Well — I do — all right? — thank everybody! And forgive me for ever wanting to be anything at all! (*Pursuing him on her knees across the floor.*) FORGIVE ME, FORGIVE ME, FORGIVE ME!

RUTH: Please stop it! Your mama'll hear you.

WALTER: Who the hell told you you had to be a doctor? If you so crazy 'bout messing 'round with sick people — then go be a nurse like other women — or just get married and be quiet . . .

BENEATHA: Well — you finally got it said . . . It took you three years but you finally got it said. Walter, give up; leave me alone — it's Mama's money.

WALTER: *He was my father, too!*

BENEATHA: So what? He was mine, too — and Travis' grandfather — but the insurance money belongs to Mama. Picking on me is not going to make her give it to you to invest in any liquor stores — (*underbreath, dropping into a chair*) — and I for one say, God bless Mama for that!

WALTER (*to Ruth*): See — did you hear? Did you hear!

RUTH: Honey, please go to work.

WALTER: Nobody in this house is ever going to understand me.

BENEATHA: Because you're a nut.

WALTER: Who's a nut?

BENEATHA: You — you are a nut. Thee is mad, boy.

WALTER (*looking at his wife and his sister from the door, very sadly*): The world's most backward race of people, and that's a fact.

BENEATHA (*turning slowly in her chair*): And then there are all those prophets who would lead us out of the wilderness — (*Walter slams out of the house*) — into the swamps!

RUTH: Bennie, why you always gotta be pickin' on your brother? Can't you be a little sweeter sometimes? (*Door opens. Walter walks in. He fumbles with his cap, starts to speak, clears throat, looks everywhere but at Ruth. Finally.*)

WALTER (*to Ruth*): I need some money for carfare.

RUTH (*looks at him, then warms; teasing, but tenderly*):

Fifty cents? (*She goes to her bag and gets money.*) Here — take a taxi!

(*Walter exits. Mama enters. She is a woman in her early sixties, full-bodied and strong. She is one of those women of a certain grace and beauty who wear it so unobtrusively that it takes a while to notice. Her dark brown face is surrounded by the total whiteness of her hair, and, being a woman who has adjusted to many things in life and overcome many more, her face is full of strength. She has, we can see, wit and faith of a kind that keep her eyes lit and full of interest and expectancy. She is, in a word, a beautiful woman. Her bearing is perhaps most like the noble bearing of the women of the Hereros of Southwest Africa — rather as if she imagines that as she walks she still bears a basket or a vessel upon her head. Her speech, on the other hand, is as careless as her carriage is precise — she is inclined to slur everything — but her voice is perhaps not so much quiet as simply soft.*)

MAMA: Who that 'round here slamming doors at this hour?

(*She crosses through the room, goes to the window, opens it, and brings in a feeble little plant growing doggedly in a small pot on the window sill. She feels the dirt and puts it back out.*)

RUTH: That was Walter Lee. He and Bennie was at it again.

MAMA: My children and they tempers. Lord, if this little old plant don't get more sun than it's been getting it ain't never going to see spring again. (*She turns from the window.*) What's the matter with you this morning, Ruth? You looks right peaked. You aiming to iron all them things? Leave some for me. I'll get to 'em this afternoon. Bennie honey, it's too drafty for you to be sitting 'round half dressed. Where's your robe?

BENEATHA: In the cleaners.

MAMA: Well, go get mine and put it on.

BENEATHA: I'm not cold, Mama, honest.

MAMA: I know — but you so thin . . .

BENEATHA (*irritably*): Mama, I'm not cold.

MAMA (*seeing the make-down bed as Travis has left it*): Lord have mercy, look at that poor bed. Bless his heart — he tries, don't he?

(*She moves to the bed Travis has sloppily made up.*)

RUTH: No — he don't half try at all 'cause he knows you going to come along behind him and fix everything. That's just how come he don't know how to do nothing right now — you done spoiled that boy so.

MAMA (*folding bedding*): Well — he's a little boy. Ain't supposed to know 'bout housekeeping. My baby, that's what he is. What you fix for his breakfast this morning?

RUTH (*angrily*): I feed my son, Lena!

MAMA: I ain't meddling — (*Underbreath; busybodyish.*) I just noticed all last week he had cold cereal, and when it starts getting this chilly in the fall a child ought to have some hot grits or something when he goes out in the cold —

RUTH (*furious*): I gave him hot oats — is that all right!

MAMA: I ain't meddling. (*Pause.*) Put a lot of nice butter on it? (*Ruth shoots her an angry look and does not reply.*) He likes lots of butter.

RUTH (*exasperated*): Lena —

MAMA (*To Beneatha. Mama is inclined to wander conversationally sometimes.*): What was you and your brother fussing 'bout this morning?

BENEATHA: It's not important, Mama.

(*She gets up and goes to look out at the bathroom, which is apparently free, and she picks up her towels and rushes out.*)

MAMA: What was they fighting about?

RUTH: Now you know as well as I do.

MAMA (*shaking her head*): Brother still worrying hisself sick about that money?

RUTH: You know he is.

MAMA: You had breakfast?

RUTH: Some coffee.

MAMA: Girl, you better start eating and looking after yourself better. You almost thin as Travis.

RUTH: Lena —

MAMA: Un-hunh?

RUTH: What are you going to do with it?

MAMA: Now don't you start, child. It's too early in the morning to be talking about money. It ain't Christian.

RUTH: It's just that he got his heart set on that store —

MAMA: You mean that liquor store that Willy Harris want him to invest in?

RUTH: Yes —

MAMA: We ain't no business people, Ruth. We just plain working folks.

RUTH: Ain't nobody business people till they go into business. Walter Lee say colored people ain't never going to start getting ahead till they start gambling on some different kinds of things in the world — investments and things.

MAMA: What done got into you, girl? Walter Lee done finally sold you on investing.

RUTH: No. Mama, something is happening between Walter and me. I don't know what it is — but he needs something — something I can't give him anymore. He needs this chance, Lena.

MAMA (*frowning deeply*): But liquor, honey —

RUTH: Well — like Walter say — I spec people going to always be drinking themselves some liquor.

MAMA: Well — whether they drinks it or not ain't none of my business. But whether I go into business selling it to 'em *is*, and I don't want that on my ledger this late in life. (*Stopping suddenly and studying her daughter-in-law.*) Ruth Younger, what's the matter with you today? You look like you could fall over right there.

RUTH: I'm tired.

MAMA: Then you better stay home from work today.

RUTH: I can't stay home. She'd be calling up the agency and screaming at them, "My girl didn't come in today — send me somebody! My girl didn't come in!" Oh, she just have a fit . . .

MAMA: Well, let her have it. I'll just call her up and say you got the flu —

RUTH (*laughing*): Why the flu?

MAMA: 'Cause it sounds respectable to 'em. Something white people get, too. They know 'bout the flu. Otherwise they think you been cut up or something when you tell 'em you sick.

RUTH: I got to go in. We need the money.

MAMA: Somebody would of thought my children done all but starved to death the way they talk about money here late. Child, we got a great big old check coming tomorrow.

RUTH (*sincerely, but also self-righteously*): Now that's your money. It ain't got nothing to do with me. We all feel like that — Walter and Bennie and me — even Travis.

MAMA (*thoughtfully, and suddenly very far away*): Ten thousand dollars —

RUTH: Sure is wonderful.

MAMA: Ten thousand dollars.

RUTH: You know what you should do, Miss Lena? You should take yourself a trip somewhere. To Europe or South America or someplace —

MAMA (*throwing up her hands at the thought*): Oh, child!

RUTH: I'm serious. Just pack up and leave! Go on away and enjoy yourself some. Forget about the family and have yourself a ball for once in your life —

MAMA (*drily*): You sound like I'm just about ready to die. Who'd go with me? What I look like wandering 'round Europe by myself?

RUTH: Shoot — these here rich white women do it all the time. They don't think nothing of packing up they suitcases and piling on one of them big steamships and — swoosh! — they gone, child.

MAMA: Something always told me I wasn't no rich white woman.

RUTH: Well — what are you going to do with it then?

MAMA: I ain't rightly decided. (*Thinking. She speaks now with emphasis.*) Some of it got to be put away for Beneatha and her schoolin' — and ain't nothing going to touch that part of it. Nothing. (*She waits several seconds, trying to make up her mind about something, and looks at Ruth a little tentatively before going on.*) Been thinking that we maybe could meet the notes on a little old two-story somewhere, with a yard where Travis could play in the summertime, if we use part of the insurance for a down payment and everybody kind of pitch in. I could maybe take on a little day work again, few days a week —

RUTH (*studying her mother-in-law furtively and concentrating on her ironing, anxious to encourage without seeming to*): Well, Lord knows, we've put enough rent into this here rat trap to pay for four houses by now . . .

MAMA (*looking up at the words "rat trap" and then looking around and leaning back and sighing — in a suddenly reflective mood —*): "Rat trap" — yes, that's all it is. (*Smiling.*) I remember just as well the day me and Big Walter moved in here. Hadn't been married but two weeks and wasn't planning on living here no more than a year. (*She shakes her head at the dissolved dream.*) We was going to set away, little by little, don't you know, and buy a little place out in Morgan Park. We had even picked out the house. (*Chuckling a little.*) Looks right dumpy today. But Lord, child, you should know all the dreams I had 'bout buying that house and fixing it up and making me a little garden in the back — (*She waits and stops smiling.*) And didn't none of it happen.

(*Dropping her hands in a futile gesture.*)

RUTH (*keeps her head down, ironing*): Yes, life can be a barrel of disappointments, sometimes.

MAMA: Honey, Big Walter would come in here some nights back then and slump down on that couch there and just look at the rug, and look at me and look at the rug and then back at me — and I'd know he was down then . . . really down. (*After a second very long and thoughtful pause; she is seeing back to times that only she can see.*) And then, Lord, when I lost that baby — little Claude — I almost thought I was going to lose Big Walter too. Oh, that man grieved hisself! He was one man to love his children.

RUTH: Ain't nothin' can tear at you like losin' your baby.

MAMA: I guess that's how come that man finally worked hisself to death like he done. Like he was fighting his own war with this here world that took his baby from him.

RUTH: He sure was a fine man, all right. I always liked Mr. Younger.

MAMA: Crazy 'bout his children! God knows there was plenty wrong with Walter Younger — hardheaded, mean, kind of wild with women — plenty wrong with him. But he sure loved his children. Always wanted them to have something — be something. That's where Brother gets all these notions, I reckon. Big Walter used to say, he'd get right wet in the eyes sometimes, lean his head back with the water standing in his eyes and say, "Seem like God didn't see fit to give the black man nothing but dreams — but He did give us children to make them dreams seem worthwhile." (*She smiles.*) He could talk like that, don't you know.

RUTH: Yes, he sure could. He was a good man, Mr. Younger.

MAMA: Yes, a fine man — just couldn't never catch up with his dreams, that's all.

(*Beneatha comes in, brushing her hair and looking up to the ceiling, where the sound of a vacuum cleaner has started up.*)

BENEATHA: What could be so dirty on that woman's rugs that she has to vacuum them every single day?

RUTH: I wish certain young women 'round here who I could name would take inspiration about certain rugs in a certain apartment I could also mention.

BENEATHA (*shrugging*): How much cleaning can a house need, for Christ's sakes.

MAMA (*not liking the Lord's name used thus*): Bennie!

RUTH: Just listen to her — just listen!

BENEATHA: Oh, God!

MAMA: If you use the Lord's name just one more time —

BENEATHA (*a bit of a whine*): Oh, Mama —

RUTH: Fresh — just fresh as salt, this girl!

BENEATHA (*drily*): Well — if the salt loses its savor —

MAMA: Now that will do. I just ain't going to have you 'round here reciting the scriptures in vain — you hear me?

BENEATHA: How did I manage to get on everybody's wrong side by just walking into a room?

RUTH: If you weren't so fresh —

BENEATHA: Ruth, I'm twenty years old.

MAMA: What time you be home from school today?

BENEATHA: Kind of late. (*With enthusiasm.*) Madeline is going to start my guitar lessons today.

(*Mama and Ruth look up with the same expression.*)

MAMA: Your *what* kind of lessons?

BENEATHA: Guitar.

RUTH: Oh, Father!

MAMA: How come you done taken it in your mind to learn to play the guitar?

BENEATHA: I just want to, that's all.

MAMA (*smiling*): Lord, child, don't you know what to do with yourself? How long it going to be before you get tired of this now — like you got tired of that little play-acting group you joined last year? (*Looking at Ruth.*) And what was it the year before that?

RUTH: The horseback-riding club for which she bought that fifty-five-dollar riding habit that's been hanging in the closet ever since!

MAMA (*to Beneatha*): Why you got to flit so from one thing to another, baby?

BENEATHA (*sharply*): I just want to learn to play the guitar. Is there anything wrong with that?

MAMA: Ain't nobody trying to stop you. I just wonders sometimes why you has to flit so from one thing to another all the time. You ain't never done nothing with all that camera equipment you brought home —

BENEATHA: I don't flit! I — I experiment with different forms of expression —

RUTH: Like riding a horse?

BENEATHA: — People have to express themselves one way or another.

MAMA: What is it you want to express?

BENEATHA (*angrily*): Me! (*Mama and Ruth look at each other and burst into raucous laughter.*) Don't worry — I don't expect you to understand.

MAMA (*to change the subject*): Who you going out with tomorrow night?

BENEATHA (*with displeasure*): George Murchison again.

MAMA (*pleased*): Oh — you getting a little sweet on him?

RUTH: You ask me, this child ain't sweet on nobody but herself — (*Underbreath.*) Express herself!

(*They laugh.*)

BENEATHA: Oh — I like George all right, Mama. I mean I like him enough to go out with him and stuff, but —

RUTH (*for devilment*): What does *and stuff* mean?

BENEATHA: Mind your own business.

MAMA: Stop picking at her now, Ruth. (*She chuckles — then a suspicious sudden look at her daughter as she turns in her chair for emphasis.*) What DOES it mean?

BENEATHA (*wearily*): Oh, I just mean I couldn't ever really be serious about George. He's — he's so shallow.

RUTH: Shallow — what do you mean he's shallow? He's *Rich!*

MAMA: Hush, Ruth.

BENEATHA: I know he's rich. He knows he's rich, too.

RUTH: Well — what other qualities a man got to have to satisfy you, little girl?

BENEATHA: You wouldn't even begin to understand. Anybody who married Walter could not possibly understand.

MAMA (*outraged*): What kind of way is that to talk about your brother?

BENEATHA: Brother is a flip — let's face it.

MAMA (*To Ruth, helplessly*): What's a flip?

RUTH (*glad to add kindling*): She's saying he's crazy.

BENEATHA: Not crazy. Brother isn't really crazy yet — he — he's an elaborate neurotic.

MAMA: Hush your mouth!

BENEATHA: As for George. Well. George looks good — he's got a beautiful car and he takes me to nice places and, as my sister-in-law says, he is probably the richest boy I will ever get to know and I even like him sometimes — but if the Youngers are sitting around waiting to see if their little Bennie is going to tie up the family with the Murchisons, they are wasting their time.

RUTH: You mean you wouldn't marry George Murchison if he asked you someday? That pretty, rich thing? Honey, I knew you was odd —

BENEATHA: No I would not marry him if all I felt for him was what I feel now. Besides, George's family wouldn't really like it.

MAMA: Why not?

BENEATHA: Oh, Mama — The Murchisons are honest-to-God-real-*live*-rich colored people, and the only people in the world who are more snobbish than rich white people are rich colored people. I thought everybody knew that. I've met Mrs. Murchison. She's a scene!

MAMA: You must not dislike people 'cause they well off, honey.

BENEATHA: Why not? It makes just as much sense as disliking people 'cause they are poor, and lots of people do that.

RUTH (*A wisdom-of-the-ages manner. To Mama.*): Well, she'll get over some of this —

BENEATHA: Get over it? What are you talking about, Ruth? Listen, I'm going to be a doctor. I'm not worried about who I'm going to marry yet — if I ever get married.

MAMA AND RUTH: *If!*

MAMA: Now, Bennie —

BENEATHA: Oh, I probably will . . . but first I'm going to be a doctor, and George, for one, still thinks that's pretty funny. I couldn't be bothered with that. I am going to be a doctor and everybody around here better understand that!

MAMA (*kindly*): 'Course you going to be a doctor, honey, God willing.

BENEATHA (*drily*): God hasn't got a thing to do with it.

MAMA: Beneatha — that just wasn't necessary.

BENEATHA: Well — neither is God. I get sick of hearing about God.

MAMA: Beneatha!

BENEATHA: I mean it! I'm just tired of hearing about God all the time. What has He got to do with anything? Does he pay tuition?

MAMA: You 'bout to get your fresh little jaw slapped!

RUTH: That's just what she needs, all right!

BENEATHA: Why? Why can't I say what I want to around here, like everybody else?

MAMA: It don't sound nice for a young girl to say things like that — you wasn't brought up that way. Me and your father went to trouble to get you and Brother to church every Sunday.

BENEATHA: Mama, you don't understand. It's all a matter of ideas, and God is just one idea I don't accept. It's not important. I am not going out and be immoral or commit crimes because I don't believe in God. I don't even think about it. It's just that I get tired of Him getting credit for all the things the human race achieves through its own stubborn effort. There simply is no blasted God — there is only man and it is *he* who makes miracles!

(*Mama absorbs this speech, studies her daughter and rises slowly and crosses to Beneatha and slaps her powerfully across the face. After, there is only silence and the daughter drops her eyes from her mother's face, and Mama is very tall before her.*)

MAMA: Now — you say after me, in my mother's house there is still God. (*There is a long pause and Beneatha stares at the floor wordlessly. Mama repeats the phrase with precision and cool emotion.*) In my mother's house there is still God.

BENEATHA: In my mother's house there is still God.

(*A long pause.*)

MAMA (*Walking away from Beneatha, too disturbed for triumphant posture. Stopping and turning back to her daughter.*): There are some ideas we ain't going to have in this house. Not long as I am at the head of this family.

BENEATHA: Yes, ma'am.

(*Mama walks out of the room.*)

RUTH (*almost gently, with profound understanding*): You think you a woman, Bennie — but you still a little girl. What you did was childish — so you got treated like a child.

BENEATHA: I see. (*Quietly.*) I also see that everybody thinks it's all right for Mama to be a tyrant. But

all the tyranny in the world will never put a God in the heavens!

(*She picks up her books and goes out. Pause.*)

RUTH (*goes to Mama's door*): She said she was sorry.

MAMA (*coming out, going to her plant*): They frightens me, Ruth. My children.

RUTH: You got good children, Lena. They just a little off sometimes — but they're good.

MAMA: No — there's something come down between me and them that don't let us understand each other and I don't know what it is. One done almost lost his mind thinking 'bout money all the time and the other done commence to talk about things I can't seem to understand in no form or fashion. What is it that's changing, Ruth.

RUTH (*soothingly, older than her years*): Now . . . you taking it all too seriously. You just got strong-willed children and it takes a strong woman like you to keep 'em in hand.

MAMA (*looking at her plant and sprinkling a little water on it*): They spirited all right, my children. Got to admit they got spirit — Bennie and Walter. Like this little old plant that ain't never had enough sunshine or nothing — and look at it . . .

(*She has her back to Ruth, who has had to stop ironing and lean against something and put the back of her hand to her forehead.*)

RUTH (*trying to keep Mama from noticing*): You . . . sure . . . loves that little old thing, don't you? . . .

MAMA: Well, I always wanted me a garden like I used to see sometimes at the back of the houses down home. This plant is close as I ever got to having one. (*She looks out of the window as she replaces the plant.*) Lord, ain't nothing as dreary as the view from this window on a dreary day, is there? Why ain't you singing this morning, Ruth? Sing that "No Ways Tired." That song always lifts me up so — (*She turns at last to see that Ruth has slipped quietly to the floor, in a state of semiconsciousness.*) Ruth! Ruth honey — what's the matter with you . . . Ruth!

Scene II

(*It is the following morning; a Saturday morning, and house cleaning is in progress at the Youngers'. Furniture has been shoved hither and yon and Mama is giving the kitchen-area walls a washing down. Beneatha, in dungarees, with a handkerchief tied around her face, is spraying insecticide into the cracks in the walls. As they work, the radio is on and a Southside disk jockey program is inappropriately filling the house with a rather exotic saxophone blues. Travis, the sole idle one, is leaning on his arms, looking out of the window.*)

TRAVIS: Grandmama, that stuff Bennie is using smells awful. Can I go downstairs, please?

MAMA: Did you get all them chores done already? I ain't seen you doing much.

TRAVIS: Yes'm — finished early. Where did Mama go this morning?

MAMA (*looking at Beneatha*): She had to go on a little errand.

(*The phone rings. Beneatha runs to answer it and reaches it before Walter, who has entered from bedroom.*)

TRAVIS: Where?

MAMA: To tend to her business.

BENEATHA: Haylo . . . (*Disappointed.*) Yes, he is. (*She tosses the phone to Walter, who barely catches it.*) It's Willie Harris again.

WALTER (*as privately as possible under Mama's gaze*): Hello, Willie. Did you get the papers from the lawyer? . . . No, not yet. I told you the mailman doesn't get here till ten-thirty . . . No, I'll come there . . . Yeah! Right away. (*He hangs up and goes for his coat.*)

BENEATHA: Brother, where did Ruth go?

WALTER (*as he exits*): How should I know!

TRAVIS: Aw come on, Grandma. Can I go outside?

MAMA: Oh, I guess so. You stay right in front of the house, though, and keep a good lookout for the postman.

TRAVIS: Yes'm. (*He darts into bedroom for stickball and bat, reenters, and sees Beneatha on her knees spraying under sofa with behind upraised. He edges closer to the target, takes aim, and lets her have it. She screams.*) Leave them poor little cockroaches alone, they ain't bothering you none! (*He runs as she swings the spraygun at him viciously and playfully.*) Grandma! Grandma!

MAMA: Look out there, girl, before you be spilling some of that stuff on that child!

TRAVIS (*safely behind the bastion of Mama*): That's right — look out, now! (*He exits.*)

BENEATHA (*drily*): I can't imagine that it would hurt him — it has never hurt the roaches.

MAMA: Well, little boys' hides ain't as tough as Southside roaches. You better get over there behind the bureau. I seen one marching out of there like Napoleon yesterday.

BENEATHA: There's really only one way to get rid of them, Mama —

MAMA: How?

BENEATHA: Set fire to this building! Mama, where did Ruth go?

MAMA (*looking at her with meaning*): To the doctor, I think.

BENEATHA: The doctor? What's the matter? (*They exchange glances.*) You don't think —

MAMA (*with her sense of drama*): Now I ain't saying what I think. But I ain't never been wrong 'bout a woman neither.

(*The phone rings.*)

BENEATHA (*at the phone*): Hay-lo . . . (*Pause, and a moment of recognition.*) Well — when did you get back! . . . And how was it? . . . Of course I've missed you — in my way . . . This morning? No . . . house cleaning and all that and Mama hates it if I let people come over when the house is like this . . . You *have*? Well, that's different . . . What is it — Oh, what the hell, come on over . . . Right, see you then. *Arrivederci.*

(*She hangs up.*)

MAMA (*who has listened vigorously, as is her habit*): Who is that you inviting over here with this house looking like this? You ain't got the pride you was born with!

BENEATHA: Asagai doesn't care how houses look, Mama — he's an intellectual.

MAMA: *Who?*

BENEATHA: Asagai — Joseph Asagai. He's an African boy I met on campus. He's been studying in Canada all summer.

MAMA: What's his name?

BENEATHA: Asagai, Joseph. Ah-sah-guy . . . He's from Nigeria.

MAMA: Oh, that's the little country that was founded by slaves way back . . .

BENEATHA: No, Mama — that's Liberia.

MAMA: I don't think I never met no African before.

BENEATHA: Well, do me a favor and don't ask him a whole lot of ignorant questions about Africans. I mean, do they wear clothes and all that —

MAMA: Well, now, I guess if you think we so ignorant 'round here maybe you shouldn't bring your friends here —

BENEATHA: It's just that people ask such crazy things. All anyone seems to know about when it comes to Africa is Tarzan —

MAMA (*indignantly*): Why should I know anything about Africa?

BENEATHA: Why do you give money at church for the missionary work?

MAMA: Well, that's to help save people.

BENEATHA: You mean save them from *heathenism* —

MAMA (*innocently*): Yes.

BENEATHA: I'm afraid they need more salvation from the British and the French.

(*Ruth comes in forlornly and pulls off her coat with dejection. They both turn to look at her.*)

RUTH (*dispiritedly*): Well, I guess from all the happy faces — everybody knows.

BENEATHA: You pregnant?

MAMA: Lord have mercy, I sure hope it's a little old girl. Travis ought to have a sister.

(*Beneatha and Ruth give her a hopeless look for this grandmotherly enthusiasm.*)

BENEATHA: How far along are you?

RUTH: Two months.

BENEATHA: Did you mean to? I mean did you plan it or was it an accident?

MAMA: What do you know about planning or not planning?

BENEATHA: Oh, Mama.

RUTH (*wearily*): She's twenty years old, Lena.

BENEATHA: Did you plan it, Ruth?

RUTH: Mind your own business.

BENEATHA: It is my business — where is he going to live, on the *roof*? (*There is silence following the remark as the three women react to the sense of it.*) Gee — I didn't mean that, Ruth, honest. Gee, I don't feel like that at all. I — I think it is wonderful.

RUTH (*dully*): Wonderful.

BENEATHA: Yes — really.

MAMA (*looking at Ruth, worried*): Doctor say everything going to be all right?

RUTH (*far away*): Yes — she says everything is going to be fine . . .

MAMA (*immediately suspicious*): "She" — What doctor you went to?

(*Ruth folds over, near hysteria.*)

MAMA (*worriedly hovering over Ruth*): Ruth honey — what's the matter with you — you sick?

(*Ruth has her fists clenched on her thighs and is fighting hard to suppress a scream that seems to be rising in her.*)

BENEATHA: What's the matter with her, Mama?

MAMA (*working her fingers in Ruth's shoulders to relax her*): She be all right. Women gets right depressed sometimes when they get her way. (*Speaking softly, expertly, rapidly.*) Now you just relax. That's right . . . just lean back, don't think 'bout nothing at all . . . nothing at all —

RUTH: I'm all right . . .

(*The glassy-eyed look melts and then she collapses into a fit of heavy sobbing. The bell rings.*)

BENEATHA: Oh, my God — that must be Asagai.

MAMA (*to Ruth*): Come on now, honey. You need to lie down and rest awhile . . . then have some nice hot food.

(*They exit, Ruth's weight on her mother-in-law. Beneatha, herself profoundly disturbed, opens the door to admit a rather dramatic-looking young man with a large package.*)

ASAGAI: Hello, Alaiyo —

BENEATHA (*holding the door open and regarding him with pleasure*): Hello . . . (*Long pause.*) Well — come in. And please excuse everything. My mother was very upset about my letting anyone come here with the place like this.

ASAGAI (*coming into the room*): You look disturbed too . . . Is something wrong?

BENEATHA (*still at the door, absently*): Yes . . . we've all got acute ghetto-itus. (*She smiles and comes toward him, finding a cigarette and sitting.*) So — sit down! No! Wait! (*She whips the spraygun off sofa where she had left it and puts the cushions back. At last perches on arm of sofa. He sits.*) So, how was Canada?

ASAGAI (*a sophisticate*): Canadian.

BENEATHA (*looking at him*): Asagai, I'm very glad you are back.

ASAGAI (*looking back at her in turn*): Are you really?

BENEATHA: Yes — very.

ASAGAI: Why? — you were quite glad when I went away. What happened?

BENEATHA: You went away.

ASAGAI: Ahhhhhhhh.

BENEATHA: Before — you wanted to be so serious before there was time.

ASAGAI: How much time must there be before one knows what one feels?

BENEATHA (*Stalling this particular conversation. Her hands pressed together, in a deliberately childish gesture.*): What did you bring me?

ASAGAI (*handing her the package*): Open it and see.

BENEATHA (*eagerly opening the package and drawing out some records and the colorful robes of a Nigerian woman*): Oh, Asagai! . . . You got them for me! . . . How beautiful . . . and the records too! (*She lifts out the robes and runs to the mirror with them and holds the drapery up in front of herself.*)

ASAGAI (*coming to her at the mirror*): I shall have to teach you how to drape it properly. (*He flings the material about her for the moment and stands back to look at her.*) Ah — Oh-pay-gay-day, oh-gbah-mu-shay. (*A Yoruba exclamation for admiration.*) You wear it well . . . very well . . . mutilated hair and all.

BENEATHA (*turning suddenly*): My hair — what's wrong with my hair?

ASAGAI (*shrugging*): Were you born with it like that?

BENEATHA (*reaching up to touch it*): No . . . of course not.

(*She looks back to the mirror, disturbed.*)

ASAGAI (*smiling*): How then?

BENEATHA: You know perfectly well how . . . as crinkly as yours . . . that's how.

ASAGAI: And it is ugly to you that way?

BENEATHA (*quickly*): Oh, no — not ugly . . . (*More slowly, apologetically.*) But it's so hard to manage when it's, well — raw.

ASAGAI: And so to accommodate that — you mutilate it every week?

BENEATHA: It's not mutilation!

ASAGAI (*laughing aloud at her seriousness*): Oh . . . please! I am only teasing you because you are so very serious about these things. (*He stands back from her and folds his arms across his chest as he watches her pulling at her hair and frowning in the mirror.*) Do you remember the first time you met me at school? . . . (*He laughs.*) You came up to me and you said — and I thought you were the most serious little thing I had ever seen — you said: (*He imitates her.*) "Mr. Asagai — I want very much to talk with you. About Africa. You see, Mr. Asagai, I am looking for my *identity!*"

(*He laughs.*)

BENEATHA (*turning to him, not laughing*): Yes —

(*Her face is quizzical, profoundly disturbed.*)

ASAGAI (*still teasing and reaching out and taking her face in his hands and turning her profile to him*): Well . . . it is true that this is not so much a profile of a Hollywood queen as perhaps a queen of the Nile — (*A mock dismissal of the importance of the question.*) But what does it matter? Assimilationism is so popular in your country.

BENEATHA (*wheeling, passionately, sharply*): I am not an assimilationist!

ASAGAI (*the protest hangs in the room for a moment and Asagai studies her, his laughter fading*): Such a serious one. (*There is a pause.*) So — you like the robes? You must take excellent care of them — they are from my sister's personal wardrobe.

BENEATHA (*with incredulity*): You — you sent all the way home — for me?

ASAGAI (*with charm*): For you — I would do much more . . . Well, that is what I came for. I must go.

BENEATHA: Will you call me Monday?

ASAGAI: Yes . . . We have a great deal to talk about. I mean about identity and time and all that.

BENEATHA: Time?

ASAGAI: Yes. About how much time one needs to know what one feels.

BENEATHA: You see! You never understood that there is more than one kind of feeling which can exist between a man and a woman — or, at least, there should be.

ASAGAI (*shaking his head negatively but gently*): No. Between a man and a woman there need be only one kind of feeling. I have that for you . . . Now even . . . right this moment . . .

BENEATHA: I know — and by itself — it won't do. I can find that anywhere.

ASAGAI: For a woman it should be enough.

BENEATHA: I know — because that's what it says in all the novels that men write. But it isn't. Go ahead and laugh — but I'm not interested in being someone's little episode in America or — (*with feminine vengeance*) — one of them! (*Asagai has burst into laughter again.*) That's funny as hell, huh!

ASAGAI: It's just that every American girl I have known has said that to me. White — black — in this you are all the same. And the same speech, too!

BENEATHA (*angrily*): Yuk, yuk, yuk!

ASAGAI: It's how you can be sure that the world's most liberated women are not liberated at all. You all talk about it too much!

(*Mama enters and is immediately all social charm because of the presence of a guest.*)

BENEATHA: Oh — Mama — this is Mr. Asagai.

MAMA: How do you do?

ASAGAI (*total politeness to an elder*): How do you do, Mrs. Younger. Please forgive me for coming at such an outrageous hour on a Saturday.

MAMA: Well, you are quite welcome. I just hope you understand that our house don't always look like this. (*Chatterish.*) You must come again. I would love to hear all about — (*not sure of the name*) — your country. I think it's so sad the way our American Negroes don't know nothing about Africa 'cept Tarzan and all that. And all that money they pour into these churches when they ought to be helping you people over there drive out them French and Englishmen done taken away your land.

(*The mother flashes a slightly superior look at her daughter upon completion of the recitation.*)

ASAGAI (*taken aback by this sudden and acutely unrelated expression of sympathy*): Yes . . . yes . . .

MAMA (*smiling at him suddenly and relaxing and looking him over*): How many miles is it from here to where you come from?

ASAGAI: Many thousands.

MAMA (*looking at him as she would Walter*): I bet you don't half look after yourself, being away from your mama either. I spec you better come 'round here from time to time to get yourself some decent home-cooked meals . . .

ASAGAI (*moved*): Thank you. Thank you very much.

(*They are all quiet, then* —) Well . . . I must go. I will call you Monday, Alaiyo.

MAMA: What's that he call you?

ASAGAI: Oh — "Alaiyo." I hope you don't mind. It is what you would call a nickname, I think. It is a Yoruba word. I am a Yoruba.

MAMA (*looking at Beneatha*): I — I thought he was from — (*Uncertain.*)

ASAGAI (*understanding*): Nigeria is my country. Yoruba is my tribal origin —

BENEATHA: You didn't tell us what Alaiyo means . . . for all I know, you might be calling me Little Idiot or something . . .

ASAGAI: Well . . . let me see . . . I do not know how just to explain it . . . The sense of a thing can be so different when it changes languages.

BENEATHA: You're evading.

ASAGAI: No — really it is difficult . . . (*Thinking.*) It means . . . it means One for Whom Bread — Food — Is Not Enough. (*He looks at her.*) Is that all right?

BENEATHA (*understanding, softly*): Thank you.

MAMA (*looking from one to the other and not understanding any of it*): Well . . . that's nice . . . You must come see us again — Mr. ——

ASAGAI: Ah-sah-guy . . .

MAMA: Yes . . . Do come again.

ASAGAI: Good-bye.

(*He exits.*)

MAMA (*after him*): Lord, that's a pretty thing just went out here! (*Insinuatingly, to her daughter.*) Yes, I guess I see why we done commence to get so interested in Africa 'round here. Missionaries my aunt Jenny!

(*She exits.*)

BENEATHA: Oh, Mama! . . .

(*She picks up the Nigerian dress and holds it up to her in front of the mirror again. She sets the headdress on haphazardly and then notices her hair again and clutches at it and then replaces the headdress and frowns at herself. Then she starts to wriggle in front of the mirror as she thinks a Nigerian woman might. Travis enters and stands regarding her.*)

TRAVIS: What's the matter, girl, you cracking up?

BENEATHA: Shut up.

(*She pulls the headdress off and looks at herself in the mirror and clutches at her hair again and squinches her eyes as if trying to imagine something. Then, suddenly, she gets her raincoat and kerchief and hurriedly prepares for going out.*)

MAMA (*coming back into the room*): She's resting now. Travis, baby, run next door and ask Miss Johnson to please let me have a little kitchen cleanser. This here can is empty as Jacob's kettle.

TRAVIS: I just came in.

MAMA: Do as you told. (*He exits and she looks at her daughter.*) Where you going?

BENEATHA (*halting at the door*): To become a queen of the Nile!

(*She exits in a breathless blaze of glory. Ruth appears in the bedroom doorway.*)

MAMA: Who told you to get up?

RUTH: Ain't nothing wrong with me to be lying in no bed for. Where did Bennie go?

MAMA (*drumming her fingers*): Far as I could make out — to Egypt. (*Ruth just looks at her.*) What time is it getting to?

RUTH: Ten twenty. And the mailman going to ring that bell this morning just like he done every morning for the last umpteen years.

(*Travis comes in with the cleanser can.*)

TRAVIS: She say to tell you that she don't have much.

MAMA (*angrily*): Lord, some people I could name sure is tight-fisted! (*Directing her grandson.*) Mark two cans of cleanser down on the list there. If she that hard up for kitchen cleanser, I sure don't want to forget to get her none!

RUTH: Lena — maybe the woman is just short on cleanser —

MAMA (*not listening*): — Much baking powder as she done borrowed from me all these years, she could of done gone into the baking business!

(*The bell sounds suddenly and sharply and all three are stunned — serious and silent — mid-speech. In spite of all the other conversations and distractions of the morning, this is what they have been waiting for, even Travis, who looks helplessly from his mother to his grandmother. Ruth is the first to come to life again.*)

RUTH (*to Travis*): Get down them steps, boy!

(*Travis snaps to life and flies out to get the mail.*)

MAMA (*her eyes wide, her hand to her breast*): You mean it done really come?

RUTH (*excited*): Oh, Miss Lena!

MAMA (*collecting herself*): Well . . . I don't know what we all so excited about 'round here for. We known it was coming for months.

RUTH: That's a whole lot different from having it come and being able to hold it in your hands . . . a piece of paper worth ten thousand dollars . . . (*Travis bursts back into the room. He holds the envelope high above his head, like a little dancer, his face is radiant and he is breathless. He moves to his grandmother with sudden slow ceremony and puts the envelope into her hands. She accepts it, and then merely holds it and looks at it.*) Come on! Open it . . . Lord have mercy, I wish Walter Lee was here!

TRAVIS: Open it, Grandmama!

MAMA (*staring at it*): Now you all be quiet. It's just a check.

RUTH: Open it . . .

MAMA (*still staring at it*): Now don't act silly . . . We ain't never been no people to act silly 'bout no money —

RUTH (*swiftly*): We ain't never had none before — OPEN IT!

(*Mama finally makes a good strong tear and pulls out the thin blue slice of paper and inspects it closely. The boy and his mother study it raptly over Mama's shoulders.*)

MAMA: *Travis!* (*She is counting off with doubt.*) Is that the right number of zeros.

TRAVIS: Yes'm . . . ten thousand dollars. Gaalee, Grandmama, you rich.

MAMA (*She holds the check away from her, still looking at it. Slowly her face sobers into a mask of unhappiness.*): Ten thousand dollars. (*She hands it to Ruth.*) Put it away somewhere, Ruth. (*She does not look at Ruth; her eyes seem to be seeing something somewhere very far off.*) Ten thousand dollars they give you. Ten thousand dollars.

TRAVIS (*to his mother, sincerely*): What's the matter with Grandmama — don't she want to be rich?

RUTH (*distractedly*): You go on out and play now, baby. (*Travis exits. Mama starts wiping dishes absently, humming intently to herself. Ruth turns to her, with kind exasperation.*) You've gone and got yourself upset.

MAMA (*not looking at her*): I spec if it wasn't for you all . . . I would just put that money away or give it to the church or something.

RUTH: Now what kind of talk is that. Mr. Younger would just be plain mad if he could hear you talking foolish like that.

MAMA (*stopping and staring off*): Yes . . . he sure would. (*Sighing.*) We got enough to do with that money, all right. (*She halts then, and turns and looks at her daughter-in-law hard; Ruth avoids her eyes and Mama wipes her hands with finality and starts to speak firmly to Ruth.*) Where did you go today, girl?

RUTH: To the doctor.

MAMA (*impatiently*): Now, Ruth . . . you know better than that. Old Doctor Jones is strange enough in his way but there ain't nothing 'bout him make

somebody slip and call him "she" — like you done this morning.

RUTH: Well, that's what happened — my tongue slipped.

MAMA: You went to see that woman, didn't you?

RUTH (*defensively, giving herself away*): What woman you talking about?

MAMA (*angrily*): That woman who —

(*Walter enters in great excitement.*)

WALTER: Did it come?

MAMA (*quietly*): Can't you give people a Christian greeting before you start asking about money?

WALTER (*to Ruth*): Did it come? (*Ruth unfolds the check and lays it quietly before him, watching him intently with thoughts of her own. Walter sits down and grasps it close and counts off the zeros.*) Ten thousand dollars — (*He turns suddenly, frantically to his mother and draws some papers out of his breast pocket.*) Mama — look. Old Willy Harris put everything on paper —

MAMA: Son — I think you ought to talk to your wife . . . I'll go on out and leave you alone if you want —

WALTER: I can talk to her later — Mama, look —

MAMA: Son —

WALTER: WILL SOMEBODY PLEASE LISTEN TO ME TODAY!

MAMA (*quietly*): I don't 'low no yellin' in this house, Walter Lee, and you know it — (*Walter stares at them in frustration and starts to speak several times.*) And there ain't going to be no investing in no liquor stores.

WALTER: But, Mama, you ain't even looked at it.

MAMA: I don't aim to have to speak on that again.

(*A long pause.*)

WALTER: You ain't looked at it and you don't aim to have to speak on that again? You ain't even looked at it and *you* have decided — (*Crumpling his papers.*) Well, *you* tell that to my boy tonight when you put him to sleep on the living room couch . . . (*Turning to Mama and speaking directly to her.*) Yeah — and tell it to my wife, Mama, tomorrow when she has to go out of here to look after somebody else's kids. And tell it to *me*, Mama, every time we need a new pair of curtains and I have to watch *you* go out and work in somebody's kitchen. Yeah, you tell me then!

(*Walter starts out.*)

RUTH: Where you going?

WALTER: I'm going out!

RUTH: Where?

WALTER: Just out of this house somewhere —

RUTH (*getting her coat*): I'll come too.

WALTER: I don't want you to come!

RUTH: I got something to talk to you about, Walter.

WALTER: That's too bad.

MAMA (*still quietly*): Walter Lee — (*She waits and he finally turns and looks at her.*) Sit down.

WALTER: I'm a grown man, Mama.

MAMA: Ain't nobody said you wasn't grown. But you still in my house and my presence. And as long as you are — you'll talk to your wife civil. Now sit down.

RUTH (*suddenly*): Oh, let him go on out and drink himself to death! He makes me sick to my stomach! (*She flings her coat against him and exits to bedroom.*)

WALTER (*violently flinging the coat after her*): And you turn mine too, baby! (*The door slams behind her.*) That was my biggest mistake —

MAMA (*still quietly*): Walter, what is the matter with you?

WALTER: Matter with me? Ain't nothing the matter with *me*!

MAMA: Yes there is. Something eating you up like a crazy man. Something more than me not giving you this money. The past few years I been watching it happen to you. You get all nervous acting and kind of wild in the eyes — (*Walter jumps up impatiently at her words.*) I said sit there now, I'm talking to you!

WALTER: Mama — I don't need no nagging at me today.

MAMA: Seem like you getting to a place where you always tied up in some kind of knot about something. But if anybody ask you 'bout it you just yell at 'em and bust out the house and go out and drink somewheres. Walter Lee, people can't live with that. Ruth's a good, patient girl in her way — but you getting to be too much. Boy, don't make the mistake of driving that girl away from you.

WALTER: Why — what she do for me?

MAMA: She loves you.

WALTER: Mama — I'm going out. I want to go off somewhere and be by myself for a while.

MAMA: I'm sorry 'bout your liquor store, son. It just wasn't the thing for us to do. That's what I want to tell you about —

WALTER: I got to go out, Mama —

(*He rises.*)

MAMA: It's dangerous, son.

WALTER: What's dangerous?

MAMA: When a man goes outside his home to look for peace.

WALTER (*beseechingly*): Then why can't there never be no peace in this house then?

MAMA: You done found it in some other house?

WALTER: No — there ain't no woman! Why do women always think there's a woman somewhere when a man gets restless. (*Picks up the check.*) Do you know what this money means to me? Do you know what this money can do for us? (*Puts it back.*) Mama — Mama — I want so many things . . .

MAMA: Yes, son —

WALTER: I want so many things that they are driving me kind of crazy . . . Mama — look at me.

MAMA: I'm looking at you. You a good-looking boy. You got a job, a nice wife, a fine boy and —

WALTER: A job. (*Looks at her.*) Mama, a job? I open and close car doors all day long. I drive a man around in his limousine and I say, "Yes, sir; no, sir; very good, sir; shall I take the Drive, sir?" Mama, that ain't no kind of job . . . that ain't nothing at all. (*Very quietly.*) Mama, I don't know if I can make you understand.

MAMA: Understand what, baby?

WALTER (*quietly*): Sometimes it's like I can see the future stretched out in front of me — just plain as day. The future, Mama. Hanging over there at the edge of my days. Just waiting for me — a big, looming blank space — full of *nothing*. Just waiting for *me*. But it don't have to be. (*Pause. Kneeling beside her chair.*) Mama — sometimes when I'm downtown and I pass them cool, quiet-looking restaurants where them white boys are sitting back and talking 'bout things . . . sitting there turning deals worth millions of dollars . . . sometimes I see guys don't look much older than me —

MAMA: Son — how come you talk so much 'bout money?

WALTER (*with immense passion*): Because it is life, Mama!

MAMA (*quietly*): Oh — (*Very quietly.*) So now it's life. Money is life. Once upon a time freedom used to be life — now it's money. I guess the world really do change . . .

WALTER: No — it was always money, Mama. We just didn't know about it.

MAMA: No . . . something has changed. (*She looks at him.*) You something new, boy. In my time we was worried about not being lynched and getting to the North if we could and how to stay alive and still have a pinch of dignity too . . . Now here come you and Beneatha — talking 'bout things we ain't never even thought about hardly, me and your daddy. You ain't satisfied or proud of nothing we done. I mean that you had a home; that we kept you out of trouble till you was grown; that you don't have to ride to work on the back of nobody's streetcar — You my children — but how different we done become.

WALTER (*A long beat. He pats her hand and gets up.*):

You just don't understand, Mama, you just don't understand.

MAMA: Son — do you know your wife is expecting another baby? (*Walter stands, stunned, and absorbs what his mother has said.*) That's what she wanted to talk to you about. (*Walter sinks down into a chair.*) This ain't for me to be telling — but you ought to know. (*She waits.*) I think Ruth is thinking 'bout getting rid of that child.

WALTER (*slowly understanding*): — No — no — Ruth wouldn't do that.

MAMA: When the world gets ugly enough — a woman will do anything for her family. *The part that's already living.*

WALTER: You don't know Ruth, Mama, if you think she would do that.

(*Ruth opens the bedroom door and stands there a little limp.*)

RUTH (*beaten*): Yes I would too, Walter. (*Pause.*) I gave her a five-dollar down payment.

(*There is total silence as the man stares at his wife and the mother stares at her son.*)

MAMA (*presently*): Well — (*Tightly.*) Well — son, I'm waiting to hear you say something . . . (*She waits.*) I'm waiting to hear how you be your father's son. Be the man he was . . . (*Pause. The silence shouts.*) Your wife says she going to destroy your child. And I'm waiting to hear you talk like him and say we a people who give children life, not who destroys them — (*She rises.*) I'm waiting to see you stand up and look like your daddy and say we done give up one baby to poverty and that we ain't going to give up nary another one . . . I'm waiting.

WALTER: Ruth — (*He can say nothing.*)

MAMA: If you a son of mine, tell her! (*Walter picks up his keys and his coat and walks out. She continues, bitterly.*) You . . . you are a disgrace to your father's memory. Somebody get me my hat!

ACT II • Scene I

(*Time: Later the same day.*)

(*At rise: Ruth is ironing again. She has the radio going. Presently Beneatha's bedroom door opens and Ruth's mouth falls and she puts down the iron in fascination.*)

RUTH: What have we got on tonight!

BENEATHA (*emerging grandly from the doorway so that we can see her thoroughly robed in the costume Asagai brought*): You are looking at what a well-dressed Nigerian woman wears — (*She parades for Ruth, her hair completely hidden by the headdress; she is coquettishly fanning herself with an ornate oriental fan, mistakenly more like Butterfly° than any Nigerian that ever was.*) Isn't it beautiful? (*She promenades to the radio and, with an arrogant flourish, turns off the good loud blues that is playing.*) Enough of this assimilationist junk! (*Ruth follows her with her eyes as she goes to the phonograph and puts on a record and turns and waits ceremoniously for the music to come up. Then, with a shout —*) OCOMOGOSIAY!

(*Ruth jumps. The music comes up, a lovely Nigerian melody. Beneatha listens, enraptured, her eyes far away — "back to the past." She begins to dance. Ruth is dumfounded.*)

RUTH: What kind of dance is that?

BENEATHA: A folk dance.

RUTH (*Pearl Bailey*): What kind of folks do that, honey?

BENEATHA: It's from Nigeria. It's a dance of welcome.

RUTH: Who you welcoming?

BENEATHA: The men back to the village.

RUTH: Where they been?

BENEATHA: How should I know — out hunting or something. Anyway, they are coming back now . . .

RUTH: Well, that's good.

BENEATHA (*with the record*): Alundi, alundi
Alundi alunya
Jop pu a jeepua
Ang gu sooooooooooo

Ai yai yae . . .
Ayehaye — alundi . . .

(*Walter comes in during this performance; he has obviously been drinking. He leans against the door heavily and watches his sister, at first with distaste. Then his eyes look off — "back to the past" — as he lifts both his fists to the roof, screaming.*)

WALTER: YEAH . . . AND ETHIOPIA STRETCH FORTH HER HANDS AGAIN! . . .

RUTH (*drily, looking at him*): Yes — and Africa sure is claiming her own tonight. (*She gives them both up and starts ironing again.*)

WALTER (*all in a drunken, dramatic shout*): Shut up! . . . I'm digging them drums . . . them drums move me! . . . (*He makes his weaving way to his wife's face and leans in close to her.*) In my *heart of hearts* — (*He thumps his chest*) — I am much warrior!

RUTH (*without even looking up*): In your heart of hearts you are much drunkard.

Butterfly: Madame Butterfly, the title character in the opera by Puccini.

WALTER (*coming away from her and starting to wander around the room, shouting*): Me and Jomo ... (*Intently, in his sister's face. She has stopped dancing to watch him in this unknown mood.*) That's my man, Kenyatta. (*Shouting and thumping his chest.*) FLAMING SPEAR! HOT DAMN! (*He is suddenly in possession of an imaginary spear and actively spearing enemies all over the room.*) OCOMOGOSIAY ...

BENEATHA (*to encourage Walter, thoroughly caught up with this side of him*): OCOMOGOSIAY, FLAMING SPEAR!

WALTER: THE LION IS WAKING ... OWIMOWEH! (*He pulls his shirt open and leaps up on the table and gestures with his spear.*)

BENEATHA: OWIMOWEH!

WALTER (*On the table, very far gone, his eyes pure glass sheets. He sees what we cannot, that he is a leader of his people, a great chief, a descendant of Chaka, and that the hour to march has come.*): Listen, my black brothers —

BENEATHA: OCOMOGOSIAY!

WALTER: — Do you hear the waters rushing against the shores of the coastlands —

BENEATHA: OCOMOGOSIAY!

WALTER: — Do you hear the screeching of the cocks in yonder hills beyond where the chiefs meet in council for the coming of the mighty war —

BENEATHA: OCOMOGOSIAY!

(*And now the lighting shifts subtly to suggest the world of Walter's imagination, and the mood shifts from pure comedy. It is the inner Walter speaking: the Southside chauffeur has assumed an unexpected majesty.*)

WALTER: — Do you hear the beating of the wings of the birds flying low over the mountains and the low places of our land —

BENEATHA: OCOMOGOSIAY!

WALTER: — Do you hear the singing of the women, singing the war songs of our fathers to the babies in the great houses? Singing the sweet war songs! (*The doorbell rings.*) OH, DO YOU HEAR, MY BLACK BROTHERS!

BENEATHA (*completely gone*): We hear you, Flaming Spear —

(*Ruth shuts off the phonograph and opens the door. George Murchison enters.*)

WALTER: Telling us to prepare for the GREATNESS OF THE TIME! (*Lights back to normal. He turns and sees George.*) Black Brother!

(*He extends his hand for the fraternal clasp.*)

GEORGE: Black Brother, hell!

RUTH (*having had enough, and embarrassed for the family*): Beneatha, you got company — what's the matter with you? Walter Lee Younger, get down off that table and stop acting like a fool ...

(*Walter comes down off the table suddenly and makes a quick exit to the bathroom.*)

RUTH: He's had a little to drink ... I don't know what her excuse is.

GEORGE (*to Beneatha*): Look honey, we're going *to* the theater — we're not going to be *in* it ... so go change, huh?

(*Beneatha looks at him and slowly, ceremoniously, lifts her hands and pulls off the headdress. Her hair is close-cropped and unstraightened. George freezes mid-sentence and Ruth's eyes all but fall out of her head.*)

GEORGE: What in the name of —

RUTH (*touching Beneatha's hair*): Girl, you done lost your natural mind? Look at your head!

GEORGE: What have you done to your head — I mean your hair!

BENEATHA: Nothing — except cut it off.

RUTH: Now that's the truth — it's what ain't been done to it! You expect this boy to go out with you with your head all nappy like that?

BENEATHA (*looking at George*): That's up to George. If he's ashamed of his heritage —

GEORGE: Oh, don't be so proud of yourself, Bennie — just because you look eccentric.

BENEATHA: How can something that's natural be eccentric?

GEORGE: That's what being eccentric means — being natural. Get dressed.

BENEATHA: I don't like that, George.

RUTH: Why must you and your brother make an argument out of everything people say?

BENEATHA: Because I hate assimilationist Negroes!

RUTH: Will somebody please tell me what assimila-whoever means!

GEORGE: Oh, it's just a college girl's way of calling people Uncle Toms — but that isn't what it means at all.

RUTH: Well, what does it mean?

BENEATHA (*cutting George off and staring at him as she replies to Ruth*): It means someone who is willing to give up his own culture and submerge himself completely in the dominant, and in this case *oppressive* culture!

GEORGE: Oh, dear, dear, dear! Here we go! A lecture on the African past! On our Great West African Heritage! In one second we will hear all about the great Ashanti empires; the great Songhay civilizations; and the great sculpture of Bénin — and then some poetry in the Bantu — and the whole monologue will end with the word *heritage*! (*Nastily.*) Let's face it, baby, your heritage is nothing but a bunch of raggedy-assed spirituals and some grass huts!

BENEATHA: GRASS HUTS! (*Ruth crosses to her and forcibly pushes her toward the bedroom.*) See there . . . you are standing there in your splendid ignorance talking about people who were the first to smelt iron on the face of the earth! (*Ruth is pushing her through the door.*) The Ashanti were performing surgical operations when the English — (*Ruth pulls the door to, with Beneatha on the other side, and smiles graciously at George. Beneatha opens the door and shouts the end of the sentence defiantly at George*) — were still tatooing themselves with blue dragons! (*She goes back inside.*)

RUTH: Have a seat, George. (*They both sit. Ruth folds her hands rather primly on her lap, determined to demonstrate the civilization of the family.*) Warm, ain't it? I mean for September. (*Pause.*) Just like they always say about Chicago weather: If it's too hot or cold for you, just wait a minute and it'll change. (*She smiles happily at this cliché of clichés.*) Everybody say it's got to do with them bombs and things they keep setting off. (*Pause.*) Would you like a nice cold beer?

GEORGE: No, thank you. I don't care for beer. (*He looks at his watch.*) I hope she hurries up.

RUTH: What time is the show?

GEORGE: It's an eight-thirty curtain. That's just Chicago, though. In New York standard curtain time is eight forty.

(*He is rather proud of this knowledge.*)

RUTH (*properly appreciating it*): You get to New York a lot?

GEORGE (*offhand*): Few times a year.

RUTH: Oh — that's nice. I've never been to New York.

(*Walter enters. We feel he has relieved himself, but the edge of unreality is still with him.*)

WALTER: New York ain't got nothing Chicago ain't. Just a bunch of hustling people all squeezed up together — being "Eastern."

(*He turns his face into a screw of displeasure.*)

GEORGE: Oh — you've been?

WALTER: *Plenty* of times.

RUTH (*shocked at the lie*): Walter Lee Younger!

WALTER (*staring her down*): Plenty! (*Pause.*) What we got to drink in this house? Why don't you offer this man some refreshment. (*To George.*) They don't know how to entertain people in this house, man.

GEORGE: Thank you — I don't really care for anything.

WALTER (*feeling his head; sobriety coming*): Where's Mama?

RUTH: She ain't come back yet.

WALTER (*looking Murchison over from head to toe, scrutinizing his carefully casual tweed sports jacket over cashmere V-neck sweater over soft eyelet shirt and tie, and soft slacks, finished off with white buckskin shoes*): Why all you college boys wear them faggoty-looking white shoes?

RUTH: Walter Lee!

(*George Murchison ignores the remark.*)

WALTER (*to Ruth*): Well, they look crazy as hell — white shoes, cold as it is.

RUTH (*crushed*): You have to excuse him —

WALTER: No he don't! Excuse me for what? What you always excusing me for! I'll excuse myself when I needs to be excused! (*A pause.*) They look as funny as them black knee socks Beneatha wears out of here all the time.

RUTH: It's the college *style*, Walter.

WALTER: Style, hell. She looks like she got burnt legs or something!

RUTH: Oh, Walter —

WALTER (*an irritable mimic*): Oh, Walter! Oh, Walter! (*To Murchison.*) How's your old man making out? I understand you all going to buy that big hotel on the Drive? (*He finds a beer in the refrigerator, wanders over to Murchison, sipping and wiping his lips with the back of his hand, and straddling a chair backward to talk to the other man.*) Shrewd move. Your old man is all right, man. (*Tapping his head and half winking for emphasis.*) I mean he knows how to operate. I mean he thinks *big*, you know what I mean, I mean for a *home*, you know? But I think he's kind of running out of ideas now. I'd like to talk to him. Listen, man, I got some plans that could turn this city upside down. I mean think like he does. *Big*. Invest big, gamble big, hell, lose *big* if you have to, you know what I mean. It's hard to find a man on this whole Southside who understands my kind of thinking — you dig? (*He scrutinizes Murchison again, drinks his beer, squints his eyes, and leans in close, confidential, man to man.*) Me and you ought to sit down and talk sometimes, man. Man, I got me some ideas . . .

MURCHISON (*with boredom*): Yeah — sometimes we'll have to do that, Walter.

WALTER (*understanding the indifference, and offended*): Yeah — well, when you get the time, man. I know you a busy little boy.

RUTH: Walter, please —

WALTER (*bitterly, hurt*): I know ain't nothing in this world as busy as you colored college boys with your fraternity pins and white shoes . . .

RUTH (*covering her face with humiliation*): Oh, Walter Lee —

WALTER: I see you all all the time — with the books tucked under your arms — going to your (*British A — a mimic*) "clahsses." And for what! What the hell you learning over there? Filling up your heads — (*counting off on his fingers*) — with the sociology and the psychology — but they teaching you how to be a man? How to take over and run the world? They teaching you how to run a rubber plantation or a steel mill? Naw — just to talk proper and read books and wear them faggoty-looking white shoes . . .

GEORGE (*looking at him with distaste, a little above it all*): You're all wacked up with bitterness, man.

WALTER (*intently, almost quietly, between the teeth, glaring at the boy*): And you — ain't you bitter, man? Ain't you just about had it yet? Don't you see no stars gleaming that you can't reach out and grab? You happy? — You contented son-of-a-bitch — you happy? You got it made? Bitter? Man, I'm a volcano. Bitter? Here I am a giant — surrounded by ants! Ants who can't even understand what it is the giant is talking about.

RUTH (*passionately and suddenly*): Oh, Walter — ain't you with nobody!

WALTER (*violently*): No! 'Cause ain't nobody with me! Not even my own mother!

RUTH: Walter, that's a terrible thing to say!

(*Beneatha enters, dressed for the evening in a cocktail dress and earrings, hair natural.*)

GEORGE: Well — hey — (*Crosses to Beneatha; thoughtful, with emphasis, since this is a reversal.*) You look great!

WALTER (*seeing his sister's hair for the first time*): What's the matter with your head?

BENEATHA (*tired of the jokes now*): I cut it off, Brother.

WALTER (*coming close to inspect it and walking around her*): Well, I'll be damned. So that's what they mean by the African bush . . .

BENEATHA: Ha ha. Let's go, George.

GEORGE (*looking at her*): You know something? I like it. It's sharp. I mean it really is. (*Helps her into her wrap.*)

RUTH: Yes — I think so, too. (*She goes to the mirror and starts to clutch at her hair.*)

WALTER: Oh no! You leave yours alone, baby. You might turn out to have a pin-shaped head or something!

BENEATHA: See you all later.

RUTH: Have a nice time.

GEORGE: Thanks. Good night. (*Half out the door, he reopens it. To Walter.*) Good night, Prometheus!°

(*Beneatha and George exit.*)

WALTER (*to Ruth*): Who is Prometheus?

RUTH: I don't know. Don't worry about it.

WALTER (*in fury, pointing after George*): See there — they get to a point where they can't insult you man to man — they got to go talk about something ain't nobody never heard of!

RUTH: How do you know it was an insult? (*To humor him.*) Maybe Prometheus is a nice fellow.

WALTER: Prometheus! I bet there ain't even no such thing! I bet that simple-minded clown —

RUTH: Walter —

(*She stops what she is doing and looks at him.*)

WALTER (*yelling*): Don't start!

RUTH: Start what?

WALTER: Your nagging! Where was I? Who was I with? How much money did I spend?

RUTH (*plaintively*): Walter Lee — why don't we just try to talk about it . . .

WALTER (*not listening*): I been out talking with people who understand me. People who care about the things I got on my mind.

RUTH (*wearily*): I guess that means people like Willy Harris.

WALTER: Yes, people like Willy Harris.

RUTH (*with a sudden flash of impatience*): Why don't you all just hurry up and go into the banking business and stop talking about it!

WALTER: Why? You want to know why? 'Cause we all tied up in a race of people that don't know how to do nothing but moan, pray, and have babies!

(*The line is too bitter even for him and he looks at her and sits down.*)

RUTH: Oh, Walter . . . (*Softly.*) Honey, why can't you stop fighting me?

WALTER (*without thinking*): Who's fighting you? Who even cares about you?

(*This line begins the retardation of his mood.*)

RUTH: Well — (*She waits a long time, and then with resignation starts to put away her things.*) I guess I might as well go on to bed . . . (*More or less to herself.*) I don't know where we lost it . . . but we have . . . (*Then, to him.*) I — I'm sorry about this

Prometheus: A shrewd and inventive god noted for stealing fire from the heavens and giving it to humans.

new baby, Walter. I guess maybe I better go on and do what I started . . . I guess I just didn't realize how bad things was with us . . . I guess I just didn't really realize — (*She starts out to the bedroom and stops.*) You want some hot milk?

WALTER: Hot milk?

RUTH: Yes — hot milk.

WALTER: Why hot milk?

RUTH: 'Cause after all that liquor you come home with you ought to have something hot in your stomach.

WALTER: I don't want no milk.

RUTH: You want some coffee then?

WALTER: No, I don't want no coffee. I don't want nothing hot to drink. (*Almost plaintively.*) Why you always trying to give me something to eat?

RUTH (*standing and looking at him helplessly*): What else can I give you, Walter Lee Younger?

(*She stands and looks at him and presently turns to go out again. He lifts his head and watches her going away from him in a new mood which began to emerge when he asked her "Who cares about you?"*)

WALTER: It's been rough, ain't it, baby? (*She hears and stops but does not turn around and he continues to her back.*) I guess between two people there ain't never as much understood as folks generally thinks there is. I mean like between me and you — (*She turns to face him.*) How we gets to the place where we scared to talk softness to each other. (*He waits, thinking hard himself.*) Why you think it got to be like that? (*He is thoughtful, almost as a child would be.*) Ruth, what is it gets into people ought to be close?

RUTH: I don't know, honey. I think about it a lot.

WALTER: On account of you and me, you mean? The way things are with us. The way something done come down between us.

RUTH: There ain't so much between us, Walter . . . Not when you come to me and try to talk to me. Try to be with me . . . a little even.

WALTER (*total honesty*): Sometimes . . . sometimes . . . I don't even know how to try.

RUTH: Walter —

WALTER: Yes?

RUTH (*coming to him, gently and with misgiving, but coming to him*): Honey . . . life don't have to be like this. I mean sometimes people can do things so that things are better . . . You remember how we used to talk when Travis was born . . . about the way we were going to live . . . the kind of house . . . (*She is stroking his head.*) Well, it's all starting to slip away from us . . .

(*He turns her to him and they look at each other and*

kiss, tenderly and hungrily. The door opens and Mama enters — Walter breaks away and jumps up. A beat.*)

WALTER: Mama, where have you been?

MAMA: My — them steps is longer than they used to be. Whew! (*She sits down and ignores him.*) How you feeling this evening, Ruth?

(*Ruth shrugs, disturbed at having been interrupted and watching her husband knowingly.*)

WALTER: Mama, where have you been all day?

MAMA (*still ignoring him and leaning on the table and changing to more comfortable shoes*): Where's Travis?

RUTH: I let him go out earlier and he ain't come back yet. Boy, is he going to get it!

WALTER: Mama!

MAMA (*as if she has heard him for the first time*): Yes, son?

WALTER: Where did you go this afternoon?

MAMA: I went downtown to tend to some business that I had to tend to.

WALTER: What kind of business?

MAMA: You know better than to question me like a child, Brother.

WALTER (*rising and bending over the table*): Where were you, Mama? (*Bringing his fists down and shouting.*) Mama, you didn't go do something with that insurance money, something crazy?

(*The front door opens slowly, interrupting him, and Travis peeks his head in, less than hopefully.*)

TRAVIS (*to his mother*): Mama, I —

RUTH: "Mama I" nothing! You're going to get it, boy! Get on in that bedroom and get yourself ready!

TRAVIS: But I —

MAMA: Why don't you all never let the child explain hisself.

RUTH: Keep out of it now, Lena.

(*Mama clamps her lips together, and Ruth advances toward her son menacingly.*)

RUTH: A thousand times I have told you not to go off like that —

MAMA (*holding out her arms to her grandson*): Well — at least let me tell him something. I want him to be the first one to hear . . . Come here, Travis. (*The boy obeys, gladly.*) Travis — (*she takes him by the shoulder and looks into his face*) — you know that money we got in the mail this morning?

TRAVIS: Yes'm —

MAMA: Well — what you think your grandmama gone and done with that money?

TRAVIS: I don't know, Grandmama.

MAMA (*putting her finger on his nose for emphasis*):

She went out and she bought you a house! (*The explosion comes from Walter at the end of the revelation and he jumps up and turns away from all of them in a fury. Mama continues, to Travis.*) You glad about the house? It's going to be yours when you get to be a man.

TRAVIS: Yeah — I always wanted to live in a house.

MAMA: All right, gimme some sugar then — (*Travis puts his arms around her neck as she watches her son over the boy's shoulder. Then, to Travis, after the embrace.*) Now when you say your prayers tonight, you thank God and your grandfather — 'cause it was him who give you the house — in his way.

RUTH (*taking the boy from Mama and pushing him toward the bedroom*): Now you get out of here and get ready for your beating.

TRAVIS: Aw, Mama —

RUTH: Get on in there — (*Closing the door behind him and turning radiantly to her mother-in-law.*) So you went and did it!

MAMA (*quietly, looking at her son with pain*): Yes, I did.

RUTH (*raising both arms classically*): PRAISE GOD! (*Looks at Walter a moment, who says nothing. She crosses rapidly to her husband.*) Please, honey — let me be glad . . . you be glad too. (*She has laid her hands on his shoulders, but he shakes himself free of her roughly, without turning to face her.*) Oh, Walter . . . a home . . . a home. (*She comes back to Mama.*) Well — where is it? How big is it? How much it going to cost?

MAMA: Well —

RUTH: When we moving?

MAMA (*smiling at her*): First of the month.

RUTH (*throwing back her head with jubilance*): *Praise God!*

MAMA (*tentatively, still looking at her son's back turned against her and Ruth*): It's — it's a nice house too . . . (*She cannot help speaking directly to him. An imploring quality in her voice, her manner, makes her almost like a girl now.*) Three bedrooms — nice big one for you and Ruth . . . Me and Beneatha still have to share our room, but Travis have one of his own — and (*with difficulty*) I figure if the — new baby — is a boy, we could get one of them double-decker outfits . . . And there's a yard with a little patch of dirt where I could maybe get to grow me a few flowers . . . And a nice big basement . . .

RUTH: Walter honey, be glad —

MAMA (*still to his back, fingering things on the table*): 'Course I don't want to make it sound fancier than it is . . . It's just a plain little old house — but it's made good and solid — and it will be *ours*. Walter

Lee — it makes a difference in a man when he can walk on floors that belong to *him* . . .

RUTH: Where is it?

MAMA (*frightened at this telling*): Well — well — it's out there in Clybourne Park —

(*Ruth's radiance fades abruptly, and Walter finally turns slowly to face his mother with incredulity and hostility.*)

RUTH: Where?

MAMA (*matter-of-factly*): Four o six Clybourne Street, Clybourne Park.

RUTH: Clybourne Park? Mama, there ain't no colored people living in Clybourne Park.

MAMA (*almost idiotically*): Well, I guess there's going to be some now.

WALTER (*bitterly*): So that's the peace and comfort you went out and bought for us today!

MAMA (*raising her eyes to meet his finally*): Son — I just tried to find the nicest place for the least amount of money for my family.

RUTH (*trying to recover from the shock*): Well — well — 'course I ain't one never been 'fraid of no crackers,° mind you — but — well, wasn't there no other houses nowhere?

MAMA: Them houses they put up for colored in them areas way out all seem to cost twice as much as other houses. I did the best I could.

RUTH (*struck senseless with the news, in its various degrees of goodness and trouble, she sits a moment, her fists propping her chin in thought, and then she starts to rise, bringing her fists down with vigor, the radiance spreading from cheek to cheek again*): Well — well — All I can say is — if this is my time in life — MY TIME — to say good-bye — (*and she builds with momentum as she starts to circle the room with an exuberant, almost tearfully happy release*) — to these Goddamned cracking walls! — (*she pounds the walls*) — and these marching roaches! — (*she wipes at an imaginary army of marching roaches*) — and this cramped little closet which ain't now or never was no kitchen! . . . then I say it loud and good, HALLELUJAH! AND GOOD-BYE MISERY . . . I DON'T NEVER WANT TO SEE YOUR UGLY FACE AGAIN! (*She laughs joyously, having practically destroyed the apartment, and flings her arms up and lets them come down happily, slowly, reflectively, over her abdomen, aware for the first time perhaps that the life therein pulses with happiness and not despair.*) Lena?

MAMA (*moved, watching her happiness*): Yes, honey?

---

crackers: White people, often used to refer disparagingly to poor whites.

RUTH (*looking off*): Is there — is there a whole lot of sunlight?

MAMA (*understanding*): Yes, child, there's a whole lot of sunlight.

(*Long pause.*)

RUTH (*collecting herself and going to the door of the room Travis is in*): Well — I guess I better see 'bout Travis. (*To Mama.*) Lord, I sure don't feel like whipping nobody today!

(*She exits.*)

MAMA (*the mother and son are left alone now and the mother waits a long time, considering deeply, before she speaks*): Son — you — you understand what I done, don't you? (*Walter is silent and sullen.*) I — I just seen my family falling apart today . . . just falling to pieces in front of my eyes . . . We couldn't of gone on like we was today. We was going backwards 'stead of forwards — talking 'bout killing babies and wishing each other was dead . . . When it gets like that in life — you just got to do something different, push on out and do something bigger . . . (*She waits.*) I wish you say something, son . . . I wish you'd say how deep inside you you think I done the right thing —

WALTER (*crossing slowly to his bedroom door and finally turning there and speaking measuredly*): What you need me to say you done right for? *You* the head of this family. You run our lives like you want to. It was your money and you did what you wanted with it. So what you need for me to say it was all right for? (*Bitterly, to hurt her as deeply as he knows is possible.*) So you butchered up a dream of mine — you — who always talking 'bout your children's dreams . . .

MAMA: Walter Lee —

(*He just closes the door behind him. Mama sits alone, thinking heavily.*)

Scene II

(*Time: Friday night. A few weeks later.*)

(*At rise: Packing crates mark the intention of the family to move. Beneatha and George come in, presumably from an evening out again.*)

GEORGE: O.K. . . . O.K., whatever you say . . . (*They both sit on the couch. He tries to kiss her. She moves away.*) Look, we've had a nice evening; let's not spoil it, huh? . . .

(*He again turns her head and tries to nuzzle in and she turns away from him, not with distaste but with momentary lack of interest; in a mood to pursue what they were talking about.*)

BENEATHA: I'm *trying* to talk to you.

GEORGE: We always talk.

BENEATHA: Yes — and I love to talk.

GEORGE (*exasperated; rising*): I know it and I don't mind it sometimes . . . I want you to cut it out, see — The moody stuff, I mean. I don't like it. You're a nice-looking girl . . . all over. That's all you need, honey, forget the atmosphere. Guys aren't going to go for the atmosphere — they're going to go for what they see. Be glad for that. Drop the Garbo routine. It doesn't go with you. As for myself, I want a nice — (*groping*) — simple (*thoughtfully*) — sophisticated girl . . . not a poet — O.K.?

(*He starts to kiss her, she rebuffs him again, and he jumps up.*)

BENEATHA: Why are you angry, George?

GEORGE: Because this is stupid! I don't go out with you to discuss the nature of "quiet desperation" or to hear all about your thoughts — because the world will go on thinking what it thinks regardless —

BENEATHA: Then why read books? Why go to school?

GEORGE (*with artificial patience, counting on his fingers*): It's simple. You read books — to learn facts — to get grades — to pass the course — to get a degree. That's all — it has nothing to do with thoughts.

(*A long pause.*)

BENEATHA: I see. (*He starts to sit.*) Good night, George.

(*George looks at her a little oddly and starts to exit. He meets Mama coming in.*)

GEORGE: Oh — hello, Mrs. Younger.

MAMA: Hello, George, how you feeling?

GEORGE: Fine — fine, how are you?

MAMA: Oh, a little tired. You know them steps can get you after a day's work. You all have a nice time tonight?

GEORGE: Yes — a fine time. A fine time.

MAMA: Well, good night.

GEORGE: Good night. (*He exits. Mama closes the door behind her.*)

MAMA: Hello, honey. What you sitting like that for?

BENEATHA: I'm just sitting.

MAMA: Didn't you have a nice time?

BENEATHA: No.

MAMA: No? What's the matter?

BENEATHA: Mama, George is a fool — honest. (*She rises.*)

MAMA (*Hustling around unloading the packages she has entered with. She stops.*): Is he, baby?

BENEATHA: Yes.

(*Beneatha makes up Travis' bed as she talks.*)

MAMA: You sure?

BENEATHA: Yes.

MAMA: Well — I guess you better not waste your time with no fools.

(*Beneatha looks up at her mother, watching her put groceries in the refrigerator. Finally she gathers up her things and starts into the bedroom. At the door she stops and looks back at her mother.*)

BENEATHA: Mama —

MAMA: Yes, baby —

BENEATHA: Thank you.

MAMA: For what?

BENEATHA: For understanding me this time.

(*She exits quickly and the mother stands, smiling a little, looking at the place where Beneatha just stood. Ruth enters.*)

RUTH: Now don't you fool with any of this stuff, Lena —

MAMA: Oh, I just thought I'd sort a few things out. Is Brother here?

RUTH: Yes.

MAMA (*with concern*): Is he —

RUTH (*reading her eyes*): Yes.

(*Mama is silent and someone knocks on the door. Mama and Ruth exchange weary and knowing glances and Ruth opens it to admit the neighbor, Mrs. Johnson,° who is a rather squeaky wide-eyed lady of no particular age, with a newspaper under her arm.*)

MAMA (*changing her expression to acute delight and a ringing cheerful greeting*): Oh — hello there, Johnson.

JOHNSON (*this is a woman who decided long ago to be enthusiastic about EVERYTHING in life and she is inclined to wave her wrist vigorously at the height of her exclamatory comments*): Hello there, yourself! H'you this evening, Ruth?

RUTH (*not much of a deceptive type*): Fine, Mis' Johnson, h'you?

JOHNSON: Fine. (*Reaching out quickly, playfully, and patting Ruth's stomach.*) Ain't you starting to poke out none yet! (*She mugs with delight at the overfamiliar remark and her eyes dart around looking*

Mrs. Johnson: This character and the scene of her visit were cut from the original production and early editions of the play.

at the crates and packing preparation; Mama's face is a cold sheet of endurance.*) Oh, ain't we getting ready round here, though! Yessir! Lookathere! I'm telling you the Youngers is really getting ready to "move on up a little higher!" — Bless God!

MAMA (*a little drily, doubting the total sincerity of the Blesser*): Bless God.

JOHNSON: He's good, ain't He?

MAMA: Oh yes, He's good.

JOHNSON: I mean sometimes He works in mysterious ways . . . but He works, don't He!

MAMA (*the same*): Yes, he does.

JOHNSON: I'm just sooooooo happy for y'all. And this here child — (*about Ruth*) looks like she could just pop open with happiness, don't she. Where's all the rest of the family?

MAMA: Bennie's gone to bed —

JOHNSON: Ain't no . . . (*the implication is pregnancy*) sickness done hit you — I hope . . . ?

MAMA: No — she just tired. She was out this evening.

JOHNSON (*all is a coo, an emphatic coo*): Aw — ain't that lovely. She still going out with the little Murchison boy?

MAMA (*drily*): Ummmm huh.

JOHNSON: That's lovely. You sure got lovely children, Younger. Me and Isaiah talks all the time 'bout what fine children you was blessed with. We sure do.

MAMA: Ruth, give Mis' Johnson a piece of sweet potato pie and some milk.

JOHNSON: Oh honey, I can't stay hardly a minute — I just dropped in to see if there was anything I could do. (*Accepting the food easily.*) I guess y'all seen the news what's all over the colored paper this week . . .

MAMA: No — didn't get mine yet this week.

JOHNSON (*lifting her head and blinking with the spirit of catastrophe*): You mean you ain't read 'bout them colored people that was bombed out their place out there?

(*Ruth straightens with concern and takes the paper and reads it. Johnson notices her and feeds commentary.*)

JOHNSON: Ain't it something how bad these here white folks is getting here in Chicago! Lord, getting so you think you right down in Mississippi! (*With a tremendous and rather insincere sense of melodrama.*) 'Course I thinks it's wonderful how our folks keeps on pushing out. You hear some of these Negroes round here talking 'bout how they don't go where they ain't wanted and all that — but not me, honey! (*This is a lie.*) Wilhemenia Othella Johnson goes anywhere, any time she feels like it!

(*With head movement for emphasis.*) Yes I do! Why if we left it up to these here crackers, the poor niggers wouldn't have nothing — (*She clasps her hand over her mouth.*) Oh, I always forgets you don't 'low that word in your house.

MAMA (*quietly, looking at her*): No — I don't 'low it.

JOHNSON (*vigorously again*): Me neither! I was just telling Isaiah yesterday when he come using it in front of me — I said, "Isaiah, it's just like Mis' Younger says all the time —"

MAMA: Don't you want some more pie?

JOHNSON: No — no thank you; this was lovely. I got to get on over home and have my midnight coffee. I hear some people say it don't let them sleep but I finds I can't close my eyes right lessen I done had that laaaast cup of coffee . . . (*She waits. A beat. Undaunted.*) My Good-night coffee, I calls it!

MAMA (*with much eye-rolling and communication between herself and Ruth*): Ruth, why don't you give Mis' Johnson some coffee.

(*Ruth gives Mama an unpleasant look for her kindness.*)

JOHNSON (*accepting the coffee*): Where's Brother tonight?

MAMA: He's lying down.

JOHNSON: Mmmmmmm, he sure gets his beauty rest, don't he? Good-looking man. Sure is a good-looking man! (*Reaching out to pat Ruth's stomach again.*) I guess that's how come we keep on having babies around here. (*She winks at Mama.*) One thing 'bout Brother, he always know how to have a *good* time. And sooooo ambitious! I bet it was his idea y'all moving out to Clybourne Park. Lord — I bet this time next month y'all's names will have been in the papers plenty — (*Holding up her hands to mark off each word of the headline she can see in front of her.*) "NEGROES INVADE CLYBOURNE PARK — BOMBED!"

MAMA (*she and Ruth look at the woman in amazement*): We ain't exactly moving out there to get bombed.

JOHNSON: Oh, honey — you know I'm praying to God every day that don't nothing like that happen! But you have to think of life like it is — and these here Chicago peckerwoods is some baaaad peckerwoods.

MAMA (*wearily*): We done thought about all that Mis' Johnson.

(*Beneatha comes out of the bedroom in her robe and passes through to the bathroom. Mrs. Johnson turns.*)

JOHNSON: Hello there, Bennie!

BENEATHA (*crisply*): Hello, Mrs. Johnson.

JOHNSON: How is school?

BENEATHA (*crisply*): Fine, thank you. (*She goes out.*)

JOHNSON (*insulted*): Getting so she don't have much to say to nobody.

MAMA: The child was on her way to the bathroom.

JOHNSON: I know — but sometimes she act like ain't got time to pass the time of day with nobody ain't been to college. Oh — I ain't criticizing her none. It's just — you know how some of our young people gets when they get a little education. (*Mama and Ruth say nothing, just look at her.*) Yes — well. Well, I guess I better get on home. (*Unmoving.*) 'Course I can understand how she must be proud and everything — being the only one in the family to make something of herself. I know just being a chauffeur ain't never satisfied Brother none. He shouldn't feel like that, though. Ain't nothing wrong with being a chauffeur.

MAMA: There's plenty wrong with it.

JOHNSON: What?

MAMA: Plenty. My husband always said being any kind of a servant wasn't a fit thing for a man to have to be. He always said a man's hands was made to make things, or to turn the earth with — not to drive nobody's car for 'em — or — (*she looks at her own hands*) carry they slop jars. And my boy is just like him — he wasn't meant to wait on nobody.

JOHNSON (*rising, somewhat offended*): Mmmmmm-mmm. The Youngers is too much for me! (*She looks around.*) You sure one proud-acting bunch of colored folks. Well — I always thinks like Booker T. Washington said that time — "Education has spoiled many a good plow hand" —

MAMA: Is that what old Booker T. said?

JOHNSON: He sure did.

MAMA: Well, it sounds just like him. The fool.

JOHNSON (*indignantly*): Well — he was one of our great men.

MAMA: Who said so?

JOHNSON (*nonplussed*): You know, me and you ain't never agreed about some things, Lena Younger. I guess I better be going —

RUTH (*quickly*): Good night.

JOHNSON: Good night. Oh — (*Thrusting it at her.*) You can keep the paper! (*With a trill.*) 'Night.

MAMA: Good night, Mis' Johnson.

(*Mrs. Johnson exits.*)

RUTH: If ignorance was gold . . .

MAMA: Shush. Don't talk about folks behind their backs.

RUTH: You do.

MAMA: I'm old and corrupted. (*Beneatha enters.*) You was rude to Mis' Johnson, Beneatha, and I don't like it at all.

BENEATHA (*at her door*): Mama, if there are two things we, as a people, have got to overcome, one is the Klu Klux Klan — and the other is Mrs. Johnson. (*She exits.*)

MAMA: Smart aleck.

(*The phone rings.*)

RUTH: I'll get it.

MAMA: Lord, ain't this a popular place tonight.

RUTH (*at the phone*): Hello — Just a minute. (*Goes to door.*) Walter, it's Mrs. Arnold. (*Waits. Goes back to the phone. Tense.*) Hello. Yes, this is his wife speaking . . . He's lying down now. Yes . . . well, he'll be in tomorrow. He's been very sick. Yes — I know we should have called, but we were so sure he'd be able to come in today. Yes — yes, I'm very sorry. Yes . . . Thank you very much. (*She hangs up. Walter is standing in the doorway of the bedroom behind her.*) That was Mrs. Arnold.

WALTER (*indifferently*): Was it?

RUTH: She said if you don't come in tomorrow that they are getting a new man . . .

WALTER: Ain't that sad — ain't that crying sad.

RUTH: She said Mr. Arnold has had to take a cab for three days . . . Walter, you ain't been to work for three days! (*This is a revelation to her.*) Where you been, Walter Lee Younger? (*Walter looks at her and starts to laugh.*) You're going to lose your job.

WALTER: That's right . . . (*He turns on the radio.*)

RUTH: Oh, Walter, and with your mother working like a dog every day —

(*A steamy, deep blues pours into the room.*)

WALTER: That's sad too — Everything is sad.

MAMA: What you been doing for these three days, son?

WALTER: Mama — you don't know all the things a man what got leisure can find to do in this city . . . What's this — Friday night? Well — Wednesday I borrowed Willy Harris' car and I went for a drive . . . just me and myself and I drove and drove . . . Way out . . . way past South Chicago, and I parked the car and I sat and looked at the steel mills all day long. I just sat in the car and looked at them big black chimneys for hours. Then I drove back and I went to the Green Hat. (*Pause.*) And Thursday — Thursday I borrowed the car again and I got in it and I pointed it the other way and I drove the other way — for hours — way, way up to Wisconsin, and I looked at the farms. I just drove and looked at the farms. Then I drove back and I went to the Green Hat. (*Pause.*) And today — today I didn't get the car. Today I just walked. All over the Southside. And I looked at the Negroes and they looked at me and finally I just sat down on the curb at Thirty-ninth and South Parkway and I just sat there and watched the Negroes go by. And then I went to the Green Hat. You all sad? You all depressed? And you know where I am going right now —

(*Ruth goes out quietly.*)

MAMA: Oh, Big Walter, is this the harvest of our days?

WALTER: You know what I like about the Green Hat? I like this little cat they got there who blows a sax . . . He blows. He talks to me. He ain't but 'bout five feet tall and he's got a conked head and his eyes is always closed and he's all music —

MAMA (*rising and getting some papers out of her handbag*): Walter —

WALTER: And there's this other guy who plays the piano . . . and they got a sound. I mean they can work on some music . . . They got the best little combo in the world in the Green Hat . . . You can just sit there and drink and listen to them three men play and you realize that don't nothing matter worth a damn, but just being there —

MAMA: I've helped do it to you, haven't I, son? Walter I been wrong.

WALTER: Naw — you ain't never been wrong about nothing, Mama.

MAMA: Listen to me, now. I say I been wrong, son. That I been doing to you what the rest of the world been doing to you. (*She turns off the radio.*) Walter — (*She stops and he looks up slowly at her and she meets his eyes pleadingly.*) What you ain't never understood is that I ain't got nothing, don't own nothing, ain't never really wanted nothing that wasn't for you. There ain't nothing as precious to me . . . There ain't nothing worth holding on to, money, dreams, nothing else — if it means — if it means it's going to destroy my boy. (*She takes an envelope out of her handbag and puts it in front of him and he watches her without speaking or moving.*) I paid the man thirty-five hundred dollars down on the house. That leaves sixty-five hundred dollars. Monday morning I want you to take this money and take three thousand dollars and put it in a savings account for Beneatha's medical schooling. The rest you put in a checking account — with your name on it. And from now on any penny that come out of it or that go in it is for you to look after. For you to decide. (*She drops her hands a little helplessly.*) It ain't much, but it's all I got in the world and I'm putting it in your hands. I'm telling you to be the head of this family from now on like you supposed to be.

WALTER (*stares at the money*): You trust me like that, Mama?

MAMA: I ain't never stop trusting you. Like I ain't never stop loving you.

(*She goes out, and Walter sits looking at the money on the table. Finally, in a decisive gesture, he gets up and, in mingled joy and desperation, picks up the money. At the same moment, Travis enters for bed.*)

TRAVIS: What's the matter, Daddy? You drunk?

WALTER (*sweetly, more sweetly than we have ever known him*): No, Daddy ain't drunk. Daddy ain't going to never be drunk again . . .

TRAVIS: Well, good night, Daddy.

(*The father has come from behind the couch and leans over, embracing his son.*)

WALTER: Son, I feel like talking to you tonight.

TRAVIS: About what?

WALTER: Oh, about a lot of things. About you and what kind of man you going to be when you grow up. . . . Son — son, what do you want to be when you grow up?

TRAVIS: A bus driver.

WALTER (*laughing a little*): A what? Man, that ain't nothing to want to be!

TRAVIS: Why not?

WALTER: 'Cause, man — it ain't big enough — you know what I mean.

TRAVIS: I don't know then. I can't make up my mind. Sometimes Mama asks me that too. And sometimes when I tell her I just want to be like you — she says she don't want me to be like that and sometimes she says she does. . . .

WALTER (*gathering him up in his arms*): You know what, Travis? In seven years you going to be seventeen years old. And things is going to be very different with us in seven years, Travis. . . . One day when you are seventeen I'll come home — home from my office downtown somewhere —

TRAVIS: You don't work in no office, Daddy.

WALTER: No — but after tonight. After what your daddy gonna do tonight, there's going to be offices — a whole lot of offices. . . .

TRAVIS: What you gonna do tonight, Daddy?

WALTER: You wouldn't understand yet, son, but your daddy's gonna make a transaction . . . a business transaction that's going to change our lives. . . . That's how come one day when you 'bout seventeen years old I'll come home and I'll be pretty tired, you know what I mean, after a day of conferences and secretaries getting things wrong the way they do . . . 'cause an executive's life is hell, man — (*The more he talks the farther away he gets.*) And I'll pull the car up on the driveway . . . just a plain black Chrysler, I think, with white walls — no — black tires. More elegant. Rich people don't have

to be flashy . . . though I'll have to get something a little sportier for Ruth — maybe a Cadillac convertible to do her shopping in. . . . And I'll come up the steps to the house and the gardener will be clipping away at the hedges and he'll say, "Good evening, Mr. Younger." And I'll say, "Hello, Jefferson, how are you this evening?" And I'll go inside and Ruth will come downstairs and meet me at the door and we'll kiss each other and she'll take my arm and we'll go up to your room to see you sitting on the floor with the catalogues of all the great schools in America around you. . . . All the great schools in the world! And — and I'll say, all right son — it's your seventeenth birthday, what is it you've decided? . . . Just tell me where you want to go to school and you'll go. Just tell me, what it is you want to be — and you'll *be* it. . . . Whatever you want to be — Yessir! (*He holds his arms open for Travis.*) You just name it, son . . . (*Travis leaps into them*) and I hand you the world!

(*Walter's voice has risen in pitch and hysterical promise and on the last line he lifts Travis high.*)

Scene III

(*Time: Saturday, moving day, one week later.*)

(*Before the curtain rises, Ruth's voice, a strident, dramatic church alto, cuts through the silence.*)

(*It is, in the darkness, a triumphant surge, a penetrating statement of expectation: "Oh, Lord, I don't feel no ways tired! Children, oh, glory hallelujah!"*)

(*As the curtain rises we see that Ruth is alone in the living room, finishing up the family's packing. It is moving day. She is nailing crates and tying cartons. Beneatha enters, carrying a guitar case, and watches her exuberant sister-in-law.*)

RUTH: Hey!

BENEATHA (*putting away the case*): Hi.

RUTH (*pointing at a package*): Honey — look in that package there and see what I found on sale this morning at the South Center. (*Ruth gets up and moves to the package and draws out some curtains.*) Lookahere — hand-turned hems!

BENEATHA: How do you know the window size out there?

RUTH (*who hadn't thought of that*): Oh — Well, they bound to fit something in the whole house. Anyhow, they was too good a bargain to pass up. (*Ruth slaps her head, suddenly remembering something.*) Oh, Bennie — I meant to put a special note on that carton over there. That's your mama's good china and she wants 'em to be very careful with it.

BENEATHA: I'll do it.

(*Beneatha finds a piece of paper and starts to draw large letters on it.*)

RUTH: You know what I'm going to do soon as I get in that new house?

BENEATHA: What?

RUTH: Honey — I'm going to run me a tub of water up to here . . . (*With her fingers practically up to her nostrils.*) And I'm going to get in it — and I am going to sit . . . and sit . . . and sit in that hot water and the first person who knocks to tell *me* to hurry up and come out —

BENEATHA: Gets shot at sunrise.

RUTH (*laughing happily*): You said it, sister! (*Noticing how large Beneatha is absent-mindedly making the note.*) Honey, they ain't going to read that from no airplane.

BENEATHA (*laughing herself*): I guess I always think things have more emphasis if they are big, somehow.

RUTH (*looking up at her and smiling*): You and your brother seem to have that as a philosophy of life. Lord, that man — done changed so 'round here. You know — you know what we did last night? Me and Walter Lee?

BENEATHA: What?

RUTH (*smiling to herself*): We went to the movies. (*Looking at Beneatha to see if she understands.*) We went to the movies. You know the last time me and Walter went to the movies together?

BENEATHA: No.

RUTH: Me neither. That's how long it been. (*Smiling again.*) But we went last night. The picture wasn't much good, but that didn't seem to matter. We went — and we held hands.

BENEATHA: Oh, Lord!

RUTH: We held hands — and you know what?

BENEATHA: What?

RUTH: When we come out of the show it was late and dark and all the stores and things was closed up . . . and it was kind of chilly and there wasn't many people on the streets . . . and we was still holding hands, me and Walter.

BENEATHA: You're killing me.

(*Walter enters with a large package. His happiness is deep in him; he cannot keep still with his newfound exuberance. He is singing and wiggling and snapping his fingers. He puts his package in a corner and puts a phonograph record, which he has brought in with him, on the record player. As the music, soulful and sensuous, comes up he dances over to Ruth and tries to get her to dance with him. She gives in at last to his raunchiness and in a fit of giggling allows herself to be drawn into his mood. They dip and she melts into his arms in a classic, body-melding "slow drag."*)

BENEATHA (*regarding them a long time as they dance, then drawing in her breath for a deeply exaggerated comment which she does not particularly mean*): Talk about — olddddddddddd-fashionedddddddd — Negroes!

WALTER (*stopping momentarily*): What kind of Negroes?

(*He says this in fun. He is not angry with her today, nor with anyone. He starts to dance with his wife again.*)

BENEATHA: Old-fashioned.

WALTER (*as he dances with Ruth*): You know, when these *New Negroes* have their convention — (*pointing at his sister*) — that is going to be the chairman of the Committee on Unending Agitation. (*He goes on dancing, then stops.*) Race, race, race! . . . Girl, I do believe you are the first person in the history of the entire human race to successfully brainwash yourself. (*Beneatha breaks up and he goes on dancing. He stops again, enjoying his tease.*) Damn, even the N double A C P takes a holiday sometimes! (*Beneatha and Ruth laugh. He dances with Ruth some more and starts to laugh and stops and pantomimes someone over an operating table.*) I can just see that chick someday looking down at some poor cat on an operating table and before she starts to slice him, she says . . . (*pulling his sleeves back maliciously*) "By the way, what are your views on civil rights down there? . . ."

(*He laughs at her again and starts to dance happily. The bell sounds.*)

BENEATHA: Sticks and stones may break my bones but . . . words will never hurt me!

(*Beneatha goes to the door and opens it as Walter and Ruth go on with the clowning. Beneatha is somewhat surprised to see a quiet-looking middle-aged white man in a business suit holding his hat and a briefcase in his hand and consulting a small piece of paper.*)

MAN: Uh — how do you do, miss. I am looking for a Mrs. — (*he looks at the slip of paper*) Mrs. Lena Younger? (*He stops short, struck dumb at the sight of the oblivious Walter and Ruth.*)

BENEATHA (*smoothing her hair with slight embarrassment*): Oh — yes, that's my mother. Excuse me. (*She closes the door and turns to quiet the other two.*) Ruth! Brother! (*Enunciating precisely but soundlessly: "There's a white man at the door!" They stop dancing, Ruth cuts off the phonograph, Beneatha opens the door. The man casts a curious quick glance at all of them.*) Uh — come in please.

MAN (*coming in*): Thank you.

BENEATHA: My mother isn't here just now. Is it business?

MAN: Yes . . . well, of a sort.

WALTER (*freely, the Man of the House*): Have a seat. I'm Mrs. Younger's son. I look after most of her business matters.

(*Ruth and Beneatha exchange amused glances.*)

MAN (*regarding Walter, and sitting*): Well — My name is Karl Lindner . . .

WALTER (*stretching out his hand*): Walter Younger. This is my wife — (*Ruth nods politely*) — and my sister.

LINDNER: How do you do.

WALTER (*amiably, as he sits himself easily on a chair, leaning forward on his knees with interest and looking expectantly into the newcomer's face*): What can we do for you, Mr. Lindner!

LINDNER (*some minor shuffling of the hat and briefcase on his knees*): Well — I am a representative of the Clybourne Park Improvement Association —

WALTER (*pointing*): Why don't you sit your things on the floor?

LINDNER: Oh — yes. Thank you. (*He slides the briefcase and hat under the chair.*) And as I was saying — I am from the Clybourne Park Improvement Association and we have had it brought to our attention at the last meeting that you people — or at least your mother — has bought a piece of residential property at — (*he digs for the slip of paper again*) — four o six Clybourne Street . . .

WALTER: That's right. Care for something to drink? Ruth, get Mr. Lindner a beer.

LINDNER (*upset for some reason*): Oh — no, really. I mean thank you very much, but no thank you.

RUTH (*innocently*): Some coffee?

LINDNER: Thank you, nothing at all.

(*Beneatha is watching the man carefully.*)

LINDNER: Well, I don't know how much you folks know about our organization. (*He is a gentle man; thoughtful and somewhat labored in his manner.*) It is one of these community organizations set up to look after — oh, you know, things like block upkeep and special projects and we also have what we call our New Neighbors Orientation Committee . . .

BENEATHA (*drily*): Yes — and what do they do?

LINDNER (*turning a little to her and then returning the main force to Walter*): Well — it's what you might call a sort of welcoming committee, I guess. I mean they, we — I'm the chairman of the committee — go around and see the new people who move into the neighborhood and sort of give them the lowdown on the way we do things out in Clybourne Park.

BENEATHA (*with appreciation of the two meanings, which escape Ruth and Walter*): Un-huh.

LINDNER: And we also have the category of what the association calls — (*he looks elsewhere*) — uh — special community problems . . .

BENEATHA: Yes — and what are some of those?

WALTER: Girl, let the man talk.

LINDNER (*with understated relief*): Thank you. I would sort of like to explain this thing in my own way. I mean I want to explain to you in a certain way.

WALTER: Go ahead.

LINDNER: Yes. Well. I'm going to try to get right to the point. I'm sure we'll all appreciate that in the long run.

BENEATHA: Yes.

WALTER: Be still now!

LINDNER: Well —

RUTH (*still innocently*): Would you like another chair — you don't look comfortable.

LINDNER (*more frustrated than annoyed*): No, thank you very much. Please. Well — to get right to the point I — (*a great breath, and he is off at last*) I am sure you people must be aware of some of the incidents which have happened in various parts of the city when colored people have moved into certain areas — (*Beneatha exhales heavily and starts tossing a piece of fruit up and down in the air.*) Well — because we have what I think is going to be a unique type of organization in American community life — not only do we deplore that kind of thing — but we are trying to do something about it. (*Beneatha stops tossing and turns with a new and quizzical interest to the man.*) We feel — (*gaining confidence in his mission because of the interest in the faces of the people he is talking to*) — we feel that most of the trouble in this world, when you come right down to it — (*he hits his knee for emphasis*) — most of the trouble exists because people just don't sit down and talk to each other.

RUTH (*nodding as she might in church, pleased with the remark*): You can say that again, mister.

LINDNER (*more encouraged by such affirmation*): That we don't try hard enough in this world to understand the other fellow's problem. The other guy's point of view.

RUTH: Now that's right.

(*Beneatha and Walter merely watch and listen with genuine interest.*)

LINDNER: Yes — that's the way we feel out in Clybourne Park. And that's why I was elected to come here this afternoon and talk to you people. Friendly like, you know, the way people should talk to each other and see if we couldn't find some way to work this thing out. As I say, the whole business is a matter of *caring* about the other fellow. Anybody can see that you are a nice family of folks, hard-working and honest I'm sure. (*Beneatha frowns slightly, quizzically, her head tilted regarding him.*) Today everybody knows what it means to be on the outside of *something*. And of course, there is always somebody who is out to take advantage of people who don't always understand.

WALTER: What do you mean?

LINDNER: Well — you see our community is made up of people who've worked hard as the dickens for years to build up that little community. They're not rich and fancy people; just hard-working, honest people who don't really have much but those little homes and a dream of the kind of community they want to raise their children in. Now, I don't say we are perfect and there is a lot wrong in some of the things they want. But you've got to admit that a man, right or wrong, has the right to want to have the neighborhood he lives in a certain kind of way. And at the moment the overwhelming majority of our people out there feel that people get along better, take more of a common interest in the life of the community, when they share a common background. I want you to believe me when I tell you that race prejudice simply doesn't enter into it. It is a matter of the people of Clybourne Park believing, rightly or wrongly, as I say, that for the happiness of all concerned that our Negro families are happier when they live in their *own* communities.

BENEATHA (*with a grand and bitter gesture*): This, friends, is the Welcoming Committee!

WALTER (*dumfounded, looking at Lindner*): Is this what you came marching all the way over here to tell us?

LINDNER: Well, now we've been having a fine conversation. I hope you'll hear me all the way through.

WALTER (*tightly*): Go ahead, man.

LINDNER: You see — in the face of all the things I have said, we are prepared to make your family a very generous offer . . .

BENEATHA: Thirty pieces and not a coin less!

WALTER: Yeah!

LINDNER (*putting on his glasses and drawing a form out of the briefcase*): Our association is prepared, through the collective effort of our people, to buy the house from you at a financial gain to your family.

RUTH: Lord have mercy, ain't this the living gall!

WALTER: All right, you through?

LINDNER: Well, I want to give you the exact terms of the financial arrangement —

WALTER: We don't want to hear no exact terms of no arrangements. I want to know if you got any more to tell us 'bout getting together?

LINDNER (*taking off his glasses*): Well — I don't suppose that you feel . . .

WALTER: Never mind how I feel — you got any more to say 'bout how people ought to sit down and talk to each other? . . . Get out of my house, man.

(*He turns his back and walks to the door.*)

LINDNER (*looking around at the hostile faces and reaching and assembling his hat and briefcase*): Well — I don't understand why you people are reacting this way. What do you think you are going to gain by moving into a neighborhood where you just aren't wanted and where some elements — well — people can get awful worked up when they feel that their whole way of life and everything they've ever worked for is threatened.

WALTER: Get out.

LINDNER (*at the door, holding a small card*): Well — I'm sorry it went like this.

WALTER: Get out.

LINDNER (*almost sadly regarding Walter*): You just can't force people to change their hearts, son.

(*He turns and put his card on a table and exits. Walter pushes the door to with stinging hatred, and stands looking at it. Ruth just sits and Beneatha just stands. They say nothing. Mama and Travis enter.*)

MAMA: Well — this all the packing got done since I left out of here this morning. I testify before God that my children got all the energy of the *dead!* What time the moving men due?

BENEATHA: Four o'clock. You had a caller, Mama.

(*She is smiling, teasingly.*)

MAMA: Sure enough — who?

BENEATHA (*her arms folded saucily*): The Welcoming Committee.

(*Walter and Ruth giggle.*)

MAMA (*innocently*): Who?

BENEATHA: The Welcoming Committee. They said they're sure going to be glad to see you when you get there.

WALTER (*devilishly*): Yeah, they said they can't hardly wait to see your face.

(*Laughter.*)

MAMA (*sensing their facetiousness*): What's the matter with you all?

WALTER: Ain't nothing the matter with us. We just telling you 'bout the gentleman who came to see you this afternoon. From the Clybourne Park Improvement Association.

MAMA: What he want?

RUTH (*in the same mood as Beneatha and Walter*): To welcome you, honey.

WALTER: He said they can't hardly wait. He said the one thing they don't have, that they just *dying* to have out there is a fine family of fine colored people! (*To Ruth and Beneatha.*) Ain't that right!

RUTH (*mockingly*): Yeah! He left his card —

BENEATHA (*handing card to Mama*): In case.

(*Mama reads and throws it on the floor — understanding and looking off as she draws her chair up to the table on which she has put her plant and some sticks and some cord.*)

MAMA: Father, give us strength. (*Knowingly — and without fun.*) Did he threaten us?

BENEATHA: Oh — Mama — they don't do it like that anymore. He talked Brotherhood. He said everybody ought to learn how to sit down and hate each other with good Christian fellowship.

(*She and Walter shake hands to ridicule the remark.*)

MAMA (*sadly*): Lord, protect us . . .

RUTH: You should hear the money those folks raised to buy the house from us. All we paid and then some.

BENEATHA: What they think we going to do — eat 'em?

RUTH: No, honey, marry 'em.

MAMA (*shaking her head*): Lord, Lord, Lord . . .

RUTH: Well — that's the way the crackers crumble. (*A beat.*) Joke.

BENEATHA (*laughingly noticing what her mother is doing*): Mama, what are you doing?

MAMA: Fixing my plant so it won't get hurt none on the way . . .

BENEATHA: Mama, you going to take *that* to the new house?

MAMA: Un-huh —

BENEATHA: That raggedy-looking old thing?

MAMA (*stopping and looking at her*): It expresses ME!

RUTH (*with delight, to Beneatha*): So there, Miss Thing!

(*Walter comes to Mama suddenly and bends down behind her and squeezes her in his arms with all his strength. She is overwhelmed by the suddenness of it and, though delighted, her manner is like that of Ruth and Travis.*)

MAMA: Look out now, boy! You make me mess up my thing here!

WALTER (*his face lit, he slips down on his knees beside her, his arms still about her*): Mama . . . you know what it means to climb up in the chariot?

MAMA (*gruffly, very happy*): Get on away from me now . . .

RUTH (*near the gift-wrapped package, trying to catch Walter's eye*): Psst —

WALTER: What the old song say, Mama . . .

RUTH: Walter — Now?

(*She is pointing at the package.*)

WALTER (*speaking the lines, sweetly, playfully, in his mother's face*): I got wings . . . you got wings . . .
All God's Children got wings . . .

MAMA: Boy — get out of my face and do some work . . .

WALTER: When I get to heaven gonna put on my wings,
Gonna fly all over God's heaven . . .

BENEATHA (*teasingly, from across the room*): Everybody talking 'bout heaven ain't going there!

WALTER (*to Ruth, who is carrying the box across to them*): I don't know, you think we ought to give her that . . . Seems to me she ain't been very appreciative around here.

MAMA (*eyeing the box, which is obviously a gift*): What is that?

WALTER (*taking it from Ruth and putting it on the table in front of Mama*): Well — what you all think? Should we give it to her?

RUTH: Oh — she was pretty good today.

MAMA: I'll good you —

(*She turns her eyes to the box again.*)

BENEATHA: Open it, Mama.

(*She stands up, looks at it, turns, and looks at all of them, and then presses her hands together and does not open the package.*)

WALTER (*sweetly*): Open it, Mama. It's for you. (*Mama looks in his eyes. It is the first present in her life without its being Christmas. Slowly she opens her package and lifts out, one by one, a brand-new sparkling set of gardening tools. Walter continues, prodding.*) Ruth made up the note — read it . . .

MAMA (*picking up the card and adjusting her glasses*): "To our own Mrs. Miniver — Love from Brother, Ruth and Beneatha." Ain't that lovely . . .

TRAVIS (*tugging at his father's sleeve*): Daddy, can I give her mine now?

WALTER: All right, son. (*Travis flies to get his gift.*)

MAMA: Now I don't have to use my knives and forks no more . . .

WALTER: Travis didn't want to go in with the rest of us, Mama. He got his own. (*Somewhat amused.*) We don't know what it is . . .

TRAVIS (*racing back in the room with a large hatbox and putting it in front of his grandmother*): Here!

MAMA: Lord have mercy, baby. You done gone and bought your grandmother a hat?

TRAVIS (*very proud*): Open it!

(*She does and lifts out an elaborate, but very elaborate, wide gardening hat, and all the adults break up at the sight of it.*)

RUTH: Travis, honey, what is that?

TRAVIS (*who thinks it is beautiful and appropriate*): It's a gardening hat! Like the ladies always have on in the magazines when they work in their gardens.

BENEATHA (*giggling fiercely*): Travis — we were trying to make Mama Mrs. Miniver — not Scarlett O'Hara!

MAMA (*indignantly*): What's the matter with you all! This here is a beautiful hat! (*Absurdly.*) I always wanted me one just like it!

(*She pops it on her head to prove it to her grandson, and the hat is ludicrous and considerably oversized.*)

RUTH: Hot dog! Go, Mama!

WALTER (*doubled over with laughter*): I'm sorry, Mama — but you look like you ready to go out and chop you some cotton sure enough!

(*They all laugh except Mama, out of deference to Travis' feelings.*)

MAMA (*gathering the boy up to her*): Bless your heart — this is the prettiest hat I ever owned — (*Walter, Ruth, and Beneatha chime in — noisily, festively, and insincerely congratulating Travis on his gift.*) What are we all standing around here for? We ain't finished packin' yet. Bennie, you ain't packed one book.

(*The bell rings.*)

BENEATHA: That couldn't be the movers . . . it's not hardly two good yet —

(*Beneatha goes into her room. Mama starts for door.*)

WALTER (*turning, stiffening*): Wait — wait — I'll get it.

(*He stands and looks at the door.*)

MAMA: You expecting company, son?

WALTER (*just looking at the door*): Yeah — yeah . . .

(*Mama looks at Ruth, and they exchange innocent and unfrightened glances.*)

MAMA (*not understanding*): Well, let them in, son.

BENEATHA (*from her room*): We need some more string.

MAMA: Travis — you run to the hardware and get me some string cord.

(*Mama goes out and Walter turns and looks at Ruth. Travis goes to a dish for money.*)

RUTH: Why don't you answer the door, man?

WALTER (*suddenly bounding across the floor to embrace her*): 'Cause sometimes it hard to let the future begin! (*Stooping down in her face.*)

I got wings! You got wings!

All God's children got wings!

(*He crosses to the door and throws it open. Standing there is a very slight little man in a not too prosperous business suit and with haunted frightened eyes and a hat pulled down tightly, brim up, around his forehead. Travis passes between the men and exits. Walter leans deep in the man's face, still in his jubilance.*)

When I get to heaven gonna put on my wings, Gonna fly all over God's heaven . . .

(*The little man just stares at him.*)

Heaven —

(*Suddenly he stops and looks past the little man into the empty hallway.*) Where's Willy, man?

BOBO: He ain't with me.

WALTER (*not disturbed*): Oh — come on in. You know my wife.

BOBO (*dumbly, taking off his hat*): Yes — h'you, Miss Ruth.

RUTH (*quietly, a mood apart from her husband already, seeing Bobo*): Hello, Bobo.

WALTER: You right on time today . . . Right on time. That's the way! (*He slaps Bobo on his back.*) Sit down . . . lemme hear.

(*Ruth stands stiffly and quietly in back of them, as though somehow she senses death, her eyes fixed on her husband.*)

BOBO (*his frightened eyes on the floor, his hat in his hands*): Could I please get a drink of water, before I tell you about it, Walter Lee?

(*Walter does not take his eyes off the man. Ruth goes blindly to the tap and gets a glass of water and brings it to Bobo.*)

WALTER: There ain't nothing wrong, is there?

BOBO: Lemme tell you —

WALTER: Man — didn't nothing go wrong?

BOBO: Lemme tell you — Walter Lee. (*Looking at Ruth and talking to her more than to Walter.*) You know how it was. I got to tell you how it was. I mean first I got to tell you how it was all the way . . . I mean about the money I put in, Walter Lee . . .

WALTER (*with taut agitation now*): What about the money you put in?

BOBO: Well — it wasn't much as we told you — me

and Willy — (*He stops.*) I'm sorry, Walter. I got a bad feeling about it. I got a real bad feeling about it . . .

WALTER: Man, what you telling me about all this for? . . . Tell me what happened in Springfield . . .

BOBO: Springfield.

RUTH (*like a dead woman*): What was supposed to happen in Springfield?

BOBO (*to her*): This deal that me and Walter went into with Willy — Me and Willy was going to go down to Springfield and spread some money 'round so's we wouldn't have to wait so long for the liquor license . . . That's what we were going to do. Everybody said that was the way you had to do, you understand, Miss Ruth?

WALTER: Man — what happened down there?

BOBO (*a pitiful man, near tears*): I'm trying to tell you, Walter.

WALTER (*screaming at him suddenly*): THEN TELL ME, GODDAMMIT . . . WHAT'S THE MATTER WITH YOU?

BOBO: Man . . . I didn't go to no Springfield, yesterday.

WALTER (*halted, life hanging in the moment*): Why not?

BOBO (*the long way, the hard way to tell*): 'Cause I didn't have no reasons to . . .

WALTER: Man, what are you talking about!

BOBO: I'm talking about the fact that when I got to the train station yesterday morning — eight o'clock like we planned . . . Man — *Willy didn't never show up.*

WALTER: Why . . . where was he . . . where is he?

BOBO: That's what I'm trying to tell you . . . I don't know . . . I waited six hours . . . I called his house . . . and I waited . . . six hours . . . I waited in that train station six hours . . . (*Breaking into tears.*) That was all the extra money I had in the world . . . (*Looking up at Walter with the tears running down his face.*) Man, *Willy is gone.*

WALTER: Gone, what you mean Willy is gone? Gone where? You mean he went by himself. You mean he went off to Springfield by himself — to take care of getting the license — (*Turns and looks anxiously at Ruth.*) You mean maybe he didn't want too many people in on the business down there? (*Looks to Ruth again, as before.*) You know Willy got his own ways. (*Looks back to Bobo.*) Maybe you was late yesterday and he just went on down there without you. Maybe — maybe — he's been callin' you at home tryin' to tell you what happened or something. Maybe — maybe — he just got sick. He's somewhere — he's got to be somewhere. We just got to find him — me and you got to find him. (*Grabs Bobo senselessly by the collar and starts to shake him.*) We got to!

BOBO (*in sudden angry, frightened agony*): What's the matter with you, Walter! *When a cat take off with your money he don't leave you no road maps!*

WALTER (*turning madly, as though he is looking for Willy in the very room*): Willy! . . . Willy . . . don't do it . . . Please don't do it . . . Man, not with that money . . . Man, please, not with that money . . . Oh, God . . . Don't let it be true . . . (*He is wandering around, crying out for Willy and looking for him or perhaps for help from God.*) Man . . . I trusted you . . . Man, I put my life in your hands . . . (*He starts to crumple down on the floor as Ruth just covers her face in horror. Mama opens the door and comes into the room, with Beneatha behind her.*) Man . . . (*He starts to pound the floor with his fists, sobbing wildly.*) THAT MONEY IS MADE OUT OF MY FATHER'S FLESH ——

BOBO (*standing over him helplessly*): I'm sorry, Walter . . . (*Only Walter's sobs reply. Bobo puts on his hat.*) I had my life staked on this deal, too . . .

(*He exits.*)

MAMA (*to Walter*): Son — (*She goes to him, bends down to him, talks to his bent head.*) Son . . . Is it gone? Son, I gave you sixty-five hundred dollars. Is it gone? All of it? Beneatha's money too?

WALTER (*lifting his head slowly*): Mama . . . I never . . . went to the bank at all . . .

MAMA (*not wanting to believe him*): You mean . . . your sister's school money . . . you used that too . . . Walter? . . .

WALTER: Yessss! All of it . . . It's all gone . . .

(*There is total silence. Ruth stands with her face covered with her hands; Beneatha leans forlornly against a wall, fingering a piece of red ribbon from the mother's gift. Mama stops and looks at her son without recognition and then, quite without thinking about it, starts to beat him senselessly in the face. Beneatha goes to them and stops it.*)

BENEATHA: Mama!

(*Mama stops and looks at both of her children and rises slowly and wanders vaguely, aimlessly away from them.*)

MAMA: I seen . . . him . . . night after night . . . come in . . . and look at that rug . . . and then look at me . . . the red showing in his eyes . . . the veins moving in his head . . . I seen him grow thin and old before he was forty . . . working and working and working like somebody's old horse . . . killing himself . . . and you — you give it all away in a day — (*She raises her arms to strike him again.*)

BENEATHA: Mama —

MAMA: Oh, God . . . (*She looks up to Him.*) Look down here — and show me the strength.

BENEATHA: Mama —
MAMA (*folding over*): Strength . . .
BENEATHA (*plaintively*): Mama . . .
MAMA: Strength!

ACT III

(*An hour later.*)

(*At curtain, there is a sullen light of gloom in the living room, gray light not unlike that which began the first scene of Act I. At left we can see Walter within his room, alone with himself. He is stretched out on the bed, his shirt out and open, his arms under his head. He does not smoke, he does not cry out, he merely lies there, looking up at the ceiling, much as if he were alone in the world.*)

(*In the living room Beneatha sits at the table, still surrounded by the now almost ominous packing crates. She sits looking off. We feel that this is a mood struck perhaps an hour before, and it lingers now, full of the empty sound of profound disappointment. We see on a line from her brother's bedroom the sameness of their attitudes. Presently the bell rings and Beneatha rises without ambition or interest in answering. It is Asagai, smiling broadly, striding into the room with energy and happy expectation and conversation.*)

ASAGAI: I came over . . . I had some free time. I thought I might help with the packing. Ah, I like the look of packing crates! A household in preparation for a journey! It depresses some people . . . but for me . . . it is another feeling. Something full of the flow of life, do you understand? Movement, progress . . . It makes me think of Africa.

BENEATHA: Africa!

ASAGAI: What kind of a mood is this? Have I told you how deeply you move me?

BENEATHA: He gave away the money, Asagai . . .

ASAGAI: Who gave away what money?

BENEATHA: The insurance money. My brother gave it away.

ASAGAI: Gave it away?

BENEATHA: He made an investment! With a man even Travis wouldn't have trusted with his most worn-out marbles.

ASAGAI: And it's gone?

BENEATHA: Gone!

ASAGAI: I'm very sorry . . . And you, now?

BENEATHA: Me? . . . Me? . . . Me, I'm nothing . . . Me. When I was very small . . . we used to take our sleds out in the wintertime and the only hills we had were the ice-covered stone steps of some houses down the street. And we used to fill them in with snow and make them smooth and slide down them all day . . . and it was very dangerous, you know

. . . far too steep . . . and sure enough one day a kid named Rufus came down too fast and hit the sidewalk and we saw his face just split open right there in front of us . . . And I remember standing there looking at his bloody open face thinking that was the end of Rufus. But the ambulance came and they took him to the hospital and they fixed the broken bones and they sewed it all up . . . and the next time I saw Rufus he just had a little line down the middle of his face . . . I never got over that . . .

ASAGAI: What?

BENEATHA: That that was what one person could do for another, fix him up — sew up the problem, make him all right again. That was the most marvelous thing in the world . . . I wanted to do that. I always thought it was the one concrete thing in the world that a human being could do. Fix up the sick, you know — and make them whole again. This was truly being God . . .

ASAGAI: You wanted to be God?

BENEATHA: No — I wanted to cure. It used to be so important to me. I wanted to cure. It used to matter. I used to care. I mean about people and how their bodies hurt . . .

ASAGAI: And you've stopped caring?

BENEATHA: Yes — I think so.

ASAGAI: Why?

BENEATHA (*bitterly*): Because it doesn't seem deep enough, close enough to what ails mankind! It was a child's way of seeing things — or an idealist's.

ASAGAI: Children see things very well sometimes — and idealists even better.

BENEATHA: I know that's what you think. Because you are still where I left off. You with all your talk and dreams about Africa! You still think you can patch up the world. Cure the Great Sore of Colonialism — (*loftily, mocking it*) with the Penicillin of Independence —!

ASAGAI: Yes!

BENEATHA: Independence *and then what?* What about all the crooks and thieves and just plain idiots who will come into power and steal and plunder the same as before — only now they will be black and do it in the name of the new Independence — WHAT ABOUT THEM?!

ASAGAI: That will be the problem for another time. First we must get there.

BENEATHA: And where does it end?

ASAGAI: End? Who even spoke of an end? To life? To living?

BENEATHA: An end to misery! To stupidity! Don't you see there isn't any real progress, Asagai, there is only one large circle that we march in, around and around, each of us with our own little picture in front of us — our own little mirage that we think is the future.

ASAGAI: That is the mistake.

BENEATHA: What?

ASAGAI: What you just said — about the circle. It isn't a circle — it is simply a long line — as in geometry, you know, one that reaches into infinity. And because we cannot see the end — we also cannot see how it changes. And it is very odd but those who see the changes — who dream, who will not give up — are called idealists . . . and those who see only the circle — we call *them* the "realists"!

BENEATHA: Asagai, while I was sleeping in that bed in there, people went out and took the future right out of my hands! And nobody asked me, nobody consulted me — they just went out and changed my life!

ASAGAI: Was it your money?

BENEATHA: What?

ASAGAI: Was it your money he gave away?

BENEATHA: It belonged to all of us.

ASAGAI: But did you earn it? Would you have had it at all if your father had not died?

BENEATHA: No.

ASAGAI: Then isn't there something wrong in a house — in a world — where all dreams, good or bad, must depend on the death of a man? I never thought to see *you* like this, Alaiyo. You! Your brother made a mistake and you are grateful to him so that now you can give up the ailing human race on account of it! You talk about what good is struggle, what good is anything! Where are we all going and why are we bothering!

BENEATHA: AND YOU CANNOT ANSWER IT!

ASAGAI (*shouting over her*): I LIVE THE ANSWER! (*Pause.*) In my village at home it is the exceptional man who can even read a newspaper . . . or who ever sees a book at all. I will go home and much of what I will have to say will seem strange to the people of my village. But I will teach and work and things will happen, slowly and swiftly. At times it will seem that nothing changes at all . . . and then again the sudden dramatic events which make history leap into the future. And then quiet again. Retrogression even. Guns, murder, revolution. And I even will have moments when I wonder if the quiet was not better than all that death and hatred. But I will look about my village at the illiteracy and disease and ignorance and I will not wonder long. And perhaps . . . perhaps I will be a great man . . . I mean perhaps I will hold on to the substance of truth and find my way always with the right course . . . and perhaps for it I will be butchered in my bed some night by the servants of empire . . .

BENEATHA: *The martyr!*

ASAGAI (*he smiles*): . . . or perhaps I shall live to be a very old man, respected and esteemed in my new nation . . . And perhaps I shall hold office and this is what I'm trying to tell you, Alaiyo: Perhaps the things I believe now for my country will be wrong and outmoded, and I will not understand and do terrible things to have things my way or merely to keep my power. Don't you see that there will be young men and women — not British soldiers then, but my own black countrymen — to step out of the shadows some evening and slit my then useless throat? Don't you see they have always been there . . . that they always will be. And that such a thing as my own death will be an advance? They who might kill me even . . . actually replenish all that I was.

BENEATHA: Oh, Asagai, I know all that.

ASAGAI: Good! Then stop moaning and groaning and tell me what you plan to do.

BENEATHA: Do?

ASAGAI: I have a bit of a suggestion.

BENEATHA: What?

ASAGAI (*rather quietly for him*): That when it is all over — that you come home with me —

BENEATHA (*staring at him and crossing away with exasperation*): Oh — Asagai — at this moment you decide to be romantic!

ASAGAI (*quickly understanding the misunderstanding*): My dear, young creature of the New World — I do not mean across the city — I mean across the ocean: home — to Africa.

BENEATHA (*slowly understanding and turning to him with murmured amazement*): To Africa?

ASAGAI: Yes! . . . (*Smiling and lifting his arms playfully.*) Three hundred years later the African Prince rose up out of the seas and swept the maiden back across the middle passage over which her ancestors had come —

BENEATHA (*unable to play*): To — to Nigeria?

ASAGAI: Nigeria. Home. (*Coming to her with genuine romantic flippancy.*) I will show you our mountains and our stars; and give you cool drinks from gourds and teach you the old songs and the ways of our people — and, in time, we will pretend that — (*very softly*) — you have only been away for a day. Say that you'll come — (*He swings her around and takes her full in his arms in a kiss which proceeds to passion.*)

BENEATHA (*pulling away suddenly*): You're getting me all mixed up —

ASAGAI: Why?

BENEATHA: Too many things — too many things have happened today. I must sit down and think. I don't know what I feel about anything right this minute.

(*She promptly sits down and props her chin on her fist.*)

ASAGAI (*charmed*): All right, I shall leave you. No — don't get up. (*Touching her, gently, sweetly.*) Just sit awhile and think . . . Never be afraid to sit awhile and think. (*He goes to door and looks at her.*) How often I have looked at you and said, "Ah — so this is what the New World hath finally wrought . . ."

(*He exits. Beneatha sits on alone. Presently Walter enters from his room and starts to rummage through things, feverishly looking for something. She looks up and turns in her seat.*)

BENEATHA (*hissingly*): Yes — just look at what the New World hath wrought! . . . Just look! (*She gestures with bitter disgust.*) There he is! *Monsieur le petit bourgeois noir°* — himself! There he is — Symbol of a Rising Class! Entrepreneur! Titan° of the system! (*Walter ignores her completely and continues frantically and destructively looking for something and hurling things to floor and tearing things out of their place in his search. Beneatha ignores the eccentricity of his actions and goes on with the monologue of insult.*) Did you dream of yachts on Lake Michigan, Brother? Did you see yourself on that Great Day sitting down at the Conference Table, surrounded by all the mighty bald-headed men in America? All halted, waiting, breathless, waiting for your pronouncements on industry? Waiting for you — Chairman of the Board! (*Walter finds what he is looking for — a small piece of white paper — and pushes it in his pocket and puts on his coat and rushes out without ever having looked at her. She shouts after him.*) I look at you and I see the final triumph of stupidity in the world!

(*The door slams and she returns to just sitting again. Ruth comes quickly out of Mama's room.*)

RUTH: Who was that?
BENEATHA: Your husband.
RUTH: Where did he go?
BENEATHA: Who knows — maybe he has an appointment at U.S. Steel.
RUTH (*anxiously, with frightened eyes*): You didn't say nothing bad to him, did you?
BENEATHA: Bad? Say anything bad to him? No — I told him he was a sweet boy and full of dreams and everything is strictly peachy keen, as the ofay° kids say!

Monsieur . . . noir: Mr. Black Middle Class.
Titan: Person of great power.
ofay: White person, usually used disparagingly.

(*Mama enters from her bedroom. She is lost, vague, trying to catch hold, to make some sense of her former command of the world, but it still eludes her. A sense of waste overwhelms her gait; a measure of apology rides on her shoulders. She goes to her plant, which has remained on the table, looks at it, picks it up and takes it to the window sill and sits it outside, and she stands and looks at it a long moment. Then she closes the window, straightens her body with effort, and turns around to her children.*)

MAMA: Well — ain't it a mess in here, though? (*A false cheerfulness, a beginning of something.*) I guess we all better stop moping around and get some work done. All this unpacking and everything we got to do. (*Ruth raises her head slowly in response to the sense of the line; and Beneatha in similar manner turns very slowly to look at her mother.*) One of you all better call the moving people and tell 'em not to come.
RUTH: Tell 'em not to come?
MAMA: Of course, baby. Ain't no need in 'em coming all the way here and having to go back. They charges for that too. (*She sits down, fingers to her brow, thinking.*) Lord, ever since I was a little girl, I always remembers people saying, "Lena — Lena Eggleston, you aims too high all the time. You needs to slow down and see life a little more like it is. Just slow down some." That's what they always used to say down home — "Lord, that Lena Eggleston is a high-minded thing. She'll get her due one day!"
RUTH: No, Lena . . .
MAMA: Me and Big Walter just didn't never learn right.
RUTH: Lena, no! We gotta go. Bennie — tell her . . . (*She rises and crosses to Beneatha with her arms outstretched. Beneatha doesn't respond.*) Tell her we can still move . . . the notes ain't but a hundred and twenty-five a month. We got four grown people in this house — we can work . . .
MAMA (*to herself*): Just aimed too high all the time —
RUTH (*turning and going to Mama fast — the words pouring out with urgency and desperation*): Lena — I'll work . . . I'll work twenty hours a day in all the kitchens in Chicago . . . I'll strap my baby on my back if I have to and scrub all the floors in America and wash all the sheets in America if I have to — but we got to MOVE! We got to get OUT OF HERE!!

(*Mama reaches out absently and pats Ruth's hand.*)

MAMA: No — I sees things differently now. Been thinking 'bout some of the things we could do to fix this place up some. I seen a second-hand bureau over on Maxwell Street just the other day that could fit right there. (*She points to where the new furniture might go. Ruth wanders away from her.*) Would need some new handles on it and then a little varnish and it look like something brand-new. And — we can put up them new curtains in the kitchen . . . Why this place be looking fine. Cheer us all up so that we forget trouble ever come . . . (*To Ruth.*) And you could get some nice screens to put up in your room round the baby's bassinet . . . (*She looks at both of them, pleadingly.*) Sometimes you just got to know when to give up some things . . . and hold on to what you got. . . .

(*Walter enters from the outside, looking spent and leaning against the door, his coat hanging from him.*)

MAMA: Where you been, son?

WALTER (*breathing hard*): Made a call.

MAMA: To who, son?

WALTER: To The Man. (*He heads for his room.*)

MAMA: What man, baby?

WALTER (*stops in the door*): The Man, Mama. Don't you know who The Man is?

RUTH: Walter Lee?

WALTER: *The Man.* Like the guys in the streets say — The Man. Captain Boss — Mistuh Charley . . . Old Cap'n Please Mr. Bossman . . .

BENEATHA (*suddenly*): Lindner!

WALTER: That's right! That's good. I told him to come right over.

BENEATHA (*fiercely, understanding*): For what? What do you want to see him for!

WALTER (*looking at his sister*): We going to do business with him.

MAMA: What you talking 'bout, son?

WALTER: Talking 'bout life, Mama. You all always telling me to see life like it is. Well — I laid in there on my back today . . . and I figured it out. Life just like it is. Who gets and who don't get. (*He sits down with his coat on and laughs.*) Mama, you know it's all divided up. Life is. Sure enough. Between the takers and the "tooken." (*He laughs.*) I've figured it out finally. (*He looks around at them.*) Yeah. Some of us always getting "tooken." (*He laughs.*) People like Willy Harris, they don't never get "tooken." And you know why the rest of us do? 'Cause we all mixed up. Mixed up bad. We get to looking 'round for the right and the wrong; and we worry about it and cry about it and stay up nights trying to figure out 'bout the wrong and the right of things all the time . . . And all the time, man, them takers is out there operating, just taking and taking. Willy Harris? Shoot — Willy Harris don't even count. He don't even count in the big

scheme of things. But I'll say one thing for old Willy Harris . . . he's taught me something. He's taught me to keep my eye on what counts in this world. Yeah — (*Shouting out a little.*) Thanks, Willy!

RUTH: What did you call that man for, Walter Lee?

WALTER: Called him to tell him to come on over to the show. Gonna put on a show for the man. Just what he wants to see. You see, Mama, the man came here today and he told us that them people out there where you want us to move — well they so upset they willing to pay us *not* to move! (*He laughs again.*) And — and oh, Mama — you would of been proud of the way me and Ruth and Bennie acted. We told him to get out . . . Lord have mercy! We told the man to get out! Oh, we was some proud folks this afternoon, yeah. (*He lights a cigarette.*) We were still full of that old-time stuff . . .

RUTH (*coming toward him slowly*): You talking 'bout taking them people's money to keep us from moving in that house?

WALTER: I ain't just talking 'bout it, baby — I'm telling you that's what's going to happen!

BENEATHA: Oh, God! Where is the bottom! Where is the real honest-to-God bottom so he can't go any farther!

WALTER: See — that's the old stuff. You and that boy that was here today. You all want everybody to carry a flag and a spear and sing some marching songs, huh? You wanna spend your life looking into things and trying to find the right and the wrong part, huh? Yeah. You know what's going to happen to that boy someday — he'll find himself sitting in a dungeon, locked in forever — and the takers will have the key! Forget it, baby! There ain't no causes — there ain't nothing but taking in this world, and he who takes most is smartest — and it don't make a damn bit of difference *how.*

MAMA: You making something inside me cry, son. Some awful pain inside me.

WALTER: Don't cry, Mama. Understand. That white man is going to walk in that door able to write checks for more money than we ever had. It's important to him and I'm going to help him . . . I'm going to put on the show, Mama.

MAMA: Son — I come from five generations of people who was slaves and sharecroppers — but ain't nobody in my family never let nobody pay 'em no money that was a way of telling us we wasn't fit to walk the earth. We ain't never been that poor. (*Raising her eyes and looking at him.*) We ain't never been that — dead inside.

BENEATHA: Well — we are dead now. All the talk about dreams and sunlight that goes on in this house. It's all dead now.

WALTER: What's the matter with you all! I didn't make this world! It was give to me this way! Hell, yes, I want me some yachts someday! Yes, I want to hang some real pearls 'round my wife's neck. Ain't she supposed to wear no pearls? Somebody tell me — tell me, who decides which women is suppose to wear pearls in this world. I tell you I am a *man* — and I think my wife should wear some pearls in this world!

(*This last line hangs a good while and Walter begins to move about the room. The word "Man" has penetrated his consciousness; he mumbles it to himself repeatedly between strange agitated pauses as he moves about.*)

MAMA: Baby, how you going to feel on the inside?

WALTER: Fine! . . . Going to feel fine . . . a man . . .

MAMA: You won't have nothing left then, Walter Lee.

WALTER (*coming to her*): I'm going to feel fine, Mama. I'm going to look that son-of-a-bitch in the eyes and say — (*he falters*) — and say, "All right, Mr. Lindner — (*he falters even more*) — that's *your* neighborhood out there! You got the right to keep it like you want! You got the right to have it like you want! Just write the check and — the house is yours." And — and I am going to say — (*His voice almost breaks.*) "And you — you people just put the money in my hand and you won't have to live next to this bunch of stinking niggers! . . ." (*He straightens up and moves away from his mother, walking around the room.*) And maybe — maybe I'll just get down on my black knees . . . (*He does so; Ruth and Bennie and Mama watch him in frozen horror.*) "Captain, Mistuh, Bossman — (*Groveling and grinning and wringing his hands in profoundly anguished imitation of the slow-witted movie stereotype.*) A-hee-hee-hee! Oh, yassuh boss! Yasssssuh! Great white — (*voice breaking, he forces himself to go on*) — Father, just gi' ussen de money, fo' God's sake, and we's — we's ain't gwine come out deh and dirty up yo' white folks neighborhood . . ." (*He breaks down completely.*) And I'll feel fine! Fine! FINE! (*He gets up and goes into the bedroom.*)

BENEATHA: That is not a man. That is nothing but a toothless rat.

MAMA: Yes — death done come in this here house. (*She is nodding, slowly, reflectively.*) Done come walking in my house on the lips of my children. You what supposed to be my beginning again. You — what supposed to be my harvest. (*To Beneatha.*) You — you mourning your brother?

BENEATHA: He's no brother of mine.

MAMA: What you say?

BENEATHA: I said that that individual in that room is no brother of mine.

MAMA: That's what I thought you said. You feeling like you better than he is today? (*Beneatha does not answer.*) Yes? What you tell him a minute ago? That he wasn't a man? Yes? You give him up for me? You done wrote his epitaph too — like the rest of the world? Well, who give you the privilege?

BENEATHA: Be on my side for once! You saw what he just did, Mama! You saw him — down on his knees. Wasn't it you who taught me to despise any man who would do that? Do what he's going to do?

MAMA: Yes — I taught you that. Me and your daddy. But I thought I taught you something else too . . . I thought I taught you to love him.

BENEATHA: Love him? There is nothing left to love.

MAMA: There is *always* something left to love. And if you ain't learned that, you ain't learned nothing. (*Looking at her.*) Have you cried for that boy today? I don't mean for yourself and for the family 'cause we lost the money. I mean for him: what he been through and what it done to him. Child, when do you think is the time to love somebody the most? When they done good and made things easy for everybody? Well then, you ain't through learning — because that ain't the time at all. It's when he's at his lowest and can't believe in hisself 'cause the world done whipped him so! When you starts measuring somebody, measure him right, child, measure him right. Make sure you done taken into account what hills and valleys he come through before he got to wherever he is.

(*Travis bursts into the room at the end of the speech, leaving the door open.*)

TRAVIS: Grandmama — the moving men are downstairs! The truck just pulled up.

MAMA (*turning and looking at him*): Are they, baby? They downstairs?

(*She sighs and sits. Lindner appears in the doorway. He peers in and knocks lightly, to gain attention, and comes in. All turn to look at him.*)

LINDNER (*hat and briefcase in hand*): Uh — hello . . .

(*Ruth crosses mechanically to the bedroom door and opens it and lets it swing open freely and slowly as the lights come up on Walter within, still in his coat, sitting at the far corner of the room. He looks up and out through the room to Lindner.*)

RUTH: He's here.

(*A long minute passes and Walter slowly gets up.*)

LINDNER (*coming to the table with efficiency, putting his briefcase on the table and starting to unfold papers and unscrew fountain pens*): Well, I certainly was glad to hear from you people. (*Walter has begun the trek out of the room, slowly and awkwardly, rather like a small boy, passing the back of his sleeve across his mouth from time to time.*) Life can really be so much simpler than people let it be most of the time. Well — with whom do I negotiate? You, Mrs. Younger, or your son here? (*Mama sits with her hands folded on her lap and her eyes closed as Walter advances. Travis goes closer to Lindner and looks at the papers curiously.*) Just some official papers, sonny —

RUTH: Travis, you go downstairs —

MAMA (*opening her eyes and looking into Walter's*): No. Travis, you stay right here. And you make him understand what you doing, Walter Lee. You teach him good. Like Willy Harris taught you. You show where our five generations done come to. (*Walter looks from her to the boy, who grins at him innocently.*) Go ahead, son — (*She folds her hands and closes her eyes.*) Go ahead.

WALTER (*at last crosses to Lindner, who is reviewing the contract*): Well, Mr. Lindner. (*Beneatha turns away.*) We called you — (*there is a profound, simple groping quality in his speech*) — because, well, me and my family (*he looks around and shifts from one foot to the other*) Well — we are very plain people . . .

LINDNER: Yes —

WALTER: I mean — I have worked as a chauffeur most of my life — and my wife here, she does domestic work in people's kitchens. So does my mother. I mean — we are plain people . . .

LINDNER: Yes, Mr. Younger —

WALTER (*really like a small boy, looking down at his shoes and then up at the man*): And — uh — well, my father, well, he was a laborer most of his life. . . .

LINDNER (*absolutely confused*): Uh, yes — yes, I understand. (*He turns back to the contract.*)

WALTER (*a beat; staring at him*): And my father — (*With sudden intensity.*) My father almost *beat a man to death* once because this man called him a bad name or something, you know what I mean?

LINDNER (*looking up, frozen*): No, no, I'm afraid I don't —

WALTER (*A beat. The tension hangs; then Walter steps back from it.*): Yeah. Well — what I mean is that we come from people who had a lot of *pride*. I mean — we are very proud people. And that's my sister over there and she's going to be a doctor — and we are very proud —

LINDNER: Well — I am sure that is very nice, but —

WALTER: What I am telling you is that we called you over here to tell you that we are very proud and that this — (*Signaling to Travis.*) Travis, come here. (*Travis crosses and Walter draws him before him facing the man.*) This is my son, and he makes the sixth generation our family in this country. And we have all thought about your offer —

LINDNER: Well, good . . . good —

WALTER: And we have decided to move into our house because my father — my father — he earned it for us brick by brick. (*Mama has her eyes closed and is rocking back and forth as though she were in church, with her head nodding the Amen yes.*) We don't want to make no trouble for nobody or fight no causes, and we will try to be good neighbors. And that's *all* we got to say about that. (*He looks the man absolutely in the eyes.*) We don't want your money. (*He turns and walks away.*)

LINDNER (*looking around at all of them*): I take it then — that you have decided to occupy . . .

BENEATHA: That's what the man said.

LINDNER (*to Mama in her reverie*): Then I would like to appeal to you, Mrs. Younger. You are older and wiser and understand things better I am sure . . .

MAMA: I am afraid you don't understand. My son said we was going to move and there ain't nothing left for me to say. (*Briskly.*) You know how these young folks is nowadays, mister. Can't do a thing with 'em! (*As he opens his mouth, she rises.*) Goodbye.

LINDNER (*folding up his materials*): Well — if you are that final about it . . . there is nothing left for me to say. (*He finishes, almost ignored by the family, who are concentrating on Walter Lee. At the door Lindner halts and looks around.*) I sure hope you people know what you're getting into.

(*He shakes his head and exits.*)

RUTH (*looking around and coming to life*): Well, for God's sake — if the moving men are here — LET'S GET THE HELL OUT OF HERE!

MAMA (*into action*): Ain't it the truth! Look at all this here mess. Ruth, put Travis' good jacket on him . . . Walter Lee, fix your tie and tuck your shirt in, you look like somebody's hoodlum! Lord have mercy, where is my plant? (*She flies to get it amid the general bustling of the family, who are deliberately trying to ignore the nobility of the past moment.*) You all start on down . . . Travis child, don't go empty-handed . . . Ruth, where did I put that box with my skillets in it? I want to be in charge of it myself . . . I'm going to make us the biggest dinner we ever ate tonight . . . Beneatha, what's the matter with them stockings? Pull them things up, girl . . .

(*The family starts to file out as two moving men appear and begin to carry out the heavier pieces of furniture, bumping into the family as they move about.*)

BENEATHA: Mama, Asagai asked me to marry him today and go to Africa —

MAMA (*in the middle of her getting-ready activity*): He did? You ain't old enough to marry nobody — (*Seeing the moving men lifting one of her chairs precariously.*) Darling, that ain't no bale of cotton, please handle it so we can sit in it again! I had that chair twenty-five years . . .

(*The movers sigh with exasperation and go on with their work.*)

BENEATHA (*girlishly and unreasonably trying to pursue the conversation*): To go to Africa, Mama — be a doctor in Africa . . .

MAMA (*distracted*): Yes, baby —

WALTER: *Africa!* What he want you to go to Africa for?

BENEATHA: To practice there . . .

WALTER: Girl, if you don't get all them silly ideas out your head! You better marry yourself a man with some loot . . .

BENEATHA (*angrily, precisely as in the first scene of the play*): What have you got to do with who I marry!

WALTER: Plenty. Now I think George Murchison —

BENEATHA: *George Murchison!* I wouldn't marry him if he was Adam and I was Eve!

(*Walter and Beneatha go out yelling at each other vigorously and the anger is loud and real till their voices diminish. Ruth stands at the door and turns to Mama and smiles knowingly.*)

MAMA (*fixing her hat at last*): Yeah — they something all right, my children . . .

RUTH: Yeah — they're something. Let's go, Lena.

MAMA (*stalling, starting to look around at the house*): Yes — I'm coming. Ruth —

RUTH: Yes?

MAMA (*quietly, woman to woman*): He finally come into his manhood today, didn't he? Kind of like a rainbow after the rain . . .

RUTH (*biting her lip lest her own pride explode in front of Mama*): Yes, Lena.

(*Walter's voice calls for them raucously.*)

WALTER (*offstage*): Y'all come on! These people charges by the hour, you know!

MAMA (*waving Ruth out vaguely*): All right, honey — go on down. I be down directly.

(*Ruth hesitates, then exits. Mama stands, at last alone in the living room, her plant on the table before her as the lights start to come down. She looks around at all the walls and ceilings and suddenly, despite herself, while the children call below, a great heaving thing rises in her and she puts her fist to her mouth to stifle it, takes a final desperate look, pulls her coat about her, pats her hat, and goes out. The lights dim down. The door opens and she comes back in, grabs her plant, and goes out for the last time.*)

Contemporary Drama

Experimentation

The experimentation in drama in the first half of the twentieth century has continued in contemporary drama. The achievements of Tennessee Williams, Arthur Miller, Harold Pinter, and other mid-century playwrights encouraged playwrights of the 1960s and 1970s to experiment more daringly. Performance pieces — plays that used texts only as starting points and improvised from them — were extremely popular in this period. Mixing media such as film, video, opera, rock, and other music with live actors was and still is an option for playwrights in the latter part of the twentieth century. However, most plays that have been celebrated by critics and audiences have been relatively traditional, building on the achievement of nineteenth-century realism and twentieth-century expressionism.

Since the 1960s, drama has developed in many different directions simultaneously. During the upheaval of the Vietnam War artists in every medium produced protests, and in drama the protests were especially powerful. Innumerable plays attacked the war, using some highly innovative techniques. Some of these techniques were drawn, directly or indirectly, from Brecht and involved short, detached scenes, barren stage settings, and music. Megan Terry's *Viet Rock* (1966) was a successful example of such antiwar plays.

Most of the interesting experimental theater was done in groups such as Richard Schechner's Performance Group, which created what Schechner called ENVIRONMENTAL THEATER in New York City in the late 1960s, and Jerzy Grotowski's Polish Laboratory Theatre in Wroclaw, Poland, during the same period. Ensembles like the Bread and Puppet Theatre, San Francisco Mime Troupe, and El Teatro Campesino on the West Coast, combined a radical political message with theatrical experimentation. The work of these groups is effective primarily at the level of performance; their texts are not representative of their impact on audiences.

Environmental
Theater

Schechner's most famous production, based on Euripides's *The Bacchae*, was *Dionysus in 69* (1969), in which Pentheus is torn to pieces in an impassioned frenzy. Part of the point of Schechner's production was to inspire the audience so much that they took the stage, becoming indistinguishable from the actors. Usually, such inspiration took control of everyone in the Garage, the performing space made from a garage in Greenwich Village where the group performed. The stage included the audience, so the actors could use all spaces available in the room and interact with audience members as they chose or as the performance called for. Jerry Rojo designed this innovative space, the Mobius Theater, with many levels, a central acting well that could be lighted, with the audience on all sides of the actors. The design has been adapted by many theatrical groups who were influenced by the theories of environmental drama.

Dionysus in 69 was an effort to draw on the same spiritual energies tapped by Greek drama by connecting with the feasts of Dionysus, god of wine and ecstasy. The play was a spontaneous and partly improvised performance piece rather than a text meant to be read. At one point the audience and actors disrobed in a simulation of a Greek religious orgy. Ordinarily, only a few audience members held back, and Schechner's goal of involving audience and actors in a pagan ritual was realized night after night during the run.

In a similar way, Julian Beck and Judith Malina's Living Theatre maintained a special relationship with the audience. Beck's plays were designed to break down the absolutes of dramatic space and audience space by having the actors roam through the audience and interact apparently at random with audience members. *Paradise Now* (1968) is his best-known play. Like Schechner's *Dionysus in 69*, it was essentially a performance piece. Certain segments were improvised; therefore, as a reading text, it has relatively little power.

But the Living Theatre normally worked with carefully written texts. Their first success was Jack Gelber's *The Connection* (1959), which created the illusion of a group of people working on a documentary film about drug addicts. The film crew interacted with the addicts sitting and waiting for their drug dealer to show up. In the audience, the filmmaker complained from time to time that the players were changing his script. A notable success, the play was followed by a string of further successes that toured all over the world. Although Beck did not know Antonin Artaud's theories when he began working in the Living Theatre, much of what he has done echoes Artaud's ideas. Beck made an effort to break down the rigid distinctions between audience and players and to avoid purely realistic theater, despite the early success of *The Connection*, which was largely but not entirely realistic. Beck's efforts to make individuals in the audience unsettled enough to feel occasionally threatened was also in keeping with Artaud's ideas.

"Poor Theater"

Grotowski's theater was called the "poor theater" because it was meant to contrast with the "rich theater" of the commercial stage, with its expensive lighting, decorated stages, rich costumes, numerous props, and elaborate settings. Grotowski had none of these. He deliberately avoided any of the trappings of the commercial stage because he was interested in stimulating the imagination of his audience. He was also interested in seeing how little he needed in order to produce a dramatic experience on stage. He followed the views of Artaud, whose notion of a theater of cruelty influenced much of the experimental theater of this period.

Grotowski's Laboratory Theatre, begun in 1959, relied on pre-existing texts but interpreted them broadly through a total reconception of their meaning. For example, Grotowski's *The Tragical Life of Doctor Faustus* (1963) took Marlowe's basic concepts and reinvented the play. For Grotowski, Faustus was a rebel saint, a character whose nobility was emotional and intellectual. Like every production of the Laboratory Theatre, the play was thought of as a developing drama around which training in acting — the cornerstone of Grotowski's achievement in theater — was structured.

One of Grotowski's best works, *Akropolis* (1962; revised frequently from 1963 to 1975) adapted an older Polish drama by Wyspianski (1904) and reset it in modern times in Auschwitz, with the actors, dressed in ragged sackcloth prison uniforms, looking wretched and starving. At the end of the play the prisoners follow a headless puppet-corpse, Christ, into an afterlife. They march in an eerie ritual procession offstage into the waiting prison camp ovens.

Grotowski's theater has been influential worldwide. When the Polish government clamped down on the Solidarity movement in the late 1970s, Grotowski left Poland. After 1970 Grotowski shifted his focus from public performances to small intense group workshops and, more recently, to the ritual performances of cultures from all over the world. The first phase of his work with the Laboratory Theatre has remained the most influential. One of his actors, Richard Cieslak, has traveled widely training people in Grotowski's methods.

Theater in the Round

Schechner's work depended on a stage space that merged audience and actors, but other companies have worked with a circular theater that, with variations, harks back to the Greeks' performing space. Theaters in the round have been built all over the world since the mid-1960s. These have not become the norm but rather an alternative to the eighteenth-century proscenium stage and the contemporary THRUST STAGE that has the audience on three sides. All of these are in active use in modern theater, both commercial and experimental.

The range of effects of the theater in the round is extraordinary. Peter Weiss's *Persecution and Assassination of Jean-Paul Marat as Per-*

formed by the Inmates of the Asylum of Charenton Under the Direction of the Marquis de Sade (1964), popularly known as *Marat/Sade*, was an especially notable success in such a theater. It was presented as a play within a play, and the actors, playing the insane, tried to establish relationships with nearby audience members and made them feel very uncomfortable. The action shifted in such a way that there was no "front" to the stage; all sides of the circle were appropriate focal points for viewing the drama.

Theater of Images

Robert Wilson has been experimenting in the 1970s and 1980s with repetitive narratives that sometimes take eight hours to perform. His multi-media dramas involve huge casts and ordinarily cover an immense historic range (Figure 8). One of his most extraordinary successes has been *Einstein on the Beach* (1976), an opera written in collaboration with composer Philip Glass. It is eight hours long and was originally produced in a conventional theater, but it uses dramatic techniques that involve extensive patterns of repetition, the creation of enigmatic and evocative images, and characters who are cartoon-like caricatures of historical people. The overall effect is hypnotic; one of the points of Wilson's work seems to be to induce a trancelike state in his audience.

Experimentation Within the Tradition

It is too soon to assess the direction in which current drama is heading, but playwrights are expressing more interest in traditional staging and traditional techniques. Within the Chekhovian/Brechtian traditions of modern drama, current playwrights have been finding considerable range of expression. Marsha Norman, who wrote *'night, Mother*, has said that her plays are "wildly traditional. I'm a purist about structure. Plays are like plane rides. You [the audience] buy the ticket and you have to get where the ticket takes you. Or else you've been had."

Yet these plays are not strictly traditional. Their level of realism is capable of surprising a middle class audience, especially since many of the best plays of this period have been by or about "outsiders" in the culture. Women, Blacks, Hispanics, Asian Americans, homosexuals, and others excluded from the mainstream of society have been producing extraordinary drama in English language theater.

Sam Shepard, one of the most prolific modern playwrights, certainly experiments with his material, much of which premiered in small theaters in Greenwich Village, such as the La Mama Experimental Theater. But his most widely known plays, among them *True West* (1980), are produced easily on conventional stages. Shepard's work is wide-ranging and challenging. His language is coarse, a representation of the way he has heard people speak, and the violence he portrays onstage is strong enough to alienate many in the audience. Shepard, important as he is, has not found a popular commercial audience for his plays. Much of Shepard's

Figure 8. Multi-media effects in Robert Wilson's CIVIL warS

early work uses rock and roll music and situations combining his own musical performance ability with his skills as a dramatist. At root, his work is always experimental.

True West, typical of his best work, presents a family that seems savagely split and unable to love or relate to one another. The scenes of physical and psychological violence are rather frightening. While they can be easily played in a proscenium theater or in a modern thrust stage, the audience does not enjoy the sense of security and comfort such staging usually provides.

Athol Fugard, the South African playwright, writes powerful plays that also work well on conventional proscenium stages. Like Shepard's, his subject matter is not the kind that permits an audience to sit back relaxed and appreciate the drama with a sense of detachment. Instead, the plays usually disturb audiences. His primary subject matter is the racial distress caused by apartheid in South Africa. Fugard's work with black actors in South Africa produced a vital experimental theater out of which his best early work grew.

The Blood Knot (1961) and *Boesman and Lena* (1969), part of a trilogy on South Africa, are based on the theme of racial discrimination. But other plays, such as *A Lesson from Aloes* (1978) and *The Road to Mecca* (1984), are involved with problems of individuals in relation to their political world. Fugard is in many ways a traditional playwright, except for his subject matter. His characters are thoroughly developed but with great economy; in *"MASTER HAROLD" . . . and the boys*, for example, we are given a deep understanding of Hally and Sam, whose relationship, past, present, and future, is the center of the play. Fugard is not writing the well-made play, any more than the other contemporary playwrights in this collection are. There is nothing "mechanical" in Fugard's work but rather a sense of organic growth, of actions arising from perceptible conditions and historical circumstances. These contribute to the sense of integrity that his plays communicate.

Some of Caryl Churchill's plays, emphasizing themes of socialism and feminism, were developed in workshops and collaborations with actors and directors. She experiments early in the first stages of preparation by spending time in the environments her plays depict. When she worked on *Top Girls* (1982) she came up with the idea of the employment agency after talking with many people whose lives are wrapped up in business. When she worked on *Serious Money* (1987), she and the group developing the play spent time at the London Stock Exchange, absorbing the atmosphere of frenetic buying and selling.

Churchill's plays emphasize experimentation within the tradition of the proscenium theater in which most of her work is produced. Actors sometimes play characters of the opposite sex, as in *Cloud Nine* (1979). Characters often speak simultaneously, as in *Top Girls,* producing something of the effect desired by the Dadaists. In some cases Churchill experiments with verse drama as a way of underscoring powerful disjunctions of expectation — as when, for example, her prosaic stockbrokers explain themselves in *Serious Money.*

Though she claims to be a traditionalist, Marsha Norman has written experimental plays. Her first success, *Getting Out* (1977), portrays the same character at two periods in her life — as an adolescent and as an adult — on separate parts of the stage at the same time. The effect is startling, but the structure of the play is clear and simple: Arlene is trying to start life over after leaving prison, while Arlie, her younger, rebellious self, is still with her, commenting on what she is doing. The play ends with a reconciliation of the two parts of the character.

In *'night, Mother*, Norman has produced another traditionally structured play. It respects the Aristotelian unities of time, place, and action, and it is confrontational. Thelma and her daughter, Jessie, are in a power struggle over Jessie's right to commit suicide. *'Night, Mother*'s technique is naturalistic, and its subject matter, as in the plays of Strindberg and Ibsen, is discomforting to its contemporary audiences.

The levels of shock in Martin Sherman's *Bent* (1979) may be so multilayered as to be difficult to sort out. The play begins with the homosexual lifestyle of Max and his lover Rudy, boldly treating the world of transvestites and gay clubs in prewar Nazi Germany. When Max and Rudy are discovered by the Nazis and suffer the fate that Hitler decreed for homosexuals, the play shifts to the madness of the concentration camp, where survival is the primary instinct of everyone.

It is possible that some audiences may react more in shock to the gay lifestyle than to the horrors of the concentration camp. Yet the concentration camp is almost unimaginable in its terror. Torture, murder, necrophilia, and the loss of one's humanity are all treated in the play, and they all reflect — in the traditional sense of social commentary — the realities of modern life. Perhaps, despite its relatively traditional structure, this is also an example of the theater of cruelty. Certainly the cruelty depicted in the play is such that no one can watch and be unmoved.

August Wilson has been working on a series of ten plays on the subject of growing up black in twentieth-century America. So far he has written four of those plays, and each has won the New York Drama Critics' Circle Award for best play of the year. Wilson's plays show the pain endured by blacks in an America that is supposed to be the land of opportunity. The frustration, exploitation, and suffering that is the lot of blacks are presented in powerful characters such as Troy Maxson in *Fences* (1985). Troy Maxson is a garbage man who was a star baseball player at a time when blacks were forced to play in their own league. The major leagues were exclusively white until 1947, when Jackie Robinson joined the Brooklyn Dodgers and the game began to be integrated. The play centers on Maxson's anger, but it also shows his pride for his family and his concerns for his son's growing up into a world in which he must empower himself to achieve what he most wants for himself.

Cory, Troy's son, does not see the same kind of discrimination and has not felt the unfairness that was Troy's primary experience in growing up. He does not understand the world from Troy Maxson's point of view. Showing the world as Troy Maxson sees it is one of the functions of the play.

All of Wilson's plays have explored the heritage of blacks to help them live intelligently in the present, with understanding and dignity. People in his plays have lost touch with the past and, for that reason, risk a loss of self-understanding.

August Wilson's plays have a naturalistic surface, but they also allude to the supernatural. The effects are achieved in a proscenium theater, using traditional methods of DRAMATURGY. Much of the powerful and lasting drama of the 1980s has followed a similar technical path. Contemporary dramatists are by no means shy of experimentation, but they are also sensitive to the continuing resources of the traditional stage as it was conceived by Chekhov and Ibsen and modified by Brecht.

Martin Sherman

Martin Sherman (b. 1941) is a Philadelphia-born playwright whose work has been produced largely in Off-Broadway theaters. He studied at Boston University, where he earned an M.F.A., and has been a playwright in residence at Mills College in Oakland, California. He has won numerous awards for his writing, among them a residency grant from the Wurlitzer Foundation of New Mexico in 1973; the Elizabeth Hull–Kate Warriner Award from Dramatists Guild in 1979; a Tony Award nomination for *Bent*; a fellowship from the National Endowment for the Arts in 1980; and, most recently, a grant from the Rockefeller Foundation.

Sherman's first play produced in New York was *Next Year in Jerusalem* (1968). Among his early plays are *The Night Before Paris* (1970), first produced in Scotland; *Things Went Badly in Westphalia* (1970), produced at the University of Connecticut in an ambitious performance and later included in Chilton's *The Best Short Plays of 1970*. *Passing By* (1974), a one-act play, was produced in London and New York and included in *Gay Plays* (1984). His two-act play *Cracks* was developed at the Eugene O'Neill Theater at Waterford, Connecticut, under the guidance of Lloyd Richards, the director of *Fences* and head of the Yale Repertory Theatre. *Soaps* (1975) and *Rio Grande* (1976) were both produced Off-Off Broadway. His first Broadway and international success was *Bent* (1979). It was developed in 1978 in the Eugene O'Neill Theater at Waterford and then at the Royal Court Theatre in London, both of which are testing grounds for new work.

Bent is the kind of play that implies immense risks for producer and theater owner: it is serious, concerned with themes that are not central to pure entertainment, and frankly homosexual in subject matter. Yet the play moved immediately from the Royal Court Theatre to a full-scale production at the Criterion Theatre in London's West End, the center of popular theater in England. Its success there was duplicated on Broadway, and since its initial run it has been produced in thirty countries, establishing Sherman as a major voice in contemporary theater.

Sherman, like many current playwrights, aligned with small theater groups as a way of developing his work. London's Royal Court Theatre and the O'Neill Theater in Connecticut discover important new theatrical talent and offer a place where playwrights can see their plays in active staged readings (something between a full-scale production and a reading, rather than a performance, by actors).

Since *Bent*, Sherman has written *Messiah* (1982), which was produced at the prestigious Aldwych Theatre in London's West End and at the Manhattan Theater Club in New York (1984). His *When She Danced* was produced at the Yvonne Arnaud Theatre in Guildford, England. *A Madhouse in Goa* was produced in 1987. In addition to working for legitimate theater, Sherman has done a number of television plays for British Broadcasting Company (BBC) and Columbia Broadcasting Company (CBS), among them *Don't Call Me Mama Any More*.

Critics are divided about the success of his work, but most point to the energy and power of his writing, especially in *Bent*, the only play of his to receive much notice in the popular press. Because he is a controversial playwright, it is likely to be some time before a consensus about his work is reached. It is also likely that he will remain problematic for the theater establishment, but it is clear that his voice will be heard in American theater.

BENT

Bent (1979) was first produced at the Royal Court Theatre in London and then at the New Apollo Theater on Broadway. The reviews were mixed, but most reviewers admitted that despite its flaws the play has an energy and power that hold its audience and demand attention. The most common critical complaint was that he did not observe the unity of plot: His play tells several stories simultaneously.

It is difficult to know exactly why such a raw and painful play as *Bent* would stimulate modern critics to call on the Aristotelian "rules" of the unities in their criticism. *New Yorker* critic Brendan Gill complained of a flaw in the unity of action, saying, "Mr. Sherman has tried to tell two or three stories at once, and sometimes the working out of their plots leads not to enlightenment but to collision." Walter Kerr, the *New York Times* critic, was sympathetic to the play but complained of a failure in the unity of character. "There is a character problem," he wrote. "We have first met [Max] as openly, candidly, even ostentatiously 'queer.' Somewhere during the nightmare he has dropped the identification; he *will* not acknowledge it." Complaining about the unity of time, Gill pointed to the opening of the play as flawed because "the playwright seeks to conceal from us" that the setting is not in the present but is in 1934. The critic Robert Brustein said in the *New Republic* that "the scene might be Greenwich Village in 1979," which in one sense only points out the play's timelessness.

In the play Sherman explores a particular type of homosexual, one who is incapable of steadiness in a relationship. Max is a thirty-four-year-old flirt who, in Sherman's words, "leads a dissolute life of drink, drugs, and sporadic sex." His relationship with his friend Rudy the dancer, who is played in a campy way as a "gushy, effusive, homebody type," is marked by superficiality and selfishness. Max does not know whether it is possible for him to love anyone.

The situation is daring. It portrays a homosexual relationship that verges on the stereotypical, almost suggesting what popular prejudice would say: that homosexual relationships are indulgent, promiscuous, and not lasting. But Sherman works hard to show the audience how much their own feelings can resemble those of the officials in Nazi Germany, where the action, we learn slowly, takes place. It is not 1979, but 1934, and the point is that the same prejudices are present in a modern American or British audience as were present in Nazi officials.

Some members of the audience will feel revulsion at the prospect of Max and Rudy's relationship, but Sherman presses on to reveal horrors of such an order that any audience would pale. One question the play raises is whether an audience that is programmed to be revulsed by homosexuality is equally revulsed by murder, especially when murders are regularly served up galore to TV and film viewers.

Act 2 has been described as "another play" by some critics, and to an extent it is. Max has moved from one world that makes it difficult for him to feel love to another world that does the same: He has been sent to Dachau. Eventually he establishes a relationship that rehabilitates him emotionally so that he can reclaim at least the shards of his humanity before he dies.

The combination of themes — homosexuality and the horrors of Dachau — may be overwhelming. The critics may be correct that the play bears too much material for its structure, that it is essentially overloaded. Sherman bases his story on historical fact and implies as he unfolds it that our liberated Western society is not really much different in its attitude toward homosexuals than Nazi Germany was in 1934.

One reason Sherman wrote the play with such an overtly sexual tone, describing necrophilia and orgasm and using extremely raw and direct language about sex, was to make audiences sense in their reactions the degree to which they have repressed their feelings about sex. Modern psychiatrists have described the ways in which the Nazis repressed their fears about sex and preached a strict morality in matters of sex and fidelity. In the Nazis' case, repression went hand in hand with dark, mangled psyches playing out brutal programs of starvation and dehumanization in concentration camps. The very people who committed the crimes depicted in act 2 would have been outraged by the themes, language, and frank portrayals throughout this play.

Martin Sherman (b. 1941)

BENT

1979

Characters

MAX	FREDDIE
RUDY	HORST
WOLF	GUARD ON TRAIN
LIEUTENANT	OFFICER
SECOND LIEUTENANT	KAPO
GRETA	CORPORAL
VICTOR	CAPTAIN

ACT I · Scene I ⸻

(*The living room of an apartment. It is small and sparsely furnished. There is a table with plants on it. A door on the left leads to the outside hall. Nearby is an exit to the kitchen. On the right is an exit to the bedroom and nearby one to the bathroom.*)

(*Max enters, wearing a bathrobe. He is thirty-four. He is very hung over. He stares into space.*)

MAX: Oh God!

(*He goes into the bathroom. Pause.*)

(*Off.*) Oh God!

(*He returns to the living room and sits down. Rudy enters, wearing a bathrobe. He is thirty and wears glasses. He carries a cup.*)

RUDY: Here.

(*He hands Max the cup. Max stares and doesn't take it.*)

Here. Coffee!

(*Max takes the cup.*)

MAX: Thanks.

(*They kiss. Max sips the coffee.*)

RUDY: It's late. It's almost three. We really slept. I missed class. I hate to dance when I miss class. Bad for the muscles. And there's no place to warm up at the club. I hate that nightclub anyhow. The floor's no good. It's cement. You shouldn't dance on cement. It ruins my ankle. They've covered it with wood. Last night, before the show, I pounded on the wood — really hard — and I could hear the cement. I'm going to complain. I really am.

(*He goes into the kitchen. Max sits in silence and stares.*)

MAX: Oh God.

(*Rudy returns from the kitchen with a jug of water and waters the plants.*)

RUDY: The plants are dying. The light's bad in this flat.° I wish we had a decent place. I wish one of your deals would come through again. Oh, listen to me, wanting a bigger place. Rosen's gonna be knocking on our door any minute now, you know that, wanting his rent. We're three weeks overdue. He always comes on a Sunday. Slimy Jew, that's what he is, only cares about money — just what everyone always says about them. What's three weeks? He can wait. Well, at least I got the new job. I'll get paid on Thursday. If Greta keeps the club open. Business stinks. Well, I suppose it means I can't complain about the cement. The thing is, I don't want to dance with a bad ankle. More coffee?

(*Max shakes his head yes. Rudy goes into the kitchen. Max stares into space. He puts his hand on his head and takes a deep breath, then closes his eyes.*)

MAX: One. Two. Three. Four. Five. (*He opens his eyes and takes another deep breath.*) Six. Seven. Eight. Nine. Ten.

(*Rudy returns from the kitchen and hands Max another cup of coffee. Rudy resumes watering the plants. Max watches him for a moment.*)

OK. Tell me.
RUDY: What?
MAX: You know.
RUDY: No.
MAX: Come on.
RUDY: I *don't* know. Listen, do you think I should ask Lena for the rent? She's such a good person. No feeling for music, though, which is daft, she's got such a good line. Perfect legs. Teddy wants to do a dance for her in total silence. You think that's a good idea? There's no place to do it, though. There's no work. Lena lost that touring job. So she

flat: Apartment.

must be broke. So she can't lend us the money.
Want some food?

MAX: Just tell me.

RUDY: What?

MAX: Must really be bad.

RUDY: What must?

MAX: That's why you won't tell me.

RUDY: Tell you what?

MAX: Don't play games.

RUDY: I'm not playing anything.

MAX: I'll hate myself, won't I? (*Silence.*) Won't I?

RUDY: I'll make something to eat.

MAX: Was I really rotten?

RUDY: Eggs.

MAX: I don't want eggs.

RUDY: Well, we're lucky to have them. I stole them from the club. They don't need eggs. People go there to drink. And see a terrific show — which is a bit sad because the show's hopeless. You know, I'm so embarrassed, I have to think of other things while I'm dancing. I have to think of grocery lists. And that's cheating. If you're thinking of grocery lists, they can tell out there that you're not thinking about straw hats or water lilies — I mean, it really shows, particularly when it's grocery lists. Your face looks really depressed, when you can't afford groceries . . .

(*Max rises and puts his hand on Rudy's mouth.*)

MAX: Stop it.

(*Rudy tries to speak.*)

Stop it!

(*They struggle. Max keeps his hand over Rudy's mouth.*)

I want to know what I did.

(*He releases Rudy. Rudy smiles.*)

RUDY: I love you.

(*He goes into the kitchen.*)

MAX: Rudy! Your plants. I'll pull the little buggers out unless you tell me.

(*Rudy comes back in. Max stands over the plants.*)

RUDY: No you won't.

MAX: Like to bet? I did last month.

RUDY: You killed one. That was mean.

MAX: I'll do it again.

RUDY: Don't touch them. You have to be nice to plants. They can hear you and everything. (*To the plants.*) He's sorry. He didn't mean it. He's just hung over.

MAX: What did I do?

(*Silence.*)

RUDY: Nothing much.

MAX: I can't remember a thing. And when I can't remember, it means . . .

RUDY: It doesn't mean anything. You drank a lot. That's all. The usual.

MAX: How'd I get this?

(*He pulls his robe off his shoulder and shows a mark on his skin.*)

RUDY: What's that?

MAX: Ouch! Don't touch it.

RUDY: I want to see it.

MAX: So *look*. You don't have to touch.

RUDY: What is it?

MAX: What does it look like? A big black and blue mark. There's another one here.

(*He shows a mark on his arm.*)

RUDY: Oh.

MAX: How did I get them?

RUDY: You fell.

MAX: How?

RUDY: Someone pushed you.

MAX: Who?

RUDY: Some bloke.°

MAX: What bloke?

RUDY: Nicky's friend.

MAX: Who's Nicky?

RUDY: One of the waiters at the club.

MAX: Which one?

RUDY: The redhead.

MAX: I don't remember him.

RUDY: He's a little fat.

MAX: Why'd Nicky's friend push me?

RUDY: You asked Nicky to come home with us.

MAX: I did?

RUDY: Yes.

MAX: But he's *fat*.

RUDY: Only a little.

MAX: A threesome with a fat person?

RUDY: Not a threesome, a twelvesome. You asked *all* the waiters. All at the same time too. You were standing on a table, making a general offer.

MAX: Oh. Then what?

RUDY: Nicky's friend pushed you off the table.

MAX: And . . .

RUDY: You landed on the floor, on top of some boy in leather.

MAX: What was he doing on the floor?

RUDY: I don't know.

MAX: Was Greta mad?

bloke: Fellow or guy.

RUDY: Greta wasn't *happy.* (*Pause.*) It was late. Almost everyone had gone. And you were very drunk. People like you drunk. (*Pause.*) I'll make some food.

MAX: I don't want food. Why didn't you stop me?

RUDY: How can I stop you?

MAX: Don't let me drink.

RUDY: Oh. Sure. When you're depressed?

MAX: Was I depressed?

RUDY: Of course.

MAX: I don't remember why.

RUDY: Then drinking worked, didn't it?

(*He returns to the kitchen. A blond man [Wolf] enters, bleary-eyed, from the bedroom. He is in his early twenties. He is naked.*)

WOLF: Good morning.

(*He stumbles into the bathroom.*)

MAX: Rudy!

RUDY (*coming out of the kitchen*): What?

MAX: Who was that?

RUDY: Who was what?

MAX: That! That person!

RUDY: Oh. Yes. Blond?

MAX: Yes.

RUDY: And big?

MAX: Yes.

RUDY: That's the one you fell on.

MAX: The boy in leather?

RUDY: Yes. You brought him home.

(*He goes into the kitchen.*)

MAX: Rudy! Your plants!

RUDY (*returning from the kitchen*): You brought him home, that's all. He got you going. All that leather, all those chains. You called him your own little storm trooper. You insulted all his friends. They left. I don't know why they didn't beat you up, but they didn't. They left. And you brought him home.

MAX: And we had a threesome?

RUDY: Maybe the two of you had a threesome. Max, there is no such thing. You pick boys up. You think you're doing it for me too. You're not. I don't like it. You and the other bloke always end up ignoring me anyhow. Besides, last night you and your own little storm trooper began to get rough with each other, and I know pain is very chic just now, but I don't like it, 'cause pain hurts, so I went to sleep. (*He takes Max's cup and pours the coffee onto the plants.*) Here Walter, have some coffee.

MAX: Walter?

RUDY: I'm naming the plants. They're my friends.

(*He goes into the kitchen. Wolf comes out of the bathroom, wearing a towel. He grins at Max.*)

MAX: Rudy!

(*Rudy returns from the kitchen. He looks at Wolf.*)

RUDY: Oh. There's a bathrobe in there — in the bedroom.

(*Wolf goes into the bedroom. Pause.*)

MAX: I'm sorry.

RUDY: It's OK.

MAX: I'm a rotten person. Why am I so rotten? Why do I do these things? He's gorgeous, though, isn't he? I don't remember anything. I don't remember what we did in bed. Why don't I ever remember?

RUDY: You were drunk. And high on coke.

MAX: That too?

RUDY: Yes.

MAX: Whose coke?

RUDY: Anna's.

MAX: I don't remember.

RUDY: You made arrangements to pick up a shipment to sell.

MAX: A *shipment?*

RUDY: Yes.

MAX: Christ! When?

RUDY: I don't know.

MAX: That can pay the rent for months.

RUDY: Anna will remember.

MAX: Right. Hey — rent. Maybe . . . do you think . . . ?

RUDY: What?

MAX: We can ask him.

RUDY: Who?

MAX: Him!

RUDY: You must be joking.

MAX: Why?

RUDY: We don't know him.

MAX: I slept with him. I think. I wonder what it was like.

RUDY: You picked him up one night and you're going to ask him to lend you the rent?

MAX: Well, you know how I am.

RUDY: Yes.

MAX: I can talk people into things.

RUDY: Yes!

MAX: I can try.

RUDY: It won't work. He thinks you're rich.

MAX: Rich?

RUDY: You told him you were rich.

MAX: Wonderful.

RUDY: And Polish.

MAX: Polish!

RUDY: You had an accent.

(*Rudy laughs and returns to the kitchen. Wolf walks out, in a short bathrobe. He stands and looks at Max. There is an embarrassed silence.*)

MAX: Hello.

WOLF: Hello. The dressing gown is short. I look silly.
MAX: You look fine.
WOLF: Yes? You too.

(*He goes to Max and kisses him, then starts to pull Max's robe off. He bites Max on the chest.*)

   Ummm . . .
MAX: Hey. Not now.
WOLF: Later then.
MAX: Yes.
WOLF: In the country.
MAX: The country?
WOLF: Your voice is better.
MAX: Oh?
WOLF: You don't have an accent.
MAX: Only when I'm drunk.
WOLF: Oh.
MAX: Last night — was it good?
WOLF: What do you think?
MAX: I'm asking.
WOLF: Do you have to ask?

(*Rudy comes in with a cup of coffee.*)

RUDY: Some coffee?
WOLF: Yes. Thank you.

(*Rudy hands him the cup. Silence.*)

   This place . . .
MAX: Yes?
WOLF: It's really . . .

(*He stops. Silence.*)

MAX: Small?
WOLF: Yes. Exactly.
MAX: I suppose it is.
WOLF: You people are strange, keeping places like this in town. I don't meet people like you too much. But you interest me, your kind.
MAX: Listen . . .
WOLF: Oh look, it doesn't matter, who you are, who I am. I'm on holiday. *That* matters. The country will be nice.
MAX: What's the country?
WOLF: The house. Your house. Your country house.
MAX (*to Rudy*): My country house?
RUDY: Oh, that. I forgot to tell you about that. We're driving there this afternoon.
MAX: To our country house?
RUDY: *Your* country house.
MAX: How do we get there?
RUDY: Car.
MAX: Mine?
RUDY: Right.
MAX: Why don't we stay here?
WOLF: Don't make jokes. You promised me two days in the country.

MAX: Your name.
WOLF: Yes?
MAX: I forgot your name.
WOLF: Wolf.
MAX: Wolf?
WOLF: I didn't forget yours.
MAX: Look, Wolf, I don't have a car.
WOLF: Of course you do.
MAX: No.
WOLF: You showed me. In the street. Pointed it out.
MAX: Did I? It wasn't mine.
WOLF: Not yours?
MAX: No. I don't have a house in the country either.
WOLF: You do. You told me all about it.
MAX: I was joking.
WOLF: I don't like jokes. You don't want me with you, is that it? Maybe I'm not good enough for you. Not rich enough. My father made watches. That's not so wonderful. Is it, Baron?

(*Pause.*)

MAX: Baron?
RUDY: Don't look at me. *That* one I didn't know about.
MAX: Baron.

(*He begins to laugh. There is a loud knock at the front door.*)

RUDY: Rosen!
MAX: Shit.

WOLF: You like to laugh at me, Baron?

(*The knocking continues.*)

MAX: Listen, Wolf, darling, you're really very sweet and very pretty and I like you a lot, but you see, I'm not very sweet, because I have a habit of getting drunk and stoned and grand and making things up. Believe me, I'm not a Baron. There is no country house. There is no money. I don't have *any* money. Sometimes I do. Sometimes I sell cocaine, sometimes I find people to invest in business deals, sometimes . . . well, I scrounge, see, and I'm good at it, and in a few weeks, I will have some money again. But right now, nothing. Rudy and I can't pay our rent. This rent. Right here. This bloody flat.° That's all we have. And that man knocking at our door is our landlord. And he's going to throw us out. Because we can't pay our rent. Out into the streets, Wolf, the streets. Filled with filth, vermin. And lice. And . . . urine. Urine! Unless someone can help us out. Unless someone gives us a hand. *That's* the truth. Look, you don't believe me, I'll show you. Right out there we have, just like in the flicks, the

---

bloody flat: Lousy apartment.

greedy landlord. (*He puts his hand on the doorknob.*) Fanfare please.

(*Rudy simulates a trumpet call.*)

Here he is, the one and only — Abraham Rosen!

(*Max swings the door open with a flourish. Two men are standing outside — Gestapo officers — in full Nazi uniform, both holding guns. The Lieutenant points to Wolf.*)

LIEUTENANT: Him!
WOLF: No!

(*Wolf throws the coffee cup at the Lieutenant and runs into the bathroom. The Lieutenant and the Second Lieutenant run after him. Rudy starts toward the bathroom but Max pulls him back.*)

MAX: Idiot! Run!

(*Max grabs Rudy and they run out of the front door.*)
   (*The lights black out on the left side of the stage. A shot rings out in the bathroom. Wolf screams.*)
   (*The lights rise on the left side of the stage as Greta enters. Greta is a man dressed as a woman. He wears a silver dress, high green leather boots, and a top hat and carries a silver cane. He is both elegant and bizarre.*)
   (*The Lieutenant watches as the Second Lieutenant drags Wolf out of the bathroom. He is bleeding but still alive. He looks up at the Lieutenant and crawls slowly toward him.*)

WOLF: Bastard!
LIEUTENANT: Wolfgang Granz, we have an order for your arrest. You resisted. Too bad.

(*The Lieutenant grabs Wolf by the neck, takes out a knife, and slits his throat.*)
   (*Greta tugs at a rope above him and pulls down a trapeze. He thrusts himself up onto the trapeze bar and sits there.*)
   (*A projection in the center of the stage reads:* BERLIN — 1934.)
   (*Lights out on the apartment. Full spotlight on Greta.*)

Scene II

(*Greta sits on the trapeze. He sings in a smoky, seductive voice.*)

GRETA: Streets of Berlin
   I must leave you soon
   Ah!
   Will you forget me?
   Was I ever really here?

   Find me a bar
   On the cobblestoned streets

Where the boys are pretty.
I cannot love
For more than one day
But one day is enough in this city.
One day is enough in this city.

Find me a boy
With two ocean blue eyes
And show him no pity.
Take out his eyes
He never need see
How they eat you alive in this city.
They eat you alive in this city.

Streets of Berlin
Will you miss me?
Streets of Berlin
Do you care?
Streets of Berlin
Will you cry out
If I vanish
Into thin air?

(*Silence.*)

OK, Victor, cut the spot.

(*The spotlight dims. Lights rise on Greta's Club. The stage is to the left. Greta's dressing room is on the right. It has a chair facing a mirror and a screen to change behind.*)

I want the song to be perfect tonight. Tomorrow, I cut it.

(*Victor comes out and helps Greta off the trapeze.*)

Jesus Christ! Careful!

(*Victor pulls the trapeze down.*)

Take some time off. We're opening late this evening. (*Walking to the dressing room.*) And Victor! I don't want to be disturbed.

(*Greta enters the dressing room. The lights fade on the rest of the club.*)

My heroes! Where are you?

(*Max and Rudy come from behind the screen. They are dressed in trousers and shirts, pieces of nightclub costumes. Greta looks at them.*)
   (*Max sits on a stool, lost in thought. Greta sits in the chair, adjusting his costume in the mirror.*)

I'm getting rid of all the rough songs. Who am I kidding? I'm getting rid of the club. Well — maybe. Maybe not. I'll turn it into something else. We'll see.
RUDY: Is it safe?
GRETA: What?
RUDY: For us to go home?

GRETA: You fucking queers, don't you have any brains at all? No, it's not safe.

RUDY: I want to go home.

GRETA: You can't. You can't go anywhere.

RUDY: I have to get my plants.

GRETA: Oh God! Forget your plants. You can't go home. You certainly can't stay here. And you can't contact friends, so don't try to see Lena, she's a nice girl, you'll get her into a lot of trouble. You understand? You have to leave Berlin.

RUDY: Why? I live here, I work here.

GRETA: No, you don't. You're sacked.

RUDY: I *don't* understand. What did we do? Why should we leave?

GRETA: Don't leave. Stay. Be *dead* queers. Who cares? I don't.

(*Max looks up.*)

MAX: Who was he?

GRETA: Who was who?

MAX: The blond?

GRETA: Wolfgang Granz.

MAX: What's that mean?

GRETA: He was Karl Ernst's boyfriend.

MAX: Who's Karl Ernst?

GRETA: What kind of world do you live in? Aren't you boys ever curious about what's going on?

MAX: Greta, don't lecture. Who's Karl Ernst?

GRETA: Von Helldorf's deputy. You know Von Helldorf?

MAX: The head of the storm troopers in Berlin.

GRETA: I don't believe it. You've actually *heard* of someone. Right. Second in command at the SA, immediately under Ernst Röhm.

RUDY: Oh. Ernst Röhm. I know him.

(*Max and Greta stare at him.*)

He's that fat queen, with those awful scars on his face, a real big shot, friend of Hitler's, runs around with a lot of beautiful boys. Goes to all the clubs. I sat at his table once. He's been *here* too, hasn't he?

MAX: Rudy, shut up.

RUDY: Why?

MAX: Just shut up. (*To Greta.*) So?

GRETA: So Hitler had Röhm arrested last night.

MAX: I don't believe it. He's Hitler's right-hand man.

GRETA: Was. He's dead. Just about anyone who's high up in the SA is dead. Your little scene on top of that table was *not* the big event of the evening. It was a bloody night. The city's in a panic. Didn't you see the soldiers on the streets — the SS? How'd you get here in your bathrobes? You're bloody lucky, that's all. The talk is that Röhm and his storm troopers — Von Helldorf, Ernst, your blond friend — the lot — were planning a coup. I don't

believe it. What the hell, let them kill each other, who cares? Except, it's the end of the club. As long as Röhm was around, a queer club was still OK. Anyhow, that's who you had — Wolfgang Granz. I hope he was a good fuck. He was a real dummy too, or didn't you notice? What's the difference? You picked up the wrong bloke, that's all.

RUDY: We can explain to somebody. It's not as if we knew him.

GRETA: Of course. Explain it all to the SS. You don't explain. Not any more. You know, you queers are not very popular anyhow. It was just Röhm keeping you all safe. Now you're like Jews. Unloved, darling, unloved.

RUDY: How about you?

GRETA: Me? Everyone knows I'm not queer. I've got a wife and kids. Of course that doesn't mean much these days, does it? But — I'm still not queer. As for this. (*He fingers his costume.*) I go where the money is.

MAX (*getting up*): Money.

GRETA: Right.

MAX: Money. Ah! Greta!

GRETA: What?

MAX: How much?

GRETA: How much what?

MAX: How much did they give you?

(*Greta laughs.*)

GRETA: Oh (*He takes out a roll of money.*) This much.

MAX: And you told them where Granz was?

GRETA: Told them darling! I showed them your building.

RUDY: Greta, you didn't.

GRETA: Why not? You don't play games with the SS. Anyway, it's just what he would do, your big shot here. He likes money too. He just isn't very good at it. I, on the other hand, have quite a knack. Here (*He holds out the money.*) Take it.

RUDY: No.

GRETA: It will help.

RUDY: We don't want it.

MAX: Shut up, Rudy.

RUDY: Stop telling me to . . .

MAX: Shut up! It's not enough.

GRETA: It's all they gave me.

MAX: We need more.

GRETA: So get more.

MAX: If they catch us, it won't help you.

GRETA: Oh? A threat? (*Pause.*) I'll do you a favor. Take some more. (*He holds out some more money.*) Here. How's that? I've made a lot off your kind, so I'm giving a little back.

RUDY: Don't take it.

MAX: OK.

(*He takes the money.*)

GRETA: Now get out.

MAX (*to Rudy*): Come on . . .

RUDY: Where? I'm not leaving Berlin.

MAX: We have to.

RUDY: We don't have to.

MAX: They're looking for us.

RUDY: But I live here.

MAX: Come on . . .

RUDY: I've paid up for dance class for the next two weeks. I can't leave. And my plants . . .

MAX: Jesus! Come on!

RUDY: If you hadn't been so drunk . . .

MAX: Don't.

RUDY: Why'd you have to take him home?

MAX: How do I know? I don't remember!

RUDY: You've ruined everything.

MAX: Right. I always do. So you go off on your own, OK? Go back to dance class. They can shoot you in the middle of an arabesque. Take half.

(*He holds out some money.*)

RUDY: I don't want it.

MAX: Then fuck it!

(*He starts to leave.*)

RUDY: Max!

GRETA: Max. He can't manage alone. Stick together.

(*Max turns back.*)

Take his hand, darling.

(*Rudy takes Max's hand.*)

That's right.

RUDY: Where are we going to go?

GRETA: Don't! Don't say anything in front of me. Get out.

(*Max stares at Greta. Then he tugs at Rudy and pulls him out of the room. Greta removes his wig. He stares at his face in the mirror.*)

(*Blackout.*)

Scene III

(*Lights up on a park in Cologne.*)

(*A middle-aged man [Freddie], well dressed, sits on a bench. He is reading a newspaper. Max enters. He sees the man and goes to the bench. The man looks up.*)

FREDDIE: Sit down.

(*Max sits.*)

Pretend we're strangers. Having a little conversation

in the park. Perfectly normal. (*He folds the newspaper.*) Do something innocent. Feed the pigeons.

MAX: There aren't any pigeons.

FREDDIE: Here.

(*He hands Max an envelope.*)

MAX: You're looking well.

FREDDIE: You're looking older.

MAX: Everything in here?

FREDDIE: Your papers and a ticket to Amsterdam.

MAX: Just one?

FREDDIE: Yes.

MAX: Shit.

FREDDIE: Keep your voice down. Remember, we're strangers. Just a casual conversation. Perfectly normal.

MAX: One ticket. I told you on the phone . . .

FREDDIE: *One* ticket. That's all.

MAX: I can't take it. Damn. Here. (*He gives the envelope back.*) Thanks anyway.

(*He gets up.*)

FREDDIE: Sit down. It wasn't easy getting new papers for you. If the family finds out . . .

(*Max sits.*)

I have to be careful. They've passed a law you know. We're not allowed to be fluffs any more. We're not even allowed to kiss or embrace or fantasize. They can arrest you if you have fluff thoughts.

(*Max laughs.*)

MAX: Oh, Uncle Freddie.

FREDDIE: It's not funny.

MAX: It is.

FREDDIE: The family takes care of me. But you. Throwing it in everyone's face. No wonder they don't want anything to do with you. Why couldn't you have been quiet about it? Settled down, got married, paid for a few boys on the side. No one would have known. Ach! Take this.

MAX: I can't. Stop giving it to me.

(*Silence.*)

FREDDIE: Look over there.

MAX: Where?

FREDDIE: Over there. See him?

MAX: Who?

FREDDIE: With the mustache.

MAX: Yes.

FREDDIE: Rather sweet.

MAX: Yes.

FREDDIE: Think he's a fluff?

MAX: I really don't know.

FREDDIE: You've been running for two years now. Haven't you? With that dancer. The family knows

all about it. You can't live like that. Take this
ticket.

MAX: I need two.

FREDDIE: I can't get two.

MAX: Of course you can.

FREDDIE: Yes. I think he is a fluff. You have to be so
careful now. What is it? Do you love him?

MAX: What?

FREDDIE: The dancer.

MAX: Christ!

FREDDIE: Do you?

MAX: Don't be stupid. What's love? Love! I'm a grown-
up now. I just feel responsible.

FREDDIE: Fluffs can't afford that kind of responsibility.
Why are you laughing?

MAX: That word. Fluffs. Look, do you think it's been
a holiday? We've tramped right across this country.
We settle in somewhere, and then suddenly they're
checking papers, and we have to leave — rather
quickly. Now we're living outside Cologne, in the
goddamn forest! In a colony of *tents* — can you
believe that? *Me* in a tent! With hundreds of very
boring unemployed people. Except most of them
are just unemployed; they're not running from the
Gestapo. I'm not cut out for this, Uncle Freddie.
I was brought up to be comfortable. Like you. OK.
I've been playing around for too long. You're right.
The family and I should make up. So. How about
a deal? *Two* tickets to Amsterdam. And two new
sets of identity papers. Once we get to Amsterdam,
I'll ditch him. And they can have me back.

FREDDIE: Maybe they don't want you back. It's been
ten years.

MAX: They want me. It's good business. I'm an only
son. (*Pause.*) Remember that marriage father wanted
to arrange? Her father had button factories too, I
just read about her in the paper; she's an eligible
widow, living in Brussels. Make the arrangements
again. I'll marry her. Our button factories can sleep
with her button factories. It's a good deal. You
know it. And eventually, when all this blows over,
you can get me back to Germany. If I want a boy,
I'll rent him, like you. I'll be a discreet, quiet . . .
fluff. Fair enough? It's what father always wanted.
Just get us *both* out alive.

FREDDIE: I'll have to ask your father.

MAX: Do it. Then ask him.

FREDDIE: I can't do things on my own. Not now. (*He
holds out the envelope.*) Just this.

MAX: I can't take it.

FREDDIE: He's looking this way. He might be the police.
No. He's a fluff. He has fluff eyes. Still. You can't
tell. You'd better leave. Just be casual. Perfectly
normal. I'll ask your father.

MAX: Soon?

FREDDIE: Yes. Can I telephone you?

MAX: In the *forest?*

FREDDIE: Telephone me. On Friday.

(*Freddie puts the envelope away. Max gets up.*)

MAX: You're looking well, Uncle Freddie.

(*Max leaves. Freddie picks up his newspaper, glances
at it, puts it down, and turns to look again at the
man with the mustache.*)

(*Blackout.*)

Scene IV

(*The forest. In front of a tent. Rudy sits in front of
a fire. He has some apples, cheese and a knife. He
calls back to the tent.*)

RUDY: Cheese! Max!

(*Max comes out of the tent and sits down.*)

Here. Eat.

MAX: No.

RUDY: It's good.

MAX: I want some wine.

RUDY: There is no wine.

MAX: Where d'you get the cheese? Steal it?

RUDY: I don't steal. I dug a ditch.

MAX: You *what?*

RUDY: Dug a ditch. Right outside of Cologne. They're
building a road. You can sign on each morning if
you get there in time. They don't check your papers.
It's good exercise too, for your shoulders. I'm getting
nice shoulders. But my feet . . . no more dancing
feet. Oh God. Here. Have some.

MAX: I don't want to eat. You shouldn't have to dig
ditches. I want some real food, for Christ's sake.
I want some wine. (*He takes the cheese.*) Look at
this cheese. It's awful. You don't know anything
about cheese. Look at all these tents. There's no
one to talk to in any of them. (*He eats a piece of
cheese.*) It has no flavor.

RUDY: Then don't eat it. I'll eat it. I have apples too.

MAX: I hate apples.

RUDY: Then starve. What did you do today, while I
was ditch digging?

MAX: Nothing.

RUDY: You had to do something.

MAX: Nothing.

RUDY: You weren't here when I got back.

MAX: Went to town.

RUDY: Have fun?

MAX: I'm working on something.

RUDY: Really?

MAX: Yes, a deal.

(*He takes an apple.*)

RUDY: Oh. A deal. Wonderful.

MAX: I might get us new papers and tickets to Amsterdam.

RUDY: You said that in Hamburg.

MAX: It didn't work out in Hamburg.

RUDY: You said that in Stuttgart.

MAX: Are you going to recite the list?

RUDY: Why not? I'm tired of your deals. You're right. This cheese is awful. I don't want to eat it.

(*He pushes the food aside.*)

MAX: You have to eat.

RUDY: Throw it out.

MAX: You'll be ill if you don't eat.

RUDY: So what?

MAX: All right. Be ill.

RUDY: No. I don't want to be ill. (*He eats a piece of cheese.*) If I'm ill, you'll leave me behind. You're just waiting for me to be ill.

MAX: Oh — here we go.

RUDY: You'd love it if I died.

MAX: Rudy!

RUDY: I know you would. Cheese makes me thirsty. Why didn't *you* buy wine?

MAX: I don't have any money. *You* dug the ditch.

RUDY: Of course. I dug the ditch. *I* make the money. If you call it money. You know how much they paid me? Enough for cheese and apples. You know what I keep asking myself?

MAX: What?

RUDY: If we had just talked to the SS that day and explained everything — could it have been worse than this?

MAX: Maybe not.

RUDY: Maybe not? You're supposed to say yes, *much* worse. Don't tell me maybe not. I'll kill myself if I believe maybe not. That's what you want. You want me to kill myself.

MAX: I just want to get us out of here. These awful tents. There's no air. We're *in* the air, but there's still no air. I can't breathe. I've got to get us across the border.

RUDY: Why don't we just cross it?

MAX: What do you mean?

RUDY: This bloke, on the job today, was telling me it's easy to cross the border.

MAX: Oh, yes, it's simple. You just walk across. Of course, they shoot you.

RUDY: He said he knew spots.

MAX: Spots.

RUDY: Spots to get through. I told him to come talk to you.

MAX: Here?

RUDY: Yes.

MAX: I told you we don't want anyone to know we're here, or that we're trying to cross the border. How can you be so thick?

RUDY: I'm not thick.

MAX: He could tell the police.

RUDY: OK. So I *am* thick. Why don't we try it anyway?

MAX: Because . . .

RUDY: Why?

MAX: I'm working on something.

RUDY: Who with?

MAX: I can't tell you.

RUDY: Why not?

MAX: It spoils it. I can't talk about it before it happens. Then it won't happen. I'm superstitious.

RUDY: Then why'd you bring it up?

MAX: So you'd know that . . .

RUDY: What?

MAX: That I'm trying.

RUDY: This is madness. We're in the middle of the jungle . . .

MAX: Forest.

RUDY: Jungle. I'm a dancer, not Mowgli. I can't dance any more. I've walked my feet away. But you don't mind. You're working on something. You worked on something in Berlin, you work on something in the jungle.

MAX: Forest.

RUDY: Jungle. I want to get out of here. I could have. I met a man in Frankfurt. You were in town "working on a deal." He gave me a lift. He was an old man, rich too. He was numb on his left side, he must have had a stroke, he shouldn't have been driving. I could have stayed with him. I could have got him to get me out of the country. He really fancied me, I could tell. But no, I had to think about you. It wasn't fair to *you.* I'm thick, you're right. You would have grabbed the chance. You're just hanging around, waiting for me to die. I think you've poisoned the cheese.

MAX: It's *your* cheese. Choke on it. Please, choke on it. I can't tell you how much I want you to choke on it. Christ! (*He picks up a knife and cuts the apple into pieces.*) Listen . . . I think I *can* get us out of here. Just hold on.

RUDY: What are you working on? Who with?

MAX: No.

RUDY: Come on.

MAX: No. Absolutely not! Trust me, just trust me.

RUDY: Why should I?

(*Max throws the knife down and gets up.*)

Where are you going?

MAX: I have to get out of here. I can't breathe. I'm going for a walk.

RUDY: You can't. There's no place to walk. Just tents and jungle.

MAX: I've got a temperature.

RUDY: What?
MAX: I've got a temperature! I'm burning.
RUDY: It's a trick.

(*He gets up and goes to him. He tries to feel his forehead. Max pulls away.*)

MAX: I know. I'm lying. Get away.
RUDY: Let me feel. (*He feels Max's forehead.*) You have got a temperature.
MAX: It's the cheese. You poisoned *me*. What the hell. I'll die in the jungle.

(*He sits down again.*)

RUDY: Forest.

(*He sits down. Silence.*)

MAX: Well . . . what do we talk about now?
RUDY: I don't know.

(*Silence.*)

MAX: Remember cocaine?
RUDY: Yes.
MAX: I'd like cocaine.
RUDY: Yes.
MAX: What would you like?
RUDY: New glasses.
MAX: What?
RUDY: My eyes have changed. I need a new prescription. I'd like new glasses.
MAX: In Amsterdam.
RUDY: Sure.
MAX: In *Amsterdam*. Cocaine and new glasses. Trust me. Plants. You'll have plants. Wonderful Dutch plants. And Dutch dance classes. Your feet will come back. And you won't dig ditches. You'll have to give up your new shoulders though. And you know what? We can buy a Dutch dog. Everyone should have a dog. I don't know why we didn't have a dog in Berlin. We'll have one in Amsterdam. (*Silence.*) Trust me.

(*Rudy looks at Max and smiles. Silence.*)

Well? What do we talk about now?
RUDY: Let's sing.
MAX: Sing?
RUDY: Well, we're sitting around a campfire; that's when people sing.
MAX: You think they sing in the Hitler Youth?
RUDY: I don't know.
MAX: They always sit around campfires.
RUDY: I never joined. How're you feeling?
MAX: Burning.

(*Rudy touches Max's forehead. He keeps his hand there.*)

Don't.

RUDY: I'm sorry, Max.

(*He strokes Max's forehead.*)

MAX: Don't.
RUDY: I really love you.
MAX: Don't! (*He pulls Rudy's hand away.*) If they see us . . . from the other tents . . . they're always looking . . . they could throw us out . . . for touching . . . we have to be careful . . . we have to be very careful . . .
RUDY: OK.

(*Pause. He starts to sing.*)

> Streets of Berlin
> I must leave you soon
> Ah!

MAX: What are you doing?
RUDY: Singing. This must be the way the Hitler Youth does it. They sing old favorites. I'm sure they're not allowed to touch either.
MAX: Don't be so sure.
RUDY: Well, it's unfair if they can and we can't.

(*He starts to sing again.*)

> Streets of Berlin
> I must leave you soon
> Ah!

(*Max takes Rudy's hand, holds it on the ground where it can't be seen, and smiles.*)

MAX: Shh!

(*They laugh. They both sing.*)

RUDY AND MAX: Find me a bar
> On the cobblestoned streets.
> Where the boys are pretty.
> I cannot love
> For more than one day
> But one day is enough in this city.
> One day is enough in this city.

FIRST VOICE (*from the darkness*): There! That's them!

(*A bright light shines on Max and Rudy.*)

SECOND VOICE (*from the darkness*): Maximilian Berber. Rudolph Hennings. Hands high in the air. You are under arrest.

(*Blackout.*)

Scene V

(*A train whistle is heard. Sound of a train running through the night. A train whistle again.*)
  (*A circle of light comes up. It is a prisoner transport train. We see one small corner. Five prisoners are in the light — two men in civilian dress, then Rudy and*

Max, then a man wearing a striped uniform with a pink triangle sewn onto it.)

   (A guard walks through the circle of light. He carries a rifle. Silence.)

RUDY: Where do you think they're taking us?

(Silence. The other prisoners look away. The Guard walks through the circle of light. Silence.)

   (To the prisoner next to him.) Did you have a trial?

(The prisoner doesn't answer.)

MAX: Rudy!

(Silence. Rudy and Max look at each other. They are both terrified. Rudy starts to extend his hand, then withdraws it. A scream is heard — off, beyond the circle. Rudy and Max look at each other, then turn away. Silence.)

   (The Guard walks through the circle of light. Silence. Another scream. Silence.)

   (The Guard walks through the circle of light.)

   (An SS Officer enters. The circle slightly expands. The Officer looks at the prisoners one by one. He stops at Rudy.)

OFFICER: Glasses. *(Silence.)* Give me your glasses.

(Rudy hands the Officer his glasses. The Officer examines them.)

   Horn-rimmed. Intelligentsia.

RUDY: What?

(The Officer smiles.)

OFFICER: Stand up.

(The Guard pulls Rudy up.)

   Step on your glasses.

(Rudy stands — petrified.)

   Step on them.

(Rudy steps on the glasses.)

   Take him.

RUDY: Max!

(Rudy looks at Max. The Guard pulls Rudy off — out of the circle. The Officer smiles.)

OFFICER: Glasses.

(He kicks the glasses away.)

   (The Officer leaves the circle of light. The light narrows. Max stares ahead.)

   (The Guard walks through the circle of light. Silence. A scream is heard — off, beyond the circle. Rudy's scream. Max stiffens. Silence. Rudy screams again. Max moves, as to get up. The man wearing the pink triangle [Horst] moves toward Max. He touches him.)

HORST: Don't.

(He removes his hand from Max and looks straight ahead.)

   (The Guard walks through the circle of light.)

   Don't move. You can't help him.

(Rudy screams. Silence.)

   (The Guard walks through the circle of light.)

MAX: This isn't happening.

HORST: It's happening.

MAX: Where are they taking us?

HORST: Dachau.

MAX: How do you know?

HORST: I've been through transport before. They took me to Cologne for a propaganda film. Pink triangle in good health. Now it's back to Dachau.

MAX: Pink triangle? What's that for?

HORST: Queer. If you're queer, that's what you wear. If you're a Jew, a yellow star. Political — a red triangle. Criminal — green. Pink's the lowest.

(He looks straight ahead.)

   (The Guard walks through the circle of light. Rudy screams. Max starts.)

MAX: This isn't happening.

(Silence.)

   This can't be happening.

(Silence.)

HORST: Listen to me. If you survive the train, you stand a chance. Here's where they break you. You can do nothing for your friend. Nothing. If you try to help him, they will kill you. If you try to care for his wounds, they will kill you. If you even *see* — see what they do to him, *hear* — hear what they do to him — they will kill you. If you want to stay alive, he cannot exist.

(Rudy screams.)

MAX: It isn't happening.

(Rudy screams.)

HORST: He hasn't a chance. He wore glasses.

(Rudy screams.)

   If you want to stay alive, he cannot exist.

(Rudy screams.)

   It *is* happening.

(Horst moves away. The light focuses in on Max's face. Rudy screams. Max stares ahead, mumbling to himself.)

MAX: It isn't happening . . . it isn't happening . . .

(*The Guard drags Rudy in. Rudy is semiconscious. His body is bloody and mutilated. The Guard holds him up. The Officer enters the circle. Max looks away. The Officer looks at Max. Max is still mumbling to himself.*)

OFFICER (*to Max*): Who is this man?
MAX: I don't know.

(*Max stops mumbling. He looks straight ahead.*)

OFFICER: Your friend?

(*Silence.*)

MAX: No.

(*Rudy moans.*)

OFFICER: Look at him.

(*Max stares straight ahead.*)

Look!

(*Max looks at Rudy. The Officer hits Rudy on the chest. Rudy screams.*)

Your friend?
MAX: No.

(*The Officer hits Rudy on the chest. Rudy screams.*)

OFFICER: Your friend?
MAX: No.

(*Silence.*)

OFFICER: Hit him.

(*Max stares at the Officer.*)

Like this.

(*The Officer hits Rudy on the chest. Rudy screams.*)

Hit him.

(*Max doesn't move.*)

Your friend?

(*Max doesn't move.*)

Your friend?
MAX: No.

(*Max closes his eyes. He hits Rudy on the chest. Rudy screams.*)

OFFICER: Open your eyes.

(*Max opens his eyes.*)

Again.

(*Max hits Rudy in the chest.*)

Again!

(*Max hits Rudy again and again and again . . .*)

Enough.

(*The Officer pushes Rudy down to the ground, at Max's feet.*)

Your friend?

MAX: No.

(*The Officer smiles.*)

OFFICER: No.

(*The Officer leaves the circle of light. The Guard follows him.*)

(*The light focuses in — on Max's face. The train is heard running through the night. The train whistles. Rudy is heard — moaning — and calling Max's name. Max stares ahead. Rudy calls Max's name. The name merges with the whistle. Max takes a deep breath. Rudy calls Max's name.*)

MAX: One. Two. Three. Four. Five. (*He takes another deep breath.*) Six. Seven. Eight. Nine. Ten.

(*Rudy is silent. Max stares ahead.*)

(*Blackout.*)

Scene VI

(*Lights up, on one side of the stage. A large barrel is on the ground. A prisoner-foreman [Kapo] stands behind the barrel, with a huge ladle. He stirs it. The Kapo wears a green triangle on his prison uniform. Prisoners come up, one by one, with bowls in their hand, to be fed. They all wear prison uniforms.*)

KAPO: It's soup tonight.

(*A prisoner with a yellow star enters. The Kapo stirs the soup.*)

Here. Let me stir it. Get the meat. There.

(*He fills the prisoner's bowl. The prisoner leaves. A prisoner with a red triangle enters. The Kapo stirs the soup.*)

Here. Lots of vegetables.

(*He fills the prisoner's bowl. The prisoner leaves. Horst enters. The Kapo does not stir the soup.*)

Here.

(*He fills Horst's bowl.*)

HORST: Soup.
KAPO: What?
HORST: Only soup. You skimmed it from the top. There's nothing in it but water. No meat, no vegetables. Nothing.
KAPO: Take what you get.

(*Horst reaches for the ladle.*)

HORST: Give me some meat.

(*The Kapo pushes him back.*)

KAPO: Fucking queer! Take what you get!

(*Blackout.*)

(*Lights rise on other side of the stage. A tight little corner at the end of the barracks. Horst crawls in and sits huddled with his bowl. He drinks the soup. Max enters, crawling in next to Horst. He carries a bowl. He wears the prison uniform. On it is a yellow star.*)

MAX: Hello.

(*Horst looks at him but says nothing. Max holds up his bowl.*)

Here.

HORST: Leave me alone.

MAX: I got extra. Some vegetables. Here.

(*He drops some vegetables from his bowl into Horst's bowl.*)

HORST: Thanks.

(*They eat in silence. Horst looks up. He stares at Max's uniform.*)

Yellow star?

MAX: What?

HORST: Jew?

MAX: Oh. Yes.

HORST: I wouldn't have thought it.

(*Silence.*)

I'm sorry about your friend.

MAX: Who?

HORST: Your friend.

MAX: Oh.

(*Silence.*)

HORST: It's not very sociable in these barracks. (*He laughs.*) Is it?

MAX: It's all right.

HORST: Right. You got a yellow star.

MAX (*pointing to Horst's pink triangle*): How'd you get that?

HORST: I signed a petition.

MAX: And?

HORST: That was it.

MAX: What kind of petition?

HORST: For Magnus Hirschfield.

MAX: Oh yes. I remember him. Berlin.

HORST: Berlin.

MAX: He wanted to . . .

HORST: Make queers legal.

MAX: Right. I remember.

HORST: Looked like he would too, for a while. It was quite a movement. Then the Nazis came in. Well. I was a nurse. They said a queer couldn't be a nurse. Suppose I had to touch a patient's penis! God forbid. They said rather than be a nurse, I should be a prisoner. A more suitable occupation. So. That's how I got my pink triangle. How'd you get the yellow star?

MAX: I'm Jewish.

HORST: You're not Jewish, you're a queer.

(*Silence.*)

MAX: I didn't want one.

HORST: Didn't want what?

MAX: A pink triangle.

HORST: Didn't *want* one?

MAX: You told me it was the lowest.

HORST: In here, it is.

MAX: So I didn't want one.

HORST: So?

MAX: So I worked a deal.

HORST: A deal?

MAX: Yes. I'm good at that.

HORST: With the Gestapo?

MAX: Yes.

HORST: You're full of shit.

(*Silence.*)

MAX: I'm going to work a lot of deals. They can't keep us here forever. Sooner or later they'll release us. I'm only under protective custody, that's what they told me. I'm going to stay alive.

HORST: I don't doubt it.

MAX: Sure. I'm good at that.

HORST: Thanks for the vegetables.

(*He starts to crawl away.*)

MAX: Where you going?

HORST: To sleep. We get up at four in the morning. I'm on stone detail. I chop stones up. It's fun. Excuse me . . .

MAX: Don't go.

HORST: I'm tired.

MAX: I don't have anyone to talk to.

HORST: Talk to your rabbi.

MAX: I'm not Jewish.

HORST: Then why are you wearing that?

MAX: It's better to be a Jew than a queer. In this place.

HORST: I think it's relative.

MAX: You told me pink was the lowest.

HORST: It is, but only because the *other* prisoners hate us so much. Except for a queer, no one is treated worse than a Jew.

MAX: I got meat in my soup.

HORST: Good for you.

MAX: I'm going to stay alive.

HORST: Good. You do that.

MAX: Don't go.

HORST: Look, friendships last about twelve hours in this place. We had ours on the train. Why don't you go and bother someone else.

MAX: You didn't think I'd make it, did you? Off the train.

HORST: I wasn't sure.

MAX: I'm going to stay alive.

HORST: Yes.

MAX: Because of you. You told me how.

HORST: Yes. (*Pause.*) I did. (*Pause.*) I'm sorry.

MAX: About what?

HORST: I don't know. Your friend.

MAX: Oh. (*Silence.*) He wasn't my friend.

(*Silence.*)

HORST: You should be wearing a pink triangle.

MAX: I made a deal.

HORST: You don't make deals here.

MAX: I did. I made a deal.

HORST: Yes.

(*He starts to leave again.*)

MAX: They said if I . . . I could . . . they said . . .

HORST: What?

MAX: Nothing.

(*Horst crawls past Max.*)

  I could prove . . . I don't know how . . .

HORST: What?

(*He stops and sits next to Max.*)

MAX: Nothing.

(*Silence.*)

HORST: Try. (*Silence.*) I think you'd better. (*Silence.*) Try to tell me.

MAX: Nothing.

(*Silence.*)

HORST: OK.

(*He moves away.*)

MAX: I made . . . they took me . . . into that room . . .

(*Horst stops.*)

HORST: Where?

MAX: Into that room.

HORST: On the train?

MAX: On the train. And they said . . . prove that you're . . . and I did . . .

HORST: Prove that you're what?

MAX: Not.

HORST: Not what?

MAX: Queer.

HORST: How?

MAX: Her.

HORST: Her?

MAX: They said, if you . . . and I did . . .

HORST: Did what?

MAX: Her. Made . . .

HORST: Made what?

MAX: Love.

HORST: Who to?

MAX: Her.

HORST: Who was she?

MAX: Only . . . maybe . . . maybe only thirteen . . . she was maybe . . . she was dead.

HORST: Oh.

MAX: Just. Just dead, minutes . . . bullet . . . in her . . . they said . . . prove that you're . . . and I did . . . prove that you're . . . lots of them, watching . . . drinking . . . "He's a bit bent," they said, "he can't . . ." But I did . . .

HORST: How?

MAX: I don't . . . I don't . . . know. I wanted . . .

HORST: To stay alive.

MAX: And there was something . . .

HORST: Something . . .

MAX: Exciting . . .

HORST: Oh God.

MAX: I hit him, you know. I kissed her. Dead lips. I killed him. Sweet lips. Angel.

HORST: God.

MAX: She was . . . like an angel . . . to save my life . . . just beginning . . . her breasts . . . just beginning . . . they said he can't . . . he's a bit bent . . . but I did . . . and I proved . . . I proved that I wasn't . . . (*Silence.*) And they enjoyed it.

HORST: Yes.

MAX: And I said, "I'm not queer." And they laughed. And I said, "Give me a yellow star." And they said, "Sure, make him a Jew. He's not queer." And they laughed. They were having fun. But . . . I . . . got . . . my . . . star . . .

HORST (*gently*): Oh yes.

MAX: I got my star.

HORST: Yes.

(*He reaches out and touches Max's face.*)

MAX: Don't do that! (*He pulls away.*) You mustn't do that. For your own sake. You mustn't touch me. I'm a rotten person.

HORST: No.

(*He touches Max again. Max hits him.*)

MAX: Rotten.

(*Horst stares at Max.*)

HORST: No.

(*Horst crawls away and leaves. Max is alone. He takes a deep breath. He closes his eyes then takes another deep breath. He opens his eyes.*)

MAX: One. Two. Three. Four. Five. (*He takes another deep breath.*) Six. Seven. Eight. Nine. Ten.

(*Blackout.*)

ACT II • Scene I ————————————

(*One month later.*)

(*A large fence extends across the stage. In front of the fence, on one side, lies a pile of rocks. On the other side — far over — a deep pit.*)

(*Max is moving rocks. He carries one rock from the pile to the other side, and starts a new pile. He returns and takes another rock. The rocks are carried one by one. He wears a prison hat. A Corporal enters with Horst. Horst also wears a prison hat. The Corporal is very officious.*)

CORPORAL: Here. You will work here.
HORST: Yes sir.
CORPORAL: He'll explain.
HORST: Yes sir.
CORPORAL: I'm up there.

(*He points off and up.*)

HORST: Yes sir.
CORPORAL: I see everything.
HORST: Yes sir.
CORPORAL: No slacking.
HORST: No sir.
CORPORAL: I see everything.
HORST: Yes sir.
CORPORAL (*to Max*): You.

(*Max puts down his rock.*)

MAX: Yes sir.
CORPORAL: Tell him what to do.
MAX: Yes sir.
CORPORAL: No slacking.
MAX: No sir.
CORPORAL: I see everything.
MAX: Yes sir.
CORPORAL (*to Horst*): You.
HORST: Yes sir.
CORPORAL: Every two hours there is a rest period.
HORST: Yes sir.
CORPORAL: For three minutes.
HORST: Yes sir.
CORPORAL: Stand at attention.

HORST: Yes sir.
CORPORAL: Don't move.
HORST: No sir.
CORPORAL: Rest.
HORST: Yes sir.
CORPORAL: Three minutes.
HORST: Yes sir.
CORPORAL: A bell rings.
HORST: Yes sir.
CORPORAL (*to Max*): You.
MAX: Yes sir.
CORPORAL: Explain it to him.
MAX: Yes sir.
CORPORAL: No slacking.
MAX: No sir.
CORPORAL (*to Horst*): You.
HORST: Yes sir.
CORPORAL: When the bell rings.
HORST: Yes sir.
CORPORAL: Don't move.
HORST: No sir.
CORPORAL: Three minutes.
HORST: Yes sir.
CORPORAL: He'll explain.
HORST: Yes sir.
CORPORAL (*to Max*): You.
MAX: Yes sir.
CORPORAL: You're responsible.
MAX: Yes sir.
CORPORAL: I'm up there.
MAX: Yes sir.
CORPORAL (*to Horst*): You.
HORST: Yes sir.
CORPORAL: I see everything.
HORST: Yes sir.

(*The Corporal leaves. Horst watches carefully until he has gone.*)

We had a boy like that in school. Used to lead us in Simon Says.
MAX: OK. I'll explain.
HORST: OK.
MAX: We have to move rocks.
HORST: Yes sir.
MAX: You see those . . .
HORST: Yes sir.
MAX: You take one rock at a time.
HORST: Yes sir.
MAX: And move it over there.
HORST: Yes sir.
MAX: And then when the entire pile is over there, you take one rock at a time, and move it back.

(*Horst looks at Max. Silence.*)

HORST: And move it back?

MAX: Yes.

HORST: We move the rocks from there to there, and then back from there to there?

MAX: Yes sir.

HORST: Why?

MAX: Start moving. He's watching.

(*Max continues to move rocks. Horst does the same. They do so in different rhythms, at times passing each other.*)

HORST: OK.

MAX: It's supposed to drive us mad.

HORST: These are heavy!

MAX: You get used to it.

HORST: What do you mean, drive us mad?

MAX: Just that. It makes no sense. It serves no purpose. I worked it out. They do it to drive us mad.

HORST: They probably know what they're doing.

MAX: No, they don't. I worked it out. It's the best job to have. That's why I got you here.

HORST: What!

(*He puts down his rock.*)

MAX: Don't stop. Keep moving.

(*Horst picks up the rock and moves it.*)

A couple more things. That fence.

HORST: Yes.

MAX: It's electric. Don't touch it. You fry.

HORST: I won't touch it.

MAX: And over there — that pit.

HORST: Where?

MAX: There.

HORST: Oh yes. It smells awful.

MAX: Bodies.

HORST: In the pit?

MAX: Yes. Sometimes we have to throw them in.

HORST: Oh. Well, it will break the routine. What do you mean you got me here?

MAX: Don't walk so fast.

HORST: Why?

MAX: You'll tire yourself. Pace it. Nice and slow.

HORST: OK. This better?

MAX: Yes. Sometimes they let us change the pattern.

HORST: That's kind of them. What do you mean you got me here?

MAX: I worked a deal.

HORST: I don't want to hear.

(*Silence.*)

Yes, I do. What's going on? You *got* me here? What right do you have . . . ?

MAX: Careful.

HORST: What?

MAX: You'll drop the rock.

HORST: No I won't. I'm holding it, I'm holding it. What right do you have . . . ?

MAX: You were at the stones?

HORST: Yes.

MAX: Was it harder than this?

HORST: I suppose so.

MAX: People became ill?

HORST: Yes.

MAX: Die?

HORST: Yes.

MAX: Guards beat you if you didn't work hard enough?

HORST: Yes.

MAX (*proudly*): So?

HORST: So? So what?

MAX: So, it was dangerous.

HORST: This isn't?

MAX: No. No one gets ill here. Look at all those blokes moving rocks over there. (*He points off.*) They look healthier than most. No one dies. The guards don't beat you, because the work is totally nonessential. All it can do is drive you mad.

HORST: That's all?

MAX: Yes.

HORST: Then maybe the other was better.

MAX: No, I worked it out! This is the best work in the camp, if you keep your head, if you have someone to talk to.

HORST: Ah! I see! Someone to talk to! Don't you think you should have asked me . . . ?

MAX: Asked you what?

HORST: If I wanted to move rocks, if I wanted to talk to you . . .

MAX: Didn't have a chance. They moved you.

HORST: Thank heaven.

MAX: Your new barracks, is it all pink triangles?

HORST: Yes. They're arresting more queers each day; they keep pouring into the camp. Is yours all yellow stars now?

MAX: Yes.

HORST: Good. You might go all religious. There was an old man at the stones. A rabbi. Really kind. It's not easy being kind here. He was. Kind to me. None of the other yellow stars want to acknowledge a pink triangle. We're not good enough to suffer with them. But this man was so godly. I thought of you.

MAX: Why?

HORST: Maybe if you knew him you could be proud of your star. You should be proud of *something*.

MAX: Don't keep looking at me. As long as they don't see us looking at each other, they can't tell we're talking.

(*Silence.*)

HORST: Where do the bodies come from?

MAX: What bodies?

HORST: The ones in the pit.

MAX: The fence. The hat trick.

HORST: Oh. What's that?

MAX: Sometimes a guard throws a prisoner's hat against the fence. He orders him to get the hat. If he doesn't get the hat, the guard will shoot him. If he does get the hat, he'll be electrocuted.

HORST: I'm really going to like it here. Thanks a lot.

MAX: I'm really doing you a favor.

HORST: A favor! You just want someone to talk to so you won't go mad. And I'm the only one who knows your secret.

MAX: What secret?

HORST: That you're a pink triangle.

MAX: It's not a secret.

HORST: If it's not a secret, wear one.

MAX: No. I'm a Jew now.

HORST: You are not.

MAX: They think I am.

HORST: But it's a lie.

MAX: It's a clever lie.

HORST: You're mad.

MAX: I thought you'd be grateful.

HORST: That's why you like this job. It can't drive you mad. You're already there.

MAX: I spent money getting you here.

HORST: Money?

MAX: Yes. I bribed the guard.

HORST: Where'd you get money?

MAX: My uncle sent me some. First letter I ever got from him. He didn't sign it, but it had money in it.

HORST: And you bribed the guard?

MAX: Yes.

HORST: For me?

MAX: Yes.

HORST: Used *your* money.

MAX: Yes.

HORST: You'll probably never get money again.

MAX: Probably not.

HORST: You are mad.

MAX: I thought you'd be grateful.

HORST: You should have asked me first.

MAX: How could I ask you? We're in separate barracks. Do you think it's easy to bribe a guard? It's complicated. It's dangerous. He could have turned on me. I took a risk. Do you think I didn't? I took a risk. I thought you'd be grateful.

HORST: I'm *not* grateful. I liked cutting stones. I liked that old rabbi. This is insane. Twelve hours of this a day? I'll be crazy in a week. Like you. Jesus!

MAX: I'm sorry I did it.

HORST: *You're* sorry.

MAX: You haven't got this camp sorted out, that's all. You don't know what's good for you. This is the best job to have.

HORST: Moving rocks back and forth for no reason. Next to a pit with dead bodies and a fence that can burn you to dust. The *best* job to have?

MAX: Yes! Why don't you understand?

HORST: I don't want to understand. I don't want to talk to you.

MAX: You have to talk to me.

HORST: Why?

MAX: I got you here to talk.

HORST: Well, hard luck. I don't want to talk. Move your rocks, and I'll move mine. Just don't speak to me.

(*They both move their rocks. A long silence.*)

MAX: I thought you'd be grateful.

(*Blackout*)

Scene II

(*The same. Three days later.*)
(*Max and Horst are moving rocks. It is very hot. Their shirts lie on the ground. A long silence.*)

HORST: It's so hot. Burning hot.

(*Silence.*)

MAX: You talked to me.

HORST: Weather talk, that's all.

MAX: After three days of silence.

HORST: *Weather* talk. Everyone talks about the weather. (*Silence.*) Anyhow.

(*Silence.*)

MAX: Did you say something?

HORST: No.

(*Silence.*)

    Anyhow.

MAX: Anyhow?

HORST: Anyhow. Anyhow, I'm sorry. (*He stands still.*) Sometimes in this place, I behave like everyone else — bloody awful. Cut off, mean, not human, I'm sorry. You were doing me a favor. This is a good place to be. And the favor won't work unless we talk, will it?

MAX: Move!

HORST: What?

MAX: Talk while you're moving. Don't stop. They can see us.

HORST (*starting to move the rock again*): It's hard to talk when you're going one way and I'm going the other. God, it's hot. (*Silence.*) Somebody died last night.

MAX: Where?

HORST: In my barracks. A Moslem.

MAX: An Arab?

HORST: No. A Moslem. That's what they call a dead person who walks. You know, one of those blokes who won't eat any more, won't talk any more, just wanders around waiting to really die.

MAX: I've seen them.

HORST: So one really died. In my barracks. (*Silence.*) God, it's hot.

(*Silence.*)

MAX: We'll miss the Olympics.

HORST: The what?

MAX: Olympics. Next month. In Berlin.

HORST: I knew there was a reason I didn't want to be here.

MAX: Perhaps they'll release us?

HORST: For the *Olympics?*

MAX: As a good will gesture. It *is* possible, don't you think?

HORST: I think it's not.

(*Silence.*)

MAX: Heard a rumor.

HORST: What?

MAX: Sardines tonight.

HORST: Don't like sardines.

MAX: It's only a rumor.

(*Silence.*)

HORST: God, it's hot.

(*Silence.*)

MAX: Very.

(*Silence.*)

HORST: Very what?

(*Silence.*)

MAX: Very hot.

(*Silence.*)

HORST: Suppose . . .

(*Silence.*)

MAX: What?

(*Silence.*)

HORST: Suppose after all this . . . (*Silence.*) We have nothing to talk about.

(*A loud bell rings. Max and Horst put down their rocks and stand at attention, staring straight ahead.*)

Shit! I'd rather be moving rocks than standing in the sun. Some rest period.

MAX: It's part of their plan.

HORST: What plan.

MAX: To drive us mad.

(*Silence.*)

Was I awful to bring you here?

HORST: No.

MAX: I was, wasn't I?

HORST: No.

MAX: I had no right . . .

HORST: Stop it. Stop thinking how awful you are. Come on, don't get depressed. Smile. (*Silence.*) You're not smiling.

MAX: You can't see me.

HORST: I can feel you.

MAX: I wish we could look at each other.

HORST: I can feel you.

MAX: They hate it if anyone looks at each other.

HORST: I've been looking at you all morning.

MAX: Yeah?

HORST: You look sexy.

MAX: Me?

HORST: Without your shirt.

MAX: No.

HORST: Come off it. You know you're sexy.

MAX: No.

HORST: Liar.

(*Max smiles.*)

MAX: Of course I'm a liar.

HORST: Sure.

MAX: I've always been sexy.

HORST: Uh-huh.

MAX: Since I was a kid.

HORST: Yes?

MAX: Twelve. I got into a lot of trouble when I was . . .

HORST: Twelve?

MAX: Twelve.

HORST: Your body's beautiful.

MAX: I take care of it. I exercise.

HORST: What?

MAX: At night I do press-ups and knee bends in the barracks.

HORST: After twelve hours of moving rocks?

MAX: Yes. I worked it out. You got to keep your entire body strong. By yourself. That's how you survive here. You should do it.

HORST: I don't like to exercise.

MAX: You're a nurse.

HORST: For other people, not myself.

MAX: But you have to think of survival.

HORST: Sleep. I think of sleep. That's how I survive.

Or I think of nothing. (*Silence.*) That frightens me.
When I think of nothing.

(*Silence.*)

MAX: Your body's nice too.
HORST: It's OK. Not great.
MAX: No, it's nice.
HORST: Not as nice as yours.
MAX: No. But it's OK.
HORST: How do you know?
MAX: I've been looking too.
HORST: When?
MAX: All day.
HORST: Yes?
MAX: Yes.

(*Silence.*)

HORST: Listen, do you . . . ?
MAX: What?
HORST: Miss . . .
MAX: What?
HORST: You know.
MAX: No I don't.
HORST: Everyone misses it.
MAX: No.
HORST: Everyone in the camp.
MAX: No.
HORST: They go crazy missing it.
MAX: No.
HORST: Come on. No one can hear us. You're not a
   yellow star with me, remember? Do you miss it?
MAX: I don't want . . .
HORST: What?
MAX: To miss it.
HORST: But do you?

(*Silence.*)

MAX: Yes.
HORST: Me too. (*Silence.*) We don't have to.
MAX: What?
HORST: Miss it. (*Silence.*) We're here together. We
   don't have to miss it.
MAX: We can't look at each other. We can't touch.
HORST: We can feel . . .
MAX: Feel what?
HORST: Each other. Without looking. Without touching.
   I can feel you right now. Next to me. Can you feel
   me?
MAX: No.
HORST: Come on. Don't be afraid. No one can hear
   us. Can you feel me?
MAX: Maybe.
HORST: No one's going to know. It's all right. Feel
   me.

MAX: Maybe.
HORST: Feel me.
MAX: It's so hot.
HORST: I'm touching you.
MAX: No.
HORST: I'm touching you.
MAX: It's burning.
HORST: I'm kissing you.
MAX: Burning.
HORST: Kissing your eyes.
MAX: Hot.
HORST: Kissing your lips.
MAX: Yes.
HORST: Mouth.
MAX: Yes.
HORST: Inside your mouth.
MAX: Yes.
HORST: Neck.
MAX: Yes.
HORST: Down . . .
MAX: Yes.
HORST: Down . . .
MAX: Yes.
HORST: Chest. My tongue . . .
MAX: Burning.
HORST: Your chest.
MAX: Your mouth.
HORST: I'm kissing your chest.
MAX: Yes.
HORST: Hard.
MAX: Yes.
HORST: Down . . .
MAX: Yes.
HORST: Down . . .
MAX: Yes.
HORST: Your cock.
MAX: Yes.
HORST: Do you feel my mouth?
MAX: Yes. Do you feel my cock?
HORST: Yes. Do you feel . . . ?
MAX: Do you feel . . . ?
HORST: Mouth.
MAX: Cock.
HORST: Cock.
MAX: Mouth.
HORST: Do you feel my cock?
MAX: Do you feel my mouth?
HORST: Yes.
MAX: Do you know what I'm doing?
HORST: Yes. Can you taste what I'm doing?
MAX: Yes.
HORST: Taste.
MAX: Feel.
HORST: Together . . .

MAX: Together . . .
HORST: Do you feel me?
MAX: I feel you.
HORST: I see you.
MAX: I feel you.
HORST: I have you.
MAX: I want you.
HORST: Do you feel me inside you?
MAX: I want you inside me.
HORST: Feel . . .
MAX: I have you inside me.
HORST: Inside . . .
MAX: Strong.
HORST: Do you feel me thrust . . . ?
MAX: Hold.
HORST: Stroke . . .
MAX: Strong . . .
HORST: Oh . . .
MAX: Strong . . .
HORST: Oh . . .
MAX: Strong . . .
HORST: I'm going to . . .
MAX: Strong . . .
HORST: Do you feel . . . ? I'm going to . . .
MAX: I feel us both.
HORST: Do you . . . ?
MAX: Oh yes . . .
HORST: Do you . . . ?
MAX: Yes. Yes.
HORST: Feel . . .
MAX: Yes. Strong . . .
HORST: Feel . . .
MAX: More . . .
HORST: Ohh . . .
MAX: Now . . .
HORST: Yes . . .
MAX: Now! (*He gasps.*) Oh! Oh! My God!

(*He has an orgasm.*)

HORST: Ohh . . . ! Now! Ohh . . . !

(*He has an orgasm. Silence.*)

   Oh. (*Silence.*) Did you?
MAX: Yes. You?
HORST: Yes.

(*Silence.*)

MAX: You're a good fuck.
HORST: So are you. (*Silence.*) Max?
MAX: What?
HORST: We did it — fucking guards, fucking camp
   — we did it! They're not going to kill us. We made
   love. We were real. We were human. We made
   love. They're not going to kill us.

(*Silence.*)

MAX: I never . . .
HORST: What?
MAX: Thought we'd . . .
HORST: What?
MAX: Do it in three minutes.

(*They laugh. The bell rings. They pick up their rocks
and resume moving them from one side to the other.*)

   (*Blackout.*)

Scene III

(*The same. Two months later.*)
   (*Max and Horst are moving rocks. They are both
walking slowly.*)

HORST: I'm going insane.

(*Silence.*)

   I'm going insane.

(*Silence.*)

   I'm going insane. I dream about rocks. I close my
   eyes and I'm moving rocks. Rocks never end. Never
   end.

(*Silence.*)

   I'm going insane.
MAX: Think of something else.
HORST: I can't think. I've been up all night. *That's*
   why I'm going insane.
MAX: Up all night?
HORST: Come on, didn't you hear? Our barracks had
   to stand outside all night.
MAX: No.
HORST: Yes. We stood at attention all night long.
   Punishment.
MAX: What for?
HORST: Someone in our barracks killed himself.
MAX: A Moslem?
HORST: Of course not. It doesn't mean anything if a
   Moslem kills himself, but if a person who's still a
   person commits suicide, well . . . it's a kind of
   defiance, isn't it? They hate that. It's an act of free
   will. Not my way. But for some. So we were all
   punished.
MAX: I'm sorry.
HORST: Sure. Yellow star is sorry.

(*Silence.*)

MAX: Heard a rumor.
HORST: Sardines?

MAX: Yes.

HORST: I hate sardines! I hate all food. Scraps. Sardine scraps. That's all we get anyhow. Not worth eating. Didn't know you could have sardine scraps. (*Silence.*) I'm going insane.

MAX: All right. You're going insane. I'm sorry. It's my fault.

HORST: What do you mean, *your* fault?

MAX: For bringing you here. Because you make me feel so guilty. And you should. This job *is* the worst. I got it wrong. I'm sorry.

HORST: I'm glad to be here.

MAX: Of course.

HORST: I am.

MAX: How can you be?

HORST: That's my secret. (*Pause.*) Maybe if I closed my eyes . . .

MAX: Heard a rumor.

HORST: What?

MAX: We may get potatoes.

HORST: When?

MAX: Tomorrow.

HORST: I don't believe it.

MAX: They said so in my barracks.

HORST: Who's they?

MAX: Some blokes.

HORST: Are they sexy?

MAX: Shut up.

HORST: You should be with us, where you belong.

MAX: No. But you shouldn't be *here*.

HORST: I want to be here.

MAX: Why would you want to be here — are you insane?

HORST: Of course I'm insane. I'm trying to tell you I'm insane. And I want to be here.

MAX: Why?

HORST: Because. Because I love rocks. (*Pause.*) Because I love you. (*Silence.*) I do. I love you. Isn't that silly? When I'm not dreaming about rocks, I'm dreaming about you. For the past six weeks, I've dreamt about you. It helps me get up. It helps me make sure my bed is perfectly made so I'm not punished. It helps me push to get a place in the toilet line. It helps me eat the stinking food. It helps me put up with the constant fights in the barracks. Knowing I'll see you. At least out of the corner of my eyes. In passing. It's a reason to live. So I'm glad I'm here.

(*Max is at one pile of rocks, moving them into symmetrical piles.*)

What are you doing?

MAX: Arranging these neatly. We've become sloppy. They can beat you for it. (*Silence.*) Don't love me.

HORST: It makes me happy. It doesn't harm anyone. It's my secret.

MAX: Don't love me.

HORST: It's my secret. And I have a signal. No one knows it. When I rub my left eyebrow at you, like this . . . (*He rubs his left eyebrow.*) It means I love you. Bet you didn't know that. I can even do it in front of the guards. No one knows. It's my secret. (*He starts to cough.*) It's cold. It was better hot. I don't like it cold.

MAX: Don't love me.

HORST: I can't help it.

MAX: I don't want anybody to love me.

HORST: Too bad.

MAX: I can't love anybody back.

HORST: Who's asking you to?

MAX: Queers aren't meant to love. I know. I thought I loved someone once. He worked in my father's factory. My father paid him to go away. He went. Queers aren't meant to love. They don't want us to. You know who loved me? That boy. That dancer, I don't remember his name. But I killed him. See — queers aren't meant to love. I'll kill you too. Hate me. That's better. Hate me. Don't love me.

HORST: I'll do what I want to do. It isn't any of your business, anyhow. I'm sorry I told you.

MAX: I'm sorry I brought you here.

(*He finishes arranging the rocks. He returns to moving the rocks. Silence. Horst starts to cough again.*)

Why are you coughing?

HORST: Because I like to.

MAX: Are you catching cold?

HORST: Probably. Up all night. In the wind.

MAX: Winter's coming.

HORST: I know. (*Silence.*) I just want to close my eyes . . .

MAX: Heard a rumor.

HORST: I don't care.

MAX: Don't you want to hear it?

HORST: Stuff your rumors.

(*He coughs again. He slips. He drops the rock and falls to the ground.*)

MAX: Horst!

(*He puts down his rock.*)

HORST: Shit.

(*Max starts toward him.*)

Don't move! He's watching. The guard. Don't help me. If you help me, they'll kill you. Get back to your rock. Do you hear me, get back!

(*Max returns, picks up his rock, but stands looking at Horst. Horst is coughing. He looks up at Max.*)

Move!

(*Max moves the rock.*)

Right. I'm all right. I'll get up. I'll get up. Don't ever help me. (*He pulls himself up.*) I'm up. It's all right. (*He picks up his rock.*) These bloody things get heavier and heavier. (*He starts to move the rock.*) The guard was watching. He'd kill you if you helped me. Never notice. Never watch. Remember? I love you. But I won't help you if *you* fall. Don't you dare help me. You don't even love me, so why are you going to help? We save *ourselves*. Do you understand? Do you?

MAX: Yes. I understand.

HORST: Promise me. Come on. Promise me. We save ourselves.

MAX: All right.

HORST: Promise me!

MAX: Yes!

HORST: You're a fool. I don't love you anymore. It was just a passing fancy. I love myself. Poor you, you don't love anybody. (*Silence.*) It's getting cold. Winter's coming.

(*They walk, moving the rocks in silence.*)

(*Blackout.*)

Scene IV

(*The same. Two months later.*)

(*Max and Horst are moving rocks. They wear jackets. Horst is slower than ever, as if dazed. He is holding the rocks with difficulty. He has a coughing spell.*)

MAX: You have a barracks leader.

(*Horst's coughing continues.*)

He can get you medicine.

(*The coughing continues.*)

He can try to get you medicine.

(*The coughing continues.*)

You must ask him.

(*The coughing continues.*)

You must get help.

(*The coughing continues.*)

You must stop coughing . . . !

(*The coughing spell slowly subsides.*)

HORST: It doesn't matter.

MAX: If you're nice to the Kapo . . .

HORST: It doesn't matter.

MAX: Some sort of medicine.

HORST: What for? The cough? How about the hands?

MAX: I told you what to do. Exercise.

HORST: They're frostbitten.

MAX: So exercise.

HORST: It doesn't matter.

MAX: Every night, I move my fingers up and down, one at a time, for a half hour. I don't do press-ups any more. Just fingers.

HORST: It doesn't matter.

MAX: You're losing weight.

HORST: I don't like sardines.

MAX: I don't know what's happening. I don't understand you.

HORST: It doesn't matter.

MAX: I can't talk you into anything. I can do that. I can talk people into things.

HORST: Can't talk me into sardines.

(*Horst starts to cough again. It goes on for a minute, then subsides.*)

MAX: It's getting worse.

HORST: It's getting colder.

MAX: You need medicine.

HORST: Stop nagging me.

MAX: See your Kapo.

HORST: He doesn't care.

MAX: Ask him.

HORST: He wants money.

MAX: Are you sure?

HORST: It doesn't matter.

MAX: I thought you cared about yourself.

HORST: You don't know anything.

MAX: I thought you loved yourself.

HORST: It's too cold.

MAX: You know what? (*Silence.*) You know what? You're turning into a Moslem.

HORST: You turned into a Jew. I turned into a Moslem.

MAX: It's not funny.

HORST: Moslems don't make jokes. So I'm not a Moslem. I'm just cold.

MAX: I'm scared.

HORST: Who isn't?

MAX: For you.

HORST: Be scared for yourself.

MAX: Why don't you listen to me?

HORST: Moslems don't listen.

MAX: You're not a Moslem.

HORST: Who said I was?

MAX: I didn't mean it. You're not a Moslem.

HORST: You're not a Jew.

MAX: Can't you ever forget that?

HORST: If I forget that . . . then . . . I am a Moslem.

(*The bell rings. They both drop their rocks and stand at attention, side by side, looking straight ahead.*)

    Look, I'm just cold. My fingers are numb. I can't stop coughing. I hate food. That's all. Nothing special. Don't get upset.

MAX: I want you to care.

HORST: I would. If I was warm.

MAX: I'll warm you.

HORST: You can't.

MAX: I know how.

HORST: No. You don't.

MAX: I do. I'm good at it. You said so.

HORST: When?

MAX: I'm next to you.

HORST: Don't start.

MAX: I'll make love to you.

HORST: Not now.

MAX: Yes. Now.

HORST: I have a headache. I can't.

MAX: Don't joke.

HORST: Moslems don't joke.

MAX: You're not a Moslem.

HORST: You're not a Jew.

MAX: Forget that.

HORST: No.

MAX: I'll make love to you.

HORST: No.

MAX: I'll make you warm.

(*Pause.*)

HORST: You can't.

MAX: You'll feel the warm . . .

HORST: I can't.

MAX: You'll *feel* it.

(*Pause.*)

HORST: In my fingers?

MAX: All over.

HORST: I can't.

MAX: I'm kissing your fingers.

HORST: They're numb.

MAX: My mouth is hot.

HORST: They're cold.

MAX: My mouth is on fire.

HORST: My fingers . . .

MAX: Are getting warm.

HORST: Are they?

MAX: They're getting warm.

HORST: I can't tell.

MAX: They're getting warm.

HORST: A little.

MAX: They're getting warm.

HORST: Yes.

MAX: My mouth is on fire. Your fingers are on fire. Your body's on fire.

HORST: Yes.

MAX: My mouth is all over you.

HORST: Yes.

MAX: My mouth is on your chest . . .

HORST: Yes.

MAX: Kissing your chest.

HORST: Yes.

MAX: Making it warm.

HORST: Yes.

MAX: Biting your nipple.

HORST: Yes.

MAX: Biting . . . into it . . .

HORST: Yes.

MAX: Harder . . . harder . . . harder . . .

HORST: Stop it! That hurts!

MAX: Harder . . .

HORST: No, stop it. I'm serious. You're hurting me.

(*A pause. Max catches his breath.*)

MAX: You pulled away.

HORST: Yes, I did.

MAX: It was exciting.

HORST: For *you* maybe. I don't try to hurt you.

MAX: I like being hurt. It's exciting.

HORST: It's not. Not when you're rough.

MAX: I'm not being rough.

HORST: Yes you are. Sometimes you are.

MAX: OK. So what? It's exciting.

HORST: Why'd you have to spoil it? You were making me warm. Why can't you be gentle?

MAX: I am.

HORST: You're not. You try to hurt me. You make me warm, and then you hurt me. I hurt enough. I don't want to feel *more* pain. Why can't you be gentle?

MAX: I am.

HORST: No, you're not. You're like them. You're like the guards. You're like the Gestapo. We stopped being gentle. I watched it, when we were on the outside. People made pain and called it love. I don't want to be like that. You don't make love to hurt.

MAX: I wanted to make you warm. That's all I wanted. I can't do anything right. I don't understand you. I used to do things right.

HORST: You still can.

MAX: People liked it when I got rough. Most. Not everybody. He didn't.

HORST: Who?

MAX: The dancer. But everyone else did. Just a little rough.

HORST: Did you like it?

MAX: I don't remember. I could never remember. I was always drunk. There was always coke. Nothing seemed to matter that much.

HORST: But some things do matter.

MAX: Not to you.

HORST: They do.

MAX: I don't understand you. All day long you've been saying nothing matters . . . your cough, your fingers . . .

HORST: They matter.

MAX: I don't understand anything anymore.

HORST: They all matter. I'm not a Moslem. You're not a Jew. My fingers are cold.

MAX: I want you to be happy.

HORST: Is that true?

MAX: I think so. I don't know. (*Pause.*) Yes.

HORST: Then be gentle with me.

MAX: I don't know how.

HORST: You know how.

MAX: You told me I don't.

HORST: I love you gentle. Love me gentle.

MAX: I don't know how.

HORST: Just hold me.

MAX: I'm afraid to hold you.

HORST: Don't be.

MAX: I'm afraid.

HORST: Don't be.

MAX: I'm going to drown.

HORST: Hold me. Please. Hold me.

MAX: OK. I'm holding you.

HORST: Are you?

MAX: Yes. You're in my arms.

HORST: Am I?

MAX: You're here in my arms. I promise. I'm holding you. You're here . . .

HORST: Touch me.

MAX: No.

HORST: Gently . . .

MAX: Here.

HORST: Are you?

MAX: Yes. Touching.

HORST: Gently.

MAX: Touching. Softly.

HORST: Warm me.

MAX: Softly.

HORST: Warm me . . . gently . . .

MAX: Softly . . . I'm touching you softly . . . gently . . . you're safe . . . I'll keep you safe . . . and warm . . . you're with me now . . . you'll never be cold again . . . I'm holding you now . . . safe . . . and warm . . . as long as you're here, as long as you're with me, as long as I'm holding you, you're safe . . .

(*Blackout.*)

Scene V

(*The same. Three days later.*)

(*Max is moving rocks. Horst is putting the rock pile into neat order.*)

HORST: The air is fresh today. Clean.

(*Horst starts to cough. He continues coughing, then stops.*)

MAX: It sounds better.

HORST: It does.

MAX: Loosening up.

HORST: It is.

MAX: The medicine is helping.

HORST: Yes. (*Silence.*) Thank you. (*Silence.*) Why don't you tell me?

MAX: Tell you what?

HORST: How you got it.

MAX: Told you. Spoke to my barracks leader. He took me to an officer.

HORST: Which one?

MAX: Some captain. The new one.

HORST: He's rotten.

MAX: You know him?

HORST: I've heard about him. You gave him money?

MAX: Yes.

HORST: I don't believe you.

MAX: Why?

HORST: You don't have any money.

MAX: My uncle sent me some.

HORST: No he didn't. He only wrote to you once.

MAX: He wrote to me again.

HORST: No. He didn't.

MAX: I didn't tell you.

HORST: Why not?

MAX: Because no one writes to *you*.

HORST: Your uncle wrote to you once.

MAX: He wrote to me again.

HORST: You're a liar.

MAX: Why don't you ever believe me?

HORST: Because I can tell when you're lying. You think you're so good at it. You're not. Your voice changes.

MAX: It what!

HORST: Changes. Sounds different.

MAX: Rubbish.

HORST: How'd you get it?

MAX: I gave him money.

HORST: Liar.

(*Silence.*)

MAX: Hey . . .

HORST: What?

MAX: Guess who I saw?

HORST: Where?

MAX: In my barracks.

HORST: Marlene Dietrich.

MAX: No. My landlord. From Berlin. Rosen.

HORST: Oh.

MAX: Nice man.

HORST: I thought you hated him.

MAX: Yes, I used to think he was what I was supposed to think he was.

HORST: What was that?

MAX: A lousy Jew.

HORST: He probably thought you were a lousy queer.

MAX: Probably.

HORST: Now he thinks you're not a queer. It's a shame.

MAX: It's not a shame. Don't start again.

(*Horst has a coughing spell.*)

You *are* taking the medicine?

(*The coughing subsides.*)

HORST: Of course I am. (*Silence.*) Of course I am, Max, I'm glad you got it.

MAX: So am I.

(*Silence.*)

HORST: Wish I knew how, though.

MAX: I told you.

HORST: You're a liar.

MAX: I am not.

HORST: It's just that . . . you don't have any money. Your uncle doesn't write to you. I know. It's silly for us to have secrets.

(*Silence.*)

MAX: Higher or lower?

HORST: What?

MAX: Does my voice get higher or lower?

HORST: Just different.

(*Silence.*)

MAX: I never met anyone like you. Can't make you believe anything.

HORST: How'd you get it?

MAX: You're never going to let up, are you?

HORST: Probably not.

MAX: Won't just be grateful.

HORST: Am I ever?

MAX: Suppose you don't like the answer.

HORST: I'll chance it.

MAX: Then when I tell you, you'll nag me about *that*.

HORST: You chance it.

MAX: I went down on him.

HORST: What?

MAX: You heard me?

HORST: No I didn't.

MAX: You wanted to know. I told you you wouldn't like it.

HORST: That SS captain?

MAX: Uh-huh.

HORST: He's the worst bastard in the . . .

MAX: I know.

HORST: You went down on him?

MAX: I had to. I didn't have any money.

HORST: You touched him?

MAX: No. I just went down on him. That's what he wanted. And I needed the medicine.

HORST: I'd rather cough.

MAX: No you wouldn't.

HORST: That bastard?

MAX: Yes.

HORST: Is he queer?

MAX: Who knows? Just felt like it, maybe. Of course, he could be queer. You don't like to think about that, do you? You don't want *them* to be queer.

HORST: No, I don't.

MAX: That's silly.

(*Silence.*)

HORST: Well, for once, you're right. It is silly. There *are* queer Nazis. And queer saints. And queer geniuses. And queer mediocrities. No better, no worse. Just people. I really believe that. That's why I signed Hirschfield's petition. That's why I ended up here. That's why I'm wearing this triangle. That's why you should be wearing it.

MAX: Do you think that captain would let a queer go down on him? Of course not. Somebody straight, yes. Even a Jew. But not a queer. That would mean maybe he was a queer. And even though maybe he *is*, he hates them more than . . .

HORST: Jews.

MAX: Yes. He'd kill me if he knew I was queer. My yellow star got your medicine.

HORST: Who needs it?

MAX: Then give it back. Throw it away. Throw it away, why don't you? And die. And you *will* die. In time. The cough will start it . . . I'm tired of being told I should have a pink triangle.

HORST: Well . . . (*Silence.*) He remember you?

MAX: Who?

HORST: Rosen?

MAX: Yes. He said I owed him rent.

HORST: What's Berlin like? Did he say?

MAX: Worse.

HORST: I miss it.

MAX: Yes. (*Pause.*) Ever go to the Silhouette?

HORST: Yes.

MAX: I never saw you there.

HORST: You weren't looking.

MAX: Greta's Club?
HORST: No.
MAX: Good. You had taste. The White Mouse?
HORST: Sometimes.
MAX: Surprised you never saw me.
HORST: What were you wearing?
MAX: Things that came off. I was conspicuous.
HORST: Why?
MAX: Because I was always making a fool of myself.
    I'm told. I don't remember. Did you sunbathe?
HORST: I loved to sunbathe.
MAX: In the nude?
HORST: Of course.
MAX: By the river.
HORST: That's right.
MAX: And you *never* saw me?
HORST: Well, actually, I did. I saw you by the river.
    You were making a fool of yourself. And I said
    some day, I'll be at Dachau with that man, moving
    rocks.
MAX: I didn't like Berlin. I mean, I wasn't happy. I
    was poor. I wasn't used to that. And always in a
    daze. And always scared. But I like it now. I miss
    it.

(*He finishes straightening the rocks and resumes moving
them.*)

HORST: We'll go back some day.
MAX: When we get out of here?
HORST: Yes.
MAX: We will, won't we?
HORST: We have to. Don't we?
MAX: Yes. Horst?
HORST: What?
MAX: We can go back together.

(*An SS Captain enters. The Corporal is with him. Max
and Horst look up for a second, then continue with
their task. The Captain stares at Max for a long time,
then Horst, then Max again.*)

CAPTAIN (*to Max*): You. Jew.

(*Max stands still.*)

MAX: Yes sir?
CAPTAIN: Feeling better?
MAX: Sir?
CAPTAIN: Your cold?
MAX: Yes sir.
CAPTAIN: Remarkable.
MAX: Yes sir.
CAPTAIN: You seem so strong.
MAX: Yes sir.
CAPTAIN: Not ill at all.
MAX: No sir.

CAPTAIN: No?
MAX: Not now, sir.
CAPTAIN: Carry on.

(*Max resumes moving rocks. The Captain watches
Max and Horst. He paces up and down. Max and
Horst move the rocks. The Captain paces. Horst coughs.
He catches himself, and tries to stifle it.*)

    Ah.

(*Horst stops the cough.*)

    You. Pervert.

(*Horst stiffens and stands still.*)

HORST: Yes sir?
CAPTAIN: Are you ill?
HORST: No sir.
CAPTAIN: You have a cough.
HORST: No sir.
CAPTAIN: I heard you cough.
HORST: Yes sir.
CAPTAIN: Something caught in your throat?
HORST: Yes sir.
CAPTAIN: From breakfast?
HORST: Yes sir.
CAPTAIN: Ah. Carry on.

(*Horst resumes his work. Max and Horst move the
rocks. The Captain stands watching them. He takes
out a cigarette. The Corporal lights it. The Captain
smokes the cigarette and watches Max and Horst.
Max and Horst continue moving rocks. Horst coughs
again, attempting to strangle it, but the cough comes
through.*)

CAPTAIN: You. Pervert.

(*Horst stands still.*)

HORST: Yes sir.
CAPTAIN: You coughed.
HORST: Yes sir.
CAPTAIN: You're not well.
HORST: I am, sir.
CAPTAIN: I see. (*To Max.*) You. Jew.

(*Max stands still.*)

MAX: Yes sir.
CAPTAIN: Watch.
MAX: Watch, sir?
CAPTAIN: Yes. Watch. (*To Horst.*) You.
HORST: Yes sir.
CAPTAIN: Put down that rock.
HORST: Yes sir.

(*He puts down the rock.*)

CAPTAIN: Good. Now take off your hat.

(*A long pause.*)

HORST: My hat, sir?
CAPTAIN: Yes. Your hat.
HORST: My hat, sir?
CAPTAIN: Your hat.
HORST: Yes sir.

(*Horst removes his hat. Max's hand moves. Horst shoots him a warning stare.*)

CAPTAIN (*to Max*): You.
MAX: Yes sir.
CAPTAIN: Relax.
MAX: Yes sir.
CAPTAIN: And watch.
MAX: Yes sir.
CAPTAIN (*to Horst*): You.
HORST: Yes sir.
CAPTAIN: Throw your hat away.

(*Horst flings his hat on the ground.*)

　　Not there.
HORST: Not there, sir?
CAPTAIN: No. Pick it up.
HORST: Yes sir.

(*He picks up his hat.*)

CAPTAIN: Throw it on the fence.
HORST: The fence, sir?
CAPTAIN: The fence.

(*Horst starts to cough.*)

　　That's all right. We'll wait.

(*The cough subsides.*)

　　Are you better?
HORST: Yes sir.
CAPTAIN: Nasty cough.
HORST: Yes sir.
CAPTAIN: On the fence. Now.
HORST: On the fence. Yes sir.

(*Horst glances at Max — another warning stare — then throws his hat on the fence. The fence sparks.*)

CAPTAIN (*to Max*): You.
MAX: Yes sir.
CAPTAIN: Are you watching?
MAX: Yes sir.
CAPTAIN: Good. (*To Horst.*) You.
HORST: Yes sir.
CAPTAIN: Get your hat. (*Silence.*) Did you hear me?
HORST: Yes sir.
CAPTAIN: Get your hat.

(*The Captain motions to the Corporal. The Corporal points his rifle at Horst.*)

HORST: Now, sir?
CAPTAIN: Now.
HORST: Are you sure, sir?
CAPTAIN: Quite.
HORST: Could I do without my hat, sir?
CAPTAIN: No.

(*Horst is silent for a moment. He feels Max watching and gives him another quick glance, his eyes saying, "don't move." He turns to the Captain.*)

HORST: Yes sir.

(*Horst looks at Max. He takes his hand and rubs his left eyebrow. He turns and stares at the Captain. The Captain waits. The Corporal is pointing his rifle. Horst turns toward the fence. He starts to walk very slowly to his hat. He almost reaches the fence when, suddenly, he turns and rushes at the Captain. He screams in fury. The Corporal shoots Horst. Horst continues to lunge at the Captain. His hand is out. He scratches the Captain's face. The Corporal shoots Horst in the back. He falls, dead.*)
　　(*Silence.*)
　　(*The Captain holds his face.*)

CAPTAIN (*to Max*): You. Jew.

(*Max is silent.*)

　　You!
MAX: Yes sir.
CAPTAIN: I hope the medicine helped. (*He turns to leave, then turns back.*) Get rid of the body.

(*Silence.*)

MAX: Yes sir.

(*The Captain leaves. The Corporal points the rifle at Max, lowers it, then walks off, after the Captain.*)
　　(*Max stares at Horst.*)
　　(*Silence.*)
　　(*Max opens his mouth to cry out. He can't.*)
　　(*Silence.*)
　　(*Max walks to Horst's body. He tries to lift it. It is heavy. He manages to pull the body partly up, Horst's head resting against Max's chest. He looks away. He takes Horst, feet dragging on the ground, toward the pit.*)
　　(*The bell rings.*)

　　No!

(*He looks up — off — at the Corporal, then back at Horst. He stands at attention. Horst starts to fall. Max pulls him up. He stands still, staring in front of him, holding on to Horst.*)

It's OK. I won't drop you. I'll hold you. If I stand at attention, I can hold you. They'll let me hold you. I won't let you down.

(*Silence.*)

I never held you before.

(*Silence.*)

You're safe. I won't drop you.

(*Silence.*)

Don't worry about the rocks. I'll do yours too. I'll move twice as many each day. I'll do yours too. You don't have to worry about them.

(*Silence.*)

I won't drop you.

(*Silence.*)

You know what?

(*Silence.*)

Horst?

(*Silence.*)

You know what?

(*Silence.*)

I think . . .

(*Silence.*)

I think I love you.

(*Silence.*)

Shh! Don't tell anyone. Don't worry about the rocks. I won't drop you. I promise . . . I think I loved . . . I can't remember his name. A dancer. I think I loved him too. Don't be jealous. Will I forget your name? No one else will touch the rocks. I think I loved . . . some boy, a long time ago. In my father's factory. Hans. That was his name. But the dancer. I don't remember. Don't be jealous. I won't let you drop.

(*Silence.*)

If I walk a little faster, I can do twice as many rocks a day. I won't let you down.

(*Silence.*)

I won't let you drop.

(*Silence.*)

I love you.

(*Silence.*)

What's wrong with that?

(*Silence.*)

I won't let you drop. I won't let you drop.

(*Silence.*)

You know what I did? I got your medicine.

(*Silence.*)

Hey —

(*Silence.*)

I don't remember your name.

(*Silence.*)

Oh my God! This can't be happening.

(*He starts to cry. The bell rings. He drags Horst's body to the pit. He throws it in the pit. He turns and looks at the rocks. He takes a deep breath. He walks over to the rocks and picks one up. He moves it across to the other side. He takes another deep breath. He stands still.*)

One. Two. Three. Four. Five. (*He takes another deep breath.*) Six. Seven. Eight. Nine. Ten.

(*He picks up a rock. He moves it across to the other side.*)
(*He moves another rock.*)
(*He moves another rock.*)
(*He moves another rock.*)
(*He pauses. He takes a deep breath.*)
(*He moves another rock.*)
(*He moves another rock.*)
(*He stops. He tries to take another deep breath. He can't. His hand is trembling. He steadies his hand. He picks up another rock and starts to move it.*)
(*He stops. He drops the rock. He moves toward the pit.*)
(*He jumps into the pit.*)
(*He disappears.*)
(*A long pause.*)
(*He climbs out of the pit.*)
(*He holds Horst's jacket, with the pink triangle on it. He takes off his own jacket. He puts Horst's jacket on.*)
(*He turns and looks at the fence.*)
(*He walks into the fence.*)
(*The fence lights up. It grows brighter and brighter, until the light consumes the stage.*)
(*And blinds the audience.*)

Sam Shepard

Samuel Shepard Rogers, Jr., was born in Illinois in 1943, but his father was a career man in the army and, like most "army brats," Shepard found himself essentially uprooted, moving from base to base around the country. If he has roots as a writer, they are clearly in the American West, but not necessarily the West created by writers of westerns, comic books, and second-rate movies. Shepard's plays often have a surreal quality, as if they are set in a world of the imagination rather than in a real place like Paris, Texas.

Shepard is one of America's most important playwrights, but without the broad popular appeal that would land his work on Broadway. He has, however, won numerous awards, including ten Obie Awards (given to off-Broadway plays) between 1966 and 1979, an Obie Award for sustained achievement in 1980, the New York Drama Critics' Circle Award for *A Lie of the Mind* in 1985, and a Pulitzer Prize for *Buried Child* in 1979. His work has been produced primarily in the experimental theater of downtown New York in places such as La Mama that are known for their artistic integrity but not for their capacity to reach a broad spectrum of theatergoers. In his way, Shepard has been an underground playwright who has won the respect of most theater people, including the best playwrights.

Shepard's love for and frustrations with music have found their way into a major theme of his work. He plays drums and guitar and has never realized an early desire for a career in rock music. But the subversive qualities of rock and roll — the critique of middle-class life implied in jazz and rock — appear in his plays in his analyses of the middle-class family. His primary themes center on the family and its complications, the nature of the person alone, set apart from everyone else, and the myth of the Old West. In each theme, Shepard expresses a deep sense of longing and of loss, emotions that his audiences have found significant.

Because his father began to drink and family life became intolerable, Shepard left home after a year at college and toured with the Bishops Company Repertory Players. At nineteen he wound up in New York working in one of the best jazz clubs of the time, the Village Gate. During this time in Greenwich Village he began to write one-act plays with extraordinary energy. Like Jack Kerouac, he almost never revised his work. He wrote it in a burst of energy and then had it performed to audiences whose admiration grew.

In the 1970s Shepard began acting in major motion pictures. One of the ironies of his life is that he has become a matinee idol after appearing in movies such as *The Right Stuff, Fool for Love, Country,* and *Crimes of the Heart.* The critic Harry Haun has said of him, "He is the Recluse as Superstar, the man who has arrived on his own terms, carefully sculpting a special myth for himself."

His output for the stage has been prodigious, with dozens of one-act plays that have not been revived after an initial run. But he has a central body of work that has gained him an enviable reputation. *Operation Sidewinder* (1970) was performed at the Vivian Beaumont Theater — a public theater at Lincoln Center in New York City — to mixed reviews. The play, set in the West, involves a giant mechanical snake designed to make contact with outer space travelers and includes Hopi snake dances as well as military scenes. *The Tooth of Crime* (1972) is about turf wars between an aging rock star and an up-and-coming young star. It has a brutality and directness that make it intense, exciting, and revealing of the way things really were in California rock and roll in the early 1970s.

Curse of the Starving Class (1977) and *Buried Child* (1978) both helped solidify Shepard's reputation. *Suicide in B-flat* (1976) and *True West* (1980) only made it clearer that his work was developing in a consistent vein of black humor and dark criticism of the sanctity of family life. *A Lie of the Mind* (1985), like *Buried Child*, is about disturbed family life. It is filled with secrets: incest, murder, and sin. *New York Times* critic Mel Gussow said it explores "the damage that one does to filial, fraternal and marital bonds." Incest — or potential incest — is also a theme in *A Fool for Love* (1983), in which Shepard starred on film. The play is set in the West and contains all the themes for which his work is known.

Shepard began his work with a sense of the West drawn from popular literature, reshaped it, and sent it back to us in a new form. If the American West has a reality that survived its mythicization in the dime novel and John Wayne's movies, then Shepard is partly responsible for the way we now see it. Whether it is more realistic or less — or even whether that concept applies — is something that must concern anyone who sees or reads his work.

TRUE WEST

True West (1980) portrays a family, or part of a family, shattered by unknown circumstances into individuals isolated in their inability to understand and express their feelings for one another. The past is a strange, silent land that no one seems to be able to discover. The image of the desert that lingers throughout the play — in contrast with the cricket-drenched suburban setting — is an image of a pure, strange, and liberating environment. In some plays it might represent a nostalgia for a happy past. Instead, in *True West* it seems to imply a place where a person, like the religious hermits of the early Christian church, can be alone and somehow commune with an inner self.

The theme of loneliness is woven in complex ways into the play. The father is in a desert somewhere drinking himself into oblivion. Mom goes vacationing alone to Alaska, a cold glacial desert that leaves her with a sense of longing not for people but for her plants. When the play opens, Austin, the screenwriter, has taken Mom's house while she is away so he can be alone and write in peace and quiet. Lee, the older, outsider brother, breaks in on his peace and quiet in the same manner that he breaks into houses in the neighborhood and steals TVs. But when he visits Mom's house and finds Austin, it is not a TV he ends up stealing: He steals Austin's livelihood and, in a fascinating way, his identity.

The struggle between Austin and Lee has a profound psychological quality that implies an almost unnatural terror. Lee and Austin are like two halves of the same person, but two halves that express totally antagonistic qualities. In their efforts to be one another, they are both trying to join the intellectual and violent sides of their nature. Early in the play Lee tells Austin "I always wondered what'd be like to be you." Austin's surprised response is to tell Lee that he has always pictured him somewhere — which is to say that he has felt much the same way.

In their aloneness Austin and Lee acknowledge a sense of incompleteness. Such an awareness is not expressed by Mom, nor is it implied about the father. In this sense, Lee and Austin are very different from their parents. Whether that difference represents a hopeful sign is an unanswered question. The play ends with a power struggle between the brothers, but a struggle not so much for ultimate control as for a successful merger of their identities. The outcome of the action is in every sense in doubt as the play ends.

The title of the play carries special irony. Saul, the producer, tells Austin that Lee's outline for a story has the ring of truth to it. Austin knows the Hollywood scene, the dishonesty that produces three hundred thousand dollar deals. Sam Shepard knows it, too. His commentary is on the Hollywood shams that pretend to be true pictures of the American West. Lee and Austin represent a portrait of the true West; and to an extent the loneliness of the Mojave Desert represents the true West. But paying attention to the truth is painful. The true West is not a B movie; it is not a piece of escapist claptrap. It is an almost schizoid disunity, a play of opposites and painful discords.

Sam Shepard (b. 1943)
TRUE WEST

1980

Characters

AUSTIN, *early thirties, light blue sports shirt, light tan cardigan sweater, clean blue jeans, white tennis shoes*

LEE, *his older brother, early forties, filthy white t-shirt, tattered brown overcoat covered with dust, dark blue baggy pants from the Salvation Army, pink suede belt, pointed black forties dress shoes scuffed up, holes in the soles, no socks, no hat, long pronounced sideburns, "Gene Vincent" hairdo, two days' growth of beard, bad teeth*

SAUL KIMMER, *late forties, Hollywood producer, pink and white flower print sports shirt, white sports coat with matching polyester slacks, black and white loafers*

MOM, *early sixties, mother of the brothers, small woman, conservative white skirt and matching jacket, red shoulder bag, two pieces of matching red luggage.*

Scene: *All nine scenes take place on the same set; a kitchen and adjoining alcove of an older home in a Southern California suburb, about 40 miles east of Los Angeles. The kitchen takes up most of the playing area to stage left. The kitchen consists of a sink, upstage center, surrounded by counter space, a wall telephone, cupboards, and a small window just above it bordered by neat yellow curtains. Stage left of sink is a stove. Stage right, a refrigerator. The alcove adjoins the kitchen to stage right. There is no wall division or door to the alcove. It is open and easily accessible from the kitchen and defined only by the objects in it: a small round glass breakfast table mounted on white iron legs, two matching white iron chairs set across from each other. The two exterior walls of the alcove which prescribe a corner in the upstage right are composed*

of many small windows, beginning from a solid wall about three feet high and extending to the ceiling. The windows look out to bushes and citrus trees. The alcove is filled with all sorts of house plants in various pots, mostly Boston ferns hanging in planters at different levels. The floor of the alcove is composed of green synthetic grass.

All entrances and exits are made stage left from the kitchen. There is no door. The actors simply go off and come onto the playing area.

Note on Set and Costume: *The set should be constructed realistically with no attempt to distort its dimensions, shapes, objects, or colors. No objects should be introduced which might draw special attention to themselves other than the props demanded by the script. If a stylistic "concept" is grafted onto the set design it will only serve to confuse the evolution of the characters' situation, which is the most important focus of the play.*

Likewise, the costumes should be exactly representative of who the characters are and not added on to for the sake of making a point to the audience.

Note on Sound: *The coyote of Southern California has a distinct yapping, doglike bark, similar to a hyena. This yapping grows more intense and maniacal as the pack grows in numbers, which is usually the case when they lure and kill pets from suburban yards. The sense of growing frenzy in the pack should be felt in the background, particularly in Scenes VII and VIII. In any case, these coyotes never make the long, mournful, solitary howl of the Hollywood stereotype.*

The sound of crickets can speak for itself.

These sounds should also be treated realistically even though they sometimes grow in volume and numbers.

ACT I • Scene I ─────────────

(*Night. Sound of crickets in dark. Candlelight appears in alcove, illuminating Austin, seated at glass table hunched over a writing notebook, pen in hand, cigarette burning in ashtray, cup of coffee, typewriter on table, stacks of paper, candle burning on table.*)

(*Soft moonlight fills kitchen illuminating Lee, beer in hand, six-pack on counter behind him. He's leaning against the sink, mildly drunk; takes a slug of beer.*)

LEE: So, Mom took off for Alaska, huh?

AUSTIN: Yeah.

LEE: Sorta' left you in charge.

AUSTIN: Well, she knew I was coming down here so she offered me the place.

LEE: You keepin' the plants watered?

AUSTIN: Yeah.

LEE: Keepin' the sink clean? She don't like even a single tea leaf in the sink ya' know.

AUSTIN (*trying to concentrate on writing*): Yeah, I know.

(*Pause.*)

LEE: She gonna' be up there a long time?

AUSTIN: I don't know.

LEE: Kinda' nice for you, huh? Whole place to yourself.

AUSTIN: Yeah, it's great.

LEE: Ya' got crickets anyway. Tons a' crickets out there. (*Looks around kitchen.*) Ya' got groceries? Coffee?

AUSTIN (*looking up from writing*): What?

LEE: You got coffee?

AUSTIN: Yeah.

LEE: At's good. (*Short pause.*) Real coffee? From the bean?

AUSTIN: Yeah. You want some?

LEE: Naw. I brought some uh — (*Motions to beer.*)

AUSTIN: Help yourself to whatever's — (*Motions to refrigerator.*)

LEE: I will. Don't worry about me. I'm not the one to worry about. I mean I can uh — (*Pause.*) You always work by candlelight?

AUSTIN: No — uh — Not always.

LEE: Just sometimes?

AUSTIN (*puts pen down, rubs his eyes*): Yeah. Sometimes it's soothing.

LEE: Isn't that what the old guys did?

AUSTIN: What old guys?

LEE: The Forefathers. You know.

AUSTIN: Forefathers?

LEE: Isn't that what they did? Candlelight burning into the night? Cabins in the wilderness.

AUSTIN (*rubs hand through his hair*): I suppose.

LEE: I'm not botherin' you am I? I mean I don't wanna break into yer uh — concentration or nothin'.

AUSTIN: No, it's all right.

LEE: That's good. I mean I realize that yer line a' work demands a lota' concentration.

AUSTIN: It's okay.

LEE: You probably think that I'm not fully able to comprehend somethin' like that, huh?

AUSTIN: Like what?

LEE: That stuff yer doin'. That art. You know. Whatever you call it.

AUSTIN: It's just a little research.

LEE: You may not know it but I did a little art myself once.

AUSTIN: You did?

LEE: Yeah! I did some a' that. I fooled around with it. No future in it.

AUSTIN: What'd you do?

LEE: Never mind what I did! Just never mind about that. (*Pause.*) It was ahead of its time.

(*Pause.*)

AUSTIN: So, you went out to see the old man, huh?

LEE: Yeah, I seen him.

AUSTIN: How's he doing?

LEE: Same. He's doin' just about the same.

AUSTIN: I was down there too, you know.

LEE: What d'ya' want, an award? You want some kinda' medal? You were down there. He told me all about you.

AUSTIN: What'd he say?

LEE: He told me. Don't worry.

(*Pause.*)

AUSTIN: Well —

LEE: You don't have to say nothin'.

AUSTIN: I wasn't.

LEE: Yeah, you were gonna' make somethin' up. Somethin' brilliant.

(*Pause.*)

AUSTIN: You going to be down here very long, Lee?

LEE: Might be. Depends on a few things.

AUSTIN: You got some friends down here?

LEE (*laughs*): I know a few people. Yeah.

AUSTIN: Well, you can stay here as long as I'm here.

LEE: I don't need your permission do I?

AUSTIN: No.

LEE: I mean she's my mother too, right?

AUSTIN: Right.

LEE: She might've just as easily asked me to take care of her place as you.

AUSTIN: That's right.

LEE: I mean I know how to water plants.

(*Long pause.*)

AUSTIN: So you don't know how long you'll be staying then?

LEE: Depends mostly on houses, ya' know.

AUSTIN: Houses?

LEE: Yeah. Houses. Electric devices. Stuff like that. I gotta' make a little tour first.

(*Short pause.*)

AUSTIN: Lee, why don't you just try another neighborhood, all right?

LEE (*laughs*): What'sa matter with this neighborhood? This is a great neighborhood. Lush. Good class a' people. Not many dogs.

AUSTIN: Well, our uh — Our mother just happens to live here. That's all.

LEE: Nobody's gonna' know. All they know is somethin's missing. That's all. She'll never even hear about it. Nobody's gonna' know.

AUSTIN: You're going to get picked up if you start walking around here at night.

LEE: Me? I'm gonna' git picked up? What about you? You stick out like a sore thumb. Look at you. You think yer regular lookin'?

AUSTIN: I've got too much to deal with here to be worrying about —

LEE: Yer not gonna' have to worry about me! I've been doin' all right without you. I haven't been anywhere near you for five years! Now isn't that true?

AUSTIN: Yeah.

LEE: So you don't have to worry about me. I'm a free agent.

AUSTIN: All right.

LEE: Now all I wanna' do is borrow yer car.

AUSTIN: No!

LEE: Just fer a day. One day.

AUSTIN: No!

LEE: I won't take it outside a twenty mile radius. I promise ya'. You can check the speedometer.

AUSTIN: You're not borrowing my car! That's all there is to it.

(*Pause.*)

LEE: Then I'll just take the damn thing.

AUSTIN: Lee, look — I don't want any trouble, all right?

LEE: That's a dumb line. That is a dumb fuckin' line. You git paid fer dreamin' up a line like that?

AUSTIN: Look, I can give you some money if you need money.

(*Lee suddenly lunges at Austin, grabs him violently by the shirt, and shakes him with tremendous power.*)

LEE: Don't you say that to me! Don't you ever say that to me! (*Just as suddenly he turns him loose, pushes him away, and backs off.*) You may be able to git away with that with the Old Man. Git him tanked up for a week! Buy him off with yer Hol-

lywood blood money, but not me! I can git my own money my own way. Big money!

AUSTIN: I was just making an offer.

LEE: Yeah, well keep it to yourself!

(*Long pause.*)

Those are the most monotonous fuckin' crickets I ever heard in my life.

AUSTIN: I kinda' like the sound.

LEE: Yeah. Supposed to be able to tell the temperature by the number a' pulses. You believe that?

AUSTIN: The temperature?

LEE: Yeah. The air. How hot it is.

AUSTIN: How do you do that?

LEE: I don't know. Some woman told me that. She was a Botanist. So I believed her.

AUSTIN: Where'd you meet her?

LEE: What?

AUSTIN: The woman Botanist?

LEE: I met her on the desert. I been spendin' a lota' time on the desert.

AUSTIN: What were you doing out there?

LEE: (*pause, stares in space*): I forgit. Had me a Pit Bull there for a while but I lost him.

AUSTIN: Pit Bull?

LEE: Fightin' dog. Damn I made some good money off that little dog. Real good money.

(*Pause.*)

AUSTIN: You could come up north with me, you know.

LEE: What's up there?

AUSTIN: My family.

LEE: Oh, that's right, you got the wife and kiddies now don't ya'. The house, the car, the whole slam. That's right.

AUSTIN: You could spend a couple of days. See how you like it. I've got an extra room.

LEE: Too cold up there.

(*Pause.*)

AUSTIN: You want to sleep for a while?

LEE (*pause, stares at Austin*): I don't sleep.

(*Lights to black.*)

Scene II

(*Morning. Austin is watering plants with a vaporizer, Lee sits at glass table in alcove drinking beer.*)

LEE: I never realized the old lady was so security-minded.

AUSTIN: How do you mean?

LEE: Made a little tour this morning. She's got locks on everything. Locks and double locks and chain locks and — What's she got that's so valuable?

AUSTIN: Antiques I guess. I don't know.

LEE: Antiques? Brought everything with her from the old place, huh. Just the same crap we always had around. Plates and spoons.

AUSTIN: I guess they have personal value to her.

LEE: Personal value. Yeah. Just a lota' junk. Most of it's phony anyway. Idaho decals. Now who in the hell wants to eat offa' plate with the State of Idaho starin' ya in the face. Every time ya' take a bite ya' get to see a little bit more.

AUSTIN: Well it must mean something to her or she wouldn't save it.

LEE: Yeah, well personally I don't wann' be invaded by Idaho when I'm eatin'. When I'm eatin' I'm home. Ya' know what I'm sayin'? I'm not driftin', I'm home. I don't need my thoughts swept off to Idaho. I don't need that!

(*Pause.*)

AUSTIN: Did you go out last night?

LEE: Why?

AUSTIN: I thought I heard you go out.

LEE: Yeah, I went out. What about it?

AUSTIN: Just wondered.

LEE: Damn coyotes kept me awake.

AUSTIN: Oh yeah, I heard them. They must've killed somebody's dog or something.

LEE: Yappin' their fool heads off. They don't yap like that on the desert. They howl. These are city coyotes here.

AUSTIN: Well, you don't sleep anyway do you?

(*Pause, Lee stares at him.*)

LEE: You're pretty smart aren't ya?

AUSTIN: How do you mean?

LEE: I mean you never had any more on the ball than I did. But here you are gettin' invited into prominent people's houses. Sittin' around talkin' like you know somethin'.

AUSTIN: They're not so prominent.

LEE: They're a helluva' lot more prominent than the houses I get invited into.

AUSTIN: Well you invite yourself.

LEE: That's right. I do. In fact I probably got a wider range a' choices than you do, come to think of it.

AUSTIN: I wouldn't doubt it.

LEE: In fact I been inside some pretty classy places in my time. And I never even went to an Ivy League school either.

AUSTIN: You want some breakfast or something?

LEE: Breakfast?

AUSTIN: Yeah. Don't you eat breakfast?

LEE: Look, don't worry about me pal. I can take care a' myself. You just go ahead as though I wasn't even here, all right?

(*Austin goes into kitchen, makes coffee.*)

AUSTIN: Where'd you walk to last night?

(*Pause.*)

LEE: I went up in the foothills there. Up in the San Gabriels. Heat was drivin' me crazy.

AUSTIN: Well, wasn't it hot out on the desert?

LEE: Different kinda' heat. Out there it's clean. Cools off at night. There's a nice little breeze.

AUSTIN: Where were you, the Mojave?

LEE: Yeah. The Mojave. That's right.

AUSTIN: I haven't been out there in years.

LEE: Out past Needles there.

AUSTIN: Oh yeah.

LEE: Up here it's different. This country's real different.

AUSTIN: Well, it's been built up.

LEE: Built up? Wiped out is more like it. I don't even hardly recognize it.

AUSTIN: Yeah. Foothills are the same though, aren't they?

LEE: Pretty much. It's funny goin' up in there. The smells and everything. Used to catch snakes up there, remember?

AUSTIN: You caught snakes.

LEE: Yeah. And you'd pretend you were Geronimo or some damn thing. You used to go right out to lunch.

AUSTIN: I enjoyed my imagination.

LEE: That what you call it? Looks like yer still enjoyin' it.

AUSTIN: So you just wandered around up there, huh?

LEE: Yeah. With a purpose.

AUSTIN: See any houses?

(*Pause.*)

LEE: Couple. Couple a' real nice ones. One of 'em didn't even have a dog. Walked right up and stuck my head in the window. Not a peep. Just a sweet kinda' suburban silence.

AUSTIN: What kind of a place was it?

LEE: Like a paradise. Kinda' place that sorta' kills ya' inside. Warm yellow lights. Mexican tile all around. Copper pots hangin' over the stove. Ya' know like they got in the magazines. Blond people movin' in and outa' the rooms, talkin' to each other. (*Pause.*) Kinda' place you wish you sorta' grew up in, ya' know.

AUSTIN: That's the kind of place you wish you'd grown up in?

LEE: Yeah, why not?

AUSTIN: I thought you hated that kind of stuff.

LEE: Yeah, well you never knew too much about me did ya'?

(*Pause.*)

AUSTIN: Why'd you go out to the desert in the first place?

LEE: I was on my way to see the old man.

AUSTIN: You mean you just passed through there?

LEE: Yeah. That's right. Three months of passin' through.

AUSTIN: Three months?

LEE: Somethin' like that. Maybe more. Why?

AUSTIN: You lived on the Mojave for three months?

LEE: Yeah. What'sa matter with that?

AUSTIN: By yourself?

LEE: Mostly. Had a couple a' visitors. Had that dog for a while.

AUSTIN: Didn't you miss people?

LEE (*laughs*): People?

AUSTIN: Yeah. I mean I go crazy if I have to spend three nights in a motel by myself.

LEE: Yer not in a motel now.

AUSTIN: No, I know. But sometimes I have to stay in motels.

LEE: Well, they got people in motels don't they?

AUSTIN: Strangers.

LEE: Yer friendly aren't ya'? Aren't you the friendly type?

(*Pause.*)

AUSTIN: I'm going to have somebody coming by here later, Lee.

LEE: Ah! Lady friend?

AUSTIN: No, a producer.

LEE: Aha! What's he produce?

AUSTIN: Film. Movies. You know.

LEE: Oh, movies. Motion Pictures! A Big Wig Huh?

AUSTIN: Yeah.

LEE: What's he comin' by here for?

AUSTIN: We have to talk about a project.

LEE: Whadya' mean, "a project"? What's "a project"?

AUSTIN: A script.

LEE: Oh. That's what yer doin' with all these papers?

AUSTIN: Yeah.

LEE: Well, what's the project about?

AUSTIN: We're uh — it's a period piece.

LEE: What's "a period piece"?

AUSTIN: Look, it doesn't matter. The main thing is we need to discuss this alone. I mean —

LEE: Oh, I get it. You want me outa' the picture.

AUSTIN: Not exactly. I just need to be alone with him for a couple of hours. So we can talk.

LEE: Yer afraid I'll embarrass ya' huh?

AUSTIN: I'm not afraid you'll embarrass me!

LEE: Well, I tell ya' what — Why don't you just gimme the keys to yer car and I'll be back here around six o'clock or so. That give ya enough time?

AUSTIN: I'm not loaning you my car, Lee.

LEE: You want me to just git lost huh? Take a hike? Is that it? Pound the pavement for a few hours while you bullshit yer way into a million bucks.

AUSTIN: Look, it's going to be hard enough for me to face this character on my own without —

LEE: You don't know this guy?

AUSTIN: No I don't know — He's a producer. I mean I've been meeting with him for months but you never get to know a producer.

LEE: Yer tryin' to hustle him? Is that it?

AUSTIN: I'm not trying to hustle him! I'm trying to work out a deal! It's not easy.

LEE: What kinda' deal?

AUSTIN: Convince him it's a worthwhile story.

LEE: He's not convinced? How come he's comin' over here if he's not convinced? I'll convince him for ya'.

AUSTIN: You don't understand the way things work down here.

LEE: How do things work down here?

(*Pause.*)

AUSTIN: Look, if I loan you my car will you have it back here by six?

LEE: On the button. With a full tank a' gas.

AUSTIN: (*digging in his pocket for keys*): Forget about the gas.

LEE: Hey, these days gas is gold, old buddy.

(*Austin hands the keys to Lee.*)

You remember that car I used to loan you?

AUSTIN: Yeah.

LEE: Forty Ford. Flathead.

AUSTIN: Yeah.

LEE: Sucker hauled ass didn't it?

AUSTIN: Lee, it's not that I don't want to loan you my car —

LEE: You are loanin' me yer car.

(*Lee gives Austin a pat on the shoulder, pause.*)

AUSTIN: I know. I just wish —

LEE: What? You wish what?

AUSTIN: I don't know. I wish I wasn't — I wish I didn't have to be doing business down here. I'd like to just spend some time with you.

LEE: I thought it was "Art" you were doin'.

(*Lee moves across kitchen toward exit, tosses keys in his hand.*)

AUSTIN: Try to get back here by six, okay?

LEE: No sweat. Hey, ya' know, if that uh — story of yours doesn't go over with the guy — tell him I got a couple a' "projects" he might be interested in. Real commercial. Full a' suspense. True-to-life stuff.

(*Lee exits, Austin stares after Lee then turns, goes to papers at table, leafs through pages, lights fade to black.*)

Scene III

(*Afternoon. Alcove, Saul Kimmer and Austin seated across from each other at table.*)

SAUL: Well, to tell you the truth Austin, I have never felt so confident about a project in quite a long time.

AUSTIN: Well, that's good to hear, Saul.

SAUL: I am absolutely convinced we can get this thing off the ground. I mean we'll have to make a sale to television and that means getting a major star. Somebody bankable. But I think we can do it. I really do.

AUSTIN: Don't you think we need a first draft before we approach a star?

SAUL: No, no, not at all. I don't think it's necessary. Maybe a brief synopsis. I don't want you to touch the typewriter until we have some seed money.

AUSTIN: That's fine with me.

SAUL: I mean it's a great story. Just the story alone. You've really managed to capture something this time.

AUSTIN: I'm glad you like it, Saul.

(*Lee enters abruptly into kitchen carrying a stolen television set, short pause.*)

LEE: Aw shit, I'm sorry about that. I am really sorry Austin.

AUSTIN (*standing*): That's all right.

LEE (*moving toward them*): I mean I thought it was way past six already. You said to have it back here by six.

AUSTIN: We were just finishing up. (*To Saul.*) This is my, uh — brother, Lee.

SAUL (*standing*): Oh, I'm very happy to meet you.

(*Lee sets T.V. on sink counter, shakes hands with Saul.*)

LEE: I can't tell ya' how happy I am to meet you sir.

SAUL: Saul Kimmer.

LEE: Mr. Kipper.

SAUL: Kimmer.

AUSTIN: Lee's been living out on the desert and he just uh —

SAUL: Oh, that's terrific! (*To Lee.*) Palm Springs?

LEE: Yeah. Yeah, right. Right around in that area. Near uh — Bob Hope Drive there.

SAUL: Oh I love it out there. I just love it. The air is wonderful.

LEE: Yeah. Sure is. Healthy.

SAUL: And the golf. I don't know if you play golf, but the golf is just about the best.

LEE: I play a lota' golf.

SAUL: Is that right?

LEE: Yeah. In fact I was hoping I'd run into somebody out here who played a little golf. I've been lookin' for a partner.

SAUL: Well, I uh —

AUSTIN: Lee's just down for a visit while our mother's in Alaska.

SAUL: Oh, your mother's in Alaska?

AUSTIN: Yes. She went up there on a little vacation. This is her place.

SAUL: I see. Well isn't that something. Alaska.

LEE: What kinda' handicap do ya' have, Mr. Kimmer?

SAUL: Oh I'm just a Sunday duffer really. You know.

LEE: That's good 'cause I haven't swung a club in months.

SAUL: Well we ought to get together sometime and have a little game. Austin, do you play?

(*Saul mimes a Johnny Carson golf swing for Austin.*)

AUSTIN: No. I don't uh — I've watched it on T.V.

LEE (*to Saul*): How 'bout tomorrow morning? Bright and early. We could get out there and put in eighteen holes before breakfast.

SAUL: Well, I've got uh — I have several appointments—

LEE: No, I mean real early. Crack a' dawn. While the dew's still thick on the fairway.

SAUL: Sounds really great.

LEE: Austin could be our caddie.

SAUL: Now that's an idea. (*Laughs.*)

AUSTIN: I don't know the first thing about golf.

LEE: There's nothin' to it. Isn't that right, Saul? He'd pick it up in fifteen minutes.

SAUL: Sure. Doesn't take long. 'Course you have to play for years to find your true form. (*Chuckles.*)

LEE (*to Austin*): We'll give ya' a quick run-down on the club faces. The irons, the woods. Show ya' a couple pointers on the basic swing. Might even let ya' hit the ball a couple times. Whadya' think, Saul?

SAUL: Why not. I think it'd be great. I haven't had any exercise in weeks.

LEE: 'At's the spirit! We'll have a little orange juice right afterwards.

(*Pause.*)

SAUL: Orange juice?

LEE: Yea! Vitamin C! Nothin' like a shot a' orange juice after a round a' golf. Hot shower. Snappin' towels at each others' privates. Real sense a' fraternity.

SAUL (*smiles at Austin*): Well, you make it sound very inviting, I must say. It really does sound great.

LEE: Then it's a date.

SAUL: Well, I'll call the country club and see if I can arrange something.

LEE: Great! Boy, I sure am sorry that I busted in on ya' all in the middle of yer meeting.

SAUL: Oh that's quite all right. We were just about finished anyway.

LEE: I can wait out in the other room if you want.

SAUL: No really —

LEE: Just got Austin's color T.V. back from the shop. I can watch a little amateur boxing now.

(*Lee and Austin exchange looks.*)

SAUL: Oh — Yes.

LEE: You don't fool around in Television, do you Saul?

SAUL: Uh — I have in the past. Produced some T.V. Specials. Network stuff. But it's mainly features now.

LEE: That's where the big money is, huh?

SAUL: Yes. That's right.

AUSTIN: Why don't I call you tomorrow, Saul and we'll get together. We can have lunch or something.

SAUL: That'd be terrific.

LEE: Right after the golf.

(*Pause.*)

SAUL: What?

LEE: You can have lunch right after the golf.

SAUL: Oh, right.

LEE: Austin was tellin' me that yer interested in stories.

SAUL: Well, we develop certain projects that we feel have commercial potential.

LEE: What kinda' stuff do ya' go in for?

SAUL: Oh, the usual. You know. Good love interest. Lots of action. (*Chuckles at Austin.*)

LEE: Westerns?

SAUL: Sometimes.

AUSTIN: I'll give you a ring, Saul.

(*Austin tries to move Saul across the kitchen but Lee blocks their way.*)

LEE: I got a Western that'd knock yer lights out.

SAUL: Oh really?

LEE: Yeah. Contemporary Western. Based on a true story. 'Course I'm not a writer like my brother here. I'm not a man of the pen.

SAUL: Well —

LEE: I mean I can tell ya' a story off the tongue but I can't put it down on paper. That don't make any difference though does it?

SAUL: No, not really.

LEE: I mean plenty a' guys have stories don't they? True-life stories. Musta' been a lota' movies made from real life.

SAUL: Yes, I suppose so.

LEE: I haven't seen a good Western since *Lonely Are the Brave.* You remember that movie?

SAUL: No, I'm afraid I —

LEE: Kirk Douglas. Helluva' movie. You remember that movie, Austin?

AUSTIN: Yes.

LEE (*to Saul*): The man dies for the love of a horse.

SAUL: Is that right.

LEE: Yeah. Ya' hear the horse screamin' at the end of it. Rain's comin' down. Horse is screamin'. Then there's a shot. BLAM! Just a single shot like that. Then nothin' but the sound of rain. And Kirk Douglas is ridin' in the ambulance. Ridin' away from the scene of the accident. And when he hears that shot he knows that his horse has died. He knows. And you see his eyes. And his eyes die. Right inside his face. And then his eyes close. And you know that he's died too. You know that Kirk Douglas has died from the death of his horse.

SAUL (*eyes Austin nervously*): Well, it sounds like a great movie. I'm sorry I missed it.

LEE: Yeah, you shouldn't a' missed that one.

SAUL: I'll have to try to catch it some time. Arrange a screening or something. Well, Austin, I'll have to hit the freeway before rush hour.

AUSTIN: (*ushers him toward exit*): It's good seeing you, Saul.

(*Austin and Saul shake hands.*)

LEE: So ya' think there's room for a real Western these days? A true-to-life Western?

SAUL: Well, I don't see why not. Why don't you uh — tell the story to Austin and have him write a little outline.

LEE: You'd take a look at it then?

SAUL: Yes. Sure. I'll give it a read-through. Always eager for new material. (*Smiles at Austin.*)

LEE: That's great! You'd really read it then huh?

SAUL: It would just be my opinion of course.

LEE: That's all I want. Just an opinion. I happen to think it has a lota' possibilities.

SAUL: Well, it was great meeting you and I'll —

(*Saul and Lee shake.*)

LEE: I'll call you tomorrow about the golf.

SAUL: Oh. Yes, right.

LEE: Austin's got your number, right?

SAUL: Yes.

LEE: So long Saul. (*Gives Saul a pat on the back.*)

(*Saul exits, Austin turns to Lee, looks at T.V. then back to Lee.*)

AUSTIN: Give me the keys.

(*Austin extends his hand toward Lee, Lee doesn't move, just stares at Austin, smiles, lights to black.*)

Scene IV

(*Night. Coyotes in distance, fade, sound of typewriter in dark, crickets, candlelight in alcove, dim light in kitchen, lights reveal Austin at glass table typing, Lee sits across from him, foot on table, drinking beer and whiskey, the T.V. is still on sink counter, Austin types for a while, then stops.)*

LEE: All right, now read it back to me.

AUSTIN: I'm not reading it back to you, Lee. You can read it when we're finished. I can't spend all night on this.

LEE: You got better things to do?

AUSTIN: Let's just go ahead. Now what happens when he leaves Texas?

LEE: Is he ready to leave Texas yet? I didn't know we were that far along. He's not ready to leave Texas.

AUSTIN: He's right at the border.

LEE (*sitting up*): No, see this is one a' the crucial parts. Right here. (*Taps paper with beer can.*) We can't rush through this. He's not right at the border. He's a good fifty miles from the border. A lot can happen in fifty miles.

AUSTIN: It's only an outline. We're not writing an entire script now.

LEE: Well ya' can't leave things out even if it is an outline. It's one a' the most important parts. Ya' can't go leavin' it out.

AUSTIN: Okay, okay. Let's just — get it done.

LEE: All right. Now. He's in the truck and he's got his horse trailer and his horse.

AUSTIN: We've already established that.

LEE: And he sees this other guy comin' up behind him in another truck. And that truck is pullin' a gooseneck.

AUSTIN: What's a gooseneck?

LEE: Cattle trailer. You know the kind with a gooseneck, goes right down in the bed a' the pick-up.

AUSTIN: Oh. All right. (*Types.*)

LEE: It's important.

AUSTIN: Okay. I got it.

LEE: All these details are important.

(*Austin types as they talk.*)

AUSTIN: I've got it.

LEE: And this other guy's got his horse all saddled up in the back a' the gooseneck.

AUSTIN: Right.

LEE: So both these guys have got their horses right along with 'em, see.

AUSTIN: I understand.

LEE: Then this first guy suddenly realizes two things.

AUSTIN: The guy in front?

LEE: Right. The guy in front realizes two things almost at the same time. Simultaneous.

AUSTIN: What were the two things?

LEE: Number one, he realizes that the guy behind him is the husband of the woman he's been —

(*Lee makes gesture of screwing by pumping his arm.*)

AUSTIN (*sees Lee's gesture*): Oh. Yeah.

LEE: And number two, he realizes he's in the middle of Tornado Country.

AUSTIN: What's "Tornado Country"?

LEE: Panhandle.

AUSTIN: Panhandle?

LEE: Sweetwater. Around in that area. Nothin'. Nowhere, and number three —

AUSTIN: I thought there was only two.

LEE: There's three. There's a third unforeseen realization.

AUSTIN: And what's that?

LEE: That he's runnin' outa' gas.

AUSTIN (*stops typing*): Come on, Lee.

(*Austin gets up, moves to kitchen, gets a glass of water.*)

LEE: Whadya' mean, "come on"? That's what it is. Write it down! He's runnin' outa' gas.

AUSTIN: It's too —

LEE: What? It's too what? It's too real! That's what ya' mean isn't it? It's too much like real life!

AUSTIN: It's not like real life! It's not enough like real life. Things don't happen like that.

LEE: What! Men don't fuck other men's women?

AUSTIN: Yes. But they don't end up chasing each other across the Panhandle. Through "Tornado Country."

LEE: They do in this movie!

AUSTIN: And they don't have horses conveniently along with them when they run out of gas! And they don't run out of gas either!

LEE: These guys run outa' gas! This is my story and one a' these guys runs outa' gas!

AUSTIN: It's just a dumb excuse to get them into a chase scene. It's contrived.

LEE: It is a chase scene! It's already a chase scene. They been chasin' each other fer days.

AUSTIN: So now they're supposed to abandon their trucks, climb on their horses, and chase each other into the mountains?

LEE (*standing suddenly*): There aren't any mountains in the Panhandle! It's flat!

(*Lee turns violently toward windows in alcove and throws beer can at them.*)

LEE: Goddamn these crickets! (*Yells at crickets.*) Shut up out there! (*Pause, turns back toward table.*) This place is like a fuckin' rest home here. How're you supposed to think!

AUSTIN: You wanna' take a break?

LEE: No, I don't wanna' take a break! I wanna' get this done! This is my last chance to get this done.

AUSTIN (*moves back into alcove*): All right. Take it easy.

LEE: I'm gonna' be leavin' this area. I don't have time to mess around here.

AUSTIN: Where are you going?

LEE: Never mind where I'm goin'! That's got nothin' to do with you. I just gotta' get this done. I'm not like you. Hangin' around bein' a parasite offa' other fools. I gotta' do this thing and get out.

(*Pause.*)

AUSTIN: A parasite? Me?

LEE: Yeah, you!

AUSTIN: After you break into people's houses and take their televisions!

LEE: They don't need their televisions! I'm doin' them a service.

AUSTIN: Give me back my keys, Lee.

LEE: Not until you write this thing! You're gonna' write this outline thing for me or that car's gonna' wind up in Arizona with a different paint job.

AUSTIN: You think you can force me to write this? I was doing you a favor.

LEE: Git off yer high horse will ya'! Favor! Big favor. Handin' down favors from the mountain top.

AUSTIN: Let's just write it, okay? Let's sit down and not get upset and see if we can just get through this.

(*Austin sits at typewriter.*)
(*Long pause.*)

LEE: Yer not gonna' even show it to him, are ya'?

AUSTIN: What?

LEE: This outline. You got no intention of showin' it to him. Yer just doin' this 'cause yer afraid a' me.

AUSTIN: You can show it to him yourself.

LEE: I will, boy! I'm gonna' read it to him on the golf course.

AUSTIN: And I'm not afraid of you either.

LEE: Then how come yer doin' it?

AUSTIN (*pause*): So I can get my keys back.

(*Pause as Lee takes keys out of his pocket slowly and throws them on table, long pause, Austin stares at keys.*)

LEE: There. Now you got yer keys back.

(*Austin looks up at Lee but doesn't take keys.*)

LEE: Go ahead. There's yer keys.

(*Austin slowly takes keys off table and puts them back in his own pocket.*)

Now what're you gonna' do? Kick me out?

AUSTIN: I'm not going to kick you out, Lee.

LEE: You couldn't kick me out, boy.

AUSTIN: I know.

LEE: So you can't even consider that one. (*Pause.*) You could call the police. That'd be the obvious thing.

AUSTIN: You're my brother.

LEE: That don't mean a thing. You go down to the L.A. Police Department there and ask them what kinda' people kill each other the most. What do you think they'd say?

AUSTIN: Who said anything about killing?

LEE: Family people. Brothers. Brothers-in-law. Cousins. Real American-type people. They kill each other in the heat mostly. In the Smog-Alerts. In the Brush Fire Season. Right about this time a' year.

AUSTIN: This isn't the same.

LEE: Oh no? What makes it different?

AUSTIN: We're not insane. We're not driven to acts of violence like that. Not over a dumb movie script. Now sit down.

(*Long pause, Lee considers which way to go with it.*)

LEE: Maybe not. (*He sits back down at table across from Austin.*) Maybe you're right. Maybe we're too intelligent, huh? (*Pause.*) We got our heads on our shoulders. One of us has even got a Ivy League diploma. Now that means somethin' don't it? Doesn't that mean somethin'?

AUSTIN: Look, I'll write this thing for you, Lee. I don't mind writing it. I just don't want to get all worked up about it. It's not worth it. Now, come on. Let's just get through it, okay?

LEE: Nah. I think there's easier money. Lotsa' places I could pick up thousands. Maybe millions. I don't need this shit. I could go up to Sacramento Valley and steal me a diesel. Ten thousand a week dismantling one a' those suckers. Ten thousand a week!

(*Lee opens another beer, puts his foot back up on table.*)

AUSTIN: No, really, look, I'll write it out for you. I think it's a great idea.

LEE: Nah, you got yer own work to do. I don't wanna' interfere with yer life.

AUSTIN: I mean it'd be really fantastic if you could sell this. Turn it into a movie. I mean it.

(*Pause.*)

LEE: Ya' think so huh?

AUSTIN: Absolutely. You could really turn your life around, you know. Change things.

LEE: I could get a house maybe.

AUSTIN: Sure you could get a house. You could get a whole ranch if you wanted to.

LEE (*laughs*): A ranch? I could get a ranch?

AUSTIN: 'Course you could. You know what a screenplay sells for these days?

LEE: No. What's it sell for?

AUSTIN: A lot. A whole lot of money.

LEE: Thousands?

AUSTIN: Yeah. Thousands.

LEE: Millions?

AUSTIN: Well —

LEE: We could get the old man outa' hock then.

AUSTIN: Maybe.

LEE: Maybe? Whadya' mean, maybe?

AUSTIN: I mean it might take more than money.

LEE: You were just tellin' me it'd change my whole life around. Why wouldn't it change his?

AUSTIN: He's different.

LEE: Oh, he's of a different ilk huh?

AUSTIN: He's not gonna' change. Let's leave the old man out of it.

LEE: That's right. He's not gonna' change but I will. I'll just turn myself right inside out. I could be just like you then, huh? Sittin' around dreamin' stuff up. Gettin' paid to dream. Ridin' back and forth on the freeway just dreamin' my fool head off.

AUSTIN: It's not all that easy.

LEE: It's not, huh?

AUSTIN: No. There's a lot of work involved.

LEE: What's the toughest part? Deciding whether to jog or play tennis?

(*Long pause.*)

AUSTIN: Well, look. You can stay here — do whatever you want to. Borrow the car. Come in and out. Doesn't matter to me. It's not my house. I'll help you write this thing or — not. Just let me know what you want. You tell me.

LEE: Oh. So now suddenly you're at my service. Is that it?

AUSTIN: What do you want to do Lee?

(*Long pause, Lee stares at him then turns and dreams at windows.*)

LEE: I tell ya' what I'd do if I still had that dog. Ya' wanna' know what I'd do?

AUSTIN: What?

LEE: Head out to Ventura. Cook up a little match. God that little dog could bear down. Lota' money in dog fightin'. Big money.

(*Pause.*)

AUSTIN: Why don't we try to see this through, Lee. Just for the hell of it. Maybe you've really got something here. What do you think?

(*Pause, Lee considers.*)

LEE: Maybe so. No harm in tryin' I guess. You think it's such a hot idea. Besides, I always wondered what'd be like to be you.

AUSTIN: You did?

LEE: Yeah, sure. I used to picture you walkin' around some campus with yer arms fulla' books. Blondes chasin' after ya'.

AUSTIN: Blondes? That's funny.

LEE: What's funny about it?

AUSTIN: Because I always used to picture you somewhere.

LEE: Where'd you picture me?

AUSTIN: Oh, I don't know. Different places. Adventures. You were always on some adventure.

LEE: Yeah.

AUSTIN: And I used to say to myself, "Lee's got the right idea. He's out there in the world and here I am. What am I doing?"

LEE: Well you were settin' yourself up for somethin'.

AUSTIN: I guess.

LEE: We better get started on this thing then.

AUSTIN: Okay.

(*Austin sits up at typewriter, puts new paper in.*)

LEE: Oh. Can I get the keys back before I forget?

(*Austin hesitates.*)

You said I could borrow the car if I wanted, right? Isn't that what you said?

AUSTIN: Yeah. Right.

(*Austin takes keys out of his pocket, sets them on table, Lee takes keys slowly, plays with them in his hand.*)

LEE: I could get a ranch, huh?

AUSTIN: Yeah. We have to write it first though.

LEE: Okay. Let's write it.

(*Lights start dimming slowly to end of scene as Austin types, Lee speaks.*)

So they take off after each other straight into an endless black prairie. The sun is just comin' down and they can feel the night on their backs. What they don't know is that each one of 'em is afraid, see. Each one separately thinks that he's the only one that's afraid. And they keep ridin' like that straight into the night. Not knowing. And the one who's chasin' doesn't know where the other one is taking him. And the one who's being chased doesn't know where he's going.

(*Lights to black, typing stops in the dark, crickets fade.*)

Act II · Scene V

(*Morning. Lee at the table in alcove with a set of golf clubs in a fancy leather bag, Austin at sink washing a few dishes.*)

AUSTIN: He really liked it, huh?

LEE: He wouldn't a' gave me these clubs if he didn't like it.

AUSTIN: He gave you the clubs?

LEE: Yeah. I told ya' he gave me the clubs. The bag too.

AUSTIN: I thought he just loaned them to you.

LEE: He said it was part a' the advance. A little gift like. Gesture of his good faith.

AUSTIN: He's giving you an advance?

LEE: Now what's so amazing about that? I told ya' it was a good story. You even said it was a good story.

AUSTIN: Well that is really incredible Lee. You know how many guys spend their whole lives down here trying to break into this business? Just trying to get in the door?

LEE (*pulling clubs out of bag, testing them*): I got no idea. How many?

(*Pause.*)

AUSTIN: How much of an advance is he giving you?

LEE: Plenty. We were talkin' big money out there. Ninth hole is where I sealed the deal.

AUSTIN: He made a firm commitment?

LEE: Absolutely.

AUSTIN: Well, I know Saul and he doesn't fool around when he says he likes something.

LEE: I thought you said you didn't know him.

AUSTIN: Well, I'm familiar with his tastes.

LEE: I let him get two up on me goin' into the back nine. He was sure he had me cold. You shoulda' seen his face when I pulled out the old pitching wedge and plopped it pin-high, two feet from the cup. He 'bout shit his pants. "Where'd a guy like you ever learn how to play golf like that?" he says.

(*Lee laughs, Austin stares at him.*)

AUSTIN: 'Course there's no contract yet. Nothing's final until it's on paper.

LEE: It's final, all right. There's no way he's gonna' back out of it now. We gambled for it.

AUSTIN: Saul, gambled?

LEE: Yeah, sure. I mean he liked the outline already so he wasn't risking that much. I just guaranteed it with my short game.

(*Pause.*)

AUSTIN: Well, we should celebrate or something. I think Mom left a bottle of champagne in the refrigerator. We should have a little toast.

(*Austin gets glasses from cupboard, goes to refrigerator, pulls out bottle of champagne.*)

LEE: You shouldn't oughta' take her champagne, Austin. She's gonna' miss that.

AUSTIN: Oh, she's not going to mind. She'd be glad we put it to good use. I'll get her another bottle. Besides, it's perfect for the occasion.

(*Pause.*)

LEE: Yer gonna' get a nice fee fer writin' the script a' course. Straight fee.

(*Austin stops, stares at Lee, puts glasses and bottle on table, pause.*)

AUSTIN: I'm writing the script?

LEE: That's what he said. Said we couldn't hire a better screenwriter in the whole town.

AUSTIN: But I'm already working on a script. I've got my own project. I don't have time to write two scripts.

AUSTIN: No, he said he was gonna' drop that other one.

(*Pause.*)

AUSTIN: What? You mean mine? He's going to drop mine and do yours instead?

LEE (*smiles*): Now look, Austin, it's jest beginner's luck ya' know. I mean I sank a fifty foot putt for this deal. No hard feelings.

(*Austin goes to phone on wall, grabs it, starts dialing.*)

He's not gonna' be in, Austin. Told me he wouldn't be in 'til late this afternoon.

AUSTIN (*stays on phone, dialing, listens*): I can't believe this. I just can't believe it. Are you sure he said that? Why would he drop mine?

LEE: That's what he told me.

AUSTIN: He can't do that without telling me first. Without talking to me at least. He wouldn't just make a decision like that without talking to me!

LEE: Well I was kinda' surprised myself. But he was real enthusiastic about my story.

(*Austin hangs up phone violently, paces.*)

AUSTIN: What'd he say! Tell me everything he said!

LEE: I been tellin' ya'! He said he liked the story a whole lot. It was the first authentic Western to come along in a decade.

AUSTIN: He liked that story! Your story?

LEE: Yeah! What's so surprisin' about that?

AUSTIN: It's stupid! It's the dumbest story I ever heard in my life.

LEE: Hey, hold on! That's my story yer talkin' about!

AUSTIN: It's a bullshit story! It's idiotic. Two lamebrains chasing each other across Texas! Are you kidding? Who do you think's going to go see a film like that?

LEE: It's not a film! It's a movie. There's a big difference. That's somethin' Saul told me.

AUSTIN: Oh he did, huh?

LEE: Yeah, he said, "In this business we make movies, American movies. Leave the films to the French."

AUSTIN: So you got real intimate with old Saul huh? He started pouring forth his vast knowledge of Cinema.

LEE: I think he liked me a lot, to tell ya' the truth. I think he felt I was somebody he could confide in.

AUSTIN: What'd you do, beat him up or something?

LEE (*stands fast*): Hey, I've about had it with the insults buddy! You think yer the only one in the brain department here? Yer the only one that can sit around and cook things up? There's other people got ideas too, ya' know!

AUSTIN: You must've done something. Threatened him or something. Now what'd you do Lee?

LEE: I convinced him!

(*Lee makes sudden menacing lunge toward Austin, wielding golf club above his head, stops himself, frozen moment, long pause, Lee lowers club.*)

AUSTIN: Oh, Jesus. You didn't hurt him did you?

(*Long silence, Lee sits back down at table.*)

Lee! Did you hurt him?

LEE: I didn't do nothin' to him! He liked my story. Pure and simple. He said it was the best story he'd come across in a long, long time.

AUSTIN: That's what he told me about my story! That's the same thing he said to me.

LEE: Well, he musta' been lyin'. He musta' been lyin' to one of us anyway.

AUSTIN: You can't come into this town and start pushing people around. They're gonna put you away!

LEE: I never pushed anybody around! I beat him fair and square. (*Pause.*) They can't touch me anyway. They can't put a finger on me. I'm gone. I can come in through the window and go out through the door. They never knew what hit 'em. You, yer stuck. Yer the one that's stuck. Not me. So don't be warnin' me what to do in this town.

(*Pause, Austin crosses to table, sits at typewriter, rests.*)

AUSTIN: Lee, come on, level with me will you? It doesn't make any sense that suddenly he'd throw my idea out the window. I've been talking to him for months. I've got too much at stake. Everything's riding on this project.

LEE: What's yer idea?

AUSTIN: It's just a simple love story.

LEE: What kinda' love story?

AUSTIN (*stands, crosses into kitchen*): I'm not telling you!

LEE: Ha! 'Fraid I'll steal it huh? Competition's gettin' kinda' close to home isn't it?

AUSTIN: Where did Saul say he was going?

LEE: He was gonna' take my story to a couple studios.

AUSTIN: That's *my* outline you know! I wrote that outline! You've got no right to be peddling it around.

LEE: You weren't ready to take credit for it last night.

AUSTIN: Give me my keys!

LEE: What?

AUSTIN: The keys! I want my keys back!

LEE: Where you goin'?

AUSTIN: Just give me my keys! I gotta' take a drive. I gotta' get out of here for a while.

LEE: Where you gonna' go, Austin?

AUSTIN (*pause*): I might just drive out to the desert for a while. I gotta' think.

LEE: You can think here just as good. This is the perfect setup for thinkin'. We got some writin' to do here, boy. Now let's just have us a little toast. Relax. We're partners now.

(*Lee pops the cork of the champagne bottle, pours two drinks as the lights fade to black.*)

Scene VI

(*Afternoon. Lee and Saul in kitchen, Austin in alcove.*)

LEE: Now you tell him. You tell him, Mr. Kipper.

SAUL: Kimmer.

LEE: Kimmer. You tell him what you told me. He don't believe me.

AUSTIN: I don't want to hear it.

SAUL: It's really not a big issue, Austin. I was simply amazed by your brother's story and —

AUSTIN: Amazed? You lost a bet! You gambled with my material!

SAUL: That's really beside the point, Austin. I'm ready to go all the way with your brother's story. I think it has a great deal of merit.

AUSTIN: I don't want to hear about it, okay? Go tell it to the executives! Tell it to somebody who's going to turn it into a package deal or something. A T.V. series. Don't tell it to me.

SAUL: But I want to continue with your project too, Austin. It's not as though we can't do both. We're big enough for that aren't we?

AUSTIN: "We"? *I* can't do both! I don't know about "we."

LEE (*to Saul*): See, what'd I tell ya'. He's totally unsympathetic.

SAUL: Austin, there's no point in our going to another screenwriter for this. It just doesn't make sense. You're brothers. You know each other. There's a familiarity with the material that just wouldn't be possible otherwise.

AUSTIN: There's no familiarity with the material! None! I don't know what "Tornado Country" is. I don't know what a "gooseneck" is. And I don't want to know! (*Pointing to Lee.*) He's a hustler! He's a bigger hustler than you are! If you can't see that, then —

LEE (*to Austin*): Hey, now hold on. I didn't have to bring this bone back to you, boy. I persuaded Saul here that you were the right man for the job. You don't have to go throwin' up favors in my face.

AUSTIN: Favors! I'm the one who wrote the fuckin' outline! You can't even spell.

SAUL (*to Austin*): Your brother told me about the situation with your father.

(*Pause.*)

AUSTIN: What? (*Looks at Lee.*)

SAUL: That's right. Now we have a clear-cut deal here, Austin. We have big studio money standing behind this thing. Just on the basis of your outline.

AUSTIN (*to Saul*): What'd he tell you about my father?

SAUL: Well — that he's destitute. He needs money.

LEE: That's right. He does.

(*Austin shakes his head, stares at them both.*)

AUSTIN (*to Lee*): And this little assignment is supposed to go toward the old man? A charity project? Is that what this is? Did you cook this up on the ninth green too?

SAUL: It's a big slice, Austin.

AUSTIN (*to Lee*): I gave him money! I already gave him money. You know that. He drank it all up!

LEE: This is a different deal here.

SAUL: We can set up a trust for your father. A large sum of money. It can be doled out to him in parcels so he can't misuse it.

AUSTIN: Yeah, and who's doing the doling?

SAUL: Your brother volunteered.

(*Austin laughs.*)

LEE: That's right. I'll make sure he uses it for groceries.

AUSTIN (*to Saul*): I'm not doing this script! I'm not writing this crap for you or anybody else. You can't blackmail me into it. You can't threaten me into it. There's no way I'm doing it. So just give it up. Both of you.

(*Long pause.*)

SAUL: Well, that's it then. I mean this is an easy three hundred grand. Just for a first draft. It's incredible, Austin. We've got three different studios all trying to cut each other's throats to get this material. In one morning. That's how hot it is.

AUSTIN: Yeah, well you can afford to give me a percentage on the outline then. And you better get the genius here an agent before he gets burned.

LEE: Saul's gonna' be my agent. Isn't that right, Saul?

SAUL: That's right. (*To Austin.*) Your brother has really got something, Austin. I've been around too long not to recognize it. Raw talent.

AUSTIN: He's got a lota' balls is what he's got. He's taking you right down the river.

SAUL: Three hundred thousand, Austin. Just for a first draft. Now you've never been offered that kind of money before.

AUSTIN: I'm not writing it.

(*Pause.*)

SAUL: I see. Well —

LEE: We'll just go to another writer then. Right, Saul? Just hire us somebody with some enthusiasm. Somebody who can recognize the value of a good story.

SAUL: I'm sorry about this, Austin.

AUSTIN: Yeah.

SAUL: I mean I was hoping we could continue both things but now I don't see how it's possible.

AUSTIN: So you're dropping my idea altogether. Is that it? Just trade horses in midstream? After all these months of meetings.

SAUL: I wish there was another way.

AUSTIN: I've got everything riding on this, Saul. You know that. It's my only shot. If this falls through —

SAUL: I have to go with what my instincts tell me —

AUSTIN: Your instincts!

SAUL: My gut reaction.

AUSTIN: You lost! That's your gut reaction. You lost a gamble. Now you're trying to tell me you like his story? How could you possibly fall for that story? It's as phony as Hopalong Cassidy. What do you see in it? I'm curious.

SAUL: It has the ring of truth, Austin.

AUSTIN (*laughs*): Truth?

LEE: It is true.

SAUL: Something about the real West.

AUSTIN: Why? Because it's got horses? Because it's got grown men acting like little boys?

SAUL: Something about the land. Your brother is speaking from experience.

AUSTIN: So am I!

SAUL: But nobody's interested in love these days, Austin. Let's face it.

LEE: That's right.

AUSTIN (*to Saul*): He's been camped out on the desert for three months. Talking to cactus. What's he know about what people wanna' see on the screen! I drive on the freeway every day. I swallow the smog. I watch the news in color. I shop in the Safeway. I'm the one who's in touch! Not him!

SAUL: I have to go now, Austin.

(*Saul starts to leave.*)

AUSTIN: There's no such thing as the West anymore!
It's a dead issue! It's dried up, Saul, and so are
you.

(*Saul stops and turns to Austin.*)

SAUL: Maybe you're right. But I have to take the
gamble, don't I?

AUSTIN: You're a fool to do this, Saul.

SAUL: I've always gone on my hunches. Always. And
I've never been wrong. (*To Lee.*) I'll talk to you
tomorrow, Lee.

LEE: All right, Mr. Kimmer.

SAUL: Maybe we could have some lunch.

LEE: Fine with me. (*Smiles at Austin.*)

SAUL: I'll give you a ring.

(*Saul exits, lights to black as brothers look at each
other from a distance.*)

Scene VII

(*Night. Coyotes, crickets, sound of typewriter in dark,
candlelight up on Lee at typewriter struggling to type
with one finger system, Austin sits sprawled out on
kitchen floor with whiskey bottle, drunk.*)

AUSTIN (*singing, from floor*): "Red sails in the sunset
Way out on the blue
Please carry my loved one
Home safely to me

Red sails in the sunset —"

LEE (*slams fist on table*): Hey! Knock it off will ya'!
I'm tryin' to concentrate here.

AUSTIN (*laughs*): You're tryin' to concentrate?

LEE: Yeah. That's right.

AUSTIN: Now you're tryin' to concentrate.

LEE: Between you, the coyotes, and the crickets a
thought don't have much of a chance.

AUSTIN: "Between me, the coyotes, and the crickets."
What a great title.

LEE: I don't need a title! I need a thought.

AUSTIN (*laughs*): A thought! Here's a thought for
ya' —

LEE: I'm not askin' fer yer thoughts! I got my own.
I can do this thing on my own.

AUSTIN: You're going to write an entire script on your
own?

LEE: That's right.

(*Pause.*)

AUSTIN: Here's a thought. Saul Kimmer —

LEE: Shut up will ya'!

AUSTIN: He thinks we're the same person.

LEE: Don't get cute.

AUSTIN: He does! He's lost his mind. Poor old Saul.
(*Giggles.*) Thinks we're one and the same.

LEE: Why don't you ease up on that champagne.

AUSTIN (*holding up bottle*): This isn't champagne anymore. We went through the champagne a long time
ago. This is serious stuff. The days of champagne
are long gone.

LEE: Well, go outside and drink it.

AUSTIN: I'm enjoying your company, Lee. For the first
time since your arrival I am finally enjoying your
company. And now you want me to go outside
and drink alone?

LEE: That's right.

(*Lee reads through paper in typewriter, makes an
erasure.*)

AUSTIN: You think you'll make more progress if you're
alone? You might drive yourself crazy.

LEE: I could have this thing done in a night if I had
a little silence.

AUSTIN: Well you'd still have the crickets to contend
with. The coyotes. The sounds of the Police Heli-
copters prowling above the neighborhood. Slashing
their searchlights down through the streets. Hunting
for the likes of you.

LEE: I'm a screenwriter now! I'm legitimate.

AUSTIN (*laughing*): A screenwriter!

LEE: That's right. I'm on salary. That's more'n I can
say for you. I got an advance coming.

AUSTIN: This is true. This is very true. An advance.
(*Pause.*) Well, maybe I oughta' go out and try my
hand at your trade. Since you're doing so good at
mine.

LEE: Ha!

(*Lee attempts to type some more but gets the ribbon
tangled up, starts trying to rethread it as they continue
talking.*)

AUSTIN: Well why not? You don't think I've got what
it takes to sneak into people's houses and steal
their T.V.s?

LEE: You couldn't steal a toaster without losin' yer
lunch.

(*Austin stands with a struggle, supports himself by
the sink.*)

AUSTIN: You don't think I could sneak into somebody's
house and steal a toaster?

LEE: Go take a shower or somethin' will ya!

(*Lee gets more tangled up with the typewriter ribbon,
pulling it out of the machine as though it was fishing
line.*)

AUSTIN: You really don't think I could steal a crumby
toaster? How much you wanna' bet I can't steal a

toaster! How much? Go ahead! You're a gambler aren't you? Tell me how much yer willing to put on the line. Some part of your big advance? Oh, you haven't got that yet have you. I forgot.

LEE: All right. I'll bet you your car that you can't steal a toaster without gettin' busted.

AUSTIN: You already got my car!

LEE: Okay, your house then.

AUSTIN: What're you gonna' give me! I'm not talkin' about my house and my car, I'm talkin' about what are you gonna' give me. You don't have nothin' to give me.

LEE: I'll give you — shared screen credit. How 'bout that? I'll have it put in the contract that this was written by both of us.

AUSTIN: I don't want my name on that piece of shit! I want something of value. You got anything of value? You got any tidbits from the desert? Any Rattlesnake bones? I'm not a greedy man. Any little personal treasure will suffice.

LEE: I'm gonna' just kick yer ass out in a minute.

AUSTIN: Oh, so now you're gonna' kick me out! Now I'm the intruder. I'm the one who's invading your precious privacy.

LEE: I'm trying to do some screenwriting here!!

(*Lee stands, picks up typewriter, slams it down hard on table, pause, silence except for crickets.*)

AUSTIN: Well, you got everything you need. You got plenty a' coffee? Groceries. You got a car. A contract. (*Pause.*) Might need a new typewriter ribbon but other than that you're pretty well fixed. I'll just leave ya' alone for a while.

(*Austin tries to steady himself to leave, Lee makes a move toward him*).

LEE: Where you goin'?

AUSTIN: Don't worry about me. I'm not the one to worry about.

(*Austin weaves toward exit, stops.*)

LEE: What're you gonna' do? Just go wander out into the night?

AUSTIN: I'm gonna' make a little tour.

LEE: Why don't ya' just go to bed for Christ's sake. Yer makin' me sick.

AUSTIN: I can take care a' myself. Don't worry about me.

(*Austin weaves badly in another attempt to exit, he crashes to the floor, Lee goes to him but remains standing.*)

LEE: You want me to call your wife for ya' or something?

AUSTIN (*from floor*): My wife?

LEE: Yeah. I mean maybe she can help ya' out. Talk to ya' or somethin'.

AUSTIN (*struggles to stand again*): She's five hundred miles away. North. North of here. Up in the North country where things are calm. I don't need any help. I'm gonna' go outside and I'm gonna' steal a toaster. I'm gonna' steal some other stuff too. I might even commit bigger crimes. Bigger than you ever dreamed of. Crimes beyond the imagination!

(*Austin manages to get himself vertical, tries to head for exit again.*)

LEE: Just hang on a minute, Austin.

AUSTIN: Why? What for? You don't need my help, right? Besides, I'm lookin' forward to the smell of the night. The bushes. Orange blossoms. Dust in the driveways. Rain bird sprinklers. Lights in people's houses. You're right about the lights, Lee. Everybody else is livin' the life. Indoors. Safe. This is a Paradise down here. You know that? We're livin' in a Paradise. We've forgotten about that.

LEE: You sound just like the old man now.

AUSTIN: Yeah, well we all sound alike when we're sloshed. We just sorta' echo each other.

LEE: Maybe if we could work on this together we could bring him back out here. Get him settled down someplace.

(*Austin turns violently toward Lee, takes a swing at him, misses, and crashes to the floor again. Lee stays standing.*)

AUSTIN: I don't want him out here! I've had it with him! I went all the way out there! I went out of my way. I gave him money and all he did was play Al Jolson records and spit at me! I gave him money!

(*Pause.*)

LEE: Just help me a little with the characters, all right? You know how to do it, Austin.

AUSTIN (*on floor, laughs*): The characters!

LEE: Yeah. You know. The way they talk and stuff. I can hear it in my head but I can't get it down on paper.

AUSTIN: What characters?

LEE: The guys. The guys in the story.

AUSTIN: Those aren't characters.

LEE: Whatever you call 'em then. I need to write somethin' out.

AUSTIN: Those are illusions of characters.

LEE: I don't give a damn what ya' call 'em! You know what I'm talkin' about!

AUSTIN: Those are fantasies of a long lost boyhood.

LEE: I gotta' write somethin' out on paper!!

(*Pause.*)

AUSTIN: What for? Saul's gonna' get you a fancy
  screenwriter isn't he?
LEE: I wanna' do it myself!
AUSTIN: Then do it! Yer on your own now, old buddy.
  You bulldogged yer way into contention. Now you
  gotta' carry it through.
LEE: I will but I need some advice. Just a couple a'
  things. Come on, Austin. Just help me get 'em
  talkin' right. It won't take much.
AUSTIN: Oh, now you're having a little doubt huh?
  What happened? The pressure's on, boy. This is
  it. You gotta' come up with it now. You don't
  come up with a winner on your first time out they
  just cut your head off. They don't give you a second
  chance ya' know.
LEE: I got a good story! I know it's a good story. I
  just need a little help is all.
AUSTIN: Not from me. Not from yer little old brother.
  I'm retired.
LEE: You could save this thing for me, Austin. I'd
  give ya' half the money. I would. I only need half
  anyway. With this kinda' money I could be a long
  time down the road. I'd never bother ya' again. I
  promise. You'd never even see me again.
AUSTIN (*still on floor*): You'd disappear?
LEE: I would for sure.
AUSTIN: Where would you disappear to?
LEE: That don't matter. I got plenty a' places.
AUSTIN: Nobody can disappear. The old man tried
  that. Look where it got him. He lost his teeth.
LEE: He never had any money.
AUSTIN: I don't mean that. I mean his teeth! His real
  teeth. First he lost his real teeth, then he lost his
  false teeth. You never knew that did ya? He never
  confided in you.
LEE: Nah, I never knew that.
AUSTIN: You wanna' drink?

(*Austin offers bottle to Lee, Lee takes it, sits down
on kitchen floor with Austin, they share the bottle.*)

  Yeah, he lost his real teeth one at a time. Woke
  up every morning with another tooth lying on the
  mattress. Finally, he decides he's gotta' get 'em all
  pulled but he doesn't have any money. Middle
  of Arizona with no money and no insurance and
  every morning another tooth is lying on the mattress.
  (*Takes a drink*). So what does he do?
LEE: I dunno'. I never knew about that.
AUSTIN: He begs the government. G.I. Bill or some
  damn thing. Some pension plan he remembers in
  the back of his head. And they send him out the
  money.
LEE: They did?

(*They keep trading the bottle between them, taking
drinks.*)

AUSTIN: Yeah. They send him the money but it's not
  enough money. Costs a lot to have all yer teeth
  yanked. They charge by the individual tooth, ya'
  know. I mean one tooth isn't equal to another
  tooth. Some are very expensive. Like the big ones
  in the back —
LEE: So what happened?
AUSTIN: So he locates a Mexican dentist in Juarez
  who'll do the whole thing for a song. And he takes
  off hitchhiking to the border.
LEE: Hitchhiking?
AUSTIN: Yeah. So how long you think it takes him to
  get to the border? A man his age.
LEE: I dunno.
AUSTIN: Eight days it takes him. Eight days in the rain
  and the sun and every day he's droppin' teeth on
  the blacktop and nobody'll pick him up 'cause his
  mouth's full a' blood.

(*Pause, they drink.*)

  So finally he stumbles into the dentist. Dentist takes
  all his money and all his teeth. And there he is, in
  Mexico, with his gums sewed up and his pockets
  empty.

(*Long silence, Austin drinks.*)

LEE: That's it?
AUSTIN: Then I go out to see him, see. I go out there
  and I take him out for a nice Chinese dinner. But
  he doesn't eat. All he wants to do is drink Martinis
  outa' plastic cups. And he takes his teeth out and
  lays 'em on the table 'cause he can't stand the feel
  of 'em. And we ask the waitress for one a' those
  doggie bags to take the Chop Suey home in. So he
  drops his teeth in the doggie bag along with the
  Chop Suey. And then we go out to hit all the bars
  up and down the highway. Says he wants to introduce me to all his buddies. And in one a' those
  bars, in one a' those bars up and down the highway,
  he left that doggie bag with his teeth laying in the
  Chop Suey.
LEE: You never found it?
AUSTIN: We went back but we never did find it. (*Pause.*)
  Now that's a true story. True to life.

(*They drink as lights fade to black.*)

Scene VIII

(*Very early morning, between night and day. No crickets, coyotes yapping feverishly in distance before light
comes up, a small fire blazes up in the dark from
alcove area, sound of Lee smashing typewriter with*

a golf club, lights coming up, Lee seen smashing type-writer methodically then dropping pages of his script into a burning bowl set on the floor of alcove, flames leap up, Austin has a whole bunch of stolen toasters lined up on the sink counter along with Lee's stolen T.V., the toasters are of a wide variety of models, mostly chrome, Austin goes up and down the line of toasters, breathing on them and polishing them with a dish towel, both men are drunk, empty whiskey bottles and beer cans litter floor of kitchen, they share a half empty bottle on one of the chairs in the alcove, Lee keeps periodically taking deliberate ax-chops at the typewriter using a nine-iron as Austin speaks, all of their mother's house plants are dead and drooping.)

AUSTIN *(polishing toasters)*: There's gonna' be a general lack of toast in the neighborhood this morning. Many, many unhappy, bewildered breakfast faces. I guess it's best not to even think of the victims. Not to even entertain it. Is that the right psychology?

LEE *(pauses)*: What?

AUSTIN: Is that the correct criminal psychology? Not to think of the victims?

LEE: What victims?

(Lee takes another swipe at typewriter with nine-iron, adds pages to the fire.)

AUSTIN: The victims of crime. Of breaking and entering. I mean is it a prerequisite for a criminal not to have a conscience?

LEE: Ask a criminal.

(Pause, Lee stares at Austin.)

What're you gonna' do with all those toasters? That's the dumbest thing I ever saw in my life.

AUSTIN: I've got hundreds of dollars worth of household appliances here. You may not realize that.

LEE: Yeah, and how many hundreds of dollars did you walk right past?

AUSTIN: It was toasters you challenged me to. Only toasters. I ignored every other temptation.

LEE: I never challenged you! That's no challenge. Anybody can steal a toaster.

(Lee smashes typewriter again.)

AUSTIN: You don't have to take it out on my typewriter ya' know. It's not the machine's fault that you can't write. It's a sin to do that to a good machine.

LEE: A sin?

AUSTIN: When you consider all the writers who never even had a machine. Who would have given an eyeball for a good typewriter. Any typewriter.

(Lee smashes typewriter again.)

AUSTIN *(polishing toasters)*: All the ones who wrote on matchbook covers. Paper bags. Toilet paper. Who had their writing destroyed by their jailers. Who persisted beyond all odds. Those writers would find it hard to understand your actions.

(Lee comes down on typewriter with one final crushing blow of the nine-iron then collapses in one of the chairs, takes a drink from bottle, pause.)

AUSTIN *(after pause)*: Not to mention demolishing a perfectly good golf club. What about all the struggling golfers? What about Lee Trevino? What do you think he would've said when he was batting balls around with broomsticks at the age of nine. Impoverished.

(Pause.)

LEE: What time is it anyway?

AUSTIN: No idea. Time stands still when you're havin' fun.

LEE: Is it too late to call a woman? You know any women?

AUSTIN: I'm a married man.

LEE: I mean a local woman.

(Austin looks out at light through window above sink.)

AUSTIN: It's either too late or too early. You're the nature enthusiast. Can't you tell the time by the light in the sky? Orient yourself around the North Star or something?

LEE: I can't tell anything.

AUSTIN: Maybe you need a little breakfast. Some toast! How 'bout some toast?

(Austin goes to cupboard, pulls out loaf of bread, and starts dropping slices into every toaster, Lee stays sitting, drinks, watches Austin.)

LEE: I don't need toast. I need a woman.

AUSTIN: A woman isn't the answer. Never was.

LEE: I'm not talkin' about permanent. I'm talkin about temporary.

AUSTIN *(putting toast in toasters)*: We'll just test the merits of these little demons. See which brands have a tendency to burn. See which one can produce a perfectly golden piece of fluffy toast.

LEE: How much gas you got in yer car?

AUSTIN: I haven't driven my car for days now. So I haven't had an opportunity to look at the gas gauge.

LEE: Take a guess. You think there's enough to get me to Bakersfield?

AUSTIN: Bakersfield? What's in Bakersfield?

LEE: Just never mind what's in Bakersfield! You think there's enough goddamn gas in the car!

AUSTIN: Sure.

LEE: Sure. You could care less, right. Let me run outa' gas on the Grapevine. You could give a shit.

AUSTIN: I'd say there was enough gas to get you just about anywhere, Lee. With your determination and guts.

LEE: What the hell time is it anyway?

(*Lee pulls out his wallet, starts going through dozens of small pieces of paper with phone numbers written on them, drops some on the floor, drops others in the fire.*)

AUSTIN: Very early. This is the time of morning when the coyotes kill people's cocker spaniels. Did you hear them? That's what they were doing out there. Luring innocent pets away from their homes.

LEE (*searching through his papers*): What's the area code for Bakersfield? You know?

AUSTIN: You could always call the operator.

LEE: I can't stand that voice they give ya'.

AUSTIN: What voice?

LEE: That voice that warns you that if you'd only tried harder to find the number in the phone book you wouldn't have to be calling the operator to begin with.

(*Lee gets up, holding a slip of paper from his wallet, stumbles toward phone on wall, yanks receiver, starts dialing.*)

AUSTIN: Well I don't understand why you'd want to talk to anybody else anyway. I mean you can talk to me. I'm your brother.

LEE (*dialing*): I wanna' talk to a woman. I haven't heard a woman's voice in a long time.

AUSTIN: Not since the Botanist?

LEE: What?

AUSTIN: Nothing. (*Starts singing as he tends toast.*)
"Red sails in the sunset
Way out on the blue
Please carry my loved one
Home safely to me."

LEE: Hey, knock it off will ya'! This is long distance here.

AUSTIN: Bakersfield?

LEE: Yeah, Bakersfield. It's Kern County.

AUSTIN: Well, what County are *we* in?

LEE: You better get yourself a 7-Up, boy.

AUSTIN: One County's as good as another.

(*Austin hums "Red Sails" softly as Lee talks on phone.*)

LEE (*to phone*): Yeah, operator look — first off I wanna' know the area code for Bakersfield. Right. Bakersfield! Okay. Good. Now I wanna' know if you can help me track somebody down. (*Pause.*) No, no I mean a phone number. Just a phone number. Okay. (*Holds a piece of paper up and reads it.*) Okay, the name is Melly Ferguson. Melly. (*Pause.*) I dunno'. Melly. Maybe. Yeah. Maybe Melanie. Yeah. Melanie Ferguson. Okay. (*Pause.*)

What? I can't hear ya' so good. Sounds like yer under the ocean. (*Pause.*) You got ten Melanie Fergusons? How could that be? Ten Melanie Fergusons in Bakersfield? Well gimme all of 'em then. (*Pause.*) What d'ya mean? Gimme all ten Melanie Fergusons! That's right. Just a second. (*To Austin.*) Gimme a pen.

AUSTIN: I don't have a pen.

LEE: Gimme a pencil then!

AUSTIN: I don't have a pencil.

LEE (*to phone*): Just a second, operator. (*To Austin.*) Yer a writer and ya' don't have a pen or a pencil!

AUSTIN: I'm not a writer. You're a writer.

LEE: I'm on the phone here! Get me a pen or a pencil.

AUSTIN: I gotta' watch the toast.

LEE (*to phone*): Hang on a second, operator.

(*Lee lets the phone drop then starts pulling all the drawers in the kitchen out on the floor and dumping the contents, searching for a pencil, Austin watches him casually.*)

LEE (*crashing through drawers, throwing contents around kitchen*): This is the last time I try to live with people, boy! I can't believe it. Here I am! Here I am again in a desperate situation! This would never happen out on the desert. I would never be in this kinda' situation out on the desert. Isn't there a pen or a pencil in this house! Who lives in this house anyway!

AUSTIN: Our mother.

LEE: How come she don't have a pen or a pencil! She's a social person isn't she? Doesn't she have to make shopping lists? She's gotta' have a pencil. (*Finds a pencil.*) Aaha! (*He rushes back to phone, picks up receiver.*) All right operator. Operator? Hey! Operator! Goddamnit!

(*Lee rips the phone off the wall and throws it down, goes back to chair and falls into it, drinks, long pause.*)

AUSTIN: She hung up?

LEE: Yeah, she hung up. I knew she was gonna' hang up. I could hear it in her voice.

(*Lee starts going through his slips of paper again.*)

AUSTIN: Well, you're probably better off staying here with me anyway. I'll take care of you.

LEE: I don't need takin' care of! Not by you anyway.

AUSTIN: Toast is almost ready.

(*Austin starts buttering all the toast as it pops up.*)

LEE: I don't want any toast!

(*Long pause*)

AUSTIN: You gotta' eat something. Can't just drink. How long have we been drinking anyway?

LEE (*looking through slips of paper*): Maybe it was

Fresno. What's the area code for Fresno? How could I have lost that number! She was beautiful.

(*Pause.*)

AUSTIN: Why don't you just forget about that, Lee. Forget about the woman.

LEE: She had green eyes. You know what green eyes do to me?

AUSTIN: I know but you're not gonna' get it on with her now anyway. It's dawn already. She's in Bakersfield for Christ's sake.

(*Long pause, Lee considers the situation.*)

LEE: Yeah. (*Looks at windows.*) It's dawn?

AUSTIN: Let's just have some toast and —

LEE: What is this bullshit with the toast anyway! You make it sound like salvation or something. I don't want any goddamn toast! How many times I gotta' tell ya'! (*Lee gets up, crosses upstage to windows in alcove, looks out, Austin butters toast.*)

AUSTIN: Well it is like salvation sort of. I mean the smell. I love the smell of toast. And the sun's coming up. It makes me feel like anything's possible. Ya' know?

LEE (*back to Austin, facing windows upstage*): So go to church why don't ya'.

AUSTIN: Like a beginning. I love beginnings.

LEE: Oh yeah. I've always been kinda' partial to endings myself.

AUSTIN: What if I come with you, Lee?

LEE (*pause as Lee turns toward Austin*): What?

AUSTIN: What if I come with you out to the desert?

LEE: Are you kiddin'?

AUSTIN: No. I'd just like to see what it's like.

LEE: You wouldn't last a day out there pal.

AUSTIN: That's what you said about the toasters. You said I couldn't steal a toaster either.

LEE: A toaster's got nothin' to do with the desert.

AUSTIN: I could make it, Lee. I'm not that helpless. I can cook.

LEE: Cook?

AUSTIN: I can.

LEE: So what! You can cook. Toast.

AUSTIN: I can make fires. I know how to get fresh water from condensation.

(*Austin stacks buttered toast up in a tall stack on plate.*)
    (*Lee slams table.*)

LEE: It's not somethin' you learn out of a Boy Scout handbook!

AUSTIN: Well how do you learn it then! How're you supposed to learn it!

(*Pause.*)

LEE: Ya' just learn it, that's all. Ya' learn it 'cause ya' have to learn it. You don't *have* to learn it.

AUSTIN: You could teach me.

LEE (*stands*): What're you, crazy or somethin'? You went to college. Here, you are down here, rollin' in bucks. Floatin' up and down in elevators. And you wanna' learn how to live on the desert!

AUSTIN: I do, Lee. I really do. There's nothin' down here for me. There never was. When we were kids here it was different. There was a life here then. But now — I keep comin' down here thinkin' it's the fifties or somethin'. I keep finding myself getting off the freeway at familiar landmarks that turn out to be unfamiliar. On the way to appointments. Wandering down streets I thought I recognized that turn out to be replicas of streets I remember. Streets I misremember. Streets I can't tell if I lived on or saw in a postcard. Fields that don't even exist anymore.

LEE: There's no point cryin' about that now.

AUSTIN: There's nothin' real down here, Lee! Least of all me!

LEE: Well I can't save you from that!

AUSTIN: You can let me come with you.

LEE: No dice, pal.

AUSTIN: You could let me come with you, Lee!

LEE: Hey, do you actually think I chose to live out in the middle a' nowhere? Do ya'? Ya' think it's some kinda' philosophical decision I took or somethin'? I'm livin' out there 'cause I can't make it here! And yer bitchin' to me about all yer success!

AUSTIN: I'd cash it all in in a second. That't the truth.

LEE (*pause, shakes his head*): I can't believe this.

AUSTIN: Let me go with you.

LEE: Stop sayin' that will ya'! Yer worse than a dog.

(*Austin offers out the plate of neatly stacked toast to Lee.*)

AUSTIN: You want some toast?

(*Lee suddenly explodes and knocks the plate out of Austin's hand, toast goes flying, long frozen moment where it appears Lee might go all the way this time when Austin breaks it by slowly lowering himself to his knees and begins gathering the scattered toast from the floor and stacking it back on the plate, Lee begins to circle Austin in a slow, predatory way, crushing pieces of toast in his wake, no words for a while, Austin keeps gathering toast, even the crushed pieces.*)

LEE: Tell ya' what I'll do, little brother. I might just consider makin' you a deal. Little trade. (*Austin continues gathering toast as Lee circles him through this.*) You write me up this screenplay thing just like I tell ya'. I mean you can use all yer usual tricks and stuff. Yer fancy language. Yer artistic hocus pocus. But ya' gotta' write everything like I

say. Every move. Every time they run outa' gas,
they run outa' gas. Every time they wanna' jump
on a horse, they do just that. If they wanna' stay
in Texas, by God they'll stay in Texas! (*Keeps
circling.*) And you finish the whole thing up for
me. Top to bottom. And you put my name on it.
And I own all the rights. And every dime goes in
my pocket. You do that and I'll sure enough take
ya' with me to the desert. (*Lee stops, pause, looks
down at Austin.*) How's that sound?

(*Pause as Austin stands slowly holding plate of demol-
ished toast, their faces are very close, pause.*)

AUSTIN: It's a deal.

(*Lee stares straight into Austin's eyes, then he slowly
takes a piece of toast off the plate, raises it to his
mouth, and takes a huge crushing bite never taking
his eyes off Austin's, as Lee crunches into the toast
the lights black out.*)

Scene IX

(*Midday. No sound, blazing heat, the stage is ravaged;
bottles, toasters, smashed typewriter, ripped out telephone, etc. All the debris from previous scene is now
starkly visible in intense yellow light, the effect should
be like a desert junkyard at high noon, the coolness
of the preceding scenes is totally obliterated. Austin
is seated at table in alcove, shirt open, pouring with
sweat, hunched over a writing notebook, scribbling
notes desperately with a ballpoint pen. Lee with no
shirt, beer in hand, sweat pouring down his chest, is
walking a slow circle around the table, picking his
way through the objects, sometimes kicking them aside.*)

LEE (*as he walks*): All right, read it back to me. Read
it back to me!
AUSTIN (*scribbling at top speed*): Just a second.
LEE: Come on, come on! Just read what ya' got.
AUSTIN: I can't keep up! It's not the same as if I had
a typewriter.
LEE: Just read what we got so far. Forget about the
rest.
AUSTIN: All right. Let's see — okay — (*wipes sweat
from his face, reads as Lee circles*) Luke says
uh —
LEE: Luke?
AUSTIN: Yeah.
LEE: His name's Luke? All right, all right — we can
change the names later. What's he say? Come on,
come on.
AUSTIN: He says uh — (*reading*) "I told ya' you were
a fool to follow me in here. I know this prairie
like the back a' my hand."

LEE: No, no no! That's not what I said. I never said
that.
AUSTIN: That's what I wrote.
LEE: It's not what I said. I never said "like the back
a' my hand." That's stupid. That's one a' those —
whadya' call it? Whadya' call that?
AUSTIN: What?
LEE: Whadya' call it when somethin's been said a
thousand times before. Whadya' call that?
AUSTIN: Um — a cliché?
LEE: Yeah. That's right. Cliché. That's what that is.
A cliché. "The back a' my hand." That's stupid.
AUSTIN: That's what you said.
LEE: I never said that! And even if I did, that's where
yer supposed to come in. That's where yer supposed
to change it to somethin' better.
AUSTIN: Well how am I supposed to do that and write
down what you say at the same time?
LEE: Ya' just do, that's all! You hear a stupid line
you change it. That's yer job.
AUSTIN: All right (*Makes more notes.*)
LEE: What're you changin' it to?
AUSTIN: I'm not changing it. I'm just trying to catch
up.
LEE: Well change it! We gotta' change that, we can't
leave that in there like that. ". . . the back a' my
hand." That's dumb.
AUSTIN (*stops writing, sits back*): All right.
LEE (*pacing*): So what'll we change it to?
AUSTIN: Um — How 'bout — "I'm on intimate terms
with this prairie."
LEE (*to himself considering line as he walks*): "I'm on
intimate terms with this prairie." Intimate terms,
intimate terms. Intimate — that means like uh —
sexual right?
AUSTIN: Well — yeah — or —
LEE: He's on sexual terms with the prairie? How dya'
figure that?
AUSTIN: Well it doesn't necessarily have to mean sexual.
LEE: What's it mean then?
AUSTIN: It means uh — close — personal —
LEE: All right. How's it sound? Put it into the uh —
the line there. Read it back. Let's see how it sounds.
(*To himself.*) "Intimate terms."
AUSTIN (*scribbles in notebook*): Okay. It'd go something
like this: (*reads*) "I told ya' you were a fool to
follow me in here. I'm on intimate terms with this
prairie."
LEE: That's good. I like that. That's real good.
AUSTIN: You do?
LEE: Yeah. Don't you?
AUSTIN: Sure.
LEE: Sounds original now. "Intimate terms." That's
good. Okay. Now we're cookin! That has a real
ring to it.

(*Austin makes more notes, Lee walks around, pours beer on his arms and rubs it over his chest feeling good about the new progress, as he does this Mom enters unobtrusively down left with her luggage, she stops and stares at the scene still holding luggage as the two men continue, unaware of her presence, Austin absorbed in his writing, Lee cooling himself off with beer.*)

LEE (*continues*): "He's on intimate terms with this prairie." Sounds real mysterious and kinda threatening at the same time.

AUSTIN (*writing rapidly*): Good.

LEE: Now — (*Lee turns and suddenly sees Mom, he stares at her for a while, she stares back, Austin keeps writing feverishly, not noticing, Lee walks slowly over to Mom and takes a closer look, long pause.*)

LEE: Mom?

(*Austin looks up suddenly from his writing, sees Mom, stands quickly, long pause, Mom surveys the damage.*)

AUSTIN: Mom. What're you doing back?

MOM: I'm back.

LEE: Here, lemme take those for ya.

(*Lee sets beer on counter then takes both her bags but doesn't know where to set them down in the sea of junk so he just keeps holding them.*)

AUSTIN: I wasn't expecting you back so soon. I thought uh — How was Alaska?

MOM: Fine.

LEE: See any igloos?

MOM: No. Just glaciers.

AUSTIN: Cold huh?

MOM: What?

AUSTIN: It must've been cold up there?

MOM: Not really.

LEE: Musta' been colder than this here. I mean we're havin' a real scorcher here.

MOM: Oh? (*She looks at damage.*)

LEE: Yeah. Must be in the hundreds.

AUSTIN: You wanna' take your coat off, Mom?

MOM: No. (*Pause, she surveys space.*) What happened in here?

AUSTIN: Oh um — Me and Lee were just sort of celebrating and uh —

MOM: Celebrating?

AUSTIN: Yeah. Uh — Lee sold a screenplay. A story, I mean.

MOM: Lee did?

AUSTIN: Yeah.

MOM: Not you?

AUSTIN: No. Him.

MOM (*to Lee*): You sold a screenplay?

LEE: Yeah. That's right. We're sorta' finishing it up right now. That's what we're doing here.

AUSTIN: Me and Lee are going out to the desert to live.

MOM: You and Lee?

AUSTIN: Yeah. I'm taking off with Lee.

MOM (*she looks back and forth at each of them, pause*): You gonna go live with your father?

AUSTIN: No. We're going to a different desert Mom.

MOM: I see. Well, you'll probably wind up on the same desert sooner or later. What're all these toasters doing here?

AUSTIN: Well — we had kind of a contest.

MOM: Contest?

LEE: Yeah.

AUSTIN: Lee won.

MOM: Did you win a lot of money, Lee?

LEE: Well not yet. It's comin' in any day now.

MOM (*to Lee*): What happened to your shirt?

LEE: Oh. I was sweatin' like a pig and I took it off.

(*Austin grabs Lee's shirt off the table and tosses it to him, Lee sets down suitcases and puts his shirt on.*)

MOM: Well, it's one hell of a mess in here isn't it?

AUSTIN: Yeah, I'll clean it up for you, Mom. I just didn't know you were coming back so soon.

MOM: I didn't either.

AUSTIN: What happened?

MOM: Nothing. I just started missing all my plants.

(*She notices dead plants.*)

AUSTIN: Oh.

MOM: Oh, they're all dead aren't they. (*She crosses toward them, examines them closely.*) You didn't get a chance to water I guess.

AUSTIN: I was doing it and then Lee came and —

LEE: Yeah I just distracted him a whole lot here, Mom. It's not his fault.

(*Pause, as Mom stares at plants.*)

MOM: Oh well, one less thing to take care of I guess. (*Turns toward brothers.*) Oh, that reminds me — You boys will probably never guess who's in town. Try and guess.

(*Long pause, brothers stare at her.*)

AUSTIN: Whadya' mean, Mom?

MOM: Take a guess. Somebody very important has come to town. I read it, coming down on the Greyhound.

LEE: Somebody very important?

MOM: See if you can guess. You'll never guess.

AUSTIN: Mom — we're trying to uh — (*Points to writing pad.*)

MOM: Picasso. (*Pause.*) Picasso's in town. Isn't that incredible? Right now.

(*Pause.*)

AUSTIN: Picasso's dead, Mom.

MOM: No, he's not dead. He's visiting the museum. I read it on the bus. We have to go down there and see him.

AUSTIN: Mom —

MOM: This is the chance of a lifetime. Can you imagine? We could all go down and meet him. All three of us.

LEE: Uh — I don't think I'm really up fer meetin' anybody right now. I'm uh — What's his name?

MOM: Picasso! Picasso! You've never heard of Picasso? Austin, you've heard of Picasso.

AUSTIN: Mom, we're not going to have time.

MOM: It won't take long. We'll just hop in the car and go down there. An opportunity like this doesn't come along every day.

AUSTIN: We're gonna' be leavin' here, Mom!

(*Pause.*)

MOM: Oh.

LEE: Yeah.

(*Pause.*)

MOM: You're both leaving?

LEE (*looks at Austin*): Well we were thinkin' about that before but now I —

AUSTIN: No, we are! We're both leaving. We've got it all planned.

MOM (*to Austin*): Well you can't leave. You have a family.

AUSTIN: I'm leaving. I'm getting out of here.

LEE (*to Mom*): I don't really think Austin's cut out for the desert do you?

MOM: No. He's not.

AUSTIN: I'm going with you, Lee!

MOM: He's too thin.

LEE: Yeah, he'd just burn up out there.

AUSTIN (*to Lee*): We just gotta' finish this screenplay and then we're gonna' take off. That's the plan. That's what you said. Come on, let's get back to work, Lee.

LEE: I can't work under these conditions here. It's too hot.

AUSTIN: Then we'll do it on the desert.

LEE: Don't be tellin' me what we're gonna' do!

MOM: Don't shout in the house.

LEE: We're just gonna' have to postpone the whole deal.

AUSTIN: I can't postpone it! It's gone past postponing! I'm doing everything you said. I'm writing down exactly what you tell me.

LEE: Yeah, but you were right all along see. It is a dumb story. "Two lamebrains chasin' each other across Texas." That's what you said, right?

AUSTIN: I never said that.

(*Lee sneers in Austin's face then turns to Mom.*)

LEE: I'm gonna' just borrow some a' your antiques, Mom. You don't mind do ya'? Just a few plates and things. Silverware.

(*Lee starts going through all the cupboards in kitchen pulling out plates and stacking them on counter as Mom and Austin watch.*)

MOM: You don't have any utensils on the desert?

LEE: Nah, I'm fresh out.

AUSTIN (*to Lee*): What're you doing?

MOM: Well some of those are very old. Bone China.

LEE: I'm tired of eatin' outa' my bare hands, ya' know. It's not civilized.

AUSTIN (*to Lee*): What're you doing? We made a deal!

MOM: Couldn't you borrow the plastic ones instead? I have plenty of plastic ones.

LEE (*as he stacks plates*): It's not the same. Plastic's not the same at all. What I need is somethin' authentic. Somethin' to keep me in touch. It's easy to get outa' touch out there. Don't worry I'll get em' back to ya'.

(*Austin rushes up to Lee, grabs him by shoulders.*)

AUSTIN: You can't just drop the whole thing, Lee!

(*Lee turns, pushes Austin in the chest knocking him backward into the alcove, Mom watches numbly, Lee returns to collecting the plates, silverware, etc.*)

MOM: You boys shouldn't fight in the house. Go outside and fight.

LEE: I'm not fightin'. I'm leavin'.

MOM: There's been enough damage done already.

LEE (*his back to Austin and Mom, stacking dishes on counter*): I'm clearin' outa' here once and for all. All this town does is drive a man insane. Look what it's done to Austin there. I'm not lettin' that happen to me. Sell myself down the river. No sir. I'd rather be a hundred miles from nowhere than let that happen to me.

(*During this Austin has picked up the ripped-out phone from the floor and wrapped the cord tightly around his hands, he lunges at Lee whose back is still to him, wraps the cord around Lee's neck, plants a foot in Lee's back and pulls back on the cord, tightening it, Lee chokes desperately, can't speak and can't reach Austin with his arms, Austin keeps applying pressure on Lee's back with his foot, bending him into the sink, Mom watches.*)

AUSTIN (*tightening cord*): You're not goin' anywhere!
You're not takin' anything with you. You're not
takin' my car! You're not takin' the dishes! You're
not takin' anything! You're stayin' right here!

MOM: You'll have to stop fighting in the house. There's
plenty of room outside to fight. You've got the
whole outdoors to fight in.

(*Lee tries to tear himself away, he crashes across the
stage like an enraged bull dragging Austin with him,
he snorts and bellows but Austin hangs on and manages
to keep clear of Lee's attempts to grab him, they crash
into the table, to the floor, Lee is face down thrashing
wildly and choking, Austin pulls cord tighter, stands
with one foot planted on Lee's back and the cord
stretched taut.*)

AUSTIN (*holding cord*): Gimme back my keys, Lee!
Take the keys out! Take 'em out!

(*Lee desperately tries to dig in his pockets, searching
for the car keys, Mom moves closer.*)

MOM (*calmly to Austin*): You're not killing him are
you?

AUSTIN: I don't know. I don't know if I'm killing him.
I'm stopping him. That's all. I'm just stopping him.

(*Lee thrashes but Austin is relentless.*)

MOM: You oughta' let him breathe a little bit.
AUSTIN: Throw the keys out, Lee!

(*Lee finally gets keys out and throws them on floor
but out of Austin's reach, Austin keeps pressure on
cord, pulling Lee's neck back, Lee gets one hand to
the cord but can't relieve the pressure.*)

Reach me those keys would ya', Mom.
MOM (*not moving*): Why are you doing this to him?
AUSTIN: Reach me the keys!
MOM: Not until you stop choking him.
AUSTIN: I can't stop choking him! He'll kill me if I
stop choking him!
MOM: He won't kill you. He's your brother.
AUSTIN: Just get me the keys would ya'!

(*Pause. Mom picks keys up off floor, hands them to
Austin.*)

AUSTIN (*to Mom*): Thanks.
MOM: Will you let him go now?
AUSTIN: I don't know. He's not gonna' let me get
outa' here.
MOM: Well you can't kill him.
AUSTIN: I can kill him! I can easily kill him. Right
now. Right here. All I gotta' do is just tighten up.
See? (*He tightens cord, Lee thrashes wildly, Austin
releases pressure a little, maintaining control.*) Ya'
see that?

MOM: That's a savage thing to do.
AUSTIN: Yeah well don't tell me I can't kill him because
I can. I can just twist. I can just keep twisting.
(*Austin twists the cord tighter, Lee weakens, his
breathing changes to a short rasp.*)
MOM: Austin!

(*Austin relieves pressure, Lee breathes easier but Austin
keeps him under control.*)

AUSTIN (*eyes on Lee, holding cord*): I'm goin' to the
desert. There's nothing stopping me. I'm going by
myself to the desert.

(*Mom moving toward her luggage.*)

MOM: Well, I'm going to go check into a motel. I
can't stand this anymore.
AUSTIN: Don't go yet!

(*Mom pauses.*)

MOM: I can't stay here. This is worse than being
homeless.
AUSTIN: I'll get everything fixed up for you, Mom. I
promise. Just stay for a while.
MOM (*picking up luggage*): You're going to the desert.
AUSTIN: Just wait!

(*Lee thrashes, Austin subdues him, Mom watches
holding luggage, pause.*)

MOM: It was the worst feeling being up there. In
Alaska. Staring out a window. I never felt so desperate before. That's why when I saw that article
on Picasso I thought —
AUSTIN: Stay here, Mom. This is where you live.

(*She looks around the stage.*)

MOM: I don't recognize it at all.

(*She exits with luggage, Austin makes a move toward
her but Lee starts to struggle and Austin subdues him
again with cord, pause.*)

AUSTIN (*holding cord*): Lee? I'll make ya' a deal. You
let me get outa' here. Just let me get to my car.
All right, Lee? Gimme a little headstart and I'll
turn you loose. Just gimme a little headstart. All
right?

(*Lee makes no response, Austin slowly releases tension
cord, still nothing from Lee.*)

AUSTIN: Lee?

(*Lee is motionless, Austin very slowly begins to stand,
still keeping a tenuous hold on the cord and his eyes
riveted to Lee for any sign of movement, Austin slowly
drops the cord and stands, he stares down at Lee who
appears to be dead.*)

AUSTIN (*whispers*): Lee?

(*Pause, Austin considers, looks toward exit, back to Lee, then makes a small movement as if to leave. Instantly Lee is on his feet and moves toward exit, blocking Austin's escape. They square off to each other, keeping a distance between them. Pause, a single coyote heard in distance, lights fade softly into moonlight, the figures of the brothers now appear to be caught in a vast desertlike landscape, they are very still but watchful for the next move, lights go slowly to black as the after-image of the brothers pulses in the dark, coyote fades.*)

Athol Fugard

Athol Fugard (b. 1932) was an actor before a playwright. In 1956, he began working with a theater group called the Circle Players in Cape Town, South Africa. The group was extremely unusual because it included both black and white actors as participants at a time when racial mixing was illegal (as it still is in many places). Fugard's wife, the actress Sheila Meiring, stimulated his interest in theater in 1956 and in developing the theater company, which sustained itself to produce fine plays and to make an ultimate contribution to world drama.

Fugard, who is white, met Zakes Mokae, a black musician and actor, in the early days of the Circle Players, and the two collaborated on several works. Mokae has said that the tradition in Africa was not so much for a solitary playwright to compose a work that others would act out as it was for people to develop a communal approach to drama, crafting a dramatic piece through their interaction. To some extent, Fugard in his early efforts did just that. He worked with actors, watched how things developed, and then shaped the drama around them.

In 1960, he began to write a two-person play called *The Blood Knot* while he was in England trying to establish a theater group there. This play was part of a trilogy called *The Family*, with *Hello and Goodbye* (1965) and *Boesman and Lena* (1969). *The Blood Knot* was given its first performance in Dorkay House in Johannesburg late in 1961. As Fugard has said, the entire production, which starred Fugard and Mokae, was put together so quickly that the government never had time to stop it. The play is about two brothers, one black, the other light-skinned enough to pass for white. It is exceptionally powerful and in its first performances in Johannesburg, it was a sensation. As a result of its success, it toured South Africa and it had a revival in New Haven and in New York in 1984 and 1985.

While they toured South Africa, Fugard and Mokae were victims of the country's apartheid policies. They could not travel in the same train car: Fugard went first class and Mokae had to go in the special cars for blacks. After *The Blood Knot*'s success the government passed laws making it all but impossible to have black and white actors working together on the stage.

Fugard has had a considerable number of plays produced in New York and London in recent years. *Sizwe Banzi Is Dead* (1972), which is about a man who exchanges identity with a corpse as a way of avoiding the racial laws of South Africa, was well received. *The Island*

(1975) starred two black actors, John Kani and Winston Ntshona, who have become associated with Fugard and his work. They portray prisoners who are putting on *Antigone* and who become immersed in the political themes of the play, seeing it as an example of the political repression they experience in their own lives.

His plays *A Lesson from Aloes* (1978) and *The Road to Mecca* (1984) were successful in their first American productions at the Yale Repertory Theatre and on Broadway. Fugard's themes are not always concerned with racial problems, but they usually center on political issues and the stress that individuals feel in trying to be themselves in an intolerant society.

Fugard is now in a somewhat anomalous position in South Africa. Blacks have criticized him for dealing with themes that they feel are more properly developed by black writers. At the same time, he is ostracized by white South African society because of his sympathies toward blacks. He himself feels he is writing what he knows about, and he does not apologize for its revealing his own limitations and his own point of view. And his attachment and commitment to South Africa remain deep and lifelong. He always returns to his homeland from his travels abroad because, as he says, he learned in South Africa everything he knows about how to develop deep feelings. His gravesite is in South Africa, a fact that he says gives him great pleasure.

"MASTER HAROLD" . . . AND THE BOYS

Athol Fugard (b. 1932) has said that *"MASTER HAROLD"... and the boys* (1982) is a very personal play in which he exorcises personal guilt (Fugard's entire name is Athol Harold Lannigan Fugard). As a white South African he has written numerous plays that represent the racial circumstances of life in that troubled nation. This play has won international distinction and has made a reputation for its stars, especially Zakes Mokae, with whom Fugard has worked for more than thirty years.

Hally reveals throughout the play that he is more attached emotionally to Sam, the black waiter in his parents' restaurant who has befriended him, than he is even to his own parents. His attitude toward his father is complicated by his father's alcoholism and lameness. Even such an alcoholic invalid is considered, in South Africa, automatically superior to a black man such as Sam, who is intelligent, quick, thoughtful, and generous. When Hally reveals his anxiety about his father, Sam warns him that it is dishonorable to treat one's father the way he does, but Sam's presumption in admonishing Hally triggers Hally's mean outburst toward him.

Zakes Mokae, who created the role of Sam in the first performance of the play at the Yale Repertory Theatre, has commented extensively about his role and the character of Sam. He has observed that some black audience members called out during a performance that he should beat Hally up the minute Hally demands that Sam call him Master Harold. But other black audience members spoke with him after the performance and agreed that, because Sam had never taken that kind of stand against Harold or his father, he was getting what he deserved. Mokae himself has pointed out that Sam is probably not living in Port Elizabeth legally and that to have taken action, even if he wanted to, would have ended with his removal from the town into exile.

Zakes Mokae understands the character from his perspective as a black South African, and he realizes Sam's limits. But he has said that if he had written the play Sam would give Hally a beating and "suffer the consequences." He points out, however, that he is an urban South African, unlike Sam, and his attitude is quite different from anything that Sam would have understood. As an urban black, Mokae could not have been sent into exile, although he could certainly have been punished, for beating a white boy.

About the question of whether the play makes a positive contribution to white-black relations in South Africa, Mokae feels that a play cannot change people's minds. Audiences are not likely to seek to change the government of South Africa simply because they have seen a play. But at the same time, he feels that it is productive to talk about the apartheid and racial distrust in South Africa.

Unfortunately, the government of South Africa decided that the play was too inflammatory for performance in its country, and the play is currently banned from performance in Johannesburg and other theatrical centers in South Africa. This suggests that while Zakes Mokae does not feel that one play will have much impact on injustices in South Africa, it is likely that the government fears otherwise.

In an important way, *"MASTER HAROLD" . . . and the boys* is a personal statement by Fugard that establishes the extent to which apartheid can damage even a person sympathetic to black rights. It is astonishing in retrospect to think, as his interviewer, Heinrich Von Staden, once said, that Hally could grow up to be Athol himself. If this is true, then it is also true that the play is hopeful.

One sign of hope is that the violence in the play is restrained. Sam does not beat Hally for his humiliation of him, although he probably would like to. And no one in the play makes a move to be physically threatening to Sam. Faint as they are, such signs are signs of hope. And as Zakes Mokae has said about the situation in his homeland, "One is always optimistic. It can't go on forever."

Athol Fugard (b. 1932)
"MASTER HAROLD" . . . AND THE BOYS   1982

(*The St. George's Park Tea Room on a wet and windy Port Elizabeth afternoon.*)

(*Tables and chairs have been cleared and are stacked on one side except for one which stands apart with a single chair. On this table a knife, fork, spoon and side plate in anticipation of a simple meal, together with a pile of comic books.*)

(*Other elements: a serving counter with a few stale cakes under glass and a not very impressive display of sweets, cigarettes and cool drinks, etc.; a few cardboard advertising handouts — Cadbury's Chocolate, Coca-Cola — and a blackboard on which an untrained hand has chalked up the prices of Tea, Coffee, Scones, Milkshakes — all flavors — and Cool Drinks; a few sad ferns in pots; a telephone; an old-style jukebox.*)

(*There is an entrance on one side and an exit into a kitchen on the other.*)

(*Leaning on the solitary table, his head cupped in one hand as he pages through one of the comic books, is Sam. A black man in his mid-forties. He wears the white coat of a waiter. Behind him on his knees, mopping down the floor with a bucket of water and a rag, is Willie. Also black and about the same age as Sam. He has his sleeves and trousers rolled up.*)

(*The year: 1950.*)

WILLIE (*singing as he works*): "She was scandalizin' my name,
She took my money
She called me honey
But she was scandalizin' my name.
Called it love but was playin' a game. . . ."

(*He gets up and moves the bucket. Stands thinking for a moment, then, raising his arms to hold an imaginary partner, he launches into an intricate ballroom dance step. Although a mildly comic figure, he reveals a reasonable degree of accomplishment.*)

Hey, Sam.

(*Sam, absorbed in the comic book, does not respond.*)

Hey, Boet° Sam!

(*Sam looks up.*)

I'm getting it. The quickstep. Look now and tell me. (*He repeats the step.*) Well?
SAM (*encouragingly*): Show me again.
WILLIE: Okay, count for me.
SAM: Ready?
WILLIE: Ready.
SAM: Five, six, seven, eight. . . . (*Willie starts to dance.*) A-n-d one two three four . . . and one two three four. . . . (*Ad libbing as Willie dances.*) Your shoulders, Willie . . . your shoulders! Don't look down! Look happy, Willie! Relax, Willie!
WILLIE (*desperate but still dancing*): I am relax.
SAM: No, you're not.
WILLIE (*he falters*): Ag no man, Sam! Mustn't talk. You make me make mistakes.
SAM: But you're stiff.
WILLIE: Yesterday I'm not straight . . . today I'm too stiff!
SAM: Well, you are. You asked me and I'm telling you.
WILLIE: Where?
SAM: Everywhere. Try to glide through it.
WILLIE: Glide?
SAM: Ja, make it smooth. And give it more style. It must look like you're enjoying yourself.
WILLIE (*emphatically*): I wasn't.
SAM: Exactly.
WILLIE: How can I enjoy myself? Not straight, too stiff and now it's also glide, give it more style, make

---

Boet: Brother.

it smooth. . . . Haai! Is hard to remember all those things, Boet Sam.

SAM: That's your trouble. You're trying too hard.

WILLIE: I try hard because it *is* hard.

SAM: But don't let me see it. The secret is to make it look easy. Ballroom must look happy, Willie, not like hard work. It must. . . . Ja! . . . it must look like romance.

WILLIE: Now another one! What's romance?

SAM: Love story with happy ending. A handsome man in tails, and in his arms, smiling at him, a beautiful lady in evening dress!

WILLIE: Fred Astaire, Ginger Rogers.

SAM: You got it. Tapdance or ballroom, it's the same. Romance. In two weeks' time when the judges look at you and Hilda, they must see a man and a woman who are dancing their way to a happy ending. What I saw was you holding her like you were frightened she was going to run away.

WILLIE: Ja! Because that is what she wants to do! I got no romance left for Hilda anymore, Boet Sam.

SAM: Then pretend. When you put your arms around Hilda, imagine she is Ginger Rogers.

WILLIE: With no teeth? You try.

SAM: Well, just remember, there's only two weeks left.

WILLIE: I know, I know! (*To the jukebox.*) I do it better with music. You got sixpence for Sarah Vaughan?

SAM: That's a slow foxtrot. You're practicing the quickstep.

WILLIE: I'll practice slow foxtrot.

SAM (*shaking his head*): It's your turn to put money in the jukebox.

WILLIE: I only got bus fare to go home. (*He returns disconsolately to his work.*) Love story and happy ending! She's doing it all right, Boet Sam, but is not me she's giving happy endings. Fuckin' whore! Three nights now she doesn't come practice. I wind up gramophone, I get record ready and I sit and wait. What happens? Nothing. Ten o'clock I start dancing with my pillow. You try and practice romance by yourself, Boet Sam. Struesgod, she doesn't come tonight I take back my dress and ballroom shoes and I find me new partner. Size twenty-six. Shoes size seven. And now she's also making trouble for me with the baby again. Reports me to Child Wellfed, that I'm not giving her money. She lies! Every week I am giving her money for milk. And how do I know is my baby? Only his hair looks like me. She's fucking around all the time I turn my back. Hilda Samuels is a bitch! (*Pause.*) Hey, Sam!

SAM: Ja.

WILLIE: You listening?

SAM: Ja.

WILLIE: So what you say?

SAM: About Hilda?

WILLIE: Ja.

SAM: When did you last give her a hiding?

WILLIE (*reluctantly*): Sunday night.

SAM: And today is Thursday.

WILLIE (*he knows what's coming*): Okay.

SAM: Hiding on Sunday night, then Monday, Tuesday, and Wednesday she doesn't come to practice . . . and you are asking me why?

WILLIE: I said okay, Boet Sam!

SAM: You hit her too much. One day she's going to leave you for good.

WILLIE: So? She makes me the hell-in too much.

SAM (*emphasizing his point*): *Too* much and *too* hard. You had the same trouble with Eunice.

WILLIE: Because she also make the hell-in, Boet Sam. She never got the steps right. Even the waltz.

SAM: Beating her up every time she makes a mistake in the waltz? (*Shaking his head.*) No, Willie! That takes the pleasure out of ballroom dancing.

WILLIE: Hilda is not too bad with the waltz, Boet Sam. Is the quickstep where the trouble starts.

SAM (*teasing him gently*): How's your pillow with the quickstep?

WILLIE (*ignoring the tease*): Good! And why? Because it got no legs. That's her trouble. She can't move them quick enough, Boet Sam. I start the record and before halfway Count Basie is already winning. Only time we catch up with him is when gramophone runs down. (*Sam laughs.*) Haaikona, Boet Sam, is not funny.

SAM (*snapping his fingers*): I got it! Give her a handicap.

WILLIE: What's that?

SAM: Give her a ten-second start and then let Count Basie go. Then I put my money on her. Hot favorite in the Ballroom Stakes: Hilda Samuels ridden by Willie Malopo.

WILLIE (*turning away*): I'm not talking to you no more.

SAM (*relenting*): Sorry, Willie. . . .

WILLIE: It's finish between us.

SAM: Okay, okay . . . I'll stop.

WILLIE: You can also fuck off.

SAM: Willie, listen! I want to help you!

WILLIE: No more jokes?

SAM: I promise.

WILLIE: Okay. Help me.

SAM (*his turn to hold an imaginary partner*): Look and learn. Feet together. Back straight. Body relaxed. Right hand placed gently in the small of her back and wait for the music. Don't start worrying about making mistakes or the judges or the other competitors. It's just you, Hilda and the music, and you're going to have a good time. What Count Basie do you play?

WILLIE: "You the cream in my coffee, you the salt in my stew."

SAM: Right. Give it to me in strict tempo.

WILLIE: Ready?

SAM: Ready.

WILLIE: A-n-d . . . (*Singing.*)
"You the cream in my coffee.
You the salt in my stew.
You will always be my necessity.
I'd be lost without you. . . ." (*etc.*)

(*Sam launches into the quickstep. He is obviously a much more accomplished dancer than Willie. Hally enters. A seventeen-year-old white boy. Wet raincoat and school case. He stops and watches Sam. The demonstration comes to an end with a flourish. Applause from Hally and Willie.*)

HALLY: Bravo! No question about it. First place goes to Mr. Sam Semela.

WILLIE (*in total agreement*): You was gliding with style, Boet Sam.

HALLY (*cheerfully*): How's it, chaps?

SAM: Okay, Hally.

WILLIE (*springing to attention like a soldier and saluting*): At your service, Master Harold!

HALLY: Not long to the big event, hey!

SAM: Two weeks.

HALLY: You nervous?

SAM: No.

HALLY: Think you stand a chance?

SAM: Let's just say I'm ready to go out there and dance.

HALLY: It looked like it. What about you, Willie?

(*Willie groans.*)

What's the matter?

SAM: He's got leg trouble.

HALLY (*innocently*): Oh, sorry to hear that, Willie.

WILLIE: Boet Sam! You promised. (*Willie returns to his work.*)

(*Hally deposits his school case and takes off his raincoat. His clothes are a little neglected and untidy: black blazer with school badge, gray flannel trousers in need of an ironing, khaki shirt and tie, black shoes. Sam has fetched a towel for Hally to dry his hair.*)

HALLY: God, what a lousy bloody day. It's coming down cats and dogs out there. Bad for business, chaps. . . . (*Conspiratorial whisper.*) . . . but it also means we're in for a nice quiet afternoon.

SAM: You can speak loud. Your Mom's not here.

HALLY: Out shopping?

SAM: No. The hospital.

HALLY: But it's Thursday. There's no visiting on Thursday afternoons. Is my Dad okay?

SAM: Sounds like it. In fact, I think he's going home.

HALLY (*stopped short by Sam's remark*): What do you mean?

SAM: The hospital phoned.

HALLY: To say what?

SAM: I don't know. I just heard your Mom talking.

HALLY: So what makes you say he's going home?

SAM: It sounded as if they were telling her to come and fetch him.

(*Hally thinks about what Sam has said for a few seconds.*)

HALLY: When did she leave?

SAM: About an hour ago. She said she would phone you. Want to eat?

(*Hally doesn't respond.*)

Hally, want your lunch?

HALLY: I suppose so. (*His mood has changed.*) What's on the menu? . . . as if I don't know.

SAM: Soup, followed by meat pie and gravy.

HALLY: Today's?

SAM: No.

HALLY: And the soup?

SAM: Nourishing pea soup.

HALLY: Just the soup. (*The pile of comic books on the table.*) And these?

SAM: For your Dad. Mr. Kempston brought them.

HALLY: You haven't been reading them, have you?

SAM: Just looking.

HALLY (*examining the comics*): Jungle Jim . . . Batman and Robin . . . Tarzan . . . God, what rubbish! Mental pollution. Take them away.

(*Sam exits waltzing into the kitchen. Hally turns to Willie.*)

HALLY: Did you hear my Mom talking on the telephone, Willie?

WILLIE: No, Master Hally. I was at the back.

HALLY: And she didn't say anything to you before she left?

WILLIE: She said I must clean the floors.

HALLY: I mean about my Dad.

WILLIE: She didn't say nothing to me about him, Master Hally.

HALLY (*with conviction*): No! It can't be. They said he needed at least another three weeks of treatment. Sam's definitely made a mistake. (*Rummages through his school case, finds a book and settles down at the table to read.*) So, Willie!

WILLIE: Yes, Master Hally! Schooling okay today?

HALLY: Yes, okay. . . . (*He thinks about it.*) . . . No, not really. Ag, what's the difference? I don't care. And Sam says you've got problems.

WILLIE: Big problems.

HALLY: Which leg is sore?

(*Willie groans.*)

Both legs.

WILLIE: There is nothing wrong with my legs. Sam is just making jokes.

HALLY: So then you *will* be in the competition.

WILLIE: Only if I can find a partner.

HALLY: But what about Hilda?

SAM (*returning with a bowl of soup*): She's the one who's got trouble with her legs.

HALLY: What sort of trouble, Willie?

SAM: From the way he describes it, I think the lady has gone a bit lame.

HALLY: Good God! Have you taken her to see a doctor?

SAM: I think a vet would be better.

HALLY: What do you mean?

SAM: What do you call it again when a racehorse goes very fast?

HALLY: Gallop?

SAM: That's it!

WILLIE: Boet Sam!

HALLY: "A gallop down the homestretch to the winning post." But what's that got to do with Hilda?

SAM: Count Basie always gets there first.

(*Willie lets fly with his slop rag. It misses Sam and hits Hally.*)

HALLY (*furious*): For Christ's sake, Willie! What the hell do you think you're doing?

WILLIE: Sorry, Master Hally, but it's him. . . .

HALLY: Act your bloody age! (*Hurls the rag back at Willie.*) Cut out the nonsense now and get on with your work. And you too, Sam. Stop fooling around.

(*Sam moves away.*)

No. Hang on. I haven't finished! Tell me exactly what my Mom said.

SAM: I have. "When Hally comes, tell him I've gone to the hospital and I'll phone him."

HALLY: She didn't say anything about taking my Dad home?

SAM: No. It's just that when she was talking on the phone. . . .

HALLY (*interrupting him*): No, Sam. They can't be discharging him. She would have said so if they were. In any case, we saw him last night and he wasn't in good shape at all. Staff nurse even said there was talk about taking more X-rays. And now suddenly today he's better? If anything, it sounds more like a bad turn to me . . . which I sincerely hope it isn't. Hang on . . . how long ago did you say she left?

SAM: Just before two . . . (*His wrist watch.*) . . . hour and a half.

HALLY: I know how to settle it. (*Behind the counter to the telephone. Talking as he dials.*) Let's give her ten minutes to get to the hospital, ten minutes to load him up, another ten, at the most, to get home, and another ten to get him inside. Forty minutes. They should have been home for at least half an hour already. (*Pause — he waits with the receiver to his ear.*) No reply, chaps. And you know why? Because she's at his bedside in hospital helping him pull through a bad turn. You definitely heard wrong.

SAM: Okay.

(*As far as Hally is concerned, the matter is settled. He returns to his table, sits down, and divides his attention between the book and his soup. Sam is at his school case and picks up a textbook.*)

Modern Graded Mathematics for Standards Nine and Ten. (*Opens it at random and laughs at something he sees.*) Who is this supposed to be?

HALLY: Old fart-face Prentice.

SAM: Teacher?

HALLY: Thinks he is. And believe me, that is not a bad likeness.

SAM: Has he seen it?

HALLY: Yes.

SAM: What did he say?

HALLY: Tried to be clever, as usual. Said I was no Leonardo da Vinci and that bad art had to be punished. So, six of the best, and his are bloody good.

SAM: On your bum?

HALLY: Where else? The days when I got them on my hands are gone forever, Sam.

SAM: With your trousers down!

HALLY: No. He's not quite that barbaric.

SAM: That's the way they do it in jail.

HALLY (*flicker of morbid interest*): Really?

SAM: Ja. When the magistrate sentences you to "strokes with a light cane."

HALLY: Go on.

SAM: They make you lie down on a bench. One policeman pulls down your trousers and holds your ankles, another one pulls your shirt over your head and holds your arms. . . .

HALLY: Thank you! That's enough.

SAM: ... and the one that gives you the strokes talks to you gently and for a long time between each one. (*He laughs.*)

HALLY: I've heard enough, Sam! Jesus! It's a bloody awful world when you come to think of it. People can be real bastards.

SAM: That's the way it is, Hally.

HALLY: It doesn't *have* to be that way. There is something called progress, you know. We don't exactly burn people at the stake anymore.

SAM: Like Joan of Arc.

HALLY: Correct. If she was captured today, she'd be given a fair trial.

SAM: And then the death sentence.

HALLY (*a world-weary sigh*): I know, I know! I oscillate between hope and despair for this world as well, Sam. But things will change, you wait and see. One day somebody is going to get up and give history a kick up the backside and get it going again.

SAM: Like who?

HALLY (*after thought*): They're called social reformers. Every age, Sam, has got its social reformer. My history book is full of them.

SAM: So where's ours?

HALLY: Good question. And I hate to say it, but the answer is: I don't know. Maybe he hasn't even been born yet. Or is still only a babe in arms at his mother's breast. God, what a thought.

SAM: So we just go on waiting.

HALLY: Ja, looks like it. (*Back to his soup and the book.*)

SAM (*reading from the textbook*): "Introduction: In some mathematical problems only the magnitude...." (*He mispronounces the word "magnitude."*)

HALLY (*correcting him without looking up*): Magnitude.

SAM: What's it mean?

HALLY: How big it is. The size of the thing.

SAM (*reading*): "... magnitude of the quantities is of importance. In other problems we need to know whether these quantities are negative or positive. For example, whether there is a debit or credit bank balance ..."

HALLY: Whether you're broke or not.

SAM: "... whether the temperature is above or below Zero...."

HALLY: Naught degrees. Cheerful state of affairs! No cash and you're freezing to death. Mathematics won't get you out of that one.

SAM: "All these quantities are called ..." (*spelling the word*) ... s-c-a-l.....

HALLY: Scalars.

SAM: Scalars! (*Shaking his head with a laugh.*) You understand all that?

HALLY (*turning a page*): No. And I don't intend to try.

SAM: So what happens when the exams come?

HALLY: Failing a maths exam isn't the end of the world, Sam. How many times have I told you that examination results don't measure intelligence?

SAM: I would say about as many times as you've failed one of them.

HALLY (*mirthlessly*): Ha, ha, ha.

SAM (*simultaneously*): Ha, ha, ha.

HALLY: Just remember Winston Churchill didn't do particularly well at school.

SAM: You've also told me that one many times.

HALLY: Well, it just so happens to be the truth.

SAM (*enjoying the word*): Magnitude! Magnitude! Show me how to use it.

HALLY (*after thought*): An intrepid social reformer will not be daunted by the magnitude of the task he has undertaken.

SAM (*impressed*): Couple of jaw-breakers in there!

HALLY: I gave you three for the price of one. Intrepid, daunted, and magnitude. I did that once in an exam. Put five of the words I had to explain in one sentence. It was half a page long.

SAM: Well, I'll put my money on you in the English exam.

HALLY: Piece of cake. Eighty percent without even trying.

SAM (*another textbook from Hally's case*): And history?

HALLY: So-so. I'll scrape through. In the fifties if I'm lucky.

SAM: You didn't do too badly last year.

HALLY: Because we had World War One. That at least has some action. You try to find that in the South African Parliamentary system.

SAM (*reading from the history textbook*): "Napoleon and the principle of equality." Hey! This sounds interesting. "After concluding peace with Britain in 1802, Napoleon used a brief period of calm to in-sti-tute ..."

HALLY: Introduce.

SAM: "... many reforms. Napoleon regarded all people as equal before the law and wanted them to have equal opportunities for advancement. All ves-ti-ges of the feu-dal sys-tem with its oppression of the poor were abol-ished." Vestiges, feudal system, and abolished. I'm all right on oppression.

HALLY: I'm thinking. He swept away ... abolished ... the last remains ... vestiges ... of the bad old days ... feudal system.

SAM: Ha! There's the social reformer we're waiting for. He sounds like a man of some magnitude.

HALLY: I'm not so sure about that. It's a damn good title for a book, though. A man of magnitude!

SAM: He sounds pretty big to me, Hally.

HALLY: Don't confuse historical significance with greatness. But maybe I'm being a bit prejudiced. Have a look in there and you'll see he's two chapters long. And hell!... has he only got dates, Sam, all of which you've got to remember! This campaign and that campaign, and then, because of all the fighting, the next thing is we get Peace Treaties all over the place. And what's the end of the story? Battle of Waterloo, which he loses. Wasn't worth it. No, I don't know about him as a man of magnitude.

SAM: Then who would you say was?

HALLY: To answer that, we need a definition of greatness, and I suppose that would be somebody who ... somebody who benefited all mankind.

SAM: Right. But like who?

HALLY (*he speaks with total conviction*): Charles Darwin. Remember him? That big book from the library. *The Origin of the Species*.

SAM: Him?

HALLY: Yes. For his Theory of Evolution.

SAM: You didn't finish it.

HALLY: I ran out of time. I didn't finish it because my two weeks was up. But I'm going to take it out again after I've digested what I read. It's safe. I've hidden it away in the Theology section. Nobody ever goes in there. And anyway who are you to talk? You hardly even looked at it.

SAM: I tried. I looked at the chapters in the beginning and I saw one called "The Struggle for an Existence." Ah ha, I thought. At last! But what did I get? Something called the mistiltoe which needs the apple tree and there's too many seeds and all are going to die except one ... ! No, Hally.

HALLY (*intellectually outraged*): What do you mean, No! The poor man had to start somewhere. For God's sake, Sam, he revolutionized science. Now we know.

SAM: What?

HALLY: Where we come from and what it all means.

SAM: And that's a benefit to mankind? Anyway, I still don't believe it.

HALLY: God, you're impossible. I showed it to you in black and white.

SAM: Doesn't mean I got to believe it.

HALLY: It's the likes of you that kept the Inquisition in business. It's called bigotry. Anyway, that's my man of magnitude. Charles Darwin! Who's yours?

SAM (*without hesitation*): Abraham Lincoln.

HALLY: I might have guessed as much. Don't get sentimental, Sam. You've never been a slave, you know. And anyway we freed your ancestors here in South Africa long before the Americans. But if you want to thank somebody on their behalf, do it to Mr. William Wilberforce.° Come on. Try again. I want a real genius.

(*Now enjoying himself, and so is Sam. Hally goes behind the counter and helps himself to a chocolate.*)

SAM: William Shakespeare.

HALLY (*no enthusiasm*): Oh. So you're also one of them, are you? You're basing that opinion on only one play, you know. You've only read my *Julius Caesar* and even I don't understand half of what they're talking about. They should do what they did with the old Bible: bring the language up to date.

SAM: That's all you've got. It's also the only one *you've* read.

HALLY: I know. I admit it. That's why I suggest we reserve our judgment until we've checked up on a few others. I've got a feeling, though, that by the end of this year one is going to be enough for me, and I can give you the names of twenty-nine other chaps in the Standard Nine class of the Port Elizabeth Technical College who feel the same. But if you want him, you can have him. My turn now. (*Pacing.*) This is a damned good exercise, you know! It started off looking like a simple question and here it's got us really probing into the intellectual heritage of our civilization.

SAM: So who is it going to be?

HALLY: My next man ... and he gets the title on two scores: social reform and literary genius ... is Leo Nikolaevich Tolstoy.

SAM: That Russian.

HALLY: Correct. Remember the picture of him I showed you?

SAM: With the long beard.

HALLY (*trying to look like Tolstoy*): And those burning, visionary eyes. My God, the face of a social prophet if ever I saw one! And remember my words when I showed it to you? Here's a *man*, Sam!

SAM: Those were words, Hally.

HALLY: Not many intellectuals are prepared to shovel manure with the peasants and then go home and write a "little book" called *War and Peace*. Incidentally, Sam, he was somebody else who, to quote, "... did not distinguish himself scholastically."

SAM: Meaning?

HALLY: He was also no good at school.

SAM: Like you and Winston Churchill.

HALLY (*mirthlessly*): Ha, ha, ha.

Mr. William Wilberforce: (1759–1833), British statesman who supported a bill outlawing the slave trade and suppressing slavery in the British Empire.

SAM (*simultaneously*): Ha, ha, ha.

HALLY: Don't get clever, Sam. That man freed his serfs of his own free will.

SAM: No argument. He was a somebody, all right. I accept him.

HALLY: I'm sure Count Tolstoy will be very pleased to hear that. Your turn. Shoot. (*Another chocolate from behind the counter.*) I'm waiting, Sam.

SAM: I've got him.

HALLY: Good. Submit your candidate for examination.

SAM: Jesus.

HALLY (*stopped dead in his tracks*): Who?

SAM: Jesus Christ.

HALLY: Oh, come on, Sam!

SAM: The Messiah.

HALLY: Ja, but still . . . No, Sam. Don't let's get started on religion. We'll just spend the whole afternoon arguing again. Suppose I turn around and say Mohammed?

SAM: All right.

HALLY: You can't have them both on the same list!

SAM: Why not? You like Mohammed, I like Jesus.

HALLY: I *don't* like Mohammed. I never have. I was merely being hypothetical. As far as I'm concerned, the Koran is as bad as the Bible. No. Religion is out! I'm not going to waste my time again arguing with you about the existence of God. You know perfectly well I'm an atheist . . . and I've got homework to do.

SAM: Okay, I take him back.

HALLY: You've got time for one more name.

SAM (*after thought*): I've got one I know we'll agree on. A simple straightforward great Man of Magnitude . . . and no arguments. And *he* really *did* benefit all mankind.

HALLY: I wonder. After your last contribution I'm beginning to doubt whether anything in the way of an intellectual agreement is possible between the two of us. Who is he?

SAM: Guess.

HALLY: Socrates? Alexandre Dumas? Karl Marx, Dostoevsky? Nietzsche?

(*Sam shakes his head after each name.*)

Give me a clue.

SAM: The letter *P* is important. . . .

HALLY: Plato!

SAM: . . . and his name begins with an *F*.

HALLY: I've got it. Freud and Psychology.

SAM: No. I didn't understand him.

HALLY: That makes two of us.

SAM: Think of moldy apricot jam.

HALLY (*after a delighted laugh*): Penicillin and Sir Alexander Fleming! And the title of the book: *The Microbe Hunters.* (*Delighted.*) Splendid, Sam! Splendid. For once we are in total agreement. The major breakthrough in medical science in the Twentieth Century. If it wasn't for him, we might have lost the Second World War. It's deeply gratifying, Sam, to know that I haven't been wasting my time in talking to you. (*Strutting around proudly.*) Tolstoy may have educated his peasants, but I've educated you.

SAM: Standard Four to Standard Nine.

HALLY: Have we been at it as long as that?

SAM: Yep. And my first lesson was geography.

HALLY (*intrigued*): Really? I don't remember.

SAM: My room there at the back of the old Jubilee Boarding House. I had just started working for your Mom. Little boy in short trousers walks in one afternoon and asks me seriously: "Sam, do you want to see South Africa?" Hey man! Sure I wanted to see South Africa!

HALLY: Was that me?

SAM: . . . So the next thing I'm looking at a map you had just done for homework. It was your first one and you were very proud of yourself.

HALLY: Go on.

SAM: Then came my first lesson. "Repeat after me, Sam: Gold in the Transvaal, mealies in the Free State, sugar in Natal, and grapes in the Cape." I still know it!

HALLY: Well, I'll be buggered. So that's how it all started.

SAM: And your next map was one with all the rivers and the mountains they came from. The Orange, the Vaal, the Limpopo, the Zambezi. . . .

HALLY: You've got a phenomenal memory!

SAM: You should be grateful. That is why you started passing your exams. You tried to be better than me.

(*They laugh together. Willie is attracted by the laughter and joins them.*)

HALLY: The old Jubilee Boarding House. Sixteen rooms with board and lodging, rent in advance and one week's notice. I haven't thought about it for donkey's years . . . and I don't think that's an accident. God, was I glad when we sold it and moved out. Those years are not remembered as the happiest ones of an unhappy childhood.

WILLIE (*knocking on the table and trying to imitate a woman's voice*): "Hally, are you there?"

HALLY: Who's that supposed to be?

WILLIE: "What you doing in there, Hally? Come out at once!"

HALLY (*to Sam*): What's he talking about?

SAM: Don't you remember?

WILLIE: "Sam, Willie . . . is he in there with you boys?"

SAM: Hiding away in our room when your mother was looking for you.

HALLY (*another good laugh*): Of course! I used to crawl and hide under your bed! But finish the story, Willie. Then what used to happen? You chaps would give the game away by telling her I was in there with you. So much for friendship.

SAM: We couldn't lie to her. She knew.

HALLY: Which meant I got another rowing for hanging around the "servants' quarters." I think I spent more time in there with you chaps than anywhere else in that dump. And do you blame me? Nothing but bloody misery wherever you went. Somebody was always complaining about the food, or my mother was having a fight with Micky Nash because she'd caught her with a petty officer in her room. Maud Meiring was another one. Remember those two? They were prostitutes, you know. Soldiers and sailors from the troopships. Bottom fell out of the business when the war ended. God, the flotsam and jetsam that life washed up on our shores! No joking, if it wasn't for your room, I would have been the first certified ten-year-old in medical history. Ja, the memories are coming back now. Walking home from school and thinking: "What can I do this afternoon?" Try out a few ideas, but sooner or later I'd end up in there with you fellows. I bet you I could still find my way to your room with my eyes closed. (*He does exactly that.*) Down the corridor . . . telephone on the right, which my Mom keeps locked because somebody is using it on the sly and not paying . . . past the kitchen and unappetizing cooking smells . . . around the corner into the backyard, hold my breath again because there are more smells coming when I pass your lavatory, then into that little passageway, first door on the right and into your room. How's that?

SAM: Good. But, as usual, you forgot to knock.

HALLY: Like that time I barged in and caught you and Cynthia . . . at it. Remember? God, was I embarrassed! I didn't know what was going on at first.

SAM: Ja, that taught you a lesson.

HALLY: And about a lot more than knocking on doors, I'll have you know, and I don't mean geography either. Hell, Sam, couldn't you have waited until it was dark?

SAM: No.

HALLY: Was it that urgent?

SAM: Yes, and if you don't believe me, wait until your time comes.

HALLY: No, thank you. I am not interested in girls. (*Back to his memories. . . . Using a few chairs he re-creates the room as he lists the items.*) A gray little room with a cold cement floor. Your bed against that wall . . . and I now know why the mattress sags so much! . . . Willie's bed . . . it's propped up on bricks because one leg is broken . . . that wobbly little table with the washbasin and jug of water . . . Yes! . . . stuck to the wall above it are some pin-up pictures from magazines. Joe Louis. . . .

WILLIE: Brown Bomber. World Title. (*Boxing pose.*) Three rounds and knockout.

HALLY: Against who?

SAM: Max Schmeling.

HALLY: Correct. I can also remember Fred Astaire and Ginger Rogers, and Rita Hayworth in a bathing costume which always made me hot and bothered when I looked at it. Under Willie's bed is an old suitcase with all his clothes in a mess, which is why I never hide there. Your things are neat and tidy in a trunk next to your bed, and on it there is a picture of you and Cynthia in your ballroom clothes, your first silver cup for third place in a competition and an old radio which doesn't work anymore. Have I left out anything?

SAM: No.

HALLY: Right, so much for the stage directions. Now the characters. (*Sam and Willie move to their appropriate positions in the bedroom.*) Willie is in bed, under his blankets with his clothes on, complaining nonstop about something, but we can't make out a word of what he's saying because he's got his head under the blankets as well. You're on your bed trimming your toenails with a knife — not a very edifying sight — and as for me. . . . What am I doing?

SAM: You're sitting on the floor giving Willie a lecture about being a good loser while you get the checkerboard and pieces ready for a game. Then you go to Willie's bed, pull off the blankets and make him play with you first because you know you're going to win, and that gives you the second game with me.

HALLY: And you certainly were a bad loser, Willie!

WILLIE: Haai!

HALLY: Wasn't he, Sam? And so slow! A game with you almost took the whole afternoon. Thank God I gave up trying to teach you how to play chess.

WILLIE: You and Sam cheated.

HALLY: I never saw Sam cheat, and mine were mostly the mistakes of youth.

WILLIE: Then how is it you two was always winning?

HALLY: Have you ever considered the possibility, Willie, that it was because we were better than you?

WILLIE: Every time better?

HALLY: Not every time. There were occasions when we deliberately let you win a game so that you would stop sulking and go on playing with us. Sam used to wink at me when you weren't looking to show me it was time to let you win.

WILLIE: So then you two didn't play fair.

HALLY: It was for your benefit, Mr. Malopo, which is more than being fair. It was an act of self-sacrifice. (*To Sam.*) But you know what my best memory is, don't you?

SAM: No.

HALLY: Come on, guess. If your memory is so good, you must remember it as well.

SAM: We got up to a lot of tricks in there, Hally.

HALLY: This one was special, Sam.

SAM: I'm listening.

HALLY: It started off looking like another of those useless nothing-to-do afternoons. I'd already been down to Main Street looking for adventure, but nothing had happened. I didn't feel like climbing trees in the Donkin Park or pretending I was a private eye and following a stranger . . . so as usual: See what's cooking in Sam's room. This time it was you on the floor. You had two thin pieces of wood and you were smoothing them down with a knife. It didn't look particularly interesting, but when I asked you what you were doing, you just said, "Wait and see, Hally. Wait . . . and see" . . . in that secret sort of way of yours, so I knew there was a surprise coming. You teased me, you bugger, by being deliberately slow and not answering my questions!

(*Sam laughs.*)

And whistling while you worked away! God, it was infuriating! I could have brained you! It was only when you tied them together in a cross and put that down on the brown paper that I realized what you were doing. "Sam is making a kite?" And when I asked you and you said "Yes" . . . ! (*Shaking his head with disbelief.*) The sheer audacity of it took my breath away. I mean, seriously, what the hell does a black man know about flying a kite? I'll be honest with you, Sam, I had no hopes for it. If you think I was excited and happy, you got another guess coming. In fact, I was shit-scared that we were going to make fools of ourselves. When we left the boarding house to go up onto the hill, I was praying quietly that there wouldn't be any other kids around to laugh at us.

SAM (*enjoying the memory as much as Hally*): Ja, I could see that.

HALLY: I made it obvious, did I?

SAM: Ja. You refused to carry it.

HALLY: Do you blame me? Can you remember what the poor thing looked like? Tomato-box wood and brown paper! Flour and water for glue! Two of my mother's old stockings for a tail, and then all those bits and pieces of string you made me tie together so that we could fly it! Hell, no, that was now only asking for a miracle to happen.

SAM: Then the big argument when I told you to hold the string and run with it when I let go.

HALLY: I was prepared to run, all right, but straight back to the boarding house.

SAM (*knowing what's coming*): So what happened?

HALLY: Come on, Sam, you remember as well as I do.

SAM: I want to hear it from you.

(*Hally pauses. He wants to be as accurate as possible.*)

HALLY: You went a little distance from me down the hill, you held it up ready to let it go. . . . "This is it," I thought. "Like everything else in my life, here comes another fiasco." Then you shouted, "Go, Hally!" and I started to run. (*Another pause.*) I don't know how to describe it, Sam. Ja! The miracle happened! I was running, waiting for it to crash to the ground, but instead suddenly there was something alive behind me at the end of the string, tugging at it as if it wanted to be free. I looked back . . . (*Shakes his head.*) . . . I still can't believe my eyes. It was flying! Looping around and trying to climb even higher into the sky. You shouted to me to let it have more string. I did, until there was none left and I was just holding that piece of wood we had tied it to. You came up and joined me. You were laughing.

SAM: So were you. And shouting, "It works, Sam! We've done it!"

HALLY: And we had! I was so proud of us! It was the most splendid thing I had ever seen. I wished there were hundreds of kids around to watch us. The part that scared me, though, was when you showed me how to make it dive down to the ground and then just when it was on the point of crashing, swoop up again!

SAM: You didn't want to try yourself.

HALLY: Of course not! I would have been suicidal if anything had happened to it. Watching you do it made me nervous enough. I was quite happy just to see it up there with its tail fluttering behind it. You left me after that, didn't you? You explained how to get it down, we tied it to the bench so that I could sit and watch it, and you went away. I wanted you to stay, you know. I was a little scared of having to look after it by myself.

SAM (*quietly*): I had work to do, Hally.

HALLY: It was sort of sad bringing it down, Sam. And it looked sad again when it was lying there on the ground. Like something that had lost its soul. Just tomato-box wood, brown paper and two of my mother's old stockings! But, hell, I'll never forget that first moment when I saw it up there. I had a stiff neck the next day from looking up so much.

(*Sam laughs. Hally turns to him with a question he never thought of asking before.*)

Why did you make that kite, Sam?

SAM (*evenly*): I can't remember.

HALLY: Truly?

SAM: Too long ago, Hally.

HALLY: Ja, I suppose it was. It's time for another one, you know.

SAM: Why do you say that?

HALLY: Because it feels like that. Wouldn't be a good day to fly it, though.

SAM: No. You can't fly kites on rainy days.

HALLY (*He studies Sam. Their memories have made him conscious of the man's presence in his life.*): How old are you, Sam?

SAM: Two score and five.

HALLY: Strange, isn't it?

SAM: What?

HALLY: Me and you.

SAM: What's strange about it?

HALLY: Little white boy in short trousers and a black man old enough to be his father flying a kite. It's not every day you see that.

SAM: But why strange? Because the one is white and the other black?

HALLY: I don't know. Would have been just as strange, I suppose, if it had been me and my Dad . . . cripple man and a little boy! Nope! There's no chance of me flying a kite without it being strange. (*Simple statement of fact — no self-pity.*) There's a nice little short story there. "The Kite-Flyers." But we'd have to find a twist in the ending.

SAM: Twist?

HALLY: Yes. Something unexpected. The way it ended with us was too straightforward . . . me on the bench and you going back to work. There's no drama in that.

WILLIE: And me?

HALLY: You?

WILLIE: Yes me.

HALLY: You want to get into the story as well, do you? I got it! Change the title: "Afternoons in Sam's Room" . . . expand it and tell all the stories. It's on its way to being a novel. Our days in the old Jubilee. Sad in a way that they're over. I almost wish we were still in that little room.

SAM: We're still together.

HALLY: That's true. It's just that life felt the right size in there . . . not too big and not too small. Wasn't

so hard to work up a bit of courage. It's got so bloody complicated since then.

(*The telephone rings. Sam answers it.*)

SAM: St. George's Park Tea Room . . . Hello, Madam . . . Yes, Madam, he's here. . . . Hally, it's your mother.

HALLY: Where is she phoning from?

SAM: Sounds like the hospital. It's a public telephone.

HALLY (*relieved*): You see! I told you. (*The telephone.*) Hello, Mom . . . Yes . . . Yes no fine. Everything's under control here. How's things with poor old Dad? . . . Has he had a bad turn? . . . What? . . . Oh, God! . . . Yes, Sam told me, but I was sure he'd made a mistake. But what's this all about, Mom? He didn't look at all good last night. How can he get better so quickly? . . . Then very obviously you must say no. Be firm with him. You're the boss. . . . You know what it's going to be like if he comes home. . . . Well then, don't blame me when I fail my exams at the end of the year. . . . Yes! How am I expected to be fresh for school when I spend half the night massaging his gammy leg? . . . So am I! . . . So tell him a white lie. Say Dr. Colley wants more X-rays of his stump. Or bribe him. We'll sneak in double tots of brandy in future. . . . What? . . . Order him to get back into bed at once! If he's going to behave like a child, treat him like one. . . . All right, Mom! I was just trying to . . . I'm sorry. . . . I said I'm sorry. . . . Quick, give me your number. I'll phone you back. (*He hangs up and waits a few seconds.*) Here we go again! (*He dials.*) I'm sorry, Mom. . . . Okay. . . . But now listen to me carefully. All it needs is for you to put your foot down. Don't take no for an answer. . . . Did you hear me? And whatever you do, don't discuss it with him. . . . Because I'm frightened you'll give in to him. . . . Yes, Sam gave me lunch. . . . I ate all of it! . . . No, Mom not a soul. It's still raining here. . . . Right, I'll tell them. I'll just do some homework and then lock up. . . . But remember now, Mom. Don't listen to anything he says. And phone me back and let me know what happens. . . . Okay. Bye, Mom. (*He hangs up. The men are staring at him.*) My Mom says that when you're finished with the floors you must do the windows. (*Pause.*) Don't misunderstand me, chaps. All I want is for him to get better. And if he was, I'd be the first person to say: "Bring him home." But he's not, and we can't give him the medical care and attention he needs at home. That's what hospitals are there for. (*Brusquely.*) So don't just stand there! Get on with it!

(*Sam clears Hally's table.*)

You heard right. My Dad wants to go home.

SAM: Is he better?

HALLY (*sharply*): No! How the hell can he be better when last night he was groaning with pain? This is not an age of miracles!

SAM: Then he should stay in hospital.

HALLY (*seething with irritation and frustration*): Tell me something I don't know, Sam. What the hell do you think I was saying to my Mom? All I can say is fuck-it-all.

SAM: I'm sure he'll listen to your Mom.

HALLY: You don't know what she's up against. He's already packed his shaving kit and pajamas and is sitting on his bed with his crutches, dressed and ready to go. I know him when he gets in that mood. If she tries to reason with him, we've had it. She's no match for him when it comes to a battle of words. He'll tie her up in knots. (*Trying to hide his true feelings.*)

SAM: I suppose it gets lonely for him in there.

HALLY: With all the patients and nurses around? Regular visits from the Salvation Army? Balls! It's ten times worse for him at home. I'm at school and my mother is here in the business all day.

SAM: He's at least got you at night.

HALLY (*before he can stop himself*): And we've got him! Please! I don't want to talk about it anymore. (*Unpacks his school case, slamming down books on the table.*) Life is just a plain bloody mess, that's all. And people are fools.

SAM: Come on, Hally.

HALLY: Yes, they are! They bloody well deserve what they get.

SAM: Then don't complain.

HALLY: Don't try to be clever, Sam. It doesn't suit you. Anybody who thinks there's nothing wrong with this world needs to have his head examined. Just when things are going along all right, without fail someone or something will come along and spoil everything. Somebody should write that down as a fundamental law of the Universe. The principle of perpetual disappointment. If there is a God who created this world, he should scrap it and try again.

SAM: All right, Hally, all right. What you got for homework?

HALLY: Bullshit, as usual. (*Opens an exercise book and reads.*) "Write five hundred words describing an annual event of cultural or historical significance."

SAM: That should be easy enough for you.

HALLY: And also plain bloody boring. You know what he wants, don't you? One of their useless old ceremonies. The commemoration of the landing of the 1820 Settlers, or if it's going to be culture, Carols by Candlelight every Christmas.

SAM: It's an impressive sight. Make a good description, Hally. All those candles glowing in the dark and the people singing hymns.

HALLY: And it's called religious hysteria. (*Intense irritation.*) Please, Sam! Just leave me alone and let me get on with it. I'm not in the mood for games this afternoon. And remember my Mom's orders . . . you're to help Willie with the windows. Come on now, I don't want any more nonsense in here.

SAM: Okay, Hally, okay.

(*Hally settles down to his homework; determined preparations . . . pen, ruler, exercise book, dictionary, another cake . . . all of which will lead to nothing.*)

(*Sam waltzes over to Willie and starts to replace tables and chairs. He practices a ballroom step while doing so. Willie watches. When Sam is finished, Willie tries.*)

Good! But just a little bit quicker on the turn and only move in to her after she's crossed over. What about this one?

(*Another step. When Sam is finished, Willie again has a go.*)

Much better. See what happens when you just relax and enjoy yourself? Remember that in two weeks' time and you'll be all right.

WILLIE: But I haven't got partner, Boet Sam.

SAM: Maybe Hilda will turn up tonight.

WILLIE: No, Boet Sam. (*Reluctantly.*) I gave her a good hiding.

SAM: You mean a bad one.

WILLIE: Good bad one.

SAM: Then you mustn't complain either. Now you pay the price for losing your temper.

WILLIE: I also pay two pounds ten shilling entrance fee.

SAM: They'll refund you if you withdraw now.

WILLIE (*appalled*): You mean, don't dance?

SAM: Yes.

WILLIE: No! I wait too long and I practice too hard. If I find me new partner, you think I can be ready in two weeks? I ask Madam for my leave now and we practice every day.

SAM: Quickstep nonstop for two weeks. World record, Willie, but you'll be mad at the end.

WILLIE: No jokes, Boet Sam.

SAM: I'm not joking.

WILLIE: So then what?

SAM: Find Hilda. Say you're sorry and promise you won't beat her again.

WILLIE: No.

SAM: Then withdraw. Try again next year.

WILLIE: No.

SAM: Then I give up.

WILLIE: Haaikona, Boet Sam, you can't.

SAM: What do you mean, I can't? I'm telling you: I give up.

WILLIE (*adamant*): No! (*Accusingly.*) It was you who start me ballroom dancing.

SAM: So?

WILLIE: Before that I use to be happy. And is you and Miriam who bring me to Hilda and say here's partner for you.

SAM: What are you saying, Willie?

WILLIE: You!

SAM: But me what? To blame?

WILLIE: Yes.

SAM: Willie . . . ? (*Bursts into laughter.*)

WILLIE: And now all you do is make jokes at me. You wait. When Miriam leaves you is my turn to laugh. Ha! Ha! Ha!

SAM (*he can't take Willie seriously any longer*): She can leave me tonight! I know what to do. (*Bowing before an imaginary partner.*) May I have the pleasure? (*He dances and sings.*)
"Just a fellow with his pillow . . .
Dancin' like a willow . . .
In an autumn breeze. . . ."

WILLIE: There you go again!

(*Sam goes on dancing and singing.*)

Boet Sam!

SAM: There's the answer to your problem! Judges' announcement in two weeks' time: "Ladies and gentlemen, the winner in the open section . . . Mr. Willie Malopo and his pillow!"

(*This is too much for a now really angry Willie. He goes for Sam, but the latter is too quick for him and puts Hally's table between the two of them.*)

HALLY (*exploding*): For Christ's sake, you two!

WILLIE (*still trying to get at Sam*): I donner you, Sam! Struesgod!

SAM (*still laughing*): Sorry, Willie . . . Sorry. . . .

HALLY: Sam! Willie! (*Grabs his ruler and gives Willie a vicious whack on the bum.*) How the hell am I supposed to concentrate with the two of you behaving like bloody children!

WILLIE: Hit him too!

HALLY: Shut up, Willie.

WILLIE: He started jokes again.

HALLY: Get back to your work. You too, Sam. (*His ruler.*) Do you want another one, Willie?

(*Sam and Willie return to their work. Hally uses the opportunity to escape from his unsuccessful attempt at homework. He struts around like a little despot, ruler in hand, giving vent to his anger and frustration.*)

Suppose a customer had walked in then? Or the Park Superintendent. And seen the two of you be-having like a pair of hooligans. That would have been the end of my mother's license, you know. And your jobs? Well, this is the end of it. From now on there will be no more of your ballroom nonsense in here. This is a business establishment, not a bloody New Brighton dancing school. I've been far too lenient with the two of you. (*Behind the counter for a green cool drink and a dollop of ice cream. He keeps up his tirade as he prepares it.*) But what really makes me bitter is that I allow you chaps a little freedom in here when business is bad and what do you do with it? The foxtrot! Specially you, Sam. There's more to life than trotting around a dance floor and I thought at least you knew it.

SAM: It's a harmless pleasure, Hally. It doesn't hurt anybody.

HALLY: It's also a rather simple one, you know.

SAM: You reckon so? Have you ever tried?

HALLY: Of course not.

SAM: Why don't you? Now.

HALLY: What do you mean? Me dance?

SAM: Yes. I'll show you a simple step — the waltz — then you try it.

HALLY: What will that prove?

SAM: That it might not be as easy as you think.

HALLY: I didn't say it was easy. I said it was simple — like in simple-minded, meaning mentally retarded. You can't exactly say it challenges the intellect.

SAM: It does other things.

HALLY: Such as?

SAM: Make people happy.

HALLY (*the glass in his hand*): So do American cream sodas with ice cream. For God's sake, Sam, you're not asking me to take ballroom dancing serious, are you?

SAM: Yes.

HALLY (*sigh of defeat*): Oh, well, so much for trying to give you a decent education. I've obviously achieved nothing.

SAM: You still haven't told me what's wrong with admiring something that's beautiful and then trying to do it yourself.

HALLY: Nothing. But we happen to be talking about a foxtrot, not a thing of beauty.

SAM: But that is just what I'm saying. If you were to see two champions doing, two masters of the art . . . !

HALLY: Oh God, I give up. So now it's also art!

SAM: Ja.

HALLY: There's a limit, Sam. Don't confuse art and entertainment.

SAM: So then what is art?

HALLY: You want a definition?

SAM: Ja.

HALLY (*He realizes he has got to be careful. He gives*

the matter a lot of thought before answering.): Philosophers have been trying to do that for centuries. What is Art? What is Life? But basically I suppose it's . . . the giving of meaning to matter.

SAM: Nothing to do with beautiful?

HALLY: It goes beyond that. It's the giving of form to the formless.

SAM: Ja, well, maybe it's not art, then. But I still say it's beautiful.

HALLY: I'm sure the word you mean to use is entertaining.

SAM (*adamant*): No. Beautiful. And if you want proof come along to the Centenary Hall in New Brighton in two weeks' time.

(*The mention of the Centenary Hall draws Willie over to them.*)

HALLY: What for? I've seen the two of you prancing around in here often enough.

SAM (*he laughs*): This isn't the real thing, Hally. We're just playing around in here.

HALLY: So? I can use my imagination.

SAM: And what do you get?

HALLY: A lot of people dancing around and having a so-called good time.

SAM: That all?

HALLY: Well, basically it is that, surely.

SAM: No, it isn't. Your imagination hasn't helped you at all. There's a lot more to it than that. We're getting ready for the championships, Hally, not just another dance. There's going to be a lot of people, all right, and they're going to have a good time, but they'll only be spectators, sitting around and watching. It's just the competitors out there on the dance floor. Party decorations and fancy lights all around the walls! The ladies in beautiful evening dresses!

HALLY: My mother's got one of those, Sam, and, quite frankly, it's an embarrassment every time she wears it.

SAM (*undeterred*): Your imagination left out the excitement.

(*Hally scoffs.*)

Oh, yes. The finalists are not going to be out there just to have a good time. One of those couples will be the 1950 Eastern Province Champions. And your imagination left out the music.

WILLIE: Mr. Elijah Gladman Guzana and his Orchestral Jazzonions.

SAM: The sound of the big band, Hally. Trombone, trumpet, tenor and alto sax. And then, finally, your imagination also left out the climax of the evening when the dancing is finished, the judges have stopped

whispering among themselves and the Master of Ceremonies collects their scorecards and goes up onto the stage to announce the winners.

HALLY: All right. So you make it sound like a bit of a do. It's an occasion. Satisfied?

SAM (*victory*): So you admit that!

HALLY: Emotionally yes, intellectually no.

SAM: Well, I don't know what you mean by that, all I'm telling you is that it is going to be *the* event of the year in New Brighton. It's been sold out for two weeks already. There's only standing room left. We've got competitors coming from Kingwilliamstown, East London, Port Alfred.

(*Hally starts pacing thoughtfully.*)

HALLY: Tell me a bit more.

SAM: I thought you weren't interested . . . intellectually.

HALLY (*mysteriously*): I've got my reasons.

SAM: What do you want to know?

HALLY: It takes place every year?

SAM: Yes. But only every third year in New Brighton. It's East London's turn to have the championships next year.

HALLY: Which, I suppose, makes it an even more significant event.

SAM: Ah ha! We're getting somewhere. Our "occasion" is now a "significant event."

HALLY: I wonder.

SAM: What?

HALLY: I wonder if I would get away with it.

SAM: But what?

HALLY (*to the table and his exercise book*): "Write five hundred words describing an annual event of cultural or historical significance." Would I be stretching poetic license a little too far if I called your ballroom championships a cultural event?

SAM: You mean . . . ?

HALLY: You think we could get five hundred words out of it, Sam?

SAM: Victor Sylvester has written a whole book on ballroom dancing.

WILLIE: You going to write about it, Master Hally?

HALLY: Yes, gentlemen, that is precisely what I am considering doing. Old Doc Bromely — he's my English teacher — is going to argue with me, of course. He doesn't like natives. But I'll point out to him that in strict anthropological terms the culture of a primitive black society includes its dancing and singing. To put my thesis in a nutshell: The war-dance has been replaced by the waltz. But it still amounts to the same thing: the release of primitive emotions through movement. Shall we give it a go?

SAM: I'm ready.

WILLIE: Me also.

HALLY: Ha! This will teach the old bugger a lesson. (*Decision taken.*) Right. Let's get ourselves organized. (*This means another cake on the table. He sits.*) I think you've given me enough general atmosphere, Sam, but to build the tension and suspense I need facts. (*Pencil poised.*)

WILLIE: Give him facts, Boet Sam.

HALLY: What you called the climax ... how many finalists?

SAM: Six couples.

HALLY (*making notes*): Go on. Give me the picture.

SAM: Spectators seated right around the hall. (*Willie becomes a spectator.*)

HALLY: ... and it's a full house.

SAM: At one end, on the stage, Gladman and his Orchestral Jazzonions. At the other end is a long table with the three judges. The six finalists go onto the dance floor and take up their positions. When they are ready and the spectators have settled down, the Master of Ceremonies goes to the microphone. To start with, he makes some jokes to get people laughing. ...

HALLY: Good touch. (*As he writes.*) "... creating a relaxed atmosphere which will change to one of tension and drama as the climax is approached."

SAM (*onto a chair to act out the M.C.*): "Ladies and gentlemen, we come now to the great moment you have all been waiting for this evening. ... The finals of the 1950 Eastern Province Open Ballroom Dancing Championships. But first let me introduce the finalists! Mr. and Mrs. Welcome Tchabalala from Kingwilliamstown ..."

WILLIE (*he applauds after every name*): Is when the people clap their hands and whistle and make a lot of noise, Master Hally.

SAM: "Mr. Mulligan Njikelane and Miss Nomhle Nkonyeni of Grahamstown; Mr. and Mrs. Norman Nchinga from Port Alfred; Mr. Fats Bokolane and Miss Dina Plaatjies from East London; Mr. Sipho Dugu and Mrs. Mable Magada from Peddie; and from New Brighton our very own Mr. Willie Malopo and Miss Hilda Samuels."

(*Willie can't believe his ears. He abandons his role as spectator and scrambles into position as a finalist.*)

WILLIE: Relaxed and ready to romance!

SAM: The applause dies down. When everybody is silent, Gladman lifts up his sax, nods at the Orchestral Jazzonions. ...

WILLIE: Play the jukebox please, Boet Sam!

SAM: I also only got bus fare, Willie.

HALLY: Hold it, everybody. (*Heads for the cash register behind the counter.*) How much is in the till, Sam?

SAM: Three shillings. Hally ... Your Mom counted it before she left.

(*Hally hesitates.*)

HALLY: Sorry, Willie. You know how she carried on the last time I did it. We'll just have to pool our combined imaginations and hope for the best. (*Returns to the table.*) Back to work. How are the points scored, Sam?

SAM: Maximum of ten points each for individual style, deportment, rhythm, and general appearance.

WILLIE: Must I start?

HALLY: Hold it for a second, Willie. And penalties?

SAM: For what?

HALLY: For doing something wrong. Say you stumble or bump into somebody ... do they take off any points?

SAM (*aghast*): Hally ... !

HALLY: When you're dancing. If you and your partner collide into another couple.

(*Hally can get no further. Sam has collapsed with laughter. He explains to Willie.*)

SAM: If me and Miriam bump into you and Hilda. ...

(*Willie joins him in another good laugh.*)

Hally, Hally ... !

HALLY (*perplexed*): Why? What did I say?

SAM: There's no collisions out there, Hally. Nobody trips or stumbles or bumps into anybody else. That's what that moment is all about. To be one of those finalists on that dance floor is like ... like being in a dream about a world in which accidents don't happen.

HALLY (*genuinely moved by Sam's image*): Jesus, Sam! That's beautiful!

WILLIE (*can endure waiting no longer*): I'm starting!

(*Willie dances while Sam talks.*)

SAM: Of course it is. That's what I've been trying to say to you all afternoon. And it's beautiful because that is what we want life to be like. But instead, like you said, Hally, we're bumping into each other all the time. Look at the three of us this afternoon: I've bumped into Willie, the two of us have bumped into you, you've bumped into your mother, she bumping into your Dad. ... None of us knows the steps and there's no music playing. And it doesn't stop with us. The whole world is doing it all the time. Open a newspaper and what do you read? America has bumped into Russia, England is bumping into India, rich man bumps into poor man. Those are big collisions, Hally. They make for a lot of bruises. People get hurt in all that bumping, and we're sick and tired of it now. It's been going on for too long. Are we never going to get it right? ... Learn to dance life like champions instead of always being just a bunch of beginners at it?

HALLY (*deep and sincere admiration of the man*): You've got a vision, Sam!

SAM: Not just me. What I'm saying to you is that everybody's got it. That's why there's only standing room left for the Centenary Hall in two weeks' time. For as long as the music lasts, we are going to see six couples get it right, the way we want life to be.

HALLY: But is that the best we can do, Sam ... watch six finalists dreaming about the way it should be?

SAM: I don't know. But it starts with that. Without the dream we won't know what we're going for. And anyway I reckon there are a few people who have got past just dreaming about it and are trying for something real. Remember that thing we read once in the paper about the Mahatma Gandhi? Going without food to stop those riots in India?

HALLY: You're right. He certainly was trying to teach people to get the steps right.

SAM: And the Pope.

HALLY: Yes, he's another one. Our old General Smuts° as well, you know. He's also out there dancing. You know, Sam, when you come to think of it, that's what the United Nations boils down to ... a dancing school for politicians!

SAM: And let's hope they learn.

HALLY (*a little surge of hope*): You're right. We mustn't despair. Maybe there's some hope for mankind after all. Keep it up, Willie. (*Back to his table with determination.*) This is a lot bigger than I thought. So what have we got? Yes, our title: "A World Without Collisions."

SAM: That sounds good! "A World Without Collisions."

HALLY: Subtitle: "Global Politics on the Dance Floor." No. A bit too heavy, hey? What about "Ballroom Dancing as a Political Vision"?

(*The telephone rings. Sam answers it.*)

SAM: St. George's Park Tea Room ... Yes, Madam ... Hally, it's your Mom.

HALLY (*back to reality*): Oh, God, yes! I'd forgotten all about that. Shit! Remember my words, Sam? Just when you're enjoying yourself, someone or something will come along and wreck everything.

General Smuts: (1870–1950), South African statesman who fought the British in the Boer War in 1899, was instrumental in forming the Union of South Africa in 1910, and was active in the creation of the United Nations.

SAM: You haven't heard what she's got to say yet.

HALLY: Public telephone?

SAM: No.

HALLY: Does she sound happy or unhappy?

SAM: I couldn't tell. (*Pause.*) She's waiting, Hally.

HALLY (*to the telephone*): Hello, Mom ... No, everything is okay here. Just doing my homework.... What's your news? ... You've what? ... (*Pause. He takes the receiver away from his ear for a few seconds. In the course of Hally's telephone conversation, Sam and Willie discreetly position the stacked tables and chairs. Hally places the receiver back to his ear.*) Yes, I'm still here. Oh, well, I give up now. Why did you do it, Mom? ... Well, I just hope you know what you've let us in for.... (*Loudly.*) I said I hope you know what you've let us in for! It's the end of the peace and quiet we've been having. (*Softly.*) Where is he? (*Normal voice.*) He can't hear us from in there. But for God's sake, Mom, what happened? I told you to be firm with him.... Then you and the nurses should have held him down, taken his crutches away.... I know only too well he's my father! ... I'm not being disrespectful, but I'm sick and tired of emptying stinking chamber pots full of phlegm and piss.... Yes, I do! When you're not there, he asks *me* to do it.... If you really want to know the truth, that's why I've got no appetite for my food.... Yes! There's a lot of things you don't know about. For your information, I still haven't got that science textbook I need. And you know why? He borrowed the money you gave me for it.... Because I didn't want to start another fight between you two.... He says that every time.... All right, Mom! (*Viciously.*) Then just remember to start hiding your bag away again, because he'll be at your purse before long for money for booze. And when he's well enough to come down here, you better keep an eye on the till as well, because that is also going to develop a leak.... Then don't complain to me when he starts his old tricks.... Yes, you do. I get it from you on one side and from him on the other, and it makes life hell for me. I'm not going to be the peacemaker anymore. I'm warning you now: when the two of you start fighting again, I'm leaving home.... Mom, if you start crying, I'm going to put down the receiver.... Okay.... (*Lowering his voice to a vicious whisper.*) Okay, Mom. I heard you. (*Desperate.*) No.... Because I don't want to. I'll see him when I get home! Mom! ... (*Pause. When he speaks again, his tone changes completely. It is not simply pretense. We sense a genuine emotional conflict.*) Welcome home, chum! ... What's that? ... Don't be silly, Dad. You being

home is just about the best news in the world. . . .
I bet you are. Bloody depressing there with everybody
going on about their ailments, hey! . . . How you
feeling? . . . Good. . . . Here as well, pal. Coming
down cats and dogs. . . . That's right. Just the day
for a kip° and a toss in your old Uncle Ned. . . .
Everything's just hunky-dory on my side, Dad. . . .
Well, to start with, there's a nice pile of comics
for you on the counter. . . . Yes, old Kemple brought
them in. *Batman and Robin, Submariner* . . . just
your cup of tea. . . . I will. . . . Yes, we'll spin a
few yarns tonight. . . . Okay, chum, see you in a
little while. . . . No, I promise. I'll come straight
home. . . . (*Pause — his mother comes back on the
phone.*) Mom? Okay. I'll lock up now. . . . What?
. . . Oh, the brandy . . . Yes, I'll remember! . . . I'll
put it in my suitcase now, for God's sake. I know
well enough what will happen if he doesn't get it.
. . . (*Places a bottle of brandy on the counter.*) I
was kind to him, Mom. I didn't say anything nasty!
. . . All right. Bye. (*End of telephone conversation.
A desolate Hally doesn't move. A strained silence.*)

SAM (*quietly*): That sounded like a bad bump, Hally.

HALLY (*Having a hard time controlling his emotions.
He speaks carefully.*): Mind your own business,
Sam.

SAM: Sorry. I wasn't trying to interfere. Shall we carry
on? Hally? (*He indicates the exercise book. No
response from Hally.*)

WILLIE (*also trying*): Tell him about when they give
out the cups, Boet Sam.

SAM: Ja! That's another big moment. The presentation
of the cups after the winners have been announced.
You've got to put that in.

(*Still no response from Hally.*)

WILLIE: A big silver one, Master Hally, called floating
trophy for the champions.

SAM: We always invite some big-shot personality to
hand them over. Guest of honor this year is going
to be His Holiness Bishop Jabulani of the All African
Free Zionist Church.

(*Hally gets up abruptly, goes to his table, and tears
up the page he was writing on.*)

HALLY: So much for a bloody world without collisions.

SAM: Too bad. It was on its way to being a good
composition.

HALLY: Let's stop bullshitting ourselves, Sam.

SAM: Have we been doing that?

HALLY: Yes! That's what all our talk about a decent
world has been . . . just so much bullshit.

kip: Nap.

SAM: We did say it was still only a dream.

HALLY: And a bloody useless one at that. Life's a
fuckup and it's never going to change.

SAM: Ja, maybe that's true.

HALLY: There's no maybe about it. It's a blunt and
brutal fact. All we've done this afternoon is waste
our time.

SAM: Not if we'd got your homework done.

HALLY: I don't give a shit about my homework, so,
for Christ's sake, just shut up about it. (*Slamming
books viciously into his school case.*) Hurry up now
and finish your work. I want to lock up and get
out of here. (*Pause.*) And then go where? Home-
sweet-fucking-home. Jesus, I hate that word.

(*Hally goes to the counter to put the brandy bottle
and comics in his school case. After a moment's hesitation, he smashes the bottle of brandy. He abandons
all further attempts to hide his feelings. Sam and Willie
work away as unobtrusively as possible.*)

Do you want to know what is really wrong with
your lovely little dream, Sam? It's not just that we
are all bad dancers. That does happen to be perfectly
true, but there's more to it than just that. You left
out the cripples.

SAM: Hally!

HALLY (*now totally reckless*): Ja! Can't leave them
out, Sam. That's why we always end up on our
backsides on the dance floor. They're also out there
dancing . . . like a bunch of broken spiders trying
to do the quickstep! (*An ugly attempt at laughter.*)
When you come to think of it, it's a bloody comical
sight. I mean, it's bad enough on two legs . . . but
one and a pair of crutches! Hell, no, Sam. That's
guaranteed to turn that dance floor into a shambles.
Why you shaking your head? Picture it, man. For
once this afternoon let's use our imaginations
sensibly.

SAM: Be careful, Hally.

HALLY: Of what? The truth? I seem to be the only
one around here who is prepared to face it. We've
had the pretty dream, it's time now to wake up
and have a good long look at the way things really
are. Nobody knows the steps, there's no music,
the cripples are also out there tripping up everybody and trying to get into the act, and it's all
called the All-Comers-How-to-Make-a-Fuckup-of-
Life Championships. (*Another ugly laugh.*) Hang
on, Sam! The best bit is still coming. Do you know
what the winner's trophy is? A beautiful big chamber
pot with roses on the side, and it's full to the brim
with piss. And guess who I think is going to be
this year's winner.

SAM (*almost shouting*): Stop now!

HALLY (*suddenly appalled by how far he has gone*): Why?

SAM: Hally? It's your father you're talking about.

HALLY: So?

SAM: Do you know what you've been saying?

(*Hally can't answer. He is rigid with shame. Sam speaks to him sternly.*)

No, Hally, you mustn't do it. Take back those words and ask for forgiveness! It's a terrible sin for a son to mock his father with jokes like that. You'll be punished if you carry on. Your father is your father, even if he is a . . . cripple man.

WILLIE: Yes, Master Hally. Is true what Sam say.

SAM: I understand how you are feeling, Hally, but even so. . . .

HALLY: No, you don't!

SAM: I think I do.

HALLY: And I'm telling you you don't. Nobody does. (*Speaking carefully as his shame turns to rage at Sam.*) It's your turn to be careful, Sam. Very careful! You're treading on dangerous ground. Leave me and my father alone.

SAM: I'm not the one who's been saying things about him.

HALLY: What goes on between me and my Dad is none of your business!

SAM: Then don't tell me about it. If that's all you've got to say about him, I don't want to hear.

(*For a moment Hally is at loss for a response.*)

HALLY: Just get on with your bloody work and shut up.

SAM: Swearing at me won't help you.

HALLY: Yes, it does! Mind your own fucking business and shut up!

SAM: Okay. If that's the way you want it, I'll stop trying.

(*He turns away. This infuriates Hally even more.*)

HALLY: Good. Because what you've been trying to do is meddle in something you know nothing about. All that concerns you in here, Sam, is to try and do what you get paid for — keep the place clean and serve the customers. In plain words, just get on with your job. My mother is right. She's always warning me about allowing you to get too familiar. Well, this time you've gone too far. It's going to stop right now.

(*No response from Sam.*)

You're only a servant in here, and don't forget it.

(*Still no response. Hally is trying hard to get one.*)

And as far as my father is concerned, all you need to remember is that he is your boss.

SAM (*needled at last*): No, he isn't. I get paid by your mother.

HALLY: Don't argue with me, Sam!

SAM: Then don't say he's my boss.

HALLY: He's a white man and that's good enough for you.

SAM: I'll try to forget you said that.

HALLY: Don't! Because you won't be doing me a favor if you do. I'm telling you to remember it.

(*A pause. Sam pulls himself together and makes one last effort.*)

SAM: Hally, Hally . . . ! Come on now. Let's stop before it's too late. You're right. We *are* on dangerous ground. If we're not careful, somebody is going to get hurt.

HALLY: It won't be me.

SAM: Don't be so sure.

HALLY: I don't know what you're talking about, Sam.

SAM: Yes, you do.

HALLY (*furious*): Jesus, I wish you would stop trying to tell me what I do and what I don't know.

(*Sam gives up. He turns to Willie.*)

SAM: Let's finish up.

HALLY: Don't turn your back on me! I haven't finished talking.

(*He grabs Sam by the arm and tries to make him turn around. Sam reacts with a flash of anger.*)

SAM: Don't do that, Hally! (*Facing the boy.*) All right, I'm listening. Well? What do you want to say to me?

HALLY (*pause as Hally looks for something to say*): To begin with, why don't you also start calling me Master Harold, like Willie.

SAM: Do you mean that?

HALLY: Why the hell do you think I said it?

SAM: And if I don't?

HALLY: You might just lose your job.

SAM (*quietly and very carefully*): If you make me say it once, I'll never call you anything else again.

HALLY: So? (*The boy confronts the man.*) Is that meant to be a threat?

SAM: Just telling you what will happen if you make me do that. You must decide what it means to you.

HALLY: Well, I have. It's good news. Because that is exactly what Master Harold wants from now on. Think of it as a little lesson in respect, Sam, that's long overdue, and I hope you remember it as well as you do your geography. I can tell you now that somebody who will be glad to hear I've finally given it to you will be my Dad. Yes! He agrees with my Mom. He's always going on about it as well. "You must teach the boys to show you more respect, my son."

SAM: So now you can stop complaining about going home. Everybody is going to be happy tonight.

HALLY: That's perfectly correct. You see, you mustn't get the wrong idea about me and my Dad, Sam. We also have our good times together. Some bloody good laughs. He's got a marvelous sense of humor. Want to know what our favorite joke is? He gives out a big groan, you see, and says: "It's not fair, is it, Hally?" Then I have to ask: "What, chum?" And then he says: "A nigger's arse" . . . and we both have a good laugh.

(*The men stare at him with disbelief.*)

What's the matter, Willie? Don't you catch the joke? You always were a bit slow on the uptake. It's what is called a pun. You see, fair means both light in color and to be just and decent. (*He turns to Sam.*) I thought *you* would catch it, Sam.

SAM: Oh ja, I catch it all right.

HALLY: But it doesn't appeal to your sense of humor.

SAM: Do you really laugh?

HALLY: Of course.

SAM: To please him? Make him feel good?

HALLY: No, for heavens sake! I laugh because I think it's a bloody good joke.

SAM: You're really trying hard to be ugly, aren't you? And why drag poor old Willie into it? He's done nothing to you except show you the respect you want so badly. That's also not being fair, you know . . . and *I* mean just or decent.

WILLIE: It's all right, Sam. Leave it now.

SAM: It's me you're after. You should just have said "Sam's arse" . . . because that's the one you're trying to kick. Anyway, how do you know it's not fair? You've never seen it. Do you want to? (*He drops his trousers and underpants and presents his backside for Hally's inspection.*) Have a good look. A real Basuto arse . . . which is about as nigger as they can come. Satisfied? (*Trousers up.*) Now you can make your Dad even happier when you go home tonight. Tell him I showed you my arse and he is quite right. It's not fair. And if it will give him an even better laugh next time, I'll also let *him* have a look. Come, Willie, let's finish up and go.

(*Sam and Willie start to tidy up the tea room. Hally doesn't move. He waits for a moment when Sam passes him.*)

HALLY (*quietly*): Sam . . .

(*Sam stops and looks expectantly at the boy. Hally spits in his face. A long and heartfelt groan from Willie. For a few seconds Sam doesn't move.*)

SAM (*taking out a handkerchief and wiping his face*): It's all right, Willie.

(*To Hally.*)

Ja, well, you've done it . . . Master Harold. Yes, I'll start calling you that from now on. It won't be difficult anymore. You've hurt yourself, Master Harold. I saw it coming. I warned you, but you wouldn't listen. You've just hurt yourself *bad.* And you're a coward, Master Harold. The face you should be spitting in is your father's . . . but you used mine, because you think you're safe inside your fair skin . . . and this time I don't mean just or decent. (*Pause, then moving violently toward Hally.*) Should I hit him, Willie?

WILLIE (*stopping Sam*): No, Boet Sam.

SAM (*violently*): Why not?

WILLIE: It won't help, Boet Sam.

SAM: I don't want to help! I want to hurt him.

WILLIE: You also hurt yourself.

SAM: And if he had done it to you, Willie?

WILLIE: Me? Spit at me like I was a dog? (*A thought that had not occurred to him before. He looks at Hally.*) Ja. Then I want to hit him. I want to hit him hard!

(*A dangerous few seconds as the men stand staring at the boy. Willie turns away, shaking his head.*)

But maybe all I do is go cry at the back. He's little boy, Boet Sam. Little *white* boy. Long trousers now, but he's still little boy.

SAM (*his violence ebbing away into defeat as quickly as it flooded*): You're right. So go on, then: groan again, Willie. You do it better than me. (*To Hally.*) You don't know all of what you've just done . . . Master Harold. It's not just that you've made me feel dirtier than I've ever been in my life . . . I mean, how do I wash off yours and your father's filth? . . . I've also failed. A long time ago I promised myself I was going to try and do something, but you've just shown me . . . Master Harold . . . that I've failed. (*Pause.*) I've also got a memory of a little white boy when he was still wearing short trousers and a black man, but they're not flying a kite. It was the old Jubilee days, after dinner one night. I was in my room. You came in and just stood against the wall, looking down at the ground, and only after I'd asked you what you wanted, what was wrong, I don't know how many times, did you speak and even then so softly I almost didn't hear you. "Sam, please help me to go and fetch my Dad." Remember? He was dead drunk on the floor of the Central Hotel Bar. They'd phoned for your Mom, but you were the only one at home. And do you remember how we did it? You went in first by yourself to ask permission for me to go into the bar. Then I loaded him onto my back like a baby and carried him back to the boarding house with you following behind carrying his crutches. (*Shaking his head as he remembers.*) A crowded Main Street with all the people watching a little white boy following his drunk father on a nigger's back! I felt for that little boy . . . Master Harold. I felt for him. After that we still had to clean him up, remember? He'd messed in his trousers, so we had to clean him up and get him into bed.

HALLY (*great pain*): I love him, Sam.

SAM: I know you do. That's why I tried to stop you from saying these things about him. It would have been so simple if you could have just despised him for being a weak man. But he's your father. You love him and you're ashamed of him. You're ashamed of so much! . . . And now that's going to include yourself. That was the promise I made to myself: to try and stop that happening. (*Pause.*) After we got him to bed you came back with me to my room and sat in a corner and carried on just looking down at the ground. And for days after that! You hadn't done anything wrong, but you went around as if you owed the world an apology for being alive. I didn't like seeing that! That's not the way a boy grows up to be a man! . . . But the one person who should have been teaching you what that means was the cause of your shame. If you really want to know, that's why I made you that kite. I wanted you to look up, be proud of something, of yourself . . . (*bitter smile at the memory*) . . . and you certainly were that when I left you with it up there on the hill. Oh, ja . . . something else! . . . If you ever do write it as a short story, there *was* a twist in our ending. I couldn't sit down there and stay with you. It was a "Whites Only" bench. You were too young, too excited to notice then. But not anymore. If you're not careful . . . Master Harold . . . you're going to be sitting up there by yourself for a long time to come, and there won't be a kite in the sky. (*Sam has got nothing more to say. He exits into the kitchen, taking off his waiter's jacket.*)

WILLIE: Is bad. Is all bad in here now.

HALLY (*books into his school case, raincoat on*): Willie . . . (*It is difficult to speak.*) Will you lock up for me and look after the keys?

WILLIE: Okay.

(*Sam returns. Hally goes behind the counter and collects the few coins in the cash register. As he starts to leave. . . .*)

SAM: Don't forget the comic books.

(*Hally returns to the counter and puts them in his case. He starts to leave again.*)

SAM (*to the retreating back of the boy*): Stop . . . Hally. . . .

(*Hally stops, but doesn't turn to face him.*)

Hally . . . I've got no right to tell you what being a man means if I don't behave like one myself, and I'm not doing so well at that this afternoon. Should we try again, Hally?

HALLY: Try what?

SAM: Fly another kite, I suppose. It worked once, and this time I need it as much as you do.

HALLY: It's still raining, Sam. You can't fly kites on rainy days, remember.

SAM: So what do we do? Hope for better weather tomorrow?

HALLY (*helpless gesture*): I don't know. I don't know anything anymore.

SAM: You sure of that, Hally? Because it would be pretty hopeless if that was true. It would mean nothing has been learnt in here this afternoon, and there was a hell of a lot of teaching going on . . . one way or the other. But anyway, I don't believe you. I reckon there's one thing you know. You don't *have* to sit up there by yourself. You know what that bench means now, and you can leave it any time you choose. All you've got to do is stand up and walk away from it.

(*Hally leaves. Willie goes up quietly to Sam.*)

WILLIE: Is okay, Boet Sam. You see. Is . . . (*he can't find any better words*) . . . is going to be okay tomorrow. (*Changing his tone.*) Hey, Boet Sam! (*He is trying hard.*) You right. I think about it and you right. Tonight I find Hilda and say sorry. And make promise I won't beat her no more. You hear me, Boet Sam?

SAM: I hear you, Willie.

WILLIE: And when we practice I relax and romance with her from beginning to end. Nonstop! You watch! Two weeks' time: "First prize for promising newcomers: Mr. Willie Malopo and Miss Hilda Samuels." (*Sudden impulse.*) To hell with it! I walk home. (*He goes to the jukebox, puts in a coin and selects a record. The machine comes to life in the gray twilight, blushing its way through a spectrum of soft, romantic colors.*) How did you say it, Boet Sam? Let's dream. (*Willie sways with the music and gestures for Sam to dance.*)

(*Sarah Vaughan sings.*)

"Little man you're crying,
I know why you're blue,
Someone took your kiddy car away;
Better go to sleep now,
Little man you've had a busy day." (*etc., etc.*)
You lead. I follow.

(*The men dance together.*)

"Johnny won your marbles,
Tell you what we'll do;
Dad will get you new ones right away;
Better go to sleep now,
Little man you've had a busy day."

Caryl Churchill

Caryl Churchill (b. 1938) is in many ways a conventional middle-class citizen. She was born in London to a comfortable family: Her father was a political cartoonist and her mother a model. During the war, her family emigrated to Canada, and much of her growing up was done in Montreal. She returned to England for college and took her degree in English literature at Oxford in Lady Margaret Hall.

Churchill says that through all these years she did all the right things. She was a proper intellectual, a proper student, a proper person. She began writing plays in Oxford, where they were produced by students. After college, she married David Harter, also from Oxford, who became a lawyer in London. She raised three sons and at the same time tried to keep alive her dream of being a writer. Most of her early work was written for radio, and many of the plays were short. With so many children in the house, she says, it was difficult to sustain a long project.

Churchill's social conscience has been a significant part of her play-writing and her life. She found herself sometimes depressed by the dullness of the middle-class life demanded of the wife of a barrister, and much of her early drama is satire directed at what many people thought was an enviable lifestyle.

In the early 1970s her husband left a very lucrative practice and has since devoted himself to helping the poor at a nearby legal aid center. She has become involved in theater groups, among them a group of women called Monstrous Regiment. She is closely aligned with the notable Royal Court Theatre in London, noted for producing satiric, biting, experimental drama with a punch.

Her first play staged at the Royal Court Theatre was a farcical but serious play called *Owners* (1972). It is an attack on the way the concept of ownership destroys the relationships that might be possible among people. Churchill's basic socialist views are very apparent in the play, which is a critique of the values that most capitalists take for granted: being aggressive, getting ahead, doing well. Although this play is not explicitly feminist, Churchill combines socialism and feminism in most of her plays, thus producing an often unusual approach to her subject matter. *Owners* has been criticized for its Brechtian use of disconnected scenes and its loose plot, but when it was produced Off Broadway in 1973 it attracted attention for Churchill as a serious playwright.

After a year as a playwright in residence at the Royal Court Theatre, Churchill produced *Objections to Sex and Violence* (1975). The play was not immensely successful but it introduced themes of feminism into her work. Among other themes, the play examines in depth the domination of women by men and the relationship of violence to sex roles.

In 1976, Churchill produced *Vinegar Tom*, a play about witch hunts set in the seventeenth century. After researching witch trials, Churchill concluded that women were convenient scapegoats for men when times became difficult. A companion play also set in the seventeenth century is *Light Shining in Buckinghamshire*, which studies revolutions. The play was developed by the Joint Stock Theatre Group and produced at the Royal Court Theatre to uniformly positive reviews.

Her first play to receive wide notice was *Cloud Nine* (1979). It treats several themes simultaneously, among them colonization. The first act is set in the Victorian era in a British colony of Africa. The play is broadly satirical, involving farcical moments in the relationships of colonialist and native, master/servant, and man/woman. Churchill cast certain parts of the play in a cross-gender fashion: a woman plays a sensitive schoolboy, a man plays an unfulfilled wife. The effect is both comic and instructive, since one of her most important purposes is to cast some light on gender distinctions. She said that she saw "parallels between the way colonizers treat the colonized and the way men tended to treat women in our own society." *Cloud Nine* was produced in the Lucille Lortel Theatre, where it ran for two years Off Broadway and won an Obie award.

Top Girls (1982) played at the Royal Court Theatre in London and at the Public Theatre in New York, where the reviews were mixed. The play, essentially feminist in theme, was praised in England for being "the best British play ever from a woman dramatist." *Fen* (1983) was also warmly praised by critics and audiences alike. A study of the effects of poverty on women, the play was developed with the Joint Stock Theatre Group and researched in the area of England called the Fens, where women work the fields and most of the people are poor.

Churchill's *Serious Money* (1987) is a verse play (like her first Oxford play) about the London stock market. It ran on Broadway to exceptional acclaim, partly because it played just after the stock market crash of October 1987. The play is a satiric study of those for whom only greed and getting ahead matter. Its success indicates that Caryl Churchill has been recognized as a major writer.

TOP GIRLS

Top Girls (1982) was commissioned by the Royal Court Theatre in London and was first performed there under the direction of Max Stafford-Clark. Like many of the explosive Royal Court playwrights, Churchill had produced experimental, socially conscious plays that challenged the normal London and Broadway styles of production. She had established herself as a serious, significant writer.

The play has been produced in England and America by both important commercial theaters and smaller experimental and regional theaters and is widely considered a feminist drama. However, Churchill is quick to point out that the play is often misunderstood; it is a critique not only of the dominance of males in the workplace but of women who are satisfied to dominate the workplace in their turn and behave essentially as males. Churchill, an ardent socialist as well as a feminist, has said that *Top Girls* is an indictment of people, male or female, who get ahead at the cost of their humanity and their capacity to care for others.

The play opens with important legendary women gathering to share Marlene's celebration of her promotion with the Top Girls employment agency. The assembled group includes Pope Joan, a woman who posed as a man and became pope; Lady Nijo, a Japanese courtesan of the thirteenth century; Isabella Bird, a Victorian traveler who had many interesting adventures; Dull Gret, a figure from a Brueghel painting who led an attack on hell; and Patient Griselda, the obedient wife who inspired Chaucer.

Churchill creates characters who could be from a medieval allegory: Pope Joan succeeds by imitating a man physically; Lady Nijo succeeds by satisfying men; Isabella Bird attracts attention by displacing men (who were the legendary travelers); and Dull Gret and Patient Griselda, allegorical characters borrowed from other works of art, have their own ways of getting on in a "man's" world. Marlene is also allegorical: she stands for the woman who will succeed at all costs, including abandoning her own daughter.

Churchill alludes to medieval practice in another way. It was common in medieval poetic literature to tell stories about important historical and biblical women (as well as men). Such collections included incisive portraits of Eve, Cleopatra, the Witch of Endor, and Dalila. In the misogynist medieval period, such compilations of "top girls" focused on women who had caused scandal and harm to society. Such literature portrayed "bad girls."

One would think that the tables would be turned at the hands of a modern feminist, but Churchill's analysis is subtle. She demonstrates that Marlene and the other contemporary women have settled for demeaning themselves rather than demanding to re-create themselves. Most of the women in Act II — Marlene, her co-workers, clients, and family — reveal their callousness, their indifference, and their basic incapacity to love. Marlene is unable to feel deeply even about those closest to her — her sister, her mother, and her daughter.

The ending of the play is a study of family relations. The failure of the two sisters is part of the message of the play. Marlene has paid an extraordinary price for her success. The play leaves us with the question of whether Marlene sees what she has done to herself and to her daughter and her sister. The play does not pull punches; it tries to illuminate the ways in which we make ourselves less human, less fulfilled, when we are driven to a success that is illusory and values that are false.

Caryl Churchill (b. 1938)
TOP GIRLS

1982

Characters

MARLENE
WAITRESS/KIT/SHONA
ISABELLA BIRD/JOYCE/MRS. KIDD
LADY NIJO/WIN
DULL GRET/ANGIE
POPE JOAN/LOUISE
PATIENT GRISELDA/NELL/JEANINE

Act I
Scene I: *A Restaurant.*
Scene II: *Top Girls' Employment Agency, London.*
Scene III: *Joyce's backyard in Suffolk.*

Act II
Scene I: *Top Girls' Employment Agency.*
Scene II: *A Year Earlier. Joyce's kitchen.*

Production Note: *The seating order for Act I, Scene I in the original production at the Royal Court was (from right) Gret, Nijo, Marlene, Joan, Griselda, Isabella.*

The Characters

ISABELLA BIRD (1831–1904): Lived in Edinburgh, traveled extensively between the ages of forty and seventy.

LADY NIJO (b. 1258): Japanese, was an Emperor's courtesan and later a Buddhist nun who traveled on foot through Japan.

DULL GRET: Is the subject of the Brueghel painting *Dulle Griet*, in which a woman in an apron and armor leads a crowd of women charging through hell and fighting the devils.

POPE JOAN: Disguised as a man, is thought to have been pope between 854 and 856.

PATIENT GRISELDA: Is the obedient wife whose story is told by Chaucer in "The Clerk's Tale" of *The Canterbury Tales.*

The Layout: *A speech usually follows the one immediately before it but: (1) When one character starts speaking before the other has finished, the point of interruption is marked* * . *E.g.,*

ISABELLA: This is the Emperor of Japan? / I once met the Emperor of Morocco.
NIJO: In fact he was the ex-Emperor.

(2) A character sometimes continues speaking right through another's speech. E.g.,

ISABELLA: When I was forty I thought my life was over. / Oh I was pitiful. I was
NIJO: I didn't say I felt it for twenty years. Not every minute.
ISABELLA: sent on a cruise for my health and felt even worse. Pains in my bones, pins and needles . . . etc.

(3) Sometimes a speech follows on from a speech earlier than the one immediately before it, and continuity is marked *. *E.g.,*

GRISELDA: I'd seen him riding by, we all had. And he'd seen me in the fields with the sheep.*

ISABELLA: I would have been well suited to minding sheep.

NIJO: And Mr. Nugent went riding by.

ISABELLA: Of course not, Nijo, I mean a healthy life in the open air.

JOAN: *He just rode up while you were minding the sheep and asked you to marry him?

where "in the fields with the sheep" is the cue to both "I would have been" and "He just rode up."

ACT I • Scene I _____

(Restaurant. Saturday night. There is a table with a white cloth set for dinner with six places. The lights come up on Marlene and the Waitress.)

MARLENE: Excellent, yes, table for six. One of them's going to be late but we won't wait. I'd like a bottle of Frascati straight away if you've got one really cold. (*The Waitress goes. Isabella Bird arrives.*) Here we are. Isabella.

ISABELLA: Congratulations, my dear.

MARLENE: Well, it's a step. It makes for a party. I haven't time for a holiday. I'd like to go somewhere exotic like you but I can't get away. I don't know how you could bear to leave Hawaii. / I'd like to lie

ISABELLA: I did think of settling.

MARLENE: in the sun forever, except of course I can't bear sitting still.

ISABELLA: I sent for my sister Hennie to come and join me. I said, Hennie we'll live here forever and help the natives. You can buy two sirloins of beef for what a pound of chops cost in Edinburgh. And Hennie wrote back, the dear, that yes, she would come to Hawaii if I wished, but I said she had far better stay where she was. Hennie was suited to life in Tobermory.

MARLENE: Poor Hennie.

ISABELLA: Do you have a sister?

MARLENE: Yes in fact.

ISABELLA: Hennie was happy. She was good. I did miss its face, my own pet. But I couldn't stay in Scotland. I loathed the constant murk.

(Lady Nijo arrives.)

MARLENE (*seeing her*): Ah! Nijo! (*The Waitress enters with the wine.*)

NIJO: Marlene! (*To Isabella.*) So excited when Marlene told me / you were coming.

ISABELLA: I'm delighted / to meet you.

MARLENE: I think a drink while we wait for the others. I think a drink anyway. What a week. (*Marlene seats Nijo. The Waitress pours the wine.*)

NIJO: It was always the men who used to get so drunk. I'd be one of the maidens, passing the sake.

ISABELLA: I've had sake.° Small hot drink. Quite fortifying after a day in the wet.

NIJO: One night my father proposed three rounds of three cups, which was normal, and then the Emperor should have said three rounds of three cups, but he said three rounds of nine cups, so you can imagine. Then the Emperor passed his sake cup to my father and said, "Let the wild goose come to me this spring."

MARLENE: Let the what?

NIJO: It's a literary allusion to a tenth-century epic, / His Majesty was very cultured.

ISABELLA: This is the Emperor of Japan? / I once met the Emperor of Morocco.

NIJO: In fact he was the ex-Emperor.

MARLENE: But he wasn't old? / Did you, Isabella?

NIJO: Twenty-nine.

ISABELLA: Oh it's a long story.

MARLENE: Twenty-nine's an excellent age.

NIJO: Well I was only fourteen and I knew he meant something but I didn't know what. He sent me an eight-layered gown and I sent it back. So when the time came I did nothing but cry. My thin gowns were badly ripped. But even that morning when he left / he'd a green

MARLENE: Are you saying he raped you?

NIJO: robe with a scarlet lining and very heavily embroidered trousers, I already felt different about him. It made me uneasy. No, of course not, Marlene, I belonged to him, it was what I was brought up for from a baby. I soon found I was sad if he stayed away. It was depressing day after day not knowing when he would come. I never enjoyed taking other women to him.

ISABELLA: I certainly never saw my father drunk. He was a clergyman. / And I didn't get married till I was fifty. (*The Waitress brings the menus.*)

NIJO: Oh, my father was a very religious man. Just before he died he said to me, "Serve His Majesty, be respectful, if you lose his favor enter holy orders."

MARLENE: But he meant stay in a convent, not go wandering round the country.

NIJO: Priests were often vagrants, so why not a nun?

sake: Japanese rice wine.

You think I shouldn't? / I still did what my father wanted.

MARLENE: No no, I think you should. / I think it was wonderful.

(*Dull Gret arrives.*)

ISABELLA: I tried to do what my father wanted.

MARLENE: Gret, good. Nijo. Gret / I know Griselda's going to be late, but should we wait for Joan? / Let's get you a drink.

ISABELLA: Hello, Gret! (*She continues to Nijo.*) I tried to be a clergyman's daughter. Needlework, music, charitable schemes. I had a tumor removed from my spine and spent a great deal of time on the sofa. I studied the metaphysical poets and hymnology. / I thought I enjoyed intellectual pursuits.

NIJO: Ah, you like poetry. I come of a line of eight generations of poets. Father had a poem / in the anthology.

ISABELLA: My father taught me Latin although I was a girl. / But really I was

MARLENE: They didn't have Latin at my school.

ISABELLA: more suited to manual work. Cooking, washing, mending, riding horses. / Better than reading

NIJO: Oh but I'm sure you're very clever.

ISABELLA: books, eh Gret? A rough life in the open air.

NIJO: I can't say I enjoyed my rough life. What I enjoyed most was being the Emperor's favorite / and wearing thin silk.

ISABELLA: Did you have any horses, Gret?

GRET: Pig.

(*Pope Joan arrives.*)

MARLENE: Oh Joan, thank God, we can order. Do you know everyone? We were just talking about learning Latin and being clever girls. Joan was by way of an infant prodigy. Of course you were. What excited you when you were ten?

JOAN: Because angels are without matter they are not individuals. Every angel is a species.

MARLENE: There you are. (*They laugh. They look at the menus.*)

ISABELLA: Yes, I forgot all my Latin. But my father was the mainspring of my life and when he died I was so grieved. I'll have the chicken, please, / and the soup.

NIJO: Of course you were grieved. My father was saying his prayers and he dozed off in the sun. So I touched his knee to rouse him. "I wonder what will happen," he said, and then he was dead before he finished the sentence. / If he'd

MARLENE: What a shock.

NIJO: died saying his prayers he would have gone straight to heaven. / Waldorf salad.

JOAN: Death is the return of all creatures to God.

NIJO: I shouldn't have woken him.

JOAN: Damnation only means ignorance of the truth. I was always attracted by the teachings of John the Scot, though he was inclined to confuse / God and the world.

ISABELLA: Grief always overwhelmed me at the time.

MARLENE: What I fancy is a rare steak. Gret?

ISABELLA: I am of course a member of the / Church of England.

MARLENE: Gret?

GRET: Potatoes.

MARLENE: I haven't been to church for years. / I like Christmas carols.

ISABELLA: Good works matter more than church attendance.

MARLENE: Make that two steaks and a lot of potatoes. Rare. But I don't do good works either.

JOAN: Canelloni, please, / and a salad.

ISABELLA: Well, I tried, but oh dear. Hennie did good works.

NIJO: The first half of my life was all sin and the second / all repentance.*

MARLENE: Oh what about starters?

GRET: Soup.

JOAN: *And which did you like best?

MARLENE: Were your travels just a penance? Avocado vinaigrette. Didn't you / enjoy yourself?

JOAN: Nothing to start with for me, thank you.

NIJO: Yes, but I was very unhappy. / It hurt to remember the past.

MARLENE: And the wine list.

NIJO: I think that was repentance.

MARLENE: Well I wonder.

NIJO: I might have just been homesick.

MARLENE: Or angry.

NIJO: Not angry, no, / why angry?

GRET: Can we have some more bread?

MARLENE: Don't you get angry? I get angry.

NIJO: But what about?

MARLENE: Yes let's have two more Frascati. And some more bread, please. (*The Waitress exits.*)

ISABELLA: I tried to understand Buddhism when I was in Japan but all this birth and death succeeding each other through eternities just filled me with the most profound melancholy. I do like something more active.

NIJO: You couldn't say I was inactive. I walked every day for twenty years.

ISABELLA: I don't mean walking. / I mean in the head.

NIJO: I vowed to copy five Mahayana sutras. / Do you know how long they are?

MARLENE: I don't think religious beliefs are something we have in common. Activity yes. (*Gret empties the bread basket into her apron.*)

NIJO: My head was active. / My head ached.

JOAN: It's no good being active in heresy.

ISABELLA: What heresy? She's calling the Church of England / a heresy.

JOAN: There are some very attractive / heresies.

NIJO: I had never heard of Christianity. Never / heard of it. Barbarians.

MARLENE: Well I'm not a Christian. / And I'm not a Buddhist.

ISABELLA: You have heard of it?

MARLENE: We don't all have to believe the same.

ISABELLA: I knew coming to dinner with a Pope we should keep off religion.

JOAN: I always enjoy a theological argument. But I won't try to convert you, I'm not a missionary. Anyway I'm a heresy myself.

ISABELLA: There are some barbaric practices in the east.

NIJO: Barbaric?

ISABELLA: Among the lower classes.

NIJO: I wouldn't know.

ISABELLA: Well theology always made my head ache.

MARLENE: Oh good, some food. (*The Waitress brings the first course, serves it during the following, then exits.*)

NIJO: How else could I have left the court if I wasn't a nun? When father died I had only His Majesty. So when I fell out of favor I had nothing. Religion is a kind of nothing / and I dedicated what was left of me to nothing.

ISABELLA: That's what I mean about Buddhism. It doesn't brace.

MARLENE: Come on, Nijo, have some wine.

NIJO: Haven't you ever felt like that? You've all felt / like that. Nothing will ever happen again. I am dead already.

ISABELLA: You thought your life was over but it wasn't.

JOAN: You wish it was over.

GRET: Sad.

MARLENE: Yes, when I first came to London I sometimes . . . and when I got back from America I did. But only for a few hours. Not twenty years.

ISABELLA: When I was forty I thought my life was over. / Oh I was pitiful. I was sent

NIJO: I didn't say I felt it for twenty years. Not every minute.

ISABELLA: on a cruise for my health and I felt even worse. Pains in my bones, pins and needles in my hands, swelling behind the ears, and — oh, stupidity. I shook all over, indefinable terror. And Australia seemed to me a hideous country, the acacias stank like drains. / I

NIJO: You were homesick. (*Gret steals a bottle of wine.*)

ISABELLA: had a photograph taken for Hennie but I told her I wouldn't send it, my hair had fallen out and my clothes were crooked, I looked completely insane and suicidal.

NIJO: So did I, exactly, dressed as a nun. / I was wearing walking shoes for the first time.

ISABELLA: I longed to go home, / but home to what? Houses are so perfectly dismal.*

NIJO: I longed to go back ten years.

MARLENE: *I thought traveling cheered you both up.

ISABELLA: Oh it did / of course. It was on

NIJO: I'm not a cheerful person, Marlene. I just laugh a lot.

ISABELLA: the trip from Australia to the Sandwich Isles, I fell in love with the sea. There were rats in the cabin and ants in the food but suddenly it was like a new world. I woke up every morning happy, knowing there would be nothing to annoy me. No nervousness. No dressing.

NIJO: Don't you like getting dressed? I adored my clothes. / When I was chosen

MARLENE: You had prettier colors than Isabella.

NIJO: to give sake to His Majesty's brother, the Emperor Kameyana, on his formal visit, I wore raw silk pleated trousers and a seven-layered gown in shades of red, and two outer garments, / yellow lined with green

MARLENE: Yes, all that silk must have been very — (*The Waitress enters, clears the first course and exits.*)

JOAN: I dressed as a boy when I left home.*

NIJO: and a light green jacket. Lady Betto had a five-layered gown in shades of green and purple.

ISABELLA: *You dressed as a boy?

MARLENE: Of course, / for safety.

JOAN: It was easy, I was only twelve. / Also women weren't allowed in the library. We wanted to study in Athens.

MARLENE: You ran away alone?

JOAN: No, not alone, I went with my friend. / He was

NIJO: Ah, an elopement.

JOAN: sixteen but I thought I knew more science than he did and almost as much philosophy.

ISABELLA: Well I always traveled as a lady and I repudiated strongly any suggestion in the press that I was other than feminine.

MARLENE: I don't wear trousers in the office. / I could but I don't.

ISABELLA: There was no great danger to a woman of my age and appearance.

MARLENE: And you got away with it, Joan?

JOAN: I did then. (*The Waitress brings in the main course.*)

MARLENE: And nobody noticed anything?

JOAN: They noticed I was a very clever boy. / And

MARLENE: I couldn't have kept pretending for so long.

JOAN: when I shared a bed with my friend, that was ordinary — two poor students in a lodging house. I think I forgot I was pretending.

ISABELLA: Rocky Mountain Jim, Mr. Nugent, showed me no disrespect. He found it interesting, I think, that I could make scones and also lasso cattle. Indeed he declared his love for me, which was most distressing.

NIJO: What did he say? / We always sent poems first.

MARLENE: What did you say?

ISABELLA: I urged him to give up whiskey, / but he said it was too late.

MARLENE: Oh Isabella.

ISABELLA: He had lived alone in the mountains for many years.

MARLENE: But did you —? (*The Waitress goes.*)

ISABELLA: Mr. Nugent was a man that any woman might love but none could marry. I came back to England.

NIJO: Did you write him a poem when you left? / Snow on the mountains. My sleeves

MARLENE: Did you never see him again?

ISABELLA: No, never.

NIJO: are wet with tears. In England no tears, no snow.

ISABELLA: Well, I say never. One morning very early in Switzerland, it was a year later, I had a vision of him as I last saw him / in his trapper's clothes with his

NIJO: A ghost!

ISABELLA: hair round his face, and that was the day, / I learned later, he died with a

NIJO: Ah!

ISABELLA: bullet in his brain. / He just bowed to me and vanished.

MARLENE: Oh Isabella.

NIJO: When your lover dies — One of my lovers died. / The priest Ariake.

JOAN: My friend died. Have we all got dead lovers?

MARLENE: Not me, sorry.

NIJO (*to Isabella*): I wasn't a nun, I was still at court, but he was a priest, and when he came to me he dedicated his whole life to hell. / He knew that when he died he would fall into one of the three lower realms. And he died, he did die.

JOAN (*to Marlene*): I'd quarreled with him over the teachings of John the Scot, who held that our ignorance of God is the same as his ignorance of himself. He only knows what he creates because he creates everything he knows but he himself is above being — do you follow?

MARLENE: No, but go on.

NIJO: I couldn't bear to think / in what shape would he be reborn.*

JOAN: St. Augustine maintained that the Neo-Platonic Ideas are indivisible

ISABELLA: *Buddhism is really most uncomfortable.

JOAN: from God, but I agreed with John that the created world is essences derived from Ideas which derived from God. As Denys the Areopagite said — the pseudo-Denys — first we give God a name, then deny it, / then reconcile the contradiction

NIJO: In what shape would he return?

JOAN: by looking beyond / those terms —

MARLENE: Sorry, what? Denys said what?

JOAN: Well we disagreed about it, we quarreled. And next day he was ill, / I was so annoyed with him

NIJO: Misery in this life and worse in the next, all because of me.

JOAN: all the time I was nursing him I kept going over the arguments in my mind. Matter is not a means of knowing the essence. The source of the species is the Idea. But then I realized he'd never understand my arguments again, and that night he died. John the Scot held that the individual disintegrates / and there is no personal immortality.

ISABELLA: I wouldn't have you think I was in love with Jim Nugent. It was yearning to save him that I felt.

MARLENE (*to Joan*): So what did you do?

JOAN: First I decided to stay a man. I was used to it. And I wanted to devote my life to learning. Do you know why I went to Rome? Italian men didn't have beards.

ISABELLA: The loves of my life were Hennie, my own pet, and my dear husband the doctor, who nursed Hennie in her last illness. I knew it would be terrible when Hennie died but I didn't know how terrible. I felt half of myself had gone. How could I go on my travels without that sweet soul waiting at home for my letters? It was Doctor Bishop's devotion to her in her last illness that made me decide to marry him. He and Hennie had the same sweet character. I had not.

NIJO: I thought His Majesty had sweet character because when he found out about Ariake he was so kind. But really it was because he no longer cared for me. One night he even sent me out to a man who had been pursuing me. / He lay awake on the other side of the screens and listened.

ISABELLA: I did wish marriage had seemed more of a step. I tried very hard to cope with the ordinary drudgery of life. I was ill again with carbuncles on the spine and nervous prostration. I ordered a tricycle, that was my idea of adventure then. And John himself fell ill, with erysipelas and anemia. I began to love him with my whole heart but it was too late. He was a skeleton with transparent white hands. I wheeled him on various seafronts in a bathchair. And he faded and left me. There was nothing in my life. The doctors said I had gout / and my heart was much affected.

NIJO: There was nothing in my life, nothing, without the Emperor's favor. The Empress had always been my enemy, Marlene, she said I had no right to wear three-layered gowns. / But I was the adopted daughter of my grandfather the Prime Minister. I had been publicly granted permission to wear thin silk.

JOAN: There was nothing in my life except my studies. I was obsessed with pursuit of the truth. I taught at the Greek School in Rome, which St. Augustine had made famous. I was poor, I worked hard, I spoke apparently brilliantly, I was still very young, I was a stranger, suddenly I was quite famous, I was everyone's favorite. Huge crowds came to hear me. The day after they made me cardinal I fell ill and lay two weeks without speaking, full of terror and regret. / But then I got up determined to

MARLENE: Yes, success is very . . .

JOAN: go on. I was seized again / with a desperate longing for the absolute.

ISABELLA: Yes, yes, to go on. I sat in Tobermory among Hennie's flowers and sewed a complete outfit in Jaeger flannel. / I was fifty-six years old.

NIJO: Out of favor but I didn't die. I left on foot, nobody saw me go. For the next twenty years I walked through Japan.

GRET: Walking is good. (Meanwhile, the Waitress enters, pours lots of wine, then shows Marlene the empty bottle.)

JOAN: Pope Leo died and I was chosen. All right then. I would be Pope. I would know God. I would know everything.

ISABELLA: I determined to leave my grief behind and set off for Tibet.

MARLENE: Magnificent all of you. We need some more wine, please, two bottles I think, Griselda isn't even here yet, and I want to drink a toast to you all. (The Waitress exits.)

ISABELLA: To yourself surely, / we're here to celebrate your success.

NIJO: Yes, Marlene.

JOAN: Yes, what is it exactly, Marlene?

MARLENE: Well it's not Pope but it is managing director.*

JOAN: And you find work for people.

MARLENE: Yes, an employment agency.

NIJO: *Over all the women you work with. And the men.

ISABELLA: And very well deserved too. I'm sure it's just the beginning of something extraordinary.

MARLENE: Well it's worth a party.

ISABELLA: To Marlene.*

MARLENE: And all of us.

JOAN: *Marlene.

NIJO: Marlene.

GRET: Marlene.

MARLENE: We've all come a long way. To our courage and the way we changed our lives and our extraordinary achievements. (They laugh and drink a toast.)

ISABELLA: Such adventures. We were crossing a mountain pass at seven thousand feet, the cook was all to pieces, the muleteers suffered fever and snow blindness. But even though my spine was agony I managed very well.*

MARLENE: Wonderful.

NIJO: *Once I was ill for four months lying alone at an inn. Nobody to offer a horse to Buddha. I had to live for myself, and I did live.

ISABELLA: Of course you did. It was far worse returning to Tobermory. I always felt dull when I was stationary. / That's why I could never stay anywhere.

NIJO: Yes, that's it exactly. New sights. The shrine by the beach, the moon shining on the sea. The goddess had vowed to save all living things. / She would even save the fishes. I was full of hope.

JOAN: I had thought the Pope would know everything. I thought God would speak to me directly. But of course he knew I was a woman.

MARLENE: But nobody else even suspected? (The Waitress brings more wine and then exits.)

JOAN: In the end I did take a lover again.*

ISABELLA: In the Vatican?

GRET: *Keep you warm.

NIJO: *Ah, lover.

MARLENE: *Good for you.

JOAN: He was one of my chamberlains. There are such a lot of servants when you're Pope. The food's very good. And I realized I did know the truth. Because whatever the Pope says, that's true.

NIJO: What was he like, the chamberlain?*

GRET: Big cock.

ISABELLA: Oh, Gret.

MARLENE: *Did he fancy you when he thought you were a fella?

NIJO: What was he like?

JOAN: He could keep a secret.

MARLENE: So you did know everything.

JOAN: Yes, I enjoyed being Pope. I consecrated bishops and let people kiss my feet. I received the King of England when he came to submit to the church. Unfortunately there were earthquakes, and some village reported it had rained blood, and in France there was a plague of giant grasshoppers, but I don't think that can have been my fault, do you?*

(*Laughter.*) The grasshoppers fell on the English Channel / and were washed up on shore.

NIJO: I once went to sea. It was very lonely. I realized it made very little difference where I went.

JOAN: and their bodies rotted and poisoned the air and everyone in those parts died. (*Laughter.*)

ISABELLA: *Such superstition! I was nearly murdered in China by a howling mob. They thought the barbarians ate babies and put them under railway sleepers to make the tracks steady, and ground up their eyes to make the lenses of cameras. / So they were shouting,

MARLENE: And you had a camera!

ISABELLA: "Child-eater, child-eater." Some people tried to sell girl babies to Europeans for cameras or stew! (*Laughter.*)

MARLENE: So apart from the grasshoppers it was a great success.

JOAN: Yes, if it hadn't been for the baby I expect I'd have lived to an old age like Theodora of Alexandria, who lived as a monk. She was accused by a girl / who fell in love with her of being the father of her child and —

NIJO: But tell us what happened to your baby. I had some babies.

MARLENE: Didn't you think of getting rid of it?

JOAN: Wouldn't that be a worse sin than having it? / But a Pope with a child was about as bad as possible.

MARLENE: I don't know, you're the Pope.

JOAN: But I wouldn't have known how to get rid of it.

MARLENE: Other Popes had children, surely.

JOAN: They didn't give birth to them.

NIJO: Well you were a woman.

JOAN: Exactly and I shouldn't have been a woman. Women, children, and lunatics can't be Pope.

MARLENE: So the only thing to do / was to get rid of it somehow.

NIJO: You had to have it adopted secretly.

JOAN: But I didn't know what was happening. I thought I was getting fatter, but then I was eating more and sitting about, the life of a Pope is quite luxurious. I don't think I'd spoken to a woman since I was twelve. The chamberlain was the one who realized.

MARLENE: And by then it was too late.

JOAN: Oh I didn't want to pay attention. It was easier to do nothing.

NIJO: But you had to plan for having it. You had to say you were ill and go away.

JOAN: That's what I should have done I suppose.

MARLENE: Did you want them to find out?

NIJO: I too was often in embarrassing situations, there's no need for a scandal. My first child was His Majesty's, which unfortunately died, but my second was Akebono's. I was seventeen. He was in love with me when I was thirteen, he was very upset when I had to go to the Emperor, it was very romantic, a lot of poems. Now His Majesty hadn't been near me for two months so he thought I was four months pregnant when I was really six, so when I reached the ninth month / I announced I was seriously ill,

JOAN: I never knew what month it was.

NIJO: and Akebono announced he had gone on a religious retreat. He held me round the waist and lifted me up as the baby was born. He cut the cord with a short sword, wrapped the baby in white and took it away. It was only a girl but I was sorry to lose it. Then I told the Emperor that the baby had miscarried because of my illness, and there you are. The danger was past.

JOAN: But, Nijo, I wasn't used to having a woman's body.

ISABELLA: So what happened?

JOAN: I didn't know of course that it was near the time. It was Rogation Day, there was always a procession. I was on the horse dressed in my robes and a cross was carried in front of me, and all the cardinals were following, and all the clergy of Rome, and a huge crowd of people. / We set off from St. Peter's to go

MARLENE: Total Pope. (*Gret pours the wine and steals the bottle.*)

JOAN: to St. John's. I had felt a slight pain earlier, I thought it was something I'd eaten, and then it came back, and came back more often. I thought when this is over I'll go to bed. There were still long gaps when I felt perfectly all right and I didn't want to attract attention to myself and spoil the ceremony. Then I suddenly realized what it must be. I had to last out till I could get home and hide. Then something changed, my breath started to catch, I couldn't plan things properly anymore. We were in a little street that goes between St. Clement's and the Colosseum, and I just had to get off the horse and sit down for a minute. Great waves of pressure were going through my body, I heard sounds like a cow lowing, they came out of my mouth. Far away I heard people screaming, "The Pope is ill, the Pope is dying." And the baby just slid out on to the road.*

MARLENE: The cardinals / won't have known where to put themselves.

NIJO: Oh dear, Joan, what a thing to do! In the street!

ISABELLA: *How embarrassing.

GRET: In a field, yah. (*They are laughing.*)

JOAN: One of the cardinals said, "The Antichrist!" and fell over in a faint. (*They all laugh.*)

MARLENE: So what did they do? They weren't best pleased.

JOAN: They took me by the feet and dragged me out of town and stoned me to death. (*They stop laughing.*)

MARLENE: Joan, how horrible.

JOAN: I don't really remember.

NIJO: And the child died too?

JOAN: Oh yes, I think so, yes. (*The Waitress enters to clear the plates. Pause. They start talking very quietly.*)

ISABELLA (*to Joan*): I never had any children. I was very fond of horses.

NIJO (*to Marlene*): I saw my daughter once. She was three years old. She wore a plum-red / small sleeved gown. Akebono's wife

ISABELLA: Birdie was my favorite. A little Indian bay mare I rode in the Rocky Mountains.

NIJO: had taken the child because her own died. Everyone thought I was just a visitor. She was being brought up carefully so she could be sent to the palace like I was. (*Gret steals her empty plate.*)

ISABELLA: Legs of iron and always cheerful, and such a pretty face. If a stranger led her she reared up like a bronco.

NIJO: I never saw my third child after he was born, the son of Ariake the priest. Ariake held him on his lap the day he was born and talked to him as if he could understand, and cried. My fourth child was Ariake's too. Ariake died before he was born. I didn't want to see anyone, I stayed alone in the hills. It was a boy again, my third son. But oddly enough I felt nothing for him.

MARLENE: How many children did you have, Gret?

GRET: Ten.

ISABELLA: Whenever I came back to England I felt I had so much to atone for. Hennie and John were so good. I did no good in my life. I spent years in self-gratification. So I hurled myself into committees, I nursed the people of Tobermory in the epidemic of influenza, I lectured the Young Women's Christian Association on Thrift. I talked and talked explaining how the East was corrupt and vicious. My travels must do good to someone besides myself. I wore myself out with good causes.

MARLENE (*pause*): Oh God, why are we all so miserable?

JOAN (*pause*): The procession never went down that street again.

MARLENE: They rerouted it specially?

JOAN: Yes they had to go all round to avoid it. And they introduced a pierced chair.

MARLENE: A pierced chair?

JOAN: Yes, a chair made out of solid marble with a hole in the seat / and it was

MARLENE: You're not serious.

JOAN: in the Chapel of the Savior, and after he was elected the Pope had to sit in it.

MARLENE: And someone looked up his skirts? / Not really!

ISABELLA: What an extraordinary thing.

JOAN: Two of the clergy / made sure he was a man.

NIJO: On their hands and knees!

MARLENE: A pierced chair!

GRET: Balls!

(*Griselda arrives unnoticed.*)

NIJO: Why couldn't he just pull up his robe?

JOAN: He had to sit there and look dignified.

MARLENE: You could have made all your chamberlains sit in it.*

GRET: Big one. Small one.

NIJO: Very useful chair at court.

ISABELLA: *Or the Laird of Tobermory in his kilt.

(*They are quite drunk. They get the giggles. Marlene notices Griselda and gets up to welcome her. The others go on talking and laughing. Gret crosses to Joan and Isabella and pours them wine from her stolen bottles. The Waitress gives out the menus.*)

MARLENE: Griselda! / There you are. Do you want to eat?

GRISELDA: I'm sorry I'm so late. No, no, don't bother.

MARLENE: Of course it's no bother. / Have you eaten?

GRISELDA: No really, I'm not hungry.

MARLENE: Well have some pudding.

GRISELDA: I never eat pudding.

MARLENE: Griselda, I hope you're not anorexic. We're having pudding, I am, and getting nice and fat.

GRISELDA: Oh if everyone is. I don't mind.

MARLENE: Now who do you know? This is Joan who was Pope in the ninth century, and Isabella Bird, the Victorian traveler, and Lady Nijo from Japan, Emperor's concubine and Buddhist nun, thirteenth century, nearer your own time, and Gret who was painted by Brueghel. Griselda's in Boccaccio and Petrarch and Chaucer because of her extraordinary marriage. I'd like profiteroles because they're disgusting.

JOAN: Zabaglione, please.

ISABELLA: Apple pie / and cream.

NIJO: What's this?

MARLENE: Zabaglione, it's Italian, it's what Joan's having, / it's delicious.

NIJO: A Roman Catholic / dessert? Yes please.

MARLENE: Gret?

GRET: Cake.

GRISELDA: Just cheese and biscuits, thank you. (*The Waitress exits.*)

MARLENE: Yes, Griselda's life is like a fairy story, except it starts with marrying the prince.

GRISELDA: He's only a marquis, Marlene.

MARLENE: Well everyone for miles around is his liege

and he'd absolute lord of life and death and you were the poor but beautiful peasant girl and he whisked you off. / Near enough a prince.

NIJO: How old were you?

GRISELDA: Fifteen.

NIJO: I was brought up in court circles and it was still a shock. Had you ever seen him before?

GRISELDA: I'd seen him riding by, we all had. And he'd seen me in the fields with the sheep.*

ISABELLA: I would have been well suited to minding sheep.

NIJO: And Mr. Nugent riding by.

ISABELLA: Of course not, Nijo, I mean a healthy life in the open air.

JOAN: *He just rode up while you were minding the sheep and asked you to marry him?

GRISELDA: No, no, it was on the wedding day. I was waiting outside the door to see the procession. Everyone wanted him to get married so there'd be an heir to look after us when he died, / and at last he

MARLENE: I don't think Walter wanted to get married. It is Walter? Yes.

GRISELDA: announced a day for the wedding but nobody knew who the bride was, we thought it must be a foreign princess, we were longing to see her. Then the carriage stopped outside our cottage and we couldn't see the bride anywhere. And he came and spoke to my father.

NIJO: And your father told you to serve the Prince.

GRISELDA: My father could hardly speak. The Marquis said it wasn't an order, I could say no, but if I said yes I must always obey him in everything.

MARLENE: That's when you should have suspected.

GRISELDA: But of course a wife must obey her husband. / And of course I must obey the Marquis.*

ISABELLA: I swore to obey dear John, of course, but it didn't seem to arise. Naturally I wouldn't have wanted to go abroad while I was married.

MARLENE: *Then why bother to mention it at all? He'd got a thing about it, that's why.

GRISELDA: I'd rather obey the Marquis than a boy from the village.

MARLENE: Yes, that's a point.

JOAN: I never obeyed anyone. They all obeyed me.

NIJO: And what did you wear? He didn't make you get married in your own clothes? That would be perverse.*

MARLENE: Oh, you wait.

GRISELDA: *He had ladies with him who undressed me and they had a white silk dress and jewels for my hair.

MARLENE: And at first he seemed perfectly normal?

GRISELDA: Marlene, you're always so critical of him. / Of course he was normal, he was very kind.

MARLENE: But, Griselda, come on, he took your baby.

GRISELDA: Walter found it hard to believe I loved him. He couldn't believe I would always obey him. He had to prove it.

MARLENE: I don't think Walter likes women.

GRISELDA: I'm sure he loved me, Marlene, all the time.

MARLENE: He just had a funny way / of showing it.

GRISELDA: It was hard for him too.

JOAN: How do you mean he took away your baby?

NIJO: Was it a boy?

GRISELDA: No, the first one was a girl.

NIJO: Even so it's hard when they take it away. Did you see it at all?

GRISELDA: Oh yes, she was six weeks old.

NIJO: Much better to do it straight away.

ISABELLA: But why did your husband take the child?

GRISELDA: He said all the people hated me because I was just one of them. And now I had a child they were restless. So he had to get rid of the child to keep them quiet. But he said he wouldn't snatch her, I had to agree and obey and give her up. So when I was feeding her a man came in and took her away. I thought he was going to kill her even before he was out of the room.

MARLENE: But you let him take her? You didn't struggle?

GRISELDA: I asked him to give her back so I could kiss her. And I asked him to bury her where no animals could dig her up. / It was Walter's child to do what he

ISABELLA: Oh, my dear.

GRISELDA: liked with.*

MARLENE: Walter was bonkers.

GRET: Bastard.

ISABELLA: *But surely, murder.

GRISELDA: I had promised.

MARLENE: I can't stand this. I'm going for a pee.

(Marlene goes out. The Waitress brings the dessert, serves it during the following, then exits.)

NIJO: No, I understand. Of course you had to, he was your life. And were you in favor after that?

GRISELDA: Oh yes, we were very happy together. We never spoke about what had happened.

ISABELLA: I can see you were doing what you thought was your duty. But didn't it make you ill?

GRISELDA: No, I was very well, thank you.

NIJO: And you had another child?

GRISELDA: Not for four years, but then I did, yes, a boy.

NIJO: Ah a boy. / So it all ended happily.

GRISELDA: Yes he was pleased. I kept my son till he was two years old. A peasant's grandson. It made the people angry. Walter explained.

ISABELLA: But surely he wouldn't kill his children / just because —

GRISELDA: Oh it wasn't true. Walter would never give in to the people. He wanted to see if I loved him enough.

JOAN: He killed his children / to see if you loved him enough?

NIJO: Was it easier the second time or harder?

GRISELDA: It was always easy because I always knew I would do what he said. (*Pause. They start to eat.*)

ISABELLA: I hope you didn't have any more children.

GRISELDA: Oh no, no more. It was twelve years till he tested me again.

ISABELLA: So whatever did he do this time? / My poor John, I never loved him enough, and he would never have dreamt . . .

GRISELDA: He sent me away. He said the people wanted him to marry someone else who'd give him an heir and he'd got special permission from the Pope. So I said I'd go home to my father. I came with nothing / so I went with nothing. I took

NIJO: Better to leave if your master doesn't want you.

GRISELDA: off my clothes. He let me keep a slip so he wouldn't be shamed. And I walked home barefoot. My father came out in tears. Everyone was crying except me.

NIJO: At least your father wasn't dead. / I had nobody.

ISABELLA: Well it can be a relief to come home. I loved to see Hennie's sweet face again.

GRISELDA: Oh yes, I was perfectly content. And quite soon he sent for me again.

JOAN: I don't think I would have gone.

GRISELDA: But he told me to come. I had to obey him. He wanted me to help prepare his wedding. He was getting married to a young girl from France / and nobody except me knew how to arrange things the way he liked them.

NIJO: It's always hard taking him another woman. (*Marlene comes back.*)

JOAN: I didn't live a woman's life. I don't understand it.

GRISELDA: The girl was sixteen and far more beautiful than me. I could see why he loved her. / She had her younger brother with her as a page. (*The Waitress enters.*)

MARLENE: Oh God, I can't bear it. I want some coffee. Six coffees. Six brandies. / Double brandies. Straightaway. (*The Waitress exits.*)

GRISELDA: They all went into the feast I'd prepared. And he stayed behind and put his arms round me and kissed me. / I felt half asleep with the shock.

NIJO: Oh, like a dream.

MARLENE: And he said, "This is your daughter and your son."

GRISELDA: Yes.

JOAN: What?

NIJO: Oh. Oh I see. You got them back.

ISABELLA: I did think it was remarkably barbaric to kill them but you learn not to say anything. / So he had them brought up secretly I suppose.

MARLENE: Walter's a monster. Weren't you angry? What did you do?

GRISELDA: Well I fainted. Then I cried and kissed the children. / Everyone was making a fuss of me.

NIJO: But did you feel anything for them?

GRISELDA: What?

NIJO: Did you feel anything for the children?

GRISELDA: Of course, I loved them.

JOAN: So you forgave him and lived with him?

GRISELDA: He suffered so much all those years.

ISABELLA: Hennie had the same sweet nature.

NIJO: So they dressed you again?

GRISELDA: Cloth of gold.

JOAN: I can't forgive anything.

MARLENE: You really are exceptional, Griselda.

NIJO: Nobody gave me back my children. (*She cries.*)

(*The Waitress brings the brandies and then exits. During the following, Joan goes to Nijo.*)

ISABELLA: I can never be like Hennie. I was always so busy in England, a kind of business I detested. The very presence of people exhausted my emotional reserves. I could not be like Hennie however I tried. I tried and was as ill as could be. The doctor suggested a steel net to support my head, the weight of my own head was too much for my diseased spine. It is dangerous to put oneself in depressing circumstances. Why should I do it?

JOAN (*to Nijo*): Don't cry.

NIJO: My father and the Emperor both died in the autumn. So much pain.

JOAN: Yes, but don't cry.

NIJO: They wouldn't let me into the palace when he was dying. I hid in the room with his coffin, then I couldn't find where I'd left my shoes, I ran after the funeral procession in bare feet, I couldn't keep up. When I got there it was over, a few wisps of smoke in the sky, that's all that was left of him. What I want to know is, if I'd still been at court, would I have been allowed to wear full mourning?

MARLENE: I'm sure you would.

NIJO: Why do you say that? You don't know anything about it. Would I have been allowed to wear full mourning?

ISABELLA: How can people live in this dim pale island and wear our hideous clothes? I cannot and will not live the life of a lady.

NIJO: I'll tell you something that made me angry. I was eighteen, at the Full Moon Ceremony. They make a special rice gruel and stir it with their sticks,

and then they beat their women across the loins
so they'll have sons and not daughters. So the Emperor beat us all / very hard as

MARLENE: What a sod. (*The Waitress enters with th*
coffees.)

NIJO: usual — that's not it, Marlene, that's normal,
what made us angry he told his attendants they
could beat us too. Well they had a wonderful
time. / So Lady Genki and I made a plan, and the
ladies

MARLENE: I'd like another brandy, please. Better make
it six. (*The Waitress exits.*)

NIJO: all hid in his rooms, and Lady Mashimizu stood
guard with a stick at the door, and when His Majesty
came in Genki seized him and I beat him till he
cried out and promised he would never order anyone
to hit us again. Afterward there was a terrible fuss.
The nobles were horrified. "We wouldn't even dream
of stepping on Your Majesty's shadow." And I had
hit him with a stick. Yes, I hit him with a stick.

(*The Waitress brings the brandy bottle and tops up
the glasses. Joan crosses in front of the table and back
to her place while drunkenly reciting:*)

JOAN: Suave, mari magno turantibus aequora
   ventis,
   e terra magnum alterius spectare laborem;
   non quia vexari quemquamst iucunda voluptas,
   sed quibus ipse malis careas quia cernere suave
   est.
   Suave etiam belli certamina magna tueri
   per campos instructa tua sine parte pericli.
   Sed nil dulcius est, bene quam munita tenere
   edita doctrina sapientum templa serena, /
   despicere unde queas alios passimque videre
   errare atque viam palantis quaerere vitae,

GRISELDA: I do think — I do wonder — it would have
been nicer if Walter hadn't had to.

ISABELLA: Why should I? Why should I?

MARLENE: Of course not.

NIJO: I hit him with a stick.

JOAN: certare ingenio, contendere nobilitate,
   noctes atque dies niti praestante labore
   ad summas emergere opes rerumque potiri.
   O miseras hominum mentis, / o pectora caeca!*°

ISABELLA: O miseras!

NIJO: *Pectora caeca!

JOAN: qualibus in tenebris vitae quantisque periclis
   degitur hoc aevi quodcumquest! / none videre
   nil aliud sibi naturam latrare, nisi utqui
   corpore seiunctus dolor absit, mente fruatur° . . .
   (*She subsides.*)

GRET: We come to hell through a big mouth. Hell's
black and red. / It's

MARLENE (*to Joan*): Shut up, pet.

GRISELDA: Hush, please.

ISABELLA: Listen, she's been to hell.

GRET: like the village where I come from. There's a
river and a bridge and houses. There's places on
fire like when the soldiers come. There's a big devil
sat on a roof with a big hole in his arse and he's
scooping stuff out of it with a big ladle and it's
falling down on us, and it's money, so a lot of the
women stop and get some. But most of us is fighting
the devils. There's lots of little devils, our size, and
we get them down all right and give them a beating.
There's lots of funny creatures round your feet,
you don't like to look, like rats and lizards, and
nasty things, a bum with a face, and fish with legs,
and faces on things that don't have faces on. But
they don't hurt, you just keep going. Well we'd
had worse, you see, we'd had the Spanish. We'd
all had family killed. My big son die on a wheel.
Birds eat him. My baby, a soldier run her through
with a sword. I'd had enough, I was mad, I hate
the bastards. I come out of my front door that
morning and shout till my neighbors come out and
I said, "Come on, we're going where the evil come
from and pay the bastards out." And they all come
out just as they was / from baking or

NIJO: All the ladies come.

GRET: washing in their aprons, and we push down
the street and the ground opens up and we go
through a big mouth into a street just like ours
but in hell. I've got a sword in my hand from
somewhere and I fill a basket with gold cups they

Suave, . . . o pectora caeca!: Joan's speech is from the Second
Book of *On the Nature of Things* by Titus Lucretius Carus
(97?–54 B.C.), the Latin poet and philosopher. The following
translation of the passage is by Cyril Bailey: Sweet it is, when
on the great sea the winds are buffeting the waters, to gaze
from the land on another's great struggles; not because it is
pleasure or joy that any one should be distressed, but because
it is sweet to perceive from what misfortune you yourself
are free. Sweet is it too, to behold great contests of war in
full array over the plains, when you have no part in the
danger. But nothing is more gladdening than to dwell in the
calm high places, firmly embattled on the heights by the
teaching of the wise, whence you can look down on others,
and see them wandering hither and thither, going astray as
they seek the way of life, in strife matching their wits or
rival claims of birth, struggling night and day by surpassing
effort to rise up to the height of power and gain possession
of the world. Ah! miserable minds of men, blind hearts!
qualibus . . . fruatur: in what darkness of life, in what great
dangers ye spend this little span of years! to think that ye
should not see that nature cries aloud for nothing else but
that pain may be kept far sundered from the body, and that,
withdrawn from care and fear, she may enjoy in mind the
sense of pleasure!

drink out of down there. You just keep running on and fighting, / you didn't stop for nothing. Oh we give them devils such a beating.*

NIJO: Take that, take that.

JOAN: *Something something something mortisque timores

tum vacuum pectus° — damn.

Quod si ridicula —

something something on and on and on

and something splendorem purpureai.

ISABELLA: I thought I would have a last jaunt up the west river in China. Why not? But the doctors were so very grave I just went to Morocco. The sea was so wild I had to be landed by ship's crane in a coal bucket. / My horse was a terror to me, a powerful black charger.

GRET: Coal bucket good.

JOAN: nos in luce timemus

something

terrorem°

(*Nijo is laughing and crying. Joan gets up and is sick. Griselda looks after her.*)

GRISELDA: Can I have some water, please? (*The Waitress exits.*)

ISABELLA: So off I went to visit the Berber sheikhs in full blue trousers and great brass spurs. I was the only European woman ever to have seen the Emperor of Morocco. I was (*the Waitress brings the water*) seventy years old. What lengths to go to for a last chance of joy. I knew my return of vigor was only temporary, but how marvelous while it lasted.

Scene II

(*"Top Girls" Employment Agency. Monday morning. The lights come up on Marlene and Jeanine.*)

MARLENE: Right, Jeanine, you are Jeanine aren't you? Let's have a look. O's and A's°. / No A's, all those

Something . . . pectus: Fragments from Lucretius meaning "the dread of death leaves your heart empty . . ."

Quod . . . purpureai. . . . nos in luce . . . terrorem: Fragments from the following passage by Lucretius: But if we see that these thoughts are mere mirth and mockery, and in very truth the fears of men and the cares that dog them fear not the clash of arms nor the weapons of war, but pass boldly among kings and lords of the world, nor dread the glitter that comes from gold nor the bright sheen of the purple robe, can you doubt that all such power belongs to reason alone, above all when the whole of life is but a struggle in darkness? For even as children tremble and fear everything in blinding darkness, so we sometimes dread in the light things that are no whit more to be feared than what children shudder at in the dark.

O's and A's: O-level and A-level examinations in the British education system. An O-level is a public examination for

JEANINE: Six O's.

MARLENE: O's you probably could have got an A. / Speeds, not brilliant, not too bad.

JEANINE: I wanted to go to work.

MARLENE: Well, Jeanine, what's your present job like?

JEANINE: I'm a secretary.

MARLENE: Secretary or typist?

JEANINE: I did start as a typist but the last six months I've been a secretary.

MARLENE: To?

JEANINE: To three of them, really, they share me. There's Mr. Ashford, he's the office manager, and Mr. Philby / is sales, and —

MARLENE: Quite a small place?

JEANINE: A bit small.

MARLENE: Friendly?

JEANINE: Oh it's friendly enough.

MARLENE: Prospects?

JEANINE: I don't think so, that's the trouble. Miss Lewis is secretary to the managing director and she's been there forever, and Mrs. Bradford / is —

MARLENE: So you want a job with better prospects?

JEANINE: I want a change.

MARLENE: So you'll take anything comparable?

JEANINE: No, I do want prospects. I want more money.

MARLENE: You're getting —?

JEANINE: Hundred.

MARLENE: It's not bad you know. You're what? Twenty?

JEANINE: I'm saving to get married.

MARLENE: Does that mean you don't want a long-term job, Jeanine?

JEANINE: I might do.

MARLENE: Because where do the prospects come in? No kids for a bit?

JEANINE: Oh no, not kids, not yet.

MARLENE: So you won't tell them you're getting married?

JEANINE: Had I better not?

MARLENE: It would probably help.

JEANINE: I'm not wearing a ring. We thought we wouldn't spend on a ring.

MARLENE: Saves taking it off.

JEANINE: I wouldn't take it off.

MARLENE: There's no need to mention it when you go for an interview. / Now, Jeanine, do you have a feel

JEANINE: But what if they ask?

MARLENE: for any particular kind of company?

secondary-school students testing basic knowledge in various subjects; it is required before advancement to more specialized courses of study. A-level exams require advanced knowledge in a subject and are taken at the end of secondary school, usually two years after O-levels.

JEANINE: I thought advertising.

MARLENE: People often do think advertising. I have got a few vacancies but I think they're looking for something glossier.

JEANINE: You mean how I dress? / I can

MARLENE: I mean experience.

JEANINE: dress different. I dress like this on purpose for where I am now.

MARLENE: I have a marketing department here of a knitwear manufacturer. / Marketing is near enough

JEANINE: Knitwear?

MARLENE: advertising. Secretary to the marketing manager, he's thirty-five, married, I've sent him a girl before and she was happy, left to have a baby, you won't want to mention marriage there. He's very fair I think, good at his job, you won't have to nurse him along. Hundred and ten, so that's better than you're doing now.

JEANINE: I don't know.

MARLENE: I've a fairly small concern here, father and two sons, you'd have more say potentially, secretarial and reception duties, only a hundred but the job's going to grow with the concern and then you'll be in at the top with new girls coming in underneath you.

JEANINE: What is it they do?

MARLENE: Lampshades. / This would be my first choice for you.

JEANINE: Just lampshades?

MARLENE: There's plenty of different kinds of lampshade. So we'll send you there, shall we, and the knitwear second choice. Are you free to go for an interview any day they call you?

JEANINE: I'd like to travel.

MARLENE: We don't have any foreign clients. You'd have to go elsewhere.

JEANINE: Yes I know. I don't really . . . I just mean . . .

MARLENE: Does your fiancé want to travel?

JEANINE: I'd like a job where I was here in London and with him and everything but now and then — I expect it's silly. Are there jobs like that?

MARLENE: There's personal assistant to a top executive in a multinational. If that's the idea you need to be planning ahead. Is that where you want to be in ten years?

JEANINE: I might not be alive in ten years.

MARLENE: Yes but you will be. You'll have children.

JEANINE: I can't think about ten years.

MARLENE: You haven't got the speeds anyway. So I'll send you to these two shall I? You haven't been to any other agency? Just so we don't get crossed wires. Now, Jeanine, I want you to get one of these jobs, all right? If I send you that means I'm putting myself on the line for you. Your presentation's OK, you look fine, just be confident and go in there convinced that this is the best job for you and you're the best person for the job. If you don't believe it they won't believe it.

JEANINE: Do you believe it?

MARLENE: I think you could make me believe it if you put your mind to it.

JEANINE: Yes, all right.

Scene III

(*Joyce's back yard. Sunday afternoon. The house with a back door is upstage. Downstage is a shelter made of junk, made by children. The lights come up on two girls, Angie and Kit, who are squashed together in the shelter. Angie is sixteen, Kit is twelve. They cannot be seen from the house.*)

JOYCE (*off, calling from the house*): Angie. Angie, are you out there?

(*Silence. They keep still and wait. When nothing else happens they relax.*)

ANGIE: Wish she was dead.

KIT: Wanna watch *The Exterminator*?

ANGIE: You're sitting on my leg.

KIT: There's nothing on telly. We can have an ice cream. Angie?

ANGIE: Shall I tell you something?

KIT: Do you wanna watch *The Exterminator*?

ANGIE: It's X, innit?

KIT: I can get into Xs.

ANGIE: Shall I tell you something?

KIT: We'll go to something else. We'll go to Ipswich. What's on the Odeon?

ANGIE: She won't let me, will she.

KIT: Don't tell her.

ANGIE: I've no money.

KIT: I'll pay.

ANGIE: She'll moan though, won't she.

KIT: I'll ask her for you if you like.

ANGIE: I've no money, I don't want you to pay.

KIT: I'll ask her.

ANGIE: She don't like you.

KIT: I still got three pounds birthday money. Did she say she don't like me? I'll go by myself then.

ANGIE: Your mum don't let you. I got to take you.

KIT: She won't know.

ANGIE: You'd be scared who'd sit next to you.

KIT: No I wouldn't. She does like me anyway. Tell me then.

ANGIE: Tell you what?

KIT: It's you she doesn't like.

ANGIE: Well I don't like her so tough shit.

JOYCE (*off*): Angie. Angie. Angie. I know you're out

there. I'm not coming out after you. You come in here. (*Silence. Nothing happens.*)

ANGIE: Last night when I was in bed. I been thinking yesterday could I make things move. You know, make things move by thinking about them without touching them. Last night I was in bed and suddenly a picture fell down off the wall.

KIT: What picture?

ANGIE: My gran, that picture. Not the poster. The photograph in the frame.

KIT: Had you done something to make it fall down?

ANGIE: I must have done.

KIT: But were you thinking about it?

ANGIE: Not about it, but about something.

KIT: I don't think that's very good.

ANGIE: You know the kitten?

KIT: Which one?

ANGIE: There only is one. The dead one.

KIT: What about it?

ANGIE: I heard it last night.

KIT: Where?

ANGIE: Out here. In the dark. What if I left you here in the dark all night?

KIT: You couldn't. I'd go home.

ANGIE: You couldn't.

KIT: I'd / go home.

ANGIE: No you couldn't, not if I said.

KIT: I could.

ANGIE: Then you wouldn't see anything. You'd just be ignorant.

KIT: I can see in the daytime.

ANGIE: No you can't. You can't hear it in the daytime.

KIT: I don't want to hear it.

ANGIE: You're scared that's all.

KIT: I'm not scared of anything.

ANGIE: You're scared of blood.

KIT: It's not the same kitten anyway. You just heard an old cat, / you just heard some old cat.

ANGIE: You don't know what I heard. Or what I saw. You don't know nothing because you're a baby.

KIT: You're sitting on me.

ANGIE: Mind my hair / you silly cunt.

KIT: Stupid fucking cow, I hate you.

ANGIE: I don't care if you do.

KIT: You're horrible.

ANGIE: I'm going to kill my mother and you're going to watch.

KIT: I'm not playing.

ANGIE: You're scared of blood. (*Kit puts her hand under dress, brings it out with blood on her finger.*)

KIT: There, see, I got my own blood, so. (*Angie takes Kit's hand and licks her finger.*)

ANGIE: Now I'm a cannibal. I might turn into a vampire now.

KIT: That picture wasn't nailed up right.

ANGIE: You'll have to do that when I get mine.

KIT: I don't have to.

ANGIE: You're scared.

KIT: I'll do it, I might do it. I don't have to just because you say. I'll be sick on you.

ANGIE: I don't care if you are sick on me, I don't mind sick. I don't mind blood. If I don't get away from here I'm going to die.

KIT: I'm going home.

ANGIE: You can't go through the house. She'll see you.

KIT: I won't tell her.

ANGIE: Oh great, fine.

KIT: I'll say I was by myself. I'll tell her you're at my house and I'm going there to get you.

ANGIE: She knows I'm here, stupid.

KIT: Then why can't I go through the house?

ANGIE: Because I said not.

KIT: My mum don't like you anyway.

ANGIE: I don't want her to like me. She's a slag.

KIT: She is not.

ANGIE: She does it with everyone.

KIT: She does not.

ANGIE: You don't even know what it is.

KIT: Yes I do.

ANGIE: Tell me then.

KIT: We get it all at school, cleverclogs. It's on television. You haven't done it.

ANGIE: How do you know?

KIT: Because I know you haven't.

ANGIE: You know wrong then because I have.

KIT: Who with?

ANGIE: I'm not telling you / who with.

KIT: You haven't anyway.

ANGIE: How do you know?

KIT: Who with?

ANGIE: I'm not telling you.

KIT: You said you told me everything.

ANGIE: I was lying wasn't I.

KIT: Who with? You can't tell me who with be- cause / you never —

ANGIE: Sh.

(*Joyce has come out of the house. She stops halfway across the yard and listens. They listen.*)

JOYCE: You there Angie? Kit? You there Kitty? Want a cup of tea? I've got some chocolate biscuits. Come on now I'll put the kettle on. Want a choccy biccy, Angie? (*They all listen and wait.*) Fucking rotten little cunt. You can stay there and die. I'll lock the door.

(*They all wait. Joyce goes back to the house. Angie and Kit sit in silence for a while.*)

KIT: When there's a war, where's the safest place?

ANGIE: Nowhere.

KIT: New Zealand is, my mum said. Your skin's burned right off. Shall we go to New Zealand?

ANGIE: I'm not staying here.

KIT: Shall we go to New Zealand?

ANGIE: You're not old enough.

KIT: You're not old enough.

ANGIE: I'm old enough to get married.

KIT: You don't want to get married.

ANGIE: No but I'm old enough.

KIT: I'd find out where they were going to drop it and stand right in the place.

ANGIE: You couldn't find out.

KIT: Better than walking round with your skin dragging on the ground. Eugh. / Would you like walking round with your skin dragging on the ground?

ANGIE: You couldn't find out, stupid, it's a secret.

KIT: Where are you going?

ANGIE: I'm not telling you.

KIT: Why?

ANGIE: It's a secret.

KIT: But you tell me all your secrets.

ANGIE: Not the true secrets.

KIT: Yes you do.

ANGIE: No I don't.

KIT: I want to go somewhere away from the war.

ANGIE: Just forget the war.

KIT: I can't.

ANGIE: You have to. It's so boring.

KIT: I'll remember it at night.

ANGIE: I'm going to do something else anyway.

KIT: What? Angie, come on. Angie.

ANGIE: It's a true secret.

KIT: It can't be worse than the kitten. And killing your mother. And the war.

ANGIE: Well I'm not telling you so you can die for all I care.

KIT: My mother says there's something wrong with you playing with someone my age. She says why haven't you got friends your own age. People your own age know there's something funny about you. She says you're a bad influence. She says she's going to speak to your mother. (*Angie twists Kit's arm till she cries out.*)

ANGIE: Say you're a liar.

KIT: She said it not me.

ANGIE: Say you eat shit.

KIT: You can't make me. (*Angie lets go.*)

ANGIE: I don't care anyway. I'm leaving.

KIT: Go on then.

ANGIE: You'll all wake up one morning and find I've gone.

KIT: Good.

ANGIE: I'm not telling you when.

KIT: Go on then.

ANGIE: I'm sorry I hurt you.

KIT: I'm tired.

ANGIE: Do you like me?

KIT: I don't know.

ANGIE: You do like me.

KIT: I'm going home. (*She gets up.*)

ANGIE: No you're not.

KIT: I'm tired.

ANGIE: She'll see you.

KIT: She'll give me a chocolate biscuit.

ANGIE: Kitty.

KIT: Tell me where you're going.

ANGIE: Sit down.

KIT (*sitting down again*): Go on then.

ANGIE: Swear?

KIT: Swear.

ANGIE: I'm going to London. To see my aunt.

KIT: And what?

ANGIE: That's it.

KIT: I see my aunt all the time.

ANGIE: I don't see my aunt.

KIT: What's so special?

ANGIE: It is special. She's special.

KIT: Why?

ANGIE: She is.

KIT: Why?

ANGIE: She is.

KIT: Why?

ANGIE: My mother hates her.

KIT: Why?

ANGIE: Because she does.

KIT: Perhaps she's not very nice.

ANGIE: She is nice.

KIT: How do you know?

ANGIE: Because I know her.

KIT: You said you never see her.

ANGIE: I saw her last year. You saw her.

KIT: Did I?

ANGIE: Never mind.

KIT: I remember her. That aunt. What's so special?

ANGIE: She gets people jobs.

KIT: What's so special?

ANGIE: I think I'm my aunt's child. I think my mother's really my aunt.

KIT: Why?

ANGIE: Because she goes to America, now shut up.

KIT: I've been to London.

ANGIE: Now give us a cuddle and shut up because I'm sick.

KIT: You're sitting on my arm.

(*They curl up in each other's arms. Silence. Joyce comes out of the house and comes up to them quietly.*)

JOYCE: Come on.

KIT: Oh hello.

JOYCE: Time you went home.

KIT: We want to go to the Odeon.

JOYCE: What time?

KIT: Don't know.

JOYCE: What's on?

KIT: Don't know.

JOYCE: Don't know much do you?

KIT: That all right then?

JOYCE: Angie's got to clean her room first.

ANGIE: No I don't.

JOYCE: Yes you do, it's a pigsty.

ANGIE: Well I'm not.

JOYCE: Then you're not going. I don't care.

ANGIE: Well I am going.

JOYCE: You've no money, have you?

ANGIE: Kit's paying anyway.

JOYCE: No she's not.

KIT: I'll help you with your room.

JOYCE: That's nice.

ANGIE: No you won't. You wait here.

KIT: Hurry then.

ANGIE: I'm not hurrying. You just wait. (*Angie goes slowly into the house. Silence.*)

JOYCE: I don't know. (*Silence.*) How's school then?

KIT: All right.

JOYCE: What are you now? Third year?

KIT: Second year.

JOYCE: Your mum says you're good at English. (*Silence.*) Maybe Angie should've stayed on.

KIT: She didn't like it.

JOYCE: I didn't like it. And look at me. If your face fits at school it's going to fit other places too. It wouldn't make no difference to Angie. She's not going to get a job when jobs are hard to get. I'd be sorry for anyone in charge of her. She'd better get married. I don't know who'd have her, mind. She's one of those girls might never leave home. What do you want to be when you grow up, Kit?

KIT: Physicist.

JOYCE: What?

KIT: Nuclear physicist.

JOYCE: Whatever for?

KIT: I could, I'm clever.

JOYCE: I know you're clever, pet. (*Silence.*) I'll make a cup of tea. (*Silence.*) Looks like it's going to rain. (*Silence.*) Don't you have friends your own age?

KIT: Yes.

JOYCE: Well then.

KIT: I'm old for my age.

JOYCE: And Angie's simple is she? She's not simple.

KIT: I love Angie.

JOYCE: She's clever in her own way.

KIT: You can't stop me.

JOYCE: I don't want to.

KIT: You can't, so.

JOYCE: Don't be cheeky, Kitty. She's always kind to little children.

KIT: She's coming so you better leave me alone.

(*Angie comes out. She has changed into an old best dress, slightly small for her.*)

JOYCE: What you put that on for? Have you done your room? You can't clean you room in that.

ANGIE: I looked in the cupboard and it was there.

JOYCE: Of course it was there, it's meant to be there. Is that why it was a surprise, finding something in the right place? I should think she's surprised, wouldn't you, Kit, to find something in her room in the right place.

ANGIE: I decided to wear it.

JOYCE: Not today, why? To clean your room? You're not going to the pictures till you've done your room. You can put your dress on after if you like. (*Angie picks up a brick.*) Have you done your room? You're not getting out of it, you know.

KIT: Angie, let's go.

JOYCE: She's not going till she's done her room.

KIT: It's starting to rain.

JOYCE: Come on, come on then. Hurry and do your room, Angie, and then you can go to the cinema with Kit. Oh it's wet, come on. We'll look up the time in the paper. Does your mother know, Kit, it's going to be a late night for you, isn't it? Hurry up, Angie. You'll spoil your dress. You make me sick. (*Joyce and Kit run into the house. Angie stays where she is. There is the sound of rain. Kit comes out of the house.*)

KIT (*shouting*): Angie. Angie, come on, you'll get wet. (*She comes back to Angie.*)

ANGIE: I put on this dress to kill my mother.

KIT: I suppose you thought you'd do it with a brick.

ANGIE: You can kill people with a brick. (*She puts the brick down.*)

KIT: Well you didn't, so.

ACT II · Scene I

(*"Top Girls" Employment Agency. Monday morning. There are three desks in the main office and a separate small interviewing area. The lights come up in the main office on Win and Nell who have just arrived for work.*)

NELL: Coffee coffee coffee coffee / coffee.

WIN: The roses were smashing. / Mermaid.

NELL: Ohhh.

WIN: Iceberg. He taught me all their names. (*Nell has some coffee now.*)

NELL: Ah. Now then.

WIN: He has one of the finest rose gardens in West Sussex. He exhibits.

NELL: He what?

WIN: His wife was visiting her mother. It was like living together.

NELL: Crafty, you never said.

WIN: He rang on Saturday morning.

NELL: Lucky you were free.

WIN: That's what I told him.

NELL: Did you hell.

WIN: Have you ever seen a really beautiful rose garden?

NELL: I don't like flowers. / I like swimming pools.

WIN: Marilyn. Esther's Baby. They're all called after birds.

NELL: Our friend's late. Celebrating all weekend I bet you.

WIN: I'd call a rose Elvis. Or John Conteh.

NELL: Is Howard in yet?

WIN: If he is he'll be bleeping us with a problem.

NELL: Howard can just hang on to himself.

WIN: Howard's really cut up.

NELL: Howard thinks because he's a fella the job was his as of right. Our Marlene's got far more balls than Howard and that's that.

WIN: Poor little bugger.

NELL: He'll live.

WIN: He'll move on.

NELL: I wouldn't mind a change of air myself.

WIN: Serious?

NELL: I've never been a staying-put lady. Pastures new.

WIN: So who's the pirate?

NELL: There's nothing definite.

WIN: Inquiries?

NELL: There's always inquiries. I'd think I'd got bad breath if there stopped being inquiries. Most of them can't afford me. Or you.

WIN: I'm all right for the time being. Unless I go to Australia.

NELL: There's not a lot of room upward.

WIN: Marlene's filled it up.

NELL: Good luck to her. Unless there's some prospects moneywise.

WIN: You can but ask.

NELL: Can always but ask.

WIN: So what have we got? I've got a Mr. Holden I saw last week.

NELL: Any use?

WIN: Pushy. Bit of a cowboy.

NELL: Goodlooker?

WIN: Good dresser.

NELL: High flyer?

WIN: That's his general idea certainly but I'm not sure he's got it up there.

NELL: Prestel wants six flyers and I've only seen two and a half.

WIN: He's making a bomb on the road but he thinks it's time for an office. I sent him to IBM but he didn't get it.

NELL: Prestel's on the road.

WIN: He's not overbright.

NELL: Can he handle an office?

WIN: Provided his secretary can punctuate he should go far.

NELL: Bear Prestel in mind then, I might put my head round the door. I've got that poor little nerd I should never had said I could help. Tender heart me.

WIN: Tender like old boots. How old?

NELL: Yes well forty-five.

WIN: Say no more.

NELL: He knows his place, he's not after calling himself a manager, he's just a poor little bod wants a better commission and a bit of sunshine.

WIN: Don't we all.

NELL: He's just got to relocate. He's got a bungalow in Dymchurch.

WIN: And his wife says.

NELL: The lady wife wouldn't care to relocate. She's going through the change.

WIN: It's his funeral, don't waste your time.

NELL: I don't waste a lot.

WIN: Good weekend you?

NELL: You could say.

WIN: Which one?

NELL: One Friday, one Saturday.

WIN: Aye — aye.

NELL: Sunday night I watched telly.

WIN: Which of them do you like best really?

NELL: Sunday was best, I like the Ovaltine.

WIN: Holden, Barker, Gardner, Duke.

NELL: I've a lady here thinks she can sell.

WIN: Taking her on?

NELL: She's had some jobs.

WIN: Services?

NELL: No, quite heavy stuff, electric.

WIN: Tough bird like us.

NELL: We could do with a few more here.

WIN: There's nothing going here.

NELL: No but I always want the tough ones when I see them. Hang on to them.

WIN: I think we're plenty.

NELL: Derek asked me to marry him again.

WIN: He doesn't know when he's beaten.

NELL: I told him I'm not going to play house, not even in Ascot.

WIN: Mind you, you could play house.

NELL: If I chose to play house I would play house ace.

WIN: You could marry him and go on working.

NELL: I could go on working and not marry him.

(*Marlene arrives.*)

MARLENE: Morning ladies. (*Win and Nell cheer and whistle.*) Mind my head.

NELL: Coffee coffee coffee.

WIN: We're tactfully not mentioning you're late.

MARLENE: Fucking tube.

WIN: We've heard that one.

NELL: We've used that one.

WIN: It's the top executive doesn't come in as early as the poor working girl.

MARLENE: Pass the sugar and shut your face, pet.

WIN: Well I'm delighted.

NELL: Howard's looking sick.

WIN: Howard is sick. He's got ulcers and heart. He told me.

NELL: He'll have to stop then, won't he?

WIN: Stop what?

NELL: Smoking, drinking, shouting. Working.

WIN: Well, working.

NELL: We're just looking through the day.

MARLENE: I'm doing some of Pam's ladies. They've been piling up while she's away.

NELL: Half a dozen little girls and an arts graduate who can't type.

WIN: I spent the whole weekend at his place in Sussex.

NELL: She fancies his rose garden.

WIN: I had to lie down in the back of the car so the neighbors wouldn't see me go in.

NELL: You're kidding.

WIN: It was funny.

NELL: Fuck that for a joke.

WIN: It was funny.

MARLENE: Anyway they'd see you in the garden.

WIN: The garden has extremely high walls.

NELL: I think I'll tell the wife.

WIN: Like hell.

NELL: She might leave him and you could have the rose garden.

WIN: The minute it's not a secret I'm out on my ear.

NELL: Don't know why you bother.

WIN: Bit of fun.

NELL: I think it's time you went to Australia.

WIN: I think it's pushy Mr. Holden time.

NELL: If you've any really pretty bastards, Marlene, I want some for Prestel.

MARLENE: I might have one this afternoon. This morning it's all Pam's secretarial.

NELL: Not long now and you'll be upstairs watching over us all.

MARLENE: Do you feel bad about it?

NELL: I don't like coming second.

MARLENE: Who does?

WIN: We'd rather it was you than Howard. We're glad for you, aren't we, Nell?

NELL: Oh yes. Aces.

(*Louise enters the interviewing area. The lights crossfade to Win and Louise in the interviewing area. Nell exits.*)

WIN: Now, Louise, hello, I have your details here. You've been very loyal to the one job I see.

LOUISE: Yes I have.

WIN: Twenty-one years is a long time in one place.

LOUISE: I feel it is. I feel it's time to move on.

WIN: And you are what age now?

LOUISE: I'm in my early forties.

WIN: Exactly?

LOUISE: Forty-six.

WIN: It's not necessarily a handicap, well it is of course we have to face that, but it's not necessarily a disabling handicap, experience does count for something.

LOUISE: I hope so.

WIN: Now between ourselves is there any trouble, any reason why you're leaving that wouldn't appear on the form?

LOUISE: Nothing like that.

WIN: Like what?

LOUISE: Nothing at all.

WIN: No long-term understandings come to a sudden end, making for an insupportable atmosphere?

LOUISE: I've always completely avoided anything like that at all.

WIN: No personality clashes with your immediate superiors or inferiors?

LOUISE: I've always taken care to get on very well with everyone.

WIN: I only ask because it can affect the reference and it also affects your motivation, I want to be quite clear why you're moving on. So I take it the job itself no longer satisfies you. Is it the money?

LOUISE: It's partly the money. It's not so much the money.

WIN: Nine thousand is very respectable. Have you dependants?

LOUISE: No, no dependants. My mother died.

WIN: So why are you making a change?

LOUISE: Other people make changes.

WIN: But why are you, now, after spending most of your life in the one place?

LOUISE: There you are, I've lived for that company, I've given my life really you could say because I haven't had a great deal of social life, I've worked in the evenings. I haven't had office entanglements for the very reason you just mentioned and if you are committed to your work you don't move in many other circles. I had management status from the age of twenty-seven and you'll appreciate what that means. I've built up a department. And there it is, it works extremely well, and I feel I'm stuck there. I've spent twenty years in middle management. I've seen young men who I trained go on, in my

own company or elsewhere, to higher things. Nobody notices me, I don't expect it, I don't attract
attention by making mistakes, everybody takes it
for granted that my work is perfect. They will
notice me when I go, they will be sorry I think to
lose me, they will offer me more money of course,
I will refuse. They will see when I've gone what I
was doing for them.

WIN: If they offer you more money you won't stay?

LOUISE: No I won't.

WIN: Are you the only woman?

LOUISE: Apart from the girls of course, yes. There was
one, she was my assistant, it was the only time I
took on a young woman assistant, I always had
my doubts. I don't care greatly for working with
women, I think I pass as a man at work. But I did
take on this young woman, her qualifications were
excellent, and she did well, she got a department
of her own, and left the company for a competitor
where she's now on the board and good luck to
her. She has a different style, she's a new kind of
attractive well dressed — I don't mean I don't dress
properly. But there is a kind of woman who is
thirty now who grew up in a different climate. They
are not so careful. They take themselves for granted.
I have had to justify my existence every minute,
and I have done so, I have proved — well.

WIN: Let's face it, vacancies are ones where you'll be
in competition with younger men. And there are
companies that will value your experience enough
that you'll be in with a chance. There are also fields
that are easier for a woman, there is a cosmetic
company here where your experience might be relevant. It's eight and a half, I don't know if that
appeals.

LOUISE: I've proved I can earn money. It's more important to get away. I feel it's now or never. I
sometimes / think —

WIN: You shouldn't talk too much at an interview.

LOUISE: I don't. I don't normally talk about myself.
I know very well how to handle myself in an office
situation. I only talk to you because it seems to
me this is different, it's your job to understand me,
surely. You asked the questions.

WIN: I think I understand you sufficiently.

LOUISE: Well good, that's good.

WIN: Do you drink?

LOUISE: Certainly not. I'm not a teetotaler, I think
that's very suspect, it's seen as being an alcoholic
if you're teetotal. What do you mean? I don't drink.
Why?

WIN: I drink.

LOUISE: I don't.

WIN: Good for you.

(*The lights crossfade to the main office with Marlene*

*sitting at her desk. Win and Louise exit. Angie arrives
in the main office.*)

ANGIE: Hello.

MARLENE: Have you an appointment?

ANGIE: It's me. I've come.

MARLENE: What? It's not Angie?

ANGIE: It was hard to find this place. I got lost.

MARLENE: How did you get past the receptionist? The
girl on the desk, didn't she try to stop you?

ANGIE: What desk?

MARLENE: Never mind.

ANGIE: I just walked in. I was looking for you.

MARLENE: Well you found me.

ANGIE: Yes.

MARLENE: So where's your mum? Are you up in town
for the day?

ANGIE: Not really.

MARLENE: Sit down. Do you feel all right?

ANGIE: Yes thank you.

MARLENE: So where's Joyce?

ANGIE: She's at home.

MARLENE: Did you come up on a school trip then?

ANGIE: I've left school.

MARLENE: Did you come up with a friend?

ANGIE: No. There's just me.

MARLENE: You came up by yourself, that's fun. What
have you been doing? Shopping? Tower of London?

ANGIE: No, I just come here. I come to you.

MARLENE: That's very nice of you to think of paying
your aunty a visit. There's not many nieces make
that the first port of call. Would you like a cup of
coffee?

ANGIE: No thank you.

MARLENE: Tea, orange?

ANGIE: No thank you.

MARLENE: Do you feel all right?

ANGIE: Yes thank you.

MARLENE: Are you tired from the journey?

ANGIE: Yes, I'm tired from the journey.

MARLENE: You sit there for a bit then. How's Joyce?

ANGIE: She's all right.

MARLENE: Same as ever.

ANGIE: Oh yes.

MARLENE: Unfortunately you've picked a day when
I'm rather busy, if there's ever a day when I'm not,
or I'd take you out to lunch and we'd go to Madame
Tussaud's. We could go shopping. What time do
you have to be back? Have you got a day return?

ANGIE: No.

MARLENE: So what train are you going back on?

ANGIE: I came on the bus.

MARLENE: So what bus are you going back on? Are
you staying the night?

ANGIE: Yes.

MARLENE: Who are you staying with? Do you want me to put you up for the night, is that it?

ANGIE: Yes please.

MARLENE: I haven't got a spare bed.

ANGIE: I can sleep on the floor.

MARLENE: You can sleep on the sofa.

ANGIE: Yes please.

MARLENE: I do think Joyce might have phoned me. It's like her.

ANGIE: This is where you work is it?

MARLENE: It's where I have been working the last two years but I'm going to move into another office.

ANGIE: It's lovely.

MARLENE: My new office is nicer than this. There's just the one big desk in it for me.

ANGIE: Can I see it?

MARLENE: Not now, no, there's someone else in it now. But he's leaving at the end of next week and I'm going to do his job.

ANGIE: Is that good?

MARLENE: Yes, it's very good.

ANGIE: Are you going to be in charge?

MARLENE: Yes I am.

ANGIE: I knew you would be.

MARLENE: How did you know?

ANGIE: I knew you'd be in charge of everything.

MARLENE: Not quite everything.

ANGIE: You will be.

MARLENE: Well we'll see.

ANGIE: Can I see it next week then?

MARLENE: Will you still be here next week?

ANGIE: Yes.

MARLENE: Don't you have to go home?

ANGIE: No.

MARLENE: Why not?

ANGIE: It's all right.

MARLENE: Is it all right?

ANGIE: Yes, don't worry about it.

MARLENE: Does Joyce know where you are?

ANGIE: Yes of course she does.

MARLENE: Well does she?

ANGIE: Don't worry about it.

MARLENE: How long are you planning to stay with me then?

ANGIE: You know when you came to see us last year?

MARLENE: Yes, that was nice wasn't it.

ANGIE: That was the best day of my whole life.

MARLENE: So how long are you planning to stay?

ANGIE: Don't you want me?

MARLENE: Yes yes, I just wondered.

ANGIE: I won't stay if you don't want me.

MARLENE: No, of course you can stay.

ANGIE: I'll sleep on the floor. I won't be any bother.

MARLENE: Don't get upset.

ANGIE: I'm not, I'm not. Don't worry about it.

(*Mrs. Kidd comes in.*)

MRS. KIDD: Excuse me.

MARLENE: Yes.

MRS. KIDD: Excuse me.

MARLENE: Can I help you?

MRS. KIDD: Excuse me bursting in on you like this but I have to talk to you.

MARLENE: I am engaged at the moment. / If you could go to reception —

MRS. KIDD: I'm Rosemary Kidd, Howard's wife, you don't recognize me but we did meet, I remember you of course / but you wouldn't —

MARLENE: Yes of course, Mrs. Kidd, I'm sorry, we did meet. Howard's about somewhere I expect, have you looked in his office?

MRS. KIDD: Howard's not about, no. I'm afraid it's you I've come to see if I could have a minute or two.

MARLENE: I do have an appointment in five minutes.

MRS. KIDD: This won't take five minutes. I'm very sorry. It is a matter of some urgency.

MARLENE: Well of course. What can I do for you?

MRS. KIDD: I just wanted a chat, an informal chat. It's not something I can simply — I'm sorry if I'm interrupting your work. I know office work isn't like housework / which is all interruptions.

MARLENE: No no, this is my niece. Angie. Mrs. Kidd.

MRS. KIDD: Very pleased to meet you.

ANGIE: Very well thank you.

MRS. KIDD: Howard's not in today.

MARLENE: Isn't he?

MRS. KIDD: He's feeling poorly.

MARLENE: I didn't know. I'm sorry to hear that.

MRS. KIDD: The fact is he's in a state of shock. About what's happened.

MARLENE: What has happened?

MRS. KIDD: You should know if anyone. I'm referring to you been appointed managing director instead of Howard. He hasn't been at all well all weekend. He hasn't slept for three nights. I haven't slept.

MARLENE: I'm sorry to hear that, Mrs. Kidd. Has he thought of taking sleeping pills?

MRS. KIDD: It's very hard when someone has worked all these years.

MARLENE: Business life is full of little setbacks. I'm sure Howard knows that. He'll bounce back in a day or two. We all bounce back.

MRS. KIDD: If you could see him you'd know what I'm talking about. What's it going to do to him working for a woman? I think if it was a man he'd get over it as something normal.

MARLENE: I think he's going to have to get over it.

MRS. KIDD: It's me that bears the brunt. I'm not the one that's been promoted. I put him first every inch of the way. And now what do I get? You women this, you women that. It's not my fault. You're going to have to be very careful how you handle him. He's very hurt.

MARLENE: Naturally I'll be tactful and pleasant to him, you don't start pushing someone around. I'll consult him over any decisions affecting his department. But that's no different, Mrs. Kidd, from any of my other colleagues.

MRS. KIDD: I think it is different, because he's a man.

MARLENE: I'm not quite sure why you came to see me.

MRS. KIDD: I had to do something.

MARLENE: Well you've done it, you've seen me. I think that's probably all we've time for. I'm sorry he's been taking it out on you. He really is a shit, Howard.

MRS. KIDD: But he's got a family to support. He's got three children. It's only fair.

MARLENE: Are you suggesting I give up the job to him then?

MRS. KIDD: It had crossed my mind if you were unavailable after all for some reason, he would be the natural second choice I think, don't you? I'm not asking.

MARLENE: Good.

MRS. KIDD: You mustn't tell him I came. He's very proud.

MARLENE: If he doesn't like what's happening here he can go and work somewhere else.

MRS. KIDD: Is that a threat?

MARLENE: I'm sorry but I do have some work to do.

MRS. KIDD: It's not that easy, a man of Howard's age. You don't care. I thought he was going too far but he's right. You're one of these ballbreakers, / that's what you

MARLENE: I'm sorry but I do have some work to do.

MRS. KIDD: are. You'll end up miserable and lonely. You're not natural.

MARLENE: Could you please piss off?

MRS. KIDD: I thought if I saw you at least I'd be doing something. (*Mrs. Kidd goes.*)

MARLENE: I've got to go and do some work now. Will you come back later?

ANGIE: I think you were wonderful.

MARLENE: I've got to go and do some work now.

ANGIE: You told her to piss off.

MARLENE: Will you come back later?

ANGIE: Can't I stay here?

MARLENE: Don't you want to go sightseeing?

ANGIE: I'd rather stay here.

MARLENE: You can stay here I suppose, if it's not boring.

ANGIE: It's where I most want to be in the world.

MARLENE: I'll see you later then.

(*Marlene goes. Shona and Nell enter the interviewing area. Angie sits at Win's desk. The lights crossfade to Nell and Shona in the interviewing area.*)

NELL: Is this right? You are Shona?

SHONA: Yeh.

NELL: It says here you're twenty-nine.

SHONA: Yeh.

NELL: Too many late nights, me. So you've been where you are for four years, Shona, you're earning six basic and three commission. So what's the problem?

SHONA: No problem.

NELL: Why do you want a change?

SHONA: Just a change.

NELL: Change of product, change of area?

SHONA: Both.

NELL: But you're happy on the road?

SHONA: I like driving.

NELL: You're not after management status?

SHONA: I would like management status.

NELL: You'd be interested in titular management status but not come off the road?

SHONA: I want to be on the road, yeh.

NELL: So how many calls have you been making a day?

SHONA: Six.

NELL: And what proportion of those are successful?

SHONA: Six.

NELL: That's hard to believe.

SHONA: Four.

NELL: You find it easy to get the initial interest do you?

SHONA: Oh yeh, I get plenty of initial interest.

NELL: And what about closing?

SHONA: I close, don't I?

NELL: Because that's what an employer is going to have doubts about with a lady as I needn't tell you, whether she's got the guts to push through to a closing situation. They think we're too nice. They think we listen to the buyer's doubts. They think we consider his needs and his feelings.

SHONA: I never consider people's feelings.

NELL: I was selling for six years, I can sell anything, I've sold in three continents, and I'm jolly as they come but I'm not very nice.

SHONA: I'm not very nice.

NELL: What sort of time do you have on the road with the other reps? Get on all right? Handle the chat?

SHONA: I get on. Keep myself to myself.

NELL: Fairly much of a loner are you?

SHONA: Sometimes.

NELL: So what field are you interested in?

SHONA: Computers.

NELL: That's a top field as you know and you'll be

up against some very slick fellas there, there's some very pretty boys in computers, it's an American-style field.

SHONA: That's why I want to do it.

NELL: Video systems appeal? That's a high-flying situation.

SHONA: Video systems appeal OK.

NELL: Because Prestel have half a dozen vacancies I'm looking to fill at the moment. We're talking in the area of ten to fifteen thousand here and upwards.

SHONA: Sounds OK.

NELL: I've half a mind to go for it myself. But it's good money here if you've got the top clients. Could you fancy it do you think?

SHONA: Work here?

NELL: I'm not in a position to offer, there's nothing officially going just now, but we're always on the lookout. There's not that many of us. We could keep in touch.

SHONA: I like driving.

NELL: So the Prestel appeals?

SHONA: Yeh.

NELL: What about ties?

SHONA: No ties.

NELL: So relocation wouldn't be a problem.

SHONA: No problem.

NELL: So just fill me in a bit more could you about what you've been doing.

SHONA: What I've been doing. It's all down there.

NELL: The bare facts are down here but I've got to present you to an employer.

SHONA: I'm twenty-nine years old.

NELL: So it says here.

SHONA: We look young. Youngness runs in the family in our family.

NELL: So just describe your present job for me.

SHONA: My present job at present. I have a car. I have a Porsche. I go up the M1 a lot. Burn up the M1 a lot. Straight up the M1 in the fast lane to where the clients are, Staffordshire, Yorkshire, I do a lot in Yorkshire. I'm selling electric things. Like dishwashers, washing machines, stainless steel tubs are a feature and the reliability of the program. After sales service, we offer a very good after sales service, spare parts, plenty of spare parts. And fridges, I sell a lot of fridges specially in the summer. People want to buy fridges in the summer because of the heat melting the butter and you get fed up standing the milk in a basin of cold water with a cloth over, stands to reason people don't want to do that in this day and age. So I sell a lot of them. Big ones with big freezers. Big freezers. And I stay in hotels at night when I'm away from home. On my expense account. I stay in various hotels. They know me, the ones I go to. I check in, have a bath,

have a shower. Then I go down to the bar, have a gin and tonic, have a chat. Then I go into the dining room and have dinner. I usually have fillet steak and mushrooms, I like mushrooms. I like smoked salmon very much. I like having a salad on the side. Green salad. I don't like tomatoes.

NELL: Christ what a waste of time.

SHONA: Beg your pardon?

NELL: Not a word of this is true, is it?

SHONA: How do you mean?

NELL: You just filled in the form with a pack of lies.

SHONA: Not exactly.

NELL: How old are you?

SHONA: Twenty-nine.

NELL: Nineteen?

SHONA: Twenty-one.

NELL: And what jobs have you done? Have you done any?

SHONA: I could though, I bet you.

(*The lights crossfade to the main office with Angie sitting as before. Win comes in to the main office. Shona and Nell exit.*)

WIN: Who's sitting in my chair?

ANGIE: What? Sorry.

WIN: Who's been eating my porridge?

ANGIE: What?

WIN: It's all right, I saw Marlene. Angie, isn't it? I'm Win. And I'm not going out for lunch because I'm knackered. I'm going to set me down here and have a yogurt. Do you like yogurt?

ANGIE: No.

WIN: That's good because I've only got one. Are you hungry?

ANGIE: No.

WIN: There's a café on the corner.

ANGIE: No thank you. Do you work here?

WIN: How did you guess?

ANGIE: Because you look as if you might work here and you're sitting at the desk. Have you always worked here?

WIN: No I was headhunted. That means I was working for another outfit like this and this lot came and offered me more money. I broke my contract, there was a hell of a stink. There's not many top ladies about. Your aunty's a smashing bird.

ANGIE: Yes I know.

MARLENE: Fan are you? Fan of your aunty's?

ANGIE: Do you think I could work here?

WIN: Not at the moment.

ANGIE: How do I start?

WIN: What can you do?

ANGIE: I don't know. Nothing.

WIN: Type?

ANGIE: Not very well. The letters jump up when I do

capitals. I was going to do a CSE° in commerce but I didn't.

WIN: What have you got?

ANGIE: What?

WIN: CSE's, O's.

ANGIE: Nothing, none of that. Did you do all that?

WIN: Oh yes, all that, and a science degree funnily enough. I started out doing medical research but there's no money in it. I thought I'd go abroad. Did you know they sell Coca Cola in Russia and Pepsi-Cola in China? You don't have to be qualified as much as you might think. Men are awful bull-shitters, they like to make out jobs are harder than they are. Any job I ever did I started doing it better than the rest of the crowd and they didn't like it. So I'd get unpopular and I'd have a drink to cheer myself up. I lived with a fella and supported him for four years, he couldn't get work. After that I went to California. I like the sunshine. Americans know how to live. This country's too slow. Then I went to Mexico, still in sales, but it's no country for a single lady. I came home, went bonkers for a bit, thought I was five different people, got over that all right, the psychiatrist said I was perfectly sane and highly intelligent. Got married in a moment of weakness and he's inside now, he's been inside four years, and I've not been to see him too much this last year. I like this better than sales, I'm not really that aggressive. I started thinking sales was a good job if you want to meet people, but you're meeting people that don't want to meet you. It's no good if you like being liked. Here your clients want to meet you because you're the one doing them some good. They hope. (*Angie has fallen asleep. Nell comes in.*)

NELL: You're talking to yourself, sunshine.

WIN: So what's new?

NELL: Who is this?

WIN: Marlene's little niece.

NELL: What's she got, brother, sister? She never talks about her family.

WIN: I was telling her my life story.

NELL: Violins?

WIN: No, success story.

NELL: You've heard Howard's had a heart attack?

WIN: No, when?

NELL: I heard just now. He hadn't come in, he was at home, he's gone to hospital. He's not dead. His wife was here, she rushed off in a cab.

WIN: Too much butter, too much smoke. We must send him some flowers. (*Marlene comes in.*) You've heard about Howard?

MARLENE: Poor sod.

CSE: Certificate of Secondary Education.

NELL: Lucky he didn't get the job if that's what his health's like.

MARLENE: Is she asleep?

WIN: She wants to work here.

MARLENE: Packer in Tesco more like.

WIN: She's a nice kid. Isn't she?

MARLENE: She's a bit thick. She's a bit funny.

WIN: She thinks you're wonderful.

MARLENE: She's not going to make it.

Scene II

(*Joyce's kitchen. Sunday evening, a year earlier. The lights come up on Joyce, Angie, and Marlene. Marlene is taking presents out of bright carrier bag. Angie has already opened a box of chocolates.*)

MARLENE: Just a few little things. / I've

JOYCE: There's no need.

MARLENE: no memory for birthdays have I, and Christmas seems to slip by. So I think I owe Angie a few presents.

JOYCE: What do you say?

ANGIE: Thank you very much. Thank you very much, Aunty Marlene. (*She opens a present. It is the dress from Act I, new.*) Oh look, Mum, isn't it lovely?

MARLENE: I don't know if it's the right size. She's grown up since I saw her. / I knew she was always

ANGIE: Isn't it lovely?

MARLENE: tall for her age.

JOYCE: She's a big lump.

MARLENE: Hold it up, Angie, let's see.

ANGIE: I'll put it on, shall I?

MARLENE: Yes, try it on.

JOYCE: Go on to your room then, we don't want / a strip show thank you.

ANGIE: Of course I'm going to my room, what do you think. Look, Mum, here's something for you. Open it, go on. What is it? Can I open it for you?

JOYCE: Yes, you open it, pet.

ANGIE: Don't you want to open it yourself? / Go on.

JOYCE: I don't mind, you can do it.

ANGIE: It's something hard. It's — what is it? A bottle. Drink is it? No, it's what? Perfume, look. What a lot. Open it, look, let's smell it. Oh it's strong. It's lovely. Put it on me. How do you do it? Put it on me.

JOYCE: You're too young.

ANGIE: I can play wearing it like dressing up.

JOYCE: And you're too old for that. Here, give it here, I'll do it, you'll tip the whole bottle over your-self / and we'll have you smelling all summer.

ANGIE: Put it on you. Do I smell? Put it on Aunty too. Put it on Aunty too. Let's all smell.

MARLENE: I didn't know what you'd like.

JOYCE: There's no danger I'd have it already, / that's one thing.

ANGIE: Now we all smell the same.

MARLENE: It's a bit of nonsense.

JOYCE: It's very kind of you Marlene, you shouldn't.

ANGIE: Now I'll put on the dress and then we'll see. (*Angie goes.*)

JOYCE: You've caught me on the hop with the place in the mess. / If you'd let me

MARLENE: That doesn't matter.

JOYCE: know you was coming I'd have got something in to eat. We had our dinner dinnertime. We're just going to have a cup of tea. You could have an egg.

MARLENE: No, I'm not hungry. Tea's fine.

JOYCE: I don't expect you take sugar.

MARLENE: Why not?

JOYCE: You take care of yourself.

MARLENE: How do you mean you didn't know I was coming?

JOYCE: You could have written. I know we're not on the phone but we're not completely in the dark ages, / we do have a postman.

MARLENE: But you asked me to come.

JOYCE: How did I ask you to come?

MARLENE: Angie said when she phoned up.

JOYCE: Angie phoned up, did she.

MARLENE: Was it just Angie's idea?

JOYCE: What did she say?

MARLENE: She said you wanted me to come and see you. / It was a couple of

JOYCE: Ha.

MARLENE: weeks ago. How was I to know that's a ridiculous idea? My diary's always full a couple of weeks ahead so we fixed it for this weekend. I was meant to get here earlier but I was held up. She gave me messages from you.

JOYCE: Didn't you wonder why I didn't phone you myself?

MARLENE: She said you didn't like using the phone. You're shy on the phone and can't use it. I don't know what you're like, do I?

JOYCE: Are there people who can't use the phone?

MARLENE: I expect so.

JOYCE: I haven't met any.

MARLENE: Why should I think she was lying?

JOYCE: Because she's like what she's like.

MARLENE: How do I know / what she's like?

JOYCE: It's not my fault you don't know what she's like. You never come and see her.

MARLENE: Well I have now / and you don't seem over the moon.*

JOYCE: Good. *Well I'd have got a cake if she'd told me. (*Pause.*)

MARLENE: I did wonder why you wanted to see me.

JOYCE: I didn't want to see you.

MARLENE: Yes, I know. Shall I go?

JOYCE: I don't mind seeing you.

MARLENE: Great, I feel really welcome.

JOYCE: You can come and see Angie any time you like, I'm not stopping you. / You

MARLENE: Ta ever so.

JOYCE: know where we are. You're the one went away, not me. I'm right here where I was. And will be a few years yet I shouldn't wonder.

MARLENE: All right. All right. (*Joyce gives Marlene a cup of tea.*)

JOYCE: Tea.

MARLENE: Sugar? (*Joyce passes Marlene the sugar.*) It's very quiet down here.

JOYCE: I expect you'd notice it.

MARLENE: The air smells different too.

JOYCE: That's the scent.

MARLENE: No, I mean walking down the lane.

JOYCE: What sort of air you get in London then?

(*Angie comes in, wearing the dress. It fits.*)

MARLENE: Oh, very pretty. / You do look pretty, Angie.

JOYCE: That fits all right.

MARLENE: Do you like the color?

ANGIE: Beautiful. Beautiful.

JOYCE: You better take it off, / you'll get it dirty.

ANGIE: I want to wear it. I want to wear it.

MARLENE: It is for wearing after all. You can't just hang it up and look at it.

ANGIE: I love it.

JOYCE: Well if you must you must.

ANGIE: If someone asks me what's my favorite color I'll tell them it's this. Thank you very much, Aunty Marlene.

MARLENE: You didn't tell your mum you asked me down.

ANGIE: I wanted it to be a surprise.

JOYCE: I'll give you a surprise / one of these days.

ANGIE: I thought you'd like to see her. She hasn't been here since I was nine. People do see their aunts.

MARLENE: Is it that long? Doesn't time fly.

ANGIE: I wanted to.

JOYCE: I'm not cross.

ANGIE: Are you glad?

JOYCE: I smell nicer anyhow, don't I?

(*Kit comes in without saying anything, as if she lived there.*)

MARLENE: I think it was a good idea, Angie, about time. We are sisters after all. It's a pity to let that go.

JOYCE: This is Kitty, / who lives up the road. This is Angie's Aunty Marlene.

KIT: What's that?

ANGIE: It's a present. Do you like it?

KIT: It's all right. / Are you coming out?*

MARLENE: Hello, Kitty.

ANGIE: *No.

KIT: What's that smell?

ANGIE: It's a present.

KIT: It's horrible. Come on.*

MARLENE: Have a chocolate.

ANGIE: *No, I'm busy.

KIT: Coming out later?

ANGIE: No.

KIT (*to Marlene*): Hello. (*Kit goes without a chocolate.*)

JOYCE: She's a little girl Angie sometimes plays with because she's the only child lives really close. She's like a little sister to her really. Angie's good with little children.

MARLENE: Do you want to work with children, Angie? / Be a teacher or a nursery nurse?

JOYCE: I don't think she's ever thought of it.

MARLENE: What do you want to do?

JOYCE: She hasn't an idea in her head what she wants to do. / Lucky to get anything.

MARLENE: Angie?

JOYCE: She's not clever like you. (*Pause.*)

MARLENE: I'm not clever, just pushy.

JOYCE: True enough. (*Marlene takes a bottle of whiskey out of the bag.*) I don't drink spirits.

ANGIE: You do at Christmas.

JOYCE: It's not Christmas, is it?

ANGIE: It's better than Christmas.

MARLENE: Glasses?

JOYCE: Just a small one then.

MARLENE: Do you want some, Angie?

ANGIE: I can't, can I?

JOYCE: Taste it if you want. You won't like it. (*Angie tastes it.*)

ANGIE: Mmm.

MARLENE: We got drunk together the night your grandfather died.

JOYCE: We did not get drunk.

MARLENE: I got drunk. You were just overcome with grief.

JOYCE: I still keep up the grave with flowers.

MARLENE: Do you really?

JOYCE: Why wouldn't I?

MARLENE: Have you seen Mother?

JOYCE: Of course I've seen Mother.

MARLENE: I mean lately.

JOYCE: Of course I've seen her lately, I go every Thursday.

MARLENE (*to Angie*): Do you remember your grandfather?

ANGIE: He got me out of the bath one night in a towel.

MARLENE: Did he? I don't think he ever gave me a bath. Did he give you a bath, Joyce? He probably got soft in his old age. Did you like him?

ANGIE: Yes of course.

MARLENE: Why?

ANGIE: What?

MARLENE: So what's the news? How's Mrs. Paisley? Still going crazily? / And Dorothy. What happened to Dorothy?*

ANGIE: Who's Mrs. Paisley?

JOYCE: *She went to Canada.

MARLENE: Did she? What to do?

JOYCE: I don't know. She just went to Canada.

MARLENE: Well / good for her.

ANGIE: Mr. Connolly killed his wife.

MARLENE: What, Connolly at Whitegates?

ANGIE: They found her body in the garden. / Under the cabbages.

MARLENE: He was always so proper.

JOYCE: Stuck up git, Connolly. Best lawyer money could buy but he couldn't get out of it. She was carrying on with Matthew.

MARLENE: How old's Matthew then?

JOYCE: Twenty-one. / He's got a motorbike.

MARLENE: I think he's about six.

ANGIE: How can he be six? He's six years older than me. / If he was six I'd be nothing, I'd be just born this minute.

JOYCE: Your aunty knows that, she's just being silly. She means it's so long since she's been here she's forgotten about Matthew.

ANGIE: You were here for my birthday when I was nine. I had a pink cake. Kit was only five then, she was four, she hadn't started school yet. She could read already when she went to school. You remember my birthday? / You remember me?

MARLENE: Yes, I remember the cake.

ANGIE: You remember me?

MARLENE: Yes, I remember you.

ANGIE: And Mum and Dad was there, and Kit was.

MARLENE: Yes, how is your dad? Where is he tonight? Up the pub?

JOYCE: No, he's not here.

MARLENE: I can see he's not here.

JOYCE: He moved out.

MARLENE: What? When did he? / Just recently?*

ANGIE: Didn't you know that? You don't know much.

JOYCE: *No, it must be three years ago. Don't be rude, Angie.

ANGIE: I'm not, am I, Aunty? What else don't you know?

JOYCE: You was in America or somewhere. You sent a postcard.

ANGIE: I've got that in my room. It's the Grand Canyon. Do you want to see it? Shall I get it? I can get it for you.

MARLENE: Yes, all right. (*Angie goes.*)

JOYCE: You could be married with twins for all I know. You must have affairs and break up and I don't need to know about any of that so I don't see what the fuss is about.

MARLENE: What fuss? (*Angie comes back with the postcard.*)

ANGIE: "Driving across the states for a new job in L.A. It's a long way but the car goes very fast. It's very hot. Wish you were here. Love from Aunty Marlene."

JOYCE: Did you make a lot of money?

MARLENE: I spent a lot.

ANGIE: I want to go to America. Will you take me?

JOYCE: She's not going to America, she's been to America, stupid.

ANGIE: She might go again, stupid. It's not something you do once. People who go keep going all the time, back and forth on jets. They go on Concorde and Laker and get jet lag. Will you take me?

MARLENE: I'm not planning a trip.

ANGIE: Will you let me know?

JOYCE: Angie, / you're getting silly.

ANGIE; I want to be American.

JOYCE: It's time you were in bed.

ANGIE: No it's not. / I don't have to go to bed at all tonight.

JOYCE: School in the morning.

ANGIE: I'll wake up.

JOYCE: Come on now, you know how you get.

ANGIE: How do I get? / I don't get anyhow.*

JOYCE: Angie. *Are you staying the night?

MARLENE: Yes, if that's all right. / I'll see you in the morning.

ANGIE: You can have my bed. I'll sleep on the sofa.

JOYCE: You will not, you'll sleep in your bed. / Think

ANGIE: Mum.

JOYCE: I can't see through that? I can just see you going to sleep / with us talking.

ANGIE: I would, I would go to sleep, I'd love that.

JOYCE: I'm going to get cross, Angie.

ANGIE: I want to show her something.

JOYCE: Then bed.

ANGIE: It's a secret.

JOYCE: Then I expect it's in your room so off you go. Give us a shout when you're ready for bed and your aunty'll be up and see you.

ANGIE: Will you?

MARLENE: Yes of course. (*Angie goes. Silence.*) It's cold tonight.

JOYCE: Will you be all right on the sofa? You can / have my bed.

MARLENE: The sofa's fine.

JOYCE: Yes the forecast said rain tonight but it's held off.

MARLENE: I was going to walk down to the estuary but I've left it a bit late. Is it just the same?

JOYCE: They cut down the hedges a few years back. Is that since you were here?

MARLENE: But it's not changed down the end, all the mud? And the reeds? We used to pick them up when they were bigger than us. Are there still lapwings?

JOYCE: You get strangers walking there on a Sunday. I expect they're looking at the mud and the lapwings, yes.

MARLENE: You could have left.

JOYCE: Who says I wanted to leave?

MARLENE: Stop getting at me then, you're really boring.

JOYCE: How could I have left?

MARLENE: Did you want to?

JOYCE: I said how, / how could I?

MARLENE: If you'd wanted to you'd have done it.

JOYCE: Christ.

MARLENE: Are we getting drunk?

JOYCE: Do you want something to eat?

MARLENE: No, I'm getting drunk.

JOYCE: Funny time to visit, Sunday evening.

MARLENE: I came this morning. I spent the day —

ANGIE (*off*): Aunty! Aunty Marlene!

MARLENE: I'd better go.

JOYCE: Go on then.

MARLENE: All right.

ANGIE (*off*): Aunty! Can you hear me? I'm ready.

(*Marlene goes. Joyce goes on sitting, clears up, sits again. Marlene comes back.*)

JOYCE: So what's the secret?

MARLENE: It's a secret.

JOYCE: I know what it is anyway.

MARLENE: I bet you don't. You always said that.

JOYCE: It's her exercise book.

MARLENE: Yes, but you don't know what's in it.

JOYCE: It's some game, some secret society she has with Kit.

MARLENE: You don't know the password. You don't know the code.

JOYCE: You're really in it, aren't you. Can you do the handshake?

MARLENE: She didn't mention a handshake.

JOYCE: I thought they'd have a special handshake. She spends hours writing that but she's useless at school. She copies things out of books about black magic, and politicians out of the paper. It's a bit childish.

MARLENE: I think it's a plot to take over the world.

JOYCE: She's been in the remedial class the last two years.

MARLENE: I came up this morning and spent the day in Ipswich. I went to see Mother.

JOYCE: Did she recognize you?

MARLENE: Are you trying to be funny?

JOYCE: No, she does wander.

MARLENE: She wasn't wandering at all, she was very lucid thank you.

JOYCE: You were very lucky then.

MARLENE: Fucking awful life she's had.

JOYCE: Don't tell me.

MARLENE: Fucking waste.

JOYCE: Don't talk to me.

MARLENE: Why shouldn't I talk? Why shouldn't I talk to you? / Isn't she my mother too?

JOYCE: Look, you've left, you've gone away, / we can do without you.

MARLENE: I left home, so what, I left home. People do leave home / it is normal.

JOYCE: We understand that, we can do without you.

MARLENE: We weren't happy. Were you happy?

JOYCE: Don't come back.

MARLENE: So it's just your mother is it, your child, you never wanted me round, / you were jealous

JOYCE: Here we go.

MARLENE: of me because I was the little one and I was clever.

JOYCE: I'm not clever enough for all this psychology / if that's what it is.

MARLENE: Why can't I visit my own family / without

JOYCE: Aah.

MARLENE: all this?

JOYCE: Just don't go on about Mum's life when you haven't been to see her for how many years. / I go

MARLENE: It's up to me.

JOYCE: and see her every week.

MARLENE: Then don't go and see her every week.

JOYCE: Somebody has to.

MARLENE: No they don't. / Why do they?

JOYCE: How would I feel if I didn't go?

MARLENE: A lot better.

JOYCE: I hope you feel better.

MARLENE: It's up to me.

JOYCE: You couldn't get out of here fast enough. (*Pause.*)

MARLENE: Of course I couldn't get out of here fast enough. What was I going to do? Marry a dairyman who'd come home pissed? / Don't you fucking this

JOYCE: Christ.

MARLENE: fucking that fucking bitch fucking tell me what to fucking do fucking.

JOYCE: I don't know how you could leave your own child.

MARLENE: You were quick enough to take her.

JOYCE: What does that mean?

MARLENE: You were quick enough to take her.

JOYCE: Or what? Have her put in a home? Have some stranger / take her would you rather?

MARLENE: You couldn't have one so you took mine.

JOYCE: I didn't know that then.

MARLENE: Like hell, / married three years.

JOYCE: I didn't know that. Plenty of people / take that long.

MARLENE: Well it turned out lucky for you, didn't it?

JOYCE: Turned out all right for you by the look of you. You'd be getting a few less thousand a year.

MARLENE: Not necessarily.

JOYCE: You'd be stuck here / like you said.

MARLENE: I could have taken her with me.

JOYCE: You didn't want to take her with you. It's no good coming back now, Marlene, / and saying —

MARLENE: I know a managing director who's got two children, she breastfeeds in the board room, she pays a hundred pounds a week on domestic help alone and she can afford that because she's an extremely high-powered lady earning a great deal of money.

JOYCE: So what's that got to do with you at the age of seventeen?

MARLENE: Just because you were married and had somewhere to live —

JOYCE: You could have lived at home. / Or live

MARLENE: Don't be stupid.

JOYCE: with me and Frank. / You

MARLENE: You never suggested.

JOYCE: said you weren't keeping it. You shouldn't have had it / if you wasn't

MARLENE: Here we go.

JOYCE: going to keep it. You was the most stupid, / for someone so clever you was the most stupid, get yourself pregnant, not go to the doctor, not tell.

MARLENE: You wanted it, you said you were glad, I remember the day, you said I'm glad you never got rid of it, I'll look after it, you said that down by the river. So what are you saying, sunshine, you don't want her?

JOYCE: Course I'm not saying that.

MARLENE: Because I'll take her, / wake her up and pack now.

JOYCE: You wouldn't know how to begin to look after her.

MARLENE: Don't you want her?

JOYCE: Course I do, she's my child.

MARLENE: Then what are you going on about / why did I have her?

JOYCE: You said I got her off you / when you didn't —

MARLENE: I said you were lucky / the way it —

JOYCE: Have a child now if you want one. You're not old.

MARLENE: I might do.

JOYCE: Good. (*Pause.*)

MARLENE: I've been on the pill so long / I'm probably sterile.

JOYCE: Listen when Angie was six months I did get pregnant and I lost it because I was so tired looking after your fucking baby / because she cried so

MARLENE: You never told me.

JOYCE: much — yes I did tell you — / and the doctor

MARLENE: Well I forgot.

JOYCE: said if I'd sat down all day with my feet up I'd've kept it / and that's the only chance I ever had because after that —

MARLENE: I've had two abortions, are you interested? Shall I tell you about them? Well I won't, it's boring, it wasn't a problem. I don't like messy talk about blood / and what a bad time we all had. I

JOYCE: If I hadn't had your baby. The doctor said.

MARLENE: don't want a baby. I don't want to talk about gynecology.

JOYCE: Then stop trying to get Angie off of me.

MARLENE: I come down here after six years. All night you've been saying I don't come often enough. If I don't come for another six years she'll be twenty-one, will that be OK?

JOYCE: That'll be fine, yes, six years would suit me fine. (*Pause.*)

MARLENE: I was afraid of this. I only came because I thought you wanted . . . I just want . . . (*She cries.*)

JOYCE: Don't grizzle, Marlene, for God's sake. Marly? Come on, pet. Love you really. Fucking stop it, will you? (*She goes to Marlene.*)

MARLENE: No, let me cry. I like it. (*They laugh, Marlene begins to stop crying.*) I knew I'd cry if I wasn't careful.

JOYCE: Everyone's always crying in this house. Nobody takes any notice.

MARLENE: You've been wonderful looking after Angie.

JOYCE: Don't get carried away.

MARLENE: I can't write letters but I do think of you.

JOYCE: You're getting drunk. I'm going to make some tea.

MARLENE: Love you. (*Joyce goes to make tea.*)

JOYCE: I can see why you'd want to leave. It's a dump here.

MARLENE: So what's this about you and Frank?

JOYCE: He was always carrying on, wasn't he. And if I wanted to go out in the evening he'd go mad, even if it was nothing, a class, I was going to go to an evening class. So he had this girlfriend, only twenty-two poor cow, and I said go on, off you go, hoppit. I don't think he even likes her.

MARLENE: So what about money?

JOYCE: I've always said I don't want your money.

MARLENE: No, does he send you money?

JOYCE: I've got four different cleaning jobs. Adds up. There's not a lot round here.

MARLENE: Does Angie miss him?

JOYCE: She doesn't say.

MARLENE: Does she see him?

JOYCE: He was never that fond of her to be honest.

MARLENE: He tried to kiss me once. When you were engaged.

JOYCE: Did you fancy him?

MARLENE: No, he looked like a fish.

JOYCE: He was lovely then.

MARLENE: Ugh.

JOYCE: Well I fancied him. For about three years.

MARLENE: Have you got someone else?

JOYCE: There's not a lot round here. Mind you, the minute you're on your own, you'd be amazed how your friends' husbands drop by. I'd sooner do without.

MARLENE: I don't see why you couldn't take my money.

JOYCE: I do, so don't bother about it.

MARLENE: Only got to ask.

JOYCE: So what about you? Good job?

MARLENE: Good for a laugh. / Got back

JOYCE: Good for more than a laugh I should think.

MARLENE: from the US of A a bit wiped out and slotted into this speedy employment agency and still there.

JOYCE: You can always find yourself work then?

MARLENE: That's right.

JOYCE: And men?

MARLENE: Oh there's always men.

JOYCE: No one special?

MARLENE: There's fellas who like to be seen with a high-flying lady. Shows they've got something really good in their pants. But they can't take the day to day. They're waiting for me to turn into the little woman. Or maybe I'm just horrible of course.

JOYCE: Who needs them.

MARLENE: Who needs them. Well I do. But I need adventures more. So on on into the sunset. I think the eighties are going to be stupendous.

JOYCE: Who for?

MARLENE: For me. / I think I'm going up up up.

JOYCE: Oh for you. Yes, I'm sure they will.

MARLENE: And for the country, come to that. Get the economy back on its feet and whoosh. She's a tough lady, Maggie. I'd give her a job. / She just needs to hang

JOYCE: You voted for them, did you?

MARLENE: in there. This country needs to stop whining. / Monetarism is not

JOYCE: Drink your tea and shut up, pet.

MARLENE: stupid. It takes time, determination. No more slop. / And

JOYCE: Well I think they're filthy bastards.

MARLENE: who's got to drive it on? First woman prime minister. Terrifico. Aces. Right on. / You must admit. Certainly gets my vote.

JOYCE: What good's first woman if it's her? I suppose

you'd have liked Hitler if he was a woman. Ms. Hitler. Got a lot done, Hitlerina. / Great adventures.

MARLENE: Bosses still walking on the worker's faces? Still dadda's little parrot? Haven't you learned to think for yourself? I believe in the individual. Look at me.

JOYCE: I am looking at you.

MARLENE: Come on, Joyce, we're not going to quarrel over politics.

JOYCE: We are though.

MARLENE: Forget I mentioned it. Not a word about the slimy unions will cross my lips. (*Pause.*)

JOYCE: You say Mother had a wasted life.

MARLENE: Yes I do. Married to that bastard.

JOYCE: What sort of life did he have? /

MARLENE: Violent life?

JOYCE: Working in the fields like an animal. / Why

MARLENE: Come off it.

JOYCE: wouldn't he want a drink? You want a drink. He couldn't afford whiskey.

MARLENE: I don't want to talk about him.

JOYCE: You started, I was talking about her. She had a rotten life because she had nothing. She went hungry.

MARLENE: She was hungry because he drank the money. / He used to hit her.

JOYCE: It's not all down to him / Their

MARLENE: She didn't hit him.

JOYCE: lives were rubbish. They were treated like rubbish. He's dead and she'll die soon and what sort of life / did they have?

MARLENE: I saw him one night. I came down.

JOYCE: Do you think I didn't? / They

MARLENE: I still have dreams.

JOYCE: didn't get to America and drive across it in a fast car. / Bad nights, they had bad days.

MARLENE: America, America, you're jealous. / I had to get out, I knew when I

JOYCE: Jealous?

MARLENE: was thirteen, out of their house, out of them, never let that happen to me, / never let him, make my own way, out.

JOYCE: Jealous of what you've done, you'd be ashamed of me if I came to your office, your smart friends, wouldn't you, I'm ashamed of you, think of nothing but yourself, you've got on, nothing's changed for most people, / has it?

MARLENE: I hate the working class / which is what

JOYCE: Yes you do.

MARLENE: you're going to go on about now, it doesn't exist any more, it means lazy and stupid. / I don't

JOYCE: Come on, now we're getting it.

MARLENE: like the way they talk. I don't like beer guts and football vomit and saucy tits / and brothers and sisters —

JOYCE: I spit when I see a Rolls Royce, scratch it with my ring / Mercedes it was.

MARLENE: Oh very mature —

JOYCE: I hate the cows I work for / and their dirty dishes with blanquette of fucking veau.

MARLENE: and I will not be pulled down to their level by a flying picket and I won't be sent to Siberia / or a loony bin just because I'm original. And I support

JOYCE: No, you'll be on a yacht, you'll be head of Coca Cola and you wait, the eighties is going to be stupendous all right because we'll get you lot off our backs —

MARLENE: Reagan even if he is a lousy movie star because the reds are swarming up his map and I want to be free in a free world —

JOYCE: What? / What?

MARLENE: I know what I mean / by that — not shut up here.

JOYCE: So don't be round here when it happens because if someone's kicking you I'll just laugh. (*Silence.*)

MARLENE: I don't mean anything personal. I don't believe in class. Anyone can do anything if they've got what it takes.

JOYCE: And if they haven't?

MARLENE: If they're stupid or lazy or frightened, I'm not going to help them get a job, why should I?

JOYCE: What about Angie?

MARLENE: What about Angie?

JOYCE: She's stupid, lazy, and frightened, so what about her?

MARLENE: You run her down too much. She'll be all right.

JOYCE: I don't expect so, no. I expect her children will say what a wasted life she had. If she has children. Because nothing's changed and it won't with them in.

MARLENE: Them, them. / Us and them?

JOYCE: And you're one of them.

MARLENE: And you're us, wonderful us, and Angie's us / and Mum and Dad's us.

JOYCE: Yes, that's right, and you're them.

MARLENE: Come on, Joyce, what a night. You've got what it takes.

JOYCE: I know I have.

MARLENE: I didn't really mean all that.

JOYCE: I did.

MARLENE: But we're friends anyway.

JOYCE: I don't think so, no.

MARLENE: Well it's lovely to be out in the country. I really must make the effort to come more often. I want to go to sleep. I want to go to sleep. (*Joyce gets blankets for the sofa.*)

JOYCE: Goodnight then. I hope you'll be warm enough.

MARLENE: Goodnight. Joyce —

JOYCE: No, pet. Sorry. (*Joyce goes. Marlene sits wrapped*

in a blanket and has another drink. Angie comes in.)

ANGIE: Mum?

MARLENE: Angie? What's the matter?

ANGIE: Mum?

MARLENE: No, she's gone to bed. It's Aunty Marlene.

ANGIE: Frightening.

MARLENE: Did you have a bad dream? What happened in it? Well you're awake now, aren't you, pet?

ANGIE: Frightening.

Marsha Norman

Marsha Norman was born in Louisville, Kentucky, in 1947. Because her mother was a deeply religious woman, she did not allow television in her house, and radios, though available, were never used. Movies were also forbidden. But Norman explains that her mother "did not know the dangers of books because she didn't read," so books were Marsha Norman's world for most of her childhood.

But they were not the only influence. Norman spent much of her youth playing the piano, and she enjoyed the children's productions of the Actors' Theatre of Louisville. The Actors' Theatre and its director, Jon Jory, later became influential on Norman's early career as a writer.

Norman has said many times that the best thing for a writer is to be able to see drama during childhood. She has intense memories of *The Glass Menagerie*, Peter Shaffer's *The Royal Hunt of the Sun*, which is about the last day of Montezuma's life, and Archibald MacLeish's *J.B.*, an adaptation of the Book of Job. The vigor and the violence of these plays were explicitly attractive to her. Some of the excitement of that kind of theatricality is present in her first play, *Getting Out* (1977), which had its first performance at the Actors' Theatre.

Norman was a philosophy major at Agnes Scott College in Georgia, but she spent a good deal of her energy in theater there. Yet when she left college she did not expect to do any writing. As she said, she was sure that she would have to work for a living. But a combination of circumstances changed that.

Norman had worked with disturbed teenagers in a Kentucky state hospital and had met a thirteen-year-old girl who was violent, reckless, and frightening. Later when she was working in children's TV in Louisville, Jon Jory offered to commission her to write a play, but initially she was not interested. When she talked over her feelings, Jory advised her to reflect on a moment when she was truly frightened. It was then that she remembered the thirteen-year-old girl, and thus began the gestation of *Getting Out*.

Her unusual approach in that play was to present two views of the same woman: Arlie as an imprisoned adolescent and Arlene as an adult trying to begin a reasonable life for herself in a shabby apartment. The two parts of the character share the stage simultaneously. The ultimate problem is how Arlene will learn to integrate the separate parts of her personality. It is a very effective work and ran for eight months Off Broadway after a successful opening with the Actors' Theatre.

Norman also wrote some one-act plays for the Actors' Theatre — *The Laundromat* and *The Pool Hall* — and a full-length play, *Circus Valentine* (1979). She won the Pulitzer Prize for *'night, Mother* (1983), currently her most successful play. *Traveler in the Dark* (1984) premiered at the American Repertory Theatre in Cambridge, Massachusetts, starring Sam Waterston as a cancer surgeon suffering from the strain of guilt.

Norman has frequently talked about the structure of her plays, which follow a very traditional pattern. She has linked them often to a "ski lift. When you get in it, you must feel absolutely secure; you must know that this thing can hold you up." Her sense of the play as resembling a machine is based in part on her awareness of the audience's needs and expectations. She has said that a good play should follow several simple rules: "You must state the issue at the beginning of the play. The audience must know what is at stake; they must know when they will be able to go home."

Norman is deeply concerned with giving language to those who are inarticulate. The most important characters in her best plays have been women who would not have been able to express themselves clearly without someone like Marsha Norman to give them a voice. Such an ambition may owe something to her youthful desire "to save the world," the same desire that led her to work in the Kentucky hospital that provided the material for her first play.

'NIGHT, MOTHER

Marsha Norman's best-known and most successful play, *'night, Mother* (1983), has won numerous awards including the Pulitzer Prize. Its subject — a middle-aged woman's determination to commit suicide and leave her mother behind — is not the uplifting fare usually offered to Broadway audiences. Such a play would seem to spell horror for a New York theater, and while it ran for ten months after a shaky start, Norman had to accept a fifty percent reduction in her standard royalties to keep the play open.

Her strategy in the play was to face the issue of suicide squarely and directly. She chose not to have Jessie deal with her decision alone and merely leave a note, as had been done in many such plays in the past. Rather, she chose to make the play a dialogue, with Jessie having to confront the one person who loves her most and who most wants her to live and to give up her thoughts of killing herself.

Norman also made the play more difficult for popular audiences because she did not take the obvious path of giving Jessie a terminal disease, as some plays had done. She felt it was imperative that the issues of life and death, of personal choice and motive, be explored directly onstage, with the characters facing as squarely as possible the ramifications of their choices.

The ethical issues that suicide raises are naturally complex, and the play does not broach them directly. But such issues are always in the minds of the audience. In no sense does the play offer anyone reasons for committing suicide. Jessie's discussion with her mother is not equivalent to a debate: She has made up her mind based on her personal feelings about life, and she makes her decision seem inevitable. Nothing Thelma can say will change it.

Jessie is not a deep thinker, not a reflective person, and she does not concern herself with spiritual issues in making her decision. Her last evening's concerns are limited to the physical, material, and psychological comfort of her mother.

Marsha Norman (b. 1947)
'NIGHT, MOTHER   *1983*

Characters

JESSIE CATES, *in her late thirties or early forties, is pale and vaguely unsteady physically. It is only in the last year that Jessie has gained control of her mind and body, and tonight she is determined to hold on to that control. She wears pants and a long black sweater with deep pockets, which contain scraps of paper, and there may be a pencil behind her ear or a pen clipped to one of the pockets of the sweater.*

As a rule, Jessie doesn't feel much like talking. Other people have rarely found her quirky sense of humor amusing. She has a peaceful energy on this night, a sense of purpose, but is clearly aware of the time passing moment by moment. Oddly enough, Jessie has never been as communicative or as enjoyable as she is on this evening, but we must know she has not always been this way. There is a familiarity between these two women that comes from having lived together for a long time. There is a shorthand to the talk and a sense of routine comfort in the way they relate to each other physically. Naturally, there are also routine aggravations.

THELMA CATES, "MAMA," *is Jessie's mother, in her late fifties or early sixties. She has begun to feel her age and so takes it easy when she can, or when it serves her purpose to let someone help her. But she speaks quickly and enjoys talking. She believes that things are what she says they are. Her sturdiness is more a mental quality than a physical one, finally. She is chatty and nosy, and this is her house.*

(The play takes place in a relatively new house built way out on a country road, with a living room and connecting kitchen, and a center hall that leads off to the bedrooms. A pull cord in the hall ceiling releases a ladder which leads to the attic. One of these bedrooms opens directly onto the hall, and its entry should be visible to everyone in the audience. It should be, in fact, the focal point of the entire set, and the lighting should make it disappear completely at times and draw the entire set into it at others. It is a point of both threat and promise. It is an ordinary door that opens onto absolute nothingness. That door is the point of all the action, and the utmost care should be given to its design and construction.)

(The living room is cluttered with magazines and needlework catalogues, ashtrays and candy dishes. Ex-

amples of Mama's needlework are everywhere — pillows, afghans, and quilts, doilies and rugs, and they are quite nice examples. The house is more comfortable than messy, but there is quite a lot to keep in place here. It is more personal than charming. It is not quaint. Under no circumstances should the set and its dressing make a judgment about the intelligence or taste of Jessie and Mama. It should simply indicate that they are very specific real people who happen to live in a particular part of the country. Heavy accents, which would further distance the audience from Jessie and Mama, are also wrong.)

(The time is the present, with the action beginning about 8:15. Clocks onstage in the kitchen and on a table in the living room should run throughout the performance and be visible to the audience.)

(Mama stretches to reach the cupcakes in a cabinet in the kitchen. She can't see them, but she can feel around for them, and she's eager to have one, so she's working pretty hard at it. This may be the most serious exercise Mama ever gets. She finds a cupcake, the coconut-covered, raspberry-and-marshmallow-filled kind known as a snowball, but sees that there's one missing from the package. She calls to Jessie, who is apparently somewhere else in the house.)

MAMA (unwrapping the cupcake): Jessie, it's the last snowball, sugar. Put it on the list, O.K.? And we're out of Hershey bars, and where's that peanut brittle? I think maybe Dawson's been in it again. I ought to put a big mirror on the refrigerator door. That'll keep him out of my treats, won't it? You hear me, honey? (Then more to herself.) I hate it when the coconut falls off. Why does the coconut fall off?

(Jessie enters from her bedroom, carrying a stack of newspapers.)

JESSIE: We got any old towels?

MAMA: There you are!

JESSIE (holding a towel that was on the stack of newspapers): Towels you don't want anymore. (Picking up Mama's snowball wrapper.) How about this swimming towel Loretta gave us? Beach towel, that's the name of it. You want it? (Mama shakes her head no.)

MAMA: What have you been doing in there?

JESSIE: And a big piece of plastic like a rubber sheet or something. Garbage bags would do if there's enough.

MAMA: Don't go making a big mess, Jessie. It's eight o'clock already.

JESSIE: Maybe an old blanket or towels we got in a soap box sometime?

MAMA: I said don't make a mess. You hair is black enough, hon.

JESSIE (continuing to search the kitchen cabinets, finding two or three more towels to add to her stack): It's not for my hair, Mama. What about some old pillows anywhere, or a foam cushion out of a yard chair would be real good.

MAMA: You haven't forgot what night it is, have you? (Holding up her fingernails.) They're all chipped, see? I've been waiting all week, Jess. It's Saturday night, sugar.

JESSIE: I know. I got it on the schedule.

MAMA (crossing to the living room): You want me to wash 'em now or are you making your mess first? (Looking at the snowball.) We're out of these. Did I say that already?

JESSIE: There's more coming tomorrow. I ordered you a whole case.

MAMA (checking the TV Guide): A whole case will go stale, Jessie.

JESSIE: They can go in the freezer till you're ready for them. Where's Daddy's gun?

MAMA: In the attic.

JESSIE: Where in the attic? I looked your whole nap and couldn't find it anywhere.

MAMA: One of his shoeboxes, I think.

JESSIE: Full of shoes. I looked already.

MAMA: Well, you didn't look good enough, then. There's that box from the ones he wore to the hospital. When he died, they told me I could have them back, but I never did like those shoes.

JESSIE (pulling them out of her pocket): I found the bullets. They were in an old milk can.

MAMA (as Jessie starts for the hall): Dawson took the shotgun, didn't he? Hand me that basket, hon.

JESSIE (getting the basket for her): Dawson better not've taken that pistol.

MAMA (stopping her again): Now my glasses, please. (Jessie returns to get the glasses.) I told him to take those rubber boots, too, but he said they were for fishing. I told him to take up fishing.

(Jessie reaches for the cleaning spray and cleans Mama's glasses for her)

JESSIE: He's just too lazy to climb up there, Mama. Or maybe he's just being smart. That floor's not very steady.

MAMA (getting out a piece of knitting): It's not a floor at all, hon, it's a board now and then. Measure this for me. I need six inches.

JESSIE (as she measures): Dawson could probably use some of those clothes up there. Somebody should have them. You ought to call the Salvation Army before the whole thing falls in on you. Six inches exactly.

MAMA: It's plenty safe! As long as you don't go up there.

JESSIE (*turning to go again*): I'm careful.

MAMA: What do you want the gun for, Jess?

JESSIE (*Not returning this time. Opening the ladder in the hall.*): Protection. (*She steadies the ladder as Mama talks.*)

MAMA: You take the TV way too serious, hon. I've never seen a criminal in my life. This is way too far to come for what's out here to steal. Never seen a one.

JESSIE (*taking her first step up*): Except for Ricky.

MAMA: Ricky is mixed up. That's not a crime.

JESSIE: Get your hands washed. I'll be right back. And get 'em real dry. You dry your hands till I get back or it's no go, all right?

MAMA: I thought Dawson told you not to go up those stairs.

JESSIE (*going up*): He did.

MAMA: I don't like the idea of a gun, Jess.

JESSIE (*calling down from the attic*): Which shoebox, do you remember?

MAMA: Black.

JESSIE: The box was black?

MAMA: The shoes were black.

JESSIE: That doesn't help much, Mother.

MAMA: I'm not trying to help, sugar. (*No answer.*) We don't have anything anybody'd want, Jessie. I mean, I don't even want what we got, Jessie.

JESSIE: Neither do I. Wash your hands. (*Mama gets up and crosses to stand under the ladder.*)

MAMA: You come down from there before you have a fit. I can't come up and get you, you know.

JESSIE: I know.

MAMA: We'll just hand it over to them when they come, how's that? Whatever they want, the criminals.

JESSIE: That's a good idea, Mama.

MAMA: Ricky will grow out of this and be a real fine boy, Jess. But I have to tell you, I wouldn't want Ricky to know we had a gun in the house.

JESSIE: Here it is. I found it.

MAMA: It's just something Ricky's going through. Maybe he's in with some bad people. He just needs some time, sugar. He'll get back in school or get a job or one day you'll get a call and he'll say he's sorry for all the trouble he's caused and invite you out for supper someplace dress-up.

JESSIE (*coming back down the steps*): Don't worry. It's not for him, it's for me.

MAMA: I didn't think you would shoot your own boy, Jessie. I know you've felt like it, well, we've all felt like shooting somebody, but we don't do it. I just don't think we need . . .

JESSIE (*interrupting*): Your hands aren't washed. Do you want a manicure or not?

MAMA: Yes, I do, but . . .

JESSIE (*crossing to the chair*): Then wash your hands and don't talk to me any more about Ricky. Those two rings he took were the last valuable things *I* had, so now he's started in on other people, door to door. I hope they put him away sometime. I'd turn him in myself if I knew where he was.

MAMA: You don't mean that.

JESSIE: Every word. Wash your hands and that's the last time I'm telling you.

(*Jessie sits down with the gun and starts cleaning it, pushing the cylinder out, checking to see that the chambers and barrel are empty, then putting some oil on a small patch of cloth and pushing it through the barrel with the push rod that was in the box. Mama goes to the kitchen and washes her hands, as instructed, trying not to show her concern about the gun.*)

MAMA: I shoulda got you to bring down that milk can. Agnes Fletcher sold hers to somebody with a flea market for forty dollars apiece.

JESSIE: I'll go back and get it in a minute. There's a wagon wheel up there, too. There's even a churn. I'll get it all if you want.

MAMA (*coming over, now, taking over now*): What are you doing?

JESSIE: The barrel has to be clean, Mama. Old powder, dust gets in it . . .

MAMA: What for?

JESSIE: I told you.

MAMA (*reaching for the gun*): And I told you, we don't get criminals out here.

JESSIE (*quickly pulling it to her*): And I told you . . . (*Then trying to be calm.*) The gun is for me.

MAMA: Well, you can have it if you want. When I die, you'll get it all, anyway.

JESSIE: I'm going to kill myself, Mama.

MAMA (*returning to the sofa*): Very funny. Very funny.

JESSIE: I am.

MAMA: You are not! Don't even say such a thing, Jessie.

JESSIE: How would you know if I didn't say it? You want it to be a surprise? You're lying there in your bed or maybe you're just brushing your teeth and you hear this . . . noise down the hall?

MAMA: Kill yourself.

JESSIE: Shoot myself. In a couple of hours.

MAMA: It must be time for your medicine.

JESSIE: Took it already.

MAMA: What's the matter with you?

JESSIE: Not a thing. Feel fine.

MAMA: You feel fine. You're just going to kill yourself.

JESSIE: Waited until I felt good enough, in fact.

MAMA: Don't make jokes, Jessie. I'm too old for jokes.

JESSIE: It's not a joke, Mama.

(*Mama watches for a moment in silence.*)

MAMA: That gun's no good, you know. He broke it right before he died. He dropped it in the mud one day.

JESSIE: Seems O.K. (*She spins the chamber, cocks the pistol, and pulls the trigger. The gun is not yet loaded, so all we hear is the click, but it will definitely work. It's also obvious that Jessie knows her way around a gun. Mama cannot speak.*) I had Cecil's all ready in there, just in case I couldn't find this one, but I'd rather use Daddy's.

MAMA: Those bullets are at least fifteen years old.

JESSIE (*pulling out another box*): These are from last week.

MAMA: Where did you get those?

JESSIE: Feed store Dawson told me about.

MAMA: Dawson!

JESSIE: I told him I was worried about prowlers. He said he thought it was a good idea. He told me what kind to ask for.

MAMA: If he had any idea . . .

JESSIE: He took it as a compliment. He thought I might be taking an interest in things. He got through telling me all about the bullets and then he said we ought to talk like this more often.

MAMA: And where was I while this was going on?

JESSIE: On the phone with Agnes. About the milk can, I guess. Anyway, I asked Dawson if he thought they'd send me some bullets and he said he'd just call for me, because he knew they'd send them if he told them to. And he was absolutely right. Here they are.

MAMA: How could he do that?

JESSIE: Just trying to help, Mama.

MAMA: And then I told you where the gun was.

JESSIE (*smiling, enjoying this joke*): See? Everybody's doing what they can.

MAMA: You told me it was for protection!

JESSIE: It *is!* I'm still doing your nails, though. Want to try that new Chinaberry color?

MAMA: Well, I'm calling Dawson right now. We'll just see what he has to say about this little stunt.

JESSIE: Dawson doesn't have any more to do with this.

MAMA: He's your brother.

JESSIE: And that's all.

MAMA (*stands up, moves toward the phone*): Dawson will put a stop to this. Yes he will. He'll take the gun away.

JESSIE: If you call him, I'll just have to do it before he gets here. Soon as you hang up the phone, I'll just walk in the bedroom and lock the door. Dawson will get here just in time to help you clean up. Go ahead, call him. Then call the police. Then call the funeral home. Then call Loretta and see if *she'll* do your nails.

MAMA: You will not! This is crazy talk, Jessie!

(*Mama goes directly to the telephone and starts to dial, but Jessie is fast, coming up behind her and taking the receiver out of her hand, putting it back down.*)

JESSIE (*firm and quiet*): I said no. This is private. Dawson is not invited.

MAMA: Just me.

JESSIE: I don't want anybody else over here. Just you and me. If Dawson comes over, it'll make me feel stupid for not doing it ten years ago.

MAMA: I think we better call the doctor. Or how about the ambulance. You like that one driver, I know. What's his name, Timmy? Get you somebody to talk to.

JESSIE (*going back to her chair*): I'm through talking, Mama. You're it. No more.

MAMA: We're just going to sit around like every other night in the world and then you're going to kill yourself? (*Jessie doesn't answer.*) You'll miss. (*Again there is no response.*) You'll just wind up a vegetable. How would you like that? Shoot your ear off? You know what the doctor said about getting excited. You'll cock the pistol and have a fit.

JESSIE: I think I can kill myself, Mama.

MAMA: You're not going to kill yourself, Jessie. You're not even upset! (*Jessie smiles, or laughs quietly, and Mama tries a different approach.*) People don't really kill themselves, Jessie. No, mam, doesn't make sense, unless you're retarded or deranged, and you're as normal as they come, Jessie, for the most part. We're all *afraid* to die.

JESSIE: I'm not, Mama. I'm cold all the time, anyway.

MAMA: That's ridiculous.

JESSIE: It's exactly what I want. It's dark and quiet.

MAMA: So is the back yard, Jessie! Close your eyes. Stuff cotton in your ears. Take a nap! It's quiet in your room. I'll leave the TV off all night.

JESSIE: So quiet I don't know it's quiet. So nobody can get me.

MAMA: You don't know what dead is like. It might not be quiet at all. What if it's like an alarm clock and you can't wake up so you can't shut it off. Ever.

JESSIE: Dead is everybody and everything I ever knew, gone. Dead is dead quiet.

MAMA: It's a sin. You'll go to hell.

JESSIE: Uh-huh.

MAMA: You will!

JESSIE: Jesus was a suicide, if you ask me.

MAMA: You'll go to hell just for saying that. Jessie!

JESSIE (*with genuine surprise*): I didn't know I thought that.

MAMA: Jessie!

(*Jessie doesn't answer. She puts the now-loaded gun*

back in the box and crosses to the kitchen. But Mama is afraid she's headed for the bedroom.)

MAMA (*in a panic*): You can't use my towels! They're my towels. I've had them for a long time. I like my towels.

JESSIE: I asked you if you wanted that swimming towel and you said you didn't.

MAMA: And you can't use your father's gun, either. It's mine now, too. And you can't do it in my house.

JESSIE: Oh, come on.

MAMA: No. You can't do it. I won't let you. The house is in my name.

JESSIE: I have to go in the bedroom and lock the door behind me so they won't arrest you for killing me. They'll probably test your hands for gunpowder, anyway, but you'll pass.

MAMA: Not in my house!

JESSIE: If I'd known you were going to act like this, I wouldn't have told you.

MAMA: How am I supposed to act? Tell you to go ahead? O.K. by me, sugar? Might try it myself. What took you so long?

JESSIE: There's just no point in fighting me over it, that's all. Want some coffee?

MAMA: Your birthday's coming up, Jessie. Don't you want to know what we got you?

JESSIE: You got me dusting powder, Loretta got me a new housecoat, pink probably, and Dawson got me new slippers, too small, but they go with the robe, he'll say. (*Mama cannot speak.*) Right? (*Apparently Jessie is right.*) Be back in a minute.

(Jessie takes the gun box, puts it on top of the stack of towels and garbage bags, and takes them into her bedroom. Mama, alone for a moment, goes to the phone, picks up the receiver, looks toward the bedroom, starts to dial, and then replaces the receiver in its cradle as Jessie walks back into the room. Jessie wonders, silently. They have lived together for so long there is very rarely any reason for one to ask what the other was about to do.)

MAMA: I started to, but I didn't. I didn't call him.

JESSIE: Good. Thank you.

MAMA (*starting over, a new approach*): What's this all about, Jessie?

JESSIE: About?

(Jessie now begins the next task she had "on the schedule," which is refilling all the candy jars, taking the empty papers out of the boxes of chocolates, etc. Mama generally snitches when Jessie does this. Not tonight, though. Nevertheless, Jessie offers.)

MAMA: What did I do?

JESSIE: Nothing. Want a caramel?

MAMA (*ignoring the candy*): You're mad at me.

JESSIE: Not a bit. I am worried about you, but I'm going to do what I can before I go. We're not just going to sit around tonight. I made a list of things.

MAMA: What things?

JESSIE: How the washer works. Things like that.

MAMA: I know how the washer works. You put the clothes in. You put the soap in. You turn it on. You wait.

JESSIE: You do something else. You don't just wait.

MAMA: Whatever else you find to do, you're still mainly waiting. The waiting's the worst part of it. The waiting's what you pay somebody else to do, if you can.

JESSIE (*nodding*): O.K. Where do we keep the soap?

MAMA: I could find it.

JESSIE: See?

MAMA: If you're mad about doing the wash, we can get Loretta to do it.

JESSIE: Oh now, that might be worth staying to see.

MAMA: She'd never in her life, would she?

JESSIE: Nope.

MAMA: What's the matter with her?

JESSIE: She thinks she's better than we are. She's not.

MAMA: Maybe if she didn't wear that yellow all the time.

JESSIE: The washer repair number is on a little card taped to the side of the machine.

MAMA: Loretta doesn't ever have to come over here again. Dawson can just leave her at home when he comes. And we don't ever have to see Dawson either if he bothers you. Does he bother you?

JESSIE: Sure he does. Be sure you clean out the lint tray every time you use the dryer. But don't ever put your house shoes in, it'll melt the soles.

MAMA: What does Dawson do, that bothers you?

JESSIE: He just calls me Jess like he knows who he's talking to. He's always wondering what I do all day. I mean, I wonder that myself, but it's my day, so it's mine to wonder about, not his.

MAMA: Family is just accident, Jessie. It's nothing personal, hon. They don't mean to get on your nerves. They don't even mean to be your family, they just are.

JESSIE: They know too much.

MAMA: About what?

JESSIE: They know things about you, and they learned it before you had a chance to say whether you wanted them to know it or not. They were there when it happened and it don't belong to them, it belongs to you, only they got it. Like my mail-order bra got delivered to their house.

MAMA: By accident!

JESSIE: All the same . . . they opened it. They saw the

little rosebuds on it. (*Offering her another candy.*) Chewy mint?

MAMA (*shaking her head no*): What do they know about you? I'll tell them never to talk about it again. Is it Ricky or Cecil or your fits or your hair is falling out or you drink too much coffee or you never go out of the house or what?

JESSIE: I just don't like their talk. The account at the grocery is in Dawson's name when you call. The number's on a whole list of numbers on the back cover of the phone book.

MAMA: Well! Now we're getting somewhere. They're none of them ever setting foot in this house again.

JESSIE: It's not them, Mother. I wouldn't kill myself just to get away from them.

MAMA: You leave the room when they come over, anyway.

JESSIE: I stay as long as I can. Besides, it's you they come to see.

MAMA: That's because I stay in the room when they come.

JESSIE: It's not them.

MAMA: Then what is it?

JESSIE (*checking the list on her note pad*): The grocery won't deliver on Saturday anymore. And if you want your order the same day, you have to call before ten. And they won't deliver less than fifteen dollars' worth. What I do is tell them what we need and tell them to add on cigarettes until it gets to fifteen dollars.

MAMA: It's Ricky. You're trying to get through to him.

JESSIE: If I thought I could do that, I would stay.

MAMA: Make him sorry he hurt you, then. That's it, isn't it?

JESSIE: He's hurt me, I've hurt him. We're about even.

MAMA: You'll be telling him killing is O.K. with you, you know. Want him to start killing next? Nothing wrong with it. Mom did it.

JESSIE: Only a matter of time, anyway, Mama. When the call comes, you let Dawson handle it.

MAMA: Honey, nothing says those calls are always going to be some new trouble he's into. You could get one that he's got a job, that he's getting married, or how about he's joined the army, wouldn't that be nice?

JESSIE: If you call the Sweet Tooth before you call the grocery, that Susie will take your fudge next door to the grocery and it'll all come out together. Be sure you talk to Susie, though. She won't let them put it in the bottom of a sack like that one time, remember?

MAMA: Ricky could come over, you know. What if he calls us?

JESSIE: It's not Ricky, Mama.

MAMA: Or anybody could call us, Jessie.

JESSIE: Not on Saturday night, Mama.

MAMA: Then what is it? Are you sick? If your gums are swelling again, we can get you to the dentist in the morning.

JESSIE: No. Can you order your medicine or do you want Dawson to? I've got a note to him. I'll add that to it if you want.

MAMA: Your eyes don't look right. I thought so yesterday.

JESSIE: That was just the ragweed. I'm not sick.

MAMA: Epilepsy is sick, Jessie.

JESSIE: It won't kill me. (*A pause.*) If it would, I wouldn't have to.

MAMA: You don't *have* to.

JESSIE: No, I don't. That's what I like about it.

MAMA: Well, I won't let you!

JESSIE: It's not up to you.

MAMA: Jessie!

JESSIE: I want to hang a big sign around my neck, like Daddy's on the barn. GONE FISHING.

MAMA: You don't like it here.

JESSIE (*smiling*): Exactly.

MAMA: I meant here in my house.

JESSIE: I know you did.

MAMA: You never should have moved back in here with me. If you'd kept your little house or found another place when Cecil left you, you'd have made some new friends at least. Had a life to lead. Had your own things around you. Give Ricky a place to come see you. You never should've come here.

JESSIE: Maybe.

MAMA: But I didn't force you, did I?

JESSIE: If it was a mistake, we made it together. You took me in. I appreciate that.

MAMA: You didn't have any business being by yourself right then, but I can see how you might want a place of your own. A grown woman should . . .

JESSIE: Mama . . . I'm just not having a very good time and I don't have any reason to think it'll get anything but worse. I'm tired. I'm hurt. I'm sad. I feel used.

MAMA: Tired of what?

JESSIE: It all.

MAMA: What does that mean?

JESSIE: I can't say it any better.

MAMA: Well, you'll have to say it better because I'm not letting you alone till you do. What were those other things? Hurt . . . (*Before Jessie can answer.*) You had this all ready to say to me, didn't you? Did you write this down? How long have you been thinking about this?

JESSIE: Off and on, ten years. On all the time, since Christmas.

MAMA: What happened at Christmas?

JESSIE: Nothing.

MAMA: So why Christmas?

JESSIE: That's it. On the nose.

(*A pause. Mama knows exactly what Jessie means. She was there, too, after all.*)

JESSIE (*putting the candy sacks away*): See where all this is? Red hots up front, sour balls and horehound mixed together in this one sack. New packages of toffee and licorice right in back there.

MAMA: Go back to your list. You're hurt by what?

JESSIE (*Mama knows perfectly well*): Mama . . .

MAMA: O.K. Sad about what? There's nothing real sad going on right now. If it was after your divorce or something, that would make sense.

JESSIE (*looking at her list, then opening the drawer*): Now, this drawer has everything in it that there's no better place for. Extension cords, batteries for the radio, extra lighters, sandpaper, masking tape, Elmer's glue, thumbtacks, that kind of stuff. The mousetraps are under the sink, but you call Dawson if you've got one and let him do it.

MAMA: Sad about what?

JESSIE: The way things are.

MAMA: Not good enough. What things?

JESSIE: Oh, everything from you and me to Red China.

MAMA: I think we can leave the Chinese out of this.

JESSIE (*crosses back into the living room*): There's extra light bulbs in a box in the hall closet. And we've got a couple of packages of fuses in the fuse box. There's candles and matches in the top of the broom closet, but if the lights go out, just call Dawson and sit tight. But don't open the refrigerator door. Things will stay cool in there as long as you keep the door shut.

MAMA: I asked you a question.

JESSIE: I read the paper. I don't like how things are. And they're not any better out there than they are in here.

MAMA: If you're doing this because of the newspapers, I can sure fix that!

JESSIE: There's just more of it on TV.

MAMA (*kicking the television set*): Take it out, then!

JESSIE: You wouldn't do that.

MAMA: Watch me.

JESSIE: What would you do all day?

MAMA (*desperately*): Sing. (*Jessie laughs.*) I would, too. You want to watch? I'll sing till morning to keep you alive, Jessie, please!

JESSIE: No. (*Then affectionately.*) It's a funny idea, though. What do you sing?

MAMA (*has no idea how to answer this*): We've got a good life here!

JESSIE (*going back into the kitchen*): I called this morning and canceled the papers, except for Sunday, for your puzzles; you'll still get that one.

MAMA: Let's get another dog, Jessie! You liked a big dog, now, didn't you? That King dog, didn't you?

JESSIE (*washing her hands*): I did like that King dog, yes.

MAMA: I'm so dumb. He's the one run under the tractor.

JESSIE: That makes him dumb, not you.

MAMA: For bringing it up.

JESSIE: It's O.K. Handi-Wipes and sponges under the sink.

MAMA: We could get a new dog and keep him in the house. Dogs are cheap!

JESSIE (*getting big pill jars out of the cabinet*): No.

MAMA: Something for you to take care of.

JESSIE: I've had you, Mama.

MAMA (*frantically starting to fill pill bottles*): You do too much for me. I can fill pill bottles all day, Jessie, and change the shelf paper and wash the floor when I get through. You just watch me. You don't have to do another thing in this house if you don't want to. You don't have to take care of me, Jessie.

JESSIE: I know that. You've just been letting me do it so I'll have something to do, haven't you?

MAMA (*realizing this was a mistake*): I don't do it as well as you. I just meant if it tires you out or makes you feel used . . .

JESSIE: Mama, I know you used to ride the bus. Riding the bus and it's hot and bumpy and crowded and too noisy and more than anything in the world you want to get off and the only reason in the world you don't get off is it's still fifty blocks from where you're going? Well, I can get off right now if I want to, because even if I ride fifty more years and get off then, it's the same place when I step down to it. Whenever I feel like it, I can get off. As soon as I've had enough, it's my stop. I've had enough.

MAMA: You're feeling sorry for yourself!

JESSIE: The plumber's helper is under the sink, too.

MAMA: You're not having a good time! Whoever promised you a good time? Do you think I've had a good time?

JESSIE: I think you're pretty happy, yeah. You have things you like to do.

MAMA: Like what?

JESSIE: Like crochet.

MAMA: I'll teach you to crochet.

JESSIE: I can't do any of that nice work, Mama.

MAMA: Good time don't come looking for you, Jessie. You could work some puzzles or put in a garden or go to the store. Let's call a taxi and go to the A&P!

JESSIE: I shopped you up for about two weeks already.

You're not going to need toilet paper till Thanksgiving.

MAMA (*interrupting*): You're acting like some little brat, Jessie. You're mad and everybody's boring and you don't have anything to do and you don't like me and you don't like going out and you don't like staying in and you never talk on the phone and you don't watch TV and you're miserable and it's your own sweet fault.

JESSIE: And it's time I did something about it.

MAMA: Not something like killing yourself. Something like . . . buying us all new dishes! I'd like that. Or maybe the doctor would let you get a driver's license now, or I know what let's do right this minute, let's rearrange the furniture.

JESSIE: I'll do that. If you want. I always thought if the TV was somewhere else, you wouldn't get such a glare on it during the day. I'll do whatever you want before I go.

MAMA (*badly frightened by those words*): You could get a job!

JESSIE: I took that telephone sales job and I didn't even make enough money to pay the phone bill, and I tried to work at the gift shop at the hospital and they said I made people real uncomfortable smiling at them the way I did.

MAMA: You could keep books. You kept your dad's books.

JESSIE: But nobody ever checked them.

MAMA: When he died, they checked them.

JESSIE: And that's when they took the books away from me.

MAMA: That's because without him there wasn't any business, Jessie!

JESSIE (*putting the pill bottles away*): You know I couldn't work. I can't do anything. I've never been around people my whole life except when I went to the hospital. I could have a seizure any time. What good would a job do? The kind of job I could get would make me feel worse.

MAMA: Jessie!

JESSIE: It's true!

MAMA: It's what you think is true!

JESSIE (*struck by the clarity of that*): That's right. It's what I think is true.

MAMA (*hysterically*): But I can't do anything about that!

JESSIE (*quietly*): No. You can't. (*Mama slumps, if not physically, at least emotionally.*) And I can't do anything either, about my life, to change it, make it better, make me feel better about it. Like it better, make it work. But I can stop it. Shut it down, turn it off like the radio when there's nothing on I want to listen to. It's all I really have that belongs to me and I'm going to say what happens to it. And it's

going to stop. And I'm going to stop it. So. Let's just have a good time.

MAMA: Have a good time.

JESSIE: We can't go on fussing all night. I mean, I could ask you things I always wanted to know and you could make me some hot chocolate. The old way.

MAMA (*in despair*): It takes cocoa, Jessie.

JESSIE (*gets it out of the cabinet*): I bought cocoa, Mama. And I'd like to have a caramel apple and do your nails.

MAMA: You didn't eat a bite of supper.

JESSIE: Does that mean I can't have a caramel apple?

MAMA: Of course not. I mean . . . (*Smiling a little.*) Of course you can have a caramel apple.

JESSIE: I thought I could.

MAMA: I make the best caramel apples in the world.

JESSIE: I know you do.

MAMA: Or used to. And you don't get cocoa like mine anywhere anymore.

JESSIE: It takes time, I know, but . . .

MAMA: The salt is the trick.

JESSIE: Trouble and everything.

MAMA (*backing away toward the stove*): It's no trouble. What trouble? You put it in the pan and stir it up. All right. Fine. Caramel apples. Cocoa. O.K.

(*Jessie walks to the counter to retrieve her cigarettes as Mama looks for the right pan. There are brief near-smiles, and maybe Mama clears her throat. We have a truce, for the moment. A genuine but nevertheless uneasy one. Jessie, who has been in constant motion since the beginning, now seems content to sit.*)

(*Mama starts looking for a pan to make the cocoa, getting out all the pans in the cabinets in the process. It looks like she's making a mess on purpose so Jessie will have to put them all away again. Mama is buying time, or trying to, and entertaining.*)

JESSIE: You talk to Agnes today?

MAMA: She's calling me from a pay phone this week. God only knows why. She has a perfectly good Trimline at home.

JESSIE (*laughing*): Well, how is she?

MAMA: How is she every day, Jessie? Nuts.

JESSIE: Is she really crazy or just silly?

MAMA: No, she's really crazy. She was probably using the pay phone because she had another little fire problem at home.

JESSIE: Mother . . .

MAMA: I'm serious! Agnes Fletcher's burned down every house she ever lived in. Eight fires, and she's due for a new one any day now.

JESSIE (*laughing*): No!

MAMA: Wouldn't surprise me a bit.

JESSIE (*laughing*): Why didn't you tell me this before? Why isn't she locked up somewhere?

MAMA: 'Cause nobody ever got hurt, I guess. Agnes woke everybody up to watch the fires as soon as she set 'em. One time she set out porch chairs and served lemonade.

JESSIE (*shaking her head*): Real lemonade?

MAMA: The houses they lived in, you knew they were going to fall down anyway, so why wait for it, is all I could ever make out about it. Agnes likes a feeling of accomplishment.

JESSIE: Good for her.

MAMA (*finding the pan she wants*): Why are you asking about Agnes? One cup or two?

JESSIE: One. She's your friend. No marshmallows.

MAMA (*getting the milk, etc.*): You have to have marshmallows. That's the old way, Jess. Two or three? Three is better.

JESSIE: Three, then. Her whole house burns up? Her clothes and pillows and everything? I'm not sure I believe this.

MAMA: When she was a girl, Jess, not now. Long time ago. But she's still got it in her, I'm sure of it.

JESSIE: She wouldn't burn her house down now. Where would she go? She can't get Buster to build her a new one, he's dead. How could she burn it up?

MAMA: Be exciting, though, if she did. You never know.

JESSIE: You do too know, Mama. She wouldn't do it.

MAMA (*forced to admit, but reluctant*): I guess not.

JESSIE: What else? Why does she wear all those whistles around her neck?

MAMA: Why does she have a house full of birds?

JESSIE: I didn't know she had a house full of birds!

MAMA: Well, she does. And she says they just follow her home. Well, I know for a fact she's still paying on the last parrot she bought. You gotta keep your life filled up, she says. She says a lot of stupid things. (*Jessie laughs, Mama continues, convinced she's getting somewhere.*) It's all that okra she eats. You can't just willy-nilly eat okra two meals a day and expect to get away with it. Made her crazy.

JESSIE: She really eats okra twice a day? Where does she get it in the winter?

MAMA: Well, she eats it a lot. Maybe not two meals, but . . .

JESSIE: More than the average person.

MAMA (*beginning to get irritated*): I don't know how much okra the average person eats.

JESSIE: Do you know how much okra Agnes eats?

MAMA: No.

JESSIE: How many birds does she have?

MAMA: Two.

JESSIE: Then what are the whistles for?

MAMA: They're not real whistles. Just little plastic ones on a necklace she won playing Bingo, and I only told you about it because I thought I might get a laugh out of you for once even if it wasn't the truth, Jessie. Things don't have to be true to talk about 'em, you know.

JESSIE: Why won't she come over here?

(*Mama is suddenly quiet, but the cocoa and milk are in the pan now, so she lights the stove and starts stirring.*)

MAMA: Well now, what a good idea. We should've had more cocoa. Cocoa is perfect.

JESSIE: Except you don't like milk.

MAMA (*another attempt, but not as energetic*): I hate milk. Coats your throat as bad as okra. Something just downright disgusting about it.

JESSIE: It's because of me, isn't it?

MAMA: No, Jess.

JESSIE: Yes, Mama.

MAMA: O.K. Yes, then, but she's crazy. She's as crazy as they come. She's a lunatic.

JESSIE: What is it exactly? Did I say something, sometime? Or did she see me have a fit and's afraid I might have another one if she came over, or what?

MAMA: I guess.

JESSIE: You guess what? What's she ever said? She must've given you some reason.

MAMA: Your hands are cold.

JESSIE: What difference does that make?

MAMA: "Like a corpse," she says, "and I'm gonna be one soon enough as it is."

JESSIE: That's crazy.

MAMA: That's Agnes. "Jessie's shook the hand of death and I can't take the chance it's catching, Thelma, so I ain't comin' over, and you can understand or not, but I ain't comin'. I'll come up the driveway, but that's as far as I go."

JESSIE (*laughing, relieved*): I thought she didn't like me! She's scared of me! How about that! Scared of me.

MAMA: I could make her come over here, Jessie. I could call her up right now and she could bring the birds and come visit. I didn't know you ever thought about her at all. I'll tell her she just has to come and she'll come, all right. She owes me one.

JESSIE: No, that's all right. I just wondered about it. When I'm in the hospital, does she come over here?

MAMA: Her kitchen is just a tiny thing. When she comes over here, she feels like . . . (*Toning it down a little.*) Well, we all like a change of scene, don't we?

JESSIE (*playing along*): Sure we do. Plus there's no birds diving around.

MAMA: I hate those birds. She says I don't understand them. What's there to understand about birds?

JESSIE: Why Agnes likes them, for one thing. Why they stay with her when they could be outside with the other birds. What their singing means. How they fly. What they think Agnes is.

MAMA: Why do you have to know so much about things, Jessie? There's just not that much *to* things that I could ever see.

JESSIE: That you could ever *tell*, you mean. You didn't have to lie to me about Agnes.

MAMA: I didn't lie. You never asked before!

JESSIE: You lied about setting fire to all those houses and about how many birds she has and how much okra she eats and why she won't come over here. If I have to keep dragging the truth out of you, this is going to take all night.

MAMA: That's fine with me. I'm not a bit sleepy.

JESSIE: Mama . . .

MAMA: All right. Ask me whatever you want. Here.

(They come to an awkward stop, as the cocoa is ready and Mama pours it into the cups Jessie has set on the table.)

JESSIE (*as Mama takes her first sip*): Did you love Daddy?

MAMA: No.

JESSIE (*pleased that Mama understands the rules better now*): I didn't think so. Were you really fifteen when you married him?

MAMA: The way he told it? I'm sitting in the mud, he comes along, drags me in the kitchen, "She's been there ever since"?

JESSIE: Yes.

MAMA: No. It was a big fat lie, the whole thing. He just thought it was funnier that way. God, this milk in here.

JESSIE: The cocoa helps.

MAMA (*pleased that they agree on this, at least*): Not enough, though, does it? You can still taste it, can't you?

JESSIE: Yeah, it's pretty bad. I thought it was my memory that was bad, but it's not. It's the milk, all right.

MAMA: It's a real waste of chocolate. You don't have to finish it.

JESSIE (*putting her cup down*): Thanks, though.

MAMA: I should've known not to make it. I knew you wouldn't like it. You never did like it.

JESSIE: You didn't ever love him, or he did something and you stopped loving him, or what?

MAMA: He felt sorry for me. He wanted a plain country woman and that's what he married, and then he held it against me the rest of my life like I was supposed to change and surprise him somehow.

Like I remember this one day he was standing on the porch and I told him to get a shirt on and he went in and got one and then he said, real peaceful, but to the point, "You're right, Thelma. If God had meant for people to go around without any clothes on, they'd have been born that way."

JESSIE (*sees Mama's hurt*): He didn't mean anything by that, Mama.

MAMA: He never said a word he didn't have to, Jessie. That was probably all he'd said to me all day, Jessie. So if he said it, there was something to it, but I never did figure that one out. What did that mean?

JESSIE: I don't know. I liked him better than you did, but I didn't know him any better.

MAMA: How could I love him, Jessie. I didn't have a thing he wanted. (*Jessie doesn't answer.*) He got his share, though. You loved him enough for both of us. You followed him around like some . . . Jessie, all the man ever did was farm and sit . . . and try to think of somebody to sell the farm to.

JESSIE: Or make me a boyfriend out of pipe cleaners and sit back and smile like the stick man was about to dance and wasn't I going to get a kick out of that. Or sit up with a sick cow all night and leave me a chain of sleepy stick elephants on my bed in the morning.

MAMA: Or just sit.

JESSIE: I liked him sitting. Big old faded blue man in the chair. Quiet.

MAMA: Agnes gets more talk out of her birds than I got from the two of you. He could've had that GONE FISHING sign around his neck in that chair. I saw him stare off at the water. I saw him look at the weather rolling in. I got where I could practically see the boat myself. But you, you knew what he was thinking about and you're going to tell me.

JESSIE: I don't know, Mama! His life, I guess. His corn. His boots. Us. Things. You know.

MAMA: No, I don't know, Jessie! You had those quiet little conversations after supper every night. What were you whispering about?

JESSIE: We weren't whispering, you were just across the room.

MAMA: What did you talk about?

JESSIE: We talked about why black socks are warmer than blue socks. Is that something to go tell Mother? You were just jealous because I'd rather talk to him than wash the dishes with you.

MAMA: I was jealous because you'd rather talk to him than anything! (*Jessie reaches across the table for the small clock and starts to wind it.*) If I had died instead of him, he wouldn't have taken you in like I did.

JESSIE: I wouldn't have expected him to.

MAMA: Then what would you have done?

JESSIE: Come visit.

MAMA: Oh, I see. He died and left you stuck with me and you're mad about it.

JESSIE (*getting up from the table*): Not anymore. He didn't mean to. I didn't have to come here. We've been through this.

MAMA: He felt sorry for you, too, Jessie, don't kid yourself about that. He said you were a runt and he said it from the day you were born and he said you didn't have a chance.

JESSIE (*getting the canister of sugar and starting to refill the sugar bowl*): I know he loved me.

MAMA: What if he did? It didn't change anything.

JESSIE: It didn't have to. I miss him.

MAMA: He never really went fishing, you know. Never once. His tackle box was full of chewing tobacco and all he ever did was drive out to the lake and sit in his car. Dawson told me. And Bennie at the bait shop, he told Dawson. They all laughed about it. And he'd come back from fishing and all he'd have to show for it was . . . a whole pipe-cleaner *family* — chickens, pigs, a dog with a bad leg — it was creepy strange. It made me sick to look at them and I hid his pipe cleaners a couple of times but he always had more somewhere.

JESSIE: I thought it might be better for you after he died. You'd get interested in things. Breathe better. Change somehow.

MAMA: Into what? The Queen? A clerk in a shoe store? Why should I? Because he said to? Because you said to? (*Jessie shakes her head.*) Well I wasn't here for his entertainment and I'm not here for yours either, Jessie. I don't know what I'm here for, but then I don't think about it. (*Realizing what all this means.*) But I bet you wouldn't be killing yourself if he were still alive. That's a fine thing to figure out, isn't it?

JESSIE (*filling the honey jar now*): That's not true.

MAMA: Oh no? Then what were you asking about him for? Why did you want to know if I loved him?

JESSIE: I didn't think you did, that's all.

MAMA: Fine then. You were right. Do you feel better now?

JESSIE (*cleaning the honey jar carefully*): It feels good to be right about it.

MAMA: It didn't matter whether I loved him. It didn't matter to me and it didn't matter to him. And it didn't mean we didn't get along. It wasn't important. We didn't talk about it. (*Sweeping the pots off the cabinet.*) Take all these pots out to the porch!

JESSIE: What for?

MAMA: Just leave me this one pan. (*She jerks the silverware drawer open.*) Get me one knife, one fork, one big spoon, and the can opener, and put them out where I can get them. (*Starts throwing knives and forks in one of the pans.*)

JESSIE: Don't do that! I just straightened that drawer!

MAMA (*throwing the pan in the sink*): And throw out all the plates and cups. I'll use paper. Loretta can have what she wants and Dawson can sell the rest.

JESSIE (*calmly*): What are you doing?

MAMA: I'm not going to cook. I never liked it, anyway. I like candy. Wrapped in plastic or coming in sacks. And tuna. I like tuna. I'll eat tuna, thank you.

JESSIE (*taking the pan out of the sink*): What if you want to make apple butter? You can't make apple butter in that little pan. What if you leave carrots on cooking and burn up that pan?

MAMA: I don't like carrots.

JESSIE: What if the strawberries are good this year and you want to go picking with Agnes.

MAMA: I'll tell her to bring a pan. You said you would do whatever I wanted! I don't want a bunch of pans cluttering up my cabinets I can't get down to, anyway. Throw them out. Every last one.

JESSIE (*gathering up the pots*): I'm putting them all back in. I'm not taking them to the porch. If you want them, they'll be here. You'll bend down and get them, like you got the one for the cocoa. And if somebody else comes over here to cook, they'll have something to cook in, and that's the end of it!

MAMA: Who's going to come cook here?

JESSIE: Agnes.

MAMA: In my pots. Not on your life.

JESSIE: There's no reason why the two of you couldn't just live here together. Be cheaper for both of you and somebody to talk to. And if the birds bothered you, well, one day when Agnes is out getting her hair done, you could take them all for a walk!

MAMA (*as Jessie straightens the silverware*): So that's why you're pestering me about Agnes. You think you can rest easy if you get me a new babysitter? Well, I don't want to live with Agnes. I barely want to talk with Agnes. She's just around. We go back, that's all. I'm not letting Agnes near this place. You don't get off as easy as that, child.

JESSIE: O.K., then. It's just something to think about.

MAMA: I don't like things to think about. I like things to go on.

JESSIE (*closing the silverware drawer*): I want to know what Daddy said to you the night he died. You came storming out of his room and said I could wait it out with him if I wanted to, but you were going to watch *Gunsmoke*. What did he say to you?

MAMA: He didn't have *anything* to say to me, Jessie. That's why I left. He didn't say a thing. It was his last chance not to talk to me and he took full advantage of it.

JESSIE (*after a moment*): I'm sorry you didn't love him. Sorry for you, I mean. He seemed like a nice man.

MAMA (*as Jessie walks to the refrigerator*): Ready for your apple now?

JESSIE: Soon as I'm through here, Mama.

MAMA: You won't like the apple, either. It'll be just like the cocoa. You never liked eating at all, did you? Any of it! What have you been living on all these years, toothpaste?

JESSIE (*as she starts to clean out the refrigerator*): Now, you know the milkman comes on Wednesdays and Saturdays, and he leaves the order blank in an egg box, and you give the bills to Dawson once a month.

MAMA: Do they still make that orangeade?

JESSIE: It's not orangeade, it's just orange.

MAMA: I'm going to get some. I thought they stopped making it. You just stopped ordering it.

JESSIE: You should drink milk.

MAMA: Not anymore, I'm not. That hot chocolate was the last. Hooray.

JESSIE (*getting the garbage can from under the sink*): I told them to keep delivering a quart a week no matter what you said. I told them you'd run out of Cokes and you'd have to drink it. I told them I knew you wouldn't pour it on the ground . . .

MAMA (*finishing her sentence*): And you told them you weren't going to be ordering anymore?

JESSIE: I told them I was taking a little holiday and to look after you.

MAMA: And they didn't think something was funny about that? You who doesn't go to the front steps? You, who only sees the driveway looking down from a stretcher passed out cold?

JESSIE (*enjoying this, but not laughing*): They said it was about time, but why didn't I take you with me? And I said I didn't think you'd want to go, and they said, "Yeah, everybody's got their own idea of vacation."

MAMA: I guess you think that's funny.

JESSIE (*pulling jars out of the refrigerator*): You know there never was any reason to call the ambulance for me. All they ever did for me in the emergency room was let me wake up. I could've done that here. Now, I'll just call them out and you say yes or no. I know you like pickles. Ketchup?

MAMA: Keep it.

JESSIE: We've had this since last Fourth of July.

MAMA: Keep the ketchup. Keep it all.

JESSIE: Are you going to drink ketchup from the bottle or what? How can you want your food and not want your pots to cook it in? This stuff will all spoil in here, Mother.

MAMA: Nothing I ever did was good enough for you and I want to know why.

JESSIE: That's not true.

MAMA: And I want to know why you've lived here this long feeling the way you do.

JESSIE: You have no earthly idea how I feel.

MAMA: Well, how could I? You're real far back there, Jessie.

JESSIE: Back where?

MAMA: What's it like over there, where you are? Do people always say the right thing or get whatever they want, or what?

JESSIE: What are you talking about?

MAMA: Why do you read the newspaper? Why don't you wear that sweater I made for you? Do you remember how I used to look, or am I just any old woman now? When you have a fit, do you see stars or what? How did you fall off the horse, really? Why did Cecil leave you? Where did you put my old glasses?

JESSIE (*stunned by Mama's intensity*): They're in the bottom drawer of your dresser in an old Milk of Magnesia box. Cecil left me because he made me choose between him and smoking.

MAMA: Jessie, I know he wasn't that dumb.

JESSIE: I never understood why he hated it so much when it's so good. Smoking is the only thing I know that's always just what you think it's going to be. Just like it was the last time, right there when you want it and real quiet.

MAMA: Your fits made him sick and you know it.

JESSIE: Say seizures, not fits. Seizures.

MAMA: It's the same thing. A seizure in the hospital is a fit at home.

JESSIE: They didn't bother him at all. Except he did feel responsible for it. It *was* his idea to go horseback riding that day. It was his idea I could do *anything* if I just made up my mind to. I fell off the horse because I didn't know how to hold on. Cecil left for pretty much the same reason.

MAMA: He had a girl, Jessie. I walked right in on them in the toolshed.

JESSIE (*after a moment*): O.K. That's fair. (*Lighting another cigarette.*) Was she very pretty?

MAMA: She was Agnes's girl, Carlene. Judge for yourself.

JESSIE (*as she walks to the living room*): I guess you and Agnes had a good talk about that, huh?

MAMA: I never thought he was good enough for you. They moved here from Tennessee, you know.

JESSIE: What are you talking about? You liked him better than I did. You flirted him out here to build your porch or I'd never even met him at all. You thought maybe he'd help you out around the place, come in and get some coffee and talk to you. God knows what you thought. All that curly hair.

MAMA: He's the best carpenter I ever saw. That little house of yours will still be standing at the end of the world, Jessie.

JESSIE: You didn't need a porch, Mama.

MAMA: All right! I wanted you to have a husband.

JESSIE: And I couldn't get one on my own, of course.

MAMA: How were you going to get a husband never opening your mouth to a living soul?

JESSIE: So I was quiet about it, so what?

MAMA: So I should have let you just sit here? Sit like your daddy? Sit here?

JESSIE: Maybe.

MAMA: Well, I didn't think so.

JESSIE: Well, what did you know?

MAMA: I never said I knew much. How was I supposed to learn anything living out here? I didn't know enough to do half the things I did in my life. Things happen. You do what you can about them and you see what happens next. I married you off to the wrong man, I admit that. So I took you in when he left. I'm sorry.

JESSIE: He wasn't the wrong man.

MAMA: He didn't love you, Jessie, or he wouldn't have left.

JESSIE: He wasn't the wrong man, Mama. I loved Cecil so much. And I tried to get more exercise and I tried to stay awake. I tried to learn to ride a horse. And I tried to stay outside with him, but he always knew I was trying, so it didn't work.

MAMA: He was a selfish man. He told me once he hated to see people move into his houses after he built them. He knew they'd mess them up.

JESSIE: I loved that bridge he built over the creek in back of the house. It didn't have to be anything special, a couple of boards would have been just fine, but he used that yellow pine and rubbed it so smooth . . .

MAMA: He had responsibilities here. He had a wife and son here and he failed you.

JESSIE: Or that baby bed he built for Ricky. I told him he didn't have to spend so much time on it, but he said it had to last, and the thing ended up weighing two hundred pounds and I couldn't move it. I said, "How long does a baby bed have to last, anyway?" But maybe he thought if it was strong enough, it might keep Ricky a baby.

MAMA: Ricky is too much like Cecil.

JESSIE: He is not. Ricky is as much like me as it's possible for any human to be. We even wear the same size pants. These are his, I think.

MAMA: That's just the same size. That's not you're the same person.

JESSIE: I see it on his face. I hear it when he talks. We look out at the world and we see the same thing: Not Fair. And the only difference between us is Ricky's out there trying to get even. And he knows not to trust anybody and he got it straight from me. And he knows not to try to get work, and guess where he got that. He walks around like there's loose boards in the floor, and you know who laid that floor, I did.

MAMA: Ricky isn't through yet. You don't know how he'll turn out!

JESSIE (*going back to the kitchen*): Yes I do and so did Cecil. Ricky is the two of us together for all time in too small a space. And we're tearing each other apart, like always, inside that boy, and if you don't see it, then you're just blind.

MAMA: Give him time, Jess.

JESSIE: Oh, he'll have plenty of that. Five years for forgery, ten years for armed assault . . .

MAMA (*furious*): Stop that! (*Then pleading.*) Jessie, Cecil might be ready to try it again, honey, that happens sometimes. Go downtown. Find him. Talk to him. He didn't know what he had in you. Maybe he sees things different now, but you're not going to know that till you go see him. Or call him up! Right now! He might be home.

JESSIE: And say what? Nothing's changed, Cecil, I'd just like to look at you, if you don't mind? No. He loved me, Mama. He just didn't know how things fall down around me like they do. I think he did the right thing. He gave himself another chance, that's all. But I did beg him to take me with him. I did tell him I would leave Ricky and you and everything I loved out here if only he would take me with him, but he couldn't and I understood that. (*Pause.*) I wrote that note I showed you. I wrote it. Not Cecil. I said "I'm sorry, Jessie, I can't fix it all for you." I said I'd always love me, not Cecil. But that's how he felt.

MAMA: Then he should've taken you with him!

JESSIE (*picking up the garbage bag she has filled*): Mama, you don't pack your garbage when you move.

MAMA: You will not call yourself garbage, Jessie.

JESSIE (*taking the bag to the big garbage can near the back door*): Just a way of saying it, Mama. Thinking about my list, that's all. (*Opening the can, putting the garbage in, then securing the lid.*) Well, a little more than that. I was trying to say it's all right that Cecil left. It was . . . a relief in a way. I never was what he wanted to see, so it was better when he wasn't looking at me all the time.

MAMA: I'll make your apple now.

JESSIE: No thanks. You get the manicure stuff and I'll be right there.

(*Jessie ties up the big garbage bag in the can and replaces the small garbage bag under the sink, all the time trying desperately to regain her calm. Mama watches, from a distance, her hand reaching unconsciously for the phone. Then she has a better idea. Or rather she thinks of the only other thing left and is willing to try it. Maybe she is even convinced it will work.*)

MAMA: Jessie, I think your daddy had little . . .

JESSIE (*interrupting her*): Garbage night is Tuesday. Put it out as late as you can. The Davis's dogs get in it if you don't. (*Replacing the garbage bag in the can under the sink.*) And keep ordering the heavy black bags. It doesn't pay to buy the cheap ones. And I've got all the ties here with the hammers and all. Take them out of the box as soon as you open a new one and put them in this drawer. They'll get lost if you don't, and rubber bands or something else won't work.

MAMA: I think your daddy had fits, too. I think he sat in his chair and had little fits. I read this a long time ago in a magazine, how little fits go, just little blackouts where maybe their eyes don't even close and people just call them "thinking spells."

JESSIE (*getting the slipcover out of the laundry basket*): I don't think you want this manicure we've been looking forward to. I washed this cover for the sofa, but it'll take both of us to get it back on.

MAMA: I watched his eyes. I know that's what it was. The magazine said some people don't even know they've had one.

JESSIE: Daddy would've known if he'd had fits, Mama.

MAMA: The lady in this story had kept track of hers and she'd had eighty thousand of them in the last eleven years.

JESSIE: Next time you wash this cover, it'll dry better if you put it on wet.

MAMA: Jessie, listen to what I'm telling you. This lady had anywhere between five and five hundred fits a day and they lasted maybe fifteen seconds apiece, so that out of her life, she'd only lost about two weeks altogether, and she had a full-time secretary job and an IQ of 120.

JESSIE (*amused by Mama's approach*): You want to talk about fits, is that it?

MAMA: Yes. I do. I want to say . . .

JESSIE (*interrupting*): Most of the time I wouldn't even know I'd had one, except I wake up with different clothes on, feeling like I've been run over. Sometimes I feel my head start to turn around or hear myself scream. And sometimes there *is* this dizzy stupid feeling a little before it, but if the TV's on, well, it's easy to miss.

(*As Jessie and Mama replace the slipcover on the sofa and the afghan on the chair, the physical struggle somehow mirrors the emotional one in the conversation.*)

MAMA: I can tell when you're about to have one. Your eyes get this big! But, Jessie, you haven't . . .

JESSIE (*taking charge of this*): What do they look like? The seizures.

MAMA (*reluctant*): Different each time, Jess.

JESSIE: O.K. Pick one, then. A good one. I think I want to know now.

MAMA: There's not much to tell. You just . . . crumple, in a heap, like a puppet and somebody cut the strings all at once, or like the firing squad in some Mexican movie, you just slide down the wall, you know. You don't know what happens? How can you not know what happens?

JESSIE: I'm busy.

MAMA: That's not funny.

JESSIE: I'm not laughing. My head turns around and I fall down and then what?

MAMA: Well, your chest squeezes in and out, and you sound like you're gagging, sucking air in and out like you can't breathe.

JESSIE: Do it for me. Make the sound for me.

MAMA: I will not. It's awful-sounding.

JESSIE: Yeah. It felt like it might be. What's next?

MAMA: Your mouth bites down and I have to get your tongue out of the way fast, so you don't bite yourself.

JESSIE: Or you. I bite you, too, don't I?

MAMA: You got me once real good. I had to get a tetanus! But I know what to watch for now. And then you turn blue and the jerks start up. Like I'm standing there poking you with a cattle prod or you're sticking your finger in a light socket as fast as you can . . .

JESSIE: Foaming like a mad dog the whole time.

MAMA: It's bubbling, Jess, not foam like the washer overflowed, for God's sake; it's bubbling like a baby spitting up. I go get a wet washcloth, that's all. And then the jerks slow down and you wet yourself and it's over. Two minutes tops.

JESSIE: How do I get to the bed?

MAMA: How do you think?

JESSIE: I'm too heavy for you now. How do you do it?

MAMA: I call Dawson. But I get you cleaned up before he gets here and I make him leave before you wake up.

JESSIE: You could just leave me on the floor.

MAMA: I want you to wake up someplace nice, O.K.? (*Then making a real effort.*) But, Jessie, and this is the reason I even brought this up! You haven't had a seizure for a solid year. A whole year, do you realize that?

JESSIE: Yeah, the phenobarb's about right now, I guess.

MAMA: You bet it is. You might never have another one, ever! You might be through with it for all time!

JESSIE: Could be.

MAMA: You are. I know you are!

JESSIE: I sure am feeling good. I really am. The double vision's gone and my gums aren't swelling. No rashes or anything. I'm feeling as good as I ever felt in my life. I'm even feeling like worrying or getting mad and I'm not afraid it will start a fit if I do, I just go ahead.

MAMA: Of course you do! You can even scream at me, if you want to. I can take it. You don't have to act like you're just visiting here, Jessie. This is your house, too.

JESSIE: The best part is, my memory's back.

MAMA: Your memory's always been good. When couldn't you remember things? You're always reminding me what . . .

JESSIE: Because I've made lists for everything. But now I remember what things mean on my lists. I see "dish towels," and I used to wonder whether I was supposed to wash them, buy them, or look for them because I wouldn't remember where I put them after I washed them, but now I know it means wrap them up, they're a present for Loretta's birthday.

MAMA (*finished with the sofa now*): You used to go looking for your lists, too, I've noticed that. You always know where they are now! (*Then suddenly worried.*) Loretta's birthday isn't coming up, is it?

JESSIE: I made a list of all the birthdays for you. I even put yours on it. (*A small smile.*) So you can call Loretta and remind her.

MAMA: Let's take Loretta to Howard Johnson's and have those fried clams. I *know* you love that clam roll.

JESSIE (*slight pause*): I won't be here, Mama.

MAMA: What have we just been talking about? You'll be here. You're well, Jessie. You're starting all over. You said it yourself. You're remembering things and . . .

JESSIE: I won't be here. If I'd ever had a year like this, to think straight and all, before now, I'd be gone already.

MAMA (*not pleading, commanding*): No, Jessie.

JESSIE (*folding the rest of the laundry*): Yes, Mama.

Once I started remembering, I could see what it all added up to.

MAMA: The fits are over!

JESSIE: It's not the fits, Mama.

MAMA: Then it's me for giving them to you, but I didn't do it!

JESSIE: It's not the fits! You said it yourself, the medicine takes care of the fits.

MAMA (*interrupting*): Your daddy gave you those fits, Jessie. He passed it down to you like your green eyes and your straight hair. It's not my fault!

JESSIE: So what if he had little fits? It's not inherited. I fell off the horse. It was an accident.

MAMA: The horse wasn't the first time, Jessie. You had a fit when you were five years old.

JESSIE: I did not.

MAMA: You did! You were eating a popsicle and down you went. He gave it to you. It's *his* fault, not mine.

JESSIE: Well, you took your time telling me.

MAMA: How do you tell that to a five-year-old?

JESSIE: What did the doctor say?

MAMA: He said kids have them all the time. He said there wasn't anything to do but wait for another one.

JESSIE: But I didn't have another one.

(*Now there is a real silence.*)

JESSIE: You mean to tell me I had fits all the time as a kid and you just told me I fell down or something and it wasn't till I had the fit when Cecil was looking that anybody bothered to find out what was the matter with me?

MAMA: It wasn't *all the time*, Jessie. And they changed when you started to school. More like your daddy's. Oh, that was some swell time, sitting here with the two of you turning off and on like light bulbs some nights.

JESSIE: How many fits did I have?

MAMA: You never hurt yourself. I never let you out of my sight. I caught you every time.

JESSIE: But you didn't tell anybody.

MAMA: It was none of their business.

JESSIE: You were ashamed.

MAMA: I didn't want anybody to know. Least of all you.

JESSIE: Least of all me. Oh, right. That was mine to know, Mama, not yours. Did Daddy know?

MAMA: He thought you were . . . you fell down a lot. That's what he thought. You were careless. Or maybe he thought I beat you. I don't know what he thought. He didn't think about it.

JESSIE: Because you didn't tell him!

MAMA: If I told him about you, I'd have to tell him about him!

JESSIE: I don't like this. I don't like this one bit.

MAMA: I didn't think you'd like it. That's why I didn't tell you.

JESSIE: If I'd known I was an epileptic, Mama, I wouldn't have ridden any horses.

MAMA: Make you feel like a freak, is that what I should have done?

JESSIE: Just get the manicure tray and sit down!

MAMA (*throwing it to the floor*): I don't want a manicure!

JESSIE: Doesn't look like you do, no.

MAMA: Maybe I did drop you, you don't know.

JESSIE: If you say you didn't, you didn't.

MAMA (*beginning to break down*): Maybe I fed you the wrong thing. Maybe you had a fever sometime and I didn't know it soon enough. Maybe it's a punishment.

JESSIE: For what?

MAMA: I don't know. Because of how I felt about your father. Because I didn't want any more children. Because I smoked too much or didn't eat right when I was carrying you. It has to be something I did.

JESSIE: It does not. It's just a sickness, not a curse. Epilepsy doesn't mean anything. It just is.

MAMA: I'm not talking about the fits here, Jessie! I'm talking about this killing yourself. It has to be me that's the matter here. You wouldn't be doing this if it wasn't. I didn't tell you things or I married you off to the wrong man or I took you in and let your life get away from you or all of it put together. I don't know what I did, but I did it, I know. This is all my fault, Jessie, but I don't know what to do about it now!

JESSIE (*exasperated at having to say this again*): It doesn't have anything to do with you!

MAMA: Everything you do has to do with me, Jessie. You can't do *anything,* wash your face or cut your finger, without doing it to me. That's right! You might as well kill me as you, Jessie, it's the same thing. This has to do with me, Jessie.

JESSIE: Then what if it does! What if it has everything to do with you! What if you are all I have and you're not enough? What if I could take all the rest of it if only I didn't have you here? What if the only way I can get away from you for good is to kill myself? What if it is? I can *still* do it!

MAMA (*in desperate tears*): Don't leave me, Jessie! (*Jessie stands for a moment, then turns for the bedroom.*) No! (*She grabs Jessie's arm.*)

JESSIE (*carefully taking her arm away*): I have a box of things I want people to have. I'm just going to go get it for you. You . . . just rest a minute.

(*Jessie is gone. Mama heads for the telephone, but she can't even pick up the receiver this time and, instead, stoops to clean up the bottles that have spilled out of the manicure tray.*)

(*Jessie returns, carrying a box that groceries were delivered in. It probably says Hershey Kisses or Starkist Tuna. Mama is still down on the floor cleaning up, hoping that maybe if she just makes it look nice enough, Jessie will stay.*)

MAMA: Jessie, how can I live here without you? I need you! You're supposed to tell me to stand up straight and say how nice I look in my pink dress, and drink my milk. You're supposed to go around and lock up so I know we're safe for the night, and when I wake up, you're supposed to be out there making the coffee and watching me get older every day, and you're supposed to help me die when the time comes. I can't do that by myself, Jessie. I'm not like you, Jessie. I hate the quiet and I don't want to die and I don't want you to go, Jessie. How can I . . . (*Has to stop a moment.*) How can I get up every day knowing you had to kill yourself to make it stop hurting and I was here all the time and I never even saw it. And then you gave me this chance to make it better, convince you to stay alive, and I couldn't do it. How can I live with myself after this, Jessie?

JESSIE: I only told you so I could explain it, so you wouldn't blame yourself, so you wouldn't feel bad. There wasn't anything you could say to change my mind. I didn't want you to save me. I just wanted you to know.

MAMA: Stay with me just a little longer. Just a few more years. I don't have that many more to go, Jessie. And as soon as I'm dead, you can do whatever you want. Maybe with me gone, you'll have all the quiet you want, right here in the house. And maybe one day you'll put in some begonias up the walk and get just the right rain for them all summer. And Ricky will be married by then and he'll bring your grandbabies over and you can sneak them a piece of candy when their daddy's not looking and then be real glad when they've gone home and left you to your quiet again.

JESSIE: Don't you see, Mama, everything I do winds up like this. How could I think you would understand? How could I think you would want a manicure? We could hold hands for an hour and then I could go shoot myself? I'm sorry about tonight, Mama, but it's exactly why I'm doing it.

MAMA: If you've got the guts to kill yourself, Jessie, you've got the guts to stay alive.

JESSIE: I know that. So it's really just a matter of where I'd rather be.

MAMA: Look, maybe I can't think of what you should do, but that doesn't mean there isn't something that would help. *You* find it. *You* think of it. You can keep trying. You can get brave and try some more. You don't have to give up!

JESSIE: I'm *not* giving up! This *is* the other thing I'm trying. And I'm sure there are some other things that might work, but *might* work isn't good enough anymore. I need something that *will* work. *This* will work. That's why I picked it.

MAMA: But something might happen. Something that could change everything. Who knows what it might be, but it might be worth waiting for! (*Jessie doesn't respond.*) Try it for two more weeks. We could have more talks like tonight.

JESSIE: No, Mama.

MAMA: I'll pay more attention to you. Tell the truth when you ask me. Let you have your say.

JESSIE: No, Mama! We wouldn't have more talks like tonight, because it's this next part that's made this last part so good, Mama. No, Mama. *This* is how I have my say. This is how I say what I thought about it *all* and I say no. To Dawson and Loretta and the Red Chinese and epilepsy and Ricky and Cecil and my Daddy. And me. And hope. I say no! (*Then going to Mama on the sofa.*) Just let me go easy, Mama.

MAMA: How can I let you go?

JESSIE: You can because you have to. It's what you've always done.

MAMA: You are my child!

JESSIE: I am what became of your child. (*Mama cannot answer.*) I found an old baby picture of me. And it was somebody else, not me. It was somebody pink and fat who never heard of sick or lonely, somebody who cried and got fed, and reached up and got held and kicked but didn't hurt anybody, and slept whenever she wanted to, just by closing her eyes. Somebody who mainly just laid there and laughed at the colors waving around over her head and chewed on a polka-dot whale and woke up knowing some new trick nearly every day, and rolled over and drooled on the sheet and felt your hand pulling my quilt back up over me. That's who I started out and this is who is left. (*There is no self-pity here.*) That's what this is about. It's somebody I lost, all right, it's my own self. Who I never was. Or who I tried to be and never got there. Somebody I waited for who never came. And never will. So, see, it doesn't much matter what else happens in the world or in this house, even. I'm what was worth waiting for and I didn't make it. Me . . . who might have made a difference to me . . . I'm not going to show up, so there's no reason to stay, except to keep you company, and

that's . . . not reason enough because I'm not . . . very good company. (*Pause.*) Am I.

MAMA (*knowing she must tell the truth*): No. And neither am I.

JESSIE: I had this strange little thought, well, maybe it's not so strange. Anyway, after Christmas, after I decided to do this, I would wonder, sometimes, what might keep me here, what might be worth staying for, and you know what it was? It was maybe if there was something I really liked, like maybe if I really liked rice pudding or cornflakes for breakfast or something, that might be enough.

MAMA: Rice pudding is good.

JESSIE: Not to me.

MAMA: And you're not afraid?

JESSIE: Afraid of what?

MAMA: I'm afraid of it, for me, I mean. When my time comes. I know it's coming, but . . .

JESSIE: You don't know when. Like in a scary movie.

MAMA: Yeah, sneaking up on me like some killer on the loose, hiding out in the back yard just waiting for me to have my hands full someday and how am I supposed to protect myself anyhow when I don't know what he looks like and I don't know how he sounds coming up behind me like that or if it will hurt or take very long or what I don't get done before it happens.

JESSIE: You've got plenty of time left.

MAMA: I forget what for, right now.

JESSIE: For whatever happens, I don't know. For the rest of your life. For Agnes burning down one more house or Dawson losing his hair or . . .

MAMA (*quickly*): Jessie, I can't just sit here and say O.K., kill yourself if you want to.

JESSIE: Sure you can. You just did. Say it again.

MAMA (*really startled*): Jessie! (*Quiet horror.*) How dare you! (*Furious.*) How dare you! You think you can just leave whenever you want, like you're watching television here? No, you can't, Jessie. You make me feel like a fool for being alive, child, and you are so wrong! I like it here, and I will stay here until they make me go, until they drag me screaming and I mean screeching into my grave, and you're real smart to get away before then because, I mean, honey, you've never heard noise like that in your life. (*Jessie turns away.*) Who am I talking to? You're gone already, aren't you? I'm looking right through you! I can't stop you because you're already gone! I guess you think they'll all have to talk about you now! I guess you think this will really confuse them. Oh yes, ever since Christmas you've been laughing to yourself and thinking, "Boy, are they all in for a surprise." Well, nobody's going to be a bit surprised, sweetheart. This is just like you. Do it the hard way, that's my girl, all right.

(*Jessie gets up and goes into the kitchen, but Mama follows her.*) You know who they're going to feel sorry for? Me! How about that! Not you, me! They're going to be *ashamed* of you. Yes. *Ashamed!* If somebody asks Dawson about it, he'll change the subject as fast as he can. He'll talk about how much he has to pay to park his car these days.

JESSIE: Leave me alone.

MAMA: It's the truth!

JESSIE: I should've just left you a note!

MAMA (*screaming*): Yes! (*Then suddenly understanding what she has said, nearly paralyzed by the thought of it, she turns slowly to face Jessie, nearly whispering.*) No. No. I . . . might not have thought of all the things you've said.

JESSIE: It's O.K., Mama.

(*Mama is nearly unconscious from the emotional devastation of these last few moments. She sits down at the kitchen table, hurt and angry and desperately afraid. But she looks almost numb. She is so far beyond what is known as pain that she is virtually unreachable and Jessie knows this, and talks quietly, watching for signs of recovery.*)

JESSIE (*washes her hands in the sink*): I remember you liked that preacher who did Daddy's, so if you want to ask him to do the service, that's O.K. with me.

MAMA (*not an answer, just a word*): What.

JESSIE (*putting on hand lotion as she talks*): And pick some songs you like or let Agnes pick, she'll know exactly which ones. Oh, and I had your dress cleaned that you wore to Daddy's. You looked real good in that.

MAMA: I don't remember, hon.

JESSIE: And it won't be so bad once your friends start coming to the funeral home. You'll probably see people you haven't seen for years, but I thought about what you should say to get you over that nervous part when they first come in.

MAMA (*simply repeating*): Come in.

JESSIE: Take them up to see their flowers, they'd like that. And when they say, "I'm so sorry, Thelma," you just say, "I appreciate your coming, Connie." And then ask how their garden was this summer or what they're doing for Thanksgiving or how their children . . .

MAMA: I don't think I should ask about their children. I'll talk about what they have on, that's always good. And I'll have some crochet work with me.

JESSIE: And Agnes will be there, so you might not have to talk at all.

MAMA: Maybe if Connie Richards does come, I can get her to tell me where she gets that Irish yarn, she calls it. I know it doesn't come from Ireland. I think it just comes with a green wrapper.

JESSIE: And be sure to invite enough people home afterward so you get enough food to feed them all and have some left for you. But don't let anybody take anything home, especially Loretta.

MAMA: Loretta will get all the food set up, honey. It's only fair to let her have some macaroni or something.

JESSIE: No, Mama. You have to be more selfish from now on. (*Sitting at the table with Mama.*) Now, somebody's bound to ask you why I did it and you just say you don't know. That you loved me and you know I loved you and we just sat around tonight like every other night of our lives, and then I came over and kissed you and said, " 'Night, Mother," and you heard me close my bedroom door and the next thing you heard was the shot. And whatever reasons I had, well, you guess I just took them with me.

MAMA (*quietly*): It was something personal.

JESSIE: Good. That's good, Mama.

MAMA: That's what I'll say, then.

JESSIE: Personal. Yeah.

MAMA: Is that what I tell Dawson and Loretta, too? We sat around, you kissed me, " 'Night, Mother"? They'll want to know more, Jessie. They won't believe it.

JESSIE: Well, then, tell them what we did. I filled up the candy jars. I cleaned out the refrigerator. We made some hot chocolate and put the cover back on the sofa. You had no idea. All right? I really think it's better that way. If they know we talked about it, they really won't understand how you let me go.

MAMA: I guess not.

JESSIE: It's private. Tonight is private, yours and mine, and I don't want anybody else to have any of it.

MAMA: O.K., then.

JESSIE (*standing behind Mama now, holding her shoulders*): Now, when you hear the shot, I don't want you to come in. First of all, you won't be able to get in by yourself, but I don't want you trying. Call Dawson, then call the police, and then call Agnes. And then you'll need something to do till somebody gets here, so wash the hot-chocolate pan. You wash that pan till you hear the doorbell ring and I don't care if it's an hour, you keep washing that pan.

MAMA: I'll make my calls and then I'll just sit. I won't need something to do. What will the police say?

JESSIE: They'll do that gunpowder test, I guess, and ask you what happened, and by that time, the ambulance will be here and they'll come in and get me and you know how that goes. You stay out here with Dawson and Loretta. You keep Dawson out here. I want the police in the room first, not Dawson, O.K.?

MAMA: What if Dawson and Loretta want me to go home with them?

JESSIE (*returning to the living room*): That's up to you.

MAMA: I think I'll stay here. All they've got is Sanka.

JESSIE: Maybe Agnes could come stay with you for a few days.

MAMA (*standing up, looking into the living room*): I'd rather be by myself, I think. (*Walking toward the box Jessie brought in earlier.*) You want me to give people those things?

JESSIE (*they sit down on the sofa, Jessie holding the box on her lap*): I want Loretta to have my little calculator. Dawson bought it for himself, you know, but then he saw one he liked better and he couldn't bring both of them home with Loretta counting every penny the way she does, so he gave the first one to me. Be funny for her to have it now, don't you think? And all my house slippers are in a sack for her in my closet. Tell her I know they'll fit and I've never worn any of them, and make sure Dawson hears you tell her that. I'm glad he loves Loretta so much, but I wish he knew not everybody has her size feet.

MAMA (*taking the calculator*): O.K.

JESSIE (*reaching into the box again*): This letter is for Dawson, but it's mostly about you, so read it if you want. There's a list of presents for you for at least twenty more Christmases and birthdays, so if you want anything special you better add it to this list before you give it to him. Or if you want to be surprised, just don't read that page. This Christmas, you're getting mostly stuff for the house, like a new rug in your bathroom and needlework, but next Christmas, you're really going to cost him next Christmas. I think you'll like it a lot and you'd never think of it.

MAMA: And you think he'll go for it?

JESSIE: I think he'll feel like a real jerk if he doesn't. Me telling him to, like this and all. Now, this number's where you call Cecil. I called it last week and he answered, so I know he still lives there.

MAMA: What do you want me to tell him?

JESSIE: Tell him we talked about him and I only had good things to say about him, but mainly tell him to find Ricky and tell him what I did, and tell Ricky you have something for him, out here, from me, and to come get it. (*Pulls a sack out of the box.*)

MAMA (*the sack feels empty*): What is it?

JESSIE (*taking it off*): My watch. (*Putting it in the sack and taking a ribbon out of the sack to tie around the top of it.*)

MAMA: He'll sell it!

JESSIE: That's the idea. I appreciate him not stealing it already. I'd like to buy him a good meal.

MAMA: He'll buy dope with it!

JESSIE: Well, then, I hope he gets some good dope with it, Mama. And the rest of this is for you. (*Handing Mama the box now. Mama picks up the things and looks at them.*)

MAMA (*surprised and pleased*): When did you do all this? During my naps, I guess.

JESSIE: I guess. I tried to be quiet about it. (*As Mama is puzzled by the presents.*) Those are just little presents. For whenever you need one. They're not bought presents, just things I thought you might like to look at, pictures or things you think you've lost. Things you didn't know you had, even. You'll see.

MAMA: I'm not sure I want them. They'll make me think of you.

JESSIE: No they won't. They're just things, like a free tube of toothpaste I found hanging on the door one day.

MAMA: Oh. All right, then.

JESSIE: Well, maybe there's one nice present in there somewhere. It's Granny's ring she gave me and I thought you might like to have it, but I didn't think you'd wear it if I gave it to you right now.

MAMA (*taking the box to a table nearby*): No. Probably not. (*Turning back to face her.*) I'm ready for my manicure, I guess. Want me to wash my hands again?

JESSIE (*standing up*): It's time for me to go, Mama.

MAMA (*starting for her*): No, Jessie, you've got all night!

JESSIE (*as Mama grabs her*): No, Mama.

MAMA: It's not even ten o'clock.

JESSIE (*very calm*): Let me go, Mama.

MAMA: I can't. You can't go. You can't do this. You didn't say it would be so soon, Jessie. I'm scared. I love you.

JESSIE (*takes her hands away*): Let go of me, Mama. I've said everything I had to say.

MAMA (*standing still a minute*): You said you wanted to do my nails.

JESSIE (*taking a small step backward*): I can't. It's too late.

MAMA: It's not too late!

JESSIE: I don't want you to wake Dawson and Loretta when you call. I want them to still be up and dressed so they can get right over.

MAMA (*as Jessie backs up, Mama moves in on her, but carefully*): They wake up fast, Jessie, if they have to. They don't matter here, Jessie. You do. I do. We're not through yet. We've got a lot of things to take care of here. I don't know where my prescriptions are and you didn't tell me what to tell Dr. Davis when he calls or how much you want me to tell Ricky or who I call to rake the leaves or . . .

JESSIE: Don't try and stop me, Mama, you can't do it.

MAMA (*grabbing her again, this time hard*): I can too! I'll stand in front of this hall and you can't get past me. (*They struggle.*) You'll have to knock me down to get away from me, Jessie. I'm not about to let you . . .

(*Mama struggles with Jessie at the door and in the struggle Jessie gets away from her and —*)

JESSIE (*almost a whisper*): 'Night, Mother. (*She vanishes into her bedroom and we hear the door lock just as Mama gets to it.*)

MAMA (*screams*): Jessie! (*Pounding on the door.*) Jessie, you let me in there. Don't you do this, Jessie. I'm not going to stop screaming until you open this door, Jessie. Jessie! Jessie! What if I don't do any of the things you told me to do! I'll tell Cecil what a miserable man he was to make you feel the way he did and I'll give Ricky's watch to Dawson if I feel like it and the only way you can make sure I do what you want is you come out here and make me, Jessie! (*Pounding again.*) Jessie! Stop this! I didn't know! I was here with you all the time. How could I know you were so alone?

(*And Mama stops for a moment, breathless and frantic, putting her ear to the door, and when she doesn't hear anything, she stands up straight again and screams once more.*)

Jessie! Please!

(*And we hear the shot, and it sounds like an answer, it sounds like No.*)

(*Mama collapses against the door, tears streaming down her face, but not screaming anymore. In shock now.*)

Jessie, Jessie, child . . . Forgive me. (*Pause.*) I thought you were mine.

(*And she leaves the door and makes her way through the living room, around the furniture, as though she didn't know where it was, not knowing what to do. Finally, she goes to the stove in the kitchen and picks up the hot-chocolate pan and carries it with her to the telephone and holds on to it while she dials the number. She looks down at the pan, holding it tight like her life depended on it. She hears Loretta answer.*)

MAMA: Loretta, let me talk to Dawson, honey.

August Wilson

August Wilson was born in Pittsburgh in 1945, the son of a white father who never lived with his family and a black mother who had come from North Carolina to a Pittsburgh slum where she worked to keep her family together. Wilson's early childhood was spent in an environment very similar to that of his play *Fences*, and Troy Maxson seems to be patterned somewhat on Wilson's stepfather.

Wilson's writing is rooted to a large extent in music, specifically the blues. As a poet, writing over several years, Wilson found himself interested in the speech patterns and rhythms that were familiar to him from black neighborhoods, but the value of those patterns became clearer to him when he grew older and moved from Pittsburgh to Minneapolis. From a distance, he was able to see more clearly what had attracted him to the language and to begin to use the language more fully in his work.

In the 1960s and 1970s Wilson became involved in the civil rights movement and began to describe himself as a black nationalist, a term he has recently said he feels comfortable with. He began writing plays in the 1960s in Pittsburgh and then took a job in St. Paul writing dramatic skits for the Science Museum of Minnesota. He founded the Playwrights Center in Minneapolis and began writing a play, *Jitney*, about a gypsy cab station, which was produced in 1982. *Fullerton Street*, about Pittsburgh, was another play written in this early period. Wilson's first commercial success, *Ma Rainey's Black Bottom*, eventually premiered at the Yale Repertory Theatre in 1984 and then went to Broadway, where it enjoyed 275 performances and won the New York Drama Critics' Circle Award.

Ma Rainey's Black Bottom is the first of a planned sequence of ten plays based on the black American experience. As Wilson has said, "I think the black Americans have the most dramatic story of all mankind to tell." The concept of such a vast project echoes O'Neill's projected group of eleven plays based on the Irish-American experience. Unfortunately, O'Neill destroyed all but *A Touch of the Poet* in his series. Wilson's project, however, is ongoing and intense and so far has produced some of the most successful plays in the recent American theater.

Ma Rainey is about the legendary black blues singer who preceded Bessie Smith and Billie Holiday. The play is about the way in which she was exploited by white managers and recording executives and the way in which she knowingly dealt with her exploitation. In the cast of the play are several black musicians in the backup band. Levee, the trumpet player, has a dream of leading his own band and establishing himself as an important jazz musician. But he is haunted by memories of seeing his mother raped by a gang of white men when he was a boy. He wants to "improve" the session he's playing by making the old jazz tune "Black Bottom" swing in the new jazz style, but Ma Rainey keeps him in tow and demands that they play the tune in the old way. Levee finally cracks under the pressure, and the play ends painfully.

Fences opened at the Yale Repertory Theatre in 1985 and in New York in early 1987, where it won the Pulitzer Prize as well as the New York Drama Critics' Circle Award. This long-running success has established Wilson firmly as an important writer. *Joe Turner's Come and Gone* opened at the Yale Repertory Theatre in late 1986 and moved to New York in early 1988, where it too has been hailed as an important play, winning its author the New York Drama Critics' Circle Award once again. *Joe Turner* is set in a rooming house in Pittsburgh in 1911 and is a study of the children of former slaves. They have come North to find work and some of them have been found by the legendary bounty hunter Joe Turner. As a study of a people in transition, the play is a quiet masterpiece. It incorporates a number of important African traditions, especially religious rituals of healing as performed by Bynum, the "bone man," a seer and a medicine man. In this play and others, Wilson makes a special effort to highlight the elements of African heritage that white society strips away from blacks.

The next play in Wilson's projected series, *The Piano Lesson*, which premiered at the Yale Repertory Theatre in 1987, also portrays the complexity of black attitudes toward the past and black heritage. The piano represents two kinds of culture: the white culture that produced it and the black culture, in the form of Papa Boy Willie, who carved into it images from black Africa. The central question in the play is whether Boy Willie should sell the piano and use the money for a down payment on a house and therefore on the future. Or should he follow his wife Berneice's advice and keep it because it is too precious to sell? The conflict is deep and the play ultimately focuses on a profound moment of spiritual exorcism. How one exorcises the past — how one lives with it or without it — is a central theme in Wilson's work, which has established him as a major figure in American theater.

FENCES

Fences (1985), like most of August Wilson's recent plays, was directed by Lloyd Richards, who also directed the first production of Lorraine Hansberry's *A Raisin in the Sun*. Richards is the dean of the School of Drama at Yale University and runs the Yale Repertory Theatre, where he has directed all of the plays Wilson has written in his projected ten-play cycle about black American life.

Fences presents a slice of life in a black tenement in Pittsburgh in the 1950s. Its main character, Troy Maxson, is a garbage collector who has taken great pride in keeping his family together and providing for them. When the play opens he and his friend Bono are talking about Troy's challenge to the company and the union about blacks' ability to do the same "easy" work as whites. Troy's rebellion and frustration set the tone of the entire play: He is looking for his rights and, at age fifty-three, he has missed many opportunities to get what he deserves.

Troy's struggle for fairness becomes virtually mythic as he describes his wrestling with death during a bout with pneumonia in 1941. He describes a three-day struggle in which he eventually overcame his foe. Troy — a good baseball player who was relegated to the Negro leagues — sees death as nothing but a fastball, and he could always deal with a fastball. Both Bono and Troy's wife, Rose, show an intense admiration for him as he describes his ordeal.

The father-son relationship that begins to take a central role in the drama is complicated by strong feelings of pride and independence on both sides. Troy's son Cory wants to play football and Troy wants him to work on the fence he's mending. Cory's youthful enthusiasm probably echoes Troy's own youthful innocence, but Troy resents it in Cory, seeing it as partly responsible for his own predicament. Cory cannot see his father's point of view and feels that he is exempt from the kind of prejudice his father suffered.

The agony of the father-son relationship, their misperceptions of each other, persist through the play. Rose's capacity to cope with the deepest of Troy's anxieties — his fear of death — is one of her most important achievements in the play. At the end of the play Rose demands that Cory give Troy the respect he deserves, although Cory's anger and inexperience make it all but impossible for him to see his father as anything other than an oppressor. Cory feels that he must say no to his father once, but Rose will not let him deny his father. When the play ends with Gabe's fantastic ritualistic dance, the audience feels a sense of closure, of spiritual finish and a final seal.

August Wilson (b. 1946)

FENCES

Characters

TROY MAXSON
JIM BONO, *Troy's friend*
ROSE, *Troy's wife*
LYONS, *Troy's oldest son by previous marriage*
GABRIEL, *Troy's brother*
CORY, *Troy and Rose's son*
RAYNELL, *Troy's daughter*

Setting: *The setting is the yard which fronts the only entrance to the Maxson household, an ancient two-story brick house set back off a small alley in a big-city neighborhood. The entrance to the house is gained by two or three steps leading to a wooden porch badly in need of paint.*

A relatively recent addition to the house and running its full width, the porch lacks congruence. It is a sturdy porch with a flat roof. One or two chairs of dubious value sit at one end where the kitchen window opens onto the porch. An old-fashioned icebox stands silent guard at the opposite end.

The yard is a small dirt yard, partially fenced, except for the last scene, with a wooden sawhorse, a pile of lumber, and other fence-building equipment set off to the side. Opposite is a tree from which hangs a ball made of rags. A baseball bat leans against the tree. Two oil drums serve as garbage receptacles and sit near the house at right to complete the setting.

The Play: *Near the turn of the century, the destitute of Europe sprang on the city with tenacious claws and an honest and solid dream. The city devoured them. They swelled its belly until it burst into a thousand furnaces and sewing machines, a thousand butcher shops and bakers' ovens, a thousand churches and hospitals and funeral parlors and money-lenders. The city grew. It nourished itself and offered each man a partnership limited only by his talent, his guile, and his willingness and capacity for hard work. For the immigrants of Europe, a dream dared and won true.*

The descendants of African slaves were offered no such welcome or participation. They came from places called the Carolinas and the Virginias, Georgia, Alabama, Mississippi, and Tennessee. They came strong, eager, searching. The city rejected them and they fled and settled along the riverbanks and under bridges in shallow, ramshackle houses made of sticks and tarpaper.

They collected rags and wood. They sold the use of their muscles and their bodies. They cleaned houses and washed clothes, they shined shoes, and in quiet desperation and vengeful pride, they stole, and lived in pursuit of their own dream. That they could breathe free, finally, and stand to meet life with the force of dignity and whatever eloquence the heart could call upon.

By 1957, the hard-won victories of the European immigrants had solidified the industrial might of America. War had been confronted and won with new energies that used loyalty and patriotism as its fuel. Life was rich, full, and flourishing. The Milwaukee Braves won the World Series, and the hot winds of change that would make the sixties a turbulent, racing, dangerous, and provocative decade had not yet begun to blow full.

ACT I · Scene I

(It is 1957. Troy and Bono enter the yard, engaged in conversation. Troy is fifty-three years old, a large man with thick, heavy hands; it is this largeness that he strives to fill out and make an accommodation with. Together with his blackness, his largeness informs his sensibilities and the choices he has made in his life.

(Of the two men, Bono is obviously the follower. His commitment to their friendship of thirty-odd years is rooted in his admiration of Troy's honesty, capacity for hard work, and his strength, which Bono seeks to emulate.)

(It is Friday night, payday, and the one night of the week the two men engage in a ritual of talk and drink. Troy is usually the most talkative and at times he can be crude and almost vulgar, though he is capable of rising to profound heights of expression. The men carry lunch buckets and wear or carry burlap aprons and are dressed in clothes suitable to their jobs as garbage collectors.)

BONO: Troy, you ought to stop that lying!
TROY: I ain't lying! The nigger had a watermelon this big.

(He indicates with his hands.)

Talking about . . . "What watermelon, Mr. Rand?"

I liked to fell out! "What watermelon, Mr. Rand?" . . . And it sitting there big as life.

BONO: What did Mr. Rand say?

TROY: Ain't said nothing. Figure if the nigger too dumb to know he carrying a watermelon, he wasn't gonna get much sense out of him. Trying to hide that great big old watermelon under his coat. Afraid to let the white man see him carry it home.

BONO: I'm like you . . . I ain't got no time for them kind of people.

TROY: Now what he look like getting mad cause he see the man from the union talking to Mr. Rand?

BONO: He come to me talking about . . . "Maxson gonna get us fired." I told him to get away from me with that. He walked away from me calling you a troublemaker. What Mr. Rand say?

TROY: Ain't said nothing. He told me to go down the Commissioner's office next Friday. They called me down there to see them.

BONO: Well, as long as you got your complaint filed, they can't fire you. That's what one of them white fellows tell me.

TROY: I ain't worried about them firing me. They gonna fire me cause I asked a question? That's all I did. I went to Mr. Rand and asked him, "Why? Why you got the white mens driving and the colored lifting?" Told him, "what's the matter, don't I count? You think only white fellows got sense enough to drive a truck. That ain't no paper job! Hell, anybody can drive a truck. How come you got all whites driving and the colored lifting?" He told me "take it to the union." Well, hell, that's what I done! Now they wanna come up with this pack of lies.

BONO: I told Brownie if the man come and ask him any questions . . . just tell the truth! It ain't nothing but something they done trumped up on you cause you filed a complaint on them.

TROY: Brownie don't understand nothing. All I want them to do is change the job description. Give everybody a chance to drive the truck. Brownie can't see that. He ain't got that much sense.

BONO: How you figure he be making out with that gal be up at Taylors' all the time . . . that Alberta gal?

TROY: Same as you and me. Getting just as much as we is. Which is to say nothing.

BONO: It is, huh? I figure you doing a little better than me . . . and I ain't saying what I'm doing.

TROY: Aw, nigger, look here . . . I know you. If you had got anywhere near that gal, twenty minutes later you be looking to tell somebody. And the first one you gonna tell . . . that you gonna want to brag to . . . is gonna be me.

BONO: I ain't saying that. I see where you be eyeing her.

TROY: I eye all the women. I don't miss nothing. Don't never let nobody tell you Troy Maxson don't eye the women.

BONO: You been doing more than eyeing her. You done bought her a drink or two.

TROY: Hell yeah, I bought her a drink! What that mean? I bought you one, too. What that mean cause I buy her a drink? I'm just being polite.

BONO: It's all right to buy her one drink. That's what you call being polite. But when you wanna be buying two or three . . . that's what you call eyeing her.

TROY: Look here, as long as you known me . . . you ever known me to chase after women?

BONO: Hell yeah! Long as I done known you. You forgetting I knew you when.

TROY: Naw, I'm talking about since I been married to Rose?

BONO: Oh, not since you been married to Rose. Now, that's the truth, there. I can say that.

TROY: All right then! Case closed.

BONO: I see you be walking up around Alberta's house. You supposed to be at Taylors' and you be walking up around there.

TROY: What you watching where I'm walking for? I ain't watching after you.

BONO: I seen you walking around there more than once.

TROY: Hell, you liable to see me walking anywhere! That don't mean nothing cause you see me walking around there.

BONO: Where she come from anyway? She just kinda showed up one day.

TROY: Tallahassee. You can look at her and tell she one of them Florida gals. They got some big healthy women down there. Grow them right up out the ground. Got a little bit of Indian in her. Most of them niggers down in Florida got some Indian in them.

BONO: I don't know about that Indian part. But she damn sure big and healthy. Woman wear some big stockings. Got them great big old legs and hips as wide as the Mississippi River.

TROY: Legs don't mean nothing. You don't do nothing but push them out of the way. But them hips cushion the ride!

BONO: Troy, you ain't got no sense.

TROY: It's the truth! Like you riding on Goodyears!

(*Rose enters from the house. She is ten years younger than Troy, her devotion to him stems from her recognition of the possibilities of her life without him: a succession of abusive men and their babies, a life of partying and running the streets, the Church, or aloneness with its attendant pain and frustration. She recognizes Troy's spirit as a fine and illuminating one*

*and she either ignores or forgives his faults, only some
of which she recognizes. Though she doesn't drink,
her presence is an integral part of the Friday night
rituals. She alternates between the porch and the kitchen,
where supper preparations are under way.)*

ROSE: What you all out here getting into?

TROY: What you worried about what we getting into
for? This is men talk, woman.

ROSE: What I care what you all talking about? Bono,
you gonna stay for supper?

BONO: No, I thank you, Rose. But Lucille say she
cooking up a pot of pigfeet.

TROY: Pigfeet! Hell, I'm going home with you! Might
even stay the night if you got some pigfeet. You
got something in there to top them pigfeet, Rose?

ROSE: I'm cooking up some chicken. I got some chicken
and collard greens.

TROY: Well, go on back in the house and let me and
Bono finish what we was talking about. This is
men talk. I got some talk for you later. You know
what kind of talk I mean. You go on and powder
it up.

ROSE: Troy Maxson, don't you start that now!

TROY (*puts his arm around her*): Aw, woman . . . come
here. Look here, Bono . . . when I met this
woman . . . I got out that place, say, "Hitch up my
pony, saddle up my mare . . . there's a woman out
there for me somewhere. I looked here. Looked
there. Saw Rose and latched on to her." I latched
on to her and told her — I'm gonna tell you the
truth — I told her, "Baby, I don't wanna marry,
I just wanna be your man." Rose told me . . . tell
him what you told me, Rose.

ROSE: I told him if he wasn't the marrying kind, then
move out the way so the marrying kind could find
me.

TROY: That's what she told me. "Nigger, you in my
way. You blocking the view! Move out the way
so I can find me a husband." I thought it over two
or three days. Come back —

ROSE: Ain't no two or three days nothing. You was
back the same night.

TROY: Come back, told her . . . "Okay, baby . . . but
I'm gonna buy me a banty rooster and put him
out there in the backyard . . . and when he see a
stranger come, he'll flap his wings and crow . . ."
Look here, Bono, I could watch the front door by
myself . . . it was that back door I was worried
about.

ROSE: Troy, you ought not talk like that. Troy ain't
doing nothing but telling a lie.

TROY: Only thing is . . . when we first got married . . . forget the rooster . . . we ain't had no yard!

BONO: I hear you tell it. Me and Lucille was staying
down there on Logan Street. Had two rooms with
the outhouse in the back. I ain't mind the outhouse
none. But when that goddamn wind blow through
there in the winter . . . that's what I'm talking about!
To this day I wonder why in the hell I ever stayed
down there for six long years. But see, I didn't
know I could do no better. I thought only white
folks had inside toilets and things.

ROSE: There's a lot of people don't know they can
do no better than they doing now. That's just something you got to learn. A lot of folks still shop at
Bella's.

TROY: Ain't nothing wrong with shopping at Bella's.
She got fresh food.

ROSE: I ain't said nothing about if she got fresh food.
I'm talking about what she charge. She charge ten
cents more than the A&P.

TROY: The A&P ain't never done nothing for me. I
spends my money where I'm treated right. I go
down to Bella, say, "I need a loaf of bread, I'll
pay you Friday." She give it to me. What sense
that make when I got money to go and spend it
somewhere else and ignore the person who done
right by me? That ain't in the Bible.

ROSE: We ain't talking about what's in the Bible. What
sense it make to shop there when she overcharge?

TROY: You shop where you want to. I'll do my shopping
where the people been good to me.

ROSE: Well, I don't think it's right for her to overcharge.
That's all I was saying.

BONO: Look here . . . I got to get on. Lucille going be
raising all kind of hell.

TROY: Where you going, nigger? We ain't finished this
pint. Come here, finish this pint.

BONO: Well, hell, I am . . . if you ever turn the bottle
loose.

TROY (*hands him the bottle*): The only thing I say
about the A&P is I'm glad Cory got that job down
there. Help him take care of his school clothes and
things. Gabe done moved out and things getting
tight around here. He got that job. . . . He can start
to look out for himself.

ROSE: Cory done went and got recruited by a college
football team.

TROY: I told that boy about that football stuff. The
white man ain't gonna let him get nowhere with
that football. I told him when he first come to me
with it. Now you come telling me he done went
and got more tied up in it. He ought to go and
get recruited in how to fix cars or something where
he can make a living.

ROSE: He ain't talking about making no living playing
football. It's just something the boys in school do.

They gonna send a recruiter by to talk to you. He'll tell you he ain't talking about making no living playing football. It's a honor to be recruited.

TROY: It ain't gonna get him nowhere. Bono'll tell you that.

BONO: If he be like you in the sports . . . he's gonna be all right. Ain't but two men ever played baseball as good as you. That's Babe Ruth and Josh Gibson.° Them's the only two men ever hit more home runs than you.

TROY: What it ever get me? Ain't got a pot to piss in or a window to throw it out of.

ROSE: Times have changed since you was playing baseball, Troy. That was before the war. Times have changed a lot since then.

TROY: How in hell they done changed?

ROSE: They got lots of colored boys playing ball now. Baseball and football.

BONO: You right about that, Rose. Times have changed, Troy. You just come along too early.

TROY: There ought not never have been no time called too early! Now you take that fellow . . . what's that fellow they had playing right field for the Yankees back then? You know who I'm talking about, Bono. Used to play right field for the Yankees.

ROSE: Selkirk?

TROY: Selkirk! That's it! Man batting .269, understand? .269. What kind of sense that make? I was hitting .432 with thirty-seven home runs! Man batting .269 and playing right field for the Yankees! I saw Josh Gibson's daughter yesterday. She walking around with raggedy shoes on her feet. Now I bet you Selkirk's daughter ain't walking around with raggedy shoes on her feet! I bet you that!

ROSE: They got a lot of colored baseball players now. Jackie Robinson was the first. Folks had to wait for Jackie Robinson.

TROY: I done seen a hundred niggers play baseball better than Jackie Robinson. Hell, I know some teams Jackie Robinson couldn't even make! What you talking about Jackie Robinson. Jackie Robinson wasn't nobody. I'm talking about if you could play ball then they ought to have let you play. Don't care what color you were. Come telling me I come along too early. If you could play . . . then they ought to have let you play.

(Troy takes a long drink from the bottle.)

ROSE: You gonna drink yourself to death. You don't need to be drinking like that.

TROY: Death ain't nothing. I done seen him. Done

wrassled with him. You can't tell me nothing about death. Death ain't nothing but a fastball on the outside corner. And you know what I'll do to that! Lookee here, Bono . . . am I lying? You get one of them fastballs, about waist high, over the outside corner of the plate where you can get the meat of the bat on it . . . and good god! You can kiss it goodbye. Now, am I lying?

BONO: Naw, you telling the truth there. I seen you do it.

TROY: If I'm lying . . . that 450 feet worth of lying!

(Pause.)

That's all death is to me. A fastball on the outside corner.

ROSE: I don't know why you want to get on talking about death.

TROY: Ain't nothing wrong with talking about death. That's part of life. Everybody gonna die. You gonna die, I'm gonna die. Bono's gonna die. Hell, we all gonna die.

ROSE: But you ain't got to talk about it. I don't like to talk about it.

TROY: You the one brought it up. Me and Bono was talking about baseball . . . you tell me I'm gonna drink myself to death. Ain't that right, Bono? You know I don't drink this but one night out of the week. That's Friday night. I'm gonna drink just enough to where I can handle it. Then I cuts it loose. I leave it alone. So don't you worry about me drinking myself to death. 'Cause I ain't worried about Death. I done seen him. I done wrestled with him.

Look here, Bono . . . I looked up one day and Death was marching straight at me. Like Soldiers on Parade! The Army of Death was marching straight at me. The middle of July, 1941. It got real cold just like it be winter. It seem like Death himself reached out and touched me on the shoulder. He touch me just like I touch you. I got cold as ice and Death standing there grinning at me.

ROSE: Troy, why don't you hush that talk.

TROY: I say . . . What you want, Mr. Death? You be wanting me? You done brought your army to be getting me? I looked him dead in the eye. I wasn't fearing nothing. I was ready to tangle. Just like I'm ready to tangle now. The Bible say be ever vigilant. That's why I don't get but so drunk. I got to keep watch.

ROSE: Troy was right down there in Mercy Hospital. You remember he had pneumonia? Laying there with a fever talking plumb out of his head.

TROY: Death standing there staring at me . . . carrying that sickle in his hand. Finally he say, "You want

Josh Gibson: (1911–1947), powerful, black baseball player known in the 1930s as the Babe Ruth of the Negro leagues.

bound over for another year?" See, just like that . . . "You want bound over for another year?" I told him, "Bound over hell! Let's settle this now!"

It seem like he kinda fell back when I said that, and all the cold went out of me. I reached down and grabbed that sickle and threw it just as far as I could throw it . . . and me and him commenced to wrestling.

We wrestled for three days and three nights. I can't say where I found the strength from. Every time it seemed like he was gonna get the best of me, I'd reach way down deep inside myself and find the strength to do him one better.

ROSE: Every time Troy tell that story he find different ways to tell it. Different things to make up about it.

TROY: I ain't making up nothing. I'm telling you the facts of what happened. I wrestled with Death for three days and three nights and I'm standing here to tell you about it.

(Pause.)

All right. At the end of the third night we done weakened each other to where we can't hardly move. Death stood up, throwed on his robe . . . had him a white robe with a hood on it. He throwed on that robe and went off to look for his sickle. Say, "I'll be back." Just like that. "I'll be back." I told him, say, "Yeah, but . . . you gonna have to find me!" I wasn't no fool. I wan't going looking for him. Death ain't nothing to play with. And I know he's gonna get me. I know I got to join his army . . . his camp followers. But as long as I keep my strength and see him coming . . . as long as I keep up my vigilance . . . he's gonna have to fight to get me. I ain't going easy.

BONO: Well, look here, since you got to keep up your vigilance . . . let me have the bottle.

TROY: Aw hell, I shouldn't have told you that part. I should have left out that part.

ROSE: Troy be talking that stuff and half the time don't even know what he be talking about.

TROY: Bono know me better than that.

BONO: That's right. I know you. I know you got some Uncle Remus° in your blood. You got more stories than the devil got sinners.

TROY: Aw hell, I done seen him too! Done talked with the devil.

ROSE: Troy, don't nobody wanna be hearing all that stuff.

(Lyons enters the yard from the street. Thirty-four

Uncle Remus: Black storyteller who recounts traditional black tales in the book by Joel Chandler Harris.

years old, Troy's son by a previous marriage, he sports a neatly trimmed goatee, sport coat, white shirt, tieless and buttoned at the collar. Though he fancies himself a musician, he is more caught up in the rituals and "idea" of being a musician than in the actual practice of the music. He has come to borrow money from Troy, and while he knows he will be successful, he is uncertain as to what extent his lifestyle will be held up to scrutiny and ridicule.)

LYONS: Hey, Pop.

TROY: What you come "Hey, Popping" me for?

LYONS: How you doing, Rose?

(He kisses her.)

Mr. Bono. How you doing?

BONO: Hey, Lyons . . . how you been?

TROY: He must have been doing all right. I ain't seen him around here last week.

ROSE: Troy, leave your boy alone. He come by to see you and you wanna start all that nonsense.

TROY: I ain't bothering Lyons.

(Offers him the bottle.)

Here . . . get you a drink. We got an understanding. I know why he come by to see me and he know I know.

LYONS: Come on, Pop . . . I just stopped by to say hi . . . see how you was doing.

TROY: You ain't stopped by yesterday.

ROSE: You gonna stay for supper, Lyons? I got some chicken cooking in the oven.

LYONS: No, Rose . . . thanks. I was just in the neighborhood and thought I'd stop by for a minute.

TROY: You was in the neighborhood all right, nigger. You telling the truth there. You was in the neighborhood cause it's my payday.

LYONS: Well, hell, since you mentioned it . . . let me have ten dollars.

TROY: I'll be damned! I'll die and go to hell and play blackjack with the devil before I give you ten dollars.

BONO: That's what I wanna know about . . . that devil you done seen.

LYONS: What . . . Pop done seen the devil? You too much, Pops.

TROY: Yeah, I done seen him. Talked to him too!

ROSE: You ain't seen no devil. I done told you that man ain't had nothing to do with the devil. Anything you can't understand, you want to call it the devil.

TROY: Look here, Bono . . . I went down to see Hertzberger about some furniture. Got three rooms for two-ninety-eight. That what it say on the radio. "Three rooms . . . two-ninety-eight." Even made up a little song about it. Go down there . . . man tell me I can't get no credit. I'm working every day and can't get no credit. What to do? I got an empty house with some raggedy furniture in it. Cory ain't got no bed. He's sleeping on a pile of rags on the floor. Working every day and can't get no credit. Come back here — Rose'll tell you — madder than hell. Sit down . . . try to figure what I'm gonna do. Come a knock on the door. Ain't been living here but three days. Who know I'm here? Open the door . . . devil standing there bigger than life. White fellow . . . got on good clothes · and everything. Standing there with a clipboard in his hand. I ain't had to say nothing. First words come out of his mouth was . . . "I understand you need some furniture and can't get no credit." I liked to fell over. He say, "I'll give you all the credit you want, but you got to pay the interest on it." I told him, "Give me three rooms worth and charge whatever you want." Next day a truck pulled up here and two men unloaded them three rooms. Man what drove the truck give me a book. Say send ten dollars, first of every month to the address in the book and everything will be all right. Say if I miss a payment the devil was coming back and it'll be hell to pay. That was fifteen years ago. To this day . . . the first of the month I send my ten dollars, Rose'll tell you.

ROSE: Troy lying.

TROY: I ain't never seen that man since. Now you tell me who else that could have been but the devil? I ain't sold my soul or nothing like that, you understand. Naw, I wouldn't have truck with the devil about nothing like that. I got my furniture and pays my ten dollars the first of the month just like clockwork.

BONO: How long you say you been paying this ten dollars a month?

TROY: Fifteen years!

BONO: Hell, ain't you finished paying for it yet? How much the man done charged you.

TROY: Ah hell, I done paid for it. I done paid for it ten times over! The fact is I'm scared to stop paying it.

ROSE: Troy lying. We got that furniture from Mr. Glickman. He ain't paying no ten dollars a month to nobody.

TROY: Aw hell, woman. Bono know I ain't that big a fool.

LYONS: I was just getting ready to say . . . I know where there's a bridge for sale.

TROY: Look here, I'll tell you this . . . it don't matter to me if he was the devil. It don't matter if the devil give credit. Somebody has got to give it.

ROSE: It ought to matter. You going around talking about having truck with the devil . . . God's the one

you gonna have to answer to. He's the one gonna be at the Judgment.

LYONS: Yeah, well, look here, Pop . . . let me have that ten dollars. I'll give it back to you. Bonnie got a job working at the hospital.

TROY: What I tell you, Bono? The only time I see this nigger is when he wants something. That's the only time I see him.

LYONS: Come on, Pop, Mr. Bono don't want to hear all that. Let me have the ten dollars. I told you Bonnie working.

TROY: What that mean to me? "Bonnie working." I don't care if she working. Go ask her for the ten dollars if she working. Talking about "Bonnie working." Why ain't you working?

LYONS: Aw, Pop, you know I can't find no decent job. Where am I gonna get a job at? You know I can't get no job.

TROY: I told you I know some people down there. I can get you on the rubbish if you want to work. I told you that the last time you came by here asking me for something.

LYONS: Naw, Pop . . . thanks. That ain't for me. I don't wanna be carrying nobody's rubbish. I don't wanna be punching nobody's time clock.

TROY: What's the matter, you too good to carry people's rubbish? Where you think that ten dollars you talking about come from? I'm just supposed to haul people's rubbish and give my money to you cause you too lazy to work. You too lazy to work and wanna know why you ain't got what I got.

ROSE: What hospital Bonnie working at? Mercy?

LYONS: She's down at Passavant working in the laundry.

TROY: I ain't got nothing as it is. I give you that ten dollars and I got to eat beans the rest of the week. Naw . . . you ain't getting no ten dollars here.

LYONS: You ain't got to be eating no beans. I don't know why you wanna say that.

TROY: I ain't got no extra money. Gabe done moved over to Miss Pearl's paying her the rent and things done got tight around here. I can't afford to be giving you every payday.

LYONS: I ain't asked you to give me nothing. I asked you to loan me ten dollars. I know you got ten dollars.

TROY: Yeah, I got it. You know why I got it? Cause I don't throw my money away out there in the streets. You living the fast life . . . wanna be a musician . . . running around in them clubs and things . . . then, you learn to take care of yourself. You ain't gonna find me going and asking nobody for nothing. I done spent too many years without.

LYONS: You and me is two different people, Pop.

TROY: I done learned my mistake and learned to do what's right by it. You still trying to get something for nothing. Life don't owe you nothing. You owe it to yourself. Ask Bono. He'll tell you I'm right.

LYONS: You got your way of dealing with the world . . . I got mine. The only thing that matters to me is the music.

TROY: Yeah, I can see that! It don't matter how you gonna eat . . . where your next dollar is coming from. You telling the truth there.

LYONS: I know I got to eat. But I got to live too. I need something that gonna help me to get out of the bed in the morning. Make me feel like I belong in the world. I don't bother nobody. I just stay with my music cause that's the only way I can find to live in the world. Otherwise there ain't no telling what I might do. Now I don't come criticizing you and how you live. I just come by to ask you for ten dollars. I don't wanna hear all that about how I live.

TROY: Boy, your mamma did a hell of a job raising you.

LYONS: You can't change me, Pop. I'm thirty-four years old. If you wanted to change me, you should have been there when I was growing up. I come by to see you . . . ask for ten dollars and you want to talk about how I was raised. You don't know nothing about how I was raised.

ROSE: Let the boy have ten dollars, Troy.

TROY (*to Lyons*): What the hell you looking at me for? I ain't got no ten dollars. You know what I do with my money.

(*To Rose.*)

Give him ten dollars if you want him to have it.

ROSE: I will. Just as soon as you turn it loose.

TROY (*handing Rose the money*): There it is. Seventy-six dollars and forty-two cents. You see this, Bono? Now, I ain't gonna get but six of that back.

ROSE: You ought to stop telling that lie. Here, Lyons. (*She hands him the money.*)

LYONS: Thanks, Rose. Look . . . I got to run . . . I'll see you later.

TROY: Wait a minute. You gonna say, "thanks, Rose" and ain't gonna look to see where she got that ten dollars from? See how they do me, Bono?

LYONS: I know she got it from you, Pop. Thanks. I'll give it back to you.

TROY: There he go telling another lie. Time I see that ten dollars . . . he'll be owing me thirty more.

LYONS: See you, Mr. Bono.

BONO: Take care, Lyons!

LYONS: Thanks, Pop. I'll see you again.

(*Lyons exits the yard.*)

TROY: I don't know why he don't go and get him a decent job and take care of that woman he got.

BONO: He'll be all right, Troy. The boy is still young.

TROY: The *boy* is thirty-four years old.

ROSE: Let's not get off into all that.

BONO: Look here . . . I got to be going. I got to be getting on. Lucille gonna be waiting.

TROY (*puts his arm around Rose*): See this woman, Bono? I love this woman. I love this woman so much it hurts. I love her so much . . . I done run out of ways of loving her. So I got to go back to basics. Don't you come by my house Monday morning talking about time to go to work . . . 'cause I'm still gonna be stroking!

ROSE: Troy! Stop it now!

BONO: I ain't paying him no mind, Rose. That ain't nothing but gin-talk. Go on, Troy. I'll see you Monday.

TROY: Don't you come by my house, nigger! I done told you what I'm gonna be doing.

(*The lights go down to black.*)

Scene II

(*The lights come up on Rose hanging up clothes. She hums and sings softly to herself. It is the following morning.*)

ROSE (*Sings*): Jesus, be a fence all around me every day
Jesus, I want you to protect me as I travel on my way.
Jesus, be a fence all around me every day.

(*Troy enters from the house.*)

Jesus, I want you to protect me
As I travel on my way.
(*To Troy.*) 'Morning. You ready for breakfast? I can fix it soon as I finish hanging up these clothes?

TROY: I got the coffee on. That'll be all right. I'll just drink some of that this morning.

ROSE: That 651 hit yesterday. That's the second time this month. Miss Pearl hit for a dollar . . . seem like those that need the least always get lucky. Poor folks can't get nothing.

TROY: Them numbers don't know nobody. I don't know why you fool with them. You and Lyons both.

ROSE: It's something to do.

TROY: You ain't doing nothing but throwing your money away.

ROSE: Troy, you know I don't play foolishly. I just play a nickel here and a nickel there.

TROY: That's two nickels you done thrown away.

ROSE: Now I hit sometimes . . . that makes up for it. It always comes in handy when I do hit. I don't hear you complaining then.

TROY: I ain't complaining now. I just say it's foolish. Trying to guess out of six hundred ways which way the number gonna come. If I had all the money niggers, these Negroes, throw away on numbers for one week — just one week — I'd be a rich man.

ROSE: Well, you wishing and calling it foolish ain't gonna stop folks from playing numbers. That's one thing for sure. Besides . . . some good things come from playing numbers. Look where Pope done bought him that restaurant off of numbers.

TROY: I can't stand niggers like that. Man ain't had two dimes to rub together. He walking around with his shoes all run over bumming money for cigarettes. All right. Got lucky there and hit the numbers . . .

ROSE: Troy, I know all about it.

TROY: Had good sense, I'll say that for him. He ain't throwed his money away. I seen niggers hit the numbers and go through two thousand dollars in four days. Man bought him that restaurant down there . . . fixed it up real nice . . . and then didn't want nobody to come in it! A Negro go in there and can't get no kind of service. I seen a white fellow come in there and order a bowl of stew. Pope picked all the meat out the pot for him. Man ain't had nothing but a bowl of meat! Negro come behind him and ain't got nothing but the potatoes and carrots. Talking about what numbers do for people, you picked a wrong example. Ain't done nothing but make a worser fool out of him than he was before.

ROSE: Troy, you ought to stop worrying about what happened at work yesterday.

TROY: I ain't worried. Just told me to be down there at the Commissioner's office on Friday. Everybody think they gonna fire me. I ain't worried about them firing me. You ain't got to worry about that.

(*Pause.*)

Where's Cory? Cory in the house? (*Calls.*) Cory?

ROSE: He gone out.

TROY: Out, huh? He gone out 'cause he know I want him to help me with this fence. I know how he is. That boy scared of work.

(*Gabriel enters. He comes halfway down the alley and, hearing Troy's voice, stops.*)

TROY (*continues*): He ain't done a lick of work in his life.

ROSE: He had to go to football practice. Coach wanted them to get in a little extra practice before the season start.

TROY: I got his practice . . . running out of here before he get his chores done.

ROSE: Troy, what is wrong with you this morning?

Don't nothing set right with you. Go on back in there and go to bed . . . get up on the other side.

TROY: Why something got to be wrong with me? I ain't said nothing wrong with me.

ROSE: You got something to say about everything. First it's the numbers . . . then it's the way the man runs his restaurant . . . then you done got on Cory. What's it gonna be next? Take a look up there and see if the weather suits you . . . or is it gonna be how you gonna put up the fence with the clothes hanging in the yard.

TROY: You hit the nail on the head then.

ROSE: I know you like I know the back of my hand. Go on in there and get you some coffee . . . see if that straighten you up. 'Cause you ain't right this morning.

(*Troy starts into the house and sees Gabriel. Gabriel starts singing. Troy's brother, he is seven years younger than Troy. Injured in World War II, he has a metal plate in his head. He carries an old trumpet tied around his waist and believes with every fiber of his being that he is the Archangel Gabriel. He carries a chipped basket with an assortment of discarded fruits and vegetables he has picked up in the strip district and which he attempts to sell.*)

GABRIEL (*Singing*): Yes, ma'am, I got plums
You ask me how I sell them
Oh ten cents apiece
Three for a quarter
Come and buy now
'Cause I'm here today
And tomorrow I'll be gone

(*Gabriel enters.*)

Hey, Rose!

ROSE: How you doing, Gabe?

GABRIEL: There's Troy . . . Hey, Troy!

TROY: Hey, Gabe.

(*Exit into kitchen.*)

ROSE (*to Gabriel*): What you got there?

GABRIEL: You know what I got, Rose. I got fruits and vegetables.

ROSE (*looking in basket*): Where's all these plums you talking about?

GABRIEL: I ain't got no plums today, Rose. I was just singing that. Have some tomorrow. Put me in a big order for plums. Have enough plums tomorrow for St. Peter and everybody.

(*Troy reenters from kitchen, crosses to steps.*)
(*To Rose.*)

Troy's mad at me.

TROY: I ain't mad at you. What I got to be mad at you about? You ain't done nothing to me.

GABRIEL: I just moved over to Miss Pearl's to keep out from in your way. I ain't mean no harm by it.

TROY: Who said anything about that? I ain't said anything about that.

GABRIEL: You ain't mad at me, is you?

TROY: Naw . . . I ain't mad at you, Gabe. If I was mad at you I'd tell you about it.

GABRIEL: Got me two rooms. In the basement. Got my own door too. Wanna see my key?

(He holds up a key.)

That's my own key! Ain't nobody else got a key like that. That's my key! My two rooms!

TROY: Well, that's good, Gabe. You got your own key . . . that's good.

ROSE: You hungry, Gabe? I was just fixing to cook Troy his breakfast.

GABRIEL: I'll take some biscuits. You got some biscuits? Did you know when I was in heaven . . . every morning me and St. Peter would sit down by the gate and eat some big fat biscuits? Oh, yeah! We had us a good time. We'd sit there and eat us them biscuits and then St. Peter would go off to sleep and tell me to wake him up when it's time to open the gates for the judgment.

ROSE: Well, come on . . . I'll make up a batch of biscuits.

(Rose exits into the house.)

GABRIEL: Troy . . . St. Peter got your name in the book. I seen it. It say . . . Troy Maxson. I say . . . I know him! He got the same name like what I got. That's my brother!

TROY: How many times you gonna tell me that, Gabe?

GABRIEL: Ain't got my name in the book. Don't have to have my name. I done died and went to heaven. He got your name though. One morning St. Peter was looking at his book . . . marking it up for the judgment . . . and he let me see your name. Got it in there under M. Got Rose's name . . . I ain't seen it like I seen yours . . . but I know it's in there. He got a great big book. Got everybody's name what was ever been born. That's what he told me. But I seen your name. Seen it with my own eyes.

TROY: Go on in the house there. Rose going to fix you something to eat.

GABRIEL: Oh, I ain't hungry. I done had breakfast with Aunt Jemimah. She come by and cooked me up a whole mess of flapjacks. Remember how we used to eat them flapjacks?

TROY: Go on in the house and get you something to eat now.

GABRIEL: I got to go sell my plums. I done sold some tomatoes. Got me two quarters. Wanna see?

(He shows Troy his quarters.)

I'm gonna save them and buy me a new horn so St. Peter can hear me when it's time to open the gates.

(Gabriel stops suddenly. Listens.)

Hear that? That's the hellhounds. I got to chase them out of here. Go on get out of here! Get out!

(Gabriel exits singing.)

Better get ready for the judgment
Better get ready for the judgment
My Lord is coming down

(Rose enters from the house.)

TROY: He gone off somewhere.

GABRIEL (offstage): Better get ready for the judgment
Better get ready for the judgment morning
Better get ready for the judgment
My God is coming down

ROSE: He ain't eating right. Miss Pearl say she can't get him to eat nothing.

TROY: What you want me to do about it, Rose? I done did everything I can for the man. I can't make him get well. Man got half his head blown away . . . what you expect?

ROSE: Seem like something ought to be done to help him.

TROY: Man don't bother nobody. He just mixed up from that metal plate he got in his head. Ain't no sense for him to go back into the hospital.

ROSE: Least he be eating right. They can help him take care of himself.

TROY: Don't nobody wanna be locked up, Rose. What you wanna lock him up for? Man go over there and fight the war . . . messin' around with them Japs, get half his head blown off . . . and they give him a lousy three thousand dollars. And I had to swoop down on that.

ROSE: Is you fixing to go into that again?

TROY: That's the only way I got a roof over my head . . . cause of that metal plate.

ROSE: Ain't no sense you blaming yourself for nothing. Gabe wasn't in no condition to manage that money. You done what was right by him. Can't nobody say you ain't done what was right by him. Look how long you took care of him . . . till he wanted to have his own place and moved over there with Miss Pearl.

TROY: That ain't what I'm saying, woman! I'm just stating the facts. If my brother didn't have that metal plate in his head . . . I wouldn't have a pot to piss in or a window to throw it out of. And I'm fifty-three years old. Now see if you can understand that!

(*Troy gets up from the porch and starts to exit the yard.*)

ROSE: Where you going off to? You been running out of here every Saturday for weeks. I thought you was gonna work on this fence?

TROY: I'm gonna walk down to Taylors'. Listen to the ball game. I'll be back in a bit. I'll work on it when I get back.

(*He exits the yard. The lights go to black.*)

Scene III

(*The lights come up on the yard. It is four hours later. Rose is taking down the clothes from the line. Cory enters carrying his football equipment.*)

ROSE: Your daddy like to had a fit with you running out of here this morning without doing your chores.

CORY: I told you I had to go to practice.

ROSE: He say you were supposed to help him with this fence.

CORY: He been saying that the last four or five Saturdays, and then he don't never do nothing, but go down to Taylors'. Did you tell him about the recruiter?

ROSE: Yeah, I told him.

CORY: What he say?

ROSE: He ain't said nothing too much. You get in there and get started on your chores before he gets back. Go on and scrub down them steps before he gets back here hollering and carrying on.

CORY: I'm hungry. What you got to eat, Mama?

ROSE: Go on and get started on your chores. I got some meat loaf in there. Go on and make you a sandwich . . . and don't leave no mess in there.

(*Cory exits into the house. Rose continues to take down the clothes. Troy enters the yard and sneaks up and grabs her from behind.*)

Troy! Go on, now. You liked to scared me to death. What was the score of the game? Lucille had me on the phone and I couldn't keep up with it.

TROY: What I care about the game? Come here, woman. (*He tries to kiss her.*)

ROSE: I thought you went down Taylors' to listen to the game. Go on, Troy! You supposed to be putting up this fence.

TROY (*attempting to kiss her again*): I'll put it up when I finish with what is at hand.

ROSE: Go on, Troy. I ain't studying you.

TROY (*chasing after her*): I'm studying you . . . fixing to do my homework!

ROSE: Troy, you better leave me alone.

TROY: Where's Cory? That boy brought his butt home yet?

ROSE: He's in the house doing his chores.

TROY (*calling*): Cory! Get your butt out here, boy!

(*Rose exits into the house with the laundry. Troy goes over to the pile of wood, picks up a board, and starts sawing. Cory enters from the house.*)

TROY: You just now coming in here from leaving this morning?

CORY: Yeah, I had to go to football practice.

TROY: Yeah, what?

CORY: Yessir.

TROY: I ain't but two seconds off you noway. The garbage sitting in there overflowing . . . you ain't done none of your chores . . . and you come in here talking about "Yeah."

CORY: I was just getting ready to do my chores now, Pop . . .

TROY: Your first chore is to help me with this fence on Saturday. Everything else come after that. Now get that saw and cut them boards.

(*Cory takes the saw and begins cutting the boards. Troy continues working. There is a long pause.*)

CORY: Hey, Pop . . . why don't you buy a TV?

TROY: What I want with a TV? What I want one of them for?

CORY: Everybody got one. Earl, Ba Bra . . . Jesse!

TROY: I ain't asked you who had one. I say what I want with one?

CORY: So you can watch it. They got lots of things on TV. Baseball games and everything. We could watch the World Series.

TROY: Yeah . . . and how much this TV cost?

CORY: I don't know. They got them on sale for around two hundred dollars.

TROY: Two hundred dollars, huh?

CORY: That ain't that much, Pop.

TROY: Naw, it's just two hundred dollars. See that roof you got over your head at night? Let me tell you something about that roof. It's been over ten years since that roof was last tarred. See now . . . the snow come this winter and sit up there on that roof like it is . . . and it's gonna seep inside. It's just gonna be a little bit . . . ain't gonna hardly notice it. Then the next thing you know, it's gonna be leaking all over the house. Then the wood rot from all that water and you gonna need a whole new roof. Now, how much you think it cost to get that roof tarred?

CORY: I don't know.

TROY: Two hundred and sixty-four dollars . . . cash money. While you thinking about a TV, I got to be thinking about the roof . . . and whatever else go wrong around here. Now if you had two hundred dollars, what would you do . . . fix the roof or buy a TV?

CORY: I'd buy a TV. Then when the roof started to leak . . . when it needed fixing . . . I'd fix it.

TROY: Where you gonna get the money from? You done spent it for a TV. You gonna sit up and watch the water run all over your brand new TV.

CORY: Aw, Pop. You got money. I know you do.

TROY: Where I got it at, huh?

CORY: You got it in the bank.

TROY: You wanna see my bankbook? You wanna see that seventy-three dollars and twenty-two cents I got sitting up in there.

CORY: You ain't got to pay for it all at one time. You can put a down payment on it and carry it on home with you.

TROY: Not me. I ain't gonna owe nobody nothing if I can help it. Miss a payment and they come and snatch it right out your house. Then what you got? Now, soon as I get two hundred dollars clear, then I'll buy a TV. Right now, as soon as I get two hundred and sixty-four dollars, I'm gonna have this roof tarred.

CORY: Aw . . . Pop!

TROY: You go on and get you two hundred dollars and buy one if ya want it. I got better things to do with my money.

CORY: I can't get no two hundred dollars. I ain't never seen two hundred dollars.

TROY: I'll tell you what . . . you get you a hundred dollars and I'll put the other hundred with it.

CORY: All right, I'm gonna show you.

TROY: You gonna show me how you can cut them boards right now.

(*Cory begins to cut the boards. There is a long pause.*)

CORY: The Pirates won today. That makes five in a row.

TROY: I ain't thinking about the Pirates. Got an all-white team. Got that boy . . . that Puerto Rican boy . . . Clemente. Don't even half-play him. That boy could be something if they give him a chance. Play him one day and sit him on the bench the next.

CORY: He gets a lot of chances to play.

TROY: I'm talking about playing regular. Playing every day so you can get your timing. That's what I'm talking about.

CORY: They got some white guys on the team that don't play every day. You can't play everybody at the same time.

TROY: If they got a white fellow sitting on the bench . . . you can bet your last dollar he can't play! The colored guy got to be twice as good

before he get on the team. That's why I don't want you to get all tied up in them sports. Man on the team and what it get him? They got colored on the team and don't use them. Same as not having them. All them teams the same.

CORY: The Braves got Hank Aaron and Wes Covington. Hank Aaron hit two home runs today. That makes forty-three.

TROY: Hank Aaron ain't nobody. That's what you supposed to do. That's how you supposed to play the game. Ain't nothing to it. It's just a matter of timing . . . getting the right follow-through. Hell, I can hit forty-three home runs right now!

CORY: Not off no major-league pitching, you couldn't.

TROY: We had better pitching in the Negro leagues. I hit seven home runs off of Satchel Paige.° You can't get no better than that!

CORY: Sandy Koufax. He's leading the league in strikeouts.

TROY: I ain't thinking of no Sandy Koufax.

CORY: You got Warren Spahn and Lew Burdette. I bet you couldn't hit no home runs off of Warren Spahn.

TROY: I'm through with it now. You go on and cut them boards.

(*Pause.*)

Your mama tell me you done got recruited by a college football team? Is that right?

CORY: Yeah. Coach Zellman say the recruiter gonna be coming by to talk to you. Get you to sign the permission papers.

TROY: I thought you supposed to be working down there at the A&P. Ain't you suppose to be working down there after school?

CORY: Mr. Stawicki say he gonna hold my job for me until after the football season. Say starting next week I can work weekends.

TROY: I thought we had an understanding about this football stuff? You suppose to keep up with your chores and hold that job down at the A&P. Ain't been around here all day on a Saturday. Ain't none of your chores done . . . and now you telling me you done quit your job.

CORY: I'm gonna be working weekends.

TROY: You damn right you are! And ain't no need for nobody coming around here to talk to me about signing nothing.

CORY: Hey, Pop . . . you can't do that. He's coming all the way from North Carolina.

TROY: I don't care where he coming from. The white man ain't gonna let you get nowhere with that

Satchell Paige: (1906?–1982), legendary black pitcher in the Negro leagues.

football noway. You go on and get your book-learning so you can work yourself up in that A&P or learn how to fix cars or build houses or something, get you a trade. That way you have something can't nobody take away from you. You go on and learn how to put your hands to some good use. Besides hauling people's garbage.

CORY: I get good grades, Pop. That's why the recruiter wants to talk with you. You got to keep up your grades to get recruited. This way I'll be going to college. I'll get a chance . . .

TROY: First you gonna get your butt down there to the A&P and get your job back.

CORY: Mr. Stawicki done already hired somebody else 'cause I told him I was playing football.

TROY: You a bigger fool than I thought . . . to let somebody take away your job so you can play some football. Where you gonna get your money to take out your girlfriend and whatnot? What kind of foolishness is that to let somebody take away your job?

CORY: I'm still gonna be working weekends.

TROY: Naw . . . naw. You getting your butt out of here and finding you another job.

CORY: Come on, Pop! I got to practice. I can't work after school and play football too. The team needs me. That's what Coach Zellman say . . .

TROY: I don't care what nobody else say. I'm the boss . . . you understand? I'm the boss around here. I do the only saying what counts.

CORY: Come on, Pop!

TROY: I asked you . . . did you understand?

CORY: Yeah . . .

TROY: What?!

CORY: Yessir.

TROY: You go on down there to that A&P and see if you can get your job back. If you can't do both . . . then you quit the football team. You've got to take the crookeds with the straights.

CORY: Yessir.

(*Pause.*)

Can I ask you a question?

TROY: What the hell you wanna ask me? Mr. Stawicki the one you got the questions for.

CORY: How come you ain't never liked me?

TROY: Liked you? Who the hell say I got to like you? What law is there say I got to like you? Wanna stand up in my face and ask a damn fool-ass question like that. Talking about liking somebody. Come here, boy, when I talk to you.

(*Cory comes over to where Troy is working. He stands slouched over and Troy shoves him on his shoulder.*)

Straighten up, goddammit! I asked you a question . . . what law is there say I got to like you?

CORY: None.

TROY: Well, all right then! Don't you eat every day?

(*Pause.*)

Answer me when I talk to you! Don't you eat every day?

CORY: Yeah.

TROY: Nigger, as long as you in my house, you put that sir on the end of it when you talk to me!

CORY: Yes . . . sir.

TROY: You eat every day.

CORY: Yessir!

TROY: Got a roof over your head.

CORY: Yessir!

TROY: Got clothes on your back.

CORY: Yessir.

TROY: Why you think that is?

CORY: Cause of you.

TROY: Ah, hell I know it's 'cause of me . . . but why do you think that is?

CORY (*hesitant*): Cause you like me.

TROY: Like you? I go out of here every morning . . . bust my butt . . . putting up with them crackers° every day . . . cause I like you? You about the biggest fool I ever saw.

(*Pause.*)

It's my job. It's my responsibility! You understand that? A man got to take care of his family. You live in my house . . . sleep you behind on my bed-clothes . . . fill you belly up with my food . . . cause you my son. You my flesh and blood. Not 'cause I like you! Cause it's my duty to take care of you. I owe a responsibility to you! Let's get this straight right here . . . before it go along any further . . . I ain't got to like you. Mr. Rand don't give me my money come payday cause he likes me. He gives me cause he owe me. I done give you everything I had to give you. I gave you your life! Me and your mama worked that out between us. And liking your black ass wasn't part of the bargain. Don't you try and go through life worrying about if somebody like you or not. You best be making sure they doing right by you. You understand what I'm saying, boy?

CORY: Yessir.

TROY: Then get the hell out of my face, and get on down to that A&P.

(*Rose has been standing behind the screen door for much of the scene. She enters as Cory exits.*)

crackers: White people, often used to refer disparagingly to poor whites.

ROSE: Why don't you let the boy go ahead and play football, Troy? Ain't no harm in that. He's just trying to be like you with the sports.

TROY: I don't want him to be like me! I want him to move as far away from my life as he can get. You the only decent thing that ever happened to me. I wish him that. But I don't wish him a thing else from my life. I decided seventeen years ago that boy wasn't getting involved in no sports. Not after what they did to me in the sports.

ROSE: Troy, why don't you admit you was too old to play in the major leagues? For once . . . why don't you admit that?

TROY: What do you mean too old? Don't come telling me I was too old. I just wasn't the right color. Hell, I'm fifty-three years old and can do better than Selkirk's .269 right now!

ROSE: How's was you gonna play ball when you were over forty? Sometimes I can't get no sense out of you.

TROY: I got good sense, woman. I got sense enough not to let my boy get hurt over playing no sports. You been mothering that boy too much. Worried about if people like him.

ROSE: Everything that boy do . . . he do for you. He wants you to say "Good job, son." That's all.

TROY: Rose, I ain't got time for that. He's alive. He's healthy. He's got to make his own way. I made mine. Ain't nobody gonna hold his hand when he get out there in that world.

ROSE: Times have changed from when you was young, Troy. People change. The world's changing around you and you can't even see it.

TROY (slow, methodical): Woman . . . I do the best I can do. I come in here every Friday. I carry a sack of potatoes and a bucket of lard. You all line up at the door with your hands out. I give you the lint from my pockets. I give you my sweat and my blood. I ain't got no tears. I done spent them. We go upstairs in that room at night . . . and I fall down on you and try to blast a hole into forever. I get up Monday morning . . . find my lunch on the table. I go out. Make my way. Find my strength to carry me through to the next Friday.

(Pause.)

That's all I got, Rose. That's all I got to give. I can't give nothing else.

(Troy exits into the house. The lights go down to black.)

Scene IV

(It is Friday. Two weeks later. Cory starts out of the house with his football equipment. The phone rings.)

CORY (calling): I got it!

(He answers the phone and stands in the screen door talking.)

Hello? Hey, Jesse. Naw . . . I was just getting ready to leave now.

ROSE (calling): Cory!

CORY: I told you, man, them spikes is all tore up. You can use them if you want, but they ain't no good. Earl got some spikes.

ROSE (calling): Cory!

CORY (calling to Rose): Mam? I'm talking to Jesse.

(Into phone.)

When she say that? (Pause.) Aw, you lying, man. I'm gonna tell her you said that.

ROSE (calling): Cory, don't you go nowhere!

CORY: I got to go to the game, Ma!

(Into the phone.)

Yeah, hey, look, I'll talk to you later. Yeah, I'll meet you over Earl's house. Later. Bye, Ma.

(Cory exits the house and starts out the yard.)

ROSE: Cory, where you going off to? You got that stuff all pulled out and thrown all over your room.

CORY (in the yard): I was looking for my spikes. Jesse wanted to borrow my spikes.

ROSE: Get up there and get that cleaned up before your daddy get back in here.

CORY: I got to go to the game! I'll clean it up when I get back.

(Cory exits.)

ROSE: That's all he need to do is see that room all messed up.

(Rose exits into the house. Troy and Bono enter the yard. Troy is dressed in clothes other than his work clothes.)

BONO: He told him the same thing he told you. Take it to the union.

TROY: Brownie ain't got that much sense. Man wasn't thinking about nothing. He wait until I confront them on it . . . then he wanna come crying seniority.

(Calls.)

Hey, Rose!

BONO: I wish I could have seen Mr. Rand's face when he told you.

TROY: He couldn't get it out of his mouth! Liked to bit his tongue! When they called me down there to the Commissioner's office . . . he thought they was gonna fire me. Like everybody else.

BONO: I didn't think they was gonna fire you. I thought they was gonna put you on the warning paper.

TROY: Hey, Rose!

(*To Bono.*)

Yeah, Mr. Rand like to bit his tongue.

(*Troy breaks the seal on the bottle, takes a drink, and hands it to Bono.*)

BONO: I see you run right down to Taylors' and told that Alberta gal.

TROY (*calling*): Hey Rose! (*To Bono*) I told everybody. Hey, Rose! I went down there to cash my check.

ROSE (*entering from the house*): Hush all that hollering, man! I know you out here. What they say down there at the Commissioner's office?

TROY: You supposed to come when I call you, woman. Bono'll tell you that.

(*To Bono.*)

Don't Lucille come when you call her?

ROSE: Man, hush your mouth. I ain't no dog . . . talk about "come when you call me."

TROY (*puts his arm around Rose*): You hear this, Bono? I had me an old dog used to get uppity like that. You say, "C'mere, Blue!" . . . and he just lay there and look at you. End up getting a stick and chasing him away trying to make him come.

ROSE: I ain't studying you and your dog. I remember you used to sing that old song.

TROY (*he sings*): Hear it ring! Hear it ring! I had a dog his name was Blue.

ROSE: Don't nobody wanna hear you sing that old song.

TROY (*sings*): You know Blue was mighty true.

ROSE: Used to have Cory running around here singing that song.

BONO: Hell, I remember that song myself.

TROY (*sings*): You know Blue was a good old dog.
Blue treed a possum in a hollow log.
That was my daddy's song. My daddy made up that song.

ROSE: I don't care who made it up. Don't nobody wanna hear you sing it.

TROY (*makes a song like calling a dog*): Come here, woman.

ROSE: You come in here carrying on, I reckon they ain't fired you. What they say down there at the Commissioner's office?

TROY: Look here, Rose . . . Mr. Rand called me into his office today when I got back from talking to them people down there . . . it come from up top . . . he called me in and told me they was making me a driver.

ROSE: Troy, you kidding!

TROY: No I ain't. Ask Bono.

ROSE: Well, that's great, Troy. Now you don't have to hassle them people no more.

(*Lyons enters from the street.*)

TROY: Aw hell, I wasn't looking to see you today. I thought you was in jail. Got it all over the front page of the *Courier* about them raiding Sefus' place . . . where you be hanging out with all them thugs.

LYONS: Hey, Pop . . . that ain't got nothing to do with me. I don't go down there gambling. I go down there to sit in with the band. I ain't got nothing to do with the gambling part. They got some good music down there.

TROY: They got some rogues . . . is what they got.

LYONS: How you been, Mr. Bono? Hi, Rose.

BONO: I see where you playing down at the Crawford Grill tonight.

ROSE: How come you ain't brought Bonnie like I told you. You should have brought Bonnie with you, she ain't been over in a month of Sundays.

LYONS: I was just in the neighborhood . . . thought I'd stop by.

TROY: Here he come . . .

BONO: Your daddy got a promotion on the rubbish. He's gonna be the first colored driver. Ain't got to do nothing but sit up there and read the paper like them white fellows.

LYONS: Hey, Pop . . . if you knew how to read you'd be all right.

BONO: Naw . . . naw . . . you mean if the nigger knew how to *drive* he'd be all right. Been fighting with them people about driving and ain't even got a license. Mr. Rand know you ain't got no driver's license?

TROY: Driving ain't nothing. All you do is point the truck where you want it to go. Driving ain't nothing.

BONO: Do Mr. Rand know you ain't got no driver's license? That's what I'm talking about. I ain't asked if driving was easy. I asked if Mr. Rand know you ain't got no driver's license.

TROY: He ain't got to know. The man ain't got to know my business. Time he find out, I have two or three driver's licenses.

LYON (*going into his pocket*): Say, look here, Pop . . .

TROY: I knew it was coming. Didn't I tell you, Bono? I know what kind of "Look here, Pop" that was. The nigger fixing to ask me for some money. It's Friday night. It's my payday. All them rogues down there on the avenue . . . the ones that ain't in jail . . . and Lyons is hopping in his shoes to get down there with them.

LYONS: See, Pop . . . if you give somebody else a chance to talk sometime, you'd see that I was fixing to pay you back your ten dollars like I told you. Here . . . I told you I'd pay you when Bonnie got paid.

TROY: Naw . . . you go ahead and keep that ten dollars.

Put it in the bank. The next time you feel like you wanna come by here and ask me for something . . . you go on down there and get that.

LYONS: Here's your ten dollars, Pop. I told you I don't want you to give me nothing. I just wanted to borrow ten dollars.

TROY: Naw . . . you go on and keep that for the next time you want to ask me.

LYONS: Come on, Pop . . . here go your ten dollars.

ROSE: Why don't you go on and let the boy pay you back, Troy?

LYONS: Here you go, Rose. If you don't take it I'm gonna have to hear about it for the next six months.

(*He hands her the money.*)

ROSE: You can hand yours over here too, Troy.

TROY: You see this, Bono. You see how they do me.

BONO: Yeah, Lucille do me the same way.

(*Gabriel is heard singing offstage. He enters.*)

GABRIEL: Better get ready for the Judgment! Better get ready for . . . Hey! . . . Hey! . . . There's Troy's boy!

LYONS: How are you doing, Uncle Gabe?

GABRIEL: Lyons . . . The King of the Jungle! Rose . . . hey, Rose. Got a flower for you.

(*He takes a rose from his pocket.*)

Picked it myself. That's the same rose like you is!

ROSE: That's right nice of you, Gabe.

LYONS: What you been doing, Uncle Gabe?

GABRIEL: Oh, I been chasing hellhounds and waiting on the time to tell St. Peter to open the gates.

LYONS: You been chasing hellhounds, huh? Well . . . you doing the right thing, Uncle Gabe. Somebody got to chase them.

GABRIEL: Oh, yeah . . . I know it. The devil's strong. The devil ain't no pushover. Hellhounds snipping at everybody's heels. But I got my trumpet waiting on the judgment time.

LYONS: Waiting on the Battle of Armageddon, huh?

GABRIEL: Ain't gonna be too much of a battle when God get to waving that Judgment sword. But the people's gonna have a hell of a time trying to get into heaven if them gates ain't open.

LYONS (*putting his arm around Gabriel*): You hear this, Pop. Uncle Gabe, you all right!

GABRIEL (*laughing with Lyons*): Lyons! King of the Jungle.

ROSE: You gonna stay for supper, Gabe. Want me to fix you a plate?

GABRIEL: I'll take a sandwich, Rose. Don't want no plate. Just wanna eat with my hands. I'll take a sandwich.

ROSE: How about you, Lyons? You staying? Got some short ribs cooking.

LYONS: Naw, I won't eat nothing till after we finished playing.

(*Pause.*)

You ought to come down and listen to me play, Pop.

TROY: I don't like that Chinese music. All that noise.

ROSE: Go on in the house and wash up, Gabe . . . I'll fix you a sandwich.

GABRIEL (*to Lyons, as he exits*): Troy's mad at me.

LYONS: What you mad at Uncle Gabe for, Pop.

ROSE: He thinks Troy's mad at him cause he moved over to Miss Pearl's.

TROY: I ain't mad at the man. He can live where he want to live at.

LYONS: What he move over there for? Miss Pearl don't like nobody.

ROSE: She don't mind him none. She treats him real nice. She just don't allow all that singing.

TROY: She don't mind that rent he be paying . . . that's what she don't mind.

ROSE: Troy, I ain't going through that with you no more. He's over there cause he want to have his own place. He can come and go as he please.

TROY: Hell, he could come and go as he please here. I wasn't stopping him. I ain't put no rules on him.

ROSE: It ain't the same thing, Troy. And you know it.

(*Gabriel comes to the door.*)

Now, that's the last I wanna hear about that. I don't wanna hear nothing else about Gabe and Miss Pearl. And next week . . .

GABRIEL: I'm ready for my sandwich, Rose.

ROSE: And next week . . . when that recruiter come from that school . . . I want you to sign that paper and go on and let Cory play football. Then that'll be the last I have to hear about that.

TROY (*to Rose as she exits into the house*): I ain't thinking about Cory nothing.

LYONS: What . . . Cory got recruited? What school he going to?

TROY: That boy walking around here smelling his piss . . . thinking he's grown. Thinking he's gonna do what he want, irrespective of what I say. Look here, Bono . . . I left the Commissioner's office and went down to the A&P . . . that boy ain't working down there. He lying to me. Telling me he got his job back . . . telling me he working weekends . . . telling me he working after school . . . Mr. Stawicki tell me he ain't working down there at all!

LYONS: Cory just growing up. He's just busting at the seams trying to fill out your shoes.

TROY: I don't care what he's doing. When he get to the point where he wanna disobey me . . . then it's time for him to move on. Bono'll tell you that. I bet he ain't never disobeyed his daddy without paying the consequences.

BONO: I ain't never had a chance. My daddy came on through . . . but I ain't never knew him to see him . . . or what he had on his mind or where he went. Just moving on through. Searching out the New Land. That's what the old folks used to call it. See a fellow moving around from place to place . . . woman to woman . . . called it searching out the New Land. I can't say if he ever found it. I come along, didn't want no kids. Didn't know if I was gonna be in one place long enough to fix on them right as their daddy. I figured I was going searching too. As it turned out I been hooked up with Lucille near about as long as your daddy been with Rose. Going on sixteen years.

TROY: Sometimes I wish I hadn't known my daddy. He ain't cared nothing about no kids. A kid to him wasn't nothing. All he wanted was for you to learn how to walk so he could start you to working. When it come time for eating . . . he ate first. If there was anything left over, that's what you got. Man would sit down and eat two chickens and give you the wing.

LYONS: You ought to stop that, Pop. Everybody feed their kids. No matter how hard times is . . . everybody care about their kids. Make sure they have something to eat.

TROY: The only thing my daddy cared about was getting them bales of cotton in to Mr. Lubin. That's the only thing that mattered to him. Sometimes I used to wonder why he was living. Wonder why the devil hadn't come and got him. "Get them bales of cotton in to Mr. Lubin" and find out he owe him money . . .

LYONS: He should have just went on and left when he saw he couldn't get nowhere. That's what I would have done.

TROY: How he gonna leave with eleven kids? And where he gonna go? He ain't knew how to do nothing but farm. No, he was trapped and I think he knew it. But I'll say this for him . . . he felt a responsibility toward us. Maybe he ain't treated us the way I felt he should have . . . but without that responsibility he could have walked off and left us . . . made his own way.

BONO: A lot of them did. Back in those days what you talking about . . . they walk out their front door and just take on down one road or another and keep on walking.

LYONS: There you go! That's what I'm talking about.

BONO: Just keep on walking till you come to something else. Ain't you never heard of nobody having the walking blues? Well, that's what you call it when you just take off like that.

TROY: My daddy ain't had them walking blues! What you talking about? He stayed right there with his family. But he was just as evil as he could be. My mama couldn't stand him. Couldn't stand that evilness. She run off when I was about eight. She sneaked off one night after he had gone to sleep. Told me she was coming back for me. I ain't never seen her no more. All his women run off and left him. He wasn't good for nobody.

When my turn come to head out, I was fourteen and got to sniffing around Joe Canewell's daughter. Had us an old mule we called Greyboy. My daddy sent me out to do some plowing and I tied up Greyboy and went to fooling around with Joe Canewell's daughter. We done found us a nice little spot, got real cozy with each other. She about thirteen and we done figured we was grown anyway . . . so we down there enjoying ourselves . . . ain't thinking about nothing. We didn't know Greyboy had got loose and wandered back to the house and my daddy was looking for me. We down there by the creek enjoying ourselves when my daddy come up on us. Surprised us. He had them leather straps off the mule and commenced to whupping me like there was no tomorrow. I jumped up, mad and embarrassed. I was scared of my daddy. When he commenced to whupping on me . . . quite naturally I run to get out of the way.

(*Pause.*)

Now I thought he was mad cause I ain't done my work. But I see where he was chasing me off so he could have the gal for himself. When I see what the matter of it was, I lost all fear of my daddy. Right there is where I become a man . . . at fourteen years of age.

(*Pause.*)

Now it was my turn to run him off. I picked up them same reins that he had used on me. I picked up them reins and commenced to whupping on him. The gal jumped up and run off . . . and when my daddy turned to face me, I could see why the devil had never come to get him . . . cause he was the devil himself. I don't know what happened. When I woke up, I was laying right there by the creek, and Blue . . . this old dog we had . . . was licking my face. I thought I was blind. I couldn't see nothing. Both my eyes were swollen shut. I layed there and cried. I didn't know what I was gonna do. The only thing I knew was the time had come for me to leave my daddy's house. And right there the world suddenly got big. And it was a long time before I could cut it down to where I could handle it.

Part of that cutting down was when I got to the place where I could feel him kicking in my blood and knew that the only thing that separated us was the matter of a few years.

(*Gabriel enters from the house with a sandwich.*)

LYONS: What you got there, Uncle Gabe?

GABRIEL: Got me a ham sandwich. Rose gave me a ham sandwich.

TROY: I don't know what happened to him. I done lost touch with everybody except Gabriel. But I hope he's dead. I hope he found some peace.

LYONS: That's a heavy story, Pop. I didn't know you left home when you was fourteen.

TROY: And didn't know nothing. The only part of the world I knew was the forty-two acres of Mr. Lubin's land. That's all I knew about life.

LYONS: Fourteen's kinda young to be out on your own. (*Phone rings.*) I don't even think I was ready to be out on my own at fourteen. I don't know what I would have done.

TROY: I got up from the creek and walked on down to Mobile. I was through with farming. Figured I could do better in the city. So I walked the two hundred miles to Mobile.

LYONS: Wait a minute . . . you ain't walked no two hundred miles, Pop. Ain't nobody gonna walk no two hundred miles. You talking about some walking there.

BONO: That's the only way you got anywhere back in them days.

LYONS: Shhh. Damn if I wouldn't have hitched a ride with somebody!

TROY: Who you gonna hitch it with? They ain't had no cars and things like they got now. We talking about 1918.

ROSE (*entering*): What you all out here getting into?

TROY (*to Rose*): I'm telling Lyons how good he got it. He don't know nothing about this I'm talking.

ROSE: Lyons, that was Bonnie on the phone. She say you supposed to pick her up.

LYONS: Yeah, okay, Rose.

TROY: I walked on down to Mobile and hitched up with some of them fellows that was heading this way. Got up here and found out . . . not only couldn't you get a job . . . you couldn't find no place to live. I thought I was in freedom. Shhh. Colored folks living down there on the riverbanks in whatever kind of shelter they could find for themselves. Right down there under the Brady Street Bridge. Living in shacks made of sticks and tarpaper. Messed around there and went from bad to worse. Started stealing. First it was food. Then I figured, hell, if I steal money I can buy me some food. Buy me some shoes too! One thing led to another. Met your mama. I was young and anxious to be a man. Met your mama and had you. What I do that for? Now I got to worry about feeding you and her. Got to steal three times as much. Went out one day looking for somebody to rob . . . that's what I was, a robber. I'll tell you the truth. I'm ashamed of it today. But it's the truth. Went to rob this fellow . . . pulled out my knife . . . and he pulled out a gun. Shot me in the chest. It felt just like somebody had taken a hot branding iron and laid it on me. When he shot me I jumped at him with my knife. They told me I killed him and they put me in the penitentiary and locked me up for fifteen years. That's where I met Bono. That's where I learned how to play baseball. Got out that place and your mama had taken you and went on to make life without me. Fifteen years was a long time for her to wait. But that fifteen years cured me of that robbing stuff. Rose'll tell you. She asked me when I met her if I had gotten all that foolishness out of my system. And I told here, "Baby, it's you and baseball all what count with me." You hear me, Bono? I meant it too. She say, "Which one comes first?" I told her, "Baby, ain't no doubt it's baseball . . . but you stick and get old with me and we'll both outlive this baseball." Am I right, Rose? And it's true.

ROSE: Man, hush your mouth. You ain't said no such thing. Talking about, "Baby, you know you'll always be number one with me." That's what you was talking.

TROY: You hear that, Bono. That's why I love her.

BONO: Rose'll keep you straight. You get off the track, she'll straighten you up.

ROSE: Lyons, you better get on up and get Bonnie. She waiting on you.

LYONS (*gets up to go*): Hey, Pop, why don't you come on down to the Grill and hear me play?

TROY: I ain't going down there. I'm too old to be sitting around in them clubs.

BONO: You got to be good to play down at the Grill.

LYONS: Come on, Pop . . .

TROY: I got to get up in the morning.

LYONS: You ain't got to stay long.

TROY: Naw, I'm gonna get my supper and go on to bed.

LYONS: Well, I got to go. I'll see you again.

TROY: Don't you come around my house on my payday.

ROSE: Pick up the phone and let somebody know you

coming. And bring Bonnie with you. You know I'm always glad to see her.

LYONS: Yeah, I'll do that, Rose. You take care now. See you, Pop. See you, Mr. Bono. See you, Uncle Gabe.

GABRIEL: Lyons! King of the Jungle!

(*Lyons exits.*)

TROY: Is supper ready, woman? Me and you got some business to take care of. I'm gonna tear it up too.

ROSE: Troy, I done told you now!

TROY (*puts his arm around Bono*): Aw hell, woman . . . this is Bono. Bono like family. I done known this nigger since . . . how long I done know you?

BONO: It's been a long time.

TROY: I done known this nigger since Skippy was a pup. Me and him done been through some times.

BONO: You sure right about that.

TROY: Hell, I done know him longer than I known you. And we still standing shoulder to shoulder. Hey, look here, Bono . . . a man can't ask for no more than that.

(*Drinks to him.*)

I love you, nigger.

BONO: Hell, I love you too . . . but I got to get home see my woman. You got yours in hand. I got to go get mine.

(*Bono starts to exit as Cory enters the yard, dressed in his football uniform. He gives Troy a hard, uncompromising look.*)

CORY: What you do that for, Pop?

(*He throws his helmet down in the direction of Troy.*)

ROSE: What's the matter? Cory . . . what's the matter?

CORY: Papa done went up to the school and told Coach Zellman I can't play football no more. Wouldn't even let me play the game. Told him to tell the recruiter not to come.

ROSE: Troy . . .

TROY: What you Troying me for. Yeah, I did it. And the boy know why I did it.

CORY: Why you wanna do that to me? That was the one chance I had.

ROSE: Ain't nothing wrong with Cory playing football, Troy.

TROY: The boy lied to me. I told the nigger if he wanna play football . . . to keep up his chores and hold down that job at the A&P. That was the conditions. Stopped down there to see Mr. Stawicki . . .

CORY: I can't work after school during the football season, Pop! I tried to tell you that Mr. Stawicki's

holding my job for me. You don't never want to listen to nobody. And then you wanna go and do this to me!

TROY: I ain't done nothing to you. You done it to yourself.

CORY: Just cause you didn't have a chance! You just scared I'm gonna be better than you, that's all.

TROY: Come here.

ROSE: Troy . . .

(*Cory reluctantly crosses over to Troy.*)

TROY: All right! See. You done made a mistake.

CORY: I didn't even do nothing!

TROY: I'm gonna tell you what your mistake was. See . . . you swung at the ball and didn't hit it. That's strike one. See, you in the batter's box now. You swung and you missed. That's strike one. Don't you strike out!

(*Lights fade to black.*)

ACT II • Scene I _____

(*The following morning. Cory is at the tree hitting the ball with the bat. He tries to mimic Troy, but his swing is awkward, less sure. Rose enters from the house.*)

ROSE: Cory, I want you to help me with this cupboard.

CORY: I ain't quitting the team. I don't care what Poppa say.

ROSE: I'll talk to him when he gets back. He had to go see about your Uncle Gabe. The police done arrested him. Say he was disturbing the peace. He'll be back directly. Come on in here and help me clean out the top of this cupboard.

(*Cory exits into the house. Rose sees Troy and Bono coming down the alley.*)

Troy . . . what they say down there?

TROY: Ain't said nothing. I give them fifty dollars and they let him go. I'll talk to you about it. Where's Cory?

ROSE: He's in there helping me clean out these cupboards.

TROY: Tell him to get his butt out here.

(*Troy and Bono go over to the pile of wood. Bono picks up the saw and begins sawing.*)

TROY (*to Bono*): All they want is the money. That makes six or seven times I done went down there and got him. See me coming they stick out their *hands*.

BONO: Yeah. I know what you mean. That's all they care about . . . that money. They don't care about what's right.

(*Pause.*)

Nigger, why you got to go and get some hard wood? You ain't doing nothing but building a little old fence. Get you some soft pine wood. That's all you need.

TROY: I know what I'm doing. This is outside wood. You put pine wood inside the house. Pine wood is inside wood. This here is outside wood. Now you tell me where the fence is gonna be?

BONO: You don't need this wood. You can put it up with pine wood and it'll stand as long as you gonna be here looking at it.

TROY: How you know how long I'm gonna be here, nigger? Hell, I might just live forever. Live longer than old man Horsely.

BONO: That's what Magee used to say.

TROY: Magee's a damn fool. Now you tell me who you ever heard of gonna pull their own teeth with a pair of rusty pliers.

BONO: The old folks . . . my granddaddy used to pull his teeth with pliers. They ain't had no dentists for the colored folks back then.

TROY: Get clean pliers! You understand? Clean pliers! Sterilize them! Besides we ain't living back then. All Magee had to do was walk over to Doc Goldblum's.

BONO: I see where you and that Tallahassee gal . . . that Alberta . . . I see where you all done got tight.

TROY: What you mean "got tight"?

BONO: I see where you be laughing and joking with her all the time.

TROY: I laughs and jokes with all of them, Bono. You know me.

BONO: That ain't the kind of laughing and joking I'm talking about.

(*Cory enters from the house.*)

CORY: How you doing, Mr. Bono?

TROY: Cory? Get that saw from Bono and cut some wood. He talking about the wood's too hard to cut. Stand back there, Jim, and let that young boy show you how it's done.

BONO: He's sure welcome to it.

(*Cory takes the saw and begins to cut the wood.*)

Whew-e-e! Look at that. Big old strong boy. Look like Joe Louis. Hell, must be getting old the way I'm watching that boy whip through that wood.

CORY: I don't see why Mama want a fence around the yard noways.

TROY: Damn if I know either. What the hell she keeping out with it? She ain't got nothing nobody want.

BONO: Some people build fences to keep people out . . . and other people build fences to keep people in. Rose wants to hold on to you all. She loves you.

TROY: Hell, nigger, I don't need nobody to tell me my wife loves me, Cory . . . go on in the house and see if you can find that other saw.

CORY: Where's it at?

TROY: I said find it! Look for it till you find it!

(*Cory exits into the house.*)

What's that supposed to mean? Wanna keep us in?

BONO: Troy . . . I done known you seem like damn near my whole life. You and Rose both. I done know both of you all for a long time. I remember when you met Rose. When you was hitting them baseball out the park. A lot of them old gals was after you then. You had the pick of the litter. When you picked Rose, I was happy for you. That was the first time I knew you had any sense. I said . . . My man Troy knows what he's doing . . . I'm gonna follow this nigger . . . he might take me somewhere. I been following you too. I done learned a whole heap of things about life watching you. I done learned how to tell where the shit lies. How to tell it from the alfalfa. You done learned me a lot of things. You showed me how to not make the same mistakes . . . to take life as it comes along and keep putting one foot in front of the other.

(*Pause.*)

Rose a good woman, Troy.

TROY: Hell, nigger, I know she a good woman. I been married to her for eighteen years. What you got on your mind, Bono?

BONO: I just say she a good woman. Just like I say anything. I ain't got to have nothing on my mind.

TROY: You just gonna say she a good woman and leave it hanging out there like that? Why you telling me she a good woman?

BONO: She loves you, Troy. Rose loves you.

TROY: You saying I don't measure up. That's what you trying to say. I don't measure up cause I'm seeing this other gal. I know what you trying to say.

BONO: I know what Rose means to you, Troy. I'm just trying to say I don't want to see you mess up.

TROY: Yeah, I appreciate that, Bono. If you was messing around on Lucille I'd be telling you the same thing.

BONO: Well, that's all I got to say. I just say that because I love you both.

TROY: Hell, you know me . . . I wasn't out there looking for nothing. You can't find a better woman than Rose. I know that. But seems like this woman just stuck onto me where I can't shake her loose. I done wrestled with it, tried to throw her off me . . . but she just stuck on tighter. Now she's stuck on for good.

BONO: You's in control . . . that's what you tell me all the time. You responsible for what you do.

TROY: I ain't ducking the responsibility of it. As long as it sets right in my heart . . . then I'm okay. Cause that's all I listen to. It'll tell me right from wrong every time. And I ain't talking about doing Rose no bad turn. I love Rose. She done carried me a long ways and I love and respect her for that.

BONO: I know you do. That's why I don't want to see you hurt her. But what you gonna do when she find out? What you got then? If you try and juggle both of them . . . sooner or later you gonna drop one of them. That's common sense.

TROY: Yeah, I hear what you saying, Bono. I been trying to figure a way to work it out.

BONO: Work it out right, Troy. I don't want to be getting all up between you and Rose's business . . . but work it so it come out right.

TROY: Ah hell, I get all up between you and Lucille's business. When you gonna get that woman that refrigerator she been wanting? Don't tell me you ain't got no money now. I know who your banker is. Mellon don't need that money bad as Lucille want that refrigerator. I'll tell you that.

BONO: Tell you what I'll do . . . when you finish building this fence for Rose . . . I'll buy Lucille that refrigerator.

TROY: You done stuck your foot in your mouth now!

(*Troy grabs up a board and begins to saw. Bono starts to walk out the yard.*)

Hey, nigger . . . where you going?

BONO: I'm going home. I know you don't expect me to help you now. I'm protecting my money. I wanna see you put that fence up by yourself. That's what I want to see. You'll be here another six months without me.

TROY: Nigger, you ain't right.

BONO: When it comes to my money . . . I'm right as fireworks on the Fourth of July.

TROY: All right, we gonna see now. You better get out your bankbook.

(*Bono exits, and Troy continues to work. Rose enters from the house.*)

ROSE: What they say down there? What's happening with Gabe?

TROY: I went down there and got him out. Cost me fifty dollars. Say he was disturbing the peace. Judge set up a hearing for him in three weeks. Say to show cause why he shouldn't be recommitted.

ROSE: What was he doing that cause them to arrest him?

TROY: Some kids was teasing him and he run them off home. Say he was howling and carrying on. Some folks seen him and called the police. That's all it was.

ROSE: Well, what's you say? What'd you tell the judge?

TROY: Told him I'd look after him. It didn't make no sense to recommit the man. He stuck out his big greasy palm and told me to give him fifty dollars and take him on home.

ROSE: Where's he at now? Where'd he go off to?

TROY: He's gone on about his business. He don't need nobody to hold his hand.

ROSE: Well, I don't know. Seem like that would be the best place for him if they did put him into the hospital. I know what you're gonna say. But that's what I think would be best.

TROY: The man done had his life ruined fighting for what? And they wanna take and lock him up. Let him be free. He don't bother nobody.

ROSE: Well, everybody got their own way of looking at it I guess. Come on and get your lunch. I got a bowl of lima beans and some cornbread in the oven. Come on get something to eat. Ain't no sense you fretting over Gabe.

(*Rose turns to go into the house.*)

TROY: Rose . . . got something to tell you.

ROSE: Well, come on . . . wait till I get this food on the table.

TROY: Rose!

(*She stops and turns around.*)

I don't know how to say this.

(*Pause.*)

I can't explain it none. It just sort of grows on you till it gets out of hand. It starts out like a little bush . . . and the next thing you know it's a whole forest.

ROSE: Troy . . . what is you talking about?

TROY: I'm talking, woman, let me talk. I'm trying to find a way to tell you . . . I'm gonna be a daddy. I'm gonna be somebody's daddy.

ROSE: Troy . . . you're not telling me this? You're gonna be . . . what?

TROY: Rose . . . now . . . see . . .

ROSE: You telling me you gonna be somebody's daddy? You telling your *wife* this?

(*Gabriel enters from the street. He carries a rose in his hand.*)

GABRIEL: Hey, Troy! Hey, Rose!

ROSE: I have to wait eighteen years to hear something like this.

GABRIEL: Hey, Rose . . . I got a flower for you.

(*He hands it to her.*)

That's a rose. Same rose like you is.

ROSE: Thanks, Gabe.

GABRIEL: Troy, you ain't mad at me is you? Them bad mens come and put me away. You ain't mad at me is you?

TROY: Naw, Gabe, I ain't mad at you.

ROSE: Eighteen years and you wanna come with this.

GABRIEL (*takes a quarter out of his pocket*): See what I got? Got a brand new quarter.

TROY: Rose . . . it's just . . .

ROSE: Ain't nothing you can say, Troy. Ain't no way of explaining that.

GABRIEL: Fellow that give me this quarter had a whole mess of them. I'm gonna keep this quarter till it stop shining.

ROSE: Gabe, go on in the house there. I got some watermelon in the frigidaire. Go on and get you a piece.

GABRIEL: Say, Rose . . . you know I was chasing hellhounds and them bad mens come and get me and take me away. Troy helped me. He come down there and told them they better let me go before he beat them up. Yeah, he did!

ROSE: You go on and get you a piece of watermelon, Gabe. Them bad mens is gone now.

GABRIEL: Okay, Rose . . . gonna get me some watermelon. The kind with the stripes on it.

(*Gabriel exits into the house.*)

ROSE: Why, Troy? Why? After all these years to come dragging this in to me now. It don't make no sense at your age. I could have expected this ten or fifteen years ago, but not now.

TROY: Age ain't got nothing to do with it, Rose.

ROSE: I done tried to be everything a wife should be. Everything a wife could be. Been married eighteen years and I got to live to see the day you tell me you been seeing another woman and done fathered a child by her. And you know I ain't never wanted no half nothing in my family. My whole family is half. Everybody got different fathers and mothers . . . my two sisters and my brother. Can't hardly tell who's who. Can't never sit down and talk about Papa and Mama. It's your papa and your mama and my papa and my mama . . .

TROY: Rose . . . stop it now.

ROSE: I ain't never wanted that for none of my children. And now you wanna drag your behind in here and tell me something like this.

TROY: You ought to know. It's time for you to know.

ROSE: Well, I don't want to know, goddamn it!

TROY: I can't just make it go away. It's done now. I can't wish the circumstance of the thing away.

ROSE: And you don't want to either. Maybe you want to wish me and my boy away. Maybe that's what you want? Well, you can't wish us away. I've got eighteen years of my life invested in you. You ought to have stayed upstairs in my bed where you belong.

TROY: Rose . . . now listen to me . . . we can get a handle on this thing. We can talk this out . . . come to an understanding.

ROSE: All of a sudden it's "we." Where was "we" at when you was down there rolling around with some godforsaken woman? "We" should have come to an understanding before you started making a damn fool of yourself. You're a day late and a dollar short when it comes to an understanding with me.

TROY: It's just . . . She gives me a different idea . . . a different understanding about myself. I can step out of this house and get away from the pressures and problems . . . be a different man. I ain't got to wonder how I'm gonna pay the bills or get the roof fixed. I can just be a part of myself that I ain't never been.

ROSE: What I want to know . . . is do you plan to continue seeing her. That's all you can say to me.

TROY: I can sit up in her house and laugh. Do you understand what I'm saying. I can laugh out loud . . . and it feels good. It reaches all the way down to the bottom of my shoes.

(*Pause.*)

Rose, I can't give that up.

ROSE: Maybe you ought to go on and stay down there with her . . . if she's a better woman than me.

TROY: It ain't about nobody being a better woman or nothing. Rose, you ain't the blame. A man couldn't ask for no woman to be a better wife than you've been. I'm responsible for it. I done locked myself into a pattern trying to take care of you all that I forgot about myself.

ROSE: What the hell was I there for? That was my job, not somebody else's.

TROY: Rose, I done tried all my life to live decent . . . to live a clean . . . hard . . . useful life. I tried to be a good husband to you. In every way I knew how. Maybe I come into the world backwards, I don't know. But . . . you born with two strikes on you before you come to the plate. You got to guard it closely . . . always looking for the curve ball on the inside corner. You can't afford to let none get past you. You can't afford a call strike. If you going down . . . you going down swinging. Everything lined up against you. What you gonna do. I fooled them,

ROSE. I bunted. When I found you and Cory and a halfway decent job . . . I was safe. Couldn't nothing touch me. I wasn't gonna strike out no more. I wasn't going back to the penitentiary. I wasn't gonna lay in the streets with a bottle of wine. I was safe. I had me a family. A job. I wasn't gonna get that last strike. I was on first looking for one of them boys to knock me in. To get me home.

ROSE: You should have stayed in my bed, Troy.

TROY: Then when I saw that gal . . . she firmed up my backbone. And I got to thinking that if I tried . . . I just might be able to steal second. Do you understand after eighteen years I wanted to steal second.

ROSE: You should have held me tight. You should have grabbed me and held on.

TROY: I stood on first base for eighteen years and I thought . . . well, goddamn it . . . go on for it!

ROSE: We're not talking about baseball! We're talking about you going off to lay in bed with another woman . . . and then bring it home to me. That's what we're talking about. We ain't talking about no baseball.

TROY: Rose, you're not listening to me. I'm trying the best I can to explain it to you. It's not easy for me to admit that I been standing in the same place for eighteen years.

ROSE: I been standing with you! I been right here with you, Troy. I got a life too. I gave eighteen years of my life to stand in the same spot with you. Don't you think I ever wanted other things? Don't you think I had dreams and hopes? What about my life? What about me. Don't you think it ever crossed my mind to want to know other men? That I wanted to lay up somewhere and forget about my responsibilities? That I wanted someone to make me laugh so I could feel good? You not the only one who's got wants and needs. But I held on to you, Troy. I took all my feelings, my wants and needs, my dreams . . . and I buried them inside you. I planted a seed and watched and prayed over it. I planted myself inside you and waited to bloom. And it didn't take me no eighteen years to find out the soil was hard and rocky and it wasn't never gonna bloom.

But I held on to you, Troy. I held you tighter. You was my husband. I owed you everything I had. Every part of me I could find to give you. And upstairs in that room . . . with the darkness falling in on me . . . I gave everything I had to try and erase the doubt that you wasn't the finest man in the world. And wherever you was going . . . I wanted to be there with you. Cause you was my husband. Cause that's the only way I was gonna survive as your wife. You always talking about

what you give . . . and what you don't have to give. But you take too. You take . . . and don't even know nobody's giving!

(*Rose turns to exit into the house; Troy grabs her arm.*)

TROY: You say I take and don't give!

ROSE: Troy! You're hurting me!

TROY: You say I take and don't give.

ROSE: Troy . . . you're hurting my arm! Let go!

TROY: I done give you everything I got. Don't you tell that lie on me.

ROSE: Troy!

TROY: Don't you tell that lie on me!

(*Cory enters from the house.*)

CORY: Mama!

ROSE: Troy. You're hurting me.

TROY: Don't you tell me about no taking and giving.

(*Cory comes up behind Troy and grabs him. Troy, surprised, is thrown off balance just as Cory throws a glancing blow that catches him on the chest and knocks him down. Troy is stunned, as is Cory.*)

ROSE: Troy. Troy. No!

(*Troy gets to his feet and starts at Cory.*)

Troy . . . no. Please! Troy!

(*Rose pulls on Troy to hold him back. Troy stops himself.*)

TROY (*to Cory*): All right. That's strike two. You stay away from around me, boy. Don't you strike out. You living with a full count. Don't you strike out.

(*Troy exits out the yard as the lights go down.*)

Scene II

(*It is six months later, early afternoon. Troy enters from the house and starts to exit the yard. Rose enters from the house.*)

ROSE: Troy, I want to talk to you.

TROY: All of a sudden, after all this time, you want to talk to me, huh? You ain't wanted to talk to me for months. You ain't wanted to talk to me last night. You ain't wanted no part of me then. What you wanna talk to me about now?

ROSE: Tomorrow's Friday.

TROY: I know what day tomorrow is. You think I don't know tomorrow's Friday? My whole life I ain't done nothing but look to see Friday coming and you got to tell me it's Friday.

ROSE: I want to know if you're coming home.

TROY: I always come home, Rose. You know that. There ain't never been a night I ain't come home.

ROSE: That ain't what I mean . . . and you know it. I want to know if you're coming straight home after work.

TROY: I figure I'd cash my check . . . hang out at Taylors' with the boys . . . maybe play a game of checkers . . .

ROSE: Troy, I can't live like this. I won't live like this. You livin' on borrowed time with me. It's been going on six months now you ain't been coming home.

TROY: I be here every night. Every night of the year. That's 365 days.

ROSE: I want you to come home tomorrow after work.

TROY: Rose . . . I don't mess up my pay. You know that now. I take my pay and I give it to you. I don't have no money but what you give me back. I just want to have a little time to myself . . . a little time to enjoy life.

ROSE: What about me? When's my time to enjoy life?

TROY: I don't know what to tell you, Rose. I'm doing the best I can.

ROSE: You ain't been home from work but time enough to change your clothes and run out . . . and you wanna call that the best you can do?

TROY: I'm going over to the hospital to see Alberta. She went into the hospital this afternoon. Look like she might have the baby early. I won't be gone long.

ROSE: Well, you ought to know. They went over to Miss Pearl's and got Gabe today. She said you told them to go ahead and lock him up.

TROY: I ain't said no such thing. Whoever told you that is telling a lie. Pearl ain't doing nothing but telling a big fat lie.

ROSE: She ain't had to tell me. I read it on the papers.

TROY: I ain't told them nothing of the kind.

ROSE: I saw it right there on the papers.

TROY: What it say, huh?

ROSE: It said you told them to take him.

TROY: Then they screwed that up, just the way they screw up everything. I ain't worried about what they got on the paper.

ROSE: Say the government send part of his check to the hospital and the other part to you.

TROY: I ain't got nothing to do with that if that's the way it works. I ain't made up the rules about how it work.

ROSE: You did Gabe just like you did Cory. You wouldn't sign the paper for Cory . . . but you signed for Gabe. You signed that paper.

(*The telephone is heard ringing inside the house.*)

TROY: I told you I ain't signed nothing, woman! The only thing I signed was the release form. Hell, I can't read, I don't know what they had on that paper! I ain't signed nothing about sending Gabe away.

ROSE: I said send him to the hospital . . . you said let him be free . . . now you done went down there and signed him to the hospital for half his money. You went back on yourself, Troy. You gonna have to answer for that.

TROY: See now . . . you been over there talking to Miss Pearl. She done got mad cause she ain't getting Gabe's rent money. That's all it is. She's liable to say anything.

ROSE: Troy, I seen where you signed the paper.

TROY: You ain't seen nothing I signed. What she doing got papers on my brother anyway? Miss Pearl telling a big fat lie. And I'm gonna tell her about it too! You ain't seen nothing I signed. Say . . . you ain't seen nothing I signed.

(*Rose exits into the house to answer the telephone. Presently she returns.*)

ROSE: Troy . . . that was the hospital. Alberta had the baby.

TROY: What she have? What is it?

ROSE: It's a girl.

TROY: I better get on down to the hospital to see her.

ROSE: Troy . . .

TROY: Rose . . . I got to go see her now. That's only right . . . what's the matter . . . the baby's all right, ain't it?

ROSE: Alberta died having the baby.

TROY: Died . . . you say she's dead? Alberta's dead?

ROSE: They said they done all they could. They couldn't do nothing for her.

TROY: The baby? How's the baby?

ROSE: They say it's healthy. I wonder who's gonna bury her.

TROY: She had family, Rose. She wasn't living in the world by herself.

ROSE: I know she wasn't living in the world by herself.

TROY: Next thing you gonna want to know if she had any insurance.

ROSE: Troy, you ain't got to talk like that.

TROY: That's the first thing that jumped out your mouth. "Who's gonna bury her?" Like I'm fixing to take on that task for myself.

ROSE: I am your wife. Don't push me away.

TROY: I ain't pushing nobody away. Just give me some space. That's all. Just give me some room to breathe.

(*Rose exits into the house. Troy walks about the yard.*)

TROY (*with a quiet rage that threatens to consume him*): All right . . . Mr. Death. See now . . . I'm gonna tell you what I'm gonna do. I'm gonna take and build me a fence around this yard. See? I'm gonna build me a fence around what belongs to me. And then I want you to stay on the other side. See? You stay over there until you're ready for me. Then you come on. Bring your army. Bring your sickle. Bring your wrestling clothes. I ain't gonna fall down on my vigilance this time. You ain't gonna sneak up on me no more. When you ready for me . . . when the top of your list say Troy Maxson . . . that's when you come around here. You come up and knock on the front door. Ain't nobody else got nothing to do with this. This is between you and me. Man to man. You stay on the other side of that fence until you ready for me. Then you come up and knock on the front door. Anytime you want. I'll be ready for you.

(*The lights go down to black.*)

Scene III

(*The lights come up on the porch. It is late evening three days later. Rose sits listening to the ball game waiting for Troy. The final out of the game is made and Rose switches off the radio. Troy enters the yard carrying an infant wrapped in blankets. He stands back from the house and calls.*)
(*Rose enters and stands on the porch. There is a long, awkward silence, the weight of which grows heavier with each passing second.*)

TROY: Rose . . . I'm standing here with my daughter in my arms. She ain't but a wee bittie little old thing. She don't know nothing about grownups' business. She innocent . . . and she ain't got no mama.

ROSE: What you telling me for, Troy?

(*She turns and exits into the house.*)

TROY: Well . . . I guess we'll just sit out here on the porch.

(*He sits down on the porch. There is an awkward indelicateness about the way he handles the baby. His largeness engulfs and seems to swallow it. He speaks loud enough for Rose to hear.*)

A man's got to do what's right for him. I ain't sorry for nothing I done. It felt right in my heart.

(*To the baby.*)

What you smiling at? Your daddy's a big man. Got these great big old hands. But sometimes he's scared. And right now your daddy's scared cause we sitting out here and ain't got no home. Oh, I been homeless before. I ain't had no little baby with me. But I been homeless. You just be out on the road by

your lonesome and you see one of them trains coming and you just kinda go like this . . .

(*He sings as a lullaby.*)

Please, Mr. Engineer let a man ride the line
Please, Mr. Engineer let a man ride the line
I ain't got no ticket please let me ride the blinds

(*Rose enters from the house. Troy hearing her steps behind him, stands and faces her.*)

She's my daughter, Rose. My own flesh and blood. I can't deny her no more than I can deny them boys.

(*Pause.*)

You and them boys is my family. You and them and this child is all I got in the world. So I guess what I'm saying is . . . I'd appreciate it if you'd help me take care of her.

ROSE: Okay, Troy . . . you're right. I'll take care of your baby for you . . . cause . . . like you say . . . she's innocent . . . and you can't visit the sins of the father upon the child. A motherless child has got a hard time.

(*She takes the baby from him.*)

From right now . . . this child got a mother. But you a womanless man.

(*Rose turns and exits into the house with the baby. Lights go down to black.*)

Scene IV

(*It is two months later. Lyons enters from the street. He knocks on the door and calls.*)

LYONS: Hey, Rose! (*Pause.*) Rose!

ROSE (*from inside the house*): Stop that yelling. You gonna wake up Raynell. I just got her to sleep.

LYONS: I just stopped by to pay Papa this twenty dollars I owe him. Where's Papa at?

ROSE: He should be here in a minute. I'm getting ready to go down to the church. Sit down and wait on him.

LYONS: I got to go pick up Bonnie over her mother's house.

ROSE: Well, sit it down there on the table. He'll get it.

LYONS (*enters the house and sets the money on the table*): Tell Papa I said thanks. I'll see you again.

ROSE: All right, Lyons. We'll see you.

(*Lyons starts to exit as Cory enters.*)

CORY: Hey, Lyons.

LYONS: What's happening, Cory. Say man, I'm sorry

I missed your graduation. You know I had a gig and couldn't get away. Otherwise, I would have been there, man. So what you doing?

CORY: I'm trying to find a job.

LYONS: Yeah I know how that go, man. It's rough out here. Jobs are scarce.

CORY: Yeah, I know.

LYONS: Look here, I got to run. Talk to Papa . . . he know some people. He'll be able to help get you a job. Talk to him . . . see what he say.

CORY: Yeah . . . all right, Lyons.

LYONS: You take care. I'll talk to you soon. We'll find some time to talk.

(*Lyons exits the yard. Cory wanders over to the tree, picks up the bat, and assumes a batting stance. He studies an imaginary pitcher and swings. Dissatisfied with the result, he tries again. Troy enters. They eye each other for a beat. Cory puts the bat down and exits the yard. Troy starts into the house as Rose exits with Raynell. She is carrying a cake.*)

TROY: I'm coming in and everybody's going out.

ROSE: I'm taking this cake down to the church for the bake sale. Lyons was by to see you. He stopped by to pay you your twenty dollars. It's laying in there on the table.

TROY (*going into his pocket*): Well . . . here go this money.

ROSE: Put it in there on the table, Troy. I'll get it.

TROY: What time you coming back?

ROSE: Ain't no use in you studying me. It don't matter what time I come back.

TROY: I just asked you a question, woman. What's the matter . . . can't I ask you a question?

ROSE: Troy, I don't want to go into it. Your dinner's in there on the stove. All you got to do is heat it up. And don't you be eating the rest of them cakes in there. I'm coming back for them. We having a bake sale at the church tomorrow.

(*Rose exits the yard. Troy sits down on the steps, takes a pint bottle from his pocket, opens it, and drinks. He begins to sing.*)

TROY: Hear it ring! Hear it ring!
   Had an old dog his name was Blue
   You know Blue was mighty true
   You know Blue as a good old dog
   Blue trees a possum in a hollow log
   You know from that he was a good old dog

(*Bono enters the yard.*)

BONO: Hey, Troy.

TROY: Hey, what's happening, Bono?

BONO: I just thought I'd stop by to see you.

TROY: What you stop by and see me for? You ain't stopped by in a month of Sundays. Hell, I must owe you money or something.

BONO: Since you got your promotion I can't keep up with you. Used to see you every day. Now I don't even know what route you working.

TROY: They keep switching me around. Got me out in Greentree now . . . hauling white folks' garbage.

BONO: Greentree, huh? You lucky, at least you ain't got to be lifting them barrels. Damn if they ain't getting heavier. I'm gonna put in my two years and call it quits.

TROY: I'm thinking about retiring myself.

BONO: You got it easy. You can *drive* for another five years.

TROY: It ain't the same, Bono. It ain't like working the back of the truck. Ain't got nobody to talk to . . . feel like you working by yourself. Naw, I'm thinking about retiring. How's Lucille?

BONO: She all right. Her arthritis get to acting up on her sometime. Saw Rose on my way in. She going down to the church, huh?

TROY: Yeah, she took up going down there. All them preachers looking for somebody to fatten their pockets.

(*Pause.*)

Got some gin here.

BONO: Naw, thanks. I just stopped by to say hello.

TROY: Hell, nigger . . . you can take a drink. I ain't never known you to say no to a drink. You ain't got to work tomorrow.

BONO: I just stopped by. I'm fixing to go over to Skinner's. We got us a domino game going over at his house every Friday.

TROY: Nigger, you can't play no dominoes. I used to whup you four games out of five.

BONO: Well, that learned me. I'm getting better.

TROY: Yeah? Well, that's all right.

BONO: Look here . . . I got to be getting on. Stop by sometime, huh?

TROY: Yeah, I'll do that, Bono. Lucille told Rose you bought her a new refrigerator.

BONO: Yeah, Rose told Lucille you had finally built your fence . . . so I figured we'd call it even.

TROY: I knew you would.

BONO: Yeah . . . okay. I'll be talking to you.

TROY: Yeah, take care, Bono. Good to see you. I'm gonna stop over.

BONO: Yeah. Okay, Troy

(*Bono exits. Troy drinks from the bottle.*)

TROY: Old Blue died and I dig his grave
   Let him down with a golden chain

Every night when I hear old Blue bark
I know Blue treed a possum in Noah's Ark.
Hear it ring! Hear it ring!

(*Cory enters the yard. They eye each other for a beat. Troy is sitting in the middle of the steps. Cory walks over.*)

CORY: I got to get by.

TROY: Say what? What's you say?

CORY: You in my way. I got to get by.

TROY: You got to get by where? This is my house. Bought and paid for. In full. Took me fifteen years. And if you wanna go in my house and I'm sitting on the steps . . . you say excuse me. Like your mama taught you.

CORY: Come on, Pop . . . I got to get by.

(*Cory starts to maneuver his way past Troy. Troy grabs his leg and shoves him back.*)

TROY: You just gonna walk over top of me?

CORY: I live here too!

TROY (*advancing toward him*): You just gonna walk over top of me in my own house?

CORY: I ain't scared of you.

TROY: I ain't asked if you was scared of me. I asked you if you was fixing to walk over top of me in my own house? That's the question. You ain't gonna say excuse me? You just gonna walk over top of me?

CORY: If you wanna put it like that.

TROY: How else am I gonna put it?

CORY: I was walking by you to go into the house cause you sitting on the steps drunk, singing to yourself. You can put it like that.

TROY: Without saying excuse me???

(*Cory doesn't respond.*)

I asked you a question. Without saying excuse me???

CORY: I ain't got to say excuse me to you. You don't count around here no more.

TROY: Oh, I see . . . I don't count around here no more. You ain't got to say excuse me to your daddy. All of a sudden you done got so grown that your daddy don't count around here no more . . . Around here in his own house and yard that he done paid for with the sweat of his brow. You done got so grown to where you gonna take over. You gonna take over my house. Is that right? You gonna wear my pants. You gonna go in there and stretch out on my bed. You ain't got to say excuse me cause I don't count around here no more. Is that right?

CORY: That's right. You always talking this dumb stuff. Now, why don't you just get out my way.

TROY: I guess you got someplace to sleep and something to put in your belly. You got that, huh? You got that? That's what you need. You got that, huh?

CORY: You don't know what I got. You ain't got to worry about what I got.

TROY: You right! You one hundred percent right! I done spent the last seventeen years worrying about what you got. Now it's your turn, see? I'll tell you what to do. You grown . . . we done established that. You a man. Now, let's see you act like one. Turn your behind around and walk out this yard. And when you get out there in the alley . . . you can forget about this house. See? 'Cause this is my house. You go on and be a man and get your own house. You can forget about this. 'Cause this is mine. You go on and get yours 'cause I'm through with doing for you.

CORY: You talking about what you did for me . . . what'd you ever give me?

TROY: Them feet and bones! That pumping heart, nigger! I give you more than anybody else is ever gonna give you.

CORY: You ain't never gave me nothing! You ain't never done nothing but hold me back. Afraid I was gonna be better than you. All you ever did was try and make me scared of you. I used to tremble every time you called my name. Every time I heard your footsteps in the house. Wondering all the time . . . what's Papa gonna say if I do this? . . . What's he gonna say if I do that? . . . What's Papa gonna say if I turn on the radio? And Mama, too . . . she tries . . . but she's scared of you.

TROY: You leave your mama out of this. She ain't got nothing to do with this.

CORY: I don't know how she stand you . . . after what you did to her.

TROY: I told you to leave your mama out of this!

(*He advances toward Cory.*)

CORY: What you gonna do . . . give me a whupping? You can't whup me no more. You're too old. You just an old man.

TROY (*shoves him on his shoulder*): Nigger! That's what you are. You just another nigger on the street to me!

CORY: You crazy! You know that?

TROY: Go on now! You got the devil in you. Get on away from me!

CORY: You just a crazy old man . . . talking about I got the devil in me.

TROY: Yeah, I'm crazy! If you don't get on the other side of that yard . . . I'm gonna show you how crazy I am! Go on . . . get the hell out of my yard.

CORY: It ain't your yard. You took Uncle Gabe's money

he got from the army to buy this house and then you put him out.

TROY (*Troy advances on Cory*): Get your black ass out of my yard!

(*Troy's advance backs Cory up against the tree. Cory grabs up the bat.*)

CORY: I ain't going nowhere! Come on . . . put me out! I ain't scared of you.

TROY: That's my bat!

CORY: Come on!

TROY: Put my bat down!

CORY: Come on, put me out.

(*Cory swings at Troy, who backs across the yard.*)

What's the matter? You so bad . . . put me out!

(*Troy advances toward Cory.*)

CORY (*backing up*): Come on! Come on!

TROY: You're gonna have to use it! You wanna draw that bat back on me . . . you're gonna have to use it.

CORY: Come on! . . . Come on!

(*Cory swings the bat at Troy a second time. He misses. Troy continues to advance toward him.*)

TROY: You're gonna have to kill me! You wanna draw that bat back on me. You're gonna have to kill me.

(*Cory, backed up against the tree, can go no farther. Troy taunts him. He sticks out his head and offers him a target.*)

Come on! Come on!

(*Cory is unable to swing the bat. Troy grabs it.*)

TROY: Then I'll show you.

(*Cory and Troy struggle over the bat. The struggle is fierce and fully engaged. Troy ultimately is the stronger and takes the bat from Cory and stands over him ready to swing. He stops himself.*)

Go on and get away from around my house.

(*Cory, stung by his defeat, picks himself up, walks slowly out of the yard and up the alley.*)

CORY: Tell Mama I'll be back for my things.

TROY: They'll be on the other side of that fence.

(*Cory exits.*)

TROY: I can't taste nothing. Helluljah! I can't taste nothing no more. (*Troy assumes a batting posture and begins to taunt Death, the fastball on the outside corner.*) Come on! It's between you and me now!

Come on! Anytime you want! Come on! I be ready for you . . . but I ain't gonna be easy.

(*The lights go down on the scene.*)

Scene V

(*The time is 1965. The lights come up in the yard. It is the morning of Troy's funeral. A funeral plaque with a light hangs beside the door. There is a small garden plot off to the side. There is noise and activity in the house as Rose, Gabriel, and Bono have gathered. The door opens and Raynell, seven years old, enters dressed in a flannel nightgown. She crosses to the garden and pokes around with a stick. Rose calls from the house.*)

ROSE: Raynell!

RAYNELL: Mam?

ROSE: What you doing out there?

RAYNELL: Nothing.

(*Rose comes to the door.*)

ROSE: Girl, get in here and get dressed. What you doing?

RAYNELL: Seeing if my garden growed.

ROSE: I told you it ain't gonna grow overnight. You got to wait.

RAYNELL: It don't look like it never gonna grow. Dag!

ROSE: I told you a watched pot never boils. Get in here and get dressed.

RAYNELL: This ain't even no pot, Mama.

ROSE: You just have to give it a chance. It'll grow. Now you come on and do what I told you. We got to be getting ready. This ain't no morning to be playing around. You hear me?

RAYNELL: Yes, mam.

(*Rose exits into the house. Raynell continues to poke at her garden with a stick. Cory enters. He is dressed in a Marine corporal's uniform, and carries a duffel bag. His posture is that of a military man, and his speech has a clipped sternness.*)

CORY (*to Raynell*): Hi.

(*Pause.*)

I bet your name is Raynell.

RAYNELL: Uh huh.

CORY: Is your mama home?

(*Raynell runs up on the porch and calls through the screendoor.*)

RAYNELL: Mama . . . there's some man out here. Mama?

(*Rose comes to the door.*)

ROSE: Cory? Lord have mercy! Look here, you all!

(Rose and Cory embrace in a tearful reunion as Bono and Lyons enter from the house dressed in funeral clothes.)

BONO: Aw, looka here . . .

ROSE: Done got all grown up!

CORY: Don't cry, Mama. What you crying about?

ROSE: I'm just so glad you made it.

CORY: Hey Lyons. How you doing, Mr. Bono.

(Lyons goes to embrace Cory.)

LYONS: Look at you, man. Look at you. Don't he look good, Rose. Got them Corporal stripes.

ROSE: What took you so long.

CORY: You know how the Marines are, Mama. They got to get all their paperwork straight before they let you do anything.

ROSE: Well, I'm sure glad you made it. They let Lyons come. Your Uncle Gabe's still in the hospital. They don't know if they gonna let him out or not. I just talked to them a little while ago.

LYONS: A Corporal in the United States Marines.

BONO: Your daddy knew you had it in you. He used to tell me all the time.

LYONS: Don't he look good, Mr. Bono?

BONO: Yeah, he remind me of Troy when I first met him.

(Pause.)

Say, Rose, Lucille's down at the church with the choir. I'm gonna go down and get the pallbearers lined up. I'll be back to get you all.

ROSE: Thanks, Jim.

CORY: See you, Mr. Bono.

LYONS *(with his arm around Raynell)*: Cory . . . look at Raynell. Ain't she precious? She gonna break a whole lot of hearts.

ROSE: Raynell, come and say hello to your brother. This is your brother, Cory. You remember Cory.

RAYNELL: No, Mam.

CORY: She don't remember me, Mama.

ROSE: Well, we talk about you. She heard us talk about you. *(To Raynell.)* This is your brother, Cory. Come on and say hello.

RAYNELL: Hi.

CORY: Hi. So you're Raynell. Mama told me a lot about you.

ROSE: You all come on into the house and let me fix you some breakfast. Keep up your strength.

CORY: I ain't hungry, Mama.

LYONS: You can fix me something, Rose. I'll be in there in a minute.

ROSE: Cory, you sure you don't want nothing. I know they ain't feeding you right.

CORY: No, Mama . . . thanks. I don't feel like eating. I'll get something later.

ROSE: Raynell . . . get on upstairs and get that dress on like I told you.

(Rose and Raynell exit into the house.)

LYONS: So . . . I hear you thinking about getting married.

CORY: Yeah, I done found the right one, Lyons. It's about time.

LYONS: Me and Bonnie been split up about four years now. About the time Papa retired. I guess she just got tired of all them changes I was putting her through.

(Pause.)

I always knew you was gonna make something out yourself. Your head was always in the right direction. So . . . you gonna stay in . . . make it a career . . . put in your twenty years?

CORY: I don't know. I got six already, I think that's enough.

LYONS: Stick with Uncle Sam and retire early. Ain't nothing out here. I guess Rose told you what happened with me. They got me down the workhouse. I thought I was being slick cashing other people's checks.

CORY: How much time you doing?

LYONS: They give me three years. I got that beat now. I ain't got but nine more months. It ain't so bad. You learn to deal with it like anything else. You got to take the crookeds with the straights. That's what Papa used to say. He used to say that when he struck out. I seen him strike out three times in a row . . . and the next time up he hit the ball over the grandstand. Right out there in Homestead Field. He wasn't satisfied hitting in the seats . . . he want to hit it over everything! After the game he had two hundred people standing around waiting to shake his hand. You got to take the crookeds with the straights. Yeah, Papa was something else.

CORY: You still playing?

LYONS: Cory . . . you know I'm gonna do that. There's some fellows down there we got us a band . . . we gonna try and stay together when we get out . . . but yeah, I'm still playing. It still helps me to get out of bed in the morning. As long as it do that I'm gonna be right there playing and trying to make some sense out of it.

ROSE *(calling)*: Lyons, I got these eggs in the pan.

LYONS: Let me go on and get these eggs, man. Get ready to go bury Papa.

(*Pause.*)

How you doing? You doing all right?

(*Cory nods. Lyons touches him on the shoulder and they share a moment of silent grief. Lyons exits into the house. Cory wanders about the yard. Raynell enters.*)

RAYNELL: Hi.
CORY: Hi.
RAYNELL: Did you used to sleep in my room?
CORY: Yeah . . . that used to be my room.
RAYNELL: That's what Papa call it. "Cory's room." It got your football in the closet.

(*Rose comes to the door.*)

ROSE: Raynell, get in there and get them good shoes on.
RAYNELL: Mama, can't I wear these. Them other one hurt my feet.
ROSE: Well, they just gonna have to hurt your feet for a while. You ain't said they hurt your feet when you went down to the store and got them.
RAYNELL: They didn't hurt then. My feet done got bigger.
ROSE: Don't you give me no backtalk now. You get in there and get them shoes on.

(*Raynell exits into the house.*)

Ain't too much changed. He still got that piece of rag tied to that tree. He was out here swinging that bat. I was just ready to go back in the house. He swung that bat and then he just fell over. Seem like he swung it and stood there with this grin on his face . . . and then he just fell over. They carried him on down to the hospital, but I knew there wasn't no need . . . why don't you come on in the house?
CORY: Mama . . . I got something to tell you. I don't know how to tell you this . . . but I've got to tell you . . . I'm not going to Papa's funeral.
ROSE: Boy, hush your mouth. That's your daddy you talking about. I don't want hear that kind of talk this morning. I done raised you to come to this? You standing there all healthy and grown talking about you ain't going to your daddy's funeral?
CORY: Mama . . . listen . . .
ROSE: I don't want to hear it, Cory. You just get that thought out of your head.
CORY: I can't drag Papa with me everywhere I go. I've got to say no to him. One time in my life I've got to say no.
ROSE: Don't nobody have to listen to nothing like that. I know you and your daddy ain't seen eye to eye, but I ain't got to listen to that kind of talk this morning. Whatever was between you and your

daddy . . . the time has come to put it aside. Just take it and set it over there on the shelf and forget about it. Disrespecting your daddy ain't gonna make you a man, Cory. You got to find a way to come to that on your own. Not going to your daddy's funeral ain't gonna make you a man.
CORY: The whole time I was growing up . . . living in his house . . . Papa was like a shadow that followed you everywhere. It weighed on you and sunk into your flesh. It would wrap around you and lay there until you couldn't tell which one was you anymore. That shadow digging in your flesh. Trying to crawl in. Trying to live through you. Everywhere I looked, Troy Maxson was staring back at me . . . hiding under the bed . . . in the closet. I'm just saying I've got to find a way to get rid of that shadow, Mama.
ROSE: You just like him. You got him in you good.
CORY: Don't tell me that, Mama.
ROSE: You Troy Maxson all over again.
CORY: I don't want to be Troy Maxson. I want to be me.
ROSE: You can't be nobody but who you are, Cory. That shadow wasn't nothing but you growing into yourself. You either got to grow into it or cut it down to fit you. But that's all you got to make life with. That's all you got to measure yourself against that world out there. Your daddy wanted you to be everything he wasn't . . . and at the same time he tried to make you into everything he was. I don't know if he was right or wrong . . . but I do know he meant to do more good than he meant to do harm. He wasn't always right. Sometimes when he touched he bruised. And sometimes when he took me in his arms he cut.

When I first met your daddy I thought . . . Here is a man I can lay down with and make a baby. That's the first thing I thought when I seen him. I was thirty years old and had done seen my share of men. But when he walked up to me and said, "I can dance a waltz that'll make you dizzy," I thought, Rose Lee, here is a man that you can open yourself up to and be filled to bursting. Here is a man that can fill all them empty spaces you been tipping around the edges of. One of them empty spaces was being somebody's mother.

I married your daddy and settled down to cooking his supper and keeping clean sheets on the bed. When your daddy walked through the house he was so big he filled it up. That was my first mistake. Not to make him leave some room for me. For my part in the matter. But at that time I wanted that. I wanted a house that I could sing in. And that's what your daddy gave me. I didn't know to keep up his strength I had to give up little pieces of mine. I did that. I took on his life as mine and mixed up the pieces so that you couldn't hardly tell which was which anymore. It was my choice. It was my life and I didn't have to live it like that. But that's what life offered me in the way of being a woman and I took it. I grabbed hold of it with both hands.

By the time Raynell came into the house, me and your daddy had done lost touch with one another. I didn't want to make my blessing off of nobody's misfortune . . . but I took on to Raynell like she was all them babies I had wanted and never had.

(*The phone rings.*)

Like I'd been blessed to relive a part of my life. And if the Lord see fit to keep up my strength . . . I'm gonna do her just like your daddy did you . . . I'm gonna give her the best of what's in me.
RAYNELL (*entering, still with her old shoes*): Mama . . . Reverend Tollivier on the phone.

(*Rose exits into the house.*)

RAYNELL: Hi.
CORY: Hi.
RAYNELL: You in the Army or the Marines?
CORY: Marines.
RAYNELL: Papa said it was the Army. Did you know Blue?
CORY: Blue? Who's Blue?
RAYNELL: Papa's dog what he sing about all the time.
CORY (*singing*): Hear it ring! Hear it ring!
  I had a dog his name was Blue
  You know Blue was mighty true
  You know Blue was a good old dog
  Blue treed a possum in a hollow log
  You know from that he was a good old dog.
  Hear it ring! Hear it ring!

(*Raynell joins in singing.*)

CORY AND RAYNELL: Blue treed a possum out on a limb
  Blue looked at me and I looked at him
  Grabbed that possum and put him in a sack
  Blue stayed there till I came back
  Old Blue's feets was big and round
  Never allowed a possum to touch the ground.

  Old Blue died and I dug his grave
  I dug his grave with a silver spade
  Let him down with a golden chain
  And every night I call his name
  Go on Blue, you good dog you
  Go on Blue, you good dog you
RAYNELL: Blue laid down and died like a man
  Blue laid down and died . . .

BOTH: Blue laid down and died like a man
  Now he's treeing possums in the Promised Land
  I'm gonna tell you this to let you know
  Blue's gone where the good dogs go
  When I hear old Blue bark
  When I hear old Blue bark
  Blue treed a possum in Noah's Ark
  Blue treed a possum in Noah's Ark.

(*Rose comes to the screen door.*)

ROSE: Cory, we gonna be ready to go in a minute.
CORY (*to Raynell*): You go on in the house and change them shoes like Mama told you so we can go to Papa's funeral.
RAYNELL: Okay, I'll be back.

(*Raynell exits into the house. Cory gets up and crosses over to the tree. Rose stands in the screen door watching him. Gabriel enters from the alley.*)

GABRIEL (*calling*): Hey, Rose!
ROSE: Gabe?
GABRIEL: I'm here, Rose. Hey Rose, I'm here!

(*Rose enters from the house.*)

ROSE: Lord . . . Look here, Lyons!
LYONS: See, I told you, Rose . . . I told you they'd let him come.
CORY: How you doing, Uncle Gabe?
LYONS: How you doing, Uncle Gabe?
GABRIEL: Hey, Rose. It's time. It's time to tell St. Peter to open the gates. Troy, you ready? You ready, Troy. I'm gonna tell St. Peter to open the gates. You get ready now.

(*Gabriel, with great fanfare, braces himself to blow. The trumpet is without a mouthpiece. He puts the end of it into his mouth and blows with great force, like a man who has been waiting some twenty-odd years for this single moment. No sound comes out of the trumpet. He braces himself and blows again with the same result. A third time he blows. There is a weight of impossible description that falls away and leaves him bare and exposed to a frightful realization. It is a trauma that a sane and normal mind would be unable to withstand. He begins to dance. A slow, strange dance, eerie and life-giving. A dance of atavistic signature and ritual. Lyons attempts to embrace him. Gabriel pushes Lyons away. He begins to howl in what is an attempt at song, or perhaps a song turning back into itself in an attempt at speech. He finishes his dance and the gates of heaven stand open as wide as God's closet.*)

That's the way that go!

COMMENTARIES

In the interviews that follow — with Athol Fugard, Caryl Churchill, Marsha Norman, and August Wilson — playwrights comment on their plays and on how their work developed. They also talk about how their plays have been received. Sam Shepard's biographer comments on the playwright's ambitions and on the nature of his work from the perspective of a critic. In the selection from Athol Fugard's *Notebooks*, we find the source of the personal pain revealed in *"MASTER HAROLD"* . . . *and the boys*. All these commentaries show us the vitality and range of our contemporary playwrights.

Ellen Oumano (b. 1943)
SAM SHEPARD: *TRUE WEST*

Ellen Oumano subtitled her biography of Sam Shepard "The Life of an American Dreamer." The American dream may have always been connected with the West, and if so, Sam Shepard has shown us that we have to rethink that dream. In True West *(1980), the American dream turns into a nightmare. Oumano discusses the fundamental interests of Shepard, the role of the artist in society and the fate of the family.*

More than ever, Shepard was becoming a man's man, a true son of the West, preferring the rodeo and the fights to literary cocktail parties and screenings. In 1980, writer Robert Coe spent two weeks with Shepard in preparation for an article he was writing for the *New York Times Magazine*. When the two men played golf, Shepard displayed a surprising sense of decorum: "At one point someone threw a club across the fairway to another person and that disgusted him; it was inappropriate behavior," relates Coe. They attended the Sugar Ray Leonard–Roberto Duran fight with Robert Woodruff: "He was pretty excited and liked Duran. He didn't like the pretty boy, the face in the 7-Up commercials — he was for the savage. He had it all articulated: 'I always pull for the savage.' It was a great fight. We drank a lot of beer and he had this whole lavish betting system set up for us. It was an amazing fight. I remember we were just wrung out afterward, exhausted." The next day Woodruff used the fight to coach the two actors playing the combative brothers, Lee and Austin, in Shepard's new play, *True West*, "locked together and somehow feeling one another's rhythm. In that fight they were so tuned to what the other one was doing it was a complicated, savage, violent dance."

Shepard told Coe that he was still going to rodeos with a partner named Slim, who had a great way of talking. "Shepard could rope a calf, things like that," Coe continues. "The whole time I was with him he had a big bandage on his thumb because he caught it in the door of his horse trailer. He said of the rodeo, 'Some of these guys at the rodeo are really cowboys and then there's these other guys, TWA pilots, who like to come and get their hats knocked off.' He has a deep admiration for real cowboys — he thinks it's a more authentic way of life." . . .

Coe was surprised to hear Shepard not only dismiss the off-off-Broadway scene of the Sixties as totally crazy, but renounce his play *The Tooth of Crime* as well. "He says it's totally irresponsible — crazy, wacked out, violent — just heaving a bunch of baboons out into the street." Not surprisingly, Coe was impressed by Shepard's genuinely "secret, retiring personality. It's not a pose — he doesn't like the spotlight, being the center of attention.

"I asked him why he doesn't write more women characters. He said he thinks men are more interesting: The real mystery in American life lies between men, not between men and women."

True West certainly explored that mystery — more shatteringly and pointedly than any of his other plays. Through a storyline more accessible and straightforward than any of his previous work, Shepard brought together and explored his two concerns: the corruption of the artist and the disintegration of the family. Austin, a successful Hollywood screenwriter, is house-sitting for his mother when he is visited by his brother, Lee, a petty burglar and vagrant with a vague but powerfully menacing air. Lee manages to sell his clichéd idea for a "real" Western for a huge fee to the producer Austin had been courting, thus calling into question what makes art, at least movie art, authentic.

Shepard was extremely pleased with the Magic's [a theater company] production of the play he had reworked so painstakingly: "This is the first one of my plays I've been able to sit through night after night and not have my stomach ball up in embarrassment," he told one interviewer. "I worked longer on this than any other play. I rewrote it thirteen times. *True West* is the first play I've truly lived up to."

Heinrich von Staden (b. 1939)
INTERVIEW WITH ATHOL FUGARD

When "MASTER HAROLD" . . . and the boys was first produced at the Yale Repertory Theatre, Athol Fugard had the chance to respond to some questions about its significance to him. He revealed that the play was deeply personal and that through it he had been able to exorcise a demon that had haunted him for some time. In this interview, Fugard detailed his involvement with South African drama and black actors in South Africa. He also commented on the extent to which censorship and other political pressures in South Africa have made it difficult for his work to be produced in his own country.

von Staden: The bombs of fiction — Athol, aren't they more explosive than TNT?

Fugard: I'd like to believe that. You understand I've got to be careful about that one. I've got to be careful about flattering myself about the potency of the one area of activity which I've got, which is theater and being a writer.

von Staden: How often have there been productions of your plays for non-segregated audiences in South Africa?

Fugard: I've had to change my tactics in terms of that over the years. At a period when the policy on segregated audiences in South Africa was rigid and very strictly enforced, I had to make a decision whether to take on an act of silence, just be silent because I couldn't go into a theater that was decent in my terms, or whether to take on the compromising circumstances of segregated audiences simply because I felt that if a play has got something to say, at least say it. And there were years when I decided to do the latter. I did perform before segregated audiences. In a sense I regret that decision now. I think I might possibly have looked after myself — and maybe the situation — better by not accepting that compromise. But I did.

von Staden: But do you think you had a genuine choice at that time?

Fugard: I had a choice between silence or being heard.

von Staden: Let me ask you along similar lines, when you are writing a play or a novel like *Tsotsi*, do you sense constraints on the way you are writing in view of the fact that certain things are anathema to the government, also in fiction?

Fugard: I would like to believe that I have operated at the table at which I sit and write, that I have operated totally without self-censorship. Maybe some awareness of what is possible and is not possible has operated subconsciously and is deciding choices I make in terms of what I favor. I think it may be pertinent to the conversation we are having, that *"MASTER HAROLD"* . . . *and the boys* is the first play of mine in twenty-four years of writing that will have its premiere outside of South Africa. And one of the reasons why I'm doing that this time is that there are elements in *"MASTER HAROLD"* . . . *and the boys* that might have run into censorship problems. . . .

von Staden: Here you are, a person who, critics say, has achieved exceptional insight into human nature, and you never obtained a university degree. What institutions, what processes do you think contributed most to the insights you have?

Fugard: Well, I think to be a South African is in a way to be at a university that teaches you about that. The South African experience is certainly one in which, if you're prepared to keep your eyes open and look, you're going to see a lot of suffering. But then, in terms of personal specifics, I suppose for me there was a very, very important relationship, a friendship, with a black man in what I suppose is any person's most formative and definitive years, the age between eleven, ten up until the age of twenty-one. It was a black man in Port Elizabeth, and my play *"MASTER HAROLD"* . . . *and the boys* reflects something of that friendship, tries to talk about it, look at it. I left South Africa, hitchhiked through the African continent, ended up as a sailor on a ship which, apart from the officers and engineers, had a totally nonwhite, had a totally black crew, and I was a sailor in a totally black crew. There was that, I think I can't nail down any one specific traumatic incident as being totally decisive. But I could be certain that *"MASTER HAROLD"* . . . *and the boys* deals with one specific moment which I'm trying to exorcise out of my soul.

von Staden: In all of your plays and in the novel you always have a South African setting. Yet your plays and your novels, though so rooted in the specifics of the South African situation, seem to have a tremendous appeal to audiences that are largely ignorant of the situation there. To what do you ascribe that?

Fugard: You take a chance. As a storyteller one year ago, I took a chance . . . I realized that it was finally time to deal with the story of a seventeen-year-old boy and his friendship with two black men. And it's a gamble. There's no formula. There is no way that you can make or decide or guarantee before the event that that story is going to resonate outside of its specific context. You just take a bloody chance.

Athol Fugard (b. 1932)
From NOTEBOOKS 1960–1977

Like most playwrights, Athol Fugard is a journal writer. In his notebooks, he has written scraps of memory that have special meaning to him. In one entry for March 1961, long before he began to write "MASTER HAROLD" . . . and the boys (1982), he describes one of his childhood memories. It concerns the real-life Sam, and it reveals — very painfully — exactly what the personal crime was that his play deals with. His gesture of contempt for the man who was like a grandfather to him became a demon that had to be exorcised.

Sam Semela — Basuto — with the family fifteen years. Meeting him again when he visited Mom set off string of memories.

The kite which he produced for me one day during those early years when Mom ran the Jubilee Hotel and he was a waiter there. He had made it himself: brown paper, its ribs fashioned from thin strips of tomato-box plank which he had smoothed down, a paste of flour and water for glue. I was surprised and bewildered that he had made it for me.

I vaguely recall shyly "haunting" the servants' quarters in the well of the hotel — cold, cement-gray world — the pungent mystery of the dark little rooms — a world I didn't understand. Frightened to enter any of the rooms. Sam, broad-faced, broader based — he smelled of woodsmoke. The "kaffir smell" of South Africa is the smell of poverty — woodsmoke and sweat.

Later, when he worked for her at the Park café, Mom gave him the sack: ". . . he became careless. He came late for work. His work went to hell. He didn't seem to care no more." I was about thirteen and served behind the counter while he waited on table.

Realize now he was the most significant — the only — friend of my boyhood years. On terrible windy days when no one came to swim or walk in the park, we would sit together and talk. Or I was reading — Introductions to Eastern Philosophy or Plato and Socrates — and when I had finished he would take the book back to New Brighton.

Can't remember now what precipitated it, but one day there was a rare quarrel between Sam and myself. In a truculent silence we closed the café, Sam set off home to New Brighton on foot and I followed a few minutes later on my bike. I saw him walking ahead of me and, coming out of a spasm of acute loneliness, as I rode up behind him I called his name, he turned in mid-stride to look back and, as I cycled past, I spat in his face. Don't suppose I will ever deal with the shame that overwhelmed me the second after I had done that.

Now he is thin. We had a long talk. He told about the old woman ("Ma") whom he and his wife have taken in to look after their house while he goes to work — he teaches ballroom dancing. "Ma" insists on behaving like a domestic — making Sam feel guilty and embarrassed. She brings him an early morning cup of coffee. Sam: "No, Ma, you mustn't, man." Ma: "I must." Sam: "Look, Ma, if I want it, I can make it." Ma: "No, I must."

Occasionally, when she is doing something, Sam feels like a cup of tea but is too embarrassed to ask her, and daren't make one for himself. Similarly, with his washing. After three days or a week away in other towns, giving dancing lessons, he comes back with underclothes that are very dirty. He is too shy to give them out to be washed so washes them himself. When Ma sees this she goes and complains to Sam's wife that he doesn't trust her, that it's all wrong for him to do the washing.

Of tsotsis, he said: "They grab a old man, stick him with a knife and ransack him. And so he must go to hospital and his kids is starving with hungry." Of others: "He's some little moneys. So he is facing starvation for the weekend."

Of township snobs, he says there are the educational ones: "If you haven't been to the big school, like Fort Hare, what you say isn't true." And the money ones: "If you aren't selling shops or got a business or a big car, man, you're nothing."

Sam's incredible theory about the likeness of those "with the true seed of love." Starts with Plato and Socrates — they were round. "Man is being shrinking all the time. An Abe Lincoln, him too, taller, but that's because man is shrinking." Basically, those with the true seed of love look the same — "It's in the eyes."

He spoke admiringly of one man, a black lawyer in East London, an educated man — university background — who was utterly without snobbery, looking down on no one — any man, educated or ignorant, rich or poor, was another *man* to him, another human being, to be respected, taken seriously, to be talked to, listened to.

"They" won't allow Sam any longer to earn a living as a dancing teacher. "You must get a job!" One of his fellow teachers was forced to work at Fraser's Quarries.

Kathleen Betsko, Rachel Koenig, and Emily Mann
Interview with Caryl Churchill

Kathleen Betsko and Rachel Koenig interviewed Caryl Churchill in February 1984 and then later that year playwright Emily Mann continued the interview. Churchill discusses the process of writing plays and the differing themes that prevail in the United States and in England. She also touches on drama as making moral and political statements, and on feminist and socialist influences in Top Girls.

Betsko and Koenig: Is there a female aesthetic? And we'd like you to wrap this question up once and for all. [Laughter]

Churchill: I don't see how you can tell until there are so many plays by women that you can begin to see what they have in common that's different from the way men have written, and there are still relatively so few. And we have things in common with male playwrights who are worried about similar things in their particular country and who have worked in the same theaters with the same directors. So it's hard to separate out and think of "women playwrights" rather than just "playwrights." Though I do remember before I wrote *Top Girls* thinking about women barristers — how they were in a minority and had to imitate men to succeed — and I was thinking of them as different from me. And then I thought, "Wait a minute, my whole concept of what plays might be is from plays written by men. I don't have to put on a wig, speak in a special voice, but how far do I assume things that have been defined by men?" There isn't a simple answer to that. And I remember long before that thinking of the "maleness" of the traditional structure of plays, with conflict and building in a certain way to a climax. But it's not something I think about very often. Playwriting will change not just because more women are doing it but because more women are doing other things as well. And of course men will be influenced by that too. So maybe you'll still be no nearer to defining a female aesthetic.

Betsko and Koenig: In Laurie Stone's *Village Voice* interview [March 1, 1983], you talked about women becoming Coca-Cola executives and you said, "Well, that's not what I mean by feminism." What exactly do you mean by feminism?

Churchill: When I was in the States in '79 I talked to some women who were saying how well things were going for women in America now with far more top executives being women, and I was struck by the difference between that and the feminism I was used to in England, which is far more closely connected with socialism. And that was one of the ideas behind writing *Top Girls*, that achieving things isn't necessarily good, it matters *what* you achieve.

Thatcher had just become prime minister; there was talk about whether it was an advance to have a woman prime minister if it was someone with policies like hers: She may be a woman but she isn't a sister, she may be a sister but she isn't a comrade. And, in fact, things have got much worse for women under Thatcher. So that's the context of that remark. I do find it hard to conceive of a right-wing feminism. Of course, socialism and feminism aren't synonymous, but I feel strongly about both and wouldn't be interested in a form of one that didn't include the other.

Betsko and Koenig: Do you think it's odd, given the fact that there is at best indifference, at worst hostility, to political plays in America, that your works are so popular here?

Churchill: Is it true that on the whole plays here tend to be more family-centered, personal, individual-centered?

Betsko and Koenig: Yes, more psychological.

Churchill: Whereas I've been quite heavily exposed to a tradition of looking at the larger context of groups of people. It doesn't mean you don't look at families or individuals within that, but you are also looking at bigger things. Like with the kind of work Joint Stock Theatre Group has done, where you go and research a subject and where you have a lot of characters, even if played by only a few people. It tends to open things out.

Betsko and Koenig: Could you talk a little about working with Joint Stock?

Churchill: I've worked with them three times, on *Light Shining in Buckinghamshire* [1976], *Cloud Nine* [1979], and *Fen* [1983]. The company was started in 1974 by several people, including Max Stafford-Clark, who directed *Light Shining* and *Cloud Nine*. There's usually a workshop of three or four weeks when the writer, director, and actors research a subject, then about ten weeks when the writer goes off and writes the play, then a six-week rehearsal when you're usually finishing writing the play. Everyone's paid the same wage each week they're working and everyone makes decisions about the budget and the affairs of the company, and because of that responsibility and the workshop everyone is much more involved than usual in the final play. It's not perfect, but it is good, and I do notice the contrast with more hierarchical organizations and feel uncomfortable in them. Because everyone is involved it's taken for granted that everyone will have good parts, so you can't write a couple of main characters and give everyone else very little to do. And usually because of the subject matter, the plays tend to have a large cast of characters, although the company is about six or eight, and the actors double. It's very pressured because the tour's booked and the posters printed long before the play is finished. It's a very intense way of working.

Betsko and Koenig: Do you find collaboration difficult?

Churchill: No, I like it. I'd always been very solitary as a writer before and I like working that closely with other people. You don't collaborate on writing the play, you still go away and write it yourself, so to that extent it's the same as usual. What's different is that you've had a period of researching something together, not just information, but your attitudes to it, and possible ways of showing things, which means that when you come back with the writing you're much more open to suggestions.

Betsko and Koenig: Does the playwright have an obligation to take a moral and political stance?

Churchill: It's almost impossible not to take one, whether you intend to or not. Most plays can be looked at from a political perspective and have said something, even if it isn't what you set out to say. If you wrote a West End comedy relying on conventional sexist jokes, that's taking a moral and political stance, though the person who wrote it might say, "I was just writing an entertaining show." Whatever you do your point of view is going to show somewhere. It usually only gets noticed and called "political" if it's against the status quo. There are times when I feel I want to deal with immediate issues and times when I don't. I do like the stuff of theater, in the same way people who are painting like paint; and of course when you say "moral and political" that doesn't have to imply reaching people logically or overtly, because theater can reach people on all kinds of other levels too. Sometimes one side or the other is going to have more weight. Sometimes it's going to be about images, more like a dream to people, and sometimes it's going to be more like reading an article. And there's room for all that. But either way, the issues you feel strongly about are going to come through, and they're going to be a moral and political stance in some form. Sometimes more explicitly, sometimes less.

Mann: Let's talk about your play *Top Girls*.

Churchill: When I wrote *Top Girls* I was writing it by myself and not for a company. I wanted to write about women doing different kinds of work and didn't feel I knew enough about it. Then I thought, this is ridiculous, if you were with a company you'd go out and talk to people, so I did. Which is how I came up with the employment agency in the second act.

Mann: Are there specific characters in *Top Girls* that have their real life counterparts?

Churchill: Quite a few of the things Win tells Angie about her life are things different people said to me. And of course the dead women at the dinner are all based on someone [from art, literature, or history]. But apart from that, it's imaginary.

Mann: Tell me about the ways in which *Top Girls* has been misunderstood.

Churchill: What I was intending to do was make it first look as though it was celebrating the achievements of women and then — by showing the main character, Marlene, being successful in a very competitive, destructive, capitalist way — ask, what kind of achievement is that? The idea was that it would start out looking like a feminist play and turn into a socialist one, as well. And I think on the whole it's mostly been understood like that. A lot of people have latched on to Marlene leaving her child, which interestingly was something that came very late. Originally the idea was just that Marlene was "writing off" her niece, Angie, because she'd never make it; I didn't yet have the plot idea that Angie was actually Marlene's own child. Of course women are pressured to make choices between working and having children in a way that men aren't, so it *is* relevant, but it isn't the main point of it.

There's another thing that I've recently discovered with other productions of *Top Girls*. In Greece, for example, where fewer women go out to work, the attitude from some men seeing it was, apparently, that the women in the play who'd gone out to work weren't very nice, weren't happy, and they abandoned their children. They felt the play was obviously saying women *shouldn't* go out to work — they took it to mean what they were wanting to say about women themselves, which is depressing. Highly depressing. [Laughter] Another example of its being open to misunderstanding was a production in Cologne, Germany, where the women characters were played as miserable and quarrelsome and competitive at the dinner, and the women in the office were neurotic and incapable. The waitress slunk about in a catsuit like a bunnygirl and Win changed her clothes on stage in the office. It just turned into a complete travesty of what it was supposed to be. So that's the sort of moment when you think you'd rather write novels, because the productions can't be changed.

Kathleen Betsko and Rachel Koenig
INTERVIEW WITH MARSHA NORMAN

Marsha Norman speaks freely in this interview about 'night, Mother *and her concepts of how a play ought to work. She discusses some of her feelings about the characters in her play, revealing some of the dimensions of the struggle she envisioned between Thelma and Jessie. She also deals with the question of how Thelma is to cope with life after Jessie dies.*

Norman: I like to talk about plays as pieces of machinery. A ski lift. When you get in it, you must feel absolutely secure; you must know that this thing can hold you up. And the first movement of it must be so smooth that whatever residual fears you had about the machine or the mountain are allayed. The journey up the mountain on the ski lift must be continuous. You can't stop and just dangle. If you do, people will realize how far down it is, and they will suddenly get afraid and start grasping the corners of their chairs, which you don't want them to do.

Betsko and Koenig: You've said the main character must want something. Is *'night, Mother,* then, Thelma's play? It seems that Jessie, the suicidal daughter, has lost all desire.

Norman: Well, Jessie certainly doesn't want to have anything more to do with *her* life, but she does want Mama to be able to go on, and that's a very strong desire on Jessie's part. She *wants* Mama to be able to do the wash and know where everything is. She wants Mama to live, and to live free of the guilt that Mama might have felt had Jessie just left her a note. Jessie's desires are so strong in the piece. The play exists because Jessie wants something for Mama. Then, of course, Mama wants Jessie to stay. So you have two conflicting goals. And at that point it is a real struggle. It might as well be armed warfare. Only very late in the piece do they realize that both goals are achievable given some moderation. What Mama does understand, finally, is that there wasn't anything she could do. And so Jessie does win. Mama certainly loses in the battle to keep her alive, but Mama does gain other things in the course of the evening.

Betsko and Koenig: For instance?

Norman: They have never been so close as they are on this evening. It is calling the question that produces the closeness.

Betsko and Koenig: What happens to a woman like Thelma Cates after her daughter has committed suicide?

Norman: Well, what's very clear about Thelma from the beginning is that she lives in an intense network of both things and people. Her friend Agnes says, "You have to keep your life filled up." That's what Thelma has done. She is devoted to her candy and her *TV Guide* and her handwork; she loves talking on the phone to her friends. After Jessie's suicide, Thelma's physical life continues pretty much the way it always was. Thelma is not weak and sick and old. She has only seemed weak and sick and old so that Jessie would feel useful. Jessie, of course, saw right through that. One of the things I think is new in Thelma's life is the experience of this evening, which will belong only to her forever. Probably for the first time, Thelma has something that is securely hers, that she does not need for anybody else to understand and would not dare tell anybody. She has a holy object: this evening that they spent together. And that probably makes for some change in Thelma. But it's probably not a change any of her friends would notice.

Betsko and Koenig: Is the holy object The Truth?

Norman: It's the moment of connection between them. Basically, it is a moment when two people are willing to go as far as they can with each other. That doesn't happen very often, and we are lucky if we have two or three moments in our lives when we know that, with this person, we have gone as far as it is possible to go. After a lifetime of missing this daughter, of somehow just living in the same space, they finally had a moment when they actually lived together, when the issues of their lives were standing there with them, in silent witness of their meeting. This is exactly the kind of meeting the theater can document, can present and preserve. In an odd way, writing for the theater is like nominating people for the archives of human history. As playwright, I select a person to nominate for permanent memory by the race. The audience, the worldwide audience, does the voting. Some of my nominations make it and some of them don't. But it seems that Jessie and Thelma are going to make it. They are going to be remembered for what they did that night.

Betsko and Koenig: Writing for the theater is an attempt to immortalize your characters?

Norman: Preserve is more like it. We preserve valuable things because they will be needed, because they are the heritage of the people who come after us. We have benefited from that preservation effort up till now — I am grateful that King Lear was preserved, that he is here for me, and I can look at his life and know what he did. We all have a responsibility to preserve those people from our own time who deserve to be remembered or must be remembered for some reason. It's the struggle that makes them memorable. Because on that night, Thelma does as good a job as anybody could do. It's that effort that gives her a place.

Betsko and Koenig: Why doesn't Thelma go a bit further? Why doesn't she attack her daughter physically to prevent the suicide?

Norman: Well, there is that final moment at the door, and it posed an interesting dilemma. At that moment in the script, Thelma is reaching for something to hit Jessie with. In the early versions of the script, there was a line that said, "I'll knock you out cold before I'll let you . . ." In my mind I saw Thelma reaching for the frying pan. Like, "I am going to hurt you now. And we will straighten this out when you wake up." [Laughter.] Then Tom Moore, the director, pointed out that while it may be tragedy to pick up a frying pan, it is farce when you put it down.

Betsko and Koenig: You weren't willing then to risk humor at that point?

Norman: Right. And you can't leave Thelma standing there at the door holding the frying pan.

Betsko and Koenig: But did you try it that way during rehearsal?

Norman: We tried to make the fight as violent as we could. Thelma only has one thing left to try and that is physical harm. But I don't know if the audience ever understands that effort.

Betsko and Koenig: Did the fact that you could not demonstrate Thelma's passion in a physical way put more weight on her final verbal plea to Jessie?

Norman: The struggle at the door is one of the most difficult moments for both of them. The actress, Anne Pitoniak, as a human being inside that character, realizes she must fight and she must lose.

Betsko and Koenig: Does she let go of Jessie in that moment?

Norman: Thelma's crucial letting go has occurred earlier in the piece. This fight is pure instinct. This has nothing to do with thinking or feeling, this is just physical. This is that last moment when you realize you're cornered, and you're not going to try to talk to the grizzly bear anymore. . . . She *does* know that she has lost. Jessie is simply too powerful. But that doesn't mean that Thelma is just going to stand there.

Betsko and Koenig: You've said it's important to you to confront life and death issues. Many writers have done it through metaphor, while you confronted it literally. Not that the play is without metaphor — but the central issue is very concrete. How did you come to that decision?

Norman: Suicide is not a new issue onstage. I had seen a couple of pieces that treated it obliquely. Pieces that did not have, for example, the person that loved you most standing there across the room saying *No* to you. I felt that if you were going to talk about suicide, there was really no way to talk about it without having someone argue back. It wasn't that I wanted to work in such a naturalistic way, it was that the issue required it. We're talking about a real gun, a real fight, a real death. One of the interesting attempts that I had seen was a play that a friend of mine, Vaughan McBride, had written. Vaughan and I both had seen a newspaper article about a man who knew that he had terminal cancer and was going to commit suicide. This man went to stay with his friend over a weekend, the idea being that they would spend this weekend talking and being together; then on Sunday morning the friend would go off to get milk and the paper, he would come back, and the other man would have had his opportunity to kill himself. Vaughan showed the evening of talking, the going to bed, and the friend going off to get the newspaper in the morning. Then the man who was going to kill himself walked back up the stairs and the play was over. There was never a mention of the suicide or the friend's agreement to this plan. There was a note in the program that said the man killed himself the next morning, and this had all been arranged. I found it unsatisfying, because I wanted them to deal with it. I didn't want to read it in the program. What I came to with *'night, Mother* was a kind of final submission to the naturalistic form. I simply felt that the subject required that it be treated in a naturalistic manner.

David Savran (*b.* 1950)
INTERVIEW WITH MARSHA NORMAN

As Marsha Norman says at the end of the previous interview, her dissatisfaction with other plays about suicide led her to be very direct in her own play and to confront the issue directly. Here she discusses how that decision changed her entire concept of the play and helped her shape the dramatic action.

Savran: How do you begin a play? With an outline, a character, a line of dialogue?

Norman: . . . With *'night, Mother* I knew I wanted to tell the story of this woman who kills herself, but I didn't have any idea how. At the time, in '81, there were a number of other plays on the subject. But I kept saying that these plays — particularly *Whose Life Is It Anyway?* — are tantrums. I wanted to put somebody in the room with this woman, somebody who cares deeply, wildly, madly, who will fight this person to the death to save her own life. This is a gladiator contest where the point is to keep the other person alive. And once I had that, I had all these parallels — gladiators and world heavyweight boxing championships — and I understood immediately how this has to work. You have to have a closed ring, nobody can get out or in, you can have only two people.

I knew going into *'night, Mother* that it was going to be the most treacherous act of my writing life. So I went to the world of music. I was in a mad Glenn

Gould state at the time — I've spent my life at the piano. Okay, I thought, what if I do a little sonata form, a three-act play with no intermission? You can actually feel the moment when the orchestra stops and the conductor raises his hands and Jessie says, "You talked to Agnes today," and the second movement starts. The second movement ends when Jessie goes in to get the box of presents, Mama just having said, "Don't leave me, Jessie." The actors would come on stage knowing, "We don't have to go all the way to the end. We just have to get to the Agnes section." And then you start in on Agnes and think, "Great, I'll just get to 'Don't leave me, Jessie,' then I can take a breath" — this is from Mama's point of view — "and get down and wash the floor." And then all they have to do is go to the end. *'Night, Mother* would be undoable if it weren't for that. People would fall out of it all the time. But they don't. So I think that if you don't have structure, you might as well not have anything to put in it. If you don't have the bookshelves, you don't have the books.

I have a great trick during that period of thinking about the play. I say, "I'm not writing until I absolutely have to, till I can no longer contain it." I build up the piece in a pressure cooker, as it were. All that time I'm writing myself notes in the form of questions. What did Daddy do? How long ago did he die? Where did he die? What did he ever do for Jessie? Those kinds of questions. Curiously enough, you'll find that just from asking the questions, you'll get all the answers during the next weeks. It's internal research into the lives of these people. From those questions will come lines of dialogue — you begin to hear the voicing, what they can talk about, what they think is funny. The first line of dialogue I wrote for *'night, Mother* was Jessie's line "We got any old towels?" As soon as I wrote it down, I understood that it was a ritual piece, that Jessie was coming in to celebrate this requiem mass, that she has these stacks of towels: here are the witnesses, the household objects. She comes in as though she is the altar boy.

I wait until I cannot avoid it anymore and by that time, I already know what the beginning is, because of all this scribbling down. Then it's really very easy. I keep two kinds of notebooks, one that has structure and information in it and the other that has my own thoughts — "Can we really have this? What about that? What would happen if this?" I have a wonderful piece of paper upstairs that says, "Have I written something that anybody will want to see? Have I written something that will last? Have I written something that will humiliate me?" This comes from a pretty grim moment in the writing of *'night, Mother.* I thought, "What is this that I've written?" Humiliation is easily a possibility.

Savran: What is the European reaction to *'night, Mother*?

Norman: *'Night, Mother* is done all over the world. Any list that New Guinea is on is a long list. It's still running in Spain, four and a half years later, with all of the jokes taken out. Curiously enough, my work has always been popular in Eastern Europe. But this time I've caught the Mediterranean crowd. What strikes you as you watch it in a foreign country, in another language, is that the play seems to contain this other culture. In Italy you get enormous "Mama mia" Mamas, and the Jessies are always Ariels, little sprites. In Scandinavian countries it's quite the opposite. The mothers are really small, like the old woman who lived in the shoe, and the daughters are Valkyries, towering over these little Mamas. In the Latin American countries Mama and Jessie look like sisters.

David Savran (b. 1950)
INTERVIEW WITH AUGUST WILSON

August Wilson is interested not only in the characters in his plays but also in their political circumstances. One of his primary efforts has been to help strip away the black male stereotypes so that his audiences can see his people as he sees them. In this interview, he discusses the social conditions of black Americans and the relationship between Troy Maxson and his son Cory. Wilson's views about their relationship may be surprising, since he interprets it in a way that differs from many of the critics' interpretations.

Savran: In reading *Fences,* I came to view Troy more and more critically as the play progressed, sharing Rose's point of view. We see that Troy has been crippled by his father. That's being replayed in Troy's relationship with Cory. Do you think there's a way out of that cycle?

Wilson: Surely. First of all, we're all like our parents. The things we are taught early in life, how to respond to the world, our sense of morality — everything, we get from them. Now you can take that legacy and do with it anything you want to do. It's in your hands. Cory is Troy's son. How can he be Troy's son without sharing Troy's values? I was trying to get at why Troy made the choices he made, how they have influenced his values and how he attempts to pass those along to his son. Each generation gives the succeeding generation what they think they need. One question in the play is "Are the tools we are given sufficient to compete in a world that is different from the one our parents knew?" I think they are — it's just that we have to do different things with the tools. That's all Troy has to give. Troy's flaw is that he does not recognize that the world was changing. That's because he spent fifteen years in a penitentiary.

As African-Americans, we should demand to participate in society as Africans. That's the way out of the vicious cycle of poverty and neglect that exists in 1987 in America, where you have a huge percentage of blacks living in the equivalent of South African townships, in housing projects. No one is inviting these people to participate in society. Look at the poverty levels — $8,500 for a family of four, if you have $8,501 you're not counted. Those statistics would go up enormously if we had an honest assessment of the cost of living in America. I don't know how anybody can support a family of four on $8,500. What I'm saying is that 85 or 90 percent of blacks in America are living in abject poverty and, for the most part, are crowded into what amount to concentration camps. The situation for blacks in America is worse than it was forty years ago. Some sociologists will tell you about the tremendous progress we've made. They didn't put me out when I walked in the door. And you can always point to someone who works on Wall Street, or is a doctor. But they don't count in the larger scheme of things.

Savran: Do you have any idea how these political changes could take place?

Wilson: I'm not sure. I know that blacks must be allowed their cultural differences. I think the process of assimilation to white American society was a big mistake. We don't want to be like you. Blacks living in housing projects are isolated from the society, for the most part — living as they choose, as

Africans. Only they don't realize the value in what they're doing because they have accepted their victimization. They've marked themselves as victims. Once they recognize that, they can begin to move through society in a different manner, from a stronger position, and claim what is theirs.

Savran: A project of yours is to point up what happens when oppression is internalized.

Wilson: Yes, transfer of aggression to the wrong target. I think it's interesting that the two roads open to blacks for "full participation" are entertainment and sports. *Ma Rainey* and *Fences*, and I didn't plan it that way. I don't think that they're the correct roads. I think Troy's right. Now with the benefit of historical perspective, I can say that the athletic scholarship was actually a way of exploiting. Now you've got two million kids who think they're going to play in the NBA. In the sixties the universities made a lot of money off of athletics. You had kids playing for free who, by and large, were not getting educated, were taking courses in basketweaving. Some of them could barely read.

Savran: Troy may be right about that issue, but it seems that he has passed on certain destructive traits in spite of himself. Take the hostility between father and son.

Wilson: I think every generation says to the previous generation: you're in my way, I've got to get by. The father-son conflict is actually a normal generational conflict that happens all the time.

Savran: So it's a healthy and a good thing?

Wilson: Oh, sure. Troy is seeing this boy walk around, smelling his piss. Two men cannot live in the same household. Troy would have been tremendously disappointed if Cory had not challenged him. Troy knows that this boy has to go out and do battle with that world: "So I had best prepare him because I know that's a harsh, cruel place out there. But that's going to be easy compared to what he's getting here. Ain't nobody gonna whip your ass like I'm gonna whip it." He has a tremendous love for the kid. But he's not going to say, "I love you," he's going to demonstrate it. He's carrying garbage for seventeen years just for the kid. The only world Troy knows is the one that he made. Cory's going to go on to find another one, he's going to arrive at the same place as Troy. I think one of the most important lines in the play is when Troy is talking about his father: "I got to the place where I could feel him kicking in my blood and knew that the only thing that separated us was the matter of a few years."

Hopefully, Cory will do things a bit differently with his son. For Troy, sports was not the way to go, the white man wouldn't let him get away with that. "Get you a job, with your hands, something that nobody can take away from you." The idea of school — he doesn't know what that is. That's for white folks. Very few blacks had paperwork jobs. But if you knew how to fix cars, you could always make some money. That's what Troy wants for Cory. There aren't many people who ever jumped up in Troy's face. So he's proud of the kid at the same time that he expresses a hurt that all men feel. You got to cut your kid loose at some point. There's that sense of loss and separation. You find out how Troy left his father's house and you see how Cory leaves his house. I suspect with Cory it will repeat with some differences and maybe, after five or six generations, they'll find a different way to do it.

Savran: Where Cory ends up is very ambiguous, as a marine in 1965.

Wilson: Yes. For the average black kid on the street, that was an alternative.

You went into the army because you could learn how to do something. I can remember my parents talking about the son of some friends: "He's in the navy. He *did* something" — as opposed to standing on the street corner, shooting drugs, drinking wine, and robbing stores. Lyons says to Cory, "I always knew you were going to make something out of yourself." It really wounds me. He's a corporal in the marines. For blacks, that is a sense of accomplishment. Therein lies one of the tragedies of blacks in America. Cory says, "I don't know. I put in six years. That's enough." Anyone who goes into the army and makes a career out of it is a loser. They sit there and are nurtured by the army and they don't have to confront life. Then they get out of the army and find there's nothing to do. They didn't learn any skills. And if they did, they can't find a job. Four months later, they're shooting dope. In the sixties a whole bunch of blacks went over, fought and died in the Vietnam War. The survivors came back to the same street corners and found out nothing had changed. They still couldn't get a job.

At the end of *Fences* every person, with the exception of Raynell, is institutionalized. Rose is in a church. Lyons is in a penitentiary. Gabriel's in a mental hospital and Cory's in the marines. The only free person is the girl, Troy's daughter, the hope for the future. That was conscious on my part because in '57 that's what I saw. Blacks have relied on institutions which are really foreign — except for the black church, which has been our saving grace. I have some problems with it but I recognize it as a central social organization and sometimes an economic organization for the black community. I would like to see blacks develop their own institutions that respond to their needs.

Writing About Drama

Why Write About Drama?

One of the best reasons for writing about drama is that the act of writing involves making a commitment to ideas, and that commitment helps clarify your thinking. Your writing forces you to examine the details, the elements of a play that might otherwise pass unnoticed, and it helps you develop creative interpretations that enrich your appreciation of the plays you read. On one level, you can expect that your writing will deepen your understanding, and on another level you can hope that your writing can help deepen the understanding of your peers and readers, as the commentaries in this book are meant to do.

Since every reader of plays has a unique experience and background, every reader can contribute something to the experience and awareness of others. You will see things that others do not. You will interpret things in a way that others will not. Naturally, every reader's aim is to respect the text, but it is not reasonable to think that there is only one way to interpret a text. Nor is it reasonable to think that only a few people can give "correct" interpretations. One of the most interesting aspects of writing about drama is that it is usually preceded by discussion, through which a range of possible interpretations begins to appear. When you start to write, you commit yourself to working with certain ideas, and you begin to deepen your thinking about those ideas as you write.

Conventions in Writing Criticism About Drama

Ordinarily, when you are asked to write about a play, you are expected to produce a critical and analytical study. A critical essay will go beyond any subjective experience and include a discussion of what the play achieves and how it does so. If you have a choice, you should choose a play that you admire and enjoy. If you have special background material on that play, such as a playbill or newspaper article, it will be especially useful to you in writing.

For a critical study you will need to go far beyond retelling the narrative of the play. You may have to describe what you feel happens in a given scene or moment in a play, but simply rewriting the plot of the play in your own words does not constitute an interpretation. A critical reading of the play demands that you isolate evidence and comment on it. For example, you may want to quote passages of dialogue or stage direction to point out an idea that plays a key role in the play. When you do so, quote in moderation. A critical essay that is merely a string of quotations linked together with a small amount of your commentary will not suffice. Further, make sure that the quotations you use are illustrations of the point you are making or that you explain clearly what their importance to your discussion is.

Approaches to Criticism

Many critical approaches are available to the reader of drama. One approach might emphasize the response of audience members or readers, recognizing that the audience brings a great deal to the play even before the action begins. The audience's or reader's previous experience with drama influences expectations about what will happen on stage and about how the central characters will behave. Personal and cultural biases also influence how an audience member reacts to the unfolding drama. Reader response criticism pays close attention to these responses and to what causes them.

Another critical approach might treat the play as the coherent work of a playwright who intends the audience to perceive certain meanings in the play. This approach assumes that a careful analysis, or close reading, of the play will reveal the author's meanings. Either approach can lead to engaging essays on drama. In the pages that follow, you will find directions on how to pay attention to your responses as an audience member or reader and advice about how to read a play with close attention to dialogue, images, and patterns of action.

Reader Response Criticism

Response criticism depends on a full experience of the text — a good understanding of its meaning as well as of its conventions of staging and performance.

Your responses to various elements of the drama, whether to the characters, the setting, the theme, or the dialogue, may change and grow as you see a play or read it through. You might have a very different reaction to a play during a second reading or viewing of it. Keeping a careful record of your responses as you read is a first step in response criticism.

However, there is a big difference between recording your responses and examining them. Douglas Atkins of the University of Kansas speaks not only of reader response in criticism, but of reader responsibility, by which he means that readers have the responsibility to respond on more than a superficial level when they read drama. This book helps you reach deeper critical levels because it informs you about the history of drama so that you can read each play in light of its historical development.

The book also gives you important background material and commentary from the playwrights and from professional critics. Reading such criticism helps you understand what the critic's role is and what a critic can say about drama.

Reading drama in a historical perspective is important because it can highlight similarities between plays of different eras. Anyone who has read *Oedipus Rex* and *Antigone* will be better prepared to respond to *Hamlet*. In addition to the history and criticism of drama presented in this book, the variety of style, subject matter, and scope of the plays in this volume gives you the opportunity to read and respond to a broad range of drama. The more plays you read carefully, the better you will become at responding to drama and writing about it.

When you write response criticism, keep these guidelines in mind:

1. As you read, make note of the important effects the text has on you. Annotate in the margins moments that are especially effective. Do you find yourself alarmed, disturbed, sympathetic, or unsympathetic to a character? Do you sense suspense, or are you confused about what is happening? Do you feel personally involved with the action, or is it very distant? Do you find the situation funny? What overall response do you find yourself giving the play?

2. By analyzing the following two elements of your response, establish why the play had the effects you observe. Do you think it would have those effects on others? Have you observed that it does?

First, determine what it is about the play that causes you to have the response you do. Is it the structure of the play, the way the characters behave, their talk? Is it an unusual use of language, allusions to literature you know (or don't know)? Is the society portrayed especially familiar (or especially unfamiliar) to you? What does the author seem to expect the audience to know before the play begins?

Second, determine what it is about you the reader that causes you to respond as you do. Were you prepared for the dramatic conventions of the play, in terms of its genre as tragedy, comedy, tragicomedy or in terms of its place in the history of drama? How does your preparation affect your response? Did you have difficulty interpreting the language of the play because of unfamiliarity? Are you especially responsive to certain kinds of plays because of familiarity?

3. What do your responses to the play tell you about your own limitations, your own expertise, your own values, and your own attitudes toward social behavior, uses of language, and your sense of what is "normal"? Be sure to be willing to face your limitations as well as your strengths.[1]

---

[1]Adapted from Kathleen McCormick, "Theory in the Reader: Bleich, Holland, and Beyond," *College English* 47 (1985): 838.

Reader response criticism is flexible and useful in the way it allows you to explore all the possibilities of a text. Its main strengths are that everyone is capable of responding to drama and that everyone will respond somewhat differently depending on his or her preparation and background.

Close Reading

The method of analyzing a play by close reading involves examining the text in detail, looking for patterns that imply a meaning that might not be evident with a less attentive approach to the text. Annotation is the key to close reading, since the critic's job is to keep track of elements in the play that, innocent though they may seem alone, imply a greater significance when seen together.

Close reading may also be thought of as close rereading, since you do not know the first time through a text just what will be meaningful as the play unfolds, and you will want to read it again to confirm and deepen your impressions. You will usually make only a few discoveries the first time through. However, it is important to annotate the text even the first time you read it.

The following guidelines will be helpful for annotating a play:

1. Underline all the speeches and images you think are important. Look for dialogue that you think reveals the play's themes, the true nature of the characters, and the position of the playwright.

2. Watch for repetition of imagery (such as the garden and weed imagery in *Hamlet*) and keep track of it through annotation. Do the same for repeated ideas in the dialogue, repeated comments on government or religion or psychology. Such repetitions will reveal their importance to the playwright.

3. Color-code or number-code various patterns in the text and then gather them either in photocopies or in lists for examination before you begin to plan your essay.

Criticism that uses the techniques of close reading pays very careful attention to the elements of drama — plot, characterization, setting, dialogue (use of language), movement, and theme — which were discussed earlier in relation to Lady Gregory's *The Rising of the Moon*. As you read a play, keep track of its chief elements because often they will give you useful ideas for your paper. You may find it helpful to refer to the earlier discussion of the elements in *The Rising of the Moon* since a short critical essay about that play is presented here.

Annotation of the special use of any of the elements will help you decide how important they are and whether a close study of them can contribute to an interesting interpretation of the play. You may not want to discuss all the elements in an essay, or if you do only one may be truly dominant, but you should be aware of them in any play you write about.

**From Prewriting
to Final Draft:
A Sample Essay on
*The Rising of the
Moon***

Most good writing results from good planning. When you write criticism about drama, consider these important stages:

1. When possible, choose a play that you enjoy.
2. Annotate the play very carefully.
3. Spend time prewriting.
4. Write a good first draft, then revise for content, organization, style, and mechanics.

The essay on Lady Gregory's *The Rising of the Moon* at the end of this section involved several stages of writing. First, the writer read and annotated the play. In the process of doing so, she noticed the unusual stage direction beginning the play, *Moonlight,* and noticed also that when the two policemen leave the Sergeant they take the lantern, but the Sergeant reminds them that it is very lonely waiting there "with nothing but the moon." Second, she used the stage directions regarding moonlight to guide her in several important techniques of prewriting, including brainstorming, clustering, freewriting, drafting a trial thesis, and outlining.

The first stage, brainstorming, involved listing ideas, words, or phrases suggested by reading the play. The idea of moonlight and the moon recurred often. Then the writer practiced clustering: beginning with *moon,* a key term developed from brainstorming, then radiating from it all the associations that naturally suggest themselves.

Next the student chose the term *romance*, because it had generated a number of responses, and performed a freewriting exercise around that term. Freewriting is a technique in which a writer takes four or five minutes to write whatever comes to mind. The technique is designed to be done quickly so the conscious censor has to be turned off. Anything you write in freewriting may be useful because you may produce ideas you did not know you had.

The following passage is part of the freewriting exercise the student wrote using *romance* as a key term. The passage is also an example of invisible writing because the writing was done on a computer and the writer turned off the monitor so that she could not censor or erase what she was writing. The writer could only go forward, as fast as possible.

THE SETTING OF THE PLAY IS COMPLETELY ROMANTIC, AND IN A LOT OF WAYS THE PLAY WOULD NOT WORK AT ALL IF IT WERE IN A DIFFERENT SETTING. WHEN YOU THINK ABOUT IT THE MOON IN THE TITLE OF THE PLAY IS WHAT MAKES ALL THE ACTION POSSIBLE. BECAUSE THE MOON IS ASSOCIATED WITH THE DARKNESS, WITH THE UNDERWORLD--IN IRELAND EVEN THE WORLD OF THE FAIRIES--THEN YOU CAN SEE THAT THE MOON IS WHAT MAKES ALL THE ACTION POSSIBLE. IT IS WHAT MAKES IT POSSIBLE FOR THE SERGEANT TO LOOK AT THINGS DIFFERENTLY. THE MOON IS THE REBEL MOON-- THAT'S WHAT THE TITLE MEANS. THE REBEL MOON IS RISING, ALWAYS RISING. SO THAT MEANS THAT THE WORLD THE POLICEMAN LIVES IN--WITH A SUN THAT LIGHTS UP EVERYTHING SO YOU CAN SEE IT IN A PRACTICAL AND NONROMANTIC WAY--IS A LOT LIKE THE LANTERN THAT THE SECOND POLICEMAN BRINGS AROUND TO THE DOCKSIDE. IT SHOWS THINGS IN A HARSH LIGHT. THE MOON SHOWS THINGS IN A SOFT LIGHT. WITHOUT IT THERE WOULD HAVE TO BE A DIFFERENT PLAY.

The freewriting gave the writer a new direction — discussing the setting of the play, especially the role of light. The clustering began with the moon, veered off to the concept of the romantic elements in the play, and then came back to the way the moon and the lantern function in the play. The writer was now ready to work up a trial thesis:

> Lady Gregory uses light to give us a romantic setting that helps us understand the relationship between the rebel and the Sergeant and the values that they each stand for.

Because the thesis is drafted before the essay is written, the thesis is like a trial balloon. It may work or it may not. At this point it gives the writer direction.

Next, the student outlined the essay. Since the writer did not know the outcome of the essay yet, the outline was necessarily sketchy:

I. Moonlight is associated with romance and rebellion; harsh light of lantern is associated with repressiveness of police.
   A. Rebel is associated with romance.
   B. Sergeant is associated with practicality and the law.
II. Without the lantern, the Sergeant is under the influence of the romantic moon and the rebel.
   A. Sergeant feels resentment about his job.
   B. Rebel sings forbidden song, and Sergeant reveals his former sympathies.
   C. Sergeant admits he was romantic when young.
III. Sergeant must choose between moon and lantern.
   A. Sergeant seems ready to arrest rebel.
   B. When police return with lantern, the Sergeant sends them away.
   C. Rebel escapes and Sergeant remains in moonlight.

The prewriting strategies of brainstorming, clustering, freewriting, drafting a thesis, and outlining helped the student generate ideas and material for her first draft. After writing this draft, she revised it carefully for organization, clarity of ideas, expression, punctuation, and format. What follows is her final draft.

Andrea James

Professor Jacobus

English 233

10 October 1988

The Use of Light in <u>The Rising of the Moon</u>

Lady Gregory uses light imagery in <u>The Rising of the Moon</u> to contrast rebellion and repressiveness. Her initial stage direction is basic: <u>Moonlight</u>. She suggests some of the values associated with moonlight, such as rebellion and romance, caution and secrecy, daring exploits, and even the underworld. All these are set against the policemen, who are governed not by the moon, which casts shadows and makes the world look magical, but by the lantern, which casts a harsh light that even the Sergeant eventually rejects.

The ballad singer, the rebel, is associated with romance from the start: "Dark hair--dark eyes, smooth face, height, five feet five. . . .   There isn't another man in Ireland would have broken jail the way he did." He is dark, handsome, and, for Ireland at the turn of the century, fairly tall. The Sergeant, by contrast, is a practical man, no romantic. He sees that he might have a chance to arrest the rebel and gain the reward for his capture if he stays right on the quay, a likely place for the rebel to escape from. But he unknowingly spoils his chances by refusing to keep the lantern the policemen offer. He tells the policemen, "You can take the lantern. Don't be too long now. It's very lonesome here with nothing but the moon." What he does not realize is that with the lantern as his guiding light, he will behave like a proper Sergeant. But with the moon to guide him, he will side with the rebel.

It takes only a few minutes for the rebel to show

up on the scene. At first, the Sergeant is very tough
and abrupt with the rebel, who is disguised as "Jimmy
Walsh, a ballad singer." The rebel tells the Sergeant
that he is a traveler, that he is from Ennis, and that
he has been to Cork. Unlike the Sergeant, who has
stayed in one place and is a family man, the ballad
singer appears as a romantic figure, in the sense that
he follows his mind to go where he wants to, sings what
he wants to, and does what he wants to.

When the ballad singer begins singing, the Sergeant
reacts badly, telling the singer, "Stop that noise."
Perhaps he is envious of the ballad singer's freedom.
When the Sergeant tries to make the rebel leave, the
rebel instead begins telling stories about the man the
Sergeant is looking for. He reminds the Sergeant of
deeds done that would frighten anyone. "It was after
the time of the attack on the police barrack at
Kilmallock. . . . Moonlight . . . just like this." The
moonlight of the tale and the moonlight of the setting
combine to add mystery and suspense to the situation.

The effect of the rebel's talk--and of the
moonlight--is to make the Sergeant feel sorry for
himself in a thankless job. "It's little we get but
abuse from the people, and no choice but to obey our
orders," he says bitterly while sitting on the barrel
sharing a pipe with the singer. When the rebel sings an
illegal song, the Sergeant corrects a few words,
revealing his former sympathies with the people. The
rebel realizes this, telling the Sergeant, "It was with
the people you were, and not with the law you were, when
you were a young man." The Sergeant admits that when he
was young he too was a romantic, but now that he is
older he is practical and law-abiding: "Well, if I was
foolish then, that time's gone. . . . I have my duties
and I know them."

The ballad singer's song "The Rising of the Moon" is the signal that tells his friend to come and get him, and it forces the Sergeant to decide what action to take. He must decide whether his heart is with the world of moonlight or the world of the lantern. He seizes the rebel's hat and wig and seems about to arrest him when the policemen, with their lantern, come back. The Sergeant orders the policemen back to the station, and they offer to leave the lantern with him. But the Sergeant refuses. We know that he will not turn the rebel in. He has chosen the world of moonlight, of the rebel.

The policemen try to make the world of the lantern seem the right choice. Policeman B says:

> Well, I thought it might be a comfort to you.
> I often think when I have it in my hand and
> can be flashing it about into every dark
> corner (doing so) that it's the same as being
> beside the fire at home, and the bits of
> bogwood blazing up now and again.
> (Flashes it about, now on the barrel, now on
> Sergeant.)

The Sergeant reacts furiously and tells them to get out--"yourselves and your lantern!"

The play ends with the Sergeant giving the hat and wig back to the rebel, obviously having chosen the side of the people. When the rebel leaves, the Sergeant wonders if he himself was crazy for losing his chance at the reward. But as the curtain goes down, the Sergeant is still in the moonlight.

Glossary of Dramatic Terms

Absurd, theater of the. A type of twentieth-century drama presenting the human condition as meaningless, absurd, and illogical. An example of the genre is Samuel Beckett's *Waiting for Godot*.

Act. A major division in the action of a play. Most plays from the Elizabethan era until the nineteenth century were divided into five acts by the playwrights or by later editors. In the nineteenth century many writers began to write four-act plays. Today one-, two-, and three-act plays are most common.

Action. What happens in a play; the events that make up the **plot**.

Agon. The Greek word for contest. In Greek tragedy the *agon* was often a formal debate in which the **chorus** divided and took the sides of the disputants.

Alienation effect. In his **epic theater**, Bertolt Brecht (1898–1956) tried to make the familiar unfamiliar (or to alienate it), in order to show the audience that familiar, seemingly "natural," and therefore unalterable, social conditions could be changed. Different devices achieved the alienation effect by calling attention to the theater as theater, for example, stage lights brought in front of the curtain, musicians put on stage instead of hidden in an orchestra pit, placards indicating scene changes and interrupting the linear flow of the action, and actors distancing themselves from their characters in order to invite the audience to analyze and criticize the characters instead of empathizing with them. These alienating devices prevent the audience from losing itself in the illusion of reality. (See **epic theater**.)

Allegory. A literary work that is coherent on at least two levels simultaneously: a literal level consisting of recognizable characters and events and an allegorical level in which the literal characters and events represent moral, political, religious, or other ideas and meanings.

Anagnorisis. Greek term for a character's discovery or recognition of someone or something previously unknown. *Anagnorisis* often paves the way for a reversal of fortune (see **peripeteia**). An example in *Oedipus Rex* is Oedipus's discovery of his true identity.

Antagonist. A character or force in conflict with the **protagonist**. The antagonist is often another character but may also be an intangible force such as nature or society. The dramatic conflict can also take the form of a struggle with the protagonist's own character.

Anticlimax. See **plot**.

Antimasque. See **masque**.

Antistrophe. The second of the three parts of the verse ode sung by the **chorus** in Greek drama. While singing the **strophe** the chorus moves in a dance rhythm from right to left; during the antistrophe it moves from left to right back to its original position. The third part, the **epode**, was sung standing still.

Apron stage. The apron is the part of the stage extending in front of the **proscenium arch**. A stage is an apron stage if all or most of it is in front of any framing structures. The Elizabethan stage, which the audience surrounded on three sides, is an example of an apron stage.

Arena stage. A stage surrounded on all sides by the audience; actors make exits and entrances through the aisles. Usually used in **theater-in-the-round**.

Arras. A curtain hung at the back of the Elizabethan playhouse to partition off an alcove or booth. The curtain could be pulled back to reveal a room or a cave.

Aside. A short speech made by a character to the audience which, by **convention**, the other characters onstage cannot hear.

Atellan farce. Broad and sometimes coarse popular humor indigenous to the town of Atella in Italy. By the third century B.C., the Romans had imported the Atellan farce, which they continued to modify and develop.

Blank verse. An unrhymed verse form often used in writing drama. Blank verse is composed of ten-syllable lines accented on the second, fourth, sixth, eighth, and tenth syllables (iambic pentameter).

Bombast. A loud, pompous speech whose inflated diction is disproportionate to the subject matter it expresses.

Bourgeois drama. Drama that treats middle-class subject matter or characters rather than the lives of the rich and powerful.

Braggart soldier. A **stock character** in comedy who is usually cowardly, parasitical, pompous, and easily victimized by practical jokers. Sir John Falstaff in Shakespeare's *Henry IV* (1, 2) is an example of this type.

Burla. (plural, *burle*). Jests or practical jokes that were part of the comic **stage business** in the *commedia dell'arte*.

Buskin. A thick-soled boot worn by Greek tragedians to increase their stature. Later called a *cothurnes*.

Catastrophe. See **plot**.

Catharsis. The feeling of emotional purgation or release that, according to Aristotle, an audience should feel after watching a tragedy.

Ceremonial drama. Egyptian passion play about the god Osiris.

Character. Any person appearing in a drama or narrative.

Stock character. A stereotypical character type whose behavior, qualities, or beliefs conform to familiar dramatic **conventions**, such as the clever servant or the **braggart soldier**. (Also called type character.)

Chiton. Greek tunic worn by Roman actors.

Choragos. An influential citizen chosen to pay for the training and costuming of the **chorus** in Greek drama competitions. He probably also paid for the musicians and met other financial production demands not paid for by the state. *Choragos* also refers to the leader of the chorus.

Chorus. A masked group that sang and danced in Greek tragedy. The chorus usually chanted in unison, offering advice and commentary on the action, but rarely participating. See also **strophe**, **antistrophe**, and **epode**.

City Dionysia. See **Dionysus**.

Climax. See **plot**.

Closet drama. A drama, usually in verse, meant for reading rather than for performance. Percy Bysshe Shelley's *Prometheus Unbound* and John Milton's *Samson Agonistes* are examples.

Comedy. A type of drama intended to interest and amuse rather than to concern the audience deeply. Although characters experience various discomfitures, the audience feels confident that they will overcome their ill fortune and find happiness at the end.

Comedy of humors. Form of comedy developed by Ben Jonson in the seventeenth century in which characters' actions are determined by the preponderance in their systems of one of the four bodily fluids or humors—blood, phlegm, choler (yellow bile), and melancholy (black bile). Characters' dispositions are exaggerated and stereotyped; common types are the melancholic and the belligerent bully.

Comedy of manners. Realistic, often satiric comedy concerned with the manners and conventions of high society. Usually refers to the Restoration comedies of late-seventeenth-century England, which feature witty dialogue or **repartee**. An example is William Congreve's *The Way of the World*.

Drawing room comedy. A type of comedy of manners concerned with life in polite society. The action generally takes place in a drawing room.

Farce. A short dramatic work that depends on exaggerated, improbable situations, incongruities, coarse wit, and horseplay for its comic effect.

High comedy. Comedy that appeals to the intellect, often focusing on the pretensions, foolishness, and incongruity of human behavior. **Comedy of manners** with its witty dialogue is a type of high comedy.

Low comedy. Comedy that lacks the intellectual appeal of **high comedy**, depending instead on boisterous buffoonery, "gags," and jokes for its comic effect.

New Comedy. Emerging between the fourth and third centuries B.C. in ancient Greece, New Comedy replaced the farcical **Old Comedy**. New Comedy, usually associated with Menander, is witty and intellectually engaging; it is often thought of as the first **high comedy**.

Old Comedy. Greek comedy of the fifth century B.C. that used stock characters and bawdy farce to attack satirically social, religious, and political institutions. Old Comedy is usually associated with Aristophanes.

Slapstick. **Low comedy** that involves little plot or character development but consists of physical horseplay or practical jokes.

Comic relief. The use of humorous characters, speeches, or scenes in an otherwise serious or tragic drama.

Commedia dell'arte. Italian **low comedy** dating from around the mid-sixteenth century in which professional actors playing **stock characters** improvised dialogue to fit a given **scenario.**

Complication. See **plot.**

Conflict. See **plot.**

Convention. Any feature of a literary work that has become standardized over time, such as the **aside** or the **stock character.** Often refers to an unrealistic device (such as Danish characters speaking English in *Hamlet*) that the audience tacitly agrees to accept.

Coryphaeus. See *koryphaios.*

Cosmic irony. See **irony.**

Cothurnus. See **buskin.**

Craft play. Medieval sacred drama based on Old and New Testament stories. Craft plays were performed outside the church by members of a particular trade guild, and their subject matter often reflected the guild's trade. The fisherman's guild, for example, might present the story of Noah and the flood.

Crisis. Same as **climax.** See **plot.**

Cruelty, theater of. A type of drama created by Antonin Artaud in the 1930s that uses shock techniques to expose the audience's primitive obsessions with cruelty and sexuality. The purpose was to overwhelm spectators' rational minds, leading them to understand and even participate in the cycle of cruelty and ritual purgation dramatized in the performance.

Cycle. A group of medieval **mystery plays** written in the vernacular (in English rather than Latin) for performance outside the church. Cycles, each of which treated biblical stories from creation through the last judgment, are named after the town in which they were produced. Most extant mystery plays are from the York, Chester, Wakefield (Towneley), and N-Town cycles.

Decorum. A quality that exists when the style of a work is appropriate to the speaker, the occasion, and the subject matter. Kings should speak in a "high style" and clowns in a "low style," according to many Renaissance authors. Decorum was a guiding critical principle in **neoclassicism.**

Denouement. See **plot.**

Deus ex machina. Latin for "a god out of a machine." In Greek drama, a mechanical device that could lower "gods" onto the stage to solve the seemingly unsolvable problems of mortal characters. Also used to describe a playwright's use of a forced or improbable solution to plot complications—for example, the discovery of a lost will or inheritance that will pay off the evil landlord.

Dialogue. Spoken interchange or conversation between two or more characters.

Diction. A playwright's choice of words or the match between language and subject matter. Also refers collectively to an actor's phrasing, enunciation, and manner of speaking.

Dionysus. Greek nature god of wine, mystic revelry, and irrational impulse. Greek tragedy probably sprang from dramatized ritual choral celebrations in his honor.

City Dionysia. (Also called Great or Greater Dionysia.) The most important of the four Athenian festivals in honor of Dionysus. This spring festival sponsored the first tragedy competitions; comedy was associated with the winter festival, the Lenaea.

Director. The person responsible for a play's interpretation and staging and for the guidance of the actors.

Disguising. Medieval entertainment featuring a masked procession of actors performing short plays in pantomime; probably the origin of the court **masque.**

Dithyramb. Ancient Greek choral hymn sung and danced to honor **Dionysus;** originally divided into an improvised story sung by a choral leader and a traditional refrain sung by the **chorus.** Believed to be the origin of Greek tragedy.

Domestic tragedy. A serious play usually focusing on the family and depicting the fall of a middle-class **protagonist** rather than of a powerful or noble hero. Also called bourgeois tragedy. An example is Arthur Miller's *Death of a Salesman,* which traces the emotional collapse and eventual suicide of Willy Loman, a traveling salesman.

Double plot. See **plot.**

Drama. A play written in prose or verse that tells a story through **dialogue** and actions performed by actors impersonating the characters of the story.

Dramatic illusion. The illusion of reality created by drama and accepted by the audience for the duration of the play.

Dramatic irony. See **irony.**

Dramatist. The author of a play; playwright.

Dramaturgy. The art of writing plays.

Drawing room comedy. See **comedy.**

Empathy. The sense of feeling *with* a character. (Distinct from sympathy, which is feeling *for* a character.)

Ensemble acting. Performance by a group of actors, usually members of a **repertory** company, in which the integrated acting of all members is emphasized over individual star performances. The famous nineteenth-century director Konstantin Stanislavski promoted this type of acting in the Moscow Art Theatre.

Environmental theater. A term used by Richard Schechner, director of the Performance Group in the late 60s and early 70s, to describe his work and the work of other theater companies, including the Bread and Puppet Theatre, Open Theatre, and Living Theatre. He also used the term to describe the indigenous theater of Africa and Asia. Environmental theater occupies the whole of a performance space; it is not confined to a stage separated from the audience. Action can take place in and around the audience, and audience members are often encouraged to participate in the theater event.

Epic theater. A type of theater first associated with German director Erwin Piscator (1893–1966). Bertolt Brecht (1898–1956) used the term to distinguish his own theater from the "dramatic" theater that created the illusion of reality and invited the audience to identify and empathize with the characters. Brecht criticized the dramatic theater for encouraging the audience to believe that social conditions were "natural," and therefore unalterable. According to Brecht, the theater should show human beings as dependent on certain political and economic factors, and at the same time as capable of altering them. "The spectator is given the chance to criticize human behavior from a social point of view, and the scene is played as a piece of history." Epic theater calls attention to itself as theater, bringing the stage lights in front of the curtain and interrupting the linear flow of the action in order to help the audience analyze the action and characters on stage. (See **alienation effect.**)

Epilogue. A final speech added to the end of a play. An example is Puck's "If we shadows have offended . . ." speech that ends Shakespeare's *A Midsummer Night's Dream.*

Epitasis. Ancient term for the **rising action** of a plot. (See also **plot.**)

Epode. The third of three parts of the verse ode sung by the **chorus** in a Greek drama. The epode follows the **strophe** and **antistrophe.**

Exodos. The concluding scene, which includes the exit of all characters and the **chorus,** of a Greek drama.

Exposition. See **plot.**

Expressionism. Early-twentieth-century literary movement in Germany that posited that art should represent powerful emotional states and moods. Expressionists abandon **realism** and **verisimilitude,** producing distorted, nightmarish images of the individual unconscious.

Falling action. See **plot.**

Farce. See **comedy.**

First Folio. The first collected edition of thirty-six of Shakespeare's plays, collected by two of his fellow actors and published posthumously in 1623.

Foil. A character who, through difference or similarity, brings out a particular aspect of another character. Laertes, reacting to the death of his father, acts as a foil for Hamlet.

Foreshadowing. Ominous hints of events to come that help to create an air of suspense in a drama.

Frons scaena. The elaborately decorated facade of the *scaena* or stage house used in presenting Roman drama. (Also called *scaena frons.*)

Hamartia. An error or wrong act through which the fortunes of the **protagonist** are reversed in a tragedy.

High comedy. See **comedy.**

History play. A drama set in a time other than that in which it was written. The term usually refers to late Elizabethan drama, such as Shakespeare's Henry plays, that draws its plots from English historical materials such as Holinshed's *Chronicles.*

Hubris. (or *hybris.*) Excessive pride or ambition. In ancient Greek tragedy *hubris* often causes the **protagonist's** fall.

Humor character. A stereotyped character in the **comedy of humors** (see **comedy**). Clever plots often play on the characters' personality distortions (caused by an imbalance of humors), revealing their absurdity.

Iambic pentameter. A poetic meter that divides a line into five parts (or feet), each part containing an unaccented syllable followed by an accented syllable. The line "When I consider everything that grows" is an example of iambic pentameter verse.

Imitation. See **mimesis.**

Impressionism. A highly personal style of writing in which the author presents characters, scenes, or moods as they appear to him or her at a particular moment rather than striving for an objectively re-alistic description.

Interlude. A short play, usually either farcical or mor-alistic, performed between the courses of a feast or between the acts of a longer play. The interlude thrived during the late fifteenth and early sixteenth centuries in England.

Irony. The use of words to suggest a meaning that is the opposite of the literal meaning, as in "I can't wait to take the exam." Irony is present in a literary work that gives expression to contradictory attitudes or impulses in order to entertain ambiguity or maintain detachment.

Cosmic irony. (same as irony of fate.) Irony present when destiny or the gods seem to be in favor of the **protagonist** but they actually are engineering his or her downfall.

Dramatic irony. Irony present when the outcome of an event or situation is the opposite of what a character expects.

Tragic irony. Irony that exists when a character's lack of complete knowledge or understanding (which the audience possesses) results in his or her fall or has tragic consequences for loved ones. An example from *Oedipus Rex* is Oedipus's declaration that he will stop at nothing to banish King Laios's murderer, whom the audience knows to be Oedipus himself.

Jongleur. A French term referring to early medieval musical entertainers who recited lyrics, ballads, and stories. Forerunners of the minstrel.

Koryphaios. The leader of the **chorus** in Greek drama.

Kothurnus. See **buskin**.

Lazzo. (plural, *lazzi*.) Comic routines or **stage business** associated with the stock situations and characters of the Italian **commedia dell'arte**. A scenario might, for example, call for the *lazzo* of fear.

Liturgical drama. Short dramatized sections of the medieval church service. Some scholars believe that these playlets evolved into the vernacular **mystery plays**, which were performed outside the church by lay people.

Low comedy. See **comedy**.

Mansion. Scenic structures used in medieval drama to indicate the locale or scene of the action. Mansions were areas inside the church used for performing liturgical drama; later more elaborate structures were built on pageant wagons to present mystery plays outside the church.

Mask. A covering used to disguise or ornament the face; used by actors in Greek drama and revived in the later **commedia dell'arte** and court **masque** to heighten dramatic effect.

Masque. (also mask). A short but elaborately staged court drama, often mythological and allegorical, principally acted and danced by masked courtiers. (Professional actors often performed the major speaking and singing roles.) Popular in England during the late sixteenth and early seventeenth centuries, masques were often commissioned to honor a particular person or occasion. Ben Jonson was the most important masque writer; the genre's most elaborate sets and costumes were designed by Jonson's occasional partner Inigo Jones.

Antimasque. A parody of the court **masque** developed by Ben Jonson featuring broad humor, grotesque characters, and ludicrous actions.

Melodrama. A suspenseful play filled with situations that appeal excessively to the audience's emotions. Justice triumphs in a happy ending: the good characters (completely virtuous) are rewarded and the bad characters (thoroughly villainous) are punished.

Method acting. A naturalistic technique of acting developed by the Russian director Konstantin Stanislavsky and adapted for American actors by Lee Strasberg, among others. The method actor identifies with the **character** he or she portrays and experiences the emotions called for by the play in an effort to render the character with emotional **verisimilitude**.

Mimesis. The Greek word for imitation. Aristotle used the term to define the role of art as an "imitation of nature."

Miracle play. A type of medieval sacred drama that depicts the lives of saints, focusing especially on the miracles performed by saints. The term is often used interchangeably with **mystery play**.

Mise-en-scène. The stage setting of a play, including the use of scenery and props.

Moira. Greek word for fate.

Morality play. Didactic late medieval drama (flourishing in England c. 1400–1550) that uses **allegory** to dramatize some aspects of the Christian moral life. Abstract qualities or entities such as Virtue, Vice, Good Deeds, Knowledge, and Death are cast as characters who discuss with the **protagonist** issues related to salvation and the afterlife. *Everyman* is an example.

Motivation. The reasons for a character's actions in a drama. For drama to be effective, the audience must believe that a character's actions are justified and plausible given what they know about him or her.

Mouth of Hell. A stage prop in medieval drama suggesting the entrance to hell. Often in the shape of an open-mouthed monster's head, the Mouth of Hell was positioned over a smoke-and-fire-belching pit in the stage that appeared to swallow up sinners.

Mystery play. A sacred medieval play dramatizing biblical events such as the creation, the fall of Adam and Eve, and Christ's birth and resurrection. The genre probably evolved from **liturgical drama**; mystery plays were often incorporated into larger **cycles of plays.**

Naturalism. Literary philosophy popularized during the nineteenth century that casts art's role as the scientifically accurate reflection of a "slice of life." Aligned with the belief that each person is a product of heredity and environment driven by internal and external forces beyond his or her control. August Strindberg's *Miss Julie,* with its focus on reality's sordidness and humankind's powerlessness, draws on naturalism.

Neoclassicism. A movement in sixteenth-century France to revive and emulate classical attitudes toward art based on principles of order, harmony, unity, restrained wit, and **decorum.** The neoclassical movement in France gave rise to a corresponding movement in England during the Restoration and eighteenth century.

New Comedy. See **comedy.**

Ode. A dignified Greek three-part song sung by the **chorus** in Greek drama. The parts are the **strophe,** the **antistrophe,** and the **epode.**

Old Comedy. See **comedy.**

Orchestra. Literally the "dancing place"; the circular stage where the Greek **chorus** performed.

Pageant. A movable stage or wagon (often called a pageant wagon) on which a set was built for the performance of medieval drama. The term can also refer to the spectacle itself.

Pallium. Long white cloak or mantle worn by Roman actors.

Pantomime. Silent acting using facial expression, body movement, and gesture to convey the plot and the characters' feelings.

Parodos. The often stately entrance song of the **chorus** in Greek drama. The term also refers to the aisles (plural, *paradoi*) on either side of the orchestra by which the chorus entered the Greek theater.

Pastoral drama. A dramatic form glorifying shepherds and rural life in an idealized natural setting; usually implies a negative comparison to urban life.

Pathos. The quality of evoking pity.

Peripeteia. A reversal of fortune, for better or worse, for the **protagonist.** Used especially to describe the main character's fall in Greek tragedy.

Phallus. An appendage added to the front of blatantly comic male characters' costumes in some Greek comedy; associated chiefly with the Greek **satyr play.**

Play. A literary genre whose plot is usually presented dramatically by actors portraying characters before an audience.

Play-within-the-play. A brief secondary drama presented to or by the characters of a play that reflects or comments on the larger work. An example is the Pyramus and Thisby episode in Shakespeare's *A Midsummer Night's Dream.*

Plot. The events of a play or narrative. The sequence and relative importance a **dramatist** assigns to these events.

Anticlimax. An unexpectedly trivial or significant conclusion to a series of significant events; an unsatisfying resolution that often occurs in place of a conventional **climax.**

Catastrophe. The outcome or conclusion of a play; usually applied specifically to tragedy. (**Denouement** is a parallel term applied to both comedy and tragedy.)

Climax. The turning point in a drama's action, preceded by the **rising action** and followed by the **falling action.** Same as crisis.

Complication. The part of the plot preceding the **climax** that establishes the entanglements to be untangled in the **denouement.** Part of the **rising action.**

Conflict. The struggle between the **protagonist** and the **antagonist** that propels the **rising action** of the plot and is resolved in the **denouement.**

Denouement. The "unknotting" of the plot's **complication**; the resolution of a drama's action. See **catastrophe.**

Double plot. A dramatic structure in which two related plots function simultaneously.

Exposition. The presentation of essential information, especially about events that have occurred prior to the first scene of a play. The exposition appears early in the play and initiates the **rising action.**

Falling action. The events of the plot following the **climax** and ending in the **castastrophe** or resolution.

Rising action. The events of the plot leading up to the **climax.**

Subplot. A secondary plot intertwined with the main plot, often reflecting or commenting on the main plot.

Underplot. Same as **subplot.**

Problem play. A drama that argues a point or presents a problem (usually a social problem). Ibsen is a notable writer of problem plays.

Prologos. In Greek drama, an introductory scene for actor or actors that precedes the entrance of the **chorus.** This **convention,** invented by Euripides, has evolved into the modern dramatic introductory monologue or **prologue.**

Prologue. A preface or introduction preceding the play proper.

Proscaena. The space in front of the *scaena* in a Roman theater.

Proscenium arch. An arched structure over the front of the stage from which a curtain often hangs. The arch frames the action onstage and separates the audience from the action.

Proskenion. The facade of the *skene* or scene building in Greek drama. May also have referred to the playing space in front of the building.

Protagonist. The main character in a drama. This character is usually the most interesting and sympathetic and is the person involved in the **conflict** driving the **plot.**

Protasis. Classical term for the introductory act or **exposition** of a drama.

Quem quaeritis trope. A brief dramatized section of the medieval church's Easter liturgy. The oldest extant **trope** and the probable origin of liturgical drama, it enacts the visit of the three Marys to Christ's empty tomb (*quem quaeritis* means "whom do you seek?" in Latin).

Rising action. See **plot.**

Realism. The literary philosophy that holds that art should accurately reproduce an image of life. Avoids the use of dramatic **conventions** such as asides and soliloquies to depict ordinary people in ordinary situations. Ibsen's *A Doll's House* is an example of realism in drama.

Recognition. See *anagnorisis.*

Repartee. Witty and pointed verbal exchanges usually found in the **comedy of manners.**

Repertory. A theater company or group of actors that presents a set of plays alternately throughout a season. The term also refers to the set of plays itself.

Restoration comedy. A type of **comedy of manners** (see **comedy**) that developed in England in the late seventeenth century. Often features **repartee** in the service of complex romantic plots. William Congreve's *The Way of the World* is an example.

Revenge tragedy. Sensational tragedy popularized during the Elizabethan age that is notable for bloody plots involving such elements as murder, ghosts, insanity, and crimes of lust.

Reversal. See **peripeteia.**

Riposte. A quick or sharp reply; similar to **repartee.**

Rising action. See **plot.**

Ritual. Repeated formalized or ceremonial practices, many of which have their roots in primitive cultures. Certain theorists hold that primitive ritual evolved into drama.

Satire. A work that makes fun of a social institution or human foible, often in an intellectually sophisticated way, to persuade the audience to share the author's views. Molière's *The Misanthrope* contains social satire.

Satyr play. A comic play performed after the tragic trilogy in Greek tragedy competitions. The satyr play provided **comic relief** and was usually a farcical, boisterous treatment of mythological material.

Scaena. The stage house in Roman drama; the facade of the *scaena* (called the *frons scaena*) was often elaborately ornamented.

Scenario. The plot outline around which professional actors of the *commedia dell'arte* improvised their plays. Most scenarios specified the action's sequence and the entrances of the main characters.

Scene. Division of an **act** in a drama. By traditional definition a scene has no major shift in place or time frame, and it is performed by a static group of actors onstage (if an actor enters or exits, the group is altered and the scene, technically, should change). The term also refers to the physical surroundings or locale in which a play's action is set.

Scenery. The backdrop and set (furniture and so on) onstage that suggest to the audience the surroundings in which a play's **action** takes place.

Senecan tragedy. Tragic drama modeled on plays written by Seneca. The genre usually has five acts and features a chorus; it is notable for its thematic concern with bloodshed, revenge, and unnatural crimes. (See also **revenge tragedy.**)

Sentimental. Refers to tender emotions in excess of what the situation calls for.

Sentimental comedy. Comedy populated by stereotypical virtuous **protagonists** and villainous **antagonists** that resolves the domestic trials of middle-class people in a pat, happy ending.

Skene. The building or "scene house" in the Greek theater that probably began as a dressing room and eventually was incorporated into the action as part of the scenery.

Slapstick. See **comedy.**

Slice of life. See **naturalism.**

Social problem play. Same as **problem play.**

Sock. Derived from the Latin *soccus,* the term refers to a light slipper or sock worn by Roman comic actors.

Soliloquy. A speech in which an actor, usually alone onstage, utters his or her thoughts aloud, revealing personal feelings. Hamlet's "To be, or not to be" speech is an example.

Spectacle. In Aristotle's terms, the costumes and scenery in a drama—the elements that appeal to the eye.

Stage business. Minor physical action, including an actor's posture and facial expression, and the use of props, all of which make up a particular interpretation of a character.

Stichomythia. Dialogue in which two speakers engage in a verbal duel in alternating lines.

Stock character. See **character.**

Strophe. The first of three parts of the verse **ode** sung by the Greek **chorus.** While singing the strophe the chorus moves in a dancelike pattern from right to left. See also **antistrophe** and **epode.**

Subplot. See **plot.**

Subtext. A level of meaning implicit in or underlying the surface meaning of a text.

Surrealism. A literary movement flourishing in France during the early twentieth century that valued the unwilled expression of the unconscious (usually as revealed in dreams) over a rendering of "reality" structured by the conscious mind.

Suspense. The sense of tension aroused by an audience's uncertainty about the resolution of dramatic conflicts.

Suspension of disbelief. An audience's willingness to accept the world of the drama as reality during the course of a play.

Symbolism. A literary device in which an object, event, or action is used to suggest a meaning beyond its literal meaning. The guns in *Hedda Gabler* have a symbolic function.

Theater. The building in which a play is performed. Also used to refer to drama as an art form.

Theater-in-the-round. The presentation of a play on an **arena stage** surrounded by the audience.

Three unities. Aristotle specified that a play's action should occur within one day (unity of time) and in a single locale (unity of place) and should reveal clearly ordered actions and plot incidents moving toward the plot's resolution (unity of action). Later scholars and critics, especially those in the neo-classical tradition, interpreted Aristotle's ideas as rules and established them as standards for drama.

Thrust stage. A stage extending beyond the **proscenium arch,** usually surrounded on three sides by the audience.

Tiring house. The backstage space in Elizabethan public theaters used for storage and possibly as a dressing room ("attiring house"). The term also refers to the changing space beneath the medieval pageant wagon.

Total theater. A concept of the theater as an experience synthesizing all the expressive arts including music, dance, lighting, and so on.

Tragedy. Serious drama in which a **protagonist,** traditionally of noble position, suffers a series of unhappy events culminating in a **catastrophe** such as death or spiritual breakdown. Shakespeare's *Hamlet,* which ends with the prince's death, is an example of Renaissance tragedy.

Tragicomedy. A play that combines elements of tragedy and comedy. Chekhov's *The Cherry Orchard* is an example. Tragicomedies often include a serious plot in which the expected tragic **catastrophe** is replaced by a happy ending.

Trope. Interpolation into or expansion of an existing medieval liturgical text. These expansions, such as the *quem quaeritis trope*, gave rise to **liturgical drama.**

Underplot. See **plot.**

Unity. The sense that the events of a play and the actions of the characters follow one another naturally to form one complete action. Unity is present when characters' behavior seems **motivated** and the work is perceived to be a connected artistic whole. See also **three unities.**

Verfremdung. German term coined by Bertolt Brecht to mean alienation. See also **alienation effect.**

Verisimilitude. The degree to which a dramatic representation approximates an appearance of reality.

Well-made play. Drama that relies for effect on the suspense generated by its logical, cleverly constructed plot rather than on characterization. Plots often involve a withheld secret, a battle of wits between hero and villain, and a **resolution** in which the secret is revealed and the **protagonist** saved.

Selected Bibliography

Selected References for Periods of Drama

GREEK DRAMA

Bieber, Margaret. *The History of the Greek and Roman Theater.* 2nd ed. Princeton: Princeton UP, 1961.

Hamilton, Edith. *The Greek Way.* New York: Norton, 1983.

Kitto, H. D. F. *Greek Tragedy: A Literary Study.* 3rd ed. London: Methuen, 1966.

———. *Form and Meaning in Drama: A Study of Six Greek Plays and of Hamlet.* 2nd ed. New York: Barnes, 1968.

Knox, Bernard M. *Word and Action: Essays on the Ancient Theater.* Baltimore: Johns Hopkins UP, 1979.

Pickard-Cambridge, Arthur W. *Dramatic Festivals of Athens.* 2nd ed. Revised by John Gould and D. M. Lewis. Oxford: Clarendon, 1962.

Steiner, George. *The Death of Tragedy.* New York: Knopf, 1961.

Taplin, Oliver. *Greek Tragedy in Action.* Berkeley: U of California P, 1978.

Trendall, A. D. and T. B. L. Webster. *Illustrations of Greek Drama.* London: Phaidon, 1971.

Vickers, Brian. *Towards Greek Tragedy: Drama, Myth, Society.* London: Longman, 1973.

Walcot, Peter. *Greek Drama in Its Theatrical and Social Context.* Cardiff: U of Wales P, 1976.

Webster, T. B. L. *Greek Theater Production.* 2nd ed. London: Methuen, 1970.

ROMAN DRAMA

Beare, William. *The Roman Stage.* 3rd ed. London: Methuen, 1969.

Bieber, Margaret. *The History of the Greek and Roman Theater.* 2nd ed. Princeton: Princeton UP, 1961.

Duckworth, George E. *The Nature of Roman Comedy: A Study in Popular Entertainment.* Princeton: Princeton UP, 1952.

Hunter, R. L. *The New Comedy of Greece and Rome.* New York: Cambridge UP, 1985.

Kenney, E. J., ed. *The Cambridge History of Classical Literature.* 2 vols. New York: Cambridge UP, 1982.

Konstan, David. *Roman Comedy.* Ithaca: Cornell UP, 1983.

Segal, Erich. *Roman Laughter.* Cambridge: Harvard UP, 1968.

MEDIEVAL DRAMA

Axton, Richard. *European Drama of the Early Middle Ages.* London: Hutchinson, 1974.

Bevington, David, ed. *Medieval Drama.* Boston: Houghton, 1975.

Chambers, Edmund K. *English Literature at the Close of the Middle Ages.* Oxford: Clarendon, 1945.

———. *The Medieval Stage.* 2 vols. London: Oxford UP, 1967.

Craig, Hardin. *English Religious Drama of the Middle Ages.* Westport, CT: Greenwood, 1978 (rpt. of 1968 ed.).

Davidson, Clifford, et al., eds. *Drama in the Middle Ages.* New York: Aims, 1982.

Gassner, John, ed. *Medieval and Tudor Drama.* New York: Bantam, 1971.

Hardison, O. B., Jr. *Christian Rite and Christian Drama in the Middle Ages: Essays in the Origin and Early History of Modern Drama.* Baltimore: Johns Hopkins UP, 1965.

Vince, Ronald W. *Ancient and Medieval Theatre: A Historiographical Handbook.* Westport, CT: Greenwood, 1984.

Wickham, Glynne. *The Medieval Theatre.* 3rd ed. New York: Cambridge UP, 1987.

Woolf, Rosemary. *The English Mystery Plays.* Berkeley: U of California P, 1972.

RENAISSANCE DRAMA

Adams, John C. *The Globe Playhouse.* 2nd ed. New York: Barnes, 1961.

Altman, Joel B. *The Tudor Play of Mind: Rhetorical Inquiry and the Development of Elizabethan Drama.* Berkeley: U of California P, 1978.

Bevington, David. *From Mankind to Marlowe: Growth of Structure in the Popular Drama of Tudor England.* Cambridge: Harvard UP, 1962.

Bradbrook, Muriel C. *The Growth and Structure of Elizabethan Comedy.* London: Chatto, 1955.

Bush, Douglas. *The Renaissance and English Humanism.* Toronto: U of Toronto P, 1939.

Chambers, E. K. *The Elizabethan Stage.* 4 vols. Oxford: Clarendon, 1923.

Farnham, W. *The Medieval Heritage of Elizabethan Tragedy.* Berkeley: U of California P, 1936.

Hussey, Maurice. *The World of Shakespeare and His Contemporaries, A Visual Approach.* New York: Viking, 1972.

Kernodle, George. *From Art to Theatre: Form and Convention in the Renaissance.* Chicago: U of Chicago P, 1944.

Lea, Kathleen M. *Italian Popular Comedy: A Study of the Commedia dell'Arte, 1560–1620.* 2 vols. Oxford: Clarendon, 1934.

Nicoll, Allardyce. *The World of Harlequin.* Cambridge: Cambridge UP, 1963.

Welsford, Enid. *The Court Masque.* Cambridge: Cambridge UP, 1927.

Wind, Edgar. *Pagan Mysteries in the Renaissance.* New Haven: Yale UP, 1958.

Woodbridge, Linda. *Woman and the English Renaissance: Literature and the Nature of Womankind 1540–1620.* Urbana and Chicago: U of Illinois P, 1984.

Yates, Frances A. *Theatre of the World.* Chicago: U of Chicago P, 1969.

RESTORATION AND EIGHTEENTH-CENTURY DRAMA

Barber, Charles L. *The Idea of Honour in the English Drama, 1591–1700.* Stockholm: Göteborg, 1957.

Cox, Jeffrey N. *In the Shadows of Romance.* Athens: Ohio UP, 1987.

Grene, Nicholas. *Shakespeare, Jonson, Molière, the Comic Contract.* Totowa, NJ: Barnes, 1980.

Holland, Norman N. *The First Modern Comedies: The Significance of Etherege, Wycherley, and Congreve.* Cambridge: Harvard UP, 1959.

Loftis, John, ed. *Restoration Drama.* New York; Oxford UP, 1966.

Lynch, Kathleen M. *The Social Mode of Restoration Comedy.* New York: Farrar, 1975.

Marshall, Geoffrey. *Restoration Serious Drama.* Norman: U of Oklahoma P, 1975.

Nicoll, Allardyce. *A History of Restoration Drama, 1600–1700.* Cambridge UP, 1923.

Powell, Jocelyn. *Restoration Theatre Production.* Boston: Routledge, 1984.

Price, Cecil. *Theatre in the Age of Garrick.* Oxford: Oxford UP, 1973.

Richards, K. R., ed. *Essays on the Eighteenth Century English Stage.* London: Methuen, 1972.

Stynan, J. L. *Restoration Comedy in Performance.* New York: Cambridge UP, 1986.

Turnell, Martin. *The Classical Movement: Studies in Corneille, Molière, and Racine.* New York: New Directions, 1948.

NINETEENTH-CENTURY DRAMA TO THE TURN OF THE CENTURY

Bentley, Eric. *The Playwright as Thinker: A Study of Drama in Modern Times.* New York: Harcourt, 1967.

Bogard, Travis, ed. *Modern Drama: Essays in Criticism.* New York: Oxford UP, 1965.

Booth, Michael. *English Melodrama.* London: Jenkins, 1965.

Brustein, Robert. *The Theatre of Revolt.* Boston: Little, Brown, 1964.

Cole, Toby, ed. *Playwrights on Playwriting: The Meaning and Making of Modern Drama from Ibsen to Ionesco.* New York: Hill, 1960.

Driver, Tom Faw. *Romantic Quest and Modern Query: A History of the Modern Theatre.* New York: Delacorte, 1970.

Gilman, Richard. *The Making of Modern Drama: A Study of Buchner, Isben, Strindberg, Chekhov, Pirandello, Brecht, Beckett, Handke.* New York: Farrar, 1974.

Stynan, J. L. *Modern Drama in Theory and Practice.* 3 vols. New York: Cambridge UP, 1980.

Valency, Maurice Jacques. *The Flower and the Castle: An Introduction to Modern Drama.* New York: Schocken, 1982.

Whitaker, Thomas R. *Fields of Play in Modern Drama.* Princeton: Princeton UP, 1977.

Williams, Raymond. *Drama from Ibsen to Eliot.* New York: Oxford UP, 1953.

DRAMA IN THE EARLY AND MID-TWENTIETH CENTURY

Artaud, Antonin. *The Theatre and Its Double.* Trans. Mary C. Richards. New York: Grove, 1958.

Bentley, Eric. *The Theatre of Commitment, and Other Essays on Drama in Our Society.* New York: Atheneum, 1967.

Blau, Herbert. *The Impossible Theatre: A Manifesto.* New York: Macmillan, 1964.

Bogard, Travis, and William I. Oliver, eds. *Modern Drama: Essays in Criticism.* New York: Oxford UP, 1965.

Brockett, Oscar G. *History of the Theatre.* 5th ed. Boston: Allyn, 1987.

Brook, Peter. *The Empty Space.* New York: Avon, 1968.

Cohn, Ruby. *From Desire to Godot: Pocket Theater of Postwar Paris.* Berkeley: U of California P, 1987.

Esslin, Martin. *The Theatre of the Absurd.* Woodstock, NY: Overlook, 1973.

Gassner, John. *Theatre at the Crossroads.* New York: Holt, 1960.

Goldberg, RosaLee. *Performance: Live Art 1909 to the Present.* New York: Abrams, 1979.

Kernan, Alvin B., ed. *The Modern American Theater: A Collection of Critical Essays.* Englewood Cliffs: Prentice, 1967.

Piscator, Erwin, *The Political Theatre: A History, 1914–1929.* Trans. Hugh Rorrison. London: Eyre Methuen, 1980.

Roose-Evans, James. *Experimental Theatre: From Stanislavsky to Today.* New Revised Edition. London: Studio Vista, 1973.

CONTEMPORARY DRAMA

Betsko, Kathleen, and Rachel Koenig. *Interviews with Contemporary Women Playwrights.* New York: Beech Tree, 1987.

Blau, Herbert. *Eye of Prey: Subversions of the Postmodern.* Bloomington: Indiana UP, 1987.

Blumenthal, Eileen. *Joseph Chaikin: Exploring at the Boundaries of Theatre.* New York: Cambridge UP, 1984.

Brecht, Stefan. *The Theatre of Visions: Robert Wilson.* Frankfurt am Main: Suhrkamp, 1978.

Cheney, Sheldon. *New Movement in the Theatre.* Westport, CT: Greenwood, 1971.

The Drama Review [journal]. New York University.

Grotowski, Jerzy. *Towards a Poor Theatre.* New York: Simon, 1968.

Hayman, Ronald. *Theatre and Anti-Theatre: New Movements Since Beckett.* New York: Oxford UP, 1979.

Hill, Errol, ed. *The Theatre of Black Americans.* 2 vols. Englewood Cliffs: Prentice, 1980.

Lahr, John. *Up Against the Fourth Wall: Essays on Modern Theatre.* New York: Grove, 1968.

Marranca, Bonnie, ed. *The Theatre of Images.* New York: Drama Book Specialists, 1977.

Schechner, Richard. *Environmental Theater.* New York: Hawthorn, 1973.

Wellworth, George E. *The Theater of Protest and Paradox.* New York: New York UP, 1971.

Selected References for Playwrights and Plays

ARISTOPHANES

Deardon, C. W. *The Stage of Aristophanes.* London: Athlone, 1976.

Dover, K. J. *Aristophanic Comedy.* Berkeley: U of California P, 1972.

Harriott, Rosemary. *Aristophanes: Poet and Dramatist.* Baltimore: Johns Hopkins UP, 1986.

McLeish, Kenneth. *The Theatre of Aristophanes.* New York: Taplinger, 1980.

Murray, Gilbert. *Aristophanes.* Oxford: Clarendon, 1933.

Reckford, Kenneth. *Aristophanes' Old-and-New Comedy.* Chapel Hill: U of North Carolina P, 1987.

Ussher, Robert Glenn. *Aristophanes.* New York: Oxford UP, 1979.

SAMUEL BECKETT

List of Plays

Waiting for Godot, 1952
All That Fall, 1957
Endgame, 1958
Act Without Words: A Mime for One Player, 1958
Krapp's Last Tape, 1958
Embers, 1959
Act Without Words II, 1959
Happy Days, 1961
Words and Music, 1962
Cascando, 1963
Play, 1963
Come and Go: Dramaticule, 1965
Film, 1965
Breath, 1970
Not I, 1973
That Time, 1976
Footfalls, 1976

Rough for Theatre I, 1976
Rough for Theatre II, 1976
A Piece of Monologue, 1979
Rockaby, 1981
Ohio Impromptu, 1981
Catastrophe, 1982
What Where, 1984

Brater, Enoch, ed. *Beckett at 80: Beckett in Context.* New York: Oxford UP, 1986.
Cohn, Ruby. *Just Play: Beckett's Theater.* Princeton: Princeton UP, 1980.
———, ed. *Samuel Beckett: A Collection of Criticism.* New York: McGraw, 1975.
Dearlove, J. E. *Accommodating the Chaos: Samuel Beckett's Nonrelational Art.* Durham: Duke UP, 1982.
Esslin, Martin, ed. *Samuel Beckett: A Collection of Critical Essays.* Englewood Cliffs, NJ: Prentice, 1965.
Fletcher, Beryl S., et al. *A Student's Guide to the Plays of Samuel Beckett.* 2nd ed. Boston: Faber, 1985.
Fletcher, John. *Beckett, the Playwright.* New York: Hill, 1985.
Gidal, Peter. *Understanding Beckett.* New York: St. Martin's, 1986.
Gontarski, S. E. *On Beckett: Essays and Criticism.* New York: Grove, 1986.
Kenner, Hugh. *A Reader's Guide to Samuel Beckett.* New York: Farrar, 1973.
Lyons, Charles R. *Samuel Beckett.* New York: Grove, 1983.
Rosen, Steven J. *Samuel Beckett and the Pessimistic Tradition.* New Brunswick: Rutgers UP, 1976.

Beckett's *Krapp's Last Tape*

Brustein, Robert. "Listening to the Past." *Seasons of Discontent.* New York: Simon, 1965. 26–29.
Clurman, Harold. "The Zoo Story and Beckett's *Krapp's Last Tape.*" *The Naked Image.* New York: Macmillan, 1966. 13–15.
Tynan, Kenneth. "*Krapp's Last Tape* and the Endgame." *Curtains.* New York: Atheneum, 1961. 225–228.

Beckett's *Happy Days*

Brustein, Robert S. "Déjà Vu." *Seasons of Discontent.* New York: Simon, 1965. 53–56.
Clurman, Harold. "Samuel Beckett." *The Divine Pastime.* New York: Macmillan, 1977. 119–124.
———"Happy Days." *The Naked Image.* New York: Macmillan, 1966. 40–42.
Gassner, John. "Foray into the Absurd." *Dramatic Soundings.* New York: Crown, 1968. 503–507.

Gilman, Richard. "Beckett's *Happy Days.*" *Common and Uncommon Masks.* New York: Random, 1971. 90–92.

BERTOLT BRECHT

Brecht, Bertolt. *Brecht on Theatre: The Development of an Aesthetic.* Ed. and trans. John Willett. New York: Hill, 1964.
Demetz, Peter, ed. *Brecht: A Collection of Critical Essays.* Englewood Cliffs: Prentice, 1962.
Esslin, Martin. *Brecht, The Man and His Works.* Garden City: Doubleday, 1971.
Ewen, Frederick. *Bertolt Brecht: His Life, His Art and His Times.* New York: Citadel, 1967.
Feugi, John. *Bertolt Brecht: Chaos, According to Plan.* New York: Cambridge UP, 1987.
Gray. Ronald. *Bertolt Brecht.* New York: Grove, 1967.
Hill, Claude. *Bertolt Brecht.* New York: Twayne, 1975.
Spalter, Max. *Brecht's Tradition.* Baltimore: Johns Hopkins UP, 1967.
Speirs, Ronald. *Bertolt Brecht.* New York: St. Martin's, 1987.
Willett, John. *The Theatre of Bertolt Brecht.* New York, 1959.

ANTON CHEKHOV

List of Plays

Platonov, 1881?
On the High Road, 1887
The Swan Song, 1887
The Bear, 1888
The Proposal, 1889
A Tragic Role, 1889
The Wedding, 1889
Ivanov, 1889
The Wood Demon, 1889
The Seagull, 1896
Uncle Vanya, 1899
Three Sisters, 1901
The Cherry Orchard, 1903

Barricelli, Jean-Pierre, ed. *Chekhov's Great Plays: A Critical Anthology.* New York: New York UP, 1981.
Emeljanow, Victor. *Chekhov: The Critical Heritage.* Boston: Routledge, 1981.
Hingley, Ronald. *Chekhov: A Biographical and Critical Study.* New York: Barnes, 1966.
Jackson, Robert Louis. *Chekhov: A Collection of Critical Essays.* Englewood Cliffs: Prentice, 1967.
Karlinsky, Simon and Michael Heim, eds. *Anton Chekhov's Life and Thought: Selected Letters and Commentary.* Berkeley: U of California P, 1975.

Magarshak, David. *Chekhov the Dramatist*. New York: Hill, 1960.

Peace, Richard. *Chekhov: A Study of the Four Major Plays*. New Haven: Yale UP, 1983.

Stanislavsky, Konstantin. *My Life in Art*. Boston, 1924.

Stynan, J. L. *Chekhov in Performance*. Cambridge: Cambridge UP, 1971.

Toumanova, Princess Nina Andronikova. *Anton Chekov, The Voice of Twilight Russia*. New York: Columbia UP, 1960.

Valency, Maurice. *The Breaking String: The Plays of Anton Chekhov*. New York; Oxford UP, 1966.

Welleck, Rene, and Nonna D. Welleck, eds. *Chekhov: New Perspectives*. Englewood Cliffs: Prentice, 1984.

Chekhov's *Three Sisters*

Babula, William. "Three Sisters, Time, and the Audience." *Modern Drama* 18 (1975): 365–370.

Hahn, Beverly. "Chekhov: *The Three Sisters*." *Critical Review* 15 (1972): 3–22.

LeMaster, J. R. "The Condition of Talk in Chekhov's *Three Sisters*." *New Laurel Review* 4 (1975): 9–16.

Moss, Howard. "*Three Sisters*." *Hudson Review* 30 (1977–78): 525–543.

Parker, David. "Three Men in Chekhov's *Three Sisters*." *Critical Review* 21 (1978): 11–23.

Chekhov's *The Cherry Orchard*

Barricelli, Jean-Pierre. "Counterpoint of the Snapping String: Chekhov's *The Cherry Orchard*." *Chekhov's Great Plays: A Critical Anthology*. New York: New York UP, 1981, 111–128.

Bely, Andrei. "*The Cherry Orchard*." *Russian Dramatic Theory from Pushkin to the Symbolists: An Anthology*. Ed. and trans. L. Senelick. Austin: U of Texas P, 1981. 89–92.

Deer, Irving. "Speech as Action in Chekhov's *The Cherry Orchard*." *Educational Theatre Journal* 10 (1959): 30–34.

Hahn, Beverly. "Chekhov's *The Cherry Orchard*." *Critical Review* 16 (1973): 56–72.

Remaley, Peter B. "Chekhov's *The Cherry Orchard*." *South Atlantic Bulletin* 38 (1973): 16–20.

CARYL CHURCHILL

Jennifer Allen. "The Man on the High Horse." *Esquire* (Nov. 1988): 141 +.

Betsko, Kathleen, and Rachel Koenig. "Caryl Churchill." *Interviews with Contemporary Women Playwrights*. New York: Beech Tree, 1987. 75–84.

Brustein, Robert. "Robert Brustein on Theater." *New Republic* 14 Feb. 1983: 27–28.

Gilman, Richard. "Theater." *Nation* 12 Feb. 1983: 186–187.

Randall, Phyllis R., ed. *Caryl Churchill: A Casebook*. New York: Garland, 1989.

EVERYMAN

Bevington, David M. *From Mankind to Marlowe: Growth of Structure in the Popular Drama of Tudor England*. Cambridge: Harvard UP, 1962.

Cawley, A.C. *Everyman*. Manchester: Manchester UP, 1977.

———, ed. *Everyman and Medieval Miracle Plays*. New York: Dutton, 1977.

Ryan, Lawrence V. "Doctrine and Dramatic Structure in *Everyman*," *Mississippi Quarterly* 14 (1961): 3–13.

ATHOL FUGARD

Benson, Mary. "Keeping an Appointment with the Future: The Theatre of Athol Fugard." *Theatre Quarterly* 7 (1977/78): 77–83.

Bragg, Melvyn. "Athol Fugard, Playwright—a Conversation with Melvyn Bragg." *Listener* 5 Dec. 1974: 734.

Fugard, Athol. "Fugard on Actors, Actors on Fugard." *Theatre Quarterly* 7 (1977/78): 83–87.

———. "Fugard on Fugard." *Yale Theatre* 1 (Winter 1973): 41–54.

———. "Letter from Athol Fugard." *Classic* 1 (1966): 78–80.

———. *Notebooks 1960–1977*. New York: Knopf, 1983.

Gray, Stephen, ed. *Athol Fugard*. Southern Africa Literature Series 1. Johannesburg: McGraw, 1982.

Heywood, Christopher. *Aspects of South African Literature*. London: Heinemann, 1976.

Kavanagh, Robert Mshengu. *Theatre and Cultural Struggle in South Africa*. London: Zed, 1985.

Seidenspinner, Margarete. *Exploring the Labyrinth; Athol Fugard's Approach to South African Drama*. Essen: Verlag Die Blaue Eule, 1986.

Walder, Dennis. *Athol Fugard*. New York: Grove, 1985.

LADY GREGORY (ISABELLA AUGUSTA GREGORY)

Adams, Hazard. *Lady Gregory*. Lewisburg: Bucknell UP, 1973.

Coxhead, Elizabeth. *Lady Gregory, A Literary Portrait*. New York: Harcourt, 1961.

Gregory, Isabella Augusta. *Lady Gregory's Journals, 1910–1930*. New York: Oxford UP, 1978.

————. *Our Irish Theatre*. Gerrards Cross: Smythe, 1972.

Kohfeldt, Mary Lou. *Lady Gregory: The Woman Behind the Irish Renaissance*. New York: Atheneum, 1985.

Maxwell, D. E. S. *A Critical History of Modern Irish Drama: 1891–1980*. New York: Cambridge UP, 1984.

O'Connor, Ulick. *All the Olympians*. New York: Atheneum, 1984.

Saddlemyer, Ann. *In Defense of Lady Gregory, Playwright*. Dublin: Dolmen, 1966.

————. *Lady Gregory, Fifty Years After*. Totowa, NJ: Barnes, 1987.

LORRAINE HANSBERRY

Brown, Lloyd W. "Lorraine Hansberry as Ironist: A Reappraisal of *A Raisin in the Sun*." *Journal of Black Studies* 4 (March 1974): 237–247.

Cheney, Anne. *Lorraine Hansberry*. Boston: Twayne, 1984.

Freedman, Morris. *American Drama in Social Context*. Carbondale: Southern Illinois UP, 1971.

Miller, Jeanne-Marie A. "Images of Black Women in Plays by Black Playwrights." *CLA Journal* 20 (June 1977): 498–499.

Nemiroff, Robert. *To Be Young, Gifted, and Black: A Portrait of Lorraine Hansberry in Her Own Words*. Englewood Cliffs: Prentice, 1969.

HENRIK IBSEN

List of Plays

Catiline, 1850
Grouse in Justedal, 1850
The Burial Mound, 1850
Norma, 1851
St. John's Night, 1853
Lady Inger of Öteraad, 1855
The Feast at Solhoug, 1856
Olaf Liljekrans, 1857
The Vikings in Helgeland, 1858
Love's Comedy, 1862
The Pretenders, 1863
Brand, 1866
Peer Gynt, 1867
The League of Youth, 1869
Emperor and Galilean, 1873
The Pillars of Society, 1877
A Doll's House, 1879
Quicksands, 1880
Ghosts, 1881

The Child Wife, 1882
An Enemy of the People, 1882
The Wild Duck, 1884
Rosmersholm, 1886
The Lady from the Sea, 1888
Hedda Gabler, 1890
The Master Builder, 1892
Little Eyolf, 1894
John Gabriel Borkman, 1896
When We Dead Awaken, 1899

Chamberlain, John S. *Ibsen: The Open Vision*. London: Athlone, 1982.

Egan, Michael, ed. *Ibsen: The Critical Heritage*. London: Routledge, 1972.

Fjelde, Rolf, ed. *Ibsen: A Collection of Critical Essays*. Englewood Cliffs: Prentice, 1965.

Gaskell, Ronald. *Drama and Reality: The European Theatre Since Ibsen*. London: Routledge, 1972.

McFarlane, James, ed. *Discussions of Henrik Ibsen*. Boston: Heath, 1962.

Meyer, Michael, *Henrik Ibsen: A Biography*. 3 vols. Garden City: Doubleday, 1971.

Noreng, Harald, et al., eds. *Contemporary Approaches to Ibsen*. Oslo: Universitetsforlaget, 1977.

Northam, John. *Ibsen: A Critical Study*. Cambridge: Cambridge UP, 1973.

Shaw, Bernard. *The Quintessence of Ibsenism*. New York: Hill, 1957.

Thomas, David. *Henrik Ibsen*. New York: Grove, 1984.

Ibsen's *A Doll's House*

Bradbrook, M. C. "*A Doll's House* and the Unweaving of the Web." *Women and Literature, 1779–1982*. 2 vols. Totowa, NJ: Barnes, 1982. 2: 81–92.

Downs, R. B. "Birth of the New Woman." *Molders of the Modern Mind*. New York: Barnes, 1961. 311–314.

Gassner, John. "An Ibsen Revival: Too Much Doll." *Dramatic Soundings*. New York: Crown, 1968. 290–294.

Hardwick, Elizabeth. "*A Doll's House*." *Seduction and Betrayal*. New York: Random, 1974. 33–48.

Ibsen, Henrik. "Doll's House." [Ibsen's notes on *A Doll's House*] *Playwrights on Playwriting*. Ed. Toby Cole. New York: Hill, 1960. 151–154.

Sprinchorn, E. M. "Ibsen and the Actors." *Ibsen and the Theatre*. Ed. Errol Durbach. New York: New York UP, 1980. 118–130.

Ibsen's *Hedda Gabler*

Braunmiller, A. R. "Hedda Gabler and the Sources of Symbolism." *Drama and Symbolism*. Ed. James

Redmond. New York: Cambridge UP, 1982. 57–70.

Ibsen, Henrik. "*Hedda Gabler.*" [Ibsen's notes on *Hedda Gabler*] *Playwrights on Playwriting.* Ed. Toby Cole. New York: Hill, 1960. 156–170.

Mayer, H. "Judith as Bourgeois Heroine." *Outsiders.* Cambridge: MIT P, 1982. 53–75.

Suzman. Janet. "*Hedda Gabler:* The Play in Performance." *Ibsen and the Theatre.* Ed. Errol Durbach. New York: New York UP, 1980. 83–104.

Tynan, Kenneth. "*Hedda Gabler.*" *Curtains.* New York: Atheneum, 1961. 77–78.

Watson, George J. "Ibsen and Miller: The Individual and Society." *Drama: An Introduction.* New York: St. Martin's, 1983. 112–131.

CHRISTOPHER MARLOWE

Bloom, Harold, ed. *Christopher Marlowe.* New York: Chelsea, 1986.

Cole, Douglas. *Suffering and Evil in the Plays of Christopher Marlowe.* Princeton: Princeton UP, 1962.

Cutts, John P. *The Left Hand of God.* Haddonfield, NJ: Haddonfield, 1973.

Ellis-Fermor, Una Mary. *Christopher Marlowe.* Hamden, CT: Anchor, 1967.

Farnham, Willard, comp. *Twentieth-Century Interpretations of Doctor Faustus: A Collection of Critical Essays.* Englewood Cliffs: Prentice, 1969.

Godshalk, W. L. *The Marlovian World Picture.* The Hague: Mouton, 1974.

Leech, Clifford, ed. *Marlowe: A Collection of Critical Essays.* Englewood Cliffs: Prentice, 1964.

Levin, Harry. *The Overreacher, A Study of Christopher Marlowe.* Boston: Beacon, 1964.

Marlowe, Christopher. *Complete Plays.* Ed., intro, and notes Irving Ribner. New York: Odyssey, 1963.

Steane, J. B. *Marlowe: A Critical Study.* Cambridge: Cambridge UP, 1964.

ARTHUR MILLER

Bloom, Harold, ed. *Arthur Miller's Death of a Salesman.* New York: Chelsea, 1988.

Carson, Neil. *Arthur Miller.* New York: Grove, 1982.

Corrigan, Robert W., ed. *Arthur Miller: A Collection of Critical Essays.* Englewood Cliffs: Prentice, 1969.

Huftel, Sheila, *Arthur Miller: The Burning Glass.* New York: Citadel, 1965.

Koon, Helene Wickham. *Twentieth Century Interpretations of Death of a Salesman.* Englewood Cliffs: Prentice, 1983.

Martin, Robert A., ed. *Arthur Miller: New Perspectives.* Englewood Cliffs: Prentice, 1982.

Miller, Arthur. *Collected Plays.* New York: Viking, 1957.

———. *The Theater Essays of Arthur Miller.* Ed. and intro. Robert A. Martin. New York: Viking, 1978.

———. *Timebends: A Life.* New York: Grove, 1987.

Roudane, Matthew C., ed. *Conversations with Arthur Miller.* Jackson: UP of Mississippi, 1987.

Schlueter, June, and James K. Flanagan. *Arthur Miller.* New York: Ungar, 1987.

Vidal, Gore, et al. "*Death of a Salesman:* A Symposium." *Tulane Drama Review* 2 (May 1958); 63–69.

MOLIÈRE (JEAN BAPTISTE POQUELIN)

Gaines, James F. *Molière's Theater.* Columbus: Ohio State UP, 1984.

Gross, Nathan. *From Gesture to Idea: Esthetics and Ethics in Molière's Comedy.* New York: Columbia UP, 1982.

Guicharnaud, Jacques. *Molière: A Collection of Critical Essays.* Englewood Cliffs: Prentice, 1964.

Hall, H. Gaston. *Comedy in Context: Essays on Molière.* Jackson: UP of Mississippi, 1984.

Jagendorf, Zvi. *The Happy End of Comedy: Jonson, Molière, and Shakespeare.* Newark: U of Delaware P, 1984.

Knutson, Harold C. *The Triumph of Wit: Molière and Restoration Comedy.* Columbus: Ohio State UP, 1988.

Molière. *Tartuffe: Comedy in Five Acts.* Trans. Richard Wilbur. New York: Harcourt, 1963.

MARSHA NORMAN

Betsko, Kathleen and Rachel Koenig. "Marsha Norman." *Interviews with Contemporary Women Playwrights.* New York: Beech Tree, 1987.

Brustein, Robert. "Robert Brustein on Theater." *New Republic* 2 May 1983: 25–26.

Denby, David. "Stranger in a Strange Land." *Atlantic* Jan. 1983: 44–45.

Gill, Brendan. "The Theatre." *New Yorker* 11 April 1983: 109–110+.

Gilman, Richard. "Theater." *Nation* 7 May 1983: 586.

Kauffmann, Stanley. "More Trick than Tragedy." *Saturday Review* Oct. 1983: 47–48.

Sauvage, Leo. "Different Kinds of Kin." *New Leader* 18 April 1983: 21–22.

Savran, David. *In Their Own Words.* New York: Theater Communications Group, 1988.

Weales, Gerald. "Really 'Going On.' " *Commonweal* 17 June 1983: 370–371.

EUGENE O'NEILL

Ahuja, Chaman. *Tragedy, Modern Temper and O'Neill.* Atlantic Highlands, NJ: Humanities, 1984.

Berlin, Normand. *Eugene O'Neill.* New York: Grove, 1987.

Bogard, Travis. *Contour in Time: The Plays of Eugene O'Neill.* New York: Oxford UP, 1988.

Cargill, Oscar, N. Bryllion Fagan, and William J. Fisher, eds. *O'Neill and His Plays: Four Decades of Criticism.* New York: New York UP, 1961.

Gassner, John, ed. *O'Neill: A Collection of Critical Essays.* Englewood Cliffs: Prentice, 1964.

Floyd, Virginia. *The Plays of Eugene O'Neill: A New Assessment.* New York: Ungar, 1985.

Leech, Clifford. *Eugene O'Neill.* New York: Grove, 1963.

Miller, Jordan Yale, *Eugene O'Neill and American Criticism: A Bibliographical Checklist.* 2nd ed. Hamden, CT: Anchor, 1973.

O'Neill, Eugene. *The Plays of Eugene O'Neill.* 3 vols. New York: Modern Library, 1982.

———. *Long Day's Journey Into Night.* New Haven: Yale UP, 1956.

HAROLD PINTER

Bloom, Harold, ed. *Harold Pinter.* New York: Chelsea, 1987.

Burkman, Katherine H. *The Dramatic World of Harold Pinter.* Columbia: Ohio State UP, 1971.

Dukore, Bernard Frank. *Harold Pinter.* New York: Grove, 1982.

Esslin, Martin. *Pinter: A Study of His Plays.* Expanded ed. New York: Norton, 1976.

Ganz, Arthur F., ed. *Pinter: A Collection of Critical Essays.* Englewood Cliffs: Prentice, 1979.

Hayman, Ronald. *Harold Pinter.* New York: Ungar, 1973.

Hinchliffe, Arnold P. *Harold Pinter.* Boston: Twayne, 1981.

Kerr, Walter. *Harold Pinter.* New York: Columbia UP, 1967.

Pinter, Harold. *Complete Works.* 3 vols. New York: Grove, 1977–78.

Quigley, Austin E. *The Pinter Problem.* Princeton: Princeton UP, 1975.

Sykes, Arlene, *Harold Pinter.* New York: Humanities, 1970.

LUIGI PIRANDELLO

Bassnet-McGuire, Susan. *Luigi Pirandello.* New York: Grove, 1983.

Bentley, Eric. *The Pirandello Commentaries.* Evanston, IL: Northwestern UP, 1986.

Büdel, Oscar. *Pirandello.* New York: Hillary, 1969.

Cambon, Glauco, ed. *Pirandello: A Collection of Critical Essays.* Englewood Cliffs: Prentice, 1967.

Guidice, Gaspare. *Pirandello: A Biography.* Trans. Alastair Hamilton. New York: Oxford UP, 1975.

Oliver, Roger W. *Dreams of Passion: The Theater of Luigi Pirandello.* New York: New York UP, 1979.

Paolucci, Anne. *Pirandello's Theater.* Carbondale: Southern Illinois UP, 1974.

Pirandello, Luigi. *Naked Masks, Five Plays.* Ed. Eric Bentley. New York: Dutton, 1952.

———. *Short Stories.* Ed. and trans. Frederick May. New York: Oxford UP, 1965.

Starkie, Walter. *Luigi Pirandello, 1867–1936.* 3rd ed. Berkeley: U of California P, 1965.

WILLIAM SHAKESPEARE

List of Plays

Comedies
The Comedy of Errors, 1592–94
The Taming of the Shrew, 1593–94
The Two Gentlemen of Verona, 1594
Love's Labor's Lost, 1594–95
A Midsummer Night's Dream, 1595–96
The Merchant of Venice, 1596–97
The Merry Wives of Windsor, 1597
Much Ado About Nothing, 1598–99
As You Like It, 1599
Twelfth Night, or What You Will, 1601-02
All's Well That Ends Well, 1602–03
Measure for Measure, 1604
Histories
Henry the Sixth, Part One, 1589–90
Henry the Sixth, Part Two, 1590–91
Henry the Sixth, Part Three, 1590–91
Richard the Third, 1592–93
King John, 1594–96
Richard the Second, 1595
Henry the Fourth, Part One, 1596–97
Henry the Fourth, Part Two, 1598
Henry the Fifth, 1599
Henry the Eighth, 1612–13
Tragedies
The Tragedy of Titus Andronicus, 1593
The Tragedy of Romeo and Juliet, 1595–96
The Tragedy of Julius Caesar, 1599
The Tragedy of Hamlet, 1600–01
The History of Troilus and Cressida, 1601–02
The Tragedy of Othello, the Moor of Venice, 1604

The Tragedy of King Lear, 1605
The Tragedy of Macbeth, 1606
The Tragedy of Antony and Cleopatra, 1606
The Tragedy of Coriolanus, 1607
The Life of Timon of Athens, 1607
Romances
Pericles, Prince of Tyre, 1607–08
Cymbeline, 1609–10
The Winter's Tale, 1610–11
The Tempest, 1611
Two Noble Kinsmen, 1613

Bamber, Linda. *Comic Women, Tragic Men; A Study of Gender and Genre in Shakespeare.* Stanford: Stanford UP, 1982.

Barber, C. L. *Shakespeare's Festive Comedy.* Princeton: Princeton UP, 1968.

Bradley, A. C. *Shakespearean Tragedy.* New York: Meridian, 1955.

Bullough, Geoffrey, ed. *Narrative and Dramatic Sources of Shakespeare.* 8 vols. New York: Columbia UP, 1957–75.

Chute, Marchette. *Shakespeare of London.* New York: Dutton, 1949.

Doran, Madeleine. *Shakespeare's Dramatic Language.* Madison: U of Wisconsin P, 1976.

Drakakis, John, ed. *Alternative Shakespeares.* New York: Methuen, 1985.

Dusinberre, Juliet. *Shakespeare and the Nature of Women.* London: Macmillan, 1975.

Eagleton, Terry. *William Shakespeare.* New York: Basil Blackwell, 1986.

Frye, Northrop. *On Shakespeare.* New Haven: Yale UP, 1986.

Goddard, Harold C. *The Meaning of Shakespeare.* Chicago: U of Chicago P, 1951.

Granville-Barker, H. *Prefaces to Shakespeare.* Princeton: Princeton UP, 1946.

Greene, G., et al., eds. *The Women's Part: Feminist Criticism of Shakespeare.* Urbana: U of Illinois P, 1980.

Jardine, Lisa. *Still Harping on Daughters: Women and Drama in the Age of Shakespeare.* Totowa, NJ: Barnes, 1983.

Kermode, Frank, ed. *Four Centuries of Shakespearean Criticism.* New York: Avon, 1974.

Kott, Jan. *Shakespeare Our Contemporary.* New York: Norton, 1974.

Righter, Anne. *Shakespeare and the Idea of the Play.* London: Chatto, 1962.

Schoenbaum, Samuel. *William Shakespeare: A Documentary Life.* New York: Oxford UP, 1975.

Schwartz, Murray M. and Coppelia Kahn, eds. *Representing Shakespeare: New Psychoanalytic Essays.* Baltimore: Johns Hopkins UP, 1981.

Shakespeare Quarterly. Annual Bibliography.

Shakespeare Survey.

Shakespeare's *Hamlet*

Bloom, Harold, ed. *William Shakespeare's Hamlet.* New York: Chelsea, 1986.

Calderwood, James. *To Be and Not To Be: Negation and Metadrama in Hamlet.* New York: Columbia UP, 1983.

Frye, Northrop. *Fools of Time: Studies in Shakespearean Tragedy.* Buffalo: U of Toronto P, 1973.

Jones, Ernest. *Hamlet and Oedipus.* New York: Norton, 1976.

Lacan, Jacques. "Desire and the Interpretation of Desire in *Hamlet*." *Literature and Psychoanalysis: The Question of Reading Otherwise.* Ed. Shoshana Felman. Baltimore: Johns Hopkins UP, 1982.

Levin, Harry. *The Question of Hamlet.* New York: Oxford UP, 1959.

Mack, Maynard. "The World of Hamlet." *Yale Review* 41 (1952): 502–523.

Mills, John A. *Hamlet on Stage: The Great Tradition.* Westport, CT: Greenwood, 1985.

Prosser, Eleanor. *Hamlet and Revenge.* Stanford, CT: Stanford UP, 1967.

Ribner, Irving. *Patterns in Shakespearean Tragedy.* New York: Barnes, 1960.

Shakespeare Survey 9 (1956).

Showalter, Elaine. "Representing Ophelia: Women, Madness, and the Responsibilities of Feminist Criticism." *Shakespeare and the Question of Theory.* Eds. Patricia Parker and Geoffrey Hartman. New York: Methuen, 1985.

Wilson, John Dover. *What Happens in Hamlet.* Cambridge: Cambridge UP, 1967.

Shakespeare's *A Midsummer Night's Dream*

Bloom, Harold, ed. *William Shakespeare's A Midsummer Night's Dream.* New York: Chelsea, 1987.

Brown, John Russell. *Shakespeare and His Comedies.* London: Methuen, 1968.

Doran, Madeleine. "Pyramus and Thisbe Once More." *Essays on Shakespeare and Elizabethan Drama in Honor of Hardin Craig.* Ed. Richard Hosley. Columbia: U of Missouri P, 1962. 449–462.

Garber, Marjorie. *Dream in Shakespeare: From Metaphor to Metamorphosis.* New Haven, CT: Yale UP, 1974.

Kermode, Frank. "The Mature Comedies." *Stratford-Upon-Avon Studies 3: Early Shakespeare.* Eds. John

Russell Brown and Bernard Harris. London: Edward Arnold, 1961. 211–227.

Latham, Minor White. *The Elizabethan Fairies: The Fairies of Folklore and the Fairies of Shakespeare.* New York: Columbia UP, 1930.

Schanzer, Ernest. "The Central Theme of *A Midsummer Night's Dream.*" *University of Toronto Quarterly* 20 (1957): 233–238.

Young, David P. *Something of Great Constancy: The Art of 'A Midsummer Night's Dream.'* New Haven: Yale UP, 1966.

BERNARD SHAW

Bentley, Eric. *Bernard Shaw.* 2nd ed. London: Methuen, 1967.

Berst, Charles A. *Bernard Shaw and the Art of Drama.* Urbana: U of Illinois P, 1973.

Brown, John Ivor. *Shaw in His Time.* London: Nelson, 1965.

Evans, T. F. *Shaw: The Critical Heritage.* Boston: Routledge, 1976.

Ganz, Arthur F. *George Bernard Shaw.* New York: Grove, 1983.

Gibbs, A. M. *The Art and Mind of Shaw: Essays in Criticism.* New York: St. Martin's, 1983.

Greene, Nicholas. *Bernard Shaw, A Critical View.* New York: St. Martin's, 1984.

Kaufman, R. J., ed. *G. B. Shaw: A Collection of Critical Essays.* Englewood Cliffs: Prentice, 1965.

May, Keith M. *Ibsen and Shaw.* New York: St. Martin's, 1985.

Shaw, Bernard. *An Autobiography.* 2 vols. Ed. Stanley Weintraub. New York: Weybright, 1969.

———. *Collected Letters.* Ed. Dan H. Laurence. New York: Dodd, 1972.

———. *Complete Plays with Prefaces.* New York: Dodd, 1962.

———. *Plays and Players: Essays on the Theatre.* Ed. A. C. Ward. New York: Oxford UP, 1963.

———. *Shaw on Shakespeare: An Anthology of Bernard Shaw's Writings on the Plays and Production of Shakespeare.* Ed. Edwin Wilson. New York: Dutton, 1961.

Zimbardo, Rose, ed. *Twentieth Century Interpretations of Major Barbara.* Englewood Cliffs: Prentice, 1970.

SAM SHEPARD

Cohn, Ruby. *New American Dramatists: 1960–1980.* New York: Grove, 1982.

Hart, Lynda. *Sam Shepard's Metaphorical Stages.* Westport, CT: Greenwood, 1987.

King, Kimball, ed. *Sam Shepard: A Casebook.* New York: Garland, 1988.

Marranca, Bonnie, ed. *American Dreams: The Imagination of Sam Shepard.* New York: Performing Arts Journal, 1981.

Mottram, Ron. *Inner Landscapes: The Theater of Sam Shepard.* Columbia: U of Missouri P, 1984.

Orbison, Tucker. "Mythic Levels in Sam Shepard's *True West.*" *Modern Drama* 27 (Dec. 1984): 506–519.

Oumano, Ellen. *Sam Shepard: The Life and Work of an American Dreamer.* New York: St. Martin's, 1986.

Sessums, Kevin. "Geography of a Horse Dreamer: Playwright, Actor, and Movie Director Sam Shepard. *Interview* (Sept. 1988): 70–78.

Sam Shepard. "Metaphors, Mad Dogs and Old-Time Cowboys." *Theatre Quarterly* 15 (Aug.-Oct. 1974): 3–16.

———. "Visualization, Language, and the Inner Library." *Drama Review* 4 (Dec. 1977): 49–58.

Shewey, Don. *Sam Shepard.* New York: Dell, 1985.

MARTIN SHERMAN

Arkatov, Janice. "A Gay Ground-Breaker." *Los Angeles Times* 3 April 1987, sec. 8: 1+.

Brustein, Robert. "A Theatre for Clever Journalists." *New Republic* 5 Jan. 1980: 23–24.

Gill, Brendan. "Surviving." *New Yorker* 17 Dec. 1979: 100–102.

Schiff, Ellen. "Plays About the Holocaust—Ashes into Art." *New York Times* 2 Dec. 1979, sec. 2: 1+.

Simon, John. "Campy Dachau, Plywood Mahogany." *New York* 17 Dec. 1979: 110–111.

SOPHOCLES

List of Plays (Sophocles wrote in the fifth century B.C. The exact dates for his plays are unknown.)

Oedipus Rex
Antigone
Oedipus at Colonus
Philoctetes
Ajax
Trachiniae
Elektra
Ichneutai
Aleadae

Bowra, Sir Maurice. *Sophoclean Tragedy.* Oxford: Clarendon, 1944.

Burton, Reginald William Boteler. *The Chorus in Sophocles' Tragedies.* New York: Oxford UP, 1980.

Gardiner, Cynthia P. *The Sophoclean Chorus: A Study*

of Character and Function. Iowa City: U of Iowa P, 1987.

Kitto, H. D. F. *Sophocles, Dramatist and Philosopher.* London: Oxford UP, 1958.

Knox, Bernard M. *Sophocles at Thebes: Sophocles' Tragic Hero and His Time.* New York: Norton, 1971.

Reinhardt, Karl. *Sophokles.* Trans. D. and H. Harvey. New York: Barnes, 1978.

Segal, Charles. *Tragedy and Civilization: An Interpretation of Sophocles.* Cambridge: Harvard UP, 1981.

Waldock, A. J. A. *Sophocles the Dramatist.* Cambridge: Cambridge UP, 1951.

Winnington-Ingram, R. P. *Sophocles: An Interpretation.* New York: Cambridge UP, 1980.

Woodard, T. M., ed. *Sophocles: A Collection of Critical Essays.* Englewood Cliffs: Prentice, 1966.

Sophocles's *Oedipus Rex*

Bloom, Harold. *Sophocles's Oedipus Rex.* New York: Chelsea, 1988.

Cameron, Alister. *The Identity of Oedipus the King: Five Essays on the Oedipus Tyrannus.* New York: New York UP, 1968.

Edmonds, Lowell. *Oedipus: The Ancient Legend and Its Later Analogues.* Baltimore: Johns Hopkins UP, 1985.

Fergusson, Francis. *The Idea of a Theater.* Princeton: Princeton UP, 1949. 14–53.

O'Brien, M. J., ed. *Twentieth-Century Interpretations of Oedipus Rex.* Englewood Cliffs: Prentice, 1968.

Sophocles's *Antigone*

Brown, Andrew. *A New Companion to Greek Tragedy.* Totowa, NJ: Barnes, 1983.

Goheen, R. F. *The Imagery of Sophocles' Antigone: A Study of Poetic Language and Structure.* Princeton: Princeton UP, 1951.

Linforth, I. M. *Antigone and Creon.* Berkeley: U of California P, 1961.

AUGUST STRINDBERG

Carlson, Harry Gilbert. *Strindberg and the Poetry of Myth.* Berkeley: U of California P, 1982.

Lucas, F. L. *The Drama of Ibsen and Strindberg.* London: Cassell, 1962.

Reinert, Otto, ed. *Strindberg: A Collection of Critical Essays.* Englewood Cliffs: Prentice, 1971.

Steene, Birgitta. *The Greatest Fire: A Study of August Strindberg.* Carbondale: Southern Illinois UP, 1973.

Sprinchorn, Evert. *Strindberg as Dramatist.* New Haven: Yale UP, 1982.

JOHN MILLINGTON SYNGE

Benson, Eugene. *J. M. Synge.* New York: Grove, 1983.

Corkery, Daniel. *Synge and Anglo-Irish Literature.* Cork: Cork UP, 1955.

Gerstenberger, Donna. *John Millington Synge.* New York: Twayne, 1965.

Green, David H. and Edward M. Stephens, *J. M. Synge 1871–1909.* New York: Macmillan, 1959.

Kiberd, Declan. *Synge and the Irish Language.* London: Macmillan, 1979.

King, Mary C. *The Drama of J. M. Synge.* Syracuse: Syracuse UP, 1985.

Price, Alan. *Synge and Anglo-Irish Drama.* London: Methuen, 1961.

Skelton, Robin. *The Writings of J. M. Synge.* London: Thames, 1971.

———. *J. M. Synge and His World.* New York: Viking, 1971.

TENNESSEE WILLIAMS

Boxill, Roger. *Tennessee Williams,* New York: St. Martin's, 1987.

Devlin, Albert J., ed. *Conversations with Tennessee Williams.* Jackson, MS: UP of Mississippi, 1986.

Falk, Signi Lenea. *Tennessee Williams.* 2nd ed. Boston: Twayne, 1978.

Leavitt, Richard Freeman, ed. *The World of Tennessee Williams.* New York: Putnam, 1978.

Parker, R. B., ed. *The Glass Menagerie: A Collection of Critical Essays.* Englewood Cliffs: Prentice, 1983.

Stanton, Stephen, ed. *Tennessee Williams: A Collection of Critical Essays.* Englewood Cliffs: Prentice, 1977.

Williams, Tennessee, *Memoirs.* Garden City: Doubleday, 1975.

AUGUST WILSON

Freedman, Samuel G. "Wilson's New *Fences* Nurtures a Partnership." *New York Times* 5 May 1985: I, 80.

———. "A Voice from the Streets." *New York Times Magazine* 15 March 1987: 33+.

Gerard, Jeremy. "Waterford to Broadway: Well-Traveled *Fences.*" *New York Times* 9 April 1987: III, 21.

Henderson, Heather. "Building *Fences:* An Interview with Mary Alice and James Earl Jones." *Yale Theater* 12 (Summer/Fall 1985): 67–70.

Kelley, Kevin. "August Wilson an Heir to O'Neill." *Boston Globe* 24 Jan. 1988: A1+.

Rich, Frank. "Theater: Family Ties in Wilson's *Fences.*" *New York Times* 27 March 1987: II, 1.

Selected List of Films, Videos, and Recordings of the Plays

Films, Videos, and Recordings

Anonymous, *Everyman*
55 min., color, 1971.
16 mm film.
Distributed by Paul Lewison.

Aristophanes, *Lysistrata* [Recording]
With Hermione Gingold and Stanley Holloway.
Caedmon Records.

Samuel Beckett, *Happy Days* [recording]
With Irene Worth and George Voscovec.
Caedmon Records.

Samuel Beckett, *Krapp's Last Tape* [recording]
Read by Donald Davis.
Spoken Arts Records.

Anton Chekhov, *The Cherry Orchard*
43 min., color and B/W, 1967
16 mm film.
Distributed by the Encyclopaedia Britannica Educational Corp.

Anton Chekhov, *The Cherry Orchard*
The Cherry Orchard I
22 min., color, 1968.
Beta, VHS, 3/4" U-matic cassette.
With Norris Houghton. Important scenes with discussion.
Distributed by the Encyclopaedia Britannica Educational Corp.

Anton Chekhov, *The Cherry Orchard*
Cherry Orchard II, Comedy or Tragedy?
22 min., color, 1968.
Beta, VHS, 3/4" U-matic cassette.
Norris Houghton examines whether the characters' words mask their feelings. Important scenes with discussion.
Distributed by the Encyclopaedia Britannica Educational Corp.

Anton Chekhov, *Three Sisters*
166 min., B/W, 1965.
Beta, VHS.
With Kim Stanley, Geraldine Page, Sandy Dennis, Shelley Winters, Kevin McCarthy. Directed by Paul Bogart.
Distributed by Budget Films.

Anton Chekhov, *Three Sisters*
165 min., color, 1973.
16 mm film.
With Alan Bates. Directed by Sir Laurence Olivier.
Distributed by Films, Inc.

Anton, Chekhov, *Three Sisters*
136 min., color, 1976.
Videotape.
With Janet Suzman. British.
Distributed by Films, Inc.

Athol Fugard, *"MASTER HAROLD" . . . and the boys*
90 min., color, 1984.
Beta, VHS.
With Matthew Broderick. A made-for-cable production.
Distributed by Lorimar Home Video.

Lorraine Hansberry, *A Raisin in the Sun*
128 min., B/W, 1961.

Beta, VHS.
With Sidney Poitier, Claudia McNeil, and Ruby Dee. Directed by Daniel Petrie.
Distributed by RCA/Columbia Pictures.

Lorraine Hansberry, *A Raisin in the Sun*
The Black Experience in the Creation of Drama
35 min., color, 1975.
VHS.
With Ruby Dee, Sidney Poitier, Claudia McNeil, and others. Traces Hansberry's artistic growth in her own words.
Distributed by Films for the Humanities.

Henrik Ibsen, *A Doll's House*
89 min., B/W, 1959.
Beta, VHS.
With Julie Harris, Christopher Plummer, Jason Robards, Hume Cronyn, Eileen Heckart, and Richard Thomas.
Distributed by MGM/UA Home Video.

Henrik Ibsen, *A Doll's House*
98 min., color, 1973.
VHS.
With Jane Fonda, Edward Fox, Trevor Howard, and David Warner.
Distributed by Prism Entertainment.

Henrik Ibsen, *Hedda Gabler*
114 min., color, 1976.
Videotape.
With Janet Suzman.
Distributed by Films, Inc.

Christopher Marlowe, *Doctor Faustus*
93 min., color, 1968.
Beta, VHS.
With Richard Burton, Andreas Teuber, Elizabeth Taylor, and Ian Marter.
Distributed by RCA/Columbia Pictures Home Video.

Arthur Miller, *Death of a Salesman*
115 min., B/W, 1951.
16 mm.
With Frederick March and Mildred Dunnock.
Distributed by many rental agencies throughout the United States.

Arthur Miller, *Death of a Salesman*
135 min., color, 1985.
Beta, VHS.
With Dustin Hoffman, John Malkovich, Charles

Dunning, and Stephen Lary. Directed by Volker Schlondorff. A made-for-TV production. Distributed by Lorimar Home Video.

Molière (Jean Baptiste Poquelin), *The Misanthrope*
16 mm film.
Distributed by Films for the Humanities.

Marsha Norman, *'night, Mother*
97 min., color, 1986.
Beta, VHS, laser optical videodisc.
With Sissy Spacek and Anne Bancroft. Directed by Tom Moore.
Distributed by MCA Home Video.

Eugene O'Neill, *Desire Under the Elms*
111 min., B/W, 1958.
Beta, VHS.
With Sophia Loren, Burl Ives, and Anthony Perkins. Directed by Delbert Mann. Adapted for the screen by Irwin Shaw.
Distributed by Films, Inc.

Luigi Pirandello, *Six Characters in Search of an Author*
60 min., color, 1978.
Beta, VHS, 3/4" U-matic cassette.
Hosted by Jose Ferrar. With Ossie Davis.
Distributed by Miami Dade Community College.

William Shakespeare, *Hamlet*
142 min., B/W, 1948.
16 mm film.
With Sir Laurence Olivier, Jean Simmons, Stanley Holloway, and Eileen Herlie. Directed by Olivier.
Distributed by Budget Films; Films, Inc.; and Learning Corp. of America.

William Shakespeare, *Hamlet*
150 min., color, 1979.
Beta, VHS, 3/4" U-matic cassette, other formats by special arrangement.
With Derek Jacobi. British.
Distributed by Time-Life Video.

William Shakespeare, *Hamlet*
114 min., color, 1969.
16 mm film.
With Nicol Williamson and Marianne Faithfull. Directed by Tony Richardson. British.
Distributed by Budget Films; Films, Inc.; and Learning Corp. of America.

William Shakespeare, *Hamlet*
104 min., color, 1970.
16 mm film.
With Richard Chamberlain and Michael Redgrave.
    Directed by Peter Wood.
Distributed by Films, Inc.

William Shakespeare, *Hamlet*
Hamlet: The Age of Elizabeth, I
30 min., color, 1959.
Beta, VHS, 3/4" U-matic cassette.
An introduction to Elizabethan theater.
Distributed by the Encyclopaedia Britannica Educa-
    tional Corp.

William Shakespeare, *A Midsummer Night's Dream*
124 min., color, 1968.
16 mm film.
With David Warner, Diana Rigg, Paul Rogers, and
    Bill Travers. Directed by Peter Hall. British.
Distributed by Films, Inc.

William Shakespeare, *A Midsummer Night's Dream*
120 min., color, 1982.
Beta, VHS.
With Helen Mirren, Peter McEnry, and Brian Clo-
    ver. British.
Distributed by Key Video and Time-Life Video.

William Shakespeare, *A Midsummer Night's Dream*
165 min., color, 1983
Beta, VHS, 3/4" U-matic cassette.
With William Hurt and Michele Shay.
Distributed by Films for the Humanities.

William Shakespeare, *A Midsummer Night's Dream*
132 min., B/W, 1935.
Beta, VHS.
With James Cagney, Mickey Rooney, Olivia de
    Haviland, Dick Powell, and Joe E. Brown. Di-
    rected by William Dieterle and Max Reinhardt.
Distributed by Key Video.

Bernard Shaw, *Major Barbara*
145 min., B/W, 1941.
Beta, VHS, 3/4" U-matic cassette.
With Wendy Hiller, Rex Harrison, Robert Morley,
    and Sybil Thorndike. British.
Distributed by Learning Corp. of America.

Sam Shepard, *True West*
110 min., color, 1986.
Beta, VHS
With John Malkovich and Gary Sinise.
Distributed by Academy Home Entertainment.

Sophocles, *Antigone*
88 min., B/W, 1962.
16 mm film.
With Irene Papas. Directed by George Tzavellas. In
    Greek, with subtitles.
Distributed by Films, Inc.

Sophocles, *Oedipus Tyrranus*
60 min, color, 1978.
Beta, VHS, 3/4" U-matic cassette.
Hosted by Jose Ferrar. Shown from the point when
    Oedipus is told of his father's death.
Distributed by Films, Inc.

Sophocles, *Oedipus the King*
97 min., color, 1968.
16 mm film.
With Christopher Plummer and Orson Wells. Di-
    rected by Philip Saville.
Distributed by Swank Motion Pictures, Inc.

Sophocles, *Oedipus Rex*
Oedipus the King
29 min., color, 1976.
3/4" U-matic cassette.
Examines classical Greek theater in general and this
    play in particular.
Distributed by Dallas County Community College.

Sophocles, *Oedipus Rex*
Oedipus Rex
90 mins., 3 parts, color, 1959.
Beta, VHS, 3/4" U-matic cassette.
Important scenes with discussion.
Distributed by the Encyclopaedia Britannica Educa-
    tional Corp.

August Strindberg, *Miss Julie*
90 min., B/W, 1950.
Beta, VHS.
With Anita Bjork and Ulf Palme.
Distributed by Embassy Home Entertainment.

John Millington Synge, *Riders to the Sea*
    [Recording]
Radio Eireann Players of Dublin.
Spoken Arts Records.

Tennessee Williams, *The Glass Menagerie*
134 min., color, 1988.
Videotape.
With John Malkovich, Joanne Woodward, and
    Karen Allen.
Distributed by MCA Home Video.

Directory of Film Distributors

Academy Home Entertainment
1 Pine Haven Shore Rd.
P.O. Box 788
Shelburne, VT 05482
(802) 985-8403
(800) 972-0001

Budget Films
4590 Santa Monica Blvd.
Los Angeles, CA 90029
(213) 660-0187

Caedmon Records
1995 Broadway
New York, NY 10023
(212) 580-3400

Embassy Home Entertainment
1901 Avenue of the Stars
Los Angeles, CA 90067
(213) 460-7200

Encyclopaedia Britannica Educational Corp.
425 Michigan Ave.
Chicago, Il 60611
(312) 347-7900

Films for the Humanities
P.O. Box 2053
Princeton, NJ 08540
(609) 452-1128

Films, Inc.
4420 Oakton St.
Skokie, IL 60076
(312) 878-2600, ext. 44
(800) 323-4222. ext. 44

Key Video
1211 Avenue of the Americas
Second Floor
New York, NY 10036
(212) 819-3238

Learning Corporation of America
1350 Avenue of the Americas
New York, NY 10019
(312) 940-1260
(800) 621-2131

Paul Lewison
8899 Beverly Blvd.
Suite 101
Los Angeles, CA 90048

Lorimar Home Video
17942 Cowan Ave.
Irvine, CA 92714
(714) 474-0355

MCA Home Video
70 Universal City Plaza
Universal City, CA 91608
(818) 777-4300

MGM/UA Home Video
1350 Avenue of the Americas
New York, NY 10019
(212) 408-0600

Miami-Dade Community College
11011 SW 104 St.
Miami, FL 33176
(305) 596-1364

Prism Entertainment
1888 Century Park East
Suite 1000
Los Angeles, CA 90067
(213) 277-3270

RCA/Columbia Pictures Home Video
350 West Olive Ave.
Burbank, CA 91505
(818) 953-7900

Spoken Arts Records
310 North Ave.
New Rochelle, NY 10801
(914) 636-5482

Swank Motion Pictures, Inc.
201 South Jefferson Ave.
St. Louis, Mo 63166
(314) 534-6300

Time-Life Video
1271 Avenue of the Americas
New York, NY 10020
(212) 484-5940

Acknowledgments (*continued from p. iv*)

The Oedipus Rex of Sophocles: An English Version by Dudley Fitts and Robert Fitzgerald, copyright 1949 by Harcourt Brace Jovanovich, Inc.; renewed 1977 by Cornelia Fitts and Robert Fitzgerald, reprinted by permission of the publisher. CAUTION: All rights, including professional, amateur, motion picture, recitation, lecturing, performance, public reading, radio broadcasting, and television, are strictly reserved. Inquiries on all rights should be addressed to Harcourt Brace Jovanovich, Inc., Copyrights and Permissions Department, Orlando, Florida 32887. *Photo:* The Guthrie Theater.

The Antigone of Sophocles: An English Version by Dudley Fitts and Robert Fitzgerald, copyright 1939 by Harcourt Brace Jovanovich, Inc.; renewed 1967 by Dudley Fitts and Robert Fitzgerald, reprinted by permission of the publisher. CAUTION: All rights, including professional, amateur, motion picture, recitation, lecturing, performance, public reading, radio broadcasting, and television, are strictly reserved. Inquiries on all rights should be addressed to Harcourt Brace Jovanovich, Inc., Copyrights and Permissions Department, Orlando, Florida 32887. *Photos:* © Martha Swope.

"Poetics: Comedy and Epic and Tragedy" by Aristotle, from *Poetics,* translated by Gerald F. Else, (1967), reprinted by permission of The University of Michigan Press.

Excerpt from "The Structural Study of Myth" by Claude Lévi-Strauss. Reprinted from *The Bibliographical and Special Series of the American Folklore Society, Vol. 5,* (1955) by permission of The American Folklore Society.

Excerpt from *Antigone* by Jean Anouilh, translated by Lewis Galantiere. Copyright 1946 by Random House, Inc. and renewed 1974 by Lewis Galantiere. Reprinted by permission of Random House, Inc.

Lysistrata: An English Version by Dudley Fitts, copyright 1954 by Harcourt Brace Jovanovich, Inc., reprinted by permission of the publisher. CAUTION: All rights, including professional, amateur, motion picture, recitation, lecturing, performance, public reading, radio broadcasting, and television, are strictly reserved. Inquiries on all rights should be addressed to Harcourt Brace Jovanovich, Inc., Copyrights and Permissions Department, Orlando, Florida 32887.

Roman Drama

Figure 2. Theater of Marcellus from *The History of the Greek and Roman Theater* by Margarete Bieber. Copyright 1939, 1961 by Princeton University Press. Fig. 641 (after Peruzzi; redrawn by Mrs. Wadhams). Reprinted by permission of Princeton University Press.

Medieval Drama

Figure 3. Pageant wagon from *Early English Stages 1300 to 1660* by Glynne William Gladstone Wickham. Reprinted by permission of Columbia University Press and Routledge & Kegan Paul Ltd.

Everyman edited by A.C. Cawley from *Everyman & Other Miracle Plays,* Everyman's Library. Reprinted by permission of J.M. Dent & Sons Ltd. Publishers

Renaissance Drama

Figure 4. Swan Theatre from *Essai sur L'Histoire du Théâtre* by Germain Bapst. Reprinted by courtesy of the Trustees of the Boston Public Library.

Christopher Marlowe's DR. FAUSTUS; Text and Major Criticism, edited, with notes, by Irving Ribner. Reprinted with permission of Macmillan Publishing Company. Copyright © 1985, 1966 by Macmillan Publishing Company. © Roslyn G. Ribner 1963.

Footnotes to accompany *Hamlet* and *A Midsummer Night's Dream* from *The Complete Works of Shakespeare* by David Bevington. Copyright © 1980, 1973 by Scott, Foresman and Company. Reprinted by permission. *Photos: A Midsummer Night's Dream,* Richard M. Feldman; *Hamlet* © Donald Cooper/Photostage.

"Masque Elements in *A Midsummer Night's Dream*" by Enid Welsford, from *The Court Masque* by Enid Welsford. Cambridge: Cambridge University Press; New York: The Macmillan Company, 1927. Reprinted by permission of Cambridge University Press.

"Fancy's Image," excerpt from *Comic Transformation in Shakespeare* by Ruth Nevo. Reprinted by permission of Methuen & Co.

"Broken Nuptials," excerpt from *Broken Nuptials in Shakespeare's Plays* by Carol Thomas Neely. Reprinted by permission of Yale University Press.

"On *A Midsummer Night's Dream*" by Linda Bamber. Reprinted from *Comic Women, Tragic Men: A Study of Gender and Genre in Shakespeare* by Linda Bamber with the permission of the publishers, Stanford University Press. © 1982 by the Board of Trustees of the Leland Stanford Junior University.

"The Play is the Message . . . " by Peter Brook from *The Shifting Point* by Peter Brook. Copyright © 1987 by Peter Brook. Reprinted by permission of Harper & Row, Publishers, Inc.

"Hamlet and His problems" from "Hamlet" in *Selected Essays* by T.S. Eliot, copyright 1950 by Harcourt Brace Jovanovich, Inc., renewed 1978 by Esme Valerie Eliot, reprinted by permission of Harcourt Brace Jovanovich, Inc., Methuen London, and Faber and Faber Ltd.

"Hamlet's Ghost," illustration of "Suggested Elizabethan Staging of the Ghost Scenes" by C. Walter Hodges from *The New Cambridge Shakespeare: Hamlet,* edited by Philip Edwards (Cambridge University Press).

Restoration and Eighteenth-Century Drama

Figure 5. Proscenium arch from *The American Playhouse in the Eighteenth Century* by Brooks McNamara.

The Misanthrope translated by Richard Wilbur, copyright 1954, 1955 by Richard Wilbur, reprinted by permission of Harcourt Brace Jovanovich, Inc. CAUTION: Professionals and amateurs are hereby warned that this translation, being fully protected under the copyright laws of the United States, the British Commonwealth, including Canada, and all other countries which are signatories to the Universal Copyright Convention, is subject to royalty. All rights, including professional, amateur, motion picture, recitation, lecturing, public reading, radio broadcasting, and television, are strictly reserved. Particular emphasis is laid on the question of readings, permission for which must be secured from the author's agent in writing. Inquiries on professional rights (except for amateur rights) should be addressed to Curtis Brown, Ltd., Ten Astor Place, New York, NY 10003. The amateur acting rights of *The Misanthrope* are controlled exclusively by the Dramatists Play Service, Inc., 440 Park Avenue South, New York, NY 10016. No amateur performance of the play may be given without obtaining in advance the written permission of the Dramatists Play Service, Inc. and paying the requisite fee.

Nineteenth-Century Drama to the Turn of the Century

Figure 6. Realistic setting in Anton Chekhov's *Three Sisters,* © 1987 Martha Swope.

A Doll's House by Henrik Ibsen, translated by Michael Meyer, © 1965 by Michael Meyer. Reprinted by permission of Harold Ober Associates Incorporated.

Hedda Gabler by Henrik Ibsen, translated by Michael Meyer, © 1962, 1974 by Michael Meyer. Reprinted by permission of Harold Ober Associates Incorporated.

CAUTION: Both of these plays are fully protected, in whole, in part, or in any form under the copyright laws of the United States of America, the British Empire including the Dominion of Canada, and all other countries of the Copyright Union, and are subject to royalty. All rights including motion picture, radio, television, recitation, public readings, are strictly reserved. For professional rights and amateur rights all inquiries should be addressed to the Author's Agent: Robert A. Freedman Dramatic Agency Inc., 1501 Broadway, New York, NY 10036. *Photos: A Doll's House,* © 1984 Martha Swope; *Hedda Gabler,* © T. Charles Erickson.

"*A Doll's House:* Ibsen the Moralist" by Muriel C. Bradbrook from *Ibsen: The Norwegian* by Muriel C. Bradbrook. Reprinted by permission of the author and Chatto & Windus.

"Notes for *Hedda Gabler,*" selection from Ibsen's Notes on *Hedda Gabler* translated by Evert Sprinchorn, from *Playwrights on Playwriting,* edited by Toby Cole. Copyright © 1960 by Toby Cole. Reprinted by permission of Hill and Wang, a division of Farrar, Straus and Giroux, Inc.

Excerpt from *Preface to Ibsen's Hedda Gabler* by Eva Le Gallienne. Copyright © 1961 by Eva Le Gallienne. Reprinted by permission of International Creative Management, Inc.

"Thematic Symbols in *Hedda Gabler*" by Caroline Mayerson. Reprinted by permission of the author.

"On *Hedda Gabler,*" excerpt from "Ibsen Read Anew" by Jan Kott from *The Theatre of Essence and Other Essays* by Jan Kott, © 1984 by Jan Kott. Reprinted by permission of the author and the Yale School of Drama.

Miss Julie by August Strindberg, from *Strindberg: Five Plays,* Harry Carlson, translator, © 1983 The Regents of the University of California. Reprinted by permission of the University of California Press.

Three Sisters by Anton Chekhov, translated by Constance Garnett, reprinted by permission of the estate of Constance Garnett and Chatto & Windus. *Photos:* Joe Giannetti/The Guthrie Theater.

The Cherry Orchard by Anton Chekhov, translated by Constance Garnett, reprinted by permission of the estate of Constance Garnett and Chatto & Windus. *Photos:* © 1987 Martha Swope.

"From Chekhov's Letters," two letters from *Letters of Anton Chekhov* translated by Michael Henry Heim with Simon Karlinsky. Copyright © 1973 by Harper & Row, Publishers, Inc. Reprinted by permission of Harper & Row, Publishers, Inc.

"On the First Production of *The Three Sisters*" by Konstantin Stanislavsky from *My Life in Art.* Reprinted by permission of the publishers, Routledge, Chapman and Hall.

Excerpt from "Recollections" by Maxim Gorky from *Reminiscences of Tolstoy, Chekhov and Andreyev* by Maxim Gorky. Reprinted by permission of the estate of Maxim Gorky and The Hogarth Press.

"The Women in *Three Sisters*" by Beverly Hahn from *Chekhov: A Study of the Major Stories and Plays* by Beverly Hahn. Copyright © 1976 by Cambridge University Press. Reprinted by permission of Cambridge University Press.

"On Chekhov" by Peter Brook from *The Shifting Point* by Peter Brook. Copyright © 1987 by Peter Brook. Reprinted by permission of Harper & Row, Publishers, Inc.

Major Barbara and authorized excerpt from the "Preface to Major Barbara" by Bernard Shaw. Copyright 1907, 1913, 1930, 1941 George Bernard Shaw. Copyright: 1957 The Public Trustees as Executor of the Estate of George Bernard Shaw. Reprinted by permission of The Society of Authors on behalf of the Estate of Bernard Shaw.

Drama in the Early and Mid-Twentieth Century

Figure 7. Expressionistic setting in Arthur Miller's *Death of a Salesman,* the New York Public Library at Lincoln Center.

Dreamer by Ellen Oumano. Copyright © 1986 by Ellen Oumano. Reprinted by permission of St. Martin's Press, Incorporated.

"Interview with Athol Fugard" by Henrich von Staden from *Theater* (Yale) Vol. 14, #1, Winter 1982. Reprinted by permission of the author and the Yale School of Drama.

Excerpt from *Notebooks 1960–1977* by Athol Fugard. Copyright © 1983 by Athol Fugard. Reprinted by permission of Alfred A. Knopf, Inc.

"Interview with Caryl Churchill" by Emily Mann from *Interviews with Contemporary Women Playwrights* by Kathleen Betsko and Rachel Koenig. Copyright © 1987 by Kathleen Betsko and Rachel Koenig. Reprinted by permission of William Morrow & Co., Inc.

"Interview with Marsha Norman" by Kathleen Betsko and Rachel Koenig from *Interviews with Contemporary Women Playwrights* by Kathleen Betsko and Rachel Koenig. Copyright © 1987 by Kathleen Betsko and Rachel Koenig. Reprinted by permission of Beech Tree Books (a division of William Morrow & Co., Inc.).

"Interview with Marsha Norman" and "Interview with August Wilson" by David Savran from *In Their Own Voices* by David Savran. Reprinted by permission of Theatre Communications Group.